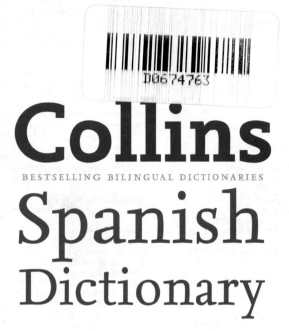

Collins

BESTSELLING BILINGUAL DICTIONARIES

Spanish
Dictionary

HarperCollins Publishers
Westerhill Road
Bishopbriggs
Glasgow
G64 2QT
Great Britain

First Edition 2011

Reprint 10 9 8 7 6 5 4 3 2 1 0

© HarperCollins Publishers 2011

ISBN 978-0-00-738237-8

Collins® is a registered trademark of
HarperCollins Publishers Limited

www.collinslanguage.com

A catalogue record for this book is
available from the British Library

Typeset by Davidson Publishing
Solutions, Glasgow

Printed in Italy by
LEGO S.p.A., Lavis (Trento)

Acknowledgements
We would like to thank those authors
and publishers who kindly gave
permission for copyright material to
be used in the Collins Word Web.
We would also like to thank Times
Newspapers Ltd for providing valuable
data.

Entered words that we have reason to
believe constitute trademarks have
been designated as such. However,
neither the presence nor absence of
such designation should be regarded
as affecting the legal status of any
trademark.

HarperCollins does not warrant that
www.collinsdictionary.com,
www.collinslanguage.com or any other
website mentioned in this title will be
provided uninterrupted, that any
website will be error free, that defects
will be corrected, or that the website or
the server that makes it available are
free of viruses or bugs. For full terms
and conditions please refer to the site
terms provided on the website.

EDITORIAL MANAGEMENT
Gaëlle Amiot-Cadey, Ruth O'Donovan

PROJECT MANAGEMENT
Genevieve Gerrard

CONTRIBUTORS
Jeremy Butterfield, Mike González,
Gerry Breslin, Teresa Álvarez García,
Brian Steel, Ana Cristina Llompart,
José Miguel Galván Déniz, Val McNulty,
Sharon Hunter, Tracy Lomas,
Enrique González Sandinero,
Caitlin McMahon, José Martín Galera,
Lydia Batanaz, Wendy Lee,
Cordelia Lilly, José María Ruiz Vaca,
Malihé Sanatian, Horst Kopleck

TECHNICAL SUPPORT
Thomas Callan

SERIES EDITOR
Rob Scriven

Introduction

You may be starting Spanish for the first time, or you may wish to extend your knowledge of the language. Perhaps you want to read and study Spanish books, newspapers and magazines, or perhaps simply have a conversation with Spanish speakers. Whatever the reason, whether you're a student, a tourist or want to use Spanish for business, this is the ideal book to help you understand and communicate. This modern, user-friendly dictionary gives priority to everyday vocabulary and the language of current affairs, business, computing and tourism, and, as in all Collins dictionaries, the emphasis is firmly placed on contemporary language and expressions.

How to use the dictionary
Below you will find an outline of how information is presented in your dictionary. Our aim is to give you the maximum amount of detail in the clearest and most helpful way.

Entries
A typical entry in your dictionary will be made up of the following elements:

Phonetic transcription
Phonetics appear in square brackets immediately after the headword. They are shown using the International Phonetic Alphabet (IPA), and a complete list of the symbols used in this system can be found on page x. The pronunciation given is for Castilian Spanish except where a word is solely used in Latin America, when we give the Latin American pronunciation. A further guide to the differences in types of Spanish pronunciation is given on page x.

Grammatical information
All words belong to one of the following parts of speech: noun, verb, adjective, adverb, pronoun, article, conjunction, preposition, abbreviation. Nouns can be singular or plural and, in Spanish, masculine or feminine. Verbs can be transitive, intransitive, reflexive or impersonal. Parts of speech appear in *italics* immediately after the phonetic spelling of the headword. The gender of the translation also appears in *italics* immediately following the key element of the translation, except where this is a regular masculine singular noun ending in "o", or a regular feminine singular noun ending in "a".

Often a word can have more than one part of speech. Just as the English word **chemical** can be an adjective or a noun, the Spanish word **conocido** can be an adjective ("(well-)known") or a noun ("acquaintance"). In the same way the verb **to walk** is sometimes transitive, ie it takes an object ("to walk the dog") and sometimes intransitive, ie it doesn't take an object ("to walk to school"). To help you find the meaning you are looking for quickly and for clarity of presentation, the different part of speech categories are separated by a triangle ▷.

Meaning divisions

Most words have more than one meaning. Take, for example, **punch** which can be, amongst other things, a blow with the fist or an object used for making holes. Other words are translated differently depending on the context in which they are used. The transitive verb **to put on**, for example, can be translated by "ponerse", "encender" etc depending on *what* it is you are putting on. To help you select the most appropriate translation in every context, entries are divided according to meaning. Each different meaning is introduced by an "indicator" in *italics* and in brackets. Thus, the examples given above will be shown as follows:

> **punch** [pʌntʃ] *n* (*blow*) golpe *m*, puñetazo; (*tool*) punzón *m*

Likewise, some words can have a different meaning when used to talk about a specific subject area or field. For example **bishop**, which in a religious context means a high-ranking clergyman, is also the name of a chess piece. To show English speakers which translation to use, we have added "subject field labels" in brackets, in this case (*Chess*):

> **bishop** [ˈbɪʃəp] *n* obispo; (*Chess*) alfil *m*

Field labels are often shortened to save space. You will find a complete list of abbreviations used in the dictionary on pages viii and ix.

Translations

Most English words have a direct translation in Spanish and vice versa, as shown in the examples given above. Sometimes, however, no exact equivalent exists in the target language. In such cases we have given an approximate equivalent, indicated by the sign ≈. An example is **Health Service**, the Spanish equivalent of which is "Insalud". There is no exact equivalent since the bodies in the two countries are quite different:

> **Health Service** *n* (*Brit*) servicio de salud pública, ≈ Insalud *m* (*SP*)

On occasion it is impossible to find even an approximate equivalent. This may be the case, for example, with the names of types of food:

> **fabada** [faˈβaða] *nf bean and sausage stew*

Here the translation (which doesn't exist) is replaced by an explanation. For increased clarity, the explanation, or "gloss", is shown in *italics*.

It is often the case that a word, or a particular meaning of a word, cannot be translated in isolation. The translation of **Dutch**, for example, is "holandés(-esa)". However, the phrase **to go Dutch** is rendered by "pagar a escote". Even an expression as simple as **washing powder** needs a separate translation since it translates as "detergente (en polvo)", not

Índice de materias

Contents

William Collins' dream of knowledge for all began with the publication of his first book in 1819. A self-educated mill worker, he not only enriched millions of lives, but also founded a flourishing publishing house. Today, staying true to this spirit, Collins books are packed with inspiration, innovation, and practical expertise. They place you at the centre of a world of possibility and give you exactly what you need to explore it.

Language is the key to this exploration, and at the heart of Collins Dictionaries is language as it is really used. New words, phrases, and meanings spring up every day, and all of them are captured and analysed by the Collins Word Web. Constantly updated, and with over 2.5 billion entries, this living language resource is unique to our dictionaries.

Words are tools for life. And a Collins Dictionary makes them work for you.

Collins. Do more.

"polvo para lavar". This is where your dictionary will prove to be particularly informative and useful since it contains an abundance of compounds, phrases and idiomatic expressions.

Levels of formality and familiarity

In English you instinctively know when to say **I'm broke** or **I'm a bit short of cash** and when to say **I don't have any money**. When you are trying to understand someone who is speaking Spanish, however, or when you yourself try to speak Spanish, it is important to know what is polite and what is less so, and what you can say in a relaxed situation but not in a formal context. To help you with this, on the Spanish-English side we have added the label *(fam)* to show that a Spanish meaning or expression is colloquial, while those meanings or expressions which are vulgar are given an exclamation mark *(fam!)*, warning you they can cause serious offence. Note also that on the English-Spanish side, translations which are vulgar are followed by an exclamation mark in brackets.

Keywords

Words labelled in the text as KEYWORD in English and PALABRA CLAVE in Spanish, such as **have** and **do** or their Spanish equivalents **tener** and **hacer**, have been given special treatment because they form the basic elements of the language. This extra help will ensure that you know how to use these complex words with confidence.

Highlighting

Words that appear with a shaded background, such as ability and abrigo are words that are specified by or commonly associated with GCSE exams and other exams of a similar level. The highlighting helps you spot your essential exam vocabulary quickly.

Cultural information

Entries which are marked in the main text by a column of dots explain aspects of culture in Spanish and English-speaking countries. Subject areas covered include politics, education, media and national festivals.

Spanish alphabetical order

In 1994 the **Real Academia Española** and the Spanish American language academies jointly decided to stop treating CH and LL as separate letters in Spanish, thereby bringing it into line with European spelling norms. This means that **chapa** and **lluvia** will appear in letters C and L respectively. Of course, it should also be remembered that words like **cancha** and **callado**, with **ch** and **ll** in the middle of the words, will also have changed places alphabetically, now being found after **cáncerígeno** and **caliza** respectively. Spanish, however still has one more letter than English with Ñ treated separately, between N and O.

Abreviaturas   Abbreviations

abreviatura	*ab(b)r*	abbreviation
adjetivo, locución adjetiva	*adj*	adjective, adjectival phrase
administración, lenguaje administrativo	*Admin*	administration
adverbio, locución adverbial	*adv*	adverb, adverbial phrase
agricultura	*Agr*	agriculture
alguien	*algn*	
América Latina	*Am*	Latin America
anatomía	*Anat*	anatomy
arquitectura	*Arq, Arch*	architecture
astrología, astronomía	*Astro*	astrology, astronomy
el automóvil	*Aut(o)*	the motor car and motoring
aviación, viajes en avión	*Aviat*	flying, air travel
biología	*Bio(l)*	biology
botánica, flores	*Bot*	botany
inglés británico	*Brit*	British English
química	*Chem*	chemistry
cine	*Cine*	cinema
comercio, finanzas, banca	*Com(m)*	commerce, finance, banking
informática	*Comput*	computing
conjunción	*conj*	conjunction
construcción	*Constr*	building
compuesto	*cpd*	compound element
cocina	*Culin*	cookery
economía	*Econ*	economics
electricidad, electrónica	*Elec*	electricity, electronics
enseñanza, sistema escolar	*Escol*	schooling, schools
España	*Esp*	Spain
especialmente	*esp*	especially
exclamación, interjección	*excl*	exclamation, interjection
femenino	*f*	feminine
lenguaje familiar (! vulgar)	*fam (!)*	informal usage (! particularly offensive)
ferrocarril	*Ferro*	railways
uso figurado	*fig*	figurative use
fotografía	*Foto*	photography
(verbo inglés) del cual la partícula es inseparable	*fus*	(phrasal verb) where the particle is inseparable
generalmente	*gen*	generally
geografía, geología	*Geo*	geography, geology
geometría	*Geom*	geometry
lenguaje familiar (! vulgar)	*inf (!)*	informal usage (! particularly offensive)
informática	*Inform*	computing
invariable	*inv*	invariable
irregular	*irreg*	irregular
lo jurídico	*Jur*	law
América Latina	*LAm*	Latin America
gramática, lingüística	*Ling*	grammar, linguistics

literatura	*Lit*	literature
masculino	*m*	masculine
matemáticas	*Mat(h)*	mathematics
medicina	*Med*	medical term, medicine
masculino/femenino	*m/f*	masculine/feminine
lo militar, el ejército	*Mil*	military matters
música	*Mus*	music
sustantivo	*n*	noun
navegación, náutica	*Naut*	sailing, navigation
sustantivo no empleado en el plural	*no pl*	collective (uncountable) noun, not used in plural
sustantivo numérico	*num*	numeral noun
complemento	*obj*	(grammatical) object
	o.s.	oneself
peyorativo	*pey, pej*	derogatory, pejorative
fotografía	*Phot*	photography
fisiología	*Physiol*	physiology
plural	*pl*	plural
política	*Pol*	politics
participio de pasado	*pp*	past participle
prefijo	*pref*	prefix
preposición	*prep*	preposition
pronombre	*pron*	pronoun
psicología, psiquiatría	*Psico, Psych*	psychology, psychiatry
tiempo pasado	*pt*	past tense
ferrocarril	*Rail*	railways
religión, lo eclesiástico	*Rel*	religion, church service
	sb	somebody
enseñanza, sistema escolar	*Scol*	schooling, schools
singular	*sg*	singular
España	*Sp*	Spain
	sth	something
subjuntivo	*subjun*	subjunctive
sujeto	*su(b)j*	(grammatical) subject
sufijo	*suff*	suffix
tauromaquia	*Taur*	bullfighting
también	*tb*	also
teatro	*Teat*	
técnica, tecnología	*Tec(h)*	technical term, technology
telecomunicaciones	*Telec, Tel*	telecommunications
	Theat	theatre
imprenta, tipografía	*Tip, Typ*	typography, printing
televisión	*TV*	television
sistema universitario	*Univ*	universities
inglés norteamericano	*US*	American English
verbo	*vb*	verb
verbo intransitivo	*vi*	intransitive verb
verbo pronominal	*vr*	reflexive verb
verbo transitivo	*vt*	transitive verb
zoología, animales	*Zool*	zoology
marca registrada	®	registered trademark
indica un equivalente cultural	≈	introduces a cultural equivalent

Spanish Pronunciation

Consonants

b	[b]	See notes on *v* below	bomba
	[β]		labor
c	[k]	*c* before *a, o* or *u* is pronounced as in *cat*	caja
ce, ci	[θe,θi]	*c* before *e* or *i* is pronounced as in *thin* and as *s*	cero, cielo
	[se,si']	in *sin* in Latin America and parts of Spain	vocero, noticiero
ch	[tʃ]	*ch* is pronounced as *ch* in *chair*	chiste
d	[d]	at the beginning of a word or after *l* or *n*,	danés
	[ð]	*d* is pronounced as in English. In any other position it is like *th* in *the*	ciudad
g	[g]	*g* before *a, o* or *u* is pronounced as in *gap* if	gafas, guerra
	[ɣ]	at the beginning of a word or after *n*. In other positions the sound is softened.	paga
ge, gi	[xe, xi]	*g* before *e* or *i* is pronounced similar to *ch* in Scottish *loch*	gente, girar
h		*h* is always silent in Spanish	haber
j	[x]	*j* is pronounced like *ch* in Scottish *loch*	jugar
ll	[ʎ]	*ll* is pronounced like the *lli* in *million*	talle
ñ	[ɲ]	*ñ* is pronounced like the *ni* in *onion*	niño
q	[k]	*q* is pronounced as *k* in *king*	que
r, rr	[r]	*r* is always pronounced in Spanish, unlike	quitar
	[rr]	the *r* in *dancer*. *rr* and *r* at the beginning of a word are trilled, like a Scottish *r*	garra
s	[s]	*s* is usually pronounced as in *pass*, but before	quizás
	[z]	*b, d, g, l, m* or *n* it is pronounced as in *rose*	isla
v	[b]	*v* is pronounced something like *b*. At the	vía
	[β]	beginning of a word or after *m* or *n* it is pronounced as *b* in *boy*. In any other position it is pronounced with the lips in position to pronounce *b* of *boy*, but not meeting	dividir
w	[b]	pronounced either like Spanish *b*, or like	wáter
	[w]	English *w*	whiskey
z	[θ]	*z* is pronounced as *th* in *thin* and as *s* in *sin* in	tenaz
	[s']	Latin America and parts of Spain	izada
	[ks]	*x* is pronounced as in *toxin* except in informal	tóxico
	[s]	Spanish or at the beginning of a word	xenofobia

f, k, l, m, n, p and *t* are pronounced as in English
' Only shown in Latin American entries.

Vowels

a	[a]	Not as long as *a* in far. When followed by a consonant in the same syllable (ie in a closed syllable), as in am*a*nte, the *a* is short as in b*a*t	p*a*ta
e	[e]	like *e* in th*e*y. In a closed syllable, as in g*e*nte, the *e* is short as in p*e*t	m*e*
i	[i]	as in m*ea*n or machi*n*e	p*i*no
o	[o]	as in l*o*cal. In a closed syllable, as in c*o*ntr*o*l, the *o* is short as in c*o*t	l*o*
u	[u]	As in r*u*le. It is silent after *q*, and in g*u*e, g*u*i, unless marked g*ü*e, g*ü*i eg antig*ü*edad, when it is pronounced like *w* in w*o*lf	l*u*nes

Semi-vowels

i, y	[j]	pronounced like *y* in *y*es	b*i*en, h*i*elo, *y*unta
u	[w]	unstressed *u* between consonant and vowel is pronounced like *w* in *w*ell. See also notes on *u* above	h*u*evo, f*u*ente, antig*ü*edad

Diphthongs

ai, ay	[ai]	as *i* in r*i*de	b*ai*le
au	[au]	as *ou* in sh*ou*t	*au*to
ei, ey	[ei]	as *ey* in gr*ey*	bu*ey*
eu	[eu]	both elements pronounced independently [e] + [u]	d*eu*da
oi, oy	[oi]	as *oy* in t*oy*	h*oy*

Stress

The rules of stress in Spanish are as follows:

(a) when a word ends in a vowel or in *n* or *s*, the second last syllable is stressed: pat*a*ta, pat*a*tas, c*o*me, c*o*men

(b) when a word ends in a consonant other than *n* or *s*, the stress falls on the last syllable: par*e*d, habl*a*r

(c) when the rules set out in (a) and (b) are not applied, an acute accent appears over the stressed vowel: com*ú*n, geograf*í*a, ingl*é*s

In the phonetic transcription, the symbol ['] precedes the syllable on which the stress falls.

In general, we give the pronunciation of each entry in square brackets after the word in question.

Spanish Verb Forms

1 Gerund **2** Imperative **3** Present **4** Preterite **5** Future **6** Present subjunctive
7 Imperfect subjunctive **8** Past participle **9** Imperfect

acertar 2 acierta **3** acierto, aciertas, acierta, aciertan **6** acierte, aciertes, acierte, acierten

acordar 2 acuerda **3** acuerdo, acuerdas, acuerda, acuerdan **6** acuerde, acuerdes, acuerde, acuerden

advertir 1 advirtiendo **2** advierte **3** advierto, adviertes, advierte, advierten **4** advirtió, advirtieron **6** advierta, adviertas, advierta, advirtamos, advirtáis, adviertan **7** advirtiera *etc*

agradecer 3 agradezco **6** agradezca *etc*

andar 4 anduve, anduviste, anduvo, anduvimos, anduvisteis, anduvieron **7** anduviera *or* anduviese *etc*

aparecer 3 aparezco **6** aparezca *etc*

aprobar 2 aprueba **3** apruebo, apruebas, aprueba, aprueban **6** apruebe, apruebes, apruebe, aprueben

atravesar 2 atraviesa **3** atravieso, atraviesas, atraviesa, atraviesan **6** atraviese, atravieses, atraviese, atraviesen

caber 3 quepo **4** cupe, cupiste, cupo, cupimos, cupisteis, cupieron **5** cabré *etc* **6** quepa *etc* **7** cupiera *etc*

caer 1 cayendo **3** caigo **4** cayó, cayeron **6** caiga *etc* **7** cayera *etc*

calentar 2 calienta **3** caliento, calientas, calienta, calientan **6** caliente, calientes, caliente, calienten

cerrar 2 cierra **3** cierro, cierras, cierra, cierran **6** cierre, cierres, cierre, cierren

COMER 1 comiendo **2** come, comed **3** como, comes, come, comemos, coméis, comen **4** comí, comiste, comió, comimos, comisteis, comieron **5** comeré, comerás, comerá, comeremos, comeréis, comerán **6** coma, comas, coma, comamos, comáis, coman **7** comiera, comieras, comiera, comiéramos, comierais, comieran **8** comido **9** comía, comías, comía, comíamos, comíais, comían

conocer 3 conozco **6** conozca *etc*

contar 2 cuenta **3** cuento, cuentas, cuenta, cuentan **6** cuente, cuentes, cuente, cuenten

costar 2 cuesta **3** cuesto, cuestas, cuesta, cuestan **6** cueste, cuestes, cueste, cuesten

dar 3 doy **4** di, diste, dio, dimos, disteis, dieron **7** diera *etc*

decir 2 di **3** digo **4** dije, dijiste, dijo, dijimos, dijisteis, dijeron **5** diré *etc* **6** diga *etc* **7** dijera *etc* **8** dicho

despertar 2 despierta **3** despierto, despiertas, despierta, despiertan **6** despierte, despiertes, despierte, despierten

divertir 1 divirtiendo **2** divierte **3** divierto, diviertes, divierte, divierten **4** divirtió, divirtieron **6** divierta, diviertas, divierta, divirtamos, divirtáis, diviertan **7** divirtiera *etc*

dormir 1 durmiendo **2** duerme **3** duermo, duermes, duerme, duermen **4** durmió, durmieron **6** duerma, duermas, duerma, durmamos, durmáis, duerman **7** durmiera *etc*

empezar 2 empieza **3** empiezo, empiezas, empieza, empiezan **4** empecé **6** empiece, empieces, empiece, empecemos, empecéis, empiecen

entender 2 entiende **3** entiendo, entiendes, entiende, entienden **6** entienda, entiendas, entienda, entiendan

ESTAR 2 está **3** estoy, estás, está, están **4** estuve, estuviste, estuvo, estuvimos, estuvisteis, estuvieron **6** esté, estés, esté, estén **7** estuviera *etc*

HABER 3 he, has, ha, hemos, habéis, han **4** hube, hubiste, hubo, hubimos, hubisteis, hubieron **5** habré *etc* **6** haya *etc* **7** hubiera *etc*

HABLAR 1 hablando **2** habla, hablad **3** hablo, hablas, habla, hablamos, habláis, hablan **4** hablé, hablaste, habló, hablamos, hablasteis, hablaron **5** hablaré, hablarás, hablará, hablaremos, hablaréis, hablarán **6** hable, hables, hable, hablemos, habléis, hablen **7** hablara or hablase, hablaras or hablases, habláramos or hablásemos, hablarais or hablaseis, hablaran or hablasen **8** hablado **9** hablaba, hablabas, hablaba, hablábamos, hablabais, hablaban

hacer 2 haz **3** hago **4** hice, hiciste, hizo, hicimos, hicisteis, hicieron **5** haré etc **6** haga etc **7** hiciera etc **8** hecho

instruir 1 instruyendo **2** instruye **3** instruyo, instruyes, instruye, instruyen **4** instruyó, instruyeron **6** instruya etc **7** instruyera etc

ir 1 yendo **2** ve **3** voy, vas, va, vamos, vais, van **4** fui, fuiste, fue, fuimos, fuisteis, fueron **6** vaya, vayas, vaya, vayamos, vayáis, vayan **7** fuera etc **9** iba, ibas, iba, íbamos, ibais, iban

jugar 2 juega **3** juego, juegas, juega, juegan **4** jugué **6** juegue etc

leer 1 leyendo **4** leyó, leyeron **7** leyera etc

morir 1 muriendo **2** muere **3** muero, mueres, muere, mueren **4** murió, murieron **6** muera, mueras, muera, muramos, muráis, mueran **7** muriera etc **8** muerto

mostrar 2 muestra **3** muestro, muestras, muestra, muestran **6** muestre, muestres, muestre, muestren

mover 2 mueve **3** muevo, mueves, mueve, mueven **6** mueva, muevas, mueva, muevan

negar 2 niega **3** niego, niegas, niega, niegan **4** negué **6** niegue, niegues, niegue, neguemos, neguéis, nieguen

ofrecer 3 ofrezco **6** ofrezca etc

oír 1 oyendo **2** oye **3** oigo, oyes, oye, oyen **4** oyó, oyeron **6** oiga etc **7** oyera etc

oler 2 huele **3** huelo, hueles, huele, huelen **6** huela, huelas, huela, huelan

parecer 3 parezco **6** parezca etc

pedir 1 pidiendo **2** pide **3** pido, pides, pide, piden **4** pidió, pidieron **6** pida etc **7** pidiera etc

pensar 2 piensa **3** pienso, piensas, piensa, piensan **6** piense, pienses, piense, piensen

perder 2 pierde **3** pierdo, pierdes, pierde, pierden **6** pierda, pierdas, pierda, pierdan

poder 1 pudiendo **2** puede **3** puedo, puedes, puede, pueden **4** pude, pudiste, pudo, pudimos, pudisteis, pudieron **5** podré etc **6** pueda, puedas, pueda, puedan **7** pudiera etc

poner 2 pon **3** pongo **4** puse, pusiste, puso, pusimos, pusisteis, pusieron **5** pondré etc **6** ponga etc **7** pusiera etc **8** puesto

preferir 1 prefiriendo **2** prefiere **3** prefiero, prefieres, prefiere, prefieren **4** prefirió, prefirieron **6** prefiera, prefieras, prefiera, prefiramos, prefiráis, prefieran **7** prefiriera etc

querer 2 quiere **3** quiero, quieres, quiere, quieren **4** quise, quisiste, quiso, quisimos, quisisteis, quisieron **5** querré etc **6** quiera, quieras, quiera, quieran **7** quisiera etc

reír 2 ríe **3** río, ríes, ríe, ríen **4** rió, rieron **6** ría, rías, ría, riamos, riáis, rían **7** riera etc

repetir 1 repitiendo **2** repite **3** repito, repites, repite, repiten **4** repitió, repitieron **6** repita etc **7** repitiera etc

rogar 2 ruega **3** ruego, ruegas, ruega, ruegan **4** rogué **6** ruegue, ruegues, ruegue, roguemos, roguéis, rueguen

saber 3 sé **4** supe, supiste, supo, supimos, supisteis, supieron **5** sabré etc **6** sepa etc **7** supiera etc

salir 2 sal **3** salgo **5** saldré etc **6** salga etc

seguir 1 siguiendo **2** sigue **3** sigo, sigues, sigue, siguen **4** siguió, siguieron **6** siga etc **7** siguiera etc

sentar 2 sienta **3** siento, sientas, sienta, sientan **6** siente, sientes, siente, sienten

sentir 1 sintiendo **2** siente **3** siento, sientes, siente, sienten **4** sintió, sintieron **6** sienta, sientas, sienta, sintamos, sintáis, sientan **7** sintiera *etc*

SER 2 sé **3** soy, eres, es, somos, sois, son **4** fui, fuiste, fue, fuimos, fuisteis, fueron **6** sea *etc* **7** fuera *etc* **9** era, eras, era, éramos, erais, eran

servir 1 sirviendo **2** sirve **3** sirvo, sirves, sirve, sirven **4** sirvió, sirvieron **6** sirva *etc* **7** sirviera *etc*

soñar 2 sueña **3** sueño, sueñas, sueña, sueñan **6** sueñe, sueñes, sueñe, sueñen

tener 2 ten **3** tengo, tienes, tiene, tienen **4** tuve, tuviste, tuvo, tuvimos, tuvisteis, tuvieron **5** tendré *etc* **6** tenga *etc* **7** tuviera *etc*

traer 1 trayendo **3** traigo **4** traje, trajiste, trajo, trajimos, trajisteis, trajeron **6** traiga *etc* **7** trajera *etc*

valer 2 val **3** valgo **5** valdré *etc* **6** valga *etc*

venir 2 ven **3** vengo, vienes, viene, vienen **4** vine, viniste, vino, vinimos, vinisteis, vinieron **5** vendré *etc* **6** venga *etc* **7** viniera *etc*

ver 3 veo **6** vea *etc* **8** visto **9** veía *etc*

vestir 1 vistiendo **2** viste **3** visto, vistes, viste, visten **4** vistió, vistieron **6** vista *etc* **7** vistiera *etc*

VIVIR 1 viviendo **2** vive, vivid **3** vivo, vives, vive, vivimos, vivís, viven **4** viví, viviste, vivió, vivimos, vivisteis, vivieron **5** viviré, vivirás, vivirá, viviremos, viviréis, vivirán **6** viva, vivas, viva, vivamos, viváis, vivan **7** viviera *or* viviese, vivieras *or* vivieses, viviera *or* viviese, viviéramos *or* viviésemos, vivierais *or* vivieseis, vivieran *or* viviesen **8** vivido **9** vivía, vivías, vivía, vivíamos, vivías, vivían

volcar 2 vuelca **3** vuelco, vuelcas, vuelca, vuelcan **4** volqué **6** vuelque, vuelques, vuelque, volquemos, volquéis, vuelquen

volver 2 vuelve **3** vuelvo, vuelves, vuelve, vuelven **6** vuelva, vuelvas, vuelva, vuelvan **8** vuelto

For additional information on Spanish verb formation, see pp 6 – 161 of the Grammar section.

Números

Numbers

uno (un, una)*	1	one
dos	2	two
tres	3	three
cuatro	4	four
cinco	5	five
seis	6	six
siete	7	seven
ocho	8	eight
nueve	9	nine
diez	10	ten
once	11	eleven
doce	12	twelve
trece	13	thirteen
catorce	14	fourteen
quince	15	fifteen
dieciséis	16	sixteen
diecisiete	17	seventeen
dieciocho	18	eighteen
diecinueve	19	nineteen
veinte	20	twenty
veintiuno(-un, -una)*	21	twenty-one
veintidós	22	twenty-two
treinta	30	thirty
treinta y uno(un, una)*	31	thirty-one
treinta y dos	32	thirty-two
cuarenta	40	forty
cincuenta	50	fifty
sesenta	60	sixty
setenta	70	seventy
ochenta	80	eighty
noventa	90	ninety
cien(ciento)**	100	a hundred, one hundred
ciento uno(un, una)*	101	a hundred and one
ciento dos	102	a hundred and two
ciento cincuenta y seis	156	a hundred and fifty-six
doscientos(-as)	200	two hundred
trescientos(-as)	300	three hundred
quinientos(-as)	500	five hundred
mil	1,000	a thousand
mil tres	1,003	a thousand and three
dos mil	2,000	two thousand
un millón	1,000,000	a million

*'uno' (+'veintiuno' etc) agrees in gender (but not number) with its noun: **treinta y una personas**; the masculine form is shortened to 'un' unless it stands alone: **veintiún caballos, veintiuno**.

'ciento' is used in compound numbers, except when it multiplies: **ciento diez, but **cien mil**. 'Cien' is used before nouns: **cien hombres, cien casas**.

Números

primero (primer, primera) 1°, 1er/1^a, 1^{era}
segundo(-a) 2°/2^a
tercero (tercer, tercera) 3°, 3er/3^a, 3^{era}
cuarto(-a) 4°/4^a
quinto(-a)
sexto(-a)
séptimo(-a)
octavo(-a)
noveno(-a); nono(-a)
décimo(-a)
undécimo(-a)
duodécimo(-a)
decimotercero(-a)
decimocuarto(-a)
decimoquinto(-a)
decimosexto(-a)
decimoséptimo(-a)
decimoctavo(-a)
decimonoveno(-a)
vigésimo(-a)
vigésimo(-a) primero(-a)
vigésimo(-a) segundo(-a)
trigésimo(-a)
trigésimo(-a) primero(-a)
trigésimo(-a) segundo(-a)
cuadragésimo(-a)
quincuagésimo(-a)
sexagésimo(-a)
septuagésimo(-a)
octogésimo(-a)
nonagésimo(-a)
centésimo(-a)
centésimo(-a) primero(-a)
milésimo(-a)

Numbers

first, 1st
second, 2nd
third, 3rd
fourth, 4th
fifth, 5th
sixth, 6th
seventh
eighth
ninth
tenth
eleventh
twelfth
thirteenth
fourteenth
fifteenth
sixteenth
seventeenth
eighteenth
nineteenth
twentieth
twenty-first
twenty-second
thirtieth
thirty-first
thirty-second
fortieth
fiftieth
sixtieth
seventieth
eightieth
ninetieth
hundredth
hundred-and-first
thousandth

La hora

The time

¿qué hora es?	*what time is it?*
es la una	it's one o'clock
son las cuatro	it's four o'clock
medianoche, las doce de la noche	midnight
la una (de la madrugada)	one o'clock (in the morning), one (a.m.)
la una y cinco	five past one
la una y diez	ten past one
la una y cuarto *or* quince	a quarter past one, one fifteen
la una y veinticinco	twenty-five past one, one twenty-five
la una y media *or* treinta	half past one, one thirty
las dos menos veinticinco, la una treinta y cinco	twenty-five to two, one thirty-five
las dos menos veinte, la una cuarenta	twenty to two, one forty
las dos menos cuarto, la una cuarenta y cinco	a quarter to two, one forty-five
las dos menos diez, la una cincuenta	ten to two, one fifty
mediodía, las doce (de la mañana)	twelve o'clock, midday, noon
la dos (de la tarde)	two o'clock (in the afternoon) two (p.m.)
la siete (de la tarde), seven o'clock (in the evening)	seven (p.m.)
¿a qué hora?	*at what time?*
a medianoche	at midnight
a las siete	at seven o'clock
a la una	at one o'clock
en veinte minutos	in twenty minutes
hace diez minutos	ten minutes ago

La fecha

The date

hoy	today
mañana	tomorrow
pasado mañana	the day after tomorrow
ayer	yesterday
antes de ayer, anteayer	the day before yesterday
la víspera	the day before, the previous day
el día siguiente	the next *or* following day
la mañana	morning
la tarde	evening

esta mañana	this morning
esta tarde	this evening, this afternoon
ayer por la mañana	yesterday morning
ayer por la tarde	yesterday evening
mañana por la mañana	tomorrow morning
mañana por la tarde	tomorrow evening, tomorrow afternoon
en la noche del sábado al domingo	during Saturday night, during the night of Saturday to Sunday
vendrá el sábado	he's coming on Saturday
los sábados	on Saturdays
todos los sábados	every Saturday
el sábado pasado	last Saturday
el sábado que viene, el próximo sábado	next Saturday
ocho días a partir del sábado	a week on Saturday
quince días a partir del sábado	a fortnight or two weeks on Saturday
de lunes a sábado	from Monday to Saturday
todos las días	every day
una vez a la semana	once a week
una vez al mes	once a month
dos veces a la semana	twice a week
hace una semana u ocho días	a week ago
hace quince días	a fortnight or two weeks ago
el año pasado	last year
dentro de dos días	in two days
dentro de ocho días o una semana	in a week
dentro de quince días	in a fortnight or two weeks
el mes que viene, el próximo mes	next month
el año que viene, el próximo año	next year
¿a qué o a cuántos estamos?	*what day is it?*
el 1/22 octubre de 2008	the 1st/22nd of October 2008, October 1st/22nd 2008
en 2008	in 2008
mil novicientos noventa y cinco	nineteen ninety-five
44 a. de J.C.	44 BC
14 d. de J.C.	14 AD
en el (siglo) XIX	in the nineteenth century
en los años treinta	in the thirties
érase una vez ...	once upon a time ...

a

10 (*tras ciertos verbos*): **voy a verle** I'm going to see him; **empezó a trabajar** he started working *o* to work; **sabe a queso** it tastes of cheese
11 (*+infin*): **al verle, le reconocí inmediatamente** when I saw him I recognized him at once; **el camino a recorrer** the distance we *etc* have to travel; **¡a callar!** keep quiet!; **¡a comer!** let's eat!
12: **a que**: **¡a que llueve!** I bet it's going to rain!; **¿a qué viene eso?** what's the meaning of this?; **¿a que sí va a venir?** he IS coming, isn't he?; **¿a que no lo haces?** — **¡a que sí!** bet you don't do it! — yes, I WILL!

abad, esa [a'βað, 'ðesa] *nm/f* abbot/abbess
abadía [aβa'ðia] *nf* abbey
abajo [a'βaxo] *adv* (*situación*) (down) below, underneath; (*en edificio*) downstairs; (*dirección*) down, downwards; **~ de** *prep* below, under; **el piso de ~** the downstairs flat; **la parte de ~** the lower part; **¡~ el gobierno!** down with the government!; **cuesta/río ~** downhill/downstream; **de arriba ~** from top to bottom; **el ~ firmante** the undersigned; **más ~** lower *o* further down
abalanzarse [aβalan'θarse] *vr*: **~ sobre** *o* **contra** to throw o.s. at
abalorios [aβa'lorjos] *nmpl* (*chucherías*) trinkets
abanderado, -a [aβande'rado, a] *nm/f* (*portaestandarte*) standard bearer; (*de un movimiento*) champion, leader; (*Am: linier*) linesman, assistant referee
abandonado, -a [aβando'naðo, a] *adj* derelict; (*desatendido*) abandoned; (*desierto*) deserted; (*descuidado*) neglected
abandonar [aβando'nar] *vt* to leave; (*persona*) to abandon, desert; (*cosa*) to abandon, leave behind; (*descuidar*) to neglect; (*renunciar a*) to give up; (*Inform*) to quit; **abandonarse** *vr*: **~se a** to abandon o.s. to; **~se al alcohol** to take to drink
abandono [aβan'dono] *nm* (*acto*) desertion, abandonment; (*estado*) abandon, neglect; (*renuncia*) withdrawal, retirement; **ganar por ~** to win by default
abanicar [aβani'kar] *vt* to fan
abanico [aβa'niko] *nm* fan; (*Naut*) derrick; **en ~** fan-shaped
abaratar [aβara'tar] *vt* to lower the price of ▷ *vi*, **abaratarse** *vr* to go *o* come down in price
abarcar [aβar'kar] *vt* to include, embrace; (*contener*) to comprise; (*Am*) to monopolize; **quien mucho abarca poco aprieta** don't bite off more than you can chew
abarrotado, -a [aβarro'taðo, a] *adj* packed; **~ de** packed *o* bursting with
abarrotar [aβarro'tar] *vt* (*local, estadio, teatro*) to fill, pack

⭕ **PALABRA CLAVE**

a [a] *prep* (**a + el = al**) **1** (*dirección*) to; **fueron a Madrid/Grecia** they went to Madrid/Greece; **me voy a casa** I'm going home
2 (*distancia*): **está a 15 km de aquí** it's 15 km from here
3 (*posición*): **estar a la mesa** to be at table; **al lado de** next to, beside; **a la derecha/izquierda** on the right/left; *ver tb* **puerta**
4 (*tiempo*): **a las 10/a medianoche** at 10/midnight; **¿a qué hora?** (at) what time?; **a la mañana siguiente** the following morning; **a los pocos días** after a few days; **estamos a 9 de julio** it's the 9th of July; **a los 24 años** at the age of 24; **ocho horas al día** eight hours a day; **al año/a la semana** (*Am*) a year/week later
5 (*manera*): **a la francesa** the French way; **a caballo** on horseback; **a oscuras** in the dark; **a rayas** striped; **le echaron a patadas** they kicked him out
6 (*medio, instrumento*): **a lápiz** in pencil; **a mano** by hand; **cocina a gas** gas stove
7 (*razón*): **a dos euros el kilo** at two euros a kilo; **a más de 50 km por hora** at more than 50 km per hour; **poco a poco** little by little
8 (*dativo*): **se lo di a él** I gave it to him; **se lo compré a él** I bought it from him
9 (*complemento directo*): **vi al policía** I saw the policeman

abarrote [aβaˈrrote] *nm* packing; **abarrotes** *nmpl* (*Am*) groceries; **tienda de ~s** (*Am*) grocery store

abarrotero, -a [aβarroˈtero, a] *nm/f* (*Am*) grocer

abastecer [aβasteˈθer] *vt*: **~ (de)** to supply (with)

abastecimiento [aβasteθiˈmjento] *nm* supply

abasto [aˈβasto] *nm* supply; (*abundancia*) abundance; **no dar ~ a algo** not to be able to cope with sth

abatible [aβaˈtiβle] *adj*: **asiento ~** tip-up seat; (*Auto*) reclining seat

abatido, -a [aβaˈtiðo, a] *adj* dejected, downcast; **estar muy ~** to be very depressed

abatimiento [aβatiˈmjento] *nm* (*depresión*) dejection, depression

abatir [aβaˈtir] *vt* (*muro*) to demolish; (*pájaro*) to shoot o bring down; (*fig*) to depress; **abatirse** *vr* to get depressed; **~se sobre** to swoop o pounce on

abdicación [aβðikaˈθjon] *nf* abdication

abdicar [aβðiˈkar] *vi* to abdicate; **~ en algn** to abdicate in favour of sb

abdomen [aβˈðomen] *nm* abdomen

abdominal [aβðomiˈnal] *adj* abdominal ▷ *nm*: **~es** abdominals, stomach muscles; (*Deporte*: *tb*: **ejercicios ~es**) sit-ups

abecedario [aβeθeˈðarjo] *nm* alphabet

abedul [aβeˈðul] *nm* birch

abeja [aˈβexa] *nf* bee; (*fig*: *hormiguita*) hard worker

abejorro [aβeˈxorro] *nm* bumblebee

aberración [aβerraˈθjon] *nf* aberration

abertura [aβerˈtura] *nf* = **apertura**

abertzale [aβerˈtʃale] *adj*, *nm/f* Basque nationalist

abeto [aˈβeto] *nm* fir

abierto, -a [aˈβjerto, a] *pp de* **abrir** ▷ *adj* open; (*fig*: *carácter*) frank

abigarrado, -a [aβiɣaˈrraðo, a] *adj* multicoloured; (*fig*) motley

abismal [aβisˈmal] *adj* (*fig*) vast, enormous

abismo [aˈβismo] *nm* abyss; **de sus ideas a las mías hay un ~** our views are worlds apart

abjurar [aβxuˈrar] *vt* to abjure, forswear ▷ *vi*: **~ de** to abjure, forswear

ablandar [aβlanˈdar] *vt* to soften; (*conmover*) to touch; (*Culin*) to tenderize ▷ *vi*, **ablandarse** *vr* to get softer

abnegación [aβneɣaˈθjon] *nf* self-denial

abnegado, -a [aβneˈɣaðo, a] *adj* self-sacrificing

abocado, -a [aβoˈkaðo, a] *adj*: **verse ~ al desastre** to be heading for disaster

abochornar [aβotʃorˈnar] *vt* to embarrass; **abochornarse** *vr* to get flustered; (*Bot*) to wilt; **~se de** to get embarrassed about

abofetear [aβofeteˈar] *vt* to slap (in the face)

abogacía [aβoɣaˈθia] *nf* legal profession; (*ejercicio*) practice of the law

abogado, -a [aβoˈɣaðo, a] *nm/f* lawyer; (*notario*) solicitor; (*asesor*) counsel; (*en tribunal*) barrister, advocate, attorney (*US*); **~ defensor** defence lawyer (*Brit*), defense attorney (*US*); **~ del diablo** devil's advocate

abogar [aβoˈɣar] *vi*: **~ por** to plead for; (*fig*) to advocate

abolengo [aβoˈlengo] *nm* ancestry, lineage

abolición [aβoliˈθjon] *nf* abolition

abolir [aβoˈlir] *vt* to abolish; (*cancelar*) to cancel

abolladura [aβoʎaˈðura] *nf* dent

abollar [aβoˈʎar] *vt* to dent

abombarse [aβomˈbarse] (*Am*) *vr* to go bad

abominable [aβomiˈnaβle] *adj* abominable

abominación [aβominaˈθjon] *nf* abomination

abonado, -a [aβoˈnaðo, a] *adj* (*deuda*) paid(-up) ▷ *nm/f* subscriber

abonar [aβoˈnar] *vt* to pay; (*deuda*) to settle; (*terreno*) to fertilize; (*idea*) to endorse; **abonarse** *vr* to subscribe; **~ dinero en una cuenta** to pay money into an account, credit money to an account

abono [aˈβono] *nm* payment; fertilizer; subscription

abordar [aβorˈðar] *vt* (*barco*) to board; (*asunto*) to broach; (*individuo*) to approach

aborigen [aβoˈrixen] *nm/f* aborigine

aborrecer [aβorreˈθer] *vt* to hate, loathe

abortar [aβorˈtar] *vi* (*malparir*) to have a miscarriage; (*deliberadamente*) to have an abortion

aborto [aˈβorto] *nm* miscarriage; abortion

abotagado, -a [aβotaˈɣaðo, a] *adj* swollen

abotonar [aβotoˈnar] *vt* to button (up), do up

abovedado, -a [aβoβeˈðaðo, a] *adj* vaulted, domed

abrasar [aβraˈsar] *vt* to burn (up); (*Agr*) to dry up, parch

abrazadera [aβraθaˈðera] *nf* bracket

abrazar [aβraˈθar] *vt* to embrace, hug; **abrazarse** *vr* to embrace, hug each other

abrazo [aˈβraθo] *nm* embrace, hug; **un ~** (*en carta*) with best wishes

abrebotellas [aβreβoˈteʎas] *nm inv* bottle opener

abrecartas [aβreˈkartas] *nm inv* letter opener

abrelatas [aβreˈlatas] *nm inv* tin (*Brit*) o can (*US*) opener

abreviar [aβreˈβjar] *vt* to abbreviate; (*texto*) to abridge; (*plazo*) to reduce ▷ *vi*: **bueno, para ~** well, to cut a long story short

abreviatura [aβreβjaˈtura] *nf* abbreviation

abridor [aβriˈðor] *nm* (*de botellas*) bottle opener; (*de latas*) tin (*Brit*) o can (*US*) opener

abrigador, a [aβriɣaˈðor, a] *adj* (*Am*) warm

abrigar [aβriˈɣar] *vt* (*proteger*) to shelter; (*suj*: *ropa*) to keep warm; (*fig*) to cherish; **abrigarse** *vr* (*con ropa*) to cover (o.s.) up; **~se (de)** to take shelter (from), protect o.s. (from); **¡abrígate bien!** wrap up well!

abrigo [a'βriɣo] nm (prenda) coat, overcoat; (lugar protegido) shelter; **al ~ de** in the shelter of

abril [a'βril] nm April; ver tb **julio**

abrillantador [aβriʎanta'ðor] nm polish

abrillantar [aβriʎan'tar] vt (pulir) to polish; (fig) to enhance

abrir [a'βrir] vt to open (up); (camino etc) to open up; (apetito) to whet; (lista) to head ▷ vi to open; **abrirse** vr to open (up); (extenderse) to open out; (cielo) to clear; **~ un negocio** to start up a business; **en un ~ y cerrar de ojos** in the twinkling of an eye; **~se paso** to find o force a way through

abrochar [aβro'tʃar] vt (con botones) to button (up); (zapato, con broche) to do up; **abrocharse** vr: **~se los zapatos** to tie one's shoelaces

abrumar [aβru'mar] vt to overwhelm; (sobrecargar) to weigh down

abrupto, -a [a'βrupto, a] adj abrupt; (empinado) steep

absceso [aβs'θeso] nm abscess

absentismo [aβsen'tismo] nm (de obreros) absenteeism

absolución [aβsolu'θjon] nf (Rel) absolution; (Jur) acquittal

absoluto, -a [aβso'luto, a] adj absolute; (total) utter, complete; **en ~** not at all

absolver [aβsol'βer] vt to absolve; (Jur) to pardon; (: acusado) to acquit

absorbente [aβsor'βente] adj absorbent; (interesante) absorbing, interesting; (exigente) demanding

absorber [aβsor'βer] vt to absorb; (embeber) to soak up; **absorberse** vr to become absorbed

absorción [aβsor'θjon] nf absorption; (Com) takeover

absorto, -a [aβ'sorto, a] pp de **absorber** ▷ adj absorbed, engrossed

abstemio, -a [aβs'temjo, a] adj teetotal

abstención [aβsten'θjon] nf abstention

abstenerse [aβste'nerse] vr: **~ (de)** to abstain o refrain (from)

abstinencia [aβsti'nenθja] nf abstinence; (ayuno) fasting

abstracción [aβstrak'θjon] nf abstraction

abstracto, -a [aβ'strakto, a] adj abstract; **en ~** in the abstract

abstraer [aβstra'er] vt to abstract; **abstraerse** vr to be o become absorbed

abstraído, -a [aβstra'iðo, a] adj absent-minded

absuelto [aβ'swelto] pp de **absolver**

absurdo, -a [aβ'surðo, a] adj absurd ▷ nm absurdity; **lo ~ es que ...** the ridiculous thing is that ...

abuchear [aβutʃe'ar] vt to boo

abuela [a'βwela] nf grandmother; **¡cuéntaselo a tu ~!** (fam!) do you think I was born yesterday? (fam); **no tener/necesitar ~** (fam) to be full of o.s./blow one's own trumpet

abuelo [a'βwelo] nm grandfather; (antepasado) ancestor; **abuelos** nmpl grandparents

abulia [a'βulja] nf lethargy

abúlico, -a [a'βuliko, a] adj lethargic

abultado, -a [aβul'taðo, a] adj bulky

abultar [aβul'tar] vt to enlarge; (aumentar) to increase; (fig) to exaggerate ▷ vi to be bulky

abundancia [aβun'danθja] nf: **una ~ de** plenty of; **en ~** in abundance

abundante [aβun'dante] adj abundant, plentiful

abundar [aβun'dar] vi to abound, be plentiful; **~ en una opinión** to share an opinion

aburguesarse [aβurɣe'sarse] vr to become middle-class

aburrido, -a [aβu'rriðo, a] adj (hastiado) bored; (que aburre) boring

aburrimiento [aβurri'mjento] nm boredom, tedium

aburrir [aβu'rrir] vt to bore; **aburrirse** vr to be bored, get bored; **~se como una almeja** u **ostra** to be bored stiff

abusado, -a [aβu'saðo, a] adj (Am: fam: astuto) sharp, cunning ▷ excl: **¡~!** (inv) look out!, careful!

abusar [aβu'sar] vi to go too far; **~ de** to abuse

abusivo, -a [aβu'siβo, a] adj (precio) exorbitant

abuso [a'βuso] nm abuse; **~ de confianza** betrayal of trust

a/c abr (= al cuidado de) c/o; (= a cuenta) on account

acá [a'ka] adv (lugar) here; **pasearse de ~ para allá** to walk up and down; **¡vente para ~!** come over here!; **¿de cuándo ~?** since when?

acabado, -a [aka'βaðo, a] adj finished, complete; (perfecto) perfect; (agotado) worn out; (fig) masterly ▷ nm finish

acabar [aka'βar] vt (llevar a su fin) to finish, complete; (consumir) to use up; (rematar) to finish off ▷ vi to finish, end; (morir) to die; **acabarse** vr to finish, stop; (terminarse) to be over; (agotarse) to run out; **~ con** to put an end to; **~ mal** to come to a sticky end; **esto ~á conmigo** this will be the end of me; **~ de llegar** to have just arrived; **acababa de hacerlo** I had just done it; **~ haciendo** o **por hacer algo** to end up (by) doing sth; **¡se acabó!** (¡basta!) that's enough!; (se terminó) it's all over!; **se me acabó el tabaco** I ran out of cigarettes

acabose [aka'βose] nm: **esto es el ~** this is the last straw

acacia [a'kaθja] nf acacia

academia [aka'ðemja] nf academy; (Escol) private school; **~ de idiomas** language school; ver tb **colegio**

académico, -a [aka'ðemiko, a] adj academic

acaecer [akae'θer] vi to happen, occur

acallar [aka'ʎar] vt *(silenciar)* to silence; *(calmar)* to pacify

acalorado, -a [akalo'raðo, a] adj *(discusión)* heated

acalorarse [akalo'rarse] vr *(fig)* to get heated

acampada [akam'paða] nf: **ir de ~** to go camping

acampanado, -a [akampa'naðo, a] adj flared

acampar [akam'par] vi to camp

acanalar [akana'lar] vt to groove; *(ondular)* to corrugate

acantilado [akanti'laðo] nm cliff

acaparar [akapa'rar] vt to monopolize; *(acumular)* to hoard

acariciar [akari'θjar] vt to caress; *(esperanza)* to cherish

acarrear [akarre'ar] vt to transport; *(fig)* to cause, result in; **le acarreó muchos disgustos** it brought him lots of problems

acaso [a'kaso] adv perhaps, maybe ▷ nm chance; **¿~ es mi culpa?** *(Am: fam)* what makes you think it's my fault?; **(por) si ~** (just) in case

acatamiento [akata'mjento] nm respect; *(de la ley)* observance

acatar [aka'tar] vt to respect; *(ley)* to obey, observe

acatarrarse [akata'rrarse] vr to catch a cold

acaudalado, -a [akauða'laðo, a] adj well-off

acaudillar [akauði'ʎar] vt to lead, command

acceder [akθe'ðer] vi to accede, agree; **~ a** *(petición etc)* to agree to; *(tener acceso a)* to have access to; *(Inform)* to access

accesible [akθe'siβle] adj accessible; **~ a** open to

acceso [ak'θeso] nm access, entry; *(camino)* access road; *(Med)* attack, fit; *(de cólera)* fit; *(Pol)* accession; *(Inform)* access; **~ aleatorio/directo/secuencial** o **en serie** *(Inform)* random/direct/sequential o serial access; **de ~ múltiple** multi-access

accesorio, -a [akθe'sorjo, a] adj accessory ▷ nm accessory; **accesorios** nmpl *(Auto)* accessories, extras; *(Teat)* props

accidentado, -a [akθiðen'taðo, a] adj uneven; *(montañoso)* hilly; *(azaroso)* eventful ▷ nm/f accident victim

accidental [akθiðen'tal] adj accidental; *(empleo)* temporary

accidentarse [akθiðen'tarse] vr to have an accident

accidente [akθi'ðente] nm accident; **por ~** by chance; **accidentes** nmpl *(de terreno)* unevenness sg, roughness sg; **~ laboral** o **de trabajo/de tráfico** industrial/road o traffic accident

acción [ak'θjon] nf action; *(acto)* action, act; *(Teat)* plot; *(Com)* share; *(Jur)* action, lawsuit; **capital en acciones** share capital; **~ liberada/ordinaria/preferente** fully-paid/ordinary/preference share

accionar [akθjo'nar] vt to work, operate; *(ejecutar)* to activate

accionista [akθjo'nista] nm/f shareholder

acebo [a'θeβo] nm holly; *(árbol)* holly tree

acechanza [aθe'tʃanθa] nf = **acecho**

acechar [aθe'tʃar] vt to spy on; *(aguardar)* to lie in wait for

acecho [a'θetʃo] nm: **estar al ~ (de)** to lie in wait (for)

aceite [a'θeite] nm oil; **~ de girasol/oliva** olive/sunflower oil; **~ de hígado de bacalao** cod-liver oil

aceitera [aθei'tera] nf oilcan

aceitoso, -a [aθei'toso, a] adj oily

aceituna [aθei'tuna] nf olive; **~ rellena** stuffed olive

acelerador [aθelera'ðor] nm accelerator

acelerar [aθele'rar] vt to accelerate; **acelerarse** vr to hurry

acelga [a'θelɣa] nf chard, beet

acento [a'θento] nm accent; *(acentuación)* stress; **~ cerrado** strong o thick accent

acentuar [aθen'twar] vt to accent; to stress; *(fig)* to accentuate

acepción [aθep'θjon] nf meaning

aceptable [aθep'taβle] adj acceptable

aceptación [aθepta'θjon] nf acceptance; *(aprobación)* approval

aceptar [aθep'tar] vt to accept; *(aprobar)* to approve; **~ hacer algo** to agree to do sth

acequia [a'θekja] nf irrigation ditch

acera [a'θera] nf pavement *(Brit)*, sidewalk *(US)*

acerado, -a [aθe'raðo, a] adj steel; *(afilado)* sharp; *(fig: duro)* steely; *(: mordaz)* biting

acerbo, -a [a'θerβo, a] adj bitter; *(fig)* harsh

acerca [a'θerka]: **~ de** prep about, concerning

acercar [aθer'kar] vt to bring o move nearer; **acercarse** vr to approach, come near

acerico [aθe'riko] nm pincushion

acero [a'θero] nm steel; **~ inoxidable** stainless steel

acérrimo, -a [a'θerrimo, a] adj *(partidario)* staunch; *(enemigo)* bitter

acertado, -a [aθer'taðo, a] adj correct; *(apropiado)* apt; *(sensato)* sensible

acertar [aθer'tar] vt *(blanco)* to hit; *(solución)* to get right; *(adivinar)* to guess ▷ vi to get it right, be right; **~ a** to manage to; **~ con** to happen o hit on

acertijo [aθer'tixo] nm riddle, puzzle

acervo [a'θerβo] nm heap; **~ común** undivided estate

achacar [atʃa'kar] vt to attribute

achacoso, -a [atʃa'koso, a] adj sickly

achaque etc [a'tʃake] vb ver **achacar** ▷ nm ailment

achicar [atʃi'kar] vt to reduce; *(humillar)* to humiliate; *(Naut)* to bale out; **achicarse** vr *(ropa)* to shrink; *(fig)* to humble o.s.

achicharrar [atʃitʃa'rrar] vt to scorch, burn

achichincle [atʃi'tʃinkle] nm/f *(Am: fam)* minion

achicoria [atʃi'korja] *nf* chicory
achuras [a'tʃuras] *nf* (*Am: Culin*) offal
aciago, -a [a'θjaɣo, a] *adj* ill-fated, fateful
acicalar [aθika'lar] *vt* to polish; (*adornar*) to bedeck; **acicalarse** *vr* to get dressed up
acicate [aθi'kate] *nm* spur; (*fig*) incentive
acidez [aθi'ðeθ] *nf* acidity
ácido, -a ['aθiðo, a] *adj* sour, acid ▷ *nm* acid; (*fam: droga*) LSD
acierto *etc* [a'θjerto] *vb ver* **acertar** ▷ *nm* success; (*buen paso*) wise move; (*solución*) solution; (*habilidad*) skill, ability; (*al adivinar*) good guess; **fue un ~ suyo** it was a sensible choice on his part
acitronar [aθitro'nar] (*Am*) *vt* (*fam*) to brown
aclamación [aklama'θjon] *nf* acclamation; (*aplausos*) applause
aclamar [akla'mar] *vt* to acclaim; (*aplaudir*) to applaud
aclaración [aklara'θjon] *nf* clarification, explanation
aclarar [akla'rar] *vt* to clarify, explain; (*ropa*) to rinse ▷ *vi* to clear up; **aclararse** *vr* (*suj: persona: explicarse*) to understand; (*fig: asunto*) to become clear; **~se la garganta** to clear one's throat
aclaratorio, -a [aklara'torjo, a] *adj* explanatory
aclimatación [aklimata'θjon] *nf* acclimatization
aclimatar [aklima'tar] *vt* to acclimatize; **aclimatarse** *vr* to become *o* get acclimatized; **~se a algo** to get used to sth
acné [ak'ne] *nm* acne
acobardar [akoβar'ðar] *vt* to daunt, intimidate; **acobardarse** *vr* (*atemorizarse*) to be intimidated; (*echarse atrás*): **~se (ante)** to shrink back (from)
acodarse [ako'ðarse] *vr*: **~ en** to lean on
acogedor, a [akoxe'ðor, a] *adj* welcoming; (*hospitalario*) hospitable
acoger [ako'xer] *vt* to welcome; (*abrigar*) to shelter; **acogerse** *vr* to take refuge; **~se a** (*pretexto*) to take refuge in; (*ley*) to resort to
acogida [ako'xiða] *nf* reception; refuge
acolchar [akol'tʃar] *vt* to pad; (*fig*) to cushion
acomedido, -a [akome'ðiðo, a] (*Am*) *adj* helpful, obliging
acometer [akome'ter] *vt* to attack; (*emprender*) to undertake
acometida [akome'tiða] *nf* attack, assault
acomodado, -a [akomo'ðaðo, a] *adj* (*persona*) well-to-do
acomodador, a [akomoða'ðor, a] *nm/f* usher(ette)
acomodar [akomo'ðar] *vt* to adjust; (*alojar*) to accommodate; **acomodarse** *vr* to conform; (*instalarse*) to install o.s.; (*adaptarse*) to adapt o.s.; **~se (a)** to adapt (to); **¡acomódese a su gusto!** make yourself comfortable!

acomodaticio, -a [akomoða'tiθjo, a] *adj* (*pey*) accommodating, obliging; (*manejable*) pliable
acompañante, -a [akompa'ɲante, a] *nm/f* companion
acompañar [akompa'ɲar] *vt* to accompany, go with; (*documentos*) to enclose; **¿quieres que te acompañe?** do you want me to come with you?; **~ a algn a la puerta** to see sb to the door *o* out; **le acompaño en el sentimiento** please accept my condolences
acomplejar [akomple'xar] *vt* to give a complex to; **acomplejarse** *vr*: **~se (con)** to get a complex (about)
acondicionado, -a [akondiθjo'naðo, a] *adj* (*Tec*) in good condition
acondicionar [akondiθjo'nar] *vt* to get ready, prepare; (*pelo*) to condition
acongojar [akongo'xar] *vt* to distress, grieve
aconsejar [akonse'xar] *vt* to advise, counsel; **~ a algn hacer** *o* **que haga algo** to advise sb to do sth; **aconsejarse** *vr*: **~se con** *o* **de** to consult
acontecer [akonte'θer] *vi* to happen, occur
acontecimiento [akonteθi'mjento] *nm* event
acopio [a'kopjo] *nm* store, stock
acoplamiento [akopla'mjento] *nm* coupling, joint
acoplar [ako'plar] *vt* to fit; (*Elec*) to connect; (*vagones*) to couple
acorazado, -a [akora'θaðo, a] *adj* armour-plated, armoured ▷ *nm* battleship
acordar [akor'ðar] *vt* (*resolver*) to agree, resolve; (*recordar*) to remind; **acordarse** *vr* to agree; **~ hacer algo** to agree to do sth; **~se (de algo)** to remember (sth)
acorde [a'korðe] *adj* (*Mus*) harmonious ▷ *nm* chord; **~ con** (*medidas etc*) in keeping with
acordeón [akorðe'on] *nm* accordion
acordonado, -a [akorðo'naðo, a] *adj* (*calle*) cordoned-off
acorralar [akorra'lar] *vt* to round up, corral; (*fig*) to intimidate
acortar [akor'tar] *vt* to shorten; (*duración*) to cut short; (*cantidad*) to reduce; **acortarse** *vr* to become shorter
acosar [ako'sar] *vt* to pursue relentlessly; (*fig*) to hound, pester; **~ a algn a preguntas** to pester sb with questions
acoso [a'koso] *nm* relentless pursuit; (*fig*) harassment; **~ sexual** sexual harassment
acostar [akos'tar] *vt* (*en cama*) to put to bed; (*en suelo*) to lay down; (*barco*) to bring alongside; **acostarse** *vr* to go to bed; to lie down; **~se con algn** to sleep with sb
acostumbrado, -a [akostum'braðo, a] *adj* (*habitual*) usual; **estar ~ a (hacer) algo** to be used to (doing) sth
acostumbrar [akostum'brar] *vt*: **~ a algn a algo** to get sb used to sth ▷ *vi*: **~ (a hacer algo)** to be in the habit (of doing sth); **acostumbrarse** *vr*: **~se a** to get used to

acotación [akota'θjon] nf (apunte) marginal note; (Geo) elevation mark; (de límite) boundary mark; (Teat) stage direction

acotamiento [akota'mjento] (Am) nm hard shoulder (Brit), berm (US)

ácrata ['akrata] adj, nm/f anarchist

acre ['akre] adj (sabor) sharp, bitter; (olor) acrid; (fig) biting ▷ nm acre

acrecentar [akreθen'tar] vt to increase, augment

acreditar [akreði'tar] vt (garantizar) to vouch for, guarantee; (autorizar) to authorize; (dar prueba de) to prove; (Com: abonar) to credit; (embajador) to accredit; **acreditarse** vr to become famous; (demostrar valía) to prove one's worth; **~se de** to get a reputation for

acreedor, a [akree'ðor, a] adj: **~ a** worthy of ▷ nm/f creditor; **común/diferido/con garantía** (Com) unsecured/deferred/secured creditor

acribillar [akriβi'ʎar] vt: **~ a balazos** to riddle with bullets

acróbata [a'kroβata] nm/f acrobat

acta ['akta] nf certificate; (de comisión) minutes pl, record; **~ de nacimiento/de matrimonio** birth/marriage certificate; **~ notarial** affidavit; **levantar ~** (Jur) to make a formal statement o deposition

actitud [akti'tuð] nf attitude; (postura) posture; **adoptar una ~ firme** to take a firm stand

activar [akti'βar] vt to activate; (acelerar) to speed up

actividad [aktiβi'ðað] nf activity; **estar en plena ~** to be in full swing

activo, -a [ak'tiβo, a] adj active; (vivo) lively ▷ nm (Com) assets pl; **~ y pasivo** assets and liabilities; **~ circulante/fijo/inmaterial/ invisible** (Com) current/fixed/intangible/ invisible assets; **~ realizable** liquid assets; **~s congelados o bloqueados** frozen assets; **~ tóxico** toxic asset; **estar en ~** (Mil) to be on active service

acto ['akto] nm act, action; (ceremonia) ceremony; (Teat) act; **en el ~** immediately; **hacer ~ de presencia** (asistir) to attend (formally)

actor [ak'tor] nm actor; (Jur) plaintiff ▷ adj: **parte ~** prosecution

actriz [ak'triθ] nf actress

actuación [aktwa'θjon] nf action; (comportamiento) conduct, behaviour; (Jur) proceedings pl; (desempeño) performance

actual [ak'twal] adj present(-day), current; **el 6 del ~** the 6th of this month

actualidad [aktwali'ðað] nf present; **actualidades** nfpl (noticias) news sg; **en la ~** at present; (hoy día) nowadays, at present; **ser de gran ~** to be current

actualizar [aktwali'θar] vt to update, modernize

actualmente [aktwal'mente] adv at present;

(hoy día) nowadays

actuar [ak'twar] vi (obrar) to work, operate; (actor) to act, perform ▷ vt to work, operate; **~ de** to act as

acuarela [akwa'rela] nf watercolour

acuario [a'kwarjo] nm aquarium; **A~** (Astro) Aquarius

acuartelar [akwarte'lar] vt (Mil: alojar) to quarter

acuático, -a [a'kwatiko, a] adj aquatic

acuchillar [akutʃi'ʎar] vt (Tec) to plane (down), smooth

acuciar [aku'θjar] vt to urge on

acuclillarse [akukli'ʎarse] vr to crouch down

acudir [aku'ðir] vi to attend, turn up; (ir) to go; **~ a** to turn to; **~ en ayuda de** to go to the aid of; **~ a una cita** to keep an appointment; **~ a una llamada** to answer a call; **no tener a quién ~** to have nobody to turn to

acuerdo [a'kwerðo] vb ver **acordar** ▷ nm agreement; (Pol) resolution; **~ de pago respectivo** (Com) knock-for-knock agreement; **A~ general sobre aranceles aduaneros y comercio** (Com) General Agreement on Tariffs and Trade; **tomar un ~** to pass a resolution; **¡de ~!** agreed!; **de ~ con** (persona) in agreement with; (acción, documento) in accordance with; **de común ~** by common consent; **estar de ~** (persona) to agree; **llegar a un ~** to come to an understanding

acumular [akumu'lar] vt to accumulate, collect

acuñar [aku'nar] vt (moneda) to mint; (frase) to coin

acuoso, -a [a'kwoso, a] adj watery

acupuntura [akupun'tura] nf acupuncture

acurrucarse [akurru'karse] vr to crouch; (ovillarse) to curl up

acusación [akusa'θjon] nf accusation

acusar [aku'sar] vt to accuse; (revelar) to reveal; (denunciar) to denounce; (emoción) to show; **~ recibo** to acknowledge receipt; **su rostro acusó extrañeza** his face registered surprise; **acusarse** vr: **~se (de)** to confess (to)

acuse [a'kuse] nm: **~ de recibo** acknowledgement of receipt

acústico, -a [a'kustiko, a] adj acoustic ▷ nf (de una sala etc) acoustics pl; (ciencia) acoustics sg

adagio [a'ðaxjo] nm adage; (Mus) adagio

adaptación [aðapta'θjon] nf adaptation

adaptador [aðapta'ðor] nm (Elec) adapter; **~ universal** universal adapter

adaptar [aðap'tar] vt to adapt; (acomodar) to fit; (convertir) **~ (para)** to convert (to)

adecuado, -a [aðe'kwaðo, a] adj (apto) suitable; (oportuno) appropriate; **el hombre ~ para el puesto** the right man for the job

adecuar [aðe'kwar] vt (adaptar) to adapt; (hacer apto) to make suitable

a. de J.C. abr (= antes de Jesucristo) B.C.

a

adelantado, -a [aðelan'taðo, a] *adj* advanced; *(reloj)* fast; **pagar por ~** to pay in advance

adelantamiento [aðelanta'mjento] *nm* advance, advancement; *(Auto)* overtaking

adelantar [aðelan'tar] *vt* to move forward; *(avanzar)* to advance; *(acelerar)* to speed up; *(Auto)* to overtake ▷ *vi* *(ir delante)* to go ahead; *(progresar)* to improve; **adelantarse** *vr* *(tomar la delantera: corredor)* to move forward; **~se a algn** to get ahead of sb; **~se a los deseos de algn** to anticipate sb's wishes

adelante [aðe'lante] *adv* forward(s), onward(s), ahead ▷ *excl* come in!; **de hoy en ~** from now on; **más ~** later on; *(más allá)* further on

adelanto [aðe'lanto] *nm* advance; *(mejora)* improvement; *(progreso)* progress; *(dinero)* advance; **los ~s de la ciencia** the advances of science

adelgazar [aðelɣa'θar] *vt* to thin (down); *(afilar)* to taper ▷ *vi* to get thin; *(con régimen)* to slim down, lose weight

ademán [aðe'man] *nm* gesture; **ademanes** *nmpl* manners; **en ~ de** as if to

además [aðe'mas] *adv* besides; *(por otra parte)* moreover; *(también)* also; **~ de** besides, in addition to

adentrarse [aðen'trarse] *vr*: **~ en** to go into, get inside; *(penetrar)* to penetrate (into)

adentro [a'ðentro] *adv* inside, in; **mar ~** out at sea; **tierra ~** inland ▷ *nm*: **dijo para sus ~s** he said to himself

adepto, -a [a'ðepto, a] *nm/f* supporter

aderezar [aðere'θar] *vt* *(ensalada)* to dress; *(comida)* to season

aderezo [aðe'reθo] *nm* dressing; seasoning

adeudar [aðeu'ðar] *vt* to owe; **adeudarse** *vr* to run into debt; **~ una suma en una cuenta** to debit an account with a sum

adherirse [aðe'rirse] *vr*: **~ a** to adhere to; *(partido)* to join; *(fig)* to follow

adhesión [aðe'sjon] *nf* adhesion; *(fig)* adherence

adicción [aðik'θjon] *nf* addiction

adición [aði'θjon] *nf* addition

adicionar [aðiθjo'nar] *vt* to add

adicto, -a [a'ðikto, a] *adj*: **~ a** *(droga etc)* addicted to; *(dedicado)* devoted to ▷ *nm/f* supporter, follower; *(toxicómano etc)* addict

adiestrar [aðjes'trar] *vt* to train, teach; *(conducir)* to guide, lead; **adiestrarse** *vr* to practise; *(aprender)* to train o.s.

adinerado, -a [aðine'raðo, a] *adj* wealthy

adiós [a'ðjos] *excl* *(para despedirse)* goodbye!, cheerio!; *(al pasar)* hello!

aditivo [aði'tiβo] *nm* additive

adivinanza [aðiβi'nanθa] *nf* riddle

adivinar [aðiβi'nar] *vt* *(profetizar)* to prophesy; *(conjeturar)* to guess

adivino, -a [aði'βino, a] *nm/f* fortune-teller

adj *abr* (= *adjunto*) encl; (= *adjetivo*) adj

adjetivo [aðxe'tiβo] *nm* adjective

adjudicación [aðxuðika'θjon] *nf* award; *(Com)* adjudication

adjudicar [aðxuði'kar] *vt* to award; **adjudicarse** *vr*: **~se algo** to appropriate sth

adjuntar [aðxun'tar] *vt* to attach, enclose

adjunto, -a [að'xunto, a] *adj* attached, enclosed ▷ *nm/f* assistant

administración [aðministra'θjon] *nf* administration; *(dirección)* management; **~ pública** civil service; **A~ de Correos** General Post Office

administrador, a [aðministra'ðor, a] *nm/f* administrator; manager(ess)

administrar [aðminis'trar] *vt* to administer

administrativo, -a [aðministra'tiβo, a] *adj* administrative

admirable [aðmi'raβle] *adj* admirable

admiración [aðmira'θjon] *nf* admiration; *(asombro)* wonder; *(Ling)* exclamation mark

admirar [aðmi'rar] *vt* to admire; *(extrañar)* to surprise; **admirarse** *vr* to be surprised; **se admiró de saberlo** he was amazed to hear it; **no es de ~ que ...** it's not surprising that ...

admisible [aðmi'siβle] *adj* admissible

admisión [aðmi'sjon] *nf* admission; *(reconocimiento)* acceptance

admitir [aðmi'tir] *vt* to admit; *(aceptar)* to accept; *(dudas)* to leave room for; **esto no admite demora** this must be dealt with immediately

admonición [aðmoni'θjon] *nf* warning

ADN *nm abr* (= *ácido desoxirribonucleico*) DNA

adobar [aðo'βar] *vt* *(preparar)* to prepare; *(cocinar)* to season

adobe [a'ðoβe] *nm* adobe, sun-dried brick

adoctrinar [aðoktri'nar] *vt* to indoctrinate

adolecer [aðole'θer] *vi*: **~ de** to suffer from

adolescente [aðoles'θente] *nm/f* adolescent, teenager ▷ *adj* adolescent, teenage

adonde [conj] (to) where

adónde [a'ðonde] *adv* = **dónde**

adopción [aðop'θjon] *nf* adoption

adoptar [aðop'tar] *vt* to adopt

adoptivo, -a [aðop'tiβo, a] *adj* *(padres)* adoptive; *(hijo)* adopted

adoquín [aðo'kin] *nm* paving stone

adorar [aðo'rar] *vt* to adore

adormecer [aðorme'θer] *vt* to put to sleep; **adormecerse** *vr* to become sleepy; *(dormirse)* to fall asleep

adornar [aðor'nar] *vt* to adorn

adorno [a'ðorno] *nm* *(objeto)* ornament; *(decoración)* decoration

adosado, -a [aðo'saðo, a] *adj* *(casa)* semidetached

adosar [aðo'sar] *(Am)* *vt* *(adjuntar)* to attach, enclose *(with a letter)*

adquiera *etc* [að'kjera] *vb ver* **adquirir**

adquirir [aðki'rir] *vt* to acquire, obtain

adquisición [aðkisi'θjon] *nf* acquisition; *(compra)* purchase

adrede [a'ðreðe] *adv* on purpose
adscribir [aðskri'βir] *vt* to appoint; **estuvo adscrito al servicio de ...** he was attached to ...
adscrito [að'skrito] *pp de* **adscribir**
ADSL *nm abbr* ADSL
aduana [a'ðwana] *nf* customs *pl*; (*impuesto*) (customs) duty
aduanero, -a [aðwa'nero, a] *adj* customs *cpd* ▷ *nm/f* customs officer
aducir [aðu'θir] *vt* to adduce; (*dar como prueba*) to offer as proof
adueñarse [aðwe'parse] *vr*: **~ de** to take possession of
adulación [aðula'θjon] *nf* flattery
adular [aðu'lar] *vt* to flatter
adulterar [aðulte'rar] *vt* to adulterate ▷ *vi* to commit adultery
adulterio [aðul'terjo] *nm* adultery
adúltero, -a [a'ðultero, a] *adj* adulterous ▷ *nm/f* adulterer/adulteress
adulto, -a [a'ðulto, a] *adj, nm/f* adult
adusto, -a [a'ðusto, a] *adj* stern; (*austero*) austere
advenedizo, -a [aðβene'ðiθo, a] *nm/f* upstart
advenimiento [aðβeni'mjento] *nm* arrival; (*al trono*) accession
adverbio [að'βerβjo] *nm* adverb
adversario, -a [aðβer'sarjo, a] *nm/f* adversary
adversidad [aðβersi'ðað] *nf* adversity; (*contratiempo*) setback
adverso, -a [að'βerso, a] *adj* adverse; (*suerte*) bad
advertencia [aðβer'tenθja] *nf* warning; (*prefacio*) preface, foreword
advertir [aðβer'tir] *vt* (*observar*) to notice; (*avisar*): **~ a algn de** to warn sb about o of
Adviento [að'βjento] *nm* Advent
advierta *etc* [að'βjerta], **advirtiendo** *etc* [aðβir'tjendo] *vb ver* **advertir**
adyacente [aðja'θente] *adj* adjacent
aéreo, -a [a'ereo, a] *adj* aerial; (*tráfico*) air *cpd*
aerobic *nm*, **aerobics** (*LAm*) [ae'roβik(s)] *nmpl* aerobics *sg*
aerodeslizador [aeroðesliða'ðor] *nm* hovercraft
aerodinámico, -a [aeroði'namiko, a] *adj* aerodynamic
aeromodelismo [aeromoðe'lismo] *nm* model aircraft making, aeromodelling
aeromozo, -a [aero'moθo, a] *nm/f* (*Am*) flight attendant, air steward(ess)
aeronáutica [aero'nautika] *nf* aeronautics *sg*
aeronáutico, -a [aero'nautiko, a] *adj* aeronautical
aeronave [aero'naβe] *nm* spaceship
aeroplano [aero'plano] *nm* aeroplane
aeropuerto [aero'pwerto] *nm* airport
aerosol [aero'sol] *nm* aerosol, spray

afabilidad [afaβili'ðað] *nf* affability, pleasantness
afable [a'faβle] *adj* affable, pleasant
afamado, -a [afa'maðo, a] *adj* famous
afán [a'fan] *nm* hard work; (*deseo*) desire; **con ~** keenly
afanador, a [afana'ðor, a] (*Am*) *nm/f* (*de limpieza*) cleaner
afanar [afa'nar] *vt* to harass; (*fam*) to pinch; **afanarse** *vr*: **~se por** to strive to
afanoso, -a [afa'noso, a] *adj* (*trabajo*) hard; (*trabajador*) industrious
afear [afe'ar] *vt* to disfigure
afección [afek'θjon] *nf* affection; (*Med*) disease
afectación [afekta'θjon] *nf* affectation
afectado, -a [afek'taðo, a] *adj* affected
afectar [afek'tar] *vt* to affect, have an effect on; (*Am: dañar*) to hurt; **por lo que afecta a esto** as far as this is concerned
afectísimo, -a [afek'tisimo, a] *adj* affectionate; **suyo ~** yours truly
afectivo, -a [afek'tiβo, a] *adj* (*problema etc*) emotional
afecto, -a [a'fekto, a] *adj*: **~ a** fond of; (*Jur*) subject to ▷ *nm* affection; **tenerle ~ a algn** to be fond of sb
afectuoso, -a [afek'twoso, a] *adj* affectionate
afeitar [afei'tar] *vt* to shave; **afeitarse** *vr* to shave
afeminado, -a [afemi'naðo, a] *adj* effeminate
aferrar [afe'rrar] *vt* to moor; (*fig*) to grasp ▷ *vi* to moor; **aferrarse** *vr* (*agarrarse*) to cling on; **~se a un principio** to stick to a principle; **~se a una esperanza** to cling to a hope
Afganistán [afɣanis'tan] *nm* Afghanistan
afianzamiento [afjanθa'mjento] *nm* strengthening; security
afianzar [afjan'θar] *vt* to strengthen, secure; **afianzarse** *vr* to steady o.s.; (*establecerse*) to become established
afiche [a'fitʃe] *nm* (*Am*) poster
afición [afi'θjon] *nf*: **~ a** a fondness o liking for; **la ~** the fans *pl*; **pinto por ~** I paint as a hobby
aficionado, -a [afiθjo'naðo, a] *adj* keen, enthusiastic; (*no profesional*) amateur ▷ *nm/f* enthusiast, fan; amateur; **ser ~ a algo** to be very keen on o fond of sth
aficionar [afiθjo'nar] *vt*: **~ a algn a algo** to make sb like sth; **aficionarse** *vr*: **~se a algo** to grow fond of sth
afilado, -a [afi'laðo, a] *adj* sharp
afilar [afi'lar] *vt* to sharpen; **afilarse** *vr* (*cara*) to grow thin
afiliarse [afi'ljarse] *vr* to affiliate
afín [a'fin] *adj* (*parecido*) similar; (*conexo*) related
afinar [afi'nar] *vt* (*Tec*) to refine; (*Mus*) to tune ▷ *vi* (*tocar*) to play in tune; (*cantar*) to sing in tune

afincarse [afin'karse] vr to settle
afinidad [afini'ðað] nf affinity; (parentesco) relationship; **por ~** by marriage
afirmación [afirma'θjon] nf affirmation
afirmar [afir'mar] vt to affirm, state; (sostener) to strengthen; **afirmarse** vr (recuperar el equilibrio) to steady o.s.; **~se en lo dicho** to stand by what one has said
afirmativo, -a [afirma'tiβo, a] adj affirmative
aflicción [aflik'θjon] nf affliction; (dolor) grief
afligir [afli'xir] vt to afflict; (apenar) to distress; **afligirse** vr: **~se (por o con o de)** to grieve (about o at); **no te aflijas tanto** you must not let it affect you like this
aflojar [aflo'xar] vt to slacken; (desatar) to loosen, undo; (relajar) to relax ▷ vi (amainar) to drop; (bajar) to go down; **aflojarse** vr to relax
aflorar [aflo'rar] vi (Geo, fig) to come to the surface, emerge
afluente [aflu'ente] adj flowing ▷ nm (Geo) tributary
afluir [aflu'ir] vi to flow
afmo., -a. abr (= afectísimo/a suyo/a) Yours
afónico, -a [a'foniko, a] adj: **estar ~** to have a sore throat; to have lost one's voice
aforo [a'foro] nm (Tec) gauging; (de teatro etc) capacity; **el teatro tiene un ~ de 2,000** the theatre can seat 2,000
afortunado, -a [afortu'naðo, a] adj fortunate, lucky
afortunadamente [afortunaða'mente] adv fortunately, luckily
afrancesado, -a [afranθe'saðo, a] adj francophile; (pey) Frenchified
afrenta [a'frenta] nf affront, insult; (deshonra) dishonour (Brit), dishonor (US), shame
África ['afrika] nf Africa; **~ del Sur** South Africa
africano, -a [afri'kano, a] adj, nm/f African
afrontar [afron'tar] vt to confront; (poner cara a cara) to bring face to face
afrutado, -a [afru'taðo, a] adj fruity
after ['after] (pl **afters** o **after**) nm, **afterhours** ['afterauars] nm inv after-hours club
afuera [a'fwera] adv out, outside; **por ~** on the outside; **afueras** nfpl outskirts
agachar [aɣa'tʃar] vt to bend, bow; **agacharse** vr to stoop, bend
agalla [a'ɣaʎa] nf (Zool) gill; **agallas** nfpl (Med) tonsillitis sg; (Anat) tonsils; **tener ~s** (fam) to have guts
agarradera [aɣarra'ðera] (Am) nf, **agarradero** [aɣarra'ðero] nm handle; **agarraderas** nfpl pull sg, influence sg
agarrado, -a [aɣa'rraðo, a] adj mean, stingy
agarrar [aɣa'rrar] vt to grasp, grab; (Am: tomar) to take, catch; (recoger) to pick up ▷ vi

(planta) to take root; **agarrarse** vr to hold on (tightly); (meterse uno con otro) to grapple (with each other); **agarró y se fue** (esp Am: (fam)) he upped and went
agarrotar [aɣarro'tar] vt (lío) to tie tightly; (persona) to squeeze tightly; (reo) to garrotte; **agarrotarse** vr (motor) to seize up; (Med) to stiffen
agasajar [aɣasa'xar] vt to treat well, fête
agencia [a'xenθja] nf agency; **~ de créditos/publicidad/viajes** credit/advertising/travel agency; **~ inmobiliaria** estate agent's (office) (Brit), real estate office (US); **~ matrimonial** marriage bureau
agenciar [axen'θjar] vt to bring about; **agenciarse** vr to look after o.s.; **~se algo** to get hold of sth
agenda [a'xenda] nf diary; **~ electrónica** PDA; **~ telefónica** telephone directory
agente [a'xente] nm/f agent; (tb: **~ de policía**) policeman/policewoman; **~ de bolsa** stockbroker; **~ de negocios** (Com) business agent; **~ de seguros** insurance broker; **~ de tránsito** (Am) traffic cop; **~ de viajes** travel agent; **~ inmobiliario** estate agent (Brit), realtor (US); **~s sociales** social partners
ágil ['axil] adj agile, nimble
agilidad [axili'ðað] nf agility, nimbleness
agilizar [axili'θar] vt (trámites) to speed up
agiotista [axjo'tista] (Am) nm/f (usurero) usurer
agitación [axita'θjon] nf (de mano etc) shaking, waving; (de líquido etc) stirring; agitation
agitado, -a [axi'aðo, a] adj hectic; (viaje) bumpy
agitar [axi'tar] vt to wave, shake; (líquido) to stir; (fig) to stir up, excite; **agitarse** vr to get excited; (inquietarse) to get worried o upset
aglomeración [aɣlomera'θjon] nf: **~ de tráfico/gente** traffic jam/mass of people
aglomerar [aɣlome'rar] vt, **aglomerarse** vr to crowd together
agnóstico, -a [aɣ'nostiko, a] adj, nm/f agnostic
agobiar [aɣo'βjar] vt to weigh down; (oprimir) to oppress; (cargar) to burden; **sentirse agobiado por** to be overwhelmed by
agolparse [aɣol'parse] vr to crowd together
agonía [aɣo'nia] nf death throes pl; (fig) agony, anguish
agonizante [aɣoni'θante] adj dying
agonizar [aɣoni'θar] vi to be dying
agosto [a'ɣosto] nm August; (fig) harvest; **hacer su ~** to make one's pile; ver tb **julio**
agotado, -a [aɣo'taðo, a] adj (persona) exhausted; (acabado) finished; (Com) sold out; (: libros) out of print; (pila) flat
agotador, a [aɣota'ðor, a] adj exhausting
agotamiento [aɣota'mjento] nm exhaustion

agotar [aɣo'tar] vt to exhaust; (*consumir*) to drain; (*recursos*) to use up, deplete; **agotarse** vr to be exhausted; (*acabarse*) to run out; (*libro*) to go out of print

agraciado, -a [aɣra'θjaðo, a] adj (*atractivo*) attractive; (*en sorteo etc*) lucky

agraciar [aɣra'θjar] vt (*Jur*) to pardon; (*con premio*) to reward; (*hacer más atractivo*) to make more attractive

agradable [aɣra'ðaβle] adj pleasant, nice

agradar [aɣra'ðar] vt, vi to please; **él me agrada** I like him; **agradarse** vr to like each other

agradecer [aɣraðe'θer] vt to thank; (*favor etc*) to be grateful for; **le ~ía me enviara ...** I would be grateful if you would send me ...; **agradecerse** vr: ¡**se agradece!** much obliged!

agradecido, -a [aɣraðe'θiðo, a] adj grateful; ¡**muy ~!** thanks a lot!

agradecimiento [aɣraðeθi'mjento] nm thanks pl; gratitude

agradezca etc [aɣra'ðeθka] vb ver **agradecer**

agrado [a'ɣraðo] nm: **ser de tu** etc ~ to be to your etc liking

agrandar [aɣran'dar] vt to enlarge; (*fig*) to exaggerate; **agrandarse** vr to get bigger

agrario, -a [a'ɣrarjo, a] adj agrarian, land cpd; (*política*) agricultural, farming cpd

agravante [aɣra'βante] adj aggravating ▷ nm of complication; **con el** or **la - de que ...** with the further difficulty that ...

agravar [aɣra'βar] vt (*pesar sobre*) to make heavier; (*irritar*) to aggravate; **agravarse** vr to worsen, get worse

agraviar [aɣra'βjar] vt to offend; (*ser injusto con*) to wrong; **agraviarse** vr to take offence

agravio [a'ɣraβjo] nm offence; wrong; (*Jur*) grievance

agredir [aɣre'ðir] vt to attack

agregado [aɣre'ɣaðo] nm aggregate; (*persona*) attaché; (*profesor*) assistant professor; **A~** = teacher (*who is not head of department*)

agregar [aɣre'ɣar] vt to gather; (*añadir*) to add; (*persona*) to appoint

agresión [aɣre'sjon] nf aggression; (*ataque*) attack

agresivo, -a [aɣre'siβo, a] adj aggressive

agriar [a'ɣrjar] vt (*fig*) to (turn) sour; **agriarse** vr to turn sour

agrícola [a'ɣrikola] adj farming cpd, agricultural

agricultor, a [aɣrikul'tor, a] nm/f farmer

agricultura [aɣrikul'tura] nf agriculture, farming

agridulce [aɣri'ðulθe] adj bittersweet; (*Culin*) sweet and sour

agrietarse [aɣrje'tarse] vr to crack; (*la piel*) to chap

agrimensor, a [aɣrimen'sor, a] nm/f surveyor

agrio, -a [a'ɣrjo, a] adj bitter

agronomía [aɣrono'mia] nf agronomy, agriculture

agropecuario, -a [aɣrope'kwarjo, a] adj farming cpd, agricultural

agrupación [aɣrupa'θjon] nf group; (*acto*) grouping

agrupar [aɣru'par] vt to group; (*Inform*) to block; **agruparse** vr (*Pol*) to form a group; (*juntarse*) to gather

agua ['aɣwa] nf water; (*Naut*) wake; (*Arq*) slope of a roof; **aguas** nfpl (*Med*) water sg, urine sg; (*Naut*) waters; **~s abajo/arriba** downstream/upstream; **~ bendita/ destilada/potable** holy/distilled/drinking water; **~ caliente** hot water; **~ corriente** running water; **~ de colonia** eau de cologne; **~ mineral (con/sin gas)** (fizzy/non-fizzy) mineral water; **~ oxigenada** hydrogen peroxide; **~s jurisdiccionales** territorial waters; **~s mayores** excrement sg; **~ pasada no mueve molino** it's no use crying over spilt milk; **estar con el ~ al cuello** to be up to one's neck; **venir como ~ de mayo** to be a godsend

aguacate [aɣwa'kate] nm avocado (pear)

aguacero [aɣwa'θero] nm (heavy) shower, downpour

aguado, -a [a'ɣwaðo, a] adj watery, watered down ▷ nf (*Agr*) watering place; (*Naut*) water supply; (*Arte*) watercolour

aguafiestas [aɣwa'fjestas] nm/f inv spoilsport

aguafuerte [aɣwa'fwerte] nf etching

aguamiel [aɣwa'mjel] (*Am*) nf fermented maguey o agave juice

aguanieve [aɣwa'njeβe] nf sleet

aguantar [aɣwan'tar] vt to bear, put up with; (*sostener*) to hold up ▷ vi to last; **aguantarse** vr to restrain o.s.; **no sé cómo aguanta** I don't know how he can take it

aguante [a'ɣwante] nm (*paciencia*) patience; (*resistencia*) endurance; (*Deporte*) stamina

aguar [a'ɣwar] vt to water down; (*fig*): **~ la fiesta a algn** to spoil sb's fun

aguardar [aɣwar'ðar] vt to wait for

aguardiente [aɣwar'ðjente] nm brandy, liquor

aguarrás [aɣwa'rras] nm turpentine

aguaviva [aɣwa'biβa] (*RPl*) nf jellyfish

agudeza [aɣu'ðeθa] nf sharpness; (*ingenio*) wit

agudizar [aɣuði'θar] vt to sharpen; (*crisis*) to make worse; **agudizarse** vr to worsen, deteriorate

agudo, -a [a'ɣuðo, a] adj sharp; (*voz*) high-pitched, piercing; (*dolor, enfermedad*) acute

agüero [a'ɣwero] nm: **buen/mal ~** good/bad omen; **ser de buen ~** to augur well; **pájaro de mal ~** bird of ill omen

aguijón [aɣi'xon] nm sting; (*fig*) spur

águila ['aɣila] nf eagle; (*fig*) genius

aguileño, -a [aɣi'leɲo, a] adj (*nariz*) aquiline; (*rostro*) sharp-featured

aguinaldo [aɣi'naldo] nm Christmas box

aguja [a'ɣuxa] *nf* needle; (*de reloj*) hand; (*Arq*) spire; (*Tec*) firing-pin; **agujas** *nfpl* (*Zool*) ribs; (*Ferro*) points

agujerear [aɣuxere'ar] *vt* to make holes in; (*penetrar*) to pierce

agujero [aɣu'xero] *nm* hole; (*Com*) deficit

agujetas [aɣu'xetas] *nfpl* stitch *sg*; (*rigidez*) stiffness *sg*

aguzar [aɣu'θar] *vt* to sharpen; (*fig*) to incite; ~ **el oído** to prick up one's ears

ahí [a'i] *adv* there; (*allá*) over there; **de ~ que** so that, with the result that; ~ **llega** here he comes; **por ~** (*dirección*) that way; **¡hasta ~ hemos llegado!** so it has come to this!; **¡~ va!** (*objeto*) here it comes!; (*individuo*) there he goes!; ~ **donde le ve** as sure as he's standing there; **200 o por ~** 200 or so

ahijado, -a [ai'xaðo, a] *nm/f* godson(-daughter)

ahínco [a'inko] *nm* earnestness; **con ~** eagerly

ahogar [ao'ɣar] *vt* (*en agua*) to drown; (*asfixiar*) to suffocate, smother; (*fuego*) to put out; **ahogarse** *vr* (*en agua*) to drown; (*por asfixia*) to suffocate

ahogo [a'oɣo] *nm* (*Med*) breathlessness; (*fig*) distress; (*problema económico*) financial difficulty

ahondar [aon'dar] *vt* to deepen, make deeper; (*fig*) to study thoroughly ▷ *vi*: ~ **en** to study thoroughly

ahora [a'ora] *adv* now; (*hace poco*) a moment ago, just now; (*dentro de poco*) in a moment; ~ **voy** I'm coming; ~ **mismo** right now; ~ **bien** now then; **por ~** for the present

ahorcar [aor'kar] *vt* to hang; **ahorcarse** *vr* to hang o.s.

ahorita [ao'rita], **ahoritita** [aori'tita] *adv* (*esp Am*: *fam*: *en este momento*) right now; (*Am*: *hace poco*) just now; (: *dentro de poco*) in a minute

ahorrar [ao'rrar] *vt* (*dinero*) to save; (*esfuerzos*) to save, avoid; **ahorrarse** *vr*: ~**se molestias** to save o.s. trouble

ahorro [a'orro] *nm* (*acto*) saving; (*frugalidad*) thrift; **ahorros** *nmpl* (*dinero*) savings

ahuecar [awe'kar] *vt* to hollow (out); (*voz*) to deepen ▷ *vi*: **¡ahueca!** (*fam*) beat it! (*fam*); **ahuecarse** *vr* to give o.s. airs

ahumar [au'mar] *vt* to smoke, cure; (*llenar de humo*) to fill with smoke ▷ *vi* to smoke; **ahumarse** *vr* to fill with smoke

ahuyentar [aujen'tar] *vt* to drive off, frighten off; (*fig*) to dispel

airado, -a [ai'raðo, a] *adj* angry

airar [ai'rar] *vt* to anger; **airarse** *vr* to get angry

aire ['aire] *nm* air; (*viento*) wind; (*corriente*) draught; (*Mus*) tune; **aires** *nmpl*: **darse ~s** to give o.s. airs; **al ~ libre** in the open air; ~ **aclimatizado** *o* **acondicionado** air conditioning; **tener ~ de** to look like; **estar de buen/mal ~** to be in a good/bad mood;

estar en el ~ (*Radio*) to be on the air; (*fig*) to be up in the air

airear [aire'ar] *vt* to ventilate; (*fig*: *asunto*) to air; **airearse** *vr* to get some fresh air

airoso, -a [ai'roso, a] *adj* windy; draughty; (*fig*) graceful

aislado, -a [ais'laðo, a] *adj* (*remoto*) isolated; (*incomunicado*) cut off; (*Elec*) insulated

aislar [ais'lar] *vt* to isolate; (*Elec*) to insulate; **aislarse** *vr* to cut o.s. off

ajar [a'xar] *vt* to spoil; (*fig*) to abuse; **ajarse** *vr* to get crumpled; (*fig*: *piel*) to get wrinkled

ajardinado, -a [axarði'naðo, a] *adj* landscaped

ajedrez [axe'ðreθ] *nm* chess

ajeno, -a [a'xeno, a] *adj* (*que pertenece a otro*) somebody else's; ~ **a** foreign to; ~ **de** free from, devoid of; **por razones ajenas a nuestra voluntad** for reasons beyond our control

ajetreado, -a [axetre'aðo, a] *adj* busy

ajetreo [axe'treo] *nm* bustle

ají [a'xi] *nm* chil(l)i, red pepper; (*salsa*) chil(l)i sauce

ajillo [a'xiʎo] *nm*: **gambas al ~** garlic prawns

ajo ['axo] *nm* garlic; ~ **porro** *o* **puerro** leek; **(tieso) como un ~** (*fam*) snobbish; **estar en el ~** to be mixed up in it

ajuar [a'xwar] *nm* household furnishings *pl*; (*de novia*) trousseau; (*de niño*) layette

ajustado, -a [axus'taðo, a] *adj* (*tornillo*) tight; (*cálculo*) right; (*ropa*) tight(-fitting); (*Deporte*: *resultado*) close

ajustar [axus'tar] *vt* (*adaptar*) to adjust; (*encajar*) to fit; (*Tec*) to engage; (*Tip*) to make up; (*apretar*) to tighten; (*concertar*) to agree (on); (*reconciliar*) to reconcile; (*cuenta, deudas*) to settle ▷ *vi* to fit; **ajustarse** *vr*: ~**se a** (*precio etc*) to be in keeping with, fit in with; ~ **las cuentas a algn** to get even with sb

ajuste [a'xuste] *nm* adjustment; (*Costura*) fitting; (*acuerdo*) compromise; (*de cuenta*) settlement

al [al] = **a+el**; **véase a**

ala ['ala] *nf* wing; (*de sombrero*) brim; (*futbolista*) winger; ~ **delta** hang-glider; **andar con el ~ caída** to be downcast; **cortar las ~s a algn** to clip sb's wings; **dar ~s a algn** to encourage sb

alabanza [ala'βanθa] *nf* praise

alabar [ala'βar] *vt* to praise

alacena [ala'θena] *nf* cupboard (*Brit*), closet (*US*)

alacrán [ala'kran] *nm* scorpion

alado, -a [a'laðo, a] *adj* winged

alambique *etc* [alam'bike] *vb ver* **alambicar** ▷ *nm* still

alambrada [alam'braða] *nf*, **alambrado** [alam'braðo] *nm* wire fence; (*red*) wire netting

alambre [a'lambre] *nm* wire; ~ **de púas** barbed wire

alameda [ala'meða] nf (plantío) poplar grove; (lugar de paseo) avenue, boulevard

álamo ['alamo] nm poplar; **~ temblón** aspen

alarde [a'larðe] nm show, display; **hacer ~ de** to boast of

alargador [alarɣa'ðor] nm extension cable o lead

alargar [alar'ɣar] vt to lengthen, extend; (paso) to hasten; (brazo) to stretch out; (cuerda) to pay out; (conversación) to spin out; **alargarse** vr to get longer

alarido [ala'riðo] nm shriek

alarma [a'larma] nf alarm; **voz de ~** warning note; **dar la ~** to raise the alarm; **~ de incendios** fire alarm

alarmante [alar'mante] adj alarming

alarmar [alar'mar] vt to alarm; **alarmarse** vr to get alarmed

alba ['alβa] nf dawn

albacea [alβa'θea] nm/f executor/executrix

albahaca [al'βaka] nf (Bot) basil

Albania [al'βanja] nf Albania

albañil [alβa'ɲil] nm bricklayer; (cantero) mason

albarán [alβa'ran] nm (Com) delivery note, invoice

albaricoque [alβari'koke] nm apricot

albedrío [alβe'ðrio] nm: **libre ~** free will

alberca [al'βerka] nf reservoir; (Am) swimming pool

albergar [alβer'ɣar] vt to shelter; (esperanza) to cherish; **albergarse** vr (refugiarse) to shelter; (alojarse) to lodge

albergue [al'βerɣe] vb ver **albergar** ▷ nm shelter, refuge; **~ juvenil** youth hostel

albóndiga [al'βondiɣa] nf meatball

albornoz [alβor'noθ] nm (de los árabes) burnous; (para el baño) bathrobe

alborotar [alβoro'tar] vi to make a row ▷ vt to agitate, stir up; **alborotarse** vr to get excited; (mar) to get rough

alboroto [alβo'roto] nm row, uproar

alborozar [alβoro'θar] vt to gladden; **alborozarse** vr to rejoice, be overjoyed

alborozo [alβo'roθo] nm joy

álbum ['alβum] (pl **álbums** o **álbumes**) nm album; **~ de recortes** scrapbook

albumen [al'βumen] nm egg white, albumen

albur [al'βur] (Am) nm (juego de palabras) pun; (doble sentido) double entendre

alcachofa [alka'tʃofa] nf (globe) artichoke; (Tip) golf ball; (de ducha) shower head

alcalde, -esa [al'kalde, alkal'desa] nm/f mayor(ess)

alcaldía [alkal'dia] nf mayoralty; (lugar) mayor's office

alcance [al'kanθe] vb ver **alcanzar** ▷ nm (Mil, Radio) range; (fig) scope; (Com) adverse balance, deficit; **estar al/fuera del ~ de algn** to be within/beyond sb's reach; (fig) to be within sb's powers/over sb's head; **de gran ~** (Mil) long-range; (fig) far-reaching

alcancía [alkan'θia] (Am) nf (para ahorrar) money box; (para colectas) collection box

alcantarilla [alkanta'riʎa] nf (de aguas cloacales) sewer; (en la calle) gutter

alcanzar [alkan'θar] vt (algo: con la mano, el pie) to reach; (alguien: en el camino etc) to catch up (with); (autobús) to catch; (suj: bala) to hit, strike ▷ vi (ser suficiente) to be enough; **~ algo a algn** to hand sth to sb; **alcánzame la sal, por favor** pass the salt please; **~ a hacer** to manage to do

alcaparra [alka'parra] nf (Bot) caper

alcatraz [alka'traθ] nm gannet

alcayata [alka'jata] nf hook

alcázar [al'kaθar] nm fortress; (Naut) quarter-deck

alcoba [al'koβa] nf bedroom

alcohol [al'kol] nm alcohol; **no bebe ~** he doesn't drink (alcohol); **~ metílico** methylated spirits pl (Brit), wood alcohol (US)

alcoholemia [alkoo'lemia] nf blood alcohol level; **prueba de la ~** breath test

alcohólico, -a [al'koliko, a] adj, nm/f alcoholic

alcoholímetro [alko'limetro] nm Breathalyser®, drunkometer (US)

alcoholismo [alko'lismo] nm alcoholism

alcornoque [alkor'noke] nm cork tree; (fam) idiot

alcurnia [al'kurnja] nf lineage

aldaba [al'daβa] nf (door) knocker

aldea [al'dea] nf village

aldeano, -a [alde'ano, a] adj village cpd ▷ nm/f villager

ale ['ale] excl come on!, let's go!

aleación [alea'θjon] nf alloy

aleatorio, -a [alea'torjo, a] adj random, contingent; **acceso ~** (Inform) random access

aleccionar [alekθjo'nar] vt to instruct; (adiestrar) to train

alegación [aleɣa'θjon] nf allegation

alegar [ale'ɣar] vt (dificultad etc) to plead; (Jur) to allege ▷ vi (Am) to argue; **~ que ...** to give as an excuse that ...

alegato [ale'ɣato] nm (Jur) allegation; (escrito) indictment; (declaración) statement; (Am) argument

alegoría [aleɣo'ria] nf allegory

alegrar [ale'ɣrar] vt (causar alegría) to cheer (up); (fuego) to poke; (fiesta) to liven up; **alegrarse** vr (fam) to get merry o tight; **~se de** to be glad about

alegre [a'leɣre] adj happy, cheerful; (fam) merry, tight; (chiste) risqué, blue

alegría [ale'ɣria] nf happiness; merriment; **~ vital** joie de vivre

alejamiento [alexa'mjento] nm removal; (distancia) remoteness

alejar [ale'xar] vt to move away, remove; (fig) to estrange; **alejarse** vr to move away

aleluya [ale'luja] nm (canto) hallelujah

alemán, -ana [ale'man, ana] adj, nm/f German ▷ nm (lengua) German

Alemania [ale'manja] *nf* Germany

alentador, a [alenta'ðor, a] *adj* encouraging

alentar [alen'tar] *vt* to encourage

alergia [a'lerxja] *nf* allergy

alero [a'lero] *nm* (*de tejado*) eaves *pl*; (*de foca, Deporte*) flipper; (*Auto*) mudguard

alerta [a'lerta] *adj inv, nm* alert

aleta [a'leta] *nf* (*de pez*) fin; (*de ave*) wing; (*de foca, Deporte*) flipper; (*de coche*) mudguard

aletargar [aletar'ɣar] *vt* to make drowsy; (*entumecer*) to make numb; **aletargarse** *vr* to grow drowsy; to become numb

aletear [alete'ar] *vi* to flutter; (*ave*) to flap its wings; (*individuo*) to wave one's arms

alevín [ale'βin] *nm* fry, young fish

alevosía [aleβo'sia] *nf* treachery

alfabeto [alfa'βeto] *nm* alphabet

alfalfa [al'falfa] *nf* alfalfa, lucerne

alfarería [alfare'ria] *nf* pottery; (*tienda*) pottery shop

alfarero, -a [alfa'rero, a] *nm/f* potter

alféizar [al'feiðar] *nm* window-sill

alférez [al'fereθ] *nm* (*Mil*) second lieutenant; (*Naut*) ensign

alfil [al'fil] *nm* (*Ajedrez*) bishop

alfiler [alfi'ler] *nm* pin; (*broche*) clip; (*pinza*) clothes peg (*Brit*) o pin (*US*); **~ de gancho** (*Am*) safety pin; **prendido con ~es** shaky

alfiletero [alfile'tero] *nm* needle case

alfombra [al'fombra] *nf* carpet; (*más pequeña*) rug

alfombrar [alfom'brar] *vt* to carpet

alfombrilla [alfom'briʎa] *nf* rug, mat; (*Inform*) mouse mat o pad

alforja [al'forxa] *nf* saddlebag

algarabía [alɣara'βia] *nf* (*fam*) gibberish; (*griterío*) hullabaloo

algarroba [alɣa'rroβa] *nf* carob

algarrobo [alɣa'rroβo] *nm* carob tree

algas ['alɣas] *nfpl* seaweed *sg*

algazara [alɣa'θara] *nf* din, uproar

álgebra ['alxeβra] *nf* algebra

álgido, -a ['alxiðo, a] *adj* icy; (*momento etc*) crucial, decisive

algo ['alɣo] *pron* something; (*en frases interrogativas*) anything ▷ *adv* somewhat, rather; **¿~ más?** anything else?; (*en tienda*) is that all?; **por ~ será** there must be some reason for it; **es ~ difícil** it's a bit awkward

algodón [alɣo'ðon] *nm* cotton; (*planta*) cotton plant; **~ de azúcar** candy floss (*Brit*), cotton candy (*US*); **~ hidrófilo** cotton wool (*Brit*), absorbent cotton (*US*)

algodonero, -a [alɣoðo'nero, a] *adj* cotton *cpd* ▷ *nm/f* cotton grower ▷ *nm* cotton plant

alguacil [alɣwa'θil] *nm* bailiff; (*Taur*) mounted official

alguien ['alɣjen] *pron* someone, somebody; (*en frases interrogativas*) anyone, anybody

alguno, -a [al'ɣuno, a] *adj* (*antes de nmsg* **algún**) some; (*después de n*): **no tiene talento ~** he has no talent, he doesn't have any talent ▷ *pron* (*alguien*) someone, somebody; **algún que otro libro** some book or other; **algún día iré** I'll go one o some day; **sin interés ~** without the slightest interest; **~ que otro** an occasional one; **~s piensan** some (people) think; **~ de ellos** one of them

alhaja [a'laxa] *nf* jewel; (*tesoro*) precious object, treasure

alhelí [ale'li] *nm* wallflower, stock

aliado, -a [a'ljaðo, a] *adj* allied

alianza [a'ljanθa] *nf* (*Pol etc*) alliance; (*anillo*) wedding ring

aliar [a'ljar] *vt* to ally; **aliarse** *vr* to form an alliance

alias ['aljas] *adv* alias

alicatado [alika'taðo] (*Esp*) *nm* tiling

alicatar [alika'tar] *vt* to tile

alicate [ali'kate] *nm*, **alicates** [ali'kates] *nmpl* pliers *pl*; **~(s) de uñas** nail clippers

aliciente [ali'θjente] *nm* incentive; (*atracción*) attraction

alienación [aljena'θjon] *nf* alienation

aliento [a'ljento] *vb ver* **alentar** ▷ *nm* breath; (*respiración*) breathing; **sin ~** breathless; **de un ~** in one breath; (*fig*) in one go

aligerar [alixe'rar] *vt* to lighten; (*reducir*) to shorten; (*aliviar*) to alleviate; (*mitigar*) to ease; (*paso*) to quicken

alijo [a'lixo] *nm* (*Naut: descarga*) unloading; (*contrabando*) consignment (of smuggled goods)

alimaña [ali'maɲa] *nf* pest

alimentación [alimenta'θjon] *nf* (*comida*) food; (*acción*) feeding; (*tienda*) grocer's (shop); **~ continua** (*en fotocopiadora etc*) stream feed

alimentador [alimenta'ðor] *nm*: **~ de papel** sheet-feeder

alimentar [alimen'tar] *vt* to feed; (*nutrir*) to nourish; **alimentarse** *vr*: **~se (de)** to feed (on)

alimenticio, -a [alimen'tiθjo, a] *adj* food *cpd*; (*nutritivo*) nourishing, nutritious

alimento [ali'mento] *nm* food; (*nutrición*) nourishment; **alimentos** *nmpl* (*Jur*) alimony *sg*

alineación [alinea'θjon] *nf* alignment; (*Deporte*) line-up

alinear [aline'ar] *vt* to align; (*Tip*) to justify; (*Deporte*) to select, pick; **alinearse** *vr* to line up; **~se en** to fall in with

aliñar [ali'ɲar] *vt* (*Culin*) to season; (*ensalada*) to dress

aliño [a'liɲo] *nm* (*Culin*) dressing

alioli [ali'oli] *nm* garlic mayonnaise

alisar [ali'sar] *vt* to smooth

aliso [a'liso] *nm* alder

alistar [alis'tar] *vt* to recruit; **alistarse** *vr* to enlist; (*inscribirse*) to enrol; (*Am: prepararse*) to get ready

aliviar [ali'βjar] *vt* (*carga*) to lighten; (*persona*) to relieve; (*dolor*) to relieve, alleviate

alivio [a'liβjo] *nm* alleviation, relief; **~ de luto** half-mourning

aljibe [al'xiβe] *nm* cistern

allá [a'ʎa] *adv* (*lugar*) there; (*por ahí*) over there; (*tiempo*) then; ~ **abajo** down there; **más ~** further on; **más ~ de** beyond; **¡~ tú!** that's your problem!

allanamiento [aʎana'mjento] *nm* (*Am Policía*) raid, search; ~ **de morada** breaking and entering

allanar [aʎa'nar] *vt* to flatten, level (out); (*igualar*) to smooth (out); (*fig*) to subdue; (*Jur*) to burgle, break into; (*Am Policía*) to raid, search; **allanarse** *vr* to fall down; **~se a** to submit to, accept

allegado, -a [aʎe'ɣaðo, a] *adj* near, close ▷ *nm/f* relation

allí [a'ʎi] *adv* there; ~ **mismo** right there; **por ~** over there; (*por ese camino*) that way

alma ['alma] *nf* soul; (*persona*) person; (*Tec*) core; **se le cayó el ~ a los pies** he became very disheartened; **entregar el ~** to pass away; **estar con el ~ en la boca** to be scared to death; **lo siento en el ~** I am truly sorry; **tener el ~ en un hilo** to have one's heart in one's mouth; **estar como ~ en pena** to suffer; **ir como ~ que lleva el diablo** to go at breakneck speed

almacén [alma'θen] *nm* (*depósito*) warehouse, store; (*Mil*) magazine; (*Am*) grocer's shop, food store, grocery store (*US*); **(grandes) almacenes** *nmpl* department store *sg*; **~ depositario** (*Com*) depository

almacenaje [almaθe'naxe] *nm* storage; **~ secundario** backup storage

almacenar [almaθe'nar] *vt* to store, put in storage; (*Inform*) to store; (*proveerse*) to stock up with

almanaque [alma'nake] *nm* almanac

almeja [al'mexa] *nf* clam

almendra [al'mendra] *nf* almond

almendro [al'mendro] *nm* almond tree

almíbar [al'miβar] *nm* syrup

almidón [almi'ðon] *nm* starch

almidonar [almiðo'nar] *vt* to starch

almirantazgo [almiran'taθɣo] *nm* admiralty

almirante [almi'rante] *nm* admiral

almirez [almi'reθ] *nm* mortar

almizcle [al'miθkle] *nm* musk

almohada [almo'aða] *nf* pillow; (*funda*) pillowcase

almohadilla [almoa'ðiʎa] *nf* cushion; (*Tec*) pad; (*Am*) pincushion; (*Inform*) hash key

almohadón [almoa'ðon] *nm* large pillow

almorranas [almo'rranas] *nfpl* piles, haemorrhoids (*Brit*), hemorrhoids (*US*)

almorzar [almor'θar] *vt*: ~ **una tortilla** to have an omelette for lunch ▷ *vi* to (have) lunch

almuerzo [al'mwerθo] *vb ver* **almorzar** ▷ *nm* lunch

alocado, -a [alo'kaðo, a] *adj* crazy

alojamiento [aloxa'mjento] *nm* lodging(s)

(*pl*); (*viviendas*) housing

alojar [alo'xar] *vt* to lodge; **alojarse** *vr*: ~ **se en** to stay at; (*bala*) to lodge in

alondra [a'londra] *nf* lark, skylark

alpaca [al'paka] *nf* alpaca

alpargata [alpar'ɣata] *nf* rope-soled shoe, espadrille

Alpes ['alpes] *nmpl*: **los ~** the Alps

alpinismo [alpi'nismo] *nm* mountaineering, climbing

alpinista [alpi'nista] *nm/f* mountaineer, climber

alpino, -a [al'pino, a] *adj* alpine

alpiste [al'piste] *nm* (*semillas*) birdseed; (*Am fam: dinero*) dough; (*fam: alcohol*) booze

alquilar [alki'lar] *vt* (*suj: propietario: inmuebles*) to let, rent (out); (*: coche*) to hire out; (*: TV*) to rent (out); (*suj: alquilador: inmuebles, TV*) to rent; (*: coche*) to hire; **"se alquila casa"** "house to let (*Brit*) o for rent (*US*)"

alquiler [alki'ler] *nm* renting; letting; hiring; (*arriendo*) rent; hire charge; **de ~** for hire; **~ de automóviles** car hire

alquimia [al'kimja] *nf* alchemy

alquitrán [alki'tran] *nm* tar

alrededor [alreðe'ðor] *adv* around, about; **alrededores** *nmpl* surroundings; **~ de** *prep* around, about; **mirar a su ~** to look (round) about one

alta ['alta] *nf* (certificate of) discharge; **dar a algn de ~** to discharge sb; **darse de ~** (*Mil*) to join, enrol; (*Deporte*) to declare o.s. fit

altanería [altane'ria] *nf* haughtiness, arrogance

altanero, -a [alta'nero, a] *adj* haughty, arrogant

altar [al'tar] *nm* altar

altavoz [alta'βoθ] *nm* loudspeaker; (*amplificador*) amplifier

alteración [altera'θjon] *nf* alteration; (*alboroto*) disturbance; **~ del orden público** breach of the peace

alterar [alte'rar] *vt* to alter; to disturb; **alterarse** *vr* (*persona*) to get upset

altercado [alter'kaðo] *nm* argument

alternar [alter'nar] *vt* to alternate ▷ *vi* to alternate; (*turnar*) to take turns; **alternarse** *vr* to alternate; (*turnar*) to take turns; **~ con** to mix with

alternativo, -a [alterna'tiβo, a] *adj* alternative; (*alterno*) alternating ▷ *nf* alternative; (*elección*) choice; **alternativas** *nfpl* ups and downs; **tomar la alternativa** (*Taur*) to become a fully-qualified bullfighter

alterno, -a [al'terno, a] *adj* (*Bot, Mat*) alternate; (*Elec*) alternating

Alteza [al'teθa] *nf* (*tratamiento*) Highness

altibajos [alti'βaxos] *nmpl* ups and downs

altiplanicie [altipla'niθje] *nf*, **altiplano** [alti'plano] *nm* high plateau

altisonante [altiso'nante] *adj* high-flown, high-sounding

altitud [alti'tuð] nf height; (Aviat, Geo) altitude; **a una ~ de** at a height of

altivo, -a [al'tiβo, a] adj haughty, arrogant

alto, -a ['alto, a] adj high; (persona) tall; (sonido) high, sharp; (noble) high, lofty; (Geo, clase) upper ▷ nm halt; (Mus) alto; (Geo) hill; (Am) pile ▷ adv (estar) high; (hablar) loud, loudly ▷ excl halt!; **la pared tiene dos metros de ~** the wall is two metres high; **en alta mar** on the high seas; **en voz alta** in a loud voice; **las altas horas de la noche** the small (Brit) o wee (US) hours; **en lo ~ de** at the top of; **pasar por ~** to overlook; **~s y bajos** ups and downs; **poner la radio más ~** to turn the radio up; **¡más ~, por favor!** louder, please!

altoparlante [altopar'lante] nm (Am) loudspeaker

altruismo [al'truismo] nm altruism

altura [al'tura] nf height; (Naut) depth; (Geo) latitude; **la pared tiene 1.80 de ~** the wall is 1 metre 80 (cm) high; **a estas ~s** at this stage; **a esta ~ del año** at this time of the year; **estar a la ~ de las circunstancias** to rise to the occasion; **ha sido un partido de gran ~** it has been a terrific match

alubia [a'luβja] nf bean; (judía verde) French bean; (judía blanca) kidney bean

alucinación [aluθina'θjon] nf hallucination

alucinante [aluθi'nante] adj (fam: estupendo) great, super

alucinar [aluθi'nar] vi to hallucinate ▷ vt to deceive; (fascinar) to fascinate

alud [a'luð] nm avalanche; (fig) flood

aludir [alu'ðir] vi: **~ a** to allude to; **darse por aludido** to take the hint; **no te des por aludido** don't take it personally

alumbrado [alum'braðo] nm lighting

alumbramiento [alumbra'mjento] nm lighting; (Med) childbirth, delivery

alumbrar [alum'brar] vt to light (up) ▷ vi (iluminar) to give light; (Med) to give birth

aluminio [alu'minjo] nm aluminium (Brit), aluminum (US)

alumno, -a [a'lumno, a] nm/f pupil, student

alusión [alu'sjon] nf allusion

alusivo, -a [alu'siβo, a] adj allusive

aluvión [alu'βjon] nm (Geo) alluvium; (fig) flood; **~ de improperios** torrent of abuse

alverja [al'βerxa] (Am) nf pea

alza ['alθa] nf rise; (Mil) sight; **~s fijas/ graduables** fixed/adjustable sights; **al** o **en ~** (precio) rising; **jugar al ~** to speculate on a rising o bull market; **cotizarse** o **estar en ~** to be rising

alzamiento [alθa'mjento] nm (aumento) rise, increase; (acción) lifting, raising; (mejor postura) higher bid; (rebelión) rising; (Com) fraudulent bankruptcy

alzar [al'θar] vt to lift (up); (precio, muro) to raise; (cuello de abrigo) to turn up; (Agr) to gather in; (Tip) to gather; **alzarse** vr to get

up, rise; (rebelarse) to revolt; (Com) to go fraudulently bankrupt; (Jur) to appeal; **~se con el premio** to carry off the prize

ama ['ama] nf lady of the house; (dueña) owner; (institutriz) governess; (madre adoptiva) foster mother; **~ de casa** housewife; **~ de cría** o **de leche** wet-nurse; **~ de llaves** housekeeper

amabilidad [amaβili'ðað] nf kindness; (simpatía) niceness

amable [a'maβle] adj kind; nice; **es usted muy ~** that's very kind of you

amaestrado, -a [amaes'traðo, a] adj (animal) trained; (: en circo etc) performing

amaestrar [amaes'trar] vt to train

amagar [ama'ɣar] vt, vi to threaten

amago [a'maɣo] nm threat; (gesto) threatening gesture; (Med) symptom

amainar [amai'nar] vt (Naut) to lower, take in; (fig) to calm ▷ vi (viento) to die down; **amainarse** vr to drop, die down; **el viento amaina** the wind is dropping

amalgama [amal'ɣama] nf amalgam

amalgamar [amalɣa'mar] vt to amalgamate; (combinar) to combine, mix

amamantar [amaman'tar] vt to suckle, nurse

amanecer [amane'θer] vi to dawn; (fig) to appear, begin to show ▷ nm dawn; **~ afiebrado** to wake up with a fever

amanerado, -a [amane'raðo, a] adj affected

amansar [aman'sar] vt to tame; (persona) to subdue; **amansarse** vr (persona) to calm down

amante [a'mante] adj: **~ de** fond of ▷ nm/f lover

amapola [ama'pola] nf poppy

amar [a'mar] vt to love

amargado, -a [amar'ɣaðo, a] adj bitter; embittered

amargar [amar'ɣar] vt to make bitter; (fig) to embitter; **amargarse** vr to become embittered

amargo, -a [a'marɣo, a] adj bitter

amargura [amar'ɣura] nf = **amargor**

amarillento, -a [amari'ʎento, a] adj yellowish; (tez) sallow

amarillo, -a [ama'riʎo, a] adj, nm yellow

amarra [a'marra] nf (Naut) mooring line; **amarras** nfpl (fig) protection sg; **tener buenas ~s** to have good connections; **soltar ~s** (Naut) to set sail

amarrado, -a [ama'rraðo, a] (Am) adj (fam) mean, stingy

amarrar [ama'rrar] vt to moor; (sujetar) to tie up

amartillar [amarti'ʎar] vt (fusil) to cock

amasar [ama'sar] vt (masa) to knead; (mezclar) to mix, prepare; (confeccionar) to concoct

amasijo [ama'sixo] nm kneading; mixing; (fig) hotchpotch

amateur ['amatur] nm/f amateur
amatista [ama'tista] nf amethyst
amazona [ama'θona] nf horsewoman
Amazonas [ama'θonas] nm: **el (Río)** ~ the Amazon
ambages [am'baxes] nmpl: **sin** ~ in plain language
ámbar ['ambar] nm amber
ambición [ambi'θjon] nf ambition
ambicionar [ambiθjo'nar] vt to aspire to
ambicioso, -a [ambi'θjoso, a] adj ambitious
ambidextro, -a [ambi'ðekstro, a] adj ambidextrous
ambientación [ambjenta'θjon] nf (Cine, Lit etc) setting; (Radio etc) sound effects pl
ambientador [ambjenta'ðor] nm air freshener
ambiente [am'bjente] nm (tb fig) atmosphere; (medio) environment; (Am) room
ambigüedad [ambiɣwe'ðað] nf ambiguity
ambiguo, -a [am'biɣwo, a] adj ambiguous
ámbito ['ambito] nm (campo) field; (fig) scope
ambos, -as ['ambos, as] adj pl, pron pl both
ambulancia [ambu'lanθja] nf ambulance
ambulante [ambu'lante] adj travelling, itinerant; (biblioteca) mobile
ambulatorio [ambula'torio] nm state health-service clinic
ameba [a'meβa] nf amoeba
amedrentar [ameðren'tar] vt to scare
amén [a'men] excl amen; ~ **de** prep besides, in addition to; **en un decir** ~ in the twinkling of an eye; **decir** ~ **a todo** to have no mind of one's own
amenaza [ame'naθa] nf threat
amenazar [amena'θar] vt to threaten ▷ vi: ~ **con hacer** to threaten to do
amenidad [ameni'ðað] nf pleasantness
ameno, -a [a'meno, a] adj pleasant
América [a'merika] nf (continente) America, the Americas; (EEUU) America; (Hispanoamérica) Latin o South America; ~ **del Norte/del Sur** North/South America; ~ **Central/Latina** Central/Latin America
americano, -a [ameri'kano, a] adj, nm/f American; Latin o South American ▷ nf (abrigo) coat; (chaqueta) jacket
amerindio, -a [ame'rindjo, a] adj, nm/f Amerindian, American Indian
amerizar [ameri'θar] vi (Aviat) to land (on the sea)
ametralladora [ametraʎa'ðora] nf machine gun
amianto [a'mjanto] nm asbestos
amigable [ami'ɣaβle] adj friendly
amígdala [a'miɣðala] nf tonsil
amigdalitis [amiɣða'litis] nf tonsillitis
amigo, -a [a'miɣo, a] adj friendly ▷ nm/f friend; (amante) lover; ~ **de lo ajeno** thief; ~ **corresponsal** penfriend; **hacerse** ~**s** to become friends; **ser** ~ **de** to like, be fond of; **ser muy** ~**s** to be close friends

amilanar [amila'nar] vt to scare; **amilanarse** vr to get scared
aminorar [amino'rar] vt to diminish; (reducir) to reduce; ~ **la marcha** to slow down
amistad [amis'tað] nf friendship; **amistades** nfpl (amigos) friends
amistoso, -a [ami'stoso, a] adj friendly
amnesia [am'nesja] nf amnesia
amnistía [amnis'tia] nf amnesty
amo ['amo] nm owner; (jefe) boss
amodorrarse [amoðo'rrarse] vr to get sleepy
amolar [amo'lar] vt to annoy; (Mex: fam) to ruin, damage
amoldar [amol'dar] vt to mould; (adaptar) to adapt
amonestación [amonesta'θjon] nf warning; **amonestaciones** nfpl marriage banns
amonestar [amone'star] vt to warn; (Rel) to publish the banns of
amoniaco [amo'njako] nm ammonia
amontonar [amonto'nar] vt to collect, pile up; **amontonarse** vr (gente) to crowd together; (acumularse) to pile up; (datos) to accumulate; (desastres) to come one on top of another
amor [a'mor] nm love; (amante) lover; **hacer el** ~ to make love; ~ **interesado** cupboard love; ~ **propio** self-respect; **por (el)** ~ **de Dios** for God's sake; **estar al** ~ **de la lumbre** to be close to the fire
amoratado, -a [amora'taðo, a] adj purple, blue with cold; (con cardenales) bruised
amordazar [amorða'θar] vt to muzzle; (fig) to gag
amorfo, -a [a'morfo, a] adj amorphous, shapeless
amorío [amo'rio] nm (fam) love affair
amoroso, -a [amo'roso, a] adj affectionate, loving
amortajar [amorta'xar] vt (fig) to shroud
amortiguador [amortiɣwa'ðor] nm shock absorber; (parachoques) bumper; (silenciador) silencer; **amortiguadores** nmpl (Auto) suspension sg
amortiguar [amorti'ɣwar] vt to deaden; (ruido) to muffle; (color) to soften
amortización [amortiθa'θjon] nf redemption; repayment; (Com) capital allowance
amotinar [amoti'nar] vt to stir up, incite (to riot); **amotinarse** vr to mutiny
amparar [ampa'rar] vt to protect; **ampararse** vr to seek protection; (de la lluvia etc) to shelter
amparo [am'paro] nm help, protection; **al** ~ **de** under the protection of
amperio [am'perjo] nm ampère, amp
ampliación [amplja'θjon] nf enlargement; (extensión) extension
ampliar [am'pljar] vt to enlarge; to extend
amplificación [amplifika'θjon] nf enlargement
amplificador [amplifika'ðor] nm amplifier

a

amplificar [amplifi'kar] vt to amplify

amplio, -a ['ampljo, a] adj spacious; (falda etc) full; (extenso) extensive; (ancho) wide

amplitud [ampli'tuð] nf spaciousness; extent; (fig) amplitude; **~ de miras** broadmindedness; **de gran ~** far-reaching

ampolla [am'poʎa] nf blister; (Med) ampoule

ampuloso, -a [ampu'loso, a] adj bombastic, pompous

amputar [ampu'tar] vt to cut off, amputate

amueblar [amwe'βlar] vt to furnish

amuleto [amu'leto] nm (lucky) charm

amurallar [amura'ʎar] vt to wall up o in

anacronismo [anakro'nismo] nm anachronism

ánade ['anaðe] nm duck

anagrama [ana'ɣrama] nm anagram

anales [a'nales] nmpl annals

analfabetismo [analfaβe'tismo] nm illiteracy

analfabeto, -a [analfa'βeto, a] adj, nm/f illiterate

analgésico [anal'xesiko] nm painkiller, analgesic

análisis [a'nalisis] nm inv analysis; **~ de costos-beneficios** cost-benefit analysis; **~ de mercados** market research; **~ de sangre** blood test

analista [ana'lista] nm/f (gen) analyst; (Pol, Hist) chronicler; **~ de sistemas** (Inform) systems analyst

analizar [anali'θar] vt to analyse

analogía [analo'xia] nf analogy; **por ~ con** on the analogy of

analógico, -a [ana'loxiko, a] adj (Inform) analog; (reloj) analogue (Brit), analog (US)

análogo, -a [a'naloɣo, a] adj analogous, similar

ananá [ana'na], **ananás** [ana'nas] nm pineapple

anaquel [ana'kel] nm shelf

anarquía [anar'kia] nf anarchy

anarquismo [anar'kismo] nm anarchism

anarquista [anar'kista] nm/f anarchist

anatomía [anato'mia] nf anatomy

anca ['anka] nf rump, haunch; **ancas** nfpl (fam) behind sg; **llevar a algn en ~s** to carry sb behind one

ancestral [anθes'tral] adj (costumbre) age-old

ancho, -a ['antʃo, a] adj wide; (falda) full; (fig) liberal ▷ nm width; (Ferro) gauge; **le viene muy ~ el cargo** (fig) the job is too much for him; **ponerse ~** to get conceited; **quedarse tan ~** to go on as if nothing had happened; **estar a sus anchas** to be at one's ease

anchoa [an'tʃoa] nf anchovy

anchura [an'tʃura] nf width; (amplitud) wideness

anciano, -a [an'θjano, a] adj old, aged ▷ nm/f old man/woman ▷ nm elder

ancla ['ankla] nf anchor; **levar ~s** to weigh anchor

ancladero [ankla'ðero] nm anchorage

anclar [an'klar] vi to (drop) anchor

andadura [anda'ðura] nf gait; (de caballo) pace

Andalucía [andalu'θia] nf Andalusia

andaluz, a [anda'luθ, a] adj, nm/f Andalusian

andamiaje [anda'mjaxe], **andamio** [an'damjo] nm scaffold(ing)

andar [an'dar] vt to go, cover, travel ▷ vi to go, walk, travel; (funcionar) to go, work; (estar) to be ▷ nm walk, gait, pace; **andarse** vr (irse) to go away o off; **~ a pie/a caballo/en bicicleta** to go on foot/on horseback/by bicycle; **¡anda!** (sorpresa) go on!; **anda en o por los 40** he's about 40; **¿en qué andas?** what are you up to?; **andamos mal de dinero/tiempo** we're badly off for money/we're short of time; **~se por las ramas** to beat about the bush; **no ~se con rodeos** to call a spade a spade (fam); **todo se ~á** all in good time; **anda por aquí** it's round here somewhere; **~ haciendo algo** to be doing sth

andariego, -a [anda'rjeɣo, a] adj fond of travelling

andén [an'den] nm (Ferro) platform; (Naut) quayside; (Am: acera) pavement (Brit), sidewalk (US)

Andes ['andes] nmpl: **los ~** the Andes

andinismo [andin'ismo] nm (Am) mountaineering, climbing

Andorra [an'dorra] nf Andorra

andrajo [an'draxo] nm rag

andrajoso, -a [andra'xoso, a] adj ragged

andurriales [andu'rrjales] nmpl out-of-the-way place sg, the sticks; **en esos ~** in that godforsaken spot

anduve [an'duβe], **anduviera** etc [andu'βjera] vb ver **andar**

anécdota [a'nekðota] nf anecdote, story

anegar [ane'ɣar] vt to flood; (ahogar) to drown; **anegarse** vr to drown; (hundirse) to sink

anejo, -a [a'nexo, a] adj attached ▷ nm (Arq) annexe

anemia [a'nemja] nf anaemia

anestesia [anes'tesja] nf anaesthetic; **~ general/local** general/local anaesthetic

anestesiar [aneste'sjar] vt to anaesthetize (Brit), anesthetize (US)

anexar [anek'sar] vt to annex; (documento) to attach; (Inform) to append

anexión [anek'sjon] nf, **anexionamiento** [aneksjona'mjento] nm annexation

anexionar [aneksjo'nar] vt to annex; **anexionarse** vr: **~se un país** to annex a country

anexo, -a [a'nekso, a] adj attached ▷ nm annexe

anfetamina [anfeta'mina] nf amphetamine

anfibio, -a [an'fiβjo, a] adj amphibious ▷ nm amphibian

anfiteatro [anfite'atro] nm amphitheatre; (Teat) dress circle

anfitrión, -ona [anfi'trjon, ona] nm/f
host(ess)

ánfora ['anfora] nf (cántaro) amphora; (Am
Pol) ballot box

ángel ['anxel] nm angel; **~ de la guarda**
guardian angel; **tener ~** to have charm

angélico, -a [an'xeliko, a], **angelical**
[anxeli'kal] adj angelic(al)

angina [an'xina] nf (Med) inflammation of
the throat; **~ de pecho** angina; **tener ~s** to
have tonsillitis, have a sore throat

anglicano, -a [angli'kano, a] adj, nm/f
Anglican

anglicismo [angli'θismo] nm anglicism

anglosajón, -ona [anglosa'xon, 'xona] adj,
nm/f Anglo-Saxon

angosto, -a [an'gosto, a] adj narrow

anguila [an'gila] nf eel; **anguilas** nfpl
slipway sg

angula [an'gula] nf elver, baby eel

ángulo ['angulo] nm angle; (esquina) corner;
(curva) bend

angustia [an'gustja] nf anguish

angustiar [angus'tjar] vt to distress, grieve;
angustiarse vr: **~se (por)** to be distressed (at,
on account of)

anhelante [ane'lante] adj eager; (deseoso)
longing

anhelar [ane'lar] vt to be eager for; (desear) to
long for, desire ▷ vi to pant, gasp

anhelo [a'nelo] nm eagerness; desire

anhídrido [a'niðriðo] nm: **~ carbónico**
carbon dioxide

anidar [ani'ðar] vt (acoger) to take in, shelter
▷ vi to nest; (fig) to make one's home

anilla [a'niʎa] nf ring; **(las) ~s** (Deporte) the rings

anillo [a'niʎo] nm ring; **~ de boda** wedding
ring; **~ de compromiso** engagement ring;
venir como ~ al dedo to suit to a tee

ánima ['anima] nf soul; **las ~s** the Angelus
(bell) sg

animación [anima'θjon] nf liveliness;
(vitalidad) life; (actividad) bustle

animado, -a [ani'maðo, a] adj (vivo) lively;
(vivaz) animated; (concurrido) bustling; (alegre)
in high spirits; **dibujos ~s** cartoon sg

animador, a [anima'ðor, a] nm/f (TV)
host(ess), compère ▷ nf (Deporte) cheerleader

animadversión [animaðβer'sjon] nf ill-will,
antagonism

animal [ani'mal] adj animal; (fig) stupid
▷ nm animal; (fig) fool; (bestia) brute

animar [ani'mar] vt (Bio) to animate, give life
to; (fig) to liven up, brighten up, cheer up;
(estimular) to stimulate; **animarse** vr to cheer
up, feel encouraged; (decidirse) to make up
one's mind

ánimo ['animo] nm (alma) soul; (mente) mind;
(valentía) courage ▷ excl cheer up!; **cobrar ~**
to take heart; **dar ~(s) a** to encourage

animoso, -a [ani'moso, a] adj brave;
(vivo) lively

aniquilar [aniki'lar] vt to annihilate, destroy

anís [a'nis] nm (grano) aniseed; (licor) anisette

aniversario [aniβer'sarjo] nm anniversary

anoche [a'notʃe] adv last night; **antes de ~**
the night before last

anochecer [anotʃe'θer] vi to get dark ▷ nm
nightfall, dark; **al ~** at nightfall

anodino, -a [ano'ðino, a] adj dull, anodyne

anomalía [anoma'lia] nf anomaly

anonadado, -a [anona'ðaðo, a] adj: **estar ~**
to be stunned

anonimato [anoni'mato] nm anonymity

anónimo, -a [a'nonimo, a] adj anonymous;
(Com) limited ▷ nm (carta) anonymous letter;
(: maliciosa) poison-pen letter

anorak [ano'rak] (pl **anoraks**) nm anorak

anorexia [ano'reksja] nf anorexia

anormal [anor'mal] adj abnormal

anotación [anota'θjon] nf note; annotation

anotar [ano'tar] vt to note down; (comentar)
to annotate

anquilosamiento [ankilosa'mjento] nm
(fig) paralysis, stagnation

ansia ['ansja] nf anxiety; (añoranza) yearning

ansiar [an'sjar] vt to long for

ansiedad [ansje'ðað] nf anxiety

ansioso, -a [an'sjoso, a] adj anxious;
(anhelante) eager; **~ de o por algo** greedy
for sth

antagónico, -a [anta'ɣoniko, a] adj
antagonistic; (opuesto) contrasting

antagonista [antaɣo'nista] nm/f antagonist

antaño [an'taɲo] adv in years gone by, long ago

Antártico [an'tartiko] nm: **el (océano) ~** the
Antarctic (Ocean)

ante ['ante] prep before, in the presence of;
(encarado con) faced with ▷ nm (piel) suede;
~ todo above all

anteanoche [antea'notʃe] adv the night
before last

anteayer [antea'jer] adv the day before
yesterday

antebrazo [ante'βraθo] nm forearm

antecedente [anteθe'ðente] adj previous
▷ nm antecedent; **~s** nmpl (profesionales)
background sg; **~s penales** criminal record;
no tener ~s to have a clean record; **estar en
~s** to be well-informed; **poner a algn en ~s**
to put sb in the picture

anteceder [anteθe'ðer] vt to precede,
go before

antecesor, a [anteθe'sor, a] nm/f
predecessor

antedicho, -a [ante'ðitʃo, a] adj
aforementioned

antelación [antela'θjon] nf: **con ~** in advance

antemano [ante'mano]: **de ~** adv
beforehand, in advance

antena [an'tena] nf antenna; (de televisión etc)
aerial; **~ parabólica** satellite dish

antenoche [ante'notʃe] (Am) adv the night
before last

anteojo [ante'oxo] *nm* eyeglass; **anteojos**
nmpl (*esp Am*) glasses, spectacles

antepasados [antepa'saðos] *nmpl* ancestors

anteponer [antepo'ner] *vt* to place in front;
(*fig*) to prefer

anteproyecto [antepro'jekto] *nm*
preliminary sketch; (*fig*) blueprint; (*Pol*):
~ **de ley** draft bill

anterior [ante'rjor] *adj* preceding, previous

anterioridad [anterjori'ðað] *nf*: **con ~ a** prior
to, before

antes ['antes] *adv* sooner; (*primero*) first; (*con
anterioridad*) before; (*hace tiempo*) previously,
once; (*más bien*) rather ▷ *prep*: ~ **de** before
▷ *conj*: ~ **(de) que** before; ~ **bien** (but) rather;
dos días ~ two days before o previously;
mucho/poco ~ long/shortly before;
~ **muerto que esclavo** better dead than
enslaved; **no quiso venir** ~ she didn't want
to come any earlier; **tomo el avión ~ que el
barco** I take the plane rather than the boat;
~ **de** o **que nada** (*en el tiempo*) first of all;
(*indicando preferencia*) above all; ~ **que yo**
before me; **cuanto** ~, **lo** ~ **posible** as soon as
possible; **cuanto** ~ **mejor** the sooner the
better

antesala [ante'sala] *nf* anteroom

antiaéreo, -a [antia'ereo, a] *adj* anti-aircraft

antibalas [anti'βalas] *adj inv*: **chaleco ~**
bulletproof jacket

antibiótico [anti'βjotiko] *nm* antibiotic

anticaspa [anti'kaspa] *adj inv* anti-
dandruff *cpd*

anticiclón [antiθi'klon] *nm* (*Meteorología*)
anti-cyclone

anticipación [antiθipa'θjon] *nf*
anticipation; **con 10 minutos de ~** 10
minutes early

anticipado, -a [antiθi'paðo, a] *adj* (in)
advance; **por ~** in advance

anticipar [antiθi'par] *vt* to anticipate;
(*adelantar*) to bring forward; (*Com*) to
advance; **anticiparse** *vr*: ~**se a su época** to
be ahead of one's time

anticipo [anti'θipo] *nm* (*Com*) advance; *ver tb*
anticipación

anticonceptivo, -a [antikonθep'tiβo, a] *adj,
nm* contraceptive; **métodos ~s** methods of
birth control

anticongelante [antikonxe'lante] *nm*
antifreeze

anticuado, -a [anti'kwaðo, a] *adj* out-of-
date, old-fashioned; (*desusado*) obsolete

anticuario [anti'kwarjo] *nm* antique dealer

anticuerpo [anti'kwerpo] *nm* (*Med*) antibody

antidepresivo [antiðepre'siβo] *nm*
antidepressant

antidoping [anti'ðopin] *adj inv* anti-drug;
control ~ drugs test

antídoto [an'tiðoto] *nm* antidote

antiestético, -a [anties'tetiko, a] *adj*
unsightly

antifaz [anti'faθ] *nm* mask; (*velo*) veil

antiglobalización [antiglobaliθa'θjon] *nf*
anti-globalization; **manifestantes ~** anti-
globalization protesters

antiglobalizador, a [antiglobaliθa'ðor, a]
adj anti-globalization *cpd*

antigualla [anti'ɣwaʎa] *nf* antique; (*reliquia*)
relic; **antiguallas** *nfpl* old things

antiguamente [antiɣwa'mente] *adv*
formerly; (*hace mucho tiempo*) long ago

antigüedad [antiɣwe'ðað] *nf* antiquity;
(*artículo*) antique; (*rango*) seniority

antiguo, -a [an'tiɣwo, a] *adj* old, ancient;
(*que fue*) former; **a la antigua** in the old-
fashioned way

antillano, -a [anti'ʎano, a] *adj, nm/f* West
Indian

Antillas [an'tiʎas] *nfpl*: **las ~** the West Indies,
the Antilles; **el mar de las ~** the Caribbean
Sea

antílope [an'tilope] *nm* antelope

antinatural [antinatu'ral] *adj* unnatural

antipatía [antipa'tia] *nf* antipathy, dislike

antipático, -a [anti'patiko, a] *adj*
disagreeable, unpleasant

antirrobo [anti'rroβo] *nm* (*tb*: **dispositivo ~**:
para casas etc) burglar alarm; (: *para coches*) car
alarm ▷ *adj inv* (*alarma etc*) anti-theft

antisemita [antise'mita] *adj* anti-Semitic
▷ *nm/f* anti-Semite

antiséptico, -a [anti'septiko, a] *adj*
antiseptic ▷ *nm* antiseptic

antiterrorismo [antiterro'rismo] *nm*
counterterrorism

antiterrorista [antiterro'rista] *adj*
antiterrorist, counterterrorist; **la lucha ~**
the fight against terrorism

antítesis [an'titesis] *nf inv* antithesis

antivirus [anti'birus] *nm inv* (*Comput*)
antivirus program

antojadizo, -a [antoxa'ðiθo, a] *adj*
capricious

antojarse [anto'xarse] *vr* (*desear*): **se me
antoja comprarlo** I have a mind to buy it;
(*pensar*): **se me antoja que ...** I have a feeling
that ...

antojo [an'toxo] *nm* caprice, whim; (*rosa*)
birthmark; (*lunar*) mole; **hacer a su ~** to do
as one pleases

antología [antolo'xia] *nf* anthology

antonomasia [antono'masja] *nf*: **por ~** par
excellence

antorcha [an'tortʃa] *nf* torch

antro ['antro] *nm* cavern; ~ **de corrupción**
(*fig*) den of iniquity

antropófago, -a [antro'pofaɣo, a] *adj, nm/f*
cannibal

antropología [antropolo'xia] *nf*
anthropology

antropólogo, -a [antro'poloɣo, a] *nm/f*
anthropologist

anual [a'nwal] *adj* annual

anualidad [anwali'ðað] *nf* annuity, annual payment; **~ vitalicia** life annuity

anuario [a'nwarjo] *nm* yearbook

anublado, -a [anu'βlaðo, a] *adj* overcast

anudar [anu'ðar] *vt* to knot, tie; (*unir*) to join; **anudarse** *vr* to get tied up; **se me anudó la voz** I got a lump in my throat

anulación [anula'θjon] *nf* (*de un matrimonio*) annulment; (*cancelación*) cancellation; (*de una ley*) repeal

anular [anu'lar] *vt* (*contrato*) to annul, cancel; (*suscripción*) to cancel; (*ley*) to repeal ▷ *nm* ring finger

anunciación [anunθja'θjon] *nf* announcement; **A~** (*Rel*) Annunciation

anunciante [anun'θjante] *nm/f* (*Com*) advertiser

anunciar [anun'θjar] *vt* to announce; (*proclamar*) to proclaim; (*Com*) to advertise

anuncio [a'nunθjo] *nm* announcement; (*señal*) sign; (*Com*) advertisement; (*cartel*) poster; (*Teat*) bill; **~s por palabras** classified ads

anzuelo [an'θwelo] *nm* hook; (*para pescar*) fish hook; **tragar el ~** to swallow the bait

añadido [aɲa'ðiðo] *nm* addition

añadidura [aɲaði'ðura] *nf* addition, extra; **por ~** besides, in addition

añadir [aɲa'ðir] *vt* to add

añejo, -a [a'ɲexo, a] *adj* old; (*vino*) mature; (*jamón*) well-cured

añicos [a'ɲikos] *nmpl*: **hacer ~** to smash, shatter; **hacerse ~** to smash, shatter

añil [a'ɲil] *nm* (*Bot, color*) indigo

año ['aɲo] *nm* year; **¡Feliz A~ Nuevo!** Happy New Year!; **tener ... ~s** to be 15 (years old); **los ~s 80** the eighties; **~ bisiesto/escolar/fiscal/sabático** leap/school/tax/sabbatical year; **~ fiscal** o tax year; **estar de buen ~** to be in good shape; **en el ~ de la nana** in the year dot; **el ~ que viene** next year

añoranza [aɲo'ranθa] *nf* nostalgia; (*anhelo*) longing

añorar [aɲo'rar] *vt* to long for

apa ['apa] *excl* (*Am*) goodness me!, good gracious!

apabullar [apaβu'ʎar] *vt* (*lit: fig*) to crush

apacentar [apaθen'tar] *vt* to pasture, graze

apacible [apa'θiβle] *adj* gentle, mild

apaciguar [apaθi'ɣwar] *vt* to pacify, calm (down)

apadrinar [apaðri'nar] *vt* to sponsor, support; (*Rel: niño*) to be godfather to

apagado, -a [apa'ɣaðo, a] *adj* (*volcán*) extinct; (*color*) dull; (*voz*) quiet; (*sonido*) muted, muffled; (*persona*) *apático*) listless; **estar ~** (*fuego, luz*) to be out; (*radio, TV etc*) to be off

apagar [apa'ɣar] *vt* to put out; (*color*) to tone down; (*sonido*) to silence, muffle; (*sed*) to quench; (*Elec, Radio, TV*) to turn off; (*Inform*) to toggle off; **apagarse** *vr* (*luz, fuego*) to go out; (*sonido*) to die away; (*pasión*) to wither; **~ el sistema** (*Inform*) to close o shut down

apagón [apa'ɣon] *nm* blackout, power cut

apaisado, -a [apai'saðo, a] *adj* (*papel*) landscape *cpd*

apalabrar [apala'βrar] *vt* to agree to; (*obrero*) to engage

apalear [apale'ar] *vt* to beat, thrash; (*Agr*) to winnow

apañado, -a [apa'ɲaðo, a] *adj* (*mañoso*) resourceful; (*arreglado*) tidy; (*útil*) handy

apañar [apa'ɲar] *vt* to pick up; (*asir*) to take hold of, grasp; (*reparar*) to mend, patch up; **apañarse** *vr* to manage, get along; **apañárselas por su cuenta** to look after number one (*fam*)

apantallar [apanta'ʎar] *vt* (*Am*) to impress

apapachar [apapa'tʃar] *vt* (*Am: fam*) to cuddle, hug

aparador [apara'ðor] *nm* sideboard; (*Am: escaparate*) shop window

aparato [apa'rato] *nm* apparatus; (*máquina*) machine; (*doméstico*) appliance; (*boato*) ostentation; (*Inform*) device; **al ~** (*Telec*) speaking; **~ de facsímil** facsimile (machine), fax; **~ respiratorio** respiratory system; **~ digestivo** digestive system; **~s de mando** (*Aviat etc*) controls

aparatoso, -a [apara'toso, a] *adj* showy, ostentatious

aparcamiento [aparka'mjento] *nm* car park (*Brit*), parking lot (*US*)

aparcar [apar'kar] *vt, vi* to park

aparear [apare'ar] *vt* (*objetos*) to pair, match; (*animales*) to mate; **aparearse** *vr* to form a pair; to mate

aparecer [apare'θer] *vi* to appear; **aparecerse** *vr* to appear; **apareció borracho** he turned up drunk

aparejado, -a [apare'xaðo, a] *adj* fit, suitable; **ir ~ con** to go hand in hand with; **llevar** o **traer ~** to involve

aparejador, a [aparexa'ðor, a] *nm/f* (*Arq*) quantity surveyor

aparejo [apa'rexo] *nm* preparation; (*de caballo*) harness; (*Naut*) rigging; (*de poleas*) block and tackle

aparentar [aparen'tar] *vt* (*edad*) to look; (*fingir*): **~ tristeza** to pretend to be sad

aparente [apa'rente] *adj* apparent; (*adecuado*) suitable

aparezca *etc* [apa'reθka] *vb ver* **aparecer**

aparición [apari'θjon] *nf* appearance; (*de libro*) publication; (*de fantasma*) apparition

apariencia [apa'rjenθja] *nf* (outward) appearance; **en ~** outwardly, seemingly

apartado, -a [apar'taðo, a] *adj* separate; (*lejano*) remote ▷ *nm* (*tipográfico*) paragraph; **~ de correos** (*Esp*), **~ postal** (*Am*) post office box

apartamento [aparta'mento] *nm* apartment, flat (*Brit*)

apartamiento [aparta'mjento] *nm* separation; (*aislamiento*) remoteness; (*Am*) apartment, flat (*Brit*)

apartar [apar'tar] *vt* to separate; *(quitar)* to remove; *(Mineralogía)* to extract; **apartarse** *vr* *(separarse)* to separate, part; *(irse)* to move away; *(mantenerse aparte)* to keep away

aparte [a'parte] *adv* *(separadamente)* separately; *(además)* besides ▷ *prep:* ~ **de** apart from ▷ *nm* (Teat) aside; *(tipográfico)* new paragraph; **"punto y ~"** "new paragraph"

aparthotel [aparto'tel] *nm* serviced apartments

apasionado, -a [apasjo'naðo, a] *adj* passionate; *(pey)* biassed, prejudiced ▷ *nm/f* admirer

apasionante [apasjo'nante] *adj* exciting

apasionar [apasjo'nar] *vt* to excite; **apasionarse** *vr* to get excited; **le apasiona el fútbol** she's crazy about football

apatía [apa'tia] *nf* apathy

apático, -a [a'patiko, a] *adj* apathetic

apátrida [a'patriða] *adj* stateless

Apdo. *nm abr* (= *Apartado (de Correos)*) P.O. Box

apeadero [apea'ðero] *nm* halt, stopping place

apearse [ape'arse] *vr* *(jinete)* to dismount; *(bajarse)* to get down o out; *(de coche)* to get out, alight; **no ~ del burro** to refuse to climb down

apechugar [apetʃu'ɣar] *vi:* ~ **con algo** to face up to sth

apedrear [apeðre'ar] *vt* to stone

apegarse [ape'ɣarse] *vr:* ~ **a** to become attached to

apego [a'peɣo] *nm* attachment, devotion

apelación [apela'θjon] *nf* appeal

apelar [ape'lar] *vi* to appeal; ~ **a** *(fig)* to resort to

apellidar [apeʎi'ðar] *vt* to call, name; **apellidarse** *vr:* **se apellida Pérez** her (sur)name's Pérez

apellido [ape'ʎiðo] *nm* surname

apenar [ape'nar] *vt* to grieve, trouble; *(Am: avergonzar)* to embarrass; **apenarse** *vr* to grieve; *(Am: avergonzarse)* to be embarrassed

apenas [a'penas] *adv* scarcely, hardly ▷ *conj* as soon as, no sooner

apéndice [a'pendiθe] *nm* appendix

apendicitis [apendi'θitis] *nf* appendicitis

aperitivo [aperi'tiβo] *nm* *(bebida)* aperitif; *(comida)* appetizer

apertura [aper'tura] *nf* *(gen)* opening; *(Pol)* openness, liberalization; *(Teat etc)* beginning; ~ **de un juicio hipotecario** *(Com)* foreclosure

apesadumbrar [apesaðum'brar] *vt* to grieve, sadden; **apesadumbrarse** *vr* to distress o.s.

apestar [apes'tar] *vt* to infect ▷ *vi:* ~ **(a)** to stink (of)

apetecer [apete'θer] *vt:* **¿te apetece una tortilla?** do you fancy an omelette?

apetecible [apete'θiβle] *adj* desirable; *(comida)* appetizing

apetito [ape'tito] *nm* appetite

apetitoso, -a [apeti'toso, a] *adj* *(gustoso)* appetizing; *(fig)* tempting

apiadarse [apja'ðarse] *vr:* ~ **de** to take pity on

ápice ['apiθe] *nm* apex; *(fig)* whit, iota; **ni un ~** not a whit; **no ceder un ~** not to budge an inch

apilar [api'lar] *vt* to pile o heap up; **apilarse** *vr* to pile up

apiñar [api'ɲar] *vt* to crowd; **apiñarse** *vr* to crowd o press together

apio ['apjo] *nm* celery

apisonadora [apisona'ðora] *nf* *(máquina)* steamroller

aplacar [apla'kar] *vt* to placate; **aplacarse** *vr* to calm down

aplanar [apla'nar] *vt* to smooth, level; *(allanar)* to roll flat, flatten; **aplanarse** *vr* *(edificio)* to collapse; *(persona)* to get discouraged

aplastante [aplas'tante] *adj* overwhelming; *(lógica)* compelling

aplastar [aplas'tar] *vt* to squash (flat); *(fig)* to crush

aplatanarse [aplata'narse] *vr* to get lethargic

aplaudir [aplau'ðir] *vt* to applaud

aplauso [a'plauso] *nm* applause; *(fig)* approval, acclaim

aplazamiento [aplaθa'mjento] *nm* postponement

aplazar [apla'θar] *vt* to postpone, defer

aplicación [aplika'θjon] *nf* application; *(esfuerzo)* effort; **aplicaciones de gestión** business applications

aplicado, -a [apli'kaðo, a] *adj* diligent, hard-working

aplicar [apli'kar] *vt* *(ejecutar)* to apply; *(poner en vigor)* to put into effect; *(esfuerzos)* to devote; **aplicarse** *vr* to apply o.s.

aplique *etc* [a'plike] *vb ver* **aplicar** ▷ *nm* wall light o lamp

aplomo [a'plomo] *nm* aplomb, self-assurance

apocado, -a [apo'kaðo, a] *adj* timid

apocamiento [apoka'mjento] *nm* timidity; *(depresión)* depression

apocarse [apo'karse] *vr* to feel small o humiliated

apócope [a'pokope] *nf* apocopation; **gran es ~ de grande** "gran" is the shortened form of "grande"

apodar [apo'ðar] *vt* to nickname

apoderado [apoðe'raðo] *nm* agent, representative

apoderar [apoðe'rar] *vt* to authorize, empower; *(Jur)* to grant (a) power of attorney to; **apoderarse** *vr:* ~ **se de** to take possession of

apodo [a'poðo] *nm* nickname

apogeo [apo'xeo] *nm* peak, summit

apolillarse [apoli'ʎarse] *vr* to get moth-eaten

apología [apolo'xia] *nf* eulogy; *(defensa)* defence

apoltronarse [apoltro'narse] vr to get lazy
apoplejía [apople'xia] nf apoplexy, stroke
apoquinar [apoki'nar] vt (fam) to cough up,
fork out
aporrear [aporre'ar] vt to beat (up)
aportar [apor'tar] vt to contribute ▷ vi to
reach port; **aportarse** vr (Am: llegar) to
arrive, come
aposentar [aposen'tar] vt to lodge, put up
aposento [apo'sento] nm lodging;
(habitación) room
apósito [a'posito] nm (Med) dressing
aposta [a'posta] adv deliberately, on purpose
apostar [apos'tar] vt to bet, stake; (tropas etc)
to station, post ▷ vi to bet
a posteriori [aposte'rjori] adv at a later date o
stage; (Lógica) a posteriori
apostilla [apos'tiʎa] nf note, comment
apóstol [a'postol] nm apostle
apóstrofo [a'postrofo] nm apostrophe
apoyar [apo'jar] vt to lean, rest; (fig) to
support, back; **apoyarse** vr: ~**se en** to lean
on
apoyo [a'pojo] nm support, backing
apreciable [apre'θjaβle] adj considerable;
(fig) esteemed
apreciación [apreθja'θjon] nf appreciation;
(Com) valuation
apreciar [apre'θjar] vt to evaluate, assess;
(Com) to appreciate, value; (persona) to
respect; (tamaño) to gauge, assess; (detalles) to
notice ▷ vi (Econ) to appreciate
aprecio [a'preθjo] nm valuation, estimate;
(fig) appreciation
aprehender [apreen'der] vt to apprehend,
detain; (ver) to see, observe
aprehensión [apreen'sjon] nf detention,
capture
apremiante [apre'mjante] adj urgent,
pressing
apremiar [apre'mjar] vt to compel, force ▷ vi
to be urgent, press
apremio [a'premjo] nm urgency; ~ **de pago**
demand note
aprender [apren'der] vt, vi to learn; ~ **a
conducir** to learn to drive; **aprenderse** vr:
~**se algo de memoria** to learn sth (off) by
heart
aprendiz, a [apren'diθ, a] nm/f apprentice;
(principiante) learner, trainee; ~ **de comercio**
business trainee
aprendizaje [aprendi'θaxe] nm
apprenticeship
aprensión [apren'sjon] nm apprehension,
fear
aprensivo, -a [apren'siβo, a] adj
apprehensive
apresar [apre'sar] vt to seize; (capturar) to
capture
aprestar [apres'tar] vt to prepare, get ready;
(Tec) to prime, size; **aprestarse** vr to get
ready

apresurado, -a [apresu'raðo, a] adj hurried,
hasty
apresuramiento [apresura'mjento] nm
hurry, haste
apresurar [apresu'rar] vt to hurry,
accelerate; **apresurarse** vr to hurry, make
haste; **me apresuré a sugerir que ...**
I hastily suggested that ...
apretado, -a [apre'taðo, a] adj tight;
(escritura) cramped
apretar [apre'tar] vt to squeeze, press; (mano)
to clasp; (dientes) to grit; (Tec) to tighten;
(presionar) to press together, pack ▷ vi to be
too tight; **apretarse** vr to crowd together;
~ **la mano a algn** to shake sb's hand; ~ **el
paso** to quicken one's step
apretón [apre'ton] nm squeeze; ~ **de manos**
handshake
aprieto [a'prjeto] vb ver **apretar** ▷ nm
squeeze; (dificultad) difficulty, predicament;
estar en un ~ to be in a fix; **ayudar a algn
a salir de un** ~ to help sb out of trouble
a priori [apri'ori] adv beforehand; (Lógica)
a priori
aprisa [a'prisa] adv quickly, hurriedly
aprisionar [aprisjo'nar] vt to imprison
aprobación [aproβa'θjon] nf approval
aprobado [apro'βaðo] nm (nota) pass mark
aprobar [apro'βar] vt to approve (of);
(examen, materia) to pass ▷ vi to pass
apropiación [apropja'θjon] nf appropriation
apropiado, -a [apro'pjaðo, a] adj
appropriate, suitable
apropiarse [apro'pjarse] vr: ~ **de** to appropriate
aprovechado, -a [aproβe'tʃaðo, a] adj
industrious, hardworking; (económico)
thrifty; (pey) unscrupulous
aprovechamiento [aproβetʃa'mjento] nm
use, exploitation
aprovechar [aproβe'tʃar] vt to use; (explotar)
to exploit; (experiencia) to profit from; (oferta,
oportunidad) to take advantage of ▷ vi to
progress, improve; **aprovecharse** vr: ~**se de**
to make use of; (pey) to take advantage of;
¡que aproveche! enjoy your meal!
aproximación [aproksima'θjon] nf
approximation; (de lotería) consolation prize
aproximadamente [aproksimaða'mente]
adv approximately
aproximado, -a [aproksi'maðo, a] adj
approximate
aproximar [aproksi'mar] vt to bring nearer;
aproximarse vr to come near, approach
apruebe etc [a'prweβe] vb ver **aprobar**
aptitud [apti'tuð] nf aptitude; (capacidad)
ability; ~ **para los negocios** business sense
apto, -a ['apto, a] adj (hábil) capable;
(apropiado): ~ **(para)** fit (for), suitable (for);
~/**no ~ para menores** (Cine) suitable/
unsuitable for children
apuesto, -a etc [a'pwesto, a] vb ver **apostar**
▷ adj neat, elegant ▷ nf bet, wager

apuntador [apunta'ðor] *nm* prompter

apuntalar [apunta'lar] *vt* to prop up

apuntar [apun'tar] *vt* (*con arma*) to aim at; (*con dedo*) to point at o to; (*anotar*) to note (down); (*datos*) to record; (*Teat*) to prompt; **apuntarse** *vr* (*Deporte: tanto, victoria*) to score; (*Escol*) to enrol; **~ una cantidad en la cuenta de algn** to charge a sum to sb's account; **~se en un curso** to enrol on a course; **¡yo me apunto!** count me in!

apunte [a'punte] *nm* note; (*Teat: voz*) prompt; (*: texto*) prompt book

apuñalar [apuɲa'lar] *vt* to stab

apurado, -a [apu'raðo, a] *adj* needy; (*difícil*) difficult; (*peligroso*) dangerous; (*Am: con prisa*) hurried, rushed; **estar en una situación apurada** to be in a tight spot; **estar ~** to be in a hurry

apurar [apu'rar] *vt* (*agotar*) to drain; (*recursos*) to use up; (*molestar*) to annoy; **apurarse** *vr* (*preocuparse*) to worry; (*esp Am: darse prisa*) to hurry

apuro [a'puro] *nm* (*aprieto*) fix, jam; (*escasez*) want, hardship; (*vergüenza*) embarrassment; (*Am: prisa*) haste, urgency

aquejado, -a [ake'xaðo, a] *adj*: **~ de** (*Med*) afflicted by

aquel, aquella, aquellos, -as [a'kel, a'keʎa, a'keʎos, -as] *adj* that, those *pl* ▷ *pron* that (one), those (ones) *pl*

aquél, aquélla, aquéllos, -as [a'kel, a'keʎa, a'keʎos, -as] *pron* that (one), those (ones) *pl*

aquello [a'keʎo] *pron* that, that business

aquí [a'ki] *adv* (*lugar*) here; (*tiempo*) now; **~ arriba** up here; **~ mismo** right here; **~ yace** here lies; **de ~ a siete días** a week from now

aquietar [akje'tar] *vt* to quieten (down), calm (down)

ara ['ara] *nf* (*altar*) altar; **en ~s de** for the sake of

árabe ['araβe] *adj* Arab, Arabian, Arabic ▷ *nm/f* Arab ▷ *nm* (*Ling*) Arabic

Arabia [a'raβja] *nf* Arabia; **~ Saudí** o **Saudita** Saudi Arabia

arado [a'raðo] *nm* plough

Aragón [ara'ɣon] *nm* Aragon

aragonés, -esa [araɣo'nes, esa] *adj, nm/f* Aragonese ▷ *nm* (*Ling*) Aragonese

arancel [aran'θel] *nm* tariff, duty; **~ de aduanas** (customs) duty

arandela [aran'dela] *nf* (*Tec*) washer; (*chorrera*) frill

araña [a'raɲa] *nf* (*Zool*) spider; (*lámpara*) chandelier

arañar [ara'ɲar] *vt* to scratch

arañazo [ara'ɲaθo] *nm* scratch

arar [a'rar] *vt* to plough, till

arbitraje [arβi'traxe] *nm* arbitration

arbitrar [arβi'trar] *vt* to arbitrate in; (*recursos*) to bring together; (*Deporte*) to referee ▷ *vi* to arbitrate

arbitrariedad [arβitrarje'ðað] *nf* arbitrariness; (*acto*) arbitrary act

arbitrario, -a [arβi'trarjo, a] *adj* arbitrary

arbitrio [ar'βitrjo] *nm* free will; (*Jur*) adjudication, decision; **dejar al ~ de algn** to leave to sb's discretion

árbitro ['arβitro] *nm* arbitrator; (*Deporte*) referee; (*Tenis*) umpire

árbol ['arβol] *nm* (*Bot*) tree; (*Naut*) mast; (*Tec*) axle, shaft; **~ de Navidad** Christmas tree

arbolado, -a [arβo'laðo, a] *adj* wooded; (*camino*) tree-lined ▷ *nm* woodland

arboladura [arβola'ðura] *nf* rigging

arbolar [arβo'lar] *vt* to hoist, raise

arboleda [arβo'leða] *nf* grove, plantation

arbusto [ar'βusto] *nm* bush, shrub

arca ['arka] *nf* chest, box; **A~ de la Alianza** Ark of the Covenant; **A~ de Noé** Noah's Ark

arcada [ar'kaða] *nf* arcade; (*de puente*) arch, span; **arcadas** *nfpl* (*náuseas*) retching *sg*

arcaico, -a [ar'kaiko, a] *adj* archaic

arce ['arθe] *nm* maple tree

arcén [ar'θen] *nm* (*de autopista*) hard shoulder; (*de carretera*) verge

archipiélago [artʃi'pjelaɣo] *nm* archipelago

archivador [artʃiβa'ðor] *nm* filing cabinet; **~ colgante** suspension file

archivar [artʃi'βar] *vt* to file (away); (*Inform*) to archive

archivo [ar'tʃiβo] *nm* archive(s) (*pl*); (*Inform*) file; **A~ Nacional** Public Record Office; **~s policíacos** police files; **nombre de ~** (*Inform*) filename; **~ adjunto** (*Inform*) attachment; **~ de seguridad** (*Inform*) backup file

arcilla [ar'θiʎa] *nf* clay

arco ['arko] *nm* arch; (*Mat*) arc; (*Mil, Mus*) bow; (*Am Deporte*) goal; **~ iris** rainbow

arder [ar'ðer] *vti* to burn; **~ sin llama** to smoulder; **estar que arde** (*persona*) to fume

ardid [ar'ðið] *nm* ploy, trick

ardiente [ar'ðjente] *adj* ardent

ardilla [ar'ðiʎa] *nf* squirrel

ardor [ar'ðor] *nm* (*calor*) heat, warmth; (*fig*) ardour; **~ de estómago** heartburn

ardoroso, -a [arðo'roso, a] *adj* passionate

arduo, -a ['arðwo, a] *adj* arduous

área ['area] *nf* area; (*Deporte*) penalty area

arena [a'rena] *nf* sand; (*de una lucha*) arena

arenal [are'nal] *nm* (*terreno arenoso*) sandy area; (*arena movediza*) quicksand

arengar [aren'gar] *vt* to harangue

arenisca [are'niska] *nf* sandstone; (*cascajo*) grit

arenoso, -a [are'noso, a] *adj* sandy

arenque [a'renke] *nm* herring

arete [a'rete] *nm* (*Am*) earring

argamasa [arɣa'masa] *nf* mortar, plaster

Argel [ar'xel] *n* Algiers

Argelia [ar'xelja] *nf* Algeria

argelino, -a [arxe'lino, a] *adj, nm/f* Algerian

Argentina [arxen'tina] *nf*: **(la) ~** Argentina, the Argentine

argentino, -a [arxen'tino, a] *adj* Argentinian; (*de plata*) silvery ▷ *nm/f* Argentinian

argolla [ar'goʎa] nf (large) ring; (Am: de matrimonio) wedding ring

argot [ar'ɣo] nm (pl **argots**) [ar'ɣo, ar'ɣos] slang

argucia [ar'ɣuθja] nf subtlety, sophistry

argüir [ar'ɣwir] vt to deduce; (discutir) to argue; (indicar) to indicate, imply; (censurar) to reproach ▷ vi to argue

argumentación [arɣumenta'θjon] nf (line of) argument

argumentar [arɣumen'tar] vt, vi to argue

argumento [arɣu'mento] nm argument; (razonamiento) reasoning; (de novela etc) plot; (Cine, TV) storyline

aria ['arja] nf aria

aridez [ari'ðeθ] nf aridity, dryness

árido, -a ['ariðo, a] adj arid, dry; **áridos** nmpl dry goods

Aries ['arjes] nm Aries

ariete [a'rjete] nm battering ram

ario, -a ['arjo, a] adj Aryan

arisco, -a [a'risko, a] adj surly; (insociable) unsociable

aristocracia [aristo'kraθja] nf aristocracy

aristócrata [aris'tokrata] nm/f aristocrat

aritmética [arit'metika] nf arithmetic

arma ['arma] nf arm; **armas** nfpl arms; **~ blanca** blade, knife; (espada) sword; **~ de doble filo** double-edged sword; **~ de fuego** firearm; **~s cortas** small arms; **~s de destrucción masiva** weapons of mass destruction; **rendir las ~s** to lay down one's arms; **ser de ~s tomar** to be somebody to be reckoned with

armada [ar'maða] nf armada; (flota) fleet; ver tb **armado**

armadillo [arma'ðiʎo] nm armadillo

armado, -a [ar'maðo, a] adj armed; (Tec) reinforced

armador [arma'ðor] nm (Naut) shipowner

armadura [arma'ðura] nf (Mil) armour; (Tec) framework; (Zool) skeleton; (Física) armature

armamento [arma'mento] nm armament; (Naut) fitting-out

armar [ar'mar] vt (soldado) to arm; (máquina) to assemble; (navío) to fit out; **~la**, **~ un lío** to start a row, kick up a fuss; **armarse** vr: **~se de valor** to summon up one's courage

armario [ar'marjo] nm wardrobe; (de cocina, baño) cupboard; **~ empotrado** built-in cupboard; **salir del ~** to come out (of the closet)

armatoste [arma'toste] nm (mueble) monstrosity; (máquina) contraption

armazón [arma'θon] nf o m body, chassis; (de mueble etc) frame; (Arq) skeleton

armiño [ar'miɲo] nm stoat; (piel) ermine

armisticio [armis'tiθjo] nm armistice

armonía [armo'nia] nf harmony

armónica [ar'monika] nf harmonica

armonioso, -a [armo'njoso, a] adj harmonious

armonizar [armoni'θar] vt to harmonize; (diferencias) to reconcile ▷ vi to harmonize; **~ con** (fig) to be in keeping with; (colores) to tone in with

arnés [ar'nes] nm armour; **arneses** nmpl harness sg

aro ['aro] nm ring; (tejo) quoit; (Am: pendiente) earring; **entrar por el ~** to give in

aroma [a'roma] nm aroma

aromaterapia [aromate'rapja] nf aromatherapy

aromático, -a [aro'matiko, a] adj aromatic

arpa ['arpa] nf harp

arpía [ar'pia] nf (fig) shrew

arpillera [arpi'ʎera] nf sacking, sackcloth

arpón [ar'pon] nm harpoon

arquear [arke'ar] vt to arch, bend; **arquearse** vr to arch, bend

arqueo [ar'keo] nm (gen) arching; (Naut) tonnage

arqueología [arkeolo'xia] nf archaeology

arqueólogo, -a [arke'oloɣo, a] nm/f archaeologist

arquero [ar'kero] nm archer, bowman; (Am Deporte) goalkeeper

arquetipo [arke'tipo] nm archetype

arquitecto, -a [arki'tekto, a] nm/f architect; **~ paisajista** o **de jardines** landscape gardener

arquitectura [arkitek'tura] nf architecture

arrabal [arra'βal] nm suburb; (LAm) slum; **arrabales** nmpl (afueras) outskirts

arraigado, -a [arrai'ɣaðo, a] adj deep-rooted; (fig) established

arraigar [arrai'ɣar] vt to establish ▷ vi, **arraigarse** vr to take root; (persona) to settle

arrancar [arran'kar] vt (sacar) to extract, pull out; (arrebatar) to snatch (away); (pedazo) to tear off; (página) to rip out; (suspiro) to heave; (Auto) to start; (Inform) to boot; (fig) to extract ▷ vi (Auto, máquina) to start; (ponerse en marcha) to get going; **~ información a algn** to extract information from sb; **~ de** to stem from

arranque etc [a'rranke] vb ver **arrancar** ▷ nm sudden start; (Auto) start; (fig) fit, outburst

arras ['arras] nfpl pledge sg, security sg

arrasar [arra'sar] vt (aplanar) to level, flatten; (destruir) to demolish

arrastrado, -a [arras'traðo, a] adj poor, wretched

arrastrar [arras'trar] vt to drag (along); (fig) to drag down, degrade; (suj: agua, viento) to carry away ▷ vi to drag, trail on the ground; **arrastrarse** vr to crawl; (fig) to grovel; **llevar algo arrastrado** to drag sth along

arrastre [a'rrastre] nm drag, dragging; (Deporte) crawl; **estar para el ~** (fig) to have had it

arre ['arre] excl gee up!

arrear [arre'ar] vt to drive on, urge on ▷ vi to hurry along

a

arrebatado, -a [arreβa'taðo, a] *adj* rash, impetuous; (*repentino*) sudden, hasty

arrebatar [arreβa'tar] *vt* to snatch (away), seize; (*fig*) to captivate; **arrebatarse** *vr* to get carried away, get excited

arrebato [arre'βato] *nm* fit of rage, fury; (*éxtasis*) rapture; **en un ~ de cólera** in an outburst of anger

arrecife [arre'θife] *nm* reef

arredrar [arreð'rar] *vt* (*hacer retirarse*) to drive back; **arredrarse** *vr* (*apartarse*) to draw back; **~se ante algo** to shrink away from sth

arreglado, -a [arre'ɣlaðo, a] *adj* (*ordenado*) neat, orderly; (*moderado*) moderate, reasonable

arreglar [arre'ɣlar] *vt* (*poner orden*) to tidy up; (*algo roto*) to fix, repair; (*problema*) to solve; **arreglarse** *vr* to reach an understanding; **arreglárselas** (*fam*) to get by, manage

arreglo [a'rreɣlo] *nm* settlement; (*orden*) order; (*acuerdo*) agreement; (*Mus*) arrangement, setting; (*Inform*) array; **con ~ a** in accordance with; **llegar a un ~** to reach a compromise

arrellanarse [arreʎa'narse] *vr* to sprawl; **~ en el asiento** to lie back in one's chair

arremangar [arreman'gar] *vt* to roll up, turn up; **arremangarse** *vr* to roll up one's sleeves

arremeter [arreme'ter] *vt* to attack, assault ▷ *vi*: **~ contra algn** to attack sb

arrendador, a [arrenda'ðor, a] *nm/f* landlord/lady

arrendamiento [arrenda'mjento] *nm* letting; (*el alquiler*) hiring; (*contrato*) lease; (*alquiler*) rent

arrendar [arren'dar] *vt* to let; to hire; to lease; to rent

arrendatario, -a [arrenda'tarjo, a] *nm/f* tenant

arreos [a'rreos] *nmpl* (*de caballo*) harness *sg*, trappings

arrepentido, -a [arrepen'tiðo, a] *nm/f* (*Pol*) reformed terrorist

arrepentimiento [arrepenti'mjento] *nm* regret, repentance

arrepentirse [arrepen'tirse] *vr* to repent; **~ de (haber hecho) algo** to regret (doing) sth

arrestar [arres'tar] *vt* to arrest; (*encarcelar*) to imprison

arresto [a'rresto] *nm* arrest; (*Mil*) detention; (*audacia*) boldness, daring; **~ domiciliario** house arrest

arriar [a'rrjar] *vt* (*velas*) to haul down; (*bandera*) to lower, strike; (*un cable*) to pay out

⊙ **PALABRA CLAVE**

arriba [a'rriβa] *adv* **1** (*posición*) above; **desde arriba** from above; **arriba del todo** at the very top, right on top; **Juan está arriba** Juan is upstairs; **lo arriba mencionado** the aforementioned; **aquí/allí arriba** up here/

there; **está hasta arriba de trabajo** (*fam*) he's up to his eyes in work (*fam*)

2 (*dirección*) up, upwards; **más arriba** higher o further up; **calle arriba** up the street

3: **de arriba abajo** from top to bottom; **mirar a algn de arriba abajo** to look sb up and down

4: **para arriba**: **de 50 euros para arriba** from 50 euros up(wards); **de la cintura (para) arriba** from the waist up

▷ *adj*: **de arriba**: **el piso de arriba** the upstairs flat (*Brit*) o apartment; **la parte de arriba** the top o upper part

▷ *prep*: **arriba de** (*Am: por encima de*) above; **arriba de 200 dólares** more than 200 dollars

▷ *excl*: **¡arriba!** up!; **¡manos arriba!** hands up!; **¡arriba España!** long live Spain!

arribar [arri'βar] *vi* to put into port; (*esp Am*: *llegar*) to arrive

arribista [arri'βista] *nm/f* parvenu(e), upstart

arriendo *etc* [a'rrjendo] *vb ver* **arrendar** ▷ *nm* = **arrendamiento**

arriero [a'rrjero] *nm* muleteer

arriesgado, -a [arrjes'ɣaðo, a] *adj* (*peligroso*) risky; (*audaz*) bold, daring

arriesgar [arrjes'ɣar] *vt* to risk; (*poner en peligro*) to endanger; **arriesgarse** *vr* to take a risk

arrimar [arri'mar] *vt* (*acercar*) to bring close; (*poner de lado*) to set aside; **arrimarse** *vr* to come close o closer; **~se a** to lean on; (*fig*) to keep company with; (*buscar ayuda*) to seek the protection of; **arrímate a mí** cuddle up to me

arrinconar [arrinko'nar] *vt* (*colocar*) to put in a corner; (*enemigo*) to corner; (*fig*) to put on one side; (*abandonar*) to push aside

arroba [a'rroβa] *nf* (*peso*) 25 pounds; (*Inform*: *en dirección electrónica*) at sign, @; **tiene talento por ~s** he has loads o bags of talent

arrodillarse [arroði'ʎarse] *vr* to kneel (down)

arrogancia [arro'ɣanθja] *nf* arrogance

arrogante [arro'ɣante] *adj* arrogant

arrojar [arro'xar] *vt* to throw, hurl; (*humo*) to emit, give out; (*Com*) to yield, produce; **arrojarse** *vr* to throw o hurl o.s.

arrojo [a'rroxo] *nm* daring

arrollador, a [arroʎa'ðor, a] *adj* crushing, overwhelming

arrollar [arro'ʎar] *vt* (*enrollar*) to roll up; (*suj*: *inundación*) to wash away; (*Auto*) to run over; (*Deporte*) to crush

arropar [arro'par] *vt* to cover (up), wrap up; **arroparse** *vr* to wrap o.s. up

arrostrar [arros'trar] *vt* to face (up to); **arrostrarse** *vr*: **~se con algn** to face up to sb

arroyo [a'rrojo] *nm* stream; (*de la calle*) gutter; **poner a algn en el ~** to turn sb onto the streets

arroz [a'rroθ] *nm* rice; **~ con leche** rice pudding

arrozal [arro'θal] *nm* paddy field
arruga [a'rruɣa] *nf* fold; (*de cara*) wrinkle; (*de vestido*) crease
arrugar [arru'ɣar] *vt* to fold; to wrinkle; to crease; **arrugarse** *vr* to get wrinkled; to get creased
arruinar [arrwi'nar] *vt* to ruin, wreck; **arruinarse** *vr* to be ruined
arrullar [arru'ʎar] *vi* to coo ▷ *vt* to lull to sleep
arrumaco [arru'mako] *nm* (*caricia*) caress; (*halago*) piece of flattery
arsenal [arse'nal] *nm* naval dockyard; (*Mil*) arsenal
arsénico [ar'seniko] *nm* arsenic
arte ['arte] *nm* (*gen m en sg, f en pl*) art; (*maña*) skill, guile; **por ~ de magia** (as if) by magic; **no tener ~ ni p~ en algo** to have nothing whatsoever to do with sth; **artes** *nfpl* arts; **Bellas A~s** Fine Art *sg*; **~s y oficios** arts and crafts
artefacto [arte'fakto] *nm* appliance; (*Arqueología*) artefact
arteria [ar'terja] *nf* artery
arterial [arte'rjal] *adj* arterial; (*presión*) blood *cpd*
artesanía [artesa'nia] *nf* craftsmanship; (*artículos*) handicrafts *pl*
artesano, -a [arte'sano, a] *nm/f* artisan, craftsman/woman
ártico, -a ['artiko, a] *adj* Arctic ▷ *nm*: **el (océano) Á~** the Arctic (Ocean)
articulación [artikula'θjon] *nf* articulation; (*Med, Tec*) joint
articulado, -a [artiku'laðo, a] *adj* articulated; jointed
articular [artiku'lar] *vt* to articulate; to join together
artículo [ar'tikulo] *nm* article; (*cosa*) thing, article; (*TV*) feature, report; **~ de fondo** leader, editorial; **artículos** *nmpl* goods; **~s de marca** (*Com*) proprietary goods; **~s de escritorio** stationery
artífice [ar'tifiθe] *nm/f* artist, craftsman; (*fig*) architect
artificial [artifi'θjal] *adj* artificial
artificio [arti'fiθjo] *nm* art, skill; (*artesanía*) craftsmanship; (*astucia*) cunning
artillería [artiʎe'ria] *nf* artillery
artillero [arti'ʎero] *nm* artilleryman, gunner
artilugio [arti'luxjo] *nm* gadget
artimaña [arti'maɲa] *nf* trap, snare; (*astucia*) cunning
artista [ar'tista] *nm/f* (*pintor*) artist, painter; (*Teat*) artist, artiste; **~ de cine** film actor/actress
artístico, -a [ar'tistiko, a] *adj* artistic
artritis [ar'tritis] *nf* arthritis
arveja [ar'βexa] *nf* (*Am*) pea
arzobispo [arθo'βispo] *nm* archbishop
as [as] *nm* ace; **as del fútbol** star player
asa ['asa] *nf* handle; (*fig*) lever

asado [a'saðo] *nm* roast (meat); (*Am: barbacoa*) barbecue

● **ASADO**
●
● Traditional Latin American barbecues,
● especially in the River Plate area, are
● celebrated in the open air around a large
● grill which is used to grill mainly beef
● and various kinds of spicy pork sausage.
● They are usually very common during
● the summer and can go on for several days.

asador [asa'ðor] *nm* (*varilla*) spit; (*aparato*) spit roaster
asadura, asaduras [asa'ðura(s)] *nf(pl)* entrails *pl*, offal *sg*; (*Culin*) chitterlings *pl*
asalariado, -a [asala'rjaðo, a] *adj* paid, wage-earning, salaried ▷ *nm/f* wage earner
asaltador, a [asalta'ðor, a], **asaltante** [asal'tante] *nm/f* assailant
asaltar [asal'tar] *vt* to attack, assault; (*fig*) to assail
asalto [a'salto] *nm* attack, assault; (*Deporte*) round
asamblea [asam'blea] *nf* assembly; (*reunión*) meeting
asar [a'sar] *vt* to roast; **~ al horno/a la parrilla** to bake/grill; **asarse** *vr* (*fig*): **me aso de calor** I'm roasting; **aquí se asa uno vivo** it's boiling hot here
asbesto [as'βesto] *nm* asbestos
ascendencia [asθen'denθja] *nf* ancestry; (*Am: influencia*) ascendancy; **de ~ francesa** of French origin
ascender [asθen'der] *vi* (*subir*) to ascend, rise; (*ser promovido*) to gain promotion ▷ *vt* to promote; **~ a** to amount to
ascendiente [asθen'djente] *nm* influence ▷ *nm/f* ancestor
ascensión [asθen'sjon] *nf* ascent; **la A~** the Ascension
ascenso [as'θenso] *nm* ascent; (*promoción*) promotion
ascensor [asθen'sor] *nm* lift (*Brit*), elevator (*US*)
ascético, -a [as'θetiko, a] *adj* ascetic
asco ['asko] *nm*: **el ajo me da ~** I hate o loathe garlic; **hacer ~s de algo** to turn up one's nose at sth; **estar hecho un ~** to be filthy; **poner a algn de ~** to call sb all sorts of names o every name under the sun; **¡qué ~!** how revolting o disgusting!
ascua ['askwa] *nf* ember; **arrimar el ~ a su sardina** to look after number one; **estar en ~s** to be on tenterhooks
aseado, -a [ase'aðo, a] *adj* clean; (*arreglado*) tidy; (*pulcro*) smart
asear [ase'ar] *vt* (*lavar*) to wash; (*ordenar*) to tidy (up)
asediar [ase'ðjar] *vt* (*Mil*) to besiege, lay siege to; (*fig*) to chase, pester
asedio [a'seðjo] *nm* siege; (*Com*) run

asegurado, a [aseɣu'raðo, a] *adj* insured

asegurador, -a [aseɣura'ðor, a] *nm/f* insurer

asegurar [aseɣu'rar] *vt* (*consolidar*) to secure, fasten; (*dar garantía de*) to guarantee; (*preservar*) to safeguard; (*afirmar: dar por cierto*) to assure, affirm; (*tranquilizar*) to reassure; (*hacer un seguro*) to insure; **asegurarse** *vr* to assure o.s., make sure

asemejarse [aseme'xarse] *vr* to be alike; **~ a** to be like, resemble

asentado, -a [asen'taðo, a] *adj* established, settled

asentar [asen'tar] *vt* (*sentar*) to seat, sit down; (*poner*) to place, establish; (*alisar*) to level, smooth down *o* out; (*anotar*) to note down ▷ *vi* to be suitable, suit

asentir [asen'tir] *vi* to assent, agree; **~ con la cabeza** to nod (one's head)

aseo [a'seo] *nm* cleanliness; **aseos** *nmpl* toilet *sg* (*Brit*), cloakroom *sg* (*Brit*), restroom *sg* (*US*)

aséptico, -a [a'septiko, a] *adj* germ-free, free from infection

asequible [ase'kiβle] *adj* (*precio*) reasonable; (*meta*) attainable; (*persona*) approachable

aserradero [aserra'ðero] *nm* sawmill

aserrar [ase'rrar] *vt* to saw

asesinar [asesi'nar] *vt* to murder; (*Pol*) to assassinate

asesinato [asesi'nato] *nm* murder; assassination

asesino, -a [ase'sino, a] *nm/f* murderer, killer; (*Pol*) assassin

asesor, a [ase'sor, a] *nm/f* adviser, consultant; (*Com*) assessor, consultant; **~ administrativo** management consultant

asesorar [aseso'rar] *vt* (*Jur*) to advise, give legal advice to; (*Com*) to act as consultant to; **asesorarse** *vr*: **~se con** *o* **de** to take advice from, consult

asesoría [aseso'ria] *nf* (*cargo*) consultancy; (*oficina*) consultant's office

asestar [ases'tar] *vt* (*golpe*) to deal; (*arma*) to aim; (*tiro*) to fire

asfalto [as'falto] *nm* asphalt

asfixia [as'fiksja] *nf* asphyxia, suffocation

asfixiar [asfik'sjar] *vt* to asphyxiate, suffocate; **asfixiarse** *vr* to be asphyxiated, suffocate

así [a'si] *adv* (*de esta manera*) in this way, like this, thus; (*aunque*) although; (*tan pronto como*) as soon as; **~ que** so; **~ como** as well as; **~ y todo** even so; **¿no es ~?** isn't it?, didn't you? *etc*; **~ de grande** this big; **¡~ sea!** so be it!; **~ es la vida** such is life, that's life

Asia ['asja] *nf* Asia

asiático, -a [a'sjatiko, a] *adj, nm/f* Asian, Asiatic

asidero [asi'ðero] *nm* handle

asiduidad [asiðwi'ðað] *nf* assiduousness

asiduo, -a [a'siðwo, a] *adj* assiduous; (*frecuente*) frequent ▷ *nm/f* regular (customer)

asiento [a'sjento] *vb ver* **asentar**, **asentir**

▷ *nm* (*mueble*) seat, chair; (*de coche, en tribunal etc*) seat; (*localidad*) seat, place; (*fundamento*) site; **~ delantero/trasero** front/back seat

asignación [asiɣna'θjon] *nf* (*atribución*) assignment; (*reparto*) allocation; (*sueldo*) salary; (*Com*) allowance; **~ (semanal)** (weekly) pocket money; **~ de presupuesto** budget appropriation

asignar [asiɣ'nar] *vt* to assign, allocate

asignatura [asiɣna'tura] *nf* subject; (*curso*) course; **~ pendiente** (*fig*) matter pending

asilado, -a [asi'laðo, a] *nm/f* refugee

asilo [a'silo] *nm* (*refugio*) asylum, refuge; (*establecimiento*) home, institution; **~ político** political asylum

asimilación [asimila'θjon] *nf* assimilation

asimilar [asimi'lar] *vt* to assimilate

asimismo [asi'mismo] *adv* in the same way, likewise

asir [a'sir] *vt* to seize, grasp; **asirse** *vr* to take hold; **~se a** *o* **de** to seize

asistencia [asis'tenθja] *nf* presence; (*Teat*) audience; (*Med*) attendance; (*ayuda*) assistance; **~ social** social *o* welfare work; **~ en carretera** roadside assistance

asistente, -a [asis'tente, a] *nm/f* assistant ▷ *nm* (*Mil*) orderly ▷ *nf* daily help; **los ~s** those present; **~ social** social worker

asistido, -a [asis'tiðo, a] *adj* (*Auto: dirección*) power-assisted; **~ por ordenador** computer-assisted

asistir [asis'tir] *vt* to assist, help ▷ *vi*: **~ a** to attend, be present at

asma ['asma] *nf* asthma

asno ['asno] *nm* donkey; (*fig*) ass

asociación [asoθja'θjon] *nf* association; (*Com*) partnership

asociado, -a [aso'θjaðo, a] *adj* associate ▷ *nm/f* associate; (*Com*) partner

asociar [aso'θjar] *vt* to associate; **asociarse** *vr* to become partners

asolar [aso'lar] *vt* to destroy

asomar [aso'mar] *vt* to show, stick out ▷ *vi* to appear; **asomarse** *vr* to appear, show up; **~ la cabeza por la ventana** to put one's head out of the window

asombrar [asom'brar] *vt* to amaze, astonish; **asombrarse** *vr*: **~se (de)** (*sorprenderse*) to be amazed (at); (*asustarse*) to be frightened (at)

asombro [a'sombro] *nm* amazement, astonishment; (*susto*) fright

asombroso, -a [asom'broso, a] *adj* amazing, astonishing

asomo [a'somo] *nm* hint, sign; **ni por ~** by no means

aspa ['aspa] *nf* (*cruz*) cross; (*de molino*) sail; **en ~** X-shaped

aspaviento [aspa'βjento] *nm* exaggerated display of feeling; (*fam*) fuss

aspecto [as'pekto] *nm* (*apariencia*) look, appearance; (*fig*) aspect; **bajo ese ~** from that point of view

aspereza [aspe'reθa] nf roughness; (de fruta) sharpness; (de carácter) surliness

áspero, -a ['aspero, a] adj (al tacto) rough; (al gusto) sharp, sour; (voz) harsh

aspersión [asper'sjon] nf sprinkling; (Agr) spraying

aspersor [asper'sor] nm sprinkler

aspiración [aspira'θjon] nf breath, inhalation; (Mus) short pause; **aspiraciones** nfpl (ambiciones) aspirations

aspirador [aspira'ðor] nm = **aspiradora**

aspiradora [aspira'ðora] nf vacuum cleaner, Hoover®

aspirante [aspi'rante] nm/f (candidato) candidate; (Deporte) contender

aspirar [aspi'rar] vt to breathe in ▷ vi: ~ **a** to aspire to

aspirina [aspi'rina] nf aspirin

asquear [aske'ar] vt to sicken ▷ vi to be sickening; **asquearse** vr to feel disgusted

asqueroso, -a [aske'roso, a] adj disgusting, sickening

asta ['asta] nf lance; (arpón) spear; (mango) shaft, handle; (Zool) horn; **a media ~** at half mast

asterisco [aste'risko] nm asterisk

asteroide [aste'roiðe] nm asteroid

astigmatismo [astiɣma'tismo] nm astigmatism

astilla [as'tiʎa] nf splinter; (pedacito) chip; **astillas** nfpl (leña) firewood sg

astillero [asti'ʎero] nm shipyard

astringente [astrin'xente] adj, nm astringent

astro ['astro] nm star

astrología [astrolo'xia] nf astrology

astrólogo, -a [as'troloɣo, a] nm/f astrologer

astronauta [astro'nauta] nm/f astronaut

astronave [astro'naβe] nm spaceship

astronomía [astrono'mia] nf astronomy

astronómico, -a [astro'nomiko, a] adj (tb fig) astronomical

astrónomo, -a [as'tronomo, a] nm/f astronomer

astucia [as'tuθja] nf astuteness; (destreza) clever trick

asturiano, -a [astu'rjano, a] adj, nm/f Asturian

astuto, -a [as'tuto, a] adj astute; (taimado) cunning

asueto [a'sweto] nm holiday; (tiempo libre) time off; **día de ~** day off; **tarde de ~** (trabajo) afternoon off; (Escol) half-holiday

asumir [asu'mir] vt to assume

asunción [asun'θjon] nf assumption; (Rel): **A~** Assumption

asunto [a'sunto] nm (tema) matter, subject; (negocio) business; **¡eso es ~ mío!** that's my business!; **~s exteriores** foreign affairs; **~s a tratar** agenda sg

asustar [asus'tar] vt to frighten; **asustarse** vr to be/become frightened

atacar [ata'kar] vt to attack

atadura [ata'ðura] nf bond, tie

atajar [ata'xar] vt (enfermedad, mal) to stop; (ruta de fuga) to cut off; (discurso) to interrupt ▷ vi (persona) to take a short cut

atajo [a'taxo] nm short cut; (Deporte) tackle

atañer [ata'ɲer] vi: ~ **a** to concern; **en lo que atañe a eso** with regard to that

ataque etc [a'take] vb ver **atacar** ▷ nm attack; **~ cardíaco** heart attack

atar [a'tar] vt to tie, tie up; **~ la lengua a algn** (fig) to silence sb

atarantado, -a [ataran'taðo, a] adj (Am: aturdido) dazed

atardecer [atarðe'θer] vi to get dark ▷ nm evening; (crepúsculo) dusk

atareado, -a [atare'aðo, a] adj busy

atascar [atas'kar] vt to clog up; (obstruir) to jam; (fig) to hinder; **atascarse** vr to stall; (cañería) to get blocked up; (fig) to get bogged down; (en discurso) to dry up

atasco [a'tasko] nm obstruction; (Auto) traffic jam

ataúd [ata'uð] nm coffin

ataviar [ata'βjar] vt to deck, array; **ataviarse** vr to dress up

atavío [ata'βio] nm attire, dress; **atavíos** nmpl finery sg

atemorizar [atemori'θar] vt to frighten, scare; **atemorizarse** vr to get frightened o scared

Atenas [a'tenas] nf Athens

atención [aten'θjon] nf attention; (bondad) kindness ▷ excl (be) careful!, look out!; **en ~ a esto** in view of this

atender [aten'der] vt to attend to, look after; (Tec) to service; (enfermo) to care for; (ruego) to comply with; (Tel) to answer ▷ vi to pay attention; **~ a** to attend to; (detalles) to take care of

atenerse [ate'nerse] vr: ~ **a** to abide by, adhere to

atentado [aten'taðo] nm crime, illegal act; (asalto) assault; (tb: **~ terrorista**) terrorist attack; **~ contra la vida de algn** attempt on sb's life; **~ golpista** attempted coup; **~ suicida** suicide bombing, suicide attack

atentamente [atenta'mente] adv: **Le saluda ~** Yours faithfully

atentar [aten'tar] vi: ~ **a** o **contra** to commit an outrage against

atento, -a [a'tento, a] adj attentive, observant; (cortés) polite, thoughtful; **estar ~ a** (explicación) to pay attention to; **su atenta (carta)** (Com) your letter

atenuante [ate'nwante] adj: **circunstancias ~s** extenuating o mitigating circumstances ▷ nfpl: **~s** extenuating o mitigating circumstances

atenuar [ate'nwar] vt to attenuate; (disminuir) to lessen, minimize

ateo, -a [a'teo, a] adj atheistic ▷ nm/f atheist

aterciopelado, -a [aterθjope'laðo, a] *adj* velvety

aterido, -a [ate'riðo, a] *adj*: **~ de frío** frozen stiff

aterrador, a [aterra'ðor, a] *adj* frightening

aterrar [ate'rrar] *vt* to frighten; (*aterrorizar*) to terrify; **aterrarse** *vr* to be frightened; to be terrified

aterrizaje [aterri'θaxe] *nm* landing; **~ forzoso** emergency o forced landing

aterrizar [aterri'θar] *vi* to land

aterrorizar [aterrori'θar] *vt* to terrify

atesorar [ateso'rar] *vt* to hoard, store up

atestado, -a [ates'taðo, a] *adj* packed ▷ *nm* (*Jur*) affidavit

atestar [ates'tar] *vt* to pack, stuff; (*Jur*) to attest, testify to

atestiguar [atesti'ɣwar] *vt* to testify to, bear witness to

atiborrar [atiβo'rrar] *vt* to fill, stuff; **atiborrarse** *vr* to stuff o.s.

ático ['atiko] *nm* (*desván*) attic; **~ de lujo** penthouse flat

atildar [atil'dar] *vt* to criticize; (*Tip*) to put a tilde over; **atildarse** *vr* to spruce o.s. up

atinado, -a [ati'naðo, a] *adj* correct; (*sensato*) wise, sensible

atinar [ati'nar] *vi* (*acertar*) to be right; **~ con** o **en** (*solución*) to hit upon; **~ al blanco** to hit the target; (*fig*) to be right; **~ a hacer** to manage to do

atípico, -a [a'tipiko, a] *adj* atypical

atisbar [atis'βar] *vt* to spy on; (*echar ojeada*) to peep at

atizar [ati'θar] *vt* to poke; (*horno etc*) to stoke; (*fig*) to stir up, rouse

atlántico, -a [at'lantiko, a] *adj* Atlantic ▷ *nm*: **el (océano) A~** the Atlantic (Ocean)

atlas ['atlas] *nm inv* atlas

atleta [at'leta] *nm/f* athlete

atlético, -a [at'letiko, a] *adj* athletic

atletismo [atle'tismo] *nm* athletics *sg*

atmósfera [at'mosfera] *nf* atmosphere

atmosférico, -a [atmos'feriko, a] *adj* atmospheric

atolladero [atoʎa'ðero] *nm*: **estar en un ~** to be in a jam

atollarse [ato'ʎarse] *vr* to get stuck; (*fig*) to get into a jam

atolondrado, -a [atolon'draðo, a] *adj* scatterbrained

atolondramiento [atolondra'mjento] *nm* bewilderment; (*insensatez*) silliness

atómico, -a [a'tomiko, a] *adj* atomic

atomizador [atomiθa'ðor] *nm* atomizer

átomo ['atomo] *nm* atom

atónito, -a [a'tonito, a] *adj* astonished, amazed

atontado, -a [aton'taðo, a] *adj* stunned; (*bobo*) silly, daft

atontar [aton'tar] *vt* to stun; **atontarse** *vr* to become confused

atormentar [atormen'tar] *vt* to torture; (*molestar*) to torment; (*acosar*) to plague, harass

atornillar [atorni'ʎar] *vt* to screw on o down

atosigar [atosi'ɣar] *vt* to harass, pester

atracador, a [atraka'ðor, a] *nm/f* robber

atracar [atra'kar] *vt* (*Naut*) to moor; (*robar*) to hold up, rob ▷ *vi* to moor; **atracarse** *vr*: **~se (de)** to stuff o.s. (with)

atracción [atrak'θjon] *nf* attraction

atraco [a'trako] *nm* holdup, robbery

atracón [atra'kon] *nm*: **darse** o **pegarse un ~ (de)** (*fam*) to stuff o.s. (with)

atractivo, -a [atrak'tiβo, a] *adj* attractive ▷ *nm* appeal; (*belleza*) attractiveness

atraer [atra'er] *vt* to attract; **dejarse ~ por** to be tempted by

atragantarse [atraɣan'tarse] *vr*: **~ (con algo)** to choke (on sth); **se me ha atragantado el chico ese/el inglés** I can't stand that boy/English

atrancar [atran'kar] *vt* (*con tranca, barra*) to bar, bolt

atrapar [atra'par] *vt* to trap; (*resfriado etc*) to catch

atrás [a'tras] *adv* (*movimiento*) back(wards); (*lugar*) behind; (*tiempo*) previously; **ir hacia ~** to go back(wards); to go to the rear; **estar ~** to be behind o at the back

atrasado, -a [atra'saðo, a] *adj* slow; (*pago*) overdue, late; (*país*) backward

atrasar [atra'sar] *vi* to be slow; **atrasarse** *vr* to stay behind; (*tren*) to be o run late; (*llegar tarde*) to be late

atraso [a'traso] *nm* slowness; lateness, delay; (*de país*) backwardness; **atrasos** *nmpl* (*Com*) arrears

atravesado, -a [atraβe'saðo, a] *adj*: **un tronco ~ en la carretera** a tree trunk lying across the road

atravesar [atraβe'sar] *vt* (*cruzar*) to cross (over); (*traspasar*) to pierce; (*período*) to go through; (*poner al través*) to lay o put across; **atravesarse** *vr* to come in between; (*intervenir*) to interfere

atraviese *etc* [atra'βjese] *vb ver* **atravesar**

atrayente [atra'jente] *adj* attractive

atreverse [atre'βerse] *vr* to dare; (*insolentarse*) to be insolent

atrevido, -a [atre'βiðo, a] *adj* daring; insolent

atrevimiento [atreβi'mjento] *nm* daring; insolence

atribución [atriβu'θjon] *nf* (*Lit*) attribution; **atribuciones** *nfpl* (*Pol*) powers, functions; (*Admin*) responsibilities

atribuir [atriβu'ir] *vt* to attribute; (*funciones*) to confer

atributo [atri'βuto] *nm* attribute

atril [a'tril] *nm* (*para libro*) lectern; (*Mus*) music stand

atrincherarse [atrintʃe'rarse] *vr* (*Mil*) to dig (o.s.) in; **~ en** (*fig*) to hide behind

atrocidad [atroθi'ðað] *nf* atrocity, outrage

atrofiarse [atro'fjarse] *vr* (*tb fig*) to atrophy

atropellar [atrope'ʎar] *vt* (*derribar*) to knock over *o* down; (*empujar*) to push (aside); (*Auto*) to run over *o* down; (*agraviar*) to insult; **atropellarse** *vr* to act hastily

atropello [atro'peʎo] *nm* (*Auto*) accident; (*empujón*) push; (*agravio*) wrong; (*atrocidad*) outrage

atroz [a'troθ] *adj* atrocious, awful

A.T.S. *nm/f abr* (= *Ayudante Técnico Sanitario*) nurse

atuendo [a'twendo] *nm* attire

atún [a'tun] *nm* tuna, tunny

aturdir [atur'ðir] *vt* to stun; (*suj: ruido*) to deafen; (*fig*) to dumbfound, bewilder

atusar [atu'sar] *vt* (*cortar*) to trim; (*alisar*) to smooth (down)

audacia [au'ðaθja] *nf* boldness, audacity

audaz [au'ðaθ] *adj* bold, audacious

audible [au'ðiβle] *adj* audible

audición [auði'θjon] *nf* hearing; (*Teat*) audition; ~ **radiofónica** radio concert

audiencia [au'ðjenθja] *nf* audience; (*Jur*) high court; (*Pol*): ~ **pública** public inquiry

audífono [au'ðifono] *nm* (*para sordos*) hearing aid

audiovisual [auðjoβi'swal] *adj* audio-visual

auditivo, -a [auði'tiβo, a] *adj* hearing *cpd*; (*conducto, nervio*) auditory

auditor [auði'tor] *nm* (*Jur*) judge advocate; (*Com*) auditor

auditoría [auðito'ria] *nf* audit; (*profesión*) auditing

auditorio [auði'torjo] *nm* audience; (*sala*) auditorium

auge ['auxe] *nm* boom; (*clímax*) climax; (*Econ*) expansion; **estar en** ~ to thrive

augurar [auɣu'rar] *vt* to predict; (*presagiar*) to portend

augurio [au'ɣurjo] *nm* omen

aula ['aula] *nf* classroom; (*en universidad etc*) lecture room

aullar [au'ʎar] *vi* to howl, yell

aullido [au'ʎiðo] *nm* howl, yell

aumentar [aumen'tar] *vt* to increase; (*precios*) to put up; (*producción*) to step up; (*con microscopio, anteojos*) to magnify ▷ *vi*, **aumentarse** to increase, be on the increase ▷ *vr* to increase, be on the increase

aumento [au'mento] *nm* increase; rise

aún [a'un] *adv* still, yet; ~ **está aquí** he's still here; ~ **no lo sabemos** we don't know yet; *¿no ha venido ~?* hasn't she come yet?

aun [a'un] *adv* even; ~ **así** even so; ~ **más** even *o* yet more

aunque [a'unke] *conj* though, although, even though

aúpa [a'upa] *excl* up!, come on!; (*fam*): **una función de** ~ a slap-up do; **una paliza de** ~ a good hiding

aureola [aure'ola] *nf* halo

auricular [auriku'lar] *nm* (*Tel*) earpiece, receiver; **auriculares** *nmpl* (*cascos*) headphones

aurora [au'rora] *nf* dawn; ~ **boreal(is)** northern lights *pl*

auscultar [auskul'tar] *vt* (*Med: pecho*) to listen to, sound

ausencia [au'senθja] *nf* absence

ausentarse [ausen'tarse] *vr* to go away; (*por poco tiempo*) to go out

ausente [au'sente] *adj* absent ▷ *nm/f* (*Escol*) absentee; (*Jur*) missing person

auspicios [aus'piθjos] *nmpl* auspices; (*protección*) protection *sg*

austeridad [austeri'ðað] *nf* austerity

austero, -a [aus'tero, a] *adj* austere

austral [aus'tral] *adj* southern ▷ *nm* monetary unit of Argentina (1985-1991)

Australia [aus'tralja] *nf* Australia

australiano, -a [austra'ljano, a] *adj, nm/f* Australian

Austria ['austrja] *nf* Austria

austriaco, -a [aus'trjako, a], **austríaco, -a** [aus'triako, a] *adj* Austrian ▷ *nm/f* Austrian

auténtico, -a [au'tentiko, a] *adj* authentic

autentificar [autentifi'kar] *vt* to authenticate

auto ['auto] *nm* (*coche*) car; (*Jur*) edict, decree; (*: orden*) writ; **autos** *nmpl* (*Jur*) proceedings; (*: acta*) court record *sg*; ~ **de comparecencia** summons, subpoena; ~ **de ejecución** writ of execution

autoadhesivo, -a [autoaðe'siβo, a] *adj* self-adhesive; (*sobre*) self-sealing

autobiografía [autoβjoɣra'fia] *nf* autobiography

autobomba [auto'bomba] *nm* (*RPl*) fire engine

autobronceador, a [autoβronθea'ðor, a] *adj* (self-)tanning

autobús [auto'βus] *nm* bus; ~ **de línea** long-distance coach

autocar [auto'kar] *nm* coach (*Brit*), (passenger) bus (*US*); ~ **de línea** intercity coach *or* bus

autóctono, -a [au'toktono, a] *adj* native, indigenous

autodefensa [autoðe'fensa] *nf* self-defence

autodeterminación [autoðetermina'θjon] *nf* self-determination

autodidacta [autoði'ðakta] *adj* self-taught ▷ *nm/f*: **ser un(a)** ~ to be self-taught

autoescuela [autoes'kwela] *nf* (*Esp*) driving school

autogestión [autoxes'tjon] *nf* self-management

autógrafo [au'toɣrafo] *nm* autograph

autómata [au'tomata] *nm* automaton

automáticamente [auto'matikamente] *adv* automatically

automático, -a [auto'matiko, a] *adj* automatic ▷ *nm* press stud

automatización [automatiθa'θjon] *nf*: **~ de fábricas** factory automation; **~ de oficinas** office automation

automotor, -triz [automo'tor, 'triz] *adj* self-propelled ▷ *nm* diesel train

automóvil [auto'moβil] *nm* (motor) car (Brit), automobile (US)

automovilismo [automoβi'lismo] *nm* (*actividad*) motoring; (*Deporte*) motor racing

automovilista [automoβi'lista] *nm/f* motorist, driver

automovilístico, -a [automoβi'listiko, a] *adj* (*industria*) car *cpd*

autonomía [autono'mia] *nf* autonomy; (*Esp Pol*) autonomy, self-government; (: *comunidad*) autonomous region

autonómico, -a [auto'nomiko, a] *adj* (*Esp Pol*) relating to autonomy, autonomous; **gobierno ~** autonomous government

autónomo, -a [au'tonomo, a], (*Esp*) **autonómico** *adj* autonomous; (*Inform*) stand-alone, offline

autopista [auto'pista] *nf* motorway (Brit), freeway (US); **~ de cuota** (*Am*) o **peaje** (*Esp*) toll (Brit) o turnpike (US) road

autopsia [au'topsja] *nf* post-mortem, autopsy

autor, a [au'tor, a] *nm/f* author; **los ~es del atentado** those responsible for the attack

autoridad [autori'ðað] *nf* authority; **~ local** local authority

autoritario, -a [autori'tarjo, a] *adj* authoritarian

autorización [autoriθa'θjon] *nf* authorization

autorizado, -a [autori'θaðo, a] *adj* authorized; (*aprobado*) approved

autorizar [autori'θar] *vt* to authorize; to approve

autorretrato [autorre'trato] *nm* self-portrait

autoservicio [autoser'βjeθjo] *nm* (*tienda*) self-service shop o store; (*restaurante*) self-service restaurant

autostop [auto'stop] *nm* hitch-hiking; **hacer ~** to hitch-hike

autostopista [autosto'pista] *nm/f* hitch-hiker

autosuficiencia [autosufi'θjenθja] *nf* self-sufficiency

autosuficiente [autosufi'θjente] *adj* self-sufficient; (*pey*) smug

autosugestión [autosuxes'tjon] *nf* autosuggestion

autovía [auto'βia] *nf* ≈ dual carriageway (Brit), ≈ divided highway (US)

auxiliar [auksi'ljar] *vt* to help ▷ *nm/f* assistant

auxilio [auk'siljo] *nm* assistance, help; **primeros ~s** first aid *sg*

Av *abr* (= Avenida) Av(e)

aval [a'βal] *nm* guarantee; (*persona*) guarantor

avalancha [aβa'lantʃa] *nf* avalanche > afe

avalar [aβa'lar] *vt* (*Com etc*) to underwrite; (*fig*) to endorse

avance [a'βanθe] *vb ver* **avanzar** ▷ *nm* advance; (*pago*) advance payment; (*Cine*) trailer

avanzado, -a [aβan'θaðo, a] *adj* advanced; **de edad avanzada**, **~ de edad** elderly

avanzar [aβan'θar] *vt, vi* to advance

avaricia [aβa'riθja] *nf* avarice, greed

avaricioso, -a [aβari'θjoso, a] *adj* avaricious, greedy

avaro, -a [a'βaro, a] *adj* miserly, mean ▷ *nm/f* miser

avasallar [aβasa'ʎar] *vt* to subdue, subjugate

Avda *abr* (= Avenida) Av(e)

AVE ['aβe] *nm abr* (= Alta Velocidad Española) ≈ bullet train

ave ['aβe] *nf* bird; **~ de rapiña** bird of prey

avecinarse [aβeθi'narse] *vr* (*tormenta, fig*) to approach, be on the way

avellana [aβe'ʎana] *nf* hazelnut

avellano [aβe'ʎano] *nm* hazel tree

avemaría [aβema'ria] *nm* Hail Mary, Ave Maria

avena [a'βena] *nf* oats *pl*

avenida [aβe'niða] *nf* (*calle*) avenue

avenir [aβe'nir] *vt* to reconcile; **avenirse** *vr* to come to an agreement, reach a compromise

aventajado, -a [aβenta'xaðo, a] *adj* outstanding

aventajar [aβenta'xar] *vt* (*sobrepasar*) to surpass, outstrip

aventón [aβen'ton] *nm* (*Am*) push; **pedir ~** to hitch a lift, hitch a ride (US)

aventura [aβen'tura] *nf* adventure; **~ sentimental** love affair

aventurado, -a [aβentu'raðo, a] *adj* risky

aventurero, -a [aβentu'rero, a] *adj* adventurous

avergonzar [aβerɣon'θar] *vt* to shame; (*desconcertar*) to embarrass; **avergonzarse** *vr* to be ashamed; to be embarrassed

avería [aβe'ria] *nf* (*Tec*) breakdown, fault

averiado, -a [aβe'rjaðo, a] *adj* broken-down; **"~"** "out of order"

averlar [aβe'rjar] *vt* to break; **averiarse** *vr* to break down

averiguación [aβeriɣwa'θjon] *nf* investigation

averiguar [aβeri'ɣwar] *vt* to investigate; (*descubrir*) to find out, ascertain

aversión [aβer'sjon] *nf* aversion, dislike; **cobrar ~ a** to take a strong dislike to

avestruz [aβes'truθ] *nm* ostrich

aviación [aβja'θjon] *nf* aviation; (*fuerzas aéreas*) air force

aviador, a [aβja'ðor, a] *nm/f* aviator, airman/woman

aviar [a'βjar] *vt* to prepare, get ready

avícola [a'βikola] *adj* poultry *cpd*

avicultura [aβikul'tura] nf poultry farming

avidez [aβi'ðeθ] nf avidity, eagerness

ávido, -a ['aβiðo, a] adj avid, eager

avinagrado, -a [aβina'ɣraðo, a] adj sour, acid

avinagrarse [aβina'ɣrarse] vr to go o turn sour

avío [a'βio] nm preparation; **avíos** nmpl gear sg, kit sg

avión [a'βjon] nm aeroplane; (ave) martin; **~ de reacción** jet (plane); **por ~** (Correos) by air mail

avioneta [aβjo'neta] nf light aircraft

avisar [aβi'sar] vt (advertir) to warn, notify; (informar) to tell; (aconsejar) to advise, counsel

aviso [a'βiso] nm warning; (noticia) notice; (Com) demand note; (Inform) prompt; **~ escrito** notice in writing; **sin previo ~** without warning; **estar sobre ~** to be on the look-out

avispa [a'βispa] nf wasp

avispado, -a [aβis'paðo, a] adj sharp, clever

avispero [aβis'pero] nm wasp's nest

avispón [aβis'pon] nm hornet

avistar [aβis'tar] vt to sight, spot

avituallar [aβitwa'ʎar] vt to supply with food

avivar [aβi'βar] vt to strengthen, intensify; **avivarse** vr to revive, acquire new life

axila [ak'sila] nf armpit

axioma [ak'sjoma] nm axiom

ay [ai] excl (dolor) ow!, ouch!; (aflicción) oh!, oh dear!; **¡ay de mí!** poor me!

aya ['aja] nf governess; (niñera) nanny

ayer [a'jer] adv, nm yesterday; **antes de ~** the day before yesterday; **~ por la tarde** yesterday afternoon/evening; **~ mismo** only yesterday

ayo ['ajo] nm tutor

ayote [a'jote] nm (Am) pumpkin

ayuda [a'juða] nf help, assistance; (Med) enema ▷ nm page; **~ humanitaria** humanitarian aid

ayudante, -a [aju'ðante, a] nm/f assistant, helper; (Escol) assistant; (Mil) adjutant

ayudar [aju'ðar] vt to help, assist

ayunar [aju'nar] vi to fast

ayunas [a'junas] nfpl: **estar en ~** (no haber comido) to be fasting; (ignorar) to be in the dark

ayuno [a'juno] nm fast; fasting

ayuntamiento [ajunta'mjento] nm (consejo) town/city council; (edificio) town/city hall; (cópula) sexual intercourse

azabache [aθa'βatʃe] nm jet

azada [a'θaða] nf hoe

azafata [aθa'fata] nf air hostess (Brit) o stewardess

azafrán [aθa'fran] nm saffron

azahar [aθa'ar] nm orange/lemon blossom

azalea [aθa'lea] nf azalea

azar [a'θar] nm (casualidad) chance, fate; (desgracia) misfortune, accident; **por ~** by chance; **al ~** at random

azogue [a'θoɣe] nm mercury

azoramiento [aθora'mjento] nm alarm; (confusión) confusion

azorar [aθo'rar] vt to alarm; **azorarse** vr to get alarmed

Azores [a'θores] nfpl: **las (Islas) ~** the Azores

azotar [aθo'tar] vt to whip, beat; (pegar) to spank

azote [a'θote] nm (látigo) whip; (latigazo) lash, stroke; (en las nalgas) spank; (calamidad) calamity

azotea [aθo'tea] nf (flat) roof

azteca [aθ'teka] adj, nm/f Aztec

azúcar [a'θukar] nm sugar

azucarado, -a [aθuka'raðo, a] adj sugary, sweet

azucarero, -a [aθuka'rero, a] adj sugar cpd ▷ nm sugar bowl

azucena [aθu'θena] nf white lily

azufre [a'θufre] nm sulphur

azul [a'θul] adj, nm blue; **~ celeste/marino** sky/navy blue

azulejo [aθu'lexo] nm tile

azuzar [aθu'θar] vt to incite, egg on

B.A. *abr* (= *Buenos Aires*) B.A.

baba ['baβa] *nf* spittle, saliva; **se le caía la ~** (*fig*) he was thrilled to bits

babear [baβe'ar] *vi* (*echar saliva*) to slobber; (*niño*) to dribble; (*fig*) to drool, slaver

babel [ba'βel] *nm o f* bedlam

babero [ba'βero] *nm* bib

babor [ba'βor] *nm* port (side); **a ~** to port

babosada [baβo'saða] *nf*: **decir ~s** (*Am: fam*) to talk rubbish

baboso, -a [ba'βoso, a] *adj* slobbering; (*Zool*) slimy; (*Am*) silly ▷ *nm/f* (*Am*) fool

babucha [ba'βutʃa] *nf* slipper

baca ['baka] *nf* (*Auto*) luggage o roof rack

bacalao [baka'lao] *nm* cod(fish)

bache ['batʃe] *nm* pothole, rut; (*fig*) bad patch

bachillerato [batʃiʎe'rato] *nm* two-year *advanced secondary school course; ver tb* **sistema educativo**

bacinica [baθi'nika], **bacinilla** [baθi'niʎa] *nf* potty

bacteria [bak'terja] *nf* bacterium, germ

bacteriológico, -a [bakterjo'loxiko, a] *adj* bacteriological; **guerra bacteriológica** germ warfare

báculo ['bakulo] *nm* stick, staff; (*fig*) support

bádminton ['baðminton] *nm* badminton

bafle ['bafle], **baffle** ['bafle] *nm* (*Elec*) speaker

bagaje [ba'ɣaxe] *nm* baggage; (*fig*) background

bagatela [baɣa'tela] *nf* trinket, trifle

Bahama [ba'ama]: **las (Islas) ~**, **las ~s** *nfpl* the Bahamas

bahía [ba'ia] *nf* bay

bailar [bai'lar] *vt, vi* to dance

bailarín, -ina [baila'rin, ina] *nm/f* dancer; (*de ballet*) ballet dancer

baile ['baile] *nm* dance; (*formal*) ball

baja ['baxa] *nf* drop, fall; (*Econ*) slump; (*Mil*) casualty; (*paro*) redundancy; **dar de ~** (*soldado*) to discharge; (*empleado*) to dismiss, sack; **darse de ~** (*retirarse*) to drop out; (*Med*) to go sick; (*dimitir*) to resign; **estar de ~** (*enfermo*) to be off sick; (*Bolsa*) to be dropping o falling; **jugar a la ~** (*Econ*) to speculate on a fall in prices; *ver tb* **bajo**

bajada [ba'xaða] *nf* descent; (*camino*) slope; (*de aguas*) ebb

bajamar [baxa'mar] *nf* low tide

bajar [ba'xar] *vi* to go o come down; (*temperatura, precios*) to drop, fall ▷ *vt* (*cabeza*) to bow; (*escalera*) to go o come down; (*radio etc*) to turn down; (*precio, voz*) to lower; (*llevar abajo*) to take down; **bajarse** *vr* (*de vehículo*) to get out; (*de autobús*) to get off; **~ de** (*coche*) to get out of; (*autobús*) to get off; **~le los humos a algn** (*fig*) to cut sb down to size; **~se algo de Internet** to download sth from the internet

bajeza [ba'xeθa] *nf* baseness; (*una bajeza*) vile deed

bajío [ba'xio] *nm* shoal, sandbank; (*Am*) lowlands *pl*

bajo, -a ['baxo, a] *adj* (*terreno*) low(-lying); (*mueble, número, precio*) low; (*piso*) ground *cpd*; (*de estatura*) small, short; (*color*) pale; (*sonido*) faint, soft, low; (*voz, tono*) deep; (*metal*) base; (*humilde*) low, humble ▷ *adv* (*hablar*) softly, quietly; (*volar*) low ▷ *prep* under, below, underneath ▷ *nm* (*Mus*) bass; **hablar en voz baja** to whisper; **~ la lluvia** in the rain

bajón [ba'xon] *nm* fall, drop

bakalao [baka'lao] *nm* (*Mus*) rave music

bala ['bala] *nf* bullet; **~ de goma** plastic bullet

balacear [balaθe'ar] *vt* (*Am, CAm*) to shoot

baladí [bala'ði] *adj* trivial

balance [ba'lanθe] *nm* (*Com*) balance; (: *libro*) balance sheet; (: *cuenta general*) stocktaking; **~ de comprobación** trial balance; **~ consolidado** consolidated balance sheet; **hacer ~** to take stock

balancear [balanθe'ar] *vt* to balance ▷ *vi* to swing (to and fro); (*vacilar*) to hesitate; **balancearse** *vr* to swing (to and fro); (*vacilar*) to hesitate

balanceo [balan'θeo] *nm* swinging

balanza [ba'lanθa] *nf* scales *pl*, balance; **~ comercial** balance of trade; **~ de pagos/de poder(es)** balance of payments/of power; (*Astro*): **B~** Libra

balar [ba'lar] *vi* to bleat

balaustrada [balaus'traða] *nf* balustrade; (*pasamanos*) banister

balazo [ba'laθo] *nm* (*tiro*) shot; (*herida*) bullet wound

balbucear [balβuθe'ar] *vi, vt* to stammer, stutter

balbuceo [balβu'θeo] *nm* stammering, stuttering

balbucir [balβu'θir] *vi, vt* to stammer, stutter

balcánico, -a [bal'kaniko, a] *adj* Balkan

balcón [bal'kon] *nm* balcony

baldar [bal'dar] *vt* to cripple; (*agotar*) to exhaust

balde ['balde] *nm* (*esp Am*) bucket, pail; **de ~** *adv* (for) free, for nothing; **en ~** *adv* in vain

baldío, -a [bal'dio, a] *adj* uncultivated; (*terreno*) waste; (*inútil*) vain ▷ *nm* wasteland

baldosa [bal'dosa] *nf* (*azulejo*) floor tile; (*grande*) flagstone

baldosín [baldo'sin] *nm* tile

Baleares [bale'ares] *nfpl*: **las (Islas) ~** the Balearics, the Balearic Islands

balero [ba'lero] *nm* (*Am: juguete*) cup-and-ball toy

balido [ba'liðo] *nm* bleat, bleating

balín [ba'lin] *nm* pellet; **balines** *nmpl* buckshot *sg*

balística [ba'listika] *nf* ballistics *pl*

baliza [ba'liθa] *nf* (*Aviat*) beacon; (*Naut*) buoy

ballena [ba'ʎena] *nf* whale

ballesta [ba'ʎesta] *nf* crossbow; (*Auto*) spring

ballet (*pl* **ballets**) [ba'le ba'les] *nm* ballet

balneario, -a [balne'arjo, a] *adj*: **estación balnearia** (*bathing*) resort ▷ *nm* spa, health resort; (*Am: en la costa*) seaside resort

balón [ba'lon] *nm* ball

baloncesto [balon'θesto] *nm* basketball

balonmano [balon'mano] *nm* handball

balonred [balon'reð] *nm* netball

balonvolea [balombo'lea] *nm* volleyball

balsa ['balsa] *nf* raft; (*Bot*) balsa wood

bálsamo ['balsamo] *nm* balsam, balm

baluarte [ba'lwarte] *nm* bastion, bulwark

bambolearse [bambole'arse] *vr* to swing, sway; (*silla*) to wobble

bamboleo [bambo'leo] *nm* swinging, swaying; wobbling

bambú [bam'bu] *nm* bamboo

banana [ba'nana] *nf* (*Am*) banana

banano [ba'nano] *nm* (*Am*) banana tree; (*fruta*) banana

banca ['banka] *nf* (*asiento*) bench; (*Com*) banking

bancario, -a [ban'karjo, a] *adj* banking *cpd*, bank *cpd*; **giro ~** bank draft

bancarrota [banka'rrota] *nf* bankruptcy; **declararse en** *o* **hacer ~** to go bankrupt

banco ['banko] *nm* bench; (*Escol*) desk; (*Com*) bank; (*Geo*) stratum; **~ comercial** *o* **mercantil** commercial bank; **~ por acciones** joint-stock bank; **~ de crédito/de ahorros** credit/savings bank; **~ de arena** sandbank; **~ de datos** (*Inform*) data bank; **~ de hielo** iceberg

banda ['banda] *nf* band; (*cinta*) ribbon; (*pandilla*) gang; (*Mus*) brass band; (*Naut*) side, edge; **la ~ ancha** broadband; **la B~ Oriental** Uruguay; **~ sonora** soundtrack; **~ transportadora** conveyor belt

bandada [ban'daða] *nf* (*de pájaros*) flock; (*de peces*) shoal

bandazo [ban'daθo] *nm*: **dar ~s** (*coche*) to veer from side to side

bandeja [ban'dexa] *nf* tray; **~ de entrada/salida** in-tray/out-tray

bandera [ban'dera] *nf* (*de tela*) flag; (*estandarte*) banner; **izar la ~** to hoist the flag

banderilla [bande'riʎa] *nf* banderilla; (*tapa*) savoury appetizer (*served on a cocktail stick*)

banderín [bande'rin] *nm* pennant, small flag

banderola [bande'rola] *nf* (*Mil*) pennant

bandido [ban'diðo] *nm* bandit

bando ['bando] *nm* (*edicto*) edict, proclamation; (*facción*) faction; **pasar al otro ~** to change sides; **los ~s** (*Rel*) the banns

bandolera [bando'lera] *nf*: **llevar en ~** to wear across one's chest; **bolsa de ~** shoulder bag

bandolero [bando'lero] *nm* bandit, brigand

banquero [ban'kero] *nm* banker

banqueta [ban'keta] *nf* stool; (*Am: acera*) pavement (*Brit*), sidewalk (*US*)

banquete [ban'kete] *nm* banquet; (*para convidados*) formal dinner; **~ de boda** wedding reception

banquillo [ban'kiʎo] *nm* (*Jur*) dock, prisoner's bench; (*banco*) bench; (*para los pies*) footstool

banquina [ban'kina] *nf* (*RPl*) hard shoulder (*Brit*), berm (*US*)

bañadera [baɲa'ðera] *nf* (*Am*) bath(tub)

bañador [baɲa'ðor] *nm* swimming costume (*Brit*), bathing suit (*US*)

bañar [ba'ɲar] *vt* (*niño*) to bath, bathe; (*objeto*) to dip; (*de barniz*) to coat; **bañarse** *vr* (*en el mar*) to bathe, swim; (*en la bañera*) to have a bath

bañera [ba'ɲera] *nf* (*Esp*) bath(tub)

bañero, -a [ba'ɲero, a] *nm/f* lifeguard ▷ *nf* bath(tub)

bañista [ba'ɲista] *nm/f* bather

baño ['baɲo] *nm* (*en bañera*) bath; (*en río, mar*) dip, swim; (*cuarto*) bathroom; (*bañera*) bath(tub); (*capa*) coating; **darse** *o* **tomar un ~** (*en bañera*) to have *o* take a bath; (*en mar, piscina*) to have a swim; **~ María** bain-marie

baptista [bap'tista] *nm/f* Baptist

baqueta [ba'keta] *nf* (*Mus*) drumstick

bar [bar] *nm* bar

barahúnda [bara'unda] *nf* uproar, hubbub

baraja [ba'raxa] *nf* pack (of cards)

barajar [bara'xar] *vt* (*naipes*) to shuffle; (*fig*) to jumble up

baranda [ba'randa], **barandilla** [baran'diʎa] *nf* rail, railing

barata [ba'rata] *nf* (*Am*) (bargain) sale

baratija [bara'tixa] *nf* trinket; *(fig)* trifle; **baratijas** *nfpl (Com)* cheap goods

baratillo [bara'tiʎo] *nm (tienda)* junk shop; *(subasta)* bargain sale; *(conjunto de cosas)* second-hand goods *pl*

barato, -a [ba'rato, a] *adj* cheap ▷ *adv* cheap, cheaply

baraúnda [bara'unda] *nf* = **barahúnda**

barba ['barβa] *nf (mentón)* chin; *(pelo)* beard; **tener ~** to be unshaven; **hacer algo en las ~s de algn** to do sth under sb's very nose; **reírse en las ~s de algn** to laugh in sb's face

barbacoa [barβa'koa] *nf (parrilla)* barbecue; *(carne)* barbecued meat

barbaridad [barβari'ðað] *nf* barbarity; *(acto)* barbarism; *(atrocidad)* outrage; **una ~ de** *(fam)* loads of; **¡qué ~!** *(fam)* how awful!; **cuesta una ~** *(fam)* it costs a fortune

barbarie [bar'βarje] *nf*, **barbarismo** [barβa'rismo] *nm* barbarism; *(crueldad)* barbarity

bárbaro, -a ['barβaro, a] *adj* barbarous, cruel; *(grosero)* rough, uncouth ▷ *nm/f* barbarian ▷ *adv*: **lo pasamos ~** *(fam)* we had a great time; **¡qué ~!** *(fam)* how marvellous!; **un éxito ~** *(fam)* a terrific success; **es un tipo ~** *(fam)* he's a great bloke

barbecho [bar'βetʃo] *nm* fallow land

barbero [bar'βero] *nm* barber, hairdresser

barbilla [bar'βiʎa] *nf* chin, tip of the chin

barbitúrico [barβi'turiko] *nm* barbiturate

barbo ['barβo] *nm*: **~ de mar** red mullet

barbudo, -a [bar'βuðo, a] *adj* bearded

barca ['barka] *nf (small)* boat; **~ pesquera** fishing boat; **~ de pasaje** ferry

barcaza [bar'kaθa] *nf* barge; **~ de desembarco** landing craft

Barcelona [barθe'lona] *nf* Barcelona

barcelonés, -esa [barθelo'nes, esa] *adj* of o from Barcelona ▷ *nm/f* native o inhabitant of Barcelona

barco ['barko] *nm* boat; *(buque)* ship; *(Com etc)* vessel; **~ de carga** cargo boat; **~ de guerra** warship; **~ de vela** sailing ship; **ir en ~** to go by boat

barda ['barða] *nf (Am: de madera)* fence

baremo [ba'remo] *nm* scale; *(tabla de cuentas)* ready reckoner

barítono [ba'ritono] *nm* baritone

barman ['barman] *nm* barman

barniz [bar'niθ] *nm* varnish; *(en la loza)* glaze; *(fig)* veneer

barnizar [barni'θar] *vt* to varnish; *(loza)* to glaze

barómetro [ba'rometro] *nm* barometer

barón [ba'ron] *nm* baron

baronesa [baro'nesa] *nf* baroness

barquero [bar'kero] *nm* boatman

barquillo [bar'kiʎo] *nm* cone, cornet

barra ['barra] *nf* bar, rod; *(Jur)* rail; *(: banquillo)* dock; *(de un bar, café)* bar; *(de pan)* French loaf; *(palanca)* lever; **~ de carmín** o **de labios** lipstick; **~ de herramientas** *(Inform)* toolbar; **~ de espaciado** *(Inform)* space bar; **~ inversa** backslash; **~ libre** free bar; **no pararse en ~s** to stick o stop at nothing

barraca [ba'rraka] *nf* hut, cabin; *(en Valencia)* thatched farmhouse; *(en feria)* booth

barranca [ba'rranka] *nf* ravine, gully

barranco [ba'rranko] *nm* ravine; *(fig)* difficulty

barrena [ba'rrena] *nf* drill

barrenar [barre'nar] *vt* to drill (through), bore

barrendero, -a [barren'dero, a] *nm/f* street-sweeper

barreno [ba'rreno] *nm* large drill

barrer [ba'rrer] *vt* to sweep; *(quitar)* to sweep away; *(Mil, Naut)* to sweep, rake (with gunfire) ▷ *vi* to sweep up

barrera [ba'rrera] *nf* barrier; *(Mil)* barricade; *(Ferro)* crossing gate; **poner ~s a** to hinder; **~ arancelaria** *(Com)* tariff barrier; **~ comercial** *(Com)* trade barrier

barriada [ba'rrjaða] *nf* quarter, district

barricada [barri'kaða] *nf* barricade

barrida [ba'rriða] *nf*, **barrido** [ba'rriðo] *nm* sweep, sweeping

barriga [ba'rriɣa] *nf* belly; *(panza)* paunch; *(vientre)* guts *pl*; **echar ~** to get middle-age spread

barrigón, -ona [barri'ɣon, ona], **barrigudo, -a** [barri'ɣuðo, a] *adj* potbellied

barril [ba'rril] *nm* barrel, cask; **cerveza de ~** draught beer

barrio ['barrjo] *nm (vecindad)* area, neighborhood (US); *(en las afueras)* suburb; **~s bajos** poor quarter *sg*; **~ chino** red-light district

barro ['barro] *nm (lodo)* mud; *(objetos)* earthenware; *(Med)* pimple

barroco, -a [ba'rroko, a] *adj* Baroque; *(fig)* elaborate ▷ *nm* Baroque

barrote [ba'rrote] *nm (de ventana etc)* bar

barruntar [barrun'tar] *vt (conjeturar)* to guess; *(presentir)* to suspect

barrunto [ba'rrunto] *nm* guess; suspicion

bartola [bar'tola] *nf*: **a la ~**, **tirarse a la ~** to take it easy, be lazy

bártulos ['bartulos] *nmpl* things, belongings

barullo [ba'ruʎo] *nm* row, uproar

basar [ba'sar] *vt* to base; **basarse** *vr*: **~se en** to be based on

basca ['baska] *nf* nausea

báscula ['baskula] *nf (platform)* scales *pl*

base ['base] *nf* base; **a ~ de** on the basis of, based on; *(mediante)* by means of; **a ~ de bien** in abundance; **~ de conocimiento** knowledge base; **~ de datos** database

básico, -a ['basiko, a] *adj* basic

basílica [ba'silika] *nf* basilica

basket, básquet ['basket] *nm* basketball

básquetbol ['basketbol] *nm (Am)* basketball

◯ PALABRA CLAVE

bastante [bas'tante] adj 1 (suficiente) enough; **bastante dinero** enough o sufficient money; **bastantes libros** enough books 2 (valor intensivo): **bastante gente** quite a lot of people; **tener bastante calor** to be rather hot; **hace bastante tiempo que ocurrió** it happened quite o rather a long time ago ▷ adv: **bastante bueno/malo** quite good/ rather bad; **bastante rico** pretty rich; **(lo) bastante inteligente (como) para hacer algo** clever enough o sufficiently clever to do sth; **voy a tardar bastante** I'm going to be a while o quite some time

bastar [bas'tar] vi to be enough o sufficient; **bastarse** vr to be self-sufficient; **~ para** to be enough to; **¡basta!** (that's) enough!
bastardilla [bastar'ðiʎa] nf italics pl
bastardo, -a [bas'tarðo, a] adj, nm/f bastard
bastidor [basti'ðor] nm frame; (de coche) chassis; (Arte) stretcher; (Teat) wing; **entre ~es** behind the scenes
basto, -a ['basto, a] adj coarse, rough ▷ nmpl: **~s** (Naipes) one of the suits in the Spanish card deck
bastón [bas'ton] nm stick, staff; (para pasear) walking stick; **~ de mando** baton
bastoncillo [baston'θiʎo] nm (tb: **~ de algodón**) cotton bud
basura [ba'sura] nf rubbish, refuse (Brit), garbage (US) ▷ adj: **comida/televisión ~** junk food/TV
basurero [basu'rero] nm (hombre) dustman (Brit), garbage collector o man (US); (lugar) rubbish dump; (cubo) (rubbish) bin (Brit), trash can (US)
bata ['bata] nf (gen) dressing gown; (cubretodo) smock, overall; (Med, Tec etc) lab(oratory) coat
batalla [ba'taʎa] nf battle; **de ~** for everyday use; **~ campal** pitched battle
batallar [bata'ʎar] vi to fight
batallón [bata'ʎon] nm battalion
batata [ba'tata] nf (Am: Culin) sweet potato
bate ['bate] nm (Deporte) bat
bateador [batea'ðor] nm (Deporte) batter, batsman
batería [bate'ria] nf battery; (Mus) drums pl; (Teat) footlights pl; **~ de cocina** kitchen utensils pl
batido, -a [ba'tiðo, a] adj (camino) beaten, well-trodden ▷ nm (Culin) batter; **~ (de leche)** milk shake ▷ nf (Am) (police) raid
batidora [bati'ðora] nf beater, mixer; **~ eléctrica** food mixer, blender
batir [ba'tir] vt to beat, strike; (vencer) to beat, defeat; (revolver) to beat, mix; (pelo) to back-comb; **batirse** vr to fight; **~ palmas** to clap, applaud
baturro, -a [ba'turro, a] nm/f Aragonese peasant

batuta [ba'tuta] nf baton; **llevar la ~** (fig) to be the boss
baúl [ba'ul] nm trunk; (Am Auto) boot (Brit), trunk (US)
bautismo [bau'tismo] nm baptism, christening
bautizar [bauti'θar] vt to baptize, christen; (fam: diluir) to water down; (dar apodo) to dub
bautizo [bau'tiθo] nm baptism, christening
bayeta [ba'jeta] nf (trapo) floor cloth; (Am: pañal) nappy (Brit), diaper (US)
bayo, -a ['bajo, a] adj bay
bayoneta [bajo'neta] nf bayonet
baza ['baθa] nf trick; **meter ~** to butt in
bazar [ba'θar] nm bazaar
bazo ['baθo] nm spleen
bazofia [ba'θofja] nf pigswill (Brit), hogwash (US); (libro etc) rubbish
BCE nm abr (= Banco Central Europeo) ECB
be [be] nf name of the letter B; **be chica/grande** (Am) V/B; **be larga** (Am) B
beatificar [beatifi'kar] vt to beatify
beato, -a [be'ato, a] adj blessed; (piadoso) pious
bebé (pl **bebés**) [be'βe, be'βes], **bebe** (Am: pl **bebes**) ['beβe, 'beβes] nm baby; **~ de diseño** designer baby
bebedero, -a [beβe'ðero, a] nm (para animales) drinking trough
bebedor, a [beβe'ðor, a] adj hard-drinking
bebé-probeta [beβe-pro'βeta] (pl **bebés-probeta**) nm/f test-tube baby
beber [be'βer] vt, vi to drink; **~ a sorbos/tragos** to sip/gulp; **se lo bebió todo** he drank it all up
bebido, -a [be'βiðo, a] adj drunk ▷ nf drink
beca ['beka] nf grant, scholarship
becado, -a [be'kaðo, a] nm/f = **becario**
becario, -a [be'karjo, a] nm/f scholarship holder, grant holder
bechamel [betʃa'mel] nf = **besamel**
bedel [be'ðel] nm porter, janitor; (Univ) porter
beduino, -a [be'ðwino, a] adj, nm/f Bedouin
beige ['beix], **beis** ['beis] adj, nm beige
béisbol ['beisβol] nm baseball
beldad [bel'dað] nf beauty
Belén [be'len] nm Bethlehem; **belén** (de Navidad) nativity scene, crib
belga ['belɣa] adj, nm/f Belgian
Bélgica ['belxika] nf Belgium
Belice [be'liθe] nm Belize
bélico, -a ['beliko, a] adj (actitud) warlike
belicoso, -a [beli'koso, a] adj (guerrero) warlike; (agresivo) aggressive, bellicose
beligerante [belixe'rante] adj belligerent
bellaco, -a [be'ʎako, a] adj sly, cunning ▷ nm villain, rogue
bellaquería [beʎake'ria] nf (acción) dirty trick; (calidad) wickedness
belleza [be'ʎeθa] nf beauty
bello, -a ['beʎo, a] adj beautiful, lovely; **Bellas Artes** Fine Art sg

bellota [be'ʎota] *nf* acorn
bemol [be'mol] *nm* (*Mus*) flat; **esto tiene ~es** (*fam*) this is a tough one
bencina [ben'sina] *nf* (*Am: gasolina*) petrol (*Brit*), gas (*US*)
bendecir [bende'θir] *vt* to bless; **~ la mesa** to say grace
bendición [bendi'θjon] *nf* blessing
bendito, -a [ben'dito, a] *pp de* **bendecir** ▷ *adj* (*santo*) blessed; (*agua*) holy; (*afortunado*) lucky; (*feliz*) happy; (*sencillo*) simple ▷ *nm/f* simple soul; **¡~ sea Dios!** thank goodness!; **es un ~** he's sweet; **dormir como un ~** to sleep like a log
benedictino, -a [beneðik'tino, a] *adj, nm* Benedictine
beneficencia [benefi'θenθja] *nf* charity
beneficiario, -a [benefi'θjarjo, a] *nm/f* beneficiary; (*de cheque*) payee
beneficio [bene'fiθjo] *nm* (*bien*) benefit, advantage; (*Com*) profit, gain; **a ~ de** for the benefit of; **en ~ propio** to one's own advantage; **~ bruto/neto** gross/net profit; **~ por acción** earnings *pl* per share
beneficioso, -a [benefi'θjoso, a] *adj* beneficial
benéfico, -a [be'nefiko, a] *adj* charitable; **sociedad benéfica** charity (organization)
beneplácito [bene'plaθito] *nm* approval, consent
benevolencia [beneβo'lenθja] *nf* benevolence, kindness
benévolo, -a [be'neβolo, a] *adj* benevolent, kind
benigno, -a [be'niɣno, a] *adj* kind; (*suave*) mild; (*Med: tumor*) benign, non-malignant
beodo, -a [be'oðo, a] *adj* drunk ▷ *nm/f* drunkard
berberecho [berβe'retʃo] *nm* cockle
berenjena [beren'xena] *nf* aubergine (*Brit*), eggplant (*US*)
Berlín [ber'lin] *nm* Berlin
berlinés, -esa [berli'nes, esa] *adj* of o from Berlin ▷ *nm/f* Berliner
berlinesa [berli'nesa] *nf* (*Am*) doughnut, donut (*US*)
bermejo, -a [ber'mexo, a] *adj* red
bermudas [ber'muðas] *nfpl* Bermuda shorts
berrear [berre'ar] *vi* to bellow, low
berrido [be'rriðo] *nm* bellow(ing)
berrinche [be'rrintʃe] *nm* (*fam*) temper, tantrum
berro ['berro] *nm* watercress
berza ['berθa] *nf* cabbage; **~ lombarda** red cabbage
besamel [besa'mel], **besamela** [besa'mela] *nf* (*Culin*) white sauce, bechamel sauce
besar [be'sar] *vt* to kiss; (*fig: tocar*) to graze; **besarse** *vr* to kiss (one another)
beso ['beso] *nm* kiss
bestia ['bestja] *nf* beast, animal; (*fig*) idiot; **~ de carga** beast of burden; **¡~!** you idiot!;

¡no seas ~! (*bruto*) don't be such a brute!; (*idiota*) don't be such an idiot!
bestial [bes'tjal] *adj* bestial; (*fam*) terrific
bestialidad [bestjali'ðað] *nf* bestiality; (*fam*) stupidity
besugo [be'suɣo] *nm* sea bream; (*fam*) idiot
besuquear [besuke'ar] *vt* to cover with kisses; **besuquearse** *vr* to kiss and cuddle
betabel [beta'bel] *nm* (*Am*) beetroot (*Brit*), beet (*US*)
betún [be'tun] *nm* shoe polish; (*Química*) bitumen, asphalt
biberón [biβe'ron] *nm* feeding bottle
Biblia ['biβlja] *nf* Bible
bibliografía [biβljoɣra'fia] *nf* bibliography
biblioteca [biβljo'teka] *nf* library; (*estantes*) bookcase, bookshelves *pl*; **~ de consulta** reference library
bibliotecario, -a [biβljote'karjo, a] *nm/f* librarian
bicarbonato [bikarβo'nato] *nm* bicarbonate
bíceps ['biθeps] *nm inv* biceps
bicho ['bitʃo] *nm* (*animal*) small animal; (*sabandija*) bug, insect; (*Taur*) bull; **~ raro** (*fam*) queer fish
bici ['biθi] *nf* (*fam*) bike
bicicleta [biθi'kleta] *nf* bicycle, cycle; **ir en ~** to cycle; **~ estática/de montaña** exercise/mountain bike
bidé [bi'ðe] *nm* bidet
bidón [bi'ðon] *nm* (*grande*) drum; (*pequeño*) can

PALABRA CLAVE

bien [bjen] *nm* **1** (*bienestar*) good; **te lo digo por tu bien** I'm telling you for your own good; **el bien y el mal** good and evil
2 (*posesión*): **bienes** goods; **bienes de consumo/equipo** consumer/capital goods; **bienes inmuebles** o **raíces/bienes muebles** real estate *sg*/personal property *sg*
▷ *adv* **1** (*de manera satisfactoria, correcta etc*) well; **trabaja/come bien** she works/eats well; **contestó bien** he answered correctly; **oler bien** to smell nice o good; **me siento bien** I feel fine; **no me siento bien** I don't feel very well; **se está bien aquí** it's nice here
2 (*frases*): **hiciste bien en llamarme** you were right to call me
3 (*valor intensivo*) very; **un cuarto bien caliente** a nice warm room; **bien de veces** lots of times; **bien se ve que ...** it's quite clear that ...
4: **estar bien**: **estoy muy bien aquí** I feel very happy here; **¿te encuentras bien?** are you all right?; **te está bien la falda** (*ser la talla*) the skirt fits you; (*sentar*) the skirt suits you; **el libro está muy bien** the book is really good; **está bien que vengan** it's all right for them to come; **¡está bien! lo haré** oh all right, I'll do it; **ya está bien de quejas** that's quite enough complaining

5 (de buena gana): **yo bien que iría pero ...** I'd gladly go but ...
▷ excl: **¡bien!** (aprobación) OK!; **¡muy bien!** well done!; **¡qué bien!** great!; **bien, gracias, ¿y usted?** fine thanks, and you?
▷ adj inv: **niño bien** rich kid; **gente bien** posh people
▷ conj 1: **bien ... bien: bien en coche bien en tren** either by car or by train
2: no bien (esp Am): **no bien llegue te llamaré** as soon as I arrive I'll call you
3: si bien even though; ver tb **más**

bienal [bje'nal] adj biennial
bienaventurado, -a [bjenaβentu'raðo, a] adj (feliz) happy; (afortunado) fortunate; (Rel) blessed
bienestar [bjenes'tar] nm well-being; **estado de** ~ welfare state
bienhechor, a [bjene'tʃor, a] adj beneficent
▷ nm/f benefactor/benefactress
bienvenido, -a [bjembe'niðo, a] adj welcome ▷ excl welcome! ▷ nf welcome; **dar la bienvenida a algn** to welcome sb
bies ['bjes] nm: **falda al** ~ bias-cut skirt; **cortar al** ~ to cut on the bias
bife ['bife] nm (Am) steak
bifocal [bifo'kal] adj bifocal
bifurcación [bifurka'θjon] nf fork; (Ferro, Inform) branch
bifurcarse [bifur'karse] vr to fork
bigamia [bi'ɣamja] nf bigamy
bígamo, -a ['biɣamo, a] adj bigamous ▷ nm/f bigamist
bigote [bi'ɣote] nm (tb: ~s) moustache
bigotudo, -a [biɣo'tuðo, a] adj with a big moustache
bikini [bi'kini] nm bikini; (Culin) toasted cheese and ham sandwich
bilateral [bilate'ral] adj bilateral
bilingüe [bi'lingwe] adj bilingual
billar [bi'ʎar] nm billiards sg; **billares** nmpl (lugar) billiard hall; (galería de atracciones) amusement arcade; ~ **americano** pool
billete [bi'ʎete] nm ticket; (de banco) banknote (Brit), bill (US); (carta) note; ~ **sencillo, ~ de ida solamente/~ de ida y vuelta** single (Brit) o one-way (US) ticket/return (Brit) o round-trip (US) ticket; **sacar (un) ~** to get a ticket; **un ~ de cinco libras** a five-pound note; ~ **electrónico** e-ticket
billetera [biʎe'tera] nf, **billetero** [biʎe'tero] nm wallet
billón [bi'ʎon] nm billion
bimensual [bimen'swal] adj twice monthly
bimotor, a [bimo'tor, a] adj twin-engined
▷ nm twin-engined plane
bingo ['bingo] nm (juego) bingo; (sala) bingo hall
binóculo [bi'nokulo] nm pince-nez
binomio [bi'nomjo] nm (Mat) binomial

biodegradable [bioðeɣra'ðaβle] adj biodegradable
biodiversidad [bioðiβersi'ðað] nf biodiversity
biografía [bjoɣra'fia] nf biography
biográfico, -a [bio'ɣrafiko, a] adj biographical
biógrafo, -a [bi'oɣrafo, a] nm/f biographer
biología [biolo'xia] nf biology
biológico, -a [bio'loxiko, a] adj biological; (cultivo, producto) organic; **guerra biológica** biological warfare
biólogo, -a [bi'oloɣo, a] nm/f biologist
biométrico, -a [bio'metriko, a] adj biometric
biombo ['bjombo] nm (folding) screen
biopsia [bi'opsja] nf biopsy
biosfera [bios'fera] nf biosphere
bioterrorismo [bioterro'rismo] nm bioterrorism
biquini [bi'kini] nm = **bikini**
birlar [bir'lar] vt (fam) to pinch
Birmania [bir'manja] nf Burma
birome [bi'rome] nf (Am) ballpoint (pen)
birria ['birrja] nf (fam): **ser una** ~ (película, libro) to be rubbish; **ir hecho una** ~ to be o look a sight
bis [bis] excl encore! ▷ nm encore ▷ adv (dos veces) twice; **viven en el 27** ~ they live at 27a
bisabuelo, -a [bisa'βwelo, a] nm/f great-grandfather/mother; **bisabuelos** nmpl great-grandparents
bisagra [bi'saɣra] nf hinge
bisbisar [bisβi'sar], **bisbisear** [bisβise'ar] vt to mutter, mumble
bisexual [bisek'swal] adj, nm/f bisexual
bisiesto [bi'sjesto] adj: **año** ~ leap year
bisnieto, -a [bis'njeto, a] nm/f great-grandson/daughter; **bisnietos** nmpl great-grandchildren
bisonte [bi'sonte] nm bison
bistec [bis'tek], **bisté** [bis'te] nm steak
bisturí [bistu'ri] nm scalpel
bisutería [bisute'ria] nf imitation o costume jewellery
bit [bit] nm (Inform) bit; ~ **de parada** stop bit; ~ **de paridad** parity bit
bitácora [bi'takora] nf: **cuaderno de** ~ logbook, ship's log
bizco, -a ['biθko, a] adj cross-eyed
bizcocho [biθ'kotʃo] nm (Culin) sponge cake
biznieto, -a [biθ'njeto, a] nm/f = **bisnieto**
bizquear [biθke'ar] vi to squint
blanco, -a ['blanko, a] adj white ▷ nm/f white man/woman, white ▷ nm (color) white; (en texto) blank; (Mil, fig) target ▷ nf (Mus) minim; **en** ~ blank; **cheque en** ~ blank cheque; **votar en** ~ to spoil one's vote; **quedarse en** ~ to be disappointed; **noche en** ~ sleepless night; **ser el** ~ **de las burlas** to be the butt of jokes; **estar sin blanca** to be broke

blancura [blan'kura] *nf* whiteness

blandir [blan'dir] *vt* to brandish

blando, -a ['blando, a] *adj* soft; *(tierno)* tender, gentle; *(carácter)* mild; *(fam)* cowardly ▷ *nm/f (Pol etc)* soft-liner

blandura [blan'dura] *nf* softness; tenderness; mildness

blanqueador [blankea'ðor] *nm (Am)* bleach

blanquear [blanke'ar] *vt* to whiten; *(fachada)* to whitewash; *(paño)* to bleach; *(dinero)* to launder ▷ *vi* to turn white

blanquecino, -a [blanke'θino, a] *adj* whitish

blanqueo [blan'keo] *nm (de pared)* whitewashing; *(de dinero)* laundering

blanquillo [blan'kiʎo] *nm (Am, CAm)* egg

blasfemar [blasfe'mar] *vi* to blaspheme; *(fig)* to curse

blasfemia [blas'femja] *nf* blasphemy

blasón [bla'son] *nm* coat of arms; *(fig)* honour

blasonar [blaso'nar] *vt* to emblazon ▷ *vi* to boast, brag

bledo ['bleðo] *nm*: **(no) me importa un ~** I couldn't care less

blindado, -a [blin'daðo, a] *adj (Mil)* armour-plated; *(antibalas)* bulletproof; **coche** o *(Am)* **carro ~** armoured car; **puertas blindadas** security doors

blindaje [blin'daxe] *nm* armour, armour-plating

bloc *(pl* **blocs)** [blok, blos] *nm* writing pad; *(Escol)* jotter; **~ de dibujos** sketch pad

blof [blof] *nm (Am)* bluff

blofear [blofe'ar] *vi (Am)* to bluff

blog [bloɣ] *(pl* **blogs)** *nm* blog

bloque ['bloke] *nm (tb Inform)* block; *(Pol)* bloc; **~ de cilindros** cylinder block

bloquear [bloke'ar] *vt (Naut etc)* to blockade; *(aislar)* to cut off; *(Com, Econ)* to freeze; **fondos bloqueados** frozen assets

bloqueo [blo'keo] *nm* blockade; *(Com)* freezing, blocking; **~ mental** mental block

blusa ['blusa] *nf* blouse

boa ['boa] *nf* boa

boato [bo'ato] *nm* show, ostentation

bobada [bo'βaða] *nf* foolish action *(o* statement); **decir ~s** to talk nonsense

bobería [boβe'ria] *nf* = **bobada**

bobina [bo'βina] *nf (Tec)* bobbin; *(Foto)* spool; *(Elec)* coil, winding

bobo, -a ['boβo, a] *adj (tonto)* daft, silly; *(cándido)* naïve ▷ *nm/f* fool, idiot ▷ *nm (Teat)* clown, funny man

boca ['boka] *nf* mouth; *(de crustáceo)* pincer; *(de cañón)* muzzle; *(entrada)* mouth, entrance; **bocas** *nfpl (de río)* mouth *sg*; **~ abajo/arriba** face down/up; **a ~ jarro** point-blank; **se me hace la ~ agua** my mouth is watering; **todo salió a pedir de ~** it all turned out perfectly; **en ~ de** *(esp Am)* according to; **la cosa anda de ~ en ~** the story is going the rounds; **¡cállate la ~!** *(fam)* shut up!; **quedarse con la ~ abierta** to be dumbfounded; **no abrir la ~** to keep quiet; **~ de incendios** hydrant; **~ del estómago** pit of the stomach; **~ de metro** tube *(Brit)* o subway *(US)* entrance

bocacalle [boka'kaʎe] *nf* side street; **la primera ~** the first turning o street

bocadillo [boka'ðiʎo] *nm* sandwich

bocado [bo'kaðo] *nm* mouthful, bite; *(de caballo)* bridle; **~ de Adán** Adam's apple

bocajarro [boka'xarro]: **a ~** *adv (Mil)* at point-blank range; **decir algo a ~** to say sth bluntly

bocanada [boka'naða] *nf (de vino)* mouthful, swallow; *(de aire)* gust, puff

bocata [bo'kata] *nm (fam)* sandwich

bocazas [bo'kaθas] *nm/f inv (fam)* bigmouth

boceto [bo'θeto] *nm* sketch, outline

bocha ['botʃa] *nf* bowl; **bochas** *nfpl* bowls *sg*

bochinche [bo'tʃintʃe] *nm (fam)* uproar

bochorno [bo'tʃorno] *nm (vergüenza)* embarrassment; *(calor)*: **hace ~** it's very muggy

bochornoso, -a [botʃor'noso, a] *adj* muggy; embarrassing

bocina [bo'θina] *nf (Mus)* trumpet; *(Auto)* horn; *(para hablar)* megaphone; **tocar la ~** *(Auto)* to sound o blow one's horn

boda ['boða] *nf (tb:* **~s)** wedding, marriage; *(fiesta)* wedding reception; **~s de plata/de oro** silver/golden wedding *sg*

bodega [bo'ðeɣa] *nf (de vino)* (wine) cellar; *(bar)* bar; *(restaurante)* restaurant; *(depósito)* storeroom; *(de barco)* hold

bodegón [boðe'ɣon] *nm (Arte)* still life

bofe ['bofe] *nm (tb:* **~s:** *de res)* lights *pl*; **echar los ~s** to slave (away)

bofetada [bofe'taða] *nf* slap (in the face); **dar de ~s a algn** to punch sb

bofetón [bofe'ton] *nm* = **bofetada**

boga ['boɣa] *nf*: **en ~** in vogue

bogar [bo'ɣar] *vi (remar)* to row; *(navegar)* to sail

bogavante [boɣa'βante] *nm (Naut)* stroke, first rower; *(Zool)* lobster

Bogotá [boɣo'ta] *n* Bogota

bogotano, -a [boɣo'tano, a] *adj* of o from Bogota ▷ *nm/f* native o inhabitant of Bogota

bohemio, -a [bo'emjo, a] *adj, nm/f* Bohemian

bohío [bo'io] *nm (Am)* shack, hut

boicot [boi'ko(t)] *(pl* **boicots)** *nm* boycott

boicotear [boikote'ar] *vt* to boycott

boicoteo [boiko'teo] *nm* boycott

bóiler ['boiler] *nm (Am)* boiler

boina ['boina] *nf* beret

bola ['bola] *nf* ball; *(canica)* marble; *(Naipes)* (grand) slam; *(betún)* shoe polish; *(mentira)* tale, story; **bolas** *nfpl (Am)* bolas; **~ de billar** billiard ball; **~ de nieve** snowball

bolchevique [boltʃe'βike] *adj, nm/f* Bolshevik

boleadoras [bolea'ðoras] *nfpl (Am)* bolas *sg*

bolear [bole'ar] *vt (Am: zapatos)* to polish, shine

bolera [bo'lera] *nf* skittle o bowling alley

bolero, -a [bo'lero, a] *nm* bolero ▷ *nm/f* (*Am: limpiabotas*) shoeshine boy/girl

boleta [bo'leta] *nf* (*Am: permiso*) pass, permit; (*de rifa*) ticket; (*recibo*) receipt; (*para votar*) ballot; **~ de calificaciones** report card

boletería [bolete'ria] *nf* (*Am*) ticket office

boletín [bole'tin] *nm* bulletin; (*periódico*) journal, review; **~ escolar** (*Esp*) school report; **~ de noticias** news bulletin; **~ de pedido** application form; **~ de precios** price list; **~ de prensa** press release

boleto [bo'leto] *nm* (*esp Am*) ticket; **~ de apuestas** betting slip; **~ de ida y vuelta** (*Am*) round trip ticket; **~ electrónico** (*Am*) e-ticket; **~ redondo** (*Am*) round trip ticket

boli ['boli] *nm* Biro®

boliche [bo'litʃe] *nm* (*bola*) jack; (*juego*) bowls *sg*; (*lugar*) bowling alley; (*Am: tienda*) small grocery store

bólido ['boliðo] *nm* meteorite; (*Auto*) racing car

bolígrafo [bo'liɣrafo] *nm* ball-point pen, Biro®

bolilla [bo'liʎa] *nf* (*Am*) topic

bolillo [bo'liʎo] *nm* (*Costura*) bobbin (for lacemaking); (*Am*) (bread) roll

bolita [bo'lita] *nf* (*Am*) marble

bolívar [bo'liβar] *nm* monetary unit of Venezuela

Bolivia [bo'liβja] *nf* Bolivia

boliviano, -a [boli'βjano, a] *adj, nm/f* Bolivian

bollería [boʎe'ria] *nf* cakes *pl* and pastries *pl*

bollo ['boʎo] *nm* (*de pan*) roll; (*dulce*) scone; (*chichón*) bump, lump; (*abolladura*) dent; **bollos** *nmpl* (*Am*) troubles

bolo ['bolo] *nm* skittle; (*píldora*) (large) pill; **(juego de)~s** skittles *sg*

bolsa ['bolsa] *nf* (*cartera*) purse; (*saco*) bag; (*Am*) pocket; (*de mujer*) handbag; (*Anat*) cavity, sac; (*Com*) stock exchange; (*Minería*) pocket; **~ de agua caliente** hot water bottle; **~ de aire** air pocket; **~ de (la) basura** bin-liner; **~ de dormir** (*Am*) sleeping bag; **~ de papel** paper bag; **~ de plástico** plastic (*o* carrier) bag; **~ de la compra** shopping bag; **"B~ de la propiedad"** "Property Mart"; **~ de trabajo** employment bureau; **jugar a la ~** to play the market

bolsillo [bol'siʎo] *nm* pocket; (*cartera*) purse; **de ~** pocket *cpd*; **meterse a algn en el ~** to get sb eating out of one's hand

bolsista [bol'sista] *nm/f* stockbroker

bolso ['bolso] *nm* (*bolsa*) bag; (*de mujer*) handbag

boludo, -a [bo'luðo, a] (*Am fam!*) *adj* stupid ▷ *nm/f* prat (!)

bomba ['bomba] *nf* (*Mil*) bomb; (*Tec*) pump; (*Am: borrachera*) drunkenness ▷ *adj* (*fam*): **noticia ~** bombshell ▷ *adv* (*fam*): **pasarlo ~** to have a great time; **~ atómica/de humo/de retardo** atomic/smoke/time bomb; **~ de gasolina** petrol pump; **~ de incendios** fire engine

bombacha [bom'batʃa] *nf* (*Am*) panties *pl*

bombardear [bombarðe'ar] *vt* to bombard; (*Mil*) to bomb

bombardeo [bombar'ðeo] *nm* bombardment; bombing

bombardero [bombar'ðero] *nm* bomber

bombazo [bom'baθo] *nm* (*Am: explosión*) explosion; (*fam: notición*) bombshell; (: *éxito*) smash hit

bombear [bombe'ar] *vt* (*agua*) to pump (out *o* up); (*Mil*) to bomb; (*Fútbol*) to lob; **bombearse** *vr* to warp

bombero [bom'bero] *nm* fireman; **(cuerpo de) ~s** fire brigade

bombilla [bom'biʎa] (*Esp*) *nf*, **bombillo** [bom'biʎo] (*Am*) *nm* (light) bulb

bombita [bom'bita] *nf* (*Am*) (light) bulb

bombín [bom'bin] *nm* bowler hat

bombo ['bombo] *nm* (*Mus*) bass drum; (*Tec*) drum; (*fam*) exaggerated praise; **hacer algo a ~ y platillo** to make a great song and dance about sth; **tengo la cabeza hecha un ~** I've got a splitting headache

bombón [bom'bon] *nm* chocolate; (*Am: de caramelo*) marshmallow; (*belleza*) gem

bombona [bom'bona] *nf*: **~ de butano** gas cylinder

bonachón, -ona [bona'tʃon, ona] *adj* good-natured

bonaerense [bonae'rense] *adj* of *o* from Buenos Aires ▷ *nm/f* native *o* inhabitant of Buenos Aires

bonanza [bo'nanθa] *nf* (*Naut*) fair weather; (*fig*) bonanza; (*Minería*) rich pocket *o* vein

bondad [bon'dað] *nf* goodness, kindness; **tenga la ~ de** (please) be good enough to

bondadoso, -a [bonda'ðoso, a] *adj* good, kind

bonito, -a [bo'nito, a] *adj* (*lindo*) pretty; (*agradable*) nice ▷ *adv* (*Am fam*) well ▷ *nm* (*atún*) tuna (fish)

bono ['bono] *nm* voucher; (*Finanzas*) bond; **~ de billetes de metro** booklet of metro tickets; **~ del Tesoro** treasury bill

bonobús [bono'βus] *nm* (*Esp*) bus pass

Bono Loto, bonoloto [bono'loto] *nm o f* (*Esp*) state-run weekly lottery; *ver tb* **lotería**

boom (*pl* **booms**) [bum, bums] *nm* boom

boquear [boke'ar] *vi* to gasp

boquerón [boke'ron] *nm* (*pez*) (kind of) anchovy; (*agujero*) large hole

boquete [bo'kete] *nm* gap, hole

boquiabierto, -a [bokia'βjerto, a] *adj* open-mouthed (in astonishment); **quedarse ~** to be amazed *o* flabbergasted

boquilla [bo'kiʎa] *nf* (*de riego*) nozzle; (*de cigarro*) cigarette holder; (*Mus*) mouthpiece

borbotón [borβo'ton] *nm*: **salir a borbotones** to gush out

borda ['borða] *nf* (*Naut*) gunwale, rail; **echar *o* tirar algo por la ~** to throw sth overboard

bordado [bor'ðaðo] *nm* embroidery

bordar [bor'ðar] *vt* to embroider

borde ['borðe] *nm* edge, border; (*de camino etc*) side; (*en la costura*) hem; **al ~ de** (*fig*) on the verge o brink of ▷ *adj*: **ser ~** (*Esp*: (*fam*)) to be rude

bordear [borðe'ar] *vt* to border

bordillo [bor'ðiʎo] *nm* kerb (*Brit*), curb (*US*)

bordo ['borðo] *nm* (*Naut*) side; **a ~** on board

borla ['borla] *nf* (*gen*) tassel; (*de gorro*) pompon

borlote [bor'lote] *nm* (*Am*) row, uproar

borrachera [borra'tʃera] *nf* (*ebriedad*) drunkenness; (*orgía*) spree, binge

borracho, -a [bo'rratʃo, a] *adj* drunk ▷ *nm/f* (*que bebe mucho*) drunkard, drunk; (*temporalmente*) drunk, drunk man/woman ▷ *nm* (*Culin*) cake soaked in liqueur or spirit

borrador [borra'ðor] *nm* (*escritura*) first draft, rough sketch; (*cuaderno*) scribbling pad; (*goma*) rubber (*Brit*), eraser; (*Com*) daybook; (*para pizarra*) duster; **hacer un nuevo ~ de** (*Com*) to redraft

borrar [bo'rrar] *vt* to erase, rub out; (*tachar*) to delete; (*cinta*) to wipe out; (*Inform*: *archivo*) to delete, erase; (*Pol etc*: *eliminar*) to deal with

borrasca [bo'rraska] *nf* (*Meteorología*) storm

borrego, -a [bo'rreɣo, a] *nm/f* lamb; (*oveja*) sheep; (*fig*) simpleton ▷ *nm* (*Am*: *fam*) false rumour

borrico, -a [bo'rriko, a] *nm* donkey; (*fig*) stupid man ▷ *nf* she-donkey; (*fig*) stupid woman

borrón [bo'rron] *nm* (*mancha*) stain; **~ y cuenta nueva** let bygones be bygones

borroso, -a [bo'rroso, a] *adj* vague, unclear; (*escritura*) illegible; (*escrito*) smudgy; (*Foto*) blurred

Bosnia ['bosnja] *nf* Bosnia

bosnio, -a ['bosnjo, a] *adj, nm/f* Bosnian

bosque ['boske] *nm* wood; (*grande*) forest

bosquejar [boske'xar] *vt* to sketch

bosquejo [bos'kexo] *nm* sketch

bostezar [boste'θar] *vi* to yawn

bostezo [bos'teθo] *nm* yawn

bota ['bota] *nf* (*calzado*) boot; (*de vino*) leather wine bottle; **~s de agua** o **goma** Wellingtons; **ponerse las ~s** (*fam*) to strike it rich

botánico, -a [bo'taniko, a] *adj* botanical ▷ *nm/f* botanist ▷ *nf* botany

botar [bo'tar] *vt* to throw, hurl; (*Naut*) to launch; (*esp Am fam*) to throw out ▷ *vi* to bounce

bote ['bote] *nm* (*salto*) bounce; (*golpe*) thrust; (*vasija*) tin, can; (*embarcación*) boat; (*Am*: *pey*: *cárcel*) jail; **de ~ en ~** packed, jammed full; **~ salvavidas** lifeboat; **dar un ~** to jump; **dar ~s** (*Auto etc*) to bump; **~ de la basura** (*Am*) dustbin (*Brit*), trash can (*US*)

botella [bo'teʎa] *nf* bottle; **~ de vino** (*contenido*) bottle of wine; (*recipiente*) wine bottle

botellín [bote'ʎin] *nm* small bottle

botellón [bote'ʎon] *nm* (*Esp*: *fam*) outdoor drinking session (*involving groups of young people*)

botica [bo'tika] *nf* chemist's (shop) (*Brit*), pharmacy

boticario, -a [boti'karjo, a] *nm/f* chemist (*Brit*), pharmacist

botijo [bo'tixo] *nm* (earthenware) jug; (*tren*) excursion train

botín [bo'tin] *nm* (*calzado*) half boot; (*polaina*) spat; (*Mil*) booty; (*de ladrón*) loot

botiquín [boti'kin] *nm* (*armario*) medicine chest; (*portátil*) first-aid kit

botón [bo'ton] *nm* button; (*Bot*) bud; (*de florete*) tip; **~ de arranque** (*Auto etc*) starter; **~ de oro** buttercup; **pulsar el ~** to press the button

botones [bo'tones] *nm inv* bellboy, bellhop (*US*)

bóveda [bo'βeða] *nf* (*Arq*) vault

boxeador [boksea'ðor] *nm* boxer

boxear [bokse'ar] *vi* to box

boxeo [bok'seo] *nm* boxing

boya ['boja] *nf* (*Naut*) buoy; (*flotador*) float

boyante [bo'jante] *adj* (*Naut*) buoyant; (*feliz*) buoyant; (*próspero*) prosperous

bozal [bo'θal] *nm* (*de caballo*) halter; (*de perro*) muzzle

bracear [braθe'ar] *vi* (*agitar los brazos*) to wave one's arms

bracero [bra'θero] *nm* labourer; (*en el campo*) farmhand

braga ['braɣa] *nf* (*cuerda*) sling, rope; (*de bebé*) nappy, diaper (*US*); **bragas** *nfpl* (*de mujer*) panties

bragueta [bra'ɣeta] *nf* fly (*Brit*), flies *pl* (*Brit*), zipper (*US*)

braille [breil] *nm* braille

bramar [bra'mar] *vi* to bellow, roar

bramido [bra'miðo] *nm* bellow, roar

brasa ['brasa] *nf* live o hot coal; **carne a la ~** grilled meat; **dar la ~** (*col*: *dar la lata, molestar*) to be a pain (*col*); **dar la ~ a algn** to go on at sb (*col*); **¡deja de darme la ~!** stop going on at me! (*col*)

brasero [bra'sero] *nm* brazier; (*Am*: *chimenea*) fireplace

brasier [bra'sjer] *nm* (*Am*) bra

Brasil [bra'sil] *nm*: **(el) ~** Brazil

brasileño, -a [brasi'leɲo, a] *adj, nm/f* Brazilian

brassier [bra'sjer] *nm* (*Am*) *ver* **brasier**

bravata [bra'βata] *nf* boast

braveza [bra'βeθa] *nf* (*valor*) bravery; (*ferocidad*) ferocity

bravío, -a [bra'βio, a] *adj* wild; (*feroz*) fierce

bravo, -a ['braβo, a] *adj* (*valiente*) brave; (*bueno*) fine, splendid; (*feroz*) ferocious; (*salvaje*) wild; (*mar etc*) rough, stormy; (*Culin*) hot, spicy ▷ *excl* bravo!

bravura [bra'βura] *nf* bravery; ferocity; (*pey*) boast

braza ['braθa] *nf* fathom; **nadar a la ~** to swim (the) breast-stroke

brazada [bra'θaða] *nf* stroke

brazalete [braθa'lete] *nm* (*pulsera*) bracelet; (*banda*) armband

brazo ['braθo] *nm* arm; (*Zool*) foreleg; (*Bot*) limb, branch; **brazos** *nmpl* (*braceros*) hands, workers; **~ derecho** (*fig*) right-hand man; **a ~ partido** hand-to-hand; **cogidos** *etc* **del ~** arm in arm; **no dar su ~ a torcer** not to give way easily; **huelga de ~s caídos** sit-down strike

brea ['brea] *nf* pitch, tar

brebaje [bre'βaxe] *nm* potion

brecha ['bretʃa] *nf* (*hoyo, vacío*) gap, opening; (*Mil, fig*) breach

brega ['breɣa] *nf* (*lucha*) struggle; (*trabajo*) hard work

breva ['breβa] *nf* (*Bot*) early fig; (*puro*) flat cigar; **¡no caerá esa ~!** no such luck!

breve ['breβe] *adj* short, brief; **en ~** (*pronto*) shortly; (*en pocas palabras*) in short ▷ *nf* (*Mus*) breve

brevedad [breβe'ðað] *nf* brevity, shortness; **con** *o* **a la mayor ~** as soon as possible

brezal [bre'θal] *nm* moor(land), heath

brezo ['breθo] *nm* heather

bribón, -ona [bri'βon, ona] *adj* idle, lazy ▷ *nm/f* (*vagabundo*) vagabond; (*pícaro*) rascal, rogue

bricolaje [briko'laxe] *nm* do-it-yourself, DIY

brida ['briða] *nf* bridle, rein; (*Tec*) clamp; **a toda ~** at top speed

bridge [britʃ] *nm* (*Naipes*) bridge

brigada [bri'ɣaða] *nf* (*unidad*) brigade; (*trabajadores*) squad, gang ▷ *nm* ≈ sergeant major

brillante [bri'ʎante] *adj* brilliant; (*color*) bright; (*joya*) sparkling ▷ *nm* diamond

brillar [bri'ʎar] *vi* (*tb fig*) to shine; (*joyas*) to sparkle; **~ por su ausencia** to be conspicuous by one's absence

brillo ['briʎo] *nm* shine; (*brillantez*) brilliance; (*fig*) splendour; **sacar ~ a** to polish

brincar [brin'kar] *vi* to skip about, hop about, jump about; **está que brinca** he's hopping mad

brinco ['brinko] *nm* jump, leap; **a ~s** by fits and starts; **de un ~** at one bound

brindar [brin'dar] *vi*: **~ a** *o* **por** to drink (a toast) to ▷ *vt* to offer, present; **le brinda la ocasión de** it offers *o* affords him the opportunity to; **brindarse** *vr*: **~se a hacer algo** to offer to do sth

brindis ['brindis] *nm inv* toast; (*Taur*) (ceremony of) dedication

brío ['brio] *nm* spirit, dash

brioso, -a [bri'oso, a] *adj* spirited, dashing

brisa ['brisa] *nf* breeze

británico, -a [bri'taniko, a] *adj* British ▷ *nm/f* Briton, British person; **los ~s** the British

brizna ['briθna] *nf* (*hebra*) strand, thread; (*de hierba*) blade; (*de tabaco*) leaf; (*trozo*) piece

broca ['broka] *nf* (*Costura*) bobbin; (*Tec*) drill bit; (*clavo*) tack

brocal [bro'kal] *nm* rim

brocha ['brotʃa] *nf* (*large*) paintbrush; **~ de afeitar** shaving brush; **pintor de ~ gorda** painter and decorator; (*fig*) poor painter

broche ['brotʃe] *nm* brooch

broma ['broma] *nf* joke; (*inocentada*) practical joke; **en ~** in fun, as a joke; **gastar una ~ a algn** to play a joke on sb; **tomar algo a ~** to take sth as a joke; **~ pesada** practical joke

bromear [brome'ar] *vi* to joke

bromista [bro'mista] *adj* fond of joking ▷ *nm/f* joker, wag

bronca ['bronka] *nf* row; (*regañada*) ticking-off; **armar una ~** to kick up a fuss; **echar una ~ a algn** to tell sb off

bronce ['bronθe] *nm* bronze; (*latón*) brass

bronceado, -a [bronθe'aðo, a] *adj* bronze *cpd*; (*por el sol*) tanned ▷ *nm* (*sun*)tan; (*Tec*) bronzing

bronceador [bronθea'ðor] *nm* suntan lotion

broncearse [bronθe'arse] *vr* to get a suntan

bronco, -a ['bronko, a] *adj* (*manera*) rude, surly; (*voz*) harsh

bronquios ['bronkjos] *nmpl* bronchial tubes

bronquitis ['bron'kitis] *nf inv* bronchitis

brotar [bro'tar] *vt* (*tierra*) to produce ▷ *vi* (*Bot*) to sprout; (*aguas*) to gush (forth); (*lágrimas*) to well up; (*Med*) to break out

brote ['brote] *nm* (*Bot*) shoot; (*Med, fig*) outbreak

bruces ['bruθes]: **de ~** *adv*: **caer** *o* **dar de ~** to fall headlong, fall flat

bruja ['bruxa] *nf* witch

brujería [bruxe'ria] *nf* witchcraft

brujo ['bruxo] *nm* wizard, magician

brújula ['bruxula] *nf* compass

bruma ['bruma] *nf* mist

brumoso, -a [bru'moso, a] *adj* misty

bruñido [bru'ɲiðo] *nm* polish

bruñir [bru'ɲir] *vt* to polish

brusco, -a ['brusko, a] *adj* (*súbito*) sudden; (*áspero*) brusque

Bruselas [bru'selas] *nf* Brussels

brutal [bru'tal] *adj* brutal

brutalidad [brutali'ðað] *nf* brutality

bruto, -a ['bruto, a] *adj* (*idiota*) stupid; (*bestial*) brutish; (*peso*) gross ▷ *nm* brute; **a la bruta**, **a lo ~** roughly; **en ~** raw, unworked

Bs.As. *abr* = **Buenos Aires**

bucal [bu'kal] *adj* oral; **por vía ~** orally

bucear [buθe'ar] *vi* to dive ▷ *vt* to explore

buceo [bu'θeo] *nm* diving; (*fig*) investigation

bucle ['bukle] *nm* curl; (*Inform*) loop

budismo [bu'ðismo] *nm* Buddhism

budista [bu'ðista] *adj, nm/f* Buddhist

buen [bwen] *adj ver* **bueno**

buenamente [bwena'mente] *adv* (*fácilmente*) easily; (*voluntariamente*) willingly

buenaventura [bwenaβen'tura] *nf* (*suerte*) good luck; (*adivinación*) fortune; **decir** *o* **echar la ~ a algn** to tell sb's fortune

buenmozo [bwen'moθo] *adj* (*Am*) handsome

⭕ **PALABRA CLAVE**

bueno, -a ['bweno, a] (*antes de nmsg* **buen**) *adj*
1 (*excelente etc*) good; (*Med*) well; **es un libro bueno, es un buen libro** it's a good book; **hace bueno, hace buen tiempo** the weather is fine, it is fine; **es buena persona** he's a good sort; **el bueno de Paco** good old Paco; **fue muy bueno conmigo** he was very nice o kind to me; **ya está bueno** he's fine now
2 (*apropiado*) **ser bueno para** to be good for; **creo que vamos por buen camino** I think we're on the right track
3 (*irónico*) **le di un buen rapapolvo** I gave him a good o real ticking off; **¡buen conductor estás hecho!** some driver o a fine driver you are!; **¡estaría bueno que ...!** a fine thing it would be if ...!
4 (*atractivo, sabroso*) **está bueno este bizcocho** this sponge is delicious; **Julio está muy bueno** (*fam*) Julio's gorgeous
5 (*saludos*) **¡buen día!** (*Am*), **¡buenos días!** (good) morning!; **¡buenas (tardes)!** good afternoon!; (*más tarde*) good evening!; **¡buenas noches!** good night!
6 (*otras locuciones*) **estar de buenas** to be in a good mood; **por las buenas o por las malas** by hook or by crook; **de buenas a primeras** all of a sudden
7 (*grande*) good, big; **un buen número de ...** a good number of ...; **un buen trozo de ...** a nice big piece of ...
▷ *excl:* **¡bueno!** all right!; **bueno, ¿y qué?** well, so what?; **bueno, lo que pasa es que ...** well, the thing is ...; **pero ¡bueno!** well, I like that!; **bueno, pues ...** right, (then) ...

Buenos Aires [bweno'saires] *nm* Buenos Aires
buey [bwei] *nm* ox
búfalo ['bufalo] *nm* buffalo
bufanda [bu'fanda] *nf* scarf
bufar [bu'far] *vi* to snort
bufete [bu'fete] *nm* (*despacho de abogado*) lawyer's office; **establecer su ~** to set up in legal practice
buffer ['bufer] *nm* (*Inform*) buffer
bufón [bu'fon] *nm* clown
buhardilla [buar'ðiʎa] *nf* attic
búho ['buo] *nm* owl; (*fig*) hermit, recluse
buhonero [buo'nero] *nm* pedlar
buitre ['bwitre] *nm* vulture
bujía [bu'xia] *nf* (*vela*) candle; (*Elec*) candle (power); (*Auto*) spark plug
bula ['bula] *nf* (*papal*) bull
bulbo ['bulβo] *nm* (*Bot*) bulb
bulevar [bule'βar] *nm* boulevard
Bulgaria [bul'ɣarja] *nf* Bulgaria

búlgaro, -a ['bulɣaro, a] *adj, nm/f* Bulgarian
bulimia [bu'limja] *nf* bulimia
bulla ['buʎa] *nf* (*ruido*) uproar; (*de gente*) crowd; **armar** o **meter ~** to kick up a row
bullicio [bu'ʎiθjo] *nm* (*ruido*) uproar; (*movimiento*) bustle
bullir [bu'ʎir] *vi* (*hervir*) to boil; (*burbujear*) to bubble; (*moverse*) to move, stir; (*insectos*) to swarm; **~ de** (*fig*) to teem o seethe with
bulto ['bulto] *nm* (*paquete*) package; (*fardo*) bundle; (*tamaño*) size, bulkiness; (*Med*) swelling, lump; (*silueta*) vague shape; (*estatua*) bust, statue; **hacer ~** to take up space; **escurrir el ~** to make o.s. scarce; (*fig*) to dodge the issue
buñuelo [bu'ɲwelo] *nm* ≈ doughnut, ≈ donut (US); (*fruta de sartén*) fritter
buque ['buke] *nm* ship, vessel; **~ de guerra** warship; **~ mercante** merchant ship; **~ de vela** sailing ship
burbuja [bur'βuxa] *nf* bubble; **hacer ~s** to bubble; (*gaseosa*) to fizz
burbujear [burβuxe'ar] *vi* to bubble
burdel [bur'ðel] *nm* brothel
burdo, -a ['burðo, a] *adj* coarse, rough
burgués, -esa [bur'ɣes, esa] *adj* middle-class, bourgeois; **pequeño ~** lower middle-class; (*Pol, pey*) petty bourgeois
burguesía [burɣe'sia] *nf* middle class, bourgeoisie
burla ['burla] *nf* (*mofa*) gibe; (*broma*) joke; (*engaño*) trick; **hacer ~ de** to make fun of
burladero [burla'ðero] *nm* (bullfighter's) refuge
burlador, a [burla'ðor, a] *adj* mocking ▷ *nm/f* mocker; (*bromista*) joker ▷ *nm* (*libertino*) seducer
burlar [bur'lar] *vt* (*engañar*) to deceive; (*seducir*) to seduce ▷ *vi* to joke; **burlarse** *vr* to joke; **~se de** to make fun of
burlesco, -a [bur'lesko, a] *adj* burlesque
burlón, -ona [bur'lon, ona] *adj* mocking
buró [bu'ro] *nm* bureau
burocracia [buro'kraθja] *nf* bureaucracy
burócrata [bu'rokrata] *nm/f* bureaucrat
buromática [buro'matika] *nf* office automation
burrada [bu'rraða] *nf* stupid act; **decir ~s** to talk nonsense; **hacer ~s** to act stupid; **una ~** (*Esp: mucho*) a (hell of a) lot
burro, -a ['burro, a] *nm/f* (*Zool*) donkey; (*fig*) ass, idiot ▷ *adj* stupid; **caerse del ~** to realise one's mistake; **no ver tres en un ~** to be as blind as a bat
bursátil [bur'satil] *adj* stock-exchange *cpd*
bus [bus] *nm* bus
busca ['buska] *nf* search, hunt ▷ *nm* bleeper, pager; **en ~ de** in search of
buscador, a [buska'ðor, a] *nm/f* searcher ▷ *nm* (*Internet*) search engine
buscar [bus'kar] *vt* to look for; (*objeto perdido*) to have a look for; (*beneficio*) to seek; (*enemigo*)

to seek out; (*traer*) to bring, fetch; (*provocar*) to provoke; (*Inform*) to search ▷ *vi* to look, search, seek; **ven a ~me a la oficina** come and pick me up at the office; **~le 3 o 4 pies al gato** to split hairs; **"~ y reemplazar"** (*Inform*) "search and replace"; **se busca secretaria** secretary wanted; **se la buscó** he asked for it

buscona [bus'kona] *nf* whore

busque *etc* ['buske] *vb ver* **buscar**

búsqueda ['buskeða] *nf* = **busca**

busto ['busto] *nm* (*Anat, Arte*) bust

butaca [bu'taka] *nf* armchair; (*de cine, teatro*) stall, seat

butano [bu'tano] *nm* butane (gas); **bombona de ~** gas cylinder

buzo ['buθo] *nm* diver; (*Am: chandal*) tracksuit

buzón [bu'θon] *nm* (*gen*) letter box; (*en la calle*) pillar box (*Brit*); (*Telec*) mailbox; **echar al ~** to post

buzonear [buθone'ar] *vt* to leaflet

C. *abr* (= *centígrado*) C.; (= *compañía*) Co

c. *abr* (= *capítulo*) ch

C/ *abr* (= *calle*) St, Rd

c.a. *abr* (= *corriente alterna*) A.C.

cabal [ka'βal] *adj* (*exacto*) exact; (*correcto*) right, proper; (*acabado*) finished, complete; **cabales** *nmpl*: **estar en sus ~es** to be in one's right mind

cábala ['kaβala] *nf* (*Rel*) cab(b)ala; (*fig*) cabal, intrigue; **cábalas** *nfpl* guess *sg*, supposition *sg*; **hacer ~s** to guess

cabalgadura [kaβalɣa'ðura] *nf* mount, horse

cabalgar [kaβal'ɣar] *vt, vi* to ride

cabalgata [kaβal'ɣata] *nf* procession; *ver tb* **Reyes Magos**

caballa [ka'βaʎa] *nf* mackerel

caballeresco, -a [kaβaʎe'resko, a] *adj* noble, chivalrous

caballería [kaβaʎe'ria] *nf* mount; (*Mil*) cavalry

caballeriza [kaβaʎe'riθa] *nf* stable

caballerizo [kaβaʎe'riθo] *nm* groom, stableman

caballero [kaβa'ʎero] *nm* gentleman; (*de la orden de caballería*) knight; (*trato directo*) sir; **"C~s"** "Gents"

caballerosidad [kaβaʎerosi'ðað] *nf* chivalry

caballete [kaβa'ʎete] *nm* (*Agr*) ridge; (*Arte*) easel; (*Tec*) trestle

caballito [kaβa'ʎito] *nm* (*caballo pequeño*) small horse, pony; (*juguete*) rocking horse;

caballitos *nmpl* merry-go-round *sg*; ~ **de mar** seahorse; ~ **del diablo** dragonfly

caballo [ka'βaʎo] *nm* horse; (*Ajedrez*) knight; (*Naipes*) ≈ queen; **ir en** ~ to ride; ~ **de carreras** racehorse; ~ **de vapor** *o* **de fuerza** horsepower; **es su** ~ **de batalla** it's his hobby-horse; ~ **blanco** (*Com*) backer; *ver tb* **Baraja Española**

cabaña [ka'βaɲa] *nf* (*casita*) hut, cabin

cabaré, cabaret (*pl* **cabarets**) [kaβa're, kaβa'res] *nm* cabaret

cabecear [kaβeθe'ar] *vt, vi* to nod

cabecera [kaβe'θera] *nf* (*gen*) head; (*de distrito*) chief town; (*de cama*) headboard; (*Imprenta*) headline

cabecilla [kaβe'θiʎa] *nm* ringleader

cabellera [kaβe'ʎera] *nf* (head of) hair; (*de cometa*) tail

cabello [ka'βeʎo] *nm* (*tb*: ~**s**) hair *sg*; ~ **de ángel** confectionery and pastry filling made of pumpkin and syrup

cabelludo [kaβe'ʎuðo] *adj ver* **cuero**

caber [ka'βer] *vi* (*entrar*) to fit, go; **caben tres más** there's room for three more; **cabe preguntar si...** one might ask whether...; **cabe que venga más tarde** he may come later

cabestrillo [kaβes'triʎo] *nm* sling

cabestro [ka'βestro] *nm* halter

cabeza [ka'βeθa] *nf* head; (*Pol*) chief, leader; ~ **de ajo** bulb of garlic; ~ **de familia** head of the household; ~ **rapada** skinhead; **caer de** ~ to fall head first; **sentar la** ~ to settle down; ~ **de lectura/escritura** read/write head; ~ **impresora** *o* **de impresión** printhead

cabezada [kaβe'θaða] *nf* (*golpe*) butt; **dar una** ~ to nod off

cabezazo [kaβe'θaθo] *nm* (*golpe*) headbutt; (*Fútbol*) header

cabezón, -ona [kaβe'θon, ona] *adj* with a big head; (*vino*) heady; (*obstinado*) pig-headed

cabezota [kaβe'θota] *adj inv* obstinate, stubborn

cabida [ka'βiða] *nf* space; **dar ~ a** to make room for; **tener ~ para** to have room for

cabildo [ka'βildo] *nm* (*de iglesia*) chapter; (*Pol*) town council

cabina [ka'βina] *nf* cabin; (*de avión*) cockpit; (*de camión*) cab; ~ **telefónica** (tele)phone box (*Brit*) *o* booth

cabizbajo, -a [kaβiθ'βaxo, a] *adj* crestfallen, dejected

cable ['kaβle] *nm* cable; (*de aparato*) lead; ~ **aéreo** (*Elec*) overhead cable; **conectar con** ~ (*Inform*) to hardwire

cabo ['kaβo] *nm* (*de objeto*) end, extremity; (*Mil*) corporal; (*Naut*) rope, cable; (*Geo*) cape; (*Tec*) thread; **al ~ de tres días** after three days; **de ~ a rabo** *o* ~ from beginning to end; (*libro: leer*) from cover to cover; **llevar a ~ to** carry out; **atar ~s** to tie up the loose ends;

C~ **de Buena Esperanza** Cape of Good Hope; C~ **de Hornos** Cape Horn; **las Islas de C~ Verde** the Cape Verde Islands

cabra ['kaβra] *nf* goat; **estar como una ~** (*fam*) to be nuts

cabré *etc* [ka'βre] *vb ver* **caber**

cabrear [kaβre'ar] *vt* to annoy; **cabrearse** *vr* (*enfadarse*) to fly off the handle

cabrío, -a [ka'βrio, a] *adj* goatish; **macho ~** (he-)goat, billy goat

cabriola [ka'βrjola] *nf* caper

cabritilla [kaβri'tiʎa] *nf* kid, kidskin

cabrito [ka'βrito] *nm* kid

cabrón [ka'βron] *nm* cuckold; (*fam!*) bastard (!)

cabronada [kaβro'naða] *nf* (*fam!*): **hacer una ~ a algn** to be a bastard to sb

caca ['kaka] *nf* (*palabra de niños*) pooh ▷ *excl*: **no toques, ¡~!** don't touch, it's dirty!

cacahuete [kaka'wete] *nm* (*Esp*) peanut

cacao [ka'kao] *nm* cocoa; (*Bot*) cacao

cacarear [kakare'ar] *vi* (*persona*) to boast; (*gallina*) to cluck; (*gallo*) to crow

cacarizo, -a [kaka'riθo, a] *adj* (*Am*) pockmarked

cacería [kaθe'ria] *nf* hunt

cacerola [kaθe'rola] *nf* pan, saucepan

cachalote [katʃa'lote] *nm* sperm whale

cacharro [ka'tʃarro] *nm* (*cazo*) pot; (*cerámica*) piece of pottery; (*fam*) useless object; **cacharros** *nmpl* pots and pans

cachear [katʃe'ar] *vt* to search, frisk

cachemir [katʃe'mir] *nm* cashmere

cacheo [ka'tʃeo] *nm* searching, frisking

cachetada [katʃe'taða] *nf* (*Am: fam: bofetada*) slap

cachete [ka'tʃete] *nm* (*Anat*) cheek; (*bofetada*) slap (in the face)

cachimba [ka'tʃimba] *nf*, **cachimbo** [ka'tʃimbo] *nm* (*Am*) pipe

cachiporra [katʃi'porra] *nf* truncheon

cachivache [katʃi'βatʃe] *nm* piece of junk; **cachivaches** *nmpl* trash *sg*, junk *sg*

cacho ['katʃo] *nm* (small) bit; (*Am: cuerno*) horn

cachondearse [katʃonde'arse] *vr*: ~ **de algn** to tease sb

cachondeo [katʃon'deo] *nm* (*fam*) farce, joke; (*guasa*) laugh

cachondo, -a [ka'tʃondo, a] *adj* (*Zool*) on heat; (*caliente*) randy, sexy; (*gracioso*) funny

cachorro, -a [ka'tʃorro, a] *nm/f* (*de perro*) pup, puppy; (*de león*) cub

cachucha [ka'tʃutʃa] (*Méx: fam*) *nf* cap

cacique [ka'θike] *nm* chief, local ruler; (*Pol*) local party boss; (*fig*) despot

caco ['kako] *nm* pickpocket

cacto ['kakto] *nm*, **cactus** ['kaktus] *nm inv* cactus

cada ['kaða] *adj inv* each; (*antes de número*) every; ~ **día** each day, every day; ~ **dos días** every other day; ~ **uno/a** each one, every one; ~ **vez más/menos** more and more/less and less; **~ vez que** ... whenever, every time (that) ...; **uno de ~ diez** one out of every ten; **¿~ cuánto?** how often?

cadalso [ka'ðalso] nm scaffold

cadáver [ka'ðaβer] nm (dead) body, corpse

cadena [ka'ðena] nf chain; (TV) channel; **reacción en ~** chain reaction; **trabajo en ~** assembly line work; **~ midi/mini** (Mus) midi/mini system; **~ montañosa** mountain range; **~ perpetua** (Jur) life imprisonment; **~ de caracteres** (Inform) character string

cadencia [ka'ðenθja] nf cadence, rhythm

cadera [ka'ðera] nf hip

cadete [ka'ðete] nm cadet

caducar [kaðu'kar] vi to expire

caducidad [kaðuθi'ðað] nf: **fecha de ~** expiry date; (de comida) sell-by date

caduco, -a [ka'ðuko, a] adj (idea etc) outdated, outmoded; **de hoja caduca** deciduous

caer [ka'er] vi to fall; (premio) to go; (sitio) to be, lie; (pago) to fall due; **caerse** vr to fall (down); **dejar ~** to drop; **estar al ~** to be due to happen; (persona) to be about to arrive; **me cae bien/mal** I like/don't like him; **~ en la cuenta** to catch on; **su cumpleaños cae en viernes** her birthday falls on a Friday; **se me ha caído el guante** I've dropped my glove

café (pl **cafés**) [ka'fe, ka'fes] nm (bebida, planta) coffee; (lugar) café ▷ adj (color) brown; **~ con leche** white coffee; **~ solo, ~ negro** (Am) (small) black coffee

cafeína [kafe'ina] nf caffein(e)

cafetal [kafe'tal] nm coffee plantation

cafetera [kafe'tera] nf ver **cafetero**

cafetería [kafete'ria] nf cafe

cafetero, -a [kafe'tero, a] adj coffee cpd ▷ nf coffee pot; **ser muy ~** to be a coffee addict

cagalera [kaɣa'lera] nf (fam!): **tener ~** to have the runs

cagar [ka'ɣar] (fam!) vt to shit (!); (fig) to bungle, mess up ▷ vi to have a shit (!); **cagarse** vr: **¡me cago en diez** etc! Christ! (!)

caído, -a [ka'iðo, a] adj fallen; (Inform) down ▷ nf fall; (declive) slope; (disminución) fall, drop; **~ del cielo** out of the blue; **a la caída del sol** at sunset; **sufrir una caída** to have a fall

caiga etc ['kaiɣa] vb ver **caer**

caimán [kai'man] nm alligator

caja ['kaxa] nf box; (ataúd) coffin, casket (US); (para reloj) case; (de ascensor) shaft; (Com) cash box; (Econ) fund; (donde se hacen los pagos) cashdesk; (en supermercado) checkout, till; (Tip) case; (de parking) pay station; **~ de ahorros** savings bank; **~ de cambios** gearbox; **~ de fusibles** fuse box; **~ fuerte** o **de caudales** safe, strongbox; **ingresar en ~** to be paid in

cajero, -a [ka'xero, a] nm/f cashier; (en banco) (bank) teller ▷ nm: **~ automático** cash dispenser, automatic telling machine, ATM

cajetilla [kaxe'tiʎa] nf (de cigarrillos) packet

cajón [ka'xon] nm big box; (de mueble) drawer

cajuela [kax'wela] (Méx) nf (Auto) boot (Brit), trunk (US)

cal [kal] nf lime; **cerrar algo a ~ y canto** to shut sth firmly

cala [kala] nf (Geo) cove, inlet; (de barco) hold

calabacín [kalaβa'θin] nm (Bot) baby marrow; (: más pequeño) courgette (Brit), zucchini (US)

calabacita (Am) [kalaβa'θita] nf courgette (Brit), zucchini (US)

calabaza [kala'βaθa] nf (Bot) pumpkin; **dar ~s a** (candidato) to fail

calabozo [kala'βoθo] nm (cárcel) prison; (celda) cell

calado, -a [ka'laðo, a] adj (prenda) lace cpd ▷ nm (Tec) fretwork; (Naut) draught ▷ nf (de cigarrillo) puff; **estar ~ (hasta los huesos)** to be soaked (to the skin)

calamar [kala'mar] nm squid

calambre [ka'lambre] nm (Elec) shock; (tb: **~s**) cramp

calamidad [kalami'ðað] nf calamity, disaster; (persona) **es una ~** he's a dead loss

calamina [kala'mina] nf calamine

calaña [ka'laɲa] nf model, pattern; (fig) nature, stamp

calar [ka'lar] vt to soak, drench; (penetrar) to pierce, penetrate; (comprender) to see through; (vela, red) to lower; **calarse** vr (Auto) to stall; **~se las gafas** to stick one's glasses on

calavera [kala'βera] nf skull

calcañal [kalka'ɲal], **calcañar** [kalka'ɲar] nm heel

calcar [kal'kar] vt (reproducir) to trace; (imitar) to copy

calceta [kal'θeta] nf (knee-length) stocking; **hacer ~** to knit

calcetín [kalθe'tin] nm sock

calcinar [kalθi'nar] vt to burn, blacken

calcio ['kalθjo] nm calcium

calco ['kalko] nm tracing

calcomanía [kalkoma'nia] nf transfer

calculador, a [kalkula'ðor, a] adj calculating ▷ nf calculator

calcular [kalku'lar] vt (Mat) to calculate, compute; **~ que** ... to reckon that ...

cálculo ['kalkulo] nm calculation; (Med) (gall) stone; (Mat) calculus; **~ de costo** costing; **~ diferencial** differential calculus; **obrar con mucho ~** to act cautiously

caldear [kalde'ar] vt to warm (up), heat (up); (metales) to weld

caldera [kal'dera] nf boiler

calderilla [kalde'riʎa] nf (moneda) small change

caldero [kal'dero] nm small boiler

caldo ['kaldo] nm stock; (consomé) consommé; **~ de cultivo** (Bio) culture medium; **poner a ~ a algn** to tear sb off a strip; **los ~s jerezanos** sherries

caldoso, -a [kal'doso, a] adj (guisado) juicy; (sopa) thin

calefacción [kalefak'θjon] *nf* heating; **~ central** central heating

calefón [kale'fon] *nm* (RPl) boiler

caleidoscopio [kaleiðos'kopjo] *nm* kaleidoscope

calendario [kalen'darjo] *nm* calendar

calentador [kalenta'ðor] *nm* heater

calentamiento [kalenta'mjento] *nm* (Deporte) warm-up; **~ global** global warming

calentar [kalen'tar] *vt* to heat (up); (fam: excitar) to turn on; (Am: enfurecer) to anger; **calentarse** *vr* to heat up, warm up; (fig: discusión etc) to get heated

calentón, -ona [kalen'ton, ona] (RPl: fam) *adj* (sexualmente) horny, randy (Brit)

calentura [kalen'tura] *nf* (Med) fever, (high) temperature; (de boca) mouth sore

calenturiento, -a [kalentu'rjento, a] *adj* (mente) overactive

calesita [kale'sita] *nf* (Am) merry-go-round, carousel

calibrar [kali'βrar] *vt* to gauge, measure

calibre [ka'liβre] *nm* (de cañón) calibre, bore; (diámetro) diameter; (fig) calibre

calidad [kali'ðað] *nf* quality; **de ~** quality *cpd*; **~ de borrador** (Inform) draft quality; **~ de carta** o **de correspondencia** (Inform) letter quality; **~ texto** (Inform) text quality; **~ de vida** quality of life; **en ~ de** in the capacity of

cálido, -a ['kaliðo, a] *adj* hot; (fig) warm

caliente [ka'ljente] *vb ver* **calentar** ⊳ *adj* hot; (fig) fiery; (disputa) heated; (fam: cachondo) randy

califa [ka'lifa] *nm* caliph

calificación [kalifika'θjon] *nf* qualification; (de alumno) grade, mark; **~ de sobresaliente** first-class mark

calificado, -a [kalifi'kado, a] *adj* (Am: competente) qualified; (obrero) skilled

calificar [kalifi'kar] *vt* to qualify; (alumno) to grade, mark; **~ de** to describe as

caligrafía [kaliɣra'fia] *nf* calligraphy

calima [ka'lima] *nf* (cerca del mar) mist

cáliz ['kaliθ] *nm* (Bot) calyx; (Rel) chalice

caliza [ka'liθa] *nf* limestone

callado, -a [ka'ʎaðo, a] *adj* quiet, silent

callar [ka'ʎar] *vt* (asunto delicado) to keep quiet about, say nothing about; (omitir) to pass over in silence; (persona, oposición) to silence ⊳ *vi*, **callarse** *vr* to keep quiet, be silent; (dejar de hablar) to stop talking; **¡calla!** be quiet!; **¡cállate!, ¡cállese!** shut up!; **¡cállate la boca!** shut your mouth!

calle ['kaʎe] *nf* street; (Deporte) lane; **~ arriba/abajo** up/down the street; **~ de sentido único** one-way street; **~ mayor** (Esp) high (Brit) o main (US) street; **~ peatonal** pedestrianized o pedestrian street; **~ principal** (Am) high (Brit) o main (US) street; **poner a algn (de patitas) en la ~** to kick sb out

calleja [ka'ʎexa] *nf* alley, narrow street

callejear [kaʎexe'ar] *vi* to wander (about) the streets

callejero, -a [kaʎe'xero, a] *adj* street *cpd* ⊳ *nm* street map

callejón [kaʎe'xon] *nm* alley, passage; (Geo) narrow pass; **~ sin salida** cul-de-sac; (fig) blind alley

callejuela [kaʎe'xwela] *nf* side-street, alley

callista [ka'ʎista] *nm/f* chiropodist

callo ['kaʎo] *nm* callus; (en el pie) corn; **callos** *nmpl* (Culin) tripe *sg*

callosidad [kaʎosi'ðað] *nf* (de pie) corn; (de mano) callus

calloso, -a [ka'ʎoso, a] *adj* horny, rough

calma ['kalma] *nf* calm; (pachorra) slowness; (Com, Econ) calm, lull; **~ chicha** dead calm; **¡~!, ¡con ~!** take it easy!

calmante [kal'mante] *adj* soothing ⊳ *nm* sedative, tranquillizer

calmar [kal'mar] *vt* to calm, calm down; (dolor) to relieve ⊳ *vi*, **calmarse** *vr* (tempestad) to abate; (mente etc) to become calm

calmoso, -a [kal'moso, a] *adj* calm, quiet

calor [ka'lor] *nm* heat; (calor agradable) warmth; **entrar en ~** to get warm; **tener ~** to be o feel hot

caloría [kalo'ria] *nf* calorie

calorífero, -a [kalo'rifero, a] *adj* heat-producing, heat-giving ⊳ *nm* heating system

calumnia [ka'lumnja] *nf* slander; (por escrito) libel

calumnioso, -a [kalum'njoso, a] *adj* slanderous; libellous

caluroso, -a [kalu'roso, a] *adj* hot; (sin exceso) warm; (fig) enthusiastic

calva ['kalβa] *nf* bald patch; (en bosque) clearing

calvario [kal'βarjo] *nm* stations *pl* of the cross; (fig) cross, heavy burden

calvicie [kal'βiθje] *nf* baldness

calvo, -a ['kalβo, a] *adj* bald; (terreno) bare, barren; (tejido) threadbare ⊳ *nm* bald man

calza ['kalθa] *nf* wedge, chock

calzado, -a [kal'θaðo, a] *adj* shod ⊳ *nm* footwear ⊳ *nf* roadway, highway

calzador [kalθa'ðor] *nm* shoehorn

calzar [kal'θar] *vt* (zapatos etc) to wear; (un mueble) to put a wedge under; (Tec: rueda etc) to scotch; **calzarse** *vr*: **~se los zapatos** to put on one's shoes; **¿qué (número) calza?** what size do you take?

calzón [kal'θon] *nm* (tb: **calzones**) shorts *pl*; (Am: de hombre) pants *pl*; (: de mujer) panties *pl*

calzoncillos [kalθon'θiʎos] *nmpl* underpants

cama ['kama] *nf* bed; (Geo) stratum; **~ individual/de matrimonio** single/double bed; **hacer la ~** to make the bed; **guardar ~** to be ill in bed

camada [ka'maða] *nf* litter; (de personas) gang, band

camafeo [kama'feo] *nm* cameo

camaleón [kamale'on] *nm* chameleon

cámara ['kamara] *nf* (*Pol etc*) chamber; (*habitación*) room; (*sala*) hall; (*Cine*) cine camera; (*fotográfica*) camera; **~ de aire** inner tube; **~ alta/baja** upper/lower house; **a ~ lenta** in slow motion; **~ de comercio** chamber of commerce; **~ digital** digital camera; **~ de gas** gas chamber; **~ de vídeo** video camera; **a ~ lenta** in slow motion; **~ frigorífica** cold-storage room

camarada [kama'raða] *nm* comrade, companion

camarero, -a [kama'rero, a] *nm* waiter ▷ *nf* (*en restaurante*) waitress; (*en casa, hotel*) maid

camarilla [kama'riʎa] *nf* (*clan*) clique; (*Pol*) lobby

camarín [kama'rin] *nm* (*Teat*) dressing room

camarógrafo, -a [kama'rografo, a] *nm/f* (*Am*) cameraman/camerawoman

camarón [kama'ron] *nm* shrimp

camarote [kama'rote] *nm* (*Naut*) cabin

cambiable [kam'bjaβle] *adj* (*variable*) changeable, variable; (*intercambiable*) interchangeable

cambiante [kam'bjante] *adj* variable

cambiar [kam'bjar] *vt* to change; (*trocar*) to exchange ▷ *vi* to change; **cambiarse** *vr* (*mudarse*) to move; (*de ropa*) to change; **~ de idea** *u* **opinión** to change one's mind; **~se de ropa** to change (one's clothes)

cambiazo [kam'bjaθo] *nm*: **dar el ~ a algn** to swindle sb

cambio ['kambjo] *nm* change; (*trueque*) exchange; (*Com*) rate of exchange; (*oficina*) bureau de change; (*dinero menudo*) small change; **a ~ de** in return o exchange for; **en ~** on the other hand; (*en lugar de eso*) instead; **~ climático** climate change; **~ de divisas** (*Com*) foreign exchange; **~ de línea** (*Inform*) line feed; **~ de página** (*Inform*) form feed; **~ a término** (*Com*) forward exchange; **~ de velocidades** gear lever; **~ de vía** points *pl*

cambista [kam'bista] *nm* (*Com*) exchange broker

camelar [kame'lar] *vt* (*con mujer*) to flirt with; (*persuadir*) to sweet-talk

camelia [ka'melia] *nf* camellia

camello [ka'meʎo] *nm* camel; (*fam: traficante*) pusher

camelo [ka'melo] *nm*: **me huele a ~** it smells fishy

camerino [kame'rino] *nm* (*Teat*) dressing room

camilla [ka'miʎa] *nf* (*Med*) stretcher

caminante [kami'nante] *nm/f* traveller

caminar [kami'nar] *vi* (*marchar*) to walk, go; (*viajar*) to travel, journey ▷ *vt* (*recorrer*) to cover, travel

caminata [kami'nata] *nf* long walk; (*por el campo*) hike

camino [ka'mino] *nm* way, road; (*sendero*) track; **a medio ~** halfway (there); **en el ~** on the way, en route; **~ de** on the way to;

~ particular private road; **~ vecinal** country road; **C~s, Canales y Puertos** (*Univ*) Civil Engineering; **ir por buen ~** (*fig*) to be on the right track; **C~ de Santiago** Way of St James; *see note*

⬤ **CAMINO DE SANTIAGO**
⬤
⬤ The *Camino de Santiago* is a medieval
⬤ pilgrim route stretching from the
⬤ Pyrenees to Santiago de Compostela in
⬤ north-west Spain, where tradition has it
⬤ the body of the Apostle James is buried.
⬤ Nowadays it is a popular tourist route as
⬤ well as a religious one. The *concha*
⬤ (cockleshell) is a symbol of the *Camino de*
⬤ *Santiago*, because it is said that when St
⬤ James' body was found it was covered in
⬤ shells.

camión [ka'mjon] *nm* lorry, truck (*US*); (*Am: autobús*) bus; **~ cisterna** tanker; **~ de la basura** dustcart, refuse lorry; **~ de mudanzas** removal (*Brit*) o moving (*US*) van; **~ de bomberos** fire engine

camionero [kamjo'nero] *nm* lorry o truck (*US*) driver, trucker (*esp US*)

camioneta [kamjo'neta] *nf* van, small truck

camionista [kamjo'nista] *nm/f* (*Am*) lorry o truck driver

camisa [ka'misa] *nf* shirt; (*Bot*) skin; **~ de dormir** nightdress; **~ de fuerza** straitjacket

camiseta [kami'seta] *nf* tee-shirt; (*ropa interior*) vest; (*de deportista*) top

camisón [kami'son] *nm* nightdress, nightgown

camorra [ka'morra] *nf*: **armar ~** to kick up a row; **buscar ~** to look for trouble

camorrista [kamo'rrista] *nm/f* thug

camote [ka'mote] *nm* (*Am*) sweet potato; (*bulbo*) tuber, bulb; (*fam: enamoramiento*) crush

campal [kam'pal] *adj*: **batalla ~** pitched battle

campamento [kampa'mento] *nm* camp

campana [kam'pana] *nf* bell

campanada [kampa'naða] *nf* peal

campanario [kampa'narjo] *nm* belfry

campanilla [kampa'niʎa] *nf* (*campana*) small bell

campaña [kam'paɲa] *nf* (*Mil, Pol*) campaign; **hacer ~ (en pro de/contra)** to campaign (for/against); **~ de venta** sales campaign; **~ electoral** election campaign

campechano, -a [kampe'tʃano, a] *adj* (*franco*) open

campeón, -ona [kampe'on, ona] *nm/f* champion

campeonato [kampeo'nato] *nm* championship

cámper ['kamper] *nm o f* (*Am*) caravan (*Brit*), trailer (*US*)

campera [kam'pera] *nf* (*RPl*) anorak

campesino, -a [kampe'sino, a] *adj* country *cpd*, rural; *(gente)* peasant *cpd* ▷ *nm/f* countryman/woman; *(agricultor)* farmer

campestre [kam'pestre] *adj* country *cpd*, rural

camping ['kampin] *nm* camping; *(lugar)* campsite; **ir de** *o* **hacer ~** to go camping

campiña [kam'piɲa] *nf* countryside

campista [kam'pista] *nm/f* camper

campo ['kampo] *nm (fuera de la ciudad)* country, countryside; *(Agr, Elec, Inform)* field; *(de fútbol)* pitch; *(de golf)* course; *(Mil)* camp; **~ de batalla** battlefield; **~ de minas** minefield; **~ petrolífero** oilfield; **~ visual** field of vision; **~ de concentración/de internación/de trabajo** concentration/internment/labour camp; **~ de deportes** sports ground, playing field

camposanto [kampo'santo] *nm* cemetery

campus ['kampus] *nm inv (Univ)* campus

camuflaje [kamu'flaxe] *nm* camouflage

camuflar [kamu'flar] *vt* to camouflage

cana ['kana] *nf ver* **cano**

Canadá [kana'ða] *nm* Canada

canadiense [kana'ðjense] *adj, nm/f* Canadian ▷ *nf* fur-lined jacket

canal [ka'nal] *nm* canal; *(Geo)* channel, strait; *(de televisión)* channel; *(de tejado)* gutter; **C~ de la Mancha** English Channel; **C~ de Panamá** Panama Canal

canaleta [kana'leta] *nf (Am: de tejado)* gutter

canalizar [kanali'θar] *vt* to channel

canalla [ka'naʎa] *nf* rabble, mob ▷ *nm* swine

canalón [kana'lon] *nm (conducto vertical)* drainpipe; *(del tejado)* gutter; **canalones** *nmpl (Culin)* cannelloni

canapé *(pl* **canapés)** [kana'pe, kana'pes] *nm* sofa, settee; *(Culin)* canapé

Canarias [ka'narjas] *nfpl:* **las (Islas) ~** the Canaries, the Canary Isles

canario, -a [ka'narjo, a] *adj o* from the Canary Isles ▷ *nm/f* native *o* inhabitant of the Canary Isles ▷ *nm (Zool)* canary

canasta [ka'nasta] *nf (round)* basket

canastilla [kanas'tiʎa] *nf* small basket; *(de niño)* layette

canasto [ka'nasto] *nm* large basket

cancela [kan'θela] *nf* (wrought-iron) gate

cancelación [kanθela'θjon] *nf* cancellation

cancelar [kanθe'lar] *vt* to cancel; *(una deuda)* to write off

cáncer ['kanθer] *nm (Med)* cancer; **C~** *(Astro)* Cancer

cancerígeno, -a [kanθe'rixeno, a] *adj* carcinogenic

cancha ['kantʃa] *nf (de baloncesto, tenis etc)* court; *(Am: de fútbol etc)* pitch; **~ de tenis** *(Am)* tennis court

canciller [kanθi'ʎer] *nm* chancellor; **C~** *(Am)* Foreign Minister, ≈ Foreign Secretary *(Brit)*

canción [kan'θjon] *nf* song; **~ de cuna** lullaby

cancionero [kanθjo'nero] *nm* song book

candado [kan'daðo] *nm* padlock

candela [kan'dela] *nf* candle

candelero [kande'lero] *nm (para vela)* candlestick; *(de aceite)* oil lamp

candente [kan'dente] *adj* red-hot; *(tema)* burning

candidato, -a [kandi'ðato, a] *nm/f* candidate; *(para puesto)* applicant

candidez [kandi'ðeθ] *nf (sencillez)* simplicity; *(simpleza)* naiveté

cándido, -a ['kandiðo, a] *adj* simple; naive

candil [kan'dil] *nm* oil lamp

candilejas [kandi'lexas] *nfpl (Teat)* footlights

candor [kan'dor] *nm (sinceridad)* frankness; *(inocencia)* innocence

canela [ka'nela] *nf* cinnamon

canelones [kane'lones] *nmpl* cannelloni

cangrejo [kan'grexo] *nm* crab

canguro [kan'guro] *nm (Zool)* kangaroo; *(de niños)* baby-sitter; **hacer de ~** to baby-sit

caníbal [ka'niβal] *adj, nm/f* cannibal

canica [ka'nika] *nf* marble

canijo, -a [ka'nixo, a] *adj* frail, sickly

canilla [ka'niʎa] *nf (Tec)* bobbin; *(Am)* tap *(Brit)*, faucet *(US)*

canino, -a [ka'nino, a] *adj* canine ▷ *nm* canine (tooth)

canjear [kanxe'ar] *vt* to exchange; *(trocar)* to swap

cano, -a ['kano, a] *adj* grey-haired, white-haired ▷ *nf (tb:* **canas)** white *o* grey hair; **tener canas** to be going grey

canoa [ka'noa] *nf* canoe

canon ['kanon] *nm* canon; *(pensión)* rent; *(Com)* tax

canónico, -a [ka'noniko, a] *adj:* **derecho ~** canon law

canónigo [ka'noniɣo] *nm* canon

canonizar [kanoni'θar] *vt* to canonize

canoso, -a [ka'noso, a] *adj (pelo)* grey *(Brit)*, gray *(US)*; *(persona)* grey-haired

cansado, -a [kan'saðo, a] *adj* tired, weary; *(tedioso)* tedious, boring; **estoy ~ de hacerlo** I'm sick of doing it

cansancio [kan'sanθjo] *nm* tiredness, fatigue

cansar [kan'sar] *vt (fatigar)* to tire, tire out; *(aburrir)* to bore; *(fastidiar)* to bother; **cansarse** *vr* to tire, get tired; *(aburrirse)* to get bored

cantábrico, -a [kan'taβriko, a] *adj* Cantabrian; **Mar C~** Bay of Biscay; **(Montes) C~s, Cordillera Cantábrica** Cantabrian Mountains

cantante [kan'tante] *adj* singing ▷ *nm/f* singer

cantar [kan'tar] *vt* to sing ▷ *vi* to sing; *(insecto)* to chirp; *(rechinar)* to squeak; *(fam: criminal)* to squeal ▷ *nm (acción)* singing; *(canción)* song; *(poema)* poem; **~ a algn las cuarenta** to tell sb a few home truths; **~ a dos voces** to sing a duet

cántara ['kantara] *nf* large pitcher

cántaro ['kantaro] *nm* pitcher, jug; **llover a ~s** to rain cats and dogs

cantautor, a [kantau'tor, a] *nm/f* singer-songwriter

cante ['kante] *nm* Andalusian folk song; **~ jondo** flamenco singing

cantera [kan'tera] *nf* quarry

cantero [kan'tero] *nm* (*Am: arriate*) border

cantidad [kanti'ðað] *nf* quantity, amount; (*Econ*) sum ▷ *adv* (*fam*) a lot; **~ alzada** lump sum; **~ de** lots of

cantilena [kanti'lena] *nf* = **cantinela**

cantimplora [kantim'plora] *nf* water bottle, canteen

cantina [kan'tina] *nf* canteen; (*de estación*) buffet; (*esp Am*) bar

cantinela [kanti'nela] *nf* ballad, song

cantinero, -a [kanti'nero, a] *nm/f* (*Am*) barman/barmaid, bartender (*US*)

canto ['kanto] *nm* singing; (*canción*) song; (*borde*) edge, rim; (*de un cuchillo*) back; **~ rodado** boulder

cantor, a [kan'tor, a] *nm/f* singer

canturrear [kanturre'ar] *vi* to sing softly

canutas [ka'nutas] *nfpl*: **pasarlas ~** (*fam*) to have a rough time (of it)

canuto [ka'nuto] *nm* (*tubo*) small tube; (*fam: porro*) joint

caña ['kaɲa] *nf* (*Bot: tallo*) stem, stalk; (*carrizo*) reed; (*vaso*) tumbler; (*de cerveza*) glass of beer; (*Anat*) shinbone; (*Am: aguardiente*) cane liquor; **~ de azúcar** sugar cane; **~ de pescar** fishing rod

cañada [ka'ɲaða] *nf* (*entre dos montañas*) gully, ravine; (*camino*) cattle track

cáñamo [ka'ɲamo] *nm* (*Bot*) hemp

cañería [kaɲe'ria] *nf* piping; (*tubo*) pipe

caño ['kaɲo] *nm* (*tubo*) tube, pipe; (*de aguas servidas*) sewer; (*Mus*) pipe; (*Naut*) navigation channel; (*de fuente*) jet

cañón [ka'ɲon] *nm* (*Mil*) cannon; (*de fusil*) barrel; (*Geo*) canyon, gorge

cañonera [kaɲo'nera] *nf* (*tb:* **lancha ~**) gunboat

caoba [ka'oβa] *nf* mahogany

caos ['kaos] *nm* chaos

caótico, -a [ka'otiko, a] *adj* chaotic

cap. *abr* (= *capítulo*) ch.

capa ['kapa] *nf* cloak, cape; (*Culin*) coating; (*Geo*) layer, stratum; (*de pintura*) coat; **de ~ y espada** cloak-and-dagger; **so ~ de** under the pretext of; **~ de ozono** ozone layer; **~s sociales** social groups

capacidad [kapaθi'ðað] *nf* (*medida*) capacity; (*aptitud*) capacity, ability; **una sala con ~ para 900** a hall seating 900; **~ adquisitiva** purchasing power

capacitación [kapaθita'θjon] *nf* training

capacitar [kapaθi'tar] *vt*: **~ a algn para algo** to qualify sb for sth; (*Tec*) to train sb for sth; **capacitarse** *vr*: **~se para algo** to qualify for sth

capar [ka'par] *vt* to castrate, geld

caparazón [kapara'θon] *nm* (*Zool*) shell

capataz [kapa'taθ] *nm* foreman, charge hand

capaz [ka'paθ] *adj* able, capable; (*amplio*) capacious, roomy; **es ~ que venga mañana** (*Am*) he'll probably come tomorrow

capcioso, -a [kap'θjoso, a] *adj* wily, deceitful; **pregunta capciosa** trick question

capea [ka'pea] *nf* (*Taur*) bullfight with young bulls

capear [kape'ar] *vt* (*dificultades*) to dodge; **~ el temporal** to weather the storm

capellán [kape'ʎan] *nm* chaplain; (*sacerdote*) priest

caperuza [kape'ruθa] *nf* hood; (*de bolígrafo*) cap

capicúa [kapi'kua] *adj inv* (*número, fecha*) reversible ▷ *nf* reversible number, e.g. 1441

capilar [kapi'lar] *adj* hair *cpd*

capilla [ka'piʎa] *nf* chapel

capital [kapi'tal] *adj* capital ▷ *nm* (*Com*) capital ▷ *nf* (*de nación*) capital (city); (*tb:* **~ de provincia**) provincial capital, ≈ county town; **~ activo/en acciones** working/share o equity capital; **~ arriesgado** venture capital; **~ autorizado** o **social** authorised capital; **~ emitido** issued capital; **~ improductivo** idle money; **~ invertido** o **utilizado** capital employed; **~ pagado** paid-up capital; **~ de riesgo** risk capital; **~ social** equity o share capital; **inversión de ~es** capital investment; *ver tb* **provincia**

capitalismo [kapita'lismo] *nm* capitalism

capitalista [kapita'lista] *adj, nm/f* capitalist

capitalizar [kapitali'θar] *vt* to capitalize

capitán [kapi'tan] *nm* captain; (*fig*) leader

capitanear [kapitane'ar] *vt* to captain

capitolio [kapi'toljo] *nm* capitol

capitulación [kapitula'θjon] *nf* (*rendición*) capitulation, surrender; (*acuerdo*) agreement, pact; **capitulaciones matrimoniales** marriage contract *sg*

capitular [kapitu'lar] *vi* to come to terms, make an agreement; (*Mil*) to surrender

capítulo [ka'pitulo] *nm* chapter

capó [ka'po] *nm* drugs baron

capó [ka'po] *nm* (*Auto*) bonnet (*Brit*), hood (*US*)

capón [ka'pon] *nm* (*gallo*) capon

caporal [kapo'ral] *nm* chief, leader

capota [ka'pota] *nf* (*de mujer*) bonnet; (*Auto*) hood (*Brit*), top (*US*)

capote [ka'pote] *nm* (*abrigo: de militar*) greatcoat; (*de torero*) cloak

capricho [ka'pritʃo] *nm* whim, caprice

caprichoso, -a [kapri'tʃoso, a] *adj* capricious

Capricornio [kapri'kornjo] *nm* Capricorn

cápsula ['kapsula] *nf* capsule; **~ espacial** space capsule

captar [kap'tar] *vt* (*comprender*) to understand; (*Radio*) to pick up; (*atención, apoyo*) to attract

captura [kap'tura] *nf* capture; (*Jur*) arrest; **~ de pantalla** screenshot

capturar [kaptu'rar] vt to capture; (Jur) to arrest; (datos) to input

capucha [ka'putʃa] nf hood, cowl

capuchón [kapu'tʃon] nm (Esp: de bolígrafo) cap

capullo [ka'puʎo] nm (Zool) cocoon; (Bot) bud; (fam!) idiot

caqui ['kaki] nm khaki

cara ['kara] nf (Anat, de moneda) face; (aspecto) appearance; (de disco) side; (fig) boldness; (descaro) cheek, nerve ▷ prep: ~ **a** facing; **de ~ a** opposite, facing; **dar la ~** to face the consequences; **echar algo en ~ a** algn to reproach sb for sth; **¿~ o cruz?** heads or tails?; **¡qué ~ más dura!** what a nerve!; **de una ~** (disquete) single-sided

carabina [kara'βina] nf carbine, rifle; (persona) chaperone

Caracas [ka'rakas] nm Caracas

caracol [kara'kol] nm (Zool) snail; (concha) (sea)shell; **escalera de ~** spiral staircase

caracolear [karakole'ar] vi (caballo) to prance about

carácter (pl **caracteres**) [ka'rakter, karak'teres] nm character; **caracteres de imprenta** (Tip) type(face) sg; **~ libre** (Inform) wildcard character; **tener buen/mal ~** to be good-natured/bad tempered

característico, -a [karakte'ristiko, a] adj characteristic ▷ nf characteristic

caracterizar [karakteri'θar] vt (distinguir) to characterize, typify; (honrar) to confer a distinction on

caradura [kara'ðura] nm/f cheeky person; **es un ~** he's got a nerve

carajillo [kara'xiʎo] nm black coffee with brandy

carajo [ka'raxo] nm (esp Am fam!): **¡~!** shit! (!); **¡qué ~!** what the hell!; **me importa un ~** I don't give a damn

caramba [ka'ramba] excl well!, good gracious!

carámbano [ka'rambano] nm icicle

caramelo [kara'melo] nm (dulce) sweet; (azúcar fundido) caramel

carantoñas [karan'toɲas] nfpl: **hacer ~ a** algn to (try to) butter sb up

caraqueño, -a [kara'keɲo, a] adj of o from Caracas ▷ nm/f native o inhabitant of Caracas

carátula [ka'ratula] nf (máscara) mask; (Teat): **la ~** the stage

caravana [kara'βana] nf caravan; (fig) group; (de autos) tailback

carbo ['carβo] nm (inf: = carbohidrato) carb

carbón [kar'βon] nm coal; **~ de leña** charcoal; **papel ~** carbon paper

carboncillo [karβon'θiʎo] nm (Arte) charcoal

carbonilla [karβo'niʎa] nf coal dust

carbonizar [karβoni'θar] vt to carbonize; (quemar) to char; **quedar carbonizado** (Elec) to be electrocuted

carbono [kar'βono] nm carbon; **~ neutral** carbon-neutral

carburador [karβura'ðor] nm carburettor

carburante [karβu'rante] nm fuel

carca ['karka] adj, nm/f inv reactionary

carcajada [karka'xaða] nf (loud) laugh, guffaw

carcajearse [karkaxe'arse] vr to roar with laughter

cárcel ['karθel] nf prison, jail; (Tec) clamp

carcelero, -a [karθe'lero, a] adj prison cpd ▷ nm/f warder

carcoma [kar'koma] nf woodworm

carcomer [karko'mer] vt to bore into, eat into; (fig) to undermine; **carcomerse** vr to become worm-eaten; (fig) to decay

carcomido, -a [karko'miðo, a] adj worm-eaten; (fig) rotten

cardar [kar'ðar] vt (Tec) to card, comb; (pelo) to backcomb

cardenal [karðe'nal] nm (Rel) cardinal; (Med) bruise

cárdeno, -a ['karðeno, a] adj purple; (lívido) livid

cardiaco, -a [kar'ðjako, a], **cardíaco, a** [kar'ðiako, a] adj cardiac; (ataque) heart cpd

cardinal [karði'nal] adj cardinal

cardo ['karðo] nm thistle

carear [kare'ar] vt to bring face to face; (comparar) to compare; **carearse** vr to come face to face, meet

carecer [kare'θer] vi: **~ de** to lack, be in need of

carencia [ka'renθja] nf lack; (escasez) shortage; (Med) deficiency

carente [ka'rente] adj: **~ de** lacking in, devoid of

carestía [kares'tia] nf (escasez) scarcity, shortage; (Com) high cost; **época de ~** period of shortage

careta [ka'reta] nf mask

carga ['karɣa] nf (peso, Elec) load; (de barco) cargo, freight; (Finanzas) tax, duty; (Mil) charge; (Inform) loading; (obligación, responsabilidad) duty, obligation; **~ aérea** (Com) air cargo; **~ útil** (Com) payload; **la ~ fiscal** the tax burden

cargado, -a [kar'ɣaðo, a] adj loaded; (Elec) live; (café, té) strong; (cielo) overcast

cargamento [karɣa'mento] nm (acción) loading; (mercancías) load, cargo

cargar [kar'ɣar] vt (barco, arma) to load; (Elec) to charge; (impuesto) to impose; (Com: algo en cuenta) to charge, debit; (Mil: enemigo) to charge; (Inform) to load ▷ vi (Auto) to load (up); (inclinarse) to lean; **~ con** to pick up, carry away; (peso: fig) to shoulder, bear; **cargarse** vr (fam: estropear) to break; (: matar) to bump off; (Elec) to become charged

cargo ['karɣo] nm (Com etc) charge, debit; (puesto) post, office; (responsabilidad) duty, obligation; (fig) weight, burden; (Jur) charge; **altos ~s** high-ranking officials; **una cantidad en ~ a** algn a sum chargeable to sb;

hacerse ~ de to take charge of *o* responsibility for

carguero [kar'ɣero] *nm* freighter, cargo boat; *(avión)* freight plane

Caribe [ka'riβe] *nm*: **el ~** the Caribbean; **del ~** Caribbean

caribeño, -a [kari'βeɲo, a] *adj* Caribbean

caricatura [karika'tura] *nf* caricature

caricia [ka'riθja] *nf* caress; *(a animal)* pat, stroke

caridad [kari'ðað] *nf* charity

caries ['karjes] *nf inv (Med)* tooth decay

cariño [ka'riɲo] *nm* affection, love; *(caricia)* caress; *(en carta)* love ...; **tener ~ a** to be fond of

cariñoso, -a [kari'ɲoso, a] *adj* affectionate

carisma [ka'risma] *nm* charisma

carismático, -a [karis'matiko, a] *adj* charismatic

caritativo, -a [karita'tiβo, a] *adj* charitable

cariz [ka'riθ] *nm*: **tener** *o* **tomar buen/mal ~** to look good/bad

carmesí [karme'si] *adj, nm* crimson

carmín [kar'min] *nm (color)* carmine; *(tb:* **~ de labios)** lipstick

carnal [kar'nal] *adj* carnal; **primo ~** first cousin

carnaval [karna'βal] *nm* carnival; *see note*

○ CARNAVAL
○
○ The 3 days before *miércoles de ceniza* (Ash
○ Wednesday), when fasting traditionally
○ starts, are the time for *carnaval*, an
○ exuberant celebration which dates back
○ to pre-Christian times. Although in
○ decline during the Franco years, the
○ *carnaval* has grown in popularity recently
○ in Spain, Cádiz and Tenerife being
○ particularly well-known for their
○ celebrations. El *martes de carnaval* (Shrove
○ Tuesday) is the biggest day, with
○ colourful street parades, fancy dress,
○ fireworks and a general party
○ atmosphere.

carne ['karne] *nf* flesh; *(Culin)* meat; **se me pone la ~ de gallina sólo verlo** I get the creeps just seeing it; **~ de cerdo/de cordero/ de ternera/de vaca** pork/lamb/veal/beef; **~ molida** *(LAm)* Brit, ground meat *(US)*; **~ picada** *(Esp)* mince *(Brit)*, ground meat *(US)*; **~ de gallina** *(fig)* gooseflesh

carné [kar'ne] *(pl* **carnés)** *(Esp) nm*: **~ de conducir** driving licence *(Brit)*, driver's license *(US)*; **~ de identidad** identity card; **~ de socio** membership card

carnero [kar'nero] *nm* sheep, ram; *(carne)* mutton

carnet *(pl* **carnets)** [kar'ne, kar'nes] *nm (Esp)* = **carné**

carnicería [karniθe'ria] *nf* butcher's (shop); *(fig: matanza)* carnage, slaughter

carnicero, -a [karni'θero, a] *adj* carnivorous ▷ *nm/f (tb fig)* butcher ▷ *nm* carnivore

carnívoro, -a [kar'niβoro, a] *adj* carnivorous ▷ *nm* carnivore

carnoso, -a [kar'noso, a] *adj* beefy, fat

caro, -a ['karo, a] *adj* dear; *(Com)* dear, expensive ▷ *adv* dear, dearly; **vender ~** to sell at a high price

carpa ['karpa] *nf (pez)* carp; *(de circo)* big top; *(Am: de camping)* tent

carpeta [kar'peta] *nf* folder, file

carpintería [karpinte'ria] *nf* carpentry, joinery

carpintero [karpin'tero] *nm* carpenter; **pájaro ~** woodpecker

carraspear [karraspe'ar] *vi (aclararse la garganta)* to clear one's throat

carraspera [karras'pera] *nf* hoarseness

carrera [ka'rrera] *nf (acción)* run(ning); *(espacio recorrido)* run; *(certamen)* race; *(trayecto)* course; *(profesión)* career; *(Escol, Univ)* course; *(de taxi)* ride; *(en medias)* ladder; **a la ~** at (full) speed; **caballo de ~(s)** racehorse; **~ de obstáculos** *(Deporte)* steeplechase; **~ de armamentos** arms race

carreta [ka'rreta] *nf* wagon, cart

carrete [ka'rrete] *nm* reel, spool; *(Tec)* coil

carretera [karre'tera] *nf* (main) road, highway; **~ nacional** ≈ A road *(Brit)*, ≈ state highway *(US)*; **~ de circunvalación** ring road

carretilla [karre'tiʎa] *nf* trolley; *(Agr)* (wheel) barrow

carril [ka'rril] *nm* furrow; *(de autopista)* lane; *(Ferro)* rail

carril bici *(pl* **carriles bici)** [karil'βiθi, kariles'βiθi] *nm* cycle lane, bikeway *(US)*

carrillo [ka'rriʎo] *nm (Anat)* cheek; *(Tec)* pulley

carrito [ka'rrito] *nm* trolley

carro ['karro] *nm* cart, wagon; *(Mil)* tank; *(Am: coche)* car; *(Tip)* carriage; **~ blindado** armoured car; **~ patrulla** *(Am)* patrol *o* panda *(Brit)* car

carrocería [karroθe'ria] *nf* body, bodywork *no pl (Brit)*

carroña [ka'rroɲa] *nf* carrion *no pl*

carroza [ka'rroθa] *nf (vehículo)* coach ▷ *nm/f (fam)* old fogey

carruaje [ka'rrwaxe] *nm* carriage

carrusel [karru'sel] *nm* merry-go-round, roundabout *(Brit)*

carta ['karta] *nf* letter; *(Culin)* menu; *(naipe)* card; *(mapa)* map; *(Jur)* document; **~ de crédito** credit card; **~ de crédito documentaria** *(Com)* documentary letter of credit; **~ de crédito irrevocable** *(Com)* irrevocable letter of credit; **~ certificada/ urgente** registered/special delivery letter; **~ marítima** chart; **~ de pedido** *(Com)* order; **~ verde** *(Auto)* green card; **~ de vinos** wine list; **echar una ~ al correo** to post a letter; **echar las ~s a algn** to tell sb's fortune

---

cartabón [karta'βon] nm set square
cartearse [karte'arse] vr to correspond
cartel [kar'tel] nm (anuncio) poster, placard; (Escol) wall chart; (Com) cartel
cartelera [karte'lera] nf hoarding, billboard; (en periódico etc) listings pl, entertainments guide; **"en ~"** "showing"
cartera [kar'tera] nf (de bolsillo) wallet; (de colegial, cobrador) satchel; (Am: de señora) handbag (Brit), purse (US); (para documentos) briefcase; (Com) portfolio; **ministro sin ~** (Pol) minister without portfolio; **ocupa la ~ de Agricultura** he is Minister of Agriculture; **~ de pedidos** (Com) order book; **efectos en ~** (Econ) holdings
carterista [karte'rista] nm/f pickpocket
cartero [kar'tero] nm postman
cartilla [kar'tiλa] nf (Escol) primer, first reading book; **~ de ahorros** savings book
cartografía [kartoɣra'fia] nf cartography
cartón [kar'ton] nm cardboard; **~ piedra** papier-mâché
cartucho [kar'tutʃo] nm (Mil) cartridge; (bolsita) paper cone; **~ de datos** (Inform) data cartridge; **~ de tinta** ink cartridge
cartulina [kartu'lina] nf fine cardboard, card
casa ['kasa] nf house; (hogar) home; (edificio) building; (Com) firm, company; **~ consistorial** town hall; **~ de huéspedes** boarding house; **~ de socorro** first aid post; **~ de citas** (fam) brothel; **~ independiente** detached house; **~ rural** (de alquiler) holiday cottage; (pensión) rural B&B; **~ rodante** (CS) caravan (Brit), trailer (US); **en ~** at home; **ir a ~** to go home; **salir de ~** to go out; (para siempre) to leave home; **echar la ~ por la ventana** (gastar) to spare no expense; ver tb **hotel**
casadero, -a [kasa'ðero, a] adj marriageable
casado, -a [ka'saðo, a] adj married ⊳ nm/f married man/woman
casamiento [kasa'mjento] nm marriage, wedding
casar [ka'sar] vt to marry; (Jur) to quash, annul; **casarse** vr to marry, get married; **~se por lo civil** to have a civil wedding, get married in a registry office (Brit)
cascabel [kaska'βel] nm (small) bell; (Zool) rattlesnake
cascada [kas'kaða] nf waterfall
cascanueces [kaska'nweθes] nm inv (a pair of) nutcrackers, nutcracker sg
cascar [kas'kar] vt to split; (nuez) to crack ⊳ vi to chatter; **cascarse** vr to crack, split, break (open)
cáscara ['kaskara] nf (de huevo, fruta seca) shell; (de fruta) skin; (de limón) peel
casco ['kasko] nm (de bombero, soldado) helmet; (cráneo) skull; (Naut: de barco) hull; (Zool: de caballo) hoof; (botella) empty bottle; (de ciudad): **el ~ antiguo** the old part; **el ~ urbano** the town centre; **los ~s azules** the UN peace-keeping force, the blue helmets

cascote [kas'kote] nm piece of rubble; **cascotes** nmpl rubble sg
caserío [kase'rio] nm hamlet, group of houses; (casa) farmhouse
casero, -a [ka'sero, a] adj (pan etc) home-made; (Am: de señora) home-loving; **"comida casera"** "home cooking" ⊳ nm/f (propietario) landlord/lady; (Com) house agent
caseta [ka'seta] nf hut; (para bañista) cubicle; (de feria) stall
casete [ka'sete] nm o f cassette; **~ digital** digital audio tape, DAT
casi ['kasi] adv almost; **~ nunca** hardly ever, almost never; **~ nada** next to nothing; **~ te caes** you almost o nearly fell
casilla [ka'siλa] nf (casita) hut, cabin; (Teat) box office; (para cartas) pigeonhole; (Ajedrez) square; **C~ postal** o **de Correo(s)** (Am) P.O. Box; **sacar a algn de sus ~s** to drive sb round the bend (fam), make sb lose his temper
casillero [kasi'λero] nm (para cartas) pigeonholes
casino [ka'sino] nm club; (de juego) casino
caso ['kaso] nm case; (suceso) event; **en ~ de ...** in case of ...; **el ~ es que** the fact is that; **en el mejor de los ~s** at best; **en ese ~** in that case; **en todo ~** in any case; **en último ~** as a last resort; **hacer ~ a** to pay attention to; **hacer ~ omiso de** to fail to mention, pass over; **hacer o venir al ~** to be relevant
caspa ['kaspa] nf dandruff
casquillo [kas'kiλo] nm (de bombilla) fitting; (de bala) cartridge case
cassette [ka'set] nf o m = **casete**
casta ['kasta] nf caste; (raza) breed
castaña [kas'taɲa] nf ver **castaño**
castañetear [kastaɲete'ar] vi (dientes) to chatter
castaño, -a [kas'taɲo, a] adj chestnut(-coloured), brown ⊳ nm chestnut tree ⊳ nf chestnut; (fam: golpe) punch; **~ de Indias** horse chestnut tree
castañuelas [kasta'ɲwelas] nfpl castanets
castellano, -a [kaste'λano, a] adj Castilian; (fam) Spanish ⊳ nm/f Castilian; (fam) Spaniard ⊳ nm (Ling) Castilian, Spanish; see note

◉ CASTELLANO
◉
◉ The term *castellano* is now the most
◉ widely used term in Spain and Spanish
◉ America to refer to the Spanish language,
◉ since *español* is too closely associated
◉ with Spain as a nation. Of course some
◉ people maintain that *castellano* should
◉ only refer to the type of Spanish spoken
◉ in Castilla.

castidad [kasti'ðað] nf chastity, purity
castigar [kasti'ɣar] vt to punish; (Deporte) to penalize; (afligir) to afflict

castigo [kas'tiɣo] nm punishment; *(Deporte)* penalty

Castilla [kas'tiʎa] nf Castile

castillo [kas'tiʎo] nm castle

castizo, -a [kas'tiθo, a] adj *(Ling)* pure; *(de buena casta)* purebred, pedigree; *(auténtico)* genuine

casto, -a ['kasto, a] adj chaste, pure

castor [kas'tor] nm beaver

castrar [kas'trar] vt to castrate; *(gato)* to doctor; *(Bot)* to prune

castrense [kas'trense] adj army cpd, military

casual [ka'swal] adj chance, accidental

casualidad [kaswali'ðað] nf chance, accident; *(combinación de circunstancias)* coincidence; **da la ~ de que ...** it (just) so happens that ...; **¡qué ~!** what a coincidence!

cataclismo [kata'klismo] nm cataclysm

catador [kata'ðor] nm taster

catalán, -ana [kata'lan, ana] adj, nm/f Catalan ▷ nm *(Ling)* Catalan

catalejo [kata'lexo] nm telescope

catalizador [kataliθa'ðor] nm catalyst; *(Auto)* catalytic converter

catalogar [katalo'ɣar] vt to catalogue; **~ (de)** *(fig)* to classify as

catálogo [ka'taloɣo] nm catalogue

Cataluña [kata'luŋa] nf Catalonia

cataplasma [kata'plasma] nf *(Med)* poultice

catapulta [kata'pulta] nf catapult

catar [ka'tar] vt to taste, sample

catarata [kata'rata] nf *(Geo)* (water)fall; *(Med)* cataract

catarro [ka'tarro] nm catarrh; *(constipado)* cold

catarsis [ka'tarsis] nf catharsis

catastro [ka'tastro] nm property register

catástrofe [ka'tastrofe] nf catastrophe

catear [kate'ar] vt *(fam: examen, alumno)* to fail

catecismo [kate'θismo] nm catechism

cátedra ['kateðra] nf *(Univ)* chair, professorship; *(Escol)* principal teacher's post; **sentar ~ sobre un argumento** to take one's stand on an argument

catedral [kate'ðral] nf cathedral

catedrático, -a [kate'ðratiko, a] nm/f professor; *(Escol)* principal teacher

categoría [kateɣo'ria] nf category; *(rango)* rank, standing; *(calidad)* quality; **de ~** *(hotel)* top-class; **de baja ~** *(oficial)* low-ranking; **de segunda ~** second-rate; **no tiene ~** he has no standing

categórico, -a [kate'ɣoriko, a] adj categorical

catequesis [kate'kesis] nf catechism lessons

cateto, -a [ka'teto, a] nm/f yokel

catolicismo [katoli'θismo] nm Catholicism

católico, -a [ka'toliko, a] adj, nm/f Catholic

catorce [ka'torθe] num fourteen

catre ['katre] nm camp bed *(Brit)*, cot *(US)*; *(fam)* pit

cauce ['kauθe] nm *(de río)* riverbed; *(fig)* channel

caucho ['kautʃo] nm rubber; *(Am: llanta)* tyre

caución [kau'θjon] nf bail

caudal [kau'ðal] nm *(de río)* volume, flow; *(fortuna)* wealth; *(abundancia)* abundance

caudaloso, -a [kauða'loso, a] adj *(río)* large; *(persona)* wealthy, rich

caudillo [kau'ðiʎo] nm leader, chief

causa ['kausa] nf cause; *(razón)* reason; *(Jur)* lawsuit, case; **a o por ~ de** because of, on account of

causar [kau'sar] vt to cause

cautela [kau'tela] nf caution, cautiousness

cauteloso, -a [kaute'loso, a] adj cautious, wary

cautivar [kauti'βar] vt to capture; *(fig)* to captivate

cautiverio [kauti'βerjo] nm, **cautividad** [kautiβi'ðað] nf captivity

cautivo, -a [kau'tiβo, a] adj, nm/f captive

cauto, -a ['kauto, a] adj cautious, careful

cava ['kaβa] nf *(bodega)* wine cellar ▷ nm *(vino)* champagne-type wine

cavar [ka'βar] vt to dig; *(Agr)* to dig over

caverna [ka'βerna] nf cave, cavern

caviar [ka'βjar] nm caviar(e)

cavidad [kaβi'ðað] nf cavity

cavilar [kaβi'lar] vt to ponder

cayado [ka'jaðo] nm *(de pastor)* crook; *(de obispo)* crozier

cayendo etc [ka'jendo] vb ver **caer**

caza ['kaθa] nf *(acción: gen)* hunting; *(: con fusil)* shooting; *(una caza)* hunt, chase; *(animales)* game; **coto de ~** hunting estate ▷ nm *(Aviat)* fighter; **ir de ~** to go hunting; **~ mayor** game hunting

cazador, a [kaθa'ðor, a] nm/f hunter/ huntress ▷ nf jacket

cazar [ka'θar] vt to hunt; *(perseguir)* to chase; *(prender)* to catch; **~las al vuelo** to be pretty sharp

cazo ['kaθo] nm saucepan

cazuela [ka'θwela] nf *(vasija)* pan; *(guisado)* casserole

CC abr (= compensación de carbono) carbon offsetting

CC.OO. nfpl abr = **Comisiones Obreras**

CD nm abr (= compact disc) CD; *(Pol: = Cuerpo Diplomático)* CD (= Diplomatic Corps)

CD-ROM [θeðe'rom] nm abr CD-ROM

CE nm abr (= Consejo de Europa) Council of Europe

cebada [θe'βaða] nf barley

cebar [θe'βar] vt *(animal)* to fatten (up); *(anzuelo)* to bait; *(Mil, Tec)* to prime; **cebarse** vr: **~se en** to vent one's fury on, take it out on

cebo ['θeβo] nm *(gen: para animales)* feed, food; *(para peces, fig)* bait; *(de arma)* charge

cebolla [θe'βoʎa] nf onion

cebolleta [θebo'ʎeta] nf spring onion

cebra ['θeβra] nf zebra; **paso de ~** zebra crossing

cecear [θeθe'ar] vi to lisp

ceceo [θe'θeo] nm lisp

cedazo [θe'ðaθo] *nm* sieve

ceder [θe'ðer] *vt* (*entregar*) to hand over; (*renunciar a*) to give up, part with ▷ *vi* (*renunciar*) to give in, yield; (*disminuir*) to diminish, decline; (*romperse*) to give way; (*viento*) to drop; (*fiebre etc*) to abate; **"ceda el paso"** (*Auto*) "give way"

cederom [θeðe'rom] *nm* CD-ROM

cedro ['θeðro] *nm* cedar

cédula ['θeðula] *nf* certificate, document; **~ de identidad** (*Am*) identity card; **~ electoral** (*Am*) ballot; **~ en blanco** blank cheque; *ver tb* **Documento Nacional de Identidad**

cegar [θe'ɣar] *vt* to blind; (*tubería etc*) to block up, stop up ▷ *vi* to go blind; **cegarse** *vr*: **~se (de)** to be blinded (by)

ceguera [θe'ɣera] *nf* blindness

ceja ['θexa] *nf* eyebrow; **~s pobladas** bushy eyebrows; **arquear las ~s** to raise one's eyebrows; **fruncir las ~s** to frown

cejar [θe'xar] *vi* (*fig*) to back down; **no ~** to keep it up, stick at it

celada [θe'laða] *nf* ambush, trap

celador, a [θela'ðor, a] *nm/f* (*de edificio*) watchman; (*de museo etc*) attendant; (*de cárcel*) warder

celda ['θelda] *nf* cell

celebración [θeleβra'θjon] *nf* celebration

celebrar [θele'βrar] *vt* to celebrate; (*alabar*) to praise ▷ *vi* to be glad; **celebrarse** *vr* to occur, take place

célebre ['θeleβre] *adj* famous

celebridad [θeleβri'ðað] *nf* fame; (*persona*) celebrity

celeste [θe'leste] *adj* sky-blue; (*cuerpo etc*) heavenly ▷ *nm* sky blue

celestial [θeles'tjal] *adj* celestial, heavenly

celibato [θeli'βato] *nm* celibacy

célibe ['θeliβe] *adj, nm/f* celibate

celo[1] ['θelo] *nm* zeal; (*Rel*) fervour; (*pey*) envy; **celos** *nmpl* jealousy *sg*; **dar ~s a algn** to make sb jealous; **tener ~s de algn** to be jealous of sb; **en ~** (*animales*) on heat

celo[2] ['θelo] *nm* Sellotape®

celofán [θelo'fan] *nm* Cellophane®

celoso, -a [θe'loso, a] *adj* (*envidioso*) jealous; (*trabajador*) zealous; (*desconfiado*) suspicious

celta ['θelta] *adj* Celtic ▷ *nm/f* Celt

célula ['θelula] *nf* cell

celular [θelu'lar] *nm* (*LAm*) mobile (phone) (*Brit*), cellphone (*US*)

celulitis [θelu'litis] *nf* (*enfermedad*) cellulitis; (*grasa*) cellulite

celuloide [θelu'loiðe] *nm* celluloid

celulosa [θelu'losa] *nf* cellulose

cementerio [θemen'terjo] *nm* cemetery, graveyard; **~ de coches** scrap yard

cemento [θe'mento] *nm* cement; (*hormigón*) concrete; (*Am: cola*) glue

cena ['θena] *nf* evening meal, dinner

cenagal [θena'ɣal] *nm* bog, quagmire

cenar [θe'nar] *vt* to have for dinner, dine on ▷ *vi* to have dinner, dine

cenicero [θeni'θero] *nm* ashtray

cenit [θe'nit] *nm* zenith

ceniza [θe'niθa] *nf* ash, ashes *pl*

censar [θen'sar] *vt* to take a census of

censo ['θenso] *nm* census; **~ electoral** electoral roll

censura [θen'sura] *nf* (*Pol*) censorship; (*moral*) censure, criticism

censurar [θensu'rar] *vt* (*idea*) to censure; (*cortar: película*) to censor

centella [θen'teʎa] *nf* spark

centellear [θenteʎe'ar] *vi* (*metal*) to gleam; (*estrella*) to twinkle; (*fig*) to sparkle

centelleo [θente'ʎeo] *nm* gleam(ing); twinkling; sparkling

centena [θen'tena] *nf* hundred

centenar [θente'nar] *nm* hundred

centenario, -a [θente'narjo, a] *adj* hundred-year-old ▷ *nm* centenary; **ser ~** to be one hundred years old

centeno [θen'teno] *nm* rye

centésimo, -a [θen'tesimo, a] *adj, nm* hundredth

centígrado [θen'tiɣraðo] *adj* centigrade

centímetro [θen'timetro] *nm* centimetre (*Brit*), centimeter (*US*)

céntimo, -a ['θentimo, a] *adj* hundredth ▷ *nm* cent

centinela [θenti'nela] *nm* sentry, guard

centollo, -a [θen'toʎo, a] *nm/f* large (*o* spider) crab

central [θen'tral] *adj* central ▷ *nf* head office; (*Tec*) plant; (*Telec*) exchange; **~ eléctrica** power station; **~ nuclear** nuclear power station; **~ telefónica** telephone exchange

centralita [θentra'lita] *nf* switchboard

centralización [θentraliθa'θjon] *nf* centralization

centralizar [θentrali'θar] *vt* to centralize

centrar [θen'trar] *vt* to centre

céntrico, -a ['θentriko, a] *adj* central

centrifugar [θentrifu'ɣar] *vt* (*ropa*) to spin-dry

centrífugo, -a [θen'trifuɣo, a] *adj* centrifugal

centrista [θen'trista] *adj* centre *cpd*

centro ['θentro] *nm* centre; **ser de ~** (*Pol*) to be a moderate; **~ de acogida (para niños)** children's home; **~ de beneficios** (*Com*) profit centre; **~ cívico** community centre; **~ comercial** shopping centre; **~ de informática** computer centre; **~ (de determinación) de costos** (*Com*) cost centre; **~ delantero** (*Deporte*) centre forward; **~ de atención al cliente** call centre; **~ de salud** health centre; **~ docente** teaching institution; **~ escolar** school; **~ juvenil** youth club; **~ social** community centre; **~ turístico** (*lugar muy visitado*) tourist centre; **~ urbano** urban area, city

centroamericano, -a [θentroameri'kano, a] *adj, nm/f* Central American

ceñido, -a [θe'niðo, a] *adj* tight

ceñir [θe'nir] *vt* (*rodear*) to encircle, surround; (*ajustar*) to fit (tightly); (*apretar*) to tighten; **ceñirse** *vr*: **~se algo** to put sth on; **~se al asunto** to stick to the matter in hand

ceño ['θeno] *nm* frown, scowl; **fruncir el ~** to frown, knit one's brow

CEOE *nf abr* (= *Confederación Española de Organizaciones Empresariales*) ≈ CBI (Brit)

cepillar [θepi'ʎar] *vt* to brush; (*madera*) to plane (down)

cepillo [θe'piʎo] *nm* brush; (*para madera*) plane; (*Rel*) poor box, alms box; **~ de dientes** toothbrush

cepo ['θepo] *nm* (*de caza*) trap

cera ['θera] *nf* wax; **~ de abejas** beeswax

cerámica [θe'ramika] *nf* pottery; (*arte*) ceramics *sg*

cerca ['θerka] *nf* fence ▷ *adv* near, nearby, close; **por aquí ~** nearby ▷ *prep*: **~ de** (*cantidad*) nearly, about; (*distancia*) near, close to ▷ *nmpl*: **~s** foreground *sg*

cercanía [θerka'nia] *nf* nearness, closeness; **cercanías** *nfpl* outskirts, suburbs; **tren de ~s** commuter o local train

cercano, -a [θer'kano, a] *adj* close, near; (*pueblo etc*) nearby; **C~ Oriente** Near East

cercar [θer'kar] *vt* to fence in; (*rodear*) to surround

cerciorar [θerθjo'rar] *vt* (*asegurar*) to assure; **cerciorarse** *vr*: **~se (de)** (*descubrir*) to find out (about); (*asegurarse*) to make sure (of)

cerco ['θerko] *nm* (*Agr*) enclosure; (*Am*) fence; (*Mil*) siege

cerda ['θerða] *nf* (*de cepillo*) bristle; (*Zool*) sow

cerdada [θer'ðaða] *nf* (*fam*): **hacer una ~ a algn** to play a dirty trick on sb

cerdo ['θerðo] *nm* pig; **carne de ~** pork

cereal [θere'al] *nm* cereal; **cereales** *nmpl* cereals, grain *sg*

cerebral [θere'βral] *adj* (*tb fig*) cerebral; (*tumor*) brain *cpd*

cerebro [θe'reβro] *nm* brain; (*fig*) brains *pl*; **ser un ~** (*fig*) to be brilliant

ceremonia [θere'monja] *nf* ceremony; **reunión de ~** formal meeting; **hablar sin ~** to speak plainly

ceremonial [θeremo'njal] *adj, nm* ceremonial

ceremonioso, -a [θeremo'njoso, a] *adj* ceremonious; (*cumplido*) formal

cereza [θe'reθa] *nf* cherry

cerilla [θe'riʎa] *nf*, **cerillo** [se'riʎo] *nm* (*Am*) match

cerner [θer'ner] *vt* to sift, sieve; **cernerse** *vr* to hover

cero ['θero] *nm* nothing, zero; (*Deporte*) nil; **8 grados bajo ~** 8 degrees below zero; **a partir de ~** from scratch

cerquillo [θer'kiʎo] *nm* (*Am*) fringe (Brit), bangs *pl* (US)

cerrado, -a [θe'rraðo, a] *adj* closed, shut; (*con llave*) locked; (*tiempo*) cloudy, overcast; (*curva*) sharp; (*acento*) thick, broad; **a puerta cerrada** (*Jur*) in camera

cerradura [θerra'ðura] *nf* (*acción*) closing; (*mecanismo*) lock

cerrajero, -a [θerra'xero, a] *nm/f* locksmith

cerrar [θe'rrar] *vt* to close, shut; (*paso, carretera*) to close; (*grifo*) to turn off; (*trato, cuenta, negocio*) to close ▷ *vi* to close, shut; (*la noche*) to come down; **~ con llave** to lock; **~ el sistema** (*Inform*) to close o shut down the system; **~ un trato** to strike a bargain; **cerrarse** *vr* to close, shut; (*herida*) to heal

cerro ['θerro] *nm* hill; **andar por las ~s de Úbeda** to wander from the point, digress

cerrojo [θe'rroxo] *nm* (*herramienta*) bolt; (*de puerta*) latch

certamen [θer'tamen] *nm* competition, contest

certero, -a [θer'tero, a] *adj* accurate

certeza [θer'teθa], **certidumbre** [θerti'ðumbre] *nf* certainty

certidumbre [θerti'ðumbre] *nf* = **certeza**

certificado, -a [θertifi'kaðo, a] *adj* certified; (*Correos*) registered ▷ *nm* certificate; **~ médico** medical certificate

certificar [θertifi'kar] *vt* (*asegurar, atestar*) to certify

cervatillo [θerβa'tiʎo] *nm* fawn

cervecería [θerβeθe'ria] *nf* (*fábrica*) brewery; (*taberna*) public house, pub

cerveza [θer'βeθa] *nf* beer; **~ de barril** draught beer

cervical [θerβi'kal] *adj* cervical

cesación [θesa'θjon] *nf* cessation, suspension

cesante [θe'sante] *adj* redundant; (*Am*) unemployed; (*ministro*) outgoing; (*diplomático*) recalled ▷ *nm/f* redundant worker

cesar [θe'sar] *vi* to cease, stop; (*de un trabajo*) to leave ▷ *vt* (*en el trabajo*) to dismiss; (*alto cargo*) to remove from office

cesárea [θe'sarea] *nf* Caesarean (section)

cese ['θese] *nm* (*de trabajo*) dismissal; (*de pago*) suspension

césped ['θespeð] *nm* grass, lawn

cesta ['θesta] *nf* basket

cesto ['θesto] *nm* (large) basket, hamper

cetro ['θetro] *nm* sceptre

CFC *nm abr* (= *clorofluorocarbono*) CFC

cfr *abr* (= *confróntese, compárese*) cf

Ch, ch [tʃe] *nf former letter in the Spanish alphabet*

chabacano, -a [tʃaβa'kano, a] *adj* vulgar, coarse

chabola [tʃa'βola] *nf* shack; **barriada** or **barrio de ~s** shanty town

chacal [tʃa'kal] *nm* jackal

chacha ['tʃatʃa] *nf* (*fam*) maid

cháchara ['tʃatʃara] *nf* chatter; **estar de ~** to chatter away

chacra ['tʃakra] *nf* (*Am*) smallholding

chafa ['tʃafa] *adj* (*Am: fam*) useless, dud

chafar [tʃa'far] *vt* (*aplastar*) to crush, flatten; (*arruinar*) to ruin

chal [tʃal] *nm* shawl

chalado, -a [tʃa'laðo, a] *adj* (*fam*) crazy

chalé (*pl* **chalés**) [tʃa'le, tʃa'les] *nm* = **chalet**

chaleco [tʃa'leko] *nm* waistcoat, vest (*US*); ~ **antibala** bulletproof vest; ~ **salvavidas** life jacket; ~ **de seguridad**, ~ **reflectante** (*Aut*) high-visibility vest

chalet (*pl* **chalets**) [tʃa'le, tʃa'les] *nm* villa, = detached house; ~ **adosado** semi-detached house

chalupa [tʃa'lupa] *nf* launch, boat

chamaco, -a [tʃa'mako, a] *nm/f* (*Am*) kid

champán [tʃam'pan], **champaña** [tʃam'paɲa] *nm* champagne

champiñón [tʃampi'ɲon] *nm* mushroom

champú [tʃam'pu] (*pl* **champúes** *o* **champús**) *nm* shampoo

chamuscar [tʃamus'kar] *vt* to scorch, singe

chance ['tʃanθe] *nm* (*a veces nf*) (*Am*) chance, opportunity

chancho, -a ['tʃantʃo, a] *nm/f* (*Am*) pig

chanchullo [tʃan'tʃuʎo] *nm* (*fam*) fiddle, wangle

chandal [tʃan'dal] *nm* tracksuit; ~ **(de tactel)** shellsuit

chantaje [tʃan'taxe] *nm* blackmail; **hacer ~ a uno** to blackmail sb

chapa ['tʃapa] *nf* (*de metal*) plate, sheet; (*de madera*) board, panel; (*de botella*) bottle top; (*insignia*) (lapel) badge; (*Am: Auto: tb*: ~ **de matrícula**) number (*Brit*) *o* license (*US*) plate; (*Am: cerradura*) lock; **de 3 ~s** (*madera*) 3-ply

chapado, -a [tʃa'paðo, a] *adj* (*metal*) plated; (*muebles etc*) finished; ~ **en oro** gold-plated

chaparrón [tʃapa'rron] *nm* downpour, cloudburst

chaperón [tʃape'ron] *nm* (*Am*): **hacer de ~** to play gooseberry

chaperona [tʃape'rona] *nf* (*Am*): **hacer de ~** to play gooseberry

chapotear [tʃapote'ar] *vt* to sponge down ▷ *vi* (*fam*) to splash about

chapucero, -a [tʃapu'θero, a] *adj* rough, crude ▷ *nm/f* bungler

chapulín [tʃapu'lin] *nm* (*Am*) grasshopper

chapurrar [tʃapurr'ar], **chapurrear** [tʃapurre'ar] *vt* (*idioma*) to speak badly

chapuza [tʃa'puθa] *nf* botched job

chapuzón [tʃapu'θon] *nm*: **darse un ~** to go for a dip

chaqué [tʃa'ke] *nm* morning coat

chaqueta [tʃa'keta] *nf* jacket; **cambiar la ~** (*fig*) to change sides

chaquetón [tʃake'ton] *nm* (three-quarter-length) coat

charca ['tʃarka] *nf* pond, pool

charco ['tʃarko] *nm* pool, puddle

charcutería [tʃarkute'ria] *nf* (*tienda*) shop selling chiefly pork meat products; (*productos*) cooked pork meats *pl*

charla ['tʃarla] *nf* talk, chat; (*conferencia*) lecture

charlar [tʃar'lar] *vi* to talk, chat

charlatán, -ana [tʃarla'tan, ana] *nm/f* chatterbox; (*estafador*) trickster

charol¹ [tʃa'rol] *nm* varnish; (*cuero*) patent leather

charol² [tʃa'rol] *nm*, **charola** [tʃa'rola] *nf* (*Am*) tray

charro, -a ['tʃarro [a] *adj* Salamancan; (*Am*) Mexican; (*ropa*) loud, gaudy; (*costumbres*) traditional ▷ *nm/f* Salamancan ▷ *nm* (*vaquero*) typical Mexican

chárter ['tʃarter] *adj inv*: **vuelo ~** charter flight

chascarrillo [tʃaska'rriʎo] *nm* (*fam*) funny story

chasco ['tʃasko] *nm* (*broma*) trick, joke; (*desengaño*) disappointment

chasis ['tʃasis] *nm inv* (*Auto*) chassis; (*Foto*) plate holder

chasquear [tʃaske'ar] *vt* (*látigo*) to crack; (*lengua*) to click

chasquido [tʃas'kiðo] *nm* (*de lengua*) click; (*de látigo*) crack

chat [tʃat] *nm* (*Internet*) chat room

chatarra [tʃa'tarra] *nf* scrap (metal)

chatear [tʃate'ar] *vi* (*Internet*) to chat

chato, -a ['tʃato, a] *adj* flat; (*nariz*) snub ▷ *nm* wine tumbler; **beber unos ~s** to have a few drinks

chaucha (*Am*) ['tʃautʃa] *nf* runner (*Brit*) *o* pole (*US*) bean

chaval, a [tʃa'βal, a] *nm/f* kid (*fam*), lad/lass

chavo, -a ['tʃaβo, a] *nm/f* (*Am: fam*) guy/girl

checar [tʃe'kar] *vt* (*Am*): ~ **tarjeta** (*al entrar*) to clock in *o* on; (*al salir*) to clock off *o* out

checo, -a ['tʃeko, a] *adj*, *nm/f* Czech ▷ *nm* (*Ling*) Czech

checoeslovaco, -a [tʃekoeslo'βako, a], **checoslovaco, -a** [tʃekoslo'βako, a] *adj*, *nm/f* Czech, Czechoslovak

Checoeslovaquia [tʃekoeslo'βakja], **Checoslovaquia** [tʃekoslo'βakja] *nf* Czechoslovakia

cheque ['tʃeke] *nm* cheque (*Brit*), check (*US*); **cobrar un ~** to cash a cheque; ~ **abierto/en blanco/cruzado** open/blank/crossed cheque; ~ **al portador** cheque payable to bearer; ~ **de viajero** traveller's cheque

chequeo [tʃe'keo] *nm* (*Med*) check-up; (*Auto*) service

chequera [tʃe'kera] *nf* (*Am*) chequebook (*Brit*), checkbook (*US*)

chévere ['tʃeβere] *adj* (*Am*) great, fabulous (*fam*)

chicano, -a [tʃi'kano, a] *adj*, *nm/f* chicano, Mexican-American

chícharo ['tʃitʃaro] *nm* (*Am*) pea

chicharrón [tʃitʃa'rron] *nm* (pork) crackling

chichón [tʃi'tʃon] nm bump, lump

chicle [tʃikle] nm chewing gum

chico, -a ['tʃiko, a] adj small, little ▷ nm/f child; (muchacho) boy; (muchacha) girl

chiflado, -a [tʃi'flaðo, a] adj (fam) crazy, round the bend ▷ nm/f nutcase

chiflar [tʃi'flar] vt to hiss, boo ▷ vi (esp Am) to whistle

chilango, -a [tʃi'lango, a] adj (Am) of o from Mexico City

Chile ['tʃile] nm Chile

chile ['tʃile] nm chilli pepper

chileno, -a [tʃi'leno, a] adj, nm/f Chilean

chillar [tʃi'ʎar] vi (persona) to yell, scream; (animal salvaje) to howl; (cerdo) to squeal; (puerta) to creak

chillido [tʃi'ʎiðo] nm (de persona) yell, scream; (de animal) howl; (de frenos) screech(ing)

chillón, -ona [tʃi'ʎon, ona] adj (niño) noisy; (color) loud, gaudy

chimenea [tʃime'nea] nf chimney; (hogar) fireplace

China ['tʃina] nf: (**la**) ~ China

china ['tʃina] nf pebble

chinche ['tʃintʃe] nf bug; (Tec) drawing pin (Brit), thumbtack (US) ▷ nm/f nuisance, pest

chincheta [tʃin'tʃeta] nf drawing pin (Brit), thumbtack (US)

chingado, -a [tʃin'gaðo, a] adj (esp Am fam!) lousy, bloody (!); **hijo de la chingada** bastard (!), son of a bitch (US) (!)

chingar [tʃin'gar] vt (Am: fam!) to fuck (up) (!), screw (up) (!); **chingarse** vr (Am: emborracharse) to get pissed (Brit), get plastered; (: fracasar) to fail

chino, -a ['tʃino, a] adj, nm/f Chinese ▷ nm (Ling) Chinese

chipirón [tʃipi'ron] nm squid

Chipre ['tʃipre] nf Cyprus

chipriota [tʃi'prjota], **chipriote** [tʃi'prjote] adj Cypriot, Cyprian ▷ nm/f Cypriot

chiquillo, -a [tʃi'kiʎo, a] nm/f kid (fam), youngster, child

chiquito, -a [tʃi'kito, a] adj very small, tiny ▷ nm/f kid (fam)

chirimoya [tʃiri'moja] nf custard apple

chiringuito [tʃirin'gito] nm small open-air bar

chiripa [tʃi'ripa] nf fluke; **por ~** by chance

chirriar [tʃi'rrjar] vi (goznes) to creak, squeak; (pájaros) to chirp, sing

chirrido [tʃi'rriðo] nm creak(ing), squeak(ing); (de pájaro) chirp(ing)

chis [tʃis] excl sh!

chisme ['tʃisme] nm (habladurías) piece of gossip; (fam: objeto) thingummyjig

chismoso, -a [tʃis'moso, a] adj gossiping ▷ nm/f gossip

chispa ['tʃispa] nf spark; (fig) sparkle; (ingenio) wit; (fam) drunkenness

chispeante [tʃispe'ante] adj (tb fig) sparkling

chispear [tʃispe'ar] vi to spark; (lloviznar) to drizzle

chisporrotear [tʃisporrote'ar] vi (fuego) to throw out sparks; (leña) to crackle; (aceite) to hiss, splutter

chiste ['tʃiste] nm joke, funny story; **~ verde** blue joke

chistera [tʃis'tera] nf top hat

chistoso, -a [tʃis'toso, a] adj (gracioso) funny, amusing; (bromista) witty

chivatazo [tʃiβa'taθo] nm (fam) tip-off; **dar ~** to inform

chivo, -a ['tʃiβo, a] nm/f (billy/nanny-)goat; **~ expiatorio** scapegoat

chocante [tʃo'kante] adj startling; (extraño) odd; (ofensivo) shocking

chocar [tʃo'kar] vi (coches etc) to collide, crash; (Mil, fig) to clash ▷ vt to shock; (sorprender) to startle; **~ con** to collide with; (fig) to run into, run up against; **¡chócala!** (fam) put it there!

chochear [tʃotʃe'ar] vi to dodder, be senile

chocho, -a ['tʃotʃo, a] adj doddering, senile; (fig) soft, doting

choclo (Am) ['tʃoklo] nm (grano) sweetcorn; (mazorca) corn on the cob

chocolate [tʃoko'late] adj chocolate ▷ nm chocolate; (fam) dope, marijuana

chocolatina [tʃokola'tina] nf chocolate

chófer ['tʃofer], **chofer** [tʃo'fer] (esp Am) nm driver

chollo ['tʃoʎo] nm (fam) bargain, snip

choque ['tʃoke] vb ver **chocar** ▷ nm (impacto) impact; (golpe) jolt; (Auto) crash; (fig) conflict; **~ frontal** head-on collision

chorizo [tʃo'riθo] nm hard pork sausage (type of salami); (ladrón) crook

chorrada [tʃo'rraða] nf (fam): **¡es una ~!** that's crap! (!); **decir ~s** to talk crap (!)

chorrear [tʃorre'ar] vt to pour ▷ vi to gush (out), spout (out); (gotear) to drip, trickle

chorro ['tʃorro] nm jet; (caudalito) dribble, trickle; (fig) stream; **salir a ~s** to gush forth; **con propulsión a ~** jet-propelled

choza ['tʃoθa] nf hut, shack

chubasco [tʃu'βasko] nm squall

chubasquero [tʃuβas'kero] nm cagoule, raincoat

chuchería [tʃutʃe'ria] nf trinket

chuleta [tʃu'leta] nf chop, cutlet; (Escol etc: fam) crib

chulo, -a ['tʃulo, a] adj (encantador) charming; (aire) proud; (pey) fresh; (fam: estupendo) great, fantastic ▷ nm (pícaro) rascal; (madrileño) working-class person from Madrid; (rufián: tb: **~ de putas**) pimp

chungo, -a ['tʃungo, a] (fam) adj lousy ▷ nf: **estar de chunga** to be in a merry mood

chupa ['tʃupa] nf (fam) jacket

chupado, -a [tʃu'paðo, a] adj (delgado) skinny, gaunt; **está ~** (fam) it's simple, it's dead easy

chupaleta [tʃupa'leta] nf lollipop

chupar [tʃu'par] vt to suck; (absorber) to absorb; **chuparse** vr to grow thin; **para ~se los dedos** mouthwatering

chupete [tʃu'pete] *nm* dummy (Brit), pacifier (US)

chupetín [tʃupe'tin] *nf* (Am) lollipop

chupetón [tʃupe'ton] *nm* suck

chupito [tʃu'pito] *nm* (fam) shot

chupón [tʃu'pon] *nm* (piruleta) lollipop; (Am: *chupete*) dummy (Brit), pacifier (US)

churrasco [tʃu'rrasko] *nm* (Am) barbecue, barbecued meat

churrería [tʃurre'ria] *nf* stall or shop which sells "churros"

churretón [tʃurre'ton] *nm* stain

churro, -a ['tʃurro, a] *adj* coarse ▷ *nm* (Culin) (type of) fritter; *see note*; (chapuza) botch, mess

○ CHURRO
○
○ Churros, long fritters made with flour and
○ water, are very popular in much of Spain
○ and are often eaten with thick hot
○ chocolate, either for breakfast or as a
○ snack. In Madrid, they eat a thicker
○ variety of churro called porra.

chusco, -a ['tʃusko, a] *adj* funny

chusma ['tʃusma] *nf* rabble, mob

chutar [tʃu'tar] *vi* (Deporte) to shoot (at goal); **esto va que chuta** it's going fine

Cía *abr* (= compañía) Co.

cianuro [θja'nuro] *nm* cyanide

cibercafé [θiβerka'fe] *nm* cybercafé

cibernauta [θiβer'nauta] *nm/f* cybernaut

cibernética [θiβer'netika] *nf* cybernetics *sg*

ciberterrorista [θiβerterro'rista] *nm/f* cyberterrorist

cicatriz [θika'triθ] *nf* scar

cicatrizar [θikatri'θar] *vt* to heal; **cicatrizarse** *vr* to heal (up), form a scar

ciclismo [θi'klismo] *nm* cycling

ciclista [θi'klista] *adj* cycle *cpd* ▷ *nm/f* cyclist

ciclo ['θiklo] *nm* cycle

ciclomotor [θiklomo'tor] *nm* moped

ciclón [θi'klon] *nm* cyclone

cicloturismo [θiklotu'rismo] *nm* touring by bicycle

ciego, -a *etc* a ['θjeɣo, a] *vb ver* **cegar** ▷ *adj* blind ▷ *nm/f* blind man/woman; **a ciegas** blindly; **me puse ciega mariscos** (fam) I stuffed myself with seafood

cielo ['θjelo] *nm* sky; (Rel) heaven; (Arq: tb: **~ raso**) ceiling; **¡~s!** good heavens!; **ver el ~ abierto** to see one's chance

ciempiés [θjem'pjes] *nm inv* centipede

cien [θjen] *num ver* **ciento**

ciénaga ['θjenaɣa] *nf* marsh, swamp

ciencia ['θjenθja] *nf* science; **ciencias** *nfpl* science *sg*; **saber algo a ~ cierta** to know sth for certain

ciencia-ficción ['θjenθjafik'θjon] *nf* science fiction

científico, -a [θjen'tifiko, a] *adj* scientific ▷ *nm/f* scientist

ciento ['θjento], **cien** *num* hundred; **pagar al 10 por ~** to pay at 10 per cent

cierne *etc* ['θjerne] *vb ver* **cerner** ▷ *nm*: **en ~** in blossom; **en ~(s)** (fig) in its infancy

cierre ['θjerre] *vb ver* **cerrar** ▷ *nm* closing, shutting; (con llave) locking; (Radio, TV) close-down; **~ de cremallera** zip (fastener); **precios de ~** (Bolsa) closing prices; **~ del sistema** (Inform) system shutdown

cierro *etc vb ver* **cerrar**

cierto, -a ['θjerto, a] *adj* sure, certain; (un tal) a certain; (correcto) right, correct; **~ hombre** a certain man; **ciertas personas** certain o some people; **sí, es ~** yes, that's correct; **por ~** by the way; **lo ~ es que ...** the fact is that ...; **estar en lo ~** to be right

ciervo ['θjerβo] *nm* (Zool) deer; (: macho) stag

cierzo ['θjerθo] *nm* north wind

cifra ['θifra] *nf* number, figure; (cantidad) number, quantity; (secreta) code; **~ global** lump sum; **~ de negocios** (Com) turnover; **en ~s redondas** in round figures; **~ de referencia** (Com) bench mark; **~ de ventas** (Com) sales figures

cifrar [θi'frar] *vt* to code, write in code; (resumir) to abridge; (calcular) to reckon

cigala [θi'ɣala] *nf* Norway lobster

cigarra [θi'ɣarra] *nf* cicada

cigarrillo [θiɣa'rriʎo] *nm* cigarette

cigarro [θi'ɣarro] *nm* cigarette; (puro) cigar

cigüeña [θi'ɣweɲa] *nf* stork

cilíndrico, -a [θi'lindriko, a] *adj* cylindrical

cilindro [θi'lindro] *nm* cylinder

cima ['θima] *nf* (de montaña) top, peak; (de árbol) top; (fig) height

címbalo ['θimbalo] *nm* cymbal

cimbrear [θimbre'ar] *vt* to brandish; **cimbrearse** *vr* to sway

cimentar [θimen'tar] *vt* to lay the foundations of; (fig: reforzar) to strengthen; (: fundar) to found

cimiento *etc* [θi'mjento] *vb ver* **cimentar** ▷ *nm* foundation

cinc [θink] *nm* zinc

cincel [θin'θel] *nm* chisel

cincelar [θinθe'lar] *vt* to chisel

cinco ['θinko] *num* five; (fecha) fifth; **las ~** five o'clock; **no estar en sus ~** (fam) to be off one's rocker

cincuenta [θin'kwenta] *num* fifty

cine ['θine] *nm* cinema; **el ~ mudo** silent films *pl*; **hacer ~** to make films

cineasta [θine'asta] *nm/f* (director de cine) film-maker o director

cinematográfico, -a [θinemato'ɣrafiko, a] *adj* cine-, film *cpd*

cínico, -a ['θiniko, a] *adj* cynical; (descarado) shameless ▷ *nm/f* cynic

cinismo [θi'nismo] *nm* cynicism

cinta ['θinta] *nf* band, strip; (de tela) ribbon; (película) reel; (de máquina de escribir) ribbon; (métrica) tape measure; (magnetofónica) tape;

~ **adhesiva** sticky tape; ~ **aislante** insulating tape; ~ **de vídeo** videotape; ~ **de carbón** carbon ribbon; ~ **magnética** (*Inform*) magnetic tape; ~ **métrica** tape measure; ~ **de múltiples impactos** (*en impresora*) multistrike ribbon; ~ **de tela** (*para máquina de escribir*) fabric ribbon; ~ **transportadora** conveyor belt

cinto ['θinto] *nm* belt, girdle

cintura [θin'tura] *nf* waist; (*medida*) waistline

cinturón [θintu'ron] *nm* belt; (*fig*) belt, zone; ~ **salvavidas** lifebelt; ~ **de seguridad** safety belt

ciprés [θi'pres] *nm* cypress (tree)

circo ['θirko] *nm* circus

circuito [θir'kwito] *nm* circuit; (*Deporte*) lap; **TV por ~ cerrado** closed-circuit TV; ~ **experimental** (*Inform*) breadboard; ~ **impreso** printed circuit; ~ **lógico** (*Inform*) logical circuit

circulación [θirkula'θjon] *nf* circulation; (*Auto*) traffic; **"cerrado a la ~ rodada"** "closed to vehicles"

circular [θirku'lar] *adj, nf* circular ▷ *vt* to circulate ▷ *vi* to circulate; (*dinero*) to be in circulation; (*Auto*) to drive; (*autobús*) to run; **"circule por la derecha"** "keep (to the) right"

círculo ['θirkulo] *nm* circle; (*centro*) clubhouse; (*Pol*) political group; ~ **vicioso** vicious circle

circuncidar [θirkunθi'dar] *vt* to circumcise

circundar [θirkun'dar] *vt* to surround

circunferencia [θirkunfe'renθja] *nf* circumference

circunscribir [θirkunskri'βir] *vt* to circumscribe; **circunscribirse** *vr* to be limited

circunscripción [θirkunskrip'θjon] *nf* division; (*Pol*) constituency

circunspecto, -a [θirkuns'pekto, a] *adj* circumspect, cautious

circunstancia [θirkuns'tanθja] *nf* circumstance; ~**s agravantes/extenuantes** aggravating/extenuating circumstances; **estar a la altura de las ~s** to rise to the occasion

circunvalación [θirkumbala'θjon] *nf*: **carretera de ~** ring road

cirio ['θirjo] *nm* (wax) candle

cirrosis [θi'rrosis] *nf* cirrhosis (of the liver)

ciruela [θi'rwela] *nf* plum; ~ **pasa** prune

cirugía [θiru'xia] *nf* surgery; ~ **estética** o **plástica** plastic surgery

cirujano [θiru'xano] *nm* surgeon

cisne ['θisne] *nm* swan; **canto de ~** swan song

cisterna [θis'terna] *nf* cistern, tank

cita ['θita] *nf* appointment, meeting; (*de novios*) date; (*referencia*) quotation; **acudir/faltar a una ~** to turn up for/miss an appointment

citación [θita'θjon] *nf* (*Jur*) summons *sg*

citar [θi'tar] *vt* to make an appointment with, arrange to meet; (*Jur*) to summons; (*un autor, texto*) to quote; **citarse** *vr*: ~**se con algn** to arrange to meet sb; **se ~on en el cine** they arranged to meet at the cinema

citología [θitolo'xia] *nf* smear test

cítrico, -a ['θitriko, a] *adj* citric ▷ *nm*: ~**s** citrus fruits

ciudad [θju'ðað] *nf* town; (*capital de país etc*) city; ~ **universitaria** university campus; **C~ del Cabo** Cape Town; **la C~ Condal** Barcelona

ciudadanía [θjuðaða'nia] *nf* citizenship

ciudadano, -a [θjuða'ðano, a] *adj* civic ▷ *nm/f* citizen

cívico, -a ['θiβiko, a] *adj* civic; (*fig*) public-spirited

civil [θi'βil] *adj* civil ▷ *nm* (*guardia*) policeman

civilización [θiβiliθa'θjon] *nf* civilization

civilizar [θiβili'θar] *vt* to civilize

civismo [θi'βismo] *nm* public spirit

cizaña [θi'θaɲa] *nf* (*fig*) discord; **sembrar ~** to sow discord

cl *abr* (= *centilitro*) cl.

clamar [kla'mar] *vt* to clamour for, cry out for ▷ *vi* to cry out, clamour

clamor [kla'mor] *nm* (*grito*) cry, shout; (*fig*) clamour, protest

clan [klan] *nm* clan; (*de gángsters*) gang

clandestino, -a [klandes'tino, a] *adj* clandestine; (*Pol*) underground

clara ['klara] *nf* (*de huevo*) egg white

claraboya [klara'βoja] *nf* skylight

clarear [klare'ar] *vi* (*el día*) to dawn; (*el cielo*) to clear up, brighten up; **clarearse** *vr* to be transparent

clarete [kla'rete] *nm* rosé (wine)

claridad [klari'ðað] *nf* (*del día*) brightness; (*de estilo*) clarity

clarificar [klarifi'kar] *vt* to clarify

clarín [kla'rin] *nm* bugle

clarinete [klari'nete] *nm* clarinet

clarividencia [klariβi'ðenθja] *nf* clairvoyance; (*fig*) far-sightedness

claro, -a ['klaro, a] *adj* clear; (*luminoso*) bright; (*color*) light; (*evidente*) clear, evident; (*poco espeso*) thin ▷ *nm* (*en bosque*) clearing ▷ *adv* clearly ▷ *excl*: **¡~ que sí!** of course!; **¡~ que no!** of course not!; **hablar ~** (*fig*) to speak plainly; **a las claras** openly; **no sacamos nada en ~** we couldn't get anything definite

clase ['klase] *nf* class; (*tipo*) kind, sort; (*Escol etc*) class; (: *aula*) classroom; ~ **alta/media/obrera** upper/middle/working class; **dar ~s** to teach; ~**s particulares** private lessons o tuition *sg*

clásico, -a ['klasiko, a] *adj* classical; (*fig*) classic

clasificación [klasifika'θjon] *nf* classification; (*Deporte*) league (table); (*Com*) ratings *pl*

clasificar [klasifi'kar] vt to classify; (Inform) to sort; **clasificarse** vr (Deporte: en torneo) to qualify

claudicar [klauði'kar] vi (fig) to back down

claustro ['klaustro] nm cloister; (Univ) staff; (junta) senate

claustrofobia [klaustro'foβja] nf claustrophobia

cláusula ['klausula] nf clause; ~ **de exclusión** (Com) exclusion clause

clausura [klau'sura] nf closing, closure

clausurar [klausu'rar] vt (congreso etc) to close, bring to a close; (Pol etc) to adjourn; (cerrar) to close (down)

clavar [kla'βar] vt (tablas etc) to nail (together); (con alfiler) to pin; (clavo) to hammer in; (cuchillo) to stick, thrust; (mirada) to fix; (fam: estafar) to cheat

clave ['klaβe] nf key; (Mus) clef ▷ adj inv key cpd; ~ **de acceso** password; ~ **lada** (Am) dialling (Brit) o area (US) code

clavel [kla'βel] nm carnation

clavícula [kla'βikula] nf collar bone

clavija [kla'βixa] nf peg, pin; (Mus) peg; (Elec) plug

clavo ['klaβo] nm (de metal) nail; (Bot) clove; **dar en el** ~ (fig) to hit the nail on the head

claxon ['klakson] (pl **claxons**) nm horn; **tocar el** ~ to sound one's horn

clemencia [kle'menθja] nf mercy, clemency

cleptómano, -a [klep'tomano, a] nm/f kleptomaniac

clerical [kleri'kal] adj clerical

clérigo ['kleriɣo] nm priest, clergyman

clero ['klero] nm clergy

clicar [kli'kar] vi (Inform) to click; **clica en el icono** click on the icon; ~ **dos veces** to double-click

cliché [kli'tʃe] nm cliché; (Tip) stencil; (Foto) negative

cliente, -a ['kljente, a] nm/f client, customer

clientela [kljen'tela] nf clientele, customers pl; (Com) goodwill; (Med) patients pl

clima ['klima] nm climate

climatizado, -a [klimati'θaðo, a] adj air-conditioned

clímax ['klimaks] nm inv climax

clínico, -a ['kliniko, a] adj clinical ▷ nf clinic; (particular) private hospital

clip (pl **clips**) [klip, klis] nm paper clip

clítoris ['klitoris] nm inv clitoris

cloaca [klo'aka] nf sewer, drain

clonación [klona'θjon] nf cloning

clonar [klo'nar] vt to clone

clorhídrico, -a [klo'riðriko, a] adj hydrochloric

cloro ['kloro] nm chlorine

clorofila [kloro'fila] nf chlorophyl(l)

club (pl **clubs** o **clubes**) [klub, klus, 'kluβes] nm club; ~ **de jóvenes** youth club; ~ **nocturno** night club

cm abr (= centímetro) cm

C.N.T. nf abr (Esp: = Confederación Nacional de Trabajo) Anarchist Union Confederation; (Am) = **Confederación Nacional de Trabajadores**

coacción [koak'θjon] nf coercion, compulsion

coaccionar [koakθjo'nar] vt to coerce, compel

coagular [koaɣu'lar] vt, **coagularse** vr (sangre) to clot; (leche) to curdle

coágulo [ko'aɣulo] nm clot

coalición [koali'θjon] nf coalition

coartada [koar'taða] nf alibi

coartar [koar'tar] vt to limit, restrict

coba ['koβa] nf: **dar ~ a algn** (adular) to suck up to sb

cobarde [ko'βarðe] adj cowardly ▷ nm/f coward

cobardía [koβar'ðia] nf cowardice

cobaya [ko'βaja] nf guinea pig

cobertizo [koβer'tiθo] nm shelter

cobertor [koβer'tor] nm bedspread

cobertura [koβer'tura] nf cover; (Com) coverage; ~ **de dividendo** (Com) dividend cover; **no tengo** ~ (Telec) I can't get a signal

cobija [ko'βixa] nf (Am) blanket

cobijar [koβi'xar] vt (cubrir) to cover; (abrigar) to shelter; **cobijarse** vr to take shelter

cobijo [ko'βixo] nm shelter

cobra ['koβra] nf cobra

cobrador, a [koβra'ðor, a] nm/f (de autobús) conductor/conductress; (de impuestos, gas) collector

cobrar [ko'βrar] vt (cheque) to cash; (sueldo) to collect, draw; (objeto) to recover; (precio) to charge; (deuda) to collect ▷ vi to be paid; **cobrarse** vr to recover, get on well; **cóbrese al entregar** cash on delivery (COD) (Brit), collect on delivery (COD) (US); **a ~** (Com) receivable; **cantidades por ~** sums due; **¿me cobra, por favor?** (en tienda) how much do I owe you?; (en restaurante) can I have the bill, please?

cobre ['koβre] nm copper; (Am fam) cent; **cobres** nmpl (Mús) brass instruments

cobro ['koβro] nm (de cheque) cashing; (pago) payment; **presentar al** ~ to cash; ver tb **llamada**

cocaína [koka'ina] nf cocaine

cocción [kok'θjon] nf (Culin) cooking; (el hervir) boiling

cocear [koθe'ar] vi to kick

cocer [ko'θer] vt, vi to cook; (en agua) to boil; (en horno) to bake

coche ['kotʃe] nm (Auto) car, automobile (US); (de tren, de caballos) coach, carriage; (para niños) pram (Brit), baby carriage (US); **ir en** ~ to drive; ~ **de bomberos** fire engine; ~ **celular** police van, patrol wagon (US); ~ **(comedor)** (Ferro) (dining) car; ~ **de carreras** racing car; ~**-escuela** learner car; ~ **fúnebre** hearse

coche-bomba ['kotʃe'βomba] (pl **coches-bomba**) nm car bomb

coche-cama ['kotʃe'kama] (*pl* **coches-cama**) *nm* (*Ferro*) sleeping car, sleeper

cochera [ko'tʃera] *nf* garage; (*de autobuses, trenes*) depot

coche-restaurante ['kotʃerestau'rante] (*pl* **coches-restaurante**) *nm* (*Ferro*) dining-car, diner

cochinillo [kotʃi'niʎo] *nm* piglet, suckling pig

cochino, -a [ko'tʃino, a] *adj* filthy, dirty ▷ *nm/f* pig

cocido, -a [ko'θiðo, a] *adj* boiled; (*fam*) plastered ▷ *nm* stew

cociente [ko'θjente] *nm* quotient

cocina [ko'θina] *nf* kitchen; (*aparato*) cooker, stove; (*actividad*) cookery; **~ casera** home cooking; **~ eléctrica** electric cooker; **~ francesa** French cuisine; **~ de gas** gas cooker

cocinar [koθi'nar] *vt, vi* to cook

cocinero, -a [koθi'nero, a] *nm/f* cook

coco ['koko] *nm* coconut; (*fantasma*) bogeyman; (*fam: cabeza*) nut; **comer el ~ a algn** (*fam*) to brainwash sb

cocodrilo [koko'ðrilo] *nm* crocodile

cocotero [koko'tero] *nm* coconut palm

cóctel ['koktel] *nm* (*bebida*) cocktail; (*reunión*) cocktail party; **~ Molotov** Molotov cocktail, petrol bomb

codazo [ko'ðaθo] *nm*: **dar un ~ a algn** to nudge sb

codear [koðe'ar] *vi* to elbow, jostle; **codearse** *vr*: **~se con** to rub shoulders with

codicia [ko'ðiθja] *nf* greed; (*fig*) lust

codiciar [koðiθ'jar] *vt* to covet

codicioso, -a [koðiθ'josо, a] *adj* covetous

codificar [koðifi'kar] *vt* (*mensaje*) to (en)code; (*leyes*) to codify

código ['koðiɣo] *nm* code; **~ de barras** (*Com*) bar code; **~ binario** binary code; **~ de caracteres** (*Inform*) character code; **~ de (la) circulación** highway code; **~ de la zona** (*Am*) dialling (*Brit*) o area (*US*) code; **~ postal** postcode; **~ civil** common law; **~ de control** (*Inform*) control code; **~ máquina** (*Inform*) machine code; **~ militar** military law; **~ de operación** (*Inform*) operational o machine code; **~ penal** penal code; **~ de práctica** code of practice

codillo [ko'ðiʎo] *nm* (*Zool*) knee; (*Tec*) elbow (joint)

codo ['koðo] *nm* (*Anat, de tubo*) elbow; (*Zool*) knee; **hablar por los ~s** to talk nineteen to the dozen

codorniz [koðor'niθ] *nf* quail

coerción [koer'θjon] *nf* coercion

coetáneo, -a [koe'taneo, a] *nm/f*: **~s** contemporaries

coexistir [koeksis'tir] *vi* to coexist

cofradía [kofra'ðia] *nf* brotherhood, fraternity; *ver tb* **Semana Santa**

cofre ['kofre] *nm* (*baúl*) trunk; (*de joyas*) box; (*de dinero*) chest; (*Am Auto*) bonnet (*Brit*), hood (*US*)

coger [ko'xer] *vt* (*Esp*) to take (hold of); (*objeto caído*) to pick up; (*frutas*) to pick, harvest; (*resfriado, ladrón, pelota*) to catch; (*Am fam!*) to lay (!) ▷ *vi*: **~ por el buen camino** to take the right road; **cogerse** *vr* (*el dedo*) to catch; **~ a algn desprevenido** to take sb unawares; **~se a algo** to get hold of sth

cogollo [ko'ɣoʎo] *nm* (*de lechuga*) heart; (*fig*) core, nucleus

cogorza [ko'ɣorθa] *nf* (*fam*): **agarrar una ~** to get smashed

cogote [ko'ɣote] *nm* back o nape of the neck

cohabitar [koaβi'tar] *vi* to live together, cohabit

cohecho [ko'etʃo] *nm* (*acción*) bribery; (*soborno*) bribe

coherencia [koe'renθja] *nf* coherence

coherente [koe'rente] *adj* coherent

cohesión [koe'sjon] *nm* cohesion

cohete [ko'ete] *nm* rocket

cohibido, -a [koi'βiðo, a] *adj* (*Psico*) inhibited; (*tímido*) shy; **sentirse ~** to feel embarrassed

cohibir [koi'βir] *vt* to restrain, restrict; **cohibirse** *vr* to feel inhibited

coima ['koima] *nf* (*Am fam*) bribe

coincidencia [koinθi'ðenθja] *nf* coincidence

coincidir [koinθi'ðir] *vi* (*en idea*) to coincide, agree; (*en lugar*) to coincide

coito ['koito] *nm* intercourse, coitus

coja *etc vb ver* **coger**

cojear [koxe'ar] *vi* (*persona*) to limp, hobble; (*mueble*) to wobble, rock

cojera [ko'xera] *nf* lameness; (*andar cojo*) limp

cojín [ko'xin] *nm* cushion

cojinete [koxi'nete] *nm* small cushion, pad; (*Tec*) (ball) bearing

cojo, -a *etc* ['koxo, a] *vb ver* **coger** ▷ *adj* (*que no puede andar*) lame, crippled; (*mueble*) wobbly ▷ *nm/f* lame person, cripple

cojón [ko'xon] *nm* (*fam!*) ball (!), testicle; **¡cojones!** shit! (!)

cojonudo, -a [koxo'nuðo, a] *adj* (*Esp fam*) great, fantastic

col [kol] *nf* cabbage; **~es de Bruselas** Brussels sprouts

cola ['kola] *nf* tail; (*de gente*) queue; (*lugar*) end, last place; (*para pegar*) glue, gum; (*de vestido*) train; **hacer ~** to queue (up)

colaboración [kolaβora'θjon] *nf* (*gen*) collaboration; (*en periódico*) contribution

colaborador, a [kolaβora'ðor, a] *nm/f* collaborator; contributor

colaborar [kolaβo'rar] *vi* to collaborate

colado, -a [ko'laðo, a] *adj* (*metal*) cast ▷ *nf*: **hacer la colada** to do the washing

colador [kola'ðor] *nm* (*de té*) strainer; (*para verduras etc*) colander

colapsar [kolap'sar] vt (tráfico etc) to bring to a standstill

colapso [ko'lapso] nm collapse; ~ **nervioso** nervous breakdown

colar [ko'lar] vt (líquido) to strain off; (metal) to cast ▷ vi to ooze, seep (through); **colarse** vr to jump the queue; (en mitin) to sneak in; (equivocarse) to slip up; ~**se en** to get into without paying; (en una fiesta) to gatecrash

colateral [kolate'ral] adj collateral

colcha ['koltʃa] nf bedspread

colchón [kol'tʃon] nm mattress; ~ **inflable** air bed, inflatable mattress

colchoneta [koltʃo'neta] nf (en gimnasio) mat; ~ **hinchable** air bed, inflatable mattress

colear [kole'ar] vi (perro) to wag its tail

colección [kolek'θjon] nf collection

coleccionar [kolekθjo'nar] vt to collect

coleccionista [kolekθjo'nista] nm/f collector

colecta [ko'lekta] nf collection

colectivo, -a [kolek'tiβo, a] adj collective, joint ▷ nm (Am: autobús) (small) bus; (taxi) collective taxi

colector [kolek'tor] nm collector; (sumidero) sewer

colega [ko'leɣa] nm/f colleague; (Esp: amigo) mate

colegiado, -a [kole'xjaðo, a] adj (profesional) registered ▷ nm/f referee

colegial, a [kole'xjal, a] adj (Escol etc) school cpd, college cpd ▷ nm/f schoolboy/girl

colegio [ko'lexjo] nm college; (escuela) school; (de abogados etc) association; ~ **de internos** boarding school; **ir al** ~ to go to school; ~ **electoral** polling station; ~ **mayor** (Esp) hall of residence; see note

COLEGIO

A *colegio* is normally a private primary or
secondary school. In the state system it
means a primary school although these
are also called *escuela*. State secondary
schools are called *institutos*.
Extracurricular subjects, such as
computing or foreign languages, are
offered in private schools called *academias*.

colegir [kole'xir] vt (juntar) to collect, gather; (deducir) to infer, conclude

cólera ['kolera] nf (ira) anger; **montar en** ~ to get angry ▷ nm (Med) cholera

colérico, -a [ko'leriko, a] adj angry, furious

colesterol [koleste'rol] nm cholesterol

coleta [ko'leta] nf pigtail

coletilla [kole'tiʎa] nf (en carta) postscript; (en conversación) filler phrase

colgante [kol'ɣante] adj hanging; ver **puente** ▷ nm (joya) pendant

colgar [kol'ɣar] vt to hang (up); (tender: ropa) to hang out ▷ vi to hang; (teléfono) to hang up; **no cuelgue** please hold

cólico ['koliko] nm colic

coliflor [koli'flor] nf cauliflower

colilla [ko'liʎa] nf cigarette end, butt

colina [ko'lina] nf hill

colindante [kolin'dante] adj adjacent, neighbouring

colindar [kolin'dar] vi to adjoin, be adjacent

colisión [koli'sjon] nf collision; ~ **frontal** head-on crash

collar [ko'ʎar] nm necklace; (de perro) collar

colmado, -a [kol'maðo, a] adj full ▷ nm grocer's (shop) (Brit), grocery store (US)

colmar [kol'mar] vt to fill to the brim; (fig) to fulfil, realize

colmena [kol'mena] nf beehive

colmillo [kol'miʎo] nm (diente) eye tooth; (de elefante) tusk; (de perro) fang

colmo ['kolmo] nm height, summit; **para ~ de desgracias** to cap it all; ¡**eso es ya el ~!** that's beyond a joke!

colocación [koloka'θjon] nf (acto) placing; (empleo) job, position; (situación) place, position; (Com) placement

colocar [kolo'kar] vt to place, put, position; (poner en empleo) to find a job for; ~ **dinero** to invest money; **colocarse** vr to place o.s.; (conseguir trabajo) to find a job

Colombia [ko'lombja] nf Colombia

colombiano, -a [kolom'bjano, a] adj, nm/f Colombian

colonia [ko'lonja] nf colony; (de casas) housing estate; (agua de colonia) cologne; ~ **escolar** summer camp (for schoolchildren); ~ **proletaria** (Am) shantytown

colonización [koloniθa'θjon] nf colonization

colonizador, a [koloniθa'ðor, a] adj colonizing ▷ nm/f colonist, settler

colonizar [koloni'θar] vt to colonize

colono [ko'lono] nm (Pol) colonist, settler; (Agr) tenant farmer

coloquial [kolo'kjal] adj colloquial

coloquio [ko'lokjo] nm conversation; (congreso) conference

color [ko'lor] nm colour; **a todo** ~ in full colour; **verlo todo ~ de rosa** to see everything through rose-coloured spectacles; **le salieron los ~es** she blushed

colorado, -a [kolo'raðo, a] adj (rojo) red; (Am: chiste) rude, blue; **ponerse** ~ to blush

colorante [kolo'rante] nm colouring (matter)

colorar [kolo'rar] vt to colour; (teñir) to dye

colorear [kolore'ar] vt to colour

colorete [kolo'rete] nm blusher

colorido [kolo'riðo] nm colour(ing)

coloso [ko'loso] nm colossus

columna [ko'lumna] nf column; (pilar) pillar; (apoyo) support; ~ **blindada** (Mil) armoured column; ~ **vertebral** spine, spinal column; (fig) backbone

columpiar [kolum'pjar] *vt* to swing; **columpiarse** *vr* to swing
columpio [ko'lumpjo] *nm* swing
colza ['kolθa] *nf* rape; **aceite de ~** rapeseed oil
coma ['koma] *nf* comma ▷ *nm* (*Med*) coma
comadre [ko'maðre] *nf* (*madrina*) godmother; (*vecina*) neighbour; (*chismosa*) gossip
comadrear [komaðre'ar] *vi* (*esp Am*) to gossip
comadrona [koma'ðrona] *nf* midwife
comal [ko'mal] *nm* (*Am*) griddle
comandancia [koman'danθja] *nf* command
comandante [koman'dante] *nm* commandant; (*grado*) major
comandar [koman'dar] *vt* to command
comarca [ko'marka] *nf* region; *ver tb* **provincia**
comba ['komba] *nf* (*curva*) curve; (*en viga*) warp; (*cuerda*) skipping rope; **saltar a la ~** to skip
combar [kom'bar] *vt* to bend, curve
combate [kom'bate] *nm* fight; (*fig*) battle; **fuera de ~** out of action
combatiente [komba'tjente] *nm* combatant
combatir [komba'tir] *vt* to fight, combat
combi ['kombi] *nm* fridge-freezer
combinación [kombina'θjon] *nf* combination; (*Química*) compound; (*bebida*) cocktail; (*plan*) scheme, setup; (*prenda*) slip
combinar [kombi'nar] *vt* to combine; (*colores*) to match
combustible [kombus'tiβle] *nm* fuel
combustión [kombus'tjon] *nf* combustion
comedia [ko'meðja] *nf* comedy; (*Teat*) play, drama; (*fig*) farce
comediante [kome'ðjante] *nm/f* (*comic*) actor/actress
comedido, -a [kome'ðiðo, a] *adj* moderate
comedor, a [kome'ðor, a] *nm/f* (*persona*) glutton ▷ *nm* (*habitación*) dining room; (*restaurante*) restaurant; (*cantina*) canteen
comensal [komen'sal] *nm/f* fellow guest/diner
comentar [komen'tar] *vt* to comment on; (*fam*) to discuss; **comentó que...** he made the comment that...
comentario [komen'tarjo] *nm* comment, remark; (*Lit*) commentary; **comentarios** *nmpl* gossip *sg*; **dar lugar a ~s** to cause gossip
comentarista [komenta'rista] *nm/f* commentator
comenzar [komen'θar] *vt, vi* to begin, start, commence; **~ a hacer algo** to begin o start doing o to do sth
comer [ko'mer] *vt* to eat; (*Damas, Ajedrez*) to take, capture ▷ *vi* to eat; (*almorzar*) to have lunch; **comerse** *vr* to eat up; (*párrafo etc*) to skip; **~ el coco** (*fam*) to brainwash; **¡a ~!** food's ready!
comercial [komer'θjal] *adj* commercial; (*relativo al negocio*) business *cpd*

comercializar [komerθjali'θar] *vt* (*producto*) to market; (*pey*) to commercialize
comerciante [komer'θjante] *nm/f* trader, merchant; (*tendero*) shopkeeper; **~ exclusivo** (*Com*) sole trader
comerciar [komer'θjar] *vi* to trade, do business
comercio [ko'merθjo] *nm* commerce, trade; (*tienda*) shop, store; (*negocio*) business; (*grandes empresas*) big business; (*fig*) dealings *pl*; **~ autorizado** (*Com*) licensed trade; **~ electrónico** e-commerce; **~ exterior** foreign trade
comestible [komes'tiβle] *adj* eatable, edible ▷ *nm*: **~s** food *sg*, foodstuffs; (*Com*) groceries
cometa [ko'meta] *nm* comet ▷ *nf* kite
cometer [kome'ter] *vt* to commit
cometido [kome'tiðo] *nm* (*misión*) task, assignment; (*deber*) commitment
comezón [kome'θon] *nf* itch, itching
cómic (*pl* **cómics**) ['komik, 'komiks] *nm* comic
comicios [ko'miθjos] *nmpl* elections; (*voto*) voting *sg*
cómico, -a ['komiko, a] *adj* comic(al) ▷ *nm/f* comedian; (*de teatro*) (comic) actor/actress
comida [ko'miða] *nf* (*alimento*) food; (*almuerzo, cena*) meal; (*de mediodía*) lunch; (*Am*) dinner; **~ basura** junk food; **~ chatarra** (*Am*) junk food
comidilla [komi'ðiʎa] *nf*: **ser la ~ del barrio** *o* **pueblo** to be the talk of the town
comienzo [ko'mjenθo] *vb ver* **comenzar** ▷ *nm* beginning, start; **dar ~ a un acto** to begin a ceremony; **~ del archivo** (*Inform*) top-of-file
comillas [ko'miʎas] *nfpl* quotation marks
comilón, -ona [komi'lon, ona] *adj* greedy ▷ *nf* (*fam*) blow-out
comino [ko'mino] *nm* cumin (seed); **no me importa un ~** I don't give a damn!
comisaría [komisa'ria] *nf* police station, precinct (*US*); (*Mil*) commissariat
comisario [komi'sarjo] *nm* (*Mil etc*) commissary; (*Pol*) commissar
comisión [komi'sjon] *nf* (*Com: pago*) commission, rake-off (*fam*); (*:junta*) board; (*encargo*) assignment; **~ mixta/permanente** joint/standing committee; **Comisiones Obreras** (*Esp: formerly*) Communist Union Confederation
comité (*pl* **comités**) [komi'te, komi'tes] *nm* committee; **~ de empresa** works council
comitiva [komi'tiβa] *nf* suite, retinue
como ['komo] *adv* as; (*tal como*) like; (*aproximadamente*) about, approximately ▷ *conj* (*ya que, puesto que*) as, since; (*en seguida que*) as soon as; (*si: +subjun*) if; **¡~ no!** of course!; **~ no lo haga hoy** unless he does it today; **~ si** as if; **es tan alto ~ ancho** it is as high as it is wide
cómo ['komo] *adv* how?, why? ▷ *excl* what?, I beg your pardon? ▷ *nm*: **el ~ y el porqué**

the whys and wherefores; **¿~ está Ud?** how are you?; **¿~ no?** why not?; **¡~ no!** (*esp Am*) of course!; **¿~ son?** what are they like?

cómoda ['komoða] *nf* chest of drawers

comodidad [komoði'ðað] *nf* comfort; **venga a su ~** come at your convenience

comodín [komo'ðin] *nm* joker; (*Inform*) wild card; **símbolo ~** wild-card character

cómodo, -a ['komoðo, a] *adj* comfortable; (*práctico, de fácil uso*) convenient

comodón, -ona [komo'ðon, ona] *adj* comfort-loving ▷ *nm/f*: **ser un(a) ~/-ona** to like one's home comforts

compact [kom'pakt] (*pl* **compacts**) *nm* (*tb*: **~ disc**) compact disk player

compacto, -a [kom'pakto, a] *adj* compact

compadecer [kompaðe'θer] *vt* to pity, be sorry for; **compadecerse** *vr*: **~se de** to pity, be sorry for

compadre [kom'paðre] *nm* (*padrino*) godfather; (*esp Am*: *amigo*) friend, pal

compaginar [kompaxi'nar] *vt*: **~ A con B** to bring A into line with B; **compaginarse** *vr*: **~se con** to tally with, square with

compañerismo [kompaɲe'rismo] *nm* comradeship

compañero, -a [kompa'ɲero, a] *nm/f* companion; (*novio*) boyfriend/girlfriend; **~ de clase** classmate

compañía [kompa'ɲia] *nf* company; **~ afiliada** associated company; **~ concesionaria** franchiser; **~ (no) cotizable** (un)listed company; **~ inversionista** investment trust; **hacer ~ a algn** to keep sb company

comparación [kompara'θjon] *nf* comparison; **en ~ con** in comparison with

comparar [kompa'rar] *vt* to compare

comparativo, -a [kompara'tiβo, a] *adj* comparative

comparecer [kompare'θer] *vi* to appear (in court)

comparsa [kom'parsa] *nm/f* extra

compartimento [komparti'mento], **compartimiento** [komparti'mjento] *nm* (*Ferro*) compartment; (*de mueble, cajón*) section; **~ estanco** (*fig*) watertight compartment

compartir [kompar'tir] *vt* to share; (*dinero, comida etc*) to divide (up), share (out)

compás [kom'pas] *nm* (*Mus*) beat, rhythm; (*Mat*) compasses *pl*; (*Naut etc*) compass; **al ~** in time

compasión [kompa'sjon] *nf* compassion, pity

compasivo, -a [kompa'siβo, a] *adj* compassionate

compatibilidad [kompatiβili'ðað] *nf* (*tb Inform*) compatibility

compatible [kompa'tiβle] *adj* compatible

compatriota [kompa'trjota] *nm/f* compatriot, fellow countryman/woman

compendiar [kompen'djar] *vt* to summarize; (*libro*) to abridge

compendio [kom'pendjo] *nm* summary; abridgement

compenetrarse [kompene'trarse] *vr* to be in tune; (*fig*): **~ (muy) bien** to get on (very) well together

compensación [kompensa'θjon] *nf* compensation; (*Jur*) damages *pl*; (*Com*) clearing; **~ de carbono** carbon offsetting

compensar [kompen'sar] *vt* to compensate; (*pérdida*) to make up for

competencia [kompe'tenθja] *nf* (*incumbencia*) domain, field; (*Com*) receipt; (*Jur, habilidad*) competence; (*rivalidad*) competition

competente [kompe'tente] *adj* (*Jur, persona*) competent; (*conveniente*) suitable

competición [kompeti'θjon] *nf* competition

competir [kompe'tir] *vi* to compete

competitivo, -a [kompeti'tiβo, a] *adj* competitive

compilar [kompi'lar] *vt* to compile

compinche [kom'pintʃe] *nm/f* (*LAm: fam*) mate, buddy (*US*)

complacencia [kompla'θenθja] *nf* (*placer*) pleasure; (*satisfacción*) satisfaction; (*buena voluntad*) willingness

complacer [kompla'θer] *vt* to please; **complacerse** *vr* to be pleased

complaciente [kompla'θjente] *adj* kind, obliging, helpful

complejo, -a [kom'plexo, a] *adj, nm* complex

complementario, -a [komplemen'tarjo, a] *adj* complementary

complemento [komple'mento] *nm* (*de moda, diseño*) accessory; (*Ling*) complement

completar [komple'tar] *vt* to complete

completo, -a [kom'pleto, a] *adj* complete; (*perfecto*) perfect; (*lleno*) full ▷ *nm* full complement

complexión [komple'ksjon] *nf* constitution

complicación [komplika'θjon] *nf* complication

complicado, -a [kompli'kaðo, a] *adj* complicated; **estar ~ en** to be mixed up in

complicar [kompli'kar] *vt* to complicate

cómplice ['kompliθe] *nm/f* accomplice

complot (*pl* **complots**) [kom'plo(t), kom'plos] *nm* plot; (*conspiración*) conspiracy

componente [kompo'nente] *adj, nm* component

componer [kompo'ner] *vt* to make up, put together; (*Mus, Lit, Imprenta*) to compose; (*algo roto*) to mend, repair; (*adornar*) to adorn; (*arreglar*) to arrange; (*reconciliar*) to reconcile; **componerse** *vr*: **~se de** to consist of; **componérselas para hacer algo** to manage to do sth

comportamiento [komporta'mjento] *nm*
behaviour, conduct
comportarse [kompor'tarse] *vr* to behave
composición [komposi'θjon] *nf*
composition
compositor, a [komposi'tor, a] *nm/f*
composer
compostura [kompos'tura] *nf (reparación)*
mending, repair; *(composición)*
composition; *(acuerdo)* agreement; *(actitud)*
composure
compra ['kompra] *nf* purchase; **compras** *nfpl*
purchases, shopping *sg*; **hacer la ~/ir de ~s**
to do the/go shopping; **~ a granel** *(Com)* bulk
buying; **~ proteccionista** *(Com)* support
buying
comprador, a [kompra'ðor, a] *nm/f* buyer,
purchaser
comprar [kom'prar] *vt* to buy, purchase;
~ deudas *(Com)* to factor
comprender [kompren'der] *vt* to
understand; *(incluir)* to comprise, include
comprensible [kompren'siβle] *adj*
understandable
comprensión [kompren'sjon] *nf*
understanding; *(totalidad)*
comprehensiveness
comprensivo, -a [kompren'siβo, a] *adj*
comprehensive; *(actitud)* understanding
compresa [kom'presa] *nf* compress;
~ higiénica sanitary towel *(Brit)* o napkin
(US)
comprimido, -a [kompri'miðo, a] *adj*
compressed ▷ *nm* *(Med)* pill, tablet; **en
caracteres ~s** *(Tip)* condensed
comprimir [kompri'mir] *vt* to compress; *(fig)*
to control; *(Inform)* to compress, zip
comprobante [kompro'βante] *nm* proof;
(Com) voucher; **~ (de pago)** receipt; **~ de
compra** proof of purchase
comprobar [kompro'βar] *vt* to check; *(probar)*
to prove; *(Tec)* to check, test
comprometer [komprome'ter] *vt* to
compromise; *(exponer)* to endanger;
comprometerse *vr* to compromise o.s.;
(involucrarse) to get involved
compromiso [kompro'miso] *nm (obligación)*
obligation; *(cita)* engagement, date;
(cometido) commitment; *(convenio)*
agreement; *(dificultad)* awkward situation;
libre de ~ *(Com)* without obligation
compuesto, -a [kom'pwesto, a] *pp de*
componer ▷ *adj*: **~ de** composed of, made up
of ▷ *nm* compound; *(Med)* preparation
compungido, -a [kompun'xiðo, a] *adj*
remorseful
computador [komputa'ðor] *nm*,
computadora [komputa'ðora] *nf*
computer; **~ central** mainframe computer;
~ especializado dedicated computer;
~ personal personal computer
cómputo ['komputo] *nm* calculation

comulgar [komul'ɣar] *vi* to receive
communion
común [ko'mun] *adj (gen)* common; *(corriente)*
ordinary; **por lo ~** generally ▷ *nm*: **el ~** the
community
comunicación [komunika'θjon] *nf*
communication; *(informe)* report
comunicado [komuni'kaðo] *nm*
announcement; **~ de prensa** press release
comunicar [komuni'kar] *vt* to
communicate; *(Arq)* to connect ▷ *vi* to
communicate; to send a report;
comunicarse *vr* to communicate; **está
comunicando** *(Telec)* the line's engaged *(Brit)*
o busy *(US)*
comunicativo, -a [komunika'tiβo, a] *adj*
communicative
comunidad [komuni'ðað] *nf* community;
~ autónoma *(Esp)* autonomous region; **~ de
vecinos** residents' association;
C~ Económica Europea (CEE) European
Economic Community (EEC)
comunión [komu'njon] *nf* communion
comunismo [komu'nismo] *nm* communism
comunista [komu'nista] *adj, nm/f*
communist
comunitario, -a [komuni'tarjo, a] *adj (de la
CE)* Community *cpd*, EC *cpd*

PALABRA CLAVE

con [kon] *prep* **1** *(medio, compañía, modo)* with;
comer con cuchara to eat with a spoon;
café con leche white coffee; **estoy con un
catarro** I've got a cold; **pasear con algn** to
go for a walk with sb; **con habilidad**
skilfully
2 *(a pesar de)*: **con todo, merece nuestros
respetos** all the same o even so, he deserves
our respect
3 *(para con)*: **es muy bueno para con los
niños** he's very good with (the) children
4 *(+infin)*: **con llegar tan tarde se quedó sin
comer** by arriving o because he arrived so
late he missed out on eating; **con estudiar
un poco apruebas** with a bit of studying
you should pass
5 *(queja)*: **¡con las ganas que tenía de ir!** and
I really wanted to go (too)!
▷ *conj*: **con que**: **será suficiente con que le
escribas** it will be enough if you write to her

conato [ko'nato] *nm* attempt; **~ de robo**
attempted robbery
concebir [konθe'βir] *vt* to conceive; *(imaginar)*
to imagine ▷ *vi* to conceive
conceder [konθe'ðer] *vt* to concede
concejal, a [konθe'xal, a] *nm/f* town
councillor
concejo [kon'θexo] *nm* council
concentración [konθentra'θjon] *nf*
concentration

concentrar [konθen'trar] vt to concentrate; **concentrarse** vr to concentrate

concéntrico, -a [kon'θentriko, a] adj concentric

concepción [konθep'θjon] nf conception

concepto [kon'θepto] nm concept; **por ~ de** as, by way of; **tener buen ~ de algn** to think highly of sb; **bajo ningún ~** under no circumstances

concernir [konθer'nir] vi to concern; **en lo que concierne a ...** with regard to ...; **en lo que a mí concierne** as far as I'm concerned

concertar [konθer'tar] vt (Mus) to harmonize; (acordar: precio) to agree; (: tratado) to conclude; (trato) to arrange, fix up; (combinar: esfuerzos) to coordinate; (reconciliar: personas) to reconcile ▷ vi to harmonize, be in tune

concesión [konθe'sjon] nf concession; (Com: fabricación) licence

concesionario, -a [konθesjo'narjo, a] nm/f (Com) (licensed) dealer, agent, concessionaire; (: de venta) franchisee; (: de transportes etc) contractor

concha ['kontʃa] nf shell; (Am fam!) cunt (!)

conchabarse [kontʃa'βarse] vr: **~ contra** to gang up on

conciencia [kon'θjenθja] nf (moral) conscience; (conocimiento) awareness; **libertad de ~** freedom of worship; **tener/tomar ~ de** to be/become aware of; **tener la ~ limpia o tranquila** to have a clear conscience; **tener plena ~ de** to be fully aware of

concienciar [konθjen'θjar] vt to make aware; **concienciarse** vr to become aware

concienzudo, -a [konθjen'θuðo, a] adj conscientious

concierto [kon'θjerto] vb ver **concertar** ▷ nm concert; (obra) concerto

conciliar [konθi'ljar] vt to reconcile ▷ adj (Rel) council cpd; **~ el sueño** to get to sleep

concilio [kon'θiljo] nm council

conciso, -a [kon'θiso, a] adj concise

conciudadano, -a [konθjuða'ðano, a] nm/f fellow citizen

concluir [konklu'ir] vt (acabar) to conclude; (inferir) to infer, deduce ▷ vi, **concluirse** vr to conclude; **todo ha concluido** it's all over

conclusión [konklu'sjon] nf conclusion; **llegar a la ~ de que ...** to come to the conclusion that ...

concluyente [konklu'jente] adj (prueba, información) conclusive

concordar [konkor'ðar] vt to reconcile ▷ vi to agree, tally

concordia [kon'korðja] nf harmony

concretar [konkre'tar] vt to make concrete, make more specific; (problema) to pinpoint; **concretarse** vr to become more definite

concreto, -a [kon'kreto, a] adj, nm (Am) concrete; **en ~** (en resumen) to sum up; (específicamente) specifically; **no hay nada en ~** there's nothing definite

concurrencia [konku'rrenθja] nf turnout

concurrido, -a [konku'rriðo, a] adj (calle) busy; (local: reunión) crowded

concurrir [konku'rrir] vi (juntarse: ríos) to meet, come together; (: personas) to gather, meet

concursante [konkur'sante] nm competitor

concursar [konkur'sar] vi to compete

concurso [kon'kurso] nm (de público) crowd; (Escol, Deporte, competición) competition; (Com) invitation to tender; (examen) open competition; (TV etc) quiz; (ayuda) help, cooperation

condal [kon'dal] adj: **la ciudad ~** Barcelona

conde ['konde] nm count

condecoración [kondekora'θjon] nf (Mil) medal, decoration

condecorar [kondeko'rar] vt to decorate

condena [kon'dena] nf sentence; **cumplir una ~** to serve a sentence

condenación [kondena'θjon] nf condemnation; (Rel) damnation

condenar [konde'nar] vt to condemn; (Jur) to convict; **condenarse** vr (Jur) to confess (one's guilt); (Rel) to be damned

condensar [konden'sar] vt to condense

condesa [kon'desa] nf countess

condescender [kondesθen'der] vi to acquiesce, comply

condición [kondi'θjon] nf (gen) condition; (rango) social class; **condiciones** nfpl (cualidades) qualities; (estado) condition; **a ~ de que ...** on condition that ...; **las condiciones del contrato** the terms of the contract; **condiciones de trabajo** working conditions; **condiciones de venta** conditions of sale

condicional [kondiθjo'nal] adj conditional

condicionar [kondiθjo'nar] vt (acondicionar) to condition; **~ algo a algo** to make sth conditional o dependent on sth

condimento [kondi'mento] nm seasoning

condolerse [kondo'lerse] vr to sympathize

condominio [kondo'minjo] nm (Com) joint ownership; (Am) condominium, apartment

condón [kon'don] nm condom

conducir [kondu'θir] vt to take, convey; (Elec etc) to carry; (Auto) to drive; (negocio) to manage ▷ vi to drive; (fig) to lead; **conducirse** vr to behave

conducta [kon'dukta] nf conduct, behaviour

conducto [kon'dukto] nm pipe, tube; (fig) channel; (Elec) lead; **por ~ de** through

conductor, a [konduk'tor, a] adj leading, guiding ▷ nm (Física) conductor; (de vehículo) driver

conduje etc [kon'duxe] vb ver **conducir**

conduzco etc [kon'duθko] vb ver **conducir**

conectado, -a [konek'taðo, a] adj (Elec) connected, plugged in; (Inform) on-line

conectar [konek'tar] *vt* to connect (up); *(enchufar)* plug in; *(Inform)* to toggle on; **conectarse** *vr (Inform)* to log in *or* on

conejillo [kone'xiʎo] *nm*: **~ de Indias** guinea pig

conejo [ko'nexo] *nm* rabbit

conexión [konek'sjon] *nf* connection; *(Inform)* logging in *or* on

confección [konfek'θjon] *nf (preparación)* preparation, making-up; *(industria)* clothing industry; *(producto)* article; **de ~** *(ropa)* off-the-peg

confeccionar [konfekθjo'nar] *vt* to make (up)

confederación [konfeðera'θjon] *nf* confederation

conferencia [konfe'renθja] *nf* conference; *(lección)* lecture; *(Telec)* call; **~ de cobro revertido** *(Telec)* reversed-charge *(Brit)* o collect *(US)* call; **~ cumbre** summit (conference); **~ de prensa** press conference

conferir [konfe'rir] *vt* to award

confesar [konfe'sar] *vt (admitir)* to confess, admit; *(error)* to acknowledge; *(crimen)* to own up to

confesión [konfe'sjon] *nf* confession

confesionario [konfesjo'narjo] *nm* confessional

confeti [kon'feti] *nm* confetti

confiado, -a [kon'fjaðo, a] *adj (crédulo)* trusting; *(seguro)* confident; *(presumido)* conceited, vain

confianza [kon'fjanθa] *nf* trust; *(aliento, confidencia)* confidence; *(familiaridad)* intimacy, familiarity; *(pey)* vanity, conceit; **margen ~** credibility gap; **tener ~ con algn** to be on close terms with sb

confiar [kon'fjar] *vt* to entrust ▷ *vi (fiarse)* to trust; *(contar con)* to rely; **confiarse** *vr* to put one's trust in; **~ en algn** to trust sb; **~ en que ...** to hope that ...

confidencia [konfi'ðenθja] *nf* confidence

confidencial [konfiðen'θjal] *adj* confidential

confidente [konfi'ðente] *nm/f* confidant/confidante; *(policial)* informer

configurar [konfiɣu'rar] *vt* to shape, form

confín [kon'fin] *nm* limit; **confines** *nmpl* confines, limits

confinar [konfi'nar] *vi* to confine; *(desterrar)* to banish

confirmación [konfirma'θjon] *nf* confirmation; *(Rel)* Confirmation

confirmar [konfir'mar] *vt* to confirm; *(Jur etc)* to corroborate; **la excepción confirma la regla** the exception proves the rule

confiscar [konfis'kar] *vt* to confiscate

confite [kon'fite] *nm* sweet *(Brit)*, candy *(US)*

confitería [konfite'ria] *nf* confectionery; *(tienda)* confectioner's (shop)

confitura [konfi'tura] *nf* jam

conflictivo, -a [konflik'tiβo, a] *adj (asunto, propuesta)* controversial; *(país, situación)* troubled

conflicto [kon'flikto] *nm* conflict; *(fig)* clash; *(: dificultad)*: **estar en un ~** to be in a jam; **~ laboral** labour dispute

confluir [konflu'ir] *vi (ríos etc)* to meet; *(gente)* to gather

conformar [konfor'mar] *vt* to shape, fashion ▷ *vi* to agree; **conformarse** *vr* to conform; *(resignarse)* to resign o.s.; **~se con algo** to be happy with sth

conforme [kon'forme] *adj* alike, similar; *(correspondiente)*: **~ con** in line with; *(de acuerdo)* agreed, in agreement; *(satisfecho)* satisfied ▷ *adv* as ▷ *excl* agreed! ▷ *nm* agreement ▷ *prep*: **~ a** in accordance with; **estar ~s (con algo)** to be in agreement (with sth); **quedarse ~ (con algo)** to be satisfied (with sth)

conformidad [konformi'ðað] *nf (semejanza)* similarity; *(acuerdo)* agreement; *(resignación)* resignation; **de/en ~ con** in accordance with; **dar su ~** to consent

conformista [konfor'mista] *nm/f* conformist

confort *(pl* **conforts)** [kon'for, kon'for(t)s] *nm* comfort

confortable [konfor'taβle] *adj* comfortable

confortar [konfor'tar] *vt* to comfort

confraternizar [konfraterni'θar] *vi* to fraternize

confrontar [konfron'tar] *vt* to confront; *(dos personas)* to bring face to face; *(cotejar)* to compare ▷ *vi* to border

confundir [konfun'dir] *vt (borrar)* to blur; *(equivocar)* to mistake, confuse; *(mezclar)* to mix; *(turbar)* to confuse; **confundirse** *vr (hacerse borroso)* to become blurred; *(turbarse)* to get confused; *(equivocarse)* to make a mistake; *(mezclarse)* to mix

confusión [konfu'sjon] *nf* confusion

confuso, -a [kon'fuso, a] *adj (gen)* confused; *(recuerdo)* hazy; *(estilo)* obscure

congelado, -a [konxe'laðo, a] *adj* frozen ▷ *nmpl*: **~s** frozen food *sg* o foods

congelador [konxela'ðor] *nm* freezer, deep freeze

congelar [konxe'lar] *vt* to freeze; **congelarse** *vr (sangre, grasa)* to congeal

congénere [kon'xenere] *nm/f*: **sus ~s** his peers

congeniar [konxe'njar] *vi* to get on *(Brit)* o along *(US)* (well)

congestión [konxes'tjon] *nf* congestion

congestionar [konxestjo'nar] *vt* to congest; **congestionarse** *vr* to become congested; **se le congestionó la cara** his face became flushed

congoja [kon'goxa] *nf* distress, grief

congraciarse [kongra'θjarse] *vr* to ingratiate o.s.

congratular [kongratu'lar] *vt* to congratulate

congregación [kongreɣa'θjon] *nf* congregation

congregar [kongre'ɣar] *vt* to gather together; **congregarse** *vr* to gather together

congresista [kongre'sista] *nm/f* delegate, congressman/woman

congreso [kon'greso] *nm* congress; **C~ de los Diputados** (*Esp Pol*) = House of Commons (*Brit*), House of Representatives (*US*); *ver tb* **Cortes**

conífera [ko'nifera] *nf* conifer

conjetura [konxe'tura] *nf* guess; (*Com*) guesstimate

conjeturar [konxetu'rar] *vt* to guess

conjugación [konxuɣa'θjon] *nf* conjugation

conjugar [konxu'ɣar] *vt* to combine, fit together; (*Ling*) to conjugate

conjunción [konxun'θjon] *nf* conjunction

conjunto, -a [kon'xunto, a] *adj* joint, united ▷ *nm* whole; (*Mus*) band; (*de ropa*) ensemble; (*Inform*) set; **en ~** as a whole; **~ integrado de programas** (*Inform*) integrated software suite

conjurar [konxu'rar] *vt* (*Rel*) to exorcise; (*peligro*) to ward off ▷ *vi* to plot

conmemoración [konmemora'θjon] *nf* commemoration

conmemorar [konmemo'rar] *vt* to commemorate

conmigo [kon'miɣo] *pron* with me

conminar [konmi'nar] *vt* to threaten

conmoción [konmo'θjon] *nf* shock; (*Pol*) disturbance; (*fig*) upheaval; **~ cerebral** (*Med*) concussion

conmovedor, a [konmoβe'ðor, a] *adj* touching, moving; (*emocionante*) exciting

conmover [konmo'βer] *vt* to shake, disturb; (*fig*) to move; **conmoverse** *vr* (*fig*) to be moved

conmutador [konmuta'ðor] *nm* switch; (*Am Telec*) switchboard; (: *central*) telephone exchange

connotación [konnota'θjon] *nf* connotation

cono ['kono] *nm* cone; **C~ Sur** Southern Cone

conocedor, a [konoθe'ðor, a] *adj* expert, knowledgeable ▷ *nm/f* expert, connoisseur

conocer [kono'θer] *vt* to know; (*por primera vez*) to meet, get to know; (*entender*) to know about; (*reconocer*) to recognize; **conocerse** *vr* (*una persona*) to know o.s.; (*dos personas*) to (get to) know each other; **~ a algn de vista** to know sb by sight; **darse a ~** (*presentarse*) to make o.s. known; **se conoce que ...** (*parece*) apparently ...

conocido, -a [kono'θiðo, a] *adj* (well-)known ▷ *nm/f* acquaintance

conocimiento [konoθi'mjento] *nm* knowledge; (*Med*) consciousness; (*Naut*: *tb*: **~ de embarque**) bill of lading; **conocimientos** *nmpl* (*personas*)

acquaintances; (*saber*) knowledge *sg*; **hablar con ~ de causa** to speak from experience; **~ (de embarque) aéreo** (*Com*) air waybill

conozco *etc* [ko'noθko] *vb ver* **conocer**

conque ['konke] *conj* and so, so then

conquista [kon'kista] *nf* conquest

conquistador, a [konkista'ðor, a] *adj* conquering ▷ *nm* conqueror

conquistar [konkis'tar] *vt* (*Mil*) to conquer; (*puesto, simpatía*) to win; (*enamorar*) to win the heart of

consagrar [konsa'ɣrar] *vt* (*Rel*) to consecrate; (*fig*) to devote

consciente [kons'θjente] *adj* conscious; **ser** *o* **estar ~ de** to be aware of

consecución [konseku'θjon] *nf* acquisition; (*de fin*) attainment

consecuencia [konse'kwenθja] *nf* consequence, outcome; (*firmeza*) consistency; **de ~** of importance

consecuente [konse'kwente] *adj* consistent

consecutivo, -a [konseku'tiβo, a] *adj* consecutive

conseguir [konse'ɣir] *vt* to get, obtain; (*sus fines*) to attain

consejería [konsexe'ria] *nf* (*Pol*) ministry (*in a regional government*)

consejero, -a [konse'xero, a] *nm/f* adviser, consultant; (*Pol*) minister (*in a regional government*); (*Com*) director; (*en comisión*) member

consejo [kon'sexo] *nm* advice; (*Pol*) council; (*Com*) board; **un ~** a piece of advice; **~ de administración** board of directors; **~ de guerra** court-martial; **~ de ministros** cabinet meeting; **C~ de Europa** Council of Europe

consenso [kon'senso] *nm* consensus

consentimiento [konsenti'mjento] *nm* consent

consentir [konsen'tir] *vt* (*permitir, tolerar*) to consent to; (*mimar*) to pamper, spoil; (*aguantar*) to put up with ▷ *vi* to agree, consent; **~ que algn haga algo** to allow sb to do sth

conserje [kon'serxe] *nm* caretaker; (*portero*) porter

conserva [kon'serβa] *nf*: **en ~** (*alimentos*) tinned (*Brit*), canned; **conservas** (*tb*: **~s alimenticias**) tinned (*Brit*) *o* canned foods

conservación [konserβa'θjon] *nf* conservation; (*de alimentos, vida*) preservation

conservador, a [konserβa'ðor, a] *adj* (*Pol*) conservative ▷ *nm/f* conservative

conservante [konser'βante] *nm* preservative

conservar [konser'βar] *vt* (*gen*) to preserve; (*recursos*) to conserve, keep; (*alimentos, vida*) to preserve; **conservarse** *vr* to survive

conservatorio [konserβa'torjo] *nm* (*Mus*) conservatoire, conservatory; (*Am*) greenhouse

considerable [konsiðe'raβle] *adj*
considerable

consideración [konsiðera'θjon] *nf*
consideration; *(estimación)* respect; **de ~**
important; **De mi** *o* **nuestra (mayor) ~** *(Am)*
Dear Sir(s) *o* Madam; **tomar en ~** to take into
account

considerado, -a [konsiðe'raðo, a] *adj*
(atento) considerate; *(respetado)* respected

considerar [konsiðe'rar] *vt (gen)* to consider;
(meditar) to think about; *(tener en cuenta)* to
take into account

consigna [kon'siɣna] *nf (orden)* order,
instruction; *(para equipajes)* left-luggage
office *(Brit)*, checkroom *(US)*

consigo [kon'siɣo] *vb ver* **conseguir** ▷ *pron (m)*
with him; *(f)* with her; *(usted)* with you;
(reflexivo) with o.s.

consiguiendo *etc* [konsi'ɣjendo] *vb ver*
conseguir

consiguiente [konsi'ɣjente] *adj* consequent;
por ~ and so, therefore, consequently

consistente [konsis'tente] *adj* consistent;
(sólido) solid, firm; *(válido)* sound; **~ en**
consisting of

consistir [konsis'tir] *vi*: **~ en** *(componerse de)*
to consist of; *(ser resultado de)* to be due to

consola [kon'sola] *nf* console, control panel;
(mueble) console table; **~ de juegos** games
console; **~ de mandos** *(Inform)* control
console; **~ de visualización** visual display
console

consolación [konsola'θjon] *nf*
consolation

consolar [konso'lar] *vt* to console

consolidar [konsoli'ðar] *vt* to consolidate

consomé *(pl* **consomés)** [konso'me,
konso'mes] *nm* consommé, clear soup

consonante [konso'nante] *adj* consonant,
harmonious ▷ *nf* consonant

consorcio [kon'sorθjo] *nm (Com)* consortium,
syndicate

conspiración [konspira'θjon] *nf* conspiracy

conspirador, a [konspira'ðor, a] *nm/f*
conspirator

conspirar [konspi'rar] *vi* to conspire

constancia [kons'tanθja] *nf (gen)* constancy;
(certeza) certainly; **dejar ~ de algo** to put sth
on record

constante [kons'tante] *adj, nf* constant

constar [kons'tar] *vi (evidenciarse)* to be
clear *o* evident; **~ (en)** to appear (in); **~ de** to
consist of; **hacer ~** to put on record; **me
consta que ...** I have evidence that ...; **que
conste que lo hice por ti** believe me, I did it
for your own good

constatar [konsta'tar] *vt (controlar)* to check;
(observar) to note

constelación [konstela'θjon] *nf*
constellation

consternación [konsterna'θjon] *nf*
consternation

constipado, -a [konsti'paðo, a] *adj*: **estar ~**
to have a cold ▷ *nm* cold

constiparse [konsti'parse] *vr* to catch a cold

constitución [konstitu'θjon] *nf*
constitution; **Día de la C~** *(Esp)* Constitution
Day *(6th December)*

constitucional [konstituθjo'nal] *adj*
constitutional

constituir [konstitu'ir] *vt (formar, componer)*
to constitute, make up; *(fundar, erigir, ordenar)*
to constitute, establish; *(ser)* to be;
constituirse *vr (Pol etc: cuerpo)* to be
composed; *(: fundarse)* to be established

constitutivo, -a [konstitu'tiβo, a] *adj*
constitutive, constituent

constituyente [konstitu'jente] *adj*
constituent

constreñir [konstre'ɲir] *vt (obligar)* to
compel, oblige; *(restringir)* to restrict

construcción [konstruk'θjon] *nf*
construction, building

constructivo, -a [konstruk'tiβo, a] *adj*
constructive

constructor, a [konstruk'tor, a] *nm/f*
builder

construir [konstru'ir] *vt* to build, construct

construyendo *etc* [konstru'jendo] *vb ver*
construir

consuelo *etc* [kon'swelo] *vb ver* **consolar** ▷ *nm*
consolation, solace

cónsul ['konsul] *nm* consul

consulado [konsu'laðo] *nm (sede)* consulate;
(cargo) consulship

consulta [kon'sulta] *nf* consultation; *(Med:
consultorio)* consulting room; *(Inform)* enquiry;
horas de ~ surgery hours; **obra de ~**
reference book

consultar [konsul'tar] *vt* to consult; **~ un
archivo** *(Inform)* to interrogate a file; **~ algo
con algn** to discuss sth with sb

consultorio [konsul'torjo] *nm (Med)*
surgery

consumar [konsu'mar] *vt* to complete,
carry out; *(crimen)* to commit; *(sentencia)*
to carry out

consumición [konsumi'θjon] *nf*
consumption; *(bebida)* drink; *(comida)* food;
~ mínima cover charge

consumidor, a [konsumi'ðor, a] *nm/f*
consumer

consumir [konsu'mir] *vt* to consume;
consumirse *vr* to be consumed; *(persona)*
to waste away

consumismo [konsu'mismo] *nm (Com)*
consumerism

consumo [kon'sumo] *nm* consumption;
bienes de ~ consumer goods

contabilidad [kontaβili'ðað] *nf* accounting,
book-keeping; *(profesión)* accountancy; *(Com)*:
~ analítica variable costing; **~ de costos** cost
accounting; **~ de doble partida** double-
entry book-keeping; **~ de gestión**

management accounting; **~ por partida simple** single-entry book-keeping

contabilizar [kontaβi'liθar] vt to enter in the accounts

contable [kon'taβle] nm/f bookkeeper; (licenciado) accountant; **~ de costos** (Com) cost accountant

contactar [kontak'tar] vi: **~ con algn** to contact sb

contacto [kon'takto] nm contact; (Auto) ignition; **lentes de ~** contact lenses; **estar en ~ con** to be in touch with

contado, -a [kon'taðo, a] adj: **~s** (escasos) numbered, scarce, few ▷ nm: **al ~** for cash; **pagar al ~** to pay (in) cash; **precio al ~** cash price

contador [konta'ðor] nm (aparato) meter; (Am: contable) accountant

contagiar [konta'xjar] vt (enfermedad) to pass on, transmit; (persona) to infect; **contagiarse** vr to become infected

contagio [kon'taxjo] nm infection

contagioso, -a [konta'xjoso, a] adj infectious; (fig) catching

contaminación [kontamina'θjon] nf (gen) contamination; (del ambiente etc) pollution

contaminar [kontami'nar] vt (gen) to contaminate; (aire, agua) to pollute; (fig) to taint

contante [kon'tante] adj: **dinero ~ (y sonante)** hard cash

contar [kon'tar] vt (páginas, dinero) to count; (anécdota etc) to tell ▷ vi to count; **contarse** vr to be counted, figure; **~ con** to rely on, count on; **sin ~** not to mention; **le cuento entre mis amigos** I reckon him among my friends

contemplación [kontempla'θjon] nf contemplation; **no andarse con contemplaciones** not to stand on ceremony

contemplar [kontem'plar] vt to contemplate; (mirar) to look at

contemporáneo, -a [kontempo'raneo, a] adj, nm/f contemporary

contendiente [konten'djente] nm/f contestant

contenedor [kontene'ðor] nm container; (de escombros) skip; **~ de (la) basura** wheelie-bin (Brit); **~ de vidrio** bottle bank

contener [konte'ner] vt to contain, hold; (risa etc) to hold back, contain; **contenerse** vr to control o restrain o.s.

contenido, -a [konte'niðo, a] adj (moderado) restrained; (risa etc) suppressed ▷ nm contents pl, content

contentar [konten'tar] vt (satisfacer) to satisfy; (complacer) to please; (Com) to endorse; **contentarse** vr to be satisfied

contento, -a [kon'tento, a] adj contented, content; (alegre) pleased; (feliz) happy

contestación [kontesta'θjon] nf answer, reply; **~ a la demanda** (Jur) defence plea

contestador [kontesta'ðor] nm: **~ automático** answering machine

contestar [kontes'tar] vt to answer (back), reply; (Jur) to corroborate, confirm

contestatario, -a [kontesta'tarjo, a] adj anti-establishment, nonconformist

contexto [kon'teksto] nm context

contienda [kon'tjenda] nf contest, struggle

contigo [kon'tiɣo] pron with you

contiguo, -a [kon'tiɣwo, a] adj (de al lado) next; (vecino) adjacent, adjoining

continental [kontinen'tal] adj continental

continente [konti'nente] adj, nm continent

contingencia [kontin'xenθja] nf contingency; (riesgo) risk; (posibilidad) eventuality

contingente [kontin'xente] adj contingent ▷ nm contingent; (Com) quota

continuación [kontinwa'θjon] nf continuation; **a ~** then, next

continuamente [kon'tinwamente] adv (sin interrupción) continuously; (a todas horas) constantly

continuar [konti'nwar] vt to continue, go on with; (reanudar) to resume ▷ vi to continue, go on; **~ hablando** to continue talking o to talk

continuidad [kontinwi'ðað] nf continuity

continuo, -a [kon'tinwo, a] adj (sin interrupción) continuous; (acción perseverante) continual

contorno [kon'torno] nm outline; (Geo) contour; **contornos** nmpl neighbourhood sg, surrounding area sg

contorsión [kontor'sjon] nf contortion

contra ['kontra] prep against; (Com: giro) on ▷ adv against ▷ adj, nm/f (Pol fam) counter-revolutionary ▷ nm con ▷ nf: **la C~ (nicaragüense)** the Contras pl

contraataque [kontraa'take] nm counterattack

contrabajo [kontra'βaxo] nm double bass

contrabandista [kontraβan'dista] nm/f smuggler

contrabando [kontra'βando] nm (acción) smuggling; (mercancías) contraband; **~ de armas** gun-running

contracción [kontrak'θjon] nf contraction

contrachapado [kontratʃa'paðo] nm plywood

contracorriente [kontrako'rrjente] nf cross-current

contradecir [kontraðe'θir] vt to contradict

contradicción [kontraðik'θjon] nf contradiction; **espíritu de ~** contrariness

contradictorio, -a [kontraðik'torjo, a] adj contradictory

contraer [kontra'er] vt to contract; (hábito) to acquire; (limitar) to restrict; **contraerse** vr to contract; (limitarse) to limit o.s.

contraespionage [kontraespjo'naxe] nm counter-espionage

contrafuerte [kontra'fwerte] *nm* (*Arq*) buttress

contragolpe [kontra'ɣolpe] *nm* backlash

contraluz [kontra'luθ] *nm o f* view against the light; (*Foto etc*) back lighting; **a ~** against the light

contramaestre [kontrama'estre] *nm* foreman

contraofensiva [kontraofen'siβa] *nf* counteroffensive

contrapartida [kontrapar'tiða] *nf* (*Com*) balancing entry; **como ~ (de)** in return (for), as o in compensation (for)

contrapelo [kontra'pelo]: **a ~** *adv* the wrong way

contrapesar [kontrape'sar] *vt* to counterbalance; (*fig*) to offset

contrapeso [kontra'peso] *nm* counterweight; (*fig*) counterbalance; (*Com*) makeweight

contraportada [kontrapor'taða] *nf* (*de revista*) back cover

contraproducente [kontraproðu'θente] *adj* counterproductive

contrariar [kontra'rjar] *vt* (*oponerse*) to oppose; (*poner obstáculo*) to impede; (*enfadar*) to vex

contrariedad [kontrarje'ðað] *nf* (*oposición*) opposition; (*obstáculo*) obstacle, setback; (*disgusto*) vexation, annoyance

contrario, -a [kon'trarjo, a] *adj* contrary; (*persona*) opposed; (*sentido, lado*) opposite ▷ *nm/f* enemy, adversary; (*Deporte*) opponent; **al ~, por el ~** on the contrary; **de lo ~** otherwise

contrarreloj [kontrarre'lo(x)] *nf* (*tb:* **prueba ~**) time trial

contrarrestar [kontrarres'tar] *vt* to counteract

contrasentido [kontrasen'tiðo] *nm* contradiction; **es un ~ que él ...** it doesn't make sense for him to ...

contraseña [kontra'seɲa] *nf* countersign; (*frase*) password

contrastar [kontras'tar] *vt* to verify ▷ *vi* to contrast

contraste [kon'traste] *nm* contrast

contrata [kon'trata] *nf* (*Jur*) written contract; (*empleo*) hiring

contratar [kontra'tar] *vt* (*firmar un acuerdo para*) to contract for; (*empleados, obreros*) to hire, engage; (*Deporte*) to sign up; **contratarse** *vr* to sign on

contratiempo [kontra'tjempo] *nm* (*revés*) setback; (*accidente*) mishap; **a ~** (*Mus*) off-beat

contratista [kontra'tista] *nm/f* contractor

contrato [kon'trato] *nm* contract; **~ de compraventa** contract of sale; **~ a precio fijo** fixed-price contract; **~ a término** forward contract; **~ de trabajo** contract of employment o service

contravenir [kontraβe'nir] *vi*: **~ a** to contravene, violate

contraventana [kontraβen'tana] *nf* shutter

contribución [kontriβu'θjon] *nf* (*municipal etc*) tax; (*ayuda*) contribution; **exento de contribuciones** tax-free

contribuir [kontriβu'ir] *vt, vi* to contribute; (*Com*) to pay (in taxes)

contribuyente [kontriβu'jente] *nm/f* (*Com*) taxpayer; (*que ayuda*) contributor

contrincante [kontrin'kante] *nm* opponent, rival

control [kon'trol] *nm* control; (*inspección*) inspection, check; (*Com*): **~ de calidad** quality control; **~ de cambios** exchange control; **~ de costos** cost control; **~ de créditos** credit control; **~ de existencias** stock control; **~ de precios** price control; **~ de pasaportes** passport inspection

controlador, a [kontrola'ðor, a] *nm/f* controller; **~ aéreo** air-traffic controller

controlar [kontro'lar] *vt* to control; to inspect, check; (*Com*) to audit

controversia [kontro'βersja] *nf* controversy

contundente [kontun'dente] *adj* (*prueba*) conclusive; (*fig: argumento*) convincing; **instrumento ~** blunt instrument

contusión [kontu'sjon] *nf* bruise

convalecencia [kombale'θenθja] *nf* convalescence

convalecer [kombale'θer] *vi* to convalesce, get better

convaleciente [kombale'θjente] *adj, nm/f* convalescent

convalidar [kombali'ðar] *vt* (*título*) to recognize

convencer [komben'θer] *vt* to convince; (*persuadir*) to persuade

convencimiento [kombenθi'mjento] *nm* (*acción*) convincing; (*persuasión*) persuasion; (*certidumbre*) conviction; **tener el ~ de que ...** to be convinced that ...

convención [komben'θjon] *nf* convention

convencional [kombenθjo'nal] *adj* conventional

conveniencia [kombe'njenθja] *nf* suitability; (*conformidad*) agreement; (*utilidad, provecho*) usefulness; **conveniencias** *nfpl* conventions; (*Com*) property *sg*; **ser de la ~ de algn** to suit sb

conveniente [kombe'njente] *adj* suitable; (*útil*) useful; (*correcto*) fit, proper; (*aconsejable*) advisable

convenio [kom'benjo] *nm* agreement, treaty; **~ de nivel crítico** threshold agreement

convenir [kombe'nir] *vi* (*estar de acuerdo*) to agree; (*ser conveniente*) to suit, be suitable: **"sueldo a ~"** "salary to be agreed"; **conviene recordar que ...** it should be remembered that ...

convento [kom'bento] nm monastery; (de monjas) convent

convenza etc [kom'benθa] vb ver **convencer**

convergencia [komber'xenθja] nf convergence

converger [komber'xer], **convergir** [komber'xir] vi to converge; **sus esfuerzos convergen a un fin común** their efforts are directed towards the same objective

conversación [kombersa'θjon] nf conversation

conversar [komber'sar] vi to talk, converse

conversión [komber'sjon] nf conversion

convertir [komber'tir] vt to convert; (transformar) to transform, turn; (Com) to (ex) change; **convertirse** vr (Rel) to convert

convexo, -a [kom'bekso, a] adj convex

convicción [kombik'θjon] nf conviction

convicto, -a [kom'bikto, a] adj convicted; (condenado) condemned

convidado, -a [kombi'ðaðo, a] nm/f guest

convidar [kombi'ðar] vt to invite; **~ a algn a una cerveza** to buy sb a beer

convincente [kombin'θente] adj convincing

convite [kom'bite] nm invitation; (banquete) banquet

convivencia [kombi'βenθja] nf coexistence, living together

convivir [kombi'βir] vi to live together; (Pol) to coexist

convocar [kombo'kar] vt to summon, call (together)

convocatoria [komboka'torja] nf summons sg; (anuncio) notice of meeting; (Escol) examination session

convulsión [kombul'sjon] nf convulsion; (Pol etc) upheaval

conyugal [konju'ɣal] adj conjugal; **vida ~** married life

cónyuge ['konyuxe] nm/f spouse, partner

coñac (pl **coñacs**) ['koɲa(k), 'koɲas] nm cognac, brandy

coñazo [ko'ɲaθo] nm (fam) pain; **dar el ~** to be a real pain

coño ['koɲo] (fam!) nm cunt (!); (Am pey) Spaniard ▷ excl (enfado) shit (!); (sorpresa) bloody hell (!); **¡qué ~!** what a pain in the arse! (!)

cool [kul] adj (fam) cool

cooperación [koopera'θjon] nf cooperation

cooperar [koope'rar] vi to cooperate

cooperativo, -a [koopera'tiβo, a] adj cooperative ▷ nf cooperative

coordinador, a [koorðina'ðor, a] nm/f coordinator ▷ nf coordinating committee

coordinar [koorði'nar] vt to coordinate

copa ['kopa] nf (tb Deporte) cup; (vaso) glass; (de árbol) top; (de sombrero) crown; **copas** nfpl (Naipes) one of the suits in the Spanish card deck; **(tomar una) ~** (to have a) drink; **ir de ~s** to go out for a drink; ver tb **Baraja Española**

copar [ko'par] vt (puestos) to monopolize

copia ['kopja] nf copy; (Arte) replica; (Com etc) duplicate; (Inform): **~ impresa** hard copy; **~ de respaldo** o **de seguridad** backup copy; **hacer ~ de seguridad** to back up; **~ de trabajo** working copy

copiar [ko'pjar] vt to copy; **~ al pie de la letra** to copy word for word

copiloto [kopi'loto] nm (Aviat) co-pilot; (Auto) co-driver

copioso, -a [ko'pjoso, a] adj copious, plentiful

copla ['kopla] nf verse; (canción) (popular) song

copo ['kopo] nm: **~s de maíz** cornflakes; **~ de nieve** snowflake

coqueta [ko'keta] adj flirtatious, coquettish ▷ nf (mujer) flirt

coquetear [kokete'ar] vi to flirt

coraje [ko'raxe] nm courage; (ánimo) spirit; (ira) anger

coral [ko'ral] adj choral ▷ nf choir ▷ nm (Zool) coral

coraza [ko'raθa] nf (armadura) armour; (blindaje) armour-plating

corazón [kora'θon] nm heart; (Bot) core; **corazones** nmpl (Naipes) hearts; **de buen ~** kind-hearted; **de todo ~** wholeheartedly; **estar mal del ~** to have heart trouble

corazonada [koraθo'naða] nf impulse; (presentimiento) presentiment, hunch

corbata [kor'βata] nf tie

corchea [kor'tʃea] nf quaver

corchete [kor'tʃete] nm catch, clasp; **corchetes** nmpl (Tip) square brackets

corcho ['kortʃo] nm cork; (Pesca) float

cordel [kor'ðel] nm cord, line

cordero [kor'ðero] nm lamb; (piel) lambskin

cordial [kor'ðjal] adj cordial ▷ nm cordial, tonic

cordialidad [korðjali'ðað] nf warmth, cordiality

cordillera [korði'ʎera] nf range (of mountains)

Córdoba ['korðoβa] nf Cordova

cordón [kor'ðon] nm (cuerda) cord, string; (de zapatos) lace; (Elec) flex, wire (US); (Mil etc) cordon; **~ umbilical** umbilical cord

cordura [kor'ðura] nf (Med) sanity; (fig) good sense; **con ~** (obrar, hablar) sensibly

coreografía [koreoɣra'fia] nf choreography

córner (pl **córners**) ['korner, 'korners] nm corner (kick)

corneta [kor'neta] nf bugle

cornisa [kor'nisa] nf cornice

coro ['koro] nm chorus; (conjunto de cantores) choir

corona [ko'rona] nf crown; (de flores) garland

coronación [korona'θjon] nf coronation

coronar [koro'nar] vt to crown

coronel [koro'nel] nm colonel

coronilla [koro'niʎa] nf (Anat) crown (of the head); **estar hasta la ~ (de)** to be utterly fed up (with)

corporación [korpora'θjon] *nf* corporation

corporal [korpo'ral] *adj* corporal, bodily

corporativo, -a [korpora'tiβo, a] *adj* corporate

corpulento, -a [korpu'lento, a] *adj* (*persona*) heavily-built

corral [ko'rral] *nm* (*patio*) farmyard; (*Agr: de aves*) poultry yard; (*redil*) pen

correa [ko'rrea] *nf* strap; (*cinturón*) belt; (*de perro*) lead, leash; **~ transportadora** conveyor belt; **~ del ventilador** (*Auto*) fan belt

corrección [korrek'θjon] *nf* correction; (*represión*) rebuke; (*cortesía*) good manners; (*Inform*): **~ por líneas** line editing; **~ en pantalla** screen editing; **~ (de pruebas)** (*Tip*) proofreading

correccional [korrekθjo'nal] *nm* reformatory

correcto, -a [ko'rrekto, a] *adj* correct; (*persona*) well-mannered

corrector, a [korrek'tor, a] *nm/f*: **~ de pruebas** proofreader

corredizo, -a [korre'ðiθo, a] *adj* (*puerta etc*) sliding; (*nudo*) running

corredor, a [korre'ðor, a] *adj* running; (*rápido*) fast ▷ *nm/f* (*Deporte*) runner ▷ *nm* (*pasillo*) corridor; (*balcón corrido*) gallery; (*Com*) agent, broker; **~ de bienes raíces** real-estate broker; **~ de bolsa** stockbroker; **~ de seguros** insurance broker

corregir [korre'xir] *vt* (*error*) to correct; (*amonestar, reprender*) to rebuke, reprimand; **corregirse** *vr* to reform

correo [ko'rreo] *nm* post, mail; (*persona*) courier; **Correos** *nmpl* Post Office *sg*; **~ aéreo** airmail; **~ basura** (*por carta*) junk mail; (*por Internet*) spam; **~ certificado** registered mail; **~ electrónico** email, electronic mail; **~ urgente** special delivery; **~ web** webmail; **a vuelta de ~** by return (of post)

correr [ko'rrer] *vt* to run; (*viajar*) to cover, travel; (*riesgo*) to run; (*aventura*) to have; (*cortinas*) to draw; (*cerrojo*) to shoot ▷ *vi* to run; (*líquido*) to run, flow; (*rumor*) to go round; **correrse** *vr* to slide, move; (*colores*) to run; (*fam: tener orgasmo*) to come; **echar a ~** to break into a run; **~ con los gastos** to pay the expenses; **eso corre de mi cuenta** I'll take care of that

correspondencia [korrespon'denθja] *nf* correspondence; (*Ferro*) connection; (*reciprocidad*) return; **~ directa** (*Com*) direct mail

corresponder [korrespon'der] *vi* to correspond; (*convenir*) to be suitable; (*pertenecer*) to belong; (*tocar*) to concern; (*favor*) to repay; **corresponderse** *vr* (*por escrito*) to correspond; (*amarse*) to love one another; **"a quien corresponda"** "to whom it may concern"

correspondiente [korrespon'djente] *adj* corresponding; (*respectivo*) respective

corresponsal [korrespon'sal] *nm/f* (*newspaper*) correspondent; (*Com*) agent

corrido, -a [ko'rriðo, a] *adj* (*avergonzado*) abashed; (*fluido*) fluent ▷ *nf* run, dash; (*de toros*) bullfight; **de ~** fluently; **tres noches corridas** three nights running; **un kilo ~** a good kilo

corriente [ko'rrjente] *adj* (*agua*) running; (*fig*) flowing; (*dinero, cuenta etc*) current; (*común*) ordinary, normal ▷ *nf* current; (*fig: tendencia*) course ▷ *nm* current month; **~ de aire** draught; **~ eléctrica** electric current; **las ~s modernas del arte** modern trends in art; **estar al ~ de** to be informed about

corrija *etc* [ko'rrixa] *vb ver* **corregir**

corrillo [ko'rriλo] *nm* ring, circle (of people); (*fig*) clique

corro ['korro] *nm* ring, circle (of people); (*baile*) ring-a-ring-a-roses; **la gente hizo ~** the people formed a ring

corroborar [korroβo'rar] *vt* to corroborate

corroer [korro'er] *vt* (*tb fig*) to corrode, eat away; (*Geo*) to erode

corromper [korrom'per] *vt* (*madera*) to rot; (*fig*) to corrupt

corrosivo, -a [korro'siβo, a] *adj* corrosive

corrupción [korrup'θjon] *nf* rot, decay; (*fig*) corruption

corrupto, -a [ko'rrupto, a] *adj* corrupt

corsé [kor'se] *nm* corset

cortacésped [korta'θespeð] *nm* lawn mower

cortado, -a [kor'taðo, a] *adj* (*con cuchillo*) cut; (*leche*) sour; (*confuso*) confused; (*desconcertado*) embarrassed; (*tímido*) shy ▷ *nm* white coffee (with a little milk)

cortafuegos [korta'fweyos] *nm inv* (*en el bosque*) firebreak, fire lane (*US*); (*Internet*) firewall

cortalápices [korta'lapiθes], **cortalápiz** [korta'lapiθ] *nm inv* (pencil) sharpener

cortar [kor'tar] *vt* to cut; (*suministro*) to cut off; (*un pasaje*) to cut out; (*comunicación, teléfono*) to cut off ▷ *vi* to cut; (*Am Telec*) to hang up; **cortarse** *vr* (*turbarse*) to become embarrassed; (*leche*) to turn, curdle; **~ por lo sano** to settle things once and for all; **~se el pelo** to have one's hair cut; **se cortó la línea** *o* **el teléfono** I got cut off

cortauñas [korta'uɲas] *nm inv* nail clippers *pl*

corte ['korte] *nm* cut, cutting; (*filo*) edge; (*de tela*) piece, length; (*Costura*) tailoring ▷ *nf* (*real*) (royal) court; **~ y confección** dressmaking; **~ de corriente** *o* **luz** power cut; **~ de pelo** haircut; **me da ~ pedírselo** I'm embarrassed to ask him for it; **¡qué ~ le di!** I left him with no comeback!; **C~ Internacional de Justicia** International Court of Justice; **las C~s** the Spanish Parliament *sg*; **hacer la ~ a** to woo, court; *see note*

cortejar [korte'xar] *vt* to court

cortejo [kor'texo] *nm* entourage; **~ fúnebre** funeral procession, cortège

cortés [kor'tes] *adj* courteous, polite

cortesía [korte'sia] *nf* courtesy

corteza [kor'teθa] *nf* (*de árbol*) bark; (*de pan*) crust; (*de fruta*) peel, skin; (*de queso*) rind

cortijo [kor'tixo] *nm* (*Esp*) farm, farmhouse

cortina [kor'tina] *nf* curtain; **~ de humo** smoke screen

corto, -a ['korto, a] *adj* (*breve*) short; (*tímido*) bashful; **~ de luces** not very bright; **~ de oído** hard of hearing; **~ de vista** short-sighted; **estar ~ de fondos** to be short of funds

cortocircuito [kortoθir'kwito] *nm* short-circuit

cortometraje [kortome'traxe] *nm* (*Cine*) short

corvo, -a ['korβo, a] *adj* curved; (*nariz*) hooked ▷ *nf* back of knee

cosa ['kosa] *nf* thing; (*asunto*) affair; **~ de** about; **eso es ~ mía** that's my business; **es poca ~** it's not important; **¡qué ~ más rara!** how strange!

coscorrón [kosko'rron] *nm* bump on the head

cosecha [ko'setʃa] *nf* (*Agr*) harvest; (*acto*) harvesting; (*de vino*) vintage; (*producción*) yield

cosechar [kose'tʃar] *vt* to harvest, gather (in)

coser [ko'ser] *vt* to sew; (*Med*) to stitch (up)

cosmético, -a [kos'metiko, a] *adj, nm* cosmetic ▷ *nf* cosmetics *pl*

cosmos ['kosmos] *nm* cosmos

cosquillas [kos'kiʎas] *nfpl*: **hacer ~** to tickle; **tener ~** to be ticklish

costa ['kosta] *nf* (*Geo*) coast; **C~ Brava** Costa Brava; **C~ Cantábrica** Cantabrian Coast; **C~ de Marfil** Ivory Coast; **C~ del Sol** Costa del Sol; **a ~** (*Com*) at cost; **a ~ de** at the expense of; **a toda ~** at any price

costado [kos'taðo] *nm* side; **de ~** (*dormir*) on one's side; **español por los 4 ~s** Spanish through and through

costal [kos'tal] *nm* sack

costanera [kostaˈnera] *nf* (*Am*) promenade, sea front

costar [kos'tar] *vt* (*valer*) to cost; **me cuesta hablarle** I find it hard to talk to him; **¿cuánto cuesta?** how much does it cost?

Costa Rica [kosta'rika] *nf* Costa Rica

costarricense [kostarri'θense], **costarriqueño, -a** [kostarri'keɲo, a] *adj, nm/f* Costa Rican

coste ['koste] *nm* (*Com*): **~ promedio** average cost; **~s fijos** fixed costs; *ver* **costo**

costear [koste'ar] *vt* to pay for; (*Com etc*) to finance; (*Naut*) to sail along the coast of; **costearse** *vr* (*negocio*) to pay for itself, cover its costs

costero [kos'tero, a] *adj* coastal, coast *cpd*

costilla [kos'tiʎa] *nf* rib; (*Culin*) cutlet

costo ['kosto] *nm* cost, price; **~ directo** direct cost; **~ de expedición** shipping charges; **~ de sustitución** replacement cost; **~ unitario** unit cost; **~ de la vida** cost of living

costoso, -a [kos'toso, a] *adj* costly, expensive

costra ['kostra] *nf* (*corteza*) crust; (*Med*) scab

costumbre [kos'tumbre] *nf* custom, habit; **como de ~** as usual

costura [kos'tura] *nf* sewing, needlework; (*confección*) dressmaking; (*zurcido*) seam

costurera [kostu'rera] *nf* dressmaker

costurero [kostu'rero] *nm* sewing box *o* case

cota ['kota] *nf* (*Geo*) height above sea level; (*fig*) height

cotarro [ko'tarro] *nm*: **dirigir el ~** (*fam*) to rule the roost

cotejar [kote'xar] *vt* to compare

cotidiano, -a [koti'ðjano, a] *adj* daily, day to day

cotilla [ko'tiʎa] *nf* busybody, gossip

cotillear [kotiʎe'ar] *vi* to gossip

cotilleo [koti'ʎeo] *nm* gossip(ing)

cotización [kotiθa'θjon] *nf* (*Com*) quotation, price; (*de club*) dues *pl*

cotizar [koti'θar] *vt* (*Com*) to quote, price; **cotizarse** *vr* (*fig*) to be highly prized; **~se a** to sell at, fetch; (*Bolsa*) to stand at, be quoted at

coto ['koto] *nm* (*terreno cercado*) enclosure; (*de caza*) reserve; (*Com*) price-fixing agreement; **poner ~ a** to put a stop to

cotorra [ko'torra] *nf* (*Zool: loro*) parrot; (*fam: persona*) windbag

coyote [ko'jote] *nm* coyote, prairie wolf

coyuntura [kojun'tura] *nf* (*Anat*) joint; (*fig*) juncture, occasion; **esperar una ~ favorable** to await a favourable moment

coz [koθ] *nf* kick

crack [krak] *nm* (*droga*) crack

cráneo ['kraneo] *nm* skull, cranium

cráter ['krater] *nm* crater

crayón [kra'jon] *nm* (*Am: lápiz*) (coloured) pencil; (*cera*) crayon

creación [krea'θjon] *nf* creation

creador, a [krea'ðor, a] *adj* creative ▷ *nm/f* creator

crear [kre'ar] *vt* to create, make; (*originar*) to originate; (*Inform: archivo*) to create; **crearse** *vr* (*comité etc*) to be set up

creativo, -a [krea'tiβo, a] *adj* creative

crecer [kre'θer] *vi* to grow; (*precio*) to rise; **crecerse** *vr* (*engreírse*) to get cocky

creces ['kreθes]: **con ~** *adv* amply, fully

crecido, -a [kre'θiðo, a] *adj* (*persona, planta*) full-grown; (*cantidad*) large ▷ *nf* (*de río*) spate, flood

creciente [kre'θjente] *adj* growing; (*cantidad*) increasing; (*luna*) crescent ▷ *nm* crescent

crecimiento [kreθi'mjento] *nm* growth; (*aumento*) increase; (*Com*) rise

credencial [kreðen'θjal] *nf* (*Am: tarjeta*) card; **credenciales** *nfpl* credentials; **~ de socio** (*Am*) membership card

crédito ['kreðito] *nm* credit; **a ~** on credit; **dar ~ a** to believe (in); **~ al consumidor** consumer credit; **~ rotativo** *o* **renovable** revolving credit

credo ['kreðo] *nm* creed

crédulo, -a ['kreðulo, a] *adj* credulous

creencia [kre'enθja] *nf* belief

creer [kre'er] *vt, vi* to think, believe; (*considerar*) to think, consider; **creerse** *vr* to believe o.s. (to be); **~ en** to believe in; **creo que sí/no** I think/don't think so; **¡ya lo creo!** I should think so!

creíble [kre'iβle] *adj* credible, believable

creído, -a [kre'iðo, a] *adj* (*engreído*) conceited

crema ['krema] *adj inv* cream (coloured) ▷ *nf* cream; (*natillas*) custard; **~ batida** (*Am*) whipped cream; **~ pastelera** (confectioner's) custard; **la ~ de la sociedad** the cream of society

cremallera [krema'ʎera] *nf* zip (fastener) (*Brit*), zipper (*US*)

crematorio [krema'torjo] *nm* crematorium (*Brit*), crematory (*US*)

crepe ['krepe] *nf* (*Esp*) pancake

crepitar [krepi'tar] *vi* (*fuego*) to crackle

crepúsculo [kre'puskulo] *nm* twilight, dusk

crespo, -a ['krespo, a] *adj* (*pelo*) curly

crespón [kres'pon] *nm* crêpe

cresta ['kresta] *nf* (*Geo, Zool*) crest

cretino, -a [kre'tino, a] *adj* cretinous ▷ *nm/f* cretin

creyendo *etc* [kre'jendo] *vb ver* **creer**

creyente [kre'jente] *nm/f* believer

creyó *etc* [kre'jo] *vb ver* **creer**

crezco *etc vb ver* **crecer**

cría ['kria] *vb ver* **criar** ▷ *nf* (*de animales*) rearing, breeding; (*animal*) young; *ver tb* **crío**

criada [kri'aða] *nf ver* **criado, a**

criadero [kria'ðero] *nm* nursery; (*Zool*) breeding place

criado, -a [kri'aðo, a] *nm* servant ▷ *nf* servant, maid

criador [kria'ðor] *nm* breeder

crianza [kri'anθa] *nf* rearing, breeding; (*fig*) breeding; (*Med*) lactation

criar [kri'ar] *vt* (*amamantar*) to suckle, feed; (*educar*) to bring up; (*producir*) to grow, produce; (*animales*) to breed; **criarse** *vr* to grow (up); **~ cuervos** to nourish a viper in one's bosom; **Dios los cría y ellos se juntan** birds of a feather flock together

criatura [kria'tura] *nf* creature; (*niño*) baby, (small) child

criba ['kriβa] *nf* sieve

cribar [kri'βar] *vt* to sieve

crimen ['krimen] *nm* crime; **~ pasional** crime of passion

criminal [krimi'nal] *adj, nm/f* criminal

crin [krin] *nf* (*tb:* **~es**) mane

crío, -a ['krio, a] *nm/f* (*fam: chico*) kid ▷ *nf* (*de animales*) rearing, breeding; (*animal*) young

cripta ['kripta] *nf* crypt

crisis ['krisis] *nf inv* crisis; **~ nerviosa** nervous breakdown

crisma ['krisma] *nf*: **romperle la ~ a algn** (*fam*) to knock sb's block off

crismas ['krismas] *nm inv* (*Esp*) Christmas card

crispación [krispa'θjon] *nf* tension

crispar [kris'par] *vt* (*músculo*) to cause to contract; (*nervios*) to set on edge

cristal [kris'tal] *nm* crystal; (*de ventana*) glass, pane; (*lente*) lens; **de ~** glass *cpd*; **~ ahumado/tallado** smoked/cut glass

cristalino, -a [krista'lino, a] *adj* crystalline; (*fig*) clear ▷ *nm* lens of the eye

cristalizar [kristali'θar] *vt, vi* to crystallize

cristiandad [kristjan'dað] *nf*, **cristianismo** [kristja'nismo] *nm* Christianity

cristianismo [kristja'nismo] *nm* Christianity

cristiano, -a [kris'tjano, a] *adj, nm/f* Christian; **hablar en ~** to speak proper Spanish; (*fig*) to speak clearly

Cristo ['kristo] *nm* (*dios*) Christ; (*crucifijo*) crucifix

criterio [kri'terjo] *nm* criterion; (*juicio*) judgement; (*enfoque*) attitude, approach; (*punto de vista*) view, opinion; **~ de clasificación** (*Inform*) sort criterion

criticar [kriti'kar] *vt* to criticize

crítico, -a ['kritiko, a] *adj* critical ▷ *nm* critic ▷ *nf* criticism; (*Teat etc*) review, notice; **la crítica** the critics *pl*

Croacia [kro'aθja] *nf* Croatia

croar [kro'ar] *vi* to croak

croata [kro'ata] *adj, nm/f* Croat(ian) ▷ *nm* (*Ling*) Croat(ian)

croissant, croissant [krwa'san] *nm* croissant

crol ['krol] *nm* crawl

cromo ['kromo] *nm* chrome; (*Tip*) coloured print

cromosoma [kromo'soma] *nm* chromosome

crónico, -a ['kroniko, a] *adj* chronic ▷ *nf* chronicle, account; (*de periódico*) feature, article

cronología [kronolo'xia] *nf* chronology

cronológico, -a [krono'loxiko, a] *adj* chronological

cronometrar [kronome'trar] *vt* to time

cronómetro [kro'nometro] *nm* (*Deporte*) stopwatch; (*Tec etc*) chronometer

croqueta [kro'keta] *nf* croquette, rissole

cruce ['kruθe] *vb ver* **cruzar** ▷ *nm* (*para peatones*) crossing; (*de carreteras*) crossroads; (*Auto etc*) junction, intersection; (*Bio: proceso*) crossbreeding; **luces de ~** dipped headlights

crucero [kru'θero] *nm* (*Naut: barco*) cruise ship; (*: viaje*) cruise

crucial [kru'θjal] *adj* crucial

crucificar [kruθifi'kar] *vt* to crucify; (*fig*) to torment

crucifijo [kruθi'fixo] *nm* crucifix

crucigrama [kruθi'ɣrama] *nm* crossword (puzzle)

cruda ['kruða] *nf* (*Am: fam*) hangover

crudo, -a ['kruðo, a] *adj* raw; (*no maduro*) unripe; (*petróleo*) crude; (*rudo, cruel*) cruel; (*agua*) hard; (*clima etc*) harsh ▷ *nm* crude (oil)

cruel [krwel] *adj* cruel

crueldad [krwel'ðað] *nf* cruelty

crujido [kru'xiðo] *nm* (*de madera etc*) creak

crujiente [kru'xjente] *adj* (*galleta etc*) crunchy

crujir [kru'xir] *vi* (*madera etc*) to creak; (*dedos*) to crack; (*dientes*) to grind; (*nieve, arena*) to crunch

cruz [kruθ] *nf* cross; (*de moneda*) tails *sg*; (*fig*) burden; **~ gamada** swastika; **C~ Roja** Red Cross

cruzado, -a [kru'θaðo, a] *adj* crossed ▷ *nm* crusader ▷ *nf* crusade

cruzar [kru'θar] *vt* to cross; (*palabras*) to exchange; **cruzarse** *vr* (*líneas etc*) to cross, intersect; (*personas*) to pass each other; **~se de brazos** to fold one's arms; (*fig*) not to lift a finger to help; **~se con algn en la calle** to pass sb in the street

cuaderno [kwa'ðerno] *nm* notebook; (*de escuela*) exercise book; (*Naut*) logbook

cuadra ['kwaðra] *nf* (*caballeriza*) stable; (*Am*) (city) block

cuadrado, -a [kwa'ðraðo, a] *adj* square ▷ *nm* (*Mat*) square

cuadrar [kwa'ðrar] *vt* to square; (*Tip*) to justify ▷ *vi*: **~ con** (*cuenta*) to square with, tally with; **cuadrarse** *vr* (*soldado*) to stand to attention; **~ por la derecha/izquierda** to right-/left-justify

cuadriculado, -a [kwaðriku'laðo, a] *adj*: **papel ~** squared *o* graph paper

cuadrilátero [kwaðri'latero] *nm* (*Deporte*) boxing ring; (*Geom*) quadrilateral

cuadrilla [kwa'ðriʎa] *nf* (*de amigos*) party, group; (*de delincuentes*) gang; (*de obreros*) team

cuadro ['kwaðro] *nm* square; (*Pintura*) painting; (*Teat*) scene; (*diagrama: tb:* **~ sinóptico**) chart, table, diagram; (*Deporte, Med*) team; (*Pol*) executive; **~ de mandos** control panel; **a ~s** check *cpd*; **tela a ~s** checked (*Brit*) *o* chequered (*US*) material

cuádruplo, -a [ˈkwaðruplo, a], **cuádruple** [ˈkwaðruple] *adj* quadruple

cuajar [kwa'xar] *vt* to thicken; (*leche*) to curdle; (*sangre*) to congeal; (*adornar*) to adorn; (*Culin*) to set ▷ *vi* (*nieve*) to lie; (*fig*) to become set, become established; (*idea*) to be received, be acceptable; **cuajarse** *vr* to curdle; to congeal; (*llenarse*) to fill up

cuajo ['kwaxo] *nm*: **de ~** (*arrancar*) by the roots; (*cortar*) completely; **arrancar algo de ~** to tear sth out by its roots

cual [kwal] *adv* like, as ▷ *pron*: **el ~** *etc* which; (*persona: sujeto*) who; (*: objeto*) whom; **lo ~** (*relativo*) which; **allá cada ~** every man to his own taste; **son a ~ más gandul** each is as idle as the other; **cada ~** each one ▷ *adj* such as; **tal ~** just as it is

cuál [kwal] *pron interrogativo* which (one), what

cualesquier [kwales'kjer], **cualesquiera** [kwales'kjera] *adj pl, pron pl de* **cualquier**; **cualquiera**

cualidad [kwali'ðað] *nf* quality

cualquier [kwal'kjer], **cualquiera** [kwal'kjera] (*pl* **cualesquier(a)**) *adj* any ▷ *pron* anybody, anyone; (*quienquiera*) whoever; **en ~ momento** any time; **~ día/ libro** any day/book; **en ~ parte** anywhere; **~a que sea** whichever it is; (*persona*) whoever it is; **un coche ~a servirá** any car will do; **no es un hombre ~a** he isn't just anybody; **eso ~a lo sabe hacer** anybody can do that; **es un ~a** he's a nobody

cuando ['kwando] *adv* when; (*aún si*) if, even if ▷ *conj* (*puesto que*) since ▷ *prep*: **yo, ~ niño ...** when I was a child *o* as a child I ...; **~ no sea así** even if it is not so; **~ más** at the (most); **~ menos** at least; **~ no** if not, otherwise; **de ~ en ~** from time to time; **ven ~ quieras** come when(ever) you like

cuándo ['kwando] *adv* when; **¿desde ~?**, **¿de ~ acá?** since when?

cuantía [kwan'tia] *nf* (*importe: de pérdidas, deuda, daños*) extent; (*importancia*) importance

cuantioso, -a [kwan'tjoso, a] *adj* substantial

⊙ **PALABRA CLAVE**

cuanto, -a ['kwanto, a] *adj* **1** (*todo*): **tiene todo cuanto desea** he's got everything he wants; **le daremos cuantos ejemplares necesite** we'll give him as many copies as *o* all the copies he needs; **cuantos hombres la ven** all the men who see her

2 unos cuantos: **había unos cuantos periodistas** there were (quite) a few journalists

3 (+*más*): **cuanto más vino bebas peor te sentirás** the more wine you drink the worse

you'll feel; **cuantos más, mejor** the more the merrier
▷ *pron*: **tiene cuanto desea** he has everything he wants; **tome cuanto/ cuantos quiera** take as much/many as you want
▷ *adv*: **en cuanto**: **en cuanto profesor** as a teacher; **en cuanto a mí** as for me; *ver tb* **antes**
▷ *conj* **1**: **cuanto más gana menos gasta** the more he earns the less he spends; **cuanto más joven se es más se es confiado** the younger you are the more trusting you are
2: **en cuanto**: **en cuanto llegue/llegué** as soon as I arrive/arrived

cuánto, -a ['kwanto, a] *adj (exclamación)* what a lot of; *(interrogativo: sg)* how much?; *(: pl)* how many? ▷ *pron, adv* how; *(interrogativo: sg)* how much?; *(: pl)* how many? ▷ *excl*: **¡~ me alegro!** I'm so glad!; **¡cuánta gente!** what a lot of people!; **¿~ tiempo?** how long?; **¿~ cuesta?** how much does it cost?; **¿a ~s estamos?** what's the date?; **¿~ hay de aquí a Bilbao?** how far is it from here to Bilbao?; **Señor no sé ~s** Mr. So-and-So

cuarenta [kwa'renta] *num* forty

cuarentena [kwaren'tena] *nf (Med etc)* quarantine; *(conjunto)* forty(-odd)

cuaresma [kwa'resma] *nf* Lent

cuarta ['kwarta] *nf ver* **cuarto**

cuartear [kwarte'ar] *vt* to quarter; *(dividir)* to divide up; **cuartearse** *vr* to crack, split

cuartel [kwar'tel] *nm (de ciudad)* quarter, district; *(Mil)* barracks *pl*; **~ de bomberos** *(Am)* fire station; **~ general** headquarters *pl*

cuarteto [kwar'teto] *nm* quartet

cuartilla [kwar'tiʎa] *nf (hoja)* sheet (of paper); **cuartillas** *nfpl (Tip)* copy *sg*

cuarto, -a ['kwarto, a] *adj* fourth ▷ *nm (Mat)* quarter, fourth; *(habitación)* room ▷ *nf (Mat)* quarter, fourth; *(palmo)* span; **~ de baño** bathroom; **~ de estar** living room; **~ de hora** quarter (of an) hour; **~ de kilo** quarter kilo; **~s final** quarter finals; **no tener un ~** to be broke *(fam)*

cuarzo ['kwarθo] *nm* quartz

cuatrimestre [kwatri'mestre] *nm* four-month period

cuatro ['kwatro] *num* four; **las ~** four o'clock; **el ~ de octubre** (on) the fourth of October; *ver tb* **seis**

cuatrocientos, -as [kwatro'θjentos, as] *num* four hundred; *ver tb* **seiscientos**

Cuba ['kuβa] *nf* Cuba

cuba ['kuβa] *nf* cask, barrel; **estar como una ~** *(fam)* to be sloshed

cubalibre [kuβa'liβre] *nm* (white) rum and coke®

cubano, -a [ku'βano, a] *adj, nm/f* Cuban

cubata [ku'βata] *nm* = **cubalibre**

cubeta [ku'βeta] *nf (balde)* bucket, tub

cúbico, -a ['kuβiko, a] *adj* cubic

cubierto, -a [ku'βjerto, a] *pp de* **cubrir** ▷ *adj* covered; *(cielo)* overcast ▷ *nm* cover; *(en la mesa)* place ▷ *nf* cover, covering; *(neumático)* tyre; *(Naut)* deck; **cubiertos** *nmpl* cutlery *sg*; **a ~** under cover; **a ~ de** covered with *o* in; **precio del ~** cover charge

cubil [ku'βil] *nm* den

cubilete [kuβi'lete] *nm (en juegos)* cup

cubito [ku'βito] *nm*: **~ de hielo** ice cube

cubo ['kuβo] *nm* cube; *(balde)* bucket, tub; *(Tec)* drum; **~ de (la) basura** dustbin (Brit), trash can (US)

cubrecama [kuβre'kama] *nm* bedspread

cubrir [ku'βrir] *vt* to cover; *(vacante)* to fill; *(Bio)* to mate with; *(gastos)* to meet; **cubrirse** *vr (cielo)* to become overcast; *(Com: gastos)* to be met *o* paid; *(: deuda)* to be covered; **~ las formas** to keep up appearances; **lo cubrieron las aguas** the waters closed over it; **el agua casi me cubría** I was almost out of my depth

cucaracha [kuka'ratʃa] *nf* cockroach

cuchara [ku'tʃara] *nf* spoon; *(Tec)* scoop

cucharada [kutʃa'raða] *nf* spoonful; **~ colmada** heaped spoonful

cucharadita [kutʃara'ðita] *nf* teaspoonful

cucharilla [kutʃa'riʎa] *nf* teaspoon

cucharón [kutʃa'ron] *nm* ladle

cuchichear [kutʃitʃe'ar] *vi* to whisper

cuchilla [ku'tʃiʎa] *nf (large)* knife; *(de arma blanca)* blade; **~ de afeitar** razor blade; **pasar a ~** to put to the sword

cuchillada [kutʃi'ʎaða] *nf (golpe)* stab; *(herida)* knife *o* stab wound

cuchillo [ku'tʃiʎo] *nm* knife

cuchitril [kutʃi'tril] *nm* hovel; *(habitación etc)* pigsty

cuclillas [ku'kliʎas] *nfpl*: **en ~** squatting

cuco, -a ['kuko, a] *adj* pretty; *(astuto)* sharp ▷ *nm* cuckoo

cucurucho [kuku'rutʃo] *nm* paper cone, cornet

cueca ['kweka] *nf* Chilean national dance

cuello ['kweʎo] *nm (Anat)* neck; *(de vestido, camisa)* collar

cuenca ['kwenka] *nf (Anat)* eye socket; *(Geo: valle)* bowl, deep valley; *(: fluvial)* basin

cuenco ['kwenko] *nm* (earthenware) bowl

cuenta ['kwenta] *vb ver* **contar** ▷ *nf (cálculo)* count, counting; *(en café, restaurante)* bill (Brit), check (US); *(Com)* account; *(de collar)* bead; *(fig)* account; **a fin de ~s** in the end; **en resumidas ~s** in short; **caer en la ~** to catch on; **dar ~ a algn de sus actos** to account to sb for one's actions; **darse ~ de** to realize; **tener en ~** to bear in mind; **echar ~s** to take stock; **~ atrás** countdown; **~ corriente/de ahorros/a plazo (fijo)** current/savings/ deposit account; **~ de caja** cash account; **~ de capital** capital account; **~ por cobrar** account receivable; **~ de correo** (Internet) email account; **~ de crédito** credit o loan account; **~ de gastos e ingresos** income and expenditure account; **~ por pagar** account payable; **abonar una cantidad en ~ a algn** to credit a sum to sb's account; **ajustar** o **liquidar una ~** to settle an account; **pasar la ~** to send the bill

cuentakilómetros [kwentaki'lometros] *nm inv* (*de distancias*) ≈ milometer, clock; (*velocímetro*) speedometer

cuento ['kwento] *vb ver* contar ▷ *nm* story; (*Lit*) short story; **~ chino** tall story; **~ de hadas** fairy tale o story; **es el ~ de nunca acabar** it's an endless business; **eso no viene a ~** that's irrelevant

cuerda ['kwerða] *nf* rope; (*hilo*) string; (*de reloj*) spring; (*Mus: de violín etc*) string; (*Mat*) chord; (*Anat*) cord; **~ floja** tightrope; **~s vocales** vocal cords; **dar ~ a un reloj** to wind up a clock

cuerdo, -a ['kwerðo, a] *adj* sane; (*prudente*) wise, sensible

cuerno ['kwerno] *nm* (*Zool: gen*) horn; (*: de ciervo*) antler; **poner los ~s a** (*fam*) to cuckold; **saber a ~ quemado** to leave a nasty taste

cuero ['kwero] *nm* (*Zool*) skin, hide; (*Tec*) leather; **en ~s** stark naked; **~ cabelludo** scalp

cuerpo ['kwerpo] *nm* body; (*cadáver*) corpse; (*fig*) main part; **~ de bomberos** fire brigade; **~ diplomático** diplomatic corps; **luchar ~ a ~** to fight hand-to-hand; **tomar ~** (*plan etc*) to take shape

cuervo ['kwerβo] *nm* (*Zool*) raven, crow; *ver* criar

cuesta ['kwesta] *vb ver* costar ▷ *nf* slope; (*en camino etc*) hill; **~ arriba/abajo** uphill/downhill; **a ~s** on one's back

cueste *etc vb ver* costar

cuestión [kwes'tjon] *nf* matter, question, issue; (*riña*) quarrel, dispute; **eso es otra ~** that's another matter

cuestionario [kwestjo'narjo] *nm* questionnaire

cuete ['kwete] *adj* (*Am: fam*) drunk ▷ *nm* (*cohete*) rocket; (*fam: embriaguez*) drunkenness; (*Am: fam*) steak

cueva ['kweβa] *nf* cave

cuidado [kwi'ðaðo] *nm* care, carefulness; (*preocupación*) care, worry ▷ *excl* careful!, look out!; **eso me tiene sin ~** I'm not worried about that

cuidadoso, -a [kwiða'ðoso, a] *adj* careful; (*preocupado*) anxious

cuidar [kwi'ðar] *vt* (*Med*) to care for; (*ocuparse de*) to take care of, look after; (*detalles*) to pay attention to ▷ *vi*: **~ de** to take care of, look after; **cuidarse** *vr* to look after o.s.; **~se de hacer algo** to take care to do sth

culata [ku'lata] *nf* (*de fusil*) butt

culebra [ku'leβra] *nf* snake; **~ de cascabel** rattlesnake

culebrón [kule'βron] *nm* (*fam*) soap (opera)

culinario, -a [kuli'narjo, a] *adj* culinary, cooking *cpd*

culminación [kulmina'θjon] *nf* culmination

culminar [kulmi'nar] *vi* to culminate

culo ['kulo] *nm* (*fam: asentaderas*) bottom, backside, bum (*Brit*); (*: ano*) arse(hole) (*Brit!*), ass(hole) (*US!*); (*de vaso*) bottom

culpa ['kulpa] *nf* fault; (*Jur*) guilt; **culpas** *nfpl* sins; **por ~ de** through, because of; **echar la ~ a algn** to blame sb for sth; **tener la ~ (de)** to be to blame (for)

culpabilidad [kulpaβili'ðað] *nf* guilt

culpable [kul'paβle] *adj* guilty ▷ *nm/f* culprit; **confesarse ~** to plead guilty; **declarar ~ a algn** to find sb guilty

culpar [kul'par] *vt* to blame; (*acusar*) to accuse

cultivar [kulti'βar] *vt* to cultivate; (*cosecha*) to raise; (*talento*) to develop

cultivo [kul'tiβo] *nm* (*acto*) cultivation; (*plantas*) crop; (*Bio*) culture

culto, -a ['kulto, a] *adj* (*cultivado*) cultivated; (*que tiene cultura*) cultured, educated ▷ *nm* (*homenaje*) worship; (*religión*) cult; (*Pol etc*) cult

cultura [kul'tura] *nf* culture

cultural [kultu'ral] *adj* cultural

culturismo [kultu'rismo] *nm* body-building

cumbia ['kumbja] *nf* popular Colombian dance

cumbre ['kumbre] *nf* summit, top; (*fig*) top, height; **conferencia (en la) ~** summit (conference)

cumpleaños [kumple'aɲos] *nm inv* birthday

cumplido, -a [kum'pliðo, a] *adj* complete, perfect; (*abundante*) plentiful; (*cortés*) courteous ▷ *nm* compliment; **visita de ~** courtesy call

cumplidor, a [kumpli'ðor, a] *adj* reliable

cumplimentar [kumplimen'tar] *vt* to congratulate; (*órdenes*) to carry out

cumplimiento [kumpli'mjento] *nm* (*de un deber*) fulfilment, execution, performance; (*acabamiento*) completion; (*Com*) expiry, end

cumplir [kum'plir] *vt* (*orden*) to carry out, obey; (*promesa*) to carry out, fulfil; (*condena*) to serve; (*años*) to reach, attain ▷ *vi* (*pago*) to fall due; (*plazo*) to expire; **cumplirse** *vr* (*plazo*) to expire; (*plan etc*) to be fulfilled; (*vaticinio*) to come true; **hoy cumple dieciocho años** he is eighteen today; **~ con** (*deber*) to carry out, fulfil

cúmulo ['kumulo] *nm* (*montón*) heap; (*nube*) cumulus

cuna ['kuna] *nf* cradle, cot; **canción de ~** lullaby

cundir [kun'dir] *vi* (*noticia, rumor, pánico*) to spread; (*rendir*) to go a long way

cuneta [ku'neta] *nf* ditch

cuña ['kuɲa] *nf* (*Tec*) wedge; (*Com*) advertising spot; (*Med*) bedpan; **tener ~s** to have influence

cuñado, -a [ku'ɲaðo, a] *nm/f* brother/sister-in-law

cuota ['kwota] *nf (parte proporcional)* share; *(cotización)* fee, dues *pl*; **~ inicial** *(Com)* down payment

cupe *etc* ['kupe] *vb ver* **caber**

cupiera *etc* [ku'pjera] *vb ver* **caber**

cupo *etc* ['kupo] *vb ver* **caber** ▷ *nm* quota, share; *(Com)*: **~ de importación** import quota; **~ de ventas** sales quota

cupón [ku'pon] *nm* coupon; **~ de la ONCE** *o* **de los ciegos** ONCE lottery ticket; *ver tb* **lotería**

cúpula ['kupula] *nf (Arq)* dome

cura ['kura] *nf (curación)* cure; *(método curativo)* treatment ▷ *nm* priest; **~ de emergencia** emergency treatment

curación [kura'θjon] *nf* cure; *(acción)* curing

curandero, -a [kuran'dero, a] *nm/f* healer; *(pej)* quack

curar [ku'rar] *vt (Med: herida)* to treat, dress; *(: enfermo)* to cure; *(Culin)* to cure, salt; *(cuero)* to tan ▷ *vi*, **curarse** *vr* to get well, recover

curiosear [kurjose'ar] *vt* to glance at, look over ▷ *vi* to look round, wander round; *(explorar)* to poke about

curiosidad [kurjosi'ðað] *nf* curiosity

curioso, -a [ku'rjoso, a] *adj* curious; *(aseado)* neat ▷ *nm/f* bystander, onlooker; **¡qué ~!** how odd!

curita [ku'rita] *nf (Am)* sticking plaster

currante [ku'rrante] *nm/f (fam)* worker

currar [ku'rrar] *vi (fam)*, **currelar** [kurre'lar] *vi (fam)* to work

currículo [ku'rrikulo], **currículum** [ku'rrikulum] *nm* curriculum vitae

curro ['kurro] *nm (fam)* work, job

cursar [kur'sar] *vt (Escol)* to study

cursi ['kursi] *adj (fam)* pretentious; *(: amanerado)* affected

cursilada [kursi'laða] *nf*: **¡qué ~!** how tacky!

cursillo [kur'siʎo] *nm* short course

cursiva [kur'siβa] *nf* italics *pl*

curso ['kurso] *nm (dirección)* course; *(fig)* progress; *(Escol)* school year; *(Univ)* academic year; **en ~** *(año)* current; *(proceso)* going on, under way; **moneda de ~ legal** legal tender

cursor [kur'sor] *nm (Inform)* cursor; *(Tec)* slide

curtido, -a [kur'tiðo, a] *adj (cara etc)* weather-beaten; *(fig: persona)* experienced

curtir [kur'tir] *vt (piel)* to tan; *(fig)* to harden

curul [ku'rul] *nm (Am: escaño)* seat

curvo, -a ['kurβo, a] *adj (gen)* curved; *(torcido)* bent ▷ *nf (gen)* curve, bend; **curva de rentabilidad** *(Com)* break-even chart

cúspide ['kuspiðe] *nf (Geo)* summit, peak; *(fig)* top, pinnacle

custodia [kus'toðja] *nf (cuidado)* safekeeping; *(Jur)* custody

custodiar [kusto'ðjar] *vt (conservar)* to keep, take care of; *(vigilar)* to guard

custodio [kus'toðjo] *nm* guardian, keeper

cutáneo, -a [ku'taneo, a] *adj* skin *cpd*

cutícula [ku'tikula] *nf* cuticle

cutis ['kutis] *nm inv* skin, complexion

cutre ['kutre] *adj (fam: lugar)* grotty; *(: persona)* naff

cuyo, -a ['kujo, a] *pron (de quien)* whose; *(de que)* whose, of which; **la señora en cuya casa me hospedé** the lady in whose house I stayed; **el asunto ~s detalles conoces** the affair the details of which you know; **por ~ motivo** for which reason; **en ~ caso** in which case

C.V. *abr* (= Curriculum Vitae) CV; (= caballos de vapor) H.P.

d

D. *abr* (= *Don*) Esq

dádiva ['daðiβa] *nf* (*donación*) donation; (*regalo*) gift

dadivoso, -a [daði'βoso, a] *adj* generous

dado, -a ['daðo, a] *pp de* **dar** ▷ *nm* die; **dados** *nmpl* dice ▷ *adj*: **en un momento ~** at a certain point; **ser ~ a (hacer algo)** to be very fond of (doing sth); **~ que** *conj* given that

daltónico, -a [dal'toniko, a] *adj* colour-blind

dama ['dama] *nf* (*gen*) lady; (*Ajedrez*) queen; **damas** *nfpl* draughts; **primera ~** (*Teat*) leading lady; (*Pol*) president's wife, first lady (*US*); **~ de honor** (*de reina*) lady-in-waiting; (*de novia*) bridesmaid

damasco [da'masko] *nm* (*tela*) damask; (*Am: drbol*) apricot tree; (: *fruta*) apricot

damnificar [damnifi'kar] *vt* to harm; (*persona*) to injure

danés, -esa [da'nes, esa] *adj* Danish ▷ *nm/f* Dane ▷ *nm* (*Ling*) Danish

danza ['danθa] *nf* (*gen*) dancing; (*una danza*) dance

danzar [dan'θar] *vt, vi* to dance

dañar [da'ɲar] *vt* (*objeto*) to damage; (*persona*) to hurt; (*estropear*) to spoil; **dañarse** *vr* (*objeto*) to get damaged

dañino, -a [da'ɲino, a] *adj* harmful

daño ['daɲo] *nm* (*a un objeto*) damage; (*a una persona*) harm, injury; **~s y perjuicios** (*Jur*) damages; **hacer ~ a** to damage; (*persona*) to hurt, injure; **hacerse ~** to hurt o.s.

dañoso, -a [da'ɲoso, a] *adj* harmful

dar [dar] *vt* **1** (*gen*) to give; (*obra de teatro*) to put on; (*film*) to show; (*fiesta*) to have; **dar algo a algn** to give sb sth *o* sth to sb; **dar una patada a algn/algo** to kick sb/sth, give sb/ sth a kick; **dar un susto a algn** to give sb a fright; **dar de beber a algn** to give sb a drink; **dar de comer** to feed

2 (*producir: intereses*) to yield; (: *fruta*) to produce

3 (*locuciones +n*): **da gusto escucharle** it's a pleasure to listen to him; **me da pena/asco** it frightens/sickens me; *ver tb* **paseo** *y otros sustantivos*

4 (*+ n. = perífrasis de verbo*): **me da asco** it sickens me

5 (*considerar*): **dar algo por descontado/ entendido** to take sth for granted/as read; **dar algo por concluido** to consider sth finished; **le dieron por desaparecido** they gave him up as lost

6 (*hora*): **el reloj dio las seis** the clock struck six (o'clock)

7: **me da lo mismo** it's all the same to me; *ver tb* **igual; más**

8: **¡y dale!** (*¡otra vez!*) not again!; **estar/seguir dale que dale** *o* **dale que te pego** *o* (*Am*) **dale y dale** to go/keep on and on

▷ *vi* **1**: **dar a** (*habitación*) to overlook, look on to; (*accionar: botón etc*) to press, hit

2: **dar con: dimos con él dos horas más tarde** we came across him two hours later; **al final di con la solución** I eventually came up with the answer

3: **dar en** (*blanco, suelo*) to hit; **el sol me da en la cara** the sun is shining (right) in my face

4: **dar de sí** (*zapatos etc*) to stretch, give

5: **dar para** to be enough for; **nuestro presupuesto no da para más** our budget's really tight

6: **dar por**: **le ha dado por estudiar música** now he's into studying music

7: **dar que hablar** to set people talking; **una película que da que pensar** a thought-provoking film

darse *vr* **1**: **darse un baño** to have a bath; **darse un golpe** to hit o.s.

2: **darse por vencido** to give up; **con eso me doy por satisfecho** I'd settle for that

3 (*ocurrir*): **se han dado muchos casos** there have been a lot of cases

4: **darse a**: **se ha dado a la bebida** he's taken to drinking

5: **se me dan bien/mal las ciencias** I'm good/bad at science

6: **dárselas de**: **se las da de experto** he fancies himself *o* poses as an expert

dardo ['darðo] *nm* dart

dársena ['darsena] *nf* (*Naut*) dock

datar [da'tar] *vi*: **~ de** to date from

dátil ['datil] *nm* date
dato ['dato] *nm* fact, piece of information; (*Mat*) datum; **datos** *nmpl* (*Inform*) data; **~s de entrada/salida** input/output data; **~s personales** personal details
dcha. *abr* (= *derecha*) r (= *right*)
d. de C. *abr* (= *después de Cristo*) A.D. (= *Anno Domini*)

○ **PALABRA CLAVE**

de [de] *prep* (**de + el = del**) 1 (*posesión, pertenencia*) of; **la casa de Isabel/mis padres** Isabel's/my parents' house; **es de ellos/ella** it's theirs/hers; **un libro de Unamuno** a book by Unamuno
2 (*origen, distancia, con números*) from; **soy de Gijón** I'm from Gijón; **de 8 a 20** from 8 to 20; **5 metros de largo** 5 metres long; **salir del cine** to go out o leave the cinema; **de ... en ...** from ... to ...; **de 2 en 2** 2 by 2, 2 at a time; **9 de cada 10** 9 out of every 10
3 (*valor descriptivo*) **una copa de vino** a glass of wine; **una silla de madera** a wooden chair; **la mesa de la cocina** the kitchen table; **un viaje de dos días** a two-day journey; **un billete de 50 euros** a 50-euro note; **un niño de tres años** a three-year-old (child); **una máquina de coser** a sewing machine; **la ciudad de Madrid** the city of Madrid; **el tonto de Juan** that idiot Juan; **ir vestido de gris** to be dressed in grey; **la niña del vestido azul** the girl in the blue dress; **la chica del pelo largo** the girl with long hair; **trabaja de profesora** she works as a teacher; **de lado** sideways; **de atrás/delante** rear/front
4 (*hora, tiempo*) **a las 8 de la mañana** at 8 o'clock in the morning; **de día/noche** by day/night; **de hoy en ocho días** a week from now; **de niño era gordo** as a child he was fat
5 (*comparaciones*) **más/menos de cien personas** more/less than a hundred people; **el más caro de la tienda** the most expensive in the shop; **menos/más de lo pensado** less/more than expected
6 (*causa*) **del calor** from the heat; **de puro tonto** out of sheer stupidity
7 (*tema*) about; **clases de inglés** English classes; **¿sabes algo de él?** do you know anything about him?; **un libro de física** a physics book
8 (*adj+de+infin*) **fácil de entender** easy to understand
9 (*oraciones pasivas*) **fue respetado de todos** he was loved by all
10 (*condicional+infin*) if; **de ser posible** if possible; **de no terminarlo hoy** if I *etc* don't finish it today

dé [de] *vb ver* **dar**
deambular [deambu'lar] *vi* to stroll, wander

debajo [de'βaxo] *adv* underneath; **~ de** below, under; **por ~ de** beneath
debate [de'βate] *nm* debate
debatir [deβa'tir] *vt* to debate; **debatirse** *vr* to struggle
deber [de'βer] *nm* duty ▷ *vt* to owe ▷ *vi*: **debe (de)** it must, it should; **deberse** *vr*: **~se a** to be owing o due to; **deberes** *nmpl* (*Escol*) homework *sg*; **debo hacerlo** I must do it; **debe de ir** he should go; **¿qué o cuánto le debo?** how much is it?
debido, -a [de'βiðo, a] *adj* proper, due; **~ a** due to, because of; **en debida forma** duly
débil ['deβil] *adj* weak; (*persona: físicamente*) feeble; (*salud*) poor; (*voz, ruido*) faint; (*luz*) dim
debilidad [deβili'ðað] *nf* weakness; feebleness; dimness; **tener ~ por algn** to have a soft spot for sb
debilitar [deβili'tar] *vt* to weaken; **debilitarse** *vr* to grow weak
débito ['deβito] *nm* debit; (*deuda*) debt; **~ bancario** (*Am*) direct debit (*Brit*) o billing (*US*)
debutar [deβu'tar] *vi* to make one's debut
década ['dekaða] *nf* decade
decadencia [deka'ðenθja] *nf* (*estado*) decadence; (*proceso*) decline, decay
decaer [deka'er] *vi* (*declinar*) to decline; (*debilitarse*) to weaken; (*salud*) to fail; (*negocio*) to fall off
decaído, -a [deka'iðo, a] *adj*: **estar ~** (*persona*) to be down
decaimiento [dekai'mjento] *nm* (*declinación*) decline; (*desaliento*) discouragement; (*Med: depresión*) depression
decano, -a [de'kano, a] *nm/f* (*Univ etc*) dean; (*de grupo*) senior member
decapitar [dekapi'tar] *vt* to behead
decena [de'θena] *nf*: **una ~** ten (or so)
decencia [de'θenθja] *nf* (*modestia*) modesty; (*honestidad*) respectability
decente [de'θente] *adj* decent
decepción [deθep'θjon] *nf* disappointment
decepcionar [deθepθjo'nar] *vt* to disappoint
decidir [deθi'ðir] *vt* (*persuadir*) to convince, persuade; (*resolver*) to decide ▷ *vi* to decide; **decidirse** *vr*: **~se a** to make up one's mind to; **~se por** to decide o settle on, choose
decimal [deθi'mal] *adj, nm* decimal
décimo, -a ['deθimo, a] *num* tenth ▷ *nf* (*Mat*) tenth; **tiene unas décimas de fiebre** he has a slight temperature
decimoctavo, -a [deθimok'taβo, a] *num* eighteenth; *ver tb* **sexto**
decimocuarto, -a [deθimo'kwarto, a] *num* fourteenth; *ver tb* **sexto**
decimonoveno, -a [deθimono'βeno, a] *num* nineteenth; *ver tb* **sexto**
decimoquinto, -a [deθimo'kinto, a] *num* fifteenth; *ver tb* **sexto**
decimoséptimo, -a [deθimo'septimo, a] *num* seventeenth; *ver tb* **sexto**

decimosexto, -a [deθimo'seksto, a] *num*
sixteenth; *ver tb* **sexto**

decimotercero, -a [deθimoter'θero, a] *num*
thirteenth; *ver tb* **sexto**

decir [de'θir] *vt* (*expresar*) to say; (*contar*) to tell;
(*hablar*) to speak; (*indicar*) to show; (*revelar*) to
reveal; (*fam: nombrar*) to call ▷ *nm* saying;
decirse *vr*: **se dice** it is said, they say; (*se
cuenta*) the story goes; **¿cómo se dice en
inglés "cursi"?** what's the English for
"cursi"?; **~ para** *o* **entre sí** to say to o.s.;
~ por ~ to talk for talking's sake; **dar que ~
(a la gente)** to make people talk; **querer ~**
to mean; **es ~** that is to say, namely; **ni que ~
tiene que ...** it goes without saying that ...;
como quien dice so to speak; **¡quién lo
diría!** would you believe it!; **el qué dirán**
gossip; **¡diga!, ¡dígame!** (*en tienda etc*) can I
help you?; (*Telec*) hello?; **le dije que fuera
más tarde** I told her to go later; **es un ~** it's
just a phrase

decisión [deθi'sjon] *nf* decision; (*firmeza*)
decisiveness; (*voluntad*) determination

decisivo, -a [deθi'siβo, a] *adj* decisive

declamar [dekla'mar] *vt, vi* to declaim; (*versos
etc*) to recite

declaración [deklara'θjon] *nf* (*manifestación*)
statement; (*de amor*) declaration; (*explicación*)
explanation; (*Jur: testimonio*) evidence; **~ de
derechos** (*Pol*) bill of rights; **~ de impuestos**
(*Com*) tax return; **~ de ingresos** *o* **de la renta**
income tax return; **~ jurada** affidavit;
falsa ~ (*Jur*) misrepresentation

declarar [dekla'rar] *vt* to declare ▷ *vi* to
declare; (*Jur*) to testify; **declararse** *vr* (*a una
chica*) to propose; (*guerra, incendio*) to break
out; **~ culpable/inocente a algn** to find sb
guilty/not guilty; **~se culpable/inocente** to
plead guilty/not guilty

declinar [dekli'nar] *vt* (*gen, Ling*) to decline;
(*Jur*) to reject ▷ *vi* (*el día*) to draw to a close

declive [de'kliβe] *nm* (*cuesta*) slope;
(*inclinación*) incline; (*fig*) decline; (*Com: tb:
~ económico*) slump

decolorarse [dekolo'rarse] *vr* to become
discoloured

decomiso [deko'miso] *nm* seizure

decoración [dekora'θjon] *nf* decoration;
(*Teat*) scenery, set; **~ de escaparates** window
dressing

decorado [deko'raðo] *nm* (*Cine, Teat*)
scenery, set

decorador, a [dekora'ðor, a] *nm/f* (*de
interiores*) (interior) decorator; (*Teat*) stage *o*
set designer

decorar [deko'rar] *vt* to decorate

decorativo, -a [dekora'tiβo, a] *adj*
ornamental, decorative

decoro [de'koro] *nm* (*respeto*) respect;
(*dignidad*) decency; (*recato*) propriety

decoroso, -a [deko'roso, a] *adj* (*decente*)
decent; (*modesto*) modest; (*digno*) proper

decrecer [dekre'θer] *vi* to decrease, diminish;
(*nivel de agua*) to go down; (*días*) to draw in

decrépito, -a [de'krepito, a] *adj* decrepit

decretar [dekre'tar] *vt* to decree

decreto [de'kreto] *nm* decree; (*Pol*) act

decreto-ley [dekreto'lei] (*pl* **decretos-leyes**)
nm decree

dedal [de'ðal] *nm* thimble

dedicación [deðika'θjon] *nf* dedication;
con ~ exclusiva *o* **plena** full-time

dedicar [deði'kar] *vt* (*libro*) to dedicate;
(*tiempo, dinero*) to devote; (*palabras: decir,
consagrar*) to dedicate, devote; **dedicarse** *vr*:
~se a (hacer algo) to devote o.s. to (doing
sth); (*carrera, estudio*) to go in for (doing sth),
take up (doing sth); **¿a qué se dedica usted?**
what do you do (for a living)?

dedicatoria [deðika'torja] *nf* (*de libro*)
dedication

dedo ['deðo] *nm* finger; (*de vino etc*) drop;
~ (del pie) toe; **~ pulgar** thumb; **~ índice**
index finger; **~ mayor** *o* **cordial** middle
finger; **~ anular** ring finger; **~ meñique**
little finger; **contar con los ~s** to count on
one's fingers; **comerse los ~s** to get very
impatient; **entrar a ~** to get a job by pulling
strings; **hacer ~** (*fam*) to hitch (a lift); **poner
el ~ en la llaga** to put one's finger on it;
no tiene dos ~s de frente he's pretty dim

deducción [deðuk'θjon] *nf* deduction

deducir [deðu'θir] *vt* (*concluir*) to deduce,
infer; (*Com*) to deduct

defecto [de'fekto] *nm* defect, flaw; (*de cara*)
imperfection; (*de pronunciación*) speech
defect; **por ~** (*Inform*) default; **~ latente** (*Com*)
latent defect

defectuoso, -a [defek'twoso, a] *adj*
defective, faulty

defender [defen'der] *vt* to defend; (*ideas*) to
uphold; (*causa*) to champion; (*amigos*) to
stand up for; **defenderse** *vr* to defend o.s.;
~se bien to give a good account of o.s.; **me
defiendo en inglés** (*fig*) I can get by in
English

defensa [de'fensa] *nf* defence; (*Naut*) fender
▷ *nm* (*Deporte*) defender, back; **en ~ propia** in
self-defence

defensivo, -a [defen'siβo, a] *adj* defensive
▷ *nf*: **a la defensiva** on the defensive

defensor, -a [defen'sor, a] *adj* defending
▷ *nm/f* (*abogado defensor*) defending counsel;
(*protector*) protector; **~ del pueblo** (*Esp*)
≈ ombudsman

deferente [defe'rente] *adj* deferential

deficiencia [defi'θjenθja] *nf* deficiency

deficiente [defi'θjente] *adj* (*defectuoso*)
defective; **~ en** lacking *o* deficient in ▷ *nm/f*:
ser un ~ mental to be mentally
handicapped

déficit (*pl* **déficits**) ['defiθit] *nm* (*Com*) deficit;
(*fig*) lack, shortage; **~ presupuestario**
budget deficit

deficitario, -a [defiθi'tarjo, a] adj (Com) in deficit; (: empresa) loss-making
definición [defini'θjon] nf definition; (Inform: de pantalla) resolution
definir [defi'nir] vt (determinar) to determine, establish; (decidir, Inform) to define; (aclarar) to clarify
definitivo, -a [defini'tiβo, a] adj (edición, texto) definitive; (fecha) definite; **en definitiva** definitively; (en conclusión) finally; (en resumen) in short
deforestación [deforesta'θjon] nf deforestation
deformación [deforma'θjon] nf (alteración) deformation; (Radio etc) distortion
deformar [defor'mar] vt (gen) to deform; **deformarse** vr to become deformed
deforme [de'forme] adj (informe) deformed; (feo) ugly; (mal hecho) misshapen
defraudar [defrau'ðar] vt (decepcionar) to disappoint; (estafar) to cheat; to defraud; **~ impuestos** to evade tax
defunción [defun'θjon] nf death, demise
degeneración [dexenera'θjon] nf (de las células) degeneration; (moral) degeneracy
degenerar [dexene'rar] vi to degenerate; (empeorar) to get worse
degollar [deɣo'ʎar] vt to slaughter
degradar [deɣra'ðar] vt to debase, degrade; (Inform: datos) to corrupt; **degradarse** vr to demean o.s.
degustación [deɣusta'θjon] nf sampling, tasting
deificar [deifi'kar] vt (persona) to deify
dejadez [dexa'ðeθ] nf (negligencia) neglect; (descuido) untidiness, carelessness
dejado, -a [de'xaðo, a] adj (desaliñado) slovenly; (negligente) careless; (indolente) lazy
dejar [de'xar] vt (gen) to leave; (permitir) to allow, let; (abandonar) to abandon, forsake; (actividad, empleo) to give up; (beneficios) to produce, yield ▷ vi: **~ de** (parar) to stop; (no hacer) to fail to; **dejarse** vr (abandonarse) to let o.s. go; **no puedo ~ de fumar** I can't give up smoking; **no dejes de visitarles** don't fail to visit them; **no dejes de comprar un billete** make sure you buy a ticket; **~ a un lado** to leave o set aside; **~ caer** to drop; **~ entrar/salir** to let in/out; **~ pasar** to let through; **¡déjalo!** (no te preocupes) don't worry about it; **te dejo en tu casa** I'll drop you off at your place; **deja mucho que desear** it leaves a lot to be desired; **~se persuadir** to allow o.s. to o let o.s. be persuaded; **¡déjate de tonterías!** stop messing about!
dejo ['dexo] nm (Ling) accent
del [del] = **de + el**; ver **de**
delantal [delan'tal] nm apron
delante [de'lante] adv in front; (enfrente) opposite; (adelante) ahead ▷ prep: **~ de** in front of, before; **la parte de ~** the front part; **estando otros ~** with others present

delantero, -a [delan'tero, a] adj front; (patas de animal) fore ▷ nm (Deporte) forward, striker ▷ nf (de vestido, casa etc) front part; (Teat) front row; (Deporte) forward line; **llevar la delantera (a algn)** to be ahead (of sb)
delatar [dela'tar] vt to inform on o against, betray; **los delató a la policía** he reported them to the police
delator, -a [dela'tor, a] nm/f informer
delegación [deleɣa'θjon] nf (acción, delegados) delegation; (Com: oficina) district office, branch; **~ de poderes** (Pol) devolution; **~ de policía** (Am) police station
delegado, -a [dele'ɣaðo, a] nm/f delegate; (Com) agent
delegar [dele'ɣar] vt to delegate
deletrear [deletre'ar] vt (tb fig) to spell (out)
deleznable [deleθ'naβle] adj (frágil) fragile; (fig: malo) poor; (: excusa) feeble
delfín [del'fin] nm dolphin
delgadez [delɣa'ðeθ] nf thinness, slimness
delgado, -a [del'ɣaðo, a] adj thin; (persona) slim, thin; (tierra) poor; (tela etc) light, delicate ▷ adv: **hilar (muy) ~** (fig) to split hairs
deliberación [deliβera'θjon] nf deliberation
deliberar [deliβe'rar] vt to debate, discuss ▷ vi to deliberate
delicadeza [delika'ðeθa] nf delicacy; (refinamiento, sutileza) refinement
delicado, -a [deli'kaðo, a] adj delicate; (sensible) sensitive; (rasgos) dainty; (gusto) refined; (situación: difícil) tricky; (: violento) embarrassing; (punto, tema) sore; (persona: difícil de contentar) hard to please; (: sensible) touchy, hypersensitive; (: atento) considerate
delicia [de'liθja] nf delight
delicioso, -a [deli'θjoso, a] adj (gracioso) delightful; (exquisito) delicious
delimitar [delimi'tar] vt to delimit; (función, responsabilidades) to define
delincuencia [delin'kwenθja] nf: **~ juvenil** juvenile delinquency; **cifras de la ~** crime rate
delincuente [delin'kwente] nm/f delinquent; (criminal) criminal; **~ sin antecedentes** first offender; **~ habitual** hardened criminal
delineante [deline'ante] nm/f draughtsman/draughtswoman; (US) draftsman/draftswoman
delinear [deline'ar] vt to delineate; (dibujo) to draw; (contornos, fig) to outline; **~ un proyecto** to outline a project
delinquir [delin'kir] vi to commit an offence
delirante [deli'rante] adj delirious
delirar [deli'rar] vi to be delirious, rave; (fig: desatinar) to talk nonsense
delirio [de'lirjo] nm (Med) delirium; (palabras insensatas) ravings pl; **~ de grandeza** megalomania; **~ de persecución** persecution mania; **con ~** (fam) madly; **¡fue el ~!** (fam) it was great!

delito [de'lito] nm (gen) crime; (infracción) offence

delta ['delta] nm delta

demacrado, -a [dema'kraðo, a] adj emaciated; **estar ~** to look pale and drawn, be wasted away

demagogia [dema'ɣoxja] nf demagogy, demagoguery

demagogo [dema'ɣoɣo] nm demagogue

demanda [de'manda] nf (pedido, Com) demand; (petición) request; (pregunta) inquiry; (reivindicación) claim; (Jur) action, lawsuit; (Teat) call; (Elec) load; **~ de pago** demand for payment; **escribir en ~ de ayuda** to write asking for help; **entablar ~** (Jur) to sue; **presentar ~ de divorcio** to sue for divorce; **~ final** final demand; **~ indirecta** derived demand; **~ de mercado** market demand

demandante [deman'dante] nm/f claimant; (Jur) plaintiff

demandar [deman'dar] vt (gen) to demand; (Jur) to sue, file a lawsuit against, start proceedings against; **~ a algn por calumnia/daños y perjuicios** to sue sb for libel/damages

demarcación [demarka'θjon] nf (de terreno) demarcation

demás [de'mas] adj: **los ~ niños** the other children, the remaining children ▷ pron: **los/las ~** the others, the rest (of them); **lo ~** the rest (of it); **por ~** moreover; (en vano) in vain; **y ~** etcetera

demasía [dema'sia] nf (exceso) excess, surplus; **comer en ~** to eat to excess

demasiado, -a [dema'sjaðo, a] adj: **~ vino** too much wine ▷ adv (antes de adj, adv) too; **~s libros** too many books; **¡es ~!** it's too much!; **es ~ pesado para levantar** it is too heavy to lift; **~ lo sé** I know it only too well; **hace ~ calor** it's too hot; **~ despacio** too slowly; **~s** too many

demencia [de'menθja] nf (locura) madness

demente [de'mente] adj mad, insane ▷ nm/f lunatic

democracia [demo'kraθja] nf democracy

demócrata [de'mokrata] nm/f democrat

democrático, -a [demo'kratiko, a] adj democratic

demoler [demo'ler] vt to demolish; (edificio) to pull down

demolición [demoli'θjon] nf demolition

demonio [de'monjo] nm devil, demon; **¡~s!** hell!, damn!; **¿cómo ~s?** how the hell?; **¿qué ~s será?** what the devil can it be?; **¿dónde ~ lo habré dejado?** where the devil can I have left it?; **tener el ~ en el cuerpo** (no parar) to be always on the go

demora [de'mora] nf delay

demorar [demo'rar] vt (retardar) to delay, hold back; (dilatar) to hold up ▷ vi to linger, stay on; **demorarse** vr to linger, stay on; (retrasarse) to take a long time; **~se en hacer algo** (esp Am) to take time doing sth

demos ['demos] vb ver **dar**

demostración [demostra'θjon] nf (gen) demonstration; (de cariño, fuerza) show; (de teorema) proof; (de amistad) gesture; (de cólera, gimnasia) display; **~ comercial** commercial exhibition

demostrar [demos'trar] vt (probar) to prove; (mostrar) to show; (manifestar) to demonstrate

demostrativo, -a [demostra'tiβo, a] adj demonstrative

demudado, -a [demu'ðaðo, a] adj (rostro) pale; (fig) upset; **tener el rostro ~** to look pale

den [den] vb ver **dar**

denegar [dene'ɣar] vt (rechazar) to refuse; (negar) to deny; (Jur) to reject

denigrar [deni'ɣrar] vt (desacreditar) to denigrate; (injuriar) to insult

denominación [denomina'θjon] nf (acto) naming; (clase) denomination; see note

● DENOMINACIÓN

The **denominación de origen**, often abbreviated to **D.O.**, is a prestigious product classification given to designated regions by the awarding body, the **Consejo Regulador de la Denominación de Origen**, when their produce meets the required quality and production standards. It is often associated with **manchego** cheeses and many of the wines from the Rioja and Ribera de Duero regions.

denominador [denomina'ðor] nm: **~ común** common denominator

denotar [deno'tar] vt (indicar) to indicate, denote

densidad [densi'ðað] nf (Física) density; (fig) thickness

denso, -a ['denso, a] adj (apretado) solid; (espeso, pastoso) thick, dense; (fig) heavy

dentadura [denta'ðura] nf (set of) teeth pl; **~ postiza** false teeth pl

dental [den'tal] adj dental

dentera [den'tera] nf (sensación desagradable) the shivers pl; (grima): **dar ~ a algn** to set sb's teeth on edge

dentífrico, -a [den'tifriko, a] adj dental, tooth cpd ▷ nm toothpaste; **pasta dentífrica** toothpaste

dentista [den'tista] nm/f dentist

dentro ['dentro] adv inside ▷ prep: **~ de** in, inside, within; **por ~** (on the) inside; **allí ~** in there; **mirar por ~** to look inside; **~ de lo posible** as far as possible; **~ de todo** all in all; **~ de tres meses** within three months

denuncia [de'nunθja] nf (delación) denunciation; (acusación) accusation; (de accidente) report; **hacer o poner una ~** to report an incident to the police

denunciar [denun'θjar] vt to report; (*delatar*) to inform on o against

departamento [departa'mento] nm (*sección*) department, section; (*Am: piso*) flat (*Brit*), apartment (*US*); (*distrito*) department, province; **~ de envíos** (*Com*) dispatch department; **~ de máquinas** (*Naut*) engine room

departir [depar'tir] vi to talk, converse

dependencia [depen'denθja] nf dependence; (*Pol*) dependency; (*Com*) office, section; (*sucursal*) branch office; (*Arq: cuarto*) room; **dependencias** nfpl outbuildings

depender [depen'der] vi: **~ de** to depend on; (*contar con*) to rely on; (*autoridad*) to be under, be answerable to; **depende** it (all) depends; **no depende de mí** it's not up to me

dependienta [depen'djenta] nf saleswoman, shop assistant

dependiente [depen'djente] adj dependent ▷ nm salesman, shop assistant

depilar [depi'lar] vt (*con cera: piernas*) to wax; (*cejas*) to pluck

depilatorio, -a [depila'torjo, a] adj depilatory ▷ nm hair remover

deplorable [deplo'raβle] adj deplorable

deplorar [deplo'rar] vt to deplore

deponer [depo'ner] vt (*armas*) to lay down; (*rey*) to depose; (*gobernante*) to oust; (*ministro*) to remove from office ▷ vi (*Jur*) to give evidence; (*declarar*) to make a statement

deportar [depor'tar] vt to deport

deporte [de'porte] nm sport; **hacer ~** to play sports

deportista [depor'tista] adj sports cpd ▷ nm/f sportsman(-woman)

deportivo, -a [depor'tiβo, a] adj (*club, periódico*) sports cpd ▷ nm sports car

depositante [deposi'tante] nm/f depositor

depositar [deposi'tar] vt (*dinero*) to deposit; (*mercaderías*) to put away, store; **depositarse** vr to settle; **~ la confianza en algn** to place one's trust in sb

depositario, -a [deposi'tarjo, a] nm/f trustee; **~ judicial** official receiver

depósito [de'posito] nm (*gen*) deposit; (*de mercaderías*) warehouse, store; (*de animales, coches*) pound; (*de agua, gasolina etc*) tank; (*en retrete*) cistern; **~ afianzado** bonded warehouse; **~ bancario** bank deposit; **~ de cadáveres** mortuary; **~ de maderas** timber yard; **~ de suministro** feeder bin

depravar [depra'βar] vt to deprave, corrupt; **depravarse** vr to become depraved

depreciar [depre'θjar] vt to depreciate, reduce the value of; **depreciarse** vr to depreciate, lose value

depredador, a [depreða'ðor, a] (*Zool*) adj predatory ▷ nm predator

depresión [depre'sjon] nf (*gen, Med*) depression; (*hueco*) hollow; (*en horizonte, camino*) dip; (*merma*) drop; (*Econ*) slump, recession; **~ nerviosa** nervous breakdown

deprimido, -a [depri'miðo, a] adj depressed

deprimir [depri'mir] vt to depress; **deprimirse** vr (*persona*) to become depressed

deprisa [de'prisa] adv quickly, hurriedly

depuración [depura'θjon] nf purification; (*Pol*) purge

depuradora [depura'ðora] nf (*de agua*) water-treatment plant; (*tb: ~ de aguas residuales*) sewage farm

depurar [depu'rar] vt to purify; (*purgar*) to purge

derecha [de'retʃa] nf ver **derecho**

derecho, -a [de'retʃo, a] adj right, right-hand ▷ nm (*privilegio*) right; (*título*) claim, title; (*lado*) right(-hand) side; (*leyes*) law ▷ nf right(-hand) side; (*Pol*) right ▷ adv straight, directly; **derechos** nmpl dues; (*profesionales*) fees; (*impuestos*) taxes; (*de autor*) royalties; **la(s) derecha(s)** (*Pol*) the Right; **~s civiles** civil rights; **~s de patente** patent rights; **~s portuarios** (*Com*) harbour dues; **~ de propiedad literaria** copyright; **~ de timbre** (*Com*) stamp duty; **~ de votar** right to vote; **~ a voto** voting right; **Facultad de D~** Faculty of Law; **a derechas** rightly, correctly; **de derechas** (*Pol*) right-wing; **"reservados todos los ~s"** "all rights reserved"; **¡no hay ~!** it's not fair!; **tener ~ a** to have a right to; **a la derecha** on the right; (*dirección*) to the right; **siga todo ~** carry o (*Brit*) go straight on

deriva [de'riβa] nf: **ir o estar a la ~** to drift, be adrift

derivado, -a [deri'βaðo, a] adj derived ▷ nm (*Ling*) derivative; (*Industria, Química*) by-product

derivar [deri'βar] vt to derive; (*desviar*) to direct ▷ vi to derive, be derived; (*Naut*) to drift; **derivarse** vr to derive, be derived; **~(se) de** (*consecuencia*) to spring from

dermoprotector, a [dermoprotek'tor, a] adj protective

derramamiento [derrama'mjento] nm (*dispersión*) spilling; (*fig*) squandering; **~ de sangre** bloodshed

derramar [derra'mar] vt to spill; (*verter*) to pour out; (*esparcir*) to scatter; **derramarse** vr to pour out; **~ lágrimas** to weep

derrame [de'rrame] nm (*de líquido*) spilling; (*de sangre*) shedding; (*de tubo etc*) overflow; (*pérdida*) leakage; (*Med*) discharge; (*declive*) slope; **~ cerebral** brain haemorrhage; **~ sinovial** water on the knee

derrapar [derra'par] vi to skid

derredor [derre'ðor] adv: **al** o **en ~ de** around, about

derretido, -a [derre'tiðo, a] adj melted; (*metal*) molten; **estar ~ por algn** (*fig*) to be crazy about sb

derretir [derre'tir] vt (*gen*) to melt; (*nieve*) to thaw; (*fig*) to squander; **derretirse** vr to melt

derribar [derri'βar] vt to knock down; (*construcción*) to demolish; (*persona, gobierno, político*) to bring down

derrocar [derro'kar] vt (gobierno) to bring down, overthrow; (ministro) to oust

derrochar [derro'tʃar] vt (dinero, recursos) to squander; (energía, salud) to be bursting with o full of

derroche [de'rrotʃe] nm (despilfarro) waste, squandering; (exceso) extravagance; **con un ~ de buen gusto** with a fine display of good taste

derrota [de'rrota] nf (Naut) course; (Mil) defeat, rout; **sufrir una grave ~** (fig) to suffer a grave setback

derrotar [derro'tar] vt (gen) to defeat

derrotero [derro'tero] nm (rumbo) course; **tomar otro ~** (fig) to adopt a different course

derruir [derru'ir] vt to demolish, tear down

derrumbar [derrum'bar] vt to throw down; (despeñar) to fling o hurl down; (edificio) to knock down; (volcar) to upset; **derrumbarse** vr (hundirse) to collapse; (: techo) to fall in, cave in; (fig: esperanzas) to collapse

des [des] vb ver **dar**

desabotonar [desaβoto'nar] vt to unbutton, undo ▷ vi (flores) to blossom; **desabotonarse** vr to come undone

desabrido, -a [desa'βriðo, a] adj (comida) insipid, tasteless; (persona: soso) dull; (: antipático) rude, surly; (respuesta) sharp; (tiempo) unpleasant

desabrochar [desaβro'tʃar] vt (botones, broches) to undo, unfasten; **desabrocharse** vr (ropa etc) to come undone

desacato [desa'kato] nm (falta de respeto) disrespect; (Jur) contempt

desacertado, -a [desaθer'taðo, a] adj (equivocado) mistaken; (inoportuno) unwise

desacierto [desa'θjerto] nm (error) mistake, error; (dicho) unfortunate remark

desaconsejado, -a [desakonse'xaðo, a] adj ill-advised

desaconsejar [desakonse'xar] vt: **~ algo a algn** to advise sb against sth

desacorde [desa'korðe] adj (Mus) discordant; (fig: opiniones) conflicting; **estar ~ con algo** to disagree with sth

desacreditar [desakreði'tar] vt (desprestigiar) to discredit, bring into disrepute; (denigrar) to run down

desacuerdo [desa'kwerðo] nm (conflicto) disagreement, discord; (error) error, blunder; **en ~** out of keeping

desafiar [desa'fjar] vt (retar) to challenge; (enfrentarse a) to defy

desafilado, -a [desafi'laðo, a] adj blunt

desafinado, -a [desafi'naðo, a] adj: **estar ~** to be out of tune

desafinar [desafi'nar] vi to be out of tune; **desafinarse** vr to go out of tune

desafío [desa'fio] nm (reto) challenge; (combate) duel; (resistencia) defiance

desaforado, -a [desafo'raðo, a] adj (grito) ear-splitting; (comportamiento) outrageous

desafortunadamente [desafortunaða'mente] adv unfortunately

desafortunado, -a [desafortu'naðo, a] adj (desgraciado) unfortunate, unlucky

desagradable [desaɣra'ðaβle] adj (fastidioso, enojoso) unpleasant; (irritante) disagreeable; **ser ~ con algn** to be rude to sb

desagradar [desaɣra'ðar] vi (disgustar) to displease; (molestar) to bother

desagradecido, -a [desaɣraðe'θiðo, a] adj ungrateful

desagrado [desa'ɣraðo] nm (disgusto) displeasure; (contrariedad) dissatisfaction; **con ~** unwillingly

desagraviar [desaɣra'βjar] vt to make amends to

desagravio [desa'ɣraβjo] nm (satisfacción) amends; (compensación) compensation

desagüe [de'saɣwe] nm (de un líquido) drainage; (cañería: tb: **tubo de ~**) drainpipe; (salida) outlet, drain

desaguisado, -a [desaɣi'saðo, a] adj illegal ▷ nm outrage

desahogado, -a [desao'ɣaðo, a] adj (holgado) comfortable; (espacioso) roomy

desahogar [desao'ɣar] vt (aliviar) to ease, relieve; (ira) to vent; **desahogarse** vr (distenderse) to relax; (desfogarse) to let off steam (fam); (confesarse) to confess, get sth off one's chest (fam)

desahogo [desa'oɣo] nm (alivio) relief; (comodidad) comfort, ease; **vivir con ~** to be comfortably off

desahuciar [desau'θjar] vt (enfermo) to give up hope for; (inquilino) to evict

desahucio [de'sauθjo] nm eviction

desairar [desai'rar] vt (menospreciar) to slight, snub; (cosa) to disregard; (Com) to default on

desaire [des'aire] nm (menosprecio) slight; (falta de garbo) unattractiveness; **dar o hacer un ~ a algn** to offend sb; **¿me va usted a hacer ese ~?** I won't take no for an answer!

desajustar [desaxus'tar] vt (desarreglar) to disarrange; (desconcertar) to throw off balance; (fig: planes) to upset; **desajustarse** vi to get out of order; (aflojarse) to loosen

desajuste [desa'xuste] nm (de máquina) disorder; (avería) breakdown; (situación) imbalance; (desacuerdo) disagreement

desalentador, -a [desalenta'ðor, a] adj discouraging

desalentar [desalen'tar] vt (desanimar) to discourage; **desalentarse** vr to get discouraged

desaliento etc [desa'ljento] vb ver **desalentar** ▷ nm discouragement; (abatimiento) depression

desaliño [desa'liɲo] nm (descuido) slovenliness; (negligencia) carelessness

desalmado, -a [desal'maðo, a] adj (cruel) cruel, heartless

desalojar [desalo'xar] vt (gen) to remove, expel; (expulsar, echar) to eject; (abandonar) to move out of ▷ vi to move out; **la policía**

desalojó el local the police cleared people out of the place

desamarrar [desama'rrar] *vt* to untie; (*Naut*) to cast off

desamor [desa'mor] *nm* (*frialdad*) indifference; (*odio*) dislike

desamparado, -a [desampa'raðo, a] *adj* (*persona*) helpless; (*lugar: expuesto*) exposed; (: *desierto*) deserted

desamparar [desampa'rar] *vt* (*abandonar*) to desert, abandon; (*Jur*) to leave defenceless; (*barco*) to abandon

desandar [desan'dar] *vt*: ~ **lo andado** *o* **el camino** to retrace one's steps

desangrar [desan'grar] *vt* to bleed; (*fig: persona*) to bleed dry; (*lago*) to drain; **desangrarse** *vr* to lose a lot of blood; (*morir*) to bleed to death

desanimado, -a [desani'maðo, a] *adj* (*persona*) downhearted; (*espectáculo, fiesta*) dull

desanimar [desani'mar] *vt* (*desalentar*) to discourage; (*deprimir*) to depress; **desanimarse** *vr* to lose heart

desapacible [desapa'θiβle] *adj* unpleasant

desaparecer [desapare'θer] *vi* to disappear; (*el sol, la luz*) to vanish; (*desaparecer de vista*) to drop out of sight; (*efectos, señales*) to wear off ▷ *vt* (*esp Am Pol*) to cause to disappear; (: *eufemismo*) to murder

desaparecido, -a [desapare'θiðo, a] *adj* missing; (*especie*) extinct ▷ *nm/f* (*Am Pol*) kidnapped *o* missing person

desaparición [desapari'θjon] *nf* disappearance; (*de especie etc*) extinction

desapasionado, -a [desapasjo'naðo, a] *adj* dispassionate, impartial

desapego [desa'peɣo] *nm* (*frialdad*) coolness; (*distancia*) detachment

desapercibido, -a [desaperθi'βiðo, a] *adj* unnoticed; (*desprevenido*) unprepared; **pasar ~** to go unnoticed

desaprensivo, -a [desapren'siβo, a] *adj* unscrupulous

desaprobar [desapro'βar] *vt* (*reprobar*) to disapprove of; (*condenar*) to condemn; (*no consentir*) to reject

desaprovechado, -a [desaproβe'tʃaðo, a] *adj* (*oportunidad, tiempo*) wasted; (*estudiante*) slack

desaprovechar [desaproβe'tʃar] *vt* to waste; (*talento*) not to use to the full ▷ *vi* (*perder terreno*) to lose ground

desarmador [desarma'ðor] *nm* (*Am*) screwdriver

desarmar [desar'mar] *vt* (*Mil, fig*) to disarm; (*Tec*) to take apart, dismantle

desarme [de'sarme] *nm* disarmament

desarraigar [desarrai'ɣar] *vt* to uproot; (*fig: costumbre*) to root out; (: *persona*) to banish

desarraigo [desa'rraiɣo] *nm* uprooting

desarreglado, -a [desarre'ɣlaðo, a] *adj* (*desordenado*) disorderly, untidy; (*hábitos*) irregular

desarreglar [desarre'ɣlar] *vt* to mess up; (*desordenar*) to disarrange; (*trastocar*) to upset, disturb

desarreglo [desa'rreɣlo] *nm* (*de casa, persona*) untidiness; (*desorden*) disorder; (*Tec*) trouble; (*Med*) upset; **viven en el mayor ~** they live in complete chaos

desarrollar [desarro'ʎar] *vt* (*gen*) to develop; (*extender*) to unfold; (*teoría*) to explain; **desarrollarse** *vr* to develop; (*ocurrir*) to take place; (*extenderse*) to open (out); (*film*) to develop; (*fig*) to grow; (*tener lugar*) to take place; **aquí desarrollan un trabajo muy importante** they carry on *o* out very important work here; **la acción se desarrolla en Roma** (*Cine etc*) the scene is set in Rome

desarrollo [desa'rroʎo] *nm* development; (*de acontecimientos*) unfolding; (*de industria, mercado*) expansion, growth; **país en vías de ~** developing country; **la industria está en pleno ~** industry is expanding steadily; **~ sostenible** sustainable development

desarticular [desartiku'lar] *vt* (*huesos*) to dislocate, put out of joint; (*objeto*) to take apart; (*grupo terrorista etc*) to break up

desaseo [desa'seo] *nm* (*suciedad*) dirtiness; (*desarreglo*) untidiness

desasir [desa'sir] *vt* to loosen; **desasirse** *vr* to extricate o.s.; **~se de** to let go, give up

desasosegar [desasose'ɣar] *vt* (*inquietar*) to disturb, make uneasy; **desasosegarse** *vr* to become uneasy

desasosiego *etc* [desaso'sjeɣo] *vb ver* **desasosegar** ▷ *nm* (*intranquilidad*) uneasiness, restlessness; (*ansiedad*) anxiety; (*Pol etc*) unrest

desastrado, -a [desas'traðo, a] *adj* (*desaliñado*) shabby; (*sucio*) dirty

desastre [de'sastre] *nm* disaster; **¡un ~!** how awful!; **la función fue un ~** the show was a shambles

desastroso, -a [desas'troso, a] *adj* disastrous

desatado, -a [desa'taðo, a] *adj* (*desligado*) untied; (*violento*) violent, wild

desatar [desa'tar] *vt* (*nudo*) to untie; (*paquete*) to undo; (*perro, odio*) to unleash; (*misterio*) to solve; (*separar*) to detach; **desatarse** *vr* (*zapatos*) to come untied; (*tormenta*) to break; (*perder control de sí mismo*) to lose self-control; **~se en injurias** to pour out a stream of insults

desatascar [desatas'kar] *vt* (*cañería*) to unblock, clear

desatender [desaten'der] *vt* (*no prestar atención a*) to disregard; (*abandonar*) to neglect

desatento, -a [desa'tento, a] *adj* (*distraído*) inattentive; (*descortés*) discourteous

desatinado, -a [desati'naðo, a] *adj* foolish, silly

desatino [desa'tino] *nm* (*idiotez*) foolishness, folly; (*error*) blunder; **desatinos** *nmpl* nonsense *sg*; **¡qué ~!** how silly!, what rubbish!

desatornillar [desatorni'ʎar] *vt* to unscrew

desatrancar [desatran'kar] *vt* (*puerta*) to unbolt; (*cañería*) to unblock

desautorizado, -a [desautori'θaðo, a] *adj* unauthorized

desautorizar [desautori'θar] *vt* (*oficial*) to deprive of authority; (*informe*) to deny

desavenencia [desaβe'nenθja] *nf* (*desacuerdo*) disagreement; (*discrepancia*) quarrel

desaventajado, -a [desaβenta'xaðo, a] *adj* (*inferior*) inferior; (*poco ventajoso*) disadvantageous

desayunar [desaju'nar] *vi*, **desayunarse** *vr* to have breakfast ▷ *vt* to have for breakfast; **~ con café** to have coffee for breakfast; **~ con algo** (*fig*) to get the first news of sth

desayuno [desa'juno] *nm* breakfast

desazón [desa'θon] *nf* (*angustia*) anxiety; (*Med*) discomfort; (*fig*) annoyance

desazonar [desaθo'nar] *vt* (*fig*) to annoy, upset; **desazonarse** *vr* (*enojarse*) to be annoyed; (*preocuparse*) to worry, be anxious

desbandarse [desβan'darse] *vr* (*Mil*) to disband; (*fig*) to flee in disorder

desbarajuste [desβara'xuste] *nm* confusion, disorder; **¡qué ~!** what a mess!

desbaratar [desβara'tar] *vt* (*gen*) to mess up; (*plan*) to spoil; (*deshacer, destruir*) to ruin ▷ *vi* to talk nonsense; **desbaratarse** *vr* (*máquina*) to break down; (*persona: irritarse*) to fly off the handle (*fam*)

desbloquear [desβloke'ar] *vt* (*negociaciones, tráfico*) to get going again; (*Com: cuenta*) to unfreeze

desbocado, -a [desβo'kaðo, a] *adj* (*caballo*) runaway; (*herramienta*) worn

desbordar [desβor'ðar] *vt* (*sobrepasar*) to go beyond; (*exceder*) to exceed ▷ *vi*, **desbordarse** *vr* (*líquido, río*) to overflow; (*entusiasmo*) to erupt; (*persona: exaltarse*) to get carried away

descabalgar [deskaβal'ɣar] *vi* to dismount

descabellado, -a [deskaβe'ʎaðo, a] *adj* (*disparatado*) wild, crazy; (*insensato*) preposterous

descabellar [deskaβe'ʎar] *vt* to ruffle; (*Taur: toro*) to give the coup de grace to

descafeinado, -a [deskafei'naðo, a] *adj* decaffeinated ▷ *nm* decaffeinated coffee, de-caff

descalabro [deska'laβro] *nm* blow; (*desgracia*) misfortune

descalificación [deskalifika'θjon] *nf* disqualification; **descalificaciones** *nfpl* discrediting *sg*

descalificar [deskalifi'kar] *vt* to disqualify; (*desacreditar*) to discredit

descalzar [deskal'θar] *vt* (*zapato*) to take off; (*persona*) to take the shoes off

descalzo, -a [des'kalθo, a] *adj* barefoot(ed); (*fig*) destitute; **estar (con los pies) ~(s)** to be barefooted

descambiar [deskam'bjar] *vt* to exchange

descaminado, -a [deskami'naðo, a] *adj* (*equivocado*) on the wrong road; (*fig*) misguided; **en eso no anda usted muy ~** you're not far wrong there

descampado [deskam'paðo] *nm* open space, piece of empty ground; **comer al ~** to eat in the open air

descansado, -a [deskan'saðo, a] *adj* (*gen*) rested; (*que tranquiliza*) restful

descansar [deskan'sar] *vt* (*gen*) to rest; (*apoyar*): **~ (sobre)** to lean (on) ▷ *vi* to rest, have a rest; (*echarse*) to lie down; (*cadáver, restos*) to lie; **¡que usted descanse!** sleep well!; **~ en** (*argumento*) to be based on

descansillo [deskan'siʎo] *nm* (*de escalera*) landing

descanso [des'kanso] *nm* (*reposo*) rest; (*alivio*) relief; (*pausa*) break; (*Deporte*) interval, half time; **día de ~** day off; **~ de enfermedad/ maternidad** sick/maternity leave; **tomarse unos días de ~** to take a few days' leave o rest

descapotable [deskapo'taβle] *nm* (*tb*: **coche ~**) convertible

descarado, -a [deska'raðo, a] *adj* (*sin vergüenza*) shameless; (*insolente*) cheeky

descarga [des'karɣa] *nf* (*Arq, Elec, Mil*) discharge; (*Naut*) unloading; (*Inform*) download

descargable [deskar'ɣaβle] *adj* downloadable

descargar [deskar'ɣar] *vt* to unload; (*golpe*) to let fly; (*arma*) to fire; (*Elec*) to discharge; (*pila*) to run down; (*conciencia*) to relieve; (*Com*) to take up; (*persona: de una obligación*) to release; (: *de una deuda*) to free; (*Jur*) to clear ▷ *vi* (*río*): **~ (en)** to flow (into); **descargarse** *vr* to unburden o.s.; **~se de algo** to get rid of sth; **~se algo de Internet** to download sth from the internet

descargo [des'karɣo] *nm* (*de obligación*) release; (*Com: recibo*) receipt; (: *de deuda*) discharge; (*Jur*) evidence; **~ de una acusación** acquittal on a charge

descarnado, -a [deskar'naðo, a] *adj* scrawny; (*fig*) bare; (*estilo*) straightforward

descaro [des'karo] *nm* nerve

descarriar [deska'rrjar] *vt* (*descaminar*) to misdirect; (*fig*) to lead astray; **descarriarse** *vr* (*perderse*) to lose one's way; (*separarse*) to stray; (*pervertirse*) to err, go astray

descarrilamiento [deskarrila'mjento] *nm* (*de tren*) derailment

descarrilar [deskarri'lar] *vi* to be derailed

descartar [deskar'tar] *vt* (*rechazar*) to reject; (*eliminar*) to rule out; **descartarse** *vr* (*Naipes*) to discard; **~se de** to shirk

descascarillado, -a [deskaskari'ʎaðo, a] *adj* (*paredes*) peeling

descendencia [desθen'denθja] *nf* (*origen*) origin, descent; (*hijos*) offspring; **morir sin dejar ~** to die without issue

descender [desθen'der] vt (bajar: escalera) to go down ▷ vi to descend; (temperatura, nivel) to fall, drop; (líquido) to run; (cortina etc) to hang; (fuerzas, persona) to fail, get weak; ~ **de** to be descended from

descendiente [desθen'djente] nm/f descendant

descenso [des'θenso] nm descent; (de temperatura) (de producción) downturn; (de calidad) decline; (Minería) collapse; (bajada) slope; (fig: decadencia) decline; (de empleado etc) demotion

descifrar [desθi'frar] vt (escritura) to decipher; (mensaje) to decode; (problema) to puzzle out; (misterio) to solve

descodificador [deskoðifika'ðor] nm decoder

descodificar [deskoðifi'kar] vt to decode

descolgar [deskol'ɣar] vt (bajar) to take down; (desde una posición alta) to lower; (de una pared etc) to unhook; (teléfono) to pick up; **descolgarse** vr to let o.s. down; **~se por** (bajar escurriéndose) to slip down; (pared) to climb down; **dejó el teléfono descolgado** he left the phone off the hook

descollar [desko'ʎar] vi (sobresalir) to stand out; (montaña etc) to rise; **la obra que más descuella de las suyas** his most outstanding work

descolorido, -a [deskolo'riðo, a] adj (color, tela) faded; (pálido) pale; (fig: estilo) colourless

descompaginar [deskompaxi'nar] vt (desordenar) to disarrange, mess up

descompasado, -a [deskompa'saðo, a] adj (sin proporción) out of all proportion; (excesivo) excessive; (hora) unearthly

descomponer [deskompo'ner] vt (gen, Ling, Mat) to break down; (desordenar) to disarrange, disturb; (materia orgánica) to rot, decompose; (Tec) to put out of order; (facciones) to distort; (estómago etc) to upset; (: planes) to mess up; (persona: molestar) to upset; (irritar) to annoy; **descomponerse** vr (corromperse) to rot, decompose; (estómago) to get upset; (el tiempo) to change (for the worse); (Tec) to break down

descomposición [deskomposi'θjon] nf (de un objeto) breakdown; (de fruta etc) decomposition; (putrefacción) rotting; (de cara) distortion; **~ de vientre** (Med) stomach upset, diarrhoea, diarrhea (US)

descompostura [deskompos'tura] nf (Tec) breakdown, fault; (desorganización) disorganization; (desorden) untidiness; (Am: diarrea) diarrhoea, diarrhea (US)

descompuesto, -a [deskom'pwesto, a] pp de **descomponer** ▷ adj (corrompido) decomposed; (roto) broken (down)

descomunal [deskomu'nal] adj (enorme) huge; (fam: excelente) fantastic

desconcertado, -a [deskonθer'taðo, a] adj disconcerted, bewildered

desconcertar [deskonθer'tar] vt (confundir) to baffle; (incomodar) to upset, put out; (orden) to disturb; **desconcertarse** vr (turbarse) to be upset; (confundirse) to be bewildered

desconchado, -a [deskon'tʃaðo, a] adj (pintura) peeling

desconcierto etc [deskon'θjerto] vb ver **desconcertar** ▷ nm (gen) disorder; (desorientación) uncertainty; (inquietud) uneasiness; (confusión) bewilderment

desconectar [deskonek'tar] vt to disconnect; (desenchufar) to unplug; (radio, televisión) to switch off; (Inform) to toggle off

desconfianza [deskon'fjanθa] nf distrust

desconfiar [deskon'fjar] vi to be distrustful; **~ de** (sospechar) to mistrust, suspect; (no tener confianza en) to have no faith o confidence in; **desconfío de ello** I doubt it; **desconfíe de las imitaciones** (Com) beware of imitations

descongelar [deskonxe'lar] vt (nevera) to defrost; (comida) to thaw; (Auto) to de-ice; (Com, Pol) to unfreeze

descongestionar [deskonxestjo'nar] vt (cabeza, tráfico) to clear; (calle, ciudad) to relieve congestion in; (fig: despejar) to clear

desconocer [deskono'θer] vt (ignorar) not to know, be ignorant of; (no aceptar) to deny; (repudiar) to disown

desconocido, -a [deskono'θiðo, a] adj unknown; (que no se conoce) unfamiliar; (no reconocido) unrecognized ▷ nm/f stranger; (recién llegado) newcomer; **está ~** he is hardly recognizable

desconocimiento [deskonoθi'mjento] nm (falta de conocimientos) ignorance; (repudio) disregard

desconsiderado, -a [deskonsiðe'raðo, a] adj inconsiderate; (insensible) thoughtless

desconsolar [deskonso'lar] vt to distress; **desconsolarse** vr to despair

desconsuelo [deskon'swelo] vb ver **desconsolar** ▷ nm (tristeza) distress; (desesperación) despair

descontado, -a [deskon'taðo, a] adj: **por ~** of course; **dar por ~ (que)** to take it for granted (that)

descontar [deskon'tar] vt (deducir) to take away, deduct; (rebajar) to discount

descontento, -a [deskon'tento, a] adj dissatisfied ▷ nm dissatisfaction, discontent

descontrol [deskon'trol] nm (fam) lack of control

descontrolarse [deskontro'larse] vr (persona) to lose control

desconvocar [deskombo'kar] vt to call off

descorazonar [deskoraθo'nar] vt to discourage, dishearten; **descorazonarse** vr to get discouraged, lose heart

descorchar [deskor'tʃar] vt to uncork, open

descorrer [desko'rrer] vt (cortina, cerrojo) to draw back; (velo) to remove

descortés [deskor'tes] adj (mal educado)

discourteous; (*grosero*) rude

descoser [desko'ser] *vt* to unstitch;
descoserse *vr* to come apart (at the seams);
(*fam: descubrir un secreto*) to blurt out a secret;
~**se de risa** to split one's sides laughing

descosido, -a [desko'siðo, a] *adj* (*costura*)
unstitched; (*desordenado*) disjointed ▷ *nm*:
como un ~ (*obrar*) wildly; (*beber, comer*) to
excess; (*estudiar*) like mad

descrédito [des'kreðito] *nm* discredit; **caer
en** ~ to fall into disrepute; **ir en** ~ **de** to be to
the discredit of

descreído, -a [deskre'iðo, a] *adj* (*incrédulo*)
incredulous; (*falto de fe*) unbelieving

descremado, -a [deskre'maðo, a] *adj*
skimmed

describir [deskri'βir] *vt* to describe

descripción [deskrip'θjon] *nf* description

descrito [des'krito] *pp de* **describir**

descuartizar [deskwarti'θar] *vt* (*animal*) to
carve up, cut up; (*fig: hacer pedazos*) to tear
apart

descubierto, -a [desku'βjerto, a] *pp de*
descubrir ▷ *adj* uncovered, bare; (*persona*)
bare-headed; (*cielo*) clear; (*coche*) open;
(*campo*) treeless ▷ *nm* (*lugar*) open space;
(*Com: en el presupuesto*) shortage; (: *bancario*)
overdraft; **al** ~ in the open; **poner al** ~ to lay
bare; **quedar al** ~ to be exposed; **estar en** ~
to be overdrawn

descubrimiento [deskuβri'mjento] *nm*
(*hallazgo*) discovery; (*de criminal, fraude*)
detection; (*revelación*) revelation; (*de secreto
etc*) disclosure; (*de estatua etc*) unveiling

descubrir [desku'βrir] *vt* to discover, find;
(*petróleo*) to strike; (*inaugurar*) to unveil;
(*vislumbrar*) to detect; (*sacar a luz: crimen*) to
bring to light; (*revelar*) to reveal, show; (*poner
al descubierto*) to expose to view; (*naipes*) to lay
down; (*quitar la tapa de*) to uncover; (*cacerola*)
to take the lid off; (*enterarse de: causa, solución*)
to find out; (*divisar*) to see, make out; (*delatar*)
to give away, betray; **descubrirse** *vr* to reveal
o.s.; (*quitarse sombrero*) to take off one's hat;
(*confesar*) to confess; (*fig: salir a luz*) to come
out o to light

descuento [des'kwento] *vb ver* **descontar**
▷ *nm* discount; ~ **del 3%** 3% off; **con** ~ at a
discount; ~ **por pago al contado** (*Com*) cash
discount; ~ **por volumen de compras** (*Com*)
volume discount

descuidado, -a [deskwi'ðaðo, a] *adj* (*sin
cuidado*) careless; (*desordenado*) untidy;
(*olvidadizo*) forgetful; (*dejado*) neglected;
(*desprevenido*) unprepared

descuidar [deskwi'ðar] *vt* (*dejar*) to neglect;
(*olvidar*) to overlook ▷ *vi*, **descuidarse** *vr*
(*distraerse*) to be careless; (*estar desaliñado*) to
let o.s. go; (*desprevenirse*) to drop one's guard;
¡descuida! don't worry!

descuido [des'kwiðo] *nm* (*dejadez*)
carelessness; (*olvido*) negligence; (*un descuido*)

oversight; **al** ~ casually; (*sin cuidado*)
carelessly; **al menor** ~ if my *etc* attention
wanders for a minute; **con** ~ thoughtlessly;
por ~ by an oversight

 PALABRA CLAVE

desde ['desðe] *prep* **1** (*lugar*) from; **desde
Burgos hasta mi casa hay 30 km** it's 30 km
from Burgos to my house; **desde lejos** from
a distance

2 (*posición*): **hablaba desde el balcón** she was
speaking from the balcony

3 (*tiempo: +adv, n*): **desde ahora** from now on;
desde entonces/la boda since then/the
wedding; **desde niño** since I *etc* was a child;
desde tres años atrás since three years ago

4 (*tiempo: +vb*): **nos conocemos
desde 1978/desde hace 20 años** we've
known each other since 1978/for 20 years; **no
le veo desde 1983/desde hace 5 años** I
haven't seen him since 1983/for 5 years;
¿desde cuándo vives aquí? how long have
you lived here?

5 (*gama*): **desde los más lujosos hasta los
más económicos** from the most luxurious
to the most reasonably priced

6: **desde luego (que no)** of course (not)
▷ *conj*: **desde que**: **desde que recuerdo** for
as long as I can remember; **desde que llegó
no ha salido** he hasn't been out since he
arrived

desdecir [desðe'θir] *vi*: ~ **de** (*no merecer*) to be
unworthy of; (*no corresponder*) to clash with;
desdecirse *vr*: ~**se de** to go back on

desdén [des'ðen] *nm* scorn

desdeñar [desðe'ɲar] *vt* (*despreciar*) to scorn

desdicha [des'ðitʃa] *nf* (*desgracia*) misfortune;
(*infelicidad*) unhappiness

desdichado, -a [desði'tʃaðo, a] *adj* (*sin suerte*)
unlucky; (*infeliz*) unhappy; (*día*) ill-fated
▷ *nm/f* (*pobre desgraciado*) poor devil

desdoblar [desðo'βlar] *vt* (*extender*) to spread
out; (*desplegar*) to unfold

desear [dese'ar] *vt* to want, desire, wish for;
¿qué desea la señora? (*tienda etc*) what can I
do for you, madam?; **estoy deseando que
esto termine** I'm longing for this to finish

desecar [dese'kar] *vt*, **desecarse** *vr* to dry up

desechar [dese'tʃar] *vt* (*basura*) to throw out o
away; (*ideas*) to reject, discard; (*miedo*) to cast
aside; (*plan*) to drop

desecho [de'setʃo] *nm* (*desprecio*) contempt; (*lo
peor*) dregs *pl*; **desechos** *nmpl* rubbish *sg*,
waste *sg*; **de** ~ (*hierro*) scrap; (*producto*) waste;
(*ropa*) cast-off

desembalar [desemba'lar] *vt* to unpack

desembarazado, -a [desemba'raðo, a]
adj (*libre*) clear, free; (*desenvuelto*) free and easy

desembarazar [desembara'θar] *vt*
(*desocupar*) to clear; (*desenredar*) to free;

desembarazarse vr: ~**se de** to free o.s. of, get rid of

desembarcar [desembar'kar] vt (personas) to land; (mercancías etc) to unload ▷ vi, **desembarcarse** vr (de barco, avión) to disembark

desembocadura [desemboka'ðura] nf (de río) mouth; (de calle) opening

desembocar [desembo'kar] vi: ~ **en** to flow into; (fig) to result in

desembolso [desem'bolso] nm payment

desembragar [desembra'ɣar] vt (Tec) to disengage, release ▷ vi (Auto) to declutch

desembrollar [desembro'ʎar] vt (madeja) to unravel; (asunto, malentendido) to sort out

desemejanza [deseme'xanθa] nf dissimilarity

desempaquetar [desempake'tar] vt (regalo) to unwrap; (mercancía) to unpack

desempatar [desempa'tar] vi to break a tie; **volvieron a jugar para ~** they held a play-off

desempate [desem'pate] nm (Fútbol) replay, play-off; (Tenis) tie-break(er)

desempeñar [desempe'ɲar] vt (cargo) to hold; (papel) to play; (deber, función) to perform, carry out; (lo empeñado) to redeem; **desempeñarse** vr to get out of debt; ~ **un papel** (fig) to play (a role)

desempeño [desem'peɲo] nm occupation; (de lo empeñado) redeeming; **de mucho ~** very capable

desempleado, -a [desemple'aðo, a] adj unemployed, out of work ▷ nm/f unemployed person

desempleo [desem'pleo] nm unemployment

desempolvar [desempol'βar] vt (muebles etc) to dust; (lo olvidado) to revive

desencadenar [desenkaðe'nar] vt to unchain; (ira) to unleash; (provocar) to cause, set off; **desencadenarse** vr to break loose; (tormenta) to burst; (guerra) to break out; **se desencadenó una lucha violenta** a violent struggle ensued

desencajar [desenka'xar] vt (hueso) to put out of joint; (mandíbula) to dislocate; (mecanismo, pieza) to disconnect, disengage

desencanto [desen'kanto] nm disillusionment, disenchantment

desenchufar [desentʃu'far] vt to unplug, disconnect

desenfadado, -a [desenfa'ðaðo, a] adj (desenvuelto) uninhibited; (descarado) forward; (en el vestir) casual

desenfado [desen'faðo] nm (libertad) freedom; (comportamiento) free and easy manner; (descaro) forwardness; (desenvoltura) self-confidence

desenfocado, -a [desenfo'kaðo, a] adj (Foto) out of focus

desenfrenado, -a [desenfre'naðo, a] adj (descontrolado) uncontrolled; (inmoderado) unbridled

desenfreno [desen'freno] nm (vicio) wildness; (falta de control) lack of self-control; (de pasiones) unleashing

desenganchar [desengan'tʃar] vt (gen) to unhook; (Ferro) to uncouple; (Tec) to disengage

desengañar [desenga'ɲar] vt to disillusion; (abrir los ojos a) to open the eyes of; **desengañarse** vr to become disillusioned; **¡desengáñate!** don't you believe it!

desengaño [desen'gaɲo] nm disillusionment; (decepción) disappointment; **sufrir un ~ amoroso** to be disappointed in love

desenlace etc [desen'laθe] nm outcome; (Lit) ending

desenmarañar [desenmara'ɲar] vt (fig) to unravel

desenmascarar [desenmaska'rar] vt to unmask, expose

desenredar [desenre'ðar] vt (pelo) to untangle; (problema) to sort out

desenroscar [desenros'kar] vt (tornillo etc) to unscrew

desentenderse [desenten'derse] vr: ~ **de** to pretend not to know about; (apartarse) to have nothing to do with

desenterrar [desente'rrar] vt to exhume; (tesoro, fig) to unearth, dig up

desentonar [desento'nar] vi (Mus) to sing (o play) out of tune; (no encajar) to be out of place; (color) to clash

desentrañar [desentra'ɲar] vt (misterio) to unravel

desentumecer [desentume'θer] vt (pierna etc) to stretch; (Deporte) to loosen up

desenvoltura [desenbol'tura] nf (libertad, gracia) ease; (descaro) free and easy manner; (al hablar) fluency

desenvolver [desenbol'βer] vt (paquete) to unwrap; (fig) to develop; **desenvolverse** vr (desarrollarse) to unfold, develop; (suceder) to go off; (prosperar) to prosper; (arreglárselas) to cope

deseo [de'seo] nm desire, wish; ~ **de saber** thirst for knowledge; **buen ~** good intentions pl; **arder en ~s de algo** to yearn for sth

deseoso, -a [dese'oso, a] adj: **estar ~ de hacer** to be anxious to do

desequilibrado, -a [desekili'βraðo, a] adj unbalanced ▷ nm/f unbalanced person; ~ **mental** mentally disturbed person

desertar [deser'tar] vt (Jur: derecho de apelación) to forfeit ▷ vi to desert; ~ **de sus deberes** to neglect one's duties

desértico, -a [de'sertiko, a] adj desert cpd; (vacío) deserted

desertor, a [deser'tor, a] nm/f deserter

desesperación [desespera'θjon] nf desperation, despair; (irritación) fury; **es una ~** it's maddening; **es una ~ tener que ...** it's infuriating to have to ...

desesperado, -a [desespe'raðo, a] *adj*
(*persona: sin esperanza*) desperate; (*caso, situación*)
hopeless; (*esfuerzo*) furious ▷ *nm*: **como un ~**
like mad ▷ *nf*: **hacer algo a la desesperada**
to do sth as a last resort o in desperation

desesperar [desespe'rar] *vt* to drive to
despair; (*exasperar*) to drive to distraction ▷ *vi*:
~ de to despair of; **desesperarse** *vr* to
despair, lose hope

desestabilizar [desestaβili'θar] *vt* to
destabilize

desestimar [desesti'mar] *vt* (*menospreciar*)
to have a low opinion of; (*rechazar*) to reject

desfachatez [desfatʃa'teθ] *nf* (*insolencia*)
impudence; (*descaro*) rudeness

desfalco [des'falko] *nm* embezzlement

desfallecer [desfaʎe'θer] *vi* (*perder las fuerzas*)
to become weak; (*desvanecerse*) to faint

desfasado, -a [desfa'saðo, a] *adj* (*anticuado*)
old-fashioned; (*Tec*) out of phase

desfase [des'fase] *nm* (*diferencia*) gap

desfavorable [desfaβo'raβle] *adj*
unfavourable

desfigurar [desfiɣu'rar] *vt* (*cara*) to disfigure;
(*cuerpo*) to deform; (*cuadro, monumento*) to
deface; (*Foto*) to blur; (*sentido*) to twist;
(*suceso*) to misrepresent

desfiladero [desfila'ðero] *nm* gorge, defile

desfilar [desfi'lar] *vi* to parade; **~on ante el
general** they marched past the general

desfile [des'file] *nm* procession; (*Mil*) parade;
~ de modelos fashion show

desfogar [desfo'ɣar] *vt* (*fig*) to vent ▷ *vi* (*Naut*:
tormenta) to burst; **desfogarse** *vr* (*fig*) to let
off steam

desgajar [desɣa'xar] *vt* (*arrancar*) to tear off;
(*romper*) to break off; (*naranja*) to split into
segments; **desgajarse** *vr* to come off

desgana [des'ɣana] *nf* (*falta de apetito*) loss of
appetite; (*renuencia*) unwillingness; **hacer
algo a ~** to do sth unwillingly

desganado, -a [desɣa'naðo, a] *adj*: **estar ~**
(*sin apetito*) to have no appetite; (*sin entusiasmo*)
to have lost interest

desgarrador, a [desɣarra'ðor, a] *adj*
heartrending

desgarrar [desɣa'rrar] *vt* to tear (up); (*fig*) to
shatter

desgarro [des'ɣarro] *nm* (*en tela*) tear;
(*aflicción*) grief; (*descaro*) impudence

desgastar [desɣas'tar] *vt* (*deteriorar*) to wear
away o down; (*estropear*) to spoil;
desgastarse *vr* to get worn out

desgaste [des'ɣaste] *nm* wear (and tear); (*de
roca*) erosion; (*de cuerda*) fraying; (*de metal*)
corrosion; **~ económico** drain on one's
resources

desglosar [desɣlo'sar] *vt* to detach; (*factura*)
to break down

desgracia [des'ɣraθja] *nf* misfortune;
(*accidente*) accident; (*vergüenza*) disgrace;
(*contratiempo*) setback; **por ~** unfortunately;

**en el accidente no hay que lamentar ~s
personales** there were no casualties in the
accident; **caer en ~** to fall from grace; **tener
la ~ de** to be unlucky enough to

desgraciado, -a [desɣra'θjaðo, a] *adj*
(*sin suerte*) unlucky, unfortunate; (*miserable*)
wretched; (*infeliz*) miserable ▷ *nm/f* (*malvado*)
swine; (*infeliz*) poor creature; **¡esa radio
desgraciada!** (*esp Am*) that lousy radio!

desgravación [desɣraβa'θjon] *nf* (*Com*):
~ de impuestos tax relief; **~ personal**
personal allowance

desgravar [desɣra'βar] *vt* (*producto*) to reduce
the tax o duty on

desgreñado, -a [desɣre'ɲaðo, a] *adj*
dishevelled

desguace [des'ɣwaθe] *nm* (*de coches*)
scrapping; (*lugar*) scrapyard

desguazar [desɣwa'θar] *vt* (*coche*) to scrap

deshabitado, -a [desaβi'taðo, a] *adj*
uninhabited

deshacer [desa'θer] *vt* (*lo hecho*) to undo,
unmake; (*proyectos: arruinar*) to spoil; (*casa*)
to break up; (*Tec*) to take apart; (*enemigo*) to
defeat; (*diluir*) to melt; (*contrato*) to break;
(*intriga*) to solve; (*cama*) to strip; (*maleta*) to
unpack; (*paquete*) to unwrap; (*nudo*) to untie;
(*costura*) to unpick; **deshacerse** *vr* (*desatarse*)
to come undone; (*estropearse*) to be spoiled;
(*descomponerse*) to fall to pieces; (*disolverse*) to
melt; (*despedazarse*) to come apart o undone;
~se de to get rid of; (*Com*) to dump, unload;
~se en (*cumplidos, elogios*) to be lavish with;
~se en lágrimas to burst into tears; **~se por
algo** to be crazy about sth

deshecho, -a [de'setʃo, a] *pp de* **deshacer**
▷ *adj* (*lazo, nudo*) undone; (*roto*) smashed;
(*despedazado*) in pieces; (*cama*) unmade; (*Med*:
persona) weak, emaciated; (: *salud*) broken;
estoy ~ I'm shattered

deshelar [dese'lar] *vt* (*cañería*) to thaw;
(*heladera*) to defrost

desheredar [desere'ðar] *vt* to disinherit

deshidratar [desiðra'tar] *vt* to dehydrate

deshielo *etc* [des'jelo] *vb ver* **deshelar** ▷ *nm*
thaw

deshinchar [desin'tʃar] *vt* (*neumático*) to let
down; (*herida etc*) to reduce the swelling of);
deshincharse *vr* (*neumático*) to go flat;
(*hinchazón*) to go down

deshonesto, -a [deso'nesto, a] *adj* (*no
honrado*) dishonest; (*indecente*) indecent

deshonra [de'sonra] *nf* (*deshonor*) dishonour;
(*vergüenza*) shame

deshonrar [deson'rar] *vt* to dishonour

deshora [de'sora]: **a ~** *adv* at the wrong time;
(*llegar*) unexpectedly; (*acostarse*) at some
unearthly hour

deshuesadero [deswesa'ðero] *nm* (*Am*)
junkyard

deshuesar [deswe'sar] *vt* (*carne*) to bone;
(*fruta*) to stone

desierto, -a [de'sjerto, a] *adj* (*casa, calle, negocio*) deserted; (*paisaje*) bleak ▷ *nm* desert

designar [desiɣ'nar] *vt* (*nombrar*) to designate; (*indicar*) to fix

designio [de'siɣnjo] *nm* plan; **con el ~ de** with the intention of

desigual [desi'ɣwal] *adj* (*lucha*) unequal; (*diferente*) different; (*terreno*) uneven; (*tratamiento*) unfair; (*cambiadizo: tiempo*) changeable; (*: carácter*) unpredictable

desigualdad [desiɣwal'ðað] *nf* (*Econ, Pol*) inequality; (*de carácter, tiempo*) unpredictability; (*de escritura*) unevenness; (*de terreno*) roughness

desilusión [desilu'sjon] *nf* disillusionment; (*decepción*) disappointment

desilusionar [desilusjo'nar] *vt* to disillusion; (*decepcionar*) to disappoint; **desilusionarse** *vr* to become disillusioned

desinfectar [desinfek'tar] *vt* to disinfect

desinflar [desin'flar] *vt* to deflate; **desinflarse** *vr* (*neumático*) to go down o flat

desintegración [desinteɣra'θjon] *nf* disintegration; **~ nuclear** nuclear fission

desinterés [desinte'res] *nm* (*desgana*) lack of interest; (*altruismo*) unselfishness

desintoxicar [desintoksi'kar] *vt* to detoxify; **desintoxicarse** *vr* (*drogadicto*) to undergo detoxification; **~se de** (*ruṭina, trabajo*) to get away from

desistir [desis'tir] *vi* (*renunciar*) to stop, desist; **~ de** (*empresa*) to give up; (*derecho*) to waive

desleal [desle'al] *adj* (*infiel*) disloyal; (*Com: competencia*) unfair

deslealtad [desleal'tað] *nf* disloyalty

desleír [desle'ir] *vt* (*líquido*) to dilute; (*sólido*) to dissolve

deslenguado, -a [deslen'gwaðo, a] *adj* (*grosero*) foul-mouthed

desligar [desli'ɣar] *vt* (*desatar*) to untie, undo; (*separar*) to separate; **desligarse** *vr* (*de un compromiso*) to extricate o.s.

desliz [des'liθ] *nm* (*fig*) lapse; **~ de lengua** slip of the tongue; **cometer un ~** to slip up

deslizar [desli'θar] *vt* to slip, slide; **deslizarse** *vr* (*escurrirse: persona*) to slip, slide; (*: coche*) to skid; (*aguas mansas*) to flow gently; (*error*) to creep in; (*tiempo*) to pass; (*persona: irse*) to slip away; **~se en un cuarto** to slip into a room

deslucido, -a [deslu'θiðo, a] *adj* dull; (*torpe*) awkward, graceless; (*deslustrado*) tarnished; (*fracasado*) unsuccessful; **quedar ~** to make a poor impression

deslucir [deslu'θir] *vt* (*deslustrar*) to tarnish; (*estropear*) to spoil, ruin; (*persona*) to discredit; **la lluvia deslució el acto** the rain ruined the ceremony

deslumbrar [deslum'brar] *vt* (*con la luz*) to dazzle; (*cegar*) to blind; (*impresionar*) to dazzle; (*dejar perplejo a*) to puzzle, confuse

desmadrarse [desma'ðrarse] *vr* (*fam: descontrolarse*) to run wild; (*divertirse*) to let one's hair down

desmadre [des'maðre] *nm* (*fam: desorganización*) chaos; (*: jaleo*) commotion

desmán [des'man] *nm* (*exceso*) outrage; (*abuso de poder*) abuse

desmandarse [desman'darse] *vr* (*portarse mal*) to behave badly; (*excederse*) to get out of hand; (*caballo*) to bolt

desmano [des'mano]: **a ~** *adv*: **me coge** o **pilla a ~** it's out of my way

desmantelar [desmante'lar] *vt* (*deshacer*) to dismantle; (*casa*) to strip; (*organización*) to disband; (*Mil*) to raze; (*andamio*) to take down; (*Naut*) to unrig

desmaquillador [desmakiʎa'ðor] *nm* make-up remover

desmaquillarse [desmaki'ʎarse] *vr* to take off one's make-up

desmarcarse [desmar'karse] *vr*: **~ de** (*Deporte*) to get clear of; (*fig*) to distance o.s. from

desmayado, -a [desma'jaðo, a] *adj* (*sin sentido*) unconscious; (*carácter*) dull; (*débil*) faint, weak; (*color*) pale

desmayar [desma'jar] *vi* to lose heart; **desmayarse** *vr* (*Med*) to faint

desmayo [des'majo] *nm* (*Med: acto*) faint; (*estado*) unconsciousness; (*depresión*) dejection; (*de voz*) faltering; **sufrir un ~** to have a fainting fit

desmedido, -a [desme'ðiðo, a] *adj* excessive; (*ambición*) boundless

desmejorar [desmexo'rar] *vt* (*dañar*) to impair, spoil; (*Med*) to weaken

desmembrar [desmem'brar] *vt* (*Med*) to dismember; (*fig*) to separate

desmemoriado, -a [desmemo'rjaðo, a] *adj* forgetful, absent-minded

desmentir [desmen'tir] *vt* (*contradecir*) to contradict; (*refutar*) to deny; (*rumor*) to scotch ▷ *vi*: **~ de** to refute; **desmentirse** *vr* to contradict o.s.

desmenuzar [desmenu'θar] *vt* (*deshacer*) to crumble; (*carne*) to chop; (*examinar*) to examine closely

desmerecer [desmere'θer] *vt* to be unworthy of ▷ *vi* (*deteriorarse*) to deteriorate

desmesurado, -a [desmesu'raðo, a] *adj* (*desmedido*) disproportionate; (*enorme*) enormous; (*ambición*) boundless; (*descarado*) insolent

desmontable [desmon'taβle] *adj* (*que se quita*) detachable; (*en compartimientos*) sectional; (*que se puede plegar etc*) collapsible, folding

desmontar [desmon'tar] *vt* (*deshacer*) to dismantle; (*motor*) to strip down; (*máquina*) to take apart; (*escopeta*) to uncock; (*tienda de campaña*) to take down; (*tierra*) to level; (*quitar los árboles a*) to clear; (*jinete*) to throw ▷ *vi* to dismount

desmoralizar [desmorali'θar] *vt* to demoralize

desmoronar [desmoro'nar] *vt* to wear away, erode; **desmoronarse** *vr* (*edificio, dique*) to collapse; (*economía*) to decline

desnatado, -a [desna'taðo, a] *adj* skimmed; (*yogur*) low-fat

desnivel [desni'βel] *nm* (*de terreno*) unevenness; (*Pol*) inequality; (*diferencia*) difference

desnudar [desnu'ðar] *vt* (*desvestir*) to undress; (*despojar*) to strip; **desnudarse** *vr* (*desvestirse*) to get undressed

desnudez [desnu'ðeθ] *nf* (*de persona*) nudity; (*fig*) bareness

desnudo, -a [des'nuðo, a] *adj* (*cuerpo*) naked; (*árbol, brazo*) bare; (*paisaje*) flat; (*estilo*) unadorned; (*verdad*) plain ▷ *nm/f* nude; **~ de** devoid o bereft of; **la retrató al ~** he painted her in the nude; **poner al ~** to lay bare

desnutrición [desnutri'θjon] *nf* malnutrition

desnutrido, -a [desnu'triðo, a] *adj* undernourished

desobedecer [desoβcðc'θer] *vt, vi* to disobey

desobediencia [desoβe'ðjenθja] *nf* disobedience

desobediente [desoβe'ðjente] *adj* disobedient

desocupado, -a [desoku'paðo, a] *adj* at leisure; (*desempleado*) unemployed; (*deshabitado*) empty, vacant

desocupar [desoku'par] *vt* to vacate; **desocuparse** *vr* (*quedar libre*) to be free; **se ha desocupado aquella mesa** that table's free now

desodorante [desoðo'rante] *nm* deodorant

desolación [desola'θjon] *nf* (*de lugar*) desolation; (*fig*) grief

desolar [deso'lar] *vt* to ruin, lay waste

desorbitado, -a [desorβi'taðo, a] *adj* (*excesivo: ambición*) boundless; (*deseos*) excessive; (*precio*) exorbitant; **con los ojos ~s** pop-eyed

desorden [de'sorðen] *nm* confusion; (*de casa, cuarto*) mess; (*político*) disorder; **desórdenes** *nmpl* (*alborotos*) disturbances; (*excesos*) excesses; **en ~** (*gente*) in confusion

desordenado, -a [desorðe'naðo, a] *adj* (*habitación, persona*) untidy; (*objetos revueltos*) in a mess, jumbled; (*conducta*) disorderly

desorganización [desoryaniθa'θjon] *nf* (*de persona*) disorganization; (*en empresa, oficina*) disorder, chaos

desorganizar [desoryani'θar] *vt* to disorganize

desorientar [desorjen'tar] *vt* (*extraviar*) to mislead; (*confundir, desconcertar*) to confuse; **desorientarse** *vr* (*perderse*) to lose one's way

desovar [deso'βar] *vi* (*peces*) to spawn; (*insectos*) to lay eggs

despabilado, -a [despaβi'laðo, a] *adj* (*despierto*) wide-awake; (*fig*) alert, sharp

despabilar [despaβi'lar] *vt* (*despertar*) to wake up; (*fig: persona*) to liven up; (*trabajo*) to get through quickly ▷ *vi*, **despabilarse** *vr* to wake up; (*fig*) to get a move on

despachar [despa'tʃar] *vt* (*negocio*) to do, complete; (*resolver: problema*) to settle; (*correspondencia*) to deal with; (*fam: comida*) to polish off; (: *bebida*) to knock back; (*enviar*) to send, dispatch; (*vender*) to sell, deal in; (*Com: cliente*) to attend to; (*despojar*) to issue; (*mandar ir*) to send away ▷ *vi* (*decidirse*) to get things settled; (*apresurarse*) to hurry up; **despacharse** *vr* to finish off; (*apresurarse*) to hurry up; **~se de algo** to get rid of sth; **~se a su gusto con algn** to give sb a piece of one's mind; **¿quién despacha?** is anybody serving?

despacho [des'patʃo] *nm* (*oficina*) office; (: *en una casa*) study; (*de paquetes*) dispatch; (*Com: venta*) sale (of goods); (*comunicación*) message; **~ de billetes** o **boletos** (*Am*) booking office; **~ de localidades** box office; **géneros sin ~** unsaleable goods; **tener buen ~** to find a ready sale

despacio [des'paθjo] *adv* (*lentamente*) slowly; (*esp Am: en voz baja*) softly; **¡~!** take it easy!

desparpajo [despar'paxo] *nm* (*desenvoltura*) self-confidence; (*pey*) nerve

desparramar [desparra'mar] *vt* (*esparcir*) to scatter; (*líquido*) to spill

despavorido, -a [despaβo'riðo, a] *adj* terrified

despecho [des'petʃo] *nm* spite; **a ~ de** in spite of; **por ~** out of (sheer) spite

despectivo, -a [despek'tiβo, a] *adj* (*despreciativo*) derogatory; (*Ling*) pejorative

despedazar [despeða'θar] *vt* to tear to pieces

despedida [despe'ðiða] *nf* (*adiós*) goodbye, farewell; (*antes de viaje*) send-off; (*en carta*) closing formula; (*de obrero*) sacking; (*Inform*) logout; **cena/función de ~** farewell dinner/performance; **regalo de ~** parting gift; **~ de soltero/soltera** stag/hen party

despedir [despe'ðir] *vt* (*visita*) to see off, show out; (*empleado*) to dismiss; (*inquilino*) to evict; (*objeto*) to hurl; (*olor etc*) to give out o off; **despedirse** *vi* (*dejar un empleo*) to give up one's job; (*Inform*) to log out o off; **~se de** to say goodbye to; **se despidieron** they said goodbye to each other

despegar [despe'ɣar] *vt* to unstick; (*sobre*) to open ▷ *vi* (*avión*) to take off; (*cohete*) to blast off; **despegarse** *vr* to come loose, come unstuck; **sin ~ los labios** without uttering a word

despego [des'peɣo] *nm* detachment

despegue etc [des'peɣe] *vb* ver **despegar** ▷ *nm* takeoff; (*de cohete*) blast-off

despeinado, -a [despei'naðo, a] *adj* dishevelled, unkempt

despeinar [despei'nar] *vt* (*pelo*) to ruffle; **¡me has despeinado todo!** you've completely ruined my hairdo!

despejado, -a [despe'xaðo, a] adj (lugar) clear, free; (cielo) clear; (persona) wide-awake, bright

despejar [despe'xar] vt (gen) to clear; (misterio) to clarify, clear up; (Mat: incógnita) to find ▷ vi (el tiempo) to clear; **despejarse** vr (tiempo, cielo) to clear (up); (misterio) to become clearer; (cabeza) to clear; **¡despejen!** (moverse) move along!; (salirse) everybody out!

despellejar [despeʎe'xar] vt (animal) to skin; (criticar) to criticize unmercifully; (fam: arruinar) to fleece

despenalizar [despenali'θar] vt to decriminalize

despensa [des'pensa] nf (armario) larder; (Naut) storeroom; (provisión de comestibles) stock of food

despeñadero [despeɲa'ðero] nm (Geo) cliff, precipice

despeñar [despe'ɲar] vt (arrojar) to fling down; **despeñarse** vr to fling o.s. down; (caer) to fall headlong; (coche) to tumble over

desperdicio [desper'ðiθjo] nm (despilfarro) squandering; (residuo) waste; **desperdicios** nmpl (basura) rubbish sg, refuse sg, garbage sg (US); (residuos) waste sg; **~s de cocina** kitchen scraps; **el libro no tiene ~** the book is excellent from beginning to end

desperezarse [despere'θarse] vr to stretch

desperfecto [desper'fekto] nm (deterioro) slight damage; (defecto) flaw, imperfection

despertador [desperta'ðor] nm alarm clock; **~ de viaje** travelling clock

despertar [desper'tar] vt (persona) to wake up; (recuerdos) to revive; (esperanzas) to raise; (sentimiento) to arouse ▷ vi to awaken, wake up; **despertarse** vr to awaken, wake up ▷ nm awakening; **~se a la realidad** to wake up to reality

despido etc [des'piðo] vb ver **despedir** ▷ nm dismissal, sacking; **~ improcedente o injustificado** wrongful dismissal; **~ injusto** unfair dismissal; **~ libre** right to hire and fire; **~ voluntario** voluntary redundancy

despierto, -a [des'pjerto, a] pp de **despertar** ▷ adj awake; (fig) sharp, alert

despilfarrar [despilfa'rrar] vt (gen) to waste; (dinero) to squander

despilfarro [despil'farro] nm (derroche) squandering; (lujo desmedido) extravagance

despistado, -a [despis'taðo, a] adj (distraído) vague, absent-minded; (poco práctico) unpractical; (confuso) confused; (desorientado) off the track ▷ nm/f (persona distraída) scatterbrain, absent-minded person

despistar [despis'tar] vt to throw off the track o scent; (fig) to mislead, confuse; **despistarse** vr to take the wrong road; (fig) to become confused

despiste [des'piste] nm (Auto etc) swerve; (error) slip; (distracción) absent-mindedness; **un ~** a mistake o slip; **tiene un terrible ~** he's terribly absent-minded

desplazamiento [desplaθa'mjento] nm displacement; (viaje) journey; (de opinión, votos) shift, swing; (Inform) scrolling; **~ hacia arriba/abajo** (Inform) scroll up/down

desplazar [despla'θar] vt (gen) to move; (Física, Naut, Tec) to displace; (tropas) to transfer; (suplantar) to take the place of; (fig) to oust; (Inform) to scroll; **desplazarse** vr (persona, vehículo) to travel, go; (objeto) to move, shift; (votos, opinión) to shift, swing

desplegable [desple'ɣable] adj (libro, tb Inform) pop-up

desplegar [desple'ɣar] vt (tela, papel) to unfold, open out; (bandera) to unfurl; (alas) to spread; (Mil) to deploy; (manifestar) to display

despliegue etc [des'pljeɣe] vb ver **desplegar** ▷ nm unfolding, opening; deployment, display

desplomarse [desplo'marse] vr (edificio, gobierno, persona) to collapse; (derrumbarse) to topple over; (precios) to slump; **se ha desplomado el techo** the ceiling has fallen in

desplumar [desplu'mar] vt (ave) to pluck; (fam: estafar) to fleece

despoblado, -a [despo'βlaðo, a] adj (sin habitantes) uninhabited; (con pocos habitantes) depopulated; (con insuficientes habitantes) underpopulated ▷ nm deserted spot

despojar [despo'xar] vt (a alguien: de sus bienes) to divest of, deprive of; (casa) to strip, leave bare; (de su cargo) to strip of; **despojarse** vr (desnudarse) to undress; **~se de** (ropa, hojas) to shed; (poderes) to relinquish

despojo [des'poxo] nm (acto) plundering; (objetos) plunder, loot; **despojos** nmpl (de ave, res) offal sg

desposado, -a [despo'saðo, a] adj, nm/f newly-wed

desposar [despo'sar] vt (sacerdote: pareja) to marry; **desposarse** vr (casarse) to marry, get married

desposeer [despose'er] vt (despojar) to dispossess; **~ a algn de su autoridad** to strip sb of his authority

déspota ['despota] nm/f despot

despotismo [despo'tismo] nm despotism

despotricar [despotri'kar] vi: **~ contra** to moan o complain about

despreciar [despre'θjar] vt (desdeñar) to despise, scorn; (afrentar) to slight

desprecio [des'preθjo] nm scorn, contempt; slight

desprender [despren'der] vt (soltar) to loosen; (separar) to separate; (desatar) to unfasten; (olor) to give off; **desprenderse** vr (botón: caerse) to fall off; (broche) to come unfastened; (olor, perfume) to be given off; **~se de** to follow from; **~se de algo** (ceder) to give sth up; (desembarazarse) to get rid of sth; **~se de algo que ...** to draw from sth that ...; **se desprende que ...** it transpires that ...

desprendimiento [desprendi'mjento] *nm*
(*gen*) loosening; (*generosidad*)
disinterestedness; (*indiferencia*) detachment;
(*de gas*) leak; (*de tierra, rocas*) landslide; **~ de
retina** detachment of the retina

despreocupado, -a [despreoku'paðo, a] *adj*
(*sin preocupación*) unworried, unconcerned;
(*tranquilo*) nonchalant; (*en el vestir*) casual;
(*negligente*) careless

despreocuparse [despreoku'parse] *vr* to be
carefree, not to worry; (*dejar de inquietarse*) to
stop worrying; (*ser indiferente*) to be
unconcerned; **~ de** to have no interest in

desprestigiar [despresti'xjar] *vt* (*criticar*) to
run down, disparage; (*desacreditar*) to discredit

desprevenido, -a [despreβe'niðo, a] *adj* (*no
preparado*) unprepared, unready; **coger** (*Esp*) *o*
agarrar a algn ~ (*Am*) to catch sb unawares

desproporcionado, -a [desproporθjo'naðo,
a] *adj* disproportionate, out of proportion

desprovisto, -a [despro'βisto, a] *adj*: **~ de**
devoid of; **estar ~ de** to lack

después [des'pwes] *adv* afterwards, later;
(*desde entonces*) since (then); (*próximo paso*)
next; **poco ~** soon after; **un año ~** a year
later; **~ se debatió el tema** next the matter
was discussed ▷ *prep*: **~ de** (*tiempo*) after,
since; (*orden*) next (to); **~ de comer** after
lunch; **~ de corregido el texto** after the text
had been corrected; **~ de esa fecha** (*pasado*)
since that date; (*futuro*) from *o* after that date;
~ de todo after all; **~ de verlo** after seeing it,
after I *etc* saw it; **mi nombre está ~ del tuyo**
my name comes next to yours ▷ *conj*: **~ (de)
que** after; **~ (de) que lo escribí** after *o* since
I wrote it, after writing it

desquiciado, -a [deski'θjaðo, a] *adj* deranged

desquite [des'kite] *nm* (*satisfacción*)
satisfaction; (*venganza*) revenge

destacado, -a [desta'kaðo, a] *adj* outstanding

destacar [desta'kar] *vt* (*Arte: hacer resaltar*) to
make stand out; (*subrayar*) to emphasize,
point up; (*Mil*) to detach, detail; (*Inform*) to
highlight ▷ *vi* (*resaltarse*) to stand out;
(*persona*) to be outstanding *o* exceptional;
destacarse *vr* (*resaltarse*) to stand out;
(*persona*) to be outstanding *o* exceptional;
quiero ~ que… I wish to emphasize that…;
~(se) contra *o* **en** *o* **sobre** to stand out *o* be
outlined against

destajo [des'taxo] *nm*: **a ~** (*por pieza*) by the job;
(*con afán*) eagerly; **trabajar a ~** to do piecework;
(*fig*) to work one's fingers to the bone

destapar [desta'par] *vt* (*botella*) to open;
(*cacerola*) to take the lid off; (*descubrir*) to
uncover; **destaparse** *vr* (*descubrirse*) to get
uncovered; (*revelarse*) to reveal one's true
character

destartalado, -a [destarta'laðo, a] *adj*
(*desordenado*) untidy; (*casa etc: grande*)
rambling; (*ruinoso*) tumbledown

destello [des'teʎo] *nm* (*de diamante*) sparkle;

(*de metal*) glint; (*de estrella*) twinkle; (*de faro*)
signal light; **no tiene un ~ de verdad**
there's not a grain of truth in it

destemplado, -a [destem'plaðo, a] *adj* (*Mus*)
out of tune; (*voz*) harsh; (*Med*) out of sorts;
(*Meteorología*) unpleasant, nasty

desteñir [deste'ɲir] *vt* to fade ▷ *vi*, **desteñirse**
vr to fade; **esta tela no destiñe** this fabric
will not run

desternillarse [desterni'ʎarse] *vr*: **~ de risa**
to split one's sides laughing

desterrar [deste'rrar] *vt* (*exilar*) to exile; (*fig*)
to banish, dismiss

destetar [deste'tar] *vt* to wean

destiempo [des'tjempo]: **a ~** *adv* at the
wrong time

destierro *etc* [des'tjerro] *vb ver* **desterrar** ▷ *nm*
exile; **vivir en el ~** to live in exile

destilar [desti'lar] *vt* to distil; (*pus, sangre*) to
ooze; (*fig: rebosar*) to exude; (: *revelar*) to reveal
▷ *vi* (*gotear*) to drip

destilería [destile'ria] *nf* distillery; **~ de
petróleo** oil refinery

destinar [desti'nar] *vt* (*funcionario*) to appoint,
assign; (*fondos*) to set aside; **es un libro
destinado a los niños** it is a book (intended
o meant) for children; **una carta que viene
destinada a usted** a letter for you, a letter
addressed to you

destinatario, -a [destina'tarjo, a] *nm/f*
addressee; (*Com*) payee

destino [des'tino] *nm* (*suerte*) destiny;
(*de viajero*) destination; (*función*) use; (*puesto*)
post, placement; **~ público** public
appointment; **salir con ~ a** to leave for;
con ~ a Londres (*avión, barco*) (bound) for
London; (*carta*) to London

destituir [destitu'ir] *vt* (*despedir*) to dismiss;
(: *ministro, funcionario*) to remove from office

destornillador [destorniʎa'ðor] *nm*
screwdriver

destornillar [destorni'ʎar] *vt* (*tornillo*) to
unscrew; **destornillarse** *vr* to unscrew

destreza [des'treθa] *nf* (*habilidad*) skill; (*maña*)
dexterity

destrozar [destro'θar] *vt* (*romper*) to smash,
break (up); (*estropear*) to ruin; (*nervios*) to
shatter; **~ a algn en una discusión** to crush
sb in an argument

destrozo [des'troθo] *nm* (*acción*) destruction;
(*desastre*) smashing; **destrozos** *nmpl* (*pedazos*)
pieces; (*daños*) havoc *sg*

destrucción [destruk'θjon] *nf* destruction

destruir [destru'ir] *vt* to destroy; (*casa*) to
demolish; (*equilibrio*) to upset; (*proyecto*) to spoil;
(*esperanzas*) to dash; (*argumento*) to demolish

desuso [de'suso] *nm* disuse; **caer en ~** to fall
into disuse, become obsolete; **una
expresión caída en ~** an obsolete expression

desvalido, -a [desβa'liðo, a] *adj* (*desprotegido*)
destitute; (*sin fuerzas*) helpless; **niños ~s**
waifs and strays

desvalijar [desβali'xar] vt (persona) to rob; (casa, tienda) to burgle; (coche) to break into

desván [des'βan] nm attic

desvanecer [desβane'θer] vt (disipar) to dispel; (recuerdo, temor) to banish; (borrar) to blur; **desvanecerse** vr (humo etc) to vanish, disappear; (duda) to be dispelled; (color) to fade; (recuerdo, sonido) to fade away; (Med) to pass out

desvanecimiento [desβaneθi'mjento] nm (desaparición) disappearance; (de dudas) dispelling; (de colores) fading; (evaporación) evaporation; (Med) fainting fit

desvariar [desβa'rjar] vi (enfermo) to be delirious; (delirar) to talk nonsense

desvarío [desβa'rio] nm delirium; (desatino) absurdity; **desvaríos** nmpl ravings

desvelar [desβe'lar] vt to keep awake; **desvelarse** vr (no poder dormir) to stay awake; (vigilar) to be vigilant o watchful; **~se por algo** (inquietarse) to be anxious about sth; (poner gran cuidado) to take great care over sth

desvencijado, -a [desβenθi'xaðo, a] adj (silla) rickety; (máquina) broken-down

desventaja [desβen'taxa] nf disadvantage; (inconveniente) drawback

desventura [desβen'tura] nf misfortune

desvergonzado, -a [desβerɣon'θaðo, a] adj (sin vergüenza) shameless; (descarado) insolent ▷ nm/f shameless person

desvergüenza [desβer'ɣwenθa] nf (descaro) shamelessness; (insolencia) impudence; (mala conducta) effrontery; **esto es una ~** this is disgraceful; **¡qué ~!** what a nerve!

desvestir [desβes'tir] vt to undress; **desvestirse** vr to undress

desviación [desβja'θjon] nf deviation; (Auto: rodeo) diversion, detour; (: carretera de circunvalación) ring road (Brit), circular route (US); **~ de la circulación** traffic diversion; **es una ~ de sus principios** it is a departure from his usual principles

desviar [des'βjar] vt to turn aside; (balón, flecha, golpe) to deflect; (pregunta) to parry; (ojos) to avert, turn away; (río) to alter the course of; (navío) to divert, re-route; (conversación) to sidetrack; **desviarse** vr (apartarse del camino) to turn aside; (: barco) to go off course; (Auto: dar un rodeo) to make a detour; **~se de un tema** to get away from the topic

desvío [des'βio] vb ver **desviar** ▷ nm (desviación) detour, diversion; (fig) indifference

desvirgar [desβir'ɣar] vt to deflower

desvirtuar [desβir'twar] vt (estropear) to spoil; (argumento, razonamiento) to detract from; (efecto) to counteract; (sentido) to distort; **desvirtuarse** vr to spoil

desvitalizar [desβitali'θar] vt (nervio) to numb

desvivirse [desβi'βirse] vr: **~ por** to long for, crave for; **~ por los amigos** to do anything for one's friends

detallar [deta'ʎar] vt to detail; (asunto por asunto) to itemize

detalle [de'taʎe] nm detail; (fig) gesture, token; **al ~** in detail; (Com) retail cpd; **comercio al ~** retail trade; **vender al ~** to sell retail; **no pierde ~** he doesn't miss a trick; **me observaba sin perder ~** he watched my every move; **tiene muchos ~s** she is very considerate

detallista [deta'ʎista] nm/f retailer ▷ adj (meticuloso) meticulous; **comercio ~** retail trade

detectar [detek'tar] vt to detect

detective [detek'tiβe] nm/f detective; **~ privado** private detective

detector [detek'tor] nm (Naut, Tec etc) detector; **~ de mentiras/de minas** lie/mine detector

detención [deten'θjon] nf (acción) stopping; (estancamiento) stoppage; (retraso) holdup, delay; (Jur: arresto) arrest; (prisión) detention; (cuidado) care; **~ de juego** (Deporte) stoppage of play; **~ ilegal** unlawful detention

detener [dete'ner] vt (gen) to stop; (Jur: arrestar) to arrest; (: encarcelar) to detain; (objeto) to keep; (retrasar) to hold up, delay; (aliento) to hold; **detenerse** vr to stop; **~se en** (demorarse) to delay over, linger over

detenidamente [deteniða'mente] adv (minuciosamente) carefully; (extensamente) at great length

detenido, -a [dete'niðo, a] adj (arrestado) under arrest; (minucioso) detailed; (examen ~) thorough; (tímido) timid ▷ nm/f person under arrest, prisoner

detenimiento [deteni'mjento] nm care; **con ~** thoroughly; (observar, considerar) carefully

detergente [deter'xente] adj, nm detergent

deteriorar [deterjo'rar] vt to spoil, damage; **deteriorarse** vr to deteriorate

deterioro [dete'rjoro] nm deterioration

determinación [determina'θjon] nf (empeño) determination; (decisión) decision; (de fecha, precio) settling, fixing

determinado, -a [determi'naðo, a] adj (preciso) certain; (Ling: artículo) definite; (persona: resuelto) determined; **un día ~** on a certain day; **no hay ningún tema ~** there is no particular theme

determinar [determi'nar] vt (plazo) to fix; (precio) to settle; (daños, impuestos) to assess; (pleito) to decide; (causar) to cause; **determinarse** vr to decide; **el reglamento determina que ...** the rules lay it down or state that ...; **aquello determinó la caída del gobierno** that brought about the fall of the government; **esto le determinó** this decided him

detestar [detes'tar] vt to detest

detonación [detona'θjon] nf detonation; (sonido) explosion

detonante [deto'nante] nm (fig) trigger

d

detonar [deto'nar] vi to detonate

detractor, a [detrak'tor, a] adj disparaging ▷ nm/f detractor

detrás [de'tras] adv (tb: **por ~**) behind; (atrás) at the back ▷ prep: **~ de** behind; **por ~ de algn** (fig) behind sb's back; **salir de ~** to come out from behind; **por ~** behind

detrimento [detri'mento] nm: **en ~ de** to the detriment of

deuda [de'uða] nf (condición) indebtedness, debt; (cantidad) debt; **~ a largo plazo** long-term debt; **~ exterior/pública** foreign/ national debt; **~ incobrable** o **morosa** bad debt; **~s activas/pasivas** assets/liabilities; **contraer ~s** to get into debt

deudor, a [deu'ðor, a] nm/f debtor; **~ hipotecario** mortgager; **~ moroso** slow payer

devaluación [deβalwa'θjon] nf devaluation

devaluar [deβalu'ar] vt to devalue

devastar [deβas'tar] vt (destruir) to devastate

devengar [deβeŋ'gar] vt (salario: ganar) to earn; (: tener que cobrar) to be due; (intereses) to bring in, accrue, earn

deveras [de'βeras] nf inv (Am): **un amigo de (a) ~** a true o real friend

devoción [deβo'θjon] nf devotion; (afición) strong attachment

devolución [deβolu'θjon] nf (reenvío) return, sending back; (reembolso) repayment; (Jur) devolution

devolver [deβol'βer] vt to return; (lo extraviado, prestado) to give back; (a su sitio) to put back; (carta al correo) to send back; (Com) to repay, refund; (visita, la palabra) to return; (salud, vista) to restore; (fam: vomitar) to throw up ▷ vi (fam) to be sick; **devolverse** vr (Am) to return; **~ mal por bien** to return ill for good; **~ la pelota a algn** to give sb tit for tat

devorar [deβo'rar] vt to devour; (comer ávidamente) to gobble up; (fig: fortuna) to run through; **todo lo devoró el fuego** the fire consumed everything; **le devoran los celos** he is consumed with jealousy

devoto, -a [de'βoto, a] adj (Rel: persona) devout; (: obra) devotional; (amigo): **~ (de algn)** devoted (to sb) ▷ nm/f admirer; **los devotos** nmpl (Rel) the faithful; **su muy ~** your devoted servant

devuelto [de'βwelto], **devuelva** etc [de'βwelβa] vb ver **devolver**

di [di] vb ver **dar, decir**

día ['dia] nm day; **~ de asueto** day off; **~ feriado** (Am) o **festivo** (public) holiday; **~ hábil/inhábil** working/non-working day; **~ lunes** (Am) Monday; **~ lectivo** teaching day; **~ libre** day off; **D~ de Reyes** Epiphany (6 January); **D~ de la Independencia** Independence Day; **¿qué ~ es?** what's the date?; **estar/poner al ~** to be/keep up to date; **el ~ de hoy/de mañana** today/tomorrow; **el ~ menos pensado** when you least expect

it; **al ~ siguiente** on the following day; **todos los ~s** every day; **un ~ sí y otro no** every other day; **vivir al ~** to live from hand to mouth; **de ~** during the day, by day; **es de ~** it's daylight; **del ~** (estilos) fashionable; (menú) today's; **de un ~ para otro** any day now; **en pleno ~** in full daylight; **en su ~** in due time; **¡hasta otro ~!** so long!

diabetes [dja'betes] nf diabetes sg

diabético, -a [dja'betiko, a] adj, nm/f diabetic

diablo ['djaβlo] nm (tb fig) devil; **pobre ~** poor devil; **hace un frío de todos los ~s** it's hellishly cold

diablura [dja'βlura] nf prank; (travesura) mischief

diadema [dja'ðema] nf (para el pelo) Alice band, headband; (joya) tiara

diafragma [dja'fraɣma] nm diaphragm

diagnosis [djaɣ'nosis] nf inv, **diagnóstico** [djaɣ'nostiko] nm diagnosis

diagnosticar [djaɣnosti'kar] vt to diagnose

diagnóstico [djaɣ'nostiko] nm = **diagnosis**

diagonal [djaɣo'nal] adj diagonal ▷ nf (Geom) diagonal; **en ~** diagonally

diagrama [dja'ɣrama] nm diagram; **~ de barras** (Com) bar chart; **~ de dispersión** (Com) scatter diagram; **~ de flujo** (Inform) flowchart

dial [di'al] nm dial

dialecto [dja'lekto] nm dialect

dialogar [djalo'ɣar] vt to write in dialogue form ▷ vi (conversar) to have a conversation; **~ con** (Pol) to hold talks with

diálogo ['djaloɣo] nm dialogue

diamante [dja'mante] nm diamond

diámetro [di'ametro] nm diameter; **~ de giro** (Auto) turning circle; **faros de gran ~** wide-angle headlights

diana ['djana] nf (Mil) reveille; (de blanco) centre, bull's-eye

diapositiva [djaposi'tiβa] nf (Foto) slide, transparency

diario, -a ['djarjo, a] adj daily ▷ nm newspaper; (libro diario) diary; (: Com) daybook; (Com: gastos) daily expenses; **~ de navegación** (Naut) logbook, **~ hablado** (Radio) news (bulletin); **~ de sesiones** parliamentary report; **a ~** daily; **de** o **para ~** everyday

diarrea [dja'rrea] nf diarrhoea

dibujante [diβu'xante] nm/f (de bosquejos) sketcher; (de dibujos animados) cartoonist; (de moda) designer; **~ de publicidad** commercial artist

dibujar [diβu'xar] vt to draw, sketch; **dibujarse** vr (emoción) to show; **~se contra** to be outlined against

dibujo [di'βuxo] nm drawing; (Tec) design; (en papel, tela) pattern; (en periódico) cartoon; (fig) description; **~s animados** cartoons; **~ del natural** drawing from life

diccionario [dikθjo'narjo] nm dictionary

dice etc vb ver **decir**

dicho, -a ['ditʃo, a] pp de **decir** ▷ adj (susodicho) aforementioned ▷ nm saying; (proverbio) proverb; (ocurrencia) bright remark ▷ nf (buena suerte) good luck; **mejor ~** rather; **~ y hecho** no sooner said than done

dichoso, -a [di'tʃoso, a] adj (feliz) happy; (afortunado) lucky; **¡aquel ~ coche!** (fam) that blessed car!

diciembre [di'θjembre] nm December; ver tb **julio**

dictado [dik'taðo] nm dictation; **escribir al ~** to take dictation; **los ~s de la conciencia** (fig) the dictates of conscience

dictador [dikta'ðor] nm dictator

dictadura [dikta'ðura] nf dictatorship

dictamen [dik'tamen] nm (opinión) opinion; (informe) report; **~ contable** auditor's report; **~ facultativo** (Med) medical report

dictar [dik'tar] vt (carta) to dictate; (Jur: sentencia) to pass; (decreto) to issue; (Am: clase) to give; (: conferencia) to deliver

didáctico, -a [di'ðaktiko, a] adj didactic; (material) teaching cpd; (juguete) educational

diecinueve [djeθinu'eβe] num nineteen; (fecha) nineteenth; ver tb **seis**

dieciocho [djeθi'otʃo] num eighteen; (fecha) eighteenth; ver tb **seis**

dieciséis [djeθi'seis] num sixteen; (fecha) sixteenth; ver tb **seis**

diecisiete [djeθi'sjete] num seventeen; (fecha) seventeenth; ver tb **seis**

diente ['djente] nm (Anat, Tec) tooth; (Zool) fang; (: de elefante) tusk; (de ajo) clove; **~ de león** dandelion; **~s postizos** false teeth; **enseñar los ~s** (fig) to show one's claws; **hablar entre ~s** to mutter, mumble; **hincar el ~ en** (comida) to bite into

diera etc ['djera] vb ver **dar**

diesel ['disel] adj: **motor ~** diesel engine

diestro, -a ['djestro, a] adj (derecho) right; (hábil) skilful; (: con las manos) handy ▷ nm (Taur) matador ▷ nf right hand; **a ~ y siniestro** (sin método) wildly

dieta ['djeta] nf diet; **dietas** nfpl expenses; **estar a ~** to be on a diet

dietético, -a [dje'tetiko, a] adj dietetic ▷ nm/f dietician ▷ nf dietetics sg

diez [djeθ] num ten; (fecha) tenth; **hacer las ~ de últimas** (Naipes) to sweep the board; ver tb **seis**

diezmar [djeθ'mar] vt to decimate

difamación [difama'θjon] nf slander; libel

difamar [difa'mar] vt (Jur: hablando) to slander; (: por escrito) to libel

diferencia [dife'renθja] nf difference; **a ~ de** unlike; **hacer ~ entre** to make a distinction between; **~ salarial** (Com) wage differential

diferenciar [diferen'θjar] vt to differentiate between ▷ vi to differ; **diferenciarse** vr to differ, be different; (distinguirse) to distinguish o.s.

diferente [dife'rente] adj different

diferido [dife'riðo] nm: **en ~** (TV etc) recorded

diferir [dife'rir] vt to defer

difícil [di'fiθil] adj difficult; (tiempos, vida) hard; (situación) delicate; **es un hombre ~** he's a difficult man to get on with

dificultad [difikul'taθ] nf difficulty; (problema) trouble; (objeción) objection

dificultar [difikul'tar] vt (complicar) to complicate, make difficult; (estorbar) to obstruct; **las restricciones dificultan el comercio** the restrictions hinder trade

difundir [difun'dir] vt (calor, luz) to diffuse; (Radio) to broadcast; **difundirse** vr to spread (out); **~ una noticia** to spread a piece of news

difunto, a [di'funto, a] adj dead, deceased ▷ nm/f deceased (person); **el ~** the deceased

difusión [difu'sjon] nf (de calor, luz) diffusion; (de noticia, teoría) dissemination; (de programa) broadcasting; (programa) broadcast

difuso, -a [di'fuso, a] adj (luz) diffused; (conocimientos) widespread; (estilo, explicación) wordy

diga etc ['diɣa] vb ver **decir**

digerir [dixe'rir] vt to digest; (fig) to absorb; (reflexionar sobre) to think over

digestión [dixes'tjon] nf digestion; **corte de ~** indigestion

digestivo, -a [dixes'tiβo, a] adj digestive ▷ nm (bebida) liqueur, digestif

digital [dixi'tal] adj (Inform) digital; (dactilar) finger cpd ▷ nf (Bot) foxglove; (droga) digitalis

dignarse [diɣ'narse] vr to deign to

dignidad [diɣni'ðað] nf dignity; (honra) honour; (rango) rank; (persona) dignitary; **herir la ~ de algn** to hurt sb's pride

digno, -a ['diɣno, a] adj worthy; (persona: honesto) honourable; **~ de elogio** praiseworthy; **~ de mención** worth mentioning; **es ~ de verse** it is worth seeing; **poco ~** unworthy

digo etc vb ver **decir**

dije etc ['dixe], **dijera** etc [di'xera] vb ver **decir**

dilapidar [dilapi'ðar] vt to squander, waste

dilatado, -a [dila'taðo, a] adj dilated; (período) long drawn-out; (extenso) extensive

dilatar [dila'tar] vt (gen) to dilate; (prolongar) to prolong; (aplazar) to delay; **dilatarse** vr (pupila etc) to dilate; (agua) to expand

dilema [di'lema] nm dilemma

diligencia [dili'xenθja] nf diligence; (rapidez) speed; (ocupación) errand, job; (carruaje) stagecoach; **diligencias** nfpl (Jur) formalities; **~s judiciales** judicial proceedings; **~s previas** inquest sg

diligente [dili'xente] adj diligent; **poco ~** slack

diluir [dilu'ir] vt to dilute; (aguar, fig) to water down

diluvio [di'luβjo] nm deluge, flood; **un ~ de cartas** (fig) a flood of letters

dimensión [dimen'sjon] nf dimension; **dimensiones** nfpl size sg; **tomar las**

dimensiones de to take the measurements of
diminutivo [diminu'tiβo] *nm* diminutive
diminuto, -a [dimi'nuto, a] *adj* tiny, diminutive
dimisión [dimi'sjon] *nf* resignation
dimitir [dimi'tir] *vt* (*cargo*) to give up; (*despedir*) to sack ▷ *vi* to resign
dimos ['dimos] *vb ver* **dar**
Dinamarca [dina'marka] *nf* Denmark
dinámico, -a [di'namiko, a] *adj* dynamic ▷ *nf* dynamics *sg*
dinamita [dina'mita] *nf* dynamite
dinamo [di'namo], **dínamo** ['dinamo] *nf, nm en Am* dynamo
dinastía [dinas'tia] *nf* dynasty
dineral [dine'ral] *nm* fortune
dinero [di'nero] *nm* money; (*dinero en circulación*) currency; **~ caro** (*Com*) dear money; **~ contante (y sonante)** hard cash; **~ de curso legal** legal tender; **~ efectivo** *o* **metálico** cash, ready cash; **~ suelto** (*loose*) change; **es hombre de ~** he is a man of means; **andar mal de ~** to be short of money; **ganar ~ a espuertas** to make money hand over fist
dinosaurio [dino'saurjo] *nm* dinosaur
dio [djo] *vb ver* **dar**
diócesis ['djoθesis] *nf inv* diocese
dios [djos] *nm* god; **D~** God; **D~ mediante** God willing; **a D~ gracias** thank heaven; **a la buena de D~** any old how; **una de D~ es Cristo** an almighty row; **D~ los cría y ellos se juntan** birds of a feather flock together; **como D~ manda** as is proper; **¡D~ mío!** (oh) my God!; **¡por D~!** for God's sake!
diosa ['djosa] *nf* goddess
diploma [di'ploma] *nm* diploma
diplomacia [diplo'maθja] *nf* diplomacy; (*fig*) tact
diplomado, -a [diplo'maðo, a] *adj* qualified ▷ *nm/f* holder of a diploma; (*Univ*) graduate; *ver tb* **licenciado**
diplomático, -a [diplo'matiko, a] *adj* (*cuerpo*) diplomatic; (*que tiene tacto*) tactful ▷ *nm/f* diplomat
diptongo [dip'tongo] *nm* diphthong
diputación [diputa'θjon] *nf* deputation; (*tb: ~ provincial*) ≈ county council; **~ permanente** (*Pol*) standing committee
diputado, -a [dipu'taðo, a] *nm/f* delegate; (*Pol*) ≈ member of parliament (*Brit*), ≈ representative (*US*); *ver tb* **Corte**
dique ['dike] *nm* dyke; (*rompeolas*) breakwater; **~ de contención** dam
diré *etc* [di're] *vb ver* **decir**
dirección [direk'θjon] *nf* direction; (*fig: tendencia*) trend; (*señas, tb Inform*) address; (*Auto*) steering; (*gerencia*) management; (*de periódico*) editorship; (*en escuela*) headship; (*Pol*) leadership; (*junta*) board of directors; (*despacho*) director's/manager's/

headmaster's/editor's office; **~ administrativa** office management; **~ asistida** power-assisted steering; **D~ General de Seguridad/Turismo** State Security/Tourist Office; **"~ única"** "one-way street"; **"~ prohibida"** "no entry"; **tomar la ~ de una empresa** to take over the running of a company
direccional [direkθjo'nal] *nf* (*Am: Auto*) indicator
directa [di'rekta] *nf* (*Auto*) top gear
directivo, -a [direk'tiβo, a] *adj* (*junta*) managing; (*función*) administrative ▷ *nm/f* (*Com*) manager ▷ *nf* (*norma*) directive; (*tb: junta directiva*) board of directors
directo, -a [di'rekto, a] *adj* direct; (*línea*) straight; (*inmediato*) immediate; (*tren*) through; (*TV*) live; **programa en ~** live programme; **transmitir en ~** to broadcast live
director, a [direk'tor, a] *adj* leading ▷ *nm/f* director; (*Escol*) head (teacher) (*Brit*), principal (*US*); (*gerente*) manager/ manageress; (*de compañía*) president; (*jefe*) head; (*Prensa*) editor; (*de prisión*) governor; (*Mus*) conductor; **~ adjunto** assistant manager; **~ de cine** film director; **~ comercial** marketing manager; **~ ejecutivo** executive director; **~ de empresa** company director; **~ general** general manager; **~ gerente** managing director; **~ de sucursal** branch manager
directorio [direk'torjo] *nm* (*Inform*) directory; (*Am: telefónico*) phone book
dirigente [diri'xente] *adj* leading ▷ *nm/f* (*Pol*) leader; **los ~s del partido** the party leaders
dirigir [diri'xir] *vt* to direct; (*acusación*) to level; (*carta*) to address; (*obra de teatro, film*) to direct; (*Mus*) to conduct; (*comercio*) to manage; (*expedición*) to lead; (*sublevación*) to head; (*periódico*) to edit; (*guiar*) to guide; **dirigirse** *vr*: **~se a** to go towards, make one's way towards; (*hablar con*) to speak to; **~se a algn solicitando algo** to apply to sb for sth; **"diríjase a ..."** "apply to ..."
dirija *etc* [di'rixa] *vb ver* **dirigir**
discernir [disθer'nir] *vt* to discern ▷ *vi* to distinguish
disciplina [disθi'plina] *nf* discipline
discípulo, -a [dis'θipulo, a] *nm/f* disciple; (*seguidor*) follower; (*Escol*) pupil
Discman® ['diskman] *nm* Discman®, personal CD player
disco ['disko] *nm* disc (*Brit*), disk (*US*); (*Deporte*) discus; (*Telec*) dial; (*Auto: semáforo*) light; (*Mus*) record; (*Inform*) disk; **~ de arranque** boot disk; **~ compacto** compact disc; **~ de densidad sencilla/doble** single/double density disk; **~ de larga duración** long-playing record (LP); **~ flexible** *o* **floppy** floppy disk; **~ de freno** brake disc; **~ maestro** master disk; **~ de reserva** backup

disk; ~ **rígido** hard disk; ~ **de una cara/dos caras** single-/double-sided disk; ~ **virtual** RAMdisk

discográfico, -a [disko'ɣrafiko, a] *adj* record *cpd*; **casa discográfica** record company; **sello** ~ label

disconforme [diskon'forme] *adj* differing; **estar** ~ **(con)** to be in disagreement (with)

discontinuo, -a [diskon'tinwo, a] *adj* discontinuous; *(Auto: línea)* broken

discordia [dis'korðja] *nf* discord

discoteca [disko'teka] *nf* disco(theque)

discreción [diskre'θjon] *nf* discretion; *(reserva)* prudence; **¡a ~!** *(Mil)* stand easy!; **añadir azúcar a** ~ *(Culin)* add sugar to taste; **comer a** ~ to eat as much as one wishes

discrecional [diskreθjo'nal] *adj* *(facultativo)* discretionary; **parada** ~ request stop

discrepancia [diskre'panθja] *nf* *(diferencia)* discrepancy; *(desacuerdo)* disagreement

discrepar [diskre'par] *vi* to disagree

discreto, -a [dis'kreto, a] *adj* *(diplomático)* discreet; *(sensato)* sensible; *(reservado)* quiet; *(sobrio)* sober; *(mediano)* fair, fairly good; **le daremos un plazo** ~ we'll allow him a reasonable time

discriminación [diskrimina'θjon] *nf* discrimination

discriminar [diskrimi'nar] *vt* to discriminate against; *(diferenciar)* to discriminate between

disculpa [dis'kulpa] *nf* excuse; *(pedir perdón)* apology; **pedir ~s a/por** to apologize to/for

disculpar [diskul'par] *vt* to excuse, pardon; **disculparse** *vr* to excuse o.s.; to apologize

discurrir [disku'rrir] *vt* *(pensar, reflexionar)* to think, meditate; *(recorrer)* to roam, wander; *(río)* to flow; *(el tiempo)* to pass, flow by

discurso [dis'kurso] *nm* speech; ~ **de clausura** closing speech; **pronunciar un** ~ to make a speech; **en el** ~ **del tiempo** with the passage of time

discusión [disku'sjon] *nf* *(diálogo)* discussion; *(riña)* argument; **tener una** ~ to have an argument

discutible [disku'tiβle] *adj* debatable; **de mérito** ~ of dubious worth

discutir [disku'tir] *vt* *(debatir)* to discuss; *(pelear)* to argue about; *(contradecir)* to argue against ▷ *vi* to discuss; *(disputar)* to argue; ~ **de política** to argue about politics; **¡no discutas!** don't argue!

disecar [dise'kar] *vt* *(para conservar: animal)* to stuff; *(: planta)* to dry

diseminar [disemi'nar] *vt* to disseminate, spread

disentir [disen'tir] *vi* to dissent, disagree

diseñador, a [diseɲa'dor, a] *nm/f* designer

diseñar [dise'ɲar] *vt, vi* to design

diseño [di'seɲo] *nm* *(Tec)* design; *(Arte)* drawing; *(Costura)* pattern; **de ~ italiano** Italian-designed; ~ **asistido por ordenador** computer-assisted design, CAD

disfraz [dis'fraθ] *nm* *(máscara)* disguise; *(traje)* fancy dress; *(excusa)* pretext; **bajo el** ~ **de** under the cloak of

disfrazar [disfra'θar] *vt* to disguise; **disfrazarse** *vr* to dress (o.s.) up; **~se de** to disguise o.s. as

disfrutar [disfru'tar] *vt* to enjoy ▷ *vi* to enjoy o.s.; **¡que disfrutes!** have a good time!; ~ **de** to enjoy, possess; ~ **de buena salud** to enjoy good health

disgregar [disɣre'ɣar] *vt* *(desintegrar)* to disintegrate; *(manifestantes)* to disperse; **disgregarse** *vr* to disintegrate, break up

disgustar [disɣus'tar] *vt* *(no gustar)* to displease; *(contrariar, enojar)* to annoy; to upset; **disgustarse** *vr* to get upset; *(dos personas)* to fall out; **estaba muy disgustado con el asunto** he was very upset about the affair

disgusto [dis'ɣusto] *nm* *(repugnancia)* disgust; *(contrariedad)* annoyance; *(desagrado)* displeasure; *(tristeza)* grief; *(riña)* quarrel; *(desgracia)* misfortune; **hacer algo a** ~ to do sth unwillingly; **matar a algn a ~s** to drive sb to distraction

disidente [disi'ðente] *nm* dissident

disimular [disimu'lar] *vt* *(ocultar)* to hide, conceal ▷ *vi* to dissemble

disipar [disi'par] *vt* *(duda, temor)* to dispel; *(esperanza)* to destroy; *(fortuna)* to squander; **disiparse** *vr* *(nubes)* to vanish; *(dudas)* to be dispelled; *(indisciplinarse)* to dissipate

diskette [dis'ket] *nm* *(Inform)* diskette, floppy disk

dislexia [dis'leksja] *nf* dyslexia

dislocar [dislo'kar] *vt* *(gen)* to dislocate; *(tobillo)* to sprain; **dislocarse** *vr* *(articulación)* to sprain, dislocate

disminución [disminu'θjon] *nf* decrease, reduction

disminuido, -a [disminu'iðo, a] *nm/f*: ~ **mental/físico** mentally/physically-handicapped person

disminuir [disminu'ir] *vt* to decrease, diminish; *(estrechar)* to lessen; *(temperatura)* to lower; *(gastos, raciones)* to cut down; *(dolor)* to relieve; *(autoridad, prestigio)* to weaken; *(entusiasmo)* to damp ▷ *vi* *(días)* to grow shorter; *(precios, temperatura)* to drop, fall; *(velocidad)* to slacken; *(población)* to decrease; *(beneficios, número)* to fall off; *(memoria, vista)* to fail

disolución [disolu'θjon] *nf* *(acto)* dissolution; *(Química)* solution; *(Com)* liquidation; *(moral)* dissoluteness

disolvente [disol'βente] *nm* solvent, thinner

disolver [disol'βer] *vt* *(gen)* to dissolve; *(manifestación)* to break up; **disolverse** *vr* to dissolve; *(Com)* to go into liquidation

dispar [dis'par] *adj* *(distinto)* different; *(irregular)* uneven

disparar [dispa'rar] vt, vi to shoot, fire; **dispararse** vr (arma de fuego) to go off; (persona: marcharse) to rush off; (: enojarse) to lose control; (caballo) to bolt

disparatado, -a [dispara'taðo, a] adj crazy

disparate [dispa'rate] nm (tontería) foolish remark; (error) blunder; **decir ~s** to talk nonsense; **¡qué ~!** how absurd!; **costar un ~** to cost a hell of a lot

disparo [dis'paro] nm shot; (acto) firing; **disparos** nmpl shooting sg, exchange sg of shots, shots; **~ inicial** (de cohete) blast-off

dispensar [dispen'sar] vt to dispense; (ayuda) to give; (honores) to grant; (disculpar) to excuse; **¡usted dispense!** I beg your pardon!; **~ a algn de hacer algo** to excuse sb from doing sth

dispersar [disper'sar] vt to disperse; (manifestación) to break up; **dispersarse** vr to scatter

disperso, -a [dis'perso, a] adj scattered

disponer [dispo'ner] vt (arreglar) to arrange; (ordenar) to put in order; (preparar) to prepare, get ready ⊳ vi: **~ de** to have, own; **disponerse** vr: **~se para** to prepare to, prepare for; **la ley dispone que ...** the law provides that ...; **no puede ~ de esos bienes** she cannot dispose of those properties

disponible [dispo'niβle] adj available; (tiempo) spare; (dinero) on hand

disposición [disposi'θjon] nf arrangement, disposition; (voluntad) willingness; (de casa, Inform) layout; (ley) order; (cláusula) provision; (aptitud) aptitude; **~ de ánimo** attitude of mind; **última ~** last will and testament; **a la ~ de** at the disposal of; **a su ~** at your service

dispositivo [disposi'tiβo] nm device, mechanism; **~ de alimentación** hopper; **~ de almacenaje** storage device; **~ periférico** peripheral (device); **~ de seguridad** safety catch; (fig) security measure

dispuesto, -a [dis'pwesto, a] pp de **disponer** ⊳ adj (arreglado) arranged; (preparado) disposed; (persona: dinámico) bright; **estar ~/poco ~ a hacer algo** to be inclined/reluctant to do sth

disputa [dis'puta] nf (discusión) dispute, argument; (controversia) controversy

disputar [dispu'tar] vt (discutir) to dispute, question; (contender) to contend for; (carrera) to compete in ⊳ vi to argue

disquete [dis'kete] nm (Inform) diskette, floppy disk

disquetera [diske'tera] nf disk drive

distancia [dis'tanθja] nf distance; (de tiempo) interval; **~ de parada** braking distance; **~ del suelo** (Auto etc) height off the ground; **a gran** o **a larga ~** long-distance; **mantenerse a ~** to keep one's distance; (fig) to remain aloof; **guardar las ~s** to keep one's distance

distanciar [distan'θjar] vt to space out; **distanciarse** vr to become estranged

distante [dis'tante] adj distant

distar [dis'tar] vi: **dista 5 km de aquí** it is 5 km from here; **¿dista mucho?** is it far?; **dista mucho de la verdad** it's very far from the truth

diste ['diste], **disteis** ['disteis] vb ver **dar**

distensión [disten'sjon] nf distension; (Pol) détente; **~ muscular** (Med) muscular strain

distinción [distin'θjon] nf distinction; (elegancia) elegance; (honor) honour; **a ~ de** unlike; **sin ~** indiscriminately; **sin ~ de edades** irrespective of age

distinguido, -a [distin'giðo, a] adj distinguished; (famoso) prominent, well-known; (elegante) elegant

distinguir [distin'gir] vt to distinguish; (divisar) to make out; (escoger) to single out; (caracterizar) to mark out; **distinguirse** vr to be distinguished; (destacarse) to distinguish o.s.; **a lo lejos no se distingue** it's not visible from a distance

distintivo, -a [distin'tiβo, a] adj distinctive; (signo) distinguishing ⊳ nm (de policía etc) badge; (fig) characteristic

distinto, -a [dis'tinto, a] adj different; (claro) clear; **~s** several, various

distorsión [distor'sjon] nf (Anat) twisting; (Radio etc) distortion

distorsionar [distorsjo'nar] vt, vi to distort

distracción [distrak'θjon] nf distraction; (pasatiempo) hobby, pastime; (olvido) absent-mindedness, distraction

distraer [distra'er] vt (atención) to distract; (divertir) to amuse; (fondos) to embezzle ⊳ vi to be relaxing; **distraerse** vr (entretenerse) to amuse o.s.; (perder la concentración) to allow one's attention to wander; **~ a algn de su pensamiento** to divert sb from his train of thought; **el pescar distrae** fishing is a relaxation

distraído, -a [distra'iðo, a] adj (gen) absent-minded; (desatento) inattentive; (entretenido) amusing ⊳ nm: **hacerse el ~** to pretend not to notice; **con aire ~** idly; **me miró distraída** she gave me a casual glance

distribuidor, a [distriβui'ðor, a] nm/f (persona: gen) distributor; (: Correos) sorter; (: Com) dealer, agent; **su ~ habitual** your regular dealer

distribuir [distriβu'ir] vt to distribute; (prospectos) to hand out; (cartas) to deliver; (trabajo) to allocate; (premios) to award; (dividendos) to pay; (peso) to distribute; (Arq) to plan

distrito [dis'trito] nm (sector, territorio) region; (barrio) district; **~ electoral** constituency; **~ postal** postal district; **D~ Federal** (Am) Federal District

disturbio [dis'turβjo] nm disturbance; (desorden) riot; **los disturbios** nmpl the troubles

disuadir [diswa'ðir] vt to dissuade

disuelto [di'swelto] pp de **disolver**

disyuntiva [disjun'tiβa] nf (dilema) dilemma

DIU ['dju] nm abr (= dispositivo intrauterino) IUD

diurno, -a ['djurno, a] adj day cpd, diurnal

divagar [diβa'γar] vi (desviarse) to digress

diván [di'βan] nm divan

divergencia [diβer'xenθja] nf divergence

diversidad [diβersi'ðað] nf diversity, variety

diversificar [diβersifi'kar] vt to diversify

diversión [diβer'sjon] nf (gen) entertainment; (actividad) hobby, pastime

diverso, -a [di'βerso, a] adj diverse; (diferente) different ▷ nm: **~s** (Com) sundries; **~s libros** several books

divertido, -a [diβer'tiðo, a] adj (chiste) amusing, funny; (fiesta etc) enjoyable; (película, libro) entertaining; **está ~** (irónico) this is going to be fun

divertir [diβer'tir] vt (entretener, recrear) to amuse, entertain; **divertirse** vr (pasarlo bien) to have a good time; (distraerse) to amuse o.s.

dividendo [diβi'ðendo] nm (Com) usu pl dividend, dividends; **~ definitivo** final dividend; **~s por acción** earnings per share

dividir [diβi'ðir] vt (gen) to divide; (separar) to separate; (distribuir) to distribute, share out

divierta etc [di'βjerta] vb ver **divertir**

divino, -a [di'βino, a] adj divine; (fig) lovely

divirtiendo etc [diβir'tjendo] vb ver **divertir**

divisa [di'βisa] nf (emblema) emblem, badge; **divisas** nfpl currency sg; (Com) foreign exchange sg; **control de ~s** exchange control; **~ de reserva** reserve currency

divisar [diβi'sar] vt to make out, distinguish

división [diβi'sjon] nf division; (de partido) split; (de país) partition

divorciado, -a [diβor'θjaðo, a] adj divorced; (opinión) split ▷ nm/f divorcé(e)

divorciar [diβor'θjar] vt to divorce; **divorciarse** vr to get divorced

divorcio [di'βorθjo] nm divorce; (fig) split

divulgar [diβul'γar] vt (desparramar) to spread; (popularizar) to popularize; (hacer circular) to divulge, circulate; **divulgarse** vr (secreto) to leak out; (rumor) to get about

DNI nm abr (Esp) = **Documento Nacional de Identidad**

● **DNI**

● The Documento Nacional de Identidad is a
● Spanish ID card which must be carried at
● all times and produced on request for the
● police. It contains the holder's photo,
● fingerprints and personal details. It is
● also known as the DNI or carnet de identidad.

Dña. abr (= Doña) Mrs

do [do] nm (Mus) C

dobladillo [doβla'ðiʎo] nm (de vestido) hem; (de pantalón: vuelta) turn-up (Brit), cuff (US)

doblaje [do'βlaxe] nm (Cine) dubbing

doblar [do'βlar] vt to double; (papel) to fold; (caño) to bend; (la esquina) to turn, go round; (film) to dub ▷ vi to turn; (campana) to toll; **doblarse** vr (plegarse) to fold (up), crease; (encorvarse) to bend; **~ a la derecha/ izquierda** to turn right/left

doble ['doβle] adj (gen) double; (de dos aspectos) dual; (cuerda) thick; (fig) two-faced ▷ nm/f (Teat) double, stand-in; **dobles** nmpl (Deporte) doubles sg; **~ o nada** double or quits; **~ página** double-page spread; **con ~ sentido** with a double meaning; **el ~** twice the quantity o as much; **su sueldo es el ~ del mío** his salary is twice (as much as) mine; (Inform): **~ cara** double-sided; **~ densidad** double density; **~ espacio** double spacing

doblegar [doβle'γar] vt to fold, crease; **doblegarse** vr to yield

doblez [do'βleθ] nm (pliegue) fold, hem ▷ nf (falsedad) duplicity

doce ['doθe] num twelve; (fecha) twelfth; **las ~** twelve o'clock; ver tb **seis**

docena [do'θena] nf dozen; **por ~s** by the dozen

docente [do'θente] adj: **personal ~** teaching staff; **centro ~** educational institution

dócil ['doθil] adj (pasivo) docile; (manso) gentle; (obediente) obedient

doctor, a [dok'tor, a] nm/f doctor; **~ en filosofía** Doctor of Philosophy

doctorado [dokto'raðo] nm doctorate

doctrina [dok'trina] nf doctrine, teaching

documentación [dokumenta'θjon] nf documentation; (de identidad etc) papers pl

documental [dokumen'tal] adj, nm documentary

documentar [dokumen'tar] vt to document; **documentarse** vr to gather information

documento [doku'mento] nm (certificado) document; (Jur) exhibit; **documentos** nmpl papers; **~ adjunto** (Inform) attachment; **~ justificativo** voucher; **D~ Nacional de Identidad** national identity card; ver **DNI**

dogma ['doγma] nm dogma

dogmático, -a [doγ'matiko, a] adj dogmatic

dólar ['dolar] nm dollar

doler [do'ler] vt, vi to hurt; (fig) to grieve; **dolerse** vr (de su situación) to grieve, feel sorry; (de las desgracias ajenas) to sympathize; (quejarse) to complain; **me duele el brazo** my arm hurts; **no me duele el dinero** I don't mind about the money; **¡ahí le duele!** you've put your finger on it!

dolor [do'lor] nm pain; (fig) grief, sorrow; **~ de cabeza** headache; **~ de estómago** stomach ache; **~ de oídos** earache; **~ sordo** dull ache

dolorido, -a [dolo'riðo, a] adj (Med) sore; **la parte dolorida** the part which hurts

doloroso, -a [dolo'roso, a] adj (Med) painful; (fig) distressing

domar [do'mar] *vt* to tame
domesticar [domesti'kar] *vt* to tame
doméstico, -a [do'mestiko, a] *adj* domestic; (*vida, servicio*) home; (*tareas*) household; (*animal*) tame, pet ▷ *nm/f* servant; **economía doméstica** home economy; **gastos ~s** household expenses
domiciliación [domiθilja'θjon] *nf*: ~ **de pagos** (*Com*) direct debit
domiciliar [domiθi'ljar] *vt* to domicile; **domiciliarse** *vr* to take up (one's) residence
domicilio [domi'θiljo] *nm* home; ~ **particular** private residence; ~ **social** (*Com*) head office, registered office; **servicio a ~** delivery service; **sin ~ fijo** of no fixed abode
dominante [domi'nante] *adj* dominant; (*persona*) domineering
dominar [domi'nar] *vt* (*gen*) to dominate; (*países*) to rule over; (*adversario*) to overpower; (*caballo, nervios, emoción*) to control; (*incendio, epidemia*) to bring under control; (*idiomas*) to be fluent in ▷ *vi* to dominate, prevail; **dominarse** *vr* to control o.s.
domingo [do'miŋgo] *nm* Sunday; **D~ de Ramos** Palm Sunday; **D~ de Resurrección** Easter Sunday; *ver tb* **sábado**; **Semana Santa**
dominguero, -a [domiŋ'gero, a] *adj* Sunday *cpd*
dominical [domini'kal] *adj* Sunday *cpd*; **periódico ~** Sunday newspaper
dominicano, -a [domini'kano, a] *adj, nm/f* Dominican
dominio [do'minjo] *nm* (*tierras*) domain; (*Pol*) dominion; (*autoridad*) power, authority; (*supremacía*) supremacy; (*de las pasiones*) grip, hold; (*de idioma*) command; **ser del ~ público** to be widely known
don [don] *nm* (*talento*) gift; **D~ Juan Gómez** Mr Juan Gómez, Juan Gómez Esq. (*Brit*); **tener ~ de gentes** to know how to handle people; ~ **de lenguas** gift for languages; ~ **de mando** (qualities of) leadership; ~ **de palabra** gift of the gab; *see note*

● **DON**
●
● Don or doña is a term used before
● someone's first name – eg Don Diego,
● Doña Inés – when showing respect or
● being polite to someone of a superior
● social standing or to an older person. It is
● becoming somewhat rare, but it does
● however continue to be used with names
● and surnames in official documents and
● in correspondence: eg Sr. D. Pedro
● Rodríguez Hernández, Sra. Dña Inés
● Rodríguez Hernández.

dona ['dona] *nf* (*Am*) doughnut, donut (*US*)
donación [dona'θjon] *nf* donation
donaire [do'naire] *nm* charm

donante [do'nante] *nm/f* donor; ~ **de sangre** blood donor
donar [do'nar] *vt* to donate
donativo [dona'tiβo] *nm* donation
doncella [don'θeʎa] *nf* (*criada*) maid
donde ['donde] *adv* where ▷ *prep*: **el coche está allí ~ el farol** the car is over there by the lamppost *o* where the lamppost is; **por ~** through which; **a ~** to where, to which; **en ~** where, in which; **es a ~ vamos nosotros** that's where we're going
dónde ['donde] *adv interrogativo* where?; *¿a ~ vas?* where are you going (to)?; *¿de ~ vienes?* where have you been?; *¿en ~?* where?; *¿por ~?* where?, whereabouts?; *¿por ~ se va al estadio?* how do you get to the stadium?
dondequiera [donde'kjera] *adv* anywhere ▷ *conj*: ~ **que** wherever; **por ~** everywhere, all over the place
donut® [do'nut] *nm* (*Esp*) doughnut, donut (*US*)
doña ['dona] *nf*: ~ **Alicia** Alicia; **D~ Carmen Gómez** Mrs Carmen Gómez; *ver tb* **don**
dopar [do'par] *vt* to dope, drug
doping ['dopin] *nm* doping, drugging
dorado, -a [do'raðo, a] *adj* (*color*) golden; (*Tec*) gilt
dorar [do'rar] *vt* (*Tec*) to gild; (*Culin*) to brown, cook lightly; ~ **la píldora** to sweeten the pill
dormir [dor'mir] *vt*: ~ **la siesta** to have an afternoon nap ▷ *vi* to sleep; **dormirse** *vr* (*persona, brazo, pierna*) to fall asleep; ~**la** (*fam*) to sleep it off; ~ **la mona** (*fam*) to sleep off a hangover; ~ **como un lirón** *o* **tronco** to sleep like a log; ~ **a pierna suelta** to sleep soundly
dormitar [dormi'tar] *vi* to doze
dormitorio [dormi'torjo] *nm* bedroom; ~ **común** dormitory
dorsal [dor'sal] *adj* dorsal ▷ *nm* (*Deporte*) number
dorso [dorso] *nm* (*de mano*) back; (*de hoja*) other side; **escribir algo al ~** to write sth on the back; **"véase al ~"** "see other side", "please turn over"
dos [dos] *num* two; (*fecha*) second; **los ~** the two of them, both of them; **cada ~ por tres** every five minutes; **de ~ en ~** in twos; **estamos a ~** (*Tenis*) the score is deuce; *ver tb* **seis**
doscientos, -as [dos'θjentos, as] *num* two hundred
dosis ['dosis] *nf inv* dose, dosage
dossier [do'sjer] *nm* dossier, file
dotado, -a [do'taðo, a] *adj* gifted; ~ **de** (*persona*) endowed with; (*máquina*) equipped with
dotar [do'tar] *vt* to endow; (*Tec*) to fit; (*barco*) to man; (*oficina*) to staff
dote ['dote] *nf* (*de novia*) dowry; **dotes** *nfpl* (*talentos*) gifts
doy [doj] *vb ver* **dar**
dragón [dra'ɣon] *nm* dragon

drama ['drama] nm drama; (obra) play
dramático, -a [dra'matiko, a] adj dramatic
▷ nm/f dramatist; (actor) actor; **obra
  dramática** play
dramaturgo, -a [drama'turɣo, a] nm/f
  dramatist, playwright
drástico, -a ['drastiko, a] adj drastic
drenaje [dre'naxe] nm drainage
droga ['droɣa] nf drug; (Deporte) dope;
  el problema de la ~ the drug problem
drogadicto, -a [droɣa'ðikto, a] nm/f drug
  addict
drogar [dro'ɣar] vt to drug; (Deporte) to dope;
  drogarse vr to take drugs
drogodependencia [droɣoðepen'denθja] nf
  drug addiction
droguería [droɣe'ria] nf ≈ hardware shop
  (Brit) o store (US)
dromedario [drome'ðarjo] nm dromedary
ducha ['dutʃa] nf (baño) shower; (Med) douche
ducharse [du'tʃarse] vr to take a shower
duda ['duða] nf doubt; **sin ~** no doubt,
  doubtless; **¡sin ~!** of course!; **no cabe ~** there
  is no doubt about it; **no le quepa ~** make no
  mistake about it; **no quiero poner en ~ su
  conducta** I don't want to call his behaviour
  into question; **sacar a algn de la ~** to settle
  sb's doubts; **tengo una ~** I have a query
dudar [du'ðar] vt to doubt ▷ vi to doubt, have
  doubts; **~ acerca de algo** to be uncertain
  about sth; **dudó en comprarlo** he hesitated
  to buy it; **dudan que sea verdad** they doubt
  whether o if it's true
dudoso, -a [du'ðoso, a] adj (incierto) hesitant;
  (sospechoso) doubtful; (conducta) dubious
duela etc vb ver **doler**
duelo ['dwelo] vb ver **doler** ▷ nm (combate)
  duel; (luto) mourning; **batirse en ~** to fight
  a duel
duende ['dwende] nm imp, goblin; **tiene ~**
  he's got real soul
dueño, -a ['dweɲo, a] nm/f (propietario) owner;
  (de pensión, taberna) landlord(-lady); (de casa,
  perro) master/mistress; (empresario) employer;
  ser ~ de sí mismo to have self-control; (libre)
  to be one's own boss; **eres ~ de hacer como
  te parezca** you're free to do as you think fit;
  hacerse ~ de una situación to take
  command of a situation
duerma etc ['dwerma] vb ver **dormir**
dulce ['dulθe] adj sweet; (carácter, clima)
  gentle, mild ▷ adv gently, softly ▷ nm sweet
dulcería [dulθe'ria] nf (Am) confectioner's
  (shop)
dulzón, -ona [dul'θon, ona] adj (alimento)
  sickly-sweet, too sweet; (canción etc) gooey
dulzura [dul'θura] nf sweetness; (ternura)
  gentleness
duna ['duna] nf dune
dúo ['duo] nm duet, duo
duodécimo, -a [duo'ðeθimo, a] adj twelfth;
  ver tb **sexto, a**

dúplex ['dupleks] nm inv (piso) duplex
  (apartment); (Telec) link-up; (Inform):
  ~ integral full duplex
duplicar [dupli'kar] vt (hacer el doble de) to
  duplicate; (cantidad) to double; **duplicarse** vr
  to double
duque ['duke] nm duke
duquesa [du'kesa] nf duchess
durable [du'raβle] adj durable
duración [dura'θjon] nf (de película, disco etc)
  length; (de pila etc) life; (curso: de
  acontecimientos etc) duration; **~ media de la
  vida** average life expectancy; **de larga ~**
  (enfermedad) lengthy; (pila) long-life; (disco)
  long-playing; **de poca ~** short
duradero, -a [dura'ðero, a] adj (tela) hard-
  wearing; (fe, paz) lasting
durante [du'rante] adv during; **~ toda la
  noche** all night long; **habló ~ una hora** he
  spoke for an hour
durar [du'rar] vi (permanecer) to last; (recuerdo)
  to remain; (ropa) to wear (well)
durazno [du'rasno] nm (Am: fruta) peach;
  (: árbol) peach tree
durex ['dureks] nm (Am: tira adhesiva)
  Sellotape® (Brit), Scotch tape® (US)
dureza [du'reθa] nf (cualidad) hardness;
  (de carácter) toughness
durmiente [dur'mjente] adj sleeping ▷ nm/f
  sleeper
duro, -a ['duro, a] adj hard; (carácter) tough;
  (pan) stale; (cuello, puerta) stiff; (clima, luz)
  harsh ▷ adv hard ▷ nm (moneda) five peseta
  coin; **el sector ~ del partido** the hardliners
  pl in the party; **ser ~ con algn** to be tough
  with o hard on sb; **~ de mollera** (torpe) dense;
  ~ de oído hard of hearing; **trabajar ~** to
  work hard; **estar sin un ~** to be broke
DVD nm abr (= disco de vídeo digital) DVD

e

E *abr* (= este) E

e [e] *conj* (*delante de* **i-** *e* **hi-** *pero no* **hie-**) and; *ver tb* **y**

ebanista [eβa'nista] *nm/f* cabinetmaker

ébano ['eβano] *nm* ebony

e-book ['ibuk] *nm* e-book

ebrio, -a ['eβrjo, a] *adj* drunk

ebullición [eβuʎi'θjon] *nf* boiling; **punto de ~** boiling point

e-card ['ikard] *nf* e-card

eccema [ek'θema] *nm* (*Med*) eczema

echar [e'tʃar] *vt* to throw; (*agua, vino*) to pour (out); (*Culin*) to put in, add; (*dientes*) to cut; (*discurso*) to give; (*empleado: despedir*) to fire, sack; (*hojas*) to sprout; (*cartas*) to post; (*humo*) to emit, give out; (*reprimenda*) to deal out; (*cuenta*) to make up; (*freno*) to put on ▷ *vi*: **~ a correr** to start running *o* to run, break into a run; **~ a llorar** to burst into tears; **~ a reír** to burst out laughing; **echarse** *vr* to lie down; **~ llave a** to lock (up); **~ abajo** (*gobierno*) to overthrow; (*edificio*) to demolish; **~ mano a** to lay hands on; **~ una mano a algn** (*ayudar*) to give sb a hand; **~ la buenaventura a algn** to tell sb's fortune; **~ la culpa a** to lay the blame on; **~ de menos** to miss; **~ una mirada** to give a look; **~ sangre** to bleed; **~se atrás** to throw o.s. back(wards); (*fig*) to back out; **~se una novia** to get o.s. a girlfriend; **~se una siestecita** to have a nap

eclesiástico, -a [ekle'sjastiko, a] *adj* ecclesiastical; (*autoridades etc*) church *cpd* ▷ *nm* clergyman

eclipsar [eklip'sar] *vt* to eclipse; (*fig*) to outshine, overshadow

eclipse [e'klipse] *nm* eclipse

eco ['eko] *nm* echo; **encontrar un ~ en** to produce a response from; **hacerse ~ de una opinión** to echo an opinion; **tener ~** to catch on

ecografía [ekoɣra'fia] *nf* ultrasound

ecología [ekolo'xia] *nf* ecology

ecológico, -a [eko'loxiko, a] *adj* ecological; (*producto, método*) environmentally-friendly; (*agricultura*) organic

ecologista [ekolo'xista] *adj* environmental, conservation *cpd* ▷ *nm/f* environmentalist

economato [ekono'mato] *nm* cooperative store

economía [ekono'mia] *nf* (*sistema*) economy; (*carrera*) economics; (*cualidad*) thrift; **~ dirigida** planned economy; **~ doméstica** housekeeping; **~ de mercado** market economy; **~ mixta** mixed economy; **~ sumergida** black economy; **hacer ~s** to economize; **~s de escala** economies of scale

económico, -a [eko'nomiko, a] *adj* (*barato*) cheap, economical; (*persona*) thrifty; (*Com: año etc*) financial; (*: situación*) economic

economista [ekono'mista] *nm/f* economist

ecosistema [ekosis'tema] *nm* ecosystem

ecu ['eku] *nm* ecu

ecuación [ekwa'θjon] *nf* equation

Ecuador [ekwa'ðor] *nm* Ecuador

ecuador [ekwa'ðor] *nm* equator

ecuánime [e'kwanime] *adj* (*carácter*) level-headed; (*estado*) calm

ecuatoriano, -a [ekwato'rjano, a] *adj, nm/f* Ecuador(i)an

ecuestre [e'kwestre] *adj* equestrian

eczema [ek'θema] *nm* = **eccema**

edad [e'ðað] *nf* age; **¿qué ~ tienes?** how old are you?; **tiene ocho años de ~** he is eight (years old); **de ~ corta** young; **ser de ~ mediana/avanzada** to be middle-aged/ getting on; **ser mayor de ~** to be of age; **llegar a mayor ~** to come of age; **ser menor de ~** to be under age; **la E~ Media** the Middle Ages; **la E~ de Oro** the Golden Age

edición [eði'θjon] *nf* (*acto*) publication; (*ejemplar*) edition; **"al cerrar la ~"** (*Tip*) "stop press"

edicto [e'ðikto] *nm* edict, proclamation

edificar [eðifi'kar] *vt, vi* to build

edificio [eði'fiθjo] *nm* building; (*fig*) edifice, structure

Edimburgo [eðim'burɣo] *nm* Edinburgh

editar [eði'tar] *vt* (*publicar*) to publish; (*preparar textos, tb Inform*) to edit

editor, a [eði'tor, a] *nm/f* (*que publica*) publisher; (*redactor*) editor ▷ *adj*: **casa ~a** publishing company

editorial [eðito'rjal] *adj* editorial ⊳ *nm* leading article, editorial; (*tb*: **casa ~**) publisher

edredón [eðre'ðon] *nm* eiderdown, quilt; **~ nórdico** continental quilt, duvet

educación [eðuka'θjon] *nf* education; (*crianza*) upbringing; (*modales*) (good) manners *pl*; (*formación*) training; **sin ~** ill-mannered; **¡qué falta de ~!** how rude!

educado, -a [eðu'kaðo, a] *adj* well-mannered; **mal ~** ill-mannered

educar [eðu'kar] *vt* to educate; (*criar*) to bring up; (*voz*) to train

educativo, -a [eðuka'tiβo, a] *adj* educational; (*política*) education *cpd*

EE.UU. *nmpl abr* (= *Estados Unidos*) USA

efectista [efek'tista] *adj* sensationalist

efectivamente [efektiβa'mente] *adv* (*como respuesta*) exactly, precisely; (*verdaderamente*) really; (*de hecho*) in fact

efectivo, -a [efek'tiβo, a] *adj* effective; (*real*) actual, real ⊳ *nm*: **pagar en ~** to pay (in) cash; **hacer ~ un cheque** to cash a cheque

efecto [e'fekto] *nm* effect, result; (*objetivo*) purpose, end; **efectos** *nmpl* (*personales*) effects; (*bienes*) goods; (*Com*) assets; (*Econ*) bills, securities; **~ 2000** millennium bug; **~ invernadero** greenhouse effect; **~s de consumo** consumer goods; **~s a cobrar** bills receivable; **~s especiales** special effects; **~s personales** personal effects; **~s secundarios** side effects; **~s sonoros** sound effects; **hacer** *o* **surtir ~** to have the desired effect; **hacer ~** (*impresionar*) to make an impression; **llevar algo a ~** to carry sth out; **en ~** in fact; (*respuesta*) exactly, indeed

efectuar [efek'twar] *vt* to carry out; (*viaje*) to make

eficacia [efi'kaθja] *nf* (*de persona*) efficiency; (*de medicamento etc*) effectiveness

eficaz [efi'kaθ] *adj* (*persona*) efficient; (*acción*) effective

eficiente [efi'θjente] *adj* efficient

efusivo, -a [efu'siβo, a] *adj* effusive; **mis más efusivas gracias** my warmest thanks

EGB *nf abr* (*Esp Escol*: = *Educación General Básica*) primary education for six- to fourteen-year olds; *ver tb* **sistema educativo**

egipcio, -a [e'xipθjo, a] *adj, nm/f* Egyptian

Egipto [e'xipto] *nm* Egypt

egoísmo [eɣo'ismo] *nm* egoism

egoísta [eɣo'ista] *adj* egoistical, selfish ⊳ *nm/f* egoist

egregio, -a [e'ɣrexjo, a] *adj* eminent, distinguished

Eire ['eire] *nm* Eire

ej. *abr* (= *ejemplo*) eg

eje ['exe] *nm* (*Geo, Mat*) axis; (*Pol, fig*) axis, main line; (*de rueda*) axle; (*de máquina*) shaft, spindle

ejecución [exeku'θjon] *nf* execution; (*cumplimiento*) fulfilment; (*actuación*) performance; (*Jur*: *embargo de deudor*) attachment

ejecutar [exeku'tar] *vt* to execute, carry out; (*matar*) to execute; (*cumplir*) to fulfil; (*Mus*) to perform; (*Jur*: *embargar*) to attach, distrain; (*deseos*) to fulfil; (*Inform*) to run

ejecutivo, -a [exeku'tiβo, a] *adj, nm/f* executive; **el (poder) ~** the executive (power)

ejemplar [exem'plar] *adj* exemplary ⊳ *nm* example; (*Zool*) specimen; (*de libro*) copy; (*de periódico*) number, issue; **~ de regalo** complimentary copy; **sin ~** unprecedented

ejemplo [e'xemplo] *nm* example; (*caso*) instance; **por ~** for example; **dar ~** to set an example

ejercer [exer'θer] *vt* to exercise; (*funciones*) to perform; (*negocio*) to manage; (*influencia*) to exert; (*un oficio*) to practise; (*poder*) to wield ⊳ *vi*: **~ de** to practise as

ejercicio [exer'θiθjo] *nm* exercise; (*Mil*) drill; (*Com*) fiscal *o* financial year; (*período*) tenure; **~ acrobático** (*Aviat*) stunt; **~ comercial** business year; **~s espirituales** (*Rel*) retreat *sg*; **hacer ~** to take exercise

ejercitar [exerθi'tar] *vt* to exercise; (*Mil*) to drill

ejército [e'xerθito] *nm* army; **E~ del Aire/de Tierra** Air Force/Army; **~ de ocupación** army of occupation; **~ permanente** standing army; **entrar en el ~** to join the army, join up

ejote [e'xote] *nm* (*Am*) green bean

PALABRA CLAVE

el [el] (*fem* **la**, *neutro* **lo**, *pl* **los**, **las**) *artículo definido* **1** the; **el libro/la mesa/los estudiantes/las flores** the book/table/students/flowers; **me gusta el fútbol** I like football; **está en la cama** she's in bed

2 (*con n abstracto o propio: no se traduce*): **el amor/ la juventud** love/youth; **el Conde Drácula** Count Dracula

3 (*posesión: se traduce a menudo por adj posesivo*): **romperse el brazo** to break one's arm; **levantó la mano** he put his hand up; **se puso el sombrero** she put her hat on

4 (*valor descriptivo*): **tener la boca grande/los ojos azules** to have a big mouth/blue eyes

5 (*con días*) on; **me iré el viernes** I'll leave on Friday; **los domingos suelo ir a nadar** on Sundays I generally go swimming

6 (*lo + adj*): **lo difícil/caro** what is difficult/ expensive; (*cuán*): **no se da cuenta de lo pesado que es** he doesn't realize how boring he is

⊳ *pron demostrativo* **1**: **mi libro y el de usted** my book and yours; **las de Pepe son mejores** Pepe's are better; **no la(s) blanca(s) sino la(s) gris(es)** not the white one(s) but the grey one(s)

2: **lo de**: **lo de ayer** what happened

yesterday; **lo de las facturas** that business about the invoices

▷ *pron relativo*: **el que** etc **1** *(indef)*: **el (los) que quiera(n) que se vaya(n)** anyone who wants to can leave; **llévese el/la que más le guste** take the one you like best

2 *(def)*: **el que compré ayer** the one I bought yesterday; **los que se van** those who leave

3: **lo que: lo que pienso yo/más me gusta** what I think/like most

▷ *conj*: **el que**: **el que lo diga** the fact that he says so; **el que sea tan vago me molesta** his being so lazy bothers me

▷ *excl*: **¡el susto que me diste!** what a fright you gave me!

▷ *pron personal* **1** *(persona: m)* him; *(: f)* her; *(: pl)* them; **lo/las veo** I can see him/them

2 *(animal, cosa: sg)* it; **lo** *(o* **la***) veo* I can see it; **los** *(o* **las***) veo* I can see them

3: **lo** *(como sustituto de frase)*: **no lo sabía** I didn't know; **ya lo entiendo** I understand now

él [el] *pron (persona)* he; *(cosa)* it; *(después de prep: persona)* him; *(: cosa)* it; **mis libros y los de él** my books and his

elaboración [elaβora'θjon] *nf (producción)* manufacture; **~ de presupuestos** *(Com)* budgeting

elaborar [elaβo'rar] *vt (producto)* to make, manufacture; *(preparar)* to prepare; *(madera, metal etc)* to work; *(proyecto etc)* to work on o out

elasticidad [elastiθi'ðað] *nf* elasticity

elástico, -a [e'lastiko, a] *adj* elastic; *(flexible)* flexible ▷ *nm* elastic; *(gomita)* elastic band

elección [elek'θjon] *nf* election; *(selección)* choice, selection; **elecciones parciales** by-election *sg*; **elecciones generales** general election *sg*

electorado [elekto'raðo] *nm* electorate, voters *pl*

electoral [elekto'ral] *adj* electoral

electricidad [elektriθi'ðað] *nf* electricity

electricista [elektri'θista] *nm/f* electrician

eléctrico, -a [e'lektriko, a] *adj* electric

electrificar [elektrifi'kar] *vt* to electrify

electrizar [elektri'θar] *vt (Ferro, fig)* to electrify

electro... [elektro] *pref* electro-

electrocardiograma [elektrokarðjo'ɣrama] *nm* electrocardiogram

electrocución [elektroku'θjon] *nf* electrocution

electrocutar [elektroku'tar] *vt* to electrocute

electrodo [elek'troðo] *nm* electrode

electrodomésticos [elektroðo'mestikos] *nmpl* (electrical) household appliances; *(Com)* white goods

electroimán [electroi'man] *nm* electromagnet

electromagnético, -a [elektromaɣ'netiko, a] *adj* electromagnetic

electrón [elek'tron] *nm* electron

electrónico, -a [elek'troniko, a] *adj* electronic ▷ *nf* electronics *sg*

electrotecnia [elektro'teknja] *nf* electrical engineering

electrotécnico, -a [elektro'tekniko, a] *nm/f* electrical engineer

electrotren [elektro'tren] *nm* express electric train

elefante [ele'fante] *nm* elephant

elegancia [ele'ɣanθja] *nf* elegance, grace; *(estilo)* stylishness

elegante [ele'ɣante] *adj* elegant, graceful; *(estiloso)* stylish, fashionable; *(traje etc)* smart; *(decoración)* tasteful

elegía [ele'xia] *nf* elegy

elegir [ele'xir] *vt (escoger)* to choose, select; *(optar)* to opt for; *(presidente)* to elect

elemental [elemen'tal] *adj (claro, obvio)* elementary; *(fundamental)* elemental, fundamental

elemento [ele'mento] *nm* element; *(fig)* ingredient; *(Am)* person, individual; *(tipo raro)* odd person; *(de pila)* cell; **elementos** *nmpl* elements, rudiments; **estar en su ~** to be in one's element; **vino a verle un ~** someone came to see you

elepé [ele'pe] *nm* LP

elevación [eleβa'θjon] *nf* elevation; *(acto)* raising, lifting; *(de precios)* rise; *(Geo etc)* height, altitude

elevado, -a [ele'βaðo, a] *pp de* **elevar** ▷ *adj* high

elevador [eleβa'ðor] *nm (Am)* lift *(Brit)*, elevator *(US)*

elevar [ele'βar] *vt* to raise, lift (up); *(precio)* to put up; *(producción)* to step up; *(informe etc)* to present; **elevarse** *vr (edificio)* to rise; *(precios)* to go up; *(transportarse, enajenarse)* to get carried away; **la cantidad se eleva a ...** the total amounts to ...

eligiendo etc [eli'xjenðo], **elija** etc [e'lixa] *vb ver* **elegir**

eliminar [elimi'nar] *vt* to eliminate, remove; *(olor, persona)* to get rid of; *(Deporte)* to eliminate, knock out

eliminatoria [elimina'torja] *nf* heat, preliminary (round)

elite [e'lite], **élite** [e'lite] *nf* elite, élite

elitista [eli'tista] *adj* elitist

elixir [elik'sir] *nm* elixir; *(tb: ~ bucal)* mouthwash

ella ['eʎa] *pron (persona)* she; *(cosa)* it; *(después de prep: persona)* her; *(cosa)* it; **de ~** hers

ellas ['eʎas] *pron ver* **ellos**

ello ['eʎo] *pron neutro* it; **es por ~ que ...** that's why ...

ellos, -as ['eʎos, as] *pron personal pl* they; *(después de prep)* them; **de ~** theirs

elocuencia [elo'kwenθja] *nf* eloquence

elocuente [elo'kwente] adj eloquent; (fig) significant; **un dato ~** a fact which speaks for itself

elogiar [elo'xjar] vt to praise, eulogize

elogio [e'loxjo] nm praise; **queda por encima de todo ~** it's beyond praise; **hacer ~ de** to sing the praises of

elote [e'lote] nm (Am) corn on the cob

eludir [elu'ðir] vt (evitar) to avoid, evade; (escapar) to escape, elude

email ['imeil] nm (gen) e-mail m; (dirección) e-mail address; **mandar un ~ a algn** to e-mail sb, send sb an e-mail

emanar [ema'nar] vi: **~ de** to emanate from, come from; (derivar de) to originate in

emancipar [emanθi'par] vt to emancipate; **emanciparse** vr to become emancipated, free o.s.

embadurnar [embaður'nar] vt to smear

embajada [emba'xaða] nf embassy

embajador, a [embaxa'ðor, a] nm/f ambassador/ambassadress

embalar [emba'lar] vt (envolver) to parcel, wrap (up); (envasar) to package ▷ vi to sprint; **embalarse** vr to go fast

embalsamar [embalsa'mar] vt to embalm

embalse [em'balse] nm (presa) dam; (lago) reservoir

embarazada [embara'θaða] adj f pregnant ▷ nf pregnant woman

embarazar [embara'θar] vt to obstruct, hamper; **embarazarse** vr (aturdirse) to become embarrassed; (confundirse) to get into a mess

embarazo [emba'raθo] nm (de mujer) pregnancy; (impedimento) obstacle, obstruction; (timidez) embarrassment

embarazoso, -a [embara'θoso, a] adj (molesto) awkward; (violento) embarrassing

embarcación [embarka'θjon] nf (barco) boat, craft; (acto) embarkation; **~ de arrastre** trawler; **~ de cabotaje** coasting vessel

embarcadero [embarka'ðero] nm pier, landing stage

embarcar [embar'kar] vt (cargamento) to ship, stow; (persona) to embark, put on board; (fig): **~ a algn en una empresa** to involve sb in an undertaking; **embarcarse** vr to embark, go on board; (marinero) to sign on; (Am: en tren etc) to get on, get in

embargar [embar'ɣar] vt (frenar) to restrain; (sentidos) to overpower; (Jur) to seize, impound

embargo [em'barɣo] nm (Jur) seizure; (Com etc) embargo; **sin ~** still, however, nonetheless

embargue etc [em'barɣe] vb ver **embargar**

embarque etc [em'barke] vb ver **embarcar** ▷ nm shipment, loading

embaucar [embau'kar] vt to trick, fool

embeber [embe'βer] vt (absorber) to absorb, soak up; (empapar) to saturate ▷ vi to shrink;

embeberse vr: **~se en un libro** to be engrossed o absorbed in a book

embellecer [embeʎe'θer] vt to embellish, beautify

embestida [embes'tiða] nf attack, onslaught; (carga) charge

embestir [embes'tir] vt to attack, assault; to charge, attack ▷ vi to attack

emblema [em'blema] nm emblem

embobado, -a [embo'βaðo, a] adj (atontado) stunned, bewildered

embolia [em'bolja] nf (Med) clot, embolism; **~ cerebral** clot on the brain

émbolo [em'bolo] nm (Auto) piston

embolsar [embol'sar] vt to pocket

emborrachar [emborra'tʃar] vt to make drunk, intoxicate; **emborracharse** vr to get drunk

emboscada [embos'kaða] nf (celada) ambush

embotar [embo'tar] vt to blunt, dull; **embotarse** vr (adormecerse) to go numb

embotellamiento [emboteʎa'mjento] nm (Auto) traffic jam

embotellar [embote'ʎar] vt to bottle; **embotellarse** vr (circulación) to get into a jam

embragar [embra'ɣar] vt (Auto, Tec) to engage; (partes) to connect ▷ vi to let in the clutch

embrague etc [em'braɣe] vb ver **embragar** ▷ nm (tb: **pedal de ~**) clutch

embriagar [embrja'ɣar] vt (emborrachar) to make drunk; (alegrar) to delight; **embriagarse** vr (emborracharse) to get drunk

embriaguez [embrja'ɣeθ] nf (borrachera) drunkenness

embrión [em'brjon] nm embryo

embrollar [embro'ʎar] vt (asunto) to confuse, complicate; (persona) to involve, embroil; **embrollarse** vr (confundirse) to get into a muddle o mess

embrollo [em'broʎo] nm (enredo) muddle, confusion; (aprieto) fix, jam

embromar [embro'mar] vt (burlarse de) to tease, make fun of; (Am fam: molestar) to annoy

embrujado, -a [embru'xaðo, a] adj (persona) bewitched; **casa embrujada** haunted house

embrujo [em'bruxo] nm (de mirada etc) charm, magic

embrutecer [embrute'θer] vt (atontar) to stupefy; **embrutecerse** vr to be stupefied

embudo [em'buðo] nm funnel

embuste [em'buste] nm trick; (mentira) lie; (humorístico) fib

embustero, -a [embus'tero, a] adj lying, deceitful ▷ nm/f (tramposo) cheat; (mentiroso) liar; (humorístico) fibber

embutido [embu'tiðo] nm (Culin) sausage; (Tec) inlay

embutir [embu'tir] vt to insert; (Tec) to inlay; (llenar) to pack tight, cram

emergencia [emer'xenθja] nf emergency; (surgimiento) emergence

emerger [emer'xer] vi to emerge, appear

emigración [emiɣra'θjon] nf emigration; (de pájaros) migration

emigrante [emi'ɣrante] adj, nm/f emigrant

emigrar [emi'ɣrar] vi (personas) to emigrate; (pájaros) to migrate

eminencia [emi'nenθja] nf eminence; (en títulos): **Su E~** His Eminence; **Vuestra E~** Your Eminence

eminente [emi'nente] adj eminent, distinguished; (elevado) high

emisario [emi'sarjo] nm emissary

emisión [emi'sjon] nf (acto) emission; (Com etc) issue; (Radio, TV: acto) broadcasting; (: programa) broadcast, programme, program (US); ~ **de acciones** (Com) share issue; ~ **gratuita de acciones** (Com) rights issue; ~ **de valores** (Com) flotation

emisor, a [emi'sor, a] nm transmitter ▷ nf radio o broadcasting station

emitir [emi'tir] vt (olor etc) to emit, give off; (moneda etc) to issue; (opinión) to express; (voto) to cast; (señal) to send out; (Radio) to broadcast; ~ **una señal sonora** to beep

emoción [emo'θjon] nf emotion; (excitación) excitement; (sentimiento) feeling; **¡qué ~!** how exciting!; (irónico) what a thrill!

emocionado, -a [emoθjo'naðo, a] adj deeply moved, stirred

emocionante [emoθjo'nante] adj (excitante) exciting, thrilling

emocionar [emoθjo'nar] vt (excitar) to excite, thrill; (conmover) to move, touch; (impresionar) to impress; **emocionarse** vr to get excited

emoticón [emoti'kon], **emoticono** [emoti'kono] nm smiley, emoticon

emotivo, -a [emo'tiβo, a] adj emotional

empacar [empa'kar] vt (gen) to pack; (en caja) to bale, crate

empacho [em'patʃo] nm (Med) indigestion; (fig) embarrassment

empadronarse [empaðro'narse] vr (Pol: como elector) to register

empalagoso, -a [empala'ɣoso, a] adj cloying; (fig) tiresome

empalmar [empal'mar] vt to join, connect ▷ vi (dos caminos) to meet, join

empalme [em'palme] nm joint, connection; (de vías) junction; (de trenes) connection

empanada [empa'naða] nf pie, pasty

empantanarse [empanta'narse] vr to get swamped; (fig) to get bogged down

empañarse [empa'narse] vr (nublarse) to get misty, steam up

empapar [empa'par] vt (mojar) to soak, saturate; (absorber) to soak up, absorb; **empaparse** vr: **~se de** to soak up

empapelar [empape'lar] vt (paredes) to paper

empaquetar [empake'tar] vt to pack, parcel up; (Com) to package

emparedado [empare'ðaðo] nm sandwich

emparejar [empare'xar] vt to pair ▷ vi to catch up

empastar [empas'tar] vt (embadurnar) to paste; (diente) to fill

empaste [em'paste] nm (de diente) filling

empatar [empa'tar] vi to draw, tie; **~on a dos** they drew two-all

empate [em'pate] nm draw, tie; **un ~ a cero** a no-score draw

empecé [empe'θe], **empecemos** etc [empe'θemos] vb ver **empezar**

empedernido, -a [empeðer'niðo, a] adj hard, heartless; (fijado) hardened, inveterate; **un fumador ~** a heavy smoker

empedrado, -a [empe'ðraðo, a] adj paved ▷ nm paving

empedrar [empe'ðrar] vt to pave

empeine [em'peine] nm (de pie, zapato) instep

empellón [empe'ʎon] nm push, shove; **abrirse paso a empellones** to push o shove one's way past o through

empeñado, -a [empe'naðo, a] adj (persona) determined; (objeto) pawned

empeñar [empe'nar] vt (objeto) to pawn, pledge; (persona) to compel; **empeñarse** vr (obligarse) to bind o.s., pledge o.s.; (endeudarse) to get into debt; **~se en hacer** to be set on doing, be determined to do

empeño [em'peno] nm (determinación) determination; (cosa prendada) pledge; **casa de ~s** pawnshop; **con ~** insistently; (con celo) eagerly; **tener ~ en hacer algo** to be bent on doing sth

empeorar [empeo'rar] vt to make worse, worsen ▷ vi to get worse, deteriorate

empequeñecer [empekene'θer] vt to dwarf; (fig) to belittle

emperador [empera'ðor] nm emperor

emperatriz [empera'triθ] nf empress

empezar [empe'θar] vt, vi to begin, start; **empezó a llover** it started to rain; **bueno, para ~** well, to start with

empiece etc [em'pjeθe] vb ver **empezar**

empiezo etc [em'pjeθo] vb ver **empezar**

empinar [empi'nar] vt to raise; (botella) to tip up; **empinarse** vr (persona) to stand on tiptoe; (animal) to rear up; (camino) to climb steeply; **~ el codo** to booze (fam)

empírico, -a [em'piriko, a] adj empirical

emplaste [em'plaste], **emplasto** [em'plasto] nm (Med) plaster

emplasto [em'plasto] nm (Med) plaster

emplazamiento [emplaθa'mjento] nm site, location; (Jur) summons sg

emplazar [empla'θar] vt (ubicar) to site, place, locate; (Jur) to summons; (convocar) to summon

empleado, -a [emple'aðo, a] nm/f (gen) employee; (de banco etc) clerk; ~ **público** civil servant

emplear [emple'ar] vt (usar) to use, employ; (dar trabajo a) to employ; **emplearse** vr (conseguir trabajo) to be employed; (ocuparse) to occupy o.s.; ~ **mal el tiempo** to waste time; **¡te está bien empleado!** it serves you right!

empleo [em'pleo] *nm* (*puesto*) job; (*puestos: colectivamente*) employment; (*uso*) use, employment; **"modo de ~"** "instructions for use"

empobrecer [empoβre'θer] *vt* to impoverish; **empobrecerse** *vr* to become poor *o* impoverished

empollar [empo'ʎar] *vt* to incubate; (*Escol fam*) to swot (up) ▷ *vi* (*gallina*) to brood; (*Escol fam*) to swot

empollón, -ona [empo'ʎon, ona] *nm/f* (*Escol fam*) swot

emporio [em'porjo] *nm* emporium, trading centre; (*Am: gran almacén*) department store

empotrado, -a [empo'traðo, a] *adj* (*armario etc*) built-in

emprendedor, a [emprende'ðor, a] *adj* enterprising

emprender [empren'der] *vt* to undertake; (*empezar*) to begin, embark on; (*acometer*) to tackle, take on; **~ marcha a** to set out for

empresa [em'presa] *nf* enterprise; (*Com: sociedad*) firm, company; (*: negocio*) business; (*esp Teat*) management; **~ filial** (*Com*) affiliated company; **~ matriz** (*Com*) parent company

empresariales [empresa'rjales] *nfpl* business studies

empresario, -a [empre'sarjo, a] *nm/f* (*Com*) businessman(-woman), entrepreneur; (*Tec*) manager; (*Mus: de ópera etc*) impresario; **~ de pompas fúnebres** undertaker (*Brit*), mortician (*US*)

empréstito [em'prestito] *nm* (public) loan; (*Com*) loan capital

empujar [empu'xar] *vt* to push, shove

empuje [em'puxe] *nm* thrust; (*presión*) pressure; (*fig*) vigour, drive

empujón [empu'xon] *nm* push, shove; **abrirse paso a empujones** to shove one's way through

empuñar [empu'ɲar] *vt* (*asir*) to grasp, take (firm) hold of; **~ las armas** (*fig*) to take up arms

emular [emu'lar] *vt* to emulate; (*rivalizar*) to rival

emulsión [emul'sjon] *nf* emulsion

PALABRA CLAVE

en [en] *prep* **1** (*posición*) in; (*: sobre*) on; **está en el cajón** it's in the drawer; **en Argentina/La Paz** in Argentina/La Paz; **en el colegio/la oficina** at school/the office; **en casa** at home; **está en el suelo/quinto piso** it's on the floor/the fifth floor; **en el periódico** in the paper

2 (*dirección*) into; **entró en el aula** she went into the classroom; **meter algo en el bolso** to put sth into one's bag; **ir de puerta en puerta** to go from door to door

3 (*tiempo*) in; on; **en 1605/3 semanas/**

invierno in 1605/3 weeks/winter; **en (el mes de) enero** in (the month of) January; **en aquella ocasión/época** on that occasion/at that time

4 (*precio*) for; **lo vendió en 20 dólares** he sold it for 20 dollars

5 (*diferencia*) by; **reducir/aumentar en una tercera parte/un 20 por ciento** to reduce/increase by a third/20 per cent

6 (*manera, forma*): **en avión/autobús** by plane/bus; **escrito en inglés** written in English; **en serio** seriously; **en espiral/círculo** in a spiral/circle

7 (*después de vb que indica gastar etc*) on; **han cobrado demasiado en dietas** they've charged too much to expenses; **se le va la mitad del sueldo en comida** half his salary goes on food

8 (*tema, ocupación*): **experto en la materia** expert on the subject; **trabaja en la construcción** he works in the building industry

9 (*adj + en + infin*): **lento en reaccionar** slow to react

enagua, enaguas [ena'ɣwa(s)] *nf(pl)* (*esp Am*) petticoat *sg*, underskirt *sg*

enajenación [enaxena'θjon] *nf*, **enajenamiento** [enaxena'mjento] *nm* alienation; (*fig: distracción*) absent-mindedness; (*: embelesamiento*) rapture, trance; **~ mental** mental derangement

enajenar [enaxe'nar] *vt* to alienate; (*fig*) to carry away

enamorado, -a [enamo'raðo, a] *adj* in love ▷ *nm/f* lover; **estar ~ (de)** to be in love (with)

enamorar [enamo'rar] *vt* to win the love of; **enamorarse** *vr*: **~se (de)** to fall in love (with)

enano, -a [e'nano, a] *adj* tiny, dwarf ▷ *nm/f* dwarf; (*pey*) runt

enardecer [enarðe'θer] *vt* (*pasiones*) to fire, inflame; (*persona*) to fill with enthusiasm; **enardecerse** *vr* to get excited; **~se por** to get enthusiastic about

encabezamiento [enkaβeθa'mjento] *nm* (*de carta*) heading; (*Com*) billhead, letterhead; (*de periódico*) headline; (*preámbulo*) foreword, preface; **~ normal** (*Tip etc*) running head

encabezar [enkaβe'θar] *vt* (*movimiento, revolución*) to lead, head; (*lista*) to head; (*carta*) to put a heading to; (*libro*) to entitle

encadenar [enkaðe'nar] *vt* to chain (together); (*poner grilletes a*) to shackle

encajar [enka'xar] *vt* (*ajustar*): **~ en** to fit (into); (*meter a la fuerza*) to push in; (*máquina etc*) to house; (*partes*) to join; (*fam: golpe*) to give, deal; (*entremeter*) to insert ▷ *vi* to fit (well); (*fig: corresponder a*) to match; **encajarse** *vr*: **~se en un sillón** to squeeze into a chair

encaje [en'kaxe] *nm* (*labor*) lace

encalar [enka'lar] *vt* (*pared*) to whitewash

encallar [enka'ʎar] *vi* (*Naut*) to run aground

encaminar [enkami'nar] *vt* to direct, send; **encaminarse** *vr*: ~**se a** to set out for; ~ **por** (*expedición etc*) to route via

encandilar [enkandi'lar] *vt* to dazzle; (*persona*) to daze, bewilder

encantado, -a [enkan'taðo, a] *adj* (*hechizado*) bewitched; (*muy contento*) delighted; ¡~! how do you do!, pleased to meet you

encantador, a [enkanteθa'ðor, a] *adj* charming, lovely ▷ *nm/f* magician, enchanter/enchantress

encantar [enkan'tar] *vt* to charm, delight; (*cautivar*) to fascinate; (*hechizar*) to bewitch, cast a spell on; **me encanta eso** I love that

encanto [en'kanto] *nm* (*magia*) spell, charm; (*fig*) charm, delight; (*expresión de ternura*) sweetheart; **como por** ~ as if by magic

encarcelar [enkarθe'lar] *vt* to imprison, jail

encarecer [enkare'θer] *vt* to put up the price of ▷ *vi*, **encarecerse** *vr* to get dearer

encarecimiento [enkareθi'mjento] *nm* price increase

encargado, -a [enkar'ɣaðo, a] *adj* in charge ▷ *nm/f* agent, representative; (*responsable*) person in charge

encargar [enkar'ɣar] *vt* to entrust; (*Com*) to order; (*recomendar*) to urge, recommend; **encargarse** *vr*: ~**se de** to look after, take charge of; ~ **algo a algn** to put sb in charge of sth

encargo [en'karɣo] *nm* (*pedido*) assignment, job; (*responsabilidad*) responsibility; (*recomendación*) recommendation; (*Com*) order

encariñarse [enkari'narse] *vr*: ~ **con** to grow fond of, get attached to

encarnación [enkarna'θjon] *nf* incarnation, embodiment

encarnizado, -a [enkarni'θaðo, a] *adj* (*lucha*) bloody, fierce

encarrilar [enkarri'lar] *vt* (*tren*) to put back on the rails; (*fig*) to correct, put on the right track

encasillar [enkasi'ʎar] *vt* (*Teat*) to typecast; (*clasificar: pey*) to pigeonhole

encasquetar [enkaske'tar] *vt* (*sombrero*) to pull down o on; **encasquetarse** *vr*: ~**se el sombrero** to pull one's hat down o on; ~ **algo a algn** to offload sth onto sb

encauzar [enkau'θar] *vt* to channel; (*fig*) to direct

encendedor [enθende'ðor] *nm* lighter

encender [enθen'der] *vt* (*con fuego*) to light; (*incendiar*) to set fire to; (*luz, radio*) to put on, switch on; (*Inform*) to toggle on, switch on; (*avivar: pasiones etc*) to inflame; (*despertar: entusiasmo*) to arouse; (*odio*) to awaken; **encenderse** *vr* to catch fire; (*excitarse*) to get excited; (*de cólera*) to flare up; (*el rostro*) to blush

encendido, -a [enθen'diðo, a] *adj* alight; (*aparato*) (switched) on; (*mejillas*) glowing; (*cara: por el vino etc*) flushed; (*mirada*)
passionate ▷ *nm* (*Auto*) ignition; (*de faroles*) lighting

encerado, -a [enθe'raðo, a] *adj* (*suelo*) waxed, polished ▷ *nm* (*Escol*) blackboard; (*hule*) oilcloth

encerar [enθe'rar] *vt* (*suelo*) to wax, polish

encerrar [enθe'rrar] *vt* (*confinar*) to shut in o up; (*con llave*) to lock in o up; (*comprender, incluir*) to include, contain; **encerrarse** *vr* to shut o lock o.s. up o in

encestar [enθes'tar] *vi* to score a basket

encharcado, -a [entʃar'kaðo, a] *adj* (*terreno*) flooded

encharcar [entʃar'kar] *vt* to swamp, flood; **encharcarse** *vr* to become flooded

enchufado, -a [entʃu'faðo, a] *nm/f* (*fam*) well-connected person

enchufar [entʃu'far] *vt* (*Elec*) to plug in; (*Tec*) to connect, fit together; (*Com*) to merge

enchufe [en'tʃufe] *nm* (*Elec: clavija*) plug; (*: toma*) socket; (*de dos tubos*) joint, connection; (*fam: influencia*) contact, connection; (*puesto*) cushy job; ~ **de clavija** jack plug; **tiene un ~ en el ministerio** he can pull strings at the ministry

encía [en'θia] *nf* (*Anat*) gum

enciclopedia [enθiklo'peðja] *nf* encyclopaedia

encienda *etc* [en'θjenda] *vb ver* **encender**

encierro *etc* [en'θjerro] *vb ver* **encerrar** ▷ *nm* shutting in o up; (*calabozo*) prison; (*Agr*) pen; (*Taur*) penning

encima [en'θima] *adv* (*sobre*) above, over; (*además*) besides; ~ **de** (*en*) on, on top of; (*sobre*) above, over; (*además de*) besides, on top of; **por** ~ **de** over; ¿**llevas dinero** ~? have you (got) any money on you?; **se me vino** ~ it took me by surprise

encina [en'θina] *nf* (holm) oak

encinta [en'θinta] *adj f* pregnant

enclave [en'klaβe] *nm* enclave

enclenque [en'klenke] *adj* weak, sickly

encoger [enko'xer] *vt* (*gen*) to shrink, contract; (*fig: asustar*) to scare; (*: desanimar*) to discourage; **encogerse** *vr* to shrink, contract; (*fig*) to cringe; ~**se de hombros** to shrug one's shoulders

encolar [enko'lar] *vt* (*engomar*) to glue, paste; (*pegar*) to stick down

encolerizar [enkoleri'θar] *vt* to anger, provoke; **encolerizarse** *vr* to get angry

encomendar [enkomen'dar] *vt* to entrust, commend; **encomendarse** *vr*: ~**se a** to put one's trust in

encomiar [enko'mjar] *vt* to praise, pay tribute to

encomienda *etc* [enko'mjenda] *vb ver* **encomendar** ▷ *nf* (*encargo*) charge, commission; (*elogio*) tribute; (*Am*) parcel, package; ~ **postal** (*Am: servicio*) parcel post

encono [en'kono] *nm* (*rencor*) rancour, spite

encontrado, -a [enkon'traðo, a] *adj*
(*contrario*) contrary, conflicting; (*hostil*)
hostile

encontrar [enkon'trar] *vt* (*hallar*) to find;
(*inesperadamente*) to meet, run into;
encontrarse *vr* to meet (each other);
(*situarse*) to be (situated); (*persona*) to find o.s.,
be; (*entrar en conflicto*) to crash, collide; **~se
con** to meet; **~se bien (de salud)** to feel well;
no se encuentra aquí en este momento
he's not in at the moment

encorvar [enkor'βar] *vt* to curve; (*inclinar*) to
bend (down); **encorvarse** *vr* to bend down,
bend over

encrespar [enkres'par] *vt* (*cabellos*) to curl;
(*fig*) to anger, irritate; **encresparse** *vr* (*el mar*)
to get rough; (*fig*) to get cross o irritated

encrucijada [enkruθi'xaða] *nf* crossroads *sg*;
(*empalme*) junction

encuadernación [enkwaðerna'θjon] *nf*
binding; (*taller*) binder's

encuadernador, a [enkwaðerna'ðor, a] *nm/f*
bookbinder

encuadrar [enkwa'ðrar] *vt* (*retrato*) to frame;
(*ajustar*) to fit, insert; (*encerrar*) to contain

encubrir [enku'βrir] *vt* (*ocultar*) to hide,
conceal; (*criminal*) to harbour, shelter;
(*ayudar*) to be an accomplice in

encuentro [en'kwentro] *vb ver* **encontrar**
▷ *nm* (*de personas*) meeting; (*Auto etc*) collision,
crash; (*Deporte*) match, game; (*Mil*)
encounter

encuerado, -a [enkwe'raðo, a] *adj* (*Am*)
nude, naked

encuesta [en'kwesta] *nf* inquiry,
investigation; (*sondeo*) public opinion poll;
~ judicial post-mortem

encumbrado, -a [enkum'braðo, a] *adj*
eminent, distinguished

encumbrar [enkum'brar] *vt* (*persona*) to
exalt; **encumbrarse** *vr* (*fig*) to become
conceited

endeble [en'deβle] *adj* (*argumento, excusa,
persona*) weak

endémico, -a [en'demiko, a] *adj* endemic

endemoniado, -a [endemo'njaðo, a] *adj*
possessed (of the devil); (*travieso*) devilish

enderezar [endere'θar] *vt* (*poner derecho*) to
straighten (out); (*: verticalmente*) to set
upright; (*fig*) to straighten o sort out; (*dirigir*)
to direct; **enderezarse** *vr* (*persona sentada*) to
sit up straight

endeudarse [endeu'ðarse] *vr* to get into
debt

endiablado, -a [endja'βlaðo, a] *adj* devilish,
diabolical; (*humorístico*) mischievous

endibia [en'diβja] *nf* endive

endilgar [endil'ɣar] *vt* (*fam*): **~ algo a algn** to
lumber sb with sth; **~ un sermón a algn** to
give sb a lecture

endiñar [endi'ɲar] *vt*: **~ algo a algn** to land
sth on sb

endomingarse [endomin'garse] *vr* to dress
up, put on one's best clothes

endosar [endo'sar] *vt* (*cheque etc*) to endorse

endulzar [endul'θar] *vt* to sweeten; (*suavizar*)
to soften

endurecer [endure'θer] *vt* to harden;
endurecerse *vr* to harden, grow hard

endurecido, -a [endure'θiðo, a] *adj* (*duro*)
hard; (*fig*) hardy, tough; **estar ~ a algo** to be
hardened o used to sth

enema [e'nema] *nm* (*Med*) enema

enemigo, -a [ene'miɣo, a] *adj* enemy,
hostile ▷ *nm/f* enemy ▷ *nf* enmity, hostility;
ser ~ de (*persona*) to dislike; (*tendencia*) to be
inimical to

enemistad [enemis'tað] *nf* enmity

enemistar [enemis'tar] *vt* to make enemies
of, cause a rift between; **enemistarse** *vr* to
become enemies; (*amigos*) to fall out

energía [ener'xia] *nf* (*vigor*) energy, drive;
(*empuje*) push; (*Tec, Elec*) energy, power;
~ atómica/eléctrica/eólica atomic/electric/
wind power; **~ solar** solar energy o power;
~s renovables renewable energy sources

enérgico, -a [e'nerxiko, a] *adj* (*gen*)
energetic; (*ataque*) vigorous; (*ejercicio*)
strenuous; (*medida*) bold; (*voz, modales*)
forceful

energúmeno, -a [ener'ɣumeno, a] *nm/f*
madman(-woman); **ponerse como un ~
con algn** to get furious with sb

enero [e'nero] *nm* January; *ver tb* **julio**

enésimo, -a [e'nesimo, a] *adj* (*Mat*) nth;
por enésima vez (*fig*) for the umpteenth
time

enfadado, -a [enfa'ðaðo, a] *adj* angry,
annoyed

enfadar [enfa'ðar] *vt* to anger, annoy;
enfadarse *vr* to get angry o annoyed

enfado [en'faðo] *nm* (*enojo*) anger,
annoyance; (*disgusto*) trouble, bother

énfasis ['enfasis] *nm* emphasis, stress;
poner ~ en to stress

enfático, -a [en'fatiko, a] *adj* emphatic

enfermar [enfer'mar] *vt* to make ill ▷ *vi* to
fall ill, be taken ill; **su actitud me enferma**
his attitude makes me sick; **~ del corazón** to
develop heart trouble

enfermedad [enferme'ðað] *nf* illness;
~ venérea venereal disease

enfermera [enfer'mera] *nf ver* **enfermero**

enfermería [enferme'ria] *nf* infirmary;
(*de colegio etc*) sick bay

enfermero, -a [enfer'mero, a] *nm* (male)
nurse ▷ *nf* nurse; **enfermera jefa** matron

enfermizo, -a [enfer'miθo, a] *adj* (*persona*)
sickly, unhealthy; (*fig*) unhealthy

enfermo, -a [en'fermo, a] *adj* ill, sick ▷ *nm/f*
invalid, sick person; (*en hospital*) patient;
caer o ponerse ~ to fall ill

enflaquecer [enflake'θer] *vt* (*adelgazar*) to
make thin; (*debilitar*) to weaken

enfocar [enfo'kar] vt (foto etc) to focus; (problema etc) to consider, look at

enfoque etc [en'foke] vb ver **enfocar** ▷ nm focus; (acto) focusing; (óptica) approach

enfrascarse [enfras'karse] vr: ~ **en un libro** to bury o.s. in a book

enfrentamiento [enfrenta'mjento] nm confrontation

enfrentar [enfren'tar] vt (peligro) to face (up to), confront; (oponer) to bring face to face; **enfrentarse** vr (dos personas) to face o confront each other; (Deporte: dos equipos) to meet; ~**se a** o **con** to face up to, confront

enfrente [en'frente] adv opposite; ~ **de** prep opposite, facing; **la casa de** ~ the house opposite, the house across the street

enfriamiento [enfria'mjento] nm chilling, refrigeration; (Med) cold, chill

enfriar [enfri'ar] vt (alimentos) to cool, chill; (algo caliente) to cool down; (habitación) to air, freshen; (entusiasmo) to dampen; **enfriarse** vr to cool down; (Med) to catch a chill; (amistad) to cool

enfurecer [enfure'θer] vt to enrage, madden; **enfurecerse** vr to become furious, fly into a rage; (mar) to get rough

engalanar [engala'nar] vt (adornar) to adorn; (ciudad) to decorate; **engalanarse** vr to get dressed up

enganchar [engan'tʃar] vt to hook; (ropa) to hang up; (dos vagones) to hitch up; (Tec) to couple, connect; (Mil) to recruit; (fam: atraer: persona) to rope into; **engancharse** vr (Mil) to enlist, join up; ~**se (a)** (drogas) to get hooked (on)

enganche [en'gantʃe] nm hook; (Tec) coupling, connection; (acto) hooking (up); (Mil) recruitment, enlistment; (Am: depósito) deposit

engañar [enga'ɲar] vt to deceive; (estafar) to cheat, swindle ▷ vi: **las apariencias engañan** appearances are deceptive; **engañarse** vr (equivocarse) to be wrong; (asimismo) to deceive o kid o.s.; **engaña a su mujer** he's unfaithful to o cheats on his wife

engaño [en'gaɲo] nm deceit; (estafa) trick, swindle; (error) mistake, misunderstanding; (ilusión) delusion

engañoso, -a [enga'ɲoso, a] adj (tramposo) crooked; (mentiroso) dishonest, deceitful; (aspecto) deceptive; (consejo) misleading

engarzar [engar'θar] vt (joya) to set, mount; (fig) to link, connect

engatusar [engatu'sar] vt (fam) to coax

engendrar [enxen'drar] vt to breed; (procrear) to beget; (fig) to cause, produce

engendro [en'xendro] nm (Bio) foetus; (fig) monstrosity; (: idea) brainchild

englobar [englo'βar] vt (comprender) to include, comprise; (incluir) to lump together

engomar [engo'mar] vt to glue, stick

engordar [engor'ðar] vt to fatten ▷ vi to get fat, put on weight

engorroso, -a [engo'rroso, a] adj bothersome, trying

engranaje [engra'naxe] nm (Auto) gear; (juego) gears pl

engrandecer [engrande'θer] vt to enlarge, magnify; (alabar) to praise, speak highly of; (exagerar) to exaggerate

engrasar [engra'sar] vt (Tec: poner grasa) to grease; (: lubricar) to lubricate, oil; (manchar) to make greasy

engreído, -a [engre'iðo, a] adj vain, conceited

engrosar [engro'sar] vt (ensanchar) to enlarge; (aumentar) to increase; (hinchar) to swell

enhebrar [ene'βrar] vt to thread

enhorabuena [enora'βwena] excl: ¡~! congratulations! ▷ nf: **dar la ~ a** to congratulate

enigma [e'niɣma] nm enigma; (problema) puzzle; (misterio) mystery

enjabonar [enxaβo'nar] vt to soap; (barba) to lather; (fam: adular) to soft-soap; (: regañar) to tick off

enjambre [en'xambre] nm swarm

enjaular [enxau'lar] vt to (put in a) cage; (fam) to jail, lock up

enjuagar [enxwa'ɣar] vt (ropa) to rinse (out)

enjuague etc [en'xwaɣe] vb ver **enjuagar** ▷ nm (Med) mouthwash; (de ropa) rinse, rinsing

enjugar [enxu'ɣar] vt to wipe (off); (lágrimas) to dry; (déficit) to wipe out

enjuiciar [enxwi'θjar] vt (Jur: procesar) to prosecute, try; (fig) to judge

enjuto, -a [en'xuto, a] adj dry, dried up; (fig) lean, skinny

enlace etc [en'laθe] vb ver **enlazar** ▷ nm link, connection; (relación) relationship; (tb: ~ **matrimonial**) marriage; (de trenes) connection; ~ **de datos** data link; ~ **sindical** shop steward; **telefónico** telephone link-up

enlatado, -a [enla'taðo, a] adj (alimentos, productos) tinned, canned

enlazar [enla'θar] vt (unir con lazos) to bind together; (atar) to tie; (conectar) to link, connect; (Am) to lasso

enlodar [enlo'ðar] vt to cover in mud; (fig: manchar) to stain; (: rebajar) to debase

enloquecer [enloke'θer] vt to drive mad ▷ vi, **enloquecerse** vr to go mad

enlutado, -a [enlu'taðo, a] adj (persona) in mourning

enmarañar [enmara'ɲar] vt (enredar) to tangle up, entangle; (complicar) to complicate; (confundir) to confuse; **enmarañarse** vr (enredarse) to become entangled; (confundirse) to get confused

enmarcar [enmar'kar] vt (cuadro) to frame; (fig) to provide a setting for

enmascarar [enmaska'rar] vt to mask; (intenciones) to disguise; **enmascararse** vr to put on a mask

enmendar [enmen'dar] *vt* to emend, correct; (*constitución etc*) to amend; (*comportamiento*) to reform; **enmendarse** *vr* to reform, mend one's ways

enmienda *etc* [en'mjenda] *vb ver* **enmendar**
▷ *nf* correction; amendment; reform

enmohecerse [enmoe'θerse] *vr* (*metal*) to rust, go rusty; (*muro, plantas*) to go mouldy

enmudecer [enmuðe'θer] *vt* to silence ▷ *vi*, **enmudecerse** *vr* (*perder el habla*) to fall silent; (*guardar silencio*) to remain silent; (*por miedo*) to be struck dumb

ennegrecer [enneɣre'θer] *vt* (*poner negro*) to blacken; (*oscurecer*) to darken; **ennegrecerse** *vr* to turn black; (*oscurecerse*) to get dark, darken

ennoblecer [ennoβle'θer] *vt* to ennoble

enojadizo, -a [enoxa'ðiθo, a] *adj* irritable, short-tempered

enojado, -a [eno'xaðo, a] *adj* (*Am*) angry

enojar [eno'xar] (*esp Am*) *vt* (*encolerizar*) to anger; (*disgustar*) to annoy, upset; **enojarse** *vr* to get angry; to get annoyed

enojo [e'noxo] *nm* (*esp Am: cólera*) anger; (*irritación*) annoyance; **enojos** *nmpl* trials, problems

enojoso, -a [eno'xoso, a] *adj* annoying

enorgullecerse [enorɣuʎe'θerse] *vr* to be proud; ~ **de** to pride o.s. on, be proud of

enorme [e'norme] *adj* enormous, huge; (*fig*) monstrous

enormidad [enormi'ðað] *nf* hugeness, immensity

enraizar [enrai'θar] *vi* to take root

enrarecido, -a [enrare'θiðo, a] *adj* rarefied

enredadera [enreða'ðera] *nf* (*Bot*) creeper, climbing plant

enredar [enre'ðar] *vt* (*cables, hilos etc*) to tangle (up), entangle; (*situación*) to complicate, confuse; (*meter cizaña*) to sow discord among *o* between; (*implicar*) to embroil, implicate; **enredarse** *vr* to get entangled, get tangled (up); (*situación*) to get complicated; (*persona*) to get embroiled; (*Am: fam*) to meddle

enredo [en'reðo] *nm* (*maraña*) tangle; (*confusión*) mix-up, confusion; (*intriga*) intrigue; (*apuro*) jam; (*amorío*) love affair

enrevesado, -a [enreβe'saðo, a] *adj* (*asunto*) complicated, involved

enriquecer [enrike'θer] *vt* to make rich; (*fig*) to enrich; **enriquecerse** *vr* to get rich

enrojecer [enroxe'θer] *vt* to redden ▷ *vi* (*persona*) to blush; **enrojecerse** *vr* to blush

enrolar [enro'lar] *vt* (*Mil*) to enlist; (*reclutar*) to recruit; **enrolarse** *vr* (*Mil*) to join up; (*afiliarse*) to enrol, sign on

enrollar [enro'ʎar] *vt* to roll (up), wind (up); **enrollarse** *vr*: ~**se con algn** to get involved with sb

enroscar [enros'kar] *vt* (*torcer, doblar*) to twist; (*arrollar*) to coil (round), wind; (*tornillo, rosca*) to screw in; **enroscarse** *vr* to coil, wind

ensalada [ensa'laða] *nf* salad; (*lío*) mix-up

ensaladilla [ensala'ðiʎa] *nf* (*tb*: ~ **rusa**) ≈ Russian salad

ensalzar [ensal'θar] *vt* (*alabar*) to praise, extol; (*exaltar*) to exalt

ensambladura [ensambla'ðura] *nf*, **ensamblaje** [ensam'blaxe] *nm* assembly; (*Tec*) joint

ensamblar [ensam'blar] *vt* (*montar*) to assemble; (*madera etc*) to join

ensanchar [ensan'tʃar] *vt* (*hacer más ancho*) to widen; (*agrandar*) to enlarge, expand; (*Costura*) to let out; **ensancharse** *vr* to get wider, expand; (*pey*) to give o.s. airs

ensanche [en'santʃe] *nm* (*de calle*) widening; (*de negocio*) expansion

ensangrentar [ensangren'tar] *vt* to stain with blood

ensañarse [ensa'ɲarse] *vr*: ~ **con** to treat brutally

ensartar [ensar'tar] *vt* (*gen*) to string (together); (*carne*) to spit, skewer

ensayar [ensa'jar] *vt* to test, try (out); (*Teat*) to rehearse

ensayista [ensa'jista] *nm/f* essayist

ensayo [en'sajo] *nm* test, trial; (*Química*) experiment; (*Teat*) rehearsal; (*Deporte*) try; (*Escol, Lit*) essay; **pedido de** ~ (*Com*) trial order; ~ **general** (*Teat*) dress rehearsal; (*Mus*) full rehearsal

enseguida [ense'ɣuiða] *adv* at once, right away; ~ **termino** I've nearly finished, I shan't be long now

ensenada [ense'naða] *nf* inlet, cove

enseñanza [ense'ɲanθa] *nf* (*educación*) education; (*acción*) teaching; (*doctrina*) teaching, doctrine; ~ **primaria/secundaria/ superior** primary/secondary/higher education

enseñar [ense'ɲar] *vt* (*educar*) to teach; (*instruir*) to teach, instruct; (*mostrar, señalar*) to show

enseres [en'seres] *nmpl* belongings

ensillar [ensi'ʎar] *vt* to saddle (up)

ensimismarse [ensimis'marse] *vr* (*abstraerse*) to become lost in thought; (*estar absorto*) to be lost in thought; (*Am*) to become conceited

ensordecer [ensorðe'θer] *vt* to deafen ▷ *vi* to go deaf

ensortijado, -a [ensorti'xaðo, a] *adj* (*pelo*) curly

ensuciar [ensu'θjar] *vt* (*manchar*) to dirty, soil; (*fig*) to defile; **ensuciarse** *vr* (*mancharse*) to get dirty; (*niño*) to dirty one's nappy

ensueño [en'sweɲo] *nm* (*sueño*) dream, fantasy; (*ilusión*) illusion; (*soñando despierto*) daydream; **de** ~ dream-like

entablado [enta'βlaðo] *nm* (*piso*) floorboards *pl*; (*armazón*) boarding

entablar [enta'βlar] *vt* (*recubrir*) to board (up); (*Ajedrez, Damas*) to set up; (*conversación*) to strike up; (*Jur*) to file ▷ *vi* to draw

entablillar [entaβli'ʎar] vt (Med) to (put in a) splint

entallado, -a [enta'ʎaðo, a] adj waisted

entallar [enta'ʎar] vt (traje) to tailor ▷ vi: **el traje entalla bien** the suit fits well

ente ['ente] nm (organización) body, organization; (compañía) company; (fam: persona) odd character; (ser) being; ~ **público** (Esp) state(-owned) body

entender [enten'der] vt (comprender) to understand; (darse cuenta) to realize; (querer decir) to mean ▷ vi to understand; (creer) to think, believe ▷ nm: **a mi** ~ in my opinion; ~ **de** to know all about; ~ **algo de** to know a little about; ~ **en** to deal with, have to do with; **entenderse** vr (comprenderse) to be understood; (2 personas) to get on together; (ponerse de acuerdo) to agree, reach an agreement; **dar a** ~ **que** ... to lead to believe that ...; ~**se mal** to get on badly; **¿entiendes?** (do you) understand?

entendido, -a [enten'diðo, a] adj (comprendido) understood; (hábil) skilled; (inteligente) knowledgeable ▷ nm/f (experto) expert ▷ excl agreed!

entendimiento [entendi'mjento] nm (comprensión) understanding; (inteligencia) mind, intellect; (juicio) judgement

enterado, -a [ente'raðo, a] adj well-informed; **estar** ~ **de** to know about, be aware of; **no darse por** ~ to pretend not to understand

enteramente [entera'mente] adv entirely, completely

enterar [ente'rar] vt (informar) to inform, tell; **enterarse** vr to find out, get to know; **para que te enteres** ... (fam) for your information ...

entereza [ente'reθa] nf (totalidad) entirety; (fig: de carácter) strength of mind; (honradez) integrity

enterito [ente'rito] nm (Am) boiler suit (Brit), overalls (US)

enternecer [enterne'θer] vt (ablandar) to soften; (apiadar) to touch, move; **enternecerse** vr to be touched, be moved

entero, -a [en'tero, a] adj (total) whole, entire; (fig: recto) honest; (: firme) firm, resolute ▷ nm (Mat) integer; (Com: punto) point; (Am: pago) payment; **las acciones han subido dos ~s** the shares have gone up two points

enterrador [enterra'ðor] nm gravedigger

enterrar [ente'rrar] vt to bury; (fig) to forget

entibiar [enti'βjar] vt (enfriar) to cool; (calentar) to warm; **entibiarse** vr (fig) to cool

entidad [enti'ðað] nf (empresa) firm, company; (organismo) body; (sociedad) society; (Filosofía) entity

entienda etc [en'tjenda] vb ver **entender**

entierro [en'tjerro] vb ver **enterrar** ▷ nm (acción) burial; (funeral) funeral

entomología [entomolo'xia] nf entomology

entonación [entona'θjon] nf (Ling) intonation; (fig) conceit

entonar [ento'nar] vt (canción) to intone; (colores) to tone; (Med) to tone up ▷ vi to be in tune; **entonarse** vr (engreírse) to give o.s. airs

entonces [en'tonθes] adv then, at that time; **desde** ~ since then; **en aquel** ~ at that time; **(pues)** ~ and so; **el** ~ **embajador de España** the then Spanish ambassador

entornar [entor'nar] vt (puerta, ventana) to half close, leave ajar; (los ojos) to screw up

entorno [en'torno] nm setting, environment; ~ **de redes** (Inform) network environment

entorpecer [entorpe'θer] vt (entendimiento) to dull; (impedir) to obstruct, hinder; (: tránsito) to slow down, delay

entrado, -a [en'traðo, a] adj: ~ **en años** elderly; **(una vez)** ~ **el verano** in the summer(time), when summer comes ▷ nf (acción) entry, access; (sitio) entrance, way in; (principio) beginning; (Com) receipts pl, takings pl; (Culin) entrée; (Deporte) innings sg; (Teat) house, audience; (para el cine etc) ticket; (Inform) input; (Econ): **entradas** nfpl income sg; **entradas brutas** gross receipts; **entradas y salidas** (Com) income and expenditure; **entrada de aire** (Tec) air intake o inlet; **de entrada** from the outset; **"entrada gratis"** "admission free"; **tiene entradas** he's losing his hair

entramparse [entram'parse] vr to get into debt

entrante [en'trante] adj next, coming; (Pol) incoming ▷ nm inlet; (Culin) starter; **entrantes** nmpl starters; **mes/año** ~ next month/year

entraña [en'traɲa] nf (fig: centro) heart, core; (raíz) root; **entrañas** nfpl (Anat) entrails; (fig) heart sg

entrañable [entra'ɲaβle] adj (persona, lugar) dear; (relación) close; (acto) intimate

entrañar [entra'ɲar] vt to entail

entrar [en'trar] vt (introducir) to bring in; (persona) to show in; (Inform) to input ▷ vi (meterse) to go o come in, enter; (comenzar): ~ **diciendo** to begin by saying; **entré en** o **a** (Am) **la casa** I went into the house; **le** ~**on ganas de reír** he felt a sudden urge to laugh; **me entró sed/sueño** I started to feel thirsty/sleepy; **no me entra** I can't get the hang of it

entre ['entre] prep (dos) between; (en medio de) among(st); (por): **se abrieron paso** ~ **la multitud** they forced their way through the crowd; ~ **una cosa y otra** what with one thing and another; ~ **más estudia más aprende** (Am) the more he studies the more he learns

entreabrir [entrea'βrir] vt to half-open, open halfway

entrecejo [entre'θexo] nm: **fruncir el** ~ to frown

entrecortado, -a [entrekor'taðo, a] *adj* (*respiración*) laboured, difficult; (*habla*) faltering

entredicho [entre'ðitʃo] *nm* (*Jur*) injunction; **poner en ~** to cast doubt on; **estar en ~** to be in doubt

entrega [en'treɣa] *nf* (*de mercancías*) delivery; (*de premios*) presentation; (*de novela etc*) instalment; **"~ a domicilio"** "door-to-door delivery service"

entregar [entre'ɣar] *vt* (*dar*) to hand (over), deliver; (*ejercicios*) to hand in; **entregarse** *vr* (*rendirse*) to surrender, give in, submit; **~se a** (*dedicarse*) to devote o.s. to; **a ~** (*Com*) to be supplied

entrelazar [entrela'θar] *vt* to entwine

entremeses [entre'meses] *nmpl* hors d'œuvres

entremeter [entreme'ter] *vt* to insert, put in; **entremeterse** *vr* to meddle, interfere

entremetido, -a [entreme'tiðo, a] *adj* meddling, interfering

entremezclar [entremeθ'klar] *vt* to intermingle; **entremezclarse** *vr* to intermingle

entrenador, a [entrena'ðor, a] *nm/f* trainer, coach

entrenamiento [entrena'mjento] *nm* training

entrenar [entre'nar] *vt* (*Deporte*) to train; (*caballo*) to exercise ▷ *vi*, **entrenarse** *vr* to train

entrepierna [entre'pjerna] *nf* (*tb: ~s*) crotch, crutch

entresacar [entresa'kar] *vt* to pick out, select

entresuelo [entre'swelo] *nm* mezzanine, entresol; (*Teat*) dress o first circle

entretanto [entre'tanto] *adv* meanwhile, meantime

entretecho [entre'tetʃo] *nm* (*Am*) attic

entretejer [entrete'xer] *vt* to interweave

entretener [entrete'ner] *vt* (*divertir*) to entertain, amuse; (*detener*) to hold up, delay; (*mantener*) to maintain; **entretenerse** *vr* (*divertirse*) to amuse o.s.; (*retrasarse*) to delay, linger; **no le entretengo más** I won't keep you any longer

entretenido, -a [entrete'niðo, a] *adj* entertaining, amusing

entretenimiento [entreteni'mjento] *nm* entertainment, amusement; (*mantenimiento*) upkeep, maintenance

entretiempo [entre'tjempo] *nm*: **ropa de ~** *clothes for spring and autumn*

entrever [entre'βer] *vt* to glimpse, catch a glimpse of

entrevista [entre'βista] *nf* interview

entrevistador, a [entreβista'ðor, a] *nm/f* interviewer

entrevistar [entreβis'tar] *vt* to interview; **entrevistarse** *vr*: **~se con** to have an interview with, see; **el ministro se entrevistó con el Rey ayer** the minister had an audience with the King yesterday

entristecer [entriste'θer] *vt* to sadden, grieve; **entristecerse** *vr* to grow sad

entrometerse [entrome'terse] *vr*: **~ (en)** to interfere (in o with)

entroncar [entron'kar] *vi* to be connected o related

entumecer [entume'θer] *vt* to numb, benumb; **entumecerse** *vr* (*por el frío*) to go o become numb

entumecido, -a [entume'θiðo, a] *adj* numb, stiff

enturbiar [entur'βjar] *vt* (*el agua*) to make cloudy; (*fig*) to confuse; **enturbiarse** *vr* (*oscurecerse*) to become cloudy; (*fig*) to get confused, become obscure

entusiasmar [entusjas'mar] *vt* to excite, fill with enthusiasm; (*gustar mucho*) to delight; **entusiasmarse** *vr*: **~se con** o **por** to get enthusiastic o excited about

entusiasmo [entu'sjasmo] *nm* enthusiasm; (*excitación*) excitement

entusiasta [entu'sjasta] *adj* enthusiastic ▷ *nm/f* enthusiast

enumerar [enume'rar] *vt* to enumerate

enunciación [enunθja'θjon] *nf*, **enunciado** [enun'θjaðo] *nm* enunciation; (*declaración*) declaration, statement

envainar [embai'nar] *vt* to sheathe

envalentonar [embalento'nar] *vt* to give courage to; **envalentonarse** *vr* (*pey: jactarse*) to boast, brag

envanecer [embane'θer] *vt* to make conceited; **envanecerse** *vr* to grow conceited

envasar [emba'sar] *vt* (*empaquetar*) to pack, wrap; (*enfrascar*) to bottle; (*enlatar*) to can; (*embolsar*) to pocket

envase [em'base] *nm* packing, wrapping; bottling; canning; pocketing; (*recipiente*) container; (*paquete*) package; (*botella*) bottle; (*lata*) tin (*Brit*), can

envejecer [embexe'θer] *vt* to make old, age ▷ *vi*, **envejecerse** *vr* (*volverse viejo*) to grow old; (*parecer viejo*) to age

envenenar [embene'nar] *vt* to poison; (*fig*) to embitter

envergadura [emberɣa'ðura] *nf* (*expansión*) expanse; (*Naut*) breadth; (*fig*) scope; **un programa de gran ~** a wide-ranging programme

envés [em'bes] *nm* (*de tela*) back, wrong side

enviar [em'bjar] *vt* to send; **~ un mensaje a algn** (*por móvil*) to text sb, send sb a text message

enviciar [embi'θjar] *vt* to corrupt ▷ *vi* (*trabajo etc*) to be addictive; **enviciarse** *vr*: **~se (con** o **en)** to get addicted (to)

envidia [em'biðja] *nf* envy; **tener ~ a** to envy, be jealous of

envidiar [embi'ðjar] vt (*desear*) to envy; (*tener celos de*) to be jealous of

envío [em'bio] nm (*acción*) sending; (*de mercancías*) consignment; (*de dinero*) remittance; (*en barco*) shipment; **gastos de ~** postage and packing; **~ contra reembolso** COD shipment

enviudar [embju'ðar] vi to be widowed

envoltorio [embol'torjo] nm package

envoltura [embol'tura] nf (*cobertura*) cover; (*embalaje*) wrapper, wrapping

envolver [embol'βer] vt to wrap (up); (*cubrir*) to cover; (*enemigo*) to surround; (*implicar*) to involve, implicate

envuelto [em'bwelto], **envuelva** etc [em'bwelβa] vb ver **envolver**

enyesar [enje'sar] vt (*pared*) to plaster; (*Med*) to put in plaster

enzarzarse [enθar'θarse] vr: **~ en algo** to get mixed up in sth; (*disputa*) to get involved in sth

epicentro [epi'θentro] nm epicentre

épico, -a ['epiko, a] adj epic ▷ nf epic (poetry)

epidemia [epi'ðemja] nf epidemic

epidermis [epi'ðermis] nf epidermis

epilepsia [epi'lepsja] nf epilepsy

epiléptico, -a [epi'leptiko, a] adj, nm/f epileptic

epílogo [e'piloɣo] nm epilogue

episodio [epi'soðjo] nm episode; (*suceso*) incident

epístola [e'pistola] nf epistle

epíteto [e'piteto] nm epithet

época ['epoka] nf period, time; (*temporada*) season; (*Historia*) age, epoch; **hacer ~** to be epoch-making

equidad [eki'ðað] nf equity, fairness

equilibrar [ekili'βrar] vt to balance

equilibrio [eki'liβrjo] nm balance, equilibrium; **mantener/perder el ~** to keep/lose one's balance; **~ político** balance of power

equilibrista [ekili'βrista] nm/f (*funámbulo*) tightrope walker; (*acróbata*) acrobat

equipaje [eki'paxe] nm luggage (Brit), baggage (US); (*avíos*) equipment, kit; **~ de mano** hand luggage; **hacer el ~** to pack

equipar [eki'par] vt (*proveer*) to equip

equiparar [ekipa'rar] vt (*igualar*) to put on the same level; (*comparar*): **~ con** to compare with; **equipararse** vr: **~se con** to be on a level with

equipo [e'kipo] nm (*conjunto de cosas*) equipment; (*Deporte, grupo*) team; (*de obreros*) shift; (*de máquinas*) plant; (*turbinas etc*) set; **~ de caza** hunting gear; **~ de música** music centre; **~ físico** (Inform) hardware; **~ manos libres** hands-free kit; **~ médico** medical team

equis ['ekis] nf (the letter) X

equitación [ekita'θjon] nf (*acto*) riding; (*arte*) horsemanship

equitativo, -a [ekita'tiβo, a] adj equitable, fair

equivalente [ekiβa'lente] adj, nm equivalent

equivaler [ekiβa'ler] vi: **~ a** to be equivalent o equal to; (*en rango*) to rank as

equivocación [ekiβoka'θjon] nf mistake, error; (*malentendido*) misunderstanding

equivocado, -a [ekiβo'kaðo, a] adj wrong, mistaken

equivocarse [ekiβo'karse] vr to be wrong, make a mistake; **~ de camino** to take the wrong road

equívoco, -a [e'kiβoko, a] adj (*dudoso*) suspect; (*ambiguo*) ambiguous ▷ nm ambiguity; (*malentendido*) misunderstanding

era ['era] vb ver **ser** ▷ nf era, age; (*Agr*) threshing floor

erais ['erais], **éramos** ['eramos], **eran** ['eran] vb ver **ser**

erario [e'rarjo] nm exchequer, treasury

eras ['eras], **eres** ['eres] vb ver **ser**

e-reader ['irider] nm e-reader

erección [erek'θjon] nf erection

erguir [er'ɣir] vt to raise, lift; (*poner derecho*) to straighten; **erguirse** vr to straighten up

erigir [eri'xir] vt to erect, build; **erigirse** vr: **~se en** to set o.s. up as

erizado, -a [eri'θaðo, a] adj bristly

erizarse [eri'θarse] vr (*pelo: de perro*) to bristle; (*: de persona*) to stand on end

erizo [e'riθo] nm hedgehog; **~ de mar** sea urchin

ermita [er'mita] nf hermitage

ermitaño, -a [ermi'taɲo, a] nm/f hermit

erosión [ero'sjon] nf erosion

erosionar [erosjo'nar] vt to erode

erótico, -a [e'rotiko, a] adj erotic

erotismo [ero'tismo] nm eroticism

erradicar [erraði'kar] vt to eradicate

errante [e'rrante] adj wandering, errant

errar [e'rrar] vi (*vagar*) to wander, roam; (*equivocarse*) to be mistaken ▷ vt: **~ el camino** to take the wrong road; **~ el tiro** to miss

errata [e'rrata] nf misprint

erróneo, -a [e'rroneo, a] adj (*equivocado*) wrong, mistaken; (*falso*) false, untrue

error [e'rror] nm error, mistake; (Inform) bug; **~ de imprenta** misprint; **~ de lectura/escritura** (Inform) read/write error; **~ sintáctico** syntax error; **~ judicial** miscarriage of justice

eructar [eruk'tar] vt to belch, burp

eructo [e'rukto] nm belch

erudito, -a [eru'ðito, a] adj erudite, learned ▷ nm/f scholar; **los ~s en esta materia** the experts in this field

erupción [erup'θjon] nf eruption; (Med) rash; (*de violencia*) outbreak; (*de ira*) outburst

es [es] vb ver **ser**

esa ['esa], **esas** ['esas] adj demostrativo, pron ver **ese**

ésa ['esa], **ésas** ['esas] pron ver **ése**

esbelto, -a [es'βelto, a] *adj* slim, slender

esbozo [es'βoθo] *nm* sketch, outline

escabeche [eska'βetʃe] *nm* brine; *(de aceitunas etc)* pickle; **en ~** pickled

escabroso, -a [eska'βroso, a] *adj (accidentado)* rough, uneven; *(fig)* tough, difficult; *(: atrevido)* risqué

escabullirse [eskaβu'ʎirse] *vr* to slip away; *(largarse)* to clear out

escacharrar [eskatʃa'rrar] *vt (fam)* to break; **escacharrarse** *vr* to get broken

escafandra [eska'fandra] *nf (buzo)* diving suit; *(escafandra espacial)* spacesuit

escala [es'kala] *nf (proporción, Mus)* scale; *(de mano)* ladder; *(de colores etc)* range; **~ de tiempo** time scale; **~ de sueldos** salary scale; **una investigación a ~ nacional** a nationwide inquiry; **reproducir a ~** to reproduce to scale; **hacer ~ en** *(gen)* to stop off at o call in at; *(Aviat)* to stop over in

escalafón [eskala'fon] *nm (escala de salarios)* salary scale, wage scale

escalar [eska'lar] *vt* to climb, scale ▷ *vi (Mil, Pol)* to escalate

escalera [eska'lera] *nf* stairs *pl*, staircase; *(escala)* ladder; *(Naipes)* run; *(de camión)* tailboard; **~ mecánica** escalator; **~ de caracol** spiral staircase; **~ de incendios** fire escape

escalerilla [eskale'riʎa] *nf (de avión)* steps *pl*

escalfar [eskal'far] *vt (huevos)* to poach

escalinata [eskali'nata] *nf* staircase

escalofriante [eskalo'frjante] *adj* chilling

escalofrío [eskalo'frio] *nm (Med)* chill; **escalofríos** *nmpl (fig)* shivers

escalón [eska'lon] *nm* step, stair; *(de escalera)* rung; *(fig: paso)* step; *(al éxito)* ladder

escalope [eska'lope] *nm (Culin)* escalope

escama [es'kama] *nf (de pez, serpiente)* scale; *(de jabón)* flake; *(fig)* resentment

escamar [eska'mar] *vt (pez)* to scale; *(producir recelo)* to make wary

escamotear [eskamote'ar] *vt (fam: robar)* to lift, swipe; *(hacer desaparecer)* to make disappear

escampar [eskam'par] *vb impersonal* to stop raining

escanciar [eskan'θjar] *vt (vino)* to pour (out)

escandalizar [eskandali'θar] *vt* to scandalize, shock; **escandalizarse** *vr* to be shocked; *(ofenderse)* to be offended

escándalo [es'kandalo] *nm* scandal; *(alboroto, tumulto)* row, uproar; **armar un ~** to make a scene; **¡es un ~!** it's outrageous!

escandaloso, -a [eskanda'loso, a] *adj* scandalous, shocking; *(risa)* hearty; *(niño)* noisy

escandinavo, -a [eskandi'naβo, a] *adj, nm/f* Scandinavian

escanear [eskane'ar] *vt* to scan

escaneo [es'kaneo] *nm* scanning

escáner [es'kaner] *nm* scanner

escaño [es'kaɲo] *nm* bench; *(Pol)* seat

escapar [eska'par] *vi (gen)* to escape, run away; *(Deporte)* to break away; **escaparse** *vr* to escape, get away; *(agua, gas, noticias)* to leak (out); **se me escapa su nombre** his name escapes me

escaparate [eskapa'rate] *nm* shop window; *(Com)* showcase; **ir de ~s** to go window shopping

escape [es'kape] *nm (huida)* escape; *(de agua, gas)* leak; *(de motor)* exhaust; **salir a ~** to rush out

escaquearse [eskake'arse] *vr (fam)* to duck out

escarabajo [eskara'βaxo] *nm* beetle

escaramuza [eskara'muθa] *nf* skirmish; *(fig)* brush

escarbar [eskar'βar] *vt (gallina)* to scratch; *(fig)* to inquire into, investigate

escarceos [eskar'θeos] *nmpl*: **en sus ~ con la política** in his occasional forays into politics; **~ amorosos** love affairs

escarcha [es'kartʃa] *nf* frost

escarchado, -a [eskar'tʃaðo, a] *adj (Culin: fruta)* crystallized

escarlata [eskar'lata] *adj inv* scarlet

escarlatina [eskarla'tina] *nf* scarlet fever

escarmentar [eskarmen'tar] *vt* to punish severely ▷ *vi* to learn one's lesson; **¡para que escarmientes!** that'll teach you!

escarmiento *etc* [eskar'mjento] *vb ver* **escarmentar** ▷ *nm (ejemplo)* lesson; *(castigo)* punishment

escarnio [es'karnjo] *nm* mockery; *(injuria)* insult

escarola [eska'rola] *nf (Bot)* endive

escarpado, -a [eskar'paðo, a] *adj (pendiente)* sheer, steep; *(rocas)* craggy

escasear [eskase'ar] *vi* to be scarce

escasez [eska'seθ] *nf (falta)* shortage, scarcity; *(pobreza)* poverty; **vivir con ~** to live on the breadline

escaso, -a [es'kaso, a] *adj (poco)* scarce; *(raro)* rare; *(ralo)* thin, sparse; *(limitado)* limited; *(recursos)* scanty; *(público)* sparse; *(posibilidad)* slim; *(visibilidad)* poor

escatimar [eskati'mar] *vt (limitar)* to skimp (on), be sparing with; **no ~ esfuerzos (para)** to spare no effort to

escayola [eska'jola] *nf* plaster

escayolar [eskajo'lar] *vt* to put in plaster

escena [es'θena] *nf* scene; *(decorado)* scenery; *(escenario)* stage; **poner en ~** to put on

escenario [esθe'narjo] *nm (Teat)* stage; *(Cine)* set; *(fig)* scene; **el ~ del crimen** the scene of the crime; **el ~ político** the political scene

escenografía [esθenoɣra'fia] *nf* set o stage design

escepticismo [esθepti'θismo] *nm* scepticism

escéptico, -a [es'θeptiko, a] *adj* sceptical ▷ *nm/f* sceptic

escisión [esθi'sjon] *nf (Med)* excision; *(fig, Pol)* split; **~ nuclear** nuclear fission

e

esclarecer [esklare'θer] vt (*iluminar*) to light up, illuminate; (*misterio, problema*) to shed light on

esclavitud [esklaβi'tuð] nf slavery

esclavizar [esklaβi'θar] vt to enslave

esclavo, -a [es'klaβo, a] nm/f slave

esclusa [es'klusa] nf (*de canal*) lock; (*compuerta*) floodgate

escoba [es'koβa] nf broom; **pasar la ~** to sweep up

escobilla [esko'βiʎa] nf brush

escocer [esko'θer] vi to burn, sting; **escocerse** vr to chafe, get chafed

escocés, -esa [esko'θes, esa] adj Scottish; (*whisky*) Scotch ⊳ nm/f Scotsman(-woman), Scot ⊳ nm (*Ling*) Scots sg; **tela escocesa** tartan

Escocia [es'koθja] nf Scotland

escoger [esko'xer] vt to choose, pick, select

escogido, -a [esko'xiðo, a] adj chosen, selected; (*calidad*) choice, select; (*persona*): **ser muy ~** to be very fussy

escolar [esko'lar] adj school cpd ⊳ nm/f schoolboy(-girl), pupil

escollo [es'koʎo] nm (*arrecife*) reef, rock; (*fig*) pitfall

escolta [es'kolta] nf escort

escoltar [eskol'tar] vt to escort; (*proteger*) to guard

escombros [es'kombros] nmpl (*basura*) rubbish sg; (*restos*) debris sg

esconder [eskon'der] vt to hide, conceal; **esconderse** vr to hide

escondidas [eskon'diðas] nfpl (*Am*) hide-and-seek sg; **a ~** secretly; **hacer algo a ~ de algn** to do sth behind sb's back

escondite [eskon'dite] nm hiding place; (*juego*) hide-and-seek

escondrijo [eskon'drixo] nm hiding place, hideout

escopeta [esko'peta] nf shotgun; **~ de aire comprimido** air gun

escoria [es'korja] nf (*desecho mineral*) slag; (*fig*) scum, dregs pl

Escorpio [es'korpjo] nm (*Astro*) Scorpio

escorpión [eskor'pjon] nm scorpion

escotado, -a [esko'taðo, a] adj low-cut

escote [es'kote] nm (*de vestido*) low neck; **pagar a ~** to share the expenses

escotilla [esko'tiʎa] nf (*Naut*) hatchway

escozor [esko'θor] nm (*dolor*) sting(ing)

escribano, -a [eskri'βano, a], **escribiente** [eskri'βjente] nm/f clerk; (*secretario judicial*) court o lawyer's clerk

escribible [eskri'βiβle] adj writable

escribir [eskri'βir] vt, vi to write; **~ a máquina** to type; **¿cómo se escribe?** how do you spell it?

escrito, -a [es'krito, a] pp de **escribir** ⊳ adj written, in writing; (*examen*) written ⊳ nm (*documento*) document; (*manuscrito*) text, manuscript; **por ~** in writing

escritor, a [eskri'tor, a] nm/f writer

escritorio [eskri'torjo] nm desk; (*oficina*) office; (*Inform*) desktop

escritura [eskri'tura] nf (*acción*) writing; (*caligrafía*) (hand)writing; (*Jur: documento*) deed; (*Com*) indenture; **~ de propiedad** title deed; **Sagrada E-** (Holy) Scripture; **~ social** articles pl of association

escrúpulo [es'krupulo] nm scruple; (*minuciosidad*) scrupulousness

escrupuloso, -a [eskrupu'loso, a] adj scrupulous

escrutar [eskru'tar] vt to scrutinize, examine; (*votos*) to count

escrutinio [eskru'tinjo] nm (*examen atento*) scrutiny; (*Pol: recuento de votos*) count(ing)

escuadra [es'kwaðra] nf (*Tec*) square; (*Mil etc*) squad; (*Naut*) squadron; (*de buques*) fleet

escuadrilla [eskwa'ðriʎa] nf (*de aviones*) squadron; (*Am: de obreros*) gang

escuadrón [eskwa'ðron] nm squadron

escuálido, -a [es'kwaliðo, a] adj skinny, scraggy; (*sucio*) squalid

escucha [es'kutʃa] nf (*acción*) listening ⊳ nm (*Telec: sistema*) monitor; (*oyente*) listener; **estar a la ~** to listen in; **estar de ~** to spy; **~s telefónicas** (phone)tapping sg

escuchar [esku'tʃar] vt to listen to; (*consejo*) to heed; (*esp Am: oír*) to hear ⊳ vi to listen; **escucharse** vr: **se escucha muy mal** (*Telec*) it's a very bad line

escudarse [esku'ðarse] vr: **~ en** (*fig*) to hide behind

escudilla [esku'ðiʎa] nf bowl, basin

escudo [es'kuðo] nm shield; **~ de armas** coat of arms

escudriñar [eskuðri'nar] vt (*examinar*) to investigate, scrutinize; (*mirar de lejos*) to scan

escuela [es'kwela] nf (*tb fig*) school; **~ normal** teacher training college; **~ técnica superior** *university offering five-year courses in engineering and technical subjects*; **~ universitaria** *university offering three-year diploma courses*; **~ de párvulos** kindergarten; **~ de artes y oficios** (*Esp*) ≈ technical college; **~ de choferes** (*Am*) driving school; **~ de manejo** (*Am*) driving school; *ver tb* **colegio**

escueto, -a [es'kweto, a] adj plain; (*estilo*) simple; (*explicación*) concise

escuincle [es'kwinkle] nm (*Am fam*) kid

esculpir [eskul'pir] vt to sculpt; (*grabar*) to engrave; (*tallar*) to carve

escultor, a [eskul'tor, a] nm/f sculptor

escultura [eskul'tura] nf sculpture

escupidera [eskupi'ðera] nf spittoon

escupir [esku'pir] vt to spit (out) ⊳ vi to spit

escupitajo [eskupi'taxo] nm (*fam*) gob of spit

escurreplatos [eskurre'platos] nm inv plate rack

escurridero [eskurri'ðero] nm (*Am*) draining board (*Brit*), drainboard (*US*)

escurridizo, -a [eskurri'ðiθo, a] adj slippery

escurridor [eskurri'ðor] nm colander

escurrir [esku'rrir] vt (ropa) to wring out; (verduras, platos) to drain ▷ vi (los líquidos) to drip; **escurrirse** vr (secarse) to drain; (resbalarse) to slip, slide; (escaparse) to slip away

ese¹ ['ese] nf (the letter) S; **hacer ~s** (carretera) to zigzag; (borracho) to reel about

ese² ['ese], **esa** ['esa], **esos** ['esos], **esas** ['esas] adj demostrativo that sg, those pl ▷ pron that (one) sg, those (ones) pl

ése ['ese], **ésa** ['esa], **ésos** ['esos], **ésas** ['esas] pron that (one) sg, those (ones) pl; ~ ... **éste** ... the former ... the latter ...; **¡no me vengas con ésas!** don't give me any more of that nonsense!

esencia [e'senθja] nf essence

esencial [esen'θjal] adj essential; (principal) chief; **lo ~** the main thing

esfera [es'fera] nf sphere; (de reloj) face; **~ de acción** scope; **~ terrestre** globe

esférico, -a [es'feriko, a] adj spherical

esforzado, -a [esfor'θaðo, a] adj (enérgico) energetic, vigorous

esforzarse [esfor'θarse] vr to exert o.s., make an effort

esfuerzo [es'fwerθo] vb ver **esforzarse** ▷ nm effort; **sin ~** effortlessly

esfumarse [esfu'marse] vr (apoyo, esperanzas) to fade away; (persona) to vanish

esgrima [es'ɣrima] nf fencing

esgrimir [esɣri'mir] vt (arma) to brandish; (argumento) to use ▷ vi to fence

esguince [es'ɣinθe] nm (Med) sprain

eslabón [esla'βon] nm link; **~ perdido** (Bio, fig) missing link

eslálom [es'lalom] nm slalom

eslavo, -a [es'laβo, a] adj Slav, Slavonic ▷ nm/f Slav ▷ nm (Ling) Slavonic

eslip [ez'lip] nm pants pl (Brit), briefs pl

eslogan [es'loɣan] nm (pl **eslógans**) slogan

eslovaco, -a [eslo'βako, a] adj, nm/f Slovak, Slovakian ▷ nm (Ling) Slovak, Slovakian

Eslovaquia [eslo'βakja] nf Slovakia

esmaltar [esmal'tar] vt to enamel

esmalte [es'malte] nm enamel; **~ de uñas** nail varnish o polish

esmerado, -a [esme'raðo, a] adj careful, neat

esmeralda [esme'ralda] nf emerald

esmerarse [esme'rarse] vr (aplicarse) to take great pains, exercise great care; (afanarse) to work hard; (hacer lo mejor) to do one's best

esmero [es'mero] nm (great) care

esnob [es'nob] adj inv (persona) snobbish; (coche etc) posh ▷ nm/f snob

esnobismo [esno'βismo] nm snobbery

eso ['eso] pron that, that thing o matter; **~ de su coche** that business about his car; **~ de ir al cine** all that about going to the cinema; **a ~ de las cinco** at about five o'clock; **en ~** thereupon, at that point; **por ~** therefore; **~ es** that's it; **nada de ~** far from it; **¡~ sí que es vida!** now this is really living!; **por ~ te lo dije** that's why I told you; **y ~ que llovía** in spite of the fact it was raining

esófago [e'sofaɣo] nm (Anat) oesophagus

esos ['esos] adj demostrativo ver **ese**

ésos ['esos] pron ver **ése**

esotérico, -a [eso'teriko, a] adj esoteric

espabilado, -a [espaβi'laðo, a] adj quick-witted

espabilar [espaβi'lar] vt, **espabilarse** vr = **despabilar(se)**

espachurrar [espatʃu'rrar] vt to squash; **espachurrarse** vr to get squashed

espacial [espa'θjal] adj (del espacio) space cpd

espaciar [espa'θjar] vt to space (out)

espacio [es'paθjo] nm space; (Mus) interval; (Radio, TV) programme, program (US); **el ~** space; **ocupar mucho ~** to take up a lot of room; **a dos ~s, a doble ~** (Tip) double-spaced; **por ~ de** during, for; **~ aéreo/exterior** air/outer space

espacioso, -a [espa'θjoso, a] adj spacious, roomy

espada [es'paða] nf sword ▷ nm swordsman; (Taur) matador; **espadas** nfpl (Naipes) one of the suits in the Spanish card deck; **estar entre la ~ y la pared** to be between the devil and the deep blue sea

espaguetis [espa'ɣetis] nmpl spaghetti sg

espalda [es'palda] nf (gen) back; (Natación) backstroke; **~s** nfpl (hombros) shoulders; **a ~s de algn** behind sb's back; **estar de ~s** to have one's back turned; **tenderse de ~s** to lie (down) on one's back; **volver la ~ a algn** to cold-shoulder sb

espaldilla [espal'ðiʎa] nf shoulder blade

espantadizo, -a [espanta'ðiθo, a] adj timid, easily frightened

espantajo [espan'taxo] nm, **espantapájaros** [espanta'paxaros] nm inv scarecrow

espantar [espan'tar] vt (asustar) to frighten, scare; (ahuyentar) to frighten off; (asombrar) to horrify, appal; **espantarse** vr to get frightened o scared; to be appalled

espanto [es'panto] nm (susto) fright; (terror) terror; (asombro) astonishment; **¡qué ~!** how awful!

espantoso, -a [espan'toso, a] adj frightening, terrifying; (ruido) dreadful

España [es'paɲa] nf Spain; **la ~ de pandereta** touristy Spain

español, a [espa'ɲol, a] adj Spanish ▷ nm/f Spaniard ▷ nm (Ling) Spanish; ver tb **castellano**

esparadrapo [espara'ðrapo] nm surgical tape

esparcimiento [esparθi'mjento] nm (dispersión) spreading; (derramamiento) scattering; (fig) cheerfulness

esparcir [espar'θir] vt to spread; (derramar) to scatter; **esparcirse** vr to spread (out); to scatter; (divertirse) to enjoy o.s.

espárrago [es'parrayo] nm (tb: ~**s**) asparagus; **estar hecho un** ~ to be as thin as a rake; **¡vete a freír** ~**s!** (fam) go to hell!

esparto [es'parto] nm esparto (grass)

espasmo [es'pasmo] nm spasm

espátula [es'patula] nf (Med) spatula; (Arte) palette knife; (Culin) fish slice

especia [es'peθja] nf spice

especial [espe'θjal] adj special

especialidad [espeθjali'ðað] nf speciality, specialty (US); (Escol: ramo) specialism

especialista [espeθja'lista] nm/f specialist; (Cine) stuntman(-woman)

especializado, -a [espeθjali'θaðo, a] adj specialized; (obrero) skilled

especialmente [espeθjal'mente] adv particularly, especially

especie [es'peθje] nf (Bio) species; (clase) kind, sort; **pagar en** ~ to pay in kind

especificar [espeθifi'kar] vt to specify

específico, -a [espe'θifiko, a] adj specific

espécimen [es'peθimen] (pl **especímenes**) nm specimen

espectáculo [espek'takulo] nm (gen) spectacle; (Teat etc) show; (función) performance; **dar un** ~ to make a scene

espectador, a [espekta'ðor, a] nm/f spectator; (de incidente) onlooker; **los espectadores** nmpl (Teat) the audience sg

espectro [es'pektro] nm ghost; (fig) spectre

especulación [espekula'θjon] nf speculation; ~ **bursátil** speculation on the Stock Market

especular [espeku'lar] vt, vi to speculate

espejismo [espe'xismo] nm mirage

espejo [es'pexo] nm mirror; (fig) model; ~ **retrovisor** rear-view mirror; **mirarse al** ~ to look (at o.s.) in the mirror

espeleología [espeleolo'xia] nf potholing

espeluznante [espeluθ'nante] adj horrifying, hair-raising

espera [es'pera] nf (pausa, intervalo) wait; (Jur: plazo) respite; **en** ~ **de** waiting for; (con expectativa) expecting; **en** ~ **de su contestación** awaiting your reply

esperanza [espe'ranθa] nf (confianza) hope; (expectativa) expectation; **hay pocas** ~**s que venga** there is little prospect of his coming; ~ **de vida** life expectancy

esperanzar [esperan'θar] vt to give hope to

esperar [espe'rar] vt (aguardar) to wait for; (tener expectativa de) to expect; (desear) to hope for ▷ vi to wait; to expect; to hope; **esperarse** vr: **como podía** ~**se** as was to be expected; **hacer** ~ **a algn** to keep sb waiting; **ir a** ~ **a algn** to go and meet sb; ~ **un bebé** to be expecting (a baby)

esperma [es'perma] nf sperm

espermatozoide [espermato'θoiðe] nm spermatozoid

espesar [espe'sar] vt to thicken; **espesarse** vr to thicken, get thicker

espeso, -a [es'peso, a] adj thick; (bosque) dense; (nieve) deep; (sucio) dirty

espesor [espe'sor] nm thickness; (de nieve) depth

espía [es'pia] nm/f spy

espiar [espi'ar] vt (observar) to spy on ▷ vi: ~ **para** to spy for

espiga [es'piya] nf (Bot: de trigo etc) ear; (: de flores) spike

espigón [espi'yon] nm (Bot) ear; (Naut) breakwater

espina [es'pina] nf thorn; (de pez) bone; ~ **dorsal** (Anat) spine; **me da mala** ~ I don't like the look of it

espinaca [espi'naka] nf (tb: ~**s**) spinach

espinazo [espi'naθo] nm spine, backbone

espinilla [espi'niλa] nf (Anat: tibia) shin(bone); (: en la piel) blackhead

espino [es'pino] nm hawthorn

espinoso, -a [espi'noso, a] adj (planta) thorny, prickly; (fig) bony; (asunto) difficult; (problema) knotty

espionaje [espjo'naxe] nm spying, espionage

espiral [espi'ral] adj, nf spiral; **la** ~ **inflacionista** the inflationary spiral

espirar [espi'rar] vt, vi to breathe out, exhale

espiritista [espiri'tista] adj, nm/f spiritualist

espíritu [es'piritu] nm spirit; (mente) mind; (inteligencia) intelligence; (Rel) spirit, soul; **E~ Santo** Holy Ghost; **con** ~ **amplio** with an open mind

espiritual [espiri'twal] adj spiritual

espita [es'pita] nf tap (Brit), faucet (US)

espléndido, -a [es'plendiðo, a] adj (magnífico) magnificent, splendid; (generoso) generous, lavish

esplendor [esplen'dor] nm splendour

espolear [espole'ar] vt to spur on

espoleta [espo'leta] nf (de bomba) fuse

espolvorear [espolβore'ar] vt to dust, sprinkle

esponja [es'ponxa] nf sponge; (fig) sponger

esponjoso, -a [espon'xoso, a] adj spongy

espontaneidad [espontanei'ðað] nf spontaneity

espontáneo, -a [espon'taneo, a] adj spontaneous; (improvisado) impromptu; (persona) natural

esporádico, -a [espo'raðiko, a] adj sporadic

esposa [es'posa] nf ver **esposo**

esposar [espo'sar] vt to handcuff

esposo, -a [es'poso, a] nm husband ▷ nf wife; **esposas** nfpl handcuffs

espray [es'prai] nm spray

espuela [es'pwela] nf spur; (fam: trago) one for the road

espuma [es'puma] nf foam; (de cerveza) froth, head; (de jabón) lather; (de olas) surf; ~ **de afeitar** shaving foam

espumadera [espuma'ðera] nf skimmer
espumoso, -a [espu'moso, a] adj frothy, foamy; (vino) sparkling
esqueje [es'kexe] nm (Bot) cutting
esquela [es'kela] nf: ~ **mortuoria** announcement of death
esquelético, -a [eske'letiko, a] adj (fam) skinny
esqueleto [eske'leto] nm skeleton; (lo esencial) bare bones (of a matter); **en ~** unfinished
esquema [es'kema] nm (diagrama) diagram; (dibujo) plan; (plan) scheme; (Filosofía) schema
esquemático, -a [eske'matiko, a] adj schematic; **un resumen ~** a brief outline
esquí [es'ki] (pl **esquís**) nm (objeto) ski; (deporte) skiing; ~ **acuático** water-skiing; **hacer ~** to go skiing
esquiar [es'kjar] vi to ski
esquilar [eski'lar] vt to shear
esquimal [eski'mal] adj, nm/f Eskimo
esquina [es'kina] nf corner; **doblar la ~** to turn the corner
esquinazo [eski'naθo] nm: **dar ~ a algn** to give sb the slip
esquirol [eski'rol] nm (Esp) strikebreaker, blackleg
esquivar [eski'βar] vt to avoid; (evadir) to dodge, elude
esquivo, -a [es'kiβo, a] adj (altanero) aloof; (desdeñoso) scornful, disdainful
esta ['esta] adj demostrativo, pron ver **este**
ésta ['esta] pron ver **éste**
está [es'ta] vb ver **estar**
estabilidad [estaβili'ðað] nf stability
estabilizador, a [estabiliθa'ðor, a] adj (Foto) antishake
estabilizar [estaβili'θar] vt to stabilize; (fijar) to make steady; (precios) to peg; **estabilizarse** vr to become stable
estable [es'taβle] adj stable
establecer [estaβle'θer] vt to establish; (fundar) to set up; (colonos) to settle; (récord) to set (up); **establecerse** vr to establish o.s.; (echar raíces) to settle (down); (Com) to start up
establecimiento [estaβleθi'mjento] nm establishment; (fundación) institution; (de negocio) start-up; (de colonias) settlement; (local) establishment; ~ **comercial** business house
establo [es'taβlo] nm (Agr) stall; (para vacas) cowshed; (para caballos) stable; (: esp Am) barn
estaca [es'taka] nf stake, post; (de tienda de campaña) peg
estacada [esta'kaða] nf (cerca) fence, fencing; (palenque) stockade; **dejar a algn en la ~** to leave sb in the lurch
estación [esta'θjon] nf station; (del año) season; ~ **de autobuses/ferrocarril** bus/railway station; ~ **balnearia (de turistas)** seaside resort; ~ **de servicio** service station; ~ **terminal** terminus; ~ **de trabajo** (Com)

work station; ~ **transmisora** transmitter; ~ **de visualización** display unit
estacionamiento [estaθjona'mjento] nm (Auto) parking; (Mil) stationing
estacionar [estaθjo'nar] vt (Auto) to park; (Mil) to station
estacionario, -a [estaθjo'narjo, a] adj stationary; (Com: mercado) slack
estada [es'taða], **estadía** [esta'ðia] nf (Am) stay
estadio [es'taðjo] nm (fase) stage, phase; (Deporte) stadium
estadista [esta'ðista] nm (Pol) statesman; (Estadística) statistician
estadística [esta'ðistika] nf (una estadística) figure, statistic; (ciencia) statistics sg
estado [es'taðo] nm (Pol: condición) state; ~ **civil** marital status; ~ **de ánimo** state of mind; ~ **de cuenta(s)** bank statement, statement of accounts; ~ **de excepción** (Pol) state of emergency; ~ **financiero** (Com) financial statement; ~ **mayor** (Mil) staff; ~ **de pérdidas y ganancias** (Com) profit and loss statement, operating statement; **E~s Unidos (EE.UU.)** United States (of America) (USA); **estar en ~ (de buena esperanza)** to be pregnant
estadounidense [estaðouni'ðense] adj United States cpd, American ▷ nm/f United States citizen, American
estafa [es'tafa] nf swindle, trick; (Com etc) racket
estafar [esta'far] vt to swindle, defraud
estafeta [esta'feta] nf (oficina de correos) post office; ~ **diplomática** diplomatic bag
estáis vb ver **estar**
estallar [esta'ʎar] vi to burst; (bomba) to explode, go off; (volcán) to erupt; (vidrio) to shatter; (látigo) to crack; (epidemia, guerra, rebelión) to break out; ~ **en llanto** to burst into tears
estallido [esta'ʎiðo] nm explosion; (de látigo, trueno) crack; (fig) outbreak
Estambul [estam'bul] nm Istanbul
estampa [es'tampa] nf (impresión, imprenta) print, engraving; (imagen, figura: de persona) appearance
estampado, -a [estam'paðo, a] adj printed ▷ nm (impresión: acción) printing; (: efecto) print; (marca) stamping
estampar [estam'par] vt (imprimir) to print; (marcar) to stamp; (metal) to engrave; (poner sello en) to stamp; (fig) to stamp, imprint
estampida [estam'piða] nf stampede
estampido [estam'piðo] nm bang, report
estampilla [estam'piʎa] nf (sello de goma) (rubber) stamp; (Am) (postage) stamp
están [es'tan] vb ver **estar**
estancado, -a [estan'kaðo, a] adj (agua) stagnant
estancar [estan'kar] vt (aguas) to hold up, hold back; (Com) to monopolize; (fig) to

block, hold up; **estancarse** *vr* to stagnate
estancia [es'tanθja] *nf (permanencia)* stay;
(sala) room; *(Am)* farm, ranch
estanciero [estan'sjero] *nm (Am)* farmer,
rancher
estanco, -a [es'tanko, a] *adj* watertight ▷ *nm*
tobacconist's (shop); *see note*

● **ESTANCO**
●
● Cigarettes, tobacco, postage stamps and
● official forms are all sold under state
● monopoly and usually through a shop
● called an *estanco*. Tobacco products are
● also sold in *quioscos* and bars but are
● generally more expensive. The number of
● *estanco* licences is regulated by the state.

estándar [es'tandar] *adj, nm* standard
estandarizar [estandari'θar] *vt* to
standardize
estandarte [estan'darte] *nm* banner,
standard
estanque *etc* [es'tanke] *vb ver* **estancar** ▷ *nm*
(lago) pool, pond; *(Agr)* reservoir
estanquero, -a [estan'kero, a] *nm/f*
tobacconist
estante [es'tante] *nm (armario)* rack, stand;
(biblioteca) bookcase; *(anaquel)* shelf; *(Am)*
prop
estantería [estante'ria] *nf* shelving,
shelves *pl*
estaño [es'taɲo] *nm* tin

○ **PALABRA CLAVE**

estar [es'tar] *vi* **1** *(posición)* to be; **está en la
plaza** it's in the square; **¿está Juan?** is Juan
in?; **estamos a 30 km de Junín** we're 30 km
from Junín
2 *(+ adj o adv: estado)* to be; **estar enfermo** to
be ill; **está muy elegante** he's looking very
smart; **estar lejos** to be far (away); **¿cómo
estás?** how are you keeping?
3 *(+ gerundio)* to be; **estoy leyendo** I'm reading
4 *(uso pasivo)* to be; **está condenado a muerte** he's
been condemned to death; **está envasado
en ...** it's packed in ...
5: estar a: ¿a cuántos estamos? what's the
date today?; **estamos a 9 de mayo** it's the
9th of May; **las manzanas están a 1,50
euros** apples are (selling at) 1.5 euros;
estamos a 25 grados it's 25 degrees today
6 *(locuciones)*: **¿estamos?** *(¿de acuerdo?)* okay?;
(¿listo?) ready?; **¡ya está bien!** that's enough!;
¿está la comida? is dinner ready?; **¡ya está!,
¡ya estuvo!** *(Am)* that's it!
7: estar con: está con gripe he's got (the) flu
8: estar de: estar de vacaciones/viaje to be
on holiday/away *o* on a trip; **está de
camarero** he's working as a waiter
9: estar para: está para salir he's about to

leave; **no estoy para bromas** I'm not in the
mood for jokes
10: estar por *(propuesta etc)* to be in favour of;
(persona etc) to support, side with; **está por
limpiar** it still has to be cleaned; **¡estoy por
dejarlo!** I think I'm going to leave this!
11: estar sin: estar sin dinero to have no
money; **está sin terminar** it isn't finished
yet
estarse *vr*: **se estuvo en la cama toda la
tarde** he stayed in bed all afternoon; **¡estáte
quieto!** stop fidgeting!
12 *(+ que)*: **está que rabia** *(fam)* he's hopping
mad *(fam)*; **estoy que me caigo de sueño**
I'm terribly sleepy, I can't keep my eyes open

estárter [es'tarter] *nm (Auto)* choke
estas ['estas] *adj demostrativo, pron ver* **este**
éstas ['estas] *pron ver* **éste**
estatal [esta'tal] *adj* state *cpd*
estático, -a [es'tatiko, a] *adj* static
estatua [es'tatwa] *nf* statue
estatura [esta'tura] *nf* stature, height
estatus [es'tatus] *nm inv* status
estatuto [esta'tuto] *nm (Jur)* statute; *(de
ciudad)* bye-law; *(de comité)* rule; **~s sociales**
(Com) articles of association
este¹ ['este] *adj (lado)* east; *(dirección)* easterly
▷ *nm* east; **en la parte del ~** in the eastern
part
este² ['este], **esta** ['esta], **estos** ['estos],
estas ['estas] *adj demostrativo* this *sg*, these *pl*;
(Am: como muletilla) er, um ▷ *pron* this (one) *sg*,
these (ones) *pl*
éste ['este], **ésta** ['esta], **éstos** ['estos], **éstas**
['estas] *pron* this (one) *sg*, these (ones) *pl*;
ése ... ~ ... the former ... the latter ...
esté [es'te] *vb ver* **estar**
estela [es'tela] *nf* wake, wash; *(fig)* trail
estelar [este'lar] *adj (Astro)* stellar; *(Teat)* star
cpd
estén [es'ten] *vb ver* **estar**
estenografía [estenoɣra'fia] *nf* shorthand
estepa [es'tepa] *nf (Geo)* steppe
estera [es'tera] *nf (alfombra)* mat; *(tejido)*
matting
estéreo [es'tereo] *adj inv, nm* stereo
estereotipo [estereo'tipo] *nm* stereotype
estéril [es'teril] *adj* sterile, barren; *(fig)* vain,
futile
esterilizar [esterili'θar] *vt* to sterilize
esterlina [ester'lina] *adj*: **libra ~** pound
sterling
estés [es'tes] *vb ver* **estar**
estético, -a [es'tetiko, a] *adj* aesthetic ▷ *nf*
aesthetics *sg*
estiércol [es'tjerkol] *nm* dung, manure
estigma [es'tiɣma] *nm* stigma
estilarse [esti'larse] *vr (estar de moda)* to be in
fashion; *(usarse)* to be used
estilo [es'tilo] *nm* style; *(Tec)* stylus; *(Natación)*
stroke; **~ de vida** lifestyle; **al ~ de** in the style

of; **algo por el ~** something along those lines

estima [es'tima] *nf* esteem, respect

estimación [estima'θjon] *nf* (*evaluación*) estimation; (*aprecio, afecto*) esteem, regard

estimado, -a [esti'maðo, a] *adj* esteemed; **"E~ Señor"** "Dear Sir"

estimar [esti'mar] *vt* (*evaluar*) to estimate; (*valorar*) to value; (*apreciar*) to esteem, respect; (*pensar, considerar*) to think, reckon

estimulante [estimu'lante] *adj* stimulating ▷ *nm* stimulant

estimular [estimu'lar] *vt* to stimulate; (*excitar*) to excite; (*animar*) to encourage

estímulo [es'timulo] *nm* stimulus; (*ánimo*) encouragement

estío [es'tio] *nm* summer

estipulación [estipula'θjon] *nf* stipulation, condition

estipular [estipu'lar] *vt* to stipulate

estirado, -a [esti'raðo, a] *adj* (*tenso*) (stretched *o* drawn) tight; (*fig: persona*) stiff, pompous; (*engreído*) stuck-up

estirar [esti'rar] *vt* to stretch; (*dinero, suma etc*) to stretch out; (*cuello*) to crane; (*discurso*) to spin out; **~ la pata** (*fam*) to kick the bucket; **estirarse** *vr* to stretch

estirón [esti'ron] *nm* pull, tug; (*crecimiento*) spurt, sudden growth; **dar un ~** (*niño*) to shoot up

estirpe [es'tirpe] *nf* stock, lineage

estival [esti'βal] *adj* summer *cpd*

esto ['esto] *pron* this, this thing *o* matter; (*como muletilla*) er, um; **~ de la boda** this business about the wedding; **en ~** at this *o* that point; **por ~** for this reason

Estocolmo [esto'kolmo] *nm* Stockholm

estofa [es'tofa] *nf*: **de baja ~** poor-quality

estofado [esto'faðo] *nm* stew

estofar [esto'far] *vt* (*bordar*) to quilt; (*Culin*) to stew

estómago [es'tomaɣo] *nm* stomach; **tener ~** to be thick-skinned

estorbar [estor'βar] *vt* to hinder, obstruct; (*fig*) to bother, disturb ▷ *vi* to be in the way

estorbo [es'torβo] *nm* (*molestia*) bother, nuisance; (*obstáculo*) hindrance, obstacle

estornudar [estornu'ðar] *vi* to sneeze

estornudo [estor'nuðo] *nm* sneeze

estos ['estos] *adj demostrativo ver* **este**

éstos ['estos] *pron ver* **éste**

estoy [es'toi] *vb ver* **estar**

estrado [es'traðo] *nm* (*tarima*) platform; (*Mus*) bandstand; **estrados** *nmpl* law courts

estrafalario, -a [estrafa'larjo, a] *adj* odd, eccentric; (*desarreglado*) slovenly, sloppy

estrago [es'traɣo] *nm* ruin, destruction; **hacer ~s en** to wreak havoc among

estragón [estra'ɣon] *nm* (*Culin*) tarragon

estrambótico, -a [estram'botiko, a] *adj* odd, eccentric; (*peinado, ropa*) outlandish

estrangulador, -a [estrangula'ðor, a] *nm/f*

strangler ▷ *nm* (*Tec*) throttle; (*Auto*) choke

estrangulamiento [estrangula'mjento] *nm* (*Auto*) bottleneck

estrangular [estrangu'lar] *vt* (*persona*) to strangle; (*Med*) to strangulate

estraperlo [estra'perlo] *nm* black market

estratagema [estrata'xema] *nf* (*Mil*) stratagem; (*astucia*) cunning

estrategia [estra'texja] *nf* strategy

estratégico, -a [estra'texiko, a] *adj* strategic

estratificar [estratifi'kar] *vt* to stratify

estrato [es'trato] *nm* stratum, layer

estrechar [estre'tʃar] *vt* (*reducir*) to narrow; (*vestido*) to take in; (*persona*) to hug, embrace; **estrecharse** *vr* (*reducirse*) to narrow, grow narrow; (*2 personas*) to embrace; **~ la mano** to shake hands

estrechez [estre'tʃeθ] *nf* narrowness; (*de ropa*) tightness; (*intimidad*) intimacy; (*Com*) want *o* shortage of money; **estrecheces** *nfpl* financial difficulties

estrecho, -a [es'tretʃo, a] *adj* narrow; (*apretado*) tight; (*íntimo*) close, intimate; (*miserable*) mean ▷ *nm* strait; **~ de miras** narrow-minded; **E~ de Gibraltar** Straits of Gibraltar

estrella [es'treʎa] *nf* star; **~ fugaz** shooting star; **~ de mar** starfish; **tener (buena)/ mala ~** to be lucky/unlucky

estrellado, -a [estre'ʎaðo, a] *adj* (*forma*) star-shaped; (*cielo*) starry; (*huevos*) fried

estrellar [estre'ʎar] *vt* (*hacer añicos*) to smash (to pieces); (*huevos*) to fry; **estrellarse** *vr* to smash; (*chocarse*) to crash; (*fracasar*) to fail

estremecer [estreme'θer] *vt* to shake; **estremecerse** *vr* to shake, tremble; **~ de** (*horror*) to shudder with; (*frío*) to shiver with

estremecimiento [estremeθi'mjento] *nm* (*temblor*) trembling, shaking

estrenar [estre'nar] *vt* (*vestido*) to wear for the first time; (*casa*) to move into; (*película, obra de teatro*) to première; **estrenarse** *vr* (*persona*) to make one's début; (*película*) to have its première; (*Teat*) to open

estreno [es'treno] *nm* (*primer uso*) first use; (*Cine etc*) première

estreñido, -a [estre'ɲiðo, a] *adj* constipated

estreñimiento [estreɲi'mjento] *nm* constipation

estreñir [estre'ɲir] *vt* to constipate

estrépito [es'trepito] *nm* noise, racket; (*fig*) fuss

estrepitoso, -a [estrepi'toso, a] *adj* noisy; (*fiesta*) rowdy

estrés [es'tres] *nm* stress

estría [es'tria] *nf* groove; **~s (en el cutis)** stretchmarks

estribación [estriβa'θjon] *nf* (*Geo*) spur; **estribaciones** *nfpl* foothills

estribar [estri'βar] *vi* (*Archit*): **~ en** to rest on, be supported by; **la dificultad estriba en el texto** the difficulty lies in the text

estribillo [estri'βiʎo] nm (Lit) refrain; (Mus) chorus

estribo [es'triβo] nm (de jinete) stirrup; (de coche, tren) step; (de puente) support; (Geo) spur; **perder los ~s** to fly off the handle

estribor [estri'βor] nm (Naut) starboard

estricnina [estrik'nina] nf strychnine

estricto, -a [es'trikto, a] adj (riguroso) strict; (severo) severe

estridente [estri'ðente] adj (color) loud; (voz) raucous

estrofa [es'trofa] nf verse

estropajo [estro'paxo] nm scourer

estropeado, -a [estrope'aðo, a] adj: **está ~** it's not working

estropear [estrope'ar] vt (arruinar) to spoil; (dañar) to damage; (: máquina) to break; **estropearse** vr (objeto) to get damaged; (coche) to break down; (la piel etc) to be ruined

estructura [estruk'tura] nf structure

estruendo [es'trwendo] nm (ruido) racket, din; (fig: alboroto) uproar, turmoil

estrujar [estru'xar] vt (apretar) to squeeze; (aplastar) to crush; (fig) to drain, bleed

estuario [es'twarjo] nm estuary

estuche [es'tutʃe] nm box, case

estudiante [estu'ðjante] nm/f student

estudiantil [estuðjan'til] adj inv student cpd

estudiar [estu'ðjar] vt to study; (propuesta) to think about o over; **~ para abogado** to study to become a lawyer

estudio [es'tuðjo] nm study; (encuesta) research; (proyecto) plan; (piso) studio flat; (Cine, Arte, Radio) studio; **estudios** nmpl studies; (erudición) learning sg; **cursar** o **hacer ~s** to study; **~ de casos prácticos** case study; **~ de desplazamientos y tiempos** (Com) time and motion study; **~s de motivación** motivational research sg; **~ del trabajo** (Com) work study; **~ de viabilidad** (Com) feasibility study

estudioso, -a [estu'ðjoso, a] adj studious

estufa [es'tufa] nf heater, fire

estupefaciente [estupefa'θjente] adj, nm narcotic

estupefacto, -a [estupe'fakto, a] adj speechless, thunderstruck

estupendamente [estupenda'mente] adv (fam): **estoy ~** I feel great; **le salió ~** he did it very well

estupendo, -a [estu'pendo, a] adj wonderful, terrific; (fam) great; **¡~!** that's great!, fantastic!

estupidez [estupi'ðeθ] nf (torpeza) stupidity; (acto) stupid thing (to do); **fue una ~ mía** that was a silly thing for me to do o say

estúpido, -a [es'tupiðo, a] adj stupid, silly

estupor [estu'por] nm stupor; (fig) astonishment, amazement

estupro [es'tupro] nm rape

estuve etc [es'tuβe], **estuviera** etc [estu'βjera] vb ver **estar**

esvástica [es'βastika] nf swastika

ETA ['eta] nf abr (Pol: = Euskadi Ta Askatasuna) ETA

etapa [e'tapa] nf (de viaje) stage; (Deporte) leg; (parada) stopping place; (fig) stage, phase; **por ~s** gradually, in stages

etarra [e'tarra] adj ETA cpd ▷ nm/f member of ETA

etc. abr (= etcétera) etc

etcétera [et'θetera] adv etcetera

eternidad [eterni'ðað] nf eternity

eternizarse [eterni'θarse] vr: **~ en hacer algo** to take ages to do sth

eterno, -a [e'terno, a] adj eternal, everlasting; (despectivo) never-ending

ético, -a ['etiko, a] adj ethical ▷ nf ethics

etiqueta [eti'keta] nf (modales) etiquette; (rótulo) label, tag; **de ~** formal

etnia ['etnja] nf ethnic group

étnico, -a ['etniko, a] adj ethnic

Eucaristía [eukaris'tia] nf Eucharist

eufemismo [eufe'mismo] nm euphemism

euforia [eu'forja] nf euphoria

eunuco [eu'nuko] nm eunuch

euro ['euro] nm (moneda) euro

eurodiputado, -a [euroðipu'taðo, a] nm/f Euro MP, MEP

Europa [eu'ropa] nf Europe

europeo, -a [euro'peo, a] adj, nm/f European

Euskadi [eus'kaði] nm the Basque Provinces pl

euskera, eusquera [eus'kera] nm (Ling) Basque; ver tb **Lengua**

eutanasia [euta'nasja] nf euthanasia

evacuación [eβakwa'θjon] nf evacuation

evacuar [eβa'kwar] vt to evacuate

evadir [eβa'ðir] vt to evade, avoid; **evadirse** vr to escape

evaluación [eβalwa'θjon] nf evaluation, assessment

evaluar [eβa'lwar] vt to evaluate, assess

evangélico, -a [eβan'xeliko, a] adj evangelical

evangelio [eβan'xeljo] nm gospel

evaporar [eβapo'rar] vt to evaporate; **evaporarse** vr to vanish

evasión [eβa'sjon] nf escape, flight; (fig) evasion; **~ fiscal** o **tributaria** tax evasion; **~ de capitales** flight of capital

evasivo, -a [eβa'siβo, a] adj evasive, non-committal ▷ nf (pretexto) excuse; **contestar con evasivas** to avoid giving a straight answer

evento [e'βento] nm event; (eventualidad) eventuality

eventual [eβen'twal] adj possible, conditional (upon circumstances); (trabajador) casual, temporary

evidencia [eβi'ðenθja] nf evidence, proof; **poner en ~** to make clear; **ponerse en ~** (persona) to show o.s. up

evidenciar [eβiðen'θjar] vt (hacer patente) to make evident; (probar) to prove, show; **evidenciarse** vr to be evident

evidente [eβi'ðente] *adj* obvious, clear, evident

evitar [eβi'tar] *vt* (*evadir*) to avoid; (*impedir*) to prevent; (*peligro*) to escape; (*molestia*) to save; (*tentación*) to shun; ~ **hacer algo** to avoid doing sth; **si puedo ~lo** if I can help it

evocar [eβo'kar] *vt* to evoke, call forth

evolución [eβolu'θjon] *nf* (*desarrollo*) evolution, development; (*cambio*) change; (*Mil*) manoeuvre

evolucionar [eβoluθjo'nar] *vi* to evolve; (*Mil, Aviat*) to manoeuvre

ex [eks] *adj* ex-; **el ex ministro** the former minister, the ex-minister

exacerbar [eksaθer'βar] *vt* to irritate, annoy

exactamente [eksakta'mente] *adv* exactly

exactitud [eksakti'tuð] *nf* exactness; (*precisión*) accuracy; (*puntualidad*) punctuality

exacto, -a [ek'sakto, a] *adj* exact; accurate; punctual; **¡~!** exactly!; **eso no es del todo ~** that's not quite right; **para ser ~** to be precise

exageración [eksaxera'θjon] *nf* exaggeration

exagerar [eksaxe'rar] *vt* to exaggerate; (*exceder*) to overdo

exaltado, -a [eksal'taðo, a] *adj* (*apasionado*) over-excited, worked up; (*exagerado*) extreme; (*fanático*) hot-headed; (*discurso*) impassioned ▷ *nm/f* (*fanático*) hothead; (*Pol*) extremist

exaltar [eksal'tar] *vt* to exalt, glorify; **exaltarse** *vr* (*excitarse*) to get excited o worked up

examen [ek'samen] *nm* examination; (*de problema*) consideration; ~ **de** (*encuesta*) inquiry into; ~ **de ingreso** entrance examination; ~ **de conducir** driving test; ~ **de ingreso** entrance examination; ~ **eliminatorio** qualifying examination

examinar [eksami'nar] *vt* to examine; (*poner a prueba*) to test; (*inspeccionar*) to inspect; **examinarse** *vr* to be examined, take an examination

exasperar [eksaspe'rar] *vt* to exasperate; **exasperarse** *vr* to get exasperated, lose patience

excavador, a [ekskaβa'ðor, a] *nm/f* (*persona*) excavator ▷ *nf* (*Tec*) digger

excavar [ekska'βar] *vt* to excavate, dig (out)

excedencia [eksθe'ðenθja] *nf* (*Mil*) leave; (*Escol*) sabbatical; **estar en ~** to be on leave; **pedir** o **solicitar la ~** to ask for leave

excedente [eksθe'ðente] *adj, nm* excess, surplus

exceder [eksθe'ðer] *vt* to exceed, surpass; **excederse** *vr* (*extralimitarse*) to go too far; (*sobrepasarse*) to excel o.s.

excelencia [eksθe'lenθja] *nf* excellence; **E~** Excellency; **por ~** par excellence

excelente [eksθe'lente] *adj* excellent

excelso, -a [eks'θelso, a] *adj* lofty, sublime

excentricidad [eksθentriθi'ðað] *nf* eccentricity

excéntrico, -a [eks'θentriko, a] *adj, nm/f* eccentric

excepción [eksθep'θjon] *nf* exception; **a ~ de** with the exception of, except for; **la ~ confirma la regla** the exception proves the rule

excepcional [eksθepθjo'nal] *adj* exceptional

excepto [eks'θepto] *adv* excepting, except (for)

exceptuar [eksθep'twar] *vt* to except, exclude

excesivo, -a [eksθe'siβo, a] *adj* excessive

exceso [eks'θeso] *nm* excess; (*Com*) surplus; ~ **de equipaje/peso** excess luggage/weight; ~ **de velocidad** speeding; **en** o **por ~** excessively

excitación [eksθita'θjon] *nf* (*sensación*) excitement; (*acción*) excitation

excitado, -a [eksθi'taðo, a] *adj* excited; (*emociones*) aroused

excitar [eksθi'tar] *vt* to excite; (*incitar*) to urge; (*emoción*) to stir up; (*esperanzas*) to raise; (*pasión*) to arouse; **excitarse** *vr* to get excited

exclamación [eksklama'θjon] *nf* exclamation

exclamar [ekskla'mar] *vi* to exclaim; **exclamarse** *vr*: ~**se** (*contra*) to complain (about)

excluir [eksklu'ir] *vt* to exclude; (*dejar fuera*) to shut out; (*solución*) to reject; (*posibilidad*) to rule out

exclusión [eksklu'sjon] *nf* exclusion

exclusiva [eksklu'siβa] *nf ver* **exclusivo**

exclusivo, -a [eksklu'siβo, a] *adj* exclusive ▷ *nf* (*Prensa*) exclusive, scoop; (*Com*) sole right o agency; **derecho ~** sole o exclusive right

Excma., Excmo. *abr* (= *Excelentísima, Excelentísimo*) courtesy title

excomulgar [ekskomul'γar] *vt* (*Rel*) to excommunicate

excomunión [ekskomu'njon] *nf* excommunication

excremento [ekskre'mento] *nm* excrement

excursión [ekskur'sjon] *nf* excursion, outing; **ir de ~** to go (off) on a trip

excursionista [ekskursjo'nista] *nm/f* (*turista*) sightseer

excusa [eks'kusa] *nf* excuse; (*disculpa*) apology; **presentar sus ~s** to excuse o.s.

excusar [eksku'sar] *vt* to excuse; (*evitar*) to avoid, prevent; **excusarse** *vr* (*disculparse*) to apologize

exento, -a [ek'sento, a] *pp de* **eximir** ▷ *adj* exempt

exequias [ek'sekjas] *nfpl* funeral rites

exfoliar [eksfo'ljar] *vt* to exfoliate

exhalar [eksa'lar] *vt* to exhale, breathe out; (*olor etc*) to give off; (*suspiro*) to breathe, heave

exhaustivo, -a [eksaus'tiβo, a] *adj* (*análisis*) thorough; (*estudio*) exhaustive

exhausto, -a [ek'sausto, a] *adj* exhausted, worn-out

exhibición [eksiβi'θjon] nf exhibition; (demostración) display, show; (de película) showing; (de equipo) performance
exhibir [eksi'βir] vt to exhibit; to display, show; (cuadros) to exhibit; (artículos) to display; (película) to screen; (mostrar con orgullo) to show off; **exhibirse** vr (mostrarse en público) to show o.s. off; (fam: indecentemente) to expose o.s.
exhortación [eksorta'θjon] nf exhortation
exhortar [eksor'tar] vt: ~ **a** to exhort to
exigencia [eksi'xenθja] nf demand, requirement
exigente [eksi'xente] adj demanding; (profesor) strict; **ser ~ con algn** to be hard on sb
exigir [eksi'xir] vt (gen) to demand, require; (impuestos) to exact, levy; **~ el pago** to demand payment
exiliado, -a [eksi'ljaðo, a] adj exiled, in exile ⊳ nm/f exile
exilio [ek'siljo] nm exile
eximio, -a [ek'simjo, a] adj (eminente) distinguished, eminent
eximir [eksi'mir] vt to exempt
existencia [eksis'tenθja] nf existence; **existencias** nfpl stock sg; **~ de mercancías** (Com) stock-in-trade; **tener en ~** to have in stock; **amargar la ~ a algn** to make sb's life a misery
existir [eksis'tir] vi to exist, be
éxito ['eksito] nm (resultado) result, outcome; (triunfo) success; (Mus, Teat) hit; **~ editorial** bestseller; **~ rotundo** smash hit; **tener ~** to be successful
éxodo ['eksoðo] nm exodus; **el ~ rural** the drift from the land
exonerar [eksone'rar] vt to exonerate; **~ de una obligación** to free from an obligation
exorbitante [eksorβi'tante] adj (precio) exorbitant; (cantidad) excessive
exorcizar [eksorθi'θar] vt to exorcize
exótico, -a [ek'sotiko, a] adj exotic
expandir [ekspan'dir] vt to expand; (Com) to expand, enlarge; **expandirse** vr to expand, spread
expansión [ekspan'sjon] nf expansion; (recreo) relaxation; **la ~ económica** economic growth; **economía en ~** expanding economy
expansionarse [ekspansjo'narse] vr (dilatarse) to expand; (recrearse) to relax
expansivo, -a [ekspan'siβo, a] adj expansive; (efusivo) communicative; **onda expansiva** shock wave
expatriarse [ekspa'trjarse] vr to emigrate; (Pol) to go into exile
expectativa [ekspekta'tiβa] nf (espera) expectation; (perspectiva) prospect; **~ de vida** life expectancy; **estar a la ~** to wait and see (what will happen)
expedición [ekspeði'θjon] nf (excursión) expedition; **gastos de ~** shipping charges

expediente [ekspe'ðjente] nm expedient; (Jur: procedimiento) action, proceedings pl; (: papeles) dossier, file, record; **~ judicial** court proceedings pl; **~ académico** (student's) record
expedir [ekspe'ðir] vt (despachar) to send, forward; (pasaporte) to issue; (cheque) to make out
expedito, -a [ekspe'ðito, a] adj (libre) clear, free
expendedor, a [ekspende'ðor, a] nm/f (vendedor) dealer; (Teat) ticket agent ⊳ nm (aparato) (vending) machine; **~ de cigarrillos** cigarette machine
expendeduría [ekspendeðu'ria] nf (estanco) tobacconist's (shop) (Brit), cigar store (US)
expensas [eks'pensas] nfpl (Jur) costs; **a ~ de** at the expense of
experiencia [ekspe'rjenθja] nf experience
experimentado, -a [eksperimen'taðo, a] adj experienced
experimentar [eksperimen'tar] vt (en laboratorio) to experiment with; (probar) to test, try out; (notar, observar) to experience; (deterioro, pérdida) to suffer; (aumento) to show; (sensación) to feel
experimento [eksperi'mento] nm experiment
experto, -a [eks'perto, a] adj expert ⊳ nm/f expert
expiar [ekspi'ar] vt to atone for
expirar [ekspi'rar] vi to expire
explanada [ekspla'naða] nf (paseo) esplanade; (a orillas del mar) promenade
explayarse [ekspla'jarse] vr (en discurso) to speak at length; **~ con algn** to confide in sb
explicación [eksplika'θjon] nf explanation
explicar [ekspli'kar] vt to explain; (teoría) to expound; (Univ) to lecture in; **explicarse** vr to explain (o.s.); **no me lo explico** I can't understand it
explícito, -a [eks'pliθito, a] adj explicit
explique etc [eks'plike] vb ver **explicar**
explorador, a [eksplora'ðor, a] nm/f (pionero) explorer; (Mil) scout ⊳ nm (Med) probe; (radar) (radar) scanner
explorar [eksplo'rar] vt to explore; (Med) to probe; (radar) to scan
explosión [eksplo'sjon] nf explosion
explosivo, -a [eksplo'siβo, a] adj explosive
explotación [eksplota'θjon] nf exploitation; (de planta etc) running; (de mina) working; (de recurso) development; **~ minera** mine; **gastos de ~** operating costs
explotar [eksplo'tar] vt to exploit; (planta) to run, operate; (mina) to work ⊳ vi (bomba etc) to explode, go off
exponer [ekspo'ner] vt to expose; (cuadro) to display; (vida) to risk; (idea) to explain; (teoría) to expound; (hechos) to set out; **exponerse** vr: **~se a (hacer) algo** to run the risk of (doing) sth

exportación [eksporta'θjon] *nf* (*acción*) export; (*mercancías*) exports *pl*

exportar [ekspor'tar] *vt* to export

exposición [eksposi'θjon] *nf* (*gen*) exposure; (*de arte*) show, exhibition; (*Com*) display; (*feria*) show, fair; (*explicación*) explanation; (*de teoría*) exposition; (*narración*) account, statement

exprés [eks'pres] *adj inv* (*café*) espresso ▷ *nm* (*Ferro*) express (train)

expresamente [ekspresa'mente] *adv* (*decir*) clearly; (*concretamente*) expressly; (*a propósito*) on purpose

expresar [ekspre'sar] *vt* to express; (*redactar*) to phrase, put; (*emoción*) to show; **expresarse** *vr* to express o.s.; (*dato*) to be stated; **como abajo se expresa** as stated below

expresión [ekspre'sjon] *nf* expression; ~ **familiar** colloquialism

expresivo, -a [ekspre'siβo, a] *adj* expressive; (*cariñoso*) affectionate

expreso, -a [eks'preso, a] *adj* (*explícito*) express; (*claro*) specific, clear; (*tren*) fast ▷ *nm* (*Ferro*) fast train

express [eks'pres] *adv* (*Am*): **enviar algo ~** to send sth special delivery

exprimidor [eksprimi'ðor] *nm* (lemon) squeezer

exprimir [ekspri'mir] *vt* (*fruta*) to squeeze; (*zumo*) to squeeze out

ex profeso [ekspro'feso] *adv* expressly

expropiar [ekspro'pjar] *vt* to expropriate

expuesto, -a [eks'pwesto, a] *pp de* **exponer** ▷ *adj* exposed; (*cuadro etc*) on show, on display; **según lo ~ arriba** according to what has been stated above

expulsar [ekspul'sar] *vt* (*echar*) to eject, throw out; (*alumno*) to expel; (*despedir*) to sack, fire; (*Deporte*) to send off

expulsión [ekspul'sjon] *nf* expulsion; sending-off

exquisito, -a [ekski'sito, a] *adj* exquisite; (*comida*) delicious; (*afectado*) affected

éxtasis ['ekstasis] *nm* (*tb droga*) ecstasy

extender [eksten'der] *vt* to extend; (*los brazos*) to stretch out, hold out; (*mapa, tela*) to spread (out), open (out); (*mantequilla*) to spread; (*certificado*) to issue; (*cheque, recibo*) to make out; (*documento*) to draw up; **extenderse** *vr* to extend; (*terreno*) to stretch o spread (out); (*persona: en el suelo*) to stretch out; (*en el tiempo*) to extend, last; (*costumbre, epidemia*) to spread; (*guerra*) to escalate; **~se sobre un tema** to enlarge on a subject

extendido, -a [eksten'diðo, a] *adj* (*abierto*) spread out, open; (*brazos*) outstretched; (*costumbre etc*) widespread

extensión [eksten'sjon] *nf* (*de terreno, mar*) expanse, stretch; (*Mus*) range; (*de conocimientos*) extent; (*de programa*) scope; (*de tiempo*) length, duration; (*Telec*) extension; **~ de plazo** (*Com*) extension; **en toda la ~ de**

la palabra in every sense of the word; **de ~** (*Inform*) add-on

extenso, -a [eks'tenso, a] *adj* extensive

extenuar [ekste'nwar] *vt* (*debilitar*) to weaken

exterior [ekste'rjor] *adj* (*de fuera*) external; (*afuera*) outside, exterior; (*apariencia*) outward; (*deuda, relaciones*) foreign ▷ *nm* exterior, outside; (*aspecto*) outward appearance; (*Deporte*) wing(er); (*países extranjeros*) abroad; **asuntos ~es** foreign affairs; **al ~** outwardly, on the outside; **en el ~** abroad; **noticias del ~** foreign o overseas news

exteriorizar [eksterjori'θar] *vt* (*emociones*) to show, reveal

exterminar [ekstermi'nar] *vt* to exterminate

exterminio [ekster'minjo] *nm* extermination

externo, -a [eks'terno, a] *adj* (*exterior*) external, outside; (*superficial*) outward ▷ *nm/f* day pupil

extinguir [ekstin'gir] *vt* (*fuego*) to extinguish, put out; (*raza, población*) to wipe out; **extinguirse** *vr* (*fuego*) to go out; (*Bio*) to die out, become extinct

extinto, -a [eks'tinto, a] *adj* extinct

extintor [ekstin'tor] *nm* (*fire*) extinguisher

extirpar [ekstir'par] *vt* (*vicios*) to eradicate, stamp out; (*Med*) to remove (surgically)

extra ['ekstra] *adj inv* (*tiempo*) extra; (*vino*) vintage; (*chocolate*) good-quality; (*gasolina*) high-octane ▷ *nm/f* extra ▷ *nm* extra; (*bono*) bonus; (*periódico*) special edition

extracción [ekstrak'θjon] *nf* extraction; (*en lotería*) draw; (*de carbón*) mining

extracto [eks'trakto] *nm* extract

extractor [ekstrak'tor] *nm* (*tb*: **~ de humos**) extractor fan

extradición [ekstraði'θjon] *nf* extradition

extraer [ekstra'er] *vt* to extract, take out

extraescolar [ekstraesko'lar] *adj*: **actividad ~** extracurricular activity

extralimitarse [ekstralimi'tarse] *vr* to go too far

extranjero, -a [ekstran'xero, a] *adj* foreign ▷ *nm/f* foreigner ▷ *nm* foreign countries *pl*; **en el ~** abroad

extrañar [ekstra'ɲar] *vt* (*sorprender*) to find strange o odd; (*echar de menos*) to miss; **extrañarse** *vr* (*sorprenderse*) to be amazed, be surprised; (*distanciarse*) to become estranged, grow apart; **me extraña** I'm surprised

extrañeza [ekstra'ɲeθa] *nf* (*rareza*) strangeness, oddness; (*asombro*) amazement, surprise

extraño, -a [eks'traɲo, a] *adj* (*extranjero*) foreign; (*raro, sorprendente*) strange, odd

extraordinario, -a [ekstraorði'narjo, a] *adj* extraordinary; (*edición, número*) special ▷ *nm* (*de periódico*) special edition; **horas extraordinarias** overtime *sg*

extrarradio [ekstra'rraðjo] *nm* suburbs *pl*

extravagancia [ekstraβa'ɣanθja] nf
oddness; outlandishness; (rareza)
peculiarity; **extravagancias** nfpl (tonterías)
nonsense sg

extravagante [ekstraβa'ɣante] adj
(excéntrico) eccentric; (estrafalario) outlandish

extraviado, -a [ekstra'βjaðo, a] adj lost,
missing

extraviar [ekstra'βjar] vt to mislead,
misdirect; (perder) to lose, misplace;
extraviarse vr to lose one's way, get lost;
(objeto) to go missing, be mislaid

extravío [ekstra'βio] nm loss; (fig)
misconduct

extremar [ekstre'mar] vt to carry to
extremes; **extremarse** vr to do one's utmost,
make every effort

extremaunción [ekstremaun'θjon] nf
extreme unction, last rites pl

extremidad [ekstremi'ðað] nf (punta)
extremity; (fila) edge; **extremidades** nfpl
(Anat) extremities

extremista [ekstre'mista] adj, nm/f
extremist

extremo, -a [eks'tremo, a] adj extreme;
(más alejado) furthest; (último) last ▷ nm end;
(situación) extreme; **E~ Oriente** Far East;
en último ~ as a last resort; **pasar de un ~ a
otro** (fig) to go from one extreme to the
other; **con ~** in the extreme; **la extrema
derecha** (Pol) the far right; **~ derecho/
izquierdo** (Deporte) outside right/left

extrovertido, -a [ekstroβer'tiðo, a] adj
extrovert, outgoing ▷ nm/f extrovert

exuberancia [eksuβe'ranθja] nf exuberance

exuberante [eksuβe'rante] adj exuberant;
(fig) luxuriant, lush

eyaculación [ejakula'θjon] nf ejaculation

eyacular [ejaku'lar] vt, vi to ejaculate

f

fa [fa] nm (Mus) F

fabada [fa'βaða] nf bean and sausage stew

fábrica ['faβrika] nf factory; **~ de moneda**
mint; **marca de ~** trademark; **precio de ~**
factory price

fabricación [faβrika'θjon] nf (manufactura)
manufacture; (producción) production; **de ~
casera** home-made; **~ nacional** home
produced; **~ en serie** mass production

fabricante [faβri'kante] nm/f manufacturer

fabricar [faβri'kar] vt (manufacturar) to
manufacture, make; (construir) to build;
(cuento) to fabricate, devise; **~ en serie** to
mass-produce

fábula ['faβula] nf (cuento) fable; (chisme)
rumour; (mentira) fib

fabuloso, -a [faβu'loso, a] adj fabulous,
fantastic

facción [fak'θjon] nf (Pol) faction; **facciones**
nfpl (del rostro) features

faceta [fa'θeta] nf facet

facha ['fatʃa] (fam) nm/f fascist, right-wing
extremist ▷ nf (aspecto) look; (cara) face; **¡qué
~ tienes!** you look a sight!

fachada [fa'tʃaða] nf (Arq) façade, front; (Tip)
title page; (fig) façade, outward show

facial [fa'θjal] adj facial

fácil ['faθil] adj (simple) easy; (sencillo) simple,
straightforward; (probable) likely; (respuesta)
facile; **~ de usar** (Inform) user-friendly

facilidad [faθili'ðað] nf (capacidad) ease;
(sencillez) simplicity; (de palabra) fluency;

facilidades *nfpl* facilities; "**~es de pago**" (*Com*) "credit facilities", "payment terms"

facilitar [faθili'tar] *vt* (*hacer fácil*) to make easy; (*proporcionar*) to provide; (*documento*) to issue; **le agradecería me ~a ...** I would be grateful if you could let me have ...

fácilmente ['faθilmente] *adv* easily

facsímil [fak'simil] *nm* (*documento*) facsimile; **enviar por ~** to fax

factible [fak'tiβle] *adj* feasible

factor [fak'tor] *nm* factor; (*Com*) agent; (*Ferro*) freight clerk

factura [fak'tura] *nf* (*cuenta*) bill; (*nota de pago*) invoice; (*hechura*) manufacture; **presentar ~ a** to invoice

facturación [faktura'θjon] *nf* (*Com*) invoicing; (: *ventas*) turnover; **~ de equipajes** luggage check-in; **~ online** online check-in

facturar [faktu'rar] *vt* (*Com*) to invoice, charge for; (*Aviat*) to check in; (*equipaje*) to register, check (US)

facultad [fakul'taθ] *nf* (*aptitud, Escol etc*) faculty; (*poder*) power

facultativo, -a [fakulta'tiβo, a] *adj* optional; (*de un oficio*) professional; **prescripción facultativa** medical prescription

faena [fa'ena] *nf* (*trabajo*) work; (*quehacer*) task, job; **~s domésticas** housework *sg*

fagot [fa'ɣot] *nm* (*Mus*) bassoon

faisán [fai'san] *nm* pheasant

faja ['faxa] *nf* (*para la cintura*) sash; (*de mujer*) corset; (*de tierra*) strip

fajo ['faxo] *nm* (*de papeles*) bundle; (*de billetes*) role, wad

falange [fa'lanxe] *nf*: **la F~** (*Pol*) the Falange

falda ['falda] *nf* (*prenda de vestir*) skirt; (*Geo*) foothill; **~ pantalón** culottes *pl*, split skirt; **~ escocesa** kilt

falla ['faʎa] *nf* (*defecto*) fault, flaw; **~ humana** (*Am*) human error

fallar [fa'ʎar] *vt* (*Jur*) to pronounce sentence on; (*Naipes*) to trump ▷ *vi* (*memoria*) to fail; (*plan*) to go wrong; (*motor*) to miss; **~ a algn** to let sb down

Fallas ['faʎas] *nfpl see note*

◉ **FALLAS**
◉
◉ In the week of the 19th of March (the
◉ feast of St Joseph, San José), Valencia
◉ honours its patron saint with a
◉ spectacular *fiesta* called *las Fallas*.
◉ The *Fallas* are huge sculptures, made of
◉ wood, cardboard, paper and cloth,
◉ depicting famous politicians and other
◉ targets for ridicule, which are set alight
◉ and burned by the *falleros*, members of the
◉ competing local groups who have just
◉ spent months preparing them.

fallecer [faʎe'θer] *vi* to pass away, die

fallecimiento [faʎeθi'mjento] *nm* decease, demise

fallido, -a [fa'ʎiðo, a] *adj* vain; (*intento*) frustrated, unsuccessful

fallo ['faʎo] *nm* (*Jur*) verdict, ruling; (*decisión*) decision; (*de jurado*) findings; (*fracaso*) failure; (*Deporte*) miss; (*Inform*) bug; **~ cardíaco** heart failure; **~ humano** (*Esp*) human error

falo ['falo] *nm* phallus

falsear [false'ar] *vt* to falsify; (*firma etc*) to forge ▷ *vi* (*Mus*) to be out of tune

falsedad [false'ðaθ] *nf* falseness; (*hipocresía*) hypocrisy; (*mentira*) falsehood

falsificar [falsifi'kar] *vt* (*firma etc*) to forge; (*voto etc*) to rig; (*moneda*) to counterfeit

falso, -a ['falso, a] *adj* false; (*erróneo*) wrong, mistaken; (*firma, documento*) forged; (*moneda etc*) fake; **en ~** falsely; **dar un paso en ~** to trip; (*fig*) to take a false step

falta ['falta] *nf* (*defecto*) fault, flaw; (*privación*) lack, want; (*ausencia*) absence; (*carencia*) shortage; (*equivocación*) mistake; (*Jur*) default; (*Deporte*) foul; (*Tenis*) fault; **~ de ortografía** spelling mistake; **~ de respeto** disrespect; **echar en ~** to miss; **hacer ~ hacer algo** to be necessary to do sth; **me hace ~ una pluma** I need a pen; **~ de educación** bad manners *pl*; **~ de ortografía** spelling mistake; **sin ~** without fail; **por ~ de** through o for lack of

faltar [fal'tar] *vi* (*escasear*) to be lacking, be wanting; (*ausentarse*) to be absent, be missing; **¿falta algo?** is anything missing?; **falta mucho todavía** there's plenty of time yet; **¿falta mucho?** is there long to go?; **faltan dos horas para llegar** there are two hours to go till arrival; **~ (al respeto) a algn** to be disrespectful to sb; **~ a una cita** to miss an appointment; **~ a la verdad** to lie; **¡no faltaba más!** (*no hay de qué*) don't mention it!

falto, -a ['falto, a] *adj* (*desposeído*) deficient, lacking; (*necesitado*) poor, wretched; **estar ~ de** to be short of

fama ['fama] *nf* (*renombre*) fame; (*reputación*) reputation

famélico, -a [fa'meliko, a] *adj* starving

familia [fa'milja] *nf* family; **~ numerosa** large family; **~ política** in-laws *pl*

familiar [fami'ljar] *adj* (*relativo a la familia*) family *cpd*; (*conocido, informal*) familiar; (*estilo*) informal; (*Ling*) colloquial ▷ *nm/f* relative, relation

familiaridad [familjari'ðaθ] *nf* familiarity; (*informalidad*) homeliness

familiarizarse [familjari'θarse] *vr*: **~ con** to familiarize o.s. with

famoso, -a [fa'moso, a] *adj* (*renombrado*) famous

fan (*pl* **fans**) [fan, fans] *nm* fan

fanático, -a [fa'natiko, a] *adj* fanatical ▷ *nm/f* fanatic; (*Cine, Deporte etc*) fan

fanatismo [fana'tismo] *nm* fanaticism

fanfarrón, -ona [fanfa'rron, ona] *adj*
boastful; (*pey*) showy
fanfarronear [fanfarrone'ar] *vi* to boast
fango ['fango] *nm* mud
fangoso, -a [fan'goso, a] *adj* muddy
fantasía [fanta'sia] *nf* fantasy, imagination;
(*Mus*) fantasia; (*capricho*) whim; **joyas de ~**
imitation jewellery *sg*
fantasma [fan'tasma] *nm* (*espectro*) ghost,
apparition; (*presumido*) show-off
fantástico, -a [fan'tastiko, a] *adj* (*irreal, fam*)
fantastic
fanzine [fan'θine] *nm* fanzine
faquir [fa'kir] *nm* fakir
faraón [fara'on] *nm* Pharaoh
faraónico, -a [fara'oniko, a] *adj* Pharaonic;
(*fig*) grandiose
faringe [fa'rinxe] *nf* pharynx
faringitis [farin'xitis] *nf* pharyngitis
farmacéutico, -a [farma'θeutiko, a] *adj*
pharmaceutical ▷ *nm/f* chemist (*Brit*),
pharmacist
farmacia [far'maθja] *nf* (*ciencia*) pharmacy;
(*tienda*) chemist's (shop) (*Brit*), pharmacy,
drugstore (*US*); **~ de turno** duty chemist;
~ de guardia all-night chemist
fármaco ['farmako] *nm* medicine, drug
faro ['faro] *nm* (*Naut: torre*) lighthouse; (*señal*)
beacon; (*Auto*) headlamp; **~s antiniebla** fog
lamps; **~s delanteros/traseros** headlights/
rear lights
farol [fa'rol] *nm* (*luz*) lantern, lamp; (*Ferro*)
headlamp; (*poste*) lamppost; **echarse un ~**
(*fam*) to show off
farola [fa'rola] *nf* street lamp (*Brit*) o light
(*US*), lamppost
farra ['farra] *nf* (*Am: fam*) party; **ir de ~** to go
on a binge
farsa ['farsa] *nf* farce
farsante [far'sante] *nm/f* fraud, fake
fascículo [fas'θikulo] *nm* part, instalment
(*Brit*), installment (*US*)
fascinar [fasθi'nar] *vt* to fascinate; (*encantar*)
to captivate
fascismo [fas'θismo] *nm* fascism
fascista [fas'θista] *adj, nm/f* fascist
fase ['fase] *nf* phase
fashion ['faʃon] *adj* (*fam*) trendy
fastidiar [fasti'ðjar] *vt* (*disgustar*) to annoy,
bother; (*estropear*) to spoil; **fastidiarse** *vr*
(*disgustarse*) to get annoyed o cross; **¡no
fastidies!** you're joking!; **¡que se fastidie!**
(*fam*) he'll just have to put up with it!
fastidio [fas'tiðjo] *nm* (*disgusto*) annoyance
fastidioso, -a [fasti'ðjoso, a] *adj* (*molesto*)
annoying
fastuoso, -a [fas'twoso, a] *adj* (*espléndido*)
magnificent; (*banquete etc*) lavish
fatal [fa'tal] *adj* (*gen*) fatal; (*desgraciado*)
ill-fated; (*fam: malo, pésimo*) awful ▷ *adv*
terribly; **lo pasó ~** he had a terrible time
(of it)

fatalidad [fatali'ðað] *nf* (*destino*) fate; (*mala
suerte*) misfortune
fatiga [fa'tiɣa] *nf* (*cansancio*) fatigue,
weariness; **fatigas** *nfpl* hardships
fatigar [fati'ɣar] *vt* to tire, weary;
fatigarse *vr* to get tired
fatigoso, -a [fati'ɣoso, a] *adj* (*que cansa*)
tiring
fatuo, -a ['fatwo, a] *adj* (*vano*) fatuous;
(*presuntuoso*) conceited
fauces ['fauθes] *nfpl* (*Anat*) gullet *sg*; (*fam*)
jaws
fauna ['fauna] *nf* fauna
favor [fa'βor] *nm* favour (*Brit*), favor (*US*);
haga el ~ de ... would you be so good as to ...,
kindly ...; **por ~** please; **a ~ in favo(u)r; a ~ de**
in favo(u)r of; (*Com*) to the order of
favorable [faβo'raβle] *adj* favourable (*Brit*),
favorable (*US*); (*condiciones etc*) advantageous
favorecer [faβore'θer] *vt* to favour (*Brit*),
favor (*US*); (*amparar*) to help; (*vestido etc*) to
become, flatter; **este peinado le favorece**
this hairstyle suits him
favorito, -a [faβo'rito, a] *adj, nm/f* favourite
(*Brit*), favorite (*US*)
fax [faks] *nm inv* fax; **mandar por ~** to fax
faz [faθ] *nf* face; **la ~ de la tierra** the face of
the earth
fe [fe] *nf* (*Rel*) faith; (*confianza*) belief;
(*documento*) certificate; **de buena fe** (*Jur*) bona
fide; **prestar fe a** to believe, credit; **actuar
con buena/mala fe** to act in good/bad faith;
dar fe de to bear witness to; **fe de erratas**
errata
fealdad [feal'dað] *nf* ugliness
febrero [fe'βrero] *nm* February; *ver tb* **julio**
febril [fe'βril] *adj* feverish; (*movido*) hectic
fecha ['fetʃa] *nf* date; **~ límite** o **tope** closing
o last day; **~ límite de venta** (*de alimentos*)
sell-by date; **~ de caducidad** (*de alimentos*)
sell-by date; (*de contrato*) expiry date;
con ~ adelantada postdated; **en ~ próxima**
soon; **hasta la ~** to date, so far; **~ de
vencimiento** (*Com*) due date; **~ de vigencia**
(*Com*) effective date
fechar [fe'tʃar] *vt* to date
fechoría [fetʃo'ria] *nf* misdeed
fecundar [fekun'dar] *vt* (*generar*) to fertilize,
make fertile
fecundo, -a [fe'kundo, a] *adj* (*fértil*) fertile;
(*fig*) prolific; (*productivo*) productive
federación [feðera'θjon] *nf* federation
federal [feðe'ral] *adj* federal
felicidad [feliθi'ðað] *nf* (*satisfacción, contento*)
happiness; **felicidades** *nfpl* best wishes,
congratulations; (*en cumpleaños*) happy
birthday
felicitación [feliθita'θjon] *nf* (*tarjeta*)
greetings card; **felicitaciones** *nfpl*
(*enhorabuena*) congratulations; **~ navideña** o
de Navidad Christmas Greetings
felicitar [feliθi'tar] *vt* to congratulate

feligrés, -esa [feli'ɣres, esa] nm/f parishioner

felino, -a [fe'lino, a] adj cat-like; (Zool) feline ▷ nm feline

feliz [fe'liθ] adj (contento) happy; (afortunado) lucky

felpudo [fel'puðo] nm doormat

femenino, -a [feme'nino, a] adj feminine; (Zool etc) female ▷ nm (Ling) feminine

feminista [femi'nista] adj, nm/f feminist

fenomenal [fenome'nal] adj phenomenal; (fam) great, terrific

fenómeno [fe'nomeno] nm phenomenon; (fig) freak, accident ▷ adv: **lo pasamos ~** we had a great time ▷ excl great!, marvellous!

feo, -a ['feo, a] adj (gen) ugly; (desagradable) bad, nasty ▷ nm insult; **hacer un ~ a algn** to offend sb; **más ~ que Picio** as ugly as sin

féretro ['feretro] nm (ataúd) coffin; (sarcófago) bier

feria ['ferja] nf (gen) fair; (Am: mercado) market; (descanso) holiday, rest day; (Am: cambio) small change; (Am: mercado) village market; **~ comercial** trade fair; **~ de muestras** trade show

feriado, -a [fe'rjaðo, a] (Am) adj: **día ~** (public) holiday ▷ nm (public) holiday

fermentar [fermen'tar] vi to ferment

ferocidad [feroθi'ðað] nf fierceness, ferocity

feroz [fe'roθ] adj (cruel) cruel; (salvaje) fierce

férreo, -a ['ferreo, a] adj iron cpd; (Tec) ferrous; (fig) (of) iron

ferretería [ferrete'ria] nf (tienda) ironmonger's (shop) (Brit), hardware store

ferretero [ferre'tero] nm ironmonger

ferrocarril [ferroka'rril] nm railway, railroad (US); **~ de vía estrecha/única** narrow-gauge/single-track railway o line

ferroviario, -a [ferrovja'rjo, a] adj rail cpd, railway cpd (Brit), railroad cpd (US) ▷ nm: **~s** railway (Brit) o railroad (US) workers

ferry ['ferri] (pl **ferrys** o **ferries**) nm ferry

fértil ['fertil] adj (productivo) fertile; (rico) rich

fertilidad [fertili'ðað] nf (gen) fertility; (productividad) fruitfulness

fertilizante [fertili'θante] nm fertilizer

fertilizar [fertili'θar] vt to fertilize

ferviente [fer'βjente] adj fervent

fervor [fer'βor] nm fervour (Brit), fervor (US)

fervoroso, -a [ferβo'roso, a] adj fervent

festejar [feste'xar] vt (agasajar) to wine and dine, fête; (galantear) to court; (celebrar) to celebrate

festejo [fes'texo] nm (diversión) entertainment; (galanteo) courtship; (fiesta) celebration; **festejos** nmpl (fiestas) festivals

festín [fes'tin] nm feast, banquet

festival [festi'βal] nm festival

festividad [festiβi'ðað] nf festivity

festivo, -a [fes'tiβo, a] adj (de fiesta) festive; (fig) witty; (Cine, Lit) humorous; **día ~** holiday

fétido, -a ['fetiðo, a] adj (hediondo) foul-smelling

feto ['feto] nm foetus; (fam) monster

fiable [fi'aβle] adj (persona) trustworthy; (máquina) reliable

fiador, a [fia'ðor, a] nm/f (Jur) surety, guarantor; (Com) backer; **salir ~ por algn** to stand bail for sb

fiambre ['fjambre] adj (Culin) served cold ▷ nm (Culin) cold meat (Brit), cold cut (US); (fam) corpse, stiff

fiambrera [fjam'brera] nf ≈ lunch box, ≈ dinner pail (US)

fianza ['fjanθa] nf surety; (Jur): **libertad bajo ~** release on bail

fiar [fi'ar] vt (salir garante de) to guarantee; (Jur) to stand bail o bond (US) for; (vender a crédito) to sell on credit; (secreto) to confide ▷ vi: **~ (de)** to trust (in); **ser de ~** to be trustworthy; **fiarse** vr: **~se de** to trust (in), rely on; **~se de algn** to rely on sb

fibra ['fiβra] nf fibre (Brit), fiber (US); (fig) vigour (Brit), vigor (US); **~ óptica** (Inform) optical fibre (Brit) o fiber (US)

ficción [fik'θjon] nf fiction

ficha ['fitʃa] nf (Telec) token; (en juegos) counter, marker; (en casino) chip; (Com, Econ) tally, check (US); (Inform) file; (tarjeta) (index) card; (Elec) plug; (en hotel) registration form; **~ policíaca** police dossier

fichaje [fi'tʃaxe] nm signing(-up)

fichar [fi'tʃar] vt (archivar) to file, index; (Deporte) to sign (up) ▷ vi (deportista) to sign (up); (obrero) to clock in o on; **estar fichado** to have a record

fichero [fi'tʃero] nm card index; (archivo) filing cabinet; (Com) box file; (Inform) file, archive; (de policía) criminal records; **~ activo** (Inform) active file; **~ archivado** (Inform) archived file; **~ indexado** (Inform) index file; **~ de reserva** (Inform) backup file; **~ de tarjetas** card index; **nombre de ~** filename

ficticio, -a [fik'tiθjo, a] adj (imaginario) fictitious; (falso) fabricated

fidelidad [fiðeli'ðað] nf (lealtad) fidelity, loyalty; (exactitud: de dato etc) accuracy; **alta ~** high fidelity, hi-fi

fideos [fi'ðeos] nmpl noodles

fiebre ['fjeβre] nf (Med) fever; (fig) fever, excitement; **~ amarilla/del heno** yellow/hay fever; **~ palúdica** malaria; **tener ~** to have a temperature; **~ aftosa** foot-and-mouth disease

fiel [fjel] adj (leal) faithful, loyal; (fiable) reliable; (exacto) accurate ▷ nm (aguja) needle, pointer; **los fieles** nmpl the faithful

fieltro ['fjeltro] nm felt

fiera ['fjera] nf ver **fiero**

fiero, -a ['fjero, a] adj (cruel) cruel; (feroz) fierce; (duro) harsh ▷ nm/f (fig) fiend ▷ nf (animal feroz) wild animal o beast; (fig) dragon

fierro ['fjerro] nm (Am) iron

fiesta ['fjesta] nf party; (de pueblo) festival; **la ~ nacional** bullfighting; **(día de) ~**

(public) holiday; **mañana es ~** it's a holiday tomorrow; **~ mayor** annual festival; **~ patria** (*Am*) independence day; **~ de guardar** (*Rel*) day of obligation; *see note*

⊕ FIESTA

Fiestas can be official public holidays (such as the *Día de la Constitución*), or special holidays for each *comunidad autónoma*, many of which are religious feast days. All over Spain there are also special local *fiestas* for a patron saint or the Virgin Mary. These often last several days and can include religious processions, carnival parades, bullfights, dancing and feasts of typical local produce.

figura [fi'ɣura] *nf* (*gen*) figure; (*forma, imagen*) shape, form; (*Naipes*) face card
figurado, -a [fiɣu'raðo, a] *adj* figurative
figurante [fiɣu'rante] *nm/f* (*Teat*) walk-on part; (*Cine*) extra
figurar [fiɣu'rar] *vt* (*representar*) to represent; (*fingir*) to feign ▷ *vi* to figure; **figurarse** *vr* (*imaginarse*) to imagine; (*suponer*) to suppose; **ya me lo figuraba** I thought as much
fijador [fixa'ðor] *nm* (*Foto etc*) fixative; (*de pelo*) gel
fijar [fi'xar] *vt* (*gen*) to fix; (*cartel*) to post, put up; (*estampilla*) to affix, stick (on); (*pelo*) to set; (*fig*) to settle (on), decide; **fijarse** *vr*: **~se en** to notice; **¡fíjate!** just imagine!; **¿te fijas?** see what I mean?
fijo, -a ['fixo, a] *adj* (*gen*) fixed; (*firme*) firm; (*permanente*) permanent; (*trabajo*) steady; (*colorfast*) fast ▷ *adv*: **mirar ~** to stare
fila ['fila] *nf* row; (*Mil*) rank; (*cadena*) line; (*en marcha*) file; **~ india** single file; **ponerse en ~** to line up, get into line; **primera ~** front row
filántropo, -a [fi'lantropo, a] *nm/f* philanthropist
filatelia [fila'telja] *nf* philately, stamp collecting
filete [fi'lete] *nm* (*de carne*) fillet steak; (*de cerdo*) tenderloin; (*pescado*) fillet; (*Mecánica: rosca*) thread
filiación [filja'θjon] *nf* (*Pol etc*) affiliation; (*señas*) particulars *pl*; (*Mil, Policía*) records *pl*
filial [fi'ljal] *adj* filial ▷ *nf* subsidiary; (*sucursal*) branch
Filipinas [fili'pinas] *nfpl*: **las (Islas) ~** the Philippines
filipino, -a [fili'pino, a] *adj, nm/f* Philippine
film [film] (*pl* **films**) *nm* = **filme**
filmar [fil'mar] *vt* to film, shoot
filme ['filme] *nm* film, movie (*US*)
filo ['filo] *nm* (*gen*) edge; **sacar ~ a** to sharpen; **al ~ del medio día** at about midday; **de doble ~** double-edged

filología [filolo'xia] *nf* philology; **~ inglesa** (*Univ*) English Studies
filón [fi'lon] *nm* (*Minería*) vein, lode; (*fig*) gold mine
filosofía [filoso'fia] *nf* philosophy
filósofo, -a [fi'losofo, a] *nm/f* philosopher
filtrar [fil'trar] *vt, vi* to filter, strain; (*información*) to leak; **filtrarse** *vr* to filter; (*fig: dinero*) to dwindle
filtro ['filtro] *nm* (*Tec, utensilio*) filter
fin [fin] *nm* end; (*objetivo*) aim, purpose; **a ~ de cuentas** at the end of the day; **al ~ y al cabo** when all's said and done; **a ~ de** in order to; **por ~** finally; **en ~** (*resumiendo*) in short; **¡en ~!** (*resignación*) oh, well!; **~ de archivo** (*Inform*) end-of-file; **~ de semana** weekend; **sin ~** endless(ly)
final [fi'nal] *adj* final ▷ *nm* end, conclusion ▷ *nf* (*Deporte*) final; **al ~** in the end; **a ~es de** at the end of
finalidad [finali'ðað] *nf* finality; (*propósito*) purpose, aim
finalista [fina'lista] *nm/f* finalist
finalizar [finali'θar] *vt* to end, finish ▷ *vi* to end, come to an end; **~ la sesión** (*Inform*) to log out o off
financiar [finan'θjar] *vt* to finance
financiero, -a [finan'θjero, a] *adj* financial ▷ *nm/f* financier
finanzas [fi'nanθas] *nfpl* finances
finca ['finka] *nf* (*casa de recreo*) house in the country; (*Esp: bien inmueble*) property, land; (*Am: granja*) farm
finde ['finde] *nm abbr* (*fam*: = *fin de semana*) weekend
fingir [fin'xir] *vt* (*simular*) to simulate, feign; (*pretextar*) to sham, fake ▷ *vi* (*aparentar*) to pretend; **fingirse** *vr*: **~se dormido** to pretend to be asleep
finlandés, -esa [finlan'des, esa] *adj* Finnish ▷ *nm/f* Finn ▷ *nm* (*Ling*) Finnish
Finlandia [fin'landja] *nf* Finland
fino, -a ['fino, a] *adj* fine; (*delgado*) slender; (*de buenas maneras*) polite, refined; (*inteligente*) shrewd; (*punta*) sharp; (*gusto*) discriminating; (*oído*) sharp; (*jerez*) fino, dry ▷ *nm* (*jerez*) dry sherry
firma ['firma] *nf* signature; (*Com*) firm, company
firmamento [firma'mento] *nm* firmament
firmante [fir'mante] *adj, nm/f* signatory; **los abajo ~s** the undersigned
firmar [fir'mar] *vt* to sign; **~ un contrato** (*Com: colocarse*) to sign on; **firmado y sellado** signed and sealed
firme ['firme] *adj* firm; (*estable*) stable; (*sólido*) solid; (*constante*) steady; (*decidido*) resolute; (*duro*) hard; **¡~s!** (*Mil*) attention!; **oferta en ~** (*Com*) firm offer ▷ *nm* road (surface)
firmemente [firme'mente] *adv* firmly
firmeza [fir'meθa] *nf* firmness; (*constancia*) steadiness; (*solidez*) solidity

fiscal [fis'kal] *adj* fiscal ▷ *nm* (*Jur*) public prosecutor, ≈ district attorney (*US*); **año ~ tax** o fiscal year

fisco ['fisko] *nm* (*hacienda*) treasury, exchequer; **declarar algo al ~** to declare sth for tax purposes

fisgar [fis'ɣar] *vt* to pry into

fisgón, -ona [fis'ɣon, ona] *adj* nosey

fisgonear [fisɣone'ar] *vt* to poke one's nose into ▷ *vi* to pry, spy

físico, -a ['fisiko, a] *adj* physical ▷ *nm* physique; (*aspecto*) appearance, looks *pl* ▷ *nm/f* physicist ▷ *nf* physics *sg*

fisioterapia [fisjote'rapja] *nf* physiotherapy

fisura [fi'sura] *nf* crack; (*Med*) fracture

fláccido, -a ['flakθiðo, a], **flácido, -a** ['flaθiðo, a] *adj* flabby

flaco, -a ['flako, a] *adj* (*muy delgado*) skinny, thin; (*débil*) weak, feeble

flagrante [fla'ɣrante] *adj* flagrant

flama ['flama] *nf* (*Am*) flame

flamable [fla'maβle] *adj* (*Am*) flammable

flamante [fla'mante] *adj* (*fam*) brilliant; (: *nuevo*) brand-new

flamenco, -a [fla'menko, a] *adj* (*de Flandes*) Flemish; (*baile, música*) flamenco ▷ *nm/f* Fleming; **los ~s** the Flemish ▷ *nm* (*Ling*) Flemish; (*baile, música*) flamenco; (*Zool*) flamingo

flamingo [fla'mingo] *nm* (*Am*) flamingo

flan [flan] *nm* creme caramel

flaquear [flake'ar] *vi* (*debilitarse*) to weaken; (*persona*) to slack

flaqueza [fla'keθa] *nf* (*delgadez*) thinness, leanness; (*fig*) weakness

flash [flaʃ] (*pl* **flashes**) [flas] *nm* (*Foto*) flash; (*Inform*): **~ drive** flash drive

flauta ['flauta] (*Mus*) *nf* flute ▷ *nm/f* flautist, flute player; **¡la gran ~!** (*Am*: *fam!*) my God!; **hijo de la gran ~** (*Am*: *fam!*) bastard (!), son of a bitch (*US!*)

flecha ['fletʃa] *nf* arrow

flechazo [fle'tʃaθo] *nm* (*acción*) bowshot; (*fam*): **fue un ~** it was love at first sight

fleco ['fleko] *nm* fringe

flema ['flema] *nm* phlegm

flemón [fle'mon] *nm* (*Med*) gumboil

flequillo [fle'kiʎo] *nm* (*de pelo*) fringe, bangs (*US*)

flete ['flete] *nm* (*carga*) freight; (*alquiler*) charter; (*precio*) freightage; **~ debido** (*Com*) freight forward; **~ sobre compras** (*Com*) freight inward

flexible [flek'siβle] *adj* flexible; (*individuo*) compliant

flexión [flek'sjon] *nf* (*Deporte*) bend; (: *en el suelo*) press-up

flexo ['flekso] *nm* adjustable table lamp

flipper ['fliper] *nm* pinball machine

flirtear [flirte'ar] *vi* to flirt

flojear [floxe'ar] *vi* (*piernas*: *al andar*) to give

way; (*alumno*) to do badly; (*cosecha, mercado*) to be poor

flojera [flo'xera] *nf* (*Am*) laziness; **me da ~** I can't be bothered

flojo, -a ['floxo, a] *adj* (*gen*) loose; (*sin fuerzas*) limp; (*débil*) weak; (*viento*) light; (*bebida*) weak; (*trabajo*) poor; (*actitud*) slack; (*precio*) low; (*Com*: *mercado*) dull, slack; (*Am*) lazy

flor [flor] *nf* flower; (*piropo*) compliment; **la ~ y nata de la sociedad** (*fig*) the cream of society; **en la ~ de la vida** in the prime of life; **a ~ de** on the surface of

flora ['flora] *nf* flora

florecer [flore'θer] *vi* (*Bot*) to flower, bloom; (*fig*) to flourish

floreciente [flore'θjente] *adj* (*Bot*) in flower, flowering; (*fig*) thriving

florería [flore'ria] *nf* (*Am*) florist's (shop)

florero [flo'rero] *nm* vase

florista [flo'rista] *nm/f* florist

floristería [floriste'ria] *nf* florist's (shop)

flota ['flota] *nf* fleet

flotador [flota'ðor] *nm* (*gen*) float; (*para nadar*) rubber ring; (*de cisterna*) ballcock

flotar [flo'tar] *vi* to float

flote ['flote] *nm*: **a ~** afloat; **salir a ~** (*fig*) to get back on one's feet

fluctuar [fluk'twar] *vi* (*oscilar*) to fluctuate

fluidez [flui'ðeθ] *nf* fluidity; (*fig*) fluency

fluido, -a ['flwiðo, a] *adj* fluid; (*lenguaje*) fluent; (*estilo*) smooth ▷ *nm* (*líquido*) fluid

fluir [flu'ir] *vi* to flow

flujo ['fluxo] *nm* flow; (*Pol*) swing; (*Naut*) rising tide; **~ y reflujo** ebb and flow; **~ de sangre** (*Med*) haemorrhage (*Brit*), hemorrhage (*US*); **~ positivo/negativo de efectivo** (*Com*) positive/negative cash flow

flúor ['fluor] *nm* fluorine; (*en dentífrico*) fluoride

fluorescente [flwores'θente] *adj* fluorescent ▷ *nm* (*tb*: **tubo ~**) fluorescent tube

fluvial [fluβi'al] *adj* (*navegación, cuenca*) fluvial, river *cpd*

FMI *nm abr* (= *Fondo Monetario Internacional*) IMF

fobia ['fobja] *nf* phobia; **~ a las alturas** fear of heights

foca ['foka] *nf* seal

foco ['foko] *nm* focus; (*centro*) focal point; (*fuente*) source; (*de incendio*) seat; (*Elec*) floodlight; (*Teat*) spotlight; (*Am*) (light) bulb, light

fofo, -a ['fofo, a] *adj* (*esponjoso*) soft, spongy; (*músculo*) flabby

fogata [fo'ɣata] *nf* (*hoguera*) bonfire

fogón [fo'ɣon] *nm* (*de cocina*) ring, burner

fogoso, -a [fo'ɣoso, a] *adj* spirited

folio ['foljo] *nm* (*hoja*) sheet (of paper), page

folklore [fol'klore] *nm* folklore

folklórico, -a [fol'kloriko, a] *adj* traditional

follaje [fo'ʎaxe] *nm* foliage

follar [fo'ʎar] *vt, vi* (*fam!*) to fuck (!)

folleto [fo'ʎeto] *nm* pamphlet; (*Com*) brochure; (*prospecto*) leaflet; (*Escol etc*) handout

follón [fo'ʎon] *nm* (*fam*: *lío*) mess; (: *conmoción*) fuss, rumpus, shindy; **armar un ~** to kick up a fuss; **se armó un ~** there was a hell of a row

fomentar [fomen'tar] *vt* (*Med*) to foment; (*fig*: *promover*) to promote, foster; (*odio etc*) to stir up

fomento [fo'mento] *nm* (*fig*: *ayuda*) fostering; (*promoción*) promotion

fonda ['fonda] *nf* ≈ boarding house; *ver tb* **hotel**

fondo ['fondo] *nm* (*de caja etc*) bottom; (*medida*) depth; (*de coche, sala*) back; (*Arte etc*) background; (*reserva*) fund; (*fig*: *carácter*) nature; **fondos** *nmpl* (*Com*) funds, resources; **~ de escritorio** (*Inform*) wallpaper; **F~ Monetario Internacional** International Monetary Fund; **~ del mar** sea bed *o* floor; **una investigación a ~** a thorough investigation; **en el ~** at bottom, deep down; **tener buen ~** to be good-natured

fonética [fo'netika] *nf* phonetics *sg*

fono ['fono] *nm* (*Am*) telephone (number)

fonobuzón [fonoβu'θon] *nm* voice mail

fontanería [fontane'ria] *nf* plumbing

fontanero [fonta'nero] *nm* plumber

footing ['futin] *nm* jogging; **hacer ~** to jog

forastero, -a [foras'tero, a] *nm/f* stranger

forcejear [forθexe'ar] *vi* (*luchar*) to struggle

fórceps ['forθeps] *nm inv* forceps *pl*

forense [fo'rense] *adj* forensic ▷ *nm/f* pathologist

forestal [fores'tal] *adj* forest *cpd*

forjar [for'xar] *vt* to forge; (*formar*) to form

forma ['forma] *nf* (*figura*) form, shape; (*molde*) mould, pattern; (*Med*) fitness; (*método*) way, means; **estar en ~** to be fit; **~ de pago** (*Com*) method of payment; **las ~s** the conventions; **de ~ que ...** so that ...; **de todas ~s** in any case

formación [forma'θjon] *nf* (*gen*) formation; (*enseñanza*) training; **~ profesional** vocational training; **~ fuera del trabajo** off-the-job training; **~ en el trabajo** *o* **sobre la práctica** on-the-job training

formal [for'mal] *adj* (*gen*) formal; (*fig*: *persona*) serious; (: *ooo*: *de fiar*) reliable; (*conducta*) steady

formalidad [formali'ðað] *nf* formality; seriousness; reliability; steadiness

formalizar [formali'θar] *vt* (*Jur*) to formalize; (*plan*) to draw up; (*situación*) to put in order, regularize; **formalizarse** *vr* (*situación*) to be put in order, be regularized

formar [for'mar] *vt* (*componer*) to form, shape; (*constituir*) to make up, constitute; (*Escol*) to train, educate ▷ *vi* (*Mil*) to fall in; (*Deporte*) to line up; **formarse** *vr* (*Escol*) to be trained (*o* educated); (*cobrar forma*) to form, take form; (*desarrollarse*) to develop

formatear [formate'ar] *vt* (*Inform*) to format

formato [for'mato] *nm* (*Inform*) format; **sin ~** (*disco, texto*) unformatted; **~ de registro** record format

formidable [formi'ðaβle] *adj* (*temible*) formidable; (*asombroso*) tremendous

fórmula ['formula] *nf* formula

formular [formu'lar] *vt* (*queja*) to lodge; (*petición*) to draw up; (*pregunta*) to pose, formulate; (*idea*) to formulate

formulario [formu'larjo] *nm* form; **~ de solicitud/de pedido** (*Com*) application/order form; **llenar un ~** to fill in a form; **~ continuo desplegable** (*Inform*) fanfold paper

fornido, -a [for'niðo, a] *adj* well-built

foro ['foro] *nm* (*gen*) forum; (*Jur*) court; **~ de debate/discusión** (*Internet*) discussion forum, message board

forrar [fo'rrar] *vt* (*abrigo*) to line; (*libro*) to cover; (*coche*) to upholster; **forrarse** *vr* (*fam*) to line one's pockets

forro ['forro] *nm* (*de cuaderno*) cover; (*costura*) lining; (*de sillón*) upholstery; **~ polar** fleece

fortalecer [fortale'θer] *vt* to strengthen; **fortalecerse** *vr* to fortify o.s.; (*opinión etc*) to become stronger

fortaleza [forta'leθa] *nf* (*Mil*) fortress, stronghold; (*fuerza*) strength; (*determinación*) resolution

fortuito, -a [for'twito, a] *adj* accidental, chance *cpd*

fortuna [for'tuna] *nf* (*suerte*) fortune, (good) luck; (*riqueza*) fortune, wealth

forzar [for'θar] *vt* (*puerta*) to force (open); (*compeler*) to compel; (*violar*) to rape; (*ojos etc*) to strain

forzoso, -a [for'θoso, a] *adj* necessary; (*inevitable*) inescapable; (*obligatorio*) compulsory

fosa ['fosa] *nf* (*sepultura*) grave; (*en tierra*) pit; (*Med*) cavity; **~s nasales** nostrils

fosforescente [fosfores'θente] *adj* phosphorescent

fósforo ['fosforo] *nm* (*Química*) phosphorus; (*esp Am*: *cerilla*) match

fósil ['fosil] *adj* fossil, fossilized ▷ *nm* fossil

foso ['foso] *nm* ditch; (*Teat*) pit; (*Auto*): **~ de reconocimiento** inspection pit

foto ['foto] *nf* photo, snap(shot); **sacar una ~** to take a photo *o* picture; **~ (de) carné** passport(-size) photo

fotocopia [foto'kopja] *nf* photocopy

fotocopiadora [fotokopja'ðora] *nf* photocopier

fotocopiar [fotoko'pjar] *vt* to photocopy

fotogénico, -a [foto'xeniko, a] *adj* photogenic

fotografía [fotoɣra'fia] *nf* (*arte*) photography; (*una fotografía*) photograph

fotografiar [fotoɣra'fjar] *vt* to photograph

fotógrafo, -a [fo'toɣrafo, a] *nm/f*
photographer

fotomatón [fotoma'ton] *nm (cabina)* photo
booth

fotonovela [fotono'βela] *nf* photo-story

FP *nf abr (Esp: Escol, Com)* = **Formación
Profesional** ▷ *nm abr (Pol)* = **Frente Popular**

frac *(pl* **fracs** *o* **fraques)** [frak, 'frakes] *nm*
dress coat, tails

fracasar [fraka'sar] *vi (gen)* to fail; *(plan etc)* to
fall through

fracaso [fra'kaso] *nm (desgracia, revés)* failure;
(de negociaciones etc) collapse, breakdown

fracción [frak'θjon] *nf* fraction; *(Pol)* faction,
splinter group

fraccionamiento [fraksjona'mjento] *nm*
(Am) housing estate

fractura [frak'tura] *nf* fracture, break

fragancia [fra'ɣanθja] *nf (olor)* fragrance,
perfume

fraganti [fra'ɣanti]: **in ~** *adv:* **coger a algn in
fraganti** to catch sb red-handed

fragata [fra'ɣata] *nf* frigate

frágil ['fraxil] *adj (débil)* fragile; *(Com)*
breakable; *(fig)* frail, delicate

fragmento [fraɣ'mento] *nm* fragment;
(pedazo) piece; *(de discurso)* excerpt; *(de canción)*
snatch

fragua ['fraɣwa] *nf* forge

fraguar [fra'ɣwar] *vt* to forge; *(fig)* to concoct
▷ *vi* to harden

fraile ['fraile] *nm (Rel)* friar; *(: monje)* monk

frambuesa [fram'bwesa] *nf* raspberry

francés, -esa [fran'θes, esa] *adj* French ▷ *nm/f*
Frenchman(-woman) ▷ *nm (Ling)* French

Francia ['franθja] *nf* France

franco, -a ['franko, a] *adj (cándido)* frank,
open; *(Com: exento)* free ▷ *nm (moneda)* franc;
~ de derechos duty-free; **~ al costado del
buque** *(Com)* free alongside ship; **~ puesto
sobre vagón** *(Com)* free on rail; **~ a bordo**
free on board

francotirador, a [frankotira'ðor, a] *nm/f*
sniper

franela [fra'nela] *nf* flannel

franja ['franxa] *nf* fringe; *(de uniforme)* stripe;
(de tierra etc) strip

franquear [franke'ar] *vt (camino)* to clear;
(carta, paquete) to frank, stamp; *(obstáculo)* to
overcome; *(Com etc)* to free, exempt

franqueo [fran'keo] *nm* postage

franqueza [fran'keθa] *nf* frankness

franquismo [fran'kismo] *nm:* **el ~** *(sistema)*
the Franco system; *(período)* the Franco years;
see note

franquista [fran'kista] *adj* pro-Franco ▷ *nm/f*
supporter of Franco

frasco ['frasko] *nm* bottle, flask; **~ al vacío**
(vacuum) flask

frase ['frase] *nf* sentence; *(locución)* phrase,
expression; **~ hecha** set phrase; *(pey)*
stock phrase

fraternal [frater'nal] *adj* brotherly, fraternal

fraterno, -a [fra'terno, a] *adj* brotherly,
fraternal

fraude ['frauðe] *nm (cualidad)* dishonesty;
(acto) fraud, swindle

fraudulento, -a [frauðu'lento, a] *adj*
fraudulent

frazada [fra'saða] *nf (Am)* blanket

frecuencia [fre'kwenθja] *nf* frequency; **con
~** frequently, often; **~ de red** *(Inform)* mains
frequency; **~ del reloj** *(Inform)* clock speed;
~ telefónica voice frequency

frecuentar [frekwen'tar] *vt (lugar)* to
frequent; *(persona)* to see frequently *o* often;
~ la buena sociedad to mix in high society

frecuente [fre'kwente] *adj* frequent;
(costumbre) common; *(vicio)* rife

fregadero [freɣa'ðero] *nm (kitchen)* sink

fregar [fre'ɣar] *vt (frotar)* to scrub; *(platos)* to
wash (up); *(Am: fam: fastidiar)* to annoy;
(: malograr) to screw up

freidora [frei'ðora] *nf* deep-fat fryer

freír [fre'ir] *vt* to fry

frenar [fre'nar] *vt* to brake; *(fig)* to check

frenazo [fre'naθo] *nm:* **dar un ~** to brake
sharply

frenesí [frene'si] *nm* frenzy

frenético, -a [fre'netiko, a] *adj* frantic;
ponerse ~ to lose one's head

freno ['freno] *nm (Tec, Auto)* brake; *(de
cabalgadura)* bit; *(fig)* check; **~ de mano**
handbrake

frente ['frente] *nm (Arq, Mil, Pol)* front; *(de
objeto)* front part ▷ *nf* forehead, brow; **~ de
batalla** battle front; **hacer ~ común con
algn** to make common cause with sb; **~ a** in
front of; *(en situación opuesta a)* opposite;
chocar de ~ to crash head-on; **hacer ~ a** to
face up to

fresa ['fresa] *nf (Esp: fruta)* strawberry; *(de
dentista)* drill

fresco, -a ['fresko, a] *adj (nuevo)* fresh; *(huevo)*
newly-laid; *(frío)* cool; *(descarado)* cheeky,
bad-mannered ▷ *nm (aire)* fresh air; *(Arte)*
fresco; *(Am: bebida)* fruit juice *o* drink ▷ *nm/f*
(fam) shameless person; *(persona insolente)*
impudent person; **tomar el ~** to get some
fresh air; **ser un ~** to have a nerve; **¡qué ~!**
what a cheek!

frescura [fres'kura] *nf* freshness; *(descaro)*
cheek, nerve; *(calma)* calmness

frialdad [frjal'dað] *nf (gen)* coldness;
(indiferencia) indifference

fricción [frik'θjon] *nf (gen)* friction; *(acto)*
rub(bing); *(Med)* massage; *(Pol, fig etc)*
friction, trouble

frigidez [frixi'ðeθ] *nf* frigidity

frigo ['friɣo] *nm* fridge

frigorífico, -a [friɣo'rifiko, a] *adj*
refrigerating ▷ *nm* refrigerator; *(camión)*
freezer lorry *o* truck (US); **instalación
frigorífica** cold-storage plant

frijol [fri'xol], **fríjol** ['frixol] *nm* kidney bean

frío, -a *etc* ['frio, a] *vb ver* **freír** ▷ *adj* cold; *(fig: indiferente)* unmoved, indifferent; *(poco entusiasta)* chilly ▷ *nm* cold(ness); indifference; **hace ~** it's cold; **tener ~** to be cold; **¡qué ~!** how cold it is!

frito, -a ['frito, a] *pp de* **freír** ▷ *adj* fried ▷ *nm* fry; **me trae ~ ese hombre** I'm sick and tired of that man; **fritos** *nmpl* fried food; **~s variados** mixed grill

frívolo, -a ['friβolo, a] *adj* frivolous

frontal [fron'tal] *adj* frontal ▷ *nm*: **choque ~** head-on collision

frontera [fron'tera] *nf* frontier; *(línea divisoria)* border; *(zona)* frontier area

fronterizo, -a [fronte'riθo, a] *adj* frontier *cpd*; *(contiguo)* bordering

frontón [fron'ton] *nm* *(Deporte: cancha)* pelota court; *(: juego)* pelota

frotar [fro'tar] *vt* to rub; *(fósforo)* to strike; **frotarse** *vr*: **~se las manos** to rub one's hands

fructífero, -a [fruk'tifero, a] *adj* productive, fruitful

frugal [fru'ɣal] *adj* frugal

fruncir [frun'θir] *vt* to pucker; *(Costura)* to gather; *(ceño)* to frown; *(labios)* to purse; **~ el ceño** to knit one's brow

frustración [frustra'θjon] *nf* frustration

frustrar [frus'trar] *vt* to frustrate; **frustrarse** *vr* to be frustrated; *(plan etc)* to fail

fruta ['fruta] *nf* fruit

frutería [frute'ria] *nf* fruit shop

frutero, -a [fru'tero, a] *adj* fruit *cpd* ▷ *nm/f* fruiterer ▷ *nm* fruit dish o bowl

frutilla [fru'tiʎa] *nf* *(Am)* strawberry

fruto ['fruto] *nm* *(Bot)* fruit; *(fig: resultado)* result, outcome; *(: beneficio)* benefit; **~s secos** nuts and dried fruit

fucsia ['fuksja] *nf* fuchsia

fue [fwe] *vb ver* **ser, ir**

fuego ['fweɣo] *nm* *(gen)* fire; *(Culin: gas)* burner, ring; *(Mil)* fire; *(fig: pasión)* fire, passion; **~ amigo** friendly fire; **~s artificiales** o **de artificio** fireworks; **prender ~ a** to set fire to; **a ~ lento** on a low flame o gas; **¡alto el ~!** cease fire!; **entre dos ~s** to be in the crossfire; **¿tienes ~?** have you (got) a light?

fuente ['fwente] *nf* fountain; *(manantial, fig)* spring; *(origen)* source; *(plato)* large dish; **~ de alimentación** *(Inform)* power supply; **de ~ desconocida/fidedigna** from an unknown/ reliable source

fuera ['fwera] *vb ver* **ser, ir** ▷ *adv* out(side); *(en otra parte)* away; *(excepto, salvo)* except, save ▷ *prep*: **~ de** outside; *(fig)* besides; **~ de alcance** out of reach; **~ de combate** out of action; *(boxeo)* knocked out; **~ de sí** beside o.s.; **por ~** (on the) outside; **los de ~** strangers, newcomers; **estar ~** *(en el extranjero)* to be abroad

fuera-borda [fwera'βorða] *nm inv* *(barco)* speedboat; *(motor)* outboard engine o motor

fuero ['fwero] *nm* *(carta municipal)* municipal charter; *(leyes locales)* local o regional law code; *(privilegio)* privilege; *(autoridad)* jurisdiction; *(fig)*: **en mi** *etc* **~ interno ...** in my *etc* heart of hearts ..., deep down ...

fuerte ['fwerte] *adj* strong; *(golpe)* hard; *(ruido)* loud; *(comida)* rich; *(lluvia)* heavy; *(dolor)* intense ▷ *adv* strongly; hard; loud(ly) ▷ *nm* *(Mil)* fort, strongpoint; *(fig)*: **ser ~ en** to be good at; **el canto no es mi ~** singing is not my strong point

fuerza ['fwerθa] *vb ver* **forzar** ▷ *nf* *(fortaleza)* strength; *(Tec, Elec)* power; *(coacción)* force; *(violencia)* violence; *(Mil: tb: **~s**)* forces *pl*; **~ de arrastre** *(Tec)* pulling power; **~ de brazos** manpower; **~ mayor** force majeure; **~ bruta** brute force; **~s armadas** (FF.AA.) armed forces; **~ del orden público** (F.O.P.) police (forces); **~s aéreas** air force *sg*; **~ vital** vitality; **a ~ de** by (dint of); **cobrar ~s** to recover one's strength; **tener ~s para** to have the strength to; **hacer algo a la ~** to be forced to do sth; **con ~ legal** *(Com)* legally binding; **a la ~** forcibly, by force; **por ~** of necessity; **~ de voluntad** willpower

fuga ['fuɣa] *nf* *(huida)* flight, escape; *(de enamorados)* elopement; *(de gas etc)* leak; **~ de cerebros** *(fig)* brain drain

fugarse [fu'ɣarse] *vr* to flee, escape

fugaz [fu'ɣaθ] *adj* fleeting

fugitivo, -a [fuxi'tiβo, a] *adj* fugitive, fleeing ▷ *nm/f* fugitive

fui *etc* [fwi] *vb ver* **ser, ir**

fulano, -a [fu'lano, a] *nm/f* so-and-so, what's-his-name

fulgor [ful'ɣor] *nm* brilliance

fulminante [fulmi'nante] *adj* *(pólvora)* fulminating; *(fig: mirada)* withering; *(Med)* sudden, serious; *(fam)* terrific, tremendous; *(éxito, golpe)* sudden; **ataque ~** stroke

fulminar [fulmi'nar] *vt*: **caer fulminado por un rayo** to be struck down by lightning; **~ a algn con la mirada** to look daggers at sb

fumador, a [fuma'ðor, a] *nm/f* smoker; **no ~** non-smoker

fumar [fu'mar] *vt, vi* to smoke; **fumarse** *vr* *(disipar)* to squander; **~ en pipa** to smoke a pipe

fumigar [fumi'ɣar] *vt* to fumigate

funámbulo, -a [fu'nambulo, a], **funambulista** [funambu'lista] *nm/f* tightrope walker

función [fun'θjon] *nf* function; *(de puesto)* duties *pl*; *(Teat etc)* show; **entrar en funciones** to take up one's duties; **~ de tarde/de noche** matinée/evening performance

funcional [funθjo'nal] *adj* functional

funcionamiento [funθjona'mjento] *nm* functioning; *(Tec)* working; **en ~** *(Com)* on stream; **entrar en ~** to come into operation

funcionar [funθjo'nar] vi (gen) to function; (máquina) to work; **"no funciona"** "out of order"

funcionario, -a [funθjo'narjo, a] nm/f official; (público) civil servant

funda ['funda] nf (gen) cover; (de almohada) pillowcase; ~ **protectora del disco** (Inform) disk-jacket

fundación [funda'θjon] nf foundation

fundamental [fundamen'tal] adj fundamental, basic

fundamentalismo [fundamenta'lismo] nm fundamentalism

fundamentalista [fundamenta'lista] adj, nm/f fundamentalist

fundamentar [fundamen'tar] vt (poner base) to lay the foundations of; (establecer) to found; (fig) to base

fundamento [funda'mento] nm (base) foundation; (razón) grounds pl; **eso carece de ~** that is groundless

fundar [fun'dar] vt to found; (crear) to set up; (fig: basar): ~ **(en)** to base o found (on); **fundarse** vr: **~se en** to be founded on

fundición [fundi'θjon] nf (acción) smelting; (fábrica) foundry; (Tip) font

fundir [fun'dir] vt (gen) to fuse; (metal) to smelt, melt down; (nieve etc) to melt; (Com) to merge; (estatua) to cast; **fundirse** vr (colores etc) to merge, blend; (unirse) to fuse together; (Elec: fusible, lámpara etc) to blow; (nieve etc) to melt

fúnebre ['funeβre] adj funeral cpd, funereal

funeral [fune'ral] nm funeral

funeraria [fune'rarja] nf undertaker's (Brit), mortician's (US)

funesto, -a [fu'nesto, a] adj ill-fated; (desastroso) fatal

funicular [funiku'lar] nm (tren) funicular; (teleférico) cable car

furgón [fur'ɣon] nm wagon

furgoneta [furɣo'neta] nf (Auto, Com) (transit) van (Brit), pickup (truck) (US)

furia ['furja] nf (ira) fury; (violencia) violence

furibundo, -a [furi'βundo, a] adj furious

furioso, -a [fu'rjoso, a] adj (iracundo) furious; (violento) violent

furor [fu'ror] nm (cólera) rage; (pasión) frenzy, passion; **hacer ~** to be a sensation

furtivo, -a [fur'tiβo, a] adj furtive ▷ nm poacher

furúnculo [fu'runkulo] nm (Med) boil

fusible [fu'siβle] nm fuse

fusil [fu'sil] nm rifle

fusilar [fusi'lar] vt to shoot

fusión [fu'sjon] nf (gen) melting; (unión) fusion; (Com) merger, amalgamation

fusta ['fusta] nf (látigo) riding crop

fútbol ['futβol] nm football (Brit), soccer (US); ~ **americano** American football (Brit), football (US); ~ **sala** indoor football (Brit) o soccer (US)

futbolín [futβo'lin] nm table football

futbolista [futβo'lista] nm/f footballer

fútil ['futil] adj trifling

futilidad [futili'ðað], **futileza** [futi'leθa] nf triviality

futón [fu'ton] nm futon

futuro, -a [fu'turo, a] adj future ▷ nm future; (Ling) future tense; **futuros** nmpl (Com) futures

g

gabacho, -a [ga'βatʃo, a] *adj* Pyrenean; *(fam)* Frenchified ▷ *nm/f* Pyrenean villager; *(fam)* Frenchy
gabán [ga'βan] *nm* overcoat
gabardina [gaβar'ðina] *nf (tela)* gabardine; *(prenda)* raincoat
gabinete [gaβi'nete] *nm (Pol)* cabinet; *(estudio)* study; *(de abogados etc)* office; **~ de consulta/de lectura** consulting/reading room
gaceta [ga'θeta] *nf* gazette
gachas ['gatʃas] *nfpl* porridge *sg*
gafar [ga'far] *vt (fam: traer mala suerte)* to put a jinx on
gafas ['gafas] *nfpl* glasses; **~ oscuras** dark glasses; **~ de sol** sunglasses
gafe ['gafe] *adj*: **ser ~** to be jinxed ▷ *nm (fam)* jinx
gaita ['gaita] *nf* flute; *(tb: ~ gallega)* bagpipes *pl; (dificultad)* bother; *(cosa engorrosa)* tough job
gajes ['gaxes] *nmpl (salario)* pay *sg*; **los ~ del oficio** occupational hazards; **~ y emolumentos** perquisites
gajo ['gaxo] *nm (gen)* bunch; *(de árbol)* bough; *(de naranja)* segment
gala ['gala] *nf* full dress; *(fig: lo mejor)* cream, flower; **galas** *nfpl* finery *sg*; **estar de ~** to be in one's best clothes; **hacer ~ de** to display, show off; **tener algo a ~** to be proud of sth
galán [ga'lan] *nm* lover, gallant; *(hombre atractivo)* ladies' man; *(Teat)*: **primer ~** leading man
galante [ga'lante] *adj* gallant; *(atento)* charming; *(cortés)* polite
galantear [galante'ar] *vt (hacer la corte a)* to court, woo
galantería [galante'ria] *nf (caballerosidad)* gallantry; *(cumplido)* politeness; *(piropo)* compliment
galápago [ga'lapaɣo] *nm (Zool)* turtle, sea/freshwater turtle *(US)*
galardón [galar'ðon] *nm* award, prize
galardonar [galarðo'nar] *vt (premiar)* to reward; *(una obra)* to award a prize for
galaxia [ga'laksja] *nf* galaxy
galera [ga'lera] *nf (nave)* galley; *(carro)* wagon; *(Med)* hospital ward; *(Tip)* galley
galería [gale'ria] *nf (gen)* gallery; *(balcón)* veranda(h); *(de casa)* corridor; *(fam: público)* audience; **~ secreta** secret passage; **~ comercial** shopping mall
Gales ['gales] *nm*: **(el País de) ~** Wales
galés, -esa [ga'les, esa] *adj* Welsh ▷ *nm/f* Welshman(-woman) ▷ *nm (Ling)* Welsh
galgo, -a ['galɣo, a] *nm/f* greyhound
Galicia [ga'liθja] *nf* Galicia
galimatías [galima'tias] *nm inv (asunto)* rigmarole; *(lenguaje)* gibberish, nonsense
gallardía [gaʎar'ðia] *nf (galantería)* dash; *(gracia)* gracefulness; *(valor)* bravery; *(elegancia)* elegance; *(nobleza)* nobleness
gallego, -a [ga'ʎeɣo, a] *adj* Galician; *(Am pey)* Spanish ▷ *nm/f* Galician; *(Am pey)* Spaniard ▷ *nm (Ling)* Galician
galleta [ga'ʎeta] *nf* biscuit *(Brit)*, cookie *(US)*; *(fam: bofetada)* whack, slap
gallina [ga'ʎina] *nf* hen ▷ *nm (fam)* chicken; **~ ciega** blind man's buff; **~ llueca** broody hen
gallinero [gaʎi'nero] *nm (criadero)* henhouse; *(Teat)* gods *sg*, top gallery; *(voces)* hubbub
gallo ['gaʎo] *nm* cock, rooster; *(Mus)* false o wrong note; *(cambio de voz)* break in the voice; **en menos que canta un ~** in an instant
galón [ga'lon] *nm (Costura)* braid; *(Mil)* stripe; *(medida)* gallon
galopante [galo'pante] *adj* galloping
galopar [galo'par] *vi* to gallop
gama ['gama] *nf (Mus)* scale; *(fig)* range; *(Zool)* doe
gamba ['gamba] *nf* prawn *(Brit)*, shrimp *(US)*
gamberrada [gambe'rraða] *nf* act of hooliganism
gamberro, -a [gam'berro, a] *nm/f* hooligan, lout
gamuza [ga'muθa] *nf* chamois; *(bayeta)* duster; *(Am: piel)* suede
gana ['gana] *nf (deseo)* desire, wish; *(apetito)* appetite; *(voluntad)* will; *(añoranza)* longing; **de buena ~** willingly; **de mala ~** reluctantly; **me da ~s de** I feel like, I want to; **tener ~s de** to feel like; **no me da la (real) ~** I (really) don't feel like it; **son ~s de molestar** they're just trying to be awkward

ganadería [ganaðe'ria] nf (ganado) livestock; (ganado vacuno) cattle pl; (cría, comercio) cattle raising

ganadero, -a [gana'ðero, a] adj stock cpd ▷ nm/f (hacendado) rancher

ganado [ga'naðo] nm livestock; ~ **caballar/cabrío** horses pl/goats pl; ~ **lanar** u **ovejuno** sheep pl; ~ **porcino/vacuno** pigs pl/cattle pl

ganador, -a [gana'ðor, a] adj winning ▷ nm/f winner; (Econ) earner

ganancia [ga'nanθja] nf (lo ganado) gain; (aumento) increase; (beneficio) profit; **ganancias** nfpl (ingresos) earnings; (beneficios) profit sg, winnings; ~**s y pérdidas** profit and loss; ~ **bruta/líquida** gross/net profit; ~**s de capital** capital gains; **sacar** ~ **de** to draw profit from

ganar [ga'nar] vt (obtener) to get, obtain; (sacar ventaja) to gain; (Com) to earn; (Deporte, premio) to win; (derrotar) to beat; (alcanzar) to reach; (Mil: objetivo) to take; (apoyo) to gain, win ▷ vi (Deporte) to win; **ganarse** vr: ~**se la vida** to earn one's living; **se lo ha ganado** he deserves it; ~ **tiempo** to gain time

ganchillo [gan'tʃiʎo] nm (para croché) crochet hook; (arte) crochet

gancho ['gantʃo] nm (gen) hook; (colgador) hanger; (pey: revendedor) tout; (fam: atractivo) sex appeal; (Boxeo: golpe) hook

gandul, -a [gan'dul, a] adj, nm/f good-for-nothing, layabout

ganga ['ganga] nf (cosa) bargain; (chollo) cushy job

gangrena [gan'grena] nf gangrene

gansada [gan'saða] nf (fam) stupid thing (to do)

ganso, -a ['ganso, a] nm/f (Zool) gander/goose; (fam) idiot

ganzúa [gan'θua] nf skeleton key ▷ nm/f burglar

garabatear [garaβate'ar] vt to scribble, scrawl

garabato [gara'βato] nm (gancho) hook; (garfio) grappling iron; (escritura) scrawl, scribble; (fam) sex appeal

garaje [ga'raxe] nm garage

garajista [gara'xista] nm/f mechanic

garante [ga'rante] adj responsible ▷ nm/f guarantor

garantía [garan'tia] nf guarantee; (seguridad) pledge; (compromiso) undertaking; (Jur: caución) warranty; **de máxima** ~ absolutely guaranteed; ~ **de trabajo** job security

garantizar [garanti'θar] vt (hacerse responsable de) to vouch for; (asegurar) to guarantee

garbanzo [gar'βanθo] nm chickpea

garbo ['garβo] nm grace, elegance; (desenvoltura) jauntiness; (de mujer) glamour; **andar con** ~ to walk gracefully

garete [ga'rete] nm: **irse al** ~ to go to the dogs

garfio ['garfjo] nm grappling iron; (gancho) hook; (Alpinismo) climbing iron

garganta [gar'ɣanta] nf (interna) throat; (externa, de botella) neck; (Geo: barranco) ravine; (desfiladero) narrow pass

gargantilla [garɣan'tiʎa] nf necklace

gárgara ['garɣara] nf gargle, gargling; **hacer** ~**s** to gargle; **¡vete a hacer** ~**s!** (fam) go to blazes!

gargarear [garɣare'ar] vi (Am) to gargle

garita [ga'rita] nf cabin, hut; (Mil) sentry box; (puesto de vigilancia) lookout post

garito [ga'rito] nm (lugar) gaming house o den

garra ['garra] nf (de gato, Tec) claw; (de ave) talon; (fam) hand, paw; (fig: de canción etc) bite; **caer en las** ~**s de algn** to fall into sb's clutches

garrafa [ga'rrafa] nf carafe, decanter

garrapata [garra'pata] nf (Zool) tick

garrote [ga'rrote] nm (palo) stick; (porra) club, cudgel; (suplicio) garrotte

garza ['garθa] nf heron

gas [gas] nm gas; (vapores) fumes pl; ~**es de escape** exhaust (fumes); ~**es lacrimógenos** tear gas sg

gasa ['gasa] nf gauze; (de pañal) nappy liner

gaseoso, -a [gase'oso, a] adj gassy, fizzy ▷ nf lemonade, pop (fam)

gasoil [ga'soil], **gasóleo** [ga'soleo] nm diesel (oil)

gasolina [gaso'lina] nf petrol, gas(oline) (US); ~ **sin plomo** unleaded petrol

gasolinera [gasoli'nera] nf petrol (Brit) o gas (US) station

gastado, -a [gas'taðo, a] adj (dinero) spent; (ropa) worn out; (usado: frase etc) trite

gastar [gas'tar] vt (dinero, tiempo) to spend; (consumir) to use (up), consume; (desperdiciar) to waste; (llevar) to wear; **gastarse** vr to wear out; (terminarse) to run out; (estropearse) to waste; ~ **en** to spend on; ~ **bromas** to crack jokes; **¿qué número gastas?** what size (shoe) do you take?

gasto ['gasto] nm (desembolso) expenditure, spending; (cantidad gastada) outlay, expense; (consumo, uso) use; (desgaste) waste; **gastos** nmpl (desembolsos) expenses; (cargos) charges, costs; ~ **corriente** (Com) revenue expenditure; ~ **fijo** (Com) fixed charge; ~**s bancarios** bank charges; ~**s corrientes** running expenses; ~**s de distribución** (Com) distribution costs; ~**s generales** overheads; ~**s de mantenimiento** maintenance expenses; ~**s operacionales** operating costs; ~**s de tramitación** (Com) handling charge sg; ~**s vencidos** (Com) accrued charges; **cubrir** ~**s** to cover expenses; **meterse en** ~**s** to incur expense

gastronomía [gastrono'mia] nf gastronomy

gata ['gata] nf (Zool) she-cat; **andar a** ~**s** to go on all fours

gatear [gate'ar] vi (andar a gatas) to go on all fours

gatillo [ga'tiʎo] *nm* (*de arma de fuego*) trigger; (*de dentista*) forceps

gato ['gato] *nm* (*Zool*) cat; (*Tec*) jack; **~ de Angora** Angora cat; **~ montés** wildcat; **dar a algn ~ por liebre** to take sb in; **aquí hay ~ encerrado** there's something fishy here; **andar a gatas** to go on all fours

gaucho, -a ['gautʃo, a] *adj, nm/f* gaucho

- **GAUCHO**
-
- *Gauchos* are the herdsmen or riders of the
- Southern Cone plains. Although
- popularly associated with Argentine
- folklore, *gauchos* belong equally to the
- cattle-raising areas of Southern Brazil
- and Uruguay. *Gauchos'* traditions and
- clothing reflect their mixed ancestry and
- cultural roots. Their baggy trousers are
- Arabic in origin, while the horse and
- guitar are inherited from the Spanish
- *conquistadors*; the poncho, maté and
- *boleadoras* (strips of leather weighted at
- either end with stones) form part of the
- Indian tradition.

gaveta [ga'βeta] *nf* drawer

gaviota [ga'βjota] *nf* seagull

gay [ge] *adj, nm* gay, homosexual

gazapo [ga'θapo] *nm* young rabbit

gazpacho [gaθ'patʃo] *nm* gazpacho

gel [xel] *nm* gel; **~ de baño/ducha** bath/shower gel

gelatina [xela'tina] *nf* jelly; (*polvos etc*) gelatine

gema ['xema] *nf* gem

gemelo, -a [xe'melo, a] *adj, nm/f* twin; **gemelos** *nmpl* (*de camisa*) cufflinks; **~s de campo** field glasses, binoculars; **~s de teatro** opera glasses

gemido [xe'miðo] *nm* (*quejido*) moan, groan; (*lamento*) wail, howl

Géminis ['xeminis] *nm* (*Astro*) Gemini

gemir [xe'mir] *vi* (*quejarse*) to moan, groan; (*animal*) to whine; (*viento*) to howl

gen [xen] *nm* gene

generación [xenera'θjon] *nf* generation; **primera/segunda/tercera/cuarta ~** (*Inform*) first/second/third/fourth generation

general [xene'ral] *adj* general; (*común*) common; (*pey: corriente*) rife; (*frecuente*) usual ▷ *nm* general; **~ de brigada/de división** brigadier-/major-general; **por lo o en ~** in general

Generalitat [xenerali'tat] *nf* regional government of Catalonia; **~ Valenciana** regional government of Valencia

generalizar [xenerali'θar] *vt* to generalize; **generalizarse** *vr* to become generalized, spread; (*difundirse*) to become widely known

generalmente [xeneral'mente] *adv* generally

generar [xene'rar] *vt* to generate

género ['xenero] *nm* (*clase*) kind, sort; (*tipo*) type; (*Bio*) genus; (*Ling*) gender; (*Com*) material; **géneros** *nmpl* (*productos*) goods; **~ humano** human race; **~ chico** (*zarzuela*) Spanish operetta; **~s de punto** knitwear *sg*

generosidad [xenerosi'ðað] *nf* generosity

generoso, -a [xene'roso, a] *adj* generous

genético, -a [xe'netiko, a] *adj* genetic ▷ *nf* genetics *sg*

genial [xe'njal] *adj* inspired; (*idea*) brilliant; (*estupendo*) wonderful; (*afable*) genial

genio ['xenjo] *nm* (*carácter*) nature, disposition; (*humor*) temper; (*facultad creadora*) genius; **mal ~** bad temper; **~ vivo** quick *o* hot temper; **de mal ~** bad-tempered

genital [xeni'tal] *adj* genital ▷ *nm*: **~es** genitals, genital organs

gente ['xente] *nf* (*personas*) people *pl*; (*raza*) race; (*nación*) nation; (*parientes*) relatives *pl*; **~ bien/baja** posh/lower-class people *pl*; **~ menuda** (*niños*) children *pl*; **es buena ~** (*fam: esp Am*) he's a good sort; **una ~ como Vd** (*Am*) a person like you

gentil [xen'til] *adj* (*elegante*) graceful; (*encantador*) charming; (*Rel*) gentile

gentileza [xenti'leθa] *nf* grace; charm; (*cortesía*) courtesy; **por ~ de** by courtesy of

gentío [xen'tio] *nm* crowd, throng

genuino, -a [xe'nwino, a] *adj* genuine

geografía [xeoɣra'fia] *nf* geography

geográfico, -a [xeo'ɣrafiko, a] *adj* geographic(al)

geología [xeolo'xia] *nf* geology

geometría [xeome'tria] *nf* geometry

geranio [xe'ranjo] *nm* (*Bot*) geranium

gerencia [xe'renθja] *nf* management; (*cargo*) post of manager; (*oficina*) manager's office

gerente [xe'rente] *nm/f* (*supervisor*) manager; (*jefe*) director

geriatría [xerja'tria] *nf* (*Med*) geriatrics *sg*

geriátrico, -a [xer'jatriko, a] *adj* geriatric

germen ['xermen] *nm* germ

germinar [xermi'nar] *vi* to germinate; (*brotar*) to sprout

gerundio [xe'rundjo] *nm* (*Ling*) gerund

gestación [xesta'θjon] *nf* gestation

gesticulación [xestikula'θjon] *nf* (*ademán*) gesticulation; (*mueca*) grimace

gesticular [xestiku'lar] *vi* (*con ademanes*) to gesticulate; (*con muecas*) to make faces

gestión [xes'tjon] *nf* management; (*diligencia, acción*) negotiation; **hacer las gestiones preliminares** to do the groundwork; **~ de cartera** (*Com*) portfolio management; **~ financiera** (*Com*) financial management; **~ interna** (*Inform*) housekeeping; **~ de personal** personnel management; **~ de riesgos** (*Com*) risk management

gestionar [xestjo'nar] *vt* (*tratar de arreglar*) to try to arrange; (*llevar*) to manage

g

gesto ['xesto] nm (mueca) grimace; (ademán) gesture; **hacer ~s** to make faces

gestoría [xesto'ria] nf agency undertaking business with government departments, insurance companies etc

Gibraltar [xiβral'tar] nm Gibraltar

gibraltareño, -a [xiβralta'reɲo, a] adj of o from Gibraltar, Gibraltarian ▷ nm/f Gibraltarian

giga ['xiɣa] nm abr gig (= gigabyte)

gigabyte ['xiɣaβait] nm gigabyte

gigante [xi'ɣante] adj, nm/f giant

gigantesco, -a [xiɣan'tesko, a] adj gigantic

gilipollas [xili'poʎas] (fam) adj inv daft ▷ nm/f berk (Brit), jerk (esp US)

gilipollez [xilipo'ʎeθ] nf (fam): **es una ~** that's a load of crap (!); **decir gilipolleces** to talk crap (!)

gimnasia [xim'nasja] nf gymnastics pl; **confundir la ~ con la magnesia** to get things mixed up

gimnasio [xim'nasjo] nm gym(nasium)

gimnasta [xim'nasta] nm/f gymnast

gimnástica [xim'nastika] nf gymnastics sg

gimotear [ximote'ar] vi to whine, whimper; (lloriquear) to snivel

ginebra [xi'neβra] nf gin

ginecología [xinekolo'xia] nf gyn(a)ecology

ginecólogo, -a [xine'koloɣo, a] nm/f gyn(a)ecologist

gira ['xira] nf tour, trip

girar [xi'rar] vt (dar la vuelta) to turn (around); (: rápidamente) to spin; (Com: giro postal) to draw; (comerciar: letra de cambio) to issue ▷ vi to turn (round); (dar vueltas) to rotate; (rápido) to spin; **la conversación giraba en torno a las elecciones** the conversation centred on the election; **~ en descubierto** to overdraw

girasol [xira'sol] nm sunflower

giratorio, -a [xira'torjo, a] adj (gen) revolving; (puente) swing cpd; (silla) swivel cpd

giro ['xiro] nm (movimiento) turn, revolution; (Ling) expression; (Com) draft; (de sucesos) trend, course; **~ bancario** bank draft, bank giro; **~ de existencias** (Com) stock turnover; **~ postal** money order

gis [xis] nm (Am) chalk

gitano, -a [xi'tano, a] adj, nm/f gypsy

glacial [gla'θjal] adj icy, freezing

glaciar [gla'θjar] nm glacier

glándula ['glandula] nf (Anat, Bot) gland

global [glo'βal] adj (en conjunto) global; (completo) total; (investigación) full; (suma) lump cpd

globalización [gloβaliθa'θjon] nf globalization

globo ['gloβo] nm (esfera) globe, sphere; (aeróstato, juguete) balloon

glóbulo ['gloβulo] nm globule; (Anat) corpuscle; **~ blanco/rojo** white/red corpuscle

gloria ['glorja] nf glory; (fig) delight; (delicia) bliss

glorieta [glo'rjeta] nf (de jardín) bower, arbour, arbor (US); (Auto) roundabout (Brit), traffic circle (US); (plaza redonda) circus; (cruce) junction

glorificar [glorifi'kar] vt (enaltecer) to glorify, praise

glorioso, -a [glo'rjoso, a] adj glorious

glosa ['glosa] nf comment; (explicación) gloss

glosar [glo'sar] vt (comentar) to comment on

glosario [glo'sarjo] nm glossary

glotón, -ona [glo'ton, ona] adj gluttonous, greedy ▷ nm/f glutton

glucosa [glu'kosa] nf glucose

gobernación [goβerna'θjon] nf government, governing; (Pol) Provincial Governor's office; **Ministro de la G-** Minister of the Interior, Home Secretary (Brit)

gobernador, -a [goβerna'ðor, a] adj governing ▷ nm/f governor

gobernante [goβer'nante] adj governing ▷ nm ruler, governor ▷ nf (en hotel etc) housekeeper

gobernar [goβer'nar] vt (dirigir) to guide, direct; (Pol) to rule, govern ▷ vi to govern; (Naut) to steer; **~ mal** to misgovern

gobierno [go'βjerno] vb ver **gobernar** ▷ nm (Pol) government; (gestión) management; (dirección) guidance, direction; (Naut) steering; (puesto) governorship

goce etc ['goθe] vb ver **gozar** ▷ nm enjoyment

gol [gol] nm goal

golf [golf] nm golf

golfo, -a ['golfo, a] nm/f (pilluelo) street urchin; (vagabundo) tramp; (gorrón) loafer; (gamberro) lout ▷ nm (Geo) gulf ▷ nf (fam: prostituta) slut, whore, hooker (US)

golondrina [golon'drina] nf swallow

golosina [golo'sina] nf titbit; (dulce) sweet

goloso, -a [go'loso, a] adj sweet-toothed; (fam: glotón) greedy

golpe ['golpe] nm blow; (de puño) punch; (de mano) smack; (de remo) stroke; (Fútbol) kick; (Tenis etc) hit, shot; (mala suerte) misfortune; (fam: atraco) job, heist (US); (fig: choque) clash; **no dar ~** to be bone idle; **de un ~** with one blow; **de ~** suddenly; **~ (de estado)** coup (d'état); **~ de gracia** coup de grâce (tb fig); **~ de fortuna/maestro** stroke of luck/genius; **cerrar una puerta de ~** to slam a door

golpear [golpe'ar] vt, vi to strike, knock; (asestar) to beat; (de puño) to punch; (golpetear) to tap; (mesa) to bang

golpista [gol'pista] adj: **intentona ~** coup attempt ▷ nm/f participant in a coup (d'état)

goma ['goma] nf (caucho) rubber; (elástico) elastic; (tira) rubber o elastic (Brit) band; (fam: preservativo) condom; (droga) hashish; (explosivo) plastic explosive; **~ (de borrar)** eraser, rubber (Brit); **~ de mascar** chewing gum; **~ de pegar** gum, glue; **~ espuma** foam rubber

gomina [go'mina] nf hair gel

gomita [go'mita] nf rubber o elastic (Brit) band

gordo, -a ['gorðo, a] adj (gen) fat; (persona) plump; (agua) hard; (fam) enormous ▷ nm/f fat man o woman; **el (premio) ~** (en lotería) first prize; **¡~!** (fam) fatty!

gordura [gor'ðura] nf fat; (corpulencia) fatness, stoutness

gorila [go'rila] nm gorilla; (fam) tough, thug; (guardaespaldas) bodyguard

gorjear [gorxe'ar] vi to twitter, chirp

gorra ['gorra] nf (gen) cap; (de niño) bonnet; (militar) bearskin; **~ de montar/de paño/de punto/de visera** riding/cloth/knitted/peaked cap; **andar** o **ir** o **vivir de ~** to sponge, scrounge; **entrar de ~** (fam) to gatecrash

gorrión [go'rrjon] nm sparrow

gorro ['gorro] nm cap; (de niño, mujer) bonnet; **estoy hasta el ~** I am fed up

gorrón, -ona [go'rron, ona] nm pebble; (Tec) pivot ▷ nm/f scrounger

gorronear [gorrone'ar] vi (fam) to sponge, scrounge

gota ['gota] nf (gen) drop; (de pintura) blob; (de sudor) bead; (Med) gout; **~ a ~** drop by drop; **caer a ~s** to drip

gotear [gote'ar] vi to drip; (escurrir) to trickle; (salirse) to leak; (cirio) to gutter; (lloviznar) to drizzle

gotera [go'tera] nf leak

gótico, -a ['gotiko, a] adj Gothic

gozar [go'θar] vi to enjoy o.s.; **~ de** (disfrutar) to enjoy; (poseer) to possess; **~ de buena salud** to enjoy good health

gozne ['goθne] nm hinge

gozo ['goθo] nm (alegría) joy; (placer) pleasure; **¡mi ~ en el pozo!** that's torn it!, just my luck!

gr abr (= gramo(s)) g

grabación [graβa'θjon] nf recording

grabado, -a [gra'βaðo, a] adj (Mus) recorded; (en cinta) taped, on tape ▷ nm print, engraving; **~ al agua fuerte** etching; **~ al aguatinta** aquatint; **~ en cobre** copperplate; **~ en madera** woodcut; **~ rupestre** rock carving

grabador, -a [graβa'ðor, a] nm/f engraver ▷ nf tape-recorder; **~a de cassettes** cassette recorder; **~a de CD/DVD** CD/DVD writer

grabar [gra'βar] vt to engrave; (discos, cintas) to record; (impresionar) to impress

gracia ['graθja] nf (encanto) grace, gracefulness; (Rel) grace; (chiste) joke; (humor) humour, wit; **¡muchas ~s!** thanks very much!; **~s a** thanks to; **tener ~** (chiste etc) to be funny; **¡qué ~!** how funny!; (irónico) what a nerve!; **no me hace ~** (broma) it's not funny; (plan) I am not too keen; **con ~s anticipadas/repetidas** thanking you in advance/again; **dar las ~s a algn por algo** to thank sb for sth

gracioso, -a [gra'θjoso, a] adj (garboso) graceful; (chistoso) funny; (cómico) comical; (agudo) witty; (título) gracious ▷ nm/f (Teat) comic character, fool; **su graciosa Majestad** His/Her Gracious Majesty

grada ['graða] nf (de escalera) step; (de anfiteatro) tier, row; **gradas** nfpl (de estadio) terraces

gradación [graða'θjon] nf gradation; (serie) graded series

gradería [graðe'ria] nf (gradas) (flight of) steps pl; (de anfiteatro) tiers pl, rows pl; **~ cubierta** covered stand

grado ['graðo] nm degree; (etapa) stage, step; (nivel) rate; (de parentesco) order of lineage; (de aceite, vino) grade; (grada) step; (Escol) class, year, grade (US); (Univ) degree; (Ling) degree of comparison; (Mil) rank; **de buen ~** willingly; **en sumo ~, en ~ superlativo** in the highest degree; **~ centígrado/Fahrenheit** degree centigrade/Fahrenheit

graduación [graðwa'θjon] nf (acto) gradation; (clasificación) rating; (del alcohol) proof, strength; (Escol) graduation; (Mil) rank; **de alta ~** high-ranking

gradual [gra'ðwal] adj gradual

graduar [gra'ðwar] vt (gen) to graduate; (medir) to gauge; (Tec) to calibrate; (Univ) to confer a degree on; (Mil) to commission; **graduarse** vr to graduate; **~se la vista** to have one's eyes tested

gráfico, -a ['grafiko, a] adj graphic; (fig: vívido) vivid, lively ▷ nm diagram ▷ nf graph; **~ de barras** (Com) bar chart; **~ de sectores** o **de tarta** (Com) pie chart; **gráficos** nmpl (tb Inform) graphics; **~s empresariales** (Com) business graphics

grajo ['graxo] nm rook

Gral. abr (Mil: = General) Gen.

gramático, -a [gra'matiko, a] nm/f (persona) grammarian ▷ nf grammar

gramo ['gramo] nm gramme (Brit), gram (US)

gran [gran] adj ver **grande**

grana ['grana] nf (Bot) seedling; (color) scarlet; **ponerse como la ~** to go as red as a beetroot

granada [gra'naða] nf pomegranate; (Mil) grenade; **~ de mano** hand grenade; **~ de metralla** shrapnel shell

granate [gra'nate] adj inv maroon ▷ nm garnet; (color) maroon

Gran Bretaña [grambre'tana] nf Great Britain

grande ['grande], **gran** adj (de tamaño) big, large; (alto) tall; (distinguido) great; (impresionante) grand ▷ nm grandee; **¿cómo es de ~?** how big is it?, what size is it?; **pasarlo en ~** to have a tremendous time

grandeza [gran'deθa] nf greatness; (tamaño) bigness; (esplendor) grandness; (nobleza) nobility

grandioso, -a [gran'djoso, a] *adj* magnificent, grand

granel [gra'nel] *nm* (*montón*) heap; **a ~** (*Com*) in bulk

granero [gra'nero] *nm* granary, barn

granito [gra'nito] *nm* (*Agr*) small grain; (*roca*) granite

granizado [grani'θaðo] *nm* iced drink; **~ de café** iced coffee

granizar [grani'θar] *vi* to hail

granizo [gra'niθo] *nm* hail

granja ['granxa] *nf* (*gen*) farm; **~ avícola** chicken o poultry farm

granjear [granxe'ar] *vt* (*cobrar*) to earn; (*ganar*) to win; (*avanzar*) to gain; **granjearse** *vr* (*amistad etc*) to gain for o.s.

granjero, -a [gran'xero, a] *nm/f* farmer

grano ['grano] *nm* grain; (*semilla*) seed; (*baya*) berry; (*Med*) pimple, spot; (*partícula*) particle; (*punto*) speck; **granos** *nmpl* cereals; **~ de café** coffee bean; **ir al ~** to get to the point

granuja [gra'nuxa] *nm* rogue; (*golfillo*) urchin

grapa ['grapa] *nf* staple; (*Tec*) clamp; (*sujetador*) clip, fastener; (*Arq*) cramp

grapadora [grapa'ðora] *nf* stapler

grasa ['grasa] *nf ver* **graso**

grasiento, -a [gra'sjento, a] *adj* greasy; (*de aceite*) oily; (*mugriento*) filthy

graso, -a ['graso, a] *adj* fatty; (*aceitoso*) greasy, oily ▷ *nf* (*gen*) grease; (*de cocina*) fat, lard; (*sebo*) suet; (*mugre*) filth; (*Auto*) oil; (*lubricante*) grease; **grasa de ballena** blubber; **grasa de pescado** fish oil

gratificación [gratifika'θjon] *nf* (*propina*) tip; (*aguinaldo*) gratuity; (*bono*) bonus; (*recompensa*) reward

gratificar [gratifi'kar] *vt* (*dar propina*) to tip; (*premiar*) to reward; **"se -á"** "a reward is offered"

gratinar [grati'nar] *vt* to cook au gratin

gratis ['gratis] *adv* free, for nothing

gratitud [grati'tuð] *nf* gratitude

grato, -a ['grato, a] *adj* (*agradable*) pleasant, agreeable; (*bienvenido*) welcome; **nos es ~ informarle que ...** we are pleased to inform you that ...

gratuito, -a [gra'twito, a] *adj* (*gratis*) free; (*sin razón*) gratuitous; (*acusación*) unfounded

grava ['graβa] *nf* (*guijos*) gravel; (*piedra molida*) crushed stone; (*en carreteras*) road metal

gravamen [gra'βamen] *nm* (*carga*) burden; (*impuesto*) tax; **libre de ~** (*Econ*) free from encumbrances

gravar [gra'βar] *vt* to burden; (*Com*) to tax; (*Econ*) to assess for tax; **~ con impuestos** to burden with taxes

grave ['graβe] *adj* heavy; (*fig, Med*) grave, serious; (*importante*) important; (*herida*) severe; (*Mus*) low, deep; (*Ling: acento*) grave; **estar ~** to be seriously ill

gravedad [graβe'ðað] *nf* gravity; (*fig*)

seriousness; (*grandeza*) importance; (*dignidad*) dignity; (*Mus*) depth

gravilla [gra'βiʎa] *nf* gravel

gravitar [graβi'tar] *vi* to gravitate; **~ sobre** to rest on

gravoso, -a [gra'βoso, a] *adj* (*pesado*) burdensome; (*costoso*) costly

graznar [graθ'nar] *vi* (*cuervo*) to squawk; (*pato*) to quack; (*hablar ronco*) to croak

Grecia ['greθja] *nf* Greece

gremio ['gremjo] *nm* trade, industry; (*asociación*) professional association, guild

greña ['greɲa] *nf* (*cabellos*) shock of hair; (*maraña*) tangle; **andar a la ~** to bicker, squabble

gresca ['greska] *nf* uproar; (*trifulca*) row

griego, -a ['grjeyo, a] *adj* Greek, Grecian ▷ *nm/f* Greek ▷ *nm* (*Ling*) Greek

grieta ['grjeta] *nf* crack; (*hendidura*) chink; (*quiebra*) crevice; (*Med*) chap; (*Pol*) rift

grifo ['grifo] *nm* tap (*Brit*), faucet (*US*); (*Am*) petrol (*Brit*) o gas (*US*) station

grilletes [gri'ʎetes] *nmpl* fetters, shackles

grillo ['griʎo] *nm* (*Zool*) cricket; (*Bot*) shoot; **grillos** *nmpl* shackles, irons

gripa ['gripa] *nf* (*Am*) flu, influenza

gripe ['gripe] *nf* flu, influenza; **~ porcina** swine flu; **~ aviar** bird flu

gris [gris] *adj* grey

gritar [gri'tar] *vt, vi* to shout, yell; **¡no grites!** stop shouting!

grito ['grito] *nm* shout, yell; (*de horror*) scream; **a ~ pelado** at the top of one's voice; **poner el ~ en el cielo** to scream blue murder; **es el último ~** (*de moda*) it's all the rage

grosella [gro'seʎa] *nf* (red)currant; **~ negra** blackcurrant

grosería [grose'ria] *nf* (*actitud*) rudeness; (*comentario*) vulgar comment; (*palabrota*) swearword

grosero, -a [gro'sero, a] *adj* (*poco cortés*) rude, bad-mannered; (*ordinario*) vulgar, crude

grosor [gro'sor] *nm* thickness

grotesco, -a [gro'tesko, a] *adj* grotesque; (*absurdo*) bizarre

grúa ['grua] *nf* (*Tec*) crane; (*de petróleo*) derrick; **~ corrediza** o **móvil/de pescante/puente/de torre** travelling/jib/overhead/tower crane

grueso, -a ['grweso, a] *adj* thick; (*persona*) stout; (*calidad*) coarse ▷ *nm* bulk; (*espesor*) thickness; (*densidad*) density; (*de gente*) main body, mass; **el ~ de** the bulk of

grulla ['gruʎa] *nf* (*Zool*) crane

grumo ['grumo] *nm* (*coágulo*) clot, lump; (*masa*) dollop

gruñido [gru'ɲiðo] *nm* grunt, growl; (*fig*) grumble

gruñir [gru'ɲir] *vi* (*animal*) to grunt, growl; (*fam*) to grumble

grupa ['grupa] *nf* (*Zool*) rump

grupo ['grupo] *nm* group; (*Tec*) unit, set; (*de árboles*) cluster; **~ sanguíneo** blood group; **~ de presión** pressure group

gruta ['gruta] *nf* grotto

guacamole [gwaka'mole] *nm* (*Am*) avocado salad

guacho, -a ['gwatʃo, a] *nm/f* (*Am*) homeless child

guadaña [gwa'ðaɲa] *nf* scythe

guagua ['gwaɣwa] *nf* (*Am, Canarias*) bus; (*Am: criatura*) baby

guajolote [gwajo'lote] *nm* (*Am*) turkey

guante ['gwante] *nm* glove; **~s de goma** rubber gloves; **se ajusta como un ~** it fits like a glove; **echar el ~ a algn** to catch hold of sb; (*fig: policía*) to catch sb

guantera [gwan'tera] *nf* glove compartment

guapo, -a ['gwapo, a] *adj* good-looking; (*mujer*) pretty, attractive; (*hombre*) handsome; (*elegante*) smart ▷ *nm* lover, gallant; (*Am fam*) tough guy, bully

guarda ['gwarða] *nm/f* (*persona*) warden, keeper ▷ *nf* (*acto*) guarding; (*custodia*) custody; (*Tip*) flyleaf, endpaper; **~ forestal** game warden; **~ jurado** (*armed*) security guard

guardabarros [gwarða'βarros] *nm inv* mudguard (*Brit*), fender (*US*)

guardabosques [gwarða'βoskes] *nm inv* gamekeeper

guardacostas [gwarða'kostas] *nm inv* coastguard vessel ▷ *nm/f* guardian, protector

guardador, a [gwarða'ðor, a] *adj* protective; (*tacaño*) mean, stingy ▷ *nm/f* guardian, protector

guardaespaldas [gwardaes'paldas] *nm/f inv* bodyguard

guardameta [gwarða'meta] *nm* goalkeeper

guardapolvo [gwarða'polβo] *nm* dust cover; (*prenda de vestir*) overalls *pl*

guardar [gwar'ðar] *vt* (*gen*) to keep; (*vigilar*) to guard, watch over; (*conservar*) to put away; (*dinero: ahorrar*) to save; (*promesa etc*) to keep; (*ley*) to observe; (*rencor*) to bear, harbour; (*Inform: archivo*) to save; **guardarse** *vr* (*preservarse*) to protect o.s.; **~se de algo** (*evitar*) to avoid sth; **~ cama** to stay in bed

guardarropa [gwarða'rropa] *nm* (*armario*) wardrobe; (*en establecimiento público*) cloakroom

guardería [gwarðe'ria] *nf* nursery

guardia ['gwarðja] *nf* (*Mil*) guard; (*cuidado*) care, custody ▷ *nm/f* (*policía*) policeman(-woman); **estar de ~** to be on guard; **montar ~** to mount guard; **la G~ Civil** the Civil Guard; **~ municipal** o **urbana** municipal police; **un ~ civil** a Civil Guard(sman); **un(a) ~ nacional** a policeman(-woman); **~ urbano** traffic policeman

guardián, -ana [gwar'ðjan, ana] *nm/f* (*gen*) guardian, keeper

guarecer [gware'θer] *vt* (*proteger*) to protect; (*abrigar*) to shelter; **guarecerse** *vr* to take refuge

guarida [gwa'riða] *nf* (*de animal*) den, lair; (*de persona*) haunt, hideout; (*refugio*) refuge

guarnecer [gwarne'θer] *vt* (*equipar*) to provide; (*adornar*) to adorn; (*Tec*) to reinforce

guarnición [gwarni'θjon] *nf* (*de vestimenta*) trimming; (*de piedra*) mount; (*Culin*) garnish; (*arneses*) harness; (*Mil*) garrison

guarrada [gwa'rraða] (*fam*) *nf* (*cosa sucia*) dirty mess; (*acto o dicho obsceno*) obscenity; **hacer una ~ a algn** to do the dirty on sb

guarrería [gwarre'ria] *nf* = **guarrada**

guarro, -a ['gwarro, a] *nm/f* (*fam*) pig; (*fig*) dirty o slovenly person

guasa ['gwasa] *nf* joke; **con** o **de ~** jokingly, in fun

guasón, -ona [gwa'son, ona] *adj* witty; (*bromista*) joking ▷ *nm/f* wit; joker

Guatemala [gwate'mala] *nf* Guatemala

guay [gwai] *adj* (*fam*) super, great

gubernamental [guβernamen'tal], **gubernativo, -a** [guβerna'tiβo, a] *adj* governmental

güero, -a ['gwero, a] *adj* (*Am*) blond(e)

guerra ['gerra] *nf* war; (*arte*) warfare; (*pelea*) struggle; **~ atómica/bacteriológica/ nuclear/de guerrillas** atomic/germ/ nuclear/guerrilla warfare; **Primera/ Segunda G~ Mundial** First/Second World War; **~ de precios** (*Com*) price war; **~ civil/ fría** civil/cold war; **~ a muerte** fight to the death; **de ~** military, war *cpd*; **estar en ~** to be at war; **dar ~ a** to be a nuisance; **dar ~ a algn** to give s.o. a lot of bother

guerrear [gerre'ar] *vi* to wage war

guerrero, -a [ge'rrero, a] *adj* fighting; (*carácter*) warlike ▷ *nm/f* warrior

guerrilla [ge'rriʎa] *nf* guerrilla warfare; (*tropas*) guerrilla band o group

guerrillero, -a [gerri'ʎero, a] *nm/f* guerrilla (fighter); (*contra invasor*) partisan

gueto ['geto] *nm* ghetto

guía ['gia] *vb ver* **guiar** ▷ *nm/f* (*persona*) guide ▷ *nf* (*libro*) guidebook; (*manual*) handbook; **~ de ferrocarriles** railway timetable; **~ telefónica** telephone directory; **~ del turista/del viajero** tourist/traveller's guide

guiar [gi'ar] *vt* to guide, direct; (*dirigir*) to lead; (*orientar*) to advise; (*Auto*) to steer; **guiarse** *vr*: **~se por** to be guided by

guijarro [gi'xarro] *nm* pebble

guillotina [giʎo'tina] *nf* guillotine

guinda ['ginda] *nf* morello cherry; (*licor*) cherry liqueur

guindilla [gin'diʎa] *nf* chil(l)i pepper

guiñapo [gi'ɲapo] *nm* (*harapo*) rag; (*persona*) rogue

guiñar [gi'ɲar] *vi* to wink

guiño [gi'ɲo] *nm* (*parpadeo*) wink; (*muecas*) grimace; **hacer ~s a** (*enamorados*) to make eyes at

guión [gi'on] *nm* (*Ling*) hyphen, dash; (*esquema*) summary, outline; (*Cine*) script

guionista [gjo'nista] *nm/f* scriptwriter

guiri ['giri] *nm/f* (*fam, pey*) foreigner

guirnalda [gir'nalda] *nf* garland

guisa ['gisa] *nf*: **a ~ de** as, like

guisado [gi'saðo] *nm* stew

guisante [gi'sante] *nm* pea

guisar [gi'sar] *vt, vi* to cook; (*fig*) to arrange

guiso ['giso] *nm* cooked dish

guitarra [gi'tarra] *nf* guitar

guitarrista [gita'rrista] *nm/f* guitarist

gula ['gula] *nf* gluttony, greed

gusano [gu'sano] *nm* maggot, worm; (*de mariposa, polilla*) caterpillar; (*lombriz*) earthworm; (*fig*) worm; (*ser despreciable*) creep; **~ de seda** silk-worm

gustar [gus'tar] *vt* to taste, sample ▷ *vi* to please, be pleasing; **~ de algo** to like *o* enjoy sth; **me gustan las uvas** I like grapes; **le gusta nadar** she likes *o* enjoys swimming; **¿gusta Ud?** would you like some?; **como Ud guste** as you wish

gusto ['gusto] *nm* (*sentido, sabor*) taste; (*agrado*) liking; (*placer*) pleasure; **tiene un ~ amargo** it has a bitter taste; **tener buen ~** to have good taste; **sobre ~s no hay nada escrito** there's no accounting for tastes; **de buen/mal ~** in good/bad taste; **sentirse a ~** to feel at ease; **¡mucho *o* tanto ~ (en conocerle)!** how do you do?, pleased to meet you; **el ~ es mío** the pleasure is mine; **tomar ~ a** to take a liking to; **con ~** willingly, gladly

gustoso, -a [gus'toso, a] *adj* (*sabroso*) tasty; (*agradable*) pleasant; (*con voluntad*) willing, glad; **lo hizo ~** he did it gladly

gutural [gutu'ral] *adj* guttural

ha¹ [a] *vb ver* **haber**

ha² *abr* (= *Hectárea(s)*) ha.

haba ['aβa] *nf* bean; **son ~s contadas** it goes without saying; **en todas partes cuecen ~s** it's the same (story) the whole world over

Habana [a'βana] *nf*: **la ~** Havana

habano [a'βano] *nm* Havana cigar

habéis *vb ver* **haber**

⭕ **PALABRA CLAVE**

haber [a'βer] *vb auxiliar* **1** (*tiempos compuestos*) to have; **había comido** I have/had eaten; **antes/después de haberlo visto** before seeing/after seeing *o* having seen it; **si lo hubiera sabido habría ido** if I had known I would have gone

2: **¡haberlo dicho antes!** you should have said so before!; **¿habrase visto (cosa igual)?** have you ever seen anything like it?

3: **haber de**: **he de hacerlo** I must do it; **ha de llegar mañana** it should arrive tomorrow

▷ *vb impersonal* **1** (*existencia: sg*) there is; (: *pl*) there are; **hay un hermano/dos hermanos** there is one brother/there are two brothers; **¿cuánto hay de aquí a Sucre?** how far is it from here to Sucre?; **habrá unos 4 grados** it must be about 4 degrees; **no hay quien te entienda** there's no understanding you

2 (*obligación*): **hay que hacer algo** something must be done; **hay que apuntarlo para**

acordarse you have to write it down to remember

3: ¡hay que ver! well I never!

4: ¡no hay de o por (Am) qué! don't mention it!, not at all!

5: ¿qué hay? (¿qué pasa?) what's up?, what's the matter?; (¿qué tal?) how's it going?

haberse vr: **habérselas con algn** to have it out with sb

▷ vt: **he aquí unas sugerencias** here are some suggestions; **todos los inventos habidos y por haber** all inventions present and future; **en el encuentro habido ayer** in yesterday's game

▷ nm (en cuenta) credit side

haberes nmpl assets; ¿**cuánto tengo en el haber?** how much do I have in my account?; **tiene varias novelas en su haber** he has several novels to his credit

habichuela [aβi'tʃwela] nf kidney bean

hábil ['aβil] adj (listo) clever, smart; (capaz) fit, capable; (experto) expert; **día ~** working day

habilidad [aβili'ðað] nf (gen) skill, ability; (inteligencia) cleverness; (destreza) expertise; (Jur) competence; **~ (para)** fitness (for); **tener ~ manual** to be clever with one's hands

habilitar [aβili'tar] vt to qualify; (autorizar) to authorize; (capacitar) to enable; (dar instrumentos) to equip; (financiar) to finance

hábilmente [aβil'mente] adv skilfully, expertly

habitación [aβita'θjon] nf (cuarto) room; (casa) dwelling, abode; (Bio: morada) habitat; **~ sencilla** o **individual** single room; **~ doble** o **de matrimonio** double room

habitante [aβi'tante] nm/f inhabitant

habitar [aβi'tar] vt (residir en) to inhabit; (ocupar) to occupy ▷ vi to live

hábitat (pl **hábitats**) ['aβitat, 'aβitats] nm habitat

hábito ['aβito] nm habit; **tener el ~ de hacer algo** to be in the habit of doing sth

habitual [aβi'twal] adj habitual

habituar [aβi'twar] vt to accustom; **habituarse** vr: **~se a** to get used to

habla ['aβla] nf (capacidad de hablar) speech; (idioma) language; (dialecto) dialect; **perder el ~** to become speechless; **de ~ francesa** French-speaking; **estar al ~** to be in contact; (Telec) to be on the line; ¡**González al ~!** (Telec) Gonzalez speaking!

hablador, a [aβla'ðor, a] adj talkative ▷ nm/f chatterbox

habladuría [aβlaðu'ria] nf rumour; **habladurías** nfpl gossip sg

hablante [a'βlante] adj speaking ▷ nm/f speaker

hablar [a'βlar] vt to speak, talk ▷ vi to speak; **hablarse** vr to speak to each other; **~ con** to speak to; ¡**hable!**, ¡**puede ~!** (Telec) you're

through!; **de eso ni ~** no way, that's out of the question; **~ alto/bajo/claro** to speak loudly/quietly/plainly o bluntly; **~ de** to speak of o about; **"se habla inglés"** "English spoken here"; **no se hablan** they are not on speaking terms

habré etc [a'βre] vb ver **haber**

hacedor, a [aθe'ðor, a] nm/f maker

hacendado, -a [aθen'daðo, a] adj property-owning ▷ nm (Am) rancher, farmer; (terrateniente) large landowner

hacendoso, -a [aθen'doso, a] adj industrious, hard-working

⬤ **PALABRA CLAVE**

hacer [a'θer] vt **1** (fabricar, producir, conseguir) to make; (construir) to build; **hacer una película/un ruido** to make a film/noise; **el guisado lo hice yo** I made o cooked the stew; **hacer amigos** to make friends

2 (ejecutar: trabajo etc) to do; **hacer la colada** to do the washing; **hacer la comida** to do the cooking; ¿**qué haces?** what are you doing?; ¡**eso está hecho!** you've got it!; **hacer el tonto/indio** to act the fool/clown; **hacer el malo** o **el papel del malo** (Teat) to play the villain

3 (estudios, algunos deportes) to do; **hacer español/económicas** to do o study Spanish/economics; **hacer yoga/gimnasia** to do yoga/go to the gym

4 (transformar, incidir en): **esto lo hará más difícil** this will make it more difficult; **salir te hará sentir mejor** going out will make you feel better; **te hace más joven** it makes you look younger

5 (cálculo): **2 y 2 hacen 4** 2 and 2 make 4; **éste hace 100** this one makes 100

6 (+ sub): **esto hará que ganemos** this will make us win; **harás que no quiera venir** you'll stop him wanting to come

7 (como sustituto de vb) to do; **él bebió y yo hice lo mismo** he drank and I did likewise

8: **no hace más que criticar** all he does is criticize

▷ vb semi-auxiliar (+ infin) **1** (directo): **les hice venir** I made o had them come; **hacer trabajar a los demás** to get others to work

2 (por intermedio de otros): **hacer reparar algo** to get sth repaired

▷ vi **1**: **haz como que no lo sabes** act as if you don't know; **hiciste bien en decírmelo** you were right to tell me

2 (ser apropiado): **si os hace** if it's alright with you

3: **hacer de**: **hacer de madre para uno** to be like a mother to sb; (Teat): **hacer de Otelo** to play Othello; **la tabla hace de mesa** the board does as a table

▷ vb impersonal **1**: **hace calor/frío** it's hot/cold; ver tb **bueno**; **sol**; **tiempo**

2 (*tiempo*): **hace tres años** three years ago; **hace un mes que voy/no voy** I've been going/I haven't been for a month; **no le veo desde hace mucho** I haven't seen him for a long time

3: ¿**cómo has hecho para llegar tan rápido?** how did you manage to get here so quickly?

hacerse *vr* **1** (*volverse*) to become; **se hicieron amigos** they became friends; **hacerse viejo** to get o grow old; **se hace tarde** it's getting late

2: **hacerse algo**: **me hice un traje** I got a suit made

3 (*acostumbrarse*): **hacerse a** to get used to; **hacerse a la idea** to get used to the idea

4: **se hace con huevos y leche** it's made out of eggs and milk; **eso no se hace** that's not done

5 (*obtener*): **hacerse de** o **con algo** to get hold of sth

6 (*fingirse*): **hacerse el sordo/sueco** to turn a deaf ear/pretend not to notice

hacha ['atʃa] *nf* axe; (*antorcha*) torch
hachazo [a'tʃaθo] *nm* axe blow
hachís [a'tʃis] *nm* hashish
hacia ['aθja] *prep* (*en dirección de, actitud*) towards; (*cerca de*) near; (*actitud*) towards; ~ **adelante/atrás** forwards/backwards; ~ **arriba/abajo** up(wards)/down(wards); ~ **mediodía** about noon
hacienda [a'θjenda] *nf* (*propiedad*) property; (*finca*) farm; (*Am*) ranch; ~ **pública** public finance; (**Ministerio de) H~** Exchequer (*Brit*), Treasury Department (*US*)
hada ['aða] *nf* fairy; ~ **madrina** fairy godmother
haga *etc* ['aɣa] *vb ver* **hacer**
Haití [ai'ti] *nm* Haiti
halagar [ala'ɣar] *vt* (*lisonjear*) to flatter
halago [a'laɣo] *nm* (*adulación*) flattery
halagüeño, -a [ala'ɣweɲo, a] *adj* flattering
halcón [al'kon] *nm* falcon, hawk
hálito ['alito] *nm* breath
hallar [a'ʎar] *vt* (*gen*) to find; (*descubrir*) to discover; (*toparse con*) to run into; **hallarse** *vr* to be (situated); (*encontrarse*) to find o.s.; **se halla fuera** he is away; **no se halla** he feels out of place
hallazgo [a'ʎaθɣo] *nm* discovery; (*cosa*) find
halógeno, a [a'loxeno, a] *adj*: **faro** ~ halogen lamp
halterofilia [altero'filja] *nf* weightlifting
hamaca [a'maka] *nf* hammock
hambre ['ambre] *nf* hunger; (*carencia*) famine; (*inanición*) starvation; (*fig*) longing; **tener** ~ to be hungry; **¡me muero de** ~! I'm starving!
hambriento, -a [am'brjento, a] *adj* hungry, starving ⊳ *nm/f* starving person; **los** ~**s** the hungry; ~ **de** hungry o longing for

hambruna [am'bruna] *nf* famine
hamburguesa [ambur'ɣesa] *nf* hamburger, burger
hamburguesería [amburɣese'ria] *nf* burger bar
hampón [am'pon] *nm* thug
hámster ['xamster] *nm* hamster
han [an] *vb ver* **haber**
haragán, -ana [ara'ɣan, ana] *adj, nm/f* good-for-nothing
harapiento, -a [ara'pjento, a] *adj* tattered, in rags
harapo [a'rapo] *nm* rag
haré *etc* [a're] *vb ver* **hacer**
harina [a'rina] *nf* flour; ~ **de maíz** cornflour (*Brit*), cornstarch (*US*); ~ **de trigo** wheat flour; **eso es** ~ **de otro costal** that's another kettle of fish
hartar [ar'tar] *vt* to satiate, glut; (*fig*) to tire, sicken; **hartarse** *vr* (*de comida*) to fill o.s., gorge o.s.; (*cansarse*): ~**se de** to get fed up with
hartazgo [ar'taθɣo] *nm* surfeit, glut
harto, -a ['arto, a] *adj* (*lleno*) full; (*cansado*) fed up ⊳ *adv* (*bastante*) enough; (*muy*) very; **estar** ~ **de** to be fed up with; **¡estoy ~ de decírtelo!** I'm sick and tired of telling you (so)!
hartura [ar'tura] *nf* (*exceso*) surfeit; (*abundancia*) abundance; (*satisfacción*) satisfaction
has¹ [as] *vb ver* **haber**
has² *abr* (= *Hectáreas*) ha.
hasta ['asta] *adv* even ⊳ *prep* (*alcanzando a*) as far as, up/down to; (*de tiempo*: *a tal hora*) till, until; (: *antes de*) before ⊳ *conj*: ~ **que** until; ~ **luego** o **ahora/el sábado** (*fam*) see you soon/on Saturday; ~ **pronto** see you soon; ~ **la fecha** (up) to date; ~ **nueva orden** until further notice; ~ **en Valencia hiela a veces** even in Valencia it freezes sometimes
hastiar [as'tjar] *vt* (*gen*) to weary; (*aburrir*) to bore; **hastiarse** *vr*: ~**se de** to get fed up with
hastío [as'tio] *nm* weariness; boredom
hatillo [a'tiʎo] *nm* belongings *pl*, kit; (*montón*) bundle, heap
hay [ai] *vb ver* **haber**
Haya ['aja] *nf*: **la** ~ The Hague
haya *etc* ['aja] *vb ver* **haber** ⊳ *nf* beech tree
haz [aθ] *vb ver* **hacer** ⊳ *nm* bundle, bunch; (*rayo: de luz*) beam ⊳ *nf*: ~ **de la tierra** face of the earth
hazaña [a'θaɲa] *nf* feat, exploit; **sería una** ~ it would be a great achievement
hazmerreír [aθmerre'ir] *nm inv* laughing stock
he [e] *vb ver* **haber** ⊳ *adv*: **he aquí** here is, here are; **he aquí por qué ...** that is why ...
hebilla [e'βiʎa] *nf* buckle, clasp
hebra ['eβra] *nf* thread; (*Bot: fibra*) fibre, grain
hebreo, -a [e'βreo, a] *adj, nm/f* Hebrew ⊳ *nm* (*Ling*) Hebrew

hechicero, -a [etʃi'θero, a] *nm/f* sorcerer/sorceress

hechizar [etʃi'θar] *vt* to cast a spell on, bewitch

hechizo [e'tʃiθo] *nm* witchcraft, magic; *(acto de magia)* spell, charm

hecho, -a ['etʃo, a] *pp de* **hacer** ▷ *adj* complete; *(maduro)* mature; *(carne)* done; *(Costura)* ready-to-wear ▷ *nm* deed, act; *(dato)* fact; *(cuestión)* matter; *(suceso)* event ▷ *excl* agreed!, done!; **¡bien ~!** well done!; **de ~** in fact, as a matter of fact; *(Pol etc: adj, adv)* de facto; **de ~ y de derecho** de facto and de jure; **~ a la medida** made-to-measure; **a lo ~, pecho** it's no use crying over spilt milk; **el ~ es que ...** the fact is that ...

hechura [e'tʃura] *nf* making, creation; *(producto)* product; *(forma)* form, shape; *(de persona)* build; *(Tec)* craftsmanship

hectárea [ek'tarea] *nf* hectare

heder [e'ðer] *vi* to stink, smell; *(fig)* to be unbearable

hediondo, -a [e'ðjondo, a] *adj* stinking

hedor [e'ðor] *nm* stench

hegemonía [exemo'nia] *nf* hegemony

helada [e'laða] *nf* frost

heladera [ela'ðera] *nf (Am: refrigerador)* refrigerator

heladería [elaðe'ria] *nf* ice-cream stall *(o parlour)*

helado, -a [e'laðo, a] *adj* frozen; *(glacial)* icy; *(fig)* chilly, cold ▷ *nm* ice-cream; **dejar ~ a algn** to dumbfound sb

helar [e'lar] *vt* to freeze, ice (up); *(dejar atónito)* to amaze; *(desalentar)* to discourage ▷ *vi*, **helarse** *vr* to freeze; *(Aviat, Ferro etc)* to ice (up), freeze up; *(líquido)* to set

helecho [e'letʃo] *nm* bracken, fern

hélice ['eliθe] *nf* spiral; *(Tec)* propeller; *(Mat)* helix

helicóptero [eli'koptero] *nm* helicopter

helio ['eljo] *nm* helium

hematoma [ema'toma] *nm* bruise

hembra ['embra] *nf (Bot, Zool)* female; *(mujer)* woman; *(Tec)* nut; **un elefante ~** a she-elephant

hemiciclo [emi'θiklo] *nm*: **el ~** *(Pol)* the floor

hemisferio [emis'ferjo] *nm* hemisphere

hemorragia [emo'rraxja] *nf* haemorrhage (Brit), hemorrhage (US)

hemorroides [emo'rroiðes] *nfpl* haemorrhoids (Brit), hemorrhoids (US)

hemos ['emos] *vb ver* **haber**

hendidura [endi'ðura] *nf* crack, split; *(Geo)* fissure

heno ['eno] *nm* hay

hepatitis [epa'titis] *nf inv* hepatitis

herbicida [erβi'θiða] *nm* weedkiller

herbívoro, -a [er'βiβoro, a] *adj* herbivorous

herboristería [erβoriste'ria] *nf* herbalist's shop

heredad [ere'ðað] *nf* landed property; *(granja)* farm

heredar [ere'ðar] *vt* to inherit

heredero, -a [ere'ðero, a] *nm/f* heir(ess); **~ del trono** heir to the throne

hereditario, -a [ereði'tarjo, a] *adj* hereditary

hereje [e'rexe] *nm/f* heretic

herencia [e'renθja] *nf* inheritance; *(fig)* heritage; *(Bio)* heredity

herido, -a [e'riðo, a] *adj* injured, wounded; *(fig)* offended ▷ *nm/f* casualty ▷ *nf* wound, injury

herir [e'rir] *vt* to wound, injure; *(fig)* to offend; *(conmover)* to touch, move

hermana [er'mana] *nf ver* **hermano**

hermanación [ermana'θjon] *nf (de ciudades)* twinning

hermanado, -a [erma'naðo, a] *adj (ciudad)* twinned

hermanastro, -a [erma'nastro, a] *nm/f* stepbrother(-sister)

hermandad [erman'dað] *nf* brotherhood; *(de mujeres)* sisterhood; *(sindicato etc)* association

hermano, -a [er'mano, a] *adj* similar ▷ *nm* brother ▷ *nf* sister; **~ gemelo** twin brother; **~ político** brother-in-law; **~ primo** first cousin; **mis ~s** my brothers, my brothers and sisters; **hermana política** sister-in-law

hermético, -a [er'metiko, a] *adj* hermetic; *(fig)* watertight

hermoso, -a [er'moso, a] *adj* beautiful, lovely; *(estupendo)* splendid; *(guapo)* handsome

hermosura [ermo'sura] *nf* beauty; *(de hombre)* handsomeness

hernia ['ernja] *nf* hernia, rupture; **~ discal** slipped disc

herniarse [er'njarse] *vr* to rupture o.s.; *(fig)* to break one's back

héroe ['eroe] *nm* hero

heroína [ero'ina] *nf (mujer)* heroine; *(droga)* heroin

heroinómano, -a [eroi'nomano, a] *nm/f* heroin addict

heroísmo [ero'ismo] *nm* heroism

herradura [erra'ðura] *nf* horseshoe

herramienta [erra'mjenta] *nf* tool

herrería [erre'ria] *nf* smithy; *(Tec)* forge

herrero [e'rrero] *nm* blacksmith

herrumbre [e'rrumbre] *nf* rust

hervidero [erβi'ðero] *nm (fig)* swarm; *(Pol etc)* hotbed

hervir [er'βir] *vi* to boil; *(burbujear)* to bubble; *(fig)*: **~ de** to teem with; **~ a fuego lento** to simmer

hervor [er'βor] *nm* boiling; *(fig)* ardour, fervour

heterosexual [eterosek'swal] *adj, nm/f* heterosexual

híbrido, -a ['iβriðo, a] *adj* hybrid

hice *etc* ['iθe] *vb ver* **hacer**

hidratante [iðra'tante] *adj*: **crema ~** moisturizing cream, moisturizer
hidratar [iðra'tar] *vt* to moisturize
hidrato [i'ðrato] *nm* hydrate; **~ de carbono** carbohydrate
hidráulico, -a [i'ðrauliko, a] *adj* hydraulic ▷ *nf* hydraulics *sg*
hidro... [iðro] *pref* hydro..., water-...
hidrodeslizador [iðrodesliθa'ðor] *nm* hovercraft
hidroeléctrico, -a [iðroe'lektriko, a] *adj* hydroelectric
hidrofobia [iðro'foβja] *nf* hydrophobia, rabies
hidrógeno [i'ðroxeno] *nm* hydrogen
hiedra ['jeðra] *nf* ivy
hiel [jel] *nf* gall, bile; (*fig*) bitterness
hielo ['jelo] *vb ver* **helar** ▷ *nm* (*gen*) ice; (*escarcha*) frost; (*fig*) coldness, reserve; **romper el ~** (*fig*) to break the ice
hiena ['jena] *nf* (*Zool*) hyena
hierba ['jerβa] *nf* (*pasto*) grass; (*Culin, Med: planta*) herb; **mala ~** weed; (*fig*) evil influence
hierbabuena [jerβa'βwena] *nf* mint
hierro ['jerro] *nm* (*metal*) iron; (*objeto*) iron object; **~ acanalado** corrugated iron; **~ colado o fundido** cast iron; **de ~** iron *cpd*
hígado ['iɣaðo] *nm* liver; **hígados** *nmpl* (*fig*) guts; **echar los ~s** to wear o.s. out
higiene [i'xjene] *nf* hygiene
higiénico, -a [i'xjeniko, a] *adj* hygienic
higo ['iɣo] *nm* fig; **~ seco** dried fig; **~ chumbo** prickly pear; **de ~s a brevas** once in a blue moon
higuera [i'gera] *nf* fig tree
hijastro, -a [i'xastro, a] *nm/f* stepson(-daughter)
hijo, -a ['ixo, a] *nm/f* son/daughter, child; (*uso vocativo*) dear; **hijos** *nmpl* children, sons and daughters; **sin ~s** childless; **~/hija político/a** son-/daughter-in-law; **~ pródigo** prodigal son; **~ adoptivo** adopted child; **~ de papá/mamá** daddy's/mummy's boy; **~ de puta** (*fam!*) bastard (!), son of a bitch (!); **~ único** only child; **cada ~ de vecino** any Tom, Dick or Harry
hilar [i'lar] *vt* to spin; (*fig*) to reason, infer; **~ delgado** to split hairs
hilera [i'lera] *nf* row, file
hilo ['ilo] *nm* thread; (*Bot*) fibre; (*tela*) linen; (*de metal*) wire; (*de agua*) trickle, thin stream; (*de luz*) beam, ray; (*de conversación*) thread, theme; (*de pensamientos*) train; **~ dental** dental floss; **colgar de un ~** (*fig*) to hang by a thread; **traje de ~** linen suit
hilvanar [ilβa'nar] *vt* (*Costura*) to tack (*Brit*), baste (*US*); (*fig*) to do hurriedly
himno ['imno] *nm* hymn; **~ nacional** national anthem
hincapié [inka'pje] *nm*: **hacer ~ en** to emphasize, stress

hincar [in'kar] *vt* to drive (in), thrust (in); (*diente*) to sink; **hincarse** *vr*: **~se de rodillas** (*esp Am*) to kneel down
hincha ['intʃa] *nm/f* (*fam: Deporte*) fan
hinchado, -a [in'tʃaðo, a] *adj* (*gen*) swollen; (*persona*) pompous ▷ *nf* (group of) supporters o fans
hinchar [in'tʃar] *vt* (*gen*) to swell; (*inflar*) to blow up, inflate; (*fig*) to exaggerate; **hincharse** *vr* (*inflarse*) to swell up; (*fam: llenarse*) to stuff o.s.; (*fig*) to get conceited; **~se de reír** to have a good laugh
hinchazón [intʃa'θon] *nf* (*Med*) swelling; (*protuberancia*) bump, lump; (*altivez*) arrogance
hindú [in'du] *adj, nm/f* Hindu
hinojo [i'noxo] *nm* fennel
hipermercado [ipermer'kaðo] *nm* hypermarket, superstore
hipertensión [iperten'sjon] *nf* high blood pressure, hypertension
hípico, -a ['ipiko, a] *adj* horse *cpd*, equine; **club ~** riding club
hipnosis [ip'nosis] *nf inv* hypnosis
hipnotismo [ipno'tismo] *nm* hypnotism
hipnotizar [ipnoti'θar] *vt* to hypnotize
hipo ['ipo] *nm* hiccups *pl*; **quitar el ~ a algn** to cure sb's hiccups
hipocresía [ipokre'sia] *nf* hypocrisy
hipócrita [i'pokrita] *adj* hypocritical ▷ *nm/f* hypocrite
hipódromo [i'poðromo] *nm* racetrack
hipopótamo [ipo'potamo] *nm* hippopotamus
hipoteca [ipo'teka] *nf* mortgage; **redimir una ~** to pay off a mortgage
hipotecar [ipote'kar] *vt* to mortgage; (*fig*) to jeopardize
hipótesis [i'potesis] *nf inv* hypothesis; **es una ~ (nada más)** that's just a theory
hiriente [i'rjente] *adj* offensive, wounding
hispánico, -a [is'paniko, a] *adj* Hispanic, Spanish
hispano, -a [is'pano, a] *adj* Hispanic, Spanish, Hispano- ▷ *nm/f* Spaniard
Hispanoamérica [ispanoa'merika] *nf* Spanish o Latin America
hispanoamericano, -a [ispanoameri'kano, a] *adj, nm/f* Spanish o Latin American
histeria [is'terja] *nf* hysteria
histérico, -a [is'teriko, a] *adj* hysterical
historia [is'torja] *nf* history; (*cuento*) story, tale; **historias** *nfpl* (*chismes*) gossip *sg*; **dejarse de ~s** to come to the point; **pasar a la ~** to go down in history
historiador, a [istorja'ðor, a] *nm/f* historian
historial [isto'rjal] *nm* record; (*profesional*) curriculum vitae, c.v., résumé (*US*); (*Med*) case history
histórico, -a [is'toriko, a] *adj* historical; (*fig*) historic
historieta [isto'rjeta] *nf* tale, anecdote; (*de dibujos*) comic strip

hito ['ito] *nm* (*fig*) landmark; (*objetivo*) goal, target; (*fig*) milestone

hizo ['iθo] *vb ver* **hacer**

hocico [o'θiko] *nm* snout; (*fig*) grimace

hockey ['xoki] *nm* hockey; **~ sobre hielo** ice hockey

hogar [o'ɣar] *nm* fireplace, hearth; (*casa*) home; (*vida familiar*) home life

hogareño, -a [oɣa'reɲo, a] *adj* home *cpd*; (*persona*) home-loving

hoguera [o'ɣera] *nf* (*gen*) bonfire; (*para herejes*) stake

hoja ['oxa] *nf* (*gen*) leaf; (*de flor*) petal; (*de hierba*) blade; (*de papel*) sheet; (*página*) page; (*formulario*) form; (*de puerta*) leaf; **~ de afeitar** razor blade; **~ de cálculo electrónica** spreadsheet; **~ informativa** leaflet, handout; **~ de ruta** road map; **~ de solicitud** application form; **~ de trabajo** (*Inform*) worksheet; **de ~ ancha** broad-leaved; **de ~ caduca/perenne** deciduous/evergreen

hojalata [oxa'lata] *nf* tin(plate)

hojaldre [o'xaldre] *nm* (*Culin*) puff pastry

hojear [oxe'ar] *vt* to leaf through, turn the pages of

hojuela [o'xwela] *nf* (*Am*) flake

hola ['ola] *excl* hello!

Holanda [o'landa] *nf* Holland

holandés, -esa [olan'des, esa] *adj* Dutch ▷ *nm/f* Dutchman(-woman); **los holandeses** the Dutch ▷ *nm* (*Ling*) Dutch

holgado, -a [ol'ɣaðo, a] *adj* loose, baggy; (*rico*) well-to-do

holgar [ol'ɣar] *vi* (*descansar*) to rest; (*sobrar*) to be superfluous; **huelga decir que** it goes without saying that

holgazán, -ana [olɣa'θan, ana] *adj* idle, lazy ▷ *nm/f* loafer

holgura [ol'ɣura] *nf* looseness, bagginess; (*Tec*) play, free movement; (*vida*) comfortable living, luxury

hollín [o'ʎin] *nm* soot

hombre ['ombre] *nm* man; (*raza humana*): **el ~** man(kind) ▷ *excl*: **¡sí ~!** (*claro*) of course!; (*para énfasis*) man, old chap; **~ de negocios** businessman; **~-rana** frogman; **~ de bien** o **pro** honest man; **~ de confianza** right-hand man; **~ de estado** statesman; **el ~ medio** the average man

hombrera [om'brera] *nf* shoulder strap

hombro ['ombro] *nm* shoulder; **arrimar el ~** to lend a hand; **encogerse de ~s** to shrug one's shoulders

hombruno, -a [om'bruno, a] *adj* mannish

homenaje [ome'naxe] *nm* (*gen*) homage; (*tributo*) tribute; **un partido ~** a benefit match

homeopatía [omeopa'tia] *nf* hom(o)eopathy

homeopático, -a [omeo'patiko, a] *adj* hom(o)eopathic

homicida [omi'θiða] *adj* homicidal ▷ *nm/f* murderer

homicidio [omi'θiðjo] *nm* murder, homicide; (*involuntario*) manslaughter

homologar [omolo'ɣar] *vt* (*Com*) to standardize; (*Escol*) to officially approve; (*Deporte*) to officially recognize; (*sueldos*) to equalize

homólogo, -a [o'moloɣo, a] *nm/f* counterpart, opposite number

homosexual [omosek'swal] *adj, nm/f* homosexual

honda ['onda] *nf* (*CS*) catapult

hondo, -a ['ondo, a] *adj* deep; **lo ~** the depth(s) (*pl*), the bottom; **con ~ pesar** with deep regret

hondonada [ondo'naða] *nf* hollow, depression; (*cañón*) ravine; (*Geo*) lowland

hondura [on'dura] *nf* depth, profundity

Honduras [on'duras] *nf* Honduras

hondureño, -a [ondu'reɲo, a] *adj, nm/f* Honduran

honestidad [onesti'ðað] *nf* purity, chastity; (*decencia*) decency

honesto, -a [o'nesto, a] *adj* chaste; decent, honest; (*justo*) just

hongo ['ongo] *nm* (*Bot: gen*) fungus; (*: comestible*) mushroom; (*: venenoso*) toadstool; (*sombrero*) bowler (hat) (*Brit*), derby (*US*); **~s del pie** foot rot *sg*, athlete's foot *sg*

honor [o'nor] *nm* (*gen*) honour (*Brit*), honor (*US*); (*gloria*) glory; **~ profesional** professional etiquette; **en ~ a la verdad** to be fair

honorable [ono'raβle] *adj* honourable (*Brit*), honorable (*US*)

honorario, -a [ono'rarjo, a] *adj* honorary ▷ *nm*: **~s** fees

honra ['onra] *nf* (*gen*) honour (*Brit*), honor (*US*); (*renombre*) good name; **~s fúnebres** funeral rites; **tener algo a mucha ~** to be proud of sth

honradez [onra'ðeθ] *nf* honesty; (*de persona*) integrity

honrado, -a [on'raðo, a] *adj* honest, upright

honrar [on'rar] *vt* to honour (*Brit*) o honor (*US*); **honrarse** *vr*: **~se con algo/de hacer algo** to be honoured by sth/to do sth

honroso, -a [on'roso, a] *adj* (*honrado*) honourable (*Brit*) o honorable (*US*); (*respetado*) respectable

hora ['ora] *nf* hour; (*tiempo*) time; **¿qué ~ es?** what time is it?; **¿a qué ~?** at what time?; **media ~** half an hour; **a la ~ de comer/de recreo** at lunchtime/at playtime; **a primera ~** first thing (in the morning); **a última ~** at the last moment; **"última ~"** "stop press"; **noticias de última ~** last-minute news; **a altas ~s** in the small hours; **a la ~ en punto** on the dot; **¡a buena ~!** about time, too!; **en mala ~** unluckily; **pedir ~** to make an appointment; **dar la ~** to strike the hour; **poner el reloj en ~** to set one's watch; **~s de oficina/de trabajo** office/working hours;

~s de visita visiting times; **~s extras** o **extraordinarias** overtime sg; **~s pico** (Am) rush o peak hours; **~s punta** rush hours; **no ver la ~ de** to look forward to; **¡ya era ~!** and about time too!

horadar [ora'ðar] vt to drill, bore

horario, -a [o'rarjo, a] adj hourly, hour cpd ▷ nm timetable; **~ comercial** business hours

horca ['orka] nf gallows sg; (Agr) pitchfork

horcajadas [orka'xaðas]: **a ~** adv astride

horchata [or'tʃata] nf cold drink made from tiger nuts and water, tiger nut milk

horda ['orða] nf horde

horizontal [oriθon'tal] adj horizontal

horizonte [ori'θonte] nm horizon

horma ['orma] nf mould; **~ (de calzado)** last; **~ de sombrero** hat block

hormiga [or'miɣa] nf ant; **hormigas** nfpl (Med) pins and needles

hormigón [ormi'ɣon] nm concrete; **~ armado/pretensado** reinforced/ prestressed concrete

hormigonera [ormiɣon'era] nf cement mixer

hormigueo [ormi'ɣeo] nm (comezón) itch; (fig) uneasiness

hormiguero [ormi'ɣero] nm (Zool) ants' nest; **era un ~** it was swarming with people

hormona [or'mona] nf hormone

hornada [or'naða] nf batch of loaves (etc)

hornillo [or'niʎo] nm (cocina) portable stove; **~ de gas** gas ring

horno ['orno] nm (Culin) oven; (Tec) furnace; (para cerámica) kiln; **~ microondas** microwave (oven); **alto ~** blast furnace; **~ crematorio** crematorium

horóscopo [o'roskopo] nm horoscope

horquilla [or'kiʎa] nf hairpin; (Agr) pitchfork

horrendo, -a [o'rrendo, a] adj horrendous, frightful

horrible [o'rriβle] adj horrible, dreadful

horripilante [orripi'lante] adj hair-raising, horrifying

horror [o'rror] nm horror, dread; (atrocidad) atrocity; **¡qué ~!** (fam) how awful!; **estudia ~es** he studies a hell of a lot

horrorizar [orrori'θar] vt to horrify, frighten; **horrorizarse** vr to be horrified

horroroso, -a [orro'roso, a] adj horrifying, ghastly

hortaliza [orta'liθa] nf vegetable

hortelano, -a [orte'lano, a] nm/f (market) gardener

hortera [or'tera] adj (fam) tacky

horterada [orte'raða] nf (fam): **es una ~** it's really naff

hortofrutícola [ortofru'tikola] adj fruit and vegetable cpd

hosco, -a ['osko, a] adj dark; (persona) sullen, gloomy

hospedar [ospe'ðar] vt to put up; **hospedarse** vr: **~se (con/en)** to stay o lodge (with/at)

hospital [ospi'tal] nm hospital

hospitalario, -a [ospita'larjo, a] adj (acogedor) hospitable

hospitalidad [ospitali'ðað] nf hospitality

hospitalizar [ospitali'θar] vt to send o take to hospital, hospitalize

hostal [os'tal] nm small hotel; ver tb **hotel**

hostelería [ostele'ria] nf hotel business o trade

hostia ['ostja] nf (Rel) host, consecrated wafer; (fam: golpe) whack, punch ▷ excl: **¡~(s)!** (fam!) damn!

hostigar [osti'ɣar] vt to whip; (fig) to harass, pester

hostil [os'til] adj hostile

hostilidad [ostili'ðað] nf hostility

hotdog [ot'dog] nm (Am) hot dog

hotel [o'tel] nm hotel; see note

HOTEL

In Spain you can choose from the following categories of accommodation, in descending order of quality and price: hotel (from 5 stars to 1), hostal, pensión, casa de huéspedes, fonda. Quality can vary widely even within these categories. The State also runs luxury hotels called paradores, which are usually sited in places of particular historical interest and are often historic buildings themselves.

hotelero, -a [ote'lero, a] adj hotel cpd ▷ nm/f hotelier

hoy [oi] adv (este día) today; (en la actualidad) now(adays) ▷ nm present time; **~ (en) día** now(adays); **el día de ~, ~ día** (Am) this very day; **~ por ~** right now; **de ~ en ocho días** a week today; **de ~ en adelante** from now on

hoyo ['ojo] nm hole, pit; (tumba) grave; (Golf) hole; (Med) pockmark

hoyuelo [oj'welo] nm dimple

hoz [oθ] nf sickle

hube etc ['uβe] vb ver **haber**

hucha ['utʃa] nf money box

hueco, -a ['weko, a] adj (vacío) hollow, empty; (resonante) booming; (sonido) resonant; (persona) conceited; (estilo) pompous ▷ nm hollow, cavity; (agujero) hole; (de escalera) well; (de ascensor) shaft; (vacante) vacancy; **~ de la mano** hollow of the hand

huelga ['welɣa] vb ver **holgar** ▷ nf strike; **declararse en ~** to go on strike, come out on strike; **~ general** general strike; **~ de hambre** hunger strike; **~ oficial** official strike

huelguista [wel'ɣista] nm/f striker

huella ['weʎa] nf (acto de pisar, pisada) tread(ing); (marca del paso) footprint, footstep;

(: *de animal, máquina*) track; ~ **dactilar** *o* **digital** fingerprint; **sin dejar** ~ without leaving a trace

huelo *etc vb ver* **oler**

huérfano, -a ['werfano, a] *adj* orphan(ed); (*fig*) unprotected ▷ *nm/f* orphan

huerta ['werta] *nf* market garden (*Brit*), truck farm (*US*); (*de Murcia, Valencia*) irrigated region

huerto ['werto] *nm* kitchen garden; (*de árboles frutales*) orchard

hueso ['weso] *nm* (*Anat*) bone; (*de fruta*) stone, pit (*US*); **sin ~** (*carne*) boned; **estar en los ~s** to be nothing but skin and bone; **ser un ~** (*profesor*) to be terribly strict; **un ~ duro de roer** a hard nut to crack

huésped, a ['wespeð, a] *nm/f* (*invitado*) guest; (*habitante*) resident; (*anfitrión*) host(ess)

huesudo, -a [we'suðo, a] *adj* bony, big-boned

huevas ['weβas] *nfpl* eggs, roe *sg*; (*Am: fam!*) balls (!)

huevera [we'βera] *nf* eggcup

huevo ['weβo] *nm* egg; (*fam!*) ball (!), testicle; **~ duro/escalfado/estrellado** *o* **frito/pasado por agua** hard-boiled/poached/fried/soft-boiled egg; **~s revueltos** scrambled eggs; **~ tibio** (*Am*) soft-boiled egg; **me costó un ~** (*fam!*) it was hard work; **tener ~s** (*fam!*) to have guts

huida [u'iða] *nf* escape, flight; **~ de capitales** (*Com*) flight of capital

huidizo, -a [ui'ðiθo, a] *adj* (*tímido*) shy; (*pasajero*) fleeting

huir [u'ir] *vt* (*escapar*) to flee, escape; (*evadir*) to avoid ▷ *vi* to flee, run away

hule ['ule] *nm* (*encerado*) oilskin; (*esp Am*) rubber

hulera [u'lera] *nf* (*Am*) catapult

humanidad [umani'ðað] *nf* (*género humano*) man(kind); (*cualidad*) humanity; (*fam: gordura*) corpulence

humanitario, -a [umani'tarjo, a] *adj* humanitarian; (*benévolo*) humane

humano, -a [u'mano, a] *adj* (*gen*) human; (*humanitario*) humane ▷ *nm* human; **ser ~** human being

humareda [uma'reða] *nf* cloud of smoke

humedad [ume'ðað] *nf* (*del clima*) humidity; (*de pared etc*) dampness; **a prueba de ~** damp-proof

humedecer [umeðe'θer] *vt* to moisten, wet; **humedecerse** *vr* to get wet

húmedo, -a ['umeðo, a] *adj* (*mojado*) damp, wet; (*tiempo etc*) humid

humildad [umil'dað] *nf* humility, humbleness

humilde [u'milde] *adj* humble, modest; (*clase etc*) low, modest

humillación [umiʎa'θjon] *nf* humiliation

humillante [umi'ʎante] *adj* humiliating

humillar [umi'ʎar] *vt* to humiliate; **humillarse** *vr* to humble o.s., grovel

humo ['umo] *nm* (*de fuego*) smoke; (*gas nocivo*) fumes *pl*; (*vapor*) steam, vapour; **humos** *nmpl* (*fig*) conceit *sg*; **irse todo en ~** (*fig*) to vanish without trace; **bajar los ~s a algn** to take sb down a peg or two

humor [u'mor] *nm* (*disposición*) mood, temper; (*lo que divierte*) humour; **de buen/mal ~** in a good/bad mood

humorismo [umo'rismo] *nm* humour

humorista [umo'rista] *nm/f* comic

humorístico, -a [umo'ristiko, a] *adj* funny, humorous

hundimiento [undi'mjento] *nm* (*gen*) sinking; (*colapso*) collapse

hundir [un'dir] *vt* to sink; (*edificio, plan*) to ruin, destroy; **hundirse** *vr* to sink, collapse; (*fig: arruinarse*) to be ruined; (*desaparecer*) to disappear; **se hundió la economía** the economy collapsed; **se hundieron los precios** prices slumped

húngaro, -a ['ungaro, a] *adj, nm/f* Hungarian ▷ *nm* (*Ling*) Hungarian, Magyar

Hungría [un'gria] *nf* Hungary

huracán [ura'kan] *nm* hurricane

huraño, -a [u'rano, a] *adj* shy; (*antisocial*) unsociable

hurgar [ur'ɣar] *vt* to poke, jab; (*remover*) to stir (up); **hurgarse** *vr*: **~se (las narices)** to pick one's nose

hurón [u'ron] *nm* (*Zool*) ferret

hurtadillas [urta'ðiʎas]: **a ~** *adv* stealthily, on the sly

hurtar [ur'tar] *vt* to steal; **hurtarse** *vr* to hide, keep out of the way

hurto ['urto] *nm* theft, stealing; (*lo robado*) (piece of) stolen property, loot

husmear [usme'ar] *vt* (*oler*) to sniff out, scent; (*fam*) to pry into ▷ *vi* to smell bad

huso ['uso] *nm* (*Tec*) spindle; (*de torno*) drum

huy ['ui] *excl* (*dolor*) ow!, ouch!; (*sorpresa*) well!; (*alivio*) phew!; **¡~, perdona!** oops, sorry!

huyo *etc vb ver* **huir**

iba etc ['iβa] vb ver **ir**

ibérico, -a [i'βeriko, a] adj Iberian;
la Península ibérica the Iberian Peninsula

iberoamericano, -a [iβeroameri'kano, a]
adj, nm/f Latin American

íbice ['iβiθe] nm ibex

Ibiza [i'βiθa] nf Ibiza

iceberg [iθe'βer] nm iceberg

icono [i'kono] nm (tb Inform) icon

iconoclasta [ikono'klasta] adj iconoclastic
▷ nm/f iconoclast

ictericia [ikte'riθja] nf jaundice

I+D nf abr (= Investigación y Desarrollo) R&D

ida ['iδa] nf going, departure; **~ y vuelta**
round trip, return; **~s y ven~s** comings and
goings

idea [i'δea] nf idea; (impresión) opinion;
(propósito) intention; **~ genial** brilliant idea;
a mala ~ out of spite; **no tengo la menor ~**
I haven't a clue

ideal [iδe'al] adj, nm ideal

idealista [iδea'lista] adj idealistic ▷ nm/f
idealist

idealizar [iδeali'θar] vt to idealize

idear [iδe'ar] vt to think up; (aparato) to
invent; (viaje) to plan

ídem ['iδem] pron ditto

idéntico, -a [i'δentiko, a] adj identical

identidad [iδenti'δaδ] nf identity;
~ corporativa corporate identity o image

identificación [iδentifika'θjon] nf
identification

identificar [iδentifi'kar] vt to identify;
identificarse vr: **~se con** to identify with

ideología [iδeolo'xia] nf ideology

idilio [i'δiljo] nm love affair

idioma [i'δjoma] nm language

idiota [i'δjota] adj idiotic ▷ nm/f idiot

idiotez [iδjo'teθ] nf idiocy

idolatrar [iδola'trar] vt (fig) to idolize

ídolo ['iδolo] nm (tb fig) idol

idóneo, -a [i'δoneo, a] adj suitable

iglesia [i'ɣlesja] nf church; **~ parroquial**
parish church; **¡con la ~ hemos topado!**
now we're really up against it!

iglú [i'ɣlu] nm igloo; (contenedor) bottle bank

ignominia [iɣno'minja] nf ignominy

ignorancia [iɣno'ranθja] nf ignorance; **por ~**
through ignorance

ignorante [iɣno'rante] adj ignorant,
uninformed ▷ nm/f ignoramus

ignorar [iɣno'rar] vt not to know, be ignorant
of; (no hacer caso a) to ignore; **ignoramos su**
paradero we don't know his whereabouts

igual [i'ɣwal] adj equal; (similar) like, similar;
(mismo) (the) same; (constante) constant;
(temperatura) even ▷ nm/f equal; **al ~ que** prep,
conj like, just like; **~ que** the same as; **sin ~**
peerless; **me da o es ~** I don't care, it makes
no difference; **no tener ~** to be unrivalled;
son ~es they're the same

igualada [iɣwa'laδa] nf equalizer

igualar [iɣwa'lar] vt (gen) to equalize, make
equal; (terreno) to make even; (allanar, nivelar)
to level (off); (Com) to agree upon; **igualarse**
vr (platos de balanza) to balance out; **~se (a)**
(equivaler) to be equal (to)

igualdad [iɣwal'daδ] nf equality; (similaridad)
sameness; (uniformidad) uniformity; **en ~ de**
condiciones on an equal basis

igualmente [iɣwal'mente] adv equally;
(también) also, likewise ▷ excl the same to you!

ikurriña [iku'rriɲa] nf Basque flag

ilegal [ile'ɣal] adj illegal

ilegítimo, -a [ile'xitimo, a] adj illegitimate

ileso, -a [i'leso, a] adj unhurt, unharmed

ilícito, -a [i'liθito, a] adj illicit

ilimitado, -a [ilimi'taδo, a] adj unlimited

ilógico, -a [i'loxiko, a] adj illogical

iluminación [ilumina'θjon] nf illumination;
(alumbrado) lighting; (fig) enlightenment

iluminar [ilumi'nar] vt to illuminate, light
(up); (fig) to enlighten

ilusión [ilu'sjon] nf illusion; (quimera)
delusion; (esperanza) hope; (emoción)
excitement, thrill; **hacerse ilusiones** to
build up one's hopes; **no te hagas ilusiones**
don't build up your hopes o get too excited

ilusionado, -a [ilusjo'naδo, a] adj excited

ilusionar [ilusjo'nar] vt: **~ a algn** (falsamente)
to build up sb's hopes ▷ vi: **le ilusiona ir de**
vacaciones he's looking forward to going on
holiday; **ilusionarse** vr (falsamente) to build
up one's hopes; (entusiasmarse) to get excited;

me **ilusiona mucho el viaje** I'm really excited about the trip

ilusionista [ilusjo'nista] *nm/f* conjurer

iluso, -a [i'luso, a] *adj* gullible, easily deceived ▷ *nm/f* dreamer, visionary

ilusorio, -a [ilu'sorjo, a] *adj (de ilusión)* illusory, deceptive; *(esperanza)* vain

ilustración [ilustra'θjon] *nf* illustration; *(saber)* learning, erudition; **la I~** the Enlightenment

ilustrado, -a [ilus'traðo, a] *adj* illustrated; learned

ilustrar [ilus'trar] *vt* to illustrate; *(instruir)* to instruct; *(explicar)* to explain, make clear; **ilustrarse** *vr* to acquire knowledge

ilustre [i'lustre] *adj* famous, illustrious

imagen [i'maxen] *nf (gen)* image; *(dibujo, TV)* picture; *(Rel)* statue; **ser la viva ~ de** to be the spitting o living image of; **a su ~** in one's own image

imaginación [imaxina'θjon] *nf* imagination; *(fig)* fancy; **ni por ~** on no account; **no se me pasó por la ~ que** ... it never even occurred to me that ...

imaginar [imaxi'nar] *vt (gen)* to imagine; *(idear)* to think up; *(suponer)* to suppose; **imaginarse** *vr* to imagine; **¡imagínate!** just imagine!, just fancy!; **imagínese que** ... suppose that ...; **me imagino que sí** I should think so

imaginario, -a [imaxi'narjo, a] *adj* imaginary

imaginativo, -a [imaxina'tiβo, a] *adj* imaginative ▷ *nf* imagination

imán [i'man] *nm* magnet

imbécil [im'beθil] *nm/f* imbecile, idiot

imbuir [imbu'ir] *vi* to imbue

imitación [imita'θjon] *nf* imitation; *(parodia)* mimicry; **a ~ de** in imitation of; **desconfíe de las imitaciones** *(Com)* beware of copies o imitations

imitar [imi'tar] *vt* to imitate; *(parodiar, remedar)* to mimic, ape; *(copiar)* to follow

impaciencia [impa'θjenθja] *nf* impatience

impaciente [impa'θjente] *adj* impatient; *(nervioso)* anxious

impacto [im'pakto] *nm* impact; *(esp Am: fig)* shock

impar [im'par] *adj* odd ▷ *nm* odd number

imparcial [impar'θjal] *adj* impartial, fair

imparcialidad [imparθjali'ðað] *nf* impartiality, fairness

impartir [impar'tir] *vt* to impart, give

impasible [impa'siβle] *adj* impassive

impávido, -a [im'paβiðo, a] *adj* fearless, intrepid

impecable [impe'kaβle] *adj* impeccable

impedimento [impeði'mento] *nm* impediment, obstacle

impedir [impe'ðir] *vt (obstruir)* to impede, obstruct; *(estorbar)* to prevent; **~ a algn hacer** o **que algn haga algo** to prevent sb (from) doing sth; **~ el tráfico** to block the traffic

impeler [impe'ler] *vt* to drive, propel; *(fig)* to impel

impenetrable [impene'traβle] *adj* impenetrable; *(fig)* incomprehensible

imperar [impe'rar] *vi (reinar)* to rule, reign; *(fig)* to prevail, reign; *(precio)* to be current

imperativo, -a [impera'tiβo, a] *adj (persona)* imperious; *(urgente, Ling)* imperative

imperceptible [imperθep'tiβle] *adj* imperceptible

imperdible [imper'ðiβle] *nm* safety pin

imperdonable [imperðo'naβle] *adj* unforgivable, inexcusable

imperfección [imperfek'θjon] *nf* imperfection; *(falla)* flaw, fault

imperfecto, -a [imper'fekto, a] *adj* faulty, imperfect ▷ *nm (Ling)* imperfect tense

imperial [impe'rjal] *adj* imperial

imperialismo [imperja'lismo] *nm* imperialism

imperio [im'perjo] *nm* empire; *(autoridad)* rule, authority; *(fig)* pride, haughtiness; **vale un ~** *(fig)* it's worth a fortune

imperioso, -a [impe'rjoso, a] *adj* imperious; *(urgente)* urgent; *(imperativo)* imperative

impermeable [imperme'aβle] *adj (a prueba de agua)* waterproof ▷ *nm* raincoat, mac *(Brit)*

impersonal [imperso'nal] *adj* impersonal

impertérrito, -a [imper'territo, a] *adj* undaunted

impertinencia [imperti'nenθja] *nf* impertinence

impertinente [imperti'nente] *adj* impertinent

imperturbable [impertur'βaβle] *adj* imperturbable; *(sereno)* unruffled; *(impasible)* impassive

ímpetu ['impetu] *nm (impulso)* impetus, impulse; *(impetuosidad)* impetuosity; *(violencia)* violence

impetuoso, -a [impe'twoso, a] *adj* impetuous; *(río)* rushing; *(acto)* hasty

impío, -a [im'pio, a] *adj* impious, ungodly; *(cruel)* cruel, pitiless

implacable [impla'kaβle] *adj* implacable, relentless

implantar [implan'tar] *vt (costumbre)* to introduce; *(Bio)* to implant; **implantarse** *vr* to be introduced

implemento [imple'mento] *nm (Am)* tool, implement

implicar [impli'kar] *vt* to involve; *(entrañar)* to imply; **esto no implica que** ... this does not mean that ...

implícito, -a [im'pliθito, a] *adj (tácito)* implicit; *(sobreentendido)* implied

implorar [implo'rar] *vt* to beg, implore

imponente [impo'nente] *adj (impresionante)* impressive, imposing; *(solemne)* grand ▷ *nm/f (Com)* depositor

imponer [impo'ner] *vt (gen)* to impose; *(tarea)* to set; *(exigir)* to exact; *(miedo)* to inspire;

(Com) to deposit; **imponerse** *vr* to assert o.s.; *(prevalecer)* to prevail; *(costumbre)* to grow up; **~se un deber** to assume a duty

imponible [impo'niβle] *adj (Com)* taxable, subject to tax; *(importación)* dutiable, subject to duty; **no ~** tax-free, tax-exempt *(US)*

impopular [impopu'lar] *adj* unpopular

importación [importa'θjon] *nf (acto)* importing; *(mercancías)* imports *pl*

importancia [impor'tanθja] *nf* importance; *(valor)* value, significance; *(extensión)* size, magnitude; **no dar ~ a** to consider unimportant; *(fig)* to make light of; **no tiene ~** it's nothing

importante [impor'tante] *adj* important; valuable, significant

importar [impor'tar] *vt (del extranjero)* to import; *(costar)* to amount to; *(implicar)* to involve ▷ *vi* to be important, matter; **me importa un rábano** *or* **un bledo** I couldn't care less, I don't give a damn; **¿le importa que fume?** do you mind if I smoke?; **¿te importa prestármelo?** would you mind lending it to me?; **¿qué importa?** what difference does it make?; **no importa** it doesn't matter; **no le importa** he doesn't care, it doesn't bother him; **"no importa precio"** "cost no object"

importe [im'porte] *nm (cantidad)* amount; *(valor)* value

importunar [importu'nar] *vt* to bother, pester

imposibilidad [imposiβili'ðað] *nf* impossibility; **mi ~ para hacerlo** my inability to do it

imposibilitar [imposiβili'tar] *vt* to make impossible, prevent

imposible [impo'siβle] *adj* impossible; *(insoportable)* unbearable, intolerable; **es ~** it's out of the question; **es ~ de predecir** it's impossible to forecast *o* predict

imposición [imposi'θjon] *nf* imposition; *(Com)* tax; *(inversión)* deposit; **efectuar una ~** to make a deposit

impostor, a [impos'tor, a] *nm/f* impostor

impotencia [impo'tenθja] *nf* impotence

impotente [impo'tente] *adj* impotent

impracticable [imprakti'kaβle] *adj (irrealizable)* impracticable; *(intransitable)* impassable

imprecar [impre'kar] *vt* to curse

impreciso, -a [impre'θiso, a] *adj* imprecise, vague

impregnar [impreɣ'nar] *vt* to impregnate; *(fig)* to pervade; **impregnarse** *vr* to become impregnated

imprenta [im'prenta] *nf (acto)* printing; *(aparato)* press; *(casa)* printer's; *(letra)* print

imprescindible [impresθin'diβle] *adj* essential, vital

impresión [impre'sjon] *nf* impression; *(Imprenta)* printing; *(edición)* edition; *(Foto)* print; *(marca)* imprint; **~ digital** fingerprint

impresionable [impresjo'naβle] *adj (sensible)* impressionable

impresionante [impresjo'nante] *adj* impressive; *(tremendo)* tremendous; *(maravilloso)* great, marvellous

impresionar [impresjo'nar] *vt (conmover)* to move; *(afectar)* to impress, strike; *(película fotográfica)* to expose; **impresionarse** *vr* to be impressed; *(conmoverse)* to be moved

impreso, -a [im'preso, a] *pp de* **imprimir** ▷ *adj* printed ▷ *nm* printed paper/book *etc*; **impresos** *nmpl* printed matter *sg*; **~ de solicitud** application form

impresora [impre'sora] *nf (Inform)* printer; **~ de chorro de tinta** ink-jet printer; **~ (por) láser** laser printer; **~ de línea** line printer

imprevisto, -a [impre'βisto, a] *adj* unforeseen; *(inesperado)* unexpected ▷ *nm*: **~s** *(dinero)* incidentals, unforeseen expenses

imprimir [impri'mir] *vt* to stamp; *(textos)* to print; *(Inform)* to output, print out

improbable [impro'βaβle] *adj* improbable; *(inverosímil)* unlikely

improcedente [improθe'ðente] *adj* inappropriate; *(Jur)* inadmissible

improductivo, -a [improðuk'tiβo, a] *adj* unproductive

improperio [impro'perjo] *nm* insult; **improperios** *nmpl* abuse *sg*

impropiedad [impropje'ðað] *nf* impropriety *(of language)*

impropio, -a [im'propjo, a] *adj* improper; *(inadecuado)* inappropriate

improvisación [improβisa'θjon] *nf* improvization

improvisado, -a [improβi'saðo, a] *adj* improvised, impromptu

improvisar [improβi'sar] *vt* to improvise; *(comida)* to rustle up ▷ *vi* to improvise; *(Mus)* to extemporize; *(Teat etc)* to ad-lib

improviso [impro'βiso] *adv*: **de ~** unexpectedly, suddenly; *(Mus etc)* impromptu

imprudencia [impru'ðenθja] *nf* imprudence; *(indiscreción)* indiscretion; *(descuido)* carelessness

imprudente [impru'ðente] *adj* unwise, imprudent; *(indiscreto)* indiscreet

impúdico, -a [im'puðiko, a] *adj* shameless; *(lujurioso)* lecherous

impudor [impu'ðor] *nm* shamelessness; *(lujuria)* lechery

impuesto, -a [im'pwesto, a] *pp de* **imponer** ▷ *adj* imposed ▷ *nm* tax; **anterior al ~** pre-tax; **sujeto a ~** taxable; **~ ambiental** green tax, environmental tax; **~ de lujo** luxury tax; **~ de plusvalía** capital gains tax; **~ sobre la propiedad** property tax; **~ sobre la renta** income tax; **~ sobre la renta de las personas físicas (IRPF)** personal income tax; **~ sobre la riqueza** wealth tax; **~ de transferencia de capital** capital transfer tax; **~ de venta** sales tax; **~ sobre el valor añadido (IVA)** value added tax (VAT)

impugnar [impuɣ'nar] vt to oppose, contest; (*refutar*) to refute, impugn

impulsar [impul'sar] vt to drive; (*promover*) to promote, stimulate

impulsivo, -a [impul'siβo, a] adj impulsive

impulso [im'pulso] nm impulse; (*fuerza, empuje*) thrust, drive; (*fig: sentimiento*) urge, impulse; **a ~s del miedo** driven on by fear

impune [im'pune] adj unpunished

impureza [impu'reθa] nf impurity; (*fig*) lewdness

impuro, -a [im'puro, a] adj impure; lewd

imputar [impu'tar] vt: **~ a** to attribute to, to impute to

inacabable [inaka'βaβle] adj (*infinito*) endless; (*interminable*) interminable

inaccesible [inakθe'siβle] adj inaccessible; (*fig: precio*) beyond one's reach, prohibitive; (*individuo*) aloof

inacción [inak'θjon] nf inactivity

inaceptable [inaθep'taβle] adj unacceptable

inactividad [inaktiβi'ðað] nf inactivity; (*Com*) dullness

inactivo, -a [inak'tiβo, a] adj inactive; (*Com*) dull; (*población*) non-working

inadaptación [inaðapta'θjon] nf maladjustment

inadecuado, -a [inaðe'kwaðo, a] adj (*insuficiente*) inadequate; (*inapto*) unsuitable

inadmisible [inaðmi'siβle] adj inadmissible

inadvertido, -a [inaðβer'tiðo, a] adj (*no visto*) unnoticed

inagotable [inaɣo'taβle] adj inexhaustible

inaguantable [inaɣwan'taβle] adj unbearable

inalámbrico, -a [ina'lambriko, a] adj cordless, wireless

inalterable [inalte'raβle] adj immutable, unchangeable

inanición [inani'θjon] nf starvation

inanimado, -a [inani'maðo, a] adj inanimate

inapreciable [inapre'θjaβle] adj invaluable

inaudito, -a [inau'ðito, a] adj unheard-of

inauguración [inauɣura'θjon] nf inauguration; (*de exposición*) opening

inaugurar [inauɣu'rar] vt to inaugurate; (*exposición*) to open

inca ['inka] nm/f Inca

incaico, -a [in'kaiko, a] adj Inca

incalculable [inkalku'laβle] adj incalculable

incandescente [inkandes'θente] adj incandescent

incansable [inkan'saβle] adj tireless, untiring

incapacidad [inkapaθi'ðað] nf incapacity; (*incompetencia*) incompetence; **~ física/mental** physical/mental disability

incapacitar [inkapaθi'tar] vt (*inhabilitar*) to incapacitate, handicap; (*descalificar*) to disqualify

incapaz [inka'paθ] adj incapable; **~ de hacer algo** unable to do sth

incautación [inkauta'θjon] nf seizure, confiscation

incautarse [inkau'tarse] vr: **~ de** to seize, confiscate

incauto, -a [in'kauto, a] adj (*imprudente*) incautious, unwary

incendiar [inθen'djar] vt to set fire to; (*fig*) to inflame; **incendiarse** vr to catch fire

incendiario, -a [inθen'djarjo, a] adj incendiary ▷ nm/f fire-raiser, arsonist

incendio [in'θendjo] nm fire; **~ intencionado** arson

incentivo [inθen'tiβo] nm incentive

incertidumbre [inθerti'ðumbre] nf (*inseguridad*) uncertainty; (*duda*) doubt

incesante [inθe'sante] adj incessant

incesto [in'θesto] nm incest

incidencia [inθi'ðenθja] nf (*Mat*) incidence; (*fig*) effect

incidente [inθi'ðente] nm incident

incidir [inθi'ðir] vi: **~ en** (*influir*) to influence; (*afectar*) to affect; **~ en un error** to be mistaken

incienso [in'θjenso] nm incense

incierto, -a [in'θjerto, a] adj uncertain

incineración [inθinera'θjon] nf incineration; (*de cadáveres*) cremation

incinerar [inθine'rar] vt to burn; (*cadáveres*) to cremate

incipiente [inθi'pjente] adj incipient

incisión [inθi'sjon] nf incision

incisivo, -a [inθi'siβo, a] adj sharp, cutting; (*fig*) incisive

incitar [inθi'tar] vt to incite, rouse

incivil [inθi'βil] adj rude, uncivil

inclemencia [inkle'menθja] nf (*severidad*) harshness, severity; (*del tiempo*) inclemency

inclinación [inklina'θjon] nf (*gen*) inclination; (*de tierras*) slope, incline; (*de cabeza*) nod, bow; (*fig*) leaning, bent

inclinado, -a [inkli'naðo, a] adj (*objeto*) leaning; (*superficie*) sloping

inclinar [inkli'nar] vt to incline; (*cabeza*) to nod, bow; **inclinarse** vi to lean, slope ▷ vr to lean, slope; (*en reverencia*) to bow; (*encorvarse*) to stoop; **~se a** (*parecerse*) to take after, resemble; **~se ante** to bow down to; **me inclino a pensar que ...** I'm inclined to think that ...

incluir [inklu'ir] vt to include; (*incorporar*) to incorporate; (*meter*) to enclose; **todo incluido** (*Com*) inclusive, all-in

inclusive [inklu'siβe] adv inclusive ▷ prep including

incluso, -a [in'kluso, a] adj included ▷ adv inclusively; (*hasta*) even

incógnita [in'koɣnita] nf (*Mat*) unknown quantity; (*fig*) mystery

incógnito [in'koɣnito] nm: **de ~** incognito

incoherente [inkoe'rente] adj incoherent

incoloro, -a [inko'loro, a] *adj* colourless

incólume [in'kolume] *adj* safe; *(indemne)* unhurt, unharmed

incomodar [inkomo'ðar] *vt* to inconvenience; *(molestar)* to bother, trouble; *(fastidiar)* to annoy; **incomodarse** *vr* to put o.s. out; *(fastidiarse)* to get annoyed; **no se incomode** don't bother

incomodidad [inkomoði'ðað] *nf* inconvenience; *(fastidio, enojo)* annoyance; *(de vivienda)* discomfort

incómodo, -a [in'komoðo, a] *adj* *(inconfortable)* uncomfortable; *(molesto)* annoying; *(inconveniente)* inconvenient; **sentirse ~** to feel ill at ease

incomparable [inkompa'raβle] *adj* incomparable

incompatible [inkompa'tiβle] *adj* incompatible

incompetencia [inkompe'tenθja] *nf* incompetence

incompetente [inkompe'tente] *adj* incompetent

incompleto, -a [inkom'pleto, a] *adj* incomplete, unfinished

incomprendido, -a [inkompren'diðo, a] *adj* misunderstood

incomprensible [inkompren'siβle] *adj* incomprehensible

incomunicado, -a [inkomuni'kaðo, a] *adj* *(aislado)* cut off, isolated; *(confinado)* in solitary confinement

inconcebible [inkonθe'βiβle] *adj* inconceivable

inconcluso, -a [inkon'kluso, a] *adj* *(inacabado)* unfinished

incondicional [inkondiθjo'nal] *adj* unconditional; *(apoyo)* wholehearted; *(partidario)* staunch

inconexo, -a [inko'nekso, a] *adj* unconnected; *(desunido)* disconnected; *(incoherente)* incoherent

inconformista [inkonfor'mista] *adj, nm/f* nonconformist

inconfundible [inkonfun'diβle] *adj* unmistakable

incongruente [inkon'grwente] *adj* incongruous

inconmensurable [inkonmensu'raβle] *adj* immeasurable, vast

inconsciencia [inkons'θjenθja] *nf* unconsciousness; *(fig)* thoughtlessness

inconsciente [inkons'θjente] *adj* unconscious; thoughtless; *(ignorante)* unaware; *(involuntario)* unwitting

inconsecuente [inkonse'kwente] *adj* inconsistent

inconsiderado, -a [inkonsiðe'raðo, a] *adj* inconsiderate

inconsistente [inkonsis'tente] *adj* inconsistent; *(Culin)* lumpy; *(endeble)* weak; *(tela)* flimsy

inconstancia [inkons'tanθja] *nf* inconstancy; *(de tiempo)* changeability; *(capricho)* fickleness

inconstante [inkons'tante] *adj* inconstant; changeable; fickle

incontable [inkon'taβle] *adj* countless, innumerable

incontestable [inkontes'taβle] *adj* unanswerable; *(innegable)* undeniable

incontinencia [inkonti'nenθja] *nf* incontinence

inconveniencia [inkombe'njenθja] *nf* unsuitability, inappropriateness; *(falta de cortesía)* impoliteness

inconveniente [inkombe'njente] *adj* unsuitable; impolite ⊳ *nm* obstacle; *(desventaja)* disadvantage; **el ~ es que ...** the trouble is that ...; **no hay ~ o para hacer eso** there is no objection to doing that; **no tengo ~** I don't mind

incordiar [inkor'ðjar] *vt* *(fam)* to hassle

incorporación [inkorpora'θjon] *nf* incorporation; *(fig)* inclusion

incorporar [inkorpo'rar] *vt* to incorporate; *(abarcar)* to embody; *(Culin)* to mix; **incorporarse** *vr* to sit up; **~se a** to join

incorrección [inkorrek'θjon] *nf* incorrectness, inaccuracy; *(descortesía)* bad-mannered behaviour

incorrecto, -a [inko'rrekto, a] *adj* incorrect, wrong; *(comportamiento)* bad-mannered

incorregible [inkorre'xiβle] *adj* incorrigible

incredulidad [inkreðuli'ðað] *nf* incredulity; *(escepticismo)* scepticism

incrédulo, -a [in'kreðulo, a] *adj* incredulous, unbelieving; sceptical

increíble [inkre'iβle] *adj* incredible

incremento [inkre'mento] *nm* increment; *(aumento)* rise, increase; **~ de precio** rise in price

increpar [inkre'par] *vt* to reprimand

incruento, -a [in'krwento, a] *adj* bloodless

incrustar [inkrus'tar] *vt* to incrust; *(piedras: en joya)* to inlay; *(fig)* to graft; *(Tec)* to set

incubar [inku'βar] *vt* to incubate; *(fig)* to hatch

inculcar [inkul'kar] *vt* to inculcate

inculpar [inkul'par] *vt*: **~ de** *(acusar)* to accuse of; *(achacar, atribuir)* to charge with, blame for

inculto, -a [in'kulto, a] *adj* *(persona)* uneducated, uncultured; *(fig: grosero)* uncouth ⊳ *nm/f* ignoramus

incumplimiento [inkumpli'mjento] *nm* non-fulfilment; *(Com)* repudiation; **~ de contrato** breach of contract; **por ~** by default

incurable [inku'raβle] *adj* *(enfermedad)* incurable; *(paciente)* incurably ill

incurrir [inku'rrir] *vi*: **~ en** to incur; *(crimen)* to commit; **~ en un error** to make a mistake

indagación [indaɣa'θjon] *nf* investigation; *(búsqueda)* search; *(Jur)* inquest

indagar [inda'ɣar] vt to investigate; to search; (averiguar) to ascertain

indecencia [inde'θenθja] nf indecency; (dicho) obscenity

indecente [inde'θente] adj indecent, improper; (lascivo) obscene

indecible [inde'θiβle] adj unspeakable; (indescriptible) indescribable

indeciso, -a [inde'θiso, a] adj (por decidir) undecided; (vacilante) hesitant

indefenso, -a [inde'fenso, a] adj defenceless

indefinido, -a [indefi'niðo, a] adj indefinite; (vago) vague, undefined

indeleble [inde'leβle] adj indelible

indemne [in'demne] adj (objeto) undamaged; (persona) unharmed, unhurt

indemnizar [indemni'θar] vt to indemnify; (compensar) to compensate

independencia [indepen'denθja] nf independence

independiente [indepen'djente] adj (libre) independent; (autónomo) self-sufficient; (Inform) stand-alone

indeseable [indese'aβle] adj, nm/f undesirable

indeterminado, -a [indetermi'naðo, a] adj (tb Ling) indefinite; (desconocido) indeterminate

India ['indja] nf: **la ~** India

indicación [indika'θjon] nf indication; (dato) piece of information; (señal) sign; (sugerencia) suggestion, hint; **indicaciones** nfpl (Com) instructions

indicado, -a [indi'kaðo, a] adj (momento, método) right; (tratamiento) appropriate; (solución) likely

indicador [indika'ðor] nm indicator; (Tec) gauge, meter; (aguja) hand, pointer; (de carretera) road sign; **~ de encendido** (Inform) power-on indicator

indicar [indi'kar] vt (mostrar) to indicate, show; (suj: termómetro etc) to read, register; (señalar) to point to

indicativo, -a [indika'tiβo, a] adj indicative ▷ nm (Radio) call sign; **~ de nacionalidad** (Auto) national identification plate

índice ['indiθe] nm index; (catálogo) catalogue; (Anat) index finger, forefinger; **~ del coste de (la) vida** cost-of-living index; **~ de crédito** credit rating; **~ de materias** table of contents; **~ de natalidad** birth rate; **~ de precios al por menor (IPM)** (Com) retail price index (RPI)

indicio [in'diθjo] nm indication, sign; (en pesquisa etc) clue

indiferencia [indife'renθja] nf indifference; (apatía) apathy

indiferente [indife'rente] adj indifferent; **me es ~** it makes no difference to me

indígena [in'dixena] adj indigenous, native ▷ nm/f native

indigencia [indi'xenθja] nf poverty, need

indigestión [indixes'tjon] nf indigestion

indigesto, -a [indi'xesto, a] adj undigested; (indigerible) indigestible; (fig) turgid

indignación [indiɣna'θjon] nf indignation

indignar [indiɣ'nar] vt to anger, make indignant; **indignarse** vr: **~se por** to get indignant about

indigno, -a [in'diɣno, a] adj (despreciable) low, contemptible; (inmerecido) unworthy

indio, -a ['indjo, a] adj, nm/f Indian

indirecto, -a [indi'rekto, a] adj indirect ▷ nf insinuation, innuendo; (sugerencia) hint

indiscreción [indiskre'θjon] nf (imprudencia) indiscretion; (irreflexión) tactlessness; (acto) gaffe, faux pas; **..., si no es ~** ..., if I may say so

indiscreto, -a [indis'kreto, a] adj indiscreet

indiscriminado, -a [indiskrimi'naðo, a] adj indiscriminate

indiscutible [indisku'tiβle] adj indisputable, unquestionable

indispensable [indispen'saβle] adj indispensable, essential

indisponer [indispo'ner] vt to spoil, upset; (salud) to make ill; **indisponerse** vr to fall ill; **~se con algn** to fall out with sb

indisposición [indisposi'θjon] nf indisposition; (desgana) unwillingness

indispuesto, -a [indis'pwesto, a] pp de **indisponer** ▷ adj (enfermo) unwell, indisposed; **sentirse ~** to feel unwell o indisposed

indistinto, -a [indis'tinto, a] adj indistinct; (vago) vague

individual [indiβi'ðwal] adj individual; (habitación) single ▷ nm (Deporte) singles sg

individuo, -a [indi'βiðwo, a] adj individual ▷ nm individual

índole ['indole] nf (naturaleza) nature; (clase) sort, kind

indolencia [indo'lenθja] nf indolence, laziness

indomable [indo'maβle] adj (animal) untameable; (espíritu) indomitable

indómito, -a [in'domito, a] adj indomitable

inducir [indu'θir] vt to induce; (inferir) to infer; (persuadir) to persuade; **~ a algn en el error** to mislead sb

indudable [indu'ðaβle] adj undoubted; (incuestionable) unquestionable; **es ~ que ...** there is no doubt that ...

indulgencia [indul'xenθja] nf indulgence; (Jur etc) leniency; **proceder sin ~ contra** to proceed ruthlessly against

indultar [indul'tar] vt (perdonar) to pardon, reprieve; (librar de pago) to exempt

indulto [in'dulto] nm pardon; exemption

industria [in'dustrja] nf industry; (habilidad) skill; **~ agropecuaria** farming and fishing; **~ pesada** heavy industry; **~ petrolífera** oil industry

industrial [indus'trjal] adj industrial ▷ nm industrialist

industrializar [industrjali'θar] *vt* to industrialize; **industrializarse** *vr* to become industrialized

inédito, -a [i'neδito, a] *adj* (*libro*) unpublished; (*nuevo*) new

inefable [ine'faβle] *adj* ineffable, indescribable

ineficaz [inefi'kaθ] *adj* (*inútil*) ineffective; (*ineficiente*) inefficient

ineludible [inelu'δiβle] *adj* inescapable, unavoidable

ineptitud [inepti'tuδ] *nf* ineptitude, incompetence

inepto, -a [i'nepto, a] *adj* inept, incompetent

inequívoco, -a [ine'kiβoko, a] *adj* unequivocal; (*inconfundible*) unmistakable

inercia [i'nerθja] *nf* inertia; (*pasividad*) passivity

inerme [i'nerme] *adj* (*sin armas*) unarmed; (*indefenso*) defenceless

inerte [i'nerte] *adj* inert; (*inmóvil*) motionless

inescrutable [ineskru'taβle] *adj* inscrutable

inesperado, -a [inespe'raδo, a] *adj* unexpected, unforeseen

inestable [ines'taβle] *adj* unstable

inestimable [inesti'maβle] *adj* inestimable; **de valor ~** invaluable

inevitable [ineβi'taβle] *adj* inevitable

inexactitud [ineksakti'tuδ] *nf* inaccuracy

inexacto, -a [inek'sakto, a] *adj* inaccurate; (*falso*) untrue

inexorable [inekso'raβle] *adj* inexorable

inexperto, -a [ineks'perto, a] *adj* (*novato*) inexperienced

infalible [infa'liβle] *adj* infallible; (*indefectible*) certain, sure; (*plan*) foolproof

infame [in'fame] *adj* infamous

infamia [in'famja] *nf* infamy; (*deshonra*) disgrace

infancia [in'fanθja] *nf* infancy, childhood; **jardín de la ~** nursery school

infante [in'fante] *nm* (*hijo del rey*) infante, prince

infantería [infante'ria] *nf* infantry

infantil [infan'til] *adj* child's, children's; (*pueril, aniñado*) infantile; (*cándido*) childlike

infarto [in'farto] *nm* (*tb:* **~ de miocardio**) heart attack

infatigable [infati'ɣaβle] *adj* tireless, untiring

infección [infek'θjon] *nf* infection

infeccioso, -a [infek'θjoso, a] *adj* infectious

infectar [infek'tar] *vt* to infect; **infectarse** *vr*: **~se (de)** (*tb fig*) to become infected (with)

infeliz [infe'liθ] *adj* (*desgraciado*) unhappy, wretched; (*inocente*) gullible ▷ *nm/f* (*desgraciado*) wretch; (*inocentón*) simpleton

inferior [infe'rjor] *adj* inferior; (*situación, Mat*) lower ▷ *nm/f* inferior, subordinate; **cualquier número ~ a nueve** any number less than *o* under *o* below nine; **una cantidad ~** a lesser quantity

inferioridad [inferjori'δaδ] *nf* inferiority; **estar en ~ de condiciones** to be at a disadvantage

inferir [infe'rir] *vt* (*deducir*) to infer, deduce; (*causar*) to cause

infernal [infer'nal] *adj* infernal

infestar [infes'tar] *vt* to infest

infidelidad [infiδeli'δaδ] *nf* infidelity, unfaithfulness

infiel [in'fjel] *adj* unfaithful, disloyal; (*falso*) inaccurate ▷ *nm/f* infidel, unbeliever

infierno [in'fjerno] *nm* hell; **¡vete al ~!** go to hell; **está en el quinto ~** it's at the back of beyond

infiltrar [infil'trar] *vt* to infiltrate; **infiltrarse** *vr* to infiltrate; **~se en** to infiltrate in(to); (*persona*) to work one's way in(to)

ínfimo, -a ['infimo, a] *adj* (*vil*) vile, mean; (*más bajo*) lowest; (*peor*) worst; (*miserable*) wretched

infinidad [infini'δaδ] *nf* infinity; (*abundancia*) great quantity; **~ de** vast numbers of; **~ de veces** countless times

infinitivo [infini'tiβo] *nm* infinitive

infinito, -a [infi'nito, a] *adj* infinite; (*fig*) boundless ▷ *adv* infinitely ▷ *nm* infinite; (*Mat*) infinity; **hasta lo ~** ad infinitum

inflación [infla'θjon] *nf* (*hinchazón*) swelling; (*monetaria*) inflation; (*fig*) conceit

inflacionario, -a [inflaθjo'narjo, a] *adj* inflationary

inflamable [infla'maβle] *adj* flammable

inflamar [infla'mar] *vt* to set on fire; (*Med, fig*) to inflame; **inflamarse** *vr* to catch fire; to become inflamed

inflar [in'flar] *vt* (*hinchar*) to inflate, blow up; (*fig*) to exaggerate; **inflarse** *vr* to swell (up); (*fig*) to get conceited

inflexible [inflek'siβle] *adj* inflexible; (*fig*) unbending

infligir [infli'xir] *vt* to inflict

influencia [in'flwenθja] *nf* influence

influenciar [inflwen'θjar] *vt* to influence

influir [influ'ir] *vt* to influence ▷ *vi* to have influence, carry weight; **~ en *o* sobre** to influence, affect; (*contribuir a*) to have a hand in

influjo [in'fluxo] *nm* influence; **~ de capitales** (*Econ etc*) capital influx

influya *etc vb ver* **influir**

influyente [influ'jente] *adj* influential

información [informa'θjon] *nf* information; (*noticias*) news sg; (*informe*) report; (*Inform: datos*) data; (*Jur*) inquiry; **I~** (*oficina*) information desk; (*Telec*) Directory Enquiries (Brit), Directory Assistance (US); (*mostrador*) Information Desk; **una ~** a piece of information; **abrir una ~** (*Jur*) to begin proceedings; **~ deportiva** (*en periódico*) sports section

informal [infor'mal] *adj* informal

informante [infor'mante] *nm/f* informant

informar [infor'mar] vt (gen) to inform; (revelar) to reveal, make known ▷ vi (Jur) to plead; (denunciar) to inform; (dar cuenta de) to report on; **informarse** vr to find out; ~**se de** to inquire into

informática [infor'matika] nf ver **informático**

informático, -a [infor'matiko, a] adj computer cpd ▷ nf (Tec) information technology; computing; (Escol) computer science o studies; ~ **de gestión** commercial computing

informativo, -a [informa'tiβo, a] adj (libro) informative; (folleto) information cpd; (Radio, TV) news cpd ▷ nm (Radio, TV) news programme

informe [in'forme] adj shapeless ▷ nm report; (dictamen) statement; (Mil) briefing; (Jur) plea; **informes** nmpl information sg; (datos) data; ~ **anual** annual report; ~ **del juez** summing-up

infortunio [infor'tunjo] nm misfortune

infracción [infrak'θjon] nf infraction, infringement; (Auto) offence

in fraganti [infra'ɣanti] adv: **pillar a algn** ~ to catch sb red-handed

infranqueable [infranke'aβle] adj impassable; (fig) insurmountable

infravalorar [infraβalo'rar] vt to undervalue; (Finanzas) to underestimate

infringir [infrin'xir] vt to infringe, contravene

infructuoso, -a [infruk'twoso, a] adj fruitless, unsuccessful

infundado, -a [infun'daðo, a] adj groundless, unfounded

infundir [infun'dir] vt to infuse, instil; ~ **ánimo a algn** to encourage sb; ~ **miedo a algn** to intimidate sb

infusión [infu'sjon] nf infusion; ~ **de manzanilla** camomile tea

ingeniar [inxe'njar] vt to think up, devise; **ingeniarse** vr to manage; ~**se para** to manage to

ingeniería [inxenje'ria] nf engineering; ~ **genética** genetic engineering; ~ **de sistemas** (Inform) systems engineering

ingeniero, -a [inxe'njero, a] nm/f engineer; (Am) courtesy title; ~ **de sonido** sound engineer; ~ **de caminos** civil engineer

ingenio [in'xenjo] nm (talento) talent; (agudeza) wit; (habilidad) ingenuity, inventiveness; (Tec): ~ **azucarero** sugar refinery

ingenioso, -a [inxe'njoso, a] adj ingenious, clever; (divertido) witty

ingenuidad [inxenwi'ðað] nf ingenuousness; (sencillez) simplicity

ingenuo, -a [in'xenwo, a] adj ingenuous

ingerir [inxe'rir] vt to ingest; (tragar) to swallow; (consumir) to consume

Inglaterra [ingla'terra] nf England

ingle ['ingle] nf groin

inglés, -esa [in'gles, esa] adj English ▷ nm/f Englishman(-woman) ▷ nm (Ling) English; **los ingleses** the English

ingratitud [ingrati'tuð] nf ingratitude

ingrato, -a [in'grato, a] adj ungrateful; (tarea) thankless

ingrediente [ingre'ðjente] nm ingredient; **ingredientes** nmpl (Am: tapas) titbits

ingresar [ingre'sar] vt (dinero) to deposit ▷ vi to come o go in; ~ **a** (esp Am) to enter; ~ **en** (club) to join; (Mil, Escol) to enrol in; ~ **en el hospital** to go into hospital

ingreso [in'greso] nm (entrada) entry; (: en hospital etc) admission; (Mil, Escol) enrolment; **ingresos** nmpl (dinero) income sg; (: Com) takings pl; ~ **gravable** taxable income sg; ~**s accesorios** fringe benefits; ~**s brutos** gross receipts; ~**s devengados** earned income sg; ~**s exentos de impuestos** non-taxable income sg; ~**s personales disponibles** disposable personal income sg

inhabilitar [inaβili'tar] vt (Pol, Med): ~ **a algn (para hacer algo)** to disqualify sb (from doing sth)

inhabitable [inaβi'taβle] adj uninhabitable

inhalar [ina'lar] vt to inhale

inherente [ine'rente] adj inherent

inhibir [ini'βir] vt to inhibit; (Rel) to restrain; **inhibirse** vr to keep out

inhóspito, -a [i'nospito, a] adj (región, paisaje) inhospitable

inhumano, -a [inu'mano, a] adj inhuman

INI ['ini] nm abr = **Instituto Nacional de Industria**

inicial [ini'θjal] adj, nf initial

iniciar [ini'θjar] vt (persona) to initiate; (empezar) to begin, commence; (conversación) to start up; ~ **a algn en un secreto** to let sb into a secret; ~ **la sesión** (Inform) to log in o on

iniciativa [iniθja'tiβa] nf initiative; (liderazgo) leadership; ~ **privada** private enterprise

inicio [i'niθjo] nm start, beginning

inicuo, -a [i'nikwo, a] adj iniquitous

ininterrumpido, -a [ininterrum'piðo, a] adj uninterrupted; (proceso) continuous; (progreso) steady

injerencia [inxe'renθja] nf interference

injertar [inxer'tar] vt to graft

injerto [in'xerto] nm graft; ~ **de piel** skin graft

injuria [in'xurja] nf (agravio, ofensa) offence; (insulto) insult; **injurias** nfpl abuse sg

injuriar [inxu'rjar] vt to insult

injurioso, -a [inxu'rjoso, a] adj offensive; insulting

injusticia [inxus'tiθja] nf injustice, unfairness; **con** ~ unjustly

injusto, -a [in'xusto, a] adj unjust, unfair

inmadurez [inmaðu'reθ] nf immaturity

inmaduro, -a [inma'ðuro, a] adj immature; (fruta) unripe

inmediaciones [inmeðja'θjones] *nfpl* neighbourhood *sg*, environs
inmediatamente [in meðjata'mente] *adv* immediately
inmediato, -a [inme'ðjato, a] *adj* immediate; (*contiguo*) adjoining; (*rápido*) prompt; (*próximo*) neighbouring, next; **de ~** (*esp Am*) immediately
inmejorable [inmexo'raβle] *adj* unsurpassable; (*precio*) unbeatable
inmenso, -a [in'menso, a] *adj* immense, huge
inmerecido, -a [inmere'θiðo, a] *adj* undeserved
inmigración [inmiɣra'θjon] *nf* immigration
inmigrante [inmi'ɣrante] *adj, nm/f* immigrant
inminente [inmi'nente] *adj* imminent, impending
inmiscuirse [inmisku'irse] *vr* to interfere, meddle
inmobiliario, -a [inmoβi'ljarjo, a] *adj* real-estate *cpd*, property *cpd* ⊳ *nf* estate agency
inmolar [inmo'lar] *vt* to immolate, sacrifice
inmoral [inmo'ral] *adj* immoral
inmortal [inmor'tal] *adj* immortal
inmortalizar [inmortali'θar] *vt* to immortalize
inmóvil [in'moβil] *adj* immobile
inmovilizar [inmoβili'θar] *vt* to immobilize; (*paralizar*) to paralyse; **inmovilizarse** *vr*: **se le ha inmovilizado la pierna** her leg was paralysed
inmueble [in'mweβle] *adj*: **bienes ~s** real estate *sg*, landed property *sg* ⊳ *nm* property
inmundicia [inmun'diθja] *nf* filth
inmundo, -a [in'mundo, a] *adj* filthy
inmune [in'mune] *adj*: ~ **(a)** (*Med*) immune (to)
inmunidad [inmuni'ðað] *nf* immunity; (*fisco*) exemption; ~ **diplomática/parlamentaria** diplomatic/parliamentary immunity
inmunitario, -a [inmuni'tarjo, a] *adj*: **sistema ~** immune system
inmunización [inmuniθa'θjon] *nf* immunization
inmunizar [inmuni'θar] *vt* to immunize
inmutable [inmu'taβle] *adj* immutable; **permaneció ~** he didn't flinch
inmutarse [inmu'tarse] *vr* to turn pale; **no se inmutó** he didn't turn a hair; **siguió sin ~** he carried on unperturbed
innato, -a [in'nato, a] *adj* innate
innecesario, -a [inneθe'sarjo, a] *adj* unnecessary
innoble [in'noβle] *adj* ignoble
innovación [innoβa'θjon] *nf* innovation
innovar [inno'βar] *vt* to introduce
inocencia [ino'θenθja] *nf* innocence
inocentada [inoθen'taða] *nf* practical joke
inocente [ino'θente] *adj* (*ingenuo*) naive,

innocent; (*no culpable*) innocent; (*sin malicia*) harmless ⊳ *nm/f* simpleton; **día de los (Santos) I-s** ≈ April Fools' Day; *see note*

> ● **DÍA DE LOS INOCENTES**
> ●
> ● The 28th December, *el día de los (Santos)*
> ● *Inocentes*, is when the Church
> ● commemorates the story of Herod's
> ● slaughter of the innocent children of
> ● Judea in the time of Christ. On this day
> ● Spaniards play *inocentadas* (practical
> ● jokes) on each other, much like our April
> ● Fools' Day pranks, eg typically sticking a
> ● *monigote* (cut-out paper figure) on
> ● someone's back, or broadcasting unlikely
> ● news stories.

inodoro, -a [ino'ðoro, a] *adj* odourless ⊳ *nm* toilet (*Brit*), lavatory (*Brit*), washroom (*US*)
inofensivo, -a [inofen'siβo, a] *adj* inoffensive
inolvidable [inolβi'ðaβle] *adj* unforgettable
inoperante [inope'rante] *adj* ineffective
inopinado, -a [inopi'naðo, a] *adj* unexpected
inoportuno, -a [inopor'tuno, a] *adj* untimely; (*molesto*) inconvenient; (*inapropiado*) inappropriate
inoxidable [inoksi'ðaβle] *adj* stainless; **acero ~** stainless steel
inquebrantable [inkeβran'taβle] *adj* unbreakable; (*fig*) unshakeable
inquietar [inkje'tar] *vt* to worry, trouble; **inquietarse** *vr* to worry, get upset
inquieto, -a [in'kjeto, a] *adj* anxious, worried; **estar ~ por** to be worried about
inquietud [inkje'tuð] *nf* anxiety, worry
inquilino, -a [inki'lino, a] *nm/f* tenant; (*Com*) lessee
inquirir [inki'rir] *vt* to enquire into, investigate
insaciable [insa'θjaβle] *adj* insatiable
insalubre [insa'luβre] *adj* unhealthy; (*condiciones*) insanitary
inscribir [inskri'βir] *vt* to inscribe; (*en lista*) to put; (*en censo*) to register; **inscribirse** *vr* to register; (*Escol etc*) to enrol
inscripción [inskrip'θjon] *nf* inscription; (*Escol etc*) enrolment; (*en censo*) registration
insecticida [insekti'θiða] *nm* insecticide
insecto [in'sekto] *nm* insect
inseguridad [inseɣuri'ðað] *nf* insecurity; ~ **ciudadana** lack of safety in the streets
inseguro, -a [inse'ɣuro, a] *adj* insecure; (*inconstante*) unsteady; (*incierto*) uncertain
inseminación [insemina'θjon] *nf*: ~ **artificial** artificial insemination (A.I.)
insensato, -a [insen'sato, a] *adj* foolish, stupid
insensibilidad [insensiβili'ðað] *nf* (*gen*) insensitivity; (*dureza de corazón*) callousness

insensible [insen'siβle] adj (gen) insensitive; (movimiento) imperceptible; (sin sensación) numb

inseparable [insepa'raβle] adj inseparable

insertar [inser'tar] vt to insert

inservible [inser'βiβle] adj useless

insidioso, -a [insi'ðjoso, a] adj insidious

insignia [in'siɣnja] nf (señal distintiva) badge; (estandarte) flag

insignificante [insiɣnifi'kante] adj insignificant

insinuar [insi'nwar] vt to insinuate, imply; **insinuarse** vr: **~se con algn** to ingratiate o.s. with sb

insípido, -a [in'sipiðo, a] adj insipid

insistencia [insis'tenθja] nf insistence

insistir [insis'tir] vi to insist; **~ en algo** to insist on sth; (enfatizar) to stress sth

in situ [in'situ] adv on the spot, in situ

insociable [inso'θjaβle] adj unsociable

insolación [insola'θjon] nf (Med) sunstroke

insolencia [inso'lenθja] nf insolence

insolente [inso'lente] adj insolent

insólito, -a [in'solito, a] adj unusual

insoluble [inso'luβle] adj insoluble

insolvencia [insol'βenθja] nf insolvency

insomnio [in'somnjo] nm insomnia

insondable [inson'daβle] adj bottomless

insonorizado, -a [insonori'θaðo, a] adj (cuarto etc) soundproof

insoportable [insopor'taβle] adj unbearable

insospechado, -a [insospe'tʃaðo, a] adj (inesperado) unexpected

inspección [inspek'θjon] nf inspection, check; **I~ inspectorate**; **~ técnica (de vehículos)** ≈ MOT (test) (Brit)

inspeccionar [inspekθjo'nar] vt (examinar) to inspect, examine; (controlar) to check

inspector, a [inspek'tor, a] nm/f inspector

inspiración [inspira'θjon] nf inspiration

inspirar [inspi'rar] vt to inspire; (Med) to inhale; **inspirarse** vr: **~se en** to be inspired by

instalación [instala'θjon] nf (equipo) fittings pl, equipment; **~ eléctrica** wiring

instalar [insta'lar] vt (establecer) to instal; (erguir) to set up, erect; **instalarse** vr to establish o.s.; (en una vivienda) to move into

instancia [ins'tanθja] nf (solicitud) application; (ruego) request; (Jur) petition; **a ~ de** at the request of; **en última ~** as a last resort

instantáneo, -a [instan'taneo, a] adj instantaneous ▷ nf snap(shot); **café ~** instant coffee

instante [ins'tante] nm instant, moment; **al ~** right now; **en un ~** in a flash

instar [ins'tar] vt to press, urge

instaurar [instau'rar] vt (costumbre) to establish; (normas, sistema) to bring in, introduce; (gobierno) to install

instigar [insti'ɣar] vt to instigate

instinto [ins'tinto] nm instinct; **por ~** instinctively

institución [institu'θjon] nf institution, establishment; **~ benéfica** charitable foundation

instituir [institu'ir] vt to establish; (fundar) to found

instituto [insti'tuto] nm (gen) institute; **I~ Nacional de Enseñanza** (Esp) ≈ comprehensive (Brit) o high (US) school; **I~ Nacional de Industria (INI)** (Esp Com) ≈ National Enterprise Board (Brit)

institutriz [institu'triθ] nf governess

instrucción [instruk'θjon] nf instruction; (enseñanza) education, teaching; (Jur) proceedings pl; (Mil) training; (Deporte) coaching; (conocimientos) knowledge; (Inform) statement; **instrucciones para el uso** directions for use; **instrucciones de funcionamiento** operating instructions

instructivo, -a [instruk'tiβo, a] adj instructive

instructor [instruk'tor] nm instructor

instruir [instru'ir] vt (gen) to instruct; (enseñar) to teach, educate; (Jur: proceso) to prepare, draw up; **instruirse** vr to learn, teach o.s.

instrumento [instru'mento] nm (gen, Mus) instrument; (herramienta) tool, implement; (Com) indenture; (Jur) legal document; **~ de percusión/cuerda/viento** percussion/ string(ed)/wind instrument

insubordinarse [insuβorði'narse] vr to rebel

insuficiencia [insufi'θjenθja] nf (carencia) lack; (inadecuación) inadequacy; **~ cardíaca/ renal** heart/kidney failure

insuficiente [insufi'θjente] adj (gen) insufficient; (Escol: nota) unsatisfactory

insufrible [insu'friβle] adj insufferable

insular [insu'lar] adj insular

insulina [insu'lina] nf insulin

insultar [insul'tar] vt to insult

insulto [in'sulto] nm insult

insumisión [insumi'sjon] nf refusal to do military service or community service

insumiso, -a [insu'miso, a] adj (rebelde) rebellious ▷ nm/f (Pol) person who refuses to do military service or community service; ver tb **mili**

insuperable [insupe'raβle] adj (excelente) unsurpassable; (problema etc) insurmountable

insurgente [insur'xente] adj, nm/f insurgent

insurrección [insurrek'θjon] nf insurrection, rebellion

intachable [inta'tʃaβle] adj irreproachable

intacto, -a [in'takto, a] adj (sin tocar) untouched; (entero) intact

integral [inte'ɣral] adj integral; (completo) complete; (Tec) built-in; **pan ~** wholemeal bread

integrar [inte'ɣrar] vt to make up, compose; (Mat, fig) to integrate

integridad [inteɣri'ðað] *nf* wholeness; (*carácter, tb Inform*) integrity; **en su ~** completely

integrismo [inte'ɣrismo] *nm* fundamentalism

integrista [inte'ɣrista] *adj, nm/f* fundamentalist

íntegro, -a ['inteɣro, a] *adj* whole, entire; (*texto*) uncut, unabridged; (*honrado*) honest

intelectual [intelek'twal] *adj, nm/f* intellectual

inteligencia [inteli'xenθja] *nf* intelligence; (*ingenio*) ability; **~ artificial** artificial intelligence

inteligente [inteli'xente] *adj* intelligent

inteligible [inteli'xiβle] *adj* intelligible

intemperie [intem'perje] *nf*: **a la ~** outdoors, out in the open, exposed to the elements

intempestivo, -a [intempes'tiβo, a] *adj* untimely

intención [inten'θjon] *nf* intention, purpose; **con segundas intenciones** maliciously; **con ~** deliberately

intencionado, -a [intenθjo'naðo, a] *adj* deliberate; **bien ~** well-meaning; **mal ~** ill-disposed, hostile

intensidad [intensi'ðað] *nf* (*gen*) intensity; (*Elec, Tec*) strength; (*de recuerdo*) vividness; **llover con ~** to rain hard

intensivo, -a [inten'siβo, a] *adj* intensive; **curso ~** crash course

intenso, -a [in'tenso, a] *adj* intense; (*impresión*) vivid; (*sentimiento*) profound, deep

intentar [inten'tar] *vt* (*tratar*) to try, attempt

intento [in'tento] *nm* (*intención*) intention, purpose; (*tentativa*) attempt

interactivo, -a [interak'tiβo, a] *adj* interactive; (*Inform*): **computación interactiva** interactive computing

intercalar [interka'lar] *vt* to insert; (*Inform: archivos, texto*) to merge

intercambio [inter'kambjo] *nm* (*canje*) exchange; (*trueque*) swap

interceder [interθe'ðer] *vi* to intercede

interceptar [interθep'tar] *vt* to intercept, cut off; (*Auto*) to hold up

intercesión [interθe'sjon] *nf* intercession

interés [inte'res] *nm* (*gen, Com*) interest; (*importancia*) concern; (*parte*) share, part; (*pey*) self-interest; **~ compuesto** compound interest; **~ simple** simple interest; **con un ~ de 9 por ciento** at an interest of 9%; **dar a ~** to lend at interest; **tener ~ en** (*Com*) to hold a share in; **intereses acumulados** accrued interest *sg*; **intereses por cobrar** interest receivable *sg*; **intereses creados** vested interests; **intereses por pagar** interest payable *sg*

interesado, -a [intere'saðo, a] *adj* interested; (*prejuiciado*) prejudiced; (*pey*) mercenary, self-seeking ▷ *nm/f* person concerned; (*firmante*) the undersigned

interesante [intere'sante] *adj* interesting

interesar [intere'sar] *vt* to interest, be of interest to ▷ *vi* to interest, be of interest; (*importar*) to be important; **interesarse** *vr*: **~se en** *o* **por** to take an interest in; **no me interesan los toros** bullfighting does not appeal to me

interferencia [interfe'renθja] *nf* interference

interferir [interfe'rir] *vt* to interfere with; (*Telec*) to jam ▷ *vi* to interfere

interfón [inter'fon] *nm* (*Am*) = **interfono**

interfono [inter'fono] *nm* intercom, entry phone

interino, -a [inte'rino, a] *adj* temporary; (*empleado etc*) provisional ▷ *nm/f* temporary holder of a post; (*Med*) locum; (*Escol*) supply teacher; (*Teat*) stand-in

interior [inte'rjor] *adj* inner, inside; (*Com*) domestic, internal ▷ *nm* interior, inside; (*fig*) soul, mind; (*Deporte*) inside forward; **Ministerio del I~** = Home Office (*Brit*), ≈ Department of the Interior (*US*); **dije para mi ~** I said to myself

interjección [interxek'θjon] *nf* interjection

interlocutor, a [interloku'tor, a] *nm/f* speaker; (*al teléfono*) person at the other end (of the line); **mi ~** the person I was speaking to

intermediario, -a [interme'ðjarjo, a] *adj* (*mediador*) mediating ▷ *nm/f* intermediary, go-between; (*mediador*) mediator

intermedio, -a [inter'meðjo, a] *adj* intermediate; (*tiempo*) intervening ▷ *nm* interval; (*Pol*) recess

interminable [intermi'naβle] *adj* endless, interminable

intermitente [intermi'tente] *adj* intermittent ▷ *nm* (*Auto*) indicator

internacional [internaθjo'nal] *adj* international

internado [inter'naðo] *nm* boarding school

internar [inter'nar] *vt* to intern; (*en un manicomio*) to commit; **internarse** *vr* (*penetrar*) to penetrate; **~se en** to go into *o* right inside; **~se en un estudio** to study a subject in depth

internauta [inter'nauta] *nm/f* web surfer, internet user

Internet [inter'net] *nm o nf* internet, Internet

interno, -a [in'terno, a] *adj* internal, interior; (*Pol etc*) domestic ▷ *nm/f* (*alumno*) boarder

interponer [interpo'ner] *vt* to interpose, put in; **interponerse** *vr* to intervene

interpretación [interpreta'θjon] *nf* interpretation; (*Mus, Teat*) performance; **mala ~** misinterpretation

interpretar [interpre'tar] *vt* to interpret; (*Teat, Mus*) to perform, play

intérprete [in'terprete] *nm/f* (*Ling*) interpreter, translator; (*Mus, Teat*) performer, artist(e)

interrogación [interroɣa'θjon] *nf*
interrogation; (*Ling: tb:* **signo de ~**) question
mark; (*Telec*) polling

interrogante [interro'ɣante] *adj*
questioning ▷ *nm* question mark; (*fig*)
question mark, query

interrogar [interro'ɣar] *vt* to interrogate,
question

interrumpir [interrum'pir] *vt* to interrupt;
(*vacaciones*) to cut short; (*servicio*) to cut off;
(*tráfico*) to block

interrupción [interrup'θjon] *nf* interruption

interruptor [interrup'tor] *nm* (*Elec*) switch

intersección [intersek'θjon] *nf* intersection;
(*Auto*) junction

interurbano, -a [interur'βano, a] *adj* inter
city; (*Telec*) long-distance

intervalo [inter'βalo] *nm* interval; (*descanso*)
break; **a ~s** at intervals, every now and then

intervención [interβen'θjon] *nf*
supervision; (*Com*) audit(ing); (*Med*)
operation; (*Telec*) tapping; (*participación*)
intervention; **~ quirúrgica** surgical
operation; **la política de no ~** the policy of
non-intervention

intervenir [interβe'nir] *vt* (*controlar*) to
control, supervise; (*Com*) to audit; (*Med*) to
operate on; (*Telec*) to tap ▷ *vi* (*participar*) to
take part, participate; (*mediar*) to intervene

interventor, a [interβen'tor, a] *nm/f*
inspector; (*Com*) auditor

interviú [inter'βju] *nf* interview

intestino [intes'tino] *nm* intestine

intimar [inti'mar] *vt* to intimate, announce;
(*mandar*) to order ▷ *vi*, **intimarse** *vr* to become
friendly

intimidad [intimi'ðað] *nf* intimacy;
(*familiaridad*) familiarity; (*vida privada*) private
life; (*Jur*) privacy

íntimo, -a ['intimo, a] *adj* intimate;
(*pensamientos*) innermost; (*vida*) personal,
private; **una boda íntima** a quiet wedding

intolerable [intole'raβle] *adj* intolerable,
unbearable

intolerancia [intole'ranθja] *nf* intolerance

intoxicación [intoksika'θjon] *nf* poisoning;
~ alimenticia food poisoning

intranet [intra'net] *nf* intranet

intranquilizarse [intrankili'θarse] *vr* to get
worried *o* anxious

intranquilo, -a [intran'kilo, a] *adj* worried

intransigente [intransi'xente] *adj*
intransigent

intransitable [intransi'taβle] *adj* impassable

intransitivo, -a [intransi'tiβo, a] *adj*
intransitive

intrepidez [intrepi'ðeθ] *nf* courage, bravery

intrépido, -a [in'trepiðo, a] *adj* intrepid,
fearless

intriga [in'triɣa] *nf* intrigue; (*plan*) plot

intrigar [intri'ɣar] *vt, vi* to intrigue

intrincado, -a [intrin'kaðo, a] *adj* intricate

intrínseco, -a [in'trinseko, a] *adj* intrinsic

introducción [introðuk'θjon] *nf*
introduction; (*de libro*) foreword; (*Inform*)
input

introducir [introðu'θir] *vt* (*gen*) to introduce;
(*moneda*) to insert; (*Inform*) to input, enter

intromisión [intromi'sjon] *nf* interference,
meddling

introvertido, -a [introβer'tiðo, a] *adj, nm/f*
introvert

intruso, -a [in'truso, a] *adj* intrusive ▷ *nm/f*
intruder

intuición [intwi'θjon] *nf* intuition

intuir [intu'ir] *vt* to know by intuition, intuit

inundación [inunda'θjon] *nf* flood(ing)

inundar [inun'dar] *vt* to flood; (*fig*) to
swamp, inundate

inusitado, -a [inusi'taðo, a] *adj* unusual

inútil [i'nutil] *adj* useless; (*esfuerzo*) vain,
fruitless

inutilidad [inutili'ðað] *nf* uselessness

inutilizar [inutili'θar] *vt* to make unusable,
put out of action; (*incapacitar*) to disable;
inutilizarse *vr* to become useless

invadir [imba'ðir] *vt* to invade

invalidar [imbali'ðar] *vt* to invalidate

inválido, -a [im'baliðo, a] *adj* invalid; (*Jur*)
null and void ▷ *nm/f* invalid

invariable [imba'rjaβle] *adj* invariable

invasión [imba'sjon] *nf* invasion

invasor, a [imba'sor, a] *adj* invading ▷ *nm/f*
invader

invencible [imben'θiβle] *adj* invincible;
(*timidez, miedo*) unsurmountable

invención [imben'θjon] *nf* invention

inventar [imben'tar] *vt* to invent

inventario [imben'tarjo] *nm* inventory;
(*Com*) stocktaking

inventiva [imben'tiβa] *nf* inventiveness

invento [im'bento] *nm* invention, (*fig*)
brainchild; (*pey*) silly idea

inventor, a [imben'tor, a] *nm/f* inventor

invernadero [imberna'ðero] *nm* greenhouse

invernar [imber'nar] *vi* (*Zool*) to hibernate

inverosímil [imbero'simil] *adj* implausible

inversión [imber'sjon] *nf* (*Com*) investment;
~ de capitales capital investment;
inversiones extranjeras foreign
investment *sg*

inverso, a [im'berso, a] *adj* inverse, opposite;
en el orden ~ in reverse order; **a la inversa**
inversely, the other way round

inversor, -a [imber'sor, a] *nm/f* (*Com*)
investor

invertebrado, -a [imberte'βraðo, a] *adj, nm*
invertebrate

invertir [imber'tir] *vt* (*Com*) to invest; (*volcar*)
to turn upside down; (*tiempo etc*) to spend

investigación [imbestiɣa'θjon] *nf*
investigation; (*indagación*) inquiry; (*Univ*)
research; **~ y desarrollo** (*Com*) research and
development (R & D); **~ de los medios de**

publicidad media research; **~ del mercado** market research

investigar [imbesti'ɣar] vt to investigate; (estudiar) to do research into

investir [imbes'tir] vt: **~ a algn con algo** to confer sth on sb; **fue investido Doctor Honoris Causa** he was awarded an honorary doctorate

invicto, -a [im'bikto, a] adj unconquered

invidente [imbi'ðente] adj sightless ▷ nm/f blind person; **los ~s** the sightless

invierno [im'bjerno] nm winter

invisible [imbi'siβle] adj invisible; **exportaciones/importaciones ~s** invisible exports/imports

invitación [imbita'θjon] nf invitation

invitado, -a [imbi'taðo, a] nm/f guest

invitar [imbi'tar] vt to invite; (incitar) to entice; **~ a algn a hacer algo** to invite sb to do sth; **~ a algo** to pay for sth; **nos invitó a cenar fuera** she took us out for dinner; **invito yo** it's on me

in vitro [im'bitro] adv in vitro

invocar [imbo'kar] vt to invoke, call on

involucrar [imbolu'krar] vt: **~ algo en un discurso** to bring something irrelevant into a discussion; **~ a algn en algo** to involve sb in sth; **involucrarse** vr (interesarse) to get involved

involuntario, -a [imbolun'tarjo, a] adj involuntary; (ofensa etc) unintentional

inyección [injek'θjon] nf injection

inyectar [injek'tar] vt to inject

ión [i'on] nm ion

IPC nm abr (Esp: = índice de precios al consumo) CPI

iPod® ['ipoð] (pl **iPods**) nm iPod®

PALABRA CLAVE

ir [ir] vi **1** to go; (a pie) to walk; (viajar) to travel; **ir caminando** to walk; **fui en tren** I went o travelled by train; **voy a la calle** I'm going out; **ir en coche/en bicicleta** to drive/cycle; **ir a pie** to walk, go on foot; **ir de pesca** to go fishing; **¡(ahora) voy!** (I'm just) coming!
2: **ir (a) por**: **ir (a) por el médico** to fetch the doctor
3 (progresar: persona, cosa) to go; **el trabajo va muy bien** work is going very well; **¿cómo te va?** how are things going?; **me va muy bien** I'm getting on very well; **le fue fatal** it went awfully badly for him
4 (funcionar): **el coche no va muy bien** the car isn't running very well
5 (sentar): **me va estupendamente** (ropa, color) it suits me really well; (medicamento) it works really well for me; **ir bien con algo** to go well with sth; **te va estupendamente ese color** that colour suits you fantastically well
6 (aspecto): **iba muy bien vestido** he was very well dressed; **ir con zapatos negros** to wear black shoes

7 (locuciones): **¿vino? — ¡que va!** did he come? — of course not!; **vamos, no llores** come on, don't cry; **¡vaya coche!** (admiración) what a car!, that's some car!; (desprecio) that's a terrible car!; **¡vaya!** (regular) so so; (desagrado) come on!; **¡vamos!** come on!; **¡que le vaya bien!** (adiós) take care!
8: **no vaya a ser**: **tienes que correr, no vaya a ser que pierdas el tren** you'll have to run so as not to miss the train
9: **no me** etc **va ni me viene** I etc don't care ▷ vb auxiliar **1**: **ir a**: **voy/iba a hacerlo hoy** I am/was going to do it today
2 (+gerundio): **iba anocheciendo** it was getting dark; **todo se me iba aclarando** everything was gradually becoming clearer to me
3 (+pp = pasivo): **van vendidos 300 ejemplares** 300 copies have been sold so far

irse vr **1**: **¿por dónde se va al zoológico?** which is the way to the zoo?
2 (marcharse) to leave; **ya se habrán ido** they must already have left o gone; **¡vámonos!**, **¡nos fuimos!** (Am) let's go!; **¡vete!** go away!; **¡vete a saber!** your guess is as good as mine!, who knows!

ira ['ira] nf anger, rage

iracundo, -a [ira'kundo, a] adj irascible

Irak [i'rak] nm = **Iraq**

Irán [i'ran] nm Iran

iraní [ira'ni] adj, nm/f Iranian

Iraq [i'rak] nm Iraq

iraquí [ira'ki] adj, nm/f Iraqi

irascible [iras'θiβle] adj irascible

iris ['iris] nm inv (arco iris) rainbow; (Anat) iris

Irlanda [ir'landa] nf Ireland; **~ del Norte** Northern Ireland, Ulster

irlandés, -esa [irlan'des, esa] adj Irish ▷ nm/f Irishman(-woman) ▷ nm (Ling) Gaelic, Irish; **los irlandeses** nmpl the Irish

ironía [iro'nia] nf irony

irónico, -a [i'roniko, a] adj ironic(al)

IRPF nm abr (Esp) = **impuesto sobre la renta de las personas físicas**

irracional [irraθjo'nal] adj irrational

irreal [irre'al] adj unreal

irrecuperable [irrekupe'raβle] adj irrecoverable, irretrievable

irreflexión [irreflek'sjon] nf thoughtlessness; (ímpetu) rashness

irregular [irreɣu'lar] adj irregular; (situación) abnormal, anomalous; **margen izquierdo/derecho ~** (texto) ragged left/right (margin)

irregularidad [irreɣulari'ðað] nf irregularity

irremediable [irreme'ðjaβle] adj irremediable; (vicio) incurable

irreparable [irrepa'raβle] adj (daños) irreparable; (pérdida) irrecoverable

irreprochable [irrepro'tʃaβle] adj irreproachable

irresistible [irresis'tiβle] adj irresistible

irresoluto, -a [irreso'luto, a] *adj* irresolute, hesitant; *(sin resolver)* unresolved

irrespetuoso, -a [irrespe'twoso, a] *adj* disrespectful

irresponsable [irrespon'saβle] *adj* irresponsible

irreversible [irreβer'siβle] *adj* irreversible

irrevocable [irreβo'kaβle] *adj* irrevocable

irrigar [irri'ɣar] *vt* to irrigate

irrisorio, -a [irri'sorjo, a] *adj* derisory, ridiculous; *(precio)* bargain *cpd*

irritación [irrita'θjon] *nf* irritation

irritar [irri'tar] *vt* to irritate, annoy; **irritarse** *vr* to get angry, lose one's temper

irrupción [irrup'θjon] *nf* irruption; *(invasión)* invasion

IRTP *nm abr (Esp: = impuesto sobre el rendimiento del trabajo personal)* ≈ PAYE

isla ['isla] *nf (Geo)* island; **I~s Británicas** British Isles; **I~s Filipinas/Malvinas/Canarias** Philippines/Falklands/Canaries

Islam [is'lam] *nm* Islam

islámico, -a [is'lamiko, a] *adj* Islamic

islandés, -esa [islan'des, esa] *adj* Icelandic ▷ *nm/f* Icelander ▷ *nm (Ling)* Icelandic

Islandia [is'landja] *nf* Iceland

isleño, -a [is'leɲo, a] *adj* island *cpd* ▷ *nm/f* islander

isotónico, -a [iso'toniko, a] *adj* isotonic

Israel [isra'el] *nm* Israel

israelí [israe'li] *adj, nm/f* Israeli

istmo ['istmo] *nm* isthmus; **el I~ de Panamá** the Isthmus of Panama

Italia [i'talja] *nf* Italy

italiano, -a [ita'ljano, a] *adj, nm/f* Italian ▷ *nm (Ling)* Italian

itinerario [itine'rarjo] *nm* itinerary, route

ITV *nf abr (= Inspección Técnica de Vehículos)* ≈ MOT (test) *(Brit)*

IVA ['iβa] *nm abr (Esp Com: = Impuesto sobre el Valor Añadido)* VAT

izar [i'θar] *vt* to hoist

izdo, izq.° *abr (= izquierdo)* L, l

izquierda [iθ'kjerða] *nf ver* **izquierdo**

izquierdista [iθkjer'ðista] *adj* leftist, left-wing ▷ *nm/f* left-winger, leftist

izquierdo, -a [iθ'kjerðo, a] *adj* left ▷ *nf* left; *(Pol)* left (wing); **a la izquierda** on the left; *(torcer etc)* (to the) left; **es un cero a la izquierda** *(fam)* he is a nonentity; **conducción por la izquierda** left-hand drive

jabalí [xaβa'li] *nm* wild boar

jabalina [xaβa'lina] *nf* javelin

jabón [xa'βon] *nm* soap; *(fam: adulación)* flattery; **~ de afeitar** shaving soap; **~ de tocador** toilet soap; **dar ~ a algn** to soft-soap sb

jabonar [xaβo'nar] *vt* to soap

jaca ['xaka] *nf* pony

jacal [xa'kal] *nm (Am)* shack

jacinto [xa'θinto] *nm* hyacinth

jactarse [xak'tarse] *vr:* **~ (de)** to boast o brag (about o of)

jadear [xaðe'ar] *vi* to pant, gasp for breath

jadeo [xa'ðeo] *nm* panting, gasping

jaguar [xa'ɣwar] *nm* jaguar

jaiba ['xaiβa] *nf (Am)* crab

jalar [xa'lar] *vt (Am)* to pull

jalbegue [xal'βeɣe] *nm* whitewash

jalea [xa'lea] *nf* jelly

jaleo [xa'leo] *nm* racket, uproar; **armar un ~** to kick up a racket

jalón [xa'lon] *nm (Am)* tug

Jamaica [xa'maika] *nf* Jamaica

jamás [xa'mas] *adv* never, not ... ever; *(interrogativo)* ever; **¿~ se vio tal cosa?** did you ever see such a thing?

jamón [xa'mon] *nm* ham; **~ (de) York** boiled ham; **~ dulce/serrano** boiled/cured ham

Japón [xa'pon] *nm:* **el ~** Japan

japonés, -esa [xapo'nes, esa] *adj, nm/f* Japanese ▷ *nm (Ling)* Japanese

jaque ['xake] *nm:* **~ mate** checkmate

jaqueca [xa'keka] *nf* (very bad) headache, migraine

jarabe [xa'raβe] *nm* syrup; **~ para la tos** cough syrup *o* mixture

jarcia [xar'θja] *nf* (Naut) ropes *pl*, rigging

jardín [xar'ðin] *nm* garden; **~ botánico** botanical garden; **~ de (la) infancia** (Esp) *o* **de niños** (Am) *o* **infantil** kindergarten, nursery school

jardinaje [xarði'naxe] *nm* gardening

jardinería [xarðine'ria] *nf* gardening

jardinero, -a [xarði'nero, a] *nm/f* gardener

jarra ['xarra] *nf* jar; (jarro) jug; (de leche) churn; (de cerveza) mug; **de** *o* **en ~s** with arms akimbo

jarro ['xarro] *nm* jug

jarrón [xa'rron] *nm* vase; (Arqueología) urn

jaula ['xaula] *nf* cage; (embalaje) crate

jauría [xau'ria] *nf* pack of hounds

jazmín [xaθ'min] *nm* jasmine

J. C. *abr* = **Jesucristo**

jeans [jins, dʒins] *nmpl* (Am) jeans, denims; **unos ~** a pair of jeans

jeep® (*pl* **jeeps**) [jip, jips] *nm* jeep®

jefa ['xefa] *nf ver* **jefe**

jefatura [xefa'tura] *nf* (liderazgo) leadership; (sede) central office; **J~ de la aviación civil** ≈ Civil Aviation Authority; **~ de policía** police headquarters *sg*

jefe, -a ['xefe, a] *nm/f* (gen) chief, head; (patrón) boss; (Pol) leader; (Com) manager(ess); **~ de camareros** head waiter; **~ de cocina** chef; **~ ejecutivo** (Com) chief executive; **~ de estación** stationmaster; **~ de estado** head of state; **~ de oficina** (Com) office manager; **~ de producción** (Com) production manager; **~ supremo** commander-in-chief; **~ de estudios** (Escol) director of studies; **~ de gobierno** head of government; **ser el ~** (fig) to be the boss

jengibre [xen'xiβre] *nm* ginger

jeque ['xeke] *nm* sheik(h)

jerarquía [xerar'kia] *nf* (orden) hierarchy; (rango) rank

jerárquico, -a [xe'rarkiko, a] *adj* hierarchic(al)

jerez [xe'reθ] *nm* sherry; **J~ de la Frontera** Jerez

jerga ['xerɣa] *nf* (tela) coarse cloth; (lenguaje) jargon; **~ informática** computer jargon

jerigonza [xeri'yonθa] *nf* (jerga) jargon, slang; (galimatías) nonsense, gibberish

jeringa [xe'riŋɡa] *nf* syringe; (Am) annoyance, bother; **~ de engrase** grease gun

jeringar [xeriŋ'ɡar] *vt* to annoy, bother

jeringuilla [xeriŋ'ɡuiʎa] *nf* syringe

jeroglífico [xero'ɣlifiko] *nm* hieroglyphic

jersey [xer'sei] (*pl* **jerseys**) *nm* jersey, pullover, jumper

Jerusalén [xerusa'len] *n* Jerusalem

Jesucristo [xesu'kristo] *nm* Jesus Christ

jesuita [xe'swita] *adj, nm* Jesuit

Jesús [xe'sus] *nm* Jesus; **¡~!** good heavens!; (al estornudar) bless you!

jet (*pl* **jets**) [jet, jet] *nm* jet (plane) ▷ *nf*: **la ~** the jet set

jeta ['xeta] *nf* (Zool) snout; (fam: cara) mug; **¡que ~ tienes!** (fam: insolencia) you've got a nerve!

jilguero [xil'ɣero] *nm* goldfinch

jinete, -a [xi'nete, a] *nm/f* horseman(-woman)

jipijapa [xipi'xapa] *nm* (Am) straw hat

jirafa [xi'rafa] *nf* giraffe

jirón [xi'ron] *nm* rag, shred

jitomate [xito'mate] *nm* (Am) tomato

jocoso, -a [xo'koso, a] *adj* humorous, jocular

joder [xo'ðer] (fam!) *vt* to fuck (!), screw (!); (fig: fastidiar) to piss off (!), bug; **joderse** *vr* (fracasar) to fail; **¡~!** damn it!; **se jodió todo** everything was ruined

jogging ['joɣin] *nm* (Am) tracksuit (Brit), sweat suit (US)

jornada [xor'naða] *nf* (viaje de un día) day's journey; (camino *o* viaje entero) journey; (día de trabajo) working day; **~ de 8 horas** 8-hour day; **(trabajar a) ~ partida** (to work a) split shift

jornal [xor'nal] *nm* (day's) wage

jornalero, -a [xorna'lero, a] *nm/f* (day) labourer

joroba [xo'roβa] *nf* hump

jorobado, -a [xoro'βaðo, a] *adj* hunchbacked ▷ *nm/f* hunchback

jota ['xota] *nf* letter J; (danza) Aragonese dance; (fam) jot, iota; **no saber ni ~** to have no idea

joven ['xoβen] *adj* young ▷ *nm* young man, youth ▷ *nf* young woman, girl

jovial [xo'βjal] *adj* cheerful, jolly

jovialidad [xoβjali'ðað] *nf* cheerfulness

joya ['xoja] *nf* jewel, gem; (fig: persona) gem; **~s de fantasía** imitation jewellery *sg*

joyería [xoxe'ria] *nf* (joyas) jewellery; (tienda) jeweller's (shop)

joyero [xo'jero] *nm* (persona) jeweller; (caja) jewel case

Juan [xwan] *nm*: **Noche de San ~** *ver* **noche**

juanete [xwa'nete] *nm* (del pie) bunion

jubilación [xuβila'θjon] *nf* (retiro) retirement

jubilado, -a [xuβi'lado, a] *adj* retired ▷ *nm/f* retired person, pensioner (Brit), senior citizen

jubilar [xuβi'lar] *vt* to pension off, retire; (fam) to discard; **jubilarse** *vr* to retire

júbilo ['xuβilo] *nm* joy, rejoicing

jubiloso, -a [xuβi'loso, a] *adj* jubilant

judía [xu'ðia] *nf ver* **judío**

judicial [xuði'θjal] *adj* judicial

judío, -a [xu'ðio, a] *adj* Jewish ▷ *nm* Jew ▷ *nf* Jewess, Jewish woman; (Culin) bean; **judía blanca** haricot bean; **judía verde** French *o* string bean

judo ['juðo] *nm* judo

juego ['xweɣo] vb ver **jugar** ▷ nm (gen) play; (pasatiempo, partido) game; (en casino) gambling; (deporte) sport; (conjunto) set; (herramientas) kit; **~ de azar** game of chance; **~ de café** coffee set; **~ de caracteres** (Inform) font; **~ limpio/sucio** fair/foul o dirty play; **~ de mesa** board game; **~ de palabras** pun, play on words; **J-s Olímpicos** Olympic Games; **~ de programas** (Inform) suite of programs; **fuera de ~** (Deporte: persona) offside; (: pelota) out of play; **por ~** in fun, for fun

juerga ['xwerɣa] nf binge; (fiesta) party; **ir de ~** to go out on a binge

jueves ['xweβes] nm inv Thursday; ver tb **sábado**

juez [xweθ] nm/f judge; (Tenis) umpire; **~ de instrucción** examining magistrate; **~ de línea** linesman; **~ de paz** justice of the peace; **~ de salida** starter

jugada [xu'ɣaða] nf play; **buena ~** good move (o shot o stroke) etc

jugador, a [xuɣa'ðor, a] nm/f player; (en casino) gambler

jugar [xu'ɣar] vt to play; (en casino) to gamble; (apostar) to bet ▷ vi to play; to gamble; (Com) to speculate; **jugarse** vr to gamble (away); **~se el todo por el todo, ~ al fútbol** to play football, to stake one's all, go for bust; **¿quién juega?** whose move is it?; **¡me la han jugado!** (fam) I've been had!

juglar [xu'ɣlar] nm minstrel

jugo ['xuɣo] nm (Bot, de fruta) juice; (fig) essence, substance; **~ de naranja** (esp Am) orange juice

jugoso, -a [xu'ɣoso, a] adj juicy; (fig) substantial, important

juguete [xu'ɣete] nm toy

juguetear [xuɣete'ar] vi to play

juguetería [xuɣete'ria] nf toyshop

juguetón, -ona [xuɣe'ton, ona] adj playful

juicio ['xwiθjo] nm judgement; (sana razón) sanity, reason; (opinión) opinion; (Jur: proceso) trial; **estar fuera de ~** to be out of one's mind; **a mi ~** in my opinion

juicioso, -a [xwi'θjoso, a] adj wise, sensible

julio ['xuljo] nm July; **el uno o el primero de ~** the first of July; **en el mes de ~** during July; **en ~ del año que viene** in July of next year

jumper ['dʒumper] nm (Am) pinafore dress (Brit), jumper (US)

junco ['xunko] nm rush, reed

jungla ['xungla] nf jungle

junio ['xunjo] nm June; ver tb **julio**

junta ['xunta] nf ver **junto**

juntar [xun'tar] vt to join, unite; (maquinaria) to assemble, put together; (dinero) to collect; **juntarse** vr to join, meet; (reunirse: personas) to meet, assemble; (arrimarse) to approach, draw closer; **~se con algn** to join sb

junto, -a ['xunto, a] adj joined; (unido) united; (anexo) near, close; (contiguo, próximo)

next, adjacent ▷ nf (asamblea) meeting, assembly; (comité, consejo) board, council, committee; (Mil, Pol) junta; (articulación) joint ▷ adv: **todo ~** all at once ▷ prep: **~ a** near (to), next to; **~s** together; **~ con** (together) with; **junta constitutiva** (Com) statutory meeting; **junta directiva** (Com) board of management; **junta general extraordinaria** (Com) extraordinary general meeting

jurado [xu'raðo] nm (Jur: individuo) juror; (: grupo) jury; (de concurso: grupo) panel (of judges); (: individuo) member of a panel

juramento [xura'mento] nm oath; (maldición) oath, curse; **bajo ~** on oath; **prestar ~** to take the oath; **tomar ~ a** to swear in, administer the oath to

jurar [xu'rar] vt, vi to swear; **~ en falso** to commit perjury; **jurárselas a algn** to have it in for sb

jurídico, -a [xu'riðiko, a] adj legal, juridical

jurisdicción [xurisðik'θjon] nf (poder, autoridad) jurisdiction; (territorio) district

jurisprudencia [xurispru'ðenθja] nf jurisprudence

jurista [xu'rista] nm/f jurist

justamente [xusta'mente] adv justly, fairly; (precisamente) just, exactly

justicia [xus'tiθja] nf justice; (equidad) fairness, justice; **de ~** deservedly

justiciero, -a [xusti'θjero, a] adj just, righteous

justificación [xustifika'θjon] nf justification; **~ automática** (Inform) automatic justification

justificante [xustifi'kante] nm voucher; **~ médico** sick note

justificar [xustifi'kar] vt (tb Tip) to justify; (probar) to verify

justo, -a ['xusto, a] adj (equitativo) just, fair, right; (preciso) exact, correct; (ajustado) tight ▷ adv (precisamente) exactly, precisely; (apenas a tiempo) just in time; **¡~!** that's it!, correct!; **llegaste muy ~** you just made it; **vivir muy ~** to be hard up

juvenil [xuβe'nil] adj youthful

juventud [xuβen'tuð] nf (adolescencia) youth; (jóvenes) young people pl

juzgado [xuθ'ɣaðo] nm tribunal; (Jur) court

juzgar [xuθ'ɣar] vt to judge; **a ~ por ...** to judge by ..., judging by ...; **~ mal** to misjudge; **júzguelo usted mismo** see for yourself

k l

karaoke [kara'oke] nm karaoke
kárate ['karate], **karate** [ka'rate] nm karate
Kg, kg abr (= kilogramo(s)) K, kg
kilo ['kilo] nm kilo
kilogramo [kilo'ɣramo] nm kilogramme (Brit), kilogram (US)
kilometraje [kilome'traxe] nm distance in kilometres, ≈ mileage
kilómetro [ki'lometro] nm kilometre (Brit), kilometer (US)
kilovatio [kilo'βatjo] nm kilowatt
kiosco ['kjosko] nm = **quiosco**
kiwi ['kiwi] nm kiwi (fruit)
kleenex® [kli'neks] nm paper handkerchief, tissue
km abr (= kilómetro(s)) km
Kosovo [koso'βo] nm Kosovo
kv abr (= kilovatio) kw

l abr (= litro(s)) l; (= libro) bk
la [la] artículo definido fsg the ▷ pron her; (en relación a usted) you; (en relación a una cosa) it ▷ nm (Mus) A; **está en la cárcel** he's in jail; **la del sombrero rojo** the woman/girl/one in the red hat
laberinto [laβe'rinto] nm labyrinth
labia ['laβja] nf fluency; (pey) glibness; **tener mucha ~** to have the gift of the gab
labial [la'βjal] adj labial
labio ['laβjo] nm lip; (de vasija etc) edge, rim; **~ inferior/superior** lower/upper lip
labor [la'βor] nf labour; (Agr) farm work; (tarea) job, task; (Costura) needlework, sewing; (punto) knitting, **~ de equipo** teamwork; **~ de ganchillo** crochet; **~es domésticas** o **del hogar** household chores
laborable [laβo'raβle] adj (Agr) workable; **día ~** working day
laboral [laβo'ral] adj (accidente, conflictividad) industrial; (jornada) working; (derecho, relaciones) labour cpd
laboralista [laβora'lista] adj: **abogado ~** labour lawyer
laborar [laβo'rar] vi to work
laboratorio [laβora'torjo] nm laboratory
laborioso, -a [laβo'rjoso, a] adj (persona) hard-working; (trabajo) tough
laborista [laβo'rista] (Pol) adj: **Partido L~** Labour Party ▷ nm/f Labour Party member o supporter

labrado, -a [la'βraðo, a] adj worked; (madera) carved; (metal) wrought ▷ nm (Agr) cultivated field

labrador, a [laβra'ðor, a] adj farming cpd ▷ nm/f farmer

labranza [la'βranθa] nf (Agr) cultivation

labrar [la'βrar] vt (gen) to work; (madera etc) to carve; (fig) to cause, bring about

labriego, -a [la'βrjeɣo, a] nm/f peasant

laca ['laka] nf lacquer; (de pelo) hairspray; ~ **de uñas** nail varnish

lacayo [la'kajo] nm lackey

lacerar [laθe'rar] vt to lacerate

lacio, -a ['laθjo, a] adj (pelo) lank, straight

lacón [la'kon] nm shoulder of pork

lacónico, -a [la'koniko, a] adj laconic

lacra ['lakra] nf (defecto) blemish; ~ **social** social disgrace

lacrar [la'krar] vt (cerrar) to seal (with sealing wax)

lacre ['lakre] nm sealing wax

lacrimoso, -a [lakri'moso, a] adj tearful

lactancia [lak'tanθja] nf lactation, breast-feeding

lactar [lak'tar] vt, vi to suckle, breast-feed

lácteo, -a ['lakteo, a] adj: **productos ~s** dairy products

ladear [laðe'ar] vt to tip, tilt ▷ vi to tilt; **ladearse** vr to lean; (Deporte) to swerve; (Aviat) to bank, turn

ladera [la'ðera] nf slope

ladino, -a [la'ðino, a] adj cunning

lado ['laðo] nm (gen) side; (fig) protection; (Mil) flank; ~ **izquierdo** left(-hand) side; ~ **a** ~ side by side; **al** ~ **de** next to, beside; **hacerse a un** ~ to stand aside; **poner de** ~ to put on its side; **poner a un** ~ to put aside; **me da de** ~ I don't care; **por un** ~ ..., **por otro** ~ ... on the one hand ..., on the other (hand) ...; **por todos** ~**s** on all sides, all round (Brit)

ladrar [la'ðrar] vi to bark

ladrido [la'ðriðo] nm bark, barking

ladrillo [la'ðriʎo] nm (gen) brick; (azulejo) tile

ladrón, -ona [la'ðron, ona] nm/f thief

lagar [la'ɣar] nm (wine/oil) press

lagartija [laɣar'tixa] nf (small) lizard, wall lizard

lagarto [la'ɣarto] nm (Zool) lizard; (Am) alligator

lago ['laɣo] nm lake

lágrima ['laɣrima] nf tear

lagrimal [laɣri'mal] nm (inner) corner of the eye

laguna [la'ɣuna] nf (lago) lagoon; (en escrito, conocimientos) gap

laico, -a ['laiko, a] adj lay ▷ nm/f layman(-woman)

lamentable [lamen'taβle] adj lamentable, regrettable; (miserable) pitiful

lamentar [lamen'tar] vt (sentir) to regret; (deplorar) to lament; **lamentarse** vr to lament; **lo lamento mucho** I'm very sorry

lamento [la'mento] nm lament

lamer [la'mer] vt to lick

lámina ['lamina] nf (plancha delgada) sheet; (para estampar, estampa) plate; (grabado) engraving

laminar [lami'nar] vt (en libro) to laminate; (Tec) to roll

lámpara ['lampara] nf lamp; ~ **de alcohol/gas** spirit/gas lamp; ~ **de pie** standard lamp

lamparón [lampa'ron] nm (Med) scrofula; (mancha) (large) grease spot

lampiño, -a [lam'piɲo, a] adj (sin pelo) hairless

lana ['lana] nf wool; (tela) woollen (Brit) o woolen (US) cloth; (Am fam: dinero) dough; **(hecho) de** ~ wool cpd

lance etc ['lanθe] vb ver **lanzar** ▷ nm (golpe) stroke; (suceso) event, incident

lancha ['lantʃa] nf launch; ~ **motora** motorboat; ~ **de pesca** fishing boat; ~ **salvavidas/torpedera** lifeboat/torpedo boat; ~ **neumática** rubber dinghy

lanero, -a [la'nero, a] adj wool cpd

langosta [lan'gosta] nf (insecto) locust; (crustáceo) lobster; (: de río) crayfish

langostino [langos'tino] nm prawn; (de agua dulce) crayfish

languidecer [langiðe'θer] vi to languish

languidez [langi'ðeθ] nf languor

lánguido, -a ['langiðo, a] adj (gen) languid; (sin energía) listless

lanilla [la'niʎa] nf nap; (tela) thin flannel cloth

lanudo, -a [la'nuðo, a] adj woolly, fleecy

lanza ['lanθa] nf (arma) lance, spear; **medir** ~**s** to cross swords

lanzadera [lanθa'ðera] nf shuttle

lanzado, -a [lan'θaðo, a] adj (atrevido) forward; (decidido) determined; **ir** ~ (rápido) to fly along

lanzamiento [lanθa'mjento] nm (gen) throwing; (Naut, Com) launch, launching; ~ **de pesos** putting the shot

lanzar [lan'θar] vt (gen) to throw; (con violencia) to fling; (Deporte: pelota) to bowl, to pitch (US); (Naut, Com) to launch; (Jur) to evict; (grito) to give, utter; **lanzarse** vr to throw o.s.; (fig) to take the plunge; ~**se a** (fig) to embark upon

lapa ['lapa] nf limpet

La Paz nf La Paz

lapicero [lapi'θero] nm pencil; (Am) propelling (Brit) o mechanical (US) pencil; (: bolígrafo) ballpoint pen, Biro®

lápida ['lapiða] nf stone; ~ **conmemorativa** memorial stone; ~ **mortuoria** headstone

lapidar [lapi'ðar] vt to stone; (Tec) to polish, lap

lapidario, -a [lapi'ðarjo, a] adj, nm lapidary

lápiz ['lapiθ] nm pencil; ~ **de color** coloured pencil; ~ **de labios** lipstick; ~ **de ojos** eyebrow pencil; ~ **óptico** o **luminoso** light pen

lapón, -ona [la'pon, ona] adj Lapp ▷ nm/f Laplander, Lapp ▷ nm (Ling) Lapp

Laponia [la'ponja] nf Lapland

lapso ['lapso] nm lapse; (error) error; ~ **de tiempo** interval of time

lapsus ['lapsus] nm inv error, mistake

largar [lar'ɣar] vt (soltar) to release; (aflojar) to loosen; (lanzar) to launch; (fam) to let fly; (velas) to unfurl; (fam) to throw; **largarse** vr (fam) to beat it; **~se a** (Am) to start to

largo, -a ['larɣo, a] adj (longitud) long; (tiempo) lengthy; (persona: alta) tall; (: fig) generous ▷ nm length; (Mus) largo; **dos años ~s** two long years; **a ~ plazo** in the long term; **tiene nueve metros de ~** it is nine metres long; **a lo ~** (posición) lengthways; **a lo ~ de** along; (tiempo) all through, throughout; **a la larga** in the long run; **me dio largas con una promesa** she put me off with a promise; **¡~ de aquí!** (fam) clear off!

largometraje [larɣome'traxe] nm full-length o feature film

largura [lar'ɣura] nf length

laringe [la'rinxe] nf larynx

laringitis [larin'xitis] nf laryngitis

larva ['larβa] nf larva

las [las] artículo definido fpl the ▷ pron them; **~ que cantan** the ones/women/girls who sing

lasaña [la'saɲa] nf lasagne, lasagna

lascivo, -a [las'θiβo, a] adj lewd

láser ['laser] nm laser

lástima ['lastima] nf (pena) pity; **dar ~** to be pitiful; **es una ~ que** it's a pity that; **¡qué ~!** what a pity!; **estar hecho una ~** to be a sorry sight

lastimar [lasti'mar] vt (herir) to wound; (ofender) to offend; **lastimarse** vr to hurt o.s.

lastimero, -a [lasti'mero, a] adj pitiful, pathetic

lastre ['lastre] nm (Tec, Naut) ballast; (fig) dead weight

lata ['lata] nf (metal) tin; (envase) tin, can; (fam) nuisance; **en ~** tinned; **dar (la) ~** to be a nuisance

latente [la'tente] adj latent

lateral [late'ral] adj side, lateral ▷ nm (Teat) wings pl

latido [la'tiðo] nm (del corazón) beat; (de herida) throb(bing)

latifundio [lati'fundjo] nm large estate

latifundista [latifun'dista] nm/f owner of a large estate

latigazo [lati'ɣaθo] nm (golpe) lash; (sonido) crack; (fig: regaño) dressing-down

látigo ['latiɣo] nm whip

latín [la'tin] nm Latin; **saber (mucho) ~** (fam) to be pretty sharp

latino, -a [la'tino, a] adj Latin

Latinoamérica [latinoa'merika] nf Latin America

latinoamericano, -a [latinoameri'kano, a] adj, nm/f Latin American

latir [la'tir] vi (corazón, pulso) to beat

latitud [lati'tuð] nf (Geo) latitude; (fig) breadth, extent

latón [la'ton] nm brass

latoso, -a [la'toso, a] adj (molesto) annoying; (aburrido) boring

laúd [la'uð] nm lute

laurel [lau'rel] nm (Bot) laurel; (Culin) bay

lava ['laβa] nf lava

lavabo [la'βaβo] nm (jofaina) washbasin; (retrete) lavatory (Brit), toilet (Brit), washroom (US)

lavadero [laβa'ðero] nm laundry

lavado [la'βaðo] nm washing; (de ropa) wash, laundry; (Arte) wash; **~ de cerebro** brainwashing; **~ en seco** dry-cleaning

lavadora [laβa'ðora] nf washing machine

lavanda [la'βanda] nf lavender

lavandería [laβande'ria] nf laundry; **~ automática** launderette

lavaplatos [laβa'platos] nm inv dishwasher

lavar [la'βar] vt to wash; (borrar) to wipe away; **lavarse** vr to wash o.s.; **~se las manos** to wash one's hands; (fig) to wash one's hands of it; **~se los dientes** to brush one's teeth; **~ y marcar** (pelo) to shampoo and set; **~ en seco** to dry-clean; **~ los platos** to wash the dishes

lavarropas [laβa'rropas] nm inv (RPl) washing machine

lavavajillas [laβaβa'xiʎas] nm inv dishwasher

laxante [lak'sante] nm laxative

lazada [la'θaða] nf bow

lazarillo [laθa'riʎo] nm: **perro de ~** guide dog

lazo ['laθo] nm knot; (lazada) bow; (para animales) lasso; (trampa) snare; (vínculo) tie; **~ corredizo** slipknot

le [le] pron (directo) him (o her); (: en relación a usted) you; (indirecto) to him (o her o it); (: a usted) to you

leal [le'al] adj loyal

lealtad [leal'tað] nf loyalty

lebrel [le'βrel] nm greyhound

lección [lek'θjon] nf lesson; **~ práctica** object lesson; **dar lecciones** to teach, give lessons; **dar una ~ a algn** (fig) to teach sb a lesson

leche ['letʃe] nf milk; (fam!) semen, spunk (!); **dar una ~ a algn** (fam) to belt sb; **estar de mala ~** (fam) to be in a foul mood; **tener mala ~** (fam) to be a nasty piece of work; **~ condensada/en polvo** condensed/powdered milk; **~ desnatada** skimmed milk; **~ de magnesia** milk of magnesia; **¡~!** hell!

lechera [le'tʃera] nf ver **lechero**

lechería [letʃe'ria] nf dairy

lechero, -a [le'tʃero, a] adj milk cpd ▷ nm milkman ▷ nf (vendedora) milkwoman; (recipiente) milk pan; (para servir) milk churn

lecho ['letʃo] nm (cama, de río) bed; (Geo) layer; **~ mortuorio** deathbed

lechón [le'tʃon] nm sucking (Brit) o suckling (US) pig

lechoso, -a [le'tʃoso, a] adj milky

lechuga [le'tʃuɣa] nf lettuce

lechuza [le'tʃuθa] nf (barn) owl

lectivo, -a [lek'tiβo, a] adj (horas) teaching cpd; **año** o **curso ~** (Escol) school year; (Univ) academic year

lector, a [lek'tor, a] nm/f reader; (Escol, Univ) (conversation) assistant ▷ nm: **~ de discos compactos** CD player; **~ óptico de caracteres** (Inform) optical character reader ▷ nf: **~a de fichas** (Inform) card reader

lectura [lek'tura] nf reading; **~ de marcas sensibles** (Inform) mark sensing

leer [le'er] vt to read; **~ entre líneas** to read between the lines

legado [le'ɣaðo] nm (don) bequest; (herencia) legacy; (enviado) legate

legajo [le'ɣaxo] nm file, bundle (of papers)

legal [le'ɣal] adj legal, lawful; (persona) trustworthy

legalidad [leɣali'ðað] nf legality

legalizar [leɣali'θar] vt to legalize; (documento) to authenticate

legaña [le'ɣaɲa] nf sleep (in eyes)

legar [le'ɣar] vt to bequeath, leave

legendario, -a [lexen'darjo, a] adj legendary

legión [le'xjon] nf legion

legionario, -a [lexjo'narjo, a] adj legionary ▷ nm legionnaire

legislación [lexisla'θjon] nf legislation; (leyes) laws pl; **~ antimonopolio** (Com) antitrust legislation

legislar [lexis'lar] vt to legislate

legislativo, -a [lexisla'tiβo, a] adj: **(elecciones) legislativas** ≈ general election

legislatura [lexisla'tura] nf (Pol) period of office

legitimar [lexiti'mar] vt to legitimize

legítimo, -a [le'xitimo, a] adj (genuino) authentic; (legal) legitimate, rightful

lego, -a ['leɣo, a] adj (Rel) secular; (ignorante) ignorant ▷ nm layman

legua ['leɣwa] nf league; **se ve (o nota) a la ~** you can tell (it) a mile off

legumbres [le'ɣumbres] nfpl pulses

leído, -a [le'iðo, a] adj well-read

lejanía [lexa'nia] nf distance

lejano, -a [le'xano, a] adj far-off; (en el tiempo) distant; (fig) remote; **L~ Oriente** Far East

lejía [le'xia] nf bleach

lejos ['lexos] adv far, far away; **a lo ~** in the distance; **de** o **desde ~** from a distance; **está muy ~** it's a long way (away); **¿está ~?** is it far?; **~ de** prep far from

lelo, -a ['lelo, a] adj silly ▷ nm/f idiot

lema ['lema] nm motto; (Pol) slogan

lencería [lenθe'ria] nf (telas) linen, drapery; (ropa interior) lingerie

lengua ['lengwa] nf tongue; (Ling) language; **~ materna** mother tongue; **~ de tierra** (Geo) spit o tongue of land; **dar a la ~** to chatter; **morderse la ~** to hold one's tongue; **sacar la ~ a algn** (fig) to cock a snook at sb

lenguado [len'gwaðo] nm sole

lenguaje [len'gwaxe] nm language; (forma de hablar) (mode of) speech; **~ comercial** business language; **~ ensamblador** o **de alto nivel** (Inform) high-level language; **~ máquina** (Inform) machine language; **~ original** source language; **~ periodístico** journalese; **~ de programación** (Inform) programming language; **en ~ llano** ≈ in plain English

lengüeta [len'gweta] nf (Anat) epiglottis; (de zapatos) tongue; (Mus) reed

lente ['lente] nm o nf lens; (lupa) magnifying glass; **lentes** nmpl glasses; **~s bifocales/de sol** (Am) bifocals/sunglasses; **~s de contacto** contact lenses; **~s progresivas** varifocal lenses

lenteja [len'texa] nf lentil

lentejuela [lente'xwela] nf sequin

lentilla [len'tiʎa] nf contact lens

lentitud [lenti'tuð] nf slowness; **con ~** slowly

lento, -a ['lento, a] adj slow

leña ['leɲa] nf firewood; **dar ~ a** to thrash; **echar ~ al fuego** to add fuel to the flames

leñador, a [leɲa'ðor, a] nm/f woodcutter

leño ['leɲo] nm (trozo de árbol) log; (madera) timber; (fig) blockhead

Leo ['leo] nm (Astro) Leo

león [le'on] nm lion; **~ marino** sea lion

leona [le'ona] nf lioness

leonino, -a [leo'nino, a] adj leonine

leopardo [leo'parðo] nm leopard

leotardos [leo'tarðos] nmpl tights

lepra ['lepra] nf leprosy

leproso, -a [le'proso, a] nm/f leper

lerdo, -a ['lerðo, a] adj (lento) slow; (patoso) clumsy

les [les] pron (directo) them; (: en relación a ustedes) you; (indirecto) to them; (: a ustedes) to you

lesbiana [les'βjana] adj, nf lesbian

lesión [le'sjon] nf wound, lesion; (Deporte) injury

lesionado, -a [lesjo'naðo, a] adj injured ▷ nm/f injured person

lesionar [lesjo'nar] vt (dañar) to hurt; (herir) to wound; **lesionarse** vr to get hurt

letal [le'tal] adj lethal

letanía [leta'nia] nf litany; (retahíla) long list

letargo [le'tarɣo] nm lethargy

letra ['letra] nf letter; (escritura) handwriting; (Com) letter, bill, draft; (Mus) lyrics pl; **letras** nfpl (Univ) arts; **~ bastardilla/negrilla** italics pl/bold type; **~ de cambio** bill of exchange; **~ de imprenta** print; **~ inicial/mayúscula/minúscula** initial/capital/small letter; **lo tomó al pie de la ~** he took it literally; **~ bancaria** (Com) bank draft; **~ de patente** (Com) letters patent pl; **escribir cuatro ~s a algn** to drop a line to sb

letrado, -a [le'traðo, a] *adj* learned; *(fam)* pedantic ▷ *nm/f* lawyer
letrero [le'trero] *nm (cartel)* sign; *(etiqueta)* label
letrina [le'trina] *nf* latrine
leucemia [leu'θemja] *nf* leukaemia
leucocito [leuko'θito] *nm* white blood cell, leucocyte
levadizo, -a [leβa'ðiθo, a] *adj:* **puente ~** drawbridge
levadura [leβa'ðura] *nf* yeast, leaven; **~ de cerveza** brewer's yeast
levantamiento [leβanta'mjento] *nm* raising, lifting; *(rebelión)* revolt, rising; *(Geo)* survey; **~ de pesos** weightlifting
levantar [leβan'tar] *vt (gen)* to raise; *(del suelo)* to pick up; *(hacia arriba)* to lift (up); *(plan)* to make, draw up; *(mesa)* to clear; *(campamento)* to strike; *(fig)* to cheer up, hearten; **levantarse** *vr* to get up; *(enderezarse)* to straighten up; *(rebelarse)* to rebel; *(sesión)* to be adjourned; *(niebla)* to lift; *(viento)* to rise; **~se (de la cama)** to get up, get out of bed; **~ el ánimo** to cheer up
levante [le'βante] *nm* east; *(viento)* east wind; **el L~** *region of Spain extending from Castellón to Murcia*
levar [le'βar] *vti:* **~ (anclas)** to weigh anchor
leve ['leβe] *adj* light; *(fig)* trivial; *(mínimo)* slight
levedad [leβe'ðað] *nf* lightness; *(fig)* levity
levita [le'βita] *nf* frock coat
léxico, -a ['leksiko, a] *adj* lexical ▷ *nm (vocabulario)* vocabulary; *(Ling)* lexicon
ley [lei] *nf (gen)* law; *(metal)* standard; **decreto-~** decree law; **de buena ~** *(fig)* genuine; **según la ~** in accordance with the law, by law, in law
leyenda [le'jenda] *nf* legend; *(Tip)* inscription
leyó *etc vb ver* **leer**
liar [li'ar] *vt* to tie (up); *(unir)* to bind; *(envolver)* to wrap (up); *(enredar)* to confuse; *(cigarrillo)* to roll; **liarse** *vr (fam)* to get involved; *(confundirse)* to get mixed up; **~se a palos** to get involved in a fight
Líbano ['liβano] *nm:* **el ~** the Lebanon
libar [li'βar] *vt* to suck
libelo [li'βelo] *nm* satire, lampoon; *(Jur)* petition
libélula [li'βelula] *nf* dragonfly
liberación [liβera'θjon] *nf* liberation; *(de la cárcel)* release
liberal [liβe'ral] *adj, nm/f* liberal
liberar [liβe'rar] *vt* to liberate
libertad [liβer'tað] *nf* liberty, freedom; **~ de asociación/de culto/de prensa/de comercio/de palabra** freedom of association/of worship/of the press/of trade/of speech; **~ condicional** probation; **~ bajo palabra** parole; **~ bajo fianza** bail; **estar en ~** to be free; **poner a algn en ~** to set sb free

libertar [liβer'tar] *vt (preso)* to set free; *(de una obligación)* to release; *(eximir)* to exempt
libertinaje [liβerti'naxe] *nm* licentiousness
libertino, -a [liβer'tino, a] *adj* permissive ▷ *nm/f* permissive person
libidinoso, -a [liβiði'noso, a] *adj* lustful; *(viejo)* lecherous
libra ['liβra] *nf* pound; **L~** *(Astro)* Libra; **~ esterlina** pound sterling
librador, a [liβra'ðor, a] *nm/f* drawer
libramiento [liβra'mjento] *(Am) nm* ring road *(Brit)*, beltway *(US)*
librar [li'βrar] *vt (de peligro)* to save; *(batalla)* to wage, fight; *(de impuestos)* to exempt; *(cheque)* to make out; *(Jur)* to exempt; **librarse** *vr:* **~se de** to escape from, free o.s. from; **de buena nos hemos librado** we're well out of that
libre ['liβre] *adj (gen)* free; *(lugar)* unoccupied; *(tiempo)* spare; *(asiento)* vacant; *(de deudas)* free of debts; *(Com):* **~ a bordo** free on board; **~ de franqueo** post-free; **~ de impuestos** free of tax; **tiro ~** free kick; **los 100 metros ~** the 100 metres freestyle (race); **al aire ~** in the open air; **¿estás ~?** are you free?
librería [liβre'ria] *nf (tienda)* bookshop; *(estante)* bookcase; **~ de ocasión** secondhand bookshop
librero, -a [li'βrero, a] *nm/f* bookseller
libreta [li'βreta] *nf* notebook; *(pan)* one-pound loaf; **~ de ahorros** savings book
libro ['liβro] *nm* book; **~ de actas** minute book; **~ de bolsillo** paperback; **~ de cabecera** bedside book; **~ de caja** *(Com)* cashbook; **~ de caja auxiliar** *(Com)* petty cash book; **~ de cocina** cookery book *(Brit)*, cookbook *(US)*; **~ de consulta** reference book; **~ de cuentas** account book; **~ de cuentos** storybook; **~ de cheques** cheque *(Brit)* o check *(US)* book; **~ de entradas y salidas** *(Com)* daybook; **~ de honor** visitors' book; **~ diario** journal; **~ electrónico** e-book; **~ mayor** *(Com)* general ledger; **~ de reclamaciones** complaints book; **~ de texto** textbook
Lic. *abr* = **Licenciado, a**
licencia [li'θenθja] *nf (gen)* licence; *(permiso)* permission; **~ por enfermedad/con goce de sueldo** sick/paid leave; **~ de armas/de caza** gun/game licence; **~ de exportación** *(Com)* export licence; **~ poética** poetic licence
licenciado, -a [liθen'θjaðo, a] *adj* licensed ▷ *nm/f* graduate; **L~ en Filosofía y Letras** = Bachelor of Arts; *see note*

⬤ **LICENCIADO**
⬤
⬤ When students finish University after an
⬤ average of five years they receive the
⬤ degree of *licenciado*. If the course is only
⬤ three years such as Nursing, or if they
⬤ choose not to do the optional two-year
⬤ specialization, they are awarded the

degree of *diplomado. Cursos de posgrado*, postgraduate courses, are becoming increasingly popular, especially one-year specialist courses called *masters*.

licenciar [liθen'θjar] *vt* (*empleado*) to dismiss; (*permitir*) to allow, permit; (*soldado*) to discharge; (*estudiante*) to confer a degree upon; **licenciarse** *vr*: **~se en derecho** to graduate in law; **~se en letras** to get an arts degree

licenciatura [liθenθja'tura] *nf* (*título*) degree; (*estudios*) degree course

licencioso, -a [liθen'θjoso, a] *adj* licentious

liceo [li'θeo] *nm* (*esp Am*) (high) school

licitar [liθi'tar] *vt* to bid for ▷ *vi* to bid

lícito, -a ['liθito, a] *adj* (*legal*) lawful; (*justo*) fair, just; (*permisible*) permissible

licor [li'kor] *nm* spirits *pl* (*Brit*), liquor (*US*); (*con hierbas etc*) liqueur

licra® ['likra] *nf* Lycra®

licuadora [likwa'ðora] *nf* blender

licuar [li'kwar] *vt* to liquidize

lid [lið] *nf* combat; (*fig*) controversy

líder ['liðer] *nm/f* leader

liderato [liðe'rato] *nm* = **liderazgo**

liderazgo [liðe'raθγo] *nm* leadership

lidia ['liðja] *nf* bullfighting; (*una lidia*) bullfight; **toros de ~** fighting bulls

lidiar [li'ðjar] *vt, vi* to fight

liebre ['ljeβre] *nf* hare; **dar gato por ~** to con

lienzo ['ljenθo] *nm* linen; (*Arte*) canvas; (*Arq*) wall

liga ['liγa] *nf* (*de medias*) garter, suspender; (*confederación*) league; (*Am: gomita*) rubber band

ligadura [liγa'ðura] *nf* bond, tie; (*Med, Mus*) ligature

ligamento [liγa'mento] *nm* (*Anat*) ligament; (*atadura*) tie; (*unión*) bond

ligar [li'γar] *vt* (*atar*) to tie; (*unir*) to join; (*Med*) to bind up; (*Mus*) to slur; (*fam*) to get off with, pick up ▷ *vi* to mix, blend; (*fam*) to get off with sb; (*2 personas*) to get off with one another; (*fam*): **(él) liga mucho** he pulls a lot of women; **ligarse** *vr* (*fig*) to commit o.s.; **~ con** (*fam*) to get off with, pick up; **~se a algn** to get off with o pick up sb

ligereza [lixe'reθa] *nf* lightness; (*rapidez*) swiftness; (*agilidad*) agility; (*superficialidad*) flippancy

ligero, -a [li'xero, a] *adj* (*de peso*) light; (*tela*) thin; (*rápido*) swift, quick; (*ágil*) agile, nimble; (*de importancia*) slight; (*de carácter*) flippant, superficial ▷ *adv* quickly, swiftly; **a la ligera** superficially; **juzgar a la ligera** to jump to conclusions

light ['lait] *adj inv* (*cigarrillo*) low-tar; (*comida*) diet *cpd*

ligue *etc* ['liγe] *vb ver* **ligar** ▷ *nm/f* boyfriend/girlfriend ▷ *nm* (*persona*) pick-up

liguero [li'γero] *nm* suspender (*Brit*) o garter (*US*) belt

lija ['lixa] *nf* (*Zool*) dogfish; **(papel de) ~** sandpaper

lijar [li'xar] *vt* to sand

lila ['lila] *adj inv, nf* lilac ▷ *nm* (*fam*) twit

lima ['lima] *nf* file; (*Bot*) lime; **~ de uñas** nail file; **comer como una ~** to eat like a horse

limar [li'mar] *vt* to file; (*alisar*) to smooth over; (*fig*) to polish up

limbo ['limbo] *nm* (*Rel*) limbo; **estar en el ~** to be on another planet

limitación [limita'θjon] *nf* limitation, limit; **~ de velocidad** speed limit

limitar [limi'tar] *vt* to limit; (*reducir*) to reduce, cut down ▷ *vi*: **~ con** to border on; **limitarse** *vr*: **~se a** to limit o confine o.s. to

límite ['limite] *nm* (*gen*) limit; (*fin*) end; (*frontera*) border; **como ~** at (the) most; (*fecha*) at the latest; **no tener ~s** to know no bounds; **~ de crédito** (*Com*) credit limit; **~ de página** (*Inform*) page break; **~ de velocidad** speed limit

limítrofe [li'mitrofe] *adj* bordering, neighbouring

limón [li'mon] *nm* lemon ▷ *adj*: **amarillo ~** lemon-yellow

limonada [limo'naða] *nf* lemonade

limonero [limo'nero] *nm* lemon tree

limosna [li'mosna] *nf* alms *pl*; **pedir ~** to beg; **vivir de ~** to live on charity

limpiabotas [limpja'βotas] *nm/f inv* bootblack (*Brit*), shoeshine boy/girl

limpiador, a [limpja'ðor, a] *adj* cleaning, cleansing ▷ *nm/f* cleaner; **= limpiaparabrisas**

limpiaparabrisas [limpjapara'βrisas] *nm inv* windscreen (*Brit*) o windshield (*US*) wiper

limpiar [lim'pjar] *vt* to clean; (*con trapo*) to wipe; (*quitar*) to wipe away; (*zapatos*) to shine, polish; (*casa*) to tidy up; (*Inform*) to debug; (*fig*) to clean up; (: *purificar*) to cleanse, purify; (*Mil*) to mop up; (*fam*) to dry-clean

limpieza [lim'pjeθa] *nf* (*estado*) cleanliness; (*acto*) cleaning; (: *de las calles*) cleansing; (: *de zapatos*) polishing; (*habilidad*) skill; (*fig: Policía*) clean-up; (*pureza*) purity; (*Mil*): **operación de ~** mopping-up operation; **~ étnica** ethnic cleansing; **~ en seco** dry cleaning

limpio, -a ['limpjo, a] *adj* clean; (*moralmente*) pure; (*ordenado*) tidy; (*despejado*) clear; (*Com*) clear, net; (*fam*) honest ▷ *adv*: **jugar ~** to play fair; **pasar a ~** to make a fair copy; **sacar algo en ~** to get benefit from sth; **~ de** free from

linaje [li'naxe] *nm* lineage, family

linaza [li'naθa] *nf* linseed; **aceite de ~** linseed oil

lince ['linθe] *nm* lynx; **ser un ~** (*fig: observador*) to be very observant; (: *astuto*) to be shrewd

linchar [lin'tʃar] *vt* to lynch

lindar [lin'dar] *vi* to adjoin; **~ con** to border on; (*Arq*) to abut on

linde ['linde] *nm o nf* boundary
lindero, -a [lin'dero, a] *adj* adjoining ▷ *nm* boundary
lindo, -a ['lindo, a] *adj* pretty, lovely ▷ *adv* (*esp Am: fam*) nicely, very well; **canta muy ~** (*Am*) he sings beautifully; **se divertían de lo ~** they enjoyed themselves enormously
línea ['linea] *nf* (*gen, moral, Pol etc*) line; (*talle*) figure; (*Inform*): **en ~** on line; **fuera de ~** off line; **~ de estado** status line; **~ de formato** format line; **~ aérea** airline; **~ de alto el fuego** ceasefire line; **~ de fuego** firing line; **~ de meta** goal line; (*de carrera*) finishing line; **~ de montaje** assembly line; **~ discontinua** (*Auto*) broken line; **~ dura** (*Pol*) hard line; **~ recta** straight line; **la ~ de 2008** (*moda*) the 2008 look
lingote [lin'gote] *nm* ingot
lingüista [lin'gwista] *nm/f* linguist
lingüística [lin'gwistika] *nf* linguistics *sg*
linimento [lini'mento] *nm* liniment
lino ['lino] *nm* linen; (*Bot*) flax
linóleo [li'noleo] *nm* lino, linoleum
linterna [lin'terna] *nf* lantern, lamp; **~ eléctrica o a pilas** torch (*Brit*), flashlight (*US*)
lío ['lio] *nm* bundle; (*desorden*) muddle, mess; (*fam: follón*) fuss; (: *relación amorosa*) affair; **armar un ~** to make a fuss; **meterse en un ~** to get into a jam; **tener un ~ con algn** to be having an affair with sb
lipotimia [lipo'timja] *nf* blackout
liquen ['liken] *nm* lichen
liquidación [likiða'θjon] *nf* liquidation; (*de cuenta*) settlement; **venta de ~** clearance sale
liquidar [liki'ðar] *vt* (*Química*) to liquefy; (*Com*) to liquidate; (*deudas*) to pay off; (*empresa*) to wind up; **~ a algn** to bump sb off, rub sb out (*fam*)
liquidez [liki'ðeθ] *nf* liquidity
líquido, -a ['likiðo, a] *adj* liquid; (*ganancia*) net ▷ *nm* liquid; (*Com: efectivo*) ready cash o money; (: *ganancia*) net amount o profit; **~ imponible** net taxable income
lira ['lira] *nf* (*Mus*) lyre; (*moneda*) lira
lírico, -a ['liriko, a] *adj* lyrical
lirio ['lirjo] *nm* (*Bot*) iris
lirón [li'ron] *nm* (*Zool*) dormouse; (*fig*) sleepyhead
Lisboa [lis'βoa] *nf* Lisbon
lisiado, -a [li'sjaðo, a] *adj* injured ▷ *nm/f* cripple
lisiar [li'sjar] *vt* to maim; **lisiarse** *vr* to injure o.s.
liso, -a ['liso, a] *adj* (*terreno*) flat; (*cabello*) straight; (*superficie*) even; (*tela*) plain; **lisa y llanamente** in plain language, plainly
lisonja [li'sonxa] *nf* flattery
lisonjear [lisonxe'ar] *vt* to flatter; (*fig*) to please
lisonjero, -a [lison'xero, a] *adj* flattering; (*agradable*) gratifying, pleasing ▷ *nm/f* flatterer

lista ['lista] *nf* list; (*en escuela*) school register; (*de libros*) catalogue; (*tb*: **~ de correos**) poste restante, general delivery (*US*); (*tb*: **~ de platos**) menu; (*tb*: **~ de precios**) price list; **pasar ~** to call the roll; (*Escol*) to call the register; **~ de direcciones** mailing list; **~ electoral** electoral roll; **~ de espera** waiting list; **tela a ~s** striped material
listado, -a [lis'taðo, a] *adj* striped ▷ *nm* (*Com, Inform*) listing; **~ paginado** (*Inform*) paged listing
listo, -a ['listo, a] *adj* (*perspicaz*) smart, clever; (*preparado*) ready; **~ para usar** ready-to-use; **¿estás ~?** are you ready?; **pasarse de ~** to be too clever by half
listón [lis'ton] *nm* (*de tela*) ribbon; (*de madera, metal*) strip
litera [li'tera] *nf* (*en barco, tren*) berth; (*en dormitorio*) bunk, bunk bed
literal [lite'ral] *adj* literal
literario, -a [lite'rarjo, a] *adj* literary
literato, -a [lite'rato, a] *adj* literary ▷ *nm/f* writer
literatura [litera'tura] *nf* literature
litigar [liti'γar] *vt* to fight; (*fig*) *vi* (*Jur*) to go to law; (*fig*) to dispute, argue
litigio [li'tixjo] *nm* (*Jur*) lawsuit; (*fig*): **en ~ con** in dispute with
litografía [litoγra'fia] *nf* lithography; (*una litografía*) lithograph
litoral [lito'ral] *adj* coastal ▷ *nm* coast, seaboard
litro ['litro] *nm* litre, liter (*US*)
liviano, -a [li'βjano, a] *adj* (*persona*) fickle; (*cosa, objeto*) trivial; (*Am*) light
lívido, -a ['liβiðo, a] *adj* livid
llaga ['ʎaγa] *nf* wound
llama ['ʎama] *nf* flame; (*fig*) passion; (*Zool*) llama; **en ~s** burning, ablaze
llamada [ʎa'maða] *nf* call; (*a la puerta*) knock; (: *al timbre*) ring; **~ a cobro revertido** reverse-charge call; **~ al orden** call to order; **~ de atención** warning; **~ a pie de página** reference note; **~ a procedimiento** (*Inform*) procedure call; **~ interurbana** trunk call; **~ metropolitana** (*Esp*), **~ local** (*Am*) local call; **~ por cobrar** (*Am*) reverse-charge call
llamamiento [ʎama'mjento] *nm*; **hacer un ~ a algn para que haga algo** to appeal to sb to do sth
llamar [ʎa'mar] *vt* to call; (*convocar*) to summon; (*invocar*) to invoke; (*atraer con gesto*) to beckon; (*atención*) to attract; (*Telec: tb*: **~ por teléfono**) to call, ring up, telephone; (*Mil*) to call up ▷ *vi* (*por teléfono*) to phone; (*a la puerta*) to knock (*o* ring); (*por señas*) to beckon; **llamarse** *vr* to be called, be named; **¿cómo se llama usted?** what's your name?; **¿quién llama?** (*Telec*) who's calling?, who's that?; **no me llama la atención** (*fam*) I don't fancy it
llamarada [ʎama'raða] *nf* (*llamas*) blaze; (*rubor*) flush; (*fig*) flare-up

llamativo, -a [ʎama'tiβo, a] adj showy; (color) loud

llamear [ʎame'ar] vi to blaze

llano, -a ['ʎano, a] adj (superficie) flat; (persona) straightforward; (estilo) clear ▷ nm plain, flat ground

llanta ['ʎanta] nf (wheel) rim; (Am: neumático) tyre; (: cámara) (inner) tube; ~ **de repuesto** (Am) spare tyre

llanto ['ʎanto] nm weeping; (fig) lamentation; (canción) dirge, lament

llanura [ʎa'nura] nf (lisura) flatness, smoothness; (Geo) plain

llave ['ʎaβe] nf key; (de gas, agua) tap (Brit), faucet (US); (Mecánica) switch; (de la luz) switch; (Mus) key; ~ **inglesa** monkey wrench; ~ **maestra** master key; ~ **de contacto, ~ de encendido** (Am: Auto) ignition key; ~ **de paso** stopcock; **echar ~ a** to lock up

llavero [ʎa'βero] nm keyring

llavín [ʎa'βin] nm latchkey

llegada [ʎe'ɣaða] nf arrival

llegar [ʎe'ɣar] vt to bring up, bring over ▷ vi to arrive; (bastar) to be enough; **llegarse** vr: ~**se a** to approach; ~ **a** (alcanzar) to reach; to manage to, succeed in; ~ **a saber** to find out; ~ **a ser famoso/el jefe** to become famous/ the boss; ~ **a las manos** to come to blows; ~ **a las manos de** to come into the hands of; **no llegues tarde** don't be late; **esta cuerda no llega** this rope isn't long enough

llenar [ʎe'nar] vt to fill; (superficie) to cover; (espacio, tiempo) to fill, take up; (formulario) to fill in o out; (fig) to heap; **llenarse** vr to fill (up); ~**se de** (fam) to stuff o.s. with

lleno, -a ['ʎeno, a] adj full, filled; (repleto) full up ▷ nm (abundancia) abundance; (Teat) full house; **dar de ~ contra un muro** to hit a wall head-on

llevadero, -a [ʎeβa'ðero, a] adj bearable, tolerable

llevar [ʎe'βar] vt to take; (ropa) to wear; (cargar) to carry; (quitar) to take away; (en coche) to drive; (transportar) to transport; (ruta) to follow, keep to; (traer: dinero) to carry; (conducir) to lead; (Mat) to carry; (aguantar) to bear; (negocio) to conduct, direct; to manage ▷ vi (suj: camino etc): ~ **a** to lead to; **llevarse** vr to carry off, take away; **llevamos dos días aquí** we have been here for two days; **él me lleva dos años** he's two years older than me; ~ **adelante** (fig) to carry forward; ~ **por delante a uno** (en coche etc) to run sb over; (fig) to ride roughshod over sb; ~ **la ventaja** to be winning o in the lead; ~ **los libros** (Com) to keep the books; **llevo las de perder** I'm likely to lose; **no las lleva todas consigo** he's not all there; **nos llevó a cenar fuera** she took us out for a meal; ~**se a uno por delante** (atropellar) to run sb over; ~**se bien** to get on well (together)

llorar [ʎo'rar] vt to cry, weep ▷ vi to cry, weep; (ojos) to water; ~ **a moco tendido** to sob one's

heart out; ~ **de risa** to cry with laughter

lloriquear [ʎorike'ar] vi to snivel, whimper

lloro ['ʎoro] nm crying, weeping

llorón, -ona [ʎo'ron, ona] adj tearful ▷ nm/f cry-baby

lloroso, -a [ʎo'roso, a] adj (gen) weeping, tearful; (triste) sad, sorrowful

llover [ʎo'βer] vi to rain; ~ **a cántaros** o **a cubos** o **a mares** to rain cats and dogs, pour (down); **ser una cosa llovida del cielo** to be a godsend; **llueve sobre mojado** it never rains but it pours

llovizna [ʎo'βiθna] nf drizzle

lloviznar [ʎoβiθ'nar] vi to drizzle

llueve etc ['ʎweβe] vb ver **llover**

lluvia ['ʎuβja] nf rain; (cantidad) rainfall; (fig: de balas etc) hail, shower; ~ **radioactiva** radioactive fallout; **día de ~** rainy day; **una ~ de regalos** a shower of gifts

lluvioso, -a [ʎu'βjoso, a] adj rainy

lo [lo] artículo definido neutro: **lo bueno** the good ▷ pron (en relación a una persona) him; (en relación a una cosa) it; **lo mío** what is mine; **lo difícil es que ...** the difficult thing about it is that ...; **no saben lo aburrido que es** they don't know how boring it is; **viste a lo americano** he dresses in the American style; **lo de** that matter of; **lo que** what, that which; **toma lo que quieras** take what(ever) you want; **lo que sea** whatever; **¡toma lo que he dicho!** I stand by what I said!; ver tb **el**

loa ['loa] nf praise

loable [lo'aβle] adj praiseworthy

loar [lo'ar] vt to praise

lobato [lo'βato] nm (Zool) wolf cub

lobo ['loβo] nm wolf; ~ **de mar** (fig) sea dog; ~ **marino** seal

lóbrego, -a ['loβreɣo, a] adj dark; (fig) gloomy

lóbulo ['loβulo] nm lobe

local [lo'kal] adj local ▷ nm place, site; (oficinas) premises pl

localidad [lokali'ðað] nf (barrio) locality; (lugar) location; (Teat) seat, ticket

localizar [lokali'θar] vt (ubicar) to locate, find; (encontrar) to find, track down; (restringir) to localize; (situar) to place

loción [lo'θjon] nf lotion, wash

loco, -a ['loko, a] adj mad; (fig) wild, mad ▷ nm/f lunatic, madman(-woman); ~ **de atar, ~ de remate, ~ rematado** raving mad; **a lo ~** without rhyme or reason; **ando ~ con el examen** the exam is driving me crazy; **estar ~ con** o **por algo/por algn** to be mad about sth/sb; **estar ~ de alegría** to be overjoyed o over the moon

locomoción [lokomo'θjon] nf locomotion

locomotora [lokomo'tora] nf engine, locomotive

locuaz [lo'kwaθ] adj loquacious, talkative

locución [loku'θjon] nf expression

locura [lo'kura] nf madness; (acto) crazy act

locutor, a [loku'tor, a] nm/f (Radio)
announcer; (comentarista) commentator; (TV)
newscaster, newsreader
locutorio [loku'torjo] nm (Telec) telephone
box o booth; (negocio) shop or internet café
providing telephone services
lodo ['lodo] nm mud
lógico, -a ['loxiko, a] adj logical; (correcto)
natural; (razonable) reasonable ▷ nm logician
▷ nf logic; **es ~ que** ... it stands to reason
that ...; **ser de una lógica aplastante** to be
as clear as day
login ['loxin] nm login
logístico, -a [lo'xistiko, a] adj logistical ▷ nf
logistics pl
logotipo [loɣo'tipo] nm logo
logrado, -a [lo'ɣraðo, a] pp de **lograr** ▷ adj
(interpretación, reproducción) polished, excellent
lograr [lo'ɣrar] vt (obtener) to get, obtain;
(conseguir) to achieve, attain; **~ hacer**
to manage to do; **~ que algn venga** to manage
to get sb to come; **~ acceso a** (Inform) to access
logro ['loɣro] nm achievement, success; (Com)
profit
lóker ['loker] nm (Am) locker
loma ['loma] nf hillock, low ridge
lombriz [lom'briθ] nf (earth)worm
lomo ['lomo] nm (de animal) back; (Culin: de cerdo)
pork loin; (: de vaca) rib steak; (de libro) spine
lona ['lona] nf canvas
loncha ['lontʃa] nf = **lonja**
lonche ['lontʃe] nm (Am) lunch
lonchería [lontʃe'ria] nf (Am) snack bar,
diner (US)
Londres ['londres] nm London
longaniza [longa'niθa] nf pork sausage
longevidad [lonxeβi'ðað] nf longevity
longitud [lonxi'tuð] nf length; (Geo)
longitude; **tener tres metros de ~** to be
three metres long; **~ de onda** wavelength;
salto de ~ long jump
longitudinal [lonxituði'nal] adj longitudinal
lonja ['lonxa] nf slice; (de tocino) rasher; (Com)
market, exchange; **~ de pescado** fish market
loro ['loro] nm parrot
los [los] artículo definido mpl the ▷ pron them;
(en relación a ustedes) you; **mis libros y ~ tuyos**
my books and yours
losa ['losa] nf stone; **~ sepulcral** gravestone
lote ['lote] nm portion, share; (Com) lot;
(Inform) batch
lotería [lote'ria] nf lottery; (juego) lotto;
le tocó la ~ he won a big prize in the lottery;
(fig) he struck lucky; **~ nacional** national
lottery; **~ primitiva** (Esp) type of state-run
lottery; see note

● **LOTERÍA**
●
● Millions of euros are spent every year on
● loterías, lotteries. There is the weekly
● Lotería Nacional which is very popular

● especially at Christmas. Other weekly
● lotteries are the Bono Loto and the (Lotería)
● Primitiva. One of the most famous
● lotteries is run by the wealthy and
● influential society for the blind, la ONCE,
● and the form is called el cupón de la ONCE
● or el cupón de los ciegos.

loza ['loθa] nf crockery; **~ fina** china
lozanía [loθa'nia] nf (lujo) luxuriance
lozano, -a [lo'θano, a] adj luxuriant;
(animado) lively
lubina [lu'βina] nf (Zool) sea bass
lubricante [luβri'kante] adj, nm lubricant
lubricar [luβri'kar], **lubrificar** [luβrifi'kar] vt
to lubricate
lucero [lu'θero] nm (Astro) bright star; (fig)
brilliance; **~ del alba/de la tarde** morning/
evening star
luces ['luθes] nfpl de **luz**
lucha ['lutʃa] nf fight, struggle; **~ de clases**
class struggle; **~ libre** wrestling
luchar [lu'tʃar] vi to fight
lucidez [luθi'ðeθ] nf lucidity
lúcido, -a [lu'θiðo, a] adj (persona) lucid;
(mente) logical; (idea) crystal-clear
luciérnaga [lu'θjernaɣa] nf glow-worm
lucimiento [luθi'mjento] nm (brillo)
brilliance; (éxito) success
lucir [lu'θir] vt to illuminate, light (up);
(ostentar) to show off ▷ vi (brillar) to shine;
(Am: parecer) to look, seem; **lucirse** vr (irónico)
to make a fool of o.s.; (presumir) to show off;
la casa luce limpia the house looks clean
lucro ['lukro] nm profit, gain; **~s y daños**
(Com) profit and loss sg
lúdico, -a ['luðiko, a] adj playful; (actividad)
recreational
ludopatía [luðopa'tia] nf addiction to
gambling (o videojuegos)
luego ['lweɣo] adv (después) next; (más tarde)
later, afterwards; (Am fam: en seguida) at once,
immediately; **desde ~** of course; **¡hasta ~!**
see you later!, so long!; **¿y ~?** what next?
lugar [lu'ɣar] nm place; (sitio) spot; (pueblo)
village, town; **en ~ de** instead of; **en primer
~** in the first place, firstly; **dar ~ a** to give rise
to; **hacer ~** to make room; **fuera de ~** out of
place; **sin ~ a dudas** without doubt,
undoubtedly; **tener ~** to take place;
~ común commonplace; **yo en su ~** if I were
him; **no hay ~ para preocupaciones** there
is no cause for concern
lugareño, -a [luɣa'reɲo, a] adj village cpd
▷ nm/f villager
lugarteniente [luɣarte'njente] nm deputy
lúgubre ['luɣuβre] adj mournful
lujo ['luxo] nm luxury; (fig) profusion,
abundance; **de ~** luxury cpd, de luxe
lujoso, -a [lu'xoso, a] adj luxurious
lujuria [lu'xurja] nf lust
lumbago [lum'baɣo] nm lumbago

lumbre ['lumbre] *nf* (*luz*) light; (*fuego*) fire;
cerca de la ~ near the fire, at the fireside;
¿tienes ~? (*para cigarro*) have you got a light?
lumbrera [lum'brera] *nf* luminary; (*fig*)
leading light
luminoso, -a [lumi'noso, a] *adj* luminous,
shining; (*idea*) bright, brilliant
luna ['luna] *nf* moon; (*vidrio: escaparate*) plate
glass; (:*de un espejo*) glass; (:*de gafas*) lens; (*fig*)
crescent; **~ creciente/llena/menguante/
nueva** crescent/full/waning/new moon;
~ de miel honeymoon; **estar en la ~** to have
one's head in the clouds
lunar [lu'nar] *adj* lunar ▷ *nm* (*Anat*) mole;
tela a ~es spotted material
lunes ['lunes] *nm inv* Monday; *ver tb* **sábado**
lupa ['lupa] *nf* magnifying glass
lustrar [lus'trar] *vt* (*esp Am: mueble*) to polish;
(*zapatos*) to shine
lustre ['lustre] *nm* polish; (*fig*) lustre; **dar ~ a**
to polish
lustroso, -a [lus'troso, a] *adj* shining
luterano, -a [lute'rano, a] *adj* Lutheran
luto ['luto] *nm* mourning; (*congoja*) grief,
sorrow; **llevar el** *o* **vestirse de ~** to be in
mourning
Luxemburgo [luksem'buryo] *nm*
Luxembourg
luz [luθ] (*pl* **luces**) *nf* (*tb fig*) light; (*fam*)
electricity; **dar a ~ un niño** to give birth to a
child; **sacar a la ~** to bring to light; **dar la ~**
to switch on the light; **encender** (*Esp*) *o*
prender (*Am*)/**apagar la ~** to switch the light
on/off; **les cortaron la ~** their (electricity)
supply was cut off; **a la ~ de** in the light of;
a todas luces by any reckoning; **hacer la ~
sobre** to shed light on; **tener pocas luces** to
be dim *o* stupid; **~ de la luna/del sol** *o* **solar**
moonlight/sunlight; **~ eléctrica** electric
light; **~ roja/verde** red/green light; **~ de
cruce** (*Auto*) dipped headlight; **~ de freno**
brake light; **~ intermitente/trasera**
flashing/rear light; **luces de tráfico** traffic
lights; **el Siglo de las Luces** the Age of
Enlightenment; **traje de luces** bullfighter's
costume

m *abr* (= *metro(s)*) m; (= *minuto(s)*) min., m;
(= *masculino*) m., masc
macana [ma'kana] *nf* (*Am: porra*) club;
(: *mentira*) lie, fib; (: *tontería*) piece of nonsense
macarra [ma'karra] *nm* (*fam*) thug
macarrones [maka'rrones] *nmpl* macaroni *sg*
macedonia [maθe'ðonja] *nf*: **~ de frutas**
fruit salad
macerar [maθe'rar] *vt* (*Culin*) to soak,
macerate; **macerarse** *vr* to soak, soften
maceta [ma'θeta] *nf* (*de flores*) pot of flowers;
(*para plantas*) flowerpot
machacar [matʃa'kar] *vt* to crush, pound;
(*moler*) to grind (up); (*aplastar*) to mash ▷ *vi*
(*insistir*) to go on, keep on
machete [ma'tʃete] *nm* machete, (large) knife
machetear [matʃete'ar] *vt* (*Am*) to swot (*Brit*),
grind away (*US*)
machismo [ma'tʃismo] *nm* sexism; male
chauvinism
machista [ma'tʃista] *adj, nm* sexist; male
chauvinist
macho ['matʃo] *adj* male; (*fig*) virile ▷ *nm*
male; (*fig*) he-man, tough guy (*US*); (*Tec:
perno*) pin, peg; (*Elec*) pin, plug; (*Costura*) hook
macizo, -a [ma'θiθo, a] *adj* (*grande*) massive;
(*fuerte, sólido*) solid ▷ *nm* mass, chunk; (*Geo*)
massif
macramé [makra'me] *nm* macramé
mácula ['makula] *nf* stain, blemish
madeja [ma'ðexa] *nf* (*de lana*) skein, hank;
(*de pelo*) mass, mop

madera [ma'ðera] nf wood; (fig) nature, character; (: aptitud) aptitude; **una ~** a piece of wood; **~ contrachapada** o **laminada** plywood; **tiene buena ~** he's made of solid stuff; **tiene ~ de futbolista** he's got the makings of a footballer

madero [ma'ðero] nm beam; (fig) ship

madrastra [ma'ðrastra] nf stepmother

madre ['maðre] adj mother cpd; (Am) tremendous ▷ nf mother; (de vino etc) dregs pl; **~ adoptiva/política/soltera** foster mother/mother-in-law/unmarried mother; **la M~ Patria** the Mother Country; **sin ~** motherless; **¡~ mía!** oh dear!; **¡tu ~!** (fam!) fuck off! (!); **salirse de ~** (río) to burst its banks; (persona) to lose all self-control

madreperla [maðre'perla] nf mother-of-pearl

madreselva [maðre'selβa] nf honeysuckle

Madrid [ma'ðrið] n Madrid

madriguera [maðri'yera] nf burrow

madrileño, -a [maðri'leɲo, a] adj of o from Madrid ▷ nm/f native o inhabitant of Madrid

madrina [ma'ðrina] nf godmother; (Arq) prop, shore; (Tec) brace; **~ de boda** bridesmaid

madrugada [maðru'yaða] nf early morning, small hours; (alba) dawn, daybreak; **a las cuarto de la ~** at four o'clock in the morning

madrugador, a [maðruya'ðor, a] adj early-rising

madrugar [maðru'yar] vi to get up early; (fig) to get ahead

madurar [maðu'rar] vt, vi (fruta) to ripen; (fig) to mature

madurez [maðu'reθ] nf ripeness; (fig) maturity

maduro, -a [ma'ðuro, a] adj ripe; (fig) mature; **poco ~** unripe

maestra [ma'estra] nf ver **maestro**

maestría [maes'tria] nf mastery; (habilidad) skill, expertise; (Am) Master's Degree

maestro, -a [ma'estro, a] adj masterly; (perito) skilled, expert; (principal) main; (educado) trained ▷ nm/f master/mistress; (profesor) teacher ▷ nm (autoridad) authority; (Mus) maestro; (experto) master; (obrero) skilled workman; **~ albañil** master mason; **~ de obras** foreman

mafia ['mafja] nf mafia; **la M~** the Mafia

magdalena [mayða'lena] nf fairy cake

magia ['maxja] nf magic

mágico, -a ['maxiko, a] adj magic(al) ▷ nm/f magician

magisterio [maxis'terjo] nm (enseñanza) teaching; (profesión) teaching profession; (maestros) teachers pl

magistrado [maxis'traðo] nm magistrate; **Primer M~** (Am) President, Prime Minister

magistral [maxis'tral] adj magisterial; (fig) masterly

magnánimo, -a [may'nanimo, a] adj magnanimous

magnate [may'nate] nm magnate, tycoon; **~ de la prensa** press baron

magnético, -a [may'netiko, a] adj magnetic

magnetismo [mayne'tismo] nm magnetism

magnetizar [mayneti'θar] vt to magnetize

magnetofón [mayneto'fon], **magnetófono** [mayne'tofono], nm tape recorder

magnetofónico, -a [mayneto'foniko, a] adj: **cinta magnetofónica** recording tape

magnífico, -a [may'nifiko, a] adj splendid, magnificent

magnitud [mayni'tuð] nf magnitude

mago, -a ['mayo, a] nm/f magician, wizard; **los Reyes M~s** the Magi, the Three Wise Men; ver tb **Reyes Magos**

magro, -a ['mayro, a] adj (persona) thin, lean; (carne) lean

magullar [mayu'ʎar] vt (amoratar) to bruise; (dañar) to damage; (fam: golpear) to bash, beat

mahometano, -a [maome'tano, a] adj Mohammedan

mahonesa [mao'nesa] nf mayonnaise

maître ['metre] nm head waiter

maíz [ma'iθ] nm maize (Brit), corn (US); sweet corn

majadero, -a [maxa'ðero, a] adj silly, stupid

majestad [maxes'tað] nf majesty; **Su M~** His/Her Majesty; **(Vuestra) M~** Your Majesty

majestuoso, -a [maxes'twoso, a] adj majestic

majo, -a ['maxo, a] adj nice; (guapo) attractive, good-looking; (elegante) smart

mal [mal] adv badly; (equivocadamente) wrongly; (con dificultad) with difficulty ▷ adj = **malo** ▷ nm evil; (desgracia) misfortune; (daño) harm, damage; (Med) illness ▷ conj: **~ que le pese** whether he likes it or not; **me entendió ~** he misunderstood me; **hablar ~ de algn** to speak ill of sb; **huele ~** it smells bad; **ir de ~ en peor** to go from bad to worse; **oigo/veo ~** I can't hear/see very well; **si ~ no recuerdo** if my memory serves me right; **¡menos ~!** just as well!; **~ que bien** rightly or wrongly; **no hay ~ que por bien no venga** every cloud has a silver lining; **~ de ojo** evil eye

malabarismo [malaβa'rismo] nm juggling

malabarista [malaβa'rista] nm/f juggler

malaconsejado, -a [malakonse'xaðo, a] adj ill-advised

malaria [ma'larja] nf malaria

malcriado, -a [mal'krjaðo, a] adj (consentido) spoiled

maldad [mal'dað] nf evil, wickedness

maldecir [malde'θir] vt to curse ▷ vi: **~ de** to speak ill of

maldición [maldi'θjon] nf curse; **¡~!** curse it!, damn!

maldito, -a [mal'dito, a] adj (condenado) damned; (perverso) wicked ▷ nm: **el ~** the devil; **¡~ sea!** damn it!; **no le hace ~ (el) caso** he doesn't take a blind bit of notice

maleante [male'ante] *adj* wicked ▷ *nm/f* criminal, crook

malecón [male'kon] *nm* pier, jetty; (*rompeolas*) breakwater; (*LAm: paseo*) sea front, promenade

maledicencia [maleði'θenθja] *nf* slander, scandal

maleducado, -a [maleðu'kaðo, a] *adj* bad-mannered, rude

maleficio [male'fiθjo] *nm* curse, spell

malentendido [malenten'diðo] *nm* misunderstanding

malestar [males'tar] *nm* (*gen*) discomfort; (*enfermedad*) indisposition; (*fig: inquietud*) uneasiness; (*Pol*) unrest; **siento un ~ en el estómago** my stomach is upset

maleta [ma'leta] *nf* case, suitcase; (*Auto*) boot (*Brit*), trunk (*US*); **hacer la ~** to pack

maletera [male'tera] *nf* (*Am Auto*) boot (*Brit*), trunk (*US*)

maletero [male'tero] *nm* (*Auto*) boot (*Brit*), trunk (*US*); (*persona*) porter

maletín [male'tin] *nm* small case, bag; (*portafolio*) briefcase

malévolo, -a [ma'leβolo, a] *adj* malicious, spiteful

maleza [ma'leθa] *nf* (*malas hierbas*) weeds *pl*; (*arbustos*) thicket

malgastar [malɣas'tar] *vt* (*tiempo, dinero*) to waste; (*recursos*) to squander; (*salud*) to ruin

malhechor, a [male'tʃor, a] *nm/f* delinquent; (*criminal*) criminal

malherido, -a [male'riðo, a] *adj* badly injured

malhumorado, -a [malumo'raðo, a] *adj* bad-tempered

malicia [ma'liθja] *nf* (*maldad*) wickedness; (*astucia*) slyness, guile; (*mala intención*) malice, spite; (*carácter travieso*) mischievousness

malicioso, -a [mali'θjoso, a] *adj* wicked, evil; sly, crafty; malicious, spiteful; mischievous

maligno, -a [ma'liɣno, a] *adj* evil; (*dañino*) pernicious, harmful; (*maléolo*) malicious; (*Med*) malignant ▷ *nm*: **el ~** the devil

malla ['maʎa] *nf* (*de una red*) mesh; (*red*) network; (*Am: de buño*) swimsuit; (*de ballet, gimnasia*) leotard; **mallas** *nfpl* tights; **~ de alambre** wire mesh

Mallorca [ma'ʎorka] *nf* Majorca

malo, -a ['malo, a] *adj* (**mal** *antes de nmsg*) bad; (*calidad*) poor; (*falso*) false; (*espantoso*) dreadful; (*niño*) naughty ▷ *nm/f* villain ▷ *nm* (*Cine fam*) bad guy ▷ *nf* spell of bad luck; **estar ~** to be ill; **andar a malas con algn** to be on bad terms with sb; **estar de malas** (*mal humor*) to be in a bad mood; **lo ~ es que ...** the trouble is that ...

malograr [malo'ɣrar] *vt* to spoil; (*plan*) to upset; (*ocasión*) to waste; **malograrse** *vr* (*plan etc*) to fail, come to grief; (*persona*) to die before one's time

malparado, -a [malpa'raðo, a] *adj*: **salir ~** to come off badly

malpensado, -a [malpen'saðo, a] *adj* nasty

malsano, -a [mal'sano, a] *adj* unhealthy

Malta ['malta] *nf* Malta

malta ['malta] *nf* malt

malteada [malte'aða] *nf* (*Am*) milk shake

maltratar [maltra'tar] *vt* to ill-treat, mistreat

maltrecho, -a [mal'tretʃo, a] *adj* battered, damaged

malva ['malβa] *nf* mallow; **~ loca** hollyhock; **(de color de) ~** mauve

malvado, -a [mal'βaðo, a] *adj* evil, villainous

malvavisco [malβa'βisko] *nm* marshmallow

malversar [malβer'sar] *vt* to embezzle, misappropriate

Malvinas [mal'βinas] *nfpl*: **Islas ~** Falkland Islands

malware ['malwer] *nm* malware

mama ['mama] (*pl* **mamás**) *nf* (*de animal*) teat; (*de mujer*) breast

mamá [ma'ma] *nf* (*fam*) mum, mummy

mamar [ma'mar] *vt* (*pecho*) to suck; (*fig*) to absorb, assimilate ▷ *vi* to suck; **dar de ~** to (breast-)feed; (*animal*) to suckle

mamarracho [mama'rratʃo] *nm* sight, mess

mambo ['mambo] *nf* (*Mus*) mambo

mameluco [mameluko] (*Am*) *nm* dungarees *pl* (*Brit*), overalls *pl* (*US*)

mamífero, -a [ma'mifero, a] *adj* mammalian, mammal *cpd* ▷ *nm* mammal

mamón, -ona [ma'mon, ona] *adj* small, baby *cpd* ▷ *nm/f* small baby; (*fam!*) wanker (!)

mampara [mam'para] *nf* (*entre habitaciones*) partition; (*biombo*) screen

mampostería [mamposte'ria] *nf* masonry

mamut [ma'mut] *nm* mammoth

manada [ma'naða] *nf* (*Zool*) herd; (*: de leones*) pride; (*: de lobos*) pack; **llegaron en ~s** (*fam*) they came in droves

Managua [ma'naɣwa] *n* Managua

manantial [manan'tjal] *nm* spring; (*fuente*) fountain; (*fig*) source

manar [ma'nar] *vt* to run with, flow with ▷ *vi* to run, flow; (*abundar*) to abound

mancha ['mantʃa] *nf* stain, mark; (*de tinta*) blot; (*de vegetación*) patch; (*imperfección*) stain, blemish, blot; (*boceto*) sketch, outline; **la M~** La Mancha

manchar [man'tʃar] *vt* to stain, mark; (*Zool*) to patch; (*ensuciar*) to soil, dirty; **mancharse** *vr* to get dirty; (*fig*) to dirty one's hands

manchego, -a [man'tʃeɣo, a] *adj* of o from La Mancha ▷ *nm/f* native o inhabitant of La Mancha

mancilla [man'θiʎa] *nf* stain, blemish

manco, -a ['manko, a] *adj* (*de un brazo*) one-armed; (*de una mano*) one-handed; (*fig*) defective, faulty; **no ser ~** to be useful o active

mancomunar [mankomu'nar] *vt* to unite, bring together; (*recursos*) to pool; (*Jur*) to make jointly responsible

mancomunidad [mankomuni'ðað] *nf* union, association; (*comunidad*) community; (*Jur*) joint responsibility

mandado [man'daðo] *nm* (*orden*) order; (*recado*) commission, errand

mandamiento [manda'mjento] *nm* (*orden*) order, command; (*Rel*) commandment; **~ judicial** warrant

mandar [man'dar] *vt* (*ordenar*) to order; (*dirigir*) to lead, command; (*país*) to rule over; (*enviar*) to send; (*pedir*) to order, ask for ▷ *vi* to be in charge; (*pey*) to be bossy; **mandarse** *vr*: **~se mudar** (*Am*: *fam*) to go away, clear off; **¿mande?** pardon?, excuse me? (*US*); **¿manda usted algo más?** is there anything else?; **~ a algn a paseo** *o* **a la porra** to tell sb to go to hell; **se lo ~emos por correo** we'll post it to you; **~ hacer un traje** to have a suit made

mandarín [manda'rin] *nm* petty bureaucrat

mandarina [manda'rina] *nf* (*fruta*) tangerine, mandarin (orange)

mandatario, -a [manda'tarjo, a] *nm/f* (*representante*) agent; **primer ~** (*esp Am*) head of state

mandato [man'dato] *nm* (*orden*) order; (*Pol*: *período*) term of office; (*: territorio*) mandate; **~ judicial** (*search*) warrant

mandíbula [man'diβula] *nf* jaw

mandil [man'dil] *nm* (*delantal*) apron

mando ['mando] *nm* (*Mil*) command; (*de país*) rule; (*el primer lugar*) lead; (*Pol*) term of office; (*Tec*) control; **~ a la izquierda** left-hand drive; **los altos ~s** the high command *sg*; **~ por botón** push-button control; **~ a distancia** remote control; **al ~ de** in charge of; **tomar el ~** to take the lead

mandolina [mando'lina] *nf* mandolin(e)

mandón, -ona [man'don, ona] *adj* bossy, domineering

manejable [mane'xaβle] *adj* manageable; (*fácil de usar*) handy

manejar [mane'xar] *vt* to manage; (*máquina*) to work, operate; (*caballo etc*) to handle; (*casa*) to run, manage; (*Am Auto*) to drive ▷ *vi* (*Am Auto*) to drive; **manejarse** *vr* (*comportarse*) to act, behave; (*arreglárselas*) to manage; **"~ con cuidado"** "handle with care"

manejo [ma'nexo] *nm* (*de bicicleta*) handling; (*de negocio*) management, running; (*Auto*) driving; (*facilidad de trato*) ease, confidence; (*de idioma*) command; **manejos** *nmpl* intrigues; **tengo ~ del francés** I have a good command of French

manera [ma'nera] *nf* way, manner, fashion; (*Arte, Lit etc*: *estilo*) manner, style; **maneras** *nfpl* (*modales*) manners; **su ~ de ser** the way he is; (*aire*) his manner; **de mala ~** (*fam*) badly, unwillingly; **de ninguna ~** no way, by no means; **de otra ~** otherwise; **de todas ~s**

at any rate; **en gran ~** to a large extent; **sobre ~** exceedingly; **a mi ~ de ver** in my view; **no hay ~ de persuadirle** there's no way of convincing him

manga ['manga] *nf* (*de camisa*) sleeve; (*de riego*) hose; **de ~ corta/larga** short-/long-sleeved; **andar ~ por hombro** (*desorden*) to be topsyturvy; **tener ~ ancha** to be easy-going

mangar [man'gar] *vt* (*unir*) to plug in; (*fam*: *birlar*) to pinch, nick, swipe; (*mendigar*) to beg

mango ['mango] *nm* handle; (*Bot*) mango; **~ de escoba** broomstick

mangonear [mangone'ar] *vt* to boss about ▷ *vi* to be bossy

manguera [man'gera] *nf* (*de riego*) hose; (*tubo*) pipe; **~ de incendios** fire hose

maní [ma'ni] (*pl* **maníes** *o* **manises**) *nm* (*Am*: *cacahuete*) peanut; (*: planta*) groundnut plant

manía [ma'nia] *nf* (*Med*) mania; (*fig*: *moda*) rage, craze; (*disgusto*) dislike; (*malicia*) spite; **tiene ~s** she's a bit fussy; **coger ~ a algn** to take a dislike to sb; **tener ~ a algn** to dislike sb

maníaco, -a [ma'niako, a] *adj* maniac(al) ▷ *nm/f* maniac

maniatar [manja'tar] *vt* to tie the hands of

maniático, -a [ma'njatiko, a] *adj* maniac(al); (*loco*) crazy; (*tiquismiquis*) fussy ▷ *nm/f* maniac

manicomio [mani'komjo] *nm* mental hospital (*Brit*), insane asylum (*US*)

manicuro, -a [mani'kuro, a] *nm/f* manicurist ▷ *nf* manicure

manifestación [manifesta'θjon] *nf* (*declaración*) statement, declaration; (*demostración*) show, display; (*Pol*) demonstration; (*concentración*) mass meeting

manifestante [manifes'tante] *nm/f* demonstrator

manifestar [manifes'tar] *vt* to show, manifest; (*declarar*) to state, declare; **manifestarse** *vr* to show, become apparent; (*Pol*: *desfilar*) to demonstrate; (*: reunirse*) to hold a mass meeting

manifiesto, -a [mani'fjesto, a] *vb ver* **manifestar** ▷ *adj* clear, manifest ▷ *nm* manifesto; (*Anat, Naut*) manifest; **poner algo de ~** (*aclarar*) to make sth clear; (*revelar*) to reveal sth; **quedar ~** to be plain *o* clear

manija [ma'nixa] *nf* handle

manillar [mani'ʎar] *nm* handlebars *pl*

maniobra [ma'njoβra] *nf* manœuvring; (*manejo*) handling; (*fig*: *movimiento*) manœuvre, move; (*: estratagema*) trick, stratagem; **maniobras** *nfpl* manœuvres

maniobrar [manio'βrar] *vt* to manœuvre; (*manejar*) to handle ▷ *vi* to manœuvre

manipulación [manipula'θjon] *nf* manipulation; (*Com*) handling

manipular [manipu'lar] *vt* to manipulate; (*manejar*) to handle

maniquí [mani'ki] *nm/f* model ▷ *nm* dummy

manirroto, -a [mani'rroto, a] adj lavish, extravagant ▷ nm/f spendthrift

manitas [ma'nitas] adj inv good with one's hands ▷ nm/f inv: **ser un ~** to be very good with one's hands

manivela [mani'βela] nf crank

manjar [man'xar] nm (tasty) dish

mano¹ ['mano] nf hand; (Zool) foot, paw; (de pintura) coat; (serie) lot, series; **a ~** by hand; **a ~ derecha/izquierda** on (o to) the right(-hand side)/left(-hand side); **a ~s llenas** lavishly, generously; **hecho a ~** handmade; **robo a ~ armada** armed robbery; **darse la(s) ~(s)** to shake hands; **de primera ~** (at) first hand; **de segunda ~** (at) second hand; **echar ~ de** to make use of; **echar una ~** to lend a hand; **echar una ~ a** to lay hands on; **está en tus ~s** it's up to you; **estrechar la ~ a algn** to shake sb's hand; **~ de obra** labour, manpower; **~ de santo** sure remedy; **¡~s a la obra!** to work!; **~s libres** hands-free; **Pedro es mi ~ derecha** Pedro is my right-hand man; **se le fue la ~** his hand slipped; (fig) he went too far; **traer o llevar algo entre ~s** to deal o be busy with sth

mano² ['mano] nm (Am fam) friend, mate

manojo [ma'noxo] nm handful, bunch; **~ de llaves** bunch of keys

manopla [ma'nopla] nf (paño) flannel; **manoplas** nfpl mittens

manoseado, -a [manose'aðo, a] adj well-worn

manosear [manose'ar] vt (tocar) to handle, touch; (desordenar) to mess up, rumple; (insistir en) to overwork; (acariciar) to caress, fondle; (pey: persona) to feel o touch up

manos libres adj inv (teléfono, dispositivo) hands-free ▷ nm inv hands-free kit

manotazo [mano'taθo] nm slap, smack

mansalva [man'salβa]: **a ~** adv indiscriminately

mansedumbre [manse'ðumbre] nf gentleness, meekness; (de animal) tameness

mansión [man'sjon] nf mansion

manso, -a ['manso, a] adj gentle, mild; (animal) tame

manta ['manta] nf blanket; (Am) poncho

manteca [man'teka] nf fat; (Am) butter; **~ de cacahuete/cacao** peanut/cocoa butter; **~ de cerdo** lard

mantecado [mante'kaðo] nm (Esp: dulce navideño) Christmas sweet made from flour, almonds and lard; (helado) ice cream

mantel [man'tel] nm tablecloth

mantendré etc [manten'dre] vb ver **mantener**

mantener [mante'ner] vt to support, maintain; (alimentar) to sustain; (conservar) to keep; (Tec) to maintain, service; **mantenerse** vr (seguir de pie) to be still standing; (no ceder) to hold one's ground; (subsistir) to sustain o.s., keep going; **~ algo en equilibrio** to keep sth balanced; **~se a distancia** to keep one's distance; **~se firme** to hold one's ground

mantenimiento [manteni'mjento] nm maintenance; sustenance; (sustento) support

mantequilla [mante'kiʎa] nf butter

mantilla [man'tiʎa] nf mantilla; **mantillas** nfpl baby clothes; **estar en ~s** (persona) to be terribly innocent; (proyecto) to be in its infancy

manto ['manto] nm (capa) cloak; (de ceremonia) robe, gown

mantón [man'ton] nm shawl

mantuve etc [man'tuβe] vb ver **mantener**

manual [ma'nwal] adj manual ▷ nm manual, handbook; **habilidad ~** manual skill

manubrio [ma'nuβrio] nm (Am Auto) steering wheel

manufactura [manufak'tura] nf manufacture; (fábrica) factory

manufacturado, -a [manufaktu'raðo, a] adj manufactured

manuscrito, -a [manus'krito, a] adj handwritten ▷ nm manuscript

manutención [manuten'θjon] nf maintenance; (sustento) support

manzana [man'θana] nf apple; (Arq) block; **~ de la discordia** (fig) bone of contention

manzanilla [manθa'niʎa] nf (planta) camomile; (infusión) camomile tea; (vino) manzanilla

manzano [man'θano] nm apple tree

maña ['maɲa] nf (gen) skill, dexterity; (pey) guile; (costumbre) habit; (una maña) trick, knack; **con ~** craftily

mañana [ma'ɲana] adv tomorrow ▷ nm future ▷ nf morning; **de o por la ~** in the morning; **¡hasta ~!** see you tomorrow!; **pasado ~** the day after tomorrow; **~ por la ~** tomorrow morning

mañanero, -a [maɲa'nero, a] adj early-rising

maño, -a ['maɲo, a] adj Aragonese ▷ nm/f native o inhabitant of Aragon

mañoso, -a [ma'ɲoso, a] adj (hábil) skilful; (astuto) smart, clever

mapa ['mapa] nm map

maple ['maple] nm (Am) maple

maqueta [ma'keta] nf (scale) model

maquillador, a [makiʎa'ðor, a] nm/f (Teat etc) make-up artist ▷ nf (Am: Com) bonded assembly plant

maquillaje [maki'ʎaxe] nm make-up; (acto) making up

maquillar [maki'ʎar] vt to make up; **maquillarse** vr to put on (some) make-up

máquina ['makina] nf machine; (de tren) locomotive, engine; (Foto) camera; (Am: coche) car; (fig) machinery; (: proyecto) plan, project; **a toda ~** at full speed; **escrito a ~** typewritten; **~ de afeitar** electric razor; **~ de coser** sewing machine; **~ de escribir**

typewriter; **~ fotográfica** camera; **~ de coser/lavar** sewing/washing machine; **~ de facsímil** facsimile (machine), fax; **~ de franqueo** franking machine; **~ tragaperras** fruit machine; (*Com*) slot machine

maquinación [makinaˈθjon] *nf* machination, plot

maquinal [makiˈnal] *adj* (*fig*) mechanical, automatic

maquinaria [makiˈnarja] *nf* (*máquinas*) machinery; (*mecanismo*) mechanism, works *pl*

maquinilla [makiˈniʎa] *nf* small machine; (*torno*) winch; **~ de afeitar** razor; **~ eléctrica** electric razor

maquinista [makiˈnista] *nm/f* (*Ferro*) engine driver (*Brit*), engineer (*US*); (*Tec*) operator; (*Naut*) engineer

mar [mar] *nm* sea; **~ de fondo** groundswell; **~ llena** high tide; **~ adentro** o **afuera** out at sea; **en alta ~** on the high seas; **por ~** by sea o boat; **hacerse a la ~** to put to sea; **a ~es** in abundance; **un ~ de** lots of; **es la ~ de guapa** she is ever so pretty; **el M~ Negro/Báltico** the Black/Baltic Sea; **el M~ Muerto/Rojo** the Dead/Red Sea; **el M~ del Norte** the North Sea

maraca [maˈraka] *nf* maraca

maraña [maˈraɲa] *nf* (*maleza*) thicket; (*confusión*) tangle

maravilla [maraˈβiʎa] *nf* marvel, wonder; (*Bot*) marigold; **hacer ~s** to work wonders; **a (las mil) ~s** wonderfully well

maravillar [maraβiˈʎar] *vt* to astonish, amaze; **maravillarse** *vr* to be astonished, be amazed

maravilloso, -a [maraβiˈʎoso, a] *adj* wonderful, marvellous

marca [ˈmarka] *nf* mark; (*sello*) stamp; (*Com*) make, brand; (*de ganado*) brand; (*: acto*) branding; (*Naut*) seamark; (*: boya*) marker; (*Deporte*) record; **de ~** excellent, outstanding; **~ de fábrica** trademark; **~ propia** own brand; **~ registrada** registered trademark

marcado, -a [marˈkaðo, a] *adj* marked, strong

marcador [markaˈðor] *nm* marker; (*rotulador*) marker (pen); (*de libro*) bookmark; (*Deporte*) scoreboard; (*: persona*) scorer

marcapasos [markaˈpasos] *nm inv* pacemaker

marcar [marˈkar] *vt* to mark; (*número de teléfono*) to dial; (*gol*) to score; (*números*) to record, keep a tally of; (*el pelo*) to set; (*ganado*) to brand; (*suj: termómetro*) to read, register; (*: reloj*) to show; (*tarea*) to assign; (*Com*) to put a price on ▷ *vi* (*Deporte*) to score; (*Telec*) to dial; **mi reloj marca las dos** it's two o'clock by my watch; **~ el compás** (*Mus*) to keep time; **~ el paso** (*Mil*) to mark time

marcha [ˈmartʃa] *nf* march; (*Deporte*) walk; (*Tec*) running, working; (*Auto*) gear; (*velocidad*) speed; (*fig*) progress; (*curso*) course; **dar ~ atrás** to reverse, put into reverse; **estar en ~** to be under way, be in motion; **hacer algo sobre la ~** to do sth as you *etc* go along; **poner en ~** to put into gear; **ponerse en ~** to start, get going; **a ~s forzadas** (*fig*) with all speed; **¡en ~!** (*Mil*) forward march!; (*fig*) let's go!; **"~ moderada"** (*Auto*) "drive slowly"; **que tiene** o **de mucha ~** (*fam*) very lively

marchar [marˈtʃar] *vi* (*ir*) to go; (*funcionar*) to work, go; (*fig*) to go, proceed; **marcharse** *vr* to go (away), leave; **todo marcha bien** everything is going well

marchitar [martʃiˈtar] *vt* to wither, dry up; **marchitarse** *vr* (*Bot*) to wither; (*fig*) to fade away

marchito, -a [marˈtʃito, a] *adj* withered, faded; (*fig*) in decline

marchoso, -a [marˈtʃoso, a] *adj* (*fam: animado*) lively; (*: moderno*) modern

marcial [marˈθjal] *adj* martial, military

marciano, -a [marˈθjano, a] *adj* Martian, of o from Mars

marco [ˈmarko] *nm* frame; (*Deporte*) goalposts *pl*; (*moneda*) mark; (*fig*) setting; (*contexto*) framework; **~ de chimenea** mantelpiece

marea [maˈrea] *nf* tide; (*llovizna*) drizzle; **~ alta/baja** high/low tide; **~ negra** oil slick

mareado, -a [mareˈaðo, a] *adj*: **estar ~** (*con náuseas*) to feel sick; (*aturdido*) to feel dizzy

marear [mareˈar] *vt* (*fig: irritar*) to annoy, upset; (*Med*): **~ a algn** to make sb feel sick; **marearse** *vr* (*tener náuseas*) to feel sick; (*desvanecerse*) to feel faint; (*aturdirse*) to feel dizzy; (*fam: emborracharse*) to get tipsy

maremoto [mareˈmoto] *nm* tidal wave

mareo [maˈreo] *nm* (*náusea*) sick feeling; (*en viaje*) travel sickness; (*aturdimiento*) dizziness; (*fam: lata*) nuisance

marfil [marˈfil] *nm* ivory

margarina [marɣaˈrina] *nf* margarine

margarita [marɣaˈrita] *nf* (*Bot*) daisy; (**rueda**) **~** (*en máquina impresora*) daisy wheel

margen [ˈmarxen] *nm* (*borde*) edge, border; (*fig*) margin, space ▷ *nf* (*de río etc*) bank; **~ de beneficio** o **de ganancia** profit margin; **~ comercial** mark-up; **~ de confianza** credibility gap; **dar ~ para** to give an opportunity for; **dejar a algn al ~** to leave sb out (in the cold); **mantenerse al ~** to keep out (of things); **al ~ de lo que digas** despite what you say

marginal [marxiˈnal] *adj* (*tema, error*) minor; (*grupo*) fringe *cpd*; (*anotación*) marginal

marginar [marxiˈnar] *vt* to exclude; (*socialmente*) to marginalize, ostracize

maría [maˈria] *nf* (*fam: mujer*) housewife

mariachi [maˈrjatʃi] *nm* (*música*) mariachi music; (*grupo*) mariachi band; (*persona*) mariachi musician

Mariachi music is the musical style most characteristic of Mexico. From the state of Jalisco in the 19th century, this music spread rapidly throughout the country, until each region had its own particular style of the mariachi "sound". A mariachi band can be made up of several singers, up to eight violins, two trumpets, guitars, a *vihuela* (an old form of guitar), and a harp. The dance associated with this music is called the *zapateado*.

marica [ma'rika] *nm (fam)* sissy; *(homosexual)* queer

maricón [mari'kon] *nm (fam)* queer

marido [ma'riðo] *nm* husband

marihuana [mari'wana] *nf* marijuana, cannabis

marimacho [mari'matʃo] *nf (fam)* mannish woman

marina [ma'rina] *nf* navy; **~ mercante** merchant navy

marinero, -a [mari'nero, a] *adj* sea *cpd*; *(barco)* seaworthy ▷ *nm* sailor, seaman

marino, -a [ma'rino, a] *adj* sea *cpd*, marine ▷ *nm* sailor; **~ de agua dulce/de cubierta/de primera** landlubber/deckhand/able seaman

marioneta [marjo'neta] *nf* puppet

mariposa [mari'posa] *nf* butterfly

mariquita [mari'kita] *nm (fam)* sissy; *(homosexual)* queer ▷ *nf (Zool)* ladybird *(Brit)*, ladybug *(US)*

marisco [ma'risko] *nm (tb: ~s)* shellfish, seafood

marisma [ma'risma] *nf* marsh, swamp

marítimo, -a [ma'ritimo, a] *adj* sea *cpd*, maritime

marmita [mar'mita] *nf* pot

mármol ['marmol] *nm* marble

marqués, -esa [mar'kes, esa] *nm/f* marquis/marchioness

marranada [marra'naða] *nf (fam)*: **es una ~** that's disgusting; **hacer una ~ a algn** to do the dirty on sb

marrano, -a [ma'rrano, a] *adj* filthy, dirty ▷ *nm (Zool)* pig; *(malo)* swine; *(sucio)* dirty pig

marrón [ma'rron] *adj* brown

marroquí [marro'ki] *adj, nm/f* Moroccan ▷ *nm* Morocco (leather)

Marruecos [ma'rrwekos] *nm* Morocco

martes ['martes] *nm inv* Tuesday; **~ de carnaval** Shrove Tuesday; *ver tb* **Carnaval**; **sábado**; **~ y trece** ≈ Friday 13th

According to Spanish superstition Tuesday is an unlucky day, even more so if it falls on the 13th of the month.

martillar [marti'ʎar], **martillear** [martiʎe'ar] *vt* to hammer

martillo [mar'tiʎo] *nm* hammer; *(de presidente de asamblea, comité)* gavel; **~ neumático** pneumatic drill *(Brit)*, jackhammer *(US)*

mártir ['martir] *nm/f* martyr

martirio [mar'tirjo] *nm* martyrdom; *(fig)* torture, torment

maruja [ma'ruxa] *nf (fam)* = **maría**

marxismo [mark'sismo] *nm* Marxism

marxista [mark'sista] *adj, nm/f* Marxist

marzo ['marθo] *nm* March; *ver tb* **julio**

mas [mas] *conj* but

 PALABRA CLAVE

más [mas] *adj, adv* **1**: **más (que, de)** *(compar)* more (than), ...+ er (than); **más grande/inteligente** bigger/more intelligent; **trabaja más (que yo)** he works more (than me); **más de seis** more than six; **es más de medianoche** it's after midnight; **durar más** to last longer; *ver tb* **cada**

2 *(superl)*: **el más** the most, ...+ est; **el más grande/inteligente (de)** the biggest/most intelligent (in)

3 *(negativo)*: **no tengo más dinero** I haven't got any more money; **no viene más por aquí** he doesn't come round here any more; **no sé más** I don't know any more, that's all I know

4 *(adicional)*: **un kilómetro más** one more kilometre; **no le veo más solución que ...** I see no other solution than to ...; **¿algo más?** anything else?; *(en tienda)* will that be all?; **¿quién más?** anybody else?

5 *(+ adj: valor intensivo)*: **¡qué perro más sucio!** what a filthy dog!; **¡es más tonto!** he's so stupid!

6 *(locuciones)*: **más o menos** more or less; **los más** most people; **es más** in fact, furthermore; **más bien** rather; **¡qué más da!** what does it matter!; *ver tb* **no**

7: **por más: por más que lo intento** no matter how much o hard I try; **por más que quisiera ayudar** much as I should like to help

8: **de más: veo que aquí estoy de más** I can see I'm not needed here; **tenemos uno de más** we've got one extra

9 *(Am)*: **no más** only, just; **ayer no más** just yesterday

▷ *prep*: **2 más 2 son 4** 2 and 0 plus 2 are 4

▷ *nm inv*: **este trabajo tiene sus más y sus menos** this job's got its good points and its bad points

masa ['masa] *nf (mezcla)* dough; *(volumen)* volume, mass; *(Física)* mass; **en ~** en masse; **las ~s** *(Pol)* the masses

masacre [ma'sakre] *nf* massacre

masaje [ma'saxe] *nm* massage; **dar ~ a** to massage

m

mascar [mas'kar] vt, vi to chew; (fig) to mumble, mutter

máscara ['maskara] nf (tb Inform) mask ▷ nm/f masked person; **~ antigás** gas mask

mascarada [maska'raða] nf masquerade

mascarilla [maska'riʎa] nf mask; (vaciado) deathmask; (de maquillaje) face pack

mascota [mas'kota] nf mascot

masculino, -a [masku'lino, a] adj masculine; (Bio) male ▷ nm (Ling) masculine

mascullar [masku'ʎar] vt to mumble, mutter

masía [ma'sia] nf farmhouse

masificación [masifika'θjon] nf overcrowding

masilla [ma'siʎa] nf putty

masivo, -a [ma'siβo, a] adj (en masa) mass

masón [ma'son] nm (free)mason

masoquista [maso'kista] adj masochistic ▷ nm/f masochist

mastectomía [mastekto'mia] nf mastectomy

máster (pl **masters**) ['master, 'masters] nm master's degree; ver tb **licenciado**

masticar [masti'kar] vt to chew; (fig) to ponder over

mástil ['mastil] nm (de navío) mast; (de guitarra) neck

mastín [mas'tin] nm mastiff

masturbación [masturβa'θjon] nf masturbation

masturbarse [mastur'βarse] vr to masturbate

mata ['mata] nf (arbusto) bush, shrub; (de hierbas) tuft; (campo) field; (manojo) tuft, blade; **matas** nfpl scrub sg; **~ de pelo** mop of hair; **a salto de ~** (día a día) from day to day; (al azar) haphazardly

matadero [mata'ðero] nm slaughterhouse, abattoir

matador, a [mata'ðor, a] adj killing ▷ nm/f killer ▷ nm (Taur) matador, bullfighter

matamoscas [mata'moskas] nm inv (palo) fly swat

matanza [ma'tanθa] nf slaughter

matar [ma'tar] vt to kill; (tiempo, pelota) to kill ▷ vi to kill; **matarse** vr (suicidarse) to kill o.s., commit suicide; (morir) to be o get killed; (gastarse) to wear o.s. out; **~ el hambre** to stave off hunger; **~ a algn a disgustos** to make sb's life a misery; **~las callando** to go about things slyly; **~se trabajando** to kill o.s. with work; **~se por hacer algo** to struggle to do sth

matasellos [mata'seʎos] nm inv postmark

mate ['mate] adj (sin brillo: color) dull, matt ▷ nm (en ajedrez) (check)mate; (Am: hierba) maté; (: vasija) gourd

matemáticas [mate'matikas] nfpl mathematics

matemático, -a [mate'matiko, a] adj mathematical ▷ nm/f mathematician

materia [ma'terja] nf (gen) matter; (Tec) material; (Escol) subject; **en ~ de** on the subject of; (en cuanto a) as regards; **~ prima** raw material; **entrar en ~** to get down to business

material [mate'rjal] adj material; (dolor) physical; (real) real; (literal) literal ▷ nm material; (Tec) equipment; **~ de construcción** building material; **~es de derribo** rubble sg

materialismo [materja'lismo] nm materialism

materialista [materja'lista] adj materialist(ic)

materialmente [materjal'mente] adv materially; (fig) absolutely

maternal [mater'nal] adj motherly, maternal

maternidad [materni'ðað] nf motherhood, maternity

materno, -a [ma'terno, a] adj maternal; (lengua) mother cpd

matinal [mati'nal] adj morning cpd

matiz [ma'tiθ] nm shade; (de sentido) shade, nuance; (de ironía etc) touch

matizar [mati'θar] vt (variar) to vary; (Arte) to blend; **~ de** to tinge with

matón [ma'ton] nm bully

matorral [mato'rral] nm thicket

matraca [ma'traka] nf rattle; (fam) nuisance

matrícula [ma'trikula] nf (registro) register; (Escol: inscripción) registration; (Auto) registration number; (: placa) number plate; **~ de honor** (Univ) top marks in a subject at university with the right to free registration the following year

matricular [matriku'lar] vt to register, enrol

matrimonial [matrimo'njal] adj matrimonial

matrimonio [matri'monjo] nm (pareja) (married) couple; (acto) marriage; **~ civil/ clandestino** civil/secret marriage; **contraer ~ (con)** to marry

matriz [ma'triθ] nf (Anat) womb; (Tec) mould; (Mat) matrix; **casa ~** (Com) head office

matrona [ma'trona] nf (mujer de edad) matron; (comadrona) midwife

matufia [ma'tufja] nf (Am: fam) put-up job

maullar [mau'ʎar] vi to mew, miaow

mausoleo [mauso'leo] nm mausoleum

maxilar [maksi'lar] nm jaw(bone)

máxima ['maksima] nf ver **máximo**

máxime ['maksime] adv especially

máximo, -a ['maksimo, a] adj maximum; (más alto) highest; (más grande) greatest ▷ nm maximum ▷ nf maxim; **~ jefe o líder** (Am) President, leader; **como ~** at most; **al ~** to the utmost

maxisingle [maksi'singel] nm twelve-inch (single)

maya ['maja] adj Mayan ▷ nm/f Maya(n)

mayo ['majo] nm May; ver tb **julio**

mayonesa [majo'nesa] nf mayonnaise
mayor [ma'jor] adj main, chief; (adulto) grown-up, adult; (Jur) of age; (de edad avanzada) elderly; (Mus) major; (comparativo: de tamaño) bigger; (: de edad) older; (superlativo: de tamaño) biggest; (tb fig) greatest; (: de edad) oldest ▷ nm chief, boss; (adulto) adult; **mayores** nmpl (antepasados) ancestors; **al por ~** wholesale; **~ de edad** adult; ver tb **mayores**
mayoral [majo'ral] nm foreman
mayordomo [major'ðomo] nm butler
mayores [ma'jores] nmpl grown-ups; **llegar a ~** to get out of hand
mayoría [majo'ria] nf majority, greater part; **en la ~ de los casos** in most cases; **en su ~** on the whole
mayorista [majo'rista] nm/f wholesaler
mayoritario, -a [majori'tarjo, a] adj majority cpd; **gobierno ~** majority government
mayúsculo, -a [ma'juskulo, a] adj (fig) big, tremendous; **~ de** capital (letter); **mayúsculas** nfpl capitals; (Tip) upper case sg
mazapán [maθa'pan] nm marzipan
mazo ['maθo] nm (martillo) mallet; (de mortero) pestle; (de flores) bunch; (Deporte) bat
me [me] pron (directo) me; (indirecto) (to) me; (reflexivo) (to) myself; **¡dámelo!** give it to me!; **me lo compró** (de mí) he bought it from me; (para mí) he bought it for me
meandro [me'andro] nm meander
mear [me'ar] (fam) vt to piss on (!) ▷ vi to pee, piss (!), have a piss (!); **mearse** vr to wet o.s.
mecánica [me'kanika] nf ver **mecánico**
mecánico, -a [me'kaniko, a] adj mechanical; (repetitivo) repetitive ▷ nm/f mechanic ▷ nf (estudio) mechanics sg; (mecanismo) mechanism
mecanismo [meka'nismo] nm mechanism; (engranaje) gear
mecanografía [mekanoɣra'fia] nf typewriting
mecanógrafo, -a [meka'noɣrafo, a] nm/f (copy) typist
mecate [me'kate] nm (Am) rope
mecedor (Am) [mese'ðor] nm, **mecedora** [meθe'ðora] nf rocking chair
mecer [me'θer] vt (cuna) to rock; **mecerse** vr to rock; (rama) to sway
mecha ['metʃa] nf (de vela) wick; (de bomba) fuse; **a toda ~** at full speed; **ponerse ~s** to streak one's hair
mechero [me'tʃero] nm (cigarette) lighter
mechón [me'tʃon] nm (gen) tuft; (manojo) bundle; (de pelo) lock
medalla [me'ðaʎa] nf medal
media ['meðja] nf ver **medio**
mediación [meða'θjon] nf mediation; **por ~ de** through
mediado, -a [me'ðjaðo, a] adj half-full; (trabajo) half-completed; **a ~s de** in the middle of, halfway through

mediano, -a [me'ðjano, a] adj (regular) medium, average; (mediocre) mediocre ▷ nf (Aut) central reservation, median (US); **(de tamaño) ~** medium-sized
medianoche [meðja'notʃe] nf midnight
mediante [me'ðjante] adv by (means of), through
mediar [me'ðjar] vi (tiempo) to elapse; (interceder) to mediate, intervene; (existir) to exist; **media el hecho de que …** there is the fact that …
medicación [meðika'θjon] nf medication, treatment
medicamento [meðika'mento] nm medicine, drug
medicina [meði'θina] nf medicine
medicinal [meðiθi'nal] adj medicinal
medición [meði'θjon] nf measurement
médico, -a ['meðiko, a] adj medical ▷ nm/f doctor; **~ de cabecera** family doctor; **~ pediatra** paediatrician; **~ residente** house physician, intern (US)
medida [me'ðiða] nf measure; (medición) measurement; (de camisa, zapato etc) size, fitting; (moderación) moderation, prudence; **en cierta/gran ~** up to a point/to a great extent; **un traje a la ~** a made-to-measure suit; **~ de cuello** collar size; **a ~ de** in proportion to; (de acuerdo con) in keeping with; **con ~** with restraint; **sin ~** immoderately; **a ~ que …** (at the same time) as …; **tomar ~s** to take steps
medidor [meði'ðor] nm (Am) meter
medieval [meðje'βal] adj medieval
medio, -a ['meðjo, a] adj half (a); (punto) mid, middle; (promedio) average ▷ adv half-; (esp Am) un tanto) rather, quite ▷ nm (centro) middle, centre; (método) means, way; (ambiente) environment ▷ nf (prenda de vestir) stocking; (Am) sock; (promedio) average; **medias** nfpl tights; **media hora** half an hour; **~ litro** half a litre; **las tres y media** half past three; **M~ Oriente** Middle East; **a ~ camino** halfway (there); **~ dormido** half asleep; **~ enojado** (esp Am) rather annoyed; **lo dejó a ~s** he left it half-done; **ir a ~s** to go fifty-fifty; **~ de transporte** means of transport; **a ~ terminar** half finished; **en ~ in** the middle; (entre) in between; **por ~ de** by (means of), through; **en los ~s financieros** in financial circles; **encontrarse en su ~** to be in one's element; **~ ambiente** environment; **~ circulante** (Com) money supply; ver tb **medios**
medioambiental [meðjoambjen'tal] adj environmental
mediocre [me'ðjokre] adj middling, average; (pey) mediocre
mediodía [meðjo'ðia] nm midday, noon
medios ['meðjos] nmpl means, resources; **los ~ de comunicación** the media
medir [me'ðir] vt (gen) to measure ▷ vi to measure; **medirse** vr (moderarse) to be

m

moderate, act with restraint; **¿cuánto mides? — mido 1.50 m** how tall are you? — I am 1.50 m tall

meditabundo, -a [meði'ta'βundo, a] *adj* pensive

meditar [meði'tar] *vt* to ponder, think over, meditate on; *(planear)* to think out ▷ *vi* to ponder, think, meditate

mediterráneo, -a [meðite'rraneo, a] *adj* Mediterranean ▷ *nm*: **el (mar) M~** the Mediterranean (Sea)

médula ['meðula] *nf* (*Anat*) marrow; (*Bot*) pith; **~ espinal** spinal cord; **hasta la ~** *(fig)* to the core

medusa [me'ðusa] *nf* (*Esp*) jellyfish

megafonía [meɣafo'nia] *nf* PA o public address system

megáfono [me'ɣafono] *nm* megaphone

megalómano, -a [meɣa'lomano, a] *nm/f* megalomaniac

megapíxel [meɣa'piksel] (*pl* **megapixels** or **megapíxeles**) *nm* megapixel

mejicano, -a [mexi'kano, a] *adj, nm/f* Mexican

Méjico ['mexiko] *nm* Mexico

mejilla [me'xiʎa] *nf* cheek

mejillón [mexi'ʎon] *nm* mussel

mejor [me'xor] *adj, adv* (*comparativo*) better; (*superlativo*) best; **lo ~** the best thing; **lo ~ de la vida** the prime of life; **a lo ~** probably; (*quizá*) maybe; **~ dicho** rather; **tanto ~** so much the better; **es el ~ de todos** he's the best of all

mejora [me'xora] *nf*, **mejoramiento** [mexora'mjento] *nm* improvement

mejorar [mexo'rar] *vt* to improve, make better ▷ *vi*, **mejorarse** *vr* to improve, get better; (*Com*) to do well, prosper; **~ a** to be better than; **los negocios mejoran** business is picking up

mejunje [me'xunxe] *nm* (*pey*) concoction

melancolía [melanko'lia] *nf* melancholy

melancólico, -a [melan'koliko, a] *adj* (*triste*) sad, melancholy; (*soñador*) dreamy

melena [me'lena] *nf* (*de persona*) long hair; (*Zool*) mane

mellizo, -a [me'ʎiθo, a] *adj, nm/f* twin

melocotón [meloko'ton] *nm* (*Esp*) peach

melodía [melo'ðia] *nf* melody; (*tonada*) tune; (*de móvil*) ringtone

melodrama [melo'ðrama] *nm* melodrama

melodramático, -a [meloðra'matiko, a] *adj* melodramatic

melón [me'lon] *nm* melon

meloso, -a [me'loso, a] *adj* honeyed, sweet; (*empalagoso*) sickly, cloying; (*voz*) sweet; (*zalamero*) smooth

membrana [mem'brana] *nf* membrane

membrete [mem'brete] *nm* letterhead; **papel con ~** headed notepaper

membrillo [mem'briʎo] *nm* quince; **carne de ~** quince jelly

memorable [memo'raβle] *adj* memorable

memorándum [memo'randum] *nm* (*libro*) notebook; (*comunicación*) memorandum

memoria [me'morja] *nf* (*gen*) memory; (*artículo*) (learned) paper; **memorias** *nfpl* (*de autor*) memoirs; **~ anual** annual report; **aprender algo de ~** to learn sth by heart; **si tengo buena ~** if my memory serves me right; **venir a la ~** to come to mind; (*Inform*): **~ auxiliar** backing storage; **~ de acceso aleatorio** random access memory, RAM; **~ del teclado** keyboard memory; **~ fija** read-only memory, ROM; **~ flash** flash drive

memorizar [memori'θar] *vt* to memorize

menaje [me'naxe] *nm* (*muebles*) furniture; (*tb*: **artículos de ~**) household items *pl*; **~ de cocina** kitchenware

mención [men'θjon] *nf* mention; **digno de ~** noteworthy; **hacer ~ de** to mention

mencionar [menθjo'nar] *vt* to mention; (*nombrar*) to name; **sin ~ ...** let alone ...

mendigar [mendi'ɣar] *vt* to beg (for)

mendigo, -a [men'diɣo, a] *nm/f* beggar

mendrugo [men'druɣo] *nm* crust

menear [mene'ar] *vt* to move; (*cola*) to wag; (*cadera*) to swing; (*fig*) to handle; **menearse** *vr* to shake; (*balancearse*) to sway; (*moverse*) to move; (*fig*) to get a move on

menester [menes'ter] *nm* (*necesidad*) necessity; **menesteres** *nmpl* (*deberes*) duties; **es ~ hacer algo** it is necessary to do sth, sth must be done

menestra [me'nestra] *nf*: **~ de verduras** vegetable stew

menguante [men'gwante] *adj* decreasing, diminishing; (*luna*) waning; (*marea*) ebb *cpd*

menguar [men'gwar] *vt* to lessen, diminish; (*fig*) to discredit ▷ *vi* to diminish, decrease; (*fig*) to decline

menopausia [meno'pausja] *nf* menopause

menor [me'nor] *adj* (*más pequeño: comparativo*) smaller; (*número*) less, lesser; (: *superlativo*) smallest; (*número*) least; (*más joven: comparativo*) younger; (: *superlativo*) youngest; (*Mus*) minor ▷ *nmf* (*joven*) young person, juvenile; **Juanito es ~ que Pepe** Juanito is younger than Pepe; **ella es la ~ de todas** she is the youngest of all; **no tengo la ~ idea** I haven't the faintest idea; **al por ~** retail; **~ de edad** minor

Menorca [me'norka] *nf* Minorca

○ **PALABRA CLAVE**

menos [menos] *adj* **1**: **menos (que, de)** (*compar: cantidad*) less (than); (: *número*) fewer (than); **con menos entusiasmo** with less enthusiasm; **menos gente** fewer people; *ver tb* **cada**
2 (*superl*): **es el que menos culpa tiene** he is the least to blame; **donde menos problemas hay** where there are fewest problems

▷ *adv* **1** (*compar*): **menos (que, de)** less (than); **me gusta menos que el otro** I like it less than the other one; **menos de cinco** less than five; **menos de lo que piensas** less than you think

2 (*superl*): **es el menos listo (de su clase)** he's the least bright (in his class); **de todas ellas es la que menos me agrada** out of all of them she's the one I like least; **(por) lo menos** at (the very) least; **es lo menos que puedo hacer** it's the least I can do; **lo menos posible** as little as possible

3 (*locuciones*): **no quiero verle y menos visitarle** I don't want to see him let alone visit him; **tenemos siete (de) menos** we're seven short; **eso es lo de menos** that's the least of it; **¡todo menos eso!** anything but that!; **al/por lo menos** at (the very) least; **si al menos** if only; **¡menos mal!** thank goodness!

▷ *prep* except; (*cifras*) minus; **todos menos él** everyone except (for) him; **5 menos 2** 5 minus 2; **las 7 menos 20** (*hora*) 20 to 7

▷ *conj*: **a menos que**: **a menos que venga mañana** unless he comes tomorrow

menoscabar [menoska'βar] *vt* (*estropear*) to damage, harm; (*fig*) to discredit

menospreciar [menospre'θjar] *vt* to underrate, undervalue; (*despreciar*) to scorn, despise

mensaje [men'saxe] *nm* message; **enviar un ~ a algn** (*por móvil*) to text sb, send sb a text message; **~ de error** (*Inform*) error message; **~ de texto** text message; **~ electrónico** email

mensajero, -a [mensa'xero, a] *nm/f* messenger

menso, -a ['menso, a] *adj* (*Am: fam*) stupid

menstruación [menstrwa'θjon] *nf* menstruation

menstruar [mens'trwar] *vi* to menstruate

mensual [men'swal] *adj* monthly; **10 euros ~es** 10 euros a month

mensualidad [menswali'ðað] *nf* (*salario*) monthly salary; (*Com*) monthly payment *o* instalment

menta ['menta] *nf* mint

mental [men'tal] *adj* mental

mentalidad [mentali'ðað] *nf* mentality

mentalizar [mentali'θar] *vt* (*sensibilizar*) to make aware; (*convencer*) to convince; (*preparar mentalmente*) to prepare mentally; **mentalizarse** *vr* (*concienciarse*) to become aware; (*prepararse mentalmente*) to prepare o.s. mentally; **~se (de)** to get used to the idea (of); **~se de que ...** (*convencerse*) to get it into one's head that ...

mentar [men'tar] *vt* to mention, name; **~ la madre a algn** to swear at sb

mente ['mente] *nf* mind; (*inteligencia*) intelligence; **no tengo en ~ hacer eso** it is not my intention to do that

mentecato, -a [mente'kato, a] *adj* silly, stupid ▷ *nm/f* fool, idiot

mentir [men'tir] *vi* to lie; **¡miento!** sorry, I'm wrong!

mentira [men'tira] *nf* (*una mentira*) lie; (*acto*) lying; (*invención*) fiction; **~ piadosa** white lie; **una ~ como una casa** a whopping great lie; (*fam*) **parece ~ que ...** it seems incredible that ..., I can't believe that ...

mentiroso, -a [menti'roso, a] *adj* lying; (*falso*) deceptive ▷ *nm/f* liar

menú [me'nu] *nm* (*tb Inform*) menu; (*tb*: **~ del día**) set meal; **~ turístico** tourist menu; **guiado por ~** (*Inform*) menu-driven

menudo, -a [me'nuðo, a] *adj* (*pequeño*) small, tiny; (*sin importancia*) petty, insignificant; **¡~ negocio!** (*fam*) some deal!; **a ~** often, frequently

meñique [me'nike] *nm* little finger

meollo [me'oʎo] *nm* (*fig*) essence, core

mercadillo [merka'ðiʎo] *nm* (*Esp*) flea market

mercado [mer'kaðo] *nm* market; **~ en baja** falling market; **M~ Común** Common Market; **~ de demanda/de oferta** seller's/buyer's market; **~ laboral** labour market; **~ objetivo** target market; **~ de productos básicos** commodity market; **~ de pulgas** (*Am*) flea market; **~ de valores** stock market; **~ exterior/interior** *o* **nacional/libre** overseas/home/free market

mercancía [merkan'θia] *nf* commodity; **mercancías** *nfpl* goods, merchandise *sg*; **~s en depósito** bonded goods; **~s perecederas** perishable goods

mercantil [merkan'til] *adj* mercantile, commercial

mercenario, -a [merθe'narjo, a] *adj, nm* mercenary

mercería [merθe'ria] *nf* (*artículos*) haberdashery (*Brit*), notions *pl* (*US*); (*tienda*) haberdasher's shop (*Brit*), drapery (*Brit*), notions store (*US*)

mercurio [mer'kurjo] *nm* mercury

merecer [mere'θer] *vt* to deserve, merit ▷ *vi* to be deserving, be worthy; **merece la pena** it's worthwhile

merecido, -a [mere'θiðo, a] *adj* (well) deserved; **llevarse su ~** to get one's deserts

merendar [meren'dar] *vt* to have for tea ▷ *vi* to have tea; (*en el campo*) to have a picnic

merendero [meren'dero] *nm* ((*open-air*) *café*: *en el campo*) picnic spot

merengue [me'renge] *nm* meringue

meridiano [meri'ðjano] *nm* (*Astro, Geo*) meridian; **la explicación es de una claridad meridiana** the explanation is as clear as day

merienda [me'rjenda] *vb ver* **merendar** ▷ *nf* (*light*) tea, afternoon snack; (*de campo*) picnic; **~ de negros** free-for-all

mérito ['merito] *nm* merit; *(valor)* worth, value; **hacer ~s** to make a good impression; **restar ~ a** to detract from

merluza [mer'luθa] *nf* hake; **coger una ~** *(fam)* to get sozzled

merma ['merma] *nf* decrease; *(pérdida)* wastage

mermar [mer'mar] *vt* to reduce, lessen ▷ *vi* to decrease, dwindle

mermelada [merme'laða] *nf* jam; **~ de naranja** marmalade

mero, -a ['mero, a] *adj* mere, simple; *(Am fam)* very ▷ *adv* *(Am)* just, right ▷ *nm* *(Zool)* grouper; **el ~ ~** *(Am: (fam))* the boss

merodear [merode'ar] *vi* (Mil) to maraud; *(de noche)* to prowl (about); *(curiosear)* to snoop around

mes [mes] *nm* month; *(salario)* month's pay; **el ~ corriente** this o the current month

mesa ['mesa] *nf* table; *(de trabajo)* desk; (Com) counter; *(en mitin)* platform; (Geo) plateau; (Arq) landing; **~ de noche/de tijera/de operaciones** u **operatoria** bedside/folding/operating table; **~ electoral** *officials in charge of a polling station*; **~ redonda** *(reunión)* round table; **~ digitalizadora** (Inform) graph pad; **~ directiva** (Am); **~ y cama** bed and board; **poner/quitar la ~** to lay/clear the table

mesero, -a [me'sero, a] *nm/f* (Am) waiter/waitress

meseta [me'seta] *nf* (Geo) tableland; (Arq) landing

mesilla [me'siʎa], **mesita** [me'sita] *nf*: **~ de noche** bedside table

mesón [me'son] *nm* inn

mestizo, -a [mes'tiθo, a] *adj* mixed-race; (Zool) crossbred ▷ *nm/f* person of mixed race

mesura [me'sura] *nf* (calma) calm; *(moderación)* moderation, restraint; *(cortesía)* courtesy

meta ['meta] *nf* goal; *(de carrera)* finish; *(fig)* goal, aim, objective

metabolismo [metaβo'lismo] *nm* metabolism

metáfora [me'tafora] *nf* metaphor

metal [me'tal] *nm* (materia) metal; (Mus) brass

metálico, -a [me'taliko, a] *adj* metallic; *(de metal)* metal ▷ *nm* *(dinero contante)* cash

metalurgia [meta'lurxja] *nf* metallurgy

metedura [mete'ðura] *nf*: **~ de pata** *(fam)* blunder

meteorito [meteo'rito] *nm* meteorite

meteoro [mete'oro] *nm* meteor

meteorología [meteorolo'xia] *nf* meteorology

meter [me'ter] *vt* (colocar) to put, place; *(introducir)* to put in, insert; *(involucrar)* to involve; *(causar)* to make, cause; **meterse** *vr*: **~se en** to go into, enter; *(fig)* to interfere in, meddle in; **~se a** to start; **~se a escritor** to become a writer; **~se con algn** to provoke sb, pick a quarrel with sb; **~ prisa a algn** to hurry sb up

meticuloso, -a [metiku'loso, a] *adj* meticulous, thorough

metódico, -a [me'toðiko, a] *adj* methodical

metodismo [meto'ðismo] *nm* Methodism

método ['metoðo] *nm* method

metodología [metoðolo'xia] *nf* methodology

metralla [me'traʎa] *nf* shrapnel

metralleta [metra'ʎeta] *nf* sub-machine-gun

métrico, -a ['metriko, a] *adj* metric ▷ *nf* metrics *pl*; **cinta métrica** tape measure

metro ['metro] *nm* metre; *(tren: tb: metropolitano)* underground (Brit), subway (US); *(instrumento)* rule; **~ cuadrado/cúbico** square/cubic metre

metrópoli [me'tropoli], **metrópolis** [me'tropolis] *nf* (ciudad) metropolis; *(colonial)* mother country

metrosexual [metrosexu'al] *adj, nm* metrosexual

mexicano, -a [mexi'kano, a] *adj, nm/f* (Am) Mexican

México ['mexiko] *nm* (Am) Mexico; **Ciudad de ~** Mexico City

mezcla ['meθkla] *nf* mixture; *(fig)* blend

mezclar [meθ'klar] *vt* to mix (up); *(armonizar)* to blend; *(combinar)* to merge; **mezclarse** *vr* to mix, mingle; **~ en** to get mixed up in, get involved in

mezquino, -a [meθ'kino, a] *adj* (cicatero) mean ▷ *nm/f* (avaro) mean person; *(miserable)* petty individual

mezquita [meθ'kita] *nf* mosque

mg *abr* (= miligramo(s)) mg

mi [mi] *adj posesivo* my ▷ *nm* (Mus) E

mí [mi] *pron* me, myself; **¿y a mí qué?** so what?

mía ['mia] *pron ver* **mío**

miaja ['mjaxa] *nf* crumb; **ni una ~** *(fig)* not the least little bit

miau [mjau] *nm* miaow

michelín [mitʃe'lin] *nm* (fam) spare tyre

micro ['mikro] *nm* (Radio) mike, microphone; *(Am: pequeño)* minibus; *(: grande)* coach, bus

microbio [mi'kroβjo] *nm* microbe

microbús [mikro'βus] *nm* minibus

microfilm (pl **microfilms**) [mikro'film, mikro'films] *nm* microfilm

micrófono [mi'krofono] *nm* microphone

microonda [mikro'onda] *nf*, **microondas** [mikro'ondas] *nm inv* microwave; **(horno) ~s** microwave (oven)

microscópico, -a [mikros'kopiko, a] *adj* microscopic

microscopio [mikros'kopjo] *nm* microscope

miedo ['mjeðo] *nm* fear; *(nerviosismo)* apprehension, nervousness; **meter ~ a** to scare, frighten; **tener ~** to be afraid; **de ~** wonderful, marvellous; **¡qué ~!** *(fam)* how awful!; **me da ~** it scares me; **hace un frío de ~** *(fam)* it's terribly cold

miedoso, -a [mje'ðoso, a] *adj* fearful, timid

miel [mjel] *nf* honey; **no hay ~ sin hiel** there's no rose without a thorn

miembro ['mjembro] *nm* limb; *(socio)* member; *(de institución)* fellow; **~ viril** penis

mientes *etc* ['mjentes] *vb ver* **mentar, mentir** ▷ *nfpl*: **no parar ~ en** to pay no attention to; **traer a las ~** to recall

mientras ['mjentras] *conj* while; *(duración)* as long as ▷ *adv* meanwhile; **~ (que)** whereas; **~ tanto** meanwhile; **~ más tiene, más quiere** the more he has, the more he wants

miércoles ['mjerkoles] *nm inv* Wednesday; **~ de ceniza** Ash Wednesday; *ver tb* **Carnaval**; **sábado**

mierda ['mjerða] *nf (fam!)* shit (!), crap (!); *(fig)* filth, dirt; **¡vete a la ~!** go to hell!

miga ['miɣa] *nf* crumb; *(fig: meollo)* essence; **hacer buenas ~s** *(fam)* to get on well; **esto tiene su ~** there's more to this than meets the eye

migaja [mi'ɣaxa] *nf*: **una ~ de** *(un poquito)* a little; **migajas** *nfpl* crumbs; *(pey)* left-overs

migración [miɣra'θjon] *nf* migration

migratorio, -a [miɣra'torjo, a] *adj* migratory

mil [mil] *num* thousand; **dos ~ libras** two thousand pounds

milagro [mi'laɣro] *nm* miracle; **hacer ~s** *(fig)* to work wonders

milagroso, -a [mila'ɣroso, a] *adj* miraculous

milésima [mi'lesima] *nf (de segundo)* thousandth

milésimo, -a [mi'lesimo, a] *num* thousandth

mili ['mili] *nf*: **hacer la ~** *(fam)* to do one's military service; *see note*

---

milicia [mi'liθja] *nf (Mil)* militia; *(servicio militar)* military service

miligramo [mili'ɣramo] *nm* milligram

milímetro [mi'limetro] *nm* millimetre *(Brit)*, millimeter *(US)*

militante [mili'tante] *adj* militant

militar [mili'tar] *adj* military ▷ *nm/f* soldier ▷ *vi* to serve in the army; *(fig)* to militate, fight

militarismo [milita'rismo] *nm* militarism

milla ['miʎa] *nf* mile; **~ marina** nautical mile

millar [mi'ʎar] *num* thousand; **a ~es** in thousands

millón [mi'ʎon] *num* million

millonario, -a [miʎo'narjo, a] *nm/f* millionaire

milusos [mi'lusos] *nm inv (Am)* odd-job man

mimar [mi'mar] *vt* to spoil, pamper

mimbre ['mimbre] *nm* wicker; **de ~** wicker *cpd*, wickerwork

mímica ['mimika] *nf (para comunicarse)* sign language; *(imitación)* mimicry

mimo ['mimo] *nm (caricia)* caress; *(de niño)* spoiling; *(Teat)* mime; *(: actor)* mime artist

mina ['mina] *nf* mine; *(pozo)* shaft; *(de lápiz)* lead refill; **hullera** o **~ de carbón** coal mine

minar [mi'nar] *vt* to mine; *(fig)* to undermine

mineral [mine'ral] *adj* mineral ▷ *nm (Geo)* mineral; *(mena)* ore

minero, -a [mi'nero, a] *adj* mining *cpd* ▷ *nm/f* miner

miniatura [minja'tura] *adj inv, nf* miniature

minicadena [minika'ðena] *nf (Mus)* mini hi-fi

MiniDisc® [mini'disk] *nm* MiniDisc®

minidisco [mini'ðisko] *nm* diskette

minifalda [mini'falda] *nf* miniskirt

minifundio [mini'fundjo] *nm* smallholding, small farm

minimizar [minimi'θar] *vt* to minimize

mínimo, -a ['minimo, a] *adj* minimum; *(insignificante)* minimal ▷ *nm* minimum; **precio/salario ~** minimum price/wage; **lo ~ que pueden hacer** the least they can do

minino, -a [mi'nino, a] *nm/f (fam)* puss, pussy

ministerio [minis'terjo] *nm* ministry *(Brit)*, department *(US)*; **M~ de Asuntos Exteriores** Foreign Office *(Brit)*, State Department *(US)*; **M~ del Comercio e Industria** Department of Trade and Industry; **M~ de (la) Gobernación** o **del Interior** ≈ Home Office *(Brit)*, Ministry of the Interior; **M~ de Hacienda** Treasury *(Brit)*, Treasury Department *(US)*

ministro, -a [mi'nistro, a] *nm/f* minister, secretary *(esp US)*; **M~ de Hacienda** Chancellor of the Exchequer, Secretary of the Treasury *(US)*; **M~ de (la) Gobernación** o **del Interior** ≈ Home Secretary *(Brit)*, Secretary of the Interior *(US)*

minoría [mino'ria] *nf* minority

minorista [mino'rista] *nm* retailer

minucioso, -a [minu'θjoso, a] *adj* thorough, meticulous; *(prolijo)* very detailed

minúsculo, -a [mi'nuskulo, a] *adj* tiny, minute ▷ *nf* small letter; **minúsculas** *nfpl* *(Tip)* lower case *sg*

minusválido, -a [minus'βaliðo, a] *adj* (physically) handicapped o disabled ▷ *nm/f* disabled person

minuta [mi'nuta] *nf (de comida)* menu; *(de abogado etc)* fee

minutero [minu'tero] *nm* minute hand
minuto [mi'nuto] *nm* minute
mío, -a [mío, a] *adj, pron*: **el ~** mine; **un amigo ~** a friend of mine; **lo ~** what is mine; **los ~s** my people, my relations
miope ['mjope] *adj* short-sighted
miopía [mjo'pia] *nf* near- *o* short-sightedness
mira ['mira] *nf* (*de arma*) sight(s) *pl*; (*fig*) aim, intention; **de amplias/estrechas ~s** broad-/narrow-minded
mirada [mi'raða] *nf* look, glance; (*expresión*) look, expression; **~ de soslayo** sidelong glance; **~ fija** stare, gaze; **~ perdida** distant look; **clavar la ~ en** to stare at; **echar una ~ a** to glance at; **levantar/bajar la ~** to look up/down; **resistir la ~ de algn** to stare sb out
mirado, -a [mi'raðo, a] *adj* (*sensato*) sensible; (*considerado*) considerate; **bien/mal ~** well/not well thought of; **bien ~ ...** all things considered ...
mirador [mira'ðor] *nm* viewpoint, vantage point
mirar [mi'rar] *vt* to look at; (*observar*) to watch; (*considerar*) to consider, think over; (*vigilar, cuidar*) to watch, look after ▷ *vi* to look; (*Arq*) to face; **mirarse** *vr* (*dos personas*) to look at each other; **~ algo/a algn de reojo** *o* **de través** to look askance at sth/sb; **~ algo/a algn por encima del hombro** to look down on sth/sb; **~ bien/mal** to think highly of/have a poor opinion of; **~ fijamente** to stare *o* gaze at; **~ por** (*fig*) to look after; **~ por la ventana** to look out of the window; **~se al espejo** to look at o.s. in the mirror; **~se a los ojos** to look into each other's eyes
mirilla [mi'riʎa] *nf* (*agujero*) spyhole, peephole
mirlo ['mirlo] *nm* blackbird
misa ['misa] *nf* mass; **~ del gallo** midnight mass (*on Christmas Eve*); **~ de difuntos** requiem mass; **como en ~** in dead silence; **estos datos van a ~** (*fig*) these facts are utterly trustworthy
miserable [mise'raβle] *adj* (*avaro*) mean, stingy; (*nimio*) miserable, paltry; (*lugar*) squalid; (*fam*) vile, despicable ▷ *nm/f* (*malvado*) rogue
miseria [mi'serja] *nf* misery; (*pobreza*) poverty; (*tacañería*) meanness, stinginess; (*condiciones*) squalor; **una ~** a pittance
misericordia [miseri'korðja] *nf* (*compasión*) compassion, pity; (*perdón*) forgiveness, mercy
misil [mi'sil] *nm* missile
misión [mi'sjon] *nf* mission; (*tarea*) job, duty; (*Pol*) assignment; **misiones** *nfpl* (*Rel*) overseas missions
misionero, -a [misjo'nero, a] *nm/f* missionary
mismo, -a ['mismo, a] *adj* (*semejante*) same; (*después de pronombre*) -self; (*para énfasis*) very ▷ *adv*: **aquí/ayer/hoy ~** right here/only yesterday/this very day; **ahora ~** right now

▷ *conj*: **lo ~ que** just like, just as; **por lo ~** for the same reason; **el ~ traje** the same suit; **en ese ~ momento** at that very moment; **vino el ~ Ministro** the Minister himself came; **yo ~ lo vi** I saw it myself; **lo hizo por sí ~** he did it by himself; **lo ~** the same (thing); **da lo ~** it's all the same; **quedamos en las mismas** we're no further forward
misterio [mis'terjo] *nm* mystery; (*lo secreto*) secrecy
misterioso, -a [miste'rjoso, a] *adj* mysterious; (*inexplicable*) puzzling
mitad [mi'tað] *nf* (*medio*) half; (*centro*) middle; **~ (y)~** half-and-half; (*fig*) yes and no; **a ~ de precio** (at) half-price; **en *o* a ~ del camino** halfway along the road; **cortar por la ~** to cut through the middle
mitigar [miti'ɣar] *vt* to mitigate; (*dolor*) to relieve; (*sed*) to quench; (*ira*) to appease; (*preocupación*) to allay; (*soledad*) to alleviate
mitin ['mitin] *nm* (*esp Pol*) meeting
mito ['mito] *nm* myth
mitología [mitolo'xia] *nf* mythology
mixto, -a ['miksto, a] *adj* mixed; (*comité*) joint
ml *abr* (= *mililitro(s)*) ml
mm *abr* (= *milímetro(s)*) mm
mobiliario [moβi'ljarjo] *nm* furniture
mocasín [moka'sin] *nm* moccasin
mochila [mo'tʃila] *nf* rucksack (*Brit*), backpack
moción [mo'θjon] *nf* motion; **~ compuesta** (*Pol*) composite motion
moco ['moko] *nm* mucus; **mocos** *nmpl* (*fam*) snot; **limpiarse los ~s** to blow one's nose; **no es ~ de pavo** it's no trifle
moda ['moða] *nf* fashion; (*estilo*) style; **de *o* a la ~** in fashion, fashionable; **pasado de ~** out of fashion; **vestido a la última ~** trendily dressed
modal [mo'ðal] *adj* modal ▷ *nm*: **modales** *nmpl* manners
modalidad [moðali'ðað] *nf* (*clase*) kind, variety; (*manera*) way; (*Inform*) mode; **~ de texto** (*Inform*) text mode
modelar [moðe'lar] *vt* to model
modelo [mo'ðelo] *adj inv* model ▷ *nm/f* model ▷ *nm* (*patrón*) pattern; (*norma*) standard
módem ['moðem] *nm* (*Inform*) modem
moderado, -a [moðe'raðo, a] *adj* moderate
moderar [moðe'rar] *vt* to moderate; (*violencia*) to restrain, control; (*velocidad*) to reduce; **moderarse** *vr* to restrain o.s., · control o.s.
modernizar [moðerni'θar] *vt* to modernize; (*Inform*) to upgrade
moderno, -a [mo'ðerno, a] *adj* modern; (*actual*) present-day; (*equipo etc*) up-to-date
modestia [mo'ðestja] *nf* modesty
modesto, -a [mo'ðesto, a] *adj* modest
módico, -a ['moðiko, a] *adj* moderate, reasonable

modificar [moðifi'kar] vt to modify

modismo [mo'ðismo] nm idiom

modisto, -a [mo'ðisto, a] nm/f (diseñador) couturier, designer; (que confecciona) dressmaker

modo [moðo] nm (manera, forma) way, manner; (Inform, Mus) mode; (Ling) mood; **modos** nmpl manners; **"~ de empleo"** "instructions for use"; **~ de gobierno** form of government; **a ~ de** like; **de este ~** in this way; **de ningún ~** in no way; **de todos ~s** at any rate; **de un ~ u otro** (in) one way or another

modorra [mo'ðorra] nf drowsiness

módulo ['moðulo] nm module; (de mueble) unit

mofarse [mo'farse] vr: **~ de** to mock, scoff at

mofle ['mofle] nm (Am) silencer (Brit), muffler (US)

mogollón [moɣo'ʎon] (fam) nm: **~ de discos** etc loads of records etc ▷ adv: **un ~** a hell of a lot

moho ['moo] nm (Bot) mould, mildew; (en metal) rust

mohoso, -a [mo'oso, a] adj mouldy; rusty

mojado, -a [mo'xaðo, a] adj wet; (húmedo) damp; (empapado) drenched

mojar [mo'xar] vt to wet; (humedecer) to damp(en), moisten; (calar) to soak; **mojarse** vr to get wet; **~ el pan en el café** to dip o dunk one's bread in one's coffee

mojón [mo'xon] nm (hito) landmark; (en un camino) signpost; (tb: **~ kilométrico**) milestone

molcajete (Am) [molka'xete] nm mortar

moldavo, -a [mol'daβo, a] adj, nm/f Moldavian, Moldovan

molde ['molde] nm mould; (vaciado) cast; (de costura) pattern; (fig) model

moldeado [molde'aðo] nm soft perm

moldear [molde'ar] vt to mould; (en yeso etc) to cast

mole ['mole] nf mass, bulk; (edificio) pile

molécula [mo'lekula] nf molecule

moler [mo'ler] vt to grind, crush; (pulverizar) to pound; (trigo etc) to mill; (cansar) to tire out, exhaust; **~ a algn a palos** to give sb a beating

molestar [moles'tar] vt to bother; (fastidiar) to annoy; (incomodar) to inconvenience, put out; (perturbar) to trouble, upset ▷ vi to be a nuisance; **molestarse** vr to bother; (incomodarse) to go to a lot of trouble; (ofenderse) to take offence; **¿le molesta el ruido?** do you mind the noise?; **siento ~le** I'm sorry to trouble you

molestia [mo'lestja] nf bother, trouble; (incomodidad) inconvenience; (Med) discomfort; **es una ~** it's a nuisance; **no es ninguna ~** it's no trouble at all

molesto, -a [mo'lesto, a] adj (que fastidia) annoying; (incómodo) inconvenient; (inquieto) uncomfortable, ill at ease; (enfadado)

annoyed; **estar ~** (Med) to be in some discomfort; **estar ~ con algn** (fig) to be cross with sb; **me sentí ~** I felt embarrassed

molido, -a [mo'liðo, a] adj (machacado) ground; (pulverizado) powdered; **estar ~** (fig) to be exhausted o dead beat

molinillo [moli'niʎo] nm hand mill; **~ de carne/café** mincer/coffee grinder

molino [mo'lino] nm (edificio) mill; (máquina) grinder

molusco [mo'lusko] nm mollusc

momentáneo, -a [momen'taneo, a] adj momentary

momento [mo'mento] nm (gen) moment; (Tec) momentum; **de ~** at the moment, for the moment; **en ese ~** at that moment, just then; **por el ~** for the time being

momia ['momja] nf mummy

mona ['mona] nf ver **mono**

monaguillo [mona'ɣiʎo] nm altar boy

monarca [mo'narka] nm/f monarch, ruler

monarquía [monar'kia] nf monarchy

monárquico, -a [mo'narkiko, a] nm/f royalist, monarchist

monasterio [monas'terjo] nm monastery

mondadientes [monda'ðjentes] nm inv toothpick

mondar [mon'dar] vt (limpiar) to clean; (pelar) to peel; **mondarse** vr: **~se de risa** (fam) to split one's sides laughing

mondongo [mon'dongo] nm (Am) tripe

moneda [mo'neða] nf (tipo de dinero) currency, money; (pieza) coin; **una ~ de 50 céntimos** a 50-cent coin; **~ de curso legal** legal tender; **~ extranjera** foreign exchange; **~ única** single currency; **es ~ corriente** (fig) it's common knowledge

monedero [mone'ðero] nm purse

monetario, -a [mone'tarjo, a] adj monetary, financial

mongólico, -a [mon'goliko, a] adj, nm/f Mongol

monigote [moni'ɣote] nm (dibujo) doodle; (de papel) cut-out figure; (pey) wimp; ver tb **inocente**

monitor, a [moni'tor, a] nm/f instructor, coach ▷ nm (TV) set; (Inform) monitor; **~ en color** colour monitor

monja ['monxa] nf nun

monje ['monxe] nm monk

mono, -a ['mono, a] adj (bonito) lovely, pretty; (gracioso) nice, charming ▷ nm/f monkey, ape ▷ nm dungarees pl; (traje de faena) overalls pl; (fam: de drogadicto) cold turkey; **una chica muy mona** a very pretty girl; **dormir la ~** to sleep it off

monóculo [mo'nokulo] nm monocle

monografía [monoɣra'fia] nf monograph

monomando [mono'mando] nm (tb: **grifo ~**) mixer tap

monoparental [monoparen'tal] adj: **familia ~** single-parent family

monopatín [monopa'tin] *nm* skateboard
monopolio [mono'poljo] *nm* monopoly;
~ total absolute monopoly
monopolizar [monopoli'θar] *vt* to
monopolize
monotonía [monoto'nia] *nf* (*sonido*)
monotone; (*fig*) monotony
monótono, -a [mo'notono, a] *adj*
monotonous
monstruo ['monstrwo] *nm* monster ▷ *adj inv*
fantastic
monstruoso, -a [mons'trwoso, a] *adj*
monstrous
monta ['monta] *nf* total, sum; **de poca ~**
unimportant, of little account
montacargas [monta'karɣas] *nm inv* service
lift (*Brit*), freight elevator (*US*)
montaje [mon'taxe] *nm* assembly;
(*organización*) fitting up; (*Teat*) décor; (*Cine*)
montage
montaña [mon'taɲa] *nf* (*monte*) mountain;
(*sierra*) mountains *pl*, mountainous area;
(*Am: selva*) forest; **~ rusa** roller coaster
montañero, -a [monta'ɲero, a] *adj*
mountain *cpd* ▷ *nm/f* mountaineer, climber
montañés, -esa [monta'ɲes, esa] *adj*
mountain *cpd*; (*de Santander*) of *o* from the
Santander region ▷ *nm/f* highlander; native
o inhabitant of the Santander region
montañismo [monta'ɲismo] *nm*
mountaineering, climbing
montañoso, -a [monta'ɲoso, a] *adj*
mountainous
montar [mon'tar] *vt* (*subir a*) to mount, get
on; (*caballo etc*) to ride; (*Tec*) to assemble, put
together; (*negocio*) to set up; (*colocar*) to lift on
to; (*Cine: película*) to edit; (*Teat: obra*) to stage,
put on; (*Culin: batir*) to whip, beat ▷ *vi* to
mount, get on; (*sobresalir*) to overlap; **~ en
bicicleta** to ride a bicycle; **~ en cólera** to get
angry; **~ a caballo** to ride, go horseriding;
~ un número *o* **numerito** to make a scene;
tanto monta it makes no odds
montaraz [monta'raθ] *adj* mountain *cpd*,
highland *cpd*; (*pey*) uncivilized
monte ['monte] *nm* (*montaña*) mountain;
(*bosque*) woodland; (*área sin cultivar*) wild area,
wild country; **~ de piedad** pawnshop; **~ alto**
forest; **~ bajo** scrub(land)
monto ['monto] *nm* total, amount
montón [mon'ton] *nm* heap, pile; **un ~ de**
(*fig*) heaps of, lots of; **a montones** by the
score, galore
monumental [monumen'tal] *adj* (*tb fig*)
monumental; **zona ~** area of historical
interest
monumento [monu'mento] *nm* monument;
(*de conmemoración*) memorial
monzón [mon'θon] *nm* monsoon
moño ['moɲo] *nm* (*de pelo*) bun; **estar hasta
el ~** (*fam*) to be fed up to the back teeth
moqueta [mo'keta] *nf* fitted carpet

mora ['mora] *nf* (*Bot*) mulberry; (*: zarzamora*)
blackberry; (*Com*): **en ~** in arrears
morado, -a [mo'raðo, a] *adj* purple, violet
▷ *nm* bruise ▷ *nf* (*casa*) dwelling, abode;
pasarlas moradas to have a tough time of it
moral [mo'ral] *adj* moral ▷ *nf* (*ética*) ethics *pl*;
(*moralidad*) morals *pl*, morality; (*ánimo*)
morale; **tener baja la ~** to be in low spirits
moraleja [mora'lexa] *nf* moral
moralidad [morali'ðað] *nf* morals *pl*,
morality
moralizar [morali'θar] *vt* to moralize
moratón [mora'ton] *nm* bruise
morbo ['morβo] *nm* (*fam*) morbid pleasure
morboso, -a [mor'βoso, a] *adj* morbid
morcilla [mor'θiʎa] *nf* blood sausage, ≈ black
pudding (*Brit*)
mordaz [mor'ðaθ] *adj* (*crítica*) biting, scathing
mordaza [mor'ðaθa] *nf* (*para la boca*) gag; (*Tec*)
clamp
morder [mor'ðer] *vt* to bite; (*mordisquear*) to
nibble; (*fig: consumir*) to eat away, eat into
▷ *vi*, **morderse** *vr* to bite; **está que muerde**
he's hopping mad; **~se la lengua** to hold
one's tongue
mordisco [mor'ðisko] *nm* bite
moreno, -a [mo'reno, a] *adj* (*color*) (dark)
brown; (*de tez*) dark; (*de pelo moreno*) dark-
haired; (*negro*) black ▷ *nm/f* (*de tez*) dark-
skinned man/woman; (*de pelo*) dark-haired
man/woman
morfina [mor'fina] *nf* morphine
moribundo, -a [mori'βundo, a] *adj* dying
▷ *nm/f* dying person
morir [mo'rir] *vi* to die; (*fuego*) to die down;
(*luz*) to go out; **morirse** *vr* to die; (*fig*) to be
dying; (*Ferro etc: vías*) to end; (*calle*) to come
out; **fue muerto a tiros/en un accidente**
he was shot (dead)/was killed in an accident;
~ de frío/hambre to die of cold/starve to
death; **¡me muero de hambre!** (*fig*) I'm
starving!; **~se por algo** to be dying for sth;
~se por algn to be crazy about sb
mormón, -ona [mor'mon, ona] *nm/f*
Mormon
moro, -a ['moro, a] *adj* Moorish ▷ *nm/f* Moor;
¡hay ~s en la costa! watch out!
moroso, -a [mo'roso, a] *adj* (*lento*) slow ▷ *nm*
(*Com*) bad debtor, defaulter; **deudor ~** (*Com*)
slow payer
morral [mo'rral] *nm* haversack
morriña [mo'rriɲa] *nf* homesickness; **tener
~** to be homesick
morro ['morro] *nm* (*Zool*) snout, nose; (*Auto,
Aviat*) nose; (*fam: labio*) (thick) lip; **beber a ~**
to drink from the bottle; **caer de ~** to
nosedive; **estar de ~s (con algn)** to be in a
bad mood (with sb); **tener ~** to have a nerve
morsa ['morsa] *nf* walrus
morse ['morse] *nm* Morse (code)
mortadela [morta'ðela] *nf* mortadella,
bologna sausage

mortaja [mor'taxa] *nf* shroud; (*Tec*) mortise; (*Am*) cigarette paper

mortal [mor'tal] *adj* mortal; (*golpe*) deadly

mortalidad [mortali'ðað], **mortandad** [mortan'dað] *nf* mortality

mortero [mor'tero] *nm* mortar

mortífero, -a [mor'tifero, a] *adj* deadly, lethal

mortificar [mortifi'kar] *vt* to mortify; (*atormentar*) to torment

mosaico [mo'saiko] *nm* mosaic

mosca ['moska] *nf* fly; **por si las ~s** just in case; **estar ~** (*desconfiar*) to smell a rat; **tener la ~ en** *o* **detrás de la oreja** to be wary

Moscú [mos'ku] *nm* Moscow

mosquear [moske'ar] (*fam*) *vt* (*hacer sospechar*) to make suspicious; (*fastidiar*) to annoy; **mosquearse** *vr* (*enfadarse*) to get annoyed; (*ofenderse*) to take offence

mosquita [mos'kita] *nf*: **parece una ~ muerta** he looks as though butter wouldn't melt in his mouth

mosquitero [moski'tero] *nm* mosquito net

mosquito [mos'kito] *nm* mosquito

mostaza [mos'taθa] *nf* mustard

mosto ['mosto] *nm* unfermented grape juice

mostrador [mostra'ðor] *nm* (*de tienda*) counter; (*de café*) bar

mostrar [mos'trar] *vt* to show; (*exhibir*) to display, exhibit; (*explicar*) to explain; **mostrarse** *vr*: **~se amable** to be kind; to prove to be kind; **no se muestra muy inteligente** he doesn't seem (to be) very intelligent; **~ en pantalla** (*Inform*) to display

mota ['mota] *nf* speck, tiny piece; (*en diseño*) dot

mote ['mote] *nm* (*apodo*) nickname

motín [mo'tin] *nm* (*del pueblo*) revolt, rising; (*del ejército*) mutiny

motivación [motiβa'θjon] *nf* motivation

motivar [moti'βar] *vt* (*causar*) to cause, motivate; (*explicar*) to explain, justify

motivo [mo'tiβo] *nm* motive, reason; (*Arte, Mus*) motif; **con ~ de** (*debido a*) because of; (*en ocasión de*) on the occasion of; (*con el fin de*) in order to; **sin ~** for no reason at all

moto ['moto] *nf*, **motocicleta** [motoθi'kleta] *nf* motorbike (*Brit*), motorcycle

motociclista [motoθi'klista] *nm/f* motorcyclist, biker

motoneta [moto'neta] *nf* (*Am*) (motor) scooter

motor, a [mo'tor, a] *adj* (*Tec*) motive; (*Anat*) motor ▷ *nm* motor, engine; **~ a chorro** *o* **de reacción/de explosión** jet engine/internal combustion engine; **~ de búsqueda** (*Internet*) search engine ▷ *nf* motorboat

motorista [moto'rista] *nm/f* (*esp Am: automovilista*) motorist; (: *motociclista*) motorcyclist

motosierra [moto'sjerra] *nf* mechanical saw

motriz [mo'triz] *adj*: **fuerza ~** motive power; (*fig*) driving force

movedizo, -a [moβe'ðiθo, a] *adj* (*inseguro*) unsteady; (*fig*) unsettled, changeable; (*persona*) fickle

mover [mo'βer] *vt* to move; (*cambiar de lugar*) to shift; (*cabeza: para negar*) to shake; (: *para asentir*) to nod; (*accionar*) to drive; (*fig*) to cause, provoke; **moverse** *vr* to move; (*mar*) to get rough; (*viento*) to rise; (*fig: apurarse*) to get a move on; (: *transformarse*) to be on the move

movido, -a [mo'βiðo, a] *adj* (*Foto*) blurred; (*persona: activo*) active; (*mar*) rough; (*día*) hectic ▷ *nf* move; **la movida madrileña** the Madrid scene

móvil ['moβil] *adj* mobile; (*pieza de máquina*) moving; (*mueble*) movable ▷ *nm* (*motivo*) motive; (*teléfono*) mobile, cellphone (*US*)

movilidad [moβili'ðað] *nf* mobility

movilizar [moβili'θar] *vt* to mobilize

movimiento [moβi'mjento] *nm* (*gen, Lit, Pol*) movement; (*Tec*) motion; (*actividad*) activity; (*Mus*) tempo; **el M~** the Falangist Movement; **~ de bloques** (*Inform*) block move; **~ de mercancías** (*Com*) turnover, volume of business; **~ obrero/sindical** workers'/trade union movement; **~ sísmico** earth tremor

mozo, -a ['moθo, a] *adj* (*joven*) young; (*soltero*) single, unmarried ▷ *nm/f* (*joven*) youth, young man/girl; (*camarero*) waiter; (*camarera*) waitress; **~ de estación** porter

MP3 *nm* MP3; **reproductor (de) ~** MP3 player

mucama [mu'kama] *nf* (*Am*) maid

muchacho, -a [mu'tʃatʃo, a] *nm/f* (*niño*) boy/girl; (*criado*) servant/servant *o* maid

muchedumbre [mutʃe'ðumbre] *nf* crowd

⭕ **PALABRA CLAVE**

mucho, -a ['mutʃo, a] *adj* **1** (*cantidad*) a lot of, much; (*número*) lots of, a lot of, many; **mucho dinero** a lot of money; **hace mucho calor** it's very hot; **muchas amigas** lots *o* a lot *o* many friends

2 (*sg: fam*): **ésta es mucha casa para él** this house is much too big for him; **había mucho borracho** there were a lot *o* lots of drunks

▷ *pron*: **tengo mucho que hacer** I've got a lot to do; **muchos dicen que ...** a lot of people say that ...; *ver tb* **tener**

▷ *adv* **1**: **me gusta mucho** I like it a lot *o* very much; **lo siento mucho** I'm very sorry; **come mucho** he eats a lot; **trabaja mucho** he works hard; **¿te vas a quedar mucho?** are you going to be staying long?; **mucho más/menos** much more/less

2 (*respuesta*) very; **¿estás cansado?** — **¡mucho!** are you tired? — very!

3 (*locuciones*): **como mucho** at (the) most; **el mejor con mucho** by far the best; **¡ni mucho menos!** far from it!; **no es rico ni**

mucho menos he's far from being rich **4: por mucho que: por mucho que le creas** however much o no matter how much you believe him

muda ['muða] nf (de ropa) change of clothing; (Zool) moult; (de serpiente) slough

mudanza [mu'ðanθa] nf (cambio) change; (de casa) move; **estar de ~** to be moving

mudar [mu'ðar] vt to change; (Zool) to shed ▷ vi to change; **mudarse** vr (la ropa) to change; **~se de casa** to move house

mudo, -a ['muðo, a] adj dumb; (callado: película) silent; (Ling: letra) mute; (: consonante) voiceless; **quedarse ~ (de)** (fig) to be dumb with; **quedarse ~ de asombro** to be speechless

mueble ['mweβle] nm piece of furniture; **muebles** nmpl furniture sg

mueca ['mweka] nf face, grimace; **hacer ~s a** to make faces at

muela ['mwela] vb ver **moler** ▷ nf (diente) tooth; (: de atrás) back tooth; (de molino) millstone; (de afilar) grindstone; **~ del juicio** wisdom tooth

muelle ['mweʎe] adj (blando) soft; (fig) soft, easy ▷ nm spring; (Naut) wharf; (malecón) pier

muermo ['mwermo] nm (fam) wimp

muerte ['mwerte] nf death; (homicidio) murder; **dar ~ a** to kill; **de mala ~** (fam) lousy, rotten; **es la ~** (fam) it's deadly boring

muerto, -a ['mwerto, a] pp de **morir** ▷ adj dead; (color) dull ▷ nm/f dead man(-woman); (difunto) deceased; (cadáver) corpse; **cargar con el ~** (fam) to carry the can; **echar el ~ a algn** to pass the buck; **hacer el ~** (nadando) to float; **estar ~ de cansancio** to be dead tired; **Día de los M~s** (Am) All Souls' Day

◉ **DÍA DE LOS MUERTOS**

◉ All Souls' Day (or "Day of the Dead") in
◉ Mexico coincides with All Saints' Day,
◉ which is celebrated in the Catholic
◉ countries of Latin America on November
◉ 1st and 2nd. All Souls' Day is actually a
◉ celebration which begins in the evening
◉ of October 31st and continues until
◉ November 2nd. It is a combination of the
◉ Catholic tradition of honouring the
◉ Christian saints and martyrs, and the
◉ ancient Mexican or Aztec traditions, in
◉ which death was not something sinister.
◉ For this reason all the dead are honoured
◉ by bringing offerings of food, flowers and
◉ candles to the cemetery.

muesca ['mweska] nf nick

muestra etc ['mwestra] vb ver **mostrar** ▷ nf (señal) indication, sign; (demostración) demonstration; (prueba) proof; (estadística) sample; (modelo) model, pattern; (testimonio) token; **dar ~s de** to show signs of; **~ al azar** (Com) random sample

muestreo [mwes'treo] nm sample, sampling

muestro etc vb ver **mostrar**

muevo etc [mweβa] vb ver **mover**

mugir [mu'xir] vi (vaca) to moo

mugre ['muɣre] nf dirt, filth, muck

mugriento, -a [mu'ɣrjento, a] adj dirty, filthy, mucky

mujer [mu'xer] nf woman; (esposa) wife

mujeriego [muxe'rjeɣo] nm womaniser

mula ['mula] nf mule

mulato, -a [mu'lato, a] adj, nm/f mulatto

muleta [mu'leta] nf (para andar) crutch; (Taur) stick with red cape attached

mullido, -a [mu'ʎiðo, a] adj (cama) soft; (hierba) soft, springy

multa ['multa] nf fine; **echar** o **poner una ~ a** to fine

multar [mul'tar] vt to fine; (Deporte) to penalize

multicines [multi'θine] nmpl multiscreen cinema

multicolor [multiko'lor] adj multicoloured

multimillonario, -a [multimiʎo'narjo, a] adj (contrato) multimillion pound o dollar cpd ▷ nm/f multimillionaire/-millionairess

multinacional [multinaθjo'nal] adj, nf multinational

múltiple ['multiple] adj multiple, many pl, numerous; **de tarea ~** (Inform) multi-tasking; **de usuario ~** (Inform) multi-user

multiplicar [multipli'kar] vt (Mat) to multiply; (fig) to increase; **multiplicarse** vr (Bio) to multiply; (fig) to be everywhere at once

múltiplo ['multiplo] adj, nm multiple

multitud [multi'tuð] nf (muchedumbre) crowd; **~ de** lots of

mundano, -a [mun'dano, a] adj worldly; (de moda) fashionable

mundial [mun'djal] adj world-wide, universal; (guerra, récord) world cpd

mundo ['mundo] nm world; (ámbito) world, circle; **el otro ~** the next world; **el ~ del espectáculo** show business; **todo el ~** everybody; **tener ~** to be experienced, know one's way around; **el ~ es un pañuelo** it's a small world; **no es nada del otro ~** it's nothing special; **se le cayó el ~ (encima)** his world fell apart

munición [muni'θjon] nf (Mil: provisiones) stores pl, supplies pl; (: de armas) ammunition

municipal [muniθi'pal] adj (elección) municipal; (concejo) town cpd, local; (piscina etc) public ▷ nm (guardia) policeman

municipio [muni'θipjo] nm (ayuntamiento) town council, corporation; (territorio administrativo) town, municipality

muñeca [mu'ɲeka] nf (Anat) wrist; (juguete) doll

muñeco [mu'ɲeko] *nm* (*figura*) figure; (*marioneta*) puppet; (*fig*) puppet, pawn; (*niño*) pretty little boy; **~ de nieve** snowman

muñequera [muɲe'kera] *nf* wristband

mural [mu'ral] *adj* mural, wall *cpd* ⊳ *nm* mural

muralla [mu'raʎa] *nf* (*city*) wall(s) *pl*

murciélago [mur'θjelaɣo] *nm* bat

murmullo [mur'muʎo] *nm* murmur(ing); (*cuchicheo*) whispering; (*de arroyo*) murmur, rippling; (*de hojas, viento*) rustle, rustling; (*ruido confuso*) hum(ming)

murmuración [murmura'θjon] *nf* gossip; (*críticas*) backbiting

murmurar [murmu'rar] *vi* to murmur, whisper; (*criticar*) to criticize; (*cotillear*) to gossip

muro ['muro] *nm* wall; **~ de contención** retaining wall

mus [mus] *nm* card game

muscular [musku'lar] *adj* muscular

músculo ['muskulo] *nm* muscle

musculoso, -a [musku'loso, a] *adj* muscular

museo [mu'seo] *nm* museum; **~ de arte** *o* **de pintura** art gallery; **~ de cera** waxworks

musgo ['musɣo] *nm* moss

musical [musi'kal] *adj, nm* musical

músico, -a ['musiko, a] *adj* musical ⊳ *nm/f* musician ⊳ *nf* music; **irse con la música a otra parte** to clear off

musitar [musi'tar] *vt, vi* to mutter, mumble

muslo ['muslo] *nm* thigh; (*de pollo*) leg, drumstick

mustio, -a ['mustjo, a] *adj* (*persona*) depressed, gloomy; (*planta*) faded, withered

musulmán, -ana [musul'man, ana] *nm/f* Moslem, Muslim

mutación [muta'θjon] *nf* (*Bio*) mutation; (: *cambio*) (sudden) change

mutilar [muti'lar] *vt* to mutilate; (*a una persona*) to maim

mutismo [mu'tismo] *nm* silence

mutuamente [mutwa'mente] *adv* mutually

mutuo, -a ['mutwo, a] *adj* mutual

muy [mwi] *adv* very; (*demasiado*) too; **M~ Señor mío** Dear Sir; **~ bien** (*de acuerdo*) all right; **~ de noche** very late at night; **eso es ~ de él** that's just like him; **eso es ~ español** that's typically Spanish

n

N *abr* (= norte) N

n/ *abr* = **nuestro, a**

nabo ['naβo] *nm* turnip

nácar ['nakar] *nm* mother-of-pearl

nacer [na'θer] *vi* to be born; (*huevo*) to hatch; (*vegetal*) to sprout; (*río*) to rise; (*fig*) to begin, originate, have its origins; **nací en Barcelona** I was born in Barcelona; **nació para poeta** he was born to be a poet; **nadie nace enseñado** we all have to learn; **nació una sospecha en su mente** a suspicion formed in her mind

nacido, -a [na'θiðo, a] *adj* born; **recién ~** newborn

naciente [na'θjente] *adj* new, emerging; (*sol*) rising

nacimiento [naθi'mjento] *nm* birth; (*fig*) birth, origin; (*de Navidad*) Nativity; (*linaje*) descent, family; (*de río*) source; **ciego de ~** blind from birth

nación [na'θjon] *nf* nation; (*pueblo*) people; **Naciones Unidas** United Nations

nacional [naθjo'nal] *adj* national; (*Com, Econ*) domestic, home *cpd*

nacionalidad [naθjonali'ðað] *nf* nationality; (*Esp, Pol*) autonomous region

nacionalismo [naθjona'lismo] *nm* nationalism

nacionalista [naθjona'lista] *adj, nm/f* nationalist

nacionalizar [naθjonali'θar] *vt* to nationalize; **nacionalizarse** *vr* (*persona*) to become naturalized

nada ['naða] *pron* nothing ▷ *adv* not at all, in no way ▷ *nf* nothingness; **no decir ~ (más)** to say nothing (else), not to say anything (else); **¡~ más!** that's all; **de ~** don't mention it; **~ de eso** nothing of the kind; **antes de ~** right away; **~ como si ~** as if it didn't matter; **no ha sido ~** it's nothing; **la ~ the** void

nadador, a [naða'ðor, a] *nm/f* swimmer

nadar [na'ðar] *vi* to swim; **~ en la abundancia** *(fig)* to be rolling in money

nadie ['naðje] *pron* nobody, no-one; **~ habló** nobody spoke; **no había ~** there was nobody there, there wasn't anybody there; **es un don ~** he's a nobody *o* nonentity

nado ['naðo]: **a ~** *adv*: **pasar a ~** to swim across

nafta ['nafta] *nf (Am)* petrol *(Brit)*, gas(oline) *(US)*

náhuatl ['nawatl] *adj, nm* Nahuatl

naipe ['naipe] *nm* (playing) card; **naipes** *nmpl* cards

nalgas ['nalɣas] *nfpl* buttocks

nalguear [nalɣe'ar] *vt (Am, CAm)* to spank

nana ['nana] *nf* lullaby

napias ['napjas] *nfpl (fam)* conk *sg*

naranja [na'ranxa] *adj inv, nf* orange; **media ~** *(fam)* better half; **¡~s de la China!** nonsense!

naranjada [naran'xaða] *nf* orangeade

naranjo [na'ranxo] *nm* orange tree

narcisista [narθi'sista] *adj* narcissistic

narciso [nar'θiso] *nm* narcissus

narcótico, -a [nar'kotiko, a] *adj, nm* narcotic

narcotizar [narkoti'θar] *vt* to drug

narcotráfico [narko'trafiko] *nm* narcotics *o* drug trafficking

nardo ['narðo] *nm* lily

narigón, -ona [nari'ɣon, ona], **narigudo, -a** [nari'ɣuðo, a] *adj* big-nosed

nariz [na'riθ] *nf* nose; **narices** *nfpl* nostrils; **¡narices!** *(fam)* rubbish!; **delante de las narices de algn** under one's (very) nose; **estar hasta las narices** to be completely fed up; **meter las narices en algo** to poke one's nose into sth; **~ chata/respingona** snub/turned-up nose

narración [narra'θjon] *nf* narration

narrador, a [narra'ðor, a] *nm/f* narrator

narrar [na'rrar] *vt* to narrate, recount

narrativo, -a [narra'tiβo, a] *adj* narrative ▷ *nf* narrative, story

nata ['nata] *nf* cream *(tb fig)*; *(en leche cocida etc)* skin; **~ batida** whipped cream

natación [nata'θjon] *nf* swimming

natal [na'tal] *adj* natal; *(país)* native; **ciudad ~** home town

natalidad [natali'ðað] *nf* birth rate

natillas [na'tiʎas] *nfpl* (egg) custard *sg*

natividad [natiβi'ðað] *nf* nativity

nativo, -a [na'tiβo, a] *adj, nm/f* native

nato, -a ['nato, a] *adj* born; **un músico ~** a born musician

natural [natu'ral] *adj* natural; *(fruta etc)* fresh ▷ *nm/f* native ▷ *nm* disposition,

temperament; **buen ~** good nature; **fruta al ~** fruit in its own juice

naturaleza [natura'leθa] *nf* nature; *(género)* nature, kind; **~ muerta** still life

naturalidad [naturali'ðað] *nf* naturalness

naturalización [naturaliθa'θjon] *nf* naturalization

naturalizarse [naturali'θarse] *vr* to become naturalized; *(aclimatarse)* to become acclimatized

naturalmente [natural'mente] *adv* naturally; *(de modo natural)* in a natural way; **¡~!** of course!

naturista [natu'rista] *adj (Med)* naturopathic ▷ *nm/f* naturopath

naufragar [naufra'ɣar] *vi (barco)* to sink; *(gente)* to be shipwrecked; *(fig)* to fail

naufragio [nau'fraxjo] *nm* shipwreck

náufrago, -a ['naufraɣo, a] *nm/f* castaway, shipwrecked person

náusea ['nausea] *nf* nausea; **me da ~s** it makes me feel sick

nauseabundo, -a [nausea'βundo, a] *adj* nauseating, sickening

náutico, -a ['nautiko, a] *adj* nautical; **club ~** sailing *o* yacht club ▷ *nf* navigation, seamanship

navaja [na'βaxa] *nf (cortaplumas)* clasp knife *(Brit)*, penknife; **~ (de afeitar)** razor

navajazo [naβa'xaθo] *nm (herida)* gash; *(acto)* slash

naval [na'βal] *adj (Mil)* naval; **construcción ~** shipbuilding; **sector ~** shipbuilding industry

Navarra [na'βarra] *nf* Navarre

nave ['naβe] *nf (barco)* ship, vessel; *(Arq)* nave; **~ espacial** spaceship; **quemar las ~s** to burn one's boats; **~ industrial** factory premises *pl*

navegación [naβeɣa'θjon] *nf* navigation; *(viaje)* sea journey; **~ aérea** air traffic; **~ costera** coastal shipping; **~ fluvial** river navigation

navegador [naβeɣa'ðor] *nm (Inform)* browser; *(de coche)* sat nav

navegante [naβe'ɣante] *nm/f* navigator

navegar [naβe'ɣar] *vi (barco)* to sail; *(avión)* to fly ▷ *vt* to sail; to fly; *(dirigir el rumbo de)* to navigate; **~ por Internet** to surf the Net

Navidad [naβi'ðað] *nf* Christmas; **Navidades** *nfpl* Christmas time *sg*; **día de ~** Christmas Day; **por ~es** at Christmas (time); **¡Feliz ~!** Merry Christmas!

navideño, -a [naβi'ðeɲo, a] *adj* Christmas *cpd*

navío [na'βio] *nm* ship

nazca *etc vb ver* **nacer**

nazi ['naθi] *adj, nm/f* Nazi

nazismo [na'θismo] *nm* Nazism

NE *abr (= nor(d)este)* NE

neblina [ne'βlina] *nf* mist

nebuloso, -a [neβu'loso, a] *adj* foggy; *(calinoso)* misty; *(indefinido)* nebulous, vague ▷ *nf* nebula

necedad [neθe'ðað] *nf* foolishness; (*una necedad*) foolish act

necesario, -a [neθe'sarjo, a] *adj* necessary; **si fuera** *o* **fuese ~** if need(s) be

neceser [neθe'ser] *nm* toilet bag; (*bolsa grande*) holdall

necesidad [neθesi'ðað] *nf* need; (*lo inevitable*) necessity; (*miseria*) poverty, need; **en caso de ~** in case of need *o* emergency; **hacer sus ~es** to relieve o.s.

necesitado, -a [neθesi'taðo, a] *adj* needy, poor; **~ de** in need of

necesitar [neθesi'tar] *vt* to need, require ▷ *vi*: **~ de** to have need of; **necesitarse** *vr* to be needed; (*en anuncios*): **"necesitase coche"** "car wanted"

necio, -a ['neθjo, a] *adj* foolish ▷ *nm/f* fool

necrología [nekrolo'xia] *nf* obituary

necrópolis [ne'kropolis] *nf inv* cemetery

néctar ['nektar] *nm* nectar

nectarina [nekta'rina] *nf* nectarine

nefasto, -a [ne'fasto, a] *adj* ill-fated, unlucky

negación [neɣa'θjon] *nf* negation; (*Ling*) negative; (*rechazo*) refusal, denial

negado, -a [ne'ɣaðo, a] *adj*: **~ para** inept at, unfitted for

negar [ne'ɣar] *vt* (*renegar, rechazar*) to refuse; (*prohibir*) to refuse, deny; (*desmentir*) to deny; **negarse** *vr*: **~se a hacer algo** to refuse to do sth

negativo, -a [neɣa'tiβo, a] *adj* negative ▷ *nm* (*Foto*) negative; (*Mat*) minus ▷ *nf* (*gen*) negative; (*rechazo*) refusal, denial; **negativa rotunda** flat refusal

negligencia [neɣli'xenθja] *nf* negligence

negligente [neɣli'xente] *adj* negligent

negociable [neɣo'θjaβle] *adj* negotiable

negociación [neɣoθja'θjon] *nf* negotiation

negociado [neɣo'θjaðo] *nm* department, section

negociante [neɣo'θjante] *nm/f* businessman(-woman)

negociar [neɣo'θjar] *vt, vi* to negotiate; **~ en** to deal in, trade in

negocio [ne'ɣoθjo] *nm* (*Com*) business; (*asunto*) affair, business; (*operación comercial*) deal, transaction; (*Am*) shop, store; (*lugar*) place of business; **los ~s** business *sg*; **hacer ~** to do business; **el ~ del libro** the book trade; **~ autorizado** licensed trade; **hombre de ~s** businessman; **~ sucio** shady deal; **hacer un buen ~** to pull off a profitable deal; **¡mal ~!** it looks bad!

negra ['neɣra] *nf* (*Mus*) crotchet; *ver* **negro**

negro, -a ['neɣro, a] *adj* black; (*suerte*) awful, atrocious; (*humor etc*) sad; (*lúgubre*) gloomy ▷ *nm* (*color*) black ▷ *nm/f* black person ▷ *nf* (*Mus*) crotchet; **~ como la boca del lobo** pitch-black; **estoy ~ con esto** I'm getting desperate about it; **ponerse ~** (*fam*) to get cross

negrura [ne'ɣrura] *nf* blackness

nene, -a ['nene, a] *nm/f* baby, small child

nenúfar [ne'nufar] *nm* water lily

neologismo [neolo'xismo] *nm* neologism

neón [ne'on] *nm* neon; **luces/lámpara de ~** neon lights/lamp

neoyorquino, -a [neojor'kino, a] *adj* New York *cpd* ▷ *nm/f* New Yorker

nepotismo [nepo'tismo] *nm* nepotism

nervio ['nerβjo] *nm* (*Anat*) nerve; (*: tendón*) tendon; (*fig*) vigour; (*Tec*) rib; **crispar los ~s a algn, poner los ~s de punta a algn** to get on sb's nerves

nerviosismo [nerβjo'sismo] *nm* nervousness, nerves *pl*

nervioso, -a [ner'βjoso, a] *adj* nervous; (*sensible*) nervy, highly-strung; (*impaciente*) restless; **¡no te pongas ~!** take it easy!

neto, -a ['neto, a] *adj* clear; (*limpio*) clean; (*Com*) net

neumático, -a [neu'matiko, a] *adj* pneumatic ▷ *nm* (*Esp*) tyre (*Brit*), tire (*US*); **~ de recambio** spare tyre

neumonía [neumo'nia] *nf* pneumonia; **~ asiática** SARS

neura ['neura] (*fam*) *nm/f* (*persona*) neurotic ▷ *nf* (*obsesión*) obsession

neurálgico, -a [neu'ralxiko, a] *adj* neuralgic; (*fig: centro*) nerve *cpd*

neurastenia [neuras'tenja] *nf* neurasthenia; (*fig*) excitability

neurólogo, -a [neu'roloɣo, a] *nm/f* neurologist

neurona [neu'rona] *nf* neuron

neutral [neu'tral] *adj* neutral

neutralizar [neutrali'θar] *vt* to neutralize; (*contrarrestar*) to counteract

neutro, -a ['neutro, a] *adj* (*Bio, Ling*) neuter

neutrón [neu'tron] *nm* neutron

nevado, -a [ne'βaðo, a] *adj* snow-covered; (*montaña*) snow-capped; (*fig*) snowy, snow-white ▷ *nf* snowstorm; (*caída de nieve*) snowfall

nevar [ne'βar] *vi* to snow ▷ *vt* (*fig*) to whiten

nevera [ne'βera] *nf* (*Esp*) refrigerator (*Brit*), icebox (*US*)

nevería [neβe'ria] *nf* (*Am*) ice-cream parlour

nevisca [ne'βiska] *nf* flurry of snow

nexo ['nekso] *nm* link, connection

ni [ni] *conj* nor, neither; (*tb*: **ni siquiera**) not even; **ni que** not even if; **ni blanco ni negro** neither white nor black; **ni el uno ni el otro** neither one nor the other

Nicaragua [nika'raɣwa] *nf* Nicaragua

nicaragüense [nikara'ɣwense] *adj, nm/f* Nicaraguan

nicho ['nitʃo] *nm* niche

nicotina [niko'tina] *nf* nicotine

nido ['niðo] *nm* nest; (*fig*) hiding place; **~ de ladrones** den of thieves

niebla ['njeβla] *nf* fog; (*neblina*) mist; **hay ~** it is foggy

niego *etc* ['njeɣo], **niegue** *etc* ['njeɣe] *vb ver* **negar**

nieto, -a ['njeto, a] *nm/f* grandson/ granddaughter; **nietos** *nmpl* grandchildren

nieve ['njeβe] *vb ver* **nevar** ▷ *nf* snow; (*Am*) ice cream; **copo de ~** snowflake

Nilo ['nilo] *nm*: **el (Río) ~** the Nile

nimiedad [nimje'ðað] *nf* small-mindedness; (*trivialidad*) triviality; (*una nimiedad*) trifle, tiny detail

nimio, -a ['nimjo, a] *adj* trivial, insignificant

ninfa ['ninfa] *nf* nymph

ninfómana [nin'fomana] *nf* nymphomaniac

ningún [nin'gun] *adj ver* **ninguno**

ninguno, -a [nin'guno, a] *adj* (*antes de nmsg* **ningún**) no ▷ *pron* (*nadie*) nobody; (*ni uno*) none, not one; (*ni uno ni otro*) neither; **de ninguna manera** by no means, not at all; **no voy a ninguna parte** I'm not going anywhere

niña ['niɲa] *nf ver* **niño**

niñera [ni'ɲera] *nf* nursemaid, nanny

niñería [niɲe'ria] *nf* childish act

niñez [ni'ɲeθ] *nf* childhood; (*infancia*) infancy

niño, -a ['niɲo, a] *adj* (*joven*) young; (*inmaduro*) immature ▷ *nm* (*chico*) boy, child ▷ *nf* girl, child; (*Anat*) pupil; **los ~s** the children; **~ bien** rich kid; **~ expósito** foundling; **~ de pecho** babe-in-arms; **~ prodigio** child prodigy; **de ~** as a child; **ser el ~ mimado de algn** to be sb's pet; **ser la niña de los ojos de algn** to be the apple of sb's eye

nipón, -ona [ni'pon, ona] *adj, nm/f* Japanese; **los nipones** the Japanese

níquel ['nikel] *nm* nickel

niquelar [nike'lar] *vt* (*Tec*) to nickel-plate

níspero ['nispero] *nm* medlar

nitidez [niti'ðeθ] *nf* (*claridad*) clarity; (: *de atmósfera*) brightness; (: *de imagen*) sharpness

nítido, -a [ni'tiðo, a] *adj* bright; (*fig*) pure; (*imagen*) clear, sharp

nitrato [ni'trato] *nm* nitrate

nitrógeno [ni'troxeno] *nm* nitrogen

nitroglicerina [nitroɣliθe'rina] *nf* nitroglycerine

nivel [ni'βel] *nm* (*Geo*) level; (*norma*) level, standard; (*altura*) height; **~ de aceite** oil level; **~ de aire** spirit level; **~ de vida** standard of living; **al ~ de** on a level with, at the same height as; (*fig*) on a par with; **a 900m sobre el ~ del mar** at 900m above sea level

nivelar [niβe'lar] *vt* to level out; (*fig*) to even up; (*Com*) to balance

NN. UU. *nfpl abr* (= *Naciones Unidas*) UN *sg*

NO *abr* (= *noroeste*) NW

no [no] *adv* no; (*con verbo*) not ▷ *excl* no!; **no tengo nada** I don't have anything, I have nothing; **no es el mío** it's not mine; **ahora no** not now; **¿no lo sabes?** don't you know?; **no mucho** not much; **no bien termine, lo entregaré** as soon as I finish I'll hand it over;

ayer no más just yesterday; **¡pase no más!** come in!; **¡a que no lo sabes!** I bet you don't know!; **¡cómo no!** of course!; **pacto de no agresión** non-aggression pact; **los países no alineados** the non-aligned countries; **el no va más** the ultimate; **la no intervención** non-intervention

noble ['noβle] *adj, nm/f* noble; **los ~s** the nobility *sg*

nobleza [no'βleθa] *nf* nobility

noche ['notʃe] *nf* night, night-time; (*la tarde*) evening; (*fig*) darkness; **de ~, por la ~** at night; **ayer por la ~** last night; **esta ~** tonight; **(en) toda la ~** all night; **hacer ~ en un sitio** to spend the night in a place; **se hace de ~** it's getting dark; **es de ~** it's dark; **N~ de San Juan** *see note*

⬤ **NOCHE DE SAN JUAN**
⬤
⬤ The *Noche de San Juan* on the 24th June is a
⬤ *fiesta* coinciding with the summer
⬤ solstice and which has taken the place of
⬤ other ancient pagan festivals.
⬤ Traditionally fire plays a major part in
⬤ these festivities with celebrations and
⬤ dancing taking place around bonfires in
⬤ towns and villages across the country.

Nochebuena [notʃe'βwena] *nf* Christmas Eve; *see note*

⬤ **NOCHEBUENA**
⬤
⬤ On *Nochebuena* in Spanish homes there is
⬤ normally a large supper when family
⬤ members come from all over to be
⬤ together. The more religiously inclined
⬤ attend *la misa del gallo* at midnight. The
⬤ tradition of receiving Christmas presents
⬤ from Santa Claus that night is becoming
⬤ more and more widespread and
⬤ gradually replacing the tradition of *los*
⬤ *Reyes Magos* (the Three Wise Men) on the
⬤ 6th of January.

Nochevieja [notʃe'βjexa] *nf* New Year's Eve; *ver tb* **uvas**

noción [no'θjon] *nf* notion; **nociones** *nfpl* elements, rudiments

nocivo, -a [no'θiβo, a] *adj* harmful

noctámbulo, -a [nok'tambulo, a] *nm/f* sleepwalker

nocturno, -a [nok'turno, a] *adj* (*de la noche*) nocturnal, night *cpd*; (*de la tarde*) evening *cpd* ▷ *nm* nocturne

nogal [no'ɣal] *nm* walnut tree; (*madera*) walnut

nómada ['nomaða] *adj* nomadic ▷ *nm/f* nomad

nombramiento [nombra'mjento] *nm* naming; (*para un empleo*) appointment; (*Pol etc*) nomination; (*Mil*) commission

nombrar [nom'brar] vt (gen) to name; (mencionar) to mention; (designar) to appoint, nominate; (Mil) to commission

nombre ['nombre] nm name; (sustantivo) noun; (fama) renown; **~ y apellidos** name in full; **poner ~ a** to call, name; **~ común/ propio** common/proper noun; **~ de pila/de soltera** Christian/maiden name; **~ de fichero** (Inform) file name; **en ~ de** in the name of, on behalf of; **sin ~** nameless; **su conducta no tiene ~** his behaviour is utterly despicable

nomenclatura [nomenkla'tura] nf nomenclature

nomeolvides [nomeol'βiðes] nm inv forget-me-not

nómina ['nomina] nf (lista) list; (Com: tb: **~s**) payroll; (hoja) payslip

nominal [nomi'nal] adj nominal; (valor) face cpd; (Ling) noun cpd, substantival

nominar [nomi'nar] vt to nominate

nominativo, -a [nomina'tiβo, a] adj (Ling) nominative; (Com): **un cheque ~ a X** a cheque made out to X

non [non] adj odd, uneven ▷ nm odd number; **pares y ~es** odds and evens

nono, -a ['nono, a] num ninth

nordeste [nor'ðeste] adj north-east, north-eastern, north-easterly ▷ nm north-east; (viento) north-east wind, north-easterly

nórdico, -a ['norðiko, a] adj (del norte) northern, northerly; (escandinavo) Nordic, Norse ▷ nm/f northerner; (escandinavo) Norseman/-woman ▷ nm (Ling) Norse

noreste [no'reste] adj, nm = **nordeste**

noria ['norja] nf (Agr) waterwheel; (de carnaval) big (Brit) o Ferris (US) wheel

norma ['norma] nf standard, norm, rule; (patrón) pattern; (método) method

normal [nor'mal] adj (corriente) normal; (habitual) usual, natural; (Tec) standard; **Escuela N~** teacher training college; **(gasolina) ~** two-star petrol

normalidad [normali'ðað] nf normality

normalizar [normali'θar] vt (reglamentar) to normalize; (Com, Tec) to standardize; **normalizarse** vr to return to normal

normalmente [normal'mente] adv (con normalidad) normally; (habitualmente) usually

normando, -a [nor'mando, a] adj, nm/f Norman

normativo, -a [norma'tiβo, a] adj: **es ~ en todos los coches nuevos** it is standard in all new cars ▷ nf rules pl, regulations pl

noroeste [noro'este] adj north-west, north-western, north-westerly ▷ nm north-west; (viento) north-west wind, north-westerly

norte ['norte] adj north, northern, northerly ▷ nm north; (fig) guide

norteamericano, -a [norteameri'kano, a] adj, nm/f (North) American

Noruega [no'rweγa] nf Norway

noruego, -a [no'rweγo, a] adj, nm/f Norwegian ▷ nm (Ling) Norwegian

nos [nos] pron (directo) us; (indirecto) (to) us; (reflexivo) to ourselves; (recíproco) (to) each other; **~ levantamos a las siete** we get up at seven

nosotros, -as [no'sotros, as] pron (sujeto) we; (después de prep) us; **~ (mismos)** ourselves

nostalgia [nos'talxja] nf nostalgia, homesickness

nota ['nota] nf note; (Escol) mark; (de fin de año) report; (Univ etc) footnote; (Com) account; **~ de aviso** advice note; **~ de crédito/débito** credit/debit note; **~ de gastos** expenses claim; **~ de sociedad** gossip column; **tomar ~s** to take notes

notable [no'taβle] adj noteworthy, notable; (Escol etc) outstanding ▷ nm/f notable

notar [no'tar] vt to notice, note; (percibir) to feel; (ver) to see; **notarse** vr to be obvious; **se nota que ...** one observes that ...

notarial [nota'rjal] adj (estilo) legal; **acta ~** affidavit

notario [no'tarjo] nm notary; (abogado) solicitor

noticia [no'tiθja] nf (información) piece of news; (TV etc) news item; **las ~s** the news sg; **según nuestras ~s** according to our information; **tener ~s de algn** to hear from sb

noticiario [noti'θjarjo] nm (Cine) newsreel; (TV) news bulletin

noticiero [noti'θjero] nm newspaper, gazette; (Am: tb: **~ telediario**) news bulletin

notificación [notifika'θjon] nf notification

notificar [notifi'kar] vt to notify, inform

notoriedad [notorje'ðað] nf fame, renown

notorio, -a [no'torjo, a] adj (público) well-known; (evidente) obvious

novato, -a [no'βato, a] adj inexperienced ▷ nm/f beginner, novice

novecientos, -as [noβe'θjentos, as] num nine hundred

novedad [noβe'ðað] nf (calidad de nuevo) newness, novelty; (noticia) piece of news; (cambio) change, (new) development; (sorpresa) surprise; **novedades** nfpl (noticia) latest (news) sg

novedoso, -a [noβe'ðoso, a] adj novel

novel [no'βel] adj new; (inexperto) inexperienced ▷ nm/f beginner

novela [no'βela] nf novel; **~ policíaca** detective story

novelero, -a [noβe'lero, a] adj highly imaginative

novelesco, -a [noβe'lesko, a] adj fictional; (romántico) romantic; (fantástico) fantastic

novelista [noβe'lista] nm/f novelist

noveno, -a [no'βeno, a] num ninth

noventa [no'βenta] num ninety

novia ['noβja] nf ver **novio**

noviazgo [no'βjaθγo] nm engagement

novicio, -a [no'βiθjo, a] *nm/f* novice
noviembre [no'βjembre] *nm* November; *ver tb* **julio**
novillada [noβi'ʎaða] *nf* (*Taur*) bullfight with young bulls
novillero [noβi'ʎero] *nm* novice bullfighter
novillo [no'βiʎo] *nm* young bull, bullock; **hacer ~s** (*fam*) to play truant (*Brit*) *o* hooky (*US*)
novio, -a ['noβjo, a] *nm/f* boyfriend/girlfriend; (*prometido*) fiancé/fiancée; (*recién casado*) bridegroom/bride; **los ~s** the newly-weds
N. S. *abr* = **Nuestro Señor**
nubarrón [nuβa'rron] *nm* storm cloud
nube ['nuβe] *nf* cloud; (*Med: ocular*) cloud, film; (*fig*) mass; **una ~ de críticas** a storm of criticism; **los precios están por las ~s** prices are sky-high; **estar en las ~s** to be away with the fairies
nublado, -a [nu'βlaðo, a] *adj* cloudy ▷ *nm* storm cloud
nublar [nu'βlar] *vt* (*oscurecer*) to darken; (*confundir*) to cloud; **nublarse** *vr* to cloud over
nuboso, -a [nu'βoso, a] *adj* cloudy
nuca ['nuka] *nf* nape of the neck
nuclear [nukle'ar] *adj* nuclear
núcleo ['nukleo] *nm* (*centro*) core; (*Física*) nucleus; **~ urbano** city centre
nudillo [nu'ðiʎo] *nm* knuckle
nudista [nu'dista] *adj, nm/f* nudist
nudo ['nuðo] *nm* knot; (*unión*) bond; (*de problema*) crux; (*Ferro*) junction; (*fig*) lump; **~ corredizo** slipknot; **con un ~ en la garganta** with a lump in one's throat
nudoso, -a [nu'ðoso, a] *adj* knotty; (*tronco*) gnarled; (*bastón*) knobbly
nuera ['nwera] *nf* daughter-in-law
nuestro, -a ['nwestro, a] *adj posesivo* our ▷ *pron* ours; **~ padre** our father; **un amigo ~** a friend of ours; **es el ~** it's ours; **los ~s** our people; (*Deporte*) our *o* the local team *o* side
nueva ['nweβa] *nf ver* **nuevo**
nuevamente [nweβa'mente] *adv* (*otra vez*) again; (*de nuevo*) anew
Nueva York [-'jork] *nf* New York
Nueva Zelanda [-θe'landa], **Nueva Zelandia** [-θe'landja] *nf* New Zealand
nueve ['nweβe] *num* nine
nuevo, -a ['nweβo, a] *adj* (*gen*) new ▷ *nf* piece of news; **¿qué hay de ~?** (*fam*) what's new?; **de ~** again
nuez [nweθ] (*pl* **nueces**) *nf* nut; (*del nogal*) walnut; **~ de Adán** Adam's apple; **~ moscada** nutmeg
nulidad [nuli'ðað] *nf* (*incapacidad*) incompetence; (*abolición*) nullity; (*individuo*) nonentity; **es una ~** he's a dead loss
nulo, -a ['nulo, a] *adj* (*inepto, torpe*) useless; (*inválido*) (null and) void; (*Deporte*) drawn, tied
núm. *abr* (= *número*) no.
numeración [numera'θjon] *nf* (*cifras*) numbers *pl*; (*arábiga, romana etc*) numerals *pl*; **~ de línea** (*Inform*) line numbering

numerador [numera'ðor] *nm* (*Mat*) numerator
numeral [nume'ral] *nm* numeral
numerar [nume'rar] *vt* to number; **numerarse** *vr* (*Mil etc*) to number off
numérico, -a [nu'meriko, a] *adj* numerical
número ['numero] *nm* (*gen*) number; (*tamaño: de zapato*) size; (*ejemplar: de diario*) number, issue; (*Teat etc*) turn, act, number; **sin ~** numberless, unnumbered; **~ binario** (*Inform*) binary number; **~ de matrícula/de teléfono** registration/telephone number; **~ personal de identificación** (*Inform etc*) personal identification number; **~ impar/par** odd/even number; **~ romano** Roman numeral; **~ de serie** (*Com*) serial number; **~ atrasado** back number
numeroso, -a [nume'roso, a] *adj* numerous; **familia numerosa** large family
numerus ['numerus] *nm:* **~ clausus** (*Univ*) restricted *o* selective entry
nunca ['nunka] *adv* (*jamás*) never; (*con verbo negativo*) ever; **~ lo pensé** I never thought it; **no viene ~** he never comes; **~ más** never again; **más que ~** more than ever
nuncio ['nunθjo] *nm* (*Rel*) nuncio
nupcial [nup'θjal] *adj* wedding *cpd*
nupcias ['nupθjas] *nfpl* wedding *sg*, nuptials
nutria ['nutrja] *nf* otter
nutrición [nutri'θjon] *nf* nutrition
nutrido, -a [nu'triðo, a] *adj* (*alimentado*) nourished; (*fig: grande*) large; (*abundante*) abundant; **mal ~** undernourished; **~ de** full of
nutrir [nu'trir] *vt* (*alimentar*) to nourish; (*dar de comer*) to feed; (*fig*) to strengthen
nutritivo, -a [nutri'tiβo, a] *adj* nourishing, nutritious
nylon [ni'lon] *nm* nylon

ñango, -a ['ɲaŋgo, a] *adj* (*Am*) puny
ñapa ['ɲapa] *nf* (*Am*) extra
ñata ['ɲata] *nf* (*Am: fam*) nose; *ver tb* **ñato**
ñato, -a ['ɲato, a] *adj* (*Am*) snub-nosed
ñoñería [ɲoɲe'ria], **ñoñez** [ɲo'ɲeθ] *nf* insipidness
ñoño, -a ['ɲoɲo, a] *adj* (*fam: tonto*) silly, stupid; (*soso*) insipid; (*persona*) spineless; (*Esp: película, novela*) sentimental
ñoquis ['ɲokis] *nmpl* (*Culin*) gnocchi

O *abr* (= *oeste*) W
o [o] *conj* or; **o ... o** either ... or; **o sea** that is
o/ *nm* (*Com*: = *orden*) o
oasis [o'asis] *nm inv* oasis
obcecarse [oβθe'karse] *vr* to become obsessed; **~ en hacer** to insist on doing
obedecer [oβeðe'θer] *vt* to obey; **~ a** (*Med etc*) to yield to; (*fig*): **~ a ..., ~ al hecho de que ...** to be due to ..., arise from ...
obediencia [oβe'ðjenθja] *nf* obedience
obediente [oβe'ðjente] *adj* obedient
obertura [oβer'tura] *nf* overture
obesidad [oβesi'ðað] *nf* obesity
obeso, -a [o'βeso, a] *adj* obese
obispo [o'βispo] *nm* bishop
obituario [oβi'twarjo] *nm* (*Am*) obituary
objeción [oβxe'θjon] *nf* objection; **hacer una ~, poner objeciones** to raise objections, object
objetar [oβxe'tar] *vt, vi* to object
objetivo, -a [oβxe'tiβo, a] *adj* objective ▷ *nm* objective; (*fig*) aim; (*Foto*) lens
objeto [oβ'xeto] *nm* (*cosa*) object; (*fin*) aim
objetor, a [oβxe'tor, a] *nm/f* objector; **~ de conciencia** conscientious objector; *ver tb* **mili**
oblicuo, -a [o'βlikwo, a] *adj* oblique; (*mirada*) sidelong
obligación [oβliɣa'θjon] *nf* obligation; (*Com*) bond, debenture
obligar [oβli'ɣar] *vt* to force; **obligarse** *vr*: **~se a** to commit o.s. to

obligatorio, -a [oβliɣa'torjo, a] *adj* compulsory, obligatory

oboe [o'βoe] *nm* oboe; *(músico)* oboist

obra ['oβra] *nf* work; *(producción)* piece of work; *(Arq)* construction, building; *(libro)* book; *(Mus)* opus; *(Teat)* play; **~ de arte** work of art; **~ maestra** masterpiece; **~ de consulta** reference book; **~s completas** complete works; **~ benéfica** charity; **"~s"** *(en carretera)* "men at work"; **~s públicas** public works; **por ~ de** thanks to (the efforts of); **~s son amores y no buenas razones** actions speak louder than words

obrar [o'βrar] *vt* to work; *(tener efecto)* to have an effect on ▷ *vi* to act, behave; *(tener efecto)* to have an effect; **la carta obra en su poder** the letter is in his/her possession

obrero, -a [o'βrero, a] *adj* working; *(movimiento)* labour *cpd*; **clase obrera** working class ▷ *nm/f (gen)* worker; *(sin oficio)* labourer

obscenidad [oβsθeni'ðað] *nf* obscenity

obsceno, -a [oβs'θeno, a] *adj* obscene

obscu... *pref* = **oscu...**

obsequiar [oβse'kjar] *vt (ofrecer)* to present; *(agasajar)* to make a fuss of, lavish attention on

obsequio [oβ'sekjo] *nm (regalo)* gift; *(cortesía)* courtesy, attention

obsequioso, -a [oβse'kjoso, a] *adj* attentive

observación [oβserβa'θjon] *nf* observation; *(reflexión)* remark; *(objeción)* objection

observador, a [oβserβa'ðor, a] *adj* observant ▷ *nm/f* observer

observancia [oβser'βanθja] *nf* observance

observar [oβser'βar] *vt* to observe; *(notar)* to notice; *(leyes)* to observe, respect; *(reglas)* to abide by; **observarse** *vr* to keep to, observe

observatorio [oβserβa'torjo] *nm* observatory; **~ del tiempo** weather station

obsesión [oβse'sjon] *nf* obsession

obsesionar [oβsesjo'nar] *vt* to obsess

obsesivo, -a [obse'siβo, a] *adj* obsessive

obseso, -a [oβ'seso, a] *nm/f (sexual)* sex maniac

obsoleto, -a [oβso'leto, a] *adj* obsolete

obstaculizar [oβstakuli'θar] *vt (dificultar)* to hinder, hamper

obstáculo [oβs'takulo] *nm (gen)* obstacle; *(impedimento)* hindrance, drawback

obstante [oβs'tante]: **no ~** *adv* nevertheless; *(de todos modos)* all the same ▷ *prep* in spite of

obstetra [oβs'tetra] *nm/f* obstetrician

obstetricia [oβste'triθja] *nf* obstetrics *sg*

obstinado, -a [oβsti'naðo, a] *adj (gen)* obstinate; *(terco)* stubborn

obstinarse [oβsti'narse] *vr* to be obstinate; **~ en** to persist in

obstrucción [oβstruk'θjon] *nf* obstruction

obstruir [oβstru'ir] *vt* to obstruct; *(bloquear)* to block; *(estorbar)* to hinder

obtener [oβte'ner] *vt (conseguir)* to obtain; *(ganar)* to gain; *(premio)* to win

obturador [oβtura'ðor] *nm (Foto)* shutter

obtuso, -a [oβ'tuso, a] *adj (filo)* blunt; *(Mat, fig)* obtuse

obviar [oβ'βjar] *vt* to obviate, remove

obvio, -a ['oββjo, a] *adj* obvious

oca ['oka] *nf* goose; *(tb: juego de la ~)* ≈ snakes and ladders

ocasión [oka'sjon] *nf (oportunidad)* opportunity, chance; *(momento)* occasion, time; *(causa)* cause; **de ~** secondhand; **con ~ de** on the occasion of; **en algunas ocasiones** sometimes; **aprovechar la ~** to seize one's opportunity

ocasionar [okasjo'nar] *vt* to cause

ocaso [o'kaso] *nm* sunset; *(fig)* decline

occidental [okθiðen'tal] *adj* western ▷ *nm/f* westerner ▷ *nm* west

occidente [okθi'ðente] *nm* west; **el O~** the West

O.C.D.E. *nf abr* (= *Organización de Cooperación y Desarrollo Económicos*) OECD

océano [o'θeano] *nm* ocean; **el ~ Índico** the Indian Ocean

ochenta [o'tʃenta] *num* eighty

ocho ['otʃo] *num* eight; *(fecha)* eighth; **~ días a** week; **dentro de ~ días** within a week

ochocientos, -as [otʃo'θjentos, as] *num* eight hundred

ocio ['oθjo] *nm (tiempo)* leisure; *(pey)* idleness; **"guía del ~"** "what's on"

ociosidad [oθjosi'ðað] *nf* idleness

ocioso, -a [o'θjoso, a] *adj (inactivo)* idle; *(inútil)* useless

octanaje [okta'naxe] *nm*: **de alto ~** high octane

octano [ok'tano] *nm* octane

octavilla [okta'βiʎa] *nm* leaflet, pamphlet

octavo, -a [ok'taβo, a] *num* eighth

octogenario, -a [oktoxe'narjo, a] *adj, nm/f* octogenarian

octubre [ok'tuβre] *nm* October; *ver tb* **julio**

ocular [oku'lar] *adj* ocular, eye *cpd*; **testigo ~** eyewitness

oculista [oku'lista] *nm/f* oculist

ocultar [okul'tar] *vt (esconder)* to hide; *(callar)* to conceal; *(disfrazar)* to screen; **ocultarse** *vr* to hide (o.s.); **~se a la vista** to keep out of sight

oculto, -a [o'kulto, a] *adj* hidden; *(fig)* secret

ocupación [okupa'θjon] *nf* occupation; *(tenencia)* occupancy

ocupado, -a [oku'paðo, a] *adj (persona)* busy; *(plaza)* occupied, taken; *(teléfono)* engaged; **¿está ocupada la silla?** is that seat taken?

ocupar [oku'par] *vt (gen)* to occupy; *(puesto)* to hold, fill; *(individuo)* to engage; *(obreros)* to employ; *(confiscar)* to seize; **ocuparse** *vr*: **~se de** *o* **en** to concern o.s. with; *(cuidar)* to look after; **~se de lo suyo** to mind one's own business

ocurrencia [oku'rrenθja] *nf (ocasión)* occurrence; *(agudeza)* witticism; *(idea)* bright idea

ocurrir [oku'rrir] *vi* to happen; **ocurrirse** *vr*: **se me ocurrió que ...** it occurred to me that ...; **¿se te ocurre algo?** can you think of o come up with anything?; **¿qué ocurre?** what's going on?

odiar [o'ðjar] *vt* to hate

odio ['oðjo] *nm* (*gen*) hate, hatred; (*disgusto*) dislike

odioso, -a [o'ðjoso, a] *adj* (*gen*) hateful; (*malo*) nasty

odisea [oði'sea] *nf* odyssey

odontólogo, -a [oðon'toloyo, a] *nm/f* dentist, dental surgeon

oeste [o'este] *nm* west; **una película del ~** western

ofender [ofen'der] *vt* (*agraviar*) to offend; (*insultar*) to insult; **ofenderse** *vr* to take offence

ofensa [o'fensa] *nf* offence; (*insulto*) slight

ofensivo, -a [ofen'siβo, a] *adj* (*insultante*) insulting; (*Mil*) offensive ▷ *nf* offensive

oferta [o'ferta] *nf* offer; (*propuesta*) proposal; (*para contrato*) bid, tender; **la ~ y la demanda** supply and demand; **artículos en ~** goods on offer; **~ excedentaria** (*Com*) excess supply; **~ monetaria** money supply; **~ pública de adquisición (OPA)** (*Com*) takeover bid; **~s de trabajo** (*en periódicos*) situations vacant column

offset ['ofset] *nm* offset

oficial [ofi'θjal] *adj* official ▷ *nm* official; (*Mil*) officer

oficina [ofi'θina] *nf* office; **~ de correos** post office; **~ de empleo** employment agency; **~ de información** information bureau; **~ de objetos perdidos** lost property office (*Brit*), lost-and-found department (*US*); **~ de turismo** tourist office; **~ principal** (*Com*) head office, main branch

oficinista [ofiθi'nista] *nm/f* clerk; **los ~s** white-collar workers

oficio [o'fiθjo] *nm* (*profesión*) profession; (*puesto*) post; (*Rel*) service; (*función*) function; (*comunicado*) official letter; **ser del ~** to be an old hand; **tener mucho ~** to have a lot of experience; **~ de difuntos** funeral service; **de ~** officially

oficioso, -a [ofi'θjoso, a] *adj* (*pey*) officious; (*no oficial*) unofficial, informal

ofimática [ofi'matika] *nf* office automation

ofrecer [ofre'θer] *vt* (*dar*) to offer; (*proponer*) to propose; **ofrecerse** *vr* (*persona*) to offer o.s., volunteer; (*situación*) to present itself; **¿qué se le ofrece?, ¿se le ofrece algo?** what can I do for you?, can I get you anything?

ofrecimiento [ofreθi'mjento] *nm* offer, offering

ofrendar [ofren'dar] *vt* to offer, contribute

oftalmólogo, -a [oftal'moloyo, a] *nm/f* ophthalmologist

ofuscación [ofuska'θjon] *nf*, **ofuscamiento** [ofuska'mjento] *nm* (*fig*) bewilderment

ofuscar [ofus'kar] *vt* (*confundir*) to bewilder; (*enceguecer*) to dazzle, blind

oída [o'iða] *nf*: **de ~s** by hearsay

oído [o'iðo] *nm* (*Anat, Mus*) ear; (*sentido*) hearing; **~ interno** inner ear; **de ~** by ear; **apenas pude dar crédito a mis ~s** I could scarcely believe my ears; **hacer ~s sordos a** to turn a deaf ear to

oigo *etc vb ver* **oír**

oír [o'ir] *vt* (*gen*) to hear; (*esp Am*: *escuchar*) to listen to; **¡oye!** (*sorpresa*) I say!, say! (*US*); **¡oiga!** excuse me!; (*Telec*) hullo?; **~ misa** to attend mass; **como quien oye llover** without paying (the slightest) attention

ojal [o'xal] *nm* buttonhole

ojalá [oxa'la] *excl* if only (it were so)!, some hope! ▷ *conj* if only...!, would that...!; **~ que venga hoy** I hope he comes today; **¡~ pudiera!** I wish I could!

ojeada [oxe'aða] *nf* glance; **echar una ~ a** to take a quick look at

ojera [o'xera] *nf*: **tener ~s** to have bags under one's eyes

ojeriza [oxe'riθa] *nf* ill-will; **tener ~ a** to have a grudge against, have it in for

ojeroso, -a [oxe'roso, a] *adj* haggard

ojo ['oxo] *nm* eye; (*de puente*) span; (*de cerradura*) keyhole ▷ *excl* careful!; **tener ~ para** to have an eye for; **~s saltones** bulging o popeyes; **~ de buey** porthole; **~ por ~** an eye for an eye; **en un abrir y cerrar de ~s** in the twinkling of an eye; **a ~s vistas** openly; (*crecer etc*) before one's (very) eyes; **a ~ (de buen cubero)** roughly; **~s que no ven, corazón que no siente** out of sight, out of mind; **ser el ~ derecho de algn** (*fig*) to be the apple of sb's eye

okey ['okei] *excl* (*Am*) O.K.

okupa [o'kupa] *nm/f* (*fam*) squatter

ola ['ola] *nf* wave; **~ de calor/frío** heatwave/ cold spell; **la nueva ~** the latest fashion; (*Cine, Mus*) (the) new wave

olé [o'le] *excl* bravo!, olé!

oleada [ole'aða] *nf* big wave, swell; (*fig*) wave

oleaje [ole'axe] *nm* swell

óleo ['oleo] *nm* oil

oleoducto [oleo'ðukto] *nm* (oil) pipeline

oler [o'ler] *vt* (*gen*) to smell; (*inquirir*) to pry into; (*fig*: *sospechar*) to sniff out ▷ *vi* to smell; **~ a** to smell of; **huele mal** it smells bad, it stinks

olfatear [olfate'ar] *vt* to smell; (*fig*: *sospechar*) to sniff out; (*inquirir*) to pry into

olfato [ol'fato] *nm* sense of smell

oligarquía [oliyar'kia] *nf* oligarchy

olimpiada [olim'pjaða] *nf*: **la ~ o las ~s** the Olympics

olímpicamente [o'limpikamente] *adv*: **pasar ~ de algo** to totally ignore sth

olímpico, -a [o'limpiko, a] *adj* Olympian; (*deportes*) Olympic

oliva [o'liβa] *nf* (*aceituna*) olive; **aceite de ~** olive oil

olivo [o'liβo] *nm* olive tree
olla ['oʎa] *nf* pan; (*para hervir agua*) kettle; (*comida*) stew; ~ **a presión** pressure cooker; ~ **podrida** *type of Spanish stew*
olmo ['olmo] *nm* elm (tree)
olor [o'lor] *nm* smell
oloroso, -a [olo'roso, a] *adj* scented
olvidadizo, -a [olβiða'ðiθo, a] *adj* (*desmemoriado*) forgetful; (*distraído*) absent-minded
olvidar [olβi'ðar] *vt* to forget; (*omitir*) to omit; (*abandonar*) to leave behind; **olvidarse** *vr* (*fig*) to forget o.s.; **se me olvidó** I forgot
olvido [ol'βiðo] *nm* oblivion; (*acto*) oversight; (*descuido*) slip; (*despiste*) forgetfulness; **caer en el ~** to fall into oblivion
ombligo [om'bliɣo] *nm* navel
omelette [ome'lete] *nf* (*Am*) omelet(te)
ominoso, -a [omi'noso, a] *adj* ominous
omisión [omi'sjon] *nf* (*abstención*) omission; (*descuido*) neglect
omiso, -a [o'miso, a] *adj*: **hacer caso ~ de** to ignore, pass over
omitir [omi'tir] *vt* to leave o miss out, omit
omnipotente [omnipo'tente] *adj* omnipotent
omnívoro, -a [om'niβoro, a] *adj* omnivorous
omoplato [omo'plato], **omóplato** [o'moplato] *nm* shoulder-blade
OMS *nf abr* (= *Organización Mundial de la Salud*) WHO
once ['onθe] *num* eleven; **onces** *nfpl* tea break *sg*
onda ['onda] *nf* wave; ~ **corta/larga/media** short/long/medium wave; ~**s acústicas/hertzianas** acoustic/Hertzian waves; ~ **sonora** sound wave
ondear [onde'ar] *vi* to wave; (*tener ondas*) to be wavy; (*agua*) to ripple; **ondearse** *vr* to swing, sway
ondulación [ondula'θjon] *nf* undulation
ondulado, -a [ondu'laðo, a] *adj* wavy ▷ *nm* wave
ondulante [ondu'lante] *adj* undulating
ondular [ondu'lar] *vt* (*el pelo*) to wave ▷ *vi*, **ondularse** *vr* to undulate
oneroso, -a [one'roso, a] *adj* onerous
ONG *nf abr* (= *organización no gubernamental*) NGO
ONU ['onu] *nf abr ver* **Organización de las Naciones Unidas**
OPA ['opa] *nf abr* (= *Oferta Pública de Adquisición*) takeover bid
opaco, -a [o'pako, a] *adj* opaque; (*fig*) dull
ópalo ['opalo] *nm* opal
opción [op'θjon] *nf* (*gen*) option; (*derecho*) right, option; **no hay ~** there is no alternative
opcional [opθjo'nal] *adj* optional
O.P.E.P. [o'pep] *nf abr* (= *Organización de Países Exportadores de Petróleo*) OPEC
ópera ['opera] *nf* opera; ~ **bufa** o **cómica** comic opera

operación [opera'θjon] *nf* (*gen*) operation; (*Com*) transaction, deal; ~ **a plazo** (*Com*) forward transaction; **operaciones accesorias** (*Inform*) housekeeping; **operaciones a término** (*Com*) futures
operador, a [opera'ðor, a] *nm/f* operator; (*Cine: proyección*) projectionist; (: *rodaje*) cameraman
operar [ope'rar] *vt* (*producir*) to produce, bring about; (*Med*) to operate on ▷ *vi* (*Com*) to operate, deal; **operarse** *vr* to occur; (*Med*) to have an operation; **se han operado grandes cambios** great changes have been made o have taken place
opereta [ope'reta] *nf* operetta
opinar [opi'nar] *vt* (*estimar*) to think ▷ *vi* (*enjuiciar*) to give one's opinion; ~ **bien de** to think well of
opinión [opi'njon] *nf* (*creencia*) belief; (*criterio*) opinion; **la ~ pública** public opinion
opio ['opjo] *nm* opium
oponente [opo'nente] *nm/f* opponent
oponer [opo'ner] *vt* (*resistencia*) to put up, offer; (*negativa*) to raise; **oponerse** *vr* (*objetar*) to object; (*estar frente a frente*) to be opposed; (*dos personas*) to oppose each other; ~ **A a B** to set A against B; **me opongo a pensar que ...** I refuse to believe o think that ...
oporto [o'porto] *nm* port
oportunidad [oportuni'ðað] *nf* (*ocasión*) opportunity; (*posibilidad*) chance
oportunismo [oportu'nismo] *nm* opportunism
oportunista [oportu'nista] *nm/f* opportunist; (*infección*) opportunistic
oportuno, -a [opor'tuno, a] *adj* (*en su tiempo*) opportune, timely; (*respuesta*) suitable; **en el momento ~** at the right moment
oposición [oposi'θjon] *nf* opposition; **oposiciones** *nfpl* (*Escol*) public examinations; **ganar un puesto por oposiciones** to win a post by public competitive examination; **hacer oposiciones a, presentarse a unas oposiciones a** to sit a competitive examination for; *see note*
opositar [oposi'tar] *vi* to sit a public entrance examination
opositor, -a [oposi'tor, a] *nm/f* (*Admin*) candidate to a public examination; (*adversario*) opponent; ~ **(a)** candidate (for)
opresión [opre'sjon] *nf* oppression
opresivo, -a [opre'siβo, a] *adj* oppressive
opresor, a [opre'sor, a] *nm/f* oppressor
oprimir [opri'mir] *vt* to squeeze; (*asir*) to grasp; (*pulsar*) to press; (*fig*) to oppress
optar [op'tar] *vi* (*elegir*) to choose; ~ **a** o **por** to opt for
optativo, -a [opta'tiβo, a] *adj* optional
óptico, -a ['optiko, a] *adj* optic(al) ▷ *nm/f* optician ▷ *nf* (*ciencia*) optics *sg*; (*tienda*) optician's; (*fig*) viewpoint; **desde esta óptica** from this point of view

optimismo [opti'mismo] nm optimism
optimista [opti'mista] nm/f optimist
óptimo, -a ['optimo, a] adj (el mejor) very best
opuesto, -a [o'pwesto, a] pp de **oponer** ⊳ adj (contrario) opposite; (antagónico) opposing
opulencia [opu'lenθja] nf opulence
opulento, -a [opu'lento, a] adj opulent
oración [ora'θjon] nf (Rel) prayer; (Ling) sentence
oráculo [o'rakulo] nm oracle
orador, a [ora'ðor, a] nm/f orator; (conferenciante) speaker
oral [o'ral] adj oral; **por vía ~** (Med) orally
orangután [orangu'tan] nm orang-utan
orar [o'rar] vi (Rel) to pray
oratoria [ora'torja] nf oratory
órbita ['orβita] nf orbit; (Anat: ocular) (eye-)socket
orden ['orðen] nm (gen) order; (Inform) command; **~ público** public order, law and order; (números): **del ~ de** about; **de primer ~** first-rate; **en ~ de prioridad** in order of priority ⊳ nf (gen) order; **~ bancaria** banker's order; **~ de compra** (Com) purchase order; **~ del día** agenda; **eso ahora está a la ~ del día** that is now the order of the day; **a la ~ de usted** at your service; **dar la ~ de hacer algo** to give the order to do sth
ordenado, -a [orðe'naðo, a] adj (metódico) methodical; (arreglado) orderly
ordenador [orðena'ðor] nm computer; **~ central** mainframe computer; **~ de gestión** business computer; **~ portátil** laptop (computer); **~ de sobremesa** desktop computer
ordenamiento [orðena'mjento] nm legislation
ordenanza [orðe'nanθa] nf ordinance; **~s municipales** by-laws ⊳ nm (Com etc) messenger; (Mil) orderly; (bedel) porter
ordenar [orðe'nar] vt (mandar) to order; (poner orden) to put in order, arrange; **ordenarse** vr (Rel) to be ordained
ordeñar [orðe'ɲar] vt to milk
ordinario, -a [orði'narjo, a] adj (común) ordinary, usual; (vulgar) vulgar, common
orégano [o'reɣano] nm oregano
oreja [o'rexa] nf ear; (Mecánica) lug, flange
orfanato [orfa'nato], **orfanatorio** [orfana'torjo] nm orphanage
orfandad [orfan'dað] nf orphanhood
orfebrería [orfeβre'ria] nf gold/silver work
orgánico, -a [or'ɣaniko, a] adj organic
organigrama [orɣani'ɣrama] nm flow chart; (de organización) organization chart
organismo [orɣa'nismo] nm (Bio) organism; (Pol) organization; **O~ Internacional de Energía Atómica** International Atomic Energy Agency
organista [orɣa'nista] nm/f organist
organización [orɣaniθa'θjon] nf organization; **O~ de las Naciones Unidas** (ONU) United Nations Organization; **O~ del Tratado del Atlántico Norte** (OTAN) North Atlantic Treaty Organization (NATO)
organizar [orɣani'θar] vt to organize
órgano ['orɣano] nm organ
orgasmo [or'ɣasmo] nm orgasm
orgía [or'xia] nf orgy
orgullo [or'ɣuʎo] nm (altanería) pride; (autorrespeto) self-respect
orgulloso, -a [orɣu'ʎoso, a] adj (gen) proud; (altanero) haughty
orientación [orjenta'θjon] nf (posición) position; (dirección) direction; **~ profesional** occupational guidance
oriental [orjen'tal] adj oriental; (región etc) eastern ⊳ nm/f oriental
orientar [orjen'tar] vt (situar) to orientate; (señalar) to point; (dirigir) to direct; (guiar) to guide; **orientarse** vr to get one's bearings; (decidirse) to decide on a course of action
oriente [o'rjente] nm east; **el O~** the East, the Orient; **Cercano/Medio/Lejano O~** Near/Middle/Far East
origen [o'rixen] nm origin; (nacimiento) lineage, birth; **dar ~ a** to cause, give rise to
original [orixi'nal] adj (nuevo) original; (extraño) odd, strange ⊳ nm original; (Tip) manuscript; (Tec) master (copy)
originalidad [orixinali'ðað] nf originality
originar [orixi'nar] vt to start, cause; **originarse** vr to originate
originario, -a [orixi'narjo, a] adj (nativo) native; (primordial) original; **ser ~ de** to originate from; **país ~** country of origin
orilla [o'riʎa] nf (borde) border; (de río) bank; (de bosque, tela) edge; (de mar) shore; **a ~s de** on the banks of
orín [o'rin] nm rust
orina [o'rina] nf urine
orinal [ori'nal] nm (chamber) pot
orinar [ori'nar] vi to urinate; **orinarse** vr to wet o.s.
orines [o'rines] nmpl urine sg
oriundo, -a [o'rjundo, a] adj: **~ de** native of
ornar [or'nar] vt to adorn
ornitología [ornitolo'xia] nf ornithology, bird watching
oro ['oro] nm gold; **~ en barras** gold ingots; **de ~** gold, golden; **no es ~ todo lo que reluce** all that glitters is not gold; **hacerse de ~** to make a fortune; ver tb **oros**
oropel [oro'pel] nm tinsel
oros ['oros] nmpl (Naipes) one of the suits in the Spanish card deck
orquesta [or'kesta] nf orchestra; **~ de cámara/sinfónica** chamber/symphony orchestra; **~ de jazz** jazz band
orquestar [orkes'tar] vt to orchestrate
orquídea [or'kiðea] nf orchid

o

ortiga [or'tiɣa] nf nettle
ortodoncia [orto'ðonθja] nf orthodontics sg
ortodoxo, -a [orto'ðokso, a] adj orthodox
ortografía [ortoɣra'fia] nf spelling
ortopedia [orto'peðja] nf orthop(a)edics sg
ortopédico, -a [orto'peðiko, a] adj
    orthop(a)edic
oruga [o'ruɣa] nf caterpillar
orzuelo [or'θwelo] nm (Med) stye
os [os] pron (gen) you; (a vosotros) (to) you;
    (reflexivo) (to) yourselves; (mutuo) (to) each
    other; **vosotros os laváis** you wash
    yourselves; **¡callaros!** (fam) shut up!
osa ['osa] nf (she-)bear; **O~ Mayor/Menor**
    Great/Little Bear, Ursa Major/Minor
osadía [osa'ðia] nf daring; (descaro)
    impudence
osar [o'sar] vi to dare
oscilación [osθila'θjon] nf (movimiento)
    oscillation; (fluctuación) fluctuation;
    (vacilación) hesitation; (de columpio) swinging,
    movement to and fro
oscilar [osθi'lar] vi to oscillate; to fluctuate;
    to hesitate
oscurecer [oskure'θer] vt to darken ▷ vi
    to grow dark; **oscurecerse** vr to grow o get
    dark
oscuridad [oskuri'ðað] nf obscurity;
    (tinieblas) darkness
oscuro, -a [os'kuro, a] adj dark; (fig)
    obscure; (indefinido) confused; (cielo) overcast,
    cloudy; (futuro etc) uncertain; **a oscuras** in
    the dark
óseo, -a ['oseo, a] adj bony; (Med etc) bone cpd
oso ['oso] nm bear; **~ blanco/gris/pardo**
    polar/grizzly/brown bear; **~ de peluche**
    teddy bear; **~ hormiguero** anteater; **hacer**
    el ~ to play the fool
ostensible [osten'siβle] adj obvious
ostentación [ostenta'θjon] nf (gen)
    ostentation; (acto) display
ostentar [osten'tar] vt (gen) to show; (pey) to
    flaunt, show off; (poseer) to have, possess
ostentoso, -a [osten'toso, a] adj
    ostentatious, showy
ostión [os'tjon] nm (Am) = **ostra**
ostra ['ostra] nf oyster ▷ excl: **¡~s!** (fam)
    sugar!
OTAN ['otan] nf abr ver **Organización del**
    Tratado del Atlántico Norte
otear [ote'ar] vt to observe; (fig) to look into
otitis [o'titis] nf earache
otoñal [oto'ɲal] adj autumnal
otoño [o'toɲo] nm autumn, fall (US)
otorgamiento [otorɣa'mjento] nm
    conferring, granting; (Jur) execution
otorgar [otor'ɣar] vt (conceder) to concede;
    (dar) to grant; (poderes) to confer; (premio) to
    award
otorrinolaringólogo, -a [otorrinolarin-
    'goloɣo, a] nm/f (Med: tb: **otorrino**) ear, nose
    and throat specialist

◯ **PALABRA CLAVE**

otro, -a ['otro, a] adj **1** (distinto: sg) another;
    (: pl) other; **otra cosa/persona** something/
    someone else; **con otros amigos** with other
    o different friends; **a/en otra parte**
    elsewhere, somewhere else
    2 (adicional): **tráigame otro café (más), por**
    favor can I have another coffee please; **otros**
    10 días más another 10 days
    ▷ pron **1** (sg) another one; **el otro** the other
    one; **(los) otros** (the) others; **¡otra!** (Mus)
    more!; **de otro** somebody o someone else's;
    que lo haga otro let somebody o someone
    else do it; **ni uno ni otro** neither one nor
    the other
    2 (recíproco): **se odian (la) una a (la) otra** they
    hate one another o each other
    3: **otro tanto**: **comer otro tanto** to eat the
    same o as much again; **recibió una decena**
    de telegramas y otras tantas llamadas he
    got about ten telegrams and as many calls

ovación [oβa'θjon] nf ovation
oval [o'βal], **ovalado, -a** [oβa'laðo, a] adj oval
óvalo ['oβalo] nm oval
ovario [o'βarjo] nm ovary
oveja [o'βexa] nf sheep; **~ negra** (fig) black
    sheep (of the family)
overol [oβe'rol] nm (Am) overalls pl
ovillo [o'βiʎo] nm (de lana) ball; (fig) tangle;
    hacerse un ~ to curl up (into a ball)
OVNI ['oβni] nm abr (= objeto volante (o volador)
    no identificado) UFO
ovulación [oβula'θjon] nf ovulation
óvulo ['oβulo] nm ovum
oxidación [oksiða'θjon] nf rusting
oxidar [oksi'ðar] vt to rust; **oxidarse** vr to go
    rusty; (Tec) to oxidize
óxido ['oksiðo] nm oxide
oxigenado, -a [oksixe'naðo, a] adj (Química)
    oxygenated; (pelo) bleached
oxígeno [ok'sixeno] nm oxygen
oyente [o'jente] nm/f listener, hearer; (Escol)
    unregistered o occasional student
oyes etc vb ver **oír**
ozono [o'θono] nm ozone

P

P *abr* (*Rel*: = *padre*) Fr.; (= *pregunta*) Q; = **papa**

pabellón [paβe'ʎon] *nm* bell tent; (*Arq*) pavilion; (*de hospital etc*) block, section; (*bandera*) flag; **~ de conveniencia** (*Com*) flag of convenience; **~ de la oreja** outer ear

pábilo ['paβilo] *nm* wick

pacer [pa'θer] *vi* to graze ▷ *vt* to graze on

pachanguero, -a [patʃan'gero, a] *adj* (*pey: música*) noisy and catchy

paciencia [pa'θjenθja] *nf* patience; **¡~!** be patient!; **¡~ y barajar!** don't give up!; **perder la ~** to lose one's temper

paciente [pa'θjente] *adj, nm/f* patient

pacificación [paθifika'θjon] *nf* pacification

pacificar [paθifi'kar] *vt* to pacify; (*tranquilizar*) to calm

pacífico, -a [pa'θifiko, a] *adj* peaceful; (*persona*) peaceable; (*existencia*) peaceful; **el (Océano) P~** the Pacific (Ocean)

pacifismo [paθi'fismo] *nm* pacifism

pacifista [paθi'fista] *nm/f* pacifist

pack [pak] *nm* (*de yogures, latas*) pack; (*de vacaciones*) package

pacotilla [pako'tiʎa] *nf* trash; **de ~** shoddy

pactar [pak'tar] *vt* to agree to, agree on ▷ *vi* to come to an agreement

pacto ['pakto] *nm* (*tratado*) pact; (*acuerdo*) agreement

padecer [paðe'θer] *vt* (*sufrir*) to suffer; (*soportar*) to endure, put up with; (*ser víctima de*) to be a victim of ▷ *vi*: **~ de** to suffer from

padecimiento [paðeθi'mjento] *nm* suffering

pádel ['paðel] *nm* paddle tennis

padrastro [pa'ðrastro] *nm* stepfather

padre ['paðre] *nm* father ▷ *adj* (*fam*): **un éxito ~** a tremendous success; **padres** *nmpl* parents; **~ espiritual** confessor; **P~ Nuestro** Lord's Prayer; **~ político** father-in-law; **García ~** García senior; **¡tu ~!** (*fam!*) up yours! (*!*)

padrino [pa'ðrino] *nm* godfather; (*fig*) sponsor, patron; **padrinos** *nmpl* godparents; **~ de boda** best man

padrón [pa'ðron] *nm* (*censo*) census, roll; (*de socios*) register

padrote [pa'ðrote] (*Am: fam*) *nm* pimp

paella [pa'eʎa] *nf* paella, *dish of rice with meat, shellfish etc*

paga ['paɣa] *nf* (*dinero pagado*) payment; (*sueldo*) pay, wages *pl*

pagadero, -a [paɣa'ðero, a] *adj* payable; **~ a la entrega/a plazos** payable on delivery/in instalments

pagano, -a [pa'ɣano, a] *adj, nm/f* pagan, heathen

pagar [pa'ɣar] *vt* (*gen*) to pay; (*las compras, crimen*) to pay for; (*deuda*) to pay (off); (*fig: favor*) to repay ▷ *vi* to pay; **pagarse** *vr*: **~se con algo** to be content with sth; **~ al contado/a plazos** to pay (in) cash/in instalments; **¡me las ~ás!** I'll get you for this!

pagaré [paɣa're] *nm* I.O.U

página ['paxina] *nf* page; **~ de inicio** (*Inform*) home page; **~ personal** (*Internet*) personal web page; **~ web** (*Internet*) web page

pago ['paɣo] *nm* (*dinero*) payment; (*fig*) return; **~ anticipado/a cuenta/a la entrega/en especie/inicial** advance payment/payment on account/cash on delivery/payment in kind/down payment; **~ a título gracioso** ex gratia payment; **en ~ de** in return for

pág(s). *abr* (= *página(s)*) p(p)

pague *etc* ['paɣe] *vb ver* **pagar**

país [pa'is] *nm* (*gen*) country; (*región*) land; **los P~es Bajos** the Low Countries; **el P~ Vasco** the Basque Country

paisaje [pai'saxe] *nm* countryside, landscape; (*vista*) scenery

paisano, -a [pai'sano, a] *adj* of the same country ▷ *nm/f* (*compatriota*) fellow countryman(-woman); **vestir de ~** (*soldado*) to be in civilian clothes; (*guardia*) to be in plain clothes

paja ['paxa] *nf* straw; (*fig*) trash, rubbish; (*en libro, ensayo*) padding, waffle; **riñeron por un quítame allá esas ~s** they quarrelled over a trifle

pajar [pa'xar] *nm* hay loft

pajarita [paxa'rita] *nf* bow tie

pájaro ['paxaro] *nm* bird; (*fam: astuto*) clever fellow; **tener la cabeza a ~s** to be featherbrained; **~ carpintero** woodpecker

pajita [pa'xita] *nf* (drinking) straw

pala ['pala] *nf* (*de mango largo*) spade; (*de mango corto*) shovel; (*raqueta etc*) bat; (: *de tenis*) racquet; (*Culin*) slice; ~ **matamoscas** fly swat; ~ **mecánica** power shovel

palabra [pa'laβra] *nf* (*gen, promesa*) word; (*facultad*) (power of) speech; (*derecho de hablar*) right to speak; **faltar a su** ~ to go back on one's word; **quedarse con la** ~ **en la boca** to stop short; (*en reunión, comité etc*): **tomar la** ~ to speak, take the floor; **pedir la** ~ to ask to be allowed to speak; **tener la** ~ to have the floor; **no encuentro ~s para expresarme** words fail me

palabrería [palaβre'ria] *nf* hot air

palabrota [pala'βrota] *nf* swearword

palacio [pa'laθjo] *nm* palace; (*mansión*) mansion, large house; ~ **de justicia** courthouse; ~ **municipal** town/city hall

paladar [pala'ðar] *nm* palate

paladear [palaðe'ar] *vt* to taste

palanca [pa'lanka] *nf* lever; (*fig*) pull, influence; ~ **de cambio** (*Auto*) gear lever, gearshift (*US*); ~ **de freno** (*Auto*) brake lever; ~ **de gobierno** *o* **de control** (*Inform*) joystick

palangana [palan'gana] *nf* washbasin

palco ['palko] *nm* box

Palestina [pales'tina] *nf* Palestine

palestino, -a [pales'tino, a] *adj, nm/f* Palestinian

palestra [pa'lestra] *nf*: **salir** *o* **saltar a la** ~ to come into the spotlight

paleto, -a [pa'leto, a] *nm/f* yokel, hick (*US*) ▷ *nf* (*pala*) small shovel; (*Arte*) palette; (*Anat*) shoulder blade; (*Deporte: de ping-pong*) bat; (*Am: helado*) ice lolly (*Brit*), Popsicle® (*US*)

paliar [pa'ljar] *vt* (*mitigar*) to mitigate; (*disfrazar*) to conceal

paliativo [palja'tiβo] *nm* palliative

palidecer [paliðe'θer] *vi* to turn pale

palidez [pali'ðeθ] *nf* paleness

pálido, -a [pa'liðo, a] *adj* pale

palillo [pa'liʎo] *nm* small stick; (*para dientes*) toothpick; **~s (chinos)** chopsticks; **estar hecho un** ~ to be as thin as a rake

palio ['paljo] *nm* canopy

paliza [pa'liθa] *nf* beating, thrashing; **dar** *o* **propinar** (*fam*) **una ~ a algn** to give sb a thrashing

palma ['palma] *nf* (*Anat*) palm; (*árbol*) palm tree; **batir** *o* **dar ~s** to clap, applaud; **llevarse la** ~ to triumph, win

palmada [pal'maða] *nf* slap; **palmadas** *nfpl* clapping *sg*, applause *sg*

palmar [pal'mar] *vi* (*tb:* **~la**) to die, kick the bucket

palmarés [palma'res] *nm* (*lista*) list of winners; (*historial*) track record

palmear [palme'ar] *vi* to clap

palmera [pal'mera] *nf* (*Bot*) palm tree

palmo ['palmo] *nm* (*medida*) span; (*fig*) small amount; ~ **a** ~ inch by inch

palmotear [palmote'ar] *vi* to clap, applaud

palmoteo [palmo'teo] *nm* clapping, applause

palo ['palo] *nm* stick; (*poste*) post, pole; (*mango*) handle, shaft; (*golpe*) blow, hit; (*de golf*) club; (*de béisbol*) bat; (*Naut*) mast; (*Naipes*) suit; **vermut a** ~ **seco** straight vermouth; **de tal** ~ **tal astilla** like father like son

paloma [pa'loma] *nf* dove, pigeon; ~ **mensajera** carrier *o* homing pigeon

palomilla [palo'miʎa] *nf* moth; (*Tec: tuerca*) wing nut; (*soporte*) bracket

palomitas [palo'mitas] *nfpl* popcorn *sg*

palpar [pal'par] *vt* to touch, feel

palpitación [palpita'θjon] *nf* palpitation

palpitante [palpi'tante] *adj* palpitating; (*fig*) burning

palpitar [palpi'tar] *vi* to palpitate; (*latir*) to beat

palta ['palta] *nf* (*Am*) avocado

palúdico, -a [pa'luðiko, a] *adj* marshy

paludismo [palu'ðismo] *nm* malaria

pamela [pa'mela] *nf* sun hat

pampa ['pampa] *nf* (*Am*) pampa(s), prairie

pan [pan] *nm* bread; (*una barra*) loaf; ~ **de molde** sliced loaf; ~ **integral** wholemeal bread; ~ **rallado** breadcrumbs *pl*; ~ **tostado** (*Am: tostada*) toast; **eso es** ~ **comido** it's a cinch; **llamar al** ~ ~ **y al vino vino** to call a spade a spade

pana ['pana] *nf* corduroy

panadería [panaðe'ria] *nf* baker's (shop)

panadero, -a [pana'ðero, a] *nm/f* baker

Panamá [pana'ma] *nm* Panama

panameño, -a [pana'meɲo, a] *adj* Panamanian

pancarta [pan'karta] *nf* placard, banner

panceta [pan'θeta] *nf* bacon

pancho, -a ['pantʃo, a] *adj*: **estar tan** ~ to remain perfectly calm ▷ *nm* (*Am*) hot dog

pancito [pan'sito] *nm* (*Am*) (bread) roll

páncreas ['pankreas] *nm* pancreas

panda ['panda] *nm* panda ▷ *nf* gang

pandereta [pande'reta] *nf* tambourine

pandilla [pan'diʎa] *nf* set, group; (*de criminales*) gang; (*pey*) clique

panecillo [pane'θiʎo] *nm* (bread) roll

panel [pa'nel] *nm* panel; ~ **acústico** acoustic screen; ~ **solar** solar panel

panfleto [pan'fleto] *nm* (*Pol etc*) pamphlet; lampoon

pánico ['paniko] *nm* panic

panificadora [panifika'ðora] *nf* bakery

panorama [pano'rama] *nm* panorama; (*vista*) view

panqué [pan'ke], **panqueque** [pan'keke] *nm* (*Am*) pancake

pantalla [pan'taʎa] *nf* (*de cine*) screen; (*cubreluz*) lampshade; (*Inform*) screen, display; **servir de** ~ to be a blind for; ~ **de ayuda** help screen; ~ **de cristal líquido** liquid crystal display; ~ **de plasma** plasma screen; ~ **plana** flatscreen; ~ **táctil** touch screen

pantalón, pantalones [panta'lon(es)] *nm(pl)* trousers *pl*, pants *pl* (US); **pantalones cortos** shorts *pl*; **pantalones vaqueros** jeans *pl*

pantano [pan'tano] *nm* (*ciénaga*) marsh, swamp; (*depósito: de agua*) reservoir; (*fig*) jam, fix, difficulty

panteón [pante'on] *nm* (*monumento*) pantheon

pantera [pan'tera] *nf* panther

pantimedias [panti'meðjas] *nfpl* (*Am*) = **pantis**

pantis ['pantis] *nmpl* tights (Brit), pantyhose (US)

pantomima [panto'mima] *nf* pantomime

pantorrilla [panto'rriʎa] *nf* calf (of the leg)

pants [pants] *nmpl* (*Am*) tracksuit (Brit), sweat suit (US)

pantufla [pan'tufla] *nf* slipper

panty(s) ['panti(s)] *nm(pl)* tights (Brit), pantyhose (US)

panza ['panθa] *nf* belly, paunch

panzón, -ona [pan'θon, ona], **panzudo, -a** [pan'θuðo, a] *adj* fat, potbellied

pañal [pa'ɲal] *nm* nappy, diaper (US); (*fig*) early stages, infancy *sg*; **estar todavía en ~es** to be still wet behind the ears

pañería [paɲe'ria] *nf* (*artículos*) drapery; (*tienda*) draper's (shop), dry-goods store (US)

paño ['paɲo] *nm* (*tela*) cloth; (*pedazo de tela*) (piece of) cloth; (*trapo*) duster, rag; **~ de cocina** dishcloth; **~ higiénico** sanitary towel; **~s menores** underclothes; **~s calientes** (*fig*) half-measures; **no andarse con ~s calientes** to pull no punches

pañuelo [pa'ɲwelo] *nm* handkerchief, hanky (fam); (*para la cabeza*) (head)scarf

papa ['papa] *nf* (*Am: patata*) potato; **~s fritas** (*Am*) French fries, chips (Brit); (*de bolsa*) crisps (Brit), potato chips (US), potato ▷ *nm*: **el P~** the Pope

papá [pa'pa] *nm* (*pl* **papás**) (fam) dad, daddy, pop (US); **papás** *nmpl* parents; **hijo de ~** Hooray Henry (fam)

papada [pa'paða] *nf* double chin

papagayo [papa'ɣajo] *nm* parrot

papalote [papa'lote] *nm* (*Am*) kite

papanatas [papa'natas] *nm inv* (fam) sucker, simpleton

paparrucha [papa'rrutʃa] *nf* (*tontería*) piece of nonsense

papaya [pa'paja] *nf* papaya

papear [pape'ar] *vt, vi* (fam) to eat

papel [pa'pel] *nm* (*gen*) paper; (*hoja de papel*) sheet of paper; (*Teat*) part, role; **papeles** *nmpl* identification papers; **~ de calco/carbón/de cartas** tracing paper/carbon paper/ stationery; **~ continuo** (*Inform*) continuous stationery; **~ de arroz/envolver/fumar** rice/ wrapping/cigarette paper; **~ de aluminio/ higiénico** tinfoil/toilet paper; **~ del** o **de pagos al Estado** government bonds *pl*; **~ de**

lija sandpaper; **~ moneda** paper money; **~ plegado (en abanico** o **en acordeón)** fanfold paper; **~ pintado** wallpaper; **~ secante** blotting paper; **~ térmico** thermal paper

papeleo [pape'leo] *nm* red tape

papelera [pape'lera] *nf* (*cesto*) wastepaper basket; (*escritorio*) desk; **~ de reciclaje** (*Inform*) wastebasket

papelería [papele'ria] *nf* (*tienda*) stationer's (shop)

papeleta [pape'leta] *nf* (*pedazo de papel*) slip o bit of paper; (*Pol*) ballot paper; (*Escol*) report; **¡vaya ~!** this is a tough one!

paperas [pa'peras] *nfpl* mumps *sg*

papilla [pa'piʎa] *nf* (*de bebé*) baby food; (*pey*) mush; **estar hecho ~** to be dog-tired

paquete [pa'kete] *nm* (*caja*) packet; (*bulto*) parcel; (*Am fam*) nuisance, bore; (*Inform*) package (*of software*); (*de vacaciones*) package tour; **~ de aplicaciones** (*Inform*) applications package; **~ integrado** (*Inform*) integrated package; **~ de gestión integrado** combined management suite; **~s postales** parcel post *sg*

par [par] *adj* (*igual*) like, equal; (*Mat*) even ▷ *nm* equal; (*de guantes*) pair; (*de veces*) couple; (*título*) peer; (*Golf, Com*) par; **~es o nones** odds or evens; **abrir de ~ en ~** to open wide; **a la ~ par**; **sobre/bajo la ~** above/ below par

para ['para] *prep* for; **no es ~ comer** it's not for eating; **decir ~ sí** to say to o.s.; **¿~ qué lo quieres?** what do you want it for?; **se casaron ~ separarse otra vez** they married only to separate again; **~ entonces** by then o that time; **lo tendré ~ mañana** I'll have it for tomorrow; **ir ~ casa** to go home, head for home; **~ profesor es muy estúpido** he's very stupid for a teacher; **¿quién es usted ~ gritar así?** who are you to shout like that?; **tengo bastante ~ vivir** I have enough to live on

parabién [para'βjen] *nm* congratulations *pl*

parábola [pa'raβola] *nf* parable; (*Mat*) parabola

parabólica [para'βolika] *nf* (*tb*: **antena ~**) satellite dish

parabrisas [para'βrisas] *nm inv* windscreen, windshield (US)

paracaídas [paraka'iðas] *nm inv* parachute

paracaidista [parakai'ðista] *nm/f* parachutist; (*Mil*) paratrooper

parachoques [para'tʃokes] *nm inv* bumper, fender (US); shock absorber

parada [pa'raða] *nf ver* **parado**

paradero [para'ðero] *nm* stopping-place; (*situación*) whereabouts

parado, -a [pa'raðo, a] *adj* (*persona*) motionless, standing still; (*fábrica*) closed, at a standstill; (*coche*) stopped; (*Am: de pie*) standing (up); (*sin empleo*) unemployed, idle;

P

(confuso) confused ▷ *nf (gen)* stop; *(acto)* stopping; *(de industria)* shutdown, stoppage; *(lugar)* stopping-place; **salir bien ~** to come off well; **parada de autobús** bus stop; **parada discrecional** request stop; **parada en seco** sudden stop; **parada de taxis** taxi rank

paradoja [para'ðoxa] *nf* paradox

parador [para'ðor] *nm (Esp)* (luxury) hotel *(owned by the state)*

paráfrasis [pa'rafrasis] *nf inv* paraphrase

paragolpes [para'golpes] *nm inv (Am: Auto)* bumper, fender (US)

paraguas [pa'raɣwas] *nm inv* umbrella

Paraguay [para'ɣwai] *nm*: **el ~** Paraguay

paraguayo, -a [para'ɣwajo, a] *adj, nm/f* Paraguayan

paraíso [para'iso] *nm* paradise, heaven; **~ fiscal** *(Com)* tax haven

paraje [pa'raxe] *nm* place, spot

paralelo, -a [para'lelo, a] *adj, nm* parallel; **en ~** *(Elec, Inform)* (in) parallel

parálisis [pa'ralisis] *nf inv* paralysis; **~ cerebral** cerebral palsy; **~ progresiva** creeping paralysis

paralítico, -a [para'litiko, a] *adj, nm/f* paralytic

paralizar [parali'θar] *vt* to paralyse; **paralizarse** *vr* to become paralysed; *(fig)* to come to a standstill

paramilitar [paramili'tar] *adj* paramilitary

páramo ['paramo] *nm* bleak plateau

parangón [paran'gon] *nm*: **sin ~** incomparable

paranoia [para'noia] *nf* paranoia

paranoico, -a [para'noiko, a] *adj, nm/f* paranoid

paranormal [paranor'mal] *adj* paranormal

parapente [para'pente] *nm (deporte)* paragliding; *(aparato)* paraglider

parapléjico, -a [para'plexiko, a] *adj, nm/f* paraplegic

parar [pa'rar] *vt* to stop; *(progreso etc)* to check, halt; *(golpe)* to ward off ▷ *vi* to stop; *(hospedarse)* to stay, put up; **pararse** *vr* to stop; *(Am)* to stand up; **no ~ de hacer algo** to keep on doing sth; **ha parado de llover** it has stopped raining; **van a ~ en la comisaría** they're going to end up in the police station; **no sabemos en qué va a ~ todo esto** we don't know where all this is going to end; **~se a hacer algo** to stop to do sth; **~se en** to pay attention to

pararrayos [para'rrajos] *nm inv* lightning conductor

parásito, -a [pa'rasito, a] *nm/f* parasite

parasol [para'sol] *nm* parasol, sunshade

parcela [par'θela] *nf* plot, piece of ground, smallholding

parche ['partʃe] *nm* patch

parchís [par'tʃis] *nm* ludo

parcial [par'θjal] *adj (pago)* part-; *(eclipse)* partial; *(juez)* prejudiced, biased; *(Pol)* partisan

parcialidad [parθjali'ðað] *nf (prejuicio)* prejudice, bias

parco, -a ['parko, a] *adj (frugal)* sparing; *(moderado)* moderate

pardillo, -a [par'ðiʎo, a] *adj (pey)* provincial ▷ *nm/f (pey)* country bumpkin ▷ *nm (Zool)* linnet

pardo, -a ['parðo, a] *adj (color)* brown; *(cielo)* overcast; *(voz)* flat, dull

parear [pare'ar] *vt (juntar, hacer par)* to match, put together; *(calcetines)* to put into pairs; *(Bio)* to mate, pair

parecer [pare'θer] *nm (opinión)* opinion, view; *(aspecto)* looks *pl* ▷ *vi (tener apariencia)* to seem, look; *(asemejarse)* to look like, seem like; *(aparecer, llegar)* to appear; **parecerse** *vr* to look alike, resemble each other; **según parece** evidently, apparently; **~se a** to look like, resemble; **al ~** apparently; **me parece que** I think (that), it seems to me that

parecido, -a [pare'θiðo, a] *adj* similar ▷ *nm* similarity, likeness, resemblance; **~ a** like, similar to; **bien ~** good-looking, nice-looking

pared [pa'reð] *nf* wall; **~ divisoria/medianera** dividing/party wall; **subirse por las ~es** *(fam)* to go up the wall

parejo, -a [pa'rexo, a] *adj (igual)* equal; *(liso)* smooth, even ▷ *nf (dos)* pair; *(: de personas)* couple; *(el otro: de un par)* other one (of a pair); *(: persona)* partner; *(de Guardias)* Civil Guard patrol

parentela [paren'tela] *nf* relations *pl*

parentesco [paren'tesko] *nm* relationship

paréntesis [pa'rentesis] *nm inv* parenthesis; *(digresión)* digression; *(en escrito)* bracket

parezco *etc vb ver* **parecer**

parida [pa'riða] *nf*: **~ mental** *(fam)* dumb idea

paridad [pari'ðað] *nf (Econ)* parity

pariente, -a [pa'rjente, a] *nm/f* relative, relation

parir [pa'rir] *vt* to give birth to ▷ *vi (mujer)* to give birth, have a baby; *(yegua)* to foal; *(vaca)* to calve

París [pa'ris] *nm* Paris

paritario, -a [pari'tarjo, a] *adj* equal

parka ['parka] *nf (Am)* anorak

parking ['parkin] *nm* car park, parking lot (US)

parlamentar [parlamen'tar] *vi (negociar)* to parley

parlamentario, -a [parlamen'tarjo, a] *adj* parliamentary ▷ *nm/f* member of parliament

parlamento [parla'mento] *nm (Pol)* parliament; *(Jur)* speech

parlanchín, -ina [parlan'tʃin, ina] *adj* loose-tongued, indiscreet ▷ *nm/f* chatterbox

parlar [par'lar] *vi* to chatter (away)

parlotear [parlote'ar] *vi* to chatter, prattle

paro ['paro] nm (huelga) stoppage (of work), strike; (desempleo) unemployment; **~ cardiaco** cardiac arrest; **estar en ~** (Esp) to be unemployed; **subsidio de ~** unemployment benefit; **hay ~ en la industria** work in the industry is at a standstill; **~ del sistema** (Inform) system shutdown

parodia [pa'roðja] nf parody

parodiar [paro'ðjar] vt to parody

parpadear [parpaðe'ar] vi (los ojos) to blink; (luz) to flicker

párpado ['parpaðo] nm eyelid

parque ['parke] nm (lugar verde) park; (Am: munición) ammunition; **~ de atracciones/de bomberos/zoológico** fairground/fire station/zoo; **~ infantil/temático/zoológico** playground/theme park/zoo

parqué, parquet [par'ke] nm parquet

parquímetro [par'kimetro] nm parking meter

parra ['parra] nf grapevine

párrafo ['parrafo] nm paragraph; **echar un ~** (fam) to have a chat

parranda [pa'rranda] nf (fam) spree, binge

parrilla [pa'rriʎa] nf (Culin) grill; (Am Auto) roof-rack; **~ (de salida)** (Auto) starting grid; **(carne a la) ~** grilled meat, barbecue

parrillada [parri'ʎaða] nf barbecue

párroco ['parroko] nm parish priest

parroquia [pa'rrokja] nf parish; (iglesia) parish church; (Com) clientele, customers pl

parroquiano, -a [parro'kjano, a] nm/f parishioner; client, customer

parte ['parte] nm message; (informe) report ▷ nf part; (lado, cara) side; (de reparto) share; (Jur) party; **en alguna ~ de Europa** somewhere in Europe; **en cualquier ~** anywhere; **por ahí no se va a ninguna ~** that leads nowhere; (fig) this is getting us nowhere; **en o por todas ~s** everywhere; **en gran ~** to a large extent; **la mayor ~ de los españoles** most Spaniards; **de algún tiempo a esta ~** for some time past; **de ~ de algn** on sb's behalf; **¿de ~ de quién?** (Telec) who is speaking?; **por ~ de** on the part of; **yo por mi ~** I for my part; **por una ~ ... por otra ~** on the one hand, ... on the other (hand); **dar ~ a algn** to report to sb; **tomar ~** to take part; **~ meteorológico** weather forecast o report

partera [par'tera] nf midwife

partición [parti'θjon] nf division, sharing-out; (Pol) partition

participación [partiθipa'θjon] nf (acto) participation, taking part; (parte) share; (Com) share, stock (US); (de lotería) shared prize; (aviso) notice, notification; **~ en los beneficios** profit-sharing; **~ minoritaria** minority interest

participante [partiθi'pante] nm/f participant

participar [partiθi'par] vt to notify, inform ▷ vi to take part, participate; **~ en una empresa** (Com) to invest in an enterprise; **le participo que ...** I have to tell you that ...

partícipe [par'tiθipe] nm/f participant; **hacer ~ a algn de algo** to inform sb of sth

particular [partiku'lar] adj (especial) particular, special; (individual, personal) private, personal ▷ nm (punto, asunto) particular, point; (individuo) individual; **tiene coche ~** he has a car of his own; **no dijo mucho sobre el ~** he didn't say much about the matter

particularizar [partikulari'θar] vt to distinguish; (especificar) to specify; (detallar) to give details about

partida [par'tiða] nf (salida) departure; (Com) entry, item; (juego) game; (grupo, bando) band, group; **mala ~** dirty trick; **~ de nacimiento/matrimonio/defunción** birth/marriage/death certificate; **echar una ~** to have a game

partidario, -a [parti'ðarjo, a] adj partisan ▷ nm/f (Deporte) supporter; (Pol) partisan

partido [par'tiðo] nm (Pol) party; (encuentro) game, match; (apoyo) support; (equipo) team; **~ amistoso** (Deporte) friendly (game); **~ de fútbol** football match; **sacar ~ de** to profit from, benefit from; **tomar ~** to take sides

partir [par'tir] vt (dividir) to split, divide; (compartir, distribuir) to share (out), distribute; (romper) to break open, split open; (rebanada) to cut (off); (vi: ponerse en camino) to set off, set out; (comenzar) to start (off o out); **partirse** vr to crack o split o break (in two etc); **a ~ de** (starting) from; **~se de risa** to split one's sides (laughing)

partitura [parti'tura] nf score

parto ['parto] nm birth, delivery; (fig) product, creation; **estar de ~** to be in labour

parvulario [parβu'larjo] nm nursery school, kindergarten

pasa ['pasa] nf ver **paso**

pasable [pa'saβle] adj passable

pasacintas [pasa'θintas] nm (Am) cassette player

pasada [pa'saða] nf ver **pasado**

pasadizo [pasa'ðiθo] nm (pasillo) passage, corridor; (callejuela) alley

pasado, -a [pa'saðo, a] adj past; (malo: comida, fruta) bad; (muy cocido) overdone; (anticuado) out of date ▷ nm past; (Ling) past (tense) ▷ nf passing, passage; (acción de pulir) rub, polish; **~ mañana** the day after tomorrow; **el mes ~** last month; **~s dos días** after two days; **lo ~, ~** let bygones be bygones; **~ de moda** old-fashioned; **~ por agua** (huevo) boiled; **estar ~ de vueltas** o **de rosca** (grifo, tuerca) to be worn; **de pasada** in passing, incidentally; **una mala pasada** a dirty trick

P

pasador [pasa'ðor] *nm* (*gen*) bolt; (*de pelo*) slide; (*horquilla*) grip; **pasadores** *nmpl* (*Am: cordones*) shoelaces

pasaje [pa'saxe] *nm* (*gen*) passage; (*pago de viaje*) fare; (*los pasajeros*) passengers *pl*; (*pasillo*) passageway

pasajero, -a [pasa'xero, a] *adj* passing; (*situación, estado*) temporary; (*amor, enfermedad*) brief; (*ave*) migratory ▷ *nm/f* passenger; (*viajero*) traveller

pasamanos [pasa'manos] *nm inv* rail, handrail; (*de escalera*) banister

pasamontañas [pasamon'taɲas] *nm inv* balaclava (helmet)

pasaporte [pasa'porte] *nm* passport

pasar [pa'sar] *vt* (*gen*) to pass; (*tiempo*) to spend; (*durezas*) to suffer, endure; (*noticia*) to give, pass on; (*película*) to show; (*persona*) to take, conduct; (*río*) to cross; (*barrera*) to pass through; (*falta*) to overlook, tolerate; (*contrincante*) to surpass, do better than; (*coche*) to overtake; (*contrabando*) to smuggle (in/out); (*enfermedad*) to give, infect with ▷ *vi* (*gen*) to pass, go; (*terminarse*) to be over; (*ocurrir*) to happen; **pasarse** *vr* (*efectos*) to pass, be over; (*flores*) to fade; (*comida*) to go bad, go off; (*fig*) to overdo it, go too far *o* over the top; **- la aspiradora** to do the vacuuming *or* hoovering, to hoover; **~ de** to go beyond, exceed; **¡pase!** come in!; **nos hicieron ~** they showed us in; **~ por** to fetch; **~ por alto** to skip; **~ por una crisis** to go through a crisis; **se hace ~ por médico** he passes himself off as a doctor; **~lo bien/ bomba** *o* **de maravilla** to have a good/great time; **¡que lo pases bien!** have a good time!; **~se al enemigo** to go over to the enemy; **~se de la raya** to go too far; **¡no te pases!** don't try me!; **se me pasó** I forgot; **se me pasó el turno** I missed my turn; **no se le pasa nada** nothing escapes him, he misses nothing; **ya se te -á** you'll get over it; **¿qué pasa?** what's happening?, what's going on?, what's up?; **¿qué te pasa?** what's wrong?; **¡cómo pasa el tiempo!** time just flies!; **pase lo que pase** come what may; **el autobús pasa por nuestra casa** the bus goes past our house

pasarela [pasa'rela] *nf* footbridge; (*en barco*) gangway

pasatiempo [pasa'tjempo] *nm* pastime, hobby; (*distracción*) amusement

Pascua, pascua ['paskwa] *nf*: **~ (de Resurrección)** Easter; **~ de Navidad** Christmas; **Pascuas** *nfpl* Christmas time *sg*; **¡felices ~s!** Merry Christmas!; **de ~s a Ramos** once in a blue moon; **hacer la ~ a** (*fam*) to annoy, bug

pase ['pase] *nm* pass; (*Cine*) performance, showing; (*Com*) permit; (*Jur*) licence

pasear [pase'ar] *vt* to take for a walk; (*exhibir*) to parade, show off ▷ *vi* to walk, go for a walk; **pasearse** *vr* to walk, go for a walk; **~ en coche** to go for a drive

paseo [pa'seo] *nm* (*distancia corta*) (short) walk, stroll; (*avenida*) avenue; **~ marítimo** promenade; **dar un ~** to go for a walk; **~ en bicicleta** (bike) ride; **~ en barco** boat trip; **mandar a algn a ~** to tell sb to go to blazes; **¡vete a ~!** get lost!

pasillo [pa'siʎo] *nm* passage, corridor

pasión [pa'sjon] *nf* passion

pasional [pasjo'nal] *adj* passionate; **crimen ~** crime of passion

pasivo, -a [pa'siβo, a] *adj* passive; (*inactivo*) inactive ▷ *nm* (*Com*) liabilities *pl*, debts *pl*; (*de cuenta*) debit side; **~ circulante** current liabilities

pasma ['pasma] *nm* (*fam*) cop

pasmar [pas'mar] *vt* (*asombrar*) to amaze, astonish; **pasmarse** *vr* to be amazed *o* astonished

pasmo ['pasmo] *nm* amazement, astonishment; (*fig*) wonder, marvel

pasmoso, -a [pas'moso, a] *adj* amazing, astonishing

paso, -a ['paso, a] *adj* dried ▷ *nm* (*gen, de baile*) step; (*modo de andar*) walk; (*huella*) footprint; (*rapidez*) speed, pace, rate; (*camino accesible*) way through, passage; (*cruce*) crossing; (*pasaje*) passing, passage; (*Rel*) religious float or sculpture; (*Geo*) pass; (*estrecho*) strait; (*fig*) step, measure; (*apuro*) difficulty ▷ *nf* raisin; **pasa de Corinto /de Esmirna** currant/sultana; **~ a ~** step by step; **a ese ~** (*fig*) at that rate; **salir al ~ de** *o* **a** to waylay; **salir del ~** to get out of trouble; **dar un ~ en falso** to trip; (*fig*) to take a false step; **estar de ~** to be passing through; **~ atrás** step backwards; (*fig*) backward step; **~ elevado/subterráneo** flyover/subway, underpass (US); **prohibido el ~** no entry; **ceda el ~** give way; **~ a nivel** (*Ferro*) level-crossing; **~ (de) cebra** (*Esp*) zebra crossing; **~ de peatones** pedestrian crossing; **~ elevado** flyover

pasota [pa'sota] *adj, nm/f* (*fam*) ≈ dropout; **ser un (tipo) ~** to be a bit of a dropout; (*ser indiferente*) not to care about anything

pasta ['pasta] *nf* (*gen*) paste; (*Culin: masa*) dough; (*: de bizcochos etc*) pastry; (*fam*) money, dough; (*encuadernación*) hardback; **pastas** *nfpl* (*bizcochos*) pastries, small cakes; (*espaguetis etc*) pasta *sg*; **~ de dientes** *o* **dentífrica** toothpaste; **~ de madera** wood pulp

pastar [pas'tar] *vt, vi* to graze

pastel [pas'tel] *nm* (*dulce*) cake; (*Arte*) pastel; (*fig*) plot; **pasteles** *nmpl* pastry *sg*, confectionery *sg*; **~ de carne** meat pie

pastelería [pastele'ria] *nf* cake shop, pastry shop

pasteurizado, -a [pasteuri'θaðo, a] *adj* pasteurized

pastilla [pas'tiʎa] *nf* (*de jabón, chocolate*) cake, bar; (*píldora*) tablet, pill

pasto ['pasto] nm (hierba) grass; (lugar) pasture, field; (fig) food, nourishment

pastor, a [pas'tor, a] nm/f shepherd(ess) ▷ nm clergyman, pastor; (Zool) sheepdog; ~ **alemán** Alsatian

pata ['pata] nf (pierna) leg; (pie) foot; (de muebles) leg; ~**s arriba** upside down; **a cuatro ~s** on all fours; **meter la ~** to put one's foot in it; ~ **de cabra** (Tec) crowbar; ~**s de gallo** crow's feet; **metedura de** ~ (fam) gaffe; **tener buena/mala** ~ to be lucky/ unlucky

patada [pa'taða] nf stamp; (puntapié) kick; **a ~s** in abundance; (trato) roughly; **echar a algn a ~s** to kick sb out

patalear [patale'ar] vi to stamp one's feet

patata [pa'tata] nf potato; ~**s fritas** o **a la española** chips, French fries; (de bolsa) crisps; **ni** ~ (fam) nothing at all; **no entendió ni** ~ he didn't understand a single word

paté [pa'te] nm pâté

patear [pate'ar] vt (pisar) to stamp on, trample (on); (pegar con el pie) to kick ▷ vi to stamp (with rage), stamp one's foot

patentar [paten'tar] vt to patent

patente [pa'tente] adj obvious, evident; (Com) patent ▷ nf patent

patera [pa'tera] nf boat

paternal [pater'nal] adj fatherly, paternal

paterno, -a [pa'terno, a] adj paternal

patético, -a [pa'tetiko, a] adj pathetic, moving

patilla [pa'tiʎa] nf (de gafas) sidepiece; **patillas** nfpl sideburns

patín [pa'tin] nm skate; (de tobogán) runner; ~ **de hielo** ice skate; ~ **de ruedas** roller skate

patinaje [pati'naxe] nm skating

patinar [pati'nar] vi to skate; (resbalarse) to skid, slip; (fam) to slip up, blunder

patines de ruedas nmpl rollerskates

patineta [pati'neta] nf (Am: patinete) scooter; (monopatín) skateboard

patinete [pati'nete] nm scooter

patio ['patjo] nm (de casa) patio, courtyard; ~ **de recreo** playground

pato ['pato] nm duck; **pagar el** ~ (fam) to take the blame, carry the can

patológico, -a [pato'loxiko, a] adj pathological

patoso, -a [pa'toso, a] adj awkward, clumsy

patotero [pato'tero] nm (Am) hooligan, lout

patraña [pa'traɲa] nf story, fib

patria ['patrja] nf native land, mother country; ~ **chica** home town

patrimonio [patri'monjo] nm inheritance; (fig) heritage; (Com) net worth

patriota [pa'trjota] nm/f patriot

patriótico, -a [pa'trjotiko, a] adj patriotic

patriotismo [patrjo'tismo] nm patriotism

patrocinador, a [patroθina'ðor, a] nm/f sponsor

patrocinar [patroθi'nar] vt to sponsor; (apoyar) to back, support

patrocinio [patro'θinjo] nm sponsorship; backing, support

patrón, -ona [pa'tron, ona] nm/f (jefe) boss, chief, master/mistress; (propietario) landlord(-lady); (Rel) patron saint ▷ nm (Costura) pattern; (Tec) standard; ~ **oro** gold standard

patronal [patro'nal] adj: **la clase** ~ management; **cierre** ~ lockout

patronato [patro'nato] nm sponsorship; (acto) patronage; (Com) employers' association; (fundación) trust; **el** ~ **de turismo** the tourist board

patrulla [pa'truʎa] nf patrol

pausa ['pausa] nf pause; (intervalo) break; (interrupción) interruption; (Tec: en videograbadora) hold; **con** ~ slowly

pausado, -a [pau'saðo, a] adj slow, deliberate

pauta ['pauta] nf line, guide line

pava ['paβa] nf (Am) kettle

pavimento [paβi'mento] nm (Arq) flooring; (de losa) pavement, paving

pavo ['paβo] nm turkey; (necio) silly thing, idiot; ~ **real** peacock; **¡no seas ~!** don't be silly!

pavor [pa'βor] nm dread, terror

payaso, -a [pa'jaso, a] nm/f clown

payo, -a [pa'jo, a] adj, nm/f non-gipsy

paz [paθ] nf peace; (tranquilidad) peacefulness, tranquillity; **dejar a algn en** ~ to leave sb alone o in peace; **hacer las paces** to make peace; (fig) to make up; **¡déjame en ~!** leave me alone!; **¡haya ~!** stop it!

PC nm abr (Pol: = Partido Comunista) CP ▷ nm PC, personal computer

P.D. abr (= posdata) P.S.

peaje [pe'axe] nm toll; **autopista de** ~ toll motorway, turnpike (US)

peatón [pea'ton] nm pedestrian; **paso de peatones** pedestrian crossing, crosswalk (US)

peatonal [peato'nal] adj pedestrian

peca ['peka] nf freckle

pecado [pe'kaðo] nm sin

pecador, a [peka'ðor, a] adj sinful ▷ nm/f sinner

pecaminoso, -a [pekami'noso, a] adj sinful

pecar [pe'kar] vi (Rel) to sin; (fig): ~ **de generoso** to be too generous

pecera [pe'θera] nf fish tank; (redonda) goldfish bowl

pecho ['petʃo] nm (Anat) chest; (de mujer) breast(s pl), bosom; (corazón) heart, breast; (valor) courage, spirit; **dar el** ~ **a** to breast-feed; **tomar algo a** ~ to take sth to heart; **no le cabía en el** ~ he was bursting with happiness

pechuga [pe'tʃuɣa] nf breast

pecoso, -a [pe'koso, a] adj freckled

peculiar [peku'ljar] *adj* special, peculiar; (*característica*) typical, characteristic

peculiaridad [pekuljari'ðað] *nf* peculiarity; special feature, characteristic

pedagogía [peðaɣo'ɣia] *nf* education

pedal [pe'ðal] *nm* pedal; ~ **de embrague** clutch (pedal); ~ **de freno** footbrake

pedalear [peðale'ar] *vi* to pedal

pédalo ['peðalo] *nm* pedalo, pedal boat

pedante [pe'ðante] *adj* pedantic ▷ *nm/f* pedant

pedantería [peðante'ria] *nf* pedantry

pedazo [pe'ðaθo] *nm* piece, bit; **hacerse ~s** to fall to pieces; (*romperse*) to smash, shatter; **un ~ de pan** a scrap of bread; (*fig*) a terribly nice person

pedernal [peðer'nal] *nm* flint

pedestal [peðes'tal] *nm* base; **tener/poner a algn en un ~** to put sb on a pedestal

pediatra [pe'ðjatra] *nm/f* paediatrician (*Brit*), pediatrician (*US*)

pedicuro, -a [peði'kuro, a] *nm/f* chiropodist (*Brit*), podiatrist (*US*)

pedido [pe'ðiðo] *nm* (*Com: mandado*) order; (*petición*) request; **~s en cartera** (*Com*) backlog *sg*

pedigrí [peði'ɣri] *nm* pedigree

pedir [pe'ðir] *vt* to ask for, request; (*comida, Com: mandar*) to order; (*exigir: precio*) to ask; (*necesitar*) to need, demand, require ▷ *vi* to ask; **~ prestado** to borrow; **~ disculpas** to apologize; **me pidió que cerrara la puerta** he asked me to shut the door; **¿cuánto piden por el coche?** how much are they asking for the car?

pedo ['peðo] (*fam*) *adj inv*: **estar ~** to be pissed (!) ▷ *nm* fart (!)

pedrada [pe'ðraða] *nf* throw of a stone; (*golpe*) blow from a stone; **herir a algn de una ~** to hit sb with a stone

pega ['peɣa] *nf* (*dificultad*) snag; **de ~** false, dud; **poner ~s** to raise objections

pegadizo, -a [peɣa'ðiθo, a] *adj* (*canción etc*) catchy

pegajoso, -a [peɣa'xoso, a] *adj* sticky, adhesive

pegamento [peɣa'mento] *nm* gum, glue

pegar [pe'ɣar] *vt* (*papel, sellos*) to stick (on); (*con cola*) to glue; (*cartel*) to post, stick up; (*coser*) to sew (on); (*unir: partes*) to join, fix together; (*Inform*) to paste; (*Med*) to give, infect with; (*dar: golpe*) to give, deal ▷ *vi* (*adherirse*) to stick, adhere; (*Inform*) to paste; (*ir juntos: colores*) to match, go together; (*golpear*) to hit; (*quemar: el sol*) to strike hot, burn; **pegarse** *vr* (*gen*) to stick; (*dos personas*) to hit each other, fight; **~le a algo** to be a great one for sth; **~ un grito** to let out a yell; **~ un salto** to jump (with fright); **~ fuego** to catch fire; **~ en** to touch; **~se un tiro** to shoot o.s.; **no pega** that doesn't seem right; **ese sombrero no pega con el abrigo** that

hat doesn't go with the coat

pegatina [peɣa'tina] *nf* (*Pol etc*) sticker

pego ['peɣo] *nm*: **dar el ~** (*pasar por verdadero*) to look like the real thing

pegote [pe'ɣote] *nm* (*fam*) eyesore, sight; (*fig*) patch, ugly mend; **tirarse ~s** (*fam*) to come on strong

peinado [pei'naðo] *nm* (*en peluquería*) hairdo; (*estilo*) hair style

peinar [pei'nar] *vt* to comb sb's hair; (*con un cierto estilo*) to style; **peinarse** *vr* to comb one's hair

peine ['peine] *nm* comb

peineta [pei'neta] *nf* ornamental comb

p.ej. *abr* (= *por ejemplo*) e.g.

Pekín [pe'kin] *n* Peking

pelado, -a [pe'laðo, a] *adj* (*cabeza*) shorn; (*fruta*) peeled; (*campo, tb fig*) bare; (*fam: sin dinero*) broke

pelaje [pe'laxe] *nm* (*Zool*) fur, coat; (*fig*) appearance

pelambre [pe'lambre] *nm* long hair, mop

pelar [pe'lar] *vt* (*fruta, patatas*) to peel; (*cortar el pelo a*) to cut the hair of; (*quitar la piel: animal*) to skin; (*ave*) to pluck; (*habas etc*) to shell; **pelarse** *vr* (*la piel*) to peel off; **voy a ~me** I'm going to get my hair cut; **corre que se las pela** (*fam*) he runs like nobody's business

peldaño [pel'daɲo] *nm* step; (*de escalera portátil*) rung

pelea [pe'lea] *nf* (*lucha*) fight; (*discusión*) quarrel, row

peleado, -a [pele'aðo, a] *adj*: **estar ~ (con algn)** to have fallen out (with sb)

pelear [pele'ar] *vi* to fight; **pelearse** *vr* to fight; (*reñir*) to fall out, quarrel

pelela [pe'lela] *nf* (*Am*) potty

peletería [pelete'ria] *nf* furrier's, fur shop

peliagudo, -a [pelja'ɣuðo, a] *adj* tricky

pelícano [pe'likano] *nm* pelican

película [pe'likula] *nf* (*Cine*) film, movie (*US*); (*cobertura ligera*) film, thin covering; (*Foto: rollo*) roll o reel of film; **~ de dibujos (animados)** cartoon film; **~ muda** silent film; **de ~** (*fam*) astonishing, out of this world

peligrar [peli'ɣrar] *vi* to be in danger

peligro [pe'liɣro] *nm* danger; (*riesgo*) risk; **"~ de muerte"** "danger"; **correr ~ de** to be in danger of, run the risk of; **con ~ de la vida** at the risk of one's life

peligroso, -a [peli'ɣroso, a] *adj* dangerous; risky

pelirrojo, -a [peli'rroxo, a] *adj* red-haired, red-headed ▷ *nm/f* redhead

pellejo [pe'ʎexo] *nm* (*de animal*) skin, hide; **salvar el ~** to save one's skin

pellizcar [peʎiθ'kar] *vt* to pinch, nip

pellizco [pe'ʎiθko] *nm* pinch

pelma ['pelma] *nm/f*, **pelmazo** [pel'maθo] *nm* (*fam*) pain (in the neck)

pelo ['pelo] nm (cabellos) hair; (de barba, bigote) whisker; (de animal: piel) fur, coat; (de perro etc) hair, coat; (de ave) down; (de tejido) nap; (Tec) fibre; **a ~** bareheaded; (desnudo) naked; **al ~** just right; **venir al ~** to be exactly what one needs; **un hombre de ~ en pecho** a brave man; **por los ~s** by the skin of one's teeth; **escaparse por un ~** to have a close shave; **se me pusieron los ~s de punta** my hair stood on end; **no tener ~s en la lengua** to be outspoken, not mince words; **con ~s y señales** in minute detail; **tomar el ~ a algn** to pull sb's leg

pelón, -ona [pe'lon, ona] adj hairless, bald

pelota [pe'lota] nf ball; (fam: cabeza) nut (fam); **en ~(s)** stark naked; **~ vasca** pelota; **devolver la ~ a algn** (fig) to turn the tables on sb; **hacer la ~ (a algn)** to creep (to sb)

pelotera [pelo'tera] nf (fam) barney

pelotón [pelo'ton] nm (Mil) squad, detachment

peluca [pe'luka] nf wig

peluche [pe'lutʃe] nm: **muñeco de ~** soft toy

peludo, -a [pe'luðo, a] adj hairy, shaggy

peluquería [peluke'ria] nf hairdresser's; (para hombres) barber's (shop)

peluquero, -a [pelu'kero, a] nm/f hairdresser; barber

pelusa [pe'lusa] nf (Bot) down; (Costura) fluff

pelvis ['pelβis] nf pelvis

pena ['pena] nf (congoja) grief, sadness; (remordimiento) regret; (dificultad) trouble; (dolor) pain; (Am: vergüenza) shame; (Jur) sentence; (Deporte) penalty; **~ capital** capital punishment; **~ de muerte** death penalty; **~ pecuniaria** fine; **merecer o valer la ~** to be worthwhile; **a duras ~s** with great difficulty; **so ~ de** on pain of; **me dan ~** I feel sorry for them; **¿no te da ~ hacerlo?** (Am) aren't you ashamed doing that?; **¡qué ~!** what a shame o pity!

penal [pe'nal] adj penal ▷ nm (cárcel) prison

penalidad [penali'ðað] nf (problema, dificultad) trouble, hardship; (Jur) penalty, punishment; **penalidades** nfpl trouble sg, hardship sg

penalizar [penali'θar] vt to penalize

penalti, penalty [pe'nalti] nm (Deporte) penalty

penalty [pe'nalti] (pl **penaltys** o **penalties**) nm penalty (kick)

penar [pe'nar] vt to penalize; (castigar) to punish ▷ vi to suffer

pendiente [pen'djente] adj pending, unsettled ▷ nm earring ▷ nf hill, slope; **tener una asignatura ~** to have to resit a subject

péndulo ['pendulo] nm pendulum

pene ['pene] nm penis

penetración [penetra'θjon] nf (acto) penetration; (agudeza) sharpness, insight

penetrante [pene'trante] adj (herida) deep; (persona, arma) sharp; (sonido) penetrating,

piercing; (mirada) searching; (viento, ironía) biting

penetrar [pene'trar] vt to penetrate, pierce; (entender) to grasp ▷ vi to penetrate, go in; (entrar) to enter; (líquido) to soak in; (emoción) to pierce

penicilina [peniθi'lina] nf penicillin

península [pe'ninsula] nf peninsula; **P~ Ibérica** Iberian Peninsula

peninsular [peninsu'lar] adj peninsular

penique [pe'nike] nm penny; **peniques** nmpl pence

penitencia [peni'tenθja] nf (remordimiento) penitence; (castigo) penance; **en ~** as a penance

penitenciaría [penitenθja'ria] nf prison, penitentiary

penitenciario, -a [peniten'θjarjo, a] adj prison cpd

penoso, -a [pe'noso, a] adj laborious, difficult; (lamentable) distressing

pensador, a [pensa'ðor, a] nm/f thinker

pensamiento [pensa'mjento] nm (gen) thought; (mente) mind; (idea) idea; (Bot) pansy; **no se le pasó por el ~** it never occurred to him

pensar [pen'sar] vt to think; (considerar) to think over, think out; (proponerse) to intend, plan, propose; (imaginarse) to think up, invent ▷ vi to think; **~ en** to think of o about; (anhelar) to aim at, aspire to; **dar que ~ a algn** to give sb food for thought

pensativo, -a [pensa'tiβo, a] adj thoughtful, pensive

pensión [pen'sjon] nf (casa) ≈ guest house; (dinero) pension; (cama y comida) board and lodging; **~ de jubilación** retirement pension; **~ escalada** graduated pension; **~ completa** full board; **media ~** half board

pensionista [pensjo'nista] nm/f (jubilado) (old-age) pensioner; (el que vive en una pensión) lodger; (Escol) boarder

penúltimo, -a [pe'nultimo, a] adj penultimate, second last

penumbra [pe'numbra] nf half-light, semi darkness

penuria [pe'nurja] nf shortage, want

peña ['peɲa] nf (roca) rock; (acantilado) cliff, crag; (grupo) group, circle; (Am: club) folk club; (Deporte) supporters' club

peñasco [pe'ɲasko] nm large rock, boulder

peñón [pe'ɲon] nm crag; **el P~** the Rock (of Gibraltar)

peón [pe'on] nm labourer; (Am) farm labourer, farmhand; (Tec) spindle, shaft; (Ajedrez) pawn

peonza [pe'onθa] nf spinning top

peor [pe'or] adj (comparativo) worse; (superlativo) worst ▷ adv worse; worst; **de mal en ~** from bad to worse; **tanto ~** so much the worse; **A es ~ que B** A is worse than B; **Z es el ~ de todos** Z is the worst of all

pepinillo [pepi'niʎo] *nm* gherkin

pepino [pe'pino] *nm* cucumber; **(no) me importa un ~** I don't care one bit

pepita [pe'pita] *nf* (*Bot*) pip; (*Minería*) nugget

pepito [pe'pito] *nm* (*Esp*: *tb*: **~ de ternera**) steak sandwich

pequeñez [peke'neθ] *nf* smallness, littleness; (*trivialidad*) trifle, triviality

pequeño, -a [pe'keɲo, a] *adj* small, little; (*cifra*) small, low; (*bajo*) short; **~ burgués** lower middle-class

pera ['pera] *adj inv* classy; **niño ~** spoiled upper-class brat ▷ *nf* pear; **eso es pedir ~s al olmo** that's asking the impossible

peral [pe'ral] *nm* pear tree

percance [per'kanθe] *nm* setback, misfortune

per cápita [per'kapita] *adj*: **renta ~** per capita income

percatarse [perka'tarse] *vr*: **~ de** to notice, take note of

percebe [per'θeβe] *nm* (*Zool*) barnacle; (*fam*) idiot

percepción [perθep'θjon] *nf* (*vista*) perception; (*idea*) notion, idea; (*Com*) collection

perceptible [perθep'tiβle] *adj* perceptible, noticeable; (*Com*) payable, receivable

percha ['pertʃa] *nf* (*poste*) pole, support; (*gancho*) peg; (*de abrigos*) coat stand; (*colgador*) coat hanger; (*ganchos*) coat hooks *pl*; (*de ave*) perch

percibir [perθi'βir] *vt* to perceive, notice; (*ver*) to see; (*peligro etc*) to sense; (*Com*) to earn, receive, get

percusión [perku'sjon] *nf* percussion

perdedor, a [perðe'ðor, a] *adj* losing ▷ *nm/f* loser

perder [per'ðer] *vt* to lose; (*tiempo, palabras*) to waste; (*oportunidad*) to lose, miss; (*tren*) to miss ▷ *vi* to lose; **perderse** *vr* (*extraviarse*) to get lost; (*desaparecer*) to disappear, be lost to view; (*arruinarse*) to be ruined; **echar a ~** (*comida*) to spoil, ruin; (*oportunidad*) to waste; **tener buen ~** to be a good loser; **¡no te lo pierdas!** don't miss it!; **he perdido la costumbre** I have got out of the habit

perdición [perði'θjon] *nf* perdition; (*fig*) ruin

pérdida ['perðiða] *nf* loss; (*de tiempo*) waste; (*Com*) net loss; **pérdidas** *nfpl* (*Com*) losses; **¡no tiene ~!** you can't go wrong!; **~ contable** (*Com*) book loss

perdido, -a [per'ðiðo, a] *adj* lost; **estar ~ por** to be crazy about; **es un caso ~** he is a hopeless case

perdigón [perði'ɣon] *nm* pellet

perdiz [per'ðiθ] *nf* partridge

perdón [per'ðon] *nm* (*disculpa*) pardon, forgiveness; (*clemencia*) mercy; **¡~!** sorry!, I beg your pardon!; **con ~** if I may, if you don't mind

perdonar [perðo'nar] *vt* to pardon, forgive; (*la vida*) to spare; (*excusar*) to exempt, excuse ▷ *vi* to pardon, forgive; **¡perdone (usted)!** sorry!, I beg your pardon!; **perdone, pero me parece que ...** excuse me, but I think ...

perdurable [perðu'raβle] *adj* lasting; (*eterno*) everlasting

perdurar [perðu'rar] *vi* (*resistir*) to last, endure; (*seguir existiendo*) to stand, still exist

perecedero, -a [pereθe'ðero, a] *adj* perishable

perecer [pere'θer] *vi* to perish, die

peregrinación [pereɣrina'θjon] *nf* (*Rel*) pilgrimage

peregrino, -a [pere'ɣrino, a] *adj* (*extraño*) strange; (*singular*) rare ▷ *nm/f* pilgrim

perejil [pere'xil] *nm* parsley

perenne [pe'renne] *adj* perennial

perentorio, -a [peren'torjo, a] *adj* (*urgente*) urgent; (*terminante*) peremptory; (*fijo*) set, fixed

pereza [pe'reθa] *nf* (*flojera*) laziness; (*lentitud*) sloth, slowness

perezoso, -a [pere'θoso, a] *adj* lazy; slow, sluggish

perfección [perfek'θjon] *nf* perfection; **a la ~** to perfection

perfeccionar [perfekθjo'nar] *vt* to perfect; (*mejorar*) to improve; (*acabar*) to complete, finish

perfectamente [perfekta'mente] *adv* perfectly

perfecto, -a [per'fekto, a] *adj* perfect ▷ *nm* (*Ling*) perfect (tense)

perfidia [per'fiðja] *nf* perfidy, treachery

perfil [per'fil] *nm* (*parte lateral*) profile; (*silueta*) silhouette, outline; (*Tec*) (cross) section; **perfiles** *nmpl* features; (*fig*) social graces; **~ del cliente** (*Com*) customer profile; **en ~** from the side, in profile

perfilado, -a [perfi'laðo, a] *adj* (*bien formado*) well-shaped; (*largo: cara*) long

perfilar [perfi'lar] *vt* (*trazar*) to outline; (*dar carácter a*) to shape, give character to; **perfilarse** *vr* to be silhouetted (*en* against); **el proyecto se va perfilando** the project is taking shape

perforación [perfora'θjon] *nf* perforation; (*con taladro*) drilling

perforadora [perfora'ðora] *nf* drill; (*tb*: **~ de fichas**) card-punch

perforar [perfo'rar] *vt* to perforate; (*agujero*) to drill, bore; (*papel*) to punch a hole in ▷ *vi* to drill, bore

perfume [per'fume] *nm* perfume, scent

perfumería [perfume'ria] *nf* perfume shop

pericia [pe'riθja] *nf* skill, expertise

periferia [peri'ferja] *nf* periphery; (*de ciudad*) outskirts *pl*

periférico, -a [peri'feriko, a] *adj* peripheral ▷ *nm* (*Inform*) peripheral; (*Am*: *Auto*) ring road (*Brit*), beltway (*US*); **barrio ~** outlying district

perilla [pe'riʎa] nf (barba) goatee; (Am: de puerta) doorknob, door handle

perímetro [pe'rimetro] nm perimeter

periódico, -a [pe'rjoðiko, a] adj periodic(al) ▷ nm (news)paper; **~ dominical** Sunday (news)paper

periodismo [perjo'ðismo] nm journalism

periodista [perjo'ðista] nm/f journalist

periodo [pe'rjoðo], **período** [pe'rioðo] nm period; **~ contable** (Com) accounting period

peripecias [peri'peθjas] nfpl adventures

periquito [peri'kito] nm budgerigar, budgie (fam)

perito, -a [pe'rito, a] adj (experto) expert; (diestro) skilled, skilful ▷ nm/f expert; skilled worker; (técnico) technician

perjudicar [perxuði'kar] vt (gen) to damage, harm; (fig) to prejudice

perjudicial [perxuði'θjal] adj damaging, harmful; (en detrimento) detrimental

perjuicio [per'xwiθjo] nm damage, harm; **en/sin ~ de** to the detriment of/without prejudice to

perjurar [perxu'rar] vi to commit perjury

perla ['perla] nf pearl; **me viene de ~s** it suits me fine

permanecer [permane'θer] vi (quedarse) to stay, remain; (seguir) to continue to be

permanencia [perma'nenθja] nf (duración) permanence; (estancia) stay

permanente [perma'nente] adj (que queda) permanent; (constante) constant; (comisión etc) standing ▷ nf perm; **hacerse una ~** to have one's hair permed

permisible [permi'siβle] adj permissible, allowable

permiso [per'miso] nm permission; (licencia) permit, licence (Brit), license (US); **con ~** excuse me; **estar de ~** (Mil) to be on leave; **~ de conducir o conductor** driving licence (Brit), driver's license (US); **~ de exportación/importación** export/import licence; **~ por asuntos familiares** compassionate leave; **~ por enfermedad** (Am) sick leave

permitir [permi'tir] vt to permit, allow; **permitirse** vr: **~se algo** to allow o.s. sth; **no me puedo ~ ese lujo** I can't afford that; **¿me permite?** may I?; **si lo permite el tiempo** weather permitting

pernera [per'nera] nf trouser leg

pernicioso, -a [perni'θjoso, a] adj (maligno, Med) pernicious; (persona) wicked

perno ['perno] nm bolt

pero ['pero] conj but; (aún) yet ▷ nm (defecto) flaw, defect; (reparo) objection; **¡no hay ~ que valga!** there are no buts about it

perol [pe'rol] nm, **perola** [pe'rola] nf pan

perpendicular [perpendiku'lar] adj perpendicular; **el camino es ~ al río** the road is at right angles to the river

perpetrar [perpe'trar] vt to perpetrate

perpetuar [perpe'twar] vt to perpetuate

perpetuo, -a [per'petwo, a] adj perpetual; (Jur etc: condena) life cpd

perplejo, -a [per'plexo, a] adj perplexed, bewildered

perra ['perra] nf (Zool) bitch; (fam: dinero) money; (: manía) mania, crazy idea; (: rabieta) tantrum; **estar sin una ~** to be flat broke

perrera [pe'rrera] nf kennel

perrito [pe'rrito] nm (tb: **~ caliente**) hot dog

perro ['perro] nm dog; **~ caliente** hot dog; **"~ peligroso"** "beware of the dog"; **ser ~ viejo** to be an old hand; **tiempo de ~s** filthy weather; **~ que ladra no muerde** his bark is worse than his bite

persa ['persa] adj, nm/f Persian ▷ nm (Ling) Persian

persecución [perseku'θjon] nf pursuit, hunt, chase; (Rel, Pol) persecution

perseguir [perse'ɣir] vt to pursue, hunt; (cortejar) to chase after; (molestar) to pester, annoy; (Rel, Pol) to persecute; (Jur) to prosecute

perseverante [perseβe'rante] adj persevering, persistent

perseverar [perseβe'rar] vi to persevere, persist; **~ en** to persevere in, persist with

persiana [per'sjana] nf (Venetian) blind

persignarse [persiɣ'narse] vr to cross o.s.

persistente [persis'tente] adj persistent

persistir [persis'tir] vi to persist

persona [per'sona] nf person; **10 ~s** 10 people; **~ mayor** elderly person; **tercera ~** third party; (Ling) third person; **en ~** in person o the flesh; **por ~** a head; **es buena ~** he's a good sort

personaje [perso'naxe] nm important person, celebrity; (Teat) character

personal [perso'nal] adj (particular) personal; (para una persona) single, for one person ▷ nm (plantilla) personnel, staff; (Naut) crew; (fam: gente) people

personalidad [personali'ðað] nf personality; (Jur) status

personalizar [personali'θar] vt to personalize ▷ vi (al hablar) to name names

personarse [perso'narse] vr to appear in person; **~ en** to present o.s. at, report to

personificar [personifi'kar] vt to personify

perspectiva [perspek'tiβa] nf perspective; (vista, panorama) view, panorama; (posibilidad futura) outlook, prospect; **tener algo en ~** to have sth in view

perspicacia [perspi'kaθja] nf discernment, perspicacity

perspicaz [perspi'kaθ] adj shrewd

persuadir [perswa'ðir] vt (gen) to persuade; (convencer) to convince; **persuadirse** vr to become convinced

persuasión [perswa'sjon] nf (acto) persuasion; (convicción) conviction

persuasivo, -a [perwa'siβo, a] adj persuasive; convincing

pertenecer [pertene'θer] *vi:* ~ **a** to belong to; *(fig)* to concern

perteneciente [pertene'θjente] *adj:* ~ **a** belonging to

pertenencia [perte'nenθja] *nf* ownership; **pertenencias** *nfpl* possessions, property *sg*

pertenezca *etc* [perte'neθka] *vb ver* **pertenecer**

pértiga ['pertiɣa] *nf* pole; **salto de** ~ pole vault

pertinaz [perti'naθ] *adj (persistente)* persistent; *(terco)* obstinate

pertinente [perti'nente] *adj* relevant, pertinent; *(apropiado)* appropriate; ~ **a** concerning, relevant to

perturbación [perturβa'θjon] *nf (Pol)* disturbance; *(Med)* upset, disturbance; ~ **del orden público** breach of the peace

perturbador, a [perturβa'ðor, a] *adj (que perturba)* perturbing, disturbing; *(subversivo)* subversive

perturbar [pertur'βar] *vt (el orden)* to disturb; *(Med)* to upset, disturb; *(mentalmente)* to perturb

Perú [pe'ru] *nm:* **el** ~ Peru

peruano, -a [pe'rwano, a] *adj, nm/f* Peruvian

perversión [perβer'sjon] *nf* perversion

perverso, -a [per'βerso, a] *adj* perverse; *(depravado)* depraved

pervertido, -a [perβer'tiðo, a] *adj* perverted ▷ *nm/f* pervert

pervertir [perβer'tir] *vt* to pervert, corrupt

pesa ['pesa] *nf* weight; *(Deporte)* shot

pesadez [pesa'ðeθ] *nf (calidad de pesado)* heaviness; *(lentitud)* slowness; *(aburrimiento)* tediousness; **es una** ~ **tener que ...** it's a bind having to ...

pesadilla [pesa'ðiʎa] *nf* nightmare, bad dream; *(fig)* worry, obsession

pesado, -a [pe'saðo, a] *adj (gen)* heavy; *(lento)* slow; *(difícil, duro)* tough, hard; *(aburrido)* tedious, boring; *(bochornoso)* sultry ▷ *nm/f* bore; **tener el estómago** ~ to feel bloated; **¡no seas ~!** come off it!

pesadumbre [pesa'ðumbre] *nf* grief, sorrow

pésame ['pesame] *nm* expression of condolence, message of sympathy; **dar el** ~ to express one's condolences

pesar [pe'sar] *vt* to weigh; *(fig)* to weigh heavily on; *(afligir)* to grieve ▷ *vi* to weigh; *(ser pesado)* to weigh a lot, be heavy; *(fig: opinión)* to carry weight ▷ *nm (sentimiento)* regret; *(pena)* grief, sorrow; **no pesa mucho** it's not very heavy; **a** ~ **de (que)** in spite of, despite; **no me pesa haberlo hecho** I'm not sorry I did it

pesca ['peska] *nf (acto)* fishing; *(cantidad de pescado)* catch; ~ **de altura/en bajura** deep sea/coastal fishing; **ir de** ~ to go fishing

pescadería [peskaðe'ria] *nf* fish shop, fishmonger's

pescadilla [peska'ðiʎa] *nf* whiting

pescado [pes'kaðo] *nm* fish

pescador, a [peska'ðor, a] *nm/f* fisherman(-woman)

pescar [pes'kar] *vt (coger)* to catch; *(tratar de coger)* to fish for; *(fam: lograr)* to get hold of, land; *(conseguir: trabajo)* to manage to get; *(sorprender)* to catch unawares ▷ *vi* to fish, go fishing

pescuezo [pes'kweθo] *nm* neck

pesebre [pe'seβre] *nm* manger

peseta [pe'seta] *nf* peseta

pesimismo [pesi'mismo] *nm* pessimism

pesimista [pesi'mista] *adj* pessimistic ▷ *nm/f* pessimist

pésimo, -a ['pesimo, a] *adj* awful, dreadful

peso ['peso] *nm* weight; *(balanza)* scales *pl*; *(Am Com)* monetary unit; *(moneda)* peso; *(Deporte)* shot; ~ **bruto/neto** gross/net weight; ~ **mosca/pesado** fly-/heavyweight; **de poco** ~ light(weight); **levantamiento de** ~**s** weightlifting; **vender a** ~ to sell by weight; **argumento de** ~ weighty argument; **eso cae de su** ~ that goes without saying

pesquero, -a [pes'kero, a] *adj* fishing *cpd*

pesquisa [pes'kisa] *nf* inquiry, investigation

pestaña [pes'taɲa] *nf (Anat)* eyelash; *(borde)* rim

pestañear [pestaɲe'ar] *vi* to blink

peste ['peste] *nf* plague; *(fig)* nuisance; *(mal olor)* stink, stench; ~ **negra** Black Death; **echar ~s** to swear, fume

pesticida [pesti'θiða] *nm* pesticide

pestilencia [pesti'lenθja] *nf (mal olor)* stink, stench

pestillo [pes'tiʎo] *nm* bolt, latch; *(cerrojo)* catch; *(picaporte)* (door) handle

petaca [pe'taka] *nf (de cigarrillos)* cigarette case; *(de pipa)* tobacco pouch; *(Am: maleta)* suitcase

pétalo ['petalo] *nm* petal

petanca [pe'tanka] *nf a game in which metal bowls are thrown at a target bowl*

petardo [pe'tarðo] *nm* firework, firecracker

petición [peti'θjon] *nf (pedido)* request, plea; *(memorial)* petition; *(Jur)* plea; **a** ~ **de** at the request of; ~ **de aumento de salarios** wage demand *o* claim

peto ['peto] *nm* dungarees *pl*, overalls *pl* (US); *(corpiño)* bodice; *(Taur)* horse's padding

petrificar [petrifi'kar] *vt* to petrify

petróleo [pe'troleo] *nm* oil, petroleum

petrolero, -a [petro'lero, a] *adj* petroleum *cpd* ▷ *nm (Com)* oil man; *(buque)* (oil) tanker

peyorativo, -a [pejora'tiβo, a] *adj* pejorative

pez [peθ] *nm* fish; ~ **de colores** goldfish; ~ **espada** swordfish; **estar como el** ~ **en el agua** to feel completely at home

pezón [pe'θon] *nm* teat, nipple

pezuña [pe'θuɲa] *nf* hoof

piadoso, -a [pja'ðoso, a] *adj (devoto)* pious, devout; *(misericordioso)* kind, merciful

pianista [pja'nista] nm/f pianist
piano ['pjano] nm piano; **~ de cola** grand piano
piar [pjar] vi to cheep
PIB nm abr (Esp Com: = Producto Interno Bruto) GDP
pibe, -a ['piβe, a] nm/f (Am) boy/girl, kid, child
picadero [pika'ðero] nm riding school
picadillo [pika'ðiʎo] nm mince, minced meat
picado, -a [pi'kaðo, a] adj pricked, punctured; (Culin) minced, chopped; (mar) choppy; (diente) bad; (tabaco) cut; (enfadado) cross
picador [pika'ðor] nm (Taur) picador; (minero) faceworker
picadora [pika'ðora] nf mincer
picadura [pika'ðura] nf (pinchazo) puncture; (de abeja) sting; (de mosquito) bite; (tabaco picado) cut tobacco
picana [pi'kana] (Am) nf (Agr) cattle prod; (Pol: para tortura) electric prod
picante [pi'kante] adj (comida, sabor) hot; (comentario) racy, spicy
picaporte [pika'porte] nm (tirador) handle; (pestillo) latch
picar [pi'kar] vt (agujerear, perforar) to prick, puncture; (billete) to punch, clip; (abeja) to sting; (mosquito, serpiente) to bite; (Culin) to mince, chop; (persona) to nibble (at); (incitar) to incite, goad; (dañar, irritar) to annoy, bother; (quemar: lengua) to burn, sting ▷ vi (pez) to bite, take the bait; (el sol) to burn, scorch; (abeja, Med) to sting; (mosquito) to bite; **picarse** vr (agriarse) to turn sour, go off; (mar) to get choppy; (ofenderse) to take offence; **me pican los ojos** my eyes sting; **me pica el brazo** my arm itches
picardía [pikar'ðia] nf villainy; (astucia) slyness, craftiness; (una picardía) dirty trick; (palabra) rude/bad word o expression
pícaro, -a ['pikaro, a] adj (malicioso) villainous; (travieso) mischievous ▷ nm (astuto) sly sort; (sinvergüenza) rascal, scoundrel
pichi ['pitʃi] nm (Esp) pinafore dress (Brit), jumper (US)
pichón, -ona [pi'tʃon, ona] nm/f (de paloma) young pigeon; (apelativo) darling, dearest
pico ['piko] nm (de ave) beak; (punta agudo) peak, sharp point; (Tec) pick, pickaxe; (Geo) peak, summit; (labia) talkativeness; **no abrir el ~** to keep quiet; **~ parásito** (Elec) spike; **y ~** and a bit; **las seis y ~** six and a bit; **son las tres y ~** it's just after three; **tiene 50 libros y ~** he has 50-odd books; **me costó un ~** it cost me quite a bit
picor [pi'kor] nm itch; (ardor) sting(ing feeling)
picoso, -a (Am) [pi'koso, a] adj (comida) hot
picotear [pikote'ar] vt to peck ▷ vi to nibble, pick
picudo, -a [pi'kuðo, a] adj pointed, with a point

pidió etc vb ver **pedir**
pido etc vb ver **pedir**
pie [pje] (pl **pies**) nm (gen, Mat) foot; (de cama, página, escalera) foot, bottom; (Teat) cue; (fig: motivo) motive, basis; (: fundamento) foothold; **~s planos** flat feet; **ir a ~** to go on foot, walk; **estar de ~** to be standing (up); **ponerse de ~** to stand up; **al ~ de la letra** (citar) literally, verbatim; (copiar) exactly, word for word; **de ~s a cabeza** from head to foot; **en ~ de guerra** on a war footing; **sin ~s ni cabeza** pointless, absurd; **dar ~ a** to give cause for; **hacer ~** (en el agua) to touch (the) bottom; **no dar ~ con bola** to be no good at anything; **saber de qué ~ cojea algn** to know sb's weak spots
piedad [pje'ðað] nf (lástima) pity, compassion; (clemencia) mercy; (devoción) piety, devotion; **tener ~ de** to take pity on
piedra ['pjeðra] nf stone; (roca) rock; (de mechero) flint; (Meteorología) hailstone; **primera ~** foundation stone; **~ de afilar** grindstone; **~ arenisca/caliza** sand-/limestone; **~ preciosa** precious stone
piel [pjel] nf (Anat) skin; (Zool) skin, hide; (de oso) fur; (cuero) leather; (Bot) skin, peel ▷ nm/f: **~ roja** redskin
pienso etc ['pjenso] vb ver **pensar** ▷ nm (Agr) feed
piercing ['pjersiŋ] nm piercing
pierdo etc ['pjerðo] vb ver **perder**
pierna ['pjerna] nf leg; **en ~s** bare-legged
pieza ['pjeθa] nf piece; (esp Am: habitación) room; (Mus) piece, composition; (Teat) work, play; **~ de recambio o repuesto** spare (part), extra (US); **~ de ropa** article of clothing; **quedarse de una ~** to be dumbfounded
pigmento [piɣ'mento] nm pigment
pigmeo, -a [piɣ'meo, a] adj, nm/f pigmy
pijama [pi'xama] nm pyjamas pl
pijo, -a ['pixo, a] nm/f (fam) upper-class twit
pila ['pila] nf (Elec) battery; (montón) heap, pile; (de fuente) sink; (Rel: tb: **~ bautismal**) font; **nombre de ~** Christian o first name; **tengo una ~ de cosas que hacer** (fam) I have heaps o stacks of things to do
pilar [pi'lar] nm pillar; (de puente) pier; (fig) prop, mainstay
píldora ['pildora] nf pill; **la ~ (anticonceptiva)** the pill; **tragarse la ~** to be taken in
pileta [pi'leta] nf basin, bowl; (Am: de cocina) sink; (: piscina) swimming pool
pillaje [pi'ʎaxe] nm pillage, plunder
pillar [pi'ʎar] vt (saquear) to pillage, plunder; (fam: coger) to catch; (: agarrar) to grasp, seize; (: entender) to grasp, catch on to; (suj: coche etc) to run over; **pillarse** vr: **~se un dedo con la puerta** to catch one's finger in the door; **~ un resfriado** (fam) to catch a cold
pillo, -a ['piʎo, a] adj villainous; (astuto) sly, crafty ▷ nm/f rascal, rogue, scoundrel

pilotar [pilo'tar] vt (avión) to pilot; (barco) to steer

piloto [pi'loto] nm pilot; (de aparato) (pilot) light; (Auto) rear light, tail light; (conductor) driver ▷ adj inv: **planta ~** pilot plant; **luz ~** side light; **~ automático** automatic pilot

pimentón [pimen'ton] nm (polvo) paprika

pimienta [pi'mjenta] nf pepper

pimiento [pi'mjento] nm pepper, pimiento

pin (pl **pins**) [pin, pins] nm badge

pinacoteca [pinako'teka] nf art gallery

pinar [pi'nar] nm pinewood

pincel [pin'θel] nm paintbrush

pinchadiscos [pintʃa'diskos] nm/f inv disc jockey, DJ

pinchar [pin'tʃar] vt (perforar) to prick, pierce; (neumático) to puncture; (incitar) to prod; (Inform) to click ▷ vi (Mus fam) to be DJ; **pincharse** vr (con droga) to inject o.s.; (neumático) to burst, puncture; **no ~ ni cortar** (fam) to cut no ice; **tener un neumático pinchado** to have a puncture o a flat tyre

pinchazo [pin'tʃaθo] nm (perforación) prick; (de llanta) puncture, flat (US); (fig) prod

pincho ['pintʃo] nm point; (aguijón) spike; (Culin) savoury (snack); **~ moruno** shish kebab; **~ de tortilla** small slice of omelette

ping-pong ['pimpon] nm table tennis

pingüino [pin'gwino] nm penguin

pinitos [pi'nitos] nmpl: **hacer sus primeros ~** to take one's first steps

pino ['pino] nm pine (tree); **vivir en el quinto ~** to live at the back of beyond

pinta ['pinta] nf spot; (gota) spot, drop; (aspecto) appearance, look(s) pl; (medida) pint; **tener buena ~** to look good, look well; **por la ~** by the look of it

pintado, -a [pin'taðo, a] adj spotted; (de muchos colores) colourful ▷ nf piece of political graffiti; **pintados** nfpl political graffiti sg; **me sienta que ni ~, me viene que ni ~** it suits me a treat

pintalabios [pinta'laβjos] nm inv (Esp) lipstick

pintar [pin'tar] vt to paint ▷ vi to paint; (fam) to count, be important; **pintarse** vr to put on make-up; **pintárselas solo para hacer algo** to manage to do sth by o.s.; **no pinta nada** (fam) he has no say

pintor, a [pin'tor, a] nm/f painter; **~ de brocha gorda** house painter; (fig) bad painter

pintoresco, -a [pinto'resko, a] adj picturesque

pintura [pin'tura] nf painting; **~ a la acuarela** watercolour; **~ al óleo** oil painting; **~ rupestre** cave painting

pinza ['pinθa] nf (Zool) claw; (para colgar ropa) clothes peg, clothespin (US); (Tec) pincers pl; **pinzas** nfpl (para depilar) tweezers

piña ['piɲa] nf (fruto del pino) pine cone; (fruta) pineapple; (fig) group

piñata [pi'ɲata] nf piñata (figurine hung up at parties to be beaten with sticks until sweets or presents fall out)

piñón [pi'ɲon] nm (Bot) pine nut; (Tec) pinion

pío, -a ['pio, a] adj (devoto) pious, devout; (misericordioso) merciful ▷ nm: **no decir ni ~** not to breathe a word

piojo ['pjoxo] nm louse

pionero, -a [pjo'nero, a] adj pioneering ▷ nm/f pioneer

pipa ['pipa] nf pipe; (Bot) seed, pip; (de girasol) sunflower seed

pipí [pi'pi] nm (fam): **hacer ~** to have a wee(-wee)

pique etc ['pike] vb ver **picar** ▷ nm (resentimiento) pique, resentment; (rivalidad) rivalry, competition; **irse a ~** to sink; (familia) to be ruined; **tener un ~ con algn** to have a grudge against sb

piqueta [pi'keta] nf pick(axe)

piquete [pi'kete] nm (agujerito) small hole; (Mil) squad, party; (de obreros) picket; (Am: de insecto) bite; **~ secundario** secondary picket

pirado, -a [pi'raðo, a] adj (fam) round the bend ▷ nm/f nutter

piragua [pi'raɣwa] nf canoe

piragüismo [pira'ɣwismo] nm (Deporte) canoeing

pirámide [pi'ramiðe] nf pyramid

piraña [pi'raɲa] nf piranha

pirarse [pi'rarse] vr: **~(las)** (largarse) to beat it (fam); (Escol) to cut class

pirata [pi'rata] adj: **edición/disco ~** pirate edition/bootleg record ▷ nm pirate; (tb: **~ informático**) hacker

Pirineo, Pirineos [piri'neo(s)] nm(pl) Pyrenees pl

pirómano, -a [pi'romano, a] nm/f (Psico) pyromaniac; (Jur) arsonist

piropo [pi'ropo] nm compliment, (piece of) flattery; **echar ~s a** to make flirtatious remarks to

pirueta [pi'rweta] nf pirouette

piruleta [piru'leta] nf lollipop

pis [pis] nm (fam) pee; **hacer ~** to have a pee; (para niños) to wee-wee

pisada [pi'saða] nf (paso) footstep; (huella) footprint

pisar [pi'sar] vt (caminar sobre) to walk on, tread on; (apretar con el pie) to press; (fig) to trample on, walk all over ▷ vi to tread, step, walk; **~ el acelerador** to step on the accelerator; **~ fuerte** (fig) to act determinedly

piscifactoría [pisθifakto'ria] nf fish farm

piscina [pis'θina] nf swimming pool

Piscis ['pisθis] nm (Astro) Pisces

piso ['piso] nm (suelo: de edificio) floor; (Am) ground; (apartamento) flat, apartment; **primer ~** (Esp) first o second (US) floor; (Am) ground o first (US) floor

pisotear [pisote'ar] vt to trample (on o underfoot); (fig: humillar) to trample on

pisotón [piso'ton] *nm* (*con el pie*) stamp

pista ['pista] *nf* track, trail; (*indicio*) clue; (*Inform*) track; ~ **de auditoría** (*Com*) audit trail; ~ **de aterrizaje** runway; ~ **de baile** dance floor; ~ **de tenis** tennis court; ~ **de hielo** ice rink; **estar sobre la ~ de algn** to be on sb's trail

pisto ['pisto] *nm* (*Culin*) ratatouille; **darse ~** (*fam*) to show off

pistola [pis'tola] *nf* pistol; (*Tec*) spray-gun

pistolero, -a [pisto'lero, a] *nm/f* gunman, gangster ▷ *nf* holster

pistón [pis'ton] *nm* (*Tec*) piston; (*Mus*) key

pitar [pi'tar] *vt* (*hacer sonar*) to blow; (*partido*) to referee; (*rechiflar*) to whistle at, boo; (*actor, obra*) to hiss ▷ *vi* to whistle; (*Auto*) to sound o toot one's horn; (*Am*) to smoke; **salir pitando** to beat it

pitido [pi'tiðo] *nm* whistle; (*sonido agudo*) beep; (*sonido corto*) pip

pitillera [piti'ʎera] *nf* cigarette case

pitillo [pi'tiʎo] *nm* cigarette

pito ['pito] *nm* whistle; (*de coche*) horn; (*cigarrillo*) cigarette; (*fam: de marihuana*) joint; (*fam!*) prick (!); **me importa un ~** I don't care two hoots

pitón [pi'ton] *nm* (*Zool*) python

pitonisa [pito'nisa] *nf* fortune-teller

pitorreo [pito'rreo] *nm* joke, laugh; **estar de ~** to be in a joking mood

píxel ['piksel] *nm* (*Inform*) pixel

piyama [pi'jama] *nm* (*Am*) pyjamas *pl*, pajamas (*US*) *pl*

pizarra [pi'θarra] *nf* (*piedra*) slate; (*encerado*) blackboard; ~ **blanca** whiteboard; ~ **interactiva** interactive whiteboard

pizarrón [piθa'rron] *nm* (*Am*) blackboard

pizca ['piθka] *nf* pinch, spot; (*fig*) spot, speck, trace; **ni ~** not a bit

pizza ['pitsa] *nf* pizza

placa ['plaka] *nf* plate; (*Med*) dental plate; (*distintivo*) badge; ~ **de matrícula** number plate; ~ **madre** (*Inform*) mother board

placaje [pla'kaxe] *nm* tackle

placard [pla'kar] *nm* (*Am*) built-in cupboard, (*clothes*) closet (*US*)

placenta [pla'θenta] *nf* placenta; (*tras el parto*) afterbirth

placentero, -a [plaθen'tero, a] *adj* pleasant, agreeable

placer [pla'θer] *nm* pleasure ▷ *vt* to please; **a ~** at one's pleasure

plácido, -a ['plaθiðo, a] *adj* placid

plaga ['plaɣa] *nf* (*Zool*) pest; (*Med*) plague; (*fig*) swarm; abundance

plagar [pla'ɣar] *vt* to infest, plague; (*llenar*) to fill; **plagado de** riddled with; **han plagado la ciudad de carteles** they have plastered the town with posters

plagiar [pla'gjar] *vt* to plagiarize; (*Am*) to kidnap

plagio ['plaxjo] *nm* plagiarism; (*Am*) kidnap

plan [plan] *nm* (*esquema, proyecto*) plan; (*idea, intento*) idea, intention; (*de curso*) programme; ~ **cotizable de jubilación** contributory pension scheme; ~ **de estudios** curriculum, syllabus; ~ **de incentivos** (*Com*) incentive scheme; **tener** ~ (*fam*) to have a date; **tener un** ~ (*fam*) to have an affair; **en ~ de cachondeo** for a laugh; **en ~ económico** (*fam*) on the cheap; **vamos en ~ de turismo** we're going as tourists; **si te pones en ese ~** ... if that's your attitude ...

plana ['plana] *nf ver* **plano**

plancha ['plantʃa] *nf* (*para planchar*) iron; (*rótulo*) plate, sheet; (*Naut*) gangway; (*Culin*) grill; **pescado a la** ~ grilled fish; ~ **de pelo** straighteners; **a la** ~ (*Culin*) grilled

planchado, -a [plan'tʃaðo, a] *adj* (*ropa*) ironed; (*traje*) pressed ▷ *nm* ironing

planchar [plan'tʃar] *vt* to iron ▷ *vi* to do the ironing

planeador [planea'ðor] *nm* glider

planear [plane'ar] *vt* to plan ▷ *vi* to glide

planeta [pla'neta] *nm* planet

planicie [pla'niθje] *nf* plain

planificación [planifika'θjon] *nf* planning; ~ **corporativa** (*Com*) corporate planning; ~ **familiar** family planning; **diagrama de** ~ (*Com*) planner

plano, -a ['plano, a] *adj* flat, level, even; (*liso*) smooth ▷ *nm* (*Mat, Tec, Aviat*) plane; (*Foto*) shot; (*Arq*) plan; (*Geo*) map; (*de ciudad*) map, street plan ▷ *nf* sheet of paper, page; (*Tec*) trowel; **primer** ~ close-up; **caer de** ~ to fall flat; **rechazar algo de** ~ to turn sth down flat; **le daba el sol de** ~ (*fig*) the sun shone directly on it; **en primera plana** on the front page; **plana mayor** staff

planta ['planta] *nf* (*Bot, Tec*) plant; (*Anat*) sole of the foot, foot; (*piso*) floor; (*Am: personal*) staff; ~ **baja** ground floor

plantación [planta'θjon] *nf* (*Agr*) plantation; (*acto*) planting

plantar [plan'tar] *vt* (*Bot*) to plant; (*puesto*) to put in; (*levantar*) to erect, set up; **plantarse** *vr* to stand firm; ~ **a algn en la calle** to chuck sb out; **dejar plantado a algn** (*fam*) to stand sb up; ~**se en** to reach, get to

plantear [plante'ar] *vt* (*problema*) to pose; (*dificultad*) to raise; **se lo** ~**é** I'll put it to him

plantilla [plan'tiʎa] *nf* (*de zapato*) insole; (*personal*) personnel; **ser de** ~ to be on the staff

plantón [plan'ton] *nm* (*Mil*) guard, sentry; (*fam*) long wait; **dar (un)** ~ **a algn** to stand sb up

plañir [pla'ɲir] *vi* to mourn

plasma ['plasma] *nm* plasma

plasta ['plasta] *nm/f* (*Esp: fam*) bore ▷ *nf* soft mass, lump; (*desastre*) botch, mess ▷ *adj* (*Esp: fam*) boring

plástico, -a ['plastiko, a] *adj* plastic ▷ *nf* (art of) sculpture, modelling ▷ *nm* plastic

P

Plastilina® [plasti'lina] *nf* Plasticine®

plata ['plata] *nf* (*metal*) silver; (*cosas hechas de plata*) silverware; (*Am*) cash, dough (*fam*); **hablar en ~** to speak bluntly o frankly

plataforma [plata'forma] *nf* platform; **~ de lanzamiento/perforación** launch(ing) pad/ drilling rig

plátano ['platano] *nm* (*fruta*) banana; (*árbol*) plane tree; banana tree

platea [pla'tea] *nf* (*Teat*) pit

plateado, -a [plate'aðo, a] *adj* silver; (*Tec*) silver-plated

plática [platika] *nf* (*Am*) talk, chat; (*Rel*) sermon

platicar [plati'kar] *vi* (*Am*) to talk, chat

platillo [pla'tiʎo] *nm* saucer; (*de limosnas*) collecting bowl; **platillos** *nmpl* cymbals; **~ volador** o **volante** flying saucer; **pasar el ~** to pass the hat round

platina [pla'tina] *nf* (*Mus*) tape deck

platino [pla'tino] *nm* platinum; **platinos** *nmpl* (*Auto*) (contact) points

plato ['plato] *nm* plate, dish; (*parte de comida*) course; (*guiso*) dish; **~ frutero/sopero** fruit/ soup dish; **primer ~** first course; **~ combinado** set main course (*served on one plate*); **~ fuerte** main course; **pagar los ~s rotos** to carry the can (*fam*)

plató [pla'to] *nm* set

platónico, -a [pla'toniko, a] *adj* platonic

playa ['plaja] *nf* beach; (*costa*) seaside; **~ de estacionamiento** (*Am*) car park

playero, -a [pla'jero, a] *adj* beach *cpd* ▷ *nf* (*Am: camiseta*) T-shirt; **playeras** *nfpl* canvas shoes; (*Tenis*) tennis shoes

plaza ['plaθa] *nf* square; (*mercado*) market(place); (*sitio*) room, space; (*en vehículo*) seat, place; (*colocación*) post, job; **~ de abastos** food market; **~ mayor** main square; **~ de toros** bullring; **hacer la ~** to do the daily shopping; **reservar una ~** to reserve a seat; **el hotel tiene 100 ~s** the hotel has 100 beds

plazo ['plaθo] *nm* (*lapso de tiempo*) time, period, term; (*fecha de vencimiento*) expiry date; (*pago parcial*) instalment; **a corto/largo ~** short-/ long-term; **comprar a ~s** to buy on hire purchase, pay for in instalments; **nos dan un ~ de ocho días** they allow us a week

plazoleta [plaθo'leta], **plazuela** [pla'θwela] *nf* small square

pleamar [plea'mar] *nf* high tide

plebe ['pleβe] *nf*: **la ~** the common people *pl*, the masses *pl*; (*pey*) the plebs *pl*

plebeyo, -a [ple'βejo, a] *adj* plebeian; (*pey*) coarse, common

plebiscito [pleβis'θito] *nm* plebiscite

plegable [ple'ɣaβle] *adj* pliable; (*silla*) folding

plegar [ple'ɣar] *vt* (*doblar*) to fold, bend; (*Costura*) to pleat; **plegarse** *vr* to yield, submit

pleito ['pleito] *nm* (*Jur*) lawsuit, case; (*fig*) dispute, feud; **pleitos** *nmpl* litigation *sg*;

entablar ~ to bring an action o a lawsuit; **poner ~** to sue

plenilunio [pleni'lunjo] *nm* full moon

plenitud [pleni'tuð] *nf* plenitude, fullness; (*abundancia*) abundance

pleno, -a ['pleno, a] *adj* full; (*completo*) complete ▷ *nm* plenum; **en ~** as a whole; (*por unanimidad*) unanimously; **en ~ día** in broad daylight; **en ~ verano** at the height of summer; **en plena cara** full in the face

pletina *nf* (*Mus*) tape deck

pliego ['pljeɣo] *vb ver* **plegar** ▷ *nm* (*hoja*) sheet (of paper); (*carta*) sealed letter/document; **~ de condiciones** details *pl*, specifications *pl*

pliegue ['pljeɣe] *vb ver* **plegar** ▷ *nm* fold, crease; (*de vestido*) pleat

plisado [pli'saðo] *nm* pleating

plomería [plome'ria] *nf* (*Am*) plumbing

plomero [plo'mero] *nm* (*Am*) plumber

plomo ['plomo] *nm* (*metal*) lead; (*Elec*) fuse; **sin ~** unleaded; **caer a ~** to fall heavily o flat

pluma ['pluma] *nf* (*Zool*) feather; (*para escribir*): **~ (estilográfica)** ink pen; **~ fuente** (*Am*) fountain pen

plumero [plu'mero] *nm* (*quitapolvos*) feather duster; **ya te veo el ~** I know what you're up to

plumón [plu'mon] *nm* (*de ave*) down; (*Am*) felt-tip pen

plural [plu'ral] *adj* plural ▷ *nm*: **en ~** in the plural

pluralidad [plurali'ðað] *nf* plurality; **una ~ de votos** a majority of votes

pluriempleo [pluriem'pleo] *nm* having more than one job

plus [plus] *nm* bonus

plusvalía [plusβa'lia] *nf* (*mayor valor*) appreciation, added value; (*Com*) goodwill

plutocracia [pluto'kraθja] *nf* plutocracy

PNB *nm abr* (*Esp Com*: = Producto Nacional Bruto) GNP

población [poβla'θjon] *nf* population; (*pueblo, ciudad*) town, city; **~ activa** working population

poblado, -a [po'βlaðo, a] *adj* inhabited; (*barba*) thick; (*cejas*) bushy ▷ *nm* (*aldea*) village; (*pueblo*) (small) town; **~ de** (*lleno de*) filled with; **densamente ~** densely populated

poblador, a [poβla'ðor, a] *nm/f* settler, colonist

poblar [po'βlar] *vt* (*colonizar*) to colonize; (*fundar*) to found; (*habitar*) to inhabit; **poblarse** *vr*: **~se de** to fill up with; (*irse cubriendo*) to become covered with

pobre ['poβre] *adj* poor ▷ *nm/f* poor person; (*mendigo*) beggar; **los ~s** the poor; **¡~!** poor thing!; **~ diablo** (*fig*) poor wretch o devil

pobreza [po'βreθa] *nf* poverty; **~ energética** fuel poverty

pocilga [po'θilɣa] *nf* pigsty

pocillo [po'siʎo] *nm* (*Am*) coffee cup

pócima ['poθima], **poción** [po'θjon] *nf* potion; (*brebaje*) concoction, nasty drink

○ **PALABRA CLAVE**

poco, -a ['poko, a] *adj* 1(*sg*) little, not much; **poco tiempo** little *o* not much time; **de poco interés** of little interest, not very interesting; **poca cosa** not much
2(*pl*) few, not many; **unos pocos** a few, some; **pocos niños comen lo que les conviene** few children eat what they should
▷ *adv* 1little, not much; **cuesta poco** it doesn't cost much; **poco más o menos** more or less
2(+ *adj: negativo, antónimo*): **poco amable/inteligente** not very nice/intelligent
3: **por poco me caigo** I almost fell
4(*tiempo*): **poco después** soon after that; **dentro de poco** shortly; **hace poco** a short time ago, not long ago; **a poco de haberse casado** shortly after getting married
5: **poco a poco** little by little
6(*Am*): **¿a poco no está divino?** isn't it just divine?; **de a poco** gradually
▷ *nm* a little, a bit; **un poco triste/de dinero** a little sad/money

podar [po'ðar] *vt* to prune
podcast ['poðkast] *nm* podcast
podcastear [poðkaste'ar] *vi* to podcast
poder [po'ðer] *vi* 1(*capacidad*), can, be able to; **no puedo hacerlo** I can't do it, I'm unable to do it
2(*permiso*) can, may, be allowed to; **¿se puede?** may I (*o* we)?; **puedes irte ahora** you may go now; **no se puede fumar en este hospital** smoking is not allowed in this hospital
3(*posibilidad*) may, might, could; **puede llegar mañana** he may *o* might arrive tomorrow; **pudiste haberte hecho daño** you might *o* could have hurt yourself; **¡podías habérmelo dicho antes!** you might have told me before!
4: **puede (ser)** perhaps; **puede que lo sepa Tomás** Tomás may *o* might know
5: **¡no puedo más!** I've had enough!; **no pude menos que dejarlo** I couldn't help but leave it; **es tonto a más no ~** he's as stupid as they come
6: **~ con**: **no puedo con este crío** this kid's too much for me; **¿puedes con eso?** can you manage that?
7: **él me puede** (*fam*) he's stronger than me
▷ *nm* power; **el ~** the Government; **~ adquisitivo** purchasing power; **detentar** *u* **ocupar** *o* **estar en el ~** to be in power *o* office; **estar** *u* **obrar en ~ de** to be in the hands *o* possession of; **por ~(es)** by proxy; **~ judicial** judiciary

poderoso, -a [poðe'roso, a] *adj* powerful
podio ['poðjo] *nm* podium
podium ['poðjum] = **podio**
podólogo, -a [po'ðoloɣo, a] *nm/f* chiropodist (*Brit*), podiatrist (*US*)
podrido, -a [po'ðriðo, a] *adj* rotten, bad; (*fig*) rotten, corrupt
podrir [po'ðrir] = **pudrir**
poema [po'ema] *nm* poem
poesía [poe'sia] *nf* poetry
poeta [po'eta] *nm* poet
poético, -a [po'etiko, a] *adj* poetic(al)
poetisa [poe'tisa] *nf* (woman) poet
póker ['poker] *nm* poker
polaco, -a [po'lako, a] *adj* Polish ▷ *nm/f* Pole ▷ *nm* (*Ling*) Polish
polar [po'lar] *adj* polar
polaridad [polari'ðað] *nf* polarity
polea [po'lea] *nf* pulley
polémica [po'lemika] *nf* polemics *sg*; (*una polémica*) controversy
polémico, -a [po'lemiko, a] *adj* polemic(al)
polen ['polen] *nm* pollen
poleo [po'leo] *nm* pennyroyal
policía [poli'θia] *nm/f* policeman(-woman) ▷ *nf* police; *see note*

○ **POLICÍA**

There are two branches of the police, both armed: the *policía nacional*, in charge of national security and public order in general, and the *policía municipal*, with duties of regulating traffic and policing the local community. Catalonia and the Basque Country have their own police forces, the *Mossos d'Esquadra* and the *Ertzaintza* respectively.

policíaco, -a [poli'θiako, a] *adj* police *cpd*; **novela policíaca** detective story
policial [poli'θjal] *adj* police *cpd*
polideportivo [poliðepor'tiβo] *nm* sports centre
poliéster [poli'ester] *nm* polyester
polietileno [policti'leno] *nm* polythene (*Brit*), polyethylene (*US*)
poligamia [poli'ɣamja] *nf* polygamy
polígono [po'liɣono] *nm* (*Mat*) polygon; (*solar*) building lot; (*zona*) area; (*unidad vecina*) housing estate; **~ industrial** industrial estate
polígrafo [po'liɣrafo] *nm* polygraph
polilla [po'liʎa] *nf* moth
polio ['poljo] *nf* polio
politécnico [poli'tekniko] *nm* polytechnic
político, -a [po'litiko, a] *adj* political; (*discreto*) tactful; (*pariente*) in-law ▷ *nm/f* politician ▷ *nf* politics *sg*; (*económica, agraria*) policy; **padre ~** father-in-law; **política exterior/de ingresos y precios** foreign/prices and incomes policy

P

póliza | 228

póliza ['poliθa] nf certificate, voucher; (impuesto) tax o fiscal stamp; ~ **de seguro(s)** insurance policy

polizón [poli'θon] nm (Aviat, Naut) stowaway

pollera [po'ʎera] nf (criadero) hencoop; (Am) skirt, overskirt

pollería [poʎe'ria] nf poulterer's (shop)

pollo ['poʎo] nm chicken; (joven) young man; (señorito) playboy; ~ **asado** roast chicken

polo ['polo] nm (Geo, Elec) pole; (helado) ice lolly (Brit), Popsicle® (US); (Deporte) polo; (suéter) polo-neck; **P~ Norte/Sur** North/South Pole; **esto es el ~ opuesto de lo que dijo antes** this is the exact opposite of what he said before

Polonia [po'lonja] nf Poland

poltrona [pol'trona] nf reclining chair, easy chair

polución [polu'θjon] nf pollution; ~ **ambiental** environmental pollution

polvera [pol'βera] nf powder compact

polvo ['polβo] nm dust; (Química, Culin, Med) powder; (fam!) screw (!); **polvos** nmpl (maquillaje) powder sg; **en ~** powdered; ~ **de talco** talcum powder; **estar hecho ~** to be worn out o exhausted; **hacer algo ~** to smash sth; **hacer ~ a algn** to shatter sb; ver tb **polvos**

pólvora ['polβora] nf gunpowder; (fuegos artificiales) fireworks pl; **propagarse como la ~** (noticia) to spread like wildfire

polvoriento, -a [polβo'rjento, a] adj (superficie) dusty; (sustancia) powdery

pomada [po'maða] nf cream

pomelo [po'melo] nm grapefruit

pómez ['pomeθ] nf: **piedra ~** pumice stone

pomo ['pomo] nm knob, handle

pompa ['pompa] nf (burbuja) bubble; (bomba) pump; (esplendor) pomp, splendour; ~**s fúnebres** funeral sg

pomposo, -a [pom'poso, a] adj splendid, magnificent; (pey) pompous

pómulo ['pomulo] nm cheekbone

pon [pon] vb ver **poner**

ponchadura [pontʃa'dura] nf (Am) puncture (Brit), flat (US)

ponchar [pon'tʃar] vt (Am: llanta) to puncture

ponche ['pontʃe] nm punch

poncho ['pontʃo] nm (Am) poncho, cape

ponderar [ponde'rar] vt (considerar) to weigh up, consider; (elogiar) to praise highly, speak in praise of

pondré etc [pon'dre] vb ver **poner**

⭕ PALABRA CLAVE

poner [po'ner] vt 1 to put; (colocar) to place, set; (ropa) to put on; (problema, la mesa) to set; (interés) to show; (telegrama) to send; (obra de teatro) to put on; (película) to show; **ponlo más alto** turn it up; **¿qué ponen en el**

Excelsior? what's on at the Excelsior?; **poner algo a secar** to put sth (out) to dry; **¡no pongas esa cara!** don't look at me like that!

2 (tienda) to open; (instalar: gas etc) to put in; (radio, TV) to switch o turn on

3 (suponer): **pongamos que ...** let's suppose that ...

4 (contribuir): **el gobierno ha puesto otro millón** the government has contributed another million

5 (Telec): **póngame con el Sr. López** can you put me through to Mr. López?

6: **poner de: le han puesto de director general** they've appointed him general manager

7 (+ adj) to make; **me estás poniendo nerviosa** you're making me nervous

8 (dar nombre): **al hijo le pusieron Diego** they called their son Diego

9 (estar escrito) to say; **¿qué pone aquí?** what does it say here?

▷ vi (gallina) to lay

ponerse vr 1 (colocarse): **se puso a mi lado** he came and stood beside me; **tú ponte en esa silla** you go and sit on that chair; **ponerse en camino** to set off

2 (vestido, cosméticos) to put on; **¿por qué no te pones el vestido nuevo?** why don't you put on o wear your new dress?

3 (sol) to set

4 (+ adj) to get, become; to turn; **ponerse enfermo/gordo/triste** to get ill/fat/sad; **se puso muy serio** he got very serious; **después de lavarla la tela se puso azul** after washing it the material turned blue; **¡no te pongas así!** don't be like that!; **ponerse cómodo** to make o.s. comfortable

5: **ponerse a, se puso a llorar** he started to cry; **tienes que ponerte a estudiar** you must get down to studying; **ponerse a bien con algn** to make it up with sb; **ponerse a mal con algn** to get on the wrong side of sb

6 (Am): **se me pone que ...** it seems to me that ..., I think that ...

pongo etc ['pongo] vb ver **poner**

poniente [po'njente] nm west; (viento) west wind

pontificado [pontifi'kaðo] nm papacy, pontificate

pontífice [pon'tifiθe] nm pope, pontiff; **el Sumo P~** His Holiness the Pope

pontón [pon'ton] nm pontoon

ponzoña [pon'θoɲa] nf poison, venom

pop [pop] adj inv, nm (Mus) pop

popa ['popa] nf stern; **a ~** astern, abaft; **de ~ a proa** fore and aft

popote [po'pote] nm (Am) straw

popular [popu'lar] adj popular; (del pueblo) of the people

popularidad [populari'ðað] nf popularity

○ PALABRA CLAVE

por [por] *prep* **1** *(objetivo)* for; **luchar por la patria** to fight for one's country; **hazlo por mí** do it for my sake

2 (+ *infin*): **por no llegar tarde** so as not to arrive late; **por citar unos ejemplos** to give a few examples

3 *(causa)* out of, because of; **no es por eso** that's not the reason; **por escasez de fondos** through *o* for lack of funds

4 *(tiempo)*: **por la mañana/noche** in the morning/at night; **se queda por una semana** she's staying (for) a week

5 *(lugar)*: **pasar por Madrid** to pass through Madrid; **ir a Guayaquil por Quito** to go to Guayaquil via Quito; **caminar por la calle** to walk along the street; **por allí** over there; **se va por ahí** we have to go that way; **¿hay un banco por aquí?** is there a bank near here?; **¿por dónde?** which way?; **está por el norte** it's somewhere in the north; **por todo el país** throughout the country

6 *(cambio, precio)*: **te doy uno nuevo por el que tienes** I'll give you a new one (in return) for the one you've got; **lo vendí por 15 dólares** I sold it for 15 dollars

7 *(valor distributivo)*: **30 euros por hora/cabeza** 30 euros an *o* per hour/a *o* per head; **10 por ciento** 10 per cent; **80 (kms) por hora** 80 (km) an *o* per hour

8 *(modo, medio)* by; **por correo/avión** by post/air; **día por día** day by day; **por orden** in order; **entrar por la entrada principal** to go in through the main entrance

9 *(agente)* by; **hecho por él** done by him; **"dirigido por"** "directed by"

10: **10 por 10 son 100** 10 by 10 is 100

11 *(en lugar de)*: **vino él por su jefe** he came instead of his boss

12: **por mí que revienten** as far as I'm concerned they can drop dead

13 *(evidencia)*: **por lo que dicen** judging by *o* from what they say

14: **estar/quedar por hacer** to be still *o* remain to be done

15: **por (muy) difícil que sea** however hard it is *o* may be; **por más que lo intente** no matter how *o* however hard I try

16: **por qué** why; **¿por qué?** why?; **¿por qué no?** why not?; **¿por?** *(fam)* why (do you ask)?

porcelana [porθe'lana] *nf* porcelain; *(china)* china

porcentaje [porθen'taxe] *nm* percentage; **~ de actividad** *(Inform)* hit rate

porción [por'θjon] *nf (parte)* portion, share; *(cantidad)* quantity, amount

pordiosero, -a [porðjo'sero, a] *nm/f* beggar

porfía [por'fia] *nf* persistence; *(terquedad)* obstinacy

porfiado, -a [por'fjaðo, a] *adj* persistent; obstinate

porfiar [por'fjar] *vi* to persist, insist; *(disputar)* to argue stubbornly

pormenor [porme'nor] *nm* detail, particular

porno ['porno] *adj inv* porno ▷ *nm* porn

pornografía [pornoɣra'fia] *nf* pornography

poro ['poro] *nm* pore

pororó [poro'ro] *nm (Am)* popcorn

poroso, -a [po'roso, a] *adj* porous

poroto [po'roto] *nm (Am)* kidney bean

porque ['porke] *conj (a causa de)* because; *(ya que)* since; *(con el fin de)* so that, in order that; **~ sí** because I feel like it

porqué [por'ke] *nm* reason, cause

porquería [porke'ria] *nf (suciedad)* filth, muck, dirt; *(acción)* dirty trick; *(objeto)* small thing, trifle; *(fig)* rubbish

porra ['porra] *nf (arma)* stick, club; *(cachiporra)* truncheon; **¡~s!** oh heck!; **¡vete a la ~!** go to heck!

porrazo [po'rraθo] *nm (golpe)* blow; *(caída)* bump; **de un ~** in one go

porro ['porro] *nm (fam: droga)* joint

porrón [po'rron] *nm glass wine jar with a long spout*

portaaviones [port(a)a'βjones] *nm inv* aircraft carrier

portada [por'taða] *nf (Tip)* title page; *(: de revista)* cover

portador, a [porta'ðor, a] *nm/f* carrier, bearer; *(Com)* bearer, payee; *(Med)* carrier; **ser ~ del virus del sida** to be HIV-positive

portaequipajes [portaeki'paxes] *nm inv* boot *(Brit)*, trunk *(US)*; *(baca)* luggage rack

portafolio [porta'foljo], **portafolios** [porta'foljos] *nm (Am)* briefcase; **~(s) de inversiones** *(Com)* investment portfolio

portal [por'tal] *nm (entrada)* vestibule, hall; *(pórtico)* porch, doorway; *(puerta de entrada)* main door; *(Deporte)* goal; *(Internet)* portal; **portales** *nmpl* arcade *sg*

portamaletas [portama'letas] *nm inv (Auto: maletero)* boot; *(: baca)* roof rack

portamonedas [portamo'neðas] *nm inv (LAm)* purse

portar [por'tar] *vt* to carry, bear; **portarse** *vr* to behave, conduct o.s.; **~se mal** to misbehave; **se portó muy bien conmigo** he treated me very well

portátil [por'tatil] *adj* portable; **(ordenador) ~** laptop (computer)

portaviones [porta'βjones] *nm inv* aircraft carrier

portavoz [porta'βoθ] *nm/f* spokesman(-woman)

portazo [por'taθo] *nm*: **dar un ~** to slam the door

porte ['porte] *nm (Com)* transport; *(precio)* transport charges *pl*; *(Correos)* postage; **~ debido** *(Com)* carriage forward; **~ pagado** *(Com)* carriage paid, post-paid

portento [por'tento] *nm* marvel, wonder

portentoso, -a [porten'toso, a] *adj* marvellous, extraordinary

porteño, -a [por'teɲo, a] *adj* of *o* from Buenos Aires ▷ *nm/f* native *o* inhabitant of Buenos Aires

portería [porte'ria] *nf* (*oficina*) porter's office; (*gol*) goal

portero, -a [por'tero, a] *nm/f* porter; (*conserje*) caretaker; (*ujier*) doorman; (*Deporte*) goalkeeper; **~ automático** (*Esp*) entry phone

pórtico ['portiko] *nm* (*porche*) portico, porch; (*fig*) gateway; (*arcada*) arcade

portilla [por'tiʎa] *nf*, **portillo** [por'tiʎo] *nm* gate

portorriqueño, -a [portorri'keɲo, a] *adj, nm/f* Puerto Rican

Portugal [portu'ɣal] *nm* Portugal

portugués, -esa [portu'ɣes, esa] *adj, nm/f* Portuguese ▷ *nm* (*Ling*) Portuguese

porvenir [porβe'nir] *nm* future

pos [pos]: **en ~ de** *prep* after, in pursuit of

posada [po'saða] *nf* (*refugio*) shelter, lodging; (*mesón*) guest house; **dar ~ a** to give shelter to, take in

posaderas [posa'ðeras] *nfpl* backside *sg*, buttocks

posar [po'sar] *vt* (*en el suelo*) to lay down, put down; (*la mano*) to place, put gently ▷ *vi* to sit, pose; **posarse** *vr* to settle; (*pájaro*) to perch; (*avión*) to land, come down

posavasos [posa'βasos] *nm inv* coaster; (*para cerveza*) beermat

posdata [pos'ðata] *nf* postscript

pose ['pose] *nf* (*Arte, afectación*) pose

poseedor, a [posee'ðor, a] *nm/f* owner, possessor; (*de récord, puesto*) holder

poseer [pose'er] *vt* to have, possess, own; (*ventaja*) to enjoy; (*récord, puesto*) to hold

poseído, -a [pose'iðo, a] *adj* possessed; **estar muy ~ de** to be very vain about

posesión [pose'sjon] *nf* possession; **tomar ~ (de)** to take over

posesivo, -a [pose'siβo, a] *adj* possessive

posgrado [pos'ɣraðo] *nm* = **postgrado**

posibilidad [posiβili'ðað] *nf* possibility; (*oportunidad*) chance

posibilitar [posiβili'tar] *vt* to make possible, permit; (*hacer factible*) to make feasible

posible [po'siβle] *adj* possible; (*factible*) feasible ▷ *nm*: **~s** means; (*bienes*) funds, assets; **de ser ~** if possible; **en** *o* **dentro de lo ~** as far as possible; **lo antes ~** as quickly as possible

posición [posi'θjon] *nf* (*gen*) position; (*rango social*) status

positivo, -a [posi'tiβo, a] *adj* positive ▷ *nf* (*Foto*) print

poso ['poso] *nm* sediment; (*heces*) dregs *pl*

posoperatorio, -a [posopera'torjo, a] *adj, nm* = **postoperatorio**

posponer [pospo'ner] *vt* (*relegar*) to put behind *o* below; (*aplazar*) to postpone

posta ['posta] *nf* (*de caballos*) relay, team; **a ~** on purpose, deliberately

postal [pos'tal] *adj* postal ▷ *nf* postcard

poste ['poste] *nm* (*de telégrafos*) post, pole; (*columna*) pillar

póster (*pl* **posters**) ['poster, 'posters] *nm* poster

postergar [poster'ɣar] *vt* (*esp Am*) to put off, postpone, delay

posteridad [posteri'ðað] *nf* posterity

posterior [poste'rjor] *adj* back, rear; (*siguiente*) following, subsequent; (*más tarde*) later; **ser ~ a** to be later than

posterioridad [posterjori'ðað] *nf*: **con ~** later, subsequently

postgrado [post'ɣraðo] *nm*: **curso de ~** postgraduate course

postizo, -a [pos'tiθo, a] *adj* false, artificial; (*sonrisa*) false, phoney ▷ *nm* hairpiece

postoperatorio, -a [postopera'torjo, a] *adj* postoperative ▷ *nm* postoperative period

postor, a [pos'tor, a] *nm/f* bidder; **mejor ~** highest bidder

postrado, -a [pos'traðo, a] *adj* prostrate

postre ['postre] *nm* sweet, dessert ▷ *nf*: **a la ~** in the end, when all is said and done; **para ~** (*fam*) to crown it all; **llegar a los ~s** (*fig*) to come too late

postrero, -a [pos'trero, a] *adj* (*antes de nmsg* **postrer**) (*último*) last; (: *que viene detrás*) rear

postulado [postu'laðo] *nm* postulate

póstumo, -a ['postumo, a] *adj* posthumous

postura [pos'tura] *nf* (*del cuerpo*) posture, position; (*fig*) attitude, position

potable [po'taβle] *adj* drinkable; **agua ~** drinking water

potaje [po'taxe] *nm* thick vegetable soup

pote ['pote] *nm* pot, jar

potencia [po'tenθja] *nf* power; (*capacidad*) capacity; **~ (en caballos)** horsepower; **en ~** potential, in the making; **las grandes ~s** the great powers

potencial [poten'θjal] *adj, nm* potential

potenciar [poten'θjar] *vt* (*promover*) to promote; (*fortalecer*) to boost

potente [po'tente] *adj* powerful

potro ['potro] *nm* (*Zool*) colt; (*Deporte*) vaulting horse

pozo ['poθo] *nm* well; (*de río*) deep pool; (*de mina*) shaft; **~ negro** cesspool; **ser un ~ de ciencia** (*fig*) to be deeply learned

PP *abr* (= *por poderes*) pp; (= *porte pagado*) carriage paid ▷ *nm abr* = **Partido Popular**

práctica ['praktika] *nf ver* **práctico**

practicable [prakti'kaβle] *adj* practicable; (*camino*) passable, usable

prácticamente ['praktikamente] *adv* practically

practicante [prakti'kante] *nm/f* (*Med*: *ayudante de doctor*) medical assistant;

(: *enfermero*) nurse; (*el que practica algo*) practitioner ▷ *adj* practising

practicar [prakti'kar] *vt* to practise; (*deporte*) to go in for, play; (*ejecutar*) to carry out, perform

práctico, -a ['praktiko, a] *adj* (*gen*) practical; (*conveniente*) handy; (*instruido: persona*) skilled, expert ▷ *nf* practice; (*método*) method; (*arte, capacidad*) skill; **en la práctica** in practice

practique *etc* [prak'tike] *vb ver* **practicar**

pradera [pra'ðera] *nf* meadow; (*de Canadá*) prairie

prado ['praðo] *nm* (*campo*) meadow, field; (*pastizal*) pasture; (*Am*) lawn

Praga ['praɣa] *nf* Prague

pragmático, -a [praɣ'matiko, a] *adj* pragmatic

preámbulo [pre'ambulo] *nm* preamble, introduction; **decir algo sin ~s** to say sth without beating about the bush

precalentamiento [prekalenta'mjento] *nm* (*Deporte*) warm-up

precario, -a [pre'karjo, a] *adj* precarious

precaución [prekau'θjon] *nf* (*medida preventiva*) preventive measure, precaution; (*prudencia*) caution, wariness

precaver [preka'βer] *vt* to guard against; (*impedir*) to forestall; **precaverse** *vr*: **~se de** o **contra algo** to (be on one's) guard against sth

precavido, -a [preka'βiðo, a] *adj* cautious, wary

precedencia [preθe'ðenθja] *nf* precedence; (*prioridad*) priority; (*superioridad*) greater importance, superiority

precedente [preθe'ðente] *adj* preceding; (*anterior*) former ▷ *nm* precedent; **sin ~(s)** unprecedented; **establecer** o **sentar un ~** to establish o set a precedent

preceder [preθe'ðer] *vt, vi* to precede, go/come before

precepto [pre'θepto] *nm* precept

preciado, -a [pre'θjaðo, a] *adj* (*estimado*) esteemed, valuable

preciar [pre'θjar] *vt* to esteem, value; **preciarse** *vr* to boast; **~se de** to pride o.s. on

precintar [preθin'tar] *vt* (*local*) to seal off; (*producto*) to seal

precinto [pre'θinto] *nm* (*Com: tb:* **~ de garantía**) seal

precio ['preθjo] *nm* (*de mercado*) price; (*costo*) cost; (*valor*) value, worth; (*de viaje*) fare; **~ de coste** o **de cobertura** cost price; **~ al contado** cash price; **~ al detalle** o **al por menor** retail price; **~ al detallista** trade price; **~ de entrega inmediata** spot price; **~ de oferta** offer price, bargain price; **~ de salida** upset price; **~ tope** top price; **~ unitario** unit price; **no tener ~** (*fig*) to be priceless; **"no importa ~"** "cost no object"

preciosidad [preθjosi'ðað] *nf* (*valor*) (high) value, (great) worth; (*encanto*) charm; (*cosa bonita*) beautiful thing; **es una ~** it's lovely, it's really beautiful

precioso, -a [pre'θjoso, a] *adj* precious; (*de mucho valor*) valuable; (*fam*) lovely, beautiful

precipicio [preθi'pjeθjo] *nm* cliff, precipice; (*fig*) abyss

precipitación [preθipita'θjon] *nf* (*prisa*) haste; (*lluvia*) rainfall; (*Química*) precipitation

precipitado, -a [preθipi'taðo, a] *adj* hasty, rash; (*salida*) hasty, sudden ▷ *nm* (*Química*) precipitate

precipitar [preθipi'tar] *vt* (*arrojar*) to hurl, throw; (*apresurar*) to hasten; (*acelerar*) to speed up, accelerate; (*Química*) to precipitate; **precipitarse** *vr* to throw o.s.; (*apresurarse*) to rush; (*actuar sin pensar*) to act rashly; **~se hacia** to rush towards

precisamente [preθisa'mente] *adv* precisely; (*justo*) precisely, exactly, just; **~ por eso** for that very reason; **~ fue él quien lo dijo** as a matter of fact he said it; **no es eso ~** it's not really that

precisar [preθi'sar] *vt* (*necesitar*) to need, require; (*fijar*) to determine exactly, fix; (*especificar*) to specify; (*señalar*) to pinpoint

precisión [preθi'sjon] *nf* (*exactitud*) precision

preciso, -a [pre'θiso, a] *adj* (*exacto*) precise; (*necesario*) necessary, essential; (*estilo, lenguaje*) concise; **es ~ que lo hagas** you must do it

preconcebido, -a [prekonθe'βiðo, a] *adj* preconceived

precoz [pre'koθ] *adj* (*persona*) precocious; (*calvicie*) premature

precursor, a [prekur'sor, a] *nm/f* precursor

predecesor, a [predeθe'sor, a] *nm/f* predecessor

predecir [prede'θir] *vt* to predict, foretell, forecast

predestinado, -a [predesti'naðo, a] *adj* predestined

predeterminar [predetermi'nar] *vt* to predetermine

predicado [predi'kaðo] *nm* predicate

predicador, a [predika'ðor, a] *nm/f* preacher

predicar [predi'kar] *vt, vi* to preach

predicción [predik'θjon] *nf* prediction; (*pronóstico*) forecast; **~ del tiempo** weather forecast(ing)

predilecto, -a [predi'lekto, a] *adj* favourite

predisponer [predispo'ner] *vt* to predispose; (*pey*) to prejudice

predisposición [predisposi'θjon] *nf* predisposition, inclination; prejudice, bias; (*Med*) tendency

predominante [predomi'nante] *adj* predominant; (*preponderante*) prevailing; (*interés*) controlling

predominar [predomi'nar] *vt* to dominate ▷ *vi* to predominate; (*prevalecer*) to prevail

predominio [predo'minjo] *nm* predominance; prevalence

preescolar [preesko'lar] *adj* preschool

P

prefabricado, -a [prefaβri'kaðo, a] *adj* prefabricated

prefacio [pre'faθjo] *nm* preface

preferencia [prefe'renθja] *nf* preference; **de** ~ preferably, for preference; **localidad de** ~ reserved seat

preferible [prefe'riβle] *adj* preferable

preferido, -a [prefe'riðo, a] *adj, nm/f* favourite, favorite (US)

preferir [prefe'rir] *vt* to prefer

prefiero *etc* [pre'fjero] *vb ver* **preferir**

prefijo [pre'fixo] *nm* prefix; (*Tel*) (dialling) code

pregonar [preɣo'nar] *vt* to proclaim, announce; (*mercancía*) to hawk

pregunta [pre'ɣunta] *nf* question; ~ **capciosa** catch question; **hacer una** ~ to ask a question; **~s frecuentes** FAQs, frequently asked questions

preguntar [preɣun'tar] *vt* to ask; (*cuestionar*) to question ▷ *vi* to ask; **preguntarse** *vr* to wonder; ~ **por algn** to ask for sb; ~ **por la salud de algn** to ask after sb's health

preguntón, -ona [preɣun'ton, ona] *adj* inquisitive

prehistórico, -a [preis'toriko, a] *adj* prehistoric

prejuicio [pre'xwiθjo] *nm* prejudgement; (*preconcepción*) preconception; (*pey*) prejudice, bias

preliminar [prelimi'nar] *adj, nm* preliminary

preludio [pre'luðjo] *nm* (*Mus, fig*) prelude

premamá [prema'ma] *adj*: **vestido** ~ maternity dress

prematrimonial [prematrimo'njal] *adj*: **relaciones ~es** premarital sex

prematuro, -a [prema'turo, a] *adj* premature

premeditación [premeðita'θjon] *nf* premeditation

premeditar [premeði'tar] *vt* to premeditate

premiar [pre'mjar] *vt* to reward; (*en un concurso*) to give a prize to

premio ['premjo] *nm* reward; prize; (*Com*) premium; ~ **gordo** first prize

premisa [pre'misa] *nf* premise

premonición [premoni'θjon] *nf* premonition

premura [pre'mura] *nf* (*prisa*) haste, urgency

prenatal [prena'tal] *adj* antenatal, prenatal

prenda ['prenda] *nf* (*de ropa*) garment, article of clothing; (*garantía*) pledge; (*fam*) darling!; **prendas** *nfpl* talents, gifts; **dejar algo en** ~ to pawn sth; **no soltar** ~ to give nothing away; (*fig*) not to say a word

prendar [pren'dar] *vt* to captivate, enchant; ~**se de algo** to fall in love with sth

prendedor [prende'ðor] *nm* brooch

prender [pren'der] *vt* (*captar*) to catch, capture; (*detener*) to arrest; (*coser*) to pin, attach; (*sujetar*) to fasten; (*Am*) to switch on

▷ *vi* to catch; (*arraigar*) to take root; **prenderse** *vr* (*encenderse*) to catch fire

prendido, -a [pren'diðo, a] *adj* (*Am*: *luz*) on

prensa ['prensa] *nf* press; **la P~** the press; **tener mala** ~ to have *o* get a bad press; **la ~ nacional** the national press

prensar [pren'sar] *vt* to press

preñado, -a [pre'ɲaðo, a] *adj* (*mujer*) pregnant; ~ **de** pregnant with, full of

preocupación [preokupa'θjon] *nf* worry, concern; (*ansiedad*) anxiety

preocupado, -a [preoku'paðo, a] *adj* worried, concerned; anxious

preocupar [preoku'par] *vt* to worry; **preocuparse** *vr* to worry; ~**se de algo** (*hacerse cargo de algo*) to take care of sth; ~**se por algo** to worry about sth

preparación [prepara'θjon] *nf* (*acto*) preparation; (*estado*) preparedness, readiness; (*entrenamiento*) training

preparado, -a [prepa'raðo, a] *adj* (*dispuesto*) prepared; (*Culin*) ready (to serve) ▷ *nm* (*Med*) preparation; **¡~s, listos, ya!** ready, steady, go!

preparar [prepa'rar] *vt* (*disponer*) to prepare, get ready; (*Tec*: *tratar*) to prepare, process, treat; (*entrenar*) to teach, train; **prepararse** *vr*: ~**se a** *o* **para hacer algo** to prepare *o* get ready to do sth

preparativo, -a [prepara'tiβo, a] *adj* preparatory, preliminary ▷ *nm*: ~**s** *nmpl* preparations

preparatoria [prepara'torja] *nf* (*Am*) sixth form college (*Brit*), senior high school (US)

preposición [preposi'θjon] *nf* preposition

prepotencia [prepo'tenθja] *nf* abuse of power; (*Pol*) high-handedness; (*soberbia*) arrogance

prepotente [prepo'tente] *adj* (*Pol*) high-handed; (*soberbio*) arrogant

prerrogativa [prerroɣa'tiβa] *nf* prerogative, privilege

presa ['presa] *nf* (*cosa apresada*) catch; (*víctima*) victim; (*de animal*) prey; (*de agua*) dam; **hacer** ~ **en** to clutch (on to), seize; **ser** ~ **de** (*fig*) to be a prey to

presagiar [presa'xjar] *vt* to presage

presagio [pre'saxjo] *nm* omen

prescindir [presθin'dir] *vi*: ~ **de** (*privarse de*) to do without, go without; (*descartar*) to dispense with; **no podemos** ~ **de él** we can't manage without him

prescribir [preskri'βir] *vt* to prescribe

prescripción [preskrip'θjon] *nf* prescription; ~ **facultativa** medical prescription

presencia [pre'senθja] *nf* presence; **en** ~ **de** in the presence of

presencial [presen'θjal] *adj*: **testigo** ~ eyewitness

presenciar [presen'θjar] *vt* to be present at; (*asistir a*) to attend; (*ver*) to see, witness

presentación [presenta'θjon] *nf* presentation; (*introducción*) introduction

presentador, a [presenta'ðor, a] *nm/f*
compère
presentar [presen'tar] *vt* to present; *(ofrecer)*
to offer; *(mostrar)* to show, display; *(renuncia)*
to tender; *(moción)* to propose; *(a una persona)*
to introduce; **presentarse** *vr (llegar
inesperadamente)* to appear, turn up; *(ofrecerse:
como candidato)* to run, stand; *(aparecer)* to
show, appear; *(solicitar empleo)* to apply; **~ al
cobro** *(Com)* to present for payment; **~se a la
policía** to report to the police
presente [pre'sente] *adj* present ▷ *nm*
present; *(Ling)* present (tense); *(regalo)* gift;
los ~s those present; **hacer ~** to state,
declare; **tener ~** to remember, bear in mind;
la carta ~, la ~ this letter
presentimiento [presenti'mjento] *nm*
premonition, presentiment
presentir [presen'tir] *vt* to have a
premonition of
preservación [preserβa'θjon] *nf* protection,
preservation
preservar [preser'βar] *vt* to protect, preserve
preservativo [preserβa'tiβo] *nm* sheath,
condom
presidencia [presi'ðenθja] *nf* presidency; *(de
comité)* chairmanship; **ocupar la ~** to
preside, be in *o* take the chair
presidente [presi'ðente] *nm/f* president; *(de
comité)* chairman(-woman); *(en parlamento)*
speaker; *(Jur)* presiding magistrate
presidiario [presi'ðjarjo] *nm* convict
presidio [pre'siðjo] *nm* prison, penitentiary
presidir [presi'ðir] *vt (dirigir)* to preside at,
preside over; *(: comité)* to take the chair at;
(dominar) to dominate, rule ▷ *vi* to preside; to
take the chair
presión [pre'sjon] *nf* pressure;
~ atmosférica atmospheric *o* air pressure;
~ arterial *o* **sanguínea** blood pressure;
a ~ under pressure
presionar [presjo'nar] *vt* to press; *(botón)* to
push, press; *(fig)* to press, put pressure on
▷ *vi*: **~ para** *o* **por** to press for
preso, -a ['preso, a] *adj*: **estar ~ de terror** *o*
pánico to be panic-stricken ▷ *nm/f* prisoner;
tomar *o* **llevar ~ a algn** to arrest sb, take sb
prisoner
prestación [presta'θjon] *nf (aportación)*
lending; *(Inform)* capability; *(servicio)* service;
(subsidio) benefit; **prestaciones** *nfpl (Auto)*
performance features; **~ de juramento**
oath-taking; **~ personal** obligatory service;
P~ Social Sustitutoria community service
for conscientious objectors; *ver tb* **mili**
prestado, -a [pres'taðo, a] *adj* on loan; **dar
algo ~** to lend sth; **pedir ~** to borrow
prestamista [presta'mista] *nm/f*
moneylender
préstamo ['prestamo] *nm* loan; **~ con
garantía** loan against collateral;
~ hipotecario mortgage

prestar [pres'tar] *vt* to lend, loan; *(atención)* to
pay; *(ayuda)* to give; *(servicio)* to do, render;
(juramento) to take, swear; **prestarse** *vr
(ofrecerse)* to offer *o* volunteer
presteza [pres'teθa] *nf* speed, promptness
prestigio [pres'tixjo] *nm* prestige; *(reputación)*
face; *(renombre)* good name
prestigioso, -a [presti'xjoso, a] *adj*
(honorable) prestigious; *(famoso, renombrado)*
renowned, famous
presto, -a ['presto, a] *adj (rápido)* quick, prompt;
(dispuesto) ready ▷ *adv* at once, right away
presumido, -a [presu'miðo, a] *adj* conceited
presumir [presu'mir] *vt* to presume ▷ *vi*
(darse aires) to be conceited; **según cabe ~** as
may be presumed, presumably; **~ de listo** to
think o.s. very smart
presunción [presun'θjon] *nf* presumption;
(sospecha) suspicion; *(vanidad)* conceit
presunto, -a [pre'sunto, a] *adj (supuesto)*
supposed, presumed; *(así llamado)* so-called
presuntuoso, -a [presun'twoso, a] *adj*
conceited, presumptuous
presuponer [presupo'ner] *vt* to presuppose
presupuesto [presu'pwesto] *pp de*
presuponer ▷ *nm (Finanzas)* budget;
(estimación: de costo) estimate; **asignación
de ~** *(Com)* budget appropriation
presuroso, -a [presu'roso, a] *adj (rápido)*
quick, speedy; *(que tiene prisa)* hasty
pretencioso, -a [preten'θjoso, a] *adj*
pretentious
pretender [preten'der] *vt (intentar)* to try to,
seek to; *(reivindicar)* to claim; *(buscar)* to seek,
try for; *(cortejar)* to woo, court; **~ que** to
expect that; **¿qué pretende usted?** what are
you after?
pretendiente [preten'djente] *nm/f*
(candidato) candidate, applicant; *(amante)*
suitor; *(al trono)* pretender
pretensión [preten'sjon] *nf (aspiración)*
aspiration; *(reivindicación)* claim; *(orgullo)*
pretension
pretexto [pre'teksto] *nm* pretext; *(excusa)*
excuse; **so ~ de** under pretext of
prevalecer [preβale'θer] *vi* to prevail
prevención [preβen'θjon] *nf (preparación)*
preparation; *(estado)* preparedness,
readiness; *(medida)* prevention; *(previsión)*
foresight, forethought; *(precaución)*
precaution
prevenido, -a [preβe'niðo, a] *adj* prepared,
ready; *(cauteloso)* cautious; **estar ~** *(preparado)*
to be ready; **ser ~** *(cuidadoso)* to be cautious;
hombre ~ vale por dos forewarned is
forearmed
prevenir [preβe'nir] *vt (impedir)* to prevent;
(prever) to foresee, anticipate; *(predisponer)* to
prejudice, bias; *(avisar)* to warn; *(preparar)* to
prepare, get ready; **prevenirse** *vr* to get
ready, prepare; **~se contra** to take
precautions against

P

preventivo, -a [preβen'tiβo, a] *adj*
preventive, precautionary

prever [pre'βer] *vt* to foresee; *(anticipar)* to
anticipate

previo, -a ['preβjo, a] *adj (anterior)* previous,
prior; *(preliminar)* preliminary ▷ *prep*:
~ **acuerdo de los otros** subject to the
agreement of the others; ~ **pago de los
derechos** on payment of the fees

previsión [preβi'sjon] *nf (perspicacia)*
foresight; *(predicción)* forecast; *(prudencia)*
caution; ~ **de ventas** *(Com)* sales forecast

previsor, a [preβi'sor, a] *adj (precavido)* far-
sighted; *(prudente)* thoughtful

previsto, -a [pre'βisto, a] *pp de* **prever** ▷ *adj*
anticipated, forecast

prima ['prima] *nf ver* **primo**

primacía [prima'θia] *nf* primacy

primario, -a [pri'marjo, a] *adj* primary ▷ *nf*
primary education; *ver tb* **sistema educativo**

primavera [prima'βera] *nf (temporada)*
spring; *(período)* springtime

Primer Ministro [pri'mer-] *nm* Prime
Minister

primero, -a [pri'mero, a] *adj (antes de nmsg*
primer) first; *(fig)* prime; *(anterior)* former;
(básico) fundamental ▷ *adv* first; *(más bien)*
sooner, rather ▷ *nf (Auto)* first gear; *(Ferro)*
first class; **de primera** *(fam)* first-class, first-
rate; **de buenas a primeras** suddenly;
primera dama *(Teat)* leading lady; **primera
plana** front page

primicia [pri'miθja] *nf (Prensa)* scoop;
primicias *nfpl (tb fig)* first fruits

primitivo, -a [primi'tiβo, a] *adj* primitive;
(original) original; *(Com: acción)* ordinary ▷ *nf*:
(Lotería) Primitiva *weekly state-run lottery; ver
tb* **lotería**

primo, -a ['primo, a] *adj (Mat)* prime ▷ *nm/f*
cousin; *(fam)* fool, idiot ▷ *nf (Com)* bonus;
(de seguro) premium; *(a la exportación)* subsidy;
~ **hermano** first cousin; **materias primas**
raw materials; **hacer el** ~ to be taken for
a ride

primogénito, -a [primo'xenito, a] *adj* first-
born

primor [pri'mor] *nm (cuidado)* care; **es un** ~
it's lovely

primordial [primor'ðjal] *adj* basic,
fundamental

primoroso, -a [primo'roso, a] *adj* exquisite,
fine

princesa [prin'θesa] *nf* princess

principal [prinθi'pal] *adj* principal, main;
(más destacado) foremost; *(piso)* first, second
(US); *(Inform)* foreground ▷ *nm (jefe)* chief,
principal

príncipe ['prinθipe] *nm* prince; ~ **heredero**
crown prince; **P~ de Asturias** *King's son and
heir to the Spanish throne;* ~ **de Gales** *(tela)* check

principiante [prinθi'pjante] *nm/f* beginner;
(novato) novice

principio [prin'θipjo] *nm (comienzo)*
beginning, start; *(origen)* origin; *(base)*
rudiment, basic idea; *(moral)* principle; **a ~s
de** at the beginning of; **desde el** ~ from the
first; **en un** ~ at first

pringar [prin'gar] *vt (Culin: pan)* to dip;
(ensuciar) to dirty; **pringarse** *vr* to get
splashed *o* soiled; ~ **a algn en un asunto**
(fam) to involve sb in a matter

pringoso, -a [prin'goso, a] *adj* greasy;
(pegajoso) sticky

pringue *etc* ['pringe] *vb ver* **pringar** ▷ *nm*
(grasa) grease, fat, dripping

prioridad [priori'ðað] *nf* priority; *(Auto)* right
of way

prisa ['prisa] *nf (apresuramiento)* hurry, haste;
(rapidez) speed; *(urgencia)* (sense of) urgency; **a
o de** ~ quickly; *(urgencia)* (sense of) urgency; **a**
to hurry up; **estar de** *o* **tener** ~ to be in a
hurry

prisión [pri'sjon] *nf (cárcel)* prison; *(período de
cárcel)* imprisonment

prisionero, -a [prisjo'nero, a] *nm/f* prisoner

prismáticos [pris'matikos] *nmpl* binoculars

privación [priβa'θjon] *nf* deprivation; *(falta)*
want, privation; **privaciones** *nfpl* hardships,
privations

privado, -a [pri'βaðo, a] *adj (particular)*
private; *(Pol: favorito)* favourite (Brit), favorite
(US); **en** ~ privately, in private; "~ **y
confidencial"** "private and confidential"

privar [pri'βar] *vt* to deprive; **privarse** *vr*: ~**se
de** *(abstenerse de)* to deprive o.s. of; *(renunciar a)*
to give up

privativo, -a [priβa'tiβo, a] *adj* exclusive

privatizar [priβati'θar] *vt* to privatize

privilegiado, -a [priβile'xjaðo, a] *adj*
privileged; *(memoria)* very good ▷ *nm/f*
(afortunado) privileged person

privilegiar [priβile'xjar] *vt* to grant a
privilege to; *(favorecer)* to favour

privilegio [priβi'lexjo] *nm* privilege;
(concesión) concession

pro [pro] *nm o nf* profit, advantage ▷ *prep*:
asociación ~ **ciegos** association for the blind
▷ *pref*: ~ **soviético/americano** pro-Soviet/-
American; **en** ~ **de** on behalf of, for; **los ~s y
los contras** the pros and cons

proa ['proa] *nf (Naut)* bow, prow; **de** ~ bow *cpd*,
fore; *ver tb* **popa**

probabilidad [proβaβili'ðað] *nf* probability,
likelihood; *(oportunidad, posibilidad)* chance,
prospect

probable [pro'βaβle] *adj* probable, likely; **es
~ que** *(+subjun)* it is probable *o* likely that; **es
~ que no venga** he probably won't come

probador [proβa'ðor] *nm (persona)* taster *(of
wine etc)*; *(en una tienda)* fitting room

probar [pro'βar] *vt (demostrar)* to prove;
(someter a prueba) to test, try out; *(ropa)* to try
on; *(comida)* to taste ▷ *vi* to try; **probarse** *vr*:
~**se un traje** to try on a suit

probeta [pro'βeta] *nf* test tube

problema [pro'βlema] *nm* problem

procedencia [proθe'ðenθja] *nf* (*principio*) source, origin; (*lugar de salida*) point of departure

procedente [proθe'ðente] *adj* (*razonable*) reasonable; (*conforme a derecho*) proper, fitting; ~ **de** coming from, originating in

proceder [proθe'ðer] *vi* (*avanzar*) to proceed; (*actuar*) to act; (*ser correcto*) to be right (and proper), be fitting ▷ *nm* (*comportamiento*) behaviour, conduct; **no procede obrar así** it is not right to act like that; ~ **de** to come from, originate in

procedimiento [proθeði'mjento] *nm* procedure; (*proceso*) process; (*método*) means, method; (*trámite*) proceedings *pl*

procesado, -a [proθe'saðo, a] *nm/f* accused (person)

procesador [proθesa'ðor] *nm*: ~ **de textos** (*Inform*) word processor

procesar [proθe'sar] *vt* to try, put on trial; (*Inform*) to process

procesión [proθe'sjon] *nf* procession; **la ~ va por dentro** he keeps his troubles to himself

proceso [pro'θeso] *nm* process; (*Jur*) trial; (*lapso*) course (of time); (*Inform*): ~ **(automático) de datos** (automatic) data processing; ~ **no prioritario** background process; ~ **por pasadas** batch processing; ~ **en tiempo real** real-time programming

proclamar [prokla'mar] *vt* to proclaim

procreación [prokrea'θjon] *nf* procreation

procrear [prokre'ar] *vt, vi* to procreate

procurador, a [prokura'ðor, a] *nm/f* attorney, solicitor

procurar [proku'rar] *vt* (*intentar*) to try, endeavour; (*conseguir*) to get, obtain; (*asegurar*) to secure; (*producir*) to produce

prodigar [proði'ɣar] *vt* to lavish; **prodigarse** *vr*: ~**se en** to be lavish with

prodigio [pro'ðixjo] *nm* prodigy; (*milagro*) wonder, marvel; **niño ~** child prodigy

prodigioso, -a [proði'xjoso, a] *adj* prodigious, marvellous

pródigo, -a ['proðiɣo, a] *adj* (*rico*) rich, productive; **hijo ~** prodigal son

producción [proðuk'θjon] *nf* production; (*suma de productos*) output; (*producto*) product; ~ **en serie** mass production

producir [proðu'θir] *vt* to produce; (*generar*) to cause, bring about; (*impresión*) to give; (*Com: interés*) to bear; **producirse** *vr* (*cambio*) to come about, happen; (*hacerse*) to be produced, be made; (*estallar*) to break out; (*accidente*) to take place; (*problema etc*) to arise

productividad [proðuktiβi'ðað] *nf* productivity

productivo, -a [proðuk'tiβo, a] *adj* productive; (*provechoso*) profitable

producto [pro'ðukto] *nm* (*resultado*) product; (*producción*) production; ~ **alimenticio** foodstuff; ~ **(nacional) bruto** gross (national) product; ~ **interno bruto** gross domestic product

productor, a [proðuk'tor, a] *adj* productive, producing ▷ *nm/f* producer

proeza [pro'eθa] *nf* exploit, feat

profanar [profa'nar] *vt* to desecrate, profane

profano, -a [pro'fano, a] *adj* profane ▷ *nm/f* (*inexperto*) layman(-woman); **soy ~ en música** I don't know anything about music

profecía [profe'θia] *nf* prophecy

proferir [profe'rir] *vt* (*palabra, sonido*) to utter; (*injuria*) to hurl, let fly

profesar [profe'sar] *vt* (*declarar*) to profess; (*practicar*) to practise

profesión [profe'sjon] *nf* profession; (*en formulario*) occupation; (*confesión*) avowal; **abogado de ~, de ~ abogado** a lawyer by profession

profesional [profesjo'nal] *adj* professional

profesor, a [profe'sor, a] *nm/f* teacher; (*instructor*) instructor; ~ **de universidad** lecturer; ~ **adjunto** assistant lecturer, associate professor (US)

profesorado [profeso'raðo] *nm* (*profesión*) teaching profession; (*cuerpo*) teaching staff, faculty (US); (*cargo*) professorship

profeta [pro'feta] *nm/f* prophet

profetizar [profeti'θar] *vt, vi* to prophesy

prófugo, -a ['profuɣo, a] *nm/f* fugitive; (*desertor*) deserter

profundidad [profundi'ðað] *nf* depth; **tener una ~ de 30 cm** to be 30 cm deep

profundizar [profundi'θar] (*fig*) *vt* to go into deeply, study in depth ▷ *vi*: ~ **en** to go into deeply

profundo, -a [pro'fundo, a] *adj* deep; (*misterio, pensador*) profound; **poco ~** shallow

profusión [profu'sjon] *nf* (*abundancia*) profusion; (*prodigalidad*) wealth

progenitor [proxeni'tor] *nm* ancestor; **progenitores** *nmpl* (*fam*) parents

programa [pro'ɣrama] *nm* programme; (*Inform*) program; ~ **de estudios** curriculum, syllabus; ~ **verificador de ortografía** (*Inform*) spelling checker

programación [proɣrama'θjon] *nf* (*Inform*) programming; ~ **estructurada** structured programming

programador, a [proɣrama'ðor, a] *nm/f* (*computer*) programmer; ~ **de aplicaciones** applications programmer

programar [proɣra'mar] *vt* (*Inform*) to program

progre ['proɣre] *adj* (*fam*) liberal

progresar [proɣre'sar] *vi* to progress, make progress

progresión [proɣre'sjon] *nf*: ~ **geométrica/aritmética** geometric/arithmetic progression

progresista [proɣre'sista] *adj, nm/f* progressive

P

progresivo, -a [proɣre'siβo, a] *adj*
progressive; *(gradual)* gradual; *(continuo)*
continuous

progreso [pro'ɣreso] *nm (tb: ~s)* progress;
hacer ~s to progress, advance

prohibición [proiβi'θjon] *nf* prohibition,
ban; **levantar la ~ de** to remove the ban on

prohibir [proi'βir] *vt* to prohibit, ban, forbid;
se prohíbe fumar no smoking; **"prohibido
el paso"** "no entry"

prójimo, -a ['proximo, a] *nm* fellow man
▷ *nm/f (vecino)* neighbour

proletariado [proleta'rjaðo] *nm* proletariat

proletario, -a [prole'tarjo, a] *adj, nm/f*
proletarian

proliferación [prolifera'θjon] *nf*
proliferation; **~ de armas nucleares** spread
of nuclear arms

proliferar [prolife'rar] *vi* to proliferate

prolífico, -a [pro'lifiko, a] *adj* prolific

prolijo, -a [pro'lixo, a] *adj* long-winded,
tedious; *(Am)* neat

prólogo ['proloɣo] *nm* prologue; *(preámbulo)*
preface, introduction

prolongación [prolonga'θjon] *nf* extension

prolongado, -a [prolon'gaðo, a] *adj (largo)*
long; *(alargado)* lengthy

prolongar [prolon'gar] *vt (gen)* to extend; *(en
el tiempo)* to prolong; *(calle, tubo)* to make
longer, extend; **prolongarse** *vr (alargarse)* to
extend, go on

promedio [pro'meðjo] *nm* average; *(de
distancia)* middle, mid-point

promesa [pro'mesa] *nf* promise ▷ *adj:*
jugador ~ promising player; **faltar a una ~**
to break a promise

prometer [prome'ter] *vt* to promise ▷ *vi* to
show promise; **prometerse** *vr (dos personas)*
to get engaged

prometido, -a [prome'tiðo, a] *adj* promised;
engaged ▷ *nm/f* fiancé/fiancée

prominente [promi'nente] *adj* prominent

promiscuo, -a [pro'miskwo, a] *adj*
promiscuous

promoción [promo'θjon] *nf* promotion;
(año) class, year; **~ por correspondencia
directa** *(Com)* direct mailshot; **~ de ventas**
sales promotion *o* drive

promocionar [promoθjo'nar] *vt (Com: dar
publicidad)* to promote

promontorio [promon'torjo] *nm* promontory

promotor [promo'tor] *nm* promoter;
(instigador) instigator

promover [promo'βer] *vt* to promote;
(causar) to cause; *(juicio)* to bring; *(motín)* to
instigate, stir up

promulgar [promul'ɣar] *vt* to promulgate;
(fig) to proclaim

pronombre [pro'nombre] *nm* pronoun

pronosticar [pronosti'kar] *vt* to predict,
foretell, forecast

pronóstico [pro'nostiko] *nm* prediction,

forecast; *(profecía)* omen; *(Med: diagnóstico)*
prognosis; **de ~ leve** slight, not serious;
~ del tiempo weather forecast

pronto, -a ['pronto, a] *adj (rápido)* prompt,
quick; *(preparado)* ready ▷ *adv* quickly,
promptly; *(en seguida)* at once, right away;
(dentro de poco) soon; *(temprano)* early ▷ *nm*
urge, sudden feeling; **tener ~s de enojo** to
be quick-tempered; **al ~** at first; **de ~**
suddenly; **tiene unos ~s muy malos** he gets
ratty all of a sudden *(inf)*; **¡hasta ~!** see you
soon!; **lo más ~ posible** as soon as possible;
por lo ~ meanwhile, for the present; **tan ~
como** as soon as

pronunciación [pronunθja'θjon] *nf*
pronunciation

pronunciar [pronun'θjar] *vt* to pronounce;
(discurso) to make, deliver; *(Jur: sentencia)* to
pass, pronounce; **pronunciarse** *vr* to revolt,
rise, rebel; *(declararse)* to declare o.s.; **~se
sobre** to pronounce on

propagación [propaɣa'θjon] *nf* propagation;
(difusión) spread(ing)

propaganda [propa'ɣanda] *nf (política)*
propaganda; *(comercial)* advertising; **hacer ~
de** *(Com)* to advertise

propagar [propa'ɣar] *vt* to propagate;
(difundir) to spread, disseminate; **propagarse**
vr (Bio) to propagate; *(fig)* to spread

propano [pro'pano] *nm* propane

propasarse [propa'sarse] *vr (excederse)* to go
too far; *(sexualmente)* to take liberties

propensión [propen'sjon] *nf* inclination,
propensity

propenso, -a [pro'penso, a] *adj:* **~ a** prone *o*
inclined to; **ser ~ a hacer algo** to be inclined
o have a tendency to do sth

propiamente [propja'mente] *adv* properly;
(realmente) really, exactly; **~ dicho** real, true

propicio, -a [pro'piθjo, a] *adj* favourable,
propitious

propiedad [propje'ðað] *nf* property; *(posesión)*
possession, ownership; *(conveniencia)*
suitability; *(exactitud)* accuracy; **~ particular**
private property; **~ pública** *(Com)* public
ownership; **ceder algo a algn en ~** to
transfer to sb the full rights over sth

propietario, -a [propje'tarjo, a] *nm/f* owner,
proprietor

propina [pro'pina] *nf* tip; **dar algo de ~** to
give something extra

propio, -a ['propjo, a] *adj* own, of one's own;
(característico) characteristic, typical;
(conveniente) proper; *(mismo)* selfsame, very;
el ~ ministro the minister himself; **¿tienes
casa propia?** have you a house of your own?;
eso es muy ~ de él that's just like him;
tiene un olor muy ~ it has a smell of its own

proponer [propo'ner] *vt* to propose, put
forward; *(candidato)* to propose, nominate;
(problema) to pose; **proponerse** *vr* to propose,
plan, intend

proporción [propor'θjon] nf proportion; (Mat) ratio; (razón, porcentaje) rate; **proporciones** nfpl dimensions; (fig) size sg; **en ~ con** in proportion to

proporcionado, -a [proporθjo'naðo, a] adj proportionate; (regular) medium, middling; (justo) just right; **bien ~** well-proportioned

proporcional [proporθjo'nal] adj proportional; **~ a** proportional to

proporcionar [proporθjo'nar] vt (dar) to give, supply, provide; **esto le proporciona una renta anual de ...** this brings him in a yearly income of ...

proposición [proposi'θjon] nf proposition; (propuesta) proposal

propósito [pro'posito] nm (intención) purpose; (intento) aim, intention ▷ adv: **a ~** by the way, incidentally; (a posta) on purpose, deliberately; **a ~ de** about, with regard to

propuesto, -a [pro'pwesto, a] pp de **proponer** ▷ nf proposal

propugnar [propuɣ'nar] vt to uphold

propulsar [propul'sar] vt to drive, propel; (fig) to promote, encourage

propulsión [propul'sjon] nf propulsion; **~ a chorro o por reacción** jet propulsion

prórroga ['prorroɣa] nf (gen) extension; (Jur) stay; (Com) deferment; (Deporte) extra time

prorrogar [prorro'ɣar] vt (período) to extend; (decisión) to defer, postpone

prorrumpir [prorrum'pir] vi to burst forth, break out; **~ en gritos** to start shouting; **~ en lágrimas** to burst into tears

prosa ['prosa] nf prose

prosaico, -a [pro'saiko, a] adj prosaic, dull

proscripción [proskrip'θjon] nf prohibition, ban; banishment; proscription

proscrito, -a [pros'krito, a] adj (prohibido) banned; (desterrado) outlawed ▷ nm/f (exilado) exile; (bandido) outlaw

prosecución [proseku'θjon] nf continuation; (persecución) pursuit

proseguir [prose'ɣir] vt to continue, carry on, proceed with; (investigación, estudio) to pursue ▷ vi to continue, go on

prospección [prospek'θjon] nf exploration; (del petróleo, del oro) prospecting

prospecto [pros'pekto] nm prospectus; (folleto) leaflet, sheet of instructions

prosperar [prospe'rar] vi to prosper, thrive, flourish

prosperidad [prosperi'ðað] nf prosperity; (éxito) success

próspero, -a ['prospero, a] adj prosperous, thriving; (que tiene éxito) successful

prostíbulo [pros'tiβulo] nm brothel

prostitución [prostitu'θjon] nf prostitution

prostituir [prosti'twir] vt to prostitute; **prostituirse** vr to prostitute o.s., become a prostitute

prostituta [prosti'tuta] nf prostitute

protagonista [protaɣo'nista] nm/f protagonist; (Lit: personaje) main character, hero/heroine

protagonizar [protaɣoni'θar] vt to head, take the chief role in

protección [protek'θjon] nf protection

protector, a [protek'tor, a] adj protective, protecting; (tono) patronizing ▷ nm/f protector; (bienhechor) patron; (de la tradición) guardian

proteger [prote'xer] vt to protect; **~ contra grabación o contra escritura** (Inform) to write-protect

protegido, -a [prote'xiðo, a] nm/f protégé/ protégée

proteína [prote'ina] nf protein

prótesis ['protesis] nf (Med) prosthesis

protesta [pro'testa] nf protest; (declaración) protestation

protestante [protes'tante] adj Protestant

protestar [protes'tar] vt to protest, declare; (fe) to protest ▷ vi to protest; (objetar) to object; **cheque protestado por falta de fondos** cheque referred to drawer

protocolo [proto'kolo] nm protocol; **sin ~s** (formalismo) informal(ly)

protón [pro'ton] nm proton

prototipo [proto'tipo] nm prototype; (ideal) model

protuberancia [protuβe'ranθja] nf protuberance

prov. abr (= provincia) prov.

provecho [pro'βetʃo] nm advantage, benefit; (Finanzas) profit; **¡buen ~!** bon appétit!; **en ~ de** to the benefit of; **sacar ~ de** to benefit from, profit by

proveer [proβe'er] vt to provide, supply; (preparar) to provide, get ready; (vacante) to fill; (negocio) to transact, dispatch ▷ vi: **~ a** to provide for; **proveerse** vr: **~se de** to provide o.s. with

provenir [proβe'nir] vi: **~ de** to come from

proverbio [pro'βerβjo] nm proverb

providencia [proβi'ðenθja] nf providence; (previsión) foresight; **providencias** nfpl measures, steps

provincia [pro'βinθja] nf province; (Esp: Admin) ≈ county, ≈ region (Scot); **un pueblo de ~(s)** a country town; see note

● **PROVINCIA**
●
● Spain is divided up into 55 administrative
● provincias, including the islands, and
● territories in North Africa. Each one has a
● capital de provincia, which generally bears
● the same name. Provincias are grouped by
● geography, history and culture into
● comunidades autónomas. It should be noted
● that the term comarca normally has a
● purely geographical function in Spanish,
● but in Catalonia it designates
● administrative boundaries.

provinciano, -a [proβin'θjano, a] adj provincial; (del campo) country cpd
provisión [proβi'sjon] nf provision; (abastecimiento) provision, supply; (medida) measure, step
provisional [proβisjo'nal] adj provisional
provocación [proβoka'θjon] nf provocation
provocar [proβo'kar] vt to provoke; (alentar) to tempt, invite; (causar) to bring about, lead to; (promover) to promote; (estimular) to rouse, stir, stimulate; (protesta, explosión) to cause, spark off; (Am): ¿te provoca un café? would you like a coffee?
provocativo, -a [proβoka'tiβo, a] adj provocative
proxeneta [prokse'neta] nm/f go-between; (de prostitutas) pimp/procuress
próximamente [proksima'mente] adv shortly, soon
proximidad [proksimi'ðað] nf closeness, proximity
próximo, -a ['proksimo, a] adj near, close; (vecino) neighbouring; (el que viene) next; **en fecha próxima** at an early date; **el mes ~** next month
proyectar [projek'tar] vt (objeto) to hurl, throw; (luz) to cast, shed; (Cine) to screen, show; (planear) to plan
proyectil [projek'til] nm projectile, missile; **~ (tele)dirigido** guided missile
proyecto [pro'jekto] nm plan; (idea) project; (estimación de costo) detailed estimate; **tener algo en ~** to be planning sth; **~ de ley** (Pol) bill
proyector [projek'tor] nm (Cine) projector
prudencia [pru'ðenθja] nf (sabiduría) wisdom, prudence; (cautela) care
prudente [pru'ðente] adj sensible, wise, prudent; (cauteloso) careful
prueba ['prweβa] vb ver **probar** ⊳ nf proof; (ensayo) test, trial; (cantidad) taste, sample; (saboreo) testing, sampling; (de ropa) fitting; (Deporte) event; **a ~** on trial; (Com) on approval; **a ~ de** proof against; **a ~ de agua/fuego** waterproof/fireproof; **~ de capacitación** (Com) proficiency test; **~ de fuego** (fig) acid test; **~ de vallas** hurdles; **someter a ~** to put to the test; ¿tiene usted **~ de ello?** can you prove it?, do you have proof?
prurito [pru'rito] nm itch; (de bebé) nappy rash; (anhelo) urge
psico... [siko] pref psycho...
psicoanálisis [sikoa'nalisis] nm psychoanalysis
psicología [sikolo'xia] nf psychology
psicológico, -a [siko'loxiko, a] adj psychological
psicólogo, -a [si'koloɣo, a] nm/f psychologist
psicópata [si'kopata] nm/f psychopath
psicosis [si'kosis] nf inv psychosis

psicosomático, -a [sikoso'matiko, a] adj psychosomatic
psiquiatra [si'kjatra] nm/f psychiatrist
psiquiátrico, -a [si'kjatriko, a] adj psychiatric ⊳ nm mental hospital
psíquico, -a ['sikiko, a] adj psychic(al)
PSOE [pe'soe] nm abr = **Partido Socialista Obrero Español**
PSS nf abr (= Prestación Social Sustitutoria) community service for conscientious objectors
púa ['pua] nf sharp point; (Bot, Zool) prickle, spine; (para guitarra) plectrum; **alambre de ~s** barbed wire
pub [puβ/paβ/paf] nm bar
pubertad [puβer'tað] nf puberty
publicación [puβlika'θjon] nf publication
publicar [puβli'kar] vt (editar) to publish; (hacer público) to publicize; (divulgar) to make public, divulge
publicidad [puβliθi'ðað] nf publicity; (Com) advertising; **dar ~ a** to publicize, give publicity to; **~ gráfica** display advertising; **~ en el punto de venta** point-of-sale advertising
publicitario, -a [puβliθi'tarjo, a] adj publicity cpd; advertising cpd
público, -a ['puβliko, a] adj public ⊳ nm public; (Teat etc) audience; (Deporte) spectators pl, crowd; (en restaurantes etc) clients pl; **el gran ~** the general public; **hacer ~** to publish; (difundir) to disclose; **~ objetivo** (Com) target audience
puchero [pu'tʃero] nm (Culin: olla) cooking pot; (: guiso) stew; **hacer ~s** to pout
pucho ['putʃo] (Am: fam) nm cigarette, fag (Brit)
pude etc vb ver **poder**
púdico, -a ['puðiko, a] adj modest; (pudibundo) bashful
pudiera etc vb ver **poder**
pudiente [pu'ðjente] adj (opulento) wealthy; (poderoso) powerful
pudor [pu'ðor] nm modesty; (vergüenza) (sense of) shame
pudrir [pu'ðrir] vt to rot; (fam) to upset, annoy; **pudrirse** vr to rot, decay; (fig) to rot, languish
pueblo ['pweβlo] vb ver **poblar** ⊳ nm people; (nación) nation; (aldea) village; (plebe) common people; (población pequeña) small town, country town
puedo etc vb ver **poder**
puente ['pwente] nm (gen) bridge; (Naut: tb: **~ de mando**) bridge; (: cubierta) deck; **~ aéreo** shuttle service; **~ colgante** suspension bridge; **~ levadizo** drawbridge; **hacer (el) ~** (fam) to take a long weekend

◉ **HACER PUENTE**
◉
◉ When a public holiday in Spain falls on
◉ a Tuesday or Thursday it is common
◉ practice for employers to make the
◉ Monday or Friday a holiday as well and to

give everyone a four-day weekend. This is known as *hacer puente*. When a named public holiday such as the *Día de la Constitución* falls on a Tuesday or Thursday, people refer to the whole holiday period as e.g. the *puente de la Constitución*.

puenting ['pwentin] *nm* bungee jumping
puerco, -a ['pwerko, a] *adj* (*sucio*) dirty, filthy; (*obsceno*) disgusting ▷ *nm/f* pig/sow; **~ espín** porcupine
pueril [pwe'ril] *adj* childish
puerro ['pwerro] *nm* leek
puerta ['pwerta] *nf* door; (*de jardín*) gate; (*portal*) doorway; (*fig*) gateway; (*gol*) goal; (*Inform*) port; **a la ~** at the door; **a ~ cerrada** behind closed doors; **~ corredera/giratoria** sliding/swing o revolving door; **~ principal/ trasera** o **de servicio** front/back door; **~ (de transmisión en) paralelo/serie** (*Inform*) parallel/serial port; **tomar la ~** (*fam*) to leave
puerto ['pwerto] *nm* (*tb Inform*) port; (*de mar*) seaport; (*paso*) pass; (*fig*) haven, refuge; **llegar a ~** (*fig*) to get over a difficulty
Puerto Rico [pwerto'riko] *nm* Puerto Rico
puertorriqueño, -a [pwertorri'keno, a] *adj, nm/f* Puerto Rican
pues [pwes] *adv* (*entonces*) then; (*¡entonces!*) well, well then; (*así que*) so ▷ *conj* (*porque*) since; **¡~ sí!** yes!, certainly!; **~ ... no sé** well ... I don't know
puesto, -a ['pwesto, a] *pp de* **poner** ▷ *adj* dressed ▷ *nm* (*lugar, posición*) place; (*trabajo*) post, job; (*Mil*) post; (*Com*) stall; (*quiosco*) kiosk ▷ *conj*: **~ que** since, as ▷ *nf* (*apuesta*) bet, stake; **tener algo ~** to have sth on, be wearing sth; **~ de mercado** market stall; **~ de policía** police station; **~ de socorro** first aid post; **puesta en escena** staging; **puesta al día** updating; **puesta en marcha** starting; **puesta a punto** fine tuning; **puesta del sol** sunset; **puesta a cero** (*Inform*) reset
púgil ['puxil] *nm* boxer
pugna ['puɣna] *nf* battle, conflict
pugnar [puɣ'nar] *vi* (*luchar*) to struggle, fight; (*pelear*) to fight
pujar [pu'xar] *vt* (*precio*) to raise, push up ▷ *vi* (*en licitación*) to bid, bid up; (*fig: esforzarse*) to struggle, strain
pulcro, -a ['pulkro, a] *adj* neat, tidy
pulga ['pulɣa] *nf* flea; **tener malas ~s** to be short-tempered
pulgada [pul'ɣaða] *nf* inch
pulgar [pul'ɣar] *nm* thumb
pulir [pu'lir] *vt* to polish; (*alisar*) to smooth; (*fig*) to polish up, touch up
pulla ['puʎa] *nf* cutting remark
pulmón [pul'mon] *nm* lung; **a pleno ~** (*respirar*) deeply; (*gritar*) at the top of one's voice; **~ de acero** iron lung
pulmonía [pulmo'nia] *nf* pneumonia

pulpa ['pulpa] *nf* pulp; (*de fruta*) flesh, soft part
pulpería [pulpe'ria] *nf* (*Am*) small grocery store
púlpito ['pulpito] *nm* pulpit
pulpo ['pulpo] *nm* octopus
pulque ['pulke] *nm* pulque

PULQUE

Pulque is a thick, white, alcoholic drink which is very popular in Mexico. In ancient times it was considered sacred by the Aztecs. It is produced by fermenting the juice of the *maguey*, a Mexican cactus similar to the agave. It can be drunk by itself or mixed with fruit or vegetable juice.

pulsación [pulsa'θjon] *nf* beat, pulsation; (*Anat*) throb(bing); (*en máquina de escribir*) tap; (*de pianista, mecanógrafo*) touch; **~ (de una tecla)** (*Inform*) keystroke; **~ doble** (*Inform*) strikeover; **pulsaciones** pulse rate
pulsador [pulsa'ðor] *nm* button, push button
pulsar [pul'sar] *vt* (*tecla*) to touch, tap; (*Mus*) to play; (*botón*) to press, push ▷ *vi* to pulsate; (*latir*) to beat, throb
pulsera [pul'sera] *nf* bracelet; **reloj de ~** wristwatch
pulso ['pulso] *nm* (*Med*) pulse; (*fuerza*) strength; (*firmeza*) steadiness, steady hand; **hacer algo a ~** to do sth unaided o by one's own efforts
pulverizador [pulβeriθa'ðor] *nm* spray, spray gun
pulverizar [pulβeri'θar] *vt* to pulverize; (*líquido*) to spray
puna ['puna] *nf* (*Am Med*) mountain sickness
punición [puni'θjon] *nf* punishment
punitivo, -a [puni'tiβo, a] *adj* punitive
punki ['punki] *adj, nm/f* punk
punta ['punta] *nf* point, tip; (*extremidad*) end; (*promontorio*) headland; (*Costura*) corner; (*Tec*) small nail; (*fig*) touch, trace; **horas ~s** peak hours, rush hours; **sacar ~ a** to sharpen; **de ~** on end; **de ~ a ~** from one end to the other; **estar de ~** to be edgy; **ir de ~ en blanco** to be all dressed up to the nines; **tener algo en la ~ de la lengua** to have sth on the tip of one's tongue; **se le pusieron los pelos de ~** her hair stood on end
puntada [pun'taða] *nf* (*Costura*) stitch
puntal [pun'tal] *nm* prop, support
puntapié [punta'pje] *f* (*pl* **puntapiés**) *nm* kick; **echar a algn a ~s** to kick sb out
puntear [punte'ar] *vt* to tick, mark; (*Mus*) to pluck
puntería [punte'ria] *nf* (*de arma*) aim, aiming; (*destreza*) marksmanship
puntero, -a [pun'tero, a] *adj* leading ▷ *nm* (*señal, Inform*) pointer; (*dirigente*) leader

P

puntiagudo, -a [puntja'ɣuðo, a] *adj* sharp, pointed

puntilla [pun'tiʎa] *nf* (*Tec*) tack, braid; (*Costura*) lace edging; **(andar) de ~s** (to walk) on tiptoe

punto ['punto] *nm* (*gen*) point; (*señal diminuta*) spot, dot; (*lugar*) spot, place; (*momento*) point, moment; (*en un examen*) mark; (*tema*) item; (*Costura*) stitch; (*Inform: impresora*) pitch; (*: pantalla*) pixel; **a ~** ready; **estar a ~ de** to be on the point of o about to; **llegar a ~** to come just at the right moment; **al ~** at once; **en ~** on the dot; **estar en su ~** (*Culin*) to be done to a turn; **hasta cierto ~** to some extent; **hacer ~** to knit; **poner un motor en ~** to tune an engine; **~ de partida/de congelación/de fusión** starting/freezing/melting point; **~ de vista** point of view, viewpoint; **~ muerto** dead centre; (*Auto*) neutral (gear); **~s a tratar** matters to be discussed, agenda *sg*; **~ final** full stop; **dos ~s** colon; **~ y coma** semicolon; **~ acápite** (*Am*) full stop, new paragraph; **~ de interrogación** question mark; **~s suspensivos** suspension points; **~ de equilibrio/de pedido** (*Com*) breakeven/reorder point; **~ inicial** o **de partida** (*Inform*) home; **~ de referencia/de venta** (*Com*) benchmark point/point-of-sale

puntocom [punto'kom] *nf inv, adj inv* dotcom, dot.com

puntuación [puntwa'θjon] *nf* punctuation; (*puntos: en examen*) mark(s) *pl*; (*: Deporte*) score

puntual [pun'twal] *adj* (*a tiempo*) punctual; (*cálculo*) exact, accurate; (*informe*) reliable

puntualidad [puntwali'ðað] *nf* punctuality; exactness, accuracy; reliability

puntualizar [puntwali'θar] *vt* to fix, specify

puntuar [pun'twar] *vt* (*Ling, Tip*) to punctuate; (*examen*) to mark ▷ *vi* (*Deporte*) to score, count

punzada [pun'θaða] *nf* (*puntura*) prick; (*Med*) stitch; (*dolor*) twinge (of pain)

punzante [pun'θante] *adj* (*dolor*) shooting, sharp; (*herramienta*) sharp; (*comentario*) biting

punzar [pun'θar] *vt* to prick, pierce ▷ *vi* to shoot, stab

puñado [pu'ɲaðo] *nm* handful (*tb fig*); **a ~s** by handfuls

puñal [pu'ɲal] *nm* dagger

puñalada [puɲa'laða] *nf* stab

puñetazo [puɲe'taθo] *nm* punch

puño ['puɲo] *nm* (*Anat*) fist; (*cantidad*) fistful, handful; (*Costura*) cuff; (*de herramienta*) handle; **como un ~** (*verdad*) obvious; (*palpable*) tangible, visible; **de ~ y letra del poeta** in the poet's own handwriting

pupila [pu'pila] *nf* (*Anat*) pupil

pupitre [pu'pitre] *nm* desk

puré [pu're] (*pl* **purés**) *nm* puree; (*sopa*) (thick) soup; **~ de patatas** (*Esp*), **~ de papas** (*Am*) mashed potatoes; **estar hecho ~** (*fig*) to be knackered

pureza [pu'reθa] *nf* purity

purga ['purɣa] *nf* purge

purgante [pur'ɣante] *adj, nm* purgative

purgar [pur'ɣar] *vt* to purge; (*Pol: depurar*) to purge, liquidate; **purgarse** *vr* (*Med*) to take a purge

purgatorio [purɣa'torjo] *nm* purgatory

purificar [purifi'kar] *vt* to purify; (*refinar*) to refine

puritano, -a [puri'tano, a] *adj* (*actitud*) puritanical; (*iglesia, tradición*) puritan ▷ *nm/f* puritan

puro, -a ['puro, a] *adj* pure; (*depurado*) unadulterated; (*oro*) solid; (*cielo*) clear; (*verdad*) simple, plain ▷ *adv*: **de ~ cansado** out of sheer tiredness ▷ *nm* cigar; **por pura casualidad** by sheer chance

púrpura ['purpura] *nf* purple

purpúreo, -a [pur'pureo, a] *adj* purple

pus [pus] *nm* pus

puse *etc* ['puse] *vb ver* **poner**

pusiera *etc* *vb ver* **poder**

pústula ['pustula] *nf* pimple, sore

puta ['puta] *nf* whore, prostitute

putada [pu'taða] *nf* (*fam!*): **hacer una ~ a algn** to play a dirty trick on sb; **¡qué ~!** what a pain in the arse! (*!*)

putrefacción [putrefak'θjon] *nf* rotting, putrefaction

pútrido, -a ['putriðo, a] *adj* rotten

puzzle ['puθle] *nm* puzzle

PVP *abr* (*Esp*: = *Precio Venta al Público*) ≈ RRP

PYME ['pime] *nf abr* (= *Pequeña y Mediana Empresa*) SME

q

que [ke] *conj* **1** *(con oración subordinada: muchas veces no se traduce)* that; **dijo que vendría** he said (that) he would come; **espero que lo encuentres** I hope (that) you find it; **dile que me llame** ask him to call me; *ver tb* **el**
2 *(en oración independiente)*: **¡que entre!** send him in; **¡que aproveche!** enjoy your meal!; **¡que se mejore tu padre!** I hope your father gets better; **¡que lo haga él!** he can do it!; *(orden)* get him to do it!
3 *(enfático)*: **¿me quieres? — ¡que sí!** do you love me? — of course!; **te digo que sí** I'm telling you
4 *(consecutivo: muchas veces no se traduce)* that; **es tan grande que no lo puedo levantar** it's so big (that) I can't lift it
5 *(comparaciones)* than; **yo que tú/él** if I were you/him; *ver tb* **más; menos**
6 *(valor disyuntivo)*: **que le guste o no** whether he likes it or not; **que venga o que no venga** whether he comes or not
7 *(porque)*: **no puedo, que tengo que quedarme en casa** I can't, I've got to stay in
8: **siguió toca que toca** he kept on playing
▷ *pron* **1** *(cosa)* that, which; *(+prep)* which; **el sombrero que te compraste** the hat (that o which) you bought; **la cama en que dormí** the bed (that o which) I slept in; **el día (en) que ella nació** the day (when) she was born

2 *(persona: suj)* that, who; *(: objeto)* that, whom; **el amigo que me acompañó al museo** the friend that o who went to the museum with me; **la chica que invité** the girl (that o whom) I invited

qué [ke] *adj* what?, which? ▷ *pron* what?; **¡~ divertido/asco!** how funny/revolting!; **¡~ día más espléndido!** what a glorious day!; **¿~ edad tienes?** how old are you?; **¿de ~ me hablas?** what are you saying to me?; **¿~ tal?** how are you?, how are things?; **¿~ hay (de nuevo)?** what's new?; **¿~ más?** anything else?

quebrada [ke'βraða] *nf ver* **quebrado**
quebradero [keβra'ðero] *nm*: **~ de cabeza** headache, worry
quebradizo, -a [keβra'ðiθo, a] *adj* fragile; *(persona)* frail
quebrado, -a [ke'βraðo, a] *adj (roto)* broken; *(terreno)* rough, uneven ▷ *nm/f* bankrupt ▷ *nm (Mat)* fraction ▷ *nf* ravine; **~ rehabilitado** discharged bankrupt
quebrantar [keβran'tar] *vt (infringir)* to violate, transgress; **quebrantarse** *vr (persona)* to fail in health
quebranto [ke'βranto] *nm* damage, harm; *(decaimiento)* exhaustion; *(dolor)* grief, pain
quebrar [ke'βrar] *vt* to break, smash ▷ *vi* to go bankrupt; **quebrarse** *vr* to break, get broken; *(Med)* to be ruptured
quedar [ke'ðar] *vi* to stay, remain; *(encontrarse)* to be; *(restar)* to remain, be left; **quedarse** *vr* to remain, stay (behind); **~ en** *(acordar)* to agree on/to; *(acabar siendo)* to end up as; **~ por hacer** to be still to be done; **~ ciego/mudo** to be left blind/dumb; **no te queda bien ese vestido** that dress doesn't suit you; **quedamos a las seis** we agreed to meet at six; **eso queda muy lejos** that's a long way (away); **nos quedan 12 kms para llegar al pueblo** there are still 12 km before we get to the village; **no queda otra** there's no alternative; **~se (con) algo** to keep sth; **~se con algn** *(fam)* to swindle sb; **~se en nada** to come to nothing o nought; **~se frito** *(inf)* to fall asleep, to crash out; **~se sin** to run out of
quedo, -a ['keðo, a] *adj* still ▷ *adv* softly, gently
quehacer [kea'θer] *nm* task, job; **~es (domésticos)** household chores
queja ['kexa] *nf* complaint
quejarse [ke'xarse] *vr (enfermo)* to moan, groan; *(protestar)* to complain; **~ de que ...** to complain (about the fact) that ...
quejido [ke'xiðo] *nm* moan
quejoso, -a [ke'xoso, a] *adj* complaining
quemado, -a [ke'maðo, a] *adj* burnt; *(irritado)* annoyed
quemadura [kema'ðura] *nf* burn, scald; *(de sol)* sunburn; *(de fusible)* blow-out

q

quemar [ke'mar] vt to burn; (fig: malgastar) to burn up, squander; (Com: precios) to slash, cut; (fastidiar) to annoy, bug ▷ vi to be burning hot; **quemarse** vr (consumirse) to burn (up); (del sol) to get sunburnt

quemarropa [kema'rropa]: **a ~** adv point-blank

quemazón [kema'θon] nf burn; (calor) intense heat; (sensación) itch

quepo etc ['kepo] vb ver **caber**

querella [ke'reʎa] nf (Jur) charge; (disputa) dispute

querellarse [kere'ʎarse] vr to file a complaint

PALABRA CLAVE

querer [ke'rer] vt **1** (desear) to want; **quiero más dinero** I want more money; **quisiera** o **querría un té** I'd like a tea; **sin querer** unintentionally; **quiero ayudar/que vayas** I want to help/you to go; **como Vd quiera** as you wish, as you please; **ven cuando quieras** come when you like; **lo hizo sin querer** he didn't mean to do it; **no quiero** I don't want to; **le pedí que me dejara ir pero no quiso** I asked him to let me go but he refused

2 (preguntas: para pedir u ofrecer algo): **¿quiere abrir la ventana?** could you open the window?; **¿quieres echarme una mano?** can you give me a hand?; **¿quiere un café?** would you like some coffee?

3 (amar) to love; (tener cariño a) to be fond of; **te quiero** I love you; **quiere mucho a sus hijos** he's very fond of his children

4 (requerir): **esta planta quiere más luz** this plant needs more light

5: **querer decir** to mean; **¿qué quieres decir?** what do you mean?

querido, -a [ke'riðo, a] adj dear ▷ nm/f darling; (amante) lover; **nuestra querida patria** our beloved country

quesería [kese'ria] nf dairy; (fábrica) cheese factory

queso ['keso] nm cheese; **~ rallado** grated cheese; **~ crema** (Am), **~ de untar** (Esp) cream cheese; **~ manchego** sheep's milk cheese made in La Mancha; **dárselas con ~ a algn** (fam) to take sb in

quicio ['kiθjo] nm hinge; **estar fuera de ~** to be beside o.s.; **sacar a algn de ~** to drive sb up the wall

quiebra ['kjeβra] nf break, split; (Com) bankruptcy; (Econ) slump

quiebro etc ['kjeβro] vb ver **quebrar** ▷ nm (del cuerpo) swerve

quien [kjen] pron relativo (suj) who; (complemento) whom; (indefinido): **~ dice eso es tonto** whoever says that is a fool; **hay ~ piensa que** there are those who think that;

no hay ~ lo haga no-one will do it; **~ más, ~ menos tiene sus problemas** everybody has problems

quién [kjen] pron interrogativo who; (complemento) whom; **¿~ es?** who is it?, who's there?; (Telec) who's calling?

quienquiera [kjen'kjera] (pl **quienesquiera**) pron whoever

quiero etc ['kjero] vb ver **querer**

quieto, -a ['kjeto, a] adj still; (carácter) placid; **¡estáte ~!** keep still!

quietud [kje'tuð] nf stillness

quijada [ki'xaða] nf jaw, jawbone

quilate [ki'late] nm carat

quilla ['kiʎa] nf keel

quimera [ki'mera] nf (sueño) pipe dream

quimérico, -a [ki'meriko, a] adj fantastic

químico, -a ['kimiko, a] adj chemical ▷ nm/f chemist ▷ nf chemistry

quimioterapia [kimiote'rapja] nf chemotherapy

quincalla [kin'kaʎa] nf hardware, ironmongery (Brit)

quince ['kinθe] num fifteen; **~ días** a fortnight

quinceañero, -a [kinθea'ɲero, a] adj fifteen-year-old; (adolescente) teenage ▷ nm/f fifteen-year-old; (adolescente) teenager

quincena [kin'θena] nf fortnight; (pago) fortnightly pay

quincenal [kinθe'nal] adj fortnightly

quiniela [ki'njela] nf football pools pl; **quinielas** nfpl pools coupon sg

quinientos, -as [ki'njentos, as] num five hundred

quinina [ki'nina] nf quinine

quinqui ['kinki] nm delinquent

quinta ['kinta] nf ver **quinto**

quinteto [kin'teto] nm quintet

quinto, -a ['kinto, a] adj fifth ▷ nm (Mil) conscript, draftee ▷ nf country house; (Mil) call-up, draft

quiosco ['kjosko] nm (de música) bandstand; (de periódicos) news stand (also selling sweets, cigarettes etc)

quirófano [ki'rofano] nm operating theatre

quirúrgico, -a [ki'rurxiko, a] adj surgical

quise etc ['kise] vb ver **querer**

quisiera etc vb ver **querer**

quisquilloso [kiski'ʎoso, a] adj (susceptible) touchy; (meticuloso) pernickety

quiste ['kiste] nm cyst

quitaesmalte [kitaes'malte] nm nail polish remover

quitamanchas [kita'mantʃas] nm inv stain remover

quitanieves [kita'njeβes] nm inv snowplough (Brit), snowplow (US)

quitar [ki'tar] vt to remove, take away; (ropa) to take off; (dolor) to relieve; (vida) to take; (valor) to reduce; (hurtar) to remove, steal ▷ vi: **¡quita de ahí!** get away!; **quitarse** vr to withdraw; (*mancha*) to come off *o* out; (*ropa*) to take off; **me quita mucho tiempo** it takes up a lot of my time; **el café me quita el sueño** coffee stops me sleeping; **~ de en medio a algn** to get rid of sb; **~se algo de encima** to get rid of sth; **~se del tabaco** to give up smoking; **se quitó el sombrero** he took off his hat

quite ['kite] *nm* (*en esgrima*) parry; (*evasión*) dodge; **estar al ~** to be ready to go to sb's aid

Quito ['kito] *n* Quito

quizá [ki'θa]

quizás [ki'θas] *adv* perhaps, maybe

r

rabadilla [raβa'ðiʎa] *nf* base of the spine

rábano ['raβano] *nm* radish; **me importa un ~** I don't give a damn

rabia ['raβja] *nf* (*Med*) rabies *sg*; (*fig: ira*) fury, rage; **¡qué ~!** isn't it infuriating!; **me da ~** it maddens me; **tener ~ a algn** to have a grudge against sb

rabiar [ra'βjar] *vi* to have rabies; to rage, be furious; **~ por algo** to long for sth

rabieta [ra'βjeta] *nf* tantrum, fit of temper

rabino [ra'βino] *nm* rabbi

rabioso, -a [ra'βjoso, a] *adj* rabid; (*fig*) furious

rabo ['raβo] *nm* tail

racha ['ratʃa] *nf* gust of wind; (*serie*) string, series; **buena/mala ~** spell of good/bad luck

racial [ra'θjal] *adj* racial, race *cpd*

racimo [ra'θimo] *nm* bunch

raciocinio [raθjo'θinjo] *nm* reason; (*razonamiento*) reasoning

ración [ra'θjon] *nf* portion; **raciones** *nfpl* rations

racional [raθjo'nal] *adj* (*razonable*) reasonable; (*lógico*) rational

racionalizar [raθjonali'θar] *vt* to rationalize; (*Com*) to streamline

racionar [raθjo'nar] *vt* to ration (out)

racismo [ra'θismo] *nm* racialism, racism

racista [ra'θista] *adj, nm/f* racist

radar [ra'ðar] *nm* radar

radiactividad [raðjaktiβi'ðað] *nf* radioactivity

radiactivo, -a [raðjak'tiβo, a] *adj* radioactive

radiador [raðja'ðor] *nm* radiator

radiante [ra'ðjante] *adj* radiant

radical [raði'kal] *adj, nm/f* radical ▷ *nm* (*Ling*) root; (*Mat*) square-root sign

radicar [raði'kar] *vi* to take root; ~ **en** (*dificultad, problema*) to lie in; (*solución*) to consist in; **radicarse** *vr* to establish o.s., put down (one's) roots

radio ['raðjo] *nf* radio; (*aparato*) radio (set) ▷ *nm* (*Mat*) radius; (*Am*) radio; (*Química*) radium; ~ **de acción** extent of one's authority, sphere of influence

radioactividad [raðjoaktiβi'ðað] *nf* radioactivity

radioactivo, -a [raðjoak'tiβo, a] *adj* radioactive

radioaficionado, -a [raðjoafiθjo'naðo, a] *nm/f* radio ham

radiocasete [raðjoka'sete] *nm* radiocassette (player)

radiodifusión [raðjodifu'sjon] *nf* broadcasting

radioemisora [raðjoemi'sora] *nf* transmitter, radio station

radiografía [raðjoɣra'fia] *nf* X-ray

radionovela [raðjono'βela] *nf* radio series

radiotaxi [raðjo'taksi] *nm* radio taxi

radioterapia [raðjote'rapja] *nf* radiotherapy

radioyente [raðjo'jente] *nm/f* listener

ráfaga ['rafaɣa] *nf* gust; (*de luz*) flash; (*de tiros*) burst

raído, -a [ra'iðo, a] *adj* (*ropa*) threadbare; (*persona*) shabby

raigambre [rai'ɣambre] *nf* (*Bot*) roots *pl*; (*fig*) tradition

raíz [ra'iθ] (*pl* **raíces**) *nf* root; ~ **cuadrada** square root; **a ~ de** as a result of; (*después de*) immediately after

raja ['raxa] *nf* (*de melón etc*) slice; (*hendidura*) slit, split; (*grieta*) crack

rajar [ra'xar] *vt* to split; (*fam*) to slash; **rajarse** *vr* to split, crack; **~se de** to back out of

rajatabla [raxa'taβla]: **a ~** *adv* (*estrictamente*) strictly, to the letter

rallador [raʎa'ðor] *nm* grater

rallar [ra'ʎar] *vt* to grate

ralo, -a ['ralo, a] *adj* thin, sparse

rama ['rama] *nf* bough, branch; **andarse por las ~s** (*fig: fam*) to beat about the bush

ramaje [ra'maje] *nm* branches *pl*, foliage

ramal [ra'mal] *nm* (*de cuerda*) strand; (*Ferro*) branch line; (*Auto*) branch (road)

rambla ['rambla] *nf* (*avenida*) avenue

ramera [ra'mera] *nf* whore, hooker (*US*)

ramificación [ramifika'θjon] *nf* ramification

ramificarse [ramifi'karse] *vr* to branch out

ramillete [rami'ʎete] *nm* bouquet; (*fig*) select group

ramo ['ramo] *nm* branch, twig; (*sección*) department, section; (*sector*) field, sector

rampa ['rampa] *nf* ramp; ~ **de acceso** entrance ramp

ramplón, -ona [ram'plon, ona] *adj* uncouth, coarse

rana ['rana] *nf* frog; **salto de ~** leapfrog; **cuando las ~s críen pelos** when pigs fly

ranchero [ran'tʃero] *nm* (*Am*) rancher; (*pequeño propietario*) smallholder

rancho ['rantʃo] *nm* (*Mil*) food; (*Am: grande*) ranch; (: *pequeño*) small farm

rancio, -a ['ranθjo, a] *adj* (*comestibles*) stale, rancid; (*vino*) aged, mellow; (*fig*) ancient

rango ['rango] *nm* rank; (*prestigio*) standing

ranura [ra'nura] *nf* groove; (*de teléfono etc*) slot; ~ **de expansión** (*Inform*) expansion slot

rap [rap] *nm* (*Mus*) rap

rapar [ra'par] *vt* to shave; (*los cabellos*) to crop

rapaz [ra'paθ] (*nf* **rapaza**) *nm/f* young boy/girl ▷ *adj* (*Zool*) predatory

rapaza [ra'paθa] *nf* young girl

rape ['rape] *nm* quick shave; (*pez*) monkfish; **al ~** cropped

rapé [ra'pe] *nm* snuff

rápidamente ['rapiðarmente] *adv* quickly

rapidez [rapi'ðeθ] *nf* speed, rapidity

rápido, -a ['rapiðo, a] *adj* fast, quick ▷ *adv* quickly ▷ *nm* (*Ferro*) express; **rápidos** *nmpl* rapids

rapiña [ra'piɲa] *nm* robbery; **ave de ~** bird of prey

raptar [rap'tar] *vt* to kidnap

rapto ['rapto] *nm* kidnapping; (*impulso*) sudden impulse; (*éxtasis*) ecstasy, rapture

raqueta [ra'keta] *nf* racquet

raquítico, -a [ra'kitiko, a] *adj* stunted; (*fig*) poor, inadequate

raquitismo [raki'tismo] *nm* rickets *sg*

raramente [rara'mente] *adv* rarely

rareza [ra'reθa] *nf* rarity; (*fig*) eccentricity

raro, -a ['raro, a] *adj* (*poco común*) rare; (*extraño*) odd, strange; (*excepcional*) remarkable; **¡qué ~!** how (very) odd!; **¡(qué) cosa más rara!** how strange!

ras [ras] *nm*: **a ~ de** level with; **a ~ de tierra** at ground level

rasar [ra'sar] *vt* to level

rascacielos [raska'θjelos] *nm inv* skyscraper

rascar [ras'kar] *vt* (*con las uñas etc*) to scratch; (*raspar*) to scrape; **rascarse** *vr* to scratch (o.s.)

rasgar [ras'ɣar] *vt* to tear, rip (up)

rasgo ['rasɣo] *nm* (*con pluma*) stroke; **rasgos** *nmpl* features, characteristics; **a grandes ~s** in outline, broadly

rasguñar [rasɣu'ɲar] *vt* to scratch; (*bosquejar*) to sketch

rasguño [ras'ɣuɲo] *nm* scratch

raso, -a ['raso, a] *adj* (*liso*) flat, level; (*a baja altura*) very low ▷ *nm* satin; (*campo llano*) flat country; **cielo ~** clear sky; **al ~** in the open

raspado [ras'paðo] *nm* (*Med*) scrape

raspadura [raspa'ðura] *nf* (*acto*) scrape,

scraping; (*marca*) scratch; **raspaduras** *nfpl*
(*de papel etc*) scrapings
raspar [ras'par] *vt* to scrape; (*arañar*) to
scratch; (*limar*) to file ▷ *vi* (*manos*) to be
rough; (*vino*) to be sharp, have a rough taste
rastra ['rastra] *nf* (*Agr*) rake; **a ~s** by dragging;
(*fig*) unwillingly
rastreador [rastrea'ðor] *nm* tracker; **~ de
minas** minesweeper
rastrear [rastre'ar] *vt* (*seguir*) to track; (*minas*)
to sweep
rastrero, -a [ras'trero, a] *adj* (*Bot, Zool*)
creeping; (*fig*) despicable, mean
rastrillar [rastri'ʎar] *vt* to rake
rastrillo [ras'triʎo] *nm* rake; (*Am*) safety razor
rastro ['rastro] *nm* (*Agr*) rake; (*pista*) track,
trail; (*vestigio*) trace; (*mercado*) flea market; **el
R~** *the Madrid flea market*; **perder el ~** to lose
the scent; **desaparecer sin ~** to vanish
without trace
rastrojo [ras'troxo] *nm* stubble
rasurado [rasu'raðo] *nm* (*Am*) shaving
rasurador [rasura'ðor] *nm*, **rasuradora** (*Am*)
[rasura'ðora] *nf* electric shaver *o* razor
rasurar [ɹasu'rar] *vt* (*Am*) to shave; **rasurarse**
vr to shave
rata ['rata] *nf* rat
ratear [rate'ar] *vt* (*robar*) to steal
ratero, -a [ra'tero, a] *adj* light-fingered
▷ *nm/f* (*carterista*) pickpocket; (*ladrón*) petty
thief; (*Am: de casas*) burglar
ratificar [ratifi'kar] *vt* to ratify
rato ['rato] *nm* while, short time; **a ~s** from
time to time; **al poco ~** shortly after, soon
afterwards; **~s libres** *o* **de ocio** leisure *sg*,
spare *o* free time *sg*; **hay para ~** there's still a
long way to go; **pasar el ~** to kill time; **pasar
un buen/mal ~** to have a good/rough time
ratón [ra'ton] *nm* (*tb Inform*) mouse
ratonera [rato'nera] *nf* mousetrap
raudal [rau'ðal] *nm* torrent; **a ~es** in
abundance; **entrar a ~es** to pour in
raya ['raja] *nf* line; (*marca*) scratch; (*en tela*)
stripe; (*puntuación*) dash; (*de pelo*) parting;
(*límite*) boundary; (*pez*) ray; **a ~s** striped;
pasarse de la ~ to overstep the mark; **tener
a ~** to keep in check
rayar [ɹa'jar] *vt* to line; to scratch; (*subrayar*)
to underline ▷ *vi*: **~ en** *o* **con** to border on; **al
~ el alba** at first light; **~ a algn** (*col*) to do sb's
head in (*col*); **está siempre rayándome con
esa historia** he's doing my head in with
that business (*col*)
rayo ['rajo] *nm* (*del sol*) ray, beam; (*de luz*) shaft;
(*en una tormenta*) (flash of) lightning; **~ solar**
o **de sol** sunbeam; **~s infrarrojos** infrared
rays; **~s X** X-rays; **como un ~** like a shot; **la
noticia cayó como un ~** the news was a
bombshell; **pasar como un ~** to flash past
raza ['raθa] *nf* race; (*de animal*) breed; **~
humana** human race; **de pura ~** (*caballo*)
thoroughbred; (*perro etc*) pedigree

razón [ra'θon] *nf* reason; (*justicia*) right,
justice; (*razonamiento*) reasoning; (*motivo*)
reason, motive; (*proporción*) ratio; (*Mat*) ratio;
a ~ de 10 cada día at the rate of 10 a day;
"~: ..." "inquiries to ..."; **en ~ de** with regard
to; **perder la ~** to go out of one's mind; **dar ~
a algn** to agree that sb is right; **dar ~ de** to
give an account of, report on; **tener/no
tener ~** to be right/wrong; **~ directa/
inversa** direct/inverse proportion; **~ de ser**
raison d'être
razonable [raθo'naβle] *adj* reasonable; (*justo,
moderado*) fair
razonamiento [raθona'mjento] *nm* (*juicio*)
judgement; (*argumento*) reasoning
razonar [raθo'nar] *vt, vi* to reason, argue
RDSI *nf abr* (= *Red Digital de Servicios Integrados*)
ISDN
re [re] *nm* (*Mus*) D
reacción [reak'θjon] *nf* reaction; **avión a ~**
jet plane; **~ en cadena** chain reaction
reaccionar [reakθjo'nar] *vi* to react
reaccionario, -a [reakθjo'narjo, a] *adj*
reactionary
reacio, -a [re'aθjo, a] *adj* stubborn; **ser** *o*
estar ~ a to be opposed to
reactivar [reakti'βar] *vt* to reactivate;
(*economía*) revitalize; **reactivarse** *vr*
(*economía*) to be on the upturn
reactor [reak'tor] *nm* reactor; (*avión*) jet
plane; **~ nuclear** nuclear reactor
readaptación [reaðapta'θjon] *nf*:
~ profesional industrial retraining
readmitir [reaðmi'tir] *vt* to readmit
reajuste [rea'xuste] *nm* readjustment;
~ salarial wage increase; **~ de plantilla**
rationalization
real [re'al] *adj* real; (*del rey, fig*) royal;
(*espléndido*) grand ▷ *nm* (*de feria*) fairground
realce *etc* [re'alθe] *vb ver* **realzar** ▷ *nm* (*Tec*)
embossing; **poner de ~** to emphasize
real-decreto [re'alde'kreto] (*pl* **reales-
decretos**) *nm* royal decree
realidad [reali'ðað] *nf* reality; (*verdad*) truth;
~ virtual virtual reality; **en ~** in fact
realismo [rea'lismo] *nm* realism
realista [rea'lista] *nm/f* realist
realización [realiθa'θjon] *nf* fulfilment,
realization; (*Com*) selling up (*Brit*),
conversion into money (*US*); **~ de plusvalías**
profit-taking
realizador, a [realiθa'ðor, a] *nm/f* film
maker; (*TV etc*) producer
realizar [reali'θar] *vt* (*objetivo*) to achieve;
(*plan*) to carry out; (*viaje*) to make, undertake;
(*Com*) to realize; **realizarse** *vr* to come about,
come true; **~se como persona** to fulfil one's
aims in life
realmente [real'mente] *adv* really, actually
realojar [realo'xar] *vt* to rehouse
realquilar [realki'lar] *vt* (*subarrendar*) to
sublet; (*alquilar de nuevo*) to relet

r

realzar [real'θar] vt (Tec) to raise; (embellecer) to enhance; (acentuar) to highlight

reanimar [reani'mar] vt (revivir; (alentar) to encourage; **reanimarse** vr to revive

reanudar [reanu'ðar] vt (renovar) to renew; (historia, viaje) to resume

reaparición [reapari'θjon] nf reappearance; (vuelta) return

rearme [re'arme] nm rearmament

reavivar [reaβi'βar] vt (persona) to revive; (fig) to rekindle

rebaja [re'βaxa] nf reduction, lowering; (Com) discount; **rebajas** nfpl (Com) sale; **"grandes ~s"** "big reductions", "sale"

rebajar [reβa'xar] vt (bajar) to lower; (reducir) to reduce; (precio) to cut; (disminuir) to lessen; (humillar) to humble; **rebajarse** vr: **~se a hacer algo** to stoop to doing sth

rebanada [reβa'naða] nf slice

rebañar [reβa'ɲar] vt (comida) to scrape up; (plato) to scrape clean

rebaño [re'βaɲo] nm herd; (de ovejas) flock

rebasar [reβa'sar] vt (tb: ~ de) to exceed; (Auto) to overtake

rebatir [reβa'tir] vt to refute; (rebajar) to reduce; (ataque) to repel

rebeca [re'βeka] nf cardigan

rebelarse [reβe'larse] vr to rebel, revolt

rebelde [re'βelde] adj rebellious; (niño) unruly ▷ nm/f rebel; **ser ~ a** to be in revolt against, rebel against

rebeldía [reβel'dia] nf rebelliousness; (desobediencia) disobedience; (Jur) default

rebelión [reβe'ljon] nf rebellion

reblandecer [reβlande'θer] vt to soften

rebobinar [reβoβi'nar] vt to rewind

rebosante [reβo'sante] adj: ~ **de** (fig) brimming o overflowing with

rebosar [reβo'sar] vi to overflow; (abundar) to abound, be plentiful; ~ **de salud** to be bursting o brimming with health

rebotar [reβo'tar] vt to bounce; (rechazar) to repel ▷ vi (pelota) to bounce; (bala) to ricochet

rebote [re'βote] nm rebound; **de** ~ on the rebound

rebozado, -a [reβo'θaðo, a] adj (Culin) fried in batter o breadcrumbs o flour

rebozar [reβo'θar] vt to wrap up; (Culin) to fry in batter etc

rebuscado, -a [reβus'kaðo, a] adj (amanerado) affected; (palabra) recherché; (idea) far-fetched

rebuscar [reβus'kar] vi (en bolsillo, cajón) to fish; (en habitación) to search high and low

rebuznar [reβuθ'nar] vi to bray

recabar [reka'βar] vt (obtener) to manage to get; ~ **fondos** to collect money

recado [re'kaðo] nm message; (encargo) errand; **dejar/tomar un** ~ (Telec) to leave/take a message

recaer [reka'er] vi to relapse; ~ **en** to fall to o on; (criminal etc) to fall back into, relapse into; (premio) to go to

recaída [reka'iða] nf relapse

recalcar [rekal'kar] vt (fig) to stress, emphasize

recalcitrante [rekalθi'trante] adj recalcitrant

recalentamiento [rekalenta'mjento] nm: ~ **global** global warming

recalentar [rekalen'tar] vt (comida) to warm up, reheat; (demasiado) to overheat; **recalentarse** vr to overheat, get too hot

recámara [re'kamara] nf side room; (Am) bedroom

recambio [re'kambjo] nm spare; (de pluma) refill; **piezas de** ~ spares

recapacitar [rekapaθi'tar] vi to reflect

recapitular [rekapitu'lar] vt to recap

recargable [rekar'ɣaβle] adj (batería, pila) rechargeable; (mechero, pluma) refillable

recargado, -a [rekar'ɣaðo, a] adj overloaded; (exagerado) over-elaborate

recargar [rekar'ɣar] vt to overload; (batería) to recharge; (mechero, pluma) to refill; (tarjeta de móvil) to top up

recargo [re'karɣo] nm surcharge; (aumento) increase

recatado, -a [reka'taðo, a] adj (modesto) modest, demure; (prudente) cautious

recato [re'kato] nm (modestia) modesty, demureness; (cautela) caution

recauchutado, -a [rekautʃu'taðo, a] adj remould cpd

recaudación [rekauða'θjon] nf (acción) collection; (cantidad) takings pl; (en deporte) gate; (oficina) tax office

recaudador, a [rekauða'ðor, a] nm/f tax collector

recaudar [rekau'ðar] vt to collect

recelar [reθe'lar] vt: ~ **que** (sospechar) to suspect that; (temer) to fear that ▷ vi: ~(**se**) **de** to distrust

recelo [re'θelo] nm distrust, suspicion

receloso, -a [reθe'loso, a] adj distrustful, suspicious

recepción [reθep'θjon] nf reception; (acto de recibir) receipt

recepcionista [reθepθjo'nista] nm/f receptionist

receptáculo [reθep'takulo] nm receptacle

receptivo, -a [reθep'tiβo, a] adj receptive

receptor, a [reθep'tor, a] nm/f recipient ▷ nm (Telec) receiver; **descolgar el** ~ to pick up the receiver

recesión [reθe'sjon] nf (Com) recession

receta [re'θeta] nf (Culin) recipe; (Med) prescription

recetar [reθe'tar] vt to prescribe

rechazar [retʃa'θar] vt to repel, drive back; (idea) to reject; (oferta) to turn down

rechazo [re'tʃaθo] nm (de fusil) recoil; (rebote) rebound; (negación) rebuff; rejection

rechifla [re'tʃifla] nf hissing, booing; (fig) derision

rechinar [retʃi'nar] vi to creak; (*dientes*) to grind; (*máquina*) to clank, clatter; (*metal seco*) to grate; (*motor*) to hum

rechistar [retʃis'tar] vi: **sin ~** without complaint

rechoncho, -a [re'tʃontʃo, a] adj (*fam*) stocky, thickset (*Brit*), heavy-set (*US*)

rechupete [retʃu'pete]: **de ~** adj (*comida*) delicious

recibidor [reθiβi'ðor] nm entrance hall

recibimiento [reθiβi'mjento] nm reception, welcome

recibir [reθi'βir] vt to receive; (*dar la bienvenida*) to welcome; (*salir al encuentro de*) to go and meet ▷ vi to entertain; **recibirse** vr: **~se de** to qualify as

recibo [re'θiβo] nm receipt; **acusar ~ de** to acknowledge receipt of

reciclable [reθi'klaβle] adj recyclable

reciclaje [reθi'klaxe] nm recycling; (*de trabajadores*) retraining; **cursos de ~** refresher courses

reciclar [reθi'klar] vt to recycle; (*trabajador*) to retrain

recién [re'θjen] adv recently, newly; (*Am*) just, recently; **~ casado** newly-wed; **el ~ llegado** the newcomer; **el ~ nacido** the newborn child; **~ a las seis** only at six o'clock

reciente [re'θjente] adj recent; (*fresco*) fresh

recientemente [reθjente'mente] adv recently

recinto [re'θinto] nm enclosure; (*área*) area, place

recio, -a ['reθjo, a] adj strong, tough; (*voz*) loud ▷ adv hard; loud(ly)

recipiente [reθi'pjente] nm (*objeto*) container, receptacle; (*persona*) recipient

reciprocidad [reθiproθi'ðað] nf reciprocity

recíproco, -a [re'θiproko, a] adj reciprocal

recital [reθi'tal] nm (*Mus*) recital; (*Lit*) reading

recitar [reθi'tar] vt to recite

reclamación [reklama'θjon] nf claim, demand; (*queja*) complaint; **libro de reclamaciones** complaints book; **~ salarial** pay claim

reclamar [rekla'mar] vt to claim, demand ▷ vi: **~ contra** to complain about; **~ a algn en justicia** to take sb to court

reclamo [re'klamo] nm (*anuncio*) advertisement; (*tentación*) attraction

reclinar [rekli'nar] vt to recline, lean; **reclinarse** vr to lean back

recluir [reklu'ir] vt to intern, confine

reclusión [reklu'sjon] nf (*prisión*) prison; (*refugio*) seclusion; **~ perpetua** life imprisonment

recluta [re'kluta] nm/f recruit ▷ nf recruitment

reclutamiento [rekluta'mjento] nm recruitment

reclutar [reklu'tar] vt (*datos*) to collect; (*dinero*) to collect up

recobrar [reko'βrar] vt (*recuperar*) to recover; (*rescatar*) to get back; (*ciudad*) to recapture; (*tiempo*) to make up (for); **recobrarse** vr to recover

recochineo [rekotʃi'neo] nm (*fam*) mickey-taking

recodo [re'koðo] nm (*de río, camino*) bend

recogedor, a [rekoxe'ðor, a] nm dustpan ▷ nm(f) picker, harvester

recoger [reko'xer] vt to collect; (*Agr*) to harvest; (*fruta*) to pick; (*levantar*) to pick up; (*juntar*) to gather; (*pasar a buscar*) to come for, get; (*dar asilo*) to give shelter to; (*faldas*) to gather up; (*mangas*) to roll up; (*pelo*) to put up; **recogerse** vr (*retirarse*) to retire; **me recogieron en la estación** they picked me up at the station

recogido, -a [reko'xiðo, a] adj (*lugar*) quiet, secluded; (*pequeño*) small ▷ nf (*Correos*) collection; (*Agr*) harvest; **recogida de datos** (*Inform*) data capture

recolección [rekolek'θjon] nf (*Agr*) harvesting; (*colecta*) collection

recomendación [rekomenda'θjon] nf (*sugerencia*) suggestion, recommendation; (*referencia*) reference; **carta de ~ para** letter of introduction to

recomendar [rekomen'dar] vt to suggest, recommend; (*confiar*) to entrust

recompensa [rekom'pensa] nf reward, recompense; (*compensación*): **~ (de una pérdida)** compensation (for a loss); **como** o **en ~ por** in return for

recompensar [rekompen'sar] vt to reward, recompense

recomponer [rekompo'ner] vt to mend; (*Inform: texto*) to reformat

reconciliación [rekonθilja'θjon] nf reconciliation

reconciliar [rekonθi'ljar] vt to reconcile; **reconciliarse** vr to become reconciled

recóndito, -a [re'kondito, a] adj (*lugar*) hidden, secret

reconfortar [rekonfor'tar] vt to comfort

reconocer [rekono'θer] vt to recognize; (*registrar*) to search; (*Med*) to examine; **~ los hechos** to face the facts

reconocido, -a [rekono'θiðo, a] adj recognized; (*agradecido*) grateful

reconocimiento [rekonoθi'mjento] nm recognition; (*registro*) search; (*inspección*) examination; (*gratitud*) gratitude; (*confesión*) admission; **~ óptico de caracteres** (*Inform*) optical character recognition; **~ de la voz** (*Inform*) speech recognition

reconquista [rekon'kista] nf reconquest; **la R~** the Reconquest (of Spain)

reconstituyente [rekonstitu'jente] nm tonic

reconstruir [rekonstru'ir] vt to reconstruct

reconversión [rekomber'sjon] nf restructuring, reorganization; (*tb:* **~ industrial**) rationalization

r

recopilación [rekopila'θjon] *nf* (*resumen*) summary; (*compilación*) compilation

recopilar [rekopi'lar] *vt* to compile

récord ['rekorð] *adj inv* record; **cifras ~ record** figures ▷ *nm* (*pl* **records** *o* **récords** ['rekorð]) record; **batir el ~** to break the record

recordar [rekor'ðar] *vt* (*acordarse de*) to remember; (*traer a la memoria*) to recall; (*recordar a otro*) to remind ▷ *vi* to remember; **recuérdale que me debe cinco dólares** remind him that he owes me five dollars; **que yo recuerde** as far as I can remember; **creo ~, si mal no recuerdo** if my memory serves me right

recordatorio [rekorða'torjo] *nm* (*de fallecimiento*) in memoriam card; (*de bautizo, comunión*) commemorative card

recorrer [reko'rrer] *vt* (*país*) to cross, travel through; (*distancia*) to cover; (*registrar*) to search; (*repasar*) to look over

recorrido [reko'rriðo] *nm* run, journey; **tren de largo ~** main-line *o* inter-city (*Brit*) train

recortado, -a [rekor'taðo, a] *adj* uneven, irregular

recortar [rekor'tar] *vt* (*papel*) to cut out; (*el pelo*) to trim; (*dibujar*) to draw in outline; **recortarse** *vr* to stand out, be silhouetted

recorte [re'korte] *nm* (*acción, de prensa*) cutting; (*de telas, chapas*) trimming; **~ presupuestario** budget cut; **~ salarial** wage cut

recostado, -a [rekos'taðo, a] *adj* leaning; **estar ~** to be lying down

recostar [rekos'tar] *vt* to lean; **recostarse** *vr* to lie down

recoveco [reko'βeko] *nm* (*de camino, río etc*) bend; (*en casa*) cubbyhole

recreación [rekrea'θjon] *nf* recreation

recrear [rekre'ar] *vt* (*entretener*) to entertain; (*volver a crear*) to recreate

recreativo, -a [rekrea'tiβo, a] *adj* recreational

recreo [re'kreo] *nm* recreation; (*Escol*) break, playtime

recriminar [rekrimi'nar] *vt* to reproach ▷ *vi* to recriminate; **recriminarse** *vr* to reproach each other

recrudecer [rekruðe'θer] *vt, vi* to worsen; **recrudecerse** *vr* to worsen

recta ['rekta] *nf ver* **recto**

rectangular [rektaŋgu'lar] *adj* rectangular

rectángulo, -a [rek'taŋgulo, a] *adj* rectangular ▷ *nm* rectangle

rectificar [rektifi'kar] *vt* to rectify; (*volverse recto*) to straighten ▷ *vi* to correct o.s.

rectitud [rekti'tuð] *nf* straightness; (*fig*) rectitude

recto, -a ['rekto, a] *adj* straight; (*persona*) honest, upright; (*estricto*) strict; (*juez*) fair; (*juicio*) sound ▷ *nm* rectum; (*Atletismo*) straight ▷ *nf* straight line; **siga todo ~** go straight on; **en el sentido ~ de la palabra** in

the proper sense of the word; **recta final** *o* **de llegada** home straight

rector, a [rek'tor, a] *adj* governing ▷ *nm/f* head, chief; (*Escol*) rector, president (*US*)

recuadro [re'kwaðro] *nm* box; (*Tip*) inset

recubrir [reku'βir] *vt*: **~ (con)** (*pintura, crema*) to cover (with)

recuento [re'kwento] *nm* inventory; **hacer el ~ de** to count *o* reckon up

recuerdo [re'kwerðo] *vb ver* **recordar** ▷ *nm* souvenir; **recuerdos** *nmpl* memories; **¡~s a tu madre!** give my regards to your mother!; **"R~ de Mallorca"** "a present from Majorca"; **contar los ~s** to reminisce

recular [reku'lar] *vi* to back down

recuperable [rekupe'raβle] *adj* recoverable

recuperación [rekupera'θjon] *nf* recovery; **~ de datos** (*Inform*) data retrieval

recuperar [rekupe'rar] *vt* to recover; (*tiempo*) to make up; (*Inform*) to retrieve; **recuperarse** *vr* to recuperate

recurrir [reku'rrir] *vi* (*Jur*) to appeal; **~ a** to resort to; (*persona*) to turn to

recurso [re'kurso] *nm* resort; (*medio*) means *pl*, resource; (*Jur*) appeal; **como último ~** as a last resort; **~s económicos** economic resources; **~s naturales** natural resources

recusar [reku'sar] *vt* to reject, refuse

red [reð] *nf* net, mesh; (*Ferro, Inform*) network; (*Elec, de agua*) mains, supply system; (*de tiendas*) chain; (*trampa*) trap; **la R~** (*Internet*) the Net; **estar conectado con la ~** to be connected to the mains; **~ local** (*Inform*) local area network; **~ de transmisión** (*Inform*) data network

redacción [reðak'θjon] *nf* (*acción*) writing; (*Escol*) essay, composition; (*limpieza de texto*) editing; (*personal*) editorial staff

redactar [reðak'tar] *vt* to draw up, draft; (*periódico, Inform*) to edit

redactor, a [reðak'tor, a] *nm/f* writer; (*en periódico*) editor

redada [re'ðaða] *nf* (*Pesca*) cast, throw; (*fig*) catch; **~ policial** police raid, round-up

rededor [reðe'ðor] *nm*: **al** *o* **en ~** around, round about

redención [reðen'θjon] *nf* redemption

redentor, a [reðen'tor, a] *adj* redeeming ▷ *nm/f* (*Com*) redeemer

redescubrir [reðesku'βrir] *vt* to rediscover

redicho, -a [re'ðitʃo, a] *adj* affected

redil [re'ðil] *nm* sheepfold

redimir [reði'mir] *vt* to redeem; (*rehén*) to ransom

rédito ['reðito] *nm* interest, yield

redoblar [reðo'βlar] *vt* to redouble ▷ *vi* (*tambor*) to roll

redomado, -a [reðo'maðo, a] *adj* (*astuto*) sly, crafty; (*perfecto*) utter

redonda [re'ðonda] *nf ver* **redondo**

redondear [reðonde'ar] *vt* to round, round off; (*cifra*) to round up

redondel [reðon'del] nm (círculo) circle; (Taur) bullring, arena; (Auto) roundabout

redondo, -a [re'ðondo, a] adj (circular) round; (completo) complete ▷ nf: **a la redonda** around, round about; **en muchas millas a la redonda** for many miles around; **rehusar en ~** to give a flat refusal

reducción [reðuk'θjon] nf reduction; **~ del activo** (Com) divestment; **~ de precios** (Com) price-cutting

reducido, -a [reðu'θiðo, a] adj reduced; (limitado) limited; (pequeño) small; **quedar ~ a** to be reduced to

reducir [reðu'θir] vt to reduce, limit; (someter) to bring under control; **reducirse** vr to diminish; (Mat): **~ (a)** to reduce (to), convert (into); **~ las millas a kilómetros** to convert miles into kilometres; **~se a** (fig) to come o boil down to

reducto [re'ðukto] nm redoubt

redundancia [reðun'danθja] nf redundancy

reedición [re(e)ði'θjon] nf reissue

reeditar [re(e)ði'tar] vt to reissue

reelección [re(e)lek'θjon] nf re-election

reelegir [re(e)le'xir] vt to re-elect

reembolsar [re(e)mbol'sar] vt (persona) to reimburse; (dinero) to repay, pay back; (depósito) to refund

reembolso [re(e)m'bolso] nm reimbursement; refund; **enviar algo contra ~** to send sth cash on delivery; **contra ~ del flete** freight forward; **~ fiscal** tax rebate

reemplazar [re(e)mpla'θar] vt to replace

reemplazo [re(e)m'plaθo] nm replacement; **de ~** (Mil) reserve

reencuentro [re(e)n'kwentro] nm reunion

reengancharse [re(e)ngan'tʃarse] vr (Mil) to re-enlist

reescribible [reeskri'βiβle] adj rewritable

reestreno [re(e)s'treno] nm rerun

reestructurar [re(e)struktu'rar] vt to restructure

refacción [refak'θjon] nf (Am) repair(s); **refacciones** nfpl (piezas de repuesto) spare parts

referencia [refe'renθja] nf reference; **con ~ a** with reference to; **hacer ~ a** to refer o allude to; **~ comercial** (Com) trade reference

referéndum [refe'rendum] (pl **referéndums**) nm referendum

referente [refe'rente] adj: **~ a** concerning, relating to

réferi ['referi] nm/f (Am) referee

referir [refe'rir] vt (contar) to tell, recount; (relacionar) to refer, relate; **referirse** vr: **~se a** to refer to; **~ al lector a un apéndice** to refer the reader to an appendix; **~ a** (Com) to convert into; **por lo que se refiere a eso** as for that, as regards that

refilón [refi'lon]: **de ~** adv obliquely; **mirar a algn de ~** to look out of the corner of one's eye at sb

refinado, -a [refi'naðo, a] adj refined

refinamiento [refina'mjento] nm refinement; **~ por pasos** (Inform) stepwise refinement

refinar [refi'nar] vt to refine

refinería [refine'ria] nf refinery

reflejar [refle'xar] vt to reflect; **reflejarse** vr to be reflected

reflejo, -a [re'flexo, a] adj reflected; (movimiento) reflex ▷ nm reflection; (Anat) reflex; (en el pelo): **~s** nmpl highlights; **tiene el pelo castaño con ~s rubios** she has chestnut hair with blond streaks

reflexión [reflek'sjon] nf reflection

reflexionar [refleksjo'nar] vt to reflect on ▷ vi to reflect; (detenerse) to pause (to think); **¡reflexione!** you think it over!

reflexivo, -a [reflek'siβo, a] adj thoughtful; (Ling) reflexive

reflujo [re'fluxo] nm ebb

reforma [re'forma] nf reform; (Arq etc) repair; **~ agraria** agrarian reform

reformar [refor'mar] vt to reform; (modificar) to change, alter; (texto) to revise; (Arq) to repair; **reformarse** vr to mend one's ways

reformatorio [reforma'torjo] nm reformatory; **~ de menores** remand home

reformista [refor'mista] adj, nm/f reformist

reforzar [refor'θar] vt to strengthen; (Arq) to reinforce; (fig) to encourage

refractario, -a [refrak'tarjo, a] adj (Tec) heat-resistant; **ser ~ a una reforma** to resist o be opposed to a reform

refrán [re'fran] nm proverb, saying

refregar [refre'ɣar] vt to scrub

refrenar [refre'nar] vt to check, restrain

refrendar [refren'dar] vt (firma) to endorse, countersign; (ley) to approve

refrescante [refres'kante] adj refreshing, cooling

refrescar [refres'kar] vt to refresh ▷ vi to cool down; **refrescarse** vr to get cooler; (tomar aire fresco) to go out for a breath of fresh air; (beber) to have a drink

refresco [re'fresko] nm soft drink, cool drink; **"~s"** "refreshments"

refriega etc [re'frjeɣa] vb ver **refregar** ▷ nf scuffle, brawl

refrigeración [refrixera'θjon] nf refrigeration; (de casa) air-conditioning

refrigerador [refrixera'ðor] nm, **refrigeradora** (Am) [refrixera'ðora] nf refrigerator, icebox (US)

refrigerar [refrixe'rar] vt to refrigerate; (sala) to air-condition

refrito [re'frito] nm (Culin): **un ~ de cebolla y tomate** sautéed onions and tomatoes; **un ~** (fig) a rehash

refuerzo etc [re'fwerθo] vb ver **reforzar** ▷ nm reinforcement; (Tec) support

refugiado, -a [refu'xjaðo, a] nm/f refugee

refugiarse [refu'xjarse] vr to take refuge, shelter

refugio [re'fuxjo] *nm* refuge; (*protección*) shelter; (*Auto*) street o traffic island; **~ alpino** o **de montaña** mountain hut; **~ subterráneo** (*Mil*) underground shelter

refulgir [reful'xir] *vi* to shine, be dazzling

refunfuñar [refunfu'ɲar] *vi* to grunt, growl; (*quejarse*) to grumble

refutar [refu'tar] *vt* to refute

regadera [reɣa'ðera] *nf* watering can; (*Am*) shower; **estar como una ~** (*fam*) to be as mad as a hatter

regadío [reɣa'ðio] *nm* irrigated land

regalado, -a [reɣa'laðo, a] *adj* comfortable, luxurious; (*gratis*) free, for nothing; **lo tuvo ~** it was handed to him on a plate

regalar [reɣa'lar] *vt* (*dar*) to give (as a present); (*entregar*) to give away; (*mimar*) to pamper, make a fuss of; **regalarse** *vr* to treat o.s. to

regalía [reɣa'lia] *nf* privilege, prerogative; (*Com*) bonus; (*de autor*) royalty

regaliz [reɣa'liθ] *nm* liquorice

regalo [re'ɣalo] *nm* (*obsequio*) gift, present; (*gusto*) pleasure; (*comodidad*) comfort

regañadientes [reɣaɲa'ðjentes]: **a ~** *adv* reluctantly

regañar [reɣa'ɲar] *vt* to scold ▷ *vi* to grumble; (*dos personas*) to fall out, quarrel

regañón, -ona [reɣa'ɲon, ona] *adj* nagging

regar [re'ɣar] *vt* to water, irrigate; (*fig*) to scatter, sprinkle

regatear [reɣate'ar] *vt* (*Com*) to bargain over; (*escatimar*) to be mean with ▷ *vi* to bargain, haggle; (*Deporte*) to dribble; **no ~ esfuerzo** to spare no effort

regateo [reɣa'teo] *nm* bargaining; (*Deporte*) dribbling; (*con el cuerpo*) swerve, dodge

regazo [re'ɣaθo] *nm* lap

regencia [re'xenθja] *nf* regency

regeneración [rexenera'θjon] *nf* regeneration

regenerar [rexene'rar] *vt* to regenerate

regentar [rexen'tar] *vt* to direct, manage; (*puesto*) to hold in an acting capacity; (*negocio*) to be in charge of

regente, -a [re'xente, a] *adj* (*príncipe*) regent; (*director*) managing ▷ *nm* (*Com*) manager; (*Pol*) regent

régimen ['reximen] (*pl* **regímenes** [re'ximenes]) *nm* regime; (*reinado*) rule; (*Med*) diet; (*reglas*) (set of) rules *pl*; (*manera de vivir*) lifestyle; **estar a ~** to be on a diet

regimiento [rexi'mjento] *nm* regiment

regio, -a ['rexjo, a] *adj* royal, regal; (*fig: suntuoso*) splendid; (*Am fam*) great, terrific

región [re'xjon] *nf* region; (*área*) area

regional [rexjo'nal] *adj* regional

regir [re'xir] *vt* to govern, rule; (*dirigir*) to manage, run; (*Econ, Jur, Ling*) to govern ▷ *vi* to apply, be in force

registrador [rexistra'ðor] *nm* registrar, recorder

registrar [rexis'trar] *vt* (*buscar*) to search; (*en cajón*) to look through; (*inspeccionar*) to inspect; (*anotar*) to note, record; (*Inform*) to log; (*Mus*) to record; **registrarse** *vr* to register; (*ocurrir*) to happen

registro [re'xistro] *nm* (*acto*) registration; (*Mus, libro*) register; (*lista*) list, record; (*Inform*) record; (*inspección*) inspection, search; **~ civil** registry office; **~ electoral** voting register; **~ de la propiedad** land registry (office)

regla ['reɣla] *nf* (*ley*) rule, regulation; (*de medir*) ruler, rule; (*Med: período*) period; **en ~** in order; (*regla científica*) law, principle; **no hay ~ sin excepción** every rule has its exception

reglamentación [reɣlamenta'θjon] *nf* (*acto*) regulation; (*lista*) rules *pl*

reglamentar [reɣlamen'tar] *vt* to regulate

reglamentario, -a [reɣlamen'tarjo, a] *adj* statutory; **en la forma reglamentaria** in the properly established way

reglamento [reɣla'mento] *nm* rules *pl*, regulations *pl*; **~ del tráfico** highway code

reglar [re'ɣlar] *vt* (*acciones*) to regulate; **reglarse** *vr*: **~ se por** to be guided by

regocijarse [reɣoθi'xarse] *vr*: **~ de** o **por** to rejoice at, be glad about

regocijo [reɣo'θixo] *nm* joy, happiness

regodearse [reɣoðe'arse] *vr* to be glad, be delighted; (*pey*): **~ con** o **en** to gloat over

regodeo [reɣo'ðeo] *nm* delight; (*pey*) perverse pleasure

regrabadora [reɣraβa'ðora] *nf* rewriter; **~ de DVD** DVD rewriter

regresar [reɣre'sar] *vi* to come/go back, return; **regresarse** *vr* (*Am*) to return

regresivo, -a [reɣre'siβo, a] *adj* backward; (*fig*) regressive

regreso [re'ɣreso] *nm* return; **estar de ~** to be back, be home

reguero [re'ɣero] *nm* (*de sangre*) trickle; (*de humo*) trail

regulación [reɣula'θjon] *nf* regulation; (*Tec*) adjustment; (*control*) control; **~ de empleo** redundancies *pl*; **~ del tráfico** traffic control

regulador [reɣula'ðor] *nm* (*Tec*) regulator; (*de radio etc*) knob, control

regular [reɣu'lar] *adj* regular; (*normal*) normal, usual; (*común*) ordinary; (*organizado*) regular, orderly; (*mediano*) average; (*fam*) not bad, so-so ▷ *adv*: **estar ~** to be so-so o alright ▷ *vt* (*controlar*) to control, regulate; (*Tec*) to adjust; **por lo ~** as a rule

regularidad [reɣulari'ðað] *nf* regularity; **con ~** regularly

regularizar [reɣulari'θar] *vt* to regularize

regusto [re'ɣusto] *nm* aftertaste

rehabilitación [reaβilita'θjon] *nf* rehabilitation; (*Arq*) restoration

rehabilitar [reaβili'tar] *vt* to rehabilitate; (*Arq*) to restore; (*reintegrar*) to reinstate

rehacer [rea'θer] *vt* (*reparar*) to mend, repair; (*volver a hacer*) to redo, repeat; **rehacerse** *vr* (*Med*) to recover

rehén [re'en] *nm/f* hostage

rehogar [reo'ɣar] *vt* to sauté, toss in oil

rehuir [reu'ir] *vt* to avoid, shun

rehusar [reu'sar] *vt, vi* to refuse

reina ['reina] *nf* queen

reinado [rei'naðo] *nm* reign

reinante [rei'nante] *adj* (*fig*) prevailing

reinar [rei'nar] *vi* to reign; (*fig: prevalecer*) to prevail, be general

reincidir [reinθi'ðir] *vi* to relapse; (*criminal*) to repeat an offence

reincorporarse [reinkorpo'rarse] *vr*: ~ **a** to rejoin

reino ['reino] *nm* kingdom; ~ **animal/ vegetal** animal/plant kingdom; **el R~ Unido** the United Kingdom

reinserción [reinser'θjon] *nf* rehabilitation

reinsertar [reinser'tar] *vt* to rehabilitate

reintegrar [reinte'ɣrar] *vt* (*reconstituir*) to reconstruct; (*persona*) to reinstate; (*dinero*) to refund, pay back; **reintegrarse** *vr*: ~**se a** to return to

reír [re'ir] *vi* to laugh; **reírse** *vr* to laugh; ~**se de** to laugh at

reiterado, -a [reite'raðo, a] *adj* repeated

reiterar [reite'rar] *vt* to reiterate; (*repetir*) to repeat

reivindicación [reiβindika'θjon] *nf* (*demanda*) claim, demand; (*justificación*) vindication

reivindicar [reiβindi'kar] *vt* to claim

reja ['rexa] *nf* (*de ventana*) grille, bars *pl*; (*en la calle*) grating

rejilla [re'xiʎa] *nf* grating, grille; (*muebles*) wickerwork; (*de ventilación*) vent; (*de coche etc*) luggage rack

rejoneador [rexonea'ðor] *nm* mounted bullfighter

rejuvenecer [rexuβene'θer] *vt, vi* to rejuvenate

relación [rela'θjon] *nf* relation, relationship; (*Mat*) ratio; (*lista*) list; (*narración*) report; ~ **costo-efectivo** *o* **costo-rendimiento** (*Com*) cost-effectiveness; **relaciones** *nfpl* (*enchufes*) influential friends, connections; **relaciones carnales** sexual relations; **relaciones comerciales** business connections; **relaciones empresariales/humanas** industrial/human relations; **relaciones laborales/públicas** labour/public relations; **con ~ a, en ~ con** in relation to; **estar en** *o* **tener buenas relaciones con** to be on good terms with

relacionar [relaθjo'nar] *vt* to relate, connect; **relacionarse** *vr* to be connected *o* linked

relajación [relaxa'θjon] *nf* relaxation

relajado, -a [rela'xaðo, a] *adj* (*disoluto*) loose; (*cómodo*) relaxed; (*Med*) ruptured

relajar [rela'xar] *vt* to relax; **relajarse** *vr* to relax

relamerse [rela'merse] *vr* to lick one's lips

relamido, -a [rela'miðo, a] *adj* (*pulcro*) overdressed; (*afectado*) affected

relámpago [re'lampaɣo] *nm* flash of lightning ⊳ *adj* lightning *cpd*; **como un** ~ as quick as lightning, in a flash; **visita/huelga** ~ lightning visit/strike

relampaguear [relampaɣe'ar] *vi* to flash

relanzar [relan'θar] *vt* to relaunch

relatar [rela'tar] *vt* to tell, relate

relatividad [relatiβi'ðað] *nf* relativity

relativo, -a [rela'tiβo, a] *adj* relative; **en lo ~ a** concerning

relato [re'lato] *nm* (*narración*) story, tale

relax [re'las] *nm* rest; **"R~"** (*en un anuncio*) "Personal services"

relegar [rele'ɣar] *vt* to relegate; ~ **algo al olvido** to banish sth from one's mind

relevante [rele'βante] *adj* eminent, outstanding

relevar [rele'βar] *vt* (*sustituir*) to relieve; **relevarse** *vr* to relay; ~ **a algn de un cargo** to relieve sb of his post

relevo [re'leβo] *nm* relief; **carrera de ~s** relay race; **coger** *o* **tomar el** ~ to take over, stand in

relieve [re'ljeβe] *nm* (*Arte, Tec*) relief; (*fig*) prominence, importance; **bajo** ~ bas-relief; **un personaje de** ~ an important man; **dar** ~ **a** to highlight

religión [reli'xjon] *nf* religion

religioso, -a [reli'xjoso, a] *adj* religious ⊳ *nm/f* monk/nun

relinchar [relin'tʃar] *vi* to neigh

relincho [re'lintʃo] *nm* neigh; (*acto*) neighing

reliquia [re'likja] *nf* relic; ~ **de familia** heirloom

rellano [re'ʎano] *nm* (*Arq*) landing

rellenar [reʎe'nar] *vt* (*llenar*) to fill up; (*Culin*) to stuff; (*Costura*) to pad; (*formulario etc*) to fill in *o* out

relleno, -a [re'ʎeno, a] *adj* full up; (*Culin*) stuffed ⊳ *nm* stuffing; (*de tapicería*) padding

reloj [re'lo(x)] *nm* clock; **poner el** ~ (**en hora**) to set one's watch (*o* the clock); ~ **de pie** grandfather clock; ~ (**de pulsera**) wristwatch; ~ **de sol** sundial; ~ **despertador** alarm (clock); ~ **digital** digital watch; **como un** ~ like clockwork; **contra (el)** ~ against the clock

relojería [reloxe'ria] (*tienda*) watchmaker's (shop); **aparato de** ~ clockwork; **bomba de** ~ time bomb

relojero, -a [relo'xero, a] *nm/f* clockmaker; watchmaker

reluciente [relu'θjente] *adj* brilliant, shining

relucir [relu'θir] *vi* to shine; (*fig*) to excel; **sacar algo a** ~ to show sth off

relumbrar [relum'brar] *vi* to dazzle, shine brilliantly

r

remachar [rema'tʃar] vt to rivet; (fig) to hammer home, drive home

remache [re'matʃe] nm rivet

remanente [rema'nente] nm remainder; (Com) balance; (de producto) surplus

remangar [reman'gar] vt to roll up; **remangarse** vr to roll one's sleeves up

remanso [re'manso] nm pool

remar [re'mar] vi to row

rematado, -a [rema'taðo, a] adj complete, utter; **es un loco ~** he's a raving lunatic

rematar [rema'tar] vt to finish off; (animal) to put out of its misery; (Com) to sell off cheap ▷ vi to end, finish off; (Deporte) to shoot

remate [re'mate] nm end, finish; (punta) tip; (Deporte) shot; (Arq) top; (Com) auction sale; **de** o **para ~** to crown it all (Brit), to top it off

remedar [reme'ðar] vt to imitate

remediar [reme'ðjar] vt (gen) to remedy; (subsanar) to make good, repair; (evitar) to avoid; **sin poder ~lo** without being able to prevent it

remedio [re'meðjo] nm remedy; (alivio) relief, help; (Jur) recourse, remedy; **poner ~ a** to correct, stop; **no tener más ~** to have no alternative; **¡qué ~!** there's no choice!; **como último ~** as a last resort; **sin ~** inevitable; (Med) hopeless

remedo [re'meðo] nm imitation; (pey) parody

remendar [remen'dar] vt to repair; (con parche) to patch; (fig) to correct

remesa [re'mesa] nf remittance; (Com) shipment

remiendo etc [re'mjendo] vb ver **remendar** ▷ nm mend; (con parche) patch; (cosido) darn; (fig) correction

remilgado, -a [remil'gaðo, a] adj prim; (afectado) affected

remilgo [re'milɣo] nm primness; (afectación) affectation

reminiscencia [reminis'θenθja] nf reminiscence

remiso, -a [re'miso, a] adj slack, slow

remite [re'mite] nm (en sobre) name and address of sender

remitente [remi'tente] nm/f (Correos) sender

remitir [remi'tir] vt to remit, send ▷ vi to slacken; (en carta): **remite: X** sender: X

remo ['remo] nm (de barco) oar; (Deporte) rowing; **cruzar un río a ~** to row across a river

remojar [remo'xar] vt to steep, soak; (galleta etc) to dip, dunk; (fam) to celebrate with a drink

remojo [re'moxo] nm steeping, soaking; (por la lluvia) drenching, soaking; **dejar la ropa en ~** to leave clothes to soak

remolacha [remo'latʃa] nf beet, beetroot (Brit)

remolcador [remolka'ðor] nm (Naut) tug; (Auto) breakdown lorry

remolcar [remol'kar] vt to tow

remolino [remo'lino] nm eddy; (de agua) whirlpool; (de viento) whirlwind; (de gente) crowd

remolque etc [re'molke] vb ver **remolcar** ▷ nm tow, towing; (cuerda) towrope; **llevar a ~ to** tow

remontar [remon'tar] vt to mend; (obstáculo) to negotiate, get over; **remontarse** vr to soar; **~se a** (Com) to amount to; (en tiempo) to go back to, date from; **~ el vuelo** to soar

remorder [remor'ðer] vt to distress, disturb; **~le la conciencia a algn** to have a guilty conscience

remordimiento [remorði'mjento] nm remorse

remoto, -a [re'moto, a] adj remote

remover [remo'βer] vt to stir; (tierra) to turn over; (objetos) to move round

remozar [remo'θar] vt (Arq) to refurbish; (fig) to brighten o polish up

remuneración [remunera'θjon] nf remuneration

remunerar [remune'rar] vt to remunerate; (premiar) to reward

renacer [rena'θer] vi to be reborn; (fig) to revive

renacimiento [renaθi'mjento] nm rebirth; **el R~** the Renaissance

renacuajo [rena'kwaxo] nm (Zool) tadpole

renal [re'nal] adj renal, kidney cpd

rencilla [ren'θiʎa] nf quarrel; **rencillas** nfpl bickering sg

rencor [ren'kor] nm rancour, bitterness; (resentimiento) ill feeling, resentment; **guardar ~ a** to have a grudge against

rencoroso, -a [renko'roso, a] adj spiteful

rendición [rendi'θjon] nf surrender

rendido, -a [ren'diðo, a] adj (sumiso) submissive; (agotado) worn-out, exhausted; (enamorado) devoted

rendija [ren'dixa] nf (hendidura) crack; (abertura) aperture; (fig) rift, split; (Jur) loophole

rendimiento [rendi'mjento] nm (producción) output; (Com) yield, profit(s) (pl); (Tec, Com) efficiency; **~ de capital** (Com) return on capital

rendir [ren'dir] vt (vencer) to defeat; (producir) to produce; (dar beneficio) to yield; (agotar) to exhaust ▷ vi to pay; (Com) to yield, produce; **rendirse** vr (someterse) to surrender; (ceder) to yield; (cansarse) to wear o.s. out; **~ homenaje** o **culto a** to pay homage to; **el negocio no rinde** the business doesn't pay

renegado, -a [rene'ɣaðo, a] adj, nm/f renegade

renegar [rene'ɣar] vt (negar) to deny vigorously ▷ vi (blasfemar) to blaspheme; **~ de** (renunciar) to renounce; (quejarse) to complain about

RENFE ['renfe] nf abr (Esp: Ferro) = **Red Nacional de Ferrocarriles Españoles**

renglón [ren'glon] *nm* (*línea*) line; (*Com*) item, article; **a ~ seguido** immediately after

renombrado, -a [renom'braðo, a] *adj* renowned

renombre [re'nombre] *nm* renown

renovable [reno'βaβle] *adj* renewable

renovación [renoβa'θjon] *nf* (*de contrato*) renewal; (*Arq*) renovation

renovar [reno'βar] *vt* to renew; (*Arq*) to renovate; (*sala*) to redecorate

renta ['renta] *nf* (*ingresos*) income; (*beneficio*) profit; (*alquiler*) rent; **~ gravable** *o* **imponible** taxable income; **~ nacional (bruta)** (gross) national income; **~ no salarial** unearned income; **~ sobre el terreno** (*Com*) ground rent; **~ vitalicia** annuity; **política de ~s** incomes policy; **vivir de sus ~s** to live on one's private income

rentabilizar [rentaβili'θar] *vt* to make profitable

rentable [ren'taβle] *adj* profitable; **no ~** unprofitable

rentar [ren'tar] *vt* to produce, yield; (*Am*) to rent

renuencia [re'nwenθja] *nf* reluctance

renuncia [re'nunθja] *nf* resignation

renunciar [renun'θjar] *vt* to renounce, give up ▷ *vi* to resign; **~ a** (*tabaco, alcohol etc*) to give up; (*oferta, oportunidad*) to turn down; (*puesto*) to resign; **~ a hacer algo** to give up doing sth

reñido, -a [re'niðo, a] *adj* (*batalla*) bitter, hard-fought; **estar ~ con algn** to be on bad terms with sb; **está ~ con su familia** he has fallen out with his family

reñir [re'nir] *vt* (*regañar*) to scold ▷ *vi* (*estar peleado*) to quarrel, fall out; (*combatir*) to fight

reo ['reo] *nm/f* culprit, offender; (*Jur*) accused

reojo [re'oxo]: **de ~** *adv* out of the corner of one's eye

reparación [repara'θjon] *nf* (*acto*) mending, repairing; (*Tec*) repair; (*fig*) amends, reparation; **"reparaciones en el acto"** "repairs while you wait"

reparador, -a [repara'ðor, a] *adj* refreshing; (*comida*) fortifying ▷ *nm* repairer

reparar [repa'rar] *vt* to repair; (*fig*) to make amends for; (*suerte*) to retrieve; (*observar*) to observe ▷ *vi*: **~ en** (*darse cuenta de*) to notice; (*poner atención en*) to pay attention to; **sin ~ en los gastos** regardless of the cost

reparo [re'paro] *nm* (*advertencia*) observation; (*duda*) doubt; (*dificultad*) difficulty; (*escrúpulo*) scruple, qualm; **poner ~s (a)** to raise objections (to); (*criticar*) to criticize; **no tuvo ~ en hacerlo** he did not hesitate to do it

repartición [reparti'θjon] *nf* distribution; (*división*) division

repartidor, a [reparti'ðor, a] *nm/f* distributor; **~ de leche** milkman

repartir [repar'tir] *vt* to distribute, share out; (*Com, Correos*) to deliver; (*Mil*) to partition; (*libros*) to give out; (*comida*) to serve out;

(*Naipes*) to deal

reparto [re'parto] *nm* distribution; (*Com, Correos*) delivery; (*Teat, Cine*) cast; (*Am: urbanización*) housing estate (*Brit*), real estate development (*US*); **"~ a domicilio"** "home delivery service"

repasar [repa'sar] *vt* (*Escol*) to revise; (*Mecánica*) to check, overhaul; (*Costura*) to mend

repaso [re'paso] *nm* revision; (*Mecánica*) overhaul, checkup; (*Costura*) mending; **~ general** servicing, general overhaul; **curso de ~** refresher course

repatriar [repa'trjar] *vt* to repatriate; **repatriarse** *vr* to return home

repecho [re'petʃo] *nm* steep incline

repelente [repe'lente] *adj* repellent, repulsive

repeler [repe'ler] *vt* to repel; (*idea, oferta*) to reject

repente [re'pente] *nm* sudden movement; (*fig*) impulse; **de ~** suddenly; **~ de ira** fit of anger

repentino, -a [repen'tino, a] *adj* sudden; (*imprevisto*) unexpected

repercusión [reperku'sjon] *nf* repercussion; **de amplia** *o* **ancha ~** far-reaching

repercutir [reperku'tir] *vi* (*objeto*) to rebound; (*sonido*) to echo; **~ en** (*fig*) to have repercussions *o* effects on

repertorio [reper'torjo] *nm* list; (*Teat*) repertoire

repesca [re'peska] *nf* (*Escol fam*) resit

repetición [repeti'θjon] *nf* repetition

repetir [repe'tir] *vt* to repeat; (*plato*) to have a second helping of; (*Teat*) to give as an encore, sing *etc* again ▷ *vi* to repeat; (*sabor*) to come back; **repetirse** *vr* to repeat o.s.; (*suceso*) to recur

repetitivo, -a [repeti'tiβo, a] *adj* repetitive, repetitious

repicar [repi'kar] *vi* (*campanas*) to ring (out)

repipi [re'pipi] *adj* la-di-da ▷ *nf*: **es una ~** she's a little madam

repique *etc* [re'pike] *vb ver* **repicar** ▷ *nm* pealing, ringing

repiqueteo [repike'teo] *nm* pealing; (*de tambor*) drumming

repisa [re'pisa] *nf* ledge, shelf; **~ de chimenea** mantelpiece; **~ de ventana** windowsill

repito *etc vb ver* **repetir**

replantear [replante'ar] *vt* (*cuestión pública*) to readdress; (*problema personal*) to reconsider; (*en reunión*) to raise again; **replantearse** *vr*: **~se algo** to reconsider sth

replegarse [reple'ɣarse] *vr* to fall back, retreat

repleto, -a [re'pleto, a] *adj* replete, full up; **~ de** filled *o* crammed with

réplica ['replika] *nf* answer; (*Arte*) replica; **derecho de ~** right of *o* to reply

replicar [repli'kar] *vi* to answer; *(objetar)* to argue, answer back

repliegue *etc* [re'pljeɣe] *vb ver* **replegarse** ▷ *nm* (*Mil*) withdrawal

repoblación [repoβla'θjon] *nf* repopulation; *(de río)* restocking; ~ **forestal** reafforestation

repoblar [repo'βlar] *vt* to repopulate; to restock; *(con árboles)* to reafforest

repollito [repo'ʎito] *nm* (*Am*): ~**s de Bruselas** (Brussels) sprouts

repollo [re'poʎo] *nm* cabbage

reponer [repo'ner] *vt* to replace, put back; *(máquina)* to re-set; *(Teat)* to revive; **reponerse** *vr* to recover; ~ **que** to reply that

reportaje [repor'taxe] *nm* report, article; ~ **gráfico** illustrated report

reportero, -a [repor'tero, a] *nm/f* reporter; ~ **gráfico/a** news photographer

reposacabezas [reposaka'βeθas] *nm inv* headrest

reposado, -a [repo'saðo, a] *adj (descansado)* restful; *(tranquilo)* calm

reposar [repo'sar] *vi* to rest, repose; *(muerto)* to lie, rest

reposición [reposi'θjon] *nf* replacement; *(Cine)* second showing; *(Teat)* revival

reposo [re'poso] *nm* rest

repostar [repos'tar] *vt* to replenish; *(Auto)* to fill up (with petrol *o* gasoline)

repostería [reposte'ria] *nf (arte)* confectionery, pastry-making; *(tienda)* confectioner's (shop)

repostero, -a [repos'tero, a] *nm/f* confectioner

reprender [repren'der] *vt* to reprimand; *(niño)* to scold

represa [re'presa] *nf* dam; *(lago artificial)* lake, pool

represalia [repre'salja] *nf* reprisal; **tomar ~s** to take reprisals, retaliate

representación [representa'θjon] *nf* representation; *(Teat)* performance; **en ~ de** representing; **por ~** by proxy

representante [represen'tante] *nm/f* (*Pol, Com*) representative; *(Teat)* performer

representar [represen'tar] *vt* to represent; *(significar)* to mean; *(Teat)* to perform; *(edad)* to look; **representarse** *vr* to imagine; **tal acto ~ía la guerra** such an act would mean war

representativo, -a [representa'tiβo, a] *adj* representative

represión [repre'sjon] *nf* repression

represivo, -a [repre'siβo, a] *adj* repressive

reprimenda [repri'menda] *nf* reprimand, rebuke

reprimir [repri'mir] *vt* to repress; **reprimirse** *vr*: ~**se de hacer algo** to stop o.s. from doing sth

reprobar [repro'βar] *vt* to censure, reprove

réprobo, -a ['reproβo, a] *nm/f* reprobate

reprochar [repro'tʃar] *vt* to reproach; *(censurar)* to condemn, censure

reproche [re'protʃe] *nm* reproach

reproducción [reproðuk'θjon] *nf* reproduction

reproducir [reproðu'θir] *vt* to reproduce; **reproducirse** *vr* to breed; *(situación)* to recur

reproductor, a [reproðuk'tor, a] *adj* reproductive ▷ *nm*: ~ **de CD** CD player; ~ **MP3/MP4** MP3/MP4 player

reptil [rep'til] *nm* reptile

república [re'puβlika] *nf* republic; **R~ Dominicana** Dominican Republic; **R~ Federal Alemana (RFA)** Federal Republic of Germany

republicano, -a [repuβli'kano, a] *adj, nm/f* republican

repudiar [repu'ðjar] *vt* to repudiate; *(fe)* to renounce

repudio [re'puðjo] *nm* repudiation

repuesto [re'pwesto] *pp de* **reponer** ▷ *nm* *(pieza de recambio)* spare (part); *(abastecimiento)* supply; **rueda de** ~ spare wheel; **y llevamos otro de** ~ and we have another as a spare *o* in reserve

repugnancia [repuɣ'nanθja] *nf* repugnance

repugnante [repuɣ'nante] *adj* repugnant, repulsive

repugnar [repuɣ'nar] *vt* to disgust ▷ *vi*, **repugnarse** *vr* *(contradecirse)* to contradict each other

repujar [repu'xar] *vt* to emboss

repulsa [re'pulsa] *nf* rebuff

repulsión [repul'sjon] *nf* repulsion, aversion

repulsivo, -a [repul'siβo, a] *adj* repulsive

reputación [reputa'θjon] *nf* reputation

reputar [repu'tar] *vt* to consider, deem

requemado, -a [reke'maðo, a] *adj (quemado)* scorched; *(bronceado)* tanned

requerimiento [rekeri'mjento] *nm* request; *(demanda)* demand; *(Jur)* summons

requerir [reke'rir] *vt* *(pedir)* to ask, request; *(exigir)* to require; *(ordenar)* to call for; *(llamar)* to send for, summon

requesón [reke'son] *nm* cottage cheese

requete... [rekete] *pref* extremely

réquiem ['rekjem] *nm* requiem

requisa [re'kisa] *nf* *(inspección)* survey, inspection; *(Mil)* requisition

requisar [reki'sar] *vt* (*Mil*) to requisition; *(confiscar)* to seize, confiscate

requisito [reki'sito] *nm* requirement, requisite; ~ **previo** prerequisite; **tener los ~s para un cargo** to have the essential qualifications for a post

res [res] *nf* beast, animal

resabio [re'saβjo] *nm* *(maña)* vice, bad habit; *(dejo)* unpleasant) aftertaste

resaca [re'saka] *nf* *(en el mar)* undertow, undercurrent; *(fig)* backlash; *(fam)* hangover

resaltar [resal'tar] *vi* to project, stick out; *(fig)* to stand out

resarcir [resar'θir] *vt* to compensate; *(pagar)* to repay; **resarcirse** *vr* to make up for;

~ a algn de una pérdida to compensate sb for a loss; **~ a algn de una cantidad** to repay sb a sum

resbaladero [resβala'ðero] nm (Am) slide

resbaladizo, -a [resβala'ðiθo, a] adj slippery

resbalar [resβa'lar] vi to slip, slide; (fig) to slip (up); **resbalarse** vr to slip, slide; (fig) to slip (up); **le resbalaban las lágrimas por las mejillas** tears were trickling down his cheeks

resbalón [resβa'lon] nm (acción) slip; (deslizamiento) slide; (fig) slip

rescatar [reska'tar] vt (salvar) to save, rescue; (objeto) to get back, recover; (cautivos) to ransom

rescate [res'kate] nm rescue; (de objeto) recovery; **pagar un ~** to pay a ransom

rescindir [resθin'dir] vt (contrato) to annul, rescind

rescisión [resθi'sjon] nf cancellation

rescoldo [res'koldo] nm embers pl

resecar [rese'kar] vt to dry off, dry thoroughly; (Med) to cut out, remove; **resecarse** vr to dry up

reseco, -a [re'seko, a] adj very dry; (fig) skinny

resentido, -a [resen'tiðo, a] adj resentful; **es un ~** he's bitter

resentimiento [resenti'mjento] nm resentment, bitterness

resentirse [resen'tirse] vr (debilitarse: persona) to suffer; **~ con** to resent; **~ de** (sufrir las consecuencias de) to feel the effects of; **~ de** (o **por**) **algo** to resent sth, be bitter about sth

reseña [re'seɲa] nf (cuenta) account; (informe) report; (Lit) review

reseñar [rese'ɲar] vt to describe; (Lit) to review

reserva [re'serβa] nf reserve; (reservación) reservation; **a ~ de que ...** unless ...; **con toda ~** in strictest confidence; **de ~** spare; **tener algo de ~** to have sth in reserve; **~ de indios** Indian reservation; (Com): **~ para amortización** depreciation allowance; **~ de caja** o **en efectivo** cash reserves; **~s del Estado** government stock; **~s en oro** gold reserves

reservación [reserβa'θjon] nf (LAm) reservation

reservado, -a [reser'βaðo, a] adj reserved; (retraído) cold, distant ▷ nm private room; (Ferro) reserved compartment

reservar [reser'βar] vt (guardar) to keep; (Ferro, Teat etc) to reserve, book; **reservarse** vr to save o.s.; (callar) to keep to o.s.; **~ con exceso** to overbook

resfriado [res'friaðo] nm cold

resfriarse [res'friarse] vr to cool off; (Med) to catch (a) cold

resguardar [resɣwar'ðar] vt to protect, shield; **resguardarse** vr: **~se de** to guard against

resguardo [res'ɣwarðo] nm defence; (vale) voucher; (recibo) receipt, slip

residencia [resi'ðenθja] nf residence; (Univ) hall of residence; **~ para ancianos** o **jubilados** residential home, old people's home

residencial [resiðen'θjal] adj residential ▷ nf (urbanización) housing estate (Brit), real estate development (US)

residente [resi'ðente] adj, nm/f resident

residir [resi'ðir] vi to reside, live; **~ en** to reside o lie in; (consistir en) to consist of

residuo [re'siðwo] nm residue; **~s atmosféricos** o **radiactivos** fallout sg

resignación [resiɣna'θjon] nf resignation

resignarse [resiɣ'narse] vr: **~ a** o **con** to resign o.s. to, be resigned to

resina [re'sina] nf resin

resistencia [resis'tenθja] nf (dureza) endurance, strength; (oposición, Elec) resistance; **la R~** (Mil) the Resistance

resistente [resis'tente] adj strong, hardy; (Tec) resistant; **~ al calor** heat-resistant

resistir [resis'tir] vt (soportar) to bear; (oponerse a) to resist, oppose; (aguantar) to put up with ▷ vi to resist; (aguantar) to last, endure; **resistirse** vr: **~se a** to refuse to, resist; **no puedo ~ este frío** I can't bear o stand this cold; **me resisto a creerlo** I refuse to believe it; **se le resiste la química** chemistry escapes her

resollar [reso'ʎar] vi to breathe noisily, wheeze

resolución [resolu'θjon] nf resolution; (decisión) decision; (moción) motion; **~ judicial** legal ruling; **tomar una ~** to take a decision

resoluto, -a [reso'luto, a] adj resolute

resolver [resol'βer] vt to resolve; (solucionar) to solve, resolve; (decidir) to decide, settle; **resolverse** vr to make up one's mind

resonancia [reso'nanθja] nf (del sonido) resonance; (repercusión) repercussion; (fig) wide effect, impact

resonante [reso'nante] adj resonant, resounding; (fig) tremendous

resonar [reso'nar] vi to ring, echo

resoplar [reso'plar] vi to snort; (por cansancio) to puff

resoplido [reso'pliðo] nm heavy breathing

resorte [re'sorte] nm spring; (fig) lever

resortera [resor'tera] nf (Am) catapult

respaldar [respal'dar] vt to back (up), support; (Inform) to back up; **respaldarse** vr to lean back; **~se con** o **en** (fig) to take one's stand on

respaldo [res'paldo] nm (de sillón) back; (fig) support, backing

respectivo, -a [respek'tiβo, a] adj respective; **en lo ~ a** with regard to

respecto [res'pekto] nm: **al ~** on this matter; **con ~ a, ~ de** with regard to, in relation to

respetable [respe'taβle] *adj* respectable

respetar [respe'tar] *vt* to respect

respeto [res'peto] *nm* respect; *(acatamiento)* deference; **respetos** *nmpl* respects; **por ~ a** out of consideration for; **presentar sus ~s a** to pay one's respects to

respetuoso, -a [respe'twoso, a] *adj* respectful

respingo [res'pingo] *nm* start, jump

respiración [respira'θjon] *nf* breathing; *(Med)* respiration; *(ventilación)* ventilation; **~ asistida** artificial respiration *(by machine)*

respirar [respi'rar] *vt, vi* to breathe; **no dejar ~ a algn** to keep on at sb; **estuvo escuchándole sin ~** he listened to him in complete silence

respiratorio, -a [respira'torjo, a] *adj* respiratory

respiro [res'piro] *nm* breathing; *(fig: descanso)* respite, rest; *(Com)* period of grace

resplandecer [resplande'θer] *vi* to shine

resplandeciente [resplande'θjente] *adj* resplendent, shining

resplandor [resplan'dor] *nm* brilliance, brightness; *(del fuego)* blaze

responder [respon'der] *vt* to answer ▷ *vi* to answer; *(fig)* to respond; *(pey)* to answer back; *(corresponder)* to correspond; **~ a** *(situación etc)* to respond to; **~ a una pregunta** to answer a question; **~ a una descripción** to fit a description; **~ de** o **por** to answer for

respondón, -ona [respon'don, ona] *adj* cheeky

responsabilidad [responsaβili'ðað] *nf* responsibility; **bajo mi ~** on my authority; **~ ilimitada** *(Com)* unlimited liability

responsabilizarse [responsaβili'θarse] *vr* to make o.s. responsible, take charge

responsable [respon'saβle] *adj* responsible; **la persona ~** the person in charge; **hacerse ~ de algo** to assume responsibility for sth

respuesta [res'pwesta] *nf* answer, reply; *(reacción)* response

resquebrajar [reskeβra'xar] *vt* to crack, split; **resquebrajarse** *vr* to crack, split

resquemor [reske'mor] *nm* resentment

resquicio [res'kiθjo] *nm* chink; *(hendidura)* crack

resta ['resta] *nf* (Mat) remainder

restablecer [restaβle'θer] *vt* to re-establish, restore; **restablecerse** *vr* to recover

restallar [resta'ʎar] *vi* to crack

restante [res'tante] *adj* remaining; **lo ~** the remainder; **los ~s** the rest, those left (over)

restar [res'tar] *vt* (Mat) to subtract; *(descontar)* to deduct; *(fig)* to take away ▷ *vi* to remain, be left

restauración [restaura'θjon] *nf* restoration

restaurante [restau'rante] *nm* restaurant

restaurar [restau'rar] *vt* to restore

restitución [restitu'θjon] *nf* return, restitution

restituir [restitu'ir] *vt* *(devolver)* to return, give back; *(rehabilitar)* to restore

resto ['resto] *nm* *(residuo)* rest, remainder; *(apuesta)* stake; **restos** *nmpl* remains; *(Culin)* leftovers, scraps; **~s mortales** mortal remains

restorán [resto'ran] *nm* (Am) restaurant

restregar [restre'ɣar] *vt* to scrub, rub

restricción [restrik'θjon] *nf* restriction; **sin ~ de** without restrictions o as to; **hablar sin restricciones** to talk freely

restrictivo, -a [restrik'tiβo, a] *adj* restrictive

restringir [restrin'xir] *vt* to restrict, limit

resucitar [resuθi'tar] *vt, vi* to resuscitate, revive

resuello *etc* [re'sweʎo] *vb ver* **resollar** ▷ *nm* *(aliento)* breath

resuelto, -a [re'swelto, a] *pp de* **resolver** ▷ *adj* resolute, determined; **estar ~ a algo** to be set on sth; **estar ~ a hacer algo** to be determined to do sth

resultado [resul'taðo] *nm* result; *(conclusión)* outcome; **resultados** *nmpl* (Inform) output *sg*; **dar ~** to produce results

resultante [resul'tante] *adj* resulting, resultant

resultar [resul'tar] *vi* (ser) to be; *(llegar a ser)* to turn out to be; *(salir bien)* to turn out well; *(seguir)* to ensue; **~ a** (Com) to amount to; **~ de** to stem from; **~ en** to result in, produce; **resulta que ...** *(en consecuencia)* it follows that ...; *(parece que)* it seems that ...; **el conductor resultó muerto** the driver was killed; **no resultó** it didn't work o come off; **me resulta difícil hacerlo** it's difficult for me to do it

resumen [re'sumen] *nm* summary, résumé; **en ~** in short

resumir [resu'mir] *vt* to sum up; *(condensar)* to summarize; *(cortar)* to abridge, cut down; **resumirse** *vr*: **la situación se resume en pocas palabras** the situation can be summed up in a few words

resurgir [resur'xir] *vi* *(reaparecer)* to reappear

resurrección [resurrek'θjon] *nf* resurrection

retablo [re'taβlo] *nm* altarpiece

retaguardia [reta'ɣwarðja] *nf* rearguard

retahíla [reta'ila] *nf* series, string; *(de injurias)* volley, stream

retal [re'tal] *nm* remnant

retar [re'tar] *vt* *(gen)* to challenge; *(desafiar)* to defy, dare

retardar [retar'ðar] *vt* *(demorar)* to delay; *(hacer más lento)* to slow down; *(retener)* to hold back

retardo [re'tarðo] *nm* delay

retazo [re'taθo] *nm* snippet (Brit), fragment

retención [reten'θjon] *nf* retention; *(de pago)* deduction; *(tráfico)* hold-up; **~ fiscal** deduction for tax purposes; **~ de llamadas** (Telec) hold facility

retener [rete'ner] *vt* *(guardar)* to retain, keep; *(intereses)* to withhold

reticente [reti'θente] *adj* (*insinuador*) insinuating; (*engañoso*) deceptive; (*postura*) reluctant; **ser ~ a hacer algo** to be reluctant *o* unwilling to do sth

retina [re'tina] *nf* retina

retintín [retin'tin] *nm* jangle, jingle; **decir algo con ~** to say sth sarcastically

retirado, -a [reti'raðo, a] *adj* (*lugar*) remote; (*vida*) quiet; (*jubilado*) retired ▷ *nf* (*Mil*) retreat; (*de dinero*) withdrawal; (*de embajador*) recall; **batirse en retirada** to retreat

retirar [reti'rar] *vt* to withdraw; (*la mano*) to draw back; (*quitar*) to remove; (*dinero*) to take out, withdraw; (*jubilar*) to retire, pension off; **retirarse** *vr* to retreat, withdraw; (*jubilarse*) to retire; (*acostarse*) to retire, go to bed

retiro [re'tiro] *nm* retreat; (*jubilación, tb Deporte*) retirement; (*pago*) pension; (*lugar*) quiet place

reto ['reto] *nm* dare, challenge

retocar [reto'kar] *vt* (*fotografía*) to touch up, retouch

retoño [re'toɲo] *nm* sprout, shoot; (*fig*) offspring, child

retoque *etc* [re'toke] *vb ver* **retocar** ▷ *nm* retouching

retorcer [retor'θer] *vt* to twist; (*argumento*) to turn, twist; (*manos, lavado*) to wring; **retorcerse** *vr* to become twisted; (*persona*) to writhe; **~se de dolor** to writhe in *o* squirm with pain

retorcido, -a [retor'θiðo, a] *adj* (*tb fig*) twisted

retorcijón [retorθi'xon] *nm* (*Am: tb:* **~ de tripas**) stomach cramp

retorcimiento [retorθi'mjento] *nm* twist, twisting; (*fig*) deviousness

retórico, -a [re'toriko, a] *adj* rhetorical; (*pey*) affected, windy ▷ *nf* rhetoric; (*pey*) affectedness

retornable [retor'naβle] *adj* returnable

retornar [retor'nar] *vt* to return, give back ▷ *vi* to return, go/come back

retorno [re'torno] *nm* return; **~ del carro** (*Inform, Tip*) carriage return

retortijón [retorti'xon] *nm* twist, twisting; **~ de tripas** stomach cramp

retozar [reto'θar] *vi* (*juguetear*) to frolic, romp; (*saltar*) to gambol

retozón, -ona [reto'θon, ona] *adj* playful

retracción [retrak'θjon] *nf* retraction

retractarse [retrak'tarse] *vr* to retract; **me retracto** I take that back

retraerse [retra'erse] *vr* to retreat, withdraw

retraído, -a [retra'iðo, a] *adj* shy, retiring

retraimiento [retrai'mjento] *nm* retirement; (*timidez*) shyness

retransmisión [retransmi'sjon] *nf* repeat (broadcast)

retransmitir [retransmi'tir] *vt* (*mensaje*) to relay; (*TV etc*) to repeat, retransmit; (*: en vivo*) to broadcast live

retrasado, -a [retra'saðo, a] *adj* late; (*Med*) mentally retarded; (*país etc*) backward, underdeveloped; **estar ~** (*reloj*) to be slow; (*persona, industria*) to be *o* lag behind

retrasar [retra'sar] *vt* (*demorar*) to postpone, put off; (*retardar*) to slow down ▷ *vi* (*atrasarse*) to be late; (*reloj*) to be slow; (*producción*) to fall (off); (*quedarse atrás*) to lag behind; **retrasarse** *vr* to be late; to be slow; to fall (off); to lag behind

retraso [re'traso] *nm* (*demora*) delay; (*lentitud*) slowness; (*tardanza*) lateness; (*atraso*) backwardness; **retrasos** *nmpl* (*Com*) arrears; (*deudas*) deficit *sg*, debts; **llegar con ~** to arrive late; **llegar con 25 minutos de ~** to be 25 minutes late; **llevo un ~ de seis semanas** I'm six weeks behind (with my work *etc*); **~ mental** mental deficiency

retratar [retra'tar] *vt* (*Arte*) to paint the portrait of; (*fotografiar*) to photograph; (*fig*) to depict, describe; **retratarse** *vr* to have one's portrait painted; to have one's photograph taken

retrato [re'trato] *nm* portrait; (*Foto*) photograph; (*descripción*) portrayal, depiction; (*fig*) likeness; **ser el vivo ~ de** to be the spitting image of

retrato-robot [re'tratoro'βo(t)] (*pl* **retratos-robot**) *nm* Identikit® picture

retreta [re'treta] *nf* retreat

retrete [re'trete] *nm* toilet

retribución [retriβu'θjon] *nf* (*recompensa*) reward; (*pago*) pay, payment

retribuir [retriβu'ir] *vt* (*recompensar*) to reward; (*pagar*) to pay

retro... [retro] *pref* retro...

retroactivo, -a [retroak'tiβo, a] *adj* retroactive, retrospective; **dar efecto ~ a un pago** to backdate a payment

retroceder [retroθe'ðer] *vi* (*echarse atrás*) to move back(wards); (*fig*) to back down; **no ~** to stand firm; **la policía hizo ~ a la multitud** the police forced the crowd back

retroceso [retro'θeso] *nm* backward movement; (*Med*) relapse; (*Com*) recession, depression; (*fig*) backing down

retrógrado, -a [re'troɣraðo, a] *adj* retrograde, retrogressive; (*Pol*) reactionary

retropropulsión [retropropul'sjon] *nf* jet propulsion

retrospectivo, -a [retrospek'tiβo, a] *adj* retrospective; **mirada retrospectiva** backward glance

retrovisor [retroβi'sor] *nm* rear-view mirror

retumbar [retum'bar] *vi* to echo, resound; (*continuamente*) to reverberate

reuma ['reuma] *nm* rheumatism

reumatismo [reuma'tismo] *nm* rheumatism

reunificar [reunifi'kar] *vt* to reunify

reunión [reu'njon] *nf* (*asamblea*) meeting; (*fiesta*) party; **~ en la cumbre** summit meeting; **~ de ventas** (*Com*) sales meeting

r

reunir [reu'nir] *vt* (*juntar*) to reunite, join (together); (*recoger*) to gather (together); (*personas*) to bring o get together; (*cualidades*) to combine; **reunirse** *vr* (*personas: en asamblea*) to meet, gather; **reunió a sus amigos para discutirlo** he got his friends together to talk it over

revalidar [reβali'ðar] *vt* (*ratificar*) to confirm, ratify

revalorar [reβalo'rar] *vt* to revalue, reassess

revalorizar [reβalori'θar] *vt* to revalue, reassess

revancha [re'βantʃa] *nf* revenge; (*Deporte*) return match; (*Boxeo*) return fight

revelación [reβela'θjon] *nf* revelation

revelado [reβe'laðo] *nm* developing

revelar [reβe'lar] *vt* to reveal; (*secreto*) to disclose; (*mostrar*) to show; (*Foto*) to develop

reventa [re'βenta] *nf* resale; (*especulación*) speculation; (*de entradas*) touting

reventar [reβen'tar] *vt* to burst, explode; (*molestar*) to annoy, rile ▷ *vi*, **reventarse** *vr* (*estallar*) to burst, explode; **me revienta tener que ponérmelo** I hate having to wear it; **~ de** (*fig*) to be bursting with; **~ por** to be bursting to

reventón [reβen'ton] *nm* (*Auto*) blow-out (*Brit*), flat (*US*)

reverberación [reβerβera'θjon] *nf* reverberation

reverberar [reβerβe'rar] *vi* (*luz*) to play, be reflected; (*superficie*) to shimmer; (*nieve*) to glare; (*sonido*) to reverberate

reverencia [reβe'renθja] *nf* reverence; (*inclinación*) bow

reverenciar [reβeren'θjar] *vt* to revere

reverendo, -a [reβe'rendo, a] *adj* reverend; (*fam*) big, awful; **un ~ imbécil** an awful idiot

reverente [reβe'rente] *adj* reverent

reversa [re'βersa] *nf* (*Am*) reverse gear

reversible [reβer'siβle] *adj* reversible

reverso [re'βerso] *nm* back, other side; (*de moneda*) reverse

revertir [reβer'tir] *vi* to revert; **~ en beneficio de** to be to the advantage of; **~ en perjuicio de** to be to the detriment of

revés [re'βes] *nm* back, wrong side; (*fig*) reverse, setback; (*Deporte*) backhand; **al ~ the** wrong way round; (*de arriba abajo*) upside down; (*ropa*) inside out; **y al ~** and vice versa; **volver algo del ~** to turn sth round; (*ropa*) to turn sth inside out; **los reveses de la fortuna** the blows of fate

revestir [reβes'tir] *vt* (*poner*) to put on; (*cubrir*) to cover, coat; (*cualidad*) to have, possess; **revestirse** *vr* (*Rel*) to put on one's vestments; (*ponerse*) to put on; **~ con o de** to arm o.s. with; **el acto revestía gran solemnidad** the ceremony had great dignity

revisar [reβi'sar] *vt* (*examinar*) to check; (*texto etc*) to revise; (*Jur*) to review

revisión [reβi'sjon] *nf* revision; **~ aduanera** customs inspection; **~ de cuentas** audit; **~ salarial** wage review

revisor, a [reβi'sor, a] *nm/f* inspector; (*Ferro*) ticket collector; **~ de cuentas** auditor

revista [re'βista] *vb ver* **revestir** ▷ *nf* magazine, review; (*Teat*) revue; (*inspección*) inspection; **~ literaria** literary review; **~ de libros** book reviews (page); **~ del corazón** *magazine featuring celebrity gossip and real-life romance stories*; **pasar ~ a** to review, inspect

revivir [reβi'βir] *vt* (*recordar*) to revive memories of ▷ *vi* to revive

revocación [reβoka'θjon] *nf* repeal

revocar [reβo'kar] *vt* (*decisión*) to revoke; (*Arq*) to plaster

revolcar [reβol'kar] *vt* to knock down, send flying; **revolcarse** *vr* to roll about

revolotear [reβolote'ar] *vi* to flutter

revoltijo [reβol'tixo] *nm* mess, jumble

revoltoso, -a [reβol'toso, a] *adj* (*travieso*) naughty, unruly

revolución [reβolu'θjon] *nf* revolution

revolucionar [reβoluθjo'nar] *vt* to revolutionize

revolucionario, -a [reβoluθjo'narjo, a] *adj, nm/f* revolutionary

revolver [reβol'βer] *vt* (*desordenar*) to disturb, mess up; (*agitar*) to shake; (*líquido*) to stir; (*mover*) to move about; (*Pol*) to stir up ▷ *vi*: **~ en** to go through, rummage (about) in; **revolverse** *vr* (*en cama*) to toss and turn; (*Meteorología*) to break, turn stormy; **~se contra** to turn on o against; **han revuelto toda la casa** they've turned the whole house upside down

revólver [re'βolβer] *nm* revolver

revuelo [re'βwelo] *nm* fluttering; (*fig*) commotion; **armar o levantar un gran ~ to** cause a great stir

revuelto, -a [re'βwelto, a] *pp de* **revolver** ▷ *adj* (*mezclado*) mixed-up, in disorder; (*mar*) rough; (*tiempo*) unsettled ▷ *nf* (*motín*) revolt; (*agitación*) commotion; **todo estaba ~** everything was in disorder o was topsy-turvy

revulsivo [reβul'siβo] *nm*: **servir de ~** to have a salutary effect

rey [rei] *nm* king; **Día de R~es** Twelfth Night; **los R~es Magos** the Three Wise Men, the Magi; **los R~es** the King and Queen; *see note*

⊙ REYES MAGOS

The night before the 6th of January (the Epiphany), which is a holiday in Spain, children go to bed expecting *los Reyes Magos*, the Three Wise Men who visited the baby Jesus, to bring them presents. Twelfth night processions, known as *cabalgatas*, take place that evening, when 3 people dressed as *los Reyes Magos* arrive in the town by land or sea to the delight of the children.

reyerta [re'jerta] nf quarrel, brawl

rezagado, -a [reθa'ɣaðo, a] adj: **quedar ~** to be left behind; (estar retrasado) to be late, be behind ▷ nm/f straggler

rezagar [reθa'ɣar] vt (dejar atrás) to leave behind; (retrasar) to delay, postpone; **rezagarse** vr (atrasarse) to fall behind

rezar [re'θar] vi to pray; **~ con** (fam) to concern, have to do with

rezo ['reθo] nm prayer

rezongar [reθon'gar] vi to grumble; (murmurar) to mutter; (refunfuñar) to growl

rezumar [reθu'mar] vt to ooze ▷ vi to leak; **rezumarse** vr to leak out

ría ['ria] nf estuary

riachuelo [rja'tʃwelo] nm stream

riada [ri'aða] nf flood

ribera [ri'βera] nf (de río) bank; (: área) riverside

ribete [ri'βete] nm (de vestido) border; (fig) addition

ribetear [riβete'ar] vt to edge, border

ricino [ri'θino] nm: **aceite de ~** castor oil

rico, -a ['riko, a] adj (adinerado) rich, wealthy; (lujoso) luxurious; (comida) delicious; (niño) lovely, cute ▷ nm/f rich person; **nuevo ~** nouveau riche

rictus ['riktus] nm (mueca) sneer, grin; **~ de amargura** bitter smile

ridiculez [riðiku'leθ] nf absurdity

ridiculizar [riðikuli'θar] vt to ridicule

ridículo, -a [ri'ðikulo, a] adj ridiculous; **hacer el ~** to make a fool of o.s.; **poner a algn en ~** to make a fool of sb; **ponerse en ~** to make a fool of o.s.

riego etc ['rjeɣo] vb ver **regar** ▷ nm (aspersión) watering; (irrigación) irrigation; **~ sanguíneo** blood flow o circulation

riel [rjel] nm rail

rienda ['rjenda] nf rein; (fig) restraint, moderating influence; **dar ~ suelta a** to give free rein to; **llevar las ~s** to be in charge

riesgo ['rjesɣo] nm risk; **seguro a o contra todo ~** comprehensive insurance; **~ para la salud** health hazard; **correr el ~ de** to run the risk of

rifa ['rifa] nf (lotería) raffle

rifar [ri'far] vt to raffle

rifle ['rifle] nm rifle

rigidez [rixi'ðeθ] nf rigidity, stiffness; (fig) strictness

rígido, -a ['rixiðo, a] adj rigid, stiff; (moralmente) strict, inflexible; (cara) wooden, expressionless

rigor [ri'ɣor] nm strictness, rigour; (dureza) toughness; (inclemencia) harshness; (meticulosidad) accuracy; **el ~ del verano** the hottest part of the summer; **con todo ~ científico** with scientific precision; **de ~** de rigueur, essential; **después de los saludos de ~** after the inevitable greetings

riguroso, -a [riɣu'roso, a] adj rigorous; (Meteorología) harsh; (severo) severe

rimar [ri'mar] vi to rhyme

rimbombante [rimbom'bante] adj (fig) pompous

rímel, rímmel ['rimel] nm mascara

rímmel ['rimel] nm = **rímel**

rin [rin] nm (Am) (wheel) rim

rincón [rin'kon] nm corner (inside)

ring [riŋ] nm (Boxeo) ring

rinoceronte [rinoθe'ronte] nm rhinoceros

riña ['riɲa] nf (disputa) argument; (pelea) brawl

riñón [ri'ɲon] nm kidney; **me costó un ~** (fam) it cost me an arm and a leg; **tener riñones** to have guts

río ['rio] vb ver **reír** ▷ nm river; (fig) torrent, stream; **~ abajo/arriba** downstream/ upstream; **cuando el ~ suena, agua lleva** there's no smoke without fire; **R~ de la Plata** River Plate

rioja [ri'oxa] nm: **~ rioja wine** ▷ nf: **La R~** La Rioja

rioplatense [riopla'tense] adj of o from the River Plate region ▷ nm/f native o inhabitant of the River Plate region

riqueza [ri'keθa] nf wealth, riches pl; (cualidad) richness

risa ['risa] nf laughter; (una risa) laugh; **¡qué ~!** what a laugh!; **caerse o morirse de ~** to split one's sides laughing, die laughing; **tomar algo a ~** to laugh sth off

risco ['risko] nm crag, cliff

risible [ri'siβle] adj ludicrous, laughable

risotada [riso'taða] nf guffaw, loud laugh

ristra ['ristra] nf string

risueño, -a [ri'sweɲo, a] adj (sonriente) smiling; (contento) cheerful

ritmo ['ritmo] nm rhythm; **a ~ lento** slowly; **trabajar a ~ lento** to go slow; **~ cardíaco** heart rate

rito ['rito] nm rite

ritual [ri'twal] adj, nm ritual

rival [ri'βal] adj, nm/f rival

rivalidad [riβali'ðað] nf rivalry, competition

rivalizar [riβali'θar] vi: **~ con** to rival, vie with

rizado, -a [ri'θaðo, a] adj (pelo) curly; (superficie) ridged; (terreno) undulating; (mar) choppy ▷ nm curls pl

rizar [ri'θar] vt to curl; **rizarse** vr (el pelo) to curl; (agua) to ripple; (el mar) to become choppy

rizo ['riθo] nm curl; (en agua) ripple

RNE nf abr = **Radio Nacional de España**

robar [ro'βar] vt to rob; (objeto) to steal; (casa etc) to break into; (Naipes) to draw; (atención) to steal, capture; (paciencia) to exhaust

roble ['roβle] nm oak

robledal [roβle'ðal], **robledo** [ro'βleðo] nm oakwood

robo ['roβo] nm robbery, theft; (objeto robado) stolen article o goods pl; **¡esto es un ~!** this is daylight robbery!

r

robot [ro'βo(t)] (pl **robots**) adj, nm robot ▷ nm (tb: **~ de cocina**) food processor
robustecer [roβuste'θer] vt to strengthen
robusto, -a [ro'βusto, a] adj robust, strong
roca ['roka] nf rock; **la R~** the Rock (of Gibraltar)
roce etc ['roθe] vb ver **rozar** ▷ nm rub, rubbing; (caricia) brush; (Tec) friction; (en la piel) graze; **tener ~ con** to have a brush with
rociar [ro'θjar] vt to sprinkle, spray
rocín [ro'θin] nm nag, hack
rocío [ro'θio] nm dew
rock [rok] adj inv, nm (Mus) rock (cpd)
rockero, -a [ro'kero, a] adj rock cpd ▷ nm/f rocker
rocola [ro'kola] nf (Am) jukebox
rocoso, -a [ro'koso, a] adj rocky
rodaballo [roða'βaʎo] nm turbot
rodado, -a [ro'ðaðo, a] adj (con ruedas) wheeled ▷ nf rut
rodaja [ro'ðaxa] nf (raja) slice
rodaje [ro'ðaxe] nm (Cine) shooting, filming; (Auto): **en ~** running in
rodamiento [roða'mjento] nm (Auto) tread
rodar [ro'ðar] vt (vehículo) to wheel (along); (escalera) to roll down; (viajar por) to travel (over) ▷ vi to roll; (coche) to go, run; (Cine) to shoot, film; (persona) to move about (from place to place), drift; **echarlo todo a ~** (fig) to mess it all up
rodear [roðe'ar] vt to surround ▷ vi to go round; **rodearse** vr: **~se de amigos** to surround o.s. with friends
rodeo [ro'ðeo] nm (ruta indirecta) long way round, roundabout way; (desvío) detour; (evasión) evasion; (Am) rodeo; **dejarse de ~s** to talk straight; **hablar sin ~s** to come to the point, speak plainly
rodilla [ro'ðiʎa] nf knee; **de ~s** kneeling; **ponerse de ~s** to kneel (down)
rodillo [ro'ðiʎo] nm roller; (Culin) rolling-pin; (en máquina de escribir, impresora) platen
rododendro [roðo'ðendro] nm rhododendron
roedor, a [roe'ðor, a] adj gnawing ▷ nm rodent
roer [ro'er] vt (masticar) to gnaw; (corroer, fig) to corrode
rogar [ro'ɣar] vt (pedir) to beg, ask for ▷ vi (suplicar) to beg, plead; **rogarse** vr: **se ruega no fumar** please do not smoke; **~ que** (+ subjun) to ask to ...; **ruegue a este señor que nos deje en paz** please ask this gentleman to leave us alone; **no se hace de ~** he doesn't have to be asked twice
rojizo, -a [ro'xiθo, a] adj reddish
rojo, -a ['roxo, a] adj red ▷ nm red (colour); (Pol) red; **ponerse ~** to turn red, blush; **al ~ vivo** red-hot
rol [rol] nm list, roll; (esp Am: papel) role
rollito [ro'ʎito] nm (tb: **~ de primavera**) spring roll

rollizo, -a [ro'ʎiθo, a] adj (objeto) cylindrical; (persona) plump
rollo, -a ['roʎo, a] adj (fam) boring, tedious ▷ nm roll; (de cuerda) coil; (de madera) log; (fam) bore; (discurso) boring speech; **¡qué ~!** what a carry-on!; **la conferencia fue un ~** the lecture was a big drag
Roma ['roma] nf Rome; **por todas partes se va a ~** all roads lead to Rome
romance [ro'manθe] nm (amoroso) romance; (Ling) Romance language; (Lit) ballad; **hablar en ~** to speak plainly
románico, -a [ro'maniko, a] adj, nm Romanesque
romano, -a [ro'mano, a] adj Roman, of Rome ▷ nm/f Roman; **a la romana** in batter
romanticismo [romanti'θismo] nm romanticism
romántico, -a [ro'mantiko, a] adj romantic
rombo ['rombo] nm (Geom) rhombus; (diseño) diamond; (Tip) lozenge
romería [rome'ria] nf (Rel) pilgrimage; (excursión) trip, outing; see note

  ● **ROMERÍA**
  ●
  ● Originally a pilgrimage to a shrine or
  ● church to express devotion to Our Lady or
  ● a local Saint, the *romería* has also become
  ● a rural *fiesta* which accompanies the
  ● pilgrimage. People come from all over to
  ● attend, bringing their own food and
  ● drink, and spend the day in celebration.

romero, -a [ro'mero, a] nm/f pilgrim ▷ nm rosemary
romo, -a ['romo, a] adj blunt; (fig) dull
rompecabezas [rompeka'βeθas] nm inv riddle, puzzle; (juego) jigsaw (puzzle)
rompehielos [rompe'jelos] nm inv icebreaker
rompehuelgas (Am) [rompe'welɣas] nm inv strikebreaker, scab
rompeolas [rompe'olas] nm inv breakwater
romper [rom'per] vt to break; (hacer pedazos) to smash; (papel, tela etc) to tear, rip; (relaciones) to break off ▷ vi (olas) to break; (sol, diente) to break through; **~ un contrato** to break a contract; **~ a** to start (suddenly) to; **~ a llorar** to burst into tears; **~ con algn** to fall out with sb; **ha roto con su novio** she has broken up with her fiancé
rompimiento [rompi'mjento] nm (acto) breaking; (fig) break; (quiebra) crack; **~ de relaciones** breaking off of relations
ron [ron] nm rum
roncar [ron'kar] vi (al dormir) to snore; (animal) to roar
roncha ['rontʃa] nf (cardenal) bruise; (hinchazón) swelling
ronco, -a ['ronko, a] adj (afónico) hoarse; (áspero) raucous
ronda ['ronda] nf (de bebidas etc) round;

(*patrulla*) patrol; (*de naipes*) hand, game; **ir de ~** to do one's round

rondar [ron'dar] *vt* to patrol; (*a una persona*) to hang round; (*molestar*) to harass; (*a una chica*) to court ▷ *vi* to patrol; (*fig*) to prowl round; (*Mus*) to go serenading

ronquido [ron'kiðo] *nm* snore, snoring

ronronear [ronrone'ar] *vi* to purr

ronroneo [ronro'neo] *nm* purr

roña ['roɲa] *nf* (*en veterinaria*) mange; (*mugre*) dirt, grime; (*óxido*) rust

roñica [ro'ɲika] *nm/f* (*fam*) skinflint

roñoso, -a [ro'ɲoso, a] *adj* (*mugriento*) filthy; (*tacaño*) mean

ropa ['ropa] *nf* clothes *pl*, clothing; **~ blanca** linen; **~ de cama** bed linen; **~ de color** coloureds *pl*; **~ interior** underwear; **~ lavada o para lavar** washing; **~ planchada** ironing; **~ sucia** dirty clothes *pl*, dirty washing; **~ usada** secondhand clothes

ropaje [ro'paxe] *nm* gown, robes *pl*

ropero [ro'pero] *nm* linen cupboard; (*guardarropa*) wardrobe

rosa ['rosa] *adj inv* pink ▷ *nf* rose; (*Anat*) red birthmark; **~ de los vientos** the compass; **estar como una ~** to feel as fresh as a daisy; **(color) de ~** pink

rosado, -a [ro'saðo, a] *adj* pink ▷ *nm* rosé

rosal [ro'sal] *nm* rosebush

rosario [ro'sarjo] *nm* (*Rel*) rosary; (*fig: serie*) string; **rezar el ~** to say the rosary

rosca ['roska] *nf* (*de tornillo*) thread; (*de humo*) coil, spiral; (*pan, postre*) ring-shaped roll/ pastry; **hacer la ~ a algn** (*fam*) to suck up to sb; **pasarse de ~** (*fig*) to go too far

rosetón [rose'ton] *nm* rosette; (*Arq*) rose window

rosquilla [ros'kiʎa] *nf* ring-shaped cake; (*de humo*) ring

rostro ['rostro] *nm* (*cara*) face; (*fig*) cheek

rotación [rota'θjon] *nf* rotation; **~ de cultivos** crop rotation

rotativo, -a [rota'tiβo, a] *adj* rotary ▷ *nm* newspaper

roto, -a ['roto, a] *pp de* **romper** ▷ *adj* broken; (*en pedazos*) smashed; (*tela, papel*) torn; (*vida*) shattered ▷ *nm* (*en vestido*) hole, tear

rotonda [ro'tonda] *nf* roundabout

rótula ['rotula] *nf* kneecap; (*Tec*) ball-and-socket joint

rotulador [rotula'ðor] *nm* felt-tip pen

rotular [rotu'lar] *vt* (*carta, documento*) to head, entitle; (*objeto*) to label

rótulo ['rotulo] *nm* (*título*) heading, title; (*etiqueta*) label; (*letrero*) sign

rotundamente [rotunda'mente] *adv* (*negar*) flatly; (*responder, afirmar*) emphatically

rotundo, -a [ro'tundo, a] *adj* round; (*enfático*) emphatic

rotura [ro'tura] *nf* (*rompimiento*) breaking; (*Med*) fracture

roturar [rotu'rar] *vt* to plough

roulote [ru'lote] *nf* caravan (*Brit*), trailer (*US*)

rozadura [roθa'ðura] *nf* abrasion, graze

rozar [ro'θar] *vt* (*frotar*) to rub; (*arañar*) to scratch; (*ensuciar*) to dirty; (*Med*) to graze; (*tocar ligeramente*) to shave, skim; (*fig*) to touch o border on; **rozarse** *vr* to rub (together); **~ con** (*fam*) to rub shoulders with

Rte. *abr* = **remite; remitente**

RTVE *nf abr* (*TV*) = **Radiotelevisión Española**

rubí [ru'βi] *nm* ruby; (*de reloj*) jewel

rubio, -a ['ruβjo, a] *adj* fair-haired, blond(e) ▷ *nm/f* blond/blonde; **tabaco ~** Virginia tobacco; (**cerveza**) **rubia** lager

rubor [ru'βor] *nm* (*sonrojo*) blush; (*timidez*) bashfulness

ruborizarse [ruβori'θarse] *vr* to blush

ruboroso, -a [ruβo'roso, a] *adj* blushing

rúbrica ['ruβrika] *nf* (*título*) title, heading; (*de la firma*) flourish; **bajo la ~ de** under the heading of

rubricar [ruβri'kar] *vt* (*firmar*) to sign with a flourish; (*concluir*) to sign and seal

rudeza [ru'ðeθa] *nf* (*tosquedad*) coarseness; (*sencillez*) simplicity

rudimentario, -a [ruðimen'tarjo, a] *adj* rudimentary, basic

rudo, -a ['ruðo, a] *adj* (*sin pulir*) unpolished; (*grosero*) coarse; (*violento*) violent; (*sencillo*) simple

rueda ['rweða] *nf* wheel; (*círculo*) ring, circle; (*rodaja*) slice, round; (*en impresora etc*) sprocket; **~ de auxilio** (*Am*) spare tyre; **~ delantera/ trasera/de repuesto** front/back/spare wheel; **~ impresora** (*Inform*) print wheel; **~ de prensa** press conference; **~ gigante** (*Am*) big (*Brit*) o Ferris (*US*) wheel

ruedo *etc* ['rweðo] *vb ver* **rodar** ▷ *nm* (*contorno*) edge, border; (*de vestido*) hem; (*círculo*) circle; (*Taur*) arena, bullring; (*esterilla*) (round) mat

ruego *etc* ['rweɣo] *vb ver* **rogar** ▷ *nm* request; **a ~ de** at the request of; **"~s y preguntas"** "question and answer session"

rufián [ru'fjan] *nm* scoundrel

rugby ['ruɣβi] *nm* rugby

rugido [ru'xiðo] *nm* roar

rugir [ru'xir] *vi* to roar; (*toro*) to bellow; (*estómago*) to rumble

rugoso, -a [ru'ɣoso, a] *adj* (*arrugado*) wrinkled; (*áspero*) rough; (*desigual*) ridged

ruido ['rwiðo] *nm* noise; (*sonido*) sound; (*alboroto*) racket, row; (*escándalo*) commotion, rumpus; **~ de fondo** background noise; **hacer o meter ~** to cause a stir

ruidoso, -a [rwi'ðoso, a] *adj* noisy, loud; (*fig*) sensational

ruin [rwin] *adj* contemptible, mean

ruina ['rwina] *nf* ruin; (*hundimiento*) collapse; (*de persona*) ruin, downfall; **estar hecho una ~** to be a wreck; **la empresa le llevó a la ~** the venture ruined him (financially)

ruindad [rwin'dað] *nf* lowness, meanness; (*acto*) low o mean act

r

ruinoso, -a [rwi'noso, a] *adj* ruinous; (*destartalado*) dilapidated, tumbledown; (*Com*) disastrous

ruiseñor [rwise'ɲor] *nm* nightingale

rulero [ru'lero] *nm* (*Am*) roller

ruleta [ru'leta] *nf* roulette

rulo ['rulo] *nm* (*para el pelo*) curler

Rumania [ru'manja] *nf* Rumania

rumano, -a [ru'mano, a] *adj, nm/f* Rumanian

rumba ['rumba] *nf* rumba

rumbo ['rumbo] *nm* (*ruta*) route, direction; (*ángulo de dirección*) course, bearing; (*fig*) course of events; **con ~ a** in the direction of; **ir con ~ a** to be heading for; (*Naut*) to be bound for

rumboso, -a [rum'boso, a] *adj* (*generoso*) generous

rumiante [ru'mjante] *nm* ruminant

rumiar [ru'mjar] *vt* to chew; (*fig*) to chew over ▷ *vi* to chew the cud

rumor [ru'mor] *nm* (*ruido sordo*) low sound; (*murmuración*) murmur, buzz

rumorearse [rumore'arse] *vr*: **se rumorea que** it is rumoured that

runrún [run'run] *nm* (*de voces*) murmur, sound of voices; (*fig*) rumour; (*de una máquina*) whirr

rupestre [ru'pestre] *adj* rock *cpd*; **pintura ~** cave painting

ruptura [rup'tura] *nf* (*gen*) rupture; (*disputa*) split; (*de contrato*) breach; (*de relaciones*) breaking-off

rural [ru'ral] *adj* rural

Rusia ['rusja] *nf* Russia

ruso, -a ['ruso, a] *adj, nm/f* Russian ▷ *nm* (*Ling*) Russian

rústico, -a ['rustiko, a] *adj* rustic; (*ordinario*) coarse, uncouth ▷ *nm/f* yokel ▷ *nf*: **libro en rústica** paperback (book)

ruta ['ruta] *nf* route

rutina [ru'tina] *nf* routine; **~ diaria** daily routine; **por ~** as a matter of course

rutinario, -a [ruti'narjo, a] *adj* routine

S *abr* (= san, santo, a) St.; (= sur) S

s. *abr* (tb: **S.**: = siglo) c.; (= siguiente) foll.

S.ª *abr* (= Sierra) Mts

S.A. *abr* (= Sociedad Anónima) Ltd., Inc. (*US*); (= Su Alteza) H.H.

sábado ['saβaðo] *nm* Saturday; (*de los judíos*) Sabbath; **del ~ en ocho días** a week on Saturday; **un ~ sí y otro no, cada dos ~s** every other Saturday; **S~ Santo** Holy Saturday; *ver tb* **Semana Santa**

sábana ['saβana] *nf* sheet; **se le pegan las ~s** he can't get up in the morning

sabandija [saβan'dixa] *nf* (*bicho*) bug; (*fig*) louse

sabañón [saβa'ɲon] *nm* chilblain

sabelotodo [saβelo'toðo] *nm/f inv* know-all

saber [sa'βer] *vt* to know; (*llegar a conocer*) to find out, learn; (*tener capacidad de*) to know how to ▷ *vi*: **~ a** to taste of, taste like ▷ *nm* knowledge, learning; **saberse** *vr*: **se sabe que ...** it is known that ...; **no se sabe** nobody knows; **a ~** namely; **¿sabes conducir/nadar?** can you drive/swim?; **¿sabes francés?** do you *o* can you speak French?; **~ de memoria** to know by heart; **lo sé** I know; **hacer ~** to inform, let know; **que yo sepa** as far as I know; **vete** *o* **anda a ~** your guess is as good as mine, who knows!; **¿sabe?** (*fam*) you know (what I mean)?; **le sabe mal que otro la saque a bailar** it upsets him that anybody else should ask her to dance

sabiduría [saβiðu'ria] nf (conocimientos) wisdom; (instrucción) learning; **~ popular** folklore

sabiendas [sa'βjendas]: **a ~** adv knowingly; **a ~ de que ...** knowing full well that ...

sabio, -a ['saβjo, a] adj (docto) learned; (prudente) wise, sensible

sable [sa'βle] nm sabre

sabor [sa'βor] nm taste, flavour; (fig) flavour; **sin ~** flavourless

saborear [saβore'ar] vt to taste, savour; (fig) to relish

sabotaje [saβo'taxe] nm sabotage

saboteador, a [saβotea'ðor, a] nm/f saboteur

sabotear [saβote'ar] vt to sabotage

sabré etc [sa'βre] vb ver **saber**

sabroso, -a [sa'βroso, a] adj tasty; (fig fam) racy, salty

sacacorchos [saka'kortʃos] nm inv corkscrew

sacapuntas [saka'puntas] nm inv pencil sharpener

sacar [sa'kar] vt to take out; (fig: extraer) to get (out); (quitar) to remove, get out; (hacer salir) to bring out; (fondos: de cuenta) to draw out, withdraw; (obtener: legado etc) to get; (demostrar) to show; (conclusión) to draw; (novela etc) to publish, bring out; (ropa) to take off; (obra) to make; (premio) to receive; (entradas) to get; (Tenis) to serve; (Fútbol) to put into play; **~ adelante** (niño) to bring up; (negocio) to carry on, go on with; **~ a algn a bailar** to get sb up to dance; **~ a algn de sí** to infuriate sb; **~ una foto** to take a photo; **~ la lengua** to stick out one's tongue; **~ buenas/ malas notas** to get good/bad marks

sacarina [saka'rina] nf saccharin(e)

sacerdote [saθer'ðote] nm priest

saciar [sa'θjar] vt (hartar) to satiate; (fig) to satisfy; **saciarse** vr (de comida) to get full up; (fig) to be satisfied

saco ['sako] nm bag; (grande) sack; (contenido) bagful; (Am: chaqueta) jacket; **~ de dormir** sleeping bag

sacramento [sakra'mento] nm sacrament

sacrificar [sakrifi'kar] vt to sacrifice; (animal) to slaughter; (perro etc) to put to sleep; **sacrificarse** vr to sacrifice o.s.

sacrificio [sakri'fiθjo] nm sacrifice

sacrilegio [sakri'lexjo] nm sacrilege

sacrílego, -a [sa'krileyo, a] adj sacrilegious

sacristán [sakris'tan] nm verger

sacristía [sakris'tia] nf sacristy

sacro, -a ['sakro, a] adj sacred

sacudida [saku'ðiða] nf (agitación) shake, shaking; (sacudimiento) jolt, bump; (fig) violent change; (Pol etc) upheaval; **~ eléctrica** electric shock

sacudir [saku'ðir] vt to shake; (golpear) to hit; (ala) to flap; (alfombra) to beat; **~ a algn** (fam) to belt sb

sádico, -a ['saðiko, a] adj sadistic ▷ nm/f sadist

sadismo [sa'ðismo] nm sadism

sadomasoquismo [saðomaso'kismo] nm sadomasochism, S & M

sadomasoquista [saðomaso'kista] adj sadomasochistic ▷ nm/f sadomasochist

saeta [sa'eta] nf (flecha) arrow; (Mus) sacred song in flamenco style

safari [sa'fari] nm safari

sagacidad [saɣaθi'ðað] nf shrewdness, cleverness

sagaz [sa'ɣaθ] adj shrewd, clever

Sagitario [saxi'tarjo] nm (Astro) Sagittarius

sagrado, -a [sa'ɣraðo, a] adj sacred, holy

Sáhara ['saara] nm: **el ~** the Sahara (desert)

sal [sal] vb ver **salir** ▷ nf salt; (gracia) wit; (encanto) charm; **~es de baño** bath salts; **~ gorda** o **de cocina** kitchen o cooking salt

sala ['sala] nf (cuarto grande) large room; (tb: **~ de estar**) living room; (Teat) house, auditorium; (de hospital) ward; **~ de apelación** court; **~ de conferencias** lecture hall; **~ de espera** waiting room; **~ de embarque** departure lounge; **~ de estar** living room; **~ de juntas** (Com) boardroom; **~ VIP** (en aeropuerto, discoteca) VIP lounge

salado, -a [sa'laðo, a] adj salty; (fig) witty, amusing; **agua salada** salt water

salar [sa'lar] vt to salt, add salt to

salariado, -a [sala'rjaðo, a] adj (empleado) salaried

salarial [sala'rjal] adj (aumento, revisión) wage cpd, salary cpd, pay cpd

salario [sa'larjo] nm wage, pay

salchicha [sal'tʃitʃa] nf (pork) sausage

salchichón [saltʃi'tʃon] nm (salami-type) sausage

saldar [sal'dar] vt to pay; (vender) to sell off; (fig) to settle, resolve

saldo ['saldo] nm (pago) settlement; (de una cuenta) balance; (lo restante) remnant(s) (pl), remainder; (de móvil) credit; **saldos** nmpl (en tienda) sale; (Com): **~ anterior** balance brought forward; **~ acreedor/deudor** o **pasivo** credit/debit balance; **~ final** final balance

saldré etc [sal'dre] vb ver **salir**

salero [sa'lero] nm salt cellar; (ingenio) wit; (encanto) charm

salgo etc ['salɣa] vb ver **salir**

salida [sa'liða] nf (puerta etc) exit, way out; (acto) leaving, going out; (de tren, Aviat) departure; (Com, Tec) output, production; (fig) way out; (resultado) outcome; (Com: oportunidad) opening; (Geo, válvula) outlet; (de gas) leak; (ocurrencia) joke; **calle sin ~** cul-de-sac; **~ de baño** (Am) bathrobe; **a la ~ del teatro** after the theatre; **dar la ~** (Deporte) to give the starting signal; **~ de incendios** fire escape; **~ impresa** (Inform) hard copy; **no hay ~** there's no way out of it; **no tenemos otra ~** we have no option; **tener ~s** to be witty

salido, -a [sa'liðo, a] adj (fam) randy

S

saliente [sa'ljente] *adj* (*Arq*) projecting; (*sol*) rising; (*fig*) outstanding

🅞 **PALABRA CLAVE**

salir [sa'lir] *vi* **1** (*persona*) to come o go out; (*tren, avión*) to leave; **Juan ha salido** Juan has gone out; **salió de la cocina** he came out of the kitchen; **salimos de Madrid a las ocho** we left Madrid at eight (o'clock); **salió corriendo (del cuarto)** he ran out (of the room); **salir de un apuro** to get out of a jam **2** (*pelo*) to grow; (*diente*) to come through; (*disco, libro*) to come out; (*planta, número de lotería*) to come up; **salir a la superficie** to come to the surface; **anoche salió en la tele** she appeared o was on TV last night; **salió en todos los periódicos** it was in all the papers; **le salió un trabajo** he got a job **3** (*resultar*): **la muchacha nos salió muy trabajadora** the girl turned out to be a very hard worker; **la comida te ha salido exquisita** the food was delicious; **sale muy caro** it's very expensive; **la entrevista que hice me salió bien/mal** the interview I did turned out o went well/badly; **nos salió a 50 euros cada uno** it worked out at 50 euros each; **no salen las cuentas** it doesn't work out o add up; **salir ganando** to come out on top; **salir perdiendo** to lose out **4** (*Deporte*) to start; (*Naipes*) to lead **5**: **salir con algn** to go out with sb **6**: **salir adelante: no sé como haré para salir adelante** I don't know how I'll get by
salirse *vr* **1** (*líquido*) to spill; (*animal*) to escape **2** (*desviarse*): **salirse de la carretera** to leave o go off the road; **salirse de lo normal** to be unusual; **salirse del tema** to get off the point **3**: **salirse con la suya** to get one's own way

saliva [sa'liβa] *nf* saliva
salmo ['salmo] *nm* psalm
salmón [sal'mon] *nm* salmon
salmonete [salmo'nete] *nm* red mullet
salmuera [sal'mwera] *nf* pickle, brine
salón [sa'lon] *nm* (*de casa*) living-room, lounge; (*muebles*) lounge suite; **~ de belleza** beauty parlour; **~ de baile** dance hall; **~ de actos/sesiones** assembly hall
salpicadera [salpika'ðera] *nf* (*Am*) mudguard (*Brit*), fender (*US*)
salpicadero [salpika'ðero] *nm* (*Auto*) dashboard
salpicar [salpi'kar] *vt* (*de barro, pintura*) to splash; (*rociar*) to sprinkle, spatter; (*esparcir*) to scatter
salpicón [salpi'kon] *nm* (*acto*) splashing; (*Culin*) meat o fish salad; (*tb*: **~ de marisco**) seafood salad
salsa ['salsa] *nf* sauce; (*con carne asada*) gravy; (*fig*) spice; **~ mayonesa** mayonnaise; **estar**

en su ~ (*fam*) to be in one's element
saltamontes [salta'montes] *nm inv* grasshopper
saltar [sal'tar] *vt* to jump (over), leap (over); (*dejar de lado*) to skip, miss out ▷ *vi* to jump, leap; (*pelota*) to bounce; (*al aire*) to fly up; (*quebrarse*) to break; (*al agua*) to dive; (*fig*) to explode, blow up; (*botón*) to come off; (*corcho*) to pop out; **saltarse** *vr* (*omitir*) to skip, miss; **salta a la vista** it's obvious; **~se todas las reglas** to break all the rules
saltear [salte'ar] *vt* (*robar*) to rob (in a holdup); (*asaltar*) to assault, attack; (*Culin*) to sauté
saltimbanqui [saltim'banki] *nm/f* acrobat
salto ['salto] *nm* jump, leap; (*al agua*) dive; **a ~s** by jumping; **~ de agua** waterfall; **~ de altura** high jump; **~ de cama** negligee; **~ mortal** somersault; (*Inform*): **~ de línea** line feed; **~ de línea automático** wordwrap; **~ de página** formfeed
saltón, -ona [sal'ton, ona] *adj* (*ojos*) bulging, popping; (*dientes*) protruding
salubre [sa'luβre] *adj* healthy, salubrious
salud [sa'luð] *nf* health; **estar bien/mal de ~** to be in good/poor health; **¡(a su) ~!** cheers!, good health!; **beber a la ~ de** to drink (to) the health of
saludable [salu'ðaβle] *adj* (*de buena salud*) healthy; (*provechoso*) good, beneficial
saludar [salu'ðar] *vt* to greet; (*Mil*) to salute; **ir a ~ a algn** to drop in to see sb; **salude de mi parte a X** give my regards to X; **le saluda atentamente** (*en carta*) yours faithfully
saludo [sa'luðo] *nm* greeting; **~s** (*en carta*) best wishes, regards; **un ~ afectuoso** o **cordial** yours sincerely
salva ['salβa] *nf* (*Mil*) salvo; **una ~ de aplausos** thunderous applause
salvación [salβa'θjon] *nf* salvation; (*rescate*) rescue
salvado [sal'βaðo] *nm* bran
salvador [salβa'ðor] *nm* rescuer, saviour; **el S~** the Saviour; **El S~** El Salvador; **San S~** San Salvador
salvadoreño, -a [salβaðo'reɲo, a] *adj, nm/f* Salvadoran, Salvadorian
salvaguardar [salβaɣwar'ðar] *vt* to safeguard; (*Inform*) to back up, make a backup copy of
salvajada [salβa'xaða] *nf* savage deed, atrocity
salvaje [sal'βaxe] *adj* wild; (*tribu*) savage
salvajismo [salβa'xismo] *nm* savagery
salvamanteles [salβaman'teles] *nm inv* table mat
salvamento [salβa'mento] *nm* (*acción*) rescue; (*de naufragio*) salvage; **~ y socorrismo** life-saving
salvapantallas [salβapan'taʎas] *nm inv* screensaver

salvar [sal'βar] vt (rescatar) to save, rescue; (resolver) to overcome, resolve; (cubrir distancias) to cover, travel; (hacer excepción) to except, exclude; (un barco) to salvage; **salvarse** vr to save o.s., escape; ¡**sálvese el que pueda!** every man for himself!

salvavidas [salβa'βiðas] adj inv: **bote/ chaleco/cinturón** ~ lifeboat/lifejacket/ lifebelt

salvia ['salβja] nf sage

salvo, -a ['salβo, a] adj safe ▷ prep except (for), save; ~ **error u omisión** (Com) errors and omissions excepted; **a** ~ out of danger; ~ **que** unless

salvoconducto [salβokon'dukto] nm safe-conduct

samba ['samba] nf samba

san [san] n (apócope de **santo**) saint; ~ **Juan** St. John; ver tb **noche**

sanar [sa'nar] vt (herida) to heal; (persona) to cure ▷ vi (persona) to get well, recover; (herida) to heal

sanatorio [sana'torjo] nm sanatorium

sanción [san'θjon] nf sanction

sancionar [sanθjo'nar] vt to sanction

sancochado, -a [sanko'tʃaðo, a] adj (Am: Culin) underdone, rare

sandalia [san'dalja] nf sandal

sandez [san'deθ] nf (cualidad) foolishness; (acción) stupid thing; **decir sandeces** to talk nonsense

sandía [san'dia] nf watermelon

sandinista [sandi'nista] adj, nm/f Sandinist(a)

sandwich ['sandwitʃ] (pl **sandwichs** o **sandwiches**) nm sandwich

saneamiento [sanea'mjento] nm sanitation

sanear [sane'ar] vt to drain; (indemnizar) to compensate; (Econ) to reorganize

Sanfermines [sanfer'mines] nmpl see note

● SANFERMINES
●
● The *Sanfermines* are a week of *fiestas* in
● Pamplona, the capital of Navarre, made
● famous by Ernest Hemingway. From the
● 7th of July, the feast of San Fermín,
● crowds of mainly young people take to
● the streets drinking, singing and
● dancing. Early in the morning bulls are
● released along the narrow streets leading
● to the bullring, and people risk serious
● injury by running out in front of them,
● a custom which is also typical of many
● Spanish villages.

sangrar [san'grar] vt, vi to bleed; (texto) to indent

sangre ['sangre] nf blood; ~ **fría** sangfroid; **a** ~ **fría** in cold blood

sangría [san'gria] nf (Med) bleeding; (Culin)

sangría (sweetened drink of red wine with fruit), ≈ fruit cup

sangriento, -a [san'grjento, a] adj bloody

sanguijuela [sangi'xwela] nf (Zool, fig) leech

sanguinario, -a [sangi'narjo, a] adj bloodthirsty

sanguíneo, -a [san'gineo, a] adj blood cpd

sanidad [sani'ðað] nf sanitation; (calidad de sano) health, healthiness; ~ **pública** public health (department)

San Isidro [sani'sidro] nm patron saint of Madrid

● SAN ISIDRO
●
● *San Isidro* is the patron saint of Madrid,
● and gives his name to the week-long
● festivities which take place around the
● 15th May. Originally an 18th-century
● trade fair, the *San Isidro* celebrations now
● include music, dance, a famous *romería*,
● theatre and bullfighting.

sanitario, -a [sani'tarjo, a] adj sanitary; (de la salud) health cpd ▷ nm: ~**s** nmpl toilets (Brit), restroom sg (US)

sano, -a ['sano, a] adj healthy; (sin daños) sound; (comida) wholesome; (entero) whole, intact; ~ **y salvo** safe and sound

Santiago [san'tjayo] nm: ~ (**de Chile**) Santiago

santiamén [santja'men] nm: **en un** ~ in no time at all

santidad [santi'ðað] nf holiness, sanctity

santificar [santifi'kar] vt to sanctify

santiguarse [santi'ɣwarse] vr to make the sign of the cross

santo, -a ['santo, a] adj holy; (fig) wonderful, miraculous ▷ nm/f saint ▷ nm saint's day; **hacer su santa voluntad** to do as one jolly well pleases; **¿a** ~ **de qué ...?** why on earth ...?; **se le fue el** ~ **al cielo** he forgot what he was about to say; ~ **y seña** password; see note

● SANTO
●
● As well as celebrating their birthday
● Spaniards have traditionally celebrated el
● *santo*, their Saint's day, when the Saint
● they were called after at birth, eg San
● Pedro or la Virgen de los Dolores, is
● honoured in the Christian calendar. This
● is a custom which is gradually dying out.

santuario [san'twarjo] nm sanctuary, shrine

saña ['saɲa] nf rage, fury

sapo ['sapo] nm toad

saque etc ['sake] vb ver **sacar** ▷ nm (Tenis) service, serve; (Fútbol) throw-in; ~ **inicial** kick-off; ~ **de esquina** corner (kick); **tener buen** ~ to eat heartily

saquear [sake'ar] vt (Mil) to sack; (robar) to loot, plunder; (fig) to ransack

saqueo [sa'keo] *nm* sacking; looting, plundering; ransacking

sarampión [saram'pjon] *nm* measles *sg*

sarcasmo [sar'kasmo] *nm* sarcasm

sarcástico, -a [sar'kastiko, a] *adj* sarcastic

sarcófago [sar'kofaɣo] *nm* sarcophagus

sardina [sar'ðina] *nf* sardine

sardónico, -a [sar'ðoniko, a] *adj* sardonic; (*irónico*) ironical, sarcastic

sargento [sar'xento] *nm* sergeant

sarmiento [sar'mjento] *nm* vine shoot

sarna ['sarna] *nf* itch; (*Med*) scabies

sarpullido [sarpu'ʎiðo] *nm* (*Med*) rash

sarro ['sarro] *nm* deposit; (*en dientes*) tartar, plaque

sartén [sar'ten] *nf* frying pan; **tener la ~ por el mango** to rule the roost

sastre ['sastre] *nm* tailor

sastrería [sastre'ria] *nf* (*arte*) tailoring; (*tienda*) tailor's (shop)

Satanás [sata'nas] *nm* Satan

satélite [sa'telite] *nm* satellite

sátira ['satira] *nf* satire

satisfacción [satisfak'θjon] *nf* satisfaction

satisfacer [satisfa'θer] *vt* to satisfy; (*gastos*) to meet; (*deuda*) to pay; (*Com: letra de cambio*) to honour (*Brit*), honor (*US*); (*pérdida*) to make good; **satisfacerse** *vr* to satisfy o.s., be satisfied; (*vengarse*) to take revenge

satisfecho, -a [satis'fetʃo, a] *pp de* **satisfacer** ▷ *adj* satisfied; (*contento*) content(ed), happy; (*tb:* **~ de sí mismo**) self-satisfied, smug

saturación [satura'θjon] *nf* saturation; **llegar a la ~** to reach saturation point

saturar [satu'rar] *vt* to saturate; **saturarse** *vr* (*mercado, aeropuerto*) to reach saturation point; **¡estoy saturado de tanta televisión!** I can't take any more television!

sauce ['sauθe] *nm* willow; **~ llorón** weeping willow

saudí [sau'ði] *adj, nm/f* Saudi

sauna ['sauna] *nf* sauna

savia ['saβja] *nf* sap

saxo ['sakso] *nm* sax

saxofón [sakso'fon] *nm* saxophone

sazonado, -a [saθo'naðo, a] *adj* (*fruta*) ripe; (*Culin*) flavoured, seasoned

sazonar [saθo'nar] *vt* to ripen; (*Culin*) to flavour, season

scooter [e'skuter] *nf* (*Esp*) scooter

Scotch® [skotʃ] *nm* (*Am*) Sellotape® (*Brit*), Scotch tape® (*US*)

screenshot [es'krinʃot] *nm* screenshot

SE *abr* (= *sudeste*) SE

○ **PALABRA CLAVE**

se [se] *pron* **1** (*reflexivo: sg: m*) himself; (*: f*) herself; (*: pl*) themselves; (*: cosa*) itself; (*: de Vd*) yourself; (*: de Vds*) yourselves; (*indefinido*) oneself; **se mira en el espejo** he looks at himself in the mirror; **¡siéntese!** sit down!;

se durmió he fell asleep; **se está preparando** she's getting (herself) ready; *para usos léxicos del pron ver el vb en cuestión, p. ej.* **arrepentirse**

2 (*como complemento indirecto*) to him; to her; to them; to it; to you; **se lo dije ayer** (*a Vd*) I told you yesterday; **se compró un sombrero** he bought himself a hat; **se rompió la pierna** he broke his leg; **cortarse el pelo** to get one's hair cut; (*uno mismo*) to cut one's hair; **se comió un pastel** he ate a cake

3 (*uso recíproco*) each other, one another; **se miraron (el uno al otro)** they looked at each other o one another

4 (*en oraciones pasivas*): **se han vendido muchos libros** a lot of books have been sold; **"se vende coche"** "car for sale"

5 (*impers*): **se dice que** people say that, it is said that; **allí se come muy bien** the food there is very good, you can eat very well there

sé [se] *vb ver* **saber, ser**

sea *etc* ['sea] *vb ver* **ser**

sebo ['seβo] *nm* fat, grease

seca ['seka] *nf ver* **seco**

secador [seka'ðor] *nm:* **~ para el pelo** hairdryer

secadora [seka'ðora] *nf* tumble dryer; **~ centrífuga** spin-dryer

secano [se'kano] *nm* (*Agr: tb:* **tierra de ~**) dry land o region; **cultivo de ~** dry farming

secar [se'kar] *vt* to dry; (*superficie*) to wipe dry; (*frente, suelo*) to mop; (*líquido*) to mop up; (*tinta*) to blot; **secarse** *vr* to dry (off); (*río, planta*) to dry up

sección [sek'θjon] *nf* section; (*Com*) department; **~ deportiva** (*en periódico*) sports page(s)

seco, -a ['seko, a] *adj* dry; (*fruta*) dried; (*persona: magro*) thin, skinny; (*carácter*) cold; (*antipático*) disagreeable; (*respuesta*) sharp, curt ▷ *nm* dry season; **habrá pan a secas** there will be just bread; **decir algo a secas** to say sth curtly; **parar en ~** to stop dead

secretaría [sekreta'ria] *nf* secretariat; (*oficina*) secretary's office

secretario, -a [sekre'tarjo, a] *nm/f* secretary; **~ adjunto** (*Com*) assistant secretary

secreto, -a [se'kreto, a] *adj* secret; (*información*) confidential; (*persona*) secretive ▷ *nm* secret; (*calidad*) secrecy

secta ['sekta] *nf* sect

sectario, -a [sek'tarjo, a] *adj* sectarian

sector [sek'tor] *nm* sector (*tb Inform*); (*de opinión*) section; (*fig: campo*) area, field; **~ privado/público** (*Com: Econ*) private/public sector

secuela [se'kwela] *nf* consequence

secuencia [se'kwenθja] *nf* sequence

secuestrar [sekwes'trar] *vt* to kidnap; (*avión*) to hijack; (*bienes*) to seize, confiscate

secuestro [se'kwestro] *nm* kidnapping; hijack; seizure, confiscation

secular [seku'lar] *adj* secular

secundar [sekun'dar] *vt* to second, support

secundario, -a [sekun'darjo, a] *adj* secondary; (*carretera*) side *cpd*; (*Inform*) background *cpd* ▷ *nf* secondary education; *ver tb* **sistema educativo**

sed [seð] *nf* thirst; (*fig*) thirst, craving; **tener ~** to be thirsty

seda ['seða] *nf* silk; **~ dental** dental floss

sedal [se'ðal] *nm* fishing line

sedán [se'ðan] *nm* (*Am*) saloon (*Brit*), sedan (*US*)

sedante [se'ðante] *nm* sedative

sede ['seðe] *nf* (*de gobierno*) seat; (*de compañía*) headquarters *pl*, head office; **Santa S~** Holy See

sedentario, -a [seðen'tarjo, a] *adj* sedentary

sediento, -a [se'ðjento, a] *adj* thirsty

sedimentar [seðimen'tar] *vt* to deposit; **sedimentarse** *vr* to settle

sedimento [seði'mento] *nm* sediment

sedoso, -a [se'ðoso, a] *adj* silky, silken

seducción [seðuk'θjon] *nf* seduction

seducir [seðu'θir] *vt* to seduce; (*sobornar*) to bribe; (*cautivar*) to charm, fascinate; (*atraer*) to attract

seductor, a [seðuk'tor, a] *adj* seductive; charming, fascinating; attractive; (*engañoso*) deceptive, misleading ▷ *nm/f* seducer

segadora-trilladora [seɣa'ðoratriʎa'ðora] *nf* combine harvester

segar [se'ɣar] *vt* (*mies*) to reap, cut; (*hierba*) to mow, cut; (*esperanzas*) to ruin

seglar [se'ɣlar] *adj* secular, lay

segregación [seɣreɣa'θjon] *nf* segregation; **~ racial** racial segregation

segregar [seɣre'ɣar] *vt* to segregate, separate

seguido, -a [se'ɣiðo, a] *adj* (*continuo*) continuous, unbroken; (*recto*) straight ▷ *adv* (*directo*) straight (on); (*después*) after; (*Am: a menudo*) often ▷ *nf*: **en seguida** at once, right away; **cinco días ~s** five days running, five days in a row; **en seguida termino** I've nearly finished, I shan't be long now

seguimiento [seɣi'mjento] *nm* chase, pursuit; (*continuación*) continuation

seguir [se'ɣir] *vt* to follow; (*venir después*) to follow on, come after; (*proseguir*) to continue; (*perseguir*) to chase, pursue; (*indicio*) to follow up; (*mujer*) to court ▷ *vi* (*gen*) to follow; (*continuar*) to continue, carry o go on; **seguirse** *vr* to follow; **a ~** to be continued; **sigo sin comprender** I still don't understand; **sigue lloviendo** it's still raining; **sigue** (*en carta*) P.T.O.; (*en libro, TV*) continued; **"hágase ~"** "please forward"; **¡siga!** (*Am: pase*) come in!

según [se'ɣun] *prep* according to ▷ *adv*: **~ (y conforme)** it all depends ▷ *conj* as; **~ esté el tiempo** depending on the weather; **~ me**

consta as far as I know; **está ~ lo dejaste** it is just as you left it

segundo, -a [se'ɣundo, a] *adj* second; (*en discurso*) secondly ▷ *nm* (*gen, medida de tiempo*) second; (*piso*) second floor ▷ *nf* (*sentido*) second meaning; **~ (de a bordo)** (*Naut*) first mate; **segunda (clase)** (*Ferro*) second class; **segunda (marcha)** (*Auto*) second (gear); **de segunda mano** second hand

seguramente [seɣura'mente] *adv* surely; (*con certeza*) for sure, with certainty; (*probablemente*) probably; **¿lo va a comprar?** **— ~** is he going to buy it? — I should think so

seguridad [seɣuri'ðað] *nf* safety; (*del estado, de casa etc*) security; (*certidumbre*) certainty; (*confianza*) confidence; (*estabilidad*) stability; **~ social** social security; **~ contra incendios** fire precautions *pl*; **~ en sí mismo** (self-)confidence

seguro, -a [se'ɣuro, a] *adj* (*cierto*) sure, certain; (*fiel*) trustworthy; (*libre de peligro*) safe; (*bien defendido, firme*) secure; (*datos etc*) reliable; (*fecha*) firm ▷ *adv* for sure, certainly ▷ *nm* (*dispositivo*) safety device; (*de cerradura*) tumbler; (*de arma*) safety catch; (*Com*) insurance; **~ contra accidentes/incendios** fire/accident insurance; **~ contra terceros/a todo riesgo** third party/comprehensive insurance; **~ dotal con beneficios** with-profits endowment assurance; **S~ de Enfermedad** ≈ National Insurance; **~ marítimo** marine insurance; **~ mixto** endowment assurance; **~ temporal** term insurance; **~ de vida** life insurance; **~s sociales** social security *sg*

seis [seis] *num* six; **~ mil** six thousand; **tiene ~ años** she is six (years old); **unos ~** about six; **hoy es el ~** today is the sixth

seiscientos, -as [seis'θjentos, as] *num* six hundred

seísmo [se'ismo] *nm* tremor, earthquake

selección [selek'θjon] *nf* selection; **~ múltiple** multiple choice; **~ nacional** (*Deporte*) national team

seleccionar [selekθjo'nar] *vt* to pick, choose, select

selectividad [selektiβi'ðað] *nf* (*Univ*) entrance examination; *see note*

⬤ **SELECTIVIDAD**

School leavers wishing to go on to University sit the dreaded *selectividad* in June, with resits in September. When student numbers are too high for a particular course only the best students get their choice. Some of the others then wait a year to sit the exam again rather than do a course they don't want.

selecto, -a [se'lekto, a] *adj* select, choice; (*escogido*) selected

S

sellar [se'Λar] vt (*documento oficial*) to seal; (*pasaporte, visado*) to stamp; (*marcar*) to brand; (*pacto, labios*) to seal

sello ['seΛo] nm stamp; (*precinto*) seal; (*fig: tb:* ~ **distintivo**) hallmark; ~ **fiscal** revenue stamp; ~**s de prima** (*Com*) trading stamps

selva ['selβa] nf (*bosque*) forest, woods pl; (*jungla*) jungle; **la S~ Negra** the Black Forest

semáforo [se'maforo] nm (*Auto*) traffic lights pl; (*Ferro*) signal

semana [se'mana] nf week; ~ **inglesa** five-day (working) week; ~ **laboral** working week; **S~ Santa** Holy Week; **entre ~** during the week; *see note*

● **SEMANA SANTA**
●
● *Semana Santa* is a holiday in Spain all
● regions take *Viernes Santo*, Good Friday,
● *Sábado Santo*, Holy Saturday, and *Domingo*
● *de Resurrección*, Easter Sunday. Other
● holidays at this time vary according to
● each region. There are spectacular
● *procesiones* all over the country, with
● members of *cofradías* (brotherhoods)
● dressing in hooded robes and parading
● their *pasos* (religious floats or sculptures)
● through the streets. Seville has the most
● renowned celebrations, on account of the
● religious fervour shown by the locals.

semanal [sema'nal] adj weekly

semanario [sema'narjo] nm weekly (magazine)

semblante [sem'blante] nm face; (*fig*) look

sembrar [sem'brar] vt (*objetos*) to sow; (*objetos*) to sprinkle, scatter about; (*noticias etc*) to spread

semejante [seme'xante] adj (*parecido*) similar; (*tal*) such; ~**s** alike, similar ▷ nm fellow man, fellow creature; **son muy** ~**s** they are very much alike; **nunca hizo cosa** ~ he never did such a thing

semejanza [seme'xanθa] nf similarity, resemblance; **a** ~ **de** like, as

semejar [seme'xar] vi to seem like, resemble; **semejarse** vr to look alike, be similar

semen ['semen] nm semen

semental [semen'tal] nm (*macho*) stud

semestral [semes'tral] adj half-yearly, bi-annual

semicírculo [semi'θirkulo] nm semicircle

semiconsciente [semikons'θjente] adj semiconscious

semidesnatado, -a [semiðesna'taðo, a] adj semi-skimmed

semifinal [semifi'nal] nf semifinal

semiinconsciente [semi(i)nkons'θjente] adj semiconscious

semilla [se'miΛa] nf seed

seminario [semi'narjo] nm (*Rel*) seminary; (*Escol*) seminar

sémola ['semola] nf semolina

sempiterno, -a [sempi'terno, a] adj everlasting

Sena ['sena] nm: **el** ~ the (river) Seine

senado [se'naðo] nm senate; *ver tb* **Las Cortes (españolas)**

senador, a [sena'ðor, a] nm/f senator

sencillez [senθi'Λeθ] nf simplicity; (*de persona*) naturalness

sencillo, -a [sen'θiΛo, a] adj simple; (*carácter*) natural, unaffected; (*billete*) single ▷ nm (*disco*) single; (*Am*) small change

senda ['senda] nf, **sendero** [sen'dero] nm path, track; **Sendero Luminoso** the Shining Path (guerrilla movement)

senderismo [sende'rismo] nm hiking

sendero [sen'dero] nm path, track

sendos, -as ['sendos, as] adj pl: **les dio** ~ **golpes** he hit both of them

senil [se'nil] adj senile

seno ['seno] nm (*Anat*) bosom, bust; (*fig*) bosom; **senos** nmpl breasts; ~ **materno** womb

sensación [sensa'θjon] nf sensation; (*sentido*) sense; (*sentimiento*) feeling; **causar** o **hacer** ~ to cause a sensation

sensacional [sensaθjo'nal] adj sensational

sensatez [sensa'teθ] nf common sense

sensato, -a [sen'sato, a] adj sensible

sensibilidad [sensiβili'ðað] nf sensitivity; (*para el arte*) feel

sensibilizar [sensiβili'θar] vt: ~ **a la población/opinión pública** to raise public awareness

sensible [sen'sible] adj sensitive; (*apreciable*) perceptible, appreciable; (*pérdida*) considerable

sensiblero, -a [sensi'βlero, a] adj sentimental, slushy

sensitivo, -a [sensi'tiβo, a] adj sense cpd

sensorial [senso'rjal] adj sensory

sensual [sen'swal] adj sensual

sentado, -a [sen'taðo, a] adj (*establecido*) settled; (*carácter*) sensible ▷ nf sitting; (*Pol*) sit-in, sit-down protest; **dar por** ~ to take for granted, assume; **dejar algo** ~ to establish sth firmly; **estar** ~ to sit, be sitting (down); **de una sentada** at one sitting

sentar [sen'tar] vt to sit, seat; (*fig*) to establish ▷ vi (*vestido*) to suit; (*alimento*): ~ **bien/mal a** to agree/disagree with; **sentarse** vr (*persona*) to sit, sit down; (*el tiempo*) to settle (down); (*los depósitos*) to settle; **¡siéntese!** (do) sit down, take a seat

sentencia [sen'tenθja] nf (*máxima*) maxim, saying; (*Jur*) sentence; ~ **de muerte** death sentence

sentenciar [senten'θjar] vt to sentence

sentido, -a [sen'tiðo, a] adj (*pérdida*) regrettable; (*carácter*) sensitive ▷ nm sense; (*sentimiento*) feeling; (*significado*) sense, meaning; (*dirección*) direction; **mi más** ~ **pésame** my deepest sympathy; ~ **del humor**

sense of humour; **~ común** common sense; **en el buen ~ de la palabra** in the best sense of the word; **sin ~** meaningless; **tener ~** to make sense; **~ único** one-way (street)

sentimental [sentimen'tal] *adj* sentimental; **vida ~** love life

sentimiento [senti'mjento] *nm* (*emoción*) feeling, emotion; (*sentido*) sense; (*pesar*) regret, sorrow

sentir [sen'tir] *vt* to feel; (*percibir*) to perceive, sense; (*esp Am: oír*) to hear; (*lamentar*) to regret, be sorry for; (*música etc*) to have a feeling for ▷ *vi* to feel; (*lamentarse*) to feel sorry ▷ *nm* opinion, judgement; **sentirse** *vr* to feel; **lo siento** I'm sorry; **~se mejor/mal** to feel better/ill; **~se como en su casa** to feel at home

seña ['sena] *nf* sign; (*Mil*) password; **señas** *nfpl* address *sg*; **~s personales** personal description *sg*; **por más ~s** moreover; **dar ~s de** to show signs of

señal [se'nal] *nf* sign; (*síntoma*) symptom; (*indicio*) indication; (*Ferro: Telec*) signal; (*marca*) mark; (*Com*) deposit; (*Inform*) marker, mark; **en ~ de** as a token of, as a sign of; **dar ~es de** to show signs of; **~ de auxilio/de peligro** distress/danger signal; **~ de llamada** ringing tone; **~ para marcar** dialling tone

señalar [sena'lar] *vt* to mark; (*indicar*) to point out, indicate; (*significar*) to denote; (*referirse a*) to allude to; (*fijar*) to fix, settle; (*pey*) to criticize

señalizar [senali'θar] *vt* (*Auto*) to put up road signs on; (*Ferro*) to put signals on; (*Auto: ruta*): **está bien señalizada** it's well signposted

señor, a [se'nor, a] *adj* (*fam*) lordly ▷ *nm* (*hombre*) man; (*caballero*) gentleman; (*dueño*) owner, master; (*trato: antes de nombre propio*) Mr; (: *hablando directamente*) sir ▷ *nf* (*dama*) lady; (*trato: antes de nombre propio*) Mrs; (: *hablando directamente*) madam; (*esposa*) wife; **los ~es González** Mr and Mrs González; **S~ Don Jacinto Benavente** (*en sobre*) Mr J. Benavente, J. Benavente Esq.; **S~ Director ...** (*de periódico*) Dear Sir ...; **¡ juez** my lord, your worship (US); **~ Presidente** Mr Chairman o President; **Muy ~ mío** Dear Sir; **Muy ~es nuestros** Dear Sirs; **Nuestro S~** (*Rel*) Our Lord; **¿está la ~a?** is the lady of the house in?; **la ~a de Smith** Mrs Smith; **Nuestra S~a** (*Rel*) Our Lady

señorita [seno'rita] *nf* (*gen*) Miss; (*mujer joven*) young lady; (*maestra*) schoolteacher

señorito [seno'rito] *nm* young gentleman; (*lenguaje de criados*) master; (*pey*) toff

señuelo [se'nwelo] *nm* decoy

sepa *etc* ['sepa] *vb ver* **saber**

separación [separa'θjon] *nf* separation; (*división*) division; (*distancia*) gap, distance; **~ de bienes** division of property

separado, -a [sepa'raðo, a] *adj* separate; (*Tec*) detached; **vive ~ de su mujer** he is separated from his wife; **por ~** separately

separar [sepa'rar] *vt* to separate; (*silla (de la mesa)*) to move away; (*Tec: pieza*) to detach; (*persona: de un cargo*) to remove, dismiss; (*dividir*) to divide; **separarse** *vr* (*parte*) to come away; (*partes*) to come apart; (*persona*) to leave, go away; (*matrimonio*) to separate

separatismo [separa'tismo] *nm* (*Pol*) separatism

sepia ['sepja] *nf* cuttlefish

septentrional [septentrjo'nal] *adj* north *cpd*, northern

septiembre [sep'tjembre] *nm* September; *ver tb* **julio**

séptimo, -a ['septimo, a] *adj, nm* seventh

sepulcral [sepul'kral] *adj* sepulchral; (*fig*) gloomy, dismal; (*silencio, atmósfera*) deadly

sepulcro [se'pulkro] *nm* tomb, grave, sepulchre

sepultar [sepul'tar] *vt* to bury; (*en accidente*) to trap; **quedaban sepultados en la caverna** they were trapped in the cave

sepultura [sepul'tura] *nf* (*acto*) burial; (*tumba*) grave, tomb; **dar ~ a** to bury; **recibir ~** to be buried

sepulturero, -a [sepultu'rero, a] *nm/f* gravedigger

sequedad [seke'ðað] *nf* dryness; (*fig*) brusqueness, curtness

sequía [se'kia] *nf* drought

séquito ['sekito] *nm* (*de rey etc*) retinue; (*Pol*) followers *pl*

PALABRA CLAVE

ser [ser] *vi* **1** (*descripción, identidad*) to be; **es médica/muy alta** she's a doctor/very tall; **la familia es de Cuzco** his (o her etc) family is from Cuzco; **ser de madera** to be made of wood; **soy Ana** I'm Ana

2 (*propiedad*): **es de Joaquín** it's Joaquín's, it belongs to Joaquín

3 (*horas, fechas, números*): **es la una** it's one o'clock; **son las seis y media** it's half-past six; **es el 1 de junio** it's the first of June; **somos/son seis** there are six of us/them; **2 y 2 son 4** 2 and 2 are o make 4

4 (*suceso*): **¿qué ha sido eso?** what was that?; **la fiesta es en mi casa** the party's at my house; **¿qué será de mí?** what will become of me?; **"érase una vez ..."** "once upon a time ..."

5 (*en oraciones pasivas*): **ha sido descubierto ya** it's already been discovered

6: es de esperar que ... it is to be hoped o I etc hope that ...

7 (*locuciones con sub*): **o sea** that is to say; **sea él sea su hermana** either him or his sister; **tengo que irme, no sea que mis hijos estén esperándome** I have to go in case my

S

children are waiting for me
8: a o **de no ser por él** ... but for him ...
9: a no ser que: a no ser que tenga uno ya
unless he's got one already
▷ *nm* being; **ser humano** human being; **ser
vivo** living creature

Serbia ['serβja] *nf* Serbia
serbio, -a ['serβjo, a] *adj* Serbian ▷ *nm/f* Serb
serenarse [sere'narse] *vr* to calm down;
(*mar*) to grow calm; (*tiempo*) to clear up
serenidad [sereni'ðað] *nf* calmness
sereno, -a [se'reno, a] *adj* (*persona*) calm,
unruffled; (*tiempo*) fine, settled; (*ambiente*)
calm, peaceful ▷ *nm* night watchman
serial [se'rjal] *nm* serial
serie ['serje] *nf* series; (*cadena*) sequence,
succession; (*TV etc*) serial; (*de inyecciones*)
course; **fuera de ~** out of order; (*fig*) special,
out of the ordinary; **fabricación en ~** mass
production; **interface/impresora
en ~** serial interface/printer
seriedad [serje'ðað] *nf* seriousness;
(*formalidad*) reliability; (*de crisis*) gravity,
seriousness
serigrafía [seriɣra'fia] *nf* silk screen
printing
serio, -a ['serjo, a] *adj* serious; reliable,
dependable; grave, serious; **poco ~** (*actitud*)
undignified; (*carácter*) unreliable; **en ~**
seriously
sermón [ser'mon] *nm* (*Rel*) sermon
seropositivo, -a [seroposi'tiβo, a] *adj* HIV-
positive
serpentear [serpente'ar] *vi* to wriggle;
(*camino, río*) to wind, snake
serpentina [serpen'tina] *nf* streamer
serpiente [ser'pjente] *nf* snake; **~ boa** boa
constrictor; **~ de cascabel** rattlesnake
serranía [serra'nia] *nf* mountainous area
serrano, -a [se'rrano, a] *adj* highland *cpd*,
hill *cpd* ▷ *nm/f* highlander
serrar [se'rrar] *vt* to saw
serrín [se'rrin] *nm* sawdust
serrucho [se'rrutʃo] *nm* handsaw
service ['serβis] *nm* (*Am: Auto*) service
servicio [ser'βiθjo] *nm* service; (*Am Auto*)
service; (*Culin etc*) set; **servicios** *nmpl* toilet(s)
(*pl*); **estar de ~** to be on duty; **~ de aduana** o
de aduana customs service; **~ a domicilio**
home delivery service; **~ incluido** (*en hotel
etc*) service charge included; **~ militar**
military service; **~ público** (*Com*) public
utility
servidor, a [serβi'ðor, a] *nm/f* servant ▷ *nm*
(*Inform*) server; **su seguro ~ (s.s.s.)** yours
faithfully; **un ~** (*el que habla o escribe*) your
humble servant
servidumbre [serβi'ðumbre] *nf* (*sujeción*)
servitude; (*criados*) servants *pl*, staff
servil [ser'βil] *adj* servile
servilleta [serβi'ʎeta] *nf* serviette, napkin

servir [ser'βir] *vt* to serve; (*comida*) to serve
out o up; (*Tenis etc*) to serve ▷ *vi* to serve;
(*camarero*) to serve, wait; (*tener utilidad*) to be of
use, be useful; **servirse** *vr* to serve o help o.s.;
¿en qué puedo ~le? how can I help you?;
~ vino a algn to pour out wine for sb; **~ de
guía** to act o serve as a guide; **no sirve para
nada** it's no use at all; **~se de algo** to make
use of sth, use sth; **sírvase pasar** please
come in
sesenta [se'senta] *num* sixty
sesgo ['sesɣo] *nm* slant; (*fig*) slant, twist
sesión [se'sjon] *nf* (*Pol*) session, sitting; (*Cine*)
showing; (*Teat*) performance; **abrir/
levantar la ~** to open/close o adjourn the
meeting; **la segunda ~** the second house
seso ['seso] *nm* brain; (*fig*) intelligence; **sesos**
nmpl (*Culin*) brains; **devanarse los ~s** to rack
one's brains
sesudo, -a [se'suðo, a] *adj* sensible, wise
set (*pl* **sets**) [set, sets] *nm* (*Tenis*) set
seta ['seta] *nf* mushroom; **~ venenosa**
toadstool
setecientos, -as [sete'θjentos, as] *num*
seven hundred
setenta [se'tenta] *num* seventy
seto ['seto] *nm* fence; **~ vivo** hedge
seudo... [seuðo] *pref* pseudo...
seudónimo [seu'ðonimo] *nm* pseudonym
severidad [seβeri'ðað] *nf* severity
severo, -a [se'βero, a] *adj* severe; (*disciplina*)
strict; (*frío*) bitter
Sevilla [se'βiʎa] *nf* Seville
sevillano, -a [seβi'ʎano, a] *adj* of o from
Seville ▷ *nm/f* native o inhabitant of Seville
sexo ['sekso] *nm* sex; **el ~ femenino/
masculino** the female/male sex
sexto, -a ['seksto, a] *num* sixth; **Juan S~** John
the Sixth
sexual [sek'swal] *adj* sexual; **vida ~** sex life
sexualidad [sekswali'ðað] *nf* sexuality
si [si] *conj* if; (*en pregunta indirecta*) if, whether
▷ *nm* (*Mus*) B; **si ... si ...** whether ... or ...; **me
pregunto si ...** I wonder if o whether ...; **si
no** if not, otherwise; **¡si fuera verdad!** if
only it were true!; **por si viene** in case he
comes
sí [si] *adv* yes ▷ *nm* consent ▷ *pron* (*uso
impersonal*) oneself; (*sg: m*) himself; (*: f*)
herself; (*: de cosa*) itself; (*: de usted*) yourself;
(*pl*) themselves; (*: de ustedes*) yourselves;
(*: recíproco*) each other; **él no quiere pero yo
sí** he doesn't want to but I do; **ella sí vendrá**
she will certainly come, she is sure to come;
claro que sí of course; **creo que sí** I think so;
porque sí because that's the way it is; (*porque
lo digo yo*) because I say so; **¡sí que lo es!** I'll
say it is!; **¡eso sí que no!** never!; **se ríe de sí
misma** she laughs at herself; **cambiaron
una mirada entre sí** they gave each other a
look; **de por sí** in itself
siamés, -esa [sja'mes, esa] *adj, nm/f* Siamese

sibarita [siβa'rita] adj sybaritic ▷ nm/f sybarite

sicario [si'karjo] nm hired killer

SIDA ['siða] nm abr (= síndrome de inmunodeficiencia adquirida) AIDS

siderúrgico, -a [siðe'rurxiko, a] adj iron and steel cpd

sidra ['siðra] nf cider

siembra etc ['sjembra] vb ver **sembrar** ▷ nf sowing

siempre ['sjempre] adv always; (todo el tiempo) all the time; (Am: así y todo) still ▷ conj: ~ que ... (+indic) whenever ...; (+subjun) provided that ...; **es lo de** ~ it's the same old story; **como** ~ as usual; **para** ~ forever; ~ **me voy mañana** (Am) I'm still leaving tomorrow

sien [sjen] nf (Anat) temple

siento etc ['sjento] vb ver **sentar, sentir**

sierra ['sjerra] vb ver **serrar** ▷ nf (Tec) saw; (Geo) mountain range; **S~ Leona** Sierra Leone

siervo, -a [sjerβo, a] nm/f slave

siesta ['sjesta] nf siesta, nap; **dormir la** o **echarse una** o **tomar una** ~ to have an afternoon nap o a doze

siete ['sjete] num seven ▷ excl (Am fam): **¡la gran ~!** wow!, hell!; **hijo de la gran ~** (fam!) bastard (!), son of a bitch (US) (!)

sífilis ['sifilis] nf syphilis

sifón [si'fon] nm syphon; **whisky con ~** whisky and soda

sigilo [si'xilo] nm secrecy; (discreción) discretion

sigla ['siɣla] nf initial, abbreviation

siglo ['siɣlo] nm century; (fig) age; **S~ de las Luces** Age of Enlightenment; **S~ de Oro** Golden Age

significación [siɣnifika'θjon] nf significance

significado [siɣnifi'kaðo] nm significance; (de palabra etc) meaning

significar [siɣnifi'kar] vt to mean, signify; (notificar) to make known, express

significativo, -a [siɣnifika'tiβo, a] adj significant

signo ['siɣno] nm sign; ~ **de admiración** o **exclamación** exclamation mark; ~ **igual** equals sign; ~ **de interrogación** question mark; ~ **de más/de menos** plus/minus sign; ~**s de puntuación** punctuation marks

sigo etc vb ver **seguir**

siguiente [si'ɣjente] adj following; (próximo) next

siguió etc vb ver **seguir**

sílaba ['silaβa] nf syllable

silbar [sil'βar] vt, vi to whistle; (silbato) to blow; (Teat etc) to hiss

silbato [sil'βato] nm (instrumento) whistle

silbido [sil'βiðo] nm whistle, whistling; (abucheo) hiss

silenciador [silenθja'ðor] nm silencer

silenciar [silen'θjar] vt (persona) to silence; (escándalo) to hush up

silencio [si'lenθjo] nm silence, quiet; **en el ~ más absoluto** in dead silence; **guardar ~** to keep silent

silencioso, -a [silen'θjoso, a] adj silent, quiet

silicio [si'liθjo] nm silicon

silla ['siʎa] nf (asiento) chair; (tb: ~ **de montar**) saddle; ~ **de ruedas** wheelchair

sillín [si'ʎin] nm saddle, seat

sillón [si'ʎon] nm armchair, easy chair

silueta [si'lweta] nf silhouette; (de edificio) outline; (figura) figure

silvestre [sil'βestre] adj (Bot) wild; (fig) rustic, rural

simbólico, -a [sim'boliko, a] adj symbolic(al)

simbolizar [simboli'θar] vt to symbolize

símbolo ['simbolo] nm symbol; ~ **gráfico** (Inform) icon

simetría [sime'tria] nf symmetry

simétrico, -a [si'metriko, a] adj symmetrical

simiente [si'mjente] nf seed

similar [simi'lar] adj similar

simio ['simjo] nm ape

simpatía [simpa'tia] nf liking; (afecto) affection; (amabilidad) kindness; (de ambiente) friendliness; (de persona, lugar) charm, attractiveness; (solidaridad) mutual support, solidarity; **tener ~ a** to like; **la famosa ~ andaluza** that well-known Andalusian charm

simpático, -a [sim'patiko, a] adj nice, pleasant; (bondadoso) kind; **no le hemos caído muy ~s** she didn't much take to us

simpatizante [simpati'θante] nm/f sympathizer

simpatizar [simpati'θar] vi: ~ **con** to get on well with

simple ['simple] adj simple; (elemental) simple, easy; (mero) mere; (puro) pure, sheer ▷ nm/f simpleton; **un ~ soldado** an ordinary soldier

simpleza [sim'pleθa] nf simpleness; (necedad) silly thing

simplicidad [simpliθi'ðað] nf simplicity

simplificar [simplifi'kar] vt to simplify

simposio [sim'posjo] nm symposium

simulacro [simu'lakro] nm (apariencia) semblance; (fingimiento) sham

simular [simu'lar] vt to simulate; (fingir) to feign, sham

simultáneo, -a [simul'taneo, a] adj simultaneous

sin [sin] prep without; (a no ser por) but for ▷ conj: ~ **que** (+subjun) without; ~ **decir nada** without a word; ~ **verlo yo** without my seeing it; **platos ~ lavar** unwashed o dirty dishes; **la ropa está ~ lavar** the clothes are unwashed; ~ **que lo sepa él** without his knowing; ~ **embargo** however

sinagoga [sina'ɣoɣa] nf synagogue

sinceridad [sinθeri'ðað] nf sincerity

sincero, -a [sin'θero, a] adj sincere; (persona) genuine; (opinión) frank; (felicitaciones) heartfelt

sincronizar [sinkroni'θar] vt to synchronize

sindical [sindi'kal] adj union cpd, trade-union cpd

sindicalista [sindika'lista] adj trade-union cpd ▷ nm/f trade unionist

sindicato [sindi'kato] nm (de trabajadores) trade(s) o labor (US) union; (de negociantes) syndicate

síndrome ['sindrome] nm syndrome; ~ de abstinencia withdrawal symptoms; ~ de la clase turista economy-class syndrome

sine qua non [sine'kwanon] adj: condición ~ sine qua non

sinfín [sin'fin] nm: un ~ de a great many, no end of

sinfonía [sinfo'nia] nf symphony

sinfónico, -a [sin'foniko, a] adj (música) symphonic; orquesta sinfónica symphony orchestra

singular [singu'lar] adj singular; (fig) outstanding, exceptional; (pey) peculiar, odd ▷ nm (Ling) singular; en ~ in the singular

singularidad [singulari'ðað] nf singularity, peculiarity

singularizar [singulari'θar] vt to single out; singularizarse vr to distinguish o.s., stand out

siniestro, -a [si'njestro, a] adj left; (fig) sinister ▷ nm (accidente) accident; (desastre) natural disaster

sinnúmero [sin'numero] nm = sinfín

sino ['sino] nm fate, destiny ▷ conj (pero) but; (salvo) except, save; no son 8 ~ 9 there are not 8 but 9; todos ~ él all except him

sinónimo, -a [si'nonimo, a] adj synonymous ▷ nm synonym

sintaxis [sin'taksis] nf syntax

síntesis ['sintesis] nf inv synthesis

sintético, -a [sin'tetiko, a] adj synthetic

sintetizar [sinteti'θar] vt to synthesize

sintió vb ver sentir

síntoma ['sintoma] nm symptom

sintomático, -a [sinto'matiko, a] adj symptomatic

sintonía [sinto'nia] nf (Radio) tuning; (melodía) signature tune

sintonizar [sintoni'θar] vt (Radio) to tune (in) to, pick up

sinvergüenza [simber'ɣwenθa] nm/f rogue, scoundrel; ¡es un ~! he's got a nerve!

sionismo [sjo'nismo] nm Zionism

siquiera [si'kjera] conj even if, even though ▷ adv (esp Am) at least; ni ~ not even; ~ bebe algo at least drink something

sirena [si'rena] nf siren, mermaid; (bocina) siren, hooter

Siria ['sirja] nf Syria

sirio, -a ['sirjo, a] adj, nm/f Syrian

sirviente, -a [sir'βjente, a] nm/f servant

sirvo etc vb ver servir

sisear [sise'ar] vt, vi to hiss

sísmico, -a ['sismiko, a] adj: movimiento ~ earthquake

sismógrafo [sis'moɣrafo] nm seismograph

sistema [sis'tema] nm system; (método) method; ~ binario (Inform) binary system; ~ de alerta inmediata early-warning system; ~ de facturación (Com) invoicing system; ~ educativo educational system; ~ impositivo o tributario taxation, tax system; ~ métrico metric system; ~ operativo (en disco) (Inform) (disk-based) operating system; see note

● SISTEMA EDUCATIVO
●
● The reform of the Spanish sistema educativo
● (education system) begun in the early
● 90s has replaced the courses EGB, BUP and
● COU with the following: Primaria a
● compulsory 6 years; Secundaria a
● compulsory 4 years; Bachillerato an
● optional 2 year secondary school course,
● essential for those wishing to go on to
● higher education.

sistemático, -a [siste'matiko, a] adj systematic

sitiar [si'tjar] vt to besiege, lay siege to

sitio ['sitjo] nm (lugar) place; (espacio) room, space; (Mil) siege; ~ de taxis (Am: parada) taxi stand o rank (Brit); ~ web website; ¿hay ~? is there any room?; hay ~ de sobra there's plenty of room

situación [sitwa'θjon] nf situation, position; (estatus) position, standing

situado, -a [si'twaðo, a] adj situated, placed; estar ~ (Com) to be financially secure

situar [si'twar] vt to place, put; (edificio) to locate, situate

slip [es'lip] (pl slips) nm pants pl, briefs pl

SME nm abr (= Sistema Monetario Europeo) EMS; (mecanismo de cambios del) ~ ERM

smoking [(e)'smokin] (pl smokings) nm dinner jacket (Brit), tuxedo (US)

SMS nm (mensaje) text (message), SMS (message)

snob [es'nob] = esnob

SO abr (= suroeste) SW

so [so] excl whoa!; ¡so burro! you idiot! ▷ prep under

sobaco [so'βako] nm armpit

sobar [so'βar] vt (tela) to finger; (ropa) to rumple, mess up; (músculos) to rub, massage; (comida) to play around with

soberanía [soβera'nia] nf sovereignty

soberano, -a [soβe'rano, a] adj sovereign; (fig) supreme ▷ nm/f sovereign; los ~s the king and queen

soberbio, -a [so'βerβjo, a] *adj* (*orgulloso*) proud; (*altivo*) haughty, arrogant; (*fig*) magnificent, superb ▷ *nf* pride; haughtiness, arrogance; magnificence

sobornar [soβor'nar] *vt* to bribe

soborno [so'βorno] *nm* (*un soborno*) bribe; (*el soborno*) bribery

sobra ['soβra] *nf* excess, surplus; **sobras** *nfpl* left-overs, scraps; **de ~** surplus, extra; **lo sé de ~** I'm only too aware of it; **tengo de ~** I've more than enough

sobrado, -a [so'βraðo, a] *adj* (*más que suficiente*) more than enough; (*superfluo*) excessive ▷ *adv* too, exceedingly; **sobradas veces** repeatedly

sobrante [so'βrante] *adj* remaining, extra ▷ *nm* surplus, remainder

sobrar [so'βrar] *vt* to exceed, surpass ▷ *vi* (*tener de más*) to be more than enough; (*quedar*) to remain, be left (over)

sobrasada [soβra'saða] *nf* ≈ sausage spread

sobre ['soβre] *prep* (*gen*) on; (*encima*) on (top of); (*por encima de, arriba de*) over, above; (*más que*) more than; (*además*) in addition to, besides; (*alrededor de*) about; (*porcentaje*) in, out of; (*tema*) about, on ▷ *nm* envelope; **~ todo** above all; **3 ~ 100** 3 in a 100, 3 out of every 100; **un libro ~ Tirso** a book about Tirso; **~ de ventanilla** window envelope

sobrecama [soβre'kama] *nf* bedspread

sobrecargar [soβrekar'ɣar] *vt* (*camión*) to overload; (*Com*) to surcharge

sobrecoger [soβreko'xer] *vt* (*sobresaltar*) to startle; (*asustar*) to scare; **sobrecogerse** *vr* (*sobresaltarse*) to be startled; (*asustarse*) to get scared; (*quedar impresionado*): **~se (de)** to be overawed (by)

sobredosis [soβre'ðosis] *nf inv* overdose

sobreentender [soβreenten'der] *vt* to understand; (*adivinar*) to deduce, infer; **sobreentenderse** *vr*: **se sobreentiende que ...** it is implied that ...

sobreescribir [soβreeskri'βir] *vt* (*Inform*) to overwrite

sobrehumano, -a [soβreu'mano, a] *adj* superhuman

sobrellevar [soβreʎe'βar] *vt* (*fig*) to bear, endure

sobremesa [soβre'mesa] *nf* (*después de comer*) sitting on after a meal; (*Inform*) desktop; **durante la ~** after dinner; **conversación de ~** table talk

sobrenatural [soβrenatu'ral] *adj* supernatural

sobrenombre [soβre'nombre] *nm* nickname

sobrepasar [soβrepa'sar] *vt* to exceed, surpass

sobreponer [soβrepo'ner] *vt* (*poner encima*) to put on top; (*añadir*) to add; **sobreponerse** *vr*: **~se a** to overcome

sobresaliente [soβresa'ljente] *adj* projecting; (*fig*) outstanding, excellent; (*Univ* etc) first class ▷ *nm* (*Univ* etc) first class (mark), distinction

sobresalir [soβresa'lir] *vi* to project, jut out; (*fig*) to stand out, excel

sobresaltar [soβresal'tar] *vt* (*asustar*) to scare, frighten; (*sobrecoger*) to startle

sobresalto [soβre'salto] *nm* (*movimiento*) start; (*susto*) scare; (*turbación*) sudden shock

sobrescribir [soβreskri'βir] *vt* = **sobreescribir**

sobretodo [soβre'toðo] *nm* overcoat

sobrevenir [soβreβe'nir] *vi* (*ocurrir*) to happen (unexpectedly); (*resultar*) to follow, ensue

sobreviviente [soβreβi'βjente] *adj* surviving ▷ *nm/f* survivor

sobrevivir [soβreβi'βir] *vi* to survive; (*persona*) to outlive; (*objeto* etc) to outlast

sobrevolar [soβreβo'lar] *vt* to fly over

sobriedad [soβrje'ðað] *nf* sobriety, soberness; (*moderación*) moderation, restraint

sobrino, -a [so'βrino, a] *nm/f* nephew/niece

sobrio, -a ['soβrjo, a] *adj* sober; (*moderado*) moderate, restrained

socarrón, -ona [soka'rron, ona] *adj* (*sarcástico*) sarcastic, ironic(al)

socavar [soka'βar] *vt* to undermine; (*excavar*) to dig underneath o below

socavón [soka'βon] *nm* (*en mina*) gallery; (*hueco*) hollow; (*en la calle*) hole

sociable [so'θjaβle] *adj* (*persona*) sociable, friendly; (*animal*) social

social [so'θjal] *adj* social; (*Com*) company *cpd*

socialdemócrata [soθjalde'mokrata] *adj* social-democratic ▷ *nm/f* social democrat

socialista [soθja'lista] *adj, nm/f* socialist

socializar [soθjali'θar] *vt* to socialize

sociedad [soθje'ðað] *nf* society; (*Com*) company; **~ de ahorro y préstamo** savings and loan society; **~ anónima (S.A.)** limited company (Ltd) (Brit), incorporated company (Inc) (US); **~ de beneficiencia** friendly society (Brit), benefit association (US); **~ de cartera** investment trust; **~ comanditaria** (*Com*) co-ownership; **~ conjunta** (*Com*) joint venture; **~ de consumo** consumer society; **~ inmobiliaria** building society (Brit), savings and loan (society) (US); **~ de responsabilidad limitada** (*Com*) private limited company

socio, -a ['soθjo, a] *nm/f* (*miembro*) member; (*Com*) partner; **~ activo** active partner; **~ capitalista** o **comanditario** sleeping o silent (US) partner

sociología [soθjolo'xia] *nf* sociology

sociólogo, -a [so'θjoloɣo, a] *nm/f* sociologist

socorrer [soko'rrer] *vt* to help

socorrismo [soko'rrismo] *nm* life-saving

socorrista [soko'rrista] *nm/f* first aider; (*en piscina, playa*) lifeguard

socorro [so'korro] *nm* (*ayuda*) help, aid; (*Mil*) relief; **¡~!** help!

soda ['soða] *nf* (*sosa*) soda; (*bebida*) soda (water)

sódico, -a ['soðiko, a] *adj* sodium *cpd*
sofá [so'fa] *nm* sofa, settee
sofá-cama [so'fakama] *nm* studio couch, sofa bed
sofisticación [sofistika'θjon] *nf* sophistication
sofisticado, -a [sofisti'kaðo, a] *adj* sophisticated
sofocar [sofo'kar] *vt* to suffocate; (*apagar*) to smother, put out; **sofocarse** *vr* to suffocate; (*fig*) to blush, feel embarrassed
sofoco [so'foko] *nm* suffocation; (*azoro*) embarrassment
sofreír [sofre'ir] *vt* to fry lightly
soft ['sof], **software** ['sofwer] *nm* (*Inform*) software
soga ['soɣa] *nf* rope
sois [sois] *vb ver* **ser**
soja ['soxa] *nf* soya
sojuzgar [soxuθ'ɣar] *vt* to subdue, rule despotically
sol [sol] *nm* sun; (*luz*) sunshine, sunlight; (*Mus*) G; ~ **naciente/poniente** rising/setting sun; **tomar el** ~ to sunbathe; **hace** ~ it is sunny
solamente [sola'mente] *adv* only, just
solapa [so'lapa] *nf* (*de chaqueta*) lapel; (*de libro*) jacket
solapado, -a [sola'paðo, a] *adj* (*intenciones*) underhand; (*gestos, movimiento*) sly
solar [so'lar] *adj* solar, sun *cpd* ▷ *nm* (*terreno*) plot (of ground); (*local*) undeveloped site
solaz [so'laθ] *nm* recreation, relaxation
solazar [sola'θar] *vt* (*divertir*) to amuse; **solazarse** *vr* to enjoy o.s., relax
soldado [sol'daðo] *nm* soldier; ~ **raso** private
soldador [solda'ðor] *nm* soldering iron; (*persona*) welder
soldar [sol'dar] *vt* to solder, weld; (*unir*) to join, unite
soleado, -a [sole'aðo, a] *adj* sunny
soledad [sole'ðað] *nf* solitude; (*estado infeliz*) loneliness
solemne [so'lemne] *adj* solemn; (*tontería*) utter; (*error*) complete
solemnidad [solemni'ðað] *nf* solemnity
soler [so'ler] *vi* to be in the habit of, be accustomed to; **suele salir a las ocho** she usually goes out at 8 o'clock; **solíamos ir todos los años** we used to go every year
solfeo [sol'feo] *nm* sol-fa, singing of scales; **ir a clases de** ~ to take singing lessons
solicitar [soliθi'tar] *vt* (*permiso*) to ask for, seek; (*puesto*) to apply for; (*votos*) to canvass for; (*atención*) to attract; (*persona*) to pursue, chase after
solícito, -a [so'liθito, a] *adj* (*diligente*) diligent; (*cuidadoso*) careful
solicitud [soliθi'tuð] *nf* (*calidad*) great care; (*petición*) request; (*a un puesto*) application
solidaridad [soliðari'ðað] *nf* solidarity; **por** ~ **con** (*Pol etc*) out of o in solidarity with

solidario, -a [soli'ðarjo, a] *adj* (*participación*) joint, common; (*compromiso*) mutually binding; **hacerse** ~ **de** to declare one's solidarity with
solidarizarse [soliðari'θarse] *vr*: ~ **con algn** to support sb, sympathize with sb
solidez [soli'ðeθ] *nf* solidity
sólido, -a ['soliðo, a] *adj* solid; (*Tec*) solidly made; (*bien construido*) well built
soliloquio [soli'lokjo] *nm* soliloquy
solista [so'lista] *nm/f* soloist
solitario, -a [soli'tarjo, a] *adj* (*persona*) lonely, solitary; (*lugar*) lonely, desolate ▷ *nm/f* (*reclusa*) recluse; (*en la sociedad*) loner ▷ *nm* solitaire ▷ *nf* tapeworm
sollozar [soʎo'θar] *vi* to sob
sollozo [so'ʎoθo] *nm* sob
solo, -a ['solo, a] *adj* (*único*) single, sole; (*sin compañía*) alone; (*Mus*) solo; (*solitario*) lonely; **hay una sola dificultad** there is just one difficulty; **a solas** alone, by o.s.
sólo ['solo] *adv* only, just; (*exclusivamente*) solely; **tan** ~ only just
solomillo [solo'miʎo] *nm* sirloin
solsticio [sols'tiθjo] *nm* solstice
soltar [sol'tar] *vt* (*dejar ir*) to let go of; (*desprender*) to unfasten, loosen; (*librar*) to release, set free; (*amarras*) to cast off; (*Auto: freno etc*) to release; (*suspiro*) to heave; (*risa etc*) to let out; **soltarse** *vr* (*desanudarse*) to come undone; (*desprenderse*) to come off; (*adquirir destreza*) to become expert; (*en idioma*) to become fluent
soltero, -a [sol'tero, a] *adj* single, unmarried ▷ *nm* bachelor ▷ *nf* single woman, spinster
solterón [solte'ron] *nm* confirmed bachelor
solterona [solte'rona] *nf* spinster, maiden lady; (*pey*) old maid
soltura [sol'tura] *nf* looseness, slackness; (*de los miembros*) agility, ease of movement; (*en el hablar*) fluency, ease
soluble [so'luβle] *adj* (*Química*) soluble; (*problema*) solvable; ~ **en agua** soluble in water
solución [solu'θjon] *nf* solution; ~ **de continuidad** break in continuity
solucionar [soluθjo'nar] *vt* (*problema*) to solve; (*asunto*) to settle, resolve
solventar [solβen'tar] *vt* (*pagar*) to settle, pay; (*resolver*) to resolve
solvente [sol'βente] *adj* solvent, free of debt
sombra ['sombra] *nf* shadow; (*como protección*) shade; **sombras** *nfpl* darkness *sg*, shadows; **sin** ~ **de duda** without a shadow of doubt; **tener buena/mala** ~ (*suerte*) to be lucky/unlucky; (*carácter*) to be likeable/disagreeable
sombrero [som'brero] *nm* hat; ~ **hongo** bowler (*brit*), derby (*US*); ~ **de copa** o **de pelo** (*Am*) top hat
sombrilla [som'briʎa] *nf* parasol, sunshade

sombrío, -a [som'brio, a] *adj* (*oscuro*) dark; (*fig*) sombre, sad; (*persona*) gloomy

somero, -a [so'mero, a] *adj* superficial

someter [some'ter] *vt* (*país*) to conquer; (*persona*) to subject to one's will; (*informe*) to present, submit; **someterse** *vr* to give in, yield, submit; **~ a** to subject to; **~se a** to submit to; **~se a una operación** to undergo an operation

somier [so'mjer] (*pl* **somiers**) *nm* spring mattress

somnífero [som'nifero] *nm* sleeping pill *o* tablet

somnolencia [somno'lenθja] *nf* sleepiness, drowsiness

somos ['somos] *vb ver* **ser**

son [son] *vb ver* **ser** ▷ *nm* sound; **en ~ de broma** as a joke

sonaja [so'naxa] *nf* (*Am*) = **sonajero**

sonajero [sona'xero] *nm* (baby's) rattle

sonambulismo [sonambu'lismo] *nm* sleepwalking

sonámbulo, -a [so'nambulo, a] *nm/f* sleepwalker

sonar [so'nar] *vt* (*campana*) to ring; (*trompeta, sirena*) to blow ▷ *vi* to sound; (*hacer ruido*) to make a noise; (*Ling*) to be sounded, be pronounced; (*ser conocido*) to sound familiar; (*campana*) to ring; (*reloj*) to strike, chime; **sonarse** *vr*: **~se (la nariz)** to blow one's nose; **es un nombre que suena** it's a name that's in the news; **me suena ese nombre** that name rings a bell

sonda ['sonda] *nf* (*Naut*) sounding; (*Tec*) bore, drill; (*Med*) probe

sondear [sonde'ar] *vt* to sound; to bore (into), drill; to probe, sound; (*fig*) to sound out

sondeo [son'deo] *nm* sounding; boring, drilling; (*encuesta*) poll, enquiry; **~ de la opinión pública** public opinion poll

sónico, -a ['soniko, a] *adj* sonic, sound *cpd*

sonido [so'niðo] *nm* sound

sonoro, -a [so'noro, a] *adj* sonorous; (*resonante*) loud, resonant; (*Ling*) voiced; **efectos ~s** sound effects

sonreír [sonre'ir] *vi*, **sonreírse** *vr* to smile

sonriente [son'rjente] *adj* smiling

sonrisa [son'risa] *nf* smile

sonrojar [sonro'xar] *vt*: **~ a algn** to make sb blush; **sonrojarse** *vr*: **~se (de)** to blush (at)

sonrojo [son'roxo] *nm* blush

sonsacar [sonsa'kar] *vt* to wheedle, coax; **~ a algn** to pump sb for information

soñador, a [soɲa'ðor, a] *nm/f* dreamer

soñar [so'ɲar] *vt*, *vi* to dream; **~ con** to dream about *o* of; **soñé contigo anoche** I dreamed about you last night

soñoliento, -a [soɲo'ljento, a] *adj* sleepy, drowsy

sopa ['sopa] *nf* soup; **~ de fideos** noodle soup

sopero, -a [so'pero, a] *adj* (*plato, cuchara*) soup *cpd* ▷ *nm* soup plate ▷ *nf* soup tureen

sopesar [sope'sar] *vt* to try the weight of; (*fig*) to weigh up

soplar [so'plar] *vt* (*polvo*) to blow away, blow off; (*inflar*) to blow up; (*vela*) to blow out; (*ayudar a recordar*) to prompt; (*birlar*) to nick; (*delatar*) to split on ▷ *vi* to blow; (*delatar*) to squeal; (*beber*) to booze, bend the elbow

soplo ['soplo] *nm* blow, puff; (*de viento*) puff, gust

soplón, -ona [so'plon, ona] *nm/f* (*fam: chismoso*) telltale; (*: de policía*) informer, grass

sopor [so'por] *nm* drowsiness

soporífero, -a [sopo'rifero, a] *adj* sleep-inducing; (*fig*) soporific ▷ *nm* sleeping pill

soportable [sopor'taβle] *adj* bearable

soportal [sopor'tal] *nm* porch; **soportales** *nmpl* arcade *sg*

soportar [sopor'tar] *vt* to bear, carry; (*fig*) to bear, put up with

soporte [so'porte] *nm* support; (*fig*) pillar, support; (*Inform*) medium; **~ de entrada/salida** input/output medium

soprano [so'prano] *nf* soprano

sor [sor] *nf*: **S~ María** Sister Mary

sorber [sor'βer] *vt* (*chupar*) to sip; (*inhalar*) to sniff, inhale; (*absorber*) to soak up, absorb

sorbete [sor'βete] *nm* iced fruit drink

sorbo ['sorβo] *nm* (*trago*) gulp, swallow; (*chupada*) sip; **beber a ~s** to sip

sordera [sor'ðera] *nf* deafness

sórdido, -a ['sorðiðo, a] *adj* dirty, squalid

sordo, -a ['sorðo, a] *adj* (*persona*) deaf; (*ruido*) dull; (*Ling*) voiceless ▷ *nm/f* deaf person; **quedarse ~** to go deaf

sordomudo, -a [sorðo'muðo, a] *adj* deaf and dumb ▷ *nm/f* deaf-mute

sorna ['sorna] *nf* (*malicia*) slyness; (*tono burlón*) sarcastic tone

soroche [so'rotʃe] *nm* (*Am Med*) mountain sickness

sorprendente [sorpren'dente] *adj* surprising

sorprender [sorpren'der] *vt* to surprise; (*asombrar*) to amaze; (*sobresaltar*) to startle; (*coger desprevenido*) to catch unawares; **sorprenderse** *vr*: **~se (de)** to be surprised *o* amazed (at)

sorpresa [sor'presa] *nf* surprise

sortear [sorte'ar] *vt* to draw lots for; (*rifar*) to raffle; (*dificultad*) to dodge, avoid

sorteo [sor'teo] *nm* (*en lotería*) draw; (*rifa*) raffle

sortija [sor'tixa] *nf* ring; (*rizo*) ringlet, curl

sosegado, -a [sose'ɣaðo, a] *adj* quiet, calm

sosegar [sose'ɣar] *vt* to quieten, calm; (*el ánimo*) to reassure ▷ *vi* to rest

sosiego *etc* [so'sjeɣo] *vb ver* **sosegar** ▷ *nm* quiet(ness), calm(ness)

soslayar [sosla'jar] *vt* (*preguntas*) to get round

soslayo [sos'lajo]: **de ~** *adv* obliquely, sideways; **mirar de ~** to look out of the corner of one's eye (at)

soso, -a ['soso, a] *adj* (*Culin*) tasteless; (*fig*) dull, uninteresting

sospecha [sos'petʃa] *nf* suspicion

sospechar [sospe'tʃar] *vt* to suspect ▷ *vi*: **~ de** to be suspicious of

sospechoso, -a [sospe'tʃoso, a] *adj* suspicious; (*testimonio, opinión*) suspect ▷ *nm/f* suspect

sostén [sos'ten] *nm* (*apoyo*) support; (*sujetador*) bra; (*alimentación*) sustenance, food

sostener [soste'ner] *vt* to support; (*mantener*) to keep up, maintain; (*alimentar*) to sustain, keep going; **sostenerse** *vr* to support o.s.; (*seguir*) to continue, remain

sostenido, -a [soste'niðo, a] *adj* continuous, sustained; (*prolongado*) prolonged; (*Mus*) sharp ▷ *nm* (*Mus*) sharp

sota ['sota] *nf* (*Naipes*) ≈ jack

sotana [so'tana] *nf* (*Rel*) cassock

sótano ['sotano] *nm* basement

soviético, -a [so'βjetiko, a] *adj, nm/f* Soviet; **los ~s** the Soviets, the Russians

soy [soi] *vb ver* **ser**

soya ['soja] *nf* (*Am*) soya (bean)

spot [es'pot] (*pl* **spot**) *nm* (*publicitario*) ad

spyware [es'paiwer] *nm* spyware

squash [es'kwas] *nm* (*Deporte*) squash

Sr. *abr* (= *Señor*) Mr

Sra. *abr* (= *Señora*) Mrs

Sras. *abr* (= *Señoras*) Mrs

S.R.C. *abr* (= *se ruega contestación*) R.S.V.P.

Sres., Srs. *abr* (= *Señores*) Messrs

Srta. *abr* = **Señorita**

Sta. *abr* (= *Santa*) St; (= *Señorita*) Miss

stand (*pl* **stands**) [es'tan, es'tan(s)] *nm* (*Com*) stand

status ['status, es'tatus] *nm inv* status

Sto. *abr* (= *Santo*) St

stop (*pl* **stops**) [es'top, es'top(s)] *nm* (*Auto*) stop sign

su [su] *pron* (*de él*) his; (*de ella*) her; (*de una cosa*) its; (*de ellos, ellas*) their; (*de usted, ustedes*) your

suave ['swaβe] *adj* gentle; (*superficie*) smooth; (*trabajo*) easy; (*música, voz*) soft, sweet; (*clima, sabor*) mild

suavidad [swaβi'ðað] *nf* gentleness; (*de superficie*) smoothness; (*de música*) softness, sweetness

suavizante [swaβi'θante] *nm* (*de ropa*) softener; (*del pelo*) conditioner

suavizar [swaβi'θar] *vt* to soften; (*quitar la aspereza*) to smooth (out); (*pendiente*) to ease; (*colores*) to tone down; (*carácter*) to mellow; (*dureza*) to temper

subalimentado, -a [suβalimen'taðo, a] *adj* undernourished

subasta [su'βasta] *nf* auction; **poner en** o **sacar a pública ~** to put up for public auction; **~ a la rebaja** Dutch auction

subastar [suβas'tar] *vt* to auction (off)

subcampeón, -ona [suβkampe'on, ona] *nm/f* runner-up

subconsciente [suβkons'θjente] *adj* subconscious

subdesarrollado, -a [suβðesarro'ʎaðo, a] *adj* underdeveloped

subdesarrollo [suβðesa'rroʎo] *nm* underdevelopment

subdirector, a [suβðirek'tor, a] *nm/f* assistant o deputy manager

súbdito, -a ['suβðito, a] *nm/f* subject

subdividir [suβðiβi'ðir] *vt* to subdivide

subestimar [suβesti'mar] *vt* to underestimate, underrate

subido, -a [su'βiðo, a] *adj* (*color*) bright, strong; (*precio*) high ▷ *nf* (*de montaña etc*) ascent, climb; (*de precio*) rise, increase; (*pendiente*) slope, hill

subir [su'βir] *vt* (*objeto*) to raise, lift up; (*cuesta, calle*) to go up; (*colina, montaña*) to climb; (*precio*) to raise, put up; (*empleado etc*) to promote ▷ *vi* to go/come up; (*a un coche*) to get in; (*a un autobús, tren*) to get on; (*precio*) to rise, go up; (*en el empleo*) to be promoted; (*río, marea*) to rise; **subirse** *vr* to get up, climb; **~se a un coche** to get in(to) a car

súbito, -a ['suβito, a] *adj* (*repentino*) sudden; (*imprevisto*) unexpected

subjetivo, -a [suβxe'tiβo, a] *adj* subjective

subjuntivo [suβxun'tiβo] *nm* subjunctive (mood)

sublevación [suβleβa'θjon] *nf* revolt, rising

sublevar [suβle'βar] *vt* to rouse to revolt; **sublevarse** *vr* to revolt, rise

sublime [su'βlime] *adj* sublime

subliminal [suβlimi'nal] *adj* subliminal

submarinismo [suβmari'nismo] *nm* scuba diving

submarinista [suβmari'nista] *nm/f* underwater explorer

submarino, -a [suβma'rino, a] *adj* underwater ▷ *nm* submarine

subnormal [suβnor'mal] *adj* subnormal ▷ *nm/f* subnormal person

subordinado, -a [suβorði'naðo, a] *adj, nm/f* subordinate

subrayar [suβra'jar] *vt* to underline; (*recalcar*) to underline, emphasize

subrepticio, -a [suβrep'tiθjo, a] *adj* surreptitious

subsanar [suβsa'nar] *vt* (*reparar*) to rectify; (*perdonar*) to excuse; (*sobreponerse a*) to overcome

subscribir [suβskri'βir] *vt* = **suscribir**

subsidiariedad [suβsiðjarie'ðað] *nf* (*Pol*) subsidiarity

subsidiario, -a [suβsi'ðjarjo, a] *adj* subsidiary

subsidio [suβ'siðjo] *nm* (*ayuda*) aid, financial help; (*subvención*) subsidy, grant; (*de enfermedad, paro etc*) benefit, allowance

subsistencia [suβsis'tenθja] *nf* subsistence

subsistir [suβsis'tir] *vi* to subsist; (*vivir*) to

live; (*sobrevivir*) to survive, endure

subte ['suβte] *nm* (*RPl*) underground (*Brit*), subway (*US*)

subterráneo, -a [suβte'rraneo, a] *adj* underground, subterranean ▷ *nm* underpass, underground passage; (*Am*) underground railway, subway (*US*)

subtitulado, -a [suβtitu'laðo, a] *adj* subtitled

subtítulo [suβ'titulo] *nm* subtitle, subheading

suburbano, -a [suβur'βano, a] *adj* suburban

suburbio [su'βurβjo] *nm* (*barrio*) slum quarter; (*afueras*) suburbs *pl*

subvención [suββen'θjon] *nf* subsidy, subvention, grant; **~ estatal** state subsidy *o* support; **~ para la inversión** (*Com*) investment grant

subvencionar [suββenθjo'nar] *vt* to subsidize

subversión [suββer'sjon] *nf* subversion

subversivo, -a [suββer'siβo, a] *adj* subversive

subyugar [suβju'ɣar] *vt* (*país*) to subjugate, subdue; (*enemigo*) to overpower; (*voluntad*) to dominate

succión [suk'θjon] *nf* suction

sucedáneo, -a [suθe'ðaneo, a] *adj* substitute ▷ *nm* substitute (food)

suceder [suθe'ðer] *vi* to happen; **~ a** (*seguir*) to succeed, follow; **lo que sucede es que ...** the fact is that ...; **~ al trono** to succeed to the throne

sucesión [suθe'sjon] *nf* succession; (*serie*) sequence, series; (*hijos*) issue, offspring

sucesivamente [suθesiβa'mente] *adv*: **y así ~** and so on

sucesivo, -a [suθe'siβo, a] *adj* successive, following; **en lo ~** in future, from now on

suceso [su'θeso] *nm* (*hecho*) event, happening; (*incidente*) incident

suciedad [suθje'ðað] *nf* (*estado*) dirtiness; (*mugre*) dirt, filth

sucinto, -a [su'θinto, a] *adj* (*conciso*) succinct, concise

sucio, -a ['suθjo, a] *adj* dirty; (*mugriento*) grimy; (*manchado*) grubby; (*borroso*) smudged; (*conciencia*) bad; (*conducta*) vile; (*táctica*) dirty, unfair

Sucre ['sukre] *n* Sucre

suculento, -a [suku'lento, a] *adj* (*sabroso*) tasty; (*jugoso*) succulent

sucumbir [sukum'bir] *vi* to succumb

sucursal [sukur'sal] *nf* branch (office); (*filial*) subsidiary

sudadera [suða'ðera] *nf* sweatshirt

Sudáfrica [su'ðafrika] *nf* South Africa

Sudamérica [suða'merika] *nf* South America

sudamericano, -a [suðameri'kano, a] *adj*, *nm/f* South American

sudar [su'ðar] *vt*, *vi* to sweat; (*Bot*) to ooze

sudeste [su'ðeste] *adj* south-east(ern); (*rumbo, viento*) south-easterly ▷ *nm* south-east; (*viento*) south-east wind

sudoeste [suðo'este] *adj* south-west(ern); (*rumbo, viento*) south-westerly ▷ *nm* south-west; (*viento*) south-west wind

sudoku [su'doku] *nm* sudoku

sudor [su'ðor] *nm* sweat

sudoroso, -a [suðo'roso, a] *adj* sweaty, sweating

Suecia ['sweθja] *nf* Sweden

sueco, -a ['sweko, a] *adj* Swedish ▷ *nm/f* Swede ▷ *nm* (*Ling*) Swedish; **hacerse el ~** to pretend not to hear *o* understand

suegro, -a ['sweɣro, a] *nm/f* father-/mother-in-law; **los ~s** one's in-laws

suela ['swela] *nf* (*de zapato, tb pescado*) sole

sueldo ['sweldo] *vb ver* **soldar** ▷ *nm* pay, wage(s) (*pl*)

suelo ['swelo] *vb ver* **soler** ▷ *nm* (*tierra*) ground; (*de casa*) floor

suelto, -a *etc* ['swelto, a] *vb ver* **soltar** ▷ *adj* loose; (*libre*) free; (*separado*) detached; (*ágil*) quick, agile; (*fue corre*) fluent, flowing ▷ *nm* (*loose*) change, small change; **está muy ~ en inglés** he is very good at *o* fluent in English

sueñito [swe'ɲito] *nm* (*Am*) nap

sueño ['sweɲo] *vb ver* **soñar** ▷ *nm* sleep; (*somnolencia*) sleepiness, drowsiness; (*lo soñado, fig*) dream; **~ pesado** *o* **profundo** deep *o* heavy sleep; **tener ~** to be sleepy

suero ['swero] *nm* (*Med*) serum; (*de leche*) whey

suerte ['swerte] *nf* (*fortuna*) luck; (*azar*) chance; (*destino*) fate, destiny; (*condición*) lot; (*género*) sort, kind; **lo echaron a ~s** they drew lots *o* tossed up for it; **tener ~** to be lucky; **de otra ~** otherwise, if not; **de ~ que** so that, in such a way that

suéter ['sweter] (*pl* **suéters**) *nm* sweater

suficiente [sufi'θjente] *adj* enough, sufficient ▷ *nm* (*Escol*) pass

sufragar [sufra'ɣar] *vt* (*ayudar*) to help; (*gastos*) to meet; (*proyecto*) to pay for

sufragio [su'fraxjo] *nm* (*voto*) vote; (*derecho de voto*) suffrage

sufrido, -a [su'friðo, a] *adj* (*de carácter fuerte*) tough; (*paciente*) long-suffering, patient; (*tela*) hard-wearing; (*color*) that does not show the dirt; (*marido*) complaisant

sufrimiento [sufri'mjento] *nm* suffering

sufrir [su'frir] *vt* (*padecer*) to suffer; (*soportar*) to bear, stand, put up with; (*apoyar*) to hold up, support ▷ *vi* to suffer

sugerencia [suxe'renθja] *nf* suggestion

sugerir [suxe'rir] *vt* to suggest; (*sutilmente*) to hint; (*idea: incitar*) to prompt

sugestión [suxes'tjon] *nf* suggestion; (*sutil*) hint; (*poder*) hypnotic power

sugestionar [suxestjo'nar] *vt* to influence

S

sugestivo, -a [suxes'tiβo, a] adj stimulating; (atractivo) attractive; (fascinante) fascinating

suicida [sui'θiða] adj suicidal ▷ nm/f suicidal person; (muerto) suicide, person who has committed suicide

suicidarse [suiθi'ðarse] vr to commit suicide, kill o.s.

suicidio [sui'θiðjo] nm suicide

Suiza ['swiθa] nf Switzerland

suizo, -a ['swiθo, a] adj, nm/f Swiss ▷ nm sugared bun

sujeción [suxe'θjon] nf subjection

sujetador [suxeta'ðor] nm fastener, clip; (prenda femenina) bra, brassiere

sujetar [suxe'tar] vt (fijar) to fasten; (detener) to hold down; (fig) to subject, subjugate; (pelo etc) to keep o hold in place; (papeles) to fasten together; **sujetarse** vr to subject o.s.

sujeto, -a [su'xeto, a] adj fastened, secure ▷ nm subject; (individuo) individual; (fam: tipo) fellow, character, type, guy (US); **~ a** subject to

suma ['suma] nf (cantidad) total, sum; (de dinero) sum; (acto) adding (up), addition; **en ~** in short; **~ y sigue** (Com) carry forward

sumamente [suma'mente] adv extremely, exceedingly

sumar [su'mar] vt to add (up); (reunir) to collect, gather ▷ vi to add up

sumario, -a [su'marjo, a] adj brief, concise ▷ nm summary

sumergir [sumer'xir] vt to submerge; (hundir) to sink; (bañar) to immerse, dip; **sumergirse** vr (hundirse) to sink beneath the surface

sumidero [sumi'ðero] nm drain, sewer; (Tec) sump

suministrar [suminis'trar] vt to supply, provide

suministro [sumi'nistro] nm supply; (acto) supplying, providing

sumir [su'mir] vt to sink, submerge; (fig) to plunge; **sumirse** vr (objeto) to sink; **~se en el estudio** to become absorbed in one's studies

sumisión [sumi'sjon] nf (acto) submission; (calidad) submissiveness, docility

sumiso, -a [su'miso, a] adj submissive, docile

sumo, -a ['sumo, a] adj great, extreme; (mayor) highest, supreme ▷ nm sumo (wrestling); **a lo ~** at most

suntuoso, -a [sun'twoso, a] adj sumptuous, magnificent; (lujoso) lavish

supe etc ['supe] vb ver **saber**

supeditar [supeði'tar] vt to subordinate; (sojuzgar) to subdue; (oprimir) to oppress; **supeditarse** vr: **~se a** to subject o.s. to

super... [super] pref super..., over...

súper ['super] adj (fam) super, great ▷ nf (gasolina) four-star (petrol)

superación [supera'θjon] nf (tb: **~ personal**) self-improvement

superar [supe'rar] vt (sobreponerse a) to overcome; (rebasar) to surpass, do better than; (pasar) to go beyond; (marca, récord) to break; (etapa: dejar atrás) to get past; **superarse** vr to excel o.s.

superávit [supe'raβit] (pl **superávits**) nm surplus

superbueno, a [super'bweno, a] adj great, fantastic

superficial [superfi'θjal] adj superficial; (medida) surface cpd

superficie [super'fiθje] nf surface; (área) area; **grandes ~s** (Com) superstores

superfluo, -a [su'perflwo, a] adj superfluous

superintendente [superinten'dente] nm/f supervisor, superintendent

superior [supe'rjor] adj (piso, clase) upper; (temperatura, número, nivel) higher; (mejor: calidad, producto) superior, better ▷ nm/f superior

superioridad [superjori'ðað] nf superiority

superlativo, -a [superla'tiβo, a] adj, nm superlative

supermercado [supermer'kaðo] nm supermarket

superponer [superpo'ner] vt to superimpose; (Inform) to overstrike

supersónico, -a [super'soniko, a] adj supersonic

superstición [supersti'θjon] nf superstition

supersticioso, -a [supersti'θjoso, a] adj superstitious

supervisar [superβi'sar] vt to supervise; (Com) to superintend

supervisor, a [superβi'sor, a] nm/f supervisor

supervivencia [superβi'βenθja] nf survival

superviviente [superβi'βjente] adj surviving ▷ nm/f survivor

supiera etc vb ver **saber**

suplantar [suplan'tar] vt (persona) to supplant; (hacerse pasar por otro) to take the place of

suplementario, -a [suplemen'tarjo, a] adj supplementary

suplemento [suple'mento] nm supplement

suplente [su'plente] adj substitute; (disponible) reserve ▷ nm/f substitute

supletorio, -a [suple'torjo, a] adj supplementary; (adicional) extra ▷ nm supplement; **mesa supletoria** spare table; **teléfono ~** extension

súplica ['suplika] nf request; (Rel) supplication; (Jur: instancia) petition; **súplicas** nfpl entreaties

suplicar [supli'kar] vt (cosa) to beg (for), plead for; (persona) to beg, plead with; (Jur) to appeal to, petition

suplicio [su'pliθjo] nm torture; (tormento) torment; (emoción) anguish; (experiencia penosa) ordeal

suplir [su'plir] vt (compensar) to make good, make up for; (reemplazar) to replace, substitute ▷ vi: ~ **a** to take the place of, substitute for

supo etc ['supo] vb ver **saber**

suponer [supo'ner] vt to suppose; (significar) to mean; (acarrear) to involve ▷ vi to count, have authority; **era de ~ que ...** it was to be expected that ...

suposición [suposi'θjon] nf supposition

supositorio [suposi'torjo] nm suppository

supremacía [suprema'θia] nf supremacy

supremo, -a [su'premo, a] adj supreme

supresión [supre'sjon] nf suppression; (de derecho) abolition; (de dificultad) removal; (de palabra etc) deletion; (de restricción) cancellation, lifting

suprimir [supri'mir] vt to suppress; (derecho, costumbre) to abolish; (dificultad) to remove; (palabra etc, Inform) to delete; (restricción) to cancel, lift

supuesto, -a [su'pwesto, a] pp de **suponer** ▷ adj (hipotético) supposed; (falso) false ▷ nm assumption, hypothesis ▷ conj: ~ **que** since; **dar por ~ algo** to take sth for granted; **por ~** of course

supurar [supu'rar] vi to fester, suppurate

sur [sur] adj southern; (rumbo) southerly ▷ nm south; (viento) south wind

suramericano, -a [surameri'kano, a] adj South American ▷ nm/f South American

surcar [sur'kar] vt to plough; (superficie) to cut, score

surco ['surko] nm (en metal, disco) groove; (Agr) furrow

sureste [su'reste] = **sudeste**

surf [surf] nm surfing

surfear [surfe'ar] vt: ~ **el Internet** to surf the internet

surgir [sur'xir] vi to arise, emerge; (dificultad) to come up, crop up

suroeste [suro'este] nm south-west

surtido, -a [sur'tiðo, a] adj mixed, assorted ▷ nm (selección) selection, assortment; (abastecimiento) supply, stock

surtidor [surti'ðor] nm (chorro) jet, spout; (fuente) fountain; ~ **de gasolina** petrol (Brit) o gas (US) pump

surtir [sur'tir] vt to supply, provide; (efecto) to have, produce ▷ vi to spout, spurt; **surtirse** vr: ~**se de** to provide o.s. with

susceptible [susθep'tiβle] adj susceptible; (sensible) sensitive; ~ **de** capable of

suscitar [susθi'tar] vt to cause, provoke; (discusión) to start; (duda, problema) to raise; (interés, sospechas) to arouse

suscribir [suskri'βir] vt (firmar) to sign; (respaldar) to subscribe to, endorse; (Com: acciones) to take out an option on; **suscribirse** vr to subscribe; ~ **a algn a una revista** to take out a subscription to a journal for sb

suscripción [suskrip'θjon] nf subscription

susodicho, -a [suso'ditʃo, a] adj above-mentioned

suspender [suspen'der] vt (objeto) to hang (up), suspend; (trabajo) to stop, suspend; (Escol) to fail; (interrumpir) to adjourn; (atrasar) to postpone

suspense [sus'pense] nm suspense; **película/novela de ~** thriller

suspensión [suspen'sjon] nf suspension; (fig) stoppage, suspension; (Jur) stay; ~ **de fuego** o **de hostilidades** ceasefire, cessation of hostilities; ~ **de pagos** suspension of payments

suspenso, -a [sus'penso, a] adj hanging, suspended; (Escol) failed ▷ nm (Escol) fail(ure); **quedar** o **estar en ~** to be pending; **película** o **novela de ~** (Am) thriller

suspicacia [suspi'kaθja] nf suspicion, mistrust

suspicaz [suspi'kaθ] adj suspicious, distrustful

suspirar [suspi'rar] vi to sigh

suspiro [sus'piro] nm sigh

sustancia [sus'tanθja] nf substance; ~ **gris** (Anat) grey matter; **sin ~** lacking in substance, shallow

sustancial [sustan'θjal] adj substantial

sustancioso, -a [sustan'θjoso, a] adj substantial; (discurso) solid

sustantivo, -a [sustan'tiβo, a] adj substantive; (Ling) substantival, noun cpd ▷ nm noun, substantive

sustentar [susten'tar] vt (alimentar) to sustain, nourish; (objeto) to hold up, support; (idea, teoría) to maintain, uphold; (fig) to sustain, keep going

sustento [sus'tento] nm support; (alimento) sustenance, food

sustituir [sustitu'ir] vt to substitute, replace

sustituto, -a [susti'tuto, a] nm/f substitute, replacement

susto ['susto] nm fright, scare; **dar un ~ a algn** to give sb a fright; **darse** o **pegarse un ~** (fam) to get a fright

sustraer [sustra'er] vt to remove, take away; (Mat) to subtract

sustrato [sus'trato] nm substratum

susurrar [susu'rrar] vi to whisper

susurro [su'surro] nm whisper

sutil [su'til] adj (aroma) subtle; (tenue) thin; (hilo, hebra) fine; (olor) delicate; (brisa) gentle; (diferencia) fine, subtle; (inteligencia) sharp, keen

sutileza [suti'leθa] nf subtlety; (delgadez) thinness; (delicadeza) delicacy; (agudeza) keenness

suturar [sutu'rar] vt to suture; (juntar con puntos) to stitch

suyo, -a ['sujo, a] adj (con artículo o después del verbo **ser**: de él) his; (: de ella) hers; (: de ellos, ellas) theirs; (: de usted, ustedes) yours; (después de un nombre: de él) of his; (: de ella) of hers;

(: *de ellos, ellas*) of theirs; (: *de usted, ustedes*) of yours; **lo ~** (*what is*) his; (*su parte*) his share, what he deserves; **los ~s** (*su familia*) one's family *o* relations; (*sus partidarios*) one's own people *o* supporters; **~ afectísimo** (*en carta*) yours faithfully *o* sincerely; **de ~** in itself; **eso es muy ~** that's just like him; **hacer de las suyas** to get up to one's old tricks; **ir a la suya, ir a lo ~** to go one's own way; **salirse con la suya** to get one's way; **un amigo ~** a friend of his (*o* hers *o* theirs *o* yours)

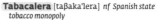

Tabacalera [taβakaˈlera] *nf Spanish state tobacco monopoly*

tabaco [taˈβako] *nm* tobacco; (*fam*) cigarettes *pl*

tábano [ˈtaβano] *nm* horsefly

tabaquería [tabakeˈria] *nf* tobacconist's (*Brit*), cigar store (*US*)

taberna [taˈβerna] *nf* bar

tabernero, -a [taβerˈnero, a] *nm/f* (*encargado*) publican; (*camarero*) barman/barmaid

tabique [taˈβike] *nm* (*pared*) thin wall; (*para dividir*) partition

tabla [ˈtaβla] *nf* (*de madera*) plank; (*estante*) shelf; (*de anuncios*) board; (*lista, catálogo*) list; (*de vestido*) pleat; (*Arte*) panel; **tablas** *nfpl* (*Taur, Teat*) boards; **estar** *o* **quedar en ~s** to draw; **~ de consulta** (*Inform*) lookup table

tablado [taˈβlaðo] *nm* (*plataforma*) platform; (*suelo*) plank floor; (*Teat*) stage

tablao [taˈβlao] *nm* (*tb:* **~ flamenco**) flamenco show

tablero [taˈβlero] *nm* (*de madera*) plank, board; (*pizarra*) blackboard; (*de ajedrez, damas*) board; (*Auto*) dashboard; **~ de gráficos** (*Inform*) graph pad; **~ de mandos** (*Am: Auto*) dashboard

tableta [taˈβleta] *nf* (*Med*) tablet; (*de chocolate*) bar

tablón [taˈβlon] *nm* (*de suelo*) plank; (*de techo*) beam; (*de anuncios*) notice board

tabú [taˈβu] *nm* taboo

tabular [taβuˈlar] *vt* to tabulate; (*Inform*) to tab

taburete [taβu'rete] *nm* stool

tacaño, -a [ta'kaɲo, a] *adj* (*avaro*) mean; (*astuto*) crafty

tacha ['tatʃa] *nf* (*defecto*) flaw, defect; (*Tec*) stud; **poner ~ a** to find fault with; **sin ~** flawless

tachar [ta'tʃar] *vt* (*borrar*) to cross out; (*corregir*) to correct; (*criticar*) to criticize; **~ de** to accuse of

tacho ['tatʃo] *nm* (*Am*) bucket, pail; **~ de la basura** rubbish bin (*Brit*), trash can (*US*)

tácito, -a ['taθito, a] *adj* (*acuerdo*) unspoken; (*Ling*) understood; (*ley*) unwritten

taciturno, -a [taθi'turno, a] *adj* (*callado*) silent; (*malhumorado*) sullen

taco ['tako] *nm* (*Billar*) cue; (*libro de billetes*) book; (*manojo de billetes*) wad; (*Am*) heel; (*tarugo*) peg; (*fam: bocado*) snack; (: *palabrota*) swear word; (: *trago de vino*) swig; (*México*) filled tortilla; **armarse** *o* **hacerse un ~** to get into a mess

tacón [ta'kon] *nm* heel; **de ~ alto** high-heeled

taconear [takone'ar] *vi* (*dar golpecitos*) to tap with one's heels; (*Mil etc*) to click one's heels

taconeo [tako'neo] *nm* (heel) tapping *o* clicking

táctico, -a ['taktiko, a] *adj* tactical ▷ *nf* tactics *pl*

tacto ['takto] *nm* touch; (*acción*) touching; (*fig*) tact

tafetán [tafe'tan] *nm* taffeta; **tafetanes** *nmpl* (*fam*) frills; **~ adhesivo** *o* **inglés** sticking plaster

tafilete [tafi'lete] *nm* morocco leather

tahona [ta'ona] *nf* (*panadería*) bakery; (*molino*) flour mill

taimado, -a [tai'maðo, a] *adj* (*astuto*) sly; (*resentido*) sullen

taita ['taita] *nm* dad, daddy

tajada [ta'xaða] *nf* slice; (*fam*) rake-off; **sacar ~** to get one's share

tajante [ta'xante] *adj* sharp; (*negativa*) emphatic; **es una persona ~** he's an emphatic person

tajar [ta'xar] *vt* to cut, slice

tajo ['taxo] *nm* (*corte*) cut; (*filo*) cutting edge; (*Geo*) cleft

tal [tal] *adj* such; **un ~ García** a man called García; **~ vez** perhaps ▷ *pron* (*persona*) someone, such a one; (*cosa*) something, such a thing; **~ como** such as; **~ para cual** tit for tat; (*dos iguales*) two of a kind; **hablábamos de que sí ~ si cual** we were talking about this, that and the other ▷ *adv*: **~ como** (*igual*) just as; **~ cual** (*como es*) just as it is; **~ el padre, cual el hijo** like father, like son; **¿qué ~?** how are things?; **¿qué ~ te gusta?** how do you like it? ▷ *conj*: **con ~ (de) que** provided that

taladradora [talaðra'ðora] *nf* drill; **~ neumática** pneumatic drill

taladrar [tala'ðrar] *vt* to drill; (*fig: ruido*) to pierce

taladro [ta'laðro] *nm* (*gen*) drill; (*hoyo*) drill hole; **~ neumático** pneumatic drill

talante [ta'lante] *nm* (*humor*) mood; (*voluntad*) will, willingness

talar [ta'lar] *vt* to fell, cut down; (*fig*) to devastate

talco ['talko] *nm* (*polvos*) talcum powder; (*Mineralogía*) talc

talega [ta'leɣa] *nf* sack

talego [ta'leɣo] *nm* sack; **tener ~** (*fam*) to have money

talento [ta'lento] *nm* talent; (*capacidad*) ability; (*don*) gift

Talgo ['talɣo] *nm abr* (*Ferro*: = *tren articulado ligero Goicoechea Oriol*) high-speed train

talismán [talis'man] *nm* talisman

talla ['taʎa] *nf* (*estatura, fig, Med*) height, stature; (*de ropa*) size, fitting; (*palo*) measuring rod; (*Arte: de madera*) carving; (*de piedra*) sculpture

tallado, -a [ta'ʎaðo, a] *adj* carved ▷ *nm* (*de madera*) carving; (*de piedra*) sculpture

tallar [ta'ʎar] *vt* (*trabajar*) to work, carve; (*grabar*) to engrave; (*medir*) to measure; (*repartir*) to deal ▷ *vi* to deal

tallarín [taʎa'rin] *nm* noodle

talle ['taʎe] *nm* (*Anat*) waist; (*medida*) size; (*física*) build; (: *de mujer*) figure; (*fig*) appearance; **de ~ esbelto** with a slim figure

taller [ta'ʎer] *nm* (*Tec*) workshop; (*fábrica*) factory; (*Auto*) garage; (*de artista*) studio

tallo ['taʎo] *nm* (*de planta*) stem; (*de hierba*) blade; (*brote*) shoot; (*col*) cabbage; (*Culin*) candied peel

talón [ta'lon] *nm* (*gen*) heel; (*Com*) counterfoil; (*cheque*) cheque (*Brit*), check (*US*); (*Tec*) rim; **~ de Aquiles** Achilles heel

talonario [talo'narjo] *nm* (*de cheques*) chequebook (*Brit*), checkbook (*US*); (*de billetes*) book of tickets; (*de recibos*) receipt book

tamaño, -a [ta'maɲo, a] *adj* (*tan grande*) such a big; (*tan pequeño*) such a small ▷ *nm* size; **de ~ natural** full-size; **¿de qué ~ es?** what size is it?

tamarindo [tama'rindo] *nm* tamarind

tambalearse [tambale'arse] *vr* (*persona*) to stagger; (*mueble*) to wobble; (*vehículo*) to sway

también [tam'bjen] *adv* (*igualmente*) also, too, as well; (*además*) besides; **estoy cansado — yo ~** I'm tired — so am I *o* me too

tambor [tam'bor] *nm* drum; (*Anat*) eardrum; **~ del freno** brake drum; **~ magnético** (*Inform*) magnetic drum

Támesis ['tamesis] *nm* Thames

tamiz [ta'miθ] *nm* sieve

tamizar [tami'θar] *vt* to sieve

tampoco [tam'poko] *adv* nor, neither; **yo ~ lo compré** I didn't buy it either

tampón [tam'pon] *nm* plug; (*Med*) tampon

t

tan [tan] *adv* so; **~ es así que** so much so that; **¡qué cosa ~ rara!** how strange!; **no es una idea ~ buena** it is not such a good idea

tanatorio [tana'torjo] *nm* (*privado*) funeral home *o* parlour; (*público*) mortuary

tanda ['tanda] *nf* (*gen*) series; (*de inyecciones*) course; (*juego*) set; (*turno*) shift; (*grupo*) gang

tanga ['tanga] *nm* (*bikini*) tanga; (*ropa interior*) tanga briefs

tangente [tan'xente] *nf* tangent; **salirse por la ~** to go off at a tangent

Tánger ['tanxer] *n* Tangier

tangerina [tanxe'rina] *nf* (*Am*) tangerine

tangible [tan'xiβle] *adj* tangible

tango ['tango] *nm* tango

tanque ['tanke] *nm* (*gen*) tank; (*Auto, Naut*) tanker

tanqueta [tan'keta] *nf* (*Mil*) small tank, armoured vehicle

tantear [tante'ar] *vt* (*calcular*) to reckon (up); (*medir*) to take the measure of; (*probar*) to test, try out; (*tomar la medida: persona*) to take the measurements of; (*considerar*) to weigh up; (*persona: opinión*) to sound out ▷ *vi* (*Deporte*) to score

tanteo [tan'teo] *nm* (*cálculo aproximado*) (rough) calculation; (*prueba*) test, trial; (*Deporte*) scoring; (*adivinanzas*) guesswork; **al ~** by trial and error

O PALABRA CLAVE

tanto, -a ['tanto, a] *adj* (*cantidad*) so much, as much; **tantos** so many, as many; **20 y tantos** 20-odd

▷ *adv* (*cantidad*) so much, as much; (*tiempo*) so long, as long; **tanto tú como yo** both you and I; **tanto como eso** as much as that; **tanto más ... cuanto que** it's all the more ... because; **tanto mejor/peor** so much the better/the worse; **tanto si viene como si va** whether he comes or whether he goes; **tanto es así que** so much so that; **por tanto, por lo tanto** therefore; **me he vuelto ronco de *o* con tanto hablar** I have become hoarse with so much talking

▷ *conj*: **con tanto que** provided (that); **en tanto que** while; **hasta tanto (que)** until such time as

▷ *nm* **1** (*suma*) certain amount; (*proporción*) so much; **un tanto perezoso** somewhat lazy
2 (*punto*) point; (*gol*) goal
3 (*locuciones*): **tanto alzado** agreed price; **tanto por ciento** percentage; **al tanto** up to date; **estar al tanto de los acontecimientos** to be fully abreast of events; **al tanto de que** because of the fact that

▷ *pron*: **cada uno paga tanto** each one pays so much; **uno de tantos** one of many; **a tantos de agosto** on such and such a day in August; **entre tanto** meanwhile

tapa ['tapa] *nf* (*de caja, olla*) lid; (*de botella*) top; (*de libro*) cover; (*de comida*) snack

tapadera [tapa'ðera] *nf* lid, cover

tapar [ta'par] *vt* (*cubrir*) to cover; (*envolver*) to wrap *o* cover up; (*la vista*) to obstruct; (*persona, falta*) to conceal; (*Am*) to fill; **taparse** *vr* to wrap o.s. up

taparrabo [tapa'rraβo] *nm* loincloth

tapete [ta'pete] *nm* table cover; **estar sobre el ~** (*fig*) to be under discussion

tapia ['tapja] *nf* (*garden*) wall

tapiar [ta'pjar] *vt* to wall in

tapicería [tapiθe'ria] *nf* tapestry; (*para muebles*) upholstery; (*tienda*) upholsterer's (shop)

tapiz [ta'piθ] *nm* (*alfombra*) carpet; (*tela tejida*) tapestry

tapizar [tapi'θar] *vt* (*pared*) to wallpaper; (*suelo*) to carpet; (*muebles*) to upholster

tapón [ta'pon] *nm* (*de botella*) top; (*corcho*) stopper; (*Tec*) plug; (*Med*) tampon; **~ de rosca *o* de tuerca** screw-top

taquigrafía [takiɣra'fia] *nf* shorthand

taquígrafo, -a [ta'kiɣrafo, a] *nm/f* shorthand writer, stenographer (US)

taquilla [ta'kiʎa] *nf* (*de estación etc*) booking office; (*de teatro*) box office; (*suma recogida*) takings *pl*; (*archivador*) filing cabinet

taquillero, -a [taki'ʎero, a] *adj*: **función taquillera** box office success ▷ *nm/f* ticket clerk

taquimecanografía [takimekanoɣra'fia] *nf* shorthand and typing

tara ['tara] *nf* (*defecto*) defect; (*Com*) tare

tarántula [ta'rantula] *nf* tarantula

tararear [tarare'ar] *vi* to hum

tardanza [tar'ðanθa] *nf* (*demora*) delay; (*lentitud*) slowness

tardar [tar'ðar] *vi* (*tomar tiempo*) to take a long time; (*llegar tarde*) to be late; (*demorar*) to delay; **¿tarda mucho el tren?** does the train take long?; **a más ~** at the (very) latest; **~ en hacer algo** to be slow *o* take a long time to do sth; **no tardes en venir** come soon, come before long

tarde ['tarðe] *adv* (*hora*) late; (*fuera de tiempo*) too late ▷ *nf* (*de día*) afternoon; (*de noche*) evening; **~ *o* temprano** sooner or later; **de ~ en ~** from time to time; **¡buenas ~s!** (*de día*) good afternoon!; (*de noche*) good evening!; **a *o* por la ~** in the afternoon; in the evening

tardío, -a [tar'ðio, a] *adj* (*retrasado*) late; (*lento*) slow (to arrive)

tardo, -a ['tarðo, a] *adj* (*lento*) slow; (*torpe*) dull; **~ de oído** hard of hearing

tarea [ta'rea] *nf* task; **tareas** *nfpl* (*Escol*) homework *sg*; **~ de ocasión** chore

tarifa [ta'rifa] *nf* (*lista de precios*) price list; (*Com*) tariff; **~ básica** basic rate; **~ completa** all-in cost; **~ a destajo** piece rate; **~ doble** double time

tarima [ta'rima] *nf* (*plataforma*) platform

tarjeta [tar'xeta] *nf* card; ~ **postal/de Navidad** postcard/credit card/Christmas card; ~ **de circuitos** (*Inform*) circuit board; ~ **cliente** loyalty card; ~ **comercial** (*Com*) calling card; ~ **dinero** cash card; ~ **gráficos** (*Inform*) graphics card; ~ **monedero** electronic purse *o* wallet; ~ **de embarque** boarding pass; ~ **de memoria** memory card; ~ **prepago** top-up card; ~ **SIM** SIM card

tarot [ta'rot] *nm* tarot

tarro ['tarro] *nm* jar, pot

tarta ['tarta] *nf* (*pastel*) cake; (*torta*) tart

tartamudear [tartamuðe'ar] *vi* to stutter, stammer

tartamudo, -a [tarta'muðo, a] *adj* stuttering, stammering ▷ *nm/f* stutterer, stammerer

tártaro, -a ['tartaro, a] *adj*: **salsa tártara** tartar(e) sauce ▷ *nm* Tartar ▷ *nm* (*Química*) tartar

tasa ['tasa] *nf* (*precio*) (fixed) price, rate; (*valoración*) valuation; (*medida, norma*) measure, standard; ~ **básica** (*Com*) basic rate; ~ **de cambio** exchange rate; **de ~ cero** (*Com*) zero-rated; ~**s de aeropuerto** airport tax; ~ **de crecimiento** growth rate; ~ **de interés/ de nacimiento** rate of interest/birth rate; ~ **de rendimiento** (*Com*) rate of return; ~**s universitarias** university fees

tasación [tasa'θjon] *nf* assessment, valuation; (*fig*) appraisal

tasador, a [tasa'ðor, a] *nm/f* valuer; (*Com: de impuestos*) assessor

tasar [ta'sar] *vt* (*arreglar el precio*) to fix a price for; (*valorar*) to value, assess; (*limitar*) to limit

tasca ['taska] *nf* (*fam*) pub

tata ['tata] *nm* (*fam*) dad(dy) ▷ *nf* (*niñera*) nanny, maid

tatarabuelo, -a [tatara'βwelo, a] *nm/f* great-great-grandfather/mother; **los ~s** one's great-great-grandparents

tatuaje [ta'twaxe] *nm* (*dibujo*) tattoo; (*acto*) tattooing

tatuar [ta'twar] *vt* to tattoo

taurino, -a [tau'rino, a] *adj* bullfighting *cpd*

Tauro ['tauro] *nm* Taurus

tauromaquia [tauro'makja] *nf* (art of) bullfighting

taxi ['taksi] *nm* taxi

taxista [tak'sista] *nm/f* taxi driver

taza ['taθa] *nf* cup; (*de retrete*) bowl; ~ **para café** coffee cup; ~ **de café** cup of coffee

tazón [ta'θon] *nm* mug, large cup; (*escudilla*) basin

te [te] *pron* (*complemento de objeto*) you; (*complemento indirecto*) (to) you; (*reflexivo*) (to) yourself; **¿te duele mucho el brazo?** does your arm hurt a lot?; **te equivocas** you're wrong; **¡cálmate!** calm yourself!

té [te] (*pl* **tés**) *nm* tea; (*reunión*) tea party

tea ['tea] *nf* (*antorcha*) torch

teatral [tea'tral] *adj* theatre *cpd*; (*fig*) theatrical

teatro [te'atro] *nm* theatre; (*Lit*) plays *pl*, drama; **el ~** (*carrera*) the theatre, acting; ~ **de aficionados/de variedades** amateur/variety theatre, vaudeville theater (*US*); **hacer ~** (*fig*) to make a fuss

tebeo [te'βeo] *nm* children's comic

techo ['tetʃo] *nm* (*externo*) roof; (*interno*) ceiling

tecla ['tekla] *nf* (*Inform, Mus, Tip*) key; (*Inform*): ~ **de anulación/de borrar** cancel/delete key; ~ **de control/de edición** control/edit key; ~ **con flecha** arrow key; ~ **programable** user-defined key; ~ **de retorno/de tabulación** return/tab key; ~ **del cursor** cursor key; ~**s de control direccional del cursor** cursor control keys

teclado [te'klaðo] *nm* keyboard (*tb Inform*); ~ **numérico** (*Inform*) numeric keypad

teclear [tekle'ar] *vi* to strum; (*fam*) to drum ▷ *vt* (*Inform*) to key (in), type in, keyboard

tecleo [te'kleo] *nm* (*Mus: sonido*) strumming; (: *forma de tocar*) fingering; (*fam*) drumming

técnico, -a ['tekniko, a] *adj* technical ▷ *nm* technician; (*experto*) expert ▷ *nf* (*procedimientos*) technique; (*tecnología*) technology; (*arte, oficio*) craft

tecnicolor [tekniko'lor] *nm* Technicolor®

tecnócrata [tek'nokrata] *nm/f* technocrat

tecnología [teknolo'xia] *nf* technology; ~ **de estado sólido** (*Inform*) solid-state technology; ~ **de la información** information technology

tecnológico, -a [tekno'loxiko, a] *adj* technological

tecolote [teko'lote] *nm* (*Am*) owl

tedio ['teðjo] *nm* (*aburrimiento*) boredom; (*apatía*) apathy; (*fastidio*) depression

tedioso, -a [te'ðjoso, a] *adj* boring; (*cansado*) wearisome, tedious

teja ['texa] *nf* (*azulejo*) tile; (*Bot*) lime (tree)

tejado [te'xaðo] *nm* (tiled) roof

tejano, -a [te'xano, a] *adj, nm/f* Texan ▷ *nmpl*: ~**s** (*vaqueros*) jeans

tejemaneje [texema'nexe] *nm* (*actividad*) bustle; (*lío*) fuss, to-do; (*intriga*) intrigue

tejer [te'xer] *vt* to weave; (*tela de araña*) to spin; (*Am*) to knit; (*fig*) to fabricate ▷ *vi*: ~ **y des**~ to chop and change

tejido [te'xiðo] *nm* fabric; (*estofa, tela*) (knitted) material; (*telaraña*) web; (*Anat*) tissue; (*textura*) texture

tel. *abr* (= *teléfono*) tel.

tela ['tela] *nf* (*material*) material; (*de fruta, en líquido*) skin; (*del ojo*) film; **hay ~ para rato** there's lots to talk about; **poner en ~ de juicio** to (call in) question; ~ **de araña** cobweb, spider's web

telar [te'lar] *nm* (*máquina*) loom; (*de teatro*) gridiron; **telares** *nmpl* textile mill *sg*

telaraña [tela'raɲa] *nf* cobweb, spider's web

tele ['tele] *nf* (*fam*) TV

tele... [tele] *pref* tele...

telebasura [teleβa'sura] *nf* trash TV

telecomunicación [telekomunika'θjon] *nf* telecommunication

teleconferencia [telekonfe'renθja] *nf* (*reunión*) teleconference; (*sistema*) teleconferencing

telecontrol [telekon'trol] *nm* remote control

telediario [tele'ðjarjo] *nm* television news

teledifusión [teleðifu'sjon] *nf* (television) broadcast

teledirigido, -a [teleðiri'xiðo, a] *adj* remote-controlled

teléf. *abr* (= *teléfono*) tel.

teleférico [tele'feriko] *nm* (*tren*) cable-railway; (*de esquí*) ski-lift

telefonear [telefone'ar] *vi* to telephone

telefónico, -a [tele'foniko, a] *adj* telephone *cpd* ▷ *nf*: **Telefónica** (*Esp*) Spanish national telephone company, ≈ British Telecom

telefonillo [telefo'niʎo] *nm* (*de puerta*) intercom

telefonista [telefo'nista] *nm/f* telephonist

teléfono [te'lefono] *nm* (tele)phone; **~ móvil** mobile phone; **está hablando por ~** he's on the phone; **llamar a algn por ~** to ring sb (up) *o* phone sb (up); **~ celular** (*Am*) mobile phone; **~ con cámara** camera phone; **~ inalámbrico** cordless phone

telegrafía [teleɣra'fia] *nf* telegraphy

telégrafo [te'leɣrafo] *nm* telegraph; (*fam: persona*) telegraph boy

telegrama [tele'ɣrama] *nm* telegram

teleimpresor [teleimpre'sor] *nm* teleprinter

telenovela [teleno'βela] *nf* soap (opera)

teleobjetivo [teleobxe'tiβo] *nm* telephoto lens

telepatía [telepa'tia] *nf* telepathy

telepático, -a [tele'patiko, a] *adj* telepathic

telerrealidad [telerreali'ðað] *nf* reality TV

telescópico, -a [tele'skopiko, a] *adj* telescopic

telescopio [tele'skopjo] *nm* telescope

telesilla [tele'siʎa] *nm* chairlift

telespectador, a [telespekta'ðor, a] *nm/f* viewer

telesquí [teles'ki] *nm* ski-lift

teletarjeta [teletar'xeta] *nf* phonecard

teletex [tele'teks], **teletexto** [tele'teksto] *nm* teletext

teletipo [tele'tipo] *nm* teletype(writer)

teletrabajador, a [teletraβaxa'ðor, a] *nm/f* teleworker

teletrabajo [teletra'βaxo] *nm* teleworking

televentas [tele'βentas] *nfpl* telesales

televidente [teleβi'ðente] *nm/f* viewer

televisar [teleβi'sar] *vt* to televise

televisión [teleβi'sjon] *nf* television; **~ en color/por satélite** colour/satellite television; **~ digital** digital television

televisor [teleβi'sor] *nm* television set

télex ['teleks] *nm* telex; **máquina ~** telex (machine); **enviar por ~** to telex

telón [te'lon] *nm* curtain; **~ de boca/ seguridad** front/safety curtain; **~ de acero** (*Pol*) iron curtain; **~ de fondo** backcloth, background

telonero, -a [telo'nero, a] *nm/f* support act; **los ~s** (*Mus*) the support band

tema ['tema] *nm* (*asunto*) subject, topic; (*Mus*) theme; **~s de actualidad** current affairs ▷ *nf* (*obsesión*) obsession; (*manía*) ill-will; **tener ~ a algn** to have a grudge against sb

temario [te'marjo] *nm* (*Escol*) set of topics; (*de una conferencia*) agenda

temático, -a [te'matiko, a] *adj* thematic ▷ *nf* subject matter

temblar [tem'blar] *vi* to shake, tremble; (*de frío*) to shiver

tembleque [tem'bleke] *adj* shaking ▷ *nm* shaking

temblón, -ona [tem'blon, ona] *adj* shaking

temblor [tem'blor] *nm* trembling; (*de tierra*) earthquake

tembloroso, -a [temblo'roso, a] *adj* trembling

temer [te'mer] *vt* to fear ▷ *vi* to be afraid; **temo que Juan llegue tarde** I am afraid Juan may be late

temerario, -a [teme'rarjo, a] *adj* (*imprudente*) rash; (*descuidado*) reckless; (*arbitrario*) hasty

temeridad [temeri'ðað] *nf* (*imprudencia*) rashness; (*audacia*) boldness

temeroso, -a [teme'roso, a] *adj* (*miedoso*) fearful; (*que inspira temor*) frightful

temible [te'miβle] *adj* fearsome

temor [te'mor] *nm* (*miedo*) fear; (*duda*) suspicion

témpano ['tempano] *nm* (*Mus*) kettledrum; **~ de hielo** ice floe

temperamento [tempera'mento] *nm* temperament; **tener ~** to be temperamental

temperatura [tempera'tura] *nf* temperature

tempestad [tempes'tað] *nf* storm; **~ en un vaso de agua** (*fig*) storm in a teacup

tempestuoso, -a [tempes'twoso, a] *adj* stormy

templado, -a [tem'plaðo, a] *adj* (*moderado*) moderate; (*: en el comer*) frugal; (*: en el beber*) abstemious; (*agua*) lukewarm; (*clima*) mild; (*Mus*) in tune, well-tuned

templanza [tem'planθa] *nf* moderation; (*en el beber*) abstemiousness; (*del clima*) mildness

templar [tem'plar] *vt* (*moderar*) to moderate; (*furia*) to restrain; (*calor*) to reduce; (*solución*) to dilute; (*afinar*) to tune (up); (*acero*) to temper; (*tuerca*) to tighten up ▷ *vi* to moderate; **templarse** *vr* to be restrained

temple ['temple] *nm* (*humor*) mood; (*coraje*) courage; (*ajuste*) tempering; (*afinación*) tuning; (*pintura*) tempera

templo ['templo] *nm* (*iglesia*) church; (*pagano etc*) temple; **~ metodista** Methodist chapel

temporada [tempo'raða] *nf* time, period; (*estación, social, Deporte*) season; **en plena ~** at the height of the season

temporal [tempo'ral] *adj* (*no permanente*) temporary; (*Rel*) temporal ▷ *nm* storm

tempranero, -a [tempra'nero, a] *adj* (*Bot*) early; (*persona*) early-rising

temprano, -a [tem'prano, a] *adj* early ▷ *adv* early; (*demasiado pronto*) too soon, too early; **lo más ~ posible** as soon as possible

ten [ten] *vb ver* **tener**

tenaces [te'naθes] *adj pl ver* **tenaz**

tenacidad [tenaθi'ðað] *nf* (*gen*) tenacity; (*dureza*) toughness; (*terquedad*) stubbornness

tenacillas [tena'θiʎas] *nfpl* (*gen*) tongs; (*para el pelo*) curling tongs; (*Med*) forceps

tenaz [te'naθ] *adj* (*material*) tough; (*persona*) tenacious; (*pegajoso*) sticky; (*terco*) stubborn

tenaza, tenazas [te'naθ(as)] *nf(pl)* (*Med*) forceps; (*Tec*) pliers; (*Zool*) pincers

tendedero [tende'ðero] *nm* (*para ropa*) drying-place; (*cuerda*) clothes line

tendencia [ten'denθja] *nf* tendency; (*proceso*) trend; **~ imperante** prevailing tendency; **~ del mercado** run of the market; **tener ~ a** to tend *o* have a tendency to

tendencioso, -a [tenden'θjoso, a] *adj* tendentious

tender [ten'der] *vt* (*extender*) to spread out; (*ropa*) to hang out; (*vía férrea, cable*) to lay; (*cuerda*) to stretch; (*trampa*) to set ▷ *vi* to tend; **tenderse** *vr* to lie down; (*fig: dejarse llevar*) to let o.s. go; (*: dejar ir*) to let things go; **~ la cama/la mesa** (*Am*) to make the bed/lay the table

tenderete [tende'rete] *nm* (*puesto*) stall; (*carretilla*) barrow; (*exposición*) display of goods

tendero, -a [ten'dero, a] *nm/f* shopkeeper

tendido, -a [ten'diðo, a] *adj* (*acostado*) lying down, flat; (*colgado*) hanging ▷ *nm* (*ropa*) washing; (*Taur*) front rows *pl* of seats; (*colocación*) laying; (*Arq: enyesado*) coat of plaster; **a galope ~** flat out

tendón [ten'don] *nm* tendon

tendré *etc* [ten'dre] *vb ver* **tener**

tenebroso, -a [tene'βroso, a] *adj* (*oscuro*) dark; (*fig*) gloomy; (*siniestro*) sinister

tenedor [tene'ðor] *nm* (*Culin*) fork; (*poseedor*) holder; **~ de libros** book-keeper; **~ de acciones** shareholder; **~ de póliza** policyholder

teneduría [teneðu'ria] *nf* keeping; **~ de libros** book-keeping

tenencia [te'nenθja] *nf* (*de casa*) tenancy; (*de oficio*) tenure; (*de propiedad*) possession; **~ asegurada** security of tenure; **~ ilícita de armas** illegal possession of weapons

⬤ **PALABRA CLAVE**

tener [te'ner] *vt* **1** (*poseer, gen*) to have; (*en la mano*) to hold; **¿tienes un boli?** have you got a pen?; **va a tener un niño** she's going to have a baby; **tiene los ojos azules** he's got blue eyes; **¡ten** (*o* **tenga**)!, **¡aquí tienes** (*o* **tiene**)!** here you are!

2 (*edad, medidas*) to be; **tiene siete años** she's seven (years old); **tiene 15 cm de largo** it's 15 cm long

3 (*sentimientos, sensaciones*): **tener sed/hambre/frío/calor** to be thirsty/hungry/cold/hot; **tener celos** to be jealous; **tener cuidado** to be careful; **tener razón** to be right; **tener suerte** to be lucky

4 (*considerar*): **lo tengo por brillante** I consider him to be brilliant; **tener en mucho a algn** to think very highly of sb

5 (*+ pp, + adj, + gerundio*): **tengo terminada ya la mitad del trabajo** I've done half the work already; **tenía el sombrero puesto** he had his hat on; **tenía pensado llamarte** I had been thinking of phoning you; **nos tiene hartos** we're fed up with him; **me ha tenido tres horas esperando** he kept me waiting three hours

6: **tener que hacer algo** to have to do sth; **tengo que acabar este trabajo hoy** I have to finish this job today

7: **¿qué tienes, estás enfermo?** what's the matter with you, are you ill?

8 (*locuciones*): **¿conque ésas tenemos?** so it's like that, then?; **no las tengo todas conmigo** I'm a bit unsure (about it); **lo tiene difícil** he'll have a hard job

tenerse *vr* **1**: **tenerse en pie** to stand up

2: **tenerse por** to think o.s.; **se tiene por un gran cantante** he thinks himself a great singer

tengo *etc* ['tengo] *vb ver* **tener**

tenia ['tenja] *nf* tapeworm

teniente [te'njente] *nm* lieutenant; (*ayudante*) deputy; **~ coronel** lieutenant colonel

tenis ['tenis] *nm* tennis; **~ de mesa** table tennis

tenista [te'nista] *nm/f* tennis player

tenor [te'nor] *nm* (*tono*) tone; (*sentido*) meaning; (*Mus*) tenor; **a ~ de** on the lines of

tensar [ten'sar] *vt* to tauten; (*arco*) to draw

tensión [ten'sjon] *nf* tension; (*Tec*) stress; (*Med*): **~ arterial** blood pressure; **~ nerviosa** nervous strain; **tener la ~ alta** to have high blood pressure

tenso, -a ['tenso, a] *adj* tense; (*relaciones*) strained

tentación [tenta'θjon] *nf* temptation

tentáculo [ten'takulo] *nm* tentacle

tentador, a [tenta'ðor, a] *adj* tempting ▷ *nm/f* tempter/temptress

tentar [ten'tar] *vt* (*tocar*) to touch, feel; (*seducir*) to tempt; (*atraer*) to attract; (*probar*) to try (out); (*Med*) to probe; **~ hacer algo** to try to do sth

t

tentativa [tenta'tiβa] nf attempt; ~ **de asesinato** attempted murder
tentempié [tentem'pje] nm (fam) snack
tenue ['tenwe] adj (delgado) thin, slender; (alambre) fine; (insustancial) tenuous; (sonido) faint; (neblina) light; (lazo, vínculo) slight
teñir [te'ɲir] vt to dye; (fig) to tinge; **teñirse** vr to dye; **~se el pelo** to dye one's hair
teología [teolo'xia] nf theology
teorema [teo'rema] nm theorem
teoría [teo'ria] nf theory; **en ~** in theory
teóricamente [te'orikamente] adv theoretically
teórico, -a [te'oriko, a] adj theoretic(al) ▷ nm/f theoretician, theorist
teorizar [teori'θar] vi to theorize
tequila [te'kila] nm o f tequila
TER [ter] nm abr (Ferro) = **tren español rápido**
terapéutico, -a [tera'peutiko, a] adj therapeutic(al) ▷ nf therapeutics sg
terapia [te'rapja] nf therapy; **~ laboral** occupational therapy
tercer [ter'θer] adj ver **tercero**
tercermundista [terθermun'dista] adj Third World cpd
tercero, -a [ter'θero, a] adj third (antes de nmsg **tercer**) ▷ nm (árbitro) mediator; (Jur) third party
terceto [ter'θeto] nm trio
terciado, -a [ter'θjaðo, a] adj slanting; **azúcar ~** brown sugar
terciar [ter'θjar] vt (Mat) to divide into three; (inclinarse) to slope; (llevar) to wear across one's chest ▷ vi (participar) to take part; (hacer de árbitro) to mediate; **terciarse** vr to arise
terciario, -a [ter'θjarjo, a] adj tertiary
tercio [ter'θjo] nm third
terciopelo [terθjo'pelo] nm velvet
terco, -a ['terko, a] adj obstinate, stubborn; (material) tough
tergal® [ter'ɣal] nm Terylene®, Dacron® (US)
tergiversar [terxiβer'sar] vt to distort ▷ vi to prevaricate
termal [ter'mal] adj thermal
termas ['termas] nfpl hot springs
térmico, -a ['termiko, a] adj thermic, thermal, heat cpd
terminación [termina'θjon] nf (final) end; (conclusión) conclusion, ending
terminal [termi'nal] adj terminal ▷ nm (Elec, Inform) terminal; **~ conversacional** interactive terminal; **~ de pantalla** visual display unit ▷ nf (Aviat, Ferro) terminal
terminante [termi'nante] adj (final) final, definitive; (tajante) categorical
terminantemente [terminante'mente] adv: **~ prohibido** strictly forbidden
terminar [termi'nar] vt (completar) to complete, finish; (concluir) to end ▷ vi (llegar a su fin) to end; (parar) to stop; (acabar) to finish; **terminarse** vr to come to an end; **~ por**

hacer algo to end up (by) doing sth
término ['termino] nm end, conclusion; (parada) terminus; (límite) boundary; (en discusión) point; (Ling, Com) term; **~ medio** average; (fig) middle way; **en otros ~s** in other words; **en último ~** (a fin de cuentas) in the last analysis; (como último recurso) as a last resort; **~ medio** average; (fig) middle way; **en ~s de** in terms of; **según los ~s del contrato** according to the terms of the contract
terminología [terminolo'xia] nf terminology
termita [ter'mita] nf termite
termo(s)® ['termo(s)] nm Thermos® (flask)
termodinámico, -a [termoði'namiko, a] adj thermodynamic ▷ nf thermodynamics sg
termómetro [ter'mometro] nm thermometer
termonuclear [termonukle'ar] adj thermonuclear
termostato [termos'tato] nm thermostat
ternero, -a [ter'nero, a] nm/f (animal) calf ▷ nf (carne) veal, beef
terno ['terno] nm (traje) three-piece suit; (conjunto) set of three
ternura [ter'nura] nf (trato) tenderness; (palabra) endearment; (cariño) fondness
terquedad [terke'ðað] nf obstinacy; (dureza) harshness
terrado [te'rraðo] nm terrace
terraplén [terra'plen] nm (Agr) terrace; (Ferro) embankment; (Mil) rampart; (cuesta) slope
terráqueo, -a [te'rrakeo, a] adj: **globo ~** globe
terrateniente [terrate'njente] nm landowner
terraza [te'rraθa] nf (balcón) balcony; (techo) flat roof; (Agr) terrace
terremoto [terre'moto] nm earthquake
terrenal [terre'nal] adj earthly
terreno, -a [te'rreno, a] adj (de la tierra) earthly, worldly ▷ nm (tierra) land; (parcela) plot; (suelo) soil; (fig) field; **un ~** a piece of land; **sobre el ~** on the spot; **ceder/perder ~** to give/lose ground; **preparar el ~ (a)** (fig) to pave the way (for)
terrestre [te'rrestre] adj terrestrial; (ruta) land cpd
terrible [te'rriβle] adj (espantoso) terrible; (aterrador) dreadful; (tremendo) awful
territorial [territo'rjal] adj territorial
territorio [terri'torjo] nm territory; **~ bajo mandato** mandated territory
terrón [te'rron] nm (de azúcar) lump; (de tierra) clod, lump; **terrones** nmpl land sg
terror [te'rror] nm terror
terrorífico, -a [terro'rifiko, a] adj terrifying
terrorismo [terro'rismo] nm terrorism
terrorista [terro'rista] adj, nm/f terrorist; **~ suicida** suicide bomber
terroso, -a [te'rroso, a] adj earthy

terruño [te'rruɲo] nm (pedazo) clod; (parcela) plot; (fig) native soil; **apego al ~** attachment to one's native soil

terso, -a ['terso, a] adj (liso) smooth; (pulido) polished; (fig: estilo) flowing

tersura [ter'sura] nf smoothness; (brillo) shine

tertulia [ter'tulja] nf (reunión informal) social gathering; (grupo) group, circle; (sala) clubroom; **~ literaria** literary circle

tesina [te'sina] nf dissertation

tesis ['tesis] nf inv thesis

tesón [te'son] nm (firmeza) firmness; (tenacidad) tenacity

tesorero, -a [teso'rero, a] nm/f treasurer

tesoro [te'soro] nm treasure; (Com, Pol) treasury; **T~ público** (Pol) Exchequer

test (pl **tests**) [tes(t), tes(t)] nm test

testaferro [testa'ferro] nm figurehead

testamentaría [testamenta'ria] nf execution of a will

testamentario, -a [testamen'tarjo, a] adj testamentary ▷ nm/f executor/executrix

testamento [testa'mento] nm will

testar [tes'tar] vi to make a will

testarudo, -a [testa'ruðo, a] adj stubborn

testículo [tes'tikulo] nm testicle

testificar [testifi'kar] vt to testify; (fig) to attest ▷ vi to give evidence

testigo [tes'tiɣo] nm/f witness; **~ de cargo/descargo** witness for the prosecution/defence; **~ ocular** eye witness; **poner a algn por ~** to cite sb as a witness

testimonial [testimo'njal] adj (prueba) testimonial; (gesto) token

testimoniar [testimo'njar] vt to testify to; (fig) to show

testimonio [testi'monjo] nm testimony; **en ~ de** as a token o mark of; **falso ~** perjured evidence, false witness

teta ['teta] nf (de biberón) teat; (Anat) nipple; (fam) breast; (fam!) tit (!)

tétanos ['tetanos] nm tetanus

tetera [te'tera] nf teapot; **~ eléctrica** (electric) kettle

tetilla [te'tiʎa] nf (Anat) nipple; (de biberón) teat

tétrico, -a ['tetriko, a] adj gloomy, dismal

textear [tekste'ar] vt (LAm) to text

textil [teks'til] adj textile

texto ['teksto] nm text

textual [teks'twal] adj textual; **palabras ~es** exact words

textura [teks'tura] nf (de tejido) texture; (de mineral) structure

tez [teθ] nf (cutis) complexion; (color) colouring

ti [ti] pron you; (reflexivo) yourself

tía ['tia] nf (pariente) aunt; (fam: mujer) girl

tibieza [ti'βjeθa] nf (temperatura) tepidness; (fig) coolness

tibio, -a ['tiβjo, a] adj lukewarm, tepid

tiburón [tiβu'ron] nm shark

tic [tik] nm (ruido) click; (de reloj) tick; **~ nervioso** (Med) nervous tic

tictac [tik'tak] nm (de reloj) tick tock

tiempo ['tjempo] nm (gen) time; (época, período) age, period; (Meteorología) weather; (Ling) tense; (edad) age; (de juego) half; **a ~** in time; **a un o al mismo ~** at the same time; **al poco ~** very soon (after); **andando el ~** in due course; **cada cierto ~** every so often; **con ~** in time; **con el ~** eventually; **se quedó poco ~** he didn't stay very long; **hace poco ~** not long ago; **mucho ~** a long time; **de ~ en ~** from time to time; **en mis ~s** in my time; **en los buenos ~s** in the good old days; **hace buen/mal ~** the weather is fine/bad; **estar a ~** to be in time; **hace ~** some time ago; **hacer ~** to while away the time; **¿qué ~ tiene?** how old is he?; **motor de 2 ~s** two-stroke engine; **~ compartido** (Inform) time sharing; **~ de ejecución** (Inform) run time; **~ inactivo** (Com) downtime; **~ libre** spare time; **~ de paro** (Com) idle time; **a ~ partido** (trabajar) part-time; **~ preferencial** (Com) prime time; **en ~ real** (Inform) real time; **primer ~** first half

tienda ['tjenda] vb ver **tender** ▷ nf shop; (más grande) store; (Naut) awning; **~ de campaña** tent; **~ de comestibles** grocer's (shop) (Brit), grocery (store) (US)

tiene etc ['tjene] vb ver **tener**

tienta ['tjenta] vb ver **tentar** ▷ nf (Med) probe; (fig) tact; **andar a ~s** to grope one's way along

tiento etc ['tjento] vb ver **tentar** ▷ nm (tacto) touch; (precaución) wariness; (pulso) steady hand; (Zool) feeler, tentacle

tierno, -a ['tjerno, a] adj (blando, dulce) tender; (fresco) fresh

tierra ['tjerra] nf earth; (suelo) soil; (mundo) world; (país) country, land; (Elec) earth, ground (US); **~ adentro** inland; **~ natal** native land; **echar ~ a un asunto** to hush an affair up; **no es de estas ~s** he's not from these parts; **la T~ Santa** the Holy Land

tieso, -a ['tjeso, a] adj (rígido) rigid; (duro) stiff; (fig: testarudo) stubborn; (fam: orgulloso) conceited ▷ adv strongly

tiesto ['tjesto] nm flowerpot; (pedazo) piece of pottery

tifoidea [tifoi'ðea] nf typhoid

tifón [ti'fon] nm (huracán) typhoon; (de mar) tidal wave

tifus ['tifus] nm typhus; **~ icteroides** yellow fever

tigre ['tiɣre] nm tiger; (Am) jaguar

tijera [ti'xera] nf (una tijera) (pair of) scissors pl; (Zool) claw; (persona) gossip; **de ~** folding; **tijeras** nfpl scissors; (para plantas) shears; **unas ~s** a pair of scissors

tijeretear [tixerete'ar] vt to snip ▷ vi (fig) to meddle

tila ['tila] nf (Bot) lime tree; (Culin) lime flower tea

t

tildar [til'dar] vt: ~ **de** to brand as
tilde ['tilde] nf (defecto) defect; (trivialidad) triviality; (Tip) tilde
tilín [ti'lin] nm tinkle
tilo ['tilo] nm lime tree
timar [ti'mar] vt (robar) to steal; (estafar) to swindle; (persona) to con; **timarse** vr (fam): ~**se con algn** to make eyes at sb
timbal [tim'bal] nm small drum
timbrar [tim'brar] vt to stamp; (sellar) to seal; (carta) to postmark
timbre ['timbre] nm (sello) stamp; (campanilla) bell; (tono) timbre; (Com) stamp duty
timidez [timi'ðeθ] nf shyness
tímido, -a ['timiðo, a] adj shy, timid
timo ['timo] nm swindle; **dar un ~ a algn** to swindle sb
timón [ti'mon] nm helm, rudder; (Am) steering wheel; **coger el ~** (fig) to take charge
timonel [timo'nel] nm helmsman
tímpano ['timpano] nm (Anat) eardrum; (Mus) small drum
tina ['tina] nf tub; (Am: baño) bath(tub)
tinaja [ti'naxa] nf large earthen jar
tinglado [tin'glaðo] nm (cobertizo) shed; (fig: truco) trick; (intriga) intrigue; **armar un ~** to lay a plot
tinieblas [ti'njeβlas] nfpl darkness sg; (sombras) shadows; **estamos en ~ sobre sus proyectos** (fig) we are in the dark about his plans
tino ['tino] nm (habilidad) skill; (Mil) marksmanship; (juicio) insight; (moderación) moderation; **sin ~** immoderately; **coger el ~** to get the feel o hang of it
tinta ['tinta] nf ink; (Tec) dye; (Arte) colour; ~ **china** Indian ink; **tintas** nfpl (fig) shades; **medias ~s** (fig) half measures; **saber algo de buena ~** to have sth on good authority
tinte ['tinte] nm dye; (acto) dyeing; (fig) tinge; (barniz) veneer
tintero [tin'tero] nm inkwell; **se le quedó en el ~** he clean forgot about it
tintinear [tintine'ar] vt to tinkle
tinto, -a ['tinto, a] nm red wine
tintorería [tintore'ria] nf dry cleaner's
tintura [tin'tura] nf (acto) dyeing; (Química) dye; (farmacéutico) tincture
tío ['tio] nm (pariente) uncle; (fam: hombre) bloke, guy (US)
tiovivo [tio'βiβo] nm merry-go-round
típico, -a ['tipiko, a] adj typical; (pintoresco) picturesque
tiple ['tiple] nm soprano (voice) ▷ nf soprano
tipo ['tipo] nm (clase) type, kind; (norma) norm; (patrón) pattern; (fam: hombre) fellow, bloke, guy (US); (Anat) build; (: de mujer) figure; (Imprenta) type; ~ **bancario/de descuento** bank/discount rate; ~ **de interés** interest rate; ~ **de interés vigente** (Com) standard rate; ~ **de cambio** exchange rate; ~ **base** (Com) base rate; ~ **a término** (Com)

forward rate; **dos ~s sospechosos** two suspicious characters; ~ **de letra** (Inform, Tip) typeface; ~ **de datos** (Inform) data type
tipografía [tipoɣra'fia] nf (tipo) printing; (lugar) printing press
tipográfico, -a [tipo'ɣrafiko, a] adj printing
tipógrafo, -a [ti'poɣrafo, a] nm/f printer
tíquet ['tiket] (pl **tíquets**) nm ticket; (en tienda) cash slip
tiquismiquis [tikis'mikis] nm fussy person ▷ nmpl (querellas) squabbling sg; (escrúpulos) silly scruples
tira ['tira] nf strip; (fig) abundance ▷ nm: ~ **y afloja** give and take; (cautela) caution; **la ~ de ...** (fam) lots of ...
tirabuzón [tiraβu'θon] nm corkscrew; (rizo) curl
tirachinas [tira'tʃinas] nm inv catapult
tiradero [tira'ðero] nm (Am) rubbish dump
tirado, -a [ti'raðo, a] adj (barato) dirt-cheap; (fam: fácil) very easy ▷ nf (acto) cast, throw; (distancia) distance; (serie) series; (Tip) printing, edition; **de una tirada** at one go; **está ~** (fam) it's a cinch
tirador, a [tira'ðor, a] nm/f (persona) shooter ▷ nm (mango) handle; (Elec) flex; ~ **certero** sniper
tiralíneas [tira'lineas] nm inv ruling-pen
tiranía [tira'nia] nf tyranny
tiránico, -a [ti'raniko, a] adj tyrannical
tiranizar [tirani'θar] vt (pueblo, empleado) to tyrannize
tirano, -a [ti'rano, a] adj tyrannical ▷ nm/f tyrant
tirante [ti'rante] adj (cuerda) tight, taut; (relaciones) strained ▷ nm (Arq) brace; (Tec) stay; (correa) shoulder strap; **tirantes** nmpl braces, suspenders (US)
tirantez [tiran'teθ] nf tightness; (fig) tension
tirar [ti'rar] vt to throw; (volcar) to upset; (derribar) to knock down o over; (tiro) to fire; (cohete) to launch; (bomba) to drop; (edificio) to pull down; (desechar) to throw out o away; (disipar) to squander; (imprimir) to print; (dar: golpe) to deal ▷ vi (disparar) to shoot; (dar un tirón) to pull; (fig) to draw; (interesar) to appeal; (fam: andar) to go; (tender a) to tend to; (Deporte) to shoot; **tirarse** vr to throw o.s.; (fig) to demean o.s.; (fam!) to screw (!); ~ **abajo** to bring down, destroy; **tira más a su padre** he takes more after his father; ~ **de algo** to pull o tug (on) sth; **ir tirando** to manage; ~ **a la derecha** to turn o go right; **a todo ~** at the most
tirita [ti'rita] nf (sticking) plaster, Band-Aid® (US)
tiritar [tiri'tar] vi to shiver
tiro ['tiro] nm (lanzamiento) throw; (disparo) shot; (tiroteo) shooting; (Deporte) shot; (Tenis, Golf) drive; (alcance) range; (de escalera) flight (of stairs); (golpe) blow; (engaño) hoax; ~ **al blanco** target practice; **caballo de ~** cart-

horse; **andar de ~s largos** to be all dressed up; **al ~** (*Am*) at once; **de a ~** (*Am: fam*) completely; **se pegó un ~** he shot himself; **le salió el ~ por la culata** it backfired on him

tiroides [ti'roiðes] *nm inv* thyroid

tirón [ti'ron] *nm* (*sacudida*) pull, tug; **de un ~** in one go; **dar un ~ a** to pull at, tug at

tiroteo [tiro'teo] *nm* exchange of shots, shooting; (*escaramuza*) skirmish

tísico, -a ['tisiko, a] *adj, nm/f* consumptive

tisis ['tisis] *nf* consumption, tuberculosis

titánico, -a [ti'taniko, a] *adj* titanic

títere ['titere] *nm* puppet; **no dejar ~ con cabeza** to turn everything upside-down

titilar [titi'lar] *vi* (*luz, estrella*) to twinkle; (*párpado*) to flutter

titiritero, -a [titiri'tero, a] *nm/f* (*acróbata*) acrobat; (*malabarista*) juggler

titubeante [tituβe'ante] *adj* (*inestable*) shaky, tottering; (*farfullante*) stammering; (*dudoso*) hesitant

titubear [tituβe'ar] *vi* to stagger; (*tartamudear*) to stammer; (*vacilar*) to hesitate

titubeo [titu'βeo] *nm* staggering; stammering; hesitation

titulado, -a [titu'laðo, a] *adj* (*libro*) entitled; (*persona*) titled

titular [titu'lar] *adj* titular ▷ *nm/f* (*de oficina*) occupant; (*de pasaporte*) holder ▷ *nm* headline ▷ *vt* to title; **titularse** *vr* to be entitled

título ['titulo] *nm* (*gen*) title; (*de diario*) headline; (*certificado*) professional qualification; (*universitario*) university degree; (*Com*) bond; (*fig*) right; **títulos** *nmpl* qualifications; **a ~ de** by way of; (*en calidad de*) in the capacity of; **a ~ de curiosidad** as a matter of interest; **~ de propiedad** title deed; **~s convertibles de interés fijo** (*Com*) convertible loan stock *sg*

tiza ['tiθa] *nf* chalk; **una ~** a piece of chalk

tiznar [tiθ'nar] *vt* to blacken; (*manchar*) to smudge, stain; (*fig*) to tarnish

tizón [ti'θon], **tizo** ['tiθo] *nm* brand; (*fig*) stain

TLC *nm abr* (= *Tratado de Libre Comercio*) NAFTA

toalla [to'aʎa] *nf* towel

tobillo [to'βiʎo] *nm* ankle

tobogán [toβo'ɣan] *nm* toboggan; (*montaña rusa*) roller-coaster; (*resbaladilla*) chute, slide

toca ['toka] *nf* headdress

tocadiscos [toka'ðiskos] *nm inv* record player

tocado, -a [to'kaðo, a] *adj* (*fruta etc*) rotten; (*fam*) touched ▷ *nm* headdress; **estar ~ de la cabeza** (*fam*) to be weak in the head

tocador [toka'ðor] *nm* (*mueble*) dressing table; (*cuarto*) boudoir; (*neceser*) toilet case; (*fam*) ladies' room

tocante [to'kante]: **~ a** *prep* with regard to; **en lo ~ a** as for, so far as concerns

tocar [to'kar] *vt* to touch; (*sentir*) to feel; (*con la mano*) to handle; (*Mus*) to play; (*campana*) to

ring; (*tambor*) to beat; (*trompeta*) to blow; (*topar con*) to run into, strike; (*referirse a*) to allude to; (*estar emparentado con*) to be related to ▷ *vi* (*a la puerta*) to knock (on *o* at the door); (*ser el turno*) to fall to, be the turn of; (*ser hora*) to be due; (*atañer*) to concern; **tocarse** *vr* (*cubrirse la cabeza*) to cover one's head; (*tener contacto*) to touch (each other); **~le a algn** to fall to sb's lot; **~ en** (*Naut*) to call at; **por lo que a mí me toca** as far as I am concerned; **te toca a ti** it's your turn; **esto toca en la locura** this verges on madness

tocateja [toka'texa] (*fam*): **a ~** *adv* in readies

tocayo, -a [to'kajo, a] *nm/f* namesake

tocino [to'θino] *nm* (*bacon*) fat; **~ de panceta** bacon

todavía [toða'βia] *adv* (*aun*) even; (*aún*) still, yet; **~ más** yet *o* still more; **~ no** not yet; **~ en 1970** as late as 1970; **está lloviendo ~** it's still raining

PALABRA CLAVE

todo, -a ['toðo, a] *adj* **1** (*sg*) all; **toda la carne** all the meat; **toda la noche** all night, the whole night; **todo el libro** the whole book; **toda una botella** a whole bottle; **todo lo contrario** quite the opposite; **está toda sucia** she's all dirty; **a toda velocidad** at full speed; **por todo el país** throughout the whole country; **es todo un hombre** he's every inch a man; **soy todo oídos** I'm all ears

2 (*pl*) all; every; **todos los libros** all the books; **todas las noches** every night; **todos los que quieran salir** all those who want to leave; **todos vosotros** all of you
▷ *pron* **1** everything, all; **todos** everyone, everybody; **lo sabemos todo** we know everything; **todos querían más tiempo** everybody *o* everyone wanted more time; **nos marchamos todos** all of us left; **corriendo y todo, no llegaron a tiempo** even though they ran, they still didn't arrive in time

2 (*con preposición*): **a pesar de todo** even so, in spite of everything; **con todo él me sigue gustando** even so I still like him; **le llamaron de todo** they called him all the names under the sun; **no me agrada del todo** I don't entirely like it
▷ *adv* all; **vaya todo seguido** keep straight on *o* ahead
▷ *nm*: **como un todo** as a whole; **arriba del todo** at the very top; **todo a cien** ≈ pound store (*Brit*), ≈ dollar store (*US*)

todopoderoso, -a [toðopoðe'roso, a] *adj* all powerful; (*Rel*) almighty

todoterreno [toðote'rreno] *nm* (*tb*: **vehículo ~**) four-wheel drive, SUV (*esp US*)

toga ['toɣa] *nf* toga; (*Escol*) gown

Tokio ['tokjo] n Tokyo
toldo ['toldo] nm (para el sol) sunshade; (en tienda) marquee; (fig) pride
tole ['tole] nm (fam) commotion
tolerancia [tole'ranθja] nf tolerance
tolerante [tole'rante] adj tolerant; (sociedad) liberal; (fig) open-minded
tolerar [tole'rar] vt to tolerate; (resistir) to endure
toma ['toma] nf (gen) taking; (Med) dose; (Elec: tb: ~ **de corriente**) socket; (Mec) inlet; ~ **de posesión** (por presidente) taking up office; ~ **de tierra** (Aviat) landing
tomacorriente [tomako'rrjente] nm (Am) socket
tomar [to'mar] vt (gen, Cine, Foto, TV) to take; (actitud) to adopt; (aspecto) to take on; (notas) to take down; (beber) to drink ▷ vi to take; (Am) to drink; **tomarse** vr to take; ~**se por** to consider o.s. to be; **¡toma!** here you are!; ~ **asiento** to sit down; ~ **a algn por loco** to think sb mad; ~ **a bien/a mal** to take well/badly; ~ **en serio** to take seriously; ~ **el pelo a algn** to pull sb's leg; **~la con algn** to pick a quarrel with sb; ~ **el sol** to sunbathe; ~ **por escrito** to write down; **toma y daca** give and take
tomate [to'mate] nm tomato
tomatera [toma'tera] nf tomato plant
tomavistas [toma'βistas] nm inv movie camera
tomillo [to'miʎo] nm thyme
tomo ['tomo] nm (libro) volume; (fig) importance
ton [ton] abr = **tonelada** ▷ nm: **sin ~ ni son** without rhyme or reason
tonada [to'naða] nf tune
tonalidad [tonali'ðað] nf tone
tonel [to'nel] nm barrel
tonelada [tone'laða] nf ton; ~**(s) métrica(s)** metric ton(s)
tonelaje [tone'laxe] nm tonnage
tonelero [tone'lero] nm cooper
tongo ['tongo] nm (Deporte) fix
tónico, -a ['toniko, a] adj tonic ▷ nm (Med) tonic ▷ nf (Mus) tonic; (fig) keynote
tonificar [tonifi'kar] vt to tone up
tono ['tono] nm (Mus) tone; (altura) pitch; (color) shade; **fuera de ~** inappropriate; ~ **de llamada** ringtone; ~ **de marcar** (Telec) dialling tone; **darse ~** to put on airs
tontería [tonte'ria] nf (estupidez) foolishness; (una tontería) silly thing; **tonterías** nfpl rubbish sg, nonsense sg
tonto, -a ['tonto, a] adj stupid; (ridículo) silly ▷ nm/f fool; (payaso) clown; **a tontas y a locas** anyhow; **hacer(se) el ~** to act the fool
topacio [to'paθjo] nm topaz
topar [to'par] vt (tropezar) to bump into; (encontrar) to find, come across; (cabra etc) to butt ▷ vi: ~ **contra** o **en** to run into; ~ **con** to run up against; **el problema topa en eso**

that's where the problem lies
tope ['tope] adj maximum ▷ nm (fin) end; (límite) limit; (Ferro) buffer; (Auto) bumper; **al ~** end to end; **fecha ~** closing date; **precio ~** top price; **sueldo ~** maximum salary; ~ **de tabulación** tab stop
tópico, -a ['topiko, a] adj topical; (Med) local ▷ nm platitude, cliché; **de uso ~** for external application
topo ['topo] nm (Zool) mole; (fig) blunderer
topografía [topoɣra'fia] nf topography
topógrafo, -a [to'poɣrafo, a] nm/f topographer; (agrimensor) surveyor
toque etc ['toke] vb ver **tocar** ▷ nm touch; (Mus) beat; (de campana) chime, ring; (Mil) bugle call; (fig) crux; **dar un ~ a** to test; **dar el último ~ a** to put the final touch to; ~ **de queda** curfew
toqué etc vb ver **tocar**
toquetear [tokete'ar] vt to finger; (fam!) to touch up
toquilla [to'kiʎa] nf (pañuelo) headscarf; (chal) shawl
tórax ['toraks] nm inv thorax
torbellino [torbe'ʎino] nm whirlwind; (fig) whirl
torcedura [torθe'ðura] nf twist; (Med) sprain
torcer [tor'θer] vt to twist; (la esquina) to turn; (Med) to sprain; (cuerda) to plait; (ropa, manos) to wring; (persona) to corrupt; (sentido) to distort ▷ vi (cambiar de dirección) to turn; (desviar) to turn off; **torcerse** vr to twist; (doblar) to bend; (desviarse) to go astray; (fracasar) to go wrong; ~ **el gesto** to scowl; ~**se un pie** to twist one's foot; **el coche torció a la derecha** the car turned right
torcido, -a [tor'θiðo, a] adj twisted; (fig) crooked ▷ nm curl
tordo, -a ['torðo, a] adj dappled ▷ nm thrush
torear [tore'ar] vt (fig: evadir) to dodge; (jugar con) to tease; (toro) to fight ▷ vi to fight bulls
toreo [to'reo] nm bullfighting
torero, -a [to'rero, a] nm/f bullfighter
tormenta [tor'menta] nf storm; (fig: confusión) turmoil
tormento [tor'mento] nm torture; (fig) anguish
tornar [tor'nar] vt (devolver) to return, give back; (transformar) to transform ▷ vi to go back; **tornarse** vr (ponerse) to become; (volver) to return
tornasolado, -a [tornaso'laðo, a] adj (brillante) iridescent; (reluciente) shimmering
torneo [tor'neo] nm tournament
tornillo [tor'niʎo] nm screw; **apretar los ~s a algn** to apply pressure on sb; **le falta un ~** (fam) he's got a screw loose
torniquete [torni'kete] nm (puerta) turnstile; (Med) tourniquet
torno ['torno] nm (Tec: grúa) winch; (: de carpintero) lathe; (tambor) drum; ~ **de banco** vice, vise (US); **en ~ (a)** round, about

toro ['toro] nm bull; (fam) he-man; **los ~s** bullfighting sg

toronja [to'ronxa] nf grapefruit

torpe ['torpe] adj (poco hábil) clumsy, awkward; (movimiento) sluggish; (necio) dim; (lento) slow; (indecente) crude; (no honrado) dishonest

torpedo [tor'peðo] nm torpedo

torpeza [tor'peθa] nf (falta de agilidad) clumsiness; (lentitud) slowness; (rigidez) stiffness; (error) mistake; (crudeza) obscenity

torre ['torre] nf tower; (de electricidad) pylon; (Ajedrez) rook; (de Aviat, Mil, Naut) turret

torrefacto, -a [torre'fakto, a] adj roasted; **café ~** high roast coffee

torrente [to'rrente] nm torrent

tórrido, -a [to'rriðo, a] adj torrid

torrija [to'rrixa] nf fried bread; **~s** French toast sg

torsión [tor'sjon] nf twisting

torso ['torso] nm torso

torta ['torta] nf cake; (fam) slap; **~ de huevos** (Am) omelette; **no entendió ni ~** he didn't understand a word of it

tortazo [tor'taθo] nm (bofetada) slap; (de coche) crash

tortícolis [tor'tikolis] nm inv stiff neck

tortilla [tor'tiʎa] nf omelette; (Am) maize pancake; **~ francesa/española** plain/potato omelette; **cambiar o volver la ~ a algn** to turn the tables on sb

tórtola ['tortola] nf turtledove

tortuga [tor'tuɣa] nf tortoise; **~ marina** turtle

tortuoso, -a [tor'twoso, a] adj winding

tortura [tor'tura] nf torture

torturar [tortu'rar] vt to torture

tos [tos] nf inv cough; **~ ferina** whooping cough

tosco, -a ['tosko, a] adj coarse

toser [to'ser] vi to cough; **no hay quien le tosa** he's in a class by himself

tostado, -a [tos'taðo, a] adj toasted; (por el sol) dark brown; (piel) tanned ▷ nf tan; (pan) piece of toast; **tostadas** nfpl toast sg

tostador [tosta'ðor] nm, **tostadora** [tosta'ðora] (Am) nf toaster

tostar [tos'tar] vt to toast; (café) to roast; (al sol) to tan; **tostarse** vr to get brown

tostón [tos'ton] nm: **ser un ~** to be a drag

total [to'tal] adj total ▷ adv in short; (al fin y al cabo) when all is said and done ▷ nm total; **en ~** in all; **~ que** to cut a long story short; **~ de comprobación** (Inform) hash total; **~ debe/haber** (Com) debit/assets total

totalidad [totali'ðað] nf whole

totalitario, -a [totali'tarjo, a] adj totalitarian

totalmente [to'talmente] adv totally

tóxico, -a ['toksiko, a] adj toxic ▷ nm poison

toxicómano, -a [toksi'komano, a] adj addicted to drugs ▷ nm/f drug addict

toxina [to'ksina] nf toxin

tozudo, -a [to'θuðo, a] adj obstinate

traba ['traβa] nf bond, tie; (cadena) fetter; **poner ~s a** to restrain

trabajador, a [traβaxa'ðor, a] nm/f worker ▷ adj hard-working; **~ autónomo o por cuenta propia** self-employed person

trabajar [traβa'xar] vt to work; (arar) to till; (empeñarse en) to work at; (empujar: persona) to push; (convencer) to persuade ▷ vi to work; (esforzarse) to strive; **¡a ~!** let's get to work!; **~ por hacer algo** to strive to do sth

trabajo [tra'βaxo] nm work; (tarea) task; (Pol) labour; (fig) effort; **tomarse el ~ de** to take the trouble to; **~ por turno/a destajo** shift work/piecework; **~ en equipo** teamwork; **~ en proceso** (Com) work-in-progress; **~s forzados** hard labour sg

trabajoso, -a [traβa'xoso, a] adj hard; (Med) pale

trabalenguas [traβa'lengwas] nm inv tongue twister

trabar [tra'βar] vt (juntar) to join, unite; (atar) to tie down, fetter; (agarrar) to seize; (amistad) to strike up; **trabarse** vr to become entangled; (reñir) to squabble; **se le traba la lengua** he gets tongue-tied

tracción [trak'θjon] nf traction; **~ delantera/trasera** front-wheel/rear-wheel drive

tractor [trak'tor] nm tractor

tradición [traði'θjon] nf tradition

tradicional [traðiθjo'nal] adj traditional

traducción [traðuk'θjon] nf translation; **~ asistida por ordenador** computer-assisted translation

traducir [traðu'θir] vt to translate; **traducirse** vr: **~se en** (fig) to entail, result in

traductor, a [traðuk'tor, a] nm/f translator

traer [tra'er] vt to bring; (llevar) to carry; (ropa) to wear; (incluir) to carry; (fig) to cause; **traerse** vr: **~se algo** to be up to sth; **~se bien/mal** to dress well/badly; **traérselas** to be annoying; **~ consigo** to involve, entail; **es un problema que se las trae** it's a difficult problem

traficar [trafi'kar] vi to trade; **~ con** (pey) to deal illegally in

tráfico ['trafiko] nm (Com) trade; (Auto) traffic

tragaluz [traɣa'luθ] nm skylight

tragamonedas [traɣamo'neðas] nm inv, **tragaperras** [traɣa'perras] nm inv slot machine

tragar [tra'ɣar] vt to swallow; (devorar) to devour, bolt down; **tragarse** vr to swallow; (tierra) to absorb, soak up; **no le puedo ~** (persona) I can't stand him

tragedia [tra'xeðja] nf tragedy

trágico, -a ['traxiko, a] adj tragic

trago ['traɣo] nm (de líquido) drink; (comido de golpe) gulp; (fam: de bebida) swig; (desgracia)

t

blow; **echar un ~** to have a drink; **~ amargo**
(fig) hard time

traición [trai'θjon] nf treachery; (Jur)
treason; (una traición) act of treachery

traicionar [traiθjo'nar] vt to betray

traicionero, -a [traiθjo'nero, a] = **traidor, a**

traidor, a [trai'ðor, a] adj treacherous ▷ nm/f
traitor

traigo etc ['traiɣo] vb ver **traer**

trailer (pl **trailers**) ['trailer, 'trailer(s)] nm
trailer

traje ['traxe] vb ver **traer** ▷ nm (gen) dress; (de
hombre) suit; (traje típico) costume; (fig) garb;
~ de baño swimsuit; **~ de luces** bullfighter's
costume; **~ hecho a la medida** made-to-
measure suit

trajera etc [tra'xera] vb ver **traer**

trajín [tra'xin] nm haulage; (fam: movimiento)
bustle; **trajines** nmpl goings-on

trajinar [traxi'nar] vt (llevar) to carry,
transport ▷ vi (moverse) to bustle about;
(viajar) to travel around

trama ['trama] nf (fig) link; (: intriga) plot; (de
tejido) weft

tramar [tra'mar] vt to plot; (Tec) to weave;
tramarse vr (fig): **algo se está tramando**
there's something going on

tramitar [trami'tar] vt (asunto) to transact;
(negociar) to negotiate; (manejar) to handle

trámite ['tramite] nm (paso) step; (Jur)
transaction; **trámites** nmpl (burocracia)
paperwork sg, procedures; (Jur) proceedings

tramo ['tramo] nm (de tierra) plot; (de escalera)
flight; (de vía) section

tramoya [tra'moja] nf (Teat) piece of stage
machinery; (fig) trick

tramoyista [tramo'jista] nm/f scene shifter;
(fig) trickster

trampa ['trampa] nf trap; (en el suelo)
trapdoor; (prestidigitación) conjuring trick;
(engaño) trick; (fam) fiddle; **caer en la ~** to fall
into the trap; **hacer ~s** (trampear) to cheat

trampear [trampe'ar] vt, vi to cheat

trampolín [trampo'lin] nm trampoline; (de
piscina etc) diving board

tramposo, -a [tram'poso, a] adj crooked,
cheating ▷ nm/f crook, cheat

tranca ['tranka] nf (palo) stick; (viga) beam;
(de puerta, ventana) bar; (borrachera) binge; **a ~s
y barrancas** with great difficulty

trancar [tran'kar] vt to bar ▷ vi to stride
along

trance ['tranθe] nm (momento difícil) difficult
moment; (situación crítica) critical situation;
(estado de hipnosis) trance; **estar en ~ de
muerte** to be at death's door

tranco ['tranko] nm stride

tranquilamente [tran'kilamente] adv (sin
preocupaciones: leer, trabajar) peacefully; (sin
enfadarse: hablar, discutir) calmly

tranquilidad [trankili'ðað] nf (calma)
calmness, stillness; (paz) peacefulness

tranquilizante [trankili'θante] nm
tranquillizer

tranquilizar [trankili'θar] vt (calmar) to calm
(down); (asegurar) to reassure; **tranquilizarse**
vr to calm down

tranquilo, -a [tran'kilo, a] adj (calmado)
calm; (apacible) peaceful; (mar) calm; (mente)
untroubled

transacción [transak'θjon] nf transaction

transatlántico, -a [transat'lantiko, a] adj
transatlantic ▷ nm (ocean) liner

transbordador [transβorða'ðor] nm ferry

transbordar [transβor'ðar] vt to transfer;
transbordarse vr to change

transbordo [trans'βorðo] nm transfer;
hacer ~ to change (trains)

transcender [transθen'der] vt = **trascender**

transcribir [transkri'βir] vt to transcribe

transcurrir [transku'rrir] vi (tiempo) to pass;
(hecho) to turn out

transcurso [trans'kurso] nm passing, lapse;
~ del tiempo lapse (of time); **en el ~ de ocho
días** in the course of a week

transeúnte [transe'unte] adj transient
▷ nm/f passer-by

transexual [transe'kswal] adj, nm/f
transsexual

transferencia [transfe'renθja] nf
transference; (Com) transfer; **~ bancaria**
banker's order; **~ de crédito** (Com) credit
transfer; **~ electrónica de fondos** (Com)
electronic funds transfer

transferir [transfe'rir] vt to transfer;
(aplazar) to postpone

transformación [transforma'θjon] nf
transformation

transformador [transforma'ðor] nm
transformer

transformar [transfor'mar] vt to transform;
(convertir) to convert

tránsfuga ['transfuɣa] nm/f (Mil) deserter;
(Pol) turncoat

transfusión [transfu'sjon] nf (tb: **~ de
sangre**) (blood) transfusion

transgénico, -a [trans'xeniko, a] adj
genetically modified

transgredir [transɣre'dir] vt to transgress

transición [transi'θjon] nf transition;
período de ~ transitional period

transido, -a [tran'siðo, a] adj overcome; **~ de
angustia** beset with anxiety; **~ de dolor**
racked with pain

transigir [transi'xir] vi to compromise;
(ceder) to make concessions

transistor [transis'tor] nm transistor

transitar [transi'tar] vi to go (from place to
place)

transitivo, -a [transi'tiβo, a] adj transitive

tránsito ['transito] nm transit; (Auto) traffic;
(parada) stop; **horas de máximo ~** rush
hours; **"se prohíbe el ~"** "no thoroughfare"

transitorio, -a [transi'torjo, a] adj transitory

transmisión [transmi'sjon] *nf* (*Radio, TV*) transmission, broadcast(ing); (*transferencia*) transfer; **~ en circuito** hookup; **~ en directo/exterior** live/outside broadcast; **~ de datos (en paralelo/en serie)** (*Inform*) (parallel/serial) data transfer *o* transmission; **plena/media ~ bidireccional** (*Inform*) full/half duplex

transmitir [transmi'tir] *vt* to transmit; (*Radio, TV*) to broadcast; (*enfermedad*) to give, pass on

transparencia [transpa'renθja] *nf* transparency; (*claridad*) clearness, clarity; (*foto*) slide

transparentar [transparen'tar] *vt* to reveal ▷ *vi* to be transparent

transparente [transpa'rente] *adj* transparent; (*aire*) clear; (*ligero*) diaphanous ▷ *nm* curtain

transpirar [transpi'rar] *vi* to perspire; (*fig*) to transpire

transponer [transpo'ner] *vt* to transpose; (*cambiar de sitio*) to move about ▷ *vi* (*desaparecer*) to disappear; (*ir más allá*) to go beyond; **transponerse** *vr* to change places; (*ocultarse*) to hide; (*sol*) to go down

transportar [transpor'tar] *vt* to transport; (*llevar*) to carry

transporte [trans'porte] *nm* transport; (*Com*) haulage; **Ministerio de T~s** Ministry of Transport

transversal [transβer'sal] *adj* transverse, cross ▷ *nf* (*tb:* **calle ~**) cross street

tranvía [tram'bia] *nm* tram, streetcar (*US*)

trapeador [trapea'ðor] *nm* (*Am*) mop

trapear [trape'ar] *vt* (*Am*) to mop

trapecio [tra'peθjo] *nm* trapeze

trapecista [trape'θista] *nm/f* trapeze artist

trapero, -a [tra'pero, a] *nm/f* ragman

trapicheos [trapi'tʃeos] *nmpl* (*fam*) schemes, fiddles

trapo ['trapo] *nm* (*tela*) rag; (*de cocina*) cloth; **trapos** *nmpl* (*fam: de mujer*) clothes, dresses; **a todo ~** under full sail; **soltar el ~** (*llorar*) to burst into tears

tráquea ['trakea] *nf* trachea, windpipe

traqueteo [trake'teo] *nm* (*crujido*) crack; (*golpeteo*) rattling

tras [tras] *prep* (*detrás*) behind; (*después*) after; **~ de** besides; **día ~ día** day after day; **uno ~ otro** one after the other

trasatlántico [trasat'lantiko] *nm* (*barco*) (cabin) cruiser

trascendencia [trasθen'denθja] *nf* (*importancia*) importance; (*en filosofía*) transcendence

trascendental [trasθenden'tal] *adj* important; transcendental

trascender [trasθen'der] *vi* (*oler*) to smell; (*noticias*) to come out, leak out; (*sucesos, sentimientos*) to spread, have a wide effect; **~ a** (*afectar*) to reach, have an effect on; (*oler a*) to

smack of; **en su novela todo trasciende a romanticismo** everything in his novel smacks of romanticism

trasegar [trase'ɣar] *vt* (*mover*) to move about; (*vino*) to decant

trasero, -a [tra'sero, a] *adj* back, rear ▷ *nm* (*Anat*) bottom; **traseros** *nmpl* ancestors

trasfondo [tras'fondo] *nm* background

trasgredir [trasɣre'ðir] *vt* to contravene

trashumante [trasu'mante] *adj* migrating

trasladar [trasla'ðar] *vt* to move; (*persona*) to transfer; (*postergar*) to postpone; (*copiar*) to copy; (*interpretar*) to interpret; **trasladarse** *vr* (*irse*) to go; (*mudarse*) to move; **~se a otro puesto** to move to a new job

traslado [tras'laðo] *nm* move; (*mudanza*) move, removal; (*de persona*) transfer; (*copia*) copy; **~ de bloque** (*Inform*) block move, cut-and-paste

traslucir [traslu'θir] *vt* to show; **traslucirse** *vr* to be translucent; (*fig*) to be revealed

trasluz [tras'luθ] *nm* reflected light; **al ~** against *o* up to the light

trasnochado, -a [trasno'tʃaðo, a] *adj* dated

trasnochador, a [trasnotʃa'ðor, a] *adj* given to staying up late ▷ *nm/f* (*fig*) night owl

trasnochar [trasno'tʃar] *vi* (*acostarse tarde*) to stay up late; (*no dormir*) to have a sleepless night; (*pasar la noche*) to stay the night

traspapelar [traspape'lar] *vt* (*documento, carta*) to mislay, misplace

traspasar [traspa'sar] *vt* (*bala*) to pierce, go through; (*propiedad*) to sell, transfer; (*calle*) to cross over; (*límites*) to go beyond; (*ley*) to break; **"traspaso negocio"** "business for sale"

traspaso [tras'paso] *nm* (*venta*) transfer, sale; (*fig*) anguish

traspié [tras'pje] (*pl* **traspiés**) *nm* (*caída*) stumble; (*tropezón*) trip; (*fig*) blunder

trasplantar [trasplan'tar] *vt* to transplant

trasplante [tras'plante] *nm* transplant

traspuesto, -a [tras'pwesto, a] *adj*: **quedarse ~** to doze off

trastada [tras'taða] *nf* (*fam*) prank

trastazo [tras'taθo] *nm* (*fam*) bump; **darse un ~** (*persona*) to bump o.s.; (*en coche*) to have a bump

traste ['traste] *nm* (*Mus*) fret; **dar al ~ con algo** to ruin sth; **ir al ~** to fall through

trastero [tras'tero] *nm* lumber room

trastienda [tras'tjenda] *nf* back room (*of shop*); **obtener algo por la ~** to get sth by underhand means

trasto ['trasto] *nm* (*mueble*) piece of furniture; (*tarro viejo*) old pot; (*pey: cosa*) piece of junk; (*: persona*) dead loss; **trastos** *nmpl* (*Teat*) scenery *sg*; **tirar los ~s a la cabeza** to have a blazing row

trastocar [trasto'kar] *vt* (*papeles*) to mix up

trastornado, -a [trastor'naðo, a] *adj* (*loco*) mad; (*agitado*) crazy

t

trastornar [trastor'nar] vt to overturn, upset; (fig: ideas) to confuse; (: nervios) to shatter; (: persona) to drive crazy; **trastornarse** vr (plan) to fall through; (volverse loco) to go mad o crazy

trastorno [tras'torno] nm (acto) overturning; (confusión) confusion; (Pol) disturbance, upheaval; (Med) upset; ~ **estomacal** stomach upset; ~ **mental** mental disorder, breakdown

trasvase [tras'βase] nm (de río) diversion

tratable [tra'taβle] adj friendly

tratado [tra'taðo] nm (Pol) treaty; (Com) agreement; (Lit) treatise

tratamiento [trata'mjento] nm treatment; (Tec) processing; (de problema) handling; ~ **de datos** (Inform) data processing; ~ **de gráficos** (Inform) graphics; ~ **de márgenes** margin settings; ~ **de textos** (Inform) word processing; ~ **por lotes** (Inform) batch processing; ~ **de tú** familiar address

tratar [tra'tar] vt (ocuparse de) to treat; (manejar, Tec) to handle; (Inform) to process; (Med) to treat; (dirigirse a: persona) to address ▷ vi: ~ **de** (hablar sobre) to deal with, be about; (intentar) to try to; **tratarse** vr to treat each other; ~ **con** (Com) to trade in; (negociar con) to negotiate with; (tener tratos con) to have dealings with; **se trata de la nueva piscina** it's about the new pool; **¿de qué se trata?** what's it about?

trato ['trato] nm dealings pl; (relaciones) relationship; (comportamiento) manner; (Com, Jur) agreement, contract; (título) (form of) address; **de ~ agradable** pleasant; **de fácil ~** easy to get on with; ~ **equitativo** fair deal; **¡~ hecho!** it's a deal!; **malos ~s** ill-treatment sg

trauma ['trauma] nm trauma

través [tra'βes] nm (contratiempo) reverse; **al ~** across, crossways; **a ~ de** across; (sobre) over; (por) through; **de ~** across; (de lado) sideways

travesaño [traβe'saɲo] nm (Arq) crossbeam; (Deporte) crossbar

travesía [traβe'sia] nf (calle) cross-street; (Naut) crossing

travesti [tra'βesti] nm/f transvestite

travesura [traβe'sura] nf (broma) prank; (ingenio) wit

travieso, -a [tra'βjeso, a] adj (niño) naughty; (adulto) restless; (ingenioso) witty ▷ nf crossing; (Arq) crossbeam; (Ferro) sleeper

trayecto [tra'jekto] nm (ruta) road, way; (viaje) journey; (tramo) stretch; (curso) course; **final del ~** end of the line

trayectoria [trajek'torja] nf trajectory; (desarrollo) development; (fig) path; **la ~ actual del partido** the party's present line

traza ['traθa] nf (Arq) plan, design; (aspecto) looks pl; (señal) sign; (engaño) trick; (habilidad) skill; (Inform) trace

trazado, -a [tra'θaðo, a] adj: **bien ~** shapely, well-formed ▷ nm (Arq) plan, design; (fig) outline; (de carretera etc) line, route

trazar [tra'θar] vt (Arq) to plan; (Arte) to sketch; (fig) to trace; (itinerario: hacer) to plot; (plan) to draw up

trazo ['traθo] nm (línea) line; (bosquejo) sketch; **trazos** nmpl (de cara) lines, features

trébol ['treβol] nm (Bot) clover; **tréboles** nmpl (Naipes) clubs

trece ['treθe] num thirteen; **estar en sus ~** to stand firm

trecho ['tretʃo] nm (distancia) distance; (de tiempo) while; (fam) piece; **de ~ en ~** at intervals

tregua ['treɣwa] nf (Mil) truce; (fig) lull, respite; **sin ~** without respite

treinta ['treinta] num thirty

tremendo, -a [tre'mendo, a] adj (terrible) terrible; (imponente: cosa) imposing; (fam: fabuloso) tremendous; (divertido) entertaining

trémulo, -a ['tremulo, a] adj quivering; (luz) flickering

tren [tren] nm (Ferro) train; ~ **de aterrizaje** undercarriage; ~ **directo/expreso/(de) mercancías/de pasajeros/suplementario** through/fast/goods o freight/passenger/relief train; ~ **de cercanías** suburban train; ~ **de vida** way of life

trenca ['trenka] nf duffel coat

trenza ['trenθa] nf (de pelo) plait

trenzar [tren'θar] vt (el pelo) to plait ▷ vi (en baile) to weave in and out; **trenzarse** vr (Am) to become involved

trepar [tre'par] vt, vi to climb; (Tec) to drill

trepidar [trepi'ðar] vi to shake, vibrate

tres [tres] num three; (fecha) third; **las ~** three o'clock

trescientos, -as [tres'θjentos, as] num three hundred

tresillo [tre'siʎo] nm three-piece suite; (Mus) triplet

treta ['treta] nf (Com etc) gimmick; (fig) trick

triangular [trjangu'lar] adj triangular

triángulo [tri'angulo] nm triangle

tribal [tri'βal] adj tribal

tribu ['triβu] nf tribe

tribuna [tri'βuna] nf (plataforma) platform; (Deporte) stand; (fig) public speaking; ~ **de la prensa** press box; ~ **del acusado** (Jur) dock; ~ **del jurado** jury box

tribunal [triβu'nal] nm (en juicio) court; (comisión, fig) tribunal; (Escol: examinadores) board of examiners; **T~ Supremo** High Court, Supreme Court (US); **T~ de Justicia de las Comunidades Europeas** European Court of Justice; ~ **popular** jury

tributar [triβu'tar] vt to pay; (las gracias) to give; (cariño) to show

tributo [tri'βuto] nm (Com) tax

triciclo [tri'θiklo] nm tricycle

tricotar [triko'tar] vi to knit

trifulca [tri'fulka] nf (fam) row, shindy

trigal [tri'ɣal] nm wheat field

trigo ['triɣo] nm wheat; **trigos** nmpl wheat field(s) (pl)

trigueño, -a [tri'ɣeɲo, a] adj (pelo) corn-coloured; (piel) olive-skinned

trillado, -a [tri'ʎaðo, a] adj threshed; (fig) trite, hackneyed

trilladora [triʎa'ðora] nf threshing machine

trillar [tri'ʎar] vt (Agr) to thresh; (fig) to frequent

trimestral [trimes'tral] adj quarterly; (Escol) termly

trimestre [tri'mestre] nm (Escol) term; (Com) quarter, financial period; (: pago) quarterly payment

trinar [tri'nar] vi (Mus) to trill; (ave) to sing, warble; (rabiar) to fume, be angry; **está que trina** he's hopping mad

trincar [trin'kar] vt (atar) to tie up; (Naut) to lash; (agarrar) to pinion

trinchar [trin'tʃar] vt to carve

trinchera [trin'tʃera] nf (fosa) trench; (para vía) cutting; (impermeable) trench-coat

trineo [tri'neo] nm sledge

trinidad [trini'ðað] nf trio; (Rel): **la T~** the Trinity

trino ['trino] nm trill

trío ['trio] nm trio

tripa ['tripa] nf (Anat) intestine; (fig: fam) belly; **tripas** nfpl (Anat) insides; (Culin) tripe sg; **tener mucha ~** to be fat; **me duelen las ~s** I have a stomach ache

triple ['triple] adj triple; (tres veces) threefold

triplicado, -a [tripli'kaðo, a] adj: **por ~** in triplicate

triplicar [tripli'kar] vt to treble

triplo, -a ['triplo, a] adj = **triple**

trípode ['tripoðe] nm tripod

tripulación [tripula'θjon] nf crew

tripulante [tripu'lante] nm/f crewman/woman

tripular [tripu'lar] vt (barco) to man; (Auto) to drive

triquiñuela [triki'ɲwela] nf trick

tris [tris] nm crack; **en un ~** in an instant; **estar en un ~ de hacer algo** to be within an inch of doing sth

triste ['triste] adj (afligido) sad; (sombrío) melancholy, gloomy; (desolado) desolate; (lamentable) sorry, miserable; (viejo) old; (único) single; **no queda sino un ~ penique** there's just one miserable penny left

tristeza [tris'teθa] nf (aflicción) sadness; (melancolía) melancholy; (de lugar) desolation; (pena) misery

triturar [tritu'rar] vt (moler) to grind; (mascar) to chew; (documentos) to shred

triunfal [triun'fal] adj triumphant; (arco) triumphal

triunfar [triun'far] vi (tener éxito) to triumph; (ganar) to win; (Naipes) to be trumps;

triunfan corazones hearts are trumps; **~ en la vida** to succeed in life

triunfo [tri'unfo] nm triumph; (Naipes) trump

trivial [tri'βjal] adj trivial

trivializar [triβjali'θar] vt to minimize, play down

triza ['triθa] nf bit, piece; **hacer algo ~s** to smash sth to bits; (papel) to tear sth to shreds

trocar [tro'kar] vt (Com) to exchange; (dinero, de lugar) to change; (palabras) to exchange; (confundir) to confuse; **trocarse** vr (confundirse) to get mixed up; (transformarse): **~se (en)** to change (into)

trocear [troθe'ar] vt to cut up

trocha ['trotʃa] nf (sendero) by-path; (atajo) short cut

troche ['trotʃe]: **a ~ y moche** adv helter-skelter, pell-mell

trofeo [tro'feo] nm (premio) trophy

trola ['trola] nf (fam) fib

tromba ['tromba] nf whirlwind; **~ de agua** downpour

trombón [trom'bon] nm trombone

trombosis [trom'bosis] nf inv thrombosis

trompa ['trompa] nf (Mus) horn; (de elefante) trunk; (trompo) humming top; (hocico) snout; (Anat) tube, duct ▷ nm (Mus) horn player; **~ de Falopio** Fallopian tube; **cogerse una ~** (fam) to get tight

trompada [trom'paða] nf = **trompazo**

trompazo [trom'paθo] nm (choque) bump, bang; (puñetazo) punch

trompeta [trom'peta] nf trumpet; (clarín) bugle ▷ nm trumpeter

trompetilla [trompe'tiʎa] nf ear trumpet

trompicón [trompi'kon]: **a trompicones** adv in fits and starts

trompo ['trompo] nm spinning top

trompón [trom'pon] nm bump

tronar [tro'nar] vt (Am) to shoot, execute; (examen) to flunk ▷ vi to thunder; (fig) to rage; (fam) to go broke

tronchar [tron'tʃar] vt (árbol) to chop down; (fig: vida) to cut short; (esperanza) to shatter; (persona) to tire out; **troncharse** vr to fall down; **~se de risa** to split one's sides with laughter

tronco ['tronko] nm (de árbol, Anat) trunk; (de planta) stem; **estar hecho un ~** to be sound asleep

trono ['trono] nm throne

tropa ['tropa] nf (Mil) troop; (soldados) soldiers pl; (soldados rasos) ranks pl; (gentío) mob

tropel [tro'pel] nm (muchedumbre) crowd; (prisa) rush; (montón) throng; **acudir (etc) en ~** to come (etc) in a mad rush

tropelía [trope'lia] nm outrage

tropezar [trope'θar] vi to trip, stumble; (fig) to slip up; **tropezarse** vr (dos personas) to run into each other; **~ con** (encontrar) to run into; (topar con) to bump into

tropezón [tro'pe'θon] *nm* trip; *(fig)* blunder; *(traspié)*: **dar un ~** to trip

tropical [tropi'kal] *adj* tropical

trópico ['tropiko] *nm* tropic

tropiezo *etc* [tro'pjeθo] *vb ver* **tropezar** ▷ *nm* *(error)* slip, blunder; *(desgracia)* misfortune; *(revés)* setback; *(obstáculo)* snag; *(discusión)* quarrel

trotamundos [trota'mundos] *nm inv* globetrotter

trotar [tro'tar] *vi* to trot; *(viajar)* to travel about

trote ['trote] *nm* trot; *(fam)* travelling; **de mucho ~** hard-wearing

trozar [tro'θar] *vt (Am)* to cut up, cut into pieces

trozo ['troθo] *nm* bit, piece; *(Lit, Mus)* passage; **a ~s** in bits

trucha ['trutʃa] *nf (pez)* trout; *(Tec)* crane

truco ['truko] *nm (habilidad)* knack; *(engaño)* trick; *(Cine)* trick effect *o* photography; **trucos** *nmpl* billiards *sg*; **~ publicitario** advertising gimmick

trueno ['trweno] *vb ver* **tronar** ▷ *nm (gen)* thunder; *(estampido)* boom; *(de arma)* bang

trueque ['trweke] *vb ver* **trocar** ▷ *nm* exchange; *(Com)* barter

trufa ['trufa] *nf (Bot)* truffle; *(fig: fam)* fib

truhán, -ana [tru'an, ana] *nm/f* rogue

truncar [trun'kar] *vt (cortar)* to truncate; *(la vida etc)* to cut short; *(el desarrollo)* to stunt

tu [tu] *adj* your

tú [tu] *pron* you

tubérculo [tu'βerkulo] *nm (Bot)* tuber

tuberculosis [tuβerku'losis] *nf inv* tuberculosis

tubería [tuβe'ria] *nf* pipes *pl*, piping; *(conducto)* pipeline

tubo ['tuβo] *nm* tube, pipe; **~ de desagüe** drainpipe; **~ de ensayo** test-tube; **~ de escape** exhaust (pipe); **~ digestivo** alimentary canal

tuerca ['twerka] *nf (Tec)* nut

tuerto, -a ['twerto, a] *adj (torcido)* twisted; *(ciego)* blind in one eye ▷ *nm/f* one-eyed person ▷ *nm (ofensa)* wrong; **a tuertas** upside-down

tuerza *etc* ['twerθa] *vb ver* **torcer**

tuétano ['twetano] *nm (Anat: médula)* marrow; *(Bot)* pith; **hasta los ~s** through and through, utterly

tufo ['tufo] *nm* vapour; *(fig: pey)* stench

tugurio [tu'ɣurjo] *nm* slum

tul [tul] *nm* tulle

tulipán [tuli'pan] *nm* tulip

tullido, -a [tu'ʎiðo, a] *adj* crippled; *(cansado)* exhausted

tumba ['tumba] *nf (sepultura)* tomb; *(sacudida)* shake; *(voltereta)* somersault; **ser (como) una ~** to keep one's mouth shut

tumbar [tum'bar] *vt* to knock down; *(doblar)* to knock over; *(fam: suj: olor)* to overpower

▷ *vi* to fall down; **tumbarse** *vr (echarse)* to lie down; *(extenderse)* to stretch out

tumbo ['tumbo] *nm (caída)* fall; *(de vehículo)* jolt; *(momento crítico)* critical moment; **dar ~s** to stagger

tumbona [tum'bona] *nf (butaca)* easy chair; *(de playa: para acostarse)* lounger; *(para sentarse)* deckchair (Brit), beach chair (US)

tumor [tu'mor] *nm* tumour

tumulto [tu'multo] *nm* turmoil; *(Pol: motín)* riot

tuna ['tuna] *nf (Mus)* student music group; *ver tb* **tuno**; *see note*

A *tuna* is made up of university students, or quite often former students, who dress up in costumes from the *Edad de Oro*, the Spanish Golden Age. These musical troupes go through the town playing their guitars, lutes and tambourines and serenade the young ladies in the halls of residence, or make impromptu appearances at weddings or parties singing traditional Spanish songs for a few pesetas.

tunante [tu'nante] *adj* rascally ▷ *nm* rogue, villain; **¡~!** you villain!

tunda ['tunda] *nf (de tela)* shearing; *(de golpes)* beating

túnel ['tunel] *nm* tunnel

Túnez ['tuneθ] *nm* Tunis

tuning ['tunin] *nm (Auto)* car styling, modding *(inf)*

tuno, -a ['tuno, a] *nm/f (fam)* rogue ▷ *nm (Mus)* member of a "tuna"; *ver* **tuna**

tuntún [tun'tun]: **al ~** *adv* thoughtlessly

tupé [tu'pe] *nm* quiff

tupido, -a [tu'piðo, a] *adj (denso)* dense; *(fig: torpe)* dim; *(tela)* close-woven

turba ['turβa] *nf (combustible)* turf; *(muchedumbre)* crowd

turbación [turβa'θjon] *nf (molestia)* disturbance; *(preocupación)* worry

turbado, -a [tur'βaðo, a] *adj (molesto)* disturbed; *(preocupado)* worried

turbante [tur'βante] *nm* turban

turbar [tur'βar] *vt (molestar)* to disturb; *(incomodar)* to upset; **turbarse** *vr* to be disturbed

turbina [tur'βina] *nf* turbine

turbio, -a ['turβjo, a] *adj (agua etc)* cloudy; *(vista)* dim, blurred; *(tema)* unclear, confused; *(negocio)* shady ▷ *adv* indistinctly

turbo ['turβo] *adj inv* turbo(-charged) ▷ *nm (tb coche)* turbo

turbulencia [turβu'lenθja] *nf* turbulence; *(fig)* restlessness

turbulento, -a [turβu'lento, a] *adj* turbulent; *(fig: intranquilo)* restless; *(: ruidoso)* noisy

turco, -a ['turko, a] *adj* Turkish ▷ *nm/f* Turk ▷ *nm* (*Ling*) Turkish

turismo [tu'rismo] *nm* tourism; (*coche*) saloon car; **hacer ~** to go travelling (abroad)

turista [tu'rista] *nm/f* tourist; (*vacacionista*) holidaymaker (*Brit*), vacationer (*US*)

turístico, -a [tu'ristiko, a] *adj* tourist *cpd*

turnar [tur'nar] *vi*, **turnarse** *vr* to take (it in) turns

turno ['turno] *nm* (*de trabajo*) shift; (*oportunidad, orden de prioridad*) opportunity; (*Deporte etc*) turn; **es su ~** it's his turn (next); **~ de día/de noche** day/night shift

turquesa [tur'kesa] *nf* turquoise

Turquía [tur'kia] *nf* Turkey

turrón [tu'rron] *nm* (*dulce*) nougat; (*fam*) sinecure, cushy job *o* number

tute ['tute] *nm* (*Naipes*) card game; **darse un ~** to break one's back

tutear [tute'ar] *vt* to address as familiar "tú"; **tutearse** *vr* to be on familiar terms

tutela [tu'tela] *nf* (*legal*) guardianship; (*Instrucción*) guidance; **estar bajo la ~ de** (*fig*) to be under the protection of

tutelar [tute'lar] *adj* tutelary ▷ *vt* to protect

tutor, a [tu'tor, a] *nm/f* (*legal*) guardian; (*Escol*) tutor; **~ de curso** form master/mistress

tuve *etc* ['tuβe] *vb ver* **tener**

tuviera *etc vb ver* **tener**

tuyo, -a ['tujo, a] *adj* yours, of yours ▷ *pron* yours; **un amigo ~** a friend of yours; **los ~s** (*fam*) your relations, your family

TV *nf abr* (= *televisión*) TV

TVE *nf abr* = **Televisión Española**

u [u] *conj* or

ubicado, -a [uβi'kaðo, a] *adj* (*esp Am*) situated

ubicar [uβi'kar] *vt* (*esp Am*) to place, situate; (: *fig*) to install in a post; (: *encontrar*) to find; **ubicarse** *vr* to be situated, be located

ubre ['uβre] *nf* udder

UCI ['uθi] *sigla f* (= *Unidad de Cuidados Intensivos*) ICU

Ud(s) *abr* = **usted(es)**

UE *nf abr* (= *Unión Europea*) EU

UEFA [w'efa] *nf abr* (= *Unión de Asociaciones de Fútbol Europeo*) UEFA

UEO *nf abr* (= *Unión Europea Occidental*) WEU

ufanarse [ufa'narse] *vr* to boast; **~ de** to pride o.s. on

ufano, -a [u'fano, a] *adj* (*arrogante*) arrogant; (*presumido*) conceited

UGT *nf abr ver* **Unión General de Trabajadores**

ujier [u'xjer] *nm* usher; (*portero*) doorkeeper

úlcera ['ulθera] *nf* ulcer

ulcerar [ulθe'rar] *vt* to make sore; **ulcerarse** *vr* to ulcerate

ulterior [ulte'rjor] *adj* (*más allá*) farther, further; (*subsecuente, siguiente*) subsequent

últimamente ['ultimamente] *adv* (*recientemente*) lately, recently; (*finalmente*) finally; (*como último recurso*) as a last resort

ultimar [ulti'mar] *vt* to finish; (*finalizar*) to finalize; (*Am*: *matar*) to kill

ultimátum [ulti'matum] *nm* (*pl* **ultimátums**) ultimatum

último, -a ['ultimo, a] adj last; (más reciente) latest, most recent; (más bajo) bottom; (más alto) top; (fig) final, extreme; **en las últimas** on one's last legs; **por ~** finally

ultra ['ultra] adj ultra ▷ nm/f extreme right-winger

ultracongelar [ultrakonxe'lar] vt to deep-freeze

ultraderecha [ultraðe'retʃa] nf extreme right (wing)

ultrajar [ultra'xar] vt (escandalizar) to outrage; (insultar) to insult, abuse

ultraje [ul'traxe] nm outrage; insult

ultraligero [ultrali'xero] nm microlight (Brit), microlite (US)

ultramar [ultra'mar] nm: **de** o **en ~** abroad, overseas; **los países de ~** the overseas countries

ultramarino, -a [ultrama'rino, a] adj overseas, foreign ▷ nmpl: **~s** groceries; **tienda de ~s** grocer's (shop)

ultranza [ul'tranθa]: **a ~** adv to the death; (a toda costa) at all costs; (completo) outright; (Pol etc) out-and-out, extreme; **un nacionalista a ~** a rabid nationalist

ultrasónico, -a [ultra'soniko, a] adj ultrasonic

ultratumba [ultra'tumba] nf: **la vida de ~** the next life; **una voz de ~** a ghostly voice

ultravioleta [ultraβjo'leta] adj inv ultraviolet

ulular [ulu'lar] vi to howl; (búho) to hoot

umbilical [umbili'kal] adj: **cordón ~** umbilical cord

umbral [um'bral] nm (gen) threshold; **~ de rentabilidad** (Com) break-even point

UME nf abr (= Unión Monetaria y Económica) EMU

🅞 PALABRA CLAVE

un, una [un, 'una] 1 artículo indefinido a; (antes de vocal) an; **una mujer/naranja** a woman/an orange

2 **unos** (o **unas**): **hay unos regalos para ti** there are some presents for you; **hay unas cervezas en la nevera** there are some beers in the fridge; ver tb **uno**

3 (enfático): **¡hace un frío!** it's so cold!; **¡tiene una casa!** he's got some house!

unánime [u'nanime] adj unanimous

unanimidad [unanimi'ðað] nf unanimity; **por ~** unanimously

unción [un'θjon] nf anointing

undécimo, -a [un'deθimo, a] adj, nm/f eleventh

UNED [u'ned] nf abr (Esp Univ: = Universidad Nacional de Enseñanza a Distancia) ≈ Open University (Brit)

ungir [un'xir] vt to rub with ointment; (Rel) to anoint

ungüento [un'gwento] nm ointment; (fig) salve, balm

únicamente ['unikamente] adv solely; (solamente) only

único, -a ['uniko, a] adj only; (solo) sole, single; (sin par) unique; **hijo ~** only child

unidad [uni'ðað] nf unity; (Tec) unit; **~ móvil** (TV) mobile unit; (Inform): **~ central** system unit, central processing unit; **~ de control** control unit; **~ de disco** disk drive; **~ de entrada/salida** input/output device; **~ de información** data item; **~ periférica** peripheral device; **~ de presentación visual** o **de visualización** visual display unit; **~ procesadora central** central processing unit

unido, -a [u'niðo, a] adj joined, linked; (fig) united

unifamiliar [unifamil'jar] adj: **vivienda ~** single-family home

unificar [unifi'kar] vt to unite, unify

uniformar [unifor'mar] vt to make uniform; (persona) to put into uniform; (Tec) to standardize

uniforme [uni'forme] adj uniform, equal; (superficie) even ▷ nm uniform

uniformidad [uniformi'ðað] nf uniformity; (llaneza) levelness, evenness

unilateral [unilate'ral] adj unilateral

unión [u'njon] nf (gen) union; (acto) uniting, joining; (calidad) unity; (Tec) joint; (fig) closeness, togetherness; **en ~ con** (together) with, accompanied by; **~ aduanera** customs union; **U~ General de Trabajadores (UGT)** (Esp) Socialist Union Confederation; **U~ Europea** European Union; **la U~ Soviética** the Soviet Union; **punto de ~** (Tec) junction

unir [u'nir] vt (juntar) to join, unite; (atar) to tie, fasten; (combinar) to combine ▷ vi (ingredientes) to mix well; **unirse** vr to join together, unite; (empresas) to merge; **les une una fuerte simpatía** they are bound by (a) strong affection; **~se en matrimonio** to marry

unisex [uni'seks] adj inv unisex

unísono [u'nisono] nm: **al ~** in unison

universal [uniβer'sal] adj universal; (mundial) world cpd; **historia ~** world history

universidad [uniβersi'ðað] nf university; **~ laboral** polytechnic, poly

universitario, -a [uniβersi'tarjo, a] adj university cpd ▷ nm/f (profesor) lecturer; (estudiante) (university) student; (graduado) graduate

universo [uni'βerso] nm universe

🅞 PALABRA CLAVE

uno, -a ['uno, a] adj one; **es todo uno** it's all one and the same; **unos pocos** a few; **unos cien** about a hundred

▷ pron 1 one; **quiero uno solo** I only want one; **uno de ellos** one of them; **una de dos** either one or the other; **no doy una hoy**

I can't do anything right today **2** (*alguien*) somebody, someone; **conozco a uno que se te parece** I know somebody o someone who looks like you; **unos querían quedarse** some (people) wanted to stay **3** (*impersonal*) one; **uno mismo** oneself; **uno nunca sabe qué hacer** one never knows what to do
4: **unos ... otros ...** some ... others; **una y otra son muy agradables** they're both very nice; **(los) uno(s) a (los) otro(s)** each other, one another
▷ *nf* one; **es la una** it's one o'clock
▷ *num* (number) one; **el día uno** the first; *ver tb* **un**

untar [un'tar] *vt* (*gen*) to rub; (*mantequilla*) to spread; (*engrasar*) to grease, oil; (*Med*) to rub (with ointment); (*fig*) to bribe; **untarse** *vr* (*fig*) to be crooked; **~ el pan con mantequilla** to spread butter on one's bread
uña ['uɲa] *nf* (*Anat*) nail; (*del pie*) toenail; (*garra*) claw; (*casco*) hoof; (*arrancaclavos*) claw; **ser ~ y carne** to be as thick as thieves; **enseñar** o **mostrar** o **sacar las ~s** to show one's claws
uperizado, -a [uperi'θaðo, a] *adj*: **leche uperizada** UHT milk
uralita® [ura'lita] *nf* corrugated asbestos cement
uranio [u'ranjo] *nm* uranium
urbanidad [urβani'ðað] *nf* courtesy, politeness
urbanismo [urβa'nismo] *nm* town planning
urbanización [urβaniθa'θjon] *nf* (*colonia, barrio*) estate, housing scheme
urbanizar [urβani'θar] *vt* (*zona*) to develop, urbanize
urbano, -a [ur'βano, a] *adj* (*de ciudad*) urban, town *cpd*; (*cortés*) courteous, polite
urbe ['urβe] *nf* large city, metropolis
urdimbre [ur'ðimbre] *nf* (*de tejido*) warp; (*intriga*) intrigue
urdir [ur'ðir] *vt* to warp; (*fig*) to plot, contrive
urgencia [ur'xenθja] *nf* urgency; (*prisa*) haste, rush; (*emergencia*) emergency; **salida de ~** emergency exit; **servicios de ~** emergency services; **"U~s"** "Casualty"
urgente [ur'xente] *adj* urgent; (*insistente*) insistent; **carta ~** registered (*Brit*) o special delivery (*US*) letter
urgir [ur'xir] *vi* to be urgent; **me urge** I'm in a hurry for it; **me urge terminarlo** I must finish it as soon as I can
urinario, -a [uri'narjo, a] *adj* urinary ▷ *nm* urinal, public lavatory, comfort station (*US*)
urna ['urna] *nf* urn; (*Pol*) ballot box; **acudir a las ~s** (*fig: persona*) to (go and) vote; (*: gobierno*) to go to the country
urología [urolo'xia] *nf* urology
urraca [u'rraka] *nf* magpie

URSS *nf abr* (*Historia*: = *Unión de Repúblicas Socialistas Soviéticas*) USSR
Uruguay [uru'ɣwai] *nm*: **El ~** Uruguay
uruguayo, -a [uru'ɣwajo, a] *adj, nm/f* Uruguayan
usado, -a [u'saðo, a] *adj* (*gen*) used; (*ropa etc*) worn; **muy ~** worn out; (*de segunda mano*) secondhand
usanza [u'sanθa] *nf* custom, usage
usar [u'sar] *vt* to use; (*ropa*) to wear; (*tener costumbre*) to be in the habit of ▷ *vi*: **~ de** to make use of; **usarse** *vr* to be used; (*ropa*) to be worn o in fashion
uso ['uso] *nm* use; (*Mecánica etc*) wear; (*costumbre*) usage, custom; (*moda*) fashion; **al ~** in keeping with custom; **al ~ de** in the style of; **de ~ externo** (*Med*) for external use; **estar en el ~ de la palabra** to be speaking, have the floor; **~ y desgaste** (*Com*) wear and tear
usted [us'teð] *pron* (*sg formal*: *abr* **Ud** o **Vd**) you *sg*; **~es** (*pl formal*: *abr* **Uds** o **Vds**) you *pl*; (*Am: formal y fam*) you *pl*
usual [u'swal] *adj* usual
usuario, -a [u'swarjo, a] *nm/f* user; **~ final** (*Com*) end user
usufructo [usu'frukto] *nm* use; **~ vitalicio (de)** life interest (in)
usura [u'sura] *nf* usury
usurero, -a [usu'rero, a] *nm/f* usurer
usurpar [usur'par] *vt* to usurp
utensilio [uten'siljo] *nm* tool; (*Culin*) utensil
útero ['utero] *nm* uterus, womb
útil ['util] *adj* useful; (*servible*) usable, serviceable ▷ *nm* tool; **día ~** working day, weekday; **es muy ~ tenerlo aquí cerca** it's very handy having it here close by
utilidad [utili'ðað] *nf* usefulness, utility; (*Com*) profit; **~es líquidas** net profit *sg*
utilizar [utili'θar] *vt* to use, utilize; (*explotar*) to harness
utopía [uto'pia] *nf* Utopia
utópico, -a [u'topiko, a] *adj* Utopian
uva ['uβa] *nf* grape; **~ pasa** raisin; **~ de Corinto** currant; **estar de mala ~** to be in a bad mood; *see note*

UVA
In Spain *las uvas* play a big part on New Years' Eve (*Nochevieja*), when on the stroke of midnight people from every part of Spain, at home, in restaurants or in the plaza mayor eat a grape for each stroke of the clock of the Puerta del Sol in Madrid. It is said to bring luck for the following year.

UVI ['uβi] *nf abr* (*Esp Med*: = *unidad de vigilancia intensiva*) ICU

V

v. abr (= voltio) v; (= ver, véase) v.; (Lit: = verso) v
va [ba] vb ver **ir**
vaca ['baka] nf (animal) cow; (carne) beef; (cuero) cowhide; **~s flacas/gordas** (fig) bad/good times
vacaciones [baka'θjones] nfpl holiday(s); **estar/irse o marcharse de ~** to be/go (away) on holiday
vacante [ba'kante] adj vacant, empty ▷ nf vacancy
vaciar [ba'θjar] vt to empty (out); (ahuecar) to hollow out; (moldear) to cast; (Inform) to dump ▷ vi (río): **~ en** to flow into; **vaciarse** vr to empty; (fig) to blab, spill the beans
vaciedad [baθje'ðað] nf emptiness
vacilación [baθila'θjon] nf hesitation
vacilante [baθi'lante] adj unsteady; (habla) faltering; (luz) flickering; (fig) hesitant
vacilar [baθi'lar] vi to be unsteady; to falter; to flicker; to hesitate, waver; (persona) to stagger, stumble; (memoria) to fail; (esp Am: divertirse) to have a great time
vacilón [baθi'lon] nm (esp Am): **estar o ir de ~** to have a great time
vacío, -a [ba'θio, a] adj empty; (puesto) vacant; (desocupado) idle; (vano) vain; (charla etc) light, superficial ▷ nm emptiness; (Física) vacuum; (un vacío) (empty) space; **hacer el ~ a algn** to send sb to Coventry
vacuna [ba'kuna] nf vaccine
vacunar [baku'nar] vt to vaccinate; **vacunarse** vr to get vaccinated

vacuno, -a [ba'kuno, a] adj bovine; **ganado ~** cattle
vacuo, -a ['bakwo, a] adj empty
vadear [baðe'ar] vt (río) to ford; (problema) to overcome; (persona) to sound out
vado ['baðo] nm ford; (solución) solution; (descanso) respite; **"~ permanente"** "keep clear"
vagabundo, -a [baɣa'βundo, a] adj wandering; (pey) vagrant ▷ nm/f (errante) wanderer; (vago) tramp, bum (US)
vagamente [baɣa'mente] adv vaguely
vagancia [ba'ɣanθja] nf (pereza) idleness, laziness; (vagabundeo) vagrancy
vagar [ba'ɣar] vi to wander; (pasear) to saunter up and down; (no hacer nada) to idle ▷ nm leisure
vagina [ba'xina] nf vagina
vago, -a ['baɣo, a] adj vague; (perezoso) lazy; (ambulante) wandering ▷ nm/f (vagabundo) tramp, bum (US); (perezoso) lazybones sg, idler
vagón [ba'ɣon] nm (de pasajeros) carriage; (de mercancías) wagon; **~ cama/restaurante** sleeping/dining car
vaguear [baɣe'ar] vi to laze around
vaguedad [baɣe'ðað] nf vagueness
vaho ['bao] nm (vapor) vapour, steam; (olor) smell; (respiración) breath; **vahos** nmpl (Med) inhalation sg
vaina ['baina] nf sheath ▷ nm (Am) nuisance
vainilla [bai'niʎa] nf vanilla
vainita [bai'nita] nf (Am) green o French bean
vais [bais] vb ver **ir**
vaivén [bai'βen] nm to-and-fro movement; (de tránsito) coming and going; **vaivenes** nmpl (fig) ups and downs
vajilla [ba'xiʎa] nf crockery, dishes pl; (una vajilla) service; **~ de porcelana** chinaware
valdré etc vb ver **valer**
vale ['bale] nm voucher; (recibo) receipt; (pagaré) I.O.U.; **~ de regalo** gift voucher o token
valedero, -a [bale'ðero, a] adj valid
valenciano, -a [balen'θjano, a] adj, nm/f Valencian ▷ nm (Ling) Valencian
valentía [balen'tia] nf courage, bravery; (pey) boastfulness; (acción) heroic deed
valentón, -ona [balen'ton, ona] adj blustering
valer [ba'ler] vt to be worth; (Mat) to equal; (costar) to cost; (amparar) to aid, protect ▷ vi (ser útil) to be useful; (ser válido) to be valid; **valerse** vr to take care of o.s. ▷ nm worth, value; **~ la pena** to be worthwhile; **¿vale?** O.K.?; **¡vale!** (¡basta!) that'll do!; **¡eso no vale!** that doesn't count!; **no vale nada** it's no good; (mercancía) it's worthless; (argumento) it's no use; **no vale para nada** he's no good at all; **más vale tarde que nunca** better late than never; **más vale que nos vayamos** we'd better go; **~se de** to make use of, take advantage of; **~se por sí mismo** to help o

manage by o.s.; **¡eso a mí no me vale!** (*Am:
fam: no importar*) I couldn't care less about that
valeroso, -a [bale'roso, a] *adj* brave, valiant
valgo *etc* ['balɣo] *vb ver* **valer**
valía [ba'lia] *nf* worth; **de gran ~** (*objeto*) very
valuable
validar [bali'ðar] *vt* to validate; (*Pol*) to ratify
validez [bali'ðeθ] *nf* validity; **dar ~ a** to
validate
válido, -a ['baliðo, a] *adj* valid
valiente [ba'ljente] *adj* brave, valiant; (*audaz*)
bold; (*pey*) boastful; (*con ironía*) fine,
wonderful ▷ *nm/f* brave man/woman
valija [ba'lixa] *nf* case; (*Am*) suitcase;
(*mochila*) satchel; (*Correos*) mailbag;
~ diplomática diplomatic bag
valioso, -a [ba'ljoso, a] *adj* valuable; (*rico*)
wealthy
valla ['baʎa] *nf* fence; (*Deporte*) hurdle; (*fig*)
barrier; **~ publicitaria** hoarding (*esp Brit*),
billboard (*esp US*)
vallar [ba'ʎar] *vt* to fence in
valle ['baʎe] *nm* valley, vale
valor [ba'lor] *nm* value, worth; (*precio*) price;
(*valentía*) valour, courage; (*importancia*)
importance; (*cara*) nerve, cheek (*fam*); **sin ~**
worthless; **~ adquisitivo** *o* **de compra**
purchasing power; **dar ~ a** to attach
importance to; **quitar ~ a** to minimize the
importance of; (*Com*): **~ según balance** book
value; **~ comercial** *o* **de mercado** market
value; **~ contable/desglosado** asset/break-
up value; **~ de escasez** scarcity value;
~ intrínseco intrinsic value; **~ a la par** par
value; **~ neto** net worth; **~ de rescate/de
sustitución** surrender/replacement value;
ver tb **valores**
valoración [balora'θjon] *nf* valuation
valorar [balo'rar] *vt* to value; (*tasar*) to price;
(*fig*) to assess
valores [ba'lores] *nmpl* (*Com*) securities; **~ en
cartera** *o* **habidos** investments
vals [bals] *nm* waltz
válvula ['balβula] *nf* valve
vamos ['bamos] *vb ver* **ir**
vampiro, -iresa [bam'piro, i'resa] *nm/ʃ*
vampire ▷ (*Cine*) vamp, femme fatale
van [ban] *vb ver* **ir**
vanagloriarse [banaɣlo'rjarse] *vr* to boast
vandalismo [banda'lismo] *nm* vandalism
vándalo, -a ['bandalo, a] *nm/f* vandal
vanguardia [ban'gwardja] *nf* vanguard; **de
~** (*Arte*) avant-garde; **estar en** *o* **ir a la ~ de**
(*fig*) to be in the forefront of
vanguardista [bangwar'ðista] *adj* avant-
garde
vanidad [bani'ðað] *nf* vanity; (*inutilidad*)
futility; (*irrealidad*) unreality
vanidoso, -a [bani'ðoso, a] *adj* vain,
conceited
vano, -a ['bano, a] *adj* (*irreal*) unreal;
(*irracional*) unreasonable; (*inútil*) vain, useless;

(*persona*) vain, conceited; (*frívolo*) frivolous
vapor [ba'por] *nm* vapour; (*vaho*) steam; (*de
gas*) fumes *pl*; (*neblina*) mist; **vapores** *nmpl*
(*Med*) hysterics; **al ~** (*Culin*) steamed; **~ de
agua** water vapour
vaporizador [baporiθa'ðor] *nm* (*de perfume
etc*) spray
vaporizar [bapori'θar] *vt* to vaporize;
(*perfume*) to spray
vaporoso, -a [bapo'roso, a] *adj* vaporous;
(*vahoso*) steamy; (*tela*) light, airy
vapulear [bapule'ar] *vt* to thrash; (*fig*) to
slate
vaquero, -a [ba'kero, a] *adj* cattle *cpd* ▷ *nm*
cowboy; **vaqueros** *nmpl* jeans
vaquilla [ba'kiʎa] *nf* heifer
vara ['bara] *nf* stick, pole; (*Tec*) rod; **~ mágica**
magic wand
variable [ba'rjaβle] *adj, nf* variable (*tb Inform*)
variación [barja'θjon] *nf* variation; **sin ~**
unchanged
variado, -a [ba'rjaðo, a] *adj* varied; (*dulces,
galletas*) assorted; **entremeses ~s** a selection
of starters
variante [ba'rjante] *adj* variant ▷ *nf*
(*alternativa*) alternative; (*Auto*) bypass
variar [ba'rjar] *vt* (*cambiar*) to change; (*poner
variedad*) to vary; (*modificar*) to modify;
(*cambiar de posición*) to switch around ▷ *vi* to
vary; **~ de** to differ from; **~ de opinión** to
change one's mind; **para ~** just for a change
varicela [bari'θela] *nf* chicken pox
varices [ba'riθes] *nfpl* varicose veins
variedad [barje'ðað] *nf* variety
varilla [ba'riʎa] *nf* stick; (*Bot*) twig; (*Tec*) rod;
(*de rueda*) spoke; **~ mágica** magic wand
vario, -a ['barjo, a] *adj* (*variado*) varied;
(*multicolor*) motley; (*cambiable*) changeable; **~s**
various, several
variopinto, -a [barjo'pinto, a] *adj* diverse;
un público ~ a mixed audience
varita [ba'rita] *nf*: **~ mágica** magic wand
varón [ba'ron] *nm* male, man
varonil [baro'nil] *adj* manly
Varsovia [bar'soβja] *nf* Warsaw
vas [bas] *vb ver* **ir**
vasco, -a ['basko, a], **vascongado a**
[baskon'gaðo, a] *adj, nm/f* Basque ▷ *nm* (*Ling*)
Basque ▷ *nfpl*: **las V~ngadas** the Basque
Country *sg* o Provinces
vascuence [bas'kwenθe] *nm* (*Ling*) Basque
vasectomía [basekto'mia] *nf* vasectomy
vaselina [base'lina] *nf* Vaseline®
vasija [ba'sixa] *nf* (earthenware) vessel
vaso ['baso] *nm* glass, tumbler; (*Anat*) vessel;
(*cantidad*) glass(ful); **~ de vino** glass of wine;
~ para vino wineglass
vástago ['bastaɣo] *nm* (*Bot*) shoot; (*Tec*) rod;
(*fig*) offspring
vasto, -a ['basto, a] *adj* vast, huge
Vaticano [bati'kano] *nm*: **el ~** the Vatican;
la Ciudad del ~ the Vatican City

V

vaticinio [bati'θinjo] nm prophecy
vatio ['batjo] nm (*Elec*) watt
vaya etc ['baja] vb ver **ir**
Vd abr = **usted**
Vds abr = **ustedes**
ve [be] vb ver **ir, ver**
vecindad [beθin'dað] nf, **vecindario**
[beθin'darjo] nm neighbourhood; (*habitantes*)
residents pl
vecino, -a [be'θino, a] adj neighbouring
▷ nm/f neighbour; (*residente*) resident; **somos
~s** we live next door to one another
vector [bek'tor] nm vector
veda ['beða] nf prohibition; (*temporada*) close
season
vedado [be'ðaðo] nm preserve
vedar [be'ðar] vt (*prohibir*) to ban, prohibit;
(*idea, plan*) to veto; (*impedir*) to stop, prevent
vega ['beɣa] nf fertile plain o valley
vegetación [bexeta'θjon] nf vegetation
vegetal [bexe'tal] adj, nm vegetable
vegetar [bexe'tar] vi to vegetate
vegetariano, -a [bexeta'rjano, a] adj, nm/f
vegetarian
vegetativo, -a [bexeta'tiβo, a] adj
vegetative
vehemencia [bee'menθja] nf (*insistencia*)
vehemence; (*pasión*) passion; (*fervor*) fervour;
(*violencia*) violence
vehemente [bee'mente] adj vehement;
passionate; fervent; violent
vehículo [be'ikulo] nm vehicle; (*Med*) carrier;
~ de servicio público public service vehicle;
~ espacial spacecraft
veía etc vb ver **ver**
veinte ['beinte] num twenty; (*orden, fecha*)
twentieth; **el siglo ~** the twentieth century
vejación [bexa'θjon] nf vexation; (*humillación*)
humiliation
vejar [be'xar] vt (*irritar*) to annoy, vex;
(*humillar*) to humiliate
vejatorio, -a [bexa'torjo, a] adj humiliating,
degrading
vejez [be'xeθ] nf old age
vejiga [be'xiɣa] nf (*Anat*) bladder
vela ['bela] nf (*de cera*) candle; (*Naut*) sail;
(*insomnio*) sleeplessness; (*vigilia*) vigil; (*Mil*)
sentry duty; (*fam*) snot; **a toda ~** (*Naut*) under
full sail; **estar a dos ~s** (*fam*) to be skint;
pasar la noche en ~ to have a sleepless night
velado, -a [be'laðo, a] adj veiled; (*sonido*)
muffled; (*Foto*) blurred ▷ nf soirée
velador [bela'ðor] nm watchman; (*candelero*)
candlestick; (*Am*) bedside table
velar [be'lar] vt (*vigilar*) to keep watch over;
(*cubrir*) to veil ▷ vi to stay awake; **~ por** to
watch over, look after
velatorio [bela'torjo] nm (funeral) wake
veleidad [belei'ðað] nf (*ligereza*) fickleness;
(*capricho*) whim
velero [be'lero] nm (*Naut*) sailing ship; (*Aviat*)
glider

veleta [be'leta] nm/f fickle person ▷ nf
weather vane
veliz [be'lis] nm (*Am*) suitcase
vello ['beʎo] nm down, fuzz
velo ['belo] nm veil; **~ de paladar** (*Anat*) soft
palate
velocidad [beloθi'ðað] nf speed; (*Tec*) rate,
pace, velocity; (*Mecánica, Auto*) gear; **¿a qué ~?**
how fast?; **de alta ~** high-speed; **cobrar ~** to
pick up o gather speed; **meter la segunda ~**
to change into second gear; **~ máxima de
impresión** (*Inform*) maximum print speed
velocímetro [belo'θimetro] nm speedometer
velorio [be'lorjo] nm (*Am*) (funeral) wake
veloz [be'loθ] adj fast, swift
ven [ben] vb ver **venir**
vena ['bena] nf vein; (*fig*) vein, disposition;
(*Geo*) seam, vein
venado [be'naðo] nm deer; (*Culin*) venison
vencedor, a [benθe'ðor, a] adj victorious
▷ nm/f victor, winner
vencer [ben'θer] vt (*dominar*) to defeat, beat;
(*derrotar*) to vanquish; (*superar, controlar*) to
overcome, master ▷ vi (*triunfar*) to win
(through), triumph; (*pago*) to fall due; (*plazo*)
to expire; **dejarse ~** to yield, give in
vencido, -a [ben'θiðo, a] adj (*derrotado*)
defeated, beaten; (*Com*) payable, due ▷ adv:
pagar ~ to pay in arrears; **le pagan por
meses ~s** he is paid at the end of the month;
darse por ~ to give up
vencimiento [benθi'mjento] nm collapse;
(*Com: de plazo*) expiration; **a su ~** when it falls
due
venda ['benda] nf bandage
vendaje [ben'daxe] nm bandage, dressing
vendar [ben'dar] vt to bandage; **~ los ojos** to
blindfold
vendaval [benda'βal] nm (*viento*) gale;
(*huracán*) hurricane
vendedor, a [bende'ðor, a] nm/f seller;
~ ambulante hawker, pedlar (*Brit*), peddler
(*US*)
vender [ben'der] vt to sell; (*comerciar*) to
market; (*traicionar*) to sell out, betray;
venderse vr (*estar a la venta*) to be on sale; **~ al
contado/al por mayor/al por menor/a
plazos** to sell for cash/wholesale/retail/on
credit; **"se vende"** "for sale"; **"véndese
coche"** "car for sale"; **~ al descubierto** to
sell short
vendimia [ben'dimja] nf grape harvest; **la ~
de 1973** the 1973 vintage
vendimiar [bendi'mjar] vi to pick grapes
vendré etc [ben'dre] vb ver **venir**
veneno [be'neno] nm poison; (*de serpiente*)
venom
venenoso, -a [bene'noso, a] adj poisonous;
venomous
venerable [bene'raβle] adj venerable
venerar [bene'rar] vt (*respetar*) to revere;
(*reconocer*) to venerate; (*adorar*) to worship

venéreo, -a [be'nereo, a] *adj* venereal; **enfermedad venérea** venereal disease

venezolano, -a [beneθo'lano, a] *adj, nm/f* Venezuelan

Venezuela [bene'θwela] *nf* Venezuela

venganza [ben'ganθa] *nf* vengeance, revenge

vengar [ben'gar] *vt* to avenge; **vengarse** *vr* to take revenge

vengativo, -a [benga'tiβo, a] *adj* (*persona*) vindictive

vengo *etc vb ver* **venir**

venia ['benja] *nf* (*perdón*) pardon; (*permiso*) consent; **con su ~** by your leave

venial [be'njal] *adj* venial

venida [be'niða] *nf* (*llegada*) arrival; (*regreso*) return; (*fig*) rashness

venidero, -a [beni'ðero, a] *adj* coming, future; **en lo ~** in (the) future

venir [be'nir] *vi* to come; (*llegar*) to arrive; (*ocurrir*) to happen; **venirse** *vr*: **~se abajo** to collapse; **a menos** (*persona*) to lose status; (*empresa*) to go downhill; **~ bien** to be suitable, come just right; (*ropa, gusto*) to suit; **~ mal** to be unsuitable o inconvenient, come awkwardly; **el año que viene** next year; **¡ven acá!** come (over) here!; **¡venga!** (*fam*) come on!

venta ['benta] *nf* (*Com*) sale; (*posada*) inn; **~ a plazos** hire purchase; **"en ~"** "for sale"; **~ al contado/al por mayor/al por menor** o **al detalle** cash sale/wholesale/retail; **~ a domicilio** door-to-door selling; **~ y arrendamiento al vendedor** sale and lease back; **~ de liquidación** clearance sale; **estar de** o **en ~** to be (up) for sale o on the market; **~s brutas** gross sales; **~s a término** forward sales

ventaja [ben'taxa] *nf* advantage; **llevar la ~** (*en carrera*) to be leading o ahead

ventajoso, -a [benta'xoso, a] *adj* advantageous

ventana [ben'tana] *nf* window; **~ de guillotina/galería** sash/bay window; **~ de la nariz** nostril

ventanilla [venta'niʎa] *nf* (*de taquilla, tb Inform*) window

ventilación [bentila'θjon] *nf* ventilation; (*corriente*) draught; (*fig*) airing

ventilador [bentila'ðor] *nm* ventilator; (*eléctrico*) fan

ventilar [benti'lar] *vt* to ventilate; (*poner a secar*) to put out to dry; (*fig*) to air, discuss

ventisca [ben'tiska] *nf* blizzard

ventisquero [bentis'kero] *nm* snowdrift

ventosidad [bentosi'ðað] *nf* flatulence

ventoso, -a [ben'toso, a] *adj* windy ▷ *nf* (*Zool*) sucker; (*instrumento*) suction pad

ventrílocuo, -a [ben'trilokwo, a] *nm/f* ventriloquist

ventura [ben'tura] *nf* (*felicidad*) happiness; (*buena suerte*) luck; (*destino*) fortune; **a la**

(buena) ~ at random

venturoso, -a [bentu'roso, a] *adj* happy; (*afortunado*) lucky, fortunate

veo *etc vb ver* **ver**

ver [ber] *vt, vi* to see; (*mirar*) to look at, watch; (*investigar*) to look into; (*entender*) to see, understand; **verse** *vr* (*encontrarse*) to meet; (*dejarse ver*) to be seen; (*hallarse: en un apuro*) to find o.s., be ▷ *nm* looks *pl*, appearance; **a ~** let's see; **a ~ si ...** I wonder if ...; **por lo que veo** apparently; **dejarse ~** to become apparent; **no tener nada que ~ con** to have nothing to do with; **a mi modo de ~** as I see it; **merece ~se** it's worth seeing; **no lo veo** I can't see it; **¡nos vemos!** see you (later)!; **¡habrase visto!** did you ever! (*fam*); **¡viera(n)** o **hubiera(n) visto qué casa!** (*Am: fam*) if only you'd seen the house!, what a house!; **ya se ve que ...** it is obvious that ...; **si te vi no me acuerdo** they *etc* just don't want to know; **ya ~emos** we'll see

vera ['bera] *nf* edge, verge; (*de río*) bank; **a la ~ de** near, next to

veracidad [beraθi'ðað] *nf* truthfulness

veraneante [berane'ante] *nm/f* holidaymaker, (summer) vacationer (US)

veranear [berane'ar] *vi* to spend the summer

veraneo [bera'neo] *nm* summer holiday; **estar de ~** to be away on (one's summer) holiday; **lugar de ~** holiday resort

veraniego, -a [bera'njeɣo, a] *adj* summer *cpd*

verano [be'rano] *nm* summer

veras ['beras] *nfpl* truth *sg*; **de ~** really, truly; **esto va de ~** this is serious

veraz [be'raθ] *adj* truthful

verbal [ber'βal] *adj* verbal; (*mensaje etc*) oral

verbena [ber'βena] *nf* street party; (*baile*) open-air dance

verbo ['berβo] *nm* verb

verboso, -a [ber'βoso, a] *adj* verbose

verdad [ber'ðað] *nf* (*lo verídico*) truth; (*fiabilidad*) reliability ▷ *adv* really; **¿~?, ¿no es ~?** isn't it?, aren't you?, don't you? *etc*; **de ~** *adj* real, proper; **a decir ~, no quiero** to tell (you) the truth, I don't want to; **la pura ~** the plain truth

verdadero, -a [berða'ðero, a] *adj* (*veraz*) true, truthful; (*fiable*) reliable; (*fig*) real

verde ['berðe] *adj* green; (*fruta etc*) green, unripe; (*chiste etc*) blue, smutty, dirty ▷ *nm* green; **viejo ~** dirty old man; **poner ~ a algn** to give sb a dressing-down

verdear [berðe'ar], **verdecer** [berðe'θer] *vi* to turn green

verdor [ber'ðor] *nm* (*lo verde*) greenness; (*Bot*) verdure; (*fig*) youthful vigour

verdugo [ber'ðuɣo] *nm* executioner; (*Bot*) shoot; (*cardenal*) weal

verdulería [berðule'ria] *nf* greengrocer's (shop)

verdulero, -a [berðu'lero, a] *nm/f* greengrocer

verdura [ber'ðura] nf greenness; **verduras** nfpl (Culin) greens

vereda [be'reða] nf path; (Am) pavement, sidewalk (US); **meter a algn en ~** to bring sb into line

veredicto [bere'ðikto] nm verdict

vergel [ber'xel] nm lush garden

vergonzoso, -a [beryon'θoso, a] adj shameful; (tímido) timid, bashful

vergüenza [ber'ɣwenθa] nf shame, sense of shame; (timidez) bashfulness; (pudor) modesty; **tener ~** to be ashamed; **me da ~ decírselo** I feel too shy o it embarrasses me to tell him; **¡qué ~!** (de situación) what a disgrace!; (a persona) shame on you!

verídico, -a [be'riðiko, a] adj true, truthful

verificar [berifi'kar] vt to check; (corroborar) to verify (tb Inform); (testamento) to prove; (llevar a cabo) to carry out; **verificarse** vr to occur, happen; (mitin etc) to be held; (profecía etc) to come o prove true

verja ['berxa] nf (cancela) iron gate; (cerca) railing(s) (pl); (rejado) grating

vermut [ber'mu] (pl **vermuts**) nm vermouth ▷ nf (esp Am) matinée

verosímil [bero'simil] adj likely, probable; (relato) credible

verruga [be'rruɣa] nf wart

versado, -a [ber'saðo, a] adj: **~ en** versed in

versátil [ber'satil] adj versatile

versión [ber'sjon] nf version; (traducción) translation

verso ['berso] nm verse; **un ~** a line of poetry; **~ libre/suelto** free/blank verse

vértebra ['berteβra] nf vertebra

vertebrado, -a [berte'βraðo, a] adj, nm/f vertebrate

vertebral [berte'βral] adj vertebral; **columna ~** spine

verter [ber'ter] vt (vaciar) to empty, pour (out); (sin querer) to spill; (basura) to dump ▷ vi to flow

vertical [berti'kal] adj vertical; (postura, piano etc) upright ▷ nf vertical

vértice ['bertiθe] nm vertex, apex

vertidos [ber'tiðos] nmpl waste sg

vertiente [ber'tjente] nf slope; (fig) aspect

vertiginoso, -a [bertixi'noso, a] adj giddy, dizzy

vértigo ['bertiɣo] nm vertigo; (mareo) dizziness; (actividad) intense activity; **de ~** (fam: velocidad) giddy; (: ruido) tremendous; (: talento) fantastic

vesícula [be'sikula] nf blister; **~ biliar** gall bladder

vespa® ['bespa] nf (motor) scooter

vespertino, -a [besper'tino, a] adj evening cpd

vespino® [bes'pino] nm o f ≈ moped

vestíbulo [bes'tiβulo] nm hall; (de teatro) foyer

vestido [bes'tiðo] nm (ropa) clothes pl, clothing; (de mujer) dress, frock

vestidor [besti'ðor] nm (Am: Deporte) changing (Brit) o locker (US) room

vestigio [bes'tixjo] nm (trazo) trace; (señal) sign; **vestigios** nmpl remains

vestimenta [besti'menta] nf clothing

vestir [bes'tir] vt (poner: ropa) to put on; (llevar: ropa) to wear; (cubrir) to clothe, cover; (pagar: la ropa) to clothe, pay for the clothing of; (sastre) to make clothes for ▷ vi (ponerse: ropa) to dress; (verse bien) to look good; **vestirse** vr to get dressed, dress o.s.; **traje de ~** (formal) formal suit; **estar vestido de** to be dressed o clad in; (como disfraz) to be dressed as

vestuario [bes'twarjo] nm clothes pl, wardrobe; (Teat: para actores) dressing room; (: para público) cloakroom; (Deporte) changing room

veta ['beta] nf (vena) vein, seam; (raya) streak; (de madera) grain

vetar [be'tar] vt to veto

veterano, -a [bete'rano, a] adj, nm/f veteran

veterinario, -a [beteri'narjo, a] nm/f vet(erinary surgeon) ▷ nf veterinary science

veto ['beto] nm veto

vetusto, -a [be'tusto, a] adj ancient

vez [beθ] nf time; (turno) turn; **a la ~ que** at the same time as; **a su ~** in its turn; **cada ~ más/menos** more and more/less and less; **una ~** once; **dos veces** twice; **de una ~** in one go; **de una ~ para siempre** once and for all; **en ~ de** instead of; **a veces** sometimes; **otra ~** again; **una y otra ~** repeatedly; **muchas veces** (con frecuencia) often; **pocas veces** seldom; **de ~ en cuando** from time to time; **7 veces 9** 7 times 9; **hacer las veces de** to stand in for; **tal ~** perhaps; **¿lo viste alguna ~?** did you ever see it?; **¿cuántas veces?** how often?; **érase una ~** once upon a time (there was)

vía ['bia] nf (calle) road; (ruta) track, route; (Ferro) line; (fig) way; (Anat) passage, tube ▷ prep via, by way of; **por ~ bucal** orally; **por ~ judicial** by legal means; **por ~ oficial** through official channels; **por ~ de** by way of; **en ~s de** in the process of; **un país en ~s de desarrollo** a developing country; **~ aérea** airway; **V~ Láctea** Milky Way; **~ pública** public highway o thoroughfare; **~ única** one-way street; **el tren está en la ~ 8** the train is (standing) at platform 8

viable ['bjaβle] adj (Com) viable; (plan etc) feasible

viaducto [bja'ðukto] nm viaduct

viajante [bja'xante] nm commercial traveller, traveling salesman (US)

viajar [bja'xar] vi to travel, journey

viaje ['bjaxe] nm (gen) tour; (Naut) voyage; (Com: carga) load; **los ~s** travel sg; **estar de ~** to be on a journey; **~ de ida y vuelta** round trip; **~ de novios** honeymoon

viajero, -a [bja'xero, a] adj travelling (Brit), traveling (US); (Zool) migratory ▷ nm/f (quien viaja) traveller; (pasajero) passenger

vial [bjal] adj road cpd, traffic cpd

víbora ['biβora] nf viper; (Am: venenoso) poisonous snake

vibración [biβra'θjon] nf vibration

vibrador [biβra'ðor] nm vibrator

vibrante [bi'βrante] adj vibrant, vibrating

vibrar [bi'βrar] vt to vibrate ▷ vi to vibrate; (pulsar) to throb, beat, pulsate

vicario [bi'karjo] nm curate

vicegerente [biθexe'rente] nm/f assistant manager

vicepresidente [biθepresi'ðente] nm/f vice president; (de comité etc) vice-chairman

viceversa [biθe'βersa] adv vice versa

viciado, -a [bi'θjaðo, a] adj (corrompido) corrupt; (contaminado) foul, contaminated

viciar [bi'θjar] vt (pervertir) to pervert; (adulterar) to adulterate; (falsificar) to falsify; (Jur) to nullify; (estropear) to spoil; (sentido) to twist; **viciarse** vr to become corrupted; (aire, agua) to be(come) polluted

vicio ['biθjo] nm (libertinaje) vice; (mala costumbre) bad habit; (mimo) spoiling; (alabeo) warp, warping; **de o por** ~ out of sheer habit

vicioso, -a [bi'θjoso, a] adj (muy malo) vicious; (corrompido) depraved; (mimado) spoiled ▷ nm/f depraved person; (adicto) addict

vicisitud [biθisi'tuð] nf vicissitude

víctima ['biktima] nf victim; (de accidente etc) casualty

victoria [bik'torja] nf victory

victorioso, -a [bikto'rjoso, a] adj victorious

vicuña [bi'kuɲa] nf vicuna

vid [bið] nf vine

vida ['biða] nf life; (duración) lifetime; (modo de vivir) way of life; ¡~!, ¡~ **mía!** (saludo cariñoso) my love!; **de por** ~ for life; **de** ~ **airada o libre** loose-living; **en la/mi** ~ never; **estar con** ~ to be still alive; **ganarse la** ~ to earn one's living; **¡esto es** ~! this is the life!; **le va la** ~ **en esto** his life depends on it

vidente [bi'ðente] nm/f (adivino) clairvoyant; (no ciego) sighted person

vídeo ['biðeo] nm video; (aparato) video (recorder); **cinta de** ~ videotape; **película de** ~ videofilm; **grabar en** ~ to record, (video) tape; ~ **compuesto/inverso** (Inform) composite/reverse video

videocámara [biðeo'kamara] nf video camera; (pequeña) camcorder

videocasete, videocassette [biðeoka'set] nm video cassette

videoclip [biðeo'klip] nm (music) video

videoclub [biðeo'klub] nm video club; (tienda) video shop

videojuego [biðeo'xweɣo] nm video game

videollamada [biðeoʎa'mada] nf video call

videoteléfono [biðeote'lefono] nf videophone

vidriero, -a [bi'ðrjero, a] nm/f glazier ▷ nf (ventana) stained-glass window; (Am: de tienda) shop window; (puerta) glass door

vidrio ['biðrjo] nm glass; (Am) window; ~ **cilindrado/inastillable** plate/splinter-proof glass

vidrioso, -a [bi'ðrjoso, a] adj glassy; (frágil) fragile, brittle; (resbaladizo) slippery

vieira ['bjeira] nf scallop

viejo, -a ['bjexo, a] adj old ▷ nm/f old man/woman; **mi** ~/**vieja** (fam) my old man/woman; **hacerse o ponerse** ~ to grow o get old

Viena ['bjena] nf Vienna

viene etc ['bjene] vb ver **venir**

vienés, -esa [bje'nes, esa] adj, nm/f Viennese

viento ['bjento] nm wind; **hacer** ~ to be windy; **contra** ~ **y marea** at all costs; **ir** ~ **en popa** to go splendidly; (negocio) to prosper

vientre ['bjentre] nm belly; (matriz) womb; **vientres** nmpl bowels; **hacer de** ~ to have a movement of the bowels

viernes ['bjernes] nm inv Friday; **V~ Santo** Good Friday; ver tb **Semana Santa**; **sábado**

Vietnam [bjet'nam] nm: **el** ~ Vietnam

vietnamita [bjetna'mita] adj, nm/f Vietnamese

viga ['biɣa] nf beam, rafter; (de metal) girder

vigencia [bi'xenθja] nf validity; (de contrato etc) term, life; **estar/entrar en** ~ to be in/come into effect o force

vigente [bi'xente] adj valid, in force; (imperante) prevailing

vigésimo, -a [bi'xesimo, a] num twentieth

vigía [bi'xia] nm look-out ▷ nf (atalaya) watchtower; (acción) watching

vigilancia [bixi'lanθja] nf vigilance; **tener a algn bajo** ~ to keep watch on sb

vigilante [bixi'lante] adj vigilant ▷ nm caretaker; (en cárcel) warder; (en almacén) shopwalker (Brit), floor-walker (US); ~ **jurado** security guard (licensed to carry a gun); ~ **nocturno** night watchman

vigilar [bixi'lar] vt to watch over; (cuidar) to look after, keep an eye on ▷ vi to be vigilant; (hacer guardia) to keep watch; ~ **por** to take care of

vigilia [vi'xilja] nf wakefulness; (Rel) vigil; fast; **comer de** ~ to fast

vigor [bi'ɣor] nm vigour, vitality; **en** ~ in force; **entrar/poner en** ~ to come/put into effect

vigoroso, -a [biɣo'roso, a] adj vigorous

VIH nm abr (= virus de inmunodeficiencia humana) HIV; ~ **negativo/positivo** HIV-negative/-positive

vil [bil] adj vile, low

vileza [bi'leθa] nf vileness; (acto) base deed

vilipendiar [bilipen'djar] vt to vilify, revile

villa ['biʎa] nf (casa) villa; (pueblo) small town; (municipalidad) municipality; **la V~** (Esp) Madrid; ~ **miseria** shanty town

villancico [bi'ʎan'θiko] *nm* (Christmas) carol
villorrio [bi'ʎorrjo] *nm* one-horse town, dump; (*Am: barrio pobre*) shanty town
vilo ['bilo]: **en ~** *adv* in the air, suspended; (*fig*) in suspense; **estar** *o* **quedar en ~** to be left in suspense
vinagre [bi'naɣre] *nm* vinegar
vinagrera [bina'ɣrera] *nf* vinegar bottle; **vinagreras** *nfpl* cruet stand *sg*
vinagreta [bina'ɣreta] *nf* vinaigrette, French dressing
vinculación [binkula'θjon] *nf* (*lazo*) link, bond; (*acción*) linking
vincular [binku'lar] *vt* to link, bind
vínculo ['binkulo] *nm* link, bond
vine *etc vb ver* **venir**
vinicultor, -a [binikul'tor, a] *nm/f* wine grower
vinicultura [binikul'tura] *nf* wine growing
viniera *etc vb ver* **venir**
vino ['bino] *vb ver* **venir** ▷ *nm* wine; **~ de solera/seco/tinto** vintage/dry/red wine; **~ de Jerez** sherry; **~ de Oporto** port (wine)
viña ['biɲa] *nf*, **viñedo** [bi'ɲeðo] *nm* vineyard
viñeta [bi'ɲeta] *nf* (*en historieta*) cartoon
viola ['bjola] *nf* viola
violación [bjola'θjon] *nf* violation; (*Jur*) offence, infringement; (*estupro*): **~ (sexual)** rape; **~ de contrato** (*Com*) breach of contract
violar [bjo'lar] *vt* to violate; (*Jur*) to infringe; (*cometer estupro*) to rape
violencia [bjo'lenθja] *nf* (*fuerza*) violence, force; (*embarazo*) embarrassment; (*acto injusto*) unjust act
violentar [bjolen'tar] *vt* to force; (*casa*) to break into; (*agredir*) to assault; (*violar*) to violate
violento, -a [bjo'lento, a] *adj* violent; (*furioso*) furious; (*situación*) embarrassing; (*acto*) forced, unnatural; (*difícil*) awkward; **me es muy ~** it goes against the grain with me
violeta [bjo'leta] *nf* violet
violín [bjo'lin] *nm* violin
violón [bjo'lon] *nm* double bass
viraje [bi'raxe] *nm* turn; (*de vehículo*) swerve; (*de carretera*) bend; (*fig*) change of direction
virar [bi'rar] *vi* to turn; to swerve; to change direction
virgen ['birxen] *adj* virgin; (*cinta*) blank ▷ *nm/f* virgin; **la Santísima V~** (*Rel*) the Blessed Virgin
virginidad [birxini'ðað] *nf* virginity
Virgo ['birɣo] *nm* Virgo
viril [bi'ril] *adj* virile
virilidad [birili'ðað] *nf* virility
virtual [bir'twal] *adj* (*real*) virtual; (*en potencia*) potential
virtud [bir'tuð] *nf* virtue; **en ~ de** by virtue of
virtuoso, -a [bir'twoso, a] *adj* virtuous ▷ *nm/f* virtuoso

viruela [bi'rwela] *nf* smallpox; **viruelas** *nfpl* pockmarks; **~s locas** chickenpox *sg*
virulento, -a [biru'lento, a] *adj* virulent
virus ['birus] *nm inv* virus
visa ['bisa] *nf*, (*Am*) **visado** [bi'saðo] *nm* visa; **~ de permanencia** residence permit
víscera ['bisθera] *nf* internal organ; **vísceras** *nfpl* entrails
visceral [bisθe'ral] *adj* (*odio*) deep-rooted; **reacción ~** gut reaction
viscoso, -a [bis'koso, a] *adj* viscous
visera [bi'sera] *nf* visor
visibilidad [bisiβili'ðað] *nf* visibility
visible [bi'siβle] *adj* visible; (*fig*) obvious; **exportaciones/importaciones ~s** (*Com*) visible exports/imports
visillo [bi'siʎo] *nm* lace curtain
visión [bi'sjon] *nf* (*Anat*) vision, (eye)sight; (*fantasía*) vision, fantasy; (*panorama*) view; **ver visiones** to see *o* be seeing things
visionario, -a [bisjo'narjo, a] *adj* (*que prevé*) visionary; (*alucinado*) deluded ▷ *nm/f* visionary; (*chalado*) lunatic
visita [bi'sita] *nf* call, visit; (*persona*) visitor; **horas/tarjeta de ~** visiting hours/card; **~ de cortesía/de cumplido/de despedida** courtesy/formal/farewell visit; **hacer una ~** to pay a visit; **ir de ~** to go visiting
visitante [bisi'tante] *adj* visiting ▷ *nm/f* visitor
visitar [bisi'tar] *vt* to visit, call on; (*inspeccionar*) to inspect
vislumbrar [bislum'brar] *vt* to glimpse, catch a glimpse of
vislumbre [bis'lumbre] *nf* glimpse; (*centelleo*) gleam; (*idea vaga*) glimmer
viso ['biso] *nm* (*de metal*) glint, gleam; (*de tela*) sheen; (*aspecto*) appearance; **hay un ~ de verdad en esto** there is an element of truth in this
visón [bi'son] *nm* mink
visor [bi'sor] *nm* (*Foto*) viewfinder
víspera ['bispera] *nf* day before; **la ~** *o* **en ~s de** on the eve of
vista ['bista] *nf* sight, vision; (*capacidad de ver*) (eye)sight; (*mirada*) look(s) (*pl*); (*Foto etc*) view; (*Jur*) hearing ▷ *nm* customs officer; **a primera ~** at first glance; **~ general** overview; **fijar** *o* **clavar la ~ en** to stare at; **hacer la ~ gorda** to turn a blind eye; **volver la ~** to look back; **está a la ~ que** it's obvious that; **a la ~** (*Com*) at sight; **en ~ de** in view of; **en ~ de que** in view of the fact that; **¡hasta la ~!** so long!, see you!; **con ~s a** with a view to; *ver tb* **visto, -a**
vistazo [bis'taθo] *nm* glance; **dar** *o* **echar un ~ a** to glance at
visto, -a *etc* ['bisto, a] *vb ver* **vestir** ▷ *pp de* **ver** ▷ *adj* seen; (*considerado*) considered ▷ *nm*: **~ bueno** approval; **"~ bueno"** "approved"; **por lo ~** apparently; **dar el ~ bueno a algo** to give sth the go-ahead; **está ~ que** it's clear

that; **está bien/mal** ~ it's acceptable/ unacceptable; **está muy** ~ it is very common; **estaba** ~ it had to be; ~ **que** *conj* since, considering that

vistoso, -a [bis'toso, a] *adj* colourful; *(alegre)* gay; *(pey)* gaudy

visual [bi'swal] *adj* visual

vital [bi'tal] *adj* life *cpd*, living *cpd*; *(fig)* vital; *(persona)* lively, vivacious

vitalicio, -a [bita'liθjo, a] *adj* for life

vitalidad [bitali'ðað] *nf* vitality; *(de persona, negocio)* energy; *(de ciudad)* liveliness

vitamina [bita'mina] *nf* vitamin

viticultor, a [bitikul'tor, a] *nm/f* vine grower

viticultura [bitikul'tura] *nf* vine growing

vitorear [bitore'ar] *vt* to cheer, acclaim

vítores ['bitores] *nmpl* cheers

vítreo, -a ['bitreo, a] *adj* vitreous

vitrina [bi'trina] *nf* glass case; *(en casa)* display cabinet; *(Am)* shop window

vituperio [bitu'perjo] *nm (condena)* condemnation; *(censura)* censure; *(insulto)* insult

viudo, -a ['bjuðo, a] *adj* widowed ▷ *nm* widower ▷ *nf* widow

viva ['biβa] *excl* hurrah! ▷ *nm* cheer; **¡- el rey!** long live the King!

vivacidad [biβaθi'ðað] *nf (vigor)* vigour; *(vida)* vivacity

vivaracho, -a [biβa'ratʃo, a] *adj* jaunty, lively; *(ojos)* bright, twinkling

vivaz [bi'βaθ] *adj (que dura)* enduring; *(vigoroso)* vigorous; *(vivo)* lively

vivencia [bi'βenθja] *nf* experience

víveres ['biβeres] *nmpl* provisions

vivero [bi'βero] *nm (Horticultura)* nursery; *(para peces)* fishpond; *(: Com)* fish farm; *(fig)* hotbed

viveza [bi'βeθa] *nf* liveliness; *(agudeza: mental)* sharpness

vivienda [bi'βjenda] *nf (alojamiento)* housing; *(morada)* dwelling; **~s protegidas** o **sociales** council housing *sg (Brit)*, public housing *sg (US)*; **(una vivienda)** house; *(piso)* flat *(Brit)*, apartment *(US)*

viviente [bi'βjente] *adj* living

vivir [bi'βir] *vt (experimentar)* to live o go through ▷ *vi (gen, Com)*: ~ **(de)** to live (by, off, on) ▷ *nm* life, living; **¡viva!** hurray!; **¡viva el rey!** long live the King!

vivo, -a ['biβo, a] *adj* living, live, alive; *(fig)* vivid; *(movimiento)* quick; *(color)* bright; *(protesta)* strong; *(persona: astuto)* smart, clever; **en** ~ *(TV etc)* live; **llegar a lo** ~ to cut to the quick

V.O. *abr* = **versión original**

vocablo [bo'kaβlo] *nm (palabra)* word; *(término)* term

vocabulario [bokaβu'larjo] *nm* vocabulary, word list

vocación [boka'θjon] *nf* vocation

vocacional [bokasjo'nal] *nf (Am)* = technical college

vocal [bo'kal] *adj* vocal ▷ *nm/f* member (of a committee *etc*) ▷ *nm* non-executive director ▷ *nf* vowel

vocalizar [bokali'θar] *vt* to vocalize

vocear [boθe'ar] *vt (para vender)* to cry; *(aclamar)* to acclaim; *(fig)* to proclaim ▷ *vi* to yell

vocerío [boθe'rio] *nm* shouting; *(escándalo)* hullabaloo

vocero, -a [bo'θero, a] *nm/f (Am)* spokesman/ woman

voces ['boθes] *pl de* **voz**

vociferar [boθife'rar] *vt* to shout; *(jactarse)* to proclaim boastfully ▷ *vi* to yell

vodka ['boðka] *nm* vodka

vol *abr* = **volumen**

volado, -a [bo'laðo, a] *adj*: **estar** ~ *(fam: inquieto)* to be worried; *(: loco)* to be crazy ▷ *adv (Am)* in a rush, hastily

volador, a [bola'ðor, a] *adj* flying

volandas [bo'landas]: **en** ~ *adv* in o through the air; *(fig)* swiftly

volante [bo'lante] *adj* flying ▷ *nm (de máquina, coche)* steering wheel; *(de reloj)* balance; *(nota)* note; **ir al** ~ to be at the wheel, be driving

volar [bo'lar] *vt (demoler)* to blow up, demolish ▷ *vi* to fly; *(fig: correr)* to rush, hurry; *(fam: desaparecer)* to disappear; **voy volando** I must dash; **¡cómo vuela el tiempo!** how time flies!

volátil [bo'latil] *adj* volatile; *(fig)* changeable

volcán [bol'kan] *nm* volcano

volcánico, -a [bol'kaniko, a] *adj* volcanic

volcar [bol'kar] *vt* to upset, overturn; *(tumbar, derribar)* to knock over; *(vaciar)* to empty out ▷ *vi* to overturn; **volcarse** *vr* to tip over; *(barco)* to capsize

voleibol [bolei'βol] *nm* volleyball

volqué [bol'ke], **volquemos** *etc* [bol'kemos] *vb ver* **volcar**

volquete [bol'kete] *nm* dumper, dump truck *(US)*

voltaje [bol'taxe] *nm* voltage

voltear [bolte'ar] *vt* to turn over; *(volcar)* to knock over; *(doblar)* to peal ▷ *vi* to roll over; **voltearse** *vr (Am)* to turn round; ~ **a hacer algo** *(Am)* to do sth again

voltereta [bolte'reta] *nf* somersault; ~ **sobre las manos** handspring; ~ **lateral** cartwheel

voltio ['boltjo] *nm* volt

voluble [bo'luβle] *adj* fickle

volumen [bo'lumen] *nm* volume; ~ **monetario** money supply; ~ **de negocios** turnover; **bajar el** ~ to turn down the volume; **poner la radio a todo** ~ to turn the radio up full

voluminoso, -a [bolumi'noso, a] *adj* voluminous; *(enorme)* massive

voluntad [bolun'tað] *nf* will, willpower; *(deseo)* desire, wish; *(afecto)* fondness; **a** ~

V

at will; (*cantidad*) as much as one likes;
buena ~ goodwill; **mala ~** ill will, malice;
por causas ajenas a mi ~ for reasons beyond
my control
voluntario, -a [bolun'tarjo, a] *adj* voluntary
▷ *nm/f* volunteer
voluntarioso, -a [bolunta'rjoso, a] *adj*
headstrong
voluptuoso, -a [bolup'twoso, a] *adj*
voluptuous
volver [bol'βer] *vt* to turn; (*boca abajo*) to turn
(over); (*voltear*) to turn round, turn upside
down; (*poner del revés*) to turn inside out;
(*devolver*) to return; (*transformar*) to change,
transform; (*manga*) to roll up ▷ *vi* to return,
go/come back; **volverse** *vr* to turn round;
(*llegar a ser*) to become; **~ la espalda** to turn
one's back; **~ bien por mal** to return good
for evil; **~ a hacer** to do again; **~ en sí** to
come to *o* round, regain consciousness; **~ la
vista atrás** to look back; **~ triste** *etc* **a algn** to
make sb sad *etc*; **~ loco a algn** to drive sb
mad; **~se loco** to go mad
vomitar [bomi'tar] *vt, vi* to vomit
vómito ['bomito] *nm* (*acto*) vomiting;
(*resultado*) vomit
voracidad [boraθi'ðað] *nf* voracity
voraz [bo'raθ] *adj* voracious; (*fig*) fierce
vórtice ['bortiθe] *nm* whirlpool; (*de aire*)
whirlwind
vos [bos] *pron* (*Am*) you
vosotros, -as [bo'sotros, as] *pron* you *pl*;
(*reflexivo*) yourselves; **entre ~** among
yourselves
votación [bota'θjon] *nf* (*acto*) voting; (*voto*)
vote; **~ a mano alzada** show of hands;
someter algo a ~ to put sth to the vote
votar [bo'tar] *vt* (*Pol: partido etc*) to vote for;
(*proyecto: aprobar*) to pass; (*Rel*) to vow ▷ *vi* to
vote
voto ['boto] *nm* vote; (*promesa*) vow; (*maldición*)
oath, curse; **votos** *nmpl* (good) wishes; **~ de
bloque/de grupo** block/card vote; **~ de
censura/de (des)confianza/de gracias** vote
of censure/(no) confidence/thanks; **dar su ~**
to cast one's vote
voy [boi] *vb ver* **ir**
voz [boθ] *nf* voice; (*grito*) shout; (*chisme*)
rumour; (*Ling: palabra*) word; (: *forma*) voice;
dar voces to shout, yell; **llamar a algn a
voces** to shout to sb; **llevar la ~ cantante**
(*fig*) to be the boss; **tener la ~ tomada** to be
hoarse; **tener ~ y voto** to have the right to
speak; **en ~ baja** in a low voice; **a ~ en cuello**
o **en grito** at the top of one's voice; **de viva ~**
verbally; **en ~ alta** aloud; **~ de mando**
command
vuelco *etc* ['bwelko] *vb ver* **volcar** ▷ *nm* spill,
overturning; (*fig*) collapse; **mi corazón dio
un ~** my heart missed a beat
vuelo ['bwelo] *vb ver* **volar** ▷ *nm* flight;
(*encaje*) lace, frill; (*de falda etc*) loose part; (*fig*)

importance; **de altos ~s** (*fig: plan*) grandiose;
(: *persona*) ambitious; **alzar el ~** to take flight;
(*fig*) to dash off; **coger al ~** to catch in flight;
~ de bajo coste low-cost flight; **~ en picado**
dive; **~ libre** hang-gliding; **~ regular**
scheduled flight; **falda de mucho ~** full *o*
wide skirt
vuelque *etc* ['bwelke] *vb ver* **volcar**
vuelta ['bwelta] *nf* turn; (*curva*) bend, curve;
(*regreso*) return; (*revolución*) revolution; (*paseo*)
stroll; (*circuito*) lap; (*de papel, tela*) reverse; (*de
pantalón*) turn-up (*Brit*), cuff (US); (*cambio*)
change; **~ a empezar** back to square one;
~ al mundo world trip; **~ ciclista** (*Deporte*)
(cycle) tour; **V~ de Francia** Tour de France;
~ cerrada hairpin bend; **a la ~** (*Esp*) on one's
return; **a la ~ de la esquina, a la ~** (*Am*)
round the corner; **a ~ de correo** by return of
post; **dar ~s** to turn, revolve; (*cabeza*) to spin;
dar(se) la ~ (*volverse*) to turn round; **dar ~s a
una idea** to turn over an idea (in one's
mind); **dar una ~** to go for a walk; (*en coche*)
to go for a drive; **dar media ~** (*Auto*) to do a
U-turn; (*fam*) to beat it; **estar de ~** (*fam*) to be
back; **poner a algn de ~ y media** to heap
abuse on sb; **no tiene ~ de hoja** there's no
alternative
vuelto ['bwelto] *pp de* **volver** ▷ *nm* (*Am:
moneda*) change
vuelvo *etc* ['bwelβo] *vb ver* **volver**
vuestro, -a ['bwestro, a] *adj* your; (*después de
n*) of yours ▷ *pron*: **el ~/la vuestra/los ~s/las
vuestras** yours; **lo ~** (what is) yours; **un
amigo ~** a friend of yours; **una idea vuestra**
an idea of yours
vulgar [bul'ɣar] *adj* (*ordinario*) vulgar; (*común*)
common
vulgaridad [bulɣari'ðað] *nf* commonness;
(*acto*) vulgarity; (*expresión*) coarse expression;
vulgaridades *nfpl* banalities
vulgarizar [bulɣari'θar] *vt* to popularize
vulgo ['bulɣo] *nm* common people
vulnerable [bulne'raβle] *adj* vulnerable
vulnerar [bulne'rar] *vt* (*Jur, Com*) to violate;
(*derechos*) to violate, to interfere with;
(*reputación*) to harm, damage
vulva ['bulβa] *nf* vulva

W X

walkie-talkie [walki'talki] *nm* walkie-talkie
walkman® ['wal(k)man] *nm* Walkman®
wáter ['bater] *nm* (*taza*) toilet; (*Am: lugar*)
  toilet (*Brit*), rest room (*US*)
waterpolo [water'polo] *nm* waterpolo
web [web] *nm o nf* (*página*) website; (*red*)
  (World Wide) Web
web site ['websait] *nm* website
webcam ['webkam] *nf* webcam
webmaster ['webmaster] *nm/f* webmaster
website ['websait] *nm* website
western ['western] (*pl* **westerns**) *nm* western
whisky ['wiski] *nm* whisky
wifi ['waifai] *nm* Wi-Fi
wiki ['wiki] *nf* wiki
windsurf ['winsurf] *nm* windsurfing;
  hacer ~ to go windsurfing

xenofobia [seno'foβja] *nf* xenophobia
xenófobo, -a [se'nofoβo, a] *adj* xenophobic
  ▷ *nm/f* xenophobe
xerografía [seroɣra'fia] *nf* xerography
xilófono [si'lofono] *nm* xylophone
xocoyote, -a [ksoko'jote, a] *nm/f* (*Am*) baby
  of the family, youngest child

yodo ['joðo] *nm* iodine
yoga ['joɣa] *nm* yoga
yogur [jo'ɣur], **yogurt** [jo'ɣurt] *nm* yogurt
yuca ['juka] *nf* (*Bot*) yucca; (*alimento*) cassava, manioc root
yudo ['juðo] *nm* judo
yugo ['juɣo] *nm* yoke
Yugoslavia [juɣos'laβja] *nf* Yugoslavia
yugular [juɣu'lar] *adj* jugular
yunque ['junke] *nm* anvil
yunta ['junta] *nf* yoke
yuntero [jun'tero] *nm* ploughman
yute ['jute] *nm* jute
yuxtaponer [jukstapo'ner] *vt* to juxtapose
yuxtaposición [jukstaposi'θjon] *nf* juxtaposition
yuyo ['jujo] *nm* (*Am*: *mala hierba*) weed

y [i] *conj* and; (*Am fam*: *pues*) well; (*hora*): **la una y cinco** five past one; **¿y eso?** why?, how so?; **¿y los demás?** what about the others?; **y bueno …** (*Am*) well …
ya [ja] *adv* (*gen*) already; (*ahora*) now; (*en seguida*) at once; (*pronto*) soon ▷ *excl* all right!; (*por supuesto*) of course! ▷ *conj* (*ahora que*) now that; **ya no** not any more, no longer; **ya lo sé** I know; **ya dice que sí, ya dice que no** first he says yes, then he says no; **¡ya, ya!** yes, yes!; (*con impaciencia*) all right!, O.K.!; **¡ya está bien!** that's (quite) enough!; **¡ya voy!** (*enfático*: *no se suele traducir*) coming!; **ya que** since
yacer [ja'θer] *vi* to lie
yacimiento [jaθi'mjento] *nm* bed, deposit; (*arqueológico*) site; **~ petrolífero** oilfield
yanqui ['janki] *adj* Yankee ▷ *nm/f* Yank, Yankee
yate ['jate] *nm* yacht
yazco *etc* ['jaθko] *vb ver* **yacer**
yedra ['jeðra] *nf* ivy
yegua ['jeɣwa] *nf* mare
yema ['jema] *nf* (*del huevo*) yolk; (*Bot*) leaf bud; (*fig*) best part; **~ del dedo** fingertip
yermo, -a ['jermo, a] *adj* barren; (*de gente*) uninhabited ▷ *nm* waste land
yerno ['jerno] *nm* son-in-law
yerto, -a ['jerto, a] *adj* stiff
yesca ['jeska] *nf* tinder
yeso ['jeso] *nm* (*Geo*) gypsum; (*Arq*) plaster
yo [jo] *pron personal* I; **soy yo** it's me, it is I; **yo que tú/usted** if I were you

Z

zafar [θa'far] *vt* (*soltar*) to untie; (*superficie*) to clear; **zafarse** *vr* (*escaparse*) to escape; (*ocultarse*) to hide o.s. away; (*Tec*) to slip off; **~se de** (*persona*) to get away from
zafio, -a ['θafjo, a] *adj* coarse
zafiro [θa'firo] *nm* sapphire
zaga ['θaɣa] *nf* rear; **a la ~** behind, in the rear
zagal [θa'ɣal] *nm* boy, lad
zaguán [θa'ɣwan] *nm* hallway
zaherir [θae'rir] *vt* (*criticar*) to criticize; (*fig: herir*) to wound
zaino, -a ['θaino, a] *adj* (*color de caballo*) chestnut; (*pérfido*) treacherous; (*animal*) vicious
zalamería [θalame'ria] *nf* flattery
zalamero, -a [θala'mero, a] *adj* flattering; (*relamido*) suave
zamarra [θa'marra] *nf* (*piel*) sheepskin; (*chaqueta*) sheepskin jacket
zambullirse [θambu'ʎirse] *vr* to dive; (*ocultarse*) to hide o.s.
zampar [θam'par] *vt* (*esconder*) to hide o put away (hurriedly); (*comer*) to gobble; (*arrojar*) to hurl ▷ *vi* to eat voraciously; **zamparse** *vr* (*chocar*) to bump; (*fig*) to gatecrash
zanahoria [θana'orja] *nf* carrot
zancada [θan'kaða] *nf* stride
zancadilla [θanka'ðiʎa] *nf* trip; (*fig*) stratagem; **echar la ~ a algn** to trip sb up
zanco ['θanko] *nm* stilt
zancudo, -a [θan'kuðo, a] *adj* long-legged ▷ *nm* (*Am*) mosquito

zángano ['θangano] *nm* drone; (*holgazán*) idler, slacker
zanja ['θanxa] *nf* (*fosa*) ditch; (*tumba*) grave
zanjar [θan'xar] *vt* (*fosa*) to ditch, trench; (*problema*) to surmount; (*conflicto*) to resolve
zapata [θa'pata] *nf* half-boot; (*Mecánica*) shoe
zapatear [θapate'ar] *vt* (*tocar*) to tap with one's foot; (*patear*) to kick; (*fam*) to ill-treat ▷ *vi* to tap with one's feet
zapatería [θapate'ria] *nf* (*oficio*) shoemaking; (*tienda*) shoe-shop; (*fábrica*) shoe factory
zapatero, -a [θapa'tero, a] *nm/f* shoemaker; **~ remendón** cobbler
zapatilla [θapa'tiʎa] *nf* slipper; (*Tec*) washer; (*de deporte*) training shoe
zapato [θa'pato] *nm* shoe
zapping ['θapin] *nm* channel-hopping; **hacer ~** to channel-hop, flick through the channels
zar [θar] *nm* tsar, czar
zarandear [θarande'ar] *vt* to sieve; (*fam*) to shake vigorously
zarpa ['θarpa] *nf* (*garra*) claw, paw; **echar la ~ a** to claw at; (*fam*) to grab
zarpar [θar'par] *vi* to weigh anchor
zarpazo [θar'paθo] *nm*: **dar un ~** to claw
zarza ['θarθa] *nf* (*Bot*) bramble
zarzal [θar'θal] *nm* (*matorral*) bramble patch
zarzamora [θarθa'mora] *nf* blackberry
zarzuela [θar'θwela] *nf* Spanish light opera; **la Z~** home of the Spanish Royal Family
zigzag [θiɣ'θaɣ] *adj* zigzag
zigzaguear [θiɣθaɣe'ar] *vi* to zigzag
zinc [θink] *nm* zinc
zíper ['siper] *nm* (*Am*) zip, zipper (*US*)
zócalo ['θokalo] *nm* (*Arq*) plinth, base; (*de pared*) skirting board
zoclo ['θoklo] *nm* (*Am*) skirting board (*Brit*), baseboard (*US*)
zoco ['θoko] *nm* (*Arab*) market, souk
zodíaco [θo'ðiako] *nm* zodiac; **signo del ~** star sign
zona ['θona] *nf* zone; **~ cero** Ground Zero; **~ euro** Eurozone; **los países de la ~ euro** the Eurozone countries; **~ fronteriza** border area; **~ del dólar** (*Com*) dollar area; **~ de fomento** o **de desarrollo** development area; **~ roja** (*Am*) red-light district
zonzo, -a ['θonθo, a] (*Am*) *adj* silly ▷ *nm/f* fool
zoo ['θoo] *nm* zoo
zoología [θoolo'xia] *nf* zoology
zoológico, -a [θoo'loxiko, a] *adj* zoological ▷ *nm* (*tb*: **parque ~**) zoo
zoólogo, -a [θo'oloɣo, a] *nm/f* zoologist
zoom [θum] *nm* zoom lens
zopenco, -a [θo'penko, a] (*fam*) *adj* dull, stupid ▷ *nm/f* clot, nitwit
zopilote [θopi'lote] *nm* (*Am*) buzzard
zoquete [θo'kete] *nm* (*de madera*) block; (*de pan*) crust; (*fam*) blockhead
zorro, -a ['θorro, a] *adj* crafty ▷ *nm/f* fox/vixen ▷ *nf* (*fam*) whore, tart, hooker (*US*)

Z

zozobra [θo'θoβra] *nf* (*fig*) anxiety
zozobrar [θoθo'βrar] *vi* (*hundirse*) to capsize; (*fig*) to fail
zueco ['θweko] *nm* clog
zumbar [θum'bar] *vt* (*burlar*) to tease; (*golpear*) to hit ▷ *vi* to buzz; (*fam*) to be very close; **zumbarse** *vr*: ~**se de** to tease; **me zumban los oídos** I have a buzzing *o* ringing in my ears
zumbido [θum'biðo] *nm* buzzing; (*fam*) punch; ~ **de oídos** buzzing *o* ringing in the ears
zumo ['θumo] *nm* juice; (*ganancia*) profit; ~ **de naranja** (fresh) orange juice
zurcir [θur'θir] *vt* (*coser*) to darn; (*fig*) to put together; **¡que las zurzan!** to blazes with them!
zurdo, -a ['θurðo, a] *adj* (*mano*) left; (*persona*) left-handed
zurrar [θu'rrar] *vt* (*Tec*) to dress; (*fam: pegar duro*) to wallop; (: *aplastar*) to flatten; (: *criticar*) to criticize harshly
zurrón [θu'rron] *nm* pouch
zutano, -a [θu'tano, a] *nm/f* so-and-so

A, a [eɪ] n (letter) A, a; (Scol: mark)
≈ sobresaliente; (Mus): **A** la m; **A for Andrew**,
(US) **A for Able** A de Antonio; **A road** n (Brit
Aut) ≈ carretera nacional

KEYWORD

a [ə] indef art (before vowel and silent h **an**) **1** un(a);
a book un libro; **an apple** una manzana;
she's a nurse (ella) es enfermera; **I haven't
got a car** no tengo coche
2 (instead of the number "one") un(a); **a year ago**
hace un año; **a hundred/thousand pounds**
cien/mil libras
3 (in expressing ratios, prices etc): **three a day/
week** tres al día/a la semana; **10 km an hour**
10 km por hora; **£5 a person** £5 por persona;
30p a kilo 30p el kilo; **three times a month**
tres veces al mes

A2 n (Brit Scol) segunda parte de los "A levels"
(módulos 4–6)
AA n abbr (Brit: = Automobile Association) ≈ RACE
m (Sp); (= Alcoholics Anonymous) A.A.; (US:
= Associate in/of Arts) título universitario; = **anti-
aircraft**
AAA n abbr (= American Automobile Association)
≈ RACE m (Sp); ['θriː'eɪz] (Brit: = Amateur Athletics
Association) asociación de atletismo amateur
aback [ə'bæk] adv: **to be taken ~** quedar(se)
desconcertado
abandon [ə'bændən] vt abandonar;

(renounce) renunciar a ▷ n abandono; (wild
behaviour): **with ~** con desenfreno; **to ~ ship**
abandonar el barco
abate [ə'beɪt] vi moderarse; (lessen)
disminuir; (calm down) calmarse
abattoir ['æbətwɑːʳ] n (Brit) matadero
abbey ['æbɪ] n abadía
abbot ['æbət] n abad m
abbreviate [ə'briːvɪeɪt] vt abreviar
abbreviation [əbriːvɪ'eɪʃən] n (short form)
abreviatura; (act) abreviación f
ABC n abbr (= American Broadcasting Company)
cadena de televisión
abdicate ['æbdɪkeɪt] vt, vi abdicar
abdication [æbdɪ'keɪʃən] n abdicación f
abdomen ['æbdəmən] n abdomen m
abduct [æb'dʌkt] vt raptar, secuestrar
abduction [æb'dʌkʃən] n rapto, secuestro
abductor [æb'dʌktəʳ] n raptor(a) m(f),
secuestrador(a) m(f)
aberration [æbə'reɪʃən] n aberración f; **in a
moment of mental ~** en un momento de
enajenación mental
abet [ə'bɛt] vt see **aid**
abeyance [ə'beɪəns] n: **in ~** (law) en desuso;
(matter) en suspenso
abide [ə'baɪd] vt: **I can't ~ it/him** no lo/le puedo
ver or aguantar; **to ~ by** vt fus atenerse a
abiding [ə'baɪdɪŋ] adj (memory etc) perdurable
ability [ə'bɪlɪtɪ] n habilidad f, capacidad f;
(talent) talento; **to the best of my ~** lo mejor
que pueda etc
abject ['æbdʒɛkt] adj (poverty) sórdido;
(apology) rastrero; (coward) vil
ablaze [ə'bleɪz] adj en llamas, ardiendo
able ['eɪbl] adj capaz; (skilled) hábil; **to be ~ to
do sth** poder hacer algo
able-bodied ['eɪbl'bɔdɪd] adj sano; **~ seaman**
marinero de primera
ably ['eɪblɪ] adv hábilmente
abnormal [æb'nɔːməl] adj anormal
aboard [ə'bɔːd] adv a bordo ▷ prep a bordo de;
~ the train en el tren
abode [ə'bəud] n (old) morada; (Law)
domicilio; **of no fixed ~** sin domicilio fijo
abolish [ə'bɔlɪʃ] vt suprimir, abolir
abolition [æbəu'lɪʃən] n supresión f,
abolición f
aborigine [æbə'rɪdʒɪnɪ] n aborigen m/f
abort [ə'bɔːt] vt abortar; (Comput)
interrumpir ▷ vi (Comput) interrumpir el
programa
abortion [ə'bɔːʃən] n aborto; **to have an ~**
abortar
abortive [ə'bɔːtɪv] adj fracasado
abound [ə'baund] vi: **to ~ (in or with)**
abundar (de or en)

KEYWORD

about [ə'baut] adv **1** (approximately) más o
menos, aproximadamente; **about a**

hundred/thousand *etc* unos(-as) *or* como cien/mil *etc*; **it takes about 10 hours** se tarda unas *or* más o menos 10 horas; **at about two o'clock** sobre las dos; **I've just about finished** casi he terminado
2 *(referring to place)* por todas partes; **to leave things lying about** dejar las cosas (tiradas) por ahí; **to run about** correr por todas partes; **to walk about** pasearse, ir y venir; **is Paul about?** ¿está por aquí Paul?; **it's the other way about** es al revés
3: **to be about to do sth** estar a punto de hacer algo; **I'm not about to do all that for nothing** no pienso hacer todo eso para nada ▷ *prep* **1** *(relating to)* de, sobre, acerca de; **a book about London** un libro sobre *or* acerca de Londres; **what is it about?** *(book, film)* ¿de qué se trata?; **we talked about it** hablamos de eso *or* ello; **what** *or* **how about doing this?** ¿qué tal si hacemos esto?
2 *(referring to place)* por; **to walk about the town** caminar por la ciudad

about face, about turn *n* *(Mil)* media vuelta; *(fig)* cambio radical
above [ə'bʌv] *adv* encima, por encima, arriba ▷ *prep* encima de; *(greater than: in number)* más de; *(: in rank)* superior a; **mentioned ~** susodicho; **~ all** sobre todo; **he's not ~ a bit of blackmail** es capaz hasta de hacer chantaje
above board *adj* legítimo
abrasive [ə'breɪzɪv] *adj* abrasivo
abreast [ə'brɛst] *adv* uno al lado de otro; **to keep ~ of** mantenerse al corriente de
abridge [ə'brɪdʒ] *vt* abreviar
abroad [ə'brɔːd] *adv* (be) en el extranjero; *(go)* al extranjero; **there is a rumour ~ that ...** corre el rumor de que ...
abrupt [ə'brʌpt] *adj* *(sudden: departure)* repentino; *(manner)* brusco
abruptly [ə'brʌptlɪ] *adv* *(leave)* repentinamente, *(speak)* bruscamente
abscess ['æbsɪs] *n* absceso
abscond [əb'skɔnd] *vi* fugarse
absence ['æbsəns] *n* ausencia; **in the ~ of** *(person)* en ausencia de; *(thing)* a falta de
absent ['æbsənt] *adj* ausente; **~ without leave (AWOL)** ausente sin permiso
absentee [æbsən'tiː] *n* ausente *m/f*
absent-minded [æbsənt'maɪndɪd] *adj* distraído
absolute ['æbsəluːt] *adj* absoluto; **~ monopoly** monopolio total
absolutely [æbsə'luːtlɪ] *adv* totalmente; **oh yes, ~!** ¡claro *or* por supuesto que sí!
absolution [æbsə'luːʃən] *n* *(Rel)* absolución *f*
absolve [əb'zɔlv] *vt*: **to ~ sb (from)** absolver a algn (de)
absorb [əb'zɔːb] *vt* absorber; **to be ~ed in a book** estar absorto en un libro
absorbent [əb'zɔːbənt] *adj* absorbente

absorbent cotton *n* (US) algodón *m* hidrófilo
absorbing [əb'zɔːbɪŋ] *adj* absorbente; *(book etc)* interesantísimo
absorption [əb'zɔːpfən] *n* absorción *f*
abstain [əb'steɪn] *vi*: **to ~ (from)** abstenerse (de)
abstention [əb'stɛnʃən] *n* abstención *f*
abstract ['æbstrækt] *adj* abstracto
absurd [əb'səːd] *adj* absurdo
ABTA ['æbtə] *n abbr* = **Association of British Travel Agents**
abundance [ə'bʌndəns] *n* abundancia
abundant [ə'bʌndənt] *adj* abundante
abuse [ə'bjuːs] *n* *(insults)* insultos *mpl*, improperios *mpl*; *(misuse)* abuso ▷ *vt* [ə'bjuːz] *(ill-treat)* maltratar; *(take advantage of)* abusar de; **open to ~** sujeto al abuso
abusive [ə'bjuːsɪv] *adj* ofensivo
abysmal [ə'bɪzməl] *adj* pésimo; *(failure)* garrafal; *(ignorance)* supino
abyss [ə'bɪs] *n* abismo
AC *abbr* (= *alternating current*) corriente *f* alterna ▷ *n abbr* (US) = **athletic club**
academic [ækə'dɛmɪk] *adj* académico, universitario; *(pej: issue)* puramente teórico ▷ *n* estudioso(-a); *(lecturer)* profesor(a) *m(f)* universitario(-a)
academic year *n* (Univ) año académico
academy [ə'kædəmɪ] *n* *(learned body)* academia; *(school)* instituto, colegio
accelerate [æk'sɛləreɪt] *vi* acelerar
acceleration [æksɛlə'reɪʃən] *n* aceleración *f*
accelerator [æk'sɛləreɪtəʳ] *n* (Brit) acelerador *m*
accent ['æksɛnt] *n* acento; *(fig)* énfasis *m*
accentuate [æk'sɛntjueɪt] *vt* *(syllable)* acentuar; *(need, difference etc)* recalcar, subrayar
accept [ək'sɛpt] *vt* aceptar; *(approve)* aprobar; *(concede)* admitir
acceptable [ək'sɛptəbl] *adj* aceptable, admisible
acceptance [ək'sɛptəns] *n* aceptación *f*; aprobación *f*; **to meet with general ~** recibir la aprobación general
access ['æksɛs] *n* acceso ▷ *vt* (Comput) acceder a; **the burglars gained ~ through a window** los ladrones lograron entrar por una ventana; **to have ~ to** tener acceso a
accessible [æk'sɛsəbl] *adj* *(place, person)* accesible; *(knowledge etc)* asequible
accessory [æk'sɛsərɪ] *n* accesorio; *(Law)*: **~ to** cómplice de; **toilet accessories** artículos *mpl* de tocador
accident ['æksɪdənt] *n* accidente *m*; *(chance)* casualidad *f*; **by ~** *(unintentionally)* sin querer; *(by coincidence)* por casualidad; **~s at work** accidentes *mpl* de trabajo; **to meet with** *or* **to have an ~** tener *or* sufrir un accidente
accidental [æksɪ'dɛntl] *adj* accidental, fortuito

accidentally [æksɪ'dentəlɪ] *adv* sin querer; por casualidad

Accident and Emergency Department *n* (Brit) Urgencias *fpl*

accident insurance *n* seguro contra accidentes

accident-prone ['æksɪdənt'prəun] *adj* propenso a los accidentes

acclaim [ə'kleɪm] *vt* aclamar, aplaudir ▷ *n* aclamación *f*, aplausos *mpl*

acclimatize [ə'klaɪmətaɪz], **acclimate** (US) [ə'klaɪmət] *vt*: **to become ~d** aclimatarse

accommodate [ə'kɔmədeɪt] *vt* alojar, hospedar; (: car, hotel etc) tener cabida para; (oblige, help) complacer; **this car ~s four people comfortably** en este coche caben cuatro personas cómodamente

accommodating [ə'kɔmədeɪtɪŋ] *adj* servicial, complaciente

accommodation *n*, **accommodations** (US) *npl* [əkɔmə'deɪʃən(z)] alojamiento; **"~ to let"** "se alquilan habitaciones"; **seating ~** asientos *mpl*

accompaniment [ə'kʌmpənɪmənt] *n* acompañamiento

accompany [ə'kʌmpənɪ] *vt* acompañar

accomplice [ə'kʌmplɪs] *n* cómplice *m/f*

accomplish [ə'kʌmplɪʃ] *vt* (finish) concluir; (aim) realizar; (task) llevar a cabo

accomplished [ə'kʌmplɪʃt] *adj* experto, hábil

accomplishment [ə'kʌmplɪʃmənt] *n* (ending) conclusión *f*; (bringing about) realización *f*; (skill) talento

accord [ə'kɔːd] *n* acuerdo ▷ *vt* conceder; **of his own ~** espontáneamente; **with one ~** de or por común acuerdo

accordance [ə'kɔːdəns] *n*: **in ~ with** de acuerdo con

according [ə'kɔːdɪŋ]: **~ to** *prep* según; (in accordance with) conforme a; **it went ~ to plan** salió según lo previsto

accordingly [ə'kɔːdɪŋlɪ] *adv* (thus) por consiguiente, en consecuencia; (appropriately) de acuerdo con esto

accordion [ə'kɔːdɪən] *n* acordeón *m*

accost [ə'kɔst] *vt* abordar, dirigirse a

account [ə'kaunt] *n* (Comm) cuenta, factura; (report) informe *m*; **accounts** *npl* (Comm) cuentas *fpl*; **"~ payee only"** "únicamente en cuenta del beneficiario"; **your ~ is still outstanding** su cuenta está todavía pendiente; **of little ~** de poca importancia; **on ~** a crédito; **to buy sth on ~** comprar algo a crédito; **on no ~** bajo ningún concepto; **on ~ of** a causa de, por motivo de; **to take into ~, take ~ of** tener en cuenta; **to keep an ~ of** llevar la cuenta de; **to bring sb to ~ for sth/for having done sth** pedirle cuentas a algn por algo/por haber hecho algo; **account for** *vt fus* (explain) explicar; **all the children were ~ed for** no faltaba ningún niño

accountability [əkauntə'bɪlɪtɪ] *n* responsabilidad *f*

accountable [ə'kauntəbl] *adj*: **~ (for)** responsable (de)

accountancy [ə'kauntənsɪ] *n* contabilidad *f*

accountant [ə'kauntənt] *n* contable *m/f*, contador(a) *m(f)* (LAm)

account number *n* (at bank etc) número de cuenta

accumulate [ə'kjuːmjuleɪt] *vt* acumular ▷ *vi* acumularse

accumulation [əkjuːmju'leɪʃən] *n* acumulación *f*

accuracy ['ækjurəsɪ] *n* (of total) exactitud *f*; (of description etc) precisión *f*

accurate ['ækjurɪt] *adj* (number) exacto; (answer) acertado; (shot) certero

accurately ['ækjurɪtlɪ] *adv* (count, shoot, answer) con precisión

accusation [ækju'zeɪʃən] *n* acusación *f*

accuse [ə'kjuːz] *vt* acusar; (blame) echar la culpa a; **to ~ sb (of sth)** acusar a algn (de algo)

accused [ə'kjuːzd] *n* acusado(-a)

accuser [ə'kjuːzəʳ] *n* acusador(a) *m(f)*

accustom [ə'kʌstəm] *vt* acostumbrar; **to ~ o.s. to sth** acostumbrarse a algo

accustomed [ə'kʌstəmd] *adj*: **~ to** acostumbrado a

AC/DC *abbr* (= alternating current/direct current) CA/CC

ace [eɪs] *n* as *m*

ache [eɪk] *n* dolor *m* ▷ *vi* doler; (yearn): **to ~ to do sth** ansiar hacer algo; **I've got stomach ~** or (US) **a stomach ~** tengo dolor de estómago, me duele el estómago; **my head ~s** me duele la cabeza

achieve [ə'tʃiːv] *vt* (reach) alcanzar; (realize) realizar; (victory, success) lograr, conseguir

achievement [ə'tʃiːvmənt] *n* (completion) realización *f*; (success) éxito

Achilles heel [ə'kɪliːz-] *n* talón *m* de Aquiles

acid ['æsɪd] *adj* ácido; (bitter) agrio ▷ *n* (Chem, inf: LSD) ácido

acid rain *n* lluvia ácida

acid test *n* (fig) prueba de fuego

acknowledge [ək'nɔlɪdʒ] *vt* (letter: also: **~ receipt of**) acusar recibo de; (fact) reconocer

acknowledgement [ək'nɔlɪdʒmənt] *n* acuse *m* de recibo; reconocimiento; **~s** (in book) agradecimientos *mpl*

acne ['æknɪ] *n* acné *m*

acorn ['eɪkɔːn] *n* bellota

acoustic [ə'kuːstɪk] *adj* acústico

acoustics [ə'kuːstɪks] *n, npl* acústica *sg*

acquaint [ə'kweɪnt] *vt*: **to ~ sb with sth** (inform) poner a algn al corriente de algo; **to be ~ed with** (person) conocer; (fact) estar al corriente de

acquaintance [ə'kweɪntəns] *n* conocimiento; (person) conocido(-a); **to make sb's ~** conocer a algn

acquiesce [ækwɪ'ɛs] vi (agree): **to ~ (in)** consentir (en), conformarse (con)

acquire [ə'kwaɪəʳ] vt adquirir

acquisition [ækwɪ'zɪʃən] n adquisición f

acquit [ə'kwɪt] vt absolver, exculpar; **to ~ o.s. well** salir con éxito

acquittal [ə'kwɪtl] n absolución f, exculpación f

acre ['eɪkəʳ] n acre m

acrid ['ækrɪd] adj (smell) acre; (fig) mordaz, sarcástico

acrobat ['ækrəbæt] n acróbata m/f

acrobatic [ækrə'bætɪk] adj acrobático

acrobatics [ækrə'bætɪks] npl acrobacia sg

acronym ['ækrənɪm] n siglas fpl

across [ə'krɔs] prep (on the other side of) al otro lado de; (crosswise) a través de ▷ adv de un lado a otro, de una parte a otra a través, al través; **to run/swim** ~ atravesar corriendo/ nadando; ~ **from** enfrente de; **the lake is 12 km** ~ el lago tiene 12 km de ancho; **to get sth** ~ **to sb** (fig) hacer comprender algo a algn

acrylic [ə'krɪlɪk] adj acrílico

act [ækt] n acto, acción f; (Theat) acto; (in music-hall etc) número; (Law) decreto, ley f ▷ vi (behave) comportarse; (Theat) actuar; (pretend) fingir; (take action) tomar medidas ▷ vt (part) hacer, representar; ~ **of God** fuerza mayor; **it's only an ~** es cuento; **to catch sb in the ~** coger a algn in fraganti or con las manos en la masa; **to ~ Hamlet** hacer el papel de Hamlet; **to ~ as** actuar or hacer de; ~**ing in my capacity as chairman, I** ... en mi calidad de presidente, yo ...; **it ~s as a deterrent** sirve para disuadir; **he's only** ~**ing** está fingiendo nada más; **act on** vt: **to ~ on sth** actuar or obrar sobre algo; **act out** vt (event) representar; (fantasies) realizar; **act up** vi (inf: person) portarse mal

acting ['æktɪŋ] n adj suplente ▷ n: **to do some** ~ hacer algo de teatro; **he is the ~ manager** es el gerente en funciones

action ['ækʃən] n acción f, acto; (Mil) acción f; (Law) proceso, demanda ▷ vt (Comm) llevar a cabo; **to put a plan into ~** poner un plan en acción or en marcha; **killed in ~** (Mil) muerto en acto de servicio or en combate; **out of ~** (person) fuera de combate; (thing) averiado, estropeado; **to take ~** tomar medidas; **to bring an ~ against sb** entablar or presentar demanda contra algn

action replay n (TV) repetición f

activate ['æktɪveɪt] vt activar

active ['æktɪv] adj activo, enérgico; (volcano) en actividad; **to play an ~ part in** colaborar activamente en

actively ['æktɪvlɪ] adv (participate) activamente; (discourage, dislike) enérgicamente

activist ['æktɪvɪst] n activista m/f

activity [æk'tɪvɪtɪ] n actividad f

activity holiday n vacaciones con actividades organizadas

actor ['æktəʳ] n actor m

actress ['æktrɪs] n actriz f

actual ['æktjuəl] adj verdadero, real

actually ['æktjuəlɪ] adv realmente, en realidad

acumen ['ækjumən] n perspicacia; **business** ~ talento para los negocios

acupuncture ['ækjupʌŋktʃəʳ] n acupuntura

acute [ə'kju:t] adj agudo

acutely [ə'kju:tlɪ] adv profundamente, extremadamente

AD adv abbr (= Anno Domini) d.C. ▷ n abbr (US Mil) = **active duty**

ad [æd] n abbr = **advertisement**

Adam ['ædəm] n Adán; ~**'s apple** n nuez f (de la garganta)

adamant ['ædəmənt] adj firme, inflexible

adapt [ə'dæpt] vt adaptar; (reconcile) acomodar ▷ vi: **to ~ (to)** adaptarse (a), ajustarse (a)

adaptability [ədæptə'bɪlɪtɪ] n (of person, device etc) adaptabilidad f

adaptable [ə'dæptəbl] adj (device) adaptable; (person) acomodadizo, que se adapta

adaptation [ædæp'teɪʃən] n adaptación f

adapter, adaptor [ə'dæptəʳ] n (Elec) adaptador m; (for several plugs) ladrón m

add [æd] vt añadir, agregar (esp LAm); (figures: also: ~ **up**) sumar ▷ vi: **to ~ to** (increase) aumentar, acrecentar ▷ n (Internet): **thanks for the ~** gracias por agregarme; **add on** vt añadir; **add up** vt (figures) sumar ▷ vi (fig): **it doesn't ~ up** no tiene sentido; **it doesn't ~ up to much** es poca cosa, no tiene gran or mucha importancia

addendum [ə'dɛndəm] n ad(d)enda m or f

adder ['ædəʳ] n víbora

addict ['ædɪkt] n (to drugs etc) adicto(-a); (enthusiast) aficionado(-a), entusiasta m/f; **heroin** ~ heroinómano(-a)

addicted [ə'dɪktɪd] adj: **to be ~ to** ser adicto a; ser aficionado a

addiction [ə'dɪkʃən] n (to drugs etc) adicción f; (enthusiasm) afición f

addictive [ə'dɪktɪv] adj que causa adicción

addition [ə'dɪʃən] n (adding up) adición f; (thing added) añadidura, añadido; **in** ~ además, por añadidura; **in ~ to** además de

additional [ə'dɪʃənl] adj adicional

additive ['ædɪtɪv] n aditivo

address [ə'drɛs] n dirección f, señas fpl; (speech) discurso; (Comput) dirección f ▷ vt (letter) dirigir; (speak to) dirigirse a, dirigir la palabra a; **form of** ~ tratamiento; **absolute/ relative** ~ (Comput) dirección f absoluta/ relativa; **to ~ o.s. to sth** (issue, problem) abordar

address book n agenda (de direcciones)

addressee [ædrɛ'si:] n destinatario(-a)

adenoids ['ædɪnɔɪdz] npl vegetaciones fpl (adenoideas)

adept ['ædɛpt] adj: ~ **at** experto or ducho en

adequate ['ædɪkwɪt] *adj* (*satisfactory*) adecuado; (*enough*) suficiente; **to feel ~ to a task** sentirse con fuerzas para una tarea
adequately ['ædɪkwɪtlɪ] *adv* adecuadamente
adhere [əd'hɪəʳ] *vi*: **to ~ to** adherirse a; (*fig: abide by*) observar
adhesive [əd'hi:zɪv] *adj, n* adhesivo
adhesive tape *n* (*Brit*) cinta adhesiva; (*US Med*) esparadrapo
ad hoc [æd'hɔk] *adj* (*decision*) ad hoc; (*committee*) formado con fines específicos ▷ *adv* ad hoc
adjacent [ə'dʒeɪsənt] *adj*: **~ to** contiguo a, inmediato a
adjective ['ædʒɛktɪv] *n* adjetivo
adjoining [ə'dʒɔɪnɪŋ] *adj* contiguo, vecino
adjourn [ə'dʒə:n] *vt* aplazar; (*session*) suspender, levantar; (*US: end*) terminar ▷ *vi* suspenderse; **the meeting has been ~ed till next week** se ha levantado la sesión hasta la semana que viene; **they ~ed to the pub** (*inf*) se trasladaron al bar
adjournment [ə'dʒə:nmənt] *n* (*period*) suspensión *f*; (*postponement*) aplazamiento
adjudicate [ə'dʒu:dɪkeɪt] *vi* sentenciar ▷ *vt* (*contest*) hacer de árbitro en, juzgar; (*claim*) decidir
adjust [ə'dʒʌst] *vt* (*change*) modificar; (*arrange*) arreglar; (*machine*) ajustar ▷ *vi*: **to ~ (to)** adaptarse (a)
adjustable [ə'dʒʌstəbl] *adj* ajustable
adjustment [ə'dʒʌstmənt] *n* adaptación *f*; arreglo; (*of prices, wages*) ajuste *m*
ad-lib [æd'lɪb] *vt, vi* improvisar ▷ *adv*: **ad lib** a voluntad, a discreción
admin ['ædmɪn] *n abbr* (*inf*) = **administration**
administer [əd'mɪnɪstəʳ] *vt* proporcionar; (*justice*) administrar
administration [ædmɪnɪ'streɪʃən] *n* administración *f*; (*government*) gobierno; **the A~** (*US*) la Administración
administrative [əd'mɪnɪstrətɪv] *adj* administrativo
administrator [əd'mɪnɪstreɪtəʳ] *n* administrador(a) *m(f)*
admirable ['ædmərəbl] *adj* admirable
admiral ['ædmərəl] *n* almirante *m*
Admiralty ['ædmərəltɪ] *n* (*Brit*) Ministerio de Marina, Almirantazgo
admiration [ædmə'reɪʃən] *n* admiración *f*
admire [əd'maɪəʳ] *vt* admirar
admirer [əd'maɪərəʳ] *n* admirador(a) *m(f)*; (*suitor*) pretendiente *m*
admiring [əd'maɪərɪŋ] *adj* (*expression*) de admiración
admissible [əd'mɪsəbl] *adj* admisible
admission [əd'mɪʃən] *n* (*to exhibition, nightclub*) entrada; (*enrolment*) ingreso; (*confession*) confesión *f*; **"~ free"** "entrada gratis or libre"; **by his own ~** él mismo reconoce que
admit [əd'mɪt] *vt* dejar entrar, dar entrada a; (*permit*) admitir; (*acknowledge*) reconocer;

"this ticket ~s two" "entrada para dos personas"; **children not ~ted** se prohíbe la entrada a (los) menores de edad; **to be ~ted to hospital** ingresar en el hospital; **I must ~ that ...** debo reconocer que ...; **admit of** *vt fus* admitir, permitir; **admit to** *vt fus* confesarse culpable de
admittance [əd'mɪtəns] *n* entrada; **"no ~"** "se prohíbe la entrada", "prohibida la entrada"
admittedly [əd'mɪtədlɪ] *adv* es cierto que
admonish [əd'mɔnɪʃ] *vt* amonestar; (*advise*) aconsejar
ad nauseam [æd'nɔ:sɪæm] *adv* hasta la saciedad
ado [ə'du:] *n*: **without (any) more ~** sin más (ni más)
adolescence [ædəu'lɛsns] *n* adolescencia
adolescent [ædəu'lɛsnt] *adj, n* adolescente *m/f*
adopt [ə'dɔpt] *vt* adoptar
adopted [ə'dɔptɪd] *adj* adoptivo
adoption [ə'dɔpʃən] *n* adopción *f*
adorable [ə'dɔ:rəbl] *adj* adorable
adore [ə'dɔ:ʳ] *vt* adorar
adoring [ə'dɔ:rɪŋ] *adj*: **to his ~ public** a un público que le adora *or* le adoraba *etc*
adorn [ə'dɔ:n] *vt* adornar
adrenalin [ə'drɛnəlɪn] *n* adrenalina
Adriatic [eɪdrɪ'ætɪk] *n*: **the ~ (Sea)** el (Mar) Adriático
adrift [ə'drɪft] *adv* a la deriva; **to come ~** (*boat*) ir a la deriva, soltarse; (*wire, rope etc*) soltarse
ADSL *n abbr* (= *asymmetrical digital subscriber line*) ADSL *m*
adult ['ædʌlt] *n* adulto(-a) ▷ *adj*: **~ education** educación *f* para adultos
adultery [ə'dʌltərɪ] *n* adulterio
advance [əd'vɑ:ns] *n* adelanto, progreso; (*money*) anticipo; (*Mil*) avance *m* ▷ *vt* avanzar, adelantar; (*money*) anticipar ▷ *vi* avanzar, adelantarse; **in ~** por adelantado; (*book*) con antelación; **to make ~s to sb** (*gen*) hacer una proposición a algn; (*amorously*) insinuarse a algn
advanced *adj* avanzado; (*Scol: studies*) adelantado; **~ in years** entrado en años
advantage [əd'vɑ:ntɪdʒ] *n* (*also Tennis*) ventaja; **to take ~ of** aprovecharse de; **it's to our ~** es ventajoso para nosotros
advantageous [ædvən'teɪdʒəs] *adj* ventajoso, provechoso
advent ['ædvənt] *n* advenimiento; **A~** Adviento
adventure [əd'vɛntʃəʳ] *n* aventura
adventure playground *n* parque *m* infantil
adventurous [əd'vɛntʃərəs] *adj* aventurero; (*bold*) arriesgado
adverb ['ædvə:b] *n* adverbio
adversary ['ædvəsərɪ] *n* adversario, contrario

adverse ['ædvə:s] *adj* adverso, contrario; ~ **to** adverso a

adversity [əd'və:sɪtɪ] *n* infortunio

advert ['ædvə:t] *n abbr* (Brit) = **advertisement**

advertise ['ædvətaɪz] *vi* hacer propaganda; (*in newspaper etc*) poner un anuncio, anunciarse; **to ~ for** (*staff*) buscar por medio de anuncios ▷ *vt* anunciar

advertisement [əd'və:tɪsmənt] *n* anuncio

advertiser ['ædvətaɪzə'] *n* anunciante *m/f*

advertising ['ædvətaɪzɪŋ] *n* publicidad *f*, propaganda; anuncios *mpl*; (*industry*) industria publicitaria

advertising agency *n* agencia de publicidad

advice [əd'vaɪs] *n* consejo, consejos *mpl*; (*notification*) aviso; **a piece of ~** un consejo; **to take legal ~** consultar a un abogado; **to ask (sb) for ~** pedir consejo (a algn)

advisable [əd'vaɪzəbl] *adj* aconsejable, conveniente

advise [əd'vaɪz] *vt* aconsejar; **to ~ sb of sth** (*inform*) informar a algn de algo; **to ~ sb against sth/doing sth** desaconsejar algo a algn/aconsejar a algn que no haga algo; **you will be well/ill ~d to go** deberías/no deberías ir

advisedly [əd'vaɪzɪdlɪ] *adv* deliberadamente

adviser [əd'vaɪzə'] *n* consejero(-a); (*business adviser*) asesor(a) *m(f)*

advisory [əd'vaɪzərɪ] *adj* consultivo; **in an ~ capacity** como asesor

advocate ['ædvəkeɪt] *vt* (*argue for*) abogar por; (*give support to*) ser partidario de ▷ *n* ['ædvəkɪt] abogado(-a); (*supporter*): ~ **of** defensor(a) *m(f)* de

Aegean [i:'dʒi:ən] *n*: **the ~** (**Sea**) el (Mar) Egeo

aerial ['ɛərɪəl] *n* antena ▷ *adj* aéreo

aerobatics [ɛərəu'bætɪks] *npl* acrobacia aérea

aerobics [ɛə'rəubɪks] *nsg* aerobic *m*, aerobismo (*LAm*)

aeroplane ['ɛərəpleɪn] *n* (Brit) avión *m*

aerosol ['ɛərəsɔl] *n* aerosol *m*

aesthetic [i:s'θɛtɪk] *adj* estético

afar [ə'fɑ:'] *adv* lejos; **from ~** desde lejos

affair [ə'fɛə'] *n* asunto; (*also*: **love ~**) aventura *f* amorosa; **~s** (*business*) asuntos *mpl*; **the Watergate ~** el asunto (de) Watergate

affect [ə'fɛkt] *vt* afectar, influir en; (*move*) conmover

affected [ə'fɛktɪd] *adj* afectado

affection [ə'fɛkʃən] *n* afecto, cariño

affectionate [ə'fɛkʃənɪt] *adj* afectuoso, cariñoso

affinity [ə'fɪnɪtɪ] *n* afinidad *f*

affirm [ə'fə:m] *vt* afirmar

affirmative [ə'fə:mətɪv] *adj* afirmativo

afflict [ə'flɪkt] *vt* afligir

affluence ['æfluəns] *n* opulencia, riqueza

affluent ['æfluənt] *adj* acomodado; **the ~ society** la sociedad opulenta

afford [ə'fɔ:d] *vt* poder permitirse; (*provide*) proporcionar; **can we ~ a car?** ¿podemos permitirnos el gasto de comprar un coche?

affordable [ə'fɔ:dəbl] *adj* asequible

Afghanistan [æf'gænɪstæn] *n* Afganistán *m*

afield [ə'fi:ld] *adv*: **far ~** muy lejos

afloat [ə'fləut] *adv* (*floating*) a flote; (*at sea*) en el mar

afoot [ə'fut] *adv*: **there is something ~** algo se está tramando

afraid [ə'freɪd] *adj*: **to be ~ of** (*person*) tener miedo a; (*thing*) tener miedo de; **to be ~ to** tener miedo de, temer; **I am ~ that** me temo que; **I'm ~ so** lo siento, pero es así, me temo que sí; **I'm ~ not** lo siento, pero no

afresh [ə'frɛʃ] *adv* de nuevo, otra vez

Africa ['æfrɪkə] *n* África

African ['æfrɪkən] *adj*, *n* africano(-a) *m(f)*

African-American *adj*, *n* afroamericano(-a)

Afro-American ['æfrəuə'mɛrɪkən] *adj*, *n* afroamericano(-a) *m(f)*

aft [ɑ:ft] *adv* (*be*) en popa; (*go*) a popa

after ['ɑ:ftə'] *prep* (*time*) después de; (*place, order*) detrás de, tras ▷ *adv* después ▷ *conj* después (de) que; **what/who are you ~?** ¿qué/a quién buscas?; **the police are ~ him** la policía le está buscando; **~ having done/he left** después de haber hecho/después de que se marchó; **~ dinner** después de cenar *or* comer; **the day ~ tomorrow** pasado mañana; **to ask ~ sb** preguntar por algn; **~ all** después de todo, al fin y al cabo; **~ you!** ¡pase usted!; **quarter ~ two** (US) las dos y cuarto

afterbirth ['ɑ:ftəbə:θ] *n* placenta

after-effects ['ɑ:ftərɪfɛkts] *npl* secuelas *fpl*, efectos *mpl*

afterlife ['ɑ:ftəlaɪf] *n* vida después de la muerte

aftermath ['ɑ:ftəmɑ:θ] *n* consecuencias *fpl*, resultados *mpl*

afternoon [ɑ:ftə'nu:n] *n* tarde *f*; **good ~!** ¡buenas tardes!

afters ['ɑ:ftəz] *n* (*inf*: *dessert*) postre *m*

after-sales service [ɑ:ftə'seɪlz-] *n* (Brit Comm: *for car, washing machine etc*) servicio de asistencia pos-venta

after-shave ['ɑ:ftəʃeɪv], **after-shave lotion** *n* loción *f* para después del afeitado, aftershave *m*

aftersun ['ɑ:ftəsʌn], **aftersun lotion** *n* aftersun *m inv*

aftertaste ['ɑ:ftəteɪst] *n* regusto

afterthought ['ɑ:ftəθɔ:t] *n* ocurrencia (tardía)

afterwards ['ɑ:ftəwədz] *adv* después, más tarde

again [ə'gɛn] *adv* otra vez, de nuevo; **to do sth ~** volver a hacer algo; **~ and ~** una y otra vez; **now and ~** de vez en cuando

against [ə'gɛnst] *prep* (*opposed*) en contra de; (*close to*) contra, junto a; **I was leaning ~ the**

desk estaba apoyado en el escritorio; **(as)** ~ frente a

age [eɪdʒ] n edad f; (old age) vejez f; (period) época ▷ vi envejecer(se) ▷ vt envejecer; **what ~ is he?** ¿qué edad or cuántos años tiene?; **he is 20 years of** ~ tiene 20 años; **under** ~ menor de edad; **to come of** ~ llegar a la mayoría de edad; **it's been ~s since I saw you** hace siglos que no te veo

aged [eɪdʒd] adj: ~ 10 de 10 años de edad ▷ npl ['eɪdʒɪd]: **the** ~ los ancianos

age group n: **to be in the same** ~ tener la misma edad; **the 40 to 50** ~ las personas de 40 a 50 años

ageing ['eɪdʒɪŋ] adj que envejece; (pej) en declive ▷ n envejecimiento

age limit n límite m de edad, edad f tope

agency ['eɪdʒənsɪ] n agencia; **through** or **by the** ~ **of** por medio de

agenda [ə'dʒɛndə] n orden m del día; **on the** ~ (Comm) en el orden del día

agent ['eɪdʒənt] n (gen) agente m/f; (representative) representante m/f delegado(-a)

aggravate ['ægrəveɪt] vt agravar; (annoy) irritar, exasperar

aggravating ['ægrəveɪtɪŋ] adj irritante, molesto

aggravation [ægrə'veɪʃən] n agravamiento

aggregate ['ægrɪgeɪt] n conjunto

aggression [ə'grɛʃən] n agresión f

aggressive [ə'grɛsɪv] adj agresivo; (vigorous) enérgico

aggressor [ə'grɛsər] n agresor(a) m(f)

aggrieved [ə'gri:vd] adj ofendido, agraviado

aggro ['ægrəu] n (inf: physical violence) bronca; (bad feeling) mal rollo; (hassle) rollo, movida

aghast [ə'gɑːst] adj horrorizado

agile ['ædʒaɪl] adj ágil

agility [ə'dʒɪlɪtɪ] n agilidad f

agitate ['ædʒɪteɪt] vt (shake) agitar; (trouble) inquietar; **to** ~ **for** hacer campaña en pro de or en favor de

agitated ['ædʒɪteɪtɪd] adj agitado

AGM n abbr = **annual general meeting**

agnostic [æg'nɔstɪk] adj, n agnóstico(-a) m(f)

ago [ə'gəu] adv: **two days** ~ hace dos días; **not long** ~ hace poco; **how long** ~? ¿hace cuánto tiempo?; **as long** ~ **as 1980** ya en 1980

agog [ə'gɔg] adj (anxious) ansioso; (excited): **(all)** ~ **(for)** (todo) emocionado (por)

agonize ['ægənaɪz] vi: **to** ~ **(over)** atormentarse (por)

agonized ['ægənaɪzd] adj angustioso

agonizing ['ægənaɪzɪŋ] adj (pain) atroz; (suspense) angustioso

agony ['ægənɪ] n (pain) dolor m atroz; (distress) angustia; **to be in** ~ retorcerse de dolor

agony aunt n (Brit inf) consejera sentimental

agree [ə'griː] vt (price) acordar, quedar en ▷ vi (statements etc) coincidir, concordar; **to** ~ **(with)** (person) estar de acuerdo (con), ponerse de acuerdo (con); **to** ~ **to do** aceptar hacer;

to ~ **to sth** consentir en algo; **to** ~ **that** (admit) estar de acuerdo en que; **it was ~d that ...** se acordó que ...; **garlic doesn't** ~ **with me** el ajo no me sienta bien

agreeable [ə'griːəbl] adj agradable; (person) simpático; (willing) de acuerdo, conforme

agreed [ə'griːd] adj (time, place) convenido

agreement [ə'griːmənt] n acuerdo; (Comm) contrato; **in** ~ de acuerdo, conforme; **by mutual** ~ de común acuerdo

agricultural [ægrɪ'kʌltʃərəl] adj agrícola

agriculture ['ægrɪkʌltʃər] n agricultura

aground [ə'graund] adv: **to run** ~ encallar, embarrancar

ahead [ə'hɛd] adv delante; ~ **of** delante de; (fig: schedule etc) antes de; ~ **of time** antes de la hora; **to be** ~ **of sb** (fig) llevar ventaja or la delantera a algn; **go right** or **straight** ~ siga adelante; **they were (right)** ~ **of us** iban (justo) delante de nosotros

aid [eɪd] n ayuda, auxilio ▷ vt ayudar, auxiliar; **in** ~ **of** a beneficio de; **with the** ~ **of** con la ayuda de; **to** ~ **and abet** (Law) ser cómplice

aide [eɪd] n (Pol) ayudante m/f

AIDS [eɪdz] n abbr (= acquired immune (or immuno-)deficiency syndrome) SIDA m, sida m

ailing ['eɪlɪŋ] adj (person, economy) enfermizo

ailment ['eɪlmənt] n enfermedad f, achaque m

aim [eɪm] vt (gun) apuntar; (missile, remark) dirigir; (blow) asestar ▷ vi (also: **take** ~) apuntar ▷ n puntería; (objective) propósito, meta; **to** ~ **at** (objective) aspirar a, pretender; **to** ~ **to do** tener la intención de hacer, aspirar a hacer

aimless ['eɪmlɪs] adj sin propósito, sin objeto

ain't [eɪnt] (inf) = **am not; aren't; isn't**

air [ɛər] n aire m; (appearance) aspecto ▷ vt (room) ventilar; (clothes, bed, grievances, ideas) airear; (views) hacer público ▷ cpd aéreo; **to throw sth into the** ~ (ball etc) lanzar algo al aire; **by** ~ (travel) en avión; **to be on the** ~ (Radio, TV: programme) estarse emitiendo; (: station) estar en antena

airbag ['ɛəbæg] n airbag m inv

air bed n (Brit) colchoneta inflable or neumática

airborne ['ɛəbɔːn] adj (in the air) en el aire; (Mil) aerotransportado; **as soon as the plane was** ~ tan pronto como el avión estuvo en el aire

air-conditioned ['ɛəkən'dɪʃənd] adj climatizado

air conditioning [-kən'dɪʃənɪŋ] n aire m acondicionado

aircraft ['ɛəkrɑːft] n pl inv avión m

aircraft carrier n porta(a)viones m inv

airfield ['ɛəfiːld] n campo de aviación

Air Force n fuerzas aéreas fpl, aviación f

air freshener n ambientador m

air gun n escopeta de aire comprimido

air hostess (Brit) n azafata, aeromoza (LAm)
airing ['eərɪŋ] n: **to give an ~ to** (linen) airear; (room) ventilar; (fig: ideas etc) airear, someter a discusión
airing cupboard n (Brit) armario m para oreo
air letter n (Brit) carta aérea
airlift ['eəlɪft] n puente m aéreo
airline ['eəlaɪn] n línea aérea
airliner ['eəlaɪnə'] n avión m de pasajeros
airmail ['eəmeɪl] n: **by ~** por avión
airplane ['eəpleɪn] n (US) avión m
air pocket n bolsa de aire
airport ['eəpɔːt] n aeropuerto
air rage n conducta agresiva de pasajeros a bordo de un avión
air raid n ataque m aéreo
air rifle n escopeta de aire comprimido
airsick ['eəsɪk] adj: **to be ~** marearse (en avión)
airspace n espacio aéreo
airspeed ['eəspiːd] n velocidad f de vuelo
airstrip ['eəstrɪp] n pista de aterrizaje
air terminal n terminal f
airtight ['eətaɪt] adj hermético
air time n (Radio, TV) tiempo en antena
air traffic control n control m de tráfico aéreo
air traffic controller n controlador(a) m(f) aéreo(-a)
airway ['eəweɪ] n (Aviat) vía aérea; (Anat) vía respiratoria
airy ['eərɪ] adj (room) bien ventilado; (manners) desenfadado
aisle [aɪl] n (of church) nave f lateral; (of theatre, plane) pasillo
aisle seat n (on plane) asiento de pasillo
ajar [ə'dʒɑː'] adj entreabierto
akin [ə'kɪn] adj: **~ to** semejante a
à la carte [ælæ'kɑːt] adv a la carta
alarm [ə'lɑːm] n alarma; (anxiety) inquietud f
▷ vt asustar, alarmar
alarm call n (in hotel etc) alarma
alarm clock n despertador m
alarmed [ə'lɑːmd] adj (person) alarmado, asustado; (house, car etc) con alarma
alarming [ə'lɑːmɪŋ] adj alarmante
alas [ə'læs] adv desgraciadamente ▷ excl ¡ay!
Albania [æl'beɪnɪə] n Albania
albatross ['ælbətrɔs] n albatros m
albeit [ɔːl'biːɪt] conj (although) aunque
album ['ælbəm] n álbum m; (L.P.) elepé m
alcohol ['ælkəhɔl] n alcohol m
alcohol-free ['ælkəhɔlfriː] adj sin alcohol
alcoholic [ælkə'hɔlɪk] adj, n alcohólico(-a) m(f)
alcoholism ['ælkəhɔlɪzəm] n alcoholismo
alcove ['ælkəuv] n nicho, hueco
ale [eɪl] n cerveza
alert [ə'lɜːt] adj alerta inv; (sharp) despierto, atento ▷ n alerta m, alarma ▷ vt poner sobre aviso; **to ~ sb (to sth)** poner sobre aviso or alertar a algn (de algo); **to ~ sb to the**

dangers of sth poner sobre aviso or alertar a algn de los peligros de algo; **to be on the ~** estar alerta or sobre aviso
A level n abbr (Brit Scol: = Advanced level) ≈ Bachillerato
algebra ['ældʒɪbrə] n álgebra
Algeria [æl'dʒɪərɪə] n Argelia
Algerian [æl'dʒɪərɪən] adj, n argelino(-a) m(f)
alias ['eɪlɪəs] adv alias, conocido por ▷ n alias m; (of criminal) apodo; (of writer) seudónimo
alibi ['ælɪbaɪ] n coartada
alien ['eɪlɪən] n (foreigner) extranjero(-a); (extraterrestrial) extraterrestre m/f ▷ adj: **~ to** ajeno a
alienate ['eɪlɪəneɪt] vt enajenar, alejar
alight [ə'laɪt] adj ardiendo ▷ vi apearse, bajar
align [ə'laɪn] vt alinear
alignment [ə'laɪnmənt] n alineación f; **the desks are out of ~** los pupitres no están bien alineados
alike [ə'laɪk] adj semejantes, iguales ▷ adv igualmente, del mismo modo; **to look ~** parecerse
alimony ['ælɪmənɪ] n (Law) pensión f alimenticia
alive [ə'laɪv] adj (gen) vivo; (lively) alegre
alkali ['ælkəlaɪ] n álcali m

KEYWORD

all [ɔːl] adj todo(-a) sg, todos(-as) pl; **all day** todo el día; **all night** toda la noche; **all men** todos los hombres; **all five came** vinieron los cinco; **all the books** todos los libros; **all the time/his life** todo el tiempo/toda su vida; **for all their efforts** a pesar de todos sus esfuerzos
▷ pron **1** todo; **I ate it all, I ate all of it** me lo comí todo; **all of them** todos (ellos); **all of us went** fuimos todos; **all the boys went** fueron todos los chicos; **is that all?** ¿eso es todo?, ¿algo más?; (in shop) ¿algo más?, ¿alguna cosa más?
2 (in phrases): **above all** sobre todo; por encima de todo; **after all** después de todo; **at all**: **anything at all** lo que sea; **not at all** (in answer to question) en absoluto; (in answer to thanks) ¡de nada!, ¡no hay de qué!; **I'm not at all tired** no estoy nada cansado(-a); **anything at all will do** cualquier cosa viene bien; **all in all** a fin de cuentas
▷ adv: **all alone** completamente solo(-a); **to be/feel all in** estar rendido; **it's not as hard as all that** no es tan difícil como lo pintas; **all the more/the better** tanto más/mejor; **all but** casi; **the score is two all** están empatados a dos

Allah ['ælə] n Alá m
all-around ['ɔːlə'raund] adj (US) = **all-round**
allay [ə'leɪ] vt (fears) aquietar; (pain) aliviar
allegation [ælɪ'geɪʃən] n alegato

allege [ə'lɛdʒ] vt pretender; **he is ~d to have said ...** se afirma que él dijo ...

alleged [ə'lɛdʒd] adj supuesto, presunto

allegedly [ə'lɛdʒɪdlɪ] adv supuestamente, según se afirma

allegiance [ə'li:dʒəns] n lealtad f

allegory ['ælɪgərɪ] n alegoría

allergic [ə'lɜ:dʒɪk] adj: **~ to** alérgico a

allergy ['ælədʒɪ] n alergia

alleviate [ə'li:vɪeɪt] vt aliviar

alley ['ælɪ] n (street) callejuela; (in garden) paseo

alleyway ['ælɪweɪ] n callejón m

alliance [ə'laɪəns] n alianza

allied ['ælaɪd] adj aliado; (related) relacionado

alligator ['ælɪgeɪtər] n caimán m

all-in ['ɔ:lɪn] adj, adv (Brit: charge) todo incluido

all-in wrestling n lucha libre

alliteration [əlɪtə'reɪʃən] n aliteración f

all-night ['ɔ:l'naɪt] adj (café) abierto toda la noche; (party) que dura toda la noche

allocate ['æləkeɪt] vt (share out) repartir; (devote) asignar

allocation [ælə'keɪʃən] n (of money) ración f, cuota; (distribution) reparto

allot [ə'lɔt] vt asignar; **in the ~ted time** en el tiempo asignado

allotment [ə'lɔtmənt] n porción f; (garden) parcela

all-out ['ɔ:laut] adj (effort etc) supremo ▷ adv: **all out** con todas las fuerzas, a fondo

allow [ə'lau] vt (permit) permitir, dejar; (a claim) admitir; (sum to spend, time estimated) dar, conceder; (concede): **to ~ that** reconocer que; **to ~ sb to do** permitir a algn hacer; **smoking is not ~ed** prohibido or se prohíbe fumar; **he is ~ed to ...** se le permite ...; **we must ~ three days for the journey** debemos dejar tres días para el viaje; **allow for** vt fus tener en cuenta

allowance [ə'lauəns] n concesión f; (payment) subvención f, pensión f; (discount) descuento, rebaja; (tax allowance) desgravación f; **to make ~s for** (person) disculpar a; (thing: take into account) tener en cuenta

alloy ['ælɔɪ] n aleación f

all right adv (feel, work) bien; (as answer) ¡de acuerdo!, ¡está bien!

all-round ['ɔ:l'raund] adj completo; (view) amplio

all-rounder ['ɔ:l'raundər] n: **to be a good ~** ser una persona que hace de todo

all-time ['ɔ:l'taɪm] adj (record) de todos los tiempos

allude [ə'lu:d] vi: **to ~ to** aludir a

alluring [ə'ljuərɪŋ] adj seductor(a), atractivo

allusion [ə'lu:ʒən] n referencia, alusión f

ally n ['ælaɪ] aliado(-a) ▷ vt [ə'laɪ]: **to ~ o.s. with** aliarse con

almighty [ɔ:l'maɪtɪ] adj todopoderoso; (row etc) imponente

almond ['ɑ:mənd] n (fruit) almendra; (tree) almendro

almost ['ɔ:lməust] adv casi; **he ~ fell** casi or por poco se cae

alms [ɑ:mz] npl limosna sg

aloft [ə'lɔft] adv arriba

alone [ə'ləun] adj solo ▷ adv solo, solamente; **to leave sb ~** dejar a algn en paz; **to leave sth ~** no tocar algo; **let ~ ...** y mucho menos ..., y no digamos ...

along [ə'lɔŋ] prep a lo largo de, por ▷ adv: **is he coming ~ with us?** ¿viene con nosotros?; **he was limping ~** iba cojeando; **~ with** junto con; **all ~** (all the time) desde el principio

alongside [ə'lɔŋ'saɪd] prep al lado de ▷ adv (Naut) de costado; **we brought our boat ~** atracamos nuestro barco

aloof [ə'lu:f] adj distante ▷ adv: **to stand ~** mantenerse a distancia

aloud [ə'laud] adv en voz alta

alphabet ['ælfəbɛt] n alfabeto

alphabetical [ælfə'bɛtɪkəl] adj alfabético; **in ~ order** por orden alfabético

alpine ['ælpaɪn] adj alpino, alpestre

Alps [ælps] npl: **the ~** los Alpes

already [ɔ:l'rɛdɪ] adv ya

alright [ɔ:l'raɪt] adv (Brit) = all right

Alsatian [æl'seɪʃən] n (dog) pastor m alemán

also ['ɔ:lsəu] adv también, además

altar ['ɔltər] n altar m

alter ['ɔltər] vt cambiar, modificar ▷ vi cambiar, modificarse

alteration [ɔltə'reɪʃən] n cambio, modificación f; (Arch) **alterations** npl (Arch) reformas fpl; (Sewing) arreglos mpl; **timetable subject to ~** el horario puede cambiar

altercation [ɔltə'keɪʃən] n altercado

alternate adj [ɔl'tɜ:nɪt] adj alterno ▷ vi ['ɔltəneɪt]: **to ~ (with)** alternar (con); **on ~ days** en días alternos

alternately [ɔl'tɜ:nɪtlɪ] adv alternativamente, por turno

alternating ['ɔltəneɪtɪŋ] adj (current) alterno

alternative [ɔl'tɜ:nətɪv] adj alternativo ▷ n alternativa; **~ medicine** medicina alternativa

alternatively [ɔl'tɜ:nətɪvlɪ] adv: **~ one could ...** por otra parte se podría ...

alternative medicine n medicina alternativa

alternator ['ɔltəneɪtər] n (Aut) alternador m

although [ɔ:l'ðəu] conj aunque, si bien

altitude ['æltɪtju:d] n altitud f, altura

alto ['æltəu] n (female) contralto f; (male) alto

altogether [ɔ:ltə'gɛðər] adv completamente, del todo; (on the whole, in all) en total, en conjunto; **how much is that ~?** ¿cuánto es todo or en total?

altruism ['æltruɪzəm] n altruismo

aluminium [ælju'mɪnɪəm], **aluminum** (US) [ə'lu:mɪnəm] n aluminio

always ['ɔ:lweɪz] adv siempre

Alzheimer's [' æltshaɪməz] n (also: **~ disease**) enfermedad f de Alzheimer

AM abbr (= amplitude modulation) A.M. f ▷ n abbr (Pol: in Wales) = **Assembly Member**

am [æm] vb see **be**

a.m. adv abbr (= ante meridiem) de la mañana

amalgamate [ə'mælgəmeɪt] vi amalgamarse ▷ vt amalgamar

amass [ə'mæs] vt amontonar, acumular

amateur ['æmətə'] n aficionado(-a), amateur m/f; **~ dramatics** dramas mpl presentados por aficionados, representación f de aficionados

amateurish ['æmətərɪʃ] adj (pej) torpe, inexperto

amaze [ə'meɪz] vt asombrar, pasmar; **to be ~d (at)** asombrarse (de)

amazed adj [ə'meɪzd] asombrado

amazement [ə'meɪzmənt] n asombro, sorpresa; **to my ~** para mi sorpresa

amazing [ə'meɪzɪŋ] adj extraordinario, asombroso; (bargain, offer) increíble

Amazon ['æməzən] n (Geo) Amazonas m; (Mythology) amazona ▷ cpd: **the ~ basin/jungle** la cuenca/selva del Amazonas

ambassador [æm'bæsədə'] n embajador(a) m(f)

amber ['æmbə'] n ámbar m; **at ~** (Brit Aut) en amarillo

ambiguity [æmbɪ'gjuːɪtɪ] n ambigüedad f; (of meaning) doble sentido

ambiguous [æm'bɪgjuəs] adj ambiguo

ambition [æm'bɪʃən] n ambición f; **to achieve one's ~** realizar su ambición

ambitious [æm'bɪʃəs] adj ambicioso; (plan) grandioso

amble ['æmbl] vi (gen: also: **~ along**) deambular, andar sin prisa

ambulance ['æmbjuləns] n ambulancia

ambush ['æmbuʃ] n emboscada ▷ vt tender una emboscada a; (fig) coger (Sp) or agarrar (LAm) por sorpresa

amen [ɑː'mɛn] excl amén

amenable [ə'miːnəbl] adj: **~ to** (advice etc) sensible a

amend [ə'mɛnd] vt (law, text) enmendar; **to make ~s** (apologize) enmendarlo, dar cumplida satisfacción

amendment [ə'mɛndmənt] n enmienda

amenities [ə'miːnɪtɪz] npl comodidades fpl

America [ə'mɛrɪkə] n América (del Norte); (USA) Estados mpl Unidos

American [ə'mɛrɪkən] adj, n (norte) americano(-a) m(f), estadounidense m/f

American football n (Brit) fútbol m americano

amiable ['eɪmɪəbl] adj (kind) amable, simpático

amicable ['æmɪkəbl] adj amistoso, amigable

amid [ə'mɪd], **amidst** [ə'mɪdst] prep entre, en medio de

amiss [ə'mɪs] adv: **to take sth ~** tomar algo a mal; **there's something ~** pasa algo

ammonia [ə'məunɪə] n amoníaco

ammunition [æmju'nɪʃən] n municiones fpl; (fig) argumentos mpl

amnesia [æm'niːzɪə] n amnesia

amnesty ['æmnɪstɪ] n amnistía; **to grant an ~ to** amnistiar (a); **A~ International** Amnistía Internacional

amok [ə'mɔk] adv: **to run ~** enloquecerse, desbocarse

among [ə'mʌŋ], **amongst** [ə'mʌŋst] prep entre, en medio de

amorous ['æmərəs] adj cariñoso

amount [ə'maunt] n (gen) cantidad f; (of bill etc) suma, importe m ▷ vi: **to ~ to** (total) sumar; (be same as) equivaler a, significar; **this ~s to a refusal** esto equivale a una negativa; **the total ~** (of money) la suma total

amp [æmp], **ampère** ['æmpeə'] n amperio; **a 13 ~ plug** un enchufe de 13 amperios

amphetamine [æm'fɛtəmiːn] n anfetamina

amphibian [æm'fɪbɪən] n anfibio

ample ['æmpl] adj (spacious) amplio; (abundant) abundante; **to have ~ time** tener tiempo de sobra

amplifier ['æmplɪfaɪə'] n amplificador m

amplify ['æmplɪfaɪ] vt amplificar, aumentar; (explain) explicar

amply ['æmplɪ] adv ampliamente

amputate ['æmpjuteɪt] vt amputar

Amtrak ['æmtræk] n (US) empresa nacional de ferrocarriles de los EEUU

amuse [ə'mjuːz] vt divertir; (distract) distraer, entretener; **to ~ o.s. with sth/by doing sth** distraerse con algo/haciendo algo; **he was ~d at the joke** le divirtió el chiste

amusement [ə'mjuːzmənt] n diversión f; (pastime) pasatiempo; (laughter) risa; **much to my ~** con gran regocijo mío

amusement arcade n salón m de juegos

amusement park n parque m de atracciones

amusing [ə'mjuːzɪŋ] adj divertido

an [æn, ən, n] indef art see **a**

anaemia [ə'niːmɪə] n anemia

anaemic [ə'niːmɪk] adj anémico; (fig) flojo

anaesthetic [ænɪs'θɛtɪk] n anestesia; **local/general ~** anestesia local/general

anaesthetist [æ'niːsθɪtɪst] n anestesista m/f

anagram ['ænəgræm] n anagrama m

anal ['eɪnl] adj anal

analogous [ə'næləgəs] adj: **~ to** or **with** análogo a

analogue, analog ['ænəlɔg] adj analógico

analogy [ə'nælədʒɪ] n analogía; **to draw an ~ between** señalar la analogía entre

analyse ['ænəlaɪz] vt (Brit) analizar

analysis (pl **analyses**) [ə'næləsɪs, -siːz] n análisis m inv

analyst ['ænəlɪst] n (political analyst, psychoanalyst) analista m/f

analyze ['ænəlaɪz] vt (US) = **analyse**

anarchic [æ'nɑːkɪk] adj anárquico

anarchist ['ænəkɪst] adj, n anarquista m/f

anarchy ['ænəkɪ] n anarquía, desorden m

anathema [əˈnæθɪmə] n: **that is ~ to him** eso es pecado para él

anatomy [əˈnætəmɪ] n anatomía

ancestor [ˈænsɪstəʳ] n antepasado

ancestry [ˈænsɪstrɪ] n ascendencia, abolengo

anchor [ˈæŋkəʳ] n ancla, áncora ▷ vi (also: **to drop ~**) anclar, echar el ancla ▷ vt (fig) sujetar, afianzar; **to weigh ~** levar anclas

anchor man, anchor woman n (Radio, TV) presentador(a) m(f)

anchovy [ˈæntʃəvɪ] n anchoa

ancient [ˈeɪnʃənt] adj antiguo; **~ monument** monumento histórico

ancillary [ænˈsɪlərɪ] adj (worker, staff) auxiliar

and [ænd] conj y; (before i, hi) e; **~ so on** etcétera; **try ~ come** procura venir; **better ~ better** cada vez mejor

Andalusia [ændəˈluːzɪə] n Andalucía

Andean [ˈændɪən] adj andino(-a); **~ high plateau** altiplanicie f, altiplano (LAm)

Andes [ˈændiːz] npl: **the ~** los Andes

Andorra [ænˈdɔːrə] n Andorra

anecdote [ˈænɪkdəʊt] n anécdota

anemia [əˈniːmɪə] n (US) = **anaemia**

anemic [əˈniːmɪk] adj (US) = **anaemic**

anesthetic [ænɪsˈθetɪk] adj, n (US) = **anaesthetic**

anesthetist [æˈniːsθɪtɪst] n (US) = **anaesthetist**

anew [əˈnjuː] adv de nuevo, otra vez

angel [ˈeɪndʒəl] n ángel m

angel dust n polvo de ángel

anger [ˈæŋgəʳ] n ira, cólera, enojo (LAm) ▷ vt enojar, enfurecer

angina [ænˈdʒaɪnə] n angina (del pecho)

angle [ˈæŋgl] n ángulo; **from their ~** desde su punto de vista

angler [ˈæŋgləʳ] n pescador(a) m(f) (de caña)

Anglican [ˈæŋglɪkən] adj, n anglicano(-a)

angling [ˈæŋglɪŋ] n pesca con caña

Anglo- [æŋgləʊ] pref anglo...

angrily [ˈæŋgrɪlɪ] adv enojado, enfadado

angry [ˈæŋgrɪ] adj enfadado, enojado (esp LAm); **to be ~ with sb/at sth** estar enfadado con algn/por algo; **to get ~** enfadarse, enojarse (esp LAm)

anguish [ˈæŋgwɪʃ] n (physical) tormentos mpl; (mental) angustia

anguished [ˈæŋgwɪʃt] adj angustioso

angular [ˈæŋgjʊləʳ] adj (shape) angular; (features) anguloso

animal [ˈænɪməl] adj, n animal m; (pej: person) bestia

animal rights [-raɪts] npl derechos mpl de los animales

animate vt [ˈænɪmeɪt] (enliven) animar; (encourage) estimular, alentar ▷ adj [ˈænɪmɪt] vivo, animado

animated [ˈænɪmeɪtɪd] adj vivo, animado

animation [ænɪˈmeɪʃən] n animación f

animosity [ænɪˈmɒsɪtɪ] n animosidad f, rencor m

aniseed [ˈænɪsiːd] n anís m

ankle [ˈæŋkl] n tobillo m

ankle sock n calcetín m

annex n [ˈæneks] (Brit: also: **annexe**: building) edificio anexo ▷ vt [æˈneks] (territory) anexionar

annihilate [əˈnaɪɪleɪt] vt aniquilar

annihilation [ənaɪəˈleɪʃən] n aniquilación f

anniversary [ænɪˈvɜːsərɪ] n aniversario

announce [əˈnaʊns] vt (gen) anunciar; (inform) comunicar; **he ~d that he wasn't going** declaró que no iba

announcement [əˈnaʊnsmənt] n (gen) anuncio; (declaration) declaración f; **I'd like to make an ~** quisiera anunciar algo

announcer [əˈnaʊnsəʳ] n (Radio) locutor(a) m(f); (TV) presentador(a) m(f)

annoy [əˈnɔɪ] vt molestar, fastidiar, fregar (LAm), embromar (LAm); **to be ~ed (at sth/ with sb)** estar enfadado or molesto (por algo/ con algn); **don't get ~ed!** ¡no se enfade!

annoyance [əˈnɔɪəns] n enojo; (thing) molestia

annoying [əˈnɔɪɪŋ] adj molesto, fastidioso, fregado (LAm), embromado (LAm); (person) pesado

annual [ˈænjʊəl] adj anual ▷ n (Bot) anual m; (book) anuario

annual general meeting n junta general anual

annually [ˈænjʊəlɪ] adv anualmente, cada año

annual report n informe m or memoria anual

annul [əˈnʌl] vt anular; (law) revocar

annum [ˈænəm] n see **per annum**

anomaly [əˈnɒməlɪ] n anomalía

anon. [əˈnɒn] abbr = **anonymous**

anonymity [ænəˈnɪmɪtɪ] n anonimato

anonymous [əˈnɒnɪməs] adj anónimo; **to remain ~** quedar en el anonimato

anorak [ˈænəræk] n anorak m

anorexia [ænəˈreksɪə] n (Med) anorexia

anorexic [ænəˈreksɪk] adj, n anoréxico(-a) m(f)

another [əˈnʌðəʳ] adj: **~ book** otro libro; **~ beer?** ¿(quieres) otra cerveza?; **in ~ five years** en cinco años más ▷ pron otro; see also **one**

answer [ˈɑːnsəʳ] n respuesta, contestación f; (to problem) solución f ▷ vi contestar, responder ▷ vt (reply to) contestar a, responder a; (problem) resolver; **to ~ the phone** contestar el teléfono; **in ~ to your letter** contestando or en contestación a su carta; **to ~ the bell** or **the door** abrir la puerta; **answer back** vi replicar, ser respondón(-ona); **answer for** vt fus responder de or por; **answer to** vt fus (description) corresponder a

answerable [ˈɑːnsərəbl] adj: **~ to sb for sth** responsable ante algn de algo

answering machine ['ɑːnsərɪŋ-] *n*
contestador *m* automático
answerphone ['ɑːnsəfəʊn] *n* (*esp Brit*)
contestador *m* (automático)
ant [ænt] *n* hormiga
antagonism [ænˈtægənɪzəm] *n*
antagonismo *m*
antagonistic [æntægəˈnɪstɪk] *adj*
antagónico; (*opposed*) contrario, opuesto
antagonize [ænˈtægənaɪz] *vt* provocar la
enemistad de
Antarctic [æntˈɑːktɪk] *adj* antártico ▷ *n*:
the ~ el Antártico
Antarctica [ænˈtɑːktɪkə] *n* Antártida
Antarctic Circle *n* Círculo Polar Antártico
Antarctic Ocean *n* Océano Antártico
antelope ['æntɪləʊp] *n* antílope *m*
antenatal [æntɪˈneɪtl] *adj* prenatal
antenna [ænˈtɛnə] (*pl* **antennae** [-niː]) *n*
antena
anthem ['ænθəm] *n*: **national** ~ himno
nacional
anthology [ænˈθɒlədʒɪ] *n* antología
anthrax ['ænθræks] *n* ántrax *m*
anthropologist [ænθrəˈpɒlədʒɪst] *n*
antropólogo(-a)
anthropology [ænθrəˈpɒlədʒɪ] *n*
antropología
anti... [æntɪ] *pref* anti...
anti-aircraft ['æntɪˈɛəkrɑːft] *adj* antiaéreo
antibiotic [æntɪbaɪˈɒtɪk] *adj, n* antibiótico
antibody ['æntɪbɒdɪ] *n* anticuerpo
anticipate [ænˈtɪsɪpeɪt] *vt* (*foresee*) prever;
(*expect*) esperar, contar con; (*forestall*)
anticiparse a, adelantarse a; **this is worse
than I** ~**d** esto es peor de lo que esperaba; **as**
~**d** según se esperaba
anticipation [æntɪsɪˈpeɪʃən] *n* previsión *f*;
esperanza; anticipación *f*
anticlimax [æntɪˈklaɪmæks] *n* decepción *f*
anticlockwise [æntɪˈklɒkwaɪz] *adv* en
dirección contraria a la de las agujas del reloj
antics ['æntɪks] *npl* gracias *fpl*
antidepressant [ˌæntɪdɪˈpresnt] *n*
antidepresivo
antidote ['æntɪdəʊt] *n* antídoto
antifreeze ['æntɪfriːz] *n* anticongelante *m*
anti-globalization ['æntɪgləʊbəlaɪˈzeɪʃən] *n*
antiglobalización *f*; ~ **protesters**
manifestantes *m/fpl* antiglobalización
antihistamine [æntɪˈhɪstəmiːn] *n*
antihistamínico
antiperspirant ['æntɪpəˈspɪrənt] *n*
antitranspirante *m*
antiquated ['æntɪkweɪtɪd] *adj* anticuado
antique [ænˈtiːk] *n* antigüedad *f* ▷ *adj*
antiguo
antique dealer *n* anticuario(-a)
antique shop *n* tienda de antigüedades
anti-Semitism [æntɪˈsɛmɪtɪzəm] *n*
antisemitismo
antiseptic [æntɪˈsɛptɪk] *adj, n* antiséptico

antishake ['æntɪʃeɪk] *adj* estabilizador
antisocial [æntɪˈsəʊʃəl] *adj* antisocial
antivirus [æntɪˈvaɪərəs] *adj* antivirus;
~ **software** antivirus *m*
antlers ['æntləz] *npl* cornamenta
anvil ['ænvɪl] *n* yunque *m*
anxiety [æŋˈzaɪətɪ] *n* (*worry*) inquietud *f*;
(*eagerness*) ansia, anhelo
anxious ['æŋkʃəs] *adj* (*worried*) inquieto; (*keen*)
deseoso; **to be** ~ **to do** tener muchas ganas
de hacer; **I'm very** ~ **about you** me tienes
muy preocupado

KEYWORD

any ['ɛnɪ] *adj* **1** (*in questions etc*) algún/alguna;
have you any butter/children? ¿tienes
mantequilla/hijos?; **if there are any
tickets left** si quedan billetes, si queda
algún billete
2 (*with negative*): **I haven't any money/books**
no tengo dinero/libros
3 (*no matter which*) cualquier; **any excuse will
do** valdrá *or* servirá cualquier excusa; **choose
any book you like** escoge el libro que
quieras; **any teacher you ask will tell you**
cualquier profesor al que preguntes te lo dirá
4 (*in phrases*): **in any case** de todas formas, en
cualquier caso; **any day now** cualquier día
(de estos); **at any moment** en cualquier
momento, de un momento a otro; **at any
rate** en todo caso; **any time: come (at) any
time** ven cuando quieras; **he might come
(at) any time** podría llegar de un momento a
otro
▷ *pron* **1** (*in questions etc*): **have you got any?**
¿tienes alguno/a?; **can any of you sing?**
¿sabe cantar alguno de vosotros/ustedes?
2 (*with negative*): **I haven't any (of them)** no
tengo ninguno
3 (*no matter which one(s)*): **take any of those
books (you like)** toma el libro que quieras de
ésos
▷ *adv* **1** (*in questions etc*): **do you want any
more soup/sandwiches?** ¿quieres más sopa/
bocadillos?; **are you feeling any better?** ¿te
sientes algo mejor?
2 (*with negative*): **I can't hear him any more**
ya no le oigo; **don't wait any longer** no
esperes más

anybody ['ɛnɪbɒdɪ] *pron* cualquiera,
cualquier persona; (*in interrogative sentences*)
alguien; (*in negative sentences*) **I don't see** ~ no
veo a nadie
anyhow ['ɛnɪhaʊ] *adv* de todos modos, de
todas maneras; (*carelessly*) de cualquier
manera; (*haphazardly*) de cualquier modo;
I shall go ~ iré de todas maneras
anyone ['ɛnɪwʌn] *pron* = **anybody**
anyplace ['ɛnɪpleɪs] *adv* (*US*) = **anywhere**
anything ['ɛnɪθɪŋ] *pron* cualquier cosa;

(in interrogative sentences) algo; (in negative sentences) nada; (everything) todo; ~ else? ¿algo más?; can you see ~? ¿ves algo?; he'll eat ~ come de todo or lo que sea; it can cost ~ between £15 and £20 puede costar entre 15 y 20 libras

anytime ['ɛnɪtaɪm] adv (at any moment) en cualquier momento, de un momento a otro; (whenever) no importa cuándo, cuando quiera

anyway ['ɛnɪweɪ] adv (at any rate) de todos modos, de todas formas; I shall go ~ iré de todos modos; (besides): ~, I couldn't come even if I wanted to además, no podría venir aunque quisiera; why are you phoning, ~? ¿entonces, por qué llamas?, ¿por qué llamas, pues?

anywhere ['ɛnɪwɛəʳ] adv dondequiera; (interrogative) en algún sitio; (negative sense) en ningún sitio; (everywhere) en o por todas partes; I don't see him ~ no le veo en ningún sitio; are you going ~? ¿vas a algún sitio?; ~ in the world en cualquier parte del mundo

apart [ə'pɑːt] adv aparte, separadamente; 10 miles ~ separados por 10 millas; to take ~ desmontar; ~ from prep aparte de

apartheid [ə'pɑːteɪt] n apartheid m

apartment [ə'pɑːtmənt] n (US) piso, departamento (LAm), apartamento; (room) cuarto

apartment block or building n (US) bloque m de apartamentos

apathetic [æpə'θɛtɪk] adj apático, indiferente

apathy ['æpəθɪ] n apatía, indiferencia

ape [eɪp] n mono ▷ vt imitar, remedar

aperitif [ə'pɛrɪtiːf] n aperitivo

aperture ['æpətʃjuəʳ] n rendija, resquicio; (Phot) abertura

APEX ['eɪpɛks] n abbr (Aviat: = advance purchase excursion) tarifa f APEX

apex ['eɪpɛks] n ápice m; (fig) cumbre f

aphorism ['æfərɪzəm] n aforismo

aphrodisiac [æfrəu'dɪzɪæk] adj, n afrodisíaco

apiece [ə'piːs] adv cada uno

apologetic [əpɔlə'dʒɛtɪk] adj (look, remark) de disculpa

apologize [ə'pɔlədʒaɪz] vi: to ~ (for sth to sb) disculparse (con algn por algo)

apology [ə'pɔlədʒɪ] n disculpa, excusa; please accept my apologies le ruego me disculpe

apostle [ə'pɔsl] n apóstol m/f

apostrophe [ə'pɔstrəfɪ] n apóstrofo m

app n abbr (Comput) = application

appal [ə'pɔːl] vt horrorizar, espantar

appalling [ə'pɔːlɪŋ] adj espantoso; (awful) pésimo; she's an ~ cook es una cocinera malísima

apparatus [æpə'reɪtəs] n (equipment) equipo; (organization) aparato; (in gymnasium) aparatos mpl

apparel [ə'pærl] n (US) indumentaria

apparent [ə'pærənt] adj aparente; (obvious) manifiesto, evidente; it is ~ that está claro que

apparently [ə'pærəntlɪ] adv por lo visto, al parecer, dizque (LAm)

appeal [ə'piːl] vi (Law) apelar ▷ n (Law) apelación f; (request) llamamiento, llamado (LAm); (plea) petición f; (charm) atractivo, encanto; to ~ for solicitar; to ~ to (person) rogar a, suplicar a; (thing) atraer, interesar; to ~ to sb for mercy rogarle misericordia a algn; it doesn't ~ to me no me atrae, no me llama la atención; right of ~ derecho de apelación

appealing [ə'piːlɪŋ] adj (nice) atractivo; (touching) conmovedor(a), emocionante

appear [ə'pɪəʳ] vi aparecer, presentarse; (Law) comparecer; (publication) salir (a luz), publicarse; (seem) parecer; to ~ on TV/in "Hamlet" salir por la tele/hacer un papel en "Hamlet"; it would ~ that parecería que

appearance [ə'pɪərəns] n aparición f; (look, aspect) apariencia, aspecto; to keep up ~s salvar las apariencias; to all ~s al parecer

appease [ə'piːz] vt (pacify) apaciguar; (satisfy) satisfacer

appendices [ə'pɛndɪsiːz] npl of appendix

appendicitis [əpɛndɪ'saɪtɪs] n apendicitis f

appendix (pl appendices) [ə'pɛndɪks, -dɪsiːz] n apéndice m; to have one's ~ out operarse de apendicitis

appetite ['æpɪtaɪt] n apetito; (fig) deseo, anhelo; that walk has given me an ~ ese paseo me ha abierto el apetito

appetizer ['æpɪtaɪzəʳ] n (drink) aperitivo; (food) tapas fpl (Sp)

applaud [ə'plɔːd] vt, vi aplaudir

applause [ə'plɔːz] n aplausos mpl

apple ['æpl] n manzana

apple pie n pastel m de manzana, pay m de manzana (LAm)

apple tree n manzano

appliance [ə'plaɪəns] n aparato; electrical ~s electrodomésticos mpl

applicable [ə'plɪkəbl] adj aplicable, pertinente; the law is ~ from January la ley es aplicable or se pone en vigor a partir de enero; to be ~ to referirse a

applicant ['æplɪkənt] n candidato(-a); solicitante m/f

application [æplɪ'keɪʃən] n (also Comput) aplicación f; (for a job, a grant etc) solicitud f

application form n solicitud f

applied [ə'plaɪd] adj (science, art) aplicado

apply [ə'plaɪ] vt: to ~ (to) aplicar (a); (fig) emplear (para) ▷ vi: to ~ to (ask) dirigirse a; (be suitable for) ser aplicable a; (be relevant to) tener que ver con; to ~ for (permit, grant, job) solicitar; to ~ the brakes echar el freno; to ~ o.s. to aplicarse a, dedicarse a

appoint [ə'pɔɪnt] vt (to post) nombrar; (date, place) fijar, señalar

appointment [ə'pɔɪntmənt] n (engagement) cita; (date) compromiso; (act) nombramiento; (post) puesto; **to make an ~ (with)** (doctor) pedir hora (con); (friend) citarse (con); **"~s"** "ofertas de trabajo"; **by ~** mediante cita

apportion [ə'pɔːʃən] vt repartir

appraisal [ə'preɪzl] n evaluación f

appreciably [ə'priːʃəblɪ] adv sensiblemente, de manera apreciable

appreciate [ə'priːʃɪeɪt] vt (like) apreciar, tener en mucho; (be grateful for) agradecer; (be aware of) comprender ▷ vi (Comm) aumentar en valor; **I ~d your help** agradecí tu ayuda

appreciation [əpriːʃɪ'eɪʃən] n apreciación f; (gratitude) reconocimiento, agradecimiento; (Comm) aumento en valor

appreciative [ə'priːʃɪətɪv] adj agradecido

apprehend [æprɪ'hɛnd] vt percibir; (arrest) detener

apprehension [æprɪ'hɛnʃən] n (fear) aprensión f

apprehensive [æprɪ'hɛnsɪv] adj aprensivo

apprentice [ə'prɛntɪs] n aprendiz(a) m(f) ▷ vt: **to be ~d to** estar de aprendiz con

apprenticeship [ə'prɛntɪsʃɪp] n aprendizaje m; **to serve one's ~** hacer el aprendizaje

approach [ə'prəʊtʃ] vi acercarse ▷ vt acercarse a; (be approximate) aproximarse a; (ask, apply to) dirigirse a; (problem) abordar ▷ n acercamiento; aproximación f; (access) acceso; (proposal) proposición f; (to problem etc) enfoque m; **to ~ sb about sth** hablar con algn sobre algo

approachable [ə'prəʊtʃəbl] adj (person) abordable; (place) accesible

appropriate [ə'prəʊprɪɪt] adj apropiado, conveniente ▷ vt [-rɪeɪt] (take) apropiarse de; (allot): **to ~ sth for** destinar algo a; **~ for or to** apropiado para; **it would not be ~ for me to comment** no estaría bien or sería pertinente que yo diera mi opinión

approval [ə'pruːvəl] n aprobación f, visto bueno; **on ~** (Comm) a prueba; **to meet with sb's ~** obtener la aprobación de algn

approve [ə'pruːv] vt aprobar; **approve of** vt fus aprobar; **they don't ~ of her** (ella) no les parece bien

approved school [ə'pruːvd-] n (Brit) correccional m

approx. abbr (= approximately) aprox

approximate [ə'prɔksɪmɪt] adj aproximado

approximately [ə'prɔksɪmɪtlɪ] adv aproximadamente, más o menos

approximation [əprɔksɪ'meɪʃən] n aproximación f

Apr. abbr (= April) abr

apr n abbr (= annual percentage rate) tasa de interés anual

apricot ['eɪprɪkɔt] n albaricoque m (Sp), damasco (LAm)

April ['eɪprəl] n abril m; see also **July**

April Fools' Day n ≈ día m de los (Santos) Inocentes

apron ['eɪprən] n delantal m; (Aviat) pista

apt [æpt] adj (to the point) acertado, oportuno; (appropriate) apropiado; **~ to do** (likely) propenso a hacer

aptitude ['æptɪtjuːd] n aptitud f, capacidad f

aquarium [ə'kwɛərɪəm] n acuario

Aquarius [ə'kwɛərɪəs] n Acuario

Arab ['ærəb] adj, n árabe m/f

Arabia [ə'reɪbɪə] n Arabia

Arabian [ə'reɪbɪən] adj árabe, arábigo

Arabian Desert n Desierto de Arabia

Arabian Sea n Mar m de Omán

Arabic ['ærəbɪk] adj (language, manuscripts) árabe, arábigo ▷ n árabe m; **~ numerals** numeración f arábiga

arable ['ærəbl] adj cultivable

Aragon ['ærəgən] n Aragón m

arbitrary ['ɑːbɪtrərɪ] adj arbitrario

arbitration [ɑːbɪ'treɪʃən] n arbitraje m; **the dispute went to ~** el conflicto laboral fue sometido al arbitraje

arbitrator ['ɑːbɪtreɪtəʳ] n árbitro

arc [ɑːk] n arco

arcade [ɑː'keɪd] n (Arch) arcada; (round a square) soportales mpl; (shopping arcade) galería comercial

arch [ɑːtʃ] n arco; (vault) bóveda; (of foot) puente m ▷ vt arquear

archaeological [ɑːkɪə'lɔdʒɪkl] adj arqueológico

archaeologist [ɑːkɪ'ɔlədʒɪst] n arqueólogo(-a)

archaeology [ɑːkɪ'ɔlədʒɪ] n arqueología

archaic [ɑː'keɪɪk] adj arcaico

archbishop [ɑːtʃ'bɪʃəp] n arzobispo

archenemy ['ɑːtʃɛnəmɪ] n enemigo jurado

archeology etc [ɑːkɪ'ɔlədʒɪ] (US) see **archaeology** etc

archery ['ɑːtʃərɪ] n tiro al arco

architect ['ɑːkɪtɛkt] n arquitecto(-a)

architectural [ɑːkɪ'tɛktʃərəl] adj arquitectónico

architecture ['ɑːkɪtɛktʃəʳ] n arquitectura

archive ['ɑːkaɪv] n often pl (also Comput) archivo; **archives** npl archivo sg

Arctic ['ɑːktɪk] adj ártico ▷ n: **the ~** el Ártico

Arctic Circle n Círculo Polar Ártico

Arctic Ocean n Océano (Glacial) Ártico

ardent ['ɑːdənt] adj (desire) ardiente; (supporter, lover) apasionado

are [ɑːʳ] vb see **be**

area ['ɛərɪə] n área; (Math etc) superficie f, extensión f; (zone) región f, zona; (of knowledge, experience) campo; **the London ~** la zona de Londres

area code n (US Tel) prefijo

arena [ə'riːnə] n arena; (of circus) pista; (for bullfight) plaza, ruedo

aren't [ɑːnt] = **are not**

Argentina [ɑːdʒən'tiːnə] n Argentina

Argentinian [ɑːdʒənˈtɪnɪən] *adj, n* argentino(-a) *m(f)*

arguable [ˈɑːgjuəbl] *adj*: **it is ~ whether ...** es dudoso que + *subjun*

arguably [ˈɑːgjuəblɪ] *adv*: **it is ~ ...** es discutiblemente ...

argue [ˈɑːgjuː] *vt* (*debate: case, matter*) mantener, argüir ▷ *vi* (*quarrel*) discutir; (*reason*) razonar, argumentar; **to ~ that** sostener que; **to ~ about sth (with sb)** pelearse (con algn) por algo

argument [ˈɑːgjumənt] *n* (*reasons*) argumento; (*quarrel*) discusión *f*; (*debate*) debate *m*; **~ for/against** argumento en pro/contra de

argumentative [ɑːgjuˈmɛntətɪv] *adj* discutidor(a)

Aries [ˈɛərɪz] *n* Aries *m*

arise [əˈraɪz] (*pt* **arose**, *pp* **arisen** [əˈrɪzn]) *vi* (*rise up*) levantarse, alzarse; (*emerge*) surgir, presentarse; **to ~ from** derivar de; **should the need ~** si fuera necesario

aristocracy [ærɪsˈtɔkrəsɪ] *n* aristocracia

aristocrat [ˈærɪstəkræt] *n* aristócrata *m/f*

aristocratic [ərɪstəˈkrætɪk] *adj* aristocrático

arithmetic [əˈrɪθmətɪk] *n* aritmética

Ark [ɑːk] *n*: **Noah's ~** el Arca *f* de Noé

arm [ɑːm] *n* (*Anat*) brazo ▷ *vt* armar; **~ in ~** cogidos del brazo; *see also* **arms**

armaments [ˈɑːməmənts] *npl* (*weapons*) armamentos *mpl*

armchair [ˈɑːmtʃɛəʳ] *n* sillón *m*, butaca

armed [ɑːmd] *adj* armado; **the ~ forces** las fuerzas armadas

armed robbery *n* robo a mano armada

Armenia [ɑːˈmiːnɪə] *n* Armenia

armour, armor (US) [ˈɑːməʳ] *n* armadura

armoured car, armored car (US) *n* coche *m* or carro (*LAm*) blindado

armpit [ˈɑːmpɪt] *n* sobaco, axila

armrest [ˈɑːmrɛst] *n* reposabrazos *m inv*, brazo

arms [ɑːmz] *npl* (*weapons*) armas *fpl*; (*Heraldry*) escudo *sg*

army [ˈɑːmɪ] *n* ejército; (*fig*) multitud *f*

A road *n* (*Brit*) ≈ carretera *f* nacional

aroma [əˈrəumə] *n* aroma *m*, fragancia

aromatherapy [ərəuməˈθɛrəpɪ] *n* aromaterapia

arose [əˈrəuz] *pt of* **arise**

around [əˈraund] *adv* alrededor; (*in the area*) a la redonda ▷ *prep* alrededor de

arousal [əˈrauzəl] *n* (*sexual*) excitación *f*; (*of feelings, interest*) despertar *m*

arouse [əˈrauz] *vt* despertar; (*anger*) provocar

arrange [əˈreɪndʒ] *vt* arreglar, ordenar; (*programme*) organizar; (*appointment*) concertar ▷ *vi*: **we have ~d for a taxi to pick you up** hemos organizado todo para que le recoja un taxi; **to ~ to do sth** quedar en hacer algo; **it was ~d that ...** se quedó en que ...

arrangement [əˈreɪndʒmənt] *n* arreglo; (*agreement*) acuerdo; **arrangements** *npl* (*plans*) planes *mpl*, medidas *fpl*; (*preparations*) preparativos *mpl*; **to come to an ~ (with sb)** llegar a un acuerdo (con algn); **by ~** a convenir; **I'll make ~s for you to be met** haré los preparativos para que le estén esperando

arrant [ˈærənt] *adj*: **~ nonsense** una verdadera tontería

array [əˈreɪ] *n* (*Comput*) matriz *f*; **~ of** (*things*) serie *f* or colección *f* de; (*people*) conjunto de

arrears [əˈrɪəz] *npl* atrasos *mpl*; **in ~** (*Comm*) en mora; **to be in ~ with one's rent** estar retrasado en el pago del alquiler

arrest [əˈrɛst] *vt* detener; (*sb's attention*) llamar ▷ *n* detención *f*; **under ~** detenido

arrival [əˈraɪvəl] *n* llegada, arribo (*LAm*); **new ~** recién llegado(-a)

arrive [əˈraɪv] *vi* llegar, arribar (*LAm*); **arrive at** *vt fus* (*decision, solution*) llegar a

arrogance [ˈærəgəns] *n* arrogancia, prepotencia (*LAm*)

arrogant [ˈærəgənt] *adj* arrogante, prepotente (*LAm*)

arrow [ˈærəu] *n* flecha

arse [ɑːs] *n* (*Brit inf!*) culo, trasero

arsenal [ˈɑːsɪnl] *n* arsenal *m*

arsenic [ˈɑːsnɪk] *n* arsénico

arson [ˈɑːsn] *n* incendio provocado

art [ɑːt] *n* arte *m*; (*skill*) destreza; (*technique*) técnica; **Arts** *npl* (*Scol*) Letras *fpl*; **work of ~** obra de arte

art college *n* escuela *f* de Bellas Artes

artefact [ˈɑːtɪfækt] *n* artefacto

artery [ˈɑːtərɪ] *n* (*Med: road etc*) arteria

artful [ˈɑːtful] *adj* (*cunning: person, trick*) mañoso

art gallery *n* pinacoteca, museo de pintura; (*Comm*) galería de arte

arthritis [ɑːˈθraɪtɪs] *n* artritis *f*

artichoke [ˈɑːtɪtʃəuk] *n* alcachofa; **Jerusalem ~** aguaturma

article [ˈɑːtɪkl] *n* artículo, objeto, cosa; (*in newspaper*) artículo; (*Brit Law: training*); **articles** *npl* contrato *sg* de aprendizaje; **~s of clothing** prendas *fpl* de vestir

articulate *adj* [ɑːˈtɪkjulɪt] (*speech*) claro; (*person*) que se expresa bien ▷ *vi* [ɑːˈtɪkjuleɪt] articular ▷ *vt* [ɑːˈtɪkjuleɪt] expresar

articulated lorry *n* (*Brit*) trailer *m*

artificial [ɑːtɪˈfɪʃəl] *adj* artificial; (*teeth etc*) postizo

artificial insemination *n* inseminación *f* artificial

artificial respiration *n* respiración *f* artificial

artillery [ɑːˈtɪlərɪ] *n* artillería

artisan [ˈɑːtɪzæn] *n* artesano(-a)

artist [ˈɑːtɪst] *n* artista *m/f*; (*Mus*) intérprete *m/f*

artistic [ɑːˈtɪstɪk] *adj* artístico

artistry [ˈɑːtɪstrɪ] *n* arte *m*, habilidad *f* (artística)

art school n escuela de bellas artes
artwork ['ɑ:twə:k] n material m gráfico

⭕ KEYWORD

as [æz] conj **1** (referring to time: while) mientras;
(: when) cuando; **she wept as she told her
story** lloraba mientras contaba lo que le
ocurrió; **as the years go by** con el paso de los
años, a medida que pasan los años; **he came
in as I was leaving** entró cuando me
marchaba; **as from tomorrow** a partir de or
desde mañana
2 (in comparisons): **as big as** tan grande como;
twice as big as el doble de grande que; **as
much money/many books as** tanto dinero/
tantos libros como; **as soon as** en cuanto, no
bien (LAm)
3 (since, because) como, ya que; **as I don't
speak German I can't understand him**
como no hablo alemán no le entiendo, no le
entiendo ya que no hablo alemán
4 (although): **much as I like them, ...** aunque
me gustan, ...
5 (referring to manner, way): **do as you wish** haz
lo que quieras; **as she said** como dijo; **he
gave it to me as a present** me lo dio de
regalo; **it's on the left as you go in** según se
entra, a la izquierda
6 (concerning): **as for** or **to that** por or en lo que
respecta a eso
7: **as if** or **though** como si; **he looked as if
he was ill** parecía como si estuviera
enfermo, tenía aspecto de enfermo; see also
long; such; well
▷ prep (in the capacity of): **he works as a
barman** trabaja de barman; **as chairman of
the company, he ...** como presidente de la
compañía, ...

a.s.a.p. abbr (= as soon as possible) cuanto antes,
lo más pronto posible
asbestos [æz'bɛstəs] n asbesto, amianto
ascend [ə'sɛnd] vt subir, ascender
ascendancy [ə'sɛndənsɪ] n ascendiente m,
dominio
ascent [ə'sɛnt] n subida; (slope) cuesta,
pendiente f; (of plane) ascenso
ascertain [æsə'teɪn] vt averiguar
ascetic [ə'sɛtɪk] adj ascético
ASCII ['æski:] n abbr (= American Standard Code for
Information Interchange) ASCII
ascribe [ə'skraɪb] vt: **to ~ sth to** atribuir
algo a
ash [æʃ] n ceniza; (tree) fresno
ashamed [ə'ʃeɪmd] adj avergonzado; **to be ~
of** avergonzarse de
ashen ['æʃn] adj pálido
ashore [ə'ʃɔ:ʳ] adv en tierra; (swim etc) a tierra
ashtray ['æʃtreɪ] n cenicero
Ash Wednesday n miércoles m de Ceniza
Asia ['eɪʃə] n Asia

Asian ['eɪʃən], **Asiatic** [eɪsɪ'ætɪk] adj, n
asiático(-a) m(f)
aside [ə'saɪd] adv a un lado ▷ n aparte m;
~ from prep (as well as) aparte or además de
ask [ɑ:sk] vt (question) preguntar; (demand)
pedir; (invite) invitar ▷ vi: **to ~ about sth**
preguntar acerca de algo; **to ~ sb sth/to do
sth** preguntar algo a algn/pedir a algn que
haga algo; **to ~ sb about sth** preguntar algo
a algn; **to ~ (sb) a question** hacer una
pregunta (a algn); **to ~ sb the time**
preguntar la hora a algn; **to ~ sb out to
dinner** invitar a cenar a algn; **ask after** vt fus
preguntar por; **ask for** vt fus pedir; **it's just
~ing for trouble** or **for it** es buscarse
problemas
askance [ə'skɑ:ns] adv: **to look ~ at sb** mirar
con recelo a algn
asking price n (Comm) precio inicial
asleep [ə'sli:p] adj dormido; **to fall ~**
dormirse, quedarse dormido
asparagus [əs'pærəgəs] n espárragos mpl
aspect ['æspɛkt] n aspecto, apariencia;
(direction in which a building etc faces)
orientación f
aspersions [əs'pə:ʃənz] npl: **to cast ~ on**
difamar a, calumniar a
asphyxiate [æs'fɪksɪeɪt] vt asfixiar
asphyxiation [aesfɪksɪ'eɪʃən] n asfixia
aspirate ['æspəreɪt] vt aspirar ▷ adj
['æspərɪt] aspirado
aspirations [æspə'reɪʃənz] npl aspiraciones
fpl; (ambition) ambición f
aspire [əs'paɪəʳ] vi: **to ~ to** aspirar a,
ambicionar
aspirin ['æsprɪn] n aspirina
aspiring [əs'paɪərɪŋ] adj: **an ~ actor** un
aspirante a actor
ass [æs] n asno, burro; (inf) imbécil m/f; (US
inf!) culo, trasero
assailant [ə'seɪlənt] n agresor(a) m(f)
assassin [ə'sæsɪn] n asesino(-a)
assassinate [ə'sæsɪneɪt] vt asesinar
assassination [əsæsɪ'neɪʃən] n asesinato
assault [ə'sɔ:lt] n (gen: attack) asalto; (Law)
agresión f ▷ vt asaltar, agredir; (sexually) violar
assemble [ə'sɛmbl] vt reunir, juntar; (Tech)
montar ▷ vi reunirse, juntarse
assembly [ə'sɛmblɪ] n (meeting) reunión f,
asamblea; (parliament) parlamento;
(construction) montaje m
assembly line n cadena de montaje
assent [ə'sɛnt] n asentimiento, aprobación f
▷ vi consentir, asentir; **to ~ (to sth)**
consentir (en algo)
assert [ə'sə:t] vt afirmar; (insist on) hacer
valer; **to ~ o.s.** imponerse
assertion [ə'sə:ʃən] n afirmación f
assertive [ə'sə:tɪv] adj enérgico, agresivo,
perentorio
assess [ə'sɛs] vt valorar, calcular; (tax,
damages) fijar; (property etc: for tax) gravar

assessment [ə'sɛsmənt] n valoración f; gravamen m; (judgment): ~ (**of**) juicio (sobre)
assessor [ə'sɛsə'] n asesor(a) m(f); (of tax) tasador(a) m(f)
asset ['æsɛt] n posesión f; (quality) ventaja; **assets** npl (funds) activo sg, fondos mpl
assiduous [ə'sɪdjuəs] adj asiduo
assign [ə'saɪn] vt (date) fijar; (task) asignar; (resources) destinar; (property) traspasar
assignment [ə'saɪnmənt] n asignación f; (task) tarea
assimilate [ə'sɪmɪleɪt] vt asimilar
assimilation [əsɪmɪ'leɪʃən] n asimilación f
assist [ə'sɪst] vt ayudar
assistance [ə'sɪstəns] n ayuda, auxilio
assistant [ə'sɪstənt] n ayudante m/f; (Brit: also: **shop ~**) dependiente(-a) m(f)
associate [adj, n ə'səʊʃɪɪt, vt, vi ə'səʊʃɪeɪt] adj asociado ▷ n socio(-a), colega m/f; (in crime) cómplice m/f; (member) miembro(-a) ▷ vt asociar; (ideas) relacionar ▷ vi: **to ~ with sb** tratar con algn; **~ director** subdirector(a) m(f); **~d company** compañía afiliada
association [əsəʊsɪ'eɪʃən] n asociación f; (Comm) sociedad f; **in ~ with** en asociación con
assorted [ə'sɔːtɪd] adj surtido, variado; **in ~ sizes** en distintos tamaños
assortment [ə'sɔːtmənt] n (of shapes, colours) surtido; (of books) colección f; (of people) mezcla
Asst. abbr = **Assistant**
assume [ə'sjuːm] vt (suppose) suponer; (responsibilities etc) asumir; (attitude, name) adoptar, tomar
assumed name [ə'sjuːmd-] n nombre m falso
assumption [ə'sʌmpʃən] n (supposition) suposición f, presunción f; (act) asunción f; **on the ~ that** suponiendo que
assurance [ə'ʃuərəns] n garantía, promesa; (confidence) confianza, aplomo; (Brit: insurance) seguro; **I can give you no ~s** no puedo hacerle ninguna promesa
assure [ə'ʃuə'] vt asegurar
assured [ə'ʃuəd] adj seguro
asterisk ['æstərɪsk] n asterisco
asteroid ['æstərɔɪd] n asteroide m
asthma ['æsmə] n asma
astonish [ə'stɔnɪʃ] vt asombrar, pasmar
astonished [ə'stɔnɪʃt] adj estupefacto, pasmado; **to be ~ (at)** asombrarse (de)
astonishing [ə'stɔnɪʃɪŋ] adj asombroso, pasmoso; **I find it ~ that** ... me asombra or pasma que ...
astonishment [ə'stɔnɪʃmənt] n asombro, sorpresa; **to my ~** con gran sorpresa mía
astound [ə'staund] vt asombrar, pasmar
astounding [ə'staundɪŋ] adj asombroso
astray [ə'streɪ] adv: **to go ~** extraviarse; **to lead ~** llevar por mal camino; **to go ~ in one's calculations** equivocarse en sus cálculos

astride [ə'straɪd] prep a caballo or horcajadas sobre
astrologer [əs'trɔlədʒə'] n astrólogo(-a)
astrology [əs'trɔlədʒɪ] n astrología
astronaut ['æstrənɔːt] n astronauta m/f
astronomer [əs'trɔnəmə'] n astrónomo(-a)
astronomical [æstrə'nɔmɪkəl] adj astronómico
astronomy [əs'trɔnəmɪ] n astronomía
astute [əs'tjuːt] adj astuto
asylum [ə'saɪləm] n (refuge) asilo; (hospital) manicomio; **to seek political ~** pedir asilo político

 KEYWORD

at [æt] prep **1** (referring to position) en; (direction) a; **at the top** en lo alto; **at home/school** en casa/la escuela; **to look at sth/sb** mirar algo/a algn
2 (referring to time): **at four o'clock** a las cuatro; **at night** por la noche; **at Christmas** en Navidad; **at times** a veces
3 (referring to rates, speed etc): **at £1 a kilo** a una libra el kilo; **two at a time** de dos en dos; **at 50 km/h** a 50 km/h
4 (referring to manner): **at a stroke** de un golpe; **at peace** en paz
5 (referring to activity): **to be at work** estar trabajando; (in office) estar en el trabajo; **to play at cowboys** jugar a los vaqueros; **to be good at sth** ser bueno en algo
6 (referring to cause): **shocked/surprised/annoyed at sth** asombrado/sorprendido/fastidiado por algo; **I went at his suggestion** fui a instancias suyas
▷ n (symbol @) arroba

ate [ɛt, eɪt] pt of **eat**
atheism ['eɪθɪɪzəm] n ateísmo
atheist ['eɪθɪɪst] n ateo(-a)
Athens ['æθɪnz] n Atenas f
athlete ['æθliːt] n atleta m/f
athletic [æθ'lɛtɪk] adj atlético
athletics [æθ'lɛtɪks] n atletismo
Atlantic [ət'læntɪk] adj atlántico ▷ n: **the ~ (Ocean)** el (Océano) Atlántico
atlas ['ætləs] n atlas m inv
A.T.M. n abbr (= Automated Telling Machine) cajero automático
atmosphere ['ætməsfɪə'] n (air) atmósfera; (fig) ambiente m
atom ['ætəm] n átomo
atom bomb n bomba atómica
atomic [ə'tɔmɪk] adj atómico
atomic bomb n bomba atómica
atomizer ['ætəmaɪzə'] n atomizador m
atone [ə'təun] vi: **to ~ for** expiar
A to Z® n guía alfabética; (map) callejero
atrocious [ə'trəuʃəs] adj atroz; (fig) horrible, infame
atrocity [ə'trɔsɪtɪ] n atrocidad f

attach [ə'tætʃ] vt sujetar; (stick) pegar; (document, email, letter) adjuntar; **to be ~ed to sb/sth** (like) tener cariño a algn/algo; **the ~ed letter** la carta adjunta

attaché [ə'tæʃeɪ] n agregado(-a)

attaché case n (Brit) maletín m

attachment [ə'tætʃmənt] n (tool) accesorio; (Comput) archivo o documento adjunto; (love): **~ (to)** apego (a), cariño (a)

attack [ə'tæk] vt (Mil) atacar; (criminal) agredir, asaltar; (criticize) criticar; (task etc) emprender ▷ n ataque m, asalto; (on sb's life) atentado; (fig: criticism) crítica; **heart ~** infarto (de miocardio)

attacker [ə'tækəʳ] n agresor(a) m(f), asaltante m/f

attain [ə'teɪn] vt (also: **~ to**) alcanzar; (achieve) lograr, conseguir

attainments [ə'teɪnmənts] npl (skill) talento sg

attempt [ə'tɛmpt] n tentativa, intento; (attack) atentado ▷ vt intentar, tratar de; **he made no ~ to help** ni siquiera intentó ayudar

attempted [ə'tɛmptɪd] adj: **~ murder/ burglary/suicide** tentativa or intento de asesinato/robo/suicidio

attend [ə'tɛnd] vt asistir a; (patient) atender; **attend to** vt fus (needs, affairs etc) ocuparse de; (speech etc) prestar atención a; (customer) atender a

attendance [ə'tɛndəns] n asistencia, presencia; (people present) concurrencia

attendant [ə'tɛndənt] n sirviente(-a) m(f), ayudante m/f; (Theat) acomodador(a) m(f) ▷ adj concomitante

attention [ə'tɛnʃən] n atención f ▷ excl (Mil) ¡firme(s)!; **for the ~ of ...** (Admin) a la atención de ...; **it has come to my ~ that ...** me he enterado de que ...

attentive [ə'tɛntɪv] adj atento; (polite) cortés

attest [ə'tɛst] vi: **to ~ to** dar fe de

attic ['ætɪk] n desván m, altillo (LAm), entretecho (LAm)

attitude ['ætɪtjuːd] n (gen) actitud f; (disposition) disposición f

attorney [ə'təːnɪ] n (US: lawyer) abogado(-a); (having proxy) apoderado

Attorney General n (Brit) ≈ Presidente m del Consejo del Poder Judicial (Sp); (US) ≈ ministro de Justicia

attract [ə'trækt] vt atraer; (attention) llamar

attraction [ə'trækʃən] n (gen) encanto, atractivo; (Physics) atracción f; (towards sth) atracción f

attractive [ə'træktɪv] adj atractivo

attribute ['ætrɪbjuːt] n atributo ▷ vt [ə'trɪbjuːt]: **to ~ sth to** atribuir algo a; (accuse) achacar algo a

attrition [ə'trɪʃən] n: **war of ~** guerra de agotamiento or desgaste

atypical [eɪ'tɪpɪkl] adj atípico

aubergine ['əubəʒiːn] n (Brit) berenjena; (colour) morado

auburn ['ɔːbən] adj color castaño rojizo

auction ['ɔːkʃən] n (also: **sale by ~**) subasta ▷ vt subastar

auctioneer [ɔːkʃə'nɪəʳ] n subastador(a) m(f)

audacious [ɔː'deɪʃəs] adj (bold) audaz, osado; (impudent) atrevido, descarado

audacity [ɔː'dæsɪtɪ] n audacia, atrevimiento; (pej) descaro

audible ['ɔːdɪbl] adj audible, que se puede oír

audience ['ɔːdɪəns] n auditorio; (gathering) público; (Radio) radioescuchas mpl; (TV) telespectadores mpl; (interview) audiencia

audio-typist ['ɔːdɪəu'taɪpɪst] n mecanógrafo(-a) de dictáfono

audiovisual [ɔːdɪəu'vɪzjuəl] adj audiovisual

audit ['ɔːdɪt] vt revisar, intervenir

audition [ɔː'dɪʃən] n audición f ▷ vi: **to ~ for the part of** hacer una audición para el papel de

auditor ['ɔːdɪtəʳ] n interventor(a) m(f), censor(a) m(f) de cuentas

auditorium [ɔːdɪ'tɔːrɪəm] n auditorio

Aug. abbr (= August) ag

augur ['ɔːɡəʳ] vi: **it ~s well** es de buen agüero

August ['ɔːɡəst] n agosto; see also **July**

aunt [ɑːnt] n tía

auntie, aunty ['ɑːntɪ] n diminutive of **aunt**

au pair ['əu'pɛəʳ] n (also: **~ girl**) chica f au pair

aura ['ɔːrə] n aura; (atmosphere) ambiente m

auspicious [ɔːs'pɪʃəs] adj propicio, de buen augurio

austere [ɔs'tɪəʳ] adj austero; (manner) adusto

austerity [ɔ'stɛrɪtɪ] n austeridad f

Australasia [ɔːstrə'leɪzɪə] n Australasia

Australia [ɔs'treɪlɪə] n Australia

Australian [ɔs'treɪlɪən] adj, n australiano(-a) m(f)

Austria ['ɔstrɪə] n Austria

Austrian ['ɔstrɪən] adj, n austríaco(-a) m(f)

authentic [ɔː'θɛntɪk] adj auténtico

authenticity [ɔːθɛn'tɪsɪtɪ] n autenticidad f

author ['ɔːθəʳ] n autor(a) m(f)

authoritarian [ɔːθɔrɪ'tɛərɪən] adj autoritario

authoritative [ɔː'θɔrɪtətɪv] adj autorizado; (manner) autoritario

authority [ɔː'θɔrɪtɪ] n autoridad f; **the authorities** npl las autoridades; **to have ~ to do sth** tener autoridad para hacer algo

authorization [ɔːθəraɪ'zeɪʃən] n autorización f

authorize ['ɔːθəraɪz] vt autorizar

auto ['ɔːtəu] n (US) coche m, carro (LAm), auto (LAm), automóvil m

autobiography [ɔːtəbaɪ'ɔɡrəfɪ] n autobiografía

autograph ['ɔːtəɡrɑːf] n autógrafo ▷ vt firmar; (photo etc) dedicar

automated ['ɔːtəmeɪtɪd] adj automatizado

automatic [ɔːtə'mætɪk] adj automático ▷ n (gun) pistola automática; (washing machine) lavadora

automatically [ɔːtə'mætɪklɪ] *adv*
automáticamente

automation [ɔːtə'meɪʃən] *n* automatización *f*

automobile ['ɔːtəməbiːl] *n* (*US*) coche *m*,
carro (*LAm*), auto (*LAm*), automóvil *m*

autonomous [ɔː'tɒnəməs] *adj* autónomo

autonomy [ɔː'tɒnəmɪ] *n* autonomía

autopsy ['ɔːtɒpsɪ] *n* autopsia

autumn ['ɔːtəm] *n* otoño

auxiliary [ɔːg'zɪlɪərɪ] *adj* auxiliar

Av. *abbr* (= *avenue*) Av., Avda

avail [ə'veɪl] *vt*: **to ~ o.s.** of aprovechar(se) de,
valerse de ▷ *n*: **to no ~** en vano, sin resultado

availability [əveɪlə'bɪlɪtɪ] *n* disponibilidad *f*

available [ə'veɪləbl] *adj* disponible;
(*obtainable*) asequible; **to make sth ~ to sb**
poner algo a la disposición de algn; **is the
manager ~?** ¿está libre el gerente?

avalanche ['ævəlɑːnʃ] *n* alud *m*, avalancha

Ave. *abbr* (= *avenue*) Av., Avda

avenge [ə'vɛndʒ] *vt* vengar

avenue ['ævənjuː] *n* avenida; (*fig*) camino, vía

average ['ævərɪdʒ] *n* promedio, media ▷ *adj*
(*mean*) medio; (*ordinary*) regular, corriente
▷ *vt* alcanzar un promedio de; **on ~** por
término medio; **average out** *vi*: **to ~ out at**
salir a un promedio de

averse [ə'vɜːs] *adj*: **to be ~ to sth/doing**
sentir aversión *or* antipatía por algo/por
hacer

aversion [ə'vɜːʃən] *n* aversión *f*, repugnancia

avert [ə'vɜːt] *vt* prevenir; (*blow*) desviar; (*one's
eyes*) apartar

aviary ['eɪvɪərɪ] *n* pajarera

aviation [eɪvɪ'eɪʃən] *n* aviación *f*

avid ['ævɪd] *adj* ávido, ansioso

avocado [ævə'kɑːdəu] *n* (*Brit: also: ~ pear*)
aguacate *m*, palta (*LAm*)

avoid [ə'vɔɪd] *vt* evitar, eludir

avoidable [ə'vɔɪdəbl] *adj* evitable, eludible

await [ə'weɪt] *vt* esperar, aguardar; **long ~ed**
largamente esperado

awake [ə'weɪk] (*pt* **awoke**, *pp* **awoken** *or*
awaked) *adj* despierto ▷ *vt* despertar ▷ *vi*
despertarse; **to be ~** estar despierto

awakening [ə'weɪknɪŋ] *n* despertar *m*

award [ə'wɔːd] *n* (*prize*) premio; (*medal*)
condecoración *f*; (*Law*) fallo, sentencia; (*act*)
concesión *f* ▷ *vt* (*prize*) otorgar, conceder;
(*Law: damages*) adjudicar

aware [ə'wɛəʳ] *adj* consciente; (*awake*)
despierto; (*informed*) enterado; **to become ~
of** darse cuenta de, enterarse de; **I am fully ~
that** sé muy bien que

awareness [ə'wɛənɪs] *n* conciencia,
conocimiento

awash [ə'wɒʃ] *adj* inundado

away [ə'weɪ] *adv* (*gen*) fuera; (*far away*) lejos;
two kilometres ~ a dos kilómetros (de
distancia); **two hours ~ by car** a dos horas
en coche; **the holiday was two weeks ~**
faltaban dos semanas para las vacaciones;

~ from lejos de, fuera de; **he's ~ for a week**
estará ausente una semana; **he's ~ in
Barcelona** está en Barcelona; **to take ~**
llevar(se); **to work/pedal ~** seguir
trabajando/pedaleando; **to fade ~**
desvanecerse; (*sound*) apagarse

away game *n* (*Sport*) partido de fuera

awe [ɔː] *n* respeto, admiración *f* respetuosa

awe-inspiring ['ɔːɪnspaɪərɪŋ] *adj*
imponente, pasmoso

awesome ['ɔːsəm] (*esp US*) *adj* (*excellent*)
formidable; = **awe-inspiring**

awful ['ɔːfəl] *adj* terrible; **an ~ lot of** (*people,
cars, dogs*) la mar de, muchísimos

awfully ['ɔːfəlɪ] *adv* (*very*) terriblemente

awhile [ə'waɪl] *adv* (durante) un rato, algún
tiempo

awkward ['ɔːkwəd] *adj* (*clumsy*) desmañado,
torpe; (*shape, situation*) incómodo; (*difficult:
question*) difícil; (*problem*) complicado

awning ['ɔːnɪŋ] *n* (*of shop*) toldo; (*of window etc*)
marquesina

awoke [ə'wəuk], **awoken** [ə'wəukən] *pt, pp*
of **awake**

AWOL ['eɪwɒl] *abbr* (*Mil etc*) = **absent without
leave**

awry [ə'raɪ] *adv*: **to be ~** estar descolocado *or*
atravesado; **to go ~** salir mal, fracasar

axe, ax (*US*) [æks] *n* hacha ▷ *vt* (*employee*)
despedir; (*project etc*) cortar; (*jobs*) reducir;
to have an ~ to grind (*fig*) tener un interés
creado *or* algún fin interesado

axes ['æksiːz] *npl* of **axis**

axis (*pl* **axes**) ['æksɪs, -siːz] *n* eje *m*

axle ['æksl] *n* eje *m*, árbol *m*

ay, aye [aɪ] *excl* (*yes*) sí; **the ayes** los que votan
a favor

azalea [ə'zeɪlɪə] *n* azalea

Azerbaijan [æzəbaɪ'dʒɑːn] *n* Azerbaiyán *m*

Aztec ['æztɛk] *adj, n* azteca *m/f*

B, b [bi:] n (letter) B, b f; (Scol: mark) N; (Mus): **B** si m; **B for Benjamin,** (US) **B for Baker** B de Barcelona; **B road** (Brit Aut) = carretera secundaria

BA n abbr = **British Academy**; (Scol) = **Bachelor of Arts**

babble ['bæbl] vi farfullar

baboon [bə'bu:n] n mandril m

baby ['beɪbɪ] n bebé m/f; (US: inf: darling) mi amor

baby carriage n (US) cochecito

baby-sit ['beɪbɪsɪt] vi hacer de canguro

baby-sitter ['beɪbɪsɪtə'] n canguro m/f

baby wipe n toallita húmeda (para bebés)

bachelor ['bætʃələ'] n soltero; **B~ of Arts/Science (BA/BSc)** licenciado(-a) en Filosofía y Letras/Ciencias

back [bæk] n (of person) espalda; (of animal) lomo; (of hand, page) dorso; (as opposed to front) parte f de atrás; (of room) fondo; (of chair) respaldo; (of page) reverso; (Football) defensa m; **to have one's ~ to the wall** (fig) estar entre la espada y la pared; **to break the ~ of a job** hacer lo más difícil de un trabajo; **~ to front** al revés; **at the ~ of my mind was the thought that ...** en el fondo tenía la idea de que ... ▷ vt (candidate: also: **~ up**) respaldar, apoyar; (horse: at races) apostar a; (car) dar marcha atrás a or con ▷ vi (car etc) dar marcha atrás ▷ adj de atrás; **~ seats/wheels** (Aut) asientos mpl traseros, ruedas fpl traseras; **~ garden/room** jardín m/habitación f de atrás; **~ payments** pagos mpl con efecto retroactivo, **~ rent** renta atrasada; **to take a ~ seat** (fig) pasar a segundo plano ▷ adv (not forward) (hacia) atrás; **he's ~ (returned)** ha vuelto; **he ran ~** volvió corriendo; **throw the ball ~ (restitution)** devuelve la pelota; **can I have it ~?** ¿me lo devuelve?; **he called ~ (again)** volvió a llamar; **~ and forth** de acá para allá; **as far ~ as the 13th century** ya en el siglo XIII; **when will you be ~?** ¿cuándo volverá?; **back down** vi echarse atrás; **back on to** vt fus: **the house ~s on to the golf course** por atrás la casa da al campo de golf; **back out** vi (of promise) volverse atrás; **back up** vt (support: person) apoyar, respaldar; (theory) defender; (car) dar marcha atrás a; (Comput) hacer una copia de reserva de

backache ['bækeɪk] n dolor m de espalda

backbencher ['bæk'bɛntʃə'] n (Brit) diputado sin cargo oficial en el gobierno o la oposición

back benches npl (Brit) ver nota

backbone ['bækbəun] n columna vertebral; **the ~ of the organization** el pilar de la organización

backcloth ['bækklɔθ] n telón m de fondo

backdate [bæk'deɪt] vt (letter) poner fecha atrasada a; **~d pay rise** aumento de sueldo con efecto retroactivo

back door n puerta f trasera

backdrop ['bækdrɔp] n = **backcloth**

backer ['bækə'] n partidario(-a); (Comm) promotor(a) m(f)

backfire [bæk'faɪə'] vi (Aut) petardear; (plans) fallar, salir mal

backgammon ['bækgæmən] n backgammon m

background ['bækgraund] n fondo; (of events) antecedentes mpl; (basic knowledge) bases fpl; (experience) conocimientos mpl, educación f ▷ cpd (noise, music) de fondo; (Comput) secundario; **~ reading** lectura de preparación; **family ~** origen m, antecedentes mpl familiares

backhand ['bækhænd] n (Tennis: also: **~ stroke**) revés m

backhanded ['bæk'hændɪd] adj (fig) ambiguo, equívoco

backhander ['bæk'hændə'] n (Brit: bribe) soborno

backing ['bækɪŋ] n (fig) apoyo, respaldo; (Comm) respaldo financiero; (Mus) acompañamiento

backlash ['bæklæʃ] n reacción f (en contra)

backlog ['bæklɔg] n: **~ of work** trabajo atrasado

back number n (of magazine etc) número atrasado

backpack ['bækpæk] n mochila

backpacker ['bækpækə'] n mochilero(-a)

back pay n atrasos mpl

backpedal ['bækpɛdl] vi (fig) volverse/echarse atrás

backseat driver ['bæksi:t-] n pasajero que se empeña en aconsejar al conductor

backside ['bæksaɪd] n (inf) trasero

backslash ['bækslæʃ] n pleca, barra inversa

backstage [bæk'steɪdʒ] adv entre bastidores

backstroke ['bækstrəʊk] n espalda

backtrack ['bæktræk] vi (fig) = **backpedal**

backup ['bækʌp] adj (train, plane) suplementario; (Comput: disk, file) de reserva ▷ n (support) apoyo; (also: **~ file**) copia de reserva; (US: congestion) embotellamiento, retención f

backward ['bækwəd] adj (movement) hacia atrás; (person, country) atrasado; (shy) tímido

backwards ['bækwədz] adv (move, go) hacia atrás; (read a list) al revés; (fall) de espaldas; **to know sth ~** or (US) **~ and forwards** (inf) saberse algo al dedillo

backwater ['bækwɔːtəʳ] n (fig) lugar m atrasado or apartado

backyard [bæk'jɑːd] n patio trasero

bacon ['beɪkən] n tocino, bacon m, beicon m

bacteria [bæk'tɪərɪə] npl bacterias fpl

bad [bæd] adj malo; (serious) grave; (meat, food) podrido, pasado; **to go ~** pasarse; **to have a ~ time of it** pasarlo mal; **I feel ~ about it** (guilty) me siento culpable; **~ debt** (Comm) cuenta incobrable; **in ~ faith** de mala fe

baddie, baddy ['bædɪ] n (inf: Cine etc) malo(-a)

bade [bæd] pt of **bid**

badge [bædʒ] n insignia; (metal badge) chapa; (of policeman) placa; (stick-on) pegatina

badger ['bædʒəʳ] n tejón m

badly ['bædlɪ] adv (work, dress etc) mal; **to reflect ~ on sb** influir negativamente en la reputación de algn; **~ wounded** gravemente herido; **he needs it ~** = le hace mucha falta; **to be ~ off (for money)** andar mal de dinero; **things are going ~** las cosas van muy mal

bad-mannered ['bæd'mænəd] adj mal educado

badminton ['bædmɪntən] n bádminton m

bad-tempered ['bæd'tɛmpəd] adj de mal genio or carácter; (temporary) de mal humor

baffle ['bæfl] vt desconcertar, confundir

baffling ['bæflɪŋ] adj incomprensible

bag [bæg] n bolsa; (handbag) bolso; (satchel) mochila; (case) maleta; (of hunter) caza ▷ vt (inf: take) coger (Sp), agarrar (LAm), pescar; **~s of** (inf: lots of) un montón de; **to pack one's ~s** hacer las maletas

baggage ['bægɪdʒ] n equipaje m

baggage allowance n límite m de equipaje

baggage (re)claim n recogida de equipajes

baggy ['bægɪ] adj (trousers) ancho, holgado

bag lady n (inf) mujer sin hogar cargada de bolsas

bagpipes ['bægpaɪps] npl gaita sg

Bahamas [bə'hɑːməz] npl: **the ~** las (Islas) Bahama

bail [beɪl] n fianza ▷ vt (prisoner: also: **grant ~ to**) poner en libertad bajo fianza; (boat: also:

~ out) achicar; **on ~** (prisoner) bajo fianza; **to be released on ~** ser puesto en libertad bajo fianza; **to ~ sb out** pagar la fianza de algn; see also **bale**

bailiff ['beɪlɪf] n alguacil m

bait [beɪt] n cebo ▷ vt poner el cebo en

bake [beɪk] vt cocer (al horno) ▷ vi (cook) cocerse; (be hot) hacer un calor terrible

baked beans npl judías fpl en salsa de tomate

baked potato n patata al horno

baker ['beɪkəʳ] n panadero(-a)

baker's dozen n docena del fraile

bakery ['beɪkərɪ] n (for bread) panadería; (for cakes) pastelería

baking ['beɪkɪŋ] n (act) cocción f; (batch) hornada

baking powder n levadura (en polvo)

balaclava [bælə'klɑːvə] n (also: **~ helmet**) pasamontañas m inv

balance ['bæləns] n equilibrio; (Comm: sum) balance m; (remainder) resto; (scales) balanza ▷ vt equilibrar; (budget) nivelar; (account) saldar; (compensate) compensar; **~ of trade/payments** balanza de comercio/pagos; **~ carried forward** balance m pasado a cuenta nueva; **~ brought forward** saldo de hoja anterior; **to ~ the books** hacer el balance

balanced ['bælənst] adj (personality, diet) equilibrado; (report) objetivo

balance sheet n balance m

balcony ['bælkənɪ] n (open) balcón m; (closed) galería; (in theatre) anfiteatro

bald [bɔːld] adj calvo; (tyre) liso

baldness ['bɔːldnɪs] n calvicie f

bale [beɪl] n (Agr) paca, fardo; **bale out** vi (of a plane) lanzarse en paracaídas ▷ vt (Naut) achicar; **to ~ sb out of a difficulty** sacar a algn de un apuro

Balearic Islands [bælɪ'ærɪk-] npl: **the ~** las (Islas) Baleares

balk [bɔːk] vi: **to ~ (at)** resistirse (a); (horse) plantarse (ante)

ball [bɔːl] n (sphere) bola; (football) balón m; (for tennis, golf etc) pelota; (of wool, string) ovillo; (dance) baile m; **to be on the ~** (fig: competent) ser un enterado; (: alert) estar al tanto; **to play ~ (with sb)** jugar a la pelota (con algn); (fig) cooperar; **to start the ~ rolling** (fig) empezar; **the ~ is in your court** (fig) le toca a usted

ballad ['bæləd] n balada, romance m

ballast ['bæləst] n lastre m

ball bearing n cojinete m de bolas

ballerina [bælə'riːnə] n bailarina

ballet ['bæleɪ] n ballet m

ballet dancer n bailarín(-ina) m(f) (de ballet)

balloon [bə'luːn] n globo; (in comic strip) bocadillo ▷ vi dispararse

ballot ['bælət] n votación f

ballot box n urna (electoral)

ballot paper n papeleta
ballpark ['bɔːlpɑːk] n (US) estadio de béisbol
ball-point pen ['bɔːlpɔɪnt-] n bolígrafo
ballroom ['bɔːlrum] n salón m de baile
balm [bɑːm] n (also fig) bálsamo
balmy ['bɑːmɪ] adj (breeze, air) suave; (inf)
= **barmy**
Baltic ['bɔːltɪk] adj báltico ▷ n: **the ~ (Sea)**
el (Mar) Báltico
bamboo [bæm'buː] n bambú m
ban [bæn] n prohibición f ▷ vt prohibir;
(exclude) excluir; **he was ~ned from driving**
le retiraron el carnet de conducir
banal [bə'nɑːl] adj banal, vulgar
banana [bə'nɑːnə] n plátano, banana (LAm)
band [bænd] n (group) banda; (gang) pandilla;
(strip) faja, tira; (at a dance) orquesta; (Mil)
banda; (rock band) grupo; **band together** vi
juntarse, asociarse
bandage ['bændɪdʒ] n venda, vendaje m ▷ vt
vendar
Band-Aid® ['bændeɪd] n (US) tirita, curita
(LAm)
B & B n abbr = **bed and breakfast**
bandit ['bændɪt] n bandido; **one-armed ~**
máquina tragaperras
bandwagon ['bændwægən] n: **to jump on**
the ~ (fig) subirse al carro
bandy ['bændɪ] vt (jokes, insults) intercambiar
bandy-legged ['bændɪ'lɛgd] adj patizambo
bang [bæŋ] n (of gun, exhaust) estallido; (of
door) portazo; (blow) golpe m ▷ vt (door) cerrar
de golpe; (one's head) golpear ▷ vi estallar
▷ adv: **to be ~ on time** (inf) llegar en punto;
to ~ the door dar un portazo; **to ~ into sth**
chocar con algo, golpearse contra algo; see
also **bangs**
banger ['bæŋəʳ] n (Brit: car: also: **old ~**)
armatoste m, cacharro; (Brit inf: sausage)
salchicha; (firework) petardo
Bangladesh [bæŋglə'dɛʃ] n Bangladesh f
bangle ['bæŋgl] n brazalete m, ajorca
bangs [bæŋz] npl (US) flequillo sg
banish ['bænɪʃ] vt desterrar
banister ['bænɪstəʳ] n, **banisters** ['bænɪstəz]
npl barandilla f, pasamanos m inv
banjo (pl **banjoes** or **banjos**) ['bændʒəu] n
banjo
bank [bæŋk] n (Comm) banco; (of river, lake)
ribera, orilla; (of earth) terraplén m ▷ vi (Aviat)
ladearse; (Comm): **to ~ with** tener una cuenta
en; **bank on** vt fus contar con
bank account n cuenta bancaria
bank balance n saldo
bank card n = **banker's card**
bank charges npl comisión f sg
bank draft n letra de cambio
banker ['bæŋkəʳ] n banquero; **~'s card** (Brit)
tarjeta bancaria; **~'s order** orden f bancaria
bank giro n giro bancario
bank holiday n (Brit) día m festivo or de
fiesta; ver nota

● **BANK HOLIDAY**
●
● El término bank holiday se aplica en el
● Reino Unido a todo día festivo oficial en
● el que cierran bancos y comercios. Los
● más destacados coinciden con Navidad,
● Semana Santa, finales de mayo y finales
● de agosto. Al contrario que en los países
● de tradición católica, no se celebran las
● festividades dedicadas a los santos.

banking ['bæŋkɪŋ] n banca
bank loan n préstamo bancario
bank manager n director(a) m(f) (de
sucursal) de banco
banknote ['bæŋknəut] n billete m de banco
bank rate n tipo de interés bancario
bankrupt ['bæŋkrʌpt] n quebrado(-a) ▷ adj
quebrado, insolvente; **to go ~** quebrar, hacer
bancarrota; **to be ~** estar en quiebra
bankruptcy ['bæŋkrʌptsɪ] n quiebra,
bancarrota
bank statement n extracto de cuenta
banner ['bænəʳ] n bandera; (in demonstration)
pancarta
bannister(s) ['bænɪstə(z)] n(pl) = **banister(s)**
banns [bænz] npl amonestaciones fpl
banquet ['bæŋkwɪt] n banquete m
banter ['bæntəʳ] n guasa, bromas fpl
baptism ['bæptɪzəm] n bautismo; (act)
bautizo
baptize [bæp'taɪz] vt bautizar
bar [bɑːʳ] n barra; (on door) tranca; (of window,
cage) reja; (of soap) pastilla; (of chocolate)
tableta; (fig: hindrance) obstáculo; (prohibition)
prohibición f; (pub) bar m, cantina (esp LAm);
(counter: in pub) barra, mostrador m; (Mus)
barra ▷ vt (road) obstruir; (window, door)
atrancar; (person) excluir; (activity) prohibir;
behind ~s entre rejas; **the B~** (Law: profession)
la abogacía; (: people) el cuerpo de abogados;
~ none sin excepción
barbarian [bɑː'bɛərɪən] n bárbaro(-a)
barbaric [bɑː'bærɪk] adj bárbaro
barbarity [bɑː'bærɪtɪ] n barbaridad f
barbecue ['bɑːbɪkjuː] n barbacoa, asado
(LAm)
barbed wire ['bɑːbd-] n alambre m de espino
barber ['bɑːbəʳ] n peluquero, barbero
barber's (shop), (US) **barber (shop)** n
peluquería
Barcelona [bɑːsɪ'ləunə] n Barcelona
bar chart n gráfico de barras
bar code n código de barras
bare [bɛəʳ] adj desnudo; (trees) sin hojas;
(head) descubierto ▷ vt desnudar; **to ~ one's**
teeth enseñar los dientes
bareback ['bɛəbæk] adv a pelo
barefaced ['bɛəfeɪst] adj descarado
barefoot ['bɛəfut] adj, adv descalzo
barely ['bɛəlɪ] adv apenas
bargain ['bɑːgɪn] n pacto; (transaction)

negocio; (*good buy*) ganga ▷ vi negociar; (*haggle*) regatear; **into the ~** además, por añadidura; **bargain for** vt fus (inf): **he got more than he ~ed for** le resultó peor de lo que esperaba

bargaining ['bɑːgənɪŋ] n negociación f, regateo; **~ table** mesa de negociaciones

barge [bɑːdʒ] n barcaza; **barge in** vi irrumpir; (*in conversation*) entrometerse; **barge into** vt fus dar contra

baritone ['bærɪtəun] n barítono

barium meal ['bɛərɪəm-] n (*Med*) sulfato de bario

bark [bɑːk] n (*of tree*) corteza; (*of dog*) ladrido ▷ vi ladrar

barley ['bɑːlɪ] n cebada

barley sugar n azúcar m cande

barmaid ['bɑːmeɪd] n camarera

barman ['bɑːmən] n camarero, barman m

barmy ['bɑːmɪ] adj (inf) chiflado, chalado

barn [bɑːn] n granero; (*for animals*) cuadra

barnacle ['bɑːnəkl] n percebe m

barometer [bəˈrɔmɪtəʳ] n barómetro

baron ['bærən] n barón m; (*fig*) magnate m; **the press ~s** los magnates de la prensa

baroness ['bærənɪs] n baronesa

baroque [bəˈrɔk] adj barroco

barrack ['bærək] vt (*Brit*) abuchear

barracks ['bærəks] npl cuartel msg

barrage ['bærɑːʒ] n (*Mil*) cortina de fuego; (*dam*) presa; (*fig: of criticism etc*) lluvia, aluvión m; **a ~ of questions** una lluvia de preguntas

barrel ['bærəl] n barril m; (*of wine*) tonel m, cuba; (*of gun*) cañón m

barren ['bærən] adj estéril

barrette [bəˈrɛt] n (US) pasador m (LAm, Sp), broche m (Mex)

barricade [bærɪˈkeɪd] n barricada ▷ vt cerrar con barricadas

barrier ['bærɪəʳ] n barrera; (*crash barrier*) barrera

barrier cream n crema protectora

barring ['bɑːrɪŋ] prep excepto, salvo

barrister ['bærɪstəʳ] n (*Brit*) abogado(-a)

barrow ['bærəu] n (*cart*) carretilla

bartender ['bɑːtɛndəʳ] n (US) camarero, barman m

barter ['bɑːtəʳ] vt: **to ~ sth for sth** trocar algo por algo

base [beɪs] n base f ▷ vt: **to ~ sth on** basar or fundar algo en ▷ adj bajo, infame; **to ~ at** (*troops*) estacionar en; **I'm ~d in London** (*work*) trabajo en Londres

baseball ['beɪsbɔːl] n béisbol m

baseball cap n gorra f de béisbol

baseline ['beɪslaɪn] n (*Tennis*) línea de fondo

basement ['beɪsmənt] n sótano

bases ['beɪsiːz] npl of **basis**; ['beɪsɪz] npl of **base**

bash [bæʃ] n: **I'll have a ~ (at it)** lo intentaré ▷ vt (inf) golpear; **bash up** vt (inf: car) destrozar; (: person) aporrear, vapulear

bashful ['bæʃful] adj tímido, vergonzoso

basic ['beɪsɪk] adj (*salary etc*) básico; (*elementary: principles*) fundamental

basically ['beɪsɪklɪ] adv fundamentalmente, en el fondo

basics npl: **the ~** los fundamentos

basil ['bæzl] n albahaca

basin ['beɪsn] n (*vessel*) cuenco, tazón m; (*Geo*) cuenca; (*also*: **wash~**) palangana, jofaina; (*in bathroom*) lavabo

basis ['beɪsɪs] (*pl* **bases** [-siːz]) n base f; **on a part-time/trial ~** a tiempo parcial/a prueba; **on the ~ of what you've said** en base a lo que has dicho

bask [bɑːsk] vi: **to ~ in the sun** tomar el sol

basket ['bɑːskɪt] n cesta, cesto

basketball ['bɑːskɪtbɔːl] n baloncesto

Basque [bæsk] adj, n vasco(-a) m(f)

Basque Country n Euskadi m, País m Vasco

bass [beɪs] n (*Mus*) bajo

bassoon [bəˈsuːn] n fagot m

bastard ['bɑːstəd] n bastardo(-a); (inf!) cabrón m, hijo de puta (!)

bat [bæt] n (*Zool*) murciélago; (*for ball games*) palo; (*for cricket, baseball*) bate m; (*Brit: for table tennis*) pala ▷ vt: **he didn't ~ an eyelid** ni pestañeó, ni se inmutó

batch [bætʃ] n lote m, remesa; (*of bread*) hornada

bated ['beɪtɪd] adj: **with ~ breath** sin respirar

bath [bɑːθ, pl bɑːðz] n (*act*) baño; (*bathtub*) bañera, tina (*esp LAm*) ▷ vt bañar; **to have a ~** bañarse, darse un baño; *see also* **baths**

bathe [beɪð] vi bañarse; (US) darse un baño, bañarse ▷ vt (*wound etc*) lavar; (US) bañar, dar un baño a

bather ['beɪðəʳ] n bañista m/f

bathing ['beɪðɪŋ] n baño

bathing cap n gorro de baño

bathing costume, bathing suit (US) n bañador m, traje m de baño

bathing trunks npl bañador msg

bathrobe ['bɑːθrəub] n albornoz m

bathroom ['bɑːθrum] n (cuarto de) baño

baths [bɑːðz] npl piscina sg

bath towel n toalla de baño

bathtub ['bɑːθtʌb] n bañera

baton ['bætən] n (*Mus*) batuta; (*weapon*) porra

battalion [bəˈtælɪən] n batallón m

batter ['bætəʳ] vt maltratar; (*wind, rain*) azotar ▷ n batido

battered ['bætəd] adj (*hat, pan*) estropeado

battery ['bætərɪ] n batería; (*of torch*) pila

battery charger n cargador m de baterías

battery farming n cría intensiva

battle ['bætl] n batalla; (*fig*) lucha ▷ vi luchar; **that's half the ~** (inf) ya hay medio camino andado; **to fight a losing ~** (*fig*) luchar por una causa perdida

battlefield ['bætlfiːld] n campo m de batalla

battleship ['bætlʃɪp] n acorazado

batty ['bætɪ] *adj* (*inf: person*) chiflado; (: *idea*) de chiflado
bauble ['bɔːbl] *n* chuchería
bawdy ['bɔːdɪ] *adj* indecente; (*joke*) verde
bawl [bɔːl] *vi* chillar, gritar
bay [beɪ] *n* (*Geo*) bahía; (*for parking*) parking *m*, estacionamiento; (*loading bay*) patio de carga; (*Bot*) laurel *m* ▷ *vi* aullar; **to hold sb at ~** mantener a alguien a raya
bay leaf *n* (hoja de) laurel *m*
bayonet ['beɪənɪt] *n* bayoneta
bay window *n* ventana saldiza
bazaar [bəˈzɑː] *n* bazar *m*
bazooka [bəˈzuːkə] *n* bazuca
BB *n abbr* (*Brit:* = *Boys' Brigade*) organización juvenil para chicos
BBC *n abbr* (= *British Broadcasting Corporation*) BBC *f*; *ver nota*

BC *adv abbr* (= *before Christ*) a. de J.C.

○ **KEYWORD**

be [biː] (*pt* **was, were**, *pp* **been**) *aux vb* **1**(*with present participle: forming continuous tenses*): **what are you doing?** ¿qué estás haciendo?, ¿qué haces?; **they're coming tomorrow** vienen mañana; **I've been waiting for you for hours** llevo horas esperándote
2 (*with pp: forming passives*) ser (*but often replaced by active or reflexive constructions*): **to be murdered** ser asesinado; **the box had been opened** habían abierto la caja; **the thief was nowhere to be seen** no se veía al ladrón por ninguna parte
3 (*in tag questions*): **it was fun, wasn't it?** fue divertido, ¿no? *or* ¿verdad?; **he's good-looking, isn't he?** es guapo, ¿no te parece?; **she's back again, is she?** entonces, ¿ha vuelto?
4 (+*to+infin*): **the house is to be sold** (*necessity*) hay que vender la casa; (*future*) van a vender la casa; **he's not to open it** no tiene que abrirlo; **he was to have come yesterday** debía de haber venido ayer; **am I to understand that ...?** ¿debo entender que ...?

▷ *vb +complement* **1**(*with n or num complement*) ser; **he's a doctor** es médico; **2 and 2 are 4** 2 y 2 son 4
2 (*with adj complement: expressing permanent or inherent quality*) ser; (: *expressing state seen as temporary or reversible*) estar; **I'm English** soy inglés(-esa); **she's tall/pretty** es alta/bonita; **he's young** es joven; **be careful/good/quiet** ten cuidado/pórtate bien/cállate; **I'm tired** estoy cansado(-a); **I'm warm** tengo calor; **it's dirty** está sucio(-a)
3 (*of health*) estar; **how are you?** ¿cómo estás?; **he's very ill** está muy enfermo; **I'm better now** ya estoy mejor
4 (*of age*) tener; **how old are you?** ¿cuántos años tienes?; **I'm sixteen (years old)** tengo dieciséis años
5 (*cost*) costar; ser; **how much was the meal?** ¿cuánto fue *or* costó la comida?; **that'll be £5.75, please** son £5.75, por favor; **this shirt is £17** esta camisa cuesta £17

▷ *vi* **1**(*exist, occur etc*) existir, haber; **the best singer that ever was** el mejor cantante que existió jamás; **is there a God?** ¿hay un Dios?, ¿existe Dios?; **be that as it may** sea como sea; **so be it** así sea
2 (*referring to place*) estar; **I won't be here tomorrow** no estaré aquí mañana
3 (*referring to movement*): **where have you been?** ¿dónde has estado?

▷ *impers vb* **1**(*referring to time*): **it's 5 o'clock** son las 5; **it's the 28th of April** estamos a 28 de abril
2 (*referring to distance*): **it's 10 km to the village** el pueblo está a 10 km
3 (*referring to the weather*): **it's too hot/cold** hace demasiado calor/frío; **it's windy today** hace viento hoy
4 (*emphatic*): **it's me** soy yo; **it was Maria who paid the bill** fue María la que pagó la cuenta

beach [biːtʃ] *n* playa ▷ *vt* varar
beacon ['biːkən] *n* (*lighthouse*) faro; (*marker*) guía; (*radio beacon*) radiofaro
bead [biːd] *n* cuenta, abalorio; (*of dew, sweat*) gota; **beads** *npl* (*necklace*) collar *m*
beak [biːk] *n* pico
beaker ['biːkə] *n* vaso
beam [biːm] *n* (*Arch*) viga; (*of light*) rayo, haz *m* de luz; (*Radio*) rayo ▷ *vi* brillar; (*smile*) sonreír; **to drive on full** *or* **main ~** conducir con las luces largas
bean [biːn] *n* judía, fríjol/frijol *m* (*esp LAm*); **runner/broad ~** habichuela/haba; **coffee ~** grano de café
beanpole ['biːnpəʊl] *n* (*inf*) espárrago
bean sprouts ['biːnsprauts] *npl* brotes *mpl* de soja
bear [beə] (*pt* **bore**, *pp* **borne**) *n* oso; (*Stock Exchange*) bajista *m* ▷ *vt* (*weight etc*) llevar; (*cost*) pagar; (*responsibility*) tener; (*traces, signs*)

mostrar; (*produce: fruit*) dar; (*Comm: interest*) devengar; (*endure*) soportar, aguantar; (*stand up to*) resistir a; (*children*) tener, dar a luz; (*fruit*) dar ▷ vi: **to ~ right/left** torcer a la derecha/izquierda; **I can't ~ him** no le puedo ver, no lo soporto; **to bring pressure to ~ on sb** ejercer presión sobre algn; **bear on** vt fus tener que ver con, referirse a; **bear out** vt fus (*suspicions*) corroborar, confirmar; (*person*) confirmar lo dicho por; **bear up** vi (*cheer up*) animarse; **he bore up well under the strain** resistió bien la presión; **bear with** vt fus (*sb's moods, temper*) tener paciencia con

beard [bɪəd] n barba

bearded ['bɪədɪd] adj con barba

bearer ['bɛərəʳ] n (*of news, cheque*) portador(a) m(f); (*of passport*) titular m/f

bearing ['bɛərɪŋ] n porte m; (*connection*) relación f; **(ball) bearings** npl cojinetes mpl a bolas; **to take a ~** marcarse; **to find one's ~s** orientarse

beast [biːst] n bestia; (*inf*) bruto, salvaje m

beastly ['biːstlɪ] adj bestial; (*awful*) horrible

beat [biːt] (pt **beat**, pp **beaten**) n (*of heart*) latido; (*Mus*) ritmo, compás m; (*of policeman*) ronda ▷ vt (*hit*) golpear, pegar; (*eggs*) batir; (*defeat*) vencer, derrotar; (*better*) sobrepasar; (*drum*) redoblar; (*rhythm*) marcar ▷ vi (*heart*) latir; **off the ~en track** aislado; **to ~ about the bush** andarse con rodeos; **to ~ it** largarse; **that ~s everything!** (*inf*) ¡eso es el colmo!; **to ~ on a door** dar golpes en una puerta; **beat down** ▷ vt (*door*) derribar a golpes; (*price*) conseguir rebajar, regatear; (*seller*) hacer rebajar el precio vi (*rain*) llover a cántaros; (*sun*) caer de plomo; **beat off** vt rechazar; **beat up** vt (*inf: person*) dar una paliza a

beating ['biːtɪŋ] n paliza, golpiza (LAm); **to take a ~** recibir una paliza

beautiful ['bjuːtɪful] adj hermoso, bello, lindo (esp LAm)

beautifully ['bjuːtɪfəlɪ] adv de maravilla

beauty ['bjuːtɪ] n belleza, hermosura; (*concept, person*) belleza; **the ~ of it is that ...** lo mejor de esto es que ...

beauty parlour, (US) beauty parlor n salón m de belleza

beauty salon n salón m de belleza

beauty sleep n: **to get one's ~** no perder horas de sueño

beauty spot n lunar m postizo; (*Brit: Tourism*) lugar m pintoresco

beaver ['biːvəʳ] n castor m

became [bɪ'keɪm] pt of **become**

because [bɪ'kɔz] conj porque; **~ of** prep debido a, a causa de

beck [bɛk] n: **to be at the ~ and call of** estar a disposición de

beckon ['bɛkən] vt (*also*: **~ to**) llamar con señas

become [bɪ'kʌm] (*irreg: like* **come**) vi + noun hacerse, llegar a ser + adj ponerse, volverse ▷ vt (*suit*) favorecer, sentar bien a; **to ~ fat** engordar; **to ~ angry** enfadarse; **it became known that ...** se descubrió que ...

becoming [bɪ'kʌmɪŋ] adj (*behaviour*) decoroso; (*clothes*) favorecedor(a)

bed [bɛd] n cama; (*of flowers*) macizo; (*of sea, lake*) fondo; (*of river*) lecho; (*of coal, clay*) capa; **to go to ~** acostarse; **bed down** vi acostarse

bed and breakfast n ≈ pensión f; ver nota

● BED AND BREAKFAST
●
● Se llama *Bed and Breakfast* a la casa de
● hospedaje particular, o granja si es en el
● campo, que ofrece cama y desayuno a
● tarifas inferiores a las de un hotel. El
● servicio se suele anunciar con carteles
● colocados en las ventanas del
● establecimiento, en el jardín o en la
● carretera y en ellos aparece a menudo
● únicamente el símbolo "B & B".

bedclothes ['bɛdkləuðz] npl ropa de cama

bedding ['bɛdɪŋ] n ropa de cama

bed linen n (*Brit*) ropa f de cama

bedraggled [bɪ'drægld] adj desastrado

bedridden ['bɛdrɪdn] adj postrado (en cama)

bedroom ['bɛdrum] n dormitorio, alcoba

bed settee n sofá-cama m

bedside ['bɛdsaɪd] n: **at sb's ~** a la cabecera de alguien

bedside lamp n lámpara de noche

bedside table n mesilla de noche

bedsit ['bɛdsɪt], **bedsitter** ['bɛdsɪtəʳ] n (*Brit*) estudio

bedspread ['bɛdsprɛd] n cubrecama m, colcha

bedtime ['bɛdtaɪm] n hora de acostarse; **it's ~** es hora de acostarse or de irse a la cama

bee [biː] n abeja; **to have a ~ in one's bonnet (about sth)** tener una idea fija (de algo)

beech [biːtʃ] n haya

beef [biːf] n carne f de vaca; **roast ~** rosbif m; **beef up** vt (*inf*) reforzar

beefburger ['biːfbəːgəʳ] n hamburguesa

beefeater ['biːfiːtəʳ] n alabardero de la Torre de Londres

beehive ['biːhaɪv] n colmena

beeline ['biːlaɪn] n: **to make a ~ for** ir derecho a

been [biːn] pp of **be**

beeper ['biːpəʳ] n (*of doctor etc*) busca m inv

beer [bɪəʳ] n cerveza

beer belly n (*inf*) barriga (de bebedor de cerveza)

beer garden n (*Brit*) terraza f de verano, jardín m (de un bar)

beet [biːt] n (*US*) remolacha

beetle ['biːtl] n escarabajo

beetroot ['biːtruːt] n (*Brit*) remolacha

before [bɪ'fɔːʳ] *prep* (*of time*) antes de; (*of space*) delante de ▷ *conj* antes (de) que ▷ *adv* (*time*) antes; (*space*) delante, adelante; ~ **going** antes de marcharse; ~ **she goes** antes de que se vaya; **the week** ~ la semana anterior; **I've never seen it** ~ no lo he visto nunca

beforehand [bɪ'fɔːhænd] *adv* de antemano, con anticipación

befriend [bɪ'frɛnd] *vt* ofrecer amistad a

beg [bɛg] *vi* pedir limosna, mendigar ▷ *vt* pedir, rogar; (*entreat*) suplicar; **to** ~ **sb to do sth** rogar a algn que haga algo; *see also* **pardon**

began [bɪ'gæn] *pt of* **begin**

beggar ['bɛgəʳ] *n* mendigo(-a)

begin (*pt* **began**, *pp* **begun**) [bɪ'gɪn, -gæn, -gʌn] *vt, vi* empezar, comenzar; **to** ~ **doing** or **to do sth** empezar a hacer algo; **I can't** ~ **to thank you** no encuentro palabras para agradecerle; **to** ~ **with, I'd like to know ...** en primer lugar, quisiera saber ...; ~**ning from Monday** a partir del lunes

beginner [bɪ'gɪnəʳ] *n* principiante *m/f*

beginning [bɪ'gɪnɪŋ] *n* principio, comienzo; **right from the** ~ desde el principio

begun [bɪ'gʌn] *pp of* **begin**

behalf [bɪ'hɑːf] *n*: **on** ~ **of** (*US*), **in** ~ **of** en nombre de, por; (*for benefit of*) en beneficio de; **on my/his** ~ por mí/él

behave [bɪ'heɪv] *vi* (*person*) portarse, comportarse; (*thing*) funcionar; (*well: also*: ~ **o.s.**) portarse bien

behaviour, behavior (*US*) [bɪ'heɪvjəʳ] *n* comportamiento, conducta

behead [bɪ'hɛd] *vt* decapitar

beheld [bɪ'hɛld] *pt, pp of* **behold**

behind [bɪ'haɪnd] *prep* detrás de ▷ *adv* detrás, por detrás, atrás ▷ *n* trasero; **to be** ~ **(schedule)** ir retrasado; ~ **the scenes** (*fig*) entre bastidores; **we're** ~ **them in technology** (*fig*) nos dejan atrás en tecnología; **to leave sth** ~ olvidar or dejarse algo; **to be** ~ **with sth** estar atrasado en algo; **to be** ~ **with payments (on sth)** estar atrasado en el pago (de algo)

behold [bɪ'həuld] (*irreg: like* **hold**) *vt* contemplar

beige [beɪʒ] *adj* (*color*) beige

Beijing ['beɪ'dʒɪŋ] *n* Pekín *m*

being ['biːɪŋ] *n* ser *m*; **to come into** ~ nacer, aparecer

Beirut [beɪ'ruːt] *n* Beirut *m*

Belarus [bɛlə'rus] *n* Bielorrusia

belated [bɪ'leɪtɪd] *adj* atrasado, tardío

belch [bɛltʃ] *vi* eructar ▷ *vt* (*also*: ~ **out**: *smoke etc*) vomitar, arrojar

belfry ['bɛlfrɪ] *n* campanario

Belgian ['bɛldʒən] *adj, n* belga *m/f*

Belgium ['bɛldʒəm] *n* Bélgica

belie [bɪ'laɪ] *vt* (*give false impression of*) desmentir, contradecir

belief [bɪ'liːf] *n* (*opinion*) opinión *f*; (*trust, faith*) fe *f*; (*acceptance as true*) creencia; **it's beyond** ~ es increíble; **in the** ~ **that** creyendo que

believable [bɪ'liːvəbl] *adj* creíble

believe [bɪ'liːv] *vt, vi* creer; **to** ~ **(that)** creer (que); **to** ~ **in** (*God, ghosts*) creer en; (*method*) ser partidario de; **he is** ~**d to be abroad** se cree que está en el extranjero; **I don't** ~ **in corporal punishment** no soy partidario del castigo corporal

believer [bɪ'liːvəʳ] *n* (*in idea, activity*) partidario(-a); (*Rel*) creyente *m/f*, fiel *m/f*

belittle [bɪ'lɪtl] *vt* despreciar

Belize [bɛ'liːz] *n* Belice *f*

bell [bɛl] *n* campana; (*small*) campanilla; (*on door*) timbre *m*; (*animal's*) cencerro; (*on toy etc*) cascabel *m*; **that rings a** ~ (*fig*) eso me suena

bellboy ['bɛlbɔɪ], **bellhop** (*US*) ['bɛlhɔp] *n* botones *m inv*

belligerent [bɪ'lɪdʒərənt] *adj* (*at war*) beligerante; (*fig*) agresivo

bellow ['bɛləu] *vi* bramar; (*person*) rugir ▷ *vt* (*orders*) gritar

bell pepper *n* (*esp US*) pimiento, pimentón *m* (*LAm*)

belly ['bɛlɪ] *n* barriga, panza

belly button *n* (*inf*) ombligo

bellyful ['bɛlɪful] *n*: **to have had a** ~ **of ...** (*inf*) estar más que harto de ...

belong [bɪ'lɔŋ] *vi*: **to** ~ **to** pertenecer a; (*club etc*) ser socio de; **this book** ~**s here** este libro va aquí

belongings [bɪ'lɔŋɪŋz] *npl* (*also*: **personal** ~) pertenencias *fpl*

Belorussia [bɛləu'rʌʃə] *n* Bielorrusia

beloved [bɪ'lʌvɪd] *adj, n* querido(-a) *m(f)*, amado(-a) *m(f)*

below [bɪ'ləu] *prep* bajo, debajo de; (*less than*) inferior a ▷ *adv* abajo, (por) debajo; **see** ~ véase más abajo

belt [bɛlt] *n* cinturón *m*; (*Tech*) correa, cinta ▷ *vt* (*thrash*) pegar con correa; **industrial** ~ cinturón industrial; **belt out** (*song*) cantar a voz en grito or a grito pelado; **belt up** *vi* (*Aut*) ponerse el cinturón de seguridad; (*fig, inf*) cerrar el pico

beltway ['bɛltweɪ] *n* (*US Aut*) carretera de circunvalación

bemused [bɪ'mjuːzd] *adj* perplejo

bench [bɛntʃ] *n* banco; (*Brit Pol*): **the Government/Opposition** ~**es** (los asientos de) los miembros del Gobierno/de la Oposición; **the B**~ (*Law*) el tribunal; (*people*) la magistratura

bend [bɛnd] (*pt, pp* **bent**) *vt* doblar; (*body, head*) inclinar ▷ *vi* inclinarse; (*road*) curvarse ▷ *n* (*Brit: in road, river*) recodo; (*in pipe*) codo; *see also* **bends**; **bend down** *vi* inclinarse, doblarse; **bend over** *vi* inclinarse

bends [bɛndz] *npl* (*Med*) apoplejía por cambios bruscos de presión

beneath [bɪ'niːθ] *prep* bajo, debajo de; (*unworthy of*) indigno de ▷ *adv* abajo, (por) debajo

benefactor ['benɪfæktəʳ] *n* bienhechor *m*

beneficial [benɪ'fɪʃəl] *adj*: ~ **to** beneficioso para

beneficiary [benɪ'fɪʃərɪ] *n* (*Law*) beneficiario(-a)

benefit ['benɪfɪt] *n* beneficio, provecho; (*allowance of money*) subsidio ▷ *vt* beneficiar ▷ *vi*: **he'll ~ from it** le sacará provecho; **unemployment ~** subsidio de desempleo

Benelux ['benɪlʌks] *n* Benelux *m*

benevolent [bɪ'nevələnt] *adj* benévolo

benign [bɪ'naɪn] *adj* (*person*) benigno; (*Med*) benigno, (*smile*) afable

bent [bent] *pt, pp of* **bend** ▷ *n* inclinación *f* ▷ *adj* (*wire, pipe*) doblado, torcido; **to be ~ on** estar empeñado en

bequest [bɪ'kwest] *n* legado

bereaved [bɪ'riːvd] *adj* afligido ▷ *n*: **the ~** los allegados *mpl* del difunto

bereavement [bɪ'riːvmənt] *n* aflicción *f*

beret ['bereɪ] *n* boina

berk [bəːk] *n* (*Brit inf*) capullo(-a) (!)

Berlin [bəː'lɪn] *n* Berlín *m*

berm [bəːm] *n* (*US Aut*) arcén *m*

Bermuda [bəː'mjuːdə] *n* las (Islas) Bermudas

berry ['berɪ] *n* baya

berserk [bə'səːk] *adj*: **to go ~** perder los estribos

berth [bəːθ] *n* (*bed*) litera; (*cabin*) camarote *m*; (*for ship*) amarradero ▷ *vi* atracar, amarrar; **to give sb a wide ~** (*fig*) evitar encontrarse con algn

beseech (*pt, pp* **besought**) [bɪ'siːtʃ, -'sɔːt] *vt* suplicar

beset (*pt, pp* **beset**) [bɪ'set] *vt* (*person*) acosar ▷ *adj*: **a policy ~ with dangers** una política rodeada de peligros

beside [bɪ'saɪd] *prep* junto a, al lado de; (*compared with*) comparado con; **to be ~ o.s. with anger** estar fuera de sí; **that's ~ the point** eso no tiene nada que ver

besides [bɪ'saɪdz] *adv* además ▷ *prep* (*as well as*) además de; (*except*) excepto

besiege [bɪ'siːdʒ] *vt* (*town*) sitiar; (*fig*) asediar

best [best] *adj* (el/la) mejor ▷ *adv* (lo) mejor; **the ~ part of** (*most*) la mayor parte de; **at ~** en el mejor de los casos; **to make the ~ of sth** sacar el mejor partido de algo; **to do one's ~** hacer todo lo posible; **to the ~ of my knowledge** que yo sepa; **to the ~ of my ability** como mejor puedo; **the ~ thing to do is ...** lo mejor (que se puede hacer) es ...; **he's not exactly patient at the ~ of times** no es que tenga mucha paciencia precisamente

best-before date *n* fecha de consumo preferente

best man *n* padrino de boda

bestow [bɪ'stəu] *vt* otorgar; (*honour, praise*) dispensar; **to ~ sth on sb** conceder *or* dar algo a algn

bestseller ['best'seləʳ] *n* éxito de ventas, bestseller *m*

bet [bet] *n* apuesta ▷ *vt, vi* (*pt, pp* **bet** *or* **betted**): **to ~ (on)** apostar (a); **it's a safe ~** (*fig*) es cosa segura

betray [bɪ'treɪ] *vt* traicionar; (*trust*) faltar a; (*inform on*) delatar

betrayal [bɪ'treɪəl] *n* traición *f*

better ['betəʳ] *adj* mejor ▷ *adv* mejor ▷ *vt* mejorar; (*record etc*) superar ▷ *n*: **to get the ~ of sb** quedar por encima de algn; **you had ~ do it** más vale que lo hagas; **he thought ~ of it** cambió de parecer; **to get ~** mejorar(se); **that's ~!** ¡eso es!; **I had ~ go** tengo que irme; **a change for the ~** una mejora; **~ off** *adj* más acomodado

betting ['betɪŋ] *n* juego, apuestas *fpl*

betting shop *n* (*Brit*) casa de apuestas

between [bɪ'twiːn] *prep* entre ▷ *adv* (*also*: **in ~**: *time*) mientras tanto; (: *place*) en medio; **the road ~ here and London** la carretera de aquí a Londres; **we only had 5 ~ us** teníamos sólo 5 entre todos

beverage ['bevərɪdʒ] *n* bebida

beware [bɪ'weəʳ] *vi*: **to ~ (of)** tener cuidado (con) ▷ *excl* ¡cuidado!; **"~ of the dog"** "perro peligroso"

bewildered [bɪ'wɪldəd] *adj* aturdido, perplejo

bewildering [bɪ'wɪldərɪŋ] *adj* desconcertante

beyond [bɪ'jɔnd] *prep* más allá de; (*past: understanding*) fuera de; (*after: date*) después de, más allá de; (*above*) superior a ▷ *adv* (*in space*) más allá; (*in time*) posteriormente; **~ doubt** fuera de toda duda; **~ repair** irreparable

bias ['baɪəs] *n* (*prejudice*) prejuicio; (*preference*) predisposición *f*

biased, biassed ['baɪəst] *adj* parcial; **to be ~ against** tener perjuicios contra

biathlon [baɪ'æθlən] *n* biatlón *m*

bib [bɪb] *n* babero

Bible ['baɪbl] *n* Biblia

bibliography [bɪblɪ'ɔgrəfɪ] *n* bibliografía

bicarbonate of soda [baɪ'kɑːbənɪt-] *n* bicarbonato sódico

biceps ['baɪseps] *n* bíceps *m*

bicker ['bɪkəʳ] *vi* reñir

bicycle ['baɪsɪkl] *n* bicicleta

bicycle pump *n* bomba de bicicleta

bid [bɪd] *n* (*at auction*) oferta, puja, postura; (*attempt*) tentativa, conato ▷ *vi* (*pt, pp* **bid**) hacer una oferta ▷ *vt* (*pt* **bade** [bæd], *pp* **bidden** ['bɪdn]) (*offer*) ofrecer; **to ~ sb good day** dar a algn los buenos días

bidder ['bɪdəʳ] *n*: **the highest ~** el mejor postor

bidding ['bɪdɪŋ] *n* (*at auction*) ofertas *fpl*, puja; (*order*) orden *f*, mandato

bide [baɪd] *vt*: **to ~ one's time** esperar el momento adecuado

bidet ['biːdeɪ] *n* bidet *m*

bifocals [baɪˈfəʊklz] *npl* gafas *fpl* or anteojos *mpl* (*LAm*) bifocales

big [bɪg] *adj* grande; (*brother, sister*) mayor; **~ business** gran negocio; **to do things in a ~ way** hacer las cosas en grande

bigamy [ˈbɪɡəmɪ] *n* bigamia

biggish [ˈbɪɡɪʃ] *adj* más bien grande; (*man*) más bien alto

bigheaded [ˈbɪɡˈhɛdɪd] *adj* engreído

bigot [ˈbɪɡət] *n* fanático(-a), intolerante *m/f*

bigoted [ˈbɪɡətɪd] *adj* fanático, intolerante

bigotry [ˈbɪɡətrɪ] *n* fanatismo, intolerancia

big toe *n* dedo gordo (del pie)

big top *n* (*circus*) circo; (*main tent*) carpa principal

big wheel *n* (*at fair*) noria

bike [baɪk] *n* bici *f*

bike lane *n* carril *m* de bicicleta, carril *m* bici

bikini [bɪˈkiːnɪ] *n* bikini *m*

bilateral [baɪˈlætərl] *adj* (*agreement*) bilateral

bilingual [baɪˈlɪŋɡwəl] *adj* bilingüe

bill [bɪl] *n* (*gen*) cuenta; (*invoice*) factura; (*Pol*) proyecto de ley; (*US: banknote*) billete *m*; (*of bird*) pico; (*notice*) cartel *m*; (*Theat*) programa *m* ▷ *vt* extender o pasar la factura a; **may I have the ~ please?** ¿puede traerme la cuenta, por favor?; **~ of exchange** letra de cambio; **~ of lading** conocimiento de embarque; **~ of sale** escritura de venta; **"post no ~s"** "prohibido fijar carteles"; **to fit** or **fill the ~** (*fig*) cumplir con los requisitos

billboard [ˈbɪlbɔːd] *n* valla publicitaria

billet [ˈbɪlɪt] *n* alojamiento ▷ *vt*: **to ~ sb (on sb)** alojar a algn (con algn)

billfold [ˈbɪlfəʊld] *n* (*US*) cartera

billiards [ˈbɪljədz] *n* billar *m*

billion [ˈbɪljən] *n* (*Brit*) billón *m*; (*US*) mil millones *mpl*

bimbo [ˈbɪmbəʊ] *n* (*inf*) tía buena sin seso

bin [bɪn] *n* (*gen*) cubo or bote *m* (*LAm*) de la basura; **litter-~** (*Brit*) papelera

binary [ˈbaɪnərɪ] *adj* (*Math*) binario; **~ code** código binario

bind (*pt, pp* **bound**) [baɪnd, baʊnd] *vt* atar, liar; (*wound*) vendar; (*book*) encuadernar; (*oblige*) obligar; **bind over** *vt* (*Law*) obligar por vía legal; **bind up** *vt* (*wound*) vendar; **to be bound up in** (*work, research etc*) estar absorto en; **to be bound up with** (*person*) estar estrechamente ligado a ▷ *n* (*inf: nuisance*) lata

binder [ˈbaɪndər] *n* (*file*) archivador *m*

binding [ˈbaɪndɪŋ] *adj* (*contract*) vinculante

binge [bɪndʒ] *n* borrachera, juerga; **to go on a ~** ir de juerga

bingo [ˈbɪŋɡəʊ] *n* bingo *m*

bin-liner [ˈbɪnlaɪnər] *n* bolsa de la basura

binoculars [bɪˈnɔkjuləz] *npl* prismáticos *mpl*, gemelos *mpl*

biochemistry [baɪəˈkɛmɪstrɪ] *n* bioquímica

biodegradable [ˈbaɪəʊdɪˈɡreɪdəbl] *adj* biodegradable

biodiversity [ˈbaɪəʊdaɪˈvəːsɪtɪ] *n* biodiversidad *f*

biographer [baɪˈɔɡrəfər] *n* biógrafo(-a)

biographical [baɪəˈɡræfɪkəl] *adj* biográfico

biography [baɪˈɔɡrəfɪ] *n* biografía

biological [baɪəˈlɔdʒɪkəl] *adj* biológico; (*products, foodstuffs etc*) orgánico(-a)

biological clock *n* reloj *m* biológico

biologist [baɪˈɔlədʒɪst] *n* biólogo(-a)

biology [baɪˈɔlədʒɪ] *n* biología

biometric [baɪəˈmɛtrɪk] *adj* biométrico

biopic [ˈbaɪəʊpɪk] *n* filme *m* biográfico

biopsy [ˈbaɪɔpsɪ] *n* biopsia

biosphere [ˈbaɪəsfɪər] *n* biosfera

bioterrorism [ˈbaɪəʊˈtɛrərɪzəm] *n* bioterrorismo

birch [bəːtʃ] *n* abedul *m*; (*cane*) vara

bird [bəːd] *n* ave *f*, pájaro; (*Brit inf: girl*) chica

birdcage [ˈbəːdkeɪdʒ] *n* jaula

bird flu *n* gripe aviar

bird of prey *n* ave *f* de presa

bird's-eye view [ˈbəːdzaɪ-] *n* vista de pájaro

bird-watcher *n* ornitólogo(-a)

bird-watching *n*: **he likes to go ~ on Sundays** los domingos le gusta ir a ver pájaros

Biro® [ˈbaɪrəʊ] *n* bolígrafo

birth [bəːθ] *n* nacimiento; (*Med*) parto; **to give ~ to** parir, dar a luz a; (*fig*) dar origen a

birth certificate *n* partida de nacimiento

birth control *n* control *m* de natalidad; (*methods*) métodos *mpl* anticonceptivos

birthday [ˈbəːθdeɪ] *n* cumpleaños *m inv*

birthmark *n* antojo, marca de nacimiento

birthplace [ˈbəːθpleɪs] *n* lugar *m* de nacimiento

birth rate *n* (tasa de) natalidad *f*

Biscay [ˈbɪskeɪ] *n*: **the Bay of ~** el Mar Cantábrico, el golfo de Vizcaya

biscuit [ˈbɪskɪt] *n* (*Brit*) galleta

bisect [baɪˈsɛkt] *vt* (*also Math*) bisecar

bisexual [baɪˈsɛksjuəl] *adj, n* bisexual *m/f*

bishop [ˈbɪʃəp] *n* obispo; (*Chess*) alfil *m*

bistro [ˈbiːstrəʊ] *n* café-bar *m*

bit [bɪt] *pt of* **bite** ▷ *n* trozo, pedazo, pedacito; (*Comput*) bit *m*; (*for horse*) freno, bocado; **a ~ of** un poco de; **a ~ mad** un poco loco; **~ by ~** poco a poco; **to come to ~s** (*break*) hacerse pedazos; **to do one's ~** aportar su granito de arena; **bring all your ~s and pieces** trae todas tus cosas

bitch [bɪtʃ] *n* (*dog*) perra; (*inf!: woman*) zorra (!)

bite [baɪt] *vt, vi* (*pt* **bit** [bɪt], *pp* **bitten** [ˈbɪtn]) morder; (*insect etc*) picar ▷ *n* (*wound: of dog, snake etc*) mordedura; (*of insect*) picadura; (*mouthful*) bocado; **to ~ one's nails** morderse las uñas; **let's have a ~ (to eat)** vamos a comer algo

bitten [ˈbɪtn] *pp of* **bite**

bitter [ˈbɪtər] *adj* amargo; (*wind, criticism*) cortante, penetrante; (*icy: weather*) glacial;

(*battle*) encarnizado ▷ n (*Brit: beer*) cerveza típica británica a base de lúpulos

bitterness ['bɪtənɪs] n amargura; (*anger*) rencor m

bizarre [bɪ'zɑːʳ] adj raro, extraño

blab [blæb] vi cantar ▷ vt (*also: ~ out*) soltar, contar

black [blæk] adj (*colour*) negro; (*dark*) oscuro ▷ n (*colour*) color m negro; (*person*): **B~** negro(-a) ▷ vt (*shoes*) lustrar; (*Brit Industry*) boicotear; **to give sb a ~ eye** ponerle a algn el ojo morado; **~ coffee** café m solo; **there it is in ~ and white** (*fig*) ahí está bien claro; **to be in the ~** (*in credit*) tener saldo positivo; **~ and blue** amoratado; **black out** vi (*faint*) desmayarse

blackberry ['blækbərɪ] n zarzamora

blackbird ['blækbəːd] n mirlo

blackboard ['blækbɔːd] n pizarra

black box n (*Aviat*) caja negra

blackcurrant ['blæk'kʌrənt] n grosella negra

black economy n economía sumergida

blacken ['blækən] vt ennegrecer; (*fig*) denigrar

black hole n (*Astro*) agujero negro

black ice n hielo invisible en la carretera

blackleg ['blækleg] n (*Brit*) esquirol m/f

blacklist ['blæklɪst] n lista negra ▷ vt poner en la lista negra

blackmail ['blækmeɪl] n chantaje m ▷ vt chantajear

black market n mercado negro, estraperlo

blackout ['blækaut] n (*Elec*) apagón m; (*TV*) bloqueo informativo; (*fainting*) desmayo, pérdida de conocimiento

black pepper n pimienta f negra

black pudding n morcilla

Black Sea n: **the ~** el Mar Negro

black sheep n oveja negra

blacksmith ['blæksmɪθ] n herrero

black spot n (*Aut*) punto negro

bladder ['blædəʳ] n vejiga

blade [bleɪd] n hoja; (*cutting edge*) filo; **a ~ of grass** una brizna de hierba

blame [bleɪm] n culpa ▷ vt: **to ~ sb for sth** echar a algn la culpa de algo; **to be to ~ (for)** tener la culpa (de); **I'm not to ~** yo no tengo la culpa; **and I don't ~ him** y lo comprendo perfectamente

blameless ['bleɪmlɪs] adj (*person*) inocente

bland [blænd] adj suave; (*taste*) soso

blank [blæŋk] adj en blanco; (*shot*) de fogueo; (*look*) sin expresión ▷ n blanco, espacio en blanco; (*cartridge*) cartucho sin bala or de fogueo; **to draw a ~** (*fig*) no conseguir nada; **my mind is a ~** no puedo recordar nada

blank cheque, blank check (*US*) n cheque m en blanco

blanket ['blæŋkɪt] n manta, frazada (*LAm*), cobija (*LAm*); (*of snow*) capa; (*of fog*) manto ▷ adj (*statement, agreement*) comprensivo, general; **to give ~ cover** (*insurance policy*) dar póliza a todo riesgo

blare [blɛəʳ] vi (*brass band, horns, radio*) resonar

blasphemous ['blæsfɪməs] adj blasfemo

blasphemy ['blæsfɪmɪ] n blasfemia

blast [blɑːst] n (*of wind*) ráfaga, soplo; (*of whistle*) toque m; (*of explosive*) explosión f; (*force*) choque m ▷ vt (*blow up*) volar; (*blow open*) abrir con carga explosiva ▷ excl (*Brit inf*) ¡maldito sea!; **(at) full ~** (*also fig*) a toda marcha; **blast off** vi (*spacecraft etc*) despegar

blast-off ['blɑːstɔf] n (*Space*) lanzamiento

blatant ['bleɪtənt] adj descarado

blaze [bleɪz] n (*fire*) fuego; (*flames*) llamarada; (*glow: of fire, sun etc*) resplandor m; (*fig*) arranque m ▷ vi (*fire*) arder en llamas; (*fig*) brillar ▷ vt: **to ~ a trail** (*fig*) abrir (un) camino; **in a ~ of publicity** bajo los focos de la publicidad

blazer ['bleɪzəʳ] n chaqueta de uniforme de colegial o de socio de club

bleach [bliːtʃ] n (*also:* **household ~**) lejía ▷ vt (*linen*) blanquear

bleached [bliːtʃt] adj (*hair*) de colorado; (*clothes*) blanqueado

bleachers ['bliːtʃəz] npl (*US Sport*) gradas fpl

bleak [bliːk] adj (*landscape*) desierto; (*landscape*) desolado, desierto; (*weather*) desapacible; (*smile*) triste; (*prospect, future*) poco prometedor(a)

bleary-eyed ['blɪərɪ'aɪd] adj: **to be ~** tener ojos de cansado

bleat [bliːt] vi balar

bled [bled] pt, pp of **bleed**

bleed (*pt, pp* **bled**) [bliːd, bled] vt sangrar; (*brakes, radiator*) desaguar ▷ vi sangrar; **my nose is ~ing** me está sangrando la nariz

bleep [bliːp] n pitido ▷ vi pitar ▷ vt llamar por el busca

bleeper ['bliːpəʳ] n (*of doctor etc*) busca m

blemish ['blemɪʃ] n marca, mancha; (*on reputation*) tacha

blend [blend] n mezcla ▷ vt mezclar ▷ vi (*colours etc*) combinarse, mezclarse

blender ['blendəʳ] n (*Culin*) batidora

bless (*pt, pp* **blessed** *or* **blest**) [bles, blest] vt bendecir; **~ you!** (*after sneeze*) ¡Jesús!

blessed ['blesɪd] adj (*Rel: holy*) santo, bendito; (*: happy*) dichoso; **every ~ day** cada santo día

blessing ['blesɪŋ] n bendición f; (*advantage*) beneficio, ventaja; **to count one's ~s** agradecer lo que se tiene; **it was a ~ in disguise** no hay mal que por bien no venga

blew [bluː] pt of **blow**

blight [blaɪt] vt (*hopes etc*) frustrar, arruinar

blimey ['blaɪmɪ] excl (*Brit inf*) ¡caray!

blind [blaɪnd] adj ciego ▷ n (*for window*) persiana ▷ vt cegar; (*dazzle*) deslumbrar; **to ~ sb to ...** (*deceive*) cegar a algn a ...; **the blind** npl los ciegos

blind alley n callejón m sin salida

blind corner n (*Brit*) esquina or curva sin visibilidad

blind date n cita a ciegas

blindfold ['blaɪndfəʊld] n venda ▷ adj, adv con los ojos vendados ▷ vt vendar los ojos a
blinding ['blaɪndɪŋ] adj (flash, light) cegador; (pain) intenso
blindingly ['blaɪndɪŋlɪ] adv: **it's ~ obvious** salta a la vista
blindly ['blaɪndlɪ] adv a ciegas, ciegamente
blindness ['blaɪndnɪs] n ceguera
blind spot n (Aut) ángulo muerto; **to have a ~ about sth** estar ciego para algo
blink [blɪŋk] vi parpadear, pestañear; (light) oscilar; **to be on the ~** (inf) estar estropeado
blinkers ['blɪŋkəz] npl (esp Brit) anteojeras fpl
blip [blɪp] n señal f luminosa; (on graph) pequeña desviación f; (fig) pequeña anomalía
bliss [blɪs] n felicidad f
blissful ['blɪsful] adj dichoso; **in ~ ignorance** feliz en la ignorancia
blister ['blɪstə'] n (on skin, paint) ampolla ▷ vi ampollarse
blistering ['blɪstərɪŋ] adj (heat) abrasador(a)
blithely ['blaɪðlɪ] adv alegremente, despreocupadamente
blizzard ['blɪzəd] n ventisca
bloated ['bləʊtɪd] adj hinchado
blob [blɔb] n (drop) gota; (stain, spot) mancha
block [blɔk] n (also Comput) bloque m; (in pipes) obstáculo; (of buildings) manzana, cuadra (LAm) ▷ vt (gen) obstruir, cerrar; (progress) estorbar; (Comput) agrupar; **~ of flats** (Brit) bloque m de pisos; **mental ~** bloqueo mental; **~ and tackle** (Tech) aparejo de polea; **3 ~s from here** a 3 manzanas or cuadras (LAm) de aquí; **block up** vt tapar, obstruir; (pipe) atascar
blockade [blɔ'keɪd] n bloqueo ▷ vt bloquear
blockage ['blɔkɪdʒ] n estorbo, obstrucción f
block booking n reserva en grupo
blockbuster ['blɔkbʌstə'] n (book) best-seller m; (film) éxito de público
block capitals npl mayúsculas fpl
block letters npl mayúsculas fpl
blog [blɔg] n (Comput) blog m ▷ vi bloguear
bloke [bləʊk] n (Brit inf) tipo, tío
blond, blonde [blɔnd] adj, n rubio(-a) m(f)
blood [blʌd] n sangre f; **new ~** (fig) gente f nueva
blood bank n banco de sangre
blood count n recuento de glóbulos rojos y blancos
blood donor n donante m/f de sangre
blood group n grupo sanguíneo
bloodhound ['blʌdhaund] n sabueso
blood poisoning n septicemia, envenenamiento de la sangre
blood pressure n tensión f, presión f sanguínea; **to have high/low ~** tener la tensión alta/baja
bloodshed ['blʌdʃed] n baño de sangre
bloodshot ['blʌdʃɔt] adj inyectado en sangre

bloodstream ['blʌdstriːm] n corriente f sanguínea
blood test n análisis m de sangre
bloodthirsty ['blʌdθəːstɪ] adj sanguinario
blood transfusion n transfusión f de sangre
blood type n grupo sanguíneo
blood vessel n vaso sanguíneo
bloody ['blʌdɪ] adj sangriento; (Brit inf!): **this ~ ...** este condenado or puñetero or fregado (LAm) ... (!) ▷ adv (Brit inf!): **~ strong/ good** terriblemente fuerte/bueno
bloody-minded ['blʌdɪ'maɪndɪd] adj (Brit inf) con malas pulgas
bloom [bluːm] n floración f; **in ~** en flor ▷ vi florecer
blossom ['blɔsəm] n flor f ▷ vi florecer; (fig) desarrollarse; **to ~ into** (fig) convertirse en
blot [blɔt] n borrón m ▷ vt (dry) secar; (stain) manchar; **to ~ out** vt (view) tapar; (memories) borrar; **to be a ~ on the landscape** estropear el paisaje; **to ~ one's copy book** (fig) manchar su reputación
blotchy ['blɔtʃɪ] adj (complexion) lleno de manchas
blotting paper ['blɔtɪŋ-] n papel m secante
blouse [blauz] n blusa
blow [bləʊ] (pt **blew**, pp **blown**) n golpe m ▷ vi soplar; (fuse) fundirse ▷ vt (glass) soplar; (fuse) quemar; (instrument) tocar; **to come to ~s** llegar a golpes; **to ~ one's nose** sonarse; **blow away** vt llevarse, arrancar; **blow down** vt derribar; **blow off** vt arrebatar; **blow out** vt apagar ▷ vi apagarse; (tyre) reventar; **blow over** vi amainar; **blow up** vi estallar ▷ vt volar; (tyre) inflar; (Phot) ampliar
blow-dry ['bləʊdraɪ] n secado con secador de mano ▷ vt secar con secador de mano
blowlamp ['bləʊlæmp] n (Brit) soplete m, lámpara de soldar
blown [bləʊn] pp of **blow**
blow-out ['bləʊaut] n (of tyre) pinchazo; (inf: big meal) banquete m, festín m
blowtorch ['bləʊtɔːtʃ] n = **blowlamp**
blue [bluː] adj azul; **~ film** película porno; **~ joke** chiste verde; **once in a ~ moon** de higos a brevas; **to come out of the ~** (fig) ser completamente inesperado; see also **blues**
bluebell ['bluːbel] n campanilla, campánula azul
blueberry n arándano
bluebottle ['bluːbɔtl] n moscarda, mosca azul
blue cheese n queso azul
blueprint ['bluːprɪnt] n proyecto; **~ (for)** (fig) anteproyecto (de)
blues [bluːz] npl: **the ~** (Mus) el blues; **to have the ~** estar triste
bluetit [bluːtɪt] n herrerillo m (común)
bluff [blʌf] vi tirarse un farol, farolear ▷ n bluff m, farol m; (Geo) precipicio, despeñadero; **to call sb's ~** coger a algn en un renuncio

blunder ['blʌndə^r] n patinazo, metedura de pata ▷ vi cometer un error, meter la pata; **to ~ into sb/sth** tropezar con algn/algo

blunt [blʌnt] adj (knife) desafilado; (person) franco, directo ▷ vt embotar, desafilar; **this pencil is ~** este lápiz está despuntado; **~ instrument** (Law) instrumento contundente

blur [blə:^r] n aspecto borroso; **to become a ~** hacerse borroso ▷ vt (vision) enturbiar; (memory) empañar

blurb [blə:b] n propaganda

blurred [blə:d] adj borroso

blurt [blə:t]: **to ~ out** vt (say) descolgarse con, dejar escapar

blush [blʌʃ] vi ruborizarse, ponerse colorado ▷ n rubor m

blusher ['blʌʃə^r] n colorete m

blustery ['blʌstərɪ] adj (weather) tempestuoso, tormentoso

BMA n abbr = **British Medical Association**

BO n abbr (inf: = body odour) olor m a sudor; (US) = **box office**

boar [bɔ:^r] n verraco, cerdo

board [bɔ:d] n tabla, tablero; (on wall) tablón m; (for chess etc) tablero; (committee) junta, consejo; (in firm) mesa or junta directiva; (Naut, Aviat): **on ~** a bordo ▷ vt (ship) embarcarse en; (train) subir a; **full ~** (Brit) pensión f completa; **half ~** (Brit) media pensión; **~ and lodging** alojamiento y comida; **to go by the ~** (fig) irse por la borda; **above ~** (fig) sin tapujos; **across the ~** (fig: adv) en todos los niveles; (: adj) general; **board up** vt (door) tapar, cegar

boarder ['bɔ:də^r] n huésped(a) m(f); (Scol) interno(-a)

board game n juego de tablero

boarding card ['bɔ:dɪŋ-] n (Brit: Aviat, Naut) tarjeta de embarque

boarding house ['bɔ:dɪŋ-] n casa de huéspedes

boarding party ['bɔ:dɪŋ-] n brigada de inspección

boarding pass ['bɔ:dɪŋ-] n (US) = **boarding card**

boarding school ['bɔ:dɪŋ-] n internado

board meeting n reunión f de la junta directiva

board room n sala de juntas

boast [bəust] vi: **to ~ (about or of)** alardear (de) ▷ vt ostentar ▷ n alarde m, baladronada

boat [bəut] n barco, buque m; (small) barca, bote m; **to go by ~** ir en barco

boater ['bəutə^r] n (hat) canotié m

boat people npl refugiados que huyen en barca

bob [bɔb] vi (boat, cork on water: also: **~ up and down**) menearse, balancearse ▷ n (Brit inf) = **shilling**; **bob up** vi (re)aparecer de repente

bobby ['bɔbɪ] n (Brit inf) poli m/f

bobby pin n (US) horquilla

bobsleigh ['bɔbsleɪ] n bob m, trineo de competición f

bode [bəud] vi: **to ~ well/ill (for)** ser de buen/mal agüero (para)

bodily ['bɔdɪlɪ] adj (comfort, needs) corporal; (pain) corpóreo ▷ adv (in person) en persona; (carry) corporalmente; (lift) en peso

body ['bɔdɪ] n cuerpo; (corpse) cadáver m; (of car) caja, carrocería; (also: **~ stocking**) body m; (fig: organization) organización f; (: public body) organismo; (: quantity) masa; (: of speech, document) parte f principal; **ruling ~** directiva; **in a ~** todos juntos, en masa

body blow n (fig) palo

body-building ['bɔdɪ'bɪldɪŋ] n culturismo

bodyguard ['bɔdɪgɑ:d] n guardaespaldas m inv

body language n lenguaje m gestual

body search n cacheo; **to carry out a ~ on sb** registrar a algn; **to submit to** or **undergo a ~** ser registrado

bodywork ['bɔdɪwə:k] n carrocería

bog [bɔg] n pantano, ciénaga ▷ vt: **to get ~ged down** (fig) empantanarse, atascarse

boggle ['bɔgl] vi: **the mind ~s!** ¡no puedo creerlo!

bogus ['bəugəs] adj falso, fraudulento; (person) fingido

boil [bɔɪl] vt hervir; (eggs) pasar por agua ▷ vi hervir; (fig: with anger) estar furioso ▷ n (Med) furúnculo, divieso; **to bring to the ~** calentar hasta que hierva; **to come to the** (Brit) or **a** (US) **~** comenzar a hervir; **~ed egg** huevo pasado por agua; **~ed potatoes** patatas fpl or papas fpl (LAm) cocidas; **boil down** vi (fig): **to ~ down to** reducirse a; **boil over** vi (liquid) salirse; (anger, resentment) llegar al colmo

boiler ['bɔɪlə^r] n caldera

boiler suit n (Brit) mono, overol m (LAm)

boiling ['bɔɪlɪŋ] adj: **I'm ~ (hot)** (inf) estoy asado

boiling point n punto de ebullición f

boil-in-the-bag [bɔɪlɪnðə'bæg] adj: **~ meals** platos que se cuecen en su misma bolsa

boisterous ['bɔɪstərəs] adj (noisy) bullicioso; (excitable) exuberante; (crowd) tumultuoso

bold [bəuld] adj (brave) valiente, audaz; (pej) descarado; (outline) grueso; (colour) llamativo; **~ type** (Typ) negrita

Bolivia [bə'lɪvɪə] n Bolivia

Bolivian [bə'lɪvɪən] adj, n boliviano(-a) m(f)

bollard ['bɔləd] n (Brit Aut) poste m

bolshy ['bɔlʃɪ] adj (Brit inf) protestón(-ona); **to be in a ~ mood** tener el día protestón

bolster ['bəulstə^r] n travesero, cabezal m; **bolster up** vt reforzar; (fig) alentar

bolt [bəult] n (lock) cerrojo; (with nut) perno, tornillo ▷ adv: **~ upright** rígido, erguido ▷ vt (door) echar el cerrojo a; (food) engullir ▷ vi fugarse; (horse) desbocarse

bomb [bɔm] n bomba ▷ vt bombardear

b

bombard [bɔm'bɑːd] vt bombardear; (fig)
asediar

bombardment [bɔm'bɑːdmənt] n
bombardeo

bombastic [bɔm'bæstɪk] adj rimbombante;
(person) pomposo

bomb disposal n desactivación f de
explosivos

bomb disposal expert n artificiero(-a)

bomber ['bɔmər] n (Aviat) bombardero;
(terrorist) persona que pone bombas

bombing ['bɔmɪŋ] n bombardeo

bomb scare n amenaza de bomba

bombshell ['bɔmʃɛl] n obús m, granada; (fig)
bomba

bomb site n lugar m donde estalló una
bomba

bona fide ['bəunə'faɪdɪ] adj genuino,
auténtico

bonanza [bə'nænzə] n bonanza

bond [bɔnd] n (binding promise) fianza;
(Finance) bono; (link) vínculo, lazo; **in ~**
(Comm) en depósito bajo fianza

bondage ['bɔndɪdʒ] n esclavitud f

bone [bəun] n hueso; (of fish) espina ▷ vt
deshuesar; quitar las espinas a; **~ of
contention** manzana de la discordia

bone idle adj gandul

bone marrow n médula; **~ transplant**
transplante m de médula

bonfire ['bɔnfaɪər] n hoguera, fogata

bonkers ['bɔŋkəz] adj (Brit inf) majareta

bonnet ['bɔnɪt] n gorra; (Brit: of car) capó m

bonus ['bəunəs] n (payment) paga
extraordinaria, plus m; (fig) bendición f

bony ['bəunɪ] adj (arm, face) huesudo; (Med:
tissue) huesudo; (meat) lleno de huesos; (fish)
lleno de espinas; (thin: person) flaco, delgado

boo [buː] excl ¡uh! ▷ vt abuchear

booby trap ['buː-bɪ-] n (Mil etc) trampa
explosiva

book [buk] n libro; (notebook) libreta;
(of stamps etc) librillo; **~s** (Comm) cuentas fpl,
contabilidad f ▷ vt (ticket, seat, room)
reservar; (driver) fichar; (Football) amonestar;
to keep the ~s llevar las cuentas or los libros;
by the ~ según las reglas; **to throw the ~
at sb** echar un rapapolvo a algn; **book in** vi
(at hotel) registrarse; **book up** vt: **all seats
are ~ed up** todas las plazas están
reservadas; **the hotel is ~ed up** el hotel está
completo

bookcase ['bukkeɪs] n librería, estante m
para libros

booking ['bukɪŋ] n reserva

booking office n (Brit: Rail) despacho de
billetes or boletos (LAm); (: Theat) taquilla,
boletería (LAm)

book-keeping ['buk'kiːpɪŋ] n contabilidad f

booklet ['buklɪt] n folleto

bookmaker ['bukmeɪkər] n corredor m de
apuestas

bookmark ['bukmɑːk] n (Comput) favorito,
marcador m

bookseller ['buksɛlər] n librero(-a)

bookshelf ['bukʃɛlf] n estante m

bookshop ['bukʃɔp] n librería

bookstall ['bukstɔːl] n quiosco de libros

book store n = **bookshop**

book token n vale m para libros

boom [buːm] n (noise) trueno, estampido; (in
prices etc) alza rápida; (Econ) boom m, auge m
▷ vi (cannon) hacer gran estruendo, retumbar;
(Econ) estar en alza

boomerang ['buːməræŋ] n bumerang m (also
fig) ▷ vi: **to ~ on sb** (fig) ser contraproducente
para algn

boon [buːn] n favor m, beneficio

boost [buːst] n estímulo, empuje m ▷ vt
estimular, empujar; (increase: sales, production)
aumentar; **to give a ~ to** (morale) levantar; **it
gave a ~ to his confidence** le dio confianza
en sí mismo

booster ['buːstər] n (Med) reinyección f; (TV)
repetidor m; (Elec) elevador m de tensión;
(also: **~ rocket**) cohete m

boot [buːt] n bota; (ankle boot) botín m,
borceguí m; (Brit: of car) maleta, maletero,
baúl m (LAm) ▷ vt dar un puntapié a; (Comput)
arrancar; **to ~** (in addition) además, por
añadidura; **to give sb the ~** (inf) despedir a
algn, poner a algn en la calle

booth [buːð] n (at fair) barraca; (telephone
booth, voting booth) cabina

booty ['buːtɪ] n botín m

booze [buːz] (inf) n bebida ▷ vi
emborracharse

border ['bɔːdər] n borde m, margen m; (of a
country) frontera; (for flowers) arriate m ▷ adj
fronterizo; **the B~s** región fronteriza entre Escocia
e Inglaterra; **border on** vt fus lindar con; (fig)
rayar en

borderline ['bɔːdəlaɪn] n (fig) frontera; **on
the ~** en el límite

bore [bɔːr] pt of **bear** ▷ vt (hole) hacer; (person)
aburrir ▷ n (person) pelmazo, pesado; (of gun)
calibre m

bored [bɔːd] adj aburrido; **he's ~ to tears** or
to death or **stiff** está aburrido como una
ostra, está muerto de aburrimiento

boredom ['bɔːdəm] n aburrimiento

boring ['bɔːrɪŋ] adj aburrido, pesado

born [bɔːn] adj: **to be ~** nacer; **I was ~ in 1960**
nací en 1960

born-again [bɔːnə'gɛn] adj: **~ Christian**
evangelista m/f

borne [bɔːn] pp of **bear**

borough ['bʌrə] n municipio

borrow ['bɔrəu] vt: **to ~ sth (from sb)** tomar
algo prestado (a alguien); **may I ~ your car?**
¿me prestas tu coche?

borrower ['bɔrəuər] n prestatario(-a)

borstal ['bɔːstl] n (Brit) reformatorio (de
menores)

Bosnia ['bozniə] n Bosnia
Bosnia-Herzegovina, Bosnia-Hercegovina ['bo:sniəherzə'gəuvi:nə] n Bosnia-Herzegovina
Bosnian ['bozniən] adj, n bosnio(-a)
bosom ['buzəm] n pecho; (fig) seno
boss [bos] n jefe(-a) m(f); (employer) patrón(-ona) m(f); (political etc) cacique m ▷ vt (also: ~ **about** or **around**) mangonear; **stop ~ing everyone about!** ¡deja de dar órdenes or de mangonear a todos!
bossy ['bosı] adj mandón(-ona)
bosun ['bəusn] n contramaestre m
botanist ['botənıst] n botanista m/f
botany ['botənı] n botánica
botch [botʃ] vt (also: ~ **up**) arruinar, estropear
both [bəuθ] adj, pron ambos(-as), los/las dos; ~ **of us went, we ~ went** fuimos los dos, ambos fuimos ▷ adv: ~ **A and B** tanto A como B
bother ['boðəʳ] vt (worry) preocupar; (disturb) molestar, fastidiar, fregar (LAm), embromar (LAm) ▷ vi (gen): **to ~ o.s.** molestarse ▷ n (trouble) dificultad f; (nuisance) molestia, lata; **what a ~!** ¡qué lata! ▷ excl ¡maldita sea!, ¡caramba!; **I'm sorry to ~ you** perdona que te moleste; **to ~ doing** tomarse la molestia de hacer; **please don't ~** no te molestes
bottle ['botl] n botella; (small) frasco; (baby's) biberón m ▷ vt embotellar; ~ **of wine/milk** botella de vino/de leche; **wine/milk ~** botella de vino/de leche; **bottle up** vt (fig) contener, reprimir
bottle bank n contenedor m de vidrio, iglú m
bottleneck ['botlnɛk] n embotellamiento
bottle-opener ['botləupnəʳ] n abrebotellas m inv
bottom ['botəm] n (of box, sea) fondo; (buttocks) trasero, culo; (of page, mountain, tree) pie m; (of list) final m ▷ adj (lowest) más bajo; (last) último; **to get to the ~ of sth** (fig) llegar al fondo de algo
bottomless ['botəmlıs] adj sin fondo, insondable
bottom line n: **the ~** lo fundamental; **the ~ is he has to go** el caso es que tenemos que despedirle
botulism ['botjulızəm] n botulismo
bough [bau] n rama
bought [bo:t] pt, pp of **buy**
boulder ['bəuldəʳ] n canto rodado
bounce [bauns] vi (ball) (re)botar; (cheque) ser rechazado ▷ vt hacer (re)botar ▷ n (rebound) (re)bote m; **he's got plenty of ~** (fig) tiene mucha energía
bouncer ['baunsəʳ] n (inf) forzudo, gorila m
bouncy castle® ['baunsı-] n castillo inflable
bound [baund] pt, pp of **bind** ▷ n (leap) salto gen pl (limit) límite m ▷ vi (leap) saltar ▷ adj: ~ **by** rodeado de; **to be ~ to do sth** (obliged) tener el deber de hacer algo; **he's ~ to come**

es seguro que vendrá; **"out of ~s to the public"** "prohibido el paso"; ~ **for** con destino a
boundary ['baundrı] n límite m, lindero
boundless ['baundlıs] adj ilimitado
bouquet ['bukeı] n (of flowers) ramo, ramillete m; (of wine) aroma m
bourbon ['buəbən] n (US: also: ~ **whiskey**) whisky m americano, bourbon m
bourgeois ['bueʒwɑ:] adj, n burgués(-esa) m(f)
bout [baut] n (of malaria etc) ataque m; (Boxing etc) combate m, encuentro
boutique [bu:'ti:k] n boutique f, tienda de ropa
bow [bəu] n (knot) lazo; (weapon) arco; (Mus) arco [bau] (of the head) reverencia; (Naut: also: ~**s**) proa ▷ vi [bau] inclinarse, hacer una reverencia; (yield): **to ~ to** or **before** ceder ante, someterse a; **to ~ to the inevitable** resignarse a lo inevitable
bowels ['bauəlz] npl intestinos mpl, vientre m; (fig) entrañas fpl
bowl [bəul] n tazón m, cuenco; (for washing) palangana, jofaina; (ball) bola; (US: stadium) estadio ▷ vi (Cricket) arrojar la pelota; see also **bowls**
bow-legged ['bəu'lɛgıd] adj estevado
bowler ['bəuləʳ] n (Cricket) lanzador m (de la pelota); (Brit: also: ~ **hat**) hongo, bombín m
bowling ['bəulıŋ] n (game) bolos mpl, bochas fpl
bowling alley n bolera
bowling green n pista para bochas
bowls [bəulz] n juego de los bolos, bochas fpl
bow tie ['bəu-] n corbata de lazo, pajarita
box [boks] n (also: **cardboard ~**) caja, cajón m; (for jewels) estuche m; (for money) cofre m; (crate) cofre m, arca; (Theat) palco ▷ vt encajonar ▷ vi (Sport) boxear
boxer ['boksəʳ] n (person) boxeador m; (dog) bóxer m
boxer shorts ['boksəʃo:ts] npl bóxers; **a pair of** ~ unos bóxers
boxing ['boksıŋ] n (Sport) boxeo, box m (LAm)
Boxing Day n (Brit) día m de San Esteban
boxing gloves npl guantes mpl de boxeo
boxing ring n ring m, cuadrilátero
box number n (for advertisements) apartado
box office n taquilla, boletería (LAm)
boxroom ['boksrum] n trastero
boy [boı] n (young) niño; (older) muchacho, chico; (son) hijo
boy band n boy band m (grupo musical de chicos)
boycott ['boıkot] n boicot m ▷ vt boicotear
boyfriend ['boıfrɛnd] n novio
boyish ['boııʃ] adj de muchacho, inmaduro
boy scout n boy scout m
bra [brɑ:] n sostén m, sujetador m, corpiño (LAm)
brace [breıs] n refuerzo, abrazadera; (Brit: on teeth) corrector m, aparato; (tool) berbiquí m

▷ vt asegurar, reforzar; **to ~ o.s. (for)** (fig)
preparase (para); see also **braces**

bracelet ['breıslıt] n pulsera, brazalete m,
pulso (LAm)

braces ['breısız] npl (on teeth) corrector m;
(Brit: for trousers) tirantes mpl, suspensores mpl
(LAm)

bracing ['breısıŋ] adj vigorizante, tónico

bracket ['brækıt] n (Tech) soporte m, puntal
m; (group) clase f, categoría; (also: **brace ~**)
soporte m, abrazadera; (also: **round ~**)
paréntesis m inv; (gen): **square ~** corchete m
▷ vt (fig: also: **~ together**) agrupar; **income ~**
nivel m económico; **in ~s** entre paréntesis

brag [bræg] vi jactarse

braid [breıd] n (trimming) galón m; (of hair)
trenza

Braille [breıl] n Braille m

brain [breın] n cerebro; **brains** npl sesos mpl;
she's got ~s es muy lista

brainchild ['breıntʃaıld] n invención f

braindead ['breındɛd] adj (Med)
clínicamente muerto; (inf) subnormal,
tarado

brainfood ['breınfu:d] n alimentos pl para el
cerebro

brainwash ['breınwɒʃ] vt lavar el cerebro a

brainwave ['breınweıv] n idea luminosa or
genial, inspiración f

brainy ['breını] adj muy listo or inteligente

braise [breız] vt cocer a fuego lento

brake [breık] n (on vehicle) freno ▷ vt, vi frenar

brake fluid n líquido de frenos

brake light n luz f de frenado

bran [bræn] n salvado

branch [brɑ:ntʃ] n rama; (fig) ramo; (Comm)
sucursal f ▷ vi ramificarse; (fig) extenderse;
branch off vi: **a small road ~es off to the
right** hay una carretera pequeña que sale
hacia la derecha; **branch out** vi (fig)
extenderse

brand [brænd] n marca; (fig: type) tipo; (iron)
hierro de marcar ▷ vt (cattle) marcar con
hierro candente

brand name n marca

brand-new ['brænd'nju:] adj flamante,
completamente nuevo

brandy ['brændı] n coñac m, brandy m

brash [bræʃ] adj (rough) tosco; (cheeky)
descarado

brass [brɑ:s] n latón m; **the ~** (Mus) los cobres

brass band n banda de metal

brassière ['bræsıə'] n sostén m, sujetador m,
corpiño (LAm)

brass tacks npl: **to get down to ~** ir al grano

brat [bræt] n (pej) mocoso(-a)

bravado [brə'vɑ:dəʊ] n fanfarronería

brave [breıv] adj valiente, valeroso ▷ n
guerrero indio ▷ vt (challenge) desafiar; (resist)
aguantar

bravery ['breıvərı] n valor m, valentía

bravo [brɑ:'vəʊ] excl ¡bravo!, ¡olé!

brawl [brɔ:l] n pelea, reyerta ▷ vi pelearse

bray [breı] n rebuzno ▷ vi rebuznar

brazen ['breızn] adj descarado, cínico ▷ vt:
to ~ it out echarle cara al asunto

brazier ['breızıə'] n brasero

Brazil [brə'zıl] n (el) Brasil

Brazilian [brə'zılıən] adj, n brasileño(-a) m(f)

breach [bri:tʃ] vt abrir brecha en ▷ n (gap)
brecha; (estrangement) ruptura; (breaking): **~ of
confidence** abuso de confianza; **~ of
contract** infracción f de contrato; **~ of the
peace** perturbación f del orden público; **in ~
of** por incumplimiento or infracción de

bread [brɛd] n pan m; (inf: money) pasta, lana
(LAm); **~ and butter** n pan con mantequilla;
(fig) pan (de cada día) ▷ adj común y
corriente; **to earn one's daily ~** ganarse el
pan; **to know which side one's ~ is
buttered (on)** saber dónde aprieta el zapato

breadbin ['brɛdbın] n panera

breadbox ['brɛdbɒks] n (US) panera

breadcrumbs ['brɛdkrʌmz] npl migajas fpl;
(Culin) pan msg rallado

breadline ['brɛdlaın] n: **on the ~** en la
miseria

breadth [brɛtθ] n anchura; (fig) amplitud f

breadwinner ['brɛdwınə'] n sostén m de la
familia

break [breık] vb (pt **broke**, pp **broken**) ▷ vt
(gen) romper; (promise) faltar a; (fall)
amortiguar; (journey) interrumpir; (law)
violar, infringir; (record) batir; (news)
comunicar ▷ vi romperse, quebrarse; (storm)
estallar; (weather) cambiar; (news etc) darse a
conocer ▷ n (gap) abertura; (crack) grieta;
(fracture) fractura; (in relations) ruptura; (rest)
descanso; (time) intervalo; (: at school)
(período de) recreo; (holiday) vacaciones fpl;
(chance) oportunidad f; (escape) evasión f,
fuga; **to ~ with sb** (fig) romper con algn;
to ~ even vi cubrir los gastos; **to ~ free** or
loose vi escaparse; **lucky ~** (inf) chiripa,
racha de buena suerte; **to have** or **take a ~**
(few minutes) descansar; **without a ~** sin
descanso or descansar; **break down** vt (door
etc) echar abajo, derribar; (resistance) vencer,
acabar con; (figures, data) analizar,
descomponer; (undermine) acabar con ▷ vi
estropearse; (Med) sufrir un colapso; (Aut)
averiarse, descomponerse (LAm); (person)
romper a llorar; (talks) fracasar; **break in** vt
(horse etc) domar ▷ vi (burglar) forzar una
entrada; **break into** vt fus (house) forzar;
break off vi (speaker) pararse, detenerse;
(branch) partir ▷ vt (talks) suspender;
(engagement) romper; **break open** vt (door etc)
abrir por la fuerza, forzar; **break out** vi
estallar; (prisoner) escaparse; **to ~ out in
spots** salir a algn granos; **break through** vi:
the sun broke through asomó el sol ▷ vt fus
(defences, barrier, crowd) abrirse paso por; **break
up** vi (marriage) deshacerse; (ship) hacerse

b

pedazos; (*crowd, meeting*) disolverse; (*Scol*) terminar (el curso); (*line*) cortarse ▷ vt (*rocks etc*) partir; (*journey*) partir; (*fight etc*) acabar con; **the line's** *or* **you're -ing up** se corta

breakable ['breɪkəbl] *adj* quebradizo ▷ *n*: **~s** cosas *fpl* frágiles

breakage ['breɪkɪdʒ] *n* rotura; **to pay for ~s** pagar por los objetos rotos

breakdown ['breɪkdaun] *n* (*Aut*) avería; (*in communications*) interrupción *f*; (*Med: also:* **nervous ~**) colapso, crisis *f* nerviosa; (*of marriage, talks*) fracaso; (*of figures*) desglose *m*

breakdown truck, breakdown van *n* (camión *m*) grúa

breaker ['breɪkəʳ] *n* rompiente *m*, ola grande

breakfast ['brɛkfəst] *n* desayuno

break-in ['breɪkɪn] *n* robo con allanamiento de morada

breaking and entering ['breɪkɪŋənd'ɛntərɪŋ] *n* (*Law*) violación *f* de domicilio, allanamiento de morada

breaking point ['breɪkɪŋ-] *n* punto de ruptura

breakthrough ['breɪkθruː] *n* ruptura; (*fig*) avance *m*, adelanto

break-up ['breɪkʌp] *n* (*of partnership, marriage*) disolución *f*

breakwater ['breɪkwɔːtəʳ] *n* rompeolas *m inv*

breast [brɛst] *n* (*of woman*) pecho, seno; (*chest*) pecho; (*of bird*) pechuga

breast-feed ['brɛstfiːd] *vt, vi* (*irreg: like* **feed**) amamantar, dar el pecho

breaststroke ['brɛststrəuk] *n* braza de pecho

breath [brɛθ] *n* aliento, respiración *f*; **to take a deep ~** respirar hondo; **out of ~** sin aliento, sofocado; **to go out for a ~ of air** salir a tomar el fresco

Breathalyser® ['brɛθəlaɪzəʳ] *n* (*Brit*) alcoholímetro *m*; **~ test** *n* prueba de alcoholemia

breathe [briːð] *vt, vi* respirar; (*noisily*) resollar; **I won't ~ a word about it** no diré ni una palabra de ello; **breathe in** *vt, ▷ vi* aspirar; **breathe out** *vt, ▷ vi* espirar

breather ['briːðəʳ] *n* respiro, descanso

breathing ['briːðɪŋ] *n* respiración *f*

breathing space *n* (*fig*) respiro, pausa

breathless ['brɛθlɪs] *adj* sin aliento, jadeante; (*with excitement*) pasmado

breathtaking ['brɛθteɪkɪŋ] *adj* imponente, pasmoso

breath test *n* prueba de la alcoholemia

bred [brɛd] *pt, pp of* **breed**

breed [briːd] (*pt, pp* **bred**) *vt* criar; (*fig: hate, suspicion*) crear, engendrar ▷ *vi* reproducirse, procrear ▷ *n* raza, casta

breeding ['briːdɪŋ] *n* (*of person*) educación *f*

breeze [briːz] *n* brisa

breezy ['briːzɪ] *adj* de mucho viento, ventoso; (*person*) despreocupado

brevity ['brɛvɪtɪ] *n* brevedad *f*

brew [bruː] *vt* (*tea*) hacer; (*beer*) elaborar; (*plot*) tramar ▷ *vi* hacerse; elaborarse; tramarse; (*fig: trouble*) prepararse; (*storm*) amenazar

brewer ['bruːəʳ] *n* cervecero, fabricante *m* de cerveza

brewery ['bruːərɪ] *n* fábrica de cerveza

briar ['braɪəʳ] *n* (*thorny bush*) zarza; (*wild rose*) escaramujo, rosa silvestre

bribe [braɪb] *n* soborno ▷ *vt* sobornar, cohechar; **to ~ sb to do sth** sobornar a algn para que haga algo

bribery ['braɪbərɪ] *n* soborno, cohecho

bric-a-brac ['brɪkəbræk] *n inv* baratijas *fpl*

brick [brɪk] *n* ladrillo

bricklayer ['brɪkleɪəʳ] *n* albañil *m*

bridal ['braɪdl] *adj* nupcial

bride [braɪd] *n* novia

bridegroom ['braɪdgruːm] *n* novio

bridesmaid ['braɪdzmeɪd] *n* dama de honor

bridge [brɪdʒ] *n* puente *m*; (*Naut*) puente *m* de mando; (*of nose*) caballete *m*; (*Cards*) bridge *m* ▷ *vt* (*river*) tender un puente sobre; (*fig*): **to ~ a gap** llenar un vacío

bridle ['braɪdl] *n* brida, freno ▷ *vt* poner la brida a; (*fig*) reprimir, refrenar ▷ *vi* (*in anger etc*) picarse

bridle path *n* camino de herradura

brief [briːf] *adj* breve, corto ▷ *n* (*Law*) escrito ▷ *vt* (*inform*) informar; (*instruct*) dar instrucciones a; **in ~ ...** en resumen ...; **to ~ sb (about sth)** informar a algn (sobre algo)

briefcase ['briːfkeɪs] *n* cartera, portafolio(s) *m inv* (*LAm*)

briefing ['briːfɪŋ] *n* (*Press*) informe *m*

briefly ['briːflɪ] *adv* (*smile, glance*) brevemente; (*explain, say*) brevemente, en pocas palabras

briefs [briːfs] *npl* (*for men*) calzoncillos *mpl*; (*for women*) bragas *fpl*

brigade [brɪ'geɪd] *n* (*Mil*) brigada

brigadier [brɪgə'dɪəʳ] *n* general *m* de brigada

bright [braɪt] *adj* brillante; (*room*) luminoso; (*day*) de sol; (*person: clever*) listo, inteligente; (*: lively*) alegre, animado; (*colour*) vivo; (*future*) prometedor(a); **to look on the ~ side** mirar el lado bueno

brighten ['braɪtn] (*also:* **~ up**) *vt* (*room*) hacer más alegre ▷ *vi* (*weather*) despejarse; (*person*) animarse, alegrarse

brill [brɪl] *adj* (*Brit inf*) guay

brilliance ['brɪljəns] *n* brillo, brillantez *f*; (*fig: of person*) inteligencia

brilliant ['brɪljənt] *adj* (*light, idea, person, success*) brillante; (*clever*) genial

brim [brɪm] *n* borde *m*; (*of hat*) ala

brine [braɪn] *n* (*Culin*) salmuera

bring (*pt, pp* **brought**) [brɪŋ, brɔːt] *vt* (*thing*) traer; (*person*) conducir; **to ~ sth to an end** terminar con algo; **I can't ~ myself to sack him** no soy capaz de echarle; **bring about** *vt* ocasionar, producir; **bring back** *vt* volver a traer; (*return*) devolver; **bring down** *vt* (*government, plane*) derribar; (*price*) rebajar; **bring forward** *vt* adelantar; (*Bookkeeping*) sumar y seguir; **bring in** *vt* (*harvest*) recoger; (*person*) hacer entrar *or* pasar; (*object*) traer; (*Pol: bill, law*) presentar; (*Law: verdict*) pronunciar; (*produce: income*) producir, rendir; **bring off** *vt* (*task, plan*) lograr, conseguir; (*deal*) cerrar; **bring on** *vt* (*illness, attack*) producir, causar; (*player, substitute*) sacar (de la reserva), hacer salir; **bring out** *vt* (*object*) sacar; (*new product*) sacar; (*book*) publicar; **bring round** *vt* (*unconscious person*) hacer volver en sí; (*convince*) convencer; **bring up** *vt* (*person*) educar, criar; (*carry up*) subir; (*question*) sacar a colación; (*food: vomit*) devolver, vomitar

brink [brɪŋk] *n* borde *m*; **on the ~ of doing sth** a punto de hacer algo; **she was on the ~ of tears** estaba al borde de las lágrimas

brisk [brɪsk] *adj* (*walk*) enérgico, vigoroso; (*speedy*) rápido; (*wind*) fresco; (*trade*) activo, animado; (*abrupt*) brusco; **business is ~** el negocio va bien *or* a paso activo

bristle ['brɪsl] *n* cerda ▷ *vi* (*fur*) erizarse; **to ~ in anger** temblar de rabia

Brit [brɪt] *n abbr* (*inf:* = *British person*) británico(-a)

Britain ['brɪtən] *n* (*also:* **Great ~**) Gran Bretaña

British ['brɪtɪʃ] *adj* británico; **the British** *npl* los británicos; **the British Isles** *npl* las Islas Británicas

British Summer Time *n* hora de verano británica

Briton ['brɪtən] *n* británico(-a)

brittle ['brɪtl] *adj* quebradizo, frágil

broach [brəutʃ] *vt* (*subject*) abordar

broad [brɔːd] *adj* ancho; (*range*) amplio; (*accent*) cerrado ▷ *n* (*US inf*) tía; **in ~ daylight** en pleno día; **the ~ outlines** las líneas generales

broadband ['brɔːdbænd] *n* banda ancha

broad bean *n* haba

broadcast ['brɔːdkɑːst] (*pt, pp* **broadcast**) *n* emisión *f* ▷ *vt* (*Radio*) emitir; (*TV*) transmitir ▷ *vi* emitir; transmitir

broadcaster ['brɔːdkɑːstər] *n* locutor(a) *m(f)*

broadcasting ['brɔːdkɑːstɪŋ] *n* radiodifusión *f*, difusión *f*

broaden ['brɔːdn] *vt* ampliar ▷ *vi* ensancharse; **to ~ one's mind** hacer más tolerante a algn

broadly ['brɔːdlɪ] *adv* en general

broad-minded ['brɔːd'maɪndɪd] *adj* tolerante, liberal

broadsheet ['brɔːdʃiːt] *n* (*Brit*) periódico de gran formato (*no sensacionalista*); *see also* **quality press**

broccoli ['brɔkəlɪ] *n* brécol *m*, bróculi *m*

brochure ['brəuʃjuər] *n* folleto

brogue [brəug] *n* (*accent*) acento regional; (*shoe*) (*tipo de*) zapato de cuero grueso

broil [brɔɪl] *vt* (*US*) asar a la parrilla

broiler ['brɔɪlər] *n* (*grill*) parilla; (*fowl*) pollo (para asar)

broke [brəuk] *pt of* **break** ▷ *adj* (*inf*) pelado, sin blanca; **to go ~** quebrar

broken ['brəukən] *pp of* **break** ▷ *adj* (*stick*) roto; (*fig: marriage*) deshecho; (*: promise, vow*) violado; **~ leg** pierna rota; **in ~ English** en un inglés chapurreado

broken-down ['brəukn'daun] *adj* (*car*) averiado; (*machine*) estropeado; (*house*) destartalado

broken-hearted ['brəukn'hɑːtɪd] *adj* con el corazón destrozado

broker ['brəukər] *n* corredor(a) *m(f)* de bolsa

brolly ['brɔlɪ] *n* (*Brit inf*) paraguas *m inv*

bronchitis [brɔŋ'kaɪtɪs] *n* bronquitis *f*

bronze [brɔnz] *n* bronce *m*

brooch [brəutʃ] *n* broche *m*

brood [bruːd] *n* camada, cría; (*children*) progenie *f* ▷ *vi* (*hen*) empollar; **to ~ over** dar vueltas a

broom [brum] *n* escoba; (*Bot*) retama

broomstick ['brumstɪk] *n* palo de escoba

Bros. *abbr* (*Comm:* = *Brothers*) Hnos

broth [brɔθ] *n* caldo

brothel ['brɔθl] *n* burdel *m*

brother ['brʌðər] *n* hermano

brotherhood ['brʌðəhud] *n* hermandad *f*

brother-in-law ['brʌðərɪn'lɔː] *n* cuñado

brought [brɔːt] *pt, pp of* **bring**

brow [brau] *n* (*forehead*) frente *f*; (*eyebrow*) ceja; (*of hill*) cumbre *f*

brown [braun] *adj* marrón; (*hair*) castaño; (*tanned*) moreno ▷ *n* (*colour*) marrón *m* ▷ *vt* (*tan*) poner moreno; (*Culin*) dorar; **to go ~** (*person*) ponerse moreno; (*leaves*) dorarse

brown bread *n* pan *m* integral

Brownie ['braunɪ] *n* niña exploradora

brown paper *n* papel *m* de estraza

brown rice *n* arroz *m* integral

brown sugar *n* azúcar *m* moreno

browse [brauz] *vi* (*animal*) pacer; (*among books*) hojear libros; **to ~ through a book** hojear un libro

browser ['brauzər] *n* (*Comput*) navegador *m*

bruise [bruːz] *n* (*on person*) cardenal *m*, moretón *m* ▷ *vt* (*leg etc*) magullar; (*fig: feelings*) herir

brunch [brʌntʃ] *n* desayuno-almuerzo

brunette [bruː'nɛt] *n* morena, morocha (*LAm*)

brunt [brʌnt] *n*: **to bear the ~ of** llevar el peso de

brush [brʌʃ] *n* cepillo, escobilla (*LAm*); (*large*) escoba; (*for painting, shaving etc*) brocha; (*artist's*) pincel *m*; (*Bot*) maleza ▷ *vt* (*sweep*) barrer; (*groom*) cepillar; (*gen*): **to ~ past, ~ against** rozar al pasar; **to have a ~ with the police** tener un roce con la policía; **brush aside** *vt* rechazar, no hacer caso a; **brush up** *vt* (*knowledge*) repasar, refrescar

brushwood ['brʌʃwud] n (*bushes*) maleza; (*sticks*) leña

Brussels ['brʌslz] n Bruselas

Brussels sprout n col f de Bruselas

brutal ['bru:tl] adj brutal

brutality [bru:'tælɪtɪ] n brutalidad f

brute [bru:t] n bruto; (*person*) bestia ▷ adj: **by ~ force** por la fuerza bruta

BSc abbr (= *Bachelor of Science*) licenciado en Ciencias

BSE n abbr (= *bovine spongiform encephalopathy*) encefalopatía espongiforme bovina

bubble ['bʌbl] n burbuja; (*in paint*) ampolla ▷ vi burbujear, borbotar

bubble bath n espuma para el baño

bubble gum n chicle m (de globo)

bubblejet printer ['bʌbldʒet-] n impresora de inyección por burbujas

bubbly ['bʌblɪ] adj (*person*) vivaracho; (*liquid*) con burbujas ▷ n (*inf*) champán m

buck [bʌk] n (*rabbit*) macho; (*deer*) gamo; (*US inf*) dólar m ▷ vi corcovear; **to pass the ~ (to sb)** echar (a algn) el muerto; **buck up** vi (*cheer up*) animarse, cobrar ánimo ▷ vt: **to ~ one's ideas up** poner más empeño

bucket ['bʌkɪt] n cubo, balde m (*esp LAm*) ▷ vi: **the rain is ~ing (down)** (*inf*) está lloviendo a cántaros

Buckingham Palace ['bʌkɪŋəm-] n el Palacio de Buckingham

buckle ['bʌkl] n hebilla ▷ vt abrochar con hebilla ▷ vi torcerse, combarse; **buckle down** vi poner empeño

bud [bʌd] n (*of plant*) brote m, yema; (*of flower*) capullo ▷ vi brotar, echar brotes

Buddhism ['budɪzm] n Budismo

Buddhist ['budɪst] adj, n budista m/f

budding ['bʌdɪŋ] adj en ciernes, en embrión

buddy ['bʌdɪ] n (*US*) compañero, compinche m

budge [bʌdʒ] vt mover; (*fig*) hacer ceder ▷ vi moverse

budgerigar ['bʌdʒərɪgɑ:ʳ] n periquito

budget ['bʌdʒɪt] n presupuesto ▷ vi: **to ~ for sth** presupuestar algo; **I'm on a tight ~** no puedo gastar mucho; **she works out her ~ every month** planea su presupuesto todos los meses

budgie ['bʌdʒɪ] n = **budgerigar**

buff [bʌf] adj (*colour*) color de ante; (*inf: person: well-muscled*) escultural ▷ n (*enthusiast*) entusiasta m/f

buffalo ['bʌfələu] (pl **buffalo** or **buffaloes**) n (*Brit*) búfalo; (*US: bison*) bisonte m

buffer ['bʌfəʳ] n amortiguador m; (*Rail*) tope m; (*Comput*) memoria intermedia, buffer m

buffer zone n zona (que sirve de) colchón

buffet ['bufeɪ] n (*Brit: bar*) bar m, cafetería; (*food*) buffet m ▷ vt ['bʌfɪt] (*strike*) abofetear; (*wind etc*) golpear

buffet car n (*Brit Rail*) coche-restaurante m

bug [bʌg] n (*insect*) chinche m; (: *gen*) bicho, sabandija; (*germ*) microbio, bacilo; (*spy device*) micrófono oculto; (*Comput*) fallo, error m ▷ vt (*annoy*) fastidiar; (*room*) poner un micrófono oculto en; (*phone*) pinchar; **I've got the travel ~** (*fig*) me encanta viajar; **it really ~s me** me fastidia or molesta mucho

bugle ['bju:gl] n corneta, clarín m

build [bɪld] n (*of person*) talle m, tipo ▷ vt (*pt, pp* **built** [bɪlt]) construir, edificar; **build on** vt fus (*fig*) basar en; **build up** vt (*morale, forces, production*) acrecentar; (*Med*) fortalecer; (*stocks*) acumular; (*establish: business*) fomentar, desarrollar; (: *reputation*) crear(se); (*increase: production*) aumentar; **don't ~ your hopes up too soon** no te hagas demasiadas ilusiones

builder ['bɪldəʳ] n constructor(a) m(f); (*contractor*) contratista m/f

building ['bɪldɪŋ] n (*act*) construcción f; (*habitation, offices*) edificio

building site n obra, solar m (*Sp*)

building society n (*Brit*) sociedad f de préstamo inmobiliario

build-up ['bɪldʌp] n (*publicity*): **to give sb/sth a good ~** hacer mucha propaganda de algn/algo

built [bɪlt] *pt, pp of* **build**

built-in ['bɪlt'ɪn] adj (*cupboard*) empotrado; (*device*) interior, incorporado; **~ obsolescence** caducidad f programada

built-up ['bɪltʌp] adj (*area*) urbanizado

bulb [bʌlb] n (*Bot*) bulbo; (*Elec*) bombilla, bombillo (*LAm*), foco (*LAm*)

Bulgaria [bʌl'gɛərɪə] n Bulgaria

Bulgarian [bʌl'gɛərɪən] adj búlgaro ▷ n búlgaro(-a); (*Ling*) búlgaro

bulge [bʌldʒ] n bulto; (*in birth rate, sales*) alza, aumento ▷ vi bombearse, pandearse; (*pocket etc*) hacer bulto; **to ~ (with)** rebosar (de)

bulimia [bə'lɪmɪə] n bulimia

bulimic [bju:'lɪmɪk] adj, n bulímico(-a) m/f

bulk [bʌlk] n (*mass*) bulto, volumen m; (*major part*) grueso; **in ~** (*Comm*) a granel; **the ~ of** la mayor parte de; **to buy in ~** comprar en grandes cantidades

bulky ['bʌlkɪ] adj voluminoso, abultado

bull [bul] n toro; (*Stock Exchange*) alcista m/f de bolsa; (*Rel*) bula

bulldog ['buldɔg] n dogo

bulldoze ['buldəuz] vt mover con excavadora; **I was ~d into doing it** (*fig, inf*) me obligaron a hacerlo

bulldozer ['buldəuzəʳ] n buldozer m, excavadora

bullet ['bulɪt] n bala; **~ wound** balazo

bulletin ['bulɪtɪn] n comunicado, parte m; (*journal*) boletín m

bulletin board n (*US*) tablón m de anuncios; (*Comput*) tablero de noticias

bulletproof ['bulɪtpru:f] adj a prueba de balas; **~ vest** chaleco antibalas

b

bullfight ['bulfaɪt] n corrida de toros
bullfighter ['bulfaɪtəʳ] n torero
bullfighting ['bulfaɪtɪŋ] n los toros mpl, el toreo; (art of bullfighting) tauromaquia
bullion ['buljən] n oro or plata en barras
bullock ['bulək] n novillo
bullring ['bulrɪŋ] n plaza de toros
bull's-eye ['bulzaɪ] n blanco, diana
bullshit ['bulʃɪt] (inf!) excl chorradas ▷ n chorradas fpl ▷ vi decir chorradas ▷ vt: **to ~ sb** quedarse con algn
bully ['bulɪ] n valentón m, matón m ▷ vt intimidar, tiranizar
bum [bʌm] n (Brit: inf: backside) culo; (: tramp) vagabundo; (inf: esp US: idler) holgazán(-ana) m(f), flojo(-a)
bumblebee ['bʌmblbiː] n abejorro
bump [bʌmp] n (blow) tope m, choque m; (jolt) sacudida; (noise) choque m, topetón m; (on road etc) bache m; (on head) chichón m ▷ vt (strike) chocar contra, topetar ▷ vi dar sacudidas; **bump into** vt fus chocar contra, tropezar con; (person) topar con; (inf: meet) tropezar con, toparse con
bumper ['bʌmpəʳ] n (Brit) parachoques m inv ▷ adj: **~ crop/harvest** cosecha abundante
bumper cars npl (US) autos or coches mpl de choque
bumpy ['bʌmpɪ] adj (road) lleno de baches; (journey, flight) agitado
bun [bʌn] n (Brit: cake) pastel m; (US: bread) bollo; (of hair) moño
bunch [bʌntʃ] n (of flowers) ramo; (of keys) manojo; (of bananas) piña; (of people) grupo; (pej) pandilla; **bunches** npl (in hair) coletas fpl
bundle ['bʌndl] n (gen) bulto, fardo; (of sticks) haz m; (of papers) legajo ▷ vt (also: **~ up**) atar, envolver; **to ~ sth/sb into** meter algo/a algn precipitadamente en
bung [bʌŋ] n tapón m, bitoque m ▷ vt (throw: also: **~ into**) arrojar; (also: **~ up**: pipe, hole) tapar; **my nose is ~ed up** (inf) tengo la nariz atascada or taponada
bungalow ['bʌŋgələu] n bungalow m, chalé m
bungee jumping ['bʌndʒiː'dʒʌmpɪŋ] n puenting m, banyi m
bungle ['bʌŋgl] vt chapucear
bunion ['bʌnjən] n juanete m
bunk [bʌŋk] n litera; **~ beds** npl literas fpl
bunker ['bʌŋkəʳ] n (coal store) carbonera; (Mil) refugio; (Golf) bunker m
bunk off vi: **to ~ school** (Brit: inf) pirarse las clases; **I'll ~ at 3 this afternoon** me voy a pirar a las 3 esta tarde
bunny ['bʌnɪ] n (also: **~ rabbit**) conejito
bunting ['bʌntɪŋ] n empavesada, banderas fpl
buoy [bɔɪ] n boya; **buoy up** vt mantener a flote; (fig) animar
buoyant ['bɔɪənt] adj (ship) capaz de flotar; (carefree) boyante, optimista; (Comm: market, prices etc) sostenido; (: economy) boyante

BUPA ['buːpə] n abbr (= British United Provident Association) seguro médico privado
burden ['bəːdn] n carga ▷ vt cargar; **to be a ~ to sb** ser una carga para algn
bureau (pl **bureaux**) ['bjuərəu, -z] n (Brit: writing desk) escritorio, buró m; (US: chest of drawers) cómoda; (office) oficina, agencia
bureaucracy [bjuə'rɔkrəsɪ] n burocracia
bureaucrat ['bjuərəkræt] n burócrata m/f
bureaucratic [bjuərə'krætɪk] adj burocrático
bureau de change [-də'ʃɑ̃ʒ] (pl **bureaux de change**) n caja f de cambio
bureaux ['bjuərəuz] npl of **bureau**
burger ['bəːgəʳ] n hamburguesa
burglar ['bəːgləʳ] n ladrón(-ona) m(f)
burglar alarm n alarma f contra robo
burglarize ['bəːgləraɪz] vt (US) robar (con allanamiento)
burglary ['bəːglərɪ] n robo con allanamiento or fractura, robo de una casa
burgle ['bəːgl] vt robar (con allanamiento)
Burgundy ['bəːgəndɪ] n Borgoña
burial ['berɪəl] n entierro
burly ['bəːlɪ] adj fornido, membrudo
Burma ['bəːmə] n Birmania
burn [bəːn] vb (pt, pp **burned** or **burnt**) ▷ vt quemar; (house) incendiar ▷ vi quemarse, arder; incendiarse; (sting) escocer ▷ n (Med) quemadura; **the cigarette ~t a hole in her dress** se ha quemado el vestido con el cigarrillo; **I've ~t myself!** ¡me he quemado!; **burn down** vt incendiar; **burn out** vt (writer etc): **to ~ o.s. out** agotarse
burner ['bəːnəʳ] n (gas) quemador m
burning ['bəːnɪŋ] adj (building, forest) en llamas; (hot: sand etc) abrasador(a); (ambition) ardiente
Burns' Night [bəːnz-] n ver nota

burnt [bəːnt] pt, pp of **burn**
burp [bəːp] (inf) n eructo ▷ vi eructar
burrow ['bʌrəu] n madriguera ▷ vt hacer una madriguera
bursary ['bəːsərɪ] n (Brit) beca
burst [bəːst] vb (pt, pp **burst**) ▷ vt (balloon, pipe) reventar; (banks etc) romper ▷ vi reventarse; romperse; (tyre) pincharse ▷ n (explosion)

estallido; (also: ~ **pipe**) reventón m; **the river has ~ its banks** el río se ha desbordado; **to ~ into flames** estallar en llamas; **to ~ out laughing** soltar la carcajada; **to ~ into tears** deshacerse en lágrimas; **to be ~ing with** reventar de; **a ~ of energy** una explosión de energía; **a ~ of applause** una salva de aplausos; **a ~ of speed** un acelerón; **to ~ open** abrirse de golpe; **burst into** vt fus (room etc) irrumpir en

bury ['bɛrɪ] vt enterrar; (body) enterrar, sepultar; **to ~ the hatchet** enterrar el hacha (de guerra), echar pelillos a la mar

bus [bʌs] n autobús m, camión m (LAm)

bus boy n (US) ayudante m/f de camarero

bus conductor n cobrador(a) m(f)

bush [buʃ] n arbusto; (scrub land) monte m bajo; **to beat about the ~** andar(se) con rodeos

bushed [buʃt] adj (inf) molido

bush fire n incendio en el monte

bushy ['buʃɪ] adj (beard, eyebrows) poblado; (hair) espeso; (fur) tupido

busily ['bɪzɪlɪ] adv afanosamente

business ['bɪznɪs] n (matter, affair) asunto; (trading) comercio, negocios mpl; (firm) empresa, casa; (occupation) oficio; **to be away on ~** estar en viaje de negocios; **it's my ~ to ...** me toca or corresponde ...; **it's none of my ~** no es asunto mío; **he means ~** habla en serio; **he's in the insurance ~** se dedica a los seguros; **I'm here on ~** estoy aquí por mi trabajo; **to do ~ with sb** hacer negocios con algn

business card n tarjeta de visita

business class n (Aviat) clase f preferente

businesslike ['bɪznɪslaɪk] adj (company) serio; (person) eficiente

businessman ['bɪznɪsmən] n hombre m de negocios

business trip n viaje m de negocios

businesswoman ['bɪznɪswumən] n mujer f de negocios

busker ['bʌskə'] n (Brit) músico(-a) ambulante

bus pass n bonobús

bus route n recorrido del autobús

bus shelter n parada cubierta

bus station n estación f or terminal f de autobuses

bus-stop ['bʌsstɔp] n parada de autobús, paradero (LAm)

bust [bʌst] n (Anat) pecho; (sculpture) busto ▷ adj (inf: broken) roto, estropeado ▷ vt (inf: Police: arrest) detener; **to go ~** quebrar

bustle ['bʌsl] n bullicio, movimiento ▷ vi menearse, apresurarse

bustling ['bʌslɪŋ] adj (town) animado, bullicioso

bust-up ['bʌstʌp] n (inf) riña

busy ['bɪzɪ] adj ocupado, atareado; (shop, street) concurrido, animado ▷ vt: **to ~ o.s. with**

ocuparse en; **he's a ~ man** (normally) es un hombre muy ocupado; (temporarily) está muy ocupado; **the line's ~** (esp US) está comunicando

busybody ['bɪzɪbɔdɪ] n entrometido(-a)

busy signal n (US Tel) señal f de comunicando

 KEYWORD

but [bʌt] conj 1 pero; **he's not very bright, but he's hard-working** no es muy inteligente, pero es trabajador

2 (in direct contradiction) sino; **he's not English but French** no es inglés sino francés; **he didn't sing but he shouted** no cantó sino que gritó

3 (showing disagreement, surprise etc): **but that's far too expensive!** ¡pero eso es carísimo!; **but it does work!** ¡(pero) sí que funciona!

▷ prep (apart from, except) menos, salvo; **we've had nothing but trouble** no hemos tenido más que problemas; **no-one but him can do it** nadie más que él puede hacerlo; **the last but one** el penúltimo; **who but a lunatic would do such a thing?** ¡sólo un loco haría una cosa así!; **but for you/your help** si no fuera por ti/tu ayuda; **anything but that** cualquier cosa menos eso

▷ adv (just, only): **she's but a child** no es más que una niña; **had I but known** si lo hubiera sabido; **I can but try** al menos lo puedo intentar; **it's all but finished** está casi acabado

butch [butʃ] adj (pej: woman) machirula, marimacho; (inf: man) muy macho

butcher ['butʃə'] n carnicero(-a) ▷ vt hacer una carnicería con; (cattle etc for meat) matar; **~'s (shop)** carnicería

butler ['bʌtlə'] n mayordomo

butt [bʌt] n (cask) tonel m; (for rain) tina; (thick end) cabo, extremo; (of gun) culata; (of cigarette) colilla; (Brit fig: target) blanco ▷ vt dar cabezadas contra, topetar; **butt in** vi (interrupt) interrumpir

butter ['bʌtə'] n mantequilla, manteca (LAm) ▷ vt untar con mantequilla

buttercup ['bʌtəkʌp] n ranúnculo

butterfly ['bʌtəflaɪ] n mariposa; (Swimming: also: ~ **stroke**) (braza de) mariposa

buttocks ['bʌtəks] npl nalgas fpl

button ['bʌtn] n botón m ▷ vt (also: ~ **up**) abotonar, abrochar ▷ vi abrocharse

buttress ['bʌtrɪs] n contrafuerte m; (fig) apoyo, sostén m

buxom ['bʌksəm] adj (woman) frescachona, rolliza

buy [baɪ] vb (pt, pp **bought**) ▷ vt comprar ▷ n compra; **to ~ sb sth/sth from sb** comprarle algo a algn; **to ~ sb a drink** invitar a algn a tomar algo; **a good/bad ~** una buena/mala compra; **buy back** vt volver a comprar;

buy in vt proveerse or abastecerse de; **buy into** vt fus comprar acciones en; **buy off** vt (inf: bribe) sobornar; **buy out** vt (partner) comprar la parte de; **buy up** vt (property) acaparar; (stock) comprar todas las existencias de

buyer ['baɪəʳ] n comprador(a) m(f); ~'s **market** mercado favorable al comprador

buy-out ['baɪaut] n (Comm) adquisición f de (la totalidad de) las acciones

buzz [bʌz] n zumbido; (inf: phone call) llamada (telefónica) ▷ vt (call on intercom) llamar; (with buzzer) hacer sonar; (Aviat: plane, building) pasar rozando ▷ vi zumbar; **my head is ~ing** me zumba la cabeza; **buzz off** vi (Brit: inf) largarse

buzzer ['bʌzəʳ] n timbre m

buzz word n palabra que está de moda

🅞 KEYWORD

by [baɪ] prep 1 (referring to cause, agent) por; de; **abandoned by his mother** abandonado por su madre; **surrounded by enemies** rodeado de enemigos; **a painting by Picasso** un cuadro de Picasso

2 (referring to method, manner, means): **by bus/ car/train** en autobús/coche/tren; **to pay by cheque** pagar con cheque; **by moonlight/ candlelight** a la luz de la luna/una vela; **by saving hard, he ...** ahorrando, ...

3 (via, through) por; **we came by Dover** vinimos por Dover

4 (close to, past): **the house by the river** la casa junto al río; **she rushed by me** pasó a mi lado como una exhalación; **I go by the post office every day** paso por delante de Correos todos los días

5 (time: not later than) para; (: during): **by daylight** de día; **by 4 o'clock** para las cuatro; **by this time tomorrow** mañana a estas horas; **by the time I got here it was too late** cuando llegué ya era demasiado tarde

6 (amount): **by the metre/kilo** por metro/ kilo; **paid by the hour** pagado por hora

7 (in measurements, sums): **to divide/multiply by 3** dividir/multiplicar por 3; **a room 3 metres by 4** una habitación de 3 metros por 4; **it's broader by a metre** es un metro más ancho; **the bus missed me by inches** no me pilló el autobús por un pelo

8 (according to) según, de acuerdo con; **it's 3 o'clock by my watch** según mi reloj, son las tres; **it's all right by me** por mí, está bien

9: **(all) by oneself** etc todo solo; **he did it (all) by himself** lo hizo él solo; **he was standing (all) by himself in a corner** estaba de pie solo en un rincón

10: **by the way** a propósito, por cierto; **this wasn't my idea, by the way** pues, no fue idea mía

▷ adv 1 see **go, pass** etc

2: **by and by** finalmente; **they'll come back by and by** acabarán volviendo; **by and large** en líneas generales, en general

bye ['baɪ], **bye-bye** ['baɪ'baɪ] excl adiós, hasta luego, chao (esp LAm)

by-election ['baɪɪlɛkʃən] n (Brit) elección f parcial; ver nota

Byelorussia [bjɛləu'rʌʃə] n Bielorrusia

bygone ['baɪgɔn] adj pasado, del pasado ▷ n: **let ~s be ~s** lo pasado, pasado está

bypass ['baɪpɑːs] n carretera de circunvalación; (Med) (operación f de) bypass m ▷ vt evitar

by-product ['baɪprɔdʌkt] n subproducto, derivado

bystander ['baɪstændəʳ] n espectador(a) m(f)

byte [baɪt] n (Comput) byte m, octeto

byword ['baɪwəːd] n: **to be a ~ for** ser sinónimo de

by-your-leave ['baɪjɔː'liːv] n: **without so much as a ~** sin decir nada, sin dar ningún tipo de explicación

C

C, c [si:] n (letter) C, c f; (Mus): **C** do m; **C for Charlie** C de Carmen

C abbr (= Celsius, centigrade) C

c abbr (= century) S.; (= circa) hacia; (US etc) = **cent(s)**

CA n abbr = **Central America**; (Brit) = **chartered accountant**

CAA n abbr (Brit: = Civil Aviation Authority) organismo de control y desarrollo de la aviación civil

cab [kæb] n taxi m; (of truck) cabina

cabaret ['kæbəreɪ] n cabaret m

cabbage ['kæbɪdʒ] n col f, berza

cabbie, cabby ['kæbɪ] n (inf) taxista m/f

cabin ['kæbɪn] n cabaña; (on ship) camarote m

cabin crew n tripulación f de cabina

cabin cruiser n yate m de motor

cabinet ['kæbɪnɪt] n (Pol) consejo de ministros; (furniture) armario; (also: **display ~**) vitrina

cabinet minister n ministro(-a) (del gabinete)

cable ['keɪbl] n cable m ▷ vt cablegrafiar

cable car n teleférico

cable television n televisión f por cable

cache [kæʃ] n (of drugs) alijo; (of arms) zulo

cackle ['kækl] vi cacarear

cactus (pl **cacti**) ['kæktəs, -taɪ] n cacto

caddie, caddy ['kædɪ] n (Golf) cadi m

cadet [kə'dɛt] n (Mil) cadete m; **police ~** cadete m de policía

cadge [kædʒ] vt gorronear

Caesarean, Cesarean (US) [si:'zɛərɪən] adj: **~ (section)** cesárea

café ['kæfeɪ] n café m

cafeteria [kæfɪ'tɪərɪə] n cafetería (con autoservicio para comer)

caffeine ['kæfi:n] n cafeína

cage [keɪdʒ] n jaula ▷ vt enjaular

cagey ['keɪdʒɪ] adj (inf) cauteloso, reservado

cagoule [kə'gu:l] n chubasquero

cahoots [kə'hu:ts] n: **to be in ~ (with sb)** estar conchabado (con algn)

cajole [kə'dʒəʊl] vt engatusar

cake [keɪk] n (large) tarta; (small) pastel m; (of soap) pastilla; **he wants to have his ~ and eat it** (fig) quiere estar en misa y repicando; **it's a piece of ~** (inf) es pan comido

caked [keɪkt] adj: **~ with** cubierto de

calamity [kə'læmɪtɪ] n calamidad f

calcium ['kælsɪəm] n calcio

calculate ['kælkjʊleɪt] vt (estimate: chances, effect) calcular; **calculate on** vt fus: **to ~ on sth/on doing sth** contar con algo/con hacer algo

calculation [kælkjʊ'leɪʃən] n cálculo, cómputo

calculator ['kælkjʊleɪtər] n calculadora

calculus ['kælkjʊləs] n cálculo

calendar ['kælındər] n calendario; **~ month/ year** n mes m/año civil

calf (pl **calves**) [kɑ:f, kɑ:vz] n (of cow) ternero, becerro; (of other animals) cría; (also: **~skin**) piel f de becerro; (Anat) pantorrilla, canilla (LAm)

calibre, caliber (US) ['kælɪbər] n calibre m

call [kɔ:l] vt (gen) llamar; (Tel) llamar; (announce: flight) anunciar; (meeting, strike) convocar ▷ vi (shout) llamar; (telephone) llamar (por teléfono), telefonear; (visit: also: **~ in, ~ round**) hacer una visita ▷ n (shout) llamada, llamado (LAm); (Tel) llamada, llamado (LAm); (of bird) canto; (appeal) llamamiento, llamada (LAm); (summons: for flight etc) llamada; (fig: lure) llamada; **to be ~ed** (person, object) llamarse; **to ~ sb names** poner verde a algn; **let's ~ it a day** (inf) ¡dejémoslo!, ¡ya está bien!; **who is ~ing?** ¿de parte de quién?; **London ~ing** (Radio) aquí Londres; **on ~** (nurse, doctor etc) de guardia; **please give me a ~ at seven** despiértame or llámeme a las siete, por favor; **long-distance ~** conferencia (interurbana); **to make a ~** llamar por teléfono; **port of ~** puerto de escala; **to pay a ~ on sb** pasarse a ver a algn; **there's not much ~ for these items** estos artículos no tienen mucha demanda; **call at** vt fus (ship) hacer escala en, tocar en; (train) parar en; **call back** vi (return) volver; (Tel) volver a llamar; **call for** vt fus (demand) pedir, exigir; (fetch) pasar a recoger; **call in** vt (doctor, expert, police) llamar; **call off** vt (cancel: meeting, race) cancelar; (: deal) anular; (: strike) desconvocar; **call on** vt fus

(visit) ir a ver; (turn to) acudir a; **call out** vi
gritar, dar voces ▷ vt (doctor) llamar; (police,
troops) hacer intervenir; **call up** vt (Mil)
llamar a filas

callbox ['kɔːlbɒks] n (Brit) cabina telefónica

call centre n (Brit) centro de atención al
cliente

caller ['kɔːlə^r] n visita f; (Tel) usuario(-a);
hold the line, ~! ¡no cuelgue!

call girl n prostituta

call-in ['kɔːlɪn] n (US) programa de línea abierta al
público

calling ['kɔːlɪŋ] n vocación f; (profession)
profesión f

calling card n tarjeta de visita

callous ['kæləs] adj insensible, cruel

calm [kɑːm] adj tranquilo; (sea) tranquilo, en
calma ▷ n calma, tranquilidad f ▷ vt calmar,
tranquilizar; **calm down** vi calmarse,
tranquilizarse ▷ vt calmar, tranquilizar

calmly ['kɑːmlɪ] adv tranquilamente, con
calma

calmness ['kɑːmnɪs] n calma

Calor gas® ['kælə^r-] n butano, camping
gas® m inv

calorie ['kælərɪ] n caloría; **low-~ product**
producto bajo en calorías

calves [kɑːvz] npl of **calf**

camber ['kæmbə^r] n (of road) combadura

Cambodia [kæm'bəudjə] n Camboya

camcorder ['kæmkɔːdə^r] n videocámara

came [keɪm] pt of **come**

camel ['kæməl] n camello

camera ['kæmərə] n cámara or máquina
fotográfica; (Cine, TV) cámara; (movie camera)
cámara, tomavistas m inv; **in ~** (Law) a puerta
cerrada

cameraman ['kæmərəmæn] n cámara m

camera phone n teléfono m con cámara

camouflage ['kæməflɑːʒ] n camuflaje m ▷ vt
camuflar

camp [kæmp] n campamento, camping m;
(Mil) campamento; (for prisoners) campo; (fig:
faction) bando ▷ vi acampar ▷ adj afectado,
afeminado; **to go ~ing** ir de or hacer
camping

campaign [kæm'peɪn] n (Mil, Pol etc)
campaña ▷ vi: **to ~ (for/against)** hacer
campaña (a favor de o en contra de)

campaigner [kæm'peɪnə^r] n: **~ for**
defensor(a) m(f) de; **~ against** persona que
hace campaña contra

campbed ['kæmpbɛd] n (Brit) cama plegable

camper ['kæmpə^r] n campista m/f; (vehicle)
caravana

campground ['kæmpgraund] n (US)
camping m, campamento

camping ['kæmpɪŋ] n camping m

campsite ['kæmpsaɪt] n camping m

campus ['kæmpəs] n campus m

can¹ [kæn] n (of oil, water) bidón m; (tin) lata,
bote m ▷ vt enlatar; (preserve) conservar en

lata; **a ~ of beer** una lata or un bote de
cerveza; **to carry the ~** (inf) pagar el pato

⊙ **KEYWORD**

can² (negative **cannot, can't**, conditional and pt
could) aux vb 1 (be able to) poder; **you can do it
if you try** puedes hacerlo si lo intentas;
I can't see you no te veo; **can you hear me?**
(not translated) ¿me oyes?
2 (know how to) saber; **I can swim/play
tennis/drive** sé nadar/jugar al tenis/
conducir; **can you speak French?** ¿hablas or
sabes hablar francés?
3 (may) poder; **can I use your phone?** ¿me
dejas or puedo usar tu teléfono?; **could I
have a word with you?** ¿podría hablar
contigo un momento?
4 (expressing disbelief, puzzlement etc): **it can't be
true!** ¡no puede ser (verdad)!; **what CAN he
want?** ¿qué querrá?
5 (expressing possibility, suggestion etc): **he could
be in the library** podría estar en la
biblioteca; **she could have been delayed**
puede que se haya retrasado

Canada ['kænədə] n Canadá m

Canadian [kə'neɪdɪən] adj, n canadiense m/f

canal [kə'næl] n canal m

canary [kə'nɛərɪ] n canario

Canary Islands, Canaries [kə'nɛərɪz] npl
las (Islas) Canarias

cancel ['kænsəl] vt cancelar; (train) suprimir;
(appointment, cheque) anular; (cross out) tachar;
cancel out vt (Math) anular; (fig)
contrarrestar; **they ~ each other out** se
anulan mutuamente

cancellation [kænsə'leɪʃən] n cancelación f;
supresión f

cancer ['kænsə^r] n cáncer m; **C~** (Astro)
Cáncer m

candid ['kændɪd] adj franco, abierto

candidate ['kændɪdeɪt] n candidato(-a)

candle ['kændl] n vela; (in church) cirio

candlelight ['kændllaɪt] n: **by ~** a la luz de
una vela

candlestick ['kændlstɪk] n (single) candelero;
(: low) palmatoria; (bigger, ornate) candelabro

candour, candor(US) ['kændə^r] n franqueza

candy ['kændɪ] n azúcar m cande; (US)
caramelo ▷ vt (fruit) escarchar

candy bar(US) n barrita (dulce)

candyfloss ['kændɪflɒs] n (Brit) algodón m
(azucarado)

cane [keɪn] n (Bot) caña; (for baskets, chairs etc)
mimbre m; (stick) vara, palmeta; (for walking)
bastón m ▷ vt (Brit Scol) castigar (con
palmeta); **~ liquor** caña

canister ['kænɪstə^r] n bote m, lata

cannabis ['kænəbɪs] n canabis m

canned [kænd] adj en lata, de lata; (inf: music)
grabado; (: drunk) mamado

cannibal ['kænɪbəl] n caníbal m/f, antropófago(-a)

cannon (pl **cannon** or **cannons**) ['kænən] n cañón m

cannot ['kænɔt] = **can not**

canoe [kə'nu:] n canoa; (Sport) piragua

canoeing [kə'nu:ɪŋ] n (Sport) piragüismo

canon ['kænən] n (clergyman) canónigo; (standard) canon m

canonize ['kænənaɪz] vt canonizar

can opener n abrelatas m inv

canopy ['kænəpɪ] n dosel m, toldo

can't [kænt] = **can not**

cantankerous [kæn'tæŋkərəs] adj arisco, malhumorado

canteen [kæn'ti:n] n (eating place) comedor m; (Brit: of cutlery) juego

canter ['kæntəʳ] n medio galope ▷ vi ir a medio galope

canvas ['kænvəs] n (material) lona; (painting) lienzo; (Naut) velamen m; **under ~** (camping) en tienda de campaña

canvass ['kænvəs] (Pol) vi: **to ~ for** solicitar votos por ▷ vt (district) hacer campaña (puerta a puerta) en; (: person) hacer campaña (puerta a puerta) a favor de; (Comm: district) sondear el mercado en; (: citizens, opinions) sondear

canyon ['kænjən] n cañón m

cap [kæp] n (hat) gorra; (for swimming) gorro; (of pen) capuchón m; (of bottle) tapón m, tapa; (: metal) chapa; (contraceptive) diafragma m ▷ vt (outdo) superar; (limit) recortar; (Brit Sport) seleccionar para el equipo nacional); **and to ~ it all, he ...** y para colmo, él ...

capability [keɪpə'bɪlɪtɪ] n capacidad f

capable ['keɪpəbl] adj capaz

capacity [kə'pæsɪtɪ] n capacidad f; (position) calidad f; **filled to ~** lleno a reventar; **this work is beyond my ~** este trabajo es superior a mí; **in an advisory ~** como asesor

cape [keɪp] n capa; (Geo) cabo

caper ['keɪpəʳ] n (Culin: also: **~s**) alcaparra; (prank) travesura

capital ['kæpɪtl] n (also: **~ city**) capital f; (money) capital m; (also: **~ letter**) mayúscula

capital gains tax n impuesto sobre la plusvalía

capitalism ['kæpɪtəlɪzəm] n capitalismo

capitalist ['kæpɪtəlɪst] adj, n capitalista m/f

capitalize ['kæpɪtəlaɪz] vt (Comm: provide with capital) capitalizar; **capitalize on** vt fus (fig) sacar provecho de, aprovechar

capital punishment n pena de muerte

Capitol ['kæpɪtl] n: **the ~** el Capitolio

capitulate [kə'pɪtjuleɪt] vi capitular, rendirse

Capricorn ['kæprɪkɔːn] n Capricornio

caps [kæps] abbr (= capital letters) may

capsize [kæp'saɪz] vt volcar, hacer zozobrar ▷ vi volcarse, zozobrar

capsule ['kæpsjuːl] n cápsula

Capt. abbr = **Captain**

captain ['kæptɪn] n capitán m ▷ vt capitanear, ser el capitán de

caption ['kæpʃən] n (heading) título; (to picture) leyenda, pie m

captivate ['kæptɪveɪt] vt cautivar, encantar

captive ['kæptɪv] adj, n cautivo(-a) m(f)

captivity [kæp'tɪvɪtɪ] n cautiverio

captor ['kæptəʳ] n captor(a) m(f)

capture ['kæptʃəʳ] vt capturar; (place) tomar; (attention) captar, llamar ▷ n captura; toma; (Comput: also: **data ~**) formulación f de datos

car [kɑːʳ] n coche m, carro (LAm), automóvil m, auto (LAm); (US Rail) vagón m; **by ~** en coche

carafe [kə'ræf] n jarra

caramel ['kærəməl] n caramelo

carat ['kærət] n quilate m; **18-~ gold** oro de 18 quilates

caravan ['kærəvæn] n (Brit) caravana, rulot m; (of camels) caravana

caravan site n (Brit) camping m para caravanas

carb [kɑːb] n abbr (inf: = carbohydrate) carbohidrato

carbohydrates [kɑːbəu'haɪdreɪts] npl (foods) hidratos mpl de carbono

car bomb n coche-bomba m

carbon ['kɑːbən] n carbono

carbon copy n copia al carbón

carbon dioxide n dióxido de carbono, anhídrido carbónico

carbon footprint n huella de carbono

carbon monoxide n monóxido de carbono

carbon-neutral [kɑːbn'njuːtrəl] adj carbono neutral

carbon offsetting [-'ɔfsetɪŋ] n compensación f de carbono

carbon paper n papel m carbón

car boot sale n mercadillo (de objetos usados expuestos en el maletero del coche)

carburettor, carburetor (US) [kɑːbju'retəʳ] n carburador m

card [kɑːd] n (thin cardboard) cartulina; (playing card) carta, naipe m; (visiting card, greetings card etc) tarjeta; (index card) ficha; **membership ~** carnet m; **to play ~s** jugar a las cartas or los naipes

cardboard ['kɑːdbɔːd] n cartón m, cartulina

cardboard city n zona de marginados sin hogar (que se refugian entre cartones)
card game n juego de naipes o cartas
cardiac ['kɑːdɪæk] adj cardíaco
cardigan ['kɑːdɪgən] n chaqueta (de punto), rebeca
cardinal ['kɑːdɪnl] adj cardinal; (importance, principal) esencial ▷ n cardenal m
cardinal number n número cardinal
card index n fichero
cardphone ['kɑːdfəʊn] n cabina que funciona con tarjetas telefónicas
care [keəʳ] n cuidado; (worry) preocupación f; (charge) cargo, custodia ▷ vi: **to ~ about** preocuparse por; **~ of (c/o)** en casa de, al cuidado de; (on letter) para (entregar a); **in sb's ~** a cargo de algn; **the child has been taken into ~** pusieron al niño bajo custodia del gobierno; **"with ~"** "¡frágil!"; **to take ~ to** cuidarse de, tener cuidado de; **to take ~ of** vt cuidar; (details, arrangements) encargarse de; **I don't ~** no me importa; **I couldn't ~ less** me trae sin cuidado; **care for** vt fus cuidar; (like) querer
career [kə'rɪəʳ] n carrera (profesional); (occupation) profesión f ▷ vi (also: **~ along**) correr a toda velocidad
carefree ['keəfriː] adj despreocupado
careful ['keəful] adj cuidadoso; (cautious) cauteloso; **(be) ~!** ¡(ten) cuidado!; **he's very ~ with his money** mira mucho el dinero; (pej) es muy tacaño
carefully ['keəfəlɪ] adv con cuidado, cuidadosamente
caregiver ['keəgɪvəʳ] n (US: professional) enfermero(-a) m/f; (unpaid) persona que cuida a un pariente o vecino
careless ['keəlɪs] adj descuidado; (heedless) poco atento
carelessness ['keəlɪsnɪs] n descuido, falta de atención
carer ['keərəʳ] n (professional) enfermero(-a) m/f; (unpaid) persona que cuida a un pariente o vecino
caress [kə'rɛs] n caricia ▷ vt acariciar
caretaker ['keəteɪkəʳ] n portero(-a), conserje m/f
car-ferry ['kɑːfɛrɪ] n transbordador m para coches
cargo (pl **cargoes**) ['kɑːgəʊ] n cargamento, carga
car hire n alquiler m de coches
Caribbean [kærɪ'biːən] adj caribe, caribeño; **the ~ (Sea)** el (Mar) Caribe
caricature ['kærɪkətjʊəʳ] n caricatura
caring ['keərɪŋ] adj humanitario
carnal ['kɑːnl] adj carnal
carnation [kɑː'neɪʃən] n clavel m
carnival ['kɑːnɪvəl] n carnaval m; (US) parque m de atracciones
carnivore ['kɑːnɪvɔːʳ] n carnívoro(-a)
carnivorous [kɑː'nɪvrəs] adj carnívoro

carol ['kærəl] n: **(Christmas) ~** villancico
carousel [kærə'sɛl] n (US) tiovivo, caballitos mpl
carp [kɑːp] n (fish) carpa; **carp at** or **about** vt fus sacar faltas de
car park n (Brit) aparcamiento, parking m, playa de estacionamiento (LAm)
carpenter ['kɑːpɪntəʳ] n carpintero(-a)
carpentry ['kɑːpɪntrɪ] n carpintería
carpet ['kɑːpɪt] n alfombra ▷ vt alfombrar; **fitted ~** moqueta
carpet bombing n bombardeo de arrasamiento
carpet slippers npl zapatillas fpl
carpet sweeper [-'swiːpəʳ] n cepillo mecánico
car phone n teléfono de coche
car rental n (US) alquiler m de coches
carriage ['kærɪdʒ] n (Brit Rail) vagón m; (horse-drawn) coche m; (for goods) transporte m; (of typewriter) carro; (bearing) porte m; **~ forward** porte m debido; **~ free** franco de porte; **~ paid** porte pagado; **~ inwards/outwards** gastos mpl de transporte a cargo del comprador/vendedor
carriageway ['kærɪdʒweɪ] n (Brit: part of road) calzada; **dual ~** autovía
carrier ['kærɪəʳ] n transportista m/f; (company) empresa de transportes; (Med) portador(a) m(f)
carrier bag n (Brit) bolsa de papel or plástico
carrot ['kærət] n zanahoria
carry ['kærɪ] vt (person) llevar; (transport) transportar; (a motion, bill) aprobar; (involve: responsibilities etc) entrañar, conllevar; (Comm: stock) tener en existencia; (interest) llevar; (Math: figure) llevarse ▷ vi (sound) oírse; **to get carried away** (fig) entusiasmarse; **this loan carries 10% interest** este empréstito devenga un interés del 10 por ciento; **carry forward** vt (Math, Comm) pasar a la página/columna siguiente; **carry on** vi (continue) seguir (adelante), continuar; (inf: complain) montar el número ▷ vt seguir, continuar; **carry out** vt (orders) cumplir; (investigation) llevar a cabo, realizar
carrycot ['kærɪkɔt] n (Brit) cuna portátil, capazo
carry-on ['kærɪ'ɔn] n (inf) follón m
cart [kɑːt] n carro, carreta ▷ vt (inf: transport) cargar con
carton ['kɑːtən] n caja (de cartón); (of milk etc) bote m; (of cigarettes) cartón m
cartoon [kɑː'tuːn] n (Press) chiste m; (comic strip) historieta, tira cómica; (film) dibujos mpl animados
cartoonist [kɑː'tuːnɪst] n humorista m/f gráfico
cartridge ['kɑːtrɪdʒ] n cartucho
cartwheel ['kɑːtwiːl] n: **to turn a ~** dar una voltereta lateral

carve [kɑːv] vt (meat) trinchar; (wood) tallar; (stone) cincelar, esculpir; (on tree) grabar; **carve up** vt dividir, repartir; (meat) trinchar

carving ['kɑːvɪŋ] n (in wood etc) escultura; (design) talla

carving knife n trinchante m

car wash n túnel m de lavado

case [keɪs] n (container) caja; (Med) caso; (for jewels etc) estuche m; (Law) causa, proceso; (Brit: also: **suit~**) maleta; **lower/upper ~** (Typ) caja baja/alta; **in ~ of** en caso de; **in any ~** en todo caso; **just in ~** por si acaso; **to have a good ~** tener buenas razones; **there's a strong ~ for reform** hay razones sólidas para exigir una reforma

cash [kæʃ] n (dinero en) efectivo; (inf: money) dinero ▷ vt cobrar, hacer efectivo; **to pay (in) ~** pagar al contado; **~ on delivery (COD)** entrega contra reembolso; **~ with order** paga al hacer el pedido; **to be short of ~** estar pelado, estar sin blanca; **cash in** vt (insurance policy etc) cobrar ▷ vi: **to ~ in on sth** sacar partido or aprovecharse de algo

cash and carry n cash and carry m, autoservicio mayorista

cashback ['kæʃ'bæk] n (discount) devolución f; (at supermarket etc) retirada de dinero en efectivo de un establecimiento donde se ha pagado con tarjeta; también dinero retirado

cashbook ['kæʃbuk] n libro de caja

cash card n tarjeta f de(l) cajero (automático)

cash desk n (Brit) caja

cash dispenser n cajero automático

cashew [kæ'ʃuː] n (also: **~ nut**) anacardo

cash flow n flujo de fondos, cash-flow m, movimiento de efectivo

cashier [kæ'ʃɪə'] n cajero(-a) ▷ vt (Mil) destituir, expulsar

cashmere ['kæʃmɪə'] n cachemir m, cachemira

cash point n cajero automático

cash register n caja

casing ['keɪsɪŋ] n revestimiento

casino [kə'siːnəu] n casino

casket ['kɑːskɪt] n cofre, estuche m; (US: coffin) ataúd m

casserole ['kæsərəul] n (food, pot) cazuela

cassette [kæ'set] n cas(s)et(t)e m or f

cassette player, cassette recorder n cas(s)et(t)e m

cast [kɑːst] (pt, pp **cast**) vt (throw) echar, arrojar, lanzar; (skin) mudar, perder; (metal) fundir; (Theat): **to ~ sb as Othello** dar a algn el papel de Otelo ▷ n (Theat) reparto; (mould) forma, molde m; (also: **plaster ~**) vaciado; **to ~ loose** soltar; **to ~ one's vote** votar; **cast aside** vt (reject) descartar, desechar; **cast away** vt desechar; **cast down** vt derribar; **cast off** vi (Naut) soltar amarras; (Knitting) cerrar los puntos ▷ vt (Knitting) cerrar; **to ~ sb off** abandonar a algn, desentenderse de algn; **cast on** vt (Knitting) montar

castanets [kæstə'nets] npl castañuelas fpl

castaway ['kɑːstəwər] n náufrago(-a)

caster sugar ['kɑːstə'-] n (Brit) azúcar m extrafino

Castile [kæs'tiːl] n Castilla

Castilian [kæs'tɪlɪən] adj, n castellano(-a) ▷ n (Ling) castellano

casting vote ['kɑːstɪŋ-] n (Brit) voto decisivo

cast iron n hierro fundido or colado

cast-iron ['kɑːstaɪən] adj (lit) (hecho) de hierro fundido or colado; (fig: alibi) irrebatible; (will) férreo

castle ['kɑːsl] n castillo; (Chess) torre f

castor ['kɑːstə'] n (wheel) ruedecilla

castor oil n aceite m de ricino

castrate [kæs'treɪt] vt castrar

casual ['kæʒjul] adj (by chance) fortuito; (irregular: work etc) eventual, temporero; (unconcerned) despreocupado; (informal: clothes) de sport

casually ['kæʒjulɪ] adv por casualidad; de manera despreocupada

casualty ['kæʒjultɪ] n víctima, herido; (dead) muerto; (Mil) baja; **heavy casualties** numerosas bajas fpl

casualty ward n urgencias fpl

cat [kæt] n gato

Catalan ['kætəlæn] adj, n catalán(-ana) m(f)

catalogue, catalog (US) ['kætəlɔg] n catálogo ▷ vt catalogar

Catalonia [kætə'ləunɪə] n Cataluña

catalyst ['kætəlɪst] n catalizador m

catalytic converter [kætə'lɪtɪkkən'vɜːtə'] n catalizador m

catapult ['kætəpʌlt] n tirachinas m inv

cataract ['kætərækt] n (Med) cataratas fpl

catarrh [kə'tɑː'] n catarro

catastrophe [kə'tæstrəfɪ] n catástrofe f

catch [kætʃ] (pt, pp **caught**) vt coger (Sp), agarrar (LAm); (arrest) atrapar, coger (Sp); (grasp) asir; (breath) recobrar; (person: by surprise) pillar; (attract: attention) captar; (Med) pillar, coger; (also: **~ up**) alcanzar ▷ vi (fire) encenderse; (in branches etc) engancharse ▷ n (fish etc) captura; (act of catching) cogida; (trick) trampa; (of lock) pestillo, cerradura; **to ~ fire** prenderse; (house) incendiarse; **to ~ sight of** divisar; **catch on** vi (understand) caer en la cuenta; (grow popular) tener éxito, cuajar; **catch out** vt (fig: with trick question) hundir; **catch up** vi (fig) ponerse al día

catching ['kætʃɪŋ] adj (Med) contagioso

catchment area ['kætʃmənt-] n (Brit) zona de captación

catch phrase n frase f de moda

catchy ['kætʃɪ] adj (tune) pegadizo

category ['kætɪgərɪ] n categoría

cater ['keɪtə'] vi: **to ~ for** (Brit) abastecer a; (needs) atender a; (consumers) proveer a

caterer ['keɪtərə'] n abastecedor(a) m(f), proveedor(a) m(f)

catering ['keɪtərɪŋ] n (trade) hostelería

caterpillar ['kætəpɪlə^r] n oruga
caterpillar track n rodado de oruga
cat flap n gatera
cathedral [kə'θi:drəl] n catedral f
catholic ['kæθəlɪk] adj católico; **C~** adj, n (Rel) católico(-a) m(f)
Catseye® ['kætsaɪ] n (Brit Aut) catadióptrico
cattle ['kætl] npl ganado sg
catty ['kætɪ] adj malicioso
catwalk ['kætwɔːk] n pasarela
caucus ['kɔːkəs] n (Pol: local committee) comité m local; (: US: to elect candidates) comité m electoral; (: group) camarilla política
caught [kɔːt] pt, pp of **catch**
cauliflower ['kɒlɪflauə^r] n coliflor f
cause [kɔːz] n causa; (reason) motivo, razón f ▷ vt causar; (provoke) provocar; **to ~ sb to do sth** hacer que algn haga algo
caution ['kɔːʃən] n cautela, prudencia; (warning) advertencia, amonestación f ▷ vt amonestar
cautious ['kɔːʃəs] adj cauteloso, prudente, precavido
cavalry ['kævəlrɪ] n caballería
cave [keɪv] n cueva, caverna ▷ vi: **to go caving** ir en una expedición espeleológica; **cave in** vi (roof etc) derrumbarse, hundirse
caveman ['keɪvmæn] n cavernícola m
caviar, caviare ['kævɪɑː^r] n caviar m
cavity ['kævɪtɪ] n hueco, cavidad f
cavort [kə'vɔːt] vi hacer cabriolades
CB n abbr (= Citizens' Band (Radio)) frecuencias de radio usadas para la comunicación privada; (Brit: = Companion of (the Order of) the Bath) título de nobleza
CBE n abbr (Brit: = Companion of (the Order of) the British Empire) título de nobleza
CBI n abbr (= Confederation of British Industry) ≈ C.E.O.E. f (Sp)
CBS n abbr (US: = Columbia Broadcasting System) cadena de radio y televisión
cc abbr (= cubic centimetres) cc, cm³; (on letter etc) = **carbon copy**
CCTV n abbr = **closed-circuit television**
CD n abbr (= compact disc) CD m; (Mil: Brit: = Civil Defence (Corps); US: = Civil Defense) defensa civil ▷ abbr (Brit: = Corps Diplomatique) CD
CD player n reproductor m de CD
CD-ROM ['siː'diː'rɒm] n abbr (= compact disc read-only memory) CD-ROM m
CD writer n grabadora f de CDs
cease [siːs] vt cesar
ceasefire ['siːsfaɪə^r] n alto m el fuego
ceaseless ['siːslɪs] adj incesante
cedar ['siːdə^r] n cedro
ceilidh ['keɪlɪ] n baile con música y danzas tradicionales escocesas o irlandesas
ceiling ['siːlɪŋ] n techo; (fig: upper limit) límite m, tope m
celebrate ['sɛlɪbreɪt] vt celebrar; (have a party) festejar ▷ vi: **let's ~!** ¡vamos a celebrarlo!
celebrated ['sɛlɪbreɪtɪd] adj célebre

celebration [sɛlɪ'breɪʃən] n celebración f, festejo
celebrity [sɪ'lɛbrɪtɪ] n celebridad f
celery ['sɛlərɪ] n apio
celibacy ['sɛlɪbəsɪ] n celibato
cell [sɛl] n celda; (Biol) célula; (Elec) elemento
cellar ['sɛlə^r] n sótano; (for wine) bodega
cello ['tʃɛləu] n violoncelo
Cellophane® ['sɛləfeɪn] n celofán m
cellphone ['sɛlfəun] n móvil
cellular ['sɛljulə^r] adj celular
Celsius ['sɛlsɪəs] adj centígrado
Celt [kɛlt, sɛlt] n celta m/f
Celtic ['kɛltɪk, 'sɛltɪk] adj celta, céltico ▷ n (Ling) celta m
cement [sə'mɛnt] n cemento ▷ vt cementar; (fig) cimentar
cement mixer n hormigonera
cemetery ['sɛmɪtrɪ] n cementerio
cenotaph ['sɛnətɑːf] n cenotafio
censor ['sɛnsə^r] n censor(a) m(f) ▷ vt (cut) censurar
censorship ['sɛnsəʃɪp] n censura
censure ['sɛnʃə^r] vt censurar
census ['sɛnsəs] n censo
cent [sɛnt] n (US: unit of dollar) centavo; (unit of euro) céntimo; see also **per**
centenary [sɛn'tiːnərɪ], **centennial** [sɛn'tɛnɪəl] (US) n centenario
center ['sɛntə^r] n (US) = **centre**
centigrade ['sɛntɪgreɪd] adj centígrado
centimetre, centimeter (US) ['sɛntɪmiːtə^r] n centímetro
centipede ['sɛntɪpiːd] n ciempiés m inv
central ['sɛntrəl] adj central; (house etc) céntrico
Central America n Centroamérica
Central American adj, n centroamericano(-a) m(f)
central heating n calefacción f central
central reservation n (Brit Aut) mediana
centre, center (US) ['sɛntə^r] n centro ▷ vt centrar; **to ~ (on)** (concentrate) concentrar (en)
centre-forward ['sɛntə'fɔːwəd] n (Sport) delantero centro
centre-half ['sɛntə'hɑːf] n (Sport) medio centro
centre-stage ['sɛntəsteɪdʒ] n: **to take ~** pasar a primer plano
century ['sɛntjurɪ] n siglo; **20th ~** siglo veinte; **in the twentieth ~** en el siglo veinte
CEO n abbr = **chief executive officer**
ceramic [sɪ'ræmɪk] adj de cerámica
cereal ['siːrɪəl] n cereal m
ceremony ['sɛrɪmənɪ] n ceremonia; **to stand on ~** hacer ceremonias, andarse con cumplidos
cert [sɜːt] n (Brit inf): **it's a dead ~** ¡es cosa segura!
certain ['sɜːtən] adj seguro; (correct) cierto; (particular) cierto; **for ~** a ciencia cierta; **a ~ Mr Smith** un tal Sr. Smith

certainly ['sə:tənlı] *adv* desde luego, por supuesto

certainty ['sə:təntı] *n* certeza, certidumbre *f*, seguridad *f*

certificate [sə'tıfıkıt] *n* certificado

certified ['sə:tıfaıd] *adj*: ~ **mail** (US) correo certificado

certified public accountant *n* (US) contable *m/f* diplomado(-a)

certify ['sə:tıfaı] *vt* certificar; (*declare insane*) declarar loco

cervical ['sə:vıkl] *adj*: ~ **cancer** cáncer *m* cervical; ~ **smear** citología

cervix ['sə:vıks] *n* cerviz *f*, cuello del útero

Cesarean [sı'zeərıən] *adj, n* (US) = **Caesarean**

cessation [sə'seıʃən] *n* cese *m*, suspensión *f*

CET *n abbr* (= *Central European Time*) hora de Europa central

cf. *abbr* (= *compare*) cfr

CFC *n abbr* (= *chlorofluorocarbon*) CFC *m*

ch. *abbr* (= *chapter*) cap

chafe [tʃeıf] *vt* (*rub*) rozar; (*irritate*) irritar; **to ~ (against)** (*fig*) irritarse *or* enojarse (con)

chain [tʃeın] *n* cadena; (*of mountains*) cordillera; (*of events*) sucesión *f* ▷ *vt* (*also*: ~ **up**) encadenar

chain reaction *n* reacción *f* en cadena

chain-smoke ['tʃeınsməuk] *vi* fumar un cigarrillo tras otro

chain store *n* tienda de una cadena, ≈ grandes almacenes *mpl*

chair [tʃeər] *n* silla; (*armchair*) sillón *m*; (*of university*) cátedra ▷ *vt* (*meeting*) presidir; **the ~** (US: *electric chair*) la silla eléctrica; **please take a ~** siéntese *or* tome asiento, por favor

chairlift ['tʃeəlıft] *n* telesilla *m*

chairman ['tʃeəmən] *n* presidente *m*

chairperson ['tʃeəpə:sn] *n* presidente(-a) *m(f)*

chairwoman ['tʃeəwumən] *n* presidenta

chalet ['ʃæleı] *n* chalet *m* (de madera)

chalice ['tʃælıs] *n* cáliz *m*

chalk [tʃɔ:k] *n* (Geo) creta; (*for writing*) tiza, gis *m* (LAm); **chalk up** *vt* apuntar; (*fig: success, victory*) apuntarse

chalkboard ['tʃɔ:kbɔ:d] (US) *n* pizarrón (LAm), pizarra (Sp)

challenge ['tʃælındʒ] *n* desafío, reto ▷ *vt* desafiar, retar; (*statement, right*) poner en duda; **to ~ sb to do sth** retar a algn a que haga algo

challenger ['tʃælındʒər] *n* (Sport) contrincante *m/f*

challenging ['tʃælındʒıŋ] *adj* que supone un reto; (*tone*) de desafío

chamber ['tʃeımbər] *n* cámara, sala

chambermaid ['tʃeımbəmeıd] *n* camarera

chamber music *n* música de cámara

champagne [ʃæm'peın] *n* champaña *m*, champán *m*

champers ['ʃæmpəz] *nsg* (*inf*) champán *m*

champion ['tʃæmpıən] *n* campeón(-ona) *m(f)*; (*of cause*) defensor(a) *m(f)*, paladín *m/f* ▷ *vt* defender, apoyar

championship ['tʃæmpıənʃıp] *n* campeonato

chance [tʃɑ:ns] *n* (*coincidence*) casualidad *f*; (*luck*) suerte *f*; (*fate*) azar *m*; (*opportunity*) ocasión *f*, oportunidad *f*, chance *m or f* (LAm); (*likelihood*) posibilidad *f*; (*risk*) riesgo ▷ *vt* arriesgar, probar ▷ *adj* fortuito, casual; **to ~ it** arriesgarse, intentarlo; **to take a ~** arriesgarse; **by ~** por casualidad; **it's the ~ of a lifetime** es la oportunidad de su vida; **the ~s are that ...** lo más probable es que ...; **to ~ to do sth** (*happen*) hacer algo por casualidad; **chance (up)on** *vt fus* tropezar(se) con

chancellor ['tʃɑ:nsələr] *n* canciller *m*; **C~ of the Exchequer** (Brit) Ministro de Economía y Hacienda; *see also* **Downing Street**

chancy ['tʃɑ:nsı] *adj* (*inf*) arriesgado

chandelier [ʃændə'lıər] *n* araña (de luces)

change [tʃeındʒ] *vt* cambiar; (*clothes, house*) cambiarse de, mudarse de; (*transform*) transformar ▷ *vi* cambiar(se); (*change trains*) hacer transbordo; (*be transformed*): **to ~ into** transformarse *in* ▷ *n* cambio; (*alteration*) modificación *f*, transformación *f*; (*coins*) suelto; (*money returned*) vuelta, vuelto (LAm); **to ~ one's mind** cambiar de opinión *or* idea; **to ~ gear** (Aut) cambiar de marcha; **she ~d into an old skirt** se puso una falda vieja; **for a ~** para variar; **can you give me ~ for £1?** ¿tiene cambio de una libra?; **keep the ~** quédese con la vuelta; **change over** *vi* (*from sth to sth*) cambiar; (*players etc*) cambiar(se) ▷ *vt* cambiar

changeable ['tʃeındʒəbl] *adj* (*weather*) cambiable; (*person*) variable

change machine *n* máquina de cambio

changeover ['tʃeındʒəuvər] *n* (*to new system*) cambio

changing ['tʃeındʒıŋ] *adj* cambiante

changing room *n* (Brit) vestuario

channel ['tʃænl] *n* (TV) canal *m*; (*of river*) cauce *m*; (*of sea*) estrecho; (*groove, fig: medium*) conducto, medio ▷ *vt* (*river etc*) encauzar; **to ~ into** (*fig: interest, energies*) encauzar a, dirigir a; **the (English) C~** el Canal (de la Mancha); **the C~ Islands** las Islas Anglonormandas; **~s of communication** canales *mpl* de comunicación; **green/red ~** (*Customs*) pasillo verde/rojo

Channel Tunnel *n*: **the ~** el túnel del Canal de la Mancha, el Eurotúnel

chant [tʃɑ:nt] *n* (*also Rel*) canto; (*of crowd*) gritos *mpl* ▷ *vt* cantar; (*slogan, word*) repetir a gritos; **the demonstrators ~ed their disapproval** los manifestantes corearon su desaprobación

chaos ['keıɔs] *n* caos *m*

chaotic [keı'ɔtık] *adj* caótico

chap [tʃæp] n (Brit inf: man) tío, tipo; **old ~**
amigo (mío)

chapel ['tʃæpəl] n capilla

chaplain ['tʃæplɪn] n capellán m

chapped ['tʃæpt] adj agrietado

chapter ['tʃæptəʳ] n capítulo

char [tʃɑ:ʳ] vt (burn) carbonizar, chamuscar

character ['kærɪktəʳ] n carácter m,
naturaleza, índole f; (in novel, film) personaje
m; (role) papel m; (individuality) carácter m;
(Comput) carácter m; **a person of good ~** una
persona de buena reputación

characteristic [kærɪktə'rɪstɪk] adj
característico ▷ n característica

characterize ['kærɪktəraɪz] vt caracterizar

charcoal ['tʃɑ:kəul] n carbón m vegetal; (Art)
carboncillo

charge [tʃɑ:dʒ] n carga; (Law) cargo,
acusación f; (cost) precio, coste m;
(responsibility) cargo; (task) encargo ▷ vt (Law):
to ~ (with) acusar (de); (gun, battery) cargar;
(Mil: enemy) cargar; (price) pedir; (customer)
cobrar; (person: with task) encargar ▷ vi
precipitarse; (make pay) cobrar; **charges** npl:
bank ~s comisiones fpl bancarias; **extra ~**
recargo, suplemento; **free of ~** gratis; **to
reverse the ~s** (Brit Tel) llamar a cobro
revertido; **to take ~ of** hacerse cargo de,
encargarse de; **to be in ~ of** estar encargado
de; **how much do you ~?** ¿cuánto cobra
usted?; **to ~ an expense (up) to sb's
account** cargar algo a cuenta de algn; **~ it
to my account** póngalo or cárguelo a mi
cuenta

charge card n tarjeta de cuenta

charge hand ['tʃɑ:dʒhænd] n capataz m

charger ['tʃɑ:dʒəʳ] n (also: **battery ~**)
cargador m (de baterías)

chariot ['tʃærɪət] n carro

charisma [kæ'rɪzmə] n carisma m

charismatic [kærɪz'mætɪk] adj carismático

charitable ['tʃærɪtəbl] adj caritativo

charity ['tʃærɪtɪ] n (gen) caridad f;
(organization) organización f benéfica; (money,
gifts) limosnas fpl

charity shop n (Brit) tienda de artículos de
segunda mano que dedica su recaudación a causas
benéficas

charm [tʃɑ:m] n encanto, atractivo; (spell)
hechizo; (object) amuleto; (on bracelet) dije m
▷ vt encantar; hechizar

charming ['tʃɑ:mɪŋ] adj encantador(a);
(person) simpático

chart [tʃɑ:t] n (table) cuadro; (graph) gráfica;
(map) carta de navegación; (weather chart)
mapa m meteorológico ▷ vt (course) trazar;
(progress) seguir; (sales) hacer una gráfica de;
to be in the ~s (record, pop group) estar en la
lista de éxitos

charter ['tʃɑ:təʳ] vt (bus) alquilar; (plane, ship)
fletar ▷ n (document) estatuto, carta; **on ~** en
alquiler, alquilado

chartered accountant n (Brit) contable m/f
diplomado(-a)

charter flight n vuelo chárter

chase [tʃeɪs] vt (pursue) perseguir; (hunt) cazar
▷ n persecución f; caza; **to ~ after** correr tras;
chase up vt (information) tratar de conseguir;
to ~ sb up about sth recordar algo a algn

chasm ['kæzəm] n abismo

chassis ['ʃæsɪ] n chasis m

chaste [tʃeɪst] adj casto

chastity ['tʃæstɪtɪ] n castidad f

chat [tʃæt] vi (also: **have a ~**) charlar; (Internet)
chatear ▷ n charla; (Internet) chat m; **chat up**
vt (inf: girl) ligar con, enrollarse con

chatline ['tʃætlaɪn] n línea (telefónica)
múltiple, party line f

chat room n (Internet) chat m, canal m de
charla

chat show n (Brit) programa m de entrevistas

chatter ['tʃætəʳ] vi (person) charlar; (teeth)
castañetear ▷ n (of birds) parloteo; (of people)
charla, cháchara

chatterbox ['tʃætəbɒks] n parlanchín(-ina)
m(f)

chattering classes ['tʃætərɪŋ'klɑ:sɪz] npl:
the ~ (inf, pej) los intelectualillos

chatty ['tʃætɪ] adj (style) informal; (person)
hablador(a)

chauffeur ['ʃəufəʳ] n chófer m

chauvinist ['ʃəuvɪnɪst] n (also: **male ~**)
machista m; (nationalist) chovinista m/f,
patriotero(-a) m(f)

cheap [tʃi:p] adj barato; (joke) de mal gusto,
chabacano; (poor quality) de mala calidad;
(reduced: ticket) económico; (: fare) barato ▷ adv
barato

cheap day return n billete de ida y vuelta el
mismo día

cheaply ['tʃi:plɪ] adv barato, a bajo precio

cheat [tʃi:t] vi hacer trampa; (in exam) copiar
▷ vt estafar, timar ▷ n trampa; estafa;
(person) tramposo(-a); **to ~ sb (out of sth)**
estafar (algo) a algn; **cheat on** vt fus
engañar; **he's been ~ing on his wife** ha
estado engañando a su esposa

check [tʃek] vt (examine) controlar; (facts)
comprobar; (count) contar; (halt) frenar;
(restrain) refrenar, restringir ▷ vi: **to ~ with
sb** consultar con algn; (official etc)
informarse por ▷ n (inspection) control m,
inspección f; (curb) freno; (bill) nota, cuenta;
(US) = **cheque**; (pattern) gen pl cuadro ▷ adj
(also: **~ed**: pattern, cloth) a cuadros; **to keep a ~
on sth/sb** controlar algo/a algn; **check in** vi
(in hotel) registrarse; (at airport) facturar ▷ vt
(luggage) facturar; **check off** vt (esp US: check)
comprobar; (cross off) tachar; **check out** vi
(of hotel) desocupar la habitación ▷ vt
(investigate: story) comprobar; (: person)
informarse sobre; **check up** vi: **to ~ up on
sth** comprobar algo; **to ~ up on sb** investigar
a algn

checkbook ['tʃɛkbuk] n (US) = **chequebook**

checked [tʃɛkt] adj a cuadros inv

checkered ['tʃɛkəd] adj (US) = **chequered**

checkers ['tʃɛkəz] n (US) damas fpl

check-in ['tʃɛkɪn] n (also: ~ **desk**: at airport) mostrador m de facturación

checking account ['tʃɛkɪŋ-] n (US) cuenta corriente

checklist ['tʃɛklɪst] n lista

checkmate ['tʃɛkmeɪt] n jaque m mate

checkout ['tʃɛkaut] n (in supermarket) caja

checkpoint ['tʃɛkpɔɪnt] n (punto de) control m, retén m (LAm)

checkroom ['tʃɛkrum] n (US) consigna

checkup ['tʃɛkʌp] n (Med) reconocimiento general; (of machine) revisión f

cheddar ['tʃɛdəʳ] n (also: ~ **cheese**) queso m cheddar

cheek [tʃiːk] n mejilla; (impudence) descaro; **what a ~!** ¡qué cara!

cheekbone ['tʃiːkbəun] n pómulo

cheeky ['tʃiːki] adj fresco, descarado

cheep [tʃiːp] n (of bird) pío ⊳ vi piar

cheer [tʃɪəʳ] vt vitorear, ovacionar; (gladden) alegrar, animar ⊳ vi dar vivas ⊳ n viva m; **cheers** npl vítores mpl; **~s!** ¡salud!; **cheer on** vt (person etc) animar con aplausos or gritos; **cheer up** vi animarse ⊳ vt alegrar, animar

cheerful ['tʃɪəful] adj alegre

cheerio [tʃɪərɪˈəu] excl (Brit) ¡hasta luego!

cheerleader ['tʃɪəliːdəʳ] n animador(a) m(f)

cheese [tʃiːz] n queso

cheeseboard ['tʃiːzbɔːd] n tabla de quesos

cheeseburger ['tʃiːzbəːgəʳ] n hamburguesa con queso

cheesecake ['tʃiːzkeɪk] n pastel m de queso

cheetah ['tʃiːtə] n guepardo

chef [ʃɛf] n jefe(-a) m(f) de cocina

chemical ['kɛmɪkəl] adj químico ⊳ n producto químico

chemist ['kɛmɪst] n (Brit: pharmacist) farmacéutico(-a); (scientist) químico(-a); **~'s (shop)** n (Brit) farmacia

chemistry ['kɛmɪstrɪ] n química

chemotherapy [kiːməuˈθɛrəpɪ] n quimioterapia

cheque, check (US) [tʃɛk] n cheque m; **to pay by ~** pagar con cheque

chequebook, checkbook (US) ['tʃɛkbuk] n talonario (de cheques), chequera (LAm)

cheque card n (Brit) tarjeta de identificación bancaria

chequered, checkered (US) ['tʃɛkəd] adj (fig) accidentado; (pattern) de cuadros

cherish ['tʃɛrɪʃ] vt (love) querer, apreciar; (protect) cuidar; (hope etc) abrigar

cherry ['tʃɛrɪ] n cereza; (also: ~ **tree**) cerezo

chess [tʃɛs] n ajedrez m

chessboard ['tʃɛsbɔːd] n tablero (de ajedrez)

chest [tʃɛst] n (Anat) pecho; (box) cofre m; **to get sth off one's ~** (inf) desahogarse; **~ of drawers** n cómoda

chestnut ['tʃɛsnʌt] n castaña; (also: ~ **tree**) castaño; (colour) castaño ⊳ adj (color) castaño inv

chesty ['tʃɛstɪ] adj (cough) de bronquios, de pecho

chew [tʃuː] vt mascar, masticar

chewing gum ['tʃuːɪŋ-] n chicle m

chic [ʃiːk] adj elegante

Chicano [tʃɪˈkɑːnəu] adj, n chicano(-a)

chick [tʃɪk] n pollito, polluelo; (US inf) chica

chicken ['tʃɪkɪn] n gallina, pollo; (food) pollo; (inf: coward) gallina m/f; **chicken out** vi (inf) rajarse; **to ~ out of doing sth** rajarse y no hacer algo

chickenpox ['tʃɪkɪnpɔks] n varicela

chickpea ['tʃɪkpiː] n garbanzo

chicory ['tʃɪkərɪ] n (for coffee) achicoria; (salad) escarola

chief [tʃiːf] n jefe(-a) m(f) ⊳ adj principal, máximo (esp LAm); **C~ of Staff** (esp Mil) Jefe m del Estado mayor

chief executive, chief executive officer (US) n director m general

chiefly ['tʃiːflɪ] adv principalmente

chiffon ['ʃɪfɔn] n gasa

chilblain ['tʃɪlbleɪn] n sabañón m

child (pl **children**) [tʃaɪld, 'tʃɪldrən] n niño(-a); (offspring) hijo(-a)

child abuse n (with violence) malos tratos mpl a niños; (sexual) abuso m sexual de niños

child benefit n (Brit) subsidio por cada hijo pequeño

childbirth ['tʃaɪldbəːθ] n parto

childcare ['tʃaɪldkɛəʳ] n cuidado de los niños

childhood ['tʃaɪldhud] n niñez f, infancia

childish ['tʃaɪldɪʃ] adj pueril, infantil

childlike ['tʃaɪldlaɪk] adj de niño, infantil

child minder n (Brit) niñera, madre f de día

child prodigy n niño(-a) prodigio inv

children ['tʃɪldrən] npl of **child**

children's home n centro de acogida para niños

Chile ['tʃɪlɪ] n Chile m

Chilean ['tʃɪlɪən] adj, n chileno(-a) m(f)

chill [tʃɪl] n frío; (Med) resfriado ⊳ adj frío ⊳ vt enfriar; (Culin) refrigerar; **chill out** vi (esp US inf) tranquilizarse

chilling ['tʃɪlɪŋ] adj escalofriante

chilly ['tʃɪlɪ] adj frío

chime [tʃaɪm] n repique m, campanada ⊳ vi repicar, sonar

chimney ['tʃɪmnɪ] n chimenea

chimney sweep n deshollinador m

chimpanzee [tʃɪmpænˈziː] n chimpancé m

chin [tʃɪn] n mentón m, barbilla

China ['tʃaɪnə] n China

china ['tʃaɪnə] n porcelana; (crockery) loza

Chinese [tʃaɪˈniːz] adj chino ⊳ n pl inv chino(-a); (Ling) chino

chink [tʃɪŋk] n (opening) rendija, hendedura; (noise) tintineo

chinwag ['tʃɪnwæg] n (Brit inf): **to have a ~** echar una parrafada

chip [tʃɪp] n gen pl (Culin: Brit) patata or (LAm) papa frita; (: US: also: **potato ~**) patata or (LAm) papa frita; (of wood) astilla; (stone) lasca; (in gambling) ficha; (Comput) chip m ▷ vt (cup, plate) desconchar; **when the ~s are down** (fig) a la hora de la verdad; **chip in** vi (inf: interrupt) interrumpir, meterse; (: contribute) contribuir

chip shop n ver nota

⊙ **CHIP SHOP**
⊙
⊙ Se denomina chip shop o fish-and-chip shop
⊙ a un tipo de tienda popular de comida
⊙ rápida en la que se despachan platos
⊙ tradicionales británicos, principalmente
⊙ filetes de pescado rebozado frito y
⊙ patatas fritas.

chiropodist [kɪˈrɔpədɪst] n (Brit) podólogo(-a)
chirp [tʃəːp] vi gorjear; (cricket) cantar ▷ n (of cricket) canto
chisel ['tʃɪzl] n (for wood) escoplo; (for stone) cincel m
chit [tʃɪt] n nota
chitchat ['tʃɪtʃæt] n chismes mpl, habladurías fpl
chivalry ['ʃɪvəlrɪ] n caballerosidad f
chives [tʃaɪvz] npl cebollinos mpl
chlorine ['klɔːriːn] n cloro
choc-ice ['tʃɒkaɪs] n (Brit) helado m cubierto de chocolate
chock-a-block ['tʃɒkəˈblɒk], **chock-full** [tʃɒkˈful] adj atestado
chocolate ['tʃɒklɪt] n chocolate m; (sweet) bombón m
choice [tʃɔɪs] n elección f; (preference) preferencia ▷ adj escogido; **I did it by** or **from ~** lo hice de buena gana; **a wide ~** un gran surtido, una gran variedad
choir ['kwaɪəʳ] n coro
choirboy ['kwaɪəbɔɪ] n niño de coro
choke [tʃəuk] vi ahogarse; (on food) atragantarse ▷ vt ahogar; (block) atascar ▷ n (Aut) estárter m
cholera ['kɒlərə] n cólera m
cholesterol [kɔˈlestərəl] n colesterol m
choose [tʃuːz] (pt **chose** [tʃəuz], pp **chosen** [tʃəuzn]) vt escoger, elegir; (team) seleccionar; **to ~ between** elegir or escoger entre; **to ~ from** escoger entre; **to ~ to do sth** optar por hacer algo
choosy ['tʃuːzɪ] adj remilgado
chop [tʃɒp] vt (wood) cortar, talar; (Culin: also: **~ up**) picar ▷ n tajo, golpe m cortante; (Culin) chuleta; **chops** npl (jaws) boca sg; **to get the ~** (inf: project) ser suprimido; (: person: be sacked) ser despedido; **chop down** vt (tree) talar; **chop off** vt cortar (de un tajo)
chopper ['tʃɒpəʳ] n (helicopter) helicóptero

choppy ['tʃɒpɪ] adj (sea) picado, agitado
chopsticks ['tʃɒpstɪks] npl palillos mpl
chord [kɔːd] n (Mus) acorde m
chore [tʃɔːʳ] n faena, tarea; (routine task) trabajo rutinario
choreographer [kɔrɪˈɔgrəfəʳ] n coreógrafo(-a)
choreography [kɔrɪˈɔgrəfɪ] n coreografía
chortle ['tʃɔːtl] vi reírse satisfecho
chorus ['kɔːrəs] n coro; (repeated part of song) estribillo
chose [tʃəuz] pt of **choose**
chosen ['tʃəuzn] pp of **choose**
Christ [kraɪst] n Cristo
christen ['krɪsn] vt bautizar
christening ['krɪsnɪŋ] n bautizo
Christian ['krɪstɪən] adj, n cristiano(-a) m(f)
Christianity [krɪstɪˈænɪtɪ] n cristianismo
Christian name n nombre m de pila
Christmas ['krɪsməs] n Navidad f; **Merry ~!** ¡Felices Navidades!
Christmas card n crismas m inv, tarjeta de Navidad
Christmas carol n villancico m
Christmas Day n día m de Navidad
Christmas Eve n Nochebuena
Christmas pudding n (esp Brit) pudín m de Navidad
Christmas tree n árbol m de Navidad
chrome [krəum] n = **chromium plating**
chromium ['krəumɪəm] n cromo; (also: **~ plating**) cromado
chromosome ['krəuməsəum] n cromosoma m
chronic ['krɒnɪk] adj crónico; (fig: liar, smoker) empedernido
chronicle ['krɒnɪkl] n crónica
chronological [krɔnəˈlɔdʒɪkəl] adj cronológico
chrysanthemum [krɪˈsænθəməm] n crisantemo
chubby ['tʃʌbɪ] adj rechoncho
chuck [tʃʌk] (inf) vt lanzar, arrojar; (Brit: also: **~ in, ~ up**) abandonar; **chuck out** vt (person) echar (fuera); (rubbish etc) tirar
chuckle ['tʃʌkl] vi reírse entre dientes
chuffed [tʃʌft] adj (inf): **to be ~ (about sth)** estar encantado (con algo)
chug [tʃʌg] vi (also: **~ along**: train) ir despacio; (: fig) ir tirando
chum [tʃʌm] n amiguete(-a) m(f), coleguilla m/f
chunk [tʃʌŋk] n pedazo, trozo
Chunnel [tʃʌnl] n = **Channel Tunnel**
church [tʃəːtʃ] n iglesia; **the C~ of England** la Iglesia Anglicana
churchyard ['tʃəːtʃjɑːd] n cementerio, camposanto
churn [tʃəːn] n (for butter) mantequera; (for milk) lechera; **churn out** vt producir en serie
chute [ʃuːt] n (also: **rubbish ~**) vertedero; (Brit: children's slide) tobogán m

chutney ['tʃʌtnɪ] n *salsa picante de frutas y especias*

CIA n abbr (US: = Central Intelligence Agency) CIA f, Agencia Central de Inteligencia

CID n abbr (Brit: = Criminal Investigation Department) ≈ B.I.C. f (Sp)

cider ['saɪdəʳ] n sidra

cigar [sɪ'gɑːʳ] n puro

cigarette [sɪgə'ret] n cigarrillo, pitillo

cigarette case n pitillera

cigarette end n colilla

cigarette lighter n mechero

Cinderella [sɪndə'relə] n Cenicienta

cinders ['sɪndəz] npl cenizas fpl

cine-camera ['sɪnɪ'kæmərə] n (Brit) cámara cinematográfica

cinema ['sɪnəmə] n cine m

cinnamon ['sɪnəmən] n canela

circle ['səːkl] n círculo; (in theatre) anfiteatro ▷ vi dar vueltas ▷ vt (surround) rodear, cercar; (move round) dar la vuelta a

circuit ['səːkɪt] n circuito; (track) pista; (lap) vuelta

circuitous [səː'kjuɪtəs] adj indirecto

circular ['səːkjuləʳ] adj circular ▷ n circular f; (as advertisement) panfleto

circulate ['səːkjuleɪt] vi circular; (person: socially) alternar, circular ▷ vt poner en circulación

circulation [səːkju'leɪʃən] n circulación f; (of newspaper etc) tirada

circumcise ['səːkəmsaɪz] vt circuncidar

circumference [sə'kʌmfərəns] n circunferencia

circumstances ['səːkəmstənsɪz] npl circunstancias fpl; (financial condition) situación f económica; **in the ~** en or dadas las circunstancias; **under no ~** de ninguna manera, bajo ningún concepto

circumvent ['səːkəmvent] vt (rule etc) burlar

circus ['səːkəs] n circo; (also: **C~**: in place names) Plaza

cirrhosis [sɪ'rəusɪs] n (also: **~ of the liver**) cirrosis f inv

CIS n abbr (= Commonwealth of Independent States) CEI f

cissy ['sɪsɪ] n = **sissy**

cistern ['sɪstən] n tanque m, depósito; (in toilet) cisterna

citation [saɪ'teɪʃən] n cita; (Law) citación f; (Mil) mención f

cite [saɪt] vt citar

citizen ['sɪtɪzn] n (Pol) ciudadano(-a); (of city) habitante m/f, vecino(-a)

Citizens' Advice Bureau n (Brit) organización voluntaria británica que aconseja especialmente en temas legales o financieros

citizenship ['sɪtɪznʃɪp] n ciudadanía; (Brit Scol) civismo

citric ['sɪtrɪk] adj: **~ acid** ácido cítrico

citrus fruits ['sɪtrəs-] npl cítricos mpl

city ['sɪtɪ] n ciudad f; **the C~** centro financiero de Londres

city centre n centro de la ciudad

City Hall n (US) ayuntamiento

City Technology College n (Brit) ≈ Centro de formación profesional

civic ['sɪvɪk] adj cívico; (authorities) municipal

civic centre n (Brit) centro de administración municipal

civil ['sɪvɪl] adj civil; (polite) atento, cortés; (well-bred) educado

civil defence n protección f civil

civil engineer n ingeniero(-a) de caminos

civil engineering n ingeniería de caminos

civilian [sɪ'vɪlɪən] adj civil; (clothes) de paisano ▷ n civil m/f

civilization [sɪvɪlaɪ'zeɪʃən] n civilización f

civilized ['sɪvɪlaɪzd] adj civilizado

civil law n derecho civil

civil liberties npl libertades fpl civiles

civil rights npl derechos mpl civiles

civil servant n funcionario(-a) (del Estado)

Civil Service n administración f pública

civil war n guerra civil

civvies ['sɪvɪz] npl: **in ~** (inf) de paisano

CJD n abbr (= Creutzfeldt-Jakob disease) enfermedad de Creutzfeldt-Jakob

clad [klæd] adj: **~ (in)** vestido (de)

claim [kleɪm] vt exigir, reclamar; (rights etc) reivindicar; (assert) pretender ▷ vi (for insurance) reclamar ▷ n (for expenses) reclamación f; (Law) demanda; (pretension) pretensión f; **to put in a ~ for sth** presentar una demanda por algo

claimant ['kleɪmənt] n (Admin, Law) demandante m/f

claim form n solicitud f

clairvoyant [kleə'vɔɪənt] n clarividente m/f

clam [klæm] n almeja; **clam up** vi (inf) cerrar el pico

clamber ['klæmbəʳ] vi trepar

clammy ['klæmɪ] adj (cold) frío y húmedo; (sticky) pegajoso

clamour, clamor (US) ['klæməʳ] n (noise) clamor m; (protest) protesta ▷ vi: **to ~ for sth** clamar por algo, pedir algo a voces

clamp [klæmp] n abrazadera; (laboratory clamp) grapa; (wheel clamp) cepo ▷ vt afianzar (con abrazadera); **clamp down on** vt fus (government, police) poner coto a

clampdown ['klæmpdaun] n restricción f; **there has been a ~ on terrorism** se ha puesto coto al terrorismo

clan [klæn] n clan m

clang [klæŋ] n estruendo ▷ vi sonar con estruendo

clanger ['klæŋəʳ] n: **to drop a ~** (Brit: (inf)) meter la pata

clap [klæp] vi aplaudir ▷ vt (hands) batir ▷ n (of hands) palmada; **to ~ one's hands** dar palmadas, batir las palmas; **a ~ of thunder** un trueno

clapping ['klæpɪŋ] n aplausos mpl
claptrap ['klæptræp] n (inf) gilipolleces fpl
claret ['klærət] n burdeos m inv
clarification [klærɪfɪ'keɪʃən] n aclaración f
clarify ['klærɪfaɪ] vt aclarar
clarinet [klærɪ'nɛt] n clarinete m
clarity ['klærɪtɪ] n claridad f
clash [klæʃ] n estruendo; (fig) choque m ▷ vi
enfrentarse; (beliefs) chocar; (disagree) estar
en desacuerdo; (colours) desentonar; (two
events) coincidir
clasp [klɑːsp] n (hold) apretón m; (of necklace,
bag) cierre m ▷ vt abrochar; (hand) apretar;
(embrace) abrazar
class [klɑːs] n (gen) clase f; (group, category)
clase f, categoría ▷ cpd de clase ▷ vt clasificar
classic ['klæsɪk] adj clásico ▷ n (work) obra
clásica, clásico; **classics** npl (Univ) clásicas fpl
classical ['klæsɪkəl] adj clásico; **~ music**
música clásica
classification [klæsɪfɪ'keɪʃən] n
clasificación f
classified ['klæsɪfaɪd] adj (information)
reservado
classified advertisement n anuncio por
palabras
classify ['klæsɪfaɪ] vt clasificar
classmate ['klɑːsmeɪt] n compañero(-a) de
clase
classroom ['klɑːsrum] n aula
classroom assistant n profesor(a) m(f) de
apoyo
classy ['klɑːsɪ] adj (inf) elegante, con estilo
clatter ['klætəʳ] n ruido, estruendo; (of hooves)
trápala ▷ vi hacer ruido or estruendo
clause [klɔːz] n cláusula; (Ling) oración f
claustrophobia [klɔːstrə'fəubɪə] n
claustrofobia
claustrophobic [klɔːstrə'fəubɪk] adj
claustrofóbico; **I feel ~** me entra
claustrofobia
claw [klɔː] n (of cat) uña; (of bird of prey) garra;
(of lobster) pinza; (Tech) garfio ▷ vi: **to ~ at**
arañar; (tear) desgarrar
clay [kleɪ] n arcilla
clean [kliːn] adj limpio; (record, reputation)
bueno, intachable; (joke) decente; (copy) en
limpio; (lines) bien definido ▷ vt limpiar;
(hands etc) lavar ▷ adv: **he ~ forgot** lo olvidó
por completo; **to come ~** (inf: admit guilt)
confesarlo todo; **to have a ~ driving licence**
tener el carnet de conducir sin sanciones; **to
~ one's teeth** lavarse los dientes; **clean off** vt
limpiar; **clean out** vt limpiar (a fondo);
clean up vt limpiar, asear ▷ vi (fig: make
profit): **to ~ up on** sacar provecho de
clean-cut ['kliːn'kʌt] adj bien definido;
(outline) nítido; (person) de buen parecer
cleaner ['kliːnəʳ] n encargado(-a) m(f) de la
limpieza; (also: **dry ~**) tintorero(-a);
(substance) producto para la limpieza
cleaning ['kliːnɪŋ] n limpieza

cleanliness ['klɛnlɪnɪs] n limpieza
cleanse [klɛnz] vt limpiar
cleanser ['klɛnzəʳ] n detergente m; (cosmetic)
loción f or crema limpiadora
clean-shaven ['kliːn'ʃeɪvn] adj bien afeitado
cleansing department ['klɛnzɪŋ-] n (Brit)
servicio municipal de limpieza
clean sweep n: **to make a ~** (Sport) arrasar,
barrer
clear [klɪəʳ] adj claro; (road, way) libre; (profit)
neto; (majority) absoluto ▷ vt (space) despejar,
limpiar; (Law: suspect) absolver; (obstacle)
salvar, saltar por encima de; (debt) liquidar;
(cheque) aceptar; (site, woodland) desmontar
▷ vi (fog etc) despejarse ▷ n: **to be in the ~**
(out of debt) estar libre de deudas; (out of
suspicion) estar fuera de toda sospecha; (out of
danger) estar fuera de peligro ▷ adv: **~ of** a
distancia de; **to make o.s. ~** explicarse
claramente; **to make it ~ to sb that …** hacer
entender a algn que …; **I have a ~ day
tomorrow** mañana tengo el día libre; **to
keep ~ of sth/sb** evitar algo/a algn; **to ~ a
profit of …** sacar una ganancia de …; **to ~
the table** recoger or quitar la mesa; **clear
away** vt (things, clothes etc) quitar (de en
medio); (dishes) retirar; **clear off** vi (inf: leave)
marcharse, mandarse mudar (LAm); **clear up**
vt limpiar; (mystery) aclarar, resolver
clearance ['klɪərəns] n (removal) despeje m;
(permission) acreditación f
clear-cut ['klɪə'kʌt] adj bien definido, claro
clearing ['klɪərɪŋ] n (in wood) claro
clearing bank n (Brit) banco central
clearly ['klɪəlɪ] adv claramente; (evidently) sin
duda
clearway ['klɪəweɪ] n (Brit) carretera en la que no
se puede estacionar
clef [klɛf] n (Mus) clave f
cleft [klɛft] n (in rock) grieta, hendedura
clemency ['klɛmənsɪ] n clemencia
clench [klɛntʃ] vt apretar, cerrar
clergy ['kləːdʒɪ] n clero
clergyman ['kləːdʒɪmən] n clérigo
clerical ['klɛrɪkəl] adj de oficina; (Rel)
clerical; (error) de copia
clerk [klɑːk, (US) kləːk] n oficinista m/f; (US)
dependiente(-a) m(f), vendedor(a) m(f); **C~ of
the Court** secretario(-a) de juzgado
clever ['klɛvəʳ] adj (mentally) inteligente, listo;
(skilful) hábil; (device, arrangement) ingenioso
clew [kluː] n (US) = **clue**
cliché ['kliːʃeɪ] n cliché m, frase f hecha
click [klɪk] vt (tongue) chasquear ▷ vi (Comput)
hacer clic; **to ~ one's heels** taconear; **to ~ on
an icon** hacer clic en un icono
client ['klaɪənt] n cliente m/f
clientele [kliːɑːn'tɛl] n clientela
cliff [klɪf] n acantilado
climate ['klaɪmɪt] n clima m; (fig) clima m,
ambiente m
climate change n cambio climático

climax ['klaɪmæks] n (of battle, career) apogeo; (of film, book) punto culminante, clímax; (sexual) orgasmo

climb [klaɪm] vi subir, trepar; (plane) elevarse, remontar el vuelo ▷ vt (stairs) subir; (tree) trepar a; (mountain) escalar ▷ n subida, ascenso; **to ~ over a wall** saltar una tapia; **climb down** vi (fig) volverse atrás

climbdown ['klaɪmdaun] n vuelta atrás

climber ['klaɪmə^r] n escalador(a) m(f)

climbing ['klaɪmɪŋ] n escalada

clinch [klɪntʃ] vt (deal) cerrar; (argument) remachar

cling [klɪŋ] (pt, pp **clung** [klʌŋ]) vi: **to ~ (to)** agarrarse (a); (clothes) pegarse (a)

clingfilm ['klɪŋfɪlm] n plástico adherente

clinic ['klɪnɪk] n clínica

clinical ['klɪnɪkl] adj clínico; (fig) frío, impasible

clink [klɪŋk] vi tintinear

clip [klɪp] n (for hair) horquilla; (also: **paper ~**) sujetapapeles m inv, clip m; (clamp) grapa ▷ vt (cut) cortar; (hedge) podar; (also: **~ together**) unir

clippers ['klɪpəz] npl (for gardening) tijeras fpl de podar; (for hair) maquinilla sg; (for nails) cortauñas m inv

clipping ['klɪpɪŋ] n (from newspaper) recorte m

clique [kliːk] n camarilla

cloak [kləuk] n capa, manto ▷ vt (fig) encubrir, disimular

cloakroom ['kləukrum] n guardarropa m; (Brit: WC) lavabo, aseos mpl, baño (esp LAm)

clock [klɔk] n reloj m; (in taxi) taxímetro; **to work against the ~** trabajar contra reloj; **around the ~** las veinticuatro horas; **to sleep round the ~** dormir un día entero; **30,000 on the ~** (Aut) treinta mil millas en el cuentakilómetros; **clock in, clock on** vi fichar, picar; **clock off, clock out** vi fichar or picar la salida; **clock up** vt hacer

clockwise ['klɔkwaɪz] adv en el sentido de las agujas del reloj

clockwork ['klɔkwəːk] n aparato de relojería ▷ adj (toy, train) de cuerda

clog [klɔg] n zueco, chanclo ▷ vt atascar ▷ vi (also: **~ up**) atascarse

cloister ['klɔɪstə^r] n claustro

clone [kləun] n clon m ▷ vt clonar

close [adj, adv kləus, vb, n kləuz] adj cercano, próximo; (near): **~ (to)** cerca (de); (print, weave) tupido, compacto; (friend) íntimo; (connection) estrecho; (examination) detallado, minucioso; (weather) bochornoso; (atmosphere) sofocante; (room) mal ventilado ▷ adv cerca; **~ by, ~ at hand** muy cerca; **~ to** prep cerca de; **to have a ~ shave** (fig) escaparse por un pelo; **how ~ is Edinburgh to Glasgow?** ¿qué distancia hay de Edimburgo a Glasgow?; **at ~ quarters** de cerca ▷ vt (end) concluir, terminar ▷ vi (shop etc) cerrar; (end) concluir(se), terminar(se) ▷ n (end) fin m, final m,

conclusión f; **to bring sth to a ~** terminar algo; **close down** vi cerrar definitivamente; **close in** vi (hunters) acercarse rodeando, rodear; (evening, night) caer; (fog) cerrarse; **to ~ in on sb** rodear or cercar a algn; **the days are closing in** los días son cada vez más cortos; **close off** vt (area) cerrar al tráfico or al público

closed [kləuzd] adj (shop etc) cerrado

closed-circuit ['kləuzd'səːkɪt] adj: **~ television** televisión f por circuito cerrado

closed shop n empresa en la que todo el personal está afiliado a un sindicato

close-knit ['kləus'nɪt] adj (fig) muy unido

closely ['kləuslɪ] adv (study) con detalle; (listen) con atención; (watch) de cerca; **we are ~ related** somos parientes cercanos; **a ~ guarded secret** un secreto rigurosamente guardado

close season [kləuz-] n (Football) temporada de descanso; (Hunting) veda

closet ['klɔzɪt] n (cupboard) armario, placar(d) m (LAm)

close-up ['kləusʌp] n primer plano

closing time n hora de cierre

closure ['kləuʒə^r] n cierre m

clot [klɔt] n (gen: also: **blood ~**) coágulo; (inf: idiot) imbécil m/f ▷ vi (blood) coagularse

cloth [klɔθ] n (material) tela, paño; (table cloth) mantel m; (rag) trapo

clothe [kləuð] vt vestir; (fig) revestir

clothes [kləuðz] npl ropa sg; **to put one's ~ on** vestirse, ponerse la ropa; **to take one's ~ off** desvestirse, desnudarse

clothes brush n cepillo (para la ropa)

clothes line n cuerda (para tender la ropa)

clothes peg, clothes pin (US) n pinza

clothing ['kləuðɪŋ] n = **clothes**

cloud [klaud] n nube f; (storm cloud) nubarrón m ▷ vt (liquid) enturbiar; **every ~ has a silver lining** no hay mal que por bien no venga; **to ~ the issue** empañar el problema; **cloud over** vi (also fig) nublarse

cloudburst ['klaudbəːst] n chaparrón m

cloudy ['klaudɪ] adj nublado; (liquid) turbio

clout [klaut] n (fig) influencia, peso ▷ vt dar un tortazo a

clove [kləuv] n clavo; **~ of garlic** diente m de ajo

clover ['kləuvə^r] n trébol m

clown [klaun] n payaso ▷ vi (also: **~ about, ~ around**) hacer el payaso

cloying ['klɔɪɪŋ] adj (taste) empalagoso

club [klʌb] n (society) club m; (weapon) porra, cachiporra; (also: **golf ~**) palo ▷ vt aporrear ▷ vi: **to ~ together** (join forces) unir fuerzas; **clubs** npl (Cards) tréboles mpl

club car n (US Rail) coche m salón

club class n (Aviat) clase f preferente

clubhouse ['klʌbhaus] n local social, sobre todo en clubs deportivos

club soda n (US) soda

cluck [klʌk] vi cloquear

clue [klu:] n pista; (in crosswords) indicación f; **I haven't a ~** no tengo ni idea

clump [klʌmp] n (of trees) grupo

clumsy ['klʌmzɪ] adj (person) torpe; (tool) difícil de manejar

clung [klʌŋ] pt, pp of **cling**

cluster ['klʌstəʳ] n grupo; (Bot) racimo ▷ vi agruparse, apiñarse

clutch [klʌtʃ] n (Aut) embrague m; (pedal) (pedal m de) embrague m; **to fall into sb's ~es** caer en las garras de algn ▷ vt agarrar

clutter ['klʌtəʳ] vt (also: **~ up**) atestar, llenar desordenadamente ▷ n desorden m, confusión f

cm abbr (= centimetre) cm

CND n abbr (Brit: = Campaign for Nuclear Disarmament) plataforma pro desarme nuclear

Co. abbr = **county; company**

c/o abbr (= care of) c/a, a/c

coach [kəutʃ] n (bus) autocar m (Sp), autobús m; (horse-drawn) coche m; (ceremonial) carroza; (of train) vagón m, coche m; (Sport) entrenador(a) m(f), instructor(a) m(f) ▷ vt (Sport) entrenar; (student) preparar, enseñar

coach station n (Brit) estación f de autobuses etc

coach trip n excursión f en autocar

coal [kəul] n carbón m

coalfield ['kəulfi:ld] n yacimiento de carbón

coalition [kəuə'lɪʃən] n coalición f

coal man n carbonero

coalmine ['kəulmaɪn] n mina de carbón

coarse [kɔ:s] adj basto, burdo; (vulgar) grosero, ordinario

coast [kəust] n costa, litoral m ▷ vi (Aut) ir en punto muerto

coastal ['kəustl] adj costero

coastguard ['kəustgɑ:d] n guardacostas m inv

coastline ['kəustlaɪn] n litoral m

coat [kəut] n (jacket) chaqueta, saco (LAm); (overcoat) abrigo; (of animal) pelo, pelaje, lana; (of paint) mano f, capa ▷ vt cubrir, revestir

coat hanger n percha, gancho (LAm)

coating ['kəutɪŋ] n capa, baño

coat of arms n escudo de armas

coax [kəuks] vt engatusar

cob [kɔb] n see **corn**

cobbled ['kɔbld] adj: **~ street** calle f empedrada, calle f adoquinada

cobbler ['kɔbləʳ] n zapatero (remendón)

cobbles ['kɔblz], **cobblestones** ['kɔblstəunz] npl adoquines mpl

cobweb ['kɔbweb] n telaraña

cocaine [kə'keɪn] n cocaína

cock [kɔk] n (rooster) gallo; (male bird) macho ▷ vt (gun) amartillar

cockerel ['kɔkərl] n gallito, gallo joven

cock-eyed ['kɔkaɪd] adj bizco; (fig: crooked) torcido; (: idea) disparatado

cockle ['kɔkl] n berberecho

cockney ['kɔknɪ] n habitante de ciertos barrios de Londres

cockpit ['kɔkpɪt] n (in aircraft) cabina

cockroach ['kɔkrəutʃ] n cucaracha

cocktail ['kɔkteɪl] n combinado, cóctel m; **prawn ~** cóctel m de gambas

cocktail cabinet n mueble-bar m

cocktail party n cóctel m

cocky ['kɔkɪ] adj farruco, flamenco

cocoa ['kəukəu] n cacao; (drink) chocolate m

coconut ['kəukənʌt] n coco

cod [kɔd] n bacalao

COD abbr (= cash on delivery, US: = collect on delivery) C.A.E.

code [kəud] n código; (cipher) clave f; (Tel) prefijo; **~ of behaviour** código de conducta; **~ of practice** código profesional

codger [kɔdʒəʳ] n (Brit inf): **an old ~** un abuelo

cod-liver oil ['kɔdlɪvəʳ-] n aceite m de hígado de bacalao

coeducational [kəuɛdju'keɪʃənl] adj mixto

coercion [kəu'ə:ʃən] n coacción f

coffee ['kɔfɪ] n café m; **white ~** (US), **~ with cream** café con leche

coffee bar n (Brit) cafetería

coffee bean n grano de café

coffee break n descanso (para tomar café)

coffee maker n máquina de hacer café, cafetera

coffeepot ['kɔfɪpɔt] n cafetera

coffee shop n café m

coffee table n mesita baja

coffin ['kɔfɪn] n ataúd m

cog [kɔg] n diente m

cogent ['kəudʒənt] adj lógico, convincente

cognac ['kɔnjæk] n coñac m

coherent [kəu'hɪərənt] adj coherente

coil [kɔɪl] n rollo; (of rope) vuelta; (of smoke) espiral f; (Aut, Elec) bobina, carrete m; (contraceptive) DIU m ▷ vt enrollar

coin [kɔɪn] n moneda ▷ vt acuñar; (word) inventar, acuñar

coinage ['kɔɪnɪdʒ] n moneda

coin-box ['kɔɪnbɔks] n (Brit) caja recaudadora

coincide [kəuɪn'saɪd] vi coincidir

coincidence [kəu'ɪnsɪdəns] n casualidad f, coincidencia

Coke® [kəuk] n Coca Cola® f

coke [kəuk] n (coal) coque m

colander ['kɔləndəʳ] n escurridor m

cold [kəuld] adj frío ▷ n frío; (Med) resfriado; **it's ~** hace frío; **to be ~** tener frío; **to catch a ~** resfriarse, acatarrarse, coger un catarro; **in ~ blood** a sangre fría; **the room's getting ~** está empezando a hacer frío en la habitación; **to give sb the ~ shoulder** tratar a algn con frialdad

cold sore n calentura, herpes m labial

cold sweat n: **to be in a ~ (about sth)** tener sudores fríos (por algo)

cold turkey n (inf) mono

Cold War *n*: **the ~** la guerra fría
coleslaw ['kəulslɔ:] *n* ensalada de col con zanahoria
colic ['kɔlɪk] *n* cólico
colicky ['kɔlɪkɪ] *adj*: **to be ~** tener un cólico
collaborate [kə'læbəreɪt] *vi* colaborar
collaboration [kəlæbə'reɪʃən] *n* colaboración *f*; (*Pol*) colaboracionismo
collapse [kə'læps] *vi* (*gen*) hundirse, derrumbarse; (*Med*) sufrir un colapso ▷ *n* (*gen*) hundimiento, derrumbamiento; (*Med*) colapso; (*of government*) caída; (*of plans, scheme*) fracaso; (*of business*) ruina
collapsible [kə'læpsəbl] *adj* plegable
collar ['kɔlər] *n* (*of coat, shirt*) cuello; (*for dog*) collar *m*; (*Tech*) collar *m* ▷ *vt* (*inf: person*) agarrar; (: *object*) birlar
collarbone ['kɔləbəun] *n* clavícula
collateral [kɔ'lætərəl] *n* (*Comm*) garantía subsidiaria
colleague ['kɔli:g] *n* colega *m/f*; (*at work*) compañero(-a) *m(f)*
collect [kə'lɛkt] *vt* reunir; (*as a hobby*) coleccionar; (*Brit*: *call and pick up*) recoger; (*wages*) cobrar; (*debts*) recaudar; (*donations, subscriptions*) colectar ▷ *vi* (*crowd*) reunirse ▷ *adv*: **to call ~** (*US Tel*) llamar a cobro revertido; **to ~ one's thoughts** reponerse, recobrar el dominio de sí mismo; **~ on delivery (COD)** (*US*) entrega contra reembolso
collection [kə'lɛkʃən] *n* colección *f*; (*of fares, wages*) cobro; (*of post*) recogida
collective [kə'lɛktɪv] *adj* colectivo
collector [kə'lɛktər] *n* coleccionista *m/f*; (*of taxes etc*) recaudador(a) *m(f)*; **~'s item** or **piece** pieza de coleccionista
college ['kɔlɪdʒ] *n* colegio; (*of technology, agriculture etc*) escuela
collide [kə'laɪd] *vi* chocar
collie ['kɔlɪ] *n* (*dog*) collie *m*, perro pastor escocés
colliery ['kɔlɪərɪ] *n* (*Brit*) mina de carbón
collision [kə'lɪʒən] *n* choque *m*, colisión *f*; **to be on a ~ course** (*also fig*) ir rumbo al desastre
colloquial [kə'ləukwɪəl] *adj* coloquial
cologne [kə'ləun] *n* (*also*: **eau de ~**) (agua de) colonia
Colombia [kə'lɔmbɪə] *n* Colombia
Colombian [kə'lɔmbɪən] *adj*, *n* colombiano(-a) *m(f)*
colon ['kəulən] *n* (*sign*) dos puntos; (*Med*) colon *m*
colonel ['kə:nl] *n* coronel *m*
colonial [kə'ləunɪəl] *adj* colonial
colonize ['kɔlənaɪz] *vt* colonizar
colony ['kɔlənɪ] *n* colonia
color ['kʌlər] *n* (*US*) = **colour**
colossal [kə'lɔsl] *adj* colosal
colour, color (*US*) ['kʌlər] *n* color *m* ▷ *vt* colorear, pintar; (*dye*) teñir; (*fig: account*) adornar; (: *judgement*) distorsionar ▷ *vi* (*blush*)

sonrojarse; **colours** *npl* (*of party, club*) colores *mpl*; **colour in** *vt* colorear
colour-blind, color-blind (*US*) ['kʌləblaɪnd] *adj* daltónico
coloured, colored (*US*) ['kʌləd] *adj* de color; (*photo*) en color; (*of race*) de color
colour film, color film (*US*) *n* película en color
colourful, colorful (*US*) ['kʌləful] *adj* lleno de color; (*person*) pintoresco
colouring, coloring (*US*) ['kʌlərɪŋ] *n* colorido, color; (*substance*) colorante *m*
colour television, color television (*US*) *n* televisión *f* en color
colt [kəult] *n* potro
column ['kɔləm] *n* columna; (*fashion column, sports column etc*) sección *f*, columna; **the editorial ~** el editorial
columnist ['kɔləmnɪst] *n* columnista *m/f*
coma ['kəumə] *n* coma *m*
comb [kəum] *n* peine *m*; (*ornamental*) peineta ▷ *vt* (*hair*) peinar; (*area*) registrar a fondo, peinar
combat ['kɔmbæt] *n* combate *m* ▷ *vt* combatir
combination [kɔmbɪ'neɪʃən] *n* (*gen*) combinación *f*
combine [kəm'baɪn] *vt* combinar; (*qualities*) reunir ▷ *vi* combinarse ▷ *n* ['kɔmbaɪn] (*Econ*) cartel *m*; (*also*: **~ harvester**) cosechadora; **a ~d effort** un esfuerzo conjunto

○ KEYWORD

come [kʌm] (*pt* **came**, *pp* **come**) *vi* 1 (*movement towards*) venir; **to come running** venir corriendo; **come with me** ven conmigo
2 (*arrive*) llegar; **he's come here to work** ha venido aquí para trabajar; **to come home** volver a casa; **we've just come from Seville** acabamos de llegar de Sevilla; **coming!** ¡voy!
3 (*reach*): **to come to** llegar a; **the bill came to £40** la cuenta ascendía a cuarenta libras
4 (*occur*): **an idea came to me** se me ocurrió una idea; **if it comes to it** llegado el caso
5 (*be, become*): **to come loose/undone** *etc* aflojarse/desabrocharse, desatarse *etc*; **I've come to like him** por fin ha llegado a gustarme
come about *vi* suceder, ocurrir
come across *vt fus* (*person*) encontrarse con; (*thing*) encontrar ▷ *vi*: **to come across well/ badly** causar buena/mala impresión
come along *vi* (*Brit*: *progress*) ir
come away *vi* (*leave*) marcharse; (*become detached*) desprenderse
come back *vi* (*return*) volver; (*reply*): **can I come back to you on that one?** volvamos sobre ese punto
come by *vt fus* (*acquire*) conseguir
come down *vi* (*price*) bajar; (*building*) derrumbarse; (*be demolished*) ser derribado

come forward vi presentarse
come from vt fus (place, source) ser de
come in vi (visitor) entrar; (train, report) llegar; (fashion) ponerse de moda; (on deal etc) entrar
come in for vt fus (criticism etc) recibir
come into vt fus (money) heredar; (be involved) tener que ver con; **to come into fashion** ponerse de moda
come off vi (button) soltarse, desprenderse; (attempt) salir bien
come on vi (pupil, work, project) marchar; (lights) encenderse; (electricity) volver; **come on!** ¡vamos!
come out vi (fact) salir a la luz; (book, sun) salir; (stain) quitarse; **to come out (on strike)** declararse en huelga; **to come out for/against** declararse a favor/en contra de
come over vt fus: **I don't know what's come over him!** ¡no sé lo que le pasa!
come round vi (after faint, operation) volver en sí
come through vi (survive) sobrevivir; (telephone call): **the call came through** recibimos la llamada
come to vi (wake) volver en sí; (total) sumar; **how much does it come to?** ¿cuánto es en total?, ¿a cuánto asciende?
come under vt fus (heading) entrar dentro de; (influence) estar bajo
come up vi (sun) salir; (problem) surgir; (event) aproximarse; (in conversation) mencionarse
come up against vt fus (resistance etc) tropezar con
come upon vt fus (find) dar con
come up to vt fus llegar hasta; **the film didn't come up to our expectations** la película no fue tan buena como esperábamos
come up with vt fus (idea) sugerir; (money) conseguir

comeback ['kʌmbæk] n (reaction) reacción f; (response) réplica; **to make a ~** (Theat) volver a las tablas
comedian [kə'mi:dɪən] n humorista m/f
comedienne [kəmi:dɪ'ɛn] n humorista
comedy ['kɔmɪdɪ] n comedia
comet ['kɔmɪt] n cometa m
comeuppance [kʌm'ʌpəns] n: **to get one's ~** llevar su merecido
comfort ['kʌmfət] n comodidad f, confort m; (well-being) bienestar m; (solace) consuelo; (relief) alivio ⊳ vt consolar
comfortable ['kʌmfətəbl] adj cómodo; (income) adecuado; (majority) suficiente; **I don't feel very ~ about it** la cosa me tiene algo preocupado
comfortably ['kʌmfətəblɪ] adv (sit) cómodamente, (live) holgadamente
comfort station n (US) servicios mpl
comic ['kɔmɪk] adj (also: **~al**) cómico, gracioso ⊳ n (comedian) cómico; (magazine) tebeo; (for adults) cómic m
comic book (US) n libro m de cómics

comic strip n tira cómica
coming ['kʌmɪŋ] n venida, llegada ⊳ adj que viene; (next) próximo; (future) venidero; **~(s) and going(s)** n(pl) ir y venir m, ajetreo; **in the ~ weeks** en las próximas semanas
comma ['kɔmə] n coma
command [kə'mɑ:nd] n orden f, mandato; (Mil: authority) mando; (mastery) dominio; (Comput) orden f, comando ⊳ vt (troops) mandar; (give orders to) mandar, ordenar; (be able to get) disponer de; (deserve) merecer; **to have at one's ~** (money, resources etc) disponer de; **to have/take ~ of** estar al/asumir el mando de
commandeer [kɔmən'dɪəʳ] vt requisar
commander [kə'mɑ:ndəʳ] n (Mil) comandante m/f, jefe(-a) m(f)
commandment [kə'mɑ:ndmənt] n (Rel) mandamiento
commando [kə'mɑ:ndəu] n comando
commemorate [kə'mɛmərɛıt] vt conmemorar
commemoration [kəmɛmə'reıʃən] n conmemoración f
commemorative [kə'mɛmərətıv] adj conmemorativo
commence [kə'mɛns] vt, vi comenzar
commencement (US) [kə'mɛnsmənt] n (Univ) (ceremonia de) graduación f
commend [kə'mɛnd] vt (praise) elogiar, alabar; (recommend) recomendar; (entrust) encomendar
commensurate [kə'mɛnʃərıt] adj: **~ with** en proporción a
comment ['kɔmɛnt] n comentario ⊳ vt: **to ~ that** comentar or observar que ⊳ vi: **to ~ (on)** comentar, hacer comentarios (sobre); **"no ~"** (written) "sin comentarios"; (spoken) "no tengo nada que decir"
commentary ['kɔməntərı] n comentario
commentator ['kɔməntɛıtəʳ] n comentarista m/f
commerce ['kɔmə:s] n comercio
commercial [kə'mə:ʃəl] adj comercial ⊳ n (TV) anuncio
commercial break n intermedio para publicidad
commercialism [kə'mə:ʃəlızəm] n comercialismo
commercial television n televisión f comercial
commiserate [kə'mızərɛıt] vi: **to ~ with** compadecerse de, condolerse de
commission [kə'mıʃən] n (committee, fee, order for work of art etc) comisión f; (act) perpetración f ⊳ vt (Mil) nombrar; (work of art) encargar; **out of ~** (machine) fuera de servicio; **~ of inquiry** comisión f investigadora; **I get 10% ~** me dan el diez por ciento de comisión; **to ~ sb to do sth** encargar a algn que haga algo; **to ~ sth from sb** (painting etc) encargar algo a algn

commissionaire [kəmɪʃəˈnɛəʳ] n (Brit) portero, conserje m

commissioner [kəˈmɪʃənəʳ] n comisario; (Police) comisario m de policía

commit [kəˈmɪt] vt (act) cometer; (resources) dedicar; (to sb's care) entregar; **to ~ o.s. (to do)** comprometerse (a hacer); **to ~ suicide** suicidarse; **to ~ sb for trial** remitir a algn al tribunal

commitment [kəˈmɪtmənt] n compromiso

committed [kəˈmɪtɪd] adj (writer, politician etc) comprometido

committee [kəˈmɪtɪ] n comité m; **to be on a ~** ser miembro(-a) de un comité

commodity [kəˈmɔdɪtɪ] n mercancía

common [ˈkɔmən] adj (gen) común; (pej) ordinario ▷ n campo común; **in ~** en común; **in ~ use** de uso corriente

common cold n: **the ~** el resfriado

common denominator n común denominador m

commoner [ˈkɔmənəʳ] n plebeyo(-a)

common land n campo comunal, ejido

common law n ley f consuetudinaria

common-law [ˈkɔmənlɔ:] adj: **~ wife** esposa de hecho

commonly [ˈkɔmənlɪ] adv comúnmente

Common Market n Mercado Común

commonplace [ˈkɔmənpleɪs] adj corriente

common room [ˈkɔmənrum] n sala de reunión

Commons [ˈkɔmənz] npl (Brit Pol): **the ~** (la Cámara de) los Comunes

common sense n sentido común

Commonwealth [ˈkɔmənwɛlθ] n: **the ~** la Comunidad (Británica) de Naciones, la Commonwealth; ver nota

> ● **COMMONWEALTH**
> ●
> ● La Commonwealth es la asociación de
> ● estados soberanos independientes y
> ● territorios asociados que formaban parte
> ● del antiguo Imperio Británico. Éste pasó a
> ● llamarse así después de la Segunda
> ● Guerra Mundial, aunque ya desde 1931 se
> ● le conocía como "British Commonwealth
> ● of Nations". Todos los estados miembros
> ● reconocen al monarca británico como
> ● "Head of the Commonwealth".

commotion [kəˈməuʃən] n tumulto, confusión f

communal [ˈkɔmju:nl] adj comunal; (kitchen) común

commune [ˈkɔmju:n] n (group) comuna ▷ vi [kəˈmju:n]: **to ~ with** comunicarse con

communicate [kəˈmju:nɪkeɪt] vt comunicar ▷ vi: **to ~ (with)** comunicarse (con); (in writing) estar en contacto (con)

communication [kəmju:nɪˈkeɪʃən] n comunicación f

communication cord n (Brit) timbre m de alarma

communion [kəˈmju:nɪən] n (also: **Holy C~**) comunión f

communiqué [kəˈmju:nɪkeɪ] n comunicado, parte m

communism [ˈkɔmjunɪzəm] n comunismo

communist [ˈkɔmjunɪst] adj, n comunista m/f

community [kəˈmju:nɪtɪ] n comunidad f; (large group) colectividad f; (local) vecindario

community centre n centro social

community chest n (US) fondo social

community service n trabajo m comunitario (prestado en lugar de cumplir una pena de prisión)

commutation ticket [kɔmju'teɪʃən-] n (US) billete m de abono

commute [kəˈmju:t] vi viajar a diario de casa al trabajo ▷ vt conmutar

commuter [kəˈmju:təʳ] n persona que viaja a diario de casa al trabajo

compact [kəmˈpækt] adj compacto; (style) conciso; (dense) apretado ▷ n [ˈkɔmpækt] (pact) pacto; (also: **powder ~**) polvera

compact disc n compact disc m, disco compacto

compact disc player n lector m or reproductor m de discos compactos

companion [kəmˈpænɪən] n compañero(-a)

companionship [kəmˈpænjənʃɪp] n compañerismo

company [ˈkʌmpənɪ] n (gen) compañía; (Comm) empresa, compañía; **to keep sb ~** acompañar a algn; **Smith and C~** Smith y Compañía

company car n coche m de la empresa

company director n director(a) m(f) de empresa

company secretary n (Brit) administrador(a) m(f) de empresa

comparable [ˈkɔmpərəbl] adj comparable

comparative [kəmˈpærətɪv] adj (freedom, luxury, cost) relativo; (study, linguistics) comparado

comparatively [kəmˈpærətɪvlɪ] adv (relatively) relativamente

compare [kəmˈpɛəʳ] vt comparar ▷ vi: **to ~ (with)** poder compararse (con); **~d with** or **to** comparado con or a; **how do the prices ~?** ¿cómo son los precios en comparación?

comparison [kəmˈpærɪsn] n comparación f; **in ~ (with)** en comparación (con)

compartment [kəmˈpɑ:tmənt] n compartim(i)ento; (Rail) departamento, compartimento

compass [ˈkʌmpəs] n brújula; **compasses** npl compás m; **within the ~ of** al alcance de

compassion [kəmˈpæʃən] n compasión f

compassionate [kəmˈpæʃənɪt] adj compasivo; **on ~ grounds** por compasión

compassionate leave n permiso por asuntos familiares

compatible [kəm'pætɪbl] adj compatible

compel [kəm'pɛl] vt obligar

compelling [kəm'pɛlɪŋ] adj (fig: argument) convincente

compensate ['kɔmpənseɪt] vt compensar ▷ vi: **to ~ for** compensar

compensation [kɔmpən'seɪʃən] n (for loss) indemnización f

compère ['kɔmpɛəʳ] n presentador(a) m(f)

compete [kəm'piːt] vi (take part) competir; (vie with) competir, hacer la competencia

competent ['kɔmpɪtənt] adj competente, capaz

competition [kɔmpɪ'tɪʃən] n (contest) concurso; (Sport) competición f; (Econ: rivalry) competencia; **in ~ with** en competencia con

competitive [kəm'pɛtɪtɪv] adj (Econ, Sport) competitivo; (spirit) competidor(a), de competencia; (selection) por concurso

competitor [kəm'pɛtɪtəʳ] n (rival) competidor(a) m(f); (participant) concursante m/f

compile [kəm'paɪl] vt recopilar

complacency [kəm'pleɪsnsɪ] n autosatisfacción f

complacent [kəm'pleɪsənt] adj autocomplaciente

complain [kəm'pleɪn] vi (gen) quejarse; (Comm) reclamar

complaint [kəm'pleɪnt] n (gen) queja; (Comm) reclamación f; (Law) demanda, querella; (Med) enfermedad f

complement ['kɔmplɪmənt] n complemento; (esp ship's crew) dotación f ▷ vt ['kɔmplɪmənt] (enhance) complementar

complementary [kɔmplɪ'mɛntərɪ] adj complementario

complete [kəm'pliːt] adj (full) completo; (finished) acabado ▷ vt (fulfil) completar; (finish) acabar; (a form) rellenar; **it's a ~ disaster** es un desastre total

completely [kəm'pliːtlɪ] adv completamente

completion [kəm'pliːʃən] n conclusión f, terminación f; **to be nearing ~** estar a punto de terminarse; **on ~ of contract** cuando se realice el contrato

complex ['kɔmplɛks] adj complejo ▷ n (gen) complejo

complexion [kəm'plɛkʃən] n (of face) tez f, cutis m; (fig) aspecto

complexity [kəm'plɛksɪtɪ] n complejidad f

compliance [kəm'plaɪəns] n (submission) sumisión f; (agreement) conformidad f; **in ~ with** de acuerdo con

complicate ['kɔmplɪkeɪt] vt complicar

complicated ['kɔmplɪkeɪtɪd] adj complicado

complication [kɔmplɪ'keɪʃən] n complicación f

compliment ['kɔmplɪmənt] n (formal) cumplido; (flirtation) piropo ▷ vt felicitar;

compliments npl saludos mpl; **to pay sb a ~** (formal) hacer cumplidos a algn; (flirt) piropear, echar piropos a algn; **to ~ sb (on sth/on doing sth)** felicitar a algn (por algo/ por haber hecho algo)

complimentary [kɔmplɪ'mɛntərɪ] adj elogioso; (copy) de regalo; **~ ticket** invitación f

comply [kəm'plaɪ] vi: **to ~ with** acatar

component [kəm'pəunənt] adj componente ▷ n (Tech) pieza, componente m

compose [kəm'pəuz] vt componer; **to be ~d of** componerse de, constar de; **to ~ o.s.** tranquilizarse

composed [kəm'pəuzd] adj sosegado

composer [kəm'pəuzəʳ] n (Mus) compositor(a) m(f)

composition [kɔmpə'zɪʃən] n composición f

compost ['kɔmpɔst] n abono

composure [kəm'pəuʒəʳ] n serenidad f, calma

compound ['kɔmpaund] n (Chem) compuesto; (Ling) término compuesto; (enclosure) recinto ▷ adj (gen) compuesto; (fracture) complicado ▷ vt [kəm'paund] (fig: problem, difficulty) agravar

comprehend [kɔmprɪ'hɛnd] vt comprender

comprehension [kɔmprɪ'hɛnʃən] n comprensión f

comprehensive [kɔmprɪ'hɛnsɪv] adj (broad) exhaustivo; (general) de conjunto; **~ (school)** n centro estatal de enseñanza secundaria, ≈ Instituto Nacional de Bachillerato (Sp); ver nota

⊜ **COMPREHENSIVE SCHOOL**
⊜
⊜ En los años 60 se creó un nuevo tipo de
⊜ centro educativo de enseñanza
⊜ secundaria (aproximadamente de los
⊜ once años en adelante) denominado
⊜ comprehensive school, abierto a todos los
⊜ alumnos independientemente de sus
⊜ capacidades, con el que se intentó poner
⊜ fin a la división tradicional entre centros
⊜ de enseñanzas teóricas para acceder a la
⊜ educación superior ("grammar schools")
⊜ y otros de enseñanzas básicamente
⊜ profesionales ("secondary modern
⊜ schools").

comprehensive insurance policy n seguro a todo riesgo

compress [kəm'prɛs] vt comprimir; (Comput) comprimir ▷ n ['kɔmprɛs] (Med) compresa

comprise [kəm'praɪz] vt (also: **be ~d of**) comprender, constar de

compromise ['kɔmprəmaɪz] n solución f intermedia; (agreement) arreglo ▷ vt comprometer ▷ vi transigir, transar (LAm) ▷ cpd (decision, solution) de término medio

compulsion [kəm'pʌlʃən] n obligación f; **under ~** a la fuerza, por obligación

compulsive [kəm'pʌlsɪv] adj compulsivo; (viewing, reading) obligado

compulsory [kəm'pʌlsərɪ] adj obligatorio

computer [kəm'pju:tə^r] n ordenador m, computador m, computadora

computer game n juego de ordenador

computerize [kəm'pju:təraɪz] vt (data) computerizar; (system) informatizar

computer literate adj: **to be ~** tener conocimientos de informática a nivel de usuario

computer programmer n programador(a) m(f)

computer programming n programación f

computer science n informática

computer studies npl informática fsg, computación fsg (LAm)

computing [kəm'pju:tɪŋ] n (activity) informática

comrade ['kɒmrɪd] n compañero(-a)

con [kɒn] vt timar, estafar ▷ n timo, estafa; **to ~ sb into doing sth** (inf) engañar a algn para que haga algo

conceal [kən'si:l] vt ocultar; (thoughts etc) disimular

concede [kən'si:d] vt (point, argument) reconocer; (game) darse por vencido en; (territory) ceder; **to ~ (defeat)** darse por vencido; **to ~ that** admitir que

conceit [kən'si:t] n orgullo, presunción f

conceited [kən'si:tɪd] adj orgulloso

conceivable [kən'si:vəbl] adj concebible; **it is ~ that ...** es posible que ...

conceive [kən'si:v] vt, vi concebir; **to ~ of sth/of doing sth** imaginar algo/imaginarse haciendo algo

concentrate ['kɒnsəntreɪt] vi concentrarse ▷ vt concentrar

concentration [kɒnsən'treɪʃən] n concentración f

concentration camp n campo de concentración

concept ['kɒnsɛpt] n concepto

conception [kən'sɛpʃən] n (idea) concepto, idea; (Biol) concepción f

concern [kən'sə:n] n (matter) asunto; (Comm) empresa; (anxiety) preocupación f ▷ vt (worry) preocupar; (involve) afectar; (relate to) tener que ver con; **to be ~ed (about)** interesarse (por), preocuparse (por)

concerning [kən'sə:nɪŋ] prep sobre, acerca de

concert ['kɒnsət] n concierto

concerted [kən'sə:təd] adj (efforts etc) concertado

concert hall n sala de conciertos

concerto [kən'tʃə:təu] n concierto

concession [kən'sɛʃən] n concesión f; (price concession) descuento; **tax ~** privilegio fiscal

conciliation [kənsɪlɪ'eɪʃən] n conciliación f

concise [kən'saɪs] adj conciso

conclude [kən'klu:d] vt (finish) concluir; (treaty etc) firmar; (agreement) llegar a; (decide): **to ~ that ...** llegar a la conclusión de que ... ▷ vi (events) concluir, terminar

concluding [kən'klu:dɪŋ] adj (remarks etc) final

conclusion [kən'klu:ʒən] n conclusión f; **to come to the ~ that** llegar a la conclusión de que

conclusive [kən'klu:sɪv] adj decisivo, concluyente

concoct [kən'kɒkt] vt (food, drink) preparar; (story) inventar; (plot) tramar

concoction [kən'kɒkʃən] n (food) mezcla; (drink) brebaje m

concourse ['kɒŋkɔ:s] n (hall) vestíbulo

concrete ['kɒnkri:t] n hormigón m ▷ adj de hormigón; (fig) concreto

concur [kən'kə:^r] vi estar de acuerdo

concurrently [kən'kʌrntlɪ] adv al mismo tiempo

concussion [kən'kʌʃən] n conmoción f cerebral

condemn [kən'dɛm] vt condenar; (building) declarar en ruina

condensation [kɒndɛn'seɪʃən] n condensación f

condense [kən'dɛns] vi condensarse ▷ vt condensar; (text) abreviar

condensed milk n leche f condensada

condescending [kɒndɪ'sɛndɪŋ] adj superior

condition [kən'dɪʃən] n condición f; (of health) estado; (disease) enfermedad f ▷ vt condicionar; **on ~ that** a condición (de) que; **weather ~s** condiciones atmosféricas; **in good/poor ~** en buenas/malas condiciones, en buen/mal estado; **~s of sale** condiciones de venta

conditional [kən'dɪʃənl] adj condicional

conditioner [kən'dɪʃənə^r] n (for hair) suavizante m, acondicionador m

condo ['kɒndəu] n abbr (US inf) = **condominium**

condolences [kən'dəulənsɪz] npl pésame msg

condom ['kɒndəm] n condón m

condominium [kɒndə'mɪnɪəm] n (US: building) bloque m de pisos or apartamentos (propiedad de quienes lo habitan), condominio (LAm); (: apartment) piso or apartamento (en propiedad), condominio (LAm)

condone [kən'dəun] vt condonar

conducive [kən'dju:sɪv] adj: **~ to** conducente a

conduct ['kɒndʌkt] n conducta, comportamiento ▷ vt [kən'dʌkt] (lead) conducir; (manage) llevar, dirigir; (Mus) dirigir ▷ vi (Mus) llevar la batuta; **to ~ o.s.** comportarse

conducted tour n (Brit) visita con guía

conductor [kən'dʌktə^r] n (of orchestra) director(a) m(f); (US: on train) revisor(a) m(f); (on bus) cobrador m; (Elec) conductor m

cone [kəun] n cono; (pine cone) piña; (for ice cream) cucurucho

confectioner [kən'fɛkʃənə^r] n (of cakes) pastelero(-a); (of sweets) confitero(-a); **~'s (shop)** n pastelería; confitería

confectionery [kən'fɛkʃənrɪ] n pasteles mpl; dulces mpl

confer [kən'fə:^r] vt: **to ~ (on)** otorgar (a) ▷ vi conferenciar; **to ~ (with sb about sth)** consultar (con algn sobre algo)

conference ['kɒnfərns] n (meeting) reunión f; (convention) congreso; **to be in ~** estar en una reunión

confess [kən'fɛs] vt confesar ▷ vi confesar; (Rel) confesarse

confession [kən'fɛʃən] n confesión f

confessional [kən'fɛʃənl] n confesionario

confessor [kən'fɛsə^r] n confesor m

confetti [kən'fɛtɪ] n confeti m

confide [kən'faɪd] vi: **to ~ in** confiar en

confidence ['kɒnfɪdns] n (gen: also: **self-~**) confianza; (secret) confidencia; **in ~** (speak, write) en confianza; **to have (every) ~ that** estar seguro or confiado de que; **motion of no ~** moción f de censura; **to tell sb sth in strict ~** decir algo a algn de manera confidencial

confidence trick n timo

confident ['kɒnfɪdənt] adj seguro de sí mismo

confidential [kɒnfɪ'dɛnʃəl] adj confidencial; (secretary) de confianza

confidentiality [kɒnfɪdɛnʃɪ'ælɪtɪ] n confidencialidad f

confine [kən'faɪn] vt (limit) limitar; (shut up) encerrar; **to ~ o.s. to doing sth** limitarse a hacer algo

confined [kən'faɪnd] adj (space) reducido

confinement [kən'faɪnmənt] n (prison) reclusión f; (Med) parto; **in solitary ~** incomunicado

confines ['kɒnfaɪnz] npl confines mpl

confirm [kən'fə:m] vt confirmar

confirmation [kɒnfə'meɪʃən] n confirmación f

confirmed [kən'fə:md] adj empedernido

confiscate ['kɒnfɪskeɪt] vt confiscar

conflict ['kɒnflɪkt] n conflicto ▷ vi [kən'flɪkt] (opinions) estar reñido; (reports, evidence) contradecirse

conflicting [kən'flɪktɪŋ] adj (reports, evidence, opinions) contradictorio

conform [kən'fɔ:m] vi: **to ~ to** (laws) someterse a; (usages, mores) amoldarse a; (standards) ajustarse a

confound [kən'faund] vt confundir; (amaze) pasmar

confront [kən'frʌnt] vt (problems) hacer frente a; (enemy, danger) enfrentarse con

confrontation [kɒnfrən'teɪʃən] n enfrentamiento, confrontación f

confuse [kən'fju:z] vt (perplex) desconcertar; (mix up) confundir; (complicate) complicar

confused [kən'fju:zd] adj confuso; (person) desconcertado; **to get ~** desconcertarse; (muddled up) hacerse un lío

confusing [kən'fju:zɪŋ] adj confuso

confusion [kən'fju:ʒən] n confusión f

congeal [kən'dʒi:l] vi coagularse

congenial [kən'dʒi:nɪəl] adj agradable

congested [kən'dʒɛstɪd] adj (gen) atestado; (telephone lines) saturado

congestion [kən'dʒɛstʃən] n congestión f

conglomerate [kən'glɒmərət] n (Comm, Geo) conglomerado

congratulate [kən'grætjuleɪt] vt felicitar

congratulations [kəngrætjuˈleɪʃənz] npl: **~ (on)** felicitaciones fpl (por); **~!** ¡enhorabuena!, ¡felicidades!

congregate ['kɒngrɪgeɪt] vi congregarse

congregation [kɒngrɪ'geɪʃən] n (in church) fieles mpl

congress ['kɒngrɛs] n congreso; (US Pol): **C~** el Congreso (de los Estados Unidos); ver nota

> ● **CONGRESS**
> ●
> ● En el Congreso de los Estados Unidos
> ● (Congress) se elaboran y aprueban las leyes
> ● federales. Consta de dos cámaras: la
> ● Cámara de Representantes ("House of
> ● Representatives"), cuyos 435 miembros
> ● son elegidos cada dos años por voto
> ● popular directo y en número
> ● proporcional a los habitantes de cada
> ● estado, y el Senado ("Senate"), con 100
> ● senadores ("senators"), 2 por estado,
> ● de los que un tercio se elige cada dos años
> ● y el resto cada seis.

congressman ['kɒngrɛsmən] n (US) diputado, miembro del Congreso

congresswoman ['kɒngrɛswumən] n (US) diputada, miembro f del Congreso

conifer ['kɒnɪfə^r] n conífera

conjecture [kən'dʒɛktʃə^r] n conjetura

conjugate ['kɒndʒugeɪt] vt conjugar

conjugation [kɒndʒə'geɪʃən] n conjugación f

conjunction [kən'dʒʌŋkʃən] n conjunción f; **in ~ with** junto con

conjunctivitis [kəndʒʌŋktɪ'vaɪtɪs] n conjuntivitis f

conjure [ˈkʌndʒə^r] vi hacer juegos de manos; **conjure up** vt (ghost, spirit) hacer aparecer; (memories) evocar

conjurer ['kʌndʒərə^r] n ilusionista m/f

conk out [kɒŋk-] vi (inf) estropearse, fastidiarse, descomponerse (LAm)

con man n timador m

connect [kə'nɛkt] vt juntar, unir; (Elec) conectar; (pipes) empalmar; (fig) relacionar, asociar ▷ vi: **to ~ with** (train) enlazar con; **to be ~ed with** (associated) estar relacionado con; (related) estar emparentado con; **I am**

trying to ~ you (Tel) estoy intentando ponerle al habla
connecting flight n vuelo m de enlace
connection [kəˈnekʃən] n juntura, unión f; (Elec) conexión f; (Tech) empalme m; (Rail) enlace m; (Tel) comunicación f; (fig) relación f; **what is the ~ between them?** ¿qué relación hay entre ellos?; **in ~ with** con respecto a, en relación a; **she has many business ~s** tiene muchos contactos profesionales; **to miss/make a ~** perder/ coger el enlace
connive [kəˈnaɪv] vi: **to ~ at** hacer la vista gorda a
connotation [kɒnəˈteɪʃən] n connotación f
conquer [ˈkɒŋkəʳ] vt (territory) conquistar; (enemy, feelings) vencer
conquest [ˈkɒŋkwest] n conquista
cons [kɒnz] npl see **convenience, pro**
conscience [ˈkɒnʃəns] n conciencia; **in all ~** en conciencia
conscientious [kɒnʃɪˈenʃəs] adj concienzudo; (objection) de conciencia
conscious [ˈkɒnʃəs] adj consciente; (deliberate: insult, error) premeditado, intencionado; **to become ~ of sth/that** darse cuenta de algo/ de que
consciousness [ˈkɒnʃəsnɪs] n conciencia; (Med) conocimiento
conscript [ˈkɒnskrɪpt] n recluta m/f
conscription [kənˈskrɪpʃən] n servicio militar (obligatorio)
consecrate [ˈkɒnsɪkreɪt] vt consagrar
consecutive [kənˈsekjʊtɪv] adj consecutivo; **on 3 ~ occasions** en 3 ocasiones consecutivas
consensus [kənˈsensəs] n consenso; **the ~ of opinion** el consenso general
consent [kənˈsent] n consentimiento ▷ vi: **to ~ to** consentir en; **by common ~** de común acuerdo
consequence [ˈkɒnsɪkwəns] n consecuencia; **in ~** por consiguiente
consequently [ˈkɒnsɪkwəntlɪ] adv por consiguiente
conservation [kɒnsəˈveɪʃən] n conservación f; (of nature) conservación, protección f
conservationist [kɒnsəˈveɪʃnɪst] n conservacionista f
conservative [kənˈsəːvətɪv] adj conservador(a); (cautious) moderado; **C~** adj, n (Brit Pol) conservador(a) m(f); **the C~ Party** el partido conservador (británico)
conservatory [kənˈsəːvətrɪ] n (greenhouse) invernadero
conserve [kənˈsəːv] vt conservar ▷ n conserva
consider [kənˈsɪdəʳ] vt considerar; (take into account) tener en cuenta; (study) estudiar, examinar; **to ~ doing sth** pensar en (la posibilidad de) hacer algo; **all things ~ed** pensándolo bien; **~ yourself lucky** ¡date por satisfecho!

considerable [kənˈsɪdərəbl] adj considerable
considerably [kənˈsɪdərəblɪ] adv bastante, considerablemente
considerate [kənˈsɪdərɪt] adj considerado
consideration [kənsɪdəˈreɪʃən] n consideración f; (reward) retribución f; **to be under ~** estar estudiándose; **my first ~ is my family** mi primera consideración es mi familia
considered [kənˈsɪdəd] adj: **it's my ~ opinion that ...** después de haber reflexionado mucho, pienso que ...
considering [kənˈsɪdərɪŋ] prep: **~ (that)** teniendo en cuenta (que)
consign [kənˈsaɪn] vt consignar
consignment [kənˈsaɪnmənt] n envío
consist [kənˈsɪst] vi: **to ~ of** consistir en
consistency [kənˈsɪstənsɪ] n (of person etc) consecuencia, coherencia; (thickness) consistencia
consistent [kənˈsɪstənt] adj (person, argument) consecuente, coherente; (results) constante
consolation [kɒnsəˈleɪʃən] n consuelo
console [kənˈsəul] vt consolar ▷ n [ˈkɒnsəul] (control panel) consola
consolidate [kənˈsɒlɪdeɪt] vt consolidar
consonant [ˈkɒnsənənt] n consonante f
consortium [kənˈsɔːtɪəm] n consorcio
conspicuous [kənˈspɪkjuəs] adj (visible) visible; (garish etc) llamativo; (outstanding) notable; **to make o.s. ~** llamar la atención
conspiracy [kənˈspɪrəsɪ] n conjura, complot m
constable [ˈkʌnstəbl] n (Brit) agente m/f (de policía); **chief ~ =** jefe m/f de policía
constabulary [kənˈstæbjulərɪ] n ≈ policía
constant [ˈkɒnstənt] adj (gen) constante; (loyal) leal, fiel
constantly [ˈkɒnstəntlɪ] adv constantemente
constellation [kɒnstəˈleɪʃən] n constelación f
consternation [kɒnstəˈneɪʃən] n consternación f
constipated [ˈkɒnstɪpeɪtəd] adj estreñido
constipation [kɒnstɪˈpeɪʃən] n estreñimiento
constituency [kənˈstɪtjuənsɪ] n (Pol) distrito electoral; (people) electorado
constituent [kənˈstɪtjuənt] n (Pol) elector(a) m(f); (part) componente m
constitute [ˈkɒnstɪtjuːt] vt constituir
constitution [kɒnstɪˈtjuːʃən] n constitución f
constitutional [kɒnstɪˈtjuːʃənl] adj constitucional; **~ monarchy** monarquía constitucional
constraint [kənˈstreɪnt] n (force) fuerza; (limit) restricción f; (restraint) reserva; (embarrassment) cohibición f
construct [kənˈstrʌkt] vt construir

construction [kənˈstrʌkʃən] n construcción f; (fig: interpretation) interpretación f; **under ~** en construcción

constructive [kənˈstrʌktɪv] adj constructivo

construe [kənˈstruː] vt interpretar

consul [ˈkɒnsl] n cónsul m/f

consulate [ˈkɒnsjulɪt] n consulado

consult [kənˈsʌlt] vt, vi consultar; **to ~ sb (about sth)** consultar a algn (sobre algo)

consultancy [kənˈsʌltənsɪ] n (Comm) consultoría; (Med) puesto de especialista

consultant [kənˈsʌltənt] n (Brit Med) especialista m/f; (other specialist) asesor(a) m(f), consultor(a) m(f)

consultation [kɒnsəlˈteɪʃən] n consulta; **in ~ with** en consulta con

consulting room n (Brit) consulta, consultorio

consume [kənˈsjuːm] vt (eat) comerse; (drink) beberse; (fire etc) consumir; (Comm) consumir

consumer [kənˈsjuːməʳ] n (of electricity, gas etc) consumidor(a) m(f)

consumer goods npl bienes mpl de consumo

consumer society n sociedad f de consumo

consumer watchdog n organización f protectora del consumidor

consummate [ˈkɒnsʌmeɪt] vt consumar

consumption [kənˈsʌmpʃən] n consumo; (Med) tisis f; **not fit for human ~** no apto para el consumo humano

cont. abbr (= continued) sigue

contact [ˈkɒntækt] n contacto; (person: pej) enchufe m ▷ vt ponerse en contacto con; **~ lenses** npl lentes fpl de contacto; **to be in ~ with sb/sth** estar en contacto con algn/algo; **business ~s** relaciones fpl comerciales

contagious [kənˈteɪdʒəs] adj contagioso

contain [kənˈteɪn] vt contener; **to ~ o.s.** contenerse

container [kənˈteɪnəʳ] n recipiente m; (for shipping etc) contenedor m

container ship n buque m contenedor, portacontenedores m inv

contaminate [kənˈtæmɪneɪt] vt contaminar

contamination [kəntæmɪˈneɪʃən] n contaminación f

cont'd abbr (= continued) sigue

contemplate [ˈkɒntəmpleɪt] vt (gen) contemplar; (reflect upon) considerar; (intend) pensar

contemplation [kɒntəmˈpleɪʃən] n contemplación f

contemporary [kənˈtempərərɪ] adj, n (of the same age) contemporáneo(-a) m(f)

contempt [kənˈtempt] n desprecio; **~ of court** (Law) desacato (a los tribunales or a la justicia)

contemptuous [kənˈtemptjuəs] adj desdeñoso

contend [kənˈtend] vt (argue) afirmar ▷ vi: **to ~ with/for** luchar contra/por; **he has a lot to ~ with** tiene que hacer frente a muchos problemas

contender [kənˈtendəʳ] n (Sport) contendiente m/f

content [kənˈtent] adj (happy) contento; (satisfied) satisfecho ▷ vt contentar; satisfacer ▷ n [ˈkɒntent] contenido; **contents** npl contenido msg; **(table of) ~s** índice m de materias; (in magazine) sumario; **to be ~ with** conformarse con; **to ~ o.s. with/with doing sth** conformarse con algo/con hacer algo

contented [kənˈtentɪd] adj contento; satisfecho

contention [kənˈtenʃən] n discusión f; (belief) argumento; **bone of ~** manzana de la discordia

contentious [kənˈtenʃəs] adj discutible

contentment [kənˈtentmənt] n satisfacción f

contest [ˈkɒntest] n contienda; (competition) concurso ▷ vt [kənˈtest] (dispute) impugnar; (Law) disputar, litigar; (Pol: election, seat) presentarse como candidato(-a) a

contestant [kənˈtestənt] n concursante m/f; (in fight) contendiente m/f

context [ˈkɒntekst] n contexto; **in/out of ~** en/fuera de contexto

continent [ˈkɒntɪnənt] n continente m; **the C~** (Brit) el continente europeo, Europa; **on the C~** en el continente europeo, en Europa

continental [kɒntɪˈnentl] adj continental; (Brit: European) europeo

continental breakfast n desayuno estilo europeo

continental quilt n (Brit) edredón m

contingency [kənˈtɪndʒənsɪ] n contingencia

contingent [kənˈtɪndʒənt] n (group) representación f

continual [kənˈtɪnjuəl] adj continuo

continually [kənˈtɪnjuəlɪ] adv continuamente

continuation [kəntɪnjuˈeɪʃən] n prolongación f; (after interruption) reanudación f; (of story, episode) continuación f

continue [kənˈtɪnjuː] vi, vt seguir, continuar; **~d on page 10** sigue en la página 10

continuing education [kənˈtɪnjuɪŋ-] n educación f continua de adultos

continuity [kɒntɪˈnjuɪtɪ] n (also Cine) continuidad f

continuous [kənˈtɪnjuəs] adj continuo; **~ performance** (Cine) sesión f continua

continuous assessment n (Brit) evaluación f continua

continuously [kənˈtɪnjuəslɪ] adv continuamente

contort [kənˈtɔːt] vt retorcer

contour [ˈkɒntuəʳ] n contorno; (also: **~ line**) curva de nivel

contraband [ˈkɒntrəbænd] n contrabando ▷ adj de contrabando

contraception [kɒntrəˈsɛpʃən] n
contracepción f
contraceptive [kɒntrəˈsɛptɪv] adj, n
anticonceptivo
contract [n ˈkɒntrækt, vb kənˈtrækt] n
contrato ▷ cpd [ˈkɒntrækt] (price, date)
contratado, de contrato; (work) bajo contrato
▷ vi (Comm): **to ~ to do sth** comprometerse
por contrato a hacer algo; (become smaller)
contraerse, encogerse ▷ vt contraer; **to be
under ~ to do sth** estar bajo contrato para
hacer algo; **~ of employment** or **of service**
contrato de trabajo; **contract in** vi tomar
parte; **contract out** vi: **to ~ out (of)** optar
por no tomar parte (en); **to ~ out of a
pension scheme** dejar de cotizar en un plan
de jubilación
contraction [kənˈtrækʃən] n contracción f
contractor [kənˈtræktəʳ] n contratista m/f
contractual [kənˈtræktjuəl] adj contractual
contradict [kɒntrəˈdɪkt] vt (declare to be wrong)
desmentir; (be contrary to) contradecir
contradiction [kɒntrəˈdɪkʃən] n
contradicción f; **to be in ~ with** contradecir
contradictory [kɒntrəˈdɪktərɪ] adj
(statements) contradictorio; **to be ~ to**
contradecir
contralto [kənˈtræltəu] n contralto f
contraption [kənˈtræpʃən] n (pej) artilugio m
contrary¹ [ˈkɒntrərɪ] adj contrario ▷ n lo
contrario; **on the ~** al contrario; **~ to what
we thought** al contrario de lo que
pensábamos; **unless you hear to the ~** a no
ser que le digan lo contrario
contrary² [kənˈtrɛərɪ] adj (perverse) terco
contrast [ˈkɒntrɑːst] n contraste m ▷ vt [kə
nˈtrɑːst] contrastar; **in ~ to** or **with a**
diferencia de
contravene [kɒntrəˈviːn] vt contravenir
contravention [kɒntrəˈvɛnʃən] n: **~ (of)**
contravención f (de)
contribute [kənˈtrɪbjuːt] vi contribuir ▷ vt:
to ~ to (gen) contribuir a; (newspaper)
colaborar en; (discussion) intervenir en
contribution [kɒntrɪˈbjuːʃən] n (money)
contribución f; (to debate) intervención f; (to
journal) colaboración f
contributor [kənˈtrɪbjutəʳ] n (to newspaper)
colaborador(a) m(f)
contrive [kənˈtraɪv] vt (invent) idear ▷ vi: **to ~
to do** lograr hacer; (try) procurar hacer
control [kənˈtrəul] vt controlar; (traffic etc)
dirigir; (machinery) manejar; (temper)
dominar; (disease, fire) dominar, controlar ▷ n
(command) control m; (of car) conducción f;
(check) freno; **controls** npl (of vehicle)
instrumentos mpl de mando; (of radio)
controles mpl; (governmental) medidas fpl de
control; **to ~ o.s.** controlarse, dominarse;
everything is under ~ todo está bajo
control; **to be in ~ of** estar al mando de; **the
car went out of ~** perdió el control del coche

control panel n (on aircraft, ship, TV etc) tablero
de instrumentos
control room n (Naut, Mil) sala de mandos;
(Radio, TV) sala de control
control tower n (Aviat) torre f de control
controversial [kɒntrəˈvəːʃl] adj polémico
controversy [ˈkɒntrəvəːsɪ] n polémica
convalesce [kɒnvəˈlɛs] vi convalecer
convector [kənˈvɛktəʳ] n calentador m de
convección
convene [kənˈviːn] vt (meeting) convocar ▷ vi
reunirse
convenience [kənˈviːnɪəns] n (comfort)
comodidad f; (advantage) ventaja; **at your
earliest ~** (Comm) tan pronto como le sea
posible; **all modern ~s** (Brit) todo confort
convenient [kənˈviːnɪənt] adj (useful) útil;
(place) conveniente; (time) oportuno; **if it is ~
for you** si le viene bien
convent [ˈkɒnvənt] n convento
convention [kənˈvɛnʃən] n convención f;
(meeting) asamblea
conventional [kənˈvɛnʃənl] adj
convencional
conversant [kənˈvəːsnt] adj: **to be ~ with**
estar familiarizado con
conversation [kɒnvəˈseɪʃən] n
conversación f
converse [ˈkɒnvəːs] n inversa ▷ vi [kənˈvəːs]
conversar; **to ~ (with sb about sth)**
conversar or platicar (LAm) (con algn de algo)
conversely [kɒnˈvəːslɪ] adv a la inversa
conversion [kənˈvəːʃən] n conversión f;
(house conversion) reforma, remodelación f
convert [kənˈvəːt] vt (Rel, Comm) convertir;
(alter) transformar ▷ n [ˈkɒnvəːt] converso(-a)
convertible [kənˈvəːtəbl] adj convertible ▷ n
descapotable m; **~ loan stock** obligaciones fpl
convertibles
convey [kənˈveɪ] vt transportar; (thanks)
comunicar; (idea) expresar
conveyancing [kənˈveɪənsɪŋ] n (Law)
preparación f de escrituras de traspaso
conveyor belt [kənˈveɪəʳ-] n cinta
transportadora
convict [kənˈvɪkt] vt (gen) condenar; (find
guilty) declarar culpable a ▷ n [ˈkɒnvɪkt]
presidiario(-a)
conviction [kənˈvɪkʃən] n condena; (belief)
creencia, convicción f
convince [kənˈvɪns] vt convencer; **to ~ sb (of
sth/that)** convencer a algn (de algo/de que)
convinced [kənˈvɪnst] adj: **~ of/that**
convencido de/de que
convincing [kənˈvɪnsɪŋ] adj convincente
convoluted [ˈkɒnvəluːtɪd] adj (argument etc)
enrevesado; (shape) enrollado, enroscado
convoy [ˈkɒnvɔɪ] n convoy m
convulse [kənˈvʌls] vt convulsionar; **to be
~d with laughter** dislocarse de risa
convulsion [kənˈvʌlʃən] n convulsión f
coo [kuː] vi arrullar

cook [kuk] vt cocinar; (*stew etc*) guisar; (*meal*) preparar ▷ vi hacerse; (*person*) cocinar ▷ n cocinero(-a); **cook up** vt (*inf: excuse, story*) inventar

cookbook ['kukbuk] n libro de cocina

cooker ['kukə^r] n cocina

cookery ['kukərɪ] n cocina

cookery book n (*Brit*) = **cookbook**

cookie ['kukɪ] n (*US*) galleta; (*Comput*) cookie f

cooking ['kukɪŋ] n cocina ▷ cpd (*apples*) para cocinar; (*utensils, salt, foil*) de cocina

cool [ku:l] adj fresco; (*not hot*) tibio; (*not afraid*) tranquilo; (*unfriendly*) frío ▷ vt enfriar ▷ vi enfriarse; **it is ~** (*weather*) hace fresco; **to keep sth ~** or **in a ~ place** conservar algo fresco or en un sitio fresco; **cool down** vi enfriarse; (*fig: person, situation*) calmarse; **cool off** vi (*become calmer*) calmarse, apaciguarse; (*lose enthusiasm*) perder (el) interés, enfriarse

coolant ['ku:lənt] n refrigerante m

coop [ku:p] n gallinero ▷ vt: **to ~ up** (*fig*) encerrar

co-op ['kəuɔp] n abbr (= *cooperative (society)*) cooperativa

cooperate [kəu'ɔpəreɪt] vi cooperar, colaborar; **will he ~?** ¿querrá cooperar?

cooperation [kəuɔpə'reɪʃən] n cooperación f, colaboración f

cooperative [kəu'ɔpərətɪv] adj cooperativo; (*person*) dispuesto a colaborar ▷ n cooperativa

coordinate [kəu'ɔ:dɪneɪt] vt coordinar ▷ n [kəu'ɔ:dɪnət] (*Math*) coordenada; **coordinates** npl (*clothes*) coordinados mpl

coordination [kəuɔ:dɪ'neɪʃən] n coordinación f

co-ownership [kəu'əunəʃɪp] n copropiedad f

cop [kɔp] n (*inf*) poli m

cope [kəup] vi: **to ~ with** poder con; (*problem*) hacer frente a

copier ['kɔpɪə^r] n (*photocopier*) (foto)copiadora

copper ['kɔpə^r] n (*metal*) cobre m; (*inf: policeman*) poli m; **coppers** npl perras fpl; (*small change*) calderilla

copy ['kɔpɪ] n copia; (*of book*) ejemplar m; (*of magazine*) número; (*material: for printing*) original m ▷ vt (*also Comput*) copiar; (*imitate*) copiar, imitar; **to make good ~** (*fig*) ser una noticia de interés; **rough ~** borrador m; **fair ~** copia en limpio; **copy out** vt copiar

copycat ['kɔpɪkæt] n (*pej*) imitador(a) m(f)

copyright ['kɔpɪraɪt] n derechos mpl de autor

coral ['kɔrəl] n coral m

coral reef n arrecife m (de coral)

cord [kɔ:d] n cuerda; (*Elec*) cable m; (*fabric*) pana; **cords** npl (*trousers*) pantalones mpl de pana

cordial ['kɔ:dɪəl] adj cordial ▷ n cordial m

cordless ['kɔ:dlɪs] adj sin hilos; **~ telephone** teléfono inalámbrico

cordon ['kɔ:dn] n cordón m; **cordon off** vt acordonar

corduroy ['kɔ:dərɔɪ] n pana

core [kɔ:^r] n (*of earth, nuclear reactor*) centro, núcleo; (*of fruit*) corazón m; (*of problem etc*) esencia, meollo ▷ vt quitar el corazón de

coriander [kɔrɪ'ændə^r] n culantro, cilantro

cork [kɔ:k] n corcho; (*tree*) alcornoque m

corkscrew ['kɔ:kskru:] n sacacorchos m inv

corn [kɔ:n] n (*Brit: wheat*) trigo; (*US: maize*) maíz m, choclo (*LAm*); (*on foot*) callo; **~ on the cob** (*Culin*) maíz en la mazorca

corned beef ['kɔ:nd-] n carne f de vaca acecinada

corner ['kɔ:nə^r] n (*outside*) esquina; (*inside*) rincón m; (*in road*) curva; (*Football*) córner m, saque m de esquina ▷ vt (*trap*) arrinconar; (*Comm*) acaparar ▷ vi (*in car*) tomar las curvas; **to cut ~s** atajar

corner shop n (*Brit*) tienda de la esquina

cornerstone ['kɔ:nəstəun] n piedra angular

cornet ['kɔ:nɪt] n (*Mus*) corneta; (*Brit: of ice cream*) cucurucho

cornflakes ['kɔ:nfleɪks] npl copos mpl de maíz, cornflakes mpl

cornflour ['kɔ:nflauə^r] n (*Brit*) harina de maíz

cornstarch ['kɔ:nsta:tʃ] n (*US*) = **cornflour**

Cornwall ['kɔ:nwəl] n Cornualles m

corny ['kɔ:nɪ] adj (*inf*) gastado

coronary ['kɔrənərɪ] n: **~ (thrombosis)** infarto

coronation [kɔrə'neɪʃən] n coronación f

coroner ['kɔrənə^r] n juez m/f de instrucción

corporal ['kɔ:pərl] n cabo ▷ adj: **~ punishment** castigo corporal

corporate ['kɔ:pərɪt] adj (*action, ownership*) colectivo; (*finance, image*) corporativo

corporation [kɔ:pə'reɪʃən] n (*of town*) ayuntamiento; (*Comm*) corporación f

corps [kɔ:^r] (*pl* **corps** [kɔ:z]) n cuerpo; **press ~** gabinete m de prensa

corpse [kɔ:ps] n cadáver m

correct [kə'rekt] adj correcto; (*accurate*) exacto ▷ vt corregir; **you are ~** tiene razón

correction [kə'rekʃən] n (*act*) corrección f; (*instance*) rectificación f; (*erasure*) tachadura

correlation [kɔrɪ'leɪʃən] n correlación f

correspond [kɔrɪs'pɔnd] vi: **to ~ (with)** (*write*) escribirse (con); (*be in accordance*) corresponder (con); (*be equivalent to*): **to ~ (to)** corresponder (a)

correspondence [kɔrɪs'pɔndəns] n correspondencia

correspondence course n curso por correspondencia

correspondent [kɔrɪs'pɔndənt] n corresponsal m/f

corresponding [kɔrɪs'pɔndɪŋ] adj correspondiente

corridor ['kɔrɪdɔ:^r] n pasillo

corroborate [kə'rɔbəreɪt] vt corroborar

corrode [kə'rəud] vt corroer ▷ vi corroerse

corrosion [kə'rəuʒən] n corrosión f

corrugated ['kɔrəgeɪtɪd] adj ondulado

corrugated iron n chapa ondulada

corrupt [kə'rʌpt] *adj* corrompido; *(person)* corrupto ▷ *vt* corromper; *(bribe)* sobornar; *(Comput: data)* degradar; **~ practices** *(dishonesty, bribery)* corrupción *f*

corruption [kə'rʌpʃən] *n* corrupción *f*; *(Comput: of data)* alteración *f*

corset ['kɔːsɪt] *n* faja; *(old-style)* corsé *m*

Corsica ['kɔːsɪkə] *n* Córcega

cortège [kɔː'teɪʒ] *n* cortejo, comitiva

cortisone ['kɔːtɪzəʊn] *n* cortisona

cosh [kɔʃ] *n* *(Brit)* cachiporra

cosmetic [kɒz'metɪk] *n* cosmético ▷ *adj* *(also fig)* cosmético

cosmetic surgery *n* cirugía *f* estética

cosmic ['kɒzmɪk] *adj* cósmico

cosmopolitan [kɒzmə'pɒlɪtn] *adj* cosmopolita

cosmos ['kɒzmɒs] *n* cosmos *m*

cosset ['kɒsɪt] *vt* mimar

cost [kɒst] *(pt, pp cost)* *n* *(gen)* coste *m*, costo, *(price)* precio; **costs** *npl* *(Law)* costas *fpl* ▷ *vi* costar, valer ▷ *vt* preparar el presupuesto de; **how much does it ~?** ¿cuánto cuesta?, ¿cuánto vale?; **what will it ~ to have it repaired?** ¿cuánto costará repararlo?; **the ~ of living** el coste *or* costo de la vida; **to ~ sb time/effort** costarle a algn tiempo/esfuerzo; **it ~ him his life** le costó la vida; **at all ~s** cueste lo que cueste

co-star ['kəʊstɑːʳ] *n* coprotagonista *m/f*

Costa Rica ['kɒstə'riːkə] *n* Costa Rica

Costa Rican ['kɒstə'riːkən] *adj, n* costarriqueño(-a) *m(f)*, costarricense *m/f*

cost-effective [kɒstɪ'fektɪv] *adj* *(Comm)* rentable

costly ['kɒstlɪ] *adj* *(expensive)* costoso

cost-of-living [kɒstəv'lɪvɪŋ] *adj:* **~ allowance** *n* plus *m* de carestía de vida; **~ index** *n* índice *m* del coste de vida

cost price *n* *(Brit)* precio de coste

costume ['kɒstjuːm] *n* traje *m*; *(Brit: also: swimming ~)* traje de baño

costume jewellery *n* bisutería

cosy, cozy (US) ['kəʊzɪ] *adj* cómodo, a gusto; *(room, atmosphere)* acogedor(a)

cot [kɒt] *n* *(Brit: child's bed)* cuna; *(US: folding bed)* cama plegable

cot death *n* muerte *f* en la cuna

Cotswolds ['kɒtswəʊldz] *npl* región de colinas del suroeste inglés

cottage ['kɒtɪdʒ] *n* casita de campo

cottage cheese *n* requesón *m*

cottage industry *n* industria artesanal

cotton ['kɒtn] *n* algodón *m*; *(thread)* hilo; **cotton on** *vi* *(inf):* **to ~ on (to sth)** caer en la cuenta (de algo)

cotton bud *n* *(Brit)* bastoncillo *m* de algodón

cotton candy *n* (US) algodón *m* (azucarado)

cotton wool *n* *(Brit)* algodón *m* (hidrófilo)

couch [kautʃ] *n* sofá *m*; *(in doctor's surgery)* camilla; *(psychiatrist's)* diván *m*

couchette [kuːʃet] *n* litera

couch potato *n* *(inf)* persona comodona que no se mueve en todo el día

cough [kɔf] *vi* toser ▷ *n* tos *f*; **cough up** *vt* escupir

cough drop *n* pastilla para la tos

cough mixture *n* jarabe *m* para la tos

could [kʊd] *pt of* **can**

couldn't ['kʊdnt] = **could not**

council ['kaʊnsl] *n* consejo; **city** *or* **town ~** ayuntamiento, consejo municipal; **C~ of Europe** Consejo de Europa

council estate *n* *(Brit)* barriada de viviendas sociales de alquiler

council house *n* *(Brit)* vivienda social de alquiler

councillor ['kaʊnsləʳ] *n* concejal *m/f*

council tax *n* *(Brit)* contribución *f* municipal *(dependiente del valor de la vivienda)*

counsel ['kaʊnsl] *n* *(advice)* consejo; *(lawyer)* abogado(-a) ▷ *vt* aconsejar; **~ for the defence/the prosecution** abogado(-a) defensor(a)/fiscal; **to ~ sth/sb to do sth** aconsejar algo/a algn que haga algo

counselling, (US) **counseling** *n* *(Psych)* asistencia *f* psicológica

counsellor, counselor (US) ['kaʊnsləʳ] *n* consejero(-a); *(US Law)* abogado(-a)

count [kaʊnt] *vt* *(gen)* contar; *(include)* incluir ▷ *vi* contar ▷ *n* cuenta; *(of votes)* escrutinio; *(nobleman)* conde *m*; *(sum)* total *m*, suma; **to ~ the cost of** calcular el coste de; **not ~ing the children** niños aparte; **10 ~ing him** diez incluyéndole a él, diez con él; **~ yourself lucky** date por satisfecho; **that doesn't ~!** ¡eso no vale!; **to ~ (up) to 10** contar hasta diez; **it ~s for very little** cuenta poco; **to keep ~ of sth** llevar la cuenta de algo; **count in** *(inf) vt:* **to ~ sb in on sth** contar con algn para algo; **count on** *vt fus* contar con; **to ~ on doing sth** contar con hacer algo; **count up** *vt* contar

countdown ['kaʊntdaʊn] *n* cuenta atrás

countenance ['kaʊntɪnəns] *n* semblante *m*, rostro ▷ *vt* *(tolerate)* aprobar, consentir

counter ['kaʊntəʳ] *n* *(in shop)* mostrador *m*; *(position: in post office, bank)* ventanilla; *(in games)* ficha; *(Tech)* contador *m* ▷ *vt* contrarrestar; *(blow)* parar; *(attack)* contestar a ▷ *adv:* **~ to** contrario a; **to buy under the ~** *(fig)* comprar de estraperlo *or* bajo mano; **to ~ sth with sth/by doing sth** contestar algo con algo/haciendo algo

counteract ['kaʊntər'ækt] *vt* contrarrestar

counterattack ['kaʊntərə'tæk] *n* contraataque *m* ▷ *vi* contraatacar

counter-clockwise ['kaʊntə'klɒkwaɪz] *adv* en sentido contrario al de las agujas del reloj

counterfeit ['kaʊntəfɪt] *n* falsificación *f* ▷ *vt* falsificar ▷ *adj* falso, falsificado

counterfoil ['kaʊntəfɔɪl] *n* *(Brit)* matriz *f*, talón *m*

countermand ['kaʊntəmɑːnd] *vt* revocar

counterpart ['kauntəpɑːt] n (of person) homólogo(-a)

countersign ['kauntəsaın] vt ratificar, refrendar

counterterrorism [kauntə'tɛrərɪzəm] n antiterrorismo

countess ['kauntıs] n condesa

countless ['kauntlıs] adj innumerable

country ['kʌntrı] n país m; (native land) patria; (as opposed to town) campo; (region) región f, tierra; **in the ~** en el campo; **mountainous ~** región f montañosa

country and western, country and western music n música country

country dancing n (Brit) baile m regional

country house n casa de campo

countryman ['kʌntrımən] n (national) compatriota m; (rural) hombre m del campo

countryside ['kʌntrısaıd] n campo

countrywide ['kʌntrı'waıd] adj nacional ▷ adv por todo el país

county ['kauntı] n condado; see also **district council**

county council n (Brit) ≈ diputación f provincial

coup [kuː] n (pl **coups** [kuːz]) n golpe m; (triumph) éxito; (also: **~ d'état**) golpe de estado

couple ['kʌpl] n (of things) par m; (of people) pareja; (married couple) matrimonio ▷ vt (ideas, names) unir, juntar; (machinery) acoplar; **a ~ of** un par de

coupon ['kuːpɔn] n cupón m; (voucher) valé m; (pools coupon) boleto (de quiniela)

courage ['kʌrɪdʒ] n valor m, valentía

courageous [kə'reɪdʒəs] adj valiente

courgette [kuə'ʒɛt] n (Brit) calabacín m

courier ['kurɪər] n mensajero(-a); (diplomatic) correo; (for tourists) guía m/f (de turismo)

course [kɔːs] n (direction) dirección f; (of river) curso; (Scol) curso; (of ship) rumbo; (fig) proceder m; (Golf) campo; (part of meal) plato; **of ~** adv desde luego, naturalmente; **of ~!** ¡claro!, ¡cómo no! (LAm); **(no) of ~ not!** ¡claro que no!, ¡por supuesto que no!; **in due ~** a su debido tiempo; **in the ~ of the next few days** durante los próximos días; **we have no other ~ but to ...** no tenemos más remedio que ...; **there are 2 ~s open to us** se nos ofrecen dos posibilidades; **the best ~ would be to ...** lo mejor sería ...; **~ of treatment** (Med) tratamiento

court [kɔːt] n (royal) corte f; (Law) tribunal m, juzgado; (Tennis) pista, cancha (LAm) ▷ vt (woman) cortejar; (fig: favour, popularity) solicitar, buscar; (: death, disaster, danger etc) buscar; **to take to ~** demandar; **~ of appeal** tribunal m de apelación

courteous ['kəːtıəs] adj cortés

courtesy ['kəːtəsı] n cortesía; **by ~ of** (por) cortesía de

courtesy bus, courtesy coach n autobús m gratuito

courthouse ['kɔːthaus] n (US) palacio de justicia

courtier ['kɔːtɪər] n cortesano

court martial (pl **courts martial**) ['kɔːt'mɑːʃəl] n consejo de guerra ▷ vt someter a consejo de guerra

courtroom ['kɔːtrum] n sala de justicia

courtyard ['kɔːtjɑːd] n patio

cousin ['kʌzn] n primo(-a); **first ~** primo(-a) carnal

cove [kəuv] n cala, ensenada

covenant ['kʌvənənt] n convenio ▷ vt: **to ~ £20 per year to a charity** concertar el pago de veinte libras anuales a una sociedad benéfica

cover ['kʌvər] vt cubrir; (with lid) tapar; (chairs etc) revestir; (distance) cubrir, recorrer; (include) abarcar; (protect) abrigar; (journalist) investigar; (issues) tratar ▷ n cubierta; (lid) tapa; (for chair etc) funda; (for bed) manta/sábana; (envelope) sobre m; (of magazine) portada; (shelter) abrigo; (insurance) cobertura; **to take ~** (shelter) protegerse, resguardarse; **under ~** (indoors) bajo techo; **under ~ of darkness** al amparo de la oscuridad; **under separate ~** (Comm) por separado; **£10 will ~ everything** con diez libras cubriremos todos los gastos; **cover up** vt (child, object) cubrir completamente, tapar; (fig: hide: truth, facts) ocultar ▷ vi: **to ~ up for sb** (fig) encubrir a algn

coverage ['kʌvərɪdʒ] n alcance m; (in media) cobertura informativa; (Insurance) cobertura

cover charge n precio del cubierto

covering ['kʌvərɪŋ] n cubierta, envoltura

covering letter, cover letter (US) n carta de explicación

cover note n (Insurance) póliza provisional

covert ['kəuvət] adj (secret) secreto, encubierto; (dissembled) furtivo

cover-up ['kʌvərʌp] n encubrimiento

covet ['kʌvɪt] vt codiciar

cow [kau] n vaca ▷ vt intimidar

coward ['kauəd] n cobarde m/f

cowardice ['kauədıs] n cobardía

cowardly ['kauədlı] adj cobarde

cowboy ['kaubɔı] n vaquero

cower ['kauər] vi encogerse (de miedo)

coy [kɔı] adj tímido

cozy ['kəuzı] adj (US) = **cosy**

CPA n abbr (US) = **certified public accountant**

CPI n abbr (= Consumer Price Index) IPC m

CPU n abbr = **central processing unit**

crab [kræb] n cangrejo

crab apple n manzana silvestre

crack [kræk] n grieta; (noise) crujido; (: of whip) chasquido; (joke) chiste m; (inf: drug) crack m; (attempt): **to have a ~ at sth** intentar algo ▷ vt agrietar, romper; (nut) cascar; (safe) forzar; (whip etc) chasquear; (knuckles) crujir; (joke) contar; (case: solve) resolver; (code) descifrar ▷ adj (athlete) de primera clase;

to ~ jokes (inf) bromear; **crack down on** vt fus reprimir fuertemente, adoptar medidas severas contra; **crack up** vi sufrir una crisis nerviosa

cracked [krækt] adj (cup, window) rajado; (wall) resquebrajado

cracker ['krækər] n (biscuit) galleta salada, cráquer m; (Christmas cracker) petardo sorpresa

crackle ['krækl] vi crepitar

crackpot ['krækpɒt] (inf) n pirado(-a) ▷ adj de pirado

cradle ['kreɪdl] n cuna ▷ vt (child) mecer, acunar; (object) abrazar

craft [krɑːft] n (skill) arte m; (trade) oficio; (cunning) astucia; (boat) embarcación f

craftsman ['krɑːftsmən] n artesano

craftsmanship ['krɑːftsmənʃip] n destreza

crafty ['krɑːftɪ] adj astuto

crag [kræg] n peñasco

cram [kræm] vt (fill): **to ~ sth with** llenar algo (a reventar) de; (put): **to ~ sth into** meter algo a la fuerza en ▷ vi (for exams) empollar

cramp [kræmp] n (Med) calambre m; (Tech) grapa ▷ vt (limit) poner trabas a

cramped [kræmpt] adj apretado; (room) minúsculo

cranberry ['krænbərɪ] n arándano agrio

crane [kreɪn] n (Tech) grúa; (bird) grulla ▷ vt, vi: **to ~ forward, to ~ one's neck** estirar el cuello

crank [kræŋk] n manivela; (person) chiflado(-a)

crankshaft ['kræŋkʃɑːft] n cigüeñal m

cranky ['kræŋkɪ] adj (eccentric) maniático; (bad-tempered) de mal genio

cranny ['krænɪ] n see **nook**

crap [kræp] n (inf!) mierda (!)

crash [kræʃ] n (noise) estrépito; (of cars, plane) accidente m; (of business) quiebra; (Stock Exchange) crac m ▷ vt (plane) estrellar ▷ vi (plane) estrellarse; (two cars) chocar; (fall noisily) caer con estrépito; **he ~ed the car into a wall** estrelló el coche contra una pared or tapia; **crash out** vi (inf: sleep) quedarse frito; (from competition) quedar eliminado

crash barrier n (Aut) barrera de protección

crash course n curso acelerado

crash helmet n casco (protector)

crash landing n aterrizaje m forzoso

crass [kræs] adj grosero, maleduçado

crate [kreɪt] n cajón m de embalaje; (for bottles) caja; (inf) armatoste m

crater ['kreɪtər] n cráter m

crave [kreɪv] vt, vi: **to ~ (for)** ansiar, anhelar

crawl [krɔːl] vi (drag o.s.) arrastrarse; (child) andar a gatas, gatear; (vehicle) avanzar (lentamente); (inf): **to ~ to sb** dar coba a algn, hacerle la pelota a algn ▷ n (Swimming) crol m

crawler lane [krɔːlə-] n (Brit Aut) carril m para tráfico lento

crayfish ['kreɪfɪʃ] n pl inv (freshwater) cangrejo (de río); (saltwater) cigala

crayon ['kreɪən] n lápiz m de color

craze [kreɪz] n manía; (fashion) moda

crazy ['kreɪzɪ] adj (person) loco; (idea) disparatado; **to go ~** volverse loco; **to be ~ about sb/sth** (inf) estar loco por algn/algo

creak [kriːk] vi crujir; (hinge etc) chirriar, rechinar

cream [kriːm] n (of milk) nata, crema; (lotion) crema; (fig) flor f y nata ▷ adj (colour) color m crema; **whipped ~** nata batida; **cream off** vt (fig: best talents, part of profits) separar lo mejor de

cream cake n pastel m de nata

cream cheese n queso blanco cremoso

creamy ['kriːmɪ] adj cremoso

crease [kriːs] n (fold) pliegue m; (in trousers) raya; (wrinkle) arruga ▷ vt (fold) doblar, plegar; (wrinkle) arrugar ▷ vi (wrinkle up) arrugarse

create [kriː'eɪt] vt (also Comput) crear; (impression) dar; (fuss, noise) hacer

creation [kriː'eɪʃən] n creación f

creative [kriː'eɪtɪv] adj creativo

creativity [kriːeɪ'tɪvɪtɪ] n creatividad f

creator [kriː'eɪtər] n creador(a) m(f)

creature ['kriːtʃər] n (living thing) criatura; (animal) animal m; (insect) bicho; (person) criatura

creature comforts npl comodidades fpl materiales

crèche, creche [krɛʃ] n (Brit) guardería (infantil)

credence ['kriːdəns] n: **to lend** or **give ~ to** creer en, dar crédito a

credentials [krɪ'dɛnʃlz] npl credenciales fpl; (letters of reference) referencias fpl

credibility [krɛdɪ'bɪlɪtɪ] n credibilidad f

credible ['krɛdɪbl] adj creíble; (witness, source) fidedigno

credit ['krɛdɪt] n (gen) crédito; (merit) honor m, mérito ▷ vt (Comm) abonar; (believe) creer, dar crédito a ▷ adj crediticio; **to be in ~** (person, bank account) tener saldo a favor; **on ~** a crédito; (inf) al fiado; **he's a ~ to his family** hace honor a su familia; **to ~ sb with** (fig) reconocer a algn el mérito de; see also **credits**

credit card n tarjeta de crédito

credit crunch n crisis f crediticia

credit note n nota de crédito

creditor ['krɛdɪtər] n acreedor(a) m(f)

credits ['krɛdɪts] npl (Cine) títulos mpl or rótulos mpl de crédito, ficha técnica

creed [kriːd] n credo

creek [kriːk] n cala, ensenada; (US) riachuelo

creep [kriːp] (pt, pp **crept** [krɛpt]) vi (animal) deslizarse; (plant) trepar; **to ~ up on sb** acercarse sigilosamente a algn; (fig: old age etc) acercarse ▷ n (inf): **he's a ~** ¡qué lameculos es!; **it gives me the ~s** me da escalofríos

creeper ['kri:pə^r] n enredadera
creepy ['kri:pɪ] adj (frightening) horripilante
cremate [krɪ'meɪt] vt incinerar
cremation [krɪ'meɪʃən] n incineración f, cremación f
crematorium [kremə'tɔ:rɪəm] (pl **crematoria**) [kremə'tɔ:rɪə] n crematorio
creosote ['krɪəsəut] n creosota
crêpe [kreɪp] n (fabric) crespón m; (also: ~ **rubber**) crep(é) m
crêpe bandage n (Brit) venda elástica
crêpe paper n papel m crep(é)
crept [krept] pt, pp of **creep**
crescent ['kresnt] n media luna; (street) calle f (en forma de semicírculo)
cress [kres] n berro
crest [krest] n (of bird) cresta; (of hill) cima, cumbre f; (of helmet) cimera; (of coat of arms) blasón m
crestfallen ['krestfɔ:lən] adj alicaído
crevice ['krevɪs] n grieta, hendedura
crew [kru:] n (of ship etc) tripulación f; (Cine etc) equipo; (gang) pandilla, banda; (Mil) dotación f
crew-cut ['kru:kʌt] n corte m al rape
crew-neck ['kru:nek] n cuello a la caja
crib [krɪb] n cuna ▷ vt (inf) plagiar; (Scol) copiar
crick [krɪk] n: ~ **in the neck** tortícolis f inv
cricket ['krɪkɪt] n (insect) grillo; (game) críquet m
cricketer ['krɪkɪtə^r] n jugador(a) m(f) de críquet
crime [kraɪm] n crimen m; (less serious) delito
criminal ['krɪmɪnl] n criminal m/f, delincuente m/f ▷ adj criminal; (law) penal
Criminal Investigation Department n ≈ Brigada de Investigación Criminal f (Sp)
crimson ['krɪmzn] adj carmesí
cringe [krɪndʒ] vi encogerse
crinkle ['krɪŋkl] vt arrugar
cripple ['krɪpl] n lisiado(-a), cojo(-a) ▷ vt lisiar, mutilar; (ship, plane) inutilizar; (production, exports) paralizar; ~**d with arthritis** paralizado por la artritis
crisis ['kraɪsɪs] (pl **crises** ['kraɪsi:z]) n crisis f
crisp [krɪsp] adj fresco; (toast, snow) crujiente; (manner) seco
crisps [krɪsps] npl (Brit) patatas fpl fritas (chips)
crispy adj crujiente
crisscross ['krɪskrɔs] adj entrelazado, entrecruzado ▷ vt entrecruzar(se)
criterion [kraɪ'tɪərɪən] (pl **criteria** [kraɪ'tɪərɪə]) n criterio
critic ['krɪtɪk] n crítico(-a)
critical ['krɪtɪkl] adj (gen) crítico; (illness) grave; **to be ~ of sb/sth** criticar a algn/algo
critically ['krɪtɪklɪ] adv (speak etc) en tono crítico; (ill) gravemente
criticism ['krɪtɪsɪzm] n crítica
criticize ['krɪtɪsaɪz] vt criticar

croak [krəuk] vi (frog) croar; (raven) graznar ▷ n (of raven) graznido
Croat ['krəuæt] adj, n = **Croatian**
Croatia [krəu'eɪʃə] n Croacia
Croatian [krəu'eɪʃən] adj, n croata m/f ▷ n (Ling) croata m
crochet ['krəuʃeɪ] n ganchillo
crockery ['krɔkərɪ] n (plates, cups etc) loza, vajilla
crocodile ['krɔkədaɪl] n cocodrilo
crocus ['krəukəs] n crocus m, croco
croft [krɔft] n granja pequeña
croissant ['krwasã] n croissant m, medialuna (esp LAm)
crony ['krəunɪ] n compinche m/f
crook [kruk] n (inf) ladrón(-ona) m(f); (of shepherd) cayado; (of arm) pliegue m
crooked ['krukɪd] adj torcido; (path) tortuoso; (inf) corrupto
crop [krɔp] n (produce) cultivo; (amount produced) cosecha; (riding crop) látigo de montar; (of bird) buche m ▷ vt cortar, recortar; (animals: grass) pacer; **crop up** vi surgir, presentarse
croquet ['krəukeɪ] n croquet m
cross [krɔs] n cruz f ▷ vt (street etc) cruzar, atravesar; (thwart: person) contrariar, ir contra ▷ vi: **the boat ~es from Santander to Plymouth** el barco hace la travesía de Santander a Plymouth ▷ adj de mal humor, enojado; **it's a ~ between geography and sociology** es una mezcla de geografía y sociología; **to ~ o.s.** santiguarse; **they've got their lines ~ed** (fig) hay un malentendido entre ellos; **to be/get ~ with sb (about sth)** estar enfadado/ enfadarse con algn (por algo); **cross off** vt tachar; **cross out** vt tachar; **cross over** vi cruzar
crossbar ['krɔsbɑ:^r] n travesaño, (of bicycle) barra
crossbow ['krɔsbəu] n ballesta
cross-Channel ferry ['krɔs'tʃænl-] n transbordador m que cruza el Canal de la Mancha
cross-country ['krɔs'kʌntrɪ], **cross-country race** n carrera a campo traviesa, cross m
cross-dressing [krɔs'dresɪŋ] n travestismo
cross-examination ['krɔsɪgzæmɪ'neɪʃən] n interrogatorio
cross-examine ['krɔsɪg'zæmɪn] vt interrogar
cross-eyed ['krɔsaɪd] adj bizco
crossfire ['krɔsfaɪə^r] n fuego cruzado
crossing ['krɔsɪŋ] n (on road) cruce m; (Rail) paso a nivel; (sea passage) travesía; (also: **pedestrian ~**) paso de peatones
crossing guard n (US) persona encargada de ayudar a los niños a cruzar la calle
crossing point n paso; (at border) paso fronterizo

cross purposes npl: **to be at ~ with sb** tener un malentendido con algn
cross-question ['krɔs'kwɛstʃən] vt interrogar
cross-reference ['krɔs'rɛfrəns] n remisión f
crossroads ['krɔsrəudz] nsg cruce m; (fig) encrucijada
cross section n corte m transversal; (of population) muestra (representativa)
crosswalk ['krɔswɔ:k] n (US) paso de peatones
crosswind ['krɔswɪnd] n viento de costado
crossword ['krɔswə:d] n crucigrama m
crotch [krɔtʃ] n (of garment) entrepierna
crotchet ['krɔtʃɪt] n (Brit Mus) negra
crouch [krautʃ] vi agacharse, acurrucarse
crouton ['kru:tɔn] n cubito de pan frito
crow [krəu] n (bird) cuervo; (of cock) canto, cacareo ▷ vi (cock) cantar; (fig) jactarse
crowbar ['krəuba:ʳ] n palanca
crowd [kraud] n muchedumbre f; (Sport) público; (common herd) vulgo ▷ vt (gather) amontonar; (fill) llenar ▷ vi (gather) reunirse; (pile up) amontonarse; **~s of people** gran cantidad de gente
crowded ['kraudɪd] adj (full) atestado; (well-attended) concurrido; (densely populated) superpoblado
crown [kraun] n corona; (of head) coronilla; (of hat) copa; (of hill) cumbre f; (for tooth) funda ▷ vt (also tooth) coronar; **and to ~ it all ...** (fig) y para colmo or remate ...
crown court n (Law) tribunal m superior
crown jewels npl joyas fpl reales
crown prince n príncipe m heredero
crow's feet ['krəuzfi:t] npl patas fpl de gallo
crucial ['kru:ʃl] adj crucial, decisivo; **his approval is ~ to the success of the project** su aprobación es crucial para el éxito del proyecto
crucifix ['kru:sɪfɪks] n crucifijo
crucifixion [kru:sɪ'fɪkʃən] n crucifixión f
crucify ['kru:sɪfaɪ] vt crucificar; (fig) martirizar
crude [kru:d] adj (materials) bruto; (fig: basic) tosco; (: vulgar) ordinario ▷ n (also ~ oil) (petróleo) crudo
cruel ['kruəl] adj cruel
cruelty ['kruəltɪ] n crueldad f
cruise [kru:z] n crucero ▷ vi (ship) navegar; (holidaymakers) hacer un crucero; (car) ir a velocidad constante
cruiser ['kru:zəʳ] n crucero
crumb [krʌm] n miga, migaja
crumble ['krʌmbl] vt desmenuzar ▷ vi (gen) desmenuzarse; (building) desmoronarse
crumbly ['krʌmblɪ] adj desmenuzable
crumpet ['krʌmpɪt] n ≈ bollo para tostar
crumple ['krʌmpl] vt (paper) estrujar; arrugar
crunch [krʌntʃ] vt (with teeth) mascar; (underfoot) ▷ n (fig) hora de la verdad

crunchy ['krʌntʃɪ] adj crujiente
crusade [kru:'seɪd] n cruzada ▷ vi: **to ~ for/ against** (fig) hacer una campaña en pro de/ en contra de
crush [krʌʃ] n (crowd) aglomeración f ▷ vt (gen) aplastar; (paper) estrujar; (cloth) arrugar; (grind, break up: garlic, ice) picar; (fruit) exprimir; (grapes) exprimir, prensar; (opposition) aplastar; (hopes) destruir; **to have a ~ on sb** estar enamorado de algn
crushing ['krʌʃɪŋ] adj aplastante; (burden) agobiante
crust [krʌst] n corteza
crusty ['krʌstɪ] adj (bread) crujiente; (person) de mal carácter; (remark) brusco
crutch [krʌtʃ] n (Med) muleta; (support) apoyo
crux [krʌks] n: **the ~** lo esencial, el quid
cry [kraɪ] vi llorar; (shout: also: ~ out) gritar ▷ n grito; (of animal) aullido; (weep): **she had a good ~** lloró a lágrima viva; **what are you ~ing about?** ¿por qué lloras?; **to ~ for help** pedir socorro a voces; **it's a far ~ from ...** (fig) dista mucho de ...; **cry off** vi retirarse; **cry out** vi (call out, shout) lanzar un grito, echar un grito ▷ vt gritar
cryptic ['krɪptɪk] adj enigmático
crystal ['krɪstl] n cristal m
crystal-clear ['krɪstl'klɪəʳ] adj claro como el agua; (fig) cristalino
CS gas n (Brit) gas m lacrimógeno
cub [kʌb] n cachorro; (also: ~ scout) niño explorador
Cuba ['kju:bə] n Cuba
Cuban ['kju:bən] adj, n cubano(-a) m(f)
cubbyhole ['kʌbɪhəul] n cuchitril m
cube [kju:b] n cubo; (of sugar) terrón m ▷ vt (Math) elevar al cubo
cubic ['kju:bɪk] adj cúbico; **~ capacity** (Aut) capacidad f cúbica
cubicle ['kju:bɪkl] n (at pool) caseta; (for bed) cubículo
cuckoo ['kuku:] n cuco
cuckoo clock n reloj m de cuco
cucumber ['kju:kʌmbəʳ] n pepino
cuddle ['kʌdl] vt abrazar ▷ vi abrazarse
cue [kju:] n (snooker cue) taco; (Theat etc) entrada
cuff [kʌf] n (Brit: of shirt, coat etc) puño; (US: of trousers) vuelta; (blow) bofetada ▷ vt bofetear; **off the ~** adv improvisado
cufflinks ['kʌflɪŋks] npl gemelos mpl
cuisine [kwɪ'zi:n] n cocina
cul-de-sac ['kʌldəsæk] n callejón m sin salida
cull [kʌl] vt (select) entresacar; (kill selectively: animals) matar selectivamente ▷ n matanza selectiva; **seal ~** matanza selectiva de foca
culminate ['kʌlmɪneɪt] vi: **to ~ in** culmina
culmination [kʌlmɪ'neɪʃən] n culminaci colmo
culottes [ku:'lɔts] npl falda f pantalón
culprit ['kʌlprɪt] n culpable m/f

cult [kʌlt] n culto; **a ~ figure** un ídolo
cultivate ['kʌltɪveɪt] vt (also fig) cultivar
cultivation [kʌltɪ'veɪʃən] n cultivo; (fig) cultura
cultural ['kʌltʃərəl] adj cultural
culture ['kʌltʃəʳ] n (also fig) cultura; (Biol) cultivo
cultured ['kʌltʃəd] adj culto
cumbersome ['kʌmbəsəm] adj voluminoso
cumin ['kʌmɪn] n (spice) comino
cunning ['kʌnɪŋ] n astucia ▷ adj astuto; (clever: device, idea) ingenioso
cup [kʌp] n taza; (prize, event) copa; **a ~ of tea** una taza de té
cupboard ['kʌbəd] n armario, placar(d) m (LAm); (in kitchen) alacena
cup final n (Football) final f de copa
cuppa ['kʌpa] n (Brit inf) (taza de) té m
cup-tie ['kʌptaɪ] n (Brit) partido de copa
curate ['kjuərɪt] n coadjutor m
curator [kjuə'reɪtəʳ] n director(a) m(f)
curb [kə:b] vt refrenar; (powers, spending) limitar ▷ n freno; (US: kerb) bordillo
curdle ['kə:dl] vi cuajarse
cure [kjuəʳ] vt curar ▷ n cura, curación f; (fig: solution) remedio; **to be ~d of sth** curarse de algo; **to take a ~** tomar un remedio
curfew ['kə:fju:] n toque m de queda
curio ['kjuərɪəu] n curiosidad f
curiosity [kjuərɪ'ɔsɪtɪ] n curiosidad f
curious ['kjuərɪəs] adj curioso; **I'm ~ about him** me intriga
curl [kə:l] n rizo; (of smoke etc) espiral f, voluta ▷ vt (hair) rizar; (paper) arrollar; (lip) fruncir ▷ vi rizarse; arrollarse; **curl up** vi arrollarse; (person) hacerse un ovillo; (inf) morirse de risa
curler ['kə:ləʳ] n bigudí m, rulo
curly ['kə:lɪ] adj rizado
currant ['kʌrnt] n pasa; (black, red) grosella
currency ['kʌrnsɪ] n moneda; **to gain ~** (fig) difundirse
current ['kʌrnt] n corriente f ▷ adj actual; **direct/alternating ~** corriente directa/alterna; **the ~ issue of a magazine** el último número de una revista; **in ~ use** de uso corriente
current account n (Brit) cuenta corriente
current affairs npl (noticias fpl de) actualidad f
currently ['kʌrntlɪ] adv actualmente
curriculum (pl **curriculums** or **curricula**) [kə'rɪkjuləm, -lə] n plan m de estudios
curriculum vitae [-'vi:taɪ] n currículum m (vitae)
curry ['kʌrɪ] n curry m ▷ vt: **to ~ favour with** buscar el favor de
curry powder n curry m en polvo
curse [kə:s] vi echar pestes, soltar palabrotas ▷ vt maldecir ▷ n maldición f; (swearword) palabrota, taco
cursor ['kə:səʳ] n (Comput) cursor m
cursory ['kə:sərɪ] adj rápido, superficial

curt [kə:t] adj seco
curtail [kə:'teɪl] vt (cut short) acortar; (restrict) restringir
curtain ['kə:tn] n cortina; (Theat) telón m; **to draw the ~s** (together) cerrar las cortinas; (apart) abrir las cortinas
curve [kə:v] n curva ▷ vi (road) hacer una curva; (line etc) curvarse
curved [kə:vd] adj curvo
cushion ['kuʃən] n cojín m; (Snooker) banda ▷ vt (seat) acolchar; (shock) amortiguar
cushy ['kuʃɪ] adj (inf): **a ~ job** un chollo; **to have a ~ time** tener la vida arreglada
custard ['kʌstəd] n (for pouring) natillas fpl
custodial sentence [kʌs'təudɪəl-] n pena de prisión
custody ['kʌstədɪ] n custodia; **to take sb into ~** detener a algn; **in the ~ of** al cuidado or cargo de
custom ['kʌstəm] n costumbre f; (Comm) clientela; see also **customs**
customary ['kʌstəmərɪ] adj acostumbrado; **it is ~ to do ...** es la costumbre hacer ...
customer ['kʌstəməʳ] n cliente m/f; **he's an awkward ~** (inf) es un tipo difícil
customized ['kʌstəmaɪzd] adj (car etc) hecho a encargo
custom-made ['kʌstəm'meɪd] adj hecho a la medida
customs ['kʌstəmz] npl aduana sg; **to go through (the) ~** pasar la aduana
customs officer n aduanero(-a), funcionario(-a) de aduanas
cut [kʌt] (pt, pp **cut**) vt cortar; (price) rebajar; (record) grabar; (reduce) reducir; (inf: avoid: class, lecture) fumarse, faltar a ▷ vi cortar; (intersect) cruzarse ▷ n corte m; (in skin) corte, cortadura; (with sword) tajo; (of knife) cuchillada; (in salary etc) rebaja; (in spending) reducción f, recorte m; (slice of meat) tajada; **to ~ one's finger** cortarse un dedo; **to ~ one's hair** cortarse el pelo; **to ~ and paste** (Comput) cortar y pegar; **to ~ sb dead** negarle el saludo or cortarle (LAm) a algn; **it ~s both ways** (fig) tiene doble filo; **to ~ a tooth** echar un diente; **power ~** (Brit) apagón m; **cut back** vt (plants) podar; (production, expenditure) reducir; **cut down** vt (tree) cortar, derribar; (consumption, expenses) reducir; **to ~ sb down to size** (fig) bajarle los humos a algn; **cut in** vi: **to ~ in (on)** (interrupt: conversation) interrumpir, intervenir (en); (Aut) cerrar el paso (a); **cut off** vt cortar; (fig) aislar, cercar; **we've been ~ off** (Tel) n... cortado la comunicación; recortar; (delete) su... (en pedazos); (ch...
cutback ['kʌtbæk]
cute [kju:t] adj lind...
cuticle ['kju:tɪkl] n c...
cutlery ['kʌtlərɪ] n cu...
cutlet ['kʌtlɪt] n chulet...

cutout ['kʌtaut] n (cardboard cutout) recortable m

cut-price ['kʌt'praɪs], **cut-rate** (US) ['kʌt'reɪt] adj a precio reducido

cutting ['kʌtɪŋ] adj (gen) cortante; (remark) mordaz ▷ n (Brit: from newspaper) recorte m; (from plant) esqueje m; (Rail) desmonte m; (Cine) montaje m

cutting edge n (of knife) filo; (fig) vanguardia; **a country on** or **at the ~ of space technology** un país puntero en tecnología del espacio

CV n abbr = **curriculum vitae**

cwt. abbr = **hundredweight**

cyanide ['saɪənaɪd] n cianuro

cybercafé ['saɪbə,kæfeɪ] n cibercafé m

cyberspace ['saɪbəspeɪs] n ciberespacio

cyberterrorism ['saɪbətɛrərɪzəm] n ciberterrorismo m

cycle ['saɪkl] n ciclo; (bicycle) bicicleta ▷ vi ir en bicicleta

cycle hire n alquiler m de bicicletas

cycle lane n carril m de bicicleta, carril m bici

cycle path n carril-bici m

cycling ['saɪklɪŋ] n ciclismo

cyclist ['saɪklɪst] n ciclista m/f

cyclone ['saɪkləun] n ciclón m

cygnet ['sɪgnɪt] n pollo de cisne

cylinder ['sɪlɪndər] n cilindro

cylinder-head gasket n junta de culata

cymbals ['sɪmblz] npl platillos mpl, címbalos mpl

cynic ['sɪnɪk] n cínico(-a)

cynical ['sɪnɪkl] adj cínico

cynicism ['sɪnɪsɪzəm] n cinismo

Cypriot ['sɪprɪət] adj, n chipriota m/f

Cyprus ['saɪprəs] n Chipre f

cyst [sɪst] n quiste m

cystitis [sɪs'taɪtɪs] n cistitis f

czar [zɑːr] n zar m

Czech [tʃɛk] adj checo ▷ n checo(-a); (Ling) checo; **the ~ Republic** la República Checa

D, d [diː] n (letter) D, d; (Mus): **D** re m; **D for David**, (US) **D for Dog** D de Dolores

D abbr (US Pol) = **democrat; democratic**

DA n abbr (US) = **district attorney**

dab [dæb] vt: **to ~ ointment onto a wound** aplicar pomada sobre una herida; **to ~ with paint** dar unos toques de pintura ▷ n (light stroke) toque m; (small amount) pizca

dabble ['dæbl] vi: **to ~ in** hacer por afición

dad [dæd], **daddy** ['dædɪ] n papá m

daddy-long-legs [dædɪ'lɔŋlɛgz] n típula

daffodil ['dæfədɪl] n narciso

daft [dɑːft] adj tonto

dagger ['dægər] n puñal m, daga; **to look ~s at sb** fulminar a algn con la mirada

daily ['deɪlɪ] adj diario, cotidiano ▷ n (paper) diario; (domestic help) asistenta ▷ adv todos los días, cada día; **twice ~** dos veces al día

dainty ['deɪntɪ] adj delicado; (tasteful) elegante

dairy ['dɛərɪ] n (shop) lechería; (on farm) vaquería; (products) lácteos pl ▷ adj (cow etc) lechero

dairy produce n productos mpl lácteos

dais ['deɪɪs] n estrado

daisy ['deɪzɪ] n margarita

dale [deɪl] n valle m

dally ['dælɪ] vi entretenerse

dam [dæm] n presa; (reservoir) embalse ▷ vt embalsar

damage ['dæmɪdʒ] n daño; (fig) perjuicio; (to machine) avería ▷ vt dañar; perjudicar;

averiar; **~ to property** daños materiales; **damages** npl (Law) daños y perjuicios; **to pay £5000 in ~s** pagar £5000 por daños y perjuicios

damaging ['dæmɪdʒɪŋ] adj: **~ (to)** perjudicial (a)

dame [deɪm] n (title) dama; (US inf) tía; (Theat) vieja; see also **pantomime**

damn [dæm] vt condenar; (curse) maldecir ▷ n (inf): **I don't give a ~** me importa un pito ▷ adj (inf: also: **~ed**) maldito, fregado (LAm); **~ (it)!** ¡maldito sea!

damnation [dæm'neɪʃən] n (Rel) condenación f ▷ excl (inf) ¡maldición!, ¡maldito sea!

damning ['dæmɪŋ] adj (evidence) irrecusable

damp [dæmp] adj húmedo, mojado ▷ n humedad f ▷ vt (also: **~en**: cloth, rag) mojar; (enthusiasm) enfriar

damper ['dæmpər] n (Mus) sordina; (of fire) regulador m de tiro; **to put a ~ on things** ser un jarro de agua fría

dampness ['dæmpnɪs] n humedad f

damson ['dæmzən] n ciruela damascena

dance [dɑ:ns] n baile m ▷ vi bailar; **to ~ about** saltar

dance floor n pista f de baile

dance hall n salón m de baile

dancer ['dɑ:nsər] n bailador(a) m(f); (professional) bailarín(-ina) m(f)

dancing ['dɑ:nsɪŋ] n baile m

dandelion ['dændɪlaɪən] n diente m de león

dandruff ['dændrəf] n caspa

D & T (Brit: Scol) n abbr (= design and technology) diseño y pretecnología

Dane [deɪn] n danés(-esa) m(f)

danger ['deɪndʒər] n peligro; (risk) riesgo; **~!** (on sign) ¡peligro!; **to be in ~ of** correr riesgo de; **out of ~** fuera de peligro

danger list n (Med): **to be on the ~** estar grave

dangerous ['deɪndʒərəs] adj peligroso

dangle ['dæŋgl] vt colgar ▷ vi pender, estar colgado

Danish ['deɪnɪʃ] adj danés(-esa) ▷ n (Ling) danés m

dapper ['dæpər] adj pulcro, apuesto

dare [dɛər] vt: **to ~ sb to do** desafiar a algn a hacer ▷ vi: **to ~ (to) do sth** atreverse a hacer algo; **I ~ say** (I suppose) puede ser, a lo mejor; **I ~ say he'll turn up** puede ser que or quizás venga; **I ~n't tell him** no me atrevo a decírselo

daredevil ['dɛədɛvl] n temerario(-a), atrevido(-a)

daring ['dɛərɪŋ] adj (person) osado; (plan, escape) atrevido ▷ n atrevimiento, osadía

dark [dɑ:k] adj oscuro; (hair, complexion) moreno; (fig: cheerless) triste, sombrío ▷ n (gen) oscuridad f; (night) tinieblas fpl; **~ chocolate** chocolate m amargo; **in the ~** a oscuras; **it is/is getting ~** es de noche/está

oscureciendo; **in the ~ about** (fig) ignorante de; **after ~** después del anochecer

darken ['dɑ:kn] vt oscurecer; (colour) hacer más oscuro ▷ vi oscurecerse; (cloud over) nublarse

dark glasses npl gafas fpl oscuras

dark horse n (fig) incógnita

darkness ['dɑ:knɪs] n (in room) oscuridad f; (night) tinieblas fpl

darkroom ['dɑ:krum] n cuarto oscuro

darling ['dɑ:lɪŋ] adj, n querido(-a) m(f)

darn [dɑ:n] vt zurcir

dart [dɑ:t] n dardo; (in sewing) pinza ▷ vi precipitarse; **to ~ away/along** salir/marchar disparado

dartboard ['dɑ:tbɔ:d] n diana

darts [dɑ:ts] n dardos mpl

dash [dæʃ] n (small quantity: of liquid) gota, chorrito; (: of solid) pizca; (sign) guión m; (: long) raya ▷ vt (break) romper, estrellar; (hopes) defraudar ▷ vi precipitarse, ir de prisa; **a ~ of soda** un poco or chorrito de sifón or soda; **dash away, dash off** vi marcharse apresuradamente

dashboard ['dæʃbɔ:d] n (Aut) salpicadero

dashing ['dæʃɪŋ] adj gallardo

data ['deɪtə] npl datos mpl

database ['deɪtəbeɪs] n base f de datos

data processing n proceso or procesamiento de datos

date [deɪt] n (day) fecha; (with friend) cita; (fruit) dátil m ▷ vt fechar; (inf: girl etc) salir con; **what's the ~ today?** ¿qué fecha es hoy?; **~ of birth** fecha de nacimiento; **closing ~** fecha tope; **to ~** adv hasta la fecha; **out of ~** pasado de moda; **up to ~** moderno; puesto al día; **to bring up to ~** (correspondence, information) poner al día; (method) actualizar; **to bring sb up to ~** poner a algn al corriente; **letter ~d 5th July** or (US) **July 5th** carta fechada el 5 de julio

dated ['deɪtɪd] adj anticuado

daub [dɔ:b] vt embadurnar

daughter ['dɔ:tər] n hija

daughter-in-law ['dɔ:tərɪnlɔ:] n nuera, hija política

daunting ['dɔ:ntɪŋ] adj desalentador(-a)

dawdle ['dɔ:dl] vi (waste time) perder el tiempo; (go slowly) andar muy despacio; **to ~ over one's work** trabajar muy despacio

dawn [dɔ:n] n alba, amanecer m; (fig) nacimiento ▷ vi amanecer; (fig): **it ~ed on him that ...** cayó en la cuenta de que ...; **at ~** al amanecer; **from ~ to dusk** de sol a sol

day [deɪ] n día m; (working day) jornada; **the ~ before** el día anterior; **the ~ after tomorrow** pasado mañana; **the ~ before yesterday** anteayer, antes de ayer; **the ~ after, the following ~** el día siguiente; **by ~** de día; **~ by ~** día a día; **(on) the ~ that ...** el día que ...; **to work an eight-hour ~** trabajar ocho horas diarias or al día; **he**

works eight hours a ~ trabaja ocho horas al día; **paid by the ~** pagado por día; **these ~s, in the present ~** hoy en día
daybreak ['deɪbreɪk] *n* amanecer *m*
day-care centre ['deɪkɛə-] *n* centro de día; (*for children*) guardería infantil
daydream ['deɪdri:m] *n* ensueño ▷ *vi* soñar despierto
daylight ['deɪlaɪt] *n* luz *f* (del día)
daylight robbery *n*: **it's ~!** (*fig, inf*) ¡es un robo descarado!
Daylight Saving Time *n* (*US*) hora de verano
day return, day return ticket *n* (*Brit*) billete *m* de ida y vuelta (en un día)
daytime ['deɪtaɪm] *n* día *m*
day-to-day ['deɪtə'deɪ] *adj* cotidiano, diario; (*expenses*) diario; **on a ~ basis** día por día
day trip *n* excursión *f* (de un día)
day tripper *n* excursionista *m/f*
daze [deɪz] *vt* (*stun*) aturdir ▷ *n*: **in a ~** aturdido
dazed [deɪzd] *adj* aturdido
dazzle ['dæzl] *vt* deslumbrar
dazzling ['dæzlɪŋ] *adj* (*light, smile*) deslumbrante; (*colour*) fuerte
DC *abbr* (*Elec*) = **direct current**
D-day ['di:deɪ] *n* (*fig*) día *m* clave
DEA *n abbr* (*US: = Drug Enforcement Administration*) *brigada especial dedicada a la lucha contra el tráfico de estupefacientes*
dead [dɛd] *adj* muerto; (*limb*) dormido; (*battery*) agotado ▷ *adv* (*completely*) totalmente; (*exactly*) justo; **he was ~ on arrival** ingresó cadáver; **to shoot sb ~** matar a algn a tiros; **~ tired** muerto (de cansancio); **to stop ~** parar en seco; **the line has gone ~** (*Tel*) se ha cortado la línea; **the ~** *npl* los muertos
deaden ['dɛdn] *vt* (*blow, sound*) amortiguar; (*pain*) calmar, aliviar
dead end *n* callejón *m* sin salida
dead-end ['dɛdɛnd] *adj*: **a ~ job** un trabajo sin porvenir
dead heat *n* (*Sport*) empate *m*
deadline ['dɛdlaɪn] *n* fecha tope; **to work to a ~** trabajar con una fecha tope
deadlock ['dɛdlɔk] *n* punto muerto
dead loss *n* (*inf*): **to be a ~** (*person*) ser un inútil; (*thing*) ser una birria
deadly ['dɛdlɪ] *adj* mortal, fatal; **~ dull** aburridísimo
deadpan ['dɛdpæn] *adj* sin expresión
Dead Sea *n*: **the ~** el Mar Muerto
deaf [dɛf] *adj* sordo; **to turn a ~ ear to sth** hacer oídos sordos a algo
deaf-and-dumb ['dɛfən'dʌm] *adj* (*person*) sordomudo; (*alphabet*) para sordomudos
deafen ['dɛfn] *vt* ensordecer
deafening ['dɛfnɪŋ] *adj* ensordecedor(-a)
deaf-mute ['dɛfmju:t] *n* sordomudo(-a)
deafness ['dɛfnɪs] *n* sordera
deal [di:l] *n* (*agreement*) pacto, convenio; (*business*) negocio, transacción *f*; (*Cards*) reparto ▷ *vt* (*pt, pp* **dealt**) (*gen*) dar; (*card*) repartir; **a great ~ (of)** bastante, mucho; **it's a ~!** (*inf*) ¡trato hecho!, ¡de acuerdo!; **to do a ~ with sb** hacer un trato con algn; **he got a bad/fair ~ from them** le trataron mal/bien; **deal in** *vt fus* tratar en, comerciar en; **deal with** *vt fus* (*people*) tratar con; (*problem*) ocuparse de; (*subject*) tratar de
dealer ['di:lə^r] *n* comerciante *m/f*; (*Cards*) mano *f*
dealership ['di:ləʃɪp] *n* concesionario
dealings ['di:lɪŋz] *npl* (*Comm*) transacciones *fpl*; (*relations*) relaciones *fpl*
dealt [dɛlt] *pt, pp of* **deal**
dean [di:n] *n* (*Rel*) deán *m*; (*Scol*) decano(-a)
dear [dɪə^r] *adj* querido; (*expensive*) caro ▷ *n*: **my ~** querido(-a); **~ me!** ¡Dios mío!; **D~ Sir/Madam** (*in letter*) Muy señor mío, Estimado señor/Estimada señora, De mi/nuestra (mayor) consideración (*esp LAm*); **D~ Mr/Mrs X** Estimado(-a) señor(a) X
dearly ['dɪəlɪ] *adv* (*love*) mucho; (*pay*) caro
dearth [də:θ] *n* (*of food, resources, money*) escasez *f*
death [dɛθ] *n* muerte *f*
deathbed ['dɛθbɛd] *n* lecho de muerte
death certificate *n* partida de defunción
deathly ['dɛθlɪ] *adj* mortal; (*silence*) profundo
death penalty *n* pena de muerte
death rate *n* tasa de mortalidad
death row *n*: **to be on ~** (*US*) estar condenado a muerte
death sentence *n* condena a muerte
death squad *n* escuadrón *m* de la muerte
death trap ['dɛθtræp] *n* lugar *m* (*or* vehículo *etc*) muy peligroso
debacle [deɪ'bɑ:kl] *n* desastre *m*, catástrofe *f*
debase [dɪ'beɪs] *vt* degradar
debatable [dɪ'beɪtəbl] *adj* discutible; **it is ~ whether ...** es discutible si ...
debate [dɪ'beɪt] *n* debate *m* ▷ *vt* discutir
debauchery [dɪ'bɔ:tʃərɪ] *n* libertinaje *m*
debenture [dɪ'bɛntʃə^r] *n* (*Comm*) bono, obligación *f*
debilitating [dɪ'bɪlɪteɪtɪŋ] *adj* (*illness etc*) debilitante
debit ['dɛbɪt] *n* debe *m* ▷ *vt*: **to ~ a sum to sb** *or* **to sb's account** cargar una suma en cuenta a algn
debit card *n* tarjeta *f* de débito
debrief [di:'bri:f] *vt* hacer dar parte
debriefing [di:'bri:fɪŋ] *n* relación *f* (de un informe)
debris ['dɛbri:] *n* escombros *mpl*
debt [dɛt] *n* deuda; **to be in ~** tener deudas; **~s of £5000** deudas de cinco mil libras; **bad ~** deuda incobrable
debt collector *n* cobrador(a) *m(f)* de deudas
debtor ['dɛtə^r] *n* deudor(a) *m(f)*
debug ['di:'bʌg] *vt* (*Comput*) depurar, limpiar

d

debunk [di:'bʌŋk] vt (inf: theory) despretigiar, desacreditar; (claim) desacreditar; (person, institution) desenmascarar

début ['deibju:] n presentación f

Dec. abbr (= December) dic

decade ['dɛkeid] n década, decenio

decadence ['dɛkədəns] n decadencia

decadent ['dɛkədənt] adj decadente

de-caff ['di:kæf] n (inf) descafeinado

decaffeinated [dɪ'kæfɪneɪtɪd] adj descafeinado

decanter [dɪ'kæntər] n jarra, decantador m

decathlon [dɪ'kæθlən] n decatlón m

decay [dɪ'keɪ] n (fig) decadencia; (of building) desmoronamiento; (of tooth) caries f inv ▷ vi (rot) pudrirse; (fig) decaer

deceased [dɪ'si:st] n: **the** ~ el/la difunto(-a) ▷ adj difunto

deceit [dɪ'si:t] n engaño

deceitful [dɪ'si:tful] adj engañoso

deceive [dɪ'si:v] vt engañar

December [dɪ'sɛmbər] n diciembre m; see also **July**

decency ['di:sənsɪ] n decencia

decent ['di:sənt] adj (proper) decente; (person) amable, bueno

deception [dɪ'sɛpʃən] n engaño

deceptive [dɪ'sɛptɪv] adj engañoso

decibel ['dɛsɪbɛl] n decibel(io) m

decide [dɪ'saɪd] vt (person) decidir; (question, argument) resolver ▷ vi decidir; **to** ~ **to do/ that** decidir hacer/que; **to** ~ **on sth** tomar una decisión sobre algo; **to** ~ **against doing sth** decidir en contra de hacer algo

decided [dɪ'saɪdɪd] adj (resolute) decidido; (clear, definite) indudable

decidedly [dɪ'saɪdɪdlɪ] adv decididamente

deciduous [dɪ'sɪdjuəs] adj de hoja caduca

decimal ['dɛsɪməl] adj decimal ▷ n decimal f; **to three** ~ **places** con tres cifras decimales

decimal point n coma decimal

decipher [dɪ'saɪfər] vt descifrar

decision [dɪ'sɪʒən] n decisión f; **to make a** ~ tomar una decisión

decisive [dɪ'saɪsɪv] adj (influence) decisivo; (manner, person) decidido; (reply) tajante

deck [dɛk] n (Naut) cubierta; (of bus) piso; (of cards) baraja; **record** ~ platina; **to go up on** ~ subir a (la) cubierta; **below** ~ en la bodega

deckchair ['dɛktʃɛər] n tumbona

declaration [dɛklə'reɪʃən] n declaración f

declare [dɪ'klɛər] vt (gen) declarar

decline [dɪ'klaɪn] n decaimiento, decadencia; (lessening) disminución f ▷ vt rehusar ▷ vi (person, business) decaer; (strength) disminuir; ~ **in living standards** disminución f del nivel de vida; **to** ~ **to do sth** rehusar hacer algo

decoder [di:'kəʊdər] n (Comput, TV) de(s)codificador m

decompose [di:kəm'pəʊz] vi descomponerse

decomposition [di:kɔmpə'zɪʃən] n descomposición f

decompression [di:kəm'prɛʃən] n descompresión f

decongestant [di:kən'dʒɛstənt] n descongestionante m

decontaminate [di:kən'tæmɪneɪt] vt descontaminar

décor ['deɪkɔ:r] n decoración f; (Theat) decorado

decorate ['dɛkəreɪt] vt (paint) pintar; (paper) empapelar; (adorn): **to** ~ **(with)** adornar (de), decorar (de)

decoration [dɛkə'reɪʃən] n adorno; (act) decoración f; (medal) condecoración f

decorator ['dɛkəreɪtər] n (workman) pintor m decorador

decoy ['di:kɔɪ] n señuelo; **police** ~ trampa or señuelo policial

decrease [n 'di:kri:s] n disminución f ▷ vt [dɪ'kri:s] disminuir, reducir ▷ vi reducirse; **to be on the** ~ ir disminuyendo

decree [dɪ'kri:] n decreto ▷ vt: **to** ~ **(that)** decretar (que); ~ **absolute/nisi** sentencia absoluta/provisional de divorcio

decrepit [dɪ'krɛpɪt] adj (person) decrépito; (building) ruinoso

dedicate ['dɛdɪkeɪt] vt dedicar

dedicated ['dɛdɪkeɪtɪd] adj dedicado; (Comput) especializado; ~ **word processor** procesador m de textos especializado or dedicado

dedication [dɛdɪ'keɪʃən] n (devotion) dedicación f; (in book) dedicatoria

deduce [dɪ'dju:s] vt deducir

deduct [dɪ'dʌkt] vt restar; (from wage etc) descontar, deducir

deduction [dɪ'dʌkʃən] n (amount deducted) descuento; (conclusion) deducción f, conclusión f

deed [di:d] n hecho, acto; (feat) hazaña; (Law) escritura; ~ **of covenant** escritura de contrato

deem [di:m] vt (formal) juzgar, considerar; **to** ~ **it wise to do** considerar prudente hacer

deep [di:p] adj profundo; (voice) bajo; (breath) profundo, a pleno pulmón ▷ adv: **the spectators stood 20** ~ los espectadores se formaron de 20 en fondo; **to be four metres** ~ tener cuatro metros de profundidad

deepen ['di:pn] vt ahondar, profundizar ▷ vi (darkness) intensificarse

deep-freeze ['di:p'fri:z] n arcón m congelador

deep-fry ['di:p'fraɪ] vt freír en aceite abundante

deeply ['di:plɪ] adv (breathe) profundamente, a pleno pulmón; (interested, moved, grateful) profundamente, hondamente; **to regret sth** ~ sentir algo profundamente

deep-rooted ['di:p'ru:tɪd] adj (prejudice, habit) profundamente arraigado; (affection) profundo

deep-sea ['di:p'si:] *adj*: ~ **diver** buzo;
~ **diving** buceo de altura
deep-seated ['di:p'si:tɪd] *adj* (*beliefs*)
(profundamente) arraigado
deer (*pl* **deer**) [dɪə'] *n* ciervo
deface [dɪ'feɪs] *vt* desfigurar, mutilar
defamation [defə'meɪʃən] *n* difamación *f*
default [dɪ'fɔ:lt] *vi* faltar al pago; (*Sport*) no
presentarse, no comparecer ▷ *n* (*Comput*)
defecto; **by** ~ (*Law*) en rebeldía; (*Sport*) por
incomparecencia; **to** ~ **on a debt** dejar de
pagar una deuda
defeat [dɪ'fi:t] *n* derrota ▷ *vt* derrotar,
vencer; (*fig: efforts*) frustrar
defecate ['defəkeɪt] *vi* defecar
defect ['di:fɛkt] *n* defecto ▷ *vi* [dɪ'fɛkt]:
to ~ **to the enemy** pasarse al enemigo;
physical ~ defecto físico; **mental** ~
deficiencia mental
defective [dɪ'fɛktɪv] *adj* (*gen*) defectuoso;
(*person*) anormal
defector [dɪ'fɛktə] *n* tránsfuga *m/f*
defence, defense (US) [dɪ'fɛns] *n* defensa;
the Ministry of D~ el Ministerio de Defensa;
witness for the ~ testigo de descargo
defenceless [dɪ'fɛnslɪs] *adj* indefenso
defend [dɪ'fɛnd] *vt* defender; (*decision, action*)
defender; (*opinion*) mantener
defendant [dɪ'fɛndənt] *n* acusado(-a); (*in civil
case*) demandado(-a)
defender [dɪ'fɛndə'] *n* defensor(a) *m(f)*;
(*Sport*) defensa *m/f*
defense [dɪ'fɛns] *n* (US) = **defence**
defensive [dɪ'fɛnsɪv] *adj* defensivo ▷ *n*
defensiva; **on the** ~ a la defensiva
defer [dɪ'fə:'] *vt* (*postpone*) aplazar; **to** ~ **to**
diferir a; (*submit*): **to** ~ **to sb/sb's opinion**
someterse a algn/a la opinión de algn
deference ['defərəns] *n* deferencia, respeto;
out of *or* **in** ~ **to** por respeto a
defiance [dɪ'faɪəns] *n* desafío; **in** ~ **of** en
contra de
defiant [dɪ'faɪənt] *adj* (*insolent*) insolente;
(*challenging*) retador(a), desafiante
deficiency [dɪ'fɪʃənsɪ] *n* (*lack*) falta; (*Comm*)
déficit *m*; (*defect*) defecto
deficient [dɪ'fɪʃənt] *adj* (*lacking*) insuficiente;
(*incomplete*) incompleto; (*defective*) defectuoso;
(*mentally*) anormal; ~ **in** deficiente en
deficit ['defɪsɪt] *n* déficit *m*
defile [dɪ'faɪl] *vt* manchar; (*violate*) violar
define [dɪ'faɪn] *vt* (*Comput*) definir; (*limits etc*)
determinar
definite ['defɪnɪt] *adj* (*fixed*) determinado;
(*clear, obvious*) claro; **he was** ~ **about it** no dejó
lugar a dudas (sobre ello)
definitely ['defɪnɪtlɪ] *adv*: **he's** ~ **mad** no cabe
duda de que está loco
definition [defɪ'nɪʃən] *n* definición *f*
deflate [di:'fleɪt] *vt* (*gen*) desinflar; (*pompous
person*) quitar *or* rebajar los humos a; (*Econ*)
deflacionar

deflect [dɪ'flɛkt] *vt* desviar
deform [dɪ'fɔ:m] *vt* deformar
deformed [dɪ'fɔ:md] *adj* deformado
deformity [dɪ'fɔ:mɪtɪ] *n* deformación *f*
defraud [dɪ'frɔ:d] *vt* estafar; **to** ~ **sb of sth**
estafar algo a algn
defrost [di:'frɔst] *vt* (*frozen food, fridge*)
descongelar
defroster [di:'frɔstə'] *n* (US) eliminador *m*
de vaho
deft [dɛft] *adj* diestro, hábil
defunct [dɪ'fʌŋkt] *adj* difunto; (*organization
etc*) ya desaparecido
defuse [di:'fju:z] *vt* desarmar; (*situation*)
calmar, apaciguar
defy [dɪ'faɪ] *vt* (*resist*) oponerse a; (*challenge*)
desafiar; (*order*) contravenir; **it defies
description** resulta imposible describirlo
degenerate [dɪ'dʒɛnəreɪt] *vi* degenerar ▷ *adj*
[dɪ'dʒɛnərɪt] degenerado
degradation [dɛgrə'deɪʃən] *n*
degradación *f*
degree [dɪ'gri:] *n* grado; (*Scol*) título; **10 ~s
below freezing** 10 grados bajo cero; **to have
a** ~ **in maths** ser licenciado(-a) en
matemáticas; **by ~s** (*gradually*) poco a poco,
por etapas; **to some** ~, **to a certain** ~ hasta
cierto punto; **a considerable** ~ **of risk** un
gran índice de riesgo
dehydrated [di:haɪ'dreɪtɪd] *adj*
deshidratado; (*milk*) en polvo
dehydration [di:haɪ'dreɪʃən] *n*
deshidratación *f*
de-ice [di:'aɪs] *vt* (*windscreen*) deshelar
de-icer [di:'aɪsə'] *n* descongelador *m*
deign [deɪn] *vi*: **to** ~ **to do** dignarse hacer
deity ['di:ɪtɪ] *n* deidad *f*, divinidad *f*
déjà vu [deɪʒɑː'vu:] *n*: **I had a sense of** ~
sentía como si ya lo hubiera vivido
dejected [dɪ'dʒɛktɪd] *adj* abatido,
desanimado
dejection [dɪ'dʒɛkʃən] *n* abatimiento
delay [dɪ'leɪ] *vt* demorar, aplazar; (*person*)
entretener; (*train*) retrasar; (*payment*) aplazar
▷ *vi* tardar ▷ *n* demora, retraso; **without** ~
en seguida, sin tardar
delectable [dɪ'lɛktəbl] *adj* (*person*)
encantador(a); (*food*) delicioso
delegate ['dɛlɪgɪt] *n* delegado(-a) ▷ *vt*
['dɛlɪgeɪt] (*person*) delegar en; (*task*) delegar;
to ~ **sth to sb/sb to do sth** delegar algo en
algn/en algn para hacer algo
delegation [dɛlɪ'geɪʃən] *n* (*of work etc*)
delegación *f*
delete [dɪ'li:t] *vt* suprimir, tachar; (*Comput*)
suprimir, borrar
deli ['dɛlɪ] *n* = **delicatessen**
deliberate [dɪ'lɪbərɪt] *adj* (*intentional*)
intencionado; (*slow*) pausado, lento ▷ *vi*
[dɪ'lɪbəreɪt] deliberar
deliberately [dɪ'lɪbərɪtlɪ] *adv* (*on purpose*)
a propósito; (*slowly*) pausadamente

deliberation [dɪlɪbə'reɪʃən] n (consideration) reflexión f; (discussion) deliberación f, discusión f

delicacy ['dɛlɪkəsɪ] n delicadeza; (choice food) manjar m

delicate ['dɛlɪkɪt] adj (gen) delicado; (fragile) frágil

delicatessen [dɛlɪkə'tɛsn] n tienda especializada en alimentos de calidad

delicious [dɪ'lɪʃəs] adj delicioso, rico

delight [dɪ'laɪt] n (feeling) placer m, deleite m; (object) encanto, delicia ▷ vt encantar, deleitar; **to take ~ in** deleitarse en

delighted [dɪ'laɪtɪd] adj: **~ (at or with/to do)** encantado (con/de hacer); **to be ~ that** estar encantado de que; **I'd be ~** con mucho or todo gusto

delightful [dɪ'laɪtful] adj encantador(a), delicioso

delinquent [dɪ'lɪŋkwənt] adj, n delincuente m/f

delirious [dɪ'lɪrɪəs] adj (Med: fig) delirante; **to be ~** delirar, desvariar

deliver [dɪ'lɪvəʳ] vt (distribute) repartir; (hand over) entregar; (message) comunicar; (speech) pronunciar; (blow) lanzar, dar; (Med) asistir al parto de

delivery [dɪ'lɪvərɪ] n reparto; entrega; (of speaker) modo de expresarse; (Med) parto, alumbramiento; **to take ~ of** recibir

delude [dɪ'lu:d] vt engañar

deluge ['dɛlju:dʒ] n diluvio ▷ vt (fig): **to ~ (with)** inundar (de)

delusion [dɪ'lu:ʒən] n ilusión f, engaño

de luxe [də'lʌks] adj de lujo

delve [dɛlv] vi: **to ~ into** hurgar en

Dem. abbr (US Pol) = **Democrat; Democratic**

demand [dɪ'mɑ:nd] vt (gen) exigir; (rights) reclamar; (need) requerir ▷ n (gen) exigencia; (claim) reclamación f; (Econ) demanda; **to ~ sth (from or of sb)** exigir algo (a algn); **to be in ~** ser muy solicitado; **on ~** a solicitud

demanding [dɪ'mɑ:ndɪŋ] adj (boss) exigente; (work) absorbente

demean [dɪ'mi:n] vt: **to ~ o.s.** rebajarse

demeanour, demeanor (US) [dɪ'mi:nəʳ] n porte m, conducta, comportamiento

demented [dɪ'mɛntɪd] adj demente

demilitarize [di:'mɪlɪtəraɪz] vt desmilitarizar; **~d zone** zona desmilitarizada

demise [dɪ'maɪz] n (death) fallecimiento

demister [di:'mɪstəʳ] n (Aut) eliminador m de vaho

demo ['dɛməu] n abbr (inf: = demonstration) manifestación f

democracy [dɪ'mɔkrəsɪ] n democracia

democrat ['dɛməkræt] n demócrata m/f

democratic [dɛmə'krætɪk] adj democrático; **the D~ Party** el partido demócrata (estadounidense)

demography [dɪ'mɔgrəfɪ] n demografía

demolish [dɪ'mɔlɪʃ] vt derribar, demoler; (fig: argument) destruir

demolition [dɛmə'lɪʃən] n derribo, demolición f

demon ['di:mən] n (evil spirit) demonio ▷ cpd temible

demonstrate ['dɛmənstreɪt] vt demostrar ▷ vi manifestarse; **to ~ (for/against)** manifestarse (a favor de/en contra de)

demonstration [dɛmən'streɪʃən] n (Pol) manifestación f; (proof) prueba, demostración f; **to hold a ~** (Pol) hacer una manifestación

demonstrator ['dɛmənstreɪtəʳ] n (Pol) manifestante m/f

demote [dɪ'məut] vt degradar

demotion [dɪ'məuʃən] n degradación f; (Comm) descenso

demure [dɪ'mjuəʳ] adj recatado

den [dɛn] n (of animal) guarida; (study) estudio

denial [dɪ'naɪəl] n (refusal) denegación f; (of report etc) desmentido

denim ['dɛnɪm] n tela vaquera; see also **denims**

denims ['dɛnɪms] npl vaqueros mpl

Denmark ['dɛnmɑ:k] n Dinamarca

denomination [dɪnɔmɪ'neɪʃən] n valor m; (Rel) confesión f

denominator [dɪ'nɔmɪneɪtəʳ] n denominador m

denote [dɪ'nəut] vt indicar, significar

denounce [dɪ'nauns] vt denunciar

dense [dɛns] adj (thick) espeso; (foliage etc) tupido; (stupid) torpe

densely [dɛnslɪ] adv: **~ populated** con una alta densidad de población

density ['dɛnsɪtɪ] n densidad f; **single/double-~ disk** n (Comput) disco de densidad sencilla/de doble densidad

dent [dɛnt] n abolladura ▷ vt (also: **make a ~ in**) abollar

dental ['dɛntl] adj dental

dental floss [-flɔs] n seda dental

dental surgeon n odontólogo(-a)

dental surgery n clínica f dental, consultorio m dental

dentist ['dɛntɪst] n dentista m/f; **~'s surgery** (Brit) consultorio dental

dentistry ['dɛntɪstrɪ] n odontología

dentures ['dɛntʃəz] npl dentadura sg (postiza)

denunciation [dɪnʌnsɪ'eɪʃən] n denuncia, denunciación f

deny [dɪ'naɪ] vt negar; (charge) rechazar; (report) desmentir; **to ~ o.s.** privarse (de); **he denies having said it** niega haberlo dicho

deodorant [di:'əudərənt] n desodorante m

depart [dɪ'pɑ:t] vi irse, marcharse; (train) salir; **to ~ from** (fig: differ from) apartarse de

departed [dɪ'pɑ:tɪd] adj (bygone: days, glory) pasado; (dead) difunto ▷ n: **the (dear) ~** el/la/los/las difunto/a/os/as

department [dɪ'pɑːtmənt] n (Comm)
sección f; (Scol) departamento; (Pol)
ministerio; **that's not my ~** (fig) no tiene
que ver conmigo; **D~ of State** (US) Ministerio
de Asuntos Exteriores
department store n grandes almacenes
mpl
departure [dɪ'pɑːtʃər] n partida, ida; (of train)
salida; **a new ~** un nuevo rumbo
departure lounge n (at airport) sala de
embarque
depend [dɪ'pɛnd] vi: **to ~ (up)on** (be dependent
upon) depender de; (rely on) contar con; **it ~s**
depende, según; **~ing on the result** según
el resultado
dependable [dɪ'pɛndəbl] adj (person) formal,
serio
dependant [dɪ'pɛndənt] n dependiente m/f
dependence [dɪ'pɛndəns] n dependencia
dependent [dɪ'pɛndənt] adj: **to be ~ (on)**
depender (de) ▷ n = **dependant**
depict [dɪ'pɪkt] vt (in picture) pintar; (describe)
representar
depleted [dɪ'pliːtɪd] adj reducido
deplorable [dɪ'plɔːrəbl] adj deplorable
deploy [dɪ'plɔɪ] vt desplegar
deport [dɪ'pɔːt] vt deportar
deportation [diːpɔː'teɪʃən] n deportación f
deportee [diːpɔː'tiː] n deportado(-a)
deposit [dɪ'pɔzɪt] n depósito; (Chem)
sedimento; (of ore, oil) yacimiento ▷ vt (gen)
depositar; **to put down a ~ of £50** dejar un
depósito de 50 libras
deposit account n (Brit) cuenta de ahorros
depot ['dɛpəu] n (storehouse) depósito;
(for vehicles) parque m
depraved [dɪ'preɪvd] adj depravado, vicioso
depravity [dɪ'prævɪti] n depravación f, vicio
depreciate [dɪ'priːʃɪeɪt] vi depreciarse,
perder valor
depreciation [dɪpriːʃɪ'eɪʃən] n
depreciación f
depress [dɪ'prɛs] vt deprimir; (press down)
apretar
depressant [dɪ'prɛsnt] n (Med) calmante m,
sedante m
depressed [dɪ'prɛst] adj deprimido; (Comm:
market, economy) deprimido; (area) deprimido
(económicamente); **to get ~** deprimirse
depressing [dɪ'prɛsɪŋ] adj deprimente
depression [dɪ'prɛʃən] n depresión f; **the
economy is in a state of ~** la economía está
deprimida
deprivation [dɛprɪ'veɪʃən] n privación f;
(loss) pérdida
deprive [dɪ'praɪv] vt: **to ~ sb of** privar a algn
de
deprived [dɪ'praɪvd] adj necesitado
dept. abbr (= department) dto
depth [dɛpθ] n profundidad f; **at a ~ of three
metres** a tres metros de profundidad; **to be
out of one's ~** (swimmer) perder pie; (fig)

sentirse perdido; **to study sth in ~** estudiar
algo a fondo; **in the ~s of** en lo más hondo de
deputize ['dɛpjutaɪz] vi: **to ~ for sb** sustituir
a algn
deputy ['dɛpjutɪ] adj: **~ head** subdirector(a)
m(f) ▷ n sustituto(-a), suplente m/f; (Pol)
diputado(-a); (agent) representante m/f
derail [dɪ'reɪl] vt: **to be ~ed** descarrilarse
deranged [dɪ'reɪndʒd] adj trastornado
derby ['dɑːbɪ] n (US) hongo
deregulation [diːrɛgju'leɪʃən] n
desreglamentación f
derelict ['dɛrɪlɪkt] adj abandonado
derision [dɪ'rɪʒən] n irrisión f, mofas fpl
derisory [dɪ'raɪzərɪ] adj (sum) irrisorio;
(laughter, person) burlón(-ona), irónico
derivative [dɪ'rɪvətɪv] n derivado ▷ adj (work)
poco original
derive [dɪ'raɪv] vt derivar; (benefit etc) obtener
▷ vi: **to ~ from** derivarse de
dermatitis [dəːmə'taɪtɪs] n dermatitis f
derogatory [dɪ'rɔgətərɪ] adj despectivo
derv [dəːv] n (Brit) gasoil m
descend [dɪ'sɛnd] vt, vi descender, bajar; **to ~
from** descender de; **in ~ing order of
importance** de mayor a menor importancia;
descend on vt fus (enemy, angry person) caer
sobre; (misfortune) sobrevenir; (gloom, silence)
invadir; **visitors ~ed on us** las visitas nos
invadieron
descendant [dɪ'sɛndənt] n descendiente m/f
descent [dɪ'sɛnt] n descenso; (Geo)
pendiente f, declive m; (origin) descendencia
describe [dɪs'kraɪb] vt describir
description [dɪs'krɪpʃən] n descripción f;
(sort) clase f, género; **of every ~** de toda clase
descriptive [dɪs'krɪptɪv] adj descriptivo
desecrate ['dɛsɪkreɪt] vt profanar
desert [n 'dɛzət, vb dɪ'zəːt] n desierto ▷ vt
abandonar, desamparar ▷ vi (Mil) desertar;
see also **deserts**
deserted [dɪ'zəːtɪd] adj desierto
deserter [dɪ'zəːtər] n desertor(-a) m(f)
desertion [dɪ'zəːʃən] n deserción f
desert island n isla desierta
deserts [dɪ'zəːts] npl: **to get one's just ~**
llevarse su merecido
deserve [dɪ'zəːv] vt merecer, ser digno de,
ameritar (LAm)
deserving [dɪ'zəːvɪŋ] adj (person) digno;
(action, cause) meritorio
design [dɪ'zaɪn] n (sketch) bosquejo; (of dress,
car) diseño; (pattern) dibujo ▷ vt (gen) diseñar;
industrial ~ diseño industrial; **to have ~s
on sb** tener la(s) mira(s) puesta(s) en algn;
to be ~ed for sb/sth estar hecho para
algn/algo
design and technology n (Brit Scol) diseño y
tecnología
designate ['dɛzɪgneɪt] vt (appoint) nombrar;
(destine) designar ▷ adj ['dɛzɪgnɪt] designado
designer [dɪ'zaɪnər] n diseñador(-a) m(f)

desirable [dɪ'zaɪərəbl] *adj* (*proper*) deseable; (*attractive*) atractivo; **it is ~ that** es conveniente que

desire [dɪ'zaɪəʳ] *n* deseo ▷ *vt* desear; **to ~ sth/ to do sth/that** desear algo/hacer algo/que

desk [dɛsk] *n* (*in office*) escritorio; (*for pupil*) pupitre *m*; (*in hotel, at airport*) recepción *f*; (*Brit: in shop, restaurant*) caja

desktop ['dɛsktɔp] *n* (*Comput*) escritorio

desktop computer *n* ordenador *m* de sobremesa

desktop publishing *n* autoedición *f*

desolate ['dɛsəlɪt] *adj* (*place*) desierto; (*person*) afligido

desolation [dɛsə'leɪʃən] *n* (*of place*) desolación *f*; (*of person*) aflicción *f*

despair [dɪs'pɛəʳ] *n* desesperación *f* ▷ *vi*: **to ~ of** desesperar de; **in ~** desesperado

despatch [dɪs'pætʃ] *n, vt* = **dispatch**

desperate ['dɛspərɪt] *adj* desesperado; (*fugitive*) peligroso; (*measures*) extremo; **we are getting ~** estamos al borde de desesperación; **to be ~ for sth/to do** necesitar urgentemente algo/hacer

desperately ['dɛspərɪtlɪ] *adv* desesperadamente; (*very*) terriblemente, gravemente; **~ ill** gravemente enfermo

desperation [dɛspə'reɪʃən] *n* desesperación *f*; **in ~** desesperado

despicable [dɪs'pɪkəbl] *adj* vil, despreciable

despise [dɪs'paɪz] *vt* despreciar

despite [dɪs'paɪt] *prep* a pesar de, pese a

despondent [dɪs'pɔndənt] *adj* deprimido, abatido

dessert [dɪ'zə:t] *n* postre *m*

dessertspoon [dɪ'zə:tspu:n] *n* cuchara (de postre)

destination [dɛstɪ'neɪʃən] *n* destino

destine ['dɛstɪn] *vt* destinar

destined ['dɛstɪnd] *adj*: **~ for London** con destino a Londres

destiny ['dɛstɪnɪ] *n* destino

destitute ['dɛstɪtju:t] *adj* desamparado, indigente

destitution [dɛstɪ'tju:ʃən] *n* indigencia, miseria

destroy [dɪs'trɔɪ] *vt* destruir; (*finish*) acabar con

destroyer [dɪs'trɔɪəʳ] *n* (*Naut*) destructor *m*

destruction [dɪs'trʌkʃən] *n* destrucción *f*; (*fig*) ruina

destructive [dɪs'trʌktɪv] *adj* destructivo, destructor(a)

detach [dɪ'tætʃ] *vt* separar; (*unstick*) despegar

detached [dɪ'tætʃt] *adj* (*attitude*) objetivo, imparcial

detached house *n* chalé *m*, chalet *m*

detachment [dɪ'tætʃmənt] *n* separación *f*; (*Mil*) destacamento; (*fig*) objetividad *f*, imparcialidad *f*

detail ['di:teɪl] *n* detalle *m*; (*Mil*) destacamento ▷ *vt* detallar; (*Mil*) destacar;

in ~ detalladamente; **to go into ~(s)** entrar en detalles

detailed ['di:teɪld] *adj* detallado

detain [dɪ'teɪn] *vt* retener; (*in captivity*) detener

detainee [di:teɪ'ni:] *n* detenido(-a)

detect [dɪ'tɛkt] *vt* (*discover*) descubrir; (*Med, Police*) identificar; (*Mil, Radar, Tech*) detectar; (*notice*) percibir

detection [dɪ'tɛkʃən] *n* descubrimiento; identificación *f*; **crime ~** investigación *f*; **to escape ~** (*criminal*) escaparse sin ser descubierto; (*mistake*) pasar inadvertido

detective [dɪ'tɛktɪv] *n* detective *m*

detective story *n* novela policíaca

detector [dɪ'tɛktəʳ] *n* detector *m*

detention [dɪ'tɛnʃən] *n* detención *f*, arresto; (*Scol*) castigo

deter [dɪ'tə:ʳ] *vt* (*dissuade*) disuadir; (*prevent*) impedir; **to ~ sb from doing sth** disuadir a algn de que haga algo

detergent [dɪ'tə:dʒənt] *n* detergente *m*

deteriorate [dɪ'tɪərɪəreɪt] *vi* deteriorarse

determination [dɪtə:mɪ'neɪʃən] *n* resolución *f*

determine [dɪ'tə:mɪn] *vt* determinar; **to ~ to do sth** decidir hacer algo

determined [dɪ'tə:mɪnd] *adj*: **to be ~ to do sth** estar decidido *or* resuelto a hacer algo; **a ~ effort** un esfuerzo enérgico

deterrent [dɪ'tɛrənt] *n* fuerza de disuasión; **to act as a ~** servir para prevenir

detest [dɪ'tɛst] *vt* aborrecer

detonate ['dɛtəneɪt] *vi* estallar ▷ *vt* hacer detonar

detonator ['dɛtəneɪtəʳ] *n* detonador *m*, fulminante *m*

detour ['di:tuəʳ] *n* (*gen, US Aut: diversion*) desvío ▷ *vt* (*US: traffic*) desviar; **to make a ~** dar un rodeo

detract [dɪ'trækt] *vt*: **to ~ from** quitar mérito a, restar valor a

detractor [dɪ'træktəʳ] *n* detractor(-a) *m(f)*

detriment ['dɛtrɪmənt] *n*: **to the ~ of** en perjuicio de; **without ~ to** sin detrimento de, sin perjuicio para

detrimental [dɛtrɪ'mɛntl] *adj*: **~ (to)** perjudicial (a)

deuce [dju:s] *n* (*Tennis*) cuarenta iguales

devaluation [dɪvælju'eɪʃən] *n* devaluación *f*

devalue [dɪ'vælju:] *vt* devaluar

devastate ['dɛvəsteɪt] *vt* devastar; **he was ~d by the news** las noticias le dejaron desolado

devastating ['dɛvəsteɪtɪŋ] *adj* devastador(-a); (*fig*) arrollador(-a)

devastation [dɛvəs'teɪʃən] *n* devastación *f*, ruina

develop [dɪ'vɛləp] *vt* desarrollar; (*Phot*) revelar; (*disease*) contraer; (*habit*) adquirir ▷ *vi* desarrollarse; (*advance*) progresar; **this land is to be ~ed** se va a construir en este terreno;

to ~ **a taste for sth** tomar gusto a algo; **to ~
into** transformarse *or* convertirse en
developer [dɪˈvɛləpəʳ] n (*property developer*)
promotor(-a) m(f)
developing country n país m en (vías de)
desarrollo
development [dɪˈvɛləpmənt] n desarrollo;
(*advance*) progreso; (*of affair, case*)
desenvolvimiento; (*of land*) urbanización f
deviant [ˈdiːvɪənt] adj anómalo, pervertido
deviate [ˈdiːvɪeɪt] vi: **to ~ (from)** desviarse
(de)
device [dɪˈvaɪs] n (*scheme*) estratagema,
recurso; (*apparatus*) aparato, mecanismo;
(*explosive device*) artefacto explosivo
devil [ˈdɛvl] n diablo, demonio
devil's advocate n: **to play (the) ~** hacer de
abogado del diablo
devious [ˈdiːvɪəs] adj intricado, enrevesado;
(*person*) taimado
devise [dɪˈvaɪz] vt idear, inventar
devoid [dɪˈvɔɪd] adj: **~ of** desprovisto de
devolution [diːvəˈluːʃən] n (*Pol*)
descentralización f
devote [dɪˈvaʊt] vt: **to ~ sth to** dedicar
algo a
devoted [dɪˈvaʊtɪd] adj (*loyal*) leal, fiel; **to be
~ to sb** querer con devoción a algn; **the book
is ~ to politics** el libro trata de política
devotee [dɛvaʊˈtiː] n devoto(-a)
devotion [dɪˈvaʊʃən] n dedicación f; (*Rel*)
devoción f
devour [dɪˈvaʊəʳ] vt devorar
devout [dɪˈvaʊt] adj devoto
dew [djuː] n rocío
dexterity [dɛksˈtɛrɪtɪ] n destreza
diabetes [daɪəˈbiːtiːz] n diabetes f
diabetic [daɪəˈbɛtɪk] n diabético(-a) ▷ adj
diabético; (*chocolate, jam*) para diabéticos
diabolical [daɪəˈbɔlɪkəl] adj diabólico; (*inf:
dreadful*) horrendo, horroroso
diagnose [ˈdaɪəgnəʊz] vt diagnosticar
diagnosis (*pl* **diagnoses**) [daɪəgˈnəʊsɪs, -siːz] n
diagnóstico
diagonal [daɪˈægənl] adj diagonal ▷ n
diagonal f
diagram [ˈdaɪəgræm] n diagrama m,
esquema m
dial [ˈdaɪəl] n esfera; (*of radio*) dial m; (*tuner*)
sintonizador m; (*of phone*) disco ▷ vt (*number*)
marcar, discar (*LAm*); **to ~ a wrong number**
equivocarse de número; **can I ~ London
direct?** ¿puedo marcar un número de
Londres directamente?
dial code n (*US*) prefijo
dialect [ˈdaɪəlɛkt] n dialecto
dialling code [ˈdaɪəlɪŋ-] n (*Brit*) prefijo
dialling tone n (*Brit*) señal f or tono de marcar
dialogue, dialog (*US*) [ˈdaɪəlɔg] n diálogo
dial tone n (*US*) señal f or tono de marcar
dialysis [daɪˈælɪsɪs] n diálisis f
diameter [daɪˈæmɪtəʳ] n diámetro

diamond [ˈdaɪəmənd] n diamante m;
diamonds npl (*Cards*) diamantes mpl
diaper [ˈdaɪəpəʳ] n (*US*) pañal m
diaphragm [ˈdaɪəfræm] n diafragma m
diarrhoea, diarrhea (*US*) [daɪəˈriːə] n
diarrea
diary [ˈdaɪərɪ] n (*daily account*) diario; (*book*)
agenda; **to keep a ~** escribir un diario
dice [daɪs] n pl inv dados mpl ▷ vt (*Culin*) cortar
en cuadritos
Dictaphone® [ˈdɪktəfəʊn] n dictáfono®
dictate [dɪkˈteɪt] vt dictar ▷ n [ˈdɪkteɪt] dictado;
dictate to vt fus (*person*) dar órdenes a; **I
won't be ~d to** no recibo órdenes de nadie
dictation [dɪkˈteɪʃən] n (*to secretary etc*)
dictado; **at ~ speed** para tomar al dictado
dictator [dɪkˈteɪtəʳ] n dictador m
dictatorship [dɪkˈteɪtəʃɪp] n dictadura
diction [ˈdɪkʃən] n dicción f
dictionary [ˈdɪkʃənrɪ] n diccionario
did [dɪd] pt of **do**
didactic [daɪˈdæktɪk] adj didáctico
diddle [ˈdɪdl] vt estafar, timar
didn't [ˈdɪdənt] = **did not**
die [daɪ] vi morir; **to ~ (of or from)** morirse
(de); **to be dying** morirse, estar muriéndose;
to be dying for sth/to do sth morirse por
algo/de ganas de hacer algo; **die away** vi
(*sound, light*) desvanecerse; **die down** vi (*gen*)
apagarse; (*wind*) amainar; **die out** vi
desaparecer, extinguirse
diehard [ˈdaɪhɑːd] n intransigente m/f
diesel [ˈdiːzl] n diesel m
diesel engine n motor m diesel
diesel fuel, diesel oil n gas-oil m
diet [ˈdaɪət] n dieta; (*restricted food*) régimen m
▷ vi (*also*: **be on a ~**) estar a dieta, hacer
régimen; **to live on a ~ of** alimentarse de
dietician [daɪəˈtɪʃən] n dietista m/f
differ [ˈdɪfəʳ] vi (*be different*) ser distinto,
diferenciarse; (*disagree*) discrepar
difference [ˈdɪfrəns] n diferencia; (*quarrel*)
desacuerdo; **it makes no ~ to me** me da
igual or lo mismo; **to settle one's ~s**
arreglarse
different [ˈdɪfrənt] adj diferente, distinto
differentiate [dɪfəˈrɛnʃɪeɪt] vt distinguir
▷ vi diferenciarse; **to ~ between** distinguir
entre
differently [ˈdɪfrəntlɪ] adv de otro modo,
en forma distinta
difficult [ˈdɪfɪkəlt] adj difícil; **~ to
understand** difícil de entender
difficulty [ˈdɪfɪkəltɪ] n dificultad f; **to have
difficulties with** (*police, landlord etc*) tener
problemas con; **to be in ~** estar en apuros
diffident [ˈdɪfɪdənt] adj tímido
dig [dɪg] vt (*pt, pp* **dug** [dʌg]) (*hole*) cavar;
(*ground*) remover; (*coal*) extraer; (*nails etc*)
clavar ▷ n (*prod*) empujón m; (*archaeological*)
excavación f; (*remark*) indirecta; **to ~ into**
(*savings*) consumir; **to ~ into one's pockets**

for sth hurgar en el bolsillo buscando algo; **to ~ one's nails into** clavar las uñas en; *see also* **digs; dig in** *vi* (*also:* ~ **o.s. in:** *Mil*) atrincherarse; (*inf: eat*) hincar los dientes ▷ *vt* (*compost*) añadir al suelo; (*knife, claw*) clavar; **to ~ in one's heels** (*fig*) mantenerse en sus trece; **dig out** *vt* (*hole*) excavar; (*survivors, car from snow*) sacar; **dig up** *vt* desenterrar; (*plant*) desarraigar

digest [daɪ'dʒɛst] *vt* (*food*) digerir; (*facts*) asimilar ▷ *n* ['daɪdʒɛst] resumen *m*

digestion [dɪ'dʒɛstʃən] *n* digestión *f*

digit ['dɪdʒɪt] *n* (*number*) dígito; (*finger*) dedo

digital ['dɪdʒɪtl] *adj* digital

digital camera *n* cámara digital

digital TV *n* televisión *f* digital

dignified ['dɪgnɪfaɪd] *adj* grave, solemne; (*action*) decoroso

dignitary ['dɪgnɪtərɪ] *n* dignatario(-a)

dignity ['dɪgnɪtɪ] *n* dignidad *f*

digress [daɪ'grɛs] *vi*: **to ~ from** apartarse de

digression [daɪ'grɛʃən] *n* digresión *f*

digs [dɪgz] *npl* (*Brit: inf*) pensión *f*, alojamiento

dilapidated [dɪ'læpɪdeɪtɪd] *adj* desmoronado, ruinoso

dilate [daɪ'leɪt] *vt* dilatar ▷ *vi* dilatarse

dilemma [daɪ'lɛmə] *n* dilema *m*; **to be in a ~** estar en un dilema

diligence ['dɪlɪdʒəns] *n* diligencia

diligent ['dɪlɪdʒənt] *adj* diligente

dill [dɪl] *n* eneldo

dilute [daɪ'luːt] *vt* diluir

dim [dɪm] *adj* (*light*) débil; (*sight*) turbio; (*outline*) borroso; (*stupid*) lerdo; (*room*) oscuro ▷ *vt* (*light*) bajar; **to take a ~ view of sth** tener una pobre opinión de algo

dime [daɪm] *n* (*US*) *moneda de diez centavos*

dimension [dɪ'mɛnʃən] *n* dimensión *f*

dimensions [dɪ'mɛnʃənz] *npl* dimensiones *fpl*

diminish [dɪ'mɪnɪʃ] *vt, vi* disminuir

diminished [dɪ'mɪnɪʃt] *adj*: **~ responsibility** (*Law*) responsabilidad *f* disminuida

diminutive [dɪ'mɪnjutɪv] *adj* diminuto ▷ *n* (*Ling*) diminutivo

dimmer ['dɪmə'] *n* (*also:* **~ switch**) regulador *m* (de intensidad); (*US Aut*) interruptor *m*

dimple ['dɪmpl] *n* hoyuelo

din [dɪn] *n* estruendo, estrépito ▷ *vt*: **to ~ sth into sb** (*inf*) meter algo en la cabeza a algn

dine [daɪn] *vi* cenar

diner ['daɪnə'] *n* (*person: in restaurant*) comensal *m/f*; (*US*) restaurante económico; (*Brit Rail*) = **dining car**

dinghy ['dɪŋgɪ] *n* bote *m*; (*also:* **rubber ~**) lancha (neumática)

dingy ['dɪndʒɪ] *adj* (*room*) sombrío; (*dirty*) sucio; (*dull*) deslucido

dining car ['daɪnɪŋ-] *n* (*Brit*) coche-restaurante *m*

dining room ['daɪnɪŋ-] *n* comedor *m*

dining table *n* mesa *f* de comedor

dinner ['dɪnə'] *n* (*evening meal*) cena, comida (*LAm*); (*lunch*) comida; (*public*) cena, banquete *m*; **~'s ready!** ¡la cena está servida!

dinner jacket *n* smoking *m*

dinner party *n* cena

dinner time *n* (*evening*) hora de cenar; (*midday*) hora de comer

dinosaur ['daɪnəsɔː'] *n* dinosaurio

dint [dɪnt] *n*: **by ~ of (doing) sth** a fuerza de (hacer) algo

diocese ['daɪəsɪs] *n* diócesis *f*

dioxide [daɪ'ɔksaɪd] *n* bióxido; **carbon ~** bióxido de carbono

Dip. *abbr* (*Brit*) = **diploma**

dip [dɪp] *n* (*slope*) pendiente *f*; (*in sea*) chapuzón *m* ▷ *vt* (*in water*) mojar; (*ladle etc*) meter; (*Brit Aut*): **to ~ one's lights** poner la luz de cruce ▷ *vi* descender, bajar

diphtheria [dɪf'θɪərɪə] *n* difteria

diphthong ['dɪfθɒŋ] *n* diptongo

diploma [dɪ'pləʊmə] *n* diploma *m*

diplomacy [dɪ'pləʊməsɪ] *n* diplomacia

diplomat ['dɪpləmæt] *n* diplomático(-a) *m(f)*

diplomatic [dɪplə'mætɪk] *adj* diplomático; **to break off ~ relations** romper las relaciones diplomáticas

diplomatic immunity *n* inmunidad *f* diplomática

dipstick ['dɪpstɪk] *n* (*Aut*) varilla de nivel (del aceite)

dipswitch ['dɪpswɪtʃ] *n* (*Brit Aut*) interruptor *m*

dire [daɪə'] *adj* calamitoso

direct [daɪ'rɛkt] *adj* (*gen*) directo; (*manner, person*) franco ▷ *vt* dirigir; **can you ~ me to ...?** ¿puede indicarme dónde está ...?; **to ~ sb to do sth** mandar a algn hacer algo

direct current *n* corriente *f* continua

direct debit *n* domiciliación *f* bancaria de recibos; **to pay by ~** domiciliar el pago

direct dialling *n* servicio automático de llamadas

direction [dɪ'rɛkʃən] *n* dirección *f*; **sense of ~** sentido de la orientación; **directions** *npl* (*advice*) órdenes *fpl*, instrucciones *fpl*; (*to a place*) señas *fpl*; **in the ~ of** hacia, en dirección a; **~s for use** modo de empleo; **to ask for ~s** preguntar el camino

directive [daɪ'rɛktɪv] *n* orden *f*, instrucción *f*; **a government ~** una orden del gobierno

directly [dɪ'rɛktlɪ] *adv* (*in straight line*) directamente; (*at once*) en seguida

directness [dɪ'rɛktnɪs] *n* (*of person, speech*) franqueza

director [dɪ'rɛktə'] *n* director(a) *m(f)*; **managing ~** director(a) *m(f)* gerente

Director of Public Prosecutions *n* ≈ fiscal *m/f* general del Estado

directory [dɪ'rɛktərɪ] *n* (*Tel*) guía (telefónica); (*street directory*) callejero; (*trade directory*) directorio de comercio; (*Comput*) directorio

directory enquiries, directory
assistance (US) *n* (*service*) (servicio *m* de)
información
dirt [dəːt] *n* suciedad *f*
dirt-cheap ['dəːt'tʃiːp] *adj* baratísimo
dirty ['dəːtɪ] *adj* sucio; (*joke*) verde, colorado
(*LAm*) ▷ *vt* ensuciar; (*stain*) manchar
disability [dɪsə'bɪlɪtɪ] *n* incapacidad *f*
disabled [dɪs'eɪbld] *adj* (*physically*)
minusválido(-a); (*mentally*) deficiente
mental
disadvantage [dɪsəd'vɑːntɪdʒ] *n* desventaja,
inconveniente *m*
disagree [dɪsə'griː] *vi* (*differ*) discrepar; **to ~**
(**with**) no estar de acuerdo (con); **I ~ with**
you no estoy de acuerdo contigo
disagreeable [dɪsə'grɪəbl] *adj* desagradable
disagreement [dɪsə'griːmənt] *n* (*gen*)
desacuerdo; (*quarrel*) riña; **to have a ~ with**
sb estar en desacuerdo con algn
disallow ['dɪsə'lau] *vt* (*goal*) anular; (*claim*)
rechazar
disappear [dɪsə'pɪəʳ] *vi* desaparecer
disappearance [dɪsə'pɪərəns] *n*
desaparición *f*
disappoint [dɪsə'pɔɪnt] *vt* decepcionar;
(*hopes*) defraudar
disappointed [dɪsə'pɔɪntɪd] *adj*
decepcionado
disappointing [dɪsə'pɔɪntɪŋ] *adj*
decepcionante
disappointment [dɪsə'pɔɪntmənt] *n*
decepción *f*
disapproval [dɪsə'pruːvəl] *n* desaprobación *f*
disapprove [dɪsə'pruːv] *vi*: **to ~ of**
desaprobar
disarm [dɪs'ɑːm] *vt* desarmar
disarmament [dɪs'ɑːməmənt] *n* desarme *m*
disarray [dɪsə'reɪ] *n*: **in ~** (*troops*)
desorganizado; (*thoughts*) confuso; (*hair,*
clothes) desarreglado; **to throw into ~**
provocar el caos
disaster [dɪ'zɑːstəʳ] *n* desastre *m*
disastrous [dɪ'zɑːstrəs] *adj* desastroso
disband [dɪs'bænd] *vt* disolver ▷ *vi*
desbandarse
disbelief [dɪsbə'liːf] *n* incredulidad *f*; **in ~** con
incredulidad
disc [dɪsk] *n* disco; (*Comput*) = **disk**
discard [dɪs'kɑːd] *vt* tirar; (*fig*) descartar
discern [dɪ'səːn] *vt* percibir, discernir;
(*understand*) comprender
discerning [dɪ'səːnɪŋ] *adj* perspicaz
discharge [dɪs'tʃɑːdʒ] *vt* (*task, duty*) cumplir;
(*ship etc*) descargar; (*patient*) dar de alta;
(*employee*) despedir; (*soldier*) licenciar;
(*defendant*) poner en libertad; (*settle: debt*)
saldar ▷ *n* ['dɪstʃɑːdʒ] (*Elec*) descarga;
(*dismissal*) despedida; (*of duty*) desempeño;
(*of debt*) pago, descargo; (*of gas, chemicals*)
escape *m*; **~d bankrupt** quebrado/a
rehabilitado/a

disciple [dɪ'saɪpl] *n* discípulo(-a)
discipline ['dɪsɪplɪn] *n* disciplina ▷ *vt*
disciplinar; **to ~ o.s. to do sth** obligarse a
hacer algo
disc jockey, DJ *n* pinchadiscos *m/f inv*
disclaim [dɪs'kleɪm] *vt* negar tener
disclaimer [dɪs'kleɪməʳ] *n* rectificación *f*;
to issue a ~ hacer una rectificación
disclose [dɪs'kləuz] *vt* revelar
disclosure [dɪs'kləuʒəʳ] *n* revelación *f*
disco ['dɪskəu] *n abbr* = **discothèque**
discoloured, discolored (US) [dɪs'kʌləd] *adj*
descolorido
discomfort [dɪs'kʌmfət] *n* incomodidad *f*;
(*unease*) inquietud *f*; (*physical*) malestar *m*
disconcert [dɪskən'səːt] *vt* desconcertar
disconnect [dɪskə'nɛkt] *vt* (*gen*) separar;
(*Elec etc*) desconectar; (*supply*) cortar (el
suministro) a
disconsolate [dɪs'kɔnsəlɪt] *adj*
desconsolado
discontent [dɪskən'tɛnt] *n* descontento
discontented [dɪskən'tɛntɪd] *adj*
descontento
discontinue [dɪskən'tɪnjuː] *vt* interrumpir;
(*payments*) suspender
discord ['dɪskɔːd] *n* discordia; (*Mus*)
disonancia
discordant [dɪs'kɔːdənt] *adj* disonante
discothèque ['dɪskəutɛk] *n* discoteca
discount ['dɪskaunt] *n* descuento ▷ *vt*
[dɪs'kaunt] descontar; (*report etc*) descartar;
at a ~ con descuento; **~ for cash** descuento
por pago en efectivo; **to give sb a ~ on sth**
hacer un descuento a algn en algo
discourage [dɪs'kʌrɪdʒ] *vt* desalentar;
(*oppose*) oponerse a; (*dissuade, deter*)
desanimar, disuadir; **to ~ sb from doing**
disuadir a algn de hacer
discouraging [dɪs'kʌrɪdʒɪŋ] *adj*
desalentador(a)
discourteous [dɪs'kəːtɪəs] *adj* descortés
discover [dɪs'kʌvəʳ] *vt* descubrir
discovery [dɪs'kʌvərɪ] *n* descubrimiento
discredit [dɪs'krɛdɪt] *vt* desacreditar
discreet [dɪ'skriːt] *adj* (*tactful*) discreto;
(*careful*) circunspecto, prudente
discrepancy [dɪ'skrɛpənsɪ] *n* (*difference*)
diferencia; (*disagreement*) discrepancia
discretion [dɪ'skrɛʃən] *n* (*tact*) discreción *f*;
(*care*) prudencia, circunspección *f*; **use your**
own ~ haz lo que creas oportuno; **at the ~ of**
a criterio de
discriminate [dɪ'skrɪmɪneɪt] *vi*: **to ~**
between distinguir entre; **to ~ against**
discriminar contra
discriminating [dɪ'skrɪmɪneɪtɪŋ] *adj*
entendido
discrimination [dɪskrɪmɪ'neɪʃən] *n*
(*discernment*) perspicacia; (*bias*)
discriminación *f*; **racial/sexual ~**
discriminación racial/sexual

d

discus ['dɪskəs] n disco

discuss [dɪ'skʌs] vt (gen) discutir; (a theme) tratar

discussion [dɪ'skʌʃən] n discusión f; **under ~** en discusión

disdain [dɪs'deɪn] n desdén m ▷ vt desdeñar

disease [dɪ'zi:z] n enfermedad f

diseased [dɪ'zi:zd] adj enfermo

disembark [dɪsɪm'ba:k] vt, vi desembarcar

disengage [dɪsɪn'geɪdʒ] vt soltar; **to ~ the clutch** (Aut) desembragar

disentangle [dɪsɪn'tæŋgl] vt desenredar

disfigure [dɪs'fɪgəʳ] vt desfigurar

disgrace [dɪs'greɪs] n ignominia; (downfall) caída; (shame) vergüenza, escándalo ▷ vt deshonrar

disgraceful [dɪs'greɪsful] adj vergonzoso; (behaviour) escandaloso

disgruntled [dɪs'grʌntld] adj disgustado, descontento

disguise [dɪs'gaɪz] n disfraz m ▷ vt disfrazar; (voice) disimular; (feelings etc) ocultar; **in ~** disfrazado; **to ~ o.s. as** disfrazarse de; **there's no disguising the fact that ...** no puede ocultarse el hecho de que ...

disgust [dɪs'gʌst] n repugnancia ▷ vt repugnar, dar asco a

disgusted [dɪs'gʌstɪd] adj indignado

disgusting [dɪs'gʌstɪŋ] adj repugnante, asqueroso

dish [dɪʃ] n (gen) plato; **to do** or **wash the ~es** fregar los platos; **dish out** vt (money, exam papers) repartir; (food) servir; (advice) dar; **dish up** vt servir

dishcloth ['dɪʃklɔθ] n (for washing) bayeta; (for drying) paño de cocina

dishearten [dɪs'ha:tn] vt desalentar

dishevelled, disheveled (US) [dɪ'ʃevəld] adj (hair) despeinado; (clothes, appearance) desarreglado

dishonest [dɪs'ɔnɪst] adj (person) poco honrado, tramposo; (means) fraudulento

dishonesty [dɪs'ɔnɪstɪ] n falta de honradez

dishonour, dishonor (US) [dɪs'ɔnəʳ] n deshonra

dishtowel ['dɪʃtauəl] n (US) bayeta

dishwasher ['dɪʃwɔʃəʳ] n lavaplatos m inv; (person) friegaplatos m/f inv

dishy ['dɪʃɪ] adj (Brit inf) buenón(-ona)

disillusion [dɪsɪ'lu:ʒən] vt desilusionar; **to become ~ed (with)** quedar desilusionado (con)

disincentive [dɪsɪn'sentɪv] n freno; **to act as a ~ (to)** actuar de freno (a); **to be a ~ to** ser un freno a

disinfect [dɪsɪn'fekt] vt desinfectar

disinfectant [dɪsɪn'fektənt] n desinfectante m

disinformation [dɪsɪnfə'meɪʃən] n desinformación f

disintegrate [dɪs'ɪntɪgreɪt] vi disgregarse, desintegrarse

disinterested [dɪs'ɪntrəstɪd] adj desinteresado

disjointed [dɪs'dʒɔɪntɪd] adj inconexo

disk [dɪsk] n (Comput) disco, disquete m; **single-/double-sided ~** disco de una cara/dos caras

disk drive n unidad f (de disco)

diskette [dɪs'ket] n diskette m, disquete m, disco flexible

disk operating system n sistema m operativo de discos

dislike [dɪs'laɪk] n antipatía, aversión f ▷ vt tener antipatía a; **to take a ~ to sb/sth** cogerle or (LAm) agarrarle antipatía a algn/algo; **I ~ the idea** no me gusta la idea

dislocate ['dɪsləkeɪt] vt dislocar; **he ~d his shoulder** se dislocó el hombro

dislodge [dɪs'lɔdʒ] vt sacar; (enemy) desalojar

disloyal [dɪs'lɔɪəl] adj desleal

dismal ['dɪzml] adj (dark) sombrío; (depressing) triste; (very bad) fatal

dismantle [dɪs'mæntl] vt desmontar, desarmar

dismay [dɪs'meɪ] n consternación f ▷ vt consternar; **much to my ~** para gran consternación mía

dismiss [dɪs'mɪs] vt (worker) despedir; (official) destituir; (idea) rechazar; (Law) rechazar; (possibility) descartar ▷ vi (Mil) romper filas

dismissal [dɪs'mɪsl] n despido; destitución f

dismount [dɪs'maunt] vi apearse; (rider) desmontar

disobedience [dɪsə'bi:dɪəns] n desobediencia

disobedient [dɪsə'bi:dɪənt] adj desobediente

disobey [dɪsə'beɪ] vt desobedecer; (rule) infringir

disorder [dɪs'ɔ:dəʳ] n desorden m; (rioting) disturbio; (Med) trastorno; (disease) enfermedad f; **civil ~** desorden m civil

disorderly [dɪs'ɔ:dəlɪ] adj (untidy) desordenado; (meeting) alborotado; **~ conduct** (Law) conducta escandalosa

disorganized [dɪs'ɔ:gənaɪzd] adj desorganizado

disorientated [dɪs'ɔ:rɪenteɪtəd] adj desorientado

disown [dɪs'əun] vt renegar de

disparaging [dɪs'pærɪdʒɪŋ] adj despreciativo; **to be ~ about sth/sb** menospreciar algo/a algn

dispassionate [dɪs'pæʃənɪt] adj (unbiased) imparcial; (unemotional) desapasionado

dispatch [dɪs'pætʃ] vt enviar; (kill) despachar; (deal with: business) despachar ▷ n (sending) envío; (speed) prontitud f; (Press) informe m; (Mil) parte m

dispel [dɪs'pel] vt disipar, dispersar

dispense [dɪs'pens] vt dispensar, repartir; (medicine) preparar; **dispense with** vt fus (make unnecessary) prescindir de

dispenser [dɪsˈpɛnsəʳ] n (container) distribuidor m automático

dispensing chemist [dɪsˈpɛnsɪŋ-] n (Brit) farmacia

disperse [dɪsˈpəːs] vt dispersar ▷ vi dispersarse

dispirited [dɪˈspɪrɪtɪd] adj desanimado, desalentado

displace [dɪsˈpleɪs] vt (person) desplazar; (replace) reemplazar

display [dɪsˈpleɪ] n (in shop window) escaparate m; (exhibition) exposición f; (Comput) visualización f; (Mil) desfile m; (of feeling) manifestación f; (pej) aparato, pompa ▷ vt exponer; manifestar; (ostentatiously) lucir; **on ~** (exhibits) expuesto, exhibido; (goods) en el escaparate

displease [dɪsˈpliːz] vt (offend) ofender; (annoy) fastidiar; **~d with** disgustado con

displeasure [dɪsˈplɛʒəʳ] n disgusto

disposable [dɪsˈpəuzəbl] adj (not reusable) desechable; **~ personal income** ingresos mpl personales disponibles

disposable nappy n pañal m desechable

disposal [dɪsˈpəuzl] n (sale) venta; (of house) traspaso; (by giving away) donación f; (arrangement) colocación f; (of rubbish) destrucción f; **at one's ~** a la disposición de algn; **to put sth at sb's ~** poner algo a disposición de algn

dispose [dɪsˈpəuz] vi: **~ of** (time, money) disponer de; (unwanted goods) deshacerse de; (Comm: sell) traspasar, vender; (throw away) tirar

disposed [dɪsˈpəuzd] adj: **~ to do** dispuesto a hacer

disposition [dɪspəˈzɪʃən] n disposición f; (temperament) carácter m

disproportionate [dɪsprəˈpɔːʃənət] adj desproporcionado

disprove [dɪsˈpruːv] vt refutar

dispute [dɪsˈpjuːt] n disputa; (verbal) discusión f; (also: **industrial ~**) conflicto (laboral) ▷ vt (argue) argüir; (question) cuestionar; **to be in** or **under ~** (matter) discutirse; (territory) estar en disputa; (Law) estar en litigio

disqualification [dɪskwɔlɪfɪˈkeɪʃən] n inhabilitación f; (Sport) descalificación f; (from driving) descalificación f

disqualify [dɪsˈkwɔlɪfaɪ] vt (Sport) desclasificar; **to ~ sb for sth/from doing sth** incapacitar a algn para algo/para hacer algo

disquiet [dɪsˈkwaɪət] n preocupación f, inquietud f

disregard [dɪsrɪˈgɑːd] vt desatender; (ignore) no hacer caso de ▷ n (indifference: to feelings, danger, money): **~ (for)** indiferencia (a); **~ (of)** (non-observance: of law, rules) violación f (de)

disrepair [dɪsrɪˈpɛəʳ] n: **to fall into ~** (building) desmoronarse; (street) deteriorarse

disreputable [dɪsˈrɛpjutəbl] adj (person, area) de mala fama; (behaviour) vergonzoso

disrespectful [dɪsrɪˈspɛktful] adj irrespetuoso

disrupt [dɪsˈrʌpt] vt (plans) desbaratar, alternar, trastornar; (meeting, public transport, conversation) interrumpir

disruption [dɪsˈrʌpʃən] n desbaratamiento; trastorno; interrupción f

disruptive [dɪsˈrʌptɪv] adj (influence) disruptivo; (strike action) perjudicial

dissatisfaction [dɪssætɪsˈfækʃən] n disgusto, descontento

dissatisfied [dɪsˈsætɪsfaɪd] adj insatisfecho

dissect [dɪˈsɛkt] vt (also fig) disecar

disseminate [dɪˈsɛmɪneɪt] vt divulgar, difundir

dissent [dɪˈsɛnt] n disensión f

dissertation [dɪsəˈteɪʃən] n (Univ) tesina; see also **master's degree**

disservice [dɪsˈsəːvɪs] n: **to do sb a ~** perjudicar a algn

dissimilar [dɪˈsɪmɪləʳ] adj distinto

dissipate [ˈdɪsɪpeɪt] vt disipar; (waste) desperdiciar

dissolute [ˈdɪsəluːt] adj disoluto

dissolve [dɪˈzɔlv] vt disolver ▷ vi disolverse

dissuade [dɪˈsweɪd] vt: **to ~ sb (from)** disuadir a algn (de)

distance [ˈdɪstns] n distancia; **in the ~** a lo lejos; **what ~ is it to London?** ¿qué distancia hay de aquí a Londres?; **it's within walking ~** se puede ir andando

distant [ˈdɪstnt] adj lejano; (manner) reservado, frío

distaste [dɪsˈteɪst] n repugnancia

distasteful [dɪsˈteɪstful] adj repugnante, desagradable

distemper [dɪsˈtɛmpəʳ] n (of dogs) moquillo

distended [dɪˈstɛndɪd] adj (stomach) hinchado

distil, distill (US) [dɪsˈtɪl] vt destilar

distillery [dɪsˈtɪlərɪ] n destilería

distinct [dɪsˈtɪŋkt] adj (different) distinto; (clear) claro; (unmistakeable) inequívoco; **as ~ from** a diferencia de

distinction [dɪsˈtɪŋkʃən] n distinción f; (in exam) sobresaliente m; **a writer of ~** un escritor destacado; **to draw a ~ between** hacer una distinción entre

distinctive [dɪsˈtɪŋktɪv] adj distintivo

distinctly [dɪsˈtɪŋktlɪ] adv claramente

distinguish [dɪsˈtɪŋgwɪʃ] vt distinguir ▷ vi: **to ~ (between)** distinguir (entre)

distinguished [dɪsˈtɪŋgwɪʃt] adj (eminent) distinguido; (career) eminente; (refined) distinguido, de categoría

distinguishing [dɪsˈtɪŋgwɪʃɪŋ] adj (feature) distintivo

distort [dɪsˈtɔːt] vt deformar; (sound) distorsionar; (account, news) tergiversar

distortion [dɪsˈtɔːʃən] n deformación f;
(of sound) distorsión f; (of truth etc)
tergiversación f; (of facts) falseamiento
distract [dɪsˈtrækt] vt distraer
distracted [dɪsˈtræktɪd] adj distraído
distraction [dɪsˈtrækʃən] n distracción f;
(confusion) aturdimiento; (amusement)
diversión f; **to drive sb to ~** (distress, anxiety)
volver loco a algn
distraught [dɪsˈtrɔːt] adj turbado,
enloquecido
distress [dɪsˈtres] n (anguish) angustia; (want)
miseria; (pain) dolor m; (danger) peligro ▷ vt
afligir; (pain) doler; **in ~** (ship etc) en peligro
distressing [dɪsˈtresɪŋ] adj angustioso,
doloroso
distribute [dɪsˈtrɪbjuːt] vt (gen) distribuir;
(share out) repartir
distribution [dɪstrɪˈbjuːʃən] n
distribución f
distributor [dɪsˈtrɪbjutəʳ] n (Aut)
distribuidor m; (Comm) distribuidora
district [ˈdɪstrɪkt] n (of country) zona, región f;
(of town) barrio; (Admin) distrito
district attorney n (US) fiscal m/f
district council n ≈ municipio; ver nota
district nurse n (Brit) enfermera que atiende a
pacientes a domicilio
distrust [dɪsˈtrʌst] n desconfianza ▷ vt
desconfiar de
disturb [dɪsˈtəːb] vt (person: bother, interrupt)
molestar; (meeting) interrumpir; (disorganize)
desordenar; **sorry to ~ you** perdone la
molestia
disturbance [dɪsˈtəːbəns] n (political etc)
disturbio; (violence) alboroto; (of mind)
trastorno; **to cause a ~** causar alboroto; **~ of
the peace** alteración f del orden público
disturbed [dɪsˈtəːbd] adj (worried, upset)
preocupado, angustiado; **to be
emotionally/mentally ~** tener problemas
emocionales/ser un trastornado mental
disturbing [dɪsˈtəːbɪŋ] adj inquietante,
perturbador(a)
disuse [dɪsˈjuːs] n: **to fall into ~** caer en
desuso
disused [dɪsˈjuːzd] adj abandonado
ditch [dɪtʃ] n zanja; (irrigation ditch) acequia
▷ vt (inf: partner) deshacerse de; (: plan, car etc)
abandonar
dither [ˈdɪðəʳ] vi vacilar
ditto [ˈdɪtəu] adv ídem, lo mismo
dive [daɪv] n (from board) salto; (underwater)
buceo; (of submarine) inmersión f; (Aviat)
picada ▷ vi (swimmer: into water) saltar; (: under
water) zambullirse, bucear; (fish, submarine)
sumergirse; (bird) lanzarse en picado; **to ~
into** (bag etc) meter la mano en; (place)
meterse de prisa en
diver [ˈdaɪvəʳ] n (Sport) saltador(a) m(f);
(underwater) buzo
diverse [daɪˈvəːs] adj diversos(-as), varios(-as)

diversification [daɪvəːsɪfɪˈkeɪʃən] n
diversificación f
diversion [daɪˈvəːʃən] n (Brit Aut)
desviación f; (distraction) diversión f; (Mil)
diversión f
diversity [daɪˈvəːsɪtɪ] n diversidad f
divert [daɪˈvəːt] vt (Brit: train, plane, traffic)
desviar; (amuse) divertir
divide [dɪˈvaɪd] vt dividir; (separate) separar
▷ vi dividirse; (road) bifurcarse; **to ~
(between, among)** repartir or dividir (entre);
40 ~d by 5 40 dividido por 5; **divide out** vt: **to
~ out (between, among)** (sweets, tasks etc)
repartir (entre)
divided [dɪˈvaɪdɪd] adj (country, couple)
dividido, separado; (opinions) en desacuerdo
divided highway n (US) carretera de doble
calzada
dividend [ˈdɪvɪdɛnd] n dividendo; (fig)
beneficio
divine [dɪˈvaɪn] adj divino ▷ vt (future)
vaticinar; (truth) alumbrar; (water, metal)
descubrir, detectar
diving [ˈdaɪvɪŋ] n (Sport) salto; (underwater)
buceo
diving board n trampolín m
divinity [dɪˈvɪnɪtɪ] n divinidad f; (Scol)
teología
division [dɪˈvɪʒən] n (also Brit Football) división
f; (sharing out) reparto; (disagreement)
diferencias fpl; (Comm) sección f; (Brit Pol)
votación f; **~ of labour** división f del trabajo
divisive [dɪˈvaɪsɪv] adj divisivo
divorce [dɪˈvɔːs] n divorcio ▷ vt divorciarse
de
divorced [dɪˈvɔːst] adj divorciado
divorcee [dɪvɔːˈsiː] n divorciado(-a)
divot [ˈdɪvət] n (Golf) chuleta
divulge [daɪˈvʌldʒ] vt divulgar, revelar
DIY adj, n abbr (Brit) = **do-it-yourself**
dizziness [ˈdɪzɪnɪs] n vértigo
dizzy [ˈdɪzɪ] adj (person) mareado; (height)
vertiginoso; **to feel ~** marearse; **I feel ~**
estoy mareado
DJ n abbr see **disc jockey**
DNA n abbr (= deoxyribonucleic acid) ADN m

○ KEYWORD

do [duː] (pt **did**, pp **done**) n **1** (inf: party etc):
we're having a little do on Saturday
damos una fiestecita el sábado; **it was
rather a grand do** fue un acontecimiento a
lo grande
2: **the dos and don'ts** lo que se debe y no se
debe hacer
▷ aux vb **1** (in negative constructions: not
translated): **I don't understand** no entiendo
2 (to form questions: not translated): **do you
speak English?** ¿habla (usted) inglés?;
didn't you know? ¿no lo sabías?; **what do
you think?** ¿qué opinas?

3 (*for emphasis, in polite expressions*): **people do make mistakes sometimes** a veces sí se cometen errores; **she does seem rather late** a mí también me parece que se ha retrasado; **do sit down/help yourself** siéntate/sírvete por favor; **do take care!** ¡ten cuidado! ¿eh?; **I DO wish I could ...** ojalá (que) pudiera ...; **but I DO like it** pero, sí (que) me gusta
4 (*used to avoid repeating vb*): **she sings better than I do** canta mejor que yo; **do you agree?** — **yes, I do/no, I don't** ¿estás de acuerdo? — sí (lo estoy)/no (lo estoy); **she lives in Glasgow — so do I** vive en Glasgow — yo también; **he didn't like it and neither did we** no le gustó a y a nosotros tampoco; **who made this mess? — I did** ¿quién hizo esta chapuza? — yo; **he asked me to help him and I did** me pidió que le ayudara y lo hice
5 (*in question tags*): **you like him, don't you?** te gusta, ¿verdad? *or* ¿no?; **I don't know him, do I?** creo que no le conozco; **he laughed, didn't he?** se rió ¿no?
▷ *vt* **1** (*gen*): **what are you doing tonight?** ¿qué haces esta noche?; **what can I do for you?** (*in shop*) ¿en qué puedo servirle?; **what does he do for a living?** ¿a qué se dedica?; **I'll do all I can** haré todo lo que pueda; **what have you done with my slippers?** ¿qué has hecho con mis zapatillas?; **to do the washing-up/cooking** fregar los platos/cocinar; **to do one's teeth/hair/nails** lavarse los dientes/arreglarse el pelo/arreglarse las uñas
2 (*Aut etc*): **the car was doing 100** el coche iba a 100; **we've done 200 km already** ya hemos hecho 200 km; **he can do 100 in that car** puede ir a 100 en ese coche
3 (*visit: city, museum*) visitar, recorrer
4 (*cook*): **a steak — well done please** un filete bien hecho, por favor
▷ *vi* **1** (*act, behave*) hacer; **do as I do** haz como yo
2 (*get on, fare*): **he's doing well/badly at school** va bien/mal en la escuela; **the firm is doing well** la empresa anda *or* va bien; **how do you do?** mucho gusto; (*less formal*) ¿qué tal?
3 (*suit*): **will it do?** ¿sirve?, ¿está *or* va bien?; **it doesn't do to upset her** cuidado en ofenderla
4 (*be sufficient*) bastar; **will £10 do?** ¿será bastante con £10?; **that'll do** así está bien; **that'll do!** (*in annoyance*) ¡ya está bien!, ¡basta ya!; **to make do (with)** arreglárselas (con)
do away with *vt fus* (*kill*) eliminar; (*eradicate: disease*) eliminar; (*abolish: law etc*) abolir; (*withdraw*) retirar
do out of *vt fus*: **to do sb out of sth** pisar algo a algn
do up *vt* (*laces*) atar; (*zip, dress, shirt*) abrochar; (*renovate: room, house*) renovar

do with *vt fus* (*need*): **I could do with a drink/some help** no me vendría mal un trago/un poco de ayuda; (*be connected with*) tener que ver con; **what has it got to do with you?** ¿qué tiene que ver contigo?
do without *vi*: **if you're late for dinner then you'll do without** si llegas tarde tendrás que quedarte sin cenar ▷ *vt fus* pasar sin; **I can do without a car** puedo pasar sin coche

DOA *abbr* = **dead on arrival**
doc [dɔk] *n* (*inf*) médico(-a)
dock [dɔk] *n* (*Naut: wharf*) dársena, muelle *m*; (*Law*) banquillo (de los acusados); **docks** *npl* muelles *mpl*, puerto *sg* ▷ *vi* (*enter dock*) atracar (en el muelle) ▷ *vt* (*pay etc*) descontar
docker ['dɔkər] *n* trabajador *m* portuario, estibador *m*
dockyard ['dɔkjɑːd] *n* astillero
doctor ['dɔktər] *n* médico; (*Ph.D. etc*) doctor(a) *m(f)* ▷ *vt* (*fig*) arreglar, falsificar; (*drink etc*) adulterar
doctorate ['dɔktərɪt] *n* doctorado
Doctor of Philosophy *n* Doctor *m* (en Filosofía y Letras)
doctrine ['dɔktrɪn] *n* doctrina
docudrama [dɔkjuˈdrɑːmə] *n* (*TV*) docudrama *m*
document ['dɔkjumənt] *n* documento ▷ *vt* documentar
documentary [dɔkjuˈmentərɪ] *adj* documental ▷ *n* documental *m*
documentation [dɔkjumenˈteɪʃən] *n* documentación *f*
doddering ['dɔdərɪŋ], **doddery** ['dɔdərɪ] *adj* vacilante
doddle ['dɔdl] *n*: **it's a ~** (*Brit*) (*inf*)) es pan comido
dodge [dɔdʒ] *n* (*of body*) regate *m*; (*fig*) truco ▷ *vt* (*gen*) evadir; (*blow*) esquivar ▷ *vi* escabullirse; (*Sport*) hacer una finta; **to ~ out of the way** echarse a un lado; **to ~ through the traffic** esquivar el tráfico
dodgems ['dɔdʒəmz] *npl* (*Brit*) autos *or* coches *mpl* de choque
dodgy ['dɔdʒɪ] *adj* (*inf: uncertain*) dudoso; (*shady*) sospechoso; (*risky*) arriesgado
doe [dəu] *n* (*deer*) cierva, gama; (*rabbit*) coneja
does [dʌz] *vb see* **do**
doesn't ['dʌznt] = **does not**
dog [dɔg] *n* perro ▷ *vt* seguir (de cerca); (*fig: memory etc*) perseguir; **to go to the ~s** (*person*) echarse a perder; (*nation etc*) ir a la ruina
dog collar *n* collar *m* de perro; (*fig*) alzacuello(s) *msg*
dog-eared ['dɔgɪəd] *adj* sobado; (*page*) con la esquina doblada
dogged ['dɔgɪd] *adj* tenaz, obstinado
doggy ['dɔgɪ] *n* (*inf*) perrito
doggy bag *n* bolsa para llevarse las sobras de la comida

dogma ['dɒgmə] *n* dogma *m*
dogmatic [dɒg'mætɪk] *adj* dogmático
dogsbody ['dɒgzbɒdɪ] *n* (Brit) burro de carga
doily ['dɒɪlɪ] *n* pañito de adorno
doings ['duːɪŋz] *npl* (events) sucesos *mpl*; (acts) hechos *mpl*
do-it-yourself [duːɪtjɔːˈsɛlf] *n* bricolaje *m*
doldrums ['dɒldrəmz] *npl*: **to be in the ~** (person) estar abatido; (business) estar estancado
dole [dəul] *n* (Brit: payment) subsidio de paro; **on the ~** parado; **dole out** *vt* repartir
doleful ['dəulful] *adj* triste, lúgubre
doll [dɒl] *n* muñeca; **doll up** *vt*: **to ~ o.s. up** ataviarse
dollar ['dɒləʳ] *n* dólar *m*
dollop ['dɒləp] *n* buena cucharada
dolphin ['dɒlfɪn] *n* delfín *m*
domain [də'meɪn] *n* (fig) campo, competencia; (land) dominios *mpl*
dome [dəum] *n* (Arch) cúpula; (shape) bóveda
domestic [də'mɛstɪk] *adj* (animal, duty) doméstico; (flight, news, policy) nacional
domestic appliance *n* aparato *m* doméstico, aparato *m* de uso doméstico
domesticated [də'mɛstɪkeɪtɪd] *adj* domesticado; (person: home-loving) casero, hogareño
dominant ['dɒmɪnənt] *adj* dominante
dominate ['dɒmɪneɪt] *vt* dominar
domination [dɒmɪ'neɪʃən] *n* dominación *f*
domineering [dɒmɪ'nɪərɪŋ] *adj* dominante
Dominican Republic [də'mɪnɪkən-] *n* República Dominicana
dominion [də'mɪnɪən] *n* dominio
domino (pl **dominoes**) ['dɒmɪnəu] *n* ficha de dominó
dominoes ['dɒmɪnəuz] *n* (game) dominó
don [dɒn] *n* (Brit) profesor(a) *m(f)* de universidad
donate [də'neɪt] *vt* donar
donation [də'neɪʃən] *n* donativo
done [dʌn] *pp of* **do**
donkey ['dɒŋkɪ] *n* burro
donor ['dəunəʳ] *n* donante *m/f*
donor card *n* carnet *m* de donante de órganos
don't [dəunt] = **do not**
donut ['dəunʌt] *n* (US) = **doughnut**
doodle ['duːdl] *n* garabato ▷ *vi* pintar dibujitos *or* garabatos
doom [duːm] *n* (fate) suerte *f*; (death) muerte *f* ▷ *vt*: **to be ~ed to failure** estar condenado al fracaso
doomsday ['duːmzdeɪ] *n* día *m* del juicio final
door [dɔːʳ] *n* puerta; (of car) portezuela; (entry) entrada; **from ~ to ~** de puerta en puerta
doorbell ['dɔːbɛl] *n* timbre *m*
door handle *n* tirador *m*; (of car) manija
doorknob *n* pomo *m* de la puerta, manilla *f* (LAm)

doorman ['dɔːmən] *n* (in hotel) portero
doormat ['dɔːmæt] *n* felpudo, estera
doorstep ['dɔːstɛp] *n* peldaño; **on your ~** en la puerta de casa; (fig) al lado de casa
doorway ['dɔːweɪ] *n* entrada, puerta; **in the ~** en la puerta
dope [dəup] *n* (inf: illegal drug) droga; (: person) imbécil *m/f*; (: information) información *f*, informes *mpl* ▷ *vt* (horse etc) drogar
dopey ['dəupɪ] *adj* atontado
dormant ['dɔːmənt] *adj* inactivo; (latent) latente
dormitory ['dɔːmɪtrɪ] *n* (Brit) dormitorio; (US: hall of residence) residencia, colegio mayor
dormouse (pl **dormice**) ['dɔːmaus, -maɪs] *n* lirón *m*
DOS [dɒs] *n abbr* = **disk operating system**
dosage ['dəusɪdʒ] *n* (on medicine bottle) dosis *f* inv, dosificación *f*
dose [dəus] *n* (of medicine) dosis *f* inv; **a ~ of flu** un ataque de gripe ▷ *vt*: **to ~ o.s. with** automedicarse con
dosser ['dɒsəʳ] *n* (Brit inf) mendigo(-a); (lazy person) vago(-a)
doss house ['dɒs-] *n* (Brit) pensión *f* de mala muerte
dossier ['dɒsɪeɪ] *n*: **~ (on)** expediente *m* (sobre)
dot [dɒt] *n* punto ▷ *vi*: **~ted with** salpicado de; **on the ~** en punto
dotcom ['dɒtkɒm] *n* puntocom *f*
dote [dəut]: **to ~ on** *vt fus* adorar, idolatrar
dot-matrix printer [dɒt'meɪtrɪks-] *n* impresora matricial *or* de matriz
dotted line ['dɒtɪd-] *n* línea de puntos; **to sign on the ~** firmar
double ['dʌbl] *adj* doble ▷ *adv* (twice): **to cost ~** costar el doble ▷ *n* (gen) doble *m* ▷ *vt* doblar; (efforts) redoblar ▷ *vi* doblarse; (have two uses etc): **to ~ as** hacer las veces de; **~ five two six (5526)** (Telec) cinco cinco dos seis; **spelt with a ~ "s"** escrito con dos "eses"; **on the ~** (Brit), **at the ~** corriendo; **double back** *vi* (person) volver sobre sus pasos; **double up** *vi* (bend over) doblarse; (share bedroom) compartir
double bass *n* contrabajo
double bed *n* cama de matrimonio
double-breasted ['dʌbl'brɛstɪd] *adj* cruzado
double-check ['dʌbl'tʃɛk] *vt* volver a revisar ▷ *vi*: **I'll ~** voy a revisarlo otra vez
double-click ['dʌbl,klɪk] (Comput) *vi* hacer doble clic
double-cross ['dʌbl'krɒs] *vt* (trick) engañar; (betray) traicionar
doubledecker ['dʌbl'dɛkəʳ] *n* autobús *m* de dos pisos
double glazing *n* (Brit) doble acristalamiento
double room *n* habitación *f* doble
doubles ['dʌblz] *n* (Tennis) juego de dobles
double whammy [-'wæmɪ] *n* (inf) palo doble

double yellow lines npl (Brit: Aut) línea doble amarilla de prohibido aparcar, ≈ línea fsg amarilla continua

doubly ['dʌblɪ] adv doblemente

doubt [daʊt] n duda ▷ vt dudar; (suspect) dudar de; **to ~ that** dudar que; **there is no ~ that** no cabe duda de que; **without (a) ~** sin duda (alguna); **beyond ~** fuera de duda; **I ~ it very much** lo dudo mucho

doubtful ['daʊtful] adj dudoso; (arousing suspicion: person) sospechoso; **to be ~ about sth** tener dudas sobre algo; **I'm a bit ~** no estoy convencido

doubtless ['daʊtlɪs] adv sin duda

dough [dəʊ] n masa, pasta; (inf: money) pasta, lana (LAm)

doughnut ['dəʊnʌt] n dónut m

douse [daʊs] vt (drench: with water) mojar; (extinguish: flames) apagar

dove [dʌv] n paloma

Dover ['dəʊvə'] n Dover

dovetail ['dʌvteɪl] vi (fig) encajar

dowdy ['daʊdɪ] adj desaliñado; (inelegant) poco elegante

down [daʊn] n (fluff) pelusa; (feathers) plumón m, flojel m; (hill) loma ▷ adv (also: **~wards**) abajo, hacia abajo; (on the ground) por/en tierra ▷ prep abajo ▷ vt (inf: drink) beberse, tragar(se); **~ with X!** ¡abajo X!; **~ there** allí abajo; **~ here** aquí abajo; **I'll be ~ in a minute** ahora bajo; **England is two goals ~** Inglaterra está perdiendo por dos tantos; **I've been ~ with flu** he estado con gripe; **the price of meat is ~** ha bajado el precio de la carne; **I've got it ~ in my diary** lo he apuntado en mi agenda; **to pay £2 ~** dejar £2 de depósito; **he went ~ the hill** fue cuesta abajo; **~ under** (in Australia etc) en Australia/Nueva Zelanda; **to ~ tools** (fig) declararse en huelga

down-and-out ['daʊnəndaʊt] n (tramp) vagabundo(-a)

down-at-heel ['daʊnət'hi:l] adj venido a menos; (appearance) desaliñado

downcast ['daʊnkɑːst] adj abatido

downfall ['daʊnfɔːl] n caída, ruina

downhearted [daʊn'hɑːtɪd] adj desanimado

downhill [daʊn'hɪl] adv: **to go ~** ir cuesta abajo; (business) estar en declive

Downing Street ['daʊnɪŋ-] n (Brit) Downing Street f; ver nota

download ['daʊnləʊd] vt (Comput) transferir, telecargar

downloadable [daʊn'ləʊdəbl] adj (Comput) descargable

down payment n entrada, pago al contado

downpour ['daʊnpɔː'] n aguacero

downright ['daʊnraɪt] adj (nonsense, lie) manifiesto; (refusal) terminante

downsize [daʊn'saɪz] vt reducir la plantilla de

Down's syndrome [daʊnz-] n síndrome m de Down

downstairs [daʊn'stɛəz] adv (below) (en el piso de) abajo; (motion) escaleras abajo; **to come (or go) ~** bajar la escalera

downstream [daʊn'striːm] adv aguas or río abajo

down-to-earth [daʊntu'ə:θ] adj práctico

downtown [daʊn'taʊn] adv en el centro de la ciudad

down under adv en Australia (or Nueva Zelanda)

downward ['daʊnwəd] adv hacia abajo; **face ~** (person) boca abajo; (object) cara abajo ▷ adj: **a ~ trend** una tendencia descendente

downwards ['daʊnwədz] adv hacia abajo; **face ~** (person) boca abajo; (object) cara abajo

dowry ['daʊrɪ] n dote f

doz. abbr = **dozen**

doze [dəʊz] vi dormitar; **doze off** vi echar una cabezada

dozen ['dʌzn] n docena; **a ~ books** una docena de libros; **~s of** cantidad de; **~s of times** cantidad de veces; **8op a ~** 8o peniques la docena

DPP n abbr (Brit) = **Director of Public Prosecutions**

Dr, Dr. abbr (= doctor) Dr

Dr. abbr (= in street names) = **Drive**

drab [dræb] adj gris, monótono

draft [drɑːft] n (first copy: of document, report) borrador m; (Comm) giro; (US: call-up) quinta ▷ vt (write roughly) hacer un borrador de; see also **draught**

drag [dræg] vt arrastrar; (river) dragar, rastrear ▷ vi arrastrarse por el suelo ▷ n (Aviat: resistance) resistencia aerodinámica; (inf) lata; (women's clothing): **in ~** vestido de mujer; **to ~ and drop** (Comput) arrastrar y soltar; **drag away** vt: **to ~ away (from)** separar a rastras (de); **drag on** vi ser interminable

dragon ['drægən] n dragón m

dragonfly ['drægənflaɪ] n libélula

drain [dreɪn] n desaguadero; (in street) sumidero; (drain cover) rejilla del sumidero

▷ vt (land, marshes) desecar; (Med) drenar; (reservoir) desecar; (fig) agotar ▷ vi escurrirse; **to be a ~ on** consumir, agotar; **to feel ~ed (of energy)** (fig) sentirse agotado

drainage ['dreɪnɪdʒ] n (act) desagüe m; (Med, Agr) drenaje m; (sewage) alcantarillado

draining board ['dreɪnɪŋ-], **drainboard** (US) ['dreɪnbɔːd] n escurridero, escurridor m

drainpipe ['dreɪnpaɪp] n tubo de desagüe

dram [dræm] n (drink) traguito, copita

drama ['drɑːmə] n (art) teatro; (play) drama m

dramatic [drə'mætɪk] adj dramático; (sudden, marked) espectacular

dramatist ['dræmətɪst] n dramaturgo(-a)

dramatize ['dræmətaɪz] vt (events etc) dramatizar; (adapt: novel: for TV, cinema) adaptar

drank [dræŋk] pt of **drink**

drape [dreɪp] vt (cloth) colocar; (flag) colgar

drapes [dreɪps] npl (US) cortinas fpl

drastic ['dræstɪk] adj (measure, reduction) severo; (change) radical

draught, draft (US) [drɑːft] n (of air) corriente f de aire; (drink) trago; (Naut) calado; **on ~** (beer) de barril

draught beer n cerveza de barril

draughtboard ['drɑːftbɔːd] (Brit) n tablero de damas

draughts [drɑːfts] n (Brit) juego de damas

draughtsman, draftsman (US) ['drɑːftsmən] n proyectista m, delineante m

draw [drɔː] (pt **drew**, pp **drawn**) ▷ vt (pull) tirar; (take out) sacar; (attract) atraer; (picture) dibujar; (money) retirar; (formulate: conclusion): **to ~ (from)** sacar (de); (comparison, distinction): **to ~ (between)** hacer (entre) ▷ vi (Sport) empatar ▷ n (Sport) empate m; (lottery) sorteo; (attraction) atracción f; **to ~ near** vi acercarse; **draw back** vi: **to ~ back (from)** echarse atrás (de); **draw in** vi (car) aparcar; (train) entrar en la estación; **draw on** vt (resources) utilizar, servirse de; (imagination, person) recurrir a; **draw out** vi (lengthen) alargarse; **draw up** vi (stop) pararse ▷ vt (document) redactar; (plan) trazar

drawback ['drɔːbæk] n inconveniente m, desventaja

drawbridge ['drɔːbrɪdʒ] n puente m levadizo

drawer [drɔː⁺] n cajón m; (of cheque) librador(a) m(f)

drawing ['drɔːɪŋ] n dibujo

drawing board n tablero (de dibujante)

drawing pin n (Brit) chincheta m

drawing room n salón m

drawl [drɔːl] n habla lenta y cansina

drawn [drɔːn] pp of **draw** ▷ adj (haggard: with tiredness) ojeroso; (: with pain) macilento

dread [drɛd] n pavor m, terror m ▷ vt temer, tener miedo or pavor a

dreadful ['drɛdful] adj espantoso; **I feel ~!** (ill) ¡me siento fatal or malísimo!; (ashamed) ¡qué vergüenza!

dream [driːm] n sueño ▷ vt, vi (pt, pp **dreamed** or **dreamt** [drɛmt]) soñar; **to have a ~ about sb/sth** soñar con algn/algo; **sweet ~s!** ¡que sueñes con los angelitos!; **dream up** vt (reason, excuse) inventar; (plan, idea) idear

dreamer ['driːmə⁺] n soñador(a) m(f)

dreamt [drɛmt] pt, pp of **dream**

dreamy ['driːmɪ] adj (person) soñador(a), distraído; (music) de sueño

dreary ['drɪərɪ] adj monótono, aburrido

dredge [drɛdʒ] vt dragar; **dredge up** vt sacar con draga; (fig: unpleasant facts) pescar, sacar a luz

dregs [drɛgz] npl heces fpl

drench [drɛntʃ] vt empapar; **~ed to the skin** calado hasta los huesos

dress [drɛs] n vestido; (clothing) ropa ▷ vt vestir; (wound) vendar; (Culin) aliñar; (shop window) decorar, arreglar ▷ vi vestirse; **to ~ o.s., get ~ed** vestirse; **she ~es very well** se viste muy bien; **dress up** vi vestirse de etiqueta; (in fancy dress) disfrazarse

dress circle n (Brit) principal m

dresser ['drɛsə⁺] n (furniture) aparador m; (: US) tocador m; (Theat) camarero(-a)

dressing ['drɛsɪŋ] n (Med) vendaje m; (Culin) aliño

dressing gown n (Brit) bata

dressing room n (Theat) camarín m; (Sport) vestuario

dressing table n tocador m

dressmaker ['drɛsmeɪkə⁺] n modista, costurera

dress rehearsal n ensayo general

drew [druː] pt of **draw**

dribble ['drɪbl] vi gotear, caer gota a gota; (baby) babear ▷ vt (ball) driblar, regatear

dried [draɪd] adj (gen) seco; (fruit) paso; (milk) en polvo

drier ['draɪə⁺] n = **dryer**

drift [drɪft] n (of current etc) flujo; (of sand) montón m; (of snow) ventisquero; (meaning) significado ▷ vi (boat) ir a la deriva; (sand, snow) amontonarse; **to catch sb's ~** cogerle el hilo a algn; **to let things ~** dejar las cosas como están; **to ~ apart** (friends) seguir su camino; (lovers) disgustarse, romper

driftwood ['drɪftwud] n madera flotante

drill [drɪl] n taladro; (bit) broca; (of dentist) fresa; (for mining etc) perforadora, barrena; (Mil) instrucción f ▷ vt perforar, taladrar; (soldiers) ejercitar; (pupils: in grammar) hacer ejercicios con ▷ vi (for oil) perforar

drink [drɪŋk] n bebida ▷ vt, vi (pt **drank**, pp **drunk**) beber, tomar (LAm); **to have a ~** tomar algo; tomar una copa or un trago; **a ~ of water** un trago de agua; **to invite sb for ~s** invitar a algn a tomar unas copas; **there's food and ~ in the kitchen** hay de comer y de beber en la cocina; **would you like something to ~?** ¿quieres beber or tomar algo?; **drink in** vt (person: fresh air) respirar; (: story, sight) beberse

drink-driving ['drɪŋk'draɪvɪŋ] n: **to be charged with** ~ ser acusado de conducir borracho or en estado de embriaguez

drinker ['drɪŋkə^r] n bebedor(a) m(f)

drinking water n agua potable

drip [drɪp] n (act) goteo; (one drip) gota; (Med) gota a gota m; (sound: of water etc) goteo; (inf: spineless person) soso(-a) ▷ vi gotear, caer gota a gota

drip-dry ['drɪp'draɪ] adj (shirt) de lava y pon

dripping ['drɪpɪŋ] n (animal fat) pringue m ▷ adj: ~ **wet** calado

drive [draɪv] (pt **drove**, pp **driven**) n paseo (en coche); (journey) viaje m (en coche); (also: ~**way**) entrada; (street) calle; (energy) energía, vigor m; (Psych) impulso; (Sport) ataque m; (Comput: also: **disk** ~) unidad f (de disco) ▷ vt (car) conducir, manejar (LAm); (nail) clavar; (push) empujar; (Tech: motor) impulsar ▷ vi (Aut: at controls) conducir, manejar (LAm); (: travel) pasearse en coche; **to go for a** ~ dar una vuelta en coche; **it's three hours' ~ from London** es un viaje de tres horas en coche desde Londres; **left-/right-hand** ~ conducción f a la izquierda/derecha; **front-/rear-wheel** ~ tracción f delantera/trasera; **sales** ~ promoción f de ventas; **to** ~ **sb mad** volverle loco a algn; **to** ~ **sb to (do) sth** empujar a algn a (hacer) algo; **he** ~**s a taxi** es taxista; **he** ~**s a Mercedes** tiene un Mercedes; **can you** ~? ¿sabes conducir or (LAm) manejar?; **to** ~ **at 50 km an hour** ir a 50km por hora; **drive at** vt fus (fig: intend, mean) querer decir, insinuar; **drive on** vi no parar, seguir adelante ▷ vt (incite, encourage) empujar; **drive out** vt (force out) expulsar, echar

drive-by ['draɪvbaɪ] n: ~ **shooting** tiroteo desde el coche

drive-in ['draɪvɪn] adj (esp US): ~ **cinema** autocine m

drivel ['drɪvl] n (inf) tonterías fpl

driven ['drɪvn] pp of **drive**

driver ['draɪvə^r] n conductor(a) m(f), chofer m (LAm); (of taxi) taxista m/f

driver's license n (US) carnet m or permiso de conducir

driveway ['draɪvweɪ] n camino de entrada

driving ['draɪvɪŋ] n conducir m, manejar m (LAm) ▷ adj (force) impulsor(a)

driving instructor n instructor(a) m(f) de autoescuela

driving lesson n clase f de conducir

driving licence n (Brit) carnet m or permiso de conducir

driving school n autoescuela

driving test n examen m de conducir

drizzle ['drɪzl] n llovizna, garúa (LAm) ▷ vi lloviznar

drone [drəun] vi (bee, aircraft, engine) zumbar; (also: ~ **on**) murmurar sin interrupción ▷ n zumbido; (male bee) zángano

drool [druːl] vi babear; **to** ~ **over sb/sth** caérsele la baba por algn/algo

droop [druːp] vi (flower) marchitarse; (shoulders) encorvarse; (head) inclinarse

drop [drɔp] n (of water) gota; (fall: in price) bajada; (: in salary) disminución f ▷ vt (allow to fall) dejar caer; (voice, eyes, price) bajar; (set down from car) dejar ▷ vi (object) caer; (price, temperature) bajar; (wind) calmarse, amainar; (numbers, attendance) disminuir; **drops** npl (Med) gotas fpl; **cough** ~**s** pastillas fpl para la tos; **a** ~ **of 10%** una bajada del 10 por ciento; **to** ~ **anchor** echar el ancla; **to** ~ **sb a line** mandar unas líneas a algn; **drop in** vi (inf: visit): **to** ~ **in (on)** pasar por casa (de); **drop off** vi (sleep) dormirse ▷ vt (passenger) bajar, dejar; **drop out** vi (withdraw) retirarse

dropout ['drɔpaut] n (from society) marginado(-a); (from university) estudiante m/f que ha abandonado los estudios

dropper ['drɔpə^r] n (Med) cuentagotas m inv

droppings ['drɔpɪŋz] npl excremento sg

dross [drɔs] n (fig) escoria

drought [draut] n sequía

drove [drəuv] pt of **drive**

drown [draun] vt (also: ~ **out**: sound) ahogar ▷ vi ahogarse

drowsy ['drauzɪ] adj soñoliento; **to be** ~ tener sueño

drudgery ['drʌdʒərɪ] n trabajo pesado or monótono

drug [drʌg] n (Med) medicamento, droga; (narcotic) droga ▷ vt drogar; **to be on** ~**s** drogarse; **he's on** ~**s** se droga

drug addict n drogadicto(-a)

drug dealer n traficante m/f de drogas

druggist ['drʌgɪst] n (US) farmacéutico(-a)

drugstore ['drʌgstɔː^r] n (US) tienda (de comestibles, periódicos y medicamentos)

drug trafficker n narcotraficante m/f

drum [drʌm] n tambor m; (large) bombo; (for oil, petrol) bidón m ▷ vi tocar el tambor; (with fingers) tamborilear ▷ vt: **to** ~ **one's fingers on the table** tamborilear con los dedos sobre la mesa; **drums** npl batería sg

drummer ['drʌmə^r] n (in military band) tambor m/f; (in jazz/pop group) batería m/f

drumstick ['drʌmstɪk] n (Mus) palillo, baqueta; (chicken leg) muslo (de pollo)

drunk [drʌŋk] pp of **drink** ▷ adj borracho ▷ n (also: ~**ard**) borracho(-a); **to get** ~ emborracharse

drunken ['drʌŋkən] adj borracho

dry [draɪ] adj seco; (day) sin lluvia; (climate) árido, seco; (humour) agudo; (uninteresting: lecture) aburrido, pesado ▷ vt secar; (tears) enjugarse ▷ vi secarse; **on** ~ **land** en tierra firme; **to** ~ **one's hands/hair/eyes** secarse las manos/el pelo/las lágrimas; **dry up** vi (*river*) secarse; (*supply, imagination etc*) agotarse; (*in speech*) atascarse

dry-clean ['draɪ'kliːn] *vt* limpiar *or* lavar en seco; **"~ only"** (*on label*) "limpieza *or* lavado en seco"

dry-cleaner's ['draɪ'kliːnəz] *n* tintorería

dry-cleaning ['draɪ'kliːnɪŋ] *n* lavado en seco

dryer ['draɪəʳ] *n* (*for hair*) secador *m*; (*for clothes*) secadora

dryness ['draɪnɪs] *n* sequedad *f*

dry rot *n* putrefacción *f*

DSS *n abbr* (*Brit*) = **Department of Social Security**; *see* **social security**

DTP *n abbr* = **desktop publishing**; (*Med: vaccination*) = **diphtheria, tetanus, pertussis**

dual ['djuəl] *adj* doble

dual carriageway *n* (*Brit*) ≈ autovía

dual nationality *n* doble nacionalidad *f*

dual-purpose ['djuəl'pəːpəs] *adj* de doble uso

dubbed [dʌbd] *adj* (*Cine*) doblado

dubious ['djuːbɪəs] *adj* indeciso; (*reputation, company*) dudoso; (*character*) sospechoso; **I'm very ~ about it** tengo mis dudas sobre ello

Dublin ['dʌblɪn] *n* Dublín

duchess ['dʌtʃɪs] *n* duquesa

duck [dʌk] *n* pato ⊳ *vi* agacharse ⊳ *vt* (*plunge in water*) zambullir

duckling ['dʌklɪŋ] *n* patito

duct [dʌkt] *n* conducto, canal *m*

dud [dʌd] *n* (*shell*) obús *m* que no estalla; (*object, tool*): **it's a ~** es una filfa ⊳ *adj*: **~ cheque** (*Brit*) cheque *m* sin fondos

due [djuː] *adj* (*proper*) debido; (*fitting*) conveniente, oportuno ⊳ *adv*: **~ north** derecho al norte; **dues** *npl* (*for club, union*) cuota *sg*; (*in harbour*) derechos *mpl*; **in ~ course** a su debido tiempo; **~ to** debido a; **to be ~ to** deberse a; **the train is ~ to arrive at 8.00** el tren tiene (prevista) la llegada a las ocho; **the rent's ~ on the 30th** hay que pagar el alquiler el día 30; **I am ~ six days' leave** me deben seis días de vacaciones; **she is ~ back tomorrow** ella debe volver mañana

duel ['djuəl] *n* duelo

duet [djuː'ɛt] *n* dúo

duffel bag ['dʌfl-] *n* macuto

duffel coat ['dʌfl-] *n* trenca

dug [dʌg] *pt, pp of* **dig**

dugout ['dʌgaʊt] *n* (*canoe*) piragua (*hecha de un solo tronco*); (*Sport*) banquillo; (*Mil*) refugio subterráneo

duke [djuːk] *n* duque *m*

dull [dʌl] *adj* (*light*) apagado; (*stupid*) torpe; (*boring*) pesado; (*sound, pain*) sordo; (*weather, day*) gris ⊳ *vt* (*pain, grief*) aliviar; (*mind, senses*) entorpecer

duly ['djuːlɪ] *adv* debidamente; (*on time*) a su debido tiempo

dumb [dʌm] *adj* mudo; (*stupid*) estúpido; **to be struck ~** (*fig*) quedar boquiabierto

dumbfounded [dʌm'faʊndɪd] *adj* pasmado

dummy ['dʌmɪ] *n* (*tailor's model*) maniquí *m*; (*Brit: for baby*) chupete *m* ⊳ *adj* falso, postizo; **~ run** ensayo

dump [dʌmp] *n* (*heap*) montón *m* de basura; (*place*) basurero, vertedero; (*inf*) tugurio; (*Mil*) depósito; (*Comput*) copia vaciada ⊳ *vt* (*put down*) dejar; (*get rid of*) deshacerse de; (*Comput*) tirar (a la papelera); (*Comm: goods*) inundar el mercado de; **to be (down) in the ~s** (*inf*) tener murria, estar deprimido

dumpling ['dʌmplɪŋ] *n* bola de masa hervida

dumpy ['dʌmpɪ] *adj* regordete(-a)

dunce [dʌns] *n* zopenco

dune [djuːn] *n* duna

dung [dʌŋ] *n* estiércol *m*

dungarees [dʌŋgə'riːz] *npl* mono *sg*, overol *msg* (*LAm*)

dungeon ['dʌndʒən] *n* calabozo

duplex ['djuːplɛks] *n* (*US: also*: **~ apartment**) dúplex *m*

duplicate ['djuːplɪkət] *n* duplicado; (*copy of letter etc*) copia ⊳ *adj* (*copy*) duplicado ⊳ *vt* ['djuːplɪkeɪt] duplicar; (*photocopy*) fotocopiar; (*repeat*) repetir; **in ~** por duplicado

durable ['djuərəbl] *adj* duradero

duration [djuə'reɪʃən] *n* duración *f*

duress [djuə'rɛs] *n*: **under ~** por coacción

during ['djuərɪŋ] *prep* durante

dusk [dʌsk] *n* crepúsculo, anochecer *m*

dust [dʌst] *n* polvo ⊳ *vt* (*furniture*) desempolvar; (*cake etc*): **to ~ with** espolvorear de; **dust off** *vt* (*also fig*) desempolvar, quitar el polvo de

dustbin ['dʌstbɪn] *n* (*Brit*) cubo de la basura, balde *m* (*LAm*)

duster ['dʌstəʳ] *n* paño, trapo; (*feather duster*) plumero

dust jacket *n* sobrecubierta

dustman ['dʌstmən] *n* (*Brit*) basurero

dustpan ['dʌstpæn] *n* cogedor *m*

dusty ['dʌstɪ] *adj* polvoriento

Dutch [dʌtʃ] *adj* holandés(-esa) ⊳ *n* (*Ling*) holandés *m* ⊳ *adv*: **to go ~** pagar a escote; **the Dutch** *npl* los holandeses

Dutchman ['dʌtʃmən], **Dutchwoman** ['dʌtʃwumən] *n* holandés(-esa) *m(f)*

dutiful ['djuːtɪful] *adj* (*child*) obediente; (*husband*) sumiso; (*employee*) cumplido

duty ['djuːtɪ] *n* deber *m*; (*tax*) derechos *mpl* de aduana; (*Med: in hospital*) servicio, guardia; **on ~** de servicio; (*at night etc*) de guardia; **off ~** libre (de servicio); **to make it one's ~ to do sth** encargarse de hacer algo sin falta; **to pay ~ on sth** pagar los derechos sobre algo

duty-free [djuːtɪ'friː] *adj* libre de impuestos; **~ shop** tienda libre de impuestos

duvet ['duːveɪ] *n* (*Brit*) edredón *m* (nórdico)

DVD *n abbr* (= *digital versatile or video disc*) DVD *m*

DVD player *n* lector *m* de DVD

DVD writer *n* grabadora de DVD

DVLA n abbr (Brit: = Driver and Vehicle Licensing Agency) organismo encargado de la expedición de permisos de conducir y matriculación de vehículos

dwarf [dwɔ:f] (pl **dwarves** [dwɔ:vz]) n enano(-a) m(f) ▷ vt empequeñecer

dwell [dwɛl] (pt, pp **dwelt** [dwɛlt]) vi morar; **dwell on** vt fus explayarse en

dwelling ['dwɛlɪŋ] n vivienda

dwelt [dwɛlt] pt, pp of **dwell**

dwindle ['dwɪndl] vi menguar, disminuir

dwindling ['dwɪndlɪŋ] adj (strength, interest) menguante; (resources, supplies) en disminución

dye [daɪ] n tinte m ▷ vt teñir; **hair** ~ tinte m para el pelo

dying ['daɪɪŋ] adj moribundo, agonizante; (moments) final; (words) último

dyke [daɪk] n (Brit) dique m; (channel) arroyo, acequia; (causeway) calzada

dynamic [daɪ'næmɪk] adj dinámico

dynamite ['daɪnəmaɪt] n dinamita ▷ vt dinamitar

dynamo ['daɪnəməu] n dinamo f, dinamo m (LAm)

dynasty ['dɪnəstɪ] n dinastía

dysentery ['dɪsɪntrɪ] n disentería

dyslexia [dɪs'lɛksɪə] n dislexia

dyslexic [dɪs'lɛksɪk] adj, n disléxico(-a) m(f)

E, e [i:] n (letter) E, e f; (Mus) mi m; **E for Edward**, (US) **E for Easy** E de Enrique

E abbr (= east) E ▷ n abbr (= Ecstasy) éxtasis m

each [i:tʃ] adj cada inv ▷ pron cada uno; (also: ~ **other**) el uno al otro; **they hate ~ other** se odian (entre ellos or mutuamente); ~ **day** cada día; **they have two books ~** tienen dos libros cada uno; **they cost £5 ~** cuestan cinco libras cada uno; ~ **of us** cada uno de nosotros

eager ['i:gəʳ] adj (gen) impaciente; (hopeful) ilusionado; (keen) entusiasmado; (pupil) apasionado; **to be ~ to do sth** estar deseoso de hacer algo; **to be ~ for** tener muchas ganas de, ansiar

eagle ['i:gl] n águila

ear [ɪəʳ] n oreja; (sense of hearing) oído; (of corn) espiga; **up to the ~s in debt** abrumado de deudas

earache ['ɪəreɪk] n dolor m de oídos

eardrum ['ɪədrʌm] n tímpano

earful ['ɪəful] n: **to give sb an** ~ (inf) echar una bronca a algn

earl [ə:l] n conde m

earlier ['ə:lɪəʳ] adj anterior ▷ adv antes

early ['ə:lɪ] adv (gen) temprano; (ahead of time) con tiempo, con anticipación ▷ adj (gen) temprano; (reply) pronto; (man) primitivo; (first: Christians, settlers) primero; **to have an ~ night** acostarse temprano; **in the** ~ or **in the spring/19th century** a principios de primavera/del siglo diecinueve; **you're ~!**

¡has llegado temprano or pronto!; ~ **in the morning/afternoon** a primeras horas de la mañana/tarde; **she's in her ~ forties** tiene poco más de cuarenta años; **at your earliest convenience** (Comm) con la mayor brevedad posible; **I can't come any earlier** no puedo llegar antes

early retirement n jubilación f anticipada

earmark ['ɪəmɑːk] vt: **to ~ for** reservar para, destinar a

earn [əːn] vt (gen) ganar; (salary) percibir; (interest) devengar; (praise) ganarse; **to ~ one's living** ganarse la vida

earnest ['əːnɪst] adj (wish) fervoroso; (person) serio, formal ⊳ n (also: ~ **money**) anticipo, señal f; **in ~** adv en serio

earnings ['əːnɪŋz] npl (personal) ingresos mpl; (of company etc) ganancias fpl

earphones ['ɪəfəunz] npl auriculares mpl

earplugs ['ɪəplʌgz] npl tapones mpl para los oídos

earring ['ɪərɪŋ] n pendiente m, arete m (LAm)

earshot ['ɪəʃɔt] n: **out of/within ~** fuera del/ al alcance del oído

earth [əːθ] n (gen) tierra; (Brit Elec) toma de tierra ⊳ vt (Brit Elec) conectar a tierra

earthenware ['əːθnwɛəʳ] n loza (de barro)

earthly ['əːθlɪ] adj terrenal, mundano; ~ **paradise** paraíso terrenal; **there is no ~ reason to think ...** no existe razón para pensar ...

earthquake ['əːθkweɪk] n terremoto

earth-shattering ['əːθʃætərɪŋ] adj trascendental

earthy ['əːθɪ] adj (fig: uncomplicated) sencillo; (coarse) grosero

ease [iːz] n facilidad f; (comfort) comodidad f ⊳ vt (task) facilitar; (problem) mitigar; (pain) aliviar; (loosen) soltar; (relieve: pressure, tension) aflojar; (weight) aligerar; (help pass): **to ~ sth in/out** meter/sacar algo con cuidado ⊳ vi (situation) relajarse; **with ~** con facilidad; **to feel at ~/ill at ~** sentirse a gusto/a disgusto; **at ~!** (Mil) ¡descansen!; **ease off, ease up** vi (work, business) aflojar; (person) relajarse

easel ['iːzl] n caballete m

easily ['iːzɪlɪ] adv fácilmente

east [iːst] n este m, oriente m ⊳ adj del este, oriental ⊳ adv al este, hacia el este; **the E~** el Oriente; (Pol) el Este

eastbound adj en dirección este

Easter ['iːstəʳ] n Pascua (de Resurrección)

Easter egg n huevo de Pascua

easterly ['iːstəlɪ] adj (to the east) al este; (from the east) del este

Easter Monday n lunes m de Pascua

eastern ['iːstən] adj del este, oriental; **E~ Europe** Europa del Este; **the E~ bloc** (Pol) los países del Este

Easter Sunday n Domingo de Resurrección

East Germany n (formerly) Alemania Oriental or del Este

easy ['iːzɪ] adj fácil; (life) holgado, cómodo; (relaxed) natural ⊳ adv: **to take it** or **things ~** (not worry) no preocuparse; (go slowly) tomarlo con calma; (rest) descansar; **payment on ~ terms** (Comm) facilidades de pago; **I'm ~** (inf) me da igual, no me importa; **easier said than done** del dicho al hecho hay buen trecho

easy chair n butaca

easy-going ['iːzɪ'gəuɪŋ] adj acomodadizo

eat (pt **ate**, pp **eaten**) [iːt, eɪt, 'iːtn] vt comer; **eat away** vt (sea) desgastar; (acid) corroer; **eat away at, eat into** vt fus corroer; **eat out** vi comer fuera; **eat up** vt (meal etc) comerse; **it ~s up electricity** devora la electricidad

eau de Cologne [əudəkə'ləun] n (agua de) colonia

eaves [iːvz] npl alero sg

eavesdrop ['iːvzdrɔp] vi: **to ~ (on sb)** escuchar a escondidas or con disimulo (a algn)

ebb [ɛb] n reflujo ⊳ vi bajar; (fig: also: ~ **away**) decaer; ~ **and flow** el flujo y reflujo; **to be at a low ~** (fig: person) estar de capa caída

ebony ['ɛbənɪ] n ébano

e-book ['iːbuk] n libro electrónico, e-book m

e-business [iːbɪznɪs] n (commerce) comercio electrónico; (company) negocio electrónico

EC n abbr (= European Community) CE f

e-card ['iːkɑːd] n tarjeta de felicitación electrónica, e-card f

ECB n abbr (= European Central Bank) BCE m

eccentric [ɪk'sɛntrɪk] adj, n excéntrico(-a)

ECG n abbr (= electrocardiogram) E.C.G. m

echo (pl **echoes**) ['ɛkəu] n eco m ⊳ vt (sound) repetir ⊳ vi resonar, hacer eco

eclipse [ɪ'klɪps] n eclipse m ⊳ vt eclipsar

eco-friendly ['iːkəufrɛndlɪ] adj ecológico

ecological [iːkə'lɔdʒɪkl] adj ecológico

ecologist [ɪ'kɔlədʒɪst] n ecologista m/f; (scientist) ecólogo(-a) m(f)

ecology [ɪ'kɔlədʒɪ] n ecología

e-commerce ['iːkɔmɜːs] n comercio electrónico

economic [iːkə'nɔmɪk] adj (profitable: price) económico; (business etc) rentable

economical [iːkə'nɔmɪkl] adj económico

economics [iːkə'nɔmɪks] n (Scol) economía ⊳ npl (financial aspects) finanzas fpl

economist [ɪ'kɔnəmɪst] n economista m/f

economize [ɪ'kɔnəmaɪz] vi economizar, ahorrar

economy [ɪ'kɔnəmɪ] n economía; **economies of scale** economías fpl de escala

economy class n (Aviat etc) clase f turista

economy class syndrome n síndrome m de la clase turista

economy size n tamaño familiar

ecosystem ['iːkəusɪstəm] n ecosistema m

eco-tourism [iːkəu'tuərɪzm] n turismo verde or ecológico

ecstasy ['ɛkstəsɪ] n éxtasis m inv; (drug) éxtasis m inv
ecstatic [ɛks'tætɪk] adj extático, extasiado
ECT n abbr (= electroconvulsive therapy) = **shock therapy**
Ecuador ['ɛkwədɔ:ʳ] n Ecuador m
ecumenical [i:kju'mɛnɪkl] adj ecuménico
eczema ['ɛksɪmə] n eczema m
edge [ɛdʒ] n (of knife etc) filo; (of object) borde m; (of lake etc) orilla ▷ vt (Sewing) ribetear ▷ vi: **to ~ past** pasar con dificultad; **on ~** (fig) = **edgy**; **to ~ away from** alejarse poco a poco de; **to ~ forward** avanzar poco a poco; **to ~ up** subir lentamente
edgeways ['ɛdʒweɪz] adv: **he couldn't get a word in ~** no pudo meter baza
edgy ['ɛdʒɪ] adj nervioso, inquieto
edible ['ɛdɪbl] adj comestible
edict ['i:dɪkt] n edicto
Edinburgh ['ɛdɪnbərə] n Edimburgo
edit ['ɛdɪt] vt (be editor of) dirigir; (re-write) redactar; (cut) cortar; (Comput) editar
edition [ɪ'dɪʃən] n (gen) edición f; (number printed) tirada
editor ['ɛdɪtəʳ] n (of newspaper) director(a) m(f); (of book) redactor(a) m(f); (also: **film ~**) montador(a) m(f)
editorial [ɛdɪ'tɔ:rɪəl] adj editorial ▷ n editorial m; **~ staff** redacción f
EDT n abbr (US: = Eastern Daylight Time) hora de verano de Nueva York
educate ['ɛdjukeɪt] vt (gen) educar; (instruct) instruir
educated ['ɛdjukeɪtɪd] adj culto
education [ɛdju'keɪʃən] n educación f; (schooling) enseñanza; (Scol: subject etc) pedagogía; **primary/secondary ~** enseñanza primaria/secundaria
educational [ɛdju'keɪʃənl] adj (policy etc) de educación, educativo; (teaching) docente; (instructive) educativo; **~ technology** tecnología educacional
eel [i:l] n anguila
eerie ['ɪərɪ] adj (sound, experience) espeluznante
effect [ɪ'fɛkt] n efecto ▷ vt efectuar, llevar a cabo; **effects** npl (property) efectos mpl; **to take ~** (law) entrar en vigor or vigencia; (drug) surtir efecto; **in ~** en realidad; **to have an ~ on sb/sth** hacerle efecto a algn/afectar algo; **to put into** (plan) llevar a la práctica; **his letter is to the ~ that ...** su carta viene a decir que ...
effective [ɪ'fɛktɪv] adj (gen) eficaz; (striking: display, outfit) impresionante; (real) efectivo; **to become ~** (law) entrar en vigor; **~ date** fecha de vigencia
effectively [ɪ'fɛktɪvlɪ] adv (efficiently) eficazmente; (strikingly) de manera impresionante; (in reality) de hecho
effectiveness [ɪ'fɛktɪvnɪs] n eficacia
effeminate [ɪ'fɛmɪnɪt] adj afeminado
effervescent [ɛfə'vɛsnt] adj efervescente

efficiency [ɪ'fɪʃənsɪ] n (gen) eficiencia; (of machine) rendimiento
efficient [ɪ'fɪʃənt] adj eficiente; (remedy, product, system) eficaz; (machine, car) de buen rendimiento
efficiently [ɪ'fɪʃəntlɪ] adv eficientemente, de manera eficiente
effort ['ɛfət] n esfuerzo; **to make an ~ to do sth** hacer un esfuerzo or esforzarse para hacer algo
effortless ['ɛfətlɪs] adj sin ningún esfuerzo
effusive [ɪ'fju:sɪv] adj efusivo
EFL n abbr (Scol) = **English as a foreign language**
e.g. adv abbr (= exempli gratia) p.ej.
egg [ɛg] n huevo; **hard-boiled/soft-boiled/ poached ~** huevo duro or (LAm) a la copa or (LAm) tibio/pasado por agua/escalfado; **scrambled ~s** huevos revueltos; **egg on** vt incitar
eggcup ['ɛgkʌp] n huevera
eggplant ['ɛgplɑ:nt] n (esp US) berenjena
eggshell ['ɛgʃɛl] n cáscara de huevo
egg white n clara de huevo
egg yolk n yema de huevo
ego ['i:gəu] n ego
egotism ['ɛgəutɪzəm] n egoísmo
egotist ['ɛgəutɪst] n egoísta m/f
Egypt ['i:dʒɪpt] n Egipto
Egyptian [ɪ'dʒɪpʃən] adj, n egipcio(-a) m(f)
eiderdown ['aɪdədaun] n edredón m
eight [eɪt] num ocho
eighteen [eɪ'ti:n] num dieciocho
eighteenth [eɪ'ti:nθ] adj decimoctavo; **the ~ floor** la planta dieciocho; **the ~ of August** el dieciocho de agosto
eighth [eɪtθ] adj octavo
eightieth ['eɪtɪɪθ] adj octogésimo
eighty ['eɪtɪ] num ochenta
Eire ['ɛərə] n Eire m
either ['aɪðəʳ] adj cualquiera de los dos ...; (both, each) cada ▷ pron: **~ (of them)** cualquiera (de los dos) ▷ adv tampoco ▷ conj: **~ yes or no** o sí o no; **on ~ side** en ambos lados; **I don't like ~** no me gusta ninguno de los dos; **no, I don't ~** no, yo tampoco
eject [ɪ'dʒɛkt] vt echar; (tenant) desahuciar ▷ vi eyectarse
eke out [i:k-] vt fus (money) hacer que llegue
EKG n abbr (US) see **electrocardiogram**
elaborate [adj ɪ'læbərɪt, vb ɪ'læbəreɪt] adj (design, pattern) complejo ▷ vt elaborar; (expand) ampliar; (refine) refinar ▷ vi explicarse con muchos detalles
elapse [ɪ'læps] vi transcurrir
elastic [ɪ'læstɪk] adj, n elástico
elastic band n (Brit) gomita
elated [ɪ'leɪtɪd] adj: **to be ~** estar eufórico
elation [ɪ'leɪʃən] n euforia
elbow ['ɛlbəu] n codo ▷ vt: **to ~ one's way through the crowd** abrirse paso a codazos por la muchedumbre

elbow grease n (inf): **to use some** or **a bit of** ~ menearse

elder ['ɛldə'] adj mayor ▷ n (tree) saúco; (person) mayor; (of tribe) anciano

elderly ['ɛldəlɪ] adj de edad, mayor ▷ npl: **the** ~ los mayores, los ancianos

eldest ['ɛldɪst] adj, n el/la mayor

elect [ɪ'lɛkt] vt elegir; (choose): **to** ~ **to do** optar por hacer ▷ adj: **the president** ~ el presidente electo

election [ɪ'lɛkʃən] n elección f; **to hold an** ~ convocar elecciones

election campaign n campaña electoral

electioneering [ɪlɛkʃə'nɪərɪŋ] n campaña electoral

elector [ɪ'lɛktə'] n elector(a) m(f)

electoral [ɪ'lɛktərəl] adj electoral

electoral college n colegio electoral

electoral roll n censo electoral

electorate [ɪ'lɛktərɪt] n electorado

electric [ɪ'lɛktrɪk] adj eléctrico

electrical [ɪ'lɛktrɪkl] adj eléctrico

electric blanket n manta eléctrica

electric chair n silla eléctrica

electric cooker n cocina eléctrica

electric current n corriente f eléctrica

electric fire n estufa eléctrica

electrician [ɪlɛk'trɪʃən] n electricista m/f

electricity [ɪlɛk'trɪsɪtɪ] n electricidad f; **to switch on/off the** ~ conectar/desconectar la electricidad

electricity board n (Brit) compañía eléctrica (estatal)

electric light n luz f eléctrica

electric shock n electrochoque m

electrify [ɪ'lɛktrɪfaɪ] vt (Rail) electrificar; (fig: audience) electrizar

electrocardiogram [ɪ'lɛktrə'ka:dɪəgræm] n electrocardiograma m

electrocute [ɪ'lɛktrəukju:t] vt electrocutar

electrode [ɪ'lɛktrəud] n electrodo

electron [ɪ'lɛktrɔn] n electrón m

electronic [ɪlɛk'trɔnɪk] adj electrónico

electronic mail n correo electrónico

electronics [ɪlɛk'trɔnɪks] n electrónica

elegance ['ɛlɪɡəns] n elegancia

elegant ['ɛlɪɡənt] adj elegante

elegy ['ɛlɪdʒɪ] n elegía

element ['ɛlɪmənt] n (gen) elemento; (of heater, kettle etc) resistencia

elementary [ɛlɪ'mɛntərɪ] adj elemental; (primitive) rudimentario; (school, education) primario

elementary school n (US) escuela de enseñanza primaria

elephant ['ɛlɪfənt] n elefante m

elevate ['ɛlɪveɪt] vt (gen) elevar; (in rank) ascender

elevation [ɛlɪ'veɪʃən] n elevación f; (rank) ascenso; (height) altitud f

elevator ['ɛlɪveɪtə'] n (US) ascensor m, elevador m (LAm)

eleven [ɪ'lɛvn] num once

elevenses [ɪ'lɛvnzɪz] npl (Brit) ≈ café m de media mañana

eleventh [ɪ'lɛvnθ] adj undécimo; **at the** ~ **hour** (fig) a última hora

elf (pl **elves**) [ɛlf, ɛlvz] n duende m

elicit [ɪ'lɪsɪt] vt: **to** ~ **sth (from sb)** obtener algo (de algn)

eligible ['ɛlɪdʒəbl] adj: **an** ~ **young man/ woman** un buen partido; **to be** ~ **for sth** llenar los requisitos para algo; **to be** ~ **for a pension** tener derecho a una pensión

eliminate [ɪ'lɪmɪneɪt] vt eliminar; (score out) suprimir; (a suspect, possibility) descartar

elite [eɪ'li:t] n élite f

elm [ɛlm] n olmo

elocution [ɛlə'kju:ʃən] n elocución f

elongated ['i:lɔŋɡeɪtɪd] adj alargado

elope [ɪ'ləup] vi fugarse

elopement [ɪ'ləupmənt] n fuga

eloquent ['ɛləkwənt] adj elocuente

else [ɛls] adv: **or** ~ si no; **something** ~ otra cosa or algo más; **somewhere** ~ en otra parte; **everywhere** ~ en todas partes menos aquí; **everyone** ~ todos los demás; **nothing** ~ nada más; **is there anything** ~ **I can do?** ¿puedo hacer algo más?; **where** ~? ¿dónde más?, ¿en qué otra parte?; **there was little** ~ **to do** apenas quedaba otra cosa que hacer; **nobody** ~ nadie más

elsewhere [ɛls'wɛə'] adv (be) en otra parte; (go) a otra parte

ELT n abbr (Scol) = **English Language Teaching**

elude [ɪ'lu:d] vt eludir; (blow, pursuer) esquivar

elusive [ɪ'lu:sɪv] adj esquivo; (answer) difícil de encontrar; **he is very** ~ no es fácil encontrarlo

elves [ɛlvz] npl of **elf**

emaciated [ɪ'meɪsɪeɪtɪd] adj escuálido

email ['i:meɪl] n abbr (= electronic mail) email m, correo electrónico ▷ vt: **to** ~ **sb** mandar un email or un correo electrónico a algn; **to** ~ **sb sth** mandar algo a algn por Internet, mandar algo a algn en un email or un correo electrónico

email address n dirección f electrónica, email m

emancipate [ɪ'mænsɪpeɪt] vt emancipar

embankment [ɪm'bæŋkmənt] n (of railway) terraplén m; (riverside) dique m

embargo (pl **embargoes**) [ɪm'ba:ɡəu] n prohibición f; (Comm, Naut) embargo; **to put an** ~ **on sth** poner un embargo en algo

embark [ɪm'ba:k] vi embarcarse ▷ vt embarcar; **to** ~ **on** (journey) emprender, iniciar; (fig) emprender

embarkation [ɛmba:'keɪʃən] n (of people) embarco; (of goods) embarque m

embarrass [ɪm'bærəs] vt avergonzar, dar vergüenza a; (financially etc) poner en un aprieto

embarrassed [ɪmˈbærəst] adj azorado, violento; **to be ~** sentirse azorado or violento

embarrassing [ɪmˈbærəsɪŋ] adj (situation) violento; (question) embarazoso

embarrassment [ɪmˈbærəsmənt] n vergüenza, azoramiento; (financial) apuros mpl

embassy [ˈɛmbəsɪ] n embajada

embed [ɪmˈbɛd] vt (jewel) empotrar; (teeth etc) clavar

embellish [ɪmˈbɛlɪʃ] vt embellecer; (fig: story, truth) adornar

embezzle [ɪmˈbɛzl] vt desfalcar, malversar

embezzlement [ɪmˈbɛzlmənt] n desfalco, malversación f

embitter [ɪmˈbɪtər] vt (person) amargar; (relationship) envenenar

emblem [ˈɛmbləm] n emblema m

embody [ɪmˈbɔdɪ] vt (spirit) encarnar; (ideas) expresar

embossed [ɪmˈbɔst] adj realzado; **~ with ...** con ... en relieve

embrace [ɪmˈbreɪs] vt abrazar, dar un abrazo a; (include) abarcar; (adopt: idea) adherirse a ▷ vi abrazarse ▷ n abrazo

embroider [ɪmˈbrɔɪdər] vt bordar; (fig: story) adornar, embellecer

embroidery [ɪmˈbrɔɪdərɪ] n bordado

embryo [ˈɛmbrɪəʊ] n (also fig) embrión m

emcee [ɛmˈsiː] n abbr (US: = master of ceremonies) presentador(a) m(f)

emend [ɪˈmɛnd] vt (text) enmendar

emerald [ˈɛmərəld] n esmeralda

emerge [ɪˈmɜːdʒ] vi (gen) salir; (arise) surgir; **it ~s that** resulta que

emergency [ɪˈmɜːdʒənsɪ] n (event) emergencia; (crisis) crisis f inv; **in an ~** en caso de urgencia; **(to declare a) state of ~** (declarar) estado de emergencia or de excepción

emergency brake n (US) freno de mano

emergency cord n (US) timbre m de alarma

emergency exit n salida de emergencia

emergency landing n aterrizaje m forzoso

emergency room (US: Med) n sala f de urgencias

emergency service n servicio de urgencia

emergent [ɪˈmɜːdʒənt] adj (nation) recientemente independizado

emery board [ˈɛmərɪ-] n lima de uñas

emigrant [ˈɛmɪɡrənt] n emigrante m/f

emigrate [ˈɛmɪɡreɪt] vi emigrar

emigration [ɛmɪˈɡreɪʃən] n emigración f

émigré [ˈɛmɪɡreɪ] n emigrado(-a)

eminence [ˈɛmɪnəns] n eminencia; **to gain** or **win ~** ganarse fama

eminent [ˈɛmɪnənt] adj eminente

emission [ɪˈmɪʃən] n emisión f

emit [ɪˈmɪt] vt emitir; (smell, smoke) despedir

emoticon [ɪˈməʊtɪkɒn] n emoticón m

emotion [ɪˈməʊʃən] n emoción f

emotional [ɪˈməʊʃənl] adj (person) sentimental; (scene) conmovedor(a), emocionante

emotive [ɪˈməʊtɪv] adj emotivo

empathy [ˈɛmpəθɪ] n empatía; **to feel ~ with sb** sentirse identificado con algn

emperor [ˈɛmpərər] n emperador m

emphasis (pl **emphases**) [ˈɛmfəsɪs, -siːz] n énfasis m inv; **to lay** or **place ~ on sth** (fig) hacer hincapié en algo; **the ~ is on sport** se da mayor importancia al deporte

emphasize [ˈɛmfəsaɪz] vt (word, point) subrayar, recalcar; (feature) hacer resaltar

emphatic [ɛmˈfætɪk] adj (condemnation) enérgico; (denial) rotundo

emphatically [ɛmˈfætɪklɪ] adv con énfasis

empire [ˈɛmpaɪər] n imperio

employ [ɪmˈplɔɪ] vt (give job to) emplear; (make use of: thing, method) emplear, usar; **he's ~ed in a bank** está empleado en un banco

employee [ɪmplɔːˈiː] n empleado(-a)

employer [ɪmˈplɔɪər] n patrón(-ona) m(f); (businessman) empresario(-a)

employment [ɪmˈplɔɪmənt] n empleo; **full ~** pleno empleo; **without ~** sin empleo; **to find ~** encontrar trabajo; **place of ~** lugar m de trabajo

employment agency n agencia de colocaciones or empleo

empower [ɪmˈpaʊər] vt: **to ~ sb to do sth** autorizar a algn para hacer algo

empress [ˈɛmprɪs] n emperatriz f

emptiness [ˈɛmptɪnɪs] n vacío

empty [ˈɛmptɪ] adj vacío; (street, area) desierto; (threat) vano ▷ n (bottle) envase m ▷ vt vaciar; (place) dejar vacío ▷ vi vaciarse; (house) quedar(se) vacío o desocupado; (place) quedar(se) desierto; **to ~ into** (river) desembocar en

empty-handed [ˈɛmptɪˈhændɪd] adj con las manos vacías

EMS n abbr (= European Monetary System) SME m

EMU n abbr (= European Monetary Union, Economic and Monetary Union) UME f

emulate [ˈɛmjʊleɪt] vt emular

emulsion [ɪˈmʌlʃən] n emulsión f

enable [ɪˈneɪbl] vt: **to ~ sb to do sth** (allow) permitir a algn hacer algo; (prepare) capacitar a algn para hacer algo

enact [ɪnˈækt] vt (law) promulgar; (play, scene, role) representar

enamel [ɪˈnæməl] n esmalte m

enamoured [ɪˈnæməd] adj: **to be ~ of** (person) estar enamorado de; (activity etc) tener gran afición a; (idea) aferrarse a

encased [ɪnˈkeɪst] adj: **~ in** (covered) revestido de

enchant [ɪnˈtʃɑːnt] vt encantar

enchanting [ɪnˈtʃɑːntɪŋ] adj encantador(a)

encl. abbr (= enclosed) adj

enclose [ɪnˈkləʊz] vt (land) cercar; (with letter etc) adjuntar; (in receptacle): **to ~ (with)**

</a

encerrar (con); **please find ~d** le mandamos adjunto

enclosure [ɪnˈkləʊʒəʳ] n cercado, recinto; (Comm) carta adjunta

encompass [ɪnˈkʌmpəs] vt abarcar

encore [ɔŋˈkɔːʳ] excl ¡otra!, ¡bis! ▷ n bis m

encounter [ɪnˈkaʊntəʳ] n encuentro ▷ vt encontrar, encontrarse con; (difficulty) tropezar con

encourage [ɪnˈkʌrɪdʒ] vt alentar, animar; (growth) estimular; **to ~ sb (to do sth)** animar a algn (a hacer algo)

encouragement [ɪnˈkʌrɪdʒmənt] n estímulo; (of industry) fomento

encouraging [ɪnˈkʌrɪdʒɪŋ] adj alentador(a)

encroach [ɪnˈkrəʊtʃ] vi: **to ~ (up)on** (gen) invadir; (time) adueñarse de

encyclopaedia, encyclopedia [ɛnsaɪkləʊˈpiːdɪə] n enciclopedia

end [ɛnd] n fin m; (of table) extremo; (of line, rope etc) cabo; (of pointed object) punta; (of town) barrio; (of street) final m; (Sport) lado ▷ vt terminar, acabar; (also: **bring to an ~, put an ~ to**) acabar con ▷ vi terminar, cabar; **to ~ (with)** terminar (con); **in the ~** al final; **to be at an ~** llegar a su fin; **at the ~ of the day** (fig) al fin y al cabo, en fin de cuentas; **to this ~, with this ~ in view** con este propósito; **from ~ to ~** de punta a punta; **on ~** (object) de punta, de cabeza; **to stand on ~** (hair) erizarse, ponerse de punta; **for hours on ~** hora tras hora; **end up** vi: **to ~ up in** terminar en; (place) ir a parar a

endanger [ɪnˈdeɪndʒəʳ] vt poner en peligro; **an ~ed species** (of animal) una especie en peligro de extinción

endearing [ɪnˈdɪərɪŋ] adj entrañable

endeavour, endeavor (US) [ɪnˈdɛvəʳ] n esfuerzo; (attempt) tentativa ▷ vi: **to ~ to do** esforzarse por hacer; (try) procurar hacer

ending [ˈɛndɪŋ] n fin m, final m; (of book) desenlace m; (Ling) terminación f

endive [ˈɛndaɪv] n (curly) escarola; (smooth, flat) endibia

endless [ˈɛndlɪs] adj interminable, inacabable; (possibilities) infinito

endorse [ɪnˈdɔːs] vt (cheque) endosar; (approve) aprobar

endorsement [ɪnˈdɔːsmənt] n (approval) aprobación f; (signature) endoso; (Brit: on driving licence) nota de sanción

endow [ɪnˈdaʊ] vt (provide with money) dotar; (found) fundar; **to be ~ed with** (fig) estar dotado de

endowment mortgage n hipoteca dotal

endowment policy n póliza dotal

endurance [ɪnˈdjʊərəns] n resistencia

endure [ɪnˈdjʊəʳ] vt (bear) aguantar, soportar; (resist) resistir ▷ vi (last) perdurar; (resist) resistir

enema [ˈɛnɪmə] n (Med) enema m

enemy [ˈɛnəmɪ] adj, n enemigo(-a) m(f); **to make an ~ of sb** enemistarse con algn

energetic [ɛnəˈdʒɛtɪk] adj enérgico

energy [ˈɛnədʒɪ] n energía

enforce [ɪnˈfɔːs] vt (law) hacer cumplir

engage [ɪnˈgeɪdʒ] vt (attention) captar; (in conversation) abordar; (worker, lawyer) contratar ▷ vi (Tech) engranar; **to ~ in** dedicarse a, ocuparse en; **to ~ sb in conversation** entablar conversación con algn; **to ~ the clutch** embragar

engaged [ɪnˈgeɪdʒd] adj (Brit: busy, in use) ocupado; (betrothed) prometido; **to get ~** prometerse; **he is ~ in research** se dedica a la investigación

engaged tone n (Brit Tel) señal f de comunicando

engagement [ɪnˈgeɪdʒmənt] n (appointment) compromiso, cita; (battle) combate m; (to marry) compromiso; (period) noviazgo; **I have a previous ~** ya tengo un compromiso

engagement ring n anillo de pedida

engaging [ɪnˈgeɪdʒɪŋ] adj atractivo, simpático

engender [ɪnˈdʒɛndəʳ] vt engendrar

engine [ˈɛndʒɪn] n (Aut) motor m; (Rail) locomotora

engine driver n (Brit: of train) maquinista m/f

engineer [ɛndʒɪˈnɪəʳ] n ingeniero(-a); (Brit: for repairs) técnico(-a); (US Rail) maquinista m/f; **civil/mechanical ~** ingeniero(-a) de caminos, canales y puertos/industrial

engineering [ɛndʒɪˈnɪərɪŋ] n ingeniería ▷ cpd (works, factory) de componentes mecánicos

England [ˈɪŋglənd] n Inglaterra

English [ˈɪŋglɪʃ] adj inglés(-esa) ▷ n (Ling) el inglés; **the English** npl los ingleses

English Channel n: **the ~** el Canal de la Mancha

Englishman [ˈɪŋglɪʃmən], **Englishwoman** [ˈɪŋglɪʃwumən] n inglés(-esa) m(f)

English-speaker [ˈɪŋglɪʃspiːkəʳ] n persona de habla inglesa

English-speaking [ˈɪŋglɪʃspiːkɪŋ] adj de habla inglesa

engrave [ɪnˈgreɪv] vt grabar

engraving [ɪnˈgreɪvɪŋ] n grabado

engrossed [ɪnˈgrəust] adj: **~ in** absorto en

engulf [ɪnˈgʌlf] vt sumergir, hundir; (fire) devorar

enhance [ɪnˈhɑːns] vt (gen) aumentar; (beauty) realzar; (position, reputation) mejorar

enigma [ɪˈnɪgmə] n enigma m

enjoy [ɪnˈdʒɔɪ] vt (have: health, fortune) disfrutar de, gozar de; (food) comer con gusto; **I ~ doing ...** me gusta hacer ...; **to ~ o.s.** divertirse, pasarlo bien

enjoyable [ɪnˈdʒɔɪəbl] adj (pleasant) agradable; (amusing) divertido

enjoyment [ɪnˈdʒɔɪmənt] n (use) disfrute m; (joy) placer m

enlarge [ɪn'lɑ:dʒ] vt aumentar; (broaden) extender; (Phot) ampliar ▷ vi: **to ~ on** (subject) tratar con más detalles

enlargement [ɪn'lɑ:dʒmənt] n (Phot) ampliación f

enlighten [ɪn'laɪtn] vt informar, instruir

enlightened [ɪn'laɪtnd] adj iluminado; (tolerant) comprensivo

Enlightenment [ɪn'laɪtnmənt] n (History): **the ~** la Ilustración, el Siglo de las Luces

enlist [ɪn'lɪst] vt alistar; (support) conseguir ▷ vi alistarse; **~ed man** (US Mil) soldado raso

enmity ['ɛnmɪtɪ] n enemistad f

enormity [ɪ'nɔ:mɪtɪ] n enormidad f

enormous [ɪ'nɔ:məs] adj enorme

enough [ɪ'nʌf] adj: **~ time/books** bastante tiempo/bastantes libros ▷ n: **have you got ~?** ¿tiene usted bastante? ▷ adv: **big ~** bastante grande; **he has not worked ~** no ha trabajado bastante; **(that's) ~!** ¡basta ya!, ¡ya está bien!; **that's ~, thanks** con eso basta, gracias; **will five be ~?** ¿bastará con cinco?; **I've had ~** estoy harto; **he was kind ~ to lend me the money** tuvo la bondad o amabilidad de prestarme el dinero; ... **which, funnily ~** ... lo que, por extraño que parezca ...

enquire [ɪn'kwaɪə'] vt, vi = **inquire**

enrage [ɪn'reɪdʒ] vt enfurecer

enrich [ɪn'rɪtʃ] vt enriquecer

enrol, enroll (US) [ɪn'rəʊl] vt (member) inscribir; (Scol) matricular ▷ vi inscribirse; (Scol) matricularse

enrolment, enrollment (US) [ɪn'rəʊlmənt] n inscripción f; matriculación f

en route [ɒn'ru:t] adv durante el viaje; **~ for/ from/to** camino de/de/a

ensconce [ɪn'skɒns] vt: **to ~ o.s.** instalarse cómodamente, acomodarse

ensue [ɪn'sju:] vi seguirse; (result) resultar

en suite [ɒn'swi:t] adj: **with ~ bathroom** con baño

ensure [ɪn'ʃʊə'] vt asegurar

entail [ɪn'teɪl] vt (imply) suponer; (result in) acarrear

entangle [ɪn'tæŋgl] vt (thread etc) enredar, enmarañar; **to become ~d in sth** (fig) enredarse en algo

enter ['ɛntə'] vt (room, profession) entrar en; (club) hacerse socio de; (army) alistarse en; (sb for a competition) inscribir; (write down) anotar, apuntar; (Comput) introducir ▷ vi entrar; **enter for** vt fus presentarse a; **enter into** vt fus (relations) establecer; (plans) formar parte de; (debate) tomar parte en; (negotiations) entablar; (agreement) llegar a, firmar; **enter (up)on** vt fus (career) emprender

enterprise ['ɛntəpraɪz] n empresa; (spirit) iniciativa; **free ~** la libre empresa; **private ~** la iniciativa privada

enterprising ['ɛntəpraɪzɪŋ] adj emprendedor(a)

entertain [ɛntə'teɪn] vt (amuse) divertir; (receive: guest) recibir (en casa); (idea) abrigar

entertainer [ɛntə'teɪnə'] n artista m/f

entertaining [ɛntə'teɪnɪŋ] adj divertido, entretenido ▷ n: **to do a lot of ~** dar muchas fiestas, tener muchos invitados

entertainment [ɛntə'teɪnmənt] n (amusement) diversión f; (show) espectáculo; (party) fiesta

enthralled [ɪn'θrɔ:ld] adj cautivado

enthralling [ɪn'θrɔ:lɪŋ] adj cautivador(a)

enthusiasm [ɪn'θu:zɪæzəm] n entusiasmo

enthusiast [ɪn'θu:zɪæst] n entusiasta m/f

enthusiastic [ɪnθu:zɪ'æstɪk] adj entusiasta; **to be ~ about sb/sth** estar entusiasmado con algn/algo

entice [ɪn'taɪs] vt tentar; (seduce) seducir

entire [ɪn'taɪə'] adj entero, todo

entirely [ɪn'taɪəlɪ] adv totalmente

entirety [ɪn'taɪərətɪ] n: **in its ~** en su totalidad

entitle [ɪn'taɪtl] vt: **to ~ sb to sth** dar a algn derecho a algo

entitled [ɪn'taɪtld] adj (book) titulado; **to be ~ to sth/to do sth** tener derecho a algo/a hacer algo

entity ['ɛntɪtɪ] n entidad f

entourage [ɒntu'rɑ:ʒ] n séquito

entrance ['ɛntrəns] n entrada ▷ vt [ɪn'trɑ:ns] encantar, hechizar; **to gain ~ to** (university etc) ingresar en

entrance examination n (to school) examen m de ingreso

entrance fee n (to a show) entrada; (to a club) cuota

entrance ramp n (US Aut) rampa de acceso

entrant ['ɛntrənt] n (in race, competition) participante m/f; (in exam) candidato(-a)

entrenched [ɛn'trɛntʃd] adj: **~ interests** intereses mpl creados

entrepreneur [ɒntrəprə'nə:'] n empresario(-a), capitalista m/f

entrust [ɪn'trʌst] vt: **to ~ sth to sb** confiar algo a algn

entry ['ɛntrɪ] n entrada; (permission to enter) acceso; (in register, diary, ship's log) apunte m; (in account book, ledger, list) partida; **no ~** prohibido el paso; (Aut) dirección prohibida; **single/double ~ book-keeping** contabilidad f simple/por partida doble

entry form n boletín m de inscripción

entry phone n (Brit) portero automático

E-number ['i:nʌmbə'] n número E

enunciate [ɪ'nʌnsɪeɪt] vt pronunciar; (principle etc) enunciar

envelop [ɪn'vɛləp] vt envolver

envelope ['ɛnvələʊp] n sobre m

enviable ['ɛnvɪəbl] adj envidiable

envious ['ɛnvɪəs] adj envidioso; (look) de envidia

environment [ɪn'vaɪərnmənt] n medio ambiente; (surroundings) entorno;

Department of the E~ ministerio del medio ambiente

environmental [ɪnvaɪərn'mɛntl] *adj* (medio) ambiental; **~ studies** (*in school etc*) ecología *sg*

environmentalist [ɪnvaɪərn'mɛntlɪst] *n* ecologista *m/f*

environmentally [ɪnvaɪərn'mɛntlɪ] *adv*: **~ sound/friendly** ecológico

envisage [ɪn'vɪzɪdʒ] *vt* (*foresee*) prever; (*imagine*) concebir

envoy ['ɛnvɔɪ] *n* enviado(-a)

envy ['ɛnvɪ] *n* envidia ▷ *vt* tener envidia a; **to ~ sb sth** envidiar algo a algn

EPA *n abbr* (US: = *Environmental Protection Agency*) *Agencia del Medio Ambiente*

epic ['ɛpɪk] *n* épica ▷ *adj* épico

epicentre, epicenter (US) ['ɛpɪsɛntəʳ] *n* epicentro

epidemic [ɛpɪ'dɛmɪk] *n* epidemia

epilepsy ['ɛpɪlɛpsɪ] *n* epilepsia

epileptic [ɛpɪ'lɛptɪk] *adj*, *n* epiléptico(-a) *m(f)*

epileptic fit [ɛpɪ'lɛptɪk-] *n* ataque *m* de epilepsia, acceso *m* epiléptico

epilogue ['ɛpɪlɔg] *n* epílogo

episode ['ɛpɪsəud] *n* episodio

epitome [ɪ'pɪtəmɪ] *n* arquetipo

epitomize [ɪ'pɪtəmaɪz] *vt* representar

epoch ['iːpɔk] *n* época

equable ['ɛkwəbl] *adj* (*climate*) estable; (*character*) ecuánime

equal ['iːkwl] *adj* (*gen*) igual; (*treatment*) equitativo ▷ *n* igual *m/f* ▷ *vt* ser igual a; (*fig*) igualar; **to be ~ to** (*task*) estar a la altura de; **the E~ Opportunities Commission** (Brit) *comisión para la igualdad de la mujer en el trabajo*

equality [iː'kwɔlɪtɪ] *n* igualdad *f*

equalize ['iːkwəlaɪz] *vt*, *vi* igualar; (*Sport*) empatar

equally ['iːkwəlɪ] *adv* igualmente; (*share etc*) a partes iguales; **they are ~ clever** son tan listos uno como otro

equanimity [ɛkwə'nɪmɪtɪ] *n* ecuanimidad *f*

equate [ɪ'kweɪt] *vt*: **to ~ sth with** equiparar algo con

equation [ɪ'kweɪʒən] *n* (*Math*) ecuación *f*

equator [ɪ'kweɪtəʳ] *n* ecuador *m*

equilibrium [iːkwɪ'lɪbrɪəm] *n* equilibrio

equip [ɪ'kwɪp] *vt* (*gen*) equipar; (*person*) proveer; **~ped with** (*machinery etc*) provisto de; **to be well ~ped** estar bien equipado; **he is well ~ped for the job** está bien preparado para este puesto

equipment [ɪ'kwɪpmənt] *n* equipo

equities ['ɛkwɪtɪz] *npl* (Brit Comm) acciones *fpl* ordinarias

equivalent [ɪ'kwɪvəlnt] *adj*, *n* equivalente *m*; **to be ~ to** equivaler a

equivocal [ɪ'kwɪvəkl] *adj* equívoco

ER *abbr* (Brit: = *Elizabeth Regina*) *la reina Isabel*; (US: *Med*) = **emergency room**

era ['ɪərə] *n* era, época

eradicate [ɪ'rædɪkeɪt] *vt* erradicar, extirpar

erase [ɪ'reɪz] *vt* (Comput) borrar

eraser [ɪ'reɪzəʳ] *n* goma de borrar

e-reader ['iːˈriːdəʳ] *n* lector de libro electrónico, e-reader *m*

erect [ɪ'rɛkt] *adj* erguido ▷ *vt* erigir, levantar; (*assemble*) montar

erection [ɪ'rɛkʃən] *n* (*of building*) construcción *f*; (*of machinery*) montaje *m*; (*structure*) edificio; (*Med*) erección *f*

Eritrea [ɛrɪ'treɪə] *n* Eritrea

ERM *n abbr* (= *Exchange Rate Mechanism*) (mecanismo de cambios del) SME *m*

erode [ɪ'rəud] *vt* (Geo) erosionar; (*metal*) corroer, desgastar

erosion [ɪ'rəuʒən] *n* erosión *f*; desgaste *m*

erotic [ɪ'rɔtɪk] *adj* erótico

err [əːʳ] *vi* errar; (Rel) pecar

errand ['ɛrnd] *n* recado, mandado (LAm); **to run ~s** hacer recados; **~ of mercy** misión *f* de caridad

erratic [ɪ'rætɪk] *adj* variable; (*results etc*) desigual, poco uniforme

error ['ɛrəʳ] *n* error *m*, equivocación *f*; **typing/ spelling ~** error de mecanografía/ortografía; **in ~** por equivocación; **~s and omissions excepted** salvo error u omisión

erupt [ɪ'rʌpt] *vi* entrar en erupción; (*Med*) hacer erupción; (*fig*) estallar

eruption [ɪ'rʌpʃən] *n* erupción *f*; (*fig: of anger, violence*) explosión *f*, estallido

escalate ['ɛskəleɪt] *vi* extenderse, intensificarse; (*costs*) aumentar vertiginosamente

escalator ['ɛskəleɪtəʳ] *n* escalera mecánica

escapade [ɛskə'peɪd] *n* aventura

escape [ɪ'skeɪp] *n* (*gen*) fuga; (Tech) escape *m*; (*from duties*) escapatoria; (*from chase*) evasión *f* ▷ *vi* (*gen*) escaparse; (*flee*) huir, evadirse ▷ *vt* evitar, eludir; (*consequences*) escapar a; **his name ~s me** no me sale su nombre; **to ~ from** (*place*) escaparse de; (*person*) huir de; (*clutches*) librarse de; **to ~ to** (*another place, freedom, safety*) huir a; **to ~ notice** pasar desapercibido

escapism [ɪ'skeɪpɪzəm] *n* escapismo, evasión *f*

eschew [ɪs'tʃuː] *vt* evitar, abstenerse de

escort ['ɛskɔːt] *n* acompañante *m/f*; (Mil) escolta; (Naut) convoy *m* ▷ *vt* [ɪ'skɔːt] acompañar; (*Mil, Naut*) escoltar

Eskimo ['ɛskɪməu] *adj* esquimal ▷ *n* esquimal *m/f*; (Ling) esquimal *m*

ESL *n abbr* (Scol) = **English as a Second Language**

esophagus [iː'sɔfəgəs] *n* (US) = **oesophagus**

ESP *n abbr* = **extrasensory perception**; (Scol: = *English for Specific (or Special) Purposes*) inglés especializado

esp. *abbr* = **especially**

especially [ɪ'spɛʃlɪ] *adv* (*gen*) especialmente; (*above all*) sobre todo; (*particularly*) en especial

espionage ['ɛspɪɑːʒ] n espionaje m
Esq. abbr (= Esquire) D.
Esquire [ɪ'skwaɪəʳ] n: **J. Brown**, ~ Sr. D. J. Brown
essay ['ɛseɪ] n (Scol) redacción f; (: longer) trabajo
essence ['ɛsns] n esencia; **in ~** esencialmente; **speed is of the ~** es esencial hacerlo con la mayor prontitud
essential [ɪ'sɛnʃl] adj (necessary) imprescindible; (basic) esencial ▷ n often pl lo esencial; **it is ~ that** es imprescindible que
essentially [ɪ'sɛnʃlɪ] adv esencialmente
EST n abbr (US: = Eastern Standard Time) hora de invierno de Nueva York
establish [ɪ'stæblɪʃ] vt establecer; (prove: fact) comprobar, demostrar; (identity) verificar; (relations) entablar
established [ɪ'stæblɪʃt] adj (business) de buena reputación; (staff) de plantilla
establishment [ɪ'stæblɪʃmənt] n establecimiento; (also: **the E~**) la clase dirigente; **a teaching ~** un centro de enseñanza
estate [ɪ'steɪt] n (land) finca, hacienda; (property) propiedad f; (inheritance) herencia, (Pol) estado; **housing ~** (Brit) urbanización f; **industrial ~** polígono industrial
estate agent n (Brit) agente m/f inmobiliario(-a)
estate car n (Brit) ranchera, coche m familiar
esteem [ɪ'stiːm] n: **to hold sb in high ~** estimar en mucho a algn ▷ vt estimar
esthetic [iːs'θɛtɪk] adj (US) = **aesthetic**
estimate ['ɛstɪmət] n estimación f; (assessment) tasa, cálculo; (Comm) presupuesto ▷ vt ['ɛstɪmeɪt] estimar; tasar, calcular; **to give sb an ~ of** presentar a algn un presupuesto de; **at a rough ~** haciendo un cálculo aproximado; **to ~ for** (Comm) hacer un presupuesto de, presupuestar
estimation [ɛstɪ'meɪʃən] n opinión f, juicio; (esteem) aprecio; **in my ~** a mi juicio
Estonia [ɛ'stəʊnɪə] n Estonia
estranged [ɪ'streɪndʒd] adj separado
e-tailing ['iːteɪlɪŋ] n venta en línea, venta vía or por Internet
et al. abbr (= et alii: and others) et al.
etc abbr (= et cetera) etc
etching ['ɛtʃɪŋ] n aguafuerte m or f
eternal [ɪ'təːnl] adj eterno
eternity [ɪ'təːnɪtɪ] n eternidad f
ethical ['ɛθɪkl] adj ético; (honest) honrado
ethics ['ɛθɪks] n ética ▷ npl moralidad f
Ethiopia [iːθɪ'əʊpɪə] n Etiopía
ethnic ['ɛθnɪk] adj étnico
ethnic cleansing [-klɛnzɪŋ] n limpieza étnica
ethnic minority n minoría étnica
ethos ['iːθɒs] n (of culture, group) sistema m de valores

e-ticket ['iːtɪkɪt] n billete electrónico, boleto electrónico (LAm)
etiquette ['ɛtɪkɛt] n etiqueta
EU n abbr (= European Union) UE f
Eucharist ['juːkərɪst] n Eucaristía
euphemism ['juːfəmɪzm] n eufemismo
euphoria [juː'fɔːrɪə] n euforia
Eurasia [juə'reɪʃə] n Eurasia
Eurasian [juə'reɪʃən] adj, n eurasiático(-a) m(f)
euro ['juərəʊ] n (currency) euro
Eurocheque ['juərəʊtʃɛk] n Eurocheque m
Euroland ['juərəʊlænd] n Eurolandia
Europe ['juərəp] n Europa
European [juərə'piːən] adj, n europeo(-a) m(f)
European Community n Comunidad f Europea
European Court of Justice n Tribunal m de Justicia de las Comunidades Europeas
European Union n Unión f Europea
Euro-sceptic [juərəʊ'skɛptɪk] n euroescéptico(-a)
Eurostar® ['juərəʊstɑːʳ] n Eurostar(r) m
Eurozone ['juərəʊzəʊn] n eurozona, zona euro
euthanasia [juːθə'neɪzɪə] n eutanasia
evacuate [ɪ'vækjueɪt] vt evacuar; (place) desocupar
evacuation [ɪvækju'eɪʃən] n evacuación f
evacuee [ɪvækju'iː] n evacuado(-a)
evade [ɪ'veɪd] vt evadir, eludir
evaluate [ɪ'væljueɪt] vt evaluar; (value) tasar; (evidence) interpretar
evangelist [ɪ'vændʒəlɪst] n evangelista m; (preacher) evangelizador(a) m(f)
evaporate [ɪ'væpəreɪt] vi evaporarse; (fig) desvanecerse ▷ vt evaporar
evaporation [ɪvæpə'reɪʃən] n evaporación f
evasion [ɪ'veɪʒən] n evasión f
evasive [ɪ'veɪsɪv] adj evasivo
eve [iːv] n: **on the ~ of** en vísperas de
even ['iːvn] adj (level) llano; (smooth) liso; (speed, temperature) uniforme; (number) par; (Sport) igual(es) ▷ adv hasta, incluso; ~ **if**, ~ **though** aunque + subjun, así + subjun (LAm); ~ **more** aun más; ~ **so** aun así; **not ~** ni siquiera; ~ **he was there** hasta él estaba allí; ~ **on Sundays** incluso los domingos; ~ **faster** aún más rápido; **to break ~** cubrir los gastos; **to get ~ with sb** ajustar cuentas con algn; **to ~ out** vi nivelarse
evening ['iːvnɪŋ] n tarde f; (dusk) atardecer m; (night) noche f; **in the ~** por la tarde; **this ~** esta tarde or noche; **tomorrow/yesterday ~** mañana/ayer por la tarde or noche
evening class n clase f nocturna
evening dress n (man's) traje m de etiqueta; (woman's) traje m de noche
event [ɪ'vɛnt] n suceso, acontecimiento; (Sport) prueba; **in the ~ of** en caso de; **in the ~** en realidad; **in the course of ~s** en el curso de los acontecimientos; **at all ~s**, **in any ~** en cualquier caso

eventful [ɪ'vɛntful] *adj* (*life*) azaroso; (*day*) ajetreado; (*game*) lleno de emoción; (*journey*) lleno de incidentes

eventual [ɪ'vɛntʃuəl] *adj* final

eventuality [ɪvɛntʃu'ælɪtɪ] *n* eventualidad f

eventually [ɪ'vɛntʃuəlɪ] *adv* (*finally*) por fin; (*in time*) con el tiempo

ever ['ɛvə'] *adv* nunca, jamás; (*at all times*) siempre; **for** ~ (para) siempre; **the best** ~ lo nunca visto; **did you** ~ **meet him?** ¿llegaste a conocerle?; **have you** ~ **been there?** ¿has estado allí alguna vez?; **have you** ~ **seen it?** ¿lo has visto alguna vez?; **better than** ~ mejor que nunca; **thank you** ~ **so much** muchísimas gracias; **yours** ~ (*in letters*) un abrazo de; ~ **since** *adv* desde entonces ⊳ *conj* después de que

evergreen ['ɛvəgriːn] *n* árbol m de hoja perenne

everlasting [ɛvə'lɑːstɪŋ] *adj* eterno, perpetuo

◯ **KEYWORD**

every ['ɛvrɪ] *adj* 1 (*each*) cada; **every one of them** (*persons*) todos ellos(-as); (*objects*) cada uno de ellos(-as); **every shop in the town was closed** todas las tiendas de la ciudad estaban cerradas
2 (*all possible*) todo(-a); **I gave you every assistance** te di toda la ayuda posible; **I have every confidence in him** tiene toda mi confianza; **we wish you every success** te deseamos toda suerte de éxitos
3 (*showing recurrence*) todo(-a); **every day/week** todos los días/todas las semanas; **every other car had been broken into** habían forzado uno de cada dos coches; **she visits me every other/third day** me visita cada dos/tres días; **every now and then** de vez en cuando

everybody ['ɛvrɪbɔdɪ] *pron* todos *pron pl*, todo el mundo; ~ **knows about it** todo el mundo lo sabe; ~ **else** todos los demás

everyday ['ɛvrɪdeɪ] *adj* (*daily: use, occurrence, experience*) diario, cotidiano; (*usual: expression*) corriente; (*common*) vulgar; (*routine*) rutinario

everyone ['ɛvrɪwʌn] *pron* = **everybody**

everything ['ɛvrɪθɪŋ] *pron* todo; ~ **is ready** todo está dispuesto; **he did** ~ **possible** hizo todo lo posible

everywhere ['ɛvrɪwɛə'] *adv* (*be*) en todas partes; (*go*) a o por todas partes; ~ **you go you meet ...** en todas partes encuentras ...

evict [ɪ'vɪkt] *vt* desahuciar

eviction [ɪ'vɪkʃən] *n* desahucio

evidence ['ɛvɪdəns] *n* (*proof*) prueba; (*of witness*) testimonio; (*facts*) datos *mpl*, hechos *mpl*; **to give** ~ prestar declaración, dar testimonio

evident ['ɛvɪdənt] *adj* evidente, manifiesto

evidently ['ɛvɪdəntlɪ] *adv* (*obviously*) obviamente, evidentemente; (*apparently*) por lo visto

evil ['iːvl] *adj* malo; (*influence*) funesto; (*smell*) horrible ⊳ *n* mal m

evoke [ɪ'vəuk] *vt* evocar; (*admiration*) provocar

evolution [iːvə'luːʃən] *n* evolución f, desarrollo

evolve [ɪ'vɔlv] *vt* desarrollar ⊳ *vi* evolucionar, desarrollarse

ewe [juː] *n* oveja

ex [ɛks] (*inf*) *n*: **my ex** mi ex

ex- [ɛks] *pref* (*former: husband, president etc*) ex-; (*out of*): **the price ~works** precio de fábrica

exact [ɪg'zækt] *adj* exacto ⊳ *vt*: **to ~ sth (from)** exigir algo (de)

exacting [ɪg'zæktɪŋ] *adj* exigente; (*conditions*) arduo

exactly [ɪg'zæktlɪ] *adv* exactamente; (*time*) en punto; ~! ¡exacto!

exaggerate [ɪg'zædʒəreɪt] *vt, vi* exagerar

exaggeration [ɪgzædʒə'reɪʃən] *n* exageración f

exalted [ɪg'zɔːltɪd] *adj* (*position*) elevado; (*elated*) enardecido

exam [ɪg'zæm] *n abbr* (*Scol*) = **examination**

examination [ɪgzæmɪ'neɪʃən] *n* (*gen*) examen m; (*Law*) interrogación f; (*Med*) reconocimiento; (*inquiry*) investigación f; **to take** or **sit an** ~ hacer un examen; **the matter is under** ~ se está examinando el asunto

examine [ɪg'zæmɪn] *vt* (*gen*) examinar; (*inspect: machine, premises*) inspeccionar; (*Scol, Law: person*) interrogar; (*at customs: luggage, passport*) registrar; (*Med*) reconocer, examinar

examiner [ɪg'zæmɪnə'] *n* examinador(a) *m(f)*

example [ɪg'zɑːmpl] *n* ejemplo; **for** ~ por ejemplo; **to set a good/bad** ~ dar buen/mal ejemplo

exasperate [ɪg'zɑːspəreɪt] *vt* exasperar, irritar; ~**d by** or **at** or **with** exasperado por or con

exasperation [ɪgzɑːspə'reɪʃən] *n* exasperación f, irritación f

excavate ['ɛkskəveɪt] *vt* excavar

excavation [ɛkskə'veɪʃən] *n* excavación f

exceed [ɪk'siːd] *vt* exceder; (*number*) pasar de; (*speed limit*) sobrepasar; (*limits*) rebasar; (*powers*) excederse en; (*hopes*) superar

exceedingly [ɪk'siːdɪŋlɪ] *adv* sumamente, sobremanera

excel [ɪk'sɛl] *vi* sobresalir; **to ~ o.s.** lucirse

excellence ['ɛksələns] *n* excelencia

Excellency ['ɛksələnsɪ] *n*: **His** ~ Su Excelencia

excellent ['ɛksələnt] *adj* excelente

except [ɪk'sɛpt] *prep* (*also*: ~ **for**, ~**ing**) excepto, salvo ⊳ *vt* exceptuar, excluir; ~ **if/when** excepto si/cuando; ~ **that** salvo que

exception [ɪkˈsɛpʃən] n excepción f; **to take ~ to** ofenderse por; **with the ~ of** a excepción de; **to make an ~** hacer una excepción

exceptional [ɪkˈsɛpʃənl] adj excepcional

exceptionally [ɪkˈsɛpʃənəlɪ] adv excepcionalmente, extraordinariamente

excerpt [ˈɛksɜːpt] n extracto

excess [ɪkˈsɛs] n exceso; **in ~ of** superior a

excess baggage n exceso de equipaje

excess fare n suplemento

excessive [ɪkˈsɛsɪv] adj excesivo

exchange [ɪksˈtʃeɪndʒ] n cambio; (of prisoners) canje m; (of ideas) intercambio; (also: **telephone ~**) central f (telefónica) ▷ vt intercambiar; **to ~ (for)** cambiar (por); **in ~ for** a cambio de; **foreign ~** (Comm) divisas fpl

exchange rate n tipo de cambio

exchequer [ɪksˈtʃɛkəʳ] n: **the ~** (Brit) Hacienda

excise [ˈɛksaɪz] n impuestos sobre el consumo interior

excite [ɪkˈsaɪt] vt (stimulate) estimular; (anger) suscitar, provocar; (move) emocionar; **to get ~d** emocionarse

excitement [ɪkˈsaɪtmənt] n emoción f

exciting [ɪkˈsaɪtɪŋ] adj emocionante

excl. abbr = **excluding; exclusive (of)**

exclaim [ɪkˈskleɪm] vi exclamar

exclamation [ɛkskləˈmeɪʃən] n exclamación f

exclamation mark, exclamation point (US) n signo de admiración

exclude [ɪkˈskluːd] vt excluir; (except) exceptuar

excluding [ɪksˈkluːdɪŋ] prep: **~ VAT** IVA no incluido

exclusion [ɪkˈskluːʒən] n exclusión f; **to the ~ of** con exclusión de

exclusion zone n zona de exclusión

exclusive [ɪkˈskluːsɪv] adj exclusivo; (club, district) selecto; **~ of tax** excluyendo impuestos; **~ of postage/service** franqueo/servicio no incluido; **from 1st to 13th March ~** del 1 al 13 de marzo exclusive

exclusively [ɪkˈskluːsɪvlɪ] adv únicamente

excommunicate [ɛkskəˈmjuːnɪkeɪt] vt excomulgar

excrement [ˈɛkskrəmənt] n excremento

excruciating [ɪkˈskruːʃɪeɪtɪŋ] adj (pain) agudísimo, atroz

excursion [ɪkˈskəːʃən] n excursión f

excuse n [ɪkˈskjuːs] disculpa, excusa; (evasion) pretexto ▷ vt [ɪkˈskjuːz] disculpar, perdonar; (justify) justificar; **to make ~s for sb** presentar disculpas por algn; **to ~ sb from doing sth** dispensar a algn de hacer algo; **to ~ o.s. (for (doing) sth)** pedir disculpas a algn (por (hacer) algo); **~ me!** ¡perdone!; (attracting attention) ¡oiga (, por favor)!; **if you will ~ me** con su permiso

ex-directory [ˈɛksdɪˈrɛktərɪ] adj (Brit): **~ (phone) number** número que no figura en la guía (telefónica)

execute [ˈɛksɪkjuːt] vt (plan) realizar; (order) cumplir; (person) ajusticiar, ejecutar

execution [ɛksɪˈkjuːʃən] n realización f; cumplimiento; ejecución f

executioner [ɛksɪˈkjuːʃənəʳ] n verdugo

executive [ɪgˈzɛkjutɪv] n (Comm) ejecutivo(-a); (Pol) poder m ejecutivo ▷ adj ejecutivo; (car, plane, position) de ejecutivo; (offices, suite) de la dirección; (secretary) de dirección

executor [ɪgˈzɛkjutəʳ] n albacea m, testamentario

exemplary [ɪgˈzɛmplərɪ] adj ejemplar

exemplify [ɪgˈzɛmplɪfaɪ] vt ejemplificar

exempt [ɪgˈzɛmpt] adj: **~ from** exento de ▷ vt: **to ~ sb from** eximir a algn de

exemption [ɪgˈzɛmpʃən] n exención f; (immunity) inmunidad f

exercise [ˈɛksəsaɪz] n ejercicio ▷ vt ejercer; (patience etc) proceder con; (dog) sacar de paseo ▷ vi hacer ejercicio

exercise bike n bicicleta estática

exercise book n cuaderno de ejercicios

exert [ɪgˈzəːt] vt ejercer; (strength, force) emplear; **to ~ o.s.** esforzarse

exertion [ɪgˈzəːʃən] n esfuerzo

exhale [ɛksˈheɪl] vt despedir, exhalar ▷ vi espirar, exhalar

exhaust [ɪgˈzɔːst] n (pipe) (tubo de) escape m; (fumes) gases mpl de escape ▷ vt agotar; **to ~ o.s.** agotarse

exhausted [ɪgˈzɔːstɪd] adj agotado

exhausting [ɪgˈzɔːstɪŋ] adj: **an ~ journey/day** un viaje/día agotador

exhaustion [ɪgˈzɔːstʃən] n agotamiento; **nervous ~** agotamiento nervioso

exhaustive [ɪgˈzɔːstɪv] adj exhaustivo

exhibit [ɪgˈzɪbɪt] n (Art) obra expuesta; (Law) objeto expuesto ▷ vt (show: emotions) manifestar; demostrar; (paintings) exponer

exhibition [ɛksɪˈbɪʃən] n exposición f

exhilarating [ɪgˈzɪləreɪtɪŋ] adj estimulante, tónico

exile [ˈɛksaɪl] n exilio; (person) exiliado(-a) ▷ vt desterrar, exiliar

exist [ɪgˈzɪst] vi existir

existence [ɪgˈzɪstəns] n existencia

existing [ɪgˈzɪstɪŋ] adj existente, actual

exit [ˈɛksɪt] n salida ▷ vi (Theat) hacer mutis; (Comput) salir (del sistema)

exit poll n encuesta a la salida de los colegios electorales

exit ramp n (US Aut) vía de acceso

exodus [ˈɛksədəs] n éxodo

exonerate [ɪgˈzɔnəreɪt] vt: **to ~ from** exculpar de

exotic [ɪgˈzɔtɪk] adj exótico

expand [ɪkˈspænd] vt ampliar, extender; (number) aumentar ▷ vi (trade etc) ampliarse, expandirse; (gas, metal) dilatarse; **to ~ on** (notes, story etc) ampliar

expanse [ɪkˈspæns] n extensión f

expansion [ɪkˈspænʃən] n ampliación f; aumento; (of trade) expansión f

expect [ɪkˈspɛkt] vt (gen) esperar; (count on) contar con; (suppose) suponer ▷ vi: **to be ~ing** estar encinta; **to ~ to do sth** esperar hacer algo; **as ~ed** como era de esperar; **I ~ so** supongo que sí

expectancy [ɪkˈspɛktənsɪ] n (anticipation) expectación f; **life ~** esperanza de vida

expectant mother [ɪkˈspɛktənt-] n futura madre f

expectation [ɛkspɛkˈteɪʃən] n (hope) esperanza; (belief) expectativa; **in ~ of** esperando; **against** or **contrary to all ~(s)** en contra de todas las previsiones; **to come** or **live up to sb's ~s** resultar tan bueno como se esperaba; **to fall short of sb's ~s** no cumplir las esperanzas de algn, decepcionar a algn

expedient [ɪkˈspiːdɪənt] adj conveniente, oportuno ▷ n recurso, expediente m

expedition [ɛkspəˈdɪʃən] n expedición f

expel [ɪkˈspɛl] vt expulsar

expend [ɪkˈspɛnd] vt gastar; (use up) consumir

expendable [ɪkˈspɛndəbl] adj prescindible

expenditure [ɪkˈspɛndɪtʃəʳ] n gastos mpl, desembolso; (of time, effort) gasto

expense [ɪkˈspɛns] n gasto, gastos mpl; (high cost) coste m; **expenses** npl (Comm) gastos mpl; **at the ~ of** a costa de; **to meet the ~ of** hacer frente a los gastos de

expense account n cuenta de gastos (de representación)

expensive [ɪkˈspɛnsɪv] adj caro, costoso

experience [ɪkˈspɪərɪəns] n experiencia ▷ vt experimentar; (suffer) sufrir; **to learn by ~** aprender con la experiencia

experienced [ɪkˈspɪərɪənst] adj experimentado

experiment [ɪkˈspɛrɪmənt] n experimento ▷ vi hacer experimentos, experimentar; **to perform** or **carry out an ~** realizar un experimento; **as an ~** como experimento; **to ~ with a new vaccine** experimentar con una vacuna nueva

experimental [ɪkspɛrɪˈmɛntl] adj experimental; **the process is still at the ~ stage** el proceso está todavía en prueba

expert [ˈɛkspəːt] adj experto, perito ▷ n experto(-a), perito(-a); (specialist) especialista m/f; **~ witness** (Law) testigo pericial; **~ in** or **at doing sth** experto or perito en hacer algo; **an ~ on sth** un experto en algo

expertise [ɛkspəːˈtiːz] n pericia

expire [ɪkˈspaɪəʳ] vi (gen) caducar, vencerse

expiry [ɪkˈspaɪərɪ] n caducidad f, vencimiento

expiry date n (of medicine, food item) fecha de caducidad

explain [ɪkˈspleɪn] vt explicar; (mystery) aclarar; **explain away** vt justificar

explanation [ɛkspləˈneɪʃən] n explicación f; aclaración f; **to find an ~ for sth** encontrarle una explicación a algo

explanatory [ɪkˈsplænətrɪ] adj explicativo; aclaratorio

explicit [ɪkˈsplɪsɪt] adj explícito

explode [ɪkˈspləud] vi estallar, explotar; (with anger) reventar ▷ vt hacer explotar; (fig: theory, myth) demoler

exploit [ˈɛksplɔɪt] n hazaña ▷ vt [ɪkˈsplɔɪt] explotar

exploitation [ɛksplɔɪˈteɪʃən] n explotación f

exploratory [ɪkˈsplɔrətrɪ] adj (fig: talks) exploratorio, preliminar

explore [ɪkˈsplɔːʳ] vt explorar; (fig) examinar, sondear

explorer [ɪkˈsplɔːrəʳ] n explorador(a) m(f)

explosion [ɪkˈspləuʒən] n explosión f

explosive [ɪkˈspləusɪv] adj, n explosivo

exponent [ɪkˈspəunənt] n partidario(-a); (of skill, activity) exponente m/f

export vt [ɛkˈspɔːt] exportar ▷ n [ˈɛkspɔːt] exportación f ▷ cpd de exportación

exporter [ɛkˈspɔːtəʳ] n exportador(a) m(f)

expose [ɪkˈspəuz] vt exponer; (unmask) desenmascarar

exposed [ɪkˈspəuzd] adj expuesto; (land, house) desprotegido; (Elec: wire) al aire; (pipe, beam) al descubierto

exposure [ɪkˈspəuʒəʳ] n exposición f; (Phot: speed) (tiempo m de) exposición f; (: shot) fotografía; **to die from ~** (Med) morir de frío

exposure meter n fotómetro

express [ɪkˈsprɛs] adj (definite) expreso, explícito; (Brit: letter etc) urgente ▷ n (train) rápido ▷ adv (send) por correo extraordinario ▷ vt expresar; (squeeze) exprimir; **to send sth ~** enviar algo por correo urgente; **to ~ o.s.** expresarse

expression [ɪkˈsprɛʃən] n expresión f

expressive [ɪkˈsprɛsɪv] adj expresivo

expressly [ɪkˈsprɛslɪ] adv expresamente

expressway [ɪkˈsprɛsweɪ] n (US: urban motorway) autopista

expulsion [ɪkˈspʌlʃən] n expulsión f

exquisite [ɛkˈskwɪzɪt] adj exquisito

ext. abbr (Tel) = **extension**

extend [ɪkˈstɛnd] vt (visit, street) prolongar; (building) ampliar; (thanks, friendship etc) extender; (Comm: credit) conceder; (deadline) prorrogar; (invitation) ofrecer ▷ vi (land) extenderse; **the contract ~s to/for ...** el contrato se prolonga hasta/por ...

extension [ɪkˈstɛnʃən] n extensión f; (building) ampliación f; (Tel: line) extensión f; (: telephone) supletorio m; (of deadline) prórroga; **~ 3718** extensión 3718

extensive [ɪkˈstɛnsɪv] adj (gen) extenso; (damage) importante; (knowledge) amplio

extensively [ɪkˈstɛnsɪvlɪ] adv (altered, damaged etc) extensamente; **he's travelled ~** ha viajado por muchos países

extent [ɪkˈstɛnt] n (breadth) extensión f; (scope: of knowledge, activities) alcance m; (degree: of damage, loss) grado; **to some ~** hasta cierto punto; **to a certain ~** hasta cierto punto; **to a large ~** en gran parte; **to the ~ of ...** hasta el punto de ...; **to such an ~ that ...** hasta tal punto que ...; **to what ~?** ¿hasta qué punto?; **debts to the ~ of £5000** deudas por la cantidad de £5000

extenuating [ɪkˈstɛnjueɪtɪŋ] adj: **~ circumstances** circunstancias fpl atenuantes

exterior [ɛkˈstɪərɪəʳ] adj exterior, externo ▷ n exterior m

exterminate [ɪkˈstəːmɪneɪt] vt exterminar

external [ɛkˈstəːnl] adj externo, exterior ▷ n: **the ~s** la apariencia exterior; **~ affairs** asuntos mpl exteriores; **for ~ use only** (Med) para uso tópico

extinct [ɪkˈstɪŋkt] adj (volcano) extinguido, apagado; (race) extinguido

extinction [ɪkˈstɪŋkʃən] n extinción f

extinguish [ɪkˈstɪŋgwɪʃ] vt extinguir, apagar

extinguisher [ɪkˈstɪŋgwɪʃəʳ] n extintor m

extol, extoll (US) [ɪkˈstəul] vt (merits, virtues) ensalzar, alabar; (person) alabar, elogiar

extort [ɪkˈstɔːt] vt sacar a la fuerza; (confession) arrancar

extortion [ɪkˈstɔːʃən] n extorsión f

extortionate [ɪkˈstɔːʃnət] adj excesivo, exorbitante

extra [ˈɛkstrə] adj adicional ▷ adv (in addition) más ▷ n (addition) extra m, suplemento; (Theat) extra m/f, comparsa m/f; (newspaper) edición f extraordinaria; **wine will cost ~** el vino se paga aparte; **~ large sizes** tallas extragrandes

extract vt [ɪkˈstrækt] sacar; (tooth) extraer; (confession) arrancar ▷ n [ˈɛkstrækt] fragmento; (Culin) extracto

extraction [ɪkˈstrækʃən] n extracción f; (origin) origen m

extracurricular [ɛkstrəkəˈrɪkjuləʳ] adj (Scol) extraescolar

extradite [ˈɛkstrədaɪt] vt extraditar

extradition [ɛkstrəˈdɪʃən] n extradición f

extramarital [ɛkstrəˈmærɪtl] adj extramatrimonial

extramural [ɛkstrəˈmjuərl] adj extraacadémico

extraneous [ɪkˈstreɪnɪəs] adj extraño, ajeno

extraordinary [ɪkˈstrɔːdnrɪ] adj extraordinario; (odd) raro; **the ~ thing is that ...** lo más extraordinario es que ...

extraordinary general meeting n junta general extraordinaria

extrasensory perception [ˈɛkstrəˈsɛnsərɪ-] n percepción f extrasensorial

extra time n (Football) prórroga

extravagance [ɪkˈstrævəgəns] n (excessive spending) derroche m; (thing bought) extravagancia

extravagant [ɪkˈstrævəgənt] adj (wasteful) derrochador(a); (taste, gift) excesivamente caro; (price) exorbitante; (praise) excesivo

extreme [ɪkˈstriːm] adj extremo; (poverty etc) extremado; (case) excepcional ▷ n extremo; **the ~ left/right** (Pol) la extrema izquierda/derecha; **~s of temperature** temperaturas extremas

extremely [ɪkˈstriːmlɪ] adv sumamente, extremadamente

extremist [ɪkˈstriːmɪst] adj, n extremista m/f

extremity [ɪkˈstrɛmətɪ] n extremidad f, punta; (need) apuro, necesidad f; **extremities** npl (hands and feet) extremidades fpl

extricate [ˈɛkstrɪkeɪt] vt: **to ~ o.s. from** librarse de

extrovert [ˈɛkstrəvəːt] n extrovertido(-a)

exuberance [ɪgˈzjuːbərns] n exuberancia

exuberant [ɪgˈzjuːbərnt] adj (person) eufórico; (style) exuberante

exude [ɪgˈzjuːd] vt rezumar

eye [aɪ] n ojo ▷ vt mirar; **to keep an ~ on** vigilar; **as far as the ~ can see** hasta donde alcanza la vista; **with an ~ to doing sth** con vistas or miras a hacer algo; **to have an ~ for sth** tener mucha vista or buen ojo para algo; **there's more to this than meets the ~** esto tiene su miga

eyeball [ˈaɪbɔːl] n globo ocular

eyebath [ˈaɪbɑːθ] n baño ocular, lavaojos m inv

eyebrow [ˈaɪbrau] n ceja

eyebrow pencil n lápiz m de cejas

eyedrops [ˈaɪdrɔps] npl gotas fpl para los ojos

eyeful [ˈaɪful] n (inf): **to get an ~ of sth** ver bien algo

eyelash [ˈaɪlæʃ] n pestaña

eyelid [ˈaɪlɪd] n párpado

eyeliner [ˈaɪlaɪnəʳ] n lápiz m de ojos

eye-opener [ˈaɪəupnəʳ] n revelación f, gran sorpresa

eyeshadow [ˈaɪʃædəu] n sombra de ojos

eyesight [ˈaɪsaɪt] n vista

eyesore [ˈaɪsɔːʳ] n monstruosidad f

eye witness n testigo m/f ocular

eyrie [ˈɪərɪ] n aguilera

f

F, f [εf] *n* (*letter*) F, f f; (*Mus*) fa *m*; **F for Frederick**, (*US*) **F for Fox** F de Francia
FA *n abbr* (*Brit*: = *Football Association*) ≈ AFE *f* (*Sp*)
fable ['feɪbl] *n* fábula
fabric ['fæbrɪk] *n* tejido, tela
fabricate ['fæbrɪkeɪt] *vt* fabricar; (*fig*) inventar
fabrication [fæbrɪ'keɪʃən] *n* fabricación *f*; (*fig*) invención *f*
fabulous ['fæbjuləs] *adj* fabuloso
façade [fə'sɑːd] *n* fachada
face [feɪs] *n* (*Anat*) cara, rostro; (*of clock*) esfera; (*side*) cara; (*surface*) superficie *f* ▷ *vt* (*direction*) estar de cara a; (*situation*) hacer frente a; (*facts*) aceptar; **~ down** (*person, card*) boca abajo; **to lose ~** desprestigiarse; **to save ~** salvar las apariencias; **to make** or **pull a ~** hacer muecas; **in the ~ of** (*difficulties etc*) en vista de, ante; **on the ~ of it** a primera vista; **~ to ~** cara a cara; **to ~ the fact that ...** reconocer que ...; **face up to** *vt fus* hacer frente a, enfrentarse a
face cloth *n* (*Brit*) toallita
face cream *n* crema (de belleza)
face lift *n* lifting *m*, estirado facial
face pack *n* (*Brit*) mascarilla
face powder *n* polvos *mpl* para la cara
facet ['fæsɪt] *n* faceta
facetious [fə'siːʃəs] *adj* chistoso
face value *n* (*of stamp*) valor *m* nominal; **to take sth at ~** (*fig*) tomar algo en sentido literal, aceptar las apariencias de algo

facial ['feɪʃəl] *adj* de la cara ▷ *n* (*also*: **beauty ~**) tratamiento facial, limpieza
facile ['fæsaɪl] *adj* superficial
facilitate [fə'sɪlɪteɪt] *vt* facilitar
facility [fə'sɪlɪtɪ] *n* facilidad *f*; **facilities** *npl* instalaciones *fpl*; **credit ~** facilidades de crédito
facing ['feɪsɪŋ] *prep* frente a ▷ *adj* de enfrente
facsimile [fæk'sɪmɪlɪ] *n* facsímil(e) *m*
fact [fækt] *n* hecho; **in ~** en realidad; **to know for a ~ that ...** saber a ciencia cierta que ...
faction ['fækʃən] *n* facción *f*
factional ['fækʃənl] *adj* (*fighting*) entre distintas facciones
factor ['fæktər] *n* factor *m*; (*Comm: person*) agente *m/f* comisionado(-a) ▷ *vi* (*Comm*) comprar deudas; **safety ~** factor de seguridad
factory ['fæktərɪ] *n* fábrica
factory floor *n* (*workers*) trabajadores *mpl*, mano *f* de obra directa; (*area*) talleres *mpl*
factual ['fæktjuəl] *adj* basado en los hechos
faculty ['fækəltɪ] *n* facultad *f*; (*US: teaching staff*) personal *m* docente
fad [fæd] *n* novedad *f*, moda
fade [feɪd] *vi* descolorarse, desteñirse; (*sound, hope*) desvanecerse; (*light*) apagarse; (*flower*) marchitarse; **fade away** *vi* (*sound*) apagarse; **fade in** *vt* (*TV, Cine*) fundir; (*Radio: sound*) mezclar ▷ *vi* (*TV, Cine*) fundirse; (*Radio*) oírse por encima; **fade out** *vt* (*TV, Cine*) fundir; (*Radio*) apagar, disminuir el volumen de ▷ *vi* (*TV, Cine*) desvanecerse; (*Radio*) apagarse, dejarse de oír
faeces, feces (*US*) ['fiːsiːz] *npl* excremento *sg*, heces *fpl*
fag [fæg] *n* (*Brit inf: cigarette*) pitillo (*Sp*), cigarro; (*US inf: homosexual*) maricón *m*
Fahrenheit ['fɑːrənhaɪt] *n* Fahrenheit *m*
fail [feɪl] *vt* suspender; (*memory etc*) fallar a ▷ *vi* suspender; (*be unsuccessful*) fracasar; (*strength, brakes, engine*) fallar; **to ~ to do sth** (*neglect*) dejar de hacer algo; (*be unable*) no poder hacer algo; **without ~** sin falta; **words ~ me!** ¡no sé qué decir!
failing ['feɪlɪŋ] *n* falta, defecto ▷ *prep* a falta de; **~ that** de no ser posible eso
failure ['feɪljər] *n* fracaso; (*person*) fracasado(-a); (*mechanical etc*) fallo; (*in exam*) suspenso; (*of crops*) pérdida, destrucción *f*; **it was a complete ~** fue un fracaso total
faint [feɪnt] *adj* débil; (*smell, breeze, trace*) leve; (*recollection*) vago; (*mark*) apenas visible ▷ *n* desmayo ▷ *vi* desmayarse; **to feel ~** estar mareado, marearse
faintest ['feɪntɪst] *adj*: **I haven't the ~ idea** no tengo la más remota idea
faintly ['feɪntlɪ] *adv* débilmente; (*vaguely*) vagamente
fair [feər] *adj* justo; (*hair, person*) rubio; (*weather*) bueno; (*good enough*) suficiente; (*sizeable*) considerable ▷ *adv*: **to play ~** jugar

limpio ▷ n feria; (Brit: *funfair*) parque m de
atracciones; **it's not ~!** ¡no es justo!, ¡no hay
derecho!; **~ copy** copia en limpio; **~ play**
juego limpio; **a ~ amount of** bastante;
~ wear and tear desgaste m natural;
trade ~ feria de muestras
fairground ['feəgraund] n recinto ferial
fair-haired [fɛə'hɛəd] *adj* (*person*) rubio
fairly ['fɛəlɪ] *adv* (*justly*) con justicia; (*equally*)
equitativamente; (*quite*) bastante; **I'm ~
sure** estoy bastante seguro
fairness ['fɛənɪs] n justicia; (*impartiality*)
imparcialidad f; **in all ~** a decir verdad
fair trade n comercio justo
fairway ['fɛəweɪ] n (*Golf*) calle f
fairy ['fɛərɪ] n hada
fairy tale n cuento de hadas
faith [feɪθ] n fe f; (*trust*) confianza; (*sect*)
religión f; **to have ~ in sb/sth** confiar en
algn/algo
faithful ['feɪθful] *adj*, *adj* (*loyal: troops etc*) leal;
(*spouse*) fiel; (*account*) exacto
faithfully ['feɪθfulɪ] *adv* fielmente; **yours ~**
(*Brit: in letters*) le saluda atentamente
fake [feɪk] n (*painting etc*) falsificación f;
(*person*) impostor(a) m(f) ▷ *adj* falso ▷ *vt*
fingir; (*painting etc*) falsificar
falcon ['fɔːlkən] n halcón m
Falkland Islands ['fɔːlklənd-] *npl* Islas *fpl*
Malvinas
fall [fɔːl] n caída; (*US*) otoño; (*decrease*)
disminución f ▷ *vi* (*pt* **fell**, *pp* **fallen** ['fɔːlən])
caer; (*accidentally*) caerse; (*price*) bajar; **falls**
npl (*waterfall*) cataratas *fpl*, salto sg de agua; **a
~ of earth** un desprendimiento de tierra; **a
~ of snow** una nevada; **to ~ flat** *vi* (*on one's face*)
caerse de bruces; (*joke, story*) no hacer gracia;
to ~ short of sb's expectations decepcionar
a algn; **to ~ in love (with sb/sth)**
enamorarse (de algn/algo); **fall apart** *vi*
deshacerse; **fall back** *vi* retroceder; **fall back
on** *vt fus* (*remedy etc*) recurrir a; **to have sth to
~ back on** tener algo a que recurrir; **fall
behind** *vi* quedarse atrás; (*fig: with payments*)
retrasarse; **fall down** *vi* (*person*) caerse;
(*building*) derrumbarse; **fall for** *vt fus* (*trick*)
tragar; (*person*) enamorarse de; **fall in** *vi* (*roof*)
hundirse; (*Mil*) alinearse; **fall in with** *vt fus*:
to ~ in with sb's plans acomodarse con los
planes de algn/algo; **fall off** *vi* caerse; (*diminish*)
disminuir; **fall out** *vi* (*friends etc*) reñir; (*hair,
teeth*) caerse; (*Mil*) romper filas; **fall over** *vi*
caer(se); **fall through** *vi* (*plan, project*) fracasar
fallacy ['fæləsɪ] n error m
fallen ['fɔːlən] *pp of* **fall**
fallible ['fæləbl] *adj* falible
fallout ['fɔːlaut] n lluvia radioactiva
fallout shelter n refugio antinuclear
fallow ['fæləu] *adj* (*land, field*) en barbecho
false [fɔːls] *adj* (*gen*) falso; (*teeth etc*) postizo;
(*disloyal*) desleal, traidor(a); **under ~
pretences** con engaños

false alarm n falsa alarma
falsehood ['fɔːlshud] n falsedad f
falsely ['fɔːlslɪ] *adv* falsamente
false teeth *npl* (*Brit*) dentadura sg postiza
falsify ['fɔːlsɪfaɪ] *vt* falsificar
falter ['fɔːltər] *vi* vacilar
fame [feɪm] n fama
familiar [fə'mɪlɪər] *adj* familiar; (*well-known*)
conocido; (*tone*) de confianza; **to be ~ with**
(*subject*) conocer (bien); **to make o.s. ~ with**
familiarizarse con; **to be on ~ terms with
sb** tener confianza con algn
familiarity [fəmɪlɪ'ærɪtɪ] n familiaridad f
familiarize [fə'mɪlɪəraɪz] *vt*: **to ~ o.s. with**
familiarizarse con
family ['fæmɪlɪ] n familia
family credit n (*Brit*) ≈ ayuda familiar
family doctor n médico(-a) de cabecera
family man n (*home-loving*) hombre m casero;
(*having family*) padre m de familia
family planning n planificación f familiar
family tree n árbol m genealógico
famine ['fæmɪn] n hambre f, hambruna
famished ['fæmɪʃt] *adj* hambriento; **I'm ~!**
(*inf*) ¡estoy muerto de hambre!, ¡tengo un
hambre canina!
famous ['feɪməs] *adj* famoso, célebre
famously ['feɪməslɪ] *adv* (*get on*)
estupendamente
fan [fæn] n abanico; (*Elec*) ventilador m;
(*person*) aficionado(-a); (*Sport*) hincha m/f; (*of
pop star*) fan m/f ▷ *vt* abanicar; (*fire, quarrel*)
atizar; **fan out** *vi* desplegarse
fanatic [fə'nætɪk] n fanático(-a)
fanatical [fə'nætɪkəl] *adj* fanático
fan belt n correa del ventilador
fanciful ['fænsɪful] *adj* (*gen*) fantástico;
(*imaginary*) fantasioso; (*design*) rebuscado
fan club n club m de fans
fancy ['fænsɪ] n (*whim*) capricho, antojo;
(*imagination*) imaginación f ▷ *adj* (*luxury*) de
lujo; (*price*) exorbitado ▷ *vt* (*feel like, want*)
tener ganas de; (*imagine*) imaginarse,
figurarse; **to take a ~ to sb** tomar cariño a
algn; **when the ~ takes him** cuando se le
antoja; **it took** *or* **caught my ~** me cayó en
gracia; **to ~ that ...** imaginarse que ...; **he
fancies her** le gusta (ella) mucho
fancy dress n disfraz m
fancy-dress ball ['fænsɪdrɛs-] n baile m de
disfraces
fang [fæŋ] n colmillo
fan heater n calefactor m de aire
fantasize ['fæntəsaɪz] *vi* fantasear, hacerse
ilusiones
fantastic [fæn'tæstɪk] *adj* fantástico
fantasy ['fæntəzɪ] n fantasía
fanzine ['fænziːn] n fanzine m
FAQs *npl abbr* (= *frequently asked questions*)
preguntas *fpl* frecuentes
far [fɑːr] *adj* (*distant*) lejano ▷ *adv* lejos; **the ~
left/right** (*Pol*) la extrema izquierda/

derecha; ~ **away**, ~ **off** (a lo) lejos; ~ **better** mucho mejor; ~ **from** lejos de; **by** ~ con mucho; **it's by** ~ **the best** es con mucho el mejor; **go as** ~ **as the farm** vaya hasta la granja; **is it** ~ **to London?** ¿estamos lejos de Londres?, ¿Londres queda lejos?; **it's not** ~ **(from here)** no está lejos (de aquí); **as** ~ **as I know** que yo sepa; **how** ~**?** ¿hasta dónde?; *(fig)* ¿hasta qué punto?; **how** ~ **have you got with your work?** ¿hasta dónde has llegado en tu trabajo?

faraway ['fɑːrəweɪ] *adj* remoto; *(look)* ausente, perdido

farce [fɑːs] *n* farsa

farcical ['fɑːsɪkəl] *adj* absurdo

fare [fɛəʳ] *n (on trains, buses)* precio (del billete); *(in taxi: cost)* tarifa; *(: passenger)* pasajero; *(food)* comida; **half/full** ~ medio billete *m*/billete *m* completo

Far East *n*: **the** ~ el Extremo *or* Lejano Oriente

farewell [fɛə'wɛl] *excl, n* adiós *m*

farm [fɑːm] *n* granja, finca, estancia *(LAm)*, chacra *(LAm)* ▷ *vt* cultivar; **farm out** *vt (work)*: **to** ~ **out (to sb)** mandar hacer fuera (a algn)

farmer ['fɑːməʳ] *n* granjero(-a), estanciero(-a) *(LAm)*

farmhand ['fɑːmhænd] *n* peón *m*

farmhouse ['fɑːmhaus] *n* granja, casa de hacienda *(LAm)*

farming ['fɑːmɪŋ] *n (gen)* agricultura; *(tilling)* cultivo; **sheep** ~ cría de ovejas

farmland ['fɑːmlænd] *n* tierra de cultivo

farm worker *n* = **farmhand**

farmyard ['fɑːmjɑːd] *n* corral *m*

far-reaching [fɑː'riːtʃɪŋ] *adj (reform, effect)* de gran alcance

fart [fɑːt] *(inf!)* *n* pedo *(!)* ▷ *vi* tirarse un pedo *(!)*

farther ['fɑːðəʳ] *adv* más lejos, más allá ▷ *adj* más lejano

farthest ['fɑːðɪst] *superlative of* **far**

fascinate ['fæsɪneɪt] *vt* fascinar

fascinated ['fæsɪneɪtəd] *adj* fascinado

fascinating ['fæsɪneɪtɪŋ] *adj* fascinante

fascination [fæsɪ'neɪʃən] *n* fascinación *f*

fascism ['fæʃɪzəm] *n* fascismo

fascist ['fæʃɪst] *adj, n* fascista *m/f*

fashion ['fæʃən] *n* moda; *(fashion industry)* industria de la moda; *(manner)* manera ▷ *vt* formar; **in** ~ a la moda; **out of** ~ pasado de moda; **in the Greek** ~ a la griega, al estilo griego; **after a** ~ *(finish, manage etc)* en cierto modo

fashionable ['fæʃnəbl] *adj* de moda; *(writer)* de moda, popular; **it is** ~ **to do ...** está de moda hacer ...

fashion show *n* desfile *m* de modelos

fast [fɑːst] *adj (also Phot: film)* rápido; *(dye, colour)* sólido; *(clock)*: **to be** ~ estar adelantado ▷ *adv* rápidamente, de prisa; *(stuck, held)* firmemente ▷ *n* ayuno ▷ *vi* ayunar; ~ **asleep** profundamente dormido; **in the** ~ **lane** *(Aut)*

en el carril de adelantamiento; **my watch is five minutes** ~ mi reloj está adelantado cinco minutos; **as** ~ **as I** *etc* **can** lo más rápido posible; **to make a boat** ~ amarrar una barca

fasten ['fɑːsn] *vt* asegurar, sujetar; *(coat, belt)* abrochar ▷ *vi* cerrarse; **fasten (up)on** *vt fus (idea)* aferrarse a

fastener ['fɑːsnəʳ] *n* cierre *m*; *(of door etc)* cerrojo; *(Brit: also:* **zip** ~) cremallera

fastening ['fɑːsnɪŋ] *n* = **fastener**

fast food *n* comida rápida, platos *mpl* preparados

fastidious [fæs'tɪdɪəs] *adj (fussy)* delicado; *(demanding)* exigente

fat [fæt] *adj* gordo; *(meat)* con mucha grasa; *(greasy)* grasiento; *(book)* grueso; *(profit)* grande, pingüe ▷ *n* grasa; *(on person)* carnes *fpl*; *(lard)* manteca; **to live off the** ~ **of the land** vivir a cuerpo de rey

fatal ['feɪtl] *adj (mistake)* fatal; *(injury)* mortal; *(consequence)* funesto

fatality [fə'tælɪtɪ] *n (road death etc)* víctima *f* mortal

fatally ['feɪtəlɪ] *adv*: ~ **injured** herido de muerte

fate [feɪt] *n* destino, sino

fateful ['feɪtful] *adj* fatídico

fat-free ['fætfriː] *adj* sin grasa

father ['fɑːðəʳ] *n* padre *m*

Father Christmas *n* Papá *m* Noel

fatherhood ['fɑːðəhud] *n* paternidad *f*

father-in-law ['fɑːðərɪnlɔː] *n* suegro

fatherly ['fɑːðəlɪ] *adj* paternal

fathom ['fæðəm] *n* braza ▷ *vt (unravel)* desentrañar; *(understand)* explicarse

fatigue [fə'tiːg] *n* fatiga, cansancio; **metal** ~ fatiga del metal

fatten ['fætn] *vt, vi* engordar; **chocolate is** ~**ing** el chocolate engorda

fatty ['fætɪ] *adj (food)* graso ▷ *n (inf)* gordito(-a), gordinflón(-ona) *m(f)*

fatuous ['fætjuəs] *adj* fatuo, necio

faucet ['fɔːsɪt] *n (US)* grifo, llave *f*, canilla *(LAm)*

fault [fɔːlt] *n (blame)* culpa; *(defect: in character)* defecto; *(in manufacture)* desperfecto; *(Geo)* falla ▷ *vt* criticar; **it's my** ~ es culpa mía; **to find** ~ **with** criticar, poner peros a; **at** ~ culpable

faulty ['fɔːltɪ] *adj* defectuoso

fauna ['fɔːnə] *n* fauna

faux pas ['fəu'pɑː] *n* desacierto

favour, favor *(US)* ['feɪvəʳ] *n* favor *m*; *(approval)* aprobación *f* ▷ *vt (proposition)* estar a favor de, aprobar; *(person etc)* preferir; *(assist)* favorecer; **to ask a** ~ **of** pedir un favor a; **to do sb a** ~ hacer un favor a algn; **to find** ~ **with sb** *(person)* caer en gracia a algn; *(: suggestion)* tener buena acogida por parte de algn; **in** ~ **of** a favor de; **to be in** ~ **of sth/of doing sth** ser partidario *or* estar a favor de algo/de hacer algo

favourable, favorable (US) ['feɪvərəbl] *adj* favorable

favourably, favorably (US) ['feɪvərəblɪ] *adv* favorablemente

favourite, favorite (US) ['feɪvərɪt] *adj*, *n* favorito(-a) *m(f)*, preferido(-a) *m(f)*

favouritism, favoritism (US) ['feɪvərɪtɪzəm] *n* favoritismo

fawn [fɔːn] *n* cervato ▷ *adj* (*also:* **~-coloured**) de color cervato, leonado ▷ *vi:* **to ~ (up)on** adular

fax [fæks] *n* fax *m* ▷ *vt* mandar *or* enviar por fax

FBI *n abbr* (US: = *Federal Bureau of Investigation*) FBI *m*

FE *n abbr* = **further education**

fear [fɪəʳ] *n* miedo, temor *m* ▷ *vt* temer; **for ~ of** por temor a; **~ of heights** vértigo; **to ~ for/that** temer por/que

fearful ['fɪəful] *adj* temeroso; (*awful*) espantoso; **to be ~ of** (*frightened*) tener miedo de

fearless ['fɪəlɪs] *adj* (*gen*) sin miedo *or* temor; (*bold*) audaz

feasibility [fiːzə'bɪlɪtɪ] *n* factibilidad *f*, viabilidad *f*

feasible ['fiːzəbl] *adj* factible, viable

feast [fiːst] *n* banquete *m*; (*Rel: also:* **~ day**) fiesta ▷ *vi* festejar

feat [fiːt] *n* hazaña

feather ['feðəʳ] *n* pluma ▷ *vt:* **to ~ one's nest** (*fig*) hacer su agosto, sacar tajada ▷ *cpd* (*mattress, bed, pillow*) de plumas

feature ['fiːtʃəʳ] *n* (*gen*) característica; (*Anat*) rasgo; (*article*) reportaje *m* ▷ *vt* (*film*) presentar ▷ *vi* figurar; **features** *npl* (*of face*) facciones *fpl*; **a (special) ~ on sth/sb** un reportaje (especial) sobre algo/algn; **it ~d prominently in ...** tuvo un papel destacado en ...

feature film *n* largometraje *m*

Feb. *abbr* (= *February*) feb

February ['februərɪ] *n* febrero; *see also* **July**

feces ['fiːsiːz] *npl* (US) = **faeces**

fed [fed] *pt*, *pp* of **feed**

federal ['fedərəl] *adj* federal

Federal Republic of Germany *n* República Federal de Alemania

federation [fedə'reɪʃən] *n* federación *f*

fed up [fed'ʌp] *adj:* **to be ~ (with)** estar harto (de)

fee [fiː] *n* (*professional*) honorarios *mpl*; (*for examination*) derechos *mpl*; (*of school*) matrícula; (*also:* **membership ~**) cuota; (*also:* **entrance ~**) entrada; **for a small ~** por poco dinero

feeble ['fiːbl] *adj* débil

feed [fiːd] *n* (*gen*) comida; (*of animal*) pienso; (*on printer*) dispositivo de alimentación ▷ *vt* (*pp, pt* **fed**) (*gen*) alimentar; (*Brit: breastfeed*) dar el pecho a; (*animal, baby*) dar de comer a ▷ *vi* (*baby, animal*) comer; **feed back** *vt* (*results*) pasar; **feed in** *vt* (*Comput*) introducir; **feed into** *vt* (*data, information*) suministrar a; **to ~ sth into a machine** introducir algo en una máquina; **feed on** *vt fus* alimentarse de

feedback ['fiːdbæk] *n* (*from person*) reacción *f*; (*Tech*) realimentación *f*, feedback *m*

feeding bottle ['fiːdɪŋ-] *n* (*Brit*) biberón *m*

feel [fiːl] *n* (*sensation*) sensación *f*; (*sense of touch*) tacto ▷ *vt* (*pt, pp* **felt**) tocar; (*cold, pain etc*) sentir; (*think, believe*) creer; **to get the ~ of sth** (*fig*) acostumbrarse a algo; **to ~ hungry/ cold** tener hambre/frío; **to ~ lonely/better** sentirse solo/mejor; **I don't ~ well** no me siento bien; **it ~s soft** es suave al tacto; **it ~s colder out here** se siente más frío aquí fuera; **to ~ like** (*want*) tener ganas de; **I'm still ~ing my way** (*fig*) todavía me estoy orientando; **I ~ that you ought to do it** creo que debes hacerlo; **feel about** *or* **around** *vi* tantear

feeler ['fiːləʳ] *n* (*of insect*) antena; **to put out ~s** (*fig*) tantear el terreno

feeling ['fiːlɪŋ] *n* (*physical*) sensación *f*; (*foreboding*) presentimiento; (*impression*) impresión *f*; (*emotion*) sentimiento; **what are your ~s about the matter?** ¿qué opinas tú del asunto?; **to hurt sb's ~s** herir los sentimientos de algn; **~s ran high about it** causó mucha controversia; **I got the ~ that ...** me dio la impresión de que ...; **there was a general ~ that ...** la opinión general fue que ...

fee-paying school ['fiːpeɪɪŋ-] *n* colegio de pago

feet [fiːt] *npl* of **foot**

feign [feɪn] *vt* fingir

fell [fel] *pt* of **fall** ▷ *vt* (*tree*) talar ▷ *adj:* **with one ~ blow** con un golpe feroz; **at one ~ swoop** de un solo golpe ▷ *n* (*Brit: mountain*) montaña; (*moorland*): **the ~** los páramos

fellow ['fɛləu] *n* tipo, tío (*Sp*); (*of learned society*) socio(-a); (*Univ*) miembro de la junta de gobierno de un colegio ▷ *cpd:* **~ students** compañeros(-as) *m(f)pl* de curso

fellow citizen *n* conciudadano(-a)

fellow countryman *n* compatriota *m*

fellow men *npl* semejantes *mpl*

fellowship ['fɛləuʃɪp] *n* compañerismo; (*grant*) beca

felony ['feləni] *n* crimen *m*, delito mayor

felt [fɛlt] *pt*, *pp* of **feel** ▷ *n* fieltro

felt-tip pen ['fɛlttɪp-] *n* rotulador *m*

female ['fiːmeɪl] *n* (*woman*) mujer *f*; (*Zool*) hembra ▷ *adj* femenino

feminine ['feminɪn] *adj* femenino

feminism ['feminɪzəm] *n* feminismo

feminist ['feminɪst] *n* feminista *m/f*

fence [fens] *n* valla, cerca; (*Racing*) valla ▷ *vt* (*also:* **~ in**) cercar ▷ *vi* hacer esgrima; **to sit on the ~** (*fig*) nadar entre dos aguas; **fence off** *vt* cercar; **fence off** *vt* separar con cerca

fencing ['fensɪŋ] *n* esgrima

fend [fɛnd] vi: **to ~ for o.s.** valerse por sí mismo; **fend off** vt (attack, attacker) rechazar, repeler; (blow) desviar; (awkward question) esquivar

fender ['fɛndər] n pantalla; (US Aut) parachoques m inv; (Rail) trompa

fennel ['fɛnl] n hinojo

ferment vi [fə'mɛnt] fermentar ▷ n ['fə:mɛnt] (fig) agitación f

fern [fə:n] n helecho

ferocious [fə'rəʊʃəs] adj feroz

ferocity [fə'rɔsɪtɪ] n ferocidad f

ferret ['fɛrɪt] n hurón m; **ferret about, ferret around** vi rebuscar; **ferret out** vt (secret, truth) desentrañar

ferry ['fɛrɪ] n (small) barca de pasaje, balsa; (large: also: **~boat**) transbordador m, ferry m ▷ vt transportar; **to ~ sth/sb across** or **over** transportar algo/a algn a la otra orilla; **to ~ sb to and fro** llevar a algn de un lado para otro

fertile ['fə:taɪl] adj fértil; (Biol) fecundo

fertility [fə'tɪlɪtɪ] n fertilidad f; fecundidad f

fertilize ['fə:tɪlaɪz] vt fertilizar; (Biol) fecundar; (Agr) abonar

fertilizer ['fə:tɪlaɪzər] n abono, fertilizante m

fervent ['fə:vənt] adj ferviente

fester ['fɛstər] vi supurar

festival ['fɛstɪvəl] n (Rel) fiesta; (Art, Mus) festival m

festive ['fɛstɪv] adj festivo; **the ~ season** (Brit: Christmas) las Navidades

festivities [fɛs'tɪvɪtɪz] npl festejos mpl

festoon [fɛs'tu:n] vt: **to ~ with** festonear or engalanar de

fetch [fɛtʃ] vt ir a buscar; (Brit: sell for) venderse por; **how much did it ~?** ¿por cuánto se vendió?; **fetch up** vi ir a parar

fetching ['fɛtʃɪŋ] adj atractivo

fête [feɪt] n fiesta

fetish ['fɛtɪʃ] n fetiche m

fetus ['fi:təs] n (US) = **foetus**

feud [fju:d] n (hostility) enemistad f; (quarrel) disputa; **a family ~** una pelea familiar

feudal ['fju:dl] adj feudal

fever ['fi:vər] n fiebre f; **he has a ~** tiene fiebre

feverish ['fi:vərɪʃ] adj febril

few [fju:] adj (not many) pocos; (some) algunos, unos ▷ pron algunos; **a ~** unos pocos; **~ people** poca gente; **a good ~, quite a ~** bastantes; **in** or **over the next ~ days** en los próximos días; **every ~ weeks** cada dos o tres semanas; **a ~ more days** unos días más

fewer ['fju:ə'] adj menos

fewest ['fju:ɪst] adj los/las menos

fiancé [fɪ'ɑ:nseɪ] n novio, prometido

fiancée [fɪ'ɑ:nseɪ] n novia, prometida

fiasco [fɪ'æskəʊ] n fiasco

fib [fɪb] n mentirijilla ▷ vi decir mentirijillas

fibre, fiber (US) ['faɪbə'] n fibra

fibreglass, fiberglass (US) ['faɪbəglɑ:s] n fibra de vidrio

fickle ['fɪkl] adj inconstante

fiction ['fɪkʃən] n (gen) ficción f

fictional ['fɪkʃənl] adj novelesco

fictitious [fɪk'tɪʃəs] adj ficticio

fiddle ['fɪdl] n (Mus) violín m; (cheating) trampa ▷ vt (Brit: accounts) falsificar; **tax ~** evasión f fiscal; **to work a ~** hacer trampa; **fiddle with** vt fus juguetear con

fiddler ['fɪdlə'] n violinista m/f

fiddly ['fɪdlɪ] adj (task) delicado, mañoso; (object) enrevesado

fidelity [fɪ'dɛlɪtɪ] n fidelidad f

fidget ['fɪdʒɪt] vi moverse (nerviosamente)

fidgety ['fɪdʒɪtɪ] adj nervioso

field [fi:ld] n (gen) campo; (Comput) campo; (fig) campo, esfera; (Sport) campo, cancha (LAm); (competitors) competidores mpl ▷ cpd: **to have a ~ day** (fig) ponerse las botas; **to lead the ~** (Sport, Comm) llevar la delantera; **to give sth a year's trial in the ~** (fig) sacar algo al mercado a prueba por un año; **my particular ~** mi especialidad

field hospital n hospital m de campaña

field marshal n mariscal m

fieldwork ['fi:ldwə:k] n (Archaeology, Geo) trabajo de campo

fiend [fi:nd] n demonio

fiendish ['fi:ndɪʃ] adj diabólico

fierce [fɪəs] adj feroz; (wind, attack) violento; (heat) intenso; (fighting, enemy) encarnizado

fiery ['faɪərɪ] adj (burning) ardiente; (temperament) apasionado

FIFA ['fi:fə] n abbr (= Fédération Internationale de Football Association) FIFA f

fifteen [fɪf'ti:n] num quince

fifteenth [fɪf'ti:nθ] adj decimoquinto; **the ~ floor** la planta quince; **the ~ of August** el quince de agosto

fifth [fɪfθ] adj quinto

fiftieth ['fɪftɪɪθ] adj quincuagésimo

fifty ['fɪftɪ] num cincuenta; **the fifties** los años cincuenta; **to be in one's fifties** andar por los cincuenta

fifty-fifty ['fɪftɪ'fɪftɪ] adj (deal, split) a medias ▷ adv: **to go ~ with sb** ir a medias con algn; **we have a ~ chance of success** tenemos un cincuenta por ciento de posibilidades de tener éxito

fig [fɪg] n higo

fight [faɪt] (pt, pp fought) n (gen) pelea; (Mil) combate m; (struggle) lucha ▷ vt luchar contra; (cancer, alcoholism) combatir; (Law): **to ~ a case** defenderse ▷ vi pelear, luchar; (quarrel): **to ~ (with sb)** pelear (con algn); (fig): **to ~ (for/against)** luchar (por/contra); **fight back** vi defenderse; (after illness) recuperarse ▷ vt (tears) contener; **fight down** vt (anger, anxiety, urge) reprimir; **fight off** vt (attack, attacker) rechazar; (disease, sleep, urge) luchar contra; **fight out** vt: **to ~ it out** decidirlo en una pelea

fighter ['faɪtə^r] n combatiente m/f; (fig) luchador(a) m(f); (plane) caza m

fighting ['faɪtɪŋ] n (gen) luchas fpl; (battle) combate m, pelea; (in streets) disturbios mpl

figment ['fɪgmənt] n: **a ~ of the imagination** un producto de la imaginación

figurative ['fɪgjurətɪv] adj (meaning) figurado; (Art) figurativo

figure ['fɪgə^r] n (Drawing, Geom) figura, dibujo; (number, cipher) cifra; (person, outline) figura; (body shape) línea; (: attractive) tipo ▷ vt (esp US: think, calculate) calcular, imaginarse ▷ vi (appear) figurar; (esp US: make sense) ser lógico; **~ of speech** (Ling) figura retórica; **public ~** personaje m; **figure on** vt fus (US) contar con; **figure out** vt (work out) resolver; (understand) comprender

figurehead ['fɪgəhed] n (fig) figura decorativa

file [faɪl] n (tool) lima; (for nails) lima de uñas; (dossier) expediente m; (folder) carpeta; (in cabinet) archivo; (Comput) fichero; (row) fila ▷ vt limar; (papers) clasificar; (Law: claim) presentar; (store) archivar; **to open/close a ~** (Comput) abrir/ cerrar un fichero; **to ~ in/out** vi entrar/salir en fila; **to ~ a suit against sb** entablar pleito contra algn; **to ~ past** desfilar ante

filing ['faɪlɪŋ] n: **to do the ~** llevar los archivos

filing cabinet n archivo

Filipino [fɪlɪ'pi:nəu] adj filipino ▷ n (person) filipino(-a) m/f; (Ling) tagalo

fill [fɪl] vt llenar; (tooth) empastar; (vacancy) cubrir ▷ n: **to eat one's ~** comer hasta hartarse; **we've already ~ed that vacancy** ya hemos cubierto esa vacante; **~ed with admiration (for)** lleno de admiración (por); **fill in** vt rellenar; (details, report) completar; **to ~ sb in on sth** (inf) poner a algn al corriente or al día sobre algo; **fill out** vt (form, receipt) rellenar; **fill up** vt llenar (hasta el borde) ▷ vi (Aut) echar gasolina

fillet ['fɪlɪt] n filete m

fillet steak n filete m de ternera

filling ['fɪlɪŋ] n (Culin) relleno; (for tooth) empaste m

filling station n estación f de servicio

fillip ['fɪlɪp] n estímulo

film [fɪlm] n película ▷ vt (scene) filmar ▷ vi rodar

film star n estrella de cine

Filofax® ['faɪləufæks] n agenda (profesional)

filter ['fɪltə^r] n filtro ▷ vt filtrar; **filter in, filter through** vi filtrarse

filter lane n (Brit) carril m de selección

filter-tipped ['fɪltətɪpt] adj con filtro

filth [fɪlθ] n suciedad f

filthy ['fɪlθɪ] adj sucio; (language) obsceno

fin [fɪn] n (gen) aleta

final ['faɪnl] adj (last) final, último; (definitive) definitivo ▷ n (Sport) final f; **finals** npl (Scol) exámenes mpl finales

finale [fɪ'nɑ:lɪ] n final m

finalist ['faɪnəlɪst] n (Sport) finalista m/f

finalize ['faɪnəlaɪz] vt ultimar

finally ['faɪnəlɪ] adv (lastly) por último, finalmente; (eventually) por fin; (irrevocably) de modo definitivo; (once and for all) definitivamente

finance [faɪ'næns] n (money, funds) fondos mpl; **finances** npl finanzas fpl ▷ cpd (page, section, company) financiero ▷ vt financiar

financial [faɪ'nænʃəl] adj financiero

financial year n ejercicio (financiero)

find [faɪnd] vt (pt, pp **found** [faund]) (gen) encontrar, hallar; (come upon) descubrir ▷ n hallazgo; descubrimiento; **to ~ sb guilty** (Law) declarar culpable a algn; **I ~ it easy** me resulta fácil; **find out** ▷ vt averiguar; (truth, secret) descubrir ▷ vi: **to ~ out about** enterarse de

findings ['faɪndɪŋz] npl (Law) veredicto sg, fallo sg; (of report) recomendaciones fpl

fine [faɪn] adj (delicate) fino; (beautiful) hermoso ▷ adv (well) bien ▷ n (Law) multa ▷ vt (Law) multar; **the weather is ~** hace buen tiempo; **he's ~** está muy bien; **you're doing ~** lo estás haciendo muy bien; **to cut it ~** (of time, money) calcular muy justo; **to get a ~ for (doing)** sth recibir una multa por (hacer) algo

fine arts npl bellas artes fpl

fine print n: **the ~** la letra pequeña or menuda

finery ['faɪnərɪ] n galas fpl

finger ['fɪŋgə^r] n dedo ▷ vt (touch) manosear; (Mus) puntear; **little/index ~** (dedo) meñique m/índice m

fingernail ['fɪŋgəneɪl] n uña

fingerprint ['fɪŋgəprɪnt] n huella dactilar

fingertip ['fɪŋgətɪp] n yema del dedo; **to have sth at one's ~s** saberse algo al dedillo

finicky ['fɪnɪkɪ] adj (fussy) delicado

finish ['fɪnɪʃ] n (end) fin m; (Sport) meta; (polish etc) acabado ▷ vt, vi acabar, terminar; **to ~ doing sth** acabar de hacer algo; **to ~ first/second/third** (Sport) llegar el primero/segundo/tercero; **I've ~ed with the paper** he terminado con el periódico; **she's ~ed with him** ha roto or acabado con él; **finish off** vt acabar, terminar; (kill) rematar; **finish up** vt acabar, terminar ▷ vi ir a parar, terminar

finishing line n línea de llegada or meta

finishing school n colegio para la educación social de señoritas

finite ['faɪnaɪt] adj finito

Finland ['fɪnlənd] n Finlandia

Finn [fɪn] n finlandés(-esa) m(f)

Finnish ['fɪnɪʃ] adj finlandés(-esa) ▷ n (Ling) finlandés m

fir [fə:^r] n abeto

fire ['faɪə^r] n fuego; (accidental, damaging) incendio; (heater) estufa ▷ vt (gun) disparar;

(set fire to) incendiar; (excite) exaltar; (interest) despertar; (dismiss) despedir ▷ vi encenderse; (Aut: engine) encender; **electric/gas** ~ estufa eléctrica/de gas; **on** ~ ardiendo, en llamas; **to be on** ~ estar ardiendo; **to catch** ~ prenderse fuego; **to set** ~ **to sth, set sth on** ~ prender fuego a algo; **insured against** ~ asegurado contra incendios; **to be/come under** ~ estar/caer bajo el fuego enemigo

fire alarm n alarma de incendios

firearm ['faɪərɑːm] n arma de fuego

fire brigade, fire department (US) n (cuerpo de) bomberos mpl

fire door n puerta contra incendios

fire engine n coche m de bomberos

fire escape n escalera de incendios

fire exit n salida de incendios

fire extinguisher n extintor m

fireman ['faɪəmən] n bombero

fireplace ['faɪəpleɪs] n chimenea

fireplug ['faɪəplʌg] n (US) boca de incendios

fireproof ['faɪəpruːf] adj a prueba de fuego; (material) incombustible

fireside ['faɪəsaɪd] n: **by the** ~ al lado de la chimenea

fire station n parque m de bomberos

firetruck n (US) = **fire engine**

firewall ['faɪəwɔːl] n (Internet) firewall m

firewood ['faɪəwʊd] n leña

fireworks ['faɪəwəːks] npl fuegos mpl artificiales

firing squad n pelotón m de ejecución

firm [fəːm] adj firme; (offer, decision) en firme ▷ n empresa; **to be a** ~ **believer in sth** ser un partidario convencido de algo; **to stand** ~ or **take a** ~ **stand on sth** (fig) mantenerse firme ante algo

firmly ['fəːmlɪ] adv firmemente

first [fəːst] adj primero ▷ adv (before others) primero; (when listing reasons etc) en primer lugar, primeramente ▷ n (person: in race) primero(-a); (Aut: also: ~ **gear**) primera; **at** ~ al principio; ~ **of all** ante todo; **the** ~ **of January** el uno or primero de enero; **in the** ~ **instance** en primer lugar; **I'll do it** ~ **thing tomorrow** lo haré mañana a primera hora; **for the** ~ **time** por primera vez; **head** ~ de cabeza; **from the (very)** ~ desde el principio

first aid n primeros auxilios mpl

first aid kit n botiquín m

first-class ['fəːst'klɑːs] adj de primera clase; ~ **ticket** (Rail etc) billete m or (LAm) boleto de primera clase; ~ **mail** correo de primera clase

first-hand [fəːst'hænd] adj de primera mano

first lady n (esp US) primera dama

firstly ['fəːstlɪ] adv en primer lugar

first name n nombre m de pila

first-rate [fəːst'reɪt] adj de primera (clase)

first-time buyer [fəːst'taɪm-] n persona que compra su primera vivienda

fiscal ['fɪskəl] adj fiscal; ~ **year** año fiscal, ejercicio

fish [fɪʃ] n pl inv pez m; (food) pescado ▷ vt pescar en ▷ vi pescar; **to go** ~**ing** ir de pesca; **fish out** vt (from water, box etc) sacar; ~ **and chips** pescado frito con patatas fritas

fish-and-chip shop n = **chip shop**

fisherman ['fɪʃəmən] n pescador m

fish farm n piscifactoría

fish fingers npl (Brit) palitos mpl de pescado (empanado)

fishing boat ['fɪʃɪŋ-] n barca de pesca

fishing industry ['fɪʃɪŋ-] n industria pesquera

fishing line ['fɪʃɪŋ-] n sedal m

fishing net ['fɪʃɪŋ-] n red f de pesca

fishing rod ['fɪʃɪŋ-] n caña (de pescar)

fishmonger ['fɪʃmʌŋgə'] n (Brit) pescadero(-a)

fishmonger's, fishmonger's shop n (Brit) pescadería

fish sticks npl (US) = **fish fingers**

fishy ['fɪʃɪ] adj (fig) sospechoso

fist [fɪst] n puño

fit [fɪt] adj (Med, Sport) en (buena) forma; (proper) adecuado, apropiado ▷ vt (clothes) quedar bien a; (try on: clothes) probar; (instal) poner; (equip) proveer; (match: facts) cuadrar or corresponder or coincidir con; (: description) estar de acuerdo con; (accommodate) ajustar, adaptar ▷ vi (clothes) quedar bien; (in space, gap) caber; (facts) coincidir ▷ n (Med) ataque m; (outburst) arranque m; ~ **to** apto para; ~ **for** apropiado para; **do as you think** or **see** ~ haz lo que te parezca mejor; **to keep** ~ mantenerse en forma; **to be** ~ **for work** (after illness) estar en condiciones para trabajar; ~ **of coughing** acceso de tos; ~ **of anger/ enthusiasm** arranque de cólera/ entusiasmo; **to have** or **suffer a** ~ tener un ataque or acceso; **this dress is a good** ~ este vestido me queda bien; **by** ~**s and starts** a rachas; **fit in** vi encajar ▷ vt (object) acomodar; (fig: appointment, visitor) encontrar un hueco para; **to** ~ **in with sb's plans** acomodarse a los planes de algn; **fit out** (Brit), **fit up** vt equipar

fitful ['fɪtful] adj espasmódico, intermitente

fitment ['fɪtmənt] n mueble m

fitness ['fɪtnɪs] n (Med) forma física; (of remark) conveniencia

fitted ['fɪtɪd] adj (jacket, shirt) entallado; (sheet) de cuatro picos

fitted carpet ['fɪtɪd-] n moqueta

fitted kitchen ['fɪtɪd-] n cocina amueblada

fitter ['fɪtə'] n ajustador(a) m(f)

fitting ['fɪtɪŋ] adj apropiado ▷ n (of dress) prueba; see also **fittings**

fitting room n (in shop) probador m

fittings ['fɪtɪŋz] npl instalaciones fpl

five [faɪv] num cinco; **she is** ~ **(years old)** tiene cinco años (de edad); **it costs** ~ **pounds** cuesta cinco libras; **it's** ~ **(o'clock)** son las cinco

fiver ['faɪvə^r] n (inf: Brit) billete m de cinco libras; (: US) billete m de cinco dólares

fix [fɪks] vt (secure) fijar, asegurar; (mend) arreglar; (make ready: meal, drink) preparar ⊳ n: **to be in a ~** estar en un aprieto; **to ~ sth in one's mind** fijar algo en la memoria; **the fight was a ~** (inf) la pelea estaba amañada; **fix on** vt (decide on) fijar; **fix up** vt (arrange: date, meeting) arreglar; **to ~ sb up with sth** conseguirle algo a algn

fixation [fɪk'seɪʃən] n (Psych) fijación f

fixed [fɪkst] adj (prices etc) fijo; **how are you ~ for money?** (inf) ¿qué tal andas de dinero?

fixture ['fɪkstʃə^r] n (Sport) encuentro; **fixtures** npl instalaciones fpl fijas

fizzle out ['fɪzl-] vi apagarse; (enthusiasm, interest) decaer; (plan) quedar en agua de borrajas

fizzy ['fɪzɪ] adj (drink) gaseoso

flabbergasted ['flæbəgɑːstɪd] adj pasmado

flabby ['flæbɪ] adj flojo (de carnes); (skin) fofo

flag [flæg] n bandera; (stone) losa ⊳ vi decaer; **~ of convenience** pabellón m de conveniencia; **flag down** vt: **to ~ sb down** hacer señas a algn para que se pare; **flag up** vt recalcar

flagpole ['flægpəʊl] n asta de bandera

flagrant ['fleɪgrənt] adj flagrante

flagship ['flægʃɪp] n buque m insignia or almirante

flair [flɛə^r] n aptitud f especial

flak [flæk] n (Mil) fuego antiaéreo; (inf: criticism) lluvia de críticas

flake [fleɪk] n (of rust, paint) desconchón m; (of snow) copo; (of soap powder) escama ⊳ vi (also: ~ off: paint) desconcharse; (skin) descamarse

flamboyant [flæm'bɔɪənt] adj (dress) vistoso; (person) extravagante

flame [fleɪm] n llama; **to burst into ~s** incendiarse; **old ~** (inf) antiguo amor m/f

flamingo [flə'mɪŋgəʊ] n flamenco

flammable ['flæməbl] adj inflamable

flan [flæn] n (Brit) tarta

flank [flæŋk] n flanco; (of person) costado ⊳ vt flanquear

flannel ['flænl] n (Brit: also: **face ~**) toallita; (fabric) franela; **flannels** npl pantalones mpl de franela

flap [flæp] n (of pocket, envelope) solapa; (of table) hoja (plegadiza); (wing movement) aletazo; (Aviat) flap m ⊳ vt (wings) batir ⊳ vi (sail, flag) ondear

flare [flɛə^r] n llamarada; (Mil) bengala; (in skirt etc) vuelo; **flares** npl (trousers) pantalones mpl de campana; **flare up** vi encenderse; (fig: person) encolerizarse; (: revolt) estallar

flash [flæʃ] n relámpago; (also: **news ~**) noticias fpl de última hora; (Phot) flash m; (US: torch) linterna ⊳ vt (light, headlights) lanzar destellos con; (torch) encender ⊳ vi brillar; (hazard light etc) lanzar destellos; **in**

a ~ en un instante; **~ of inspiration** ráfaga de inspiración; **to ~ sth about** ostentar algo, presumir con algo; **he ~ed by** or **past** pasó como un rayo

flashback ['flæʃbæk] n flashback m, escena retrospectiva

flashbulb ['flæʃbʌlb] n bombilla de flash

flash drive n (Comput) memoria flash, flash drive m

flashlight ['flæʃlaɪt] n (US: torch) linterna

flashy ['flæʃɪ] adj (pej) ostentoso

flask [flɑːsk] n petaca; (also: **vacuum ~**) termo

flat [flæt] adj llano; (smooth) liso; (tyre) desinflado; (battery) descargado; (beer) sin gas; (Mus: instrument) desafinado ⊳ n (Brit: apartment) piso (Sp), departamento (LAm), apartamento; (Aut) pinchazo; (Mus) bemol m; (to work) **~ out** (trabajar) a tope; **~ rate of pay** sueldo fijo

flatly ['flætlɪ] adv rotundamente, de plano

flatmate ['flætmeɪt] n compañero(-a) de piso

flat pack n: **it comes in a ~** viene en un paquete plano para su automontaje

flatscreen ['flætskriːn] adj pantalla plana

flatten ['flætn] vt (also: **~ out**) allanar; (smooth out) alisar; (house, city) arrasar

flatter ['flætə^r] vt adular, halagar; (show to advantage) favorecer

flattering ['flætərɪŋ] adj halagador(a); (clothes etc) que favorece, favorecedor(a)

flattery ['flætərɪ] n adulación f

flaunt [flɔːnt] vt ostentar, lucir

flavour, flavor (US) ['fleɪvə^r] n sabor m, gusto ⊳ vt sazonar, condimentar; **strawberry ~ed** con sabor a fresa

flavouring, flavoring (US) ['fleɪvərɪŋ] n (in product) aromatizante m

flaw [flɔː] n defecto

flawless ['flɔːlɪs] adj impecable

flax [flæks] n lino

flaxen ['flæksən] adj muy rubio

flea [fliː] n pulga

flea market n rastro, mercadillo

fleck [flɛk] n mota ⊳ vt (with blood, mud etc) salpicar; **brown ~ed with white** marrón con motas blancas

flee [fliː] (pt, pp **fled** [flɛd]) vt huir de, abandonar ⊳ vi huir

fleece [fliːs] n (of sheep) vellón m; (wool) lana; (top) forro polar ⊳ vt (inf) desplumar

fleet [fliːt] n flota; (of cars, lorries etc) parque m

fleeting ['fliːtɪŋ] adj fugaz

Flemish ['flɛmɪʃ] adj flamenco ⊳ n (Ling) flamenco; **the ~** los flamencos

flesh [flɛʃ] n carne f; (skin) piel f; (of fruit) pulpa; **of ~ and blood** de carne y hueso

flesh wound n herida superficial

flew [fluː] pt of **fly**

flex [flɛks] n cable m ⊳ vt (muscles) tensar

flexibility [flɛksɪ'bɪlɪtɪ] n flexibilidad f

flexible ['flɛksəbl] adj flexible; **~ working hours** horario sg flexible

flexitime ['flɛksɪtaɪm] n horario flexible

flick [flɪk] n golpecito; (with finger) capirotazo; (Brit: inf: film) película ▷ vt dar un golpecito a; **flick off** vt quitar con el dedo; **flick through** vt fus hojear

flicker ['flɪkə^r] vi (light) parpadear; (flame) vacilar ▷ n parpadeo

flier ['flaɪə^r] n aviador(a) m(f)

flies [flaɪz] npl of **fly**

flight [flaɪt] n vuelo; (escape) huida, fuga; (also: ~ **of steps**) tramo (de escaleras); **to take** ~ huir, darse a la fuga; **to put to** ~ ahuyentar; **how long does the** ~ **take?** ¿cuánto dura el vuelo?

flight attendant n (US) auxiliar m/f de vuelo

flight deck n (Aviat) cabina de mandos

flight path n trayectoria de vuelo

flight recorder n registrador m de vuelo

flimsy ['flɪmzɪ] adj (thin) muy ligero; (excuse) flojo

flinch [flɪntʃ] vi encogerse; **to ~ from** retroceder ante

fling [flɪŋ] vt (pt, pp **flung** [flʌŋ]) arrojar ▷ n (love affair) aventura amorosa

flint [flɪnt] n pedernal m; (in lighter) piedra

flip [flɪp] vt: **to ~ a coin** echar a cara o cruz; **flip over** vt dar la vuelta a; **flip through** vt fus (book) hojear; (records) ver de pasada

flip-flops ['flɪpflɒps] npl (esp Brit) chancletas fpl

flippant ['flɪpənt] adj poco serio

flipper ['flɪpə^r] n aleta

flirt [fləːt] vi coquetear, flirtear ▷ n coqueta f

flit [flɪt] vi revolotear

float [fləut] n flotador m; (in procession) carroza; (sum of money) reserva ▷ vi (Comm: currency) flotar; (swimmer) hacer la plancha ▷ vt (gen) hacer flotar; (company) lanzar; **to ~ an idea** plantear una idea

flock [flɒk] n (of sheep) rebaño; (of birds) bandada; (of people) multitud f ▷ vi: **to ~ to** acudir en tropel a

flog [flɒg] vt azotar; (inf) vender

flood [flʌd] n inundación f; (of words, tears etc) torrente m; (of letters, imports etc) avalancha ▷ vt (Aut: carburettor) inundar ▷ vi (place) inundarse; (people): **to ~ into** inundar; **to ~ the market** (Comm) inundar el mercado

flooding ['flʌdɪŋ] n inundaciones fpl

floodlight ['flʌdlaɪt] n foco ▷ vt (irreg: like **light**) iluminar con focos

floodwater ['flʌdwɔːtə^r] n aguas fpl (de la inundación)

floor [flɔː^r] n suelo, piso (LAm); (storey) piso; (of sea, valley) fondo; (dance floor) pista ▷ vt (with blow) derribar; (fig: baffle) dejar anonadado; **ground** ~ (US), **first** ~ planta baja; **first** ~ (US), **second** ~ primer piso; **top** ~ último piso; **to have the** ~ (speaker) tener la palabra

floorboard ['flɔːbɔːd] n tabla

flooring ['flɔːrɪŋ] n suelo; (material) solería

floor show n cabaret m

flop [flɒp] n fracaso ▷ vi (fail) fracasar

floppy ['flɒpɪ] adj flojo ▷ n (Comput: also: ~ **disk**) floppy m

flora ['flɔːrə] n flora

floral ['flɔːrl] adj floral; (pattern) floreado; (dress, wallpaper) de flores

florid ['flɒrɪd] adj (style) florido

florist ['flɒrɪst] n florista m/f; ~'**s (shop)** n floristería

flotation [fləu'teɪʃən] n (of shares) emisión f; (of company) lanzamiento

flounce [flauns] n volante m; **flounce in** vi entrar con gesto exagerado; **flounce out** vi salir con gesto airado

flounder ['flaundə^r] vi tropezar ▷ n (Zool) platija

flour ['flauə^r] n harina

flourish ['flʌrɪʃ] vi florecer ▷ n ademán m, movimiento (ostentoso)

flout [flaut] vt burlarse de; (order) no hacer caso de, hacer caso omiso de

flow [fləu] n (movement) flujo; (of traffic) circulación f; (direction) curso; (Elec) corriente f ▷ vi (river, blood) fluir; (traffic) circular

flow chart n organigrama m

flower ['flauə^r] n flor f ▷ vi florecer; **in ~** en flor

flower bed n macizo

flowerpot ['flauəpɒt] n tiesto

flowery ['flauərɪ] adj florido; (perfume, pattern) de flores

flown [fləun] pp of **fly**

fl. oz. abbr = **fluid ounce**

flu [fluː] n gripe f; **to have** ~ tener la gripe

fluctuate ['flʌktjueɪt] vi fluctuar

fluency ['fluːənsɪ] n fluidez f, soltura

fluent ['fluːənt] adj (speech) elocuente; **he speaks** ~ **French, he's** ~ **in French** domina el francés

fluently ['fluːəntlɪ] adv con soltura

fluff [flʌf] n pelusa

fluffy ['flʌfɪ] adj de pelo suave

fluid ['fluːɪd] adj (movement) fluido, líquido; (situation) inestable ▷ n fluido, líquido; (in diet) líquido

fluid ounce n onza f líquida

fluke [fluːk] n (inf) chiripa

flung [flʌŋ] pt, pp of **fling**

fluorescent [fluə'rɛsnt] adj fluorescente

fluoride ['fluəraɪd] n fluoruro

fluoride toothpaste n pasta de dientes con flúor

flurry ['flʌrɪ] n (of snow) ventisca; (haste) agitación f; ~ **of activity** frenesí m de actividad

flush [flʌʃ] n (on face) rubor m; (fig: of youth, beauty) resplandor m ▷ vt limpiar con agua; (also: ~ **out**: game, birds) levantar; (fig: criminal) poner al descubierto ▷ vi ruborizarse ▷ adj: ~ **with** a ras de; **to ~ the toilet** tirar de la cadena (del wáter); **hot ~es** (Med) sofocos mpl

flushed [flʌʃt] adj ruborizado

flustered ['flʌstəd] *adj* aturdido

flute [fluːt] *n* flauta travesera

flutter ['flʌtə^r] *n* (*of wings*) revoloteo, aleteo; (*inf: bet*) apuesta ▷ *vi* revolotear; **to be in a ~** estar nervioso

flux [flʌks] *n* flujo; **in a state of ~** cambiando continuamente

fly [flaɪ] (*pt* flew, *pp* flown) *n* (*insect*) mosca; (*on trousers: also:* **flies**) bragueta ▷ *vt* (*plane*) pilotar; (*cargo*) transportar (en avión); (*distance*) recorrer (en avión) ▷ *vi* volar; (*passenger*) ir en avión; (*escape*) evadirse; (*flag*) ondear; **fly away** *vi* (*bird, insect*) irse volando; **fly in** *vi* (*person*) llegar en avión; (*plane*) aterrizar; **he flew in from Bilbao** llegó en avión desde Bilbao; **fly off** *vi* irse volando; **fly out** *vi* irse en avión

fly-drive *n*: **~ holiday** vacaciones que incluyen vuelo y alquiler de coche

flying ['flaɪɪŋ] *n* (*activity*) (el) volar ▷ *adj*: **~ visit** visita relámpago; **with ~ colours** con lucimiento

flying picket *n* piquete *m* volante

flying saucer *n* platillo volante

flying squad *n* (*Police*) brigada móvil

flying start *n*: **to get off to a ~** empezar con buen pie

flyover ['flaɪəʊvə^r] *n* (*Brit: bridge*) paso elevado *or* (*LAm*) a desnivel

flysheet ['flaɪʃiːt] *n* (*for tent*) doble techo

flyweight ['flaɪweɪt] *adj* de peso mosca ▷ *n* peso mosca

FM *abbr* (*Radio: = frequency modulation*) FM; (*Brit Mil*) = **field marshal**

FO *n abbr* (*Brit: = Foreign Office*) ≈ Min. de AA. EE. (*= Ministerio de Asuntos Exteriores*)

foal [fəʊl] *n* potro

foam [fəʊm] *n* espuma ▷ *vi* hacer espuma

fob [fɔb] *n* (*also:* **watch ~**) leontina ▷ *vt*: **to ~ sb off with sth** deshacerse de algn con algo

focal ['fəʊkəl] *adj* focal; **~ point** punto focal; (*fig*) centro de atención

focus ['fəʊkəs] (*pl* **focuses**) *n* foco; (*centre*) centro ▷ *vt* (*field glasses etc*) enfocar ▷ *vi*: **to ~ (on)** enfocar (a); (*issue etc*) centrarse en; **in/ out of ~** enfocado/desenfocado

fodder ['fɔdə^r] *n* pienso

foe [fəʊ] *n* enemigo

foetus, fetus (*US*) ['fiːtəs] *n* feto

fog [fɔg] *n* niebla

foggy ['fɔgɪ] *adj*: **it's ~** hay niebla

fog lamp, fog light (*US*) *n* (*Aut*) faro antiniebla

foil [fɔɪl] *vt* frustrar ▷ *n* hoja; (*also:* **kitchen ~**) papel *m* (de) aluminio; (*Fencing*) florete *m*

fold [fəʊld] *n* (*bend, crease*) pliegue *m*; (*Agr*) redil *m* ▷ *vt* doblar; **to ~ one's arms** cruzarse de brazos; **fold up** *vi* plegarse, doblarse; (*business*) quebrar ▷ *vt* (*map etc*) plegar

folder ['fəʊldə^r] *n* (*for papers*) carpeta; (*binder*) carpeta de anillas; (*brochure*) folleto; (*Comput*) directorio

folding ['fəʊldɪŋ] *adj* (*chair, bed*) plegable

foliage ['fəʊlɪɪdʒ] *n* follaje *m*

folk [fəʊk] *npl* gente *f* ▷ *adj* popular, folklórico; **folks** *npl* familia, parientes *mpl*

folklore ['fəʊklɔː^r] *n* folklore *m*

folk music *n* música folk

folk singer *n* cantante *m/f* de música folk

folk song *n* canción *f* popular *or* folk

follow ['fɔləʊ] *vt* seguir ▷ *vi* seguir; (*result*) resultar; **he ~ed suit** hizo lo mismo; **to ~ sb's advice** seguir el consejo de algn; **I don't quite ~ you** no te comprendo muy bien; **it doesn't ~ that ...** no se deduce que ....; **follow on** *vi* seguir; (*continue*): **to ~ on from** ser la consecuencia lógica de; **follow out** *vt* (*implement: idea, plan*) realizar, llevar a cabo; **follow through** *vt* llevar hasta el fin ▷ *vi* (*Sport*) dar el remate; **follow up** *vt* (*letter, offer*) responder a; (*case*) investigar

follower ['fɔləʊə^r] *n* seguidor(a) *m(f)*; (*Pol*) partidario(-a)

following ['fɔləʊɪŋ] *adj* siguiente ▷ *n* seguidores *mpl*, afición *f*

follow-up ['fɔləʊʌp] *n* continuación *f*

folly ['fɔlɪ] *n* locura

fond [fɔnd] *adj* (*loving*) cariñoso; **to be ~ of sb** tener cariño a algn; **she's ~ of swimming** tiene afición a la natación, le gusta nadar

fondle ['fɔndl] *vt* acariciar

font [fɔnt] *n* pila bautismal

food [fuːd] *n* comida

food chain *n* cadena alimenticia

food mixer *n* batidora

food poisoning *n* intoxicación *f* alimentaria

food processor *n* robot *m* de cocina

food stamp *n* (*US*) vale *m* para comida

foodstuffs ['fuːdstʌfs] *npl* comestibles *mpl*

fool [fuːl] *n* tonto(-a); (*Culin*) puré *m* de frutas con nata ▷ *vt* engañar; **to make a ~ of o.s.** ponerse en ridículo; **you can't ~ me** a mí no me engañas; *see also* **April Fools' Day**; **fool about, fool around** *vi* hacer el tonto

foolhardy ['fuːlhɑːdɪ] *adj* temerario

foolish ['fuːlɪʃ] *adj* tonto; (*careless*) imprudente

foolproof ['fuːlpruːf] *adj* (*plan etc*) infalible

foot [fut] (*pl* **feet**) *n* (*Anat*) pie *m*; (*of page, stairs, mountain*) pie *m*; (*measure*) pie (= 304 mm); (*of animal, table*) pata ▷ *vt* (*bill*) pagar; **on ~** a pie; **to find one's feet** acostumbrarse; **to put one's ~ down** (*say no*) plantarse; (*Aut*) pisar el acelerador

footage ['futɪdʒ] *n* (*Cine*) imágenes *fpl*

foot-and-mouth [futənd'maʊθ], **foot-and-mouth disease** *n* fiebre *f* aftosa

football ['futbɔːl] *n* balón *m*; (*game: Brit*) fútbol *m*; (*US*) fútbol *m* americano

footballer ['futbɔːlə^r] *n* (*Brit*) = **football player**

football match *n* partido de fútbol

football player n futbolista m/f, jugador(a) m(f) de fútbol

footbrake ['futbreɪk] n freno de pie

footbridge ['futbrɪdʒ] n pasarela, puente m para peatones

foothills ['futhɪlz] npl estribaciones fpl

foothold ['futhəuld] n pie m firme

footing ['futɪŋ] n (fig) nivel m; **to lose one's ~** perder pie; **on an equal ~** en pie de igualdad

footlights ['futlaɪts] npl candilejas fpl

footman ['futmən] n lacayo

footnote ['futnəut] n nota (de pie de página)

footpath ['futpɑ:θ] n sendero

footprint ['futprɪnt] n huella, pisada

footsie ['futsɪ] n: **to play ~ with sb** (inf) juguetear con los pies de algn

footstep ['futstɛp] n paso

footwear ['futwɛəʳ] n calzado

KEYWORD

for [fɔ:] prep **1** (indicating destination, intention) para; **the train for London** el tren para Londres; (in announcements) el tren con destino a Londres; **he left for Rome** marchó para Roma; **he went for the paper** fue por el periódico; **is this for me?** ¿es esto para mí?; **it's time for lunch** es la hora de comer

2 (indicating purpose) para; **what('s it) for?** ¿para qué (es)?; **what's this button for?** ¿para qué sirve este botón?; **to pray for peace** rezar por la paz

3 (on behalf of, representing): **the MP for Hove** el diputado por Hove; **he works for the government/a local firm** trabaja para el gobierno/en una empresa local; **I'll ask him for you** se lo pediré por ti; **G for George** G de Gerona

4 (because of) por esta razón; **for fear of being criticized** por temor a ser criticado

5 (with regard to) para; **it's cold for July** hace frío para julio; **he has a gift for languages** tiene don de lenguas

6 (in exchange for) por; **I sold it for £5** lo vendí por £5; **to pay 50 pence for a ticket** pagar 50 peniques por un billete

7 (in favour of): **are you for or against us?** ¿estás con nosotros o contra nosotros?; **I'm all for it** estoy totalmente a favor; **vote for X** vote (a) X

8 (referring to distance): **there are roadworks for 5 km** hay obras en 5 km; **we walked for miles** caminamos kilómetros y kilómetros

9 (referring to time): **he was away for two years** estuvo fuera (durante) dos años; **it hasn't rained for three weeks** no ha llovido durante or en tres semanas; **I have known her for years** la conozco desde hace años; **can you do it for tomorrow?** ¿lo podrás hacer para mañana?

10 (with infinitive clauses): **it is not for me to decide** la decisión no es cosa mía; **it would**

be best for you to leave sería mejor que te fueras; **there is still time for you to do it** todavía te queda tiempo para hacerlo; **for this to be possible** ... para que esto sea posible ...

11 (in spite of) a pesar de; **for all his complaints** a pesar de sus quejas
▷ conj (since, as: rather formal) puesto que

forage ['fɒrɪdʒ] n forraje m

foray ['fɒreɪ] n incursión f

forbid (pt **forbad(e)**, pp **forbidden**) [fə'bɪd, -'bæd, -'bɪdn] vt prohibir; **to ~ sb to do sth** prohibir a algn hacer algo

forbidden [fə'bɪdn] pt of **forbid** ▷ adj (food, area) prohibido; (word, subject) tabú

forbidding [fə'bɪdɪŋ] adj (landscape) inhóspito; (severe) severo

force [fɔ:s] n fuerza ▷ vt obligar, forzar; **to ~ o.s. to do** hacer un esfuerzo por hacer; **the F~s** npl (Brit) las Fuerzas Armadas; **sales ~** (Comm) personal m de ventas; **a ~ 5 wind** un viento fuerza 5; **to join ~s** unir fuerzas; **in ~** (law etc) en vigor; **to ~ sb to do sth** obligar a algn a hacer algo; **force back** vt (crowd, enemy) hacer retroceder; (tears) reprimir; **force down** vt (food) tragar con esfuerzo

forced [fɔ:st] adj (smile) forzado; (landing) forzoso

force-feed ['fɔ:sfi:d] vt (animal, prisoner) alimentar a la fuerza

forceful ['fɔ:sful] adj enérgico

forceps ['fɔ:sɛps] npl fórceps m inv

forcibly ['fɔ:səblɪ] adv a la fuerza

ford [fɔ:d] n vado ▷ vt vadear

fore [fɔ:ʳ] n: **to bring to the ~** sacar a la luz pública; **to come to the ~** empezar a destacar

forearm ['fɔ:rɑ:m] n antebrazo

foreboding [fɔ:'bəudɪŋ] n presentimiento

forecast ['fɔ:kɑ:st] n pronóstico ▷ vt (irreg: like **cast**) pronosticar; **weather ~** previsión f meteorológica

forecourt ['fɔ:kɔ:t] n patio; (of garage) área de entrada

forefathers ['fɔ:fɑ:ðəz] npl antepasados mpl

forefinger ['fɔ:fɪŋgəʳ] n (dedo) índice m

forefront ['fɔ:frʌnt] n: **in the ~ of** en la vanguardia de

forego (pt **forewent**, pp **foregone**) [fɔ:'gəu, -'wɛnt, -'gɔn] vt = **forgo**

foregone ['fɔ:gɔn] pp of **forego** ▷ adj: **it's a ~ conclusion** es una conclusión inevitable

foreground ['fɔ:graund] n (also Comput) primer plano m

forehand ['fɔ:hænd] n (Tennis) derechazo directo

forehead ['fɒrɪd] n frente f

foreign ['fɒrɪn] adj extranjero; (trade) exterior

foreign currency n divisas fpl

foreigner ['fɒrɪnəʳ] n extranjero(-a)

foreign exchange n (system) cambio de divisas; (money) divisas fpl, moneda extranjera

Foreign Minister n Ministro(-a) de Asuntos Exteriores, Canciller m (LAm)

Foreign Office n (Brit) Ministerio de Asuntos Exteriores

Foreign Secretary n (Brit) Ministro(-a) de Asuntos Exteriores, Canciller m (LAm)

foreleg ['fɔːleg] n pata delantera

foreman ['fɔːmən] n capataz m; (Law: of jury) presidente m/f

foremost ['fɔːməust] adj principal ▷ adv: **first and ~** ante todo, antes que nada

forename ['fɔːneɪm] n nombre m (de pila)

forensic [fə'rɛnsɪk] adj forense; **~ scientist** forense m/f

foreplay ['fɔːpleɪ] n preámbulos mpl (de estimulación sexual)

forerunner ['fɔːrʌnə'] n precursor(a) m(f)

foresee (pt **foresaw**, pp **foreseen**) [fɔː'siː, -'sɔː, -'siːn] vt prever

foreseeable [fɔː'siːəbl] adj previsible

foreshadow [fɔː'ʃædəu] vt prefigurar, anunciar

foresight ['fɔːsaɪt] n previsión f

foreskin ['fɔːskɪn] n (Anat) prepucio

forest ['fɔrɪst] n bosque m

forestall [fɔː'stɔːl] vt anticiparse a

forestry ['fɔrɪstrɪ] n silvicultura

foretaste ['fɔːteɪst] n anticipo

foretell (pt, pp **foretold**) [fɔː'tɛl, -'təuld] vt predecir, pronosticar

forever [fə'rɛvə'] adv siempre; (for good) para siempre; (endlessly) constantemente

forewent [fɔː'wɛnt] pt of **forego**

foreword ['fɔːwəːd] n prefacio

forfeit ['fɔːfɪt] n (in game) prenda ▷ vt perder (derecho a)

forgave [fə'geɪv] pt of **forgive**

forge [fɔːdʒ] n fragua; (smithy) herrería ▷ vt (signature: Brit: money) falsificar; (metal) forjar; **forge ahead** vi avanzar mucho

forger ['fɔːdʒə'] n falsificador(a) m(f)

forgery ['fɔːdʒərɪ] n falsificación f

forget (pt **forgot**, pp **forgotten**) [fə'gɛt, -'gɔt, -'gɔtn] vt olvidar, olvidarse de ▷ vi olvidarse

forgetful [fə'gɛtful] adj olvidadizo, despistado

forget-me-not [fə'gɛtmɪnɔt] n nomeolvides f inv

forgive (pt **forgave**, pp **forgiven**) [fə'gɪv, -'geɪv, -'gɪvn] vt perdonar; **to ~ sb for sth/ for doing sth** perdonar algo a algn/a algn por haber hecho algo

forgiveness [fə'gɪvnɪs] n perdón m

forgo (pt **forwent**, pp **forgone**) [fɔː'gəu, -'wɛnt, -'gɔn] vt (give up) renunciar a; (go without) privarse de

forgot [fə'gɔt] pt of **forget**

forgotten [fə'gɔtn] pp of **forget**

fork [fɔːk] n (for eating) tenedor m; (for gardening) horca; (of roads) bifurcación f; (in tree) horcadura ▷ vi (road) bifurcarse; **fork out** vt (inf: pay) soltar

fork-lift truck ['fɔːklɪft-] n máquina elevadora

forlorn [fə'lɔːn] adj (person) triste, melancólico; (deserted: cottage) abandonado; (desperate: attempt) desesperado

form [fɔːm] n forma; (Brit Scol) curso; (document) formulario, planilla (LAm) ▷ vt formar; **in the ~ of** en forma de; **in top ~** en plena forma; **to be in good ~** (Sport: fig) estar en plena forma; **to ~ part of** sth formar parte de algo; **to ~ a circle/a queue** hacer una curva/una cola

formal ['fɔːməl] adj (offer, receipt) por escrito; (person etc) correcto; (occasion, dinner) ceremonioso; **~ dress** traje m de vestir; (evening dress) traje m de etiqueta

formalities [fɔː'mælɪtɪz] npl formalidades fpl

formality [fɔː'mælɪtɪ] n ceremonia

formally ['fɔːməlɪ] adv oficialmente

format ['fɔːmæt] n formato ▷ vt (Comput) formatear

formation [fɔː'meɪʃən] n formación f

formative ['fɔːmətɪv] adj (years) de formación

former ['fɔːmə'] adj anterior; (earlier) antiguo; (ex) ex; **the ~ ... the latter ...** aquél ... éste ...; **the ~ president** el antiguo or ex presidente; **the ~ Yugoslavia/Soviet Union** la antigua or ex Yugoslavia/Unión Soviética

formerly ['fɔːməlɪ] adv antes

formidable ['fɔːmɪdəbl] adj formidable

formula ['fɔːmjulə] n fórmula; **F~ One** (Aut) Fórmula Uno

forsake (pt **forsook**, pp **forsaken**) [fə'seɪk, -'suk, -'seɪkən] vt (gen) abandonar; (plan) renunciar a

fort [fɔːt] n fuerte m; **to hold the ~** (fig) quedarse a cargo

forte ['fɔːtɪ] n fuerte m

forth [fɔːθ] adv: **back and ~** de acá para allá; **and so ~** y así sucesivamente

forthcoming [fɔːθ'kʌmɪŋ] adj próximo, venidero; (character) comunicativo

forthright ['fɔːθraɪt] adj franco

forthwith ['fɔːθ'wɪθ] adv en el acto, acto seguido

fortieth ['fɔːtɪɪθ] adj cuadragésimo

fortify ['fɔːtɪfaɪ] vt fortalecer

fortitude ['fɔːtɪtjuːd] n (city) fortificar; (person) tortalecer

fortnight ['fɔːtnaɪt] n (Brit) quincena; **it's a ~ since ...** hace quince días que ...

fortnightly ['fɔːtnaɪtlɪ] adj quincenal ▷ adv quincenalmente

fortress ['fɔːtrɪs] n fortaleza

fortunate ['fɔːtʃənɪt] adj: **it is ~ that ...** (es una) suerte que ...

fortunately ['fɔːtʃənɪtlɪ] adv afortunadamente

fortune ['fɔːtʃən] n suerte f; (wealth) fortuna;
  to make a ~ hacer un dineral
fortune-teller ['fɔːtʃəntelə'] n adivino(-a)
forty ['fɔːtɪ] num cuarenta
forum ['fɔːrəm] n (also fig) foro
forward ['fɔːwəd] adj (position) avanzado;
  (movement) hacia delante; (front) delantero;
  (not shy) atrevido ▷ n (Sport) delantero ▷ vt
  (letter) remitir; (career) promocionar; **to
  move ~** avanzar; **"please ~"** "remítase al
  destinatario"
forwarding address n destinatario
forward planning n planificación f por
  anticipado
forward slash n barra diagonal
forwent [fɔː'went] pt of **forgo**
fossil ['fɔsl] n fósil m
foster ['fɔstə'] vt (child) acoger en familia;
  (idea) fomentar
foster child n hijo(-a) adoptivo(-a)
foster mother n madre f adoptiva
fought [fɔːt] pt, pp of **fight**
foul [faul] adj (gen) sucio, puerco; (weather,
  smell etc) asqueroso; (language) grosero;
  (temper) malísimo ▷ n (Football) falta ▷ vt
  (dirty) ensuciar; (block) atascar; (entangle:
  anchor, propeller) atascar, enredarse en; (football
  player) cometer una falta contra
foul play n (Sport) mala jugada; (Law) muerte f
  violenta
found [faund] pt, pp of **find** ▷ vt (establish)
  fundar
foundation [faun'deɪʃən] n (act) fundación f;
  (basis) base f; (also: **~ cream**) crema de base;
  foundations npl (of building) cimientos mpl
foundations [faun'deɪʃənz] npl (of building)
  cimientos mpl; **to lay the ~** poner los
  cimientos
founder ['faundə'] n fundador(a) m(f) ▷ vi
  irse a pique
foundry ['faundrɪ] n fundición f
fountain ['fauntɪn] n fuente f
fountain pen n (pluma) estilográfica,
  plumafuente f (LAm)
four [fɔː'] num cuatro; **on all ~s** a gatas
four-by-four ['fɔbaɪ'fɔ'] n todoterreno, 4x4 m
  (cuatro por cuatro)
four-letter word ['fɔːletə-] n taco
four-poster ['fɔː'pəustə'] n (also: **~ bed**) cama
  de columnas
foursome ['fɔːsəm] n grupo de cuatro
  personas
fourteen ['fɔː'tiːn] num catorce
fourteenth [fɔː'tiːnθ] adj decimocuarto
fourth [fɔːθ] adj cuarto ▷ n (Aut: also: **~ gear**)
  cuarta (velocidad)
four-wheel drive ['fɔːwiːl-] n tracción f a las
  cuatro ruedas
fowl [faul] n ave f (de corral)
fox [fɔks] n zorro ▷ vt confundir
foyer ['fɔɪeɪ] n vestíbulo
Fr. abbr (Rel: = father) P.; (= friar) Fr.

fracas ['frækɑː] n gresca, refriega
fraction ['frækʃən] n fracción f
fracture ['fræktʃə'] n fractura ▷ vt fracturar
fragile ['frædʒaɪl] adj frágil
fragment ['frægmənt] n fragmento
fragrance ['freɪɡrəns] n fragancia
fragrant ['freɪɡrənt] adj fragante, oloroso
frail [freɪl] adj (fragile) frágil, quebradizo;
  (weak) delicado
frame [freɪm] n (Tech) armazón f; (of picture,
  door etc) marco; (of spectacles: also: **~s**) montura
  ▷ vt encuadrar; (picture) enmarcar; (reply)
  formular; **to ~ sb** (inf) inculpar por engaños
  a algn
frame of mind n estado de ánimo
framework ['freɪmwəːk] n marco
France [frɑːns] n Francia
franchise ['fræntʃaɪz] n (Pol) derecho
  al voto, sufragio; (Comm) licencia,
  concesión f
frank [fræŋk] adj franco ▷ vt (Brit: letter)
  franquear
frankly ['fræŋklɪ] adv francamente
frankness ['fræŋknɪs] n franqueza
frantic ['fræntɪk] adj (desperate: need, desire)
  desesperado; (: search) frenético; (: person)
  desquiciado
fraternity [frə'təːnɪtɪ] n (club) fraternidad f;
  (US) club m de estudiantes; (guild) gremio
fraud [frɔːd] n fraude m; (person) impostor(a)
  m(f)
fraught [frɔːt] adj (tense) tenso; **~ with**
  cargado de
fray [freɪ] n combate m, lucha, refriega ▷ vi
  deshilacharse; **tempers were ~ed** el
  ambiente se ponía tenso
freak [friːk] n (person) fenómeno; (event)
  suceso anormal; (inf: enthusiast) adicto(-a)
  ▷ adj (storm, conditions) anormal; **health ~** (inf)
  maniático(-a) en cuestión de salud; **freak
  out** vi (inf: on drugs) flipar
freckle ['frekl] n peca
free [friː] adj (person: at liberty) libre; (not fixed)
  suelto; (gratis) gratuito; (unoccupied)
  desocupado; (liberal) generoso ▷ vt (prisoner
  etc) poner en libertad; (jammed object) soltar;
  to give sb a ~ hand dar carta blanca a algn;
  ~ and easy despreocupado; **is this seat ~?**
  ¿está libre este asiento?; **~ of tax** libre de
  impuestos; **admission ~** entrada libre;
  ~ (of charge), for ~ adv gratis
freedom ['friːdəm] n libertad f; **~ of
  association** libertad de asociación
Freefone® ['friːfəun] n (Brit) número
  gratuito
free-for-all ['friːfərɔːl] n riña general
free gift n regalo
freehold ['friːhəuld] n propiedad f absoluta
free kick n tiro libre
freelance ['friːlɑːns] adj independiente ▷ adv
  por cuenta propia; **to do ~ work** trabajar por
  su cuenta

freely ['fri:lɪ] *adv* libremente; (*liberally*) generosamente

free-market economy ['fri:'mɑːkɪt-] *n* economía de libre mercado

freemason ['fri:meɪsn] *n* francmasón *m*

Freepost® ['fri:pəust] *n* porte *m* pagado

free-range ['fri:'reɪndʒ] *adj* (*hen, egg*) de granja

free speech *n* libertad *f* de expresión

free trade *n* libre comercio

freeway ['fri:weɪ] *n* (US) autopista

free will *n* libre albedrío; **of one's own ~** por su propia voluntad

freeze [fri:z] (*pt* **froze**, *pp* **frozen**) *vi* helarse, congelarse ▷ *vt* helar; (*prices, food, salaries*) congelar ▷ *n* helada; (*on arms, wages*) congelación *f*; **freeze over** *vi* (*lake, river*) helarse, congelarse; (*window, windscreen*) cubrirse de escarcha; **freeze up** *vi* helarse, congelarse

freeze-dried ['fri:zdraɪd] *adj* liofilizado

freezer ['fri:zə^r] *n* congelador *m*, congeladora *f*

freezing ['fri:zɪŋ] *adj* helado

freezing point *n* punto de congelación; **3 degrees below ~** tres grados bajo cero

freight [freɪt] *n* (*goods*) carga; (*money charged*) flete *m*

freight train *n* (US) tren *m* de mercancías

French [frentʃ] *adj* francés(-esa) ▷ *n* (*Ling*) francés *m*; **the French** *npl* los franceses

French bean *n* judía verde

French bread *n* pan *m* francés

French dressing *n* (*Culin*) vinagreta

French fried potatoes, French fries (US) *npl* patatas *fpl* or (LAm) papas *fpl* fritas

French loaf *n* barra de pan

Frenchman ['frentʃmən] *n* francés *m*

French stick *n* barra de pan

French window *n* puerta ventana

Frenchwoman ['frentʃwumən] *n* francesa

frenzy ['frenzɪ] *n* frenesí *m*

frequency ['fri:kwənsɪ] *n* frecuencia

frequent *adj* ['fri:kwənt] frecuente ▷ *vt* [frɪ'kwent] frecuentar

frequently ['fri:kwəntlɪ] *adv* frecuentemente, a menudo

fresco ['freskəu] *n* fresco

fresh [freʃ] *adj* (*gen*) fresco; (*bread*) tierno; (*new*) nuevo; (*water*) dulce; **to make a ~ start** empezar de nuevo

freshen ['freʃən] *vi* (*wind*) arreciar; (*air*) refrescar; **freshen up** *vi* (*person*) arreglarse

fresher ['freʃə^r] *n* (*Brit Scol: inf*) estudiante *m/f* de primer año

freshly ['freʃlɪ] *adv*: **~ painted/arrived** recién pintado/llegado

freshman ['freʃmən] *n* (*US Scol*) = **fresher**

freshness ['freʃnɪs] *n* frescura

freshwater ['freʃwɔ:tə^r] *adj* (*fish*) de agua dulce

fret [fret] *vi* inquietarse

FRG *n abbr* (= *Federal Republic of Germany*) RFA *f*

Fri. *abbr* (= *Friday*) vier

friar ['fraɪə^r] *n* fraile *m*; (*before name*) fray

friction ['frɪkʃən] *n* fricción *f*

Friday ['fraɪdɪ] *n* viernes *m inv*; *see also* **Tuesday**

fridge [frɪdʒ] *n* (*Brit*) nevera, frigo, refrigeradora (LAm), heladera (LAm)

fridge-freezer ['frɪdʒ'fri:zə^r] *n* frigorífico-congelador *m*, combi *m*

fried [fraɪd] *pt, pp of* **fry** ▷ *adj*: **~ egg** huevo frito, huevo estrellado

friend [frend] *n* amigo(-a) ▷ *vt* (*Internet*) agregar como amigo

friendly ['frendlɪ] *adj* simpático; (*government*) amigo; (*place*) acogedor(-a); (*match*) amistoso

friendly fire *n* fuego amigo, disparos *mpl* del propio bando

friendship ['frendʃɪp] *n* amistad *f*

fries [fraɪz] *npl* (*esp US*) = **French fried potatoes**

frieze [fri:z] *n* friso

frigate ['frɪgɪt] *n* fragata

fright [fraɪt] *n* susto; **to take ~** asustarse

frighten ['fraɪtn] *vt* asustar; **frighten away, frighten off** *vt* (*birds, children etc*) espantar, ahuyentar

frightened ['fraɪtnd] *adj* asustado

frightening ['fraɪtnɪŋ] *adj*: **it's ~** da miedo

frightful ['fraɪtful] *adj* espantoso, horrible

frigid ['frɪdʒɪd] *adj* (*Med*) frígido

frill [frɪl] *n* volante *m*; **without ~s** (*fig*) sin adornos

frilly ['frɪlɪ] *adj* con volantes

fringe [frɪndʒ] *n* (Brit: *of hair*) flequillo; (*edge: of forest etc*) borde *m*, margen *m*

fringe benefits *npl* ventajas *fpl* complementarias

Frisbee® ['frɪzbɪ] *n* frisbee® *m*

frisk [frɪsk] *vt* cachear, registrar

frisky ['frɪskɪ] *adj* juguetón(-ona)

fritter ['frɪtə^r] *n* buñuelo; **fritter away** *vt* desperdiciar

frivolous ['frɪvələs] *adj* frívolo

frizzy ['frɪzɪ] *adj* crespo

fro [frəu] *see* **to**

frock [frɔk] *n* vestido

frog [frɔg] *n* rana; **to have a ~ in one's throat** tener carraspera

frogman ['frɔgmən] *n* hombre-rana *m*

frolic ['frɔlɪk] *vi* juguetear

○ **KEYWORD**

from [frɔm] *prep* **1** (*indicating starting place*) de, desde; **where do you come from?, where are you from?** ¿de dónde eres?; **where has he come from?** ¿de dónde ha venido?; **from London to Glasgow** de Londres a Glasgow; **to escape from sth/sb** escaparse de algo/algn

2 (*indicating origin etc*) de; **a letter/telephone call from my sister** una carta/llamada de

mi hermana; **tell him from me that ...**
dígale de mi parte que ...
3 (*indicating time*): **from one o'clock to** or
until or **till nine** de la una a las nueve, desde
la una hasta las nueve; **from January (on)** a
partir de enero; **(as) from Friday** a partir del
viernes
4 (*indicating distance*) de; **the hotel is 1 km
from the beach** el hotel está a 1 km de la
playa
5 (*indicating price, number etc*) de; **prices range
from £10 to £50** los precios van desde £10 a or
hasta £50; **the interest rate was increased
from 9% to 10%** el tipo de interés fue
incrementado de un 9% a un 10%
6 (*indicating difference*) de; **he can't tell red
from green** no sabe distinguir el rojo del
verde; **to be different from sb/sth** ser
diferente de algn/algo
7 (*because of, on the basis of*): **from what he says**
por lo que dice; **weak from hunger**
debilitado por el hambre

front [frʌnt] *n* (*foremost part*) parte *f* delantera;
(*of house*) fachada; (*promenade: also:* **sea ~**)
paseo marítimo; (*Mil, Pol, Meteorology*) frente
m; (*fig: appearances*) apariencia ▷ *adj* (*wheel,
leg*) delantero; (*row, line*) primero ▷ *vi:* **to ~
onto sth** dar a algo; **in ~ (of)** delante (de)
frontage ['frʌntɪdʒ] *n* (*of building*) fachada
front bench *n* (Brit: Pol) ver nota
frontbencher ['frʌnt'bɛntʃəʳ] *n* (Brit) *see*
front bench
front door *n* puerta principal
frontier ['frʌntɪəʳ] *n* frontera
front page *n* primera plana
front room *n* (Brit) salón *m*, sala
front-wheel drive ['frʌntwi:l-] *n* tracción *f*
delantera
frost [frɒst] *n* (*gen*) helada; (*also:* **hoar~**)
escarcha ▷ *vt* (US Culin) escarchar
frostbite ['frɒstbaɪt] *n* congelación *f*
frosted ['frɒstɪd] *adj* (*glass*) esmerilado; (*esp
US: cake*) glaseado
frosting ['frɒstɪŋ] *n* (*esp US: icing*) glaseado
frosty ['frɒstɪ] *adj* (*weather*) de helada; (*surface*)
cubierto de escarcha; (*welcome etc*) glacial
froth [frɒθ] *n* espuma
frothy ['frɒθɪ] *adj* espumoso
frown [fraun] *vi* fruncir el ceño ▷ *n:* **with a ~**
frunciendo el entrecejo; **frown on** *vt fus*
desaprobar
froze [frəuz] *pt of* **freeze**
frozen ['frəuzn] *pp of* **freeze** ▷ *adj* (*food*)
congelado; (*Comm*): **~ assets** activos *mpl*
congelados or bloqueados
frugal ['fru:gəl] *adj* (*person*) frugal
fruit [fru:t] *n pl inv* fruta
fruiterer ['fru:tərəʳ] *n* frutero(-a); **~'s (shop)**
frutería
fruit fly *n* mosca de la fruta
fruitful ['fru:tful] *adj* provechoso

fruition [fru:'ɪʃən] *n:* **to come to ~** realizarse
fruit juice *n* jugo or (Sp) zumo de fruta
fruitless ['fru:tlɪs] *adj* (*fig*) infructuoso, inútil
fruit machine *n* (Brit) máquina tragaperras
fruit salad *n* macedonia or (LAm) ensalada de
frutas
frustrate [frʌs'treɪt] *vt* frustrar
frustrated [frʌs'treɪtɪd] *adj* frustrado
frustrating [frʌs'treɪtɪŋ] *adj* (*job, day*)
frustrante
frustration [frʌs'treɪʃən] *n* frustración *f*
fry (*pt, pp* **fried**) [fraɪ, -d] *vt* freír ▷ *n:* **small ~**
gente *f* menuda
frying pan ['fraɪɪŋ-] *n* sartén *f*, sartén *m*
(*LAm*)
FT *n abbr* (Brit: = *Financial Times*) periódico
financiero; (= the FT index) el índice de valores del
Financial Times
ft. *abbr* = **foot; feet**
fuddy-duddy ['fʌdɪdʌdɪ] (*pej*) *n* carcamal *m*,
carroza *m/f* ▷ *adj* chapado a la antigua
fudge [fʌdʒ] *n* (*Culin*) caramelo blando ▷ *vt* (*issue,
problem*) rehuir, esquivar
fuel [fjuəl] *n* (*for heating*) combustible *m*; (*coal*)
carbón *m*; (*wood*) leña; (*for engine*) carburante
m ▷ *vt* (*furnace etc*) alimentar; (*aircraft, ship etc*)
aprovisionar de combustible
fuel oil *n* fuel oil *m*
fuel tank *n* depósito de combustible
fugitive ['fju:dʒɪtɪv] *n* (*from prison*)
fugitivo(-a)
fulfil, fulfill (US) [ful'fɪl] *vt* (*function*)
desempeñar; (*condition*) cumplir; (*wish, desire*)
realizar
full [ful] *adj* lleno; (*fig*) pleno; (*complete*)
completo; (*maximum*) máximo; (*information*)
detallado; (*price*) íntegro, sin descuento
▷ *adv:* **~ well** perfectamente; **we're ~ up for
July** estamos completos para julio; **I'm ~
(up)** estoy lleno; **~ employment** pleno
empleo; **~ name** nombre *m* completo; **a ~
two hours** dos horas enteras; **at ~ speed** a
toda velocidad; **in ~** (*reproduce, quote*)
íntegramente; **to write sth in ~** escribir
algo por extenso; **to pay in ~** pagar la deuda
entera
full-length [ful'lɛŋθ] *adj* (*portrait*) de cuerpo
entero; (*film*) de largometraje
full moon *n* luna llena, plenilunio
full-scale [fulskeɪl] *adj* (*attack, war, search,
retreat*) en gran escala; (*plan, model*) de tamaño
natural
full stop *n* punto
full-time ['fultaɪm] *adj* (*work*) de tiempo
completo ▷ *adv:* **to work ~** trabajar a tiempo
completo
fully ['fulɪ] *adv* completamente; (*at least*) al
menos
fully-fledged ['fulɪ'flɛdʒd], **full-fledged**
(US) *adj* (*teacher, barrister*) diplomado; (*bird*)
con todas sus plumas, capaz de volar; (*fig*)
de pleno derecho

fumble ['fʌmbl] *vi*: **to ~ with** manejar torpemente, manosear

fume [fjuːm] *vi* estar furioso, echar humo

fumes [fjuːmz] *npl* humo *sg*, gases *mpl*

fun [fʌn] *n* (*amusement*) diversión *f*; (*joy*) alegría; **to have ~** divertirse; **for ~** por gusto; **to make ~ of** reírse de

function ['fʌŋkʃən] *n* función *f* ▷ *vi* funcionar; **to ~ as** hacer (las veces) de, fungir de (*LAm*)

functional ['fʌŋkʃənl] *adj* funcional

fund [fʌnd] *n* fondo; (*reserve*) reserva; **funds** *npl* (*money*) fondos *mpl*

fundamental [fʌndə'mɛntl] *adj* fundamental; **fundamentals** *npl* fundamentos *mpl*

fundamentalism [fʌndə'mɛntəlɪzəm] *n* fundamentalismo, integrismo

fundamentalist [fʌndə'mɛntəlɪst] *n* fundamentalista *m/f*, integrista *m/f*

funding ['fʌndɪŋ] *n* financiación *f*

fund-raising ['fʌndreɪzɪŋ] *n* recaudación *f* de fondos

funeral ['fjuːnərəl] *n* (*burial*) entierro; (*ceremony*) funerales *mpl*

funeral director *n* director(a) *m(f)* de pompas fúnebres

funeral parlour *n* (*Brit*) funeraria

funeral service *n* misa de cuerpo presente

funfair ['fʌnfɛəʳ] *n* (*Brit*) parque *m* de atracciones; (*travelling*) feria

fungus (*pl* **fungi**) ['fʌŋɡəs, -ɡaɪ] *n* hongo; (*mould*) moho

funky ['fʌŋkɪ] *adj* (*music*) funky; (*inf*: *good*) guay

funnel ['fʌnl] *n* embudo; (*of ship*) chimenea

funny ['fʌnɪ] *adj* gracioso, divertido; (*strange*) curioso, raro

fun run *n* maratón *m* popular

fur [fəːʳ] *n* piel *f*; (*Brit*: *on tongue etc*) sarro

fur coat *n* abrigo de pieles

furious ['fjuərɪəs] *adj* furioso; (*effort*, *argument*) violento; **to be ~ with sb** estar furioso con algn

furlong ['fəːlɔŋ] *n* octava parte de una milla

furlough ['fəːləu] *n* (*US Mil*) permiso

furnace ['fəːnɪs] *n* horno

furnish ['fəːnɪʃ] *vt* amueblar; (*supply*) proporcionar; (*information*) facilitar

furnished ['fəːnɪʃt] *adj*: **~ flat** *or* (*US*) **apartment** piso amueblado

furnishings ['fəːnɪʃɪŋz] *npl* mobiliario *sg*

furniture ['fəːnɪtʃəʳ] *n* muebles *mpl*; **piece of ~** mueble *m*

furore [fjuə'rɔːrɪ] *n* (*protests*) escándalo

furrow ['fʌrəu] *n* surco ▷ *vt* (*forehead*) arrugar

furry ['fəːrɪ] *adj* peludo; (*toy*) de peluche

further ['fəːðəʳ] *adj* (*new*) nuevo; (*place*) más lejano ▷ *adv* más lejos; (*more*) más; (*moreover*) además ▷ *vt* hacer avanzar; **how much ~ is it?** ¿a qué distancia queda?; **~ to your letter**

of ... (*Comm*) con referencia a su carta de ...; **to ~ one's interests** fomentar sus intereses

further education *n* educación *f* postescolar

furthermore [fəːðə'mɔːʳ] *adv* además

furthest ['fəːðɪst] *superlative of* **far**

furtive ['fəːtɪv] *adj* furtivo

fury ['fjuərɪ] *n* furia

fuse, fuze (*US*) [fjuːz] *n* fusible *m*; (*for bomb etc*) mecha ▷ *vt* (*metal*) fundir; (*fig*) fusionar ▷ *vi* fundirse; fusionarse; (*Brit Elec*): **to ~ the lights** fundir los plomos; **a ~ has blown** se ha fundido un fusible

fuse box *n* caja de fusibles

fuse wire *n* hilo fusible

fusion ['fjuːʒən] *n* fusión *f*

fuss [fʌs] *n* (*excitement*) conmoción *f*; (*complaint*) alboroto, protesta ▷ *vi* preocuparse (por pequeñeces) ▷ *vt* (*person*) molestar; **to make a ~** armar jaleo; **fuss over** *vt fus* (*person*) contemplar, mimar

fusspot ['fʌspɔt] *n* (*inf*) quisquilloso(-a)

fussy ['fʌsɪ] *adj* (*person*) quisquilloso; **I'm not ~** (*inf*) me da igual

fusty ['fʌstɪ] *adj* (*pej*) rancio; **to smell ~** oler a cerrado

futile ['fjuːtaɪl] *adj* vano

futon ['fuːtɔn] *n* futón *m*

future ['fjuːtʃəʳ] *adj* (*gen*) futuro; (*coming*) venidero ▷ *n* futuro, porvenir; **in ~** de ahora en adelante

futures ['fjuːtʃəz] *npl* (*Comm*) operaciones *fpl* a término, futuros *mpl*

fuze [fjuːz] *n, vb* (*US*) = **fuse**

fuzzy ['fʌzɪ] *adj* (*Phot*) borroso; (*hair*) muy rizado

fwd. *abbr* = **forward**

FYI *abbr* = **for your information**

G, g [dʒiː] n (letter) G, g f; **G** (Mus) sol m; **G for George** G de Gerona

G n abbr (Brit Scol: mark: = good) N; (US Cine: = general audience) todos los públicos

g. abbr (= gram(s), gravity) g

gab [gæb] n: **to have the gift of the ~** (inf) tener mucha labia

gabble ['gæbl] vi hablar atropelladamente; (gossip) cotorrear

gable ['geɪbl] n aguilón m

gadget ['gædʒɪt] n aparato

Gaelic ['geɪlɪk] adj, n (Ling) gaélico

gag [gæg] n (on mouth) mordaza; (joke) chiste m ▷ vt (prisoner etc) amordazar ▷ vi (choke) tener arcadas

gaiety ['geɪɪtɪ] n alegría

gain [geɪn] n ganancia ▷ vt ganar ▷ vi (watch) adelantarse; **to ~ by sth** ganar con algo; **to ~ ground** ganar terreno; **to ~ 3 lbs (in weight)** engordar 3 libras; **gain (up)on** vt fus alcanzar

gainfully ['geɪnfʊlɪ] adv: **to be ~ employed** tener un trabajo remunerado

gait [geɪt] n forma de andar, andares mpl

gal., gall. abbr = **gallon(s)**

gala ['gɑːlə] n gala; **swimming ~** certamen m de natación

galaxy ['gæləksɪ] n galaxia

gale [geɪl] n (wind) vendaval m; **~ force 10** vendaval de fuerza 10

gallant ['gælənt] adj valeroso; (towards ladies) galante

gall bladder n vesícula biliar

gallery ['gælərɪ] n (Theat) galería; (for spectators) tribuna; (also: **art ~**: state-owned) pinacoteca or museo de arte; (: private) galería de arte

galley ['gælɪ] n (ship's kitchen) cocina; (ship) galera

gallon ['gæln] n galón m (= 8 pintas; Brit = 4,546 litros; US = 3,785 litros)

gallop ['gæləp] n galope m ▷ vi galopar; **~ing inflation** inflación f galopante

gallows ['gæləuz] n horca

gallstone ['gɔːlstəun] n cálculo biliar

Gallup poll ['gæləp-] n sondeo de opinión

galore [gə'lɔːʳ] adv en cantidad, en abundancia

galvanize ['gælvənaɪz] vt (metal) galvanizar; (fig): **to ~ sb into action** mover or impulsar a algn a actuar

Gambia ['gæmbɪə] n Gambia

gambit ['gæmbɪt] n (fig): **opening ~** táctica inicial

gamble ['gæmbl] n (risk) jugada arriesgada; (bet) apuesta ▷ vt: **to ~ on** apostar a; (fig) contar con, confiar en que ▷ vi jugar; (take a risk) jugárselas; (Comm) especular; **to ~ on the Stock Exchange** jugar a la bolsa

gambler ['gæmbləʳ] n jugador(a) m(f)

gambling ['gæmblɪŋ] n juego

game [geɪm] n (gen) juego; (match) partido; (of cards) partida; (Hunting) caza ▷ adj valiente; (ready): **to be ~ for anything** estar dispuesto a todo; **~s** (Scol) deportes mpl; **big ~** caza mayor

gamekeeper ['geɪmkiːpəʳ] n guardabosque m/f

game plan n (for game) plan m de juego; (gen) táctica

games console [geɪmz-] n consola de juegos

game show n programa m concurso inv, concurso

gammon ['gæmən] n (bacon) tocino ahumado; (ham) jamón m ahumado

gamut ['gæmət] n (Mus) gama; **to run the (whole) ~ of emotions** (fig) recorrer toda la gama de emociones

gang [gæŋ] n (of criminals etc) banda; (of kids) pandilla; (of colleagues) peña; (of workmen) brigada ▷ vi: **to ~ up on sb** conchabarse contra algn

gangly ['gæŋglɪ] adj desgarbado

gangrene ['gæŋgriːn] n gangrena

gangster ['gæŋstəʳ] n gángster m

gang warfare n guerra entre bandas

gangway ['gæŋweɪ] n (Brit: in theatre, bus etc) pasillo; (on ship) pasarela

gantry ['gæntrɪ] n (for crane, railway signal) pórtico; (for rocket) torre f de lanzamiento

gaol [dʒeɪl] n, vt (Brit) = **jail**

gap [gæp] n hueco; (in trees, traffic) claro; (in market, records) laguna; (in time) intervalo

gape [geɪp] vi mirar boquiabierto

gaping ['geɪpɪŋ] adj (hole) muy abierto

gap year n año sabático (*antes de empezar a estudiar en la universidad*)

garage ['gærɑ:ʒ] n garaje m; (*for repairs*) taller m

garage sale n venta de objetos usados (*en el jardín de una casa particular*)

garbage ['gɑ:bɪdʒ] n (*US*) basura; (*nonsense*) bobadas fpl; (*fig: film, book etc*) basura

garbage can n (*US*) cubo or balde m (*LAm*) or bote m (*LAm*) de la basura

garbage collector n (*US*) basurero(-a)

garbage truck n (*US*) camión m de la basura

garbled ['gɑ:bld] adj (*account, explanation*) confuso

garden ['gɑ:dn] n jardín m; **gardens** npl (*public*) parque m, jardines mpl; (*private*) huertos mpl

garden centre n (*Brit*) centro de jardinería

garden city n (*Brit*) ciudad f jardín

gardener ['gɑ:dnə'] n jardinero(-a)

gardening ['gɑ:dnɪŋ] n jardinería

gargle ['gɑ:gl] vi hacer gárgaras, gargarear (*LAm*)

garish ['gɛərɪʃ] adj chillón(-ona)

garland ['gɑ:lənd] n guirnalda

garlic ['gɑ:lɪk] n ajo

garment ['gɑ:mənt] n prenda (de vestir)

garnish ['gɑ:nɪʃ] vt adornar; (*Culin*) aderezar

garrison ['gærɪsn] n guarnición f ▷ vt guarnecer

garrulous ['gærjʊləs] adj charlatán(-ana)

garter ['gɑ:tə'] n (*US*) liga

gas [gæs] n gas m; (*US: gasoline*) gasolina ▷ vt asfixiar con gas; **Calor ~®** (gas m) butano

gas cooker n (*Brit*) cocina de gas

gas cylinder n bombona de gas

gas fire n estufa de gas

gas-fired ['gæsfaɪəd] adj de gas

gash [gæʃ] n brecha, raja; (*from knife*) cuchillada ▷ vt rajar; (*with knife*) acuchillar

gasket ['gæskɪt] n (*Aut*) junta

gas mask n careta antigás

gas meter n contador m de gas

gasoline ['gæsəli:n] n (*US*) gasolina

gasp [gɑ:sp] n grito sofocado ▷ vi (*pant*) jadear; **gasp out** vt (*say*) decir jadeando

gas pedal n (*esp US*) acelerador m

gas station n (*US*) gasolinera

gassy ['gæsɪ] adj con mucho gas

gas tank n (*US Aut*) depósito (de gasolina)

gas tap n llave f del gas

gastric ['gæstrɪk] adj gástrico

gate [geɪt] n (*also at airport*) puerta; (*Rail: at level crossing*) barrera; (*metal*) verja

gâteau (*pl* **gâteaux**) ['gætəu, z] n tarta

gatecrash ['geɪtkræʃ] vt colarse en

gateway n puerta

gather ['gæðə'] vt (*flowers, fruit*) coger (*Sp*), recoger (*LAm*); (*assemble*) reunir; (*pick up*) recoger; (*Sewing*) fruncir; (*understand*) sacar en consecuencia ▷ vi (*assemble*) reunirse; (*dust*) acumularse; (*clouds*) cerrarse; **to ~ speed** ganar velocidad; **to ~ (from/that)** deducir (por/que); **as far as I can ~** por lo que tengo entendido

gathering ['gæðərɪŋ] n reunión f, asamblea

gaudy ['gɔ:dɪ] adj chillón(-ona)

gauge, gage (*US*) [geɪdʒ] n calibre m; (*Rail*) ancho de vía, entrevía; (*instrument*) indicador m ▷ vt medir; (*fig: sb's capabilities, character*) juzgar, calibrar; **petrol ~** indicador m (del nivel) de gasolina; **to ~ the right moment** elegir el momento (oportuno)

gaunt [gɔ:nt] adj descarnado; (*fig*) adusto

gauntlet ['gɔ:ntlɪt] n (*fig*): **to run the ~ of sth** exponerse a algo; **to throw down the ~** arrojar el guante

gauze [gɔ:z] n gasa

gave [geɪv] pt of **give**

gawk [gɔ:k] vi mirar pasmado

gay [geɪ] adj (*homosexual*) gay; (*colour, person*) alegre

gaze [geɪz] n mirada fija ▷ vi: **to ~ at sth** mirar algo fijamente

gazump [gə'zʌmp] vt, vi (*Brit*) echarse atrás en la venta ya acordada de una casa por haber una oferta más alta

GB abbr (= *Great Britain*) GB

GBH n abbr (*Brit Law: inf*) = **grievous bodily harm**

GCE n abbr (*Brit*: = *General Certificate of Education*) ≈ certificado de bachillerato

GCSE n abbr (*Brit*: = *General Certificate of Secondary Education*) certificado del último ciclo de la enseñanza secundaria obligatoria

Gdns. abbr (= *gardens*) jdns

GDP n abbr (= *gross domestic product*) PIB m

GDR n abbr (= *German Democratic Republic*) RDA f

gear [gɪə'] n equipo; (*Tech*) engranaje m; (*Aut*) velocidad f, marcha ▷ vt (*fig: adapt*): **to ~ sth to** adaptar or ajustar algo a; **top** or (*US*) **high/low ~** cuarta/primera; **in ~** con la marcha metida; **our service is ~ed to meet the needs of the disabled** nuestro servicio va enfocado a responder a las necesidades de los minusválidos; **gear up** vi prepararse

gear box n caja de cambios

gear lever, gear shift (*US*) n palanca de cambio

gear stick n (*Brit*) = **gear lever**

geese [gi:s] npl of **goose**

gel [dʒɛl] n gel m

gelignite ['dʒɛlɪgnaɪt] n gelignita

gem [dʒɛm] n gema, piedra preciosa; (*fig*) joya

Gemini ['dʒɛmɪnaɪ] n Géminis m

gen [dʒɛn] n (*Brit inf*): **to give sb the ~ on sth** poner a algn al tanto de algo

Gen. abbr (*Mil*: = *General*) Gen., Gral

gen. abbr (= *general*) grl.; = **generally**

gender ['dʒɛndə'] n género

gene [dʒi:n] n gen(e) m

general ['dʒɛnərl] n general m ▷ adj general; **in ~** en general; **~ audit** auditoría general; **the ~ public** el gran público

general anaesthetic, general anesthetic (US) n anestesia general

general delivery n (US) lista de correos

general election n elecciones fpl generales

generalization [dʒɛnrəlaɪˈzeɪʃən] n generalización f

generalize [ˈdʒɛnrəlaɪz] vi generalizar

generally [ˈdʒɛnrəlɪ] adv generalmente, en general

general practitioner n médico(-a) de medicina general

general store n tienda (que vende de todo) (LAm, Sp), almacén m (SC, Sp)

general strike n huelga general

generate [ˈdʒɛnəreɪt] vt generar

generation [dʒɛnəˈreɪʃən] n (of electricity etc) generación f

generator [ˈdʒɛnəreɪtəʳ] n generador m

generosity [dʒɛnəˈrɒsɪtɪ] n generosidad f

generous [ˈdʒɛnərəs] adj generoso; (copious) abundante

genetic [dʒɪˈnɛtɪk] adj genético; ~ **engineering** ingeniería genética; ~ **fingerprinting** identificación f genética

genetically modified organism [dʒɪˈnɛtɪkəlɪ-] n organismo genéticamente modificado, organismo transgénico

genetic engineering n ingeniería genética

genetic fingerprinting [-ˈfɪŋɡəprɪntɪŋ] n identificación f genética

genetics [dʒɪˈnɛtɪks] n genética

Geneva [dʒɪˈniːvə] n Ginebra

genial [ˈdʒiːnɪəl] adj afable

genitals [ˈdʒɛnɪtlz] npl (órganos mpl) genitales mpl

genitive [ˈdʒɛnɪtɪv] n genitivo

genius [ˈdʒiːnɪəs] n genio

genocide [ˈdʒɛnəusaɪd] n genocidio

genome [ˈɡiːnəum] n genoma m

gent [dʒɛnt] n abbr (Brit inf) = **gentleman**

genteel [dʒɛnˈtiːl] adj fino, distinguido

gentle [ˈdʒɛntl] adj (sweet) dulce; (touch etc) ligero, suave

gentleman [ˈdʒɛntlmən] n señor m; (well-bred man) caballero; ~**'s agreement** acuerdo entre caballeros

gently [ˈdʒɛntlɪ] adv suavemente

gentry [ˈdʒɛntrɪ] npl pequeña nobleza sg

gents [dʒɛnts] n servicios mpl (de caballeros)

genuine [ˈdʒɛnjuɪn] adj auténtico; (person) sincero

genuinely [ˈdʒɛnjuɪnlɪ] adv sinceramente

geographic [dʒɪəˈɡræfɪk], **geographical** [dʒɪəˈɡræfɪkl] adj geográfico

geography [dʒɪˈɒɡrəfɪ] n geografía

geological [dʒɪəˈlɒdʒɪkl] adj geológico

geologist [dʒɪˈɒlədʒɪst] n geólogo(-a)

geology [dʒɪˈɒlədʒɪ] n geología

geometry [dʒɪˈɒmətrɪ] n geometría

Geordie [ˈdʒɔːdɪ] n habitante m/f de Tyneside

Georgia [ˈdʒɔːdʒə] n Georgia

geranium [dʒɪˈreɪnjəm] n geranio

gerbil [ˈdʒɛrbl] n gerbo

geriatric [dʒɛrɪˈætrɪk] adj, n geriátrico(-a) m(f)

germ [dʒəːm] n (microbe) microbio, bacteria; (seed) germen m

German [ˈdʒəːmən] adj alemán(-ana) ⊳ n alemán(-ana) m(f); (Ling) alemán m

German Democratic Republic n República Democrática Alemana

germane [dʒəːˈmeɪn] adj: ~ **(to)** pertinente (a)

German measles n rubeola, rubéola

Germany [ˈdʒəːmənɪ] n Alemania; **East/West ~** (History) Alemania Oriental or Democrática/Occidental or Federal

gesticulate [dʒɛsˈtɪkjuleɪt] vi gesticular

gesture [ˈdʒɛstjəʳ] n gesto; **as a ~ of friendship** en señal de amistad

O KEYWORD

get [ɡɛt] (pt, pp **got**, (US) pp **gotten**) vi 1 (become, be) ponerse, volverse; **to get old/tired** envejecer/cansarse; **to get drunk** emborracharse; **to get dirty** ensuciarse; **to get ready/washed** prepararse/lavarse; **to get married** casarse; **when do I get paid?** ¿cuándo me pagan or se me paga?; **it's getting late** se está haciendo tarde

2 (go): **to get to/from** llegar a/de; **to get home** llegar a casa; **he got under the fence** pasó por debajo de la barrera

3 (begin) empezar a; **to get to know sb** (llegar a) conocer a algn; **I'm getting to like him** me está empezando a gustar; **let's get going** or **started** ¡vamos a empezar!)

4 (modal aux vb): **you've got to do it** tienes que hacerlo

⊳ vt 1: **to get sth done** (finish) hacer algo; (have done) mandar hacer algo; **to get one's hair cut** cortarse el pelo; **to get the car going** or **to go** arrancar el coche; **to get sb to do sth** conseguir or hacer que algn haga algo; **to get sth/sb ready** preparar algo/a algn

2 (obtain: money, permission, results) conseguir; (find: job, flat) encontrar; (fetch: person, doctor) buscar; (object) ir a buscar, traer; **to get sth for sb** conseguir algo para algn; **get me Mr Jones, please** (Tel) póngame or (LAm) comuníqueme con el Sr. Jones, por favor; **can I get you a drink?** ¿quieres algo de beber?

3 (receive: present, letter) recibir; (acquire: reputation) alcanzar; (: prize) ganar; **what did you get for your birthday?** ¿qué te regalaron por tu cumpleaños?; **how much did you get for the painting?** ¿cuánto sacaste por el cuadro?

4 (catch) coger (Sp), agarrar (LAm); (hit: target etc) dar en; **to get sb by the arm/throat** coger or agarrar a algn por el brazo/cuello; **get him!** ¡cógelo! (Sp), ¡atrápalo! (LAm); **the bullet got him in the leg** la bala le dio en la pierna

5 (*take, move*) llevar; **to get sth to sb** hacer llegar algo a algn; **do you think we'll get it through the door?** ¿crees que lo podremos meter por la puerta?

6 (*catch, take: plane, bus etc*) coger (*Sp*), tomar (*LAm*); **where do I get the train for Birmingham?** ¿dónde se coge *or* se toma el tren para Birmingham?

7 (*understand*) entender; (*hear*) oír; **I've got it!** ¡ya lo tengo!, ¡eureka!; **I don't get your meaning** no te entiendo; **I'm sorry, I didn't get your name** lo siento, no me he enterado de tu nombre

8 (*have, possess*): **to have got** tener

9 (*inf: annoy*) molestar; (: *thrill*) chiflar

get about *vi* salir mucho; (*news*) divulgarse

get across *vt* (*message, meaning*) lograr comunicar ▷ *vi*: **to get across to sb** hacer que algn comprenda

get along *vi* (*agree*) llevarse bien; (*depart*) marcharse; (*manage*) = **get by**

get at *vt fus* (*attack*) meterse con; (*reach*) alcanzar; (*the truth*) descubrir; **what are you getting at?** ¿qué insinúas?

get away *vi* marcharse; (*escape*) escaparse

get away with *vt fus* hacer impunemente

get back *vi* (*return*) volver ▷ *vt* recobrar

get back at (*inf*): **to get back at sb (for sth)** vengarse de algn (por algo)

get by *vi* (*pass*) (lograr) pasar; (*manage*) arreglárselas; **I can get by in Dutch** me defiendo en holandés

get down *vi* bajar(se) ▷ *vt fus* bajar ▷ *vt* bajar; (*depress*) deprimir

get down to *vt fus* (*work*) ponerse a

get in *vi* entrar; (*train*) llegar; (*arrive home*) volver a casa, regresar; (*political party*) salir ▷ *vt* (*bring in: harvest*) recoger; (: *coal, shopping, supplies*) comprar, traer; (*insert*) meter

get into *vt fus* entrar en; (*vehicle*) subir a; **to get into a rage** enfadarse

get off *vi* (*from train etc*) bajar(se); (*depart: person, car*) marcharse ▷ *vt* (*remove*) quitar; (*send off*) mandar; (*have as leave: day, time*) tener libre ▷ *vt fus* (*train, bus*) bajar(se) de; **to get off to a good start** (*fig*) empezar muy bien *or* con buen pie

get on ▷ *vi* (*at exam etc*): **how are you getting on?** ¿cómo te va?; (*agree*): **to get on (with)** llevarse bien (con) ▷ *vt fus* subir(se) a

get on to *vt fus* (*deal with*) ocuparse de; (*inf: contact on phone etc*) hablar con

get out *vi* salir; (*of vehicle*) bajar(se); (*news*) saberse ▷ *vt* sacar

get out of *vt fus* salir de; (*duty etc*) escaparse de; (*gain from: pleasure, benefit*) sacar de

get over *vt fus* (*illness*) recobrarse de

get round *vt fus* rodear; (*fig: person*) engatusar a ▷ *vi*: **to get round to doing sth** encontrar tiempo para hacer algo

get through *vt fus* (*finish*) acabar ▷ *vi* (*Tel*) (lograr) comunicar

get through to *vt fus* (*Tel*) comunicar con

get together *vi* reunirse ▷ *vt* reunir, juntar

get up *vi* (*rise*) levantarse ▷ *vt fus* subir; **to get up enthusiasm for sth** cobrar entusiasmo por algo

get up to *vt fus* (*reach*) llegar a; (*prank*) hacer

getaway ['gɛtəweɪ] *n* fuga

get-together ['gɛttəgɛðər] *n* reunión *f*; (*party*) fiesta

get-up ['gɛtʌp] *n* (*Brit inf: outfit*) atavío, atuendo

get-well card [gɛt'wɛl-] *n* tarjeta en la que se desea a un enfermo que se mejore

geyser ['giːzər] *n* (*water heater*) calentador *m* de agua; (*Geo*) géiser *m*

Ghana ['gɑːnə] *n* Ghana

ghastly ['gɑːstlɪ] *adj* horrible; (*pale*) pálido

gherkin ['gəːkɪn] *n* pepinillo

ghetto ['gɛtəu] *n* gueto

ghetto blaster [-'blɑːstər] *n* radiocas(s)et(t)e *m* portátil (*de gran tamaño*)

ghost [gəust] *n* fantasma *m* ▷ *vt* (*book*) escribir por otro

ghost story *n* cuento de fantasmas

GI *n abbr* (*US inf: = government issue*) soldado del ejército norteamericano

giant ['dʒaɪənt] *n* gigante *m/f* ▷ *adj* gigantesco, gigante; **~ (size) packet** paquete *m* (de tamaño) gigante *or* familiar

giant killer *n* (*Sport*) matagigantes *m inv*

gibberish ['dʒɪbərɪʃ] *n* galimatías *m*

giblets ['dʒɪblɪts] *npl* menudillos *mpl*

Gibraltar [dʒɪ'brɔːltər] *n* Gibraltar *m*

giddy ['gɪdɪ] *adj* (*dizzy*) mareado; (*height, speed*) vertiginoso; **it makes me ~** me marea; **I feel ~** me siento mareado

gift [gɪft] *n* (*gen*) regalo; (*Comm: also: free ~*) obsequio; (*ability*) don *m*; **to have a ~ for sth** tener dotes para algo

gifted ['gɪftɪd] *adj* dotado

gift shop, gift store (*US*) *n* tienda de regalos

gift token, gift voucher *n* vale-regalo *m*

gig¹ [gɪg] *n* (*inf: concert*) actuación *f*

gig² [gɪg] *n abbr* (*inf: = gigabyte*) giga *m*

gigabyte ['gɪgəbaɪt] *n* gigabyte *m*

gigantic [dʒaɪ'gæntɪk] *adj* gigantesco

giggle ['gɪgl] *vi* reírse tontamente ▷ *n* risilla

gill [dʒɪl] *n* (*measure*) 0.25 pintas (*Brit* = 0,148 litros; *US* = 0,118 litros.)

gills [gɪlz] *npl* (*of fish*) branquias *fpl*, agallas *fpl*

gilt [gɪlt] *adj, n* dorado

gilt-edged ['gɪltɛdʒd] *adj* (*Comm: stocks, securities*) de máxima garantía

gimmick ['gɪmɪk] *n* reclamo; **sales ~** reclamo promocional

gin [dʒɪn] *n* (*liquor*) ginebra

ginger ['dʒɪndʒər] *n* jengibre *m*

ginger ale *n* ginger ale *m*

ginger beer *n* refresco *m* de jengibre

gingerbread ['dʒɪndʒəbrɛd] *n* pan *m* de jengibre

gingerly ['dʒɪndʒəlɪ] adv con pies de plomo

ginseng ['dʒɪnsɛŋ] n ginseng m

gipsy ['dʒɪpsɪ] n gitano(-a)

giraffe [dʒɪ'rɑːf] n jirafa

girder ['gəːdər] n viga

girdle ['gəːdl] n (corset) faja ▷ vt ceñir

girl [gəːl] n (small) niña; (young woman) chica, joven f, muchacha; **an English ~** una (chica) inglesa

girl band n girl band m (grupo musical de chicas)

girlfriend ['gəːlfrɛnd] n (of girl) amiga; (of boy) novia

girlish ['gəːlɪʃ] adj de niña

giro ['dʒaɪrəu] n (Brit: bank giro) giro bancario; (post office giro) giro postal

girth [gəːθ] n circunferencia; (of saddle) cincha

gist [dʒɪst] n lo esencial

give [gɪv] (pt **gave**, pp **given** [geɪv, 'gɪvn]) vt dar; (deliver) entregar; (as gift) regalar ▷ vi (break) romperse; (stretch: fabric) dar de sí; **to ~ sb sth, ~ sth to sb** dar algo a algn; **how much did you ~ for it?** ¿cuánto pagaste por él?; **12 o'clock, ~ or take a few minutes** más o menos las doce; **~ them my regards** dales recuerdos de mi parte; **I can ~ you 10 minutes** le puedo conceder 10 minutos; **to ~ way** (Brit Aut) ceder el paso; **to ~ way to despair** ceder a la desesperación; **give away** vt (give free) regalar; (betray) traicionar; (disclose) revelar; **give back** vt devolver; **give in** vi ceder ▷ vt entregar; **give off** vt despedir; **give out** vt distribuir ▷ vi (be exhausted: supplies) agotarse; (fail: engine) averiarse; (strength) fallar; **give up** vi rendirse, darse por vencido ▷ vt renunciar a; **to ~ up smoking** dejar de fumar; **to ~ o.s. up** entregarse

giveaway ['gɪvəweɪ] n (inf): **her expression was a ~** su expresión la delataba; **the exam was a ~!** ¡el examen estaba tirado! ▷ cpd: **~ prices** precios mpl de regalo

given ['gɪvn] pp of **give** ▷ adj (fixed: time, amount) determinado ▷ conj: **~ (that)** ... dado (que) ...; **~ the circumstances** ... dadas las circunstancias ...

glacier ['glæsɪər] n glaciar m

glad [glæd] adj contento; **to be ~ about sth/that** alegrarse de algo/de que; **I was ~ of his help** agradecí su ayuda

gladly ['glædlɪ] adv con mucho gusto

glamorous ['glæmərəs] adj con glamour, glam(o)uroso

glamour, glamor (US) ['glæmər] n encanto, atractivo

glance [glɑːns] n ojeada, mirada ▷ vi: **to ~ at** echar una ojeada a; **glance off** vt fus (bullet) rebotar en

glancing ['glɑːnsɪŋ] adj (blow) oblicuo

gland [glænd] n glándula

glare [glɛər] n deslumbramiento, brillo ▷ vi deslumbrar; **to ~ at** mirar con odio

glaring ['glɛərɪŋ] adj (mistake) manifiesto

glass [glɑːs] n vidrio, cristal m; (for drinking) vaso; (with stem) copa; (also: **looking ~**) espejo

glass ceiling n (fig) techo or barrera invisible (que impide ascender profesionalmente a las mujeres o miembros de minorías étnicas)

glasses ['glɑːsəs] npl gafas fpl, anteojos mpl (LAm)

glasshouse ['glɑːshaus] n invernadero

glassware ['glɑːswɛər] n cristalería

Glaswegian [glæs'wiːdʒən] adj de Glasgow ▷ n nativo(-a) or habitante m(f) de Glasgow

glaze [gleɪz] vt (window) acristalar; (pottery) vidriar; (Culin) glasear ▷ n barniz m; (Culin) glaseado

glazed [gleɪzd] adj (eye) vidrioso; (pottery) vidriado

glazier ['gleɪzɪər] n vidriero(-a)

gleam [gliːm] n destello ▷ vi relucir; **a ~ of hope** un rayo de esperanza

glean [gliːn] vt (gather: information) recoger

glee [gliː] n alegría, regocijo

glen [glɛn] n cañada

glib [glɪb] adj (person) de mucha labia; (comment) fácil

glide [glaɪd] vi deslizarse; (Aviat: bird) planear

glider ['glaɪdər] n (Aviat) planeador m

gliding ['glaɪdɪŋ] n (Aviat) vuelo sin motor

glimmer ['glɪmər] n luz f tenue; (of hope) rayo

glimpse [glɪmps] n vislumbre m ▷ vt vislumbrar, entrever; **to catch a ~ of** vislumbrar

glint [glɪnt] n destello; (in the eye) chispa ▷ vi centellear

glisten ['glɪsn] vi relucir, brillar

glitter ['glɪtər] vi relucir, brillar ▷ n brillo

gloat [gləut] vi: **to ~ over** regodearse con

global ['gləubl] adj (world-wide) mundial; (comprehensive) global

globalization ['gləubəlaɪzeɪʃən] n globalización f, mundialización f

global warming [-'wɔːmɪŋ] n (re)calentamiento global or de la tierra

globe [gləub] n globo, esfera; (model) bola del mundo; globo terráqueo

gloom [gluːm] n penumbra; (sadness) desaliento, melancolía

gloomy ['gluːmɪ] adj (dark) oscuro; (sad) triste; (pessimistic) pesimista; **to feel ~** sentirse pesimista

glorify ['glɔːrɪfaɪ] vt glorificar

glorious ['glɔːrɪəs] adj glorioso; (weather, sunshine) espléndido

glory ['glɔːrɪ] n gloria

gloss [glɔs] n (shine) brillo; (also: **~ paint**) (pintura) esmalte m; **gloss over** vt fus restar importancia a; (omit) pasar por alto

glossary ['glɔsərɪ] n glosario

glossy ['glɔsɪ] adj lustroso; (hair) brillante; (photograph) con brillo; (magazine) de papel satinado or cuché

glove [glʌv] n guante m

glove compartment n (Aut) guantera
glow [gləʊ] vi (shine) brillar ▷ n brillo
glower ['glaʊəʳ] vi: **to ~ at** mirar con ceño
glucose ['glu:kəʊs] n glucosa
glue [glu:] n pegamento, cemento (LAm) ▷ vt pegar
glum [glʌm] adj (mood) abatido; (person, tone) melancólico
glut [glʌt] n superabundancia
glutton ['glʌtn] n glotón(-ona) m(f); **~ for punishment** masoquista m/f
gluttony ['glʌtənɪ] n gula, glotonería
GM adj abbr (= genetically-modified) transgénico
gm abbr (= gram) g
GMT abbr (= Greenwich Mean Time) GMT
gnarled [nɑ:ld] adj nudoso
gnat [næt] n mosquito
gnaw [nɔ:] vt roer
gnome [nəʊm] n gnomo
GNP n abbr (= gross national product) PNB m
go [gəʊ] (pt **went**, pp **gone**) vi ir; (travel) viajar; (depart) irse, marcharse; (work) funcionar, marchar; (be sold) venderse; (time) pasar; (become) ponerse; (break etc) estropearse, romperse ▷ n (pl **goes**) **to have a go (at)** probar suerte (con); **to be on the go** no parar; **whose go is it?** ¿a quién le toca?; **to go by car/on foot** ir en coche/a pie; **he's going to do it** va a hacerlo; **to go for a walk** ir a dar un paseo; **to go dancing** ir a bailar; **to go looking for sth/sb** ir a buscar algo/a algn; **to make sth go, get sth going** poner algo en marcha; **my voice has gone** he perdido la voz; **the cake is all gone** se acabó la tarta; **the money will go towards our holiday** el dinero es para (ayuda de) nuestras vacaciones; **how did it go?** ¿qué tal salió or resultó?, ¿cómo ha ido?; **the meeting went well** la reunión salió bien; **to go and see sb** ir a ver a algn; **to go to sleep** dormirse; **I'll take whatever is going** acepto lo que haya; **... to go** (US: food) ... para llevar; **go about** vi (rumour) propagarse; (also: **go round**: wander about) andar (de un sitio para otro) ▷ vt fus: **how do I go about this?** ¿cómo me las arreglo para hacer esto?; **to go about one's business** ocuparse de sus asuntos; **go after** vt fus (pursue) perseguir; (job, record etc) andar tras; **go against** vt fus (be unfavourable to: results) ir en contra de; (be contrary to: principles) ser contrario a; **go ahead** vi seguir adelante; **go along** vi ir; **as you go along** sobre la marcha ▷ vt fus bordear; **go along with** vt fus (accompany) acompañar; (agree with: idea) estar de acuerdo con; **go around** vi = **go round**; **go away** vi irse, marcharse; **go back** vi volver; **go back on** vt fus (promise) faltar a; **go by** vi (years, time) pasar ▷ vt fus guiarse por; **go down** vi bajar; (ship) hundirse; (sun) ponerse ▷ vt fus bajar por; **that should go down well with him** eso le va a gustar; **he's gone down with flu** ha cogido la gripe;

go for vt fus (fetch) ir por; (like) gustar; (attack) atacar; **go in** vi entrar; **go in for** vt fus (competition) presentarse a; **go into** vt fus entrar en; (investigate) investigar; (embark on) dedicarse a; **go off** vi irse, marcharse; (food) pasarse; (lights etc) apagarse; (explode) estallar; (event) realizarse ▷ vt fus perder el interés por; **I'm going off the idea** ya no me gusta tanto él/la idea; **the party went off well** la fiesta salió bien; **go on** vi (continue) seguir, continuar; (lights) encenderse; (happen) pasar, ocurrir; (be guided by: evidence etc) partir de; **to go on doing sth** seguir haciendo algo; **what's going on here?** ¿qué pasa aquí?; **go on at** vt fus (nag) soltarle el rollo a; **go out** vi salir; (fire, light) apagarse; (ebb: tide) bajar, menguar; **to go out with sb** salir con algn; **go over** vi (ship) zozobrar ▷ vt fus (check) revisar; **to go over sth in one's mind** repasar algo mentalmente; **go past** vi, vt fus pasar; **go round** vi (circulate: news, rumour) correr; (suffice) alcanzar, bastar; (revolve) girar, dar vueltas; (visit): **to go round (to sb's)** pasar a ver (a algn); **to go round (by)** (make a detour) dar la vuelta (por) ▷ vt fus **to go round the back** pasar por detrás; **go through** vt fus (town etc) atravesar; (search through) revisar; (perform: ceremony) realizar; (examine: list, book) repasar; **go through with** vt fus (plan, crime) llevar a cabo; **I couldn't go through with it** no pude llevarlo a cabo; **go together** vi entenderse; **go under** vi (sink: ship, person) hundirse; (fig: business, firm) quebrar; **go up** vi subir; **to go up in flames** estallar en llamas; **go with** vt fus (accompany) ir con, acompañar a; (fit, suit) hacer juego con; **go without** vt fus pasarse sin
goad [gəʊd] vt aguijonear
go-ahead ['gəʊəhɛd] adj emprendedor(a) ▷ n luz f verde; **to give sth/sb the ~** dar luz verde a algo/algn
goal [gəʊl] n meta, arco (LAm); (score) gol m
goalkeeper ['gəʊlki:pəʳ] n portero, guardameta m/f, arquero (LAm)
goal post n poste m (de la portería)
goat [gəʊt] n cabra f
gobble ['gɔbl] vt (also: **~ down, ~ up**) engullir
go-between ['gəʊbɪtwi:n] n intermediario(-a)
goblin ['gɔblɪn] n duende m
go-cart ['gəʊkɑ:t] n = **go-kart**
god [gɔd] n dios m; **G~** Dios m
godchild ['gɔdtʃaɪld] n ahijado(-a)
goddamn ['gɔddæm] adj (inf: also: **~ed**) maldito, puñetero ▷ excl: **~!** ¡cagüen diez!
goddaughter ['gɔddɔ:təʳ] n ahijada
goddess ['gɔdɪs] n diosa
godfather ['gɔdfɑ:ðəʳ] n padrino
god-forsaken ['gɔdfəseɪkən] adj dejado de la mano de Dios
godmother ['gɔdmʌðəʳ] n madrina

godparents ['gɔdpɛərənts] *npl*: **the ~** los padrinos

godsend ['gɔdsɛnd] *n*: **to be a ~** venir como llovido del cielo

godson ['gɔdsʌn] *n* ahijado

goes [gəuz] *vb see* **go**

gofer ['gəufəʳ] *n* (*inf*) chico(-a) para todo

goggles ['gɔglz] *npl* (*Aut*) gafas *fpl*, anteojos *mpl* (*LAm*); (*diver's*) gafas *fpl* submarinas

going ['gəuɪŋ] *n* (*conditions*) cosas *fpl* ▷ *adj*: **the ~ rate** la tarifa corriente *or* en vigor; **it was slow ~** las cosas iban lentas

goings-on ['gəuɪŋz'ɔn] *npl* (*inf*) tejemanejes *mpl*

go-kart ['gəukɑːt] *n* kart *m*

gold [gəuld] *n* oro ▷ *adj* (*reserves*) de oro

golden ['gəuldn] *adj* (*made of gold*) de oro; (*colour*) dorado

golden rule *n* regla de oro

goldfish ['gəuldfɪʃ] *n* pez *m* de colores

goldmine ['gəuldmaɪn] *n* mina de oro

gold-plated ['gəuld'pleɪtɪd] *adj* chapado en oro

goldsmith ['gəuldsmɪθ] *n* orfebre *m/f*

golf [gɔlf] *n* golf *m*

golf ball *n* (*for game*) pelota de golf; (*on typewriter*) esfera impresora

golf club *n* club *m* de golf; (*stick*) palo (de golf)

golf course *n* campo de golf

golfer ['gɔlfəʳ] *n* jugador(a) *m(f)* de golf, golfista *m/f*

golfing ['gɔlfɪŋ] *n*: **to go ~** jugar al golf

gone [gɔn] *pp of* **go**

goner ['gɔnəʳ] *n* (*inf*): **to be a ~** estar en las últimas

gong [gɔŋ] *n* gong *m*

good [gud] *adj* bueno; (*before m sing n*) buen; (*well-behaved*) educado ▷ *n* bien *m*; **~!** ¡qué bien!; **he's ~ at it** se le da bien; **to be ~ for** servir para; **it's ~ for you** te hace bien; **would you be ~ enough to …?** ¿podría hacerme el favor de …?; ¿sería tan amable de …?; **that's very ~ of you** es usted muy amable; **to feel ~** sentirse bien; **it's ~ to see you** me alegro de verte; **a ~ deal (of)** mucho; **a ~ many** muchos; **to make ~** reparar; **it's no ~ complaining** no sirve de nada quejarse; **is this any ~?** (*will it do?*) ¿sirve esto?; (*what's it like?*) ¿qué tal es esto?; **it's a ~ thing you were there** menos mal que estabas allí; **for ~** (*for ever*) para siempre, definitivamente; **~ morning/afternoon** ¡buenos días/buenas tardes!; **~ evening!** ¡buenas noches!; **~ night!** ¡buenas noches!; **he's up to no ~** está tramando algo; **for the common ~** para el bien común; *see also* **goods**

goodbye [gud'baɪ] *excl* ¡adiós!; **to say ~ (to)** (*person*) despedirse (de)

Good Friday *n* Viernes *m* Santo

good-looking ['gud'lukɪŋ] *adj* guapo

good-natured ['gud'neɪtʃəd] *adj* (*person*) de

buen carácter; (*discussion*) cordial

goodness ['gudnɪs] *n* (*of person*) bondad *f*; **for ~ sake!** ¡por Dios!; **~ gracious!** ¡madre mía!

goods [gudz] *npl* bienes *mpl*; (*Comm etc*) géneros *mpl*, mercancías *fpl*, artículos *mpl*; **all his ~ and chattels** todos sus bienes

goods train *n* (*Brit*) tren *m* de mercancías

goodwill [gud'wɪl] *n* buena voluntad *f*; (*Comm*) fondo de comercio; (*customer connections*) clientela

Google® ['guːgəl] *n* Google® *m* ▷ *vi* hacer búsquedas en Internet ▷ *vt* buscar información en Internet sobre

goose (*pl* **geese**) [guːs, giːs] *n* ganso, oca

gooseberry ['guzbərɪ] *n* grosella espinosa *or* silvestre; **to play ~** hacer de carabina

gooseflesh ['guːsflɛʃ] *n*, **goosepimples** ['guːspɪmplz] *npl* carne *f* de gallina

gopher ['gəufəʳ] *n* = **gofer**

gore [gɔːʳ] *vt* dar una cornada a, cornear ▷ *n* sangre *f*

gorge [gɔːdʒ] *n* garganta ▷ *vr*: **to ~ o.s. (on)** atracarse (de)

gorgeous ['gɔːdʒəs] *adj* precioso; (*weather*) estupendo; (*person*) guapísimo

gorilla [gə'rɪlə] *n* gorila *m*

gorse [gɔːs] *n* tojo

gory ['gɔːrɪ] *adj* sangriento

gosh [gɔʃ] (*inf*) *excl* ¡cielos!

go-slow ['gəu'sləu] *n* (*Brit*) huelga de celo

gospel ['gɔspl] *n* evangelio

gossip ['gɔsɪp] *n* cotilleo; (*person*) cotilla *m/f* ▷ *vi* cotillear, comadrear (*LAm*); **a piece of ~** un cotilleo

gossip column *n* ecos *mpl* de sociedad

got [gɔt] *pt, pp of* **get**

Gothic ['gɔθɪk] *adj* gótico

gotten ['gɔtn] (*US*) *pp of* **get**

gourmet ['guəmeɪ] *n* gastrónomo(-a) *m(f)*

gout [gaut] *n* gota

govern ['gʌvən] *vt* (*gen*) gobernar; (*event, conduct*) regir

governess ['gʌvənɪs] *n* institutriz *f*

government ['gʌvnmənt] *n* gobierno; **local ~** administración *f* municipal

governor ['gʌvənəʳ] *n* gobernador(a) *m(f)*; (*of school etc*) miembro del consejo; (*of jail*) director(a) *m(f)*

gown [gaun] *n* vestido; (*of teacher*: *Brit*: *of judge*) toga

GP *n abbr* (*Med*) = **general practitioner**

GPO *n abbr* (*Brit*: *old*) = **General Post Office**; (*US*) = **Government Printing Office**

gr. *abbr* (*Comm*: = *gross*) bto

grab [græb] *vt* coger (*Sp*) *or* agarrar; **to ~ at** intentar agarrar

grace [greɪs] *n* (*Rel*) gracia; (*gracefulness*) elegancia, gracia; (*graciousness*) cortesía, gracia ▷ *vt* (*favour*) honrar; (*adorn*) adornar; **5 days' ~** un plazo de 5 días; **to say ~** bendecir la mesa; **his sense of humour is his saving ~** lo que le salva es su sentido del humor

graceful ['greisful] adj grácil, ágil; (style, shape) elegante, gracioso

gracious ['greɪʃəs] adj amable ▷ excl: **good ~!** ¡Dios mío!

grade [greɪd] n (quality) clase f, calidad f; (in hierarchy) grado; (Scol: mark) nota; (US Scol) curso; (: gradient) pendiente f, cuesta ▷ vt clasificar; **to make the ~** (fig) dar el nivel

grade crossing n (US) paso a nivel

grade school n (US) escuela primaria

gradient ['greɪdɪənt] n pendiente f

gradual ['grædjuəl] adj gradual

gradually ['grædjuəlɪ] adv gradualmente

graduate n ['grædjuɪt] licenciado(-a), graduado(-a), egresado(-a) (LAm); (US Scol) bachiller m/f ▷ vi ['grædjueɪt] licenciarse, graduarse, recibirse (LAm); (US) obtener el título de bachillerato

graduation [grædju'eɪʃən] n graduación f; (US Scol) entrega de los títulos de bachillerato

graffiti [grə'fi:tɪ] npl pintadas fpl

graft [grɑːft] n (Agr, Med) injerto; (bribery) corrupción f ▷ vt injertar; **hard ~** (inf) trabajo duro

grain [greɪn] n (single particle) grano no pl (cereals) cereales mpl; (US: corn) trigo; (in wood) veta

gram [græm] n (US) gramo

grammar ['græmə^r] n gramática

grammar school n (Brit) ≈ instituto (de segunda enseñanza); (US) escuela primaria; see also **comprehensive school**

grammatical [grə'mætɪkl] adj gramatical

gramme [græm] n = **gram**

gran [græn] n (Brit: inf) abuelita

grand [grænd] adj magnífico, imponente; (wonderful) estupendo; (gesture etc) grandioso ▷ n (US: inf) mil dólares mpl

grandad (inf) ['grændæd] n = **granddad**

grandchild ['græntʃaɪld] (pl **grandchildren**) n nieto(-a) m/f

granddad ['grændæd] n yayo, abuelito

granddaughter ['grændɔːtə^r] n nieta

grandfather ['grænfɑːðə^r] n abuelo

grand jury n (US) jurado de acusación

grandma ['grænmɑː] n yaya, abuelita

grandmother ['grænmʌðə^r] n abuela

grandpa ['grænpɑː] n = **grandad**

grandparents ['grændpɛərənts] npl abuelos mpl

grand piano n piano de cola

Grand Prix ['grɑ̃ː'pri:] n (Aut) gran premio, Grand Prix m

grandson ['grænsʌn] n nieto

grandstand ['grændstænd] n (Sport) tribuna

grand total n suma total, total m

granite ['grænɪt] n granito

granny ['grænɪ] n abuelita, yaya

grant [grɑːnt] vt (concede) conceder; (admit): **to ~ (that)** reconocer (que) ▷ n (Scol) beca; **to take sth for ~ed** dar algo por sentado

granulated sugar ['grænjuleɪtɪd-] n (Brit) azúcar m granulado

granule ['grænju:l] n gránulo

grape [greɪp] n uva; **sour ~s** (fig) envidia sg; **a bunch of ~s** un racimo de uvas

grapefruit ['greɪpfru:t] n pomelo (SC, Sp), toronja (LAm)

grapevine ['greɪpvaɪn] n vid f, parra; **I heard it on the ~** (fig) me enteré, me lo contaron

graph [grɑːf] n gráfica

graphic ['græfɪk] adj gráfico

graphic equalizer n ecualizador m gráfico

graphics ['græfɪks] n (art, process) artes fpl gráficas ▷ npl (drawings: Comput) gráficos mpl

grapple ['græpl] vi (also: **to ~ with a problem**) enfrentarse a un problema

grasp [grɑːsp] vt agarrar, asir; (understand) comprender ▷ n (grip) asimiento; (reach) alcance m; (understanding) comprensión f; **to have a good ~ of** (subject) dominar; **grasp at** vt fus (rope etc) tratar de agarrar; (fig: opportunity) aprovechar

grasping ['grɑːspɪŋ] adj avaro

grass [grɑːs] n hierba; (lawn) césped m; (pasture) pasto; (inf: informer) soplón(-ona) m(f)

grasshopper ['grɑːshɔpə^r] n saltamontes m inv

grass roots adj de base ▷ npl (Pol) bases fpl

grate [greɪt] n parrilla ▷ vi chirriar, rechinar ▷ vt (Culin) rallar

grateful ['greɪtful] adj agradecido

grater ['greɪtə^r] n rallador m

gratifying ['grætɪfaɪɪŋ] adj gratificante

grating ['greɪtɪŋ] n (iron bars) rejilla ▷ adj (noise) chirriante

gratitude ['grætɪtjuːd] n agradecimiento

gratuitous [grə'tjuːɪtəs] adj gratuito

gratuity [grə'tjuːɪtɪ] n gratificación f

grave [greɪv] n tumba ▷ adj serio, grave

gravel ['grævl] n grava

gravestone ['greɪvstəun] n lápida

graveyard ['greɪvjɑːd] n cementerio, camposanto

gravity ['grævɪtɪ] n gravedad f; (seriousness) seriedad f

gravy ['greɪvɪ] n salsa de carne

gray [greɪ] adj (US) = **grey**

graze [greɪz] vi pacer ▷ vt (touch lightly, scrape) rozar ▷ n (Med) rozadura

grease [griːs] n (fat) grasa; (lubricant) lubricante m ▷ vt engrasar; **to ~ the skids** (US: fig) engrasar el mecanismo

greaseproof ['griːspruːf] adj a prueba de grasa; (Brit: paper) de grasa

greasy ['griːsɪ] adj (hands, clothes) grasiento; (road, surface) resbaladizo

great [greɪt] adj grande; (before n sing) gran; (inf) estupendo, macanudo (LAm), regio (LAm); (pain, heat) intenso; **we had a ~ time** nos lo pasamos muy bien; **they're ~ friends** son íntimos or muy amigos; **the ~ thing is that ...** lo bueno es que ...; **it was ~!** ¡fue estupendo!

Great Barrier Reef n Gran Barrera de Coral

Great Britain n Gran Bretaña

greater ['greɪtər] *adj* mayor; **G~ London** el área metropolitana de Londres

greatest ['greɪtɪst] *adj* (el/la) mayor

great-grandchild (*pl* **-children**) [greɪt'grændtʃaɪld, 'tʃɪldrən] *n* bisnieto(-a)

great-grandfather [greɪt'grændfɑ:ðər] *n* bisabuelo

great-grandmother [greɪt'grændmʌðər] *n* bisabuela

Great Lakes *npl*: **the ~** los Grandes Lagos

greatly ['greɪtlɪ] *adv* muy; (*with verb*) mucho

greatness ['greɪtnɪs] *n* grandeza

Greece [gri:s] *n* Grecia

greed [gri:d] *n* (*also:* **~iness**) codicia; (*for food*) gula; (*for power etc*) avidez *f*

greedy ['gri:dɪ] *adj* codicioso; (*for food*) glotón(-ona)

Greek [gri:k] *adj* griego ⊳ *n* griego(-a); (*Ling*) griego; **ancient/modern ~** griego antiguo/moderno

green [gri:n] *adj* verde; (*inexperienced*) novato ⊳ *n* verde *m*; (*stretch of grass*) césped *m*; (*of golf course*) campo, green *m*; **the G~ party** (*Pol*) el partido verde; **greens** *npl* verduras *fpl*; **to have ~ fingers** (*fig*) tener buena mano para las plantas

green belt *n* cinturón *m* verde

green card *n* (*Aut*) carta verde; (*US: work permit*) permiso de trabajo para los extranjeros en EE. UU.

greenery ['gri:nərɪ] *n* vegetación *f*

greengage ['gri:ngeɪdʒ] *n* (ciruela) claudia

greengrocer ['gri:ngrəusər] *n* (*Brit*) frutero(-a), verdulero(-a)

greenhouse ['gri:nhaus] *n* invernadero

greenhouse effect *n* efecto invernadero

greenhouse gas *n* gas *m* que produce el efecto invernadero

greenish ['gri:nɪʃ] *adj* verdoso

Greenland ['gri:nlənd] *n* Groenlandia

green light *n* luz *f* verde

green pepper *n* pimiento verde

green salad *n* ensalada *f* (de lechuga, pepino, pimiento verde, etc)

green tax *n* impuesto ambiental

greet [gri:t] *vt* saludar; (*news*) recibir

greeting ['gri:tɪŋ] *n* (*gen*) saludo; (*welcome*) bienvenida; **~s** saludos *mpl*; **season's ~s** Felices Pascuas

greeting card, greetings card *n* tarjeta de felicitación

gregarious [grə'gɛərɪəs] *adj* gregario

grenade [grə'neɪd] *n* (*also:* **hand ~**) granada

grew [gru:] *pt of* **grow**

grey [greɪ] *adj* gris; **to go ~** salirle canas

grey-haired [greɪ'hɛəd] *adj* canoso

greyhound ['greɪhaund] *n* galgo

grid [grɪd] *n* rejilla; (*Elec*) red *f*

gridlock ['grɪdlɔk] *n* (*esp US*) retención *f*

grief [gri:f] *n* dolor *m*, pena; **to come to ~** (*plan*) fracasar, ir al traste; (*person*) acabar mal, desgraciarse

grievance ['gri:vəns] *n* (*cause for complaint*) motivo de queja, agravio

grieve [gri:v] *vi* afligirse, acongojarse ⊳ *vt* afligir, apenar; **to ~ for** llorar por; **to ~ for sb** (*dead person*) llorar la pérdida de algn

grievous ['gri:vəs] *adj* grave; (*loss*) cruel; **~ bodily harm** (*Law*) daños *mpl* corporales graves

grill [grɪl] *n* (*on cooker*) parrilla ⊳ *vt* (*Brit*) asar a la parrilla; (*question*) interrogar; **~ed meat** carne *f* (asada) a la parrilla *or* plancha

grille [grɪl] *n* rejilla

grim [grɪm] *adj* (*place*) lúgubre; (*person*) adusto

grimace [grɪ'meɪs] *n* mueca ⊳ *vi* hacer muecas

grime [graɪm] *n* mugre *f*

grin [grɪn] *n* sonrisa abierta ⊳ *vi*: **to ~ (at)** sonreír abiertamente (a)

grind [graɪnd] (*pt, pp* **ground**) *vt* (*coffee, pepper etc*) moler; (*US: meat*) picar; (*make sharp*) afilar; (*polish: gem, lens*) esmerilar ⊳ *vi* (*car gears*) rechinar ⊳ *n*: **the daily ~** (*inf*) la rutina diaria; **to ~ one's teeth** hacer rechinar los dientes; **to ~ to a halt** (*vehicle*) pararse con gran estruendo de frenos; (*fig: talks, scheme*) interrumpirse; (*work, production*) paralizarse

grip [grɪp] *n* (*hold*) asimiento; (*of hands*) apretón *m*; (*handle*) asidero; (*of racquet etc*) mango; (*understanding*) comprensión *f* ⊳ *vt* agarrar; **to get to ~s with** enfrentarse con; **to lose one's ~** (*fig*) perder el control; **he lost his ~ of the situation** la situación se le fue de las manos

gripping ['grɪpɪŋ] *adj* absorbente

grisly ['grɪzlɪ] *adj* horripilante, horrible

gristle ['grɪsl] *n* cartílago

grit [grɪt] *n* gravilla; (*courage*) valor *m* ⊳ *vt* (*road*) poner gravilla en; **I've got a piece of ~ in my eye** tengo una arenilla en el ojo; **to ~ one's teeth** apretar los dientes

grits [grɪts] *npl* (*US*) maíz *msg* a medio moler

groan [grəun] *n* gemido, quejido ⊳ *vi* gemir, quejarse

grocer ['grəusər] *n* tendero (de ultramarinos); **~'s (shop)** *n* tienda de ultramarinos *or* (*LAm*) de abarrotes

groceries ['grəusərɪz] *npl* comestibles *mpl*

grocery ['grəusərɪ] *n* (*shop*) tienda de ultramarinos

groin [grɔɪn] *n* ingle *f*

groom [gru:m] *n* mozo(-a) de cuadra; (*also:* **bride~**) novio ⊳ *vt* (*horse*) almohazar; (*fig*): **to ~ sb for** preparar a algn para; **well-~ed** acicalado

groove [gru:v] *n* ranura; (*of record*) surco

grope [grəup] *vi* ir a tientas; **to ~ for** buscar a tientas

gross [grəus] *adj* (*neglect, injustice*) grave; (*vulgar: behaviour*) grosero; (: *appearance*) de mal gusto; (*Comm*) bruto ⊳ *vt* (*Comm*) recaudar en bruto

gross domestic product n producto interior bruto

grossly ['grəuslɪ] adv (greatly) enormemente

gross national product n producto nacional bruto

grotesque [grə'tɛsk] adj grotesco

grotto ['grɒtəu] n gruta

grotty ['grɒtɪ] adj asqueroso

ground [graund] pt, pp of **grind** ▷ n suelo, tierra; (Sport) campo, terreno; (reason) gen pl motivo, razón f; (US: also: ~ **wire**) tierra ▷ vt (plane) mantener en tierra; (US Elec) conectar con tierra ▷ vi (ship) varar, encallar ▷ adj (coffee etc) molido; **grounds** npl (of coffee etc) poso sg; (gardens etc) jardines mpl, parque m; **on the** ~ en el suelo; **common** ~ terreno común; **to gain/lose** ~ ganar/perder terreno; **to the** ~ al suelo; **below** ~ bajo tierra; **he covered a lot of** ~ **in his lecture** abarcó mucho en la clase

ground cloth n (US) = **groundsheet**

ground floor n (Brit) planta baja

grounding ['graundɪŋ] n (in education) conocimientos mpl básicos

groundless ['graundlɪs] adj infundado, sin fundamento

ground rules npl normas básicas

groundsheet ['graundʃiːt] (Brit) n tela impermeable

ground staff n personal m de tierra

ground swell n mar m or f de fondo; (fig) ola

ground-to-air ['grauntə'ɛə] adj tierra-aire

ground-to-ground ['grauntə'graund] adj tierra-tierra

groundwork ['graundwəːk] n trabajo preliminar

group [gruːp] n grupo; (Mus: pop group) conjunto, grupo ▷ vt (also: ~ **together**) agrupar ▷ vi agruparse

grouse [graus] n pl inv (bird) urogallo ▷ vi (complain) quejarse

grove [grəuv] n arboleda

grovel ['grɒvl] vi (fig) arrastrarse

grow (pt grew, pp grown) [grəu, gruː, grəun] vi crecer; (increase) aumentar; (expand) desarrollarse; (become) volverse ▷ vt cultivar; (hair, beard) dejar crecer; **to ~ rich/weak** enriquecerse/debilitarse; **to ~ tired of waiting** cansarse de esperar; **grow apart** vi (fig) alejarse uno del otro; **grow away from** vt fus (fig) alejarse de; **grow on** vt fus: **that painting is ~ing on me** ese cuadro me gusta cada vez más; **grow out of** vt fus (habit) perder; (clothes): **I've ~n out of this shirt** esta camisa se me ha quedado pequeña; **grow up** vi crecer, hacerse hombre/mujer

grower ['grəuə*] n (Agr) cultivador(a) m(f), productor(a) m(f)

growing ['grəuɪŋ] adj creciente; ~ **pains** (also fig) problemas mpl de crecimiento

growl [graul] vi gruñir

grown [grəun] pp of **grow**

grown-up [grəun'ʌp] n adulto(-a), mayor m/f

growth [grəuθ] n crecimiento, desarrollo; (what has grown) brote m; (Med) tumor m

grub [grʌb] n gusano; (inf: food) comida

grubby ['grʌbɪ] adj sucio, mugriento, mugroso (LAm)

grudge [grʌdʒ] n rencor ▷ vt: **to ~ sb sth** dar algo a algn de mala gana; **to bear sb a ~** guardar rencor a algn; **he ~s (giving) the money** da el dinero de mala gana

gruelling, grueling (US) ['gruəlɪŋ] adj agotador

gruesome ['gruːsəm] adj horrible

gruff [grʌf] adj (voice) ronco; (manner) brusco

grumble ['grʌmbl] vi refunfuñar, quejarse

grumpy ['grʌmpɪ] adj gruñón(-ona)

grunt [grʌnt] vi gruñir ▷ n gruñido

G-string ['dʒiːstrɪŋ] n tanga m

guarantee [gærən'tiː] n garantía ▷ vt garantizar; **he can't ~ (that) he'll come** no está seguro de poder venir

guard [gɑːd] n guardia; (person) guarda m/f; (Brit Rail) jefe m de tren; (safety device: on machine) cubierta de protección; (protection) protección f; (fireguard) pantalla, (mudguard) guardabarros m inv ▷ vt guardar; **to ~ (against or from)** proteger (de); **to be on one's ~** (fig) estar en guardia; **guard against** vi: **to ~ against doing sth** guardarse de hacer algo

guarded ['gɑːdɪd] adj (fig) cauteloso

guardian ['gɑːdɪən] n guardián(-ana) m(f); (of minor) tutor(a) m(f)

guard's van n (Brit Rail) furgón m del jefe de tren

Guatemala [gwɑːtə'mɑːlə] n Guatemala

Guatemalan [gwɑːtə'mɑːlən] adj, n guatemalteco(-a) m(f)

guerrilla [gə'rɪlə] n guerrillero(-a)

guess [gɛs] vi, vt (gen) adivinar; (suppose) suponer ▷ n suposición f, conjetura; **I ~ you're right** (esp US) supongo que tienes razón; **to keep sb ~ing** mantener a algn a la expectativa; **to take** or **have a ~** tratar de adivinar; **my ~ is that ...** yo creo que ...

guesswork ['gɛswəːk] n conjeturas fpl; **I got the answer by ~** acerté a ojo de buen cubero

guest [gɛst] n invitado(-a); (in hotel) huésped(a) m(f); **be my ~** (inf) estás en tu casa

guest-house ['gɛsthaus] n casa de huéspedes, pensión f

guest room n cuarto de huéspedes

guff [gʌf] n (inf) bobadas fpl

guffaw [gʌ'fɔː] n carcajada ▷ vi reírse a carcajadas

guidance ['gaɪdəns] n (gen) dirección f; (advice) consejos mpl; **marriage/vocational ~** orientación f matrimonial/profesional

guide [gaɪd] n (person) guía m/f; (book) guía f; (fig) guía f; (also: **girl ~**) exploradora ▷ vt

guiar; **to be ~d by sb/sth** dejarse guiar por algn/algo
guidebook ['gaɪdbʊk] n guía
guide dog n perro guía
guided tour n visita f con guía
guidelines ['gaɪdlaɪnz] npl (fig) directrices fpl
guild [gɪld] n gremio
guildhall ['gɪldhɔːl] n (Brit: town hall) ayuntamiento
guile [gaɪl] n astucia
guillotine ['gɪlətiːn] n guillotina
guilt [gɪlt] n culpabilidad f
guilty ['gɪltɪ] adj culpable; **to feel ~ (about)** sentirse culpable (de); **to plead ~/not ~** declararse culpable/inocente
guinea pig n cobaya; (fig) conejillo de Indias
guise [gaɪz] n: **in** or **under the ~ of** bajo la apariencia de
guitar [gɪ'tɑːʳ] n guitarra
guitarist [gɪ'tɑːrɪst] n guitarrista m/f
gulf [gʌlf] n golfo; (abyss) abismo; **the G~** el Golfo (Pérsico)
Gulf States npl: **the ~** los países del Golfo
gull [gʌl] n gaviota
gullet ['gʌlɪt] n esófago
gullible ['gʌlɪbl] adj crédulo
gully ['gʌlɪ] n barranco
gulp [gʌlp] vi tragar saliva ▷ vt (also: **~ down**) tragarse ▷ n (of liquid) trago; (of food) bocado; **in** or **at one ~** de un trago
gum [gʌm] n (Anat) encía; (glue) goma, cemento (LAm); (sweet) gominola; (also: **chewing-~**) chicle m ▷ vt pegar con goma; **gum up** vt: **to ~ up the works** (inf) entorpecerlo todo
gumboots ['gʌmbuːts] npl (Brit) botas fpl de goma
gun [gʌn] n (small) pistola; (shotgun) escopeta; (rifle) fusil m; (cannon) cañón m ▷ vt (also: **~ down**) abatir a tiros; **to stick to one's ~s** (fig) mantenerse firme or en sus trece
gunboat ['gʌnbəʊt] n cañonero
gunfire ['gʌnfaɪəʳ] n disparos mpl
gunman ['gʌnmən] n pistolero
gunpoint ['gʌnpɔɪnt] n: **at ~** a mano armada
gunpowder ['gʌnpaʊdəʳ] n pólvora
gunshot ['gʌnʃɔt] n disparo
gurgle ['gəːgl] vi gorgotear
gush [gʌʃ] vi chorrear, salir a raudales; (fig) deshacerse en efusiones
gust [gʌst] n (of wind) ráfaga
gusto ['gʌstəʊ] n entusiasmo
gut [gʌt] n intestino; (Mus etc) cuerda de tripa ▷ vt (poultry, fish) destripar; (building): **the blaze ~ted the entire building** el fuego destruyó el edificio entero
guts [gʌts] npl (courage) agallas fpl, valor m; (inf: innards: of people, animals) tripas fpl; **to hate sb's ~** odiar a algn (a muerte)
gutted ['gʌtɪd] adj (inf: disappointed): **I was ~** me quedé hecho polvo

gutter ['gʌtəʳ] n (of roof) canalón m; (in street) cuneta; **the ~** (fig) el arroyo
gutter press n (inf): **the ~** la prensa sensacionalista or amarilla; see also **tabloid press**
guy [gaɪ] n (also: **~rope**) viento, cuerda; (inf: man) tío (Sp), tipo
Guy Fawkes' Night [gaɪ'fɔːks-] n ver nota

● **GUY FAWKES' NIGHT**
●
● La noche del cinco de noviembre,
● Guy Fawkes' Night, se celebra el fracaso de
● la conspiración de la pólvora
● ("Gunpowder Plot"), el intento fallido
● de volar el parlamento de Jaime 1 en 1605.
● Esa noche se lanzan fuegos artificiales
● y se queman en muchas hogueras
● muñecos de trapo que representan a
● "Guy Fawkes", uno de los cabecillas.
● Días antes los niños tienen por
● costumbre pedir a los viandantes
● "a penny for the guy", dinero para
● comprar los cohetes.

guzzle ['gʌzl] vi tragar ▷ vt engullir
gym [dʒɪm] n (also: **~nasium**) gimnasio; (also: **~nastics**) gimnasia
gymnasium [dʒɪm'neɪzɪəm] n gimnasio
gymnast ['dʒɪmnæst] n gimnasta m/f
gymnastics [dʒɪm'næstɪks] n gimnasia
gym shoes npl zapatillas fpl de gimnasia
gym slip n (Brit) pichi m
gynaecologist, gynecologist (US) [gaɪnɪ'kɔlədʒɪst] n ginecólogo(-a)
gynaecology, gynecology (US) [gaɪnə'kɔlədʒɪ] n ginecología
gypsy ['dʒɪpsɪ] n = gipsy

H, h [eɪtʃ] n (letter) H, h f; **H for Harry**, (US) **H for How** H de Historia

haberdashery ['hæbə'dæʃərɪ] n (Brit) mercería; (US: men's clothing) prendas fpl de caballero

habit ['hæbɪt] n hábito, costumbre f; (drug habit) adicción f; **to get out of/into the ~ of doing sth** perder la costumbre de/acostumbrarse a hacer algo

habitat ['hæbɪtæt] n hábitat m

habitual [hə'bɪtjuəl] adj acostumbrado, habitual; (drinker, liar) empedernido

hack [hæk] vt (cut) cortar; (slice) tajar ▷ n corte m; (axe blow) hachazo; (pej: writer) escritor(a) m(f) a sueldo; (old horse) jamelgo

hacker ['hækə'] n (Comput) pirata m informático

hackneyed ['hæknɪd] adj trillado, gastado

hacksaw ['hæksɔ:] n sierra para metales

had [hæd] pt, pp of **have**

haddock (pl **haddock** or **haddocks**) ['hædək] n especie de merluza

hadn't ['hædnt] = **had not**

haematology, hematology (US) ['hi:mə'tɔlədʒɪ] n hematología

haemophilia, hemophilia (US) ['hi:mə'fɪlɪə] n hemofilia

haemorrhage, hemorrhage (US) ['hemərɪdʒ] n hemorragia

haemorrhoids, hemorrhoids (US) ['hemərɔɪdz] npl hemorroides fpl, almorranas fpl

hag [hæg] n (ugly) vieja fea, tarasca; (nasty) bruja; (witch) hechicera

haggard ['hægəd] adj ojeroso

haggis ['hægɪs] n (Scottish) asadura de cordero cocida; see also **Burns' Night**

haggle ['hægl] vi (argue) discutir; (bargain) regatear

haggling ['hæglɪŋ] n regateo

Hague [heɪg] n: **The ~** La Haya

hail [heɪl] n (weather) granizo ▷ vt saludar; (call) llamar a ▷ vi granizar; **to ~ (as)** aclamar (como), celebrar (como); **he ~s from Scotland** es natural de Escocia

hailstone ['heɪlstəun] n (piedra de) granizo

hailstorm ['heɪlstɔ:m] n granizada

hair [hɛə'] n (gen) pelo, cabellos mpl; (one hair) pelo, cabello; (head of hair) pelo, cabellera; (on legs etc) vello; **to do one's ~** arreglarse el pelo; **grey ~** canas fpl

hairband ['hɛəbænd] n cinta

hairbrush ['hɛəbrʌʃ] n cepillo (para el pelo)

haircut ['hɛəkʌt] n corte m de pelo

hairdo ['hɛədu:] n peinado

hairdresser ['hɛədrɛsə'] n peluquero(-a); **~'s** peluquería

hairdryer ['hɛədraɪə'] n secador m (de pelo)

hair gel n fijador

hairgrip ['hɛəgrɪp] n horquilla

hairnet ['hɛənet] n redecilla

hairpiece ['hɛəpi:s] n trenza postiza

hairpin ['hɛəpɪn] n horquilla

hairpin bend, hairpin curve (US) n curva muy cerrada

hair-raising ['hɛəreɪzɪŋ] adj espeluznante

hair spray n laca

hairstyle ['hɛəstaɪl] n peinado

hairy ['hɛərɪ] adj peludo, velludo; (inf: frightening) espeluznante

hake [heɪk] n merluza

half [hɑ:f] n (pl **halves** [hɑ:vz]) mitad f; (Sport: of match) tiempo, parte f; (: of ground) campo; (of beer) ≈ caña (Sp), media pinta; (Rail, Bus) billete m de niño ▷ adj medio ▷ adv medio, a medias; **~-an-hour** media hora; **two and a ~** dos y media; **~ a dozen** media docena; **~ a pound** media libra, ≈ 250 gr.; **to cut sth in** cortar algo por la mitad; **to go halves (with sb)** ir a medias (con algn); **~ empty/closed** medio vacío/entreabierto; **~ asleep** medio dormido; **~ past 3** las 3 y media

half-baked ['hɑ:f'beɪkt] adj (inf: idea, scheme) mal concebido or pensado

half board n (Brit: in hotel) media pensión

half-brother ['hɑ:fbrʌðə'] n hermanastro

half-caste ['hɑ:fkɑ:st] n mestizo(-a)

half day n medio día m, media jornada

half fare n medio pasaje m

half-hearted ['hɑ:f'hɑ:tɪd] adj indiferente, poco entusiasta

half-hour [hɑ:f'auə'] n media hora

half-mast ['hɑ:f'mɑ:st] n: **at ~** (flag) a media asta

h

halfpenny ['heɪpnɪ] n medio penique m
half-price ['hɑ:f'praɪs] adj a mitad de precio
half term n (Brit Scol) vacaciones de mediados del
trimestre
half-time [hɑ:f'taɪm] n descanso
halfway ['hɑ:f'weɪ] adv a medio camino; **to
meet sb ~** (fig) llegar a un acuerdo con algn
halfway house n centro de readaptación de
antiguos presos; (fig) solución f intermedia
half-wit ['hɑ:fwɪt] n (inf) zoquete m
hall [hɔ:l] n (for concerts) sala; (entrance way)
entrada, vestíbulo
hallmark ['hɔ:lmɑ:k] n (mark) rasgo
distintivo; (seal) sello
hallo [hə'ləu] excl = **hello**
hall of residence n (Brit) colegio mayor,
residencia universitaria
Hallowe'en [hæləu'i:n] n víspera de Todos
los Santos; ver nota

⬤ **HALLOWE'EN**
⬤
⬤   .
⬤ La tradición anglosajona dice que en
⬤ la noche del 31 de octubre, Hallowe'en,
⬤ víspera de Todos los Santos, es fácil ver
⬤ a brujas y fantasmas. Es una ocasión
⬤ festiva en la que los niños se disfrazan y
⬤ van de puerta en puerta llevando un farol
⬤ hecho con una calabaza en forma de
⬤ cabeza humana. Cuando se les abre
⬤ la puerta gritan "trick or treat" para
⬤ indicar que gastarán una broma a quien
⬤ no les dé un pequeño regalo (como
⬤ golosinas o dinero).

hallucination [həlu:sɪ'neɪʃən] n alucinación
f
hallway ['hɔ:lweɪ] n vestíbulo
halo ['heɪləu] n (of saint) aureola, halo
halt [hɔ:lt] n (stop) alto, parada; (Rail)
apeadero ▷ vt parar ▷ vi pararse; (process)
interrumpirse; **to call a ~ (to sth)** (fig) poner
fin (a algo)
halve [hɑ:v] vt partir por la mitad
halves [hɑ:vz] pl of **half**
ham [hæm] n jamón m (cocido); (inf: also:
radio ~) radioaficionado(-a) m(f); (: also:
~ actor) comicastro
hamburger ['hæmbə:gə^r] n hamburguesa
hamlet ['hæmlɪt] n aldea
hammer ['hæmə^r] n martillo ▷ vt (nail)
clavar; **to ~ a point home to sb** remacharle
un punto a algn; **hammer out** vt (metal)
forjar a martillo; (fig: solution, agreement)
elaborar (trabajosamente)
hammock ['hæmək] n hamaca
hamper ['hæmpə^r] vt estorbar ▷ n cesto
hamster ['hæmstə^r] n hámster m
hamstring ['hæmstrɪŋ] n (Anat) tendón m
de la corva
hand [hænd] n mano f; (of clock) aguja,
manecilla; (writing) letra; (worker) obrero;

(measurement: of horse) palmo ▷ vt (give) dar,
pasar; (deliver) entregar; **to give sb a ~** echar
una mano a algn, ayudar a algn; **to force
sb's ~** forzarle la mano a algn; **at ~** a mano;
in ~ entre manos; **we have the matter in ~**
tenemos el asunto entre manos; **to have in
one's ~** (knife, victory) tener en la mano; **to
have a free ~** tener carta blanca; **on ~** (person,
services) a mano, al alcance; **to ~** (information
etc) a mano; **on the one ~ ..., on the other ~
...** por una parte ... por otra (parte) ...; **hand
down** vt pasar, bajar; (tradition) transmitir;
(heirloom) dejar en herencia; (US: sentence,
verdict) imponer; **hand in** vt entregar; **hand
out** vt (leaflets, advice) repartir, distribuir;
hand over vt (deliver) entregar; (surrender)
ceder; **hand round** vt (Brit: information, papers)
pasar (de mano en mano); (: chocolates etc)
ofrecer
handbag ['hændbæg] n bolso, cartera (LAm)
hand baggage n = **hand luggage**
handbasin ['hændbeɪsn] n lavabo
handbook ['hændbuk] n manual m
handbrake ['hændbreɪk] n freno de mano
hand cream n crema para las manos
handcuffs ['hændkʌfs] npl esposas fpl
handful ['hændful] n puñado
hand-held ['hændhɛld] adj de mano
handicap ['hændɪkæp] n desventaja; (Sport)
hándicap m ▷ vt estorbar
handicapped ['hændɪkæpt] adj: **to be
mentally ~** ser mentalmente m/f
discapacitado; **to be physically ~** ser
minusválido(-a)
handicraft ['hændɪkrɑ:ft] n artesanía
handiwork ['hændɪwə:k] n manualidad(es)
f(pl); (fig) obra; **this looks like his ~** (pej) es
obra de él, parece
handkerchief ['hæŋkətʃɪf] n pañuelo
handle ['hændl] n (of door etc) pomo, tirador m;
(of cup etc) asa; (of knife etc) mango; (for winding)
manivela ▷ vt (touch) tocar; (deal with)
encargarse de; (treat: people) manejar;
"~ with care" "(manéjese) con cuidado";
to fly off the ~ perder los estribos
handlebar ['hændlbɑ:^r] n, **handlebars**
['hændlbɑ:z] npl manillar msg
hand luggage n equipaje m de mano
handmade ['hændmeɪd] adj hecho a mano
handout ['hændaut] n (distribution)
repartición f; (charity) limosna; (leaflet)
folleto, octavilla; (press handout) nota
handrail ['hændreɪl] n (on staircase etc)
pasamanos m inv, barandilla
handset ['hændsɛt] n (Tel) auricular m
hands-free ['hændzfri:] adj (Tel: telephone)
manos libres; **~ kit** manos libres m inv
handshake ['hændʃeɪk] n apretón m de
manos; (Comput) coloquio
handsome ['hænsəm] adj guapo
hands-on ['hændz'ɔn] adj práctico; **she has
a very ~ approach** le gusta tomar parte

activa; ~ **experience** (*Comput*) experiencia práctica

handstand ['hændstænd] *n* voltereta, salto mortal

handwriting ['hændraıtıŋ] *n* letra

handwritten ['hændrıtn] *adj* escrito a mano, manuscrito

handy ['hændı] *adj* (*close at hand*) a mano; (*useful: machine, tool etc*) práctico; (*skilful*) hábil, diestro; **to come in ~** venir bien

handyman ['hændımæn] *n* manitas *m inv*

hang (*pt, pp* **hung**) [hæŋ, hʌŋ] *vt* colgar; (*head*) bajar; (*criminal: pt, pp* **hanged**) ahorcar; **to get the ~ of sth** (*inf*) coger el tranquillo a algo; **hang about** *or* **around** *vi* haraganear; **hang back** *vi* (*hesitate*): **to ~ back (from doing)** vacilar (en hacer); **hang down** *vi* colgar, pender; **hang on** *vi* (*wait*) esperar ▷ *vt fus* (*depend on: decision etc*) depender de; **to ~ on to** (*keep*) guardar, quedarse con; **hang out** *vt* (*washing*) tender, colgar ▷ *vi* (*inf: live*) vivir; (: *often be found*) moverse; **to ~ out of sth** colgar fuera de algo; **hang round** *vi* = **hang around**; **hang together** *vi* (*cohere: argument etc*) sostenerse; **hang up** *vt* (*coat*) colgar ▷ *vi* (*Tel*) colgar; **to ~ up on sb** colgarle a algn

hangar ['hæŋəʳ] *n* hangar *m*

hanger ['hæŋəʳ] *n* percha

hanger-on [hæŋər'ɔn] *n* parásito

hang-gliding ['hæŋglaıdıŋ] *n* vuelo con ala delta

hanging ['hæŋıŋ] *n* (*execution*) ejecución *f* (en la horca)

hangover ['hæŋəuvəʳ] *n* (*after drinking*) resaca

hang-up ['hæŋʌp] *n* complejo

hanker ['hæŋkəʳ] *vi*: **to ~ after** (*miss*) echar de menos; (*long for*) añorar

hankie, hanky ['hæŋkı] *n abbr* = **handkerchief**

Hansard ['hænsɑːd] *n actas oficiales de las sesiones del parlamento británico*

haphazard [hæp'hæzəd] *adj* fortuito

happen ['hæpən] *vi* suceder, ocurrir; (*take place*) tener lugar, realizarse; (*chance*): **he ~ed to hear/see** dió la casualidad de que oyó/vió; **as it ~s** da la casualidad de que; **what's ~ing?** ¿qué pasa?; **happen (up)on** *vt fus* tropezar *or* dar con

happening ['hæpnıŋ] *n* suceso, acontecimiento

happily ['hæpılı] *adv* (*luckily*) afortunadamente; (*cheerfully*) alegremente

happiness ['hæpınıs] *n* (*contentment*) felicidad *f*; (*joy*) alegría

happy ['hæpı] *adj* feliz; (*cheerful*) alegre; **to be ~ (with)** estar contento (con); **yes, I'd be ~ to** sí, con mucho gusto; **H~ Christmas!** ¡Feliz Navidad!; **H~ New Year!** ¡Feliz Año Nuevo!; **~ birthday!** ¡Feliz cumpleaños!

happy-go-lucky ['hæpıgəu'lʌkı] *adj* despreocupado

happy hour *n horas en las que la bebida es más barata en un bar*

harass ['hærəs] *vt* acosar, hostigar

harassed ['hærəst] *adj* agobiado, presionado

harassment ['hærəsmənt] *n* persecución *f*, acoso; (*worry*) preocupación *f*

harbour, harbor (*US*) ['hɑːbəʳ] *n* puerto ▷ *vt* (*fugitive*) dar abrigo a; (*hope etc*) abrigar; (*hide*) dar abrigo a; (*retain: grudge etc*) guardar

hard [hɑːd] *adj* duro; (*difficult*) difícil; (*work*) arduo; (*person*) severo ▷ *adv* (*work*) mucho, duro; (*think*) profundamente; **to look ~ at sb/sth** clavar los ojos en algn/algo; **to try ~** esforzarse; **no ~ feelings!** ¡sin rencor(es)!; **to be ~ of hearing** ser duro de oído; **to be ~ done by** ser tratado injustamente; **to be ~ on sb** ser muy duro con algn; **I find it ~ to believe that ...** me cuesta trabajo creer que ...

hardback ['hɑːdbæk] *n* libro de tapa dura

hardboard ['hɑːdbɔːd] *n* aglomerado *m* (*de madera*)

hard cash *n* dinero en efectivo

hard copy *n* (*Comput*) copia impresa

hard-core ['hɑːd'kɔːʳ] *adj* (*pornography*) duro; (*supporters*) incondicional

hard disk *n* (*Comput*) disco duro

harden ['hɑːdn] *vt* endurecer; (*steel*) templar; (*fig*) curtir; (: *determination*) fortalecer ▷ *vi* (*substance*) endurecerse; (*fig*) curtirse

hard-headed ['hɑːd'hedıd] *adj* poco sentimental, realista

hard-hitting ['hɑːd'hıtıŋ] *adj* (*speech, article*) contundente

hard labour *n* trabajos *mpl* forzados

hardly ['hɑːdlı] *adv* (*scarcely*) apenas; **that can ~ be true** eso difícilmente puede ser cierto; **~ ever** casi nunca; **I can ~ believe it** apenas me lo puedo creer

hard sell *n* publicidad *f* agresiva; **~ techniques** técnicas *fpl* agresivas de venta

hardship ['hɑːdʃıp] *n* (*troubles*) penas *fpl*; (*financial*) apuro

hard shoulder *n* (*Aut*) arcén *m*

hard-up [hɑːd'ʌp] *adj* (*inf*) sin un duro (*Sp*), sin plata (*LAm*)

hardware ['hɑːdwɛəʳ] *n* ferretería; (*Comput*) hardware *m*

hardware shop, hardware store (*US*) *n* ferretería

hard-wearing [hɑːd'wɛərıŋ] *adj* resistente, duradero; (*shoes*) resistente

hard-won ['hɑːd'wʌn] *adj* ganado con esfuerzo

hard-working [hɑːd'wəːkıŋ] *adj* trabajador(a)

hardy ['hɑːdı] *adj* fuerte; (*plant*) resistente

hare [hɛəʳ] *n* liebre *f*

hare-brained ['hɛəbreınd] *adj* atolondrado

harem [hɑː'riːm] *n* harén *m*

hark back [hɑːk-] *vi*: **to ~ to** (*former days, earlier occasion*) recordar

harm [hɑːm] n daño, mal m ▷ vt (person) hacer
daño a; (health, interests) perjudicar; (thing)
dañar; **out of ~'s way** a salvo; **there's no ~
in trying** no se pierde nada con intentar
harmful ['hɑːmful] adj (gen) dañino;
(reputation) perjudicial
harmless ['hɑːmlɪs] adj (person) inofensivo;
(drug) inocuo; (joke etc) inocente
harmonica [hɑː'mɔnɪkə] n armónica
harmonize ['hɑːmənaɪz] vt, vi armonizar
harmony ['hɑːmənɪ] n armonía
harness ['hɑːnɪs] n arreos mpl ▷ vt (horse)
enjaezar; (resources) aprovechar
harp [hɑːp] n arpa ▷ vi: **to ~ on (about)**
machacar (con)
harpoon [hɑː'puːn] n arpón m
harrowing ['hærəuɪŋ] adj angustioso
harsh [hɑːʃ] adj (cruel) duro, cruel; (severe)
severo; (words) hosco; (colour) chillón(-ona);
(contrast) violento
harvest ['hɑːvɪst] n (harvest time) siega;
(of cereals etc) cosecha; (of grapes) vendimia
▷ vt, vi cosechar
has [hæz] vb see **have**
has-been ['hæzbiːn] n (inf: person) persona
acabada; (: thing) vieja gloria
hash [hæʃ] n (Culin) picadillo; (fig: mess) lío
hashish ['hæʃɪʃ] n hachís m
hasn't ['hæznt] = **has not**
hassle ['hæsl] n (inf) lío, rollo ▷ vt incordiar
haste [heɪst] n prisa
hasten ['heɪsn] vt acelerar ▷ vi darse prisa;
I ~ to add that ... me apresuro a añadir
que ...
hastily ['heɪstɪlɪ] adv de prisa
hasty ['heɪstɪ] adj apresurado
hat [hæt] n sombrero
hatch [hætʃ] n (Naut: also: **~way**) escotilla ▷ vi
salir del cascarón ▷ vt incubar; (fig: scheme,
plot) idear, tramar; **5 eggs have ~ed** han
salido 5 pollos
hatchback ['hætʃbæk] n (Aut) tres or cinco
puertas m
hatchet ['hætʃɪt] n hacha
hate [heɪt] vt odiar, aborrecer ▷ n odio; **I ~ to
trouble you, but ...** siento or lamento
molestarle, pero ...
hateful ['heɪtful] adj odioso
hatred ['heɪtrɪd] n odio
hat trick n: **to score a ~** (Brit Sport) marcar
tres tantos (or triunfos) seguidos
haughty ['hɔːtɪ] adj altanero, arrogante
haul [hɔːl] vt tirar, jalar (LAm); (by lorry)
transportar ▷ n (of fish) redada; (of stolen goods
etc) botín m
haulage ['hɔːlɪdʒ] n (Brit) transporte m; (costs)
gastos mpl de transporte
haulier ['hɔːlɪəʳ], **hauler** (US) ['hɔːləʳ] n
transportista m/f
haunch [hɔːntʃ] n anca; (of meat) pierna
haunt [hɔːnt] vt (ghost) aparecer en; (frequent)
frecuentar; (obsess) obsesionar ▷ n guarida

haunted ['hɔːntɪd] adj (castle etc) embrujado;
(look) de angustia
Havana [hə'vɑːnə] n La Habana

KEYWORD

have [hæv] (pt, pp **had**) aux vb **1** (gen) haber;
to have arrived/eaten haber llegado/
comido; **having finished** or **when he had
finished, he left** cuando hubo acabado,
se fue
2 (in tag questions): **you've done it, haven't
you?** lo has hecho, ¿verdad? or ¿no?
3 (in short answers and questions): **I haven't** no;
so I have pues, es verdad; **we haven't paid
— yes we have!** no hemos pagado — ¡sí que
hemos pagado!; **I've been there before,
have you?** he estado allí antes, ¿y tú?
▷ modal aux vb (be obliged): **to have (got) to do
sth** tener que hacer algo; **you haven't to
tell her** no hay que or no debes decírselo
▷ vt **1** (possess) tener; **he has (got) blue eyes/
dark hair** tiene los ojos azules/el pelo negro
2 (referring to meals etc): **to have breakfast/
lunch/dinner** desayunar/comer/cenar; **to
have a drink/a cigarette** tomar algo/fumar
un cigarrillo
3 (receive) recibir; (obtain) obtener; **may I have
your address?** ¿puedes darme tu dirección?;
you can have it for £5 te lo puedes quedar
por £5; **I must have it by tomorrow** lo
necesito para mañana; **to have a baby** tener
un niño or bebé
4 (maintain, allow): **I won't have it!** ¡no lo
permitiré!; **I won't have this nonsense!**
¡no permitiré estas tonterías!; **we can't have
that** no podemos permitir eso
5: **to have sth done** hacer or mandar hacer
algo; **to have one's hair cut** cortarse el pelo;
to have sb do sth hacer que algn haga algo
6 (experience, suffer): **to have a cold/flu** tener
un resfriado/la gripe; **she had her bag
stolen/her arm broken** le robaron el bolso/
se rompió un brazo; **to have an operation**
operarse
7 (+ noun): **to have a swim/walk/bath/rest**
nadar/dar un paseo/darse un baño/
descansar; **let's have a look** vamos a ver;
to have a meeting/party celebrar una
reunión/una fiesta; **let me have a try**
déjame intentarlo
have in vt: **to have it in for sb** (inf) tenerla
tomada con algn
have on vt: **have you anything on
tomorrow?** ¿vas a hacer algo mañana?;
I don't have any money on me no llevo
dinero (encima); **to have sb on** (Brit: (inf))
tomarle el pelo a algn
have out vt: **to have it out with sb** (settle a
problem etc) dejar las cosas en claro con algn

haven ['heɪvn] n puerto; (fig) refugio

haven't ['hævnt] = **have not**

havoc ['hævək] n estragos mpl; **to play ~ with sth** hacer estragos en algo

Hawaii [hə'waɪiː] n (Islas fpl) Hawai m

hawk [hɔːk] n halcón m ▷ vt (goods for sale) pregonar

hawthorn ['hɔːθɔːn] n espino

hay [heɪ] n heno

hay fever n fiebre f del heno

haystack ['heɪstæk] n almiar m

haywire ['heɪwaɪər] adj (inf): **to go ~** (person) volverse loco; (plan) irse al garete

hazard ['hæzəd] n riesgo; (danger) peligro ▷ vt (remark) aventurar; (one's life) arriesgar; **to be a health ~** ser un peligro para la salud; **to ~ a guess** aventurar una respuesta or hipótesis

hazardous ['hæzədəs] adj (dangerous) peligroso; (risky) arriesgado

hazard warning lights npl (Aut) señales fpl de emergencia

haze [heɪz] n neblina

hazel ['heɪzl] n (tree) avellano ▷ adj (eyes) color m de avellano

hazelnut ['heɪzlnʌt] n avellana

hazy ['heɪzɪ] adj brumoso; (idea) vago

h & c abbr (Brit) = **hot and cold (water)**

he [hiː] pron él; **he who ...** aquél que ..., quien ...

head [hɛd] n cabeza; (leader) jefe(-a) m(f) ▷ vt (list) encabezar; (group) capitanear; **~s (or tails)** cara (o cruz); **~ first** de cabeza; **~ over heels** patas arriba; **~ over heels in love** perdidamente enamorado; **on your ~ be it!** ¡allá tú!; **they went over my ~ to the manager** fueron directamente al gerente sin hacerme caso; **it was above or over their ~s** no alcanzaron a entenderlo; **to come to a ~** (fig: situation etc) llegar a un punto crítico; **to have a ~ for business** tener talento para los negocios; **to have no ~ for heights** no resistir las alturas; **to lose/keep one's ~** perder la cabeza/mantener la calma; **to sit at the ~ of the table** sentarse a la cabecera de la mesa; **to ~ the ball** cabecear (el balón); **head for** vt fus dirigirse a; (disaster) ir camino de; **head off** vt (threat, danger) evitar

headache ['hɛdeɪk] n dolor m de cabeza; **to have a ~** tener dolor de cabeza

headband ['hɛdbænd] n cinta (para la cabeza), vincha (LAm)

headdress ['hɛddrɛs] n (of bride, Indian) tocado

header ['hɛdər] n (Brit inf: Football) cabezazo; (: fall) caída de cabeza

headhunt ['hɛdhʌnt] vt: **to be ~ed** ser seleccionado por un cazatalentos

heading ['hɛdɪŋ] n título

headlamp ['hɛdlæmp] n (Brit) = **headlight**

headland ['hɛdlənd] n promontorio

headlight ['hɛdlaɪt] n faro

headline ['hɛdlaɪn] n titular m

headlong ['hɛdlɔŋ] adv (fall) de cabeza; (rush) precipitadamente

head office n oficina central, central f

head-on [hɛd'ɔn] adj (collision) de frente

headphones ['hɛdfəʊnz] npl auriculares mpl

headquarters ['hɛdkwɔːtəz] npl sede f central; (Mil) cuartel m general

head-rest ['hɛdrɛst] n reposa-cabezas m inv

headroom ['hɛdrum] n (in car) altura interior; (under bridge) (límite m de) altura

headscarf ['hɛdskɑːf] n pañuelo

headset ['hɛdsɛt] n cascos mpl

headstrong ['hɛdstrɔŋ] adj testarudo

head teacher n director(a)

head waiter n maître m

headway ['hɛdweɪ] n: **to make ~** (fig) hacer progresos

headwind ['hɛdwɪnd] n viento contrario

heady ['hɛdɪ] adj (experience, period) apasionante; (wine) fuerte

heal [hiːl] vt curar ▷ vi cicatrizar

health [hɛlθ] n salud f

health care n asistencia sanitaria

health centre n ambulatorio, centro médico

health food n, **health foods** npl alimentos mpl orgánicos

health hazard n riesgo para la salud

Health Service n (Brit) servicio de salud pública, ≈ Insalud m (Sp)

healthy ['hɛlθɪ] adj (gen) sano; (economy, bank balance) saludable

heap [hiːp] n montón m ▷ vt amontonar; (plate) colmar; **~s of** (inf: lots) montones de; **to ~ favours/praise/gifts etc on sb** colmar a algn de favores/elogios/regalos etc

hear (pt, pp **heard**) [hɪər, hɜːd] vt oír; (perceive) sentir; (listen to) escuchar; (lecture) asistir a; (Law: case) ver ▷ vi oír; **to ~ about** oír hablar de; **to ~ from sb** tener noticias de algn; **I've never ~d of that book** nunca he oído hablar de ese libro; **hear out** vt: **to ~ sb out** dejar que algn termine de hablar

heard [hɜːd] pt, pp of **hear**

hearing ['hɪərɪŋ] n (sense) oído; (Law) vista; **to give sb a ~** dar a algn la oportunidad de hablar, escuchar a algn

hearing aid n audífono

hearsay ['hɪəseɪ] n rumores mpl, habladurías fpl

hearse [hɜːs] n coche m fúnebre

heart [hɑːt] n corazón m; (fig) valor m; (of lettuce) cogollo; **hearts** npl (Cards) corazones mpl; **at ~** en el fondo; **by ~** (learn, know) de memoria; **to have a weak ~** tener el corazón débil; **to set one's ~ on sth/on doing sth** anhelar algo/hacer algo; **I did not have the ~ to tell her** no tuve valor para decírselo; **to take ~** cobrar ánimos; **the ~ of the matter** lo esencial or el meollo del asunto

heartache ['hɑːteɪk] n angustia

heart attack n infarto (de miocardio)

heartbeat ['hɑːtbiːt] n latido (del corazón)

heartbreak ['hɑːtbreɪk] n angustia, congoja

heartbreaking ['hɑːtbreɪkɪŋ] adj
desgarrador(a)

heartbroken ['hɑːtbrəʊkən] adj: **she was ~
about it** eso le partió el corazón

heartburn ['hɑːtbəːn] n acedía

heart disease n enfermedad f cardíaca

heartfelt ['hɑːtfɛlt] adj (cordial) cordial;
(deeply felt) sincero

hearth [hɑːθ] n (gen) hogar m; (fireplace)
chimenea

heartily ['hɑːtɪlɪ] adv sinceramente,
cordialmente; (laugh) a carcajadas; (eat) con
buen apetito; **to be ~ sick of** estar
completamente harto de

heartland ['hɑːtlænd] n zona interior or
central; (fig) corazón m

heartless ['hɑːtlɪs] adj despiadado

heart-to-heart ['hɑːtə'hɑːt] n (also: **~ talk**)
conversación f íntima

heart transplant n transplante m de
corazón

hearty ['hɑːtɪ] adj (person) campechano;
(laugh) sano; (dislike, support) absoluto

heat [hiːt] n (gen) calor m; (Sport: also:
qualifying ~) prueba eliminatoria; (Zool):
in or **on ~** en celo ▷ vt calentar; **heat up** vi
(gen) calentarse ▷ vt calentar

heated ['hiːtɪd] adj caliente; (fig) acalorado

heater ['hiːtər] n calentador m, estufa

heath [hiːθ] n (Brit) brezal m

heather ['hɛðər] n brezo

heating ['hiːtɪŋ] n calefacción f

heatstroke ['hiːtstrəʊk] n insolación f

heatwave ['hiːtweɪv] n ola de calor

heave [hiːv] vt (pull) tirar; (push) empujar con
esfuerzo; (lift) levantar (con esfuerzo) ▷ vi
(water) subir y bajar ▷ n tirón m; empujón m;
(effort) esfuerzo; (throw) echada; **to ~ a sigh**
dar or echar un suspiro, suspirar; **heave to** vi
(Naut) ponerse al pairo

heaven ['hɛvn] n cielo; (Rel) paraíso; **thank
~!** ¡gracias a Dios!; **for ~'s sake!** (pleading) ¡por
el amor de Dios!, ¡por lo que más quiera!;
(protesting) ¡por Dios!

heavenly ['hɛvnlɪ] adj celestial; (Rel) divino

heavily ['hɛvɪlɪ] adv pesadamente; (drink,
smoke) en exceso; (sleep, sigh) profundamente

heavy ['hɛvɪ] adj pesado; (work) duro; (sea,
rain, meal) fuerte; (drinker, smoker)
empedernido; (eater) comilón(-ona);
(responsibility) grave; (schedule) ocupado;
(weather) bochornoso

heavy goods vehicle n (Brit) vehículo
pesado

heavyweight ['hɛvɪweɪt] n (Sport) peso
pesado

Hebrew ['hiːbruː] adj, n (Ling) hebreo

Hebrides ['hɛbrɪdiːz] npl: **the ~** las Hébridas

heck [hɛk] n (inf): **why the ~ ...?** ¿por qué
porras ...?; **a ~ of a lot of** cantidad de

heckle ['hɛkl] vt interrumpir

heckler ['hɛklər] n el/la que interrumpe a un orador

hectare ['hɛktɑːr] n (Brit) hectárea

hectic ['hɛktɪk] adj agitado; (busy) ocupado

he'd [hiːd] = **he would; he had**

hedge [hɛdʒ] n seto ▷ vt cercar (con un seto)
▷ vi contestar con evasivas; **as a ~ against
inflation** como protección contra la
inflación; **to ~ one's bets** (fig) cubrirse

hedgehog ['hɛdʒhɔg] n erizo

heed [hiːd] vt (also: **take ~ of**: pay attention)
hacer caso de; (bear in mind) tener en cuenta;
to pay (no) ~ to, take (no) ~ of (no) hacer
caso a, (no) tener en cuenta

heedless ['hiːdlɪs] adj desatento

heel [hiːl] n talón m; (of shoe) tacón m ▷ vt
(shoe) poner tacón a; **to take to one's ~s** (inf)
poner pies en polvorosa; **to bring to ~** meter
en cintura; see also **dig**

hefty ['hɛftɪ] adj (person) fornido; (piece)
grande; (price) alto

heifer ['hɛfər] n novilla, ternera

height [haɪt] n (of person) talla, estatura; (of
building) altura; (high ground) cerro; (altitude)
altitud f; **what ~ are you?** ¿cuánto mides?;
of average ~ de estatura mediana; **to be
afraid of ~s** tener miedo a las alturas; **at the
~ of summer** en los días más calurosos del
verano; **it's the ~ of fashion** es el último
grito en moda

heighten ['haɪtn] vt elevar; (fig) aumentar

heir [ɛər] n heredero

heiress ['ɛərɛs] n heredera

heirloom ['ɛəluːm] n reliquia de familia

held [hɛld] pt, pp of **hold**

helicopter ['hɛlɪkɔptər] n helicóptero

helium ['hiːlɪəm] n helio

hell [hɛl] n infierno; **oh ~!** (inf) ¡demonios!,
¡caramba!

he'll [hiːl] = **he will; he shall**

hellish ['hɛlɪʃ] adj infernal; (inf) horrible

hello [hə'ləʊ] excl ¡hola!; (to attract attention)
¡oiga!; (surprise) ¡caramba!; (Tel) ¡dígame! (esp
Sp), ¡aló! (LAm)

helm [hɛlm] n (Naut) timón m

helmet ['hɛlmɪt] n casco

help [hɛlp] n ayuda; (cleaner etc) criada,
asistenta ▷ vt ayudar; **~!** ¡socorro!; **with the
~ of** con la ayuda de; **can I ~ you?** (in shop)
¿qué desea?; **to be of ~ to sb** servir a algn; **to
~ sb (to) do sth** echarle una mano or ayudar
a algn a hacer algo; **~ yourself** sírvete; **he
can't ~ it** no lo puede evitar; **help out** vi
ayudar, echar una mano ▷ vt: **to ~ sb out**
ayudar a algn, echar una mano a algn

helper ['hɛlpər] n ayudante m/f

helpful ['hɛlpful] adj útil; (person) servicial

helping ['hɛlpɪŋ] n ración f

helping hand n: **to give sb a ~** echar una
mano a algn

helpless ['hɛlplɪs] adj (incapable) incapaz;
(defenceless) indefenso

helpline ['hɛlplaɪn] n teléfono de asistencia
al público

hem [hɛm] n dobladillo ▷ vt poner or coser el dobladillo a; **hem in** vt cercar; **to feel ~med in** (fig) sentirse acosado

hematology [hi:mə'tɔlədʒɪ] n (US) = **haematology**

hemisphere ['hɛmɪsfɪə'] n hemisferio

hemophilia [hi:mə'fɪlɪə] n (US) = **haemophilia**

hemorrhage ['hɛmərɪdʒ] n (US) = **haemorrhage**

hemorrhoids ['hɛmərɔɪdz] npl (US) = **haemorrhoids**

hen [hɛn] n gallina; (female bird) hembra

hence [hɛns] adv (therefore) por lo tanto; **two years ~** de aquí a dos años

henceforth [hɛns'fɔ:θ] adv de hoy en adelante

henchman ['hɛntʃmən] n (pej) secuaz m

hen night n (inf) despedida de soltera

hepatitis [hɛpə'taɪtɪs] n hepatitis f inv

her [hə:'] pron (direct) la; (indirect) le; (stressed, after prep) ella ▷ adj su; see also **me**; **my**

herald ['hɛrəld] n (forerunner) precursor(a) m(f) ▷ vt anunciar

heraldry ['hɛrəldrɪ] n heráldica

herb [hə:b] n hierba

herbal ['hə:bl] adj de hierbas

herbal tea n infusión f de hierbas

herbicide ['hə:bɪsaɪd] n herbicida m

herd [hə:d] n rebaño; (of wild animals, swine) piara ▷ vt (drive, gather: animals) llevar en manada; (: people) reunir; **herd together** vt agrupar, reunir ▷ vi apiñarse, agruparse

here [hɪə'] adv aquí; **~!** (present) ¡presente!; **~ is/are** aquí está/están; **~ she is** aquí está; **come ~!** ¡ven aquí or acá!; **~ and there** aquí y allá

hereafter [hɪər'ɑ:ftə'] adv en el futuro ▷ n: **the ~** el más allá

hereby [hɪə'baɪ] adv (in letter) por la presente

hereditary [hɪ'rɛdɪtrɪ] adj hereditario

heresy ['hɛrəsɪ] n herejía

heretic ['hɛrətɪk] n hereje m/f

heritage ['hɛrɪtɪdʒ] n (gen) herencia; (fig) patrimonio; **our national ~** nuestro patrimonio nacional

hermit ['hə:mɪt] n ermitaño(-a)

hernia ['hə:nɪə] n hernia

hero (pl **heroes**) ['hɪərəu] n héroe m; (in book, film) protagonista m

heroic [hɪ'rəuɪk] adj heroico

heroin ['hɛrəuɪn] n heroína

heroine ['hɛrəuɪn] n heroína; (in book, film) protagonista

heron ['hɛrən] n garza

herring ['hɛrɪŋ] n arenque m

hers [hə:z] pron (el) suyo/(la) suya etc; **a friend of ~** un amigo suyo; **this is ~** esto es suyo or de ella; see also **mine**

herself [hə:'sɛlf] pron (reflexive) se; (emphatic) ella misma; (after prep) sí (misma); see also **oneself**

he's [hi:z] = **he is**; **he has**

hesitant ['hɛzɪtənt] adj indeciso; **to be ~ about doing sth** no decidirse a hacer algo

hesitate ['hɛzɪteɪt] vi dudar, vacilar; (in speech) titubear; (be unwilling) resistirse a; **don't ~ to ask (me)** no dudes en pedírmelo

hesitation [hɛzɪ'teɪʃən] n indecisión f; **I have no ~ in saying (that)** ... no tengo el menor reparo en afirmar que ...

heterosexual [hɛtərəu'sɛksjuəl] adj, n heterosexual m/f

het up [hɛt'ʌp] adj (inf) agitado, nervioso

hew [hju:] vt cortar

hexagon ['hɛksəgən] n hexágono

hey [heɪ] excl ¡oye!, ¡oiga!

heyday ['heɪdeɪ] n: **the ~ of** el apogeo de

HGV n abbr = **heavy goods vehicle**

hi [haɪ] excl ¡hola!

hiatus [haɪ'eɪtəs] n vacío, interrupción f; (Ling) hiato

hibernate ['haɪbəneɪt] vi invernar

hibernation [haɪbə'neɪʃən] n hibernación f

hiccough, hiccup ['hɪkʌp] vi hipar; **hiccoughs** npl hipo sg

hid [hɪd] pt of **hide**

hidden ['hɪdn] pp of **hide** ▷ adj: **there are no ~ extras** no hay suplementos ocultos; **~ agenda** plan m encubierto

hide [haɪd] (pt **hid**, pp **hidden**) n (skin) piel f ▷ vt esconder, ocultar; (feelings, truth) encubrir, ocultar ▷ vi: **to ~ (from sb)** esconderse or ocultarse (de algn)

hide-and-seek ['haɪdən'si:k] n escondite m

hideaway ['haɪdəweɪ] n escondite m

hideous ['hɪdɪəs] adj horrible

hiding ['haɪdɪŋ] n (beating) paliza; **to be in ~** (concealed) estar escondido

hierarchy ['haɪərɑ:kɪ] n jerarquía

hi-fi ['haɪfaɪ] abbr = **high fidelity** ▷ n estéreo, hifi m ▷ adj de alta fidelidad

high [haɪ] adj (tall, speed, number) grande, alto; (price) elevado; (wind) fuerte; (voice) agudo; (inf: on drugs) colocado; (: on drink) borracho; (Culin: meat, game) pasado; (: spoilt) estropeado ▷ adv alto, a gran altura ▷ n: **exports have reached a new ~** las exportaciones han alcanzado niveles inusitados; **it is 20 m ~** tiene 20 m de altura; **~ in the air** en las alturas; **to pay a ~ price for sth** pagar algo muy caro

highbrow ['haɪbrau] adj culto

highchair ['haɪtʃɛə'] n silla alta (para niños)

high-class ['haɪ'klɑ:s] adj (neighbourhood) de alta sociedad; (hotel) de lujo; (person) distinguido, de categoría; (food) de alta categoría

High Court n (Law) tribunal m supremo; ver nota

higher ['haɪə'] adj (form of life, study etc) superior ▷ adv más alto ▷ n (Scottish Scol): **H~** cada una de las asignaturas que se estudian entre los 16 y los 17 años generalmente, así como el certificado de haberlas probado

higher education n educación f or enseñanza superior
high-flier, high-flyer [haɪˈflaɪəʳ] n ambicioso(-a)
high-handed [haɪˈhændɪd] adj despótico
high heels npl (heels) tacones mpl altos; (shoes) zapatos mpl de tacón
highjack [ˈhaɪdʒæk] vb, n = **hijack**
high jump n (Sport) salto de altura
highlands [ˈhaɪləndz] npl tierras fpl altas; **the H~** (in Scotland) las Tierras Altas de Escocia
highlight [ˈhaɪlaɪt] n (fig: of event) punto culminante ▷ vt subrayar; **highlights** npl (in hair) reflejos mpl
highlighter n rotulador
highly [ˈhaɪlɪ] adv sumamente; **~ paid** muy bien pagado; **to speak ~ of** hablar muy bien de; **~ strung** muy excitable
highness [ˈhaɪnɪs] n altura; **Her** or **His H~** Su Alteza
high-pitched [haɪˈpɪtʃt] adj agudo
high-rise [ˈhaɪraɪz] n (also: **~ block, ~ building**) torre f de pisos
high school n centro de enseñanza secundaria, ≈ Instituto Nacional de Bachillerato (Sp), liceo (LAm)
high season n (Brit) temporada alta
high street n (Brit) calle f mayor
high-tech (inf) adj al-tec (fam), de alta tecnología
high tide n marea alta
highway [ˈhaɪweɪ] n carretera; (US) autopista
Highway Code n (Brit) código de la circulación
hijack [ˈhaɪdʒæk] vt secuestrar ▷ n (also: **~ing**) secuestro
hijacker [ˈhaɪdʒækəʳ] n secuestrador(a) m(f)
hike [haɪk] vi (go walking) ir de excursión (a pie); (tramp) caminar ▷ n caminata; (inf: in prices etc) aumento; **hike up** vt (raise) aumentar
hiker [ˈhaɪkəʳ] n excursionista m/f
hiking [ˈhaɪkɪŋ] n senderismo
hilarious [hɪˈlɛərɪəs] adj divertidísimo
hill [hɪl] n colina; (high) montaña; (slope) cuesta
hillside [ˈhɪlsaɪd] n ladera
hilltop [ˈhɪltɔp] n cumbre f
hill walking n senderismo (de montaña)
hilly [ˈhɪlɪ] adj montañoso; (uneven) accidentado
hilt [hɪlt] n (of sword) empuñadura; **to the ~** (fig: support) incondicionalmente; **to be in debt up to the ~** estar hasta el cuello de deudas
him [hɪm] pron (direct) le, lo; (indirect) le; (stressed, after prep) él; see also **me**
Himalayas [hɪməˈleɪəz] npl: **the ~** el Himalaya
himself [hɪmˈsɛlf] pron (reflexive) se; (emphatic) él mismo; (after prep) sí (mismo); see also **oneself**

hind [haɪnd] adj posterior ▷ n cierva
hinder [ˈhɪndəʳ] vt estorbar, impedir
hindrance [ˈhɪndrəns] n estorbo, obstáculo
hindsight [ˈhaɪndsaɪt] n percepción f tardía or retrospectiva; **with ~** en retrospectiva; **with the benefit of ~** con la perspectiva del tiempo transcurrido
Hindu [ˈhɪnduː] n hindú m/f
Hinduism [ˈhɪnduːɪzm] n (Rel) hinduismo
hinge [hɪndʒ] n bisagra, gozne m ▷ vi (fig): **to ~ on** depender de
hint [hɪnt] n indirecta; (advice) consejo ▷ vt: **to ~ that** insinuar que ▷ vi: **to ~ at** aludir a; **to drop a ~** soltar or tirar una indirecta; **give me a ~** dame una pista
hip [hɪp] n cadera; (Bot) escaramujo
hippie [ˈhɪpɪ] n hippie m/f, jipi m/f
hippo [ˈhɪpəu] (pl **hippos**) n hipopótamo
hippopotamus (pl **hippopotamuses** or **hippopotami**) [hɪpəˈpɔtəməs, -ˈpɔtəmaɪ] n hipopótamo
hippy [ˈhɪpɪ] n = **hippie**
hire [ˈhaɪəʳ] vt (Brit: car, equipment) alquilar; (worker) contratar ▷ n alquiler m; **for ~** se alquila; (taxi) libre; **on ~** de alquiler; **hire out** vt alquilar, arrendar
hire car, hired car n (Brit) coche m de alquiler
hire purchase n (Brit) compra a plazos; **to buy sth on ~** comprar algo a plazos
his [hɪz] pron (el) suyo/(la) suya etc ▷ adj su; **this is ~** esto es suyo or de él; see also **my; mine**
Hispanic [hɪsˈpænɪk] adj hispánico
hiss [hɪs] vi sisear; (in protest) silbar ▷ n siseo; silbido
historian [hɪˈstɔːrɪən] n historiador(a) m(f)
historic [hɪˈstɔrɪk], **historical** [hɪˈstɔrɪkl] adj histórico
history [ˈhɪstərɪ] n historia; **there's a long ~ of that illness in his family** esa enfermedad corre en su familia
hit [hɪt] vt (pt, pp **hit**) (strike) golpear, pegar; (reach: target) alcanzar; (collide with: car) chocar contra; (fig: affect) afectar ▷ n golpe m; (success) éxito; (on website) visita; (in web search) correspondencia; **to ~ the headlines** salir en primera plana; **to ~ the road** (inf) largarse; **to ~ it off with sb** llevarse bien con algn; **hit back** vi defenderse; (fig) devolver golpe por golpe; **hit out at** vt fus asestar un golpe a; (fig) atacar; **hit (up)on** vt fus (answer) dar con; (solution) hallar, encontrar
hit-and-run driver [ˈhɪtənˈrʌn-] n conductor que tras atropellar a algn se da a la fuga
hitch [hɪtʃ] vt (fasten) atar, amarrar; (also: **~ up**) arremangarse ▷ n (difficulty) problema, pega; **to ~ a lift** hacer autostop; **technical ~** problema m técnico; **hitch up** vt (horse, cart) enganchar, uncir
hitch-hike [ˈhɪtʃhaɪk] vi hacer autostop
hitch-hiker [ˈhɪtʃhaɪkəʳ] n autostopista m/f
hitch-hiking [ˈhɪtʃhaɪkɪŋ] n autostop m
hi-tech [haɪˈtɛk] adj de alta tecnología

hitherto ['hɪðə'tu:] *adv* hasta ahora, hasta aquí

hit list *n* lista negra

hitman ['hɪtmæn] *n* asesino a sueldo

HIV *n abbr* (= *human immunodeficiency virus*) VIH *m*; **~-negative** VIH negativo; **~-positive** VIH positivo, seropositivo

hive [haɪv] *n* colmena; **the shop was a ~ of activity** (*fig*) la tienda era una colmena humana; **hive off** *vt* (*inf: separate*) separar; (: *privatize*) privatizar

HM *abbr* (= His (or Her) Majesty) S.M.

HMS *abbr* = **His (or Her) Majesty's Ship**

HMSO *n abbr* (Brit: = His (or Her) Majesty's Stationery Office) distribuidor oficial de las publicaciones del gobierno del Reino Unido

HNC *n abbr* (Brit: = Higher National Certificate) título académico

HND *n abbr* (Brit: = Higher National Diploma) título académico

hoard [hɔːd] *n* (*treasure*) tesoro; (*stockpile*) provisión *f* ⊳ *vt* acumular

hoarding ['hɔːdɪŋ] *n* (*for posters*) valla publicitaria

hoarse [hɔːs] *adj* ronco

hoax [həʊks] *n* engaño

hob [hɔb] *n* quemador *m*

hobble ['hɔbl] *vi* cojear

hobby ['hɔbɪ] *n* pasatiempo, afición *f*

hobby-horse ['hɔbɪhɔːs] *n* (*fig*) tema preferido

hobo ['həʊbəʊ] *n* (US) vagabundo

hockey ['hɔkɪ] *n* hockey *m*

hockey stick *n* palo *m* de hockey

hodge-podge ['hɔdʒpɔdʒ] *n* (US) = **hotchpotch**

hog [hɔg] *n* cerdo, puerco ⊳ *vt* (*fig*) acaparar; **to go the whole ~** echar el todo por el todo

Hogmanay [hɔgmə'neɪ] *n* (Scottish) Nochevieja; *ver nota*

⬤ HOGMANAY
⬤
⬤ La Nochevieja o "New Year's Eve" se
⬤ conoce como "Hogmanay" en Escocia,
⬤ donde se festeja de forma especial.
⬤ La familia y los amigos suelen juntar
⬤ para oír las campanadas del reloj y luego
⬤ se hace el "first-footing", costumbre que
⬤ consiste en visitar a los amigos y vecinos
⬤ llevando algo de beber (generalmente
⬤ whisky) y un trozo de carbón que se
⬤ supone que traerá buena suerte para
⬤ el año entrante.

hoist [hɔɪst] *n* (*crane*) grúa ⊳ *vt* levantar, alzar

hold [həʊld] (*pt, pp* **held**) *vt* sostener; (*contain*) contener; (*have: power, qualification*) tener; (*keep back*) retener; (*believe*) sostener; (*take hold of*) coger (Sp), agarrar (LAm); (*bear: weight*) soportar; (*meeting*) celebrar ⊳ *vi* (*withstand:*

pressure) resistir; (*be valid*) ser válido; (*stick*) pegarse ⊳ *n* (*grasp*) asimiento; (*fig*) dominio; (*Wrestling*) presa; (*Naut*) bodega; **~ the line!** (*Tel*) ¡no cuelgue!; **to ~ one's own** (*fig*) defenderse; **to ~ office** (*Pol*) ocupar un cargo; **to ~ firm** *or* **fast** mantenerse firme; **he ~s the view that …** opina *or* es su opinión que …; **to ~ sb responsible for sth** culpar *or* echarle la culpa a algn de algo; **where can I get ~ of …?** ¿dónde puedo encontrar (a) …?; **to catch** *or* **get (a) ~ of** agarrarse *or* asirse de; **hold back** *vt* retener; (*secret*) ocultar; **to ~ sb back from doing sth** impedir a algn hacer algo, impedir que algn haga algo; **hold down** *vt* (*person*) sujetar; (*job*) mantener; **hold forth** *vi* perorar; **hold off** *vt* (*enemy*) rechazar ⊳ *vi*: **if the rain ~s off** si no llueve; **hold on** *vi* agarrarse bien; (*wait*) esperar; **~ on!** (*Tel*) ¡(espere) un momento!; **hold on to** *vt fus* agarrarse a; (*keep*) guardar; **hold out** *vt* ofrecer ⊳ *vi* (*resist*) resistir; **to ~ out (against)** resistir (a), sobrevivir; **hold over** *vt* (*meeting etc*) aplazar; **hold up** *vt* (*raise*) levantar; (*support*) apoyar; (*delay*) retrasar; (: *traffic*) demorar; (*rob: bank*) asaltar, atracar

holdall ['həʊldɔːl] *n* (Brit) bolsa

holder ['həʊldər] *n* (*of ticket, record*) poseedor(a) *m(f)*; (*of passport, post, office, title etc*) titular *m/f*

holding ['həʊldɪŋ] *n* (*share*) participación *f*

holdup ['həʊldʌp] *n* (*robbery*) atraco; (*delay*) retraso; (Brit: *in traffic*) embotellamiento

hole [həʊl] *n* agujero ⊳ *vt* agujerear; **~ in the heart** (*Med*) boquete *m* en el corazón; **to pick ~s in** (*fig*) encontrar defectos en; **the ship was ~d** se abrió una vía de agua en el barco; **hole up** *vi* esconderse

holiday ['hɔlədɪ] *n* vacaciones *fpl*; (*day off*) (día *m* de) fiesta, día *m* festivo *or* feriado (LAm); **on ~** de vacaciones; **to be on ~** estar de vacaciones

holiday camp *n* colonia *or* centro vacacional; (*for children*) colonia veraniega infantil

holiday job *n* (Brit) trabajo para las vacaciones

holidaymaker ['hɔlədɪmeɪkər] *n* (Brit) turista *m/f*

holiday pay *n* paga de las vacaciones

holiday resort *n* centro turístico

Holland ['hɔlənd] *n* Holanda

holler ['hɔlər] *vi* (*inf*) gritar, vocear

hollow ['hɔləʊ] *adj* hueco; (*fig*) vacío; (*eyes*) hundido; (*sound*) sordo ⊳ *n* (*gen*) hueco; (*in ground*) hoyo ⊳ *vt*: **to ~ out** ahuecar

holly ['hɔlɪ] *n* acebo

Hollywood ['hɔlɪwʊd] *n* Hollywood *m*

holocaust ['hɔləkɔːst] *n* holocausto

hologram ['hɔləgræm] *n* holograma *m*

holster ['həʊlstər] *n* pistolera

holy ['həʊlɪ] *adj* (*gen*) santo, sagrado; (*water*) bendito; **the H~ Father** el Santo Padre

Holy Communion *n* Sagrada Comunión *f*

Holy Ghost, Holy Spirit *n* Espíritu *m* Santo

h

homage ['hɔmɪdʒ] n homenaje m; **to pay ~ to** rendir homenaje a

home [həʊm] n casa; (country) patria; (institution) asilo; (Comput) punto inicial or de partida ▷ adj (domestic) casero, de casa; (Econ, Pol) nacional; (Sport: team) de casa; (: match, win) en casa ▷ adv (direction) a casa; **at ~** en casa; **to go/come ~** ir/volver a casa; **make yourself at ~** ¡estás en tu casa!; **it's near my ~** está cerca de mi casa; **home in on** vt fus (missile) dirigirse hacia

home address n domicilio

home-brew [həʊm'bru:] n cerveza etc casera

Home Counties npl condados que rodean Londres

home economics n economía doméstica

home help n (Brit) trabajador(a) m(f) del servicio de atención domiciliaria

homeland ['həʊmlænd] n tierra natal

homeless ['həʊmlɪs] adj sin hogar, sin casa ▷ npl: **the ~** las personas sin hogar

homely ['həʊmlɪ] adj (domestic) casero; (simple) sencillo

home-made [həʊm'meɪd] adj casero

home match n partido en casa

Home Office n (Brit) Ministerio del Interior

homeopathy etc [həʊmɪ'ɔpəθɪ] (US) = **homoeopathy** etc

home owner n propietario(-a) m/f de una casa

home page n (Comput) página de inicio

home rule n autonomía

Home Secretary n (Brit) Ministro del Interior

homesick ['həʊmsɪk] adj: **to be ~** tener morriña or nostalgia

home town n ciudad f natal

home truth n: **to tell sb a few ~s** decir cuatro verdades a algn

homeward ['həʊmwəd] adj (journey) de vuelta ▷ adv hacia casa

homework ['həʊmwə:k] n deberes mpl

homicidal [hɔmɪ'saɪdl] adj homicida

homicide ['hɔmɪsaɪd] n (US) homicidio

homoeopath, homeopath (US) ['həʊmɪəʊpæθ] n homeópata m/f

homoeopathic, homeopathic (US) [həʊmɪəʊ'pæθɪk] adj homeopático

homoeopathy, homeopathy (US) [həʊmɪ'ɔpəθɪ] n homeopatía

homogeneous [hɔmə'dʒi:nɪəs] adj homogéneo

homosexual [hɔməʊ'sɛksjuəl] adj, n homosexual m/f

Hon abbr (= honourable, honorary) en títulos

Honduras [hɔn'djʊərəs] n Honduras fpl

honest ['ɔnɪst] adj honrado; (sincere) franco, sincero; **to be quite ~ with you ...** para serte franco ...

honestly ['ɔnɪstlɪ] adv honradamente; francamente, de verdad

honesty ['ɔnɪstɪ] n honradez f

honey ['hʌnɪ] n miel f; (US inf) cariño; (: to strangers) guapo, linda

honeycomb ['hʌnɪkəʊm] n panal m; (fig) laberinto

honeymoon ['hʌnɪmu:n] n luna de miel

honeysuckle ['hʌnɪsʌkl] n madreselva

Hong Kong ['hɔŋ'kɔŋ] n Hong-Kong m

honk [hɔŋk] vi (Aut) tocar la bocina

honorary ['ɔnərərɪ] adj no remunerado; (duty, title) honorífico; **~ degree** doctorado honoris causa

honour, honor (US) ['ɔnəʳ] vt honrar; (commitment, promise) cumplir con ▷ n honor m, honra; **in ~ of** en honor de; **it's a great ~** es un gran honor

honourable, honorable (US) ['ɔnərəbl] adj honrado, honorable

honours degree n (Univ) licenciatura superior

honours list n (Brit) lista de distinciones honoríficas que entrega la reina; ver nota

Hons. [ɔnz] abbr (Univ) = **hono(u)rs degree**

hood [hʊd] n capucha; (Brit Aut) capota; (US Aut) capó m; (US inf) matón m; (of cooker) campana de humos

hoodie ['hʊdɪ] n (pullover) sudadera f con capucha; (young person) capuchero(-a) m(f)

hoof (pl **hoofs** or **hooves**) [hu:f, hu:vz] n pezuña

hook [hʊk] n gancho; (on dress) corchete m, broche m; (for fishing) anzuelo ▷ vt enganchar; **~s and eyes** corchetes mpl, macho y hembra m; **by ~ or by crook** por las buenas o por las malas, cueste lo que cueste; **to be ~ed on** (inf) estar enganchado a; **hook up** vt (Radio, TV) transmitir en cadena

hooligan ['hu:lɪgən] n gamberro

hooliganism ['hu:lɪgənɪzəm] n gamberrismo

hoop [hu:p] n aro

hooray [hu:'reɪ] excl = **hurrah**

hoot [hu:t] vi (Brit Aut) tocar la bocina; (siren) sonar; (owl) ulular ▷ n bocinazo, toque m de sirena; **to ~ with laughter** morirse de risa

hooter ['hu:təʳ] n (Brit Aut) bocina; (of ship, factory) sirena

hoover® ['hu:vəʳ] (Brit) n aspiradora ▷ vt pasar la aspiradora por

hooves [hu:vz] pl of **hoof**

hop [hɔp] vi saltar, brincar; (on one foot) saltar con un pie ▷ n salto, brinco; see also **hops**

hope [həʊp] vt, vi esperar ▷ n esperanza; **I ~ so/not** espero que sí/no

hopeful ['həʊpful] adj (person) optimista; (situation) prometedor(a); **I'm ~ that she'll manage to come** confío en que podrá venir

hopefully ['həʊpfulɪ] adv con optimismo, con esperanza; **~ he will recover** esperamos que se recupere

hopeless ['həʊplɪs] adj desesperado

hops [hɔps] npl lúpulo sg

horizon [hə'raɪzn] n horizonte m

horizontal [hɔrɪ'zɔntl] adj horizontal

hormone ['hɔːməʊn] n hormona
horn [hɔːn] n cuerno, cacho (LAm); (Mus: also: **French ~**) trompa; (Aut) bocina, claxon m
hornet ['hɔːnɪt] n avispón m
horny ['hɔːnɪ] adj (material) córneo; (hands) calloso; (US inf) cachondo
horoscope ['hɔrəskəʊp] n horóscopo
horrendous [hɔ'rɛndəs] adj horrendo
horrible ['hɔrɪbl] adj horrible
horrid ['hɔrɪd] adj horrible, horroroso
horrific [hɔ'rɪfɪk] adj (accident) horroroso; (film) horripilante
horrify ['hɔrɪfaɪ] vt horrorizar
horrifying ['hɔrɪfaɪɪŋ] adj horroroso
horror ['hɔrər] n horror m
horror film n película de terror or miedo
hors d'œuvre [ɔː'dəːvrə] n entremeses mpl
horse [hɔːs] n caballo
horseback ['hɔːsbæk] n: **on ~** a caballo
horse chestnut n (tree) castaño de Indias; (nut) castaña de Indias
horseman ['hɔːsmən] n jinete m
horsepower ['hɔːspaʊər] n caballo (de fuerza), potencia en caballos
horse-racing ['hɔːsreɪsɪŋ] n carreras fpl de caballos
horseradish ['hɔːsrædɪʃ] n rábano picante
horse riding n (Brit) equitación f
horseshoe ['hɔːsʃuː] n herradura
hose [həʊz] n (also: **~pipe**) manguera; **hose down** vt limpiar con manguera
hospice ['hɔspɪs] n hospicio
hospitable ['hɔspɪtəbl] adj hospitalario
hospital ['hɔspɪtl] n hospital m
hospitality [hɔspɪ'tælɪtɪ] n hospitalidad f
host [həʊst] n anfitrión m; (TV, Radio) presentador(a) m(f); (of inn etc) mesonero; (Rel) hostia; (large number): **a ~ of** multitud de
hostage ['hɔstɪdʒ] n rehén m
hostel ['hɔstl] n hostal m; (for students, nurses etc) residencia; (also: **youth ~**) albergue m juvenil; (for homeless people) hospicio
hostess ['həʊstɪs] n anfitriona; (Brit: air hostess) azafata; (TV, Radio) presentadora; (in night-club) señorita de compañía
hostile ['hɔstaɪl] adj hostil
hostility [hɔ'stɪlɪtɪ] n hostilidad f
hot [hɔt] adj caliente; (weather) caluroso, de calor; (as opposed to only warm) muy caliente; (spicy) picante; (fig) ardiente, acalorado; **to be ~** (person) tener calor, (object) estar caliente; (weather) hacer calor; **hot up** vi (inf: situation) ponerse difícil or apurado; (: party) animarse ▷ vt (inf: pace) apretar; (: engine) aumentar la potencia de
hotbed ['hɔtbɛd] n (fig) semillero
hotchpotch ['hɔtʃpɔtʃ] n mezcolanza, baturrillo
hot dog n perrito caliente
hotel [həʊ'tɛl] n hotel m
hotelier [həʊ'tɛlɪər] n hotelero

hot-headed [hɔt'hɛdɪd] adj exaltado
hothouse ['hɔthaʊs] n invernadero
hot line n (Pol) teléfono rojo, línea directa
hotly ['hɔtlɪ] adv con pasión, apasionadamente
hotplate ['hɔtpleɪt] n (on cooker) hornillo
hot potato n (Brit inf) asunto espinoso; **to drop sth/sb like a ~** no querer saber ya nada de algo/algn
hot seat n primera fila
hotspot ['hɔtspɔt] n (Comput: also: **wireless ~**) punto de acceso inalámbrico
hot spot n (trouble spot) punto caliente; (night club etc) lugar m popular
hot-water bottle [hɔt'wɔːtə-] n bolsa de agua caliente
hot-wire ['hɔtwaɪər] vt (inf: car) hacer el puente en
hound [haʊnd] vt acosar ▷ n perro de caza
hour ['aʊər] n hora; **at 30 miles an ~** a 30 millas por hora; **lunch ~** la hora del almuerzo or de comer; **to pay sb by the ~** pagar a algn por horas
hourly ['aʊəlɪ] adj (de) cada hora; (rate) por hora ▷ adv cada hora
house n [haʊs] (pl **houses** ['haʊzɪz]) casa; (Pol) cámara; (Theat) sala ▷ vt [haʊz] (person) alojar; **at/to my ~** en/a mi casa; **the H~ of Commons/Lords** (Brit) la Cámara de los Comunes/Lores; **the H~ of Representatives** (US) la Cámara de Representantes; **it's on the ~** (fig) la casa invita
house arrest n arresto domiciliario
houseboat ['haʊsbəʊt] n casa flotante
housebound ['haʊsbaʊnd] adj confinado en casa
housebreaking ['haʊsbreɪkɪŋ] n allanamiento de morada
housecoat ['haʊskəʊt] n bata
household ['haʊshəʊld] n familia
householder ['haʊshəʊldər] n propietario(-a); (head of house) cabeza de familia
housekeeper ['haʊskiːpər] n ama de llaves
housekeeping ['haʊskiːpɪŋ] n (work) trabajos mpl domésticos; (Comput) gestión f interna; (also: **~ money**) dinero para gastos domésticos
house plant n planta de interior
house-proud ['haʊspraʊd] adj preocupado por el embellecimiento de la casa
house-warming ['haʊswɔːmɪŋ] n (also: **~ party**) fiesta de estreno de una casa
housewife ['haʊswaɪf] n ama de casa
house wine n vino m de la casa
housework ['haʊswəːk] n faenas fpl (de la casa)
housing ['haʊzɪŋ] n (act) alojamiento; (houses) viviendas fpl ▷ cpd (problem, shortage) de (la) vivienda
housing association n asociación f de la vivienda

housing benefit n (Brit) subsidio por alojamiento
housing development, housing estate (Brit) n urbanización f
hovel ['hɔvl] n casucha
hover ['hɔvəʳ] vi flotar (en el aire); (helicopter) cernerse; **to ~ on the brink of disaster** estar al borde mismo del desastre
hovercraft ['hɔvəkrɑːft] n aerodeslizador m, hovercraft m
how [hau] adv cómo; **~ are you?** ¿cómo estás?; (formal) ¿cómo está usted?; **~ do you do?** encantado, mucho gusto; **~ far is it to ...?** ¿qué distancia hay de aquí a ...?; **~ long have you been here?** ¿cuánto (tiempo) hace que estás aquí?, ¿cuánto (tiempo) llevas aquí?; **~ lovely!** ¡qué bonito!; **~ many/much?** ¿cuántos/cuánto?; **~ much does it cost?** ¿cuánto cuesta?; **~ old are you?** ¿cuántos años tienes?; **~ is school?** ¿qué tal la escuela?; **~ was the film?** ¿qué tal la película?; **~ about a drink?** ¿te gustaría algo de beber?, ¿qué te parece una copa?
however [hau'ɛvəʳ] adv de cualquier manera; (+ adjective) por muy ... que; (in questions) cómo ▷ conj sin embargo, no obstante; **~ I do it** lo haga como lo haga; **~ cold it is** por mucho frío que haga; **~ did you do it?** ¿cómo lo hiciste?
howl [haul] n aullido ▷ vi aullar; (person) dar alaridos; (wind) ulular
HP n abbr (Brit) = **hire purchase**
hp abbr (Aut) = **horsepower**
HQ n abbr = **headquarters**
HR n abbr (US) = **House of Representatives; human resources**
hr, hrs abbr (= hour(s)) h
HRH abbr (= His (or Her) Royal Highness) S.A.R.
HTML n abbr (Comput: = hypertext markup language) HTML m
hub [hʌb] n (of wheel) cubo; (fig) centro
hubbub ['hʌbʌb] n barahúnda, barullo
hubcap ['hʌbkæp] n tapacubos m inv
huddle ['hʌdl] vi: **to ~ together** amontonarse
hue [hju:] n color m, matiz m; **~ and cry** n protesta
huff [hʌf] n: **in a ~** enojado
hug [hʌg] vt abrazar ▷ n abrazo
huge [hju:dʒ] adj enorme
hulk [hʌlk] n (ship) barco viejo; (person, building etc) mole f
hull [hʌl] n (of ship) casco
hullo [hə'ləu] excl = **hello**
hum [hʌm] vt tararear, canturrear ▷ vi tararear, canturrear; (insect) zumbar ▷ n (Elec) zumbido; (of traffic, machines) zumbido, ronroneo; (of voices etc) murmullo
human ['hju:mən] adj humano ▷ n (also: **~ being**) ser m humano
humane [hju:'meɪn] adj humano, humanitario

humanitarian [hju:mænɪ'tɛərɪən] adj humanitario
humanity [hju:'mænɪtɪ] n humanidad f
human rights npl derechos mpl humanos
humble ['hʌmbl] adj humilde ▷ vt humillar
humbug ['hʌmbʌg] n patrañas fpl; (Brit: sweet) caramelo de menta
humdrum ['hʌmdrʌm] adj (boring) monótono, aburrido; (routine) rutinario
humid ['hju:mɪd] adj húmedo
humidity [hju:'mɪdɪtɪ] n humedad f
humiliate [hju:'mɪlɪeɪt] vt humillar
humiliating [hju:'mɪlɪeɪtɪŋ] adj humillante, vergonzoso
humiliation [hju:mɪlɪ'eɪʃən] n humillación f
humility [hju:'mɪlɪtɪ] n humildad f
hummus ['huməs] n humus m
humorous ['hju:mərəs] adj gracioso, divertido
humour, humor (US) ['hju:məʳ] n humorismo, sentido del humor; (mood) humor m ▷ vt (person) complacer; **sense of ~** sentido del humor; **to be in a good/bad ~** estar de buen/mal humor
hump [hʌmp] n (in ground) montículo; (camel's) giba
hunch [hʌntʃ] n (premonition) presentimiento; **I have a ~ that** tengo la corazonada or el presentimiento de que
hunchback ['hʌntʃbæk] n jorobado(-a)
hunched [hʌntʃt] adj jorobado
hundred ['hʌndrəd] num ciento; (before n) cien; **about a ~ people** unas cien personas, alrededor de cien personas; **~s of** centenares de; **~s of people** centenares de personas; **I'm a ~ per cent sure** estoy completamente seguro
hundredth ['hʌndrɪdθ] adj centésimo
hundredweight ['hʌndrədweɪt] n (Brit) = 50.8 kg; 112 lb; (US) = 45.3 kg; 100 lb
hung [hʌŋ] pt, pp of **hang**
Hungarian [hʌŋ'gɛərɪən] adj húngaro ▷ n húngaro(-a) m(f); (Ling) húngaro
Hungary ['hʌŋgərɪ] n Hungría
hunger ['hʌŋgəʳ] n hambre f ▷ vi: **to ~ for** (fig) tener hambre de, anhelar
hungover [hʌŋ'əuvəʳ] adj (inf): **to be ~** tener resaca
hungry ['hʌŋgrɪ] adj hambriento; **to be ~** tener hambre; **~ for** (fig) sediento de
hunk [hʌŋk] n (of bread etc) trozo, pedazo
hunt [hʌnt] vt (seek) buscar; (Sport) cazar ▷ vi (search): **to ~ (for)** buscar; (Sport) cazar ▷ n caza, cacería; **hunt down** vt acorralar, seguir la pista a
hunter ['hʌntəʳ] n cazador(a) m(f); (horse) caballo de caza
hunting ['hʌntɪŋ] n caza
hurdle ['hə:dl] n (Sport) valla; (fig) obstáculo
hurl [hə:l] vt lanzar, arrojar
hurling ['hə:lɪŋ] n (Sport) juego irlandés semejante al hockey

hurrah [hu'rɑː], hurray [hu'reɪ] n ¡viva!, ¡hurra!

hurricane ['hʌrɪkən] n huracán m

hurried ['hʌrɪd] adj (fast) apresurado; (rushed) hecho de prisa

hurriedly ['hʌrɪdlɪ] adv con prisa, apresuradamente

hurry ['hʌrɪ] n prisa ▷ vb (also: ~ up) ▷ vi apresurarse, darse prisa, apurarse (LAm) ▷ vt (person) dar prisa a; (work) apresurar, hacer de prisa; to be in a ~ tener prisa, tener apuro (LAm), estar apurado (LAm); to ~ back/home darse prisa en volver/volver a casa; hurry along vi pasar de prisa; hurry away, hurry off vi irse corriendo; hurry on vi: to ~ on to say apresurarse a decir; hurry up vi darse prisa, apurarse (LAm)

hurt [hɜːt] n prisa ▷ (pt, pp hurt) vt hacer daño a; (business, interests etc) perjudicar ▷ vi doler ▷ adj lastimado; I ~ my arm me lastimé el brazo; where does it ~? ¿dónde te duele?

hurtful ['hɜːtful] adj (remark etc) hiriente, dañino

hurtle ['hɜːtl] vi: to ~ past pasar como un rayo

husband ['hʌzbənd] n marido

hush [hʌʃ] n silencio ▷ vt hacer callar; (cover up) encubrir; ~! ¡chitón!, ¡cállate!; hush up vt (fact) encubrir, callar

husk [hʌsk] n (of wheat) cáscara

husky ['hʌskɪ] adj ronco; (burly) fornido ▷ n perro esquimal

hustle ['hʌsl] vt (push) empujar; (hurry) dar prisa a ▷ n bullicio, actividad f febril; ~ and bustle ajetreo

hut [hʌt] n cabaña; (shed) cobertizo

hutch [hʌtʃ] n conejera

hyacinth ['haɪəsɪnθ] n jacinto

hybrid ['haɪbrɪd] adj, n híbrido; ~ car coche híbrido; ~ engine motor híbrido

hydrangea [haɪ'dreɪnʒə] n hortensia

hydrant ['haɪdrənt] n (also: fire ~) boca de incendios

hydraulic [haɪ'drɔːlɪk] adj hidráulico

hydroelectric [haɪdrəʊɪ'lektrɪk] adj hidroeléctrico

hydrofoil ['haɪdrəfɔɪl] n aerodeslizador m

hydrogen ['haɪdrədʒən] n hidrógeno

hyena [haɪ'iːnə] n hiena

hygiene ['haɪdʒiːn] n higiene f

hygienic [haɪ'dʒiːnɪk] adj higiénico

hymn [hɪm] n himno

hype [haɪp] n (inf) bombo

hyperactive [haɪpər'æktɪv] adj hiperactivo

hyperlink ['haɪpəlɪŋk] n hiperenlace m

hypermarket ['haɪpəmɑːkɪt] n hipermercado

hyphen ['haɪfn] n guión m

hypnosis [hɪp'nəʊsɪs] n hipnosis f

hypnotic [hɪp'nɒtɪk] adj hipnótico

hypnotism ['hɪpnətɪzəm] n hipnotismo

hypnotist ['hɪpnətɪst] n hipnotista m/f

hypnotize ['hɪpnətaɪz] vt hipnotizar

hypochondriac [haɪpəʊ'kɒndrɪæk] n hipocondríaco(-a)

hypocrisy [hɪ'pɒkrɪsɪ] n hipocresía

hypocrite ['hɪpəkrɪt] n hipócrita m/f

hypocritical [hɪpə'krɪtɪkl] adj hipócrita

hypodermic [haɪpə'dɜːmɪk] adj hipodérmico ▷ n (syringe) aguja hipodérmica

hypotenuse [haɪ'pɒtɪnjuːz] n hipotenusa

hypothermia [haɪpəʊ'θɜːmɪə] n hipotermia

hypothesis, hypotheses [haɪ'pɒθɪsɪs, -siːz] n hipótesis f inv

hypothetical [haɪpə'θetɪkl] adj hipotético

hysterectomy [hɪstə'rektəmɪ] n histerectomía

hysteria [hɪ'stɪərɪə] n histeria

hysterical [hɪ'sterɪkl] adj histérico

hysterics [hɪ'sterɪks] npl histeria sg, histerismo sg; to have ~ ponerse histérico; to be in ~ (fig) morirse de risa

I, i [aɪ] n (letter) I, i f; **I for Isaac**, (US) **I for Item** I de Inés, I de Israel

I [aɪ] pron yo ▷ abbr = **island; isle**

IBA n abbr (Brit: = Independent Broadcasting Authority) see **ITV**

Iberian [aɪˈbɪərɪən] adj ibero, ibérico

Iberian Peninsula n: **the ~** la Península Ibérica

ice [aɪs] n hielo ▷ vt (cake) alcorzar ▷ vi (also: **~ over, ~ up**) helarse; **to keep sth on ~** (fig: plan, project) tener algo en reserva

iceberg [ˈaɪsbəːg] n iceberg m; **the tip of the ~** la punta del iceberg

icebox [ˈaɪsbɔks] n (Brit) congelador m; (US) nevera, refrigeradora (LAm)

ice bucket n cubo para el hielo

ice cream n helado

ice cube n cubito de hielo

iced [aɪst] adj (drink) con hielo; (cake) escarchado

ice hockey n hockey m sobre hielo

Iceland [ˈaɪslənd] n Islandia

Icelander [ˈaɪsləndə^r] n islandés(-esa) m(f)

Icelandic [aɪsˈlændɪk] adj islandés(-esa) ▷ n (Ling) islandés m

ice lolly n (Brit) polo

ice rink n pista de hielo

ice-skating [ˈaɪsskeɪtɪŋ] n patinaje m sobre hielo

icicle [ˈaɪsɪkl] n carámbano

icing [ˈaɪsɪŋ] n (Culin) alcorza; (Aviat etc) formación f de hielo

icing sugar n (Brit) azúcar m glas(eado)

icon [ˈaɪkɔn] n (gen) icono; (Comput) icono

ICT n abbr (= Information and Communication(s) Technology) TIC f, tecnología de la información; (Brit Scol) informática

ICU n abbr (= intensive care unit) UVI f

icy [ˈaɪsɪ] adj (road) helado; (fig) glacial

I'd [aɪd] = **I would; I had**

ID card n (identity card) DNI m

idea [aɪˈdɪə] n idea; **good ~!** ¡buena idea!; **to have an ~ that ...** tener la impresión de que ...; **I haven't the least ~** no tengo ni (la más remota) idea

ideal [aɪˈdɪəl] n ideal m ▷ adj ideal

idealism [aɪˈdɪəlɪzəm] n idealismo

idealist [aɪˈdɪəlɪst] n idealista m/f

ideally [aɪˈdɪəlɪ] adv: **~, the book should have ...** lo ideal sería que el libro tuviera ...

identical [aɪˈdɛntɪkl] adj idéntico

identification [aɪdɛntɪfɪˈkeɪʃən] n identificación f; **means of ~** documentos mpl personales

identify [aɪˈdɛntɪfaɪ] vt identificar ▷ vi: **to ~ with** identificarse con

Identikit® [aɪˈdɛntɪkɪt] n: **~ (picture)** retrato-robot m

identity [aɪˈdɛntɪtɪ] n identidad f

identity card n carnet m de identidad, cédula (de identidad) (LAm)

identity parade n identificación f de acusados

identity theft n robo de identidad

ideological [aɪdɪəˈlɔdʒɪkəl] adj ideológico

ideology [aɪdɪˈɔlədʒɪ] n ideología

idiom [ˈɪdɪəm] n modismo; (style of speaking) lenguaje m

idiomatic [ɪdɪəˈmætɪk] adj idiomático

idiosyncrasy [ɪdɪəuˈsɪŋkrəsɪ] n idiosincrasia

idiot [ˈɪdɪət] n (gen) idiota m/f; (fool) tonto(-a)

idiotic [ɪdɪˈɔtɪk] adj idiota; tonto

idle [ˈaɪdl] adj (inactive) ocioso; (lazy) holgazán(-ana); (unemployed) parado, desocupado; (talk) frívolo ▷ vi (machine) funcionar or marchar en vacío; **~ capacity** (Comm) capacidad f sin utilizar; **~ money** (Comm) capital m improductivo; **~ time** (Comm) tiempo de paro; **idle away** vt: **to ~ away one's time** malgastar or desperdiciar el tiempo

idol [ˈaɪdl] n ídolo

idolize [ˈaɪdəlaɪz] vt idolatrar

idyllic [ɪˈdɪlɪk] adj idílico

i.e. abbr (= id est: that is) es decir

if [ɪf] conj si ▷ n: **there are a lot of ifs and buts** hay muchas dudas sin resolver; **(even) if** aunque, si bien; **I'd be pleased if you could do it** yo estaría contento si pudieras hacerlo; **if necessary** si resultase necesario; **if I were you** yo en tu lugar; **if only** si solamente; **as if** como si

iffy [ˈɪfɪ] adj (inf) dudoso

igloo [ˈɪgluː] n iglú m

ignite [ɪgˈnaɪt] vt (set fire to) encender ▷ vi
encenderse

ignition [ɪgˈnɪʃən] n (Aut: process) ignición f;
(: mechanism) encendido; **to switch on/off
the** ~ arrancar/apagar el motor

ignition key n (Aut) llave f de contacto

ignorance [ˈɪgnərəns] n ignorancia; **to keep
sb in** ~ **of sth** ocultarle algo a algn

ignorant [ˈɪgnərənt] adj ignorante; **to be** ~
of (subject) desconocer; (events) ignorar

ignore [ɪgˈnɔːʳ] vt (person) no hacer caso de;
(fact) pasar por alto

ill [ɪl] adj enfermo, malo ▷ n mal m; (fig)
infortunio ▷ adv mal; **to take** or **be taken** ~
caer or ponerse enfermo; **to feel** ~ **(with)**
encontrarse mal (de); **to speak/think** ~ **of
sb** hablar/pensar mal de algn

I'll [aɪl] = **I will**; **I shall**

ill-advised [ɪləˈvaɪzd] adj poco
recomendable; **he was** ~ **to go** se equivocaba
al ir

ill-at-ease [ɪləˈtiːz] adj incómodo

illegal [ɪˈliːgl] adj ilegal

illegible [ɪˈlɛdʒɪbl] adj ilegible

illegitimate [ɪlɪˈdʒɪtɪmət] adj ilegítimo

ill-fated [ɪlˈfeɪtɪd] adj malogrado

ill feeling n rencor m

ill health n mala salud f; **to be in** ~ estar mal
de salud

illicit [ɪˈlɪsɪt] adj ilícito

illiterate [ɪˈlɪtərət] adj analfabeto

ill-mannered [ɪlˈmænəd] adj mal educado

illness [ˈɪlnɪs] n enfermedad f

ill-treat [ɪlˈtriːt] vt maltratar

illuminate [ɪˈluːmɪneɪt] vt (room, street)
iluminar, alumbrar; (subject) aclarar; ~**d sign**
letrero luminoso

illumination [ɪluːmɪˈneɪʃən] n alumbrado;
illuminations npl luminarias fpl, luces fpl

illusion [ɪˈluːʒən] n ilusión f; **to be under
the** ~ **that** ... estar convencido de que ...

illustrate [ˈɪləstreɪt] vt ilustrar

illustration [ɪləˈstreɪʃən] n (example) ejemplo,
ilustración f; (in book) lámina, ilustración f

illustrious [ɪˈlʌstrɪəs] adj ilustre

ill will n rencor m

I'm [aɪm] = **I am**

image [ˈɪmɪdʒ] n imagen f

imagery [ˈɪmɪdʒərɪ] n imágenes fpl

imaginary [ɪˈmædʒɪnərɪ] adj imaginario

imagination [ɪmædʒɪˈneɪʃən] n imaginación f;
(inventiveness) inventiva; (illusion) fantasía

imaginative [ɪˈmædʒɪnətɪv] adj imaginativo

imagine [ɪˈmædʒɪn] vt imaginarse; (suppose)
suponer

imbalance [ɪmˈbæləns] n desequilibrio

imbue [ɪmˈbjuː] vt: **to** ~ **sth with** imbuir
algo de

IMF n abbr (= International Monetary Fund) FMI m

imitate [ˈɪmɪteɪt] vt imitar

imitation [ɪmɪˈteɪʃən] n imitación f; (copy)
copia; (pej) remedo

immaculate [ɪˈmækjulət] adj limpísimo,
inmaculado; (Rel) inmaculado

immaterial [ɪməˈtɪərɪəl] adj incorpóreo; **it is
** ~ **whether** ... no importa si ...

immature [ɪməˈtjuəʳ] adj (person) inmaduro;
(of one's youth) joven

immaturity [ɪməˈtjuərɪtɪ] n inmadurez f

immediate [ɪˈmiːdɪət] adj inmediato;
(pressing) urgente, apremiante; (nearest:
family) próximo; (: neighbourhood) inmediato;
in the ~ **future** en un futuro próximo

immediately [ɪˈmiːdɪətlɪ] adv (at once) en
seguida; (directly) inmediatamente; ~ **next
to** justo al lado de

immense [ɪˈmɛns] adj inmenso, enorme

immensely [ɪˈmɛnslɪ] adv enormemente

immerse [ɪˈmɜːs] vt (submerge) sumergir; **to
be** ~**d in** (fig) estar absorto en

immersion heater [ɪˈmɜːʃən-] n (Brit)
calentador m de inmersión

immigrant [ˈɪmɪgrənt] n inmigrante m/f

immigrate [ˈɪmɪgreɪt] vi inmigrar

immigration [ɪmɪˈgreɪʃən] n inmigración f

imminent [ˈɪmɪnənt] adj inminente

immobilize [ɪˈməubɪlaɪz] vt inmovilizar

immoral [ɪˈmɔrl] adj inmoral

immorality [ɪməˈrælɪtɪ] n inmoralidad f

immortal [ɪˈmɔːtl] adj inmortal

immortality [ɪmɔːˈtælɪtɪ] n inmortalidad f

immortalize [ɪˈmɔːtlaɪz] vt inmortalizar

immune [ɪˈmjuːn] adj: ~ **(to)** inmune (a)

immune system n sistema m inmunitario

immunity [ɪˈmjuːnɪtɪ] n (Med: of diplomat)
inmunidad f; (Comm) exención f

immunization [ɪmjunaɪˈzeɪʃən] n
inmunización f

immunize [ˈɪmjunaɪz] vt inmunizar

imp [ɪmp] n (small devil, child) diablillo

impact [ˈɪmpækt] n (gen) impacto

impair [ɪmˈpeəʳ] vt perjudicar

impart [ɪmˈpɑːt] vt comunicar; (make known)
participar; (bestow) otorgar

impartial [ɪmˈpɑːʃl] adj imparcial

impassable [ɪmˈpɑːsəbl] adj (barrier)
infranqueable; (road) intransitable

impassive [ɪmˈpæsɪv] adj impasible

impatience [ɪmˈpeɪʃəns] n impaciencia

impatient [ɪmˈpeɪʃənt] adj impaciente;
to get or **grow** ~ impacientarse

impeccable [ɪmˈpɛkəbl] adj impecable

impede [ɪmˈpiːd] vt estorbar, dificultar

impediment [ɪmˈpɛdɪmənt] n obstáculo,
estorbo; (also: **speech** ~) defecto (del habla)

impending [ɪmˈpɛndɪŋ] adj inminente

imperative [ɪmˈpɛrətɪv] adj (tone) imperioso;
(necessary) imprescindible ▷ n (Ling)
imperativo

imperfect [ɪmˈpəːfɪkt] adj imperfecto; (goods
etc) defectuoso ▷ n (Ling: also: ~ **tense**)
imperfecto

imperfection [ɪmpəˈfɛkʃən] n (blemish)
desperfecto; (fault, flaw) defecto

imperial [ɪmˈpɪərɪəl] *adj* imperial
imperialism [ɪmˈpɪərɪəlɪzəm] *n*
imperialismo
impersonal [ɪmˈpəːsənl] *adj* impersonal
impersonate [ɪmˈpəːsəneɪt] *vt* hacerse pasar
por
impersonation [ɪmpəːsəˈneɪʃən] *n*
imitación *f*
impertinence [ɪmˈpəːtɪnəns] *n*
impertinencia, insolencia
impertinent [ɪmˈpəːtɪnənt] *adj*
impertinente, insolente
impervious [ɪmˈpəːvɪəs] *adj* impermeable;
(*fig*): ~ **to** insensible a
impetuous [ɪmˈpetjuəs] *adj* impetuoso
impetus [ˈɪmpətəs] *n* ímpetu *m*; (*fig*) impulso
impinge [ɪmˈpɪndʒ]: **to ~ on** *vt fus* (*affect*)
afectar a
implant [ɪmˈplɑːnt] *vt* (*Med*) injertar,
implantar; (*fig*: *idea*, *principle*) inculcar
implausible [ɪmˈplɔːzɪbl] *adj* implausible
implement *n* [ˈɪmplɪmənt] instrumento,
herramienta ⊳ *vt* [ˈɪmplɪment] hacer
efectivo; (*carry out*) realizar
implicate [ˈɪmplɪkeɪt] *vt* (*compromise*)
comprometer; (*involve*) enredar; **to ~ sb in**
sth comprometer a algn en algo
implication [ɪmplɪˈkeɪʃən] *n* consecuencia;
by ~ indirectamente
implicit [ɪmˈplɪsɪt] *adj* (*gen*) implícito;
(*complete*) absoluto
implicitly [ɪmˈplɪsɪtlɪ] *adv* implícitamente
imply [ɪmˈplaɪ] *vt* (*involve*) implicar, suponer;
(*hint*) insinuar
impolite [ɪmpəˈlaɪt] *adj* mal educado
import *vt* [ɪmˈpɔːt] importar ⊳ *n* [ˈɪmpɔːt]
(*Comm*) importación *f*; (: *article*) producto
importado; (*meaning*) significado, sentido
⊳ *cpd* (*duty*, *licence etc*) de importación
importance [ɪmˈpɔːtəns] *n* importancia;
to be of great/little ~ tener mucha/poca
importancia
important [ɪmˈpɔːtənt] *adj* importante; **it's
not ~** no importa, no tiene importancia; **it is
~ that** es importante que
importer [ɪmˈpɔːtə^r] *n* importador(a) *m(f)*
impose [ɪmˈpəuz] *vt* imponer ⊳ *vi*: **to ~ on sb**
abusar de algn
imposing [ɪmˈpəuzɪŋ] *adj* imponente,
impresionante
imposition [ɪmpəˈzɪʃn] *n* (*of tax etc*)
imposición *f*; **to be an ~** (*on person*)
molestar
impossible [ɪmˈpɔsɪbl] *adj* imposible; (*person*)
insoportable; **it is ~ for me to leave now** me
es imposible salir ahora
impostor [ɪmˈpɔstə^r] *n* impostor(a) *m(f)*
impotence [ˈɪmpətəns] *n* impotencia
impotent [ˈɪmpətənt] *adj* impotente
impound [ɪmˈpaund] *vt* embargar
impoverished [ɪmˈpɔvərɪʃt] *adj* necesitado;
(*land*) agotado

impractical [ɪmˈpræktɪkl] *adj* (*person*) poco
práctico
imprecise [ɪmprɪˈsaɪs] *adj* impreciso
impregnable [ɪmˈpregnəbl] *adj*
invulnerable; (*castle*) inexpugnable
impress [ɪmˈpres] *vt* impresionar; (*mark*)
estampar ⊳ *vi* causar buena impresión; **to ~
sth on sb** convencer a algn de la importancia
de algo
impression [ɪmˈpreʃən] *n* impresión *f*;
(*footprint etc*) huella; (*print run*) edición *f*; **to be
under the ~ that** tener la impresión de que;
to make a good/bad ~ on sb causar buena/
mala impresión a algn
impressionist [ɪmˈpreʃənɪst] *n*
impresionista *m/f*
impressive [ɪmˈpresɪv] *adj* impresionante
imprint [ˈɪmprɪnt] *n* (*Publishing*) pie *m* de
imprenta; (*fig*) sello
imprison [ɪmˈprɪzn] *vt* encarcelar
imprisonment [ɪmˈprɪznmənt] *n*
encarcelamiento; (*term of imprisonment*) cárcel *f*;
life ~ cadena perpetua
improbable [ɪmˈprɔbəbl] *adj* improbable,
inverosímil
impromptu [ɪmˈprɔmptjuː] *adj* improvisado
⊳ *adv* de improviso
improper [ɪmˈprɔpə^r] *adj* (*incorrect*) impropio;
(*unseemly*) indecoroso; (*indecent*) indecente;
(*dishonest*: *activities*) deshonesto
improve [ɪmˈpruːv] *vt* mejorar; (*foreign
language*) perfeccionar ⊳ *vi* mejorar; **improve
(up)on** *vt fus* (*offer*) mejorar
improvement [ɪmˈpruːvmənt] *n* mejora,
perfeccionamiento; **to make ~s to** mejorar
improvise [ˈɪmprəvaɪz] *vt*, *vi* improvisar
imprudent [ɪmˈpruːdnt] *adj* imprudente
impudent [ˈɪmpjudnt] *adj* descarado,
insolente
impulse [ˈɪmpʌls] *n* impulso; **to act on ~**
actuar sin reflexionar, dejarse llevar por el
impulso
impulsive [ɪmˈpʌlsɪv] *adj* irreflexivo,
impulsivo
impure [ɪmˈpjuə^r] *adj* (*adulterated*) adulterado;
(*morally*) impuro
impurity [ɪmˈpjuərɪtɪ] *n* impureza

🔘 KEYWORD

in [ɪn] *prep* **1** (*indicating place, position, with place
names*) en; **in the house/garden** en (la) casa/
el jardín; **in here/there** aquí/ahí *or* allí
dentro; **in London/England** en Londres/
Inglaterra; **in town** en el centro (de la
ciudad)
2 (*indicating time*) en; **in spring** en (la)
primavera; **in 1988/May** en 1988/mayo;
in the afternoon por la tarde; **at four
o'clock in the afternoon** a las cuatro de la
tarde; **I did it in three hours/days** lo hice
en tres horas/días; **I'll see you in two weeks**

or **in two weeks' time** te veré dentro de dos semanas; **once in a hundred years** una vez cada cien años
3 (*indicating manner etc*) en; **in a loud/soft voice** en voz alta/baja; **in pencil/ink** a lápiz/bolígrafo; **the boy in the blue shirt** el chico de la camisa azul; **in writing** por escrito; **to pay in dollars** pagar en dólares
4 (*indicating circumstances*): **in the sun/shade** al sol/a la sombra; **in the rain** bajo la lluvia; **a change in policy** un cambio de política; **a rise in prices** un aumento de precios
5 (*indicating mood, state*): **in tears** llorando; **in anger/despair** enfadado/desesperado; **to live in luxury** vivir lujosamente
6 (*with ratios, numbers*): **1 in 10 households, 1 household in 10** una de cada 10 familias; **20 pence in the pound** 20 peniques por libra; **they lined up in twos** se alinearon de dos en dos; **in hundreds** a *or* por centenares
7 (*referring to people, works*) entre; entre; **the disease is common in children** la enfermedad es común entre los niños; **in (the works of) Dickens** en (las obras de) Dickens
8 (*indicating profession etc*): **to be in teaching** dedicarse a la enseñanza
9 (*after superlative*) de; **the best pupil in the class** el/la mejor alumno(-a) de la clase
10 (*with present participle*): **in saying this** al decir esto
▷ *adv*: **to be in** (*person: at home*) estar en casa; (*: at work*) estar; (*train, ship, plane*) haber llegado; (*in fashion*) estar de moda; **she'll be in later today** llegará más tarde hoy; **to ask sb in** hacer pasar a algn; **to run/limp** *etc* **in** entrar corriendo/cojeando *etc*; **in that** *conj* ya que ▷ *npl*: **the ins and outs** (*of proposal, situation etc*) los detalles

in., ins *abbr* = **inch(es)**
inability [ɪnə'bɪlɪtɪ] *n*: ~ **(to do)** incapacidad *f* (de hacer)
inaccuracy [ɪn'ækjʊrəsɪ] *n* inexactitud *f*
inaccurate [ɪn'ækjʊrət] *adj* inexacto, incorrecto
inadequate [ɪn'ædɪkwət] *adj* (*insufficient*) insuficiente; (*unsuitable*) inadecuado; (*person*) incapaz
inadmissible [ɪnəd'mɪsəbl] *adj* improcedente, inadmisible
inadvertent [ɪnəd'vəːtənt] *adj* descuidado, involuntario
inadvertently [ɪnəd'vəːtntlɪ] *adv* por descuido
inadvisable [ɪnəd'vaɪzəbl] *adj* poco aconsejable
inane [ɪ'neɪn] *adj* necio, fatuo
inanimate [ɪn'ænɪmət] *adj* inanimado
inapplicable [ɪn'æplɪkəbl] *adj* inaplicable
inappropriate [ɪnə'prəuprɪət] *adj* inadecuado

inarticulate [ɪnɑː'tɪkjʊlət] *adj* (*person*) incapaz de expresarse; (*speech*) mal pronunciado
inasmuch as [ɪnəz'mʌtʃ-] *adv* en la medida en que
inaugural [ɪ'nɔːgjʊrəl] *adj* inaugural; (*speech*) de apertura
inaugurate [ɪ'nɔːgjʊreɪt] *vt* inaugurar; (*president, official*) investir
inauguration [ɪnɔːgjʊ'reɪʃən] *n* inauguración *f*; (*of official*) investidura; (*of event*) ceremonia de apertura
in-between [ɪnbɪ'twiːn] *adj* intermedio
inborn [ɪn'bɔːn] *adj* (*feeling*) innato
inbred [ɪn'brɛd] *adj* innato; (*family*) consanguíneo
Inc. *abbr* = **incorporated**
Inca ['ɪŋkə] *adj* (*also*: ~**n**) inca, de los incas ▷ *n* inca *m/f*
incapable [ɪn'keɪpəbl] *adj*: ~ **(of doing sth)** incapaz (de hacer algo)
incapacitate [ɪnkə'pæsɪteɪt] *vt*: **to** ~ **sb** incapacitar a algn
incapacity [ɪnkə'pæsɪtɪ] *n* (*inability*) incapacidad *f*
incarcerate [ɪn'kɑːsəreɪt] *vt* encarcelar
incarnate *adj* [ɪn'kɑːnɪt] en persona ▷ *vt* ['ɪnkɑːneɪt] encarnar
incarnation [ɪnkɑː'neɪʃən] *n* encarnación *f*
incendiary [ɪn'sɛndɪərɪ] *adj* incendiario ▷ *n* (*bomb*) bomba incendiaria
incense *n* ['ɪnsɛns] incienso ▷ *vt* [ɪn'sɛns] (*anger*) indignar, encolerizar
incentive [ɪn'sɛntɪv] *n* incentivo, estímulo
incessant [ɪn'sɛsnt] *adj* incesante, continuo
incessantly [ɪn'sɛsəntlɪ] *adv* constantemente
incest ['ɪnsɛst] *n* incesto
inch [ɪntʃ] *n* pulgada; **to be within an** ~ **of** estar a dos dedos de; **he didn't give an** ~ no hizo la más mínima concesión; **a few** ~**es** unas pulgadas; **inch forward** *vi* avanzar palmo a palmo
incidence ['ɪnsɪdns] *n* (*of crime, disease*) incidencia
incident ['ɪnsɪdnt] *n* incidente *m*; (*in book*) episodio
incidental [ɪnsɪ'dɛntl] *adj* circunstancial, accesorio; (*unplanned*) fortuito; ~ **to** relacionado con; ~ **expenses** (gastos *mpl*) imprevistos *mpl*
incidentally [ɪnsɪ'dɛntəlɪ] *adv* (*by the way*) por cierto
incident room *n* (*Police*) centro de coordinación
incinerate [ɪn'sɪnəreɪt] *vt* incinerar, quemar
incinerator [ɪn'sɪnəreɪtəʳ] *n* incinerador *m*, incineradora
incision [ɪn'sɪʒən] *n* incisión *f*
incisive [ɪn'saɪsɪv] *adj* (*mind*) penetrante; (*remark etc*) incisivo
incite [ɪn'saɪt] *vt* provocar, incitar

incl. *abbr* = **including; inclusive (of)**
inclination [ɪnklɪ'neɪʃən] *n* (*tendency*) tendencia, inclinación *f*
incline [*n* 'ɪnklaɪn, *vb* ɪn'klaɪn] *n* pendiente *f*, cuesta ▷ *vt* (*slope*) inclinar; (*head*) poner de lado ▷ *vi* inclinarse; **to be ~d to** (*tend*) ser propenso a; (*be willing*) estar dispuesto a
include [ɪn'kluːd] *vt* incluir, comprender; (*in letter*) adjuntar; **the tip is/is not ~d** la propina está/no está incluida
including [ɪn'kluːdɪŋ] *prep* incluso, inclusive; **~ tip** propina incluida
inclusion [ɪn'kluːʒən] *n* inclusión *f*
inclusive [ɪn'kluːsɪv] *adj* inclusivo ▷ *adv* inclusive; **~ of tax** incluidos los impuestos; **$50, ~ of all surcharges** 50 dólares, incluidos todos los recargos
incognito [ɪnkɔg'niːtəu] *adv* de incógnito
incoherent [ɪnkəu'hɪərənt] *adj* incoherente
income ['ɪnkʌm] *n* (*personal*) ingresos *mpl*; (*from property etc*) renta; (*profit*) rédito; **gross/net ~** ingresos *mpl* brutos/netos; **~ and expenditure account** cuenta de gastos e ingresos
income support *n* (Brit) ≈ ayuda familiar
income tax *n* impuesto sobre la renta
incoming ['ɪnkʌmɪŋ] *adj* (*passengers, flight*) de llegada; (*government*) entrante; (*tenant*) nuevo
incompatible [ɪnkəm'pætɪbl] *adj* incompatible
incompetence [ɪn'kɔmpɪtəns] *n* incompetencia
incompetent [ɪn'kɔmpɪtənt] *adj* incompetente
incomplete [ɪnkəm'pliːt] *adj* incompleto; (*unfinished*) sin terminar
incomprehensible [ɪnkɔmprɪ'hɛnsɪbl] *adj* incomprensible
inconceivable [ɪnkən'siːvəbl] *adj* inconcebible
inconclusive [ɪnkən'kluːsɪv] *adj* sin resultado (definitivo); (*argument*) poco convincente
incongruous [ɪn'kɔŋgruəs] *adj* discordante
inconsiderate [ɪnkən'sɪdərət] *adj* desconsiderado; **how ~ of him!** ¡qué falta de consideración (de su parte)!
inconsistency [ɪnkən'sɪstənsɪ] *n* inconsecuencia; (*of actions etc*) falta de lógica; (*of work*) carácter *m* desigual, inconsistencia; (*of statement etc*) contradicción *f*
inconsistent [ɪnkən'sɪstnt] *adj* inconsecuente; (*contradictory*) incongruente; **~ with** que no concuerda con
inconspicuous [ɪnkən'spɪkjuəs] *adj* (*discreet*) discreto; (*person*) que llama poco la atención
incontinent [ɪn'kɔntɪnənt] *adj* incontinente
inconvenience [ɪnkən'viːnjəns] *n* (*gen*) inconvenientes *mpl*; (*trouble*) molestia ▷ *vt* incomodar; **to put sb to great ~** causar mucha molestia a algn; **don't ~ yourself** no se moleste

inconvenient [ɪnkən'viːnjənt] *adj* incómodo, poco práctico; (*time, place*) inoportuno; **that time is very ~ for me** esa hora me es muy inconveniente
incorporate [ɪn'kɔːpəreɪt] *vt* incorporar; (*contain*) comprender; (*add*) agregar
incorporated [ɪn'kɔːpəreɪtɪd] *adj*: **~ company** (US) ≈ Sociedad *f* Anónima (S.A.)
incorrect [ɪnkə'rɛkt] *adj* incorrecto
increase [*n* 'ɪnkriːs, *vb* ɪn'kriːs] *n* aumento ▷ *vi* aumentar; (*grow*) crecer; (*price*) subir ▷ *vt* aumentar; (*price*) subir; **an ~ of 5%** un aumento de 5%; **to be on the ~** ir en aumento
increasing [ɪn'kriːsɪŋ] *adj* (*number*) creciente, que va en aumento
increasingly [ɪn'kriːsɪŋlɪ] *adv* cada vez más
incredible [ɪn'krɛdɪbl] *adj* increíble
incredibly [ɪn'krɛdɪblɪ] *adv* increíblemente
incredulous [ɪn'krɛdjuləs] *adj* incrédulo
increment ['ɪnkrɪmənt] *n* aumento, incremento
incriminate [ɪn'krɪmɪneɪt] *vt* incriminar
incubate ['ɪnkjubeɪt] *vt* (*egg*) incubar, empollar ▷ *vi* (*egg, disease*) incubar
incubation [ɪnkju'beɪʃən] *n* incubación *f*
incubator ['ɪnkjubeɪtə*r*] *n* incubadora
incumbent [ɪn'kʌmbənt] *n* ocupante *m/f* ▷ *adj*: **it is ~ on him to ...** le incumbe ...
incur [ɪn'kəː*r*] *vt* (*expenses*) incurrir en; (*loss*) sufrir; (*anger, disapproval*) provocar
incurable [ɪn'kjuərəbl] *adj* incurable
indebted [ɪn'dɛtɪd] *adj*: **to be ~ to sb** estar agradecido a algn
indecency [ɪn'diːsnsɪ] *n* indecencia
indecent [ɪn'diːsnt] *adj* indecente
indecent assault *n* (Brit) atentado contra el pudor
indecent exposure *n* exhibicionismo
indecision [ɪndɪ'sɪʒən] *n* indecisión *f*
indecisive [ɪndɪ'saɪsɪv] *adj* indeciso; (*discussion*) no resuelto, inconcluyente
indeed [ɪn'diːd] *adv* efectivamente, en realidad; (*in fact*) en efecto; (*furthermore*) es más; **yes ~!** ¡claro que sí!
indefinite [ɪn'dɛfɪnɪt] *adj* indefinido; (*uncertain*) incierto
indefinitely [ɪn'dɛfɪnɪtlɪ] *adv* (*wait*) indefinidamente
indemnity [ɪn'dɛmnɪtɪ] *n* (*insurance*) indemnidad *f*; (*compensation*) indemnización *f*
indent [ɪn'dent] *vt* (*text*) sangrar
independence [ɪndɪ'pendns] *n* independencia
Independence Day *n* Día *m* de la Independencia

● **INDEPENDENCE DAY**
●
● El cuatro de julio es la fiesta nacional de
● los Estados Unidos, *Independence Day*, en
● conmemoración de la Declaración de

● Independencia escrita por Thomas
● Jefferson y adoptada en 1776. En ella se
● proclamaba la ruptura total con Gran
● Bretaña de las trece colonias americanas
● que fueron el origen de los Estados
● Unidos de América.

independent [ɪndɪ'pɛndənt] *adj*
independiente; **to become ~** independizarse
independent school *n* (*Brit*) escuela *f*
privada, colegio *m* privado
in-depth ['ɪndɛpθ] *adj* en profundidad, a
fondo
index ['ɪndɛks] *n* (*pl* **indexes**: *in book*) índice *m*;
(: *in library etc*) catálogo; (*pl* **indices** ['ɪndɪsi:z]
: *ratio, sign*) exponente *m*
index card *n* ficha
index finger *n* índice *m*
index-linked ['ɪndɛks'lɪŋkt], **indexed** (*US*)
['ɪndɛkst] *adj* indexado
India ['ɪndɪə] *n* la India
Indian ['ɪndɪən] *adj, n* indio(-a) *m(f)*; (*also*:
American ~) indio(-a) *m(f)* de América,
amerindio(-a) *m(f)*; (*pej*): **Red ~** piel roja *m/f*
Indian Ocean *n*: **the ~** el Océano Índico, el
Mar de las Indias
Indian summer *n* (*fig*) veranillo de San
Martín
indicate ['ɪndɪkeɪt] *vt* indicar ▷ *vi* (*Brit Aut*):
to ~ left/right indicar a la izquierda/a la
derecha
indication [ɪndɪ'keɪʃən] *n* indicio, señal *f*
indicative [ɪn'dɪkətɪv] *adj*: **to be ~ of sth**
indicar algo ▷ *n* (*Ling*) indicativo
indicator ['ɪndɪkeɪtə*] *n* (*gen*) indicador *m*;
(*Aut*) intermitente *m*, direccional *m* (*LAm*)
indices ['ɪndɪsi:z] *npl of* **index**
indict [ɪn'daɪt] *vt* acusar
indictment [ɪn'daɪtmənt] *n* acusación *f*
indifference [ɪn'dɪfrəns] *n* indiferencia
indifferent [ɪn'dɪfrənt] *adj* indiferente; (*poor*)
regular
indigenous [ɪn'dɪdʒɪnəs] *adj* indígena
indigestion [ɪndɪ'dʒɛstʃən] *n* indigestión *f*
indignant [ɪn'dɪɡnənt] *adj*: **to be ~ about
sth** indignarse por algo
indignation [ɪndɪɡ'neɪʃən] *n* indignación *f*
indignity [ɪn'dɪɡnɪtɪ] *n* indignidad *f*
indigo ['ɪndɪɡəʊ] *adj* (*colour*) (de color) añil ▷ *n*
añil *m*
indirect [ɪndɪ'rɛkt] *adj* indirecto
indiscreet [ɪndɪ'skri:t] *adj* indiscreto,
imprudente
indiscriminate [ɪndɪ'skrɪmɪnət] *adj*
indiscriminado
indispensable [ɪndɪ'spɛnsəbl] *adj*
indispensable, imprescindible
indisputable [ɪndɪ'spju:təbl] *adj*
incontestable
indistinct [ɪndɪ'stɪŋkt] *adj* indistinto
indistinguishable [ɪndɪ'stɪŋgwɪʃəbl] *adj*
indistinguible

individual [ɪndɪ'vɪdjuəl] *n* individuo ▷ *adj*
individual; (*personal*) personal; (*particular*)
particular
individuality [ɪndɪvɪdju'ælɪtɪ] *n*
individualidad *f*
individually [ɪndɪ'vɪdjuəlɪ] *adv*
individualmente; particularmente
indoctrination [ɪndɒktrɪ'neɪʃən] *n*
adoctrinamiento
Indonesia [ɪndə'ni:zɪə] *n* Indonesia
indoor ['ɪndɔ:*] *adj* (*swimming pool*) cubierto;
(*plant*) de interior; (*sport*) bajo cubierta
indoors [ɪn'dɔ:z] *adv* dentro; (*at home*) en casa
induce [ɪn'dju:s] *vt* inducir, persuadir; (*bring
about*) producir; **to ~ sb to do sth** persuadir a
algn a que haga algo
inducement [ɪn'dju:smənt] *n* (*incentive*)
incentivo, aliciente *m*
induction [ɪn'dʌkʃən] *n* (*Med*: *of birth*)
inducción *f*
indulge [ɪn'dʌldʒ] *vt* (*whim*) satisfacer;
(*person*) complacer; (*child*) mimar ▷ *vi*: **to ~ in**
darse el gusto de
indulgence [ɪn'dʌldʒəns] *n* vicio
indulgent [ɪn'dʌldʒənt] *adj* indulgente
industrial [ɪn'dʌstrɪəl] *adj* industrial
industrial action *n* huelga
industrial estate *n* (*Brit*) polígono *or* (*LAm*)
zona industrial
industrialist [ɪn'dʌstrɪəlɪst] *n* industrial *m/f*
industrialize [ɪn'dʌstrɪəlaɪz] *vt*
industrializar
industrial park *n* (*US*) = **industrial estate**
industrial relations *npl* relaciones *fpl*
empresariales
industrious [ɪn'dʌstrɪəs] *adj* (*gen*)
trabajador(a); (*student*) aplicado
industry ['ɪndəstrɪ] *n* industria; (*diligence*)
aplicación *f*
inebriated [ɪ'ni:brɪeɪtɪd] *adj* borracho
inedible [ɪn'ɛdɪbl] *adj* incomible; (*plant etc*)
no comestible
ineffective [ɪnɪ'fɛktɪv], **ineffectual**
[ɪnɪ'fɛktʃuəl] *adj* ineficaz, inútil
inefficiency [ɪnɪ'fɪʃənsɪ] *n* ineficacia
inefficient [ɪnɪ'fɪʃənt] *adj* ineficaz,
ineficiente
ineligible [ɪn'ɛlɪdʒɪbl] *adj* inelegible
inept [ɪ'nɛpt] *adj* incompetente, incapaz
inequality [ɪnɪ'kwɒlɪtɪ] *n* desigualdad *f*
inertia [ɪ'nə:ʃə] *n* inercia; (*laziness*) pereza
inescapable [ɪnɪ'skeɪpəbl] *adj* ineludible,
inevitable
inevitable [ɪn'ɛvɪtəbl] *adj* inevitable;
(*necessary*) forzoso
inevitably [ɪn'ɛvɪtəblɪ] *adv* inevitablemente;
as ~ happens ... como siempre pasa ...
inexact [ɪnɪɡ'zaekt] *adj* inexacto
inexcusable [ɪnɪks'kju:zəbl] *adj*
imperdonable
inexhaustible [ɪnɪɡ'zɔ:stɪbl] *adj* inagotable
inexpensive [ɪnɪk'spɛnsɪv] *adj* económico

inexperience [ɪnɪk'spɪərɪəns] n falta de experiencia

inexperienced [ɪnɪk'spɪərɪənst] adj inexperto; **to be ~ in sth** no tener experiencia en algo

inexplicable [ɪnɪk'splɪkəbl] adj inexplicable

infallible [ɪn'fælɪbl] adj infalible

infamous ['ɪnfəməs] adj infame

infancy ['ɪnfənsɪ] n infancia

infant ['ɪnfənt] n niño(-a); (baby) niño(-a) pequeño(-a), bebé m/f

infantry ['ɪnfəntrɪ] n infantería

infant school n (Brit) escuela infantil

infatuated [ɪn'fætjʊeɪtɪd] adj: ~ **with** (in love) loco por; **to become ~ (with sb)** enamoriscarse (de algn), encapricharse (con algn)

infatuation [ɪnfætju'eɪʃən] n enamoramiento

infect [ɪn'fɛkt] vt (wound) infectar; (food) contaminar; (person, animal) contagiar; (fig: pej) corromper; **~ed with** (illness) contagiado de; **to become ~ed** (wound) infectarse

infection [ɪn'fɛkʃən] n infección f; (fig) contagio

infectious [ɪn'fɛkʃəs] adj contagioso; (fig) infeccioso

infer [ɪn'fəːʳ] vt deducir, inferir; **to ~ (from)** inferir (de), deducir (de)

inference ['ɪnfərəns] n deducción f, inferencia

inferior [ɪn'fɪərɪəʳ] adj, n inferior m/f; **to feel ~** sentirse inferior

inferiority [ɪnfɪərɪ'ɔrətɪ] n inferioridad f

inferiority complex n complejo de inferioridad

inferno [ɪn'fəːnəʊ] n infierno; (fig) hoguera

infertile [ɪn'fəːtaɪl] adj estéril; (person) infecundo

infertility [ɪnfəː'tɪlɪtɪ] n esterilidad f; infecundidad f

infested [ɪn'fɛstɪd] adj: ~ **(with)** plagado (de)

infidelity [ɪnfɪ'dɛlɪtɪ] n infidelidad f

in-fighting ['ɪnfaɪtɪŋ] n (fig) lucha(s) f(pl) interna(s)

infinite ['ɪnfɪnɪt] adj infinito; **an ~ amount of money/time** un sinfín de dinero/tiempo

infinitely ['ɪnfɪnɪtlɪ] adv infinitamente

infinitive [ɪn'fɪnɪtɪv] n infinitivo

infinity [ɪn'fɪnɪtɪ] n (Math) infinito; **an ~** infinidad f

infirm [ɪn'fəːm] adj enfermizo, débil

infirmary [ɪn'fəːmərɪ] n hospital m

inflamed [ɪn'fleɪmd] adj: **to become ~** inflamarse

inflammable [ɪn'flæməbl] adj (Brit) inflamable; (situation etc) explosivo

inflammation [ɪnflə'meɪʃən] n inflamación f

inflatable [ɪn'fleɪtəbl] adj inflable

inflate [ɪn'fleɪt] vt (tyre) inflar; (fig) hinchar

inflation [ɪn'fleɪʃən] n (Econ) inflación f

inflationary [ɪn'fleɪʃnərɪ] adj inflacionario

inflexible [ɪn'flɛksɪbl] adj inflexible

inflict [ɪn'flɪkt] vt: **to ~ on** infligir en; (tax etc) imponer a

influence ['ɪnfluəns] n influencia ▷ vt influir en, influenciar; **under the ~ of alcohol** en estado de embriaguez

influential [ɪnflu'ɛnʃl] adj influyente

influenza [ɪnflu'ɛnzə] n gripe f

influx ['ɪnflʌks] n afluencia

info (inf) ['ɪnfəu] n = **information**

inform [ɪn'fɔːm] vt: **to ~ sb of sth** informar a algn sobre or de algo; (warn) avisar a algn de algo; (communicate) comunicar algo a algn ▷ vi: **to ~ on sb** delatar a algn

informal [ɪn'fɔːml] adj (manner, tone) desenfadado; (dress, occasion) informal; (visit, meeting) extraoficial

informality [ɪnfɔː'mælɪtɪ] n falta de ceremonia; (intimacy) intimidad f; (familiarity) familiaridad f; (ease) afabilidad f

informant [ɪn'fɔːmənt] n informante m/f

information [ɪnfə'meɪʃən] n información f; (news) noticias fpl; (knowledge) conocimientos mpl; (Law) delación f; **a piece of ~** un dato; **for your ~** para su información

information office n información f

information science n gestión f de la información

information technology n informática

informative [ɪn'fɔːmətɪv] adj informativo

informer [ɪn'fɔːməʳ] n delator(a) m(f); (also: **police ~**) soplón(-ona) m(f)

infra-red [ɪnfrə'rɛd] adj infarrojo

infrastructure ['ɪnfrəstrʌktʃəʳ] n infraestructura

infrequent [ɪn'friːkwənt] adj infrecuente

infringe [ɪn'frɪndʒ] vt infringir, violar ▷ vi: **to ~ on** invadir

infringement [ɪn'frɪndʒmənt] n infracción f; (of rights) usurpación f; (Sport) falta

infuriate [ɪn'fjʊərɪeɪt] vt: **to become ~d** ponerse furioso

infuriating [ɪn'fjʊərɪeɪtɪŋ] adj (habit, noise) enloquecedor(a); **I find it ~** me saca de quicio

ingenious [ɪn'dʒiːnjəs] adj ingenioso

ingenuity [ɪndʒɪ'njuːɪtɪ] n ingeniosidad f

ingenuous [ɪn'dʒɛnjuəs] adj ingenuo

ingot ['ɪŋgət] n lingote m, barra

ingrained [ɪn'greɪnd] adj arraigado

ingratiate [ɪn'greɪʃɪeɪt] vt: **to ~ o.s. with** congraciarse con

ingratitude [ɪn'grætɪtjuːd] n ingratitud f

ingredient [ɪn'griːdɪənt] n ingrediente m

ingrowing ['ɪngrəʊɪŋ] adj: ~ **(toe)nail** uña encarnada

inhabit [ɪn'hæbɪt] vt vivir en; (occupy) ocupar

inhabitant [ɪn'hæbɪtənt] n habitante m/f

inhale [ɪn'heɪl] vt inhalar ▷ vi (breathe in) aspirar; (in smoking) tragar

inhaler [ɪn'heɪləʳ] n inhalador m

inherent [ɪn'hɪərənt] adj: ~ **in** or **to** inherente a

inherit [ɪn'hɛrɪt] vt heredar
inheritance [ɪn'hɛrɪtəns] n herencia; *(fig)* patrimonio
inhibit [ɪn'hɪbɪt] vt inhibir, impedir; **to ~ sb from doing sth** impedir a algn hacer algo
inhibited [ɪn'hɪbɪtɪd] adj *(person)* cohibido
inhibition [ɪnhɪ'bɪʃən] n cohibición f
in-house ['ɪnhaus] adj dentro de la empresa
inhuman [ɪn'hju:mən] adj inhumano
inhumane [ɪnhju:'meɪn] adj inhumano
inimitable [ɪ'nɪmɪtəbl] adj inimitable
initial [ɪ'nɪʃl] adj inicial; *(first)* primero ▷ n inicial f ▷ vt firmar con las iniciales; **initials** npl iniciales fpl; *(abbreviation)* siglas fpl
initially [ɪ'nɪʃəlɪ] adv en un principio
initiate [ɪ'nɪʃɪeɪt] vt *(start)* iniciar; **to ~ sb into a secret** iniciar a algn en un secreto; **to ~ proceedings against sb** *(Law)* poner una demanda contra algn
initiation [ɪnɪʃɪ'eɪʃən] n *(into secret etc)* iniciación f; *(beginning)* comienzo
initiative [ɪ'nɪʃətɪv] n iniciativa; **to take the ~** tomar la iniciativa
inject [ɪn'dʒɛkt] vt inyectar; *(money, enthusiasm)* aportar
injection [ɪn'dʒɛkʃən] n inyección f; **to have an ~** ponerse una inyección
injure ['ɪndʒər] vt herir, *(hurt)* lastimar; *(fig: reputation etc)* perjudicar; *(feelings)* herir; **to ~ o.s.** hacerse daño, lastimarse
injured ['ɪndʒəd] adj *(also fig)* herido; **~ party** *(Law)* parte f perjudicada
injury ['ɪndʒərɪ] n herida, lesión f; *(wrong)* perjuicio, daño; **to escape without ~** salir ileso
injury time n *(Sport)* descuento
injustice [ɪn'dʒʌstɪs] n injusticia; **you do me an ~** usted es injusto conmigo
ink [ɪŋk] n tinta
ink-jet printer ['ɪŋkdʒɛt-] n impresora de chorro de tinta
inkling ['ɪŋklɪŋ] n sospecha; *(idea)* idea
inlaid ['ɪnleɪd] adj *(wood)* taraceado; *(tiles)* entarimado
inland adj ['ɪnlənd] interior; *(town)* del interior ▷ adv [ɪn'lænd] tierra adentro
Inland Revenue n *(Brit)* ≈ Hacienda, ≈ Agencia Tributaria
in-laws ['ɪnlɔːz] npl suegros mpl
inlet ['ɪnlɛt] n *(Geo)* ensenada, cala; *(Tech)* admisión f, entrada
inmate ['ɪnmeɪt] n *(in prison)* preso(-a), presidiario(-a); *(in asylum)* internado(-a)
inmost ['ɪnməust] adj más íntimo, más secreto
inn [ɪn] n posada, mesón m
innate [ɪ'neɪt] adj innato
inner ['ɪnər] adj interior, interno; *(feelings)* íntimo
inner-city adj *(schools, problems)* de las zonas céntricas pobres, de los barrios céntricos pobres

inner city n barrios deprimidos del centro de una ciudad
innermost ['ɪnəməust] adj más íntimo, más secreto
inner tube n *(of tyre)* cámara, llanta *(LAm)*
inning ['ɪnɪŋ] n *(US: Baseball)* inning m, entrada; **~s** *(Cricket)* entrada, turno
innocence ['ɪnəsns] n inocencia
innocent ['ɪnəsnt] adj inocente
innocuous [ɪ'nɔkjuəs] adj inocuo
innovation [ɪnəu'veɪʃən] n novedad f
innovative ['ɪnəu'veɪtɪv] adj innovador
innuendo *(pl innuendoes)* [ɪnju'ɛndəu, -əuz] n indirecta
innumerable [ɪ'nju:mrəbl] adj innumerable
inoculate [ɪ'nɔkjuleɪt] vt: **to ~ sb with sth/ against sth** inocular or vacunar a algn con algo/contra algo
inoculation [ɪnɔkju'leɪʃən] n inoculación f
inoffensive [ɪnə'fɛnsɪv] adj inofensivo
inordinate [ɪ'nɔːdɪnət] adj excesivo, desmesurado
inordinately [ɪ'nɔːdɪnətlɪ] adv excesivamente, desmesuradamente
in-patient ['ɪnpeɪʃənt] n *(paciente m/f)* interno(-a)
input ['ɪnput] n *(Elec)* entrada; *(of resources)* inversión f; *(Comput)* entrada de datos ▷ vt *(Comput)* introducir, entrar
inquest ['ɪnkwɛst] n *(coroner's)* investigación f post-mortem
inquire [ɪn'kwaɪər] vi preguntar ▷ vt: **to ~ when/where/whether** preguntar cuándo/ dónde/si; **to ~ about** *(person)* preguntar por; *(fact)* informarse de; **inquire into** vt fus: **to ~ into sth** investigar or indagar algo
inquiry [ɪn'kwaɪərɪ] n pregunta; *(Law)* investigación f, pesquisa; *(commission)* comisión f investigadora; **to hold an ~ into sth** emprender una investigación sobre algo; **"Inquiries"** "Información"
inquiry office n *(Brit)* oficina de información
inquisition [ɪnkwɪ'zɪʃən] n inquisición f
inquisitive [ɪn'kwɪzɪtɪv] adj *(mind)* inquisitivo; *(person)* fisgón(-ona)
inroad ['ɪnrəud] n incursión f; *(fig)* invasión f; **to make ~s into** *(time)* ocupar parte de; *(savings, supplies)* agotar parte de
insane [ɪn'seɪn] adj loco; *(Med)* demente
insanity [ɪn'sænɪtɪ] n demencia, locura
inscribe [ɪn'skraɪb] vt inscribir; *(book etc)*: **to ~ (to sb)** dedicar (a algn)
inscription [ɪn'skrɪpʃən] n *(gen)* inscripción f; *(in book)* dedicatoria
inscrutable [ɪn'skru:təbl] adj inescrutable, insondable
insect ['ɪnsɛkt] n insecto
insecticide [ɪn'sɛktɪsaɪd] n insecticida m
insect repellent n loción f contra los insectos
insecure [ɪnsɪ'kjuər] adj inseguro
insecurity [ɪnsɪ'kjuərɪtɪ] n inseguridad f

insemination [ɪnsemɪ'neɪʃn] n: **artificial ~** inseminación f artificial

insensitive [ɪn'sensɪtɪv] adj insensible

inseparable [ɪn'sɛprəbl] adj inseparable; **they were ~ friends** los unía una estrecha amistad

insert vt [ɪn'sə:t] (into sth) introducir; (Comput) insertar ▷ n [ˈɪnsə:t] encarte m

insertion [ɪn'sə:ʃən] n inserción f

in-service [ɪn'sə:vɪs] adj (training, course) en el trabajo, a cargo de la empresa

inshore [ɪn'ʃɔ:r] adj: **~ fishing** pesca f costera ▷ adv (fish) a lo largo de la costa; (move) hacia la orilla

inside [ˈɪnˈsaɪd] n interior m; (lining) forro; (of road: Brit) izquierdo; (: in US, Europe etc) derecho ▷ adj interior, interno ▷ adv (within) (por) dentro, adentro (esp LAm); (with movement) hacia dentro; (inf: in prison) en chirona ▷ prep dentro de; (of time): **~ 10 minutes** en menos de 10 minutos; **insides** npl (inf) tripas fpl; **~ out** adv (turn) al revés; (know) a fondo

inside lane n (Aut: Brit) carril m izquierdo; (: in US, Europe etc) carril m derecho

insider [ɪn'saɪdər] n enterado(-a)

insider dealing, insider trading n (Stock Exchange) abuso de información privilegiada

insight [ˈɪnsaɪt] n perspicacia, percepción f; **to gain** or **get an ~ into sth** comprender algo mejor

insignificant [ɪnsɪg'nɪfɪknt] adj insignificante

insincere [ɪnsɪn'sɪər] adj poco sincero

insinuate [ɪn'sɪnjʊeɪt] vt insinuar

insinuation [ɪnsɪnjʊ'eɪʃən] n insinuación f

insist [ɪn'sɪst] vi insistir; **to ~ on doing** empeñarse en hacer; **to ~ that** insistir en que; (claim) exigir que

insistence [ɪn'sɪstəns] n insistencia; (stubbornness) empeño

insistent [ɪn'sɪstənt] adj insistente; (noise, action) persistente

insofar as [ɪnsəʊ'fɑ:-] conj en la medida en que, en tanto que

insole [ˈɪnsəʊl] n plantilla

insolence [ˈɪnsələns] n insolencia, descaro

insolent [ˈɪnsələnt] adj insolente, descarado

insolvent [ɪn'sɒlvənt] adj insolvente

insomnia [ɪn'sɒmnɪə] n insomnio

insomniac [ɪn'sɒmnɪæk] n insomne m/f

inspect [ɪn'spekt] vt inspeccionar, examinar; (troops) pasar revista a

inspection [ɪn'spekʃən] n inspección f, examen m; (of troops) revista

inspector [ɪn'spektər] n inspector(a) m(f); (Brit: on buses, trains) revisor(a) m(f)

inspiration [ɪnspə'reɪʃən] n inspiración f

inspire [ɪn'spaɪər] vt inspirar; **to ~ sb (to do sth)** alentar a algn (a hacer algo)

inspiring [ɪn'spaɪərɪŋ] adj inspirador(a)

instability [ɪnstə'bɪlɪtɪ] n inestabilidad f

install, instal (US) [ɪn'stɔ:l] vt instalar

installation [ɪnstə'leɪʃən] n instalación f

instalment, installment (US) [ɪn'stɔ:l-mənt] n plazo; (of story) entrega; (of TV serial etc) capítulo; **in ~s** (pay, receive) a plazos; **to pay in ~s** pagar a plazos or por abonos

instance [ˈɪnstəns] n ejemplo, caso; **for ~** por ejemplo; **in the first ~** en primer lugar; **in that ~** en ese caso

instant [ˈɪnstənt] n instante m, momento ▷ adj inmediato; (coffee) instantáneo

instantly [ˈɪnstəntlɪ] adv en seguida, al instante

instant message n mensaje m instantáneo

instant messaging [-'mesədʒɪŋ] n mensajería instantánea

instead [ɪn'sted] adv en cambio; **~ of** en lugar de, en vez de

instep [ˈɪnstep] n empeine m

instigate [ˈɪnstɪgeɪt] vt (rebellion, strike, crime) instigar; (new ideas etc) fomentar

instigation [ɪnstɪ'geɪʃən] n instigación f; **at sb's ~** a instigación de algn

instil [ɪn'stɪl] vt: **to ~ into** inculcar a

instinct [ˈɪnstɪŋkt] n instinto

instinctive [ɪn'stɪŋktɪv] adj instintivo

institute [ˈɪnstɪtju:t] n instituto; (professional body) colegio ▷ vt (begin) iniciar, empezar; (proceedings) entablar

institution [ɪnstɪ'tju:ʃən] n institución f; (beginning) iniciación f; (Med: home) asilo; (asylum) manicomio; (custom) costumbre f arraigada

instruct [ɪn'strʌkt] vt: **to ~ sb in sth** instruir a algn en or sobre algo; **to ~ sb to do sth** dar instrucciones a algn de or mandar a algn hacer algo

instruction [ɪn'strʌkʃən] n (teaching) instrucción f; **instructions** npl órdenes fpl; **~s (for use)** modo sg de empleo

instructor [ɪn'strʌktər] n instructor(a) m(f)

instrument [ˈɪnstrəmənt] n instrumento

instrumental [ɪnstrə'mentl] adj (Mus) instrumental; **to be ~ in** ser el artífice de; **to be ~ in sth/in doing sth** ser responsable de algo/de hacer algo

instrument panel n tablero (de instrumentos)

insufficient [ɪnsə'fɪʃənt] adj insuficiente

insular [ˈɪnsjʊlər] adj insular; (outlook) estrecho de miras

insulate [ˈɪnsjʊleɪt] vt aislar

insulating tape [ˈɪnsjʊleɪtɪŋ-] n cinta aislante

insulation [ɪnsjʊ'leɪʃən] n aislamiento

insulin [ˈɪnsjʊlɪn] n insulina

insult n [ˈɪnsʌlt] insulto; (offence) ofensa ▷ vt [ɪn'sʌlt] insultar; ofender

insulting [ɪn'sʌltɪŋ] adj insultante; ofensivo

insurance [ɪn'ʃʊərəns] n seguro; **fire/life ~** seguro contra incendios/de vida; **to take out ~ (against)** hacerse un seguro (contra)

insurance company n compañía f de seguros

insurance policy n póliza (de seguros)

insure [ɪn'ʃʊəʳ] vt asegurar; **to ~ sb** or **sb's life** hacer un seguro de vida a algn; **to ~ (against)** asegurar (contra); **to be ~d for £5000** tener un seguro de 5000 libras

insured [ɪn'ʃʊəd] n: **the ~** el/la asegurado(-a)

insurer [ɪn'ʃʊərəʳ] n asegurador(a)

intact [ɪn'tækt] adj íntegro; (untouched) intacto

intake ['ɪnteɪk] n (Tech) entrada, toma; (: pipe) tubo de admisión; (of food) ingestión f; (Brit Scol): **an ~ of 200 a year** 200 matriculados al año

integer ['ɪntɪdʒəʳ] n (número) entero

integral ['ɪntɪɡrəl] adj (whole) íntegro; (part) integrante

integrate ['ɪntɪɡreɪt] vt integrar ▷ vi integrarse

integrity [ɪn'tɛɡrɪtɪ] n honradez f, rectitud f; (Comput) integridad f

intellect ['ɪntəlɛkt] n intelecto

intellectual [ɪntə'lɛktjuəl] adj, n intelectual m/f

intelligence [ɪn'tɛlɪdʒəns] n inteligencia

Intelligence Service n Servicio de Inteligencia

intelligence test n prueba de inteligencia

intelligent [ɪn'tɛlɪdʒənt] adj inteligente

intend [ɪn'tɛnd] vt (gift etc): **to ~ sth for** destinar algo a; **to ~ to do sth** tener intención de or pensar hacer algo

intended [ɪn'tɛndɪd] adj (effect) deseado

intense [ɪn'tɛns] adj intenso; **to be ~** (person) tomárselo todo muy en serio

intensely [ɪn'tɛnslɪ] adv intensamente; (very) sumamente

intensify [ɪn'tɛnsɪfaɪ] vt intensificar; (increase) aumentar

intensity [ɪn'tɛnsɪtɪ] n (gen) intensidad f

intensive [ɪn'tɛnsɪv] adj intensivo

intensive care n: **to be in ~** estar bajo cuidados intensivos; **~ unit** n unidad f de vigilancia intensiva

intent [ɪn'tɛnt] n propósito; (Law) premeditación f ▷ adj (absorbed) absorto; (attentive) atento; **to all ~s and purposes** a efectos prácticos; **to be ~ on doing sth** estar resuelto or decidido a hacer algo

intention [ɪn'tɛnʃən] n intención f, propósito

intentional [ɪn'tɛnʃənl] adj deliberado

intently [ɪn'tɛntlɪ] adv atentamente, fijamente

interact [ɪntər'ækt] vi (substances) influirse mutuamente; (people) relacionarse

interaction [ɪntər'ækʃən] n interacción f, acción f recíproca

interactive [ɪntər'æktɪv] adj (Comput) interactivo

intercept [ɪntə'sɛpt] vt interceptar; (stop) detener

interception [ɪntə'sɛpʃən] n interceptación f; detención f

interchange n ['ɪntətʃeɪndʒ] intercambio; (on motorway) intersección f ▷ vt [ɪntə'tʃeɪndʒ] intercambiar

interchangeable [ɪntə'tʃeɪndʒəbl] adj intercambiable

intercity [ɪntə'sɪtɪ] adj: **~ (train)** (tren m) intercity m

intercom ['ɪntəkɔm] n interfono

intercourse ['ɪntəkɔ:s] n (also: **sexual ~**) relaciones fpl sexuales, contacto sexual; (social) trato

interest ['ɪntrɪst] n (Comm) interés m ▷ vt interesar; **compound/simple ~** interés compuesto/simple; **business ~s** negocios mpl; **British ~s in the Middle East** los intereses británicos en el Medio Oriente

interested ['ɪntrɪstɪd] adj interesado; **to be ~ in** interesarse por

interesting ['ɪntrɪstɪŋ] adj interesante

interest rate n tipo de interés

interface ['ɪntəfeɪs] n (Comput) junción f, interface m

interfere [ɪntə'fɪəʳ] vi: **to ~ in** (quarrel, other people's business) entrometerse en; **to ~ with** (hinder) estorbar; (damage) estropear; (Radio) interferir con

interference [ɪntə'fɪərəns] n (gen) intromisión f; (Radio, TV) interferencia

interim ['ɪntərɪm] adj provisional ▷ n: **in the ~** en el ínterin; **~ dividend** dividendo parcial

interior [ɪn'tɪərɪəʳ] n interior m ▷ adj interior

interior decorator, interior designer n interiorista m/f, diseñador(a) m(f) de interiores

interior design n interiorismo, decoración f de interiores

interjection [ɪntə'dʒɛkʃən] n interrupción f

interlock [ɪntə'lɔk] vi entrelazarse; (wheels etc) endentarse

interlude ['ɪntəlu:d] n intervalo; (rest) descanso; (Theat) intermedio

intermediary [ɪntə'mi:dɪərɪ] n intermediario(-a)

intermediate [ɪntə'mi:dɪət] adj intermedio

intermission [ɪntə'mɪʃən] n (Theat) descanso

intermittent [ɪntə'mɪtnt] adj intermitente

intern vt [ɪn'tə:n] internar; (enclose) encerrar ▷ n ['ɪntə:n] (US) médico(-a) m(f) interno(-a)

internal [ɪn'tə:nl] adj interno, interior; (injury, structure, memo) internal; **~ injuries** heridas fpl or lesiones fpl internas

internally [ɪn'tə:nəlɪ] adv interiormente; **"not to be taken ~"** "uso externo"

Internal Revenue Service n (US) ≈ Hacienda, ≈ Agencia Tributaria

international [ɪntə'næʃənl] adj internacional; **~ (game)** partido internacional; **~ (player)** jugador(a) m(f) internacional

internee [ɪntə:'ni:] n interno(-a), recluso(-a)

internet, Internet ['ɪntənɛt] *n*: **the ~** (el *or* la) Internet

internet café *n* cibercafé *m*

Internet Service Provider *n* proveedor *m* de (acceso a) Internet

internet user *n* internauta *m/f*

internment [ɪn'tə:nmənt] *n* internamiento

interplay ['ɪntəpleɪ] *n* interacción *f*

interpret [ɪn'tə:prɪt] *vt* interpretar; *(translate)* traducir; *(understand)* entender ▷ *vi* hacer de intérprete

interpretation [ɪntə:prɪ'teɪʃən] *n* interpretación *f*; traducción *f*

interpreter [ɪn'tə:prɪtə*r*] *n* intérprete *m/f*

interrelated [ɪntərɪ'leɪtɪd] *adj* interrelacionado

interrogate [ɪn'tɛrəʊgeɪt] *vt* interrogar

interrogation [ɪntɛrəʊ'geɪʃən] *n* interrogatorio

interrogative [ɪntə'rɔgətɪv] *adj* interrogativo

interrupt [ɪntə'rʌpt] *vt, vi* interrumpir

interruption [ɪntə'rʌpʃən] *n* interrupción *f*

intersect [ɪntə'sɛkt] *vt* cruzar ▷ *vi (roads)* cruzarse

intersection [ɪntə'sɛkʃən] *n* intersección *f*; *(of roads)* cruce *m*

intersperse [ɪntə'spə:s] *vt*: **to ~ with** salpicar de

interstate ['ɪntərsteɪt] *n (US)* carretera interestatal

intertwine [ɪntə'twaɪn] *vt* entrelazar ▷ *vi* entrelazarse

interval ['ɪntəvl] *n* intervalo; *(Brit Theat, Sport)* descanso; *(Scol)* recreo; **at ~s** a ratos, de vez en cuando; **sunny ~s** *(Meteorology)* claros *mpl*

intervene [ɪntə'vi:n] *vi* intervenir; *(take part)* participar; *(occur)* sobrevenir

intervention [ɪntə'vɛnʃən] *n* intervención *f*

interview ['ɪntəvju:] *n (Radio, TV etc)* entrevista ▷ *vt* entrevistar a

interviewee [ɪntəvju:'i:] *n* entrevistado(-a)

interviewer ['ɪntəvju:ə*r*] *n* entrevistador(a) *m(f)*

intestate [ɪn'tɛsteɪt] *adj* intestado

intestine [ɪn'tɛstɪn] *n*: **large/small ~** intestino grueso/delgado

intimacy ['ɪntɪməsɪ] *n* intimidad *f*; *(relations)* relaciones *fpl* íntimas

intimate *adj* ['ɪntɪmət] íntimo; *(friendship)* estrecho; *(knowledge)* profundo ▷ *vt* ['ɪntɪmeɪt] *(announce)* dar a entender

intimidate [ɪn'tɪmɪdeɪt] *vt* intimidar, amedrentar

intimidating [ɪn'tɪmɪdeɪtɪŋ] *adj* amedrentador, intimidante

intimidation [ɪntɪmɪ'deɪʃən] *n* intimidación *f*

into ['ɪntu:] *prep (gen)* en; *(towards)* a; *(inside)* hacia el interior de; **~ three pieces/French** en tres pedazos/al francés; **to change pounds ~ euros** cambiar libras por euros

intolerable [ɪn'tɔlərəbl] *adj* intolerable, insoportable

intolerant [ɪn'tɔlərənt] *adj*: **~ (of)** intolerante (con)

intoxicated [ɪn'tɔksɪkeɪtɪd] *adj* embriagado

intoxication [ɪntɔksɪ'keɪʃən] *n* embriaguez *f*

intractable [ɪn'træktəbl] *adj (person)* intratable; *(problem)* irresoluble; *(illness)* incurable

intranet ['ɪntrənet] *n* intranet *f*

intransitive [ɪn'trænsɪtɪv] *adj* intransitivo

intravenous [ɪntrə'vi:nəs] *adj* intravenoso

in-tray ['ɪntreɪ] *n* bandeja de entrada

intrepid [ɪn'trɛpɪd] *adj* intrépido

intricate ['ɪntrɪkət] *adj (design, pattern)* intrincado; *(plot, problem)* complejo

intrigue [ɪn'tri:g] *n* intriga ▷ *vt* fascinar ▷ *vi* andar en intrigas

intriguing [ɪn'tri:gɪŋ] *adj* fascinante

intrinsic [ɪn'trɪnsɪk] *adj* intrínseco

introduce [ɪntrə'dju:s] *vt* introducir, meter; *(speaker, TV show etc)* presentar; **to ~ sb (to sb)** presentar algn (a algn); **to ~ sb to** *(pastime, technique)* introducir a algn a; **may I ~ ...?** permítame presentarle a ...

introduction [ɪntrə'dʌkʃən] *n* introducción *f*; *(of person)* presentación *f*; **a letter of ~** una carta de recomendación

introductory [ɪntrə'dʌktərɪ] *adj* introductorio; **an ~ offer** una oferta introductoria; **~ remarks** comentarios *mpl* preliminares

introvert ['ɪntrəʊvə:t] *adj, n* introvertido(-a) *m(f)*

intrude [ɪn'tru:d] *vi (person)* entrometerse; **to ~ on** estorbar

intruder [ɪn'tru:də*r*] *n* intruso(-a)

intrusion [ɪn'tru:ʒən] *n* invasión *f*

intuition [ɪntju:'ɪʃən] *n* intuición *f*

intuitive [ɪn'tju:ɪtɪv] *adj* intuitivo

inundate ['ɪnʌndeɪt] *vt*: **to ~ with** inundar de

invade [ɪn'veɪd] *vt* invadir

invalid *n* ['ɪnvəlɪd] minusválido(-a) ▷ *adj* [ɪn'vælɪd] *(not valid)* inválido, nulo

invaluable [ɪn'væljuəbl] *adj* inestimable

invariably [ɪn'vɛərɪəblɪ] *adv* sin excepción, siempre; **she is ~ late** siempre llega tarde

invasion [ɪn'veɪʒən] *n* invasión *f*

invent [ɪn'vɛnt] *vt* inventar

invention [ɪn'vɛnʃən] *n* invento; *(inventiveness)* inventiva; *(lie)* invención *f*

inventive [ɪn'vɛntɪv] *adj* inventivo

inventor [ɪn'vɛntə*r*] *n* inventor(a) *m(f)*

inventory ['ɪnvəntrɪ] *n* inventario

invert [ɪn'və:t] *vt* invertir

inverted commas [ɪn'və:tɪd-] *npl (Brit)* comillas *fpl*

invest [ɪn'vɛst] *vt* invertir; *(fig: time, effort)* dedicar ▷ *vi*: **to ~ in** *(company etc)* invertir dinero en; *(fig: sth useful)* comprar; **to ~ sb with sth** conferir algo a algn

investigate [ɪn'vɛstɪɡeɪt] vt investigar; (study) estudiar, examinar

investigation [ɪnvɛstɪ'ɡeɪʃən] n investigación f, pesquisa; examen m

investigator [ɪn'vɛstɪɡeɪtəʳ] n investigador(a) m(f); **private ~** investigador(a) m(f) privado(-a)

investment [ɪn'vɛstmənt] n inversión f

investor [ɪn'vɛstəʳ] n inversor(a) m(f)

invigilator [ɪn'vɪdʒɪleɪtəʳ] n celador(a) m(f)

invigorating [ɪn'vɪɡəreɪtɪŋ] adj vigorizante

invisible [ɪn'vɪzɪbl] adj invisible

invitation [ɪnvɪ'teɪʃən] n invitación f; **at sb's ~** a invitación de algn; **by ~ only** solamente por invitación

invite [ɪn'vaɪt] vt invitar; (opinions etc) solicitar, pedir; (trouble) buscarse; **to ~ sb (to do)** invitar a algn (a hacer); **to ~ sb to dinner** invitar a algn a cenar; **invite out** vt invitar a salir; **invite over** vt invitar a casa

inviting [ɪn'vaɪtɪŋ] adj atractivo; (look) provocativo; (food) apetitoso

invoice ['ɪnvɔɪs] n factura ▷ vt facturar; **to ~ sb for goods** facturar a algn las mercancías

involuntary [ɪn'vɒləntrɪ] adj involuntario

involve [ɪn'vɒlv] vt (entail) suponer, implicar, tener que ver con; (concern, affect) corresponder a; **to ~ sb (in sth)** involucrar a algn (en algo), comprometer a algn (con algo)

involved [ɪn'vɒlvd] adj complicado; **to be ~ in sth** (take part) estar involucrado en algo; (engrossed in) estar muy metido

involvement [ɪn'vɒlvmənt] n participación f, dedicación f; (obligation) compromiso; (difficulty) apuro

inward ['ɪnwəd] adj (movement) interior, interno; (thought, feeling) íntimo ▷ adv hacia dentro

inwards ['ɪnwədz] adv hacia dentro

I/O abbr (Comput: = input/output) E/S; **~ error** error m de E/S

iodine ['aɪəʊdiːn] n yodo

ioniser ['aɪənaɪzəʳ] n ionizador m

iota [aɪ'əʊtə] n (fig) jota, ápice m

IOU n abbr (= I owe you) pagaré m

IPA n abbr (= International Phonetic Alphabet) AFI m

iPod® ['aɪpɒd] n iPod® m

IQ n abbr (= intelligence quotient) C.I. m

IRA n abbr (= Irish Republican Army) IRA m; (US) = **individual retirement account**

Iran [ɪ'rɑːn] n Irán m

Iranian [ɪ'reɪnɪən] adj iraní ▷ n iraní m/f; (Ling) iraní m

Iraq [ɪ'rɑːk] n Irak m

Iraqi [ɪ'rɑːkɪ] adj, n irakí m/f

irate [aɪ'reɪt] adj enojado, airado

Ireland ['aɪələnd] n Irlanda; **Republic of ~** República de Irlanda

iris (pl **irises**) ['aɪrɪs, -ɪz] n (Anat) iris m; (Bot) lirio

Irish ['aɪrɪʃ] adj irlandés(-esa) ▷ n (Ling) irlandés m; **the ~** npl los irlandeses

Irishman ['aɪrɪʃmən] n irlandés m

Irish Sea n: **the ~** el Mar de Irlanda

Irishwoman ['aɪrɪʃwʊmən] n irlandesa

irk [əːk] vt fastidiar

irksome ['əːksəm] adj fastidioso

IRN n abbr (= Independent Radio News) servicio de noticias en las cadenas de radio privadas

iron ['aɪən] n hierro; (for clothes) plancha ▷ adj de hierro ▷ vt (clothes) planchar; **irons** npl (chains) grilletes mpl; **iron out** vt (crease) quitar; (fig) allanar, resolver

Iron Curtain n: **the ~** el Telón de Acero

ironic [aɪ'rɒnɪk], **ironical** [aɪ'rɒnɪkl] adj irónico

ironically [aɪ'rɒnɪklɪ] adv irónicamente

ironing ['aɪənɪŋ] n (act) planchado; (ironed clothes) ropa planchada; (clothes to be ironed) ropa por planchar

ironing board n tabla de planchar

ironmonger ['aɪənmʌŋɡəʳ] n (Brit) ferretero(-a); **~'s (shop)** ferretería

irony ['aɪrənɪ] n ironía; **the ~ of it is that ...** lo irónico del caso es que ...

irrational [ɪ'ræʃənl] adj irracional

irregular [ɪ'reɡjuləʳ] adj irregular; (surface) desigual; (action, event) anómalo; (behaviour) poco ortodoxo

irrelevant [ɪ'reləvənt] adj irrelevante; **to be ~** estar fuera de lugar, no venir al caso

irresistible [ɪrɪ'zɪstɪbl] adj irresistible

irrespective [ɪrɪ'spɛktɪv]: **~ of** prep sin tener en cuenta, no importa

irresponsible [ɪrɪ'spɒnsɪbl] adj (act) irresponsable; (person) poco serio

irreverent [ɪ'rɛvərnt] adj irreverente, irrespetuoso

irrevocable [ɪ'rɛvəkəbl] adj irrevocable

irrigate ['ɪrɪɡeɪt] vt regar

irrigation [ɪrɪ'ɡeɪʃən] n riego

irritable ['ɪrɪtəbl] adj (person: temperament) irritable; (: mood) de mal humor

irritate ['ɪrɪteɪt] vt fastidiar; (Med) picar

irritating ['ɪrɪteɪtɪŋ] adj fastidioso

irritation [ɪrɪ'teɪʃən] n fastidio; picazón f, picor m

IRS n abbr (US) = **Internal Revenue Service**

is [ɪz] vb see **be**

ISA ['aɪsə] n abbr (Brit: = individual savings account) plan de ahorro personal para pequeños inversores con fiscalidad cero

ISBN n abbr (= International Standard Book Number) ISBN m

ISDN n abbr (= Integrated Services Digital Network) RDSI f

Islam ['ɪzlɑːm] n Islam m

Islamic [ɪz'læmɪk] adj islámico

island ['aɪlənd] n isla; (also: **traffic ~**) isleta

islander ['aɪləndəʳ] n isleño(-a)

isle [aɪl] n isla

isn't ['ɪznt] = **is not**

isobar ['aɪsəʊbɑːʳ] n isobara

isolate ['aɪsəleɪt] vt aislar

isolated ['aɪsəleɪtɪd] *adj* aislado
isolation [aɪsə'leɪʃən] *n* aislamiento
isotope ['aɪsəutəup] *n* isótopo
ISP *n abbr* = **Internet Service Provider**
Israel ['ɪzreɪl] *n* Israel *m*
Israeli [ɪz'reɪlɪ] *adj, n* israelí *m/f*
issue ['ɪsjuː] *n* cuestión *f*, asunto; (*outcome*) resultado; (*of banknotes etc*) emisión *f*; (*of newspaper etc*) número; (*offspring*) sucesión *f*, descendencia ▷ *vt* (*rations, equipment*) distribuir, repartir; (*orders*) dar; (*certificate, passport*) expedir; (*decree*) promulgar; (*magazine*) publicar; (*cheque*) extender; (*banknotes, stamp*) emitir ▷ *vi*: **to ~ (from)** derivar (de), brotar (de); **at ~** en cuestión; **to take ~ with sb (over)** disentir con algn (en); **to avoid the ~** andarse con rodeos; **to confuse** *or* **obscure the ~** confundir las cosas; **to make an ~ of sth** dar a algo más importancia de lo necesario; **to ~ sth to sb, ~ sb with sth** entregar algo a algn
isthmus ['ɪsməs] *n* istmo
IT *n abbr* = **information technology**

○ KEYWORD

it [ɪt] *pron* **1** (*specific subject: not generally translated*) él/ella; (*: direct object*) lo/la; (*: indirect object*) le; (*after prep*) él/ella; (*abstract concept*) ello; **it's on the table** está en la mesa; **I can't find it** no lo (*or* la) encuentro; **give it to me** dámelo (*or* dámela); **I spoke to him about it** le hablé del asunto; **what did you learn from it?** ¿qué aprendiste de él (*or* ella)?; **did you go to it?** (*party, concert etc*) ¿fuiste?
2 (*impersonal*): **it's raining** llueve, está lloviendo; **it's 6 o'clock/the 10th of August** son las 6/es el 10 de agosto; **how far is it? — it's 10 miles/2 hours on the train** ¿a qué distancia está? — a 10 millas/2 horas en tren; **who is it? — it's me** ¿quién es? — soy yo

Italian [ɪ'tæljən] *adj* italiano ▷ *n* italiano(-a); (*Ling*) italiano
italic [ɪ'tælɪk] *adj* cursivo; **italics** *npl* cursiva *sg*
Italy ['ɪtəlɪ] *n* Italia
itch [ɪtʃ] *n* picazón *f*; (*fig*) prurito ▷ *vi* (*person*) sentir *or* tener comezón; (*part of body*) picar; **to be ~ing to do sth** rabiar por *or* morirse de ganas de hacer algo
itchy ['ɪtʃɪ] *adj*: **to be ~** picar; **my hand is ~** me pica la mano
it'd ['ɪtd] = **it would; it had**
item ['aɪtəm] *n* artículo; (*on agenda*) asunto (a tratar); (*in programme*) número; (*also*: **news ~**) noticia; **~s of clothing** prendas *fpl* de vestir
itemize ['aɪtəmaɪz] *vt* detallar
itinerary [aɪ'tɪnərərɪ] *n* itinerario
it'll ['ɪtl] = **it will; it shall**
ITN *n abbr* (*Brit*) = **Independent Television News**

its [ɪts] *adj* su
it's [ɪts] = **it is; it has**
itself [ɪt'sɛlf] *pron* (*reflexive*) sí mismo(-a); (*emphatic*) él/ella mismo(-a)
ITV *n abbr* (*Brit*: = *Independent Television*)
IUD *n abbr* (= *intra-uterine device*) DIU *m*
I've [aɪv] = **I have**
ivory ['aɪvərɪ] *n* marfil *m*
ivy ['aɪvɪ] *n* hiedra
Ivy League *n* (*US*) *ver nota*

J

J, j [dʒeɪ] n (letter) J, j f; **J for Jack**, (US) **J for Jig** J de José

jab [dʒæb] vt (elbow) dar un codazo a; (punch) dar un golpe rápido a ▷ vi: **to ~ at** intentar golpear a; **to ~ sth into sth** clavar algo en algo ▷ n codazo; golpe m (rápido); (Med: inf) pinchazo

jack [dʒæk] n (Aut) gato; (Bowls) boliche m; (Cards) sota; **jack in** vt (inf) dejar; **jack up** vt (Aut) levantar con el gato

jackal ['dʒækl] n (Zool) chacal m

jackdaw ['dʒækdɔ:] n grajo(-a), chova

jacket ['dʒækɪt] n chaqueta, americana, saco (LAm); (of boiler etc) camisa; (of book) sobrecubierta

jacket potato n patata asada (con piel)

jack-in-the-box ['dʒækɪnðəbɒks] n caja sorpresa, caja de resorte

jack-knife ['dʒæknaɪf] vi colear

jack plug n (Elec) enchufe m de clavija

jackpot ['dʒækpɒt] n premio gordo

Jacuzzi® [dʒəˈkuːzɪ] n jacuzzi® m

jaded ['dʒeɪdɪd] adj (tired) cansado; (fed up) hastiado

jagged ['dʒægɪd] adj dentado

jail [dʒeɪl] n cárcel f ▷ vt encarcelar

jail sentence n pena f de cárcel

jam [dʒæm] n mermelada; (also: **traffic ~**) atasco, embotellamiento; (difficulty) apuro ▷ vt (passage etc) obstruir; (mechanism, drawer etc) atascar; (Radio) interferir ▷ vi atascarse, trabarse; **to get sb out of a ~** sacar a algn del paso or de un apuro; **to ~ sth into sth** meter algo a la fuerza en algo; **the telephone lines are ~med** las líneas están saturadas

Jamaica [dʒəˈmeɪkə] n Jamaica

jamb [dʒæm] n jamba

jammed [dʒæmd] adj atascado

Jan abbr (= January) ene

jangle ['dʒæŋgl] vi sonar (de manera) discordante

janitor ['dʒænɪtər] n (caretaker) portero, conserje m

January ['dʒænjuərɪ] n enero; see also **July**

Japan [dʒəˈpæn] n (el) Japón

Japanese [dʒæpəˈniːz] adj japonés(-esa) ▷ n pl inv japonés(-esa) m(f); (Ling) japonés m

jar [dʒɑːr] n (glass: large) jarra; (small) tarro ▷ vi (sound) chirriar; (colours) desentonar

jargon ['dʒɑːgən] n jerga

jaundice ['dʒɔːndɪs] n ictericia

jaundiced ['dʒɔːndɪst] adj (fig: embittered) amargado; (: disillusioned) desilusionado

javelin ['dʒævlɪn] n jabalina

jaw [dʒɔː] n mandíbula; **jaws** npl (Tech: of vice etc) mordaza sg

jay [dʒeɪ] n (Zool) arrendajo

jaywalker ['dʒeɪwɔːkər] n peatón(-ona) m(f) imprudente

jazz [dʒæz] n jazz m; **jazz up** vt (liven up) animar

JCB® n abbr excavadora

jealous ['dʒɛləs] adj (gen) celoso; (envious) envidioso; **to be ~** tener celos

jealousy ['dʒɛləsɪ] n celos mpl; envidia

jeans [dʒiːnz] npl (pantalones mpl) vaqueros mpl or tejanos mpl, bluejean m inv (LAm)

Jeep® [dʒiːp] n jeep m

jeer [dʒɪər] vi: **to ~ (at)** (boo) abuchear; (mock) mofarse (de)

Jello® ['dʒɛləu] n (US) gelatina

jelly ['dʒɛlɪ] n (jam) jalea; (dessert etc) gelatina

jellyfish ['dʒɛlɪfɪʃ] n medusa

jeopardize ['dʒɛpədaɪz] vt arriesgar, poner en peligro

jeopardy ['dʒɛpədɪ] n: **to be in ~** estar en peligro

jerk [dʒəːk] n (jolt) sacudida; (wrench) tirón m; (US inf) imbécil m/f, pendejo(-a) (LAm) ▷ vt dar una sacudida a; tirar bruscamente de ▷ vi (vehicle) dar una sacudida

Jersey ['dʒəːzɪ] n Jersey m

jersey ['dʒəːzɪ] n jersey m; (fabric) tejido de punto

Jesus ['dʒiːzəs] n Jesús m; **~ Christ** Jesucristo

jet [dʒɛt] n (of gas, liquid) chorro; (Aviat) avión m a reacción

jet-black [dʒɛt'blæk] adj negro como el azabache

jet engine n motor m a reacción

jet lag n desorientación f por desfase horario

jet-setter ['dʒɛtsetər] n personaje m de la jet

jet-ski ['dʒɛtskiː] vi practicar el motociclismo acuático

jettison ['dʒɛtɪsn] vt desechar

jetty ['dʒɛtɪ] n muelle m, embarcadero

Jew [dʒu:] n judío(-a)

jewel ['dʒu:əl] n joya; (in watch) rubí m

jeweller, jeweler (US) ['dʒu:ələ'] n joyero(-a); **~'s (shop)** joyería

jewellery, jewelry (US) ['dʒu:əlrɪ] n joyas fpl, alhajas fpl

Jewess ['dʒu:ɪs] n judía

Jewish ['dʒu:ɪʃ] adj judío

jibe [dʒaɪb] n mofa

jiffy ['dʒɪfɪ] n (inf): **in a ~** en un santiamén

jigsaw ['dʒɪgsɔ:] n (also: **~ puzzle**) rompecabezas m inv, puzle m; (tool) sierra de vaivén

jilt [dʒɪlt] vt dejar plantado a

jingle ['dʒɪŋgl] n (advert) musiquilla ▷ vi tintinear

jinx [dʒɪŋks] n: **there's a ~ on it** está gafado

jitters ['dʒɪtəz] npl (inf): **to get the ~** ponerse nervioso

jittery ['dʒɪtərɪ] adj (inf) agitado

job [dʒɔb] n trabajo; (task) tarea; (duty) deber m; (post) empleo; (inf: difficulty) dificultad f; **it's a good ~ that ...** menos mal que ...; **just the ~!** ¡justo lo que necesito!; **a part-time/full-time ~** un trabajo a tiempo parcial/tiempo completo; **that's not my ~** eso no me incumbe or toca a mí; **he's only doing his ~** está cumpliendo nada más

job centre n (Brit) oficina de empleo

jobless ['dʒɔblɪs] adj sin trabajo ▷ n: **the ~** los parados

job satisfaction n satisfacción f en el trabajo

job security n garantía de trabajo

jockey ['dʒɔkɪ] n jockey m/f ▷ vi: **to ~ for position** maniobrar para sacar delantera

jockstrap ['dʒɔkstræp] n suspensorio

jocular ['dʒɔkjulə'] adj (humorous) gracioso; (merry) alegre

jog [dʒɔg] vt empujar (ligeramente) ▷ vi (run) hacer footing; **to ~ along** (fig) ir tirando; **to ~ sb's memory** refrescar la memoria a algn

jogger ['dʒɔgə'] n corredor(a) m(f)

jogging ['dʒɔgɪŋ] n footing m

join [dʒɔɪn] vt (things) unir, juntar; (become member of: club) hacerse socio de; (Pol: party) afiliarse a; (meet: people) reunirse con; (fig) unirse a ▷ vi (roads) empalmar; (rivers) confluir ▷ n juntura; **will you ~ us for dinner?** ¿quieres cenar con nosotros?; **I'll ~ you later** me reuniré contigo luego; **to ~ forces (with)** aliarse (con); **join in** vi tomar parte, participar ▷ vt fus tomar parte or participar en; **join up** vi unirse; (Mil) alistarse

joiner ['dʒɔɪnə'] n carpintero(-a)

joint [dʒɔɪnt] n (Tech) juntura, unión f; (Anat) articulación f; (Brit Culin) pieza de carne (para asar); (inf: place) garito; (of cannabis) porro ▷ adj (common) común; (combined) conjunto; (responsibility) compartido; (committee) mixto

joint account n (with bank etc) cuenta común

jointly ['dʒɔɪntlɪ] adv (gen) en común; (together) conjuntamente

joist [dʒɔɪst] n viga

joke [dʒəuk] n chiste m; (also: **practical ~**) broma ▷ vi bromear; **to play a ~ on** gastar una broma a

joker ['dʒəukə'] n chistoso(-a), bromista m/f; (Cards) comodín m

jolly ['dʒɔlɪ] adj (merry) alegre; (enjoyable) divertido ▷ adv (inf) muy, la mar de ▷ vt: **to ~ sb along** animar or darle ánimos a algn; **~ good!** ¡estupendo!

jolt [dʒəult] n (shake) sacudida; (blow) golpe m; (shock) susto ▷ vt (physically) sacudir; (emotionally) asustar

Jordan ['dʒɔ:dən] n (country) Jordania; (river) Jordán m

jostle ['dʒɔsl] vt dar empujones or empellones a

jot [dʒɔt] n: **not one ~** ni pizca, ni un ápice; **jot down** vt apuntar

jotter ['dʒɔtə'] n (Brit) bloc m

journal ['dʒə:nl] n (paper) periódico; (magazine) revista; (diary) diario

journalism ['dʒə:nəlɪzəm] n periodismo

journalist ['dʒə:nəlɪst] n periodista m/f

journey ['dʒə:nɪ] n viaje m; (distance covered) trayecto ▷ vi viajar; **return ~** viaje de regreso; **a five-hour ~** un viaje de cinco horas

joy [dʒɔɪ] n alegría

joyful ['dʒɔɪful] adj alegre

joyrider ['dʒɔɪraɪdə'] n persona que se da una vuelta en un coche robado

joystick ['dʒɔɪstɪk] n (Aviat) palanca de mando; (Comput) palanca de control

JP n abbr see **Justice of the Peace**

Jr abbr = **junior**

jubilant ['dʒu:bɪlnt] adj jubiloso

judge [dʒʌdʒ] n juez m/f ▷ vt juzgar; (competition) actuar de or ser juez en; (estimate) considerar; (: weight, size etc) calcular ▷ vi: **judging** or **to ~ by his expression** a juzgar por su expresión; **as far as I can ~** por lo que puedo entender, a mi entender; **I ~d it necessary to inform him** consideré necesario informarle

judicial [dʒu:'dɪʃl] adj judicial

judiciary [dʒu:'dɪʃɪərɪ] n poder m judicial, magistratura

judo ['dʒu:dəu] n judo

jug [dʒʌg] n jarra

juggernaut ['dʒʌgənɔ:t] n (Brit: huge truck) camión m de carga pesada

juggle ['dʒʌgl] vi hacer juegos malabares

juggler ['dʒʌglə'] n malabarista m/f

juice [dʒu:s] n jugo, zumo (Sp); (of meat) jugo; (inf: petrol): **we've run out of ~** se nos acabó la gasolina

juicy ['dʒu:sɪ] adj jugoso
jukebox ['dʒu:kbɔks] n máquina de discos
Jul. abbr (= July) jul
July [dʒu:'laɪ] n julio; **the first of ~** el uno or primero de julio; **during ~** en el mes de julio; **in ~ of next year** en julio del año que viene
jumble ['dʒʌmbl] n revoltijo ▷ vt (also: **~ together, ~ up**: mix up) revolver; (: disarrange) mezclar
jumble sale n (Brit) mercadillo; ver nota

> ● JUMBLE SALE
> ●
> ● En cada jumble sale pueden comprarse todo
> ● tipo de objetos baratos de segunda mano,
> ● especialmente ropa, juguetes, libros,
> ● vajillas y muebles. Suelen organizarse en
> ● los locales de un colegio, iglesia,
> ● ayuntamiento o similar, con fines
> ● benéficos, bien en ayuda de una
> ● organización benéfica conocida o para
> ● solucionar problemas más concretos de
> ● la comunidad.

jumbo ['dʒʌmbəu], **jumbo jet** n jumbo
jump [dʒʌmp] vi saltar, dar saltos; (start) sobresaltarse; (increase) aumentar ▷ vt saltar ▷ n salto; (fence) obstáculo; (increase) aumento; **to ~ the queue** (Brit) colarse; **jump about** vi dar saltos, brincar; **jump at** vt fus (fig) apresurarse a aprovechar; **he ~ed at the offer** se apresuró a aceptar la oferta; **jump down** vi bajar de un salto, saltar a tierra; **jump up** vi levantarse de un salto
jumper ['dʒʌmpəʳ] n (Brit: pullover) jersey m, suéter m; (US: pinafore dress) pichi m; (Sport) saltador(a) m(f)
jump leads, jumper cables (US) npl cables mpl puente de batería
jump-start ['dʒʌmpsta:t] vt (car) arrancar con ayuda de otra batería or empujando; (fig: economy) reactivar
jumpy ['dʒʌmpɪ] adj nervioso
Jun. abbr = **junior**; (= June) jun
junction ['dʒʌŋkʃən] n (Brit: of roads) cruce m; (Rail) empalme m
juncture ['dʒʌŋktʃəʳ] n: **at this ~** en este momento, en esta coyuntura
June [dʒu:n] n junio; see also **July**
jungle ['dʒʌŋgl] n selva, jungla
junior ['dʒu:nɪəʳ] adj (in age) menor, más joven; (competition) juvenil; (position) subalterno ▷ n menor m/f, joven m/f; **he's ~ to me** es menor que yo
junior high school n (US) centro de educación secundaria
junior school n (Brit) escuela primaria
junk [dʒʌŋk] n (cheap goods) baratijas fpl; (lumber) trastos mpl viejos; (rubbish) basura; (ship) junco ▷ vt (esp US) deshacerse de
junk bond n (Comm) obligación f basura inv

junket ['dʒʌŋkɪt] n (Culin) dulce de leche cuajada; (Brit inf): **to go on a ~, go ~ing** viajar a costa ajena or del erario público
junk food n comida basura or de plástico
junkie ['dʒʌŋkɪ] n (inf) yonqui m/f, heroinómano(-a)
junk mail n propaganda (buzoneada), correo m basura inv
junk shop n tienda de objetos usados
Jupiter ['dʒu:pɪtəʳ] n (Mythology, Astro) Júpiter m
jurisdiction [dʒuərɪs'dɪkʃən] n jurisdicción f; **it falls** or **comes within/outside our ~** es/no es de nuestra competencia
jurisprudence [dʒuərɪs'pru:dəns] n jurisprudencia
juror ['dʒuərəʳ] n jurado
jury ['dʒuərɪ] n jurado
just [dʒʌst] adj justo ▷ adv (exactly) exactamente; (only) sólo, solamente, no más (LAm); **he's ~ done it/left** acaba de hacerlo/irse; **I've ~ seen him** acabo de verle; **~ right** perfecto; **~ two o'clock** las dos en punto; **she's ~ as clever as you** es tan lista como tú; **~ as well that ...** menos mal que ...; **it's ~ as well you didn't go** menos mal que no fuiste; **it's ~ as good (as)** es igual (que), es tan bueno (como); **~ as he was leaving** en el momento en que se marchaba; **we were ~ going** ya nos íbamos; **I was ~ about to phone** estaba a punto de llamar; **~ before/enough** justo antes/lo suficiente; **~ here** aquí mismo; **he ~ missed** falló por poco; **~ listen to this** escucha esto un momento; **~ ask someone the way** simplemente pregúntale a alguien por dónde se va; **not ~ now** ahora no
justice ['dʒʌstɪs] n justicia; (US: judge) juez m/f; **to do ~ to** (fig) hacer justicia a; **this photo doesn't do you ~** esta foto no te favorece
Justice of the Peace n juez m/f de paz; see also **Crown Court**
justification [dʒʌstɪfɪ'keɪʃən] n justificación f
justify ['dʒʌstɪfaɪ] vt justificar; (text) alinear, justificar; **to be justified in doing sth** tener motivo para o razón al hacer algo
jut [dʒʌt] vi (also: **~ out**) sobresalir
juvenile ['dʒu:vənaɪl] adj juvenil; (humour, mentality) infantil; (court) de menores ▷ n joven m/f, menor m/f de edad

K, k [keɪ] n (letter) K, k f; **K for King** K de Kilo

K n abbr (= one thousand) mil ▷ abbr (Brit: = Knight) título; (= kilobyte) K

kamikaze [kæmɪ'kɑːzɪ] adj kamikaze

kangaroo [kæŋgə'ruː] n canguro

karaoke [kɑːrə'əʊkɪ] n karaoke

karate [kə'rɑːtɪ] n karate m

Kazakhstan [kɑːzɑːk'stæn] n Kazajstán m

kebab [kə'bæb] n pincho moruno, brocheta

keel [kiːl] n quilla; **on an even ~** (fig) en equilibrio; **keel over** vi (Naut) zozobrar, volcarse; (person) desplomarse

keen [kiːn] adj (interest, desire) grande, vivo; (eye, intelligence) agudo; (competition) reñido; (edge) afilado; (Brit: eager) entusiasta; **to be ~ to do or on doing sth** tener muchas ganas de hacer algo; **to be ~ on sth/sb** interesarse por algo/algn; **I'm not ~ on going** no tengo ganas de ir

keep [kiːp] (pt, pp **kept**) vt (retain, preserve) guardar; (hold back) quedarse con; (shop) ser propietario de; (feed: family etc) mantener; (promise) cumplir; (chickens, bees etc) criar ▷ vi (food) conservarse; (remain) seguir, continuar ▷ n (of castle) torreón m; (food etc) comida, sustento; **to ~ doing sth** seguir haciendo algo; **to ~ sb from doing sth** impedir a algn hacer algo; **to ~ sth from happening** impedir que algo ocurra; **to ~ sb happy** tener a algn contento; **to ~ sb waiting** hacer esperar a algn; **to ~ a place tidy** mantener un lugar limpio; **to ~ sth to o.s.** no decirle algo a nadie; **to ~ time** (clock) mantener la hora exacta; **~ the change** quédese con la vuelta; **to ~ an appointment** acudir a una cita; **to ~ a record or note of sth** tomar nota de or apuntar algo; see also **keeps**; **keep away** vt: **to ~ sth/sb away from sb** mantener algo/a algn apartado de algn ▷ vi: **to ~ away (from)** mantenerse apartado (de); **keep back** vt (crowd, tears) contener; (money) quedarse con; (conceal: information): **to ~ sth back from sb** ocultar algo a algn ▷ vi hacerse a un lado; **keep down** vt (control: prices, spending) controlar; (retain: food) retener ▷ vi seguir agachado, no levantar la cabeza; **keep in** ▷ vt (invalid, child) impedir que salga, no dejar salir; (Scol) castigar (a quedarse en el colegio) ▷ vi (inf): **to ~ in with sb** mantener la relación con algn; **keep off** ▷ vt (dog, person) mantener a distancia ▷ vi evitar; **~ your hands off!** ¡no toques!; **"~ off the grass"** "prohibido pisar el césped"; **keep on** vi seguir, continuar; **to ~ on doing** seguir or continuar haciendo; **to ~ on (about sth)** no parar de hablar (de algo); **keep out** vi (stay out) permanecer fuera; **"~ out"** "prohibida la entrada"; **keep up** vt mantener, conservar ▷ vi no rezagarse; (fig: in comprehension) seguir (el hilo); **to ~ up with** (pace) ir al paso de; (level) mantenerse a la altura de; **to ~ up with sb** seguir el ritmo a algn; (fig) seguir a algn

keeper ['kiːpəʳ] n guarda m/f

keep-fit [kiːp'fɪt] n gimnasia (de mantenimiento)

keeping ['kiːpɪŋ] n (care) cuidado; **in ~ with** de acuerdo con

keeps [kiːps] n: **for ~** (inf) para siempre

keepsake ['kiːpseɪk] n recuerdo

keg [kɛg] n barrilete m, barril m

kennel ['kɛnl] n perrera; **kennels** npl residencia canina

Kenya ['kɛnjə] n Kenia

kept [kɛpt] pt, pp of **keep**

kerb [kəːb] n (Brit) bordillo

kerb crawler [-krɔːləʳ] n conductor en busca de prostitutas desde su coche

kernel ['kəːnl] n (nut) fruta; (fig) meollo

kerosene ['kɛrəsiːn] n keroseno

ketchup ['kɛtʃəp] n salsa de tomate, ketchup m

kettle ['kɛtl] n hervidor m

kettle drum n (Mus) timbal m

key [kiː] n (gen) llave f; (Mus) tono; (of piano, typewriter) tecla; (on map) clave f ▷ cpd (vital: position, issue, industry etc) clave ▷ vt (also: **~ in**) teclear

keyboard ['kiːbɔːd] n teclado ▷ vt (text) teclear

keyboarder ['kiːbɔːdəʳ] n teclista m/f

keyed up [kiːd-] adj (person) nervioso; **to be (all) ~** estar nervioso or emocionado

keyhole ['kiːhəʊl] n ojo (de la cerradura)

keyhole surgery n cirugía cerrada or no invasiva

keynote ['ki:nəʊt] n (Mus) tónica; (fig) idea fundamental

keypad ['ki:pæd] n teclado numérico

keyring ['ki:rɪŋ] n llavero

kg abbr (= kilogram) kg

khaki ['kɑ:kɪ] n caqui

kick [kɪk] vt (person) dar una patada a; (ball) dar un puntapié a; (habit) quitarse de ▷ vi (horse) dar coces ▷ n patada; puntapié m, tiro; (of rifle) culetazo; (inf: thrill): **he does it for ~s** lo hace por pura diversión; **kick around** vt (idea) dar vueltas a; (person) tratar a patadas a; **kick off** vi (Sport) hacer el saque inicial

kick-off ['kɪkɔf] n saque inicial; **the ~ is at 10 o'clock** el partido empieza a las diez

kid [kɪd] n (inf: child) niño(-a), chiquillo(-a); (animal) cabrito; (leather) cabritilla ▷ vi (inf) bromear

kid gloves npl: **to treat sb with ~** andarse con pies de plomo con algn

kidnap ['kɪdnæp] vt secuestrar

kidnapper ['kɪdnæpə'] n secuestrador(a) m(f)

kidnapping ['kɪdnæpɪŋ] n secuestro

kidney ['kɪdnɪ] n riñón m

kidney bean n judía, alubia

kill [kɪl] vt matar; (murder) asesinar; (fig: rumour, conversation) acabar con ▷ n matanza; **to ~ time** matar el tiempo; **kill off** vt exterminar, terminar con; (fig) echar por tierra

killer ['kɪlə'] n asesino(-a)

killer instinct n: **to have the ~** ir a por todas

killing ['kɪlɪŋ] n (one) asesinato; (several) matanza; **to make a ~** (Comm) hacer su agosto

killjoy ['kɪldʒɔɪ] n (Brit) aguafiestas m/f inv

kiln [kɪln] n horno

kilo ['ki:ləʊ] n abbr (= kilogram(me)) kilo

kilobyte ['kɪləʊbaɪt] n (Comput) kilobyte m

kilogram, kilogramme ['kɪləʊɡræm] n kilogramo

kilometre, kilometer (US) ['kɪləmi:tə'] n kilómetro

kilowatt ['kɪləʊwɔt] n kilovatio

kilt [kɪlt] n falda escocesa

kin [kɪn] n parientes mpl

kind [kaɪnd] adj (treatment) bueno, cariñoso; (person, act, word) amable, atento ▷ n clase f, especie f; (species) género; **in ~** (Comm) en especie; **a ~ of** una especie de; **to be two of a ~** ser tal para cual; **would you be ~ enough to ...?, would you be so ~ as to ...?** ¿me hace el favor de ...?; **it's very ~ of you (to do)** le agradezco mucho (el que haya hecho)

kindergarten ['kɪndəɡɑ:tn] n jardín m de infancia

kind-hearted [kaɪnd'hɑ:tɪd] adj bondadoso, de buen corazón

kindle ['kɪndl] vt encender

kindly ['kaɪndlɪ] adj bondadoso; (gentle) cariñoso ▷ adv bondadosamente, amablemente; **will you ~ ...** sería usted tan amable de ...

kindness ['kaɪndnɪs] n bondad f, amabilidad f; (act) favor m

kindred ['kɪndrɪd] n familia, parientes mpl ▷ adj: **~ spirits** almas fpl gemelas

kinetic [kɪ'nɛtɪk] adj cinético

king [kɪŋ] n rey m

kingdom ['kɪŋdəm] n reino

kingfisher ['kɪŋfɪʃə'] n martín m pescador

king-size ['kɪŋsaɪz], **king-sized** ['kɪŋsaɪzd] adj de tamaño gigante; (cigarette) extra largo; **~ bed** cama de matrimonio extragrande

kinky ['kɪŋkɪ] adj (pej) perverso

kiosk ['ki:ɔsk] n quiosco; (Brit Tel) cabina; **newspaper ~** quiosco, kiosco

kipper ['kɪpə'] n arenque m ahumado

Kirghizia [kə:'ɡɪzɪə] n Kirguizistán m

kiss [kɪs] n beso ▷ vt besar; **~ of life** (artificial respiration) respiración f boca a boca; **to ~ sb goodbye** dar un beso de despedida a algn; **to ~ (each other)** besarse

kissagram ['kɪsəɡræm] n servicio de felicitaciones mediante el que se envía a una persona vestida de manera sugerente para besar a algn

kit [kɪt] n equipo; (set of tools etc) (caja de) herramientas fpl; (assembly kit) juego de armar; **tool ~** juego or estuche m de herramientas; **kit out** vt equipar

kitchen ['kɪtʃɪn] n cocina

kitchen sink n fregadero

kite [kaɪt] n (toy) cometa

kith [kɪθ] n: **~ and kin** parientes mpl y allegados

kitten ['kɪtn] n gatito(-a)

kitty ['kɪtɪ] n (pool of money) fondo común; (Cards) bote m

kiwi ['ki:wi:] n (inf: New Zealander) neozelandés(-esa) m(f); (also: **~ fruit**) kiwi m

km abbr (= kilometre) km

km/h abbr (= kilometres per hour) km/h

knack [næk] n: **to have the ~ of doing sth** tener facilidad para hacer algo

knackered ['nækəd] adj (inf) hecho polvo

knapsack ['næpsæk] n mochila

knead [ni:d] vt amasar

knee [ni:] n rodilla

kneecap ['ni:kæp] vt destrozar a tiros la rótula de ▷ n rótula

kneel [ni:l] (pt, pp knelt) [nɛlt] vi (also: **~ down**) arrodillarse

knelt [nɛlt] pt, pp of **kneel**

knew [nju:] pt of **know**

knickers ['nɪkəz] npl (Brit) bragas fpl, calzones mpl (LAm)

knife [naɪf] (pl **knives**) n cuchillo ▷ vt acuchillar; **~, fork and spoon** cubiertos mpl

knife edge n: **to be on a ~** estar en la cuerda floja

knight [naɪt] n caballero; (Chess) caballo

knighthood ['naɪthʊd] n (title): **to get a ~** recibir el título de Sir

knit [nɪt] vt tejer, tricotar; (brows) fruncir; (fig): **to ~ together** unir, juntar ▷ vi hacer punto, tejer, tricotar; (bones) soldarse

knitting ['nɪtɪŋ] n labor f de punto

knitting needle, knit pin (US) n aguja de hacer punto or tejer

knitwear ['nɪtwɛə^r] n prendas fpl de punto

knives [naɪvz] pl of **knife**

knob [nɔb] n (of door) pomo; (of stick) puño; (on radio, TV) botón m; (lump) bulto; (fig): **a ~ of butter** (Brit) un pedazo de mantequilla

knock [nɔk] vt (strike) golpear; (bump into) chocar contra; (fig: inf) criticar ▷ vi (at door etc): **to ~ at/on** llamar a ▷ n golpe m; (on door) llamada; **knock down** vt (pedestrian) atropellar; (price) rebajar; **knock off** vi (inf: finish) salir del trabajo ▷ vt (inf: steal) birlar; (strike off) quitar; (fig: from price, record): **to ~ off £10** rebajar en £10; **knock out** vt dejar sin sentido; (Boxing) poner fuera de combate, dejar K.O.; (in competition) eliminar; (stop) estropear, dejar fuera de servicio; **knock over** vt (object) derribar, tirar; (pedestrian) atropellar

knockdown ['nɔkdaʊn] adj (price) de saldo

knocker ['nɔkə^r] n (on door) aldaba

knockout ['nɔkaʊt] n (Boxing) K.O. m, knockout m

knot [nɔt] n (gen) nudo ▷ vt anudar; **to tie a ~** hacer un nudo

knotty ['nɔtɪ] adj (fig) complicado

know [nəʊ] (pt **knew**, pp **known** [njuː, nəʊn]) vt (gen) saber; (person, author, place) conocer; (recognize) reconocer ▷ vi: **as far as I ~ ...** que yo sepa ...; **yes, I ~** sí, ya lo sé; **I don't ~** no lo sé; **to ~ how to do** saber hacer; **to ~ how to swim** saber nadar; **to ~ about** or **of sb/sth** saber de algn/algo; **to get to ~ sth** enterarse de algo; **I ~ nothing about it** no sé nada de eso; **I don't ~ him** no lo or le conozco; **to ~ right from wrong** saber distinguir el bien del mal

know-all ['nəʊɔːl] n (Brit pej) sabelotodo m/f inv, sabihondo(-a)

know-how ['nəʊhaʊ] n conocimientos mpl

knowing ['nəʊɪŋ] adj (look etc) de complicidad

knowingly ['nəʊɪŋlɪ] adv (purposely) a sabiendas; (smile, look) con complicidad

know-it-all ['nəʊɪtɔːl] n (US) = **know-all**

knowledge ['nɔlɪdʒ] n (gen) conocimiento; (learning) saber m, conocimientos mpl; **to have no ~ of** no saber nada de; **with my ~** con mis conocimientos, sabiéndolo; **to (the best of) my ~** a mi entender, que yo sepa; **not to my ~** que yo sepa, no; **it is common that ...** es del dominio público que ...; **it has come to my ~ that ...** me he enterado de que ...; **to have a working ~ of Spanish** defenderse con el español

knowledgeable ['nɔlɪdʒəbl] adj entendido, erudito

known [nəʊn] pp of **know** ▷ adj (thief, facts) conocido; (expert) reconocido

knuckle ['nʌkl] n nudillo; **knuckle down** vi (inf) ponerse a trabajar en serio; **knuckle under** vi someterse

KO abbr (= knock out) K.O. m ▷ vt (knock out) dejar K.O.

koala [kəʊ'ɑːlə] n (also: **~ bear**) koala m

Koran [kɔ'rɑːn] n Corán m

Korea [kə'rɪə] n Corea; **North/South ~** Corea del Norte/Sur

Korean [kə'rɪən] adj, n coreano(-a) m(f)

kosher ['kəʊʃə^r] adj autorizado por la ley judía

Kosovar ['kɔsəvɑː^r], **Kosovan** ['kɔsəvən] adj kosovar

Kosovo ['kɒsəvəʊ] n Kosovo m

Kremlin ['kremlɪn] n: **the ~** el Kremlin

kudos ['kjuːdɒs] n gloria, prestigio

Kuwait [ku'weɪt] n Kuwait m

kW abbr (= kilowatt) Kv

L, l [ɛl] *n (letter)* L, l *f*; **L for Lucy**, (US) **L for Love** L de Lorenzo

L *abbr (on maps etc)* = **lake**; *(size)* = **large**; *(= left)* izq.; *(Brit Aut: = learner)* L

LA *n abbr* (US) = **Los Angeles**

lab [læb] *n abbr* = **laboratory**

label ['leɪbl] *n* etiqueta; *(brand: of record)* sello (discográfico) ▷ *vt* poner una etiqueta a, etiquetar

labor ['leɪbə'] *n, vb* (US) = **labour**

laboratory [ləˈbɔrətəri] *n* laboratorio

Labor Day *n* (US) día *m* de los trabajadores *(primer lunes de septiembre)*

laborious [ləˈbɔːrɪəs] *adj* penoso

labor union (US) sindicato

Labour ['leɪbə'] *n (Brit Pol: also:* **the ~ Party**) el partido laborista, los laboristas

labour, labor (US) ['leɪbə'] *n (task)* trabajo; *(also:* **~ force**) mano *f* de obra; *(workers)* trabajadores *mpl*; *(Med) (dolores mpl de)* parto ▷ *vi*: **to ~ (at)** trabajar (en) ▷ *vt*: **to ~ a point** insistir en un punto; **hard ~** trabajos *mpl* forzados; **to be in ~** estar de parto; **the L~ party** (Brit) el partido laborista, los laboristas *mpl*

labourer, laborer (US) ['leɪbərə'] *n* peón *m*; *(on farm)* peón *m*, obrero; *(day labourer)* jornalero

labyrinth ['læbɪrɪnθ] *n* laberinto

lace [leɪs] *n* encaje *m*; *(of shoe etc)* cordón *m* ▷ *vt (shoes: also:* **~ up**) atarse; *(drink: fortify with spirits)* echar licor a

laceration [læsəˈreɪʃən] *n* laceración *f*

lack [læk] *n (absence)* falta, carencia; *(scarcity)* escasez *f* ▷ *vt* faltarle a algn, carecer de; **through** *or* **for ~ of** por falta de; **to be ~ing** faltar, no haber; **to be ~ing in sth** faltarle a algn algo

lacquer ['lækə'] *n* laca; **hair ~** laca para el pelo

lacy ['leɪsɪ] *adj (like lace)* como de encaje

lad [læd] *n* muchacho, chico; *(in stable etc)* mozo

ladder ['lædə'] *n* escalera (de mano); *(Brit: in tights)* carrera ▷ *vt (Brit: tights)* hacer una carrera en

laden ['leɪdn] *adj:* **~ (with)** cargado (de); **fully ~** *(truck, ship)* cargado hasta el tope

ladle ['leɪdl] *n* cucharón *m*

lady ['leɪdɪ] *n* señora; *(distinguished, noble)* dama; **young ~** señorita; **the ladies' (room)** los servicios de señoras; **"ladies and gentlemen ..."** "señoras y caballeros ..."

ladybird ['leɪdɪbɜːd], **ladybug** (US) ['leɪdɪbʌg] *n* mariquita

ladylike ['leɪdɪlaɪk] *adj* fino

Ladyship ['leɪdɪʃɪp] *n:* **your ~** su Señoría

LAFTA *n abbr (= Latin American Free Trade Association)* ALALC *f*

lag [læg] *vi (also:* **~ behind**) retrasarse, quedarse atrás ▷ *vt (pipes)* revestir

lager ['lɑːgə'] *n* cerveza (rubia)

lager lout *n (Brit inf)* gamberro borracho

lagoon [ləˈguːn] *n* laguna

laid [leɪd] *pt, pp of* **lay**

laid-back [leɪdˈbæk] *adj (inf)* tranquilo, relajado

laid up *adj:* **to be ~** *(person)* tener que guardar cama

lain [leɪn] *pp of* **lie**

lair [lɛə'] *n* guarida

laity ['leɪtɪ] *n* laicado

lake [leɪk] *n* lago

Lake District *n (Brit):* **the ~** la Región de los Lagos

lamb [læm] *n* cordero; *(meat)* carne *f* de cordero

lamb chop *n* chuleta de cordero

lame [leɪm] *adj* cojo, rengo (LAm); *(weak)* débil; *(excuse)* poco convincente; **~ duck** *(fig: person)* inútil *m/f*; *(: firm)* empresa en quiebra

lament [ləˈmɛnt] *n* lamento ▷ *vt* lamentarse de

laminated ['læmɪneɪtɪd] *adj* laminado

lamp [læmp] *n* lámpara

lamppost ['læmppəʊst] *n (Brit)* farola

lampshade ['læmpʃeɪd] *n* pantalla

lance [lɑːns] *n* lanza ▷ *vt (Med)* abrir con lanceta

land [lænd] *n* tierra; *(country)* país *m*; *(piece of land)* terreno; *(estate)* tierras *fpl*, finca; *(Agr)* campo ▷ *vi (from ship)* desembarcar; *(Aviat)* aterrizar; *(fig: fall)* caer ▷ *vt (obtain)* conseguir; *(passengers, goods)* desembarcar; **to go/travel by ~** ir/viajar por tierra;

to own ~ ser dueño de tierras; **to ~ on one's feet** caer de pie; (*fig: to be lucky*) salir bien parado; **to ~ sb with sth** (*inf*) hacer cargar a algn con algo; **land up** *vi*: **to ~ up in/at** ir a parar a/en
landfill site ['lændfɪl-] *n* vertedero
landing ['lændɪŋ] *n* desembarco; aterrizaje *m*; (*of staircase*) rellano
landing card *n* tarjeta de desembarque
landing gear *n* (*Aviat*) tren *m* de aterrizaje
landing strip *n* pista de aterrizaje
landlady ['lændleɪdɪ] *n* (*of boarding house*) patrona; (*owner*) dueña
landlocked ['lændlɔkt] *adj* cercado de tierra
landlord ['lændlɔːd] *n* propietario; (*of pub etc*) patrón *m*
landmark ['lændmɑːk] *n* lugar *m* conocido; **to be a** ~ (*fig*) hacer época
landowner ['lændəunəʳ] *n* terrateniente *m/f*
landscape ['lændskeɪp] *n* paisaje *m*
landscape gardener *n* diseñador(-a) *m(f)* de paisajes
landslide ['lændslaɪd] *n* (*Geo*) corrimiento de tierras; (*fig: Pol*) victoria arrolladora
lane [leɪn] *n* (*in country*) camino; (*in town*) callejón *m*; (*Aut*) carril *m*; (*in race*) calle *f*; (*for air or sea traffic*) ruta; **shipping** ~ ruta marina
language ['læŋgwɪdʒ] *n* lenguaje *m*; (*national tongue*) idioma *m*, lengua; **bad** ~ palabrotas *fpl*
language laboratory *n* laboratorio de idiomas
language school *n* academia de idiomas
language studies *npl* estudios *mpl* filológicos
languid ['læŋgwɪd] *adj* lánguido
languish ['læŋgwɪʃ] *vi* languidecer
lank [læŋk] *adj* (*hair*) lacio
lanky ['læŋkɪ] *adj* larguirucho
lantern ['læntn] *n* linterna, farol *m*
lap [læp] *n* (*of track*) vuelta; (*of body*) regazo ▷ *vi* (*waves*) chapotear; **to sit on sb's** ~ sentarse en las rodillas de algn; **lap up** *vt* beber a lengüetadas *or* con la lengua; (*fig: compliments, attention*) disfrutar; (: *lies etc*) tragarse
lapdog ['læpdɔg] *n* perro faldero
lapel [lə'pɛl] *n* solapa
Lapland ['læplænd] *n* Laponia
lapse [læps] *n* (*fault*) error *m*, fallo; (*moral*) desliz *m* ▷ *vi* (*expire*) caducar; (*morally*) cometer un desliz; (*time*) pasar, transcurrir; **to ~ into bad habits** volver a las andadas; ~ **of time** lapso, intervalo; **a ~ of memory** un lapsus de memoria
laptop ['læptɔp] *n* (*also: ~ computer*) (ordenador *m*) portátil *m*
larceny ['lɑːsənɪ] *n* latrocinio
lard [lɑːd] *n* manteca (de cerdo)
larder ['lɑːdəʳ] *n* despensa
large [lɑːdʒ] *adj* grande ▷ *adv*: **by and** ~ en general, en términos generales; **at** ~ (*free*) en libertad; (*generally*) en general; **to make ~(r)**

hacer mayor *or* más extenso; **a ~ number of people** una gran cantidad de personas; **on a ~ scale** a gran escala
largely ['lɑːdʒlɪ] *adv* (*mostly*) en su mayor parte; (*introducing reason*) en gran parte
large-scale ['lɑːdʒ'skeɪl] *adj* (*map, drawing*) a gran escala; (*reforms, business activities*) importante
lark [lɑːk] *n* (*bird*) alondra; (*joke*) broma; **lark about** *vi* bromear, hacer el tonto
larva (*pl* **larvae**) ['lɑːvə, -iː] *n* larva
laryngitis [lærɪn'dʒaɪtɪs] *n* laringitis *f*
larynx ['lærɪŋks] *n* laringe *f*
lasagne [lə'zænjə] *n* lasaña
laser ['leɪzəʳ] *n* láser *m*
laser beam *n* rayo láser
laser printer *n* impresora láser
lash [læʃ] *n* latigazo; (*punishment*) azote *m*; (*also: eye~*) pestaña ▷ *vt* azotar; (*tie*) atar; **lash down** *vt* sujetar con cuerdas ▷ *vi* (*rain*) caer a trombas; **lash out** *vi* (*inf: spend*) gastar a la loca; **to ~ out (at sb)** (*hit*) arremeter (contra algn); **to ~ out against sb** lanzar invectivas contra algn
lass [læs] *n* chica
lasso [læ'suː] *n* lazo ▷ *vt* coger con lazo
last [lɑːst] *adj* (*gen*) último; (*final*) último, final ▷ *adv* (*finally*) por último ▷ *vi* (*endure*) durar; (*continue*) continuar, seguir; ~ **night** anoche; ~ **week** la semana pasada; **at** ~ por fin; ~ **but one** penúltimo; ~ **time** la última vez; **it ~s (for) two hours** dura dos horas
last-ditch ['lɑːst'dɪtʃ] *adj* (*attempt*) de último recurso, último, desesperado
lasting ['lɑːstɪŋ] *adj* duradero
lastly ['lɑːstlɪ] *adv* por último, finalmente
last-minute ['lɑːstmɪnɪt] *adj* de última hora
latch [lætʃ] *n* picaporte *m*, pestillo; **latch on to** *vt fus* (*cling to: person*) pegarse a; (: *idea*) aferrarse a
late [leɪt] *adj* (*not on time*) tarde, atrasado; (*towards end of period, life*) tardío; (*hour*) avanzado; (*deceased*) fallecido ▷ *adv* tarde; (*behind time, schedule*) con retraso; **to be (10 minutes)** ~ llegar con (10 minutos de) retraso; **to be ~ with** estar atrasado con; ~ **delivery** entrega tardía; ~ **in life** a una edad avanzada; **of** ~ últimamente; ~ **at night** a última hora de la noche; **in ~ May** hacia fines de mayo; **the ~ Mr X** el difunto Sr. X; **to work** ~ trabajar hasta tarde
latecomer ['leɪtkʌməʳ] *n* recién llegado(-a)
lately ['leɪtlɪ] *adv* últimamente
latent ['leɪtnt] *adj* latente; ~ **defect** defecto latente
later ['leɪtəʳ] *adj* (*date etc*) posterior; (*version etc*) más reciente ▷ *adv* más tarde, después; ~ **on today** hoy más tarde
latest ['leɪtɪst] *adj* último; **at the** ~ a más tardar
latex ['leɪtɛks] *n* látex *m*
lathe [leɪð] *n* torno

lather ['lɑːðəʳ] n espuma (de jabón) ▷ vt
enjabonar
Latin ['lætɪn] n latín m ▷ adj latino
Latin America n América Latina,
Latinoamérica
Latin American adj, n latinoamericano(-a)
m(f)
Latino [læ'tiːnəu] adj, n latino(-a) m(f)
latitude ['lætɪtjuːd] n latitud f; (fig: freedom)
libertad f
latter ['lætəʳ] adj último; (of two) segundo
▷ n: **the ~** el último, éste
latterly ['lætəlɪ] adv últimamente
Latvia ['lætvɪə] n Letonia
laudable ['lɔːdəbl] adj loable
laugh [lɑːf] n risa; (loud) carcajada ▷ vi reírse,
reír; reírse a carcajadas; **(to do sth) for a ~**
(hacer algo) en broma; **laugh at** vt fus reírse
de; **laugh off** vt tomar a risa
laughable ['lɑːfəbl] adj ridículo
laughing ['lɑːfɪŋ] adj risueño ▷ n: **it's no ~
matter** no es cosa de risa
laughing stock n: **to be the ~ of the town**
ser el hazmerreír de la ciudad
laughter ['lɑːftəʳ] n risa
launch [lɔːntʃ] n (boat) lancha; see also
launching ▷ vt (ship) botar; (rocket, plan)
lanzar; (fig) comenzar; **launch forth** vi: **to ~
forth (into)** lanzarse a or en, emprender;
launch into vt fus lanzarse a; **launch out** vi
= **launch forth**
launching ['lɔːntʃɪŋ] n (of rocket etc)
lanzamiento; (inauguration) estreno
launder ['lɔːndəʳ] vt lavar
Launderette® [lɔːn'drɛt], **Laundromat**®
(US) ['lɔːndrəmæt] n lavandería (automática)
laundry ['lɔːndrɪ] n lavandería; (clothes: dirty)
ropa sucia; (clean) colada; **to do the ~** hacer
la colada
laureate ['lɔːrɪət] adj see **poet laureate**
laurel ['lɔrl] n laurel m; **to rest on one's ~s**
dormirse en or sobre los laureles
lava ['lɑːvə] n lava
lavatory ['lævətərɪ] n wáter m; **lavatories** npl
servicios mpl, aseos mpl, sanitarios mpl (LAm)
lavender ['lævəndəʳ] n lavanda
lavish ['lævɪʃ] adj abundante; (giving freely):
~ with pródigo en ▷ vt: **to ~ sth on sb** colmar
a algn de algo
law [lɔː] n ley f; (study) derecho; (of game)
regla; **against the ~** contra la ley; **to study ~**
estudiar derecho; **to go to ~** recurrir a la
justicia
law-abiding ['lɔːəbaɪdɪŋ] adj respetuoso con
la ley
law and order n orden m público
law court n tribunal m (de justicia)
lawful ['lɔːful] adj legítimo, lícito
lawless ['lɔːlɪs] adj (act) ilegal; (person)
rebelde; (country) ingobernable
Law Lord n (Brit) miembro de la Cámara de los
Lores y del más alto tribunal de apelación

lawn [lɔːn] n césped m
lawnmower ['lɔːnməuəʳ] n cortacésped m
lawn tennis n tenis m sobre hierba
law school n (US) facultad f de derecho
lawsuit ['lɔːsuːt] n pleito; **to bring a ~
against** entablar un pleito contra
lawyer ['lɔːjəʳ] n abogado(-a); (for sales, wills
etc) notario(-a)
lax [læks] adj (discipline) relajado; (person)
negligente
laxative ['læksətɪv] n laxante m
lay [leɪ] pt of **lie** ▷ adj laico; (not expert) lego
▷ vt (pt, pp **laid** [leɪd]) (place) colocar; (eggs,
table) poner; (trap) tender; (carpet) extender;
to ~ the facts/one's proposals before sb
presentar los hechos/sus propuestas a algn;
lay aside, lay by vt dejar a un lado; **lay down**
vt (pen etc) dejar; (arms) rendir; (policy) trazar;
(rules etc) establecer; **to ~ down the law**
imponer las normas; **lay in** vt abastecerse
de; **lay into** vt fus (inf: attack, scold) arremeter
contra; **lay off** vt (workers) despedir; **lay on** vt
(water, gas) instalar; (meal, facilities) proveer;
lay out vt (plan) trazar; (display) exponer;
(spend) gastar; **lay up** vt (store) guardar; (ship)
desarmar; (illness) obligar a guardar cama
layabout ['leɪəbaut] n vago(-a)
lay-by ['leɪbaɪ] n (Brit Aut) área de descanso
layer ['leɪəʳ] n capa
layman ['leɪmən] n lego
layout ['leɪaut] n (design) plan m, trazado;
(disposition) disposición f; (Press) composición f
laze [leɪz] vi no hacer nada; (pej) holgazanear
lazy ['leɪzɪ] adj perezoso, vago, flojo (LAm)
lb. abbr = **pound** (weight)
lead¹ [liːd] (pt, pp **led** [lɛd]) n (front position)
delantera; (distance, time ahead) ventaja; (clue)
pista; (Elec) cable m; (for dog) correa; (Theat)
papel m principal ▷ vt conducir; (life) llevar;
(be leader of) dirigir; (Sport) ir en cabeza de;
(orchestra: Brit) ser el primer violín en; (: US)
dirigir ▷ vi ir primero; **to be in the ~** (Sport)
llevar la delantera; (fig) ir a la cabeza; **to
take the ~** (Sport) tomar la delantera; (fig)
tomar la iniciativa; **to ~ sb to believe that
...** hacer creer a algn que ...; **to ~ sb to do sth**
llevar a algn a hacer algo; **lead astray** vt
llevar por mal camino; **lead away** vt llevar;
lead back vt hacer volver; **lead off** vt llevar
▷ vi (in game) abrir; **lead on** vt (tease) engañar;
to ~ sb on to (induce) incitar a algn a; **lead to**
vt fus producir, provocar; **lead up to** vt fus
(events) conducir a; (in conversation) preparar el
terreno para
lead² [lɛd] n (metal) plomo; (in pencil) mina
leaded ['lɛdɪd] adj: **~ windows** ventanas fpl
emplomadas
leaden ['lɛdn] adj (sky, sea) plomizo; (heavy:
footsteps) pesado
leader ['liːdəʳ] n jefe(-a) m(f), líder m; (of union
etc) dirigente m/f; (guide) guía m/f; (of
newspaper) editorial m; **they are ~s in their**

field (fig) llevan la delantera en su
especialidad
leadership ['li:dəʃɪp] n dirección f; **qualities
of** ~ iniciativa sg; **under the** ~ **of** ...
dirección de ..., al mando de ...
lead-free ['lɛdfri:] adj sin plomo
leading ['li:dɪŋ] adj (main) principal;
(outstanding) destacado; (first) primero; (front)
delantero; **a** ~ **question** una pregunta
tendenciosa
leading lady n (Theat) primera actriz f
leading light n (fig: person) figura principal
leading man n (Theat) primer actor m
lead singer [li:d-] n cantante m/f
lead-up ['li:dʌp] n: **in the** ~ **to the election**
cuando falta etc poco para las elecciones
leaf (pl **leaves**) [li:f, li:vz] n hoja; **to turn
over a new** ~ (fig) hacer borrón y cuenta
nueva; **to take a** ~ **out of sb's book** (fig)
seguir el ejemplo de algn; **leaf through** vt fus
(book) hojear
leaflet ['li:flɪt] n folleto
league [li:g] n sociedad f; (Football) liga; **to be
in** ~ **with** estar confabulado con
league table n clasificación f
leak [li:k] n (of liquid, gas) escape m, fuga;
(in pipe) agujero; (in roof) gotera; (fig: of
information, in security) filtración f ▷ vi (ship)
hacer agua; (shoes) tener un agujero; (pipe)
tener un escape; (roof) tener goteras; (also:
~ **out**: liquid, gas) escaparse, salirse; (fig: news)
trascender, divulgarse ▷ vt (gen) dejar
escapar; (fig: information) filtrar
leakage ['li:kɪdʒ] n (of water, gas etc) escape m,
fuga
lean [li:n] (pt, pp **leaned** or **leant**) adj (thin)
flaco; (meat) magro ▷ vt: **to** ~ **sth on sth**
apoyar algo en algo ▷ vi (slope) inclinarse;
(rest): **to** ~ **against** apoyarse contra; **to** ~ **on**
apoyarse en; **lean back** vi inclinarse hacia
atrás; **lean forward** vi inclinarse hacia
adelante; **lean out** vi: **to** ~ **out (of)** asomarse
(a); **lean over** vi inclinarse
leaning ['li:nɪŋ] adj inclinado ▷ n: ~
(towards) inclinación f (hacia); **the L~
Tower of Pisa** la Torre Inclinada de Pisa
leant [lɛnt] pt, pp of **lean**
leap [li:p] n salto ▷ vi (pt, pp **leaped** or **leapt**
[lɛpt]) saltar; **to** ~ **at an offer** apresurarse a
aceptar una oferta; **leap up** vi (person) saltar
leapfrog ['li:pfrɔg] n pídola ▷ vi: **to** ~ **over
sb/sth** saltar por encima de algn/algo
leapt [lɛpt] pt, pp of **leap**
leap year n año bisiesto
learn (pt, pp **learned** or **learnt**) [lə:n, -t] vt
(gen) aprender; (come to know of) enterarse de
▷ vi aprender; **to** ~ **how to do sth** aprender a
hacer algo; **to** ~ **that** ... enterarse or
informarse de que ...; **to** ~ **about sth** (Scol)
aprender algo; (hear) enterarse or informarse
de algo; **we were sorry to** ~ **that** ... nos dio
tristeza saber que ...

learned ['lə:nɪd] adj erudito
learner ['lə:nər] n principiante m/f; (Brit: also:
~ **driver**) conductor(a) m(f) en prácticas; see
also **L-plates**
learning ['lə:nɪŋ] n saber m, conocimientos
mpl
learnt [lə:nt] pp of **learn**
lease [li:s] n arriendo ▷ vt arrendar; **on** ~ en
arriendo; **lease back** vt subarrendar
leash [li:ʃ] n correa
least [li:st] adj (slightest) menor, más pequeño;
(smallest amount of) mínimo ▷ adv menos ▷ n:
the ~ lo menos; **the** ~ **expensive car** el coche
menos caro; **at** ~ por lo menos, al menos;
not in the ~ en absoluto
leather ['lɛðər] n cuero ▷ cpd: ~ **goods**
artículos mpl de cuero or piel
leave [li:v] (pt, pp **left**) vt dejar; (go away from)
abandonar ▷ vi irse; (train) salir ▷ n permiso;
to ~ **school** dejar la escuela or el colegio; ~ **it
to me!** ¡yo me encargo!; **he's already left
for the airport** ya se ha marchado al
aeropuerto; **to be left** quedar, sobrar;
there's some milk left over sobra or queda
algo de leche; **on** ~ de permiso; **to take
one's** ~ **of** despedirse de; **leave behind** vt
(on purpose) dejar (atrás); (accidentally) olvidar;
leave off vt (lid) no poner; (switch) no
encender; (inf: stop): **to** ~ **off doing sth** dejar
de hacer algo; **leave on** vt (lid) dejar puesto;
(light, fire, cooker) dejar encendido; **leave out**
vt omitir; **leave over** vt (postpone) dejar,
aplazar
leave of absence n excedencia
leaves [li:vz] pl of **leaf**
Lebanon ['lɛbənən] n: **the** ~ el Líbano
lecherous ['lɛtʃərəs] adj lascivo
lectern ['lɛktə:n] n atril m
lecture ['lɛktʃər] n conferencia; (Scol) clase f
▷ vi dar clase(s) ▷ vt (scold) sermonear;
(reprove) echar una reprimenda a; **to give a** ~
on dar una conferencia sobre
lecture hall n sala de conferencias; (Univ) aula
lecturer ['lɛktʃərər] n conferenciante m/f;
(Brit: at university) profesor(a) m(f)
lecture theatre n = **lecture hall**
LED n abbr (Elec: = light-emitting diode) LED m
led [lɛd] pt, pp of **lead**
ledge [lɛdʒ] n (on wall) repisa; (of window)
alféizar m; (of mountain) saliente m
ledger ['lɛdʒər] n libro mayor
lee [li:] n sotavento; **in the** ~ **of** al abrigo de
leech [li:tʃ] n sanguijuela
leek [li:k] n puerro
leer [lɪər] vi: **to** ~ **at sb** mirar de manera
lasciva a algn
leeway ['li:weɪ] n (fig): **to have some** ~ tener
cierta libertad de acción
left [lɛft] pt, pp of **leave** ▷ adj izquierdo;
(remaining): **there are two** ~ quedan dos ▷ n
izquierda ▷ adv a la izquierda; **on** or **to the** ~
a la izquierda; **the L~** (Pol) la izquierda

left-hand *adj*: **the ~ side** la izquierda
left-hand drive ['lɛfthænd-] *n* conducción *f* por la izquierda
left-handed [lɛft'hændɪd] *adj* zurdo; **~ scissors** tijeras *fpl* zurdas or para zurdos
left-hand side ['lɛfthænd-] *n* izquierda *f*
left-luggage [lɛft'lʌgɪdʒ], **left-luggage office** *n* (Brit) consigna
left-luggage locker *n* (Brit) consigna *f* automática
left-overs ['lɛftəuvəz] *npl* sobras *fpl*
left-wing [lɛft'wɪŋ] *adj* (Pol) de izquierda(s), izquierdista
lefty ['lɛftɪ] *n* (inf: Pol) rojillo/(-a)
leg [lɛg] *n* pierna; (of animal, chair) pata; (Culin: of meat) pierna; (of journey) etapa; **1st/2nd ~** (Sport) partido de ida/de vuelta; **to pull sb's ~** tomar el pelo a algn; **to stretch one's ~s** dar una vuelta
legacy ['lɛgəsɪ] *n* herencia; (fig) herencia, legado
legal ['li:gl] *adj* (permitted by law) lícito; (of law) legal; (inquiry etc) jurídico; **to take ~ action** or **proceedings against sb** entablar or levantar un pleito contra algn
legal holiday *n* (US) fiesta oficial
legality [lɪ'gælɪtɪ] *n* legalidad *f*
legalize ['li:gəlaɪz] *vt* legalizar
legally ['li:gəlɪ] *adv* legalmente; **~ binding** con fuerza legal
legal tender *n* moneda de curso legal
legend ['lɛdʒənd] *n* leyenda
legendary ['lɛdʒəndərɪ] *adj* legendario
leggings ['lɛgɪŋz] *npl* mallas *fpl*, leggins *mpl*
legible ['lɛdʒəbl] *adj* legible
legion ['li:dʒən] *n* legión *f*
legionnaire [li:dʒə'neəʳ] *n* legionario
legislation [lɛdʒɪs'leɪʃən] *n* legislación *f*; **a piece of ~** (bill) un proyecto de ley; (act) una ley
legislative ['lɛdʒɪslətɪv] *adj* legislativo
legislator ['lɛdʒɪsleɪtəʳ] *n* legislador(a) *m(f)*
legislature ['lɛdʒɪslətʃəʳ] *n* cuerpo legislativo
legitimacy [lɪ'dʒɪtɪməsɪ] *n* legitimidad *f*
legitimate [lɪ'dʒɪtɪmət] *adj* legítimo
legitimize [lɪ'dʒɪtɪmaɪz] *vt* legitimar
legless ['lɛglɪs] *adj* (Brit inf) mamado
leg-room ['lɛgru:m] *n* espacio para las piernas
leisure ['lɛʒəʳ] *n* ocio, tiempo libre; **at ~** con tranquilidad
leisure centre *n* polideportivo
leisurely ['lɛʒəlɪ] *adj* sin prisa; lento
lemon ['lɛmən] *n* limón *m*
lemonade [lɛmə'neɪd] *n* (fruit juice) limonada; (fizzy) gaseosa
lemon tea *n* té *m* con limón
lend [lɛnd] (*pt, pp* **lent** [lɛnt]) *vt*: **to ~ sth to sb** prestar algo a algn
lender ['lɛndəʳ] *n* prestamista *m/f*
length [lɛŋθ] *n* (size) largo, longitud *f*; (section: of road, pipe) tramo; (: of rope etc) largo; (of wood,

string) trozo; (amount of time) duración *f*; **at ~** (at last) por fin, finalmente; (lengthily) largamente; **it is two metres in ~** tiene dos metros de largo; **what ~ is it?** ¿cuánto tiene de largo?; **to fall full ~** caer de bruces; **to go to any ~(s) to do sth** ser capaz de hacer cualquier cosa para hacer algo
lengthen ['lɛŋθn] *vt* alargar ▷ *vi* alargarse
lengthways ['lɛŋθweɪz] *adv* a lo largo
lengthy ['lɛŋθɪ] *adj* largo, extenso; (meeting) prolongado
lenient ['li:nɪənt] *adj* indulgente
lens [lɛnz] *n* (of spectacles) lente *f*; (of camera) objetivo
Lent [lɛnt] *n* Cuaresma
lent [lɛnt] *pt, pp of* **lend**
lentil ['lɛntl] *n* lenteja
Leo ['li:əu] *n* Leo
leopard ['lɛpəd] *n* leopardo
leotard ['li:ətɑ:d] *n* malla
leper ['lɛpəʳ] *n* leproso(-a)
leprosy ['lɛprəsɪ] *n* lepra
lesbian ['lɛzbɪən] *adj* lesbiano ▷ *n* lesbiana
lesion ['li:ʒən] *n* (Med) lesión *f*
less [lɛs] *adj* (in size, degree etc) menor; (in quantity) menos ▷ *pron, adv* menos; **~ than half** menos de la mitad; **~ than £1/a kilo/3 metres** menos de una libra/un kilo/3 metros; **~ than ever** menos que nunca; **~ 5%** menos el cinco por ciento; **~ and ~** cada vez menos; **the ~ he works ...** cuanto menos trabaja ...
lessen ['lɛsn] *vi* disminuir, reducirse ▷ *vt* disminuir, reducir
lesser ['lɛsəʳ] *adj* menor; **to a ~ extent** or **degree** en menor grado
lesson ['lɛsn] *n* clase *f*; **a maths ~** una clase de matemáticas; **to give ~s in** dar clases de; **it taught him a ~** (fig) le sirvió de lección
lest [lɛst] *conj*: **~ it happen** para que no pase
let [lɛt] (*pt, pp* **let**) *vt* (allow) dejar, permitir; (Brit: lease) alquilar; **to ~ sb do sth** dejar que algn haga algo; **to ~ sb have sth** dar algo a algn; **to ~ sb know sth** comunicar algo a algn; **~'s go** ¡vamos!; **~ him come** que venga; **"to ~"** "se alquila"; **let down** *vt* (lower) bajar; (dress) alargar; (tyre) desinflar; (hair) soltar; (disappoint) defraudar; **let go** *vi* soltar; (fig) dejarse ir ▷ *vt* soltar; **let in** *vt* dejar entrar; (visitor etc) hacer pasar; **what have you ~ yourself in for?** ¿en qué te has metido?; **let off** *vt* dejar escapar; (firework etc) disparar; (bomb) accionar; (passenger) dejar, bajar; **to ~ off steam** (fig, inf) desahogarse, desfogarse; **let on** *vi*: **to ~ on that ...** revelar que ...; **let out** *vt* dejar salir; (dress) ensanchar; (rent out) alquilar; **let up** *vi* disminuir; (rain etc) amainar
lethal ['li:θl] *adj* (weapon) mortífero; (poison, wound) mortal
lethargic [lɛ'θɑ:dʒɪk] *adj* aletargado
letter ['lɛtəʳ] *n* (of alphabet) letra; (correspondence) carta; **letters** *npl* (literature,

learning) letras *fpl*; **small/capital ~**
minúscula/mayúscula; **covering ~** carta
adjunta
letter bomb *n* carta-bomba
letterbox ['lɛtəbɒks] *n* (*Brit*) buzón *m*
lettering ['lɛtərɪŋ] *n* letras *fpl*
letter-opener ['lɛtərəupnə'] *n* abrecartas *m*
inv
lettuce ['lɛtɪs] *n* lechuga
let-up ['lɛtʌp] *n* descanso, tregua
leukaemia, leukemia (*US*) [lu:'ki:mɪə] *n*
leucemia
level ['lɛvl] *adj* (*flat*) llano; (*flattened*) nivelado;
(*uniform*) igual ▷ *adv* a nivel ▷ *n* nivel *m*;
(*height*) altura ▷ *vt* nivelar, allanar; (*destroy*:
building) derribar; (*gun*) apuntar; (*accusation*):
to ~ (against) levantar (contra) ▷ *vi* (*inf*): **to ~
with sb** ser franco con algn; **to be ~ with**
estar a nivel de; **a ~ spoonful** (*Culin*) una
cucharada rasa; **to draw ~ with** (*team*)
igualar; (*runner, car*) alcanzar a; **A ~s** (*Brit*)
≈ exámenes *mpl* de bachillerato superior,
B.U.P.; **O ~s** *npl* (*Brit: formerly*) ≈ bachillerato
sg elemental, octavo *sg* de Básica; **on the ~**
(*fig: honest*) en serio; **talks at ministerial ~**
charlas a nivel ministerial; **level off** *or* **out**
vi (*prices etc*) estabilizarse; (*ground*) nivelarse;
(*aircraft*) ponerse en una trayectoria
horizontal
level crossing *n* (*Brit*) paso a nivel
level-headed [lɛvl'hedɪd] *adj* sensato
level playing field *n* situación *f* de igualdad;
to compete on a ~ competir en igualdad de
condiciones
lever ['li:və'] *n* palanca ▷ *vt*: **to ~ up** levantar
con palanca
leverage ['li:vərɪdʒ] *n* (*fig: influence*)
influencia
levity ['lɛvɪtɪ] *n* frivolidad *f*, informalidad *f*
levy ['lɛvɪ] *n* impuesto ▷ *vt* exigir, recaudar
lewd [lu:d] *adj* lascivo, obsceno, colorado
(*LAm*)
lexicographer [lɛksɪ'kɔgrəfə'] *n*
lexicógrafo(-a) *m(f)*
lexicography [lɛksɪ'kɔgrəfɪ] *n* lexicografía
LGV *n abbr* (= *Large Goods Vehicle*) vehículo
pesado
liability [laɪə'bɪlɪtɪ] *n* (*pej: person, thing*)
estorbo, lastre *m*; (*Law: responsibility*)
responsabilidad *f*; (*handicap*) desventaja
liable ['laɪəbl] *adj* (*subject*): **~ to** sujeto a;
(*responsible*): **~ for** responsable de; (*likely*): **~ to
do** propenso a hacer; **to be ~ to a fine**
exponerse a una multa
liaise [li:'eɪz] *vi*: **to ~ (with)** colaborar (con);
to ~ with sb mantener informado a algn
liaison [li:'eɪzɔn] *n* (*coordination*) enlace *m*;
(*affair*) relación *f*
liar ['laɪə'] *n* mentiroso(-a)
libel ['laɪbl] *n* calumnia ▷ *vt* calumniar
libellous ['laɪbləs] *adj* difamatorio,
calumnioso

liberal ['lɪbərl] *adj* (*gen*) liberal; (*generous*):
~ with generoso con ▷ *n*: **L~** (*Pol*) liberal *m/f*
Liberal Democrat *n* (*Brit*) demócrata *m/f*
liberal
liberalize ['lɪbərəlaɪz] *vt* liberalizar
liberate ['lɪbəreɪt] *vt* (*people: from poverty etc*)
librar; (*prisoner*) libertar; (*country*) liberar
liberation [lɪbə'reɪʃən] *n* liberación *f*
liberation theology *n* teología de la
liberación
liberty ['lɪbətɪ] *n* libertad *f*; **to be at ~**
(*criminal*) estar en libertad; **to be at ~ to do**
estar libre para hacer; **to take the ~ of doing
sth** tomarse la libertad de hacer algo
Libra ['li:brə] *n* Libra
librarian [laɪ'brɛərɪən] *n* bibliotecario(-a)
library ['laɪbrərɪ] *n* biblioteca
libretto [lɪ'brɛtəu] *n* libreto
Libya ['lɪbɪə] *n* Libia
lice [laɪs] *pl of* **louse**
licence, license (*US*) ['laɪsns] *n* licencia;
(*permit*) permiso; (*also*: **driving ~**, (*US*):
driver's license) carnet *m* de conducir,
permiso de manejar (*LAm*); (*excessive freedom*)
libertad *f*; **import ~** licencia *or* permiso de
importación; **produced under ~** elaborado
bajo licencia
licence number *n* (número de) matrícula
licence plate *n* (placa de) matrícula
license ['laɪsns] *n* (*US*) = **licence** ▷ *vt*
autorizar, dar permiso a; (*car*) sacar la
matrícula de *or* (*LAm*) la patente de
licensed ['laɪsnst] *adj* (*for alcohol*) autorizado
para vender bebidas alcohólicas
licensee [laɪsən'si:] *n* (*in a pub*)
concesionario(-a), dueño(-a) de un bar
license plate *n* (*US*) placa (de matrícula)
licensing hours *npl* (*Brit*) *horas durante las cuales
se permite la venta y consumo de alcohol (en un bar etc)*
lick [lɪk] *vt* lamer; (*inf: defeat*) dar una paliza a
▷ *n* lamedura; **a ~ of paint** una mano de
pintura; **to ~ one's lips** relamerse
licorice ['lɪkərɪs] *n* = **liquorice**
lid [lɪd] *n* (*of box, case, pan*) tapa, tapadera; **to
take the ~ off sth** (*fig*) exponer algo a la luz
pública
lie [laɪ] *n* mentira ▷ *vi* mentir (*pt* **lay**, *pp* **lain**
[leɪ, leɪn]) (*rest*) estar echado, estar acostado;
(*of object: be situated*) estar, encontrarse; **to
tell ~s** mentir; **to ~ low** (*fig*) mantenerse a
escondidas; **lie about, lie around** *vi* (*things*)
estar tirado; (*Brit: people*) estar acostado *or*
tumbado; **lie back** *vi* recostarse; **lie down** *vi*
echarse, tumbarse; **lie up** *vi* (*hide*) esconderse
Liechtenstein ['lɪktənstaɪn] *n*
Liechtenstein *m*
lie detector *n* detector *m* de mentiras
lie-down ['laɪdaun] *n* (*Brit*): **to have a ~**
echarse (una siesta)
lie-in ['laɪɪn] *n* (*Brit*): **to have a ~** quedarse en
la cama
lieu [lu:]: **in ~ of** *prep* en lugar de

lieutenant [lɛfˈtɛnənt, (US) luːˈtɛnənt] n (Mil) teniente m

life (pl **lives**) [laɪf, laɪvz] n vida; (of licence etc) vigencia; **to be sent to prison for ~** ser condenado a cadena perpetua; **country/city ~** la vida en el campo/en la ciudad; **true to ~** fiel a la realidad; **to paint from ~** pintar del natural; **to put** or **breathe new ~ into** (person) reanimar; (project, area etc) infundir nueva vida a

life assurance n (Brit) seguro de vida

lifebelt [ˈlaɪfbɛlt] n (Brit) cinturón m salvavidas

lifeboat [ˈlaɪfbəut] n lancha de socorro

life-buoy [ˈlaɪfbɔɪ] n boya or guindola salvavidas

life expectancy n esperanza de vida

lifeguard [ˈlaɪfgɑːd] n vigilante m/f, socorrista m/f

life insurance n = **life assurance**

life jacket n chaleco salvavidas

lifeless [ˈlaɪflɪs] adj sin vida; (dull) soso

lifelike [ˈlaɪflaɪk] adj natural

lifeline [ˈlaɪflaɪn] n (fig) cordón m umbilical

lifelong [ˈlaɪflɔŋ] adj de toda la vida

life preserver n (US) = **lifebelt**

lifer [ˈlaɪfəʳ] n (Inf) condenado(-a) m(f) a cadena perpetua

life sentence n cadena perpetua

life-sized [ˈlaɪfsaɪzd] adj de tamaño natural

life span n vida

lifestyle [ˈlaɪfstaɪl] n estilo de vida

life support system n (Med) sistema m de respiración asistida

lifetime [ˈlaɪftaɪm] n: **in his ~** durante su vida; **once in a ~** una vez en la vida; **the chance of a ~** una oportunidad única

lift [lɪft] vt levantar; (copy) plagiar ▷ vi (fog) disiparse ▷ n (Brit: elevator) ascensor m, elevador m (LAm); **to give sb a ~** (Brit) llevar a algn en coche; **lift off** vt levantar, quitar ▷ vi (rocket, helicopter) despegar; **lift out** vt sacar; (troops, evacuees etc) evacuar; **lift up** vt levantar

lift-off [ˈlɪftɔf] n despegue m

ligament [ˈlɪgəmənt] n ligamento

light [laɪt] n luz f; (flame) lumbre f; (lamp) luz f, lámpara; (daylight) luz f del día; (headlight) faro; (rear light) luz f trasera; (for cigarette etc): **have you got a ~?** ¿tienes fuego? ▷ vt (pt, pp **lighted** or **lit** [lɪt] (candle, cigarette, fire) encender; (room) alumbrar ▷ adj (colour) claro; (room) con mucha luz ▷ adv (travel) con poco equipaje; **lights** npl (traffic lights) semáforos mpl; **to turn the ~ on/off** encender/apagar la luz; **in the ~ of** a la luz de; **to come to ~** salir a la luz; **to cast** or **shed** or **throw ~ on** arrojar luz sobre; **to make ~ of sth** (fig) no dar importancia a algo; **light up** vi (smoke) encender un cigarrillo; (face) iluminarse ▷ vt (illuminate) iluminar, alumbrar; (set fire to) encender

light bulb n bombilla, bombillo (LAm), foco (LAm)

lighten [ˈlaɪtn] vi (grow light) clarear ▷ vt (give light to) iluminar; (make lighter) aclarar; (make less heavy) aligerar

lighter [ˈlaɪtəʳ] n (also: **cigarette ~**) encendedor m (LAm), mechero

light-headed [laɪtˈhɛdɪd] adj (dizzy) mareado; (excited) exaltado; (by nature) atolondrado

light-hearted [laɪtˈhɑːtɪd] adj (person) alegre; (remark etc) divertido

lighthouse [ˈlaɪthaus] n faro

lighting [ˈlaɪtɪŋ] n (act) iluminación f; (system) alumbrado

lightly [ˈlaɪtlɪ] adv ligeramente; (not seriously) con poca seriedad; **to get off ~** ser castigado con poca severidad

lightness [ˈlaɪtnɪs] n claridad f; (in weight) ligereza

lightning [ˈlaɪtnɪŋ] n relámpago, rayo

lightning conductor, lightning rod (US) n pararrayos m inv

lightweight [ˈlaɪtweɪt] adj (suit) ligero ▷ n (Boxing) peso ligero

light year n año luz

like [laɪk] vt (person) querer a; (thing): **I ~ swimming/apples** me gusta nadar/me gustan las manzanas ▷ prep como ▷ adj parecido, semejante ▷ n: **did you ever see the ~ (of it)?** ¿has visto cosa igual?; **his ~s and dislikes** sus gustos y aversiones; **the ~s of him** personas como él; **I would ~, I'd ~** me gustaría; (for purchase) quisiera; **would you ~ a coffee?** ¿te apetece un café?; **I ~ swimming** me gusta nadar; **to be** or **look ~ sb/sth** parecerse a algn/algo; **that's just ~ him** es muy de él, es típico de él; **do it ~ this** hazlo así; **it is nothing ~ ...** no tiene parecido alguno con ...; **what's he ~?** ¿cómo es (él)?; **what's the weather ~?** ¿qué tiempo hace?; **something ~ that** algo así or por el estilo; **I feel ~ a drink** me apetece algo de beber; **if you ~** si quieres

likeable [ˈlaɪkəbl] adj simpático, agradable

likelihood [ˈlaɪklɪhud] n probabilidad f; **in all ~** según todas las probabilidades

likely [ˈlaɪklɪ] adj probable, capaz (LAm); **he's ~ to leave** es probable or (LAm) capaz que se vaya; **not ~!** ¡ni hablar!

liken [ˈlaɪkən] vt: **to ~ to** comparar con

likeness [ˈlaɪknɪs] n (similarity) semejanza, parecido

likewise [ˈlaɪkwaɪz] adv igualmente; **to do ~** hacer lo mismo

liking [ˈlaɪkɪŋ] n: **~ (for)** (person) cariño (a); (thing) afición (a); **to take a ~ to sb** tomar cariño a algn; **to be to sb's ~** ser del gusto de algn

lilac [ˈlaɪlək] n (tree) lilo; (flower) lila ▷ adj (colour) de color lila

Lilo® [ˈlaɪləu] n colchoneta inflable

lily [ˈlɪlɪ] n lirio, azucena; **~ of the valley** n lirio de los valles

lily of the valley n lirio de los valles

limb [lɪm] n miembro; (of tree) rama; **to be out on a ~** (fig) estar aislado

limber up ['lɪmbər-] vi (fig) entrenarse; (Sport) hacer (ejercicios de) precalentamiento

limbo ['lɪmbəu] n: **to be in ~** (fig) quedar a la expectativa

lime [laɪm] n (tree) limero; (fruit) lima; (Geo) cal f

limelight ['laɪmlaɪt] n: **to be in the ~** (fig) ser el centro de atención

limerick ['lɪmərɪk] n quintilla humorística

limestone ['laɪmstəun] n piedra caliza

limit ['lɪmɪt] n límite m ▷ vt limitar; **weight/speed ~** peso máximo/velocidad f máxima; **within ~s** entre límites

limitation [lɪmɪ'teɪʃən] n limitación f

limited ['lɪmɪtɪd] adj limitado; **to be ~ to** limitarse a; **~ edition** edición limitada

limousine ['lɪməziːn] n limusina

limp [lɪmp] n: **to have a ~** tener cojera ▷ vi cojear, renguear (LAm) ▷ adj flojo

limpet ['lɪmpɪt] n lapa

line [laɪn] n (Comm) línea; (straight line) raya; (rope) cuerda; (for fishing) sedal m; (wire) hilo; (row, series) fila, hilera; (of writing) renglón m; (on face) arruga; (Rail) vía; (speciality) rama ▷ vt (Sewing): **to ~ (with)** forrar (de); **to ~ the streets** ocupar las aceras; **in ~ with** de acuerdo con; **she's in ~ for promotion** (fig) tiene muchas posibilidades de que la asciendan; **to bring sth into ~ with sth** poner algo de acuerdo con algo; **~ of research/business** campo de investigación/comercio; **to take the ~ that ...** ser de la opinión que ...; **hold the ~ please** (Tel) no cuelgue usted, por favor; **to draw the ~ at doing sth** negarse a hacer algo; no permitir que se haga algo; **on the right ~s** por buen camino; **a new ~ in cosmetics** una nueva línea en cosméticos; **line up** vi hacer cola ▷ vt alinear, poner en fila; **to have sth ~d up** tener algo arreglado

linear ['lɪnɪər] adj lineal

lined [laɪnd] adj (face) arrugado; (paper) rayado; (clothes) forrado

lineman ['laɪnmən] n (US) técnico de las líneas; (Football) delantero

linen ['lɪnɪn] n ropa blanca; (cloth) lino

liner ['laɪnər] n vapor m de línea transatlántico; **dustbin ~** bolsa de la basura

linesman ['laɪnzmən] n (Sport) juez m de línea

line-up ['laɪnʌp] n (US: queue) cola; (Sport) alineación f

linger ['lɪŋgər] vi retrasarse, tardar en marcharse; (smell, tradition) persistir

lingerie ['lænʒəriː] n ropa interior (de mujer), lencería

lingo (pl **lingoes**) ['lɪŋgəu, -gəuz] n (pej) jerga

linguist ['lɪŋgwɪst] n lingüista m/f

linguistic [lɪŋ'gwɪstɪk] adj lingüístico

linguistics [lɪŋ'gwɪstɪks] n lingüística

lining ['laɪnɪŋ] n forro; (Tech) revestimiento; (of brake) guarnición f

link [lɪŋk] n (of chain) eslabón m; (connection) conexión f; (relationship) relación f; (bond) vínculo, lazo; (Internet) enlace m ▷ vt vincular, unir; (associate): **to ~ with** or **to** relacionar con; **rail ~** línea de ferrocarril, servicio de trenes; **links** npl (Golf) campo de golf; **link up** vt acoplar ▷ vi unirse

lino ['laɪnəu], **linoleum** (Brit) [lɪ'nəulɪəm] n linóleo

lion ['laɪən] n león m

lioness ['laɪənɪs] n leona

lip [lɪp] n labio; (of jug) pico; (of cup etc) borde m

liposuction ['lɪpəusʌkʃən] n liposucción f

lip-read ['lɪpriːd] vi leer los labios

lip salve n crema protectora para labios

lip service n: **to pay ~ to sth** alabar algo pero sin hacer nada

lipstick ['lɪpstɪk] n lápiz m or barra de labios, carmín m

liqueur [lɪ'kjuər] n licor m

liquid ['lɪkwɪd] adj, n líquido

liquidation [lɪkwɪ'deɪʃən] n liquidación f; **o go into ~** entrar en liquidación

liquidize ['lɪkwɪdaɪz] vt (Culin) licuar

liquidizer ['lɪkwɪdaɪzər] n (Culin) licuadora

liquor ['lɪkər] n licor m, bebidas fpl alcohólicas

liquorice ['lɪkərɪs] n regaliz m

liquor store n (US) bodega, tienda de vinos y bebidas alcohólicas

Lisbon ['lɪzbən] n Lisboa

lisp [lɪsp] n ceceo ▷ vi cecear

list [lɪst] n lista; (of ship) inclinación f ▷ vt (write down) hacer una lista de; (mention) enumerar; (Comput) hacer un listado de ▷ vi (ship) inclinarse; **shopping ~** lista de las compras; see also **lists**

listed building ['lɪstɪd-] n (Arch) edificio de interés histórico-artístico

listen ['lɪsn] vi escuchar, oír; (pay attention) atender

listener ['lɪsnər] n oyente m/f

listeria [lɪs'tɪərɪə] n listeria

listing ['lɪstɪŋ] n (Comput) listado

listless ['lɪstlɪs] adj apático, indiferente

lists [lɪsts] npl (History) liza sg; **to enter the ~ (against sb/sth)** salir a la palestra (contra algn/algo)

lit [lɪt] pt, pp of **light**

litany ['lɪtənɪ] n letanía

liter ['liːtər] n (US) = **litre**

literacy ['lɪtərəsɪ] n capacidad f de leer y escribir

literal ['lɪtərl] adj literal

literally ['lɪtrəlɪ] adv literalmente

literary ['lɪtərərɪ] adj literario

literate ['lɪtərət] adj que sabe leer y escribir; (educated) culto

literature ['lɪtərɪtʃər] n literatura; (brochures etc) folletos mpl

lithe [laɪð] adj ágil

Lithuania [lɪθju'eɪnɪə] n Lituania

litigate ['lɪtɪgeɪt] vi litigar
litigation [lɪtɪ'geɪʃən] n litigio
litmus paper ['lɪtməs-] n papel m de tornasol
litre, liter (US) ['liːtəʳ] n litro
litter ['lɪtəʳ] n (rubbish) basura; (paper) papeles mpl (tirados); (young animals) camada, cría
litter bin n (Brit) papelera
littered ['lɪtəd] adj: ~ **with** lleno de
little ['lɪtl] adj (small) pequeño, chico (LAm); (not much) poco; (often translated by suffix, eg): ~ **house** casita ▷ adv poco; **a** ~ un poco (de); **a** ~ **bit** un poquito; ~ **by** ~ poco a poco; ~ **finger** (dedo) meñique m; **for a** ~ **while** (durante) un rato; **with** ~ **difficulty** sin problema or dificultad; **as** ~ **as possible** lo menos posible
little finger n dedo meñique
little-known ['lɪtl'nəun] adj poco conocido
liturgy ['lɪtədʒɪ] n liturgia
live¹ [laɪv] adj (animal) vivo; (wire) conectado; (broadcast) en directo; (issue) de actualidad; (unexploded) sin explotar
live² [lɪv] vi vivir ▷ vt (a life) llevar; (experience) vivir; **to** ~ **in London** vivir en Londres; **to** ~ **together** vivir juntos; **live down** vt hacer olvidar; **live off** vt fus (land, fish etc) vivir de; (pej: parents etc) vivir a costa de; **live on** vt fus (food) vivir de, alimentarse de; **to** ~ **on £50 a week** vivir con 50 libras semanales or a la semana; **live out** vi (student) ser externo ▷ vt: **to** ~ **out one's days** or **life** pasar el resto de la vida; **live up** vt: **to** ~ **it up** (inf) tirarse la gran vida; **live up to** vt fus (fulfil) cumplir con; (justify) justificar
livelihood ['laɪvlɪhud] n sustento
lively ['laɪvlɪ] adj (gen) vivo; (interesting: place, book etc) animado; (pace) rápido; (party, tune) alegre
liven up ['laɪvn-] vt (discussion, evening) animar ▷ vi animarse
liver ['lɪvəʳ] n hígado
lives [laɪvz] npl of **life**
livestock ['laɪvstɔk] n ganado
livid ['lɪvɪd] adj lívido; (furious) furioso
living ['lɪvɪŋ] adj (alive) vivo ▷ n: **to earn** or **make a** ~ ganarse la vida; **cost of** ~ coste m de la vida; **in** ~ **memory** que se recuerde or recuerda
living conditions npl condiciones fpl de vida
living room n sala (de estar), living m (LAm)
living standards npl nivel msg de vida
living wage n sueldo suficiente para vivir
lizard ['lɪzəd] n lagartija
llama ['lɑːmə] n llama
load [ləud] n (gen) carga; (weight) peso ▷ vt (Comput) cargar; (also: ~ **up**): **to** ~ **(with)** cargar (con or de); **a** ~ **of**, ~**s of** (fig) (gran) cantidad de, montones de
loaded ['ləudɪd] adj (dice) cargado; (question) intencionado; (inf: rich) forrado (de dinero)
loaf (pl **loaves**) [ləuf, ləuvz] n (barra de) pan m ▷ vi (also: ~ **about**, ~ **around**) holgazanear

loan [ləun] n préstamo; (Comm) empréstito ▷ vt prestar; **on** ~ (book, painting) prestado; **to raise a** ~ (money) procurar un empréstito
loath [ləuθ] adj: **to be** ~ **to do sth** ser reacio a hacer algo
loathe [ləuð] vt aborrecer; (person) odiar
loaves [ləuvz] pl of **loaf**
lob [lɔb] vt (ball) volear por alto
lobby ['lɔbɪ] n vestíbulo, sala de espera; (Pol: pressure group) grupo de presión ▷ vt presionar
lobbyist ['lɔbɪɪst] n cabildero(-a)
lobe [ləub] n lóbulo
lobster ['lɔbstəʳ] n langosta
local ['ləukl] adj local ▷ n (pub) bar m; **the locals** npl los vecinos, los del lugar
local anaesthetic, local anesthetic (US) n (Med) anestesia local
local authority n municipio, ayuntamiento (Sp)
local call n (Tel) llamada local
local government n gobierno municipal
locality [ləu'kælɪtɪ] n localidad f
locally ['ləukəlɪ] adv en la vecindad
locate [ləu'keɪt] vt (find) localizar; (situate): **to be** ~**d in** estar situado en
location [ləu'keɪʃən] n situación f; **on** ~ (Cine) en exteriores, fuera del estudio
loch [lɔx] n lago
lock [lɔk] n (of door, box) cerradura, chapa (LAm); (of canal) esclusa; (of hair) mechón m ▷ vt (with key) cerrar con llave; (immobilize) inmovilizar ▷ vi (door etc) cerrarse con llave; (wheels) trabarse; ~ **stock and barrel** (fig) por completo or entero; **on full** ~ (Aut) con el volante girado al máximo; **lock away** vt (valuables) guardar bajo llave; (criminal) encerrar; **lock in** vt encerrar; **lock out** vt (person) cerrar la puerta a; **the workers were** ~**ed out** los trabajadores tuvieron que enfrentarse con un cierre patronal; **lock up** vt (criminal) meter en la cárcel; (mental patient) encerrar; (house) cerrar (con llave) ▷ vi echar la llave
locker ['lɔkəʳ] n casillero
locker-room ['lɔkərum] n (US Sport) vestuario
locket ['lɔkɪt] n medallón m
locksmith ['lɔksmɪθ] n cerrajero(-a)
lock-up ['lɔkʌp] n (prison) cárcel f; (cell) jaula; (also: ~ **garage**) jaula, cochera
locomotive [ləukə'məutɪv] n locomotora
locum ['ləukəm] n (Med) (médico(-a)) suplente m(f)
locust ['ləukəst] n langosta
lodge [lɔdʒ] n casa del guarda; (porter's) portería; (Freemasonry) logia ▷ vi (person): **to** ~ **(with)** alojarse (en casa de) ▷ vt (complaint) presentar
lodger ['lɔdʒəʳ] n huésped m/f
lodging ['lɔdʒɪŋ] n alojamiento, hospedaje m
lodgings ['lɔdʒɪŋz] npl alojamiento sg; (house) casa sg de huéspedes

loft [lɔft] n desván m
lofty ['lɔftɪ] adj alto; (haughty) altivo,
arrogante; (sentiments, aims) elevado, noble
log [lɔg] n (of wood) leño, tronco; (written
account) diario; (book) = **logbook** ▷ n abbr
(= logarithm) log ▷ vt anotar, registrar; **log in,
log on** vi (Comput) iniciar la sesión; **log off,
log out** vi (Comput) finalizar la sesión
logarithm ['lɔgərɪðəm] n logaritmo
logbook ['lɔgbuk] n (Naut) diario de a bordo;
(Aviat) libro de vuelo; (of car) documentación f
(del coche)
logger ['lɔgəʳ] n leñador(a) m(f)
loggerheads ['lɔgəhedz] npl: **at ~ (with)** de
pique (con)
logic ['lɔdʒɪk] n lógica
logical ['lɔdʒɪkl] adj lógico
login ['lɔgɪn] n (Comput) login m
logo ['ləugəu] n logotipo
loin [lɔɪn] n (Culin) lomo, solomillo; **loins** npl
lomos mpl
loiter ['lɔɪtəʳ] vi vagar; (pej) merodear
loll [lɔl] vi (also: **~ about**) repantigarse
lollipop ['lɔlɪpɔp] n pirulí m; (iced) polo
lollipop lady n (Brit) ver nota
lollipop man, lollipop lady n (Brit) persona
encargada de ayudar a los niños a cruzar la calle
lolly ['lɔlɪ] n (inf: ice cream) polo; (: lollipop)
piruleta; (: money) guita
London ['lʌndən] n Londres m
Londoner ['lʌndənəʳ] n londinense m/f
lone [ləun] adj solitario
loneliness ['ləunlɪnɪs] n soledad f,
aislamiento
lonely ['ləunlɪ] adj (situation) solitario; (person)
solo; (place) aislado
loner ['ləunəʳ] n solitario(-a)
long [lɔŋ] adj largo ▷ adv mucho tiempo,
largamente ▷ vi: **to ~ for sth** anhelar algo
▷ n: **the ~ and the short of it is that …** (fig)
en resumidas cuentas …; **in the ~ run** a la
larga; **so** or **as ~ as** mientras, con tal de que;
don't be ~! ¡no tardes!, ¡vuelve pronto!; **how
~ is the street?** ¿cuánto tiene la calle de
largo?; **how ~ is the lesson?** ¿cuánto dura la
clase?; **six metres ~** que mide seis metros, de
seis metros de largo; **six months ~** que dura
seis meses, de seis meses de duración; **all
night ~** toda la noche; **~ ago** hace mucho
(tiempo); **he no ~er comes** ya no viene;
~ before mucho antes; **before ~** (+ future)
dentro de poco; (+ past) poco tiempo después;
at ~ last al fin, por fin; **I shan't be ~** termino
pronto
long-distance [lɔŋ'dɪstəns] adj (race) de
larga distancia; (call) interurbano
longhand ['lɔŋhænd] n escritura (corriente)
long-haul ['lɔŋhɔ:l] adj (flight) de larga
distancia
longing ['lɔŋɪŋ] n anhelo, ansia; (nostalgia)
nostalgia ▷ adj anhelante
longitude ['lɔŋgɪtju:d] n longitud f

long jump n salto de longitud
long-life ['lɔŋlaɪf] adj (batteries) de larga
duración; (milk) uperizado
long-lost ['lɔŋlɔst] adj desaparecido hace
mucho tiempo
long-playing record ['lɔŋpleɪɪŋ-] n elepé m,
disco de larga duración
long-range ['lɔŋ'reɪndʒ] adj de gran alcance;
(weather forecast) a largo plazo
long-sighted ['lɔŋ'saɪtɪd] adj (Brit) présbita
long-standing ['lɔŋ'stændɪŋ] adj de mucho
tiempo
long-suffering [lɔŋ'sʌfərɪŋ] adj sufrido
long-term ['lɔŋtə:m] adj a largo plazo
long wave n onda larga
long-winded [lɔŋ'wɪndɪd] adj prolijo
loo [lu:] n (Brit: inf) wáter m
look [luk] vi mirar; (seem) parecer; (building
etc): **to ~ south/on to the sea** dar al sur/al
mar ▷ n (glance) vistazo; (appearance)
aire m, aspecto; **looks** npl físico sg, belleza sg;
to ~ ahead mirar hacia delante; **it ~s about
four metres long** yo calculo que tiene unos
cuatro metros de largo; **it ~s all right to me**
a mí me parece que está bien; **to have a ~ at
sth** echar un vistazo a algo; **to have a ~ for
sth** buscar algo; **~ (here)!** (expressing annoyance
etc) ¡oye!; **~!** (expressing surprise) ¡mira!; **look
after** vt fus (care for) cuidar a; (deal with)
encargarse de; **look around** vi echar una
mirada alrededor; **look at** vt fus mirar;
(consider) considerar; **look back** vi mirar
hacia atrás; **to ~ back at sb/sth** mirar hacia
atrás algo/a algn; **to ~ back on** (event, period)
recordar; **look down on** vt fus (fig) despreciar,
mirar con desprecio; **look for** vt fus buscar;
look forward to vt fus esperar con ilusión;
(in letters): **we ~ forward to hearing from
you** quedamos a la espera de su respuesta or
contestación; **I'm not ~ing forward to it** no
tengo ganas de eso, no me hace ilusión; **look
in** vi: **to ~ in on sb** (visit) pasar por casa de
algn; **look into** vt fus investigar; **look on** vi
mirar (como espectador); **look out** vi
(beware): **to ~ out (for)** tener cuidado (de);
look out for vt fus (seek) buscar; (await)
esperar; **look over** vt (essay) revisar; (town,
building) inspeccionar, registrar; (person)
examinar; **look round** vi (turn) volver la
cabeza; **to ~ round for sth** buscar algo; **look
through** vt fus (papers, book) hojear; (briefly)
echar un vistazo a; (telescope) mirar por; **look
to** vt fus ocuparse de; (rely on) contar con;
look up vi mirar hacia arriba; (improve)
mejorar ▷ vt (word) buscar; (friend) visitar;
look up to vt fus admirar
look-out ['lukaut] n (tower etc) puesto de
observación; (person) vigía m/f; **to be on the ~
for sth** estar al acecho de algo
loom [lu:m] n telar m ▷ vi: **~ (up)** (threaten)
surgir, amenazar; (event: approach)
aproximarse

loony ['lu:nɪ] *adj, n* (*inf*) loco(-a) *m(f)*

loop [lu:p] *n* lazo; (*bend*) vuelta, recodo; (*Comput*) bucle *m*

loophole ['lu:phəʊl] *n* laguna

loose [lu:s] *adj* (*gen*) suelto; (*not tight*) flojo; (*wobbly etc*) movedizo; (*clothes*) ancho; (*morals, discipline*) relajado ▷ *vt* (*free*) soltar; (*slacken*) aflojar; (*also*: **~ off**: *arrow*) disparar, soltar; **~ connection** (*Elec*) hilo desempalmado; **to be at a ~ end** *or* (*US*) **at ~ ends** no saber qué hacer; **to tie up ~ ends** (*fig*) no dejar ningún cabo suelto, atar cabos

loose change *n* cambio

loose chippings [-'tʃɪpɪŋz] *npl* (*on road*) gravilla *sg* suelta

loosely ['lu:slɪ] *adv* libremente, aproximadamente

loosely-knit [-nɪt] *adj* de estructura abierta

loosen ['lu:sn] *vt* (*free*) soltar; (*untie*) desatar; (*slacken*) aflojar; **loosen up** *vi* (*before game*) hacer (ejercicios de) precalentamiento; (*inf: relax*) soltarse, relajarse

loot [lu:t] *n* botín *m* ▷ *vt* saquear

looting ['lu:tɪŋ] *n* pillaje *m*

lop-sided ['lɔp'saɪdɪd] *adj* torcido; (*fig*) desequilibrado

lord [lɔːd] *n* señor *m*; **L~ Smith** Lord Smith; **the L~** el Señor; **the (House of) L~s** (*Brit*) la Cámara de los Lores

Lordship ['lɔːdʃɪp] *n*: **your ~** su Señoría

lore [lɔːʳ] *n* saber *m* popular, tradiciones *fpl*

lorry ['lɔrɪ] *n* (*Brit*) camión *m*

lorry driver *n* camionero(-a)

lose [lu:z] (*pt, pp* **lost**) [lu:z, lɔst] *vt* perder ▷ *vi* perder, ser vencido; **to ~ (time)** (*clock*) atrasarse; **to ~ no time (in doing sth)** no tardar (en hacer algo); **to get lost** (*object*) extraviarse; (*person*) perderse; **lose out** *vi* salir perdiendo

loser ['lu:zəʳ] *n* perdedor(a) *m(f)*; **to be a bad ~** no saber perder

loss [lɔs] *n* pérdida; **heavy ~es** (*Mil*) grandes pérdidas *fpl*; **to be at a ~** no saber qué hacer; **to be a dead ~** ser completamente inútil; **to make a ~** sufrir pérdidas; **to cut one's ~es** reducir las pérdidas; **to sell sth at a ~** vender algo perdiendo dinero

lost [lɔst] *pt, pp* *of* **lose** ▷ *adj* perdido; **~ in thought** absorto, ensimismado

lost and found *n* (*US*) = **lost property**; **lost property office** *or* **department**

lost cause *n* causa perdida

lost property *n* (*Brit*) objetos *mpl* perdidos

lost property office *or* **department** *n* (*Brit*) departamento de objetos perdidos

lot [lɔt] *n* (*at auction*) lote *m*; (*destiny*) suerte *f*; **the ~** el todo, todos *mpl*, todas *fpl*; **a ~** mucho, bastante; **a ~ of, ~s of** muchos(-as), mucho(-a) *adj sg*; **I read a ~** leo bastante; **to draw ~s (for sth)** echar suertes (para decidir algo)

lotion ['ləʊʃən] *n* loción *f*

lottery ['lɔtərɪ] *n* lotería

loud [laud] *adj* (*voice, sound*) fuerte; (*laugh, shout*) estrepitoso; (*gaudy*) chillón(-ona) ▷ *adv* (*speak etc*) fuerte; **out ~** en voz alta

loudhailer [laud'heɪləʳ] *n* (*Brit*) megáfono

loudly ['laudlɪ] *adv* (*noisily*) fuerte; (*aloud*) en alta voz

loudspeaker [laud'spi:kəʳ] *n* altavoz *m*

lounge [laundʒ] *n* salón *m*, sala de estar; (*of hotel*) salón *m*; (*of airport*) sala de embarque ▷ *vi* (*also*: **~ about, ~ around**) holgazanear, no hacer nada

lounge bar *n* salón *m*

lounge suit *n* (*Brit*) traje *m* de calle

louse (*pl* **lice**) [laus, laɪs] *n* piojo; **louse up** *vt* (*inf*) echar a perder

lousy ['lauzɪ] *adj* (*fig*) vil, asqueroso; (*ill*) fatal

lout [laut] *n* gamberro(-a)

lovable ['lʌvəbl] *adj* amable, simpático

love [lʌv] *n* (*romantic, sexual*) amor *m*; (*kind, caring*) cariño ▷ *vt* amar, querer; **to send one's ~ to sb** dar sus recuerdos a algn; **~ from Anne** (*in letter*) con cariño de Anne; **I ~ to read** me encanta leer; **to be in ~ with** estar enamorado de; **to make ~** hacer el amor; **I ~ you** te quiero; **for the ~ of** por amor a; **"15 ~"** (*Tennis*) "15 a cero"; **I ~ paella** me encanta la paella; **I'd ~ to come** me gustaría muchísimo venir

love affair *n* aventura sentimental *or* amorosa

loved ones ['lʌvdwʌnz] *npl* seres *mpl* queridos

love-hate relationship ['lʌvheɪt-] *n* relación *f* de amor y odio

love life *n* vida sentimental

lovely ['lʌvlɪ] *adj* (*delightful*) precioso, encantador(a), lindo (*esp LAm*); (*beautiful*) precioso, lindo (*esp LAm*); **we had a ~ time** lo pasamos estupendo

lover ['lʌvəʳ] *n* amante *m/f*; (*amateur*): **a ~ of** un(a) aficionado(-a) *or* un(a) amante de

lovesick ['lʌvsɪk] *adj* enfermo de amor, amartelado

loving ['lʌvɪŋ] *adj* amoroso, cariñoso

low [ləʊ] *adj, adv* bajo ▷ *n* (*Meteorology*) área de baja presión ▷ *vi* (*cow*) mugir; **to feel ~** sentirse deprimido; **to turn (down) ~** bajar; **to reach a new** *or* **an all-time ~** llegar a su punto más bajo

low-alcohol [ləʊ'ælkəhɔl] *adj* bajo en alcohol

low-calorie ['ləʊ'kælərɪ] *adj* bajo en calorías

low-cut ['ləʊkʌt] *adj* (*dress*) escotado

lower ['ləʊəʳ] *adj* más bajo; (*less important*) menos importante ▷ *vt* bajar; (*reduce: price*) reducir, rebajar; (: *resistance*) debilitar; **to ~ o.s. to** (*fig*) rebajarse a ▷ *vi* ['lauəʳ]: **to ~ (at sb)** fulminar (a algn) con la mirada

Lower House *n* (*Pol*): **the ~** la Cámara baja

low-fat ['ləʊ'fæt] *adj* (*milk, yoghurt*) desnatado; (*diet*) bajo en calorías

lowland ['ləulənd] *n* tierra baja
lowly ['ləulɪ] *adj* humilde
low-tech ['ləutɛk] *adj* de baja tecnología, tradicional
loyal ['lɔɪəl] *adj* leal
loyalist ['lɔɪəlɪst] *n* legitimista *m/f*
loyalty ['lɔɪəltɪ] *n* lealtad *f*
loyalty card *n* (Brit) tarjeta cliente
lozenge ['lɒzɪndʒ] *n* (Med) pastilla
LP *n abbr* (= long-playing record) elepé *m*
L-plates ['ɛlpleɪts] *npl* (Brit) (placas *fpl* de) la L; ver nota

● **L-PLATES**
●
●
● En el Reino Unido las personas que están
● aprendiendo a conducir han de llevar
● indicativos blancos con una L en rojo
● llamados normalmente *L-plates* (de
● "learner" en la parte delantera y trasera
● de los automóviles que conducen. No
● tienen que ir a clases teóricas, sino que
● desde el principio se les entrega un carnet
● de conducir provisional ("provisional
● driving licence") para que realicen sus
● prácticas, que han de estar supervisadas
● por un conductor con carnet definitivo
● ("full driving licence"). Tampoco se les
● permite hacer prácticas en autopistas
● aunque vayan acompañados.

Lt. *abbr* (= lieutenant) Tte.
Ltd *abbr* (Comm: = limited company) S.A.
lubricant ['lu:brɪkənt] *n* lubricante *m*
lubricate ['lu:brɪkeɪt] *vt* lubricar, engrasar
lucid ['lu:sɪd] *adj* lúcido
luck [lʌk] *n* suerte *f*; **good/bad ~** buena/mala suerte; **good ~!** ¡(que tengas) suerte!; **to be in ~** estar de suerte; **to be out of ~** tener mala suerte; **bad** *or* **hard** *or* **tough ~!** ¡qué pena!
luckily ['lʌkɪlɪ] *adv* afortunadamente
lucky ['lʌkɪ] *adj* afortunado; (at cards etc) con suerte; (object) que trae suerte
lucrative ['lu:krətɪv] *adj* lucrativo
ludicrous ['lu:dɪkrəs] *adj* absurdo
lug [lʌg] *vt* (drag) arrastrar
luggage ['lʌgɪdʒ] *n* equipaje *m*
luggage rack *n* (in train) rejilla, redecilla; (on car) baca, portaequipajes *m inv*
lukewarm ['lu:kwɔ:m] *adj* tibio, templado
lull [lʌl] *n* tregua ▷ *vt* (child) acunar; (person, fear) calmar; **to ~ sb to sleep** arrullar a algn; **to ~ sb into a false sense of security** dar a algn una falsa sensación de seguridad
lullaby ['lʌləbaɪ] *n* nana
lumbago [lʌm'beɪgəu] *n* lumbago
lumber ['lʌmbəʳ] *n* (junk) trastos *mpl* viejos; (wood) maderos *mpl* ▷ *vt* (Brit inf): **to ~ sb with sth/sb** hacer que algn cargue con algo/algn ▷ *vi* (also: **~ about, ~ along**) moverse pesadamente

lumberjack ['lʌmbədʒæk] *n* maderero
luminous ['lu:mɪnəs] *adj* luminoso
lump [lʌmp] *n* terrón *m*; (fragment) trozo; (in sauce) grumo; (in throat) nudo; (swelling) bulto ▷ *vt* (also: **~ together**) juntar; (persons) poner juntos
lump sum *n* suma global
lumpy ['lʌmpɪ] *adj* (sauce) lleno de grumos
lunacy ['lu:nəsɪ] *n* locura
lunar ['lu:nəʳ] *adj* lunar
lunatic ['lu:nətɪk] *adj, n* loco(-a) *m(f)*
lunch [lʌntʃ] *n* almuerzo, comida ▷ *vi* almorzar; **to invite sb to** *or* **for ~** invitar a algn a almorzar
lunch break, lunch hour *n* hora del almuerzo
luncheon ['lʌntʃən] *n* almuerzo
luncheon meat *n* tipo de fiambre
luncheon voucher *n* vale *m* de comida
lunchtime ['lʌntʃtaɪm] *n* hora del almuerzo *or* de comer
lung [lʌŋ] *n* pulmón *m*
lunge [lʌndʒ] *vi* (also: **~ forward**) abalanzarse; **to ~ at** arremeter contra
lurch [lə:tʃ] *vi* dar sacudidas ▷ *n* sacudida; **to leave sb in the ~** dejar a algn plantado
lure [luəʳ] *n* (bait) cebo; (decoy) señuelo; (attraction) atracción *f* ▷ *vt* convencer con engaños
lurid ['luərɪd] *adj* (colour) chillón(-ona); (account) sensacional; (detail) horripilante
lurk [lə:k] *vi* (hide) esconderse; (wait) estar al acecho; (fig) acechar
luscious ['lʌʃəs] *adj* delicioso
lush [lʌʃ] *adj* exuberante
lust [lʌst] *n* lujuria; (greed) codicia; **lust after** *vt fus* codiciar
lusty ['lʌstɪ] *adj* robusto, fuerte
lute [lu:t] *n* laúd *m*
Luxembourg ['lʌksəmbə:g] *n* Luxemburgo
luxurious [lʌg'zjuərɪəs] *adj* lujoso
luxury ['lʌkʃərɪ] *n* lujo ▷ *cpd* de lujo
LV *n abbr* (Brit) = **luncheon voucher**
LW *abbr* (Radio) = **long wave**
Lycra® ['laɪkrə] *n* licra®
lying ['laɪɪŋ] *n* mentiras *fpl* ▷ *adj* (statement, story) falso; (person) mentiroso
lyric ['lɪrɪk] *adj* lírico; **lyrics** *npl* (of song) letra *sg*
lyrical ['lɪrɪkl] *adj* lírico

M, m [ɛm] *n* (*letter*) M, m *f*; **M for Mary,** (*US*) **M for Mike** M de Madrid

M *n abbr* (*Brit*: = *motorway*): **the M8** = la A8 ▷ *abbr* (= *medium*) M

m *abbr* (= *metre*) m.; = **metre; mile; million**

ma [mɑː] (*inf*) *n* mamá

MA *n abbr* (*Scol*) = **Master of Arts**; (*US*) = **Military Academy**

mac [mæk] *n* (*Brit*) impermeable *m*

macaroni [mækəˈrəʊnɪ] *n* macarrones *mpl*

Macedonia [mæsɪˈdəʊnɪə] *n* Macedonia

Macedonian [mæsɪˈdəʊnɪən] *adj* macedonio ▷ *n* macedonio(-a); (*Ling*) macedonio

machine [məˈʃiːn] *n* máquina ▷ *vt* (*dress etc*) coser a máquina; (*Tech*) trabajar a máquina

machine gun *n* ametralladora

machine language *n* (*Comput*) lenguaje *m* máquina

machinery [məˈʃiːnərɪ] *n* maquinaria; (*fig*) mecanismo

machine translation *n* traducción *f* automática

machine washable *adj* lavable a máquina

macho [ˈmætʃəʊ] *adj* macho

mackerel [ˈmækrl] *n pl inv* caballa

mackintosh [ˈmækɪntɔʃ] *n* (*Brit*) impermeable *m*

mad [mæd] *adj* loco; (*idea*) disparatado; (*angry*) furioso, enojado (*LAm*); **~ (at or with sb)** furioso (con algn); **to be ~ (keen) about** *or* **on sth** estar loco por algo; **to go ~** volverse loco, enloquecer(se)

madam [ˈmædəm] *n* señora; **can I help you, ~?** ¿le puedo ayudar, señora?; **M~ Chairman** señora presidenta

mad cow disease *n* encefalopatía espongiforme bovina

madden [ˈmædn] *vt* volver loco

made [meɪd] *pt, pp of* **make**

Madeira [məˈdɪərə] *n* (*Geo*) Madeira; (*wine*) madeira *m*

made-to-measure [ˈmeɪdtəmɛʒər] *adj* (*Brit*) hecho a la medida

made-up [ˈmeɪdʌp] *adj* (*story*) ficticio

madhouse [ˈmædhaus] *n* (*also fig*) manicomio

madly [ˈmædlɪ] *adv* locamente

madman [ˈmædmən] *n* loco

madness [ˈmædnɪs] *n* locura

Madrid [məˈdrɪd] *n* Madrid *m*

Mafia [ˈmæfɪə] *n* Mafia

mag [mæg] *n abbr* (*Brit inf*) = **magazine**

magazine [mægəˈziːn] *n* revista; (*Mil: store*) almacén *m*; (*of firearm*) recámara

maggot [ˈmægət] *n* gusano

magic [ˈmædʒɪk] *n* magia ▷ *adj* mágico

magical [ˈmædʒɪkəl] *adj* mágico

magician [məˈdʒɪʃən] *n* mago(-a)

magistrate [ˈmædʒɪstreɪt] *n* juez *m/f* (municipal)

magnesium [mægˈniːzɪəm] *n* magnesio

magnet [ˈmægnɪt] *n* imán *m*

magnetic [mægˈnɛtɪk] *adj* magnético

magnetic tape *n* cinta magnética

magnificent [mægˈnɪfɪsnt] *adj* magnífico

magnify [ˈmægnɪfaɪ] *vt* (*object*) ampliar; (*sound*) aumentar; (*fig*) exagerar

magnifying glass [ˈmægnɪfaɪɪŋ-] *n* lupa

magnitude [ˈmægnɪtjuːd] *n* magnitud *f*

magpie [ˈmægpaɪ] *n* urraca

mahogany [məˈhɔgənɪ] *n* caoba ▷ *cpd* de caoba

maid [meɪd] *n* criada; **old ~** (*pej*) solterona

maiden [ˈmeɪdn] *n* doncella ▷ *adj* (*aunt etc*) solterona; (*speech, voyage*) inaugural

maiden name *n* apellido de soltera

mail [meɪl] *n* correo; (*letters*) cartas *fpl* ▷ *vt* (*post*) echar al correo; (*send*) mandar por correo; **by ~** por correo

mailbox [ˈmeɪlbɔks] *n* (*US: for letters etc*: *Comput*) buzón *m*

mailing list [ˈmeɪlɪŋ-] *n* lista de direcciones

mailman [ˈmeɪlmæn] *n* (*US*) cartero

mail-order [ˈmeɪlɔːdər] *n* pedido postal; (*business*) venta por correo ▷ *adj*: **~ firm** or **house** casa de venta por correo

maim [meɪm] *vt* mutilar, lisiar

main [meɪn] *adj* principal, mayor ▷ *n* (*pipe*) cañería principal *or* maestra; (*US*) red *f* eléctrica; **the ~s** (*Brit Elec*) la red eléctrica; **in the ~** en general

main course *n* (*Culin*) plato principal

mainframe [ˈmeɪnfreɪm] *n* (*also*: **~ computer**) ordenador *m or* computadora central

mainland ['meɪnlənd] n continente m

mainly ['meɪnlɪ] adv principalmente, en su mayoría

main road n carretera principal

mainstay ['meɪnsteɪ] n (fig) pilar m

mainstream ['meɪnstriːm] n (fig) corriente f principal

main street n calle f mayor

maintain [meɪn'teɪn] vt mantener; (affirm) sostener; **to ~ that ...** mantener or sostener que ...

maintenance ['meɪntənəns] n mantenimiento; (alimony) pensión f alimenticia

maisonette [meɪzə'net] n dúplex m

maize [meɪz] n (Brit) maíz m, choclo (LAm)

majestic [mə'dʒestɪk] adj majestuoso

majesty ['mædʒɪstɪ] n majestad f; **Your M~** Su Majestad

major ['meɪdʒəʳ] n (Mil) comandante m ▷ adj principal; (Mus) mayor ▷ vi (US Univ): **to ~ in** especializarse en; **a ~ operation** una operación or intervención de gran importancia

Majorca [mə'jɔːkə] n Mallorca

majority [mə'dʒɔrɪtɪ] n mayoría ▷ cpd (verdict) mayoritario

make [meɪk] vt (pt, pp **made** [meɪd]) hacer; (manufacture) hacer, fabricar; (mistake) cometer; (speech) pronunciar; (cause to be): **to ~ sb sad** poner triste or entristecer a algn; (force): **to ~ sb do sth** obligar a algn a hacer algo; (equal): **2 and 2 ~ 4** 2 y 2 son 4 ▷ n marca; **to ~ a fool of sb** poner a algn en ridículo; **to ~ a profit/loss** obtener ganancias/sufrir pérdidas; **to ~ a profit of £500** sacar una ganancia de 500 libras; **to ~ it** (arrive) llegar; (achieve sth) tener éxito; **what time do you ~ it?** ¿qué hora tienes?; **to ~ do with** contentarse con; **make for** vt fus (place) dirigirse a; **make off** vi largarse; **make out** vt (decipher) descifrar; (understand) entender; (see) distinguir; (write: cheque) extender; **to ~ out (that)** (claim, imply) dar a entender (que); **to ~ out a case for sth** dar buenas razones en favor de algo; **make over** vt (assign): **to ~ over (to)** ceder or traspasar (a); **make up** vt (invent) inventar; (parcel) hacer ▷ vi reconciliarse; (with cosmetics) maquillarse; **to be made up of** estar compuesto de; **make up for** vt fus compensar

make-believe ['meɪkbɪliːv] n ficción f, fantasía

makeover ['meɪkəʊvəʳ] n cambio de imagen; **to give sb a ~** hacerle a algn un cambio de imagen

maker ['meɪkəʳ] n fabricante m/f; (of film, programme) autor(a) m(f)

makeshift ['meɪkʃɪft] adj improvisado

make-up ['meɪkʌp] n maquillaje m

make-up remover n desmaquillador m

making ['meɪkɪŋ] n (fig): **in the ~** en vías de formación; **to have the ~s of** (person) tener madera de

malaria [mə'lɛərɪə] n malaria

Malaysia [mə'leɪzɪə] n Malaisia, Malaysia

male [meɪl] n (Biol, Elec) macho ▷ adj (sex, attitude) masculino; (child etc) varón

malevolent [mə'levələnt] adj malévolo

malfunction [mæl'fʌŋkʃən] n mal funcionamiento

malice ['mælɪs] n (ill will) malicia; (rancour) rencor m

malicious [mə'lɪʃəs] adj malicioso; rencoroso

malign [mə'laɪn] vt difamar, calumniar ▷ adj maligno

malignant [mə'lɪgnənt] adj (Med) maligno

mall [mɔːl] n (US: also: **shopping ~**) centro comercial

mallet ['mælɪt] n mazo

malnutrition [mælnjuː'trɪʃən] n desnutrición f

malpractice [mæl'præktɪs] n negligencia profesional

malt [mɔːlt] n malta; (whisky) whisky m de malta

Malta ['mɔːltə] n Malta

Maltese [mɔːl'tiːz] adj maltés(-esa) ▷ n (pl inv) maltés(-esa) m(f); (Ling) maltés m

malware ['mælweəʳ] n (Comput) malware m, software m malicioso

mammal ['mæml] n mamífero

mammoth ['mæməθ] n mamut m ▷ adj gigantesco

man (pl **men**) [mæn, mɛn] n hombre m; (mankind) el hombre; (Chess) pieza ▷ vt (Naut) tripular; (Mil) defender; (operate: machine) manejar; **an old ~** un viejo; **~ and wife** marido y mujer

manage ['mænɪdʒ] vi arreglárselas ▷ vt (be in charge of) dirigir; (person etc) manejar; **to ~ to do sth** conseguir hacer algo; **to ~ without sth/sb** poder prescindir de algo/algn

manageable ['mænɪdʒəbl] adj manejable

management ['mænɪdʒmənt] n dirección f, administración f; **"under new ~"** "bajo nueva dirección"

manager ['mænɪdʒəʳ] n director(a) m(f); (of pop star) mánager m(f); (Sport) entrenador(a) m(f); **sales ~** jefe(-a) m(f) de ventas

manageress ['mænɪdʒəres] n directora; (Sport) entrenadora

managerial [mænə'dʒɪərɪəl] adj directivo

managing director ['mænɪdʒɪŋ-] n director(a) m(f) general

Mancunian [mæŋ'kjuːnɪən] adj de Manchester ▷ n nativo(-a) or habitante m(f) de Manchester

mandarin ['mændərɪn] n (also: **~ orange**) mandarina; (person) mandarín m

mandate ['mændeɪt] n mandato

mandatory ['mændətərɪ] adj obligatorio

mane [meɪn] n (of horse) crin f; (of lion) melena

maneuver [mə'nu:və^r] vb, n (US) = **manoeuvre**

manfully ['mænfəlɪ] adv resueltamente

mangetout [mɒnʒ'tu:] n tirabeque m

mangle ['mæŋgl] vt mutilar, destrozar ▷ n escurridor m

mango (pl **mangoes**) ['mæŋgəu] n mango

mangy ['meɪndʒɪ] adj roñoso; (Med) sarnoso

manhandle ['mænhændl] vt maltratar; (move by hand: goods) manipular

manhole ['mænhəul] n boca de alcantarilla

manhood ['mænhud] n edad f viril; (manliness) virilidad f

man-hour ['mæn'auə^r] n hora-hombre f

manhunt ['mænhʌnt] n caza de hombre

mania ['meɪnɪə] n manía

maniac ['meɪnɪæk] n maníaco(-a); (fig) maniático

manic ['mænɪk] adj (behaviour, activity) frenético

manicure ['mænɪkjuə^r] n manicura

manicure set n estuche m de manicura

manifest ['mænɪfest] vt manifestar, mostrar ▷ adj manifiesto ▷ n **manifiesto**

manifesto [mænɪ'festəu] n manifiesto

manipulate [mə'nɪpjuleɪt] vt manipular

mankind [mæn'kaɪnd] n humanidad f, género humano

manly ['mænlɪ] adj varonil

man-made ['mæn'meɪd] adj artificial

manner ['mænə^r] n manera, modo; (behaviour) conducta, manera de ser; (type) clase f; **manners** npl modales mpl, educación fsg; **(good) ~s** (buena) educación fsg, (buenos) modales mpl; **bad ~s** falta sg de educación, malos modales mpl; **all ~ of** toda clase or suerte de

mannerism ['mænərɪzəm] n gesto típico

manoeuvre, maneuver (US) [mə'nu:və^r] vt, vi maniobrar ▷ n maniobra; **to ~ sb into doing sth** manipular a algn para que haga algo

manor ['mænə^r] n (also: ~ **house**) casa solariega

manpower ['mænpauə^r] n mano f de obra

mansion ['mænʃən] n mansión f

manslaughter ['mænslɔ:tə^r] n homicidio involuntario

mantelpiece ['mæntlpi:s] n repisa de la chimenea

manual ['mænjuəl] adj manual ▷ n manual m; **~ worker** obrero(-a), trabajador(a) m(f) manual

manufacture [mænju'fæktʃə^r] vt fabricar ▷ n fabricación f

manufacturer [mænju'fæktʃərə^r] n fabricante m/f

manure [mə'njuə^r] n estiércol m, abono

manuscript ['mænjuskrɪpt] n manuscrito

Manx [mæŋks] adj de la Isla de Man

many ['menɪ] adj muchos(-as) ▷ pron muchos(-as); **a great ~** muchísimos, un buen número de; **~ a time** muchas veces; **too ~ difficulties** demasiadas dificultades; **twice as ~** el doble; **how ~?** ¿cuántos?

map [mæp] n mapa m ▷ vt trazar el mapa de; **map out** vt (fig: career, holiday, essay) proyectar, planear

maple ['meɪpl] n arce m, maple m (LAm)

mar [mɑ:^r] vt estropear

Mar abbr (= March) mar

marathon ['mærəθən] n maratón m ▷ adj: **a ~ session** una sesión maratoniana

marble ['mɑ:bl] n mármol m; (toy) canica

March [mɑ:tʃ] n marzo; see also **July**

march [mɑ:tʃ] vi (Mil) marchar; (demonstrators) manifestarse; (fig) caminar con resolución ▷ n marcha; (demonstration) manifestación f

mare [meə^r] n yegua

margarine [mɑ:dʒə'ri:n] n margarina

marg(e) [mɑ:dʒ] n abbr (inf) = **margarine**

margin ['mɑ:dʒɪn] n margen m; (Comm: profit margin) margen m de beneficios

marginal ['mɑ:dʒɪnl] adj marginal

marginally ['mɑ:dʒɪnəlɪ] adv ligeramente

marginal seat n (Pol) circunscripción f políticamente no definida

marigold ['mærɪgəuld] n caléndula

marijuana [mærɪ'wɑ:nə] n marihuana

marina [mə'ri:nə] n puerto deportivo

marinade [mærɪ'neɪd] n adobo

marinate ['mærɪneɪt] vt adobar

marine [mə'ri:n] adj marino ▷ n soldado de infantería de marina

marital ['mærɪtl] adj matrimonial; **~ status** estado civil

maritime ['mærɪtaɪm] adj marítimo

marjoram ['mɑ:dʒərəm] n mejorana

mark [mɑ:k] n marca, señal f; (in snow, mud etc) huella; (stain) mancha; (Brit Scol) nota; (currency) marco ▷ vt (Sport: player) marcar; (stain) manchar; (Brit Scol) calificar, corregir; **punctuation ~s** signos mpl de puntuación; **to be quick off the ~** (fig) ser listo; **up to the ~** (in efficiency) a la altura de las circunstancias; **to ~ time** marcar el paso; (fig) marcar(se) un ritmo; **mark down** vt (reduce: prices, goods) rebajar; **mark off** vt (tick) indicar, señalar; **mark out** vt trazar; **mark up** vt (price) aumentar

marked [mɑ:kt] adj marcado, acusado

marker ['mɑ:kə^r] n (sign) marcador m; (bookmark) registro

market ['mɑ:kɪt] n mercado ▷ vt (Comm) comercializar; (promote) publicitar; **open ~** mercado libre; **to be on the ~** estar en venta; **to play the ~** jugar a la bolsa

market economy n economía de mercado

market garden n (Brit) huerto

marketing ['mɑ:kɪtɪŋ] n marketing m, mercadotecnia

m

marketplace ['mɑ:kɪtpleɪs] n mercado
market research n (Comm) estudios mpl de mercado
marksman ['mɑ:ksmən] n tirador m
marmalade ['mɑ:məleɪd] n mermelada de naranja
maroon [mə'ru:n] vt: **to be ~ed** (shipwrecked) quedar aislado; (fig) quedar abandonado ▷ n (colour) granate m
marquee [mɑ:'ki:] n carpa, entoldado
marriage ['mærɪdʒ] n (state) matrimonio; (wedding) boda; (act) casamiento
marriage bureau n agencia matrimonial
marriage certificate n partida de casamiento
marriage of convenience n matrimonio de conveniencia
married ['mærɪd] adj casado; (life, love) conyugal
marrow ['mærəu] n médula; (vegetable) calabacín m
marry ['mærɪ] vt casarse con; (father, priest etc) casar ▷ vi (also: **get married**) casarse
Mars [mɑ:z] n Marte m
marsh [mɑ:ʃ] n pantano; (salt marsh) marisma
marshal ['mɑ:ʃl] n (Mil) mariscal m; (at sports meeting, demonstration etc) oficial m; (US: of police, fire department) jefe(-a) m(f) ▷ vt (facts) ordenar; (soldiers) formar
marshy ['mɑ:ʃɪ] adj pantanoso
martial arts npl artes fpl marciales
martial law n ley f marcial
martyr ['mɑ:tə*] n mártir m/f ▷ vt martirizar
martyrdom ['mɑ:tədəm] n martirio
marvel ['mɑ:vl] n maravilla, prodigio ▷ vi: **to ~ (at)** maravillarse (de)
marvellous, marvelous (US) ['mɑ:vləs] adj maravilloso
Marxism ['mɑ:ksɪzəm] n marxismo
Marxist ['mɑ:ksɪst] adj, n marxista m/f
marzipan ['mɑ:zɪpæn] n mazapán m
mascara [mæs'kɑ:rə] n rimel m
mascot ['mæskət] n mascota
masculine ['mæskjulɪn] adj masculino
mash [mæʃ] vt machacar ▷ n (mix) mezcla; (Culin) puré m; (pulp) amasijo
mashed potatoes [mæʃt-] npl puré m de patatas or (LAm) papas
mask [mɑ:sk] n máscara ▷ vt (cover): **to ~ one's face** ocultarse la cara; (hide: feelings) esconder
masochist ['mæsəukɪst] n masoquista m/f
mason ['meɪsn] n (also: **stone~**) albañil m; (also: **free~**) masón m
masonic [mə'sɔnɪk] adj masónico
masonry ['meɪsnrɪ] n masonería; (in building) mampostería
masquerade [mæskə'reɪd] n baile m de máscaras; (fig) mascarada ▷ vi: **to ~ as** disfrazarse de, hacerse pasar por

mass [mæs] n (people) muchedumbre f; (Phys) masa; (Rel) misa; (great quantity) montón m ▷ vi reunirse; (Mil) concentrarse; **the ~es** las masas; **to go to ~** ir a or oír misa
massacre ['mæsəkə*] n masacre f ▷ vt masacrar
massage ['mæsɑ:ʒ] n masaje m ▷ vt dar masajes or un masaje a
massive ['mæsɪv] adj enorme; (support, intervention) masivo
mass media npl medios mpl de comunicación de masas
mass-produce ['mæsprə'dju:s] vt fabricar en serie
mast [mɑ:st] n (Naut) mástil m; (Radio etc) torre f, antena
mastectomy [mæs'tɛktəmɪ] n mastectomía
master ['mɑ:stə*] n (of servant, animal) amo; (fig: of situation) dueño; (Art, Mus) maestro; (in secondary school) profesor m; (title for boys): **M~ X** Señorito X ▷ vt dominar
masterly ['mɑ:stəlɪ] adj magistral
mastermind ['mɑ:stəmaɪnd] n inteligencia superior ▷ vt dirigir, planear
Master of Arts n licenciatura superior en Letras; see also **master's degree**
Master of Science n licenciatura superior en Ciencias; see also **master's degree**
masterpiece ['mɑ:stəpi:s] n obra maestra
master plan n plan m rector
master's degree n máster m

  ⊚ **MASTER'S DEGREE**
  ⊚
  ⊚ Los estudios de postgrado británicos que
  ⊚ llevan a la obtención de un master's degree
  ⊚ consisten generalmente en una
  ⊚ combinación de curso(s) académico(s) y
  ⊚ tesina ("dissertation") sobre un tema
  ⊚ original, o bien únicamente la redacción
  ⊚ de una tesina. El primer caso es el más
  ⊚ frecuente para los títulos de "MA"
  ⊚ ("Master of Arts") y "MSc" ("Master of
  ⊚ Science"), mientras que los de "MLitt"
  ⊚ ("Master of Letters") o "MPhil"
  ⊚ ("Master of Philosophy") se obtienen
  ⊚ normalmente mediante tesina.
  ⊚ En algunas universidades, como las
  ⊚ escocesas, el título de master's degree no
  ⊚ es de postgrado, sino que corresponde
  ⊚ a la licenciatura.

mastery ['mɑ:stərɪ] n maestría
masturbate ['mæstəbeɪt] vi masturbarse
masturbation [mæstə'beɪʃən] n masturbación f
mat [mæt] n alfombrilla; (also: **door~**) felpudo ▷ adj = **matt**
match [mætʃ] n cerilla, fósforo; (game) partido; (fig) igual m/f ▷ vt emparejar; (go well with) hacer juego con; (equal) igualar; (correspond to) corresponderse con; (pair: also:

~ up) casar con ▷ vi hacer juego; **to be a good ~** hacer buena pareja

matchbox ['mætʃbɒks] n caja de cerillas

matching ['mætʃɪŋ] adj que hace juego

mate [meɪt] n (workmate) compañero(-a), colega m/f; (inf: friend) amigo(-a), compadre m/f (LAm); (animal) macho/hembra; (in merchant navy) primer oficial m, segundo de a bordo ▷ vi acoplarse, aparearse ▷ vt acoplar, aparear

material [mə'tɪərɪəl] n (substance) materia; (equipment) material m; (cloth) tela, tejido ▷ adj material; (important) esencial; **materials** npl materiales mpl; (equipment etc) artículos mpl

materialize [mə'tɪərɪəlaɪz] vi materializarse

maternal [mə'təːnl] adj maternal; **~ grandmother** abuela materna

maternity [mə'təːnɪtɪ] n maternidad f

maternity dress n vestido premamá

maternity hospital n hospital m de maternidad

maternity leave n baja por maternidad

math [mæθ] n abbr (US: = mathematics) matemáticas fpl

mathematical [mæθə'mætɪkl] adj matemático

mathematician [mæθəmə'tɪʃən] n matemático(-a) m(f)

mathematics [mæθə'mætɪks] n matemáticas fpl

maths [mæθs] n abbr (Brit: = mathematics) matemáticas fpl

matinée ['mætɪneɪ] n sesión f de tarde, vermú(t) m (LAm)

mating call n llamada del macho

matrices ['meɪtrɪsiːz] pl of **matrix**

matriculation [mətrɪkju'leɪʃən] n matriculación f, matrícula

matrimonial [mætrɪ'məunɪəl] adj matrimonial

matrimony ['mætrɪmənɪ] n matrimonio

matrix (pl **matrices**) ['meɪtrɪks, 'meɪtrɪsiːz] n matriz f

matron ['meɪtrən] n (in hospital) enfermera jefe; (in school) ama de llaves

matt [mæt] adj mate

matted ['mætɪd] adj enmarañado

matter ['mætə'] n cuestión f, asunto; (Physics) sustancia, materia; (content) contenido; (Med: pus) pus m ▷ vi importar; **it doesn't ~** no importa; **what's the ~?** ¿qué pasa?; **no ~ what** pase lo que pase; **as a ~ of course** por rutina; **as a ~ of fact** en realidad; **printed ~** impresos mpl; **reading ~** material m de lectura, lecturas fpl

matter-of-fact ['mætərəv'fækt] adj (style) prosaico; (person) práctico; (voice) neutro

mattress ['mætrɪs] n colchón m

mature [mə'tjuə'] adj maduro ▷ vi madurar

mature student n estudiante de más de 21 años

maturity [mə'tjuərɪtɪ] n madurez f

maul [mɔːl] vt magullar

mausoleum [mɔːsə'lɪəm] n mausoleo

mauve [məuv] adj de color malva

maverick ['mævrɪk] n (fig) inconformista m/f, persona independiente

max abbr = **maximum**

maximize ['mæksɪmaɪz] vt (profits etc) llevar al máximo; (chances) maximizar

maximum ['mæksɪməm] adj máximo ▷ n (pl **maxima** ['mæksɪmə]) máximo

May [meɪ] n mayo; see also **July**

may [meɪ] vi (conditional **might**) (indicating possibility): **he ~ come** puede que venga; (be allowed to): **~ I smoke?** ¿puedo fumar?; (wishes): **~ God bless you!** ¡que Dios le bendiga!; **~ I sit here?** ¿me puedo sentar aquí?

maybe ['meɪbiː] adv quizá(s); **~ not** quizá(s) no

May Day n el primero de Mayo

mayday ['meɪdeɪ] n señal f de socorro

mayhem ['meɪhem] n caos m total

mayonnaise [meɪə'neɪz] n mayonesa

mayor [meə'] n alcalde m

mayoress ['meəres] n alcaldesa

maze [meɪz] n laberinto

MBE n abbr (Brit: = Member of the Order of the British Empire) título ceremonial

MC n abbr (= master of ceremonies) e.p.; (US: = Member of Congress) diputado del Congreso de los Estados Unidos

MD n abbr (= Doctor of Medicine) título universitario; (Comm) = **managing director**; (= MiniDisc) MiniDisc® m, minidisc m

MD player n MiniDisc m, minidisc m

me [miː] pron (direct) me; (stressed, after pronoun) mí; **can you hear me?** ¿me oyes?; **he heard ME!** me oyó a mí; **it's me** soy yo; **give them to me** dámelos; **with/without me** conmigo/sin mí; **it's for me** es para mí

meadow ['medəu] n prado, pradera

meagre, meager (US) ['miːgə'] adj escaso, pobre

meal [miːl] n comida; (flour) harina; **to go out for a ~** salir a comer

meals on wheels nsg (Brit) servicio de alimentación a domicilio para necesitados y tercera edad

mealtime ['miːltaɪm] n hora de comer

mean [miːn] adj (with money) tacaño; (unkind) mezquino, malo; (average) medio; (US: vicious: animal) resabiado; (: person) malicioso ▷ vt (pt, pp **meant** [ment]) (signify) querer decir, significar; (intend): **to ~ to do sth** tener la intención de or pensar hacer algo ▷ n medio, término medio; **do you ~ it?** ¿lo dices en serio?; **what do you ~?** ¿qué quiere decir?; **to be meant for sb/sth** ser para algn/algo; see also **means**

meander [mɪ'ændə'] vi (river) serpentear; (person) vagar

meaning ['miːnɪŋ] n significado, sentido

meaningful ['miːnɪŋful] adj significativo

meaningless ['miːnɪŋlɪs] *adj* sin sentido
meanness ['miːnnɪs] *n* (*with money*) tacañería; (*unkindness*) maldad *f*, mezquindad *f*
means [miːnz] *npl* medio *sg*, manera *sg*; (*resource*) recursos *mpl*, medios *mpl*; **by ~ of** mediante, por medio de; **by all ~!** ¡naturalmente!, ¡claro que sí!
meant [mɛnt] *pt, pp of* **mean**
meantime ['miːntaɪm], **meanwhile** ['miːnwaɪl] *adv* (*also*: **in the ~**) mientras tanto
measles ['miːzlz] *n* sarampión *m*
measly ['miːzlɪ] *adj* (*inf*) miserable
measure ['mɛʒəʳ] *vt* medir; (*for clothes etc*) tomar las medidas a ▷ *vi* medir ▷ *n* medida; (*ruler*) cinta métrica, metro; **a litre ~** una medida de un litro; **some ~ of success** cierto éxito; **to take ~s to do sth** tomar medidas para hacer algo; **measure up** *vi*: **to ~ up (to)** estar a la altura (de)
measurement ['mɛʒəmənt] *n* (*measure*) medida; (*act*) medición *f*; **to take sb's ~s** tomar las medidas a algn
meat [miːt] *n* carne *f*; **cold ~s** fiambres *mpl*; **crab ~** carne *f* de cangrejo
meatball ['miːtbɔːl] *n* albóndiga
Mecca ['mɛkə] *n* (*city*) la Meca; (*fig*) meca
mechanic [mɪ'kænɪk] *n* mecánico(-a)
mechanical [mɪ'kænɪkl] *adj* mecánico
mechanics [mə'kænɪks] *n* mecánica ▷ *npl* mecanismo *sg*
mechanism ['mɛkənɪzəm] *n* mecanismo
medal ['mɛdl] *n* medalla
medallion [mɪ'dælɪən] *n* medallón *m*
medallist, medalist (US) ['mɛdlɪst] *n* (*Sport*) medallista *m/f*
meddle ['mɛdl] *vi*: **to ~ in** entrometerse en; **to ~ with sth** manosear algo
media ['miːdɪə] *npl* medios *mpl* de comunicación
media circus *n excesivo despliegue informativo*
mediaeval [mɛdɪ'iːvl] *adj* = **medieval**
median ['miːdɪən] *n* (US: *also*: **~ strip**) mediana
mediate ['miːdɪeɪt] *vi* mediar
mediator ['miːdɪeɪtəʳ] *n* mediador(a) *m(f)*
Medicaid ['mɛdɪkeɪd] *n* (US) *programa de ayuda médica*
medical ['mɛdɪkl] *adj* médico ▷ *n* (*also*: **~ examination**) reconocimiento médico
medical certificate *n* certificado *m* médico
Medicare ['mɛdɪkɛəʳ] *n* (US) *seguro médico del Estado*
medicated ['mɛdɪkeɪtɪd] *adj* medicinal
medication [mɛdɪ'keɪʃən] *n* (*drugs etc*) medicación *f*
medicine ['mɛdsɪn] *n* medicina; (*drug*) medicamento
medieval, mediaeval [mɛdɪ'iːvl] *adj* medieval
mediocre [miːdɪ'əukəʳ] *adj* mediocre
mediocrity [miːdɪ'ɔkrɪtɪ] *n* mediocridad *f*

meditate ['mɛdɪteɪt] *vi* meditar
meditation [mɛdɪ'teɪʃən] *n* meditación *f*
Mediterranean [mɛdɪtə'reɪnɪən] *adj* mediterráneo; **the ~ (Sea)** el (Mar *m*) Mediterráneo
medium ['miːdɪəm] *adj* mediano; (*level, height*) medio ▷ *n* (*pl* **media**: *means*) medio; (*pl* **mediums**: *person*) médium *m/f*; **happy ~** punto justo
medium-dry ['miːdɪəm'draɪ] *adj* semiseco
medium-sized ['miːdɪəm'saɪzd] *adj* de tamaño mediano; (*clothes*) de (la) talla mediana
medium wave *n* onda media
medley ['mɛdlɪ] *n* mezcla; (*Mus*) popurrí *m*
meek [miːk] *adj* manso, sumiso
meet [miːt] (*pt, pp* **met**) *vt* encontrar; (*accidentally*) encontrarse con; (*by arrangement*) reunirse con; (*for the first time*) conocer; (*go and fetch*) ir a buscar; (*opponent*) enfrentarse con; (*obligations*) cumplir; (*bill, expenses*) pagar, costear ▷ *vi* encontrarse; (*in session*) reunirse; (*join: objects*) unirse; (*get to know*) conocerse ▷ *n* (Brit Hunting) cacería; (US Sport) encuentro; **pleased to ~ you!** ¡encantado (de conocerle)!, ¡mucho gusto!; **meet up** *vi*: **to ~ up with sb** reunirse con algn; **meet with** *vt fus* reunirse con; (*difficulty*) tropezar con
meeting ['miːtɪŋ] *n* (*also Sport: rally*) encuentro; (*arranged*) cita, compromiso (LAm); (*formal session, business meeting*) reunión *f*; (Pol) mitin *m*; **to call a ~** convocar una reunión
meeting place *n* lugar *m* de reunión or encuentro
meg [mɛg] *n abbr* (*inf*: = megabyte) megabyte
megabyte ['mɛgəbaɪt] *n* (*Comput*) megabyte *m*, megaocteto
megaphone ['mɛgəfəun] *n* megáfono
megapixel ['mɛgəpɪksl] *n* megapíxel *m*
megawatt ['mɛgəwɔt] *n* megavatio
melancholy ['mɛlənkəlɪ] *n* melancolía ▷ *adj* melancólico
mellow ['mɛləu] *adj* (*wine*) añejo; (*sound, colour*) suave; (*fruit*) maduro ▷ *vi* (*person*) madurar
melody ['mɛlədɪ] *n* melodía
melon ['mɛlən] *n* melón *m*
melt [mɛlt] *vi* (*metal*) fundirse; (*snow*) derretirse; (*fig*) ablandarse ▷ *vt* (*also*: **~ down**) fundir; **~ed butter** mantequilla derretida; **melt away** *vi* desvanecerse
meltdown ['mɛltdaun] *n* (*in nuclear reactor*) fusión *f* (de un reactor nuclear)
melting pot ['mɛltɪŋ-] *n* (*fig*) crisol *m*; **to be in the ~** estar sobre el tapete
member ['mɛmbəʳ] *n* (*of political party*) miembro; (*of club*) socio(-a); **M~ of Parliament (MP)** (Brit) diputado(-a); **M~ of the European Parliament (MEP)** (Brit) eurodiputado(-a); **M~ of Congress** (US)

miembro del Congreso; **M~ of the House of Representatives (MHR)** (US) miembro *m/f* de la Cámara de Representantes; **M~ of the Scottish Parliament (MSP)** (Brit) diputado(-a) *m(f)* del Parlamento escocés

membership ['membəʃɪp] *n* (members) miembros *mpl*; socios *mpl*; (numbers) número de miembros or socios; **to seek ~ of** pedir el ingreso a

membership card *n* carnet *m* de socio

memento [mə'mentəu] *n* recuerdo

memo ['meməu] *n* apunte *m*, nota

memoirs ['memwɑ:z] *npl* memorias *fpl*

memorable ['memərəbl] *adj* memorable

memorandum (*pl* **memoranda**) [memə'rændəm, -də] *n* nota (de servicio); (Pol) memorándum *m*

memorial [mɪ'mɔ:rɪəl] *n* monumento conmemorativo ▷ *adj* conmemorativo

Memorial Day *n* (US) *día de conmemoración de los caídos en la guerra*

memorize ['meməraɪz] *vt* aprender de memoria

memory ['memərɪ] *n* memoria; (recollection) recuerdo; (Comput) memoria; **to have a good/bad ~** tener buena/mala memoria; **loss of ~** pérdida de memoria

memory card *n* tarjeta de memoria

memory stick *n* (Comput) barra de memoria

men [men] *pl of* **man**

menace ['menəs] *n* amenaza; (inf: nuisance) lata ▷ *vt* amenazar; **a public ~** un peligro público

menacing ['menɪsɪŋ] *adj* amenazador(-a)

mend [mend] *vt* reparar, arreglar; (darn) zurcir ▷ *vi* reponerse ▷ *n* (gen) remiendo; (darn) zurcido; **to be on the ~** ir mejorando; **to ~ one's ways** enmendarse

mending ['mendɪŋ] *n* arreglo, reparación *f*; (clothes) ropa por remendar

menial ['mi:nɪəl] *adj* (pej) bajo, servil

meningitis [menɪn'dʒaɪtɪs] *n* meningitis *f*

menopause ['menəupɔ:z] *n* menopausia

men's room *n* (US): **the ~** el servicio de caballeros

menstruate ['menstrueɪt] *vi* menstruar

menstruation [menstru'eɪʃən] *n* menstruación *f*

menswear ['menzweə'] *n* confección *f* de caballero

mental ['mentl] *adj* mental; **~ illness** enfermedad *f* mental

mental hospital *n* (hospital *m*) psiquiátrico

mentality [men'tælɪtɪ] *n* mentalidad *f*

mentally ['mentlɪ] *adv*: **to be ~ ill** tener una enfermedad mental

menthol ['menθɒl] *n* mentol *m*

mention ['menʃən] *n* mención *f* ▷ *vt* mencionar; (speak of) hablar de; **don't ~ it!** ¡de nada!; **I need hardly ~ that ...** huelga decir que ...; **not to ~,** **without ~ing** sin contar

menu ['menju:] *n* (set menu) menú *m*; (printed) carta; (Comput) menú *m*

MEP *n abbr* = **Member of the European Parliament**

mercenary ['mə:sɪnərɪ] *adj, n* mercenario(-a)

merchandise ['mə:tʃəndaɪz] *n* mercancías *fpl*

merchant ['mə:tʃənt] *n* comerciante *m/f*

merchant bank *n* (Brit) banco comercial

merchant navy, merchant marine (US) *n* marina mercante

merciful ['mə:sɪful] *adj* compasivo

merciless ['mə:sɪlɪs] *adj* despiadado

mercury ['mə:kjurɪ] *n* mercurio

mercy ['mə:sɪ] *n* compasión *f*; (Rel) misericordia; **at the ~ of** a la merced de

mere [mɪə'] *adj* simple, mero

merely ['mɪəlɪ] *adv* simplemente, sólo

merge [mə:dʒ] *vt* (join) unir; (mix) mezclar; (fuse) fundir; (Comput: files, text) intercalar ▷ *vi* unirse; (Comm) fusionarse

merger ['mə:dʒə'] *n* (Comm) fusión *f*

meringue [mə'ræŋ] *n* merengue *m*

merit ['merɪt] *n* mérito ▷ *vt* merecer

mermaid ['mə:meɪd] *n* sirena

merry ['merɪ] *adj* alegre; **M~ Christmas!** ¡Felices Pascuas!

merry-go-round ['merɪgəuraund] *n* tiovivo

mesh [meʃ] *n* malla; (Tech) engranaje *m* ▷ *vi* (gears) engranar; **wire ~** tela metálica

mesmerize ['mezməraɪz] *vt* hipnotizar

mess [mes] *n* confusión *f*; (of objects) revoltijo; (dirt) porquería; (tangle) lío; (Mil) comedor *m*; **to be (in) a ~** (room) estar revuelto; **to be/get o.s. in a ~** estar/meterse en un lío; **mess about, mess around** *vi* (inf) perder el tiempo; (pass the time) pasar el rato; **mess about** or **around with** *vt fus* (inf: play with) divertirse con; (: handle) manosear; **mess up** *vt* (disarrange) desordenar; (spoil) estropear; (dirty) ensuciar; **mess with** (inf) *vt fus* (challenge, confront) meterse con (fam); (interfere with) interferir con

message ['mesɪdʒ] *n* recado, mensaje *m*; **to get the ~** (fig, inf) enterarse

message board *n* (Internet) foro de debate

messenger ['mesɪndʒə'] *n* mensajero(-a)

Messiah [mɪ'saɪə] *n* Mesías *m*

Messrs, Messrs. *abbr* (on letters: = Messieurs) Sres

messy ['mesɪ] *adj* (dirty) sucio; (untidy) desordenado; (confused: situation etc) confuso

met [met] *pt, pp of* **meet** ▷ *adj abbr* = **meteorological**

metabolism [me'tæbəlɪzəm] *n* metabolismo

metal ['metl] *n* metal *m*

metallic [me'tælɪk] *adj* metálico

metaphor ['metəfə'] *n* metáfora

mete [mi:t]: **to ~ out** *vt fus* (punishment) imponer

meteor ['mi:tɪə'] *n* meteoro

meteorite ['mi:tɪəraɪt] *n* meteorito**

meteorological [mi:tɪərə'lɒdʒɪkl] *adj*
meteorológico
meteorology [mi:tɪə'rɒlədʒɪ] *n*
meteorología
meter ['mi:tər] *n* (*instrument*) contador *m*; (US:
unit) = **metre** ▷ *vt* (US Post) franquear;
parking ~ parquímetro
methane ['mi:θeɪn] *n* metano
method ['mɛθəd] *n* método; ~ **of payment**
método de pago
methodical [mɪ'θɒdɪkl] *adj* metódico
Methodist ['mɛθədɪst] *adj, n* metodista *m/f*
methodology [mɛθə'dɒlədʒɪ] *n*
metodología
meths [mɛθs] *n* (*Brit*) = **methylated spirit**
methylated spirit ['mɛθɪleɪtɪd-] *n* (*Brit*)
alcohol *m* metilado *or* desnaturalizado
meticulous [mɛ'tɪkjuləs] *adj* meticuloso
metre, meter (US) ['mi:tər] *n* metro
metric ['mɛtrɪk] *adj* métrico; **to go** ~ pasar al
sistema métrico
metropolitan [mɛtrə'pɒlɪtən] *adj*
metropolitano
Metropolitan Police *n* (*Brit*): **the** ~ la policía
londinense
mettle ['mɛtl] *n* valor *m*, ánimo
mew [mju:] *vi* (*cat*) maullar
mews [mju:z] (*Brit*) *n*: ~ **cottage** casa
acondicionada en antiguos establos o cocheras;
~ **flat** piso en antiguos establos o cocheras
Mexican ['mɛksɪkən] *adj, n* mejicano(-a) *m(f)*,
mexicano(-a) *m(f)* (*LAm*)
Mexico ['mɛksɪkəʊ] *n* Méjico, México (*LAm*)
Mexico City *n* Ciudad *f* de Méjico *or* (*LAm*)
México
mezzanine ['mɛtsəni:n] *n* entresuelo
mg *abbr* (= *milligram*) mg
Mgr *abbr* (= *Monseigneur, Monsignor*) Mons;
(*Comm*) = **manager**
MHz *abbr* (= *megahertz*) MHz
MI5 *n abbr* (*Brit*: = *Military Intelligence, section five*)
servicio de contraespionaje del gobierno británico
MI6 *n abbr* (*Brit*: = *Military Intelligence, section six*)
servicio de inteligencia del gobierno británico
MIA *abbr* (*Mil*: = *missing in action*) desaparecido
miaow [mi:'aʊ] *vi* maullar
mice [maɪs] *pl of* **mouse**
mickey ['mɪkɪ] *n*: **to take the** ~ **out of sb**
tomar el pelo a algn
micro... [maɪkrəʊ] *pref* micro...
microbe ['maɪkrəʊb] *n* microbio
microbiology [maɪkrəʊbaɪ'ɒlədʒɪ] *n*
microbiología
microchip ['maɪkrəʊtʃɪp] *n* microchip *m*,
microplaqueta
microcosm ['maɪkrəʊkɒzəm] *n* microcosmo
microfiche ['maɪkrəʊfi:ʃ] *n* microficha
microfilm ['maɪkrəʊfɪlm] *n* microfilm *m*
microlight ['maɪkrəʊlaɪt] *v* ultraligero
microphone ['maɪkrəfəʊn] *n* micrófono
microprocessor ['maɪkrəʊ'prəʊsɛsər] *n*
microprocesador *m*

microscope ['maɪkrəskəʊp] *n* microscopio;
under the ~ al microscopio
microwave ['maɪkrəʊweɪv] *n* (*also*: ~ **oven**)
horno microondas
mid [mɪd] *adj*: **in** ~ **May** a mediados de mayo;
in ~ **afternoon** a media tarde; **in** ~ **air** en
el aire; **he's in his** ~ **thirties** tiene unos
treinta y cinco años
midday [mɪd'deɪ] *n* mediodía *m*
middle ['mɪdl] *n* centro; (*half-way point*)
medio; (*waist*) cintura ▷ *adj* de en medio;
in the ~ **of the night** en plena noche; **I'm in
the** ~ **of reading it** lo estoy leyendo ahora
mismo
middle-aged [mɪdl'eɪdʒd] *adj* de mediana
edad
Middle Ages *npl*: **the** ~ la Edad *sg* Media
middle class *n*: **the** ~**(es)** la clase media
▷ *adj*: **middle-class** de clase media
Middle East *n* Oriente *m* Medio
middleman ['mɪdlmæn] *n* intermediario
middle name *n* segundo nombre *m*
middle-of-the-road ['mɪdləvðə'rəʊd] *adj*
moderado
middle school *n* (US) colegio para niños de doce a
catorce años; (*Brit*) colegio para niños de ocho o nueve
a doce o trece años
middleweight ['mɪdlweɪt] *n* (*Boxing*) peso
medio
middling ['mɪdlɪŋ] *adj* mediano
midge [mɪdʒ] *n* mosquito
midget ['mɪdʒɪt] *n* enano(-a)
midi system *n* cadena midi
Midlands ['mɪdləndz] *npl* región central de
Inglaterra
midnight ['mɪdnaɪt] *n* medianoche *f*; **at** ~ a
medianoche
midriff ['mɪdrɪf] *n* diafragma *m*
midst [mɪdst] *n*: **in the** ~ **of** entre, en medio
de; (*situation, action*) en mitad de
midsummer [mɪd'sʌmər] *n*: **a** ~ **day** un día
de pleno verano
midway [mɪd'weɪ] *adj, adv*: ~ (**between**)
a medio camino (entre); ~ **through** a la
mitad (de)
midweek [mɪd'wi:k] *adv* entre semana
midwife (*pl* **midwives**) ['mɪdwaɪf, -waɪvz] *n*
matrona, comadrona
midwinter [mɪd'wɪntər] *n*: **in** ~ en pleno
invierno
might [maɪt] *vb see* **may** ▷ *n* fuerza, poder *m*;
he ~ **be there** puede que esté allí, a lo mejor
está allí; **I** ~ **as well go** más vale que vaya;
you ~ **like to try** podría intentar
mightn't ['maɪtnt] = **might not**
mighty ['maɪtɪ] *adj* fuerte, poderoso
migraine ['mi:greɪn] *n* jaqueca
migrant ['maɪgrənt] *adj* migratorio; (*worker*)
emigrante ▷ *n* (*bird*) ave *f* migratoria; (*worker*)
emigrante *m/f*
migrate [maɪ'greɪt] *vi* emigrar
migration [maɪ'greɪʃən] *n* emigración *f*

mike [maɪk] *n abbr* (= *microphone*) micro
mild [maɪld] *adj* (*person*) apacible; (*climate*) templado; (*slight*) ligero; (*taste*) suave; (*illness*) leve
mildly ['maɪldlɪ] *adv* ligeramente; suavemente; **to put it ~** por no decir algo peor
mile [maɪl] *n* milla; **to do 20 ~s per gallon** hacer 20 millas por galón
mileage ['maɪlɪdʒ] *n* número de millas; (*Aut*) kilometraje *m*
mileometer [maɪ'lɒmɪtəʳ] *n* (*Brit*) = **milometer**
milestone ['maɪlstəʊn] *n* mojón *m*; (*fig*) hito
militant ['mɪlɪtnt] *adj, n* militante *m/f*
military ['mɪlɪtərɪ] *adj* militar
military service *n* servicio militar
militate ['mɪlɪteɪt] *vi*: **to ~ against** militar en contra de
militia [mɪ'lɪʃə] *n* milicia
milk [mɪlk] *n* leche *f* ▷ *vt* (*cow*) ordeñar; (*fig*) chupar
milk chocolate *n* chocolate *m* con leche
milkman ['mɪlkmən] *n* lechero, repartidor *m* de la leche
milk shake *n* batido, malteada (*LAm*)
milky ['mɪlkɪ] *adj* lechoso
Milky Way *n* Vía Láctea
mill [mɪl] *n* (*windmill etc*) molino; (*coffee mill*) molinillo; (*factory*) fábrica; (*spinning mill*) hilandería ▷ *vt* moler ▷ *vi* (*also*: **~ about**) arremolinarse
millennium (*pl* **millenniums** *or* **millennia**) [mɪ'lɛnɪəm, -'lɛnɪə] *n* milenio, milenario
miller ['mɪləʳ] *n* molinero
milli... ['mɪlɪ] *pref* mili...
milligram, milligramme ['mɪlɪɡræm] *n* miligramo
millilitre, milliliter (US) ['mɪlɪliːtəʳ] *n* mililitro
millimetre, millimeter (US) ['mɪlɪmiːtəʳ] *n* milímetro
millinery ['mɪlɪnərɪ] *n* sombrerería
million ['mɪljən] *n* millón *m*; **a ~ times** un millón de veces
millionaire [mɪljə'nɛəʳ] *n* millonario(-a)
millionth ['mɪljənθ] *adj* millonésimo
milometer [maɪ'lɒmɪtəʳ] *n* (*Brit*) cuentakilómetros *m inv*
mime [maɪm] *n* mímica; (*actor*) mimo(-a) ▷ *vt* remedar ▷ *vi* actuar de mimo
mimic ['mɪmɪk] *n* imitador(a) *m(f)* ▷ *adj* mímico ▷ *vt* remedar, imitar
min. *abbr* (= *minute(s)*) m.; = **minimum**
mince [mɪns] *vt* picar ▷ *vi* (*in walking*) andar con pasos menudos ▷ *n* (*Brit Culin*) carne *f* picada, picadillo
mincemeat ['mɪnsmiːt] *n* conserva de fruta picada; (*US*: *meat*) carne *f* picada
mince pie *n* pastelillo relleno de fruta picada
mincer ['mɪnsəʳ] *n* picadora de carne

mind [maɪnd] *n* (*gen*) mente *f*; (*contrasted with matter*) espíritu *m* ▷ *vt* (*attend to, look after*) ocuparse de, cuidar; (*be careful of*) tener cuidado con; (*object to*): **I don't ~ the noise** no me molesta el ruido; **it is on my ~** me preocupa; **to my ~** a mi parecer *or* juicio; **to change one's ~** cambiar de idea *or* de parecer; **to bring** *or* **call sth to ~** recordar algo; **to have sth/sb in ~** tener algo/a algn en mente; **to be out of one's ~** haber perdido el juicio; **to bear sth in ~** tomar *or* tener algo en cuenta; **to make up one's ~** decidirse; **it went right out of my ~** se me fue por completo (de la cabeza); **to be in two ~s about sth** estar indeciso *or* dudar ante algo; **I don't ~** me es igual; **~ you, ...** te advierto que ...; **never ~!** ¡es igual!, ¡no importa!; (*don't worry*) ¡no te preocupes!; **"~ the step"** "cuidado con el escalón"
minder ['maɪndəʳ] *n* guardaespaldas *m inv*
mindful ['maɪndful] *adj*: **~ of** consciente de
mindless ['maɪndlɪs] *adj* (*violence, crime*) sin sentido; (*work*) de autómata
mine [maɪn] *pron* (el) mío/(la) mía *etc*; **a friend of ~** un(a) amigo(-a) mío/mía ▷ *adj*: **this book is ~** este libro es mío ▷ *n* mina ▷ *vt* (*coal*) extraer; (*ship, beach*) minar
minefield ['maɪnfiːld] *n* campo de minas
miner ['maɪnəʳ] *n* minero(-a)
mineral ['mɪnərəl] *adj* mineral ▷ *n* mineral *m*; **minerals** *npl* (*Brit*: *soft drinks*) refrescos *mpl* con gas
mineral water *n* agua mineral
mingle ['mɪŋɡl] *vi*: **to ~ with** mezclarse con
miniature ['mɪnətʃəʳ] *adj* (en) miniatura ▷ *n* miniatura
minibar ['mɪnɪbɑːʳ] *n* minibar *m*
minibus ['mɪnɪbʌs] *n* microbús *m*
minicab ['mɪnɪkæb] *n* taxi *m* (*que sólo puede pedirse por teléfono*)
MiniDisc® ['mɪnɪdɪsk] *n* MiniDisc® *m*
minim ['mɪnɪm] *n* (*Brit Mus*) blanca
minimal ['mɪnɪml] *adj* mínimo
minimalist ['mɪnɪməlɪst] *adj, n* minimalista *m/f*
minimize ['mɪnɪmaɪz] *vt* minimizar; (*play down*) empequeñecer
minimum ['mɪnɪməm] *n* (*pl* **minima** ['mɪnɪmə]) mínimo ▷ *adj* mínimo; **to reduce to a ~** reducir algo al mínimo; **~ wage** salario mínimo
mining ['maɪnɪŋ] *n* minería ▷ *adj* minero
mini-series ['mɪnɪsɪərɪːz] *n* serie *f* de pocos capítulos, miniserie *f*
miniskirt ['mɪnɪskəːt] *n* minifalda
minister ['mɪnɪstəʳ] *n* (*Brit Pol*) ministro(-a); (*junior*) secretario(-a) de Estado; (*Rel*) pastor *m* ▷ *vi*: **to ~ to** atender a
ministerial [mɪnɪs'tɪərɪəl] *adj* (*Brit Pol*) ministerial
ministry ['mɪnɪstrɪ] *n* (*Brit Pol*) ministerio; (*Rel*) sacerdocio; **M~ of Defence** Ministerio de Defensa

m

mink [mɪŋk] n visón m
minor ['maɪnəʳ] adj (repairs, injuries) leve; (poet, planet) menor; (unimportant) secundario; (Mus) menor ▷ n (Law) menor m/f de edad
Minorca [mɪ'nɔːkə] n Menorca
minority [maɪ'nɔrɪtɪ] n minoría; **to be in a ~** estar en or ser minoría
mint [mɪnt] n (plant) menta, hierbabuena; (sweet) caramelo de menta ▷ vt (coins) acuñar; **the (Royal) M~**, (US) **the (US) M~** la Casa de la Moneda; **in ~ condition** en perfecto estado
minus ['maɪnəs] n (also: **~ sign**) signo menos ▷ prep menos; **12 ~ 6 equals 6** 12 menos 6 son 6; **~ 24°C** menos 24 grados
minuscule ['mɪnəskjuːl] adj minúsculo
minute¹ ['mɪnɪt] n minuto; (fig) momento; **minutes** npl (of meeting) actas fpl; **it is 5 ~s past 3** son las 3 y 5 (minutos); **at the last ~** a última hora; **wait a ~!** ¡espera un momento!; **up to the ~** de última hora
minute² [maɪ'njuːt] adj diminuto; (search) minucioso; **in ~ detail** con todo detalle
minutiae [mɪ'njuːʃiː] npl minucias fpl
miracle ['mɪrəkl] n milagro
miraculous [mɪ'rækjuləs] adj milagroso
mirage ['mɪrɑːʒ] n espejismo
mirror ['mɪrəʳ] n espejo; (in car) retrovisor m ▷ vt reflejar
mirth [məːθ] n alegría; (laughter) risa, risas fpl
misadventure [mɪsəd'ventʃəʳ] n desventura; **death by ~** muerte f accidental
misapprehension ['mɪsæprɪ'henʃən] n equivocación f
misappropriate [mɪsə'prəuprɪeɪt] vt (funds) malversar
misbehave [mɪsbɪ'heɪv] vi portarse mal
misbehaviour, misbehavior (US) [mɪsbɪ'heɪvjəʳ] n mala conducta
misc. abbr = **miscellaneous**
miscalculate [mɪs'kælkjuleɪt] vt calcular mal
miscalculation [mɪskælkju'leɪʃən] n error m (de cálculo)
miscarriage ['mɪskærɪdʒ] n (Med) aborto (no provocado); **~ of justice** error m judicial
miscarry [mɪs'kærɪ] vi (Med) abortar (de forma natural); (fail: plans) fracasar, malograrse
miscellaneous [mɪsɪ'leɪnɪəs] adj varios(-as), diversos(-as); **~ expenses** gastos diversos
mischief ['mɪstʃɪf] n (naughtiness) travesura; (harm) mal m, daño; (maliciousness) malicia
mischievous ['mɪstʃɪvəs] adj travieso; dañino; (playful) malicioso
misconception ['mɪskən'sepʃən] n idea equivocada; equivocación f
misconduct [mɪs'kɔndʌkt] n mala conducta; **professional ~** falta profesional
misconstrue [mɪskən'struː] vt interpretar mal

misdemeanour, misdemeanor (US) [mɪsdɪ'miːnəʳ] n delito, ofensa
misdirect [mɪsdɪ'rekt] vt (person) informar mal; (letter) poner señas incorrectas en
miser ['maɪzəʳ] n avaro(-a)
miserable ['mɪzərəbl] adj (unhappy) triste, desgraciado; (wretched) miserable; **to feel ~** sentirse triste
miserly ['maɪzəlɪ] adj avariento, tacaño
misery ['mɪzərɪ] n (unhappiness) tristeza; (wretchedness) miseria, desdicha
misfire [mɪs'faɪəʳ] vi fallar
misfit ['mɪsfɪt] n (person) inadaptado(-a)
misfortune [mɪs'fɔːtʃən] n desgracia
misgiving [mɪs'ɡɪvɪŋ], **misgivings** [mɪs'ɡɪvɪŋz] npl (mistrust) recelo; (apprehension) presentimiento; **to have ~s about sth** tener dudas sobre algo
misguided [mɪs'ɡaɪdɪd] adj equivocado
mishandle [mɪs'hændl] vt (treat roughly) maltratar; (mismanage) manejar mal
mishap ['mɪshæp] n desgracia, contratiempo
misinform [mɪsɪn'fɔːm] vt informar mal
misinterpret [mɪsɪn'təːprɪt] vt interpretar mal
misjudge [mɪs'dʒʌdʒ] vt juzgar mal
mislay [mɪs'leɪ] vt (irreg: like **lay**) extraviar, perder
mislead [mɪs'liːd] vt (irreg: like **lead**) llevar a conclusiones erróneas; (deliberately) engañar
misleading [mɪs'liːdɪŋ] adj engañoso
mismanage [mɪs'mænɪdʒ] vt administrar mal
mismanagement [mɪs'mænɪdʒmənt] n mala administración f
misnomer [mɪs'nəuməʳ] n término inapropiado or equivocado
misogynist [mɪ'sɔdʒɪnɪst] n misógino
misplace [mɪs'pleɪs] vt (lose) extraviar; **~d** (trust etc) inmerecido
misprint ['mɪsprɪnt] n errata, error m de imprenta
mispronounce [mɪsprə'nauns] vt pronunciar mal
misquote ['mɪs'kwəut] vt citar incorrectamente
misread [mɪs'riːd] vt (irreg: like **read**) leer mal
misrepresent [mɪsreprɪ'zent] vt falsificar
Miss [mɪs] n Señorita; **Dear ~ Smith** Estimada Señorita Smith
miss [mɪs] vt (train etc) perder; (target) errar; (appointment, class) faltar a; (escape, avoid) evitar; (notice loss of: money etc) notar la falta de, echar en falta; (regret the absence of): **I ~ him** le echo de menos ▷ vi fallar ▷ n (shot) tiro fallido; **the bus just ~ed the wall** faltó poco para que el autobús se estrella contra el muro; **you're ~ing the point** no has entendido la idea; **miss out** vt (Brit) omitir; **miss out on** vt fus (fun, party, opportunity) perderse
misshapen [mɪs'ʃeɪpən] adj deforme

missile ['mɪsaɪl] n (Aviat) misil m; (object thrown) proyectil m

missing ['mɪsɪŋ] adj (pupil) ausente, que falta; (thing) perdido; **to be ~** faltar; **~ person** desaparecido(-a); **~ in action** desaparecido en combate

mission ['mɪʃən] n misión f; **on a ~ for sb** en una misión para algn

missionary ['mɪʃənrɪ] n misionero(-a)

misspell [mɪs'spel] vt (irreg: like **spell**) escribir mal

misspent ['mɪs'spent] adj: **his ~ youth** su juventud disipada

mist [mɪst] n (light) neblina; (heavy) niebla; (at sea) bruma ▷ vi (also: **~ over, ~ up**: weather) nublarse; (Brit: windows) empañarse

mistake [mɪs'teɪk] n error m ▷ vt (irreg: like **take**) entender mal; **by ~** por equivocación; **to make a ~** (about sb/sth) equivocarse; (in writing, calculating etc) cometer un error; **to ~ A for B** confundir A con B

mistaken [mɪs'teɪkən] pp of **mistake** ▷ adj (idea etc) equivocado; **to be ~** equivocarse, engañarse; **~ identity** identificación f errónea

mister ['mɪstər] n (inf) señor m; see **Mr**

mistletoe ['mɪsltəu] n muérdago

mistook [mɪs'tuk] pt of **mistake**

mistreat [mɪs'triːt] vt maltratar, tratar mal

mistress ['mɪstrɪs] n (lover) amante f; (of house) señora (de la casa); (Brit: in primary school) maestra; (in secondary school) profesora; see also **Mrs**

mistrust [mɪs'trʌst] vt desconfiar de ▷ n: **~ (of)** desconfianza (de)

misty ['mɪstɪ] adj nebuloso, brumoso; (day) de niebla; (glasses) empañada

misunderstand [mɪsʌndə'stænd] vt, vi (irreg: like **understand**) entender mal

misunderstanding [mɪsʌndə'stændɪŋ] n malentendido

misunderstood [mɪsʌndə'stud] pt, pp of **misunderstand** ▷ adj (person) incomprendido

misuse n [mɪs'juːs] mal uso; (of power) abuso; (of funds) malversación f ▷ vt [mɪs'juːz] abusar de; (funds) malversar

mitigate ['mɪtɪgeɪt] vt mitigar; **mitigating circumstances** circunstancias fpl atenuantes

mitigation [mɪtɪ'geɪʃən] n mitigación f, alivio

mix [mɪks] vt (gen) mezclar; (combine) unir ▷ vi mezclarse; (people) llevarse bien ▷ n mezcla; **to ~ sth with sth** mezclar algo con algo; **to ~ business with pleasure** combinar los negocios con el placer; **cake ~** preparado para pastel; **mix in** vt (eggs etc) añadir; **mix up** vt mezclar; (confuse) confundir; **to be ~ed up in sth** estar metido en algo

mixed [mɪkst] adj (assorted) variado, surtido; (school, marriage etc) mixto; (feelings etc) encontrado

mixed grill n (Brit) parrillada mixta

mixed salad n ensalada mixta

mixed-up [mɪkst'ʌp] adj (confused) confuso, revuelto

mixer ['mɪksər] n (for food) batidora; (person): **he's a good ~** tiene don de gentes

mixer tap n (grifo) monomando

mixture ['mɪkstʃər] n mezcla

mix-up ['mɪksʌp] n confusión f

ml abbr (= millilitre(s)) ml

mm abbr (= millimetre) mm

MMS n abbr (= multimedia messaging service) MMS m

moan [məun] n gemido ▷ vi gemir; (inf: complain): **to ~ (about)** quejarse (de)

moat [məut] n foso

mob [mɔb] n multitud f; (pej): **the ~** el populacho ▷ vt acosar

mobile ['məubaɪl] adj móvil ▷ n móvil m

mobile home n caravana

mobile phone n teléfono móvil

mobility [məu'bɪlɪtɪ] n movilidad f; **~ of labour** or (US) **labor** movilidad f de la mano de obra

mobilize ['məubɪlaɪz] vt movilizar

mock [mɔk] vt (make ridiculous) ridiculizar; (laugh at) burlarse de ▷ adj fingido; **~ exams** (Brit: Scol) exámenes mpl de prueba

mockery ['mɔkərɪ] n burla; **to make a ~ of** desprestigiar

mock-up ['mɔkʌp] n maqueta

mod cons ['mɔd'kɔnz] npl abbr (= modern conveniences) see **convenience**

mode [məud] n modo; (of transport) medio; (Comput) modo, modalidad f

model ['mɔdl] n (gen) modelo; (Arch) maqueta; (person: for fashion, art) modelo m/f ▷ adj modelo inv ▷ vt modelar; **to ~ o.s. on** tomar como modelo a ▷ vi ser modelo; **~ railway** ferrocarril m de juguete; **to ~ clothes** pasar modelos, ser modelo; **to ~ on** crear a imitación de

modem ['məudəm] n módem m

moderate [adj, n 'mɔdərət, vb 'mɔdəreɪt] adj, n moderado(-a) m(f) ▷ vi moderarse, calmarse ▷ vt moderar

moderation [mɔdə'reɪʃən] n moderación f; **in ~** con moderación

moderator ['mɔdəreɪtər] n (mediator) moderador(a) m(f)

modern ['mɔdən] adj moderno; **~ languages** lenguas fpl modernas

modernize ['mɔdənaɪz] vt modernizar

modest ['mɔdɪst] adj modesto; (small) módico

modesty ['mɔdɪstɪ] n modestia

modicum ['mɔdɪkəm] n: **a ~ of** un mínimo de

modification [mɔdɪfɪ'keɪʃən] n modificación f; **to make ~s** hacer cambios or modificaciones

modify ['mɔdɪfaɪ] vt modificar

m

module ['mɔdju:l] n módulo
mogul ['məugəl] n (fig) magnate m
mohair ['məuheə^r] n mohair m
Mohammed [mə'hæmɛd] n Mahoma m
moist [mɔɪst] adj húmedo
moisten ['mɔɪsn] vt humedecer
moisture ['mɔɪstʃə^r] n humedad f
moisturize ['mɔɪstʃəraɪz] vt (skin) hidratar
moisturizer ['mɔɪstʃəraɪzə^r] n crema
  hidratante
molar ['məulə^r] n muela
molasses [məu'læsɪz] n melaza
mold [məuld] n, vt (US) = **mould**
Moldavia [mɔl'deɪvɪə], **Moldova** [mɔl'dəuvə]
  n Moldavia, Moldova
mole [məul] n (animal) topo; (spot) lunar m
molecule ['mɔlɪkju:l] n molécula
molest [məu'lɛst] vt importunar; (sexually)
  abusar sexualmente de
mollycoddle ['mɔlɪkɔdl] vt mimar
Molotov cocktail ['mɔlətɔf-] n cóctel m
  Molotov
molt [məult] vi (US) = **moult**
molten ['məultən] adj fundido; (lava)
  líquido
mom [mɔm] n (US) = **mum**
moment ['məumənt] n momento; **at** or **for
  the ~** de momento, por el momento, por
  ahora; **in a ~** dentro de un momento
momentarily ['məuməntrɪlɪ] adv
  momentáneamente; (US: very soon) de un
  momento a otro
momentary ['məuməntərɪ] adj
  momentáneo
momentous [məu'mɛntəs] adj
  trascendental, importante
momentum [məu'mɛntəm] n momento;
  (fig) ímpetu m; **to gather ~** cobrar velocidad;
  (fig) cobrar fuerza
mommy ['mɔmɪ] n (US) = **mummy**
Mon abbr (= Monday) lun
Monaco ['mɔnəkəu] n Mónaco
monarch ['mɔnək] n monarca m/f
monarchy ['mɔnəkɪ] n monarquía
monastery ['mɔnəstərɪ] n monasterio
Monday ['mʌndɪ] n lunes m inv; see also
  Tuesday
monetary ['mʌnɪtərɪ] adj monetario
money ['mʌnɪ] n dinero, plata (LAm); **to
  make ~** ganar dinero; **I've got no ~ left** no
  me queda dinero
money belt n riñonera
money order n giro
money-spinner ['mʌnɪspɪnə^r] n (inf: person,
  idea, business) filón m
mongrel ['mʌŋgrəl] n (dog) perro cruzado
monitor ['mɔnɪtə^r] n (Scol) monitor m;
  (also: **television ~**) receptor m de control;
  (of computer) monitor m ▷ vt controlar;
  (foreign station) escuchar
monk [mʌŋk] n monje m
monkey ['mʌŋkɪ] n mono

monkey nut n (Brit) cacahuete m, maní m
  (LAm)
monkey wrench n llave f inglesa
monogamous [mə'nɔgəməs] adj
  monógamo
monologue ['mɔnəlɔg] n monólogo
monopolize [mə'nɔpəlaɪz] vt monopolizar
monopoly [mə'nɔpəlɪ] n monopolio;
  Monopolies and Mergers Commission
  (Brit) comisión reguladora de monopolios y fusiones
monosyllable ['mɔnəsɪləbl] n monosílabo
monotone ['mɔnətəun] n voz f (or tono)
  monocorde
monotonous [mə'nɔtənəs] adj monótono
monotony [mə'nɔtənɪ] n monotonía
monoxide [mə'nɔksaɪd] n: **carbon ~**
  monóxido de carbono
monseigneur [mɔnseɪn'jə:^r], **monsignor**
  [mɔn'si:njə^r] n monseñor m
monsoon [mɔn'su:n] n monzón m
monster ['mɔnstə^r] n monstruo
monstrosity [mɔns'trɔsɪtɪ] n
  monstruosidad f
monstrous ['mɔnstrəs] adj (huge) enorme;
  (atrocious) monstruoso
month [mʌnθ] n mes m; **300 dollars a ~**
  300 dólares al mes; **every ~** cada mes
monthly ['mʌnθlɪ] adj mensual ▷ adv
  mensualmente ▷ n (magazine) revista,
  mensual; **twice ~** dos veces al mes;
  ~ instalment mensualidad f
monument ['mɔnjumənt] n monumento
moo [mu:] vi mugir
mood [mu:d] n humor m; **to be in a good/
  bad ~** estar de buen/mal humor
moody ['mu:dɪ] adj (changeable) de humor
  variable; (sullen) malhumorado
moon [mu:n] n luna
moonlight ['mu:nlaɪt] n luz f de la luna ▷ vi
  hacer pluriempleo
moonlighting ['mu:nlaɪtɪŋ] n
  pluriempleo
moonlit ['mu:nlɪt] adj: **a ~ night** una noche
  de luna
Moor [muə^r] n moro(-a)
moor [muə^r] n páramo ▷ vt (ship) amarrar
  ▷ vi echar las amarras
moorings ['muərɪŋz] npl (chains) amarras fpl;
  (place) amarradero sg
Moorish ['muərɪʃ] adj moro; (architecture)
  árabe
moorland ['muələnd] n páramo, brezal m
moose [mu:s] n pl inv alce m
mop [mɔp] n fregona; (of hair) melena ▷ vt
  fregar; **mop up** vt limpiar
mope [məup] vi estar deprimido; **mope
  about, mope around** vi andar abatido
moped ['məupɛd] n ciclomotor m
moral ['mɔrl] adj moral ▷ n moraleja;
  morals npl moralidad f, moral f
morale [mɔ'rɑ:l] n moral f
morality [mə'rælɪtɪ] n moralidad f

moralize ['mɔrəlaɪz] *vi*: **to ~ (about)** moralizar (sobre)

morally ['mɔrəlɪ] *adv* moralmente

moral victory *n* victoria moral

morass [mə'ræs] *n* pantano

morbid ['mɔ:bɪd] *adj* (*interest*) morboso; (*Med*) mórbido

⭕ KEYWORD

more [mɔ:ʳ] *adj* 1 (*greater in number etc*) más; **more people/work than before** más gente/trabajo que antes
2 (*additional*) más; **do you want (some) more tea?** ¿quieres más té?; **is there any more wine?** ¿queda vino?; **it'll take a few more weeks** tardará unas semanas más; **it's 2 kms more to the house** faltan 2 kms para la casa; **more time/letters than we expected** más tiempo del que/más cartas de las que esperábamos; **I have no more money, I don't have any more money** (ya) no tengo más dinero
▷ *pron* (*greater amount, additional amount*) más; **more than 10** más de 10; **it cost more than the other one/than we expected** costó más que el otro/más de lo que esperábamos; **is there any more?** ¿hay más?; **I want more** quiero más; **and what's more ...** y además ...; **many/much more** muchos(-as)/mucho(-a) más
▷ *adv* más; **more dangerous/easily (than)** más peligroso/fácilmente (que); **more and more expensive** cada vez más caro; **more or less** más o menos; **more than ever** más que nunca; **she doesn't live here any more** ya no vive aquí

moreover [mɔ:'rəuvəʳ] *adv* además, por otra parte

morgue [mɔ:g] *n* depósito de cadáveres

Mormon ['mɔ:mən] *n* mormón(-ona) *m(f)*

morning ['mɔ:nɪŋ] *n* (*gen*) mañana; (*early morning*) madrugada; **in the ~** por la mañana; **7 o'clock in the ~** las 7 de la mañana; **this ~** esta mañana

morning-after pill ['mɔ:nɪŋ'ɑ:ftə-] *n* píldora del día después

morning sickness *n* (*Med*) náuseas *fpl* del embarazo

Moroccan [mə'rɔkən] *adj, n* marroquí *m/f*

Morocco [mə'rɔkəu] *n* Marruecos *m*

moron ['mɔ:rɔn] *n* imbécil *m/f*

morphine ['mɔ:fi:n] *n* morfina

Morse [mɔ:s] *n* (*also*: **~ code**) (código) morse *m*

morsel ['mɔ:sl] *n* (*of food*) bocado

mortal ['mɔ:tl] *adj, n* mortal *m*

mortality [mɔ:'tælɪtɪ] *n* mortalidad *f*

mortar ['mɔ:təʳ] *n* argamasa; (*implement*) mortero

mortgage ['mɔ:gɪdʒ] *n* hipoteca ▷ *vt* hipotecar; **to take out a ~** sacar una hipoteca

mortgage company *n* (*US*) ≈ banco hipotecario

mortician [mɔ:'tɪʃən] *n* (*US*) director(a) *m(f)* de pompas fúnebres

mortified ['mɔ:tɪfaɪd] *adj*: **I was ~** me dio muchísima vergüenza

mortuary ['mɔ:tjuərɪ] *n* depósito de cadáveres

mosaic [məu'zeɪɪk] *n* mosaico

Moscow ['mɔskəu] *n* Moscú *m*

Moslem ['mɔzləm] *adj, n* = **Muslim**

mosque [mɔsk] *n* mezquita

mosquito (*pl* **mosquitoes**) [mɔs'ki:təu] *n* mosquito, zancudo (*LAm*)

moss [mɔs] *n* musgo

most [məust] *adj* la mayor parte de, la mayoría de ▷ *pron* la mayor parte, la mayoría ▷ *adv* el más; (*very*) muy; **the ~** (*also*: **+** *adjective*) el más; **~ of them** la mayor parte de ellos; **I saw the ~** yo fui el que más vi; **at the (very) ~** a lo sumo, todo lo más; **to make the ~ of** aprovechar (al máximo); **a ~ interesting book** un libro interesantísimo

mostly ['məustlɪ] *adv* en su mayor parte, principalmente

MOT *n abbr* (*Brit*: = *Ministry of Transport*): **the ~ (test)** ≈ la ITV

motel [məu'tel] *n* motel *m*

moth [mɔθ] *n* mariposa nocturna; (*clothes moth*) polilla

mothball ['mɔθbɔ:l] *n* bola de naftalina

mother ['mʌðəʳ] *n* madre *f* ▷ *adj* materno ▷ *vt* (*care for*) cuidar (como una madre)

motherhood ['mʌðəhud] *n* maternidad *f*

mother-in-law ['mʌðərɪnlɔ:] *n* suegra

motherly ['mʌðəlɪ] *adj* maternal

mother-of-pearl ['mʌðərəv'pə:l] *n* nácar *m*

Mother's Day *n* Día *m* de la Madre

mother tongue *n* lengua materna

motif [məu'ti:f] *n* motivo; (*theme*) tema *m*

motion ['məuʃən] *n* movimiento; (*gesture*) ademán *m*, señal *f*; (*at meeting*) moción *f*; (*Brit*: *also*: **bowel ~**) evacuación *f* intestinal ▷ *vt, vi*: **to ~ (to) sb to do sth** hacer señas a algn para que haga algo; **to be in ~** (*vehicle*) estar en movimiento; **to set in ~** poner en marcha; **to go through the ~s of doing sth** (*fig*) hacer algo mecánicamente *or* sin convicción

motionless ['məuʃənlɪs] *adj* inmóvil

motion picture *n* película

motivate ['məutɪveɪt] *vt* motivar

motivated ['məutɪveɪtɪd] *adj* motivado

motivation [məutɪ'veɪʃən] *n* motivación *f*

motive ['məutɪv] *n* motivo; **from the best ~s** con las mejores intenciones

motley ['mɔtlɪ] *adj* variopinto

motor ['məutəʳ] *n* motor *m*; (*Brit*: *inf*: *vehicle*) coche *m*, carro (*LAm*), automóvil *m*, auto *m* (*LAm*) ▷ *adj* motor/motora, motriz

motorbike ['məutəbaɪk] *n* moto *f*

motorboat ['məutəbəut] *n* lancha motora

m

motorcar ['məʊtəkɑːʳ] n (Brit) coche m, carro (LAm), automóvil m, auto m (LAm)
motorcycle ['məʊtəsaɪkl] n motocicleta
motorcycle racing n motociclismo
motorcyclist ['məʊtəsaɪklɪst] n motociclista m/f
motoring ['məʊtərɪŋ] n (Brit) automovilismo ▷ adj (accident, offence) de tráfico or tránsito
motorist ['məʊtərɪst] n conductor(a) m(f), automovilista m/f
motor racing n (Brit) carreras fpl de coches, automovilismo
motorway ['məʊtəweɪ] n (Brit) autopista
mottled ['mɔtld] adj moteado
motto (pl **mottoes**) ['mɔtəʊ] n lema m; (watchword) consigna
mould, mold (US) [məʊld] n molde m; (mildew) moho ▷ vt moldear; (fig) formar
mouldy, moldy (US) ['məʊldɪ] adj enmohecido
moult, molt (US) [məʊlt] vi mudar la piel; (bird) mudar las plumas
mound [maʊnd] n montón m, montículo
mount [maʊnt] n monte m; (horse) montura; (for jewel etc) engarce m; (for picture) marco ▷ vt montar en, subir a; (stairs) subir; (exhibition) montar; (attack) lanzar; (stamp) pegar, fijar; (picture) enmarcar ▷ vi (increase) aumentar; (also: ~ up: on horse) montar
mountain ['maʊntɪn] n montaña ▷ cpd de montaña; **to make a ~ out of a molehill** hacer una montaña de un grano de arena
mountain bike n bicicleta de montaña
mountaineer [maʊntɪ'nɪəʳ] n montañero(-a), alpinista m/f, andinista m/f (LAm)
mountaineering [maʊntɪ'nɪərɪŋ] n montañismo, alpinismo, andinismo (LAm)
mountainous ['maʊntɪnəs] adj montañoso
mountain range n sierra
mountain rescue team n equipo de rescate de montaña
mountainside ['maʊntɪnsaɪd] n ladera de la montaña
mourn [mɔːn] vt llorar, lamentar ▷ vi: **to ~ for** llorar la muerte de, lamentarse por
mourner ['mɔːnəʳ] n doliente m/f
mournful ['mɔːnful] adj triste, lúgubre
mourning ['mɔːnɪŋ] n luto ▷ cpd (dress) de luto; **in ~** de luto
mouse (pl **mice**) [maʊs, maɪs] n (also Comput) ratón m
mouse mat, mouse pad n (Comput) alfombrilla, almohadilla
mousetrap ['maʊstræp] n ratonera
mousse [muːs] n (Culin) mousse f; (for hair) espuma (moldeadora)
moustache [məs'tɑːʃ], **mustache** (US) ['mʌstæʃ] n bigote m
mousy ['maʊsɪ] adj (person) tímido; (hair) pardusco
mouth (pl **mouths**) [maʊθ, -ðz] n boca; (of river) desembocadura
mouthful ['maʊθful] n bocado
mouth organ n armónica
mouthpiece ['maʊθpiːs] n (of musical instrument) boquilla; (Tel) micrófono; (spokesman) portavoz m/f
mouthwash ['maʊθwɔʃ] n enjuague m bucal
mouth-watering ['maʊθwɔːtərɪŋ] adj apetitoso
movable ['muːvəbl] adj movible
move [muːv] n (movement) movimiento; (in game) jugada; (: turn to play) turno; (change of house) mudanza ▷ vt mover; (emotionally) conmover; (Pol: resolution etc) proponer ▷ vi (gen) moverse; (traffic) circular; (Brit: also: ~ house) trasladarse, mudarse; **to ~ sb to do sth** mover a algn a hacer algo; **to be ~d** estar conmovido; **to get a ~ on** darse prisa; **move about** or **around** vi moverse; (travel) viajar; **move along** vi (stop loitering) circular; (along seat etc) correrse; **move away** vi (leave) marcharse; **move back** vi (return) volver; **move down** vt (demote) degradar; **move forward** vi avanzar ▷ vt adelantar; **move in** vi (to a house) instalarse; **move off** vi ponerse en camino; **move on** vi seguir viaje ▷ vt (onlookers) hacer circular; **move out** vi (of house) mudarse; **move over** vi hacerse a un lado, correrse; **move up** vi subir; (employee) ascender
movement ['muːvmənt] n movimiento; (Tech) mecanismo; **~ (of the bowels)** (Med) evacuación f
movie ['muːvɪ] n película; **to go to the ~s** ir al cine
movie camera n cámara cinematográfica
movie theater n (US) cine m
moving ['muːvɪŋ] adj (emotional) conmovedor(a); (that moves) móvil; (instigating) motor(a)
mow (pt **mowed**, pp **mowed** or **mown**) [məʊ, -n] vt (grass) cortar; (corn) segar; (also: ~ **down**: shoot) acribillar
mower ['məʊəʳ] n (also: **lawn~**) cortacésped m
Mozambique [məʊzæm'biːk] n Mozambique m
MP n abbr (= Military Police) PM; (Brit) = **Member of Parliament**
mpg n abbr (= miles per gallon) 30 mpg = 9.4 l. per 100 km
mph abbr (= miles per hour) 60 mph = 96 km/h
MP3 ['empiː'θriː] n MP3 m
MP3 player n reproductor m MP3
Mr, Mr. ['mɪstəʳ] n: **Mr Smith** (el) Sr. Smith
Mrs, Mrs. ['mɪsɪz] n: **~ Smith** (la) Sra. de Smith
Ms, Ms. [mɪz] n (Miss or Mrs) abreviatura con la que se evita hacer expreso el estado civil de una mujer; **Ms Smith** (la) Sr(t)a. Smith
MSc abbr see **Master of Science**
MSP n abbr (Brit) = **Member of the Scottish Parliament**

Mt *abbr* (*Geo*: = *mount*) m
much [mʌtʃ] *adj* mucho ▷ *adv, n, pron* mucho; (*before pp*) muy; **how ~ is it?** ¿cuánto es?, ¿cuánto cuesta?; **too ~** demasiado; **so ~** tanto; **it's not ~** no es mucho; **as ~ as** tanto como; **however ~ he tries** por mucho que se esfuerce; **I like it very/so ~** me gusta mucho/tanto; **thank you very ~** muchas gracias, muy agradecido
muck [mʌk] *n* (*dirt*) suciedad *f*; (*fig*) porquería; **muck about** *or* **around** *vi* (*inf*) perder el tiempo; (*enjoy o.s.*) entretenerse; (*tinker*) manosear; **muck in** *vi* (*inf*) arrimar el hombro; **muck out** *vt* (*stable*) limpiar; **muck up** *vt* (*inf*: *dirty*) ensuciar; (*: spoil*) echar a perder; (*: ruin*) estropear
mucky ['mʌkı] *adj* (*dirty*) sucio
mucus ['mjuːkəs] *n* mucosidad *f*, moco
mud [mʌd] *n* barro, lodo
muddle ['mʌdl] *n* desorden *m*, confusión *f*; (*mix-up*) embrollo, lío ▷ *vt* (*also*: **~ up**) embrollar, confundir; **muddle along**, **muddle on** *vi* arreglárselas de alguna manera; **muddle through** *vi* salir del paso
muddy ['mʌdı] *adj* fangoso, cubierto de lodo
mudguard ['mʌdgɑːd] *n* guardabarros *m inv*
mudslide ['mʌdslaid] *n* desprendimiento de tierra
muesli ['mjuːzlı] *n* muesli *m*
muffin ['mʌfın] *n* bollo, ≈ magdalena
muffle ['mʌfl] *vt* (*sound*) amortiguar; (*against cold*) abrigar
muffled ['mʌfld] *adj* sordo, apagado; (*noise etc*) amortiguado
muffler ['mʌfləʳ] *n* (*scarf*) bufanda; (*US Aut*) silenciador *m*; (*on motorbike*) silenciador *m*, mofle *m*
mug [mʌg] *n* (*cup*) taza alta; (*for beer*) jarra; (*inf*: *face*) jeta; (*: fool*) bobo ▷ *vt* (*assault*) atracar; **it's a ~'s game** es cosa de bobos; **mug up** *vt* (*inf*: *also*: **~ up on**) empollar
mugger ['mʌgəʳ] *n* atracador(a) *m(f)*
mugging ['mʌgıŋ] *n* atraco callejero
muggins ['mʌgınz] *nsg* (*inf*) tonto(-a) el bote
muggy ['mʌgı] *adj* bochornoso
mule [mjuːl] *n* mula
mull [mʌl] **to ~ over** *vt* meditar sobre
multicoloured, multicolored (US) ['mʌltıkʌləd] *adj* multicolor
multi-level [mʌltı'lɛvl] *adj* (US) = **multistorey**
multimedia ['mʌltı'miːdıə] *adj* multimedia
multinational [mʌltı'næʃənl] *n* multinacional *f* ▷ *adj* multinacional
multiple ['mʌltıpl] *adj* múltiple ▷ *n* múltiplo; (*Brit*: *also*: **~ store**) (cadena de) grandes almacenes *mpl*
multiple choice *n* (*also*: **~ test**) examen *m* de tipo test
multiple sclerosis [-sklı'rəusıs] *n* esclerosis *f* múltiple

multiplex ['mʌltıplɛks] *n* (*also*: **~ cinema**) multicines *m inv*
multiplication [mʌltıplı'keıʃən] *n* multiplicación *f*
multiply ['mʌltıplaı] *vt* multiplicar ▷ *vi* multiplicarse
multistorey [mʌltı'stɔːrı] *adj* (*Brit*: *building, car park*) de muchos pisos
multitude ['mʌltıtjuːd] *n* multitud *f*
mum [mʌm] *n* (*Brit*) mamá ▷ *adj*: **to keep ~ (about sth)** no decir ni mu (de algo)
mumble ['mʌmbl] *vt* decir entre dientes ▷ *vi* hablar entre dientes, musitar
mummy ['mʌmı] *n* (*Brit*: *mother*) mamá; (*embalmed*) momia
mumps [mʌmps] *n* paperas *fpl*
munch [mʌntʃ] *vt, vi* mascar
mundane [mʌn'deın] *adj* mundano
municipal [mjuː'nısıpl] *adj* municipal
munitions [mjuː'nıʃənz] *npl* municiones *fpl*
mural ['mjuərl] *n* (*pintura*) mural *m*
murder ['məːdəʳ] *n* asesinato; (*in law*) homicidio ▷ *vt* asesinar, matar; **to commit ~** cometer un asesinato *or* homicidio
murderer ['məːdərəʳ] *n* asesino
murderous ['məːdərəs] *adj* homicida
murky ['məːkı] *adj* (*water, past*) turbio; (*room*) sombrío
murmur ['məːməʳ] *n* murmullo ▷ *vt, vi* murmurar; **heart ~** soplo cardíaco
muscle ['mʌsl] *n* músculo; (*fig*: *strength*) garra, fuerza; **muscle in** *vi* entrometerse
muscular ['mʌskjuləʳ] *adj* muscular; (*person*) musculoso
muscular dystrophy *n* distrofia muscular
muse [mjuːz] *vi* meditar ▷ *n* musa
museum [mjuː'zıəm] *n* museo
mushroom ['mʌʃrum] *n* (*gen*) seta, hongo; (*small*) champiñón *m* ▷ *vi* (*fig*) crecer de la noche a la mañana
music ['mjuːzık] *n* música
musical ['mjuːzıkl] *adj* musical; (*sound*) melodioso; (*person*) con talento musical ▷ *n* (*show*) (comedia) musical *m*
musical instrument *n* instrumento musical
music centre *n* equipo de música
musician [mjuː'zıʃən] *n* músico(-a)
Muslim ['mʌzlım] *adj, n* musulmán(-ana) *m(f)*
muslin ['mʌzlın] *n* muselina
mussel ['mʌsl] *n* mejillón *m*
must [mʌst] *aux vb* (*obligation*): **I ~ do it** debo hacerlo, tengo que hacerlo; (*probability*): **he ~ be there by now** ya debe (de) estar allí ▷ *n*: **it's a ~** es imprescindible
mustache ['mʌstæʃ] *n* (US) = **moustache**
mustard ['mʌstəd] *n* mostaza
muster ['mʌstəʳ] *vt* juntar, reunir; (*also*: **~ up**) reunir; (*: courage*) armarse de
mustn't ['mʌsnt] = **must not**
mutant ['mjuːtənt] *adj, n* mutante *m*

m

mutate [mju:'teɪt] *vi* sufrir mutación, transformarse

mute [mju:t] *adj, n* mudo(-a) *m(f)*

muted ['mju:tɪd] *adj* (*noise*) sordo; (*criticism*) callado

mutilate ['mju:tɪleɪt] *vt* mutilar

mutiny ['mju:tɪnɪ] *n* motín *m* ▷ *vi* amotinarse

mutter ['mʌtəʳ] *vt, vi* murmurar

mutton ['mʌtn] *n* (carne *f* de) cordero

mutual ['mju:tʃuəl] *adj* mutuo; (*friend*) común

mutually ['mju:tʃuəlɪ] *adv* mutuamente

Muzak® ['mju:zæk] *n* hilo musical

muzzle ['mʌzl] *n* hocico; (*protective device*) bozal *m*; (*of gun*) boca ▷ *vt* amordazar; (*dog*) poner un bozal a

MW *abbr* (*Radio: = medium wave*) onda media

my [maɪ] *adj* mi(s); **my house/brother/sisters** mi casa/hermano/mis hermanas; **I've washed my hair/cut my finger** me he lavado el pelo/cortado un dedo; **is this my pen or yours?** ¿este bolígrafo es mío o tuyo?

Myanmar ['maɪænmɑːʳ] *n* Myanmar

myself [maɪ'self] *pron* (*reflexive*) me; (*emphatic*) yo mismo; (*after prep*) mí (mismo); *see also* **oneself**

mysterious [mɪs'tɪərɪəs] *adj* misterioso

mystery ['mɪstərɪ] *n* misterio

mystical ['mɪstɪkl] *adj* místico

mystify ['mɪstɪfaɪ] *vt* (*perplex*) dejar perplejo; (*disconcert*) desconcertar

myth [mɪθ] *n* mito

mythical ['mɪθɪkl] *adj* mítico

mythology [mɪ'θɔlədʒɪ] *n* mitología

N, n [ɛn] *n* (*letter*) N, n *f*; **N for Nellie**, (*US*) **N for Nan** N de Navarra

N *abbr* (*= North*) N

n/a *abbr* (*= not applicable*) no interesa; (*Comm etc*) *= no account*

naan [nɑ:n] *n* **= nan bread**

nab [næb] *vt* (*inf: grab*) coger (*Sp*), agarrar (*LAm*); (*: catch out*) pillar

NAFTA ['næftə] *n abbr* (*= North Atlantic Free Trade Agreement*) TLC *m*

nag [næg] *n* (*pej: horse*) rocín *m* ▷ *vt* (*scold*) regañar; (*annoy*) fastidiar

nagging ['nægɪŋ] *adj* (*doubt*) persistente; (*pain*) continuo ▷ *n* quejas *fpl*

nail [neɪl] *n* (*human*) uña; (*metal*) clavo ▷ *vt* clavar; (*fig: catch*) coger (*Sp*), pillar; **to pay cash on the ~** pagar a tocateja; **to ~ sb down to a date/price** hacer que algn se comprometa a una fecha/un precio

nailbrush ['neɪlbrʌʃ] *n* cepillo para las uñas

nailfile ['neɪlfaɪl] *n* lima para las uñas

nail polish *n* esmalte *m or* laca para las uñas

nail polish remover *n* quitaesmalte *m*

nail scissors *npl* tijeras *fpl* para las uñas

nail varnish *n* (*Brit*) **= nail polish**

naïve [naɪ'i:v] *adj* ingenuo

naked ['neɪkɪd] *adj* (*nude*) desnudo; (*flame*) expuesto al aire; **with the ~ eye** a simple vista

name [neɪm] *n* (*gen*) nombre *m*; (*surname*) apellido; (*reputation*) fama, renombre *m* ▷ *vt* (*child*) poner nombre a; (*criminal*) identificar;

(*price, date etc*) fijar; (*appoint*) nombrar; **by ~** de nombre; **in the ~ of** en nombre de; **what's your ~?** ¿cómo se llama usted?; **my ~ is Peter** me llamo Pedro; **to give one's ~ and address** dar sus señas; **to take sb's ~ and address** apuntar las señas de algn; **to make a ~ for o.s.** hacerse famoso; **to get (o.s.) a bad ~** forjarse una mala reputación

nameless ['neɪmlɪs] *adj* anónimo, sin nombre

namely ['neɪmlɪ] *adv* a saber

namesake ['neɪmseɪk] *n* tocayo(-a)

nan bread [nɑː-] *n* pan indio sin apenas levadura

nanny ['nænɪ] *n* niñera

nap [næp] *n* (*sleep*) sueñecito, siesta; **they were caught ~ping** les pilló desprevenidos

nape [neɪp] *n*: **~ of the neck** nuca, cogote *m*

napkin ['næpkɪn] *n* (*also:* **table ~**) servilleta

nappy ['næpɪ] *n* (*Brit*) pañal *m*

nappy rash *n* prurito

narcissus (*pl* **narcissi**) [nɑː'sɪsəs, -saɪ] *n* narciso

narcotic [nɑː'kɔtɪk] *adj, n* narcótico; **narcotics** *npl* estupefacientes *mpl*, narcóticos *mpl*

narrate [nə'reɪt] *vt* narrar, contar

narrative ['nærətɪv] *n* narrativa ▷ *adj* narrativo

narrator [nə'reɪtə^r] *n* narrador(a) *m(f)*

narrow ['nærəu] *adj* estrecho; (*resources, means*) escaso ▷ *vi* estrecharse; (*diminish*) reducirse; **to have a ~ escape** escaparse por los pelos; **narrow down** *vt* (*search, investigation, possibilities*) restringir, limitar; (*list*) reducir

narrowly ['nærəlɪ] *adv* (*miss*) por poco

narrow-minded [nærəu'maɪndɪd] *adj* de miras estrechas

NASA *n abbr* (US: = *National Aeronautics and Space Administration*) NASA *f*

nasal ['neɪzl] *adj* nasal

nasty ['nɑːstɪ] *adj* (*remark*) feo; (*person*) antipático; (*revolting: taste, smell*) asqueroso; (*wound, disease etc*) peligroso, grave; **to turn ~** (*situation*) ponerse feo; (*weather*) empeorar; (*person*) ponerse negro

nation ['neɪʃən] *n* nación *f*

national ['næʃənl] *adj* nacional ▷ *n* súbdito(-a)

national anthem *n* himno nacional

National Curriculum *n* (*Brit*) plan *m* general de estudios (*en Inglaterra y Gales*)

national debt *n* deuda pública

national dress *n* traje *m* típico del país

National Guard *n* (US) Guardia Nacional

National Health Service *n* (*Brit*) servicio nacional de salud, ≈ INSALUD *m* (*Sp*)

National Insurance *n* (*Brit*) seguro social nacional, ≈ Seguridad *f* Social

nationalism ['næʃnəlɪzəm] *n* nacionalismo

nationalist ['næʃnəlɪst] *adj, n* nacionalista *m/f*

nationality [næʃə'nælɪtɪ] *n* nacionalidad *f*

nationalization [næʃnəlaɪ'zeɪʃən] *n* nacionalización *f*

nationalize ['næʃnəlaɪz] *vt* nacionalizar; **~d industry** industria nacionalizada

nationally ['næʃnəlɪ] *adv* (*nationwide*) a escala nacional; (*as a nation*) como nación

national service *n* (*Mil*) servicio militar

National Trust *n* (*Brit*) organización encargada de preservar el patrimonio histórico británico

nationwide ['neɪʃənwaɪd] *adj* a escala nacional

native ['neɪtɪv] *n* (*local inhabitant*) natural *m/f*; (*in colonies*) indígena *m/f*, nativo(-a) ▷ *adj* (*indigenous*) indígena; (*country*) natal; (*innate*) natural, innato; **a ~ of Russia** un(a) natural de Rusia; **~ language** lengua materna; **a ~ speaker of French** un hablante nativo de francés

Native American *adj, n* americano(-a) indígena *m(f)*, amerindio(-a) *m(f)*

native speaker *n* hablante *m/f* nativo(-a)

Nativity [nə'tɪvɪtɪ] *n*: **the ~** Navidad *f*

nativity play *n* auto del nacimiento

NATO ['neɪtəu] *n abbr* (= *North Atlantic Treaty Organization*) OTAN *f*

natural ['nætʃrəl] *adj* natural; **death from ~ causes** (*Law*) muerte *f* por causas naturales

natural gas *n* gas *m* natural

natural history *n* historia natural

naturalize ['nætʃrəlaɪz] *vt*: **to become ~d** (*person*) naturalizarse; (*plant*) aclimatarse

naturally ['nætʃrəlɪ] *adv* (*speak etc*) naturalmente; (*of course*) desde luego, por supuesto, ¡cómo no! (*LAm*); (*instinctively*) por naturaleza

natural resources *npl* recursos *mpl* naturales

natural selection *n* selección *f* natural

nature ['neɪtʃə^r] *n* naturaleza; (*group, sort*) género, clase *f*; (*character*) modo de ser, carácter *m*; **by ~** por naturaleza; **documents of a confidential ~** documentos *mpl* de tipo confidencial

nature reserve *n* reserva natural

naught [nɔːt] *n* = **nought**

naughty ['nɔːtɪ] *adj* (*child*) travieso; (*story, film*) picante, escabroso, colorado (*LAm*)

nausea ['nɔːsɪə] *n* náusea

nauseate ['nɔːsɪeɪt] *vt* dar náuseas a; (*fig*) dar asco a

naval ['neɪvl] *adj* naval, de marina

naval officer *n* oficial *m/f* de marina

nave [neɪv] *n* nave *f*

navel ['neɪvl] *n* ombligo

navigate ['nævɪgeɪt] *vt* (*ship*) gobernar; (*river etc*) navegar por ▷ *vi* navegar; (*Aut*) ir de copiloto

navigation [nævɪ'geɪʃən] *n* (*action*) navegación *f*; (*science*) náutica

navvy ['nævɪ] *n* (*Brit*) peón *m* caminero

navy ['neɪvɪ] n marina de guerra; (ships) armada, flota ▷ adj azul marino

Nazi ['nɑːtsɪ] adj, n nazi m/f

NB abbr (= nota bene) nótese

NBA n abbr (US) = **National Basketball Association; National Boxing Association**

NBC n abbr (US: = National Broadcasting Company) cadena de televisión

near [nɪəʳ] adj (place, relation) cercano; (time) próximo ▷ adv cerca ▷ prep (also: ~ **to**: space) cerca de, junto a; (: time) cerca de ▷ vt acercarse a, aproximarse a; ~ **here/there** cerca de aquí/de allí; **£25,000 or ~est offer** 25,000 libras o precio a discutir; **in the ~ future** en fecha próxima; **the building is ~ing completion** el edificio está casi terminado

nearby [nɪə'baɪ] adj cercano, próximo ▷ adv cerca

nearly ['nɪəlɪ] adv casi, por poco; **I ~ fell** por poco me caigo; **not ~** ni mucho menos, ni con mucho

near miss n (shot) tiro casi en el blanco; (Aviat) accidente evitado por muy poco

nearside ['nɪəsaɪd] n (Aut: right-hand drive) lado izquierdo; (: left-hand drive) lado derecho

near-sighted [nɪə'saɪtɪd] adj miope, corto de vista

neat [niːt] adj (place) ordenado, bien cuidado; (person) pulcro; (plan) ingenioso; (spirits) solo

neatly ['niːtlɪ] adv (tidily) con esmero; (skilfully) ingeniosamente

neatness ['niːtnɪs] n (tidiness) orden m; (skilfulness) destreza, habilidad f

necessarily ['nesɪsrɪlɪ] adv necesariamente; **not ~** no necesariamente

necessary ['nesɪsrɪ] adj necesario, preciso; **he did all that was ~** hizo todo lo necesario; **if ~** si es necesario

necessity [nɪ'sesɪtɪ] n necesidad f; **necessities** npl artículos mpl de primera necesidad; **in case of ~** en caso de urgencia

neck [nɛk] n (Anat) cuello; (of animal) pescuezo ▷ vi besuquearse; ~ **and ~** parejos; **to stick one's ~ out** (inf) arriesgarse

necklace ['nɛklɪs] n collar m

neckline ['nɛklaɪn] n escote m

necktie ['nɛktaɪ] n (US) corbata

nectarine ['nɛktərɪn] n nectarina

née [neɪ] adj: ~ **Scott** de soltera Scott

need [niːd] n (lack) escasez f, falta; (necessity) necesidad f ▷ vt (require) necesitar; **in case of ~** en caso de necesidad; **there's no ~ for ...** no hace(n) falta ...; **to be in ~ of, have ~ of** necesitar; **10 will meet my immediate ~s** 10 satisfarán mis necesidades más apremiantes; **the ~s of industry** las necesidades de la industria; **I ~ it** lo necesito; **a signature is ~ed** se requiere una firma; **I ~ to do it** tengo que hacerlo; **you don't ~ to go** no hace falta que vayas

needle ['niːdl] n aguja ▷ vt (fig: inf) picar, fastidiar

needless ['niːdlɪs] adj innecesario, inútil; ~ **to say** huelga decir que

needlework ['niːdlwəːk] n (activity) costura, labor f de aguja

needn't ['niːdnt] = **need not**

needy ['niːdɪ] adj necesitado

negative ['negətɪv] n (Phot) negativo; (answer) negativa; (Ling) negación f ▷ adj negativo

negative equity n situación en la que el valor de la vivienda es menor que el de la hipoteca que pesa sobre ella

neglect [nɪ'glɛkt] vt (one's duty) faltar a, no cumplir con; (child) descuidar, desatender ▷ n (state) abandono; (personal) dejadez f; (of child) desatención f; (of duty) incumplimiento; **to ~ to do sth** olvidarse de hacer algo

negligee ['neglɪʒeɪ] n (nightdress) salto de cama

negligence ['neglɪdʒəns] n negligencia

negligent ['neglɪdʒənt] adj negligente; (casual) descuidado

negligible ['neglɪdʒɪbl] adj insignificante, despreciable

negotiable [nɪ'gəʊʃɪəbl] adj: **not ~** (cheque) no trasferible

negotiate [nɪ'gəʊʃɪeɪt] vt (treaty, loan) negociar; (obstacle) franquear; (bend in road) tomar ▷ vi: **to ~ (with)** negociar (con); **to ~ with sb for sth** tratar or negociar con algn por algo

negotiating table [nɪ'gəʊʃɪeɪtɪŋ-] n mesa de negociaciones

negotiation [nɪgəʊʃɪ'eɪʃən] n negociación f, gestión f; **negotiations** npl negociaciones; **to enter into ~s with sb** entrar en negociaciones con algn

negotiator [nɪ'gəʊʃɪeɪtəʳ] n negociador(a) m(f)

neigh [neɪ] n relincho ▷ vi relinchar

neighbour, neighbor (US) ['neɪbəʳ] n vecino(-a)

neighbourhood, neighborhood (US) ['neɪbəhud] n (place) vecindad f, barrio; (people) vecindario

neighbourhood watch n (Brit: also: ~ **scheme**) vigilancia del barrio por los propios vecinos

neighbouring, neighboring (US) ['neɪbərɪŋ] adj vecino

neither ['naɪðəʳ] adj ni ▷ conj: **I didn't move and ~ did John** no me he movido, ni Juan tampoco ▷ pron ninguno; ~ **is true** ninguno(-a) de los/las dos es cierto(-a) ▷ adv: ~ **good nor bad** ni bueno ni malo

neologism [nɪ'ɔlədʒɪzəm] n neologismo

neon ['niːɔn] n neón m

neon light n lámpara de neón

Nepal [nɪ'pɔːl] n Nepal m

nephew ['nevjuː] n sobrino

nerd [nəːd] n (inf) primo(-a)

nerve [nə:v] *n* (*Anat*) nervio; (*courage*) valor *m*; (*impudence*) descaro, frescura; (*nervousness*) nerviosismo *msg*, nervios *mpl*; **a fit of ~s** un ataque de nervios; **to lose one's ~** (*self-confidence*) perder el valor

nerve centre *n* (*Anat*) centro nervioso; (*fig*) punto neurálgico

nerve-racking [nə:vrækɪŋ] *adj* angustioso

nervous [nə:vəs] *adj* (*anxious*) nervioso; (*Anat*) nervioso; (*timid*) tímido, miedoso

nervous breakdown *n* crisis *f* nerviosa

nervous wreck *n* (*inf*): **to be a ~** estar de los nervios

nervy [nə:vi] *adj*: **to be ~** estar nervioso

nest [nɛst] *n* (*of bird*) nido ▷ *vi* anidar

nest egg *n* (*fig*) ahorros *mpl*

nestle [nɛsl] *vi*: **to ~ down** acurrucarse

Net [nɛt] *n* (*Comput*) Internet *m or f*

net [nɛt] *n* (*gen*) red *f*; (*fabric*) tul *m* ▷ *adj* (*Comm*) neto, líquido; (*weight, price, salary*) neto ▷ *vt* coger (*Sp*) *or* agarrar (*LAm*) con red; (*money: person*) cobrar; (*: deal, sale*) conseguir; (*Sport*) marcar; **~ of tax** neto; **he earns £10,000 ~ per year** gana 10,000 libras netas por año; **the N~** (*Internet*) la Red

netball [nɛtbɔ:l] *n* balonred *m*

net curtain *n* visillo

Netherlands [nɛðələndz] *npl*: **the ~** los Países Bajos

net profit *n* beneficio neto

nett [nɛt] *adj* = **net**

netting [nɛtɪŋ] *n* red *f*, redes *fpl*

nettle [nɛtl] *n* ortiga

network [nɛtwə:k] *n* red *f* ▷ *vt* (*Radio, TV*) difundir por la red de emisores; **local area ~** red local; **there's no ~ coverage here** (*Tel*) aquí no hay cobertura

neurological [njuərəˈlɔdʒɪkl] *adj* neurológico

neurosis (*pl* **neuroses**) [njuəˈrəusɪs, -si:z] *n* neurosis *f inv*

neurotic [njuəˈrɔtɪk] *adj, n* neurótico(-a) *m(f)*

neuter [nju:təʳ] *adj* (*Ling*) neutro ▷ *vt* castrar, capar

neutral [nju:trəl] *adj* (*person*) neutral; (*colour etc*) neutro; (*Elec*) neutro ▷ *n* (*Aut*) punto muerto

neutralize [nju:trəlaɪz] *vt* neutralizar

neutron [nju:trɔn] *n* neutrón *m*

never [nɛvəʳ] *adv* nunca, jamás; **I ~ went** no fui nunca; **~ in my life** jamás en la vida; *see also* **mind**

never-ending [nɛvərˈɛndɪŋ] *adj* interminable, sin fin

nevertheless [nɛvəðəˈlɛs] *adv* sin embargo, no obstante

new [nju:] *adj* nuevo; (*recent*) reciente; **as good as ~** como nuevo

New Age *n* Nueva era

newborn [nju:bɔ:n] *adj* recién nacido

newcomer [nju:kʌməʳ] *n* recién venido *or* llegado

new-fangled [nju:fæŋgld] *adj* (*pej*) modernísimo

new-found [nju:faund] *adj* (*friend*) nuevo; (*enthusiasm*) recién adquirido

newly [nju:lɪ] *adv* recién

newly-weds [nju:lɪwɛdz] *npl* recién casados

new moon *n* luna nueva

news [nju:z] *n* noticias *fpl*; **a piece of ~** una noticia; **the ~** (*Radio, TV*) las noticias *fpl*, el telediario; **good/bad ~** buenas/malas noticias *fpl*; **financial ~** noticias *fpl* financieras

news agency *n* agencia de noticias

newsagent [nju:zeɪdʒənt] *n* (*Brit*) vendedor(a) *m(f)* de periódicos

newscaster [nju:zka:stəʳ] *n* presentador(a) *m(f)*, locutor(a) *m(f)*

news dealer *n* (*US*) = **newsagent**

news flash *n* noticia de última hora

newsletter [nju:zlɛtəʳ] *n* hoja informativa, boletín *m*

newspaper [nju:zpeɪpəʳ] *n* periódico, diario; **daily ~** diario; **weekly ~** periódico semanal

newsprint [nju:zprɪnt] *n* papel *m* de periódico

newsreader [nju:zri:dəʳ] *n* = **newscaster**

newsreel [nju:zri:l] *n* noticiario

newsroom [nju:zru:m] *n* (*Press, Radio, TV*) sala de redacción

news stand *n* quiosco *or* puesto de periódicos

newsworthy [nju:zwə:ðɪ] *adj*: **to be ~** ser de interés periodístico

newt [nju:t] *n* tritón *m*

new town *n* (*Brit*) ciudad *f* nueva (*construida con subsidios estatales*)

New Year *n* Año Nuevo; **Happy ~!** ¡Feliz Año Nuevo!; **to wish sb a happy ~** desear a algn un feliz año nuevo

New Year's Day *n* Día *m* de Año Nuevo

New Year's Eve *n* Nochevieja

New York [-ˈjɔ:k] *n* Nueva York

New Zealand [-ˈzi:lənd] *n* Nueva Zelanda (*Sp*), Nueva Zelandia (*LAm*) ▷ *adj* neozelandés(-esa)

New Zealander [-ˈzi:ləndəʳ] *n* neozelandés(-esa) *m(f)*

next [nɛkst] *adj* (*house, room*) vecino, de al lado; (*meeting*) próximo; (*page*) siguiente ▷ *adv* después; **the ~ day** el día siguiente; **~ time** la próxima vez; **~ year** el año próximo *or* que viene; **~ month** el mes que viene *or* entrante; **the week after ~** no la semana que viene sino la otra; **"turn to the ~ page"** "vuelva a la página siguiente"; **you're ~** le toca; **~ to** *prep* junto a, al lado de; **~ to nothing** casi nada

next door *adv* en la casa de al lado ▷ *adj* vecino, de al lado

next-of-kin [nɛkstəvˈkɪn] *n* pariente(s) *m(pl)* más cercano(s)

NHS *n abbr* (*Brit*) = **National Health Service**

NI *abbr* = **Northern Ireland**; *(Brit)* = **National Insurance**
nib [nɪb] *n* plumilla
nibble ['nɪbl] *vt* mordisquear
Nicaragua [nɪkə'ræɡjuə] *n* Nicaragua
Nicaraguan [nɪkə'ræɡjuən] *adj, n* nicaragüense *m/f*, nicaragüeño(-a) *m(f)*
nice [naɪs] *adj* *(likeable)* simpático, majo; *(kind)* amable; *(pleasant)* agradable; *(attractive)* bonito, mono; *(distinction)* fino; *(taste, smell, meal)* rico
nicely ['naɪslɪ] *adv* amablemente; *(of health etc)* bien; **that will do ~** perfecto
niceties ['naɪsɪtɪz] *npl* detalles *mpl*
niche [niːʃ] *n* *(Arch)* nicho, hornacina
nick [nɪk] *n* *(wound)* rasguño; *(cut, indentation)* mella, muesca ▷ *vt* *(cut)* cortar; *(inf)* birlar, mangar; *(: arrest)* pillar; **in the ~ of time** justo a tiempo; **in good ~** en buen estado; **to ~ o.s.** cortarse
nickel ['nɪkl] *n* níquel *m*; *(US)* moneda *de* 5 centavos
nickname ['nɪkneɪm] *n* apodo, mote *m* ▷ *vt* apodar
nicotine ['nɪkəti:n] *n* nicotina
nicotine patch *n* parche *m* de nicotina
niece [ni:s] *n* sobrina
Nigeria [naɪ'dʒɪərɪə] *n* Nigeria
Nigerian [naɪ'dʒɪərɪən] *adj, n* nigeriano(-a) *m(f)*
niggling ['nɪɡlɪŋ] *adj* *(detail: trifling)* nimio, insignificante; *(annoying)* molesto; *(doubt, pain)* constante
night [naɪt] *n* *(gen)* noche *f*; *(evening)* tarde *f*; **last ~** anoche; **the ~ before last** anteanoche, antes de ayer por la noche; **at ~, by ~** de noche, por la noche; **in the ~, during the ~** durante la noche, por la noche
nightcap ['naɪtkæp] *n* *(drink)* bebida que se toma antes de acostarse
night club *n* club nocturno, discoteca
nightdress ['naɪtdres] *n* *(Brit)* camisón *m*
nightfall ['naɪtfɔ:l] *n* anochecer *m*
nightgown ['naɪtɡaun], **nightie** ['naɪtɪ] *(Brit)* *n* = **nightdress**
nightingale ['naɪtɪŋɡeɪl] *n* ruiseñor *m*
night life *n* vida nocturna
nightly ['naɪtlɪ] *adj* de todas las noches ▷ *adv* todas las noches, cada noche
nightmare ['naɪtmɛəʳ] *n* pesadilla
night porter *n* guardián *m* nocturno
night school *n* clase(s) *f(pl)* nocturna(s)
night shift *n* turno nocturno *or* de noche
night-time ['naɪttaɪm] *n* noche *f*
night watchman *n* vigilante *m* nocturno, sereno
nil [nɪl] *n* *(Brit Sport)* cero, nada
Nile [naɪl] *n*: **the ~** el Nilo
nimble ['nɪmbl] *adj* *(agile)* ágil, ligero; *(skilful)* diestro
nine [naɪn] *num* nueve
nineteen ['naɪn'ti:n] *num* diecinueve

nineteenth [naɪn'ti:nθ] *adj* decimonoveno, decimonono
ninetieth ['naɪntɪɪθ] *adj* nonagésimo
ninety ['naɪntɪ] *num* noventa
ninth [naɪnθ] *adj* noveno
nip [nɪp] *vt* *(pinch)* pellizcar; *(bite)* morder ▷ *vi* *(Brit inf)*: **to ~ out/down/up** salir/bajar/subir un momento ▷ *n* *(drink)* trago
nipple ['nɪpl] *n* *(Anat)* pezón *m*; *(of bottle)* tetilla; *(Tech)* boquilla, manguito
nippy ['nɪpɪ] *adj* *(Brit: person)* rápido; *(taste)* picante; **it's a very ~ car** es un coche muy potente para el tamaño que tiene
nit [nɪt] *n* *(of louse)* liendre *f*; *(inf: idiot)* imbécil *m/f*
nitrogen ['naɪtrədʒən] *n* nitrógeno
NM, N. Mex. *abbr* *(US)* = **New Mexico**

🔵 KEYWORD

no [nəu] *(pl* **noes)** *adv* *(opposite of "yes")* no; **are you coming? — no (I'm not)** ¿vienes? — no; **would you like some more? — no thank you** ¿quieres más? — no gracias
▷ *adj* **1** *(not any)*: **I have no money/time/books** no tengo dinero/tiempo/libros; **no other man would have done it** ningún otro lo hubiera hecho;
2: **"no entry"** "prohibido el paso"; **"no smoking"** "prohibido fumar"
▷ *n* no *m*

no. *abbr* *(= number)* nº, núm
Nobel prize [nəu'bɛl-] *n* premio Nobel
nobility [nəu'bɪlɪtɪ] *n* nobleza
noble ['nəubl] *adj* *(person)* noble; *(title)* de nobleza
nobody ['nəubədɪ] *pron* nadie
no-claims bonus ['nəukleɪmz-] *n* bonificación *f* por carencia de reclamaciones
nod [nɔd] *vi* saludar con la cabeza; *(in agreement)* asentir con la cabeza ▷ *vt*: **to ~ one's head** inclinar la cabeza ▷ *n* inclinación *f* de cabeza; **they ~ded their agreement** asintieron con la cabeza; **nod off** *vi* cabecear
no-fly zone [nəu'flaɪ-] *n* zona de exclusión aérea
noise [nɔɪz] *n* ruido; *(din)* escándalo, estrépito
noisy ['nɔɪzɪ] *adj* *(gen)* ruidoso; *(child)* escandaloso
nominal ['nɔmɪnl] *adj* nominal
nominate ['nɔmɪneɪt] *vt* *(propose)* proponer; *(appoint)* nombrar
nomination [nɔmɪ'neɪʃən] *n* propuesta; nombramiento
nominee [nɔmɪ'ni:] *n* candidato(-a)
nonalcoholic [nɔnælkə'hɔlɪk] *adj* sin alcohol
noncommittal ['nɔnkə'mɪtl] *adj* *(reserved)* reservado; *(uncommitted)* evasivo

nondescript ['nɔndɪskrɪpt] *adj* anodino, soso
none [nʌn] *pron* ninguno(-a) ▷ *adv* de
ninguna manera; **~ of you** ninguno de
vosotros; **I've ~ left** no me queda
ninguno(-a); **he's ~ the worse for it** no le ha
perjudicado; **I have ~** no tengo ninguno; **~ at
all** (*not one*) ni uno
nonentity [nɔ'nɛntɪtɪ] *n* cero a la izquierda,
nulidad *f*
nonetheless [nʌnðə'lɛs] *adv* sin embargo,
no obstante, aún así
non-event [nɔnɪ'vɛnt] *n* acontecimiento sin
importancia; **it was a ~** no pasó
absolutamente nada
nonexistent [nɔnɪg'zɪstənt] *adj* inexistente
non-fiction [nɔn'fɪkʃən] *n* no ficción *f*
no-no ['nəunəu] *n* (*inf*): **it's a ~** de eso ni
hablar
no-nonsense [nəu'nɔnsəns] *adj* sensato
nonplussed [nɔn'plʌst] *adj* perplejo
nonsense ['nɔnsəns] *n* tonterías *fpl*,
disparates *fpl*, **~!** ¡qué tonterías!; **it is ~ to say
that ...** es absurdo decir que ...
nonsensical [nɔn'sɛnsɪkl] *adj* disparatado,
absurdo
non-smoker ['nɔn'sməukəʳ] *n* no
fumador(a) *m(f)*
non-smoking ['nɔn'sməukɪŋ] *adj* (de) no
fumador
nonstarter [nɔn'stɑ:təʳ] *n*: **it's a ~** no tiene
futuro
non-stick ['nɔn'stɪk] *adj* (*pan, surface*)
antiadherente
nonstop ['nɔn'stɔp] *adj* continuo; (*Rail*)
directo ▷ *adv* sin parar
noodles ['nu:dlz] *npl* tallarines *mpl*
nook [nuk] *n* rincón *m*; **~s and crannies**
escondrijos *mpl*
noon [nu:n] *n* mediodía *m*
no-one ['nəuwʌn] *pron* = **nobody**
noose [nu:s] *n* lazo corredizo
nor [nɔ:ʳ] *conj* = **neither** ▷ *adv see* **neither**
norm [nɔ:m] *n* norma
normal ['nɔ:ml] *adj* normal; **to return to ~**
volver a la normalidad
normality [nɔ:'mælɪtɪ] *n* normalidad *f*
normally ['nɔ:məlɪ] *adv* normalmente
Normandy ['nɔ:məndɪ] *n* Normandía
north [nɔ:θ] *n* norte *m* ▷ *adj* (del) norte ▷ *adv*
al *or* hacia el norte
North Africa *n* África del Norte
North America *n* América del Norte
North American *adj, n* norteamericano(-a)
m(f)
northbound ['nɔ:θbaund] *adj* (*traffic*) que se
dirige al norte; (*carriageway*) de dirección
norte
north-east [nɔ:θ'i:st] *n* nor(d)este *m*
northeastern [nɔ:θ'i:stən] *adj* nor(d)este,
del nor(d)este
northerly ['nɔ:ðəlɪ] *adj* (*point, direction*) hacia
el norte, septentrional; (*wind*) del norte

northern ['nɔ:ðən] *adj* norteño, del norte
Northern Ireland *n* Irlanda del Norte
North Korea *n* Corea del Norte
North Pole *n*: **the ~** el Polo Norte
North Sea *n*: **the ~** el Mar del Norte
North Sea oil *n* petróleo del Mar del Norte
north-west [nɔ:θ'wɛst] *n* noroeste *m*
northwestern ['nɔ:θ'wɛstən] *adj* noroeste,
del noroeste
Norway ['nɔ:weɪ] *n* Noruega
Norwegian [nɔ:'wi:dʒən] *adj* noruego(-a) ▷ *n*
noruego(-a); (*Ling*) noruego
nos. *abbr* (= *numbers*) núms.
nose [nəuz] *n* (*Anat*) nariz *f*; (*Zool*) hocico;
(*sense of smell*) olfato ▷ *vi*: **~ one's way**
avanzar con cautela; **to pay through the ~**
(for sth) (*inf*) pagar un dineral (por algo);
nose about, nose around *vi* curiosear
nosebleed ['nəuzbli:d] *n* hemorragia nasal
nose-dive ['nəuzdaɪv] *n* picado vertical
nosey ['nəuzɪ] *adj* curioso, fisgón(-ona)
nostalgia [nɔs'tældʒɪə] *n* nostalgia
nostalgic [nɔs'tældʒɪk] *adj* nostálgico
nostril ['nɔstrɪl] *n* ventana *or* orificio de la
nariz
nosy ['nəuzɪ] *adj* = **nosey**
not [nɔt] *adv* no; **~ at all** no ... en absoluto;
~ that ... no es que ...; **it's too late, isn't it?**
es demasiado tarde, ¿verdad?; **~ yet** todavía
no; **~ now** ahora no; **why ~?** ¿por qué no?;
I hope ~ espero que no; **~ at all** no ... nada;
(*after thanks*) de nada
notable ['nəutəbl] *adj* notable
notably ['nəutəblɪ] *adv* especialmente; (*in
particular*) sobre todo
notary ['nəutərɪ] *n* (*also:* **~ public**) notario(-a)
notation [nəu'teɪʃən] *n* notación *f*
notch [nɔtʃ] *n* muesca, corte *m*; **notch up** *vt*
(*score, victory*) apuntarse
note [nəut] *n* (*Mus: record, letter*) nota;
(*banknote*) billete *m*; (*tone*) tono ▷ *vt* (*observe*)
notar, observar; (*write down*) apuntar, anotar;
delivery ~ nota de entrega; **to compare ~s**
(*fig*) cambiar impresiones; **of ~** conocido,
destacado; **to take ~** prestar atención a; **just
a quick ~ to let you know that ...** sólo unas
líneas para informarte que ...
notebook ['nəutbuk] *n* libreta, cuaderno;
(*for shorthand*) libreta
noted ['nəutɪd] *adj* célebre, conocido
notepad ['nəutpæd] *n* bloc *m*
notepaper ['nəutpeɪpə] *n* papel *m* para
cartas
noteworthy ['nəutwə:ðɪ] *adj* notable, digno
de atención
nothing ['nʌθɪŋ] *n* nada; (*zero*) cero; **he does
~** no hace nada; **~ new** nada nuevo; **~ much**
no mucho; **for ~** (*free*) gratis; (*in vain*) en
balde; **~ at all** nada en absoluto
notice ['nəutɪs] *n* (*announcement*) anuncio;
(*warning*) aviso; (*dismissal*) despido;
(*resignation*) dimisión *f*; (*review: of play etc*)

n

reseña ▷ vt (observe) notar, observar; **to bring sth to sb's ~** (attention) llamar la atención de algn sobre algo; **to take ~ of** hacer caso de, prestar atención a; **at short ~** con poca antelación; **without ~** sin previo aviso; **advance ~** previo aviso; **until further ~** hasta nuevo aviso; **to give sb ~ of sth** avisar a algn de algo; **to give ~, hand in one's ~** dimitir, renunciar; **it has come to my ~ that ...** he llegado a saber que ...; **to escape** or **avoid ~** pasar inadvertido

noticeable ['nəutɪsəbl] adj evidente, obvio

notice board n (Brit) tablón m de anuncios

notification [nəutɪfɪ'keɪʃən] n aviso; (announcement) anuncio

notify ['nəutɪfaɪ] vt: **to ~ sb (of sth)** comunicar (algo) a algn

notion ['nəuʃən] n noción f, idea; (opinion) opinión f

notions ['nəuʃənz] npl (US) mercería

notoriety [nəutə'raɪətɪ] n notoriedad f, mala fama

notorious [nəu'tɔ:rɪəs] adj notorio, tristemente célebre

notwithstanding [nɔtwɪθ'stændɪŋ] adv no obstante, sin embargo; **~ this** a pesar de esto

nougat ['nu:gɑ:] n turrón m

nought [nɔ:t] n cero

noun [naun] n nombre m, sustantivo

nourish ['nʌrɪʃ] vt nutrir; (fig) alimentar

nourishing ['nʌrɪʃɪŋ] adj nutritivo, rico

nourishment ['nʌrɪʃmənt] n alimento, sustento

Nov. abbr (= November) nov

novel ['nɔvl] n novela ▷ adj (new) nuevo, original; (unexpected) insólito

novelist ['nɔvəlɪst] n novelista m/f

novelty ['nɔvəltɪ] n novedad f

November [nəu'vɛmbər] n noviembre m; see also **July**

novice ['nɔvɪs] n principiante m/f, novato(-a); (Rel) novicio(-a)

now [nau] adv (at the present time) ahora; (these days) actualmente, hoy día ▷ conj: **~ (that)** ya que, ahora que; **right ~** ahora mismo; **by ~** ya; **I'll do it just ~** ahora mismo lo hago; **~ and then, ~ and again** de vez en cuando; **from ~ on** de ahora en adelante; **between ~ and Monday** entre hoy y el lunes; **in 3 days from ~** de hoy en 3 días; **that's all for ~** eso es todo por ahora

nowadays ['nauədeɪz] adv hoy (en) día, actualmente

nowhere ['nəuwɛər] adv (direction) a ninguna parte; (location) en ninguna parte; **~ else** en or a ninguna otra parte

no-win situation [nəu'wɪn-] n: **I'm in a ~** haga lo que haga, llevo las de perder

nozzle ['nɔzl] n boquilla

NP n abbr = **notary public**

nr abbr (Brit) = **near**

nth [ɛnθ] adj: **for the ~ time** (inf) por enésima vez

nuclear ['nju:klɪər] adj nuclear

nuclear family n familia nuclear

nuclear-free zone ['nju:klɪə'fri:-] n zona desnuclearizada

nucleus (pl **nuclei**) ['nju:klɪəs, 'nju:klɪaɪ] n núcleo

nude [nju:d] adj, n desnudo(-a) m(f); **in the ~** desnudo

nudge [nʌdʒ] vt dar un codazo a

nudist ['nju:dɪst] n nudista m/f

nudity ['nju:dɪtɪ] n desnudez f

nuisance ['nju:sns] n molestia, fastidio; (person) pesado, latoso; **what a ~!** ¡qué lata!

null [nʌl] adj: **~ and void** nulo y sin efecto

numb [nʌm] adj entumecido; (fig) insensible ▷ vt quitar la sensación a, entumecer, entorpecer; **to be ~ with cold** estar entumecido de frío; **~ with fear/grief** paralizado de miedo/dolor

number ['nʌmbər] n número; (numeral) número, cifra; (quantity) cantidad f ▷ vt (pages etc) numerar, poner número a; (amount to) sumar, ascender a; **reference ~** número de referencia; **telephone ~** número de teléfono; **wrong ~** (Tel) número equivocado; **opposite ~** (person) homólogo(-a); **to be ~ed among** figurar entre; **a ~ of** varios, algunos; **they were ten in ~** eran diez

number plate n (Brit) matrícula, placa

Number Ten n (Brit: 10 Downing Street) residencia del primer ministro

numbskull ['nʌmskʌl] n (inf) papanatas m/f inv

numeral ['nju:mərəl] n número, cifra

numerate ['nju:mərɪt] adj competente en aritmética

numerical [nju:'mɛrɪkl] adj numérico

numerous ['nju:mərəs] adj numeroso, muchos

nun [nʌn] n monja, religiosa

nunnery ['nʌnərɪ] n convento de monjas

nurse [nə:s] n enfermero(-a); (nanny) niñera ▷ vt (patient) cuidar, atender; (baby: Brit) mecer; (: US) criar, amamantar; **male ~** enfermero

nursery ['nə:sərɪ] n (institution) guardería infantil; (room) cuarto de los niños; (for plants) criadero, semillero

nursery rhyme n canción f infantil

nursery school n escuela infantil

nursery slope n (Brit Ski) cuesta para principiantes

nursing ['nə:sɪŋ] n (profession) profesión f de enfermera; (care) asistencia, cuidado ▷ adj (mother) lactante

nursing home n clínica de reposo

nurture ['nə:tʃər] vt (child, plant) alimentar, nutrir

nut [nʌt] n (Tech) tuerca; (Bot) nuez f ▷ adj (chocolate etc) con nueces; **~s** (Culin) frutos secos

nutcrackers ['nʌtkrækəz] npl cascanueces m inv

nutmeg ['nʌtmeg] n nuez f moscada

nutrient ['nju:trɪənt] adj nutritivo ▷ n elemento nutritivo

nutrition [nju:'trɪʃən] n nutrición f, alimentación f

nutritionist [nju:'trɪʃənɪst] n dietista m/f

nutritious [nju:'trɪʃəs] adj nutritivo

nuts [nʌts] adj (inf) chiflado

nutshell ['nʌtʃel] n cáscara de nuez; **in a ~** en resumidas cuentas

nutty ['nʌtɪ] adj (flavour) a frutos secos; (inf: foolish) chalado

NVQ n abbr (Brit = national vocational qualification) título de formación profesional

NY abbr (US) = **New York**

nylon ['naɪlɒn] n nylon m, nilón m ▷ adj de nylon or nilón

O, o [əu] n (letter) O, o f; **O for Oliver**, (US) **O for Oboe** O de Oviedo

oak [əuk] n roble m ▷ adj de roble

OAP n abbr (Brit) = **old-age pensioner**

oar [ɔːʳ] n remo; **to put** or **shove one's ~ in** (fig, inf) entrometerse

oasis (pl **oases**) [əu'eɪsɪs, əu'eɪsi:z] n oasis m inv

oath [əuθ] n juramento; (swear word) palabrota; **on** (Brit) or **under ~** bajo juramento

oatmeal ['əutmiːl] n harina de avena

oats [əuts] npl avena

OBE n abbr (Brit: = Order of the British Empire) título ceremonial

obedience [ə'biːdɪəns] n obediencia; **in ~ to** de acuerdo con

obedient [ə'biːdɪənt] adj obediente

obese [əu'biːs] adj obeso

obesity [əu'biːsɪtɪ] n obesidad f

obey [ə'beɪ] vt obedecer; (instructions) cumplir

obituary [ə'bɪtjuərɪ] n necrología

object ['ɔbdʒɪkt] n (gen) objeto; (purpose) objeto, propósito; (Ling) objeto, complemento ▷ vi [əb'dʒɛkt]: **to ~ to** (attitude) estar en contra de; (proposal) oponerse a; **to ~ that** objetar que; **expense is no ~** no importa lo que cueste; **I ~!** ¡protesto!; **to ~ that** objetar que

objection [əb'dʒɛkʃən] n objeción f; **I have no ~ to ...** no tengo inconveniente en que ...

objectionable [əb'dʒekʃənəbl] *adj* (*gen*) desagradable; (*conduct*) censurable

objective [əb'dʒektɪv] *adj, n* objetivo

obligation [ɔblɪ'geɪʃən] *n* obligación *f*; (*debt*) deber *m*; **"without ~"** "sin compromiso"; **to be under an ~ to sb/to do sth** estar comprometido con algn/a hacer algo

obligatory [ə'blɪgətərɪ] *adj* obligatorio

oblige [ə'blaɪdʒ] *vt* (*do a favour for*) complacer, hacer un favor a; **to ~ sb to do sth** obligar a algn a hacer algo; **to be ~d to sb for sth** estarle agradecido a algn por algo; **anything to ~!** todo sea por complacerte

obliging [ə'blaɪdʒɪŋ] *adj* servicial, atento

oblique [ə'bliːk] *adj* oblicuo; (*allusion*) indirecto ▷ *n* (*Typ*) barra

obliterate [ə'blɪtəreɪt] *vt* arrasar; (*memory*) borrar

oblivion [ə'blɪvɪən] *n* olvido

oblivious [ə'blɪvɪəs] *adj*: **~ of** inconsciente de

oblong ['ɔblɔŋ] *adj* rectangular ▷ *n* rectángulo

obnoxious [əb'nɔkʃəs] *adj* odioso, detestable; (*smell*) nauseabundo

oboe ['əubəu] *n* oboe *m*

obscene [əb'siːn] *adj* obsceno

obscenity [əb'senɪtɪ] *n* obscenidad *f*

obscure [əb'skjuər] *adj* oscuro ▷ *vt* oscurecer; (*hide: sun*) ocultar

obscurity [əb'skjuərɪtɪ] *n* oscuridad *f*; (*obscure point*) punto oscuro; **to rise from ~** salir de la nada

observant [əb'zə:vnt] *adj* observador(a)

observation [ɔbzə'veɪʃən] *n* (*Med*) observación *f*; (*by police etc*) vigilancia

observatory [əb'zə:vətrɪ] *n* observatorio

observe [əb'zə:v] *vt* (*gen*) observar; (*rule*) cumplir

observer [əb'zə:vər] *n* observador(a) *m(f)*

obsess [əb'ses] *vt* obsesionar; **to be ~ed by** *or* **with sb/sth** estar obsesionado con algn/algo

obsession [əb'seʃən] *n* obsesión *f*

obsessive [əb'sesɪv] *adj* obsesivo

obsolescence [ɔbsə'lesns] *n* obsolescencia

obsolete ['ɔbsəliːt] *adj* obsoleto

obstacle ['ɔbstəkl] *n* obstáculo; (*nuisance*) estorbo

obstacle race *n* carrera de obstáculos

obstetrician [ɔbstə'trɪʃən] *n* obstetra *m/f*

obstinate ['ɔbstɪnɪt] *adj* terco, obstinado; (*determined*) tenaz

obstruct [əb'strʌkt] *vt* (*block*) obstruir; (*hinder*) estorbar, obstaculizar

obstruction [əb'strʌkʃən] *n* obstrucción *f*; (*object*) estorbo, obstáculo

obtain [əb'teɪn] *vt* (*get*) obtener; (*achieve*) conseguir; **to ~ sth (for o.s.)** conseguir *or* adquirir algo

obtainable [əb'teɪnəbl] *adj* asequible

obtuse [əb'tjuːs] *adj* obtuso

obvious ['ɔbvɪəs] *adj* (*clear*) obvio, evidente; (*unsubtle*) poco sutil; **it's ~ that ...** está claro que ..., es evidente que ...

obviously ['ɔbvɪəslɪ] *adv* obviamente, evidentemente; **~ not!** ¡por supuesto que no!; **he was ~ not drunk** era evidente que no estaba borracho; **he was not ~ drunk** no se le notaba que estaba borracho

occasion [ə'keɪʒən] *n* oportunidad *f*, ocasión *f*; (*event*) acontecimiento ▷ *vt* ocasionar, causar; **on that ~** esa vez, en aquella ocasión; **to rise to the ~** ponerse a la altura de las circunstancias

occasional [ə'keɪʒənl] *adj* poco frecuente, ocasional

occasionally [ə'keɪʒənlɪ] *adv* de vez en cuando; **very ~** muy de tarde en tarde, en muy contadas ocasiones

occult [ɔ'kʌlt] *adj* (*gen*) oculto

occupant ['ɔkjupənt] *n* (*of house*) inquilino(-a); (*of boat, car*) ocupante *m/f*

occupation [ɔkju'peɪʃən] *n* (*of house*) tenencia; (*job*) trabajo; (*pastime*) ocupaciones *fpl*; (*calling*) oficio

occupational hazard *n* gajes *mpl* del oficio

occupier ['ɔkjupaɪər] *n* inquilino(-a)

occupy ['ɔkjupaɪ] *vt* (*seat, post, time*) ocupar; (*house*) habitar; **to ~ o.s. with** *or* **by doing** (*as job*) dedicarse a hacer; (*to pass time*) entretenerse haciendo; **to be occupied with sth/in doing sth** estar ocupado con algo/haciendo algo

occur [ə'kə:r] *vi* ocurrir, suceder; **to ~ to sb** ocurrírsele a algn

occurrence [ə'kʌrəns] *n* suceso

ocean ['əuʃən] *n* océano; **~s of** (*inf*) la mar de

ocean-going ['əuʃəngəuɪŋ] *adj* de alta mar

o'clock [ə'klɔk] *adv*: **it is five ~** son las cinco

OCR *n abbr* = **optical character recognition/reader**

Oct. *abbr* (= *October*) oct

octane ['ɔkteɪn] *n* octano; **high ~ petrol** *or* (*US*) **gas** gasolina de alto octanaje

octave ['ɔktɪv] *n* octava

October [ɔk'təubər] *n* octubre *m*; *see also* **July**

octopus ['ɔktəpəs] *n* pulpo

odd [ɔd] *adj* (*strange*) extraño, raro; (*number*) impar; (*sock, shoe etc*) suelto; **60-~** 60 y pico; **at ~ times** de vez en cuando; **to be the ~ one out** estar de más; **if you have the ~ minute** si tienes unos minutos libres; *see also* **odds**

oddity ['ɔdɪtɪ] *n* rareza; (*person*) excéntrico(-a)

odd-job man [ɔd'dʒɔb-] *n* hombre *m* que hace chapuzas

odd jobs *npl* chapuzas *fpl*

oddly ['ɔdlɪ] *adv* extrañamente

oddments ['ɔdmənts] *npl* (*Brit Comm*) restos *mpl*

odds [ɔdz] *npl* (*in betting*) puntos *mpl* de ventaja; **it makes no ~** da lo mismo; **at ~** reñidos(-as); **to succeed against all the ~**

tener éxito contra todo pronóstico; **~ and ends** cachivaches *mpl*

odds-on [ɔdz'ɔn] *adj* (*inf*): **the ~ favourite** el máximo favorito; **it's ~ he'll come** seguro que viene

odometer [ɔ'dɔmɪtər] *n* (*US*) cuentakilómetros *m inv*

odour, odor (*US*) ['əudər] *n* olor *m*; (*unpleasant*) hedor *m*; (*perfume*) perfume *m*

oesophagus, esophagus (*US*) [i:'sɔfəgəs] *n* esófago

oestrogen, estrogen (*US*) ['i:strədʒən] *n* estrógeno

KEYWORD

of [ɔv, əv] *prep* **1** (*gen*) de; **a friend of ours** un amigo nuestro; **a boy of 10** un chico de 10 años; **that was kind of you** eso fue muy amable de tu parte

2 (*expressing quantity, amount, dates etc*) de; **a kilo of flour** un kilo de harina; **there were three of them** había tres; **three of us went** tres de nosotros fuimos; **the 5th of July** el 5 de julio; **a quarter of four** (*US*) las cuarto menos cuarto

3 (*from, out of*) de; **made of wood** (hecho) de madera

off [ɔf] *adj, adv* (*engine, light*) apagado; (*tap*) cerrado; (*Brit: food: bad*) pasado, malo; (: *milk*) cortado; (*cancelled*) suspendido; (*removed*): **the lid was ~** no estaba puesta la tapadera ▷ *prep* de; **to be ~** (*leave*) irse, marcharse; **to be ~ sick** estar enfermo *or* de baja; **a day ~** un día libre; **to have an ~ day** tener un mal día; **he had his coat ~** se había quitado el abrigo; **10% ~** (*Comm*) (con el) 10% de descuento; **it's a long way ~** está muy lejos; **5 km ~ (the road)** a 5 km (de la carretera); **~ the coast** frente a la costa; **I'm ~ meat** (*no longer eat/like it*) paso de la carne; **on the ~ chance** por si acaso; **~ and on, on and ~** de vez en cuando; **I must be ~** tengo que irme; **to be well/badly ~** andar bien/mal de dinero; **I'm afraid the chicken is ~** desgraciadamente ya no queda pollo; **that's a bit ~, isn't it?** (*fig, inf*) ¡eso no se hace!

offal ['ɔfl] *n* (*Brit Culin*) menudillos *mpl*, asaduras *fpl*

off-colour ['ɔf'kʌlər] *adj* (*Brit: ill*) indispuesto; **to feel ~** sentirse *or* estar mal

offence, offense (*US*) [ə'fɛns] *n* (*crime*) delito; (*insult*) ofensa; **to take ~ at** ofenderse por; **to commit an ~** cometer un delito

offend [ə'fɛnd] *vt* (*person*) ofender ▷ *vi*: **to ~ against** (*law, rule*) infringir

offender [ə'fɛndər] *n* delincuente *m/f*; (*against regulations*) infractor(a) *m(f)*

offense [ə'fɛns] *n* (*US*) = **offence**

offensive [ə'fɛnsɪv] *adj* ofensivo; (*smell etc*) repugnante ▷ *n* (*Mil*) ofensiva

offer ['ɔfər] *n* (*gen*) oferta, ofrecimiento; (*proposal*) propuesta ▷ *vt* ofrecer; **"on ~"** (*Comm*) "en oferta"; **to make an ~ for sth** hacer una oferta por algo; **to ~ sth to sb, ~ sb sth** ofrecer algo a algn; **to ~ to do sth** ofrecerse a hacer algo

offering ['ɔfərɪŋ] *n* (*Rel*) ofrenda

offertory ['ɔfətrɪ] *n* (*Rel*) ofertorio

offhand [ɔf'hænd] *adj* informal; (*brusque*) desconsiderado ▷ *adv* de improviso, sin pensarlo; **I can't tell you ~** no te lo puedo decir así de improviso *or* (*LAm*) así nomás

office ['ɔfɪs] *n* (*place*) oficina; (*room*) despacho; (*position*) cargo, oficio; **doctor's ~** (*US*) consultorio; **to take ~** entrar en funciones; **through his good ~s** gracias a sus buenos oficios; **O~ of Fair Trading** (*Brit*) oficina que regula normas comerciales

office automation *n* ofimática, buromática

office block, office building (*US*) *n* bloque *m* de oficinas

office hours *npl* horas *fpl* de oficina; (*US Med*) horas *fpl* de consulta

officer ['ɔfɪsər] *n* (*Mil etc*) oficial *m/f*; (*of organization*) director(a) *m(f)*; (*also*: **police ~**) agente *m/f* de policía

office work *n* trabajo de oficina

office worker *n* oficinista *m/f*

official [ə'fɪʃl] *adj* (*authorized*) oficial, autorizado; (*strike*) oficial ▷ *n* funcionario(-a)

officialdom [ə'fɪʃldəm] *n* burocracia

officiate [ə'fɪʃieɪt] *vi* (*Rel*) oficiar; **to ~ as Mayor** ejercer las funciones de alcalde; **to ~ at a marriage** celebrar una boda

officious [ə'fɪʃəs] *adj* oficioso

offing ['ɔfɪŋ] *n*: **in the ~** (*fig*) en perspectiva

off-licence ['ɔflaɪsns] *n* (*Brit: shop*) tienda de bebidas alcohólicas; *ver nota*

> ⬤ **OFF-LICENCE**
>
> ⬤ En el Reino Unido una *off-licence* es una
> ⬤ tienda especializada en la venta de
> ⬤ bebidas alcohólicas para el consumo
> ⬤ fuera del establecimiento. De ahí su
> ⬤ nombre, pues se necesita un permiso
> ⬤ especial para tal venta, que está
> ⬤ estrictamente regulada. Suelen vender
> ⬤ además bebidas sin alcohol, tabaco,
> ⬤ chocolate, patatas fritas etc y a menudo
> ⬤ son parte de grandes cadenas nacionales.

off-load ['ɔfləud] *vt* descargar, desembarcar

off-peak ['ɔf'pi:k] *adj* (*holiday*) de temporada baja; (*electricity*) de banda económica; (*ticket*) *billete de precio reducido por viajar fuera de las horas punta*

off-putting ['ɔfputɪŋ] *adj* (*Brit: person*) poco amable, difícil; (*behaviour*) chocante; (*remark*) desalentador(a)

o

off-season ['ɔf'siːzn] *adj, adv* fuera de
temporada

offset ['ɔfset] *vt* (*irreg: like* **set**) (*counteract*)
contrarrestar, compensar ▷ *n* (*also:*
~ printing) offset *m*

offshoot ['ɔfʃuːt] *n* (*Bot*) vástago; (*fig*)
ramificación *f*

offshore [ɔf'ʃɔːʳ] *adj* (*breeze, island*) costero;
(*fishing*) de bajura; **~ oilfield** campo
petrolífero submarino

offside ['ɔf'saɪd] *n* (*Aut: with right-hand drive*)
lado derecho; (: *with left-hand drive*) lado
izquierdo ▷ *adj* (*Sport*) fuera de juego; (*Aut: in
UK*) del lado derecho; (: *in US, Europe etc*) del
lado izquierdo

offspring ['ɔfsprɪŋ] *n* descendencia

offstage [ɔf'steɪdʒ] *adv* entre bastidores

off-the-cuff [ɔfðə'kʌf] *adj* espontáneo

off-the-peg [ɔfðə'pɛg], **off-the-rack** (US)
[ɔfðə'ræk] *adv* confeccionado

off-the-record [ɔfðə'rɛkɔːd] *adj* extraoficial,
confidencial ▷ *adv* extraoficialmente,
confidencialmente

off-white ['ɔfwaɪt] *adj* blanco grisáceo

often ['ɔfn] *adv* a menudo, con frecuencia,
seguido (*LAm*); **how ~ do you go?** ¿cada
cuánto vas?

ogle ['əugl] *vt* comerse con los ojos a

oh [əu] *excl* ¡ah!

oil [ɔɪl] *n* aceite *m*; (*petroleum*) petróleo
▷ *vt* (*machine*) engrasar; **fried in ~** frito en
aceite

oilcan ['ɔɪlkæn] *n* lata de aceite

oilfield ['ɔɪlfiːld] *n* campo petrolífero

oil filter *n* (*Aut*) filtro de aceite

oil painting *n* pintura al óleo

oil refinery *n* refinería de petróleo

oil rig *n* torre *f* de perforación

oilskins ['ɔɪlskɪnz] *npl* impermeable *msg*,
chubasquero *sg*

oil slick *n* marea negra

oil tanker *n* petrolero; (*truck*) camión *m*
cisterna

oil well *n* pozo (de petróleo)

oily ['ɔɪlɪ] *adj* aceitoso; (*food*) grasiento

ointment ['ɔɪntmənt] *n* ungüento

O.K., okay ['əu'keɪ] *excl* O.K., ¡está bien!,
¡vale! ▷ *adj* bien ▷ *n*: **to give sth one's ~** dar
el visto bueno a *or* aprobar algo ▷ *vt* dar el
visto bueno a; **it's ~ with** *or* **by me** estoy de
acuerdo, me parece bien; **are you ~ for
money?** ¿andas *or* vas bien de dinero?

old [əuld] *adj* viejo; (*former*) antiguo; **how ~
are you?** ¿cuántos años tienes?, ¿qué edad
tienes?; **he's 10 years ~** tiene 10 años; **~er
brother** hermano mayor; **any ~ thing will
do** sirve cualquier cosa

old age *n* vejez *f*

old-age pension ['əuldeɪdʒ-] *n* (*Brit*)
jubilación *f*, pensión *f*

old-age pensioner ['əuldeɪdʒ-] *n* (*Brit*)
jubilado(-a)

old-fashioned ['əuld'fæʃənd] *adj* anticuado,
pasado de moda

old people's home *n* (*esp Brit*) residencia *f* de
ancianos

olive ['ɔlɪv] *n* (*fruit*) aceituna; (*tree*) olivo ▷ *adj*
(*also:* **~-green**) verde oliva *inv*

olive oil *n* aceite *m* de oliva

Olympic [əu'lɪmpɪk] *adj* olímpico; **the ~
Games, the ~s** *npl* las Olimpíadas

omelette, omelet ['ɔmlɪt] *n* tortilla, tortilla
de huevo (*LAm*)

omen ['əumən] *n* presagio

ominous ['ɔmɪnəs] *adj* de mal agüero,
amenazador(-a)

omission [əu'mɪʃən] *n* omisión *f*; (*error*)
descuido

omit [əu'mɪt] *vt* omitir; (*by mistake*) olvidar,
descuidar; **to ~ to do sth** olvidarse *or* dejar
de hacer algo

🔵 **KEYWORD**

on [ɔn] *prep* **1** (*indicating position*) en; sobre; **on
the wall** en la pared; **it's on the table** está
sobre *or* en la mesa; **on the left** a la
izquierda; **I haven't got any money on me**
no llevo dinero encima

2 (*indicating means, method, condition etc*): **on
foot** a pie; **on the train/plane** (*go*) en tren/
avión; (*be*) en el tren/el avión; **on the radio/
television** por *or* en la radio/televisión;
on the telephone al teléfono; **to be on
drugs** drogarse; (*Med*) estar a tratamiento;
to be on holiday/business estar de
vacaciones/en viaje de negocios; **we're on
irregular verbs** estamos con los verbos
irregulares

3 (*referring to time*): **on Friday** el viernes; **on
Fridays** los viernes; **on June 20th** el 20 de
junio; **a week on Friday** del viernes en una
semana; **on arrival** al llegar; **on seeing this**
al ver esto

4 (*about, concerning*) sobre, acerca de; **a book
on physics** un libro de *or* sobre física

5 (*at the expense of*): **this round's on me** esta
ronda la pago yo, invito yo a esta ronda;
(*earning*): **he's on sixteen thousand pounds
a year** gana dieciséis mil libras al año

▷ *adv* **1** (*referring to dress*): **to have one's coat
on** tener *or* llevar el abrigo puesto; **she put
her gloves on** se puso los guantes

2 (*referring to covering*): **"screw the lid on
tightly"** "cerrar bien la tapa"

3 (*further, continuously*): **to walk/run** *etc* **on**
seguir caminando/corriendo *etc*; **from that
day on** desde aquel día; **it was well on in
the evening** estaba ya entrada la tarde

4 (*in phrases*): **I'm on to sth** creo haber
encontrado algo; **my father's always on at
me to get a job** (*inf*) mi padre siempre me
está dando la lata para que me ponga
a trabajar

▷ adj **1** (functioning, in operation: machine, radio, TV, light) encendido(-a) (Sp), prendido(-a) (LAm); (: tap) abierto(-a); (: brakes) echado(-a), puesto(-a); **is the meeting still on?** (in progress) ¿todavía continúa la reunión?; (not cancelled) ¿va a haber reunión al fin?; **there's a good film on at the cinema** ponen una buena película en el cine **2**: **that's not on!** (inf: not possible) ¡eso ni hablar!; (: not acceptable) ¡eso no se hace!

once [wʌns] adv una vez; (formerly) antiguamente ▷ conj una vez que; **~ he had left/it was done** una vez que se había marchado/se hizo; **at ~** en seguida, inmediatamente; (simultaneously) a la vez; **~ a week** una vez a la semana; **~ more** otra vez; **~ and for all** de una vez por todas; **~ upon a time** érase una vez; **I knew him ~** le conocía hace tiempo

oncoming ['ɔnkʌmɪŋ] adj (traffic) que viene de frente

KEYWORD

one [wʌn] num un/una; **one hundred and fifty** ciento cincuenta; **one by one** uno a uno; **it's one (o'clock)** es la una
▷ adj **1** (sole) único; **the one book which** el único libro que; **the one man who** el único que
2 (same) mismo(-a); **they came in the one car** vinieron en un solo coche
▷ pron **1**: **this one** éste/ésta; **that one** ése/ésa; (more remote) aquél/aquélla; **I've already got (a red) one** ya tengo uno(-a) (rojo(-a)); **one by one** uno por uno(-a); **to be one up on sb** llevar ventaja a algn; **to be at one (with sb)** estar completamente de acuerdo (con algn)
2: **one another** (us) nos; (you) os (Sp); (you: polite: them) se; **do you two ever see one another?** ¿os veis alguna vez? (Sp), ¿se ven alguna vez?; **the two boys didn't dare look at one another** los dos chicos no se atrevieron a mirarse (el uno al otro); **they all kissed one another** se besaron unos a otros
3 impers; **one never knows** nunca se sabe; **to cut one's finger** cortarse el dedo; **one needs to eat** hay que comer

one-day excursion ['wʌndeɪ-] n (US) billete m de ida y vuelta en un día
one-man ['wʌn'mæn] adj (business) individual
one-man band n hombre-orquesta m
one-off [wʌn'ɔf] n (Brit inf: object) artículo único; (: event) caso especial
one-parent family ['wʌnpɛərənt-] n familia monoparental
oneself [wʌn'sɛlf] pron (reflexive) se; (after prep) sí; (emphatic) uno(-a) mismo(-a); **to hurt ~**

hacerse daño; **to keep sth for ~** guardarse algo; **to talk to ~** hablar solo
one-shot [wʌn'ʃɔt] n (US) = **one-off**
one-sided [wʌn'saɪdɪd] adj (argument) parcial; (decision, view) unilateral; (game, contest) desigual
one-to-one ['wʌntəwʌn] adj (relationship) individualizado
one-upmanship [wʌn'ʌpmənʃɪp] n: **the art of ~** el arte de quedar siempre por encima
one-way ['wʌnweɪ] adj (street, traffic) de dirección única; (ticket) sencillo
ongoing ['ɔngəʊɪŋ] adj continuo
onion ['ʌnjən] n cebolla
online [ɔn'laɪn] adj, adv (Comput) en línea; (switched on) conectado
onlooker ['ɔnlʊkəʳ] n espectador(a) m(f)
only ['əʊnlɪ] adv solamente, sólo, nomás (LAm) ▷ adj único, solo ▷ conj solamente que, pero; **an ~ child** un hijo único; **not ~ ... but also ...** no sólo ... sino también ...; **I'd be ~ too pleased to help** encantado de ayudarles; **I saw her ~ yesterday** le vi ayer mismo; **I would come, ~ I'm very busy** iría, sólo que estoy muy atareado
on-screen [ɔn'skriːn] adj (Comput etc) en pantalla; (romance, kiss) cinematográfico
onset ['ɔnsɛt] n comienzo
onshore ['ɔnʃɔːʳ] adj (wind) que sopla del mar hacia la tierra
onslaught ['ɔnslɔːt] n ataque m, embestida
onto ['ɔntʊ] prep = **on to**
onus ['əʊnəs] n responsabilidad f; **the ~ is upon him to prove it** le incumbe a él demostrarlo
onward ['ɔnwəd], **onwards** ['ɔnwədz] adv (move) (hacia) adelante; **from that time ~** desde entonces en adelante
oops [ʊps] excl (also: **~-a-daisy!**) ¡huy!
ooze [uːz] vi rezumar
opaque [əʊ'peɪk] adj opaco
OPEC ['əʊpɛk] n abbr (= Organization of Petroleum-Exporting Countries) OPEP f
open ['əʊpn] adj abierto; (car) descubierto; (road, view) despejado; (meeting) público; (admiration) manifiesto ▷ vt abrir ▷ vi (flower, eyes, door, debate) abrirse; (book etc: commence) comenzar; **in the ~ (air)** al aire libre; **~ verdict** veredicto inconcluso; **~ ticket** billete m sin fecha; **~ ground** (among trees) claro; (waste ground) solar m; **to have an ~ mind (on sth)** estar sin decidirse aún (sobre algo); **to ~ a bank account** abrir una cuenta en el banco; **open on to** vt fus (room, door) dar a; **open out** vt abrir ▷ vi (person) abrirse; **open up** vt abrir; (blocked road) despejar ▷ vi abrirse
open day n (Brit) jornada de puertas abiertas or acceso público
opening ['əʊpnɪŋ] n abertura; (beginning) comienzo; (opportunity) oportunidad f; (job) puesto vacante, vacante f

O

opening hours *npl* horario de apertura
open learning *n* enseñanza flexible a tiempo parcial
openly ['əupnlɪ] *adv* abiertamente
open-minded [əupn'maɪndɪd] *adj* de amplias miras, sin prejuicios
open-necked ['əupnnɛkt] *adj* sin corbata
open-plan ['əupn'plæn] *adj* diáfano, sin tabiques
open prison *n* centro penitenciario de régimen abierto
Open University *n* (*Brit*) ≈ Universidad *f* Nacional de Enseñanza a Distancia, UNED *f*; *ver nota*

> OPEN UNIVERSITY
>
> La *Open University*, fundada en 1969, está especializada en impartir cursos a distancia y a tiempo parcial con sus propios materiales de apoyo diseñados para tal fin, entre ellos programas de radio y televisión emitidos por la "BBC". Los trabajos se envían por correo y se complementan con la asistencia obligatoria a cursos de verano. Para obtener la licenciatura es necesario estudiar un mínimo de módulos y alcanzar un determinado número de créditos.

opera ['ɔpərə] *n* ópera
opera house *n* teatro de la ópera
opera singer *n* cantante *m/f* de ópera
operate ['ɔpəreɪt] *vt* (*machine*) hacer funcionar; (*company*) dirigir ▷ *vi* funcionar; (*drug*) hacer efecto; **to ~ on sb** (*Med*) operar a algn
operatic [ɔpə'rætɪk] *adj* de ópera
operating room *n* (*US*) quirófano, sala de operaciones
operating table *n* mesa de operaciones
operating theatre *n* quirófano, sala de operaciones
operation [ɔpə'reɪʃən] *n* (*gen*) operación *f*; (*of machine*) funcionamiento; **to be in** = estar funcionando *or* en funcionamiento; **to have an** ~ (*Med*) ser operado; **to have an ~ for** operarse de; **the company's ~s during the year** las actividades de la compañía durante el año
operational [ɔpə'reɪʃənl] *adj* operacional, en buen estado; (*Comm*) en condiciones de servicio; (*ready for use or action*) en condiciones de funcionar; **when the service is fully ~** cuando el servicio esté en pleno funcionamiento
operative ['ɔpərətɪv] *adj* (*measure*) en vigor; **the ~ word** la palabra clave
operator ['ɔpəreɪtə*] *n* (*of machine*) operario(-a), maquinista *m/f*; (*Tel*) operador(a) *m(f)*, telefonista *m/f*

opinion [ə'pɪnjən] *n* (*gen*) opinión *f*; **in my ~** en mi opinión, a mi juicio; **to seek a second ~** pedir una segunda opinión
opinionated [ə'pɪnjəneɪtɪd] *adj* testarudo
opinion poll *n* encuesta, sondeo
opponent [ə'pəunənt] *n* adversario(-a), contrincante *m/f*
opportune ['ɔpətjuːn] *adj* oportuno
opportunity [ɔpə'tjuːnɪtɪ] *n* oportunidad *f*, chance *m or f* (*LAm*); **to take the ~ to do** *or* **of doing** aprovechar la ocasión para hacer
oppose [ə'pəuz] *vt* oponerse a; **to be ~d to sth** oponerse a algo; **as ~d to** en vez de; (*unlike*) a diferencia de
opposing [ə'pəuzɪŋ] *adj* (*side*) opuesto, contrario
opposite ['ɔpəzɪt] *adj* opuesto, contrario; (*house etc*) de enfrente ▷ *adv* en frente ▷ *prep* en frente de, frente a ▷ *n* lo contrario; **the ~ sex** el otro sexo, el sexo opuesto
opposite number *n* (*Brit*) homólogo(-a)
opposition [ɔpə'zɪʃən] *n* oposición *f*
oppress [ə'prɛs] *vt* oprimir
oppression [ə'prɛʃən] *n* opresión *f*
oppressive [ə'prɛsɪv] *adj* opresivo
opt [ɔpt] *vi*: **to ~ for** optar por; **to ~ to do** optar por hacer; **opt out** *vi*: **to ~ out of** optar por no hacer
optical ['ɔptɪkl] *adj* óptico
optical character reader *n* lector *m* óptico de caracteres
optical character recognition *n* reconocimiento *m* óptico de caracteres
optician [ɔp'tɪʃən] *n* óptico *m/f*
optimism ['ɔptɪmɪzəm] *n* optimismo
optimist ['ɔptɪmɪst] *n* optimista *m/f*
optimistic [ɔptɪ'mɪstɪk] *adj* optimista
optimum ['ɔptɪməm] *adj* óptimo
option ['ɔpʃən] *n* opción *f*; **to keep one's ~s open** (*fig*) mantener las opciones abiertas; **I have no ~** no tengo más *or* otro remedio
optional ['ɔpʃənl] *adj* opcional; (*course*) optativo; **~ extras** opciones *fpl* extras
or [ɔː*] *conj* o; (*before o, ho*) u; (*with negative*): **he hasn't seen or heard anything** no ha visto ni oído nada; **or else** si no; **let me go or I'll scream!** ¡suélteme, o me pongo a gritar!
oral ['ɔːrəl] *adj* oral ▷ *n* examen *m* oral
orange ['ɔrɪndʒ] *n* (*fruit*) naranja ▷ *adj* (de color) naranja
orange juice *n* jugo *m* de naranja, zumo *m* de naranja (*Sp*)
orange squash *n* bebida de naranja
orator ['ɔrətə*] *n* orador(a) *m(f)*
orbit ['ɔːbɪt] *n* órbita ▷ *vt, vi* orbitar; **to be in/ go into ~ (round)** estar en/entrar en órbita (alrededor de)
orbital ['ɔːbɪtl] *n* (*also:* **~ motorway**) autopista de circunvalación
orchard ['ɔːtʃəd] *n* huerto; **apple ~** manzanar *m*, manzanal *m*

orchestra [ˈɔːkɪstrə] n orquesta; (US: seating) platea

orchid [ˈɔːkɪd] n orquídea

ordain [ɔːˈdeɪn] vt (Rel) ordenar

ordeal [ɔːˈdiːl] n experiencia terrible

order [ˈɔːdəʳ] n orden m; (command) orden f; (type, kind) clase f; (state) estado; (Comm) pedido, encargo ▷ vt (also: **put in ~**) ordenar, poner en orden; (Comm) encargar, pedir; (command) mandar, ordenar; **in ~** (gen) en orden; (of document) en regla; **in (working) ~** en funcionamiento; **a machine in working ~** una máquina en funcionamiento; **to be out of ~** estar desordenado; (not working) no funcionar; **in ~ to do** para hacer; **in ~ that** para que + subjun; **on ~** (Comm) pedido; **to be on ~** estar pedido; **we are under ~s to do it** tenemos orden de hacerlo; **a point of ~** una cuestión de procedimiento; **to place an ~ for sth with sb** hacer un pedido de algo a algn; **made to ~** hecho a la medida; **his income is of the ~ of £24,000 per year** sus ingresos son del orden de 24 mil libras al año; **to the ~ of** (Banking) a la orden de; **to ~ sb to do sth** mandar a algn hacer algo

order form n hoja de pedido

orderly [ˈɔːdəlɪ] n (Mil) ordenanza m; (Med) auxiliar m/f (de hospital) ▷ adj ordenado

ordinary [ˈɔːdnrɪ] adj corriente, normal; (pej) común y corriente; **out of the ~** fuera de lo común, extraordinario

ordinary degree n (Brit) diploma m; ver nota

ordination [ɔːdɪˈneɪʃən] n ordenación f

Ordnance Survey n (Brit) servicio oficial de topografía y cartografía

ore [ɔːʳ] n mineral m

oregano [ɔrɪˈɡɑːnəu] n orégano

organ [ˈɔːɡən] n órgano

organic [ɔːˈɡænɪk] adj orgánico; (vegetables, produce) biológico

organism [ˈɔːɡənɪzəm] n organismo

organist [ˈɔːɡənɪst] n organista m/f

organization [ɔːɡənaɪˈzeɪʃən] n organización f

organize [ˈɔːɡənaɪz] vt organizar

organized [ˈɔːɡənaɪzd] adj organizado; **to get ~** organizarse

organized crime n crimen organizado

organizer [ˈɔːɡənaɪzəʳ] n organizador(-a) m(f)

orgasm [ˈɔːɡæzəm] n orgasmo

orgy [ˈɔːdʒɪ] n orgía

Orient [ˈɔːrɪənt] n Oriente m

oriental [ɔːrɪˈentl] adj oriental

orientation [ɔːrɪenˈteɪʃən] n orientación f

origin [ˈɔrɪdʒɪn] n origen m; (point of departure) procedencia

original [əˈrɪdʒɪnl] adj original; (first) primero; (earlier) primitivo ▷ n original m

originality [ərɪdʒɪˈnælɪtɪ] n originalidad f

originally [əˈrɪdʒɪnəlɪ] adv (at first) al principio; (with originality) con originalidad

originate [əˈrɪdʒɪneɪt] vi: **to ~ from, to ~ in** surgir de, tener su origen en

Orkneys [ˈɔːknɪz] npl: **the ~** (also: **the Orkney Islands**) las Orcadas

ornament [ˈɔːnəmənt] n adorno; (trinket) chuchería

ornamental [ɔːnəˈmentl] adj decorativo, de adorno

ornate [ɔːˈneɪt] adj recargado

ornithology [ɔːnɪˈθɔlədʒɪ] n ornitología

orphan [ˈɔːfn] n huérfano(-a) ▷ vt: **to be ~ed** quedar huérfano(-a)

orphanage [ˈɔːfənɪdʒ] n orfanato

orthodox [ˈɔːθədɔks] adj ortodoxo

orthopaedic, orthopedic (US) [ɔːθəˈpiːdɪk] adj ortopédico

Oscar [ˈɔskəʳ] n óscar m

ostensible [ɔsˈtensɪbl] adj aparente

ostensibly [ɔsˈtensɪblɪ] adv aparentemente

ostentatious [ɔstenˈteɪʃəs] adj pretencioso, aparatoso; (person) ostentativo

osteopath [ˈɔstɪəpæθ] n osteópata m/f

ostracize [ˈɔstrəsaɪz] vt hacer el vacío a

ostrich [ˈɔstrɪtʃ] n avestruz m

other [ˈʌðəʳ] adj otro ▷ pron: **the ~ one** el/la otro(-a); **~s** (other people) otros; **~ than** (apart from) aparte de; **the ~ day** el otro día; **some ~ people have still to arrive** quedan por llegar otros; **some actor or ~** un actor cualquiera; **somebody or ~** alguien, alguno; **it was no ~ than the bishop** no era otro que el obispo

otherwise [ˈʌðəwaɪz] adv, conj de otra manera; (if not) si no; **an ~ good piece of work** un trabajo que, quitando eso, es bueno

OTT abbr (inf) = **over the top**; see **top**

otter [ˈɔtəʳ] n nutria

ouch [autʃ] excl ¡ay!

ought (pt **ought**) [ɔːt] aux vb: **I ~ to do it** debería hacerlo; **this ~ to have been corrected** esto debiera de haberse corregido; **he ~ to win** (probability) debiera ganar; **you ~ to go and see it** vale la pena ir a verlo

ounce [auns] n onza (=28.35g; 16oz = 1lb)

our [ˈauəʳ] adj nuestro; see also **my**

ours [ˈauəz] pron (el) nuestro/(la) nuestra etc; see also **mine**

ourselves [auəˈselvz] pron pl (reflexive, after prep) nosotros; (emphatic) nosotros mismos; **we did it (all) by ~** lo hicimos nosotros solos; see also **oneself**

oust [aust] vt desalojar

out [aut] adv fuera, afuera; (not at home) fuera (de casa); (light, fire) apagado; (on strike) en huelga ▷ vt: **to ~ sb** revelar públicamente la homosexualidad de algn; **~ there** allí (fuera); **he's ~** (absent) no está, ha salido; **to be ~ in one's calculations** equivocarse (en sus cálculos); **to run ~** salir corriendo; **~ loud** en alta voz; **~ of** prep (outside) fuera de; (because of: anger etc) por; **to look ~ of the window** mirar por la ventana; **to drink ~**

of a cup beber de una taza; **made ~ of wood** de madera; **~ of petrol** sin gasolina; **"~ of order"** "no funciona"; **it's ~ of stock** (*Comm*) está agotado; **to be ~ and about again** estar repuesto y levantado; **the journey ~** el viaje de ida; **the boat was 10 km ~** el barco estaba a 10 kilómetros de la costa; **before the week was ~** antes del fin de la semana; **he's ~ for all he can get** busca sus propios fines, anda detrás de lo suyo

out-and-out ['autəndaut] *adj* (*liar, thief etc*) redomado, empedernido

outback ['autbæk] *n* interior *m*

outboard ['autbɔːd] *adj*: **~ motor** (motor *m*) fuera borda *m*

outbound ['autbaund] *adj* (*flight*) de salida; (*flight: not return*) de ida; **~ from/for** con salida de/hacia

outbreak ['autbreɪk] *n* (*of war*) comienzo; (*of disease*) epidemia; (*of violence etc*) ola

outburst ['autbəːst] *n* explosión *f*, arranque *m*

outcast ['autkɑːst] *n* paria *m/f*

outcome ['autkʌm] *n* resultado

outcrop ['autkrɒp] *n* (*of rock*) afloramiento

outcry ['autkraɪ] *n* protestas *fpl*

outdated [aut'deɪtɪd] *adj* anticuado

outdo [aut'duː] *vt* (*irreg: like* **do**) superar

outdoor [aut'dɔːʳ] *adj* al aire libre; (*clothes*) de calle

outdoors [aut'dɔːz] *adv* al aire libre

outer ['autəʳ] *adj* exterior, externo

outer space *n* espacio exterior

outfit ['autfɪt] *n* equipo; (*clothes*) traje *m*; (*inf: organization*) grupo, organización *f*

outgoing ['autgəuɪŋ] *adj* (*president, tenant*) saliente; (*means of transport*) que sale; (*character*) extrovertido

outgoings ['autgəuɪŋz] *npl* (*Brit*) gastos *mpl*

outgrow [aut'grəu] *vt* (*irreg: like* **grow**): **he has ~n his clothes** su ropa le queda pequeña ya

outhouse ['authaus] *n* dependencia

outing ['autɪŋ] *n* excursión *f*, paseo

outlandish [aut'lændɪʃ] *adj* estrafalario

outlaw ['autlɔː] *n* proscrito(-a) ▷ *vt* (*person*) declarar fuera de la ley; (*practice*) declarar ilegal

outlay ['autleɪ] *n* inversión *f*

outlet ['autlɛt] *n* salida; (*of pipe*) desagüe *m*; (*US Elec*) toma de corriente; (*for emotion*) desahogo; (*also:* **retail ~**) punto de venta

outline ['autlaɪn] *n* (*shape*) contorno, perfil *m*; (*sketch, plan*) esbozo ▷ *vt* (*plan etc*) esbozar; **in ~** (*fig*) a grandes rasgos

outlive ['autlɪv] *vt* sobrevivir a

outlook ['autluk] *n* (*fig: prospects*) perspectivas *fpl*; (*: for weather*) pronóstico; (*opinion*) punto de vista

outlying ['autlaɪɪŋ] *adj* remoto, aislado

outmoded [aut'məudɪd] *adj* anticuado, pasado de moda

outnumber [aut'nʌmbəʳ] *vt* exceder or superar en número

out-of-date [autəv'deɪt] *adj* (*passport*) caducado, vencido; (*theory, idea*) anticuado; (*clothes, customs*) pasado de moda

out-of-doors [autəv'dɔːz] *adv* al aire libre

out-of-the-way [autəvðə'weɪ] *adj* (*remote*) apartado; (*unusual*) poco común or corriente

out-of-town [autəv'taun] *adj* (*shopping centre etc*) en las afueras

outpatient ['autpeɪʃənt] *n* paciente *m/f* externo(-a)

outpost ['autpəust] *n* puesto avanzado

output ['autput] *n* (*volumen m* de) producción *f*, rendimiento; (*Comput*) salida ▷ *vt* (*Comput: to power*) imprimir

outrage ['autreɪdʒ] *n* (*scandal*) escándalo; (*atrocity*) atrocidad *f* ▷ *vt* ultrajar

outrageous [aut'reɪdʒəs] *adj* (*clothes*) extravagante; (*behaviour*) escandaloso

outright [aut'raɪt] *adv* (*ask, deny*) francamente; (*refuse*) rotundamente; (*win*) de manera absoluta; (*be killed*) en el acto; (*completely*) completamente ▷ *adj* ['autraɪt] completo; (*winner*) absoluto; (*refusal*) rotundo

outset ['autsɛt] *n* principio

outside [aut'saɪd] *n* exterior *m* ▷ *adj* exterior, externo ▷ *adv* fuera, afuera (*LAm*) ▷ *prep* fuera de; (*beyond*) más allá de; **at the ~** (*fig*) a lo sumo; **an ~ chance** una posibilidad remota; **~ left/right** (*esp Football*) extremo izquierdo/derecho

outside lane *n* (*Aut: in Britain*) carril *m* de la derecha; (*: in US, Europe etc*) carril *m* de la izquierda

outside line *n* (*Tel*) línea (exterior)

outsider [aut'saɪdəʳ] *n* (*stranger*) forastero(-a)

outsize ['autsaɪz] *adj* (*clothes*) de talla grande

outskirts ['autskəːts] *npl* alrededores *mpl*, afueras *fpl*

outspoken [aut'spəukən] *adj* muy franco

outstanding [aut'stændɪŋ] *adj* excepcional, destacado; (*unfinished*) pendiente

outstay [aut'steɪ] *vt*: **to ~ one's welcome** quedarse más de la cuenta

outstretched [aut'strɛtʃt] *adj* (*arm*) extendido

outstrip [aut'strɪp] *vt* (*competitors, demand: also fig*) dejar atrás, aventajar

out-tray ['auttreɪ] *n* bandeja de salida

outward ['autwəd] *adj* (*sign, appearances*) externo; (*journey*) de ida

outwardly ['autwədlɪ] *adv* por fuera

outwards [autwədz] *adj* (*esp Brit*) = **outward**

outweigh [aut'weɪ] *vt* pesar más que

outwit [aut'wɪt] *vt* ser más listo que

oval ['əuvl] *adj* ovalado ▷ *n* óvalo

ovary ['əuvərɪ] *n* ovario

ovation [əu'veɪʃən] *n* ovación *f*

oven ['ʌvn] *n* horno

oven glove *n* guante *m* para el horno, manopla para el horno

ovenproof ['ʌvnpruːf] *adj* refractario, resistente al horno

oven-ready ['ʌvnrɛdɪ] *adj* listo para el horno

over ['əuvəʳ] *adv* encima, por encima ▷ *adj* (*finished*) terminado; (*surplus*) de sobra; (*excessively*) demasiado ▷ *prep* (por) encima de; (*above*) sobre; (*on the other side of*) al otro lado de; (*more than*) más de; (*during*) durante; (*about, concerning*): **they fell out ~ money** riñeron por una cuestión de dinero; **~ here** (por) aquí; **~ there** (por) allí *or* allá; **all ~** (*everywhere*) por todas partes; **~ and ~ (again)** una y otra vez; **~ and above** además de; **to ask sb ~** invitar a algn a casa; **to bend ~** inclinarse; **now ~ to our Paris correspondent** damos la palabra a nuestro corresponsal de París; **the world ~** en todo el mundo, en el mundo entero; **she's not ~ intelligent** no es muy lista que digamos

overall ['əuvərɔːl] *adj* (*length*) total; (*study*) de conjunto ▷ *adv* [əuvər'ɔːl] en conjunto ▷ *n* (*Brit*) guardapolvo; **overalls** *npl* mono *sg*, overol *msg* (*LAm*)

overall majority *n* mayoría absoluta

overanxious [əuvər'æŋkʃəs] *adj* demasiado preocupado *or* ansioso

overawe [əuvər'ɔː] *vt* intimidar

overbalance [əuvə'bæləns] *vi* perder el equilibrio

overbearing [əuvə'bɛərɪŋ] *adj* autoritario, imperioso

overboard ['əuvəbɔːd] *adv* (*Naut*) por la borda; **to go ~ for sth** (*fig*) enloquecer por algo

overbook [əuvə'buk] *vt* sobrereservar, reservar con exceso

overcame [əuvə'keɪm] *pt of* **overcome**

overcast ['əuvəkɑːst] *adj* encapotado

overcharge [əuvə'tʃɑːdʒ] *vt*: **to ~ sb** cobrar un precio excesivo a algn

overcoat ['əuvəkəut] *n* abrigo

overcome [əuvə'kʌm] *vt* (*irreg: like* **come**) (*gen*) vencer; (*difficulty*) superar; **she was quite ~ by the occasion** la ocasión le conmovió mucho

overconfident [əuvə'kɔnfɪdənt] *adj* demasiado confiado

overcrowded [əuvə'kraudɪd] *adj* atestado de gente; (*city, country*) superpoblado

overdo [əuvə'duː] *vt* (*irreg: like* **do**) exagerar; (*overcook*) cocer demasiado; **to ~ it** (*work etc*) pasarse

overdone [əuvə'dʌn] *adj* (*vegetables*) recocido; (*steak*) demasiado hecho

overdose ['əuvədəus] *n* sobredosis *f inv*

overdraft ['əuvədrɑːft] *n* saldo deudor

overdrawn [əuvə'drɔːn] *adj* (*account*) en descubierto

overdrive ['əuvədraɪv] *n* (*Aut*) sobremarcha, superdirecta

overdue [əuvə'djuː] *adj* retrasado; (*recognition*) tardío; (*bill*) vencido y no pagado;

that change was long ~ ese cambio tenía que haberse hecho hace tiempo

overemphasis [əuvər'ɛmfəsɪs] *n*: **to put an ~ on** poner énfasis excesivo en

overestimate [əuvər'ɛstɪmeɪt] *vt* sobreestimar

overexcited [əuvərɪk'saɪtɪd] *adj* sobreexcitado

overflow [əuvə'fləu] *vi* desbordarse ▷ *n* ['əuvəfləu] (*excess*) exceso; (*of river*) desbordamiento; (*also*: **~ pipe**) (cañería de) desagüe *m*

overgrown [əuvə'grəun] *adj* (*garden*) cubierto de hierba; **he's just an ~ schoolboy** es un niño en grande

overhaul *vt* [əuvə'hɔːl] revisar, repasar ▷ *n* ['əuvəhɔːl] revisión *f*

overhead *adv* [əuvə'hɛd] por arriba *or* encima ▷ *adj* ['əuvəhɛd] (*cable*) aéreo; (*railway*) elevado, aéreo ▷ *n* ['əuvəhɛd] (*US*) = **overheads**

overhead projector *n* retroproyector

overheads ['əuvəhɛdz] *npl* (*Brit*) gastos *mpl* generales

overhear [əuvə'hɪəʳ] *vt* (*irreg: like* **hear**) oír por casualidad

overheat [əuvə'hiːt] *vi* (*engine*) recalentarse

overjoyed [əuvə'dʒɔɪd] *adj* encantado, lleno de alegría

overkill ['əuvəkɪl] *n* (*Mil*) capacidad *f* excesiva de destrucción; (*fig*) exceso

overland ['əuvəlænd] *adj, adv* por tierra

overlap *vi* [əuvə'læp] superponerse ▷ *n* ['əuvəlæp] superposición *f*

overleaf [əuvə'liːf] *adv* al dorso

overload [əuvə'ləud] *vt* sobrecargar

overlook [əuvə'luk] *vt* (*have view of*) dar a, tener vistas a; (*miss*) pasar por alto; (*excuse*) perdonar

overnight [əuvə'naɪt] *adv* durante la noche; (*fig*) de la noche a la mañana ▷ *adj* de noche; **to stay ~** pasar la noche

overnight bag *n* fin *m* de semana, neceser *m* de viaje

overpass ['əuvəpɑːs] *n* (*US*) paso elevado *or* a desnivel

overpay [əuvə'peɪ] *vt*: **to ~ sb by £50** pagar 50 libras de más a algn

overplay [əuvə'pleɪ] *vt* exagerar; **to ~ one's hand** desmedirse

overpower [əuvə'pauəʳ] *vt* dominar; (*fig*) embargar

overpowering [əuvə'pauərɪŋ] *adj* (*heat*) agobiante; (*smell*) penetrante

overrate [əuvə'reɪt] *vt* sobrevalorar

overreact [əuvərɪ'ækt] *vi* reaccionar de manera exagerada

override [əuvə'raɪd] *vt* (*irreg: like* **ride**) (*order, objection*) no hacer caso de

overriding [əuvə'raɪdɪŋ] *adj* predominante

overrule [əuvə'ruːl] *vt* (*decision*) anular; (*claim*) denegar

o

overrun [əuvə'rʌn] vt (irreg: like **run**)
(Mil: country) invadir; (time limit) rebasar,
exceder ▷ vi rebasar el límite previsto;
the town is ~ with tourists el pueblo está
inundado de turistas

overseas [əuvə'siːz] adv en ultramar; (abroad)
en el extranjero ▷ adj (trade) exterior; (visitor)
extranjero

oversee [əuvə'siː] (irreg: like **see**) vt supervisar

overshadow [əuvə'ʃædəu] vt (fig) eclipsar;
to be ~ed by estar a la sombra de

oversight ['əuvəsaɪt] n descuido; **due to an
~** a causa de un descuido or una equivocación

oversleep [əuvə'sliːp] vi (irreg: like **sleep**)
dormir más de la cuenta, no despertarse
a tiempo

overspend [əuvə'spɛnd] vi (irreg: like **spend**)
gastar más de la cuenta; **we have overspent
by five dollars** hemos excedido el
presupuesto en cinco dólares

overstate [əuvə'steɪt] vt exagerar

overstay [əuvə'steɪ] vt: **to ~ one's time** or
welcome quedarse más de lo conveniente

overstep [əuvə'stɛp] vt: **to ~ the mark** or
the limits pasarse de la raya

overt [əu'vəːt] adj abierto

overtake [əuvə'teɪk] vt (irreg: like **take**)
sobrepasar; (Brit Aut) adelantar

overthrow [əuvə'θrəu] vt (irreg: like **throw**)
(government) derrocar

overtime ['əuvətaɪm] n horas fpl
extraordinarias; **to do** or **work ~** hacer or
trabajar horas extraordinarias or extras

overtone ['əuvətəun] n (fig) tono

overtook [əuvə'tuk] pt of **overtake**

overture ['əuvətʃuəʳ] n (Mus) obertura; (fig)
propuesta

overturn [əuvə'təːn] vt volcar; (fig: plan)
desbaratar; (: government) derrocar ▷ vi volcar

overview ['əuvəvjuː] n visión f de conjunto

overweight [əuvə'weɪt] adj demasiado
gordo or pesado

overwhelm [əuvə'wɛlm] vt aplastar

overwhelming [əuvə'wɛlmɪŋ] adj (victory,
defeat) arrollador(a); (desire) irresistible;
one's ~ impression is of heat lo que más
impresiona es el calor

overwork [əuvə'wəːk] n trabajo excesivo ▷ vt
hacer trabajar demasiado ▷ vi trabajar
demasiado

overwrite [əuvə'raɪt] vt (irreg: like **write**)
(Comput: file, disk) sobre(e)scribir

overwrought [əuvə'rɔːt] adj sobreexcitado

owe [əu] vt deber; **to ~ sb sth, to ~ sth to sb**
deber algo a algn

owing to ['əuɪŋtuː] prep debido a, por causa de

owl [aul] n (also: **long-eared ~**) búho; (also:
barn ~) lechuza

own [əun] vt tener, poseer ▷ vi: **to ~ to sth/to
having done sth** confesar or reconocer algo/
haber hecho algo ▷ adj propio; **a room of
my ~** mi propia habitación; **to get one's ~**

back tomarse la revancha; **on one's ~** solo,
a solas; **can I have it for my (very) ~?**
¿puedo quedarme con él?; **to come into
one's ~** llegar a realizarse; **own up** vi
confesar

owner ['əunəʳ] n dueño(-a)

ownership ['əunəʃɪp] n posesión f; **it's
under new ~** está bajo nueva dirección

own goal n (Sport) autogol m; **to score an ~**
marcar un gol en propia puerta, marcar un
autogol

ox (pl **oxen**) [ɔks, 'ɔksn] n buey m

Oxbridge ['ɔksbrɪdʒ] n universidades de Oxford y
Cambridge; ver nota

> ● OXBRIDGE
> ●
> ● El término Oxbridge es una fusión de
> ● Ox(ford) y (Cam)bridge, las dos
> ● universidades británicas más antiguas
> ● y con mayor prestigio académico y social.
> ● Muchos miembros destacados de la clase
> ● dirigente del país son antiguos alumnos
> ● de una de las dos. El mismo término suele
> ● aplicarse a todo lo que ambas representan
> ● en cuestión de prestigio y privilegios
> ● sociales.

oxen ['ɔksən] npl of **ox**

oxide ['ɔksaɪd] n óxido

oxtail ['ɔksteɪl] n: **~ soup** sopa de rabo de
buey

oxygen ['ɔksɪdʒən] n oxígeno

oxygen mask n máscara de oxígeno

oyster ['ɔɪstəʳ] n ostra

oz. abbr = **ounce(s)**

ozone ['əuzəun] n ozono

ozone friendly adj que no daña la capa de
ozono

ozone layer n capa de ozono

P

P, p [pi:] *n* (*letter*) P, p *f*; **P for Peter** P de París

P *abbr* = **president; prince**

p *abbr* (= *page*) pág.; (*Brit*) = **penny; pence**

PA *n abbr* = **personal assistant; public address system**

pa [pɑ:] *n* (*inf*) papá *m*

p.a. *abbr* = **per annum**

pace [peɪs] *n* paso; (*rhythm*) ritmo ▷ *vi*: **to ~ up and down** pasearse de un lado a otro; **to keep ~ with** llevar el mismo paso que; (*events*) mantenerse a la altura de *or* al corriente de; **to set the ~** (*running*) marcar el paso; (*fig*) marcar la pauta; **to put sb through his ~s** (*fig*) poner a algn a prueba

pacemaker ['peɪsmeɪkəʳ] *n* (*Med*) marcapasos *m inv*; (*Sport*: *also*: **pacesetter**) liebre *f*

pacific [pə'sɪfɪk] *adj* pacífico ▷ *n*: **the P~ (Ocean)** el (Océano) Pacífico

pacifier ['pæsɪfaɪəʳ] *n* (*US*: *dummy*) chupete *m*

pacifist ['pæsɪfɪst] *n* pacifista *m/f*

pack [pæk] *n* (*packet*) paquete *m*; (*Comm*) embalaje *m*; (*of hounds*) jauría; (*of people*) manada; (*of thieves etc*) banda; (*of cards*) baraja; (*bundle*) fardo; (*US*: *of cigarettes*) paquete *m*, cajetilla ▷ *vt* (*wrap*) empaquetar; (*fill*) llenar; (*in suitcase etc*) meter, poner; (*cram*) llenar, atestar; (*fig*: *meeting etc*) llenar de partidarios; (*Comput*) comprimir; **to ~ (one's bags)** hacer las maletas; **to ~ sb off** despachar a algn; **the place was ~ed** el local estaba (lleno) hasta los topes; **to send sb ~ing** (*inf*) echar a algn con cajas destempladas; **pack in** *vi* (*break down*: *watch, car*) estropearse ▷ *vt* (*inf*) dejar; **~ it in!** ¡para!, ¡basta ya!; **pack up** *vi* (*inf*: *machine*) estropearse; (*person*) irse ▷ *vt* (*belongings, clothes*) recoger; (*goods, presents*) empaquetar, envolver

package ['pækɪdʒ] *n* paquete *m*; (*bulky*) bulto; (*Comput*) paquete *m* (*de software*); (*also*: **~ deal**) acuerdo global ▷ *vt* (*Comm*: *goods*) envasar, embalar

package holiday *n* viaje *m* organizado (con todo incluido)

package tour *n* viaje *m* organizado

packaging ['pækɪdʒɪŋ] *n* envase *m*

packed [pækt] *adj* abarrotado

packed lunch [pækt-] *n* almuerzo frío

packet ['pækɪt] *n* paquete *m*

packing ['pækɪŋ] *n* embalaje *m*

packing case *n* cajón *m* de embalaje

pact [pækt] *n* pacto

pad [pæd] *n* (*of paper*) bloc *m*; (*cushion*) cojinete *m*; (*launching pad*) plataforma (de lanzamiento); (*inf*: *flat*) casa ▷ *vt* rellenar

padded ['pædɪd] *adj* (*jacket*) acolchado; (*bra*) reforzado

padded cell *n* celda acolchada

padding ['pædɪŋ] *n* relleno; (*fig*) paja

paddle ['pædl] *n* (*oar*) canalete *m*, pala; (*US*: *for table tennis*) pala ▷ *vt* remar ▷ *vi* (*with feet*) chapotear

paddle steamer *n* vapor *m* de ruedas

paddling pool ['pædlɪŋ-] *n* (*Brit*) piscina para niños

paddock ['pædək] *n* (*field*) potrero

paddy field ['pædɪ-] *n* arrozal *m*

padlock ['pædlɔk] *n* candado ▷ *vt* cerrar con candado

paediatrician, pediatrician (*US*) [pi:dɪə'trɪʃən] *n* pediatra *m/f*

paediatrics, pediatrics (*US*) [pi:dɪ'ætrɪks] *n* pediatría

paedophile, pedophile (*US*) ['pi:dəufaɪl] *adj* de pedófilos ▷ *n* pedófilo(-a)

pagan ['peɪgən] *adj, n* pagano(-a) *m(f)*

page [peɪdʒ] *n* página; (*of newspaper*) plana; (*also*: **~ boy**) paje *m* ▷ *vt* (*in hotel etc*) llamar por altavoz a

pageant ['pædʒənt] *n* (*procession*) desfile *m*; (*show*) espectáculo

pageantry ['pædʒəntrɪ] *n* pompa

pager ['peɪdʒəʳ] *n* busca *m*

pagination [pædʒɪ'neɪʃən] *n* paginación *f*

paid [peɪd] *pt, pp* de **pay** ▷ *adj* (*work*) remunerado; (*holiday*) pagado; (*official*) a sueldo; **to put ~ to** (*Brit*) acabar con

paid-up ['peɪdʌp], **paid-in** (*US*) ['peɪdɪn] *adj* (*member*) con sus cuotas pagadas *or* al día; (*share*) liberado; **~ capital** capital *m* desembolsado

pail [peɪl] *n* cubo, balde *m*

pain [peɪn] *n* dolor *m*; **to be in ~** sufrir; **on ~ of death** so *or* bajo pena de muerte; *see also* **pains**

pained [peɪnd] *adj (expression)* afligido

painful ['peɪnful] *adj* doloroso; *(difficult)* penoso; *(disagreeable)* desagradable

painfully ['peɪnfəlɪ] *adv (fig: very)* terriblemente

painkiller ['peɪnkɪlə'] *n* analgésico

painless ['peɪnlɪs] *adj* sin dolor; *(method)* fácil

pains [peɪnz] *npl (efforts)* esfuerzos *mpl*; **to take ~ to do sth** tomarse el trabajo de hacer algo

painstaking ['peɪnzteɪkɪŋ] *adj (person)* concienzudo, esmerado

paint [peɪnt] *n* pintura ▷ *vt* pintar; **a tin of ~** un bote de pintura; **to ~ the door blue** pintar la puerta de azul

paintbrush ['peɪntbrʌʃ] *n (artist's)* pincel *m*; *(decorator's)* brocha

painter ['peɪntə'] *n* pintor(a) *m(f)*

painting ['peɪntɪŋ] *n* pintura

paintwork ['peɪntwɜːk] *n* pintura

pair [peə'] *n (of shoes, gloves etc)* par *m*; *(of people)* pareja; **a ~ of scissors** unas tijeras; **a ~ of trousers** unos pantalones, un pantalón; **pair off** *vi*: **to ~ off (with sb)** hacer pareja (con algn)

pajamas [pɪ'dʒɑːmaz] *npl (US)* pijama *msg*, piyama *msg (LAm)*

Pakistan [pɑːkɪ'stɑːn] *n* Paquistán *m*

Pakistani [pɑːkɪ'stɑːnɪ] *adj, n* paquistaní *m/f*

pal [pæl] *n (inf)* amiguete(-a) *m(f)*, colega *m/f*

palace ['pæləs] *n* palacio

palatable ['pælɪtəbl] *adj* sabroso; *(acceptable)* aceptable

palate ['pælɪt] *n* paladar *m*

pale [peɪl] *adj (gen)* pálido; *(colour)* claro ▷ *n*: **to be beyond the ~** pasarse de la raya ▷ *vi* palidecer; **to grow** *o* **turn ~** palidecer; **to ~ into insignificance (beside)** no poderse comparar (con)

Palestine ['pælɪstaɪn] *n* Palestina

Palestinian [pælɪs'tɪnɪən] *adj, n* palestino(-a) *m(f)*

palette ['pælɪt] *n* paleta

pall [pɔːl] *n (of smoke)* cortina ▷ *vi* cansar

pallet ['pælɪt] *n (for goods)* pallet *m*

pallid ['pælɪd] *adj* pálido

palm [pɑːm] *n (Anat)* palma; *(also: ~ tree)* palmera, palma ▷ *vt*: **to ~ sth off on sb** *(Brit)* *(inf)* endosarle algo a algn

Palm Sunday *n* Domingo de Ramos

palpable ['pælpəbl] *adj* palpable

paltry ['pɔːltrɪ] *adj (amount etc)* miserable; *(insignificant: person)* insignificante

pamper ['pæmpə'] *vt* mimar

pamphlet ['pæmflət] *n* folleto; *(political: handed out in street)* panfleto

pan [pæn] *n (also: sauce~)* cacerola, cazuela, olla; *(also: frying ~)* sartén *f*; *(of lavatory)* taza ▷ *vi (Cine)* tomar panorámicas; **to ~ for gold** cribar oro

pan- [pæn] *pref* pan-

Panama ['pænəmɑː] *n* Panamá *m*

Panama Canal *n* el Canal de Panamá

pancake ['pænkeɪk] *n* crepe *f*, panqueque *m (LAm)*

pancreas ['pæŋkrɪəs] *n* páncreas *m*

panda ['pændə] *n* panda *m*

panda car *n (Brit)* coche *m* de la policía

pandemonium [pændɪ'məʊnɪəm] *n (noise)*: **there was ~** se armó un tremendo jaleo; *(mess)* caos *m*

pander ['pændə'] *vi*: **to ~ to** complacer a

p & p *abbr (Brit: = postage and packing)* gastos de envío

pane [peɪn] *n* cristal *m*

panel ['pænl] *n (of wood)* panel *m*; *(of cloth)* paño; *(Radio, TV)* panel *m* de invitados

panelling, paneling (US) ['pænəlɪŋ] *n* paneles *mpl*

pang [pæŋ] *n*: **~s of conscience** remordimientos *mpl*; **~s of hunger** dolores *mpl* del hambre

panhandler ['pænhændlə'] *n (US inf)* mendigo(-a)

panic ['pænɪk] *n* pánico ▷ *vi* dejarse llevar por el pánico

panic buying [-baɪɪŋ] *n* compras masivas por miedo a futura escasez

panicky ['pænɪkɪ] *adj (person)* asustadizo

panic-stricken ['pænɪkstrɪkən] *adj* preso del pánico

panorama [pænə'rɑːmə] *n* panorama *m*

pansy ['pænzɪ] *n (Bot)* pensamiento; *(inf, pej)* maricón *m*

pant [pænt] *vi* jadear

panther ['pænθə'] *n* pantera

panties ['pæntɪz] *npl* bragas *fpl*

pantihose ['pæntɪhəʊz] *n (US)* medias *fpl*, panties *mpl*

panto ['pæntəʊ] *n (Brit inf)* = **pantomime**

pantomime ['pæntəmaɪm] *n (Brit)* representación *f* musical navideña; *ver nota*

○ **PANTOMIME**
○
○ En época navideña los teatros británicos
○ ponen en escena representaciones
○ llamadas *pantomimes*, versiones libres de
○ cuentos tradicionales como Aladino o
○ El gato con botas. En ella nunca faltan
○ personajes como la dama ("dame"), papel
○ que siempre interpreta un actor; el
○ protagonista joven ("principal boy"),
○ normalmente interpretado por una
○ actriz, y el malvado ("villain"). Es un
○ espectáculo familiar dirigido a los niños
○ pero con grandes dosis de humor para
○ adultos en el que se alienta la
○ participación del público.

pantry ['pæntrɪ] *n* despensa

pants [pænts] *npl (Brit: underwear: woman's)* bragas *fpl*; *(: man's)* calzoncillos *mpl*; *(US: trousers)* pantalones *mpl*

paparazzi [pæpə'rætsɪ] npl paparazzi mpl
paper ['peɪpəʳ] n papel m; (also: **news~**)
periódico, diario; (study, article) artículo;
(exam) examen m ▷ adj de papel ▷ vt
empapelar; (**identity**) **~s** npl papeles mpl,
documentos mpl; **a piece of ~** un papel;
to put sth down on ~ poner algo por escrito
paperback ['peɪpəbæk] n libro de bolsillo
paper bag n bolsa de papel
paper clip n clip m
paper hankie n pañuelo de papel
paper shop n (Brit) tienda de periódicos
paperweight ['peɪpəweɪt] n pisapapeles m inv
paperwork ['peɪpəwəːk] n trabajo
administrativo; (pej) papeleo
paprika ['pæprɪkə] n pimentón m
par [pɑːʳ] n par f; (Golf) par m ▷ adj a la par; **to
be on a ~ with** estar a la par con; **at ~** a la par;
to be above/below ~ estar sobre/bajo par; **to
feel under ~** sentirse en baja forma
parable ['pærəbl] n parábola
paracetamol [pærə'siːtəmɔl] n (Brit)
paracetamol m
parachute ['pærəʃuːt] n paracaídas m inv ▷ vi
lanzarse en paracaídas
parade [pə'reɪd] n desfile m ▷ vt (gen)
recorrer, desfilar por; (show off) hacer alarde
de ▷ vi desfilar; (Mil) pasar revista;
a fashion ~ un desfile de modelos
paradise ['pærədaɪs] n paraíso
paradox ['pærədɔks] n paradoja
paradoxically [pærə'dɔksɪklɪ] adv
paradójicamente
paraffin ['pærəfɪn] n (Brit): **~ (oil)** parafina
paragon ['pærəgən] n modelo
paragraph ['pærəgrɑːf] n párrafo, acápite m
(LAm); **new ~** punto y aparte, punto acápite
(LAm)
Paraguay ['pærəgwaɪ] n Paraguay m
Paraguayan [pærə'gwaɪən] adj, n
paraguayo(-a) m(f), paraguayano(-a) m(f)
parallel ['pærəlɛl] adj: **~ (with/to)** en paralelo
(con/a); (fig) semejante (a) ▷ n (line) paralela;
(fig) paralelo; (Geo) paralelo
paralysis [pə'rælɪsɪs] n parálisis f inv
paralytic [pærə'lɪtɪk] adj paralítico
paralyze ['pærəlaɪz] vt paralizar; **~d**
paralizado
paramedic [pærə'mɛdɪk] n auxiliar m/f
sanitario(-a)
parameter [pə'ræmɪtəʳ] n parámetro
paramilitary [pærə'mɪlɪtərɪ] adj (organization,
operations) paramilitar
paramount ['pærəmaunt] adj: **of ~
importance** de suma importancia
paranoia [pærə'nɔɪə] n paranoia
paranoid ['pærənɔɪd] adj (person, feeling)
paranoico
paranormal [pærə'nɔːml] adj paranormal
paraphernalia [pærəfə'neɪlɪə] n
parafernalia
paraphrase ['pærəfreɪz] vt parafrasear

parasite ['pærəsaɪt] n parásito(-a)
parasol ['pærəsɔl] n sombrilla, quitasol m
paratrooper ['pærətruːpəʳ] n paracaidista m/f
parcel ['pɑːsl] n paquete m ▷ vt (also: **~ up**)
empaquetar, embalar; **to be part and ~ of**
ser parte integrante de; **parcel out** vt
parcelar, repartir
parcel bomb n paquete m bomba
parcel post n servicio de paquetes postales
parch [pɑːtʃ] vt secar, resecar
parched [pɑːtʃt] adj (person) muerto de sed
parchment ['pɑːtʃmənt] n pergamino
pardon ['pɑːdn] n perdón m; (Law) indulto
▷ vt perdonar; indultar; **~ me!, I beg your ~!**
¡perdone usted!; (**I beg your**) **~?**, (US) **~ me?**
¿cómo (dice)?
parent ['pɛərənt] n (mother) madre f; (father)
padre m; **parents** npl padres mpl
parentage ['pɛərəntɪdʒ] n familia, linaje m;
of unknown ~ de padres desconocidos
parental [pə'rɛntl] adj paternal/maternal
parenthesis (pl **parentheses**) [pə'rɛnθɪsɪs,
-θɪsiːz] n paréntesis m inv; **in parentheses**
entre paréntesis
Paris ['pærɪs] n París m
parish ['pærɪʃ] n parroquia
parishioner [pə'rɪʃənəʳ] n feligrés(-esa) m(f)
Parisian [pə'rɪzɪən] adj, n parisino(-a) m(f),
parisiense m/f
parity ['pærɪtɪ] n paridad f, igualdad f
park [pɑːk] n parque m, jardín m público ▷ vt
aparcar, estacionar ▷ vi aparcar, estacionar
parking ['pɑːkɪŋ] n aparcamiento,
estacionamiento; **"no ~"** "prohibido aparcar
or estacionarse"
parking lot n (US) parking m, aparcamiento,
playa f de estacionamiento (LAm)
parking meter n parquímetro
parking place n sitio para aparcar,
aparcamiento
parking ticket n multa de aparcamiento
Parkinson's n (also: **~ disease**) (enfermedad f
de) Parkinson m
parkway ['pɑːkweɪ] n (US) alameda
parlance ['pɑːləns] n lenguaje m; **in
common/modern ~** en lenguaje corriente/
moderno
parliament ['pɑːləmənt] n parlamento;
(Spanish) las Cortes fpl; ver nota

P

⬤ **PARLIAMENT**
⬤
⬤ El Parlamento británico (Parliament) tiene
⬤ como sede el palacio de Westminster,
⬤ también llamado "Houses of Parliament".
⬤ Consta de dos cámaras: la Cámara de los
⬤ Comunes ("House of Commons") está
⬤ formada por 650 diputados ("Members of
⬤ Parliament") que acceden a ella tras ser
⬤ elegidos por sufragio universal en su
⬤ respectiva área o circunscripción
⬤ electoral ("constituency"). Se reúne

175 días al año y sus sesiones son presididas y moderadas por el Presidente de la Cámara ("Speaker"). La cámara alta es la Cámara de los Lores ("House of Lords") y sus miembros son nombrados por el monarca o bien han heredado su escaño. Su poder es limitado, aunque actúa como tribunal supremo de apelación, excepto en Escocia.

parliamentary [pɑːləˈmɛntərɪ] *adj* parlamentario

parlour, parlor (*US*) [ˈpɑːlə^r] *n* salón *m*, living *m* (*LAm*)

Parmesan [pɑːmɪˈzæn] *n* (*also:* ~ **cheese**) queso parmesano

parochial [pəˈrəukɪəl] *adj* parroquial; (*pej*) de miras estrechas

parody [ˈpærədɪ] *n* parodia ▷ *vt* parodiar

parole [pəˈrəul] *n*: **on** ~ en libertad condicional

parrot [ˈpærət] *n* loro, papagayo

parry [ˈpærɪ] *vt* parar

parsley [ˈpɑːslɪ] *n* perejil *m*

parsnip [ˈpɑːsnɪp] *n* chirivía

parson [ˈpɑːsn] *n* cura *m*

part [pɑːt] *n* (*gen*) parte *f*; (*Mus*) parte *f*; (*bit*) trozo; (*of machine*) pieza; (*Theat etc*) papel *m*; (*of serial*) entrega; (*US: in hair*) raya ▷ *adv* = **partly** ▷ *vt* separar; (*break*) partir ▷ *vi* (*people*) separarse; (*roads*) bifurcarse; (*crowd*) apartarse; (*break*) romperse; **to take ~ in** participar or tomar parte en; **to take sb's** ~ tomar partido por algn; **for my** ~ por mi parte; **for the most** ~ en su mayor parte; (*people*) en su mayoría; **for the better** ~ **of the day** durante la mayor parte del día; ~ **of speech** (*Ling*) categoría gramatical, parte *f* de la oración; **to take sth in good/bad** ~ aceptar algo bien/tomarse algo a mal; **part with** *vt fus* ceder, entregar; (*money*) pagar; (*get rid of*) deshacerse de

part exchange *n* (*Brit*): **in** ~ como parte del pago

partial [ˈpɑːʃl] *adj* parcial; **to be** ~ **to** (*like*) ser aficionado a

participant [pɑːˈtɪsɪpənt] *n* (*in competition*) concursante *m/f*

participate [pɑːˈtɪsɪpeɪt] *vi*: **to ~ in** participar en

participation [pɑːtɪsɪˈpeɪʃən] *n* participación *f*

participle [ˈpɑːtɪsɪpl] *n* participio

particle [ˈpɑːtɪkl] *n* partícula; (*of dust*) mota; (*fig*) pizca

particular [pəˈtɪkjulə^r] *adj* (*special*) particular; (*concrete*) concreto; (*given*) determinado; (*detailed*) detallado, minucioso; (*fussy*) quisquilloso; (*demanding*) exigente; **particulars** *npl* (*information*) datos *mpl*, detalles *mpl*; (*details*) pormenores *mpl*; **in** ~ en particular; **to be very ~ about** ser muy

exigente en cuanto a; **I'm not** ~ me es or da igual

particularly [pəˈtɪkjuləlɪ] *adv* (*in particular*) sobre todo; (*difficult, good etc*) especialmente

parting [ˈpɑːtɪŋ] *n* (*act of*) separación *f*; (*farewell*) despedida; (*Brit: in hair*) raya ▷ *adj* de despedida; ~ **shot** (*fig*) golpe *m* final

partisan [pɑːtɪˈzæn] *adj* partidista ▷ *n* partidario(-a); (*fighter*) partisano(-a)

partition [pɑːˈtɪʃən] *n* (*Pol*) división *f*; (*wall*) tabique *m* ▷ *vt* dividir; dividir con tabique

partly [ˈpɑːtlɪ] *adv* en parte

partner [ˈpɑːtnə^r] *n* (*Comm*) socio(-a); (*Sport*) pareja; (*at dance*) pareja; (*spouse*) cónyuge *m/f*; (*friend etc*) compañero(-a) ▷ *vt* acompañar

partnership [ˈpɑːtnəʃɪp] *n* (*gen*) asociación *f*; (*Comm*) sociedad *f*; **to go into** or ~ (**with**), **form a ~ (with)** asociarse (con)

partridge [ˈpɑːtrɪdʒ] *n* perdiz *f*

part-time [ˈpɑːtˈtaɪm] *adj, adv* a tiempo parcial

party [ˈpɑːtɪ] *n* (*Pol*) partido; (*celebration*) fiesta; (*group*) grupo; (*Law*) parte *f*, interesado ▷ *adj* (*Pol*) de partido; (*dress etc*) de fiesta, de gala; **to have** or **give** or **throw a ~** organizar una fiesta; **dinner ~** cena; **to be a ~ to a crime** ser cómplice *m/f* de un crimen

party line *n* (*Pol*) línea política del partido; (*Tel*) línea compartida

party political broadcast *n* ≈ espacio electoral

pass [pɑːs] *vt* (*time, object*) pasar; (*place*) pasar por; (*exam, law*) aprobar; (*overtake, surpass*) rebasar; (*approve*) aprobar ▷ *vi* pasar; (*Scol*) aprobar ▷ *n* (*permit*) permiso, pase *m*; (*membership card*) carnet *m*; (*in mountains*) puerto; (*Sport*) pase *m*; (*Scol: also:* ~ **mark**) aprobado; **to ~ sth through sth** pasar algo por algo; **to ~ the time of day with sb** pasar el rato con algn; **things have come to a pretty ~!** ¡hasta dónde hemos llegado!; **to make a ~ at sb** (*inf*) insinuársele a algn; **pass away** *vi* fallecer; **pass by** *vi* pasar ▷ *vt* (*ignore*) pasar por alto; **pass down** *vt* (*customs, inheritance*) pasar, transmitir; **pass for** *vt fus* pasar por; **she could ~ for 25** se podría creer que sólo tiene 25 años; **pass on** *vi* (*die*) fallecer, morir ▷ *vt* (*hand on*): **to ~ on (to)** transmitir (a); (*cold, illness*) pegar (a); (*benefits*) dar (a); (*price rises*) pasar (a); **pass out** *vi* desmayarse; (*Mil*) graduarse; **pass over** *vi* (*die*) fallecer ▷ *vt* omitir, pasar por alto; **pass up** *vt* (*opportunity*) dejar pasar, no aprovechar

passable [ˈpɑːsəbl] *adj* (*road*) transitable; (*tolerable*) pasable

passage [ˈpæsɪdʒ] *n* pasillo; (*act of passing*) tránsito; (*fare, in book*) pasaje *m*; (*by boat*) travesía

passenger [ˈpæsɪndʒə^r] *n* pasajero(-a), viajero(-a)

passer-by [pɑːsəˈbaɪ] *n* transeúnte *m/f*

passing ['pɑ:sɪŋ] adj (fleeting) pasajero; **in ~** de paso

passing place n (Aut) apartadero

passion ['pæʃən] n pasión f

passionate ['pæʃənɪt] adj apasionado

passion fruit n fruta de la pasión, granadilla

passion play n drama m de la Pasión

passive ['pæsɪv] adj (also Ling) pasivo

passive smoking n efectos del tabaco en fumadores pasivos

Passover ['pɑ:səuvə'] n Pascua (de los judíos)

passport ['pɑ:spɔ:t] n pasaporte m

passport control n control m de pasaporte

passport office n oficina de pasaportes

password ['pɑ:swə:d] n (also Comput) contraseña

past [pɑ:st] prep (further than) más allá de; (later than) después de ▷ adj pasado; (president etc) antiguo ▷ n (time) pasado; (of person) antecedentes mpl; **quarter/half ~ four** las cuatro y cuarto/media; **he's ~ forty** tiene más de cuarenta años; **I'm ~ caring** ya no me importa; **to be ~ it** (inf: person) estar acabado; **for the ~ few/three days** durante los últimos días/últimos tres días; **to run ~** pasar corriendo por; **in the ~** en el pasado, antes

pasta ['pæstə] n pasta

paste [peɪst] n (gen) pasta; (glue) engrudo ▷ vt (stick) pegar; (glue) engomar; **tomato ~** tomate concentrado

pastel ['pæstl] adj pastel; (painting) al pastel

pasteurized ['pæstəraɪzd] adj pasteurizado

pastille ['pæstl] n pastilla

pastime ['pɑ:staɪm] n pasatiempo

pastor ['pɑ:stə'] n pastor m

past participle [-'pɑ:tɪsɪpl] n (Ling) participio m (de) pasado or (de) pretérito or pasivo

pastry ['peɪstrɪ] n (dough) pasta; (cake) pastel m

pasture ['pɑ:stʃə'] n (grass) pasto

pasty n ['pæstɪ] empanada ▷ adj ['peɪstɪ] pastoso; (complexion) pálido

pat [pæt] vt dar una palmadita a; (dog etc) acariciar ▷ n (of butter) porción f ▷ adj: **he knows it (off) ~** se lo sabe de memoria or al dedillo; **to give sb/o.s. a ~ on the back** (fig) felicitar a algn/felicitarse

patch [pætʃ] n (of material) parche m; (mended part) remiendo; (of land) terreno; (Comput) ajuste m ▷ vt (clothes) remendar; **(to go through) a bad ~** se lo sabe de memoria or una mala racha; **patch up** vt (mend temporarily) reparar; **to ~ up a quarrel** hacer las paces

patchy ['pætʃɪ] adj desigual

pâté ['pæteɪ] n paté m

patent ['peɪtnt] n patente f ▷ vt patentar ▷ adj patente, evidente

patent leather n charol m

paternal [pə'tə:nl] adj paternal; (relation) paterno

paternity [pə'tə:nɪtɪ] n paternidad f

paternity leave n permiso m por paternidad, licencia por paternidad

path [pɑ:θ] n camino, sendero; (trail, track) pista; (of missile) trayectoria

pathetic [pə'θetɪk] adj (pitiful) penoso, patético; (very bad) malísimo; (moving) conmovedor(a)

pathname ['pɑ:θneɪm] n (Comput) nombre m del directorio

pathological [pæθə'lɔdʒɪkəl] adj patológico

pathologist [pə'θɔlədʒɪst] n patólogo(-a)

pathos ['peɪθɔs] n patetismo

pathway ['pɑ:θweɪ] n sendero, vereda

patience ['peɪʃns] n paciencia; (Brit Cards) solitario; **to lose one's ~** perder la paciencia

patient ['peɪʃnt] n paciente m/f ▷ adj paciente, sufrido; **to be ~ with sb** tener paciencia con algn

patio ['pætɪəu] n patio

patriot ['peɪtrɪət] n patriota m/f

patriotic [pætrɪ'ɔtɪk] adj patriótico

patriotism ['pætrɪətɪzəm] n patriotismo

patrol [pə'trəul] n patrulla ▷ vt patrullar por; **to be on ~** patrullar, estar de patrulla

patrol car n coche m patrulla

patrolman [pə'trəulmən] n (US) policía m

patron ['peɪtrən] n (in shop) cliente m/f; (of charity) patrocinador(a) m(f); **~ of the arts** mecenas m

patronize ['pætrənaɪz] vt (shop) ser cliente de; (look down on) tratar con condescendencia a

patronizing ['pætrənaɪzɪŋ] adj condescendiente

patron saint n santo(-a) patrón(-ona)

patter ['pætə'] n golpeteo; (sales talk) labia ▷ vi (rain) tamborilear

pattern ['pætən] n (Sewing) patrón m; (design) dibujo; (behaviour, events) esquema m; **~ of events** curso de los hechos; **behaviour ~s** modelos mpl de comportamiento

patterned ['pætənd] adj (material) estampado

paunch [pɔ:ntʃ] n panza, barriga

pauper ['pɔ:pə'] n pobre m/f

pause [pɔ:z] n pausa; (interval) intervalo ▷ vi hacer una pausa; **to ~ for breath** detenerse para tomar aliento

pave [peɪv] vt pavimentar; **to ~ the way for** preparar el terreno para

pavement ['peɪvmənt] n (Brit) acera, vereda (LAm), andén m (LAm), banqueta (LAm); (US) calzada, pavimento

pavilion [pə'vɪlɪən] n pabellón m; (Sport) vestuarios mpl

paving ['peɪvɪŋ] n pavimento, enlosado

paving stone n losa

paw [pɔ:] n pata; (claw) garra ▷ vt (animal) tocar con la pata; (pej: touch) tocar, manosear

pawn [pɔ:n] n (Chess) peón m; (fig) instrumento ▷ vt empeñar

pawnbroker ['pɔ:nbrəukə'] n prestamista m/f

pawnshop ['pɔ:nʃɔp] n casa de empeños

pay [peɪ] (*pt, pp* **paid**) *n* paga; (*wage etc*) sueldo, salario ▷ *vt* pagar; (*visit*) hacer; (*respect*) ofrecer ▷ *vi* pagar; (*be profitable*) rendir, compensar, ser rentable; **to be in sb's ~** estar al servicio de algn; **to ~ attention (to)** prestar atención (a); **I paid £5 for that record** pagué 5 libras por ese disco; **how much did you ~ for it?** ¿cuánto pagaste por él?; **to ~ one's way** (*contribute one's share*) pagar su parte; (*remain solvent: company*) ser solvente; **to ~ dividends** (*Comm*) pagar dividendos; (*fig*) compensar; **it won't ~ you to do that** no te merece la pena hacer eso; **to put paid to** (*plan, person*) acabar con; **pay back** *vt* (*money*) devolver, reembolsar; (*person*) pagar; **pay for** *vt fus* pagar; **pay in** *vt* ingresar; **pay off** *vt* liquidar; (*person*) pagar; (*debts*) liquidar, saldar; (*creditor*) cancelar, redimir; (*workers*) despedir; (*mortgage*) cancelar, redimir ▷ *vi* (*scheme, decision*) dar resultado; **to ~ sth off in instalments** pagar algo a plazos; **pay out** *vt* (*rope*) ir dando; (*money*) gastar, desembolsar; **pay up** *vt* pagar

payable ['peɪəbl] *adj* pagadero; **to make a cheque ~ to sb** extender un cheque a favor de algn

pay award *n* aumento de sueldo

pay day *n* día *m* de paga

PAYE *n abbr* (Brit: = *pay as you earn*) *sistema de retención fiscal en la parte de ingresos*

payee [peɪ'iː] *n* portador(a) *m(f)*

pay envelope *n* (US) = **pay packet**

payment ['peɪmənt] *n* pago; **advance ~** (*part sum*) anticipo, adelanto; (*total sum*) saldo; **monthly ~** mensualidad *f*; **deferred ~**, **~ by instalments** pago a plazos or diferido; **on ~ of £5** mediante pago de or pagando £5; **in ~ for** en pago de

payout ['peɪaʊt] *n* pago; (*in competition*) premio en metálico

pay packet *n* (Brit) sobre *m* (de la paga)

pay-phone ['peɪfəʊn] *n* teléfono público

payroll ['peɪrəʊl] *n* plantilla, nómina; **to be on a firm's ~** estar en la plantilla or nómina de una empresa

pay slip *n* nómina, hoja del sueldo

pay television *n* televisión *f* de pago

PC *n abbr* (= *personal computer*) PC *m*, OP *m*; (Brit) = **police constable** ▷ *adj abbr* = **politically correct**

pc *abbr* = **per cent; postcard**

PDA *n abbr* (= *personal digital assistant*) agenda electrónica

PE *n abbr* (= *physical education*) ed. física

pea [piː] *n* guisante *m*, chícharo (LAm), arveja (LAm)

peace [piːs] *n* paz *f*; (*calm*) paz *f*, tranquilidad *f*; **to be at ~ with sb/sth** estar en paz con algn/algo; **to keep the ~** (*policeman*) mantener el orden; (*citizen*) guardar el orden

peaceful ['piːsfʊl] *adj* (*gentle*) pacífico; (*calm*) tranquilo, sosegado

peacekeeping ['piːskiːpɪŋ] *adj* de pacificación ▷ *n* pacificación *f*

peacekeeping force *n* fuerza de pacificación

peach [piːtʃ] *n* melocotón *m*, durazno (LAm)

peacock ['piːkɔk] *n* pavo real

peak [piːk] *n* (*of mountain: top*) cumbre *f*, cima; (: *point*) pico; (*of cap*) visera; (*fig*) cumbre *f*

peak hours *npl*, **peak period** *n* horas *fpl* punta

peak rate *n* tarifa máxima

peal [piːl] *n* (*of bells*) repique *m*; **~ of laughter** carcajada

peanut ['piːnʌt] *n* cacahuete *m*, maní *m* (LAm)

peanut butter *n* mantequilla de cacahuete

pear [pɛəʳ] *n* pera

pearl [pəːl] *n* perla

peasant ['pɛznt] *n* campesino(-a)

peat [piːt] *n* turba

pebble ['pɛbl] *n* guijarro

peck [pɛk] *vt* (*also*: **~ at**) picotear; (*food*) comer sin ganas ▷ *n* picotazo; (*kiss*) besito

pecking order ['pɛkɪŋ-] *n* orden *m* de jerarquía

peckish ['pɛkɪʃ] *adj* (Brit inf): **I feel ~** tengo ganas de picar algo

peculiar [pɪ'kjuːlɪəʳ] *adj* (*odd*) extraño, raro; (*typical*) propio, característico; (*particular: importance, qualities*) particular; **~ to** propio de

pedal ['pɛdl] *n* pedal *m* ▷ *vi* pedalear

pedalo ['pɛdələʊ] *n* patín *m* a pedal

pedantic [pɪ'dæntɪk] *adj* pedante

peddle ['pɛdl] *vt* (*goods*) ir vendiendo or vender de puerta en puerta; (*drugs*) traficar con; (*gossip*) divulgar

peddler ['pɛdləʳ] *n* vendedor(a) *m(f)* ambulante

pedestal ['pɛdəstl] *n* pedestal *m*

pedestrian [pɪ'dɛstrɪən] *n* peatón *m* ▷ *adj* pedestre

pedestrian crossing *n* (Brit) paso de peatones

pedestrianized *adj*: **a ~ street** una calle peatonal

pedestrian precinct, pedestrian zone (US) *n* zona reservada para peatones

pediatrics [piːdɪ'ætrɪks] *n* (US) = **paediatrics**

pedigree ['pɛdɪgriː] *n* genealogía; (*of animal*) pedigrí *m* ▷ *cpd* (*animal*) de raza, de casta

pedophile ['piːdəʊfaɪl] *n* (US) = **paedophile**

pee [piː] *vi* (*inf*) mear

peek [piːk] *vi* mirar a hurtadillas; (*Comput*) inspeccionar

peel [piːl] *n* piel *f*; (*of orange, lemon*) cáscara; (: *removed*) peladuras *fpl* ▷ *vt* pelar ▷ *vi* (*paint etc*) desconcharse; (*wallpaper*) despegarse, desprenderse; (*skin*) pelar; **peel back** *vt* pelar

peep [piːp] *n* (Brit: *look*) mirada furtiva; (*sound*) pío ▷ *vi* (Brit: *look*) mirar furtivamente; **peep out** *vi* asomar la cabeza

peephole ['piːphəʊl] *n* mirilla

peer [pɪəʳ] *vi*: **to ~ at** escudriñar ▷ *n* (*noble*) par *m*; (*equal*) igual *m*; (*contemporary*) contemporáneo(-a)

peerage ['pɪərɪdʒ] *n* nobleza
peeved [pi:vd] *adj* enojado
peg [pɛg] *n* clavija; *(for coat etc)* gancho, colgador *m*; *(Brit: also:* **clothes ~**) pinza; *(also:* **tent ~**) estaca ▷ *vt (clothes)* tender; *(groundsheet)* fijar con estacas; *(fig: wages, prices)* fijar
pejorative [pɪ'dʒɒrətɪv] *adj* peyorativo
pekinese [pi:kɪ'ni:z] *n* pequinés(-esa) *m(f)*
pelican ['pɛlɪkən] *n* pelícano
pelican crossing *n (Brit Aut)* paso de peatones señalizado
pellet ['pɛlɪt] *n* bolita; *(bullet)* perdigón *m*
pelt [pɛlt] *vt:* **to ~ sb with sth** arrojarle algo a algn ▷ *vi (rain: also:* **~ down**) llover a cántaros; *(inf: run)* correr ▷ *n* pellejo
pelvis ['pɛlvɪs] *n* pelvis *f*
pen [pɛn] *n (also:* **ballpoint ~**) bolígrafo; *(also:* **fountain ~**) pluma; *(for sheep)* redil *m*; *(US inf: prison)* cárcel *f*, chirona; **to put ~ to paper** tomar la pluma
penal ['pi:nl] *adj* penal; **~ servitude** trabajos *mpl* forzados
penalize ['pi:nəlaɪz] *vt (punish)* castigar; *(Sport)* sancionar, penalizar
penalty ['pɛnltɪ] *n (gen)* pena; *(fine)* multa; *(Sport)* sanción *f*; *(also:* **~ kick:** *Football)* penalty *m*
penalty area *n (Brit Sport)* área de castigo
penalty shoot-out [-'ʃu:taut] *n (Football)* tanda de penaltis
penance ['pɛnəns] *n* penitencia
pence [pɛns] *pl of* **penny**
penchant ['pã:ʃã:ŋ] *n* predilección *f*, inclinación *f*
pencil ['pɛnsl] *n* lápiz *m*, lapicero (*LAm*) ▷ *vt (also:* **~ in**) escribir con lápiz; *(fig)* apuntar con carácter provisional
pencil case *n* estuche *m*
pencil sharpener *n* sacapuntas *m inv*
pendant ['pɛndnt] *n* pendiente *m*
pending ['pɛndɪŋ] *prep* antes de ▷ *adj* pendiente; **~ the arrival of ...** hasta que llegue ..., hasta llegar ...
pendulum ['pɛndjuləm] *n* péndulo
penetrate ['pɛnɪtreɪt] *vt* penetrar
penetration [pɛnɪ'treɪʃən] *n* penetración *f*
penfriend ['pɛnfrɛnd] *n (Brit)* amigo(-a) por correspondencia
penguin ['pɛŋgwɪn] *n* pingüino
penicillin [pɛnɪ'stlɪn] *n* penicilina
peninsula [pə'nɪnsjulə] *n* península
penis ['pi:nɪs] *n* pene *m*
penitence ['pɛnɪtns] *n* penitencia
penitentiary [pɛnɪ'tɛnʃərɪ] *n (US)* cárcel *f*, presidio
penknife ['pɛnnaɪf] *n* navaja
pen name *n* seudónimo
pennant ['pɛnənt] *n* banderola; banderín *m*
penniless ['pɛnɪlɪs] *adj* sin dinero
Pennines ['pɛnaɪnz] *npl* (Montes *mpl*) Peninos *mpl*

penny *(pl* **pennies** *or (Brit)* **pence**) ['pɛnɪ, 'pɛnɪz, pɛns] *n (Brit)* penique *m*; *(US)* centavo
penpal ['pɛnpæl] *n* amigo(-a) por correspondencia
penpusher ['pɛnpuʃər] *n (pej)* chupatintas *m/f inv*
pension ['pɛnʃən] *n (allowance, state payment)* pensión *f*; *(old-age)* jubilación *f*; **pension off** *vt* jubilar
pensioner ['pɛnʃənər] *n (Brit)* jubilado(-a)
pension fund *n* fondo de pensiones
pensive ['pɛnsɪv] *adj* pensativo; *(withdrawn)* preocupado
pentagon ['pɛntəgən] *n* pentágono; **the P~** *(US Pol)* el Pentágono

> ● **PENTAGON**
> ●
> ● Se conoce como el Pentágono *(the*
> ● *Pentagon)* al edificio de planta pentagonal
> ● que acoge las dependencias del
> ● Ministerio de Defensa estadounidense
> ● ("Department of Defense") en Arlington,
> ● Virginia. En lenguaje periodístico se
> ● aplica también a la dirección militar
> ● del país.

Pentecost ['pɛntɪkɔst] *n* Pentecostés *m*
penthouse ['pɛnthaus] *n* ático (de lujo)
pent-up ['pɛntʌp] *adj (feelings)* reprimido
penultimate [pɛ'nʌltɪmət] *adj* penúltimo
people ['pi:pl] *npl* gente *f*; *(citizens)* pueblo *sg*, ciudadanos *mpl*; *(Pol):* **the ~** el pueblo ▷ *n (nation, race)* pueblo, nación *f* ▷ *vt* poblar; **several ~ came** vinieron varias personas; **~ say that ...** dice la gente que ...; **old/young ~** los ancianos/jóvenes; **~ at large** la gente en general; **a man of the ~** un hombre del pueblo
pep [pɛp] *n (inf)* energía; **pep up** *vt* animar
pepper ['pɛpər] *n (spice)* pimienta; *(vegetable)* pimiento, ají *m* (*LAm*), chile *m* (*LAm*) ▷ *vt:* **to ~ with** *(fig)* salpicar de
peppermint ['pɛpəmɪnt] *n* menta; *(sweet)* pastilla de menta
pepperoni [pɛpə'rəunɪ] *n* ≈ salchichón *m* picante
per [pə:r] *prep* por; **~ day/person** por día/persona; **~ annum** al año; **as ~ your instructions** de acuerdo con sus instrucciones
per capita *adj, adv* per cápita
perceive [pə'si:v] *vt* percibir; *(realize)* darse cuenta de
per cent, percent (*US*) [pə'sɛnt] *n* por ciento; **a 20 ~ discount** un descuento del 20 por ciento
percentage [pə'sɛntɪdʒ] *n* porcentaje *m*; **to get a ~ on all sales** percibir un tanto por ciento sobre todas las ventas; **on a ~ basis** a porcentaje
percentage point *n* punto (porcentual)

p

perception [pə'sɛpʃən] n percepción f; (insight) perspicacia

perceptive [pə'sɛptɪv] adj perspicaz

perch [pɜːtʃ] n (fish) perca; (for bird) percha ▷ vi: **to ~ (on)** (bird) posarse (en); (person) encaramarse (en)

percolate ['pɜːkəleɪt] vt (coffee) filtrar ▷ vi (coffee) filtrarse; (fig) filtrarse

percolator ['pɜːkəleɪtəʳ] n cafetera de filtro

percussion [pə'kʌʃən] n percusión f

perennial [pə'rɛnɪəl] adj perenne

perfect adj ['pɜːfɪkt] perfecto ▷ n (also: **~ tense**) perfecto ▷ vt [pə'fɛkt] perfeccionar; **he's a ~ stranger to me** no le conozco de nada, me es completamente desconocido

perfection [pə'fɛkʃən] n perfección f

perfectly ['pɜːfɪktlɪ] adv perfectamente; **I'm ~ happy with the situation** estoy muy contento con la situación; **you know ~ well** lo sabes muy bien or perfectamente

perforate ['pɜːfəreɪt] vt perforar

perforation [pɜːfə'reɪʃən] n perforación f

perform [pə'fɔːm] vt (carry out) realizar, llevar a cabo; (Theat) representar; (piece of music) interpretar ▷ vi (Theat) actuar; (Tech) funcionar

performance [pə'fɔːməns] n (of task) realización f; (of a play) representación f; (of player etc) actuación f; (of engine) rendimiento; (of car) prestaciones fpl; (of function) desempeño; **the team put up a good ~** el equipo se defendió bien

performer [pə'fɔːməʳ] n (actor) actor m, actriz f; (Mus) intérprete m/f

performing arts npl: **the ~** las artes teatrales

perfume ['pɜːfjuːm] n perfume m

perfunctory [pə'fʌŋktərɪ] adj superficial

perhaps [pə'hæps] adv quizá(s), tal vez; **~ so/ not** puede que sí/no

peril ['pɛrɪl] n peligro, riesgo

perilous ['pɛrɪləs] adj peligroso

perimeter [pə'rɪmɪtəʳ] n perímetro

period ['pɪərɪəd] n período, periodo; (History) época; (Scol) clase f; (full stop) punto; (Med) regla, periodo; (US Sport) tiempo ▷ adj (costume, furniture) de época; **for a ~ of three weeks** durante (un período de) tres semanas; **the holiday ~** el período de vacaciones

periodical [pɪərɪ'ɔdɪkl] adj periódico ▷ n revista, publicación f periódica

periodically [pɪərɪ'ɔdɪklɪ] adv de vez en cuando, cada cierto tiempo

period pains npl dolores mpl de la regla or de la menstruación

peripheral [pə'rɪfərəl] adj periférico ▷ n (Comput) periférico, unidad f periférica

periphery [pə'rɪfərɪ] n periferia

perish ['pɛrɪʃ] vi perecer; (decay) echarse a perder

perishable ['pɛrɪʃəbl] adj perecedero

perjure ['pɜːdʒəʳ] vt: **to ~ o.s.** perjurar

perjury ['pɜːdʒərɪ] n (Law) perjurio

perk [pɜːk] n beneficio, extra m; **perk up** vi (cheer up) animarse

perky ['pɜːkɪ] adj alegre, animado

perm [pɜːm] n permanente f ▷ vt: **to have one's hair ~ed** hacerse una permanente

permanent ['pɜːmənənt] adj permanente; (job, position) fijo; (dye, ink) indeleble; **~ address** domicilio permanente; **I'm not ~ here** no estoy fijo aquí

permanently ['pɜːmənəntlɪ] adv (lastingly) para siempre, de modo definitivo; (all the time) permanentemente

permeate ['pɜːmɪeɪt] vi penetrar, trascender ▷ vt penetrar, trascender a

permissible [pə'mɪsɪbl] adj permisible, lícito

permission [pə'mɪʃən] n permiso; **to give sb ~ to do sth** autorizar a algn para que haga algo; **with your ~** con su permiso

permissive [pə'mɪsɪv] adj permisivo

permit n ['pɜːmɪt] permiso, licencia; (entrance pass) pase m ▷ vt [pə'mɪt] permitir; (accept) tolerar ▷ vi [pə'mɪt]: **weather ~ting** si el tiempo lo permite; **fishing ~** permiso de pesca; **building/export ~** licencia or permiso de construcción/exportación

perpendicular [pɜːpən'dɪkjuləʳ] adj perpendicular

perpetual [pə'pɛtjuəl] adj perpetuo

perplex [pə'plɛks] vt dejar perplejo

perplexed [pə'plɛkst] adj perplejo, confuso

persecute ['pɜːsɪkjuːt] vt (pursue) perseguir; (harass) acosar

persecution [pɜːsɪ'kjuːʃən] n persecución f

perseverance [pɜːsɪ'vɪərəns] n perseverancia

persevere [pɜːsɪ'vɪəʳ] vi perseverar

Persia ['pɜːʃə] n Persia

Persian ['pɜːʃən] adj, n persa m/f ▷ n (Ling) persa m; **the ~ Gulf** el Golfo Pérsico

persist [pə'sɪst] vi persistir; **to ~ in doing sth** empeñarse en hacer algo

persistence [pə'sɪstəns] n empeño

persistent [pə'sɪstənt] adj (lateness, rain) persistente; (determined) porfiado; (continuing) constante; **~ offender** (Law) multirreincidente m/f

person ['pɜːsn] n persona; **in ~** en persona; **on** or **about one's ~** encima; **a ~ to ~ call** una llamada (de) persona a persona

personal ['pɜːsnl] adj personal, individual; (visit) en persona; (Brit Tel) (de) persona a persona

personal assistant n ayudante m/f personal

personal column n anuncios mpl personales

personal computer n ordenador m personal

personal identification number n número personal de identificación

personality [pɜːsə'nælɪtɪ] n personalidad f

personally ['pɜːsnəlɪ] adv personalmente; (in person) en persona; **to take sth ~** tomarse algo a mal

personal organizer n agenda; (electronic) agenda electrónica

personal property n bienes mpl muebles
personal stereo n walkman® m
personify [pəˈsɒnɪfaɪ] vt encarnar, personificar
personnel [pəːsəˈnɛl] n personal m
personnel department n departamento de personal
personnel manager n jefe m de personal
perspective [pəˈspɛktɪv] n perspectiva; **to get sth into ~** ver algo en perspectiva or como es
Perspex® [ˈpəːspɛks] n (Brit) vidrio acrílico, plexiglás® m
perspiration [pəːspɪˈreɪʃən] n transpiración f, sudor m
perspire [pəˈspaɪəʳ] vi transpirar, sudar
persuade [pəˈsweɪd] vt: **to ~ sb to do sth** persuadir a algn para que haga algo; **to ~ sb of sth/that** persuadir or convencer a algn de algo/de que; **I am ~d that ...** estoy convencido de que ...
persuasion [pəˈsweɪʒən] n persuasión f; (persuasiveness) persuasiva; (creed) creencia
persuasive [pəˈsweɪsɪv] adj persuasivo
pertaining [pəːˈteɪnɪŋ]· **~ to** prep relacionado con
pertinent [ˈpəːtɪnənt] adj pertinente, a propósito
perturb [pəˈtəːb] vt perturbar
Peru [pəˈruː] n el Perú
peruse [pəˈruːz] vt (examine) leer con detención, examinar; (glance at) mirar por encima
Peruvian [pəˈruːvɪən] adj, n peruano(-a) m(f)
pervade [pəˈveɪd] vt impregnar; (influence, ideas) extenderse por
perverse [pəˈvəːs] adj perverso; (stubborn) terco; (wayward) travieso
perversion [pəˈvəːʃən] n perversión f
pervert n [ˈpəːvəːt] pervertido(-a) ▷ vt [pəˈvəːt] pervertir
pessimism [ˈpɛsɪmɪzəm] n pesimismo
pessimist [ˈpɛsɪmɪst] n pesimista m/f
pessimistic [pɛsɪˈmɪstɪk] adj pesimista
pest [pɛst] n (insect) insecto nocivo; (fig) lata, molestia; **pests** npl plaga
pester [ˈpɛstəʳ] vt molestar, acosar
pesticide [ˈpɛstɪsaɪd] n pesticida m
pet [pɛt] n animal m doméstico; (favourite) favorito(-a) ▷ vt acariciar ▷ vi (inf) besuquearse ▷ cpd: **teacher's ~** favorito(-a) (del profesor); **~ hate** manía
petal [ˈpɛtl] n pétalo
peter [ˈpiːtəʳ]: **to ~ out** vi agotarse, acabarse
petite [pəˈtiːt] adj menuda, chiquita
petition [pəˈtɪʃən] n petición f ▷ vt presentar una petición a ▷ vi: **to ~ for divorce** pedir el divorcio
petrified [ˈpɛtrɪfaɪd] adj (fig) pasmado, horrorizado
petrol [ˈpɛtrəl] (Brit) n gasolina; (for lighter) bencina; **two/four-star ~** gasolina normal/súper

petrol bomb n cóctel m Molotov
petrol can n bidón m de gasolina
petroleum [pəˈtrəʊlɪəm] n petróleo
petrol pump n (Brit: in car) bomba de gasolina; (in garage) surtidor m de gasolina
petrol station n (Brit) gasolinera
petrol tank n (Brit) depósito (de gasolina)
petticoat [ˈpɛtɪkəʊt] n combinación f, enagua(s) f(pl) (LAm)
petty [ˈpɛtɪ] adj (mean) mezquino; (unimportant) insignificante
petty cash n dinero para gastos menores
petty officer n contramaestre m
petulant [ˈpɛtjulənt] adj malhumorado
pew [pjuː] n banco
pewter [ˈpjuːtəʳ] n peltre m
PG n abbr (Cine) = **parental guidance**
pH n abbr (= pH value) pH
phantom [ˈfæntəm] n fantasma m
pharmacist [ˈfɑːməsɪst] n farmacéutico(-a)
pharmacy [ˈfɑːməsɪ] n (US) farmacia
phase [feɪz] n fase f ▷ vt: **~d withdrawal** retirada progresiva; **phase in** vt introducir progresivamente; **phase out** vt (machinery, product) retirar progresivamente; (job, subsidy) eliminar por etapas
PhD abbr = **Doctor of Philosophy**
pheasant [ˈfɛznt] n faisán m
phenomena [fəˈnɒmɪnə] npl of **phenomenon**
phenomenal [fɪˈnɒmɪnl] adj fenomenal, extraordinario
phenomenon (pl **phenomena**) [fəˈnɒmɪnən, -nə] n fenómeno
Philippines [ˈfɪlɪpiːnz] npl: **the ~** (las Islas) Filipinas
philosopher [fɪˈlɒsəfəʳ] n filósofo(-a)
philosophical [fɪləˈsɒfɪkl] adj filosófico
philosophy [fɪˈlɒsəfɪ] n filosofía
phlegm [flɛm] n flema
phobia [ˈfəʊbjə] n fobia
phone [fəʊn] n teléfono ▷ vt telefonear, llamar por teléfono; **to be on the ~** tener teléfono; (be calling) estar hablando por teléfono; **phone back** vt, ▷ vi volver a llamar; **phone up** vt, ▷ vi llamar por teléfono
phone book n guía telefónica
phone box, phone booth n cabina telefónica
phone call n llamada (telefónica)
phonecard [ˈfəʊnkɑːd] n tarjeta telefónica
phone-in [ˈfəʊnɪn] n (Brit Radio, TV) programa de radio o televisión con las líneas abiertas al público
phone number n número de teléfono
phone tapping [-tæpɪŋ] n escuchas telefónicas
phonetics [fəˈnɛtɪks] n fonética
phoney [ˈfəʊnɪ] adj, n = **phony**
phony [ˈfəʊnɪ] adj falso ▷ n (person) farsante m/f
photo [ˈfəʊtəʊ] n foto f
photo album n álbum m de fotos

photocall ['fəutəukɔːl] n sesión f fotográfica para la prensa
photocopier ['fəutəukɒpɪəʳ] n fotocopiadora
photocopy ['fəutəukɒpɪ] n fotocopia ▷ vt fotocopiar
Photofit® ['fəutəufɪt] n (also: ~ picture) retrato robot
photograph ['fəutəgræf] n fotografía ▷ vt fotografiar; **to take a ~ of sb** sacar una foto de algn
photographer [fə'tɔgrəfəʳ] n fotógrafo
photography [fə'tɔgrəfɪ] n fotografía
photo opportunity n oportunidad de salir en la foto
phrase [freɪz] n frase f ▷ vt (letter) expresar, redactar
phrase book n libro de frases
physical ['fɪzɪkl] adj físico; ~ **examination** reconocimiento médico; ~ **exercises** ejercicios mpl físicos
physical education n educación f física
physically ['fɪzɪklɪ] adv físicamente
physician [fɪ'zɪʃən] n médico(-a)
physicist ['fɪzɪsɪst] n físico(-a)
physics ['fɪzɪks] n física
physiotherapist [fɪzɪəu'θerəpɪst] n fisioterapeuta
physiotherapy [fɪzɪəu'θerəpɪ] n fisioterapia
physique [fɪ'ziːk] n físico
pianist ['pɪənɪst] n pianista m/f
piano [pɪ'ænəu] n piano
pick [pɪk] n (tool: also: ~axe) pico, piqueta ▷ vt (select) elegir, escoger; (gather) coger (Sp), recoger (LAm); (lock) abrir con ganzúa; (scab, spot) rascar ▷ vi: **to ~ and choose** ser muy exigente; **take your** ~ escoja lo que quiera; **the ~ of** lo mejor de; **to ~ one's nose/teeth** hurgarse la nariz/escarbarse los dientes; **to ~ pockets** ratear, ser carterista; **to ~ one's way through** andar a tientas, abrirse camino; **to ~ a fight/quarrel with sb** buscar pelea/camorra con algn; **to ~ sb's brains** aprovecharse de los conocimientos de algn; **pick at** vt fus: **to ~ at one's food** comer con poco apetito; **pick off** vt (kill) matar de un tiro; **pick on** vt fus (person) meterse con; **pick out** vt escoger; (distinguish) identificar; **pick up** vi (improve: sales) ir mejor; (: patient) reponerse; (: Finance) recobrarse ▷ vt (from floor) recoger; (buy) comprar; (find) encontrar; (learn) aprender; (Police: arrest) detener; (Radio, TV, Tel) captar; **to ~ up speed** acelerarse; **to ~ o.s. up** levantarse; **to ~ up where one left off** volver a empezar algo donde lo había dejado
pickaxe, pickax (US) ['pɪkæks] n pico, zapapico
picket ['pɪkɪt] n (in strike) piquete m ▷ vt hacer un piquete en, piquetear; **to be on ~ duty** estar de piquete
pickle ['pɪkl] n (also: ~s: as condiment) escabeche m; (fig: mess) apuro ▷ vt conservar

en escabeche; (in vinegar) conservar en vinagre; **in a ~** en un lío, en apuros
pickpocket ['pɪkpɒkɪt] n carterista m/f
pickup ['pɪkʌp] n (also: ~ truck, ~ van) furgoneta, camioneta
picnic ['pɪknɪk] n picnic m, merienda ▷ vi hacer un picnic
picnic area n zona de picnic; (Aut) área de descanso
picture ['pɪktʃəʳ] n cuadro; (painting) pintura; (photograph) fotografía; (film) película; (TV) imagen f; (fig: description) descripción f; (: situation) situación f ▷ vt pintar; (imagine) imaginar; **the ~s** (Brit) el cine; **we get a good ~ here** captamos bien la imagen aquí; **to take a ~ of sb/sth** hacer or sacar una foto a algn/de algo; **the garden is a ~ in June** el jardín es una preciosidad en junio; **the overall ~** la impresión general; **to put sb in the ~** poner a algn al corriente or al tanto
picture book n libro de dibujos
picture frame n marco
picture messaging n (envío de) mensajes mpl con imágenes
picturesque [pɪktʃə'resk] adj pintoresco
pie [paɪ] n (of meat etc: large) pastel m; (: small) empanada; (sweet) tarta
piece [piːs] n pedazo, trozo; (of cake) trozo; (Draughts etc) ficha; (Chess) pieza; (part of a set) pieza; (item): **a ~ of furniture/advice** un mueble/un consejo ▷ vt: **to ~ together** juntar; (Tech) armar; **to take to ~s** desmontar; **a ~ of news** una noticia; **a 10p ~** una moneda de 10 peniques; **a six-~ band** un conjunto de seis (músicos); **in one ~** (object) de una sola pieza; **~ by ~** pieza por or a pieza; **to say one's ~** decir su parecer
piecemeal ['piːsmiːl] adv poco a poco
piecework ['piːswəːk] n trabajo a destajo
pie chart n gráfico de sectores or de tarta
pier [pɪəʳ] n muelle m, embarcadero
pierce [pɪəs] vt penetrar en, perforar; **to have one's ears ~d** hacerse los agujeros de las orejas
pig [pɪg] n cerdo, puerco, chancho (LAm); (person: greedy) tragón(-ona) m(f), comilón(-ona) m(f); (nasty) cerdo(-a)
pigeon ['pɪdʒən] n paloma; (as food) pichón m
pigeonhole ['pɪdʒənhəul] n casilla
piggy bank ['pɪgɪbæŋk] n hucha (en forma de cerdito)
piglet ['pɪglɪt] n cerdito, cochinillo
pigmentation [pɪgmən'teɪʃən] n pigmentación f
pigmy ['pɪgmɪ] n = **pygmy**
pigskin ['pɪgskɪn] n piel f de cerdo
pigsty ['pɪgstaɪ] n pocilga
pigtail ['pɪgteɪl] n (girl's) trenza; (Chinese) coleta; (Taur) coleta
pike [paɪk] n (spear) pica; (fish) lucio
pilchard ['pɪltʃəd] n sardina

pile [paɪl] n (heap) montón m; (of carpet) pelo; **in a ~** en un montón; (into car) meterse en; **pile on** vt: **to ~ it on** (inf) exagerar; **pile up** vi (accumulate: work) amontonarse, acumularse ▷ vt (put in a heap: books, clothes) apilar, amontonar; (accumulate) acumular

piles [paɪlz] npl (Med) almorranas fpl, hemorroides mpl

pile-up ['paɪlʌp] n (Aut) accidente m múltiple

pilfering ['pɪlfərɪŋ] n ratería

pilgrim ['pɪlgrɪm] n peregrino(-a); **the P~ Fathers** or **P~s** los primeros colonos norteamericanos; see also **Thanksgiving**

pilgrimage ['pɪlgrɪmɪdʒ] n peregrinación f, romería

pill [pɪl] n píldora; **the ~** la píldora; **to be on the ~** tomar la píldora (anticonceptiva)

pillage ['pɪlɪdʒ] vt pillar, saquear

pillar ['pɪlə'] n pilar m, columna

pillar box n (Brit) buzón m

pillion ['pɪljən] n (of motorcycle) asiento trasero; **to ride ~** ir en el asiento trasero

pillow ['pɪləu] n almohada

pillowcase ['pɪləukeɪs], **pillowslip** ['pɪləuslɪp] n funda (de almohada)

pilot ['paɪlət] n piloto inv ▷ adj (scheme etc) piloto ▷ vt pilotar; (fig) guiar, conducir

pilot light n piloto

pimp [pɪmp] n chulo, cafiche m (LAm)

pimple ['pɪmpl] n grano

PIN n abbr (= personal identification number) PIN m

pin [pɪn] n alfiler m; (Elec: of plug) clavija; (Tech) perno; (: wooden) clavija; (drawing pin) chincheta; (in grenade) percutor m ▷ vt prender con (alfiler); sujetar con perno; **~s and needles** hormigueo sg; **to ~ sth on sb** (fig) cargar a algn con la culpa de algo; **pin down** vt (fig): **there's something strange here, but I can't quite ~ it down** aquí hay algo raro pero no puedo precisar qué es; **to ~ sb down** hacer que algn concrete

pinafore ['pɪnəfɔː'] n delantal m

pinball ['pɪnbɔːl] n (also: **~ machine**) millón m, fliper m

pincers ['pɪnsəz] npl pinzas fpl, tenazas fpl

pinch [pɪntʃ] n pellizco; (of salt etc) pizca ▷ vt pellizcar; (inf: steal) birlar ▷ vi (shoe) apretar; **at a ~** en caso de apuro; **to feel the ~** (fig) pasar apuros or estrecheces

pincushion ['pɪnkuʃən] n acerico

pine [paɪn] n (also: **~ tree**) pino ▷ vi: **to ~ for** suspirar por; **pine away** vi morirse de pena

pineapple ['paɪnæpl] n piña, ananá(s) m (LAm)

ping [pɪŋ] n (noise) sonido agudo

Ping-Pong® ['pɪŋpɔŋ] n pingpong m

pink [pɪŋk] adj (de color) rosa ▷ n (colour) rosa; (Bot) clavel m

pinpoint ['pɪnpɔɪnt] vt precisar

pint [paɪnt] n pinta (Brit = 0,57 l, US = 0,47 l); (Brit inf: of beer) pinta de cerveza, = jarra (Sp)

pin-up ['pɪnʌp] n (picture) fotografía de mujer u hombre medio desnudos; **~ (girl)** = chica de calendario

pioneer [paɪə'nɪə'] n pionero(-a) ▷ vt promover

pious ['paɪəs] adj piadoso, devoto

pip [pɪp] n (seed) pepita; **the ~s** (Brit Tel) la señal

pipe [paɪp] n tubería, cañería; (for smoking) pipa, cachimba (LAm), cachimbo (LAm) ▷ vt conducir en cañerías; **(bag)-s** npl gaita sg; **pipe down** vi (inf) callarse

pipe cleaner n limpiapipas m inv

pipe dream n sueño imposible

pipeline ['paɪplaɪn] n tubería, cañería; (for oil) oleoducto; (for natural gas) gaseoducto; **it is in the ~** (fig) está en trámite

piper ['paɪpə'] n (gen) flautista m/f; (with bagpipes) gaitero(-a)

piping ['paɪpɪŋ] adv: **to be ~ hot** estar calentito

pique [piːk] n pique m, resentimiento

pirate ['paɪərət] n pirata m/f ▷ vt (record, video, book) hacer una copia pirata de, piratear

Pisces ['paɪsiːz] n Piscis m

piss [pɪs] vi (inf) mear

pissed [pɪst] adj (inf: drunk) mamado, pedo

pistol ['pɪstl] n pistola

piston ['pɪstən] n pistón m, émbolo

pit [pɪt] n hoyo; (also: **coal ~**) mina; (in garage) foso de inspección; (also: **orchestra ~**) foso de la orquesta; (quarry) cantera ▷ vt (chickenpox) picar; (rust) comer; **to ~ A against B** oponer A a B; **pits** npl (Aut) box msg; **~ted with** (chickenpox) picado de; **to ~ one's wits against sb** medir fuerzas con algn

pitch [pɪtʃ] n (throw) lanzamiento m; (Mus) tono; (Brit Sport) campo, terreno; (tar) brea; (in market etc) puesto; (fig: degree) nivel m, grado ▷ vt (throw) arrojar, lanzar ▷ vi (fall) caer(se); (Naut) cabecear; **I can't keep working at this ~** no puedo seguir trabajando a este ritmo; **at its (highest) ~** en su punto máximo; **his anger reached such a ~ that ...** su ira or cólera llegó a tal extremo que ...; **to ~ a tent** montar una tienda (de campaña); **to ~ one's aspirations too high** tener ambiciones desmesuradas

pitch-black ['pɪtʃ'blæk] adj negro como boca de lobo

pitched battle [pɪtʃt-] n batalla campal

piteous ['pɪtɪəs] adj lastimoso

pitfall ['pɪtfɔːl] n riesgo

pith [pɪθ] n (of orange) piel f blanca; (fig) meollo

pithy ['pɪθɪ] adj jugoso

pitiful ['pɪtɪful] adj (touching) lastimoso, conmovedor(a); (contemptible) lamentable

pitiless ['pɪtɪlɪs] adj despiadado, implacable

pittance ['pɪtns] n miseria

pity ['pɪtɪ] n (compassion) compasión f, piedad f; (shame) lástima ▷ vt compadecer(se de);

to have or **take ~ on sb** compadecerse de algn; **what a ~!** ¡qué pena!; **it is a ~ that you can't come** ¡qué pena que no puedas venir!

pivot ['pɪvət] n eje m ▷ vi: **to ~ on** girar sobre; (fig) depender de

pixel ['pɪksl] n (Comput) pixel m, punto

pizza ['piːtsə] n pizza

placard ['plækɑːd] n (in march etc) pancarta

placate [plə'keɪt] vt apaciguar

place [pleɪs] n lugar m, sitio; (rank) rango; (seat) plaza, asiento; (post) puesto; (in street names) plaza; (home): **at/to his ~** en/a su casa ▷ vt (object) poner, colocar; (identify) reconocer; (find a post for) dar un puesto a, colocar; (goods) vender; **to take ~** tener lugar; **to be ~d** (in race, exam) colocarse; **out of ~** (not suitable) fuera de lugar; **in the first ~** (first of all) en primer lugar; **to change ~s with sb** cambiarse de sitio con algn; **~ of birth** lugar m de nacimiento; **from ~ to ~** de un sitio a or para otro; **all over the ~** por todas partes; **he's going ~s** (fig, inf) llegará lejos; **I feel rather out of ~ here** me encuentro algo desplazado; **to put sb in his ~** (fig) poner a algn en su lugar; **it is not my ~ to do it** no me incumbe a mí hacerlo; **to ~ an order with sb (for)** hacer un pedido a algn (de); **we are better ~d than a month ago** estamos en mejor posición que hace un mes

place mat n (wooden etc) salvamanteles m inv; (in linen etc) mantel m individual

placement ['pleɪsmənt] n colocación f; (at work) emplazamiento

placid ['plæsɪd] adj apacible, plácido

plagiarism ['pleɪdʒjərɪzm] n plagio

plague [pleɪg] n plaga; (Med) peste f ▷ vt (fig) acosar, atormentar; **to ~ sb with questions** acribillar a algn a preguntas

plaice [pleɪs] n pl inv platija

plaid [plæd] n (material) tela de cuadros

plain [pleɪn] adj (clear) claro, evidente; (simple) sencillo; (frank) franco, abierto; (not handsome) poco atractivo; (pure) natural, puro ▷ adv claramente ▷ n llano, llanura; **in ~ clothes** (police) vestido de paisano; **to make sth ~ to sb** dejar algo en claro a algn

plain chocolate n chocolate m oscuro or amargo

plainly ['pleɪnlɪ] adv claramente, evidentemente; (frankly) francamente

plaintiff ['pleɪntɪf] n demandante m/f

plaintive ['pleɪntɪv] adj (cry, voice) lastimero, quejumbroso; (look) que da lástima

plait [plæt] n trenza ▷ vt trenzar

plan [plæn] n (drawing) plano; (scheme) plan m, proyecto ▷ vt (think) pensar; (prepare) proyectar, planear; (intend) pensar, tener la intención de ▷ vi hacer proyectos; **have you any ~s for today?** ¿piensas hacer algo hoy?; **to ~ to do** pensar hacer; **how long do you ~ to stay?** ¿cuánto tiempo piensas quedarte?; **to ~ (for)** planear, proyectar; **plan out** vt planear detalladamente

plane [pleɪn] n (Aviat) avión m; (tree) plátano; (tool) cepillo; (Math) plano

planet ['plænɪt] n planeta m

plank [plæŋk] n tabla

planner ['plænəʳ] n planificador(-a) m(f); (chart) diagrama m de planificación; **town ~** urbanista m/f

planning ['plænɪŋ] n (Pol, Econ) planificación f; **family ~** planificación familiar

planning permission n licencia de obras

plant [plɑːnt] n planta; (machinery) maquinaria; (factory) fábrica ▷ vt plantar; (field) sembrar; (bomb) colocar

plantation [plæn'teɪʃən] n plantación f; (estate) hacienda

plant pot n maceta, tiesto

plaque [plæk] n placa

plasma ['plæzmə] n plasma m

plasma screen n pantalla de plasma

plaster ['plɑːstəʳ] n (for walls) yeso; (also: **~ of Paris**) yeso mate; (Med: for broken leg etc) escayola; (Brit: also: **sticking ~**) tirita, esparadrapo ▷ vt enyesar; (cover): **to ~ with** llenar or cubrir de; **to be ~ed with mud** estar cubierto de barro

plaster cast n (Med) escayola; (model, statue) vaciado de yeso

plastered ['plɑːstəd] adj (inf) borracho

plastic ['plæstɪk] n plástico ▷ adj de plástico

plastic bag n bolsa de plástico

plastic bullet n bala de goma

plastic explosive n goma 2®

plasticine® ['plæstɪsiːn] n (Brit) plastilina®

plastic surgery n cirugía plástica

plate [pleɪt] n (dish) plato; (metal, in book) lámina; (Phot) placa; (on door) placa; (Aut: also: **number ~**) matrícula; (dental plate) placa de dentadura postiza

plateau (pl **plateaus** or **plateaux**) ['plætəu, -z] n meseta, altiplanicie f

plate glass n vidrio or cristal m cilindrado

platform ['plætfɔːm] n (Rail) andén m; (stage) plataforma; (at meeting) tribuna; (Pol) programa m (electoral); **the train leaves from ~ seven** el tren sale del andén número siete

platinum ['plætɪnəm] n platino

platoon [plə'tuːn] n pelotón m

platter ['plætəʳ] n fuente f

plausible ['plɔːzɪbl] adj verosímil; (person) convincente

play [pleɪ] n (gen) juego; (Theat) obra ▷ vt (game) jugar; (compete against) jugar contra; (instrument) tocar; (Theat) representar; (: part) hacer el papel de; (fig) desempeñar ▷ vi jugar; (band) tocar; (tape, record) sonar; (frolic) juguetear; **to ~ safe** ir a lo seguro; **to bring** or **call into ~** poner en juego; **to ~ a trick on sb** gastar una broma a algn; **they're ~ing at soldiers** están jugando a (los) soldados; **to ~ for time** (fig) tratar de ganar tiempo; **to ~ into sb's hands** (fig) hacerle el juego a algn;

a smile ~ed on his lips una sonrisa le bailaba en los labios; **play about, play around** vi (person) hacer el tonto; **to ~ about** or **around with** (fiddle with) juguetear con; (idea) darle vueltas a; **play along** vi: **to ~ along with** seguirle el juego a ▷ vt: **to ~ sb along** (fig) jugar con algn; **play back** vt (tape) poner; **play down** vt quitar importancia a; **play on** vt fus (sb's feelings, credulity) aprovecharse de; **to ~ on sb's nerves** atacarle los nervios a algn; **play up** vi (cause trouble) dar guerra

playact ['pleɪækt] vi (fig) hacer comedia or teatro

playboy ['pleɪbɔɪ] n playboy m

player ['pleɪə^r] n jugador(a) m(f); (Theat) actor m, actriz f; (Mus) músico(-a) m(f)

playful ['pleɪful] adj juguetón(-ona)

playground ['pleɪgraund] n (in school) patio de recreo; (in park) parque m infantil

playgroup ['pleɪgruːp] n jardín m de infancia

playing card ['pleɪɪŋ-] n naipe m, carta

playing field n campo de deportes

playmaker ['pleɪmeɪkə^r] n (Sport) jugador encargado de facilitar buenas jugadas a sus compañeros

playmate ['pleɪmeɪt] n compañero(-a) de juego

play-off ['pleɪɔf] n (Sport) (partido de) desempate m

playpen ['pleɪpen] n corral m

playschool ['pleɪskuːl] n = **playgroup**

plaything ['pleɪθɪŋ] n juguete m

playtime ['pleɪtaɪm] n (Scol) (hora de) recreo

playwright ['pleɪraɪt] n dramaturgo(-a)

plc abbr (Brit: = public limited company) S.A.

plea [pliː] n (request) súplica, petición f; (excuse) pretexto, disculpa; (Law) alegato, defensa

plea bargaining n (Law) acuerdo entre fiscal y defensor para agilizar los trámites judiciales

plead [pliːd] vt (Law): **to ~ sb's case** defender a algn; (give as excuse) poner como pretexto ▷ vi (Law) declararse; (beg): **to ~ with sb** suplicar or rogar a algn; **to ~ guilty/not guilty** (defendant) declararse culpable/ inocente; **to ~ for sth** (beg for) suplicar algo

pleasant ['plɛznt] adj agradable

pleasantries ['plɛzntrɪz] npl (polite remarks) cortesías fpl; **to exchange ~** conversar amablemente

please [pliːz] excl ¡por favor! ▷ vt (give pleasure to) dar gusto a, agradar ▷ vi (think fit): **do as you ~** haz lo que quieras or lo que te dé la gana; **to ~ o.s.** hacer lo que le parezca; **~!** ¡por favor!; **~ yourself!** ¡haz lo que quieras!, ¡como quieras!; **~ don't cry!** ¡no llores! te lo ruego

pleased [pliːzd] adj (happy) alegre, contento; (satisfied): **~ (with)** satisfecho (de); **~ to meet you** ¡encantado!, ¡tanto or mucho gusto!; **to be ~ (about sth)** alegrarse (de algo); **we are ~ to inform you that ...** tenemos el gusto de comunicarle que ...

pleasing ['pliːzɪŋ] adj agradable, grato

pleasure ['plɛʒə^r] n placer m, gusto; (will) voluntad f ▷ cpd de recreo; **"it's a ~"** "el gusto es mío"; **it's a ~ to see him** da gusto verle; **I have much ~ in informing you that ...** tengo el gran placer de comunicarles que ...; **with ~** con mucho or todo gusto; **is this trip for business or ~?** ¿este viaje es de negocios o de placer?

pleasure cruise n crucero de placer

pleat [pliːt] n pliegue m

pleb [plɛb] n: **the ~s** la gente baja, la plebe

plebiscite ['plɛbɪsɪt] n plebiscito

plectrum ['plɛktrəm] n plectro

pledge [plɛdʒ] n (object) prenda; (promise) promesa, voto ▷ vt (pawn) empeñar; (promise) prometer; **to ~ support for sb** prometer su apoyo a algn; **to ~ sb to secrecy** hacer jurar a algn que guardará el secreto

plentiful ['plɛntɪful] adj copioso, abundante

plenty ['plɛntɪ] n abundancia; **~ of** mucho(s) (-a(s)); **we've got ~ of time to get there** tenemos tiempo de sobra para llegar

pleurisy ['pluərɪsɪ] n pleuresía

pliable ['plaɪəbl] adj flexible

pliers ['plaɪəz] npl alicates mpl, tenazas fpl

plight [plaɪt] n condición f or situación f difícil

plimsolls ['plɪmsəlz] npl (Brit) zapatillas fpl de tenis

plinth [plɪnθ] n plinto

plod [plɔd] vi caminar con paso pesado; (fig) trabajar laboriosamente

plonk [plɔŋk] (inf) n (Brit: wine) vino peleón ▷ vt: **to ~ sth down** dejar caer algo

plot [plɔt] n (scheme) complot m, conjura; (of story, play) argumento; (of land) terreno, parcela ▷ vt (mark out) trazar; (conspire) tramar, urdir ▷ vi conspirar; **a vegetable ~** un cuadro de hortalizas

plough, plow (US) [plau] n arado ▷ vt (earth) arar; **plough back** vt (Comm) reinvertir; **plough through** vt fus (crowd) abrirse paso a la fuerza por

ploughman ['plaumən] n: **~'s lunch** pan m con queso y cebolla

plow [plau] n, vb (US) = **plough**

ploy [plɔɪ] n truco, estratagema

pluck [plʌk] vt (fruit) coger (Sp), recoger (LAm); (musical instrument) puntear; (bird) desplumar ▷ n valor m, ánimo; **to ~ up courage** hacer de tripas corazón; **to ~ one's eyebrows** depilarse las cejas

plucky ['plʌkɪ] adj valiente

plug [plʌg] n tapón m; (Elec) enchufe m, clavija; (Aut: also: **spark(ing) ~**) bujía ▷ vt (hole) tapar; (inf: advertise) dar publicidad a; **to give sb/sth a ~** dar publicidad a algn/ algo; **to ~ a lead into a socket** enchufar un hilo en una toma; **plug in** vt, ▷ vi (Elec) enchufar

plughole ['plʌghəul] n desagüe m

plum [plʌm] *n* (*fruit*) ciruela; (*also:* **~ job**) chollo

plumb [plʌm] *adj* vertical ▷ *n* plomo ▷ *adv* (*exactly*) exactamente, en punto ▷ *vt* sondar; (*fig*) sondear; **plumb in** *vt* (*washing machine*) conectar

plumber ['plʌmə^r] *n* fontanero(-a), plomero(-a) (*LAm*)

plumbing ['plʌmɪŋ] *n* (*trade*) fontanería, plomería (*LAm*); (*piping*) cañerías

plummet ['plʌmɪt] *vi:* **to ~ (down)** caer a plomo

plump [plʌmp] *adj* rechoncho, rollizo ▷ *vt:* **to ~ sth (down) on** dejar caer algo en; **plump for** *vt fus* (*inf: choose*) optar por; **plump up** *vt* ahuecar

plunder ['plʌndə^r] *n* pillaje *m*; (*loot*) botín *m* ▷ *vt* saquear, pillar

plunge [plʌndʒ] *n* zambullida ▷ *vt* sumergir, hundir ▷ *vi* (*fall*) caer; (*dive*) saltar; (*person*) arrojarse; (*sink*) hundirse; **to take the ~** lanzarse; **to ~ a room into darkness** sumir una habitación en la oscuridad

plunger ['plʌndʒə^r] *n* émbolo; (*for drain*) desatascador *m*

plunging ['plʌndʒɪŋ] *adj* (*neckline*) escotado

pluperfect [pluː'pəːfɪkt] *n* pluscuamperfecto

plural ['plʊərl] *adj* plural ▷ *n* plural *m*

plus [plʌs] *n* (*also:* **~ sign**) signo más; (*fig*) punto a favor ▷ *adj:* **a ~ factor** (*fig*) un factor a favor ▷ *prep* más, y, además de; **ten/twenty ~** más de diez/veinte

plush [plʌʃ] *adj* de felpa

plus-one ['plʌs'wʌn] *n* (*inf*) acompañante *mf*

ply [plaɪ] *vt* (*a trade*) ejercer ▷ *vi* (*ship*) ir y venir; (*for hire*) ofrecerse (para alquilar); **three ~** (*wool*) de tres cabos; **to ~ sb with drink** no dejar de ofrecer copas a algn

plywood ['plaɪwʊd] *n* madera contrachapada

PM *n abbr* (*Brit*) = **Prime Minister**

p.m. *adv abbr* (= *post meridiem*) de la tarde *or* noche

PMS *n abbr* (= *premenstrual syndrome*) SPM *m*

PMT *n abbr* (= *premenstrual tension*) SPM *m*

pneumatic [njuː'mætɪk] *adj* neumático

pneumatic drill *n* taladradora neumática

pneumonia [njuː'məʊnɪə] *n* pulmonía, neumonía

PO *n abbr* (= *Post Office*) Correos *mpl*; (*Naut*) = **petty officer**

po *abbr* = **postal order**

poach [pəʊtʃ] *vt* (*cook*) escalfar; (*steal*) cazar/pescar en vedado ▷ *vi* cazar/pescar en vedado

poached [pəʊtʃt] *adj* (*egg*) escalfado

poacher ['pəʊtʃə^r] *n* cazador(a) *m(f)* furtivo(-a)

PO Box *n abbr* (= *Post Office Box*) apdo., aptdo.

pocket ['pɔkɪt] *n* bolsillo; (*of air, Geo, fig*) bolsa; (*Billiards*) tronera ▷ *vt* meter en el bolsillo; (*steal*) embolsarse; (*Billiards*) entronerar; **breast ~** bolsillo de pecho; **~ of**

resistance foco de resistencia; **~ of warm air** bolsa de aire caliente; **to be out of ~** salir perdiendo; **to be £5 in/out of ~** salir ganando/perdiendo 5 libras

pocketbook ['pɔkɪtbuk] *n* (*US: wallet*) cartera; (*: handbag*) bolso

pocket knife *n* navaja

pocket money *n* asignación *f*

pod [pɔd] *n* vaina

podcast ['pɔdkɑːst] *n* podcast *m* ▷ *vi* podcastear

podgy ['pɔdʒɪ] *adj* gordinflón(-ona)

podiatrist [pɔ'diːətrɪst] *n* (*US*) podólogo(-a)

podium ['pəʊdɪəm] *n* podio

poem ['pəʊɪm] *n* poema *m*

poet ['pəʊɪt] *n* poeta *m/f*

poetic [pəʊ'etɪk] *adj* poético

poet laureate [-'lɔːrɪɪt] *n* poeta *m* laureado

poetry ['pəʊɪtrɪ] *n* poesía

poignant ['pɔɪnjənt] *adj* conmovedor(a)

point [pɔɪnt] *n* punto; (*tip*) punta; (*purpose*) fin *m*, propósito; (*Brit Elec: also:* **power ~**) toma de corriente, enchufe *m*; (*use*) utilidad *f*; (*significant part*) lo esencial; (*place*) punto, lugar *m*; (*also:* **decimal ~**): **2 ~ 3 (2.3)** dos coma tres (2,3) ▷ *vt* (*gun etc*): **to ~ sth at sb** apuntar con algo a algn ▷ *vi:* **to ~** señalar; **points** *npl* (*Aut*) contactos *mpl*; (*Rail*) agujas *fpl*; **to be on the ~ of doing sth** estar a punto de hacer algo; **to make a ~ of doing sth** poner empeño en hacer algo; **to get the ~** comprender; **to come to the ~** ir al meollo; **there's no ~ (in doing)** no tiene sentido (hacer); **~ of departure** (*also fig*) punto de partida; **~ of order** cuestión *f* de procedimiento; **~ of sale** (*Comm*) punto de venta; **~-of-sale advertising** publicidad *f* en el punto de venta; **the train stops at Carlisle and all ~s south** el tren para en Carlisle, y en todas las estaciones al sur; **when it comes to the ~** a la hora de la verdad; **in ~ of fact** en realidad; **that's the whole ~!** ¡de eso se trata!; **to be beside the ~** no venir al caso; **you've got a ~ there!** ¡tienes razón!; **point out** *vt* señalar; **point to** *vt fus* indicar con el dedo; (*fig*) indicar, señalar

point-blank ['pɔɪnt'blæŋk] *adv* (*say, refuse*) sin más hablar; (*also:* **at ~ range**) a quemarropa

pointed ['pɔɪntɪd] *adj* (*shape*) puntiagudo, afilado; (*remark*) intencionado

pointer ['pɔɪntə^r] *n* (*stick*) puntero; (*needle*) aguja, indicador *m*; (*clue*) indicación *f*, pista; (*advice*) consejo

pointless ['pɔɪntlɪs] *adj* sin sentido

point of view *n* punto de vista

poise [pɔɪz] *n* (*of head, body*) porte *m*; (*calmness*) aplomo

poison ['pɔɪzn] *n* veneno ▷ *vt* envenenar

poisonous ['pɔɪznəs] *adj* venenoso; (*fumes etc*) tóxico; (*fig: ideas, literature*) pernicioso; (*: rumours, individual*) nefasto

poke [pəuk] vt (fire) hurgar, atizar; (jab with finger, stick etc) dar; (Comput) almacenar; (put): **to ~ sth in(to)** introducir algo en ▷ n (jab) empujoncito; (with elbow) codazo; **to ~ one's head out of the window** asomar la cabeza por la ventana; **to ~ fun at sb** ridiculizar a algn; **to give the fire a ~** atizar el fuego; **poke about** vi fisgonear; **poke out** vi (stick out) salir

poker ['pəukəʳ] n atizador m; (Cards) póker m

poky ['pəukı] adj estrecho

Poland ['pəulənd] n Polonia

polar ['pəuləʳ] adj polar

polar bear n oso polar

polarize ['pəuləraız] vt polarizar

Pole [pəul] n polaco(-a)

pole [pəul] n palo; (Geo) polo; (Tel) poste m; (flagpole) asta; (tent pole) mástil m

poleaxe ['pəulæks] vt (fig) desnucar

pole bean n (US) judía trepadora

pole star n estrella polar

pole vault n salto con pértiga

police [pə'li:s] n policía ▷ vt (streets, city, frontier) vigilar

police car n coche-patrulla m

police constable n (Brit) guardia m, policía m

police department n (US) policía

police force n cuerpo de policía

policeman [pə'li:smən] n guardia m, policía m, agente m (LAm)

police officer n guardia m, policía m

police station n comisaría

policewoman [pə'li:swumən] n mujer f policía

policy ['pɒlısı] n política; (also: **insurance ~**) póliza; (of newspaper, company) política; **it is our ~ to do that** tenemos por norma hacer eso; **to take out a ~** sacar una póliza, hacerse un seguro

polio ['pəulɪəu] n polio f

Polish ['pəulıʃ] adj polaco ▷ n (Ling) polaco

polish ['pɒlıʃ] n (for shoes) betún m; (for floor) cera (de lustrar); (for nails) esmalte m; (shine) brillo, lustre m; (fig: refinement) refinamiento ▷ vt (shoes) limpiar; (make shiny) pulir, sacar brillo a; (fig: improve) perfeccionar, refinar; **polish off** vt (work) terminar; (food) despachar; **polish up** vt (shoes, furniture etc) limpiar, sacar brillo a; (fig: language) perfeccionar

polished ['pɒlıʃt] adj (fig: person) refinado

polite [pə'laıt] adj cortés, atento; (formal) correcto; **it's not ~ to do that** es de mala educación hacer eso

politeness [pə'laıtnıs] n cortesía

political [pə'lıtıkl] adj político

politically [pə'lıtıkəlı] adv políticamente

politically correct adj políticamente correcto

politician [pɒlı'tıʃən] n político(-a)

politics ['pɒlıtıks] n política

poll [pəul] n (votes) votación f, votos mpl; (also: **opinion ~**) sondeo, encuesta ▷ vt (votes)

obtener; (in opinion poll) encuestar; **to go to the ~s** (voters) votar; (government) acudir a las urnas

pollen ['pɒlən] n polen m

pollen count n índice m de polen

polling booth n cabina de votar

polling day n día m de elecciones

polling station n centro electoral

pollster ['pəulstəʳ] n (person) encuestador(a) m(f); (organization) empresa de encuestas or sondeos

poll tax n (Brit) contribución f municipal (no progresiva)

pollutant [pə'lu:tənt] n (agente m) contaminante m

pollute [pə'lu:t] vt contaminar

pollution [pə'lu:ʃən] n contaminación f

polo ['pəuləu] n (sport) polo

polo-neck ['pəuləunɛk] adj de cuello vuelto ▷ n (sweater) suéter m de cuello vuelto

polo shirt n polo, niqui m

poly bag n (Brit inf) bolsa de plástico

polyester [pɒlı'ɛstəʳ] n poliéster m

polygraph ['pɒlıgrɑ:f] n polígrafo

polystyrene [pɒlı'staıri:n] n poliestireno

polytechnic [pɒlı'tɛknık] n escuela politécnica

polythene ['pɒlıθi:n] n (Brit) polietileno

polythene bag n bolsa de plástico

polyurethane [pɒlı'juərıθeın] n poliuretano

pomegranate ['pɒmıgrænıt] n granada

pomp [pɒmp] n pompa

pompous ['pɒmpəs] adj pomposo; (person) presumido

pond [pɒnd] n (natural) charca; (artificial) estanque m

ponder ['pɒndəʳ] vt meditar

ponderous ['pɒndərəs] adj pesado

pong [pɒŋ] n (Brit inf) peste f ▷ vi (Brit inf) apestar

pontiff ['pɒntıf] n pontífice m

pony ['pəunı] n poney m, potro

ponytail ['pəunıteıl] n coleta, cola de caballo

pony trekking n (Brit) excursión f a caballo

poodle ['pu:dl] n caniche m

pool [pu:l] n (natural) charca; (pond) estanque m; (also: **swimming ~**) piscina, alberca (LAm); (billiards) billar m americano; (Comm: consortium) consorcio; (: US: monopoly trust) trust m ▷ vt juntar; **typing ~** servicio de mecanografía; (football) **~s** npl quinielas fpl

poor [puəʳ] adj pobre; (bad) malo ▷ npl: **the ~** los pobres

poorly ['puəlı] adj mal, enfermo ▷ adv mal

pop [pɒp] n ¡pum!; (sound) ruido seco; (Mus) (música) pop m; (US inf: father) papá m; (inf: drink) gaseosa ▷ vt (burst) hacer reventar ▷ vi reventar; (cork) saltar; **she ~ped her head out (of the window)** sacó de repente la cabeza (por la ventana); **pop in** vi entrar un momento; **pop out** vi salir un momento; **pop up** vi aparecer inesperadamente

pop concert n concierto pop
popcorn ['pɒpkɔːn] n palomitas fpl (de maíz)
pope [pəup] n papa m
poplar ['pɒplər] n álamo
popper ['pɒpər] n corchete m, automático
poppy ['pɒpɪ] n amapola; see also
   Remembrance Day
Popsicle® ['pɒpsɪkl] n (US) polo
pop star n estrella del pop
popular ['pɒpjulər] adj popular; **a ~ song** una
   canción popular; **to be ~ (with)** (person) caer
   bien (a); (decision) ser popular (entre)
popularity [pɒpju'lærɪtɪ] n popularidad f
population [pɒpju'leɪʃən] n población f
pop-up ['pɒpʌp] adj desplegable, pop-up inv
   ▷ n desplegable m
pop-up book n libro desplegable
pop-up menu n (Comput) menú m
   desplegable
porcelain ['pɔːslɪn] n porcelana
porch [pɔːtʃ] n pórtico, entrada; (US) veranda
porcupine ['pɔːkjupaɪn] n puerco m espín
pore [pɔːr] n poro ▷ vi: **to ~ over** enfrascarse
   en
pork [pɔːk] n (carne f de) cerdo or chancho
   (LAm)
pork chop n chuleta de cerdo
pork pie n (Brit: Culin) empanada de carne de
   cerdo
porn [pɔːn] adj (inf) porno inv ▷ n porno
pornographic [pɔːnə'græfɪk] adj
   pornográfico
pornography [pɔː'nɔɡrəfɪ] n pornografía
porpoise ['pɔːpəs] n marsopa
porridge ['pɒrɪdʒ] n gachas fpl de avena
port [pɔːt] n (harbour) puerto; (Naut: left side)
   babor m; (wine) oporto; (Comput) puerta,
   puerto, port m; **~ of call** puerto de escala
portable ['pɔːtəbl] adj portátil
porter ['pɔːtər] n (for luggage) maletero;
   (doorkeeper) portero(-a), conserje m/f; (US Rail)
   mozo de los coches-cama
portfolio [pɔːt'fəulɪəu] n (case, of artist)
   cartera, carpeta; (Pol, Finance) cartera
porthole ['pɔːthəul] n portilla
portion ['pɔːʃən] n porción f; (helping) ración f
portly ['pɔːtlɪ] adj corpulento
portrait ['pɔːtreɪt] n retrato
portray [pɔː'treɪ] vt retratar; (in writing)
   representar
portrayal [pɔː'treɪəl] n representación f
Portugal ['pɔːtjugl] n Portugal m
Portuguese [pɔːtju'giːz] adj portugués(-esa)
   ▷ n pl inv portugués(-esa) m(f); (Ling)
   portugués m
pose [pəuz] n postura, actitud f; (pej)
   afectación f, pose f ▷ vi posar; (pretend): **to ~
   as** hacerse pasar por ▷ vt (question) plantear;
   to ~ for posar para; **to strike a ~** tomar or
   adoptar una pose or actitud
poser ['pəuzər] n problema m/pregunta
   difícil; (person) = **poseur**

poseur [pəu'zəːr] n presumido(-a), persona
   afectada
posh [pɒʃ] adj (inf) elegante, de lujo ▷ adv (inf):
   to talk ~ hablar con acento afectado
position [pə'zɪʃən] n posición f; (job) puesto
   ▷ vt colocar; **to be in a ~ to do sth** estar en
   condiciones de hacer algo
positive ['pɒzɪtɪv] adj positivo; (certain)
   seguro; (definite) definitivo; **we look
   forward to a ~ reply** (Comm) esperamos que
   pueda darnos una respuesta en firme; **he's a
   ~ nuisance** es un auténtico pelmazo; **~ cash
   flow** (Comm) flujo positivo de efectivo
positively ['pɒzɪtɪvlɪ] adv (affirmatively,
   enthusiastically) de forma positiva; (inf: really)
   absolutamente
posse ['pɒsɪ] n (US) pelotón m
possess [pə'zɛs] vt poseer; **like one ~ed**
   como un poseído; **whatever can have ~ed
   you?** ¿cómo se te ocurrió?
possessed [pə'zɛst] adj poseso, poseído
possession [pə'zɛʃən] n posesión f;
   possessions npl (belongings) pertenencias fpl;
   to take ~ of sth tomar posesión de algo
possessive [pə'zɛsɪv] adj posesivo
possessiveness [pə'zɛsɪvnɪs] n posesividad f
possibility [pɒsɪ'bɪlɪtɪ] n posibilidad f; **he's
   ~ for the part** es uno de los posibles para el
   papel
possible ['pɒsɪbl] adj posible; **as big as ~** lo
   más grande posible; **it is ~ to do it** es posible
   hacerlo; **as far as ~** en la medida de lo
   posible; **a ~ candidate** un(a) posible
   candidato(-a)
possibly ['pɒsɪblɪ] adv (perhaps) posiblemente,
   tal vez; **I cannot ~ come** me es imposible
   venir; **could you ~ ...?** ¿podrías ...?
post [pəust] n (Brit: system) correos mpl;
   (letters, delivery) correo; (job, situation) puesto;
   (trading post) factoría; (pole) poste m; (on
   internet forum) anuncio, post m ▷ vt (Brit: send
   by post) mandar por correo; (: put in mailbox)
   echar al correo; (Mil) apostar; (bills) fijar,
   pegar; (to internet) colgar; (Brit: appoint): **to ~
   to** destinar a; **by ~** por correo; **by return of ~**
   a vuelta de correo; **to keep sb ~ed** tener a
   algn al corriente
postage ['pəustɪdʒ] n porte m, franqueo
postage stamp n sello (de correo)
postal ['pəustl] adj postal, de correos
postal order n giro postal
postbox ['pəustbɒks] n (Brit) buzón m
postcard ['pəustkaːd] n (tarjeta) postal f
postcode ['pəustkəud] n (Brit) código postal
poster ['pəustər] n cartel m, afiche m (LAm)
poste restante [pəust'rɛstɔ̃nt] n (Brit) lista
   de correos
posterior [pɒs'tɪərɪər] n (inf) trasero
posterity [pɒs'tɛrɪtɪ] n posteridad f
postgraduate ['pəust'grædjuːt] n
   posgraduado(-a)
posthumous ['pɒstjuməs] adj póstumo

postman ['pəustmən] (Brit) (irreg: like **man**) n cartero

postmark ['pəustmɑːk] n matasellos m inv

post-mortem [pəust'mɔːtəm] n autopsia

post office n (building) (oficina de) correos m; (organization): **the Post Office** Dirección f General de Correos

postpone [pəs'pəun] vt aplazar, postergar (LAm)

postponement [pəs'pəunmənt] n aplazamiento

posture ['pɔstʃəʳ] n postura, actitud f

post-war [pəust'wɔːʳ] adj de la posguerra

postwoman ['pəustwumən] (irreg: like **woman**) n (Brit) cartera

posy ['pəuzɪ] n ramillete m (de flores)

pot [pɔt] n (for cooking) olla; (teapot) tetera; (coffeepot) cafetera; (for flowers) maceta; (for jam) tarro, pote m (LAm); (piece of pottery) cacharro; (inf: marijuana) costo, chocolate m ▷ vt (plant) poner en tiesto; (conserve) conservar (en tarros); **~s of** (inf) montones de; **to go to ~** (inf: work, performance) irse al traste

potato (pl **potatoes**) [pə'teɪtəu] n patata, papa (LAm)

potato crisps, potato chips (US) npl patatas fpl or papas fpl (LAm)

potato peeler n pelapatatas m inv

potent ['pəutnt] adj potente, poderoso; (drink) fuerte

potential [pə'tɛnʃl] adj potencial, posible ▷ n potencial m; **to have ~** prometer

pothole ['pɔthəul] n (in road) bache m; (Brit: underground) gruta

potholing ['pɔthəulɪŋ] n (Brit): **to go ~** dedicarse a la espeleología

potion ['pəuʃən] n poción f, pócima

potluck [pɔt'lʌk] n: **to take ~** conformarse con lo que haya

pot plant n planta de interior

potted ['pɔtɪd] adj (food) en conserva; (plant) en tiesto or maceta; (fig: shortened) resumido

potter ['pɔtəʳ] n alfarero(-a) ▷ vi: **to ~ around, ~ about** entretenerse haciendo cosillas; **to ~ round the house** estar en casa haciendo cosillas; **~'s wheel** torno de alfarero

pottery ['pɔtərɪ] n cerámica; (factory) alfarería; **a piece of ~** un objeto de cerámica

potty ['pɔtɪ] adj (inf: mad) chiflado ▷ n orinal m de niño

pouch [pautʃ] n (Zool) bolsa; (for tobacco) petaca

poultry ['pəultrɪ] n aves fpl de corral; (meat) pollo

pounce [pauns] vi: **to ~ on** precipitarse sobre ▷ n salto, ataque m

pound [paund] n libra; (for dogs) perrera; (for cars) depósito ▷ vt (beat) golpear; (crush) machacar ▷ vi (beat) dar golpes; **half a ~** media libra; **a one ~ note** un billete de una libra

pound sterling n libra esterlina

pour [pɔːʳ] vt echar; (tea) servir ▷ vi correr, fluir; (rain) llover a cántaros; **pour away, pour off** vt vaciar, verter; **to ~ sb a drink** servirle a algn una copa; **pour in** vi (people) entrar en tropel; **to come ~ing in** (water) entrar a raudales; (letters) llegar a montones; (cars, people) llegar en tropel; **pour out** vi (people) salir en tropel ▷ vt (drink) echar, servir; (fig): **to ~ out one's feelings** desahogarse

pouring ['pɔːrɪŋ] adj: **~ rain** lluvia torrencial

pout [paut] vi hacer pucheros

poverty ['pɔvətɪ] n pobreza, miseria; (fig) falta, escasez f

poverty line n: **below the ~** por debajo del umbral de pobreza

poverty-stricken ['pɔvətɪstrɪkn] adj necesitado

POW n abbr = **prisoner of war**

powder ['paudəʳ] n polvo; (also: **face ~**) polvos mpl; (also: **gun ~**) pólvora ▷ vt empolvar; **to ~ one's face** empolvarse la cara; **to ~ one's nose** empolvarse la nariz, ponerse polvos; (euphemism) ir al baño

powder compact n polvera

powdered milk ['paudəd-] n leche f en polvo

powder keg n (fig) polvorín m

powder puff n borla (para empolvarse)

powder room n aseos mpl

power ['pauəʳ] n poder m; (strength) fuerza; (nation) potencia; (drive) empuje m; (Tech) potencia; (Elec) energía ▷ vt impulsar; **to be in ~** (Pol) estar en el poder; **to do all in one's ~ to help sb** hacer todo lo posible por ayudar a algn; **the world ~s** las potencias mundiales

power cut n (Brit) apagón m

powered ['pauəd] adj: **~ by** impulsado por; **nuclear-~ submarine** submarino nuclear

power failure n = **power cut**

powerful ['pauəful] adj poderoso; (engine) potente; (strong) fuerte; (play, speech) convincente

powerless ['pauəlɪs] adj impotente

power of attorney n poder m, procuración f

power point n (Brit) enchufe m

power station n central f eléctrica

pp abbr (= per procurationem: by proxy) p.p.; = **pages**

PPS n abbr (= post postscriptum) posdata adicional; (Brit: = Parliamentary Private Secretary) ayudante de un ministro

PR n abbr see **proportional representation**; (= public relations) relaciones fpl públicas

practical ['præktɪkl] adj práctico

practicality [præktɪ'kælɪtɪ] n (of situation etc) aspecto práctico

practical joke n broma pesada

practically ['præktɪklɪ] adv (almost) casi, prácticamente

practice ['præktɪs] n (habit) costumbre f; (exercise) práctica; (training) adiestramiento; (Med: of profession) práctica, ejercicio; (Med, Law: business) consulta ▷ vt, vi (US) = **practise**; **in ~** (in reality) en la práctica; **out of ~** desentrenado; **to put sth into ~** poner algo en práctica; **it's common ~** es bastante corriente; **target ~** práctica de tiro; **he has a small ~** (doctor) tiene pocos pacientes; **to set up in ~ as** establecerse como

practise, practice (US) ['præktɪs] vt (carry out) practicar; (profession) ejercer; (train at) practicar ▷ vi ejercer; (train) practicar

practising, practicing (US) ['præktɪsɪŋ] adj (Christian etc) practicante; (lawyer) en ejercicio; (homosexual) activo

practitioner [præk'tɪʃənə[r]] n practicante m/f; (Med) médico(-a)

pragmatic [præg'mætɪk] adj pragmático

prairie ['prɛərɪ] n (US) pampa

praise [preɪz] n alabanza(s) f(pl), elogio(s) m(pl) ▷ vt alabar, elogiar

praiseworthy ['preɪswə:ðɪ] adj loable

pram [præm] n (Brit) cochecito de niño

prance [prɑ:ns] vi (horse) hacer cabriolas

prank [præŋk] n travesura

prat [præt] n (Brit inf) imbécil m/f

prawn [prɔ:n] n gamba

prawn cocktail n cóctel m de gambas

pray [preɪ] vi rezar; **to ~ for forgiveness** pedir perdón

prayer [prɛə[r]] n oración f, rezo; (entreaty) ruego, súplica

preach [pri:tʃ] vi predicar

preacher ['pri:tʃə[r]] n predicador(a) m(f); (US: minister) pastor(a) m(f)

prearrange [pri:ə'reɪndʒ] vt organizar or acordar de antemano

precarious [prɪ'kɛərɪəs] adj precario

precaution [prɪ'kɔ:ʃən] n precaución f

precede [prɪ'si:d] vt, vi preceder

precedent ['prɛsɪdənt] n precedente m; **to establish** or **set a ~** sentar un precedente

preceding [prɪ'si:dɪŋ] adj precedente

precinct ['pri:sɪŋkt] n recinto; (US: district) distrito, barrio; **precincts** npl recinto; **pedestrian ~** (Brit) zona peatonal; **shopping ~** (Brit) centro comercial

precious ['prɛʃəs] adj precioso; (treasured) querido; (stylized) afectado ▷ adv (inf): **~ little/few** muy poco/pocos; **your ~ dog** (ironic) tu querido perro

precipitate adj [prɪ'sɪpɪtɪt] (hasty) precipitado ▷ vt [prɪ'sɪpɪteɪt] precipitar

precise [prɪ'saɪs] adj preciso, exacto; (person) escrupuloso

precisely [prɪ'saɪslɪ] adv exactamente, precisamente

precision [prɪ'sɪʒən] n precisión f

preclude [prɪ'klu:d] vt excluir

precocious [prɪ'kəuʃəs] adj precoz

precondition [pri:kən'dɪʃən] n condición f previa

predator ['prɛdətə[r]] n depredador m

predecessor ['pri:dɪsɛsə[r]] n antecesor(a) m(f)

predestination [pri:dɛstɪ'neɪʃən] n predestinación f

predicament [prɪ'dɪkəmənt] n apuro

predict [prɪ'dɪkt] vt predecir, pronosticar

predictable [prɪ'dɪktəbl] adj previsible

prediction [prɪ'dɪkʃən] n pronóstico, predicción f

predominant [prɪ'dɔmɪnənt] adj predominante

predominantly [prɪ'dɔmɪnəntlɪ] adv en su mayoría

pre-eminent [pri:'ɛmɪnənt] adj preeminente

pre-empt [pri:'ɛmt] vt (Brit) adelantarse a

preen [pri:n] vt: **to ~ itself** (bird) limpiarse las plumas; **to ~ o.s.** pavonearse

prefab ['pri:fæb] n casa prefabricada

preface ['prɛfəs] n prefacio

prefect ['pri:fɛkt] n (Brit: in school) monitor(a) m(f)

prefer [prɪ'fə:[r]] vt preferir; (Law: charges, complaint) presentar; (: action) entablar; **to ~ coffee to tea** preferir el café al té

preferable ['prɛfrəbl] adj preferible

preferably ['prɛfrəblɪ] adv preferentemente, más bien

preference ['prɛfrəns] n preferencia; (priority) prioridad f; **in ~ to sth** antes que algo

preferential [prɛfə'rɛnʃəl] adj preferente

prefix ['pri:fɪks] n prefijo

pregnancy ['prɛgnənsɪ] n (of woman) embarazo; (of animal) preñez f

pregnancy test n prueba del embarazo

pregnant ['prɛgnənt] adj (woman) embarazada; (animal) preñada; **3 months ~** embarazada de tres meses; **~ with meaning** cargado de significado

prehistoric ['pri:hɪs'tɔrɪk] adj prehistórico

prejudge [pri:'dʒʌdʒ] vt prejuzgar

prejudice ['prɛdʒʊdɪs] n (bias) prejuicio; (harm) perjuicio ▷ vt (bias) predisponer; (harm) perjudicar; **to ~ sb in favour of/ against** (bias) predisponer a algn a favor de/ en contra de

prejudiced ['prɛdʒʊdɪst] adj (person) predispuesto; (view) parcial, interesado; **to be ~ against sb/sth** estar predispuesto en contra de algn/algo

preliminary [prɪ'lɪmɪnərɪ] adj preliminar

prelude ['prɛlju:d] n preludio

premarital ['pri:'mærɪtl] adj prematrimonial, premarital

premature ['prɛmətʃuə[r]] adj (arrival etc) prematuro; **you are being a little ~** te has adelantado

premeditation [pri:mɛdɪ'teɪʃən] n premeditación f

premier ['prɛmɪəʳ] adj primero, principal ▷ n
(Pol) primer(a) ministro(-a)

première ['prɛmɪɛəʳ] n estreno

Premier League [prɛmɪə'liːg] n primera
división

premise ['prɛmɪs] n premisa

premises ['prɛmɪsɪs] npl local msg; **on the ~**
en el lugar mismo; **business ~** locales mpl
comerciales

premium ['priːmɪəm] n premio; (insurance)
prima; **to be at a ~** estar muy solicitado;
to sell at a ~ (shares) vender caro

premium bond n (Brit) bono del estado que
participa en una lotería nacional; ver nota

premonition [prɛmə'nɪʃən] n
presentimiento

preoccupied [priː'ɔkjupaɪd] adj (worried)
preocupado; (absorbed) ensimismado

prep [prɛp] adj abbr: **~ school = preparatory
school** ▷ n abbr (Scol: = preparation) deberes mpl

prepaid [priː'peɪd] adj porte pagado;
~ envelope sobre m de porte pagado

preparation [prɛpə'reɪʃən] n preparación f;
preparations npl preparativos mpl; **in ~ for
sth** en preparación para algo

preparatory [prɪ'pærətərɪ] adj preparatorio,
preliminar; **~ to sth/to doing sth** como
preparación para algo/para hacer algo

preparatory school n (Brit) colegio privado de
enseñanza primaria; (US) colegio privado de
enseñanza secundaria

prepare [prɪ'pɛəʳ] vt preparar, disponer;
(Culin) preparar ▷ vi: **to ~ for** (action)
prepararse or disponerse para; (event) hacer
preparativos para

prepared [prɪ'pɛəd] adj (willing): **to be ~ to
help sb** estar dispuesto a ayudar a algn;
~ for listo para

preposition [prɛpə'zɪʃən] n preposición f

preposterous [prɪ'pɔstərəs] adj absurdo,
ridículo

prep school [prɛp-] n = **preparatory school**

prerequisite [priː'rɛkwɪzɪt] n requisito
previo

preschool ['priː'skuːl] adj (child, age)
preescolar

prescribe [prɪ'skraɪb] vt prescribir; (Med)
recetar; **~d books** (Brit Scol) libros mpl del
curso

prescription [prɪ'skrɪpʃən] n (Med) receta;
to make up a ~ (US), **fill a ~** preparar una
receta; **only available on ~** se vende
solamente con receta (médica)

presence ['prɛzns] n presencia; (attendance)
asistencia; **in sb's ~** en presencia de algn;
~ of mind aplomo

presence of mind n aplomo

present adj ['prɛznt] (in attendance) presente;
(current) actual ▷ n ['prɛznt] (gift) regalo;
(actuality): **the ~** la actualidad, el presente
▷ vt [prɪ'zɛnt] (introduce) presentar; (expound)
exponer; (give) presentar, dar, ofrecer; (Theat)

representar; **to be ~ at** asistir a, estar
presente en; **those ~** los presentes; **to give
sb a ~, make sb a ~ of sth** regalar algo a algn;
at ~ actualmente; **to ~ o.s. for an interview**
presentarse a una entrevista; **may I ~ Miss
Clark** permítame presentarle or le presento a
la Srta Clark

presentable [prɪ'zɛntəbl] adj: **to make o.s. ~**
arreglarse

presentation [prɛzn'teɪʃən] n presentación f;
(gift) obsequio; (of case) exposición f; (Theat)
representación f; **on ~ of the voucher** al
presentar el vale

present-day ['prɛzntdeɪ] adj actual

presenter [prɪ'zɛntəʳ] n (Radio, TV) locutor(a)
m(f)

presently ['prɛzntlɪ] adv (soon) dentro de
poco; (US: now) ahora

present participle n participio (de)
presente

preservation [prɛzə'veɪʃən] n conservación f

preservative [prɪ'zə:vətɪv] n conservante m

preserve [prɪ'zə:v] vt (keep safe) preservar,
proteger; (maintain) mantener; (food)
conservar; (in salt) salar ▷ n (for game) coto,
vedado often pl (jam) confitura

preside [prɪ'zaɪd] vi presidir

presidency ['prɛzɪdənsɪ] n presidencia

president ['prɛzɪdənt] n presidente m/f;
(US: of company) director(a) m(f)

presidential [prɛzɪ'dɛnʃl] adj presidencial

press [prɛs] n (tool, machine, newspapers) prensa;
(printer's) imprenta; (of hand) apretón m ▷ vt
(push) empujar; (squeeze) apretar; (grapes)
pisar; (clothes: iron) planchar; (pressure)
presionar; (doorbell) apretar, pulsar, tocar;
(insist): **to ~ sth on sb** insistir en que algn
acepte algo ▷ vi (squeeze) apretar; (pressurize)
ejercer presión; **to go to ~** (newspaper) entrar
en prensa; **to be in the ~** (being printed) estar
en prensa; (in the newspapers) aparecer en la
prensa; **we are ~ed for time** tenemos poco
tiempo; **to ~ sb to do or into doing sth** (urge,
entreat) presionar a algn para que haga algo;
to ~ sb for an answer insistir a algn para
que conteste; **to ~ charges against sb** (Law)
demandar a algn; **press ahead** vi seguir
adelante; **press on** vi avanzar; (hurry) apretar
el paso

press agency n agencia de prensa

press conference n rueda de prensa

pressing ['prɛsɪŋ] adj apremiante

press officer n jefe(-a) m(f) de prensa

press release n comunicado de prensa

press stud n (Brit) botón m de presión

press-up ['prɛsʌp] n (Brit) flexión f

pressure ['prɛʃəʳ] n presión f; (urgency)
apremio, urgencia; (influence) influencia;
high/low ~ alta/baja presión; **to put ~ on sb**
presionar a algn, hacer presión sobre algn

pressure cooker n olla a presión

pressure gauge n manómetro

pressure group n grupo de presión
pressurized ['prɛʃəraɪzd] adj (container)
a presión
prestige [prɛs'tiːʒ] n prestigio
prestigious [prɛs'tɪdʒəs] adj prestigioso
presumably [prɪ'zjuːməblɪ] adv es de
suponer que, cabe presumir que; ~ **he did it**
es de suponer que lo hizo él
presume [prɪ'zjuːm] vt: **to ~ (that)** presumir
(que), suponer (que); **to ~ to do** (dare)
atreverse a hacer
presumption [prɪ'zʌmpʃən] n suposición f;
(pretension) presunción f
presuppose [priːsə'pəʊz] vt presuponer
pretence, pretense (US) [prɪ'tɛns] n (claim)
pretensión f; (pretext) pretexto; (make-believe)
fingimiento; **on** or **under the ~ of doing sth**
bajo or con el pretexto de hacer algo; **she is
devoid of all ~** no es pretenciosa; **under
false ~s** con engaños
pretend [prɪ'tɛnd] vt (feign) fingir ▷ vi (feign)
fingir; (claim): **to ~ to sth** pretender a algo
pretense [prɪ'tɛns] n (US) = **pretence**
pretension [prɪ'tɛnʃən] n (claim) pretensión f;
to have no ~s to sth/to being sth no
engañarse en cuanto a algo/a ser algo
pretentious [prɪ'tɛnʃəs] adj pretencioso;
(ostentatious) ostentoso, aparatoso
pretext ['priːtɛkst] n pretexto; **on** or **under
the ~ of doing sth** con el pretexto de hacer
algo
pretty ['prɪtɪ] adj (gen) bonito, lindo (LAm)
▷ adv bastante
prevail [prɪ'veɪl] vi (gain mastery) prevalecer;
(be current) predominar; (persuade): **to ~ (up)on
sb to do sth** persuadir a algn para que haga
algo
prevailing [prɪ'veɪlɪŋ] adj (dominant)
predominante
prevalent ['prɛvələnt] adj (dominant)
dominante; (widespread) extendido;
(fashionable) de moda
prevent [prɪ'vɛnt] vt: **to ~ (sb) from doing
sth** impedir (a algn) hacer algo; **to ~ sth
from happening** evitar que ocurra algo
preventative [prɪ'vɛntətɪv] adj preventivo
prevention [prɪ'vɛnʃən] n prevención f
preventive [prɪ'vɛntɪv] adj preventivo
preview ['priːvjuː] n (of film) preestreno
previous ['priːvɪəs] adj previo, anterior; **he
has no ~ experience in that field** no tiene
experiencia previa en ese campo; **I have a ~
engagement** tengo un compromiso anterior
previously ['priːvɪəslɪ] adv antes
prewar [priː'wɔːr] adj antes de la guerra
prey [preɪ] n presa ▷ vi: **to ~ on** vivir a costa
de; (feed on) alimentarse de; **it was ~ing on
his mind** le obsesionaba
price [praɪs] n precio; (Betting: odds) puntos
mpl de ventaja ▷ vt (goods) fijar el precio de;
to go up or **rise in** ~ subir de precio; **what is
the ~ of ...?** ¿qué precio tiene ...?; **to put a ~**

on sth poner precio a algo; **what ~ his
promises now?** ¿para qué sirven ahora sus
promesas?; **he regained his freedom, but
at a** ~ recobró su libertad, pero le había
costado caro; **to be ~d out of the market**
(article) no encontrar comprador por ese
precio; (nation) no ser competitivo
priceless ['praɪslɪs] adj que no tiene precio;
(inf: amusing) divertidísimo
price list n tarifa
pricey ['praɪsɪ] adj (Brit inf) caro
prick [prɪk] n pinchazo; (with pin) alfilerazo;
(sting) picadura ▷ vt pinchar; (hurt) picar;
to ~ up one's ears aguzar el oído
prickle ['prɪkl] n (sensation) picor m; (Bot)
espina; (Zool) púa
prickly ['prɪklɪ] adj espinoso; (fig: person)
enojadizo
prickly heat n sarpullido causado por exceso
de calor
pride [praɪd] n orgullo; (pej) soberbia ▷ vt:
to ~ o.s. on enorgullecerse de; **to take (a) ~
in** enorgullecerse de; **her ~ and joy** su
orgullo; **to have ~ of place** tener prioridad
priest [priːst] n sacerdote m
priesthood ['priːsthud] n (practice)
sacerdocio; (priests) clero
prim [prɪm] adj (demure) remilgado; (prudish)
gazmoño
primal ['praɪməl] adj original; (important)
principal
primarily ['praɪmərɪlɪ] adv (above all) ante
todo, primordialmente
primary ['praɪmərɪ] adj primario; (first in
importance) principal ▷ n (US: also: ~ **election**)
(elección f) primaria; ver nota

○ **PRIMARY**
○
○ Las elecciones primarias (primaries) sirven
○ para preseleccionar a los candidatos de
○ los partidos Demócrata ("Democratic")
○ y Republicano ("Republican") durante
○ la campaña que precede a las elecciones
○ a presidente de los Estados Unidos.
○ Se inician en New Hampshire y tienen
○ lugar en 35 estados de febrero a junio.
○ El número de votos obtenidos por cada
○ candidato determina el número de
○ delegados que votarán en el congreso
○ general ("National Convention") de julio
○ y agosto, cuando se decide el candidato
○ definitivo de cada partido.

primary school n (Brit) escuela primaria
primate n ['praɪmɪt] (Rel) primado ▷ n
['praɪmeɪt] (Zool) primate m
prime [praɪm] adj primero, principal; (basic)
fundamental; (excellent) selecto, de primera
clase ▷ n: **in the ~ of life** en la flor de la vida
▷ vt (gun, pump) cebar; (wood: fig) preparar;
~ **example** ejemplo típico

Prime Minister n primer(a) ministro(-a);
see also **Downing Street**
primer ['praɪmə'] n (book) texto elemental;
(paint) capa preparatoria
primeval [praɪ'miːvəl] adj primitivo
primitive ['prɪmɪtɪv] adj primitivo; (crude)
rudimentario; (uncivilized) inculto
primrose ['prɪmrəuz] n primavera, prímula
prince [prɪns] n príncipe m
princess [prɪn'ses] n princesa
principal ['prɪnsɪpl] adj principal ▷ n
director(a) m(f); (in play) protagonista
principal m/f; (Comm) capital m, principal m;
see also **pantomime**
principally ['prɪnsɪplɪ] adv principalmente
principle ['prɪnsɪpl] n principio; **in ~** en
principio; **on ~** por principio
print [prɪnt] n (impression) marca, impresión f;
(footprint) huella; (fingerprint) huella dactilar;
(letters) letra de molde; (fabric) estampado;
(Art) grabado; (Phot) impresión f ▷ vt (gen)
imprimir; (on mind) grabar; (write in capitals)
escribir en letras de molde; **out of ~** agotado;
print out vt (Comput) imprimir
printed matter n impresos mpl
printer ['prɪntə'] n (person) impresor(a) m(f);
(machine) impresora
printing ['prɪntɪŋ] n (art) imprenta; (act)
impresión f; (quantity) tirada
printout ['prɪntaut] n (Comput) copia impresa
prior ['praɪə'] adj anterior, previo; (more
important) más importante ▷ n prior m; **~ to
doing** antes de or hasta hacer; **without ~
notice** sin previo aviso; **to have a ~ claim
to sth** tener prioridad en algo
priority [praɪ'ɒrɪtɪ] n prioridad f; **to have** or
take ~ over sth tener prioridad sobre algo
prise, prize (US) [praɪz] vt: **to ~ open** abrir
con palanca
prism ['prɪzəm] n prisma m
prison ['prɪzn] n cárcel f, prisión f ▷ cpd
carcelario
prisoner ['prɪznə'] n (in prison) preso(-a);
(captured person) prisionero; (under arrest)
detenido(-a); (in dock) acusado(-a); **the ~ at
the bar** el/la acusado(-a); **to take sb ~** hacer
or tomar prisionero a algn
prisoner of war n prisionero(-a) or preso(-a)
de guerra
pristine ['prɪstiːn] adj pristino
privacy ['prɪvəsɪ] n (seclusion) soledad f;
(intimacy) intimidad f; **in the strictest ~** con
el mayor secreto
private ['praɪvɪt] adj (personal) particular;
(confidential) secreto, confidencial; (property,
industry, discussion etc) privado; (person)
reservado; (place) tranquilo; (sitting etc)
a puerta cerrada ▷ n soldado raso; **"~"** (on
envelope) "confidencial"; (on door) "privado";
in ~ en privado; **in (his) ~ life** en su vida
privada; **to be in ~ practice** tener consulta
particular

private enterprise n la empresa privada
private eye n detective m/f privado(-a)
private limited company n (Brit) sociedad f
de responsabilidad limitada
privately ['praɪvɪtlɪ] adv en privado; (in o.s.)
en secreto
private property n propiedad f privada
private school n colegio privado
privatize ['praɪvɪtaɪz] vt privatizar
privet ['prɪvɪt] n alheña
privilege ['prɪvɪlɪdʒ] n privilegio; (prerogative)
prerrogativa
privy ['prɪvɪ] adj: **to be ~ to** estar enterado de
Privy Council n consejo privado (de la
Corona)
prize [praɪz] n premio ▷ adj (first class) de
primera clase ▷ vt apreciar, estimar; (US)
= **prise**
prize-giving ['praɪzgɪvɪŋ] n distribución f de
premios
prizewinner ['praɪzwɪnə'] n premiado(-a)
pro [prəu] n (Sport) profesional m/f; **the ~s
and cons** los pros y los contras
pro- [prəu] pref (in favour of) pro, en pro de;
~Soviet pro-soviético
proactive [prəu'æktɪv] adj: **to be ~** impulsar
la actividad
probability [prɔbə'bɪlɪtɪ] n probabilidad f;
in all ~ lo más probable
probable ['prɔbəbl] adj probable; **it is ~/
hardly ~ that** es probable/poco probable que
probably ['prɔbəblɪ] adv probablemente
probation [prə'beɪʃən] n: **on ~** (employee) a
prueba; (Law) en libertad condicional
probation officer n persona a cargo de los presos
en libertad condicional
probe [prəub] n (Med, Space) sonda; (enquiry)
investigación f ▷ vt sondar; (investigate)
investigar
problem ['prɔbləm] n problema m; **what's
the ~?** ¿cuál es el problema?, ¿qué pasa?; **no
~!** ¡por supuesto!; **to have ~s with the car**
tener problemas con el coche
procedure [prə'siːdʒə'] n procedimiento;
(bureaucratic) trámites mpl; **cashing a cheque
is a simple ~** cobrar un cheque es un trámite
sencillo
proceed [prə'siːd] vi proceder; (continue): **to ~
(with)** continuar (con); **to ~ against sb** (Law)
proceder contra algn; **I am not sure how to
~** no sé cómo proceder; see also **proceeds**
proceedings [prə'siːdɪŋz] npl acto sg, actos
mpl; (Law) proceso sg; (meeting) función f sg;
(records) actas fpl
proceeds ['prəusiːdz] npl ganancias fpl,
ingresos mpl
process ['prəuses] n proceso; (method)
método, sistema m; (proceeding)
procedimiento ▷ vt tratar, elaborar ▷ vi
[prə'ses] (Brit: formal: go in procession) desfilar;
in ~ en curso; **we are in the ~ of moving
to ...** estamos en vías de mudarnos a ...

P

processing ['prəusɛsɪŋ] n elaboración f
procession [prə'sɛʃən] n desfile m; **funeral ~** cortejo fúnebre
proclaim [prə'kleɪm] vt proclamar; (announce) anunciar
procrastinate [prəu'kræstɪneɪt] vi demorarse
procreation [prəukrɪ'eɪʃən] n procreación f
Procurator Fiscal ['prɔkjureɪtə-] n (Scottish) fiscal m/f
procure [prə'kjuəʳ] vt conseguir, obtener
prod [prɔd] vt (push) empujar; (with elbow) dar un codazo a ▷ n empujoncito; codazo
prodigal ['prɔdɪgl] adj pródigo
prodigious [prə'dɪdʒəs] adj prodigioso
prodigy ['prɔdɪdʒɪ] n prodigio
produce n ['prɔdjuːs] (Agr) productos mpl agrícolas ▷ vt [prə'djuːs] producir; (yield) rendir; (bring) sacar; (show) presentar, mostrar; (proof of identity) enseñar, presentar; (Theat) poner en escena; (offspring) dar a luz
producer [prə'djuːsəʳ] n (Theat) director(a) m(f); (Agr, Cine) productor(a) m(f)
product ['prɔdʌkt] n producto
production [prə'dʌkʃən] n (act) producción f; (Theat) representación f, montaje m; **to put into ~** lanzar a la producción
production line n línea de producción
productive [prə'dʌktɪv] adj productivo
productivity [prɔdʌk'tɪvɪtɪ] n productividad f
Prof. [prɔf] abbr (= professor) Prof
profane [prə'feɪn] adj profano
profess [prə'fɛs] vt profesar; **I do not ~ to be an expert** no pretendo ser experto
profession [prə'fɛʃən] n profesión f
professional [prə'fɛʃnl] n profesional m/f; (skilled person) perito ▷ adj profesional; (by profession) de profesión; **to take ~ advice** buscar un consejo profesional
professor [prə'fɛsəʳ] n (Brit) catedrático(-a) m(f); (US: teacher) profesor(a) m(f)
proficiency [prə'fɪʃənsɪ] n capacidad f, habilidad f
proficient [prə'fɪʃənt] adj experto, hábil
profile ['prəufaɪl] n perfil m; **to keep a high/low ~** tratar de llamar la atención/pasar inadvertido
profit ['prɔfɪt] n (Comm) ganancia; (fig) provecho ▷ vi: **to ~ by** or **from** aprovechar or sacar provecho de; **~ and loss account** cuenta de ganancias y pérdidas; **with ~s endowment assurance** seguro dotal con beneficios; **to sell sth at a ~** vender algo con ganancia
profitability [prɔfɪtə'bɪlɪtɪ] n rentabilidad f
profitable ['prɔfɪtəbl] adj (Econ) rentable; (beneficial) provechoso, útil
profound [prə'faund] adj profundo
profusely [prə'fjuːslɪ] adv profusamente
programme, program (US) ['prəugræm] n programa m ▷ vt programar

programmer, programer (US) ['prəugræməʳ] n programador(a) m(f)
programming, programing (US) ['prəugræmɪŋ] n programación f
progress n ['prəugrɛs] progreso; (development) desarrollo ▷ vi [prə'grɛs] progresar, avanzar; desarrollarse; **in ~** (meeting, work etc) en curso; **as the match ~ed** a medida que avanzaba el partido
progression [prə'grɛʃən] n progresión f
progressive [prə'grɛsɪv] adj progresivo; (person) progresista
prohibit [prə'hɪbɪt] vt prohibir; **to ~ sb from doing sth** prohibir a algn hacer algo; **"smoking ~ed"** "prohibido fumar"
prohibition [prəuɪ'bɪʃən] n (US) prohibicionismo
project [n 'prɔdʒɛkt, vb prə'dʒɛkt] n proyecto; (Scol, Univ: research) trabajo, proyecto ▷ vt proyectar ▷ vi (stick out) salir, sobresalir
projection [prə'dʒɛkʃən] n proyección f; (overhang) saliente m
projector [prə'dʒɛktəʳ] n proyector m
proletariat [prəulɪ'tɛərɪət] n proletariado
prolific [prə'lɪfɪk] adj prolífico
prologue, prolog (US) ['prəulɔg] n prólogo
prolong [prə'lɔŋ] vt prolongar, extender
prom [prɔm] n abbr (Brit) = **promenade**; **promenade concert**; (US: ball) baile m de gala; ver nota

● **PROM**
●
● Los conciertos de música clásica más
● conocidos en Inglaterra son los llamados
● *Proms* (o *promenade concerts*), que tienen
● lugar en el "Royal Albert Hall" de Londres,
● aunque también se llama así a cualquier
● concierto de esas características. Su
● nombre se debe al hecho de que en un
● principio el público paseaba durante las
● actuaciones; en la actualidad parte de la
● gente que acude a ellos permanece de pie.
● En Estados Unidos se llama *prom* a un
● baile de gala en un colegio o universidad.

promenade [prɔmə'nɑːd] n (by sea) paseo marítimo ▷ vi (stroll) pasearse
promenade concert n concierto (en que parte del público permanece de pie)
prominence ['prɔmɪnəns] n (fig) importancia
prominent ['prɔmɪnənt] adj (standing out) saliente; (important) eminente, importante; **he is ~ in the field of ...** destaca en el campo de ...
promiscuity [prɔmɪs'kjuːɪtɪ] n promiscuidad f
promiscuous [prə'mɪskjuəs] adj (sexually) promiscuo
promise ['prɔmɪs] n promesa ▷ vt, vi prometer; **to make sb a ~** prometer algo

a algn; **a young man of** ~ un joven con
futuro; **to ~ (sb) to do sth** prometer (a algn)
hacer algo; **to ~ well** ser muy prometedor
promising ['prɒmɪsɪŋ] adj prometedor(a)
promote [prə'məʊt] vt promover; (new
product) dar publicidad a, lanzar; (Mil)
ascender; (employee) ascender; (ideas)
fomentar; **the team was ~d to the second
division** (Brit Football) el equipo ascendió a la
segunda división
promoter [prə'məʊtə'] n (of sporting event)
promotor(a) m(f); (of company, business)
patrocinador(a) m(f)
promotion [prə'məʊʃən] n (gen) promoción f;
(Mil) ascenso
prompt [prɒmpt] adj pronto ▷ adv: **at six
o'clock** ~ a las seis en punto ▷ n (Comput)
aviso, guía f ▷ vt (urge) mover, incitar; (when
talking) instar; (Theat) apuntar; **to ~ sb to do
sth** instar a algn a hacer algo; **to be ~ to do
sth** no tardar en hacer algo; **they're very ~**
(punctual) son muy puntuales
promptly ['prɒmptlɪ] adv (punctually)
puntualmente; (rapidly) rápidamente
prone [prəʊn] adj (lying) postrado; ~ **to**
propenso a
prong [prɒŋ] n diente m, punta
pronoun ['prəʊnaʊn] n pronombre m
pronounce [prə'naʊns] vt pronunciar;
(declare) declarar ▷ vi: **to ~ (up)on**
pronunciarse sobre; **they ~d him unfit to
plead** le declararon incapaz de defenderse
pronunciation [prənʌnsɪ'eɪʃən] n
pronunciación f
proof [pru:f] n prueba; **70°** ~ graduación f del
70 por 100 ▷ adj: ~ **against** a prueba de ▷ vt
(tent, anorak) impermeabilizar
proofreader ['pru:fri:də'] n corrector(a) m(f)
de pruebas
prop [prɒp] n apoyo; (fig) sostén m; **props**
accesorios mpl, at(t)rezzo msg ▷ vt (lean): **to ~
sth against** apoyar algo contra; **prop up** vt
(roof, structure) apuntalar; (economy) respaldar
propaganda [prɒpə'gændə] n propaganda
propel [prə'pɛl] vt impulsar, propulsar
propeller [prə'pɛlə'] n hélice f
propensity [prə'pɛnsɪtɪ] n propensión f
proper ['prɒpə'] adj (suited, right) propio; (exact)
justo; (apt) apropiado, conveniente; (timely)
oportuno; (seemly) correcto, decente;
(authentic) verdadero; (inf: real) auténtico;
to go through the ~ channels (Admin) ir por
la vía oficial
properly ['prɒpəlɪ] adv (adequately)
correctamente; (decently) decentemente
proper noun n nombre m propio
property ['prɒpətɪ] n propiedad f; (estate)
finca; **lost ~** objetos mpl perdidos; **personal
~** bienes mpl muebles
prophecy ['prɒfɪsɪ] n profecía
prophesy ['prɒfɪsaɪ] vt profetizar; (fig)
predecir

prophet ['prɒfɪt] n profeta m/f
proportion [prə'pɔ:ʃən] n proporción f;
(share) parte f; **proportions** npl (size)
dimensiones fpl; **to be in/out of ~ to** or **with
sth** estar en/no guardar proporción con algo;
to see sth in ~ (fig) ver algo en su justa
medida
proportional [prə'pɔ:ʃənl] adj proporcional;
~ **(to)** en proporción (con)
proportional representation n (Pol)
representación f proporcional
proposal [prə'pəʊzl] n propuesta; (offer of
marriage) oferta de matrimonio; (plan)
proyecto; (suggestion) sugerencia
propose [prə'pəʊz] vt proponer; (have in mind):
to ~ sth/to do or **doing sth** proponer algo/
proponerse hacer algo ▷ vi declararse; **to ~
to do** tener intención de hacer
proposer [prə'pəʊzə'] n (of motion)
proponente m/f
proposition [prɒpə'zɪʃən] n propuesta,
proposición f; **to make sb a ~** proponer algo
a algn
proprietor [prə'praɪətə'] n propietario(-a),
dueño(-a)
propriety [prə'praɪətɪ] n decoro
pro rata [prəʊ'rɑ:tə] adv a prorrata
prose [prəʊz] n prosa; (Scol) traducción f
inversa
prosecute ['prɒsɪkju:t] vt (Law) procesar;
"trespassers will be ~d" (Law) "se procesará
a los intrusos"
prosecution [prɒsɪ'kju:ʃən] n proceso, causa;
(accusing side) acusación f
prosecutor ['prɒsɪkju:tə'] n acusador(a) m(f);
(also: **public ~**) fiscal m/f
prospect [n 'prɒspɛkt, vb prə'spɛkt] n (chance)
posibilidad f; (outlook) perspectiva; (hope)
esperanza ▷ vt explorar ▷ vi buscar;
prospects npl (for work etc) perspectivas fpl; **to
be faced with the ~ of** tener que enfrentarse
a la posibilidad de que ...; **we were faced
with the ~ of leaving early** se nos planteó la
posibilidad de marcharnos pronto; **there is
every ~ of an early victory** hay buenas
perspectivas de una pronta victoria
prospecting [prə'spɛktɪŋ] n prospección f
prospective [prə'spɛktɪv] adj (possible)
probable, eventual; (certain) futuro; (buyer)
presunto; (legislation, son-in-law) futuro
prospectus [prə'spɛktəs] n prospecto
prosper ['prɒspə'] vi prosperar
prosperity [prɒ'spɛrɪtɪ] n prosperidad f
prosperous ['prɒspərəs] adj próspero
prostate ['prɒsteɪt] n (also: ~ **gland**) próstata
prostitute ['prɒstɪtju:t] n prostituta; **male ~**
prostituto
prostitution [prɒstɪ'tju:ʃən] n prostitución f
prostrate ['prɒstreɪt] adj postrado; (fig)
abatido ▷ vt: **to ~ o.s.** postrarse
protagonist [prə'tægənɪst] n protagonista
m/f

P

protect [prəˈtɛkt] *vt* proteger
protection [prəˈtɛkʃən] *n* protección *f*; **to be under sb's ~** estar amparado por algn
protective [prəˈtɛktɪv] *adj* protector(a); **~ custody** (*Law*) detención *f* preventiva
protégé [ˈprəʊtɛʒeɪ] *n* protegido(-a)
protein [ˈprəʊtiːn] *n* proteína
protest [*n* ˈprəʊtɛst, *vb* prəˈtɛst] *n* protesta ▷ *vi*: **to ~ about** *or* **at/against** protestar de/contra ▷ *vt* (*affirm*) afirmar, declarar; (*insist*): **to ~ (that)** insistir en (que); **to do sth under ~** hacer algo bajo protesta; **to ~ against/about** protestar en contra de/por
Protestant [ˈprɔtɪstənt] *adj, n* protestante *m/f*
protester, protestor [prəˈtɛstəʳ] *n* (*in demonstration*) manifestante *m/f*
protocol [ˈprəʊtəkɔl] *n* protocolo
prototype [ˈprəʊtətaɪp] *n* prototipo
protracted [prəˈtræktɪd] *adj* prolongado
protractor [prəˈtræktəʳ] *n* (*Geom*) transportador *m*
protrude [prəˈtruːd] *vi* salir, sobresalir
proud [praud] *adj* orgulloso; (*pej*) soberbio, altanero ▷ *adv*: **to do sb ~** tratar a algn a cuerpo de rey; **to do o.s. ~** no privarse de nada; **to be ~ to do sth** estar orgulloso de hacer algo
prove [pruːv] *vt* probar; (*verify*) comprobar; (*show*) demostrar ▷ *vi*: **to ~ correct** resultar correcto; **to ~ o.s.** ponerse a prueba; **he was ~d right in the end** al final se vio que tenía razón
proverb [ˈprɔvəːb] *n* refrán *m*
provide [prəˈvaɪd] *vt* proporcionar, dar; **to ~ sb with sth** proveer a algn de algo; **to be ~d with** ser provisto de; **provide for** *vt fus* (*person*) mantener a; (*problem etc*) tener en cuenta
provided [prəˈvaɪdɪd] *conj*: **~ (that)** con tal de que, a condición de que
providing [prəˈvaɪdɪŋ] *conj*: **~ (that)** a condición de que, con tal de que
province [ˈprɔvɪns] *n* provincia; (*fig*) esfera
provincial [prəˈvɪnʃəl] *adj* provincial; (*pej*) provinciano
provision [prəˈvɪʒən] *n* provisión *f*; (*supply*) suministro, abastecimiento; **provisions** *npl* provisiones *fpl*, víveres *mpl*; **to make ~ for** (*one's family, future*) atender las necesidades de
provisional [prəˈvɪʒənl] *adj* provisional, provisorio (*LAm*); (*temporary*) interino ▷ *n*: **P~** (*Ireland Pol*) Provisional *m* (*miembro de la tendencia activista del IRA*)
provisional driving licence *n* (*Brit Aut*) carnet *m* de conducir provisional; *see also* **L-plates**
proviso [prəˈvaɪzəu] *n* condición *f*, estipulación *f*; **with the ~ that** a condición de que
provocation [prɔvəˈkeɪʃən] *n* provocación *f*
provocative [prəˈvɔkətɪv] *adj* provocativo

provoke [prəˈvəuk] *vt* (*arouse*) provocar, incitar; (*cause*) causar, producir; (*anger*) enojar; **to ~ sb to sth/to do sth** *or* **into doing sth** provocar a algn a algo/a hacer algo
provost [ˈprɔvəst] *n* (*Brit: of university*) rector(a) *m(f)*; (*Scottish*) alcalde(-esa) *m(f)*
prow [prau] *n* proa
prowess [ˈprauɪs] *n* (*skill*) destreza, habilidad *f*; (*courage*) valor *m*; **his ~ as a footballer** (*skill*) su habilidad como futbolista
prowl [praul] *vi* (*also*: **~ about, ~ around**) merodear ▷ *n*: **on the ~** de merodeo, merodeando
prowler [ˈprauləʳ] *n* merodeador(a) *m(f)*
proximity [prɔkˈsɪmɪtɪ] *n* proximidad *f*
proxy [ˈprɔksɪ] *n* poder *m*; (*person*) apoderado(-a); **by ~** por poderes
prudent [ˈpruːdnt] *adj* prudente
prune [pruːn] *n* ciruela pasa ▷ *vt* podar
pry [praɪ] *vi*: **to ~ into** entrometerse en
PS *abbr* (= *postscript*) P.D.
psalm [saːm] *n* salmo
PSBR *n abbr* (*Brit*: = *public sector borrowing requirement*) necesidades de endeudamiento del sector público
pseudonym [ˈsjuːdənɪm] *n* seudónimo
PSHE *n abbr* (*Brit Scol*: = *personal, social, and health education*) formación social y sanitaria para la vida adulta
psyche [ˈsaɪkɪ] *n* psique *f*
psychiatric [saɪkɪˈætrɪk] *adj* psiquiátrico
psychiatrist [saɪˈkaɪətrɪst] *n* psiquiatra *m/f*
psychiatry [saɪˈkaɪətrɪ] *n* psiquiatría
psychic [ˈsaɪkɪk] *adj* (*also*: **~al**) psíquico
psychoanalysis (*pl* **psychoanalyses**) [saɪkəuəˈnælɪsɪs, -siːz] *n* psicoanálisis *m inv*
psychoanalyst [saɪkəuˈænəlɪst] *n* psicoanalista *m/f*
psychological [saɪkəˈlɔdʒɪkl] *adj* psicológico
psychologist [saɪˈkɔlədʒɪst] *n* psicólogo(-a)
psychology [saɪˈkɔlədʒɪ] *n* psicología
psychopath [ˈsaɪkəupæθ] *n* psicópata *m/f*
psychosis (*pl* **psychoses**) [saɪˈkəusɪs, -siːz] *n* psicosis *f inv*
psychotherapy [saɪkəuˈθɛrəpɪ] *n* psicoterapia
PT *n abbr* (*Brit*: = *physical training*) Ed. Fís.
pt *abbr* = *pint(s)*; *point(s)*
PTA *n abbr* (*Brit*: = *Parent-Teacher Association*) ≈ Asociación *f* de Padres de Alumnos
PTO *abbr* (= *please turn over*) sigue
pub [pʌb] *n abbr* (= *public house*) pub *m*, bar *m*
pub crawl *n* (*inf*): **to go on a ~** ir a recorrer bares
puberty [ˈpjuːbətɪ] *n* pubertad *f*
public [ˈpʌblɪk] *adj* público ▷ *n*: **the ~** el público; **in ~** en público; **to make sth ~** revelar *or* hacer público algo; **to be ~ knowledge** ser del dominio público; **to go ~** (*Comm*) proceder a la venta pública de acciones
public address system *n* megafonía, sistema *m* de altavoces

publican ['pʌblɪkən] n dueño(-a) or encargado(-a) de un bar

publication [pʌblɪ'keɪʃən] n publicación f

public company n sociedad f anónima

public convenience n (Brit) aseos mpl públicos, sanitarios mpl (LAm)

public holiday n día m de fiesta, (día) feriado (LAm)

public house n (Brit) bar m, pub m

publicity [pʌb'lɪsɪtɪ] n publicidad f

publicize ['pʌblɪsaɪz] vt publicitar; (advertise) hacer propaganda para

public limited company n sociedad f anónima (S.A.)

publicly ['pʌblɪklɪ] adv públicamente, en público

public opinion n opinión f pública

public relations n relaciones fpl públicas

public relations officer n encargado(-a) de relaciones públicas

public school n (Brit) colegio privado; (US) instituto

public sector n sector m público

public-spirited [pʌblɪk'spɪrɪtɪd] adj cívico

public transport, public transportation (US) n transporte m público

public utility n servicio público

publish ['pʌblɪʃ] vt publicar

publisher ['pʌblɪʃər] n (person) editor(a) m(f); (firm) editorial f

publishing ['pʌblɪʃɪŋ] n (industry) industria del libro

pub lunch n almuerzo que se sirve en un pub; **to go for a ~** almorzar o comer en un pub

puck [pʌk] n (Ice Hockey) puck m

pucker ['pʌkər] vt (pleat) arrugar; (brow etc) fruncir

pudding ['pudɪŋ] n pudín m; (Brit: sweet) postre m; **black ~** morcilla; **rice ~** arroz m con leche

puddle ['pʌdl] n charco

puerile ['pjuəraɪl] adj pueril

Puerto Rican ['pwə:təu'ri:kən] adj, n puertorriqueño(-a) m(f)

Puerto Rico [-'ri:kəu] n Puerto Rico

puff [pʌf] n soplo; (of smoke) bocanada; (of breathing, engine) resoplido; (also: **powder ~**) borla ▷ vt: **to ~ one's pipe** dar chupadas a la pipa; (also: **~ out**: sails, cheeks) hinchar, inflar ▷ vi (gen) soplar; (pant) jadear; **to ~ out smoke** echar humo

puffed [pʌft] adj (inf: out of breath) sin aliento

puffin ['pʌfɪn] n frailecillo

puff pastry, puff paste (US) n hojaldre m

puffy ['pʌfɪ] adj hinchado

pull [pul] n (tug): **to give sth a ~** dar un tirón a algo; (fig: advantage) ventaja; (: influence) influencia ▷ vt tirar de, jalar (LAm); (haul) tirar, jalar (LAm), arrastrar; (strain): **to ~ a muscle** sufrir un tirón ▷ vi tirar, jalar (LAm); **to ~ to pieces** hacer pedazos; **to ~ one's punches** andarse con bromas; **to ~ one's**

weight hacer su parte; **to ~ o.s. together** tranquilizarse, sobreponerse; **to ~ sb's leg** tomar el pelo a algn; **to ~ strings (for sb)** enchufar (a algn); **pull about** vt (handle roughly: object) manosear; (: person) maltratar; **pull apart** vt (take apart) desmontar; (break) romper; **pull away** vi (vehicle: move off) salir, arrancar; (draw back) apartarse bruscamente; **pull back** vt (lever etc) tirar hacia sí; (curtains) descorrer ▷ vi (refrain) contenerse; (Mil: withdraw) retirarse; **pull down** vt (house) derribar; **pull in** vi (Aut: at the kerb) parar (junto a la acera); (Rail) llegar; **pull off** vt (deal etc) cerrar; **pull out** vi irse, marcharse; (car, train etc) salir ▷ vt sacar, arrancar; **pull over** vi (Aut) hacerse a un lado; **pull round, pull through** vi salvarse; (Med) recobrar la salud; **pull up** vi (stop) parar ▷ vt (uproot) arrancar, desarraigar; (stop) parar

pulley ['pulɪ] n polea

pull-out ['pulaut] n suplemento ▷ cpd (pages, magazine) separable

pullover ['puləuvər] n jersey m, suéter m

pulp [pʌlp] n (of fruit) pulpa; (for paper) pasta; (pej: also: **~ magazines** etc) prensa amarilla; **to reduce sth to ~** hacer algo papilla

pulpit ['pulpɪt] n púlpito

pulsate [pʌl'seɪt] vi pulsar, latir

pulse [pʌls] n (Anat) pulso; (of music, engine) pulsación f; (Bot) legumbre f; **pulses** npl legumbres; **to feel** or **take sb's ~** tomar el pulso a algn

pulverize ['pʌlvəraɪz] vt pulverizar; (fig) hacer polvo

puma ['pju:mə] n puma m

pump [pʌmp] n bomba; (shoe) zapatilla de tenis ▷ vt sacar con una bomba; (fig: inf) (son) sacar; **to ~ sb for information** (son) sacarle información a algn; **pump up** vt inflar

pumpkin ['pʌmpkɪn] n calabaza

pun [pʌn] n juego de palabras

punch [pʌntʃ] n (blow) golpe m, puñetazo; (tool) punzón m; (for paper) perforadora; (for tickets) taladro; (drink) ponche m ▷ vt (hit): **to ~ sb/sth** dar un puñetazo or golpear a algn/algo; (make a hole in) punzar; perforar

punch line n (of joke) remate m

punch-up ['pʌntʃʌp] n (Brit inf) riña

punctual ['pʌŋktjuəl] adj puntual

punctuality [pʌŋktju'ælɪtɪ] n puntualidad f

punctuate ['pʌŋktjueɪt] vt puntuar; (fig) interrumpir

punctuation [pʌŋktju'eɪʃən] n puntuación f

punctuation mark n signo de puntuación

puncture ['pʌŋktʃər] (Brit) n pinchazo ▷ vt pinchar; **to have a ~** tener un pinchazo

pundit ['pʌndɪt] n experto(-a)

pungent ['pʌndʒənt] adj acre

punish ['pʌnɪʃ] vt castigar; **to ~ sb for sth/ for doing sth** castigar a algn por algo/por haber hecho algo

punishment ['pʌnɪʃmənt] n castigo; (fig, inf): **to take a lot of ~** (boxer) recibir una paliza; (car) ser maltratado

punk [pʌŋk] n (also: **~ rocker**) punki m/f; (also: **~ rock**) música punk; (US inf: hoodlum) matón m

punt [pʌnt] n (boat) batea; (Ireland) libra irlandesa ▷ vi (bet) apostar

punter ['pʌntəʳ] n (gambler) jugador(a) m(f)

puny ['pju:nɪ] adj enclenque

pup [pʌp] n cachorro

pupil ['pju:pl] n alumno(-a); (of eye) pupila

puppet ['pʌpɪt] n títere m

puppy ['pʌpɪ] n cachorro, perrito

purchase ['pə:tʃɪs] n compra; (grip) agarre m, asidero ▷ vt comprar

purchaser ['pə:tʃɪsəʳ] n comprador(a) m(f)

pure [pjuəʳ] adj puro; **a ~ wool jumper** un jersey de pura lana; **it's laziness, ~ and simple** es pura vagancia

purée ['pjuəreɪ] n puré m

purely ['pjuəlɪ] adv puramente

purgatory ['pə:gətərɪ] n purgatorio

purge [pə:dʒ] n (Med, Pol) purga ▷ vt purgar

purify ['pjuərɪfaɪ] vt purificar, depurar

purist ['pjuərɪst] n purista m/f

puritan ['pjuərɪtən] n puritano(-a)

purity ['pjuərɪtɪ] n pureza

purple ['pə:pl] adj morado

purport [pə:'pɔ:t] vi: **to ~ to be/do** dar a entender que es/hace

purpose ['pə:pəs] n propósito; **on ~** a propósito, adrede; **to no ~** para nada, en vano; **for teaching ~s** con fines pedagógicos; **for the ~s of this meeting** para los fines de esta reunión

purposeful ['pə:pəsful] adj resuelto, determinado

purr [pə:ʳ] n ronroneo ▷ vi ronronear

purse [pə:s] n monedero; (US: handbag) bolso, cartera (LAm) ▷ vt fruncir

purser ['pə:səʳ] n (Naut) comisario(-a)

pursue [pə'sju:] vt seguir; (harass) perseguir; (profession) ejercer; (pleasures) buscar; (inquiry, matter) seguir

pursuit [pə'sju:t] n (chase) caza; (of pleasure etc) busca; (occupation) actividad f; **in (the) ~ of sth** en busca de algo

pus [pʌs] n pus m

push [puʃ] n empujón m; (Mil) ataque m; (drive) empuje m ▷ vt empujar; (button) apretar; (promote) promover; (fig: press, advance: views) fomentar; (thrust): **to ~ sth (into)** meter algo a la fuerza (en) ▷ vi empujar; (fig) hacer esfuerzos; **at a ~** (inf) a duras penas; **she is ~ing 50** (inf) raya en los 50; **to be ~ed for time/money** andar justo de tiempo/escaso de dinero; **to ~ a door open/shut** abrir/cerrar una puerta empujándola; **to ~ for** (better pay, conditions) reivindicar; **"~"** (on door) "empujar"; (on bell) "pulse"; **push aside** vt apartar con la mano; **push in** vi colarse; **push off** vi (inf) largarse;

push on vi (continue) seguir adelante; **push over** vt (cause to fall) hacer caer, derribar; (knock over) volcar; **push through** vi (crowd) abrirse paso a empujones ▷ vt (measure) despachar; **push up** vt (total, prices) hacer subir

pushchair ['puʃtʃɛəʳ] n (Brit) silla de niño

pusher ['puʃəʳ] n (also: **drug ~**) traficante m/f de drogas

pushover ['puʃəuvəʳ] n (inf): **it's a ~** está tirado

push-up ['puʃʌp] n (US) flexión f

pushy ['puʃɪ] adj (pej) agresivo

puss [pus], **pussy** ['pusɪ], **pussy-cat** ['pusɪkæt] n minino

put [put] (pt, pp **put**) vt (place) poner, colocar; (put into) meter; (express, say) expresar; (a question) hacer; (estimate) calcular; (cause to be): **to ~ sb in a good/bad mood** poner a algn de buen/mal humor; **to ~ a lot of time into sth** dedicar mucho tiempo a algo; **to ~ money on a horse** apostar dinero en un caballo; **to ~ money into a company** invertir dinero en una compañía; **to ~ sb to a lot of trouble** causar mucha molestia a algn; **we ~ the children to bed** acostamos a los niños; **how shall I ~ it?** ¿cómo puedo explicarlo o decirlo?; **I ~ it to you that ...** le sugiero que ...; **to stay ~** no moverse; **put about** vi (Naut) virar ▷ vt (rumour) hacer correr; **put across** vt (ideas etc) comunicar; **put aside** vt (lay down: book etc) dejar or poner a un lado; (save) ahorrar; (in shop) guardar; **put away** vt (store) guardar; **put back** vt (replace) devolver a su lugar; (postpone) aplazar; (set back: watch, clock) retrasar; **this will ~ us back 10 years** esto nos retrasará 10 años; **put by** vt (money) guardar; **put down** vt (on ground) poner en el suelo; (animal) sacrificar; (in writing) apuntar; (suppress: revolt etc) sofocar; (attribute) atribuir; **~ me down for £15** apúntame por 15 libras; **~ it down on my account** (Comm) póngalo en mi cuenta; **put forward** vt (ideas) presentar, proponer; (date) adelantar; **put in** vt (application, complaint) presentar; (time) dedicar; **put in for** vt fus (job) solicitar; (promotion) pedir; **put off** vt (postpone) aplazar; (discourage) desanimar, quitar las ganas a; **put on** vt (clothes, lipstick etc) ponerse; (light etc) encender; (play etc) presentar; (gain): **to ~ on weight** engordar; (brake) echar; (record, kettle etc) poner; (assume: accent, manner) afectar, fingir; (airs) adoptar, darse; (concert, exhibition etc) montar; (extra bus, train etc) poner; (inf: kid, have on: esp US) tomar el pelo a; (inform, indicate): **to ~ sb on to sb/ sth** informar a algn de algn/algo; **to ~ on weight** engordar; **put out** vt (fire, light) apagar; (rubbish etc) sacar; (cat etc) echar; (one's hand) alargar; (news, rumour) hacer circular; (tongue etc) sacar; (person: inconvenience) molestar, fastidiar; (dislocate:

shoulder, vertebra, knee) dislocar(se) ▷ vi (Naut):
to ~ out to sea hacerse a la mar; **to ~ out
from Plymouth** salir de Plymouth; **put
through** vt (call) poner; (plan etc) hacer
aprobar; **~ me through to Mr Low** póngame
or comuníqueme (LAm) con el Señor Low; **put
together** vt unir, reunir; (assemble: furniture)
armar, montar; (meal) preparar; **put up** vt
(raise) levantar, alzar; (hang) colgar; (build)
construir; (increase) aumentar; (accommodate)
alojar; (incite): **to ~ sb up to doing sth** instar
or incitar a algn a hacer algo; **to ~ sth up for
sale** poner algo a la venta; **put upon** vt fus: **to
be ~ upon** (imposed upon) dejarse explotar; **put
up with** vt fus aguantar
putt [pʌt] vt hacer un putt ▷ n putt m
putter ['pʌtə'] n putter m
putting green ['pʌtɪŋ-] n green m, minigolf m
putty ['pʌtɪ] n masilla
put-up ['putʌp] adj: **~ job** (Brit) estafa
puzzle ['pʌzl] n (riddle) acertijo; (jigsaw)
rompecabezas m inv; (also: **crossword ~**)
crucigrama m; (mystery) misterio ▷ vt dejar
perplejo, confundir ▷ vi: **to ~ about** quebrar
la cabeza por; **to ~ over** (sb's actions) quebrarse
la cabeza por; (mystery, problem) devanarse
los sesos sobre; **to be ~d about sth** no llegar
a entender algo
puzzling ['pʌzlɪŋ] adj (question) misterioso,
extraño; (attitude, instructions) extraño
PVC n abbr (= polyvinyl chloride) P.V.C. m
pygmy ['pɪgmɪ] n pigmeo(-a)
pyjamas, pajamas (US) [pɪ'dʒɑːməz] npl
pijama m, piyama m (LAm); **a pair of ~**
un pijama
pylon ['paɪlən] n torre f de conducción eléctrica
pyramid ['pɪrəmɪd] n pirámide f
Pyrenean [pɪrə'niːən] adj pirenaico
Pyrenees [pɪrə'niːz] npl: **the ~** los Pirineos
Pyrex® ['paɪreks] n pírex m ▷ cpd:
~ casserole cazuela de pírex
python ['paɪθən] n pitón m

Q, q [kjuː] n (letter) Q, q f; **Q for Queen** Q de
Quebec
QC n abbr (Brit: = Queen's Counsel) título concedido
a determinados abogados
QED abbr (= quod erat demonstrandum) Q.E.D.
qty abbr (= quantity) cantidad
quack [kwæk] n (of duck) graznido; (pej: doctor)
curandero(-a), matasanos m inv ▷ vi graznar
quad [kwɒd] abbr = **quadrangle**; **quadruple**;
quadruplet
quadrangle ['kwɒdræŋgl] n (Brit: courtyard)
patio
quadruple [kwɒ'druːpl] vt, vi cuadruplicar
quadruplet [kwɒ'druːplɪt] n cuatrillizo
quagmire ['kwægmaɪə'] n lodazal m,
cenegal m
quail [kweɪl] n (bird) codorniz f ▷ vi
amedrentarse
quaint [kweɪnt] adj extraño; (picturesque)
pintoresco
quake [kweɪk] vi temblar ▷ n abbr
= **earthquake**
qualification [kwɒlɪfɪ'keɪʃən] n (ability)
capacidad f; (often pl: diploma etc) título;
(reservation) salvedad f; (modification)
modificación f; (act) calificación f; **what are
your ~s?** ¿qué títulos tienes?
qualified ['kwɒlɪfaɪd] adj (trained) cualificado;
(fit) capacitado; (limited) limitado;
(professionally) titulado; **~ for/to do sth**
capacitado para/para hacer algo; **he's not ~
for the job** no está capacitado para ese

trabajo; **it was a ~ success** fue un éxito relativo

qualify ['kwɔlɪfaɪ] vt (Ling) calificar a; (capacitate) capacitar; (modify) matizar; (limit) moderar ▷ vi (in competition): **to ~ (for)** calificarse (para); (pass examination(s)): **to ~ (as)** calificarse (de), graduarse (en), recibirse (de) (LAm); (be eligible): **to ~ (for)** reunir los requisitos (para); **to ~ as an engineer** sacar el título de ingeniero

quality ['kwɔlɪtɪ] n calidad f; (moral) cualidad f; **of good/poor ~** de buena or alta/poca calidad

quality press n prensa seria

qualm [kwɑːm] n escrúpulo; **to have ~s about sth** sentir escrúpulos por algo

quandary ['kwɔndrɪ] n: **to be in a ~** verse en un dilema

quango ['kwæŋgəu] n abbr (Brit: = quasi-autonomous non-governmental organization) organismo semiautónomo de subvención estatal

quantifiable [kwɔntɪˈfaɪəbl] adj cuantificable

quantify ['kwɔntɪfaɪ] vt cuantificar

quantity ['kwɔntɪtɪ] n cantidad f; **in ~** en grandes cantidades

quantity surveyor n aparejador(a) m(f)

quantum leap ['kwɔntəm-] n (fig) avance m espectacular

quarantine ['kwɔrntiːn] n cuarentena

quarrel ['kwɔrl] n riña, pelea ▷ vi reñir, pelearse; **to have a ~ with sb** reñir or pelearse con algn; **I can't ~ with that** no le veo pegas

quarrelsome ['kwɔrəlsəm] adj pendenciero

quarry ['kwɔrɪ] n (for stone) cantera; (animal) presa

quart [kwɔːt] n cuarto de galón = 1.136 l

quarter ['kwɔːtəʳ] n cuarto, cuarta parte f; (US: coin) moneda de 25 centavos; (of year) trimestre m; (district) barrio ▷ vt dividir en cuartos; (Mil: lodge) alojar; **quarters** npl (barracks) cuartel m; (living quarters) alojamiento sg; **a ~ of an hour** un cuarto de hora; **to pay by the ~** pagar trimestralmente or cada tres meses; **it's a ~ to** or (US) **of three** son las tres menos cuarto; **it's a ~ past** or (US) **after three** son las tres y cuarto; **from all ~s** de todas partes; **at close ~s** de cerca

quarterback ['kwɔːtəbæk] n (US: football) mariscal m de campo

quarter final n cuarto de final

quarterly ['kwɔːtəlɪ] adj trimestral ▷ adv cada 3 meses, trimestralmente

quartet, quartette [kwɔːˈtet] n cuarteto

quartz [kwɔːts] n cuarzo

quash [kwɔʃ] vt (verdict) anular, invalidar

quaver ['kweɪvəʳ] n (Brit Mus) corchea ▷ vi temblar

quay [kiː] n (also: ~side) muelle m

queasy ['kwiːzɪ] adj: **to feel ~** tener náuseas

queen [kwiːn] n reina; (Cards etc) dama

queen mother n reina madre

Queen's Speech [kwiːnz-] n ver nota

queer [kwɪəʳ] adj (odd) raro, extraño ▷ n (pej: inf!) marica m (!)

quell [kwel] vt calmar; (put down) sofocar

quench [kwentʃ] vt (flames) apagar; **to ~ one's thirst** apagar la sed

querulous ['kwerələs] adj (person, voice) quejumbroso

query ['kwɪərɪ] n (question) pregunta; (doubt) duda ▷ vt preguntar; (disagree with, dispute) no estar conforme con, dudar de

quest [kwest] n busca, búsqueda

question ['kwestʃən] n pregunta; (matter) asunto, cuestión f ▷ vt (doubt) dudar de; (interrogate) interrogar, hacer preguntas a; **to ask sb a ~, put a ~ to sb** hacerle una pregunta a algn; **the ~ is ...** el asunto es ...; **to bring** or **call sth into ~** poner algo en (tela de) duda; **beyond ~** fuera de toda duda; **out of the ~** imposible, ni hablar

questionable ['kwestʃənəbl] adj discutible; (doubtful) dudoso

question mark n punto de interrogación

questionnaire [kwestʃəˈneəʳ] n cuestionario

queue [kjuː] (Brit) n cola ▷ vi hacer cola; **to jump the ~** colarse

quibble ['kwɪbl] vi andarse con sutilezas

quiche [kiːʃ] n quiche m

quick [kwɪk] adj rápido; (temper) vivo; (agile) ágil; (mind) listo; (eye) agudo; (ear) fino ▷ n: **cut to the ~** (fig) herido en lo más vivo; **be ~!** ¡date prisa!; **to be ~ to act** obrar con prontitud; **she was ~ to see that** se dio cuenta de eso en seguida

quicken ['kwɪkən] vt apresurar ▷ vi apresurarse, darse prisa

quick fix n (pej) parche m

quickly ['kwɪklɪ] adv rápidamente, de prisa; **we must act ~** tenemos que actuar cuanto antes

quicksand ['kwɪksænd] n arenas fpl movedizas

quick-witted [kwɪkˈwɪtɪd] adj listo, despabilado

quid [kwɪd] n pl inv (Brit: inf) libra

quiet ['kwaɪət] adj (voice, music etc) bajo; (person, place) tranquilo; (silent) callado;

(*reserved*) reservado; (*discreet*) discreto; (*not noisy: engine*) silencioso ▷ *n* silencio; (*calm*) tranquilidad *f* ▷ *vt, vi* (US) = **quieten**; **keep ~!** ¡cállate!, ¡silencio!; **business is ~ at this time of year** hay poco movimiento en esta época

quieten ['kwaɪətn] (*also: ~ **down**) *vi* (*grow calm*) calmarse; (*grow silent*) callarse ▷ *vt* calmar; hacer callar

quietly ['kwaɪətlɪ] *adv* tranquilamente; (*silently*) silenciosamente

quietness ['kwaɪətnɪs] *n* (*silence*) silencio; (*calm*) tranquilidad *f*

quilt [kwɪlt] *n* (*Brit*) edredón *m*

quin [kwɪn] *n abbr* = **quintuplet**

quintuplet [kwɪn'tjuːplɪt] *n* quintillizo

quip [kwɪp] *n* ocurrencia ▷ *vi* decir con ironía

quirk [kwɜːk] *n* peculiaridad *f*; **by some ~ of fate** por algún capricho del destino

quirky ['kwɜːkɪ] *adj* raro, estrafalario

quit (*pt, pp* **quit** *or* **quitted**) [kwɪt] *vt* dejar, abandonar; (*premises*) desocupar; (*Comput*) abandonar ▷ *vi* (*give up*) renunciar; (*go away*) irse; (*resign*) dimitir; **~ stalling!** (US: (*inf*)) ¡déjate de evasivas!

quite [kwaɪt] *adv* (*rather*) bastante; (*entirely*) completamente; **~ a few of them** un buen número de ellos; **~ (so)!** ¡así es!, ¡exactamente!; **~ new** bastante nuevo; **that's not ~ right** eso no está del todo bien; **not ~ as many as last time** no tantos como la última vez; **she's ~ pretty** es bastante guapa

quits [kwɪts] *adj*: **~ (with)** en paz (con); **let's call it ~** quedamos en paz

quiver ['kwɪvə^r] *vi* estremecerse ▷ *n* (*for arrows*) carcaj *m*

quiz [kwɪz] *n* (*game*) concurso; (*: TV, Radio*) programa-concurso; (*questioning*) interrogatorio ▷ *vt* interrogar

quizzical ['kwɪzɪkl] *adj* burlón(-ona)

quorum ['kwɔːrəm] *n* quórum *m*

quota ['kwəʊtə] *n* cuota

quotation [kwəʊ'teɪʃən] *n* cita; (*estimate*) presupuesto

quotation marks *npl* comillas *fpl*

quote [kwəʊt] *n* cita ▷ *vt* (*sentence*) citar; (*Comm: sum, figure*) cotizar ▷ *vi*: **to ~ from** citar de; **quotes** *npl* (*inverted commas*) comillas *fpl*; **in ~s** entre comillas; **the figure ~d for the repairs** el presupuesto dado para las reparaciones; **~ ... unquote** (*in dictation*) comillas iniciales ... finales

quotient ['kwəʊʃənt] *n* cociente *m*

qv *n abbr* (= *quod vide: which see*) q.v.

R, r [ɑː^r] *n* (*letter*) R, r *f*; **R for Robert**, (US) **R for Roger** R de Ramón

R *abbr* (= *right*) dcha.; (= *river*) R.; (= *Réaumur scale*) R; (*US Cine*: = *restricted*) sólo mayores; (*US Pol*) = **republican**; (*Brit*: = *Rex, Regina*) R

rabbi ['ræbaɪ] *n* rabino

rabbit ['ræbɪt] *n* conejo ▷ *vi*: **to ~ (on)** (*Brit*: (*inf*)) hablar sin ton ni son

rabbit hutch *n* conejera

rabble ['ræbl] *n* (*pej*) chusma, populacho

rabies ['reɪbiːz] *n* rabia

RAC *n abbr* (*Brit*: = *Royal Automobile Club*) ≈ RACE *m* (*Sp*)

raccoon [rə'kuːn] *n* mapache *m*

race [reɪs] *n* carrera; (*species*) raza ▷ *vt* (*horse*) hacer correr; (*person*) competir contra; (*engine*) acelerar ▷ *vi* (*compete*) competir; (*run*) correr; (*pulse*) latir a ritmo acelerado; **the arms ~** la carrera armamentista; **the human ~** el género humano; **he ~d across the road** cruzó corriendo la carretera; **to ~ in/out** entrar/salir corriendo

race car *n* (US) = **racing car**

race car driver *n* (US) = **racing driver**

racecourse ['reɪskɔːs] *n* hipódromo

racehorse ['reɪshɔːs] *n* caballo de carreras

racetrack ['reɪstræk] *n* hipódromo; (*for cars*) circuito de carreras

racial ['reɪʃl] *adj* racial

racing ['reɪsɪŋ] *n* carreras *fpl*

racing car *n* (*Brit*) coche *m* de carreras

racing driver *n* (*Brit*) piloto *m/f* de carreras

racism ['reɪsɪzəm] n racismo
racist ['reɪsɪst] adj, n racista m/f
rack [ræk] n (also: **luggage ~**) rejilla
(portaequipajes); (shelf) estante m; (also:
roof ~) baca; (also: **clothes ~**) perchero ▷ vt
(cause pain to) atormentar; **to go to ~ and
ruin** venirse abajo; **to ~ one's brains**
devanarse los sesos; **rack up** vt conseguir,
ganar
racket ['rækɪt] n (for tennis) raqueta; (noise)
ruido, estrépito; (swindle) estafa, timo
racquet ['rækɪt] n raqueta
racy ['reɪsɪ] adj picante, subido
radar ['reɪdɑːʳ] n radar m
radial ['reɪdɪəl] adj (tyre: also: **~-ply**) radial
radiant ['reɪdɪənt] adj brillante,
resplandeciente
radiate ['reɪdɪeɪt] vt (heat) radiar, irradiar ▷ vi
(lines) extenderse
radiation [reɪdɪ'eɪʃən] n radiación f
radiator ['reɪdɪeɪtəʳ] n (Aut) radiador m
radical ['rædɪkl] adj radical
radii ['reɪdɪaɪ] npl of **radius**
radio ['reɪdɪəu] n radio f ▷ vi: **to ~ to sb**
mandar un mensaje por radio a algn ▷ vt
(information) radiar, transmitir por radio;
(one's position) indicar por radio; (person)
llamar por radio; **on the ~** en or por la radio
radioactive [reɪdɪəu'æktɪv] adj radi(o)activo
radioactivity [reɪdɪəuæk'tɪvɪtɪ] n radi(o)
actividad f
radio station n emisora
radio taxi n radio taxi m
radiotherapy ['reɪdɪəuθerəpɪ] n radioterapia
radish ['rædɪʃ] n rábano
radium ['reɪdɪəm] n radio
radius (pl **radii**) ['reɪdɪəs, -ɪaɪ] n radio;
within a ~ of 50 miles en un radio de 50
millas
RAF n abbr (Brit) see **Royal Air Force**
raffle ['ræfl] n rifa, sorteo ▷ vt (object) rifar
raft [rɑːft] n (craft) balsa; (also: **life ~**) balsa
salvavidas
rafter ['rɑːftəʳ] n viga
rag [ræg] n (piece of cloth) trapo; (torn cloth)
harapo; (pej: newspaper) periodicucho; (for
charity) actividades estudiantiles benéficas ▷ vt
(Brit) tomar el pelo a; **rags** npl harapos mpl;
in ~s en harapos, hecho jirones
rag doll n muñeca de trapo
rage [reɪdʒ] n (fury) rabia, furor m ▷ vi (person)
rabiar, estar furioso; (storm) bramar; **to fly
into a ~** montar en cólera; **it's all the ~** es lo
último; (very fashionable) está muy de moda
ragged ['rægɪd] adj (edge) desigual, mellado;
(cuff) roto; (appearance) andrajoso,
harapiento; **~ left/right** (text) margen m
izquierdo/derecho irregular
rag week n ver nota
raid [reɪd] n (Mil) incursión f; (criminal) asalto;
(by police) redada, allanamiento (LAm) ▷ vt
invadir, atacar; asaltar

rail [reɪl] n (on stair) barandilla, pasamanos m
inv; (on bridge) pretil m; (of balcony, ship)
barandilla; (for train) riel m, carril m; **rails** npl
vía sg; **by ~** por ferrocarril, en tren
railcard ['reɪlkɑːd] n (Brit) tarjeta para obtener
descuentos en el tren; **Young Person's R~**
≈ Tarjeta joven (Sp)
railing ['reɪlɪŋ] n, **railings** ['reɪlɪŋz] npl verja sg
railway ['reɪlweɪ], **railroad** (US) ['reɪlrəud] n
ferrocarril m, vía férrea
railway line n (Brit) línea (de ferrocarril)
railwayman ['reɪlweɪmən] n (Brit)
ferroviario
railway station n (Brit) estación f de
ferrocarril
rain [reɪn] n lluvia ▷ vi llover; **in the ~** bajo
la lluvia; **it's ~ing** llueve, está lloviendo;
it's ~ing cats and dogs está lloviendo
a cántaros or a mares
rainbow ['reɪnbəu] n arco iris
raincoat ['reɪnkəut] n impermeable m
raindrop ['reɪndrɔp] n gota de lluvia
rainfall ['reɪnfɔːl] n lluvia
rainforest ['reɪnfɔrɪst] n selva tropical
rainstorm ['reɪnstɔːm] n temporal m (de
lluvia)
rainwater ['reɪnwɔːtəʳ] n agua de lluvia
rainy ['reɪnɪ] adj lluvioso
raise [reɪz] n aumento ▷ vt (lift) levantar;
(build) erigir, edificar; (increase) aumentar;
(improve: morale) subir; (: standards) mejorar;
(doubts) suscitar; (a question) plantear;
(cattle, family) criar; (crop) cultivar; (army)
reclutar; (funds) reunir; (loan) obtener;
(end: embargo) levantar; **to ~ one's voice** alzar
la voz; **to ~ one's glass to sb/sth** brindar por
algn/algo; **to ~ a laugh/a smile** provocar
risa/una sonrisa; **to ~ sb's hopes** dar
esperanzas a algn
raisin ['reɪzn] n pasa de Corinto
rake [reɪk] n (tool) rastrillo; (person) libertino
▷ vt (garden) rastrillar; (fire) hurgar; (with
machine gun) barrer; **rake in, rake together** vt
sacar
rally ['rælɪ] n reunión f; (Pol) mitin m; (Aut)
rallye m; (Tennis) peloteo ▷ vt reunir ▷ vi
reunirse; (sick person) recuperarse; (Stock
Exchange) recuperarse; **rally round** vt fus (fig)
dar apoyo a
RAM [ræm] n abbr (Comput: = random access
memory) RAM f
ram [ræm] n carnero; (Tech) pisón m; (also:
battering ~) ariete m ▷ vt (crash into) dar
contra, chocar con; (push: fist etc) empujar
con fuerza; (tread down) apisonar
Ramadan ['ræmədæn] n Ramadán m
ramble ['ræmbl] n caminata, excursión f en
el campo ▷ vi (pej: also: **~ on**) divagar
rambler ['ræmbləʳ] n excursionista m/f; (Bot)
trepadora
rambling ['ræmblɪŋ] adj (speech) inconexo;
(Bot) trepador(a); (house) laberíntico

ramp [ræmp] n rampa; **on/off ~** n (US Aut) vía de acceso/salida; **"~"** (Aut) "rampa"
rampage ['ræm'peɪdʒ] n: **to be on the ~** desmandarse ▷ vi: **they went rampaging through the town** recorrieron la ciudad armando alboroto
rampant ['ræmpənt] adj (disease etc): **to be ~** estar muy extendido
rampart ['ræmpɑːt] n terraplén m; (wall) muralla
ram raid vt atracar (rompiendo el escaparate con un coche)
ramshackle ['ræmʃækl] adj destartalado
ran [ræn] pt of **run**
ranch [rɑːntʃ] n (US) hacienda, estancia
rancher ['rɑːntʃər] n ganadero
rancid ['rænsɪd] adj rancio
rancour, rancor (US) ['ræŋkər] n rencor m
random ['rændəm] adj fortuito, sin orden; (Comput, Math) aleatorio ▷ n: **at ~** al azar
random access n (Comput) acceso aleatorio
randy ['rændɪ] adj (Brit inf) cachondo, caliente
rang [ræŋ] pt of **ring**
range [reɪndʒ] n (of mountains) cadena de montañas, cordillera; (of missile) alcance m; (of voice) registro; (series) serie f; (of products) surtido; (Mil: also: **shooting ~**) campo de tiro; (also: **kitchen ~**) fogón m ▷ vt (place) colocar; (arrange) arreglar ▷ vi: **to ~ over** (wander) recorrer; (extend) extenderse por; **within (firing) ~** a tiro; **do you have anything else in this price ~?** ¿tiene algo más de esta gama de precios?; **intermediate-/short-~ missile** proyectil m de medio/corto alcance; **to ~ from ... to ...** oscilar entre ... y ...; **~d left/ right** (text) alineado a la izquierda/derecha
ranger [reɪndʒər] n guardabosques m inv
rank [ræŋk] n (row) fila; (Mil) rango; (status) categoría; (Brit: also: **taxi ~**) parada ▷ vi: **to ~ among** figurar entre ▷ adj (stinking) fétido, rancio; (hypocrisy, injustice etc) manifiesto; **the ~ and file** (fig) las bases; **to close ~s** (Mil) cerrar filas; (fig) hacer un frente común; **~ outsider** participante m/f sin probabilidades de vencer; **I ~ him sixth** yo le pongo en sexto lugar
rankle ['ræŋkl] vi (insult) doler
ransack ['rænsæk] vt (search) registrar; (plunder) saquear
ransom ['rænsəm] n rescate m; **to hold sb to ~** (fig) poner a algn entre la espada y la pared
rant [rænt] vi despotricar
rap [ræp] vt golpear, dar un golpecito en ▷ n (music) rap m
rape [reɪp] n violación f; (Bot) colza ▷ vt violar
rapid ['ræpɪd] adj rápido
rapidly ['ræpɪdlɪ] adv rápidamente
rapids ['ræpɪdz] npl (Geo) rápidos mpl
rapist ['reɪpɪst] n violador m
rapport [ræ'pɔːr] n entendimiento
rapture ['ræptʃər] n éxtasis m

rapturous ['ræptʃərəs] adj extático; (applause) entusiasta; **a ~ (party)** macrofiesta con música máquina; **~ music** música máquina
rare [reər] adj raro, poco común; (Culin: steak) poco hecho; **it is ~ to find that ...** es raro descubrir que ...
rarely ['reəlɪ] adv rara vez, pocas veces
raring ['reərɪŋ] adj: **to be ~ to go** (inf) tener muchas ganas de empezar
rascal ['rɑːskl] n pillo(-a), pícaro(-a)
rash [ræʃ] adj imprudente, precipitado ▷ n (Med) sarpullido, erupción f (cutánea); **to come out in a ~** salir salpullidos
rasher ['ræʃər] n loncha
raspberry ['rɑːzbərɪ] n frambuesa
rasping ['rɑːspɪŋ] adj: **a ~ noise** un ruido áspero
rat [ræt] n rata
ratchet ['rætʃɪt] n (Tech) trinquete m
rate [reɪt] n (ratio) razón f; (percentage) tanto por ciento; (price) precio; (: of hotel) tarifa; (of interest) tipo; (speed) velocidad f ▷ vt (value) tasar; (estimate) estimar; **to ~ as** ser considerado como; **rates** npl (Brit) impuesto sg municipal; (fees) tarifa sg; **failure ~** porcentaje m de fallos; **pulse ~** pulsaciones fpl por minuto; **~ of pay** tipos mpl de sueldo; **at a ~ of 60 kph** a una velocidad de 60 kph; **~ of growth** ritmo de crecimiento; **~ of return** (Comm) tasa de rendimiento; **bank ~** tipo or tasa de interés bancario; **at any ~** en todo caso; **to ~ sb/sth highly** tener a algn/ algo en alta estima; **the house is ~d at £84 per annum** (Brit) la casa está tasada en 84 libras al año
rateable value ['reɪtəbl-] n (Brit) valor m impuesto
ratepayer ['reɪtpeɪər] n (Brit) contribuyente m/f
rather ['rɑːðər] adv antes, más bien; (somewhat) algo, un poco; (quite) bastante; **it's ~ expensive** es algo caro; (too much) es demasiado caro; **there's ~ a lot** hay bastante; **I would** or **I'd ~ go** preferiría ir; **I'd ~ not** prefiero que no; **I ~ think he won't come** me inclino a creer que no vendrá; **or ~** (more accurately) o mejor dicho
ratify ['rætɪfaɪ] vt ratificar
rating ['reɪtɪŋ] n (valuation) tasación f; (standing) posición f; (Brit Naut: sailor) marinero; **ratings** npl (Radio, TV) niveles mpl de audiencia
ratio ['reɪʃɪəu] n razón f; **in the ~ of 100 to 1** a razón de or en la proporción de 100 a 1
ration ['ræʃən] n ración f; **rations** npl víveres mpl ▷ vt racionar
rational ['ræʃənl] adj racional; (solution, reasoning) lógico, razonable; (person) cuerdo, sensato
rationale [ræʃə'nɑːl] n razón f fundamental
rationalize ['ræʃnəlaɪz] vt (reorganize: industry) racionalizar

r

rationally ['ræʃnəlı] adv racionalmente; (logically) lógicamente

ratpack ['rætpæk] n (Brit inf) periodistas que persiguen a los famosos

rat race n lucha incesante por la supervivencia

rattle ['rætl] n golpeteo; (of train etc) traqueteo; (object: of baby) sonaja, sonajero; (: of sports fan) matraca ⊳ vi (small objects) castañetear; (car, bus): **to ~ along** traquetear ⊳ vt hacer sonar agitando; (inf: disconcert) poner nervioso a

rattlesnake ['rætlsneɪk] n serpiente f de cascabel

ratty ['rætɪ] adj (inf) furioso; **to get ~** mosquearse

raucous ['rɔːkəs] adj estridente, ronco

raunchy ['rɔːntʃɪ] adj (inf) lascivo

ravage ['rævɪdʒ] vt hacer estragos en, destrozar; **ravages** npl estragos mpl

rave [reɪv] vi (in anger) encolerizarse; (with enthusiasm) entusiasmarse; (Med) delirar, desvariar ⊳ cpd: **~ review** reseña entusiasta; **a ~ (party)** macrofiesta con música máquina; **~ music** música máquina ⊳ n (inf: party) rave m

raven ['reɪvən] n cuervo

ravenous ['rævənəs] adj: **to be ~** tener un hambre canina

ravine [rə'viːn] n barranco

raving ['reɪvɪŋ] adj: **~ lunatic** loco de atar

ravioli [rævɪ'əulɪ] n ravioles mpl, ravioli mpl

ravish ['rævɪʃ] vt (charm) encantar, embelesar; (rape) violar

ravishing ['rævɪʃɪŋ] adj encantador(a)

raw [rɔː] adj (uncooked) crudo; (not processed) bruto; (sore) vivo; (inexperienced) novato, inexperto; **~ materials** materias primas

raw material n materia prima

ray [reɪ] n rayo; **~ of hope** (rayo de) esperanza

raze [reɪz] vt (also: **~ to the ground**) arrasar, asolar

razor ['reɪzə'] n (open) navaja; (safety razor) máquina de afeitar; (electric razor) máquina (eléctrica) de afeitar

razor blade n hoja de afeitar

RC abbr = **Roman Catholic**

Rd abbr = **road**

RE n abbr (Brit: = religious education)

re [riː] prep con referencia a

reach [riːtʃ] n alcance m; (Boxing) envergadura; (of river etc) extensión f entre dos recodos ⊳ vt alcanzar, llegar a; (achieve) lograr ⊳ vi extenderse; (stretch out hand: also: **~ down, ~ over, ~ across** etc) tender la mano; **within ~** al alcance (de la mano); **out of ~** fuera del alcance; **can I ~ you at your hotel?** ¿puedo localizarte en tu hotel?; **to ~ sb by phone** comunicarse con algn por teléfono; **reach out** vt (hand) tender ⊳ vi: **to ~ out for sth** alargar or tender la mano para tomar algo

react [riː'ækt] vi reaccionar

reaction [riː'ækʃən] n reacción f

reactionary [riː'ækʃənrɪ] adj, n reaccionario(-a) m(f)

reactor [riː'æktə'] n (also: **nuclear ~**) reactor m (nuclear)

read (pt, pp read) [riːd, rɛd] vi leer ⊳ vt leer; (understand) entender; (study) estudiar; **to take sth as ~** (fig) dar algo por sentado; **do you ~ me?** (Tel) ¿me escucha?; **to ~ between the lines** leer entre líneas; **read out** vt leer en alta voz; **read over** vt repasar; **read through** vt (quickly) leer rápidamente, echar un vistazo a; (thoroughly) leer con cuidado or detenidamente; **read up, read up on** vt fus documentarse sobre

readable ['riːdəbl] adj (writing) legible; (book) que merece la pena leer

reader ['riːdə'] n lector(a) m(f); (book) libro de lecturas; (Brit: at university) profesor(a) m(f)

readership ['riːdəʃɪp] n (of paper etc) número de lectores

readily ['rɛdɪlɪ] adv (willingly) de buena gana; (easily) fácilmente; (quickly) en seguida

readiness ['rɛdɪnɪs] n buena voluntad; (preparedness) preparación f; **in ~** (prepared) listo, preparado

reading ['riːdɪŋ] n lectura; (understanding) comprensión f; (on instrument) indicación f

readjustment [riːə'dʒʌstmənt] n reajuste m

ready ['rɛdɪ] adj listo, preparado; (willing) dispuesto; (available) disponible ⊳ adv: **~-cooked** listo para comer ⊳ n: **at the ~** (Mil) listo para tirar; **~ for use** listo para usar; **to be ~ to do sth** estar listo para hacer algo; **to get ~** vi prepararse ⊳ vt preparar

ready-made ['rɛdɪ'meɪd] adj confeccionado

ready money n dinero contante

ready-to-wear ['rɛdɪtə'wɛə'] adj confeccionado

reaffirm [riːə'fəːm] vt reafirmar

real [rɪəl] adj verdadero, auténtico; **in ~ terms** en términos reales; **in ~ life** en la vida real, en la realidad

real ale n cerveza elaborada tradicionalmente

real estate n bienes mpl raíces

realism ['rɪəlɪzəm] n (also Art) realismo

realist ['rɪəlɪst] n realista m/f

realistic [rɪə'lɪstɪk] adj realista

realistically [rɪə'lɪstɪklɪ] adv de modo realista

reality [rɪ'ælɪtɪ] n realidad f; **in ~** en realidad

reality TV n telerrealidad f

realization [rɪəlaɪ'zeɪʃən] n comprensión f; (of a project) realización f; (Comm: of assets) realización f

realize ['rɪəlaɪz] vt (understand) darse cuenta de; (a project) realizar; (Comm: asset) realizar; **I ~ that ...** comprendo or entiendo que ...

really ['rɪəlɪ] adv realmente; (for emphasis) verdaderamente; (actually): **what ~ happened** lo que pasó en realidad; **~?** ¿de veras?; **~!** (annoyance) ¡vamos!, ¡por favor!

realm [rɛlm] n reino; (fig) esfera

realtor ['rɪəltɔːʳ] n (US) corredor(a) m(f) de bienes raíces

reap [riːp] vt segar; (fig) cosechar, recoger

reappear [riːəˈpɪəʳ] vi reaparecer

reappraisal [riːəˈpreɪzl] n revaluación f

rear [rɪəʳ] adj trasero ▷ n parte f trasera ▷ vt (cattle, family) criar ▷ vi (also: ~ up: animal) encabritarse

rearguard ['rɪəɡɑːd] n retaguardia

rearrange [riːəˈreɪndʒ] vt ordenar or arreglar de nuevo

rear-view ['rɪəvjuː]: ~ **mirror** n (Aut) espejo retrovisor

rear-wheel drive n tracción f trasera

reason ['riːzn] n razón f ▷ vi: **to ~ with sb** tratar de que algn entre en razón; **it stands to ~ that ...** es lógico que ...; **the ~ for/why** la causa de/la razón por la cual; **she claims with good ~ that she's underpaid** dice con razón que está mal pagada; **all the more ~ why you should not sell it** razón de más para que no lo vendas

reasonable ['riːznəbl] adj razonable; (sensible) sensato

reasonably ['riːznəblɪ] adv razonablemente; **a ~ accurate report** un informe bastante exacto

reasoning ['riːznɪŋ] n razonamiento, argumentos mpl

reassurance [riːəˈʃuərəns] n consuelo

reassure [riːəˈʃuəʳ] vt tranquilizar; **to ~ sb that** tranquilizar a algn asegurándole que

rebate ['riːbeɪt] n (on product) rebaja; (on tax etc) desgravación f; (repayment) reembolso

rebel ['rɛbl] n rebelde m/f ▷ vi [rɪˈbɛl] rebelarse, sublevarse

rebellion [rɪˈbɛljən] n rebelión f, sublevación f

rebellious [rɪˈbɛljəs] adj rebelde; (child) revoltoso

rebirth [riːˈbəːθ] n renacimiento

rebound [rɪˈbaund] vi (ball) rebotar ▷ n ['riːbaund] rebote m

rebuff [rɪˈbʌf] n desaire m, rechazo ▷ vt rechazar

rebuild [riːˈbɪld] vt (irreg: like **build**) reconstruir

rebuke [rɪˈbjuːk] n reprimenda ▷ vt reprender

rebut [rɪˈbʌt] vt rebatir

recall [rɪˈkɔːl] vt (remember) recordar; (ambassador etc) retirar; (Comput) volver a llamar ▷ n recuerdo

recant [rɪˈkænt] vi retractarse

recap ['riːkæp] vt, vi recapitular

recd., rec'd abbr (= received) recibido

recede [rɪˈsiːd] vi retroceder

receding [rɪˈsiːdɪŋ] adj (forehead, chin) hundido; ~ **hairline** entradas fpl

receipt [rɪˈsiːt] n (document) recibo; (act of receiving) recepción f; **receipts** npl (Comm) ingresos mpl; **to acknowledge ~ of** acusar recibo de; **we are in ~ of ...** obra en nuestro poder ...

receive [rɪˈsiːv] vt recibir; (guest) acoger; (wound) sufrir; **"~d with thanks"** "recibí"

receiver [rɪˈsiːvəʳ] n (Tel) auricular m; (Radio) receptor m; (of stolen goods) perista m/f; (Law) administrador m jurídico

receivership [rɪˈsiːvəʃɪp] n: **to go into ~** entrar en liquidación

recent ['riːsnt] adj reciente; **in ~ years** en los últimos años

recently ['riːsntlɪ] adv recientemente, recién (LAm); ~ **arrived** recién llegado; **until ~** hasta hace poco

receptacle [rɪˈsɛptɪkl] n receptáculo

reception [rɪˈsɛpʃən] n (in building, office etc) recepción f; (welcome) acogida

reception desk n recepción f

receptionist [rɪˈsɛpʃənɪst] n recepcionista m/f

recess [rɪˈsɛs] n (in room) hueco; (for bed) nicho; (secret place) escondrijo; (Pol etc: holiday) período vacacional; (US Law: short break) descanso; (Scol: esp US) recreo

recession [rɪˈsɛʃən] n recesión f, depresión f

recharge [riːˈtʃɑːdʒ] vt (battery) recargar

recipe ['rɛsɪpɪ] n receta; (for disaster, success) fórmula

recipient [rɪˈsɪpɪənt] n recibidor(a) m(f); (of letter) destinatario(-a)

reciprocate [rɪˈsɪprəkeɪt] vt devolver, corresponder a ▷ vi corresponder

recital [rɪˈsaɪtl] n (Mus) recital m

recitation [rɛsɪˈteɪʃən] n (of poetry) recitado; (of complaints etc) enumeración f, relación f

recite [rɪˈsaɪt] vt (poem) recitar; (complaints etc) enumerar

reckless ['rɛkləs] adj temerario, imprudente; (speed) peligroso

reckon ['rɛkən] vt (calculate) calcular; (consider) considerar ▷ vi: **to ~ without sb/ sth** dejar de contar con algn/algo; **he is somebody to be ~ed with** no se le puede descartar; **I ~ that ...** me parece que ..., creo que ...; **reckon on** vt fus contar con

reckoning ['rɛkənɪŋ] n (calculation) cálculo

reclaim [rɪˈkleɪm] vt (land) recuperar; (: from sea) rescatar; (demand back) reclamar

recline [rɪˈklaɪn] vi reclinarse

reclining [rɪˈklaɪnɪŋ] adj (seat) reclinable

recluse [rɪˈkluːs] n recluso(-a)

recognition [rɛkəɡˈnɪʃən] n reconocimiento; **transformed beyond ~** irreconocible; **in ~ of** en reconocimiento de

recognize ['rɛkəɡnaɪz] vt reconocer, conocer; **to ~ (by/as)** reconocer (por/como)

recoil [rɪˈkɔɪl] vi (person): **to ~ from doing sth** retraerse de hacer algo ▷ n (of gun) retroceso

recollect [rɛkəˈlɛkt] vt recordar, acordarse de

recollection [rɛkəˈlɛkʃən] n recuerdo; **to the best of my ~** que yo recuerde

r

recommend [rɛkə'mɛnd] vt recomendar; **she has a lot to ~ her** tiene mucho a su favor
recommendation [rɛkəmɛn'deɪʃən] n recomendación f
reconcile ['rɛkənsaɪl] vt (two people) reconciliar; (two facts) conciliar; **to ~ o.s. to sth** resignarse or conformarse a algo
reconciliation [rɛkənsɪlɪ'eɪʃən] n reconciliación f
recondition [ri:kən'dɪʃən] vt (machine) reparar, reponer
reconditioned [ri:kən'dɪʃənd] adj renovado, reparado
reconnoitre, reconnoiter (US) [rɛkə'nɔɪtəʳ] vt, vi (Mil) reconocer
reconsider [ri:kən'sɪdəʳ] vt repensar
reconstruct [ri:kən'strʌkt] vt reconstruir
reconvene [ri:kən'vi:n] vt volver a convocar ▷ vi volver a reunirse
record n ['rɛkɔ:d] (Mus) disco; (of meeting etc) acta; (register) registro, partida; (file) archivo; (also: **police** or **criminal ~**) antecedentes mpl penales; (written) expediente m; (Sport) récord m; (Comput) registro ▷ vt [rɪ'kɔ:d] (set down) registrar; (Comput) registrar; (relate) hacer constar; (Mus: song etc) grabar; **in ~ time** en un tiempo récord; **public ~s** archivos mpl nacionales; **he is on ~ as saying that ...** hay pruebas de que ha dicho públicamente que ...; **Spain's excellent ~** el excelente historial de España; **off the ~** adj no oficial ▷ adv confidencialmente
record card n (in file) ficha
recorded delivery [rɪ'kɔ:dɪd-] n (Brit Post) entrega con acuse de recibo
recorder [rɪ'kɔ:dəʳ] n (Mus) flauta de pico; (Tech) contador m
record holder n (Sport) actual poseedor(a) m(f) del récord
recording [rɪ'kɔ:dɪŋ] n (Mus) grabación f
recording studio n estudio de grabación
record library n discoteca
record player n tocadiscos m inv
recount vt [rɪ'kaʊnt] contar
re-count ['ri:kaʊnt] n (Pol: of votes) segundo escrutinio, recuento ▷ vt [ri:'kaʊnt] volver a contar
recoup [rɪ'ku:p] vt: **to ~ one's losses** recuperar las pérdidas
recourse [rɪ'kɔ:s] n recurso; **to have ~ to** recurrir a
recover [rɪ'kʌvəʳ] vt recuperar; (rescue) rescatar ▷ vi recuperarse
recovery [rɪ'kʌvərɪ] n recuperación f; rescate m; (Med): **to make a ~** restablecerse
recreate [ri:krɪ'eɪt] vt recrear
recreation [rɛkrɪ'eɪʃən] n recreación f; (amusement) recreo
recreational [rɛkrɪ'eɪʃənl] adj de, recreo; **~ drug** droga recreativa
recreational vehicle n (US) caravana or roulotte f pequeña

recrimination [rɪkrɪmɪ'neɪʃən] n recriminación f
recruit [rɪ'kru:t] n recluta m/f ▷ vt reclutar; (staff) contratar
recruitment [rɪ'kru:tmənt] n reclutamiento
rectangle ['rɛktæŋgl] n rectángulo
rectangular [rɛk'tæŋgjʊləʳ] adj rectangular
rectify ['rɛktɪfaɪ] vt rectificar
rector ['rɛktəʳ] n (Rel) párroco; (Scol) rector(a) m(f)
rectum ['rɛktəm] n (Anat) recto
recuperate [rɪ'ku:pəreɪt] vi reponerse, restablecerse
recur [rɪ'kə:ʳ] vi repetirse; (pain, illness) producirse de nuevo
recurrence [rɪ'kə:rns] n repetición f
recurrent [rɪ'kə:rnt] adj repetido
recurring [rɪ'kə:rɪŋ] adj (problem) repetido, constante
recyclable [ri:'saɪkləbl] adj reciclable
recycle [ri:'saɪkl] vt reciclar
recycling [ri:'saɪklɪŋ] n reciclaje m
red [rɛd] n rojo ▷ adj rojo; (hair) pelirrojo; (wine) tinto; **to be in the ~** (account) estar en números rojos; (business) tener un saldo negativo; **to give sb the ~ carpet treatment** recibir a algn con todos los honores
red alert n alerta roja
red-blooded ['rɛd'blʌdɪd] adj (inf) viril
Red Cross n Cruz f Roja
redcurrant ['rɛdkʌrənt] n grosella roja
redden ['rɛdn] vt enrojecer ▷ vi enrojecerse
reddish ['rɛdɪʃ] adj (hair) rojizo
redecorate [ri:'dɛkəreɪt] vt pintar de nuevo; volver a decorar
redeem [rɪ'di:m] vt redimir; (promises) cumplir; (sth in pawn) desempeñar; (Rel) rescatar; (fig) rescatar
redeeming [rɪ'di:mɪŋ] adj: **~ feature** punto bueno or favorable
redefine [ri:dɪ'faɪn] vt redefinir
redemption [rɪ'dɛmpʃən] n (Rel) redención f; **to be past** or **beyond ~** no tener remedio
redeploy [ri:dɪ'plɔɪ] vt disponer de nuevo
redeployment [ri:dɪ'plɔɪmənt] n redistribución f
red-handed [rɛd'hændɪd] adj: **he was caught ~** le pillaron con las manos en la masa
redhead ['rɛdhɛd] n pelirrojo(-a)
red herring n (fig) pista falsa
red-hot [rɛd'hɔt] adj candente
redirect [ri:daɪ'rɛkt] vt (mail) reexpedir
rediscover [ri:dɪs'kʌvəʳ] vt redescubrir
redistribute [ri:dɪs'trɪbju:t] vt redistribuir, hacer una nueva distribución de
red light n: **to go through** or **jump a ~** (Aut) saltarse un semáforo
red-light district n barrio chino, zona de tolerancia
red meat n carne f roja

redo [riːˈduː] vt (irreg: like **do**) rehacer
redolent [ˈrɛdələnt] adj: ~ **of** (smell) con fragancia a; **to be ~ of** (fig) evocar
redouble [riːˈdʌbl] vt: **to ~ one's efforts** redoblar los esfuerzos
redraft [riːˈdrɑːft] vt volver a redactar
redress [rɪˈdrɛs] n reparación f ▷ vt reparar, corregir; **to ~ the balance** restablecer el equilibrio
Red Sea n: **the ~** el mar Rojo
redskin [ˈrɛdskɪn] n piel roja m/f
red tape n (fig) trámites mpl, papeleo (fam)
reduce [rɪˈdjuːs] vt reducir; (lower) rebajar; **to ~ sth by/to** reducir algo en/a; **to ~ sb to silence/despair/tears** hacer callar/ desesperarse/llorar a algn; **"~ speed now"** (Aut) "reduzca la velocidad"
reduced [rɪˈdjuːst] adj (decreased) reducido, rebajado; **at a ~ price** con rebaja or descuento; **"greatly ~ prices"** "grandes rebajas"
reduction [rɪˈdʌkʃən] n reducción f; (of price) rebaja; (discount) descuento
redundancy [rɪˈdʌndənsɪ] n despido; (unemployment) desempleo; **voluntary ~** baja voluntaria
redundant [rɪˈdʌndənt] adj (Brit: worker) parado, sin trabajo; (detail, object) superfluo; **to be made ~** quedar(se) sin trabajo, perder el empleo
reed [riːd] n (Bot) junco, caña; (Mus: of clarinet etc) lengüeta
re-educate [riːˈɛdjukeɪt] vt reeducar
reef [riːf] n (at sea) arrecife m
reek [riːk] vi: **to ~ (of)** oler or apestar (a)
reel [riːl] n carrete m, bobina; (of film) rollo ▷ vt (Tech) devanar; (also: **~ in**) sacar ▷ vi (sway) tambalear(se); **my head is ~ing** me da vueltas la cabeza; **reel off** vt recitar de memoria
ref [rɛf] n abbr (inf) = **referee**
ref. abbr (Comm: = with reference to) Ref
refectory [rɪˈfɛktərɪ] n comedor m
refer [rɪˈfəː] vt (send: patient) referir; (: matter) remitir; (ascribe) referir a, relacionar con ▷ vi: **to ~ to** (allude to) referirse a, aludir a; (apply to) relacionarse con; (consult) remitirse a; **he ~red me to the manager** me envió al gerente
referee [rɛfəˈriː] n árbitro; (Brit: for job application): **to be a ~ for sb** proporcionar referencias a algn ▷ vt (match) arbitrar en
reference [ˈrɛfrəns] n (mention: in book) referencia; (sending) remisión f; (relevance) relación f; (for job application: letter) carta de recomendación; **with ~ to** con referencia a; (Comm: in letter) me remito a
reference book n libro de consulta
reference library n biblioteca de consulta
reference number n número de referencia
referendum (pl **referenda**) [rɛfəˈrɛndəm, -də] n referéndum m

referral [rɪˈfəːrəl] n remisión f
refill vt [riːˈfɪl] rellenar ▷ n [ˈriːfɪl] repuesto, recambio
refine [rɪˈfaɪn] vt (sugar, oil) refinar
refined [rɪˈfaɪnd] adj (person, taste) refinado, fino
refinement [rɪˈfaɪnmənt] n (of person) cultura, educación f
refinery [rɪˈfaɪnərɪ] n refinería
refit (also Naut) n [ˈriːfɪt] reparación f ▷ vt [riːˈfɪt] reparar
reflect [rɪˈflɛkt] vt (light, image) reflejar ▷ vi (think) reflexionar, pensar; **it ~s badly/well on him** le perjudica/le hace honor
reflection [rɪˈflɛkʃən] n (act) reflexión f; (image) reflejo; (discredit) crítica; **on ~** pensándolo bien
reflector [rɪˈflɛktəʳ] n (Aut) catafaros m inv; (telescope) reflector m
reflex [ˈriːflɛks] adj, n reflejo
reflexive [rɪˈflɛksɪv] adj (Ling) reflexivo
reform [rɪˈfɔːm] n reforma ▷ vt reformar
reformat [riːˈfɔːmæt] vt (Comput) recomponer
Reformation [rɛfəˈmeɪʃən] n: **the ~** la Reforma
reformatory [rɪˈfɔːmətərɪ] n (US) reformatorio
refrain [rɪˈfreɪn] vi: **to ~ from doing** abstenerse de hacer ▷ n (Mus etc) estribillo
refresh [rɪˈfrɛʃ] vt refrescar
refresher course [rɪˈfrɛʃə-] n (Brit) curso de repaso
refreshing [rɪˈfrɛʃɪŋ] adj (drink) refrescante; (sleep) reparador; (change etc) estimulante; (idea, point of view) estimulante, interesante
refreshments [rɪˈfrɛʃmənts] npl (drinks) refrescos mpl
refrigeration [rɪfrɪdʒəˈreɪʃən] n refrigeración f
refrigerator [rɪˈfrɪdʒəreɪtəʳ] n frigorífico, refrigeradora (LAm), heladera (LAm)
refuel [riːˈfjuəl] vi repostar (combustible)
refuge [ˈrɛfjuːdʒ] n refugio, asilo; **to take ~ in** refugiarse en
refugee [rɛfjuˈdʒiː] n refugiado(-a)
refugee camp n campamento para refugiados
refund n [ˈriːfʌnd] reembolso ▷ vt [rɪˈfʌnd] devolver, reembolsar
refurbish [riːˈfəːbɪʃ] vt restaurar, renovar
refusal [rɪˈfjuːzəl] n negativa; **first ~** primera opción; **to have first ~ on sth** tener la primera opción a algo
refuse¹ [ˈrɛfjuːs] n basura
refuse² [rɪˈfjuːz] vt (reject) rechazar; (invitation) declinar; (permission) denegar; (say no to) negarse a ▷ vi negarse; (horse) rehusar; **to ~ to do sth** negarse a or rehusar hacer algo
refuse collection n recogida de basuras
regain [rɪˈgeɪn] vt recobrar, recuperar
regal [ˈriːgl] adj regio, real
regard [rɪˈgɑːd] n (gaze) mirada; (aspect) respecto; (esteem) respeto; (attention)

r

consideración f ▷ vt (consider) considerar;
(look at) mirar; **to give one's ~s to** saludar de
su parte a; **"(kind) ~s"** "muy atentamente";
"with kindest ~s" "con muchos recuerdos";
~s to María, please give my ~s to María
recuerdos a María, dele recuerdos a María de
mi parte; **as ~s, with ~ to** con respecto a,
en cuanto a

regarding [rɪ'gɑːdɪŋ] prep con respecto a,
en cuanto a

regardless [rɪ'gɑːdlɪs] adv a pesar de todo;
~ of sin reparar en

regatta [rɪ'gætə] n regata

regenerate [rɪ'dʒɛnəreɪt] vt regenerar

reggae ['rɛɡeɪ] n reggae m

régime [reɪ'ʒiːm] n régimen m

regiment n ['rɛdʒɪmənt] regimiento ▷ vt
['rɛdʒɪmɛnt] reglamentar

regimental [rɛdʒɪ'mɛntl] adj militar

region ['riːdʒən] n región f; **in the ~ of** (fig)
alrededor de

regional ['riːdʒənl] adj regional

register ['rɛdʒɪstəʳ] n registro ▷ vt registrar;
(birth) declarar; (car) matricular; (letter)
certificar; (instrument) marcar, indicar ▷ vi (at
hotel) registrarse; (as student) matricularse;
(sign on) inscribirse; (make impression) producir
impresión; **to ~ a protest** presentar una
queja; **to ~ for a course** matricularse or
inscribirse en un curso

registered ['rɛdʒɪstəd] adj (design) registrado;
(Brit: letter) certificado; (student) matriculado;
(voter) registrado

registered trademark n marca registrada

registrar ['rɛdʒɪstrɑːʳ] n secretario(-a) (del
registro civil)

registration [rɛdʒɪs'treɪʃən] n (act)
declaración f; (Aut: also: **~ number**) matrícula

registry ['rɛdʒɪstrɪ] n registro

registry office n (Brit) registro civil; **to get
married in a ~** casarse por lo civil

regret [rɪ'grɛt] n sentimiento, pesar m; (remorse)
remordimiento ▷ vt sentir, lamentar; (repent
of) arrepentirse de; **we ~ to inform you
that ...** sentimos informarle que ...

regretfully [rɪ'grɛtfəlɪ] adv con pesar,
sentidamente

regrettable [rɪ'grɛtəbl] adj lamentable; (loss)
sensible

regular ['rɛɡjuləʳ] adj regular; (soldier)
profesional; (inf: intensive) verdadero; (listener,
reader) asiduo; (usual) habitual ▷ n (client etc)
cliente(-a) m(f) habitual

regularity [rɛɡju'lærɪtɪ] n regularidad f

regularly ['rɛɡjuləlɪ] adv con regularidad

regulate ['rɛɡjuleɪt] vt (gen) controlar; (Tech)
regular, ajustar

regulation [rɛɡju'leɪʃən] n (rule) regla,
reglamento; (adjustment) regulación f

rehabilitate [riː'əˈbɪlɪteɪt] vt rehabilitar

rehabilitation ['riːəbɪlɪ'teɪʃən] n
rehabilitación f

rehash [riː'hæʃ] vt (inf) hacer un refrito de

rehearsal [rɪ'həːsəl] n ensayo; **dress ~**
ensayo general or final

rehearse [rɪ'həːs] vt ensayar

rehouse [riː'hauz] vt dar nueva vivienda a

reign [reɪn] n reinado; (fig) predominio ▷ vi
reinar; (fig) imperar

reigning ['reɪnɪŋ] adj (monarch) reinante,
actual; (predominant) imperante

reimburse [riːɪm'bəːs] vt reembolsar

rein [reɪn] n (for horse) rienda; **to give sb
free ~** dar rienda suelta a algn

reincarnation [riːɪnkɑː'neɪʃən] n
reencarnación f

reindeer ['reɪndɪəʳ] n pl inv reno

reinforce [riːɪn'fɔːs] vt reforzar

reinforced concrete [riːɪn'fɔːst-] n
hormigón m armado

reinforcement [riːɪn'fɔːsmənt] n (action)
refuerzo; **reinforcements** npl (Mil)
refuerzos mpl

reinstate [riːɪn'steɪt] vt (worker) reintegrar
(a su puesto); (tax, law) reinstaurar

reiterate [riː'ɪtəreɪt] vt reiterar, repetir

reject n ['riːdʒɛkt] (thing) desecho ▷ vt
[rɪ'dʒɛkt] rechazar; (proposition, offer etc)
descartar

rejection [rɪ'dʒɛkʃən] n rechazo

rejoice [rɪ'dʒɔɪs] vi: **to ~ at** or **over** regocijarse
or alegrarse de

rejuvenate [rɪ'dʒuːvəneɪt] vt rejuvenecer

relapse [rɪ'læps] n (Med) recaída; (into crime)
reincidencia

relate [rɪ'leɪt] vt (tell) contar, relatar; (connect)
relacionar ▷ vi relacionarse; **to ~ to** (connect)
relacionarse or tener que ver con

related [rɪ'leɪtɪd] adj afín; (person)
emparentado; **to be ~ to** (connected) guardar
relación con; (by family) ser pariente de

relating [rɪ'leɪtɪŋ]: **~ to** prep referente a

relation [rɪ'leɪʃən] n (person) pariente m/f;
(link) relación f; **in ~ to** en relación con, en lo
que se refiere a; **to bear a ~ to** guardar
relación con; **diplomatic ~s** relaciones fpl
diplomáticas; **relations** npl (relatives)
familiares mpl

relationship [rɪ'leɪʃənʃɪp] n relación f;
(personal) relaciones fpl; (also: **family ~**)
parentesco

relative ['rɛlətɪv] n pariente m/f, familiar m/f
▷ adj relativo

relatively ['rɛlətɪvlɪ] adv (fairly, rather)
relativamente

relax [rɪ'læks] vi descansar; (quieten down)
relajarse ▷ vt relajar; (grip) aflojar; **~!** (calm
down) ¡tranquilo!

relaxation [riːlæk'seɪʃən] n (rest) descanso;
(easing) relajación f, relajamiento m;
(amusement) recreo; (entertainment) diversión f

relaxed [rɪ'lækst] adj relajado; (tranquil)
tranquilo

relaxing [rɪ'læksɪŋ] adj relajante

relay n ['ri:leɪ] (race) carrera de relevos ▷ vt [rɪ'leɪ] (Radio, TV) retransmitir; (pass on) retransmitir

release [rɪ'li:s] n (liberation) liberación f; (discharge) puesta en libertad f; (of gas etc) escape m; (of film etc) estreno; (of record) lanzamiento ▷ vt (prisoner) poner en libertad; (film) estrenar; (book) publicar; (piece of news) difundir; (gas etc) despedir, arrojar; (free: from wreckage etc) liberar; (Tech: catch, spring etc) desenganchar; (let go) soltar, aflojar

relegate ['relǝgeɪt] vt relegar; (Sport): **to be ~d to** bajar a

relent [rɪ'lɛnt] vi ceder, ablandarse; (let up) descansar

relentless [rɪ'lɛntlɪs] adj implacable

relevance ['relǝvǝns] n relación f

relevant ['relǝvǝnt] adj (fact) pertinente; **~ to** relacionado con

reliability [rɪlaɪǝ'bɪlɪtɪ] n fiabilidad f; seguridad f; veracidad f

reliable [rɪ'laɪǝbl] adj (person, firm) de confianza, de fiar; (method, machine) seguro; (source) fidedigno

reliably [rɪ'laɪǝblɪ] adv: **to be ~ informed that ...** saber de fuente fidedigna que ...

reliance [rɪ'laɪǝns] n: **~ (on)** dependencia (de)

relic ['rɛlɪk] n (Rel) reliquia; (of the past) vestigio

relief [rɪ'li:f] n (from pain, anxiety) alivio, desahogo; (help, supplies) socorro, ayuda; (Art, Geo) relieve m; **by way of light ~** a modo de diversión

relieve [rɪ'li:v] vt (pain, patient) aliviar; (bring help to) ayudar, socorrer; (burden) aligerar; (take over from: gen) sustituir a; (: guard) relevar; **to ~ sb of sth** quitar algo a algn; **to ~ sb of his command** (Mil) relevar a algn de su mando; **to ~ o.s.** hacer sus necesidades

relieved [rɪ'li:vd] adj: **to be ~** sentir un gran alivio

religion [rɪ'lɪdʒǝn] n religión f

religious [rɪ'lɪdʒǝs] adj religioso

religious education n educación f religiosa

relinquish [rɪ'lɪŋkwɪʃ] vt abandonar; (plan, habit) renunciar a

relish ['rɛlɪʃ] n (Culin) salsa; (enjoyment) entusiasmo; (flavour) sabor m, gusto ▷ vt (food, challenge etc) saborear; **to ~ doing** gozar haciendo

relive [ri:'lɪv] vt vivir de nuevo, volver a vivir

relocate [ri:lǝu'keɪt] vt trasladar ▷ vi trasladarse

reluctance [rɪ'lʌktǝns] n desgana, renuencia

reluctant [rɪ'lʌktǝnt] adj reacio; **to be ~ to do sth** resistirse a hacer algo

reluctantly [rɪ'lʌktǝntlɪ] adv de mala gana

rely [rɪ'laɪ]: **~ on** vt fus confiar en, fiarse de; (be dependent on) depender de; **you can ~ on my discretion** puedes contar con mi discreción

remain [rɪ'meɪn] vi (survive) quedar; (be left) sobrar; (continue) quedar(se), permanecer; **to ~ silent** permanecer callado; **I ~, yours faithfully** (in letters) le saluda atentamente

remainder [rɪ'meɪndǝr] n resto

remaining [rɪ'meɪnɪŋ] adj restante, que queda(n)

remains [rɪ'meɪnz] npl restos mpl

remand [rɪ'mɑ:nd] n: **on ~** detenido (bajo custodia) ▷ vt: **to ~ in custody** mantener bajo custodia

remand home n (Brit) reformatorio

remark [rɪ'mɑ:k] n comentario ▷ vt comentar; **to ~ on sth** hacer observaciones sobre algo

remarkable [rɪ'mɑ:kǝbl] adj notable; (outstanding) extraordinario

remarry [ri:'mærɪ] vi casarse por segunda vez, volver a casarse

remedial [rɪ'mi:dɪǝl] adj: **~ education** educación f de los niños atrasados

remedy ['rɛmǝdɪ] n remedio ▷ vt remediar, curar

remember [rɪ'mɛmbǝr] vt recordar, acordarse de; (bear in mind) tener presente; **I ~ seeing it, I ~ having seen it** recuerdo haberlo visto; **she ~ed doing it** se acordó de hacerlo; **~ me to your wife and children!** ¡déle recuerdos a su familia!

remembrance [rɪ'mɛmbrǝns] n (memory, souvenir) recuerdo; **in ~ of** en conmemoración de

Remembrance Day, Remembrance Sunday n (Brit) ver nota

remind [rɪ'maɪnd] vt: **to ~ sb to do sth** recordar a algn que haga algo; **to ~ sb of sth** recordar algo a algn; **she ~s me of her mother** me recuerda a su madre; **that ~s me!** ¡a propósito!

reminder [rɪ'maɪndǝr] n notificación f; (memento) recuerdo

r

reminisce [rɛmɪ'nɪs] vi recordar (viejas historias)
reminiscent [remɪ'nɪsnt] adj: **to be ~ of** sth recordar algo
remiss [rɪ'mɪs] adj descuidado; **it was ~ of me** fue un descuido de mi parte
remission [rɪ'mɪʃən] n remisión f; (of sentence) reducción f de la pena
remit [rɪ'mɪt] vt (send: money) remitir, enviar
remittance [rɪ'mɪtns] n remesa, envío
remnant ['rɛmnənt] n resto; (of cloth) retal m, retazo; **remnants** npl (Comm) restos de serie
remorse [rɪ'mɔːs] n remordimientos mpl
remorseful [rɪ'mɔːsful] adj arrepentido
remorseless [rɪ'mɔːslɪs] adj (fig) implacable, inexorable
remote [rɪ'məut] adj remoto; (distant) lejano; (person) distante; **there is a ~ possibility that ...** hay una posibilidad remota de que ...
remote control n mando a distancia
remotely [rɪ'məutlɪ] adv remotamente; (slightly) levemente
remould ['riːməuld] n (Brit: tyre) neumático or llanta (LAm) recauchutado(-a)
removable [rɪ'muːvəbl] adj (detachable) separable
removal [rɪ'muːvəl] n (taking away) (el) quitar; (Brit: from house) mudanza; (from office: dismissal) destitución f; (Med) extirpación f
removal man n (Brit) mozo de mudanzas
removal van n (Brit) camión m de mudanzas
remove [rɪ'muːv] vt quitar; (employee) destituir; (name: from list) tachar, borrar; (doubt) disipar; (Tech) retirar, separar; (Med) extirpar; **first cousin once ~d** (parent's cousin) tío(-a) segundo(-a); (cousin's child) sobrino(-a) segundo(-a)
remuneration [rɪmjuːnə'reɪʃən] n remuneración f
Renaissance [rɪ'neɪsɔ̃ns] n: **the ~** el Renacimiento
rename [riː'neɪm] vt poner nuevo nombre a
render ['rɛndəʳ] vt (thanks) dar; (aid) proporcionar; (honour) dar, conceder; (assistance) dar, prestar; **to ~ sth +adj** volver algo + adj; **to ~ sth useless** hacer algo inútil
rendering ['rɛndərɪŋ] n (Mus etc) interpretación f
rendez-vous ['rɔndɪvuː] n cita ▷ vi reunirse, encontrarse; (spaceship) efectuar una reunión espacial
rendition [rɛn'dɪʃən] n (Mus) interpretación f
renew [rɪ'njuː] vt renovar; (resume) reanudar; (extend date) prorrogar; (negotiations) volver a
renewable [rɪ'njuːəbl] adj renovable; **~ energy, ~s** energías renovables
renewal [rɪ'njuːəl] n renovación f; reanudación f; prórroga
renounce [rɪ'nauns] vt renunciar a; (right, inheritance) renunciar
renovate ['rɛnəveɪt] vt renovar
renovation [rɛnə'veɪʃən] n renovación f

renown [rɪ'naun] n renombre m
renowned [rɪ'naund] adj renombrado
rent [rɛnt] n alquiler m; (for house) arriendo, renta ▷ vt (also: **~ out**) alquilar
rental [rɛntl] n (for television, car) alquiler m
rent boy n (Brit inf) chapero
reopen [riː'əupən] vt volver a abrir, reabrir
reorder [riː'ɔːdəʳ] vt volver a pedir, repetir el pedido de; (rearrange) volver a ordenar or arreglar
reorganization [riːɔːgənaɪ'zeɪʃən] n reorganización f
reorganize [riː'ɔːgənaɪz] vt reorganizar
rep [rɛp] n abbr (Comm) = **representative**; (Theat) = **repertory**
repair [rɪ'pɛəʳ] n reparación f, arreglo; (patch) remiendo ▷ vt reparar, arreglar; **in good/ bad ~** en buen/mal estado; **under ~** en obras
repair kit n caja de herramientas
repatriate [riː'pætrɪeɪt] vt repatriar
repay [riː'peɪ] vt (irreg: like **pay**) (money) devolver, reembolsar; (person) pagar; (debt) liquidar; (sb's efforts) devolver, corresponder a
repayment [riː'peɪmənt] n reembolso, devolución f; (sum of money) recompensa
repeal [rɪ'piːl] n revocación f ▷ vt revocar
repeat [rɪ'piːt] n (Radio, TV) reposición f ▷ vt repetir ▷ vi repetirse
repeatedly [rɪ'piːtɪdlɪ] adv repetidas veces
repeat prescription n (Brit) receta renovada
repel [rɪ'pɛl] vt repugnar
repellent [rɪ'pɛlənt] adj repugnante ▷ n: **insect ~** crema/loción f antiinsectos
repent [rɪ'pɛnt] vi: **to ~ (of)** arrepentirse (de)
repentance [rɪ'pɛntəns] n arrepentimiento
repercussion [riːpə'kʌʃən] n (consequence) repercusión f; **to have ~s** repercutir
repertoire ['rɛpətwaːʳ] n repertorio
repertory ['rɛpətərɪ] n (also: **~ theatre**) teatro de repertorio
repertory company n compañía de repertorio
repetition [rɛpɪ'tɪʃən] n repetición f
repetitive [rɪ'pɛtɪtɪv] adj (movement, work) repetitivo, reiterativo; (speech) lleno de repeticiones
rephrase [riː'freɪz] vt decir or formular de otro modo
replace [rɪ'pleɪs] vt (put back) devolver a su sitio; (take the place of) reemplazar, sustituir
replacement [rɪ'pleɪsmənt] n reemplazo; (act) reposición f; (thing) recambio; (person) suplente m/f
replay ['riːpleɪ] n (Sport) partido de desempate; (TV: playback) repetición f
replenish [rɪ'plɛnɪʃ] vt (tank etc) rellenar; (stock etc) reponer; (with fuel) repostar
replica ['rɛplɪkə] n réplica, reproducción f
reply [rɪ'plaɪ] n respuesta, contestación f ▷ vi contestar, responder; **in ~** en respuesta; **there's no ~** (Tel) no contestan
reply coupon n cupón-respuesta m

report [rɪ'pɔːt] n informe m; (Press etc)
reportaje m; (Brit: also: **school ~**) informe m
escolar; (of gun) detonación f ▷ vt informar
sobre; (Press etc) hacer un reportaje sobre;
(notify: accident, culprit) denunciar ▷ vi (make
a report) presentar un informe; (present o.s.):
to ~ (to sb) presentarse (ante algn);
annual ~ (Comm) informe m anual; **to ~
(on)** hacer un informe (sobre); **it is ~ed
from Berlin that ...** se informa desde Berlín
que ...

report card n (US, Scottish) cartilla escolar

reportedly [rɪ'pɔːtɪdlɪ] adv según se dice,
según se informa

reporter [rɪ'pɔːtə'] n (Press) periodista m/f,
reportero(-a); (Radio, TV) locutor(a) m(f)

repose [rɪ'pəuz] n: **in ~** (face, mouth) en reposo

repossession order [riːpə'zɛʃən-] n orden de
devolución de la vivienda por el impago de la hipoteca

represent [rɛprɪ'zɛnt] vt representar; (Comm)
ser agente de

representation [rɛprɪzɛn'teɪʃən] n
representación f; (petition) petición f;
representations npl (protest) quejas fpl

representative [rɛprɪ'zɛntətɪv] n (US Pol)
representante m/f, diputado(-a); (Comm)
representante m/f ▷ adj: **~ (of)** representativo
(de)

repress [rɪ'prɛs] vt reprimir

repression [rɪ'prɛʃən] n represión f

reprieve [rɪ'priːv] n (Law) indulto; (fig) alivio
▷ vt indultar; (fig) salvar

reprimand ['rɛprɪmɑːnd] n reprimenda ▷ vt
reprender

reprint ['riːprɪnt] n reimpresión f ▷ vt
[riː'prɪnt] reimprimir

reprisal [rɪ'praɪzl] n represalia; **to take ~s**
tomar represalias

reproach [rɪ'prəutʃ] n reproche m ▷ vt: **to ~
sb with sth** reprochar algo a algn; **beyond ~**
intachable

reproachful [rɪ'prəutʃful] adj de reproche, de
acusación

reproduce [riːprə'djuːs] vt reproducir ▷ vi
reproducirse

reproduction [riːprə'dʌkʃən] n
reproducción f

reproof [rɪ'pruːf] n reproche m

reptile ['rɛptaɪl] n reptil m

republic [rɪ'pʌblɪk] n república

republican [rɪ'pʌblɪkən] adj, n
republicano(-a) m(f)

repudiate [rɪ'pjuːdɪeɪt] vt (accusation)
rechazar; (obligation) negarse a reconocer

repugnant [rɪ'pʌgnənt] adj repugnante

repulsive [rɪ'pʌlsɪv] adj repulsivo

reputable ['rɛpjutəbl] adj (make etc) de
renombre

reputation [rɛpju'teɪʃən] n reputación f; **he
has a ~ for being awkward** tiene fama de
difícil

repute [rɪ'pjuːt] n reputación f, fama

reputed [rɪ'pjuːtɪd] adj supuesto; **to be ~ to
be rich/intelligent** etc tener fama de rico/
inteligente etc

reputedly [rɪ'pjuːtɪdlɪ] adv según dicen or se
dice

request [rɪ'kwɛst] n solicitud f, petición f
▷ vt: **to ~ sth of** or **from sb** solicitar algo a
algn; **at the ~ of** a petición de; **"you are ~ed
not to smoke"** "se ruega no fumar"

request stop n (Brit) parada discrecional

requiem ['rɛkwɪəm] n réquiem m

require [rɪ'kwaɪə'] vt (need: person) necesitar,
tener necesidad de; (: thing, situation) exigir,
requerir; (want) pedir; (demand) insistir en
que; **to ~ sb to do sth/sth of sb** exigir que
algn haga algo; **what qualifications are ~d?**
¿qué títulos se requieren?; **~d by law**
requerido por la ley

requirement [rɪ'kwaɪəmənt] n requisito;
(need) necesidad f

requisite ['rɛkwɪzɪt] n requisito ▷ adj
necesario, requerido

requisition [rɛkwɪ'zɪʃən] n solicitud f; (Mil)
requisa ▷ vt (Mil) requisar

reroute [riː'ruːt] vt desviar

resat [riː'sæt] pt, pp of **resit**

rescue ['rɛskjuː] n rescate m ▷ vt rescatar; **to
come/go to sb's ~** ir en auxilio de uno,
socorrer a algn; **to ~ from** librar de

rescuer ['rɛskjuə'] n salvador(a) m(f)

research [rɪ'səːtʃ] n investigaciones fpl ▷ vt
investigar; **a piece of ~** un trabajo de
investigación; **to ~ (into sth)** investigar
(algo)

researcher [rɪ'səːtʃə'] n investigador(a) m(f)

resemblance [rɪ'zɛmbləns] n parecido; **to
bear a strong ~ to** parecerse mucho a

resemble [rɪ'zɛmbl] vt parecerse a

resent [rɪ'zɛnt] vt resentirse por, ofenderse
por; **he ~s my being here** le molesta que
esté aquí

resentful [rɪ'zɛntful] adj resentido

resentment [rɪ'zɛntmənt] n resentimiento

reservation [rɛzə'veɪʃən] n reserva; (Brit:
also: **central ~**) mediana; **with ~s** con
reservas

reservation desk n (US: in hotel) recepción f

reserve [rɪ'zəːv] n reserva; (Sport) suplente m/f
▷ vt (seats etc) reservar; **reserves** npl (Mil)
reserva sg; **in ~** en reserva

reserved [rɪ'zəːvd] adj reservado

reservoir ['rɛzəvwɑː'] n (artificial lake)
embalse m, represa; (tank) depósito

reset [riː'sɛt] vt (Comput) reinicializar

reshape [riː'ʃeɪp] vt (policy) reformar, rehacer

reshuffle [riː'ʃʌfl] n: **Cabinet ~** (Pol)
remodelación f del gabinete

reside [rɪ'zaɪd] vi residir

residence ['rɛzɪdəns] n residencia; (formal:
home) domicilio; (length of stay) permanencia;
in ~ (doctor) residente; **to take up ~**
instalarse

residence permit n (Brit) permiso de residencia

resident ['rɛzɪdənt] n vecino(-a); (in hotel) huésped(a) m(f) ▷ adj residente; (population) permanente

residential [rɛzɪ'dɛnʃəl] adj residencial

residue ['rɛzɪdjuː] n resto, residuo

resign [rɪ'zaɪn] vt (gen) renunciar a ▷ vi: **to ~ (from)** dimitir (de), renunciar (a); **to ~ o.s. to** (endure) resignarse a

resignation [rɛzɪg'neɪʃən] n dimisión f; (state of mind) resignación f; **to tender one's ~** presentar la dimisión

resigned [rɪ'zaɪnd] adj resignado

resilience [rɪ'zɪlɪəns] n (of material) elasticidad f; (of person) resistencia

resilient [rɪ'zɪlɪənt] adj (person) resistente

resin ['rɛzɪn] n resina

resist [rɪ'zɪst] vt resistirse a; (temptation, damage) resistir

resistance [rɪ'zɪstəns] n resistencia

resistant [rɪ'zɪstənt] adj: **~ (to)** resistente (a)

resit ['riːsɪt] (pt, pp **resat**) vt (Brit: exam) volver a presentarse a; (: subject) recuperar, volver a examinarse de (Sp)

resolute ['rɛzəluːt] adj resuelto

resolution [rɛzə'luːʃən] n (gen) resolución f; (purpose) propósito; (Comput) definición f; **to make a ~** tomar una resolución

resolve [rɪ'zɔlv] n (determination) resolución f; (purpose) propósito ▷ vt resolver ▷ vi resolverse; **to ~ to do** resolver hacer

resolved [rɪ'zɔlvd] adj resuelto

resort [rɪ'zɔːt] n (town) centro turístico; (recourse) recurso ▷ vi: **to ~ to** recurrir a; **in the last ~** como último recurso; **seaside/winter sports ~** playa, estación f balnearia/centro de deportes de invierno

resound [rɪ'zaund] vi: **to ~ (with)** resonar (con)

resounding [rɪ'zaundɪŋ] adj sonoro; (fig) clamoroso

resource [rɪ'sɔːs] n recurso; **resources** npl recursos mpl; **natural ~s** recursos mpl naturales; **to leave sb to his/her own ~s** (fig) abandonar a algn/a sus propios recursos

resourceful [rɪ'sɔːsful] adj ingenioso

respect [rɪs'pɛkt] n (consideration) respeto; (relation) respecto; **respects** npl recuerdos mpl, saludos mpl ▷ vt respetar; **with ~ to** con respecto a; **in this ~** en cuanto a eso; **to have or show ~ for** tener or mostrar respeto a; **out of ~ for** por respeto a; **in some ~s** en algunos aspectos; **with due ~ I still think you're wrong** con el respeto debido, sigo creyendo que está equivocado

respectable [rɪs'pɛktəbl] adj respetable; (quite big: amount etc) apreciable; (passable) tolerable; (quite good: player, result etc) bastante bueno

respected [rɪs'pɛktɪd] adj respetado, estimado

respectful [rɪs'pɛktful] adj respetuoso

respective [rɪs'pɛktɪv] adj respectivo

respectively [rɪs'pɛktɪvlɪ] adv respectivamente

respiration [rɛspɪ'reɪʃən] n respiración f

respite ['rɛspaɪt] n respiro; (Law) prórroga

resplendent [rɪs'plɛndənt] adj resplandeciente

respond [rɪs'pɔnd] vi responder; (react) reaccionar

response [rɪs'pɔns] n respuesta; (reaction) reacción f; **in ~ to** como respuesta a

responsibility [rɪspɔnsɪ'bɪlɪtɪ] n responsabilidad f; **to take ~ for sth/sb** admitir responsabilidad por algo/uno

responsible [rɪs'pɔnsɪbl] adj (liable): **~ (for)** responsable (de); (character) serio, formal; (job) de responsabilidad; **to be ~ to sb (for sth)** ser responsable ante algn (de algo)

responsibly [rɪs'pɔnsɪblɪ] adv con seriedad

responsive [rɪs'pɔnsɪv] adj sensible

rest [rɛst] n descanso, reposo; (Mus) pausa, silencio; (support) apoyo; (remainder) resto ▷ vi descansar; (be supported): **to ~ on** apoyarse en ▷ vt (lean): **to ~ sth on/against** apoyar algo en or sobre/contra; **the ~ of them** (people, objects) los demás; **to set sb's mind at ~** tranquilizar a algn; **to ~ one's eyes** or **gaze on** fijar la mirada en; **it ~s with him** depende de él; **~ assured that ...** tenga por seguro que ...

restaurant ['rɛstərɔŋ] n restaurante m

restaurant car n (Brit) coche-comedor m

restful ['rɛstful] adj descansado, tranquilo

restitution [rɛstɪ'tjuːʃən] n: **to make ~ to sb for sth** restituir algo a algn; (paying) indemnizar a algn por algo

restive ['rɛstɪv] adj inquieto; (horse) rebelón(-ona)

restless ['rɛstlɪs] adj inquieto; **to get ~** impacientarse

restoration [rɛstə'reɪʃən] n restauración f; (giving back) devolución f, restitución f

restore [rɪ'stɔːʳ] vt (building) restaurar; (sth stolen) devolver, restituir; (health) restablecer

restrain [rɪs'treɪn] vt (feeling) contener, refrenar; (person): **to ~ (from doing)** disuadir (de hacer)

restrained [rɪs'treɪnd] adj (style) reservado

restraint [rɪs'treɪnt] n (restriction) freno, control m; (of style) reserva; **wage ~** control m de los salarios

restrict [rɪs'trɪkt] vt restringir, limitar

restriction [rɪs'trɪkʃən] n restricción f, limitación f

rest room n (US) aseos mpl

restructure [riː'strʌktʃəʳ] vt reestructurar

result [rɪ'zʌlt] n resultado ▷ vi: **to ~ in** terminar en, tener por resultado; **as a ~ of** a or como consecuencia de; **to ~ (from)** resultar (de)

resume [rɪ'zjuːm] vt (work, journey) reanudar; (sum up) resumir ▷ vi (meeting) continuar
résumé ['reɪzjuːmeɪ] n resumen m
resumption [rɪ'zʌmpʃən] n reanudación f
resurgence [rɪ'səːdʒəns] n resurgimiento
resurrection [rezə'rekʃən] n resurrección f
resuscitate [rɪ'sʌsɪteɪt] vt (Med) resucitar
retail ['riːteɪl] n venta al por menor ▷ cpd al por menor ▷ vt vender al por menor or al detalle ▷ vi: **to ~ at** (Comm) tener precio de venta al público de
retailer ['riːteɪləʳ] n minorista m/f, detallista m/f
retail price n precio de venta al público, precio al detalle or al por menor
retain [rɪ'teɪn] vt (keep) retener, conservar; (employ) contratar
retainer [rɪ'teɪnəʳ] n (servant) criado; (fee) anticipo
retaliate [rɪ'tælɪeɪt] vi: **to ~ (against)** tomar represalias (contra)
retaliation [rɪtælɪ'eɪʃən] n represalias fpl; **in ~ for** como represalia por
retarded [rɪ'tɑːdɪd] adj retrasado
retch [retʃ] vi darle a algn arcadas
retentive [rɪ'tentɪv] adj (memory) retentivo
reticence ['retɪsns] n reticencia, reserva
retina ['retɪnə] n retina
retire [rɪ'taɪəʳ] vi (give up work) jubilarse; (withdraw) retirarse; (go to bed) acostarse
retired [rɪ'taɪəd] adj (person) jubilado
retirement [rɪ'taɪəmənt] n jubilación f; **early ~** jubilación f anticipada
retiring [rɪ'taɪərɪŋ] adj (departing: chairman) saliente; (shy) retraído
retort [rɪ'tɔːt] n (reply) réplica ▷ vi replicar
retrace [riː'treɪs] vt: **to ~ one's steps** volver sobre sus pasos, desandar lo andado
retract [rɪ'trækt] vt (statement) retirar; (claws) retraer; (undercarriage, aerial) replegar ▷ vi retractarse
retrain [riː'treɪn] vt reciclar
retread ['riːtred] n neumático or llanta (LAm) recauchutado(-a)
retreat [rɪ'triːt] n (place) retiro; (Mil) retirada ▷ vi retirarse; (flood) bajar; **to beat a hasty ~** (fig) retirarse en desbandada
retrial ['riːtraɪəl] n nuevo proceso
retribution [retrɪ'bjuːʃən] n desquite m
retrieval [rɪ'triːvəl] n recuperación f; **information ~** recuperación f de datos
retrieve [rɪ'triːv] vt recobrar; (situation, honour) salvar; (Comput) recuperar; (error) reparar
retriever [rɪ'triːvəʳ] n perro cobrador
retrospect ['retrəspekt] n: **in ~** retrospectivamente
retrospective [retrə'spektɪv] adj retrospectivo; (law) retroactivo ▷ n exposición f retrospectiva
return [rɪ'təːn] n (going or coming back) vuelta, regreso; (of sth stolen etc) devolución f;

(recompense) recompensa; (Finance: from land, shares) ganancia, ingresos mpl; (Comm: of merchandise) devolución f ▷ cpd (journey) de regreso; (Brit: ticket) de ida y vuelta; (match) de vuelta ▷ vi (person etc: come or go back) volver, regresar; (symptoms etc) reaparecer ▷ vt devolver; (favour, love etc) corresponder a; (verdict) pronunciar; (Pol: candidate) elegir; **returns** npl (Comm) ingresos mpl; **tax ~** declaración f de la renta; **in ~ (for)** a cambio (de); **by ~ of post** a vuelta de correo; **many happy ~s (of the day)!** ¡feliz cumpleaños!
returning officer [rɪ'təːnɪŋ-] n (Brit Pol) escrutador(a) m(f)
return ticket n (esp Brit) billete m (Sp) or boleto m (LAm) de ida y vuelta, billete m redondo (Mex)
reunion [riː'juːnɪən] n (of family) reunión f; (of two people, school) reencuentro
reunite [riːjuː'naɪt] vt reunir; (reconcile) reconciliar
rev [rev] n abbr (Aut: = revolution) revolución f ▷ vt (also: ~ up) acelerar
revaluation [riːvæljuː'eɪʃən] n revalorización f
revamp [riː'væmp] vt renovar
reveal [rɪ'viːl] vt (make known) revelar
revealing [rɪ'viːlɪŋ] adj revelador(a)
reveille [rɪ'vælɪ] n (Mil) diana
revel ['revl] vi: **to ~ in sth/in doing sth** gozar de algo/haciendo algo
revelation [revə'leɪʃən] n revelación f
revelry ['revlrɪ] n jarana, juerga
revenge [rɪ'vendʒ] n venganza; (in sport) revancha; **to take ~ on** vengarse de; **to get one's ~ (for sth)** vengarse (de algo)
revenue ['revənjuː] n ingresos mpl, rentas fpl
reverberate [rɪ'vəːbəreɪt] vi (sound) resonar, retumbar
reverence ['revərəns] n reverencia
Reverend ['revərənd] adj (in titles): **the ~ John Smith** (Anglican) el Reverendo John Smith; (Catholic) el Padre John Smith; (Protestant) el Pastor John Smith
reverent ['revərənt] adj reverente
reverie ['revərɪ] n ensueño
reversal [rɪ'vəːsl] n (of order) inversión f; (of policy) cambio de rumbo; (of decision) revocación f
reverse [rɪ'vəːs] n (opposite) contrario; (back: of cloth) revés m; (: of coin) reverso; (: of paper) dorso; (Aut: also: ~ gear) marcha atrás ▷ adj (order) inverso; (direction) contrario ▷ vt (decision) dar marcha atrás a; (Aut) dar marcha atrás a; (position, function) invertir ▷ vi (Brit Aut) poner en marcha atrás; **in ~ order** en orden inverso; **the ~** lo contrario; **to go into ~** dar marcha atrás
reverse-charge call [rɪ'vəːstʃɑːdʒ-] n (Brit) llamada a cobro revertido
reversing lights [rɪ'vəːsɪŋ-] npl (Brit Aut) luces fpl de marcha atrás

revert [rɪ'vəːt] vi: **to ~** volver or revertir a

review [rɪ'vjuː] n (magazine) revista; (Mil) revista; (of book, film) reseña; (US: examination) repaso, examen m ▷ vt repasar, examinar; (Mil) pasar revista a; (book, film) reseñar; **to come under ~** ser examinado

reviewer [rɪ'vjuːəʳ] n crítico(-a)

revile [rɪ'vaɪl] vt injuriar, vilipendiar

revise [rɪ'vaɪz] vt (manuscript) corregir; (opinion) modificar; (price, procedure) revisar; (Brit: study: subject) repasar; (look over) revisar; **~d edition** edición f corregida

revision [rɪ'vɪʒən] n corrección f; modificación f; (of subject) repaso; (revised version) revisión f

revitalize [riː'vaɪtəlaɪz] vt revivificar

revival [rɪ'vaɪvəl] n (recovery) reanimación f; (Pol) resurgimiento; (of interest) renacimiento; (Theat) reestreno; (of faith) despertar m

revive [rɪ'vaɪv] vt resucitar; (custom) restablecer; (hope, courage) reanimar; (play) reestrenar ▷ vi (person) volver en sí; (from tiredness) reponerse; (business) reactivarse

revoke [rɪ'vəuk] vt revocar

revolt [rɪ'vəult] n rebelión f ▷ vi rebelarse, sublevarse ▷ vt dar asco a, repugnar; **to ~ (against sb/sth)** rebelarse (contra algn/algo)

revolting [rɪ'vəultɪŋ] adj asqueroso, repugnante

revolution [rɛvə'luːʃən] n revolución f

revolutionary [rɛvə'luːʃənrɪ] adj, n revolucionario(-a) m(f)

revolutionize [rɛvə'luːʃənaɪz] vt revolucionar

revolve [rɪ'vɔlv] vi dar vueltas, girar; **to ~ (a) round** girar en torno a

revolver [rɪ'vɔlvəʳ] n revólver m

revolving [rɪ'vɔlvɪŋ] adj (chair, door etc) giratorio

revue [rɪ'vjuː] n (Theat) revista

revulsion [rɪ'vʌlʃən] n asco, repugnancia

reward [rɪ'wɔːd] n premio, recompensa ▷ vt: **to ~ (for)** recompensar or premiar (por)

rewarding [rɪ'wɔːdɪŋ] adj (fig) gratificante; **financially ~** económicamente provechoso

rewind [riː'waɪnd] vt (tape) rebobinar; (watch) dar cuerda a; (wool etc) devanar

rewire [riː'waɪəʳ] vt (house) renovar la instalación eléctrica de

reword [riː'wəːd] vt expresar en otras palabras

rewritable [riː'raɪtəbl] adj reescribible

rewrite [riː'raɪt] vt (irreg: like **write**) reescribir

Rh abbr (= rhesus) Rh m

rheumatism ['ruːmətɪzəm] n reumatismo, reúma

rheumatoid arthritis ['ruːmətɔɪd-] n reúma m articular

Rhine [raɪn] n: **the ~** el (río) Rin

rhinoceros [raɪ'nɔsərəs] n rinoceronte m

Rhone [rəun] n: **the ~** el (río) Ródano

rhubarb ['ruːbɑːb] n ruibarbo

rhyme [raɪm] n rima; (verse) poesía ▷ vi: **to ~ (with)** rimar (con); **without ~ or reason** sin ton ni son

rhythm ['rɪðm] n ritmo

rhythm method n método (de) Ogino

RI n abbr (Brit: = religious instruction) ed. religiosa ▷ abbr

rib [rɪb] n (Anat) costilla ▷ vt (mock) tomar el pelo a

ribbon ['rɪbən] n cinta; **in ~s** (torn) hecho trizas

rice [raɪs] n arroz m

rice pudding n arroz m con leche

rich [rɪtʃ] adj rico; (soil) fértil; (food) pesado; (: sweet) empalagoso; **the rich** npl los ricos; **riches** npl riqueza sg; **to be ~ in sth** abundar en algo

rickets ['rɪkɪts] n raquitismo

rickety ['rɪkɪtɪ] adj (old) desvencijado; (shaky) tambaleante

rickshaw ['rɪkʃɔː] n carro de culí

rid (pt, pp **rid**) [rɪd] vt: **to ~ sb of sth** librar a algn de algo; **to get ~ of** deshacerse or desembarazarse de

riddance ['rɪdns] n: **good ~!** ¡y adiós muy buenas!

riddle ['rɪdl] n (conundrum) acertijo; (mystery) enigma m, misterio ▷ vt: **to be ~d with** ser lleno or plagado de

ride [raɪd] (pt **rode**, pp **ridden**) n paseo; (distance covered) viaje m, recorrido ▷ vi (on horse: as sport) montar; (go somewhere: on horse, bicycle) dar un paseo, pasearse; (journey: on bicycle, motor cycle, bus) viajar ▷ vt (a horse) montar a; (distance) recorrer; **to ~ a bicycle** andar en bicicleta; **to ~ at anchor** (Naut) estar fondeado; **can you ~ a bike?** ¿sabes montar en bici(cleta)?; **to go for a ~** dar un paseo; **to take sb for a ~** (fig) tomar el pelo a algn; **ride out** vt: **to ~ out the storm** (fig) capear el temporal

rider ['raɪdəʳ] n (on horse) jinete m; (on bicycle) ciclista m/f; (on motorcycle) motociclista m/f

ridge [rɪdʒ] n (of hill) cresta; (of roof) caballete m; (wrinkle) arruga

ridicule ['rɪdɪkjuːl] n irrisión f, burla ▷ vt poner en ridículo a, burlarse de; **to hold sth/ sb up to ~** poner algo/a algn en ridículo

ridiculous [rɪ'dɪkjuləs] adj ridículo

riding ['raɪdɪŋ] n equitación f; **I like ~** me gusta montar a caballo

riding school n escuela de equitación

rife [raɪf] adj: **to be ~** ser muy común; **to be ~ with** abundar en

riffraff ['rɪfræf] n chusma, gentuza

rifle ['raɪfl] n rifle m, fusil m ▷ vt saquear; **rifle through** vt fus saquear

rifle range n campo de tiro; (at fair) tiro al blanco

rift [rɪft] n (fig: between friends) desavenencia; (: in party) escisión f

rig [rɪg] n (also: **oil ~**: on land) torre f de perforación; (: at sea) plataforma petrolera ▷ vt (election etc) amañar los resultados de; **rig out** vt (Brit) ataviar; **rig up** vt improvisar

rigging ['rɪgɪŋ] n (Naut) aparejo

right [raɪt] adj (true, correct) correcto, exacto; (suitable) indicado, debido; (proper) apropiado, propio; (just) justo; (morally good) bueno; (not left) derecho ▷ n (title, claim) derecho; (not left) derecha ▷ adv (correctly) bien, correctamente; (straight) derecho, directamente; (not on the left) a la derecha; (to the right) hacia la derecha ▷ vt (put straight) enderezar; (correct) corregir ▷ excl ¡bueno!, ¡está bien!; **to be ~** (person) tener razón; (answer) ser correcto; **to get sth ~** acertar en algo; **you did the ~ thing** hiciste bien; **let's get it ~ - this time!** ¡a ver si esta vez nos sale bien!; **to put a mistake ~** corregir un error; **the ~ time** la hora exacta; (fig) el momento oportuno; **by ~s** en justicia; **~ and wrong** el bien y el mal; **film ~s** derechos mpl de la película; **on the ~** a la derecha; **to be in the ~** tener razón; **~ now** ahora mismo; **~ before/after** inmediatamente antes/ después; **~ in the middle** exactamente en el centro; **~ away** en seguida; **to go ~ to the end of sth** llegar hasta el final de algo; **~, who's next?** ¿y ahora, ¿quién sigue?; **all ~!** ¡vale!; **I'm/I feel all ~ now** ya estoy bien

right angle n ángulo recto

righteous ['raɪtʃəs] adj justo, honrado; (anger) justificado

rightful ['raɪtful] adj (heir) legítimo

right-hand ['raɪthænd] adj: **~ drive** conducción f por la derecha; **the ~ side** derecha

right-handed [raɪt'hændɪd] adj (person) que usa la mano derecha, diestro

right-hand man n brazo derecho

right-hand side n derecha

rightly ['raɪtlɪ] adv correctamente, debidamente; (with reason) con razón; **if I remember ~** si recuerdo bien

right of way n (on path etc) derecho de paso; (Aut) prioridad f de paso

right-wing [raɪt'wɪŋ] adj (Pol) de derechas, derechista

rigid ['rɪdʒɪd] adj rígido; (person, ideas) inflexible

rigidly ['rɪdʒɪdlɪ] adv rígidamente; (inflexibly) inflexiblemente

rigmarole ['rɪgmərəul] n galimatías m inv

rigor mortis ['rɪgə'mɔːtɪs] n rigidez f cadavérica

rigorous ['rɪgərəs] adj riguroso

rile [raɪl] vt irritar

rim [rɪm] n borde m; (of spectacles) montura, aro; (of wheel) llanta

rind [raɪnd] n (of bacon, cheese) corteza; (of lemon etc) cáscara

ring [rɪŋ] (pt **rang**, pp **rung**) n (of metal) aro; (on finger) anillo; (of people) corro; (of objects) círculo; (gang) banda; (for boxing) cuadrilátero; (of circus) pista; (bull ring) ruedo, plaza; (sound of bell) toque m; (telephone call) llamada ▷ vi (on telephone) llamar por teléfono; (large bell) repicar; (doorbell, phone) sonar; (also: **~ out**: voice, words) sonar; (ears) zumbar ▷ vt (Brit Tel: also: **~ up**) llamar; (bell etc) hacer sonar; (doorbell) tocar; **that has the ~ of truth about it** eso suena a verdad; **to give sb a ~** (Brit Tel) llamar a algn, dar un telefonazo a algn; **the name doesn't ~ a bell (with me)** el nombre no me suena; **~ back** vt, ▷ vi (Tel) devolver la llamada; **ring off** vi (Brit Tel) colgar, cortar la comunicación; **ring up** vt (Brit: Tel) llamar, telefonear

ring binder n carpeta de anillas

ringing ['rɪŋɪŋ] n (of bell) toque m, tañido; (of large bell) repique m; (in ears) zumbido

ringing tone n (Tel) tono de llamada

ringleader ['rɪŋliːdəʳ] n cabecilla m/f

ringlets ['rɪŋlɪts] npl tirabuzones mpl, bucles mpl

ring road n (Brit) carretera periférica or de circunvalación

ringtone ['rɪŋtəun] n tono de llamada

rink [rɪŋk] n (also: **ice ~**) pista de hielo; (for roller-skating) pista de patinaje

rinse [rɪns] n (of dishes) enjuague m; (of clothes) aclarado; (hair colouring) reflejo ▷ vt enjuagar, aclarar; (hair) dar reflejos a

riot ['raɪət] n motín m, disturbio ▷ vi amotinarse; **to run ~** desmandarse

riot gear n uniforme m antidisturbios inv

riotous ['raɪətəs] adj alborotado; (party) bullicioso; (uncontrolled) desenfrenado

riot police n policía antidisturbios

RIP abbr (= requiescat or requiescant in pace: rest in peace) q.e.p.d.

rip [rɪp] n rasgón m, desgarrón m ▷ vt rasgar, desgarrar ▷ vi rasgarse; **rip off** vt (inf: cheat) estafar; **rip up** vt hacer pedazos

ripcord ['rɪpkɔːd] n cabo de desgarre

ripe [raɪp] adj (fruit) maduro

ripen ['raɪpən] vt, vi madurar

rip-off ['rɪpɔf] n (inf): **it's a ~!** ¡es una estafa!, ¡es un timo!

ripple ['rɪpl] n onda, rizo; (sound) murmullo ▷ vi rizarse ▷ vt rizar

rise [raɪz] (pt **rose**, pp **risen** [rəuz, 'rɪzn]) n (slope) cuesta, pendiente f; (hill) altura; (increase: in wages: Brit) aumento; (: in prices, temperature) subida, alza; (fig: to power etc) ascenso; (: ascendancy) auge m ▷ vi (gen) elevarse; (prices) subir; (waters) crecer; (river) nacer; (sun) salir; (person: from bed etc) levantarse; (also: **~ up**: rebel) sublevarse; (in rank) ascender; **~ to power** ascenso al poder; **to give ~ to** dar lugar or origen a; **to ~ to the occasion** ponerse a la altura de las circunstancias

r

risen ['rɪzn] *pp of* **rise**

rising ['raɪzɪŋ] *adj* (*increasing: number*) creciente; (*: prices*) en aumento *or* alza; (*tide*) creciente; (*sun, moon*) naciente ▷ *n* (*uprising*) sublevación *f*

rising star *n* (*fig*) figura en alza

risk [rɪsk] *n* riesgo, peligro ▷ *vt* (*gen*) arriesgar; (*dare*) atreverse a; **to take** *or* **run the ~ of doing** correr el riesgo de hacer; **at ~** en peligro; **at one's own ~** bajo su propia responsabilidad; **fire/health/security ~** peligro de incendio/para la salud/para la seguridad

risky ['rɪskɪ] *adj* arriesgado, peligroso

risqué ['ri:skeɪ] *adj* (*joke*) subido de color

rissole ['rɪsəul] *n* croqueta

rite [raɪt] *n* rito; **last ~s** últimos sacramentos *mpl*

ritual ['rɪtjuəl] *adj* ritual ▷ *n* ritual *m*, rito

rival ['raɪvl] *n* rival *m/f*; (*in business*) competidor(a) *m(f)* ▷ *adj* rival, opuesto ▷ *vt* competir con

rivalry ['raɪvlrɪ] *n* rivalidad *f*, competencia

river ['rɪvə^r] *n* río ▷ *cpd* (*port, traffic*) de río, del río; **up/down ~** río arriba/abajo

riverbank ['rɪvəbæŋk] *n* orilla (del río)

rivet ['rɪvɪt] *n* roblón *m*, remache *m* ▷ *vt* remachar; (*fig*) fascinar

riveting ['rɪvɪtɪŋ] *adj* (*fig*) fascinante

Riviera [rɪvɪ'eərə] *n*: **the (French) ~** la Costa Azul, la Riviera (francesa); **the Italian ~** la Riviera italiana

road [rəud] *n* (*gen*) camino; (*motorway etc*) carretera; (*in town*) calle *f*; **major/minor ~** carretera general/secundaria; **main ~** carretera; **it takes four hours by ~** se tarda cuatro horas por carretera; **on the ~ to success** camino del éxito

roadblock ['rəudblɔk] *n* barricada, control *m*, retén *m* (*LAm*)

road hog ['rəudhɔg] *n* loco(-a) del volante

road map *n* mapa *m* de carreteras

road rage *n* conducta agresiva de los conductores

road safety *n* seguridad *f* vial

roadside ['rəudsaɪd] *n* borde *m* (del camino) ▷ *cpd* al lado de la carretera; **by the ~** al borde del camino

roadsign ['rəudsaɪn] *n* señal *f* de tráfico

road tax *n* (*Brit*) impuesto de rodaje

roadway ['rəudweɪ] *n* calzada

roadworks ['rəudwə:ks] *npl* obras *fpl*

roadworthy ['rəudwə:ðɪ] *adj* (*car*) en buen estado para circular

roam [rəum] *vi* vagar ▷ *vt* vagar por

roar [rɔ:^r] *n* (*of animal*) rugido, bramido; (*of crowd*) clamor *m*, rugido; (*of vehicle, storm*) estruendo; (*of laughter*) carcajada ▷ *vi* rugir, bramar; hacer estruendo; **to ~ with laughter** reírse a carcajadas

roaring ['rɔ:rɪŋ] *adj*: **a ~ success** un tremendo éxito; **to do a ~ trade** hacer buen negocio

roast [rəust] *n* carne *f* asada, asado ▷ *vt* (*meat*) asar; (*coffee*) tostar

roast beef *n* rosbif *m*

roasting ['rəustɪŋ] *n*: **to give sb a ~** (*inf*) echar una buena bronca a algn

rob [rɔb] *vt* robar; **to ~ sb of sth** robar algo a algn; (*fig: deprive*) quitar algo a algn

robber ['rɔbə^r] *n* ladrón(-ona) *m(f)*

robbery ['rɔbərɪ] *n* robo

robe [rəub] *n* (*for ceremony etc*) toga; (*also:* **bath ~**) bata, albornoz *m*

robin ['rɔbɪn] *n* petirrojo

robot ['rəubɔt] *n* robot *m*

robust [rəu'bʌst] *adj* robusto, fuerte

rock [rɔk] *n* (*gen*) roca; (*boulder*) peña, peñasco; (*Brit: sweet*) ≈ pirulí *m* ▷ *vt* (*swing gently*) mecer; (*shake*) sacudir ▷ *vi* mecerse, balancearse; sacudirse; **on the ~s** (*drink*) con hielo; **their marriage is on the ~s** su matrimonio se está yendo a pique; **to ~ the boat** (*fig*) crear problemas

rock and roll *n* rock and roll *m*, rocanrol *m*

rock-bottom ['rɔk'bɔtəm] *adj* (*fig*) por los suelos; **to reach** *or* **touch ~** (*price*) estar por los suelos; (*person*) tocar fondo

rock climbing *n* (*Sport*) escalada

rockery ['rɔkərɪ] *n* cuadro alpino

rocket ['rɔkɪt] *n* cohete *m* ▷ *vi* (*prices*) dispararse, ponerse por las nubes

rocking chair ['rɔkɪŋ-] *n* mecedora

rocking horse *n* caballo de balancín

rocky ['rɔkɪ] *adj* (*gen*) rocoso; (*unsteady: table*) inestable

rod [rɔd] *n* vara, varilla; (*Tech*) barra; (*also:* **fishing ~**) caña

rode [rəud] *pt of* **ride**

rodent ['rəudnt] *n* roedor *m*

rodeo ['rəudɪəu] *n* rodeo

roe [rəu] *n* (*species: also:* **~ deer**) corzo; (*of fish*): **hard/soft ~** hueva/lecha

rogue [rəug] *n* pícaro, pillo

role [rəul] *n* papel *m*, rol *m*

role-model ['rəulmɔdl] *n* modelo a imitar

role play *n* (*also:* **~-ing**) juego de papeles *or* roles

roll [rəul] *n* rollo; (*of bank notes*) fajo; (*also:* **bread ~**) panecillo; (*register*) lista, nómina; (*sound: of drums etc*) redoble *m*; (*movement: of ship*) balanceo ▷ *vt* hacer rodar; (*also:* **~ up:** *string*) enrollar; (*: sleeves*) arremangar; (*cigarettes*) liar; (*also:* **~ out:** *pastry*) aplanar ▷ *vi* (*gen*) rodar; (*drum*) redoblar; (*in walking*) bambolearse; (*ship*) balancearse; **cheese ~** panecillo de queso; **roll about, roll around** *vi* (*person*) revolcarse; (*of time*) pasar; **roll in** *vi* (*mail, cash*) entrar a raudales; **roll over** *vi* dar una vuelta; **roll up** *vi* (*inf: arrive*) presentarse, aparecer ▷ *vt* (*carpet, cloth, map*) arrollar; (*sleeves*) arremangar; **to ~ o.s. up into a ball** acurrucarse, hacerse un ovillo

roll call *n*: **to take a ~** pasar lista

roller ['rəulə^r] *n* rodillo; (*wheel*) rueda; (*for road*) apisonadora; (*for hair*) rulo

Rollerblades® ['rəuləbleɪdz] *npl* patines *mpl* en línea

roller coaster n montaña rusa
roller skates npl patines mpl de rueda
roller-skating ['rəuləskeitiŋ] n patinaje sobre ruedas; **to go ~** ir a patinar (sobre ruedas)
rolling ['rəuliŋ] adj (landscape) ondulado
rolling pin n rodillo (de cocina)
rolling stock n (Rail) material m rodante
ROM [rɔm] n abbr (Comput: = read-only memory) (memoria) ROM f
Roman ['rəumən] adj, n romano(-a) m(f)
Roman Catholic adj, n católico(-a) m(f) (romano(-a))
romance [rə'mæns] n (love affair) amor m, idilio; (charm) lo romántico; (novel) novela de amor
Romania [ruː'meiniə] n = **Rumania**
Romanian [ruː'meiniən] adj, n = **Rumanian**
Roman numeral n número romano
romantic [rə'mæntik] adj romántico
Rome [rəum] n Roma
romp [rɔmp] n retozo, jugueteo ▷ vi (also: **~ about**) juguetear; **to ~ home** (horse) ganar fácilmente
rompers ['rɔmpəz] npl pelele m
roof [ruːf] n (gen) techo; (of house) tejado ▷ vt techar, poner techo a; **~ of the mouth** paladar m
roofing ['ruːfiŋ] n techumbre f
roof rack n (Aut) baca, portaequipajes msg
rook [ruk] n (bird) graja; (Chess) torre f
rookie ['ruki] n (inf) novato(-a); (Mil) chivo
room [ruːm] n (in house) cuarto, habitación f, pieza (esp LAm); (also: **bed~**) dormitorio; (in school etc) sala; (space) sitio; **rooms** npl (lodging) alojamiento sg; **"~s to let"**, (US) **"~s for rent"** "se alquilan pisos or cuartos"; **single/double ~** habitación individual/doble or para dos personas; **is there ~ for this?** ¿cabe esto?; **to make ~ for sb** hacer sitio para algn; **there is ~ for improvement** podría mejorarse
rooming house ['ruːmiŋ-] n (US) pensión f
roommate ['ruːmmeit] n compañero(-a) de cuarto
room service n servicio de habitaciones
roomy ['ruːmi] adj espacioso
roost [ruːst] n percha ▷ vi pasar la noche
rooster ['ruːstə'] n gallo
root [ruːt] n (Bot, Math) raíz f ▷ vi (plant, belief) arraigar(se); **to take ~** (plant) echar raíces; (idea) arraigar(se); **the ~ of the problem is that ...** la raíz del problema es que ...; **root about** vi (fig) rebuscar; **root for** vt fus apoyar a; **root out** vt desarraigar
root beer n (US) refresco sin alcohol de extractos de hierbas
rope [rəup] n cuerda; (Naut) cable m ▷ vt (box) atar or amarrar con (una) cuerda; (climbers: also: **~ together**) encordarse; (an area: also: **~ off**) acordonar; **to ~ sb in** (fig) persuadir a algn a tomar parte; **to know the ~s** (fig) conocer los trucos (del oficio)

ropey ['rəupi] adj (inf) chungo
rosary ['rəuzəri] n rosario
rose [rəuz] pt of **rise** ▷ n rosa; (also: **~bush**) rosal m; (on watering can) roseta ▷ adj color de rosa
rosé ['rəuzei] n vino rosado, clarete m
rosebud ['rəuzbʌd] n capullo de rosa
rosebush ['rəuzbuʃ] n rosal m
rosemary ['rəuzməri] n romero
rosette [rəu'zet] n rosetón m
roster ['rɔstə'] n: **duty ~** lista de tareas
rostrum ['rɔstrəm] n tribuna
rosy ['rəuzi] adj rosado, sonrosado; **the future looks ~** el futuro parece prometedor
rot [rɔt] n (decay) putrefacción f, podredumbre f; (fig: pej) tonterías fpl ▷ vt pudrir, corromper ▷ vi pudrirse, corromperse; **it has ~ted** está podrido; **to stop the ~** (fig) poner fin a las pérdidas
rota ['rəutə] n lista (de tareas)
rotary ['rəutəri] adj rotativo
rotate [rəu'teit] vt (revolve) hacer girar, dar vueltas a; (change round: crops) cultivar en rotación; (: jobs) alternar ▷ vi (revolve) girar, dar vueltas
rotating [rəu'teitiŋ] adj (movement) rotativo
rote [rəut] n: **by ~** de memoria
rotor ['rəutə'] n rotor m
rotten ['rɔtn] adj (decayed) podrido; (: wood) carcomido; (fig) corrompido; (inf: bad) pésimo; **to feel ~** (ill) sentirse fatal; **~ to the core** completamente podrido
rotund [rəu'tʌnd] adj rotundo
rough [rʌf] adj (skin, surface) áspero; (terrain) accidentado; (road) desigual; (voice) bronco; (person, manner: coarse) tosco, grosero; (weather) borrascoso; (treatment) brutal; (sea) embravecido; (town, area) peligroso; (cloth) basto; (plan) preliminar; (guess) aproximado; (violent) violento ▷ n (Golf): **in the ~** en las hierbas altas; **to ~ it** vivir sin comodidades; **to sleep ~** (Brit) pasar la noche al raso; **the sea is ~ today** el mar está agitado hoy; **to have a ~ time (of it)** pasar una mala racha; **~ estimate** cálculo aproximado
roughage ['rʌfidʒ] n fibra(s) f(pl), forraje m
rough-and-ready ['rʌfən'redi] adj improvisado, tosco
rough copy, rough draft n borrador m
roughly ['rʌfli] adv (handle) torpemente; (make) toscamente; (approximately) aproximadamente; **~ speaking** más o menos
roughness ['rʌfnis] n aspereza; tosquedad f; brutalidad f
roulette [ruː'let] n ruleta
Roumania [ruː'meiniə] n = **Rumania**
round [raund] adj redondo ▷ n círculo; (of policeman) ronda; (of milkman) recorrido; (of doctor) visitas fpl; (game: in competition, cards) partida; (of ammunition) cartucho; (Boxing) asalto; (of talks) ronda ▷ vt (corner) doblar ▷ prep alrededor de; (surrounding): **~ his neck/**

the table en su cuello/alrededor de la mesa; (in a circular movement): **to move ~ the room/ sail ~ the world** dar una vuelta a la habitación/circumnavigar el mundo; (in various directions): **to move ~ a room/house** moverse por toda la habitación/casa ▷ adv: **all ~** por todos lados; **the long way ~** por el camino menos directo; **all the year ~** durante todo el año; **it's just ~ the corner** (fig) está a la vuelta de la esquina; **to ask sb ~** invitar a algn a casa; **I'll be ~ at six o'clock** llegaré a eso de las seis; **she arrived ~ (about) noon** llegó alrededor del mediodía; **~ the clock** day las 24 horas; **to go ~ to sb's (house)** ir a casa de algn; **to go ~ the back** pasar por atrás; **enough to go ~** bastante (para todos); **in ~ figures** en números redondos; **to go the ~s** (story) divulgarse; **a ~ of applause** una salva de aplausos; **a ~ of drinks/sandwiches** una ronda de bebidas/ bocadillos; **a ~ of toast** (Brit) una tostada; **the daily ~** la rutina cotidiana; **round off** vt (speech etc) acabar, poner término a; **round up** vt (cattle) acorralar; (people) reunir; (prices) redondear

roundabout ['raʊndəbaʊt] n (Brit: Aut) glorieta, rotonda; (: at fair) tiovivo ▷ adj (route, means) indirecto

rounders ['raʊndəz] n (Brit: game) juego similar al béisbol

roundly ['raʊndlɪ] adv (fig) rotundamente

round-shouldered ['raʊndˈʃəʊldəd] adj cargado de espaldas

round trip n viaje m de ida y vuelta

roundup ['raʊndʌp] n rodeo; (of criminals) redada; **a ~ of the latest news** un resumen de las últimas noticias

rouse [raʊz] vt (wake up) despertar; (stir up) suscitar

rousing ['raʊzɪŋ] adj (applause) caluroso; (speech) conmovedor(a)

rout [raʊt] n (Mil) derrota; (flight) desbandada ▷ vt derrotar

route [ruːt] n ruta, camino; (of bus) recorrido; (of shipping) rumbo, derrota; **the best ~ to London** el mejor camino o la mejor ruta para ir a Londres; **en ~ from ... to** en el viaje de ... a; **en ~ for** rumbo a, con destino en

route map n (Brit: for journey) mapa m de carreteras

routine [ruːˈtiːn] adj (work) rutinario ▷ n rutina; (Theat) número; (Comput) rutina; **~ procedure** trámite m rutinario

row¹ [rəʊ] n (line) fila, hilera; (Knitting) vuelta ▷ vi (in boat) remar ▷ vt (boat) conducir remando; **four days in a ~** cuatro días seguidos

row² [raʊ] n (noise) escándalo; (dispute) bronca, pelea; (fuss) jaleo; (scolding) reprimenda ▷ vi reñir(se); **to make a ~** armar un lío; **to have a ~** pelearse, reñir

rowboat ['rəʊbəʊt] n (US) bote m de remos

rowdy ['raʊdɪ] adj (person: noisy) ruidoso; (: quarrelsome) pendenciero; (occasion) alborotado ▷ n pendenciero

rowing ['rəʊɪŋ] n remo

rowing boat n (Brit) bote m or barco de remos

royal ['rɔɪəl] adj real

Royal Air Force n Fuerzas Aéreas Británicas fpl

royalist ['rɔɪəlɪst] adj, n monárquico(-a) m(f)

royalty ['rɔɪəltɪ] n (royal persons) (miembros mpl de la) familia real; (payment to author) derechos mpl de autor

rpm abbr (= revolutions per minute) r.p.m.

RSPB n abbr (Brit) = **Royal Society for the Protection of Birds**

RSPCA n abbr (Brit) = **Royal Society for the Prevention of Cruelty to Animals**

RSVP abbr (= répondez s'il vous plaît) SRC

RTA n abbr (= road traffic accident) accidente m de carretera

Rt. Hon. abbr (Brit: = Right Honourable) tratamiento honorífico de diputado

Rt. Rev. abbr (= Right Reverend) Rvdo.

rub [rʌb] vt (gen) frotar; (hard) restregar ▷ n (gen) frotamiento; (touch) roce m; **to give sth a ~** frotar algo; **to ~ sb up** or (US) **~ sb the wrong way** sacar de quicio a algn; **rub down** vt (body) secar frotando; (horse) almohazar; **rub in** vt (ointment) frotar; **rub off** vt borrarse ▷ vi quitarse (frotando); **to ~ off on sb** influir en algn, pegársele a algn; **rub out** vt borrar ▷ vi borrarse

rubber ['rʌbər] n caucho, goma; (Brit: eraser) goma de borrar

rubber band n goma, gomita

rubber bullet n bala de goma

rubber gloves npl guantes mpl de goma

rubber plant n ficus m

rubber ring n (for swimming) flotador m

rubbish ['rʌbɪʃ] (Brit) n (from household) basura; (waste) desperdicios mpl; (fig: pej) tonterías fpl; (trash) basura, porquería ▷ vt (inf) poner por los suelos; **what you've just said is ~** lo que acabas de decir es una tontería

rubbish bin n cubo o bote m (LAm) de la basura

rubbish dump n (in town) vertedero, basurero

rubble ['rʌbl] n escombros mpl

ruby ['ruːbɪ] n rubí m

RUC n abbr (= Royal Ulster Constabulary) fuerza de policía en Irlanda del Norte

rucksack ['rʌksæk] n mochila

rudder ['rʌdər] n timón m

ruddy ['rʌdɪ] adj (face) rubicundo; (inf: damned) condenado

rude [ruːd] adj (impolite: person) grosero, maleducado; (: word, manners) rudo, grosero; (indecent) indecente; **to be ~ to sb** ser grosero con algn

rudimentary [ruːdɪˈmɛntərɪ] adj rudimentario

rue [ruː] vt arrepentirse de

rueful ['ru:ful] *adj* arrepentido

ruffian ['rʌfɪən] *n* matón *m*, criminal *m*

ruffle ['rʌfl] *vt* (*hair*) despeinar; (*clothes*) arrugar; (*fig: person*) agitar

rug [rʌg] *n* alfombra *f*; (*Brit: for knees*) manta

rugby ['rʌgbɪ] *n* (*also: ~ football*) rugby *m*

rugged ['rʌgɪd] *adj* (*landscape*) accidentado; (*features*) robusto

rugger ['rʌgəʳ] *n* (*Brit inf*) rugby *m*

ruin ['ru:ɪn] *n* ruina ▷ *vt* arruinar; (*spoil*) estropear; **ruins** *npl* ruinas *fpl*, restos *mpl*; **in ~s** en ruinas

rule [ru:l] *n* (*norm*) norma, costumbre *f*; (*regulation, ruler*) regla; (*government*) dominio; (*dominion etc*): **under British ~** bajo el dominio británico ▷ *vt* (*country, person*) gobernar; (*decide*) disponer; (*draw lines*) trazar ▷ *vi* gobernar; (*Law*) fallar; **to ~ against/in favour of/on** fallar en contra de/a favor de/ sobre; **to ~ that ...** (*umpire, judge*) fallar que ...; **it's against the ~s** está prohibido; **as a ~** por regla general, generalmente; **by ~ of thumb** por experiencia; **majority ~** (*Pol*) gobierno mayoritario; **rule out** *vt* excluir

ruled [ru:ld] *adj* (*paper*) rayado

ruler ['ru:ləʳ] *n* (*sovereign*) soberano; (*for measuring*) regla

ruling ['ru:lɪŋ] *adj* (*party*) gobernante; (*class*) dirigente ▷ *n* (*Law*) fallo, decisión *f*

rum [rʌm] *n* ron *m*

Rumania [ru:'meɪnɪə] *n* Rumanía

Rumanian [ru:'meɪnɪən] *adj, n* rumano(-a) *m(f)*

rumble ['rʌmbl] *n* ruido sordo; (*of thunder*) redoble *m* ▷ *vi* retumbar, hacer un ruido sordo; (*stomach, pipe*) sonar

rummage ['rʌmɪdʒ] *vi* revolverlo todo

rumour, rumor (US) ['ru:məʳ] *n* rumor *m* ▷ *vt*: **it is ~ed that ...** se rumorea que ...; **~ has it that ...** corre la voz de que ...

rump [rʌmp] *n* (*of animal*) ancas *fpl*, grupa

rump steak *n* filete *m* de lomo

rumpus ['rʌmpəs] *n* (*inf*) lío, jaleo; (*quarrel*) pelea, riña; **to kick up a ~** armar un follón *or* armar bronca

run [rʌn] (*pt* **ran**, *pp* **run**) *n* (*Sport*) carrera; (*outing*) paseo, excursión *f*; (*distance travelled*) trayecto; (*series*) serie *f*; (*Theat*) temporada; (*Ski*) pista; (*in tights, stockings*) carrera ▷ *vt* (*operate: business*) dirigir; (*: competition, course*) organizar; (*: hotel, house*) administrar, llevar; (*Comput: program*) ejecutar; (*to pass: hand*) pasar; (*Press: feature*) publicar ▷ *vi* (*gen*) correr; (*work: machine*) funcionar, marchar; (*bus, train: operate*) circular, ir; (*: travel*) ir; (*continue: play*) seguir en cartel; (*: contract*) ser válido; (*flow: river, bath*) fluir; (*colours, washing*) desteñirse; (*in election*) ser candidato; **to go for a ~** ir a correr; **to make a ~ for it** echar(se) a correr, escapar(se), huir; **to have the ~ of sb's house** tener el libre uso de la casa de algn; **a ~ of luck** una racha de suerte; **there was a ~ on** (*meat, tickets*) hubo mucha demanda de; **in the long ~** a la larga; **on the ~** en fuga; **I'll ~ you to the station** te llevaré a la estación en coche; **to ~ a risk** correr un riesgo; **to ~ a bath** llenar la bañera; **to ~ errands** hacer recados; **it's very cheap to ~** es muy económico; **to be ~ off one's feet** estar ocupadísimo; **to ~ for the bus** correr tras el autobús; **we shall have to ~ for it** tendremos que escapar; **the train ~s between Gatwick and Victoria** el tren circula entre Gatwick y Victoria; **the bus ~s every 20 minutes** el autobús pasa cada 20 minutos; **to ~ on petrol/on diesel/off batteries** funcionar con gasolina/gasoil/ baterías; **my salary won't ~ to a car** mi sueldo no me da para comprarme un coche; **the car ran into the lamppost** el coche chocó contra el farol; **run about, run around** *vi* (*children*) correr por todos lados; **run across** *vt fus* (*find*) dar o topar con; **run after** *vt fus* (*to catch up*) correr tras; (*chase*) perseguir; **run away** *vi* huir; **run down** *vi* (*clock*) pararse ▷ *vt* (*reduce: production*) ir reduciendo; (*factory*) restringir la producción de; (*Aut*) atropellar; (*criticize*) criticar; **to be ~ down** (*person: tired*) encontrarse agotado; **run in** *vt* (*Brit: car*) rodar; **run into** *vt fus* (*meet: person, trouble*) tropezar con; (*collide with*) chocar con; **to ~ into debt** contraer deudas, endeudarse; **run off** *vt* (*water*) dejar correr ▷ *vi* huir corriendo; **run out** *vi* (*person*) salir corriendo; (*liquid*) irse; (*lease*) caducar, vencer; (*money*) acabarse; **run out of** *vt fus* quedar sin; **I've ~ out of petrol** se me acabó la gasolina; **run over** *vt* (*Aut*) atropellar ▷ *vt fus* (*revise*) repasar; **run through** *vt fus* (*instructions*) repasar; **run up** *vt* (*debt*) incurrir en; **to ~ up against** (*difficulties*) tropezar con

run-around ['rʌnəraund] *n*: **to give sb the ~** traer a algn al retortero

runaway ['rʌnəweɪ] *adj* (*horse*) desbocado; (*truck*) sin frenos; (*person*) fugitivo

rung [rʌŋ] *pp* of **ring** ▷ *n* (*of ladder*) escalón *m*, peldaño

run-in ['rʌnɪn] *n* (*inf*) altercado

runner ['rʌnəʳ] *n* (*in race: person*) corredor(a) *m(f)*; (*: horse*) caballo; (*on sledge*) patín *m*; (*wheel*) ruedecilla

runner bean *n* (*Brit*) judía verde

runner-up [rʌnər'ʌp] *n* subcampeón(-ona) *m(f)*

running ['rʌnɪŋ] *n* (*sport*) atletismo; (*race*) carrera ▷ *adj* (*costs, water*) corriente; (*commentary*) en directo; **to be in/out of the ~ for sth** tener/no tener posibilidades de ganar algo; **6 days ~** 6 días seguidos

running costs *npl* (*of business*) gastos *mpl* corrientes; (*of car*) gastos *mpl* de mantenimiento

runny ['rʌnɪ] *adj* líquido; (*eyes*) lloroso; **to have a ~ nose** tener mocos

run-of-the-mill ['rʌnəvðə'mɪl] *adj* común y corriente

runt [rʌnt] *n (also pej)* enano

run-up ['rʌnʌp] *n*: ~ **to** *(election etc)* período previo a

runway ['rʌnweɪ] *n (Aviat)* pista (de aterrizaje)

rupee [ruː'piː] *n* rupia

rupture ['rʌptʃəʳ] *n (Med)* hernia ▷ *vt*: **to ~ o.s.** causarse una hernia

rural ['ruərl] *adj* rural

rush [rʌʃ] *n* ímpetu *m*; *(hurry)* prisa, apuro *(LAm)*; *(Comm)* demanda repentina; *(Bot)* junco; *(current)* corriente *f* fuerte, ráfaga; *(of feeling)* torrente *m* ▷ *vt* apresurar; *(work)* hacer de prisa; *(attack: town etc)* asaltar ▷ *vi* correr, precipitarse; **gold ~** fiebre *f* del oro; **we've had a ~ of orders** ha habido una gran demanda; **I'm in a ~ (to do)** tengo prisa *or* apuro *(LAm)* (por hacer); **is there any ~ for this?** ¿te corre prisa esto?; **to ~ sth off** hacer algo de prisa y corriendo; **rush through** *vt fus (meal)* comer de prisa; *(book)* leer de prisa; *(work)* hacer de prisa; *(town)* atravesar a toda velocidad ▷ *vt sep (Comm: order)* despachar rápidamente

rush hour *n* horas *fpl* punta

rusk [rʌsk] *n* bizcocho tostado

Russia ['rʌʃə] *n* Rusia

Russian ['rʌʃən] *adj* ruso ▷ *n* ruso(-a); *(Ling)* ruso

rust [rʌst] *n* herrumbre *f*, moho ▷ *vi* oxidarse

rustic ['rʌstɪk] *adj* rústico

rustle ['rʌsl] *vi* susurrar ▷ *vt (paper)* hacer crujir; *(US: cattle)* hurtar, robar

rustproof ['rʌstpruːf] *adj* inoxidable

rusty ['rʌstɪ] *adj* oxidado

rut [rʌt] *n* surco; *(Zool)* celo; **to be in a ~** ser esclavo de la rutina

ruthless ['ruːθlɪs] *adj* despiadado

RV *abbr (= revised version)* traducción inglesa de la *Biblia de 1855* ▷ *n abbr (US)* = **recreational vehicle**

rye [raɪ] *n* centeno

rye bread *n* pan de centeno

S, s [ɛs] *n (letter)* S, s *f*; **S for Sugar** S de sábado

S *abbr (= Saint)* Sto.(-a.); *(US Scol: mark: = satisfactory)* suficiente; *(= south)* S; *(on clothes)* = **small**

SA *n abbr* = **South Africa**; **South America**

Sabbath ['sæbəθ] *n* domingo; *(Jewish)* sábado

sabotage ['sæbətɑːʒ] *n* sabotaje *m* ▷ *vt* sabotear

saccharin, saccharine ['sækərɪn] *n* sacarina

sachet ['sæʃeɪ] *n* sobrecito

sack [sæk] *n (bag)* saco, costal *m* ▷ *vt (dismiss)* despedir, echar; *(plunder)* saquear; **to get the ~** ser despedido; **to give sb the ~** despedir *or* echar a algn

sacking ['sækɪŋ] *n (material)* arpillera

sacrament ['sækrəmənt] *n* sacramento

sacred ['seɪkrɪd] *adj* sagrado, santo

sacrifice ['sækrɪfaɪs] *n* sacrificio ▷ *vt* sacrificar; **to make ~s (for sb)** sacrificarse (por algn)

sacrilege ['sækrɪlɪdʒ] *n* sacrilegio

sad [sæd] *adj (unhappy)* triste; *(deplorable)* lamentable

saddle ['sædl] *n* silla (de montar); *(of cycle)* sillín *m* ▷ *vt (horse)* ensillar; **to ~ sb with sth** *(inf: task, bill, name)* cargar a algn con algo; *(responsibility)* gravar a algn con algo; **to be ~d with sth** *(inf)* quedar cargado con algo

saddlebag ['sædlbæg] *n* alforja

sadist ['seɪdɪst] *n* sádico(-a)

sadistic [sə'dɪstɪk] *adj* sádico

sadly ['sædlɪ] adv tristemente; (regrettably) desgraciadamente; ~ **lacking (in)** muy deficiente (en)

sadness ['sædnɪs] n tristeza

sae abbr (Brit: = stamped addressed envelope) sobre con las propias señas de uno y con sello

safari [sə'fɑːrɪ] n safari m

safe [seɪf] adj (out of danger) fuera de peligro; (not dangerous, sure) seguro; (unharmed) ileso; (trustworthy) digno de confianza ▷ n caja de caudales, caja fuerte; ~ **and sound** sano or salvo; **(just) to be on the ~ side** para mayor seguridad; ~ **journey!** ¡buen viaje!; **it is ~ to say that ...** se puede decir con confianza que ...

safe-conduct [seɪf'kɒndʌkt] n salvoconducto

safe-deposit [seɪfdɪpɒzɪt] n (vault) cámara acorazada; (box) caja de seguridad or de caudales

safeguard ['seɪfgɑːd] n protección f, garantía ▷ vt proteger, defender

safe haven n refugio

safekeeping [seɪf'kiːpɪŋ] n custodia

safely ['seɪflɪ] adv seguramente, con seguridad; (without mishap) sin peligro; **I can ~ say** puedo decir or afirmar con toda seguridad, **to arrive** llegar bien

safe sex n sexo seguro or sin riesgo

safety ['seɪftɪ] n seguridad f ▷ cpd de seguridad; **road ~** seguridad f en carretera; ~ **first!** ¡precaución!

safety belt n cinturón m (de seguridad)

safety catch n seguro

safety pin n imperdible m, seguro (LAm)

safety valve n válvula de seguridad or de escape

saffron ['sæfrən] n azafrán m

sag [sæg] vi aflojarse

saga ['sɑːgə] n (History) saga; (fig) epopeya

sage [seɪdʒ] n (herb) salvia; (man) sabio

Sagittarius [sædʒɪ'tɛərɪəs] n Sagitario

Sahara [sə'hɑːrə] n: **the ~ (Desert)** el Sáhara

said [sɛd] pt, pp of **say**

sail [seɪl] n (on boat) vela ▷ vt (boat) gobernar ▷ vi (travel: ship) navegar; (passenger) pasear en barco; (Sport) hacer vela; (set off: also: **to set ~**) zarpar; **to go for a ~** dar un paseo en barco; **they ~ed into Copenhagen** arribaron a Copenhague; **sail through** vt fus (exam) aprobar fácilmente

sailboat ['seɪlbəut] n (US) velero, barco de vela

sailing ['seɪlɪŋ] n (Sport) vela; **to go ~** hacer vela

sailing boat n barco de vela

sailing ship n barco de vela

sailor ['seɪlər] n marinero, marino

saint [seɪnt] n santo; **S~ John** San Juan

sake [seɪk] n: **for the ~ of** por; **for the ~ of argument** digamos, es un decir; **art for art's ~** el arte por el arte

salad ['sæləd] n ensalada; **tomato ~** ensalada de tomate

salad bowl n ensaladera

salad cream n (Brit) mayonesa

salad dressing n aliño

salami [sə'lɑːmɪ] n salami m, salchichón m

salary ['sælərɪ] n sueldo

sale [seɪl] n venta; (at reduced prices) liquidación f, saldo; (auction) subasta; **sales** npl (total amount sold) ventas fpl, facturación f; **"for ~"** "se vende"; **on ~** en venta; **on ~ or return** (goods) venta por reposición; **closing-down** or (US) **liquidation ~** liquidación f; ~ **and lease back** venta y arrendamiento al vendedor

saleroom ['seɪlruːm] n sala de subastas

sales assistant n (Brit) dependiente(-a) m(f)

sales clerk n (US) dependiente(-a) m(f)

sales conference n conferencia de ventas

sales figures npl cifras fpl de ventas

sales force n personal m de ventas

salesman ['seɪlzmən] n vendedor m; (in shop) dependiente m; (representative) viajante m

salesperson ['seɪlzpə:sən] irreg n vendedor(a) m(f), dependiente(-a) m/f

sales rep n representante mf, agente m/f comercial

saleswoman ['seɪlzwumən] n vendedora; (in shop) dependienta; (representative) viajante f

saline ['seɪlaɪn] adj salino

saliva [sə'laɪvə] n saliva

sallow ['sæləu] adj cetrino

sally forth, sally out ['sælɪ-] vi salir, ponerse en marcha

salmon ['sæmən] n pl inv salmón m

salon ['sælɔn] n (hairdressing salon, beauty salon) salón m

saloon [sə'luːn] n (US) bar m, taberna; (Brit Aut) (coche m de) turismo; (ship's lounge) cámara, salón m

salt [sɔːlt] n sal f ▷ vt salar; (put salt on) poner sal en; **an old ~** un lobo de mar; **salt away** vt (inf: money) ahorrar

salt cellar n salero

saltwater ['sɔːlt'wɔːtər] adj (fish etc) de agua salada, de mar

salty ['sɔːltɪ] adj salado

salute [sə'luːt] n saludo; (of guns) salva ▷ vt saludar

salvage ['sælvɪdʒ] n (saving) salvamento, recuperación f; (things saved) objetos mpl salvados ▷ vt salvar

salvation [sæl'veɪʃən] n salvación f

Salvation Army n Ejército de Salvación

Samaritan [sə'mærɪtən] n: **to call the ~s** llamar al teléfono de la esperanza

same [seɪm] adj mismo ▷ pron: **the ~** el mismo/la misma; **the ~ book as** el mismo libro que; **on the ~ day** el mismo día; **at the ~ time** (at the same moment) al mismo tiempo; (yet) sin embargo; **all** or **just the ~** sin

embargo, aun así; **they're one and the ~**
(*person*) son la misma persona; (*thing*) son
iguales; **to do the ~ (as sb)** hacer lo mismo
(que otro); **and the ~ to you!** ¡igualmente!;
~ here! ¡yo también!; **the ~ again** (*in bar etc*)
otro igual
sample ['sɑːmpl] *n* muestra ▷ *vt* (*food, wine*)
probar; **to take a ~** tomar una muestra; **free
~** muestra gratuita
sanatorium (*pl* **sanatoria**) [sænə'tɔːrɪəm,
-rɪə] *n* (*Brit*) sanatorio
sanctimonious [sæŋktɪ'məunɪəs] *adj*
santurrón(-ona)
sanction ['sæŋkʃən] *n* sanción *f* ▷ *vt*
sancionar; **sanctions** *npl* (*Pol*) sanciones *fpl*;
to impose economic ~s on *or* **against**
imponer sanciones económicas a *or* contra
sanctity ['sæŋktɪtɪ] *n* (*gen*) santidad *f*;
(*inviolability*) inviolabilidad *f*
sanctuary ['sæŋktjuərɪ] *n* (*gen*) santuario;
(*refuge*) asilo, refugio; (*for wildlife*) reserva
sand [sænd] *n* arena; (*beach*) playa ▷ *vt* (*also:
~ down: wood etc*) lijar
sandal ['sændl] *n* sandalia
sandbag ['sændbæg] *n* saco de arena
sandbox ['sændbɒks] *n* (*US*) = **sandpit**
sandcastle ['sændkɑːsl] *n* castillo de arena
sand dune *n* duna
sandpaper ['sændpeɪpə^r] *n* papel *m* de lija
sandpit ['sændpɪt] *n* (*for children*) cajón *m* de
arena
sands [sændz] *npl* playa *sg* de arena
sandstone ['sændstəun] *n* piedra arenisca
sandstorm ['sændstɔːm] *n* tormenta de
arena
sandwich ['sændwɪtʃ] *n* bocadillo (*Sp*),
sandwich *m* (*LAm*) ▷ *vt* (*also:* **~ in**) intercalar;
to be ~ed between estar apretujado entre;
cheese/ham ~ sandwich de queso/jamón
sandy ['sændɪ] *adj* arenoso; (*colour*) rojizo
sane [seɪn] *adj* cuerdo, sensato
sang [sæŋ] *pt of* **sing**
sanitary ['sænɪtərɪ] *adj* (*system, arrangements*)
sanitario; (*clean*) higiénico
sanitary towel, sanitary napkin (*US*) *n*
paño higiénico, compresa
sanitation [sænɪ'teɪʃən] *n* (*in house*) servicios
mpl higiénicos; (*in town*) servicio de
desinfección
sanitation department *n* (*US*)
departamento de limpieza y recogida de
basuras
sanity ['sænɪtɪ] *n* cordura; (*of judgment*)
sensatez *f*
sank [sæŋk] *pt of* **sink**
Santa Claus [sæntə'klɔːz] *n* San Nicolás *m*,
Papá Noel *m*
sap [sæp] *n* (*of plants*) savia ▷ *vt* (*strength*)
minar, agotar
sapling ['sæplɪŋ] *n* árbol nuevo *or* joven
sapphire ['sæfaɪə^r] *n* zafiro
sarcasm ['sɑːkæzm] *n* sarcasmo

sarcastic [sɑː'kæstɪk] *adj* sarcástico; **to be ~**
ser sarcástico
sardine [sɑː'diːn] *n* sardina
Sardinia [sɑː'dɪnɪə] *n* Cerdeña
SARS ['sɑːz] *n abbr* (= *severe acute respiratory
syndrome*) neumonía asiática, SARS *m*
SAS *n abbr* (*Brit Mil*: = *Special Air Service*) cuerpo del
ejército británico encargado de misiones clandestinas
SASE *n abbr* (*US*: = *self-addressed stamped envelope*)
sobre con las propias señas de uno y con sello
sash [sæʃ] *n* faja
Sat. *abbr* (= *Saturday*) sáb
sat [sæt] *pt, pp of* **sit**
Satan ['seɪtn] *n* Satanás *m*
satchel ['sætʃl] *n* bolsa; (*child's*) cartera,
mochila (*LAm*)
satellite ['sætəlaɪt] *n* satélite *m*
satellite dish *n* (antena) parabólica
satellite television *n* televisión *f* por
satélite
satin ['sætɪn] *n* raso ▷ *adj* de raso; **with a ~
finish** satinado
satire ['sætaɪə^r] *n* sátira
satisfaction [sætɪs'fækʃən] *n* satisfacción *f*;
it gives me great ~ es para mí una gran
satisfacción; **has it been done to your ~?**
¿se ha hecho a su satisfacción?
satisfactory [sætɪs'fæktərɪ] *adj* satisfactorio
satisfied ['sætɪsfaɪd] *adj* satisfecho; **to be ~
(with sth)** estar satisfecho (de algo)
satisfy ['sætɪsfaɪ] *vt* satisfacer; (*pay*) liquidar;
(*convince*) convencer; **to ~ the requirements**
llenar los requisitos; **to ~ sb that** convencer
a algn de que; **to ~ o.s. of sth** convencerse de
algo
satisfying ['sætɪsfaɪɪŋ] *adj* satisfactorio
satsuma [sæt'suːmə] *n* satsuma
saturated fat [sætʃəreɪtɪd-] *n* grasa
saturada
saturation [sætʃə'reɪʃən] *n* saturación *f*
Saturday ['sætədɪ] *n* sábado; *see also* **Tuesday**
sauce [sɔːs] *n* salsa; (*sweet*) crema; (*fig: cheek*)
frescura
saucepan ['sɔːspən] *n* cacerola, olla
saucer ['sɔːsə^r] *n* platillo
saucy ['sɔːsɪ] *adj* fresco, descarado
Saudi Arabia *n* Arabia Saudí *or* Saudita
sauna ['sɔːnə] *n* sauna
saunter ['sɔːntə^r] *vi* deambular
sausage ['sɒsɪdʒ] *n* salchicha; (*salami etc*)
salchichón *m*
sausage roll *n* empanadilla de salchicha
sautéed ['səuteɪd] *adj* salteado
savage ['sævɪdʒ] *adj* (*cruel, fierce*) feroz,
furioso; (*primitive*) salvaje ▷ *n* salvaje *m/f* ▷ *vt*
(*attack*) embestir
save [seɪv] *vt* (*rescue*) salvar, rescatar; (*money,
time*) ahorrar; (*put by*) guardar; (*Comput*)
salvar (y guardar); (*avoid: trouble*) evitar;
(*Sport*) parar ▷ *vi* (*also:* **~ up**) ahorrar ▷ *n*
(*Sport*) parada ▷ *prep* salvo, excepto; **to ~ face**
salvar las apariencias; **God ~ the Queen!**

¡Dios guarde a la Reina!, ¡Viva la Reina!; **I ~d you a piece of cake** te he guardado un trozo de tarta; **it will ~ me an hour** con ello ganaré una hora

saving ['seɪvɪŋ] n (on price etc) economía ▷ adj: **the ~ grace of** el único mérito de; **savings** npl ahorros mpl; **to make ~s** economizar

savings account n cuenta de ahorros

savings and loan association n (US) sociedad f de ahorro y préstamo

savings bank n caja de ahorros

saviour, savior (US) ['seɪvjə'] n salvador(a) m(f)

savour, savor (US) ['seɪvə'] n sabor m, gusto ▷ vt saborear

savoury, savory (US) ['seɪvərɪ] adj sabroso; (dish: not sweet) salado

saw [sɔ:] pt of **see** ▷ n (tool) sierra ▷ vt (pt **sawed**, pp **sawed** or **sawn** [sɔ:n]) serrar; **to ~ sth up** (a)serrar algo

sawdust ['sɔ:dʌst] n (a)serrín m

sawmill ['sɔ:mɪl] n aserradero

sawn [sɔ:n] pp of **saw**

sawn-off ['sɔ:nɔf], **sawed-off** (US) ['sɔ:dɔf] adj: **~ shotgun** escopeta de cañones recortados

saxophone ['sæksəfəʊn] n saxófono

say [seɪ] (pt, pp **said** [sɛd]) n: **to have one's ~** expresar su opinión ▷ vt, vi decir; **to have a** or **some ~ in sth** tener voz y voto en algo; **to ~ yes/no** decir que sí/no; **my watch ~s 3 o'clock** mi reloj marca las tres; **that is to ~** es decir; **that goes without ~ing** ni que decir tiene; **she said (that) I was to give you this** me pidió que te diera esto; **I should ~ it's worth about £100** yo diría que vale unas 100 libras; **~ after me** repite lo que yo diga; **shall we ~ Tuesday?** ¿quedamos, por ejemplo, el martes?; **that doesn't ~ much for him** eso no dice nada a su favor; **when all is said and done** al fin y al cabo, a fin de cuentas; **there is something** or **a lot to be said for it** hay algo or mucho que decir a su favor

saying ['seɪɪŋ] n dicho, refrán m

say-so ['seɪsəʊ] n (inf) autorización f

scab [skæb] n costra; (pej) esquirol(a) m(f)

scaffold ['skæfəld] n (for execution) cadalso

scaffolding ['skæfəldɪŋ] n andamio, andamiaje m

scald [skɔ:ld] n escaldadura ▷ vt escaldar

scale [skeɪl] n (gen) escala; (Mus) escala; (of fish) escama; (of salaries, fees etc) escalafón m ▷ vt (mountain) escalar; (tree) trepar; **scales** npl (small) balanza sg; (large) báscula sg; **on a large ~** a gran escala; **~ of charges** tarifa, lista de precios; **pay ~** escala salarial; **to draw sth to ~** dibujar algo a escala; **scale down** vt reducir

scallion ['skæljən] n (US) cebolleta

scallop ['skɔləp] n (Zool) venera; (Sewing) festón m

scalp [skælp] n cabellera ▷ vt escalpar

scalpel ['skælpl] n bisturí m

scam [skæm] n (inf) estafa, timo

scamper ['skæmpə'] vi: **to ~ away, ~ off** escabullirse

scampi ['skæmpɪ] npl gambas fpl

scan [skæn] vt (examine) escudriñar; (glance at quickly) dar un vistazo a; (TV, Radar) explorar, registrar; (Comput) escanear ▷ n (Med) examen m ultrasónico; **to have a ~** pasar por el escáner

scandal ['skændl] n escándalo; (gossip) chismes mpl

scandalize ['skændəlaɪz] vt escandalizar

scandalous ['skændələs] adj escandaloso

Scandinavia [skændɪ'neɪvɪə] n Escandinavia

Scandinavian [skændɪ'neɪvɪən] adj, n escandinavo(-a) m(f)

scanner ['skænə'] n (Radar, Med, Comput) escáner m

scant [skænt] adj escaso

scanty ['skæntɪ] adj (meal) insuficiente; (clothes) ligero

scapegoat ['skeɪpɡəʊt] n cabeza de turco, chivo expiatorio

scar [skɑ:] n cicatriz f ▷ vt marcar con una cicatriz ▷ vi cicatrizarse

scarce [skɛəs] adj escaso; **to make o.s. ~** (inf) esfumarse

scarcely ['skɛəslɪ] adv apenas; **~ anybody** casi nadie; **I can ~ believe it** casi no puedo creerlo

scare [skɛə'] n susto, sobresalto; (panic) pánico ▷ vt asustar, espantar; **to ~ sb stiff** dar a algn un susto de muerte; **bomb ~** amenaza de bomba; **scare away, scare off** vt espantar, ahuyentar

scarecrow ['skɛəkrəʊ] n espantapájaros m inv

scared [skɛəd] adj: **to be ~** asustarse, estar asustado

scarf (pl **scarves**) [skɑ:f, skɑ:vz] n (long) bufanda; (square) pañuelo

scarlet ['skɑ:lɪt] adj escarlata

scarlet fever n escarlatina

scarper ['skɑ:pə'] vi (Brit inf) largarse

scarves [skɑ:vz] npl of **scarf**

scary ['skɛərɪ] adj (inf) de miedo; **it's ~** da miedo

scathing ['skeɪðɪŋ] adj mordaz; **to be ~ about sth** criticar algo duramente

scatter ['skætə'] vt (spread) esparcir, desparramar; (put to flight) dispersar ▷ vi desparramarse; dispersarse

scatterbrained ['skætəbreɪnd] adj ligero de cascos

scavenge ['skævɪndʒ] vi: **to ~ (for)** (person) revolver entre la basura (para encontrar); **to ~ for food** (hyenas etc) nutrirse de carroña

scavenger ['skævɪndʒə'] n (person) mendigo/a que rebusca en la basura; (Zool: animal) animal m de carroña; (: bird) ave f de carroña

S

scenario [sɪˈnɑːrɪəu] n (Theat) argumento; (Cine) guión m; (fig) escenario

scene [siːn] n (Theat) escena; (of crime, accident) escenario; (sight, view) vista, panorama; (fuss) escándalo; **the political ~ in Spain** el panorama político español; **behind the ~s** (also fig) entre bastidores; **to appear** or **come on the ~** (also fig) aparecer, presentarse; **to make a ~** (inf: fuss) armar un escándalo

scenery [ˈsiːnərɪ] n (Theat) decorado; (landscape) paisaje m

scenic [ˈsiːnɪk] adj (picturesque) pintoresco

scent [sɛnt] n perfume m, olor m; (fig: track) rastro, pista; (sense of smell) olfato ▷ vt perfumar; (suspect) presentir; **to put** or **throw sb off the ~** (fig) despistar a algn

sceptic, skeptic (US) [ˈskɛptɪk] n escéptico(-a)

sceptical, skeptical (US) [ˈskɛptɪkl] adj escéptico

schedule [ˈʃɛdjuːl, (US) ˈskɛdjuːl] n (of trains) horario; (of events) programa m; (list) lista ▷ vt (timetable) establecer el horario de; (list) catalogar; (visit) fijar la hora de; **on ~** a la hora, sin retraso; **to be ahead of/behind ~** ir adelantado/retrasado; **we are working to a very tight ~** tenemos un programa de trabajo muy apretado; **everything went according to ~** todo salió según lo previsto; **the meeting is ~d for seven** or **to begin at seven** la reunión está fijada para las siete

scheduled [ˈʃɛdjuːld, (US) ˈskɛdjuːld] adj (date, time) fijado; (visit, event, bus, train) programado; (stop) previsto; **~ flight** vuelo regular

scheme [skiːm] n (plan) plan m, proyecto; (method) esquema m; (plot) intriga; (trick) ardid m; (arrangement) disposición f; (pension scheme etc) sistema m ▷ vi proyectar ▷ vi (plan) hacer proyectos; (intrigue) intrigar; **colour ~** combinación f de colores

scheming [ˈskiːmɪŋ] adj intrigante

schism [ˈskɪzəm] n cisma m

schizophrenia [skɪtsəˈfriːnɪə] n esquizofrenia

schizophrenic [skɪtsəˈfrɛnɪk] adj esquizofrénico

scholar [ˈskɔlər] n (pupil) alumno(-a), estudiante m/f; (learned person) sabio(-a), erudito(-a)

scholarly [ˈskɔlərlɪ] adj erudito

scholarship [ˈskɔləʃɪp] n erudición f; (grant) beca

school [skuːl] n (gen) escuela, colegio; (in university) facultad f; (of fish) banco ▷ vt (animal) amaestrar; **to be at** or **go to ~** ir al colegio or a la escuela

school age n edad f escolar

schoolbook [ˈskuːlbuk] n libro de texto

schoolboy [ˈskuːlbɔɪ] n alumno

schoolchild (pl **schoolchildren**) [ˈskuːltʃaɪld, -tʃɪldrən] n alumno(-a)

schoolgirl [ˈskuːlɡəːl] n alumna

schooling [ˈskuːlɪŋ] n enseñanza

school-leaver [ˈskuːlliːvər] n (Brit) joven que ha terminado la educación secundaria

schoolmaster [ˈskuːlmɑːstər] n (primary) maestro; (secondary) profesor m

schoolmistress [ˈskuːlmɪstrɪs] n (primary) maestra; (secondary) profesora

schoolteacher [ˈskuːltiːtʃər] n (primary) maestro(-a); (secondary) profesor(a) m(f)

schoolyard [ˈskuːljɑːd] n (US) patio del colegio

sciatica [saɪˈætɪkə] n ciática

science [ˈsaɪəns] n ciencia; **the ~s** las ciencias

science fiction n ciencia-ficción f

scientific [saɪənˈtɪfɪk] adj científico

scientist [ˈsaɪəntɪst] n científico(-a)

sci-fi [ˈsaɪfaɪ] n abbr (inf) = **science fiction**

Scilly Isles [ˈsɪlɪ-], **Scillies** [ˈsɪlɪz] npl: **the ~** las Islas Sorlingas

scissors [ˈsɪzəz] npl tijeras fpl; **a pair of ~** unas tijeras

scoff [skɔf] vt (Brit inf: eat) engullir ▷ vi: **to ~ (at)** (mock) mofarse (de)

scold [skəuld] vt regañar

scone [skɔn] n pastel de pan

scoop [skuːp] n cucharón m; (for flour etc) pala; (Press) exclusiva ▷ vt (Comm: market) adelantarse a; (: profit) sacar; (Comm, Press: competitors) adelantarse a; **scoop out** vt excavar; **scoop up** vt recoger

scooter [ˈskuːtər] n (motor cycle) Vespa®; (toy) patinete m

scope [skəup] n (of plan, undertaking) ámbito; (reach) alcance m; (of person) competencia; (opportunity) libertad f (de acción); **there is plenty of ~ for improvement** hay bastante campo para efectuar mejoras

scorch [skɔːtʃ] vt (clothes) chamuscar; (earth, grass) quemar, secar

scorching [ˈskɔːtʃɪŋ] adj abrasador(a)

score [skɔːr] n (points etc) puntuación f; (Mus) partitura; (reckoning) cuenta; (twenty) veintena ▷ vt (goal, point) ganar; (mark, cut) rayar ▷ vi marcar un tanto; (Football) marcar un gol; (keep score) llevar el tanteo; **to keep (the) ~** llevar la cuenta; **to have an old ~ to settle with sb** (fig) tener cuentas pendientes con algn; **on that ~** en lo que se refiere a eso; **~s of people** (fig) muchísima gente, cantidad de gente; **to ~ 6 out of 10** obtener una puntuación de 6 sobre 10; **score out** vt tachar

scoreboard [ˈskɔːbɔːd] n marcador m

scoreline [ˈskɔːlaɪn] n (Sport) resultado final

scorer [ˈskɔːrər] n marcador m; (keeping score) encargado(-a) del marcador

scorn [skɔːn] n desprecio ▷ vt despreciar

Scorpio [ˈskɔːpɪəu] n Escorpión m

scorpion [ˈskɔːpɪən] n alacrán m, escorpión m

Scot [skɔt] n escocés(-esa) m(f)

Scotch [skɔtʃ] n whisky m escocés
scotch [skɔtʃ] vt (rumour) desmentir; (plan) frustrar
Scotch tape® n (US) cinta adhesiva, celo, scotch® m
scot-free [skɔt'fri:] adv: **to get off ~** (unpunished) salir impune; (unhurt) salir ileso
Scotland ['skɔtlənd] n Escocia
Scots [skɔts] adj escocés(-esa)
Scotsman ['skɔtsmən] n escocés m
Scotswoman ['skɔtswumən] n escocesa
Scottish ['skɔtɪʃ] adj escocés(-esa); **the ~ National Party** partido político independista escocés; **the ~ Parliament** el Parlamento escocés
scoundrel ['skaundrəl] n canalla m/f, sinvergüenza m/f
scour ['skauəʳ] vt (clean) fregar, estregar; (search) recorrer, registrar
scourge [skə:dʒ] n azote m
scout [skaut] n explorador m; **girl ~** (US) niña exploradora; **scout around** vi reconocer el terreno
scowl [skaul] vi fruncir el ceño; **to ~ at sb** mirar con ceño a algn
scrabble ['skræbl] vi (claw): **to ~ (at)** arañar ▷ n: **S~®** Scrabble® m, Intelect® m; **to ~ around for sth** revolver todo buscando algo
scram [skræm] vi (inf) largarse
scramble ['skræmbl] n (climb) subida (difícil); (struggle) pelea ▷ vi: **to ~ out/through** salir/abrirse paso con dificultad; **to ~ for** pelear por; **to go scrambling** (Sport) hacer motocrós
scrambled eggs ['skræmbld-] npl huevos mpl revueltos
scrap [skræp] n (bit) pedacito; (fig) pizca; (fight) riña, bronca; (also: **~ iron**) chatarra, hierro viejo ▷ vt (discard) desechar, descartar ▷ vi reñir, armar (una) bronca; **scraps** npl (waste) sobras fpl, desperdicios mpl; **to sell sth for ~** vender algo como chatarra
scrapbook ['skræpbuk] n álbum m de recortes
scrap dealer n chatarrero(-a)
scrape [skreip] n (fig) lío, apuro ▷ vt raspar; (skin etc) rasguñar; (also: **~ against**) rozar; **to get into a ~** meterse en un lío; **scrape through** vi (succeed) salvarse por los pelos; (exam) aprobar por los pelos
scrap heap n (fig): **on the ~** desperdiciado; **to throw sth on the ~** desechar or descartar algo
scrap merchant n (Brit) chatarrero(-a)
scrap paper n pedazos mpl de papel
scrap yard n depósito de chatarra; (for cars) cementerio de coches
scratch [skrætʃ] n rasguño; (from claw) arañazo ▷ adj: **~ team** equipo improvisado ▷ vt (paint, car) rayar; (with claw, nail) rasguñar, arañar; (Comput) borrar ▷ vi rascarse; **to start from ~** partir de cero; **to be up to ~** cumplir con los requisitos

scratch card n (Brit) tarjeta f de "rasque y gane"
scrawl [skrɔ:l] n garabatos mpl ▷ vi hacer garabatos
scrawny ['skrɔ:nɪ] adj (person, neck) flaco
scream [skri:m] n chillido ▷ vi chillar; **it was a ~** (fig, inf) fue para morirse de risa or muy divertido; **he's a ~** (fig, inf) es muy divertido or de lo más gracioso; **to ~ at sb (to do sth)** gritarle a algn (para que haga algo)
screech [skri:tʃ] vi chirriar
screen [skri:n] n (Cine, TV) pantalla; (movable) biombo; (wall) tabique m; (also: **wind~**) parabrisas m inv ▷ vt (conceal) tapar; (from the wind etc) proteger; (film) proyectar; (fig: person: for security) investigar; (: for illness) hacer una exploración a
screenful ['skri:nful] n pantalla
screening ['skri:nɪŋ] n (of film) proyección f; (for security) investigación f; (Med) exploración f
screenplay ['skri:npleɪ] n guión m
screen saver [-seɪvəʳ] n (Comput) salvapantallas m inv
screenshot ['skri:nʃɔt] n (Comput) screenshot m, captura de pantalla
screw [skru:] n tornillo; (propeller) hélice f ▷ vt atornillar; **to ~ sth to the wall** fijar algo a la pared con tornillos; **screw up** vt (paper, material etc) arrugar; (inf: ruin) fastidiar; **to ~ up one's eyes** arrugar el entrecejo; **to ~ up one's face** torcer or arrugar la cara
screwdriver ['skru:draɪvəʳ] n destornillador m
screwed-up ['skru:d'ʌp] adj (inf): **she's totally ~** está trastornada
scribble ['skrɪbl] n garabatos mpl ▷ vi garabatear ▷ vt escribir con prisa; **to ~ down** garabatear algo
script [skrɪpt] n (Cine etc) guión m; (writing) escritura, letra
Scripture ['skrɪptʃəʳ] n Sagrada Escritura
scroll [skrəul] n rollo ▷ vt (Comput) desplazar
scrotum ['skrəutəm] n escroto
scrounge [skraundʒ] (inf) vt: **to ~ sth off or from sb** gorronear algo a algn ▷ vi: **to ~ on sb** vivir a costa de algn
scrounger ['skraundʒəʳ] n gorrón(-ona) m(f)
scrub [skrʌb] n (clean) fregado; (land) maleza ▷ vt fregar, restregar; (reject) cancelar, anular
scruff [skrʌf] n: **by the ~ of the neck** por el pescuezo
scruffy ['skrʌfɪ] adj desaliñado, desaseado
scrum ['skrʌm], **scrummage** ['skrʌmɪdʒ] n (Rugby) melée f
scruple ['skru:pl] n escrúpulo; **to have no ~s about doing sth** no tener reparos en or escrúpulos para hacer algo
scrupulous ['skru:pjuləs] adj escrupuloso
scrutinize ['skru:tɪnaɪz] vt escudriñar; (votes) escrutar

S

scrutiny ['skru:tɪnɪ] *n* escrutinio, examen *m*; **under the ~ of sb** bajo la mirada *or* el escrutinio de algn

scuba diving ['sku:bə'daɪvɪŋ] *n* submarinismo

scuff [skʌf] *vt (shoes, floor)* rayar

scuffle ['skʌfl] *n* refriega

scullery ['skʌlərɪ] *n* trascocina

sculptor ['skʌlptə^r] *n* escultor(a) *m(f)*

sculpture ['skʌlptʃə^r] *n* escultura

scum [skʌm] *n (on liquid)* espuma; *(pej: people)* escoria

scupper ['skʌpə^r] *vt (Brit: boat)* hundir; (: *fig: plans etc)* acabar con

scurrilous ['skʌrɪləs] *adj* difamatorio, calumnioso

scurry ['skʌrɪ] *vi:* **to ~ off** escabullirse

scuttle ['skʌtl] *n (also: coal ~)* cubo, carbonera ▷ *vt (ship)* barrenar ▷ *vi (scamper):* **to ~ away**, **~ off** escabullirse

scythe [saɪð] *n* guadaña

sea [si:] *n* mar *m/f*; **by ~** *(travel)* en barco; **on the ~** *(boat)* en el mar; *(town)* junto al mar; **to be all at ~** *(fig)* estar despistado; **out to** *or* **at ~** en alta mar; **to go by ~** ir en barco; **heavy** *or* **rough ~** marejada; **by** *or* **beside the ~** *(holiday)* en la playa; *(village)* a orillas del mar; **a ~ of faces** una multitud de caras

sea bed *n* fondo del mar

seaboard ['si:bɔ:d] *n* litoral *m*

seafood ['si:fu:d] *n* mariscos *mpl*

sea front *n (beach)* playa; *(prom)* paseo marítimo

seagoing ['si:gəuɪŋ] *adj (ship)* de alta mar

seagull ['si:gʌl] *n* gaviota

seal [si:l] *n (animal)* foca; *(stamp)* sello ▷ *vt (close)* cerrar; (: *with seal)* sellar; *(decide: sb's fate)* decidir; (: *bargain)* cerrar; **~ of approval** sello de aprobación; **seal off** *vt* obturar

sea level *n* nivel *m* del mar

sea lion *n* león *m* marino

seam [si:m] *n* costura; *(of metal)* juntura; *(of coal)* veta, filón *m*; **the hall was bursting at the ~s** la sala rebosaba de gente

seaman ['si:mən] *n* marinero

seance ['seɪɔns] *n* sesión *f* de espiritismo

seaplane ['si:pleɪn] *n* hidroavión *m*

search [sə:tʃ] *n (for person, thing)* busca, búsqueda; *(of drawer, pockets)* registro; *(inspection)* reconocimiento ▷ *vt (look in)* buscar en; *(examine)* examinar; *(person, place)* registrar; *(Comput)* buscar ▷ *vi:* **to ~ for** buscar; **in ~ of** en busca de; **"~ and replace"** *(Comput)* "buscar y reemplazar"; **search through** *vt fus* registrar

search engine *n (Comput, Internet)* buscador *m*

searching ['sə:tʃɪŋ] *adj (question)* penetrante

searchlight ['sə:tʃlaɪt] *n* reflector *m*

search party *n* equipo de salvamento

search warrant *n* mandamiento judicial

seashore ['si:ʃɔ^r] *n* playa, orilla del mar; **on the ~** a la orilla del mar

seasick ['si:sɪk] *adj* mareado; **to be ~** marearse

seaside ['si:saɪd] *n* playa, orilla del mar; **to go to the ~** ir a la playa

seaside resort *n* centro turístico costero

season ['si:zn] *n (of year)* estación *f*; *(sporting etc)* temporada; *(gen)* época, período ▷ *vt (food)* sazonar; **to be in/out of ~** estar en sazón/fuera de temporada; **the busy ~** *(for shops, hotels etc)* la temporada alta; **the open ~** *(Hunting)* la temporada de caza *or* de pesca

seasonal ['si:znl] *adj* estacional

seasoned ['si:znd] *adj (wood)* curado; *(fig: worker, actor)* experimentado; *(troops)* curtido; **~ campaigner** veterano(-a)

seasoning ['si:znɪŋ] *n* condimento

season ticket *n* abono

seat [si:t] *n (in bus, train: place)* asiento; *(chair)* silla; *(Parliament)* escaño; *(buttocks)* trasero; *(centre: of government etc)* sede *f* ▷ *vt* sentar; *(have room for)* tener cabida para; **are there any ~s left?** ¿quedan plazas?; **to take one's ~** sentarse, tomar asiento; **to be ~ed** estar sentado, sentarse

seat belt *n* cinturón *m* de seguridad

seating ['si:tɪŋ] *n* asientos *mpl*

sea water *n* agua *m* del mar

seaweed ['si:wi:d] *n* alga marina

seaworthy ['si:wə:ðɪ] *adj* en condiciones de navegar

sec. *abbr* = **second(s)**

secluded [sɪ'klu:dɪd] *adj* retirado

seclusion [sɪ'klu:ʒən] *n* retiro

second ['sɛkənd] *adj* segundo ▷ *adv (in race etc)* en segundo lugar ▷ *n (gen)* segundo; *(Aut: also: ~ gear)* segunda; *(Comm)* artículo con algún desperfecto; *(Brit Scol: degree)* título universitario de segunda clase ▷ *vt (motion)* apoyar; [sɪ'kɔnd] *(employee)* trasladar temporalmente; **~ floor** *(Brit)* segundo piso; *(US)* primer piso; **Charles the S~** Carlos Segundo; **to ask for a ~ opinion** *(Med)* pedir una segunda opinión; **just a ~!** ¡un momento!; **to have ~ thoughts** cambiar de opinión; **on ~ thoughts** *or (US)* **~ thought** pensándolo bien; **~ mortgage** segunda hipoteca

secondary ['sɛkəndərɪ] *adj* secundario

secondary education *n* enseñanza secundaria

secondary school *n* escuela secundaria

second-class ['sɛkənd'klɑ:s] *adj* de segunda clase ▷ *adv:* **to send sth ~** enviar algo por correo de segunda clase; **to travel ~** viajar en segunda; **~ citizen** ciudadano(-a) de segunda (clase)

second cousin *n* primo(-a) segundo(-a)

second-guess ['sɛkənd'gɛs] *vt (evaluate)* juzgar (a posteriori); *(anticipate):* **to ~ sth/sb** (intentar) adivinar algo/lo que va a hacer algn

secondhand ['sɛkənd'hænd] *adj* de segunda mano, usado ▷ *adv*: **to buy sth ~** comprar algo de segunda mano; **to hear sth ~** oír algo indirectamente

second hand *n* (*on clock*) segundero

secondly ['sɛkəndlɪ] *adv* en segundo lugar

secondment [sɪ'kɔndmənt] *n* (*Brit*) traslado temporal

second-rate ['sɛkənd'reɪt] *adj* de segunda categoría

secrecy ['si:krəsɪ] *n* secreto

secret ['si:krɪt] *adj*, *n* secreto; **in ~** *adv* en secreto; **to keep sth ~ (from sb)** ocultarle algo (a algn); **to make no ~ of sth** no ocultar algo

secret agent *n* agente *m/f* secreto(-a), espía *m/f*

secretary ['sɛkrətərɪ] *n* secretario(-a); **S~ of State** (*Brit Pol*) Ministro (con cartera)

secretary-general ['sɛkrətərɪ'dʒɛnərl] *n* secretario(-a) general

secrete [sɪ'kri:t] *vt* (*Med, Anat, Bio*) secretar; (*hide*) ocultar, esconder

secretive ['si:krətɪv] *adj* reservado, sigiloso

secretly ['si:krɪtlɪ] *adv* en secreto

secret police *n* policía secreta

secret service *n* servicio secreto

sect [sɛkt] *n* secta

sectarian [sɛk'tɛərɪən] *adj* sectario

section ['sɛkʃən] *n* sección *f*; (*part*) parte *f*; (*of document*) artículo; (*of opinion*) sector *m*; **business ~** (*Press*) sección *f* de economía

sector ['sɛktə'] *n* sector *m*

secular ['sɛkjulə'] *adj* secular, seglar

secure [sɪ'kjuə'] *adj* (*free from anxiety*) seguro; (*firmly fixed*) firme, fijo ▷ *vt* (*fix*) asegurar, afianzar; (*get*) conseguir; (*Comm: loan*) garantizar; **to make sth ~** afianzar algo; **to ~ sth for sb** conseguir algo para algn

security [sɪ'kjuərɪtɪ] *n* seguridad *f*; (*for loan*) fianza; (: *object*) prenda; **securities** *npl* (*Comm*) valores *mpl*, títulos *mpl*; **~ of tenure** tenencia asegurada; **to increase/tighten ~** aumentar/estrechar las medidas de seguridad; **job ~** seguridad *f* en el empleo

Security Council *n*: **the ~** el Consejo de Seguridad

security forces *npl* fuerzas *fpl* de seguridad

security guard *n* guardia *m/f* de seguridad

sedan [sɪ'dæn] *n* (*US Aut*) sedán *m*

sedate [sɪ'deɪt] *adj* tranquilo ▷ *vt* administrar sedantes a, sedar

sedation [sɪ'deɪʃən] *n* (*Med*) sedación *f*; **to be under ~** estar bajo sedación

sedative ['sɛdɪtɪv] *n* sedante *m*, calmante *m*

sediment ['sɛdɪmənt] *n* sedimento

seduce [sɪ'dju:s] *vt* (*gen*) seducir

seduction [sɪ'dʌkʃən] *n* seducción *f*

seductive [sɪ'dʌktɪv] *adj* seductor(-a)

see [si:] (*pt* **saw**, *pp* **seen**) *vt* (*gen*) ver; (*understand*) ver, comprender; (*look at*) mirar ▷ *vi* ver ▷ *n* sede *f*; **to ~ sb to the door** acompañar a algn a la puerta; **to ~ that** (*ensure*) asegurarse de que; **~ you soon/later/tomorrow!** ¡hasta pronto/luego/mañana!; **as far as I can ~** por lo visto *or* por lo que veo; **there was nobody to be ~n** no se veía a nadie; **let me ~** (*show me*) a ver; (*let me think*) vamos a ver; **to go and ~ sb** ir a ver a algn; **~ for yourself** compruébalo tú mismo; **I don't know what she ~s in him** no sé qué le encuentra; **see about** *vt fus* atender a, encargarse de; **see off** *vt* despedir; **see out** *vt* (*take to the door*) acompañar hasta la puerta; **see through** *vt fus* calar ▷ *vt* llevar a cabo; **see to** *vt fus* atender a, encargarse de

seed [si:d] *n* semilla; (*in fruit*) pepita; (*fig*) germen *m*; (*Tennis*) preseleccionado(-a); **to go to ~** (*plant*) granar; (*fig*) descuidarse

seedling ['si:dlɪŋ] *n* planta de semillero

seedy ['si:dɪ] *adj* (*person*) desaseado; (*place*) sórdido

seeing ['si:ɪŋ] *conj*: **~ (that)** visto que, en vista de que

seek (*pt*, *pp* **sought**) [si:k, sɔ:t] *vt* (*gen*) buscar; (*post*) solicitar; **to ~ advice/help from sb** pedir consejos/solicitar ayuda a algn; **seek out** *vt* (*person*) buscar

seem [si:m] *vi* parecer; **there ~s to be ...** parece que hay ...; **it ~s (that) ...** parece que ...; **what ~s to be the trouble?** ¿qué pasa?; **I did what I ~ed best** hice lo que parecía mejor

seemingly ['si:mɪŋlɪ] *adv* aparentemente, según parece

seen [si:n] *pp* of **see**

seep [si:p] *vi* filtrarse

seesaw ['si:sɔ:] *n* balancín *m*, subibaja *m*

seethe [si:ð] *vi* hervir; **to ~ with anger** enfurecerse

see-through ['si:θru:] *adj* transparente

segment ['sɛgmənt] *n* segmento; (*of citrus fruit*) gajo

segregate ['sɛgrɪgeɪt] *vt* segregar

seize [si:z] *vt* (*grasp*) agarrar, asir; (*take possession of*) secuestrar; (: *territory*) apoderarse de; (*opportunity*) aprovecharse de; **seize up** *vi* (*Tech*) agarrotarse; **seize (up)on** *vt fus* valerse de

seizure ['si:ʒə'] *n* (*Med*) ataque *m*; (*Law*) incautación *f*

seldom ['sɛldəm] *adv* rara vez

select [sɪ'lɛkt] *adj* selecto, escogido; (*hotel, restaurant, clubs*) exclusivo ▷ *vt* escoger, elegir; (*Sport*) seleccionar; **a ~ few** una minoría selecta

selection [sɪ'lɛkʃən] *n* selección *f*, elección *f*; (*Comm*) surtido

selective [sɪ'lɛktɪv] *adj* selectivo

self [sɛlf] *n* (*pl* **selves** [sɛlvz]) uno mismo ▷ *pref* auto...; **the ~** el yo

self-appointed [sɛlfə'pɔɪntɪd] *adj* autonombrado

self-assurance [sɛlfə'ʃuərəns] *n* confianza en sí mismo

self-assured [sɛlfəˈʃuəd] *adj* seguro de sí
self-catering [sɛlfˈkeɪtərɪŋ] *adj* (Brit) sin
  pensión *or* servicio de comida; ~ **apartment**
  apartamento con cocina propia
self-centred, self-centered (US)
  [sɛlfˈsɛntəd] *adj* egocéntrico
self-confessed [sɛlfkənˈfɛst] *adj* (alcoholic etc)
  confeso
self-confidence [sɛlfˈkɒnfɪdns] *n* confianza
  en sí mismo
self-confident [sɛlfˈkɒnfɪdnt] *adj* seguro de
  sí (mismo), lleno de confianza en sí mismo
self-conscious [sɛlfˈkɒnʃəs] *adj* cohibido
self-contained [sɛlfkənˈteɪnd] *adj* (gen)
  independiente; (Brit: flat) con entrada
  particular
self-control [sɛlfkənˈtrəul] *n* autodominio
self-defence, self-defense (US) [sɛlfdɪˈfɛns]
  n defensa propia
self-discipline [sɛlfˈdɪsɪplɪn] *n*
  autodisciplina
self-employed [sɛlfɪmˈplɔɪd] *adj* que trabaja
  por cuenta propia, autónomo
self-esteem [sɛlfɪˈstiːm] *n* amor *m* propio
self-evident [sɛlfˈɛvɪdnt] *adj* patente
self-explanatory [sɛlfɪksˈplænətərɪ] *adj* que
  no necesita explicación
self-governing [sɛlfˈɡʌvənɪŋ] *adj* autónomo
self-help [sɛlfˈhɛlp] *n* autosuficiencia,
  ayuda propia
self-indulgent [sɛlfɪnˈdʌldʒənt] *adj*
  indulgente consigo mismo
self-inflicted [sɛlfɪnˈflɪktɪd] *adj* infligido a sí
  mismo
self-interest [sɛlfˈɪntrɪst] *n* egoísmo
selfish [ˈsɛlfɪʃ] *adj* egoísta
selfishness [ˈsɛlfɪʃnɪs] *n* egoísmo
selfless [ˈsɛlflɪs] *adj* desinteresado
self-pity [sɛlfˈpɪtɪ] *n* lástima de sí mismo
self-portrait [sɛlfˈpɔːtreɪt] *n* autorretrato
self-possessed [sɛlfpəˈzɛst] *adj* sereno,
  dueño de sí mismo
self-preservation [ˈsɛlfprɛzəˈveɪʃən] *n*
  propia conservación *f*
self-raising [sɛlfˈreɪzɪŋ], **self-rising** (US)
  [sɛlfˈraɪzɪŋ] *adj*: ~ **flour** harina con levadura
self-respect [sɛlfrɪˈspɛkt] *n* amor *m* propio
self-righteous [sɛlfˈraɪtʃəs] *adj*
  santurrón(-ona)
self-sacrifice [sɛlfˈsækrɪfaɪs] *n* abnegación *f*
self-same [sɛlfseɪm] *adj* mismo, mismísimo
self-satisfied [sɛlfˈsætɪsfaɪd] *adj* satisfecho
  de sí mismo
self-service [sɛlfˈsəːvɪs] *adj* de autoservicio
self-sufficient [sɛlfsəˈfɪʃənt] *adj*
  autosuficiente
self-tanning [sɛlfˈtænɪŋ] *adj*
  autobronceador
self-taught [sɛlfˈtɔːt] *adj* autodidacta
sell (pt, pp **sold**) [sɛl, səuld] *vt* vender ▷ *vi*
  venderse; **to ~ at** *or* **for £10** venderse

a 10 libras; **to ~ sb an idea** (fig) convencer a
  algn de una idea; **sell off** *vt* liquidar; **sell out**
  vi transigir, transar (LAm); **to ~ out (to sb/**
  sth) (Comm) vender su negocio (a algn/algo)
  ▷ *vt* agotar las existencias de, venderlo todo;
  the tickets are all sold out las entradas
  están agotadas; **sell up** *vi* (Comm) liquidarse
sell-by date [ˈsɛlbaɪ-] *n* fecha de caducidad
seller [ˈsɛləʳ] *n* vendedor(a) *m(f)*; **~'s market**
  mercado de demanda
selling price [ˈsɛlɪŋ-] *n* precio de venta
Sellotape® [ˈsɛləuteɪp] *n* (Brit) cinta
  adhesiva, celo, scotch® *m*
sellout [ˈsɛlaut] *n* traición *f*; **it was a ~** (Theat
  etc) fue un éxito de taquilla
selves [sɛlvz] *npl of* **self**
semblance [ˈsɛmbləns] *n* apariencia
semen [ˈsiːmən] *n* semen *m*
semester [sɪˈmɛstəʳ] *n* (US) semestre *m*
semi [ˈsɛmɪ] *n* = **semidetached house**
semi... [ˈsɛmɪ] *pref* semi..., medio...
semicircle [ˈsɛmɪsəːkl] *n* semicírculo
semicolon [sɛmɪˈkəulən] *n* punto y coma
semiconductor [sɛmɪkənˈdʌktəʳ] *n*
  semiconductor *m*
semidetached [sɛmɪdɪˈtætʃt],
  semidetached house *n* casa adosada
semi-final [sɛmɪˈfaɪnl] *n* semifinal *f*
seminar [ˈsɛmɪnɑːʳ] *n* seminario
seminary [ˈsɛmɪnərɪ] *n* (Rel) seminario
semiskilled [ˈsɛmɪskɪld] *adj* (work, worker)
  semicualificado
semi-skimmed [ˈsɛmiˈskɪmd] *adj*
  semidesnatado
semi-skimmed (milk) *n* leche
  semidesnatada
Sen., sen. *abbr* = **senator**; **senior**
senate [ˈsɛnɪt] *n* senado; *see also* **Congress**
senator [ˈsɛnɪtəʳ] *n* senador(a) *m(f)*
send (pt, pp **sent**) [sɛnd, sɛnt] *vt* mandar,
  enviar; **to ~ by post** mandar por correo; **to ~**
  sb for sth mandar a algn a buscar algo; **to ~**
  word that ... avisar *or* mandar aviso de
  que ...; **she ~s (you) her love** te manda *or*
  envía cariñosos recuerdos; **to ~ sb to sleep/**
  into fits of laughter dormir/hacer reír a
  algn; **to ~ sb flying** echar a algn; **to ~ sth**
  flying tirar algo; **send away** *vt* (letter, goods)
  despachar; **send away for** *vt fus* pedir; **send**
  back *vt* devolver; **send for** *vt fus* mandar
  traer; (by post) escribir pidiendo algo; **send in**
  vt (report, application, resignation) mandar; **send**
  off *vt* (goods) despachar; (Brit Sport: player)
  expulsar; **send on** *vt* (letter) mandar, expedir;
  (luggage etc: in advance) facturar; **send out** *vt*
  (invitation) mandar; (emit: light, heat) emitir,
  difundir; (signal) emitir; **send round** *vt*
  (letter, document etc) hacer circular; **send up** *vt*
  (person, price) hacer subir; (Brit: parody) parodiar
sender [ˈsɛndəʳ] *n* remitente *m/f*
send-off [ˈsɛndɔf] *n*: **a good ~** una buena
  despedida

send-up ['sɛndʌp] *n* (*inf*) parodia, sátira

senile ['si:naɪl] *adj* senil

senior ['si:nɪər] *adj* (*older*) mayor, más viejo; (: *on staff*) de más antigüedad; (*of higher rank*) superior ▷ *n* mayor *m*; **P. Jones ~** P. Jones padre

senior citizen *n* persona de la tercera edad

senior high school *n* (*US*) ≈ instituto de enseñanza media

seniority [si:nɪ'ɒrɪtɪ] *n* antigüedad *f*; (*in rank*) rango superior

sensation [sɛn'seɪʃən] *n* (*physical feeling, impression*) sensación *f*

sensational [sɛn'seɪʃənl] *adj* sensacional

sense [sɛns] *n* (*faculty, meaning*) sentido; (*feeling*) sensación *f*; (*good sense*) sentido común, juicio ▷ *vt* sentir, percibir; **~ of humour** sentido del humor; **it makes ~** tiene sentido; **there is no ~ in (doing) that** no tiene sentido (hacer) eso; **to come to one's ~s** (*regain consciousness*) volver en sí, recobrar el sentido; **to take leave of one's ~s** perder el juicio

senseless ['sɛnslɪs] *adj* estúpido, insensato; (*unconscious*) sin conocimiento

sense of humour *n* (*Brit*) sentido del humor

sensibility [sɛnsɪ'bɪlɪtɪ] *n* sensibilidad *f*; **sensibilities** *npl* delicadeza *sg*

sensible ['sɛnsɪbl] *adj* sensato; (*reasonable*) razonable, lógico

sensibly ['sɛnsɪblɪ] *adv* sensatamente; razonablemente, de modo lógico

sensitive ['sɛnsɪtɪv] *adj* sensible; (*touchy*) susceptible; **he is very ~ about it** es muy susceptible acerca de eso

sensitivity [sɛnsɪ'tɪvɪtɪ] *n* sensibilidad *f*; susceptibilidad *f*

sensual ['sɛnsjuəl] *adj* sensual

sensuous ['sɛnsjuəs] *adj* sensual

sent [sɛnt] *pt, pp of* **send**

sentence ['sɛntəns] *n* (*Ling*) frase *f*, oración *f*; (*Law*) sentencia, fallo ▷ *vt*: **to ~ sb to death/ to five years** condenar a algn a muerte/a cinco años de cárcel; **to pass ~ on sb** (*also fig*) sentenciar *or* condenar a algn

sentiment ['sɛntɪmənt] *n* sentimiento; (*opinion*) opinión *f*

sentimental [sɛntɪ'mɛntl] *adj* sentimental

sentry ['sɛntrɪ] *n* centinela *m*

Sep. *abbr* (= *September*) sep., set.

separate [*adj* 'sɛprɪt, *vb* 'sɛpəreɪt] *adj* separado; (*distinct*) distinto ▷ *vt* separar; (*part*) dividir ▷ *vi* separarse; **~ from** separado *or* distinto de; **under ~ cover** (*Comm*) por separado; **to ~** dividir *or* separar en; **he is ~d from his wife, but not divorced** está separado de su mujer, pero no (está) divorciado

separately ['sɛprɪtlɪ] *adv* por separado

separates ['sɛprɪts] *npl* (*clothes*) coordinados *mpl*

separation [sɛpə'reɪʃən] *n* separación *f*

September [sɛp'tɛmbər] *n* se(p)tiembre *m*; *see also* **July**

septic ['sɛptɪk] *adj* séptico; **to go ~** ponerse séptico

septic tank *n* fosa séptica

sequel ['si:kwl] *n* consecuencia, resultado; (*of story*) continuación *f*

sequence ['si:kwəns] *n* sucesión *f*, serie *f*; (*Cine*) secuencia; **in ~** en orden *or* serie

sequin ['si:kwɪn] *n* lentejuela

Serb [sə:b] *adj, n* = **Serbian**

Serbia ['sə:bɪə] *n* Serbia

Serbian ['sə:bɪən] *adj* serbio ▷ *n* serbio(-a); (*Ling*) serbio

serenade [sɛrə'neɪd] *n* serenata ▷ *vt* dar serenata a

serene [sɪ'ri:n] *adj* sereno, tranquilo

sergeant ['sɑ:dʒənt] *n* sargento

serial ['sɪərɪəl] *n* novela por entregas; (*TV*) serie *f*

serial killer *n* asesino(-a) múltiple

serial number *n* número de serie

series ['sɪəri:z] *n pl inv* serie *f*

serious ['sɪərɪəs] *adj* serio; (*grave*) grave; **are you ~ (about it)?** ¿lo dices en serio?

seriously ['sɪərɪəslɪ] *adv* en serio; (*ill, wounded etc*) gravemente; (*inf: extremely*) de verdad; **to take sth/sb ~** tomar algo/a algn en serio; **he's ~ rich** es una pasada de rico

sermon ['sə:mən] *n* sermón *m*

serpent ['sə:pənt] *n* serpiente *f*

serrated [sɪ'reɪtɪd] *adj* serrado, dentellado

serum ['sɪərəm] *n* suero

servant ['sə:vənt] *n* (*gen*) servidor(a) *m(f)*; (*also:* **house ~**) criado(-a) *m(f)*

serve [sə:v] *vt* servir; (*customer*) atender; (*train*) tener parada en; (*apprenticeship*) hacer; (*prison term*) cumplir ▷ *vi* (*servant, soldier etc*) servir; (*Tennis*) sacar ▷ *n* (*Tennis*) saque *m*; **it ~s him right** se lo merece, se lo tiene merecido; **to ~ a summons on sb** entregar una citación a algn; **it ~s my purpose** me sirve para lo que quiero; **are you being ~d?** ¿le atienden?; **the power station ~s the entire region** la central eléctrica abastece a toda la región; **to ~ as/for/to do** servir de/para/para hacer; **to ~ on a committee/ a jury** ser miembro de una comisión/un jurado; **serve out, serve up** *vt* (*food*) servir

server *n* (*Comput*) servidor *m*

service ['sə:vɪs] *n* (*gen*) servicio; (*Rel: Catholic*) misa; (: *other*) oficio (religioso); (*Aut*) mantenimiento; (*of dishes*) juego ▷ *vt* (*car, washing machine*) revisar; (: *repair*) reparar; **the S~s** las fuerzas armadas; **funeral ~** exequias *fpl*; **to hold a ~** celebrar un oficio religioso; **the essential ~s** los servicios esenciales; **medical/social ~s** servicios *mpl* médicos/ sociales; **the train ~ to London** los trenes a Londres; **to be of ~ to sb** ser útil a algn; **~ included/not included** servicio incluido/ no incluido; **services** (*Econ: tertiary sector*)

sector *m* terciario *or* (de) servicios; (*Brit: on motorway*) área de servicio

serviceable ['sə:vɪsəbl] *adj* servible, utilizable

service area *n* (*on motorway*) área de servicios

service charge *n* (*Brit*) servicio

serviceman ['sə:vɪsmən] *n* militar *m*

service station *n* estación *f* de servicio

serviette [sə:vɪ'ɛt] *n* (*Brit*) servilleta

session ['sɛʃən] *n* (*sitting*) sesión *f*; **to be in ~** estar en sesión

set [sɛt] (*pt, pp* **set**) *n* juego; (*Radio*) aparato; (*TV*) televisor *m*; (*of utensils*) batería; (*of cutlery*) cubierto; (*of books*) colección *f*; (*Tennis*) set *m*; (*group of people*) grupo; (*Cine*) plató *m*; (*Theat*) decorado; (*Hairdressing*) marcado ▷ *adj* (*fixed*) fijo; (*ready*) listo; (*resolved*) resuelto, decidido ▷ *vt* (*place*) poner, colocar; (*fix*) fijar; (*adjust*) ajustar, arreglar; (*decide: rules etc*) establecer, decidir; (*assign: task*) asignar; (*: homework*) poner ▷ *vi* (*sun*) ponerse; (*jam, jelly*) cuajarse; (*concrete*) fraguar; **a ~ of false teeth** una dentadura postiza; **a ~ of dining-room furniture** muebles *mpl* de comedor; **~ in one's ways** con costumbres arraigadas; **a ~ phrase** una frase hecha; **to be all ~ to do sth** estar listo para hacer algo; **to be ~ on doing sth** estar empeñado en hacer algo; **a novel ~ in Valencia** una novela ambientada en Valencia; **to ~ to music** poner música a; **to ~ on fire** incendiar, prender fuego a; **to ~ free** poner en libertad; **to ~ sth going** poner algo en marcha; **to ~ sail** zarpar, hacerse a la mar; **set about** *vt fus*: **to ~ about doing sth** ponerse a hacer algo; **set aside** *vt* poner aparte, dejar de lado; **set back** *vt* (*progress*): **to ~ back (by)** retrasar (por); **a house ~ back from the road** una casa apartada de la carretera; **set down** *vt* (*bus, train*) dejar; (*record*) poner por escrito; **set in** *vi* (*infection*) declararse; (*complications*) comenzar; **the rain has ~ in for the day** parece que va a llover todo el día; **set off** *vi* partir ▷ *vt* (*bomb*) hacer estallar; (*cause to start*) poner en marcha; (*show up well*) hacer resaltar; **set out** *vi* partir ▷ *vt* (*arrange*) disponer; (*state*) exponer; **to ~ out to do sth** proponerse hacer algo; **to ~ out (from)** salir (de); **set up** *vt* (*organization*) establecer

setback ['sɛtbæk] *n* (*hitch*) revés *m*, contratiempo; (*in health*) recaída

set menu *n* menú *m*

set phrase *n* frase *f* hecha

settee [sɛ'ti:] *n* sofá *m*

setting ['sɛtɪŋ] *n* (*scenery*) marco; (*of jewel*) engaste *m*, montadura

settle ['sɛtl] *vt* (*argument, matter*) resolver; (*pay: bill, accounts*) pagar, liquidar; (*colonize: land*) colonizar; (*Med: calm*) calmar, sosegar ▷ *vi* (*dust etc*) depositarse; (*weather*) estabilizarse; **to ~ for sth** convenir en

aceptar algo; **to ~ on sth** decidirse por algo; **that's ~d then** bueno, está arreglado; **to ~ one's stomach** asentar el estómago; **settle down** *vi* (*get comfortable*) ponerse cómodo, acomodarse; (*calm down*) calmarse, tranquilizarse; (*live quietly*) echar raíces; **settle in** *vi* instalarse; **settle up** *vi*: **to ~ up with sb** ajustar cuentas con algn

settlement ['sɛtlmənt] *n* (*payment*) liquidación *f*; (*agreement*) acuerdo, convenio; (*village etc*) poblado; **in ~ of our account** (*Comm*) en pago *or* liquidación de nuestra cuenta

settler ['sɛtlə^r] *n* colono(-a), colonizador(a) *m(f)*

setup ['sɛtʌp] *n* sistema *m*

seven ['sɛvn] *num* siete

seventeen [sɛvn'ti:n] *num* diez y siete, diecisiete

seventeenth [sɛvn'ti:nθ] *adj* decimoséptimo

seventh ['sɛvnθ] *adj* séptimo

seventieth ['sɛvntɪθ] *adj* septuagésimo

seventy ['sɛvntɪ] *num* setenta

sever ['sɛvə^r] *vt* cortar; (*relations*) romper

several ['sɛvərl] *adj, pron* varios(-as) *m(f)pl*, algunos(-as) *m(f)pl*; **~ of us** varios de nosotros; **~ times** varias veces

severance ['sɛvərəns] *n* (*of relations*) ruptura

severance pay *n* indemnización *f* por despido

severe [sɪ'vɪə^r] *adj* severo; (*serious*) grave; (*hard*) duro; (*pain*) intenso

severity [sɪ'vɛrɪtɪ] *n* severidad *f*; gravedad *f*; intensidad *f*

Seville [sə'vɪl] *n* Sevilla

sew (*pt* sewed, *pp* sewn) [səu, səud, səun] *vt, vi* coser; **sew up** *vt* coser

sewage ['su:ɪdʒ] *n* (*effluence*) aguas *fpl* residuales; (*system*) alcantarillado

sewer ['su:ə^r] *n* alcantarilla, cloaca

sewing ['səuɪŋ] *n* costura

sewing machine *n* máquina de coser

sewn [səun] *pp* of **sew**

sex [sɛks] *n* sexo; **the opposite ~** el sexo opuesto; **to have ~** hacer el amor

sex appeal *n* sex-appeal *m*, gancho

sex education *n* educación *f* sexual

sexism ['sɛksɪzəm] *n* sexismo

sexist ['sɛksɪst] *adj, n* sexista *m/f*

sex life *n* vida sexual

sex object *n* objeto sexual

sexual ['sɛksjuəl] *adj* sexual; **~ assault** atentado contra el pudor; **~ harassment** acoso sexual; **~ intercourse** relaciones *fpl* sexuales

sexuality [sɛksju'ælɪtɪ] *n* sexualidad *f*

sexy ['sɛksɪ] *adj* sexy

shabby ['ʃæbɪ] *adj* (*person*) desharrapado; (*clothes*) raído, gastado

shack [ʃæk] *n* choza, chabola

shackles ['ʃæklz] *npl* grillos *mpl*, grilletes *mpl*

shade [ʃeɪd] n sombra; (for lamp) pantalla; (for eyes) visera; (of colour) tono m, tonalidad f; (US: window shade) persiana ▷ vt dar sombra a; **shades** npl (US: sunglasses) gafas fpl de sol; **in the ~** a la sombra; (small quantity): **a ~ of** un poquito de; **a ~ smaller** un poquito más pequeño

shadow [ˈʃædəu] n sombra ▷ vt (follow) seguir y vigilar; **without** or **beyond a ~ of doubt** sin lugar a dudas

shadow cabinet n (Brit Pol) gobierno en la oposición

shadowy [ˈʃædəʊɪ] adj oscuro; (dim) indistinto

shady [ˈʃeɪdɪ] adj sombreado; (fig: dishonest) sospechoso; (deal) turbio

shaft [ʃɑːft] n (of arrow, spear) astil m; (Aut, Tech) eje m, árbol m; (of mine) pozo; (of lift) hueco, caja; (of light) rayo; **ventilator ~** chimenea de ventilación

shaggy [ˈʃægɪ] adj peludo

shake [ʃeɪk] (pt **shook**, pp **shaken** [ˈʃeɪkn]) vt sacudir; (building) hacer temblar; (perturb) inquietar, perturbar; (weaken) debilitar; (alarm) trastornar ▷ vi estremecerse; (tremble) temblar ▷ n (movement) sacudida; **to ~ one's head** (in refusal) negar con la cabeza; (in dismay) mover or menear la cabeza, incrédulo; **to ~ hands with sb** estrechar la mano a algn; **to ~ in one's shoes** (fig) temblar de miedo; **shake off** vt sacudirse; (fig) deshacerse de; **shake up** vt agitar

shake-up [ˈʃeɪkʌp] n reorganización f

shaky [ˈʃeɪkɪ] adj (unstable) inestable, poco firme; (trembling) tembloroso; (health) delicado; (memory) defectuoso; (person: from illness) temblando; (premise etc) incierto

shall [ʃæl] aux vb: **I ~ go** iré; **~ I help you?** ¿quieres que te ayude?; **I'll buy three, ~ I?** compro tres, ¿no te parece?

shallot [ʃəˈlɔt] n (Brit) cebollita, chalote m

shallow [ˈʃæləʊ] adj poco profundo; (fig) superficial

sham [ʃæm] n fraude m, engaño ▷ adj falso, fingido ▷ vt fingir, simular

shambles [ˈʃæmblz] n desorden m, confusión f; **the economy is (in) a complete ~** la economía está en un estado desastroso

shame [ʃeɪm] n vergüenza; (pity) lástima, pena ▷ vt avergonzar; **it is a ~ that/to do** es una lástima or pena que/hacer; **what a ~!** ¡qué lástima or pena!; **to put sth/sb to ~** (fig) ridiculizar algo/a algn

shamefaced [ˈʃeɪmfeɪst] adj avergonzado

shameful [ˈʃeɪmful] adj vergonzoso

shameless [ˈʃeɪmlɪs] adj descarado

shampoo [ʃæmˈpuː] n champú m ▷ vt lavar con champú

shamrock [ˈʃæmrɔk] n trébol m

shandy [ˈʃændɪ], **shandygaff** (US) [ˈʃændɪgæf] n clara, cerveza con gaseosa

shan't [ʃɑːnt] = **shall not**

shanty town [ˈʃæntɪ-] n barrio de chabolas

shape [ʃeɪp] n forma ▷ vt formar, dar forma a; (clay) modelar; (stone) labrar; (sb's ideas) formar; (sb's life) determinar ▷ vi (also: **~ up**: events) desarrollarse; (person) formarse; **to take ~** tomar forma; **to get o.s. into ~** ponerse en forma or en condiciones; **in the ~ of a heart** en forma de corazón; **I can't bear gardening in any ~ or form** no aguanto la jardinería de ningún modo

shapeless [ˈʃeɪplɪs] adj informe, sin forma definida

shapely [ˈʃeɪplɪ] adj bien formado or proporcionado

share [ʃeəʳ] n (part) parte f, porción f; (contribution) cuota; (Comm) acción f ▷ vt dividir; (fig: have in common) compartir; **to have a ~ in the profits** tener una proporción de las ganancias; **he has a 50% ~ in a new business venture** tiene una participación del 50% en un nuevo negocio; **to ~ in** participar en; **to ~ out (among** or **between)** repartir (entre)

share certificate n certificado or título de una acción

shareholder [ˈʃeəhəʊldəʳ] n (Brit) accionista m/f

share issue n emisión f de acciones

shark [ʃɑːk] n tiburón m

sharp [ʃɑːp] adj (razor, knife) afilado; (point) puntiagudo; (outline) definido; (pain) intenso; (Mus) desafinado; (contrast) marcado; (voice) agudo; (curve, bend) cerrado; (person: quick-witted) avispado; (: dishonest) poco escrupuloso ▷ n (Mus) sostenido ▷ adv: **at two o'clock ~** a las dos en punto; **to be ~ with sb** hablar a algn de forma brusca y tajante; **turn ~ left** tuerce del todo a la izquierda

sharpen [ˈʃɑːpn] vt afilar; (pencil) sacar punta a; (fig) agudizar

sharpener [ˈʃɑːpnəʳ] n (gen) afilador m; (also: **pencil ~**) sacapuntas m inv

sharp-eyed [ʃɑːpˈaɪd] adj de vista aguda

sharply [ˈʃɑːplɪ] adv (abruptly) bruscamente; (clearly) claramente; (harshly) severamente

shatter [ˈʃætəʳ] vt hacer añicos or pedazos; (fig: ruin) destruir, acabar con ▷ vi hacerse añicos

shattered [ˈʃætəd] adj (grief-stricken) destrozado, deshecho; (exhausted) agotado, hecho polvo

shave [ʃeɪv] vt afeitar, rasurar ▷ vi afeitarse ▷ n: **to have a ~** afeitarse

shaver [ˈʃeɪvəʳ] n (also: **electric ~**) máquina de afeitar (eléctrica)

shaving [ˈʃeɪvɪŋ] n (action) afeitado; **shavings** npl (of wood etc) virutas fpl

shaving brush n brocha (de afeitar)

shaving cream n crema (de afeitar)

shaving foam n espuma de afeitar

shawl [ʃɔːl] n chal m

S

she [ʃiː] *pron* ella; **there ~ is** allí está; **~-cat** gata

sheaf (*pl* **sheaves**) [ʃiːf, ʃiːvz] *n* (*of corn*) gavilla; (*of arrows*) haz *m*; (*of papers*) fajo

shear [ʃɪərʳ] *vt* (*pt, pp* **sheared** *or* **shorn** [ʃɔːn]) (*sheep*) esquilar, trasquilar; **shear off** *vi* romperse

shears [ʃɪəz] *npl* (*for hedge*) tijeras *fpl* de jardín

sheath [ʃiːθ] *n* vaina; (*contraceptive*) preservativo

shed [ʃed] (*pt, pp* **shed**) *n* cobertizo; (*Industry, Rail*) nave *f* ▷ *vt* (*skin*) mudar; (*tears*) derramar; (*workers*) despedir; **to ~ light on** (*problem, mystery*) aclarar, arrojar luz sobre

she'd [ʃiːd] = **she had; she would**

sheen [ʃiːn] *n* brillo, lustre *m*

sheep [ʃiːp] *n pl inv* oveja

sheepdog [ʃiːpdɔg] *n* perro pastor

sheepish [ʃiːpɪʃ] *adj* tímido, vergonzoso

sheepskin [ʃiːpskɪn] *n* piel *f* de carnero

sheer [ʃɪərʳ] *adj* (*utter*) puro, completo; (*steep*) escarpado; (*material*) diáfano ▷ *adv* verticalmente; **by ~ chance** de pura casualidad

sheet [ʃiːt] *n* (*on bed*) sábana; (*of paper*) hoja; (*of glass, metal*) lámina

sheik, sheikh [ʃeɪk] *n* jeque *m*

shelf (*pl* **shelves**) [ʃelf, ʃelvz] *n* estante *m*

shelf life *n* (*Comm*) periodo de conservación antes de la venta

shell [ʃel] *n* (*on beach*) concha, caracol (*LAm*); (*of egg, nut etc*) cáscara; (*explosive*) proyectil *m*, obús *m*; (*of building*) armazón *m* ▷ *vt* (*peas*) desenvainar; (*Mil*) bombardear; **shell out** *vi* (*inf*): **to ~ out (for)** soltar el dinero (para), desembolsar (para)

she'll [ʃiːl] = **she will; she shall**

shellfish [ʃelfɪʃ] *n pl inv* crustáceo *pl* (*as food*) mariscos *mpl*

shellsuit [ʃelsuːt] *n* chándal *m* (de tactel®)

shelter [ʃeltərʳ] *n* abrigo, refugio ▷ *vt* (*aid*) amparar, proteger; (*give lodging to*) abrigar; (*hide*) esconder ▷ *vi* abrigarse, refugiarse; **to take ~ (from)** refugiarse *o* asilarse (de); **bus ~** parada de autobús cubierta

sheltered [ʃeltəd] *adj* (*life*) protegido; (*spot*) abrigado

shelve [ʃelv] *vt* (*fig*) dar carpetazo a

shelves [ʃelvz] *npl* of **shelf**

shelving [ʃelvɪŋ] *n* estantería

shepherd [ʃepəd] *n* pastor *m* ▷ *vt* (*guide*) guiar, conducir

shepherd's pie *n* pastel de carne y puré de patatas

sheriff [ʃerɪf] *n* (*US*) sheriff *m*

sherry [ʃerɪ] *n* jerez *m*

she's [ʃiːz] = **she is; she has**

Shetland [ʃetlənd] *n* (*also*: **the ~s, the ~ Isles**) las Islas *fpl* Shetland

Shetland pony *n* pony *m* de Shetland

shield [ʃiːld] *n* escudo; (*Tech*) blindaje *m* ▷ *vt*: **to ~ (from)** proteger (de)

shift [ʃɪft] *n* (*change*) cambio; (*at work*) turno ▷ *vt* trasladar; (*remove*) quitar ▷ *vi* moverse; (*change place*) cambiar de sitio; **the wind has ~ed to the south** el viento ha virado al sur; **a ~ in demand** (*Comm*) un desplazamiento de la demanda

shift work *n* (*Brit*) trabajo por turnos; **to do ~** trabajar por turnos

shifty [ʃɪftɪ] *adj* tramposo; (*eyes*) furtivo

Shiite [ʃiːaɪt] *adj, n* shiíta *m/f*

shilling [ʃɪlɪŋ] *n* (*Brit: formerly*) chelín *m* (= 12 peniques antiguos; una libra tenía 20 chelines)

shilly-shally [ʃɪlɪʃælɪ] *vi* titubear, vacilar

shimmer [ʃɪmərʳ] *n* reflejo trémulo ▷ *vi* relucir

shin [ʃɪn] *n* espinilla ▷ *vi*: **to ~ down/up a tree** bajar de/trepar a un árbol

shine [ʃaɪn] (*pt, pp* **shone**) *n* brillo, lustre *m* ▷ *vi* brillar, relucir ▷ *vt* (*shoes*) lustrar, sacar brillo a; **to ~ a torch on sth** dirigir una linterna hacia algo

shingle [ʃɪŋgl] *n* (*on beach*) guijarras *fpl*

shingles [ʃɪŋglz] *n* (*Med*) herpes *msg*

shiny [ʃaɪnɪ] *adj* brillante, lustroso

ship [ʃɪp] *n* buque *m*, barco ▷ *vt* (*goods*) embarcar; (*oars*) desarmar; (*send*) transportar *or* enviar por vía marítima; **~'s manifest** manifiesto del buque; **on board ~** a bordo

shipbuilding [ʃɪpbɪldɪŋ] *n* construcción *f* naval

shipment [ʃɪpmənt] *n* (*act*) embarque *m*; (*goods*) envío

shipper [ʃɪpərʳ] *n* compañía naviera

shipping [ʃɪpɪŋ] *n* (*act*) embarque *m*; (*traffic*) buques *mpl*

shipwreck [ʃɪprek] *n* naufragio ▷ *vt*: **to be ~ed** naufragar

shipyard [ʃɪpjɑːd] *n* astillero

shire [ʃaɪərʳ] *n* (*Brit*) condado

shirk [ʃəːk] *vt* eludir, esquivar; (*obligations*) faltar a

shirt [ʃəːt] *n* camisa; **in ~ sleeves** en mangas de camisa

shirty [ʃəːtɪ] *adj* (*Brit inf*): **to be ~** estar de malas pulgas

shit [ʃɪt] (*inf!*) *n* mierda (!); (*nonsense*) chorradas *fpl*; **to be a ~** ser un cabrón (!) ▷ *excl* ¡mierda! (!); **tough ~!** ¡te jodes! (!)

shiver [ʃɪvərʳ] *n* escalofrío ▷ *vi* temblar, estremecerse; (*with cold*) tiritar

shoal [ʃəul] *n* (*of fish*) banco

shock [ʃɔk] *n* (*impact*) choque *m*; (*Elec*) descarga (eléctrica); (*emotional*) conmoción *f*; (*start*) sobresalto, susto; (*Med*) postración *f* nerviosa ▷ *vt* dar una sacudida a; (*offend*) escandalizar; **to get a ~** (*Elec*) sentir una sacudida eléctrica; **to give sb a ~** dar un susto a algn; **to be suffering from ~** padecer una postración nerviosa; **it came as a ~ to hear that …** me etc asombró descubrir que …

shock absorber [-əbsɔːbəʳ] *n* amortiguador *m*

shocking ['ʃɒkɪŋ] adj (awful: weather, handwriting) espantoso, horrible; (improper) escandaloso; (result) inesperado
shock wave n onda expansiva or de choque
shod [ʃɒd] pt, pp of **shoe** ▷ adj calzado
shoddy ['ʃɒdɪ] adj de pacotilla
shoe [ʃuː] n (pt, pp shod [ʃɒd]) n zapato; (for horse) herradura; (brake shoe) zapata ▷ vt (horse) herrar
shoelace ['ʃuːleɪs] n cordón m
shoe polish n betún m
shoeshop ['ʃuːʃɒp] n zapatería
shoestring ['ʃuːstrɪŋ] n (shoelace) cordón m; (fig): **on a ~** con muy poco dinero, a lo barato
shone [ʃɒn] pt, pp of **shine**
shoo [ʃuː] excl ¡fuera!; (to animals) ¡zape! ▷ vt (also: **~ away**, **~ off**) ahuyentar
shook [ʃuk] pt of **shake**
shoot [ʃuːt] (pt, pp shot) n (on branch, seedling) retoño, vástago; (shooting party) cacería; (competition) concurso de tiro; (preserve) coto de caza ▷ vt disparar; (kill) matar a tiros; (execute) fusilar; (Cine: film, scene) rodar, filmar ▷ vi (Football) chutar; **to ~ (at)** tirar (a); **to ~ past** pasar como un rayo; **to ~ in/out** vi entrar corriendo/salir disparado; **shoot down** vt (plane) derribar; **shoot up** vi (prices) dispararse
shooting ['ʃuːtɪŋ] n (shots) tiros mpl, tiroteo; (Hunting) caza con escopeta; (act: murder) asesinato (a tiros); (Cine) rodaje m
shooting star n estrella fugaz
shop [ʃɒp] n tienda; (workshop) taller m ▷ vi (also: **go ~ping**) ir de compras; **to talk ~** (fig) hablar del trabajo; **repair ~** taller m de reparaciones; **shop around** vi comparar precios
shopaholic ['ʃɒpə'hɒlɪk] n (inf) adicto(-a) a las compras
shop assistant n (Brit) dependiente(-a) m(f)
shop floor n (Brit fig) taller m, fábrica
shopkeeper ['ʃɒpkiːpəʳ] n (Brit) tendero(-a)
shoplift ['ʃɒplɪft] vi robar en las tiendas
shoplifter ['ʃɒplɪftəʳ] n ratero(-a)
shoplifting ['ʃɒplɪftɪŋ] n ratería, robo (en las tiendas)
shopper ['ʃɒpəʳ] n comprador(a) m(f)
shopping ['ʃɒpɪŋ] n (goods) compras fpl
shopping bag n bolsa (de compras)
shopping centre, **shopping center** (US) n centro comercial
shopping mall n centro comercial
shopping trolley n (Brit) carrito de la compra
shop steward n (Brit Industry) enlace m/f sindical
shop window n escaparate m, vidriera (LAm)
shore [ʃɔːʳ] n (of sea, lake) orilla ▷ vt: **to ~ (up)** reforzar; **on ~** en tierra
shorn [ʃɔːn] pp of **shear**
short [ʃɔːt] adj (not long) corto; (in time) breve, de corta duración; (person) bajo; (curt) brusco,

seco ▷ vi (Elec) ponerse en cortocircuito ▷ n (also: **~ film**) cortometraje m; (**a pair of**) **~s** (unos) pantalones mpl cortos; **to be ~ of sth** estar falto de algo; **in ~** en pocas palabras; **a ~ time ago** hace poco (tiempo); **in the ~ term** a corto plazo; **to be in ~ supply** escasear, haber escasez de; **I'm ~ of time** me falta tiempo; **~ of doing ...** a menos que hagamos etc ...; **everything ~ of ...** todo menos ...; **it is ~ for** es la forma abreviada de; **to cut ~** (speech, visit) interrumpir, terminar inesperadamente; **to fall ~ of** no alcanzar; **to run ~ of sth** acabársele algo; **to stop ~** parar en seco; **to stop ~ of** detenerse antes de
shortage ['ʃɔːtɪdʒ] n escasez f, falta
shortbread ['ʃɔːtbrɛd] n galleta de mantequilla, especie de mantecada
short-change [ʃɔːt'tʃeɪndʒ] vt: **to ~ sb** no dar el cambio completo a algn
short-circuit [ʃɔːt'səːkɪt] n cortocircuito ▷ vt poner en cortocircuito ▷ vi ponerse, en cortocircuito
shortcoming ['ʃɔːtkʌmɪŋ] n defecto, deficiencia
shortcrust pastry ['ʃɔːtkrʌst-], **short pastry** n (Brit) pasta quebradiza
shortcut ['ʃɔːtkʌt] n atajo
shorten ['ʃɔːtn] vt acortar; (visit) interrumpir
shortfall ['ʃɔːtfɔːl] n déficit m, deficiencia
shorthand ['ʃɔːthænd] n (Brit) taquigrafía; **to take sth down in ~** taquigrafiar algo
shorthand typist n (Brit) taquimecanógrafo(-a)
short list n (Brit: for job) lista de candidatos pre-seleccionados
short-lived ['ʃɔːt'lɪvd] adj efímero
shortly ['ʃɔːtlɪ] adv en breve, dentro de poco
short-sighted [ʃɔːt'saɪtɪd] adj (Brit) miope, corto de vista; (fig) imprudente
short-sleeved adj de manga corta
short-staffed [ʃɔːt'stɑːft] adj falto de personal
short story n cuento
short-tempered [ʃɔːt'tɛmpəd] adj enojadizo
short-term ['ʃɔːttəːm] adj (effect) a corto plazo
short wave n (Radio) onda corta
shot [ʃɒt] pt, pp of **shoot** ▷ n (sound) tiro, disparo; (person) tirador(a) m(f); (try) tentativa; (injection) inyección f; (Phot) toma, fotografía; (shotgun pellets) perdigones mpl; **to fire a ~ at sb/sth** tirar or disparar contra algn/algo; **to have a ~ at (doing) sth** probar suerte con algo; **like a ~** (without any delay) como un rayo; **a big ~** (inf) un pez gordo; **to get ~ of sth/sb** (inf) deshacerse de algo/ algn, quitarse algo/a algn de encima
shotgun ['ʃɒtgʌn] n escopeta
should [ʃud] aux vb: **I ~ go now** debo irme ahora; **he ~ be there now** debe de haber llegado (ya); **I ~ go if I were you** yo en tu lugar me iría; **I ~ like to** me gustaría; **~ he**

phone ... si llamara ..., en caso de que llamase ...

shoulder ['ʃəʊldəʳ] n hombro; (Brit: of road): **hard ~ arcén** m ▷ vt (fig) cargar con; **to look over one's ~** mirar hacia atrás; **to rub ~s with sb** (fig) codearse con algn; **to give sb the cold ~** (fig) dar de lado a algn

shoulder bag n bolso de bandolera

shoulder blade n omóplato

shoulder strap n tirante m

shouldn't ['ʃʊdnt] = **should not**

shout [ʃaʊt] n grito ▷ vt gritar ▷ vi gritar, dar voces; **shout down** vt hundir a gritos

shouting ['ʃaʊtɪŋ] n griterío

shouting match n (inf) discusión f a voz en grito

shove [ʃʌv] n empujón m ▷ vt empujar; (inf: put): **to ~ sth in** meter algo a empellones; **he ~d me out of the way** me quitó de en medio de un empujón; **shove off** vi (Naut) alejarse del muelle; (fig: inf) largarse

shovel ['ʃʌvl] n pala; (mechanical) excavadora ▷ vt mover con pala

show [ʃəʊ] (pt **showed**, pp **shown**) n (of emotion) demostración f; (semblance) apariencia; (Comm, Tech: exhibition) exhibición f, exposición f; (Theat) función f, espectáculo; (organization) negocio, empresa ▷ vt mostrar, enseñar; (courage etc) mostrar, manifestar; (exhibit) exponer; (film) proyectar ▷ vi mostrarse; (appear) aparecer; **on ~** (exhibits etc) expuesto; **to be on ~** estar expuesto; **it's just for ~** es sólo para impresionar; **to ask for a ~ of hands** pedir una votación a mano alzada; **who's running the ~ here?** ¿quién manda aquí?; **to ~ a profit/loss** (Comm) arrojar un saldo positivo/negativo; **I have nothing to ~ for it** no saqué ningún provecho (de ello); **to ~ sb to his seat/to the door** acompañar a algn a su asiento/a la puerta; **as ~n in the illustration** como se ve en el grabado; **it just goes to ~ that ...** queda demostrado que ...; **it doesn't ~** no se ve or nota; **show in** vt (person) hacer pasar; **show off** vi (pej) presumir ▷ vt (display) lucir; (pej) hacer alarde de; **show out** vt: **to ~ sb out** acompañar a algn a la puerta; **show up** vi (stand out) destacar; (inf: turn up) presentarse ▷ vt descubrir; (unmask) desenmascarar

showbiz ['ʃəʊbɪz] n (inf) = **show business**

show business n el mundo del espectáculo

showdown ['ʃəʊdaʊn] n crisis f, momento decisivo

shower ['ʃaʊəʳ] n (rain) chaparrón m, chubasco; (of stones etc) lluvia; (also: ~ bath) ducha ▷ vi llover ▷ vt: **to ~ sb with sth** colmar a algn de algo; **to have** or **take a ~** ducharse

shower cap n gorro de baño

shower gel n gel de ducha

showery ['ʃaʊərɪ] adj (weather) lluvioso

showing ['ʃəʊɪŋ] n (of film) proyección f

show jumping n hípica

shown [ʃəʊn] pp of **show**

show-off ['ʃəʊɒf] n (inf: person) fanfarrón(-ona) m(f)

showpiece ['ʃəʊpiːs] n (of exhibition etc) objeto más valioso, joya; **that hospital is a ~** hospital es un modelo del género

showroom ['ʃəʊruːm] n sala de muestras

show trial n juicio propagandístico

shrank [ʃræŋk] pt of **shrink**

shrapnel ['ʃræpnl] n metralla

shred [ʃred] n gen pl triza, jirón m; (fig: of truth, evidence) pizca, chispa ▷ vt hacer trizas; (documents) triturar; (Culin) desmenuzar

shredder ['ʃredəʳ] n (vegetable shredder) picadora; (document shredder) trituradora (de papel)

shrewd [ʃruːd] adj astuto

shriek [ʃriːk] n chillido ▷ vt, vi chillar

shrill [ʃrɪl] adj agudo, estridente

shrimp [ʃrɪmp] n camarón m

shrine [ʃraɪn] n santuario, sepulcro

shrink (pt **shrank**, pp **shrunk**) [ʃrɪŋk, ʃræŋk, ʃrʌŋk] vi encogerse; (be reduced) reducirse ▷ vt encoger ▷ n (inf, pej) loquero(-a); **to ~ from (doing) sth** no atreverse a hacer algo; **shrink away** vi retroceder, retirarse

shrinkage ['ʃrɪŋkɪdʒ] n encogimiento; reducción f; (Comm: in shops) pérdidas fpl

shrink-wrap ['ʃrɪŋkræp] vt empaquetar en envase termorretráctil

shrivel ['ʃrɪvl] (also: ~ **up**) vt (dry) secar; (crease) arrugar ▷ vi secarse; arrugarse

shroud [ʃraʊd] n sudario ▷ vt: **~ed in mystery** envuelto en el misterio

Shrove Tuesday ['ʃrəʊv-] n martes m de carnaval

shrub [ʃrʌb] n arbusto

shrubbery ['ʃrʌbərɪ] n arbustos mpl

shrug [ʃrʌg] n encogimiento de hombros ▷ vt, vi: **to ~ (one's shoulders)** encogerse de hombros; **shrug off** vt negar importancia a; (cold, illness) deshacerse de

shrunk [ʃrʌŋk] pp of **shrink**

shrunken ['ʃrʌŋkn] adj encogido

shudder ['ʃʌdəʳ] n estremecimiento, escalofrío ▷ vi estremecerse

shuffle ['ʃʌfl] vt (cards) barajar; **to ~ (one's feet)** arrastrar los pies

shun [ʃʌn] vt rehuir, esquivar

shunt [ʃʌnt] vt (Rail) maniobrar

shut (pt, pp **shut**) [ʃʌt] vt cerrar ▷ vi cerrarse; **shut down** vt, ▷ vi cerrar; (machine) parar; **shut off** vt (stop: power, water supply etc) interrumpir, cortar; (engine) parar; **shut out** vt (person) excluir, dejar fuera; (noise, cold) no dejar entrar; (block: view) tapar; (memory) tratar de olvidar; **shut up** vi (inf: keep quiet) callarse ▷ vt (close) cerrar; (silence) callar

shutter ['ʃʌtəʳ] n contraventana; (Phot) obturador m

shuttle [ˈʃʌtl] n lanzadera; (also: ~ **service**: Aviat) puente m aéreo ▷ vi (vehicle, person) ir y venir ▷ vt (passengers) transportar, trasladar
shuttlecock [ˈʃʌtlkɔk] n volante m
shy [ʃaɪ] adj tímido ▷ vi: **to ~ away from doing sth** (fig) rehusar hacer algo; **to be ~ of doing sth** esquivar hacer algo
Siberia [saɪˈbɪərɪə] n Siberia
sibling [ˈsɪblɪŋ] n (formal) hermano(-a)
Sicily [ˈsɪsɪlɪ] n Sicilia
sick [sɪk] adj (ill) enfermo; (nauseated) mareado; (humour) morboso; **to be ~** (Brit) vomitar; **to feel ~** tener náuseas; **to be ~ of** (fig) estar harto de; **a ~ person** un(a) enfermo(-a); **to be (off) ~** estar ausente por enfermedad; **to fall** or **take ~** ponerse enfermo
sickbag [ˈsɪkbæg] n bolsa para el mareo
sick bay n enfermería
sick building syndrome n enfermedad causada por falta de ventilación y luz natural en un edificio
sicken [ˈsɪkn] vt dar asco a ▷ vi enfermar; **to be ~ing for** (cold, flu etc) mostrar síntomas de
sickening [ˈsɪknɪŋ] adj (fig) asqueroso
sickle [ˈsɪkl] n hoz f
sick leave n baja por enfermedad
sickly [ˈsɪklɪ] adj enfermizo; (taste) empalagoso
sickness [ˈsɪknɪs] n enfermedad f, mal m; (vomiting) náuseas fpl
sick pay n prestación por enfermedad pagada por la empresa
side [saɪd] n (gen) lado; (face, surface) cara; (of paper) cara; (slice of bread) rebanada; (of body) costado; (of animal) ijar m, ijada; (of lake) orilla; (part) lado; (aspect) aspecto; (team: Sport) equipo; (: Pol etc) partido; (of hill) ladera ▷ adj (door, entrance) lateral ▷ vi: **to ~ with sb** tomar partido por algn; **by the ~ of** al lado de; **~ by ~** juntos(-as); **from all ~s** de todos lados; **to take ~s (with)** tomar partido (por); **~ of beef** flanco de vaca; **the right/wrong ~** el derecho/revés; **from ~ to ~** de un lado a otro
sideboard [ˈsaɪdbɔːd] n aparador m
sideboards [ˈsaɪdbɔːdz], **sideburns** (Brit) [ˈsaɪdbəːnz] npl patillas fpl
side effect n efecto secundario
sidelight [ˈsaɪdlaɪt] n (Aut) luz f lateral
sideline [ˈsaɪdlaɪn] n (Sport) línea de banda; (fig) empleo suplementario
sidelong [ˈsaɪdlɔŋ] adj de soslayo; **to give a ~ glance at sth** mirar algo de reojo
side road n (Brit) calle f lateral
side-saddle [ˈsaɪdsædl] adv a la amazona
side show n (stall) caseta; (fig) atracción f secundaria
sidestep [ˈsaɪdstep] vt (question) eludir; (problem) esquivar ▷ vi (Boxing etc) dar un quiebro

side street n calle f lateral
sidetrack [ˈsaɪdtræk] vt (fig) desviar (de su propósito)
sidewalk [ˈsaɪdwɔːk] n (US) acera, vereda (LAm), andén m (LAm), banqueta (LAm)
sideways [ˈsaɪdweɪz] adv de lado
siding [ˈsaɪdɪŋ] n (Rail) apartadero, vía muerta
sidle [ˈsaɪdl] vi: **to ~ up (to)** acercarse furtivamente (a)
siege [siːdʒ] n cerco, sitio; **to lay ~ to** cercar, sitiar
sieve [sɪv] n colador m ▷ vt cribar
sift [sɪft] vt cribar ▷ vi: **to ~ through** (information) examinar cuidadosamente
sigh [saɪ] n suspiro ▷ vi suspirar
sight [saɪt] n (faculty) vista; (spectacle) espectáculo; (on gun) mira, alza ▷ vt ver, divisar; **in ~** a la vista; **out of ~** fuera de (la) vista; **at ~** a la vista; **at first ~** a primera vista; **to lose ~ of sth/sb** perder algo/a algn de vista; **to catch ~ of sth/sb** divisar algo/ a algn; **I know her by ~** la conozco de vista; **to set one's ~s on (doing) sth** aspirar a or ambicionar (hacer) algo
sightseeing [ˈsaɪtsiːɪŋ] n turismo; **to go ~** hacer turismo
sign [saɪn] n (with hand) señal f, seña; (trace) huella, rastro; (notice) letrero; (written) signo; (also: **road ~**) indicador m; (: with instructions) señal f de tráfico ▷ vt firmar; (Sport) fichar; **as a ~ of** en señal de; **it's a good/bad ~** es buena/mala señal; **plus/minus ~** signo de más/de menos; **to ~ one's name** firmar; **sign away** vt (rights etc) ceder; **sign in** vi firmar el registro (al entrar); **sign off** vi (Radio, TV) cerrar el programa; **sign on** vi (Mil) alistarse; (as unemployed) apuntarse al paro; (employee) firmar un contrato ▷ vt (Mil) alistar; (employee) contratar; **to ~ on for a course** matricularse en un curso; **sign out** vi firmar el registro (al salir); **sign over** vt: **to ~ sth over to sb** traspasar algo a algn; **sign up** vi (Mil) alistarse; (for course) inscribirse ▷ vt (player) fichar; (contract) contratar
signal [ˈsɪgnl] n señal f ▷ vi (Aut) señalizar ▷ vt (person) hacer señas a; (message) transmitir; **the engaged ~** (Tel) la señal de comunicando; **the ~ is very weak** (TV) no captamos bien el canal; **to ~ a left/right turn** (Aut) indicar que se va a doblar a la izquierda/derecha; **to ~ to sb (to do sth)** hacer señas a algn (para que haga algo)
signalman [ˈsɪgnlmən] n (Rail) guardavía m
signature [ˈsɪgnətʃəʳ] n firma
signature tune n sintonía
signet ring [ˈsɪgnət-] n (anillo de) sello
significance [sɪgˈnɪfɪkəns] n significado; (importance) trascendencia; **that is of no ~** eso no tiene importancia
significant [sɪgˈnɪfɪkənt] adj significativo; (important) trascendente; **it is ~ that ...** es significativo que ...

S

signify ['sɪgnɪfaɪ] vt significar
sign language n mímica, lenguaje m por or de señas
signpost ['saɪnpəʊst] n indicador m
Sikh [siːk] adj, n sij m/f
silence ['saɪlns] n silencio ▷ vt hacer callar, acallar; (guns) reducir al silencio
silencer ['saɪlnsə^r] n silenciador m
silent ['saɪlnt] adj (gen) silencioso; (not speaking) callado; (film) mudo; **to keep** or **remain ~** guardar silencio
silent partner n (Comm) socio(-a) comanditario(-a)
silhouette [sɪluːˈet] n silueta; **~d against** destacado sobre or contra
silicon ['sɪlɪkən] n silicio
silicon chip n chip m, plaqueta de silicio
silicone ['sɪlɪkəʊn] n silicona
silk [sɪlk] n seda ▷ cpd de seda
silky ['sɪlkɪ] adj sedoso
silly ['sɪlɪ] adj (person) tonto; (idea) absurdo; **to do sth ~** hacer una tontería
silt [sɪlt] n sedimento
silver ['sɪlvə^r] n plata; (money) moneda suelta ▷ adj de plata
silver foil, silver paper (Brit) n papel m de plata
silver-plated [sɪlvə'pleɪtɪd] adj plateado
silversmith ['sɪlvəsmɪθ] n platero(-a)
silvery ['sɪlvrɪ] adj plateado
SIM card ['sɪm-] n (Tel) SIM card m of, tarjeta SIM
similar ['sɪmɪlə^r] adj: **~ to** parecido or semejante a
similarity [sɪmɪˈlærɪtɪ] n parecido, semejanza
similarly ['sɪmɪləlɪ] adv del mismo modo; (in a similar way) de manera parecida; (equally) igualmente
simile ['sɪmɪlɪ] n símil m
simmer ['sɪmə^r] vi hervir a fuego lento; **simmer down** vi (fig, inf) calmarse, tranquilizarse
simple ['sɪmpl] adj (easy) sencillo; (foolish) simple; (Comm) simple; **the ~ truth** la pura verdad
simplicity [sɪm'plɪsɪtɪ] n sencillez f; (foolishness) ingenuidad f
simplify ['sɪmplɪfaɪ] vt simplificar
simply ['sɪmplɪ] adv (in a simple way: live, talk) sencillamente; (just, merely) sólo
simulate ['sɪmjuleɪt] vt simular
simultaneous [sɪməl'teɪnɪəs] adj simultáneo
simultaneously [sɪməl'teɪnɪəslɪ] adv simultáneamente, a la vez
sin [sɪn] n pecado ▷ vi pecar
since [sɪns] adv desde entonces ▷ prep desde ▷ conj (time) desde que; (because) ya que, puesto que; **~ then, ever ~** desde entonces; **~ Monday** desde el lunes; (ever) **~ I arrived** desde que llegué

sincere [sɪn'sɪə^r] adj sincero
sincerely [sɪn'sɪəlɪ] adv sinceramente; **yours ~** (in letters) le saluda (afectuosamente); **~ yours** (US: in letters) le saluda atentamente
sincerity [sɪn'serɪtɪ] n sinceridad f
sinew ['sɪnjuː] n tendón m
sinful ['sɪnful] adj (thought) pecaminoso; (person) pecador(a)
sing (pt **sang**, pp **sung**) [sɪŋ, sæŋ, sʌŋ] vt cantar ▷ vi (gen) cantar; (bird) trinar; (ears) zumbar
Singapore [sɪŋə'pɔː^r] n Singapur m
singe [sɪndʒ] vt chamuscar
singer ['sɪŋə^r] n cantante m/f
singing ['sɪŋɪŋ] n (of person, bird) canto; (songs) canciones fpl; (in the ears) zumbido; (of kettle) silbido
single ['sɪŋgl] adj único, solo; (unmarried) soltero; (not double) individual, sencillo ▷ n (Brit: also: **~ ticket**) billete m sencillo; (record) sencillo, single m; **singles** npl (Tennis) individual msg; **not a ~ one was left** no quedaba ni uno; **every ~ day** todos los días (sin excepción); **single out** vt (choose) escoger; (point out) singularizar
single bed n cama individual
single-breasted [sɪŋgl'brestɪd] adj (jacket, suit) recto, sin cruzar
single file n: **in ~** en fila de uno
single-handed [sɪŋgl'hændɪd] adv sin ayuda
single-minded [sɪŋgl'maɪndɪd] adj resuelto, firme
single parent n (mother) madre f soltera; (father) padre m soltero; **~ family** familia monoparental
single room n habitación f individual
singly ['sɪŋglɪ] adv uno por uno
singular ['sɪŋgjulə^r] adj singular, extraordinario, raro, extraño; (outstanding) excepcional; (Ling) singular ▷ n (Ling) singular m; **in the feminine ~** en femenino singular
sinister ['sɪnɪstə^r] adj siniestro
sink [sɪŋk] (pt **sank**, pp **sunk**) n fregadero ▷ vt (ship) hundir, echar a pique; (foundations) excavar; (piles etc): **to ~ sth into** hundir algo en ▷ vi (gen) hundirse; **he sank into a chair/the mud** se dejó caer en una silla/se hundió en el barro; **the shares** or **share prices have sunk to three dollars** las acciones han bajado a tres dólares; **sink in** vi (fig) penetrar, calar; **the news took a long time to ~ in** la noticia tardó mucho en hacer mella en él (or mí etc)
sinner ['sɪnə^r] n pecador(a) m(f)
sinus ['saɪnəs] n (Anat) seno
sip [sɪp] n sorbo ▷ vt sorber, beber a sorbitos
siphon ['saɪfən] n sifón m ▷ vt (also: **~ off**: funds) desviar
sir [sə:^r] n señor m; **S~ John Smith** el Señor John Smith; **yes ~** sí, señor; **Dear S~** (in letter)

Muy señor mío, Estimado Señor; **Dear S~s** Muy señores nuestros, Estimados Señores

siren ['saɪərn] n sirena

sirloin ['sə:lɔɪn] n solomillo

sirloin steak n filete m de solomillo

sissy ['sɪsɪ] n (inf) marica m

sister ['sɪstər] n hermana; (Brit: nurse) enfermera jefe

sister-in-law ['sɪstərɪnlɔ:] n cuñada

sit (pt, pp **sat**) [sɪt, sæt] vi sentarse; (be sitting) estar sentado; (assembly) reunirse; (dress etc) caer, sentar; (for painter) posar ▷ vt (exam) presentarse a; **that jacket ~s well** esa chaqueta sienta bien; **to ~ on a committee** ser miembro de una comisión or un comité; **sit about, sit around** vi holgazanear; **sit back** vi (in seat) recostarse; **sit down** vi sentarse; **to be ~ting down** estar sentado; **sit in on** vt fus: **to ~ in on a discussion** asistir a una discusión; **sit on** vt fus (jury, committee) ser miembro de, formar parte de; **sit up** vi incorporarse; (not go to bed) no acostarse

sitcom ['sɪtkɔm] n abbr (TV: = situation comedy) telecomedia

site [saɪt] n sitio; (also: **building ~**) solar m ▷ vt situar

sit-in ['sɪtɪn] n (demonstration) sentada f

sitting ['sɪtɪŋ] n (of assembly etc) sesión f; (in canteen) turno

sitting room n sala de estar

situated ['sɪtjueɪtɪd] adj situado, ubicado (LAm)

situation [sɪtju'eɪʃən] n situación f; **"~s vacant"** (Brit) "ofertas de trabajo"

situation comedy n (TV, Radio) serie f cómica, comedia de situación

six [sɪks] num seis

sixteen [sɪks'ti:n] num dieciséis

sixteenth [sɪks'ti:nθ] adj decimosexto

sixth [sɪksθ] adj sexto; **the upper/lower ~** (Scol) el séptimo/sexto año

sixth form n (Brit) clase f de alumnos del sexto año (de 16 a 18 años de edad)

sixth-form college n instituto m para alumnos de 16 a 18 años

sixtieth ['sɪkstɪɪθ] adj sexagésimo

sixty ['sɪkstɪ] num sesenta

size [saɪz] n (gen) tamaño; (extent) extensión f; (of clothing) talla; (of shoes) número; **I take ~ 5 shoes** calzo el número cinco; **I take ~ 14** mi talla es la 42; **I'd like the small/large ~** (of soap powder etc) quisiera el tamaño pequeño/grande; **size up** vt formarse una idea de

sizeable ['saɪzəbl] adj importante, considerable

sizzle ['sɪzl] vi crepitar

skate [skeɪt] n patín m; (fish) pl inv raya ▷ vi patinar; **skate over, skate round** vt fus (problem, issue) pasar por alto

skateboard ['skeɪtbɔ:d] n monopatín m

skateboarding n monopatín m

skater ['skeɪtər] n patinador(a) m(f)

skating ['skeɪtɪŋ] n patinaje m; **figure ~** patinaje m artístico

skating rink n pista de patinaje

skeleton ['skelɪtn] n esqueleto; (Tech) armazón m; (outline) esquema m

skeleton staff n personal m reducido

skeptic etc ['skeptɪk] (US) = **sceptic** etc

sketch [sketʃ] n (drawing) dibujo; (outline) esbozo, bosquejo; (Theat) pieza corta, sketch m ▷ vt dibujar; (plan etc: also: **~ out**) esbozar

sketch book n bloc m de dibujo

sketchy ['sketʃɪ] adj incompleto

skewer ['skju:ər] n broqueta

ski [ski:] n esquí m ▷ vi esquiar

ski boot n bota de esquí

skid [skɪd] n patinazo ▷ vi patinar; **to go into a ~** comenzar a patinar

skier ['ski:ər] n esquiador(a) m(f)

skiing ['ski:ɪŋ] n esquí m; **to go ~** practicar el esquí, (ir a) esquiar

ski jump n pista para salto de esquí

skilful, skillful (US) ['skɪlful] adj diestro, experto

ski lift n telesilla m, telesquí m

skill [skɪl] n destreza, pericia; (technique) arte m, técnica; **there's a certain ~ to doing it** se necesita cierta habilidad para hacerlo

skilled [skɪld] adj hábil, diestro; (worker) cualificado

skillful ['skɪlful] (US) = **skilful**

skim [skɪm] vt (milk) desnatar; (glide over) rozar, rasar ▷ vi: **to ~ through** (book) hojear

skimmed milk [skɪmd-] n leche f desnatada or descremada

skimp [skɪmp] vt (work) chapucear; (cloth etc) escatimar; **to ~ on** (material etc) economizar; (work) escatimar

skimpy ['skɪmpɪ] adj (meagre) escaso; (skirt) muy corto

skin [skɪn] n (gen) piel f; (complexion) cutis m; (of fruit, vegetable) piel f, cáscara; (crust: on pudding, paint) nata ▷ vt (fruit etc) pelar; (animal) despellejar; **wet** or **soaked to the ~** calado hasta los huesos

skin cancer n cáncer m de piel

skin-deep ['skɪn'di:p] adj superficial

skin diving n buceo

skinhead ['skɪnhed] n cabeza m/f rapada, skin(head) m/f

skinny ['skɪnɪ] adj flaco, magro

skintight ['skɪntaɪt] adj (dress etc) muy ajustado

skip [skɪp] n brinco, salto; (container) contenedor m ▷ vi brincar; (with rope) saltar a la comba ▷ vt (pass over) omitir, saltarse

ski pants npl pantalones mpl de esquí

ski pass n forfait m (de esquí)

ski pole n bastón m de esquiar

skipper ['skɪpər] n (Naut, Sport) capitán m

skipping rope ['skɪpɪŋ-] n (Brit) comba, cuerda (de saltar)

S

skirmish | 584

skirmish ['skə:mɪʃ] n escaramuza
skirt [skə:t] n falda, pollera (LAm) ▷ vt
  (surround) ceñir, rodear; (go round) ladear
skirting board ['skə:tɪŋ-] n (Brit) rodapié m
ski slope n pista de esquí
ski suit n traje m de esquiar
skittle ['skɪtl] n bolo; **~s** (game) boliche m
skive [skaɪv] vi (Brit: inf) gandulear
skulk [skʌlk] vi esconderse
skull [skʌl] n calavera; (Anat) cráneo
skunk [skʌŋk] n mofeta
sky [skaɪ] n cielo; **to praise sb to the skies**
  poner a algn por las nubes
skydiving ['skaɪdaɪvɪŋ] n paracaidismo
  acrobático
sky-high ['skaɪ'haɪ] adj (inf) por las nubes
  ▷ adv (throw) muy alto; **prices have gone ~**
  (inf) los precios están por las nubes
skylight ['skaɪlaɪt] n tragaluz m, claraboya
skyline ['skaɪlaɪn] n (horizon) horizonte m; (of
  city) perfil m
skyscraper ['skaɪskreɪpəʳ] n rascacielos m inv
slab [slæb] n (stone) bloque m; (of wood) tabla,
  plancha; (flat) losa; (of cake) trozo; (of meat,
  cheese) tajada, trozo
slack [slæk] adj (loose) flojo; (slow) de poca
  actividad; (careless) descuidado; (Comm:
  market) poco activo; (: demand) débil; (period)
  bajo; **business is ~** hay poco movimiento en
  el negocio
slacken ['slækn] (also: **~ off**) vi aflojarse ▷ vt
  aflojar; (speed) disminuir
slacks [slæks] npl pantalones mpl
slag [slæg] n escoria, escombros mpl
slag heap n escorial m, escombrera
slain [sleɪn] pp of **slay**
slam [slæm] vt (door) cerrar de golpe; (throw)
  arrojar (violentamente); (criticize) vapulear,
  vituperar ▷ vi cerrarse de golpe; **to ~ the
  door** dar un portazo
slander ['slɑːndəʳ] n calumnia, difamación f
  ▷ vt calumniar, difamar
slang [slæŋ] n argot m; (jargon) jerga
slanging match ['slæŋɪŋ-] n (Brit inf) bronca
  gorda
slant [slɑːnt] n sesgo, inclinación f; (fig)
  punto de vista, interpretación f; **to get a
  new ~ on sth** obtener un nuevo punto de
  vista sobre algo
slanted ['slɑːntɪd], **slanting** ['slɑːntɪŋ] adj
  inclinado
slap [slæp] n palmada; (in face) bofetada ▷ vt
  dar una palmada/bofetada a; (paint etc): **to ~
  sth on sth** embadurnar algo con algo ▷ adv
  (directly) de lleno
slapdash ['slæpdæʃ] adj chapucero
slapstick ['slæpstɪk] n: **~ comedy** comedia de
  payasadas
slap-up ['slæpʌp] adj: **a ~ meal** (Brit) un
  banquetazo, una comilona
slash [slæʃ] vt acuchillar; (fig: prices) fulminar
slat [slæt] n (of wood, plastic) tablilla, listón m

slate [sleɪt] n pizarra ▷ vt (Brit: fig: criticize)
  vapulear
slaughter ['slɔːtəʳ] n (of animals) matanza;
  (of people) carnicería ▷ vt matar
slaughterhouse ['slɔːtəhaus] n matadero
Slav [slɑːv] adj eslavo
slave [sleɪv] n esclavo(-a) ▷ vi (also: **~ away**)
  trabajar como un negro; **to ~ (away) at sth**
  trabajar como un negro en algo
slave driver n (inf, pej) tirano(-a)
slavery ['sleɪvərɪ] n esclavitud f
slavish ['sleɪvɪʃ] adj (devotion) de esclavo;
  (imitation) servil
slay (pt **slew**, pp **slain**) [sleɪ, slu:, sleɪn] vt
  (literary) matar
sleazy ['sliːzɪ] adj (fig: place) sórdido
sledge [sledʒ], **sled** (US) [sled] n trineo
sledgehammer ['sledʒhæməʳ] n mazo
sleek [sliːk] adj (shiny) lustroso
sleep [sliːp] (pt, pp **slept**) n sueño ▷ vi dormir
  ▷ vt: **we can ~ 4** podemos alojar a 4, tenemos
  cabida para 4; **to go to ~** dormirse; **to have
  a good night's ~** dormir toda la noche; **to
  put to ~** (patient) dormir; (animal: euphemism:
  kill) sacrificar; **to ~ lightly** tener el sueño
  ligero; **to ~ with sb** (euphemism) acostarse
  con algn; **sleep in** vi (oversleep) quedarse
  dormido
sleeper ['sliːpəʳ] n (person) durmiente m/f;
  (Brit Rail: on track) traviesa; (: train) coche-
  cama m
sleeping bag ['sliːpɪŋ-] n saco de dormir
sleeping car n coche-cama m
sleeping partner n (Comm) socio(-a)
  comanditario(-a)
sleeping pill n somnífero
sleepless ['sliːplɪs] adj: **a ~ night** una noche
  en blanco
sleepover ['sliːpəuvəʳ] n: **we're having a ~ at
  Fiona's** nos quedamos a dormir en casa de
  Fiona
sleepwalk ['sliːpwɔːk] vi caminar dormido;
  (habitually) ser sonámbulo
sleepwalker ['sliːpwɔːkəʳ] n sonámbulo(-a)
sleepy ['sliːpɪ] adj soñoliento; (place)
  soporífero; **to be** or **feel ~** tener sueño
sleet [sliːt] n aguanieve f
sleeve [sliːv] n manga; (Tech) manguito; (of
  record) funda
sleeveless ['sliːvlɪs] adj (garment) sin mangas
sleigh [sleɪ] n trineo
sleight [slaɪt] n: **~ of hand** prestidigitación f
slender ['slendəʳ] adj delgado; (means) escaso
slept [slept] pt, pp of **sleep**
slew [sluː] vi (veer) torcerse ▷ pt of **slay**
slice [slaɪs] n (of meat) tajada; (of bread)
  rebanada; (of lemon) rodaja; (utensil) paleta
  ▷ vt cortar, tajar; rebanar; **~d bread** pan m de
  molde
slick [slɪk] adj (skilful) hábil, diestro; (clever)
  astuto ▷ n (also: **oil ~**) marea negra
slid [slɪd] pt, pp of **slide**

slide [slaɪd] (*pt, pp* **slid**) *n* (*in playground*) tobogán *m*; (*Phot*) diapositiva; (*microscope slide*) portaobjetos *m inv*, plaquilla de vidrio; (*Brit: also:* **hair ~**) pasador *m* ▷ *vt* correr, deslizar ▷ *vi* (*slip*) resbalarse; (*glide*) deslizarse; **to let things ~** (*fig*) dejar que ruede la bola

sliding ['slaɪdɪŋ] *adj* (*door*) corredizo; **~ roof** (*Aut*) techo de corredera

sliding scale *n* escala móvil

slight [slaɪt] *adj* (*slim*) delgado; (*frail*) delicado; (*pain etc*) leve; (*trifling*) insignificante; (*small*) pequeño ▷ *n* desaire *m* ▷ *vt* (*offend*) ofender, desairar; **a ~ improvement** una ligera mejora; **not in the ~est** en absoluto; **there's not the ~est possibility** no hay la menor *or* más mínima posibilidad

slightly ['slaɪtlɪ] *adv* ligeramente, un poco; **~ built** delgado

slim [slɪm] *adj* delgado, esbelto ▷ *vi* adelgazar

slime [slaɪm] *n* limo, cieno

slimming ['slɪmɪŋ] *n* adelgazamiento ▷ *adj* (*diet, pills*) adelgazante

slimy ['slaɪmɪ] *adj* cenagoso; (*covered with mud*) fangoso; (*also fig: person*) adulón, zalamero

sling [slɪŋ] (*pt, pp* **slung** [slʌŋ]) *n* (*Med*) cabestrillo; (*weapon*) honda ▷ *vt* tirar, arrojar; **to have one's arm in a ~** llevar el brazo en cabestrillo

slip [slɪp] *n* (*slide*) resbalón *m*; (*mistake*) descuido; (*underskirt*) combinación *f*; (*of paper*) papelito ▷ *vt* (*slide*) deslizar ▷ *vi* (*slide*) deslizarse; (*stumble*) resbalar(se); (*decline*) decaer; (*move smoothly*): **to ~ into/out of** (*room etc*) colarse en/salirse de; **to let a chance ~ by** dejar escapar la oportunidad; **to ~ sth on/off** ponerse/quitarse algo; **to ~ on a jumper** ponerse un jersey *or* un suéter; **it ~ped from her hand** se la cayó de la mano; **to give sb the ~** dar esquinazo a algn; **wages ~** (*Brit*) hoja del sueldo; **a ~ of the tongue** un lapsus; **slip away** *vi* escabullirse; **slip in** *vt* meter ▷ *vi* meterse, colarse; **slip out** *vi* (*go out*) salir (un momento); **slip up** *vi* (*make mistake*) equivocarse; meter la pata

slipped disc [slɪpt-] *n* vértebra dislocada

slipper ['slɪpə'] *n* zapatilla, pantufla

slippery ['slɪpərɪ] *adj* resbaladizo

slip road *n* (*Brit*) carretera de acceso

slipshod ['slɪpʃɔd] *adj* descuidado, chapucero

slip-up ['slɪpʌp] *n* (*error*) desliz *m*

slipway ['slɪpweɪ] *n* grada, gradas *fpl*

slit [slɪt] (*pt, pp* **slit**) *n* raja; (*cut*) corte *m* ▷ *vt* rajar, cortar; **to ~ sb's throat** cortarle el pescuezo a algn

slither ['slɪðə'] *vi* deslizarse

sliver ['slɪvə'] *n* (*of glass, wood*) astilla; (*of cheese, sausage*) lonja, loncha

slob [slɔb] *n* (*inf*) patán(-ana) *m(f)*, palurdo(-a) *m(f)*

slog [slɔg] (*Brit*) *vi* sudar tinta ▷ *n*: **it was a ~** costó trabajo (hacerlo)

slogan ['sləugən] *n* eslogan *m*, lema *m*

slop [slɔp] *vi* (*also:* **~ over**) derramarse, desbordarse ▷ *vt* derramar, verter

slope [sləup] *n* (*up*) cuesta, pendiente *f*; (*down*) declive *m*; (*side of mountain*) falda, vertiente *f* ▷ *vi*: **to ~ down** estar en declive; **to ~ up** subir (en pendiente)

sloping ['sləupɪŋ] *adj* en pendiente; en declive

sloppy ['slɔpɪ] *adj* (*work*) descuidado; (*appearance*) desaliñado

slot [slɔt] *n* ranura; (*fig: in timetable*) hueco; (*Radio, TV*) espacio ▷ *vt*: **to ~ into** encajar en

sloth [sləuθ] *n* (*vice*) pereza; (*Zool*) oso perezoso

slot machine *n* (*Brit: vending machine*) máquina expendedora; (*for gambling*) máquina tragaperras

slouch [slautʃ] *vi*: **to ~ about, ~ around** (*laze*) gandulear

Slovak ['sləuvæk] *adj* eslovaco ▷ *n* eslovaco(-a); (*Ling*) eslovaco; **the ~ Republic** Eslovaquia

Slovakia [sləu'vækɪə] *n* Eslovaquia

Slovakian [sləu'vækɪən] *adj, n* = **Slovak**

Slovene [sləu'viːn] *adj* esloveno ▷ *n* esloveno(-a); (*Ling*) esloveno

Slovenia [sləu'viːnɪə] *n* Eslovenia

Slovenian [sləu'viːnɪən] *adj, n* = **Slovene**

slovenly ['slʌvənlɪ] *adj* (*dirty*) desaliñado, desaseado; (*careless*) descuidado

slow [sləu] *adj* lento; (*watch*): **to be ~** ir atrasado ▷ *adv* lentamente, despacio ▷ *vt* (*also:* **~ down, ~ up**) retardar; (*engine, machine*) reducir la marcha de ▷ *vi* (*also:* **~ down, ~ up**) ir más despacio; **"~"** (*road sign*) "disminuir la velocidad"; **at a ~ speed** a una velocidad lenta; **the ~ lane** el carril derecho; **business is ~** (*Comm*) hay poca actividad; **my watch is 20 minutes ~** mi reloj lleva 20 minutos de retraso; **bake for two hours in a ~ oven** cocer *or* asar dos horas en el horno a fuego lento; **to be ~ to act/decide** tardar en obrar/decidir; **to go ~** (*driver*) conducir despacio; (*in industrial dispute*) trabajar a ritmo lento

slowly ['sləulɪ] *adv* lentamente, despacio; **to drive ~** conducir despacio; **~ but surely** lento pero seguro

slow motion *n*: **in ~** a cámara lenta

sludge [slʌdʒ] *n* lodo, fango

slug [slʌg] *n* babosa; (*bullet*) posta

sluggish ['slʌgɪʃ] *adj* (*slow*) lento; (*lazy*) perezoso; (*business, market, sales*) inactivo

sluice [sluːs] *n* (*gate*) esclusa; (*channel*) canal *m* ▷ *vt*: **to ~ down** *or* **out** regar

slum [slʌm] *n* (*area*) barrios *mpl* bajos; (*house*) casucha

slump [slʌmp] *n* (*economic*) depresión *f* ▷ *vi* hundirse; (*prices*) caer en picado; **the ~ in the price of copper** la baja repentina del precio del cobre; **he was ~ed over the wheel** se había desplomado encima del volante

slung [slʌŋ] *pt, pp of* **sling**
slur [sləːʳ] *n* calumnia ▷ *vt* calumniar, difamar; (*word*) pronunciar mal; **to cast a ~ on sb** manchar la reputación de algn, difamar a algn
slurp [sləːp] *vt, vi* sorber ruidosamente
slurred [sləːd] *adj* (*pronunciation*) poco claro
slush [slʌʃ] *n* nieve *f* a medio derretir
slush fund *n* fondos *mpl* para sobornar
slut [slʌt] *n* marrana
sly [slaɪ] *adj* (*clever*) astuto; (*nasty*) malicioso
smack [smæk] *n* (*slap*) bofetada; (*blow*) golpe *m* ▷ *vt* dar una manotada a; golpear con la mano ▷ *vi*: **to ~ of** saber a, oler a ▷ *adv*: **it fell ~ in the middle** (*inf*) cayó justo en medio
small [smɔːl] *adj* pequeño, chico (*LAm*); (*in height*) bajo, chaparro (*LAm*); (*letter*) en minúscula ▷ *n*: **~ of the back** región *f* lumbar; **~ shopkeeper** pequeño(-a) comerciante *m(f)*; **to get** *or* **grow ~er** (*stain, town*) empequeñecer; (*debt, organization, numbers*) reducir, disminuir; **to make ~er** (*amount, income*) reducir; (*garden, object, garment*) achicar
small ads *npl* (*Brit*) anuncios *mpl* por palabras
small business *n* pequeño negocio; **~es** la pequeña empresa
small change *n* suelto, cambio
smallholder [ˈsmɔːlhəʊldəʳ] *n* (*Brit*) granjero(-a), parcelero(-a)
small hours *npl*: **in the ~** a altas horas de la noche
smallpox [ˈsmɔːlpɒks] *n* viruela
small talk *n* cháchara
smarmy [ˈsmɑːmɪ] *adj* (*Brit pej*) pelotillero (*fam*)
smart [smɑːt] *adj* elegante; (*clever*) listo, inteligente; (*quick*) rápido, vivo; (*weapon*) inteligente ▷ *vi* escocer, picar; **the ~ set** la gente de buen tono; **to look ~** estar elegante; **my eyes are ~ing** me pican los ojos
smartcard [ˈsmɑːtkɑːd] *n* tarjeta inteligente
smart phone *n* smartphone *m*
smash [smæʃ] *n* (*also*: **~-up**) choque *m*; (*sound*) estrépito ▷ *vt* (*break*) hacer pedazos; (*car etc*) estrellar; (*Sport: record*) batir ▷ *vi* hacerse pedazos; (*against wall etc*) estrellarse; **smash up** *vt* (*car*) hacer pedazos; (*room*) destrozar
smashing [ˈsmæʃɪŋ] *adj* (*inf*) estupendo
smattering [ˈsmætərɪŋ] *n*: **a ~ of Spanish** algo de español
smear [smɪəʳ] *n* mancha; (*Med*) frotis *m inv* (*cervical*); (*insult*) calumnia ▷ *vt* untar; (*fig*) calumniar, difamar; **his hands were ~ed with oil/ink** tenía las manos manchadas de aceite/tinta
smear campaign *n* campaña de calumnias
smear test *n* (*Med*) citología, frotis *m inv* (*cervical*)
smell [smɛl] (*pt, pp* **smelt** *or* **smelled**) *n* olor *m*; (*sense*) olfato ▷ *vt, vi* oler; **it ~s good/of garlic** huele bien/a ajo

smelly [ˈsmɛlɪ] *adj* maloliente
smelt [smɛlt] *vt* (*ore*) fundir ▷ *pt, pp of* **smell**
smile [smaɪl] *n* sonrisa ▷ *vi* sonreír
smirk [sməːk] *n* sonrisa falsa *or* afectada
smock [smɔk] *n* blusón; (*children's*) babi *m*; (*US: overall*) guardapolvo, bata
smog [smɔg] *n* smog *m*
smoke [sməʊk] *n* humo ▷ *vi* fumar; (*chimney*) echar humo ▷ *vt* (*cigarettes*) fumar; **to go up in ~** quemarse; (*fig*) quedar en agua de borrajas
smoke alarm *n* detector *m* de humo, alarma contra incendios
smoked [sməʊkt] *adj* (*bacon, glass*) ahumado
smokeless fuel [ˈsməʊklɪs-] *n* combustible *m* sin humo
smoker [ˈsməʊkəʳ] *n* fumador(a) *m(f)*
smoke screen *n* cortina de humo
smoking [ˈsməʊkɪŋ] *n*: **"no ~"** "prohibido fumar"; **he's given up ~** ha dejado de fumar
smoky [ˈsməʊkɪ] *adj* (*room*) lleno de humo
smolder [ˈsməʊldəʳ] *vi* (*US*) = **smoulder**
smooth [smuːð] *adj* liso; (*sea*) tranquilo; (*flavour, movement*) suave; (*person: pej*) meloso ▷ *vt* alisar; (*also*: **~ out**) (*creases*) alisar; (*difficulties*) allanar; **smooth over** *vt*: **to ~ things over** (*fig*) limar las asperezas
smother [ˈsmʌðəʳ] *vt* sofocar; (*repress*) contener
smoulder, smolder (*US*) [ˈsməʊldəʳ] *vi* arder sin llama
SMS *n abbr* (= *short message service*) SMS *m*
SMS message *n* (mensaje *m*) SMS *m*
smudge [smʌdʒ] *n* mancha ▷ *vt* manchar
smug [smʌg] *adj* engreído
smuggle [ˈsmʌgl] *vt* pasar de contrabando; **to ~ in/out** (*goods etc*) meter/sacar de contrabando
smuggler [ˈsmʌgləʳ] *n* contrabandista *m/f*
smuggling [ˈsmʌglɪŋ] *n* contrabando
smutty [ˈsmʌtɪ] *adj* (*fig*) verde, obsceno
snack [snæk] *n* bocado, tentempié *m*; **to have a ~** tomar un bocado
snack bar *n* cafetería
snag [snæg] *n* problema *m*; **to run into** *or* **hit a ~** encontrar inconvenientes, dar con un obstáculo
snail [sneɪl] *n* caracol *m*
snake [sneɪk] *n* (*gen*) serpiente *f*; (*harmless*) culebra; (*poisonous*) víbora
snap [snæp] *n* (*sound*) chasquido; golpe *m* seco; (*photograph*) foto *f* ▷ *adj* (*decision*) instantáneo ▷ *vt* (*fingers etc*) castañetear; (*break*) partir, quebrar; (*photograph*) tomar una foto de ▷ *vi* (*break*) partirse, quebrarse; (*fig: person*) contestar bruscamente; **to ~ shut** cerrarse de golpe; **a cold ~** (*of weather*) una ola de frío; **snap at** *vt fus*: **to ~ (at sb)** (*person*) hablar con brusquedad a algn; (*dog*) intentar morder (a algn); **to ~ one's fingers at sth/sb** (*fig*) burlarse de algo/uno; **snap off** *vi* (*break*) partirse; **snap up** *vt* agarrar

snappy ['snæpɪ] adj (inf: answer) instantáneo; (slogan) conciso; **make it ~!** (hurry up) ¡date prisa!

snapshot ['snæpʃɒt] n foto f (instantánea)

snare [snɛəʳ] n trampa ▷ vt cazar con trampa; (fig) engañar

snarl [snɑːl] n gruñido ▷ vi gruñir; **to get ~ed up** (wool, plans) enmarañarse, enredarse; (traffic) quedar atascado

snatch [snætʃ] n (small piece) fragmento; (fig) robo; **~es of** trocitos mpl de ▷ vt (snatch away) arrebatar; (grasp) coger (Sp), agarrar; **~es of conversation** fragmentos mpl de conversación; **to ~ a sandwich** comer un bocadillo a prisa; **to ~ some sleep** buscar tiempo para dormir; **don't ~!** ¡no me lo quites!; **snatch up** vt agarrar

snazzy ['snæzɪ] adj (inf) guapo

sneak [sniːk] vi: **to ~ in/out** entrar/salir a hurtadillas ▷ vt: **to ~ a look at sth** mirar algo de reojo ▷ n (inf) soplón(-ona) m(f); **to ~ up on sb** aparecérsele de improviso a algn

sneakers ['sniːkəz] npl (US) zapatos mpl de lona, zapatillas fpl

sneer [snɪəʳ] n sonrisa de desprecio ▷ vi sonreír con desprecio; **to ~ at sth/sb** burlarse or mofarse de algo/uno

sneeze [sniːz] n estornudo ▷ vi estornudar

sniff [snɪf] vi sorber (por la nariz) ▷ vt husmear, oler; (glue, drug) esnifar; **sniff at** vt fus: **it's not to be ~ed at** no es de despreciar

sniffer dog ['snɪfə-] n (for drugs) perro antidroga; (for explosives) perro antiexplosivos

snigger ['snɪɡəʳ] n risa disimulada ▷ vi reírse con disimulo

snip [snɪp] n (piece) recorte m; (bargain) ganga ▷ vt tijeretear

sniper ['snaɪpəʳ] n francotirador(a) m(f)

snippet ['snɪpɪt] n retazo

snivelling, sniveling (US) ['snɪvlɪŋ] adj llorón(-ona)

snob [snɒb] n (e)snob m/f

snobbery ['snɒbərɪ] n (e)snobismo

snobbish ['snɒbɪʃ] adj (e)snob

snog [snɒɡ] vi (Brit inf) besuquearse, morrear; **to ~ sb** besuquear a algn

snooker ['snuːkəʳ] n snooker m, billar inglés

snoop [snuːp] vi: **to ~ about** fisgonear

snooty ['snuːtɪ] adj (inf) (e)snob

snooze [snuːz] n siesta ▷ vi echar una siesta

snore [snɔːʳ] vi roncar ▷ n ronquido

snorkel ['snɔːkl] n tubo de respiración

snort [snɔːt] n bufido ▷ vi bufar ▷ vt (inf: drugs) esnifar

snout [snaʊt] n hocico, morro

snow [snəʊ] n nieve f ▷ vi nevar ▷ vt: **to be ~ed under with work** estar agobiado de trabajo

snowball ['snəʊbɔːl] n bola de nieve ▷ vi ir aumentando

snowbound ['snəʊbaʊnd] adj bloqueado por la nieve

snowdrift ['snəʊdrɪft] n ventisquero

snowdrop ['snəʊdrɒp] n campanilla

snowfall ['snəʊfɔːl] n nevada

snowflake ['snəʊfleɪk] n copo de nieve

snowman ['snəʊmæn] n figura de nieve

snowplough, snowplow (US) ['snəʊplaʊ] n quitanieves m inv

snowshoe ['snəʊʃuː] n raqueta (de nieve)

snowstorm ['snəʊstɔːm] n tormenta de nieve, nevasca

snowy ['snəʊɪ] adj de (mucha) nieve

SNP n abbr (Brit Pol) = **Scottish National Party**

snub [snʌb] vt: **to ~ sb** desairar a algn ▷ n desaire m, repulsa

snub-nosed [snʌb'nəʊzd] adj chato

snuff [snʌf] n rapé m ▷ vt (also: ~ out: candle) apagar

snug [snʌɡ] adj (cosy) cómodo; (fitted) ajustado

snuggle ['snʌɡl] vi: **to ~ down in bed** hacerse un ovillo or acurrucarse en la cama; **to ~ up to sb** acurrucarse junto a algn

KEYWORD

so [səʊ] adv **1** (thus, likewise) así, de este modo; **if so** de ser así; **I like swimming — so do I** a mí me gusta nadar — a mí también; **I've got work to do — so has Paul** tengo trabajo que hacer — Paul también; **it's five o'clock — so it is!** son las cinco — ¡pues es verdad!; **I hope/think so** espero/creo que sí; **so far** hasta ahora; (in past) hasta este momento; **so to speak** por decirlo así

2 (in comparisons etc: to such a degree) tan; **so quickly (that)** tan rápido (que); **so big (that)** tan grande (que); **she's not so clever as her brother** no es tan lista como su hermano; **we were so worried** estábamos preocupadísimos

3: **so much** adj tanto(-a) ▷ adv tanto; **so many** tantos(-as)

4 (phrases): **10 or so** unos 10, 10 o así; **so long!** (inf: goodbye) ¡hasta luego!; **she didn't so much as send me a birthday card** no me mandó ni una tarjeta siquiera por mi cumpleaños; **so (what)?** (inf) ¿y (qué)?

▷ conj **1** (expressing purpose): **so as to do** para hacer; **so (that)** para que + subjun; **we hurried so (that) we wouldn't be late** nos dimos prisa para no llegar tarde

2 (expressing result) así que; **so you see, I could have gone** así que ya ves, (yo) podría haber ido; **so that's the reason!** ¡así que es por eso or por eso es!

soak [səʊk] vt (drench) empapar; (put in water) remojar ▷ vi remojarse, estar a remojo; **soak in** vi penetrar; **soak up** vt absorber

soaking ['səʊkɪŋ] adj (also: ~ wet) calado or empapado (hasta los huesos or el tuétano)

so-and-so ['səʊənsəʊ] n (somebody) fulano(-a) de tal

soap [səup] *n* jabón *m*
soapbox ['səupbɒks] *n* tribuna improvisada
soapflakes ['səupfleɪks] *npl* jabón *msg* en escamas
soap opera *n* (TV) telenovela; (*Radio*) radionovela
soap powder *n* jabón *m* en polvo
soapy ['səupɪ] *adj* jabonoso
soar [sɔːʳ] *vi* (*on wings*) remontarse; (*building etc*) elevarse; (*price*) dispararse; (*morale*) elevarse
sob [sɒb] *n* sollozo ⊳ *vi* sollozar
sober ['səubəʳ] *adj* (*moderate*) moderado; (*serious*) serio; (*not drunk*) sobrio; (*colour, style*) discreto; **sober up** *vi* pasársele a algn la borrachera
sob story *n* (*inf, pej*) dramón *m*
so-called ['səu'kɔːld] *adj* llamado
soccer ['sɒkəʳ] *n* fútbol *m*
sociable ['səuʃəbl] *adj* sociable
social ['səuʃl] *adj* social ⊳ *n* velada, fiesta
social club *n* club *m*
socialism ['səuʃəlɪzəm] *n* socialismo
socialist ['səuʃəlɪst] *adj, n* socialista *m/f*
socialize ['səuʃəlaɪz] *vi* hacer vida social; **to ~ with** (*colleagues*) salir con
social life *n* vida social
socially ['səuʃəlɪ] *adv* socialmente
social networking [-'nɛtwə:kɪŋ] *n* interacción *f* social a través de la red
social security *n* seguridad *f* social
social services *npl* servicios *mpl* sociales
social work *n* asistencia social
social worker *n* asistente(-a) *m(f)* social
society [sə'saɪətɪ] *n* sociedad *f*; (*club*) asociación *f*; (*also*: **high ~**) alta sociedad ⊳ *cpd* (*party, column*) social, de sociedad
sociologist [səusɪ'ɒlədʒɪst] *n* sociólogo(-a)
sociology [səusɪ'ɒlədʒɪ] *n* sociología
sock [sɒk] *n* calcetín *m*, media (*LAm*); **to pull one's ~s up** (*fig*) hacer esfuerzos, despabilarse
socket ['sɒkɪt] *n* (*Elec*) enchufe *m*
sod [sɒd] *n* (*of earth*) césped *m*; (*inf!*) cabrón(-ona) *m(f)* (!) ⊳ *excl*: **~ off!** (*inf!*) ¡vete a la porra!
soda ['səudə] *n* (*Chem*) sosa; (*also*: **~ water**) soda; (*US: also*: **~ pop**) gaseosa
sodden ['sɒdn] *adj* empapado
sodium ['səudɪəm] *n* sodio
sodium chloride *n* cloruro sódico *or* de sodio
sofa ['səufə] *n* sofá *m*
sofa bed *n* sofá-cama *m*
soft [sɒft] *adj* (*teacher, parent*) blando; (*gentle, not loud*) suave; (*stupid*) bobo; **~ currency** divisa blanda *or* débil
soft drink *n* bebida no alcohólica
soft drugs *npl* drogas *fpl* blandas
soften ['sɒfn] *vt* ablandar; suavizar ⊳ *vi* ablandarse; suavizarse
softener ['sɒfnəʳ] *n* suavizante *m*

softly ['sɒftlɪ] *adv* suavemente; (*gently*) delicadamente, con delicadeza
softness ['sɒftnɪs] *n* blandura; suavidad *f*
software ['sɒftwɛəʳ] *n* (*Comput*) software *m*
soggy ['sɒgɪ] *adj* empapado
soil [sɔɪl] *n* (*earth*) tierra, suelo ⊳ *vt* ensuciar
solace ['sɒlɪs] *n* consuelo
solar ['səuləʳ] *adj* solar
solarium (*pl* **solaria**) [sə'lɛərɪəm, -rɪə] *n* solario
solar panel *n* panel *m* solar
solar power *n* energía *f* solar
solar system *n* sistema *m* solar
sold [səuld] *pt, pp of* **sell**
solder ['səuldəʳ] *vt* soldar ⊳ *n* soldadura
soldier ['səuldʒəʳ] *n* (*gen*) soldado; (*army man*) militar *m* ⊳ *vi*: **to ~ on** seguir adelante; **toy ~** soldadito de plomo
sold out *adj* (*Comm*) agotado
sole [səul] *n* (*of foot*) planta; (*of shoe*) suela; (*fish*) *pl inv* lenguado ⊳ *adj* único; **the ~ reason** la única razón
solely ['səullɪ] *adv* únicamente, sólo, solamente; **I will hold you ~ responsible** le consideraré el único responsable
solemn ['sɒləm] *adj* solemne
sole trader *n* (*Comm*) comerciante *m/f* exclusivo(-a)
solicit [sə'lɪsɪt] *vt* (*request*) solicitar ⊳ *vi* (*prostitute*) abordar clientes
solicitor [sə'lɪsɪtəʳ] *n* (*Brit: for wills etc*) ≈ notario(-a); (*in court*) ≈ abogado(-a)
solid ['sɒlɪd] *adj* sólido; (*gold etc*) macizo; (*line*) continuo; (*vote*) unánime ⊳ *n* sólido; **we waited two ~ hours** esperamos dos horas enteras; **to be on ~ ground** estar en tierra firme; (*fig*) estar seguro
solidarity [sɒlɪ'dærɪtɪ] *n* solidaridad *f*
solid fuel *n* combustible *m* sólido
solitaire [sɒlɪ'tɛəʳ] *n* (*game, gem*) solitario
solitary ['sɒlɪtərɪ] *adj* solitario, solo; (*isolated*) apartado, aislado; (*only*) único
solitary confinement *n* incomunicación *f*; **to be in ~** estar incomunicado
solitude ['sɒlɪtjuːd] *n* soledad *f*
solo ['səuləu] *n* solo ⊳ *adv* (*fly*) en solitario
soloist ['səuləuɪst] *n* solista *m/f*
solstice ['sɒlstɪs] *n* solsticio
soluble ['sɒljubl] *adj* soluble
solution [sə'luːʃən] *n* solución *f*
solve [sɒlv] *vt* resolver, solucionar
solvency ['sɒlvənsɪ] *n* (*Comm*) solvencia
solvent ['sɒlvənt] *adj* (*Comm*) solvente ⊳ *n* (*Chem*) solvente *m*
solvent abuse *n* uso indebido de disolventes
Somalia [sə'mɑːlɪə] *n* Somalia
sombre, somber (*US*) ['sɒmbəʳ] *adj* sombrío

◯ KEYWORD

some [sʌm] *adj* **1** (*a certain amount or number of*): **some tea/water/biscuits** té/agua/(unas)

galletas; **have some tea** tómese un té;
there's some milk in the fridge hay leche
en el frigo; **there were some people
outside** había algunas personas fuera; **I've
got some money, but not much** tengo algo
de dinero, pero no mucho
2 (*certain: in contrasts*) algunos(-as); **some
people say that ...** hay quien dice que ...;
**some films were excellent, but most were
mediocre** hubo películas excelentes, pero la
mayoría fueron mediocres
3 (*unspecified*): **some woman was asking for
you** una mujer estuvo preguntando por ti;
some day algún día; **some day next week**
un día de la semana que viene; **he was
asking for some book (or other)** pedía no
se qué libro; **in some way or other** de
alguna que otra manera
4 (*considerable amount of*) bastante; **some days
ago** hace unos cuantos días; **after some
time** pasado algún tiempo; **at some length**
con mucho detalle
5 (*inf: intensive*): **that was some party!**
¡menuda fiesta!
▷ *pron* **1** (*a certain number*): **I've got some** (*books
etc*) tengo algunos(-as)
2 (*a certain amount*) algo; **I've got some** (*money,
milk*) tengo algo; algunos(-as); **some days
ago** hace unos cuantos días; **after some
time** pasado algún tiempo; **at some length**
con mucho detalle
alguno?; **could I have some of that cheese?**
¿me puede dar un poco de ese queso?; **I've
read some of the book** he leído parte del
libro
▷ *adv*: **some 10 people** unas 10 personas, una
decena de personas

somebody ['sʌmbədɪ] *pron* alguien; **~ or
other** alguien
somehow ['sʌmhau] *adv* de alguna manera;
(*for some reason*) por una u otra razón
someone ['sʌmwʌn] *pron* = **somebody**
someplace ['sʌmpleɪs] *adv* (*US*)
= **somewhere**
somersault ['sʌməsɔːlt] *n* (*deliberate*) salto
mortal; (*accidental*) vuelco ▷ *vi* dar un salto
mortal; dar vuelcos
something ['sʌmθɪŋ] *pron* algo ▷ *adv*: **he's ~
like me** es un poco como yo; **~ to do** algo que
hacer; **it's ~ of a problem** es bastante
problemático; **would you like ~ to eat/
drink?** ¿te gustaría cenar/tomar algo?
sometime ['sʌmtaɪm] *adv* (*in future*) algún
día, en algún momento; **~ last month**
durante el mes pasado; **I'll finish it ~** lo
terminaré un día de éstos
sometimes ['sʌmtaɪmz] *adv* a veces
somewhat ['sʌmwɔt] *adv* algo
somewhere ['sʌmwɛər] *adv* (*be*) en alguna
parte; (*go*) a alguna parte; **~ else** (*be*) en otra
parte; (*go*) a otra parte
son [sʌn] *n* hijo
sonar ['səunɑːr] *n* sonar *m*

song [sɔŋ] *n* canción *f*
songwriter ['sɔŋraɪtər] *n* compositor(a) *m(f)*
de canciones
sonic ['sɔnɪk] *adj* (*boom*) sónico
son-in-law ['sʌnɪnlɔː] *n* yerno
sonnet ['sɔnɪt] *n* soneto
sonny ['sʌnɪ] *n* (*inf*) hijo
soon [suːn] *adv* pronto, dentro de poco;
~ afterwards poco después; **very/quite ~**
muy/bastante pronto; **how ~ can you be
ready?** ¿cuánto tardas en prepararte?; **it's
too ~ to tell** es demasiado pronto para saber;
see you ~! ¡hasta pronto!; *see also* **as**
sooner ['suːnər] *adv* (*time*) antes, más
temprano; **I would ~ do that** preferiría
hacer eso; **~ or later** tarde o temprano; **no ~
said than done** dicho y hecho; **the ~ the
better** cuanto antes mejor; **no ~ had we left
than ...** apenas nos habíamos marchado
cuando ...
soot [sut] *n* hollín *m*
soothe [suːð] *vt* tranquilizar; (*pain*) aliviar
sophisticated [səˈfɪstɪkeɪtɪd] *adj* sofisticado
sophomore ['sɔfəmɔːr] *n* (*US*) estudiante *m/f*
de segundo año
sopping ['sɔpɪŋ] *adj*: **~ (wet)** empapado
soppy ['sɔpɪ] *adj* (*pej*) bobo, tonto
soprano [səˈprɑːnəu] *n* soprano *f*
sorbet ['sɔːbeɪ] *n* sorbete *m*
sorcerer ['sɔːsərər] *n* hechicero
sordid ['sɔːdɪd] *adj* (*place etc*) sórdido; (*motive
etc*) mezquino
sore [sɔːr] *adj* (*painful*) doloroso, que duele;
(*offended*) resentido ▷ *n* llaga; **~ throat** dolor
m de garganta; **my eyes are ~, I have ~ eyes**
me duelen los ojos; **it's a ~ point** es un
asunto delicado o espinoso
sorely *adv*: **I am ~ tempted to (do it)** estoy
muy tentado a (hacerlo)
sorrow ['sɔrəu] *n* pena, dolor *m*
sorry ['sɔrɪ] *adj* (*regretful*) arrepentido;
(*condition, excuse*) lastimoso; (*sight, failure*)
triste; **~!** ¡perdón!, ¡perdone!; **~?** ¿cómo?;
I am ~ lo siento; **I feel ~ for him** me da
lástima *or* pena; **I'm ~ to hear that ...** siento
saber que ...; **to be ~ about sth** lamentar
algo
sort [sɔːt] *n* clase *f*, género, tipo; (*make: of
coffee, car etc*) marca ▷ *vt* (*also: ~ out*) (*papers*)
clasificar; (*organize*) ordenar, organizar;
(*resolve: problem, situation etc*) arreglar,
solucionar; (*Comput*) clasificar; **what ~ do
you want?** (*make*) ¿qué marca quieres?; **what
~ of car?** ¿qué tipo de coche?; **I shall do
nothing of the ~** no pienso hacer nada
parecido; **it's ~ of awkward** (*inf*) es bastante
difícil
sorting office ['sɔːtɪŋ-] *n* oficina de
clasificación del correo
SOS *n* SOS *m*
so-so ['səusəu] *adv* regular, así así
soufflé ['suːfleɪ] *n* suflé *m*

sought [sɔ:t] *pt, pp of* **seek**

soul [səʊl] *n* alma *f*; **God rest his ~** Dios le reciba en su seno *or* en su gloria; **I didn't see a ~** no vi a nadie; **the poor ~ had nowhere to sleep** el pobre no tenía dónde dormir

soulful ['səʊlfʊl] *adj* lleno de sentimiento

sound [saʊnd] *adj* (*healthy*) sano; (*safe, not damaged*) en buen estado; (*valid: argument, policy, claim*) válido; (: *move*) acertado; (*dependable: person*) de fiar; (*sensible*) sensato, razonable ▷ *adv:* **~ asleep** profundamente dormido ▷ *n* (*noise*) sonido, ruido; (*volume: on TV etc*) volumen *m*; (*Geo*) estrecho ▷ *vt* (*alarm*) sonar; (*also:* **~ out**: *opinions*) consultar, sondear ▷ *vi* sonar, resonar; (*fig: seem*) parecer; **to ~ like** sonar a; **to be of ~ mind** estar en su sano juicio; **I don't like the ~ of it** no me gusta nada; **it ~s as if ...** parece que ...; **sound off** *vi* (*inf*): **to ~ off (about)** (*give one's opinions*) despotricar (contra)

sound barrier *n* barrera del sonido

sound bite *n* cita jugosa

sound effects *npl* efectos *mpl* sonoros

soundly ['saʊndlɪ] *adv* (*sleep*) profundamente; (*beat*) completamente

soundproof ['saʊndpru:f] *adj* insonorizado

sound system *n* equipo de sonido

soundtrack ['saʊndtræk] *n* (*of film*) banda sonora

soup [su:p] *n* (*thick*) sopa; (*thin*) caldo; **in the ~** (*fig*) en apuros

soup plate *n* plato sopero

soupspoon ['su:pspu:n] *n* cuchara sopera

sour ['saʊəʳ] *adj* agrio; (*milk*) cortado; **it's just ~ grapes!** (*fig*) ¡pura envidia!, ¡están verdes!; **to go** *or* **turn ~** (*milk*) cortarse; (*wine*) agriarse; (*fig: relationship*) agriarse; (: *plans*) irse a pique

source [sɔ:s] *n* fuente *f*; **I have it from a reliable ~ that ...** sé de fuente fidedigna que ...

south [saʊθ] *n* sur *m* ▷ *adj* del sur ▷ *adv* al sur, hacia el sur; **(to the) ~ of** al sur de; **the S~ of France** el Sur de Francia; **to travel ~** viajar hacia el sur

South Africa *n* Sudáfrica

South African *adj, n* sudafricano(-a) *m(f)*

South America *n* América del Sur, Sudamérica

South American *adj, n* sudamericano(-a) *m(f)*

southbound ['saʊθbaʊnd] *adj* (con) rumbo al sur

south-east [saʊθ'i:st] *n* sudeste *m* ▷ *adj* (*counties etc*) (del) sudeste

southeastern [saʊθ'i:stən] *adj* sureste, del sureste

southerly ['sʌðəlɪ] *adj* sur; (*from the south*) del sur

southern ['sʌðən] *adj* del sur, meridional; **the ~ hemisphere** el hemisferio sur

South Korea *n* Corea del Sur

South Pole *n* Polo Sur

southward ['saʊθwəd], **southwards** ['saʊθwədz] *adv* hacia el sur

south-west [saʊθ'wɛst] *n* suroeste *m*

southwestern [saʊθ'wɛstən] *adj* suroeste

souvenir [su:və'nɪəʳ] *n* recuerdo

sovereign ['sɔvrɪn] *adj, n* soberano(-a) *m(f)*

soviet ['səʊvɪət] *adj* soviético

sow [saʊ] *n* cerda, puerca

sow [səʊ] (*pt* **sowed**, *pp* **sown** [səʊn]) *vt* sembrar

soya ['sɔɪə], **soy** (*US*) [sɔɪ] *n* soja

sozzled ['sɔzld] *adj* (*Brit inf*) mamado

spa [spɑ:] *n* balneario

space [speɪs] *n* espacio; (*room*) sitio ▷ *vt* (*also:* **~ out**) espaciar; **to clear a ~ for sth** hacer sitio para algo; **in a confined ~** en un espacio restringido; **in a short ~ of time** en poco *or* un corto espacio de tiempo; **(with)in the ~ of an hour/three generations** en el espacio de una hora/tres generaciones

spacecraft ['speɪskrɑ:ft] *n* nave *f* espacial, astronave *f*

spaceman ['speɪsmæn] *n* astronauta *m*, cosmonauta *m*

spaceship ['speɪsʃɪp] *n* = **spacecraft**

spacesuit ['speɪssu:t] *n* traje *m* espacial

spacewoman ['speɪswʊmən] *n* astronauta, cosmonauta

spacing ['speɪsɪŋ] *n* espacio

spacious ['speɪʃəs] *adj* amplio

spade [speɪd] *n* (*tool*) pala; **spades** *npl* (*Cards: British*) picas *fpl*; (*Spanish*) espadas *fpl*

spaghetti [spə'gɛtɪ] *n* espaguetis *mpl*

Spain [speɪn] *n* España

spam [spæm] *n* (*junk email*) correo basura

span [spæn] *n* (*of bird, plane*) envergadura; (*of hand*) palmo; (*of arch*) luz *f*; (*in time*) lapso ▷ *vt* extenderse sobre, cruzar; (*fig*) abarcar

Spaniard ['spænjəd] *n* español(a) *m(f)*

spaniel ['spænjəl] *n* perro de aguas

Spanish ['spænɪʃ] *adj* español(a) ▷ *n* (*Ling*) español *m*, castellano; **the Spanish** *npl* (*people*) los españoles; **~ omelette** tortilla española *or* de patata

spank [spæŋk] *vt* zurrar, dar unos azotes a

spanner ['spænəʳ] *n* (*Brit*) llave *f* inglesa

spar [spɑ:ʳ] *n* palo, verga ▷ *vi* (*Boxing*) entrenarse (en el boxeo)

spare [spɛəʳ] *adj* de reserva; (*surplus*) sobrante, de más ▷ *n* (*part*) pieza de repuesto ▷ *vt* (*do without*) pasarse sin; (*afford to give*) tener de sobra; (*refrain from hurting*) perdonar; (*details etc*) ahorrar; **to ~** (*surplus*) sobrante, de sobra; **there are two going ~** sobran *or* quedan dos; **to ~ no expense** no escatimar gastos; **can you ~ (me) £10?** ¿puedes prestarme *or* darme 10 libras?; **can you ~ the time?** ¿tienes tiempo?; **I've a few minutes to ~** tengo unos minutos libres; **there is no time to ~** no hay tiempo que perder

spare part *n* pieza de repuesto

spare room n cuarto de los invitados

spare time n ratos mpl de ocio, tiempo libre

spare tyre, spare tire (US) n (Aut) neumático or llanta (LAm) de recambio

spare wheel n (Aut) rueda de recambio

sparing ['spɛərɪŋ] adj: **to be ~ with** ser parco en

sparingly ['spɛərɪŋlɪ] adv escasamente

spark [spɑːk] n chispa; (fig) chispazo

sparking plug ['spɑːk(ɪŋ)-] n = **spark plug**

sparkle ['spɑːkl] n centelleo, destello ▷ vi centellear; (shine) relucir, brillar

sparkler ['spɑːklə[r]] n bengala

sparkling ['spɑːklɪŋ] adj centelleante; (wine) espumoso

spark plug n bujía

sparring partner ['spɑːrɪŋ-] n sparring m; (fig) contrincante m/f

sparrow ['spærəu] n gorrión m

sparse [spɑːs] adj esparcido, escaso

spartan ['spɑːtən] adj (fig) espartano

spasm ['spæzəm] n (Med) espasmo; (fig) arranque m, ataque m

spasmodic [spæz'mɔdɪk] adj espasmódico

spastic ['spæstɪk] n espástico(-a)

spat [spæt] pt, pp of **spit** ▷ n (US) riña

spate [speɪt] n (fig): **~ of** torrente m de; **in ~** (river) crecido

spatter ['spætə[r]] vt: **to ~ with** salpicar de

spatula ['spætjulə] n espátula

spawn [spɔːn] vt (pej) engendrar ▷ vi desovar, frezar ▷ n huevas fpl

speak (pt **spoke**, pp **spoken**) [spiːk, spəuk, 'spəukn] vt (language) hablar; (truth) decir ▷ vi hablar; (make a speech) intervenir; **to ~ one's mind** hablar claro or con franqueza; **to ~ to sb/of or about sth** hablar con algn/de or sobre algo; **to ~ at a conference/in a debate** hablar en un congreso/un debate; **he has no money to ~ of** no tiene mucho dinero que digamos; **~ing!** ¡al habla!; **~ up!** ¡habla más alto!; **speak for** vt fus: **to ~ for sb** hablar por or en nombre de algn; **that picture is already spoken for** (in shop) ese cuadro está reservado

speaker ['spiːkə[r]] n (in public) orador(a) m(f); (also: **loud~**) altavoz m; (for stereo etc) bafle m; (Pol): **the S~** (Brit) el Presidente de la Cámara de los Comunes; (US) el Presidente del Congreso; **are you a Welsh ~?** ¿habla Vd galés?

spear [spɪə[r]] n lanza; (for fishing) arpón m ▷ vt alancear; arponear

spearhead ['spɪəhɛd] vt (attack etc) encabezar ▷ n punta de lanza, vanguardia

spec [spɛk] n (inf): **on ~** por si acaso; **to buy on ~** arriesgarse a comprar

special ['spɛʃl] adj especial; (edition etc) extraordinario; (delivery) urgente ▷ n (train) tren m especial; **nothing ~** nada de particular, nada extraordinario

special delivery n (Post): **by ~** por entrega urgente

special effects npl (Cine) efectos mpl especiales

specialist ['spɛʃəlɪst] n especialista m/f; **a heart ~** (Med) un(-a) especialista del corazón

speciality [spɛʃɪ'ælɪtɪ], **specialty** (US) ['spɛʃəltɪ] n especialidad f

specialize ['spɛʃəlaɪz] vi: **to ~ (in)** especializarse (en)

specially ['spɛʃlɪ] adv especialmente

special offer n (Comm) oferta especial

special school n (Brit) colegio m de educación especial

specialty ['spɛʃəltɪ] n (US) = **speciality**

species ['spiːʃiːz] n especie f

specific [spə'sɪfɪk] adj específico

specifically [spə'sɪfɪklɪ] adv (explicitly: state, warn) específicamente, expresamente; (especially: design, intend) especialmente

specification [spɛsɪfɪ'keɪʃən] n especificación f; **specifications** npl (plan) presupuesto sg; (of car, machine) descripción f técnica; (for building) plan msg detallado

specify ['spɛsɪfaɪ] vt, vi especificar, precisar; **unless otherwise specified** salvo indicaciones contrarias

specimen ['spɛsɪmən] n ejemplar m; (Med: of urine) espécimen m; (: of blood) muestra

speck [spɛk] n grano, mota

speckled ['spɛkld] adj moteado

specs [spɛks] npl (inf) gafas fpl (Sp), anteojos mpl

spectacle ['spɛktəkl] n espectáculo; **spectacles** npl (Brit: glasses) gafas fpl (Sp), anteojos mpl

spectacular [spɛk'tækjulə[r]] adj espectacular; (success) impresionante

spectator [spɛk'teɪtə[r]] n espectador(a) m(f)

spectator sport n deporte m espectáculo

spectrum (pl **spectra**) ['spɛktrəm, -trə] n espectro

speculate ['spɛkjuleɪt] vi especular; (try to guess): **to ~ about** especular sobre

speculation [spɛkju'leɪʃən] n especulación f

sped [spɛd] pt, pp of **speed**

speech [spiːtʃ] n (faculty) habla; (formal talk) discurso; (words) palabras fpl; (manner of speaking) forma de hablar; (language) idioma m, lenguaje m

speechless ['spiːtʃlɪs] adj mudo, estupefacto

speed [spiːd] (pt, pp **sped** [spɛd]) n (also Aut, Tech: gear) velocidad f; (haste) prisa; (promptness) rapidez f ▷ vi (Aut: exceed speed limit) conducir con exceso de velocidad; **at full** or **top ~** a máxima velocidad; **at a ~ of 70 km/h** a una velocidad de 70 km por hora; **at ~** a gran velocidad; **a five-~ gearbox** una caja de cambios de cinco velocidades; **shorthand/typing ~** rapidez f en taquigrafía/mecanografía; **the years sped by** los años pasaron volando; **speed up** ▷ vi acelerarse ▷ vt acelerar

speedboat ['spiːdbəut] n lancha motora

S

speedily ['spi:dɪlɪ] adv rápido, rápidamente
speeding ['spi:dɪŋ] n (Aut) exceso de velocidad
speed limit n límite m de velocidad, velocidad f máxima
speedometer [spɪ'dɒmɪtəʳ] n velocímetro
speed trap n (Aut) control m de velocidades
speedway ['spi:dweɪ] n (Sport) pista de carrera
speedy ['spi:dɪ] adj (fast) veloz, rápido; (prompt) pronto
spell [spɛl] (pt, pp **spelt** or **spelled** [spɛlt, spɛld]) n (also: **magic ~**) encanto, hechizo; (period of time) rato, período; (turn) turno ▷ vt deletrear; (fig) anunciar, presagiar; **to cast a ~ on sb** hechizar a algn; **he can't ~** no sabe escribir bien, comete faltas de ortografía; **can you ~ it for me?** ¿cómo se deletrea or se escribe?; **how do you ~ your name?** ¿cómo se escribe tu nombre?; **spell out** vt (explain): **to ~ sth out for sb** explicar algo a algn en detalle
spellbound ['spɛlbaund] adj embelesado, hechizado
spellchecker n (Comput) corrector m (ortográfico)
spelling ['spɛlɪŋ] n ortografía
spelling mistake n falta de ortografía
spelt [spɛlt] pt, pp of **spell**
spend (pt, pp **spent**) [spɛnd, spɛnt] vt (money) gastar; (time) pasar; (life) dedicar; **to ~ time/money/effort on sth** gastar tiempo/dinero/ energías en algo
spending ['spɛndɪŋ] n: **government ~** gastos mpl del gobierno
spending money n dinero para gastos
spendthrift ['spɛndθrɪft] n derrochador(a) m(f) manirroto(-a)
spent [spɛnt] pt, pp of **spend** ▷ adj (cartridge, bullets, match) usado
sperm [spə:m] n esperma
sperm bank n banco de esperma
spew [spju:] vt vomitar, arrojar
sphere [sfɪəʳ] n esfera
spice [spaɪs] n especia ▷ vt especiar
spick-and-span ['spɪkən'spæn] adj impecable
spicy ['spaɪsɪ] adj picante
spider ['spaɪdəʳ] n araña
spider's web n telaraña
spiel [ʃpi:l] n (inf) rollo
spike [spaɪk] n (point) punta; (Zool) pincho, púa; (Bot) espiga; (Elec) pico parásito ▷ vt: **to ~ a quote** cancelar una cita; **spikes** npl (Sport) zapatillas fpl con clavos
spill (pt, pp **spilt** or **spilled**) [spɪl, spɪlt, spɪld] vt derramar, verter; (blood) derramar ▷ vi derramarse; **to ~ the beans** (inf) descubrir el pastel; **spill out** vi derramarse, desparramarse; **spill over** vi desbordarse
spillage ['spɪlɪdʒ] n (event) derrame m; (substance) vertidos

spin [spɪn] (pt, pp **spun**) n (revolution of wheel) vuelta, revolución f; (Aviat) barrena; (trip in car) paseo (en coche) ▷ vt (wool etc) hilar; (wheel) girar ▷ vi girar, dar vueltas; **the car spun out of control** el coche se descontroló y empezó a dar vueltas; **spin out** vt alargar, prolongar
spina bifida ['spaɪnə'bɪfɪdə] n espina f bífida
spinach ['spɪnɪtʃ] n espinacas fpl
spinal ['spaɪnl] adj espinal
spinal cord n médula espinal
spindly ['spɪndlɪ] adj (leg) zanquivano
spin doctor n (inf) informador(a) parcial al servicio de un partido político
spin-dryer [spɪn'draɪəʳ] n (Brit) secadora centrífuga
spine [spaɪn] n espinazo, columna vertebral; (thorn) espina
spineless ['spaɪnlɪs] adj (fig) débil, flojo
spinning ['spɪnɪŋ] n (of thread) hilado; (art) hilandería; (Sport) spinning m
spinning top n peonza
spinning wheel n rueca, torno de hilar
spin-off ['spɪnɒf] n derivado, producto secundario
spinster ['spɪnstəʳ] n soltera; (pej) solterona
spiral ['spaɪərl] n espiral f ▷ adj en espiral ▷ vi (prices) dispararse; **the inflationary ~** la espiral inflacionista
spiral staircase n escalera de caracol
spire ['spaɪəʳ] n aguja, chapitel m
spirit ['spɪrɪt] n (soul) alma f; (ghost) fantasma m; (attitude) espíritu m; (courage) valor m, ánimo; **spirits** npl (drink) alcohol msg, bebidas fpl alcohólicas; **in good ~s** alegre, de buen ánimo; **Holy S~** Espíritu m Santo; **community ~, public ~** civismo
spirited ['spɪrɪtɪd] adj enérgico, vigoroso
spirit level n nivel m de aire
spiritual ['spɪrɪtjuəl] adj espiritual ▷ n (also: **Negro ~**) canción f religiosa, espiritual m
spiritualism ['spɪrɪtjuəlɪzəm] n espiritualismo
spit [spɪt] (pt, pp **spat** [spæt]) n (for roasting) asador m, espetón m; (spittle) esputo, escupitajo; (saliva) saliva ▷ vi escupir; (sound) chisporrotear
spite [spaɪt] n rencor m, ojeriza ▷ vt fastidiar; **in ~ of** a pesar de, pese a
spiteful ['spaɪtful] adj rencoroso, malévolo
spittle ['spɪtl] n saliva, baba
splash [splæʃ] n (sound) chapoteo; (of colour) mancha ▷ vt salpicar de ▷ vi (also: **~ about**) chapotear; **to ~ paint on the floor** manchar el suelo de pintura; **splash out** vi (Brit) (inf) derrochar dinero
spleen [spli:n] n (Anat) bazo
splendid ['splɛndɪd] adj espléndido
splint [splɪnt] n tablilla
splinter ['splɪntəʳ] n astilla; (in finger) espigón m ▷ vi astillarse, hacer astillas

split [splɪt] (pt, pp **split**) n hendedura, raja; (fig) división f; (Pol) escisión f ▷ vt partir, rajar; (party) dividir; (work, profits) repartir ▷ vi (divide) dividirse, escindirse; **to ~ the difference** partir la diferencia; **to do the ~s** hacer el spagat; **to ~ sth down the middle** (also fig) dividir algo en dos; **split up** vi (couple) separarse, romper; (meeting) acabarse

split personality n doble personalidad f

split second n fracción f de segundo

splutter ['splʌtər] vi chisporrotear; (person) balbucear

spoil (pt, pp **spoilt** or **spoiled**) [spɔɪl, spɔɪlt, spɔɪld] vt (damage) dañar; (ruin) estropear, echar a perder; (child) mimar, consentir; (ballot paper) invalidar ▷ vi: **to be ~ing for a fight** estar con ganas de lucha, andar con ganas de pelea

spoiled [spɔɪld] adj (US: food: bad) pasado, malo; (milk) cortado

spoils [spɔɪlz] npl despojo sg, botín msg

spoilsport ['spɔɪlspɔːt] n aguafiestas m inv

spoilt [spɔɪlt] pt, pp of **spoil** ▷ adj (child) mimado, consentido; (ballot paper) invalidado

spoke [spəʊk] pt of **speak** ▷ n rayo, radio

spoken ['spəʊkn] pp of **speak**

spokesman ['spəʊksmən] n portavoz m, vocero (LAm)

spokesperson ['spəʊkspɜːn] n portavoz m/f, vocero(-a) (LAm)

spokeswoman ['spəʊkswʊmən] n portavoz f, vocera (LAm)

sponge [spʌndʒ] n esponja; (Culin: also: **~ cake**) bizcocho ▷ vt (wash) lavar con esponja ▷ vi: **to ~ on** or (US) **off sb** vivir a costa de algn

sponge bag n (Brit) neceser m

sponsor ['spɒnsər] n (Radio, TV) patrocinador(a) m(f); (for membership) padrino/ madrina; (Comm) fiador(a) m(f), avalador(a) m(f) ▷ vt patrocinar; apadrinar; (parliamentary bill) apoyar, respaldar; (idea etc) presentar, promover; **I ~ed him at 3p a mile** (in fund-raising race) me apunté para darle 3 peniques la milla

sponsorship ['spɒnsəʃɪp] n patrocinio

spontaneous [spɒn'teɪnɪəs] adj espontáneo

spooky ['spuːkɪ] adj (inf: place, atmosphere) espeluznante, horripilante

spool [spuːl] n carrete m; (of sewing machine) canilla

spoon [spuːn] n cuchara

spoon-feed ['spuːnfiːd] vt dar de comer con cuchara a; (fig) dárselo todo mascado a

spoonful ['spuːnful] n cucharada

sporadic [spə'rædɪk] adj esporádico

sport [spɔːt] n deporte m; (person): **to be a good ~** ser muy majo; (amusement) juego, diversión f; **indoor/outdoor ~s** deportes mpl en sala cubierta/al aire libre; **to say sth in ~** decir algo en broma

sporting ['spɔːtɪŋ] adj deportivo; **to give sb a ~ chance** darle a algn su oportunidad

sport jacket n (US) = **sports jacket**

sports car n coche m sport

sports centre n (Brit) polideportivo

sports ground n campo de deportes, centro deportivo

sports jacket, sport jacket (US) n chaqueta deportiva

sportsman ['spɔːtsmən] n deportista m

sportsmanship ['spɔːtsmənʃɪp] n deportividad f

sports utility vehicle n todoterreno m inv

sportswear ['spɔːtsweər] n ropa de deporte

sportswoman ['spɔːtswʊmən] n deportista

sporty ['spɔːtɪ] adj deportivo

spot [spɒt] n sitio, lugar m; (dot: on pattern) punto, mancha; (pimple) grano; (also: **advertising ~**) spot m; (small amount): **a ~ of** un poquito de ▷ vt (notice) notar, observar ▷ adj (Comm) inmediatamente efectivo; **on the ~** en el acto; (in difficulty) en un aprieto; **to do sth on the ~** hacer algo en el acto; **to put sb on the ~** poner a algn en un apuro

spot check n reconocimiento rápido

spotless ['spɒtlɪs] adj (clean) inmaculado; (reputation) intachable

spotlight ['spɒtlaɪt] n foco, reflector m; (Aut) faro auxiliar

spot-on [spɒt'ɒn] adj (Brit inf) exacto

spotted ['spɒtɪd] adj (pattern) de puntos

spotty ['spɒtɪ] adj (face) con granos

spouse [spauz] n cónyuge m/f

spout [spaut] n (of jug) pico; (pipe) caño ▷ vi chorrear

sprain [spreɪn] n torcedura, esguince m ▷ vt: **to ~ one's ankle** torcerse el tobillo

sprang [spræŋ] pt of **spring**

sprawl [sprɔːl] vi tumbarse ▷ n: **urban ~** crecimiento urbano descontrolado; **to send sb ~ing** tirar a algn al suelo

spray [spreɪ] n rociada; (of sea) espuma; (container) atomizador m; (of paint) pistola rociadora; (of flowers) ramita ▷ vt rociar; (crops) regar ▷ cpd (deodorant) en atomizador

spread [spred] (pt, pp **spread**) n extensión f; (of idea) diseminación f; (inf: food) comilona; (Press, Typ: two pages) plana ▷ vt extender; diseminar; (butter) untar; (wings, sails) desplegar; (scatter) esparcir ▷ vi (also: **~ out:** stain) extenderse; (news) diseminarse; **middle-age ~** gordura de la mediana edad; **repayments will be ~ over 18 months** los pagos se harán a lo largo de 18 meses; **spread out** vi (move apart) separarse

spread-eagled ['spredɪːgld] adj: **to be ~** estar despatarrado

spreadsheet ['spredʃiːt] n (Comput) hoja de cálculo

spree [spriː] n: **to go on a ~** ir de juerga or farra (LAm)

sprightly ['spraɪtlɪ] adj vivo, enérgico

S

spring [sprɪŋ] (pt **sprang**, pp **sprung**) n
(season) primavera; (leap) salto, brinco;
(coiled metal) resorte m; (of water) fuente f,
manantial m; (bounciness) elasticidad f ▷ vi
(arise) brotar, nacer; (leap) saltar, brincar ▷ vt:
to ~ a leak (pipe etc) empezar a hacer agua;
he sprang the news on me de repente me
soltó la noticia; **in (the)** ~ en (la) primavera;
to walk with a ~ in one's step andar dando
saltos or brincos; **to ~ into action** lanzarse
a la acción; **spring up** vi (thing: appear)
aparecer; (problem) surgir
springboard ['sprɪŋbɔːd] n trampolín m
spring-clean [sprɪŋ'kliːn] n (also: **~ing**)
limpieza general
spring onion n cebolleta
spring roll n rollito de primavera
springtime ['sprɪŋtaɪm] n primavera
sprinkle ['sprɪŋkl] vt (pour: liquid) rociar;
(: salt, sugar) espolvorear; **to ~ water** etc **on**,
~ with water etc rociar or salpicar de agua
etc
sprinkler ['sprɪŋklər] n (for lawn) aspersor m;
(to put out fire) aparato de rociadura
automática
sprint [sprɪnt] n (e)sprint m ▷ vi (gen) correr
a toda velocidad; (Sport) esprintar; **the 200
metres ~** el (e)sprint de 200 metros
sprinter ['sprɪntər] n velocista m/f
spritzer ['sprɪtsər] n vino blanco con soda
sprout [spraut] vi brotar, retoñar ▷ n:
(Brussels) ~s npl coles fpl de Bruselas
spruce [spruːs] n (Bot) pícea ▷ adj aseado,
pulcro; **spruce up** vt (tidy) arreglar, acicalar;
(smarten up: room etc) ordenar; **to ~ o.s. up**
arreglarse
sprung [sprʌŋ] pp of **spring**
spry [spraɪ] adj ágil, activo
spun [spʌn] pt, pp of **spin**
spur [spəːr] n espuela; (fig) estímulo, aguijón
m ▷ vt (also: **~ on**) estimular, incitar; **on the ~
of the moment** de improviso
spurious ['spjʊərɪəs] adj falso
spurn [spəːn] vt desdeñar, rechazar
spurt [spəːt] n chorro; (of energy) arrebato ▷ vi
chorrear; **to put in** or **on a ~** (runner) acelerar;
(fig: in work etc) hacer un gran esfuerzo
spy [spaɪ] n espía m/f ▷ vi: **to ~ on** espiar a ▷ vt
(see) divisar, lograr ver ▷ cpd (film, story) de
espionaje
spying ['spaɪɪŋ] n espionaje m
spyware ['spaɪwɛər] n (Comput) spyware m
sq. abbr (Math etc) = **square**
squabble ['skwɔbl] n riña, pelea ▷ vi reñir,
pelear
squad [skwɔd] n (Mil) pelotón m; (Police)
brigada; (Sport) equipo; **flying ~** (Police)
brigada móvil
squaddie ['skwɔdɪ] n (Mil: inf) chivo
squadron ['skwɔdrn] n (Mil) escuadrón m;
(Aviat, Naut) escuadra
squalid ['skwɔlɪd] adj miserable

squall [skwɔːl] n (storm) chubasco; (wind)
ráfaga
squalor ['skwɔlər] n miseria
squander ['skwɔndər] vt (money) derrochar,
despilfarrar; (chances) desperdiciar
square [skwɛər] n cuadro; (in town) plaza;
(US: block of houses) manzana, cuadra (LAm);
(inf: person) carca m/f ▷ adj cuadrado; (inf:
ideas, tastes) trasnochado ▷ vt (arrange)
arreglar; (Math) cuadrar; (reconcile)
compaginar ▷ vi cuadrar, conformarse; **all ~**
igual(es); **a ~ meal** una comida decente; **two
metres ~** dos metros por dos; **one ~ metre**
un metro cuadrado; **to get one's accounts ~**
dejar las cuentas claras; **I'll ~ it with him**
(inf) yo lo arreglo con él; **can you ~ it with
your conscience?** ¿cómo se justifica ante sí
mismo?; **we're back to ~ one** (fig) hemos
vuelto al punto de partida; **square up** vi
(settle): **to ~ up (with sb)** ajustar cuentas (con
algn)
squarely ['skwɛəlɪ] adv (fully) de lleno;
(honestly, fairly) honradamente, justamente
square root n raíz f cuadrada
squash [skwɔʃ] n (vegetable) calabaza; (Sport)
squash m; (Brit: drink): **lemon/orange ~** zumo
(Sp) or jugo (LAm) de limón/naranja ▷ vt
aplastar
squat [skwɔt] adj achaparrado ▷ vi
agacharse, sentarse en cuclillas; (on property)
ocupar ilegalmente
squatter ['skwɔtər] n ocupante m/f ilegal,
okupa m/f
squawk [skwɔːk] vi graznar
squeak [skwiːk] vi (hinge, wheel) chirriar,
rechinar; (shoe, wood) crujir; (mouse) chillar
▷ n (of hinge, wheel etc) chirrido,
rechinamiento; (of shoes) crujir m; (of mouse
etc) chillido
squeaky ['skwiːkɪ] adj que cruje; **to be ~
clean** (fig) ser superhonrado
squeal [skwiːl] vi chillar, dar gritos agudos
squeamish ['skwiːmɪʃ] adj delicado,
remilgado
squeeze [skwiːz] n presión f; (of hand)
apretón m; (Comm: credit squeeze) restricción f
▷ vt (lemon etc) exprimir; (hand, arm) apretar;
a ~ of lemon unas gotas de limón; **to ~ past/
under sth** colarse al lado de/por debajo de
algo; **squeeze out** vt exprimir; (fig) excluir;
squeeze through vi abrirse paso con
esfuerzos
squelch [skwɛltʃ] vi chapotear
squid [skwɪd] n calamar m
squiggle ['skwɪgl] n garabato
squint [skwɪnt] vi bizquear, ser bizco ▷ n
(Med) estrabismo; **to ~ at sth** mirar algo
entornando los ojos
squirm [skwəːm] vi retorcerse, revolverse
squirrel ['skwɪrəl] n ardilla
squirt [skwəːt] vi salir a chorros ▷ vt chiscar
Sr abbr = **senior**; (Rel) = **sister**

Sri Lanka [srɪ'læŋkə] n Sri Lanka m
SS abbr (= steamship) M.V.
St abbr (= saint) Sto.(-a); (= street) c/
stab [stæb] n (with knife etc) puñalada; (of pain) pinchazo; **to have a ~ at (doing) sth** (inf) probar (a hacer) algo ▷ vt apuñalar; **to ~ sb to death** matar a algn a puñaladas
stability [stə'bɪlɪtɪ] n estabilidad f
stable ['steɪbl] adj estable ▷ n cuadra, caballeriza; **riding ~s** escuela hípica
stack [stæk] n montón m, pila; (inf) mar f ▷ vt amontonar, apilar; **there's ~s of time to finish it** hay cantidad de tiempo para acabarlo
stadium ['steɪdɪəm] n estadio
staff [stɑːf] n (work force) personal m, plantilla; (Brit Scol: also: **teaching ~**) cuerpo docente; (stick) bastón m ▷ vt proveer de personal; **to be ~ed by Asians/women** tener una plantilla asiática/femenina
stag [stæg] n ciervo, venado; (Brit Stock Exchange) especulador m con nuevas emisiones
stage [steɪdʒ] n escena; (point) etapa; (platform) plataforma; **the ~** el escenario, el teatro ▷ vt (play) poner en escena, representar; (organize) montar, organizar; (fig: perform: recovery etc) efectuar; **in ~s** por etapas; **in the early/final ~s** en las primeras/últimas etapas; **to go through a difficult ~** pasar una fase or etapa mala
stagecoach ['steɪdʒkəʊtʃ] n diligencia
stage manager n director(a) m(f) de escena
stagger ['stægə'] vi tambalear ▷ vt (amaze) asombrar; (hours, holidays) escalonar
staggering ['stægərɪŋ] adj (amazing) asombroso, pasmoso
stagnant ['stægnənt] adj estancado
stagnate [stæg'neɪt] vi estancarse; (fig: economy, mind) quedarse estancado
stag night, stag party n despedida de soltero
staid [steɪd] adj (clothes) serio, formal
stain [steɪn] n mancha; (colouring) tintura ▷ vt manchar; (wood) teñir
stained glass n vidrio m de color
stained glass window [steɪnd-] n vidriera de colores
stainless ['steɪnlɪs] adj (steel) inoxidable
stainless steel n acero inoxidable
stain remover n quitamanchas m inv
stair [steə'] n (step) peldaño, escalón m; **stairs** npl escaleras fpl
staircase ['steəkeɪs], **stairway** ['steəweɪ] n escalera
stake [steɪk] n estaca, poste m; (Betting) apuesta ▷ vt (bet) apostar; (also: **~ out:** area) cercar con estacas; **to be at ~** estar en juego; **to have a ~ in sth** tener interés en algo; **to ~ a claim to (sth)** presentar reclamación por or reclamar (algo)
stalactite ['stæləktaɪt] n estalactita

stalagmite ['stæləgmaɪt] n estalagmita
stale [steɪl] adj (bread) duro; (food) pasado; (smell) rancio; (beer) agrio
stalemate ['steɪlmeɪt] n tablas fpl; **to reach ~** (fig) estancarse, alcanzar un punto muerto
stalk [stɔːk] n tallo, caña ▷ vt (Aut) acechar, cazar al acecho; **to ~ off** irse airado
stall [stɔːl] n (in market) puesto; (in stable) casilla (de establo) ▷ vt (Aut) parar, calar; (fig) dar largas a ▷ vi (Aut) pararse, calarse; (fig) buscar evasivas; **stalls** npl (Brit: in cinema, theatre) butacas fpl; **a newspaper ~** un quiosco (de periódicos); **a flower ~** un puesto de flores
stallion ['stælɪən] n semental m, garañón m
stalwart ['stɔːlwət] n partidario(-a) incondicional
stamina ['stæmɪnə] n resistencia
stammer ['stæmə'] n tartamudeo, balbuceo ▷ vi tartamudear, balbucir
stamp [stæmp] n sello, estampilla (LAm); (mark) marca, huella; (on document) timbre m ▷ vi (also: **~ one's foot**) patear ▷ vt patear, golpear con el pie; (letter) poner sellos en, franquear; (with rubber stamp) marcar con sello; **~ed addressed envelope (sae)** sobre m franqueado con la dirección propia; **stamp out** vt (fire) apagar con el pie; (crime, opposition) acabar con
stamp album n álbum m para sellos
stamp collecting n filatelia
stampede [stæm'piːd] n (of cattle) estampida
stance [stæns] n postura
stand [stænd] (pt, pp stood) n (attitude) posición f, postura; (for taxis) parada; (also: **music ~**) atril m; (Sport) tribuna; (at exhibition) stand m ▷ vi (be) estar, encontrarse; (be on foot) estar de pie; (rise) levantarse; (remain) quedar en pie ▷ vt (place) poner, colocar; (tolerate, withstand) aguantar, soportar; **to make a ~** (fig) resistir, mantener una postura firme; **to take a ~ on an issue** adoptar una actitud hacia una cuestión; **to ~ for parliament** (Brit) presentarse (como candidato) a las elecciones; **nothing ~s in our way** nada nos lo impide; **to ~ still** quedarse inmóvil; **to let sth ~ as it is** dejar algo como está; **as things ~** tal como están las cosas; **to ~ sb a drink/meal** invitar a algn a una copa/a comer; **the company will have to ~ the loss** la empresa tendrá que hacer frente a las pérdidas; **I can't ~ him** no le aguanto, no le puedo ver; **to ~ guard** or **watch** (Mil) hacer guardia; **stand aside** vi apartarse, mantenerse aparte; **stand back** vi retirarse; **stand by** ▷ vi (be ready) estar listo ▷ vt fus (opinion) mantener; **stand down** vi (withdraw) ceder el puesto; (Mil, Law) retirarse; **stand for** vt fus (signify) significar; (tolerate) aguantar, permitir; **stand in for** vt fus suplir a; **stand out** vi (be prominent) destacarse; **stand up** vi (rise)

levantarse, ponerse de pie; **stand up for** *vt fus* defender; **stand up to** *vt fus* hacer frente a

standard ['stændəd] *n* patrón *m*, norma; *(flag)* estandarte *m* ▷ *adj (size etc)* normal, corriente, estándar; **standards** *npl (morals)* valores *mpl* morales; **the gold ~** (Comm) el patrón oro; **high/low ~** de alto/bajo nivel; **below** *or* **not up to ~** *(work)* de calidad inferior; **to be** *or* **come up to ~** satisfacer los requisitos; **to apply a double ~** aplicar un doble criterio

standardize ['stændədaɪz] *vt* estandarizar

standard lamp *n* (Brit) lámpara de pie

standard of living *n* nivel *m* de vida

stand-by ['stændbaɪ] *n (alert)* alerta, aviso; *(also: ~ ticket:* Theat) *entrada reducida de última hora*; *(:Aviat)* billete *m* standby; **to be on ~** estar preparado; *(doctor)* estar listo para acudir; *(Aviat)* estar en la lista de espera

stand-in ['stændɪn] *n* suplente *m/f*; *(Cine)* doble *m/f*

standing ['stændɪŋ] *adj (upright)* derecho; *(on foot)* de pie, en pie; *(permanent: committee)* permanente; *(:rule)* fijo; *(:army)* permanente, regular; *(grievance)* constante, viejo ▷ *n* reputación *f*; *(duration):* **of six months'** ~ que lleva seis meses; **of many years'** ~ que lleva muchos años; **he was given a ~ ovation** le dieron una calurosa ovación de pie; **~ joke** motivo constante de broma; **a man of some ~** un hombre de cierta posición *or* categoría

standing order *n* (Brit: at bank) giro bancario; **~s** *npl* (Mil) reglamento *sg* general

standing room *n* sitio para estar de pie

stand-off ['stændɒf] *n* punto muerto

stand-offish [stænd'ɒfɪʃ] *adj* distante

standpoint ['stændpɔɪnt] *n* punto de vista

standstill ['stændstɪl] *n:* **at a ~** *(industry, traffic)* paralizado, en un punto muerto; **to come to a ~** pararse, quedar paralizado

stank [stæŋk] *pt of* **stink**

staple ['steɪpl] *n (for papers)* grapa; *(product)* producto *or* artículo de primeva necesidad ▷ *adj (crop, industry, food etc)* básico ▷ *vt* grapar

stapler ['steɪplə] *n* grapadora

star [stɑ:] *n* estrella; *(celebrity)* estrella, astro ▷ *vi:* **to ~ in** ser la estrella de; **four-~ hotel** hotel de cuatro estrellas; **4-~ petrol** gasolina extra ▷ *vt* (Theat, Cine) ser el/la protagonista de; **the stars** *npl* (Astrology) el horóscopo

starboard ['stɑ:bəd] *n* estribor *m*

starch [stɑ:tʃ] *n* almidón *m*

stardom ['stɑ:dəm] *n* estrellato

stare [steə] *n* mirada fija ▷ *vi:* **to ~ at** mirar fijo

starfish ['stɑ:fɪʃ] *n* estrella de mar

stark [stɑ:k] *adj (bleak)* severo, escueto; *(simplicity, colour)* austero; *(reality, truth)* puro; *(poverty)* absoluto ▷ *adv:* **~ naked** en cueros

starkers ['stɑ:kəz] *adj* (Brit inf): **to be ~** estar en cueros

starling ['stɑ:lɪŋ] *n* estornino

starry ['stɑ:rɪ] *adj* estrellado

starry-eyed [stɑ:rɪ'aɪd] *adj (gullible, innocent)* inocentón(-ona), ingenuo; *(idealistic)* idealista; *(from wonder)* asombrado; *(from love)* enamoradísimo

Stars and Stripes *npl:* **the ~** las barras y las estrellas, la bandera de EEUU

star sign *n* signo del zodíaco

start [stɑ:t] *n (beginning)* principio, comienzo; *(departure)* salida; *(sudden movement)* sobresalto; *(advantage)* ventaja ▷ *vt* empezar, comenzar; *(cause)* causar; *(found: business, newspaper)* establecer, fundar; *(engine)* poner en marcha ▷ *vi (begin)* comenzar, empezar; *(with fright)* asustarse, sobresaltarse; *(train etc)* salir; **to give sb a ~** dar un susto a algn; **at the ~** al principio; **for a ~** en primer lugar; **to make an early ~** ponerse en camino temprano; **the thieves had three hours' ~** los ladrones llevaban tres horas de ventaja; **to ~ a fire** provocar un incendio; **to ~ doing** *or* **to do sth** empezar a hacer algo; **to ~ (off) with ...** *(firstly)* para empezar; *(at the beginning)* al principio; **start off** *vi* empezar, comenzar; *(leave)* salir, ponerse en camino; **start out** *vi (begin)* empezar; *(set out)* partir, salir; **start over** *vi* (US) volver a empezar; **start up** *vi* comenzar; *(car)* ponerse en marcha ▷ *vt* comenzar; *(car)* poner en marcha

starter ['stɑ:tə] *n* (Aut) botón *m* de arranque; *(Sport: official)* juez *m/f* de salida; *(:runner)* corredor(a) *m(f)*; (Brit Culin) entrada, entrante *m*

starting point ['stɑ:tɪŋ-] *n* punto de partida

startle ['stɑ:tl] *vt* sobresaltar

startling ['stɑ:tlɪŋ] *adj* alarmante

starvation [stɑ:'veɪʃən] *n* hambre *f*, hambruna *f*; *(Med)* inanición *f*

starve [stɑ:v] *vi* pasar hambre; *(to death)* morir de hambre ▷ *vt* hacer pasar hambre; *(fig)* privar; **I'm starving** estoy muerto de hambre

stash [stæʃ] *vt:* **to ~ sth away** *(inf)* poner algo a buen recaudo

state [steɪt] *n* estado; *(pomp):* **in ~** con mucha ceremonia ▷ *vt (say, declare)* afirmar; *(a case)* presentar, exponer; **~ of emergency** estado de excepción or emergencia; **~ of mind** estado de ánimo; **to lie in ~** *(corpse)* estar de cuerpo presente; **to be in a ~** estar agitado; **the S~s** los Estados Unidos

State Department *n* (US) Ministerio de Asuntos Exteriores

stately ['steɪtlɪ] *adj* majestuoso, imponente

statement ['steɪtmənt] *n* afirmación *f*; (Law) declaración *f*; (Comm) estado; **official ~** informe *m* oficial; **~ of account, bank ~** estado de cuenta

States [steɪts] *npl:* **the ~** los Estados Unidos

state school *n* escuela *or* colegio estatal

statesman ['steɪtsmən] *n* estadista *m*

static ['stætɪk] *n* (*Radio*) parásitos *mpl* ▷ *adj* estático

station ['steɪʃən] *n* (*gen*) estación *f*; (*place*) puesto, sitio; (*Radio*) emisora; (*rank*) posición *f* social ▷ *vt* colocar, situar; (*Mil*) apostar; **action ~s!** ¡a los puestos de combate!; **to be ~ed in** (*Mil*) estar estacionado en

stationary ['steɪʃnərɪ] *adj* estacionario, fijo

stationer ['steɪʃənəʳ] *n* papelero(-a)

stationer's, stationer's shop *n* (*Brit*) papelería

stationery ['steɪʃənərɪ] *n* (*writing paper*) papel *m* de escribir; (*writing materials*) artículos *mpl* de escritorio

station master *n* (*Rail*) jefe *m* de estación

station wagon *n* (*US*) coche *m* familiar con ranchera

statistic [stə'tɪstɪk] *n* estadística

statistics [stə'tɪstɪks] *n* (*science*) estadística

statue ['stætju:] *n* estatua

stature ['stætʃəʳ] *n* estatura; (*fig*) talla

status ['steɪtəs] *n* condición *f*, estado; (*reputation*) reputación *f*, estatus *m*

status quo *n* (e)statu quo *m*

status symbol *n* símbolo de prestigio

statute ['stætju:t] *n* estatuto, ley *f*

statutory ['stætjutrɪ] *adj* estatutario; **~ meeting** junta ordinaria

staunch [stɔ:ntʃ] *adj* leal, incondicional ▷ *vt* (*flow, blood*) restañar

stave [steɪv] *vt*: **to ~ off** (*attack*) rechazar; (*threat*) evitar

stay [steɪ] *n* (*period of time*) estancia; (*Law*): **~ of execution** aplazamiento de una sentencia ▷ *vi* (*remain*) quedar(se); (*as guest*) hospedarse; **to ~ put** seguir en el mismo sitio; **to ~ the night/5 days** pasar la noche/estar or quedarse 5 días; **stay away** *vi* (*from person, building*) no acercarse; (*from event*) no acudir; **stay behind** *vi* quedar atrás; **stay in** *vi* (*at home*) quedarse en casa; **stay on** *vi* quedarse; **stay out** *vi* (*of house*) no volver a casa; (*strikers*) no volver al trabajo; **stay up** *vi* (*at night*) velar, no acostarse

staycation [steɪ'keɪʃən] *n* (*inf*) vacaciones *fpl* en casa

staying power ['steɪɪŋ-] *n* resistencia, aguante *m*

STD *n abbr* (= *sexually transmitted disease*) ETS *f*

stead [stɛd] *n*: **in sb's ~** en lugar de algn; **to stand sb in good ~** ser muy útil a algn

steadfast ['stɛdfɑ:st] *adj* firme, resuelto

steadily ['stɛdɪlɪ] *adv* (*firmly*) firmemente; (*unceasingly*) sin parar; (*fixedly*) fijamente; (*drive*) a velocidad constante

steady ['stɛdɪ] *adj* (*fixed*) firme, fijo; (*regular*) regular; (*boyfriend etc*) formal, fijo; (*person, character*) sensato, juicioso ▷ *vt* (*hold*) mantener firme; (*stabilize*) estabilizar;

(*nerves*) calmar; **to ~ o.s. on** *or* **against sth** afirmarse en algo

steak [steɪk] *n* (*gen*) filete *m*; (*beef*) bistec *m*

steal (*pt* **stole**, *pp* **stolen**) [sti:l, stəul, 'stəuln] *vt, vi* robar; **steal away, steal off** *vi* marcharse furtivamente

stealth [stɛlθ] *n*: **by ~** a escondidas, sigilosamente

stealthy ['stɛlθɪ] *adj* cauteloso, sigiloso

steam [sti:m] *n* vapor *m*; (*mist*) vaho, humo ▷ *vt* (*Culin*) cocer al vapor ▷ *vi* echar vapor; (*ship*): **to ~ along** avanzar, ir avanzando; **under one's own ~** (*fig*) por sus propios medios *or* propias fuerzas; **to run out of ~** (*fig: person*) quedar(se) agotado, quemarse; **to let off ~** (*fig*) desahogarse; **steam up** *vi* (*window*) empañarse; **to get ~ed up about sth** (*fig*) ponerse negro por algo

steam engine *n* máquina de vapor

steamer ['sti:məʳ] *n* (*buque m de*) vapor *m*; (*Culin*) recipiente para cocinar al vapor

steamroller ['sti:mrəuləʳ] *n* apisonadora

steamship ['sti:mʃɪp] *n* = **steamer**

steamy ['sti:mɪ] *adj* (*room*) lleno de vapor; (*window*) empañado; (*heat, atmosphere*) bochornoso

steel [sti:l] *n* acero ▷ *adj* de acero

steelworks ['sti:lwə:ks] *n* acería, fundición *f* de acero

steep [sti:p] *adj* escarpado, abrupto; (*stair*) empinado; (*price*) exorbitante, excesivo ▷ *vt* empapar, remojar

steeple ['sti:pl] *n* aguja, campanario

steeplejack ['sti:pldʒæk] *n* reparador(a) *m(f)* de chimeneas *or* de campanarios

steer [stɪəʳ] *vt* (*car*) conducir (*Sp*), manejar (*LAm*); (*person*) dirigir, guiar ▷ *vi* conducir (*Sp*), manejar (*LAm*); **to ~ clear of sb/sth** (*fig*) esquivar a algn/evadir algo

steering ['stɪərɪŋ] *n* (*Aut*) dirección *f*

steering wheel *n* volante *m*

stem [stɛm] *n* (*of plant*) tallo; (*of glass*) pie *m*; (*of pipe*) cañón *m* ▷ *vt* detener; (*blood*) restañar; **stem from** *vt fus* ser consecuencia de

stench [stɛntʃ] *n* hedor *m*

stencil ['stɛnsl] *n* (*typed*) cliché *m*, clisé *m*; (*lettering*) plantilla ▷ *vt* hacer un cliché de

stenographer [stɛ'nɔgrəfəʳ] *n* (*US*) taquígrafo(-a)

step [stɛp] *n* paso; (*sound*) paso, pisada; (*stair*) peldaño, escalón *m* ▷ *vi*: **to ~ forward** dar un paso adelante; **steps** *npl* (*Brit*) = **stepladder**; **~ by ~** paso a paso; (*fig*) poco a poco; **to keep in ~ (with)** llevar el paso de; (*fig*) llevar el paso de, estar de acuerdo con; **to be in/out of ~ with** estar acorde con/estar en disonancia con; **to take ~s to solve a problem** tomar medidas para resolver un problema; **step down** *vi* (*fig*) retirarse; **step in** *vi* entrar; (*fig*) intervenir; **step off** *vt fus* bajar de; **step on** *vt fus* pisar; **step over** *vt fus*

S

pasar por encima de; **step up** vt (increase) aumentar

step aerobics npl step m

stepbrother ['stɛpbrʌðə'] n hermanastro

stepchild ['stɛptʃaɪld] (pl **stepchildren**) n hijastro(-a) m/f

stepdaughter ['stɛpdɔːtə'] n hijastra

stepfather ['stɛpfɑːðə'] n padrastro

stepladder ['stɛplædə'] n escalera doble or de tijera

stepmother ['stɛpmʌðə'] n madrastra

stepping stone ['stɛpɪŋ-] n pasadera

stepsister ['stɛpsɪstə'] n hermanastra

stepson ['stɛpsʌn] n hijastro

stereo ['stɛrɪəu] n estéreo ▷ adj (also: **~phonic**) estéreo, estereofónico; **in ~** en estéreo

stereotype ['stɪərɪətaɪp] n estereotipo ▷ vt estereotipar

sterile ['stɛraɪl] adj estéril

sterilization ['stɛrɪlaɪ'zeɪʃən] n esterilización f

sterilize ['stɛrɪlaɪz] vt esterilizar

sterling ['stəːlɪŋ] adj (silver) de ley ▷ n (Econ) libras fpl esterlinas; **a pound ~** una libra esterlina; **he is of ~ character** tiene un carácter excelente

stern [stəːn] adj severo, austero ▷ n (Naut) popa

steroid ['stɪərɔɪd] n esteroide m

stethoscope ['stɛθəskəup] n estetoscopio

stew [stjuː] n cocido, estofado, guisado (LAm) ▷ vt, vi estofar, guisar; (fruit) cocer; **~ed fruit** compota de fruta

steward ['stjuːəd] n (Brit: gen) camarero; (shop steward) enlace m/f sindical

stewardess ['stjuːədɛs] n azafata

stewardship ['stjuːədʃɪp] n tutela

St. Ex. abbr = **stock exchange**

stg abbr (= sterling) ester

stick [stɪk] (pt, pp **stuck**) n palo; (as weapon) porra; (also: **walking ~**) bastón m ▷ vt (glue) pegar; (inf: put) meter; (: tolerate) aguantar, soportar ▷ vi pegarse; (come to a stop) quedarse parado; (get jammed: door, lift) atascarse; **to get hold of the wrong end of the ~** entender al revés; **to ~ to** (word, principles) atenerse a, ser fiel a; (promise) cumplir; **it stuck in my mind** se me quedó grabado; **to ~ sth into** clavar or hincar algo en; **stick around** vi (inf) quedarse; **stick out** vi sobresalir ▷ vt: **to ~ it out** (inf) aguantar; **stick up** vi sobresalir; **stick up for** vt fus defender

sticker ['stɪkə'] n (label) etiqueta adhesiva; (with slogan) pegatina

sticking plaster ['stɪkɪŋ-] n (Brit) esparadrapo

sticking point n (fig) punto de fricción

stick insect n insecto palo

stickler ['stɪklə'] n: **to be a ~ for** insistir mucho en

stick shift n (US Aut) palanca de cambios

stick-up ['stɪkʌp] n asalto, atraco

sticky ['stɪkɪ] adj pegajoso; (label) adhesivo; (fig) difícil

stiff [stɪf] adj rígido, tieso; (hard) duro; (difficult) difícil; (person) inflexible; (price) exorbitante; **to have a ~ neck/back** tener tortícolis/dolor de espalda; **the door's ~** la puerta está atrancada ▷ adv: **scared/bored ~** muerto de miedo/aburrimiento

stiffen ['stɪfn] vt hacer más rígido; (limb) entumecer ▷ vi endurecerse; (grow stronger) fortalecerse

stifle ['staɪfl] vt ahogar, sofocar

stifling ['staɪflɪŋ] adj (heat) sofocante, bochornoso

stigma ['stɪgmə] n (Bot, Med, Rel, pl **stigmata** [stɪg'mɑːtə], fig: pl **stigmas**) estigma m

stile [staɪl] n escalera (para pasar una cerca)

stiletto [stɪ'lɛtəu] n (Brit: also: **~ heel**) tacón m de aguja

still [stɪl] adj inmóvil, quieto; (orange juice etc) sin gas ▷ adv (up to this time) todavía; (even) aún; (nonetheless) sin embargo, aun así ▷ n (Cine) foto f fija; **keep ~!** ¡estate quieto!, ¡no te muevas!; **he ~ hasn't arrived** todavía no ha llegado

stillborn ['stɪlbɔːn] adj nacido muerto

still life n naturaleza muerta

stilt [stɪlt] n zanco; (pile) pilar m, soporte m

stilted ['stɪltɪd] adj afectado, artificial

stimulant ['stɪmjulənt] n estimulante m

stimulate ['stɪmjuleɪt] vt estimular

stimulating ['stɪmjuleɪtɪŋ] adj estimulante

stimulation [stɪmju'leɪʃən] n estímulo

stimulus (pl **stimuli**) ['stɪmjuləs, -laɪ] n estímulo, incentivo

sting [stɪŋ] (pt, pp **stung**) n (wound) picadura; (pain) escozor m, picazón m; (organ) aguijón m; (inf: confidence trick) timo ▷ vt picar ▷ vi picar, escocer; **my eyes are ~ing** me pican or escuecen los ojos

stingy ['stɪndʒɪ] adj tacaño

stink [stɪŋk] (pt **stank**, pp **stunk** [stæŋk, stʌŋk]) n hedor m, tufo ▷ vi heder, apestar

stinking ['stɪŋkɪŋ] adj hediondo, fétido; (fig: inf) horrible

stint [stɪnt] n tarea, destajo; **to do one's ~ (at sth)** hacer su parte (de algo), hacer lo que corresponde (de algo) ▷ vi: **to ~ on** escatimar

stir [stəː'] n (fig: agitation) conmoción f ▷ vt (tea etc) remover; (fire) atizar; (move) agitar; (fig: emotions) provocar ▷ vi moverse; **to give sth a ~** remover; algo; **to cause a ~** causar conmoción or sensación; **stir up** vt excitar; (trouble) fomentar

stir-fry ['stəːfraɪ] vt sofreír removiendo ▷ n plato preparado sofriendo y removiendo los ingredientes

stirrup ['stɪrəp] n estribo

stitch [stɪtʃ] n (Sewing) puntada; (Knitting) punto; (Med) punto (de sutura); (pain) punzada ▷ vt coser; (Med) suturar

stoat [stəut] n armiño

stock [stɔk] n (Comm: reserves) existencias fpl, stock m; (: selection) surtido; (Agr) ganado, ganadería; (Culin) caldo; (fig: lineage) estirpe f, cepa; (Finance) capital m; (: shares) acciones fpl; (Rail: rolling stock) material m rodante ▷ adj (Comm: goods, size) normal, de serie; (fig: reply etc) clásico, trillado; (: greeting) acostumbrado ▷ vt (have in stock) tener existencias de; (supply) proveer, abastecer; **in** ~ en existencia or almacén; **to have sth in** ~ tener existencias de algo; **out of** ~ agotado; **to take** ~ **of** (fig) considerar, examinar; **stocks** npl (History: punishment) cepo sg; **~s and shares** acciones y valores; **government** ~ papel m del Estado; **stock up with** vt fus abastecerse de

stockbroker ['stɔkbrəukə'] n agente m/f or corredor(a) m(f) de bolsa

stock cube n pastilla or cubito de caldo

stock exchange n bolsa

stockholder ['stɔkhəuldə'] n (US) accionista m/f

stocking ['stɔkɪŋ] n media

stock market n bolsa (de valores)

stock phrase n vieja frase f

stockpile ['stɔkpaɪl] n reserva ▷ vt acumular, almacenar

stockroom ['stɔkru:m] n almacén m, depósito

stocktaking ['stɔkteɪkɪŋ] n (Brit Comm) inventario, balance m

stocky ['stɔkɪ] adj (strong) robusto; (short) achaparrado

stodgy ['stɔdʒɪ] adj indigesto, pesado

stoke [stəuk] vt atizar

stole [stəul] pt of **steal** ▷ n estola

stolen ['stəuln] pp of **steal**

stolid ['stɔlɪd] adj (person) imperturbable, impasible

stomach ['stʌmək] n (Anat) estómago; (belly) vientre m ▷ vt tragar, aguantar

stomach ache n dolor m de estómago

stone [stəun] n piedra; (in fruit) hueso; (Brit: weight) = 6.348 kg; 14lb ▷ adj de piedra ▷ vt apedrear; (fruit) deshuesar; **within a ~'s throw of the station** a tiro de piedra or a dos pasos de la estación

stone-cold ['stəun'kəuld] adj helado

stone-deaf ['stəun'dɛf] adj sordo como una tapia

stonewall [stəun'wɔ:l] vi alargar la cosa innecesariamente ▷ vt dar largas a

stonework ['stəunwə:k] n (art) cantería

stood [stud] pt, pp of **stand**

stooge [stu:dʒ] n (inf) hombre m de paja

stool [stu:l] n taburete m

stoop [stu:p] vi (also: ~ **down**) doblarse, agacharse; (also: **have a ~**) ser cargado de

espaldas; (bend) inclinarse, encorvarse; **to ~ to (doing) sth** rebajarse a (hacer) algo

stop [stɔp] n parada, alto; (in punctuation) punto ▷ vt parar, detener; (break off) suspender; (block: pay) suspender; (: cheque) invalidar; (prevent) impedir; (also: **put a ~ to**) poner término a ▷ vi pararse, detenerse; (end) acabarse; **to ~ doing sth** dejar de hacer algo; **to ~ sb (from) doing sth** impedir a algn hacer algo; **to ~ dead** pararse en seco; **~ it!** ¡basta ya!, ¡párate!; **stop by** vi pasar por; **stop off** vi interrumpir el viaje; **stop up** vt (hole) tapar

stopgap ['stɔpgæp] n interino; (person) sustituto(-a); (measure) medida provisional ▷ cpd (situation) provisional

stopover ['stɔpəuvə'] n parada intermedia; (Aviat) escala

stoppage ['stɔpɪdʒ] n (strike) paro; (temporary stop) interrupción f; (of pay) suspensión f; (blockage) obstrucción f

stopper ['stɔpə'] n tapón m

stop press n noticias fpl de última hora

stopwatch ['stɔpwɔtʃ] n cronómetro

storage ['stɔ:rɪdʒ] n almacenaje m; (Comput) almacenamiento

storage heater n acumulador m de calor

store [stɔ:'] n (stock) provisión f; (depot) almacén m; (Brit: large shop) almacén m; (US) tienda; (reserve) reserva, repuesto ▷ vt (gen) almacenar; (Comput) almacenar; (keep) guardar; (in filing system) archivar; **stores** npl víveres mpl; **who knows what is in ~ for us** quién sabe lo que nos espera; **to set great/ little ~ by sth** dar mucha/poca importancia a algo, valorar mucho/poco algo; **store up** vt acumular

storekeeper ['stɔ:ki:pə'] n (US) tendero(-a)

storeroom ['stɔ:ru:m] n despensa

storey, story (US) ['stɔ:rɪ] n piso

stork [stɔ:k] n cigüeña

storm [stɔ:m] n tormenta; (wind) vendaval m; (fig: of applause) salva; (: of criticism) nube f ▷ vi (fig) rabiar ▷ vt tomar por asalto, asaltar; **to take a town by ~** (Mil) tomar una ciudad por asalto

stormy ['stɔ:mɪ] adj tempestuoso

story ['stɔ:rɪ] n historia; (Press) artículo; (joke) cuento, chiste m; (plot) argumento; (lie) cuento; (US) = **storey**

storybook ['stɔ:rɪbuk] n libro de cuentos

stout [staut] adj (strong) sólido; (fat) gordo, corpulento ▷ n cerveza negra

stove [stəuv] n (for cooking) cocina; (for heating) estufa; **gas/electric ~** cocina de gas/eléctrica

stow [stəu] vt meter, poner; (Naut) estibar

stowaway ['stəuəweɪ] n polizón(-ona) m(f)

straddle ['strædl] vt montar a horcajadas

straggle ['strægl] vi (wander) vagar en desorden; (lag behind) rezagarse

straight [streɪt] adj (direct) recto, derecho; (plain, uncomplicated) sencillo; (frank) franco,

S

directo; (in order) en orden; (continuous)
continuo; (Theat: part, play) serio; (person:
conventional) recto, convencional;
(: heterosexual) heterosexual ▷ adv derecho,
directamente; (drink) solo; **to put** or **get sth ~**
dejar algo en claro; **10 ~ wins** 10 victorias
seguidas; **to be (all) ~** (tidy) estar en orden;
(clarified) estar claro; **I went ~ home** (me) fui
directamente a casa; **~ away, ~ off** (at once)
en seguida

straighten ['streɪtn] vt (also: **~ out**)
enderezar, poner derecho ▷ vi (also: **~ up**)
enderezarse, ponerse derecho; **to ~ things
out** poner las cosas en orden

straight-faced [streɪt'feɪst] adj serio ▷ adv
sin mostrar emoción, impávido

straightforward [streɪt'fɔ:wəd] adj (simple)
sencillo; (honest) sincero

strain [streɪn] n (gen) tensión f; (Tech) presión
f; (Med) distensión f, torcedura; (breed) raza;
(lineage) linaje m; (of virus) variedad f ▷ vt (back
etc) distender, torcerse; (resources) agotar;
(tire) cansar; (stretch) estirar; (filter) filtrar;
(meaning) tergiversar ▷ vi esforzarse; **strains**
npl (Mus) son m; **she's under a lot of ~** está
bajo mucha tensión

strained [streɪnd] adj (muscle) torcido; (laugh)
forzado; (relations) tenso

strainer ['streɪnər] n colador m

strait [streɪt] n (Geo) estrecho; **to be in dire
~s** (fig) estar en un gran aprieto

straitjacket ['streɪtdʒækɪt] n camisa de
fuerza

strait-laced [streɪt'leɪst] adj mojigato,
gazmoño

strand [strænd] n (of thread) hebra; (of rope)
ramal m; **a ~ of hair** un pelo

stranded ['strændɪd] adj (person: without
money) desamparado; (: without transport)
colgado

strange [streɪndʒ] adj (not known)
desconocido; (odd) extraño, raro

strangely adv de un modo raro; see also
enough

stranger ['streɪndʒər] n desconocido(-a);
(from another area) forastero(-a); **I'm a ~ here**
no soy de aquí

strangle ['stræŋgl] vt estrangular

stranglehold ['stræŋglhəuld] n (fig)
dominio completo

strap [stræp] n correa; (of slip, dress) tirante m
▷ vt atar con correa

strapped [stræpt] adj: **to be ~ for cash** (inf)
andar mal de dinero

strapping ['stræpɪŋ] adj robusto, fornido

strategic [strə'ti:dʒɪk] adj estratégico

strategy ['strætɪdʒɪ] n estrategia

straw [strɔ:] n paja; (also: **drinking ~**) caña,
pajita; **that's the last ~!** ¡eso es el colmo!

strawberry ['strɔ:bərɪ] n fresa, frutilla (LAm)

stray [streɪ] adj (animal) extraviado; (bullet)
perdido; (scattered) disperso ▷ vi extraviarse,

perderse; (wander: walker) vagar, ir sin rumbo
fijo; (: speaker) desvariar

streak [stri:k] n raya; (fig: of madness etc) vena
▷ vt rayar ▷ vi: **to ~ past** pasar como un rayo;
to have ~s in one's hair tener vetas en el
pelo; **a winning/losing ~** una racha de
buena/mala suerte

streaker ['stri:kər] n corredor(a) m(f)
desnudo(-a)

stream [stri:m] n riachuelo, arroyo; (jet)
chorro; (flow) corriente f; (of people) oleada
▷ vt (Scol) dividir en grupos por habilidad ▷ vi
correr, fluir; **to ~ in/out** (people) entrar/salir
en tropel; **against the ~** a contracorriente;
on ~ (new power plant etc) en funcionamiento

streamer ['stri:mər] n serpentina

streamline ['stri:mlaɪn] vt aerodinamizar;
(fig) racionalizar

streamlined ['stri:mlaɪnd] adj aerodinámico

street [stri:t] n calle f ▷ adj callejero; **the
back ~s** las callejuelas; **to be on the ~s**
(homeless) estar sin vivienda; (as prostitute)
hacer la calle

streetcar ['stri:tkɑ:] n (US) tranvía m

street lamp n farol m

street light n farol m (LAm), farola (Sp)

street map n plano (de la ciudad)

street plan n plano callejero

streetwise ['stri:twaɪz] adj (inf) pícaro

strength [streŋθ] n fuerza; (of girder, knot etc)
resistencia; (of chemical solution) potencia; (of
wine) graduación f de alcohol; (fig: power)
poder m; **on the ~ of** a base de, en base a; **to
be at full/below ~** tener/no tener completo
el cupo

strengthen ['streŋθn] vt fortalecer, reforzar

strenuous ['strenjuəs] adj (tough) arduo;
(energetic) enérgico; (opposition) firme, tenaz;
(efforts) intensivo

stress [stres] n (force, pressure) presión f;
(mental strain) estrés m, tensión f; (accent,
emphasis) énfasis m, acento; (Ling, Poetry)
acento; (Tech) tensión f, carga ▷ vt subrayar,
recalcar; **to be under ~** estar estresado; **to
lay great ~ on sth** hacer hincapié en algo

stressed [strest] adj (tense) estresado,
agobiado; (syllable) acentuado

stressful ['stresful] adj (job) estresante

stretch [stretʃ] n (of sand etc) trecho; (of road)
tramo; (of time) período, tiempo ▷ vi
estirarse; (extend): **to ~ to** or **as far as**
extenderse hasta; (be enough: money, food): **to ~
to** alcanzar para, dar de sí para ▷ vt extender,
estirar; (make demands of) exigir el máximo
esfuerzo a; **to ~ one's legs** estirar las
piernas; **stretch out** vi tenderse ▷ vt (arm
etc) extender; (spread) estirar

stretcher ['stretʃər] n camilla

strewn [stru:n] adj: **~ with** cubierto or
sembrado de

stricken ['strɪkən] adj (person) herido; (city,
industry etc) condenado; **~ with** (arthritis,

disease) afligido por; **grief-~** destrozado por el dolor

strict [strɪkt] *adj* (*order, rule etc*) estricto; (*discipline, ban*) severo; **in ~ confidence** en la más absoluta confianza

strictly ['strɪktlɪ] *adv* estrictamente; (*totally*) terminantemente; **~ confidential** estrictamente confidencial; **~ speaking** en (el) sentido estricto (de la palabra); **~ between ourselves ...** entre nosotros ...

stride [straɪd] (*pt* **strode**, *pp* **stridden** ['strɪdn]) *n* zancada, tranco ▷ *vi* dar zancadas, andar a trancos; **to take in one's ~** (*fig: changes etc*) tomar con calma

strife [straɪf] *n* lucha

strike [straɪk] (*pt, pp* **struck**) *n* huelga; (*of oil etc*) descubrimiento; (*attack*) ataque *m*; (*Sport*) golpe *m* ▷ *vt* golpear, pegar; (*oil etc*) descubrir; (*obstacle*) topar con; (*produce: coin, medal*) acuñar; (: *agreement, deal*) alcanzar ▷ *vi* declarar la huelga; (*attack: Mil etc*) atacar; (*clock*) dar la hora; **on ~** (*workers*) en huelga; **to call a ~** declarar una huelga; **to go on** or **come out on ~** ponerse or declararse en huelga; **to ~ a match** encender una cerilla; **to ~ a balance** (*fig*) encontrar un equilibrio; **to ~ a bargain** cerrar un trato; **the clock struck nine o'clock** el reloj dio las nueve; **strike back** *vi* (*Mil*) contraatacar; (*fig*) devolver el golpe; **strike down** *vt* derribar; **strike off** *vt* (*from list*) tachar; (*doctor etc*) suspender; **strike out** *vt* borrar, tachar; **strike up** *vt* (*Mus*) empezar a tocar; (*conversation*) entablar; (*friendship*) trabar

striker ['straɪkə'] *n* huelguista *m/f*; (*Sport*) delantero

striking ['straɪkɪŋ] *adj* (*colour*) llamativo; (*obvious*) notorio

Strimmer® ['strɪmə'] *n* cortacéspedes *m inv* (*especial para los bordes*)

string [strɪŋ] (*pt, pp* **strung** [strʌŋ]) *n* (*gen*) cuerda; (*row*) hilera; (*Comput*) cadena ▷ *vt*: **to ~ together** ensartar; **to ~ out** extenderse; **the strings** *npl* (*Mus*) los instrumentos de cuerda; **to pull ~s** (*fig*) mover palancas; **to get a job by pulling ~s** conseguir un trabajo por enchufe; **with no ~s attached** (*fig*) sin compromiso

string bean *n* judía verde, habichuela

stringent ['strɪndʒənt] *adj* riguroso, severo

strip [strɪp] *n* tira; (*of land*) franja; (*of metal*) cinta, lámina ▷ *vt* desnudar; (*also: ~ down: machine*) desmontar ▷ *vi* desnudarse; **strip off** *vt* (*paint etc*) quitar ▷ *vi* (*person*) desnudarse

strip cartoon *n* tira cómica, historieta (*LAm*)

stripe [straɪp] *n* raya; (*Mil*) galón *m*; **white with green ~s** blanco con rayas verdes

striped [straɪpt] *adj* a rayas, rayado

strip lighting *n* alumbrado fluorescente

stripper ['strɪpə'] *n* artista *m/f* de striptease

strip-search ['strɪpsə:tʃ] *vt*: **to ~ sb** desnudar y registrar a algn

strive (*pt* **strove**, *pp* **striven**) [straɪv, strəʊv, 'strɪvn] *vi*: **to ~ to do sth** esforzarse or luchar por hacer algo

strode [strəʊd] *pt of* **stride**

stroke [strəʊk] *n* (*blow*) golpe *m*; (*Swimming*) brazada; (*Med*) apoplejía; (*caress*) caricia; (*of pen*) trazo; (*Swimming: style*) estilo; (*of piston*) carrera ▷ *vt* acariciar; **at a ~** de golpe; **a ~ of luck** un golpe de suerte; **two-~ engine** motor *m* de dos tiempos

stroll [strəʊl] *n* paseo, vuelta ▷ *vi* dar un paseo or una vuelta; **to go for a ~**, **have** or **take a ~** dar un paseo

stroller ['strəʊlə'] *n* (*US: pushchair*) cochecito

strong [strɔŋ] *adj* fuerte; (*bleach, acid*) concentrado ▷ *adv*: **to be going ~** (*company*) marchar bien; (*person*) conservarse bien; **they are 50 ~** son 50

stronghold ['strɔŋhəʊld] *n* fortaleza; (*fig*) baluarte *m*

strongly ['strɔŋlɪ] *adv* fuertemente, con fuerza; (*believe*) firmemente; **to feel ~ about sth** tener una opinión firme sobre algo

strongroom ['strɔŋru:m] *n* cámara acorazada

stroppy ['strɔpɪ] *adj* (*Brit inf*) borde; **to get ~** ponerse borde

strove [strəʊv] *pt of* **strive**

struck [strʌk] *pt, pp of* **strike**

structural ['strʌktʃərəl] *adj* estructural

structure ['strʌktʃə'] *n* estructura; (*building*) construcción *f*

struggle ['strʌgl] *n* lucha ▷ *vi* luchar; **to have a ~ to do sth** esforzarse por hacer algo

strum [strʌm] *vt* (*guitar*) rasguear

strung [strʌŋ] *pt, pp of* **string**

strut [strʌt] *n* puntal *m* ▷ *vi* pavonearse

stub [stʌb] *n* (*of ticket etc*) matriz *f*; (*of cigarette*) colilla ▷ *vt*: **to ~ one's toe on sth** dar con el dedo del pie contra algo; **stub out** *vt* (*cigarette*) apagar

stubble ['stʌbl] *n* rastrojo; (*on chin*) barba (*incipiente*)

stubborn ['stʌbən] *adj* terco, testarudo

stuck [stʌk] *pt, pp of* **stick** ▷ *adj* (*jammed*) atascado

stuck-up [stʌk'ʌp] *adj* engreído, presumido

stud [stʌd] *n* (*shirt stud*) corchete *m*; (*of boot*) taco; (*earring*) pendiente *m* (de bolita); (*also: ~ farm*) caballeriza; (*also: ~ horse*) caballo semental ▷ *vt* (*fig*): **~ded with** salpicado de

student ▷ ['stju:dənt] *n* estudiante *m/f* ▷ *adj* estudiantil; **a law/medical ~** un(a) estudiante de derecho/medicina

student driver *n* (*US Aut*) aprendiz(a) *m(f)* de conductor

students' union *n* (*Brit: association*) sindicato de estudiantes; (: *building*) centro de estudiantes

studio ['stju:dɪəʊ] *n* estudio; (*artist's*) taller *m*

S

studio flat, studio apartment (US) *n* estudio

studious ['stju:dɪəs] *adj* estudioso; *(studied)* calculado

studiously ['stju:dɪəslɪ] *adv (carefully)* con esmero

study ['stʌdɪ] *n* estudio ▷ *vt* estudiar; *(examine)* examinar, investigar ▷ *vi* estudiar; **to make a ~ of sth** realizar una investigación de algo; **to ~ for an exam** preparar un examen

stuff [stʌf] *n* materia; *(cloth)* tela; *(substance)* material *m*, sustancia; *(things, belongings)* cosas *fpl* ▷ *vt* llenar; *(Culin)* rellenar; *(animal: for exhibition)* disecar; **my nose is ~ed up** tengo la nariz tapada; **~ed toy** juguete *m* or muñeco de trapo

stuffing ['stʌfɪŋ] *n* relleno

stuffy ['stʌfɪ] *adj (room)* mal ventilado; *(person)* de miras estrechas

stumble ['stʌmbl] *vi* tropezar, dar un traspié; **stumble across** *vt fus (fig)* tropezar con

stumbling block ['stʌmblɪŋ-] *n* tropiezo, obstáculo

stump [stʌmp] *n (of tree)* tocón *m*; *(of limb)* muñón *m* ▷ *vt*: **to be ~ed** quedarse perplejo; **to be ~ed for an answer** quedarse sin saber qué contestar

stun [stʌn] *vt* aturdir

stung [stʌŋ] *pt, pp of* **sting**

stunk [stʌŋk] *pp of* **stink**

stunned [stʌnd] *adj (dazed)* aturdido, atontado; *(amazed)* pasmado; *(shocked)* anonadado

stunning ['stʌnɪŋ] *adj (fig: news)* pasmoso; *(: outfit etc)* sensacional

stunt [stʌnt] *n (Aviat)* vuelo acrobático; *(in film)* escena peligrosa; *(also: **publicity ~**)* truco publicitario

stunted ['stʌntɪd] *adj* enano, achaparrado

stuntman ['stʌntmæn] *n* especialista *m*

stupendous [stju:'pɛndəs] *adj* estupendo, asombroso

stupid ['stju:pɪd] *adj* estúpido, tonto

stupidity [stju:'pɪdɪtɪ] *n* estupidez *f*

sturdy ['stə:dɪ] *adj* robusto, fuerte

stutter ['stʌtər] *n* tartamudeo ▷ *vi* tartamudear

sty [staɪ] *n (for pigs)* pocilga

stye [staɪ] *n (Med)* orzuelo

style [staɪl] *n* estilo; *(fashion)* moda; *(of dress etc)* hechura; *(hair style)* corte *m*; **in the latest ~** en el último modelo

stylish ['staɪlɪʃ] *adj* elegante, a la moda

stylist ['staɪlɪst] *n (hair stylist)* peluquero(-a)

stylus (*pl* **styli** *or* **styluses**) ['staɪləs, -laɪ] *n (of record player)* aguja

suave [swɑ:v] *adj* cortés, fino

sub [sʌb] *n abbr* = **submarine; subscription**

sub... [sʌb] *pref* sub...

subconscious [sʌb'kɒnʃəs] *adj* subconsciente ▷ *n* subconsciente *m*

subcontinent [sʌb'kɒntɪnənt] *n*: **the Indian ~** el subcontinente (de la India)

subcontract *n* ['sʌb'kɒntrækt] subcontrato ▷ *vt* ['sʌbkən'trækt] subcontratar

subcontractor ['sʌbkən'træktər] *n* subcontratista *m/f*

subdue [səb'dju:] *vt* sojuzgar; *(passions)* dominar

subdued [səb'dju:d] *adj (light)* tenue; *(person)* sumiso, manso

subject *n* ['sʌbdʒɪkt] súbdito; *(Scol)* tema *m*, materia; *(Grammar)* sujeto ▷ *vt* [səb'dʒɛkt]: **to ~ sb to sth** someter a algn a algo ▷ *adj* ['sʌbdʒɪkt]: **to be ~ to** *(law)* estar sujeto a; *(person)* ser propenso a; **to change the ~** cambiar de tema; **~ to confirmation in writing** sujeto a confirmación por escrito

subjective [səb'dʒɛktɪv] *adj* subjetivo

subject matter *n* materia; *(content)* contenido

subjunctive [səb'dʒʌŋktɪv] *adj, n* subjuntivo

sublet [sʌb'lɛt] *vt, vi* subarrendar, realquilar

submarine [sʌbmə'ri:n] *n* submarino

submerge [səb'mə:dʒ] *vt* sumergir; *(flood)* inundar ▷ *vi* sumergirse

submission [səb'mɪʃən] *n* sumisión *f*; *(to committee etc)* ponencia

submissive [səb'mɪsɪv] *adj* sumiso

submit [səb'mɪt] *vt* someter; *(proposal, claim)* presentar ▷ *vi* someterse; **I ~ that ...** me permito sugerir que ...

subnormal [sʌb'nɔ:məl] *adj* subnormal

subordinate [sə'bɔ:dɪnət] *adj, n* subordinado(-a) *m(f)*

subpoena [səb'pi:nə] *(Law) n* citación *f* ▷ *vt* citar

subscribe [səb'skraɪb] *vi* suscribir; **to ~ to** *(fund)* suscribir, aprobar; *(opinion)* estar de acuerdo con; *(newspaper)* suscribirse a

subscriber [səb'skraɪbər] *n (to periodical)* suscriptor(a) *m(f)*; *(to telephone)* abonado(-a)

subscription [səb'skrɪpʃən] *n (to club)* abono; *(to magazine)* suscripción *f*; **to take out a ~ to** suscribirse a

subsequent ['sʌbsɪkwənt] *adj* subsiguiente, posterior; **~ to** posterior a

subsequently ['sʌbsɪkwəntlɪ] *adv* posteriormente, más tarde

subside [səb'saɪd] *vi* hundirse; *(flood)* bajar; *(wind)* amainar

subsidence [səb'saɪdns] *n* hundimiento; *(in road)* socavón *m*

subsidiarity [səbsɪdɪ'ærɪtɪ] *n (Pol)* subsidiariedad *f*

subsidiary [səb'sɪdɪərɪ] *n* sucursal *f*, filial *f* ▷ *adj (Univ: subject)* secundario

subsidize ['sʌbsɪdaɪz] *vt* subvencionar

subsidy ['sʌbsɪdɪ] *n* subvención *f*

subsistence [səb'sɪstəns] *n* subsistencia

substance ['sʌbstəns] *n* sustancia; *(fig)* esencia; **to lack ~** *(argument)* ser poco convincente; *(accusation)* no tener fundamento; (film, book) tener poca profundidad

substance abuse n uso indebido de sustancias tóxicas

substantial [səb'stænʃl] adj sustancial, sustancioso; (fig) importante

substantially [səb'stænʃəlɪ] adv sustancialmente; **~ bigger** bastante más grande

substantiate [səb'stænʃɪeɪt] vt comprobar

substitute ['sʌbstɪtjuːt] n (person) suplente m/f; (thing) sustituto ▷ vt: **to ~ A for B** sustituir B por A, reemplazar A por B

substitution [sʌbstɪ'tjuːʃən] n sustitución f

subterranean [sʌbtə'reɪnɪən] adj subterráneo

subtitle ['sʌbtaɪtl] n subtítulo

subtle ['sʌtl] adj sutil

subtlety ['sʌtltɪ] n sutileza

subtotal [sʌb'təʊtl] n subtotal m

subtract [səb'trækt] vt restar; sustraer

subtraction [səb'trækʃən] n resta; sustracción f

suburb ['sʌbəːb] n barrio residencial; **the ~s** las afueras (de la ciudad)

suburban [sə'bəːbən] adj suburbano; (train etc) de cercanías

suburbia [sə'bəːbɪə] n barrios mpl residenciales

subversive [səb'vəːsɪv] adj subversivo

subway ['sʌbweɪ] n (Brit) paso subterráneo or inferior; (US) metro

succeed [sək'siːd] vi (person) tener éxito; (plan) salir bien ▷ vt suceder a; **to ~ in doing** lograr hacer

succeeding [sək'siːdɪŋ] adj (following) sucesivo; **~ generations** generaciones fpl futuras

success [sək'sɛs] n éxito; (gain) triunfo

successful [sək'sɛsful] adj (venture) de éxito, exitoso (esp LAm); **to be ~ (in doing)** lograr (hacer)

successfully [sək'sɛsfulɪ] adv con éxito

succession [sək'sɛʃən] n (series) sucesión f, serie f; (descendants) descendencia; **in ~** sucesivamente

successive [sək'sɛsɪv] adj sucesivo, consecutivo; **on three ~ days** tres días seguidos

successor [sək'sɛsəʳ] n sucesor(a) m(f)

succinct [sək'sɪŋkt] adj sucinto

succulent ['sʌkjulənt] adj suculento; **succulents** npl (Bot) plantas fpl carnosas

succumb [sə'kʌm] vi sucumbir

such [sʌtʃ] adj tal, semejante; (of that kind): **~ a book** tal libro; **~ books** tales libros; (so much): **~ courage** tanto valor ▷ adv tan; **~ a long trip** un viaje tan largo; **~ a lot of** tanto; **~ as** (like) tal como; **~ a noise as to** un ruido tal que; **~ books as I have** cuantos libros tengo; **I said no ~ thing** no dije tal cosa; **it's ~ a long time since we saw each

other** hace tanto tiempo que no nos vemos; **~ a long time ago** hace tantísimo tiempo; **as ~** adv como tal

such-and-such ['sʌtʃənsʌtʃ] adj tal o cual

suchlike ['sʌtʃlaɪk] pron (inf): **and ~** y cosas por el estilo

suck [sʌk] vt chupar; (bottle) sorber; (breast) mamar; (pump, machine) aspirar

sucker ['sʌkəʳ] n (Bot) serpollo; (Zool) ventosa; (inf) bobo, primo

suction ['sʌkʃən] n succión f

Sudan [su'dæn] n Sudán m

sudden ['sʌdn] adj (rapid) repentino, súbito; (unexpected) imprevisto; **all of a ~** de repente

sudden-death [sʌdn'dɛθ] n (also: **~ play off**) desempate m instantáneo, muerte f súbita

suddenly ['sʌdnlɪ] adv de repente

sudoku [su'dəukuː] n sudoku m

suds [sʌdz] npl espuma sg de jabón

sue [suː] vt demandar; **to ~ (for)** demandar (por); **to ~ for divorce** solicitar or pedir el divorcio; **to ~ for damages** demandar por daños y perjuicios

suede [sweɪd] n ante m, gamuza (LAm)

suet ['suɪt] n sebo

suffer ['sʌfəʳ] vt sufrir, padecer; (tolerate) aguantar, soportar; (undergo: loss, setback) experimentar ▷ vi sufrir, padecer; **to ~ from** padecer, sufrir; **to ~ from the effects of alcohol/a fall** sufrir los efectos del alcohol/ resentirse de una caída

sufferer ['sʌfərəʳ] n víctima f; (Med): **~ from** enfermo(-a) de

suffering ['sʌfərɪŋ] n (hardship, deprivation) sufrimiento; (pain) dolor m

suffice [sə'faɪs] vi bastar, ser suficiente

sufficient [sə'fɪʃənt] adj suficiente, bastante

sufficiently [sə'fɪʃəntlɪ] adv suficientemente, bastante

suffix ['sʌfɪks] n sufijo

suffocate ['sʌfəkeɪt] vi ahogarse, asfixiarse

sugar ['ʃugəʳ] n azúcar m ▷ vt echar azúcar a, azucarar

sugar beet n remolacha

sugar cane n caña de azúcar

suggest [sə'dʒɛst] vt sugerir; (recommend) aconsejar; **what do you ~ I do?** ¿qué sugieres que haga?; **this ~s that ...** esto hace pensar que ...

suggestion [sə'dʒɛstʃən] n sugerencia; **there's no ~ of ...** no hay indicación or evidencia de ...

suicide ['suɪsaɪd] n suicidio; (person) suicida m/f; **to commit ~** suicidarse

suicide attack n atentado suicida

suicide bomber n terrorista m/f suicida

suicide bombing n atentado m suicida

suit [suːt] n traje m; (Law) pleito; (Cards) palo ▷ vt convenir; (clothes) sentar bien a, ir bien a; (adapt): **to ~ sth** adaptar or ajustar algo a; **to be ~ed to sth** (suitable for) ser apto para algo; **well ~ed** (couple) hechos el uno para el otro; **to bring a ~ against sb** entablar demanda contra algn; **to follow ~** (Cards) seguir el palo; (fig) seguir el ejemplo (de algn); **that ~s me** me va bien

suitable ['su:təbl] adj conveniente; (apt) indicado

suitably ['su:təblɪ] adv convenientemente; (appropriately) en forma debida

suitcase ['su:tkeɪs] n maleta, valija (LAm)

suite [swi:t] n (of rooms) suite f; (Mus) suite f; (furniture): **bedroom/dining room ~** (juego de) dormitorio/comedor m; **a three-piece ~** un tresillo

suitor ['su:tə'] n pretendiente m

sulfur ['sʌlfə'] n (US) = **sulphur**

sulk [sʌlk] vi estar de mal humor

sulky ['sʌlkɪ] adj malhumorado

sullen ['sʌlən] adj hosco, malhumorado

sulphur, sulfur (US) ['sʌlfə'] n azufre m

sultana [sʌl'tɑ:nə] n (fruit) pasa de Esmirna

sultry ['sʌltrɪ] adj (weather) bochornoso; (seductive) seductor(a)

sum [sʌm] n suma; (total) total m; **sum up** vt resumir; (evaluate rapidly) evaluar ▷ vi hacer un resumen

summarize ['sʌməraɪz] vt resumir

summary ['sʌmərɪ] n resumen m ▷ adj (justice) sumario

summer ['sʌmə'] n verano ▷ adj de verano; **in (the) ~** en (el) verano

summer holidays npl vacaciones fpl de verano

summerhouse ['sʌməhaus] n (in garden) cenador m, glorieta

summertime ['sʌmətaɪm] n (season) verano

summer time n (by clock) hora de verano

summit ['sʌmɪt] n cima, cumbre f; (also: **~ conference**) (conferencia) cumbre f

summon ['sʌmən] vt (person) llamar; (meeting) convocar; **to ~ a witness** citar a un testigo; **summon up** vt (courage) armarse de

summons ['sʌmənz] n llamamiento, llamada ▷ vt citar, emplazar; **to serve a ~ on sb** citar a algn ante el juicio

sumo ['su:məu] n (also: **~ wrestling**) sumo

sump [sʌmp] n (Brit Aut) cárter m

Sun abbr (= Sunday) dom

sun [sʌn] n sol m; **they have everything under the ~** no les falta nada, tienen de todo

sunbathe ['sʌnbeɪð] vi tomar el sol

sunbed ['sʌnbɛd] n cama solar

sunblock ['sʌnblɔk] n filtro solar

sunburn ['sʌnbə:n] n (painful) quemadura del sol; (tan) bronceado

sunburnt ['sʌnbə:nt], **sunburned** ['sʌnbə:nd] adj (tanned) bronceado; (painfully) quemado por el sol

Sunday ['sʌndɪ] n domingo; see also **Tuesday**

Sunday paper n (periódico) dominical m

Sunday school n catequesis f

sundial ['sʌndaɪəl] n reloj m de sol

sundown ['sʌndaun] n anochecer m, puesta de sol

sundries ['sʌndrɪz] npl géneros mpl diversos

sundry ['sʌndrɪ] adj varios, diversos; **all and ~** todos sin excepción

sunflower ['sʌnflauə'] n girasol m

sung [sʌŋ] pp of **sing**

sunglasses ['sʌnglɑ:sɪz] npl gafas fpl de sol

sunk [sʌŋk] pp of **sink**

sunlight ['sʌnlaɪt] n luz f del sol

sunlit ['sʌnlɪt] adj iluminado por el sol

sun lounger n tumbona, perezosa (LAm)

sunny ['sʌnɪ] adj soleado; (day) de sol; (fig) alegre; **it is ~** hace sol

sunrise ['sʌnraɪz] n salida del sol

sun roof n (Aut) techo corredizo or solar; (on building) azotea, terraza

sunscreen ['sʌnskri:n] n protector m solar

sunset ['sʌnsɛt] n puesta del sol

sunshade ['sʌnʃeɪd] n (over table) sombrilla

sunshine ['sʌnʃaɪn] n sol m

sunstroke ['sʌnstrəuk] n insolación f

suntan ['sʌntæn] n bronceado

suntan lotion n bronceador m

suntanned ['sʌntænd] adj bronceado

suntan oil n aceite m bronceador

super ['su:pə'] adj (inf) genial

superannuation [su:pərænju'eɪʃən] n jubilación f, pensión f

superb [su:'pə:b] adj magnífico, espléndido

Super Bowl n (US Sport) super copa de fútbol americano

supercilious [su:pə'sɪlɪəs] adj (disdainful) desdeñoso; (haughty) altanero

superconductor [su:pəkən'dʌktə'] n superconductor m

superficial [su'pə'fɪʃəl] adj superficial

superfluous [su'pə:fluəs] adj superfluo, de sobra

superglue ['su:pəglu:] n cola de contacto, supercola

superhighway ['su:pəhaɪweɪ] n (US) superautopista; **the information ~** la superautopista de la información

superimpose ['su:pərɪm'pəuz] vt sobreponer

superintendent [su:pərɪn'tɛndənt] n director(a) m(f); (also: **police ~**) subjefe(-a) m(f)

superior [su'pɪərɪə'] adj superior; (smug: person) altivo, desdeñoso; (: smile, air) de suficiencia; (: remark) desdeñoso ▷ n superior m; **Mother S~** (Rel) madre f superiora

superiority [supɪərɪ'ɔrɪtɪ] n superioridad f; desdén m

superlative [su'pə:lətɪv] adj, n superlativo

superman ['su:pəmæn] n superhombre m

supermarket ['su:pəmɑ:kɪt] n supermercado

supermodel ['su:pəmɔdl] n top model f, supermodelo f

supernatural [su:pə'nætʃərəl] adj sobrenatural ▷ n: **the ~** lo sobrenatural

supernova [su:pə'nəuvə] n supernova
superpower ['su:pəpauə^r] n (Pol) superpotencia
supersede [su:pə'si:d] vt suplantar
supersonic ['su:pə'sɒnɪk] adj supersónico
superstar ['su:pəsta:^{r}] n superestrella ▷ adj de superestrella
superstition [su:pə'stɪʃən] n superstición f
superstitious [su:pə'stɪʃəs] adj supersticioso
superstore ['su:pəstɔ:^{r}] n (Brit) hipermercado
supervise ['su:pəvaɪz] vt supervisar
supervision [su:pə'vɪʒən] n supervisión f
supervisor ['su:pəvaɪzə^r] n supervisor(a) m(f)
supper ['sʌpə^r] n cena; **to have ~** cenar
supple ['sʌpl] adj flexible
supplement n ['sʌplɪmənt] suplemento ▷ vt [sʌplɪ'mɛnt] suplir
supplementary [sʌplɪ'mɛntərɪ] adj suplementario
supplier [sə'plaɪə^r] n suministrador(a) m(f); (Comm) distribuidor(a) m(f)
supply [sə'plaɪ] vt (provide) suministrar; (information) facilitar; (fill: need, want) suplir, satisfacer; (equip): **to ~ (with)** proveer (de) ▷ n provisión f; (of gas, water etc) suministro ▷ adj (Brit: teacher etc) suplente; **supplies** npl (food) víveres mpl; (Mil) pertrechos mpl; **office supplies** materiales mpl para oficina; **to be in short ~** escasear, haber escasez de; **the electricity/water/gas ~** el suministro de electricidad/agua/gas; **~ and demand** la oferta y la demanda
support [sə'pɔ:t] n (moral, financial etc) apoyo; (Tech) soporte m ▷ vt apoyar; (financially) mantener; (uphold) sostener; (Sport: team) seguir, ser hincha de; **they stopped work in ~ (of)** pararon de trabajar en apoyo (de); **to ~ o.s.** (financially) ganarse la vida
supporter [sə'pɔ:tə^r] n (Pol etc) partidario(-a); (Sport) aficionado(-a); (Football) hincha m/f
supporting [sə'pɔ:tɪŋ] adj (wall) de apoyo; **~ role** papel m secundario; **~ actor/actress** actor/actriz m/f secundario/a
supportive [sə'pɔ:tɪv] adj de apoyo; **I have a ~ family/wife** mi familia/mujer me apoya
suppose [sə'pəuz] vt, vi suponer; (imagine) imaginarse; **to be ~d to do sth** deber hacer algo; **I don't ~ she'll come** no creo que venga; **he's ~d to be an expert** se le supone un experto
supposedly [sə'pəuzɪdlɪ] adv según cabe suponer
supposing [sə'pəuzɪŋ] conj en caso de que; **always ~ (that) he comes** suponiendo que venga
suppress [sə'prɛs] vt suprimir; (yawn) ahogar
supreme [su'pri:m] adj supremo
Supreme Court n (US) Tribunal m Supremo, Corte f Suprema
supremo [su'pri:məu] n autoridad f máxima
surcharge ['sə:tʃa:dʒ] n sobretasa, recargo

sure [ʃuə^r] adj seguro; (definite, convinced) cierto; (aim) certero ▷ adv: **that ~ is pretty, that's ~ pretty** (US) ¡qué bonito es!; **to be ~ of sth** estar seguro de algo; **to be ~ of o.s.** estar seguro de sí mismo; **to make ~ of sth/ that** asegurarse de algo/asegurar que; **I'm not ~ how/why/when** no estoy seguro de cómo/por qué/cuándo; **~!** (of course) ¡claro!, ¡por supuesto!; **~ enough** efectivamente
sure-fire ['ʃuəfaɪə^r] adj (inf) infalible
surely ['ʃuəlɪ] adv (certainly) seguramente; **~ you don't mean that!** ¡no lo dices en serio!
surety ['ʃuərətɪ] n fianza; (person) fiador(a) m(f); **to go** or **stand ~ for sb** ser fiador de algn, salir garante por algn
surf [sə:f] n olas fpl ▷ vi hacer surf ▷ vt (Internet): **to ~ the Net** navegar por Internet
surface ['sə:fɪs] n superficie f ▷ vt (road) revestir ▷ vi salir a la superficie ▷ cpd (Mil, Naut) de (la) superficie; **on the ~ it seems that ...** (fig) a primera vista parece que ...
surface mail n vía terrestre
surfboard ['sə:fbɔ:d] n tabla (de surf)
surfeit ['sə:fɪt] n: **a ~ of** un exceso de
surfer ['sə:fə^r] n surfista m/f; **web** or **net ~** internauta m/f
surfing ['sə:fɪŋ] n surf m
surge [sə:dʒ] n oleada, oleaje m; (Elec) sobretensión f transitoria ▷ vi (wave) romper; (people) avanzar a tropel; **to ~ forward** avanzar rápidamente
surgeon ['sə:dʒən] n cirujano(-a)
surgery ['sə:dʒərɪ] n cirugía; (Brit: room) consultorio; (: Pol) horas en las que los electores pueden reunirse personalmente con su diputado; **to undergo ~** operarse
surgical ['sə:dʒɪkl] adj quirúrgico
surgical spirit n (Brit) alcohol m
surly ['sə:lɪ] adj hosco, malhumorado
surname ['sə:neɪm] n apellido
surpass [sə:'pa:s] vt superar, exceder
surplus ['sə:pləs] n excedente m; (Comm) superávit m ▷ adj (Comm) excedente, sobrante; **to have a ~ of sth** tener un excedente de algo; **it is ~ to our requirements** nos sobra; **~ stock** saldos mpl
surprise [sə'praɪz] n sorpresa ▷ vt sorprender; **to take by ~** (person) coger desprevenido or por sorpresa a, sorprender a; (Mil: town, fort) atacar por sorpresa
surprised [sə'praɪzd] adj (look, smile) de sorpresa; **to be ~** sorprenderse
surprising [sə'praɪzɪŋ] adj sorprendente
surprisingly [sə'praɪzɪŋlɪ] adv (easy, helpful) de modo sorprendente; (somewhat) ~, **he agreed** para sorpresa de todos, aceptó
surrealism [sə'rɪəlɪzəm] n surrealismo
surrender [sə'rɛndə^r] n rendición f, entrega ▷ vi rendirse, entregarse ▷ vt renunciar
surreptitious [sʌrəp'tɪʃəs] adj subrepticio
surrogate ['sʌrəgɪt] n (Brit) sustituto(-a)
surrogate mother n madre f de alquiler

S

surround [sə'raund] *vt* rodear, circundar; (*Mil etc*) cercar

surrounding [sə'raundɪŋ] *adj* circundante

surroundings [sə'raundɪŋz] *npl* alrededores *mpl*, cercanías *fpl*

surveillance [sə:'veɪləns] *n* vigilancia

survey *n* ['sə:veɪ] inspección *f* reconocimiento; (*inquiry*) encuesta; (*comprehensive view: of situation etc*) vista de conjunto ▷ *vt* [sə:'veɪ] examinar, inspeccionar; (*Surveying: building*) inspeccionar; (: *land*) hacer un reconocimiento de, reconocer; (*look at*) mirar, contemplar; (*make inquiries about*) hacer una encuesta de; **to carry out a ~ of** inspeccionar, examinar

surveyor [sə'veɪər] *n* (*Brit: of building*) perito *m/f*; (*of land*) agrimensor(a) *m(f)*

survival [sə'vaɪvl] *n* supervivencia

survive [sə'vaɪv] *vi* sobrevivir; (*custom etc*) perdurar ▷ *vt* sobrevivir a

survivor [sə'vaɪvər] *n* superviviente *m/f*

susceptible [sə'sɛptəbl] *adj* (*easily influenced*) influenciable; (*to disease, illness*): **~ to** propenso a

suspect *adj, n* ['sʌspɛkt] sospechoso(-a) *m(f)* ▷ *vt* [səs'pɛkt] sospechar

suspected [səs'pɛktɪd] *adj* presunto; **to have a ~ fracture** tener una posible fractura

suspend [səs'pɛnd] *vt* suspender

suspended animation [səs'pɛndəd-] *n*: **in a state of ~** en (estado de) hibernación

suspended sentence *n* (*Law*) libertad *f* condicional

suspender belt [səs'pɛndər-] *n* (*Brit*) liguero, portaligas *m inv* (*LAm*)

suspenders [səs'pɛndəz] *npl* (*Brit*) ligas *fpl*; (*US*) tirantes *mpl*

suspense [səs'pɛns] *n* incertidumbre *f*, duda; (*in film etc*) suspense *m*; **to keep sb in ~** mantener a algn en suspense

suspension [səs'pɛnʃən] *n* (*gen*) suspensión *f*; (*of driving licence*) privación *f*

suspension bridge *n* puente *m* colgante

suspicion [səs'pɪʃən] *n* sospecha; (*distrust*) recelo; (*trace*) traza; **to be under ~** estar bajo sospecha; **arrested on ~ of murder** detenido bajo sospecha de asesinato

suspicious [səs'pɪʃəs] *adj* (*suspecting*) receloso; (*causing suspicion*) sospechoso; **to be ~ of** or **about sb/sth** tener sospechas de algn/algo

sustain [səs'teɪn] *vt* sostener, apoyar; (*suffer*) sufrir, padecer

sustainable [səs'teɪnəbl] *adj* sostenible; **~ development** desarrollo sostenible

sustained [səs'teɪnd] *adj* (*effort*) sostenido

sustenance ['sʌstɪnəns] *n* sustento

SUV ['ɛsju:'vi:] *n abbr* (= *sports utility vehicle*) todoterreno *m inv*, vehículo para cuatro

swab [swɔb] *n* (*Med*) algodón *m*, frotis *m inv* ▷ *vt* (*Naut: also*: **~ down**) limpiar, fregar

swagger ['swægər] *vi* pavonearse

swallow ['swɔləu] *n* (*bird*) golondrina; (*of food*) bocado; (*of drink*) trago ▷ *vt* tragar; **swallow up** *vt* (*savings etc*) consumir

swam [swæm] *pt of* **swim**

swamp [swɔmp] *n* pantano, ciénaga ▷ *vt* abrumar, agobiar

swan [swɔn] *n* cisne *m*

swap [swɔp] *n* canje *m*, trueque *m* ▷ *vt*: **to ~ (for)** canjear (por), cambiar (por)

swarm [swɔ:m] *n* (*of bees*) enjambre *m*; (*fig*) multitud *f* ▷ *vi* (*bees*) formar un enjambre; (*fig*) hormiguear, pulular

swarthy ['swɔ:ðɪ] *adj* moreno

swastika ['swɔstɪkə] *n* esvástica, cruz *f* gamada

swat [swɔt] *vt* aplastar ▷ *n* (*also*: **fly ~**) matamoscas *m inv*

sway [sweɪ] *vi* mecerse, balancearse ▷ *vt* (*influence*) mover, influir en ▷ *n* (*rule, power*): **~ (over)** dominio (sobre); **to hold ~ over sb** dominar a algn, mantener el dominio sobre algn

swear (*pt* **swore**, *pp* **sworn**) [sweər, swɔ:r, swɔ:n] *vi* jurar; (*curse*) decir tacos ▷ *vt*: **to ~ an oath** prestar juramento, jurar; **to ~ to sth** declarar algo bajo juramento; **swear in** *vt* tomar juramento (a); **to be sworn in** prestar juramento

swearword ['sweəwə:d] *n* taco, palabrota

sweat [swɛt] *n* sudor *m* ▷ *vi* sudar

sweatband ['swɛtbænd] *n* (*Sport: on head*) banda; (: *on wrist*) muñequera

sweater ['swɛtər] *n* suéter *m*

sweatshirt ['swɛtʃə:t] *n* sudadera

sweaty ['swɛtɪ] *adj* sudoroso

Swede [swi:d] *n* sueco(-a)

swede [swi:d] *n* (*Brit*) nabo

Sweden ['swi:dn] *n* Suecia

Swedish ['swi:dɪʃ] *adj, n* (*Ling*) sueco

sweep [swi:p] *n* (*pt, pp* **swept**) *n* (*act*) barrida; (*of arm*) manotazo *m*; (*curve*) curva, alcance *m*; (*also*: **chimney ~**) deshollinador(a) *m(f)* ▷ *vt* barrer; (*with arm*) empujar; (*current*) arrastrar; (*disease, fashion*) recorrer ▷ *vi* barrer; **sweep away** *vt* barrer; (*rub out*) borrar; **sweep past** *vi* pasar rápidamente; (*brush by*) rozar; **sweep up** *vi* barrer

sweeper ['swi:pər] *n* (*person*) barrendero(-a); (*machine*) barredora; (*Football*) líbero, libre *m*

sweeping ['swi:pɪŋ] *adj* (*gesture*) dramático; (*generalized*) generalizado; (*changes, reforms*) radical

sweet [swi:t] *n* (*candy*) dulce *m*, caramelo; (*Brit: pudding*) postre *m* ▷ *adj* dulce; (*sugary*) azucarado; (*charming: person*) encantador(a); (: *smile, character*) dulce, amable, agradable ▷ *adv*: **to smell/taste ~** oler/saber dulce

sweet and sour *adj* agridulce

sweetcorn ['swi:tkɔ:n] *n* maíz *m* (dulce)

sweeten ['swi:tn] *vt* (*person*) endulzar; (*add sugar to*) poner azúcar a

sweetener ['swi:tnər] *n* (*Culin*) edulcorante *m*

sweetheart ['swi:tɑ:t] n amor m, novio(-a); (in speech) amor, cariño

sweetness ['swi:tnɪs] n (gen) dulzura

sweet pea n guisante m de olor

sweetshop ['swi:tʃɔp] n (Brit) confitería, bombonería

swell [swɛl] (pt swelled, pp swollen or swelled) n (of sea) marejada, oleaje m ▷ adj (US: inf: excellent) estupendo, fenomenal ▷ vt hinchar, inflar ▷ vi (also: ~ up) hincharse; (numbers) aumentar; (sound, feeling) ir aumentando

swelling ['swɛlɪŋ] n (Med) hinchazón f

sweltering ['swɛltərɪŋ] adj sofocante, de mucho calor

swept [swɛpt] pt, pp of **sweep**

swerve [swə:v] n regate m; (in car) desvío brusco ▷ vi desviarse bruscamente

swift [swɪft] n (bird) vencejo m ▷ adj rápido, veloz

swig [swɪg] n (inf: drink) trago

swill [swɪl] n bazofia ▷ vt (also: ~ out, ~ down) lavar, limpiar con agua

swim [swɪm] (pt swam, pp swum) n: **to go for a ~** ir a nadar or a bañarse ▷ vi nadar; (head, room) dar vueltas ▷ vt pasar a nado; **to go ~ming** ir a nadar; **to ~ a length** nadar or hacer un largo

swimmer ['swɪmə^r] n nadador(a) m(f)

swimming ['swɪmɪŋ] n natación f

swimming cap n gorro de baño

swimming costume n bañador m, traje m de baño

swimmingly ['swɪmɪŋlɪ] adv: **to go ~** (wonderfully) ir como una seda or sobre ruedas

swimming pool n piscina, alberca (LAm)

swimming trunks npl bañador msg

swimsuit ['swɪmsu:t] n = **swimming costume**

swindle ['swɪndl] n estafa ▷ vt estafar

swine [swaɪn] n pl inv cerdo, puerco; (inf!) canalla m (!)

swing [swɪŋ] (pt, pp swung) n (in playground) columpio; (movement) balanceo, vaivén m; (change of direction) viraje m; (rhythm) ritmo; (Pol: in votes etc): **there has been a ~ towards/away from Labour** ha habido un viraje en favor/en contra del Partido Laborista ▷ vt balancear; (on a swing) columpiar; (also: ~ round) voltear, girar ▷ vi balancearse, columpiarse; (also: ~ round) dar media vuelta; **a ~ to the left** un movimiento hacia la izquierda; **to be in full ~** estar en plena marcha; **to get into the ~ of things** meterse en situación; **the road ~s south** la carretera gira hacia el sur

swing bridge n puente m giratorio

swing door, swinging door (US) ['swɪŋɪŋ-] n puerta giratoria

swingeing ['swɪndʒɪŋ] adj (Brit) abrumador(a)

swipe [swaɪp] n golpe m fuerte ▷ vt (hit) golpear fuerte; (inf: steal) guindar; (credit card etc) pasar

swipe card [swaɪp-] n tarjeta magnética deslizante, tarjeta swipe

swirl [swə:l] vi arremolinarse

swish [swɪʃ] n (sound: of whip) chasquido; (: of skirts) frufrú m; (: of grass) crujido ▷ adj (inf: smart) elegante ▷ vi chasquear

Swiss [swɪs] adj, n pl inv suizo(-a) m(f)

switch [swɪtʃ] n (for light, radio etc) interruptor m; (change) cambio ▷ vt (change) cambiar de; (invert: also: ~ round, ~ over) intercambiar; **switch off** vt apagar; (engine) parar; **switch on** vt (Aut: ignition) encender, prender (LAm); (engine, machine) arrancar; (water supply) conectar

switchboard ['swɪtʃbɔ:d] n (Tel) centralita (de teléfonos), conmutador m (LAm)

Switzerland ['swɪtsələnd] n Suiza

swivel ['swɪvl] vi (also: ~ round) girar

swollen ['swəulən] pp of **swell**

swoon [swu:n] vi desmayarse

swoop [swu:p] n (by police etc) redada; (of bird etc) descenso en picado, calada ▷ vi (also: ~ down) caer en picado

swop [swɔp] n, vb = **swap**

sword [sɔ:d] n espada

swordfish ['sɔ:dfɪʃ] n pez m espada

swore [swɔ:^r] pt of **swear**

sworn [swɔ:n] pp of **swear** ▷ adj (statement) bajo juramento; (enemy) implacable

swot [swɔt] (Brit) vt, vi empollar ▷ n empollón(-ona) m(f)

swum [swʌm] pp of **swim**

swung [swʌŋ] pt, pp of **swing**

syllable ['sɪləbl] n sílaba

syllabus ['sɪləbəs] n programa m de estudios; **on the ~** en el programa de estudios

symbol ['sɪmbl] n símbolo

symbolic [sɪm'bɔlɪk], **symbolical** [sɪm'bɔlɪkl] adj simbólico; **to be ~ of sth** simbolizar algo

symbolism ['sɪmbəlɪzəm] n simbolismo

symbolize ['sɪmbəlaɪz] vt simbolizar

symmetrical [sɪ'mɛtrɪkl] adj simétrico

symmetry ['sɪmɪtrɪ] n simetría

sympathetic [sɪmpə'θɛtɪk] adj compasivo; (understanding) comprensivo; **to be ~ to a cause** (well-disposed) apoyar una causa; **to be ~ towards** (person) ser comprensivo con

sympathize ['sɪmpəθaɪz] vi: **to ~ with** (person) compadecerse de; (feelings) comprender; (cause) apoyar

sympathizer ['sɪmpəθaɪzə^r] n (Pol) simpatizante m/f

sympathy ['sɪmpəθɪ] n (pity) compasión f; (understanding) comprensión f; **a letter of ~** un pésame; **with our deepest ~** nuestro más sentido pésame

symphony ['sɪmfənɪ] n sinfonía

symposium [sɪm'pəuzɪəm] n simposio

symptom ['sɪmptəm] n síntoma m, indicio

synagogue ['sɪnəgɔg] n sinagoga

sync [sɪŋk] n (inf): **to be in/out of ~ (with)** ir/
no ir al mismo ritmo (que); (fig: *people*)
conectar/no conectar con
synchronized swimming ['sɪŋkrənaɪzd-] n
natación f sincronizada
syndicate ['sɪndɪkɪt] n (gen) sindicato; (Press)
agencia (de noticias)
syndrome ['sɪndrəum] n síndrome m
synonym ['sɪnənɪm] n sinónimo
synopsis, synopses [sɪ'nɔpsɪs, -siːz] n
sinopsis f inv
syntax ['sɪntæks] n sintaxis f
synthetic [sɪn'θetɪk] adj sintético ▷ n
sintético
syphilis ['sɪfɪlɪs] n sífilis f
syphon ['saɪfən] n, vb = **siphon**
Syria ['sɪrɪə] n Siria
syringe [sɪ'rɪndʒ] n jeringa
syrup ['sɪrəp] n jarabe m, almíbar m
system ['sɪstəm] n sistema m; (Anat)
organismo; **it was quite a shock to his ~**
fue un golpe para él
systematic [sɪstə'mætɪk] adj sistemático;
metódico
system disk n (Comput) disco del sistema
systems analyst n analista m/f de sistemas

T, t [tiː] n (letter) T, t f; **T for Tommy** T de
Tarragona
TA n abbr (Brit) = **Territorial Army**
ta [tɑː] excl (Brit: inf) ¡gracias!
tab [tæb] n abbr = **tabulator** ▷ n lengüeta;
(label) etiqueta; **to keep ~s on** (fig)
vigilar
tabby ['tæbɪ] n (also: ~ **cat**) gato atigrado
tabernacle ['tæbənækl] n tabernáculo
table ['teɪbl] n mesa; (chart: of statistics etc)
cuadro, tabla ▷ vt (Brit: motion etc) presentar;
to lay or **set the ~** poner la mesa; **to clear
the ~** quitar or levantar la mesa; **league ~**
(Football, Rugby) clasificación f del
campeonato; **~ of contents** índice m de
materias
tablecloth ['teɪblklɔθ] n mantel m
table d'hôte [tɑːbl'dəut] n menú m
table lamp n lámpara de mesa
tablemat ['teɪblmæt] n (for plate) posaplatos
m inv; (for hot dish) salvamantel m
tablespoon ['teɪblspuːn] n cuchara grande;
(also: ~**ful**: as measurement) cucharada
grande
tablet ['tæblɪt] n (Med) pastilla, comprimido;
(for writing) bloc m; (of stone) lápida; **~ of soap**
pastilla de jabón
table tennis n ping-pong m, tenis m de mesa
table wine n vino de mesa
tabloid ['tæblɔɪd] n (newspaper) periódico
popular sensacionalista
tabloid press n ver nota

El término genérico *tabloid press* o "tabloids" se usa para referirse a los periódicos populares británicos, por su tamaño reducido. A diferencia de la llamada *quality press*, estos periódicos se caracterizan por su lenguaje sencillo, presentación llamativa y contenido a menudo sensacionalista, con gran énfasis en noticias sobre escándalos financieros y sexuales de los famosos, por lo que también reciben el nombre peyorativo de "gutter press".

taboo [tə'bu:] *adj, n* tabú *m*
tabulate ['tæbjuleɪt] *vt* disponer en tablas
tabulator ['tæbjuleɪtəʳ] *n* tabulador *m*
tachograph ['tækəgrɑ:f] *n* tacógrafo
tacit ['tæsɪt] *adj* tácito
tack [tæk] *n* (*nail*) tachuela; (*stitch*) hilván *m*; (*Naut*) bordada ▷ *vt* (*nail*) clavar con tachuelas; (*stitch*) hilvanar ▷ *vi* virar; **to ~ sth on to (the end of) sth** (*of letter, book*) añadir algo a (*l final de*) algo
tackle ['tækl] *n* (*gear*) equipo; (*fishing tackle, for lifting*) aparejo; (*Football*) entrada, tackle *m*; (*Rugby*) placaje *m* ▷ *vt* (*difficulty*) enfrentarse a, abordar; (*challenge: person*) hacer frente a; (*grapple with*) agarrar; (*Football*) entrar a; (*Rugby*) placar
tacky ['tækɪ] *adj* pegajoso; (*inf*) hortera *inv*, de mal gusto
tact [tækt] *n* tacto, discreción *f*
tactful ['tæktful] *adj* discreto, diplomático; **to be ~** tener tacto, actuar discretamente
tactical ['tæktɪkl] *adj* táctico
tactical voting *n* voto útil
tactician [tæk'tɪʃən] *n* táctico(-a)
tactics ['tæktɪks] *n, npl* táctica *sg*
tactless ['tæktlɪs] *adj* indiscreto
tadpole ['tædpəul] *n* renacuajo
taffy ['tæfɪ] *n* (*US*) melcocha
tag [tæg] *n* (*label*) etiqueta; **price/name ~** etiqueta del precio/con el nombre; **tag along** *vi*: **to ~ along with sb** engancharse a algn
tail [teɪl] *n* cola; (*Zool*) rabo; (*of shirt, coat*) faldón *m* ▷ *vt* (*follow*) vigilar a; **heads or ~s** cara o cruz; **to turn ~** volver la espalda; **tails** *npl* (*formal suit*) levita; **tail away, tail off** *vi* (*in size, quality etc*) ir disminuyendo
tailback ['teɪlbæk] *n* (*Brit Aut*) cola
tail end *n* cola, parte *f* final
tailgate ['teɪlgeɪt] *n* (*Aut*) puerta trasera
tailor ['teɪləʳ] *n* sastre *m* ▷ *vt*: **to ~ sth (to)** confeccionar algo a medida (para); **~'s (shop)** sastrería
tailoring ['teɪlərɪŋ] *n* (*cut*) corte *m*; (*craft*) sastrería
tailor-made ['teɪlə'meɪd] *adj* (*also fig*) hecho a (la) medida
tailwind ['teɪlwɪnd] *n* viento de cola

tainted ['teɪntɪd] *adj* (*water, air*) contaminado; (*fig*) manchado
Taiwan [taɪ'wɑːn] *n* Taiwán *m*
Taiwanese [taɪwəˈniːz] *adj, n* taiwanés(-esa) *m/f*
Tajikistan [tɑːdʒɪkɪˈstɑːn] *n* Tayikistán *m*
take [teɪk] (*pt* **took**, *pp* **taken**) *vt* tomar; (*grab*) coger (*Sp*), agarrar (*LAm*); (*gain: prize*) ganar; (*require: effort, courage*) exigir; (*support weight of*) aguantar; (*hold: passengers etc*) tener cabida para; (*accompany, bring, carry*) llevar; (*exam*) presentarse a; (*conduct: meeting*) presidir ▷ *vi* (*fire*) prender; (*dye*) coger (*Sp*), agarrar, tomar ▷ *n* (*Cine*) toma; **to ~ sth from** (*drawer etc*) sacar algo de; (*person*) quitar algo a, coger algo a (*Sp*); **to ~ sb's hand** tomar de la mano a algn; **to ~ notes** tomar apuntes; **to be ~n ill** ponerse enfermo; **~ the first on the left** toma la primera a la izquierda; **I only took Russian for one year** sólo estudié ruso un año; **I took him for a doctor** le tenía por médico; **it won't ~ long** durará poco; **it will ~ at least five litres** tiene cabida por lo menos para cinco litros; **to be ~n with sb/sth** (*attracted*) tomarle cariño a algn/tomarle gusto a algo; **I ~ it that ...** supongo que ...;
take after *vt fus* parecerse a; **take apart** *vt* desmontar; **take away** *vt* (*remove*) quitar; (*carry off*) llevar ▷ *vi*: **to ~ away from** quitar mérito a; **take back** *vt* (*return*) devolver; (*one's words*) retractar; **take down** *vt* (*building*) derribar; (*dismantle: scaffolding*) desmantelar; (*message etc*) apuntar, tomar nota de; **take in** *vt* (*Brit: deceive*) engañar; (*understand*) entender; (*include*) abarcar; (*lodger*) acoger, recibir; (*orphan, stray dog*) recoger; (*Sewing*) achicar; **take off** *vi* (*Aviat*) despegar, decolar (*LAm*) ▷ *vt* (*remove*) quitar; (*imitate*) imitar, remedar; **take on** *vt* (*work*) emprender; (*employee*) contratar; (*opponent*) desafiar; **take out** *vt* sacar; (*remove*) quitar; **don't ~ it out on me!** ¡no te desquites conmigo!; **take over** *vt* (*business*) tomar posesión de ▷ *vi*: **to ~ over from sb** reemplazar a algn; **take to** *vt fus* (*person*) coger cariño a (*Sp*), encariñarse con (*LAm*); (*activity*) aficionarse a; **to ~ to doing sth** aficionarse a (hacer) algo; **take up** *vt* (*a dress*) acortar; (*occupy: time, space*) ocupar; (*engage in: hobby etc*) dedicarse a; (*absorb: liquids*) absorber; (*accept: offer, challenge*) aceptar ▷ *vi*: **to ~ up with sb** hacerse amigo de algn; **to ~ sb up on** aceptar algo de algn; **take upon** *vt*: **to ~ it upon o.s. to do sth** encargarse de hacer algo
takeaway ['teɪkəweɪ] *adj* (*Brit: food*) para llevar ▷ *n* tienda *or* restaurante *m* de comida para llevar
taken ['teɪkən] *pp of* **take**
takeoff ['teɪkɔf] *n* (*Aviat*) despegue *m*, decolaje *m* (*LAm*)
takeover ['teɪkəuvəʳ] *n* (*Comm*) absorción *f*

takeover bid n oferta pública de adquisición

takings ['teɪkɪŋz] npl (Comm) ingresos mpl

talc [tælk] n (also: **~um powder**) talco

tale [teɪl] n (story) cuento; (account) relación f; **to tell ~s** (fig) contar chismes

talent ['tælnt] n talento

talented ['tæləntɪd] adj talentoso, de talento

talisman ['tælɪzmən] n talismán m

talk [tɔːk] n charla; (gossip) habladurías fpl, chismes mpl; (conversation) conversación f ▷ vi (speak) hablar; (chatter) charlar; **talks** npl (Pol etc) conversaciones fpl; **to give a ~** dar una charla or conferencia; **to ~ about** hablar de; **to ~ sb into doing sth** convencer a algn para que haga algo; **to ~ sb out of doing sth** disuadir a algn de que haga algo; **to ~ shop** hablar del trabajo; **talking of films, have you seen ...?** hablando de películas, ¿has visto ...?; **talk over** vt discutir

talkative ['tɔːkətɪv] adj hablador(a)

talking point ['tɔːkɪŋ-] n tema m de conversación

talking-to ['tɔːkɪŋtuː] n: **to give sb a good ~** echar una buena bronca a algn

talk show n programa m magazine

tall [tɔːl] adj alto; (tree) grande; **to be 6 feet ~** = medir 1 metro 80, tener 1 metro 80 de alto; **how ~ are you?** ¿cuánto mides?

tall story n cuento chino

tally ['tælɪ] n cuenta ▷ vi: **to ~ (with)** concordar (con), cuadrar (con); **to keep a ~ of sth** llevar la cuenta de algo

talon ['tælən] n garra

tambourine [tæmbə'riːn] n pandereta

tame [teɪm] adj (mild) manso; (tamed) domesticado; (fig: story, style, person) soso, anodino

tamper ['tæmpəʳ] vi: **to ~ with** (lock etc) intentar forzar; (papers) falsificar

tampon ['tæmpən] n tampón m

tan [tæn] n (also: **sun~**) bronceado ▷ vt broncear ▷ vi ponerse moreno ▷ adj (colour) marrón; **to get a ~** broncearse, ponerse moreno

tandem ['tændəm] n tándem m

tang [tæŋ] n sabor m fuerte

tangent ['tændʒənt] n (Math) tangente f; **to go off at a ~** (fig) salirse por la tangente

tangerine [tændʒə'riːn] n mandarina

tangible ['tændʒəbl] adj tangible; **~ assets** bienes mpl tangibles

tangle ['tæŋgl] n enredo; **to get in(to) a ~** enredarse

tank [tæŋk] n (also: **water ~**) depósito, tanque m; (for fish) acuario; (Mil) tanque m

tanker ['tæŋkəʳ] n (ship) petrolero; (truck) camión m cisterna

tankini [taŋ'kiːniː] n tankini m

tanned [tænd] adj (skin) moreno, bronceado

tannoy® ['tænɔɪ] n: **over the ~** por el altavoz

tantalizing ['tæntəlaɪzɪŋ] adj tentador(a)

tantamount ['tæntəmaunt] adj: **~ to** equivalente a

tantrum ['tæntrəm] n rabieta; **to throw a ~** coger una rabieta

Tanzania [tænzə'nɪə] n Tanzania

tap [tæp] n (Brit: on sink etc) grifo, canilla (LAm); (gentle blow) golpecito; (gas tap) llave f ▷ vt (table etc) tamborilear; (shoulder etc) dar palmaditas en; (resources) utilizar, explotar; (telephone conversation) intervenir, pinchar; **on ~** (fig: resources) a mano; **beer on ~** cerveza de barril

tap dancing ['tæpdɑːnsɪŋ] n claqué m

tape [teɪp] n cinta; (also: **magnetic ~**) cinta magnética; (sticky tape) cinta adhesiva ▷ vt (record) grabar (en cinta); **on ~** (song etc) grabado (en cinta)

tape deck n pletina

tape measure n cinta métrica, metro

taper ['teɪpəʳ] n cirio ▷ vi afilarse

tape recorder n grabadora

tapestry ['tæpɪstrɪ] n (object) tapiz m; (art) tapicería

tar [tɑːʳ] n alquitrán m, brea; **low/middle ~ cigarettes** cigarrillos con contenido bajo/medio de alquitrán

target ['tɑːgɪt] n (gen) blanco; **to be on ~** (project) seguir el curso previsto

tariff ['tærɪf] n (on goods) arancel m; (Brit: in hotels etc) tarifa

tarmac ['tɑːmæk] n (Brit: on road) asfalto; (Aviat) pista (de aterrizaje)

tarnish ['tɑːnɪʃ] vt deslustrar

tarot ['tærəu] n tarot m

tarpaulin [tɑː'pɔːlɪn] n lona (impermeabilizada)

tarragon ['tærəgən] n estragón m

tart [tɑːt] n (Culin) tarta; (Brit inf: pej: woman) fulana ▷ adj (flavour) agrio, ácido; **tart up** vt (room, building) dar tono a

tartan ['tɑːtn] n tartán m, tela escocesa ▷ adj de tartán

tartar ['tɑːtəʳ] n (on teeth) sarro

tartar sauce n salsa tártara

task [tɑːsk] n tarea; **to take to ~** reprender

task force n (Mil, Police) grupo de operaciones

tassel ['tæsl] n borla

taste [teɪst] n sabor m, gusto; (also: **after~**) dejo; (sip) sorbo; (fig: glimpse, idea) muestra, idea ▷ vt probar ▷ vi: **to ~ of** or **like** (fish etc) saber a; **you can ~ the garlic (in it)** se nota el sabor a ajo; **can I have a ~ of this wine?** ¿puedo probar este vino?; **to have a ~ for sth** ser aficionado a algo; **in good/bad** or **poor ~** de buen/mal gusto; **to be in bad** or **poor ~** ser de mal gusto

tasteful ['teɪstful] adj de buen gusto

tasteless ['teɪstlɪs] adj (food) soso; (remark) de mal gusto

tasty ['teɪstɪ] adj sabroso, rico

ta-ta ['tæ'tɑː] interj (Brit inf) hasta luego, adiós

tatters ['tætəz] npl: **in ~** (also: **tattered**) hecho jirones

tattoo [tə'tuː] n tatuaje m; (spectacle) espectáculo militar ▷ vt tatuar

tatty ['tætɪ] adj (Brit inf) cochambroso

taught [tɔːt] pt, pp of **teach**

taunt [tɔːnt] n pulla ▷ vt lanzar pullas a

Taurus ['tɔːrəs] n Tauro

taut [tɔːt] adj tirante, tenso

tax [tæks] n impuesto ▷ vt gravar (con un impuesto); (fig: test) poner a prueba; (: patience) agotar; **before/after ~** impuestos excluidos/incluidos; **free of ~** libre de impuestos

taxable ['tæksəbl] adj (income) imponible, sujeto a impuestos

taxation [tæk'seɪʃən] n impuestos mpl; **system of ~** sistema m tributario

tax avoidance n evasión f de impuestos

tax disc n (Brit Aut) pegatina del impuesto de circulación

tax evasion n evasión f fiscal

tax-free ['tæksfriː] adj libre de impuestos

taxi ['tæksɪ] n taxi m ▷ vi (Aviat) rodar por la pista

taxi driver n taxista m/f

taxi rank, taxi stand (Brit) n parada de taxis

tax payer n contribuyente m/f

tax rebate n devolución f de impuestos, reembolso fiscal

tax relief n desgravación f fiscal

tax return n declaración f de la renta

TB n abbr = **tuberculosis**

tbc abbr (= to be confirmed) por confirmar

TD n abbr (US) = **Treasury Department**; (: Football) = **touchdown**

tea [tiː] n té m; (Brit: snack) = merienda; **high ~** (Brit) = merienda-cena

tea bag n bolsita de té

tea break n (Brit) descanso para el té

teach (pt, pp **taught**) [tiːtʃ, tɔːt] vt: **to ~ sb sth, ~ sth to sb** enseñar algo a algn ▷ vi enseñar; (be a teacher) ser profesor(a); **it taught him a lesson** (eso) le sirvió de escarmiento

teacher ['tiːtʃər] n (in secondary school) profesor(a) m(f); (in primary school) maestro(-a); **Spanish ~** profesor(a) m(f) de español

teaching ['tiːtʃɪŋ] n enseñanza

tea cloth n (Brit) paño de cocina, trapo de cocina (LAm)

tea cosy n cubretetera m

teacup ['tiːkʌp] n taza de té

teak [tiːk] n (madera de) teca

tea leaves npl hojas fpl de té

team [tiːm] n equipo; (of animals) pareja; **team up** vi asociarse

teamwork ['tiːmwɜːk] n trabajo en equipo

teapot ['tiːpɒt] n tetera

tear¹ [tɪər] n lágrima; **in ~s** llorando; **to burst into ~s** deshacerse en lágrimas

tear² [tɛər] (pt **tore**, pp **torn**) n rasgón m, desgarrón m ▷ vt romper, rasgar ▷ vi rasgarse; **to ~ to pieces** or **to bits** or **to shreds** (also fig) hacer pedazos, destrozar;

tear along vi (rush) precipitarse; **tear apart** vt (also fig) hacer pedazos; **tear away** vt: **to ~ o.s. away (from sth)** alejarse (de algo); **tear down** vt (building, statue) derribar; (poster, flag) arrancar; **tear off** vt (sheet of paper etc) arrancar; (one's clothes) quitarse a tirones; **tear out** vt (sheet of paper, cheque) arrancar; **tear up** vt (sheet of paper etc) romper

tearful ['tɪəful] adj lloroso

tear gas n gas m lacrimógeno

tearoom ['tɪəruːm] n salón m de té

tease [tiːz] n bromista m/f ▷ vt tomar el pelo a

tea set n servicio de té

teaspoon ['tiːspuːn] n cucharita; (also: ~ful: as measurement) cucharadita

teat [tiːt] n (of bottle) boquilla, tetilla

teatime ['tiːtaɪm] n hora del té

tea towel n (Brit) paño de cocina

technical ['tɛknɪkl] adj técnico

technical college n centro de formación profesional

technicality [tɛknɪ'kælɪtɪ] n detalle m técnico; **on a legal ~** por una cuestión formal

technically ['tɛknɪklɪ] adv técnicamente

technician [tɛk'nɪʃn] n técnico(-a)

technique [tɛk'niːk] n técnica

technological [tɛknə'lɒdʒɪkl] adj tecnológico

technology [tɛk'nɒlədʒɪ] n tecnología

teddy ['tɛdɪ], **teddy bear** n osito de peluche

tedious ['tiːdɪəs] adj pesado, aburrido

tee [tiː] n (Golf) tee m

teem [tiːm] vi: **to ~ with** rebosar de; **it is ~ing (with rain)** llueve a mares

teen [tiːn] adj = **teenage** ▷ n (US) = **teenager**

teenage ['tiːneɪdʒ] adj (fashions etc) juvenil

teenager ['tiːneɪdʒər] n adolescente m/f, quinceañero(-a)

teens [tiːnz] npl: **to be in one's ~** ser adolescente

tee-shirt ['tiːʃɜːt] n = **T-shirt**

teeter ['tiːtər] vi balancearse

teeth [tiːθ] npl of **tooth**

teethe [tiːð] vi echar los dientes

teething ring ['tiːðɪŋ-] n mordedor m

teething troubles ['tiːðɪŋ-] npl (fig) dificultades fpl iniciales

teetotal ['tiː'təutl] adj (person) abstemio

TEFL ['tɛfl] n abbr (= Teaching of English as a Foreign Language); **~ qualification** título para la enseñanza del inglés como lengua extranjera

tel. abbr (= telephone) tel

telecommunications ['tɛlɪkəmjuːnɪ] n telecomunicaciones fpl

teleconferencing ['tɛlɪkɒnfərənsɪŋ] n teleconferencias fpl

telegram ['tɛlɪgræm] n telegrama m

telegraph ['tɛlɪgrɑːf] n telégrafo

telegraph pole n poste m telegráfico

telepathic [tɛlɪ'pæθɪk] adj telepático

telephone ['tɛlɪfəun] n teléfono ▷ vt llamar por teléfono, telefonear; **to be on the ~**

(*subscriber*) tener teléfono; (*be speaking*) estar hablando por teléfono

telephone book n guía f telefónica

telephone booth, telephone box (*Brit*) n cabina telefónica

telephone call n llamada telefónica

telephone directory n guía telefónica

telephone number n número de teléfono

telephonist [tə'lɛfənɪst] n (*Brit*) telefonista m/f

telesales ['tɛlɪseɪlz] npl televentas fpl

telescope ['tɛlɪskəʊp] n telescopio

Teletext® ['tɛlɪtɛkst] n teletexto m

telethon ['tɛlɪθɒn] n telemaratón m, maratón m televisivo (*con fines benéficos*)

televise ['tɛlɪvaɪz] vt televisar

television ['tɛlɪvɪʒən] n televisión f; **to watch** ~ mirar or ver la televisión

television licence n impuesto por uso de televisor

television programme n programa m de televisión

television set n televisor m

teleworking ['tɛlɪwɜːkɪŋ] n teletrabajo

telex ['tɛlɛks] n télex m ⊳ vt (*message*) enviar por télex; (*person*) enviar un télex a ⊳ vi enviar un télex

tell (*pt, pp* **told**) [tɛl, təʊld] vt decir; (*relate: story*) contar; (*distinguish*): **to** ~ **sth from** distinguir algo de ⊳ vi (*talk*): **to** ~ **(of)** contar; (*have effect*) tener efecto; **to** ~ **sb to do sth** decir a algn que haga algo; **to** ~ **sb about sth** contar algo a algn; **to** ~ **the time** dar or decir la hora; **can you** ~ **me the time?** ¿me puedes decir la hora?; **(I)** ~ **you what ...** fíjate ...; **I couldn't** ~ **them apart** no podía distinguirlos; **tell off** vt: **to** ~ **sb off** regañar a algn; **tell on** vt fus: **to** ~ **on sb** chivarse de algn

teller ['tɛləʳ] n (*in bank*) cajero(-a)

telling ['tɛlɪŋ] adj (*remark, detail*) revelador(a)

telltale ['tɛlteɪl] adj (*sign*) indicador(a)

telly ['tɛlɪ] n (*Brit inf*) tele f

temp [tɛmp] n abbr (*Brit*: = *temporary office worker*) empleado(-a) eventual ⊳ vi trabajar como empleado(-a) eventual

temper ['tɛmpəʳ] n (*mood*) humor m; (*bad temper*) (mal) genio; (*fit of anger*) ira; (*of child*) rabieta ⊳ vt (*moderate*) moderar; **to be in a** ~ estar furioso; **to lose one's** ~ enfadarse, enojarse (*LAm*); **to keep one's** ~ contenerse, no alterarse

temperament ['tɛmprəmənt] n (*nature*) temperamento

temperamental [tɛmprə'mɛntl] adj temperamental

temperate ['tɛmprət] adj moderado; (*climate*) templado

temperature ['tɛmprətʃəʳ] n temperatura; **to have** or **run a** ~ tener fiebre

template ['tɛmplɪt] n plantilla

temple ['tɛmpl] n (*building*) templo; (*Anat*) sien f

temporary ['tɛmpərərɪ] adj provisional, temporal; (*passing*) transitorio; (*worker*) eventual; (*job*) temporal; ~ **teacher** maestro(-a) interino(-a)

tempt [tɛmpt] vt tentar; **to** ~ **sb into doing sth** tentar or inducir a algn a hacer algo; **to be** ~**ed to do sth** (*person*) sentirse tentado de hacer algo

temptation [tɛmp'teɪʃən] n tentación f

tempting ['tɛmptɪŋ] adj tentador(a); (*food*) apetitoso(-a)

ten [tɛn] num diez; ~**s of thousands** decenas fpl de miles

tenacity [tə'næsɪtɪ] n tenacidad f

tenancy ['tɛnənsɪ] n alquiler m

tenant ['tɛnənt] n (*rent-payer*) inquilino(-a); (*occupant*) habitante m/f

tend [tɛnd] vt (*sick etc*) cuidar, atender; (*cattle, machine*) vigilar, cuidar ⊳ vi: **to** ~ **to do sth** tener tendencia a hacer algo

tendency ['tɛndənsɪ] n tendencia

tender ['tɛndəʳ] adj tierno, blando; (*delicate*) delicado; (*meat*) tierno; (*sore*) sensible; (*affectionate*) tierno, cariñoso ⊳ n (*Comm: offer*) oferta; (*money*): **legal** ~ moneda de curso legal ⊳ vt ofrecer; **to put in a** ~ **(for)** hacer una oferta (para); **to put work out to** ~ ofrecer un trabajo a contrata; **to** ~ **one's resignation** presentar la dimisión

tendon ['tɛndən] n tendón m

tenement ['tɛnəmənt] n casa or bloque m de pisos or vecinos (*LAm*)

tenet ['tɛnət] n principio

tenner ['tɛnəʳ] n (*billete m de*) diez libras fpl

tennis ['tɛnɪs] n tenis m

tennis ball n pelota de tenis

tennis court n cancha de tenis

tennis match n partido de tenis

tennis player n tenista m/f

tennis racket n raqueta de tenis

tennis shoes npl zapatillas fpl de tenis

tenor ['tɛnəʳ] n (*Mus*) tenor m

tenpin bowling ['tɛnpɪn-] n bolos mpl

tense [tɛns] adj tenso; (*stretched*) tirante; (*stiff*) rígido, tieso; (*person*) nervioso ⊳ n (*Ling*) tiempo ⊳ vt (*tighten: muscles*) tensar

tension ['tɛnʃən] n tensión f

tent [tɛnt] n tienda (de campaña), carpa (*LAm*)

tentative ['tɛntətɪv] adj (*person*) indeciso; (*provisional*) provisional

tenterhooks ['tɛntəhuks] npl: **on** ~ sobre ascuas

tenth [tɛnθ] adj décimo

tent peg n clavija, estaca

tent pole n mástil m

tenuous ['tɛnjuəs] adj tenue

tenure ['tɛnjuəʳ] n posesión f, tenencia; **to have** ~ tener posesión or título de propiedad

tepid ['tɛpɪd] adj tibio

term [tɜːm] n (*limit*) límite m; (*Comm*) plazo; (*word*) término; (*period*) período; (*Scol*) trimestre m ⊳ vt llamar, calificar de; **terms**

npl (*conditions*) condiciones *fpl*; (*Comm*) precio, tarifa; **in the short/long ~** a corto/largo plazo; **during his ~ of office** bajo su mandato; **to be on good ~s with sb** llevarse bien con algn; **to come to ~s with** (*problem*) aceptar; **in ~s of ...** en cuanto a ..., en términos de ...

terminal ['tə:mɪnl] *adj* (*disease*) mortal; (*patient*) terminal ▷ *n* (*Elec*) borne *m*; (*Comput*) terminal *m*; (*also:* **air ~**) terminal *f*; (*Brit: also:* **coach ~**) (estación *f*) terminal *f*

terminate ['tə:mɪneɪt] *vt* poner término a; (*pregnancy*) interrumpir ▷ *vi:* **to ~ in** acabar en

termini ['tə:mɪnaɪ] *npl of* **terminus**

terminology [tə:mɪ'nɔlədʒɪ] *n* terminología

terminus (*pl* **termini**) ['tə:mɪnəs, 'tə:mɪnaɪ] *n* término, (estación *f*) terminal *f*

termite ['tə:maɪt] *n* termita, comején *m*

term paper *n* (*US Univ*) trabajo escrito trimestral *or* semestral

terrace ['terəs] *n* terraza; (*Brit: row of houses*) hilera de casas adosadas; **the ~s** (*Brit Sport*) las gradas *fpl*

terraced ['terəst] *adj* (*garden*) escalonado; (*house*) adosado

terracotta ['terə'kɔtə] *n* terracota

terrain [te'reɪn] *n* terreno

terrestrial [tɪ'restrɪəl] *adj* (*life*) terrestre; (*Brit: channel*) de transmisión (por) vía terrestre

terrible ['terɪbl] *adj* terrible, horrible; (*inf*) malísimo

terribly ['terɪblɪ] *adv* terriblemente; (*very badly*) malísimamente

terrier ['terɪəʳ] *n* terrier *m*

terrific [tə'rɪfɪk] *adj* fantástico, fenomenal, macanudo (*LAm*); (*wonderful*) maravilloso

terrify ['terɪfaɪ] *vt* aterrorizar; **to be terrified** estar aterrado *or* aterrorizado

terrifying ['terɪfaɪɪŋ] *adj* aterrador(a)

territorial [terɪ'tɔ:rɪəl] *adj* territorial

territory ['terɪtərɪ] *n* territorio

terror ['terəʳ] *n* terror *m*

terror attack *n* atentado (terrorista)

terrorism ['terərɪzəm] *n* terrorismo

terrorist ['terərɪst] *n* terrorista *m/f*

terrorist attack *n* atentado (terrorista)

terrorize ['terəraɪz] *vt* aterrorizar

terse [tə:s] *adj* (*style*) conciso, (*reply*) brusco

TESL [tesl] *n abbr* = **Teaching of English as a Second Language**

test [test] *n* (*trial, check*) prueba, ensayo, (: *of goods in factory*) control *m*; (*of courage etc*) prueba; (*Chem, Med*) prueba; (*of blood, urine*) análisis *m inv*; (*exam*) examen *m*, test *m*; (*also:* **driving ~**) examen *m* de conducir ▷ *vt* probar, poner a prueba; (*Med*) examinar; (: *blood*) analizar; **to put sth to the ~** someter algo a prueba; **to ~ sth for sth** analizar algo en busca de algo

testament ['testəmənt] *n* testamento; **the Old/New T~** el Antiguo/Nuevo Testamento

testicle ['testɪkl] *n* testículo

testify ['testɪfaɪ] *vi* (*Law*) prestar declaración; **to ~ to sth** atestiguar algo

testimony ['testɪmənɪ] *n* (*Law*) testimonio, declaración *f*

test match *n* partido internacional

testosterone [tes'tɔstərəun] *n* testosterona

test pilot *n* piloto *m/f* de pruebas

test tube *n* probeta

tetanus ['tetənəs] *n* tétano

tether ['teðəʳ] *vt* atar ▷ *n:* **to be at the end of one's ~** no aguantar más

text [tekst] *n* texto; (*on mobile*) mensaje *m* de texto ▷ *vt:* **to ~ sb** enviar un mensaje (de texto) a algn

textbook ['tekstbuk] *n* libro de texto

textiles ['tekstaɪlz] *npl* tejidos *mpl*

text message *n* mensaje *m* de texto

text messaging [-'mesɪdʒɪŋ] *n* (envío de) mensajes *mpl* de texto

textual ['tekstjuəl] *adj* del texto, textual

texture ['tekstʃəʳ] *n* textura

Thai [taɪ] *adj, n* tailandés(-esa) *m(f)*

Thailand ['taɪlænd] *n* Tailandia

Thames [temz] *n:* **the ~** el (río) Támesis

than [ðæn, ðən] *conj* que; (*with numerals*): **more ~ 10/once** más de 10/una vez; **I have more/less ~ you** tengo más/menos que tú; **it is better to phone ~ to write** es mejor llamar por teléfono que escribir; **no sooner did he leave ~ the phone rang** en cuanto se marchó, sonó el teléfono

thank [θæŋk] *vt* dar las gracias a, agradecer; **~ you (very much)** (muchas) gracias; **~ heavens, ~ God!** ¡gracias a Dios!, ¡menos mal!; *see also* **thanks**

thankful ['θæŋkful] *adj:* **~ for** agradecido (por)

thankfully ['θæŋkfəlɪ] *adv* (*gratefully*) con agradecimiento; (*with relief*) por suerte; **~ there were few victims** afortunadamente hubo pocas víctimas

thankless ['θæŋklɪs] *adj* ingrato

thanks [θæŋks] *npl* gracias *fpl* ▷ *excl* ¡gracias!; **many ~, ~ a lot** ¡muchas gracias!; **~ to** *prep* gracias a

Thanksgiving ['θæŋksgɪvɪŋ], **Thanksgiving Day** *n* día *m* de Acción de Gracias; *ver nota*

● **THANKSGIVING DAY**
●
● En Estados Unidos el cuarto jueves de
● noviembre es *Thanksgiving Day*, fiesta
● oficial en la que se conmemora la
● celebración que tuvieron los primeros
● colonos norteamericanos ("Pilgrims"
● o "Pilgrim Fathers") tras la estupenda
● cosecha de 1621, por la que se dan gracias
● a Dios. En Canadá se celebra una fiesta
● semejante el segundo lunes de octubre,
● aunque no está relacionada con dicha
● fecha histórica.

○ KEYWORD

that [ðæt] (pl **those**) adj (demonstrative) ese(-a), esos(-as) pl; (more remote) aquel/aquella m/f, aquellos(-as) m(f)pl; **leave those books on the table** deja esos libros sobre la mesa; **that one** ése/ésa; (more remote) aquél/aquélla; **that one over there** ése/ésa de ahí; aquél/aquélla de allí
▷ pron **1** (demonstrative) ese(-a); ése(-a), esos(-as) pl; ésos(-as) pl; (neuter) eso; (more remote) aquél/aquélla m/f; aquél/aquélla m/f, aquéllos(-as) m(f)pl; aquéllos(-as) m(f)pl, aquello neuter; **what's that?** ¿qué es eso (or aquello)?; **who's that?** ¿quién es?; (pointing etc) ¿quién es ése/a?; **is that you?** ¿eres tú?; **will you eat all that?** ¿vas a comer todo eso?; **that's my house** ésa es mi casa; **that's what he said** eso es lo que dijo; **that is (to say)** es decir; **at** or **with that she ...** en eso, ella ...; **do it like that** hazlo así
2 (relative: subject, object) que; (with preposition) (el/la) que, el/la cual; **the book (that) I read** el libro que leí; **the books that are in the library** los libros que están en la biblioteca; **all (that) I have** todo lo que tengo; **the box (that) I put it in** la caja en la que or donde lo puse; **the people (that) I spoke to** la gente con la que hablé; **not that I know of** que yo sepa, no
3 (relative: of time) que; **the day (that) he came** el día (en) que vino
▷ conj que; **he thought that I was ill** creyó que yo estaba enfermo
▷ adv (demonstrative): **I can't work that much** no puedo trabajar tanto; **I didn't realize it was that bad** no creí que fuera tan malo; **that high** así de alto

thatched [θætʃt] adj (roof) de paja; **~ cottage** casita con tejado de paja
thaw [θɔ:] n deshielo ▷ vi (ice) derretirse; (food) descongelarse ▷ vt descongelar

○ KEYWORD

the [ði:, ðə] def art **1** (gen) el, la f, los pl, las fpl; (NB = el immediately before feminine noun beginning with stressed (h)a; a+el = al; de+el = del): **the boy/girl** el chico/la chica; **the books/flowers** los libros/las flores; **to the postman/from the drawer** al cartero/del cajón; **I haven't the time/money** no tengo tiempo/dinero; **1.10 euros to the dollar** 1,10 euros por dólar; **paid by the hour** pagado por hora
2 (+adj to form noun) los; lo; **the rich and the poor** los ricos y los pobres; **to attempt the impossible** intentar lo imposible
3 (in titles, surnames): **Elizabeth the First** Isabel Primera; **Peter the Great** Pedro el Grande; **do you know the Smiths?** ¿conoce a los Smith?

4 (in comparisons): **the more he works the more he earns** cuanto más trabaja más gana

theatre, theater (US) ['θɪətər] n teatro; (also: **lecture ~**) aula; (Med: also: **operating ~**) quirófano
theatre-goer, theater-goer (US) ['θɪətəgəuər] n aficionado(-a) al teatro
theatrical [θɪˈætrɪkl] adj teatral
theft [θɛft] n robo
their [ðɛər] adj su
theirs [ðɛəz] pron (el) suyo/(la) suya etc; see also **my; mine**
them [ðɛm, ðəm] pron (direct) los/las; (indirect) les; (stressed, after prep) ellos/ellas; **I see ~** los veo; **both of ~** ambos(-as), los/las dos; **give me a few of ~** dame algunos(-as); see also **me**
theme [θi:m] n tema m
theme park n parque m temático
theme song n tema m (musical)
themselves [ðəmˈsɛlvz] pron pl (subject) ellos mismos/ellas mismas; (complement) se; (after prep) sí (mismos(-as)); see also **oneself**
then [ðɛn] adv (at that time) entonces; (next) pues; (later) luego, después; (and also) además ▷ conj (therefore) en ese caso, entonces ▷ adj: **the ~ president** el entonces presidente; **from ~ on** desde entonces; **until ~** hasta entonces; **and ~ what?** ¿y luego, qué?; **what do you want me to do, ~?** ¿entonces, qué quiere que haga?
theologian [θɪəˈləudʒən] n teólogo(-a)
theology [θɪˈɒlədʒɪ] n teología
theoretical [θɪəˈrɛtɪkl] adj teórico
theorize ['θɪəraɪz] vi teorizar
theory ['θɪərɪ] n teoría
therapist ['θɛrəpɪst] n terapeuta m/f
therapy ['θɛrəpɪ] n terapia

○ KEYWORD

there ['ðɛər] adv **1**: **there is, there are** hay; **there is no-one here** no hay nadie aquí; **there is no bread left** no queda pan; **there has been an accident** ha habido un accidente
2 (referring to place) ahí; (distant) allí; **it's there** está ahí; **put it in/on/up/down there** ponlo ahí dentro/encima/arriba/abajo; **I want that book there** quiero ese libro de ahí; **there he is!** ¡ahí está!; **there's the bus** ahí or ya viene el autobús; **back/down there** allí atrás/abajo; **over there, through there** por allí
3: **there, there** (esp to child) venga, venga, bueno

thereabouts ['ðɛərəˈbauts] adv por ahí
thereafter [ðɛərˈɑ:ftər] adv después
thereby ['ðɛəbaɪ] adv así, de ese modo
therefore ['ðɛəfɔ:r] adv por lo tanto
there's [ðɛəz] = **there is; there has**

thereupon [ðɛərə'pɒn] *adv* (*at that point*) en eso, en seguida

thermal ['θə:ml] *adj* termal; (*paper*) térmico

thermometer [θə'mɒmɪtə^r] *n* termómetro

Thermos® ['θə:məs] *n* (*also:* **~ flask**) termo

thermostat ['θə:məustæt] *n* termostato

thesaurus [θɪ'sɔ:rəs] *n* tesoro, diccionario de sinónimos

these [ði:z] *adj pl* estos(-as) ▷ *pron pl* éstos(-as)

thesis (*pl* **theses**) ['θi:sɪs, -si:z] *n* tesis *f inv*

they [ðeɪ] *pron pl* ellos/ellas; **~ say that ...** (*it is said that*) se dice que ...

they'd [ðeɪd] = **they had; they would**

they'll [ðeɪl] = **they shall; they will**

they're [ðɛə^r] = **they are**

they've [ðeɪv] = **they have**

thick [θɪk] *adj* (*wall, slice*) grueso; (*dense: liquid, smoke etc*) espeso; (*vegetation, beard*) tupido; (*stupid*) torpe ▷ *n:* **in the ~ of the battle** en lo más reñido de la batalla; **it's 20 cm ~** tiene 20 cm de espesor

thicken ['θɪkn] *vi* espesarse ▷ *vt* (*sauce etc*) espesar

thicket ['θɪkɪt] *n* espesura

thickness ['θɪknɪs] *n* espesor *m*, grueso

thickset [θɪk'sɛt] *adj* fornido

thick-skinned [θɪk'skɪnd] *adj* (*fig*) insensible

thief (*pl* **thieves**) [θi:f, θi:vz] *n* ladrón(-ona) *m(f)*

thigh [θaɪ] *n* muslo

thimble ['θɪmbl] *n* dedal *m*

thin [θɪn] *adj* delgado; (*wall, layer*) fino; (*watery*) aguado; (*light*) tenue; (*hair*) escaso; (*fog*) ligero; (*crowd*) disperso ▷ *vt:* **to ~ (down)** (*sauce, paint*) diluir ▷ *vi* (*fog*) aclararse; (*also:* **~ out:** *crowd*) dispersarse; **his hair is ~ning** se está quedando calvo

thing [θɪŋ] *n* cosa; (*object*) objeto, artículo; (*contraption*) chisme *m*; (*mania*) manía; **things** *npl* (*belongings*) cosas *fpl*; **the best ~ would be to ...** lo mejor sería ...; **the main ~ is ...** lo principal es ...; **first ~ (in the morning)** a primera hora (de la mañana); **last ~ (at night)** a última hora (de la noche); **the ~ is ...** lo que pasa es que ...; **how are ~s?** ¿qué tal van las cosas?; **she's got a ~ about mice** le dan no sé qué los ratones; **poor ~!** ¡pobre! *m/f*, ¡pobrecito(-a)!

think (*pl* **thought**) [θɪŋk, θɔ:t] *vi* pensar ▷ *vt* pensar, creer; (*imagine*) imaginar; **what did you ~ of it?** ¿qué te parece?; **what did you ~ of them?** ¿qué te parecieron?; **to ~ about sth/sb** pensar en algo/algn; **I'll ~ about it** lo pensaré; **to ~ of doing sth** pensar en hacer algo; **I ~ so/not** creo que sí/no; **~ again!** ¡piénsalo bien!; **to ~ aloud** pensar en voz alta; **to ~ well of sb** tener buen concepto de algn; **think out** *vt* (*plan*) elaborar, tramar; (*solution*) encontrar; **think over** *vt* reflexionar sobre, meditar; **I'd like to ~ things over** me gustaría pensármelo; **think through** *vt* pensar bien; **think up** *vt* imaginar

think tank *n* grupo de expertos

thinly ['θɪnlɪ] *adv* (*cut*) en lonchas finas; (*spread*) en una capa fina

third [θə:d] *adj* (*before n*) tercer(a); (*following n*) tercero(-a) ▷ *n* tercero(-a); (*fraction*) tercio; (*Brit Scol: degree*) título universitario de tercera clase

thirdly ['θə:dlɪ] *adv* en tercer lugar

third party insurance *n* (*Brit*) seguro a terceros

third-rate ['θə:d'reɪt] *adj* de poca calidad

Third World *n:* **the ~** el Tercer Mundo ▷ *cpd* tercermundista

thirst [θə:st] *n* sed *f*

thirsty ['θə:stɪ] *adj* (*person*) sediento; **to be ~** tener sed

thirteen [θə:'ti:n] *num* trece

thirteenth [θə:'ti:nθ] *adj* decimotercero ▷ *n* (*in series*) decimotercero(-a); (*fraction*) decimotercio

thirtieth ['θə:tɪəθ] *adj* trigésimo ▷ *n* (*in series*) trigésimo(-a); (*fraction*) treintavo

thirty ['θə:tɪ] *num* treinta

🔘 **KEYWORD**

this [ðɪs] (*pl* **these**) *adj* (*demonstrative*) este(-a), estos(-as) *pl*, esto *neuter;* **this man/woman** este hombre/esta mujer; **these children/flowers** estos chicos/estas flores; **this way** por aquí; **this time last year** hoy hace un año; **this one (here)** éste(-a), esto (de aquí) ▷ *pron* (*demonstrative*) este(-a); éste(-a), estos(-as) *pl;* éstos(-as) *pl,* esto *neuter;* **who is this?** ¿quién es éste/ésta?; **what is this?** ¿qué es esto?; **this is where I live** aquí vivo; **this is what he said** esto es lo que dijo; **this is Mr Brown** (*in introductions*) le presento al Sr. Brown; (*photo*) éste es el Sr. Brown; (*on telephone*) habla el Sr. Brown; **they were talking of this and that** hablaban de esto y lo otro ▷ *adv* (*demonstrative*): **this high/long** así de alto/largo; **this far** hasta aquí

thistle ['θɪsl] *n* cardo

thorn [θɔ:n] *n* espina

thorough ['θʌrə] *adj* (*search*) minucioso; (*knowledge*) profundo; (*research*) a fondo

thoroughbred ['θʌrəbrɛd] *adj* (*horse*) de pura sangre

thoroughfare ['θʌrəfɛə^r] *n* calle *f;* **"no ~"** "prohibido el paso"

thoroughly ['θʌrəlɪ] *adv* (*search*) minuciosamente; (*study*) profundamente; (*wash*) a fondo; (*utterly: bad, wet etc*) completamente, totalmente

those [ðəuz] *pron pl* ésos/ésas; (*more remote*) aquéllos(-as) ▷ *adj pl* esos/esas; aquellos(-as)

though [ðəu] *conj* aunque ▷ *adv* sin embargo, aún así; **even ~** aunque; **it's not so easy, ~** sin embargo no es tan fácil

thought [θɔ:t] *pt, pp of* **think** ▷ *n* pensamiento; (*opinion*) opinión *f;* (*intention*)

intención f; **to give sth some ~** pensar algo
detenidamente; **after much ~** después de
pensarlo bien; **I've just had a ~** se me acaba
de ocurrir una idea

thoughtful ['θɔːtful] adj pensativo;
(consecrate) atento

thoughtless ['θɔːtlɪs] adj desconsiderado

thousand ['θaʊzənd] num mil; **two ~** dos
mil; **~s of** miles de

thousandth ['θaʊzəntθ] num milésimo

thrash [θræʃ] vt dar una paliza a; **thrash
about** vi revolverse; **thrash out** vt discutir a
fondo

thread [θrɛd] n hilo; (of screw) rosca ▷ vt
(needle) enhebrar

threadbare ['θrɛdbɛəʳ] adj raído

threat [θrɛt] n amenaza; **to be under ~ of**
estar amenazado de

threaten ['θrɛtn] vi amenazar ▷ vt: **to ~ sb
with sth/to do** amenazar a algn con algo/
con hacer

threatening ['θrɛtnɪŋ] adj amenazador(a),
amenazante

three [θriː] num tres

three-dimensional [θriːdɪ'mɛnʃənl] adj
tridimensional

threefold ['θriːfəʊld] adv: **to increase ~**
triplicar

three-piece ['θriːpiːs]: **~ suit** traje m de tres
piezas; **~ suite** tresillo

three-ply [θriː'plaɪ] adj (wood) de tres capas;
(wool) triple

three-quarter [θriː'kwɔːtəʳ] adj: **~ length
sleeves** mangas fpl tres cuartos

three-quarters [θriː'kwɔːtəz] npl tres cuartas
partes; **~ full** tres cuartas partes lleno

thresh [θrɛʃ] vt (Agr) trillar

threshold ['θrɛʃhəʊld] n umbral m; **to be on
the ~ of** (fig) estar al borde de

threw [θruː] pt of **throw**

thrift [θrɪft] n economía

thrifty ['θrɪftɪ] adj económico

thrill [θrɪl] n (excitement) emoción f ▷ vt
emocionar; **to be ~ed** (with gift etc) estar
encantado

thriller ['θrɪləʳ] n película/novela de suspense

thrilling ['θrɪlɪŋ] adj emocionante

thrive (pt thrived, throve, pp thrived, thriven)
[θraɪv, θrəʊv, 'θrɪvn] vi (grow) crecer; (do well)
prosperar

thriving ['θraɪvɪŋ] adj próspero

throat [θrəʊt] n garganta; **I have a sore ~** me
duele la garganta

throb [θrɔb] n (of heart) latido; (of engine)
vibración f ▷ vi latir; vibrar; (with pain) dar
punzadas; **my head is ~bing** la cabeza me da
punzadas

throes [θrəʊz] npl: **in the ~ of** en medio de

thrombosis [θrɔm'bəʊsɪs] n trombosis f

throne [θrəʊn] n trono

throng [θrɔŋ] n multitud f, muchedumbre f
▷ vt, vi apiñarse, agolparse

throttle ['θrɔtl] n (Aut) acelerador m ▷ vt
estrangular

through [θruː] prep por, a través de; (time)
durante; (by means of) por medio de, mediante;
(owing to) gracias a ▷ adj (ticket, train) directo
▷ adv completamente, de parte a parte; de
principio a fin; **(from) Monday ~ Friday** (US)
de lunes a viernes; **to go ~ sb's papers** mirar
entre los papeles de algn; **I am halfway ~ the
book** voy por la mitad del libro; **the soldiers
didn't let us ~** los soldados no nos dejaron
pasar; **to put sb ~ to sb** (Tel) poner or pasar a
algn con algn; **to be ~** (Tel) tener comunicación;
(have finished) haber terminado; **"no ~ road"**
(Brit) "calle sin salida"

throughout [θruː'aʊt] prep (place) por todas
partes de, por todo; (time) durante todo ▷ adv
por or en todas partes

throve [θrəʊv] pt of **thrive**

throw [θrəʊ] (pt threw, pp thrown [θruː,
θrəʊn]) n tiro; (Sport) lanzamiento ▷ vt tirar,
echar, botar (LAm); (Sport) lanzar; (rider)
derribar; (fig) desconcertar; **to ~ a party** dar
una fiesta; **throw about, throw around** vt
(litter etc) tirar, esparcir; **throw away** vt tirar;
throw in vt (Sport: ball) sacar; (include) incluir;
throw off vt deshacerse de; **throw open** vt
(doors, windows) abrir de par en par; (house,
gardens etc) abrir al público; (competition, race)
abrir a todos; **throw out** vt tirar, botar (LAm);
throw together vt (clothes) amontonar;
(meal) preparar a la carrera; (essay) hacer sin
cuidado; **throw up** vi vomitar, devolver

throwaway ['θrəʊəweɪ] adj para tirar,
desechable

throw-in ['θrəʊɪn] n (Sport) saque m de banda

thrown [θrəʊn] pp of **throw**

thru [θruː] prep, adj, adv (US) = **through**

thrush [θrʌʃ] n zorzal m, tordo; (Med)
candiasis f

thrust [θrʌst] (pt, pp thrust) n (Tech) empuje
m ▷ vt empujar; (push in) introducir

thud [θʌd] n golpe m sordo

thug [θʌɡ] n gamberro(-a)

thumb [θʌm] n (Anat) pulgar m ▷ vt: **to ~ a
lift** hacer dedo; **to give sth/sb the ~s up/
down** aprobar/desaprobar algo/a algn;
thumb through vt fus (book) hojear

thumbtack ['θʌmtæk] n (US) chincheta,
chinche f

thump [θʌmp] n golpe m; (sound) ruido seco or
sordo ▷ vt, vi golpear

thunder ['θʌndəʳ] n trueno; (of applause etc)
estruendo ▷ vi tronar; (train etc): **to ~ past**
pasar como un trueno

thunderbolt ['θʌndəbəʊlt] n rayo

thunderclap ['θʌndəklæp] n trueno

thunderstorm ['θʌndəstɔːm] n tormenta

thundery ['θʌndərɪ] adj tormentoso

Thur., Thurs. abbr (= Thursday) juev

Thursday ['θəːzdɪ] n jueves m inv; see also
Tuesday

thus [ðʌs] *adv* así, de este modo

thwart [θwɔːt] *vt* frustrar

thyme [taɪm] *n* tomillo

tiara [tɪˈɑːrə] *n* tiara, diadema

Tibet [tɪˈbet] *n* el Tibet

tick [tɪk] *n* (*sound: of clock*) tictac *m*; (*mark*) señal *f* (de visto bueno), palomita (*LAm*); (*Zool*) garrapata; (*Brit*: *inf*): **to buy sth on** ~ comprar algo a crédito ▷ *vi* hacer tictac ▷ *vt* marcar, señalar; **to put a** ~ **against sth** poner una señal en algo; **tick off** *vt* marcar; (*person*) reñir; **tick over** *vi* (*Brit*: *engine*) girar en marcha lenta; (: *fig*) ir tirando

ticket [ˈtɪkɪt] *n* billete *m*, tíquet *m*, boleto (*LAm*); (*for cinema etc*) entrada, boleto (*LAm*); (*in shop: on goods*) etiqueta; (*for library*) tarjeta; (*US Pol*) lista (de candidatos); **to get a parking** ~ (*Aut*) ser multado por estacionamiento ilegal

ticket barrier *n* (*Brit*: *Rail*) barrera más allá de la cual se necesita billete/boleto

ticket collector *n* revisor/a(*m*/*f*)

ticket inspector *n* revisor/a *m*(*f*), inspector(a) *m*(*f*) de boletos (*LAm*)

ticket machine *n* máquina de billetes (*Sp*) or boletos (*LAm*)

ticket office *n* (*Theat*) taquilla, boletería (*LAm*); (*Rail*) despacho de billetes or boletos (*LAm*)

tickle [ˈtɪkl] *n*: **to give sb a** ~ hacer cosquillas a algn ▷ *vt* hacer cosquillas a ▷ *vi* hacer cosquillas

ticklish [ˈtɪklɪʃ] *adj* (*which tickles: blanket*) que pica; (: *cough*) irritante; (*fig: problem*) delicado; **to be** ~ tener cosquillas

tidal [ˈtaɪdl] *adj* de marea

tidal wave *n* maremoto

tidbit [ˈtɪdbɪt] *n* (*US*) = **titbit**

tiddlywinks [ˈtɪdlɪwɪŋks] *n* juego de la pulga

tide [taɪd] *n* marea; (*fig: of events*) curso, marcha ▷ *vt*: **to** ~ **sb over** or **through (until)** sacar a algn del apuro (hasta); **high/low** ~ marea alta/baja; **the** ~ **of public opinion** la tendencia de la opinión pública

tidy [ˈtaɪdɪ] *adj* (*room*) ordenado; (*drawing, work*) limpio; (*person*) (bien) arreglado; (: *in character*) metódico; (*mind*) claro, metódico ▷ *vt* (*also*: ~ **up**) ordenar, poner en orden

tie [taɪ] *n* (*string etc*) atadura; (*Brit: necktie*) corbata; (*fig: link*) vínculo, lazo; (*Sport: draw*) empate *m* ▷ *vt* atar ▷ *vi* (*Sport*) empatar; **family** ~**s** obligaciones *fpl* familiares; **cup** ~ (*Sport: match*) partido de copa; **to** ~ **in a bow** hacer un lazo; **to** ~ **a knot in sth** hacer un nudo en algo; **tie down** *vt* atar; (*fig*): **to** ~ **sb down to** obligar a algn a; **tie in** *vi*: **to** ~ **in (with)** (*correspond*) concordar (con); **tie on** *vt* (*Brit: label etc*) atar; **tie up** *vt* (*parcel*) envolver; (*dog*) atar; (*boat*) amarrar; (*arrangements*) concluir; **to be** ~**d up** (*busy*) estar ocupado

tier [tɪəʳ] *n* grada; (*of cake*) piso

tiger [ˈtaɪgəʳ] *n* tigre *m*

tight [taɪt] *adj* (*rope*) tirante; (*money*) escaso; (*clothes, budget*) ajustado; (*programme*) apretado; (*budget*) ajustado; (*security*) estricto; (*inf: drunk*) borracho ▷ *adv* (*squeeze*) muy fuerte; (*shut*) herméticamente; **to be packed** ~ (*suitcase*) estar completamente lleno; (*people*) estar apretados; **everybody hold** ~! ¡agárrense bien!

tighten [ˈtaɪtn] *vt* (*rope*) tensar, estirar; (*screw*) apretar ▷ *vi* estirarse; apretarse

tight-fisted [taɪtˈfɪstɪd] *adj* tacaño

tight-lipped [ˈtaɪtˈlɪpt] *adj*: **to be** ~ (*silent*) rehusar hablar; (*angry*) apretar los labios

tightly [ˈtaɪtlɪ] *adv* (*grasp*) muy fuerte

tightrope [ˈtaɪtrəup] *n* cuerda floja

tights [taɪts] *npl* (*Brit*) medias *fpl*, panties *mpl*

tile [taɪl] *n* (*on roof*) teja; (*on floor*) baldosa; (*on wall*) azulejo ▷ *vt* (*floor*) poner baldosas en; (*wall*) alicatar

tiled [taɪld] *adj* (*floor*) embaldosado; (*wall, bathroom*) alicatado; (*roof*) con tejas

till [tɪl] *n* caja (registradora) ▷ *vt* (*land*) cultivar ▷ *prep, conj* = **until**

tiller [ˈtɪləʳ] *n* (*Naut*) caña del timón

tilt [tɪlt] *vt* inclinar ▷ *vi* inclinarse ▷ *n* (*slope*) inclinación *f*; **to wear one's hat at a** ~ llevar el sombrero echado a un lado or terciado; **(at) full** ~ a toda velocidad or carrera

timber [ˈtɪmbəʳ] *n* (*material*) madera; (*trees*) árboles *mpl*

time [taɪm] *n* tiempo; (*epoch*) *often pl* época; (*by clock*) hora; (*moment*) momento; (*occasion*) vez *f*; (*Mus*) compás *m* ▷ *vt* calcular or medir el tiempo de; (*race*) cronometrar; (*remark etc*) elegir el momento para; **a long** ~ mucho tiempo; **four at a** ~ cuarto a la vez; **for the** ~ **being** de momento, por ahora; **at** ~**s** a veces, a ratos; ~ **after** ~, ~ **and again** repetidas veces, una y otra vez; **from** ~ **to** ~ de vez en cuando; **in** ~ (*soon enough*) a tiempo; (*after some time*) con el tiempo; (*Mus*) al compás; **in a week's** ~ dentro de una semana; **in no** ~ en un abrir y cerrar de ojos; **any** ~ cuando sea; **on** ~ a la hora; **to be 30 minutes behind/ ahead of** ~ llevar media hora de retraso/ adelanto; **to take one's** ~ tomárselo con calma; **he'll do it in his own** ~ (*without being hurried*) lo hará sin prisa; (*out of working hours*) lo hará en su tiempo libre; **by the** ~ **he arrived** cuando llegó; **5** ~ **s** **5** por 5; **what** ~ **is it?** ¿qué hora es?; **what** ~ **do you make it?** ¿qué hora es or tiene?; **to be behind the** ~**s** estar atrasado; **to carry three boxes at a** ~ llevar tres cajas a la vez; **to keep** ~ llevar el ritmo or el compás; **to have a good** ~ pasarlo bien, divertirse; **to** ~ **sth well/badly** elegir un buen/mal momento para algo; **the bomb was** ~**d to explode five minutes later** la bomba estaba programada para explotar cinco minutos más tarde

time bomb *n* bomba de relojería

time frame *n* plazo
time lag *n* desfase *m*
timeless ['taımlıs] *adj* eterno
time limit *n* (*gen*) límite *m* de tiempo; (*Comm*) plazo
timeline ['taimlain] *n* línea de tiempo
timely ['taımlı] *adj* oportuno
time off *n* tiempo libre
timer ['taımə^r] *n* (*also*: **~ switch**) interruptor *m*; (*in kitchen*) temporizador *m*; (*Tech*) temporizador *m*
time scale *n* escala de tiempo
time switch *n* (*Brit*) interruptor *m* (horario)
timetable ['taımteıbl] *n* horario; (*programme of events etc*) programa *m*
time zone *n* huso horario
timid ['tımıd] *adj* tímido
timing ['taımıŋ] *n* (*Sport*) cronometraje *m*; **the ~ of his resignation** el momento que eligió para dimitir
timpani ['tımpənı] *npl* tímpanos *mpl*
tin [tın] *n* estaño; (*also*: **~ plate**) hojalata; (*Brit*: *can*) lata
tinfoil ['tınfɔıl] *n* papel *m* de estaño
tinge [tındʒ] *n* matiz *m* ▷ *vt*: **~d with** teñido de
tingle ['tıŋgl] *n* hormigueo ▷ *vi* (*cheeks, skin*: *from cold*) sentir comezón; (: *from bad circulation*) sentir hormigueo; **to ~ with** estremecerse de
tinker ['tıŋkə^r] *n* calderero(-a); (*gipsy*) gitano(-a); **tinker with** *vt fus* jugar con, tocar
tinkle ['tıŋkl] *vi* tintinear
tinned [tınd] *adj* (*Brit*: *food*) en lata, en conserva
tinnitus ['tınıtəs] *n* (*Med*) acufeno
tin opener [-əupnə^r] *n* (*Brit*) abrelatas *m inv*
tinsel ['tınsl] *n* oropel *m*
tint [tınt] *n* matiz *m*; (*for hair*) tinte *m* ▷ *vt* (*hair*) teñir
tinted ['tıntıd] *adj* (*hair*) teñido; (*glass, spectacles*) ahumado
tiny ['taını] *adj* minúsculo, pequeñito
tip [tıp] *n* (*end*) punta; (*gratuity*) propina; (*Brit*: *for rubbish*) vertedero; (*advice*) consejo ▷ *vt* (*waiter*) dar una propina a; (*tilt*) inclinar; (*empty*: *also*: **~ out**) vaciar, echar; (*predict*: *winner*) pronosticar; (: *horse*) recomendar; **he ~ped out the contents of the box** volcó el contenido de la caja; **tip off** *vt* avisar, poner sobre aviso a; **tip over** *vt* volcar ▷ *vi* volcarse
tip-off ['tıpɔf] *n* (*hint*) advertencia
tipped [tıpt] *adj* (*Brit*: *cigarette*) con filtro
Tipp-Ex® ['tıpɛks] *n* Tipp-Ex® *m*
tipster ['tıpstə^r] *n* (*Racing*) pronosticador(a) *m(f)*
tipsy ['tıpsı] *adj* alegre, achispado
tiptoe ['tıptəu] *n* (*Brit*): **on ~** de puntillas
tiptop ['tıptɔp] *adj*: **in ~ condition** en perfectas condiciones
tirade [taı'reıd] *n* diatriba
tire ['taıə^r] *n* (*US*) = **tyre** ▷ *vt* cansar ▷ *vi* (*gen*) cansarse; (*become bored*) aburrirse; **tire out** *vt* agotar, rendir

tired ['taıəd] *adj* cansado; **to be ~ of sth** estar harto de algo; **to be/feel/look ~** estar/ sentirse/parecer cansado
tireless ['taıəlıs] *adj* incansable
tire pressure *n* (*US*) = **tyre pressure**
tiresome ['taıəsəm] *adj* aburrido
tiring ['taırıŋ] *adj* cansado
tissue ['tıʃuː] *n* tejido; (*paper handkerchief*) pañuelo de papel, kleenex® *m*
tissue paper *n* papel *m* de seda
tit [tıt] *n* (*bird*) herrerillo común; **to give ~ for tat** dar ojo por ojo
titbit ['tıtbıt], **tidbit** (*US*) ['tıdbıt] *n* (*food*) golosina; (*news*) pedazo
title ['taıtl] *n* título; (*Law*: *right*): **~ (to)** derecho (a)
title deed *n* (*Law*) título de propiedad
title role *n* papel *m* principal
titter ['tıtə^r] *vi* reírse entre dientes
T-junction ['tiː dʒʌŋkʃən] *n* cruce *m* en T
TM *abbr* (= *trademark*) marca de fábrica; = **transcendental meditation**

○ **KEYWORD**

to [tuː, tə] *prep* **1** (*direction*) a; **to go to France/ London/school/the station** ir a Francia/ Londres/al colegio/a la estación; **to go to Claude's/the doctor's** ir a casa de Claude/al médico; **the road to Edinburgh** la carretera de Edimburgo; **to the left/right** a la izquierda/derecha
2 (*as far as*) hasta, a; **from here to London** de aquí a *or* hasta Londres; **to count to 10** contar hasta 10; **from 40 to 50 people** entre 40 *y* 50 personas
3 (*with expressions of time*): **a quarter/twenty to five** las cuarto menos cuarto/veinte
4 (*for, of*): **the key to the front door** la llave de la puerta principal; **she is secretary to the director** es la secretaria del director; **a letter to his wife** una carta a *or* para su mujer
5 (*expressing indirect object*) a; **to give sth to sb** darle algo a algn; **give it to me** dámelo; **to talk to sb** hablar con algn; **to be a danger to sb** ser un peligro para algn; **to carry out repairs to sth** hacer reparaciones en algo
6 (*in relation to*): **3 goals to 2** 3 goles a 2; **30 miles to the gallon** ≈ 9,4 litros a los cien (kilómetros); **8 apples to the kilo** 8 manzanas por kilo
7 (*purpose, result*): **to come to sb's aid** venir en auxilio *or* ayuda de algn; **to sentence sb to death** condenar a algn a muerte; **to my great surprise** con gran sorpresa mía
▷ *infin particle* **1** (*simple infin*): **to go/eat** ir/ comer
2 (*following another vb; see also relevant vb*): **to want/try/start to do** querer/intentar/ empezar a hacer
3 (*with vb omitted*): **I don't want to** no quiero

4 (*purpose, result*) para; **I did it to help you** lo hice para ayudarte; **he came to see you** vino a verte

5 (*equivalent to relative clause*): **I have things to do** tengo cosas que hacer; **the main thing is to try** lo principal es intentarlo

6 (*after adj etc*): **ready to go** listo para irse; **too old to ...** demasiado viejo (como) para ...
▷ *adv*: **pull/push the door to** tirar de/empujar la puerta; **to go to and fro** ir y venir

toad [təud] *n* sapo

toadstool ['təudstuːl] *n* seta venenosa

toast [təust] *n* (*Culin*: *also*: **piece of ~**) tostada; (*drink, speech*) brindis *m inv* ▷ *vt* (*Culin*) tostar; (*drink to*) brindar por

toaster ['təustəʳ] *n* tostador *m*

tobacco [təˈbækəu] *n* tabaco; **pipe ~** tabaco de pipa

tobacconist [təˈbækənɪst] *n* estanquero(-a), tabaquero(-a) (*LAm*); **~'s (shop)** (*Brit*) estanco, tabaquería (*LAm*)

toboggan [təˈbɔgən] *n* tobogán *m*

today [təˈdeɪ] *adv, n* (*also fig*) hoy *m*; **what day is it ~?** ¿qué día es hoy?; **what date is it ~?** ¿a qué fecha estamos hoy?; **~ is the 4th of March** hoy es el 4 de marzo; **~'s paper** el periódico de hoy; **a fortnight ~** de hoy en 15 días, dentro de 15 días

toddler ['tɔdləʳ] *n* niño(-a) (que empieza a andar)

toe [təu] *n* dedo (del pie); (*of shoe*) punta ▷ *vt*: **to ~ the line** (*fig*) acatar las normas; **big/little ~** dedo gordo/pequeño del pie

TOEFL ['təufl] *n abbr* = **Test(ing) of English as a Foreign Language**

toenail ['təuneɪl] *n* uña del pie

toffee ['tɔfɪ] *n* caramelo

toffee apple *n* (*Brit*) manzana de caramelo

tofu ['təufuː] *n* tofu *m*

toga ['təugə] *n* toga

together [təˈgɛðəʳ] *adv* juntos; (*at same time*) al mismo tiempo, a la vez; **~ with** junto con

toil [tɔɪl] *n* trabajo duro, labor *f* ▷ *vi* esforzarse

toilet ['tɔɪlət] *n* (*Brit: lavatory*) servicios *mpl*, baño ▷ *cpd* (*bag, soap etc*) de aseo; **to go to the ~** ir al baño; *see also* **toilets**

toilet bag *n* neceser *m*, bolsa de aseo

toilet paper *n* papel *m* higiénico

toiletries ['tɔɪlətrɪz] *npl* artículos *mpl* de aseo; (*make-up etc*) artículos *mpl* de tocador

toilet roll *n* rollo de papel higiénico

toilets ['tɔɪləts] *npl* (*Brit*) servicios *mpl*

toilet water *n* (agua de) colonia

token ['təukən] *n* (*sign*) señal *f*, muestra; (*souvenir*) recuerdo; (*voucher*) vale *m*; (*disc*) ficha ▷ *cpd* (*fee, strike*) nominal, simbólico; **book/record ~** (*Brit*) vale *m* para comprar libros/discos; **by the same ~** (*fig*) por la misma razón

tokenism ['təukənɪzəm] *n* (*Pol*) política simbólica *or* de fachada

Tokyo ['təukjəu] *n* Tokio, Tokío

told [təuld] *pt, pp of* **tell**

tolerable ['tɔlərəbl] *adj* (*bearable*) soportable; (*fairly good*) pasable

tolerance ['tɔlərns] *n* (*also Tech*) tolerancia

tolerant ['tɔlərnt] *adj*: **~ of** tolerante con

tolerate ['tɔləreɪt] *vt* tolerar

toll [təul] *n* (*of casualties*) número de víctimas; (*tax, charge*) peaje *m* ▷ *vi* (*bell*) doblar

toll bridge *n* puente *m* de peaje

toll call *n* (*US Telec*) conferencia, llamada interurbana

toll-free ['tɔl'friː] *adj, adv* (*US*) gratis

tomato (*pl* **tomatoes**) [təˈmɑːtəu] *n* tomate *m*

tomato sauce *n* salsa de tomate

tomb [tuːm] *n* tumba

tomboy ['tɔmbɔɪ] *n* marimacho

tombstone ['tuːmstəun] *n* lápida

tomcat ['tɔmkæt] *n* gato

tomorrow [təˈmɔrəu] *adv, n* (*also fig*) mañana; **the day after ~** pasado mañana; **~ morning** mañana por la mañana; **a week ~** de mañana en ocho (días)

ton [tʌn] *n* tonelada; **~s of** (*inf*) montones de

tone [təun] *n* tono ▷ *vi* armonizar; **dialling ~** (*Tel*) señal *f* para marcar; **tone down** *vt* (*criticism*) suavizar; (*colour*) atenuar; **tone up** *vt* (*muscles*) tonificar

tone-deaf [təun'dɛf] *adj* sin oído musical

tongs [tɔnz] *npl* (*for coal*) tenazas *fpl*; (*for hair*) tenacillas *fpl*

tongue [tʌn] *n* lengua; **~ in cheek** en broma

tongue-tied ['tʌntaɪd] *adj* (*fig*) mudo

tongue-twister ['tʌntwɪstəʳ] *n* trabalenguas *m inv*

tonic ['tɔnɪk] *n* (*Med*) tónico; (*Mus*) tónica; (*also*: **~ water**) (agua) tónica

tonight [təˈnaɪt] *adv, n* esta noche; **I'll see you ~** nos vemos esta noche

tonsil ['tɔnsl] *n* amígdala; **to have one's ~s out** sacarse las amígdalas *or* anginas

tonsillitis [tɔnsɪ'laɪtɪs] *n* amigdalitis *f*

too [tuː] *adv* (*excessively*) demasiado; (*very*) muy; (*also*) también; **it's ~ sweet** está demasiado dulce; **I'm not ~ sure about that** no estoy muy seguro de eso; **I went ~** yo también fui; **~ much** *adv, adj* demasiado; **~ many** *adj* demasiados(-as); **~ bad!** ¡mala suerte!

took [tuk] *pt of* **take**

tool [tuːl] *n* herramienta; (*fig: person*) instrumento

tool box *n* caja de herramientas

tool kit *n* juego de herramientas

toot [tuːt] *n* (*of horn*) bocinazo; (*of whistle*) silbido ▷ *vi* (*with car horn*) tocar la bocina

tooth (*pl* **teeth**) [tuːθ, tiːθ] *n* (*Anat, Tech*) diente *m*; (*molar*) muela; **to clean one's teeth** lavarse los dientes; **to have a ~ out** sacarse una muela; **by the skin of one's teeth** por un pelo

toothache ['tu:θeɪk] n dolor m de muelas
toothbrush ['tu:θbrʌʃ] n cepillo de dientes
toothpaste ['tu:θpeɪst] n pasta de dientes
toothpick ['tu:θpɪk] n palillo
top [tɔp] n (of mountain) cumbre f, cima; (of head) coronilla; (of ladder) (lo) alto; (of cupboard, table) superficie f; (lid: of box, jar) tapa; (: of bottle) tapón m; (of list, table, queue, page) cabeza; (toy) peonza; (Dress: blouse) blusa; (: T-shirt) camiseta; (: of pyjamas) chaqueta ▷ adj de arriba; (in rank) principal, primero; (best) mejor ▷ vt (exceed) exceder; (be first in) encabezar; **on ~ of** sobre, encima de; **from ~ to bottom** de pies a cabeza; **the ~ of the milk** la nata; **at the ~ of the stairs** en lo alto de la escalera; **at the ~ of the street** al final de la calle; **at the ~ of one's voice** (fig) a voz en grito; **at ~ speed** a máxima velocidad; **a ~ surgeon** un cirujano eminente; **over the ~** (inf) excesivo, desmesurado; **to go over the ~** pasarse; **top off** (US) vt volver a llenar; **top up** vt volver a llenar; (mobile phone) recargar el saldo de
top-class [tɔp'klɑ:s] adj de primera clase
top floor n último piso
top hat n sombrero de copa
top-heavy ['tɔp'hɛvɪ] adj (object) con más peso en la parte superior
topic ['tɔpɪk] n tema m
topical ['tɔpɪkl] adj actual
topless ['tɔplɪs] adj (bather etc) topless
top-level ['tɔplɛvl] adj (talks) al más alto nivel
topmost ['tɔpməust] adj más alto
top-notch ['tɔp'nɔtʃ] adj (inf) de primerísima categoría
topping ['tɔpɪŋ] n (Culin): **with a ~ of cream** con nata por encima
topple ['tɔpl] vt volcar, derribar ▷ vi caerse
top-secret [tɔp'si:krɪt] adj de alto secreto
topsy-turvy ['tɔpsɪ'tə:vɪ] adj, adv patas arriba
top-up card n (for mobile phone) tarjeta prepago
top-up loan n (Brit) préstamo complementario
torch [tɔ:tʃ] n antorcha; (Brit: electric) linterna
tore [tɔ:r] pt of **tear**
torment n ['tɔ:mɛnt] tormento ▷ vt [tɔ:'mɛnt] atormentar; (fig: annoy) fastidiar
torn [tɔ:n] pp of **tear**
tornado (pl **tornadoes**) [tɔ:'neɪdəu] n tornado
torpedo (pl **torpedoes**) [tɔ:'pi:dəu] n torpedo
torrent ['tɔrnt] n torrente m
torrential [tɔ'rɛnʃl] adj torrencial
torrid ['tɔrɪd] adj tórrido; (fig) apasionado
torso ['tɔ:səu] n torso
tortoise ['tɔ:təs] n tortuga
torture ['tɔ:tʃər] n tortura ▷ vt torturar; (fig) atormentar
Tory ['tɔ:rɪ] adj, n (Brit Pol) conservador(a) m(f)
toss [tɔs] vt tirar, echar; (head) sacudir ▷ n (movement: of head etc) sacudida; (of coin)

tirada, echada (LAm); **to ~ a coin** echar a cara o cruz; **to ~ up for sth** jugar algo a cara o cruz; **to ~ and turn** (in bed) dar vueltas (en la cama); **to win/lose the ~** (also Sport) ganar/perder (a cara o cruz)
tot [tɔt] n (Brit: drink) copita; (child) nene(-a) m(f); **tot up** vt sumar
total ['təutl] adj total, entero; (emphatic: failure etc) completo, total ▷ n total m, suma ▷ vt (add up) sumar; (amount to) ascender a; **grand ~** cantidad f total; (cost) importe m total; **in ~** en total, en suma
totalitarian [təutælɪ'tɛərɪən] adj totalitario
totality [təu'tælɪtɪ] n totalidad f
totally ['təutəlɪ] adv totalmente
totter ['tɔtər] vi tambalearse
touch [tʌtʃ] n (sense) tacto; (contact) contacto; (Football) fuera de juego ▷ vt tocar; (emotionally) conmover; **a ~ of** (fig) una pizca or un poquito de; **to get in ~ with sb** ponerse en contacto con algn; **I'll be in ~** le llamaré/escribiré; **to lose ~** (friends) perder contacto; **to be out of ~ with events** no estar al corriente (de los acontecimientos); **the personal ~** el toque personal; **to put the finishing ~es to sth** dar el último toque a algo; **no artist in the country can ~ him** no hay artista en todo el país que le iguale; **touch down** vi (on land) aterrizar; **touch on** vt fus (topic) aludir (brevemente) a; **touch up** vt (paint) retocar
touch-and-go ['tʌtʃən'gəu] adj arriesgado
touchdown ['tʌtʃdaun] n aterrizaje m; (US Football) ensayo
touched [tʌtʃt] adj conmovido; (inf) chiflado
touching ['tʌtʃɪŋ] adj conmovedor(a)
touchline ['tʌtʃlaɪn] n (Sport) línea de banda
touch-sensitive ['tʌtʃ'sɛnsɪtɪv] adj sensible al tacto
touchy ['tʌtʃɪ] adj (person) quisquilloso
tough [tʌf] adj (meat) duro; (journey) penoso; (task, problem, situation) difícil; (resistant) resistente; (person) fuerte; (: pej) bruto ▷ n (gangster etc) gorila m; **they got ~ with the workers** se pusieron muy duros con los trabajadores
toughen ['tʌfn] vt endurecer
toupée ['tu:peɪ] n peluquín m
tour [tuər] n viaje m; (also: **package ~**) viaje m con todo incluido; (of town, museum) visita ▷ vt viajar por; **to go on a ~ of** (region, country) ir de viaje por; (museum, castle) visitar; **to go on ~** partir or ir de gira
tour guide n guía m/f turístico(-a)
tourism ['tuərɪzm] n turismo
tourist ['tuərɪst] n turista m/f ▷ cpd turístico; **the ~ trade** el turismo
tourist class n (Aviat) clase f turista
tourist office n oficina de turismo
tournament ['tuənəmənt] n torneo
tour operator n touroperador(a) m(f), operador(a) m(f) turístico(-a)

tousled ['tauzld] *adj* (*hair*) despeinado
tout [taut] *vi*: **to ~ for business** solicitar clientes ▷ *n*: **ticket ~** revendedor(a) *m(f)*
tow [təu] *n*: **to give sb a ~** (*Aut*) remolcar a algn ▷ *vt* remolcar; **"on** or (US) **in ~"** (*Aut*) "a remolque"; **tow away** *vt* llevarse a remolque
toward [tə'wɔːd], **towards** [tə'wɔːdz] *prep* hacia; (*of attitude*) respecto a, con; (*of purpose*) para; **~noon** alrededor de mediodía; **~the end of the year** hacia finales de año; **to feel friendly ~sb** sentir amistad hacia algn
towel ['tauəl] *n* toalla; **to throw in the ~** (*fig*) darse por vencido, renunciar
towelling ['tauəlɪŋ] *n* (*fabric*) felpa
towel rail, towel rack (US) *n* toallero
tower ['tauə^r] *n* torre *f* ▷ *vi* (*building, mountain*) elevarse; **to ~ above** or **over sth/sb** dominar algo/destacarse sobre algn
tower block *n* (*Brit*) bloque *m* de pisos
towering ['tauərɪŋ] *adj* muy alto, imponente
town [taun] *n* ciudad *f*; **to go to ~** ir a la ciudad; (*fig*) tirar la casa por la ventana; **in the ~** en la ciudad; **to be out of ~** estar fuera de la ciudad
town centre *n* centro de la ciudad
town council *n* Ayuntamiento, consejo municipal
town hall *n* ayuntamiento
townie ['tauni] *n* (*Brit inf*) persona de la ciudad
town plan *n* plano de la ciudad
town planning *n* urbanismo
township ['taunʃip] *n* municipio habitado sólo por negros en Sudáfrica
towrope ['təurəup] *n* cable *m* de remolque
tow truck *n* (US) camión *m* grúa
toxic ['tɔksɪk] *adj* tóxico
toxin ['tɔksɪn] *n* toxina
toy [tɔɪ] *n* juguete *m*; **toy with** *vt fus* jugar con; (*idea*) acariciar
toyshop ['tɔɪʃɔp] *n* juguetería
trace [treɪs] *n* rastro ▷ *vt* (*draw*) trazar, delinear; (*locate*) encontrar; **there was no ~ of it** no había ningún indicio de ello
tracing paper ['treɪsɪŋ-] *n* papel *m* de calco
track [træk] *n* (*mark*) huella, pista; (*path: gen*) camino, senda; (*: of bullet etc*) trayectoria; (*: of suspect, animal*) pista, rastro; (*Rail*) vía; (*Comput, Sport*) pista; (*on album*) canción *f* ▷ *vt* seguir la pista de; **to keep ~ of** mantenerse al tanto de, seguir; **a four-~ tape** una cinta de cuarto pistas; **the first ~ on the record/ tape** la primera canción en el disco/la cinta; **to be on the right ~** (*fig*) ir por buen camino; **track down** *vt* (*person*) localizar; (*sth lost*) encontrar
track meet *n* (US) concurso de carreras y saltos
track record *n*: **to have a good ~** (*fig*) tener un buen historial
tracksuit ['træksuːt] *n* chandal *m*
tract [trækt] *n* (*Geo*) región *f*; (*pamphlet*) folleto

traction ['trækʃən] *n* (*Aut: power*) tracción *f*; **in ~** (*Med*) en tracción
tractor ['træktə^r] *n* tractor *m*
trade [treɪd] *n* comercio, negocio; (*skill, job*) oficio, empleo; (*industry*) industria ▷ *vi* negociar, comerciar; **foreign ~** comercio exterior ▷ *vt* (*exchange*): **to ~ sth (for sth)** cambiar algo (por algo); **trade in** *vt* (*old car etc*) ofrecer como parte del pago
Trade Descriptions Act *n* (*Brit*) ley sobre descripciones comerciales
trade fair *n* feria de muestras
trade-in ['treɪdɪn] *adj*: **~ price/value** precio/ valor de un artículo usado que se descuenta del precio de otro nuevo
trademark ['treɪdmɑːk] *n* marca de fábrica
trade name *n* marca registrada
trade-off ['treɪdɔf] *n*: **a ~ (between)** un equilibrio (entre)
trader ['treɪdə^r] *n* comerciante *m/f*
trade secret *n* secreto profesional
tradesman ['treɪdzmən] *n* (*shopkeeper*) comerciante *m/f*
trade union *n* sindicato
trade unionist [-'juːnjənɪst] *n* sindicalista *m/f*
trading ['treɪdɪŋ] *n* comercio
tradition [trə'dɪʃən] *n* tradición *f*
traditional [trə'dɪʃənl] *adj* tradicional
traffic ['træfɪk] *n* tráfico, circulación *f*, tránsito ▷ *vi*: **to ~ in** (*pej: liquor, drugs*) traficar en; **air ~** tráfico aéreo
traffic calming [-'kɑːmɪŋ] *n* reducción *f* de la velocidad de la circulación
traffic circle *n* (US) rotonda, glorieta
traffic island *n* refugio, isleta
traffic jam *n* embotellamiento, atasco
traffic lights *npl* semáforo *sg*
traffic warden *n* guardia *m/f* de tráfico
tragedy ['trædʒədɪ] *n* tragedia
tragic ['trædʒɪk] *adj* trágico
trail [treɪl] *n* (*tracks*) rastro, pista; (*path*) camino, sendero; (*dust, smoke*) estela ▷ *vt* (*drag*) arrastrar; (*follow*) seguir la pista de; (*follow closely*) vigilar ▷ *vi* arrastrarse; (*in contest etc*) ir perdiendo; **to be on sb's ~** seguir la pista de algn; **trail away, trail off** *vi* (*sound*) desvanecerse; (*interest, voice*) desaparecer; **trail behind** *vi* quedar a la zaga
trailer ['treɪlə^r] *n* (*Aut*) remolque *m*; (*caravan*) caravana; (*Cine*) trailer *m*, avance *m*
train [treɪn] *n* tren *m*; (*of dress*) cola; (*series*): **~ of events** curso de los acontecimientos ▷ *vt* (*educate*) formar; (*teach skills to*) adiestrar; (*sportsman*) entrenar; (*dog*) adiestrar, amaestrar; (*point: gun etc*): **to ~ on** apuntar a ▷ *vi* (*Sport*) entrenarse; (*be educated, learn a skill*) formarse; **to go by ~** ir en tren; **to ~ as a teacher** *etc* estudiar para profesor *etc*; **one's ~ of thought** el razonamiento de algn; **to ~ sb to do sth** enseñar a algn a hacer algo
trained [treɪnd] *adj* (*worker*) cualificado; (*animal*) amaestrado

trainee [treɪ'niː] n trabajador(a) m(f) en prácticas ▷ cpd: **he's a ~ teacher** (primary) es estudiante de magisterio; (secondary) está haciendo las prácticas del I.C.E.

trainer ['treɪnəʳ] n (Sport) entrenador(a) m(f); (of animals) domador(a) m(f); **trainers** npl (shoes) zapatillas fpl (de deporte)

training ['treɪnɪŋ] n formación f; entrenamiento; **to be in ~** (Sport) estar entrenando; (: fit) estar en forma

training college n (gen) colegio de formación profesional; (for teachers) escuela normal

training course n curso de formación

training shoes npl zapatillas fpl (de deporte)

traipse [treɪps] vi andar penosamente

trait [treɪt] n rasgo

traitor ['treɪtəʳ] n traidor(a) m(f)

tram [træm] n (Brit: also: **~car**) tranvía m

tramp [træmp] n (person) vagabundo(-a); (inf, pej: woman) puta ▷ vi andar con pasos pesados

trample ['træmpl] vt: **to ~ (underfoot)** pisotear

trampoline ['træmpəliːn] n trampolín m

trance [trɑːns] n trance m; **to go into a ~** entrar en trance

tranquil ['træŋkwɪl] adj tranquilo

tranquillizer, tranquilizer (US) ['træŋkwɪlaɪzəʳ] n (Med) tranquilizante m

transact [træn'zækt] vt (business) tramitar

transaction [træn'zækʃən] n transacción f, operación f; **cash ~s** transacciones al contado

transatlantic ['trænzət'læntɪk] adj transatlántico

transcend [træn'sɛnd] vt rebasar

transcendental [trænsen'dɛntl] adj: **~ meditation** meditación f transcendental

transcribe [træn'skraɪb] vt transcribir, copiar

transcript ['trænskrɪpt] n copia

transcription [træn'skrɪpʃən] n transcripción f

transfer n ['trænsfəʳ] transferencia; (Sport) traspaso; (picture, design) calcomanía ▷ vt [træns'fəːʳ] trasladar, pasar; **to ~ the charges** (Brit Tel) llamar a cobro revertido; **by bank ~** por transferencia bancaria o giro bancario; **to ~ money from one account to another** transferir dinero de una cuenta a otra; **to ~ sth to sb's name** transferir algo al nombre de algn

transform [træns'fɔːm] vt transformar

transformation [trænsfə'meɪʃən] n transformación f

transfusion [træns'fjuːʒən] n transfusión f

transient ['trænzɪənt] adj transitorio

transistor [træn'zɪstəʳ] n (Elec) transistor m

transit ['trænzɪt] n: **in ~** en tránsito

transition [træn'zɪʃən] n transición f

transition period n período de transición

transitive ['trænzɪtɪv] adj (Ling) transitivo

translate [trænz'leɪt] vt: **to ~ (from/into)** traducir (de/a)

translation [trænz'leɪʃən] n traducción f

translator [trænz'leɪtəʳ] n traductor(a) m(f)

transmission [trænz'mɪʃən] n transmisión f

transmit [trænz'mɪt] vt transmitir

transmitter [trænz'mɪtəʳ] n transmisor m; (station) emisora

transparency [træns'pɛərnsɪ] n (Brit Phot) diapositiva

transparent [træns'pærnt] adj transparente

transpire [træns'paɪəʳ] vi (turn out) resultar (ser); (happen) ocurrir, suceder; (become known): **it finally ~d that ...** por fin se supo que ...

transplant vt [træns'plɑːnt] transplantar ▷ n ['trænsplɑːnt] (Med) transplante m; **to have a heart ~** hacerse un transplante de corazón

transport n ['trænspɔːt] transporte m ▷ vt [træns'pɔːt] transportar; **public ~** transporte m público

transportation [trænspɔː'teɪʃən] n transporte m; (of prisoners) deportación f

transport café n (Brit) bar-restaurante m de carretera

transsexual [trænz'sɛksjuəl] adj, n transexual m/f

transvestite [trænz'vɛstaɪt] n travesti m/f

trap [træp] n (snare, trick) trampa ▷ vt coger (Sp) or agarrar (Lam) en una trampa; (trick) engañar; (confine) atrapar; (immobilize) bloquear; (jam) atascar; **to set** or **lay a ~ (for sb)** poner(le) una trampa (a algn); **to ~ one's finger in the door** pillarse el dedo en la puerta

trap door n escotilla

trapeze [trə'piːz] n trapecio

trappings ['træpɪŋz] npl adornos mpl

trash [træʃ] n basura; (nonsense) tonterías fpl; **the book/film is ~** el libro/la película no vale nada

trash can n (US) cubo, balde m (LAm) or bote m (LAm) de la basura

trashy ['træʃɪ] adj (inf) chungo

trauma ['trɔːmə] n trauma m

traumatic [trɔː'mætɪk] adj traumático

travel ['trævl] n viaje m ▷ vi viajar ▷ vt (distance) recorrer; **this wine doesn't ~ well** este vino pierde con los viajes

travel agency n agencia de viajes

travel agent n agente m/f de viajes

travel insurance n seguro de viaje

traveller, traveler (US) ['trævləʳ] n viajero(-a); (Comm) viajante m/f

traveller's cheque, traveler's check (US) n cheque m de viaje

travelling, traveling (US) ['trævlɪŋ] n los viajes, el viajar ▷ adj (circus, exhibition) ambulante ▷ cpd (bag, clock) de viaje

travel-sick ['trævəlsɪk] adj: **to get ~** marearse al viajar

travel sickness *n* mareo
travesty ['trævəstɪ] *n* parodia
trawler ['trɔːləʳ] *n* pesquero de arrastre
tray [treɪ] *n* (*for carrying*) bandeja; (*on desk*) cajón *m*
treacherous ['trɛtʃərəs] *adj* traidor(a); **road conditions are ~** el estado de las carreteras es peligroso
treachery ['trɛtʃərɪ] *n* traición *f*
treacle ['triːkl] *n* (*Brit*) melaza
tread [trɛd] (*pt* **trod**, *pp* **trodden** [trɔd, 'trɔdn]) *n* paso, pisada; (*of tyre*) banda de rodadura ▷ *vi* pisar; **tread on** *vt fus* pisar
treason ['triːzn] *n* traición *f*
treasure ['trɛʒəʳ] *n* tesoro ▷ *vt* (*value*) apreciar, valorar
treasurer ['trɛʒərəʳ] *n* tesorero(-a)
treasury ['trɛʒərɪ] *n*: **the T~** (*US*), **the T~ Department** ≈ el Ministerio de Economía y de Hacienda
treat [triːt] *n* (*present*) regalo; (*pleasure*) placer *m* ▷ *vt* tratar; (*consider*) considerar; **to give sb a ~** hacer un regalo a algn; **to ~ sb to sth** invitar a algn a algo; **to ~ sth as a joke** tomar algo a broma
treatise ['triːtɪz] *n* tratado
treatment ['triːtmənt] *n* tratamiento; **to have ~ for sth** recibir tratamiento por algo
treaty ['triːtɪ] *n* tratado
treble ['trɛbl] *adj* triple ▷ *vt* triplicar ▷ *vi* triplicarse
treble clef *n* (*Mus*) clave *f* de sol
tree [triː] *n* árbol *m*
tree trunk *n* tronco de árbol
trek [trɛk] *n* (*long journey*) expedición *f*; (*tiring walk*) caminata
trellis ['trɛlɪs] *n* enrejado
tremble ['trɛmbl] *vi* temblar
tremendous [trɪ'mɛndəs] *adj* tremendo; (*enormous, huge*) enorme; (*excellent*) estupendo
tremor ['trɛməʳ] *n* temblor *m*; (*also*: **earth ~**) temblor *m* de tierra
trench [trɛntʃ] *n* zanja; (*Mil*) trinchera
trend [trɛnd] *n* (*tendency*) tendencia; (*of events*) curso; (*fashion*) moda; **~ towards/away from sth** tendencia hacia/en contra de algo; **to set the ~** marcar la pauta
trendy ['trɛndɪ] *adj* de moda
trepidation [trɛpɪ'deɪʃən] *n* inquietud *f*
trespass ['trɛspəs] *vi*: **to ~ on** entrar sin permiso en; **"no ~ing"** "prohibido el paso"
trestle ['trɛsl] *n* caballete *m*
trial ['traɪəl] *n* (*Law*) juicio, proceso; (*test: of machine etc*) prueba; (*hardship*) desgracia; **trials** *npl* (*Athletics*) pruebas *fpl*; (*of horses*) pruebas *fpl*; **to bring sb to ~** (*for a crime*) llevar a algn a juicio (por un delito); **~ by jury** juicio ante jurado; **to be sent for ~** ser remitido al tribunal; **by ~ and error** a fuerza de probar
trial period *n* periodo de prueba
triangle ['traɪæŋgl] *n* (*Math, Mus*) triángulo

triangular [traɪ'æŋgjuləʳ] *adj* triangular
triathlon [traɪ'æθlən] *n* triatlón *m*
tribe [traɪb] *n* tribu *f*
tribesman ['traɪbzmən] *n* miembro de una tribu
tribunal [traɪ'bjuːnl] *n* tribunal *m*
tributary ['trɪbjuːtərɪ] *n* (*river*) afluente *m*
tribute ['trɪbjuːt] *n* homenaje *m*, tributo; **to pay ~ to** rendir homenaje a
trice [traɪs] *n*: **in a ~** en un santiamén
trick [trɪk] *n* trampa; (*conjuring trick, deceit*) truco; (*joke*) broma; (*Cards*) baza ▷ *vt* engañar; **it's a ~ of the light** es una ilusión óptica; **to play a ~ on sb** gastar una broma a algn; **that should do the ~** eso servirá; **to ~ sb out of sth** quitarle algo a algn con engaños; **to ~ sb into doing sth** hacer que algn haga algo con engaños
trickery ['trɪkərɪ] *n* engaño
trickle ['trɪkl] *n* (*of water etc*) hilo ▷ *vi* gotear
tricky ['trɪkɪ] *adj* difícil; (*problem*) delicado
tricycle ['traɪsɪkl] *n* triciclo
tried [traɪd] *adj* probado
trifle ['traɪfl] *n* bagatela; (*Culin*) dulce de bizcocho, gelatina, fruta y natillas ▷ *adv*: **a ~ long** un pelín largo ▷ *vi*: **to ~ with** jugar con
trifling ['traɪflɪŋ] *adj* insignificante
trigger ['trɪgəʳ] *n* (*of gun*) gatillo; **trigger off** *vt* desencadenar
trilogy ['trɪlədʒɪ] *n* trilogía
trim [trɪm] *adj* (*elegant*) aseado; (*house, garden*) en buen estado; (*figure*): **to be ~** tener buen talle ▷ *n* (*haircut etc*) recorte *m* ▷ *vt* (*neaten*) arreglar; (*cut*) recortar; (*decorate*) adornar; (*Naut: a sail*) orientar; **to keep in (good) ~** mantener en buen estado
trimmings ['trɪmɪŋz] *npl* (*extras*) accesorios *mpl*; (*cuttings*) recortes *mpl*
Trinity ['trɪnɪtɪ] *n*: **the ~** la Trinidad
trinket ['trɪŋkɪt] *n* chuchería, baratija
trio ['triːəu] *n* trío
trip [trɪp] *n* viaje *m*; (*excursion*) excursión *f*; (*stumble*) traspié *m* ▷ *vi* (*stumble*) tropezar; (*go lightly*) andar a paso ligero; **on a ~** de viaje; **trip over** *vt fus* tropezar con; **trip up** *vi* tropezar, caerse ▷ *vt* hacer tropezar or caer
tripe [traɪp] *n* (*Culin*) callos *mpl*; (*pej: rubbish*) bobadas *fpl*
triple ['trɪpl] *adj* triple ▷ *adv*: **~ the distance/the speed** 3 veces la distancia/la velocidad
triple jump *n* triple salto
triplets ['trɪplɪts] *npl* trillizos(-as) *m(f)pl*
triplicate ['trɪplɪkət] *n*: **in ~** por triplicado
tripod ['traɪpɔd] *n* trípode *m*
tripwire ['trɪpwaɪəʳ] *n* cable *m* de trampa
trite [traɪt] *adj* trillado
triumph ['traɪʌmf] *n* triunfo ▷ *vi*: **to ~ (over)** vencer
triumphant [traɪ'ʌmfənt] *adj* triunfante
trivia ['trɪvɪə] *npl* trivialidades *fpl*
trivial ['trɪvɪəl] *adj* insignificante, trivial
trod [trɔd] *pt of* **tread**

trodden ['trɔdn] *pp of* **tread**
trolley ['trɔlɪ] *n* carrito; *(in hospital)* camilla
trolley bus *n* trolebús *m*
trombone [trɔm'bəun] *n* trombón *m*
troop [tru:p] *n* grupo, banda; **troops** *npl (Mil)* tropas *fpl*; **troop in** *vi* entrar en tropel; **troop out** *vi* salir en tropel
trophy ['trəufɪ] *n* trofeo
tropic ['trɔpɪk] *n* trópico; **the ~s** los trópicos, la zona tropical; **T~ of Cancer/Capricorn** trópico de Cáncer/Capricornio
tropical ['trɔpɪkl] *adj* tropical
trot [trɔt] *n* trote *m* ▷ *vi* trotar; **on the ~** *(Brit fig)* seguidos(-as); **trot out** *vt (excuse, reason)* volver a usar; *(names, facts)* sacar a relucir
trouble ['trʌbl] *n* problema *m*, dificultad *f*; *(worry)* preocupación *f*; *(bother, effort)* molestia, esfuerzo; *(unrest)* inquietud *f*; *(with machine etc)* fallo, avería; *(Med)*: **stomach ~** problemas *mpl* gástricos ▷ *vt* molestar; *(worry)* preocupar, inquietar ▷ *vi*: **to ~ to do sth** molestarse en hacer algo; **troubles** *npl (Pol etc)* conflictos *mpl*; **to be in ~** estar en un apuro; *(for doing wrong)* tener problemas; **to have ~ doing sth** tener dificultad en *or* para hacer algo; **to go to the ~ of doing sth** tomarse la molestia de hacer algo; **it's no ~!** ¡no es molestia (ninguna)!; **what's the ~?** ¿qué pasa?; **the ~ is …** el problema es …, lo que pasa es …; **please don't ~ yourself** por favor no se moleste
troubled ['trʌbld] *adj (person)* preocupado; *(epoch, life)* agitado
troublemaker ['trʌblmeɪkə'] *n* agitador(a) *m(f)*
troubleshooter ['trʌblʃu:tə'] *n (in conflict)* mediador(a) *m(f)*
troublesome ['trʌblsəm] *adj* molesto, inoportuno
troubling ['trʌblɪŋ] *adj (thought)* preocupante; **these are ~ times** son malos tiempos
trough [trɔf] *n (also: **drinking ~**)* abrevadero; *(also: **feeding ~**)* comedero; *(channel)* canal *m*
trounce [trauns] *vt* dar una paliza a
troupe [tru:p] *n* grupo
trousers ['trauzəz] *npl* pantalones *mpl*; **short ~** pantalones *mpl* cortos
trouser suit *n* traje *m* de chaqueta y pantalón
trout [traut] *n pl inv* trucha
trowel ['trauəl] *n* paleta
truant ['truənt] *n*: **to play ~** *(Brit)* hacer novillos
truce [tru:s] *n* tregua
truck [trʌk] *n (US)* camión *m*; *(Rail)* vagón *m*
truck driver *n* camionero(-a)
trucker ['trʌkə'] *n (esp US)* camionero(-a)
truck farm *n (US)* huerto de hortalizas
trudge [trʌdʒ] *vi* caminar penosamente
true [tru:] *adj* verdadero; *(accurate)* exacto; *(genuine)* auténtico; *(faithful)* fiel; *(wheel)* centrado; *(wall)* a plomo; *(beam)* alineado;

~ to life verídico; **to come ~** realizarse, cumplirse
truffle ['trʌfl] *n* trufa
truly ['tru:lɪ] *adv* realmente; *(faithfully)* fielmente; **yours ~** *(in letter-writing)* atentamente
trump [trʌmp] *n (Cards)* triunfo; **to turn up ~s** *(fig)* salir *or* resultar bien
trumped-up ['trʌmptʌp] *adj* inventado
trumpet ['trʌmpɪt] *n* trompeta
truncheon ['trʌntʃən] *n (Brit)* porra
trundle ['trʌndl] *vt, vi*: **to ~ along** rodar haciendo ruido
trunk [trʌŋk] *n (of tree, person)* tronco; *(of elephant)* trompa; *(case)* baúl *m*; *(US Aut)* maletero, baúl *m (LAm)*
trunks [trʌŋks] *npl (also: **swimming ~**)* bañador *m*
truss [trʌs] *n (Med)* braguero ▷ *vt*: **to ~ (up)** atar
trust [trʌst] *n* confianza; *(Comm)* trust *m*; *(Law)* fideicomiso ▷ *vt (rely on)* tener confianza en; *(entrust)*: **to ~ sth to sb** confiar algo a algn; *(hope)*: **to ~ (that)** esperar (que); **in ~** en fideicomiso; **you'll have to take it on ~** tienes que aceptarlo a ojos cerrados
trusted ['trʌstɪd] *adj* de confianza, fiable, de fiar
trustee [trʌs'ti:] *n (Law)* fideicomisario
trustful ['trʌstful] *adj* confiado
trustworthy ['trʌstwə:ðɪ] *adj* digno de confianza, fiable, de fiar
truth, truths [tru:θ, tru:ðz] *n* verdad *f*
truthful ['tru:θfəl] *adj (person)* sincero; *(account)* fidedigno
try [traɪ] *n* tentativa, intento; *(Rugby)* ensayo ▷ *vt (Law)* juzgar, procesar; *(test: sth new)* probar, someter a prueba; *(attempt)* intentar; *(strain: patience)* hacer perder ▷ *vi* probar; **to give sth a ~** intentar hacer algo; **to ~ one's (very) best** *or* **hardest** poner todo su empeño, esmerarse; **to ~ to do sth** intentar hacer algo; **~ again!** ¡vuelve a probar!; **~ harder!** ¡esfuérzate más!; **well, I tried** al menos lo intenté; **try on** *vt (clothes)* probarse; **try out** *vt* probar, poner a prueba
trying ['traɪɪŋ] *adj* cansado; *(person)* pesado
T-shirt ['ti:ʃə:t] *n* camiseta
T-square ['ti:skweə'] *n* regla en T
tub [tʌb] *n* cubo *(Sp)*, balde *m (LAm)*; *(bath)* bañera, tina *(LAm)*
tubby ['tʌbɪ] *adj* regordete
tube [tju:b] *n* tubo; *(Brit: underground)* metro; *(US inf: television)* tele *f*
tuberculosis [tjubə:kju'ləusɪs] *n* tuberculosis *f inv*
tube station *n (Brit)* estación *f* de metro
TUC *n abbr (Brit: = Trades Union Congress)* federación nacional de sindicatos
tuck [tʌk] *n (Sewing)* pliegue *m* ▷ *vt (put)* poner; **tuck away** *vt* esconder; **tuck in** *vt* meter; *(child)* arropar ▷ *vi (eat)* comer con apetito; **tuck up** *vt (child)* arropar

tuck shop n (Scol) tienda de golosinas

Tue., Tues. abbr (= Tuesday) mart

Tuesday ['tjuːzdɪ] n martes m inv; **on** ~ el
martes; **on** ~**s** los martes; **every** ~ todos los
martes; **every other** ~ cada dos martes, un
martes sí y otro no; **last/next** ~ el martes
pasado/próximo; **a week/fortnight on** ~,
~ **week/fortnight** del martes en 8/15 días,
del martes en una semana/dos semanas

tuft [tʌft] n mechón m; (of grass etc) manojo

tug [tʌg] n (ship) remolcador m ▷ vt remolcar

tug-of-love [tʌgəv'lʌv] n: ~ **children** hijos
envueltos en el litigio de los padres por su custodia

tug-of-war [tʌgəv'wɔːʳ] n : **children** juego de la cuerda

tuition [tjuː'ɪʃən] n (Brit) enseñanza; (: private
tuition) clases fpl particulares; (US: school fees)
matrícula

tulip ['tjuːlɪp] n tulipán m

tumble ['tʌmbl] n (fall) caída ▷ vi caerse,
tropezar; **to** ~ **to sth** (inf) caer en la cuenta
de algo

tumbledown ['tʌmbldaʊn] adj ruinoso

tumble dryer n (Brit) secadora

tumbler ['tʌmbləʳ] n vaso

tummy ['tʌmɪ] n (inf) barriga, vientre m

tumour, tumor (US) ['tjuːməʳ] n tumor m

tuna ['tjuːnə] n pl inv (also: ~ **fish**) atún m

tune [tjuːn] n (melody) melodía ▷ vt (Mus)
afinar; (Radio, TV, Aut) sintonizar; **to be in/
out of** ~ (instrument) estar afinado/
desafinado; (singer) afinar/desafinar; **to be
in/out of** ~ **with** (fig) armonizar/desentonar
con; **to the** ~ **of** (fig: amount) por (la) cantidad
de; **tune in** vi (Radio, TV): **to** ~ **in (to)**
sintonizar (con); **tune up** vi (musician) afinar
(su instrumento)

tuneful ['tjuːnful] adj melodioso

tuner ['tjuːnəʳ] n (radio set) sintonizador m;
piano ~ afinador(a) m(f) de pianos

tunic ['tjuːnɪk] n túnica

Tunisia [tjuː'nɪzɪə] n Túnez m

tunnel ['tʌnl] n túnel m; (in mine) galería ▷ vi
construir un túnel/una galería

tunnel vision n (Med) visión f periférica
restringida; (fig) estrechez f de miras

turbo ['tɜːbəʊ] n turbo

turbulence ['tɜːbjʊləns] n (Aviat) turbulencia

tureen [tə'riːn] n sopera

turf [tɜːf] n césped m; (clod) tepe m ▷ vt cubrir
con césped; **turf out** vt (inf) echar a la calle

turgid ['tɜːdʒɪd] adj (prose) pesado

Turk [tɜːk] n turco(-a)

Turkey ['tɜːkɪ] n Turquía

turkey ['tɜːkɪ] n pavo

Turkish ['tɜːkɪʃ] adj turco ▷ n (Ling) turco

turmoil ['tɜːmɔɪl] n desorden m, alboroto;
in ~ revuelto

turn [tɜːn] n turno; (in road) curva; (Theat)
número; (Med) ataque m ▷ vt girar, volver,
voltear (LAm); (collar, steak) dar la vuelta a;
(shape: wood, metal) tornear; (change): **to** ~ **sth
into** convertir algo en ▷ vi volver, voltearse

(LAm); (person: look back) volverse; (reverse
direction) dar la vuelta, voltear (LAm); (milk)
cortarse; (change) cambiar; (become): **to** ~ **into
sth** convertirse or transformarse en algo;
a good ~ un favor; **it gave me quite a** ~ me
dio un susto; **"no left** ~**"** (Aut) "prohibido
girar a la izquierda"; **it's your** ~ te toca a ti;
in ~ por turnos; **to take** ~**s** turnarse; **at the** ~
of the year/century a fin de año/a finales de
siglo; **to take a** ~ **for the worse** (situation,
patient) empeorar; **they** ~**ed him against us**
le pusieron en contra nuestra; **the car** ~**ed
the corner** el coche dobló la esquina; **to** ~
left (Aut) torcer or girar a la izquierda; **she
has no-one to** ~ **to** no tiene a quién recurrir;
turn around vi (person) volverse, darse la
vuelta ▷ vt (object) dar la vuelta a, voltear
(LAm); **turn away** vi apartar la vista ▷ vt
(reject: person, business) rechazar; **turn back** vi
volverse atrás ▷ vt hacer retroceder; (clock)
retrasar; **turn down** vt (refuse) rechazar;
(reduce) bajar; (fold) doblar; **turn in** vi (inf: go
to bed) acostarse ▷ vt (fold) doblar hacia
dentro; **turn off** vi (from road) desviarse ▷ vt
(light, radio etc) apagar; (engine) parar; **turn on**
vt (light, radio etc) encender, prender (LAm);
(engine) poner en marcha; **turn out** vt (light,
gas) apagar; (produce: goods, novel etc) producir
▷ vi (attend: troops) presentarse; (: doctor)
atender; **to** ~ **out to be** ... resultar ser ...;
turn over vi (person) volverse ▷ vt (mattress,
card) dar la vuelta a; (page) volver; **turn round**
vi volverse; (rotate) girar; **turn to** vt fus: **to** ~
to sb acudir a algn; **turn up** vi (person) llegar,
presentarse; (lost object) aparecer ▷ vt (radio)
subir, poner más alto; (heat, gas) poner más
fuerte

turning ['tɜːnɪŋ] n (side road) bocacalle f; (bend)
curva; **the first** ~ **on the right** la primera
bocacalle a la derecha

turning point n (fig) momento decisivo

turnip ['tɜːnɪp] n nabo

turnout ['tɜːnaʊt] n (attendance) asistencia;
(number of people attending) número de
asistentes; (spectators) público

turnover ['tɜːnəʊvəʳ] n (Comm: amount of
money) facturación f; (of goods) movimiento;
there is a rapid ~ **in staff** hay mucho
movimiento de personal

turnpike ['tɜːnpaɪk] n (US) autopista de peaje

turnstile ['tɜːnstaɪl] n torniquete m

turntable ['tɜːnteɪbl] n plato

turn-up ['tɜːnʌp] n (Brit: on trousers) vuelta

turpentine ['tɜːpəntaɪn] n (also: **turps**)
trementina

turquoise ['tɜːkwɔɪz] n (stone) turquesa ▷ adj
color turquesa

turret ['tʌrɪt] n torreón m

turtle ['tɜːtl] n tortuga (marina)

turtleneck ['tɜːtlnɛk], **turtleneck sweater**
n (jersey m de) cuello cisne

tusk [tʌsk] n colmillo

tussle ['tʌsl] n lucha, pelea
tutor ['tjuːtəʳ] n profesor(a) m(f)
tutorial [tjuːˈtɔːrɪəl] n (Scol) seminario
tuxedo [tʌkˈsiːdəu] n (US) smóking m, esmoquin m
TV [tiːˈviː] n abbr (= television) televisión f
TV dinner n cena precocinada
TV licence n licencia que se paga por el uso del televisor, destinada a financiar la BBC
twang [twæŋ] n (of instrument) tañido; (of voice) timbre m nasal
tweed [twiːd] n tweed m
tweezers ['twiːzəz] npl pinzas fpl (de depilar)
twelfth [twelfθ] num duodécimo
twelve [twelv] num doce; **at ~ o'clock** (midday) a mediodía; (midnight) a medianoche
twentieth ['twentɪɪθ] num vigésimo
twenty ['twentɪ] num veinte
twerp [twəːp] n (inf) idiota m/f
twice [twaɪs] adv dos veces; **~ as much** dos veces más, el doble; **she is ~ your age** ella te dobla la edad; **~ a week** dos veces a la o por semana
twiddle ['twɪdl] vt, vi: **to ~ (with) sth** dar vueltas a algo; **to ~ one's thumbs** (fig) estar de brazos cruzados
twig [twɪg] n ramita ▷ vi (inf) caer en la cuenta
twilight ['twaɪlaɪt] n crepúsculo; (morning) madrugada; **in the ~** en la media luz
twin [twɪn] adj, n gemelo(-a) m(f) ▷ vt hermanar
twin-bedded room ['twɪnˈbɛdɪd-] n = **twin room**
twin beds npl camas fpl gemelas
twine [twaɪn] n bramante m ▷ vi (plant) enroscarse
twinge [twɪndʒ] n (of pain) punzada; (of conscience) remordimiento
twinkle ['twɪŋkl] n centelleo ▷ vi centellear; (eyes) parpadear
twin room n habitación f con dos camas
twin town n ciudad f hermanada or gemela
twirl [twəːl] n giro ▷ vt dar vueltas a ▷ vi piruetear
twist [twɪst] n (action) torsión f; (in road, coil) vuelta; (in wire, flex) doblez f; (in story) giro ▷ vt torcer, retorcer; (roll around) enrollar; (fig) deformar ▷ vi serpentear; **to ~ one's ankle/ wrist** (Med) torcerse el tobillo/la muñeca
twisted ['twɪstɪd] adj (wire, rope) trenzado, enroscado; (ankle, wrist) torcido; (fig: logic, mind) retorcido
twit [twɪt] n (inf) tonto
twitch [twɪtʃ] n sacudida; (nervous) tic m nervioso ▷ vi moverse nerviosamente
two [tuː] num dos; **~ by ~, in ~s** de dos en dos; **to put ~ and ~ together** (fig) atar cabos
two-bit [tuːˈbɪt] adj (esp US: inf, pej) de poca monta, de tres al cuarto
two-door [tuːˈdɔːʳ] adj (Aut) de dos puertas
two-faced [tuːˈfeɪst] adj (pej: person) falso, hipócrita

twofold ['tuːfəuld] adv: **to increase ~** duplicarse ▷ adj (increase) doble; (reply) en dos partes
two-piece [tuːˈpiːs] n (also: **~ suit**) traje m de dos piezas; (also: **~ swimsuit**) dos piezas m inv, bikini m
twosome ['tuːsəm] n (people) pareja
two-way ['tuːweɪ] adj: **~ traffic** circulación f de dos sentidos; **~ radio** radio f emisora y receptora
tycoon [taɪˈkuːn] n: **(business) ~** magnate m/f
type [taɪp] n (category) tipo, género; (model) modelo; (Typ) tipo, letra ▷ vt (letter etc) escribir a máquina; **what ~ do you want?** ¿qué tipo quieres?; **in bold/italic ~** en negrita/cursiva
type-cast ['taɪpkɑːst] adj (actor) encasillado
typeface ['taɪpfeɪs] n tipo de letra
typescript ['taɪpskrɪpt] n texto mecanografiado
typesetter ['taɪpsetəʳ] n cajista m/f
typewriter ['taɪpraɪtəʳ] n máquina de escribir
typewritten ['taɪprɪtn] adj mecanografiado
typhoid ['taɪfɔɪd] n (fiebre f) tifoidea
typhoon [taɪˈfuːn] n tifón m
typhus ['taɪfəs] n tifus m
typical ['tɪpɪkl] adj típico
typically ['tɪpɪklɪ] adv típicamente
typing ['taɪpɪŋ] n mecanografía
typist ['taɪpɪst] n mecanógrafo(-a)
tyrant ['taɪərənt] n tirano(-a)
tyre, tire (US) ['taɪəʳ] n neumático, llanta (LAm)
tyre pressure n presión f de los neumáticos

U, u [ju:] *n (letter)* U, u *f;* **U for Uncle** U de Uruguay

U *n abbr (Brit Cine: = universal)* todos los públicos

U-bend ['ju:bend] *n* recodo

ubiquitous [ju:'bɪkwɪtəs] *adj* omnipresente, ubicuo

udder ['ʌdəʳ] *n* ubre *f*

UEFA [ju:'eɪfə] *n abbr (= Union of European Football Associations)* U.E.F.A. *f*

UFO ['ju:fəu] *n abbr (= unidentified flying object)* OVNI *m*

Uganda [ju:'gændə] *n* Uganda

ugh [ə:h] *excl* ¡uf!

ugly ['ʌglɪ] *adj* feo; *(dangerous)* peligroso

UHF *abbr (= ultra-high frequency)* UHF *f*

UHT *adj abbr (= ultra heat treated);* **~ milk** leche *f* uperizada

UK *n abbr (= United Kingdom)* Reino Unido, R.U.

Ukraine [ju:'kreɪn] *n* Ucrania

ulcer ['ʌlsəʳ] *n* úlcera; **mouth ~** llaga bucal

Ulster ['ʌlstəʳ] *n* Ulster *m*

ulterior [ʌl'tɪərɪəʳ] *adj* ulterior; **~ motive** segundas intenciones *fpl*

ultimate ['ʌltɪmət] *adj* último, final; *(greatest)* mayor ▷ *n:* **the ~ in luxury** el colmo del lujo

ultimately ['ʌltɪmətlɪ] *adv (in the end)* por último, al final; *(fundamentally)* a fin de cuentas

ultimatum *(pl ultimatums or ultimata)* [ʌltɪ'meɪtəm, -tə] *n* ultimátum *m*

ultrasound ['ʌltrəsaund] *n (Med)* ultrasonido

ultraviolet ['ʌltrə'vaɪəlɪt] *adj* ultravioleta

umbilical cord [ʌmbɪ'laɪkl-] *n* cordón *m* umbilical

umbrella [ʌm'brelə] *n* paraguas *m inv;* **under the ~ of** *(fig)* bajo la protección de

umlaut ['umlaut] *n* diéresis *f inv*

umpire ['ʌmpaɪəʳ] *n* árbitro ▷ *vt* arbitrar

umpteen [ʌmp'ti:n] *num* enésimos(-as); **for the ~th time** por enésima vez

UN *n abbr (= United Nations)* ONU *f*

unable [ʌn'eɪbl] *adj:* **to be ~ to do sth** no poder hacer algo; *(not know how to)* ser incapaz de hacer algo, no saber hacer algo

unacceptable [ʌnək'septəbl] *adj (proposal, behaviour, price)* inaceptable; **it's ~ that** no se puede aceptar que

unaccompanied [ʌnə'kʌmpənɪd] *adj* no acompañado; *(singing, song)* sin acompañamiento

unaccountably [ʌnə'kauntəblɪ] *adv* inexplicablemente

unaccustomed [ʌnə'kʌstəmd] *adj:* **to be ~ to** no estar acostumbrado a

unanimous [ju:'nænɪməs] *adj* unánime

unanimously [ju:'nænɪməslɪ] *adv* unánimemente

unarmed [ʌn'ɑ:md] *adj (person)* desarmado; *(combat)* sin armas

unashamed [ʌnə'feɪmd] *adj* desvergonzado

unassuming [ʌnə'sju:mɪŋ] *adj* modesto, sin pretensiones

unattached [ʌnə'tætʃt] *adj (person)* soltero; *(part etc)* suelto

unattended [ʌnə'tendɪd] *adj (car, luggage)* desatendido

unattractive [ʌnə'træktɪv] *adj* poco atractivo

unauthorized [ʌn'ɔ:θəraɪzd] *adj* no autorizado

unavailable [ʌnə'veɪləbl] *adj (article, room, book)* no disponible; *(person)* ocupado

unavoidable [ʌnə'vɔɪdəbl] *adj* inevitable

unaware [ʌnə'wɛəʳ] *adj:* **to be ~ of** ignorar

unawares [ʌnə'wɛəz] *adv:* **to catch sb ~** pillar a algn desprevenido

unbalanced [ʌn'bælənst] *adj* desequilibrado; *(mentally)* trastornado

unbearable [ʌn'bɛərəbl] *adj* insoportable

unbeatable [ʌn'bi:təbl] *adj (gen)* invencible; *(price)* inmejorable

unbeaten [ʌn'bi:tn] *adj (team)* imbatido; *(army)* invicto; *(record)* no batido

unbelievable [ʌnbɪ'li:vəbl] *adj* increíble

unbend [ʌn'bend] *vi (irreg: like bend) (fig: person)* relajarse ▷ *vt (wire)* enderezar

unborn [ʌn'bɔ:n] *adj* que va a nacer

unbreakable [ʌn'breɪkəbl] *adj* irrompible

unbroken [ʌn'brəukən] *adj (seal)* intacto; *(series)* continuo, ininterrumpido; *(record)* no batido; *(spirit)* indómito

unbutton [ʌn'bʌtn] *vt* desabrochar

uncalled-for [ʌn'kɔ:ldfɔ:ʳ] *adj* gratuito, inmerecido

u

uncanny [ʌn'kænɪ] *adj* extraño, extraordinario
unceasing [ʌn'si:sɪŋ] *adj* incesante
unceremonious ['ʌnserɪ'məʊnɪəs] *adj* (*abrupt, rude*) brusco, hosco
uncertain [ʌn'sə:tn] *adj* incierto; (*indecisive*) indeciso; **it's ~ whether** no se sabe si; **in no ~ terms** sin dejar lugar a dudas
uncertainty [ʌn'sə:tntɪ] *n* incertidumbre *f*
unchanged [ʌn'tʃeɪndʒd] *adj* sin cambiar *or* alterar
unchecked [ʌn'tʃɛkt] *adj* desenfrenado
uncivilized [ʌn'sɪvɪlaɪzd] *adj* (*gen*) inculto, poco civilizado; (*fig: behaviour etc*) bárbaro
uncle ['ʌŋkl] *n* tío
unclear [ʌn'klɪə^r] *adj* poco claro; **I'm still ~ about what I'm supposed to do** tengo muy claro lo que tengo que hacer
uncomfortable [ʌn'kʌmfətəbl] *adj* incómodo; (*uneasy*) inquieto
uncommon [ʌn'kɔmən] *adj* poco común, raro
uncompromising [ʌn'kɔmprəmaɪzɪŋ] *adj* intransigente
unconcerned [ʌnkən'sə:nd] *adj* indiferente; **to be ~ about** ser indiferente a, no preocuparse de
unconditional [ʌnkən'dɪʃənl] *adj* incondicional
unconnected [ʌnkə'nɛktɪd] *adj* (*unrelated*): **to be ~ with** no estar relacionado con
unconscious [ʌn'kɔnʃəs] *adj* sin sentido; (*unaware*) inconsciente ▷ *n*: **the ~** el inconsciente; **to knock sb ~** dejar a algn sin sentido
unconsciously [ʌn'kɔnʃəslɪ] *adv* inconscientemente
unconstitutional [ʌnkɔnstɪ'tju:ʃənl] *adj* anticonstitucional
uncontrollable [ʌnkən'trəʊləbl] *adj* (*temper*) indomable; (*laughter*) incontenible
unconventional [ʌnkən'vɛnʃənl] *adj* poco convencional
unconvinced [ʌnkən'vɪnst] *adj*: **to be** *or* **remain ~** seguir sin convencerse
uncouth [ʌn'ku:θ] *adj* grosero, inculto
uncover [ʌn'kʌvə^r] *vt* (*gen*) descubrir; (*take lid off*) destapar
undecided [ʌndɪ'saɪdɪd] *adj* (*person*) indeciso; (*question*) no resuelto, pendiente
undeniable [ʌndɪ'naɪəbl] *adj* innegable
under ['ʌndə^r] *prep* debajo de; (*less than*) menos de; (*according to*) según, de acuerdo con ▷ *adv* debajo, abajo; **~ there** ahí debajo; **~ construction** en construcción; en obras; **~ the circumstances** dadas las circunstancias; **in ~ 2 hours** en menos de dos horas; **~ anaesthetic** bajo los efectos de la anestesia; **~ discussion** en discusión, sobre el tapete
under-age [ʌndər'eɪdʒ] *adj* menor de edad
undercarriage ['ʌndəkærɪdʒ] *n* (*Brit Aviat*) tren *m* de aterrizaje

undercharge [ʌndə'tʃɑ:dʒ] *vt* cobrar de menos
underclass ['ʌndəklɑ:s] *n* clase *f* marginada
undercoat ['ʌndəkəʊt] *n* (*paint*) primera mano
undercover [ʌndə'kʌvə^r] *adj* clandestino
undercurrent ['ʌndəkʌrnt] *n* corriente *f* submarina; (*fig*) tendencia oculta
undercut ['ʌndəkʌt] *vt* (*irreg: like* **cut**) vender más barato que; fijar un precio más barato que
underdog ['ʌndədɔg] *n* desvalido(-a)
underdone [ʌndə'dʌn] *adj* (*Culin*) poco hecho
underestimate [ʌndər'ɛstɪmeɪt] *vt* subestimar
underfed [ʌndə'fɛd] *adj* subalimentado
underfoot [ʌndə'fut] *adv*: **it's wet ~** el suelo está mojado
undergo [ʌndə'gəʊ] *vt* (*irreg: like* **go**) sufrir; (*treatment*) recibir, someterse a; **the car is ~ing repairs** están reparando el coche
undergraduate ['ʌndə'grædjuət] *n* estudiante *m/f* ▷ *cpd*: **~ courses** cursos *mpl* de licenciatura
underground ['ʌndəgraund] *n* (*Brit: railway*) metro; (*Pol*) movimiento clandestino ▷ *adj* subterráneo ▷ *adv* (*work*) en la clandestinidad
undergrowth ['ʌndəgrəʊθ] *n* maleza
underlie [ʌndə'laɪ] *vt* (*irreg: like* **lie**) (*fig*) ser la razón fundamental de; **the underlying cause** la causa fundamental
underline [ʌndə'laɪn] *vt* subrayar
underling ['ʌndəlɪŋ] *n* (*pej*) subalterno(-a)
undermine [ʌndə'maɪn] *vt* socavar, minar
underneath [ʌndə'ni:θ] *adv* debajo ▷ *prep* debajo de, bajo
underpaid [ʌndə'peɪd] *adj* mal pagado
underpants ['ʌndəpænts] *npl* calzoncillos *mpl*
underpass ['ʌndəpɑ:s] *n* (*Brit*) paso subterráneo
underprivileged [ʌndə'prɪvɪlɪdʒd] *adj* desposeído
underrate [ʌndə'reɪt] *vt* infravalorar, subestimar
underscore ['ʌndəskɔ:^r] *vt* subrayar, sostener
undershirt ['ʌndəʃə:t] *n* (*US*) camiseta
undershorts ['ʌndəʃɔ:ts] *npl* (*US*) calzoncillos *mpl*
underside ['ʌndəsaɪd] *n* parte *f* inferior, revés *m*
undersigned ['ʌndəsaɪnd] *adj, n*: **the ~** el/la *etc* abajo firmante
underskirt ['ʌndəskə:t] *n* (*Brit*) enaguas *fpl*
understand [ʌndə'stænd] *vt, vi* (*irreg: like* **stand**) entender, comprender; (*assume*) tener entendido; **to make o.s. understood** hacerse entender; **I ~ you have been absent** tengo entendido que (usted) ha estado ausente

understandable [ʌndə'stændəbl] *adj* comprensible

understanding [ʌndə'stændɪŋ] *adj* comprensivo ▷ *n* comprensión *f*, entendimiento; *(agreement)* acuerdo; **to come to an ~ with sb** llegar a un acuerdo con algn; **on the ~ that** a condición de que + *subjun*

understate [ʌndə'steɪt] *vt* minimizar

understatement [ʌndə'steɪtmənt] *n* subestimación *f*; *(modesty)* modestia (excesiva); **to say it was good is quite an ~** decir que estuvo bien es quedarse corto

understood [ʌndə'stud] *pt, pp of* **understand** ▷ *adj* entendido; *(implied)*: **it is ~ that** se sobreentiende que

understudy ['ʌndəstʌdɪ] *n* suplente *m/f*

undertake [ʌndə'teɪk] *vt (irreg: like* **take**) emprender; **to ~ to do sth** comprometerse a hacer algo

undertaker ['ʌndəteɪkər] *n* director(a) *m(f)* de pompas fúnebres

undertaking ['ʌndəteɪkɪŋ] *n* empresa; *(promise)* promesa

undertone ['ʌndətəun] *n (of criticism)* connotación *f*; *(low voice)*: **in an ~** en voz baja

underwater [ʌndə'wɔːtər] *adv* bajo el agua ▷ *adj* submarino

underway [ʌndə'weɪ] *adj*: **to be ~** *(meeting)* estar en marcha; *(investigation)* estar llevándose a cabo

underwear ['ʌndəweər] *n* ropa interior *or* íntima *(LAm)*

underwent [ʌndə'went] *vb see* **undergo**

underworld ['ʌndəwəːld] *n (of crime)* hampa, inframundo

underwrite [ʌndə'raɪt] *vt (irreg: like* **write**) *(Comm)* suscribir; *(Insurance)* asegurar *(contra riesgos)*

underwriter ['ʌndəraɪtər] *n (Insurance)* asegurador(a) *m(f)*

undesirable [ʌndɪ'zaɪərəbl] *adj* indeseable

undies ['ʌndɪz] *npl (inf)* paños *mpl* menores

undiluted [ʌndaɪ'luːtɪd] *adj (concentrate)* concentrado

undiplomatic [ʌndɪplə'mætɪk] *adj* poco diplomático

undisciplined [ʌn'dɪsɪplɪnd] *adj* indisciplinado

undisputed [ʌndɪ'spjuːtɪd] *adj* incontestable

undivided [ʌndɪ'vaɪdɪd] *adj*: **I want your ~ attention** quiero su completa atención

undo [ʌn'duː] *vt (irreg: like* **do**) *(laces)* desatar; *(button etc)* desabrochar; *(spoil)* deshacer

undoing [ʌn'duːɪŋ] *n* ruina, perdición *f*

undone [ʌn'dʌn] *pp of* **undo** ▷ *adj*: **to come ~** *(clothes)* desabrocharse; *(parcel)* desatarse

undoubted [ʌn'dautɪd] *adj* indudable

undoubtedly [ʌn'dautɪdlɪ] *adv* indudablemente, sin duda

undress [ʌn'drɛs] *vi* desnudarse, desvestirse *(esp LAm)*

undue [ʌn'djuː] *adj* indebido, excesivo

undulating ['ʌndjuleɪtɪŋ] *adj* ondulante

unduly [ʌn'djuːlɪ] *adv* excesivamente, demasiado

undying [ʌn'daɪɪŋ] *adj* eterno

unearth [ʌn'əːθ] *vt* desenterrar

unearthly [ʌn'əːθlɪ] *adj*: **~ hour** *(inf)* hora intempestiva

unease [ʌn'iːz] *n* malestar *m*

uneasy [ʌn'iːzɪ] *adj* intranquilo; *(worried)* preocupado; **to feel ~ about doing sth** sentirse incómodo con la idea de hacer algo

uneducated [ʌn'ɛdjukeɪtɪd] *adj* ignorante, inculto

unemployed [ʌnɪm'plɔɪd] *adj* parado, sin trabajo ▷ *n*: **the ~** los parados

unemployment [ʌnɪm'plɔɪmənt] *n* paro, desempleo, cesantía *(LAm)*

unemployment benefit *n (Brit)* subsidio de desempleo *or* paro

unending [ʌn'ɛndɪŋ] *adj* interminable

unenviable [ʌn'ɛnvɪəbl] *adj* poco envidiable

unequal [ʌn'iːkwəl] *adj (length, objects etc)* desigual; *(amounts)* distinto; *(division of labour)* poco justo

unerring [ʌn'əːrɪŋ] *adj* infalible

uneven [ʌn'iːvn] *adj* desigual; *(road etc)* con baches

uneventful [ʌnɪ'vɛntful] *adj* sin incidentes

unexpected [ʌnɪk'spɛktɪd] *adj* inesperado

unexpectedly [ʌnɪk'spɛktɪdlɪ] *adv* inesperadamente

unexplained [ʌnɪks'pleɪnd] *adj* inexplicado

unfailing [ʌn'feɪlɪŋ] *adj (support)* indefectible; *(energy)* inagotable

unfair [ʌn'fɛər] *adj*: **~ (to sb)** injusto (con algn); **it's ~ that ...** es injusto que ..., no es justo que ...

unfaithful [ʌn'feɪθful] *adj* infiel

unfamiliar [ʌnfə'mɪlɪər] *adj* extraño, desconocido; **to be ~ with sth** desconocer *or* ignorar algo

unfashionable [ʌn'fæʃnəbl] *adj (clothes)* pasado *or* fuera de moda; *(district)* poco elegante

unfasten [ʌn'fɑːsn] *vt* desatar

unfavourable, unfavorable *(US)* [ʌn'feɪvərəbl] *adj* desfavorable

unfeeling [ʌn'fiːlɪŋ] *adj* insensible

unfinished [ʌn'fɪnɪʃt] *adj* inacabado, sin terminar

unfit [ʌn'fɪt] *adj* en baja forma; *(incompetent)* incapaz; **~ for work** no apto para trabajar

unfold [ʌn'fəuld] *vt* desdoblar; *(fig)* revelar ▷ *vi* abrirse; revelarse

unforeseen ['ʌnfɔː'siːn] *adj* imprevisto

unforgettable [ʌnfə'gɛtəbl] *adj* inolvidable

unforgivable [ʌnfə'gɪvəbl] *adj* imperdonable

unfortunate [ʌn'fɔːtʃnət] *adj* desgraciado; *(event, remark)* inoportuno

unfortunately [ʌn'fɔːtʃnətlɪ] *adv* desgraciadamente, por desgracia

u

unfounded [ʌnˈfaʊndɪd] *adj* infundado
unfriendly [ʌnˈfrɛndlɪ] *adj* antipático; *(behaviour, remark)* hostil, poco amigable
unfurl [ʌnˈfəːl] *vt* desplegar
unfurnished [ʌnˈfəːnɪʃt] *adj* sin amueblar
ungainly [ʌnˈgeɪnlɪ] *adj (walk)* desgarbado
ungodly [ʌnˈgɒdlɪ] *adj*: **at an ~ hour** a una hora intempestiva
ungrateful [ʌnˈgreɪtful] *adj* ingrato
unhappiness [ʌnˈhæpɪnɪs] *n* tristeza
unhappy [ʌnˈhæpɪ] *adj (sad)* triste; *(unfortunate)* desgraciado; *(childhood)* infeliz; **~ with** *(arrangements etc)* poco contento con, descontento de
unharmed [ʌnˈhɑːmd] *adj (person)* ileso
UNHCR *n abbr* (= *United Nations High Commission for Refugees*) ACNUR *m*
unhealthy [ʌnˈhɛlθɪ] *adj (gen)* malsano, insalubre; *(person)* enfermizo; *(interest)* morboso
unheard-of [ʌnˈhəːdɒv] *adj* inaudito, sin precedente
unhelpful [ʌnˈhɛlpful] *adj (person)* poco servicial; *(advice)* inútil
unholy [ʌnˈhəʊlɪ] *adj*: **an ~ alliance** una alianza nefasta; **he returned at an ~ hour** volvió a una hora intempestiva
unhurt [ʌnˈhəːt] *adj* ileso
unhygienic [ʌnhaɪˈdʒiːnɪk] *adj* antihigiénico
UNICEF [ˈjuːnɪsɛf] *n abbr* (= *United Nations International Children's Emergency Fund*) UNICEF *f*
unidentified [ʌnaɪˈdɛntɪfaɪd] *adj* no identificado; **~ flying object (UFO)** objeto volante no identificado
uniform [ˈjuːnɪfɔːm] *n* uniforme *m* ▷ *adj* uniforme
uniformity [juːnɪˈfɔːmɪtɪ] *n* uniformidad *f*
unify [ˈjuːnɪfaɪ] *vt* unificar, unir
unimportant [ʌnɪmˈpɔːtənt] *adj* sin importancia
uninhabited [ʌnɪnˈhæbɪtɪd] *adj* desierto; *(country)* despoblado; *(house)* deshabitado, desocupado
uninspiring [ʌnɪnˈspaɪərɪŋ] *adj* anodino
unintentional [ʌnɪnˈtɛnʃənəl] *adj* involuntario
union [ˈjuːnjən] *n* unión *f*; *(also:* **trade ~**) sindicato ▷ *cpd* sindical; **the U~** *(US)* la Unión
Union Jack *n* bandera del Reino Unido
unique [juːˈniːk] *adj* único
unisex [ˈjuːnɪsɛks] *adj* unisex
unison [ˈjuːnɪsn] *n*: **in ~** en armonía
unit [ˈjuːnɪt] *n* unidad *f*; *(team, squad)* grupo; **kitchen ~** módulo de cocina; **production ~** taller *m* de fabricación; **sink ~** fregadero
unite [juːˈnaɪt] *vt* unir ▷ *vi* unirse
united [juːˈnaɪtɪd] *adj* unido
United Kingdom *n* Reino Unido
United Nations, United Nations Organization *n* Naciones Unidas *fpl*
United States, United States of America *n* Estados Unidos *mpl* (de América)
unit trust *n* (Brit) bono fiduciario

unity [ˈjuːnɪtɪ] *n* unidad *f*
Univ. *abbr* = **university**
universal [juːnɪˈvəːsl] *adj* universal
universe [ˈjuːnɪvəːs] *n* universo
university [juːnɪˈvəːsɪtɪ] *n* universidad *f* ▷ *cpd (student, professor, education, degree)* universitario; *(year)* académico; **to be at/go to ~** estudiar en/ir a la universidad
unjust [ʌnˈdʒʌst] *adj* injusto
unkempt [ʌnˈkɛmpt] *adj* descuidado; *(hair)* despeinado
unkind [ʌnˈkaɪnd] *adj* poco amable; *(comment etc)* cruel
unknown [ʌnˈnəʊn] *adj* desconocido ▷ *adv*: **~ to me** sin saberlo yo; **~ quantity** incógnita
unlawful [ʌnˈlɔːful] *adj* ilegal, ilícito
unleaded [ʌnˈlɛdɪd] *n (also:* **~ petrol**) gasolina sin plomo
unleash [ʌnˈliːʃ] *vt* desatar
unless [ʌnˈlɛs] *conj* a menos que; **~ he comes** a menos que venga; **~ otherwise stated** salvo indicación contraria; **~ I am mistaken** si no mi equivoco
unlike [ʌnˈlaɪk] *adj* distinto ▷ *prep* a diferencia de
unlikely [ʌnˈlaɪklɪ] *adj* improbable
unlimited [ʌnˈlɪmɪtɪd] *adj* ilimitado; **~ liability** responsabilidad *f* ilimitada
unlisted [ʌnˈlɪstɪd] *adj (US Tel)* que no figura en la guía; **~ company** empresa sin cotización en bolsa
unload [ʌnˈləʊd] *vt* descargar
unlock [ʌnˈlɒk] *vt* abrir (con llave)
unlucky [ʌnˈlʌkɪ] *adj* desgraciado; *(object, number)* que da mala suerte; **to be ~** *(person)* tener mala suerte
unmarked [ʌnˈmɑːkt] *adj (unstained)* sin mancha; **~ police car** vehículo policial camuflado
unmarried [ʌnˈmærɪd] *adj* soltero
unmistakable [ʌnmɪsˈteɪkəbl] *adj* inconfundible
unmitigated [ʌnˈmɪtɪgeɪtɪd] *adj* rematado, absoluto
unnamed [ʌnˈneɪmd] *adj (nameless)* sin nombre; *(anonymous)* anónimo
unnatural [ʌnˈnætʃrəl] *adj (gen)* antinatural; *(manner)* afectado; *(habit)* perverso
unnecessary [ʌnˈnɛsəsərɪ] *adj* innecesario, inútil
unnerve [ʌnˈnəːv] *vt (accident)* poner nervioso; *(hostile attitude)* acobardar; *(long wait, interview)* intimidar
unnoticed [ʌnˈnəʊtɪst] *adj*: **to go** *or* **pass ~** pasar desapercibido
UNO [ˈjuːnəʊ] *n abbr* (= *United Nations Organization*) ONU *f*
unobtainable [ʌnəbˈteɪnəbl] *adj* inasequible; *(Tel)* inexistente
unobtrusive [ʌnəbˈtruːsɪv] *adj* discreto
unofficial [ʌnəˈfɪʃl] *adj* no oficial; **~ strike** huelga no oficial

unorthodox [ʌnˈɔːθədɒks] *adj* poco ortodoxo

unpack [ʌnˈpæk] *vi* deshacer las maletas, desempacar (*LAm*) ▷ *vt* deshacer

unpaid [ʌnˈpeɪd] *adj* (*bill, debt*) sin pagar, impagado; (*Comm*) pendiente; (*holiday*) sin sueldo; (*work*) sin pago, voluntario

unpalatable [ʌnˈpælətəbl] *adj* (*truth*) desagradable

unparalleled [ʌnˈpærəleld] *adj* (*unequalled*) sin par; (*unique*) sin precedentes

unpleasant [ʌnˈpleznt] *adj* (*disagreeable*) desagradable; (*person, manner*) antipático

unplug [ʌnˈplʌg] *vt* desenchufar, desconectar

unpopular [ʌnˈpɒpjʊləʳ] *adj* poco popular; **to be ~ with sb** (*person, law*) no ser popular con algn; **to make o.s. ~ (with)** hacerse impopular (con)

unprecedented [ʌnˈpresɪdəntɪd] *adj* sin precedentes

unpredictable [ʌnprɪˈdɪktəbl] *adj* imprevisible

unprofessional [ʌnprəˈfeʃənl] *adj* poco profesional; **~ conduct** negligencia

UNPROFOR *n abbr* (= *United Nations Protection Force*) FORPRONU f, Unprofor f

unprotected [ˈʌnprəˈtektɪd] *adj* (*sex*) sin protección

unpunished [ʌnˈpʌnɪʃt] *adj*: **to go ~** quedar sin castigo, salir impune

unqualified [ʌnˈkwɒlɪfaɪd] *adj* sin título, no cualificado; (*success*) total, incondicional

unquestionably [ʌnˈkwestʃənəblɪ] *adv* indiscutiblemente

unravel [ʌnˈrævl] *vt* desenmarañar

unreal [ʌnˈrɪəl] *adj* irreal

unrealistic [ʌnrɪəˈlɪstɪk] *adj* poco realista

unreasonable [ʌnˈriːznəbl] *adj* irrazonable; **to make ~ demands on sb** hacer demandas excesivas a algn

unrecognizable [ʌnˈrekəgnaɪzəbl] *adj* irreconocible

unrelated [ʌnrɪˈleɪtɪd] *adj* sin relación; (*family*) no emparentado

unrelenting [ʌnrɪˈlentɪŋ] *adj* implacable

unreliable [ʌnrɪˈlaɪəbl] *adj* (*person*) informal; (*machine*) poco fiable

unremitting [ʌnrɪˈmɪtɪŋ] *adj* incesante

unrepeatable [ʌnrɪˈpiːtəbl] *adj* irrepetible

unrepentant [ʌnrɪˈpentənt] *adj* (*smoker, sinner*) impenitente; **to be ~ about sth** no arrepentirse de algo

unreservedly [ʌnrɪˈzɜːvɪdlɪ] *adv* sin reserva

unrest [ʌnˈrest] *n* inquietud f, malestar m; (*Pol*) disturbios mpl

unripe [ʌnˈraɪp] *adj* verde, inmaduro

unrivalled, unrivaled (*US*) [ʌnˈraɪvəld] *adj* incomparable, sin par

unroll [ʌnˈrəʊl] *vt* desenrollar

unruly [ʌnˈruːlɪ] *adj* indisciplinado

unsafe [ʌnˈseɪf] *adj* (*journey*) peligroso; (*car etc*) inseguro; (*method*) arriesgado; **~ to drink/ eat** no apto para el consumo humano

unsaid [ʌnˈsed] *adj*: **to leave sth ~** dejar algo sin decir

unsatisfactory [ˈʌnsætɪsˈfæktərɪ] *adj* poco satisfactorio

unsavoury, unsavory (*US*) [ʌnˈseɪvərɪ] *adj* (*fig*) repugnante

unscathed [ʌnˈskeɪðd] *adj* ileso

unscrew [ʌnˈskruː] *vt* destornillar

unscrupulous [ʌnˈskruːpjʊləs] *adj* sin escrúpulos

unseat [ʌnˈsiːt] *vt* (*rider*) hacer caerse de la silla a; (*fig: official*) hacer perder su escaño a

unseeded [ʌnˈsiːdɪd] *adj* (*Sport*) no preseleccionado

unseen [ʌnˈsiːn] *adj* (*person, danger*) oculto

unselfish [ʌnˈselfɪʃ] *adj* generoso, poco egoísta; (*act*) desinteresado

unsettled [ʌnˈsetld] *adj* inquieto; (*situation*) inestable; (*weather*) variable

unsettling [ʌnˈsetlɪŋ] *adj* perturbador(a), inquietante

unshaven [ʌnˈʃeɪvn] *adj* sin afeitar

unsightly [ʌnˈsaɪtlɪ] *adj* desagradable

unskilled [ʌnˈskɪld] *adj*: **~ workers** mano f de obra no cualificada

unspeakable [ʌnˈspiːkəbl] *adj* indecible; (*awful*) incalificable

unspoiled [ˈʌnˈspɔɪld], **unspoilt** [ˈʌnˈspɔɪlt] *adj* (*place*) que no ha perdido su belleza natural

unstable [ʌnˈsteɪbl] *adj* inestable

unsteady [ʌnˈstedɪ] *adj* inestable

unstuck [ʌnˈstʌk] *adj*: **to come ~** despegarse; (*fig*) fracasar

unsubscribe [ʌnsəbˈskraɪb] *vt* (*Internet*) borrarse

unsuccessful [ʌnsəkˈsesful] *adj* (*attempt*) infructuoso; (*writer, proposal*) sin éxito; **to be ~** (*in attempting sth*) no tener éxito, fracasar

unsuitable [ʌnˈsuːtəbl] *adj* inconveniente, inapropiado; (*time*) inoportuno

unsung [ˈʌnsʌn] *adj*: **an ~ hero** un héroe desconocido

unsure [ʌnˈʃʊəʳ] *adj* inseguro, poco seguro; **to be ~ of o.s.** estar poco seguro de sí mismo

unsuspecting [ʌnsəˈspektɪŋ] *adj* confiado

unsympathetic [ʌnsɪmpəˈθetɪk] *adj* (*attitude*) poco comprensivo; (*person*) sin compasión; **~ (to)** indiferente (a)

untapped [ʌnˈtæpt] *adj* (*resources*) sin explotar

unthinkable [ʌnˈθɪŋkəbl] *adj* inconcebible, impensable

untidy [ʌnˈtaɪdɪ] *adj* (*room*) desordenado, en desorden; (*appearance*) desaliñado

untie [ʌnˈtaɪ] *vt* desatar

until [ənˈtɪl] *prep* hasta ▷ *conj* hasta que; **~ he comes** hasta que venga; **~ now** hasta ahora; **~ then** hasta entonces; **from morning ~ night** de la mañana a la noche

untimely [ʌnˈtaɪmlɪ] *adj* inoportuno; (*death*) prematuro

untold [ʌnˈtəʊld] adj (story) nunca contado; (suffering) indecible; (wealth) incalculable

untoward [ʌntəˈwɔːd] adj (behaviour) impropio; (event) adverso

untrue [ʌnˈtruː] adj (statement) falso

unused [ʌnˈjuːzd] adj sin usar, nuevo; **to be ~ to (doing) sth** no estar acostumbrado a (hacer) algo

unusual [ʌnˈjuːʒʊəl] adj insólito, poco común

unusually [ʌnˈjuːʒʊəlɪ] adv: **he arrived ~ early** llegó más temprano que de costumbre

unveil [ʌnˈveɪl] vt (statue) descubrir

unwanted [ʌnˈwɒntɪd] adj (person, effect) no deseado

unwelcome [ʌnˈwɛlkəm] adj (at a bad time) inoportuno, molesto; **to feel ~** sentirse incómodo

unwell [ʌnˈwɛl] adj: **to feel ~** estar indispuesto, sentirse mal

unwieldy [ʌnˈwiːldɪ] adj difícil de manejar

unwilling [ʌnˈwɪlɪŋ] adj: **to be ~ to do sth** estar poco dispuesto a hacer algo

unwillingly [ʌnˈwɪlɪŋlɪ] adv de mala gana

unwind [ʌnˈwaɪnd] (irreg: like **wind**) vt desenvolver ▷ vi (relax) relajarse

unwise [ʌnˈwaɪz] adj imprudente

unwitting [ʌnˈwɪtɪŋ] adj inconsciente

unwittingly [ʌnˈwɪtɪŋlɪ] adv inconscientemente, sin darse cuenta

unworkable [ʌnˈwəːkəbl] adj (plan) impracticable

unworthy [ʌnˈwəːðɪ] adj indigno; **to be ~ of sth/to do sth** ser indigno de algo/de hacer algo

unwrap [ʌnˈræp] vt desenvolver

unwritten [ʌnˈrɪtn] adj (agreement) tácito; (rules, law) no escrito

unzip [ʌnˈzɪp] vt abrir la cremallera de; (Comput) descomprimir

⊘ KEYWORD

up [ʌp] prep: **to go/be up sth** subir/estar subido en algo; **he went up the stairs/the hill** subió las escaleras/la colina; **we walked/climbed up the hill** subimos la colina; **they live further up the street** viven más arriba en la calle; **go up that road and turn left** sigue por esa calle y gira a la izquierda

▷ adv 1 (upwards, higher) más arriba; **up in the mountains** en lo alto (de la montaña); **put it a bit higher up** ponlo un poco más arriba or alto; **to stop halfway up** pararse a la mitad del camino or de la subida; **up there** ahí or allí arriba; **up above** en lo alto, por encima, arriba; **"this side up"** "este lado hacia arriba"; **to live/go up North** vivir en el norte/ir al norte

2: **to be up** (out of bed) estar levantado; (prices, level) haber subido; (building) estar construido; (tent) estar montado; (curtains,

paper etc) estar puesto; **time's up** se acabó el tiempo; **when the year was up** al terminarse el año; **he's well up in** or **on politics** (Brit: knowledgeable) está muy al día en política; **what's up?** (wrong) ¿qué pasa?; **what's up with him?** ¿qué le pasa?; **prices are up on last year** los precios han subido desde el año pasado

3: **up to** (as far as) hasta; **up to now** hasta ahora or la fecha

4: **up to** (depending on): **it's up to you** depende de ti; **he's not up to it** (job, task etc) no es capaz de hacerlo; **I don't feel up to it** no me encuentro con ánimos para ello; **his work is not up to the required standard** su trabajo no da la talla; (inf: be doing): **what is he up to?** ¿qué estará tramando?

▷ vi (inf): **she upped and left** se levantó y se marchó

▷ vt (inf: price) subir

▷ n: **ups and downs** altibajos mpl

up-and-coming [ʌpəndˈkʌmɪŋ] adj prometedor(a)

upbringing [ˈʌpbrɪŋɪŋ] n educación f

upcoming [ˈʌpkʌmɪŋ] adj próximo

update [ʌpˈdeɪt] vt poner al día

upfront [ʌpˈfrʌnt] adj claro, directo ▷ adv a las claras; (pay) por adelantado; **to be ~ about sth** admitir algo claramente

upgrade [ʌpˈɡreɪd] vt ascender; (Comput) modernizar

upheaval [ʌpˈhiːvl] n trastornos mpl; (Pol) agitación f

uphill [ʌpˈhɪl] adj cuesta arriba; (fig: task) penoso, difícil ▷ adv: **to go ~** ir cuesta arriba

uphold [ʌpˈhəʊld] vt (irreg: like **hold**) sostener

upholstery [ʌpˈhəʊlstərɪ] n tapicería

upkeep [ˈʌpkiːp] n mantenimiento

upmarket [ʌpˈmaːkɪt] adj (product) de categoría

upon [əˈpɒn] prep sobre

upper [ˈʌpəʳ] adj superior, de arriba ▷ n (of shoe: also: **~s**) pala

upper-class [ʌpəˈklaːs] adj (district, people, accent) de clase alta; (attitude) altivo

uppercut [ˈʌpəkʌt] n uppercut m, gancho a la cara

uppermost [ˈʌpəməʊst] adj el más alto; **what was ~ in my mind** lo que me preocupaba más

upright [ˈʌpraɪt] adj vertical; (fig) honrado

uprising [ˈʌpraɪzɪŋ] n sublevación f

uproar [ˈʌprɔːʳ] n tumulto, escándalo

uproarious [ʌpˈrɔːrɪəs] adj escandaloso; (hilarious) graciosísimo

uproot [ʌpˈruːt] vt desarraigar

upset n [ˈʌpsɛt] (to plan etc) revés m, contratiempo; (Med) trastorno ▷ vt [ʌpˈsɛt] (irreg: like **set**) (glass etc) volcar; (spill) derramar; (plan) alterar; (person) molestar, perturbar

▷ adj [ʌpˈsɛt] preocupado, perturbado;

(*stomach*) revuelto; **to have a stomach ~** (*Brit*) tener el estómago revuelto; **to get ~** molestarse, llevarse un disgusto

upsetting [ʌp'setɪŋ] *adj* (*worrying*) inquietante; (*offending*) ofensivo; (*annoying*) molesto

upshot ['ʌpʃɔt] *n* resultado

upside-down ['ʌpsaɪd'daun] *adv* al revés; **to turn a place ~** (*fig*) revolverlo todo

upstage ['ʌp'steɪdʒ] *vt* robar protagonismo a

upstairs [ʌp'steəz] *adv* arriba ▷ *adj* (*room*) de arriba ▷ *n* el piso superior

upstart ['ʌpstɑːt] *n* advenedizo

upstream [ʌp'striːm] *adv* río arriba

uptake ['ʌpteɪk] *n*: **he is quick/slow on the ~** es muy listo/torpe

uptight [ʌp'taɪt] *adj* tenso, nervioso

up-to-date ['ʌptə'deɪt] *adj* actual, moderno; **to bring sb ~ (on sth)** poner a algn al corriente/tanto (de algo)

uptown ['ʌptaun] *adv* (*US*) hacia las afueras ▷ *adj* exterior, de las afueras

upturn ['ʌptɜːn] *n* (*in luck*) mejora; (*Comm: in market*) resurgimiento económico; (: *in value of currency*) aumento

upward, upwards ['ʌpwəd(z)] *adv* hacia arriba; (*more than*): **~(s) of** más de

upwardly-mobile ['ʌpwədlɪ'məubaɪl] *adj*: **to be ~** mejorar socialmente

upwards ['ʌpwədz] *adv* = **upward**

uranium [juə'reɪnɪəm] *n* uranio

Uranus [juə'reɪnəs] *n* (*Astro*) Urano

urban ['ɜːbən] *adj* urbano

urbane [ə:'beɪn] *adj* cortés, urbano

urchin ['ɜːtʃɪn] *n* pilluelo, golfillo

Urdu ['uədu:] *n* urdu *m*

urge [ɜːdʒ] *n* (*force*) impulso; (*desire*) deseo ▷ *vt*: **to ~ sb to do sth** animar a algn a hacer algo; **urge on** *vt* animar

urgency ['ɜːdʒənsɪ] *n* urgencia

urgent ['ɜːdʒənt] *adj* (*earnest, persistent: plea*) insistente; (: *tone*) urgente

urinal ['juərɪnl] *n* (*building*) urinario; (*vessel*) orinal *m*

urinate ['juərɪneɪt] *vi* orinar

urine ['juərɪn] *n* orina

urn [ɜːn] *n* urna; (*also*: **tea ~**) tetera (grande)

Uruguay ['juerəgwaɪ] *n* el Uruguay

Uruguayan [juərə'gwaɪən] *adj, n* uruguayo(-a) *m(f)*

US *n abbr* (= *United States*) EE.UU. (= *Estados Unidos*)

us [ʌs] *pron* nos; (*after prep*) nosotros(-as); (*inf: me*): **give us a kiss** dame un beso; *see also* **me**

USA *n abbr* = **United States of America**; (*Mil*) = **United States Army**

usable ['ju:zəbl] *adj* utilizable

usage ['ju:zɪdʒ] *n* (*Ling*) uso; (*utilization*) utilización *f*

use *n* [ju:s] uso, empleo; (*usefulness*) utilidad *f* ▷ *vt* [ju:z] usar, emplear; **in ~** en uso; **out of ~** en desuso; **to be of ~** servir; **ready for ~** listo

(para usar); **to make ~ of sth** aprovecharse *or* servirse de algo; **it's no ~** (*pointless*) es inútil; (*not useful*) no sirve; **what's this ~d for?** ¿para qué sirve esto?; **to be ~d to** estar acostumbrado a (*Sp*), acostumbrar; **to get ~d to** acostumbrarse a; **she ~d to do it** (*ella*) solía *or* acostumbraba hacerlo; **use up** *vt* (*food*) consumir; (*money*) gastar

used [ju:zd] *adj* (*car*) usado

useful ['ju:sful] *adj* útil; **to come in ~** ser útil

usefulness ['ju:sfəlnɪs] *n* utilidad *f*

useless ['ju:slɪs] *adj* inútil; (*unusable: object*) inservible

user ['ju:zə^r] *n* usuario(-a); (*of petrol, gas etc*) consumidor(a) *m(f)*

user-friendly ['ju:zə'frendlɪ] *adj* (*Comput*) fácil de utilizar

username ['ju:zəneɪm] *n* (*Comput*) nombre *m* de usuario

usher ['ʌʃə^r] *n* (*at wedding*) ujier *m*; (*in cinema etc*) acomodador *m* ▷ *vt*: **to ~ sb in** (*into room*) hacer pasar a algn; **to ~ed in a new era** (*fig*) inició una nueva era

usherette [ʌʃə'ret] *n* (*in cinema*) acomodadora

USSR *n abbr* (*History*: = *Union of Soviet Socialist Republics*): **the (former) ~** la (antigua) U.R.S.S. (= *Unión de Repúblicas Socialistas Soviéticas*)

usu. *abbr* = **usually**

usual ['ju:ʒuəl] *adj* normal, corriente; **as ~** como de costumbre, como siempre

usually ['ju:ʒuəlɪ] *adv* normalmente

utensil [ju:'tensl] *n* utensilio; **kitchen ~s** batería de cocina

uterus ['ju:tərəs] *n* útero

utility [ju:'tɪlɪtɪ] *n* utilidad *f*; (*public utility*) (empresa de) servicio público

utility room *n* trascocina

utilize ['ju:tɪlaɪz] *vt* utilizar

utmost ['ʌtməust] *adj* mayor ▷ *n*: **to do one's ~** hacer todo lo posible; **it is of the ~ importance that …** es de la mayor importancia que …

utter ['ʌtə^r] *adj* total, completo ▷ *vt* pronunciar, proferir

utterance ['ʌtərns] *n* palabras *fpl*, declaración *f*

utterly ['ʌtəlɪ] *adv* completamente, totalmente

U-turn ['ju:'tɜːn] *n* cambio de sentido; (*fig*) giro de 180 grados

Uzbekistan [ʌzbekɪ'stɑːn] *n* Uzbekistán *m*

u

V

V, v [viː] n (letter) V, v f; **V for Victor** V de Valencia

v. abbr (= verse) vers.°; (= vide: see) V, vid., vide; (= versus) vs.; = **volt**

vac [væk] n abbr (Brit inf) = **vacation**

vacancy ['veɪkənsɪ] n (Brit: job) vacante f; (room) cuarto libro; **have you any vacancies?** ¿tiene or hay alguna habitación or algún cuarto libre?; **"no vacancies"** "completo"

vacant ['veɪkənt] adj desocupado, libre; (expression) distraído

vacate [vəˈkeɪt] vt (house) desocupar; (job) dejar (vacante)

vacation [vəˈkeɪʃən] n vacaciones fpl; **on ~** de vacaciones; **to take a ~** (esp US) tomarse unas vacaciones

vacationer [vəˈkeɪʃənəʳ], **vacationist** [vəˈkeɪʃənɪst] n (US) turista m/f

vaccinate ['væksɪneɪt] vt vacunar

vaccination [væksɪˈneɪʃən] n vacunación f

vaccine ['væksiːn] n vacuna

vacuum ['vækjum] n vacío

vacuum cleaner n aspiradora

vacuum-packed ['vækjumˈpækt] adj envasado al vacío

vagina [vəˈdʒaɪnə] n vagina

vagrant ['veɪgrənt] n vagabundo(-a)

vague [veɪg] adj vago; (blurred: memory) borroso; (uncertain) incierto; (ambiguous) impreciso; (person: absent-minded) distraído; (: evasive): **to be ~** no decir las cosas

claramente; **I haven't the ~st idea** no tengo la más remota idea

vaguely ['veɪglɪ] adv vagamente

vain [veɪn] adj (conceited) presumido; (useless) vano, inútil; **in ~** en vano

vainly ['veɪnlɪ] adv (to no effect) en vano; (conceitedly) vanidosamente

valentine ['væləntaɪn] n (also: ~ card) tarjeta del Día de los Enamorados

Valentine's Day n día de los enamorados (el 14 de febrero, día de San Valentín)

valiant ['væljənt] adj valiente

valid ['vælɪd] adj válido; (ticket) valedero; (law) vigente

valley ['vælɪ] n valle m

valour, valor (US) ['væləʳ] n valor m, valentía

valuable ['væljuəbl] adj (jewel) de valor; (time) valioso; **valuables** npl objetos mpl de valor

valuation [væljuˈeɪʃən] n tasación f, valuación f

value ['væljuː] n valor m; (importance) importancia ⊳ vt (fix price of) tasar, valorar; (esteem) apreciar; **values** npl (moral) valores mpl morales; **to lose (in) ~** (currency) bajar; (property) desvalorizarse; **to gain (in) ~** (currency) subir; (property) revalorizarse; **you get good ~ (for money) in that shop** la relación calidad-precio es muy buena en esa tienda; **to be of great ~ to sb** ser de gran valor para algn; **it is ~d at £8** está valorado en ocho libras

valued ['væljuːd] adj (appreciated) apreciado

valve [vælv] n (Anat, Tech) válvula

vampire ['væmpaɪəʳ] n vampiro

van [væn] n (Aut) furgoneta, camioneta (LAm); (Brit Rail) furgón m (de equipajes)

vandal ['vændl] n vándalo(-a)

vandalism ['vændəlɪzəm] n vandalismo

vandalize ['vændəlaɪz] vt dañar, destruir, destrozar

vanguard ['vængɑːd] n vanguardia

vanilla [vəˈnɪlə] n vainilla

vanish ['vænɪʃ] vi desaparecer, esfumarse

vanity ['vænɪtɪ] n vanidad f

vantage point ['vɑːntɪdʒ-] n posición f ventajosa

vapour, vapor (US) ['veɪpəʳ] n vapor m; (on breath, window) vaho

variable ['vɛərɪəbl] adj variable ⊳ n variable f

variance ['vɛərɪəns] n: **to be at ~ (with)** estar en desacuerdo (con), no cuadrar (con)

variant ['vɛərɪənt] n variante f

variation [vɛərɪˈeɪʃən] n variación f

varicose ['værɪkəus] adj: **~ veins** varices fpl

varied ['vɛərɪd] adj variado

variety [vəˈraɪətɪ] n variedad f, diversidad f; (quantity) surtido; **for a ~ of reasons** por varias or diversas razones

variety show n espectáculo de variedades

various ['vɛərɪəs] adj varios(-as), diversos(-as); **at ~ times** (different) en distintos momentos; (several) varias veces

varnish ['vɑːnɪʃ] n (gen) barniz m; (also: **nail ~**) esmalte m ▷ vt (gen) barnizar; (nails) pintar (con esmalte)

vary ['vɛərɪ] vt variar; (change) cambiar ▷ vi variar; (disagree) discrepar ▷ vi; **to ~ with** or **according to** variar según or de acuerdo con

vase [vɑːz] n florero, jarrón m

vasectomy [væ'sɛktəmɪ] n vasectomía

Vaseline® ['væsɪliːn] n vaselina®

vast [vɑːst] adj enorme; (success) abrumador(a), arrollador(a)

vastly ['vɑːstlɪ] adv enormemente

VAT [væt] n abbr (Brit: = value added tax) IVA m

vat [væt] n tina, tinaja

Vatican ['vætɪkən] n: **the ~** el Vaticano

vault [vɔːlt] n (of roof) bóveda; (tomb) panteón m; (in bank) cámara acorazada ▷ vt (also: **~ over**) saltar (por encima de)

vaunted ['vɔːntɪd] adj: **much ~** cacareado

VCR n abbr = **video cassette recorder**

VD n abbr = **venereal disease**

VDU n abbr (= visual display unit) UPV f

veal [viːl] n ternera

veer [vɪəʳ] vi (vehicle) virar; (wind) girar

veg. [vɛdʒ] n abbr (Brit inf) = **vegetable(s)**

vegan ['viːgən] n vegetariano(-a) estricto(-a)

vegeburger, veggieburger ['vɛdʒɪbɔːgəʳ] n hamburguesa vegetal

vegetable ['vɛdʒtəbl] n (Bot) vegetal m; (edible plant) legumbre f, hortaliza ▷ adj vegetal; **vegetables** npl (cooked) verduras fpl

vegetarian [vɛdʒɪ'tɛərɪən] adj, n vegetariano(-a) m(f)

vegetation [vɛdʒɪ'teɪʃən] n vegetación f

vegetative ['vɛdʒɪtətɪv] adj vegetativo; (Bot) vegetal

vehement ['viːɪmənt] adj vehemente, apasionado; (dislike, hatred) violento

vehicle ['viːɪkl] n vehículo; (fig) vehículo, medio

veil [veɪl] n velo ▷ vt velar; **under a ~ of secrecy** (fig) en el mayor secreto

veiled [veɪld] adj (also fig) disimulado, velado

vein [veɪn] n vena; (of ore etc) veta

Velcro® ['vɛlkrəu] n velcro® m

velour [və'luəʳ] n terciopelo

velvet ['vɛlvɪt] n terciopelo ▷ adj aterciopelado

vending machine ['vɛndɪŋ-] n máquina expendedora, expendedor m

vendor ['vɛndəʳ] n vendedor(a) m(f); **street ~** vendedor(a) m(f) callejero(-a)

veneer [və'nɪəʳ] n chapa, enchapado; (fig) barniz m

venereal [vɪ'nɪərɪəl] adj: **~ disease (VD)** enfermedad f venérea

Venetian blind [vɪ'niːʃən-] n persiana

Venezuela [vɛnɛ'zweɪlə] n Venezuela

Venezuelan [vɛnɛ'zweɪlən] adj, n venezolano(-a) m(f)

vengeance ['vɛndʒəns] n venganza; **with a ~** (fig) con creces

venison ['vɛnɪsn] n carne f de venado

venom ['vɛnəm] n veneno

venomous ['vɛnəməs] adj venenoso

vent [vɛnt] n (opening) abertura; (air-hole) respiradero; (in wall) rejilla (de ventilación) ▷ vt (fig: feelings) desahogar

ventilation [vɛntɪ'leɪʃən] n ventilación f

ventilator ['vɛntɪleɪtəʳ] n ventilador m

ventriloquist [vɛn'trɪləkwɪst] n ventrílocuo(-a)

venture ['vɛntʃəʳ] n empresa ▷ vt arriesgar; (opinion) ofrecer ▷ vi arriesgarse, lanzarse; **a business ~** una empresa comercial; **to ~ to do sth** aventurarse a hacer algo

venue ['vɛnjuː] n (meeting place) lugar m de reunión; (for concert) local m

Venus ['viːnəs] n (Astro) Venus m

verb [vəːb] n verbo

verbal ['vəːbl] adj verbal

verbatim [vəː'beɪtɪm] adj, adv al pie de la letra, palabra por palabra

verdict ['vəːdɪkt] n veredicto, fallo; (fig: opinion) opinión f, juicio; **~ of guilty/ not guilty** veredicto de culpabilidad/ inocencia

verge [vəːdʒ] n (Brit) borde m; **to be on the ~ of doing sth** estar a punto de hacer algo; **verge on** vt fus rayar en

verify ['vɛrɪfaɪ] vt comprobar, verificar; (prove the truth of) confirmar

vermin ['vəːmɪn] npl (animals) bichos mpl; (insects) sabandijas fpl; (fig) sabandijas fpl

vermouth ['vəːməθ] n vermut m

versatile ['vəːsətaɪl] adj (person) polifacético; (machine, tool etc) versátil

verse [vəːs] n versos mpl, poesía; (stanza) estrofa; (in bible) versículo; **in ~** en verso

version ['vəːʃən] n versión f

versus ['vəːsəs] prep contra

vertical ['vəːtɪkl] adj vertical

vertigo ['vəːtɪgəu] n vértigo; **to suffer from ~** tener vértigo

verve [vəːv] n brío

very ['vɛrɪ] adv muy ▷ adj: **the ~ book which** el mismo libro que; **the ~ last** el último (de todos); **at the ~ least** al menos; **~ much** muchísimo; **~ well/little** muy bien/poco; **~ high frequency** (Radio) frecuencia muy alta; **it's ~ cold** hace mucho frío; **the ~ thought (of it) alarms me** con sólo pensarlo me entra miedo

vessel ['vɛsl] n (Anat) vaso; (ship) barco; (container) vasija

vest [vɛst] n (Brit) camiseta; (US: waistcoat) chaleco

vested interests ['vɛstɪd-] npl (Comm) intereses mpl creados

vet [vɛt] n abbr = **veterinary surgeon**; (US: inf) = **veteran** ▷ vt revisar; **to ~ sb for a job** someter a investigación a algn para un trabajo

V

veteran ['vɛtərn] n veterano(-a) ▷ adj: **she is a ~ campaigner for ...** es una veterana de la campaña de ...

veterinarian [vɛtrɪ'nɛərɪən] n (US) = veterinary surgeon

veterinary surgeon n (Brit) veterinario(-a)

veto ['vi:təʊ] n (pl **vetoes**) veto ▷ vt prohibir, vedar; **to put a ~ on** vetar

vetting ['vɛtɪŋ] n: **positive ~** investigación gubernamental de los futuros altos cargos de la Administración

vex [vɛks] vt (irritate) fastidiar; (make impatient) impacientar

vexed [vɛkst] adj (question) controvertido

VG n abbr (Brit Scol etc: = very good) S (= sobresaliente)

VHF abbr (= very high frequency) VHF f

via ['vaɪə] prep por, por vía de

viable ['vaɪəbl] adj viable

vial ['vaɪəl] n frasco pequeño

vibes [vaɪbz] npl (inf): **I got good/bad ~** me dio buen/mal rollo

vibrate [vaɪ'breɪt] vi vibrar

vibration [vaɪ'breɪʃən] n vibración f

vicar ['vɪkər] n párroco

vicarage ['vɪkərɪdʒ] n parroquia

vicarious [vɪ'kɛərɪəs] adj indirecto; (responsibility) delegado

vice [vaɪs] n (evil) vicio; (Tech) torno de banco

vice- [vaɪs] pref vice...

vice-chairman ['vaɪs'tʃɛəmən] n vicepresidente m

vice versa ['vaɪsɪ'və:sə] adv viceversa

vicinity [vɪ'sɪnɪtɪ] n (area) vecindad f; (nearness) proximidad f; **in the ~ (of)** cercano (a)

vicious ['vɪʃəs] adj (remark) malicioso; (blow) brutal; (dog, horse) resabido; **a ~ circle** un círculo vicioso

victim ['vɪktɪm] n víctima; **to be the ~ of** ser víctima de

victimize ['vɪktɪmaɪz] vt (strikers etc) tomar represalias contra

victor ['vɪktər] n vencedor(a) m(f)

Victorian [vɪk'tɔ:rɪən] adj victoriano

victorious [vɪk'tɔ:rɪəs] adj vencedor(a)

victory ['vɪktərɪ] n victoria; **to win a ~ over sb** obtener una victoria sobre algn

video ['vɪdɪəʊ] cpd de vídeo ▷ n vídeo ▷ vt grabar (en vídeo)

video call n videollamada

video camera n videocámara, cámara de vídeo

video cassette n videocassette f

video cassette recorder n = video recorder

video game n videojuego

videophone ['vɪdɪəʊfəʊn] n videoteléfono, videófono

video recorder n vídeo, videocassette f

video tape n cinta de vídeo

vie [vaɪ] vi: **to ~ with** competir con

Vienna [vɪ'ɛnə] n Viena

Vietnam, Viet Nam [vjɛt'næm] n Vietnam m

Vietnamese [vjɛtnə'mi:z] adj vietnamita ▷ n pl inv vietnamita m/f; (Ling) vietnamita m

view [vju:] n vista; (landscape) paisaje m; (opinion) opinión f, criterio ▷ vt (look at) mirar; (examine) examinar; **on ~** (in museum etc) expuesto; **in full ~ of** a la vista de algn; **to be within ~ (of sth)** estar a la vista (de algo); **an overall ~ of the situation** una visión de conjunto de la situación; **in ~ of the fact that** en vista de que; **to take or hold the ~ that ...** opinar or pensar que ...; **with a ~ to doing sth** con miras or vistas a hacer algo

viewer ['vju:ər] n (small projector) visionadora; (TV) televidente m/f, telespectador(a) m(f)

viewfinder ['vju:faɪndər] n visor m de imagen

viewpoint ['vju:pɔɪnt] n punto de vista

vigil ['vɪdʒɪl] n vigilia; **to keep ~** velar

vigilant ['vɪdʒɪlənt] adj vigilante

vigilante [vɪdʒɪ'læntɪ] n vecino/a que se toma la justicia por su mano

vigorous ['vɪgərəs] adj enérgico, vigoroso

vile [vaɪl] adj (action) vil, infame; (smell) repugnante; (temper) endemoniado

villa ['vɪlə] n (country house) casa de campo; (suburban house) chalet m

village ['vɪlɪdʒ] n aldea

villager ['vɪlɪdʒər] n aldeano(-a)

villain ['vɪlən] n (scoundrel) malvado(-a); (criminal) maleante m/f; see also **pantomime**

vinaigrette [vɪneɪ'grɛt] n vinagreta

vindicate ['vɪndɪkeɪt] vt vindicar, justificar

vindictive [vɪn'dɪktɪv] adj vengativo

vine [vaɪn] n vid f

vinegar ['vɪnɪgər] n vinagre m

vineyard ['vɪnjɑ:d] n viña, viñedo

vintage ['vɪntɪdʒ] n (year) vendimia, cosecha; **the 1970 ~** la cosecha de 1970

vintage car n coche m antiguo or de época

vintage wine n vino añejo

vinyl ['vaɪnl] n vinilo

viola [vɪ'əʊlə] n (Mus) viola

violate ['vaɪəleɪt] vt violar

violation [vaɪə'leɪʃən] n violación f; **in ~ of sth** en violación de algo

violence ['vaɪələns] n violencia; **acts of ~** actos mpl de violencia

violent ['vaɪələnt] adj (gen) violento; (pain) intenso; **a ~ dislike of sb/sth** una profunda antipatía or manía a algn/algo

violet ['vaɪələt] adj violado, violeta ▷ n (plant) violeta

violin [vaɪə'lɪn] n violín m

violinist [vaɪə'lɪnɪst] n violinista m/f

VIP n abbr (= very important person) VIP m

virgin ['və:dʒɪn] n virgen m/f ▷ adj virgen; **the Blessed V~** la Santísima Virgen

virginity [və:'dʒɪnɪtɪ] n virginidad f

Virgo ['və:gəʊ] n Virgo

virile ['vɪraɪl] adj viril

virtual ['vəːtjuəl] adj (also Comput, Physics) virtual

virtually ['vəːtjuəlɪ] adv (almost) prácticamente, virtualmente; **it is ~ impossible** es prácticamente imposible

virtual reality n (Comput) realidad f virtual

virtue ['vəːtjuː] n virtud f; **by ~ of** en virtud de

virtuosity [vəːtjuˈɔsɪtɪ] n virtuosismo

virtuous ['vəːtjuəs] adj virtuoso

virus ['vaɪərəs] n virus m inv

visa ['viːzə] n visado, visa (LAm)

vise [vaɪs] n (US Tech) = **vice**

visibility [vɪzɪˈbɪlɪtɪ] n visibilidad f

visible ['vɪzəbl] adj visible; **~ exports/ imports** exportaciones fpl/importaciones fpl visibles

vision ['vɪʒən] n (sight) vista; (foresight, in dream) visión f

visit ['vɪzɪt] n visita ▷ vt (person) visitar, hacer una visita a; (place) ir a, (ir a) conocer; **to pay a ~ to** (person) visitar a; **on a private/official ~** en visita privada/oficial

visiting hours npl (in hospital etc) horas fpl de visita

visitor ['vɪzɪtər] n (gen) visitante m/f; (to one's house) visita; (tourist) turista m/f; (tripper) excursionista m/f; **to have ~s** (at home) tener visita

visitor centre, visitor center (US) n centro m de información

visitors' book n libro de visitas

visor ['vaɪzər] n visera

vista ['vɪstə] n vista, panorama

visual ['vɪzjuəl] adj visual

visual aid n medio visual

visual arts npl artes fpl plásticas

visualize ['vɪzjuəlaɪz] vt imaginarse; (foresee) prever

vital ['vaɪtl] adj (essential) esencial, imprescindible; (crucial) crítico; (person) enérgico, vivo; (organ) vital; **of ~ importance (to sb/sth)** de suma importancia (para algn/algo)

vitality [vaɪˈtælɪtɪ] n energía, vitalidad f

vitally ['vaɪtəlɪ] adv: **~ important** de suma importancia

vital statistics npl (of population) estadísticas fpl demográficas; (inf: of woman) medidas fpl (corporales)

vitamin ['vɪtəmɪn] n vitamina

vitamin pill n pastilla de vitaminas

viva ['vaɪvə] n (also: **~ voce**) examen m oral

vivacious [vɪˈveɪʃəs] adj vivaz, alegre

vivid ['vɪvɪd] adj (account) gráfico; (light) intenso; (imagination) vivo

vividly ['vɪvɪdlɪ] adv (describe) gráficamente; (remember) como si fuera hoy

viz abbr (= videlicet: namely) v.gr.

V-neck ['viːnɛk] n cuello de pico

vocabulary [vəuˈkæbjulərɪ] n vocabulario

vocal ['vəukl] adj vocal; (articulate) elocuente

vocal cords npl cuerdas fpl vocales

vocalist ['vəukəlɪst] n cantante m/f

vocation [vəuˈkeɪʃən] n vocación f

vocational [vəuˈkeɪʃənl] adj profesional; **~ guidance** orientación f profesional; **~ training** formación f profesional

vociferous [vəˈsɪfərəs] adj vociferante

vodka ['vɔdkə] n vodka m

vogue [vəug] n boga, moda; **to be in ~, be the ~** estar de moda or en boga

voice [vɔɪs] n voz f ▷ vt (opinion) expresar; **in a loud/soft ~** en voz alta/baja; **to give ~ to** expresar

voice mail n (Tel) fonobuzón m

voice-over ['vɔɪsəuvər] n voz f en off

void [vɔɪd] n vacío; (hole) hueco ▷ adj (invalid) nulo, inválido; (empty): **~ of** carente or desprovisto de

vol. abbr (= volume) t

volatile ['vɔlətaɪl] adj (situation) inestable; (person) voluble; (liquid) volátil; (Comput: memory) no permanente

volcano (pl **volcanoes**) [vɔlˈkeɪnəu] n volcán m

volition [vəˈlɪʃən] n: **of one's own ~** por su propia voluntad

volley ['vɔlɪ] n (of gunfire) descarga; (of stones etc) lluvia; (Tennis etc) volea

volleyball ['vɔlɪbɔːl] n voleibol m, balonvolea m

volt [vəult] n voltio

voltage ['vəultɪdʒ] n voltaje m; **high/low ~** alto/bajo voltaje, alta/baja tensión

volume ['vɔljuːm] n (of tank) volumen m; (book) tomo; **~ one/two** (of book) tomo primero/segundo; **volumes** npl (great quantities) cantidad fsg; **his expression spoke ~s** su expresión (lo) decía todo

voluntarily ['vɔləntrɪlɪ] adv libremente, voluntariamente

voluntary ['vɔləntərɪ] adj voluntario, espontáneo

volunteer [vɔlənˈtɪər] n voluntario(-a) ▷ vt (information) ofrecer ▷ vi ofrecerse (de voluntario); **to ~ to do** ofrecerse a hacer

vomit ['vɔmɪt] n vómito ▷ vt, vi vomitar

voracious [vəˈreɪʃəs] adj voraz; (reader) ávido

vote [vəut] n voto; (votes cast) votación f; (right to vote) derecho a votar; (franchise) sufragio ▷ vt (chairman) elegir ▷ vi votar, ir a votar; **~ of thanks** voto de gracias; **to put sth to the ~, to take a ~ on sth** someter algo a votación; **~ for** or **in favour of/against** voto a favor de/en contra de; **to ~ to do sth** votar por hacer algo; **he was ~d secretary** fue elegido secretario por votación; **to pass a ~ of confidence/no confidence** aprobar un voto de confianza/de censura

voter ['vəutər] n votante m/f

voting ['vəutɪŋ] n votación f

vouch [vautʃ]: **to ~ for** vt fus garantizar, responder de

voucher ['vautʃər] n (for meal, petrol) vale m; **luncheon/travel ~** vale m de comida/de viaje

vow [vau] n voto ▷ vi hacer voto ▷ vt: **to ~ to do/that** jurar hacer/que; **to take** or **make a ~ to do sth** jurar hacer algo, comprometerse a hacer algo

vowel ['vauəl] n vocal f

voyage ['vɔɪɪdʒ] n (journey) viaje m; (crossing) travesía

voyeur [vwɑːˈjəːr] n voyeur m/f, mirón(-ona) m(f)

vs abbr (= versus) vs

VSO n abbr (Brit: = Voluntary Service Overseas) organización que envía jóvenes voluntarios a trabajar y enseñar en los países del Tercer Mundo

vulgar ['vʌlgər] adj (rude) ordinario, grosero; (in bad taste) de mal gusto

vulnerable ['vʌlnərəbl] adj vulnerable

vulture ['vʌltʃər] n buitre m, gallinazo (LAm)

W, w ['dʌblju:] n (letter) W, w f; **W for William** W de Washington

W abbr (= west) O; (Elec: = watt) v

wad [wɔd] n (of cotton wool, paper) bolita; (of banknotes etc) fajo

waddle ['wɔdl] vi andar como un pato

wade [weɪd] vi: **to ~ through** caminar por el agua; (fig: a book) leer con dificultad

wafer ['weɪfər] n (biscuit) barquillo; (Rel) oblea; (: consecrated) hostia; (Comput) oblea, microplaqueta

waffle ['wɔfl] n (Culin) gofre m ▷ vi meter el rollo

waft [wɔft] vt llevar por el aire ▷ vi flotar

wag [wæg] vt menear, agitar ▷ vi moverse, menearse; **the dog ~ged its tail** el perro meneó la cola

wage [weɪdʒ] n (also: **~s**) sueldo, salario ▷ vt: **to ~ war** hacer la guerra; **a day's ~** el sueldo de un día

wage earner n asalariado(-a)

wage packet n sobre m de la paga

wager ['weɪdʒər] n apuesta ▷ vt apostar

waggle ['wægl] vt menear, mover

wagon, waggon ['wægən] n (horse-drawn) carro; (Brit Rail) vagón m

wail [weɪl] n gemido ▷ vi gemir

waist [weɪst] n cintura, talle m

waistcoat ['weɪstkəut] n (Brit) chaleco

waistline ['weɪstlaɪn] n talle m

wait [weɪt] n espera; (interval) pausa ▷ vi esperar; **to lie in ~ for** acechar a; **I can't ~ to**

(*fig*) estoy deseando; **to ~ for** esperar (a); **to keep sb ~ing** hacer esperar a algn; **~ a moment!** ¡un momento!, ¡un momentito!; **"repairs while you ~"** "reparaciones en el acto"; **wait behind** *vi* quedarse; **wait on** *vt fus* servir a; **wait up** *vi* esperar levantado

waiter ['weɪtəʳ] *n* camarero

waiting list *n* lista de espera

waiting room *n* sala de espera

waitress ['weɪtrɪs] *n* camarera

waive [weɪv] *vt* suspender

wake [weɪk] (*pt* **woke** *or* **waked**, *pp* **woken** *or* **waked**) *vt* (*also*: **~ up**) despertar ▷ *vi* (*also*: **~ up**) despertarse ▷ *n* (*for dead person*) velatorio; (*Naut*) estela; **to ~ up to sth** (*fig*) darse cuenta de algo; **in the ~ of** tras, después de; **to follow in sb's ~** (*fig*) seguir las huellas de algn

waken ['weɪkn] *vt*, *vi* = **wake**

Wales [weɪlz] *n* País *m* de Gales

walk [wɔːk] *n* (*stroll*) paseo; (*hike*) excursión *f* a pie, caminata; (*gait*) paso, andar *m*; (*in park etc*) paseo ▷ *vi* andar, caminar; (*for pleasure, exercise*) pasearse ▷ *vt* (*distance*) recorrer a pie, andar; (*dog*) (sacar a) pasear; **to go for a ~** ir a dar un paseo; **10 minutes' ~ from here** a 10 minutos de aquí andando; **people from all ~s of life** gente de todas las esferas; **to ~ in one's sleep** ser sonámbulo(-a); **I'll ~ you home** te acompañaré a casa; **walk out** *vi* (*go out*) salir; (*as protest*) marcharse, salirse; (*strike*) declararse en huelga; **to ~ out on sb** abandonar a algn

walkabout ['wɔːkəbaut] *n*: **to go (on a) ~** darse un baño de multitudes

walker ['wɔːkəʳ] *n* (*person*) paseante *m/f*, caminante *m/f*

walkie-talkie ['wɔːkɪ'tɔːkɪ] *n* walkie-talkie *m*

walking ['wɔːkɪŋ] *n* (el) andar; **it's within ~ distance** se puede ir andando *or* a pie

walking shoes *npl* zapatos *mpl* para andar

walking stick *n* bastón *m*

Walkman® ['wɔːkmən] *n* walkman® *m*

walkout ['wɔːkaut] *n* (*of workers*) huelga

walkover ['wɔːkəuvəʳ] *n* (*inf*) pan *m* comido

walkway ['wɔːkweɪ] *n* paseo

wall [wɔːl] *n* pared *f*; (*exterior*) muro; (*city wall etc*) muralla; **to go to the ~** (*fig*: *firm etc*) quebrar, ir a la bancarrota; **wall in** *vt* (*garden etc*) cercar con una tapia

walled [wɔːld] *adj* (*city*) amurallado; (*garden*) con tapia

wallet ['wɔlɪt] *n* cartera, billetera (*esp LAm*)

wallflower ['wɔːlflauəʳ] *n* alhelí *m*; **to be a ~** (*fig*) comer pavo

wallop ['wɔləp] *vt* (*inf*) zurrar

wallow ['wɔləu] *vi* revolcarse; **to ~ in one's grief** sumirse en su pena

wallpaper ['wɔːlpeɪpəʳ] *n* (*for walls*) papel *m* pintado; (*Comput*) fondo de escritorio ▷ *vt* empapelar

wally ['wɔlɪ] *n* (*inf*) majadero(-a)

walnut ['wɔːlnʌt] *n* nuez *f*; (*tree*) nogal *m*

walrus (*pl* **walrus** *or* **walruses**) ['wɔːlrəs] *n* morsa

waltz [wɔːlts] *n* vals *m* ▷ *vi* bailar el vals

wan [wɔn] *adj* pálido

wand [wɔnd] *n* (*also*: **magic ~**) varita (mágica)

wander ['wɔndəʳ] *vi* (*person*) vagar; deambular; (*thoughts*) divagar; (*get lost*) extraviarse ▷ *vt* recorrer, vagar por

wane [weɪn] *vi* menguar

wangle ['wæŋgl] (*Brit inf*) *vt*: **to ~ sth** agenciarse *or* conseguir algo ▷ *n* chanchullo

want [wɔnt] *vt* (*wish for*) querer, desear; (*need*) necesitar; (*lack*) carecer de ▷ *n* (*poverty*) pobreza; **for ~ of** por falta de; **wants** *npl* (*needs*) necesidades *fpl*; **to ~ to do** querer hacer; **to ~ sb to do sth** querer que algn haga algo; **you're ~ed on the phone** te llaman al teléfono; **to be in ~** estar necesitado

wanted [wɔntɪd] *adj* (*criminal*) buscado; **"~"** (*in advertisements*) "se busca"

wanting ['wɔntɪŋ] *adj*: **to be ~ (in)** estar falto (de); **to be found ~** no estar a la altura de las circunstancias

wanton ['wɔntn] *adj* (*licentious*) lascivo

war [wɔːʳ] *n* guerra; **to make ~** hacer la guerra; **the First/Second World W~** la primera/segunda guerra mundial

ward [wɔːd] *n* (*in hospital*) sala; (*Pol*) distrito electoral; (*Law*: *child*: *also*: **~ of court**) pupilo(-a); **ward off** *vt* desviar, parar; (*attack*) rechazar

warden ['wɔːdn] *n* (*Brit*: *of institution*) director(a) *m(f)*; (*of park, game reserve*) guardián(-ana) *m(f)*; (*Brit*: *also*: **traffic ~**) guardia *m/f*

warder ['wɔːdəʳ] *n* (*Brit*) guardián(-ana) *m(f)*, carcelero(-a) *m(f)*

wardrobe ['wɔːdrəub] *n* armario, guardarropa, ropero, clóset/closet *m* (*LAm*)

warehouse ['wɛəhaus] *n* almacén *m*, depósito

wares [wɛəz] *npl* mercancías *fpl*

warfare ['wɔːfɛəʳ] *n* guerra

warhead ['wɔːhɛd] *n* cabeza armada; **nuclear ~s** cabezas *fpl* nucleares

warily ['wɛərɪlɪ] *adv* con cautela, cautelosamente

warm [wɔːm] *adj* caliente; (*person, greeting, heart*) afectuoso, cariñoso; (*supporter*) entusiasta; (*thanks, congratulations, apologies*) efusivo; (*clothes etc*) que abriga; (*welcome, day*) caluroso; **it's ~** hace calor; **I'm ~** tengo calor; **to keep sth ~** mantener algo caliente; **warm up** *vi* (*room*) calentarse; (*person*) entrar en calor; (*athlete*) hacer ejercicios de calentamiento; (*discussion*) acalorarse ▷ *vt* calentar

war memorial *n* monumento a los caídos

warm-hearted [wɔːm'hɑːtɪd] *adj* afectuoso

warmly ['wɔːmlɪ] *adv* afectuosamente

W

warmth [wɔ:mθ] n calor m

warm-up ['wɔ:mʌp] n (Sport) ejercicios mpl de calentamiento

warn [wɔ:n] vt avisar, advertir; **to ~ sb not to do sth** or **against doing sth** aconsejar a algn que no haga algo

warning ['wɔ:nɪŋ] n aviso, advertencia; **gale ~** (Meteorology) aviso de vendaval; **without (any) ~** sin aviso or avisar

warning light n luz f de advertencia

warning triangle n (Aut) triángulo señalizador

warp [wɔ:p] vi (wood) combarse

warrant ['wɔrnt] n (Law: to arrest) orden f de detención; (: to search) mandamiento de registro ▷ vt (justify, merit) merecer

warranty ['wɔrəntɪ] n garantía; **under ~** (Comm) bajo garantía

warren ['wɔrən] n (of rabbits) madriguera; (fig) laberinto

warrior ['wɔrɪər] n guerrero(-a)

Warsaw ['wɔ:sɔ:] n Varsovia

warship ['wɔ:ʃɪp] n buque m or barco de guerra

wart [wɔ:t] n verruga

wartime ['wɔ:taɪm] n: **in ~** en tiempos de guerra, en la guerra

wary ['wɛərɪ] adj cauteloso; **to be ~ about** or **of doing sth** tener cuidado con hacer algo

was [wɔz] pt of **be**

wash [wɔʃ] vt lavar; (sweep, carry: sea etc) llevar ▷ vi lavarse ▷ n (clothes etc) lavado; (bath) baño; (of ship) estela; **he was ~ed overboard** fue arrastrado del barco por las olas; **to have a ~** lavarse; **wash away** vt (stain) quitar lavando; (river etc) llevarse; (fig) limpiar; **wash down** vt lavar; **wash off** vt quitar lavando; **wash up** vi (Brit) fregar los platos; (US: have a wash) lavarse

washable ['wɔʃəbl] adj lavable

washbasin ['wɔʃbeɪsn], **washbowl** (US) ['wɔʃbəul] n lavabo

washcloth ['wɔʃklɔθ] n (US) manopla

washer ['wɔʃər] n (Tech) arandela

washing ['wɔʃɪŋ] n (dirty) ropa sucia; (clean) colada

washing line n cuerda de (colgar) la ropa

washing machine n lavadora

washing powder n (Brit) detergente m (en polvo)

Washington ['wɔʃɪŋtən] n (city, state) Washington m

washing-up [wɔʃɪŋ'ʌp] n fregado; (dishes) platos mpl (para fregar); **to do the ~** fregar los platos

washing-up liquid n lavavajillas m inv

wash-out ['wɔʃaut] n (inf) fracaso

washroom ['wɔʃrum] n servicios mpl

wasn't ['wɔznt] = **was not**

wasp [wɔsp] n avispa

wastage ['weɪstɪdʒ] n desgaste m; (loss) pérdida; **natural ~** desgaste natural

waste [weɪst] n derroche m, despilfarro; (misuse) desgaste m; (of time) pérdida; (food) sobras fpl; (rubbish) basura, desperdicios mpl ▷ adj (material) de desecho; (left over) sobrante; (energy, heat) desperdiciado; (land, ground: in city) sin construir; (: in country) baldío ▷ vt (squander) malgastar, derrochar; (time) perder; (opportunity) desperdiciar; **wastes** npl (area of land) tierras fpl baldías; **to lay ~** devastar, arrasar; **it's a ~ of money** es tirar el dinero; **to go to ~** desperdiciarse; **waste away** vi consumirse

wastebasket ['weɪstbɑ:skɪt] n (esp US) = **wastepaper basket**

wasteful ['weɪstful] adj derrochador(a); (process) antieconómico

waste ground n (Brit) terreno baldío

wastepaper basket ['weɪstpeɪpə-] n papelera; (Comput) papelera de reciclaje

waste pipe n tubo de desagüe

waster ['weɪstər] n (inf) gandul m/f

watch [wɔtʃ] n reloj m; (vigil) vigilia; (vigilance) vigilancia; (Mil: guard) centinela m; (Naut: spell of duty) guardia ▷ vt (look at) mirar, observar; (: match, programme) ver; (spy on, guard) vigilar; (be careful of) cuidar, tener cuidado de ▷ vi ver, mirar; (keep guard) montar guardia; **to keep a close ~ on sth/sb** vigilar algo/a algn de cerca; **~ how you drive/what you're doing** ten cuidado al conducir/con lo que haces; **watch out** vi cuidarse, tener cuidado

watchdog ['wɔtʃdɔg] n perro guardián; (fig) organismo de control

watchful ['wɔtʃful] adj vigilante, sobre aviso

watchmaker ['wɔtʃmeɪkər] n relojero(-a)

watchman ['wɔtʃmən] n (irreg: like **man**) n guardián m; (also: **night ~**) sereno, vigilante m; (in factory) vigilante m nocturno

watch strap n pulsera (de reloj)

watchword ['wɔtʃwə:d] n consigna, contraseña

water ['wɔ:tər] n agua ▷ vt (plant) regar ▷ vi (eyes) llorar; **I'd like a drink of ~** quisiera un vaso de agua; **in British ~s** en aguas británicas; **to pass ~** orinar; **his mouth ~ed** se le hizo la boca agua; **water down** vt (milk etc) aguar; (fig: story) dulcificar, diluir

watercolour, watercolor (US) ['wɔ:təkʌlər] n acuarela

watercress ['wɔ:təkrɛs] n berro

waterfall ['wɔ:təfɔ:l] n cascada, salto de agua

water heater n calentador m de agua

watering can ['wɔ:tərɪŋ-] n regadera

water lily n nenúfar m

waterline ['wɔ:təlaɪn] n (Naut) línea de flotación

waterlogged ['wɔ:təlɔgd] adj (boat) anegado; (ground) inundado

water main n cañería del agua

watermark ['wɔ:təmɑ:k] n (on paper) filigrana

watermelon ['wɔːtəmɛlən] n sandía

waterproof ['wɔːtəpruːf] adj impermeable

watershed ['wɔːtəʃɛd] n (Geo) cuenca; (fig) momento crítico

water-skiing ['wɔːtəskiːɪŋ] n esquí m acuático

water tank n depósito de agua

watertight ['wɔːtətaɪt] adj hermético

waterway ['wɔːtəweɪ] n vía fluvial or navegable

waterworks ['wɔːtəwəːks] npl central fsg depuradora

watery ['wɔːtərɪ] adj (colour) desvaído; (coffee) aguado; (eyes) lloroso

watt [wɔt] n vatio

wave [weɪv] n ola; (of hand) señal f con la mano; (Radio) onda; (in hair) onda; (fig: of enthusiasm, strikes) oleada ▷ vi agitar la mano; (flag) ondear ▷ vt (handkerchief, gun) agitar; **short/medium/long ~** (Radio) onda corta/media/larga; **the new ~** (Cine, Mus) la nueva ola; **to ~ goodbye to sb** decir adiós a algn con la mano; **he ~d us over to his table** nos hizo señas (con las manos) para que nos acercásemos a su mesa; **wave aside, wave away** vt (person): **to ~ sb aside** apartar a algn con la mano; (fig: suggestion, objection) rechazar; (doubts) desechar

wavelength ['weɪvlɛŋθ] n longitud f de onda

waver ['weɪvəʳ] vi oscilar; (confidence) disminuir; (faith) flaquear

wavy ['weɪvɪ] adj ondulado

wax [wæks] n cera ▷ vt encerar ▷ vi (moon) crecer

waxworks ['wækswəːks] npl museo sg de cera

way [weɪ] n camino; (distance) trayecto, recorrido; (direction) dirección f, sentido; (manner) modo, manera; (habit) costumbre f; **which ~?** — **this ~** ¿por dónde? or ¿en qué dirección? — por aquí; **on the ~** (en route) en (el) camino; (expected) en camino; **to be on one's ~** estar en camino; **you pass it on your ~ home** está de camino a tu casa; **to be in the ~** bloquear el camino; (fig) estorbar; **to keep out of sb's ~** esquivar a algn; **to make ~ (for sb/sth)** dejar paso (a algn/algo); (fig) abrir camino (a algn/algo); **to go out of one's ~ to do sth** desvivirse por hacer algo; **to lose one's ~** perderse, extraviarse; **to be the wrong ~ round** estar del or al revés; **in a ~** en cierto modo or sentido; **by the ~** a propósito; **by ~ of** (via) pasando por; (as a sort of) como, a modo de; **"~ in"** (Brit) "entrada"; **"~ out"** (Brit) "salida"; **the ~ back** el camino de vuelta; **the village is rather out of the ~** el pueblo está un poco apartado or retirado; **it's a long ~ away** está muy lejos; **to get one's own ~** salirse con la suya; **"give ~"** (Brit Aut) "ceda el paso"; **no ~!** (inf) ¡ni pensarlo!; **put it the right ~ up** ponlo

boca arriba; **he's in a bad ~** está grave; **to be under ~** (work, project) estar en marcha

waylay [weɪˈleɪ] vt (irreg: like **lay**) atacar

wayward ['weɪwəd] adj díscolo, caprichoso

WC ['dʌbljuːsiː] n abbr (Brit: = water closet) wáter m

we [wiː] pron pl nosotros(-as); **we understand** (nosotros) entendemos; **here we are** aquí estamos

weak [wiːk] adj débil, flojo; (tea, coffee) flojo, aguado; **to grow ~(er)** debilitarse

weaken ['wiːkən] vi debilitarse; (give way) ceder ▷ vt debilitar

weakling ['wiːklɪŋ] n debilucho(-a)

weakness ['wiːknɪs] n debilidad f; (fault) punto débil; **to have a ~ for** tener debilidad por

wealth [wɛlθ] n (money, resources) riqueza; (of details) abundancia

wealthy ['wɛlθɪ] adj rico

wean [wiːn] vt destetar

weapon ['wɛpən] n arma; **~s of mass destruction** armas de destrucción masiva

wear [wɛəʳ] (pt wore, pp worn) n (use) uso; (deterioration through use) desgaste m; (clothing): **sports/baby~** ropa de deportes/de niños ▷ vt (clothes, beard) llevar; (shoes) calzar; (look, smile) tener; (damage: through use) gastar, usar ▷ vi (last) durar; (rub through etc) desgastarse; **evening ~** (man's) traje m de etiqueta; (woman's) traje m de noche; **to ~ a hole in sth** hacer un agujero en algo; **wear away** vt gastar ▷ vi desgastarse; **wear down** vt gastar; (strength) agotar; **wear off** vi (pain, excitement etc) pasar, desaparecer; **wear out** vt desgastar; (person, strength) agotar

wear and tear n desgaste m

weary ['wɪərɪ] adj (tired) cansado; (dispirited) abatido ▷ vt cansar ▷ vi: **to ~ of** cansarse de, aburrirse de

weasel ['wiːzl] n (Zool) comadreja

weather ['wɛðəʳ] n tiempo ▷ vt (storm, crisis) hacer frente a; **under the ~** (fig: ill) mal, pachucho; **what's the ~ like?** ¿qué tiempo hace?, ¿cómo hace?

weather-beaten ['wɛðəbiːtn] adj curtido

weathercock ['wɛðəkɔk] n veleta

weather forecast n boletín m meteorológico

weatherman ['wɛðəmæn] n hombre m del tiempo

weather vane n = **weathercock**

weave [wiːv] (pt wove, pp woven) [wiːv, wəuv, 'wəuvn] vt (cloth) tejer; (fig) entretejer ▷ vi (pt, pp weaved) (fig: move in and out) zigzaguear

weaver ['wiːvəʳ] n tejedor(a) m(f)

web [wɛb] n (of spider) telaraña; (on foot) membrana; (Comput: network) red f; **the W~** la Red

web address n dirección f de página web

webcam ['wɛbkæm] n webcam f

web page n página web

website ['wɛbsaɪt] n sitio web
wed [wɛd] (pt, pp **wedded**) vt casar ▷ vi
casarse ▷ n: **the newly-~s** los recién casados
Wed. abbr (= Wednesday) miérc
we'd [wi:d] = **we had; we would**
wedding ['wɛdɪŋ] n boda, casamiento
wedding anniversary n aniversario de
boda; **silver/golden ~** bodas fpl de plata/
de oro
wedding day n día m de la boda
wedding dress n traje m de novia
wedding present n regalo de boda
wedding ring n alianza
wedge [wɛdʒ] n (of wood etc) cuña; (of cake)
trozo ▷ vt acuñar; (push) apretar
Wednesday ['wɛdnzdɪ] n miércoles m inv;
see also **Tuesday**
wee [wi:] adj (Scottish) pequeñito
weed [wi:d] n mala hierba, maleza ▷ vt
escardar, desherbar; **weed out** vt eliminar
weedkiller ['wi:dkɪləʳ] n herbicida m
weedy ['wi:dɪ] adj (person) debilucho
week [wi:k] n semana; **a ~ today** de hoy en
ocho días; **Tuesday ~, a ~ on Tuesday** del
martes en una semana; **once/twice a ~** una
vez/dos veces a la semana; **this ~** esta
semana; **in two ~s'** time dentro de dos
semanas; **every other ~** cada dos semanas
weekday ['wi:kdeɪ] n día m laborable; **on ~s**
entre semana, en días laborables
weekend [wi:k'ɛnd] n fin m de semana
weekly ['wi:klɪ] adv semanalmente, cada
semana ▷ adj semanal ▷ n semanario;
~ newspaper semanario
weep (pt, pp **wept**) [wi:p, wɛpt] vi, vt llorar;
(Med: wound etc) supurar
weeping willow ['wi:pɪŋ-] n sauce m llorón
weepy ['wi:pɪ] n (inf: film) película
lacrimógena; (: story) historia lacrimógena
weigh [weɪ] vt, vi pesar; **to ~ anchor** levar
anclas; **to ~ the pros and cons** pesar los pros
y los contras; **weigh down** vt sobrecargar;
(fig: with worry) agobiar; **weigh out** vt (goods)
pesar; **weigh up** vt sopesar
weight [weɪt] n peso; (on scale) pesa; **to lose/
put on ~** adelgazar/engordar; **~s and
measures** pesas y medidas
weighting ['weɪtɪŋ] n (allowance): **(London) ~**
dietas (por residir en Londres)
weight lifter n levantador(a) m(f) de pesas
weightlifting ['weɪtlɪftɪŋ] n levantamiento
de pesas
weight training n musculación f (con pesas)
weighty ['weɪtɪ] adj pesado
weir [wɪəʳ] n presa
weird [wɪəd] adj raro, extraño
weirdo ['wɪədəu] n (inf) tío(-a) raro(-a)
welcome ['wɛlkəm] adj bienvenido ▷ n
bienvenida ▷ vt dar la bienvenida a; (be glad
of) alegrarse de; **to make sb ~** recibir or
acoger bien a algn; **thank you — you're ~**
gracias — de nada; **you're ~ to try** puede

intentar cuando quiera; **we ~ this step**
celebramos esta medida
weld [wɛld] n soldadura ▷ vt soldar
welfare ['wɛlfɛəʳ] n bienestar m; (social aid)
asistencia social; **W~** (US) subsidio de paro;
to look after sb's ~ cuidar del bienestar
de algn
welfare state n estado del bienestar
welfare work n asistencia social
well [wɛl] n pozo ▷ adv bien ▷ adj: **to be ~**
estar bien (de salud) ▷ excl ¡vaya!, ¡bueno!;
as ~ (in addition) además, también; **as ~ as**
además de; **you might as ~ tell me** más vale
que me lo digas; **it would be as ~ to ask** más
valdría preguntar; **~ done!** ¡bien hecho!;
get ~ soon! ¡que te mejores pronto!; **to do ~**
(business) ir bien; **I did ~ in my exams** me
han salido bien los exámenes; **they are
doing ~ now** les va bien ahora; **to think ~ of
sb** pensar bien de algn; **I don't feel ~** no me
encuentro or siento bien; **~, as I was
saying ...** bueno, como decía ...; **well up** vi
brotar
we'll [wi:l] = **we will; we shall**
well-behaved ['wɛlbɪ'heɪvd] adj: **to be ~**
portarse bien
well-being ['wɛl'bi:ɪŋ] n bienestar m
well-built ['wɛl'bɪlt] adj (person) fornido
well-deserved ['wɛldɪ'zə:vd] adj merecido
well-dressed ['wɛl'drɛst] adj bien vestido
well-heeled ['wɛl'hi:ld] adj (inf: wealthy) rico
wellies ['wɛlɪz] (inf) npl (Brit) botas de goma
wellingtons ['wɛlɪŋtənz] npl (also:
Wellington boots) botas fpl de goma
well-known ['wɛl'nəun] adj (person)
conocido
well-mannered ['wɛl'mænəd] adj educado
well-meaning ['wɛl'mi:nɪŋ] adj
bienintencionado
well-off ['wɛl'ɔf] adj acomodado
well-paid [wɛl'peɪd] adj bien pagado, bien
retribuido
well-read ['wɛl'rɛd] adj culto
well-to-do ['wɛltə'du:] adj acomodado
well-wisher ['wɛlwɪʃəʳ] n admirador(a) m(f)
Welsh [wɛlʃ] adj galés(-esa) ▷ n (Ling) galés m;
the Welsh npl los galeses; **the ~ Assembly** el
Parlamento galés
Welshman ['wɛlʃmən] n galés m
Welsh rarebit [-'rɛəbɪt] n pan m con queso
tostado
Welshwoman ['wɛlʃwumən] n galesa
went [wɛnt] pt of **go**
wept [wɛpt] pt, pp of **weep**
were [wə:ʳ] pt of **be**
we're [wɪəʳ] = **we are**
weren't [wə:nt] = **were not**
west [wɛst] n oeste m ▷ adj occidental, del
oeste ▷ adv al or hacia el oeste; **the W~**
Occidente m
westbound ['wɛstbaund] adj (traffic,
carriageway) con rumbo al oeste

West Country n: **the ~** el suroeste de Inglaterra

westerly ['wɛstəlɪ] adj (wind) del oeste

western ['wɛstən] adj occidental ▷ n (Cine) película del oeste

westerner ['wɛstənəʳ] n (Pol) occidental m/f

West German (formerly) adj de Alemania Occidental ▷ n alemán(-ana) m(f) (de Alemania Occidental)

West Germany n (formerly) Alemania Occidental

West Indian adj, n antillano(-a) m(f)

West Indies [-ˈɪndɪz] npl: **the ~** las Antillas

Westminster ['wɛstmɪnstəʳ] n el parlamento británico, Westminster m

wet [wɛt] adj (damp) húmedo; (wet through) mojado; (rainy) lluvioso ▷ vt: **to ~ one's pants** or **o.s.** mearse; **to get ~** mojarse; **"~ paint"** "recién pintado"

wet blanket n: **to be a ~** (fig) ser un/una aguafiestas

wetsuit ['wɛtsuːt] n traje m de buzo

we've [wiːv] = **we have**

whack [wæk] vt dar un buen golpe a

whale [weɪl] n (Zool) ballena

whaling ['weɪlɪŋ] n pesca de ballenas

wharf (pl **wharves**) [wɔːf, wɔːvz] n muelle m

 KEYWORD

what [wɔt] adj **1** (in direct/indirect questions) qué; **what size is he?** ¿qué talla usa?; **what colour/shape is it?** ¿de qué color/forma es?; **what books do you need?** ¿qué libros necesitas?

2 (in exclamations): **what a mess!** ¡qué desastre!; **what a fool I am!** ¡qué tonto soy!

▷ pron **1** (interrogative) qué; **what are you doing?** ¿qué haces or estás haciendo?; **what is happening?** ¿qué pasa or está pasando?; **what is it called?** ¿cómo se llama?; **what about me?** ¿y yo qué?; **what about doing ...?** ¿qué tal si hacemos ...?; **what is his address?** ¿cuáles son sus señas?; **what will it cost?** ¿cuánto costará?

2 (relative) lo que; **I saw what you did/was on the table** vi lo que hiciste/había en la mesa; **what I want is a cup of tea** lo que quiero es una taza de té; **I don't know what to do** no sé qué hacer; **tell me what you're thinking about** dime en qué estás pensando

3 (reported questions): **she asked me what I wanted** me preguntó qué quería

▷ excl (disbelieving) ¡cómo!; **what, no coffee!** ¡que no hay café!

whatever [wɔtˈɛvəʳ] adj: **~ book you choose** cualquier libro que elijas ▷ pron: **do ~ is necessary** haga lo que sea necesario; **no reason ~** ninguna razón en absoluto;

nothing ~ nada en absoluto; **~ it costs** cueste lo que cueste

whatsoever [wɔtsəʊˈɛvəʳ] adj see **whatever**

wheat [wiːt] n trigo

wheedle ['wiːdl] vt: **to ~ sb into doing sth** engatusar a algn para que haga algo; **to ~ sth out of sb** sonsacar algo a algn

wheel [wiːl] n rueda; (Aut: also: **steering ~**) volante m; (Naut) timón m ▷ vt (pram etc) empujar ▷ vi (also: **~ round**) dar la vuelta, girar; **four-~ drive** tracción f en las cuatro ruedas; **front-/rear-~ drive** tracción f delantera/trasera

wheelbarrow ['wiːlbærəʊ] n carretilla

wheelchair ['wiːltʃɛəʳ] n silla de ruedas

wheel clamp n (Aut) cepo

wheelie-bin ['wiːlɪbɪn] n (Brit) contenedor m de basura

wheeze [wiːz] vi resollar

wheezy ['wiːzɪ] adj silbante

 KEYWORD

when [wɛn] adv cuando; **when did it happen?** ¿cuándo ocurrió?; **I know when it happened** sé cuándo ocurrió

▷ conj **1** (at, during, after the time that) cuando; **be careful when you cross the road** ten cuidado al cruzar la calle; **that was when I needed you** entonces era cuando te necesitaba; **I'll buy you a car when you're 18** te compraré un coche cuando cumplas 18 años

2 (on, at which): **on the day when I met him** el día en que le conocí

3 (whereas) cuando; **you said I was wrong when in fact I was right** dijiste que no tenía razón, cuando en realidad sí la tenía

whenever [wɛnˈɛvəʳ] conj cuando; (every time) cada vez que; **I go ~ I can** voy siempre or todas las veces que puedo

where [wɛəʳ] adv dónde ▷ conj donde; **this is ~** aquí es donde; **~ possible** donde sea posible; **~ are you from?** ¿de dónde es usted?

whereabouts ['wɛərəbaʊts] adv dónde ▷ n: **nobody knows his ~** nadie conoce su paradero

whereas [wɛərˈæz] conj mientras

whereby [wɛəˈbaɪ] adv mediante el/la cual etc, por lo/la cual etc

whereupon [wɛərəˈpɔn] conj con lo cual, después de lo cual

wherever [wɛərˈɛvəʳ] adv dondequiera que; (interrogative) dónde; **sit ~ you like** siéntese donde quiera

wherewithal ['wɛərwɪðɔːl] n recursos mpl; **the ~ (to do sth)** los medios económicos (para hacer algo)

whet [wɛt] vt estimular; (appetite) abrir

W

whether ['wɛðər] *conj* si; **I don't know ~ to accept or not** no sé si aceptar o no; **~ you go or not** vayas o no vayas

O **KEYWORD**

which [wɪtʃ] *adj* **1** (*interrogative: direct, indirect*) qué; **which picture(s) do you want?** ¿qué cuadro(s) quieres?; **which one?** ¿cuál?; **which one of you?** ¿cuál de vosotros?; **tell me which one you want** dime cuál (es el que) quieres
2: **in which case** en cuyo caso; **we got there at eight pm, by which time the cinema was full** llegamos allí a las ocho, cuando el cine estaba lleno
▷ *pron* (*interrogative*) cual; **I don't mind which** el(-la) que sea; **which do you want?** ¿cuál quieres?
3 (*relative: replacing noun*) que; (*: replacing clause*) lo que; (*: after preposition*) (el(-la)) que, el(-la) cual; **the apple which you ate/which is on the table** la manzana que comiste/que está en la mesa; **the chair on which you are sitting** la silla en la que estás sentado; **he didn't believe it, which upset me** no se lo creyó, lo cual *or* lo que me disgustó; **after which** después de lo cual

whichever [wɪtʃˈɛvər] *adj*: **take ~ book you prefer** coja el libro que prefiera; **~ book you take** cualquier libro que coja
whiff [wɪf] *n* bocanada; **to catch a ~ of sth** oler algo
while [waɪl] *n* rato, momento ▷ *conj* durante; (*whereas*) mientras; (*although*) aunque ▷ *vt*: **to ~ away the time** pasar el rato; **for a ~** durante algún tiempo; **in a ~** dentro de poco; **all the ~** todo el tiempo; **we'll make it worth your ~** te compensaremos generosamente
whilst [waɪlst] *conj* = **while**
whim [wɪm] *n* capricho
whimper ['wɪmpər] *n* (*weeping*) lloriqueo; (*moan*) quejido ▷ *vi* lloriquear; quejarse
whimsical ['wɪmzɪkl] *adj* (*person*) caprichoso
whine [waɪn] *n* (*of pain*) gemido; (*of engine*) zumbido ▷ *vi* gemir; zumbar; (*fig: complain*) gimotear
whip [wɪp] *n* látigo; (*Brit: Pol*) *diputado encargado de la disciplina del partido en el parlamento* ▷ *vt* azotar; (*snatch*) arrebatar; (*US Culin*) batir; **whip up** *vt* (*cream etc*) batir (rápidamente); (*inf: meal*) preparar rápidamente; (*: stir up: support, feeling*) avivar; *ver nota*
whipped cream [wɪpt-] *n* nata montada
whip-round ['wɪpraund] *n* (*Brit*) colecta
whirl [wəːl] *n* remolino ▷ *vt* hacer girar, dar vueltas a ▷ *vi* (*dancers*) girar, dar vueltas; (*leaves, dust, water etc*) arremolinarse
whirlpool ['wəːlpuːl] *n* remolino

whirlwind ['wəːlwɪnd] *n* torbellino
whirr [wəːr] *vi* zumbar
whisk [wɪsk] *n* (*Brit Culin*) batidor *m* ▷ *vt* (*Brit Culin*) batir; **to ~ sb away** *or* **off** llevarse volando a algn
whiskers [wɪskəz] *npl* (*of animal*) bigotes *mpl*; (*of man*) patillas *fpl*
whisky, whiskey (*US, Ireland*) ['wɪskɪ] *n* whisky *m*
whisper ['wɪspər] *n* cuchicheo; (*rumour*) rumor *m*; (*fig*) susurro, murmullo ▷ *vi* cuchichear, hablar bajo; (*fig*) susurrar ▷ *vt* susurrar; **to ~ sth to sb** decirle algo al oído a algn
whistle ['wɪsl] *n* (*sound*) silbido; (*object*) silbato ▷ *vi* silbar; **to ~ a tune** silbar una melodía
white [waɪt] *adj* blanco; (*pale*) pálido ▷ *n* blanco; (*of egg*) clara; **to turn** *or* **go ~** (*person*) palidecer, ponerse blanco; (*hair*) encanecer; **the ~s** (*washing*) la ropa blanca; **tennis ~s** ropa *f* de tenis
whiteboard ['waɪtbɔːd] *n* pizarra blanca; **interactive ~** pizarra interactiva
white coffee *n* (*Brit*) café *m* con leche
white-collar worker ['waɪtkɔlə-] *n* oficinista *m/f*
white elephant *n* (*fig*) maula
White House *n* (*US*) Casa Blanca
white lie *n* mentirijilla
white paper *n* (*Pol*) libro blanco
whitewash ['waɪtwɔʃ] *n* (*paint*) cal *f*, jalbegue *m* ▷ *vt* encalar, blanquear; (*fig*) encubrir
whiting ['waɪtɪŋ] *n pl inv* (*fish*) pescadilla
Whitsun ['wɪtsn] *n* (*Brit*) Pentecostés *m*
whittle ['wɪtl] *vt*: **to ~ away**: **whittle down** ir reduciendo
whizz [wɪz] *vi*: **to ~ past** *or* **by** pasar a toda velocidad
whizz kid *n* (*inf*) prodigio(-a)
WHO *n abbr* (= *World Health Organization*) OMS *f*

O **KEYWORD**

who [huː] *pron* **1** (*interrogative*) quién; **who is it?, who's there?** ¿quién es?; **who are you looking for?** ¿a quién buscas?; **I told her who I was** le dije quién era yo
2 (*relative*) que; **the man/woman who spoke to me** el hombre/la mujer que habló conmigo; **those who can swim** los que saben *or* sepan nadar

whoever [huːˈɛvər] *pron*: **~ finds it** cualquiera *or* quienquiera que lo encuentre; **ask ~ you like** pregunta a quien quieras; **~ he marries** se case con quien se case
whole [həul] *adj* (*complete*) todo, entero; (*not broken*) intacto ▷ *n* (*total*) total *m*; (*sum*) conjunto; **~ villages were destroyed** pueblos enteros fueron destruídos; **the ~ of**

the town toda la ciudad, la ciudad entera;
on the ~, as a ~ en general
wholefood(s) [həulfu:d(z)] *n(pl)* alimento(s)
m(pl) integral(es)
wholehearted [həul'hɑ:tɪd] *adj (support,
approval)* total; *(sympathy)* todo
wholeheartedly [həul'hɑ:tɪdlɪ] *adv* con
entusiasmo
wholemeal ['həulmi:l] *adj (Brit: flour, bread)*
integral
wholesale ['həulseɪl] *n* venta al por mayor
▷ *adj* al por mayor; *(destruction)* sistemático
wholesaler ['həulseɪlər] *n* mayorista *m/f*
wholesome ['həulsəm] *adj* sano
wholewheat ['həulwi:t] *adj* = **wholemeal**
wholly ['həulɪ] *adv* totalmente,
enteramente

KEYWORD

whom [hu:m] *pron* **1** *(interrogative)*: **whom did
you see?** ¿a quién viste?; **to whom did you
give it?** ¿a quién se lo diste?; **tell me from
whom you received it** dígame de quién lo
recibiste
2 *(relative)* que; **to whom** a quien(es); **of
whom** de quien(es), del/de la que; **the man
whom I saw** el hombre qui vi; **the man to
whom I wrote** el hombre a quien escribí;
the lady about whom I was talking la
señora de (la) que hablaba; **the lady with
whom I was talking** la señora con quien *or*
(la) que hablaba

whooping cough ['hu:pɪŋ-] *n* tos *f* ferina
whoops [wu:ps] *excl (also:* **~-a-daisy!**) ¡huy!
whore [hɔ:ʳ] *n (inf: pej)* puta

KEYWORD

whose [hu:z] *adj* **1** *(possessive: interrogative)* de
quién; **whose book is this?, whose is this
book?** ¿de quién es este libro?; **whose pencil
have you taken?** ¿de quién es el lápiz que
has cogido?; **whose daughter are you?** ¿de
quién eres hija?
2 *(possessive: relative)* cuyo(-a) *m(f)*, cuyos(-as)
m(f)pl; **the man whose son they rescued** el
hombre cuyo hijo rescataron; **the girl
whose sister he was speaking to** la chica
con cuya hermana estaba hablando; **those
whose passports I have** aquellas personas
cuyos pasaportes tengo; **the woman whose
car was stolen** la mujer a quien le robaron
el coche
▷ *pron* de quién; **whose is this?** ¿de quién es
esto?; **I know whose it is** sé de quién es

KEYWORD

why [waɪ] *adv* por qué; **why not?** ¿por qué
no?; **why not do it now?** ¿por qué no lo

haces (*or* hacemos ahora?
▷ *conj*: **I wonder why he said that** me
pregunto por qué dijo eso; **that's not why
I'm here** no es por eso (por lo) que estoy aquí;
the reason why la razón por la que
▷ *excl (expressing surprise, shock, annoyance)*
¡hombre!, ¡vaya!; *(explaining)*: **why, it's you!**
¡hombre, eres tú!; **why, that's impossible**
¡pero si eso es imposible!

whyever [waɪ'ɛvəʳ] *adv* por qué
wicked ['wɪkɪd] *adj* malvado, cruel
wicket ['wɪkɪt] *n (Cricket)* palos *mpl*
wide [waɪd] *adj* ancho; *(area, knowledge)* vasto,
grande; *(choice)* amplio ▷ *adv*: **to open ~**
abrir de par en par; **to shoot ~** errar el tiro;
it is three metres ~ tiene tres metros de
ancho
wide-angle lens ['waɪdæŋgl-] *n* (objetivo)
gran angular *m*
widely ['waɪdlɪ] *adv (differing)* muy; **it is ~
believed that ...** existe la creencia
generalizada de que ...; **to be ~ read** *(author)*
ser muy leído; *(reader)* haber leído mucho
widen ['waɪdn] *vt* ensanchar; *(experience)*
ampliar ▷ *vi* ensancharse
wide open *adj* abierto de par en par
widespread ['waɪdsprɛd] *adj (belief etc)*
extendido, general
widow ['wɪdəu] *n* viuda
widowed ['wɪdəud] *adj* viudo
widower ['wɪdəuəʳ] *n* viudo
width [wɪdθ] *n* anchura; *(of cloth)* ancho;
it's seven metres in ~ tiene siete metros
de ancho
wield [wi:ld] *vt (sword)* blandir; *(power)* ejercer
wife *(pl* **wives)** [waɪf, waɪvz] *n* mujer *f*,
esposa
Wi-Fi ['waɪfaɪ] *n abbr (= wireless fidelity)* wi-fi *m*
▷ *adj (hot spot, network etc)* wi-fi
wig [wɪg] *n* peluca
wiggle ['wɪgl] *vt* menear ▷ *vi* menearse
wiki ['wɪki:] *n (Comput)* wiki *f*
wild [waɪld] *adj (animal)* salvaje; *(plant)*
silvestre; *(rough)* furioso, violento; *(idea)*
descabellado; *(rough: sea)* bravo; *(: land)*
agreste; *(: weather)* muy revuelto; *(inf: angry)*
furioso ▷ *n*: **the ~** la naturaleza; **wilds** *npl*
regiones *fpl* salvajes, tierras *fpl* vírgenes;
to be ~ about *(enthusiastic)* estar *or* andar loco
por; **in its ~ state** en estado salvaje
wild card *n (Comput)* comodín *m*
wildcat ['waɪldkæt] *n* gato montés
wilderness ['wɪldənɪs] *n* desierto; *(jungle)*
jungla
wildfire ['waɪldfaɪəʳ] *n*: **to spread like ~**
correr como un reguero de pólvora
wild-goose chase [waɪld'gu:s-] *n (fig)*
búsqueda inútil
wildlife ['waɪldlaɪf] *n* fauna
wildly ['waɪldlɪ] *adv (roughly)* violentamente;
(foolishly) locamente; *(rashly)*

W

descabelladamente; (*lash out*) a diestro y siniestro; (*guess*) a lo loco; (*happy*) a más no poder

wilful, willful (US) ['wɪlful] *adj* (*action*) deliberado; (*obstinate*) testarudo

 KEYWORD

will [wɪl] *aux vb* **1** (*forming future tense*): **I will finish it tomorrow** lo terminaré *or* voy a terminar mañana; **I will have finished it by tomorrow** lo habré terminado para mañana; **will you do it? — yes I will/no I won't** ¿lo harás? — sí/no; **you won't lose it, will you?** no lo vayas a perder *or* no lo perderás ¿verdad?
2 (*in conjectures, predictions*): **he will** *or* **he'll be there by now** ya habrá llegado, ya debe (de) haber llegado; **that will be the postman** será el cartero, debe ser el cartero
3 (*in commands, requests, offers*): **will you be quiet!** ¿quieres callarte?; **will you help me?** ¿quieres ayudarme?; **will you have a cup of tea?** ¿te apetece un té?; **I won't put up with it!** ¡no lo soporto!
4 (*habits, persistence*): **the car won't start** el coche no arranca; **accidents will happen** son cosas que pasan
▷ *vt* (*pt, pp* **willed**): **to will sb to do sth** desear que algn haga algo; **he willed himself to go on** con gran fuerza de voluntad, continuó
▷ *n* **1** (*desire*) voluntad *f*; **against sb's will** contra la voluntad de algn; **he did it of his own free will** lo hizo por su propia voluntad
2 (*Law*) testamento; **to make a** *or* **one's will** hacer su testamento

willing ['wɪlɪŋ] *adj* (*with goodwill*) de buena voluntad; (*enthusiastic*) entusiasta; **he's ~ to do it** está dispuesto a hacerlo; **to show ~** mostrarse dispuesto
willingly ['wɪlɪŋlɪ] *adv* con mucho gusto
willingness ['wɪlɪŋnɪs] *n* buena voluntad
willow ['wɪləʊ] *n* sauce *m*
willpower ['wɪlpaʊəʳ] *n* fuerza de voluntad
willy-nilly ['wɪlɪ'nɪlɪ] *adv* quiérase o no
wilt [wɪlt] *vi* marchitarse
wily ['waɪlɪ] *adj* astuto
wimp [wɪmp] *n* (*inf*) enclenque *m/f*; (*character*) calzonazos *m inv*
win [wɪn] (*pt, pp* **won**) *n* (*in sports etc*) victoria, triunfo ▷ *vt* ganar; (*obtain: contract etc*) conseguir, lograr ▷ *vi* ganar; **win over, win round** (*Brit*) *vt* convencer a
wince [wɪns] *vi* encogerse
winch [wɪntʃ] *n* torno
wind¹ [wɪnd, *n* viento; (*Med*) gases *mpl*; (*breath*) aliento *vt* (*take breath away from*) dejar sin aliento a; **into** *or* **against the ~** contra el viento; **to get ~ of sth** enterarse de algo; **to break ~** ventosear

wind² [waɪnd] (*pt, pp* **wound**) *vt* enrollar; (*wrap*) envolver; (*clock, toy*) dar cuerda a ▷ *vi* (*road, river*) serpentear; **wind down** *vt* (*car window*) bajar; (*fig: production, business*) disminuir; **wind up** *vt* (*clock*) dar cuerda a; (*debate*) concluir, terminar
windfall ['wɪndfɔ:l] *n* golpe *m* de suerte
wind farm *n* parque *m* eólico
winding ['waɪndɪŋ] *adj* (*road*) tortuoso
wind instrument *n* (*Mus*) instrumento de viento
windmill ['wɪndmɪl] *n* molino de viento
window ['wɪndəʊ] *n* ventana; (*in car, train*) ventana; (*in shop etc*) escaparate *m*, vitrina (*LAm*), vidriera (*LAm*); (*Comput*) ventana
window box *n* jardinera (de ventana)
window cleaner *n* (*person*) limpiacristales *m inv*
window ledge *n* alféizar *m*, repisa
window pane *n* cristal *m*
window seat *n* asiento junto a la ventana
window-shopping [wɪndəʊ'ʃɒpɪŋ] *n*: **to go ~** ir a ver *or* mirar escaparates
windowsill ['wɪndəʊsɪl] *n* alféizar *m*, repisa
windpipe ['wɪndpaɪp] *n* tráquea
wind power *n* energía eólica
windscreen ['wɪndskri:n], **windshield** (US) ['wɪndʃi:ld] *n* parabrisas *m inv*
windscreen washer, windshield washer (US) *n* lavaparabrisas *m inv*
windscreen wiper, windshield wiper (US) *n* limpiaparabrisas *m inv*
windsurfing ['wɪndsə:fɪŋ] *n* windsurf *m*
windswept ['wɪndswɛpt] *adj* azotado por el viento
windy ['wɪndɪ] *adj* de mucho viento; **it's ~** hace viento
wine [waɪn] *n* vino ▷ *vt*: **to ~ and dine sb** agasajar *or* festejar a algn
wine bar *n* bar especializado en vinos
wine cellar *n* bodega
wine glass *n* copa (de *or* para vino)
wine list *n* lista de vinos
wine tasting *n* degustación *f* de vinos
wine waiter *n* escanciador *m*
wing [wɪŋ] *n* ala; (*Brit Aut*) aleta; **wings** *npl* (*Theat*) bastidores *mpl*
winger ['wɪŋəʳ] *n* (*Sport*) extremo
wing mirror *n* (*espejo*) retrovisor *m*
wink [wɪŋk] *n* guiño; (*blink*) pestañeo ▷ *vi* guiñar; (*blink*) pestañear; (*light etc*) parpadear
winner ['wɪnəʳ] *n* ganador(a) *m(f)*
winning ['wɪnɪŋ] *adj* (*team*) ganador(a); (*goal*) decisivo; (*charming*) encantador(a)
winnings ['wɪnɪŋz] *npl* ganancias *fpl*
winter ['wɪntəʳ] *n* invierno ▷ *vi* invernar
winter sports *npl* deportes *mpl* de invierno
wintertime ['wɪntətaɪm] *n* invierno
wintry ['wɪntrɪ] *adj* invernal
wipe [waɪp] *n*: **to give sth a ~** pasar un trapo sobre algo ▷ *vt* limpiar; (*tape*) borrar; **to ~ one's nose** limpiarse la nariz; **wipe off** *vt*

limpiar con un trapo; **wipe out** vt (debt) liquidar; (memory) borrar; (destroy) destruir; **wipe up** vt limpiar

wire ['waɪə'] n alambre m; (Elec) cable m (eléctrico); (Tel) telegrama m ▷ vt (house) poner la instalación eléctrica en; (also: **~ up**) conectar

wireless ['waɪəlɪs] n (Brit) radio f ▷ adj inalámbrico

wire service n (US) agencia de noticias

wiring ['waɪərɪŋ] n instalación f eléctrica

wiry ['waɪərɪ] adj enjuto y fuerte

wisdom ['wɪzdəm] n sabiduría, saber m; (good sense) cordura

wisdom tooth n muela del juicio

wise [waɪz] adj sabio; (sensible) juicioso; **I'm none the ~r** sigo sin entender; **wise up** vi (inf): **to ~ up (to sth)** enterarse (de algo)

wisecrack ['waɪzkræk] n broma

wish [wɪʃ] n (desire) deseo ▷ vt desear; (want) querer; **best ~es** (on birthday etc) felicidades fpl; **with best ~es** (in letter) saludos mpl, recuerdos mpl; **he ~ed me well** me deseó mucha suerte; **to ~ sth on sb** imponer algo a algn; **to ~ to do/sb to do sth** querer hacer/ que algn haga algo; **to ~ for** desear

wishbone ['wɪʃbəun] n espoleta (de la que tiran dos personas quien se quede con el hueso más largo pide un deseo)

wishful ['wɪʃful] adj: **it's ~ thinking** eso es hacerse ilusiones

wistful ['wɪstful] adj pensativo; (nostalgic) nostálgico

wit [wɪt] n (wittiness) ingenio, gracia; (intelligence: also: **~s**) inteligencia; (person) chistoso(-a); **to have** or **keep one's ~s about one** no perder la cabeza

witch [wɪtʃ] n bruja

witchcraft ['wɪtʃkrɑːft] n brujería

○ KEYWORD

with [wɪð, wɪθ] prep **1** (accompanying, in the company of) con (con +mí, ti, sí = conmigo, contigo, consigo); **I was with him** estaba con él; **we stayed with friends** nos quedamos en casa de unos amigos

2 (descriptive, indicating manner etc) con; de; **a room with a view** una habitación con vistas; **the man with the grey hat/blue eyes** el hombre del sombrero gris/de los ojos azules; **red with anger** rojo de ira; **to shake with fear** temblar de miedo; **to fill sth with water** llenar algo de agua

3: **I'm with you/I'm not with you** (understand) ya te entiendo/no te entiendo; **to be with it** (inf: person: up-to-date) estar al tanto; (: alert) ser despabilado; **I'm not really with it today** no doy pie con bola hoy

withdraw [wɪθ'drɔː] vt (irreg: like **draw**) retirar ▷ vi retirarse; (go back on promise)

retractarse; **to ~ money (from the bank)** retirar fondos (del banco); **to ~ into o.s.** ensimismarse

withdrawal [wɪθ'drɔːəl] n retirada; (of money) reintegro

withdrawal symptoms npl síndrome m de abstinencia

withdrawn [wɪθ'drɔːn] adj (person) reservado, introvertido ▷ pp of **withdraw**

withdrew [wɪθ'druː] pt of **withdraw**

wither ['wɪðə'] vi marchitarse

withhold [wɪθ'həuld] vt (irreg: like **hold**) (money) retener; (decision) aplazar; (permission) negar; (information) ocultar

within [wɪð'ɪn] prep dentro de ▷ adv dentro; **~ reach** al alcance de la mano; **~ sight of** a la vista de; **~ the week** antes de que acabe la semana; **to be ~ the law** atenerse a la legalidad; **~ an hour from now** dentro de una hora; **~ a mile (of)** a menos de una milla (de)

without [wɪð'aut] prep sin; **to go** or **do ~ sth** prescindir de algo; **~ anybody knowing** sin saberlo nadie

withstand [wɪθ'stænd] vt (irreg: like **stand**) resistir a

witness ['wɪtnɪs] n (person) testigo m/f; (evidence) testimonio ▷ vt (event) presenciar, ser testigo de; (document) atestiguar la veracidad de; **~ for the prosecution/ defence** testigo de cargo/descargo; **to ~ to (having seen) sth** dar testimonio de (haber visto) algo; **to bear ~ to** (fig) ser testimonio de

witness box, witness stand (US) n tribuna de los testigos

witticism ['wɪtɪsɪzm] n dicho ingenioso

witty ['wɪtɪ] adj ingenioso

wives [waɪvz] npl of **wife**

wizard ['wɪzəd] n hechicero

wk abbr = **week**

wobble ['wɔbl] vi tambalearse

woe [wəu] n desgracia

woeful ['wəuful] adj (bad) lamentable; (sad) apesadumbrado

wok [wɔk] n wok m

woke [wəuk] pt of **wake**

woken ['wəukn] pp of **wake**

wolf (pl **wolves**) [wulf, wulvz] n lobo

woman (pl **women**) ['wumən, 'wɪmɪn] n mujer f; **young ~** (mujer f) joven f; **women's page** (Press) sección f de la mujer

womanly ['wumənlɪ] adj femenino

womb [wuːm] n (Anat) matriz f, útero

women ['wɪmɪn] npl of **woman**

won [wʌn] pt, pp of **win**

wonder ['wʌndə'] n maravilla, prodigio; (feeling) asombro ▷ vi: **to ~ whether** preguntarse si; **to ~ at** asombrarse de; **to ~ about** pensar sobre or en; **it's no ~ that** no es de extrañar que

wonderful ['wʌndəful] adj maravilloso

wonky ['wɔŋkɪ] *adj* (*Brit inf: unsteady*) poco seguro, cojo; (: *broken down*) estropeado

wont [wɔnt] *n*: **as is his/her ~** como tiene por costumbre

won't [wəunt] = **will not**

woo [wu:] *vt* (*woman*) cortejar

wood [wud] *n* (*timber*) madera; (*forest*) bosque *m* ▷ *cpd* de madera

wood carving *n* tallado en madera

wooded ['wudɪd] *adj* arbolado

wooden ['wudn] *adj* de madera; (*fig*) inexpresivo

woodpecker ['wudpɛkəʳ] *n* pájaro carpintero

woodwind ['wudwɪnd] *n* (*Mus*) instrumentos *mpl* de viento de madera

woodwork ['wudwə:k] *n* carpintería

woodworm ['wudwə:m] *n* carcoma

wool [wul] *n* lana; **knitting ~** lana (de hacer punto); **to pull the ~ over sb's eyes** (*fig*) dar a algn gato por liebre

woollen, woolen (*US*) ['wulən] *adj* de lana ▷ *n*: **~s** géneros *mpl* de lana

woolly, wooly (*US*) ['wulɪ] *adj* de lana; (*fig: ideas*) confuso

woozy ['wu:zɪ] *adj* (*inf*) mareado

word [wə:d] *n* palabra; (*news*) noticia; (*promise*) palabra (de honor) ▷ *vt* redactar; **~ for ~** palabra por palabra; **what's the ~ for "pen" in Spanish?** ¿cómo se dice "pen" en español?; **to put sth into ~s** expresar algo en palabras; **to have a ~ with sb** hablar (dos palabras) con algn; **in other ~s** en otras palabras; **to break/keep one's ~** faltar a la palabra/cumplir la promesa; **to leave ~ (with/for sb) that ...** dejar recado (con/para algn) de que ...; **to have ~s with sb** (*quarrel with*) discutir *or* reñir con algn

wording ['wə:dɪŋ] *n* redacción *f*

word-of-mouth [wə:dəv'mauθ] *n*: **by** *or* **through ~** de palabra, por el boca a boca

word processing *n* procesamiento *or* tratamiento de textos

word processor [-'prəusɛsəʳ] *n* procesador *m* de textos

wore [wɔ:ʳ] *pt* of **wear**

work [wə:k] *n* trabajo; (*job*) empleo, trabajo; (*Art, Lit*) obra ▷ *vi* trabajar; (*mechanism*) funcionar, marchar; (*medicine*) ser eficaz, surtir efecto ▷ *vt* (*shape*) trabajar; (*stone etc*) tallar; (*mine etc*) explotar; (*machine*) manejar, hacer funcionar; (*cause*) producir; **to go to ~** ir a trabajar *or* al trabajo; **to be at ~ (on sth)** estar trabajando (en algo); **to set to ~, start ~** ponerse a trabajar; **to be out of ~** estar parado, no tener trabajo; **his life's ~** el trabajo de su vida; **to ~ hard** trabajar mucho *or* duro; **to ~ to rule** (*Industry*) hacer una huelga de celo; **to ~ loose** (*part*) desprenderse; (*knot*) aflojarse; *see also* **works**; **work off** *vt*: **to ~ off one's feelings** desahogarse; **work on** *vt fus* trabajar en,

dedicarse a; (*principle*) basarse en; **he's ~ing on the car** está reparando el coche; **work out** *vi* (*plans etc*) salir bien, funcionar; (*Sport*) hacer ejercicios ▷ *vt* (*problem*) resolver; (*plan*) elaborar; **it ~s out at £100** asciende a 100 libras; **work up** *vt*: **he ~ed his way up in the company** ascendió en la compañía mediante sus propios esfuerzos

workable ['wə:kəbl] *adj* (*solution*) práctico, factible

workaholic [wə:kə'hɔlɪk] *n* adicto(-a) al trabajo

worked up [wə:kt-] *adj*: **to get ~** excitarse

worker ['wə:kəʳ] *n* trabajador(a) *m(f)*, obrero(-a) *m(f)*; **office ~** oficinista *m/f*

work experience *n*: **I'm going to do my ~ in a factory** voy a hacer las prácticas en una fábrica

work force *n* mano *f* de obra

working class *n* clase *f* obrera ▷ *adj*: **working-class** obrero

working order *n*: **in ~** en funcionamiento

working week *n* semana laboral

workload ['wə:kləud] *n* cantidad *f* de trabajo

workman ['wə:kmən] *n* obrero

workmanship ['wə:kmənʃɪp] *n* (*art*) hechura; (*skill*) habilidad *f*

workmate ['wə:kmeɪt] *n* compañero(-a) de trabajo

work of art *n* obra de arte

workout ['wə:kaut] *n* (*Sport*) sesión *f* de ejercicios

work permit *n* permiso de trabajo

workplace ['wə:kpleɪs] *n* lugar *m* de trabajo

works [wə:ks] *nsg* (*Brit: factory*) fábrica ▷ *npl* (*of clock, machine*) mecanismo; **road ~** obras *fpl*

worksheet ['wə:kʃi:t] *n* (*Comput*) hoja de trabajo; (*Scol*) hoja de ejercicios

workshop ['wə:kʃɔp] *n* taller *m*

work station *n* estación *f* de trabajo

work surface *n* encimera

worktop ['wə:ktɔp] *n* encimera

work-to-rule ['wə:ktə'ru:l] *n* (*Brit*) huelga de celo

world [wə:ld] *n* mundo ▷ *cpd* (*champion*) del mundo; (*power, war*) mundial; **all over the ~** por todo el mundo, en el mundo entero; **the business ~** el mundo de los negocios; **what in the ~ is he doing?** ¿qué diablos está haciendo?; **to think the ~ of sb** (*fig*) tener un concepto muy alto de algn; **to do sb a ~ of good** sentar muy bien a algn; **W~ War One/Two** la primera/segunda Guerra Mundial

World Cup *n* (*Football*): **the ~** el Mundial, los Mundiales

worldly ['wə:ldlɪ] *adj* mundano

World Series *n*: **the ~** (*US Baseball*) el campeonato nacional de béisbol de EEUU

World Service *n see* **BBC**

world-wide ['wə:ldwaɪd] *adj* mundial, universal

World-Wide Web *n*: **the ~** el World Wide Web

worm [wəːm] *n* gusano; *(earthworm)* lombriz *f*
worn [wɔːn] *pp of* **wear** ▷ *adj* usado
worn-out ['wɔːnaut] *adj (object)* gastado; *(person)* rendido, agotado
worried ['wʌrɪd] *adj* preocupado; **to be ~ about sth** estar preocupado por algo
worry ['wʌrɪ] *n* preocupación *f* ▷ *vt* preocupar, inquietar ▷ *vi* preocuparse; **to ~ about** *or* **over sth/sb** preocuparse por algo/algn
worrying ['wʌrɪɪŋ] *adj* inquietante
worse [wəːs] *adj, adv* peor ▷ *n* el peor, lo peor; **a change for the ~** un empeoramiento; **so much the ~ for you** tanto peor para ti; **he is none the ~ for it** se ha quedado tan fresco *or* tan tranquilo; **to get ~, to grow ~** empeorar
worsen ['wəːsn] *vt, vi* empeorar
worse off *adj (financially)*: **to be ~** tener menos dinero; *(fig)*: **you'll be ~ this way** de esta forma estarás peor que antes
worship ['wəːʃɪp] *n (organized worship)* culto; *(act)* adoración *f* ▷ *vt* adorar; **Your W~** (*Brit: to mayor*) su Ilustrísima; *(: to judge)* su señoría
worst [wəːst] *adj* (el/la) peor ▷ *adv* peor ▷ *n* lo peor; **at ~** en el peor de los casos; **to come off ~** llevar la peor parte; **if the ~ comes to the ~** en el peor de los casos
worth [wəːθ] *n* valor *m* ▷ *adj*: **to be ~** valer; **how much is it ~?** ¿cuánto vale?; **it's ~ it** vale *or* merece la pena; **to be ~ one's while (to do)** merecer la pena (hacer); **it's not ~ the trouble** no vale *or* merece la pena
worthless ['wəːθlɪs] *adj* sin valor; *(useless)* inútil
worthwhile ['wəːθwaɪl] *adj (activity)* que merece la pena; *(cause)* loable
worthy ['wəːðɪ] *adj (person)* respetable; *(motive)* honesto; **~ of** digno de

O **KEYWORD**

would [wud] *aux vb* **1** *(conditional tense)*: **if you asked him he would do it** si se lo pidieras, lo haría; **if you had asked him he would have done it** si se lo hubieras pedido, lo habría *or* hubiera hecho
2 *(in offers, invitations, requests)*: **would you like a biscuit?** ¿quieres una galleta?; *(formal)* ¿querría una galleta?; **would you ask him to come in?** ¿quiere hacerle pasar?; **would you open the window please?** ¿quiere *or* podría abrir la ventana, por favor?
3 *(in indirect speech)*: **I said I would do it** dije que lo haría
4 *(emphatic)*: **it WOULD have to snow today!** ¡tenía que nevar precisamente hoy!
5 *(insistence)*: **she wouldn't behave** no quiso comportarse bien
6 *(conjecture)*: **it would have been midnight** sería medianoche; **it would seem so** parece ser que sí
7 *(indicating habit)*: **he would go there on Mondays** iba allí los lunes

would-be ['wudbiː] *adj (pej)* presunto
wouldn't ['wudnt] = **would not**
wound¹ [wuːnd] *n* herida ▷ *vt* herir
wound² [waund] *pt, pp of* **wind²**
wove [wəuv] *pt of* **weave**
woven ['wəuvən] *pp of* **weave**
WP *n abbr* = **word processing; word processor** ▷ *abbr* (Brit inf: = **weather permitting**) si lo permite el tiempo
WPC *n abbr* (Brit) = **woman police constable**
wpm *abbr* (= *words per minute*) p.p.m.
wrap [ræp] *n (stole)* chal *m* ▷ *vt* (also: **~ up**) envolver; *(gift)* envolver, abrigar ▷ *vi (dress warmly)* abrigarse; **under ~s** *(fig: plan, scheme)* oculto, tapado
wrapper ['ræpə'] *n* (Brit: *of book*) sobrecubierta; *(on chocolate etc)* envoltura
wrapping paper ['ræpɪŋ-] *n* papel *m* de envolver
wrath [rɔθ] *n* cólera
wreak [riːk] *vt (destruction)* causar; **to ~ havoc (on)** hacer *or* causar estragos (en); **to ~ vengeance (on)** vengarse (en)
wreath [riːθ] *(pl* **wreaths** [riːθ, riːðz] *n (also:* **funeral ~)** corona; *(of flowers)* guirnalda
wreck [rɛk] *n (ship: destruction)* naufragio; *(: remains)* restos *mpl* del barco; *(pej: person)* ruina ▷ *vt* destrozar; *(chances)* arruinar; **to be ~ed** *(Naut)* naufragar
wreckage ['rɛkɪdʒ] *n (remains)* restos *mpl*; *(of building)* escombros *mpl*
wren [rɛn] *n (Zool)* reyezuelo
wrench [rɛntʃ] *n (Tech)* llave *f* inglesa; *(tug)* tirón *m* ▷ *vt* arrancar; **to ~ sth from sb** arrebatar algo violentamente a algn
wrestle ['rɛsl] *vi*: **to ~ (with sb)** luchar (con *or* contra algn)
wrestler ['rɛslə'] *n* luchador(a) *m(f)* (de lucha libre)
wrestling ['rɛslɪŋ] *n* lucha libre
wretched ['rɛtʃɪd] *adj* miserable
wriggle ['rɪgl] *vi* serpentear; *(also:* **~ about)** menearse, retorcerse
wring *(pt, pp* **wrung)** [rɪŋ, rʌŋ] *vt* torcer, retorcer; *(wet clothes)* escurrir; *(fig)*: **to ~ sth out of sb** sacar algo por la fuerza a algn
wrinkle ['rɪŋkl] *n* arruga ▷ *vt* arrugar ▷ *vi* arrugarse
wrist [rɪst] *n* muñeca
wrist watch *n* reloj *m* de pulsera
writ [rɪt] *n* mandato judicial; **to serve a ~ on sb** notificar un mandato judicial a algn
writable ['raɪtəbl] *adj* (CD, DVD) escribible
write *(pt* **wrote,** *pp* **written)** [raɪt, rəut, 'rɪtn] *vt* escribir; *(cheque)* extender ▷ *vi* escribir; **to ~ sb a letter** escribir una carta a algn; **write away** *vi*: **to ~ away for** *(information, goods)* pedir por escrito *or* carta; **write down** *vt* escribir; *(note)* apuntar; **write off** *vt (debt)* borrar (como incobrable); *(fig)* desechar por inútil; *(smash up: car)* destrozar; **write out** *vt* escribir; **write up** *vt* redactar

W

write-off ['raɪtɔf] n siniestro total; **the car is a ~** el coche es pura chatarra
writer ['raɪtəʳ] n escritor(a) m(f)
writhe [raɪð] vi retorcerse
writing ['raɪtɪŋ] n escritura; (handwriting) letra; (of author) obras fpl; **in ~** por escrito; **to put sth in ~** poner algo por escrito; **in my own ~** escrito por mí
writing paper n papel m de escribir
written ['rɪtn] pp of **write**
wrong [rɔŋ] adj (wicked) malo; (unfair) injusto; (incorrect) equivocado, incorrecto; (not suitable) inoportuno, inconveniente ▷ adv mal ▷ n mal m; (injustice) injusticia ▷ vt ser injusto con; (hurt) agraviar; **to be ~** (answer) estar equivocado; (in doing, saying) equivocarse; **it's ~ to steal, stealing is ~** es mal robar; **you are ~ to do it** haces mal en hacerlo; **you are ~ about that, you've got it ~** en eso estás equivocado; **to be in the ~** no tener razón; (guilty) tener la culpa; **what's ~?** ¿qué pasa?; **what's ~ with the car?** ¿qué le pasa al coche?; **there's nothing ~** no pasa nada; **you have the ~ number** (Tel) se ha equivocado de número; **to go ~** (person) equivocarse; (plan) salir mal; (machine) estropearse
wrongdoer ['rɔŋduəʳ] n malhechor(a) m(f)
wrong-foot [rɔŋ'fut] vt (Sport) hacer perder el equilibrio a; (fig) poner en un aprieto a
wrongful ['rɔŋful] adj injusto; **~ dismissal** (Industry) despido improcedente
wrongly ['rɔŋlɪ] adv (answer, do, count) incorrectamente; (treat) injustamente
wrong number n (Tel): **you've got the ~** se ha equivocado de número
wrote [rəʊt] pt of **write**
wrought [rɔːt] adj: **~ iron** hierro forjado
wrung [rʌŋ] pt, pp of **wring**
WRVS n abbr (Brit: = Women's Royal Voluntary Service) cuerpo de voluntarias al servicio de la comunidad
wry [raɪ] adj irónico
wt. abbr = **weight**
WWW n abbr (= World Wide Web) WWW m or f

X, x [eks] n (letter) X, x f; (Brit Cine: formerly) no apto para menores de 18 años; **X for Xmas** X de Xiquena; **if you earn X dollars a year** si ganas X dólares al año
X-certificate ['ɛksə'tɪfɪkɪt] adj (Brit: film: formerly) no apto para menores de 18 años
Xerox® ['zɪərɔks] n (also: **~ machine**) fotocopiadora; (photocopy) fotocopia ▷ vt fotocopiar
XL abbr = **extra large**
Xmas ['ɛksməs] n abbr = **Christmas**
X-rated ['eks'reɪtɪd] adj (US: film) no apto para menores de 18 años
X-ray [eks'reɪ] n radiografía; **X-rays** npl rayos mpl X ▷ vt radiografiar
xylophone ['zaɪləfəun] n xilófono

Y, y [waɪ] n (letter) Y, y f; **Y for Yellow**, (US) **Y for Yoke** Y de Yegua

yacht [jɔt] n yate m

yachting ['jɔtɪŋ] n (sport) balandrismo

yachtsman ['jɔtsmən] n balandrista m

Yank [jæŋk], **Yankee** ['jæŋkɪ] n (pej) yanqui m/f

yank [jæŋk] vt tirar de, jalar de (LAm) ▷ n tirón m

yap [jæp] vi (dog) aullar

yard [jɑːd] n patio; (US: garden) jardín m; (measure) yarda; **builder's ~** almacén m

yard sale n (US) venta de objetos usados (en el jardín de una casa particular)

yardstick ['jɑːdstɪk] n (fig) criterio, norma

yarn [jɑːn] n hilo; (tale) cuento (chino), historia

yawn [jɔːn] n bostezo ▷ vi bostezar

yawning ['jɔːnɪŋ] adj (gap) muy abierto

yd. abbr (= yard) yda

yeah [jɛə] adv (inf) sí

year [jɪər] n año; (Scol, Univ) curso; **this ~** este año; **~ in, ~ out** año tras año; **a or per ~** al año; **to be eight ~s old** tener ocho años; **she's three ~s old** tiene tres años; **an eight- -~-old child** un niño de ocho años (de edad)

yearly ['jɪəlɪ] adj anual ▷ adv anualmente, cada año; **twice ~** dos veces al año

yearn [jəːn] vi: **to ~ for sth** añorar algo, suspirar por algo

yeast [jiːst] n levadura

yell [jɛl] n grito, alarido ▷ vi gritar

yellow ['jɛləu] adj, n amarillo

Yellow Pages® npl páginas fpl amarillas

yelp [jɛlp] n aullido ▷ vi aullar

yeoman ['jəumən] n: **Y~ of the Guard** alabardero de la Casa Real

yes [jɛs] adv, n sí m; **to say/answer ~** decir/ contestar que sí; **to say ~ (to)** decir que sí (a), conformarse (con)

yesterday ['jɛstədɪ] adv, n ayer m; **~ morning/ evening** ayer por la mañana/tarde; **all day ~** todo el día de ayer; **the day before ~** antes de ayer, anteayer

yet [jɛt] adv todavía ▷ conj sin embargo, a pesar de todo; **~ again** de nuevo; **it is not finished ~** todavía no está acabado; **the best ~** el/la mejor hasta ahora; **as ~** hasta ahora, todavía

yew [juː] n tejo

Y-fronts® ['waɪfrʌnts] npl (Brit) calzoncillos mpl, eslip msg tradicional

Yiddish ['jɪdɪʃ] n yiddish m

yield [jiːld] n producción f; (Agr) cosecha; (Comm) rendimiento ▷ vt producir, dar; (profit) rendir ▷ vi rendirse, ceder; (US Aut) ceder el paso; **a ~ of 5%** un rédito del 5 por ciento

YMCA n abbr (= Young Men's Christian Association) Asociación f de Jóvenes Cristianos

yob ['jɔb], **yobbo** ['jɔbbəu] n (Brit inf) gamberro

yoga ['jəugə] n yoga m

yoghurt, yogurt ['jəugət] n yogur m

yoke [jəuk] n (of oxen) yunta; (on shoulders) balancín m; (fig) yugo ▷ vt (also: **~ together**: oxen) uncir

yolk [jəuk] n yema (de huevo)

yonder ['jɔndər] adv allá (a lo lejos)

yonks [jɔŋks] npl (inf): **I haven't seen him for ~** hace siglos que no lo veo

◯ KEYWORD

you [juː] pron **1** (subject: familiar: singular) tú; (: plural) vosotros(-as) (Sp), ustedes (LAm); (polite) usted, ustedes pl; **you are very kind** eres/es etc muy amable; **you French enjoy your food** a vosotros (or ustedes) los franceses os (or les) gusta la comida; **you and I will go** iremos tú y yo

2 (object: direct: familiar: singular) te; (: plural) os (Sp), les (LAm); (polite: singular masc) lo or le; (: plural masc) los or les; (singular fem) la; (plural fem) las; **I know you** te/le etc conozco

3 (object: indirect: familiar: singular) te; (: plural) os (Sp), les (LAm); (polite) le, les pl; **I gave the letter to you yesterday** te/os etc di la carta ayer

4 (stressed): **I told YOU to do it** te dije a ti que lo hicieras, es a ti a quien dije que lo hicieras; see also **3, 5**

5 (after prep: NB: con +ti = contigo: familiar: singular) ti; (: plural) vosotros(-as) (Sp), ustedes (LAm); (polite) usted, ustedes pl; **it's for you** es para ti/vosotros etc

y

6 (*comparisons: familiar: singular*) tú; (: *plural*) vosotros(-as) (*Sp*), ustedes (*LAm*); (*polite*) usted, ustedes *pl*; **she's younger than you** es más joven que tú/vosotros *etc*
7 (*impersonal: one*): **fresh air does you good** el aire puro (te) hace bien; **you never know** nunca se sabe; **you can't do that!** ¡eso no se hace!

you'd [ju:d] = **you had; you would**
you'll [ju:l] = **you will; you shall**
young [jʌŋ] *adj* joven ▷ *npl* (*of animal*) cría; (*people*): **the ~** los jóvenes, la juventud; **a ~ man/lady** un(a) joven; **my ~er brother** mi hermano menor *or* pequeño; **the ~er generation** la nueva generación
youngster ['jʌŋstə^r] *n* joven *m/f*
your [jɔː^r] *adj* tu, vuestro *pl*; (*formal*) su; **~ house** tu *etc* casa; *see also* **my**
you're [juə^r] = **you are**
yours [jɔːz] *pron* tuyo, vuestro *pl*; (*formal*) suyo; **a friend of ~** un amigo tuyo *etc*; *see also* **faithfully; mine; sincerely**
yourself [jɔːˈsɛlf] *pron* (*reflexive*) tú mismo; (*complement*) te; (*after prep*) ti (mismo); (*formal*) usted mismo; (: *complement*) se; (: *after prep*) sí (mismo); **you ~ told me** me lo dijiste tú mismo; **(all) by ~** sin ayuda de nadie, solo; *see also* **oneself**
yourselves [jɔːˈsɛlvz] *pron pl* vosotros mismos; (*after prep*) vosotros (mismos); (*formal*) ustedes (mismos); (: *complement*) se; (: *after prep*) sí mismos
youth [ju:θ] *n* juventud *f*; (*young man*) (*pl* **youths**) [ju:ðz] joven *m*; **in my ~** en mi juventud
youth club *n* club *m* juvenil
youthful ['ju:θful] *adj* juvenil
youth hostel *n* albergue *m* juvenil
you've [ju:v] = **you have**
yr *abbr* (= *year*) a
Yugoslav ['ju:gəuslɑːv] *adj, n* yugoslavo(-a) *m(f)*
Yugoslavia [ju:gəuˈslɑːvɪə] *n* Yugoslavia
yuppie ['jʌpɪ] (*inf*) *adj, n* yuppie *m/f*
YWCA *n abbr* (= *Young Women's Christian Association*) Asociación *f* de Jóvenes Cristianas

Z, z [zɛd, (*US*) zi:] *n* (*letter*) Z, z *f*; **Z for Zebra** Z de Zaragoza
zany ['zeɪnɪ] *adj* estrafalario
zap [zæp] *vt* (*Comput*) borrar
zeal [zi:l] *n* celo, entusiasmo
zebra ['zi:brə] *n* cebra
zebra crossing *n* (*Brit*) paso de peatones
zero ['zɪərəu] *n* cero; **5 degrees below ~** 5 grados bajo cero
zest [zɛst] *n* ánimo, vivacidad *f*; (*of orange*) piel *f*; **~ for living** brío
zigzag ['zɪgzæg] *n* zigzag *m* ▷ *vi* zigzaguear
Zimbabwe [zɪmˈbɑːbwɪ] *n* Zimbabwe *m*
Zimmer® ['zɪmə^r] *n* (*also:* **~ frame**) andador *m*, andaderas *fpl*
zinc [zɪŋk] *n* cinc *m*, zinc *m*
zip [zɪp] *n* (*also:* **~ fastener**, *US: also:* **~per**) cremallera, cierre *m* relámpago (*LAm*); (*energy*) energía, vigor *m* ▷ *vt* (*Comput*) comprimir; (*also:* **~ up**) cerrar la cremallera de ▷ *vi*: **to ~ along to the shops** ir de compras volando
zip code *n* (*US*) código postal
zip file *n* (*Comput*) archivo *m* comprimido
zipper ['zɪpə^r] *n* (*US*) cremallera
zit [zɪt] *n* grano
zodiac ['zəudɪæk] *n* zodíaco
zombie ['zɔmbɪ] *n* zombi *m*
zone [zəun] *n* zona
zonked [zɔŋkt] *adj* (*inf*) hecho polvo
zoo [zu:] *n* zoo, (parque *m*) zoológico
zoologist [zuˈɔlədʒɪst] *n* zoólogo(-a)

zoology [zuːˈɒlədʒɪ] *n* zoología
zoom [zuːm] *vi*: **to ~ past** pasar zumbando;
  to ~ in (on sth/sb) (*Phot, Cine*) enfocar (algo/
  a algn) con el zoom
zoom lens *n* zoom *m*
zucchini [zuːˈkiːnɪ] *n(pl)* (*US*) calabacín(-ines)
  m(pl)

Grammar
Gramática

Using the grammar

The Grammar section deals systematically and comprehensively with all the information you will need in order to communicate accurately in Spanish. The numbers, → ① etc, direct you to the relevant example in every case.

Abbreviations

cond.	*conditional*
fem.	*feminine*
masc.	*masculine*
plur.	*plural*
sing.	*singular*
subj	*subjunctive*
algn	alguien
sb	somebody
sth	something

Contents

Verbs

Simple Tenses: Formation of Regular Verbs

Simple tenses are one-word tenses formed by adding endings to a stem. The different endings identify the subject of the verb. The stem and endings of regular verbs are totally predictable. For irregular verbs see page 42 onwards.

First Conjugation

First conjugation verbs end in **-ar** e.g. **hablar** *to speak*. For the present, imperfect, preterite, present subjunctive and imperfect subjunctive, the stem is the infinitive minus **-ar** (e.g. **habl-**). For the future and conditional the stem is the infinitive (e.g. **hablar-**).

To the appropriate stem add the following endings:

		❶ PRESENT	❷ IMPERFECT	❸ PRETERITE
	1ˢᵗ person	**-o**	**-aba**	**-é**
sing.	2ⁿᵈ person	**-as**	**-abas**	**-aste**
	3ʳᵈ person	**-a**	**-aba**	**-ó**
	1ˢᵗ person	**-amos**	**-ábamos**	**-amos**
plur.	2ⁿᵈ person	**-áis**	**-abais**	**-asteis**
	3ʳᵈ person	**-an**	**-aban**	**-aron**

		❹ PRESENT SUBJUNCTIVE	❺ IMPERFECT SUBJUNCTIVE
	1ˢᵗ person	**-e**	**-ara** *or* **-ase**
sing.	2ⁿᵈ person	**-es**	**-aras** *or* **-ases**
	3ʳᵈ person	**-e**	**-ara** *or* **-ase**
	1ˢᵗ person	**-emos**	**-áramos** *or* **-ásemos**
plur.	2ⁿᵈ person	**-éis**	**-arais** *or* **-aseis**
	3ʳᵈ person	**-en**	**-aran** *or* **-asen**

		❻ FUTURE	❼ CONDITIONAL
	1ˢᵗ person	**-é**	**-ía**
sing.	2ⁿᵈ person	**-ás**	**-ías**
	3ʳᵈ person	**-á**	**-ía**
	1ˢᵗ person	**-emos**	**-íamos**
plur.	2ⁿᵈ person	**-éis**	**-íais**
	3ʳᵈ person	**-án**	**-ían**

Examples

	① PRESENT	② IMPERFECT	③ PRETERITE
(yo)	hablo	hablaba	hablé
(tú)	hablas	hablabas	hablaste
(él/ella/Vd)	habla	hablaba	habló
(nosotros/as)	hablamos	hablábamos	hablamos
(vosotros/as)	habláis	hablabais	hablasteis
(ellos/as/Vds)	hablan	hablaban	hablaron

④ PRESENT SUBJUNCTIVE	⑤ IMPERFECT SUBJUNCTIVE
(yo) hable	hablara or hablase
(tú) hables	hablaras or hablases
(él/ella/Vd) hable	hablara or hablase
(nosotros/as) hablemos	habláramos or hablásemos
(vosotros/as) habléis	hablarais or hablaseis
(ellos/as/Vds) hablen	hablaran or hablasen

⑥ FUTURE	⑦ CONDITIONAL
(yo) hablaré	hablaría
(tú) hablarás	hablarías
(él/ella/Vd) hablará	hablaría
(nosotros/as) hablaremos	hablaríamos
(vosotros/as) hablaréis	hablaríais
(ellos/as/Vds) hablarán	hablarían

Note that the subject pronouns appear in brackets because they are not normally necessary in Spanish (see page 96).

Verbs

Simple Tenses: Second Conjugation

Second conjugation verbs end in **-er** e.g. **comer** to eat. For the present, imperfect, preterite, present subjunctive and imperfect subjunctive, the stem is the infinitive minus **-er** (e.g. **com-**). For irregular verbs see 42. For the future and conditional the stem is the infinitive (e.g. **comer-**).

To the appropriate stem add the following endings:

		① PRESENT	② IMPERFECT	③ PRETERITE
	1st person	-o	-ía	-í
sing.	2nd person	-es	-ías	-iste
	3rd person	-e	-ía	-ió
	1st person	-emos	-íamos	-imos
plur.	2nd person	-éis	-íais	-isteis
	3rd person	-en	-ían	-ieron

		④ PRESENT SUBJUNCTIVE	⑤ IMPERFECT SUBJUNCTIVE
	1st person	-a	-iera or -iese
sing.	2nd person	-as	-ieras or -ieses
	3rd person	-a	-iera or -iese
	1st person	-amos	-iéramos or -iésemos
plur.	2nd person	-áis	-ierais or -ieseis
	3rd person	-an	-ieran or -iesen

		⑥ FUTURE	⑦ CONDITIONAL
	1st person	-é	-ía
sing.	2nd person	-ás	-ías
	3rd person	-á	-ía
	1st person	-emos	-íamos
plur.	2nd person	-éis	-íais
	3rd person	-án	-ían

Examples

	① PRESENT	② IMPERFECT	③ PRETERITE
(yo)	como	comía	comí
(tú)	comes	comías	comiste
(él/ella/Vd)	come	comía	comió
(nosotros/as)	comemos	comíamos	comimos
(vosotros/as)	coméis	comíais	comisteis
(ellos/as/Vds)	comen	comían	comieron

④ PRESENT SUBJUNCTIVE	⑤ IMPERFECT SUBJUNCTIVE
(yo) coma	comiera *or* comiese
(tú) comas	comieras *or* comieses
(él/ella/Vd) coma	comiera *or* comiese
(nosotros/as) comamos	comiéramos *or* comiésemos
(vosotros/as) comáis	comierais *or* comieseis
(ellos/as/Vds) coman	comieran *or* comiesen

⑥ FUTURE	⑦ CONDITIONAL
(yo) comeré	comería
(tú) comerás	comerías
(él/ella/Vd) comerá	comería
(nosotros/as) comeremos	comeríamos
(vosotros/as) comeréis	comeríais
(ellos/as/Vds) comerán	comerían

Note that the subject pronouns appear in brackets because they are not normally necessary in Spanish (see page 96).

9

Simple Tenses: Third Conjugation

Third conjugation verbs end in **-ir** e.g. **vivir** to live. For the present, imperfect, preterite, present subjunctive and imperfect subjunctive the stem is the infinitive minus **-ir** (e.g. **viv-**). For irregular verbs see 42. For the future and conditional the stem is the infinitive (e.g. **vivir-**).

To the appropriate stem add the following endings:

		❶ PRESENT	❷ IMPERFECT	❸ PRETERITE
	1st person	**-o**	**-ía**	**-í**
sing.	2nd person	**-es**	**-ías**	**-iste**
	3rd person	**-e**	**-ía**	**-ió**
	1st person	**-imos**	**-íamos**	**-imos**
plur.	2nd person	**-ís**	**-íais**	**-isteis**
	3rd person	**-en**	**-ían**	**-ieron**

		❹ PRESENT SUBJUNCTIVE	❺ IMPERFECT SUBJUNCTIVE
	1st person	**-a**	**-iera** or **-iese**
sing.	2nd person	**-as**	**-ieras** or **-ieses**
	3rd person	**-a**	**-iera** or **-iese**
	1st person	**-amos**	**-iéramos** or **-iésemos**
plur.	2nd person	**-áis**	**-ierais** or **-ieseis**
	3rd person	**-an**	**-ieran** or **-iesen**

		❻ FUTURE	❼ CONDITIONAL
	1st person	**-é**	**-ía**
sing.	2nd person	**-ás**	**-ías**
	3rd person	**-á**	**-ía**
	1st person	**-emos**	**-íamos**
plur.	2nd person	**-éis**	**-íais**
	3rd person	**-án**	**-ían**

Examples

	① PRESENT	② IMPERFECT	③ PRETERITE
(yo)	vivo	vivía	viví
(tú)	vives	vivías	viviste
(él/ella/Vd)	vive	vivía	vivió
(nosotros/as)	vivimos	vivíamos	vivimos
(vosotros/as)	vivís	vivíais	vivisteis
(ellos/as/Vds)	viven	vivían	vivieron

	④ PRESENT SUBJUNCTIVE	⑤ IMPERFECT SUBJUNCTIVE
(yo)	viva	viviera or viviese
(tú)	vivas	vivieras or vivieses
(él/ella/Vd)	viva	viviera or viviese
(nosotros/as)	vivamos	viviéramos or viviésemos
(vosotros/as)	viváis	vivierais or vivieseis
(ellos/as/Vds)	vivan	vivieran or viviesen

	⑥ FUTURE	⑦ CONDITIONAL
(yo)	viviré	viviría
(tú)	vivirás	vivirías
(él/ella/Vd)	vivirá	viviría
(nosotros/as)	viviremos	viviríamos
(vosotros/as)	viviréis	viviríais
(ellos/as/Vds)	vivirán	vivirían

Note that the subject pronouns appear in brackets because they are not normally necessary in Spanish (see page 96).

The Imperative

The imperative is the form of the verb used to give commands or orders. It can be used politely, as in English 'Shut the door, please'.

In *positive* commands, the imperative forms for **Vd**, **Vds** and **nosotros** are the same as the subjunctive. The other forms are as follows:

> **tú** (same as 3rd person singular present indicative in regular verbs)
> **vosotros** (final **-r** of infinitive changes to **-d** in regular verbs) → ❶

(tú)	**habla** speak	**come** eat	**vive** live
(Vd)	**hable** speak	**coma** eat	**viva** live
(nosotros)	**hablemos**	**comamos**	**vivamos**
	let's speak	let's eat	let's live
(vosotros)	**hablad** speak	**comed** eat	**vivid** live
(Vds)	**hablen** speak	**coman** eat	**vivan** live

In *negative* commands, all the imperative forms are exactly the same as the present subjunctive.

Position of object pronouns with the imperative:
- in *positive* commands: they follow the verb and are attached to it. An accent may be needed to show the stress (see page 127) → ❷
- in *negative* commands: they precede the verb → ❸

For reflexive verbs – e.g. **levantarse** to get up – the object pronoun is the reflexive pronoun. An accent may be needed to show the stress (see page 127). The **nosotros** and **vosotros** forms also drop the final **-s** and **-d** respectively before the pronoun → ❹

> BUT: **idos (vosotros)** go

ⓘ Note: For general instructions, the infinitive is used instead of the imperative → ❺

Examples

1 cantar — to sing
cantad — sing

2 Perdóneme — Excuse me
Enviémoselos — Let's send them to him/her/them
Elíjanos — Choose us
Explíquemelo — Explain it to me

Esperémosla — Let's wait for her/it
Devuélvaselo — Give it back to him/her/them

3 No me molestes — Don't disturb me
No se la devolvamos — Let's not give it back to him/her/them

No les castiguemos — Let's not punish them
No me lo mandes — Don't send it to me
No las conteste — Don't answer them
No nos lo hagan — Don't do it to us

4 Levántate Get up — No te levantes Don't get up
Levántese (Vd) Get up — No se levante (Vd) Don't get up
Levantémonos Let's get up — No nos levantemos Let's not get up

Levantaos Get up — No os levantéis Don't get up
Levántense (Vds) Get up — No se levanten (Vds) Don't get up

5 Ver pág ... — See page ...
No pasar — Do not pass

For the order of object pronouns, see page 100.

13

Compound Tenses: Formation of Regular Verbs

In Spanish the compound tenses of both regular and irregular verbs are formed using the past participle of the main verb together with the auxiliary verb **haber**. See opposite for the compound tenses of **hablar** as an example.

The Past Participle

For all compound tenses you need to know how to form the past participle of the verb. For regular verbs this is as follows:

First conjugation: replace the **-ar** of the infinitive by **-ado** (e.g. **cantar** *to sing* → **cantado** *sung*)

Second conjugation: replace the **-er** of the infinitive by **-ido** (e.g. **comer** *to eat* → **comido** *eaten*)

Third conjugation: replace the **-ir** of the infinitive by **-ido** (e.g. **vivir** *to live* → **vivido** *lived*)

The past participle of irregular verbs is given for each verb in the verb tables, pages 42 to 76.

Examples

	PERFECT (have/has spoken)	PLUPERFECT (had spoken)
(yo)	he hablado	había hablado
(tú)	has hablado	habías hablado
(él/ella/Vd)	ha hablado	había hablado
(nosotros/as)	hemos hablado	habíamos hablado
(vosotros/as)	habéis hablado	habíais hablado
(ellos/as/Vds)	han hablado	habían hablado

	FUTURE PERFECT (shall/will have spoken)	CONDITIONAL PERFECT (would have spoken)
(yo)	habré hablado	habría hablado
(tú)	habrás hablado	habrías hablado
(él/ella/Vd)	habrá hablado	habría hablado
(nosotros/as)	habremos hablado	habríamos hablado
(vosotros/as)	habréis hablado	habríals hablado
(ellos/as/Vds)	habrán hablado	habrían hablado

	PAST ANTERIOR (had spoken)	PERFECT SUBJUNCTIVE (have spoken/spoke)
(yo)	hube hablado	haya hablado
(tú)	hubiste hablado	hayas hablado
(él/ella/Vd)	hubo hablado	haya hablado
(nosotros/as)	hubimos hablado	hayamos hablado
(vosotros/as)	hubisteis hablado	hayáis hablado
(ellos/as/Vds)	hubieron hablado	hayan hablado

	PLUPERFECT SUBJUNCTIVE (had spoken)
(yo)	hubiera *or* hubiese hablado
(tú)	hubieras *or* hubieses hablado
(él/ella/Vd)	hubiera *or* hubiese hablado
(nosotros/as)	hubiéramos *or* hubiésemos hablado
(vosotros/as)	hubierais *or* hubieseis hablado
(ellos/as/Vds)	hubieran *or* hubiesen hablado

Verbs

Reflexive Verbs

A reflexive verb is one accompanied by a reflexive pronoun. The infinitive of a reflexive verb ends with the pronoun **se**, which is added to the verb form e.g. **lavarse** to wash (oneself).
The pronouns are:

	SINGULAR	PLURAL
1st person	**me**	**nos**
2nd person	**te**	**os**
3rd person	**se**	**se**

The reflexive pronoun is not always translated in English → ❶

The plural pronouns are sometimes translated as 'one another', 'each other' (the *reciprocal* meaning). The reciprocal meaning may be emphasized by **el uno al otro/la una a la otra** etc. → ❷

Reflexive verbs are conjugated in the same way as non-reflexive verbs, but see page 12 for an ending change needed in the imperative.

Position of reflexive pronouns

The pronoun comes before the verb, except with the infinitive, gerund and positive commands, when it is attached to the end of the verb (but see also page 98). → ❸

Use of reflexive verbs

Verbs can often be used both reflexively and non-reflexively but with a different but closely related meaning. → ❹

Often a reflexive verb can be used to avoid the passive (see page 20) or in impersonal expressions (see page 22) → ❺

Examples

① Me visto — I'm dressing (myself)
Nos lavamos — We're washing (ourselves)
Se levanta — He gets up

② Nos queremos — We love each other
Se parecen — They resemble one another
Se miraban el uno al otro — They were looking at each other

③ ¿Cómo se llama Vd? — What is your name?
No se ha despertado — He hasn't woken up
No te levantes — Don't get up
Quiero irme — I want to go away
Estoy levantándome — I am getting up
Siéntense — Sit down
Vámonos — Let's go

④

NON-REFLEXIVE	REFLEXIVE
caer to fall	caerse to fall down (by accident)
dormir to sleep	dormirse to go to sleep
enfadar to annoy	enfadarse to get annoyed
hacer to make	hacerse to become
ir to go	irse to leave, go away
lavar to wash	lavarse to get washed
levantar to raise	levantarse to get up
llamar to call	llamarse to be called
morir to die, be killed (by accident or on purpose)	morirse to die (from natural causes)
vestir to dress (someone)	vestirse to get dressed
volver to return	volverse to turn round

⑤ Se perdió la batalla — The battle was lost
No se veían las casas — The houses could not be seen
Se dice que ... — (It is said that) People say that ...
No se puede entrar — You/One can't go in
No se permite — It is not allowed

Reflexive Verbs *continued*

Conjugation of: **lavarse** to wash (oneself)

1 SIMPLE TENSES

	PRESENT	IMPERFECT
(yo)	**me** lavo	**me** lavaba
(tú)	**te** lavas	**te** lavabas
(él/ella/Vd)	**se** lava	**se** lavaba
(nosotros/as)	**nos** lavamos	**nos** lavábamos
(vosotros/as)	**os** laváis	**os** lavabais
(ellos/as/Vds)	**se** lavan	**se** lavaban

	FUTURE	CONDITIONAL
(yo)	**me** lavaré	**me** lavaría
(tú)	**te** lavarás	**te** lavarías
(él/ella/Vd)	**se** lavará	**se** lavaría
(nosotros/as)	**nos** lavaremos	**nos** lavaríamos
(vosotros/as)	**os** lavaréis	**os** lavaríais
(ellos/as/Vds)	**se** lavarán	**se** lavarían

	PRETERITE	PRESENT SUBJUNCTIVE
(yo)	**me** lavé	**me** lave
(tú)	**te** lavaste	**te** laves
(él/ella/Vd)	**se** lavó	**se** lave
(nosotros/as)	**nos** lavamos	**nos** lavemos
(vosotros/as)	**os** lavasteis	**os** lavéis
(ellos/as/Vds)	**se** lavaron	**se** laven

	IMPERFECT SUBJUNCTIVE
(yo)	**me** lavara *or* lavase
(tú)	**te** lavaras *or* lavases
(él/ella/Vd)	**se** lavara *or* lavase
(nosotros/as)	**nos** laváramos *or* lavásemos
(vosotros/as)	**os** lavarais *or* lavaseis
(ellos/as/Vds)	**se** lavaran *or* lavasen

Reflexive Verbs *continued*

Conjugation of: **lavarse** to wash (oneself)

2 COMPOUND TENSES

	PERFECT	PLUPERFECT
(yo)	me he lavado	me había lavado
(tú)	te has lavado	te habías lavado
(él/ella/Vd)	se ha lavado	se había lavado
(nosotros/as)	nos hemos lavado	nos habíamos lavado
(vosotros/as)	os habéis lavado	os habíais lavado
(ellos/as/Vds)	se han lavado	se habían lavado

	FUTURE PERFECT	PAST ANTERIOR
(yo)	me habré lavado	me hube lavado
(tú)	te habrás lavado	te hubiste lavado
(él/ella/Vd)	se habrá lavado	se hubo lavado
(nosotros/as)	nos habremos lavado	nos hubimos lavado
(vosotros/as)	os habréis lavado	os hubisteis lavado
(ellos/as/Vds)	se habrán lavado	se hubieron lavado

	PERFECT SUBJUNCTIVE
(yo)	me haya lavado
(tú)	te hayas lavado
(él/ella/Vd)	se haya lavado
(nosotros/as)	nos hayamos lavado
(vosotros/as)	os hayáis lavado
(ellos/as/Vds)	se hayan lavado

	PLUPERFECT SUBJUNCTIVE
(yo)	me hubiera *or* hubiese lavado
(tú)	te hubieras *or* hubieses lavado
(él/ella/Vd)	se hubiera *or* hubiese lavado
(nosotros/as)	nos hubiéramos *or* hubiésemos lavado
(vosotros/as)	os hubierais *or* hubieseis lavado
(ellos/as/Vds)	se hubieran *or* hubiesen lavado

Verbs

The Passive

In the passive, the subject of the verb receives the action (e.g. *I was hit*) instead of performing it (e.g. *I hit the ball*).

In the same way that English uses 'to be' with the past participle to form the passive, Spanish uses a tense of **ser** with the past participle, which agrees in number and gender with the subject → ①

The word that corresponds to 'by' in Spanish passive sentences is **por** → ②

Whereas in English an active sentence with an indirect object can be made into two passive sentences (e.g. active = *His mother gave him the book*; passive: *The book was given to him by his mother* or *He was given the book by his mother*), in Spanish only the direct object of an active verb can become the subject of a passive one → ③

Less common in Spanish than English, the passive is used where the identity of the agent is unknown or unimportant → ④

Otherwise, active constructions are generally preferred, such as specifying the subject or using the 3rd person plural (equivalent to 'they') → ⑤

When the action of the sentence is performed on a person, the reflexive form of the verb can be used in the 3rd person singular, and the person becomes the object → ⑥

When the action is performed on a thing, this becomes the subject of the sentence and the verb is made reflexive, agreeing in number with the subject → ⑦

Examples

1. Pablo ha sido despedido — Paul has been sacked
   Su madre era muy admirada — His mother was greatly admired
   El palacio será vendido — The palace will be sold
   Las puertas habían sido cerradas — The doors had been closed

2. La casa fue diseñada por mi hermano — The house was designed by my brother

3. Su madre le regaló el libro — His mother gave him the book
   BECOMES:
   El libro le fue regalado por su madre — The book was given to him by his mother

4. La ciudad fue conquistada tras un largo asedio — The city was conquered after a long siege
   Ha sido declarado el estado de excepción — A state of emergency has been declared

5. La policía interrogó al sospechoso — The suspect was questioned by the police
   RATHER THAN:
   El sospechoso fue interrogado por la policía
   Usan demasiada publicidad en la televisión — Too much advertising is used on television

6. Últimamente no se le/les ha visto mucho en público — He has/They have not been seen much in public recently

7. Esta palabra ya no se usa — This word is no longer used
   Todos los libros se han vendido — All the books have been sold

Verbal Idioms

Although we think of **gustar** as meaning *to like*, the way it is used is more like *to be pleasing to*, as the subject of the verb is the thing that pleases and it is used with an indirect object → ①

Other Spanish verbs and expressions behave similarly → ②

Impersonal Verbs

Spanish impersonal verbs are used only in the infinitive, the gerund, and in the 3rd person without a subject pronoun, e.g.

> **llueve** it's raining
> **es fácil decir que ...** it's easy to say that ...

The most common impersonal verbs are ones to do with the weather, such as **amanecer**, **anochecer**, **granizar**, **llover**, **lloviznar**, **nevar**, **tronar** → ③

Some reflexive verbs are also used impersonally:

INFINITIVE	CONSTRUCTION
creerse	**se cree que*** + *indicative* → ④
decirse	**se dice que*** + *indicative* → ⑤
poderse	**se puede** + *infinitive* → ⑥
tratarse de	**se trata de** + *noun* → ⑦
	se trata de + *infinitive* → ⑧
venderse	**se vende*** + *noun* → ⑨

*This impersonal construction conveys the same meaning as the 3rd person plural of these verbs; **creen que**, **dicen que**, **venden**.

Examples

1 Me gusta este vestido.   I like this dress (This dress pleases me)

Me gustan los animales   I like animals

2 Me gustan más estas   I prefer these
Nos encanta hacer deporte   We love doing sport
Me duele la cabeza   I have a headache
Le faltaban tres dientes   He had three teeth missing

3 Amanece/Está amaneciendo   It's daybreak
Anochece/Está anocheciendo   It's getting dark
Graniza/Está granizando   It's hailing
Llueve/Está lloviendo   It's raining
Llovizna/Está lloviznando   It's drizzling
Nieva/Está nevando   It's snowing
Truena/Está tronando   It's thundering

4 Se cree que llegarán mañana   It is thought they will arrive tomorrow

5 Se dice que ha sido el peor invierno en 50 años   People say it's been the worst winter in 50 years

6 Aquí se puede aparcar   You can park here

7 No se trata de dinero   It isn't a question/matter of money

8 Se trata de poner fin al asunto   We must put an end to the matter

9 Se vende coche   Car for sale

Verbs

The Infinitive

The infinitive is the form of the verb found in dictionary entries meaning 'to ...', e.g. **hablar** to speak, **vivir** to live. It is used in the following ways:

- After a preposition → ❶
- As a verbal noun → ❷

In this use the article may precede the infinitive, especially when the infinitive is the subject and begins the sentence → ❸

- After another verb or a verb followed by a preposition → ❹

The following construction should also be noted:
> *indefinite pronoun* + **que** + *infinitive* → ❺

Object pronouns generally follow the infinitive and are attached to it. For exceptions see page 98.

Verbs followed by an infinitive with no linking preposition

deber, **poder**, **saber**, **querer** and **tener que** (**hay que** in impersonal constructions) → ❻

verbs of seeing or hearing, e.g. **ver** *to see*, **oír** *to hear* → ❼

dejar, **hacer** → ❽

The following common verbs:

aconsejar to advise → ❾	**necesitar** to need → ⑯
conseguir to manage to → ⑩	**odiar** to hate
decidir to decide	**olvidar** to forget → ⑰
desear to wish, want → ⑪	**pensar** to think → ⑱
esperar to hope → ⑫	**preferir** to prefer → ⑲
evitar to avoid → ⑬	**procurar** to try → ⑮
impedir to prevent → ⑭	**prohibir** to forbid → ⑳
intentar to try → ⑮	**prometer** to promise → ㉑
lograr to manage to → ⑩	**proponer** to propose → ㉒

1. Me hizo daño sin saberlo — She hurt me without realizing

2. Su deporte preferido es montar a caballo — Her favourite sport is horse riding
   Ver es creer — Seeing is believing

3. El viajar tanto me resulta cansado — I find so much travelling tiring

4. ¿Quiere Vd esperar? — Would you like to wait?
   Aprenderán pronto a nadar — They will soon learn to swim
   Pronto dejará de llover — It'll stop raining soon

5. Tengo algo que decirte — I have something to tell you

6. No puede venir — She can't come

7. Nos ha visto llegar — She saw us arriving

8. No me hagas reír — Don't make me laugh

9. Le aconsejamos olvidarlo — We'd advise you to forget it

10. Aún no he conseguido/logrado entenderlo — I still haven't managed to work it out

11. No desea tener más hijos — She doesn't want to have any more children

12. Esperamos casarnos — We are hoping to get married

13. Evite beber cuando conduzca — Avoid drinking and driving

14. No pudo impedirle hablar — He couldn't prevent him from speaking

15. Intentamos/Procuramos pasar desapercibidos — We tried not to be noticed

16. Necesitaba salir a la calle — I needed to go out

17. Olvidó dejar su dirección — He forgot to leave his address

18. ¿Piensan venir? — Are you thinking of coming?

19. Preferiría elegirlo yo mismo — I'd rather choose it myself

20. Prohibió fumar a los alumnos — He forbade the pupils to smoke

21. Prometieron volver pronto — They promised to come back soon

22. Propongo salir cuanto antes — I propose to leave ASAP

Verbs

The Gerund

Formation

First conjugation:
* replace the **-ar** of the infinitive by **-ando** → ①

Second conjugation:
* replace the **-er** of the infinitive by **-iendo** → ②

Third conjugation:
* replace the **-ir** of the infinitive by **-iendo** → ③

For irregular gerunds, see irregular verbs, page 42 onwards.

Uses

After the verb **estar**, to form the continuous tenses → ④

After the verbs **seguir** and **continuar** *to continue*, and **ir** when meaning to *happen gradually* → ⑤

In time constructions, after **llevar** → ⑥

When the action in the main clause needs to be complemented by another action → ⑦

The position of object pronouns is the same as for the infinitive (see pages 24 and 98).

The gerund is invariable and strictly verbal in sense.

Examples

1. cantar to sing → cantando singing

2. temer to fear → temiendo fearing

3. partir to leave → partiendo leaving

4. Estoy escribiendo una carta   I am writing a letter
   Estaban esperándonos   They were waiting for us

5. Sigue viniendo todos los días   He/She is still coming every day
   Continuarán subiendo
   los precios   Prices will continue to go up
   El ejército iba avanzando poco   The army was advancing
   a poco   little by little

6. Lleva dos años estudiando   He/She has been studying
   inglés   English for two years

7. Pasamos el día tomando el sol   We spent the day sunbathing
   en la playa   on the beach
   Iba cojeando   He/She/I was limping
   Salieron corriendo   They ran out

Verbs

Use of Tenses

The Present

Unlike English, Spanish can use both the simple present and the continuous present to talk about what is happening now → ①

Normally, however, the continuous present is used to describe actions that are going on at this very moment → ②

Spanish uses the present tense where English uses the perfect in the following cases:
- with certain expressions of time – notably **desde** *for/since* – when an action begun in the past is continued in the present → ③
  - ⓘ Note: The perfect can be used as in English when the verb is negative → ④
- in the construction **acabar de hacer** *to have just done* → ⑤

Like English, Spanish often uses the present where a future action is implied → ⑥

The Future

The future is generally used as in English → ⑦, but note the following:

Immediate future time is often expressed by means of the present tense of **ir** + **a** + infinitive → ⑧

When 'will' or 'shall' mean 'wish to', 'are willing to', **querer** is used → ⑨

The Future Perfect

Used as in English shall/will have done → ⑩

It can also express conjecture, usually about things in the recent past → ⑪

Examples

1 Fumo
Lee
Vivimos

I smoke *or* I am smoking
He reads *or* He is reading
We live *or* We are living

2 Está fumando

He is smoking

3 Linda estudia español desde
hace seis meses
Estoy de pie desde las siete
¿Hace mucho que esperan?
Ya hace dos semanas que
estamos aquí

Linda's been learning Spanish for
six months (and still is)
I've been up since seven
Have you been waiting long?
We've been here for two
weeks now

4 No se han visto desde hace
meses

They haven't seen each other for
months

5 Isabel acaba de salir

Isabel has just left

6 Mañana voy a Madrid

I am going to Madrid tomorrow

7 Lo haré mañana

I'll do it tomorrow

8 Te vas a caer si no tienes
cuidado
Va a perder el tren
Va a llevar una media hora

You'll fall if you're not careful

He's going to miss the train
It'll take about half an hour

9 ¿Me quieres esperar un
momento, por favor?

Will you wait for me a second,
please?

10 Lo habré acabado para mañana

I will have finished it for
tomorrow

11 Ya habrán llegado a casa

They must have arrived home by
now

Use of Tenses *continued*

The Imperfect

The imperfect describes:
- an action or state in the past without definite limits in time → ❶
- habitual action(s) in the past (often expressed in English by means of *would* or *used to*) → ❷

Spanish uses the imperfect tense where English uses the pluperfect in the following cases:
- with certain expressions of time – notably **desde** *for/since* – when an action begun in the remoter past was continued in the more recent past → ❸
- ⓘ Note: The pluperfect is used as in English when the verb is negative or the action has been completed → ❹
- in the construction **acabar de hacer** *to have just done* → ❺

Both the continuous and simple forms in English can be translated by the Spanish simple imperfect, but the continuous imperfect is used when the emphasis is on the fact that an action was going on at a precise moment in the past → ❻

The Perfect

The perfect is generally used much as it is in English → ❼

The Preterite

The preterite generally corresponds to the English simple past in both written and spoken Spanish → ❽

However, while English can use the simple past to describe habitual actions or settings, Spanish uses the imperfect (see above) → ❾

The Past Anterior

This tense is only ever used in written, literary Spanish, to replace the pluperfect in time clauses where the verb in the main clause is in the preterite → ❿

Examples

1. Todos mirábamos en silencio
We were all watching in silence
Nuestras habitaciones daban a la playa
Our rooms overlooked the beach

2. En su juventud se levantaba de madrugada
In his youth he used to get up really early
Hablábamos sin parar durante horas
We would talk non-stop for hours on end
Mi hermano siempre me tomaba el pelo
My brother was always teasing me

3. Hacía dos años que vivíamos en Irlanda
We had been living in Ireland for two years
Estaba enfermo desde 2005
He had been ill since 2005
Hacía mucho tiempo que salían juntos
They had been going out together for a long time

4. Hacía un año que no le había visto
I hadn't seen him for a year
Hacía una hora que había llegado
She had arrived an hour before

5. Acababa de encontrármelos
I had just found them

6. Cuando llegué, todos estaban fumando
When I arrived, they were all smoking

7. Todavía no han salido
They haven't come out yet

8. Me desperté y salté de la cama
I woke up and jumped out of bed

9. Siempre iban en coche al trabajo
They always travelled to work by car

10. Apenas hubo acabado, se oyeron unos golpes en la puerta
She had scarcely finished when there was a knock at the door

The Subjunctive: when to use it

After verbs of:

- 'wishing'

querer que ⎤
desear que ⎦   to wish that, want → ❶

- 'emotion' (e.g. regret, surprise, shame, pleasure, etc)

sentir que   to be sorry that → ❷
sorprender que   to be surprised that → ❸
alegrarse de que   to be pleased that → ❹

- 'asking' and 'advising'

pedir que   to ask that → ❺
aconsejar que   to advise that → ❻

In all the above constructions, when the subject of the verbs in the main and subordinate clause is the same, the infinitive is used, and the conjunction **que** omitted → ❼

- 'ordering', 'forbidding', 'allowing'

mandar que* ⎤
ordenar que ⎦   to order that → ❽

permitir que* ⎤
dejar que* ⎦   to allow that → ❾

prohibir que*   to forbid that → ❿
impedir que*   to prevent that → ⓫

* With these verbs either the subjunctive or the infinitive is used when the object of the main verb is the subject of the subordinate verb → ⓬

Always after verbs expressing doubt or uncertainty, and verbs of opinion used negatively.

dudar que   to doubt that → ⓭
no creer que ⎤
no pensar que ⎦   not to think that → ⓮

Examples

①	Queremos que esté contenta	We want her to be happy (*literally*: We want that she is happy)
	¿Desea Vd que lo haga yo?	Do you want me to do it?
②	Sentí mucho que no vinieran	I was very sorry that they didn't come
③	Nos sorprendió que no les vieran Vds	We were surprised you didn't see them
④	Me alegro de que te gusten	I'm pleased that you like them
⑤	Solo les pedimos que tengan cuidado	We're only asking you to take care
⑥	Le aconsejé que no llegara tarde	I advised him not to be late
⑦	Quiero que lo termines pronto	I want you to finish it soon
	BUT:	
	Quiero terminarlo pronto	I want to finish it soon
⑧	Ha mandado que vuelvan	He has ordered them to come back
	Ordenó que fueran castigados	He ordered them to be punished
⑨	No permitas que te tomen el pelo	Don't let them pull your leg
	No me dejó que la llevara a casa	She wouldn't let me take her home
⑩	Te prohíbo que digas eso	I forbid you to say that
⑪	No les impido que vengan	I am not preventing them from coming
⑫	Les ordenó que salieran *or* Les ordenó salir	She ordered them to go out
⑬	Dudo que lo sepan hacer	I doubt they can do it
⑭	No creo que sean tan listos	I don't think they are as clever as that

33

The Subjunctive: when to use it *continued*

In impersonal constructions which express necessity, possibility, etc:

hace falta que
es necesario que ⎤ it is necessary that → ①
es posible que it is possible that → ②
más vale que it is better that → ③
es una lástima que it is a pity that → ④

ⓘ Note: In impersonal constructions which state a fact or
express certainty the indicative is used when the impersonal
verb is affirmative. When it is negative, the subjunctive is
used → ⑤

After certain conjunctions:

para que
a fin de que* ⎤ so that → ⑥
como si as if → ⑦
sin que* without → ⑧
a condición de que* ⎤
con tal (de) que* provided that,
siempre que ⎦ on condition that → ⑨
a menos que ⎤
a no ser que ⎦ unless → ⑩
antes (de) que* before → ⑪
no sea que lest/in case → ⑫
mientras (que) ⎤
siempre que ⎦ as long as → ⑬
(el) que the fact that → ⑭

* When the subject of both verbs is the same, the infinitive is
used, and the final que is omitted → ⑧

Examples

1. ¿Hace falta que vaya Jaime? — Does Jaime have to go?

2. Es posible que tengan razón — It's possible that they are right

3. Más vale que se quede Vd en su casa — You'd be better to stay at home

4. Es una lástima que haya perdido su perrito — It's a shame/pity that she has lost her puppy

5. Es verdad que va a venir — It's true that he's coming
   BUT:
   No es verdad que vayan a hacerlo — It's not true that they are going to do it

6. Átalas bien para que no se caigan — Tie them on securely so that they won't fall off

7. Hablaba como si no creyera en sus propias palabras — He talked as if he didn't believe in his own words

8. Salimos sin que nos vieran — We left without them seeing us
   BUT:
   Me fui sin esperarla — I left without waiting for her

9. Lo haré con tal de que me cuentes todo lo que pasó — I'll do it provided you tell me exactly what happened

10. Saldremos de paseo a menos que esté lloviendo — We'll go for a walk unless it's raining

11. Avísale antes de que sea demasiado tarde — Tell him before it's too late

12. Habla en voz baja, no sea que alguien nos oiga — Speak quietly in case anyone hears us

13. Eso no pasará mientras yo sea el jefe aquí — That won't happen as long as I am the boss here

14. El que no me escribiera no me importaba demasiado — The fact that he didn't write didn't bother me too much

The Subjunctive: when to use it *continued*

After the conjunctions:

de modo que ⎤
de forma que ⎬ so that (*indicating a purpose*) → ①
de manera que ⎦

ⓘ Note: When these conjunctions introduce a result rather than
a purpose the indicative is used → ②

In relative clauses with an antecedent which is:
- negative → ③
- indefinite → ④
- non-specific → ⑤

In main clauses, to express a wish or exhortation. The verb may be
preceded by expressions like **ojalá** or **que** → ⑥

In the **si** clause of conditions where the English sentence contains a
conditional tense → ⑦

In set expressions → ⑧

In the following constructions which translate *however*:
- **por** + *adjective* + **que** + *subjunctive* → ⑨
- **por** + *adverb* + **que** + *subjunctive* → ⑩
- **por** + **mucho** + **que** + *subjunctive* → ⑪

Examples

1. Vuélvanse de manera que les vea bien
   Turn round so that I can see you properly

2. No quieren hacerlo, de manera que tendré que hacerlo yo
   They won't do it, so I'll have to do it myself

3. No he encontrado a nadie que la conociera
   I haven't met anyone who knows her

   No dijo nada que no supiéramos ya
   He/She didn't say anything we didn't already know

4. Necesito alguien que sepa conducir
   I need someone who can drive

   Busco algo que me distraiga
   I'm looking for something to take my mind off it

5. Busca una casa que tenga calefacción central
   He/She's looking for a house which has central heating
   (*subjunctive used since such a house may or may not exist*)

   El que lo haya visto tiene que decírmelo
   Anyone who has seen it must tell me
   (*subjunctive used since it is not known who has seen it*)

6. ¡Ojalá haga buen tiempo!
   Let's hope the weather will be good!

   ¡Que te diviertas!
   Have a good time!

7. Si fuéramos en coche llegaríamos a tiempo
   If we went by car we'd be there in time

8. Diga lo que diga ...
   Whatever he may say ...
   Sea lo que sea ...
   Be that as it may ...
   Pase lo que pase ...
   Come what may ...
   Sea como sea ...
   One way or another ...

9. Por cansado que esté, seguirá trabajando
   No matter how/However tired he may be, he'll go on working

10. Por lejos que viva, iremos a buscarle
    No matter how/However far away he lives, we'll go and find him

11. Por mucho que lo intente, nunca lo conseguirá
    No matter how/However hard he tries, he'll never succeed

37

The Subjunctive: when to use it *continued*

Clauses taking either a subjunctive or an indicative

In certain constructions, a subjunctive is needed when the action refers to future events or hypothetical situations, whereas an indicative is used when stating a fact or experience → ①

The commonest of these are:

The conjunctions:

cuando	when → ①
en cuanto	as soon as → ②
tan pronto como	
después (de) que*	after → ③
hasta que	until → ④
mientras	while → ⑤
siempre que	whenever → ⑥
aunque	even though → ⑦

All conjunctions and pronouns ending in **-quiera** (*-ever*) → ⑧

* ⓘ Note: If the subject of both verbs is the same, the subjunctive introduced by **después (de) que** may be replaced by **después de** + *infinitive* → ⑨

Sequence of tenses in Subordinate Clauses

If the verb in the main clause is in the present, future or imperative, the verb in the dependent clause will be in the present or perfect subjunctive → ⑩

If the verb in the main clause is in the conditional or any past tense, the verb in the dependent clause will be in the imperfect or pluperfect subjunctive → ⑪

Examples

1. Le aconsejé que oyera música cuando estuviera nervioso
   I advised him to listen to music when he felt nervous

   Me gusta nadar cuando hace calor
   I like to swim when it is warm

2. Te devolveré el libro tan pronto como lo haya leído
   I'll give you back the book as soon as I have read it

3. Te lo diré después de que te hayas sentado
   I'll tell you after you've sat down

4. Quédate aquí hasta que volvamos
   Stay here until we come back

5. No hablen en voz alta mientras estén ellos aquí
   Don't speak loudly while they are here

6. Vuelvan por aquí siempre que quieran
   Come back whenever you want

7. No le creeré aunque diga la verdad
   I won't believe him even if he's telling the truth

8. La encontraré dondequiera que esté
   I will find her wherever she may be

9. Después de cenar nos fuimos al cine
   After dinner we went to the cinema

10. Quiero que lo hagas
    (*pres + pres subj*)
    I want you to do it

    Temo que no haya venido
    (*pres + perf subj*)
    I fear he hasn't come (may not have come)

    Iremos por aquí para que no nos vean (*future + pres subj*)
    We'll go this way so that they won't see us

11. Me gustaría que llegaras temprano (*cond + imperf subj*)
    I'd like you to arrive early

    Les pedí que me esperaran (*preterite + imperf subj*)
    I asked them to wait for me

    Sentiría mucho que hubiese muerto (*cond + pluperf subj*)
    I would be very sorry if he were dead

Ser and Estar

Spanish has two verbs – **ser** and **estar** – for 'to be'.

They are not interchangeable and each one is used in defined contexts.

ser is used:
- with an adjective, to express a permanent or inherent quality → ①
- to express occupation or nationality → ②
- to express possession → ③
- to express origin or the material something is made from → ④
- with a noun, pronoun or infinitive following the verb → ⑤
- to express the time and date → ⑥
- to form the passive, with the past participle (see page 20).

  ⓘ Note: This use emphasizes the action of the verb. If, however, the resultant state or condition needs to be emphasized, **estar** is used. The past participle then functions as an adjective → ⑦

estar is used:
- to indicate place or location of a person, animal or thing* → ⑧
- with an adjective or adjectival phrase, to express a quality or state seen by the speaker as subject to change or different from expected → ⑨
- when speaking of a person's state of health → ⑩
- to form the continuous tenses → ⑪
- with **de** + *noun*, to indicate a temporary occupation → ⑫

With certain adjectives both **ser** and **estar** can be used, but with a different meaning:
- **ser** will express a permanent or inherent quality → ⑬
- **estar** will express a temporary state or quality → ⑭

*To talk about where an event is taking place, use **ser** → ⑮

Examples

1. Mi hermano es alto
   María es inteligente

   My brother is tall
   María is intelligent

2. Javier es aviador
   Sus padres son italianos

   Javier is an airman
   His parents are Italian

3. La casa es de Miguel

   The house belongs to Miguel

4. Mi mujer es de Granada
   Las paredes son de ladrillo

   My wife is from Granada
   The walls are made of brick

5. Andrés es un niño travieso
   Soy yo, Enrique
   Todo es proponérselo

   Andrés is a naughty boy
   It's me, Enrique
   It's all a question of putting your mind to it

6. Son las tres y media
   Mañana es sábado

   It's half past three
   Tomorrow is Saturday

7. Las puertas eran cerradas sigilosamente

   The doors were being silently closed

   Las puertas estaban cerradas

   The doors were closed (resultant action)

8. La comida está en la mesa

   The meal is on the table

9. El lavabo está ocupado
   Hoy estoy de mal humor
   Las tiendas están cerradas

   The toilet is engaged
   I'm in a bad mood today
   The shops are closed

10. ¿Cómo están Vds?
    Estamos todos bien
    Su amigo está enfermo

    How are you?
    We are all well
    Her friend is ill

11. Estamos aprendiendo mucho

    We are learning a great deal

12. Mi primo está de camarero en un bar

    My cousin is working as a waiter in a bar

13. Su hermana es muy joven/vieja
    Mi hijo es bueno/malo
    Viajar es cansado

    His sister is very young/old
    My son is good/naughty
    Travelling is tiring

14. Está muy joven/vieja con ese vestido
    Está bueno/malo
    Hoy estoy cansada

    She looks very young/old in that dress
    He is well/ill
    I am tired today

15. La boda será en Madrid

    The wedding will be in Madrid

Irregular Verbs

The verbs on the following pages provide the main patterns for irregular verbs. They are given in their most common simple tenses, together with the imperative and the gerund. The past participle is also shown, to enable you to form all the compound tenses (see pages 14 to 15.)

Note that **escribir** and **romper** are not shown in the tables as only their past participles are irregular (**escrito** and **roto**).

Also not shown are verbs that make predictable spelling changes such as **c** to **qu** and **g** to **gu** before **e** (e.g. **sacar** and **pagar**). See page 128.

The pronouns **ella** and **Vd** take the same verb endings as **él**, while **ellas** and **Vds** take the same endings as **ellos**.

> All the verbs included in the tables differ from the three conjugations set out on pages 6 to 11. Many – e.g. **contar** – serve as models for groups of verbs, while others – e.g. **ir** – are unique.

Imperfect Subjunctive of Irregular Verbs

For verbs with an irregular root form in the preterite tense – e.g. **andar** →**anduvieron** – the imperfect subjunctive is formed by using the root form of the 3rd person plural of the preterite tense, and adding the imperfect subjunctive endings **-iera/-iese** etc where the verb has an 'i' in the preterite ending – e.g. andu**vieron** →anduv**iera/iese**. Where the verb has no 'i' in the preterite ending, add **-era/-ese** etc – e.g. produj**eron** →produj**era/ese**.

abrir (to open)

	PAST PARTICIPLE **abierto**	GERUND **abriendo**	IMPERATIVE **abre** **abrid**
	PRESENT	FUTURE	IMPERFECT
(yo)	abro	abriré	abría
(tú)	abres	abrirás	abrías
(él)	abre	abrirá	abría
(nosotros)	abrimos	abriremos	abríamos
(vosotros)	abrís	abriréis	abríais
(ellos)	abren	abrirán	abrían
	PRESENT SUBJUNCTIVE	CONDITIONAL	PRETERITE
(yo)	abra	abriría	abrí
(tú)	abras	abrirías	abriste
(él)	abra	abriría	abrió
(nosotros)	abramos	abriríamos	abrimos
(vosotros)	abráis	abriríais	abristeis
(ellos)	abran	abrirían	abrieron

actuar (to act)

	PAST PARTICIPLE **actuado**	GERUND **actuando**	IMPERATIVE **actúa** **actuad**
	PRESENT	FUTURE	IMPERFECT
(yo)	actúo	actuaré	actuaba
(tú)	actúas	actuarás	actuabas
(él)	actúa	actuará	actuaba
(nosotros)	actuamos	actuaremos	actuábamos
(vosotros)	actuáis	actuaréis	actuabais
(ellos)	actúan	actuarán	actuaban
	PRESENT SUBJUNCTIVE	CONDITIONAL	PRETERITE
(yo)	actúe	actuaría	actué
(tú)	actúes	actuarías	actuaste
(él)	actúe	actuaría	actuó
(nosotros)	actuemos	actuaríamos	actuamos
(vosotros)	actuéis	actuaríais	actuasteis
(ellos)	actúen	actuarían	actuaron

Irregular Verbs

adquirir (to acquire)

	PAST PARTICIPLE	GERUND	IMPERATIVE
	adquirido	adquiriendo	adquiere
			adquirid

	PRESENT	FUTURE	IMPERFECT
(yo)	adquiero	adquiriré	adquiría
(tú)	adquieres	adquirirás	adquirías
(él)	adquiere	adquirirá	adquiría
(nosotros)	adquirimos	adquiriremos	adquiríamos
(vosotros)	adquirís	adquiriréis	adquiríais
(ellos)	adquieren	adquirirán	adquirían

	PRESENT SUBJUNCTIVE	CONDITIONAL	PRETERITE
(yo)	adquiera	adquiriría	adquirí
(tú)	adquieras	adquirirías	adquiriste
(él)	adquiera	adquiriría	adquirió
(nosotros)	adquiramos	adquiriríamos	adquirimos
(vosotros)	adquiráis	adquiriríais	adquiristeis
(ellos)	adquieran	adquirirían	adquirieron

almorzar (to have lunch)

	PAST PARTICIPLE	GERUND	IMPERATIVE
	almorzado	almorzando	almuerza
			almorzad

	PRESENT	FUTURE	IMPERFECT
(yo)	almuerzo	almorzaré	almorzaba
(tú)	almuerzas	almorzarás	almorzabas
(él)	almuerza	almorzará	almorzaba
(nosotros)	almorzamos	almorzaremos	almorzábamos
(vosotros)	almorzáis	almorzaréis	almorzabais
(ellos)	almuerzan	almorzarán	almorzaban

	PRESENT SUBJUNCTIVE	CONDITIONAL	PRETERITE
(yo)	almuerce	almorzaría	almorcé
(tú)	almuerces	almorzarías	almorzaste
(él)	almuerce	almorzaría	almorzó
(nosotros)	almorcemos	almorzaríamos	almorzamos
(vosotros)	almorcéis	almorzaríais	almorzasteis
(ellos)	almuercen	almorzarían	almorzaron

andar (to walk)

	PAST PARTICIPLE andado	GERUND andando	IMPERATIVE anda andad
	PRESENT	FUTURE	IMPERFECT
(yo)	ando	andaré	andaba
(tú)	andas	andarás	andabas
(él)	anda	andará	andaba
(nosotros)	andamos	andaremos	andábamos
(vosotros)	andáis	andaréis	andabais
(ellos)	andan	andarán	andaban
	PRESENT SUBJUNCTIVE	CONDITIONAL	PRETERITE
(yo)	ande	andaría	anduve
(tú)	andes	andarías	anduviste
(él)	ande	andaría	anduvo
(nosotros)	andemos	andaríamos	anduvimos
(vosotros)	andéis	andaríais	anduvisteis
(ellos)	anden	andarían	anduvieron

avergonzar (to shame)

	PAST PARTICIPLE avergonzado	GERUND avergonzando	IMPERATIVE avergüenza avergonzad
	PRESENT	FUTURE	IMPERFECT
(yo)	avergüenzo	avergonzaré	avergonzaba
(tú)	avergüenzas	avergonzarás	avergonzabas
(él)	avergüenza	avergonzará	avergonzaba
(nosotros)	avergonzamos	avergonzaremos	avergonzábamos
(vosotros)	avergonzáis	avergonzaréis	avergonzabais
(ellos)	avergüenzan	avergonzarán	avergonzaban
	PRESENT SUBJUNCTIVE	CONDITIONAL	PRETERITE
(yo)	avergüence	avergonzaría	avergoncé
(tú)	avergüences	avergonzarías	avergonzaste
(él)	avergüence	avergonzaría	avergonzó
(nosotros)	avergoncemos	avergonzaríamos	avergonzamos
(vosotros)	avergoncéis	avergonzaríais	avergonzasteis
(ellos)	avergüencen	avergonzarían	avergonzaron

45

caber (to fit)

	PAST PARTICIPLE	GERUND	IMPERATIVE
	cabido	cabiendo	cabe
			cabed

	PRESENT	FUTURE	IMPERFECT
(yo)	quepo	cabré	cabía
(tú)	cabes	cabrás	cabías
(él)	cabe	cabrá	cabía
(nosotros)	cabemos	cabremos	cabíamos
(vosotros)	cabéis	cabréis	cabíais
(ellos)	caben	cabrán	cabían

	PRESENT SUBJUNCTIVE	CONDITIONAL	PRETERITE
(yo)	quepa	cabría	cupe
(tú)	quepas	cabrías	cupiste
(él)	quepa	cabría	cupo
(nosotros)	quepamos	cabríamos	cupimos
(vosotros)	quepáis	cabríais	cupisteis
(ellos)	quepan	cabrían	cupieron

caer (to fall)

	PAST PARTICIPLE	GERUND	IMPERATIVE
	caído	cayendo	cae
			caed

	PRESENT	FUTURE	IMPERFECT
(yo)	caigo	caeré	caía
(tú)	caes	caerás	caías
(él)	cae	caerá	caía
(nosotros)	caemos	caeremos	caíamos
(vosotros)	caéis	caeréis	caíais
(ellos)	caen	caerán	caían

	PRESENT SUBJUNCTIVE	CONDITIONAL	PRETERITE
(yo)	caiga	caería	caí
(tú)	caigas	caerías	caíste
(él)	caiga	caería	cayó
(nosotros)	caigamos	caeríamos	caímos
(vosotros)	caigáis	caeríais	caísteis
(ellos)	caigan	caerían	cayeron

cocer (to boil)

	PAST PARTICIPLE	GERUND	IMPERATIVE
	cocido	cociendo	cuece
			coced

	PRESENT	FUTURE	IMPERFECT
(yo)	cuezo	coceré	cocía
(tú)	cueces	cocerás	cocías
(él)	cuece	cocerá	cocía
(nosotros)	cocemos	coceremos	cocíamos
(vosotros)	cocéis	coceréis	cocíais
(ellos)	cuecen	cocerán	cocían

	PRESENT SUBJUNCTIVE	CONDITIONAL	PRETERITE
(yo)	cueza	cocería	cocí
(tú)	cuezas	cocerías	cociste
(él)	cueza	cocería	coció
(nosotros)	cozamos	coceríamos	cocimos
(vosotros)	cozáis	coceríais	cocisteis
(ellos)	cuezan	cocerían	cocieron

coger (to take)

	PAST PARTICIPLE	GERUND	IMPERATIVE
	cogido	cogiendo	coge
			coged

	PRESENT	FUTURE	IMPERFECT
(yo)	cojo	cogeré	cogía
(tú)	coges	cogerás	cogías
(él)	coge	cogerá	cogía
(nosotros)	cogemos	cogeremos	cogíamos
(vosotros)	cogéis	cogeréis	cogíais
(ellos)	cogen	cogerán	cogían

	PRESENT SUBJUNCTIVE	CONDITIONAL	PRETERITE
(yo)	coja	cogería	cogí
(tú)	cojas	cogerías	cogiste
(él)	coja	cogería	cogió
(nosotros)	cojamos	cogeríamos	cogimos
(vosotros)	cojáis	cogeríais	cogisteis
(ellos)	cojan	cogerían	cogieron

Irregular Verbs

conducir (to drive, to lead)

	PAST PARTICIPLE	GERUND	IMPERATIVE
	conducido	conduciendo	conduce
			conducid

	PRESENT	FUTURE	IMPERFECT
(yo)	conduzco	conduciré	conducía
(tú)	conduces	conducirás	conducías
(él)	conduce	conducirá	conducía
(nosotros)	conducimos	conduciremos	conducíamos
(vosotros)	conducís	conduciréis	conducíais
(ellos)	conducen	conducirán	conducían

	PRESENT SUBJUNCTIVE	CONDITIONAL	PRETERITE
(yo)	conduzca	conduciría	conduje
(tú)	conduzcas	conducirías	condujiste
(él)	conduzca	conduciría	condujo
(nosotros)	conduzcamos	conduciríamos	condujimos
(vosotros)	conduzcáis	conduciríais	condujisteis
(ellos)	conduzcan	conducirían	condujeron

construir (to build)

	PAST PARTICIPLE	GERUND	IMPERATIVE
	construido	construyendo	construye
			construid

	PRESENT	FUTURE	IMPERFECT
(yo)	construyo	construiré	construía
(tú)	construyes	construirás	construías
(él)	construye	construirá	construía
(nosotros)	construimos	construiremos	construíamos
(vosotros)	construís	construiréis	construíais
(ellos)	construyen	construirán	construían

	PRESENT SUBJUNCTIVE	CONDITIONAL	PRETERITE
(yo)	construya	construiría	construí
(tú)	construyas	construirías	construiste
(él)	construya	construiría	construyó
(nosotros)	construyamos	construiríamos	construimos
(vosotros)	construyáis	construiríais	construisteis
(ellos)	construyan	construirían	construyeron

contar (to tell, to count)

	PAST PARTICIPLE	GERUND	IMPERATIVE
	contado	contando	cuenta
			contad

	PRESENT	FUTURE	IMPERFECT
(yo)	cuento	contaré	contaba
(tú)	cuentas	contarás	contabas
(él)	cuenta	contará	contaba
(nosotros)	contamos	contaremos	contábamos
(vosotros)	contáis	contaréis	contabais
(ellos)	cuentan	contarán	contaban

	PRESENT SUBJUNCTIVE	CONDITIONAL	PRETERITE
(yo)	cuente	contaría	conté
(tú)	cuentes	contarías	contaste
(él)	cuente	contaría	contó
(nosotros)	contemos	contaríamos	contamos
(vosotros)	contéis	contaríais	contasteis
(ellos)	cuenten	contarían	contaron

crecer (to grow)

	PAST PARTICIPLE	GERUND	IMPERATIVE
	crecido	creciendo	crece
			contad

	PRESENT	FUTURE	IMPERFECT
(yo)	crezco	creceré	crecía
(tú)	creces	crecerás	crecías
(él)	crece	crecerá	crecía
(nosotros)	crecemos	creceremos	crecíamos
(vosotros)	crecéis	creceréis	crecíais
(ellos)	crecen	crecerán	crecían

	PRESENT SUBJUNCTIVE	CONDITIONAL	PRETERITE
(yo)	crezca	crecería	crecí
(tú)	crezcas	crecerías	creciste
(él)	crezca	crecería	creció
(nosotros)	crezcamos	creceríamos	crecimos
(vosotros)	crezcáis	creceríais	crecisteis
(ellos)	crezcan	crecerían	crecieron

Irregular Verbs

cruzar (to cross)

	PAST PARTICIPLE cruzado	GERUND cruzando	IMPERATIVE cruza cruzad
	PRESENT	**FUTURE**	**IMPERFECT**
(yo)	cruzo	cruzaré	cruzaba
(tú)	cruzas	cruzarás	cruzabas
(él)	cruza	cruzará	cruzaba
(nosotros)	cruzamos	cruzaremos	cruzábamos
(vosotros)	cruzáis	cruzaréis	cruzabais
(ellos)	cruzan	cruzarán	cruzaban
	PRESENT SUBJUNCTIVE	**CONDITIONAL**	**PRETERITE**
(yo)	cruce	cruzaría	crucé
(tú)	cruces	cruzarías	cruzaste
(él)	cruce	cruzaría	cruzó
(nosotros)	crucemos	cruzaríamos	cruzamos
(vosotros)	crucéis	cruzaríais	cruzasteis
(ellos)	crucen	cruzarían	cruzaron

dar (to give)

	PAST PARTICIPLE dado	GERUND dando	IMPERATIVE da dad
	PRESENT	**FUTURE**	**IMPERFECT**
(yo)	doy	daré	daba
(tú)	das	darás	dabas
(él)	da	dará	daba
(nosotros)	damos	daremos	dábamos
(vosotros)	dais	daréis	dabais
(ellos)	dan	darán	daban
	PRESENT SUBJUNCTIVE	**CONDITIONAL**	**PRETERITE**
(yo)	dé	daría	di
(tú)	des	darías	diste
(él)	dé	daría	dio
(nosotros)	demos	daríamos	dimos
(vosotros)	deis	daríais	disteis
(ellos)	den	darían	dieron

decir (to say)

	PAST PARTICIPLE	GERUND	IMPERATIVE
	dicho	diciendo	di
			decid

	PRESENT	FUTURE	IMPERFECT
(yo)	digo	diré	decía
(tú)	dices	dirás	decías
(él)	dice	dirá	decía
(nosotros)	decimos	diremos	decíamos
(vosotros)	decís	diréis	decíais
(ellos)	dicen	dirán	decían

	PRESENT SUBJUNCTIVE	CONDITIONAL	PRETERITE
(yo)	diga	diría	dije
(tú)	digas	dirías	dijiste
(él)	diga	diría	dijo
(nosotros)	digamos	diríamos	dijimos
(vosotros)	digáis	diríais	dijisteis
(ellos)	digan	dirían	dijeron

dirigir (to direct)

	PAST PARTICIPLE	GERUND	IMPERATIVE
	dirigido	dirigiendo	dirige
			dirigid

	PRESENT	FUTURE	IMPERFECT
(yo)	dirijo	dirigiré	dirigía
(tú)	diriges	dirigirás	dirigías
(él)	dirige	dirigirá	dirigía
(nosotros)	dirigimos	dirigiremos	dirigíamos
(vosotros)	dirigís	dirigiréis	dirigíais
(ellos)	dirigen	dirigirán	dirigían

	PRESENT SUBJUNCTIVE	CONDITIONAL	PRETERITE
(yo)	dirija	dirigiría	dirigí
(tú)	dirijas	dirigirías	dirigiste
(él)	dirija	dirigiría	dirigió
(nosotros)	dirijamos	dirigiríamos	dirigimos
(vosotros)	dirijáis	dirigiríais	dirigisteis
(ellos)	dirijan	dirigirían	dirigieron

Irregular Verbs

dormir (to sleep)

	PAST PARTICIPLE	GERUND	IMPERATIVE
	dormido	durmiendo	duerme
			dormid
	PRESENT	**FUTURE**	**IMPERFECT**
(yo)	duermo	dormiré	dormía
(tú)	duermes	dormirás	dormías
(él)	duerme	dormirá	dormía
(nosotros)	dormimos	dormiremos	dormíamos
(vosotros)	dormís	dormiréis	dormíais
(ellos)	duermen	dormirán	dormían
	PRESENT SUBJUNCTIVE	**CONDITIONAL**	**PRETERITE**
(yo)	duerma	dormiría	dormí
(tú)	duermas	dormirías	dormiste
(él)	duerma	dormiría	durmió
(nosotros)	durmamos	dormiríamos	dormimos
(vosotros)	durmáis	dormiríais	dormisteis
(ellos)	duerman	dormirían	durmieron

elegir (to choose)

	PAST PARTICIPLE	GERUND	IMPERATIVE
	elegido	eligiendo	elige
			elegid
	PRESENT	**FUTURE**	**IMPERFECT**
(yo)	elijo	elegiré	elegía
(tú)	eliges	elegirás	elegías
(él)	elige	elegirá	elegía
(nosotros)	elegimos	elegiremos	elegíamos
(vosotros)	elegís	elegiréis	elegíais
(ellos)	eligen	elegirán	elegían
	PRESENT SUBJUNCTIVE	**CONDITIONAL**	**PRETERITE**
(yo)	elija	elegiría	elegí
(tú)	elijas	elegirías	elegiste
(él)	elija	elegiría	eligió
(nosotros)	elijamos	elegiríamos	elegimos
(vosotros)	elijáis	elegiríais	elegisteis
(ellos)	elijan	elegirían	eligieron

empezar (to begin)

	PAST PARTICIPLE	GERUND	IMPERATIVE
	empezado	empezando	empieza
			empezad

	PRESENT	FUTURE	IMPERFECT
(yo)	empiezo	empezaré	empezaba
(tú)	empiezas	empezarás	empezabas
(él)	empieza	empezará	empezaba
(nosotros)	empezamos	empezaremos	empezábamos
(vosotros)	empezáis	empezaréis	empezabais
(ellos)	empiezan	empezarán	empezaban

	PRESENT SUBJUNCTIVE	CONDITIONAL	PRETERITE
(yo)	empiece	empezaría	empecé
(tú)	empieces	empezarías	empezaste
(él)	empiece	empezaría	empezó
(nosotros)	empecemos	empezaríamos	empezamos
(vosotros)	empecéis	empezaríais	empezasteis
(ellos)	empiecen	empezarían	empezaron

entender (to understand)

	PAST PARTICIPLE	GERUND	IMPERATIVE
	entendido	entendiendo	entiende
			entended

	PRESENT	FUTURE	IMPERFECT
(yo)	entiendo	entenderé	entendía
(tú)	entiendes	entenderás	entendías
(él)	entiende	entenderá	entendía
(nosotros)	entendemos	entenderemos	entendíamos
(vosotros)	entendéis	entenderéis	entendíais
(ellos)	entienden	entenderán	entendían

	PRESENT SUBJUNCTIVE	CONDITIONAL	PRETERITE
(yo)	entienda	entendería	entendí
(tú)	entiendas	entenderías	entendiste
(él)	entienda	entendería	entendió
(nosotros)	entendamos	entenderíamos	entendimos
(vosotros)	entendáis	entenderíais	entendisteis
(ellos)	entiendan	entenderían	entendieron

enviar (to send)

	PAST PARTICIPLE	GERUND	IMPERATIVE
	enviado	enviando	envía
			enviad

	PRESENT	FUTURE	IMPERFECT
(yo)	envío	enviaré	enviaba
(tú)	envías	enviarás	enviabas
(él)	envía	enviará	enviaba
(nosotros)	enviamos	enviaremos	enviábamos
(vosotros)	enviáis	enviaréis	enviabais
(ellos)	envían	enviarán	enviaban

	PRESENT SUBJUNCTIVE	CONDITIONAL	PRETERITE
(yo)	envíe	enviaría	envié
(tú)	envíes	enviarías	enviaste
(él)	envíe	enviaría	envió
(nosotros)	enviemos	enviaríamos	enviamos
(vosotros)	enviéis	enviaríais	enviasteis
(ellos)	envíen	enviarían	enviaron

erguir (to erect)

	PAST PARTICIPLE	GERUND	IMPERATIVE
	erguido	irguiendo	yergue
			erguid

	PRESENT	FUTURE	IMPERFECT
(yo)	yergo	erguiré	erguía
(tú)	yergues	erguirás	erguías
(él)	yergue	erguirá	erguía
(nosotros)	erguimos	erguiremos	erguíamos
(vosotros)	erguís	erguiréis	erguíais
(ellos)	yerguen	erguirán	erguían

	PRESENT SUBJUNCTIVE	CONDITIONAL	PRETERITE
(yo)	yerga	erguiría	erguí
(tú)	yergas	erguirías	erguiste
(él)	yerga	erguiría	irguió
(nosotros)	irgamos	erguiríamos	erguimos
(vosotros)	irgáis	erguiríais	erguisteis
(ellos)	yergan	erguirían	irguieron

errar (to err)

	PAST PARTICIPLE	GERUND	IMPERATIVE
	errado	errando	yerra
			errad

	PRESENT	FUTURE	IMPERFECT
(yo)	yerro	erraré	erraba
(tú)	yerras	errarás	errabas
(él)	yerra	errará	erraba
(nosotros)	erramos	erraremos	errábamos
(vosotros)	erráis	erraréis	errabais
(ellos)	yerran	errarán	erraban

	PRESENT SUBJUNCTIVE	CONDITIONAL	PRETERITE
(yo)	yerre	erraría	erré
(tú)	yerres	errarías	erraste
(él)	yerre	erraría	erró
(nosotros)	erremos	erraríamos	erramos
(vosotros)	erréis	erraríais	errasteis
(ellos)	yerren	errarían	erraron

estar (to be)

	PAST PARTICIPLE	GERUND	IMPERATIVE
	estado	estando	está
			estad

	PRESENT	FUTURE	IMPERFECT
(yo)	estoy	estaré	estaba
(tú)	estás	estarás	estabas
(él)	está	estará	estaba
(nosotros)	estamos	estaremos	estábamos
(vosotros)	estáis	estaréis	estabais
(ellos)	están	estarán	estaban

	PRESENT SUBJUNCTIVE	CONDITIONAL	PRETERITE
(yo)	esté	estaría	estuve
(tú)	estés	estarías	estuviste
(él)	esté	estaría	estuvo
(nosotros)	estemos	estaríamos	estuvimos
(vosotros)	estéis	estaríais	estuvisteis
(ellos)	estén	estarían	estuvieron

freír (to fry)

	PAST PARTICIPLE frito	GERUND friendo	IMPERATIVE fríe freíd
	PRESENT	FUTURE	IMPERFECT
(yo)	frío	freiré	freía
(tú)	fríes	freirás	freías
(él)	fríe	freirá	freía
(nosotros)	freímos	freiremos	freíamos
(vosotros)	freís	freiréis	freíais
(ellos)	fríen	freirán	freían
	PRESENT SUBJUNCTIVE	CONDITIONAL	PRETERITE
(yo)	fría	freiría	freí
(tú)	frías	freirías	freíste
(él)	fría	freiría	frio
(nosotros)	friamos	freiríamos	freímos
(vosotros)	friais	freiríais	freísteis
(ellos)	frían	freirían	frieron

haber (to have, *auxiliary*)

	PAST PARTICIPLE habido	GERUND habiendo	IMPERATIVE *not used*
	PRESENT	FUTURE	IMPERFECT
(yo)	he	habré	había
(tú)	has	habrás	habías
(él)	ha	habrá	había
(nosotros)	hemos	habremos	habíamos
(vosotros)	habéis	habréis	habíais
(ellos)	han	habrán	habían
	PRESENT SUBJUNCTIVE	CONDITIONAL	PRETERITE
(yo)	haya	habría	hube
(tú)	hayas	habrías	hubiste
(él)	haya	habría	hubo
(nosotros)	hayamos	habríamos	hubimos
(vosotros)	hayáis	habríais	hubisteis
(ellos)	hayan	habrían	hubieron

hacer (to do, to make)

	PAST PARTICIPLE	GERUND	IMPERATIVE
	hecho	haciendo	haz
			haced
	PRESENT	**FUTURE**	**IMPERFECT**
(yo)	hago	haré	hacía
(tú)	haces	harás	hacías
(él)	hace	hará	hacía
(nosotros)	hacemos	haremos	hacíamos
(vosotros)	hacéis	haréis	hacíais
(ellos)	hacen	harán	hacían
	PRESENT SUBJUNCTIVE	**CONDITIONAL**	**PRETERITE**
(yo)	haga	haría	hice
(tú)	hagas	harías	hiciste
(él)	haga	haría	hizo
(nosotros)	hagamos	haríamos	hicimos
(vosotros)	hagáis	haríais	hicisteis
(ellos)	hagan	harían	hicieron

ir (to go)

	PAST PARTICIPLE	GERUND	IMPERATIVE
	ido	yendo	ve
			id
	PRESENT	**FUTURE**	**IMPERFECT**
(yo)	voy	iré	iba
(tú)	vas	irás	ibas
(él)	va	irá	iba
(nosotros)	vamos	iremos	íbamos
(vosotros)	vais	iréis	ibais
(ellos)	van	irán	iban
	PRESENT SUBJUNCTIVE	**CONDITIONAL**	**PRETERITE**
(yo)	vaya	iría	fui
(tú)	vayas	irías	fuiste
(él)	vaya	iría	fue
(nosotros)	vayamos	iríamos	fuimos
(vosotros)	vayáis	iríais	fuisteis
(ellos)	vayan	irían	fueron

Irregular Verbs

jugar (to play)

	PAST PARTICIPLE	GERUND	IMPERATIVE
	jugado	jugando	juega
			jugad
	PRESENT	FUTURE	IMPERFECT
(yo)	juego	jugaré	jugaba
(tú)	juegas	jugarás	jugabas
(él)	juega	jugará	jugaba
(nosotros)	jugamos	jugaremos	jugábamos
(vosotros)	jugáis	jugaréis	jugabais
(ellos)	juegan	jugarán	jugaban
	PRESENT SUBJUNCTIVE	CONDITIONAL	PRETERITE
(yo)	juegue	jugaría	jugué
(tú)	juegues	jugarías	jugaste
(él)	juegue	jugaría	jugó
(nosotros)	juguemos	jugaríamos	jugamos
(vosotros)	juguéis	jugaríais	jugasteis
(ellos)	jueguen	jugarían	jugaron

leer (to read)

	PAST PARTICIPLE	GERUND	IMPERATIVE
	leído	leyendo	lee
			leed
	PRESENT	FUTURE	IMPERFECT
(yo)	leo	leeré	leía
(tú)	lees	leerás	leías
(él)	lee	leerá	leía
(nosotros)	leemos	leeremos	leíamos
(vosotros)	leéis	leeréis	leíais
(ellos)	leen	leerán	leían
	PRESENT SUBJUNCTIVE	CONDITIONAL	PRETERITE
(yo)	lea	leería	leí
(tú)	leas	leerías	leíste
(él)	lea	leería	leyó
(nosotros)	leamos	leeríamos	leímos
(vosotros)	leáis	leeríais	leísteis
(ellos)	lean	leerían	leyeron

Irregular Verbs

lucir (to shine)

	PAST PARTICIPLE	GERUND	IMPERATIVE
	lucido	luciendo	luce
			lucid

	PRESENT	FUTURE	IMPERFECT
(yo)	luzco	luciré	lucía
(tú)	luces	lucirás	lucías
(él)	luce	lucirá	lucía
(nosotros)	lucimos	luciremos	lucíamos
(vosotros)	lucís	luciréis	lucíais
(ellos)	lucen	lucirán	lucían

	PRESENT SUBJUNCTIVE	CONDITIONAL	PRETERITE
(yo)	luzca	luciría	lucí
(tú)	luzcas	lucirías	luciste
(él)	luzca	luciría	lució
(nosotros)	luzcamos	luciríamos	lucimos
(vosotros)	luzcáis	luciríais	lucisteis
(ellos)	luzcan	lucirían	lucieron

llover (to rain)

	PAST PARTICIPLE	GERUND	IMPERATIVE
	llovido	lloviendo	*not used*

	PRESENT	FUTURE	IMPERFECT
	llueve	lloverá	llovía

	PRESENT SUBJUNCTIVE	CONDITIONAL	PRETERITE
	llueva	llovería	llovió

morir (to die)

	PAST PARTICIPLE	GERUND	IMPERATIVE
	muerto	muriendo	muere
			morid

	PRESENT	FUTURE	IMPERFECT
(yo)	muero	moriré	moría
(tú)	mueres	morirás	morías
(él)	muere	morirá	moría
(nosotros)	morimos	moriremos	moríamos
(vosotros)	morís	moriréis	moríais
(ellos)	mueren	morirán	morían

	PRESENT SUBJUNCTIVE	CONDITIONAL	PRETERITE
(yo)	muera	moriría	morí
(tú)	mueras	morirías	moriste
(él)	muera	moriría	murió
(nosotros)	muramos	moriríamos	morimos
(vosotros)	muráis	moriríais	moristeis
(ellos)	mueran	morirían	murieron

mover (to move)

	PAST PARTICIPLE	GERUND	IMPERATIVE
	movido	moviendo	mueve
			moved

	PRESENT	FUTURE	IMPERFECT
(yo)	muevo	moveré	movía
(tú)	mueves	moverás	movías
(él)	mueve	moverá	movía
(nosotros)	movemos	moveremos	movíamos
(vosotros)	movéis	moveréis	movíais
(ellos)	mueven	moverán	movían

	PRESENT SUBJUNCTIVE	CONDITIONAL	PRETERITE
(yo)	mueva	movería	moví
(tú)	muevas	moverías	moviste
(él)	mueva	movería	movió
(nosotros)	movamos	moveríamos	movimos
(vosotros)	mováis	moveríais	movisteis
(ellos)	muevan	moverían	movieron

nacer (to be born)

	PAST PARTICIPLE	GERUND	IMPERATIVE
	nacido	naciendo	nace
			naced

	PRESENT	FUTURE	IMPERFECT
(yo)	nazco	naceré	nacía
(tú)	naces	nacerás	nacías
(él)	nace	nacerá	nacía
(nosotros)	nacemos	naceremos	nacíamos
(vosotros)	nacéis	naceréis	nacíais
(ellos)	nacen	nacerán	nacían

	PRESENT SUBJUNCTIVE	CONDITIONAL	PRETERITE
(yo)	nazca	nacería	nací
(tú)	nazcas	nacerías	naciste
(él)	nazca	nacería	nació
(nosotros)	nazcamos	naceríamos	nacimos
(vosotros)	nazcáis	naceríais	nacisteis
(ellos)	nazcan	nacerían	nacieron

negar (to deny)

	PAST PARTICIPLE	GERUND	IMPERATIVE
	negado	negando	niega
			negad

	PRESENT	FUTURE	IMPERFECT
(yo)	niego	negaré	negaba
(tú)	niegas	negarás	negabas
(él)	niega	negará	negaba
(nosotros)	negamos	negaremos	negábamos
(vosotros)	negáis	negaréis	negabais
(ellos)	niegan	negarán	negaban

	PRESENT SUBJUNCTIVE	CONDITIONAL	PRETERITE
(yo)	niegue	negaría	negué
(tú)	niegues	negarías	negaste
(él)	niegue	negaría	negó
(nosotros)	neguemos	negaríamos	negamos
(vosotros)	neguéis	negaríais	negasteis
(ellos)	nieguen	negarían	negaron

Irregular Verbs

oír (to hear)

	PAST PARTICIPLE	GERUND	IMPERATIVE
	oído	oyendo	oye
			oíd

	PRESENT	FUTURE	IMPERFECT
(yo)	oigo	oiré	oía
(tú)	oyes	oirás	oías
(él)	oye	oirá	oía
(nosotros)	oímos	oiremos	oíamos
(vosotros)	oís	oiréis	oíais
(ellos)	oyen	oirán	oían

	PRESENT SUBJUNCTIVE	CONDITIONAL	PRETERITE
(yo)	oiga	oiría	oí
(tú)	oigas	oirías	oíste
(él)	oiga	oiría	oyó
(nosotros)	oigamos	oiríamos	oímos
(vosotros)	oigáis	oiríais	oísteis
(ellos)	oigan	oirían	oyeron

oler (to smell)

	PAST PARTICIPLE	GERUND	IMPERATIVE
	olido	oliendo	huele
			oled

	PRESENT	FUTURE	IMPERFECT
(yo)	huelo	oleré	olía
(tú)	hueles	olerás	olías
(él)	huele	olerá	olía
(nosotros)	olemos	oleremos	olíamos
(vosotros)	oléis	oleréis	olíais
(ellos)	huelen	olerán	olían

	PRESENT SUBJUNCTIVE	CONDITIONAL	PRETERITE
(yo)	huela	olería	olí
(tú)	huelas	olerías	oliste
(él)	huela	olería	olió
(nosotros)	olamos	oleríamos	olimos
(vosotros)	oláis	oleríais	olisteis
(ellos)	huelan	olerían	olieron

pedir (to ask for)

	PAST PARTICIPLE	GERUND	IMPERATIVE
	pedido	pidiendo	pide
			pedid

	PRESENT	FUTURE	IMPERFECT
(yo)	pido	pediré	pedía
(tú)	pides	pedirás	pedías
(él)	pide	pedirá	pedía
(nosotros)	pedimos	pediremos	pedíamos
(vosotros)	pedís	pediréis	pedíais
(ellos)	piden	pedirán	pedían

	PRESENT SUBJUNCTIVE	CONDITIONAL	PRETERITE
(yo)	pida	pediría	pedí
(tú)	pidas	pedirías	pediste
(él)	pida	pediría	pidió
(nosotros)	pidamos	pediríamos	pedimos
(vosotros)	pidáis	pediríais	pedisteis
(ellos)	pidan	pedirían	pidieron

pensar (to think)

	PAST PARTICIPLE	GERUND	IMPERATIVE
	pensado	pensando	piensa
			pensad

	PRESENT	FUTURE	IMPERFECT
(yo)	pienso	pensaré	pensaba
(tú)	piensas	pensarás	pensabas
(él)	piensa	pensará	pensaba
(nosotros)	pensamos	pensaremos	pensábamos
(vosotros)	pensáis	pensaréis	pensabais
(ellos)	piensan	pensarán	pensaban

	PRESENT SUBJUNCTIVE	CONDITIONAL	PRETERITE
(yo)	piense	pensaría	pensé
(tú)	pienses	pensarías	pensaste
(él)	piense	pensaría	pensó
(nosotros)	pensemos	pensaríamos	pensamos
(vosotros)	penséis	pensaríais	pensasteis
(ellos)	piensen	pensarían	pensaron

poder (to be able)

	PAST PARTICIPLE	GERUND	IMPERATIVE
	podido	pudiendo	puede
			poded
	PRESENT	FUTURE	IMPERFECT
(yo)	puedo	podré	podía
(tú)	puedes	podrás	podías
(él)	puede	podrá	podía
(nosotros)	podemos	podremos	podíamos
(vosotros)	podéis	podréis	podíais
(ellos)	pueden	podrán	podían
	PRESENT SUBJUNCTIVE	CONDITIONAL	PRETERITE
(yo)	pueda	podría	pude
(tú)	puedas	podrías	pudiste
(él)	pueda	podría	pudo
(nosotros)	podamos	podríamos	pudimos
(vosotros)	podáis	podríais	pudisteis
(ellos)	puedan	podrían	pudieron

poner (to put)

	PAST PARTICIPLE	GERUND	IMPERATIVE
	puesto	poniendo	pon
			poned
	PRESENT	FUTURE	IMPERFECT
(yo)	pongo	pondré	ponía
(tú)	pones	pondrás	ponías
(él)	pone	pondrá	ponía
(nosotros)	ponemos	pondremos	poníamos
(vosotros)	ponéis	pondréis	poníais
(ellos)	ponen	pondrán	ponían
	PRESENT SUBJUNCTIVE	CONDITIONAL	PRETERITE
(yo)	ponga	pondría	puse
(tú)	pongas	pondrías	pusiste
(él)	ponga	pondría	puso
(nosotros)	pongamos	pondríamos	pusimos
(vosotros)	pongáis	pondríais	pusisteis
(ellos)	pongan	pondrían	pusieron

prohibir (to forbid)

	PAST PARTICIPLE	GERUND	IMPERATIVE
	prohibido	prohibiendo	prohíbe
			prohibid
	PRESENT	FUTURE	IMPERFECT
(yo)	prohíbo	prohibiré	prohibía
(tú)	prohíbes	prohibirás	prohibías
(él)	prohíbe	prohibirá	prohibía
(nosotros)	prohibimos	prohibiremos	prohibíamos
(vosotros)	prohibís	prohibiréis	prohibíais
(ellos)	prohíben	prohibirán	prohibían
	PRESENT SUBJUNCTIVE	CONDITIONAL	PRETERITE
(yo)	prohíba	prohibiría	prohibí
(tú)	prohíbas	prohibirías	prohibiste
(él)	prohíba	prohibiría	prohibió
(nosotros)	prohibamos	prohibiríamos	prohibimos
(vosotros)	prohibáis	prohibiríais	prohibisteis
(ellos)	prohíban	prohibirían	prohibieron

querer (to want)

	PAST PARTICIPLE	GERUND	IMPERATIVE
	querido	queriendo	quiere
			quered
	PRESENT	FUTURE	IMPERFECT
(yo)	quiero	querré	quería
(tú)	quieres	querrás	querías
(él)	quiere	querrá	quería
(nosotros)	queremos	querremos	queríamos
(vosotros)	queréis	querréis	queríais
(ellos)	quieren	querrán	querían
	PRESENT SUBJUNCTIVE	CONDITIONAL	PRETERITE
(yo)	quiera	querría	quise
(tú)	quieras	querrías	quisiste
(él)	quiera	querría	quiso
(nosotros)	queramos	querríamos	quisimos
(vosotros)	queráis	querríais	quisisteis
(ellos)	quieran	querrían	quisieron

rehusar (to refuse)

	PAST PARTICIPLE	GERUND	IMPERATIVE
	rehusado	rehusando	rehúsa
			rehusad
	PRESENT	FUTURE	IMPERFECT
(yo)	rehúso	rehusaré	rehusaba
(tú)	rehúsas	rehusarás	rehusabas
(él)	rehúsa	rehusará	rehusaba
(nosotros)	rehusamos	rehusaremos	rehusábamos
(vosotros)	rehusáis	rehusaréis	rehusabais
(ellos)	rehúsan	rehusarán	rehusaban
	PRESENT SUBJUNCTIVE	CONDITIONAL	PRETERITE
(yo)	rehúse	rehusaría	rehusé
(tú)	rehúses	rehusarías	rehusaste
(él)	rehúse	rehusaría	rehusó
(nosotros)	rehusemos	rehusaríamos	rehusamos
(vosotros)	rehuséis	rehusaríais	rehusasteis
(ellos)	rehúsen	rehusarían	rehusaron

reír (to laugh)

	PAST PARTICIPLE	GERUND	IMPERATIVE
	reído	riendo	ríe
			reíd
	PRESENT	FUTURE	IMPERFECT
(yo)	río	reiré	reía
(tú)	ríes	reirás	reías
(él)	ríe	reirá	reía
(nosotros)	reímos	reiremos	reíamos
(vosotros)	reís	reiréis	reíais
(ellos)	ríen	reirán	reían
	PRESENT SUBJUNCTIVE	CONDITIONAL	PRETERITE
(yo)	ría	reiría	reí
(tú)	rías	reirías	reíste
(él)	ría	reiría	rio
(nosotros)	riamos	reiríamos	reímos
(vosotros)	riais	reiríais	reísteis
(ellos)	rían	reirían	rieron

reñir (to scold)

	PAST PARTICIPLE	GERUND	IMPERATIVE
	reñido	riñendo	ríñe
			reñid

	PRESENT	FUTURE	IMPERFECT
(yo)	riño	reñiré	reñía
(tú)	riñes	reñirás	reñías
(él)	riñe	reñirá	reñía
(nosotros)	reñimos	reñiremos	reñíamos
(vosotros)	reñís	reñiréis	reñíais
(ellos)	riñen	reñirán	reñían

	PRESENT SUBJUNCTIVE	CONDITIONAL	PRETERITE
(yo)	riña	reñiría	reñí
(tú)	riñas	reñirías	reñiste
(él)	riña	reñiría	riñó
(nosotros)	riñamos	reñiríamos	reñimos
(vosotros)	riñáis	reñiríais	reñisteis
(ellos)	riñan	reñirían	riñeron

resolver (to solve)

	PAST PARTICIPLE	GERUND	IMPERATIVE
	resuelto	resolviendo	resuelve
			resolved

	PRESENT	FUTURE	IMPERFECT
(yo)	resuelvo	resolveré	resolvía
(tú)	resuelves	resolverás	resolvías
(él)	resuelve	resolverá	resolvía
(nosotros)	resolvemos	resolveremos	resolvíamos
(vosotros)	resolvéis	resolveréis	resolvíais
(ellos)	resuelven	resolverán	resolvían

	PRESENT SUBJUNCTIVE	CONDITIONAL	PRETERITE
(yo)	resuelva	resolvería	resolví
(tú)	resuelvas	resolverías	resolviste
(él)	resuelva	resolvería	resolvió
(nosotros)	resolvamos	resolveríamos	resolvimos
(vosotros)	resolváis	resolveríais	resolvisteis
(ellos)	resuelvan	resolverían	resolvieron

reunir (to put together, to gather)

	PAST PARTICIPLE	GERUND	IMPERATIVE
	reunido	reuniendo	reúne
			reunid

	PRESENT	FUTURE	IMPERFECT
(yo)	reúno	reuniré	reunía
(tú)	reúnes	reunirás	reunías
(él)	reúne	reunirá	reunía
(nosotros)	reunimos	reuniremos	reuníamos
(vosotros)	reunís	reuniréis	reuníais
(ellos)	reúnen	reunirán	reunían

	PRESENT SUBJUNCTIVE	CONDITIONAL	PRETERITE
(yo)	reúna	reuniría	reuní
(tú)	reúnas	reunirías	reuniste
(él)	reúna	reuniría	reunió
(nosotros)	reunamos	reuniríamos	reunimos
(vosotros)	reunáis	reuniríais	reunisteis
(ellos)	reúnan	reunirían	reunieron

rogar (to beg)

	PAST PARTICIPLE	GERUND	IMPERATIVE
	rogado	rogando	ruega
			rogad

	PRESENT	FUTURE	IMPERFECT
(yo)	ruego	rogaré	rogaba
(tú)	ruegas	rogarás	rogabas
(él)	ruega	rogará	rogaba
(nosotros)	rogamos	rogaremos	rogábamos
(vosotros)	rogáis	rogaréis	rogabais
(ellos)	ruegan	rogarán	rogaban

	PRESENT SUBJUNCTIVE	CONDITIONAL	PRETERITE
(yo)	ruegue	rogaría	rogué
(tú)	ruegues	rogarías	rogaste
(él)	ruegue	rogaría	rogó
(nosotros)	roguemos	rogaríamos	rogamos
(vosotros)	roguéis	rogaríais	rogasteis
(ellos)	rueguen	rogarían	rogaron

saber (to know)

	PAST PARTICIPLE	GERUND	IMPERATIVE
	sabido	sabiendo	sabe
			sabed

	PRESENT	FUTURE	IMPERFECT
(yo)	sé	sabré	sabía
(tú)	sabes	sabrás	sabías
(él)	sabe	sabrá	sabía
(nosotros)	sabemos	sabremos	sabíamos
(vosotros)	sabéis	sabréis	sabíais
(ellos)	saben	sabrán	sabían

	PRESENT SUBJUNCTIVE	CONDITIONAL	PRETERITE
(yo)	sepa	sabría	supe
(tú)	sepas	sabrías	supiste
(él)	sepa	sabría	supo
(nosotros)	sepamos	sabríamos	supimos
(vosotros)	sepáis	sabríais	supisteis
(ellos)	sepan	sabrían	supieron

salir (to go out)

	PAST PARTICIPLE	GERUND	IMPERATIVE
	salido	saliendo	sal
			salid

	PRESENT	FUTURE	IMPERFECT
(yo)	salgo	saldré	salía
(tú)	sales	saldrás	salías
(él)	sale	saldrá	salía
(nosotros)	salimos	saldremos	salíamos
(vosotros)	salís	saldréis	salíais
(ellos)	salen	saldrán	salían

	PRESENT SUBJUNCTIVE	CONDITIONAL	PRETERITE
(yo)	salga	saldría	salí
(tú)	salgas	saldrías	saliste
(él)	salga	saldría	salió
(nosotros)	salgamos	saldríamos	salimos
(vosotros)	salgáis	saldríais	salisteis
(ellos)	salgan	saldrían	salieron

satisfacer (to satisfy)

	PAST PARTICIPLE	GERUND	IMPERATIVE
	satisfecho	satisfaciendo	satisfaz/satisface
			satisfaced

	PRESENT	FUTURE	IMPERFECT
(yo)	satisfago	satisfaré	satisfacía
(tú)	satisfaces	satisfarás	satisfacías
(él)	satisface	satisfará	satisfacía
(nosotros)	satisfacemos	satisfaremos	satisfacíamos
(vosotros)	satisfacéis	satisfaréis	satisfacíais
(ellos)	satisfacen	satisfarán	satisfacían

	PRESENT SUBJUNCTIVE	CONDITIONAL	PRETERITE
(yo)	satisfaga	satisfaría	satisfice
(tú)	satisfagas	satisfarías	satisficiste
(él)	satisfaga	satisfaría	satisfizo
(nosotros)	satisfagamos	satisfaríamos	satisficimos
(vosotros)	satisfagáis	satisfaríais	satisficisteis
(ellos)	satisfagan	satisfarían	satisficieron

seguir (to follow)

	PAST PARTICIPLE	GERUND	IMPERATIVE
	seguido	siguiendo	sigue
			seguid

	PRESENT	FUTURE	IMPERFECT
(yo)	sigo	seguiré	seguía
(tú)	sigues	seguirás	seguías
(él)	sigue	seguirá	seguía
(nosotros)	seguimos	seguiremos	seguíamos
(vosotros)	seguís	seguiréis	seguíais
(ellos)	siguen	seguirán	seguían

	PRESENT SUBJUNCTIVE	CONDITIONAL	PRETERITE
(yo)	siga	seguiría	seguí
(tú)	sigas	seguirías	seguiste
(él)	siga	seguiría	siguió
(nosotros)	sigamos	seguiríamos	seguimos
(vosotros)	sigáis	seguiríais	seguisteis
(ellos)	sigan	seguirían	siguieron

sentir (to feel)

	PAST PARTICIPLE	GERUND	IMPERATIVE
	sentido	sintiendo	siente
			sentid

	PRESENT	FUTURE	IMPERFECT
(yo)	siento	sentiré	sentía
(tú)	sientes	sentirás	sentías
(él)	siente	sentirá	sentía
(nosotros)	sentimos	sentiremos	sentíamos
(vosotros)	sentís	sentiréis	sentíais
(ellos)	sienten	sentirán	sentían

	PRESENT SUBJUNCTIVE	CONDITIONAL	PRETERITE
(yo)	sienta	sentiría	sentí
(tú)	sientas	sentirías	sentiste
(él)	sienta	sentiría	sintió
(nosotros)	sintamos	sentiríamos	sentimos
(vosotros)	sintáis	sentiríais	sentisteis
(ellos)	sientan	sentirían	sintieron

ser (to be)

	PAST PARTICIPLE	GERUND	IMPERATIVE
	sido	siendo	sé
			sed

	PRESENT	FUTURE	IMPERFECT
(yo)	soy	seré	era
(tú)	eres	serás	eras
(él)	es	será	era
(nosotros)	somos	seremos	éramos
(vosotros)	sois	seréis	erais
(ellos)	son	serán	eran

	PRESENT SUBJUNCTIVE	CONDITIONAL	PRETERITE
(yo)	sea	sería	fui
(tú)	seas	serías	fuiste
(él)	sea	sería	fue
(nosotros)	seamos	seríamos	fuimos
(vosotros)	seáis	seríais	fuisteis
(ellos)	sean	serían	fueron

tener (to have)

	PAST PARTICIPLE	GERUND	IMPERATIVE
	tenido	teniendo	ten
			tened

	PRESENT	FUTURE	IMPERFECT
(yo)	tengo	tendré	tenía
(tú)	tienes	tendrás	tenías
(él)	tiene	tendrá	tenía
(nosotros)	tenemos	tendremos	teníamos
(vosotros)	tenéis	tendréis	teníais
(ellos)	tienen	tendrán	tenían

	PRESENT SUBJUNCTIVE	CONDITIONAL	PRETERITE
(yo)	tenga	tendría	tuve
(tú)	tengas	tendrías	tuviste
(él)	tenga	tendría	tuvo
(nosotros)	tengamos	tendríamos	tuvimos
(vosotros)	tengáis	tendríais	tuvisteis
(ellos)	tengan	tendrían	tuvieron

torcer (to twist)

	PAST PARTICIPLE	GERUND	IMPERATIVE
	torcido	torciendo	tuerce
			torced

	PRESENT	FUTURE	IMPERFECT
(yo)	tuerzo	torceré	torcía
(tú)	tuerces	torcerás	torcías
(él)	tuerce	torcerá	torcía
(nosotros)	torcemos	torceremos	torcíamos
(vosotros)	torcéis	torceréis	torcíais
(ellos)	tuercen	torcerán	torcían

	PRESENT SUBJUNCTIVE	CONDITIONAL	PRETERITE
(yo)	tuerza	torcería	torcí
(tú)	tuerzas	torcerías	torciste
(él)	tuerza	torcería	torció
(nosotros)	torzamos	torceríamos	torcimos
(vosotros)	torzáis	torceríais	torcisteis
(ellos)	tuerzan	torcerían	torcieron

traer (to bring)

	PAST PARTICIPLE	GERUND	IMPERATIVE
	traído	trayendo	trae
			traed

	PRESENT	FUTURE	IMPERFECT
(yo)	traigo	traeré	traía
(tú)	traes	traerás	traías
(él)	trae	traerá	traía
(nosotros)	traemos	traeremos	traíamos
(vosotros)	traéis	traeréis	traíais
(ellos)	traen	traerán	traían

	PRESENT SUBJUNCTIVE	CONDITIONAL	PRETERITE
(yo)	traiga	traería	traje
(tú)	traigas	traerías	trajiste
(él)	traiga	traería	trajo
(nosotros)	traigamos	traeríamos	trajimos
(vosotros)	traigáis	traeríais	trajisteis
(ellos)	traigan	traerían	trajeron

valer (to be worth)

	PAST PARTICIPLE	GERUND	IMPERATIVE
	valido	valiendo	vale
			valed

	PRESENT	FUTURE	IMPERFECT
(yo)	valgo	valdré	valía
(tú)	vales	valdrás	valías
(él)	vale	valdrá	valía
(nosotros)	valemos	valdremos	valíamos
(vosotros)	valéis	valdréis	valíais
(ellos)	valen	valdrán	valían

	PRESENT SUBJUNCTIVE	CONDITIONAL	PRETERITE
(yo)	valga	valdría	valí
(tú)	valgas	valdrias	valiste
(él)	valga	valdría	valió
(nosotros)	valgamos	valdríamos	valimos
(vosotros)	valgáis	valdríais	valisteis
(ellos)	valgan	valdrían	valieron

venir (to come)

	PAST PARTICIPLE	GERUND	IMPERATIVE
	venido	viniendo	ven
			venid

	PRESENT	FUTURE	IMPERFECT
(yo)	vengo	vendré	venía
(tú)	vienes	vendrás	venías
(él)	viene	vendrá	venía
(nosotros)	venimos	vendremos	veníamos
(vosotros)	venís	vendréis	veníais
(ellos)	vienen	vendrán	venían

	PRESENT SUBJUNCTIVE	CONDITIONAL	PRETERITE
(yo)	venga	vendría	vine
(tú)	vengas	vendrías	viniste
(él)	venga	vendría	vino
(nosotros)	vengamos	vendríamos	vinimos
(vosotros)	vengáis	vendríais	vinisteis
(ellos)	vengan	vendrían	vinieron

ver (to see)

	PAST PARTICIPLE	GERUND	IMPERATIVE
	visto	viendo	ve
			ved

	PRESENT	FUTURE	IMPERFECT
(yo)	veo	veré	veía
(tú)	ves	verás	veías
(él)	ve	verá	veía
(nosotros)	vemos	veremos	veíamos
(vosotros)	veis	veréis	veíais
(ellos)	ven	verán	veían

	PRESENT SUBJUNCTIVE	CONDITIONAL	PRETERITE
(yo)	vea	vería	vi
(tú)	veas	verías	viste
(él)	vea	vería	vio
(nosotros)	veamos	veríamos	vimos
(vosotros)	veáis	veríais	visteis
(ellos)	vean	verían	vieron

volcar (to overturn)

	PAST PARTICIPLE	GERUND	IMPERATIVE
	volcado	volcando	vuelca
			volcad

	PRESENT	FUTURE	IMPERFECT
(yo)	vuelco	volcaré	volcaba
(tú)	vuelcas	volcarás	volcabas
(él)	vuelca	volcará	volcaba
(nosotros)	volcamos	volcaremos	volcábamos
(vosotros)	volcáis	volcaréis	volcabais
(ellos)	vuelcan	volcarán	volcaban

	PRESENT SUBJUNCTIVE	CONDITIONAL	PRETERITE
(yo)	vuelque	volcaría	volqué
(tú)	vuelques	volcarías	volcaste
(él)	vuelque	volcaría	volcó
(nosotros)	volquemos	volcaríamos	volcamos
(vosotros)	volquéis	volcaríais	volcasteis
(ellos)	vuelquen	volcarían	volcaron

volver (to return)

	PAST PARTICIPLE	GERUND	IMPERATIVE
	vuelto	volviendo	vuelve
			volved

	PRESENT	FUTURE	IMPERFECT
(yo)	vuelvo	volveré	volvía
(tú)	vuelves	volverás	volvías
(él)	vuelve	volverá	volvía
(nosotros)	volvemos	volveremos	volvíamos
(vosotros)	volvéis	volveréis	volvíais
(ellos)	vuelven	volverán	volvían

	PRESENT SUBJUNCTIVE	CONDITIONAL	PRETERITE
(yo)	vuelva	volvería	volví
(tú)	vuelvas	volverías	volviste
(él)	vuelva	volvería	volvió
(nosotros)	volvamos	volveríamos	volvimos
(vosotros)	volváis	volveríais	volvisteis
(ellos)	vuelvan	volverían	volvieron

The Gender of Nouns

In Spanish, all nouns are either masculine or feminine, whether denoting people, animals or things. Gender is largely unpredictable and has to be learnt for each noun. However, the following guidelines will help you determine the gender for certain types of nouns:

Nouns denoting male people and animals are usually – but not always – masculine, e.g.

un hombre a man

un toro a bull

un enfermero a (*male*) nurse

un semental a stallion

Nouns denoting female people and animals are usually – but not always – feminine, e.g.

una niña a girl

una vaca a cow

una enfermera a nurse

una yegua a mare

Some nouns are masculine *or* feminine depending on the sex of the person to whom they refer, e.g.

un camarada a (*male*) comrade

una camarada a (*female*) comrade

un belga a Belgian (*man*)

una belga a Belgian (*woman*)

Other nouns referring to either men *or* women have only one gender which applies to both, e.g.

una persona a person

una visita a visitor

una víctima a victim

una estrella a star

Often the ending of a noun indicates its gender. Shown below and opposite are some of the most important to guide you.

Masculine endings

-o	**un clavo** a nail, **un plátano** a banana EXCEPTIONS: **mano** hand, **foto** photograph, **moto(cicleta)** motorbike
-r	**un tractor** a tractor, **el altar** the altar EXCEPTIONS: **coliflor** cauliflower, **flor** flower, **labor** task

Feminine endings

-a	una casa a house, la cara the face EXCEPTIONS: día day, mapa map, planeta planet, tranvía tram, and most words ending in -ma (tema subject, problema problem, *etc*)
-ión	una canción a song, una procesión a procession EXCEPTIONS: most nouns not ending in -ción or -sión, e.g. avión aeroplane, camión lorry, gorrión sparrow
-dad, -tad,	una ciudad a town, la libertad freedom
-itis	una faringitis pharyngitis, la celulitis cellulitis
-sis	una tesis a thesis, una dosis a dose EXCEPTIONS: análisis analysis, énfasis emphasis, paréntesis parenthesis

Some nouns change meaning according to gender:

	MASCULINE	FEMININE
capital	capital (*money*)	capital (*city*)
cometa	comet	kite
corte	cut	court (*royal*)
coma	coma	comma
cura	priest	cure
frente	front (*in war*)	forehead
guía	guide (*man*)	guide(book), guide (*woman*)
orden	order (*arrangement*)	order (*command*)
papa	Pope	potato
pendiente	earring	slope
policía	policeman	police, policewoman
radio	radius, radium	radio

Nouns

Gender: the Formation of Feminines

As in English, males and females are sometimes differentiated by the use of two quite separate words, e.g.

mi marido my husband   **mi mujer** my wife
un toro a bull   **una vaca** a cow

There are, however, some words in Spanish which show this distinction by the form of their ending:

Nouns ending in **-o** change to **-a** to form the feminine (e.g. **un amigo** a (*male*) friend → **una amiga** a (*female*) friend; **un gato** a cat → **una gata** a (*female*) cat).

If the masculine singular form already ends in **-a**, no further **-a** is added to the feminine (e.g. **un deportista** a sportsman → **una deportista** a sportswoman).

If the last letter of the masculine singular form is a consonant, an **-a** is normally added in the feminine (e.g. **un vendedor** a salesman → **una vendedora** a saleswoman).

* If the last syllable has an accent, it disappears in the feminine (e.g. **un león** a lion → **una leona** a lioness; see page 127)

Feminine forms to note

MASCULINE	FEMININE	
el abad	la abadesa	abbot/abbess
un actor	una actriz	actor/actress
el alcalde	la alcaldesa	mayor/mayoress
el conde	la condesa	count/countess
el duque	la duquesa	duke/duchess
el emperador	la emperatriz	emperor/empress
un poeta	una poetisa	poet/poetess
el príncipe	la princesa	prince/princess
el rey	la reina	king/queen
un sacerdote	una sacerdotisa	priest/priestess
un tigre	una tigresa	tiger/tigress
el zar	la zarina	tzar/tzarina

The Formation of Plurals

Nouns ending in an unstressed vowel add -s to the singular form
(e.g. la casa the house → las casas the houses; el libro the book →
los libros the books).

Nouns ending in a consonant or a stressed vowel add -es to the
singular form (e.g. un rumor a rumour → unos rumores (some)
rumours; un jabalí a boar → unos jabalíes (some) boars).

> (i) BUT: café coffee shop   (*plural*: cafés)
>   mamá mummy   (*plural*: mamás)
>   papá daddy   (*plural*: papás)
>   pie foot   (*plural*: pies)
>   sofá sofa   (*plural*: sofás)
>   té tea   (*plural*. tes)

and words of foreign origin ending in a consonant, e.g.:

>   coñac brandy   (*plural*: coñacs)
>   jersey jumper   (*plural*: jerseys)

(i) Note:
* nouns ending in -n or -s with an accent on the last syllable drop
  this accent in the plural (e.g. la canción the song
  → las canciones the songs; el autobús the bus
  → los autobuses the buses); see page 127.
* nouns ending in -n with the stress on the last syllable but one in
  the singular add an accent to that syllable in the plural in order
  to show the correct position for stress (e.g. un examen
  an exam → unos exámenes (some) exams; un crimen
  a crime → unos crímenes (some) crimes; see page 127)
* nouns ending in -z change this to c in the plural (e.g. la luz
  the light → las luces the lights).

Nouns with an unstressed final syllable ending in -s do not change in
the plural (e.g. un paraguas an umbrella → unos paraguas (some)
umbrellas; el lunes Monday → los lunes Mondays).

Articles

The Definite Article

	WITH MASC. NOUN	WITH FEM. NOUN	
SING.	el	la	the
PLUR.	los	las	the

The article used depends on both the gender of the noun and whether it is singular or plural → ①

> ⓘ Note: use **el** not **la** immediately before a feminine singular noun starting with a stressed **a-** or **ha-** → ②

a + el becomes **al** and **de + el** becomes **del** → ③

Uses of the Definite Article

While the Spanish definite article ususally translates as 'the', it is often used where English has no article or uses another construction:

- with abstract nouns, except when following certain prepositions → ④
- in generalizations, especially with plural or uncountable nouns → ⑤
- with parts of the body → ⑥
  Note that 'ownership' is often indicated by an indirect object pronoun or a reflexive pronoun → ⑦
- with titles/ranks/professions followed by a proper name → ⑧
  EXCEPTIONS: with **Don/Doña**, **San/Santo(a)** → ⑨
- before nouns of official, academic and religious buildings, and names of meals and games → ⑩

The definite article is *not* used with nouns in apposition unless those nouns are individualized → ⑪

Examples

① el tren the train
la estación the station
el actor the actor (*male*)
la actriz the actress
los hoteles the hotels
las mujeres the women

② el agua pura the pure water
la misma agua the same water
el hacha the axe
la mejor hacha the best axe

③ al cine
to the cinema
al hospital
to the hospital
del departamento
from/of the department
del presidente
from/of the president

④ Los precios suben
Prices are rising
El tiempo es oro
Time is money
BUT:
con pasión
with passion
sin esperanza
without hope

⑤ No me gusta el café
I don't like coffee
Los niños necesitan ser queridos
Children need to be loved

⑥ No puedo mover las piernas
I can't move my legs

⑦ Lávate las manos
Wash your hands

⑧ el doctor Ochoa
Doctor Ochoa
el señor Ramírez
Mr Ramírez

⑨ Don Arturo Ruiz
Mr Arturo Ruiz
Santa Teresa
Saint Teresa

⑩ en la cárcel
in prison
en la universidad
at university
en la iglesia
at church
la cena
dinner
el tenis
tennis

⑪ Madrid, capital de España,
es la ciudad que ...
Madrid, the capital of Spain,
is the city which ...
BUT:
Maria Callas, la famosa
cantante de ópera ...
Maria Callas, the famous opera
singer ...

The Indefinite Article

	WITH MASC. NOUN	WITH FEM. NOUN	
SING.	un	una	a
PLUR.	unos	unas	some

The indefinite article is used in Spanish largely as it is in English. However, there is no article when a person's profession is being stated → ① unless the profession is qualified by an adjective → ②

The article is not used with the following words: → ③

otro	another	cien	a hundred
cierto	certain	mil	a thousand
semejante	such (a)	sin	without
tal	such (a)	qué	what a

There is no article with a noun in apposition → ④. When an abstract noun is qualified by an adjective, the indefinite article is used, but is not translated in English → ⑤

The Article lo

This is never used with a noun. Instead, it is used in the following ways:

- as an intensifier before an adjective or adverb in the construction **lo** + adjective/adverb + **que** → ⑥
  Note: The adjective agrees with the noun it refers to → ⑦
- With an adjective or participle to form an abstract noun → ⑧
- In the phrase **lo de** to refer to a subject of which speaker and listener are already aware. → ⑨
- In certain set expressions, the commonest of which are: → ⑩
a lo mejor	maybe, perhaps	**por lo menos**	at least
a lo lejos	in the distance	**por lo tanto**	therefore, so
a lo largo de	along, through	**por lo visto**	apparently

Examples

1 Es profesor
Mi madre es enfermera

He's a teacher
My mother is a nurse

2 Es un buen médico
Se hizo una escritora célebre

He's a good doctor
She became a famous writer

3 otro libro
cierta calle
tal mentira
cien/mil años
sin casa
¡Qué sorpresa!

another book
a certain street
such a lie
a hundred/thousand years
without a house
What a surprise!

4 Baroja, gran escritor de la
Generación del 98

Baroja, a great writer of the
'Generación del 98'

5 con una gran sabiduría
Dieron pruebas de una sangre
fría increíble

with great wisdom
They showed incredible coolness

6 No sabíamos lo pequeña que
era la casa
Sé lo mucho que te gusta la
música

We didn't know how small
the house was
I know how much you like
music

7 No te imaginas lo simpáticos
que son

You can't imagine how nice
they are

8 Lo bueno de eso es que ...

The good thing about it is
that ...

9 Lo de tu hermano me
preocupa mucho

That business with your
brother worries me a lot

10 A lo mejor ha salido
A lo lejos se veían unas casas

Perhaps he's gone out
Some houses could be seen in
the distance

a lo largo de su vida
a lo largo de la carretera
Hubo por lo menos cincuenta
heridos
Por lo visto, no viene

throughout his life
along the road
At least fifty people were injured

He's not coming, it seems

Adjectives

Most adjectives agree in number and gender with the noun or pronoun.

> ⓘ Note that:
> - if the adjective refers to two or more singular nouns of the same gender, a plural ending of that gender is required → ❶
> - if the adjective refers to two or more singular nouns of different genders, a masculine plural ending is required → ❷

The Formation of Feminines

Adjectives ending in **-o** change to **-a** → ❸

Some groups of adjectives add **-a**:
- adjectives of nationality or geographical origin → ❹
- adjectives ending in **-or** (except irregular comparatives: see page 88), **-án**, **-ón**, **-ín** → ❺

> ⓘ Note: When there is an accent on the last syllable, it disappears in the feminine (see page 127).

Other adjectives do not change → ❻

The Formation of Plurals

Adjectives ending in an unstressed vowel add **-s** → ❼

Adjectives ending in a stressed vowel or a consonant add **-es** → ❽

> ⓘ Note:
> - if there is an accent on the last syllable of a word ending in a consonant, it will disappear in the plural (see page 127) → ❾
> - if the last letter is a **z**, it will become a **c** in the plural → ❿

Examples

1. la lengua y la literatura españolas — (the) Spanish language and literature
2. Nunca había visto árboles y flores tan raros — I had never seen such strange trees and flowers
3. mi hermano pequeño — my little brother
   mi hermana pequeña — my little sister
4. un chico español — a Spanish boy
   una chica española — a Spanish girl

   el equipo barcelonés — the team from Barcelona
   la vida barcelonesa — the Barcelona way of life
5. un niño encantador — a charming little boy
   una niña encantadora — a charming little girl

   un hombre holgazán — an idle man
   una mujer holgazana — an idle woman

   un gesto burlón — a mocking gesture
   una sonrisa burlona — a mocking smile

   un chico cantarín — a boy who's fond of singing
   una chica cantarina — a girl who's fond of singing
6. un final feliz — a happy ending
   una infancia feliz — a happy childhood

   mi amigo belga — my Belgian (*male*) friend
   mi amiga belga — my Belgian (*female*) friend

   el vestido verde — the green dress
   la blusa verde — the green blouse
7. el último tren — the last train
   los últimos trenes — the last trains

   una casa vieja — an old house
   unas casas viejas — (some) old houses
8. un médico iraní — an Iranian doctor
   unos médicos iraníes — (some) Iranian doctors

   un examen fácil — an easy exam
   unos exámenes fáciles — (some) easy exams
9. un río francés — a French river
   unos ríos franceses — (some) French rivers
10. un día feliz — a happy day
    unos días felices — (some) happy days

85

Adjectives

Invariable Adjectives

Some adjectives and other parts of speech used adjectivally never change in the feminine or plural. The commonest of these are:
- nouns used to denote colour → ①
- compound adjectives → ②
- nouns used as adjectives → ③

Shortening of Adjectives

The following drop the final -o before a masculine singular noun:

bueno good → ④
malo bad
alguno* some → ⑤
ninguno* none
uno one → ⑥
primero first → ⑦
tercero third
postrero last → ⑧

* ⓘ Note: An accent is required to show the correct position for stress.

Grande *big, great* is usually shortened to **gran** before a masculine *or* feminine singular noun → ⑨

Santo *Saint* changes to **San** except with saints' names beginning with **Do-** *or* **To-** → ⑩

Ciento *a hundred* is shortened to **cien** before a masculine *or* feminine plural noun → ⑪

Cualquiera drops the final -a before a singular noun → ⑫

Examples

❶	los vestidos naranja	the orange dresses
❷	las chaquetas azul marino	the navy blue jackets
❸	bebés probeta mujeres soldado	test-tube babies women soldiers
❹	un buen libro	a good book
❺	algún libro	some book
❻	cuarenta y un años	forty-one years
❼	el primer hijo	the first child
❽	un postrer deseo	a last wish
❾	un gran actor una gran decepción	a great actor a great disappointment
❿	San Antonio Santo Tomás	Saint Anthony Saint Thomas
⓫	cien años cien millones	a hundred years a hundred million
⓬	cualquier día a cualquier hora	any day any time

Adjectives

Comparatives and Superlatives

Comparatives

más ... (que) more ... (than) → ❶
menos ... (que) less ... (than) → ❷
tanto ... como as ... as → ❸
tan ... como as ... as → ❹
tan ... que so ... that → ❺

demasiado ...
bastante ... **para** too ...
suficiente ... enough ... to → ❻
enough ...

'Than' followed by a clause is translated by **de lo que** → ❼

Superlatives

el/la/los/las más ... (que) the most ... (that) → ❽
el/la/los/las menos ... (que) the least ... (that) → ❾

After a superlative, **de** is often translated as 'in' → ❿

Adjectives with irregular comparatives/superlatives

ADJECTIVE	COMPARATIVE	SUPERLATIVE
bueno/a good	**mejor** better	**el/la mejor** the best
malo/a bad	**peor** worse	**el/la peor** the worst
grande big	**mayor** or **más grande** bigger; older	**el/la más grande** the biggest; the oldest
pequeño/a small	**menor** or **más pequeño/a** smaller; younger; lesser	**el/la más pequeño/a** the smallest; the youngest; the least

While the regular comparative and superlative forms of **grande** and **pequeño** are used mainly to express physical size (→ ⓫), the irregular forms are used mainly to express age, in which case they come after the noun (→ ⓬), and abstract size and degrees of importance, in which case they come before the noun (→ ⓭)

Examples

1. una razón más seria — a more serious reason
   Es más alto que mi hermano — He's taller than my brother

2. una película menos conocida — a less well known film
   Luis es menos tímido que tú — Luis is less shy than you

3. Pablo tenía tanto miedo como yo — Pablo was as frightened as I was

4. No es tan grande como creía — It isn't as big as I thought

5. El examen era tan difícil que nadie aprobó — The exam was so difficult that nobody passed

6. No tengo suficiente dinero para comprarlo — I haven't got enough money to buy it

7. Está más cansada de lo que parece — She is more tired than she seems

8. el caballo más veloz — the fastest horse
   la casa más pequeña — the smallest house
   los días más lluviosos — the wettest days
   las manzanas más maduras — the ripest apples

9. el hombre menos simpático — the least likeable man
   la niña menos habladora — the least talkative girl
   los cuadros menos bonitos — the least attractive paintings
   las camisas menos viejas — the least old shirts

10. la estación más ruidosa de Londres — the noisiest station in London

11. Este plato es más grande que aquél — This plate is bigger than that one
    Mi casa es más pequeña que la tuya — My house is smaller than yours

12. mis hermanos mayores — my older brothers
    la hija menor — the youngest daughter

13. el menor ruido — the slightest sound
    las mayores dificultades — the biggest difficulties

Adjectives

Interrogative Adjectives

	MASCULINE	FEMININE	
SING.	¿qué?	¿qué?	what?, which?
	¿cuánto?	¿cuánta?	how much?
PLUR.	¿qué?	¿qué?	what?, which?
	¿cuántos?	¿cuántas?	how many?

Interrogative adjectives, when not invariable, agree in number and gender with the noun → ①

The forms shown above are also used in indirect questions → ②

Exclamatory Adjectives

	MASCULINE	FEMININE	
SING.	¡qué!	¡qué!	what (a)!
	¡cuánto!	¡cuánta!	what (a lot of)!
PLUR.	¡qué!	¡qué!	what!
	¡cuántos!	¡cuántas!	what (a lot of)!

Exclamatory adjectives, when not invariable, agree in number and gender with the noun → ③

Examples

1 ¿Qué libro te gustó más? — Which book did you like most?
¿Qué clase de hombre es? — What type of man is he?
¿Qué instrumentos toca Vd? — What instruments do you play?
¿Qué ofertas ha recibido Vd? — What offers have you received?
¿Cuánto dinero te queda? — How much money have you got left?

¿Cuánta lluvia ha caído? — How much rain have we had?
¿Cuántos vestidos quieres comprar? — How many dresses do you want to buy?
¿Cuántas personas van a venir? — How many people are coming?

2 No sé a qué hora llegó — I don't know what time she arrived at

Dígame cuántas postales quiere — Tell me how many postcards you'd like

3 ¡Qué pena! — What a shame!
¡Qué tiempo tan/más malo! — What lousy weather!
¡Cuánto tiempo! — What a long time!
¡Cuánta pobreza! — What poverty!
¡Cuántos autobuses! — What a lot of buses!
¡Cuántas mentiras! — What a lot of lies!

Adjectives

Possessive Adjectives

Weak forms

WITH SING. NOUN		WITH PLUR. NOUN		
MASC.	FEM.	MASC.	FEM.	
mi	mi	mis	mis	my
tu	tu	tus	tus	your
su	su	sus	sus	his; her; its; your (of **Vd**)
nuestro	nuestra	nuestros	nuestras	our
vuestro	vuestra	vuestros	vuestras	your
su	su	sus	sus	their; your (of **Vds**)

All possessive adjectives agree in number and (when applicable) in gender with the noun described, not with the owner → **1**
The weak forms always precede the noun → **1**
Since the form **su(s)** can mean his, her, your (of **Vd**, **Vds**) or their, clarification is often needed. This is done by adding **de él**, **de ella**, **de Vds** etc to the noun, and usually (but not always) changing the possessive to a definite article → **2**

Strong forms

WITH SING. NOUN		WITH PLUR. NOUN		
MASC.	FEM.	MASC.	FEM.	
mío	mía	míos	mías	my
tuyo	tuya	tuyos	tuyas	your
suyo	suya	suyos	suyas	his; her; its; your (of **Vd**)
nuestro	nuestra	nuestros	nuestras	our
vuestro	vuestra	vuestros	vuestras	your
suyo	suya	suyos	suyas	their; your (of **Vds**)

The strong forms follow the noun and are used to translate the English *of mine*, etc → **3** and to address people → **4**

Examples

1 Pilar no ha traído nuestros libros
Pilar hasn't brought our books

Antonio irá a vuestra casa
Antonio will go to your house

¿Han vendido su coche tus vecinos?
Have your neighbours sold their car?

Mi hermano y tu primo no se llevan bien
My brother and your cousin don't get on

2 su casa → la casa de él
his house

sus amigos → los amigos de Vd
your friends

sus coches → los coches de ellos
their cars

su abrigo → el abrigo de ella
her coat

3 Es un capricho suyo
It's a whim of hers

un amigo nuestro
a friend of ours

una revista tuya
a magazine of yours

4 Muy señor mío (in letters)
Dear Sir

hija mía
my daughter

¡Dios mío!
My God!

Amor mío
Darling/My love

Adjectives

Position of Adjectives

Spanish adjectives usually follow the noun → ①, ②

Note that when used figuratively or to express a quality already inherent in the noun, adjectives can precede the noun → ③

As in English, demonstrative, possessive (weak forms), numerical, interrogative and exclamatory adjectives precede the noun → ④

Indefinite adjectives such as **ambos** *both* and **cada** *each* usually precede the noun → ⑤

> ⓘ Note: **alguno** *some/any* follows the noun in negative expressions → ⑥

Some adjectives can precede or follow the noun, but their meaning varies according to their position:

	BEFORE NOUN	AFTER NOUN
antiguo	former	old, ancient → ⑦
diferente	various	different → ⑧
grande	great	big → ⑨
medio	half	average → ⑩
mismo	same	-self, very/precisely → ⑪
nuevo	new, another, fresh	brand new → ⑫
pobre	poor (wretched)	poor (not rich) → ⑬
puro	sheer, mere	pure (clear) → ⑭
varios	several	various, different → ⑮
viejo	old (long known, etc)	old (aged) → ⑯

Adjectives following the noun are linked by **y** → ⑰

Examples

1. la página siguiente — the following page
   la hora exacta — the right time

2. una corbata azul — a blue tie
   una palabra española — a Spanish word

3. un dulce sueño — a sweet dream
   un terrible desastre — a terrible disaster
   (*all disasters are terrible*)

4. este sombrero — this hat
   mi padre — my father
   ¿qué hombre? — what man?

5. cada día — every day
   otra vez — another time
   poco dinero — little money

6. sin duda alguna — without any doubt

7. un antiguo colega — a former colleague
   la historia antigua — ancient history

8. diferentes capítulos — various chapters
   personas diferentes — different people

9. un gran pintor — a great painter
   una casa grande — a big house

10. medio melón — half a melon
    velocidad media — average speed

11. la misma respuesta — the same answer
    yo mismo — myself
    eso mismo — precisely that

12. mi nuevo coche — my new car
    unos zapatos nuevos — (some) brand new shoes

13. esa pobre mujer — that poor woman
    un país pobre — a poor country

14. la pura verdad — the plain truth
    aire puro — fresh air

15. varios caminos — several ways/paths
    artículos varios — various items

16. un viejo amigo — an old friend
    esas toallas viejas — those old towels

17. una acción cobarde y falsa — a cowardly, deceitful act

Pronouns

Personal Pronouns: subject

		SUBJECT PRONOUNS		
		SINGULAR	PLURAL	
1st	person	yo I	nosotros we	(masc./masc. + fem.)
			nosotras we	(all fem.)
2nd	person	tú you	vosotros you	(masc./masc. + fem.)
			vosotras you	(all fem.)
3rd	person	él he; it	ellos they	(masc./masc. + fem.)
		ella she; it	ellas they	(all fem.)
		usted (Vd) you	ustedes (Vds) you	

Subject pronouns have a limited usage in Spanish. Normally they are only used with a verb:

- for emphasis → ❶
- for clarity → ❷

BUT: **Vd** and **Vds** should always be used for politeness, whether they are otherwise needed or not → ❸

It as subject and *they*, referring to things, are never translated into Spanish → ❹

tú/usted
As a general rule, you should use **tú** (or **vosotros**, if plural) when addressing a friend, a child, a relative, someone you know well, or when invited to do so. In all other cases, use **usted** (or **ustedes**).

nosotros/as; vosotros/as; él/ella; ellos/ellas
All these forms reflect the number and gender of the noun(s) they replace. **Nosotros**, **vosotros** and **ellos** also replace a combination of masculine and feminine nouns.

Examples

1 Ellos sí que llegaron tarde
They really did arrive late

Tú no tienes por qué venir
There is no reason for you to come

Ella jamás creería eso
She would never believe that

2 Yo estudio español pero él estudia francés
I study Spanish but he studies French

Ella era muy deportista pero él prefería jugar a las cartas
She was a sporty type but he preferred to play cards

Vosotros saldréis primero y nosotros os seguiremos
You leave first and we will follow you

3 Pase Vd por aquí
Please come this way

¿Habían estado Vds antes en esta ciudad?
Had you been to this town before?

4 ¿Qué es? — Es una sorpresa
What is it? — It's a surprise

¿Qué son? — Son abrelatas
What are they? — They are tin-openers

Personal Pronouns: object

		SINGULAR		PLURAL	
		DIRECT OBJECT PRONOUNS			
1st	person	me	me	nos	us
2nd	person	te	you	os	you
3rd	person (*masc.*)	lo	him; it; you (of Vd)	los	them; you (of Vds)
	(*fem.*)	la	her; it; you (of Vd)	las	them; you (of Vds)
		INDIRECT OBJECT PRONOUNS			
1st	person	me		nos	
2nd	person	te		os	
3rd	person	le		les	

lo sometimes functions as a 'neuter' pronoun, referring to an idea or information contained in a previous statement or question. It is often not translated → ❶

Indirect object pronouns replace the preposition **a** + noun → ❷

Use direct object pronouns instead to replace personal **a** + noun.

Position of object pronouns

In constructions other than the affirmative imperative, infinitive or gerund, the pronoun always comes before the verb → ❸
In the affirmative imperative, infinitive and gerund, the pronoun follows the verb and is attached to it. An accent is needed in certain cases to show the correct position for stress (see also page 127) → ❹
Where an infinitive or gerund depends on a previous verb, object pronouns, and also reflexive pronouns, may be used either after the infinitive or gerund, or before the main verb → ❺

For information on reflexive pronouns see page 16.

Examples

1 ¿Va a venir María? — No lo sé
Hay que regar las plantas
— Yo lo haré
Habían comido ya pero no nos
lo dijeron
Yo conduzco de prisa pero él lo
hace despacio

Is María coming? — I don't know
The plants need watering
— I'll do it
They had already eaten, but they
didn't tell us
I drive fast but he drives slowly

2 Estoy escribiendo a Teresa
Le estoy escribiendo
Da de comer al gato
Dale de comer

I am writing to Teresa
I am writing to her
Give the cat some food
Give it some food

3 Te quiero
¿Las ve Vd?
Tu hija no nos conoce
No los toques
Sofía os ha escrito
¿Os ha escrito Sofía?
¿Qué te pedían?

I love you
Can you see them?
Your daughter doesn't know us
Don't touch them
Sofía has written to you
Has Sofía written to you?
What were they asking you for?

4 Ayúdame
Acompáñenos
Quiero decirte algo
Estaban persiguiéndonos
No quería darte la noticia
todavía
Llegaron diciéndome que ...

Help me
Come with us
I want to tell you something
They were coming after us
I didn't want to tell you the news
yet
They came telling me that ...

5 Lo está comiendo *or*
Está comiéndolo
Estoy afeitándome *or*
Me estoy afeitando
Les voy a hablar *or*
Voy a hablarles

She is eating it

I'm shaving

I'm going to talk to them

Personal Pronouns *continued*

Order of object pronouns

When two object pronouns are combined, the order is: indirect before direct, i.e.

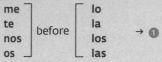

⟶ **❶**

    ⓘ Note: When two 3rd person object pronouns are combined, the first (i.e. the indirect object pronoun) becomes **se** ⟶ **❷**

Points to note on object pronouns

As **le/les** can refer to either gender, and **se** to either gender, singular or plural, sometimes clarification is needed. This is done by adding **a él** *to him*, **a ella** *to her*, **a Vd** *to you* etc to the phrase, usually after the verb ⟶ **❸**

When a noun object precedes the verb, the corresponding object pronoun must be used too ⟶ **❹**

Indirect object pronouns are often used instead of possessive adjectives with parts of the body or clothing to indicate 'ownership', and also in certain common constructions involving reflexive verbs (see also Uses of the Definite Article, page 80) ⟶ **❺**

Le and **les** are often used in Spanish instead of **lo** and **los** when referring to people. Equally **la** is sometimes used instead of **le** when referring to a feminine person or animal, although this usage is considered incorrect by some speakers of Spanish ⟶ **❻**

Examples

1. Paloma os lo mandará mañana

   ¿Te los ha enseñado mi hermana?

   No me lo digas

   Todos estaban pidiéndotelo

   No quiere prestárnosla

   Paloma is sending it to you tomorrow

   Has my sister shown them to you?

   Don't tell me (that)

   They were all asking you for it

   He won't lend it to us

2. Se lo di ayer

   I gave it to him/her/them yesterday

3. Le escriben mucho a ella

   Se lo van a mandar pronto a ellos

   They write to her often

   They will be sending it to them soon

4. A tu hermano lo conozco bien

   A María la vemos algunas veces

   I know your brother well

   We sometimes see María

5. La chaqueta le estaba ancha

   Me duele el tobillo

   Se me ha perdido el bolígrafo

   His jacket was too loose

   My ankle is aching

   I have lost my pen

6. Le *or* Lo encontraron en el cine

   Les *or* Los oímos llegar

   They met him at the cinema

   We heard them coming

Personal Pronouns *continued*

Pronouns after prepositions

These are the same as the subject pronouns, except for the forms
mí *me*, **ti** *you* (*singular*), and the reflexive **sí** *himself, herself, themselves, yourselves* → ①

Con *with* combines with **mí**, **ti** and **sí** to form

conmigo	with me → ②
contigo	with you
consigo	with himself/herself *etc*

The following prepositions always take a subject pronoun:

entre	between, among → ③
hasta **incluso**	even, including → ④
salvo **menos**	except → ⑤
según	according to → ⑥

ⓘ Note: Subject pronouns are also used in comparative
constructions → ⑦

These pronouns are used for emphasis, especially where contrast is
involved → ⑧

Ello *it, that* is used after a preposition when referring to an idea already
mentioned, but never to a concrete noun → ⑨

A él, **de él** never contract → ⑩

1. Pienso en ti — I'm thinking about you
   ¿Son para mí? — Are they for me?
   Es para ella — This is for her
   Iban hacia ellos — They were going towards them
   Volveréis sin nosotros — You'll come back without us
   Volaban sobre vosotros — They were flying above you
   Hablaba para sí — He was talking to himself

2. Venid conmigo — Come with me
   Lo trajeron consigo — They brought it/him with them
   BUT:
   ¿Hablaron con vosotros? — Did they talk to you?

3. entre tú y ella — between you and her

4. Hasta yo puedo hacerlo — Even I can do it

5. todos menos yo — everybody except me

6. según tú — according to you

7. Es más joven que yo — He is younger than me (or than I am)

8. ¿A ti no te escriben? — Don't they write to you?
   Me lo manda a mí, no a ti — She is sending it to me, not to you

9. Nunca pensaba en ello — He never thought about it
   Por todo ello me parece que … — For all those reasons it seems to me that …

10. A él no lo conozco — I don't know him
    No he sabido nada de él — I haven't heard from him

Relative Pronouns

	PEOPLE	
SINGULAR	PLURAL	
que	que	who, that (*subject*) → ①
que	que	who(m), that (*direct object*) → ②
a quien	a quienes	
a quien	a quienes	to whom, that → ③
de que	de que	of whom, that → ④
de quien	de quienes	
cuyo/a	cuyos/as	whose → ⑤

THINGS	
SINGULAR AND PLURAL	
que	which, that (*subject*) → ⑥
que	which, that (*direct object*) → ⑦
a que	to which, that → ⑧
de que	of which, that → ⑨
cuyo	whose → ⑩

cuyo agrees with the noun it accompanies → ⑤/⑩

You cannot omit the relative pronoun in Spanish as you can in English → ②/④/⑦

el cual, el que, etc
These are used when the relative is separated from the word it refers to, or when it would otherwise be unclear which word it referred to. The pronouns always agree in number and gender with the noun → ⑪
El cual may also be used when the verb in the relative clause is separated from the relative pronoun → ⑫

lo que, lo cual
The neuter form **lo** is normally used when referring to an idea, statement or abstract noun. In certain expressions, the form **lo cual** may also be used as the subject of the relative clause → ⑬

Examples

1. Mi hermano, que tiene veinte años, es el más joven
   My brother, who is twenty, is the youngest

2. Los amigos que más quiero son ...
   The friends (that) I like best are ...

   María, a quien Daniel admira tanto, es ...
   María, whom Daniel admires so much, is ...

3. Mis abogados, a quienes he escrito hace poco, están ...
   My lawyers, to whom I wrote recently, are ...

4. la chica de que te hablé
   the girl (that) I told you about

   los niños de quienes se ocupa Vd
   the children (that) you look after

5. Vendrá la mujer cuyo hijo está enfermo
   The woman whose son is ill will be coming

6. Hay una escalera que lleva a la buhardilla
   There's a staircase which leads to the loft

7. La casa que hemos comprado tiene ...
   The house (which) we've bought has ...

   Este es el regalo que me ha mandado mi amiga
   This is the present (that) my friend sent to me

8. la tienda a que siempre va
   the shop (which) she always goes to

9. las injusticias de que se quejan
   the injustices (that) they're complaining about

10. la ventana cuyas cortinas están corridas
    the window whose curtains are drawn

11. El padre de Elena, el cual tiene mucho dinero, es ...
    Elena's father, who has a lot of money, is ...

    (el cual *is used here since* que *or* quien *might equally refer to Elena*)

    Su hermana, a la cual/la que hacía mucho que no veía, estaba también allí
    His sister, whom I hadn't seen for a long time, was also there

12. Vieron a su tío, el cual, después de levantarse, salió
    They saw their uncle, who, after having got up, went out

13. Lo que dijiste fue una tontería
    What you said was foolish

    Todo estaba en silencio, lo que (*or* lo cual) me pareció muy raro
    All was silent, which I thought most odd

Relative Pronouns *continued*

Relative pronouns after prepositions

Que and **quienes** are generally used after the prepositions:

a	to	→ ①
con	with	→ ②
de	from, about, of	→ ③
en	in, on, into	→ ④

It should be noted that **en que** can sometimes be translated by:
- *where*. In this case it can also be replaced by **en donde** or **donde** → ⑤
- *when*. Sometimes here it can be replaced by **cuando** → ⑥

El que or **el cual** are used after other prepositions, and they always agree → ⑦

el que, la que; los que, las que
These mean *the one(s) who/which, those who/that* → ⑧

> ⓘ Note: **quien(es)** can replace **el que** *etc* when used in a general sense referring to a person or people → ⑨

todos los que, todas las que
These mean *all who, all those/the ones which* → ⑩

todo lo que
This translates *all that, everything that* → ⑪

el de, la de; los de, las de
These can mean:
- *the one(s) of, that/those of* → ⑫
- *the one(s) with* → ⑬

Examples

1. las tiendas a (las) que íbamos — the shops we used to go to

2. la chica con quien (or la que) sale — the girl he's going out with

3. el libro de(l) que te hablé — the book I told you about

4. el lío en (el) que te has metido — the trouble you've got yourself into

5. el sitio en que (en donde/donde) se escondía — the place where he/she was hiding

6. el año en que naciste — the year (when) you were born

7. el puente debajo del que/cual pasa el río — the bridge under which the river flows
   las obras por las cuales/que es famosa — the plays for which she is famous

8. Esa película es la que quiero ver — That film is the one I want to see
   ¿Te acuerdas de ese amigo? El que te presenté ayer — Do you remember that friend? The one I introduced you to yesterday
   Los que quieran entrar tendrán que pagar — Those who want to go in will have to pay

9. Quien (or El que) llegue antes ganará el premio — The person who arrives first will win the prize

10. Todos los que salían iban de negro — All those who were coming out were dressed in black

11. Quiero saber todo lo que ha pasado — I want to know all that has happened

12. Trae la foto de tu novio y la de tu hermano — Bring the photo of your boyfriend and the one of your brother
    Viajamos en mi coche y en el de María — We travelled in my car and María's
    Te doy estos libros y también los de mi hermana — I'll give you these books and my sister's too

13. Tu amigo, el de las gafas, me lo contó — Your friend, the one with glasses, told me

Interrogative Pronouns

> **¿qué?** what?
> **¿cuál(es)?** which?; what?
> **¿quién(es)?** who?

qué

It translates *what* → ❶

ⓘ Note: **por** + **qué** is normally translated by *why* → ❷

cuál

It normally implies a choice, and translates *which* → ❸

ⓘ However, **cúal(es)** is also used in *what is/are* questions that require specific information rather than a definition as the answer → ❹

ⓘ Note: Whilst the pronoun **qué** can also work as an adjective meaning *what* or *which*, **cuál** only works as a pronoun → ❺

quién

SUBJECT *or* AFTER PREPOSITION	**quién(es)**	who → ❻
OBJECT	**a quién(es)**	whom → ❼
	de quién(es)	whose → ❽

All the forms shown above are also used in indirect questions → ❾

Examples

1. ¿Qué estan haciendo? — What are they doing?
   ¿Qué dices? — What are you saying?
   ¿Qué es un tractor, papá? — What's a tractor, Daddy?
   ¿Qué son las alcaparras? — What are capers?
   ¿Para qué lo quieres? — What do you want it for?

2. ¿Por qué no llegaron Vds antes? — Why didn't you arrive earlier?

3. ¿Cuál de estos vestidos te gusta más? — Which of these dresses do you like best?
   ¿Cuáles viste? — Which ones did you see?

4. ¿Cuál es la capital de España? — What is the capital of Spain?
   ¿Cuál es tu consejo? — What is your advice?
   ¿Cuál es su fecha de nacimiento? — What is your date of birth?

5. ¿Qué libro es más interesante? — Which book is more interesting?
   ¿Cuál (de estos libros) es más interesante? — Which (of these books) is more interesting?

6. ¿Quién ganó la carrera? — Who won the race?
   ¿Con quiénes los viste? — Who did you see them with?
   ¿A quién se lo diste? — Who did you give it to?

7. ¿A quiénes ayudaste? — Who(m) did you help?

8. ¿De quién es este libro? — Whose book is this?

9. Le pregunté para qué lo quería — I asked him/her what he/she wanted it for
   No me dijeron cuáles preferían — They didn't tell me which ones they preferred
   No sabía a quién acudir — I didn't know who to turn to

Possessive Pronouns

These are the same as the strong forms of the possessive adjectives, but they are always accompanied by the definite article.

Singular:

MASCULINE	FEMININE	
el mío	la mía	mine
el tuyo	la tuya	yours (of tú)
el suyo	la suya	his; hers; its; yours (of Vd)
el nuestro	la nuestra	ours
el vuestro	la vuestra	yours (of vosotros)
el suyo	la suya	theirs; yours (of Vds)

Plural:

MASCULINE	FEMININE	
los míos	las mías	mine
los tuyos	las tuyas	yours (of tú)
los suyos	las suyas	his; hers; its; yours (of Vd)
los nuestros	las nuestras	ours
los vuestros	las vuestras	yours (of vosotros)
los suyos	las suyas	theirs; yours (of Vds)

The pronoun agrees in number and gender with the noun it replaces, not with the owner → ❶

Alternative translations are 'my own', 'your own' etc → ❷

After the prepositions a and de the article el is contracted in the normal way (see page 80):

    a + el mío → al mío → ❸
    de + el mío → del mío → ❹

Examples

1 Pregunta a Cristina si este bolígrafo es el suyo

Ask Cristina if this pen is hers

¿Qué equipo ha ganado, el suyo o el nuestro?

Which team won – theirs or ours?

Mi perro es más joven que el tuyo

My dog is younger than yours

Daniel pensó que esos libros eran los suyos

Daniel thought those books were his

Si no tienes discos, te prestaré los míos

If you don't have any records, I'll lend you mine

Las habitaciones son menos amplias que las vuestras

The rooms are smaller than yours

2 ¿Es su familia tan grande como la tuya?

Is his/her/their family as big as your own one?

Sus precios son más bajos que los nuestros

Their prices are lower than our own

3 ¿Por qué prefieres este sombrero al mío?

Why do you prefer this hat to mine?

Su coche se parece al vuestro

His/her/their car looks like yours

4 Mi libro está encima del tuyo

My book is on top of yours

Adverbs

Formation

Most adverbs are formed by adding **-mente** to the feminine form of the adjective. Accents on the adjective are not affected since the suffix **-mente** is stressed independently → **1**

> ⓘ Note: **-mente** is omitted:
> - in the first of two or more of these adverbs when joined by a conjunction → **2**
> - **recientemente** *recently* is replaced by **recién** immediately before a past participle → **3**

The following adverbs are formed in an irregular way:

bueno →	bien	malo →	mal
good	well	bad	badly

Adjectives used as adverbs

Certain adjectives are used adverbially. These include:
alto, bajo, barato, caro, claro, derecho, fuerte and **rápido** → **4**

> ⓘ Note: Other adjectives used where in English we would use an adverb agree with the subject, and can normally be replaced by the adverb ending in **-mente** or an adverbial phrase → **5**

Position of adverbs

When the adverb accompanies a verb, it may either immediately follow it or precede it for emphasis → **6**

> ⓘ Note: The adverb can never be placed between **haber** and the past participle in compound tenses → **7**

When the adverb accompanies an adjective or another adverb, it generally precedes the adjective or adverb → **8**

Examples

1 FEM ADJECTIVE   ADVERB

lenta slow	lentamente slowly
franca frank	francamente frankly
feliz happy	felizmente happily
fácil easy	fácilmente easily

2 Lo hicieron lenta pero   They did it slowly but efficiently
eficazmente

3 El pan estaba recién hecho   The bread had just been baked

4 hablar alto/bajo   to speak loudly/softly
cortar derecho   to cut (in a) straight (line)
costar barato/caro   to be cheap/expensive
Habla muy fuerte   He talks very loudly
ver claro   to see clearly
correr rápido   to run fast

5 Esperaban impacientes   They were waiting impatiently
(*or* impacientemente/
con impaciencia)
Vivieron muy felices (*or* muy   They lived very happily
felizmente)

6 No conocemos aún al nuevo   We still haven't met the new
médico   doctor
Aún estoy esperando   I'm still waiting
Han hablado muy bien   They spoke very well
Siempre le regalaban flores   They always gave her flowers

7 Lo he hecho ya   I've already done it
No ha estado nunca en Italia   She's never been to Italy

8 un sombrero muy bonito   a very nice hat
hablar demasiado alto   to talk too loud
mañana temprano   early tomorrow
hoy mismo   today

Comparatives and Superlatives

Comparatives

These are formed using the following constructions:

más ... (que) more ... (than) → ①
menos ... (que) less ... (than) → ②
tanto como as much as → ③
tan ... como as ... as → ④
tan ... que so ... that → ⑤
demasiado ... para too ... to → ⑥
(lo) bastante ...
(lo) suficientemente ... ⎤ **para** enough to → ⑦
cada vez más/menos more and more/less and less → ⑧

ⓘ To translate *more than/fewer than* with a number, use **más de/menos de** (e.g. **más de 10** more than 10; **menos de 100** fewer than 100).

Superlatives

These are formed by placing **más/menos** *the most/the least* before the adverb → ⑨

lo is added before a superlative which is qualified → ⑩

Adverbs with irregular comparatives/superlatives

ADVERB	COMPARATIVE	SUPERLATIVE
bien well	**mejor*** better	**(lo) mejor** (the) best
mal badly	**peor** worse	**(lo) peor** (the) worst
mucho a lot	**más** more	**(lo) más** (the) most
poco little	**menos** less	**(lo) menos** (the) least

* **más bien** also exists, meaning *rather* → ⑪

Examples

1. más de prisa — more quickly
   más abiertamente — more openly
   Mi hermana canta más fuerte que yo — My sister sings louder than me

2. menos fácilmente — less easily
   menos a menudo — less often
   Nos vemos menos frecuentemente que antes — We see each other less often than we used to

3. Daniel no lee tanto como Andrés — Daniel doesn't read as much as Andrés

4. Hágalo tan rápido como le sea posible — Do it as quickly as you can
   Ganan tan poco como nosotros — They earn as little as we do

5. Llegaron tan pronto que tuvieron que esperarnos — They arrived so early that they had to wait for us

6. Es demasiado tarde para ir al cine — It's too late to go to the cinema

7. Eres (lo) bastante grande para hacerlo solo — You're old enough to do it by yourself

8. Me gusta el campo cada vez más — I like the countryside more and more

9. María es la que corre más rápido — María is the one who runs fastest
   El que llegó menos tarde fue Miguel — Miguel was the one to arrive the least late

10. Lo hice lo más de prisa que pude — I did it as quickly as I could

11. Era un hombre más bien bajito — He was a rather short man
    Estaba más bien inquieta que impaciente — I was restless rather than impatient

115

Prepositions

It is often difficult to give an English equivalent for Spanish prepositions, since usage varies so much between the two languages and the Spanish preposition may not always be the one that the English sentence leads you to expect, and vice versa. If in doubt you will find the examples in the dictionary will help you.

Note that English verbal constructions often contain a preposition (or adverb) where none exists in Spanish, and vice versa (e.g. to look *at* something **mirar algo**).

Below are some typical examples using **en**, **a**, **de**, **por** and **para**:

Trabaja **en** Madrid	He works in Madrid
Lo compramos **en** el supermercado	We bought it at the supermarket
Vivimos **en** la planta baja	We live on the ground floor
No entró **en** el bar	He didn't go into the bar
Vamos **en** tren	We're going by train
Nació **en** 2000	She was born in 2000
Voy **al** parque	I'm going to the park
¿Cuándo llegaste **a** Londres?	When did you arrive in London?
Fuimos **a** casa	We went home
Está **a** siete kilómetros de aquí	It's seven kilometres from here
Empieza **a** las dos	It starts at two o'clock
Estamos **a** tres de julio	It's the third of July
una taza **de** té	a cup of tea/a teacup
la casa **de** Julia	Julia's house
un médico **de** Vigo	a doctor from Vigo
la mujer **del** sombrero rojo	the woman in the red hat
del 15 al 30	from the 15th to the 30th
la cuidad más/menos bonita **del** mundo	the most/least beautiful city in the world
Había más/menos **de** cien personas	There were more/fewer than a hundred people

Examples

Fue pintado **por** Velázquez	It was painted by Velázquez
Fue **por** necesidad	It was out of necessity
Me castigaron **por** mentir	I was punished for lying
¿Cuánto me darás **por** este libro?	How much will you give me for this book?
Vaya **por** ese camino	Go along that path
por el túnel	through the tunnel
Tiene que estar **por** aquí	It's got to be around here somewhere
por correo áereo	by airmail
por la tarde	in the afternoon
90 km **por** hora	90 km per hour
Lo hago **por** ellos	I'm doing it for them
Es **para** ti	It's for you
Es **para** mañana	It's for tomorrow
una habitación **para** dos noches	a room for two nights
Para ser un niño, lo hace muy bien	For a child, he is very good at it
Salen **para** Cádiz	They are leaving for Cádiz
Es demasiado torpe **para** comprenderlo	He's too stupid to understand
hablar **para** sí	to talk to oneself
Todavía tengo **para** 1 hora	I'll be another hour (at it) yet

Personal a

When the direct object of a verb is a noun referring to a person or pet animal, **a** must be placed immediately before it:

Querían mucho **a** sus hijos	They loved their children dearly
El niño miraba **a** su perro con asombro	The boy kept looking at his dog in astonishment

EXCEPTION: **tener** to have

Tienen dos hijos	They have two children

Conjunctions

Some conjunctions introduce a main clause, e.g. **y** *and*, **pero** *but*, and some introduce a subordinate clause, e.g. **porque** *because* and **mientras que** *while*. They are used in much the same way as in English, but:

> Some conjunctions in Spanish require a following subjunctive, see pages 34 to 36.

> Some conjunctions are 'split' in Spanish like 'both ... and', 'either ... or' in English:

> **tanto ... como** both ... and → ❶
> **ni ... ni** neither ... nor → ❷
> **o (bien) ... o (bien)** either ... or (else) → ❸
> **sea ... sea** either ... or, whether ... or → ❹

y
- Before words beginning with **i-** or **hi-** + consonant it becomes **e** → ❺

o
- Before words beginning with **o-** or **ho-** it becomes **u** → ❻
- Between numerals it becomes **ó** → ❼

que
- meaning *that* → ❽
- in comparisons, meaning *than* → ❾
- followed by the subjunctive, see page 32.

porque (not to be confused with **por qué** *why*)
- **como** should be used instead at the beginning of a sentence → ❿

pero, sino
- **pero** normally translates *but* → ⓫
- **sino** is used when there is a direct contrast after a negative → ⓬

Examples

1. Estas flores crecen tanto en verano como en invierno

   These flowers grow in both summer and winter

2. Ni él ni ella vinieron
   No tengo ni dinero ni comida

   Neither he nor she came
   I have neither money nor food

3. Debe de ser o ingenua o tonta
   O bien me huyen o bien no me reconocen

   She must be either naïve or stupid
   Either they're avoiding me or else they don't recognize me

4. Sea en verano, sea en invierno, siempre me gusta andar

   I always like walking, whether in summer or in winter

5. Diana e Isabel
   madre e hija
   BUT:
   árboles y hierba

   Diana and Isabel
   mother and daughter

   trees and grass

6. diez u once
   minutos u horas

   ten or eleven
   minutes or hours

7. 37 ó 38

   37 or 38

8. Dicen que te han visto
   ¿Sabías que estábamos allí?

   They say (that) they've seen you
   Did you know that we were there?

9. Le gustan más que nunca
   María es menos guapa que su hermana

   He likes them more than ever
   Maria is less attractive than her sister

10. Como estaba lloviendo no pudimos salir
    (*Compare with:* No pudimos salir porque estaba lloviendo)

    Because/As it was raining we couldn't go out

11. Me gustaría ir, pero estoy muy cansada

    I'd like to go, but I am very tired

12. No es escocesa sino irlandesa

    She isn't Scottish but Irish

Demonstrative Adjectives

	MASCULINE	FEMININE	
SING.	este	esta	this
	ese	esa	
	aquel	aquella	that
PLUR.	estos	estas	these
	esos	esas	
	aquellos	aquellas	those

Demonstrative adjectives normally precede the noun and always agree in number and in gender with it → ①

The forms **ese/a/os/as** are used:
- to indicate distance from the speaker but proximity to the person addressed → ②
- to indicate a not too remote distance → ③

The forms **aquel/la/los/las** are used to indicate distance, in space or time → ④

Demonstrative Pronouns

Demonstrative pronouns → ⑤ are identical to demonstrative adjectives with the following exceptions:
- neuter forms of the pronouns exist (**esto, eso** and **aquello**). These are used to refer to an idea or a statement or to an object when we want to identify it but don't have a specific noun in mind → ⑥
- the masculine and feminine pronouns were always written with an accent in the past (**éste, ésta, éstos, éstas; ése, ésa, ésos, ésas; aquél, aquélla, aquéllos, aquéllas**) to distinguish them from demonstrative adjectives. Nowadays the accents are only considered essential where ambiguity is otherwise possible. The neuter forms are never written with an accent.

An additional meaning of **aquel** is *the former*, and of **este** *the latter* → ⑦

Examples

① Este bolígrafo no escribe — This pen is not working

Esa revista es muy mala — That is a very bad magazine

Aquella montaña es muy alta — That mountain (over there) is very high

¿Conoces a esos señores? — Do you know those gentlemen?

Siga Vd hasta aquellos edificios — Carry on until you come to those buildings

¿Ves aquellas personas? — Can you see those people (over there)?

② Ese papel en donde escribes ... — That paper you are writing on ...

③ No me gustan esos cuadros — I don't like those pictures

④ Aquella calle parece muy ancha — That street (over there) looks very wide

Aquellos años sí que fueron felices — Those were really happy years

⑤ ¿Qué abrigo te gusta más? — Which coat do you like best?
— Este de aquí — — This one here

Aquella casa era más grande que esta — That house was bigger than this one

estos libros y aquellos — these books and those (over there)

Quiero estas sandalias y esas — I'd like these sandals and those ones

⑥ No puedo creer que esto me esté pasando a mí — I can't believe this is really happening to me

Eso de madrugar es algo que no le gusta — (This business of) getting up early is something she doesn't like

Aquello sí que me gustó — I really did like that

Esto es una bicicleta — This is a bicycle

⑦ Hablaban Jaime y Andrés, este a voces y aquel casi en un susurro — Jaime and Andrés were talking, the latter in a loud voice and the former almost in a whisper

Negatives

A sentence is made negative by adding **no** between the subject and the verb (and any preceding object pronouns) → **1**

In phrases like *not her, not now,* etc the Spanish **no** usually comes after the word it qualifies → **2**

With verbs of saying, hoping, thinking etc *not* is translated by **que no** → **3**

Double negatives

The following are the most common negative pairs:

no ... nada nothing
  (*not ... anything*)

no ... nadie nobody
  (*not ... anybody*)

no ... más no longer (*not ... any more*)

no ... nunca never (*not ... ever*)

no ... jamás never (stronger)
  (*not ... ever*)

no ... más que only
  (*not ... more than*)

no ... ningún/ninguno/a
  no (*not any*)

no ... tampoco not ... either

no ... ni ... ni neither ... nor

no ... ni siquiera not even

Word order

No precedes the verb (and any object pronouns) in both simple and compound tenses, and the second element follows the verb → **4**

Sometimes the above negatives are placed before the verb (with the exception of **más** and **más que**), and **no** is then dropped → **5**

Negatives in short replies

No is the usual negative response to a question → **6**

ⓘ Note: It is often translated as 'not' → **7**

Negative words like **nada**, **nunca** and **nadie** can also be used on their own in short replies → **8**

Examples

1 El coche no es suyo
Yo no me lo pondré

The car is not his
I won't put it on

2 ¿Quién lo ha hecho? — Ella no
Ahora no
Dame ese libro, el que está a
  tu lado no, el otro

Who did it? — Not her
Not now
Give me that book, not the one
  near you, the other one

3 Opino que no
Dijeron que no

I think not
They said not

4 No dicen nada
No han visto a nadie
No me veréis más
No te olvidaré nunca/jamás
No habían recorrido más que
  40 kms cuando ...
No se me ha ocurrido
  ninguna idea
No les estaban esperando ni
  mi hijo ni mi hija
No ha venido ni siquiera Juan
No lo haré nunca más
No se ve nunca a nadie por allí

No he hablado nunca más que
  con su mujer

They don't say anything
They haven't seen anybody
You won't see me any more
I'll never forget you
They hadn't travelled more than
  40 kms when ...
I haven't had any ideas

Neither my son nor my daughter
  was waiting for them
Even Juan hasn't come
I'll never do it again
You never see anybody around
  there
I've only ever spoken to his wife

5 Nadie ha venido hoy
Nunca me han gustado
Ni mi hermano ni mi hermana
  fuman

Nobody came today
I've never liked them
Neither my brother nor my sister
  smokes

6 ¿Quieres intentarlo? — No

Do you want to try? — No

7 ¿Vienes o no?

Are you coming or not?

8 ¿Ha venido alguien? — ¡Nadie!
¿Has ido al Japón alguna vez?
  — Nunca

Has anyone come? — Nobody!
Have you ever been to Japan?
  — Never

Sentence Stucture

Question Forms

Direct

There are two ways of forming direct questions in Spanish:

> by inverting the normal word order so that
> *subject + verb* → *verb + subject* → **1**

> by maintaining the word order *subject + verb*, but by using a rising
> intonation at the end of the sentence → **2**

> ⓘ Note: In compound tenses the auxiliary may never be
> separated from the past participle, as happens in English → **3**

Indirect

An indirect question is one that is 'reported', e.g. he asked me 'what
the time was', tell me 'which way to go'. Word order in indirect
questions can adopt one of the two following patterns:

> *interrogative word + subject + verb* → **4**

> *interrogative word + verb + subject* → **5**

¿verdad?, ¿no?

These are used wherever English would use 'isn't it?', 'don't they?',
'weren't we?', 'is it?' etc tagged on to the end of a sentence → **6**

sí

Sí is the word for 'yes' in answer to a question put either in the
affirmative or in the negative → **7**

Examples

1 ¿Vendrá tu madre?
¿Lo trajo Vd?
¿Es posible eso?
¿Cuándo volverán Vds?

Will your mother come?
Did you bring it?
Is it possible?
When will you come back?

2 El gato, ¿se bebió toda la leche?
Andrés, ¿va a venir?

Did the cat drink up all his milk?
Is Andrés coming?

3 ¿Lo ha terminado Vd?
¿Había llegado tu amigo?

Have you finished it?
Had your friend arrived?

4 Dime qué autobuses pasan
por aquí
No sé cuántas personas
vendrán

Tell me which buses come this
way
I don't know how many people
will turn up

5 Me preguntó dónde trabajaba
mi hermano
No sabemos a qué hora
empieza la película

He asked me where my brother
worked
We don't know what time the
film starts

6 Hace calor, ¿verdad?
No se olvidará Vd, ¿verdad?
Estaréis cansados, ¿no?
Te lo dijo María, ¿no?

It's warm, isn't it?
You won't forget, will you?
You must be tired, aren't you?
María told you, didn't she?

7 ¿Lo has hecho? — Sí
¿No lo has hecho? — Sí

Have you done it? — Yes (I have)
Haven't you done it? — Yes
(I have)

Pronunciation

Normal Word Stress

There are simple rules to establish which syllable in a Spanish word is stressed. When an exception to these rules occurs an acute accent (stress-mark) is needed. These rules are as follows:

- words ending in a vowel or combination of vowels, or with the consonants -s or -n are stressed on the next to last syllable (casa; casas; corre; corren; palabra; palabras; crisis)
- words ending in a consonant other than -s or -n bear the stress on the last syllable (reloj; verdad; batidor)
- a minority of words bear the stress on the second to last syllable, and these always need an accent (murciélago; pájaro)
- some nouns change their stress from singular to plural (carácter; caracteres; régimen; regímenes)

Stress in Diphthongs

In the case of diphthongs there are rules to establish which of the vowels is stressed. These rules are as follows:

- diphthongs formed by the combination of a 'weak' vowel (i, u) and a 'strong' vowel (a, e or o) bear the stress on the strong vowel (baile; boina; peine; causa; reina)
- diphthongs formed by the combination of two 'weak' vowels bear the stress on the second vowel (fui; viudo)

ⓘ Note: Two 'strong' vowels don't form a diphthong but are pronounced as two separate vowels. In these cases stress follows the normal rules (me mareo; caer; caos; correa)